ANNOTATED GUIDE TO THE INSOLVENCY L[

SEVENTH EDITION

ANNOTATED GUIDE TO THE INSOLVENCY LEGISLATION

Insolvency Acts 1986 and 2000
Insolvency Rules 1986
EC Regulation on Insolvency Proceedings 2000
Enterprise Act 2002

Seventh Edition

Len Sealy MA LLM PhD, Barrister and Solicitor (NZ)
*S J Berwin Professor Emeritus of Corporate Law,
University of Cambridge*

David Milman LLB PhD
*CMS Cameron McKenna Professor of Corporate and Insolvency Law,
University of Manchester*

Disclaimer

This publication is sold on the understanding that the publisher is not engaged in rendering legal or accounting advice or other professional services. The publisher, its editors and any authors, consultants or general editors expressly disclaim all and any liability and responsibility to any person, whether a purchaser or reader of this publication or not, in respect of anything and of the consequences of anything, done or omitted to be done by any such person in reliance, whether wholly or partially, upon the whole or any part of the contents of this publication. While this publication is intended to provide accurate information in regard to the subject matter covered, readers entering into transactions on the basis of such information should seek the services of a competent professional adviser.

The publisher advises that any statutory or other materials issued by the Crown or other relevant bodies and reproduced or quoted in this publication are not the authorised official versions of those statutory or other materials. In their preparation, however, the greatest care has been taken to ensure exact conformity with the law as enacted or other material as issued.

While copyright in all statutory and other materials resides in the Crown or other relevant body, copyright in the remaining material in this publication is vested in the publisher.

First published in 2004 by Sweet & Maxwell Ltd of
100 Avenue Road
London NW3 3PF
Typeset by MFK Information Services Limited, Stevenage, Hertfordshire
Printed in England by Ashford Colour Press, Gosport, Hants
Second (revised) reprint 2004

No natural forests were destroyed to make this product; only farmed timber was used and replanted.

A CIP catalogue record for this book is available from the British Library

ISBN 0 421 892501

First published by CCH Editions Limited 1987, Reprinted 1987
Second edition published by CCH Editions Limited 1988, Reprinted 1990, 1991
Third edition published by CCH Editions Limited 1991, Reprinted 1993
Fourth edition published by CCH Editions Limited 1994
Fifth edition published by CCH Editions Limited 1999, Reprinted by Sweet & Maxwell Ltd 2001
Sixth edition by Sweet & Maxwell Ltd 2002

© 1987, 1988, 1991, 1994, 1999 CCH Editions Limited
© 2001, 2002, 2004 Sweet & Maxwell Ltd

All rights reserved. Crown copyright material is reproduced with the permission of the Controller of HMSO and the Queen's Printer for Scotland.

No part of this publication may be reproduced or transmitted in any form or by any means, or stored in any retrieval system of any nature without prior written permission, except for permitted fair dealing under the Copyright, Designs and Patents Act 1988, or in accordance with the terms of a licence issued by the Copyright Licensing Agency in respect of photocopying and/or reprographic reproduction. Application for permission for other use of copyright material including permission to reproduce extracts in other published works shall be made to the publishers. Full acknowledgment of author, publisher and source must be given.

© Sweet & Maxwell 2004

PREFACE TO THE SEVENTH EDITION

Readers familiar with earlier editions of this book will have been struck by the fact that the sixth edition was noticeably more bulky than its predecessors. The relentless expansion of legislation has meant that this seventh edition has had to be bigger still which posed a major challenge to our publishers if the work was to continue, as everyone hoped, to be bound as a single volume. In the period of little more than a year since the previous edition went to press, the Insolvency Act 2000 has been brought fully into operation, introducing a moratorium into the company voluntary arrangement procedure for small companies, and the parts of the Enterprise Act 2002 dealing with corporate insolvency and the abolition of the Crown's preference in all insolvency procedures have also come into force—to say nothing of the numerous accompanying statutory instruments making changes to the rules and regulations. If the object of these innovations had been to substitute new laws and procedures for older ones, the increase in the volume of the legislation would have been more modest; but this is not generally the case. What much of the new legislation does is to supplement an existing procedure with one or several alternatives: the new moratorium provisions for voluntary arrangements, for instance, apply only to small, "eligible" companies, and the old law continues to apply to all other companies. So it is necessary for this book to deal with both regimes. And we also now have two corporate administration regimes running in parallel. If the style of drafting of the new laws had been as economical as the old, we would not have needed as many extra pages; but this, too, is not so. The company voluntary arrangement provisions in the original Insolvency Act of 1986 occupied just seven sections, yet the addition of a moratorium has required a Schedule of 45 paragraphs; and the new administration regime has needed a Schedule of 116 paragraphs to supplement the original Pt II, which contains only 20 sections.

In order to make some space available for all this new material, we have taken the decision to remove the Company Directors Disqualification Act 1986 and commentary from this edition. This we have done with regret; but we have done so also in recognition of the fact that almost all cases of disqualification are now dealt with administratively by disqualification undertakings and that disqualification by court order has become a relative rarity, generating virtually nothing for the law reports. Given that there is likely to be little further judicial development of this topic, readers may find it useful not to discard their sixth edition of the *Guide*, but keep it for future reference in dealing with disqualification cases.

The Enterprise Act 2002 also makes major changes to the law of personal insolvency, but these parts of the Act are not to be brought into force until April 1, 2004. Fortunately, the amending rules and much of the other supplementary material due to come into effect on the same date has already been published, and so it has been possible to provide a full commentary on the new bankruptcy provisions in this edition—subject, of course to the caveat that there may well be further statutory instruments published nearer to the operative date, for which our readers will need to be vigilant. This, we hope, will rule out any need for a further edition of the book in 2004.

In this edition of the *Guide* we have incorporated all the amendments and additions made to the Insolvency Act 1986 by the Insolvency Act 2000 and the Enterprise Act 2002 at the appropriate places in the 1986 Act, and in so far as the latter two Acts make other, "self-standing", changes in insolvency law the full text of the relevant provisions, with annotations, will be found in the separate entries for those Acts. The Insolvency Rules 1986 also incorporate all the changes made to date, including those not due to come into force until next April.

New case-law developments since the previous addition have been noted where appropriate. In particular, a number of recent cases have thrown light on the scope of the EC Regulation on Insolvency Proceedings 2000 and the meaning of some of the terms which it uses.

It is a pleasure, once again, to express our thanks to our friend and colleague Peter Bailey for his help and support, and to thank our publishers and their staff for their help at all stages of production.

The text is based on sources which were available to us up to September 15, 2003.

The need for a reprint of this edition has made it possible for us to update the text by including the changes made by the Insolvency (Amendment) Rules 2004 (SI 2004/584) and the Insolvency Proceedings (Monetary Limits) (Amendment) Order 2004 (SI 2004/584), which are due to come into force on April 1, 2004. In the interests of saving space, we have not drawn attention to these (mostly minor) modifications of the Rules at every place where they have been made.

The recent decisions of the Chancery Division in *National Westminster Bank plc v Spectrum Plus Ltd* [2004] EWHC 9 (Ch); [2004] B.C.C. 51 and of the House of Lords in *Re Leyland Daf Ltd, Buchler v Talbot* [2004] UKHL 9, each mark a major departure from long-standing rulings on aspects of the law governing floating charges.

We would like also to record our thanks to members of the Policy Unit of the Insolvency Service, who have kindly given us the benefit of their advice on a number of points.

Len Sealy
David Milman
March, 2004

ABOUT THE AUTHORS

Len Sealy MA, LLM, PhD, Barrister and Solicitor (NZ) is S J Berwin Professor Emeritus of Corporate Law at the University of Cambridge. He is an eminent commentator on company and commercial law, having written and lectured extensively in these areas.

David Milman LLB, PhD is CMS Cameron McKenna Professor of Corporate and Insolvency Law at the University of Manchester. He is the editor of leading bankruptcy and insolvency publications.

ABBREVIATIONS

The following abbreviations are used in this work:

BA 1914	Bankruptcy Act 1914
B(A)A 1926	Bankruptcy (Amendment) Act 1926
BR 1952	Bankruptcy Rules 1952
BRO	Bankruptcy restriction order
BRU	Bankruptcy restriction undertaking
CA	Companies Act (e.g. CA 1985 = Companies Act 1985)
CDDA 1986	Company Directors Disqualification Act 1986
CFCSA 1972	Companies (Floating Charges and Receivers) (Scotland) Act 1972
CJA	Criminal Justice Act (e.g. CJA 1988 = Criminal Justice Act 1988)
COMI	Centre of main interests
CPR	Civil Procedure Rules
CVA	Company voluntary arrangement
DTI	Department of Trade and Industry
EA 2002	Enterprise Act 2002
FA	Finance Act (e.g. FA 1985 = Finance Act 1985)
FSA 1986	Financial Services Act 1986
FSMA 2000	Financial Services and Markets Act 2000
IA	Insolvency Act (e.g. IA 1985 = Insolvency Act 1985)
IPA	Income payments agreement
IR 1986	Insolvency Rules 1986
I(A)R	Insolvency (Amendment) Rules (e.g. I(A)R 1993 = Insolvency Amendment Rules 1993)
IVA	Individual voluntary arrangement
LLP	Limited liability partnership
LLPA 2000	Limited Liability Partnerships Act 2000
LLPR 2001	Limited Liability Partnerships Regulations 2001 (SI 2001/1090)
LPA 1925	Law of Property Act 1925
OR	Official receiver
POCA 2002	Proceeds of Crime Act 2002
RSC	Rules of the Supreme Court
Cork Report	*Report of the Review Committee on Insolvency Law and Practice* (Cmnd 8558, 1982)
EC Regulation	EC Regulation on Insolvency Proceedings 2000
Finality Regulations	Financial Markets and Insolvency (Settlement Finality) Regulations 1999 (SI 1999/2979)
White Paper	*A Revised Framework for Insolvency Law* (Cmnd 9175, 1984)

Appendix I and Appendix II list the words and phrases which are given a special statutory definition or used in a particular sense in the legislation or the Rules, and give references to the provisions in which they and the accompanying commentary can be found.

CONTENTS

	Page
Preface to the Seventh Edition	v
About the Authors	vi
Abbreviations	vii
Case Table	xi
Statutes Table	liii
Statutory Instrument Table	lxv
Introduction	1
Insolvency Act 1986	9
Insolvency Act 2000	593
EC Regulation on Insolvency Proceedings 2000	602
Enterprise Act 2002	639
The Insolvency Rules 1986	654
Appendix I: Index to Statutory Definitions	1113
Appendix II: Index to Definitions in the Rules	1123
Appendix III: Insolvency Service Information	1126
Appendix IV: Practice Direction: Insolvency Proceedings	1127
Appendix V: Practice Direction: Applications under the Companies Act 1985 and the Insurance Companies Act 1982	1143
Index	1145

Case Table

This is a list of all cases cited, practice notes and directions in the notes to the Insolvency Acts 1986 and 2000, the Insolvency Rules 1986, the EC Regulation on Insolvency Proceedings 2000 and the Enterprise Act 2002.

Abbreviations in the provision column are to the Insolvency Act 1986 (IA), the Insolvency Act 2000 (IA 2000), the Insolvency Rules 1986 (IR), the EC Regulation on Insolvency Proceedings 2000 (ER) and the Enterprise Act 2002 (EA).

	Provision
A	
A Straume (UK) Ltd v Bradlor Developments Ltd [2000] B.C.C. 333; (2000) 2 T.C.L.R. 409	IA 11(3)
A&C Supplies Ltd, Re; sub nom. Sutton (Removal of Liquidator), Re [1998] B.C.C. 708; [1998] 1 B.C.L.C. 603	IA 29(2), 45(1),(2), 172(1),(2)
A&J Fabrications (Batley) Ltd v Grant Thornton (A Firm) (No.1) [1999] B.C.C. 807; [1998] 2 B.C.L.C. 227	IA 212(1)
ACLI Metals (London), Re (1989) 5 B.C.C. 749; [1989] B.C.L.C. 749	IA 168(5)
AE Farr Ltd, Re [1992] B.C.C. 150; [1992] B.C.L.C. 333	IA 236
AE Realisations (1985) Ltd, Re [1988] 1 W.L.R. 200; [1987] 3 All E.R. 83; (1987) 3 B.C.C. 136	IA 179, 181(1)–(3)
AI Levy (Holdings) Ltd, Re [1964] Ch. 19; [1963] 2 W.L.R. 1464	IA 127
AIB Finance Ltd v Alsop; sub nom. AIB Finance Ltd v Debtors [1998] 2 All E.R. 929; [1998] Lloyd's Rep. Bank. 102; [1998] B.C.C. 780	IR 6.5
AJ Adams (Builders), Re [1991] B.C.C. 62; [1991] B.C.L.C. 359	IA 108, 171(4)

	Provision
AMF International Ltd, Re [1995] B.C.C. 439; [1995] 2 B.C.L.C. 529	IR 4.139–4.148A
AMF International Ltd (No.2), Re; sub nom. Cohen v Ellis [1996] 1 W.L.R. 77; [1996] B.C.C. 335	IA 213(3)
ANC Clark Goldring & Page Ltd [2001] B.C.C. 479	IA Sch.4, para.6
ARV Aviation Ltd, Re (1988) 4 B.C.C. 708; [1989] B.C.L.C. 664	IA 15
AT & T Istel v Tully (No.1) [1993] A.C. 45; reversing [1992] Q.B. 315; [1992] 2 W.L.R. 112	IA 236
AV Sorge & Co, Re [1986] P.C.C. 380	IA 115
Abbey Leisure, Re; sub nom. Virdi v Abbey Leisure [1990] B.C.C. 60; [1990] B.C.L.C. 342	IA 125(2)
Abbott, Re [1997] B.C.C. 226	IA 263(5), (6)
Addlestone Linoleum Co, Re (1888) L.R. 37 Ch. D. 191	IA 74(2)(f)
Adlards Motor Group Holding, Re [1990] B.C.L.C. 68	IA 236
Aectra Refining and Manufacturing Inc v Exmar NV (The New Vanguard and The Pacifica) [1994] 1 W.L.R. 1634; [1995] 1 All E.R. 641; *The Times*, August 15, 1994	IA 251
Agnew v CIR. *See* Brumark Investments Ltd, Re	

Case	Provision
Aiglon Ltd v Gau Shan Co Ltd [1993] 1 Lloyd's Rep. 164; [1993] B.C.L.C. 321	IA 425(1)
Air Ecosse Ltd v Civil Aviation Authority 1987 S.C. 285; 1987 S.L.T. 751; (1987) 3 B.C.C. 492, 2 Div	IA 11(3)
Airlines Airspares v Handley Page [1970] Ch. 193; [1970] 2 W.L.R. 163	IA 37(1),(2)
Akers v Lomas; sub nom. Trading Partners Ltd, Re [2002] 1 B.C.L.C. 655; [2002] B.P.I.R. 606	IA 236, 236(2), 426(4),(5),(11)
Aktieselskabet Dansk Skibsfinansiering v Brothers [2001] 2 B.C.L.C. 324	IA 213
Albert v Albert [1997] 2 F.L.R. 791; [1998] 1 F.C.R. 331; [1996] B.P.I.R. 233	IA 310, 366(1)
Alipour v Ary; sub nom. Alipour v UOC Corp (No.1); UOC Corp (No.1), Re; Company (No.002180 of 1986), Re [1997] 1 W.L.R. 534; [1997] B.C.C. 377	IA 123, 124(1), 135
Alipour v UOC Corp (No.2); sub nom. UOC Corp (No.2), Re [1998] B.C.C. 191; [1997] 2 B.C.L.C. 569	IR 4.25–4.31
Allan Ellis (Transport & Packing) Services, Re (1989) 5 B.C.C. 835	IA 192(2)
Allard Holdings Ltd, Re [2001] 1 B.C.L.C. 404; [2002] B.P.I.R. 1	IR 4.73–4.85
Allen, Re. *See* Debtor (No.367 of 1992), Re	
Alman v Approach Housing Ltd [2002] B.C.C. 723; [2001] 1 B.C.L.C. 530; [2001] B.P.I.R. 203	IA 5(2), 7(3)
Alpa Lighting Ltd, Re; sub nom. Mills v Samuels [1997] B.P.I.R. 341	IA 7(4), 263(4)
Alpha Club (UK) Ltd, Re [2002] EWHC 884; [2002] 2 B.C.L.C. 612	IA 124A
Alt Landscapes, Re [1999] B.P.I.R. 459	IA 172(1),(2), IR 4.108–4.112, 6.126
AMEC Properties v Planning Research & Systems [1992] B.C.L.C. 1149; [1992] 1 E.G.L.R. 70; [1992] 13 E.G. 109, CA	IA 37(1),(2), 44(1),(2)
AMP Enterprises Ltd v Hoffman; sub nom. AMP Music Box Enterprises Ltd v Hoffman [2002] EWHC 1899; [2002] B.C.C. 996	IA 108
Anglesea Colliery Co, Re (1865–66) L.R. 1 Ch. App. 555	IA 74(1)
Anglo American Insurance Co Ltd (Disclosure), Re [2002] B.C.C. 715	IA 236
Anglo Austrian Printing and Publishing Union (No.2), Re [1894] 2 Ch. 622	IA 212(1)
Anglo French Cooperative Society Ex p. Pelly, Re (1882) L.R. 21 Ch. D. 492	IA 212
Anglo Manx Group Ltd v Aitken; sub nom. Anglo Manx Group Ltd v Lord Beaverbrook [2002] B.P.I.R. 215	IA 281(2)–(6),(8)
Antal International Ltd, Re [2003] EWHC 1339	IA 44(1),(2)
Anvil Estates Ltd, Re, unreported 1993	IA Sch.1
Application Pursuant to r.7.28 of the Insolvency Rules 1986, Re [1994] B.C.C. 369; [1994] 1 B.C.L.C. 104	IR 7.26–7.32
Applied Data Base Ltd v Secretary of State for Trade & Industry [1995] 1 B.C.L.C. 272	IR 4.7–4.14
Arbuthnot Leasing International Ltd v Havelet Leasing Ltd (No.2) [1990] B.C.C. 636	IA 423(1)–(3)
Argentum Reductions (UK) Ltd, Re [1975] 1 W.L.R. 186; [1975] 1 All E.R. 608	IA 127

Case Table

	Provision		Provision
Ariyo v Sovereign Leasing Plc [1998] B.P.I.R. 177	IA 267(1), (2), IR 6.4	Atlantic & General Investment Trust Ltd v Richbell Information Services Inc; sub nom. Richbell Information Services Inc, Re [2000] B.C.C. 111; [2000] 2 B.C.L.C. 778...	IA 220
Arrows Ltd (No.3), Re [1992] B.C.C. 131; [1992] B.C.L.C. 555	IA 8(1),(2), 236	Atlantic Computers Plc (In Administration), Re. *See* British & Commonwealth Holdings Plc (In Administration) v Barclays de Zoete Wedd Ltd (No.1)	
Arrows Ltd (No.4), Re; sub nom. Hamilton v Naviede [1995] 2 A.C. 75; [1994] 3 W.L.R. 656; [1992] B.C.C. 446; [1992] B.C.L.C. 1176	IA 236, 433(1), IR 9.1–9.6	Atlantic Computer Systems Plc (No.1), Re [1992] Ch. 505; [1992] 2 W.L.R. 367; [1990] B.C.C. 859	IA 11(3), 19(3)–(6)
Arthur Rathbone Kitchens Ltd, Re [1998] B.C.C. 450; [1997] 2 B.C.L.C. 280	IA 7(4)	Attorney General's Reference (No.7 of 2000) [2001] EWCA Civ 888; [2001] 1 W.L.R. 1879	IA 433(2)–(4)
Artman v Artman; sub nom. Bankrupt (No.622 of 1995), Re [1996] B.P.I.R. 511	IA 271(1), (2),(4), 282(1),(3)	Austintel Ltd, Re [1997] B.C.C. 362	IA 413(1), IR 7.26–7.32
Ash & Newman v Creative Devices Research [1991] B.C.L.C. 403	IA 37(1),(2)	Avatar Communications, Re (1988) 4 B.C.C. 473	IA 134(2)
Ashe v Mumford [2001] B.P.I.R. 1	IA 423(1)–(3)	Aveling Barford Ltd, Re [1989] 1 W.L.R. 360; [1988] 3 All E.R. 1019	IA 236(4)–(6), IR 9.1–9.6
Ashurst v Pollard; sub nom. Pollard v Ashurst [2001] Ch. 595; [2001] 2 W.L.R. 722; [2001] B.P.I.R. 131 affirming [2000] 2 All E.R. 772; [2001] I.L.Pr. 7; [2000] B.P.I.R. 347	IA 314(8), ER	Awan, Re; sub nom. Petitioning Creditor v Awan (A Bankrupt) [2000] B.P.I.R. 241	IR 6.14, 6.15, 7.55
Aspinalls Club Ltd v Simone Halabi [1998] B.P.I.R. 322	IA 6.22	Axis Genetics Ltd, Re. *See* Biosource Technologies Inc v Axis Genetics Plc (In Administration)	
Asset Visions Ltd, Re [2002] EWHC 756; [2003] B.P.I.R. 305	IA 34	Ayala Holdings Ltd, Re [1993] B.C.L.C. 256	IA 424
Assico Engineering Ltd (In Liquidation), Re [2002] B.C.C. 481; [2002] B.P.I.R. 15	IR 4.50–4.71	Ayala Holdings Ltd (No.2), Re [1996] 1 B.C.L.C. 467	IA 127, Sch.4, para.6
Astor Chemical Ltd v Synthetic Technology Ltd [1990] B.C.C. 97; [1990] B.C.L.C. 1	IA 9(1), 14(1), 37(1), (2), 7.26–7.32	**B**	
		B Johnson & Co (Builders) Ltd, Re [1955] Ch. 634; [1955] 3 W.L.R. 269	IA 206(3), 212(1)
Atherton v Ogunlende [2003] B.P.I.R. 21	IR 6.5		

Case Table

	Provision		Provision
BCCI, Morris v State Bank of India [1999] B.C.C. 943	IA 213	Bank of Credit and Commerce International SA (No.5), Sheik Khalid v Bank of Credit & Commerce International SA [1994] 1 B.C.L.C. 429	IR 4.50–4.71
BCCI Banque Arabe Internationale d'Investissement SA v Morris [2002] B.C.C. 407	IA 213, 213(2)	Bank of Credit and Commerce International SA (No.6) [1994] 1 B.C.L.C. 450	IR 7.1–7.18
BHT (UK) Ltd, Re; sub nom. Duckworth v Natwest Finance Ltd [2004] EWHC 201, Ch D (Companies Ct)	IA 40(1), (2)	Bank of Credit and Commerce International SA (No.7) [1994] 1 B.C.L.C. 455	IA 236(2)
BRAC Rent-A-Car International Inc, Re; sub nom. BRAC Rent-A-Car Ltd, Re [2003] EWHC 128; [2003] 1 W.L.R. 1421; [2003] B.C.C. 248	IA 8(1),(2), ER para.14, Art.3(1), IR 2.31	Bank of Credit and Commerce International SA (No.8), Morris v Rayners Enterprises Inc [1988] A.C. 214; [1997] B.C.C. 965	IR 4.90
Baars, Re [2002] EWHC 2159; [2003] B.P.I.R. 523	IA 286(1), (2)	Bank of Credit and Commerce International SA (No.10) [1997] Ch.213; [1996] B.C.C. 980	IR 4.90
Baby Moon (UK), Re [1985] P.C.C. 103	IR 12.12	Bank of Credit and Commerce International SA (In Liquidation) (No.12), Re; sub nom. Morris v Bank of America National Trust and Savings Association [1997] B.C.C. 561; [1997] 1 B.C.L.C. 526	IA 236
Bagnall v Official Receiver [2003] EWHC 1398; [2003] 3 All E.R. 613	IA 279(3)–(5)		
Bailey, Re [1977] 1 W.L.R. 278	IA 336(3)–(5)		
Banca Carige v Banco Nacional de Cuba [2001] B.P.I.R. 407	IA 423(1)–(3)	Bank of Credit and Commerce International (Overseas) Ltd (In Liquidation) v Habib Bank Ltd [1999] 1 W.L.R. 42; [1998] 4 All E.R. 753; [1998] 2 B.C.L.C. 459	IR 4.90
Banco Nacional de Cuba v Cosmos Trading Corp [2000] B.C.C. 910; [2000] 1 B.C.L.C. 813	IA 220		
Bank of Credit and Commerce International SA (In Liquidation) v BRS Kumar Brothers Ltd [1994] 1 B.C.L.C. 211	IA Pt III	Bank of Ireland v Hollicourt (Contractors) Ltd [2001] Ch.555; [2000] B.C.C. 1210	IA 127
		Bank of Scotland v Pacific Shelf. See Bank of Scotland, Petitioners	
Bank of Credit and Commerce International SA (In Liquidation) v Prince Fahd Bin Salman Abdul Aziz Al-Saud [1997] B.C.C. 63	IR 4.90	Bank of Scotland, Petitioners; sub nom. Bank of Scotland v Pacific Shelf 1988 S.L.T. 690; 1988 S.C.L.R. 487; (1988) 4 B.C.C. 457	IA 242, 243
Bank of Credit and Commerce International SA (In Liquidation) (No.2), Re [1992] B.C.C. 715; [1992] B.C.L.C. 579	IA 195, Sch.4, paras 2,3	Bankrupt (No.1273 of 1990), A, Re The Independent February 26, 1990	IR 6.46
Bank of Credit and Commerce International SA (No.4) [1994] 1 B.C.L.C. 419	IA 130(1)	Bankrupt (No.622 of 1995), A, Re The Times June 27, 1996	IA 282(1), (3)

Case Table

Case	Provision
Bankrupt Estate of Cirillo Ex p. Official Trustee in Bankruptcy (No.1), Re; sub nom. Cirillo (A Bankrupt) Ex p. Official Trustee in Bankruptcy, Re [1997] B.P.I.R. 166	IA Sch.5
Bankrupt Estate of Cirillo Ex p. Official Trustee in Bankruptcy (No.2), Re [1997] B.P.I.R. 574	IA 323
Banque des Marchands de Moscou (Koupetschesky) v Kindersley [1951] Ch. 112; [1950] 2 All E.R. 549	IA 220
Banque Nationelle de Paris plc v Montman Ltd [2000] 1 B.C.L.C. 576	IA 107
Barbor v Middleton 1988 S.L.T. 288; 1988 S.C.L.R. 178; (1988) 4 B.C.C. 681	IA 74(1)
Barclays Bank Plc v Eustice [1995] 1 W.L.R. 1238; [1995] 4 All E.R. 511; [1995] B.C.C. 978	IA 423(1)–(3)
Barclays Bank Plc v Henson [2000] B.P.I.R. 941	IR 6.105
Barclays Bank Ltd v Quistclose Investments Ltd; sub nom. Quistclose Investments Ltd v Rolls Razor Ltd (In Voluntary Liquidation) [1970] A.C. 567; [1968] 3 W.L.R. 1097	IA 107
Barclays Mercantile Business Finance Ltd v Sibec Developments Ltd; sub nom. Sibec Developments, Re [1992] 1 W.L.R. 1253; [1993] 2 All E.R. 195; [1993] B.C.C. 148	IA 11(3), 20(1)
Barings Plc (In Liquidation), Re (No.2); sub nom. Barings Plc (In Liquidation) (No.7), Re [2002] 1 B.C.L.C. 401; [2002] B.P.I.R. 653	IA 167(1)
Barings Plc (In Liquidation) (No.1), Re; sub nom. Hamilton v Law Debenture Trustees Ltd [2001] 2 B.C.L.C. 159; [2002] B.P.I.R. 85	IA 168(2)
Barleycorn Enterprises Ltd, Re; sub nom. Mathias & Davies v Down (Liquidator of Barleycorn Enterprises Ltd) [1970] Ch. 465; [1970] 2 W.L.R. 898	IA 107, 115, IR 4.218–4.220
Barlow Clowes Gilt Managers Ltd, Re (No.2), unreported July 31, 1990	IA 236
Barlow Clowes Gilt Managers Ltd, Re [1992] Ch. 208; [1992] 2 W.L.R. 36; [1991] B.C.C. 608	IA 236
Barn Crown Ltd, Re [1995] 1 W.L.R. 147; [1994] 4 All E.R. 42; [1994] B.C.C. 381	IA 127
Barrow Borough Transport Ltd, Re [1990] Ch. 227; [1989] 3 W.L.R. 858; (1989) 5 B.C.C. 646	IA 11(3)
Barton Manufacturing Co Ltd, Re [1998] B.C.C. 827; [1999] 1 B.C.L.C. 740	IA 238(4)
Bayoil SA, Re; sub nom. Seawind Tankers Corp v Bayoil SA [1999] 1 W.L.R. 147; [1999] 1 All E.R. 374; [1998] B.C.C. 988	IA 123
Beacon Leisure, Re [1990] B.C.C. 213; [1992] B.C.L.C. 565	IA 239(6)
Beck Foods Ltd. See Rees v Boston BC	
Beer v Higham [1997] B.P.I.R. 349	IA 284(1)–(3),(6)
Beesley (Audrey), Ex p.; sub nom. Beesley (Terence Jack) v Official Receiver; Beesley (Audrey) (A Bankrupt), Re [1975] 1 W.L.R. 568; [1975] 1 All E.R. 385	IA 282(1),(3)
Bell Group Finance (Pty) Ltd (In Liquidation) v Bell Group (UK) Holdings Ltd [1996] B.C.C. 505; [1996] 1 B.C.L.C. 304	IA 123, 125(1)
Bellmex International Ltd v Green [2001] B.C.C. 253	IA 236
Bendall v McWhirter [1952] 2 Q.B. 466; [1952] 1 All E.R. 1307	IA 335A

Case Table

Case	Provision
Berkeley Applegate (Investment Consultants) Ltd (No.2), Re (1988) 4 B.C.C. 279	IA 115, IR 4.127–4.131
Berkeley Applegate (Investment Consultants) (No.3), Re (1989) 5 B.C.C. 803	IA 115, IR 4.127–4.131
Berkeley Securities (Property) Ltd [1980] 1 W.L.R. 1589	IA 322(3), (4), IR 13.12(2)
Bernasconi v Nicholas Bennett & Co [2000] B.C.C. 921; [2000] B.P.I.R. 8	IA 213
Beverley Group Plc v McClue [1995] B.C.C. 751; [1995] 2 B.C.L.C. 407	IA 1(1), 5(2), IR 1.13–1.21
Bill Hennessy Associates Ltd [1992] B.C.C. 386	IR 4.7–4.14
Biosource Technologies Inc v Axis Genetics Plc (In Administration); sub nom. Axis Genetics Plc's (In Administration) Patent, Re [2000] B.C.C. 943; [2000] 1 B.C.L.C. 286	IA 11(3)
Bird v Hadkinson [2000] C.P. Rep. 21; [1999] B.P.I.R. 653	IA 366(1)
Bishopsgate Investment Management Ltd (In Provisional Liquidation) v Maxwell [1993] Ch. 1; [1992] 2 W.L.R. 991; [1992] B.C.C. 222	IA 133, 236
Bishopsgate Investment Management Ltd (In Liquidation) v Maxwell (No.2) [1994] B.C.C. 732	IA 236
Bournemouth & Boscombe Athletic Football Club Co Ltd, Re [1998] B.P.I.R. 183	IA 6(3), IR 1.13–1.21
Brabon, Re; sub nom. Treharne v Brabon [2000] B.C.C. 1171; [2001] 1 B.C.L.C. 11; [2000] B.P.I.R. 537	IA 339(1)–(3), 423(1)–(3)
Bradley-Hole (A Bankrupt), Re [1995] 1 W.L.R. 1097; [1995] 4 All E.R. 865	IA 263(5), (6)
Bramble Ex p. See Toleman Ex p. Bramble, Re	
Branston & Gothard Ltd, Re [1999] 1 All E.R. (Comm) 289; [1999] Lloyd's Rep. Bank. 251; [1999] B.P.I.R. 466	IA 127, 239(4)
Brauch (A Debtor), Ex p. Brittanic Securities & Investments, Re [1978] Ch. 316; [1977] 3 W.L.R. 354	IA 265
Brian D Pierson (Contractors) Ltd, Re; sub nom. Penn v Pierson [1999] B.C.C. 26; [2001] 1 B.C.L.C. 275	IA 214(1), 239(6)
Brian Sheridan Cars Ltd, Re [1995] B.C.C. 1035	IR 7.47
Bridgend Goldsmiths Ltd, Re [1995] B.C.C. 226; [1995] 2 B.C.L.C. 208	IA 108, 263(5),(6)
Brightlife Ltd, Re [1987] Ch. 200; [1987] 2 W.L.R. 197; (1986) 2 B.C.C. 99,359	IA 40(1), (2), 175(2)(b)
Brillouet v Hachette Magazines Ltd [1996] B.P.I.R. 518	IA 375(1)
Bristol Airport Plc v Powdrill; sub nom. Paramount Airways Ltd (No.1), Re [1990] Ch. 744; [1990] 2 W.L.R. 1362; [1990] B.C.C. 130	IA 11(3), 246, 248, 436
Bristol and West Building Society v Trustee of the Property of John Julius Back (A Bankrupt); sub nom. Melinek (A Bankrupt), Re [1998] 1 B.C.L.C. 485; [1997] B.P.I.R. 358	IA 285(3), (4)
Bristol and West Building Society v Saunders; Bearman (A Bankrupt), Re. See Saunders (A Bankrupt), Re	
Bristol Athenaeum, Re (1890) L.R. 43 Ch. D. 236	IA 220
British & Commonwealth Holdings Plc (No.3), Re [1992] 1 W.L.R. 672; [1992] B.C.C. 58	IA 14(3)

Case Table

Case	Provision
British & Commonwealth Holdings Plc (In Administration) v Barclays de Zoete Wedd Ltd (No.1); sub nom. Atlantic Computers Plc (In Administration), Re [1998] B.C.C. 200	IA 236
British & Commonwealth Holdings Plc (Joint Administrators) v Spicer and Oppenheim; sub nom. British & Commonwealth Holdings Plc (Nos.1 and 2), Re [1993] A.C. 426; [1992] 3 W.L.R. 853; [1992] B.C.C. 977	IA 236
British & Commonwealth Holdings Plc (Joint Administrators) v Spicer and Oppenheim [1992] Ch. 342; [1992] 2 W.L.R. 931	IA 236
British Eagle International Airlines Ltd v Compagnie Nationale Air France [1975] 1 W.L.R. 758; [1975] 2 All E.R. 390, HL	IA 107
Brook Martin & Co, Re [1993] B.C.L.C. 328; [1992] E.G.C.S. 138	IA 236
Brooke v Hewitt (1796) 3 Ves 253	IA 345(1)–(3)
Brooke Marine, Re [1988] B.C.L.C. 546	IA 18(2), Sch.B1, para.13
Brown v Beat [2002] B.P.I.R. 421	IA 303(1), 304(2)
Brown v City of London Corp [1996] 1 W.L.R. 1070; [1996] 1 E.G.L.R. 139	IA 44(1),(2)
Brumark Investments Ltd, Re; sub nom. Inland Revenue Commissioner v Agnew; Agnew v Inland Revenue Commissioner [2001] UKPC 28; [2001] 2 A.C. 710	IA 40(1),(2)
Bruton v Inland Revenue Commissioners; sub nom. Debtor (No.647–SD–1999), Re [2000] B.P.I.R. 946	IA 267(1),(2)
Buckingham International Plc (In Liquidation) (No.1), Re; sub nom. Mitchell v Carter [1997] B.C.C. 907; [1997] 1 B.C.L.C. 681	IA 183
Buckingham International Plc (In Liquidation) (No.2), Re; sub nom. Mitchell v Carter (No.2); Mitchell v Buckingham International Plc (In Liquidation) [1998] B.C.C. 943; [1998] 2 B.C.L.C. 369	IA 183
Budge v Budge (Contractors) Ltd [1997] B.P.I.R. 366	IR 6.5
Bullard & Taplin Ltd, Re [1996] B.C.C. 973; [1996] B.P.I.R. 526	IA 263(5),(6)
Bulmer Ex p. Greaves, Re [1937] Ch. 499	IA 301(1), IR 6.165
Burford Midland Properties Ltd v Marley Extrusions Ltd [1994] B.C.C. 604; [1995] 1 B.C.L.C. 102	IA 1(1), 5(2)
Burton v Burton [1986] 2 F.L.R. 419	IA 284(1)–(3), (6)
Burton & Deakin Ltd, Re [1977] 1 W.L.R. 390; [1977] 1 All E.R. 631	IA 127
Business Properties, Re (1988) 4 B.C.C. 684	IA 8(1),(2)
Busytoday Ltd, Re; sub nom. Popely v Lewis [1992] 1 W.L.R. 683; [1992] 4 All E.R. 61; [1992] B.C.C. 480; [1993] B.C.L.C. 43	IR 7.47
Butterworth v Soutter [2000] B.P.I.R. 582	IA 282(4)
Byford (decd), Re [2003] EWHC 1267	IA 283

C

Case	Provision
CCA v Brecht (1987) 7 A.C.L.C. 40	IA 206(3)
CE King Ltd (In Administration), Re; sub nom. CE King Ltd v Kodak [2000] 2 B.C.L.C. 297	IA 14(3)
CIL Realisations Ltd (In Liquidation), Re; sub nom. Chalk v Kahn [2001] B.C.C. 300; [2000] 2 B.C.L.C. 361	IA 40(1),(2)
CVC/Opportunity Equity Partners Ltd v Demarco Almeida [2002] UKPC 16; [2002] B.C.C. 684	IA 122(1), 125(2)

Case Table

	Provision		Provision
Cadbury Schweppes Plc v Somji; sub nom. Somji v Cadbury Schweppes Plc [2001] 1 W.L.R. 615; [2001] 1 B.C.L.C. 498; [2001] B.P.I.R. 172	IA 276(1)	Cartwright, Re [1975] 1 W.L.R. 573	IR 7.55
Cadogan Estates v McMahon [2001] B.P.I.R. 17	IA 345(1)–(3)	Cartwright v Cartwright [2002] EWCA Civ 931; [2002] B.P.I.R. 895	IR 12.3
Cadwell v Jackson [2001] B.P.I.R. 966	IR 6.105, 12.3	Cartwright v Staffordshire and Moorlands DC [1998] B.P.I.R. 328	IR 6.1
Calahurst, Re [1989] B.C.L.C. 140; [1989] P.C.C. 357	IR 7.47	Cases of Taff's Well, Re [1992] Ch.179; [1991] B.C.C. 582	IA 8(1),(2), 129
Cale v Assuidoman KPS (Harrow) Ltd [1996] B.P.I.R. 245	IR 6.5	Casterbridge Properties Ltd (No.2), Re; sub nom. Jeeves v Official Receiver [2002] B.C.C. 453; [2002] B.P.I.R. 428	IA 133, 236
Calmex, Re [1989] 1 All E.R. 485; (1988) 4 B.C.C. 761	IA 130(1), 147(1), IR 4.16–4.21A	Castle New Homes, Re [1979] 1 W.L.R. 1075; [1979] 2 All E.R. 775	IA 236
Campbell Coverings, Re (No.2) [1954] Ch. 225; [1954] 2 W.L.R. 204	IA 133	Cavco Floor, Re [1990] B.C.C. 589; [1990] B.C.L.C. 940	IA 9(1)
Cancol Ltd, Re; sub nom. Cazaly Irving Holdings Ltd v Cancol Ltd [1996] 1 All E.R. 37; [1995] B.C.C. 1133	IA 1, 6(1), IR 1.13–1.21	Celtic Extraction Ltd (In Liquidation), Re; sub nom. Official Receiver (as Liquidator of Celtic Extraction Ltd and Bluestone Chemicals Ltd) v Environment Agency [2001] Ch. 475; [2000] 2 W.L.R. 991; [2000] B.C.C. 487	IA 178
Capital Prime Properties Plc v Worthgate Ltd (In Liquidation) [2000] B.C.C. 525; [2000] 1 B.C.L.C. 647	IA 178(4)	Centralcrest Engineering Ltd, Re; sub nom. Inland Revenue Commissioners v Nelmes [2000] B.C.C. 727	IA 212(1)
Cardona, Re; sub nom. Inland Revenue Commissioners v Cardona [1997] B.C.C. 697; [1997] B.P.I.R. 604	IA 262(4)–(7)	Centrebind Ltd, Re; sub nom. Centrebind Ltd v Inland Revenue Commissioners [1967] 1 W.L.R. 377; [1966] 3 All E.R. 889	IA 166
Carman v Baron (1996) 12 I.L.&P.60	IA 310	Chalk v Kahn. *See* CIL Realisations Ltd (In Liquidation), Re	
Carr v British International Helicopters [1993] B.C.C. 855; [1994] 2 B.C.L.C. 474	IA 11(3)	Chancery plc, Re [1991] B.C.C. 171	IA 9(1)
Carreras Rothmans Ltd v Freeman Mathews Treasure Ltd (In Liquidation) [1985] Ch. 207; [1984] 3 W.L.R. 1016; [1985] 1 All E.R. 155	IA 107	Chandler v Director of Public Prosecutions [1964] A.C. 763	IA 214
Carter Commercial Developments Ltd, Re [2002] B.C.C. 803; [2002] B.P.I.R. 1053	IA 11(3)	Charnley Davies Business Services, Re (1987) 3 B.C.C. 408; 1988 P.C.C. 1	IA 18(2), 23(1), (2), 140
Carter-Knight (A Bankrupt) v Peat [2000] B.P.I.R. 968; (2000) 97(30) L.S.G. 40	IA 276(1)	Charnley Davies (No.2), Re [1990] B.C.C. 605; [1990] B.C.L.C. 760	IA 17, 17(2), 27(1)

Case Table

Case	Provision
Charterhouse Investment Trust v Tempest Diesels [1986] B.C.L.C. 1; (1985) 1 B.C.C. 99,544	IA 9(1)
Chase Manhattan Bank NA v Israel-British Bank (London) Ltd [1981] Ch. 105; [1980] 2 W.L.R. 202; [1979] 3 All E.R. 1025	IA 107
Chelmsford City Football Club (1980) Ltd, Re [1991] B.C.C. 133	IA 9(1), IR 2.9
Chesterfield Catering Co Ltd, Re [1977] Ch. 373; [1976] 3 W.L.R. 879	IA 124(2), (3)
Chohan v Saggar [1992] B.C.C. 306	IA 423(1)–(3), 425(2),(3)
Choudhury v Inland Revenue Commissioners [2000] B.P.I.R. 246	IA 282(4)
Choudri v Palta [1992] B.C.C. 787	IA 37(4)
Christofi v Barclays Bank Plc [2000] 1 W.L.R. 937; [1999] 4 All E.R. 437; [1999] B.P.I.R. 855	IA 366(1)
Church of Scientology Advanced Organisation Saint Hill Europe and South Africa v Scott [1997] B.P.I.R. 418	IA 306
Cirillo (A Bankrupt) Ex p. Official Trustee in Bankruptcy, Re. See Bankrupt Estate of Cirillo Ex p. Official Trustee in Bankruptcy (No.1), Re	
Citro (Domenico) (A Bankrupt), Re [1991] Ch. 142; [1990] 3 W.L.R. 880	IA 336(3)–(5)
City Electrical Factors v Hardingham [1996] B.P.I.R. 541	IA 267(4), (5), IR 6.5
City Logistics (In Administration), Re [2002] EWHC 757; [2002] 2 B.C.L.C. 103	IA 11(3)
City of Westminster Assurance Co Ltd v Registrar of Companies [1997] B.C.C. 960	IA Pt IV
Clarke v Coutts & Co [2002] EWCA Civ 943; [2002] B.P.I.R. 916	IA 252(2)
Clarkson v Clarkson [1994] B.C.C. 921	IA 283(4), 339(1)–(3)
Clasper Group Services, Re (1988) 4 B.C.C. 673; [1989] B.C.L.C. 143	IA 206(3)
Claughton v Charalambous [1998] B.P.I.R. 558	IA 335A
Claybridge Shipping Co SA, Re [1981] Com. L.R. 107	IA 123
Cleaver v Delta American Reinsurance Co (In Liquidation) [2001] UKPC 6; [2001] 2 A.C. 328; [2001] 1 B.C.L.C. 482	IR 4.88
Clements v Udal; sub nom. Clements v Udall [2001] B.C.C. 658; [2002] 2 B.C.L.C. 606; [2001] B.P.I.R. 454	IA 7(5), 108, 172(1), 2), 263(5),(6), 363(1)
Cloverbay Ltd (Joint Administrators) v Bank of Credit and Commerce International SA [1991] Ch. 90; [1990] 3 W.L.R. 574; [1990] B.C.C. 414	IA 236
Coath, Re [2000] B.P.I.R. 981	IA 263(5), (6)
Coe v Ashurst [1999] B.P.I.R. 662	IA 323
Cohen v Motchell (1980) 25 QBD 262	IA 307(4)
Cohen v Selby; sub nom. Simmon Box (Diamonds) Ltd, Re [2002] B.C.C. 82; [2001] 1 B.C.L.C. 176, CA	IA 213(3)
Cohen v TSB Bank Plc; sub nom. Cohen v Smith & Williamson [2002] 2 B.C.L.C. 32; [2002] B.P.I.R. 243	IA Pt III
Colgate, Re [1986] Ch.439	IA 363(1)
Colt Telecom Group Plc, Re (No.1). See Highberry Ltd v Colt Telecom Group Plc (No.1)	
Commercial Bank of South Australia, Re (1886) L.R. 33 Ch. D. 174	IA 221
Compania Merabello San Nicholas SA, Re [1973] Ch. 75; [1972] 3 W.L.R. 471; [1972] 3 All E.R. 448	IA 220, 225

Case Table

Case	Provision
Company A, Re [1985] B.C.L.C. 37	IA 123(1)
Company A, Re (No.00996 of 1979) [1980] Ch 138	IA 206(3)
Company A, Re (No.002567 of 1982) [1983] 1 W.L.R. 927	IA 125(2)
Company A, Re (No.003160 of 1986) (1986) 2 B.C.C. 99, 276	IA 124(1)
Company A, Re (No.003843 of 1986) (1987) 3 B.C.C. 624	IA 125(2)
Company A, Re (No.007523 of 1986) (1987) 3 B.C.C. 57	IA 127
Company A, Re (No.00175 of 1987) (1987) 3 B.C.C. 124	IA 9(3),(4),(5), IR 2.4–2.8, 2.10, 12.9
Company A, Re (No.00359 of 1987); sub nom. International Westminster Bank v Okeanos Maritime Corp [1988] Ch.210; 1987] 3 W.L.R. 339; (1987) 3 B.C.C. 160	IA 220, 221(5)
Company A, Re (No.00370 of 1987 [1988] 1 W.L.R. 1068; (1988) 4 B.C.C. 506	IA 122(1)
Company A, Re (No.003028 of 1987) (1987) 3 B.C.C. 575	IA 123, 124(1), 125(2)
Company A, Re (No.003318 of 1987) (Oriental Credit Ltd) [1988] Ch.204; (1987) 3 B.C.C. 564	IA 236
Company A, Re (No.005009 of 1987) (1988) 4 B.C.C. 424	IA 214(1), 240, 245(3)–(5), 249, 251
Company A, Re (No.001363 of 1988) (1989) 5 B.C.C. 18	IA 125(1)
Company A, Re (No.001992 of 1988), Re (1988) 4 B.C.C. 451; [1989] B.C.L.C. 9	IA 10(2)
Company A, Re (No.004502 of 1988) Ex p Johnson [1991] B.C.C. 234	IA 122(1)
Company A, Re (No.005685 of 1988) (1989) 5 B.C.C.79	IA 127
Company A, Re (No.007130 of 1988) [2000] 1 B.C.L.C. 582	IA 127
Company A, Re (No.001448 of 1989) (1989) 5 B.C.C. 706; [1989] B.C.L.C. 715	IA 10(1), IR 4.7–4.14
Company A, Re (No.008790 of 1990) [1992] B.C.C. 11	IA 123, 123(1)
Company A, Re (No. 0010656 of 1990) [1991] B.C.L.C. 330	IA 123
Company A, Re (No.00330 of 1991) Ex p. Holden [1991] B.C.C. 241	IA 125(2)
Company A, Re (No.00687 of 1991) [1991] B.C.C. 210	IR 4.22–4.24
Company A, Re (No.001946 of 1991) Ex p Fin Soft Holding SA [1991] B.C.L.C. 737	IA 123
Company A, Re (No.003102 of 1991) Ex p. Nyckeln Finance Co Ltd [1991] B.C.L.C. 539	IA 220
Company A, Re (No.0012209 of 1991) [1991] 1 W.L.R. 351	IA 123
Company A, Re (No. 006341 of 1992) ex p B Ltd [1994] 1 B.C.L.C. 225	IA 114(4)
Company A, Re (No.005374 of 1993) [1993] B.C.C. 734	IA 236
Company A, Re (No.004539 of 1993) [1995] B.C.C.116	IR 4.50–4.71
Company A, Re (No.002081 of 1994), Re Company A (No.002082 of 1994) [1994] B.C.C. 933	IA Pt IV
Company A, Re (No.007816 of 1994) [1997] 2 B.C.L.C. 685	IA 124A
Company A, Re (No.007923 of 1994, Re A Company (No.007924 of 1994) [1995] B.C.C. 634	IA 124A, IR 4.7–4.14
Company A, Re (No.007936 of 1994) [1995] B.C.C. 705	IA 124(2),(3)
Company A, Re (No.004415 of 1996) [1997] 1 B.C.L.C. 479	IA 125(2)
Company A, Re (No.006685 of 1996) [1997] B.C.C. 830	IA 123
Company A, Re (No.007020 of 1996) [1998] 2 B.C.L.C. 54	IR 4.22–4.24
Company A, Re (No.00514 of 1999) [2000] B.C.C. 698	IR 2.1–2.3
Company A, Re (No.005174 of 1999), Re [2000] 1 W.L.R. 502; [2000] B.C.C. 698	IA 19(3)–(6), 19(5)–(10)

Case Table

	Provision		Provision
Company A, Re (No. 2634 of 2002) [2002] EWHC 944; [2002] 2 B.C.L.C. 591	IA 123	Cosslett (Contractors) Ltd, Re; sub nom. Clark (Administrator of Cosslett (Contractors) Ltd) v Mid Glamorgan CC [1998] Ch. 495; [1998] 2 W.L.R. 131; [1997] B.C.C. 724	IA 234(1), (2)
Coney, Re [1998] B.P.I.R. 333	IA 272(1), 282(1),(3)		
Consolidated Goldfields of New Zealand, Re [1953] Ch. 689; [1953] 2 W.L.R. 584	IA 74(1)	Cosslett (Contractors) Ltd (In Administration) (No.2), Re. See Smith (Administrator of Cosslett (Contractors) Ltd) v Bridgend CBC	
Constellation, The; sub nom. Master and Crew of MV Constellation, Regency and Surveyor v Owners of MV Constellation, Regency, Surveyor and Vigia [1966] 1 W.L.R. 272; [1965] 3 All E.R. 873	IA 128	County Bookshops Ltd v Grove [2002] EWHC 1160; [2003] 1 B.C.L.C. 479; [2002] B.P.I.R. 772	IA 7(3)
Consumer and Industrial Press (No.1), Re (1988) 4 B.C.C. 68; [1988] B.C.L.C. 177	IA 8(1),(2)	Coutts & Co v Stock [2000] 1 W.L.R. 906; [2000] 2 All E.R. 56; [2000] B.C.C. 247	IA 127
Consumer & Industrial Press Ltd (No. 2), Re (1988) 4 B.C.C. 72	IA 15(5), 17(2), 18(2)	Cove (A Debtor), Re [1990] 1 W.L.R. 708; [1990] 1 All E.R. 949	IA 252(2)
Continental Assurance Co of London Plc, Re [2001] B.P.I.R. 733	IA 212(1), 214, 214(3), 214(4)	Cover Europe Ltd, Re; sub nom. Kvaerner Masa-Yards Inc v Barrett [2002] EWHC 861; [2002] 2 B.C.L.C. 61	ER Art.25, IR 7.1–7.18
Continental Assurance Co of London Plc (In Liquidation) (No.2), Re [1998] 1 B.C.L.C. 583	IR 7.55	Cozens v Customs and Excise Commissioners [2000] B.P.I.R. 252	IR 6.5
Cook, Re [1999] B.P.I.R. 881	IA 303(1)	Craig v Humberclyde Industrial Finance Group Ltd [1999] B.C.C. 378	IA Sch.4, para.6
Cooper v Fearnley; sub nom. Debtor (No.103 of 1994), Re [1997] B.P.I.R. 20	IA 255(1), (2)	Craiglaw Developments Ltd v Gordon Wilson & Co 1997 S.C. 356; 1998 S.L.T. 1046; [1998] B.C.C. 530	IA 243
Cooper v Official Receiver [2002] EWHC 1970; [2003] B.P.I.R. 55	IA 276(1)	Cranley Mansions, Re; sub nom. Saigol v Goldstein [1994] 1 W.L.R. 1610; [1994] B.C.C. 576	IA 6, 6A, IR 1.13–1.21
Copeland & Craddock Ltd, Re [1997] B.C.C. 294	IA 125(1)		
Corbenstoke (No.2), Re (1989) 5 B.C.C. 767; [1990] B.C.L.C. 60	IA 172(1), (2)	Creditnet Ltd Ex p [1996] 1 W.L.R. 1291; [1996] B.C.C. 444	IR 7.26–7.32
Cornhill Insurance v Cornhill Financial Services [1992] B.C.C. 818; [1993] B.C.L.C. 914	IA 18(2), 27(1), IR 7.47	Crigglestone Coal Co Ltd, Re [1906] 2 Ch. 327	IA 125(1)
Cornhill Insurance Plc v Improvement Services Ltd [1986] 1 W.L.R. 114; [1986] P.C.C. 204	IA 123(1)	Croftbell, Re [1990] B.C.C. 781; [1990] B.C.L.C. 844	IA 9(3), Pt III, 29(2), Sch.B1, para.14(2),(3)

Case Table

Case	Provision
Crossmore Electrical and Civil Engineering, Re (1989) 5 B.C.C. 37; [1989] B.C.L.C. 137	IA 127
Cullinane v Inland Revenue Commissioners [2000] B.P.I.R. 996	IA 268
Cumming's Trustee v Glenrinnes Farms [1993] B.C.C. 829; 1993 S.L.T. 904	IA 82(1),(2)
Cummings and Fuller v Claremont Petroleum [1998] B.P.I.R. 187	IA 306
Cupit, Re [1996] B.P.I.R. 560 (Note)	IA 253(1)–(3)
Cyona Distributors, Re [1967] Ch. 889; [1967] 2 W.L.R. 369	IA 213(2)

D

Case	Provision
D'Jan of London, Re; sub nom. Copp v D'Jan [1993] B.C.C. 646; [1994] 1 B.C.L.C. 561	IA 212(1), 213(3), 214(4)
DKG Contractors, Re [1990] B.C.C. 903	IA 212, 214, 214(4), 239(6), 240(2)
DPR Futures Ltd, Re [1989] 1 W.L.R. 778; (1989) 5 B.C.C. 603	IA 155(1)
Daisytek-ISA Ltd, Re	ER Art.3(1)
Dallhold Estates (UK), Re [1992] B.C.C. 394; [1992] B.C.L.C. 621	IA 8(1),(2), EA 254(1)
Dana (UK) Ltd, Re [1999] 2 B.C.L.C. 239	IA 24(1),(2), 25(1), Sch.B1, paras.53, 54, 68(2),(3)
Data Online Transactions (UK) Ltd, Re February 9, 2001	IA 125(2)
David Meek Plant Ltd, Re [1993] B.C.C. 175; [1994] 1 B.C.L.C. 680	IA 11(3)
Davies (Eileen) [1997] B.P.I.R. 619	IA 285(2)
Davis v Martin-Sklan. See Hussein (Essengin), Re	
Dawodu v American Express Bank [2001] B.P.I.R. 983	IR 6.25
Dear v Reeves [2001] EWCA Civ 277; [2001] B.P.I.R. 577	IA 436
Debtor (No.400 of 1940), Re; sub nom. Debtor v Dodwell [1949] Ch. 236; [1949] 1 All E.R. 510	IA 303(1)
Debtor (No.26A of 1975) [1985] 1 W.L.R. 6	IA 314(1),(2),(6)
Debtor (No.2A of 1980) [1981] Ch.148	IA 373(2)
Debtor (No.707 of 1985), The Times January 21, 1988	IA 282(1),(3)
Debtor (No.1 of 1987) [1989] 1 W.L.R. 271	IA Pt IX, 268, IR 6.5, 7.55
Debtor (No.11 of 1987), The Independent March 28, 1988	IR 6.5
Debtor (No.10 of 1988) [1989] 1 W.L.R. 405	IA 268, IR 6.5
Debtor (No.190 of 1987), The Times, May 21, 1988	IA 268, IR 6.5, 7.55
Debtor (No.83 of 1988) [1990] 1 W.L.R. 708	IA 252(2), 256(5), 257(1), 262(4)–(7)
Debtor (No.310 of 1988) [1989] 1 W.L.R. 452	IA 383(2)–(4), IR 6.1
Debtor (No.222 of 1990), A, Re Bank of Ireland (No.2), Ex p [1993] B.C.L.C. 233	IA 262, IR 4.50–4.71
Debtor (No.259 of 1990), Re [1992] 1 W.L.R. 226; [1992] 1 All E.R. 641	IA 262
Debtor (No.32 of 1991 (No.2)) [1994] B.C.C. 524	IR 6.5
Debtor (No.88 of 1991) [1993] Ch.286	IA 268
Debtor (No.234 and 236 of 1991), Re The Independent June 29, 1992	IR 6.3, 6.14
Debtor (No.51/SD/1991) [1992] 1 W.L.R. 1294	IR 6.111, IA 267(1),(2)
Debtor (No.490/SD/1991) [1992] 1 W.L.R. 271	IA 268
Debtor (No.657/SD/1991) [1993] B.C.L.C. 1280	IA 268, IR 6.5

Case Table

Case	Provision
Debtor (No.784 of 1991) [1992] Ch.554	IA 265
Debtor (No.10 of 1992), Re; sub nom. Peck v Craighead [1995] B.C.C. 525; [1995] 1 B.C.L.C. 337	IA 258(2)–(5)
Debtor (No 49 and 50 of 1992) [1995] Ch.66	IR 6.5
Debtor (No.64 of 1992)(Bradford & Bingley Building Society v A Debtor), Re [1994] 1 W.L.R. 264; [1994] B.C.C. 55	IA 260(1), (2),(2A), IR 12.16
Debtor (No.68 of 1992) [1993] T.L.R. 69	IA 282(1), (3)
Debtor (No.90 of 1992) [1993] T.L.R. 387	IR 6.5
Debtor (No.106 of 1992), *The Independent* April 20, 1992	IA 268, IR 6.1, 6.5
Debtor (No.340 of 1992) [1996] 2 All E.R. 211	IA 268, IR 7.55
Debtor (No.367 of 1992), Re; sub nom. Allen, Re [1998] B.P.I.R. 319	IA 264
Debtor (No.383/SD/1992), Re; sub nom. Neely v Inland Revenue Commissioners [1996] B.P.I.R. 473; 66 T.C. 131	IR 6.5
Debtor (No.960/SD/1992) [1993] S.T.C. 218	IR 6.5
Debtor (No.415/SD/1993) [1994] 1 W.L.R. 917	IR 6.5
Debtor (No.22 of 1993), Re (Focus Insurance v A Debtor) [1994] 1 W.L.R. 46; [1994] 2 All E.R. 105	IA 267(1), (2), IR 7.55
Debtor (No.32 of 1993), Re [1994] 1 W.L.R. 899; [1994] B.C.C. 438	IA 271(3)
Debtor (No.87 of 1993)(No.1), Re [1996] B.C.C. 74	IA 262
Debtor (No.87 of 1993)(No.2), Re [1996] B.C.C. 80	IA 262(1)–(3),(8)
Debtor (No.638 IO of 1994), Re, *The Times*, December 3, 1998	IA 263(4)
Debtor (No.13AIO and 14AIO of 1994) [1995] 1 W.L.R. 1127; [1996] B.C.C. 25	IA 252(2)
Debtor (No.50A-SD–1995), Re; sub nom. Jelly v All Type Roofing Co [1997] Ch. 310; [1997] 2 W.L.R. 57; [1997] B.C.C. 465	IA 267(1), (2)
Debtor (No.140 IO of 1995), Re; sub nom. Greystoke v Hamilton-Smith[1996] 2 B.C.L.C. 429; [1997] B.P.I.R. 24	IA 2(2), 256(1), IA 2000 2
Debtor (No.574 of 1995), Re; sub nom. National Westminster Bank Plc v Scher [1998] 2 B.C.L.C. 124; [1998] B.P.I.R. 224	IA 262
Debtor (No.488–IO of 1996), Re; sub nom. M (A Debtor), Re; J (A Debtor), Re; JP v Debtor [1999] 2 B.C.L.C. 571; [1999] 1 F.L.R. 926; [1999] 2 F.C.R. 637; [1999] Fam. Law 293	IA 260(1), (2),(2A)
Debtor (No.90 of 1997), *The Times*, July 1, 1998	IR 6.5
Debtor (No.169 of 1997), unreported, 1998	IA 282(1), (3)
Debtor (No.68–SD–1997), Re; sub nom. Galloppa v Galloppa [1998] 4 All E.R. 779; [1999] B.P.I.R. 352	IA 267(1), (2)
Debtor (No.510 of 1997), The Times June 18,1998	IR 6.8
Debtor (No.620 of 1997), *The Times* June 18, 1998	IR 6.5
Debtor (No.544/SD/98) [2001] 1 B.C.L.C. 103	IA 123(1), IR 6.5
Debtor (No.87 of 1999), Re [2000] B.P.I.R. 589	IR 6.5
Debtor (No.101 of 1999) (No.1), Re [2001] 1 B.C.L.C. 54; [2000] B.P.I.R. 998	IA 262
Debtor (No.101 of 1999) (No.2), Re [2001] B.P.I.R. 996	IA 262(4)–(7)
Debtor (No.35 of 2000), Re [2002] B.P.I.R. 75	IR 6.5

	Provision		Provision
Debtor v Dodwell. *See* Debtor (No.400 of 1940), Re		Dollar Land Holdings Plc, Re [1993] B.C.C. 823; [1994] 1 B.C.L.C. 404	IA 124(1)
Debtor v Focus Insurance (In Liquidation); sub nom. Debtor (No.22 of 1993), Re [1994] 1 W.L.R. 46; [1994] 2 All E.R. 105	IA 270	Dollar Land (Feltham) Ltd, Re [1995] B.C.C. 740; [1995] 2 B.C.L.C. 370	IR 4.16–4.21A, 7.47
Debtor A. Re [1949] Ch.236	IA 168(5)	Doorbar v Alltime Securities Ltd (Nos.1 and 2) [1996] 1 W.L.R. 456; [1996] 2 All E.R. 948; [1995] B.C.C. 1149	IA 1, 262, 262(1)–(3),(8), IR 1.13–1.21
Delfin International (SA) Ltd (No.2), Re. *See* Secretary of State for Trade and Industry v Delfin International (SA) Ltd			
Deloitte & Touche AG v Johnson [1999] 1 W.L.R. 1605; [1999] B.C.C. 992	IA 108	Dora v Simper [2000] 2 B.C.L.C. 561	IA 424
		Doreen Boards Ltd, Re [1996] 1 B.C.L.C. 501	IR 4.22–4.24
Demaglass Holdings Ltd (Winding Up Petition: Application for Adjournment), Re [2001] 2 B.C.L.C. 633	IA 125(1)	Downsview Nominees Ltd v First City Corp Ltd; sub nom. First City Corp Ltd v Downsview Nominees Ltd [1993] A.C. 295; [1993] 2 W.L.R. 86; [1993] B.C.C. 46	IA Pt III, 212(2)
Demite Ltd v Protec Health Ltd [1998] B.C.C. 638	IA 42(1)		
Dennis (A Bankrupt), Re; sub nom. Dennis v Goodman [1996] Ch. 80; [1995] 3 W.L.R. 367	IA 251	Doyle v Saville and Hardwick [2002] B.P.I.R. 947	IA 339(1)–(3)
		Drew v Lord Advocate, 1996 S.L.T. 1062	IA 206(3)
Denny v Yeldon [1995] 3 All E.R. 624; [1995] 1 B.C.L.C. 560	IA 14(1)	Dubai Bank Ltd v Galadari (1989) 5 B.C.C. 722	IA 236
Densham, Re [1975] 1 W.L.R. 1519	IA 336(3)–(5)	Duke Group Ltd v Carver [2001] B.P.I.R. 459	IA 426(4),(5),(11)
Dent (A Bankrupt), Re; [1994] 1 W.L.R. 956; [1994] 2 All E.R. 904	IA 251	Dyer v Hyslop 1994 S.C.L.R. 171	IA 242(1)
		Dynamics Corporation of America (No.2), Re [1976] 1 W.L.R. 757	IR 6.111
Dewrun Ltd, Re. *See* Royal Bank of Scotland Plc v Bhardwaj			
		E	
Devon and Somerset Farmers, Re [1994] Ch. 57; [1993] 3 W.L.R. 866	IA 29(2), 40(1),(2)	EISC Teo, Re [1991] I.L.R.M. 760	IA 40(1),(2)
		ELS Ltd, Re [1994] B.C.C. 449	IA 44(1),(2)
Dianoor Jewels Ltd (Set Aside), Re [2001] 1 B.C.L.C. 450; [2001] B.P.I.R. 234	IA 8(1),(2)	Eastern Capital Futures (In Liquidation), Re [1989] B.C.L.C. 371	IA 115
Diesels & Components Pty Ltd, Re (1985) 2 A.C.L.C. 555	IA 19(5)–(10)	Eberhardt & Co Ltd v Mair [1995] 1 W.L.R. 1180; [1995] 3 All E.R. 963; [1995] B.C.C. 845	IA 268, IR 6.25
Digginwell Plant & Construction Ltd, Re [2002] B.P.I.R. 299	IR 2.1–2.3	Ebrahimi v Westbourne Galleries Ltd; sub nom. Westbourne Galleries, Re [1973] A.C. 360; [1972] 2 W.L.R. 1289	IA 122(1)

Case Table

Case	Provision
Edennote Ltd (No.2), Re; sub nom. Ryman v Tottenham Hotspur [1997] 2 B.C.L.C. 89	IA 167(1), 168(5)
Eloc Electro-Optieck and Communicatie BV, Re [1982] Ch. 43; [1981] 3 W.L.R. 176; [1981] 2 All E.R. 1111	IA 220
Embassy Art Products, Re; sub nom. Collinson, Sherratt and Robinson v Parry, Parry and Brodie [1988] B.C.L.C. 1; [1987] P.C.C. 389; (1987) 3 B.C.C. 292	IA 236
Emmadart Ltd, Re [1979] Ch. 540; [1979] 2 W.L.R. 868	IA 124, 124(1), Sch.1
Empire Paper Ltd (In Liquidation), Re [1999] B.C.C. 406	IA 189
Empire Resolution Ltd v MPW Insurance Brokers Ltd [1999] B.P.I.R. 486	IA Sch.4, para.6
Engel v Peri; sub nom. Peri v Engel [2002] EWHC 799; [2002] B.P.I.R. 961	IA 282(1), (3), 303(1), 363(1)
England v Smith (Re Southern Equities Corp) [2001] Ch.419; [2000] B.P.I.R. 28	IA 426(4), (5),(11)
Environment Agency v Clark. *See* Rhondda Waste Disposal Ltd (In Administration), Re; sub nom. Clark v Environment Agency; Environment Agency v Clark	
Environment Agency v Stout [1998] B.P.I.R. 576	IA 306
Envis v Thakkar [1997] B.P.I.R. 189	IA Pt VIII
Equiticorp International Plc, Re [1989] 1 W.L.R. 1010; (1989) 5 B.C.C. 599	IA 9(1), 124(1)
Equity & Provident Ltd, Re; sub nom.Insolvency Act 1986, Re [2002] EWHC 186; [2002] 2 B.C.L.C. 78	IA 124A
Equity Nominees Ltd, Re [2000] B.C.C. 84; [1999] 2 B.C.L.C. 19	IA 172(1), (2), IR 4.108–4.112, 6.126
Etic Ltd, Re [1928] Ch. 861	IA 212(1)
Euro Commercial Leasing Ltd v Cartwright & Lewis [1995] B.C.C. 830; [1995] 2 B.C.L.C. 618	IA 11(3), 234(1),(2)
Ewart v Fryer. *See* Fryer v Ewart	
Excalibur Airways Ltd (In Liquidation), Re [1998] 1 B.C.L.C. 436; [1998] B.P.I.R. 598	IA 7(4)
Exchange Securities & Commodities Ltd, Re [1983] B.C.L.C. 186	IA 130(1)
Exchange Travel (Holdings) Ltd (No.1), Re [1991] B.C.L.C. 728	IA 248
Exchange Travel (Holdings) Ltd (No.2), Re [1992] B.C.C. 954; [1993] B.C.L.C. 887	IA 20(1), 140(1),(2)
Exchange Travel (Holdings) Ltd (No.4), Re; sub nom. Katz v McNally (Recovery of Preferences) [1999] B.C.C. 291	IA 239(6), Sch.4, para.6

F

Case	Provision
F v F [1994] 1 F.L.R. 359	IA 282(1), (3)
FMS Financial Management Services Ltd, Re (1989) 5 B.C.C. 191	IA 1(1), 7(4)
FSA Business Software Ltd, Re [1990] B.C.C. 465; [1990] B.C.L.C. 825	IA 123
Fairway Graphics, Re [1991] B.C.L.C. 468	IA 127
Fairway Magazines, Re [1992] B.C.C. 924; [1993] B.C.L.C. 643	IA 239(6), 245(2)
Falcon RJ Developments Ltd, Re (1987) 3 B.C.C. 146; [1987] B.C.L.C. 437	IA 124(5), 195

Case Table

Case	Provision
Farmer v Moseley (Holdings) Ltd [2001] 2 B.C.L.C. 572	IA Sch.4, para.6
Farmizer (Products) Ltd, Re; sub nom. Moore v Gadd [1997] B.C.C. 655; [1997] 1 B.C.L.C. 589	IA 214
Farnborough Aircraft.com Ltd, Re [2002] EWHC 1224; [2002] 2 B.C.L.C. 641	IR 2.9
Felixstowe Dock & Railway Co v United States Lines Inc [1989] Q.B. 360; [1989] 2 W.L.R. 109	IA 8(1),(2), EA 254(1)
First Express, Re [1991] B.C.C. 782	IA Pt III, 234(1),(2)
Fisher v Raven [1964] A.C. 210	IA 360(2)
Fitch v Official Receiver [1996] 1 W.L.R. 242; [1996] B.C.C. 328	IA 375(1)
Flack, Re [1900] 2 Q.B. 32	IA 372
Fletcher v Vooght [2000] B.P.I.R. 435; (2000) 97(12) L.S.G. 39	IA 252(1), 256A
Flightline Ltd v Edwards; sub nom. Swissair Schweizerische Luftverkehr AG, Re; Edwards v Flightline Ltd [2003] EWCA Civ 63; [2003] 1 W.L.R. 1200; [2003] B.C.C. 361	IA 130(1)
Flint, Re [1993] Ch.319	IA 284(1)–(3), (6)
Floor Fourteen Ltd, Re. *See* Lewis v Inland Revenue Commissioners	
Focus Insurance Co Ltd, Re [1996] B.C.C. 659	IA 426(4), (5),(11)
Forcesun Ltd, Re [2002] EWHC 443; [2002] 2 B.C.L.C. 302	IA 124A
Ford AG-Werke AG v Transtec Automotive (Campsie) Ltd; sub nom. TransTec Automotive (Campsie) Ltd, Re [2001] B.C.C. 403	IA 37(1),(2)
Forrester & Lamego Ltd, Re [1997] 2 B.C.L.C. 155	IA 124A
Forte (Charles) Investments v Amanda [1964] Ch. 240; [1963] 3 W.L.R. 662	IA 122(1)
Forte's (Manufacturing), Re. *See* Stanhope Pension Trust Ltd v Registrar of Companies	
Foster v Wilson (1843) 12 M.&W. 191	IA 323
Foxley v UK [2000] B.P.I.R. 1009	IA 371(1)
Freevale Ltd v Metrostore (Holdings) Ltd [1984] Ch. 199; [1984] 2 W.L.R. 496	IA 37(1),(2)
French's (Wine Bar), Re [1987] B.C.L.C. 499	IA 127
Frost v Unity Trust Bank Plc (No.1) [1998] B.P.I.R. 459	IA 252(2)
Fryer v Ewart; sub nom. Ewart v Fryer [1902] A.C. 187 affirming [1901] 1 Ch. 499	IA 130(1)
Fuller v Cyracuse Ltd; sub nom. Cyracuse Ltd, Re [2001] B.C.C. 806; [2001] 1 B.C.L.C. 187	IA 125(2)

G

Case	Provision
G&M Aldridge Pty Ltd v Walsh [2002] B.P.I.R. 482	IA 340(3)
Galileo Group Ltd, Re; sub nom. Company (No.003025 of 1997), Re; Elles v Hambros Bank Ltd [1999] Ch. 100; [1998] 2 W.L.R. 364; [1998] B.C.C. 228	IA 236
Gallard, Re [1896] 1 Q.B. 68	IR 6.165
Gallidoro Trawlers, Re [1991] B.C.C. 691; [1991] B.C.L.C. 411	IA 9(1),(4), (5)
Galloppa v Galloppa. *See* Debtor (No.68–SD–1997), Re	
Garrow v Society of Lloyd's [2000] C.L.C. 241; [1999] B.P.I.R. 885	IR 6.5
Gerald Cooper Chemicals Ltd, Re [1978] Ch. 262; [1978] 2 W.L.R. 866	IA 213(2)
German Date Coffee Co, Re (1881–82) L.R. 20 Ch. D. 169	IA 122(1)
Gerrard (Thomas) & Son, Re [1968] Ch. 455; [1967] 3 W.L.R. 84	IA 206(3)
Geveran Trading Co Ltd v Skjevesland (No.3). *See* Skjevesland v Geveran Trading Co Ltd (No.3)	
Gilmartin (a bankrupt), Re [1989] 1 W.L.R. 513	IA 271(3), IR 7.48
Glen Express Ltd, Re [2000] B.P.I.R. 456	IR 4.90

Case Table

Case	Provision
Glenister v Rowe (Costs); sub nom. Rowe v Rowe [2000] Ch. 76; [1999] 3 W.L.R. 716; [1999] B.P.I.R. 674	IA 382(3), (4)
Global Finance Recoveries Ltd v Jones [2000] B.P.I.R. 1029	IA 267(1), (2)
Globe Legal Services Ltd, Re; [2002] B.C.C. 858	IR 4.73–4.85
Glossop v Glossop [1907] 2 Ch. 370	IA 19(1)
Gold Co, Re (1879) 12 Ch.D.77	IA 236
Goldspan Ltd, Re [2003] B.P.I.R. 93	IA 260(1), (2),(2A)
Goldthorpe & Lacey, Re (1987) 3 B.C.C. 595	IR 4.16–4.21A
Gomba Holdings (UK) Ltd v Homan; Gomba Holdings (UK) Ltd v Johnson Matthey Bankers Ltd [1986] 1 W.L.R. 1301; [1986] 3 All E.R. 94; (1986) 2 B.C.C. 99,102	IA 48(5),(6)
Goodwill Merchant Financial Services Ltd, Re; sub nom. Financial Services Authority v Goodwill Merchant Financial Ltd [2001] 1 B.C.L.C. 259	IA 135
Gordon & Breach Science Publishers Ltd, Re [1995] B.C.C. 261; [1995] 2 B.C.L.C. 189	IA 124(5)
Gorman (a Bankrupt), Re [1990] 1 All E.R. 717	IA 336(3)–(5)
Gosling v Gaskell; sub nom. Gaskell v Gosling [1897] A.C. 575	IA 44(1),(2)
Gosscott (Groundworks), Re (1988) 4 B.C.C. 372; [1988] B.C.L.C. 363	IA 9(4),(5), IR 4.218–4.220
Gourlay's Trustee v Gourlay 1995 S.L.T. (Sh Ct) 7	IA 336(3)–(5)
Government of India, Ministry of Finance (Revenue Division) v Taylor [1955] A.C. 491	IR 12.3
Grady v HM Prison Service [2003] EWCA Civ 527; [2003] 3 All E.R. 745	IA 306
Gray's Inn Construction Co Ltd, Re [1980] 1 W.L.R. 711; [1980] 1 All E.R. 814	IA 127
Great Yarmouth BC v Alterman, unreported, January 28, 1998	IA 262(1)–(3),(8)
Green v Satsangi [1998] 1 B.C.L.C. 458; [1998] B.P.I.R. 55	IA 304(1)
Greene King Plc v Stanley [2001] EWCA Civ 1966; [2002] B.P.I.R. 491	IA 260(1),(2),(2A)
Greenacre Publishing Ltd, Re; sub nom. Greenacre Publishing Group v Manson Group [2000] B.C.C. 11	IA 123
Greenhaven Motors Ltd, Re [1999] B.C.C. 463; [1999] 1 B.C.L.C. 635	IA 167(1),(3), 168(5)
Grey Marlin Ltd, Re [2000] 1 W.L.R. 370; [1999] 4 All E.R. 429; [2000] B.C.C. 410	IR 4.25–4.31
Greystoke v Hamilton-Smith. See Debtor (No.140 IO of 1995), Re	
Griffin Hotel Co Ltd, Re [1941] Ch. 129; [1940] 4 All E.R. 324	IA 175(2)(b)
Griffin Trading Co, Re [2000] B.P.I.R. 256	IR 4.90
Griffiths v Civil Aviation Authority [1997] B.P.I.R. 50	IA 306
Griffiths v Yorkshire Bank Plc [1994] 1 W.L.R. 1427; (1994) 91(36) L.S.G. 36	IA 40(1),(2)
Grovewood Holdings plc v James Capel & Co Ltd [1995] Ch.80; [1995] B.C.C. 760	IA Sch.4, para.6
Guidezone Ltd, Re; sub nom. Kaneria v Patel [2001] B.C.C. 692; [2000] 2 B.C.L.C. 321	IA 122(1)
Gunningham, Re [2002] B.P.I.R. 302	IR 7.10

H

Case	Provision
H&K (Medway) Ltd, Re; sub nom. Mackay v Inland Revenue Commissioners [1997] 1 W.L.R. 1422; [1997] 2 All E.R. 321; [1997] B.C.C. 853	IA 40(1),(2)

Case Table

	Provision		Provision
HJ Tomkins, Re [1990] B.C.L.C. 76	IA 125(1)	Harris Simons Construction Ltd, Re [1989] 1 W.L.R. 368; (1989) 5 B.C.C. 11	IA 8(1),(2), 43(1),(2),Sch.B1, para.11, Sch.B1, para.39
HL Bolton Engineering Co Ltd, Re [1956] Ch. 577; [1956] 2 W.L.R. 844	IA 82(1),(2)		
Hackney LBC v Crown Estates Commissioners [1996] B.P.I.R. 428	IA 320(1)–(4)	Harrods (Buenos Aires) Ltd (No.2), Re [1992] Ch. 72; [1991] 3 W.L.R. 397; [1991] B.C.C. 249	IA 122(1), 125(1), 221
Hadjipanayi v Yeldon [2001] B.P.I.R. 487; [2000] E.G.C.S. 122	IA Pt III	Hawk Insurance Co Ltd, Re [2001] B.C.C. 57	IA Sch.4
Haig v Aitken [2001] Ch. 110; [2000] 3 W.L.R. 1117; [2000] B.P.I.R. 462	IA 311(1)	Hawking v Hafton House Ltd, 1990 S.C. 198; 1990 S.L.T. 496	IA 51(1), (2), 55(1),(2)
Halson Packaging Ltd, Re [1997] B.C.C. 993; [1997] B.P.I.R. 194	IA 7(4)	Hayward, Re [1997] Ch.45	IA 314(8), ER
Halt Garage (1964) Ltd, Re [1982] 3 All E.R. 1016	IA 238(5)	Headington Investments Ltd ex p Maxwell [1993] B.C.C. 500	IA 236
Hamblin v Field [2000] B.P.I.R. 621	IA 339(1)–(3)	Healing Research Trustee Co, Re [1992] 2 All E.R. 481; [1991] B.C.L.C. 716	IA 124(1)
Hamilton v Naviede. *See* Arrows Ltd (No.4)		Heath v Tang [1993] 1 W.L.R. 1421; [1993] 4 All E.R. 694	IA 303(1), 306
Hamilton v Naviede. *See* Arrows Ltd (No.5)		Henwood v Customs and Excise [1998] B.P.I.R. 339	IA 282(1), (3)
Hamilton v Official Receiver [1998] B.P.I.R. 602	IA 168(5)	Heritage Joinery v Krasner [1999] B.P.I.R. 683; [1999] Lloyd's Rep. P.N. 825	IA 263(1), (2)
Hans Place Ltd, Re [1992] B.C.C. 737; [1993] B.C.L.C. 768	IA 168(5), 178(2)		
Hardy v Buchler [1997] B.P.I.R. 643	IA 363(2), (4)	Hewitt Brannan (Tools), Re [1990] B.C.C. 354; [1991] B.C.L.C. 80	IA 124(5)
Hardy v Focus Insurance Co Ltd (In Liquidation) [1997] B.P.I.R. 77	IA 279(3)–(5), 303(1)	Hibernian Merchants, Re [1958] Ch. 76; [1957] 3 W.L.R. 486, Ch D	IA 221
Harmony Carpets v Chaffin-Laird [2000] B.C.C. 893; [2000] B.P.I.R. 61	IA 263(1), (2)	High Street Services Ltd v Bank of Credit & Commerce International SA [1993] B.C.C. 360	IR 4.90
Harper v O'Reilly [1997] B.P.I.R. 656	IA 284(1)–(3),(6)	Highberry Ltd v Colt Telecom Group Plc (No.1); sub nom. Colt Telecom Group Plc, Re (No.1) [2002] EWHC 2503; [2003] 1 B.C.L.C. 290	IA Sch.B1, para.11, IR 7.51, 7.60
Harrington v Bennett [2000] B.P.I.R. 630	IA 335A		
Harris v Gross [2001] B.P.I.R. 586	IA 276(1)	Hill v East and West India Dock Co; sub nom. East and West India Dock Co v Hill (1883–84) L.R. 9 App. Cas. 448	IA 181(1)–(3)
Harris Bus Co Ltd, Re [2000] B.C.C. 1151	IA 17(2)		

Case Table

Case	Provision
Hill Samuel & Co Ltd v Laing [1991] B.C.C. 665	IA 57(2),(4),(5)
Hillingdon LBC v Cutler; sub nom. Hillingdon Corp v Cutler [1968] 1 Q.B. 124; [1967] 3 W.L.R. 246	IA 9(2)
Hills v Alex Lawrie Factors [2001] B.P.I.R. 1038	IA 344(1),(2)
Hindcastle Ltd v Barbara Attenborough Associates Ltd [1997] A.C. 70; [1996] 2 W.L.R. 262; [1996] B.C.C. 636	IA 181(1)–(3), 315
Hitco 2000 Ltd, Re; sub nom. Official Receiver v Cowan [1995] B.C.C. 161; [1995] 2 B.C.L.C. 63	IR 7.49
Hoare, Re [1997] B.P.I.R. 683	IA 260(1),(2),(2A)
Hoare v Inland Revenue Commissioners [2002] EWHC 775; [2002] B.P.I.R. 986	IA 282(1),(3)
Hofer v Strawson [1999] 2 B.C.L.C. 336; [1999] B.P.I.R. 501	IR 6.5
Holdenhurst Securities Plc v Cohen [2001] 1 B.C.L.C. 460	IA 7(3)
Holliday, Re [1981] Ch. 405	IA 336(3)–(5)
Holmes v Official Receiver [1996] B.C.C. 246; [1996] B.P.I.R. 279	IA 279(3)–(5)
Home Remedies Ltd, Re [1943] Ch. 1	IA 116
Home Treat, Re [1991] B.C.C. 165; [1991] B.C.L.C. 705	IA 14(1), 206(3)
Hook v Jewson Ltd [1997] B.C.C. 752; [1997] 1 B.C.L.C. 664	IA 255(1),(2)
Hope v Premierpace (Europe) Ltd [1999] B.P.I.R. 695	IA 267(1),(2), 282(1),(3)
Horne (A Bankrupt), Re; sub nom. Dacorum BC v Horne; Horne v Dacorum BC [2000] 4 All E.R. 550; [2000] B.P.I.R. 1047	IR 6.1
Horrocks v Broome; sub nom. Broome (A Debtor), Re; Thompson v Broome [2000] B.C.C. 257; [1999] 1 B.C.L.C. 356; [1999] B.P.I.R. 66	IA 263(4)
Hough, Re (1990) 6 I.L.&P. 17	IA 420(1)
Household Mortgage Corp Plc v Whitehead; sub nom. Whitehead v Household Mortgage Corp Plc [2002] EWCA Civ 1657; [2003] 1 W.L.R. 1173	IA 260(1),(2),(2A)
Howard Holdings Inc, Re; sub nom. Coles v Thompson [1998] B.C.C. 549	IA 214
Hughes v Hannover Ruckversicherungs AG [1997] B.C.C. 921; [1997] 1 B.C.L.C. 497	IA 426(4),(5),(10),(11),(12)
Hunt v Peasegood [2001] B.P.I.R. 76	IA 282(1),(3), 306
Hunt's Trustee v Hunt [1995] S.C.L.R. 969	IA 336(3)–(5)
Hurren (a Bankrupt), Re [1983] 1 W.L.R. 183	IA 322(1)
Hurst v Bennett (No.1); sub nom. Debtor (No.303 of 1997), Re [2001] EWCA Civ 182; [2001] 2 B.C.L.C. 290; [2001] B.P.I.R. 287	IR 6.5
Hurst v Bennett (No.2) [2001] EWCA Civ 1398; [2002] B.P.I.R. 102	IA 255(1),(2), 375(1)
Hussein (Essengin), Re; sub nom. Davis v Martin-Sklan [1995] B.C.C. 1122; [1995] 2 B.C.L.C. 483	IA 263(5),(6)
Hydrodan (Corby) Ltd (In Liquidation), Re; sub nom. Hydrodam (Corby) Ltd (In Liquidation), Re [1994] B.C.C. 161; [1994] 2 B.C.L.C. 180	IA 214(1), 251

Case Table

I

	Provision
ILG Travel Ltd (In Administration), Re [1996] B.C.C. 21; [1995] 2 B.C.L.C. 128	IR 4.90
ITM Corp Ltd (In Liquidation), Re; sub nom. Stirling Estates v Pickard UK Ltd; Sterling Estates v Pickard UK Ltd [1997] B.C.C. 554; [1997] 2 B.C.L.C. 389	IA 179, 182
Imperial Land Co of Marseilles, Re; sub nom. National Bank, Re (1870) L.R. 10 Eq. 298	IA 206(3)
Imperial Motors (UK), Re [1990] B.C.L.C. 29; (1989) 5 B.C.C. 214	IA 8(1),(2)
Independent Insurance Co Ltd (In Provisional Liquidation), Re (No.1) [2002] EWHC 1577; [2002] 2 B.C.L.C. 709	IR 4.25–4.31
Independent Pension Trustee Ltd v LAW Construction Co Ltd, 1997 S.L.T. 1105; *The Times*, November 1, 1996	IA Pt III
Industrial & Commercial Securities plc (1989) 5 B.C.C. 320	IR 7.47
Industrial Diseases Compensation Ltd v Marrons [2001] B.P.I.R. 600	IA 346(1),(5)
Ing Lease (UK) Ltd v Griswold [1998] B.C.C. 905	IA 263(3)
Inland Revenue Commissioners v Adam & Partners Ltd; sub nom. Adam & Partners Ltd, Re [2002] B.C.C. 247; [2001] 1 B.C.L.C. 222; [2000] B.P.I.R. 986	IA 1(1)
Inland Revenue Commissioners v Cardona [1997] B.C.C. 697; [1997] B.P.I.R. 604	IR 8.1–8.16
Inland Revenue Commissioners v Conbeer; sub nom. Debtor (No.2021 of 1995), Re; Debtor (No.2022 of 1995), Re [1996] 2 All E.R. 345; [1996] B.C.C. 189	IR 8.1–8.6
Inland Revenue Commissioners v Debtor [1995] B.C.C. 971	IA 271(3)
Inland Revenue Commissioners v Duce [1999] B.P.I.R. 189	IA 262(1)–(3),(8), 262(4)–(7)
Inland Revenue Commissioners v Goldblatt [1972] Ch. 498; [1972] 2 W.L.R. 953	IA 40(1),(2)
Inland Revenue Commissioners v Lawrence; sub nom. FJL Realisations Ltd, Re [2001] B.C.C. 663; [2001] 1 B.C.L.C. 204	IA 19(5)–(10)
Inland Revenue Commissioners v Robinson [1999] B.P.I.R. 329	IA 282(1),(3)
Inquiry into Mirror Group Newspapers plc [2000] B.C.C. 217	IA 236
Inside Sport Ltd (In Liquidation), Re; sub nom. Inside Sports Ltd, Re [2000] B.C.C. 40; [2000] 1 B.C.L.C. 302	IA 171
Instrumentation Electrical Services Ltd, Re (1988) 4 B.C.C. 99,544	IA 9(1), 124(1)
International Bulk Commodities Ltd, Re [1993] Ch. 77; [1992] 3 W.L.R. 238; [1992] B.C.C. 463	IA 29(2), 251
International Tin Council, Re [1989] Ch. 309; [1988] 3 W.L.R. 1159; (1988) 4 B.C.C. 653	IA 117, 220(1)
Iona Hotels Ltd (In Receivership), Petitioners; sub nom. Iona Hotels Ltd v Craig 1990 S.C. 330; 1991 S.L.T. 11	IA 55(3),(4)
Islington Metal and Plating Works, Re [1984] 1 W.L.R. 14; [1983] 3 All E.R. 218; (1983) 1 B.C.C. 98,933	IR 13.12(2)
Isovel Contracts Ltd (In Administration) v ABB Building Technologies Ltd (formerly ABB Steward Ltd) [2002] 1 B.C.L.C. 390; [2002] B.P.I.R. 525	IR 4.90

J

	Provision
JE Cade & Son Ltd, Re [1991] B.C.C. 360; [1992] B.C.L.C. 213	IA 122(1)

Case Table

	Provision		Provision
JN Taylor Pty Ltd, Re [1998] B.P.I.R. 347	IA 426(40), (5),(11)	Joshua Shaw & Sons Ltd, Re (1989) 5 B.C.C. 188	IA 42(1), 153
JN2 Ltd, Re [1978] 1 W.L.R. 183; [1977] 3 All E.R. 1104	IA 124(1)	Judd v Brown [1999] B.P.I.R. 517; [1998] 1 F.L.R. 360; [1997] B.P.I.R. 470	IA 305(2), 335A
JSF Finance & Currency Exchange Co Ltd v Akma Solutions Inc; sub nom. JSF Finance v Currency Exchange [2001] 2 B.C.L.C. 307; [2002] B.P.I.R. 535	IA 123	Jyske Bank (Gibraltar) Ltd v Spjeldnaes (No.1) (1998) 95(42) L.S.G. 33; *The Times*, October 10, 1998	IR 13.7
Jackson v Bell [2001] EWCA Civ 387; [2001] B.P.I.R. 612	IA 339(1)–(3), 340(4),(5)	Jyske Bank (Gibraltar) Ltd v Spjeldnaes (No.2) [2000] B.C.C. 16; [1999] 2 B.C.L.C. 101; [1999] B.P.I.R. 525	IA 423(4),(5)
Jacobs v Official Receiver; sub nom. Jacobs (A Bankrupt), Re [1999] 1 W.L.R. 619; [1998] 3 All E.R. 250; [1998] B.P.I.R. 711	IA 279(3)–(5)		

K

	Provision
James Ex p (1874) 9 Ch App 609	IA Pt IX, Sch.B1, para.5
James McHale Automobiles Ltd, Re [1997] B.C.C. 202; [1997] 1 B.C.L.C. 273	IA 112(2), 236(2)
Jamieson, Petitioners 1997 S.C. 195; 1997 S.L.T. 821; [1997] B.C.C. 682	IA 63(1)
Janeash, Re [1990] B.C.C. 250	IA 123
Japan Leasing (Europe) Plc, Re. *See* Wallace v Shoa Leasing (Singapore) PTE Ltd	
Jay Benning Peltz (A Firm) v Deutsch [2001] B.P.I.R. 510	IR 7.51
Jayham Ltd, Re [1996] B.C.C. 224; [1995] 2 B.C.L.C. 455	IA Pt IV
Jeffrey S Levitt Ltd, Re [1992] Ch. 457; [1992] 2 W.L.R. 975; [1992] B.C.C. 137	IA 236
Jelly v All Type Roofing Co. *See* Debtor (No.50A-SD–1995), Re	
Jogia (A Bankrupt), Re; sub nom. Trustee in Bankruptcy v D Pennellier & Co [1988] 1 W.L.R. 484; [1988] 2 All E.R. 328	IR 12.12
John Dee Group Ltd v WMH (21) Ltd (formerly Magnet Ltd) [1998] B.C.C. 972	IA Pt III
John Slack Ltd, Re [1995] B.C.C. 1116	IA Sch.1
Johnson v Davies [1999] Ch. 117; [1998] 3 W.L.R. 1299; [1998] 2 B.C.L.C. 252	IA 5(2), 260(1),(2),(2A)

	Provision
Katz v McNally (Recovery of Preferences). *See* Exchange Travel (Holdings) Ltd (No.4), Re	
Kayford Ltd (In Liquidation), Re [1975] 1 W.L.R. 279; [1975] 1 All E.R. 604	IA 107, 239(3)
Kellar v BBR Graphic Engineers (Yorks) Ltd [2002] B.P.I.R. 544	IR 6.5
Keypak Homecare Ltd (No.1), Re (1987) 3 B.C.C. 588; [1987] B.C.L.C. 409	IA 108
Kahn v Inland Revenue Commissioners. *See* Toshoku Finance UK Plc (In Liquidation), Re	
Karnos Property Co (1989) 5 B.C.C. 14; [1989] B.C.L.C. 340	IA 123
Keenan, Re [1998] B.P.I.R. 205	IA 276(1)
Kent Carpets Ltd v Symes. *See* Symes (A Debtor), Re	
Kentish Homes Ltd, Re. *See* Powdrill and Lyle (Joint Liquidators of Kentish Homes Ltd) v Tower Hamlets LBC	
Khan v Breezevale Sarl; sub nom. Debtor (No.106 of 1992), Re [1996] B.P.I.R. 190	IR 6.5
Khan v Permayer [2001] B.P.I.R. 95	IA 258(2)–(5)

Case	Provision
Khan-Ghauri v Dunbar Bank Plc [2001] B.P.I.R. 618	IA 315(1), (2)
Kilvert v Flackett (A Bankrupt) [1998] 2 F.L.R. 806; [1998] B.P.I.R. 721	IA 310(1), (1A),(2),(7)
King v Anthony [1998] 2 B.C.L.C. 517; [1999] B.P.I.R. 73	IA 263(3)
King v Inland Revenue Commissioners [1996] B.P.I.R. 414	IA 271(3)
Kings v Cleghorn [1998] B.P.I.R. 463	IA 263(5), (6)
Kingscroft Insurance Co Ltd, Re [1994] B.C.C. 343; [1994] 1 B.C.L.C. 80	IA 236
Knight v Lawrence [1991] B.C.C. 411; [1993] B.C.L.C. 215	IA Pt III
Knights v Seymour Pierce Ellis Ltd (formerly Ellis & Partners Ltd); sub nom. Taylor Sinclair (Capital) Ltd (In Liquidation), Re [2001] 2 B.C.L.C. 176; [2002] B.P.I.R. 203	IA 238(4)
Knowles v Coutts & Co [1998] B.P.I.R. 96	IA 255(1), (2)
Konigsberg (a bankrupt), Re [1989] 1 W.L.R. 1257	IA 311(1)
Koutrouzas v Lombard Natwest Factors Ltd; sub nom. Lombard Natwest Factors Ltd v Koutrouzas [2002] EWHC 1084; [2003] B.P.I.R. 444	IA 260(1), (2),(2A)
Krasner v Dennison; sub nom. Lesser v Lawrence; Dennison v Krasner [2001] Ch. 76; [2000] 3 W.L.R. 720	IA 306, 310
Kubiangha v Ekpenyong [2002] EWHC 1567; [2002] 2 B.C.L.C. 597	IA 423(1)–(3)
Kudos Glass Ltd (In Liquidation), Re; sub nom. Rout v Lewis [2002] B.C.C. 416; [2001] 1 B.C.L.C. 390	IA 7(4)
Kumar, Re [1993] 1 W.L.R. 224	IA 339(1)–(3)
Kuwait Asia Bank EC v National Mutual Life Nominees [1991] 1 A.C. 187; [1990] 3 W.L.R. 297; [1990] B.C.C. 567	IA 251
Kyris v Oldham [2003] 1 B.C.L.C. 35	IA 27(1)
Kyrris (No.1), Re [1998] B.P.I.R. 103	IA 420(1)
Kyrris (No.2), Re; sub nom. Oldham v Kyrris [1998] B.P.I.R. 111	IA 420(1)

L

Case	Provision
LHF Wools, Re [1970] Ch. 27; [1969] 3 W.L.R. 100	IA 123
Ladd v Marshall [1954] 1 W.L.R. 1489; [1954] 3 All E.R. 745	IR 6.5
Land and Property Trust Co (No.1), Re [1991] B.C.C. 446; [1991] B.C.L.C. 845	IA 9(4),(5)
Land and Property Trust Co (No.2), Re [1993] B.C.C. 462; [1994] 1 B.C.L.C. 232	IA 9(4),(5)
Land and Property Trust Co (No.3), Re [1991] 1 W.L.R. 601; [1991] 3 All E.R. 409	IA 9(4),(5)
Land Rover Group Ltd v UPF (UK) Ltd (In Administrative Receivership) (2002)	IA 37(1),(2)
Landau (A Bankrupt), Re; sub nom. Pointer v Landau; L (A Bankrupt), Re [1998] Ch. 223; [1997] 3 W.L.R. 225	IA 306, 310
Langley Marketing Services, Re [1992] B.C.C. 585	IR 7.47
Lascomme Ltd v United Dominions Trust (Ireland) [1994] I.L.R.M. 227	IA Pt III
Latreefers Inc, Re. *See* Stocznia Gdanska SA v Latreefers Inc	
Law Society v Southall [2001] EWCA Civ 2001; [2002] B.P.I.R. 336	IA 423
Ledingham-Smith (A Bankrupt), Re; sub nom. Trustee of the Bankrupt v Pannel Kerr Forster [1993] B.C.L.C. 635	IA 340(3), (4),(5)
Lee v Lee (A Bankrupt); sub nom. Lee (A Bankrupt), Re [2000] B.C.C. 500; [2000] 1 F.L.R. 92; [1999] B.P.I.R. 926	IA 320(1)–(4)
Lee Behrens & Co Ltd, Re [1932] 2 Ch. 46	IA 238(5)
Legal Services Commission (formerly Legal Aid Board) v Leonard [2002] EWCA Civ 744; [2002] B.P.I.R. 994	IR 6.25

Case Table

Case	Provision
Leicester v Stevenson [2002] EWHC 2831; [2003] 2 B.C.L.C. 97	IA 147(1)
Leigh Estates (UK) Ltd, Re [1994] B.C.C. 292; [1994] R.A. 57	IA 125(1), Sch.1
Leisure Study Group Ltd, Re [1994] 2 B.C.L.C. 65	IA 1(2), 7(1),(2),(4), Pt III
Leon v York-o-Matic, Ltd [1966] 1 W.L.R. 1450; [1966] 3 All E.R. 277	IA 168(5)
Lesser v Lawrence. *See* Krasner v Dennison	
Levy v Legal Services Commission (formerly Legal Aid Board); sub nom. Levy v Legal Aid Board [2001] 1 All E.R. 895; [2001] 1 F.L.R. 435; [2000] B.P.I.R. 1065	IA 264, 267(1),(2) 382(3),(4), IR 12.3
Lewis v Hyde [1997] B.C.C. 976	IA 340(3)
Lewis v Inland Revenue Commissioners; sub nom. Floor Fourteen Ltd, Re [2001] 3 All E.R. 499; [2002] B.C.C. 198	IA 115, 175(2)(a), 238, Sch.4, para.3A, IR 4.218–4.220
Lewis v Ogwr BC [1996] R.A. 124	IA 285(1)
Lewis's of Leicester Ltd, Re [1995] B.C.C. 514; [1995] 1 B.C.L.C. 428	IA 14(3), 238(4), 239(3)
Leyland DAF Ltd, Re; sub nom. Buchler v Talbot [2004] UKHL 9; [2004] 2 W.L.R. 582; [2004] 1 All E.R. 1289; [2004] 1 B.C.L.C. 281; (2004) 101(12) L.S.G. 35; (2004) 154 N.L.J. 381; (2004) 148 S.J.L.B. 299; *The Times*, March 5, 2004, HL; [2002] EWCA Civ 228; [2003] B.C.C. 159	1A 107, 115, 175, Sch. B1, para. 65(3), para. 99(b), IR 4.127–4.131, 4.218–4.220
Leyland DAF Ltd (No.1), Re; sub nom. Talbot v Edcrest Ltd; McKillop v Edcrest Ltd [1994] B.C.C. 166; [1994] 2 B.C.L.C. 106	IA 234(1), (2)
Lichfield Freight Terminal Ltd, Re [1997] B.C.C. 11; [1997] 2 B.C.L.C. 109	IA 117
Lightning Electrical Contractors Ltd, Re [1996] B.C.C. 950; [1996] 2 B.C.L.C. 302	IA 216(3)
Lilley v American Express Europe Ltd [2000] B.P.I.R. 70	IA 267(4), (5)
Linda Marie, Re (1988) 4 B.C.C. 463	IA 156, IR 4.218–4.220
Lindop v Stewart Noble & Sons Ltd, 1999 S.C.L.R. 889; [2000] B.C.C. 747	IA 57(1A), (2A),(2D), 57(2),(4),(5), 60(1)
Lineas Navieras Bolivianas SAM, Re [1995] 1 B.C.L.C. 440	IA 130(1)
Lines Bros (In Liquidation) (No.1), Re [1983] Ch. 1; [1982] 2 W.L.R. 1010	IA 189(1), IR 4.91
Linkrealm Ltd, Re [1998] B.C.C. 478	IA 130(1)
Lipe Ltd v Leyland DAF Ltd (In Administrative Receivership) [1993] B.C.C. 385; [1994] 1 B.C.L.C. 84	IA 44(1),(2)
Lloyd's v Micklethwait; sub nom. Micklethwait, Re [2002] EWHC 1123; [2003] B.P.I.R. 101	IA 266(3), (4)
Lloyds v Waters [2001] B.P.I.R. 698	282(1),(3)
Lloyds Bank Plc v Cassidy [2002] EWCA Civ 1606; [2003] B.P.I.R. 424	IA Pt III
Lloyds Bank Plc v Ellicott [2002] EWCA Civ 1333; [2003] B.P.I.R. 632	IA 260(1), (2),(2A)
Lloyds Bank SF Nominees v Aladdin Ltd (In Liquidation) [1996] 1 B.C.L.C. 720	IA 181(1)–(3)
Loch v John Blackwood Ltd [1924] A.C. 783; [1924] All E.R. Rep. 200	IA 122(1)

Case Table

Case	Provision
Lomax Leisure Ltd, Re [2000] Ch. 502; [1999] 3 W.L.R. 652; [2000] B.C.C. 352	IA 8(1),(2), 11(3), 248, Sch.B1, para.11
Lombard Natwest Factors Ltd v Koutrouzas. *See* Koutrouzas v Lombard Natwest Factors Ltd	
Lombard North Central Plc v Brook [1999] B.P.I.R. 701	IR 1.13–1.21
London and General Bank, Re [1895] 2 Ch. 166	IA 206(3)
London City Corp v Bown, The Times October 11, 1989	IA 306, 315(1),(2)
London Iron and Steel Co, Re [1990] B.C.C. 159; [1990] B.C.L.C. 372	IA 234(1),(2)
Lord Advocate v Aero Technologies Ltd (In Receivership) 1991 S.L.T. 134	IA 57(1)
Lowrie, Re [1981] 3 All E.R. 353	IA 336(3)–(5)
Lowston, Re [1991] B.C.L.C. 570	IA 147(1)
Lummus Agricultural Services Ltd, Re; sub nom. Lummus Agriculture Services Ltd, Re [1999] B.C.C. 953; [2001] 1 B.C.L.C. 137	IA 122(1), 125(1)

M

Case	Provision
M (Restraint Order), Re; sub nom. M, Re [1992] Q.B. 377; [1992] 2 W.L.R. 340	IA 252(2)
MC Bacon Ltd (No.1), Re; sub nom. Company (No.005009 of 1987) (No.1), Re [1990] B.C.C. 78; [1990] B.C.L.C. 324	IA 214(1), 238(4), 239, 239(2), 239(5), 340(4),(5)
MC Bacon Ltd (No.2), Re; sub nom. Company (No.005009 of 1987) (No.2), Re [1991] Ch. 127; [1990] 3 W.L.R. 646; [1990] B.C.C. 430	IA 115, IR 4.218–4.220
MCH Services Ltd, Re (1987) 3 B.C.C. 179	IA 124(5)
MCI Worldcom Ltd v Primus Telecommunications Ltd; sub nom. MCI WorldCom Ltd, Re [2002] EWHC 2436; [2003] 1 B.C.L.C. 330	IA 123
MEPC plc v Scottish Amicable Life Assurance Society [1996] B.P.I.R. 447	IA 315(3),(5)
MS Fashions Ltd v Bank of Credit and Commerce International SA (In Liquidation) (No.2) [1993] Ch. 425; [1993] 3 W.L.R. 220	IR 4.90
MTI Trading Systems Ltd (In Administration), Re; sub nom. MTI Holdings Ltd, Re [1998] B.C.C. 400, CA; affirming [1997] B.C.C. 703; [1998] 2 B.C.L.C. 246	IA 8(1),(2), IR 7.47
MTI Trading Systems Ltd v Winter [1998] B.C.C. 591	IA 27(1)
McGreavy (Otherwise McGreavey), Re; sub nom. McGreavy v Benfleet Urban DC [1950] Ch. 269; [1950] 1 All E.R. 442	IA 267(1),(2)
McGuinness Bros (UK), Re (1987) 3 B.C.C. 571	IA 127
McIsaac: Petitioners: Joint Liquidators of First Tokyo Index Trust Ltd [1994] B.C.C. 410	IA 236, 366(1), IR 12.12
McKeen (A Debtor), Re [1995] B.C.C. 412	IA 263(5),(6)
McKillop and Watters, Petitioners [1994] B.C.C. 677	IA 57(1), 63(1)
McLuckie Brothers Ltd v Newhouse Contracts Ltd 1993 S.L.T. 641	IA 242(4)
McMahon's Trustee, *The Times* March 26, 1997	IA 336(3)–(5)
McMullen & Sons, ltd v Cerrone [1994] B.C.C. 25; [1994] 1 B.C.L.C. 152	IA 252(2)
Mackay, Ex p (1873) L.R. 8 Ch.App.643	IA 107

Case Table

	Provision		Provision
Mahomed v Morris (No.2) [2001] B.C.C. 233; [2000] 2 B.C.L.C. 536	IA 168(5)	Maxwell Fleet and Facilities Management Ltd (In Administration) (No.1), Re [2001] 1 W.L.R. 323; [2000] 1 All E.R. 464; [1999] 2 B.C.L.C. 721	IA 19(5)–(10)
Mander v Evans [2001] 1 W.L.R. 2378; [2001] 3 All E.R. 811; [2001] B.P.I.R. 902	IA 281(2)–(6),(8)		
Manlon Trading Ltd (Petition for Administration Order), Re (1988) 4 B.C.C. 455	IA 10(2)	Meadrealm Ltd v Transcontinental Golf Construction, unreported 1991	IA 29(2)
Manson v Smith (Liquidator of Thomas Christy Ltd) [1997] 2 B.C.L.C. 161	IA 212	Measures Brothers Ltd v Measures [1910] 2 Ch. 248	IA 91(2)
Maple Environmental Services Ltd, Re [2000] B.C.C. 93; [2001] B.P.I.R. 321	IA 7(4)	Medforth v Blake [2000] Ch. 86; [1999] 3 W.L.R. 922; [1999] B.C.C. 771	IA Pt III
Marann Brooks CSV Ltd, Re [2003] B.C.C. 239	ER Art 1	Medisco Equipment, Re (1983) 1 B.C.C. 98,944; [1983] Com. L.R. 232	IA 116, 124(5)
March Estates Plc v Gunmark Ltd [1996] 2 B.C.L.C. 1; [1996] B.P.I.R. 439	IA 1(1), 4(3), 5(2), 248, 262	Meesan Investments, Re (1988) 4 B.C.C. 788	IA 11(3)
		Memco Engineering Ltd, Re [1986] Ch. 86; [1985] 3 W.L.R. 875; (1985) 1 B.C.C. 99,460	IA 176(3)
Margart Pty Ltd, Hamilton, Re v Westpac Banking Corp (1984) 2 A.C.L.C. 709	IA 127	Menastar Finance Ltd (In Liquidation), Re; sub nom. Menastar Ltd v Simon [2002] EWHC 2610; [2003] B.C.C. 404	IR 4.73–4.85
Mark One (Oxford Street) Plc, Re [1999] 1 W.L.R. 1445; [1999] 1 All E.R. 608; [1998] B.C.C. 984	IA 18(2)		
Market Wizard Systems (UK) Ltd, Re [1998] 2 B.C.L.C. 282; [1998–99] Info T.L.R. 19	IA 124A, 206(3)	Mettoy Pension Trustees Ltd v Evans [1990] 1 W.L.R. 1587; [1991] 2 All E.R. 513	IA 247(2)
		Micklethwait, Re. See Lloyd's v Micklethwait	
Marlborough Club Co (Contributories), Re (1867–68) L.R. 5 Eq. 365	IA 149(1)	Mid East Trading Ltd, Re; sub nom. Lehman Bros Inc v Phillips; Phillips v Lehman Brothers [1998] 1 All E.R. 577; [1998] B.C.C. 726	IA 236
Martin-Coulter Enterprises Ltd, Re (1988) 4 B.C.C. 210	IA 124(2), (3)		
Masters v Leaver [2000] I.L.Pr. 387; [2000] B.P.I.R. 284	IA 281(2)–(6),(8)	Midland Counties District Bank Ltd v Attwood [1905] 1 Ch. 357	IA 91(2)
Maxwell v Bishopsgate Investment Management Ltd [1993] T.L.R. 67	IA 267(1), (2)	Migration Services International Ltd, Re; sub nom. Webster v Official Receiver [2000] B.C.C. 1095; [2000] 1 B.C.L.C. 666; (1999) 96(47) L.S.G. 29	IA 216(3)
Maxwell Communications Corporation plc, Homan v Vogel [1994] B.C.C. 741	IA 236		
Maxwell Communications Corp Plc (No.1), Re [1992] B.C.C. 372; [1992] B.C.L.C. 465	IA 8(3)	Midrome v Shaw [1993] B.C.C. 659; [1994] 1 B.C.L.C. 180	IR 7.47
Maxwell Communications Corp Plc (No.2), Re [1993] 1 W.L.R. 1402; [1994] 1 All E.R. 737	IA 14(3)	Milgate Developments, Re; sub nom. Canniford v Smith [1991] B.C.C. 24; [1993] B.C.L.C. 291	IA 122(1)

Case Table

	Provision		Provision
Miliangos v George Frank (Textiles) Ltd (No.1) [1976] A.C. 443; [1975] 3 W.L.R. 758	IR 4.91	Morphites v Bernasconi; sub nom. Morphitis v Bernasconi [2003] EWCA Civ 289; [2003] 2 W.L.R. 1521	IA 213(1), (2), 214
Miller v Bain (Director's Breach of Duty); sub nom. Pantone 485 Ltd, Re [2002] 1 B.C.L.C. 266	IA 212(1), 236	Morrice (or Rocks) v Brae Hotel (Shetland) Ltd; sub nom. Morrice v Brae Hotel (Shetland) Ltd 1997 S.L.T. 474; [1997] B.C.C. 670	IA 123
Mills v Grove Securities Ltd [1997] B.P.I.R. 243; [1996] C.C.L.R. 74	IA 267(1), (2)	Morris v Bank of America National Trust (Appeal against Striking Out) [2000] 1 All E.R. 954; [2000] B.C.C. 1076	IA 213
Mineral Resources Ltd, Re; sub nom. Insolvency Act 1986, Re; Environment Agency v Stout [1999] 1 All E.R. 746; [1999] B.C.C. 422.	IA 178	Morris v Harris [1927] A.C. 252.	IA Pt IV
Mirror Group Newspapers Plc v Maxwell (No.1) [1998] B.C.C. 324; [1998] 1 B.C.L.C. 638. . .	IA 35(1), 399(2), IR 6.138	Morris v Kanssen; sub nom. Kanssen v Rialto (West End) Ltd [1946] A.C. 459.	IA 232
		Morris v Murjani [1996] B.P.I.R. 458	IA 331(1), (3)
Mistral Finance (In Liquidation), Re [2001] B.C.C. 27.	IA 238(4), 239(4)	Morton v Confer [1963] 1 W.L.R. 763; [1963] 2 All E.R. 765 . . .	IA 206(4)
		Mott, Re [1987] C.L.Y. 212	IA 336(3)–(5)
Mitchell v Carter. *See* Buckingham International Plc (In Liquidation) (No.1), Re		Mountney v Treharne [2002] EWCA Civ 1174.	IA 283(5), 284(1)–(3),(6)
Mond v Hammond Suddards (No.2); sub nom. RS&M Engineering Co Ltd, Re [2000] Ch. 40; [1999] 3 W.L.R. 697; [2000] B.C.C. 445	IA 115, 127, 156	Movitex, Re [1992] 1 W.L.R. 303; [1992] 2 All E.R. 264; [1992] B.C.C. 101	IA 112(2), IR 4.218–4.220
Mond v Hyde [1999] Q.B. 1097; [1999] 2 W.L.R. 499	IA 400(2)	Mulkerrins (formerly Woodward) v PricewaterhouseCoopers; sub nom. Mulkerrins v Pricewaterhouse Coopers [2003] UKHL 41	IA 306
Money Markets International Stockbrokers Ltd (In Liquidation) v London Stock Exchange Ltd [2002] 1 W.L.R. 1150; [2001] 4 All E.R. 223; [2001] 2 B.C.L.C. 347	IA 107	Mulvey v Secretary of State for Social Security 1997 S.C. (H.L.) 105; 1997 S.L.T. 753; [1997] B.P.I.R. 696	IA 306
Montgomery v Wanda Modes Ltd; sub nom. Wanda Modes Ltd, Re [2002] 1 B.C.L.C. 289; [2003] B.P.I.R. 457, Ch D	IA 123	Munns v Perkins [2002] B.P.I.R. 120	IA 35(1), 36(1)
Moon v Franklin [1996] B.P.I.R. 196	IA 423(1)–(3), 424	Munro Ex p. Singer, Re v Trustee in Bankruptcy [1981] 1 W.L.R. 1358	IA 299(1), (2), IR 13.4
Mordant, Re [1996] B.P.I.R. 302	IA 284(1)–(3),(6)		
Morier Ex p; sub nom. Willis, Percival & Co, Re (1879) L.R. 12 Ch. D. 491	IR 4.90	Murjani (A Bankrupt), Re [1996] 1 W.L.R. 1498; [1996] 1 All E.R. 65; [1996] B.C.C. 278 . . .	IA 366(1)
Morley IRC [1996] B.P.I.R. 452.	IR 6.4	Muscovitch, Re [1939] Ch. 694 .	IA 9(2)

Case Table

	Provision
Myles J Callaghan Ltd (In Receivership) v Glasgow DC, 1987 S.C. 171; 1988 S.L.T. 227; (1987) 3 B.C.C. 337.....	IA 53(6), (7), 55(1),(2), IR 4.90

N

	Provision
N (A Debtor), Re [2002] B.P.I.R. 1024......................	IA 262
NG (A Bankrupt), Re; sub nom. Trustee of the Estate of NG v NG [1997] B.C.C. 507; [1998] 2 F.L.R. 386	IA 305(2), 336(3)–(5)
NS Distribution, Re [1990] B.C.L.C. 169...............	IA 17(2)
NT Gallagher & Son Ltd, Re; sub nom. NT Gallagher & Sons Ltd v Howard; Shierson v Tomlinson [2002] EWCA Civ 404; [2002] 1 W.L.R. 2380; [2002] B.P.I.R. 565	IA 7(4), 7A, 263(5),(6), IR 4.16–4.21A
Naeem (A Bankrupt) (No.18 of 1988), Re [1990] 1 W.L.R. 48; (1989) 86(46) L.S.G. 37......	IA 260(1), (2),(2A), 262
Namco UK Ltd, Re [2003] EWHC 989; [2003] 2 B.C.L.C. 78	IA 135
National Employers Mutual General Insurance Association Ltd (In Liquidation), Re [1995] B.C.C. 774; [1995] 1 B.C.L.C. 232......................	IA 130(1)
National Provincial Bank Ltd v Ainsworth [1965] A.C. 1175..	IA 335A
National Westminster Bank Ltd v Halesowen Presswork and Assemblies Ltd; sub nom. Halesowen Presswork & Assemblies v Westminster Bank Ltd [1972] A.C. 785; [1972] 2 W.L.R. 455	IA 323, IR 4.90
National Westminster Bank Ltd v Jones [2001] EWCA Civ 1541; [2002] B.P.I.R. 361	IA 423(1)–(3)
National Westminster Bank Plc v Scher. *See* Debtor (No.574 of 1995), Re	
Neely v Inland Revenue Commissioners. *See* Debtor (No.383–SD–92), Re	
Nelson v Nelson [1997] B.P.I.R. 702.......................	IA 306
Neuschild v British Equitorial Oil Co Ltd [1925] Ch. 346.......	IA 194
New Bullas Trading Ltd, Re [1994] B.C.C. 36; [1994] 1 B.C.L.C. 485...............	IA 40(1),(2)
New Cap Reinsurance Corporation Ltd v HIH Casualty & General Insurance Ltd [2002] EWCA Civ 300; [2002] 2 B.C.L.C. 228	IA 130(1)
New Hampshire Insurance Co v Rush & Tompkins Group Plc [1998] 2 B.C.L.C. 471	IA 221
Newhart Developments v Cooperative Commercial Bank [1978] Q.B. 814; [1978] 2 W.L.R. 636	IA Pt III
Newman Shopfitters (Cleveland), Re [1991] B.C.L.C. 407......	IA 15(5)
Newport County Association Football Club, Re (1987) 3 B.C.C. 635; [1987] B.C.L.C. 582......................	IA 8(1),(2), IR 2.1–2.3
Niagara Mechanical Services International Ltd (In Administration), Re; sub nom. Canary Wharf Contractors (DS6) Ltd v Niagara Mechanical Services International Ltd (In Administration)[2001] B.C.C. 393; [2000] 2 B.C.L.C. 425...	IA 107
Nicoll v Cutts [1985] P.C.C. 311; (1985) 1 B.C.C. 99,427	IA 37(1), (2), 44(1),(2)
Nicoll v Steelpress (Supplies) Ltd 1992 S.C. 119; 1993 S.L.T. 533	IA 243(1), (2)
Nolton Business Centres Ltd, Re; sub nom. Eliades v City of London Common Council [1996] B.C.C. 500; [1996] 1 B.C.L.C. 400; [1996] R.A. 116	IR 12.2
Norditrak (UK) Ltd, Re [2000] 1 W.L.R. 343; [2000] B.C.C. 441	IA 18(2), 84(1), 240(1),(3)

Case	Provision
Norfolk House Plc (in receivership) v Repsol Petroleum Ltd, 1992 S.L.T. 235	IA 72
Norglen Ltd (in liq) v Reeds Rains Prudential Ltd [1999] 2 A.C. 1; [1998] B.C.C. 44	IA Sch.4, para.6
Norman Holding Co Ltd (in liquidation), Re [1991] 1 W.L.R. 10; [1991] B.C.C. 11	IR 4.90
Norman Laurier v United Overseas Bank [1996] B.P.I.R. 635	IR 6.5
Normandy Marketing, Re [1993] B.C.C. 879	IA 220, 225, 441
North Brazilian Sugar Factories, Re (1888) L.R. 37 Ch. D. 83	IA 155(1)
North Carolina Estate Co, Re (1889) 5 T.L.R. 328	IA 183
North West Holdings Plc (In Liquidation) (Costs), Re; sub nom. Secretary of State for Trade and Industry v Backhouse [2001] EWCA Civ 67; [2002] B.C.C. 441	IA 124A
Nowmost Co Ltd, Re [1997] B.C.C. 105; [1996] 2 B.C.L.C. 492	IA 125(1)

O

Case	Provision
O'Sullivan (Julie), Re [2001] B.P.I.R. 534	IA 255(1), (2)
Oakes v Simms [1997] B.P.I.R. 499	IA 366(1)
Oasis Merchandising Services Ltd (In Liquidation), Re; sub nom. Ward v Aitken [1998] Ch. 170; [1997] 2 W.L.R. 765; [1997] B.C.C. 282	IA 212(1), 214(1), 238, Sch.4, para.6
Oben v Blackman; sub nom. Debtor (No.510 of 1997), Re; Blackman (A Debtor), Re [1999] B.C.C. 446; [2000] B.P.I.R. 302	IR 7.55
Official Custodian for Charities v Parway Estates Developments Ltd (In Liquidation) [1985] Ch. 151; [1984] 3 W.L.R. 525	IA 130(1)
Official Receiver v Brunt [1999] B.P.I.R. 560	IA 400(2)
Official Receiver v Cummings-John [2000] B.P.I.R. 320	IA 363(2), (4)
Official Receiver v Doshi [2001] 2 B.C.L.C. 235	IA 214(1)
Official Receiver v Environment Agency [1999] B.P.I.R. 986	IA 436
Official Receiver v Mulkerrins [2002] B.P.I.R. 582	IA 306
Olympia & York Canary Wharf Ltd (No.1), Re; sub nom. American Express Europe Ltd v Adamson [1993] B.C.C. 154; [1993] B.C.L.C. 453	IA 11(3)
Omgate Ltd v Gordon [2001] B.P.I.R. 909	IR 6.25, 6.26
Ord v Upton [2000] 2 W.L.R. 755	IA 306
Oriental Commercial Bank, Re; sub nom. European Bank, Ex p. (1871–72) L.R. 7 Ch. App. 99	IR 4.73–4.85
Oriental Inland Steam Co Ex p. Scinde Railway Co, Re (1873–74) L.R. 9 Ch. App. 557	IA 183
Orion Media Marketing Ltd v Media Brook Ltd [2002] 1 B.C.L.C. 184; [2003] B.P.I.R. 474	IA 123
Orleans Motor Co Ltd, Re [1911] 2 Ch. 41	IA 245(2)
Osborn v Cole [1999] B.P.I.R. 251	IA 303(1)
O'Toole v Mitcham (1978) C.L.C. 40–429	IA 236
Ouvaroff, Re [1997] B.P.I.R. 712	IA 366(1)
Oxted Financial Services Ltd v Gordon [1998] B.P.I.R. 231	IA 266(3), (4)

P

Case	Provision
P & C and R & T, Re; sub nom. Griffiths v Provincial & City Property Co [1991] B.C.C. 98; [1991] B.C.L.C. 366	IA 14(1)
PFTZM Ltd, Re; sub nom. Jourdain v Paul [1995] B.C.C. 280; [1995] 2 B.C.L.C. 354	IA 214(1), 236, 240
Pacific & General Insurance Ltd (in liquidation) v Home & Overseas Insurance Co Ltd [1997] B.C.C. 400	IA 135

Case Table

	Provision		Provision
Paget Ex p. Official Receiver, Re [1927] 2 Ch. 85.............	IA 290(3), (5)	Patel v Jones; sub nom. Jones v Patel [2001] EWCA Civ 779; [2001] B.P.I.R. 919	IA Pt IX, 306, 436
Palmer (deceased), Re [1994] Ch.316...................	IA 421A(1)	Patrick and Lyon Ltd, Re [1933] Ch. 786	IA 213
Pantmaenog Timber Co Ltd, Re; sub nom. Official Receiver v Hay; Pantmaenog Timber Co (In Liquidation), Re [2003] UKHL 49, [2003] 3 W.L.R. 767, [2003] B.C.C. 659, reversing [2001] EWCA Civ 1227; [2002] Ch. 239; [2002] B.C.C. 11	IA 236	Peake, Re [1987] C.L.Y. 215....	IA 252(2)
		Pearl Maintenance Services Ltd, Re [1995] B.C.C. 657; [1995] 1 B.C.L.C. 449..............	IA 40(1),(2)
		Peck v Craighead. See Debtor (No.10 of 1992), Re	
		Penrose v Official Receiver; sub nom. Penrose v Secretary of State for Trade and Industry [1996] 1 W.L.R. 482; [1996] 2 All E.R. 96; [1995] B.C.C. 311; [1996] 1 B.C.L.C. 389	IA 216(3)
Pantone 485 Ltd, Re. See Miller v Bain (Director's Breach of Duty)			
Paramount Airways Ltd, Re. See Bristol Airport Plc v Powdrill		Performing Rights Society v Rowland [1998] B.P.I.R. 128 .	IA 306, 436
Paramount Airways Ltd (No.2), Re; sub nom. Powdrill v Hambros Bank (Jersey) Ltd [1993] Ch. 223; [1992] 3 W.L.R. 690; [1992] B.C.C. 416	IA 238, 238(3), IR 12.12	Philip Alexander Securities & Futures Ltd, Re [1998] B.C.C. 819; [1999] 1 B.C.L.C. 124...	IA 18(2), IR 2.18–2.29, 4.50–4.71
Paramount Airways Ltd (No.3), Re. See Powdrill v Watson		Phillips (Liquidator of AJ Bekhor & Co) v Brewin Dolphin Bell Lawrie Ltd (formerly Brewin Dolphin & Co Ltd); sub nom. Phillips v Brewin Dolphin Bell Lawrie Ltd [2001] UKHL 2; [2001] 1 W.L.R. 143; [2001] B.C.C. 864.................	IA 238(4)
Park Air Services Plc, Re; sub nom. Christopher Moran Holdings Ltd v Bairstow [2000] 2 A.C. 172; [1999] 2 W.L.R. 396 reversing [1996] 1 W.L.R. 649; [1996] B.C.C. 556;	IA 11(3), 178(6), 189(1), IR 11.13		
		Phoenix Properties v Wimpole Street Nominees [1992] B.C.L.C. 737..............	IA Pt III
Park Gate Waggon Works Co, Re (1881) 17 Ch.D.234	IA Sch.4, para.6	Piccadilly Property Management Ltd, Re [2000] B.C.C. 44; [1999] 2 B.C.L.C. 145	IR 4.16–4.21A, 7.47
Parke v Daily News (No.2) [1962] Ch. 927; [1962] 3 W.L.R. 566.	IA 187	Pike v Cork Gully [1997] B.P.I.R. 723	IA 307(1), 308(1),(4)
Parkfield Group Plc (In Liquidation), Re; sub nom. Bridisco Ltd v Jordan [1997] B.C.C. 778; [1998] 1 B.C.L.C. 451	IR 4.73–4.85	Pimlico Capital Ltd, Re. See TFB Mortgages Ltd v Pimlico Capital Ltd	
		Pinecord Ltd (In Liquidation), Re; sub nom. Bennett v Rolph [1995] B.C.C. 483; [1995] 2 B.C.L.C. 57................	IR 4.90
Partizan Ltd v OJ Kilkenny & Co Ltd [1998] B.C.C. 912; [1998] 1 B.C.L.C. 157	IA 125(1)	Pinewood Joinery v Starelm Properties Ltd [1994] B.C.C. 569......................	IA 424
Pascoe, Re [1944] Ch.219	IA 307(1), IR 12.3		
Patel, Re [1986] 1 W.L.R. 221 ..	IA 267(4), (5)	Pinstripe Farming Co Ltd, Re [1996] B.C.C. 913; [1996] 2 B.C.L.C. 295...............	IA 135

xxxix

Case Table

	Provision		Provision
Pitt v Mond [2001] B.P.I.R. 624	IA 263(1), (2)	Potters Oils, Re (No.2) [1986] 1 W.L.R. 201; [1986] 1 All E.R. 890; [1986] B.C.C. 99,593	IA 36(1)
Platts v Western Trust and Savings Ltd [1996] B.P.I.R. 339	IR 6.5	Powdrill v Watson; sub nom. Paramount Airways Ltd (No.3), Re; Talbot v Cadge; Talbot v Grundy; Leyland DAF Ltd (No.2), Re[1995] 2 A.C. 394; affirming [1994] 2 All E.R. 513; [1994] B.C.C. 172	IA 19, 19(3)–(6), 19(5)–(10), 37(1),(2), 44(1),(2), 57(1A),(2A),(2D), Sch.B1, para.99
Pleatfine, Re (1983) 1 B.C.C. 98,942; *The Times*, June 15, 1983	IA 118		
Pollard v Ashurst. *See* Ashurst v Pollard			
Polly Peck International Plc Ex p the joint administrators [1994] B.C.C. 15	IA 235		
Polly Peck International Plc, Re, unreported February 8, 1999	IA 18(2)		
Polly Peck International Plc (In Administration) v Henry [1999] 1 B.C.L.C. 407; [1998] O.P.L.R. 323	IA 8(1),(2), 14(1)	Powdrill and Lyle (Joint Liquidators of Kentish Homes Ltd) v Tower Hamlets LBC; sub nom. Kentish Homes Ltd, Re [1993] B.C.C. 212; [1993] B.C.L.C. 1375	IA 115, IR 12.2, 13.12
Polly Peck International Plc (In Administration) (No.1), Re [1991] B.C.C. 503	IR 2.18–2.29, 2.32–2.46A		
Polly Peck International Plc (In Administration) (No.4), Re; sub nom. Barlow v Polly Peck International Finance Ltd [1996] 2 All E.R. 433; [1996] B.C.C. 486	IR 2.18–2.29, 4.73–4.85	Power v Sharp Investments Ltd; sub nom. Shoe Lace Ltd, Re [1993] B.C.C. 609; [1994] 1 B.C.L.C. 111	IA 245(2)
		Powerstore (Trading) Ltd, Re [1997] 1 W.L.R. 1280; [1998] 1 All E.R. 121; [1998] B.C.C. 305	IA 18(2)
Polly Peck International Plc (In Administration) (No.5), Re [1998] 3 All E.R. 812; reversing [1997] 2 B.C.L.C. 630; (1997) 94(1) L.S.G. 23	IA 11(3)	Pozzuto v Iacovides [2003] EWHC 431	IA 339(1)–(3)
		Practice Direction [1987] 1 W.L.R. 119	IR 6.5
Port v Auger. *See* Port (A Bankrupt) (No. 516 of 1987), Re		Practice Direction: Applications under the Companies Act 1985 and the Insurance Companies Act 1982 [1999] B.C.C. 741	IA 122(1), 127, App. V
Port (A Bankrupt) (No. 516 of 1987), Re; sub nom. Port v Auger [1994] 1 W.L.R. 862; [1994] 3 All E.R. 200	IA 303(1), IR 7.1–7.18	Practice Direction (Bankruptcy 1/92) [1992] 1 All E.R. 704	IR 6.28
Portbase Clothing Ltd, Re; sub nom. Mond v Taylor [1993] Ch. 388; [1993] 3 W.L.R. 14; [1993] B.C.C. 96	IA 107, 115, Pt XII, IR 4.218–4.220	Practice Direction (Bankruptcy: Voluntary Arrangements) [1992] 1 W.L.R. 120	IA Pt VIII
		Practice Direction (Insolvency Proceedings) (No.1) [1999] B.C.C. 727; [1999] B.P.I.R. 441	IA 135, Pt IX
Portman Building Society v Gallwey [1955] 1 W.L.R. 96	IA 232		

xl

Case Table

	Provision		Provision
Practice Direction (Insolvency Proceedings) (No.2) [2000] B.C.C. 927; [2000] B.P.I.R. 647	IR 4.3, 4.8(6), 4.7–4.14, 4.15, 4.19, 4.35, 4.47, 4.59, 7.11, 13.2(2),(3), App.IV	Practice Note (Bankruptcy: Substituted Service) [1987] 1 W.L.R. 82	IR 6.3, 6.14
		Practice Statement (Ch D: Administration Orders: Reports) [2002] 1 W.L.R. 1358; [2002] 3 All E.R. 95; [2002] B.C.C. 354	IR 2.1–2.3, 7.26–7.32
		Preston BC v Riley [1995] B.C.C. 700; [1999] B.P.I.R. 284	IA 267(1), (2)
Practice Direction No.1 of 1990 [1990] B.C.C. 292	IA 125(2), 127, App. V	Priceland Ltd, Re; sub nom. Waltham Forest LBC v Registrar of Companies [1997] B.C.C. 207; [1997] 1 B.C.L.C. 467; [1996] E.G.C.S. 188	IA Pt IV
Practice Note (Administration Order Applications: Content of Independent Reports); sub nom. Practice Note (Ch D: Administration Order Applications: Independent Reports); Practice Statement (Ch D: Administration Orders: Reports); Practice Statement (Administration Orders: Reports) [1994] 1 W.L.R. 160; [1994] 1 All E.R. 324; [1994] B.C.C. 35	IR 2.1–2.3	Primlaks (UK) (No.2), Re [1990] B.C.L.C. 234	IR 7.60
		Priory Garage (Walthamstow) Ltd, Re [2001] B.P.I.R. 144	IA 238, 339(1)–(3), 342(1)
		Probe Data Systems (No.3), Re; sub nom. Secretary of State for Trade and Industry v Desai [1992] B.C.C. 110; affirming [1991] B.C.C. 428; [1991] B.C.L.C. 586	IR 7.47
Practice Note (Bankruptcy) (No.2/87) [1987] 1 W.L.R. 1424	IA 268, IR 6.8	Produce Marketing Consortium (In Liquidation)(No.1), Re; sub nom. Halls v David [1989] 1 W.L.R. 745; [1989] 3 All E.R. 1; (1989) 5 B.C.C. 399	IA 214
Practice Note (Bankruptcy: Certificate of Debt) [1987] 1 W.L.R. 120	IR 6.25		
Practice Note (Bankruptcy: Petition) [1987] 1 W.L.R. 81	IA 267(1), (2), IR 6.6, 6.8	Produce Marketing Consortium (In Liquidation), Re (No.2) (1989) 5 B.C.C. 569; [1989] B.C.L.C. 520	IA 214, 214(1), 214(3)
Practice Note (Bankruptcy: Prescribed Forms) [1988] 1 W.L.R. 557	IR Sch.4	Prosser v Castle Sanderson Solicitors [2002] EWCA Civ 1140; [2003] B.C.C. 440	IA 256(1)
Practice Note (Bankruptcy: Statutory Demands) (No.2/88) [1988] 1 W.L.R. 557; [1988] 2 All E.R. 127	IR 6.1	Purpoint, Re [1991] B.C.C. 121; [1991] B.C.L.C. 491	IA 212, 214, 214(4)
Practice Note (Bankruptcy: Statutory Demand) [1987] 1 W.L.R. 85	IA 268	Purvis (Withdrawal of Bankruptcy Petitions), Re [1997] 3 All E.R. 663; [1998] B.P.I.R. 153	IA 271(5)
Practice Note (Bankruptcy: Service Abroad) (No.1/88) [1988] 1 W.L.R. 461	IR 6.3	**Q**	
Practice Note (Bankruptcy: Statutory Demand: Setting Aside) [1987] 1 W.L.R. 119	IR 6.4	QRS 1 ApS v Frandsen [1999] 1 W.L.R. 2169; [1999] 3 All E.R. 289	IR 12.3

Case Table

	Provision		Provision
Quadmost Ltd v Reprotech (Pebsham) Ltd [2001] B.P.I.R. 349	IA Sch.4, para.6	R v Shacter (Norman) [1960] 2 Q.B. 252; [1960] 2 W.L.R. 258	IA 206(3)
Quickdome Ltd, Re (1988) 4 B.C.C. 296	IA 124(1)	R (on the application of Eliades) v Institute of Chartered Accountants [2001] B.P.I.R. 363	IA 391(2)
R		RA Securities Ltd v Mercantile Credit Co Ltd [1995] 3 All E.R. 581; [1994] B.C.C. 598	IA 5(2)
R v Barnet Justices Ex p Phillippou [1997] B.P.I.R. 134	IA 252(2)		
R v Carr-Briant [1943] K.B. 607.	IA 206(4)	RBG Resources Plc, Re. *See* Shierson v Rastogi	
R v Cole, Lees & Birch [1998] B.C.C. 87	IA 216(4)	RS&M Engineering Co Ltd, Re. *See* Mond v Hammond Suddards (No.2)	
R v Daniel [2002] EWCA Crim 959; [2002] B.P.I.R. 1193	IA 352, 354(1)	Rae, Re [1995] B.C.C. 102	IA 306
R v Dickson (William Ewing) [1991] B.C.C. 719; (1992) 94 Cr. App. R. 7	IA 130(1)	Rafidain Bank (No.1), Re [1992] B.C.C. 376; [1992] B.C.L.C. 301	IA 127, Pt XII
R v Doring (Petra) [2002] EWCA Crim 1695; [2002] B.C.C. 838	IA 206(3), 216, 216(4)	Rahall v McLennan [2000] B.P.I.R. 140	IA 306
R v Faryab (Frank) [1999] B.P.I.R. 569; [2000] Crim. L.R. 180	IA 236, 433(1)	Railtrack Plc (In Administration) (No.2), Re; sub nom. Winsor v Bloom; Winsor v Special Railway Administrators of Railtrack Plc [2002] EWCA Civ 955; [2002] 1 W.L.R. 3002; [2002] 2 B.C.L.C. 755	IA 11(3)
R v Godwin (1980) 11 Cr.App.R. 97	IA 360(1)		
R v Kansal [1993] Q.B. 244; [1992] B.C.C. 615	IA 433(1)		
R v Kearns (Nicholas Gary) [2002] EWCA Crim 748	IA 354(3)	Raja v Austin Gray (A Firm) [2002] EWCA Civ 1965; [2003] B.P.I.R. 725	IA Pt III
R v Kemp (Peter David Glanville) [1988] Q.B. 645; [1988] 2 W.L.R. 975; (1988) 4 B.C.C. 203	IA 213(1)	Raja v Rubin [2000] Ch. 274; [1999] 3 W.L.R. 606; [1999] B.P.I.R. 575	IA Pt VIII, 263(4)
R v Lord Chancellor Ex p Lightfoot [2000] B.P.I.R. 120	IA 272	Rank Film Distributors Ltd v Video Information Centre [1982] A.C. 380; [1981] 2 All E.R. 76	IA 236
R v McCredie (Graeme George) [2000] B.C.C. 617; [2000] 2 B.C.L.C. 438	IA 206(1), (2), 216(4)		
		Raval, Re [1998] B.P.I.R. 389	IA 335A
R v Miller [1977] 3 All E.R. 986	IA 360(2)	Razzaq v Pala [1997] 1 W.L.R. 1336; [1998] B.C.C. 66	IA 4(3), 248, 285(3),(4), 383(2)–(4)
R.v Mungroo (Ivan Kimble) [1998] B.P.I.R. 784; (1997) 94(25) L.S.G. 33	IA 357(1), (3)		
R v Robinson [1990] B.C.C. 656; [1990] Crim. L.R. 804	IA 206(1), (2)	Real Estate Development Co, Re [1991] B.C.L.C. 210	IA 220
R v Scott [1998] B.P.I.R. 471	IA 360(1)	Rees v Boston BC; sub nom. Beck Foods Ltd, Re; Boston BC v Rees; Beck Foods Ltd v Boston Tax [2001] EWCA Civ 1934; [2002] 1 W.L.R. 1304; [2002] B.C.C. 495	IA 44(1),(2)
R v Secretary of State for Social Security Ex p. Taylor [1997] B.P.I.R. 505; [1996] C.O.D. 332	IA 285(1)		

Case Table

	Provision		Provision
Regional Collection Services Ltd v Heald; sub nom. H (In Bankruptcy), Re; H (A Debtor) (No.38–SD of 1997), Re [2000] B.P.I.R. 661	IR 6.3	Robertson (A Bankrupt), Re [1989] 1 W.L.R. 1139	IR 6.211
Reid v Hamblin [2001] B.P.I.R. 929	IA 258(2)–(5)	Rolled Steel Products (Holdings) Ltd v British Steel Corp [1986] Ch. 246; [1985] 2 W.L.R. 908.	IA 232, 238(5)
Reid v Ramlort Ltd; sub nom. Thoars (Deceased), Re; Reid v Ramlot Ltd [2002] EWHC 2416; [2003] 1 B.C.L.C. 499	IA 238(4), 339(1)–(3)	Rooney v Cardona (No.1) [1999] 1 W.L.R. 1388; [1999] 1 F.L.R. 1236; [1999] B.P.I.R. 291	IA 283(2), (3)
		Rooney v Das [1999] B.P.I.R. 404	IA 340(4), (5)
Reigate v Union Manufacturing Co (Ramsbottom) Ltd [1918] 1 K.B. 592	IA 91(2)	Ross, Re [1997] B.C.C. 29	IA 251
		Ross (A Bankrupt) (No.2), Re; sub nom. Ross v Stonewood Securities Ltd [2000] B.P.I.R. 636; (2000) 97(21) L.S.G. 40	IA 266(3), (4)
Reynolds Ex p (1882) 21 Ch D 601	IA 366(1)		
Rhondda Waste Disposal Ltd (In Administration), Re; sub nom. Clark v Environment Agency; Environment Agency v Clark [2001] Ch. 57; [2000] 3 W.L.R. 1304	IA 11(3)	Rothschild v Bell [1999] B.P.I.R. 300	IA 283(3A)
		Rottenberg v Monjack [1992] B.C.C. 688; [1993] B.C.L.C. 374	IA 37(4)
Rica Gold Washing Co Ltd, Re; sub nom. Rica Gold Washing Co, Re (1879) L.R. 11 Ch. D. 36	IA 9(1), 124(2),(3), 172(1),(2), 212(5)	Rowbotham Baxter, Re [1990] B.C.C. 113; [1990] B.C.L.C. 397	IA 8(3), 9(1), Sch.B1, para.3(1),(3)
		Rowe v Sanders [2002] EWCA Civ 242; [2002] 2 All E.R. 800 (Note); [2002] B.P.I.R. 847	IA 306, 310
Richbell Information Services Inc v Atlantic & General Investment Trust Ltd (Validation of Disposition) [1999] B.C.C. 871	IA 123, 127	Royal Bank of Canada v Chetty [1997] B.P.I.R. 137	IA 306
		Royal Bank of Scotland Plc v Bhardwaj; sub nom. Dewrun Ltd, Re [2002] B.C.C. 57	IA 127
Richbell Strategic Holdings Ltd (No.1), Re [1997] 2 B.C.L.C. 429	IA 123	Royal Bank of Scotland Plc v Binnell [1996] B.P.I.R. 352	IR 6.5
Richbell Strategic Holdings Ltd (In Liquidation) (No.2), Re [2001] B.C.C. 409; [2000] 2 B.C.L.C. 794	IA 133	Royal Bank of Scotland v Debtor [1996] B.P.I.R. 478	IA 282(1), (3)
		Royal Bank of Scotland v Farley [1996] B.P.I.R. 638	IA 282(1), (3)
Rimar Pty Ltd v Pappas (1986) 60 A.L.J.R. 309	IA 30794)		
Ringinfo Ltd, Re [2002] 1 B.C.L.C. 210	IA 123	Royal British Bank v Turquand [1843–60] All E.R. Rep. 435; 119 E.R. 886; (1856) 6 El. & Bl. 327	IA 42(3)
Rio Properties Inc v Al-Midani [2003] B.P.I.R. 302	IA 284(1)–(3),(6), IA 267(1),(2)	Runciman v Walker Runciman [1993] B.C.C. 223; [1992] B.C.L.C. 1084	IA 9(1)
Ritchie v Burns; sub nom. Burns Trustee v Burns 2001 S.L.T. 1383; [2001] B.P.I.R. 666	IA 336(3)–(5)	Russell v Russell [1998] 1 F.L.R. 936; [1999] 2 F.C.R. 137; [1998] B.P.I.R. 259	IA 264, 382(3),(4)

Case	Provision
Russian & English Bank v Baring Bros & Co Ltd (No.2); sub nom. Russian & English Bank, Re [1932] 1 Ch. 663	IA 123
Rye v Ashfield Nominees Ltd, August 2, 2001	IR 4.127–4.131

S

Case	Provision
S & A Conversions, Re (1988) 4 B.C.C. 384; (1988) 138 N.L.J. Rep. 169	IA 192(2)
SA&D Wright Ltd, Re; sub nom. Denney v John Hudson & Co Ltd [1992] B.C.C. 503; [1992] B.C.L.C. 901	IA 127
SCL Building Services, Re (1989) 5 B.C.C. 746; [1990] B.C.L.C. 98	IA 8(1),(2)
SCMLLA Ltd v Gesso Properties (BVI) Ltd [1995] B.C.C. 793; [1995] E.G.C.S. 52	IA 178(4)
SEIL Trade Finance, Re [1992] B.C.C. 538	IA 246(3)
SHV Senator Hanseatische Verwaltungs Gesellschaft mbH, Re [1997] 1 W.L.R. 515; [1997] B.C.C.112	IA 124A
SJ Smith (A Bankrupt), Re, Ex p. Braintree DC; sub nom. Smith (AP), Re; Smith v Braintree DC [1990] 2 A.C. 215; [1989] 3 W.L.R. 1317	IA Pt IX, 285(1)
SN Group Plc v Barclays Bank Plc [1993] B.C.C. 506	IR 4.7–4.14, 7.47
St Ives Windings, Re (1987) 3 B.C.C. 634	IA Pt I, 8(3), 18(2)
St James's Club (1852) De G.M. & G 383	IA 220(1)
Saini v Petroform Ltd [1997] B.P.I.R. 515	IA 306
Salcombe Hotel Development Co, Re (1989) 5 B.C.C. 807; [1991] B.C.L.C. 44	IA 99(1), 166
Salmet International Ltd (In Administration), Re. See Spring Valley Properties Ltd v Harris	
Salters Hall School Ltd (In Liquidation), Re; sub nom. Merrygold v Horton [1998] 1 B.C.L.C. 401	IR 4.127–4.131
Salvage Association, Re [2003] EWHC 1028; [2003] 3 All E.R. 246; [2003] B.C.C. 504	IA Pt I, 8(1),(2)
Salvidge v Hussein; sub nom. Debtor (No.SD8/9 of 1998), Re [2000] B.C.C. 36; [1999] B.P.I.R. 410	IR 6.5
Sameen v Abeyewickrema [1963] A.C. 597; [1963] 2 W.L.R. 1114	IA 9(2)
Sandwell Copiers, Re (1988) 4 B.C.C. 227; [1988] B.C.L.C. 209	IA 115
Sankey Furniture Ltd Ex p. Harding, Re [1995] 2 B.C.L.C. 594	IA 108, 117, 172(1),(2), IR 6.126
Sargent v Customs and Excise Commissioners [1995] 1 W.L.R. 821; [1995] S.T.C. 398; [1995] 2 B.C.L.C. 34	IA Pt III
Sasea Finance Ltd (In Liquidation), Re [1999] B.C.C. 103; [1998] 1 B.C.L.C. 559	IA 236
Sasea Finance Ltd (In Liquidation) v KPMG (formerly KPMG Peat Marwick McLintock) (No.1) [1998] B.C.C. 216	IA 236, 236(2)
Saunders (a Bankrupt), Bristol & West Building Society v Saunders [1997] Ch.60; [1997] B.C.C. 83	IA 130(1), 285(3),(4)
Saunders v United Kingdom (19187/91) [1997] B.C.C. 872; [1998] 1 B.C.L.C. 362; (1997) 23 E.H.R.R. 313	IA 236, 433(1)
Schooler v Customs and Excise Commissioners [1995] 2 B.C.L.C. 610; [1996] B.P.I.R. 207	IA 420(1), 267(1),(2)

Case Table

Case	Provision
Schuppan (A Bankrupt) (No.1), Re; sub nom. Bankrupt (No.400 of 1995), Re [1996] 2 All E.R. 664; [1997] 1 B.C.L.C. 211; [1996] B.P.I.R. 486	IA Sch.5
Schuppan (A Bankrupt) (No.2), Re; sub nom. Trustee in Bankruptcy of Schuppan v Schuppan [1997] 1 B.C.L.C. 256; [1997] B.P.I.R. 271	IA 423(1)–(3), Sch.5
Scott v Davis [2003] B.P.I.R.	IA 310(1), (1A),(2)
Scottish & Newcastle plc, Petitioners [1993] B.C.C. 634	IA 53(6), (7), 60(1)
Sea Voyager Maritime Inc v Bielecki (t/a Hughes Hooker & Co); sub nom. Bielecki, Re [1999] 1 All E.R. 628; [1999] B.C.C. 924	IA 262(1)–(3),(8)
Seagull Manufacturing Co Ltd (In Liquidation) (No.1), Re [1993] Ch. 345; [1993] 2 W.L.R. 872 affirming [1992] Ch. 128; [1991] 3 W.L.R. 307; [1990] B.C.C. 550;	IA 9(2), 133, 236, 290(1),(2), 366(1), IR 4.211–4.217, 12.12
Seagull Manufacturing Co Ltd (In Liquidation) (No.2), Re [1994] Ch. 91; [1994] 2 W.L.R. 453; [1993] B.C.C. 833	IR 12.12
Secretary of State for Trade and Industry v Aurum Marketing Ltd; sub nom. Aurum Marketing Ltd (In Liquidation), Re [2002] B.C.C. 31; [2000] 2 B.C.L.C. 645	IA 124A
Secretary of State for Trade and Industry v Delfin International (SA) Ltd; sub nom. Delfin International (SA) Ltd (No.2), Re [2000] 1 B.C.L.C. 71	IA 124A
Secretary of State for Trade and Industry v Jabble [1998] B.C.C. 39; [1998] 1 B.C.L.C. 598	IA 34
Secretary of State for Trade and Industry v Leyton Housing Trustees Ltd [2000] 2 B.C.L.C. 808	IA 124A
Secretary of State for Trade and Industry v Liquid Acquisitions Ltd [2002] EWHC 180; [2003] 1 B.C.L.C. 375	IA 124A
Secretary of State for Trade and Industry v North West Holdings Plc [1998] B.C.C. 997; [1999] 1 B.C.L.C. 425	IR 4.7–4.14
Secretary of State for Trade and Industry v Palmer [1994] B.C.C. 990; 1995 S.L.T. 188; 1995 S.C.L.R. 30	IA 9(4),(5)
Secretary of State for Trade and Industry v Travel Time (UK) Ltd; sub nom. Company (No.5669 of 1998), Re [2000] B.C.C. 792; [2000] 1 B.C.L.C. 427	IA 124A
Secure & Provide, Re [1992] B.C.C. 405	IA 124A, IR 4.25–4.31
Securum Finance Ltd v Camswell Ltd [1994] B.C.C. 434, Ch D	IA 123
Seven Eight Six Properties Ltd v Ghafoor [1997] B.P.I.R. 519	IA 306
Shamash v Inland Revenue Commissioners [2002] B.P.I.R. 189	IA 282(1), (3)
Shamji v Johnson Matthey Bankers [1991] B.C.L.C. 36	IA 34
Shapland Inc, Re; sub nom. Mills v Edict Ltd [2000] B.C.C. 106; [1999] B.P.I.R. 391	IA 238(4), 239(4), 239(6)
Share, Re [2002] B.P.I.R. 194	IA 339(1)–(3)
Sharp v Thomson; sub nom. Sharp v Woolwich Building Society, 1997 S.C. (H.L.) 66; 1997 S.L.T. 636; [1998] B.C.C. 115	IA 50, 53(6),(7)
Sharp v Woolwich Building Society. *See* Sharp v Thomson	
Sharps of Truro, Re [1990] B.C.C. 94	IA 9(1), 18(2)
Shearing & Loader Ltd, Re [1991] B.C.C. 232	IA 9(1)
Shepheard v Lamey [2001] B.P.I.R. 939	IA 171, IR 4.113–4.120

Case Table

	Provision		Provision
Shepherd v Legal Services Commission [2003] B.P.I.R. 140	IA 266(3), (4)	Skjevesland v Geveran Trading Co Ltd (No.3); sub nom. Geveran Trading Co Ltd v Skjevesland (No.3) [2003] B.C.C. 209; [2003] B.P.I.R. 73	IA 265
Sheppard & Cooper Ltd v TSB Bank Plc (No.2) [1996] 2 All E.R. 654; [1996] B.C.C. 965	IA 34	Smallman Construction, Re (1988) 4 B.C.C. 784; [1989] B.C.L.C. 420	IA 17(2), 25(1), Sch.B1, paras.54, 68(2),(3)
Sherborne Associates Ltd, Re [1995] B.C.C. 40	IA 214(2)		
Sheridan Securities, Re (1988) 4 B.C.C. 200	IA 19(3)–(6), 20(1)	Smith v UIC Insurance Co Ltd [2001] B.C.C. 11	IA 135, IR 4.25–4.31
Shierson v Rastogi; sub nom. RBG Resources Plc, Re [2002] EWCA Civ 1624; [2003] 1 W.L.R. 586; [2002] B.C.C. 1005	IA 236	Smith (Administrator of Cosslett (Contractors) Ltd) v Bridgend CBC; sub nom. Cosslett (Contractors) Ltd (In Administration) (No.2), Re [2001] UKHL 58; [2002] 1 A.C. 336; [2001] 3 W.L.R. 1347; [2001] B.C.C. 740	IA 234(1), (2), IR 4.90
Shilena Hosiery Co Ltd, Re [1980] Ch. 219; [1979] 3 W.L.R. 332	IA 423		
Shindler v Northern Raincoat Co [1960] 1 W.L.R. 1038; [1960] 2 All E.R. 239	IA 14(2)		
Shire Court Residents Ltd v Registrar of Companies [1995] B.C.C. 821	IA Pt IV	Smiths Ltd v Middleton (No.1) [1979] 3 All E.R. 842	IR 3.32
Shoe Lace Ltd, Re. See Power v Sharp Investments Ltd		Sobam BV, Re; sub nom. Satelscoop BV, Re [1996] B.C.C. 351; [1996] 1 B.C.L.C. 446; [1996] R.A. 93; [1995] E.G.C.S. 189; [1995] N.P.C. 180	IA 44(1),(2)
Sibec Developments, Re. See Barclays Mercantile Business Finance Ltd v Sibec Developments Ltd			
Siebe Gorman & Co Ltd v Barclays Bank Ltd; sub nom. Siebe Gorman & Co Ltd v RH McDonald Ltd [1979] 2 Lloyd's Rep. 142, Ch D	IA 40(1), (2)	Soden v British & Commonwealth Holdings Plc (In Administration)[1998] A.C. 298; [1997] 3 W.L.R. 840; [1997] B.C.C. 952	IA 74(2)(f)
Signland, Re [1982] 2 All E.R. 609	IR 4.7–4.14	Soden v Burns; sub nom. R. v Secretary of State for Trade and Industry Ex p. Soden [1996] 1 W.L.R. 1512; [1996] 3 All E.R. 967; [1997] B.C.C. 308	IA 236
Silven Properties Ltd v Royal Bank of Scotland Plc [2002] EWHC 1976; [2003] B.P.I.R. 171	IA Pt III		
Simmon Box (Diamonds) Ltd, Re. See Cohen v Selby		Solomon, Re [1967] Ch 573	IA 336(3)–(5)
Simms v Oakes [2002] B.P.I.R. 1244	IA 339(1)–(3)	Solomons v Williams; sub nom. Bankrupt (457/2001), Re [2001] B.P.I.R. 1123	IA 309
Singh v Official Receiver [1997] B.P.I.R. 530	IA 306		
Skarzynski v Chalford Property Co Ltd [2001] B.P.I.R. 673	IA 268, 282(1),(3), IR 12.10	Somji v Cadbury Schweppes Plc. See Cadbury Schweppes Plc v Somji	
		Southard & Co Ltd, Re [1979] 1 W.L.R. 1198; [1979] 3 All E.R. 556, CA	IA 116, 124(5)
Skjevesland v Geveran Trading (No.4) [2002] EWHC 2898; [2003] B.C.C. 391	ER Art.3(1)		

Case Table

Case	Provision
Southern Foundries (1926) Ltd v Shirlaw [1940] A.C. 701; [1940] 2 All E.R. 445	IA 14(2)
Southward v Banham [2002] B.P.I.R. 1253	IR 6.5
Sowman v Samuel (David) Trust Ltd (In Liquidation) [1978] 1 W.L.R. 22; [1978] 1 All E.R. 616	IA Pt III
Specialised Mouldings Ltd, Re, unreported, February 13, 1987	IA 44(1),(2)
Spectrum Plus Ltd, Re; sub nom. National Westminster Bank Plc v Spectrum Plus Ltd (In Creditors Voluntary Liquidation) [2004] EWHC 9; [2004] 2 W.L.R. 783; [2004] 1 All E.R. 981; [2004] 1 B.C.L.C. 335; (2004) 154 N.L.J. 93; [2004] B.C.C. 51; *The Times*, January 23, 2004, Ch D (Companies Ct)	IA 40(1),(2)
Spirit Motorsport Ltd (In Liquidation), Re [1996] 1 B.C.L.C. 684; [1997] B.P.I.R. 288	IA 181(1)–(3)
Spring Valley Properties Ltd v Harris; sub nom. Salmet International Ltd (In Administration), Re [2001] B.C.C. 796; [2001] B.P.I.R. 709	IA 19(3)–(6)
Stacey v Hill [1901] 1 Q.B. 660	IA 181(1)–(3)
Stalltow Distribution Ltd, Re [2002] B.C.C. 486	IA 9(4),(5)
Standard Chartered Bank Ltd v Walker [1982] 1 W.L.R. 1410; [1982] 3 All E.R. 938	IA Pt III
Stanhope Pension Trust Ltd v Registrar of Companies; sub nom. Forte's (Manufacturing), Re [1994] B.C.C. 84; [1994] 1 B.C.L.C. 628; (1995) 69 P. & C.R. 238; [1993] E.G.C.S. 206; [1993] N.P.C. 169	IA Pt IV
Stein v Blake (No.1) [1996] A.C. 243; [1995] 2 W.L.R. 710; [1995] B.C.C. 543	IA 323, IR 4.90
Stein v Saywell (1969) 121 C.L.R. 529	IA 175(2)(b)
Stella Metals Ltd (In Liquidation), Re [1997] B.C.C. 626; [1997] B.P.I.R. 293	IA 108, 263(5),(6)
Stern (A Bankrupt) Ex p. Keyser Ullman, Re [1982] 1 W.L.R. 860; [1982] 2 All E.R. 600	IA 290(4)
Stetzel Thomson & Co Ltd, Re (1988) 4 B.C.C. 74	IA 112(2)
Stocznia Gdanska SA v Latreefers Inc; sub nom. Latreefers Inc, Re [2000] C.P.L.R. 65; [2001] B.C.C. 174 affirming [1999] 1 B.C.L.C. 271	IA 123, 135, 220
Strongmaster Ltd v Kaye [2002] EWHC 444; [2002] B.P.I.R. 1259	IA 263(5),(6)
Structures & Computers Ltd, Re; sub nom. Structures & Computers Ltd v Ansys Inc [1998] B.C.C. 348; [1998] 1 B.C.L.C. 292	IA 8(1),(2)
Sugar Properties (Derisley Wood), Re [1988] B.C.L.C. 146	IA 127
Supperstone v Auger [1999] B.P.I.R. 152	IA 303(2)
Supperstone v Lloyd's Names Association Working Party [1999] B.P.I.R. 832	IA 307(2),(5),(7)
Sweatfield Ltd, Re [1997] B.C.C. 744; [1998] B.P.I.R. 276	IA 1(1), 6A, 262(1)–(3),(8)
Swindon Town Properties Ltd v Swindon Town Football Co Ltd [2003] B.P.I.R. 253	IA 6
Swissair Schweizerische Luftverkehr AG, Re; Edwards v Flightline Ltd. *See* Flightline Ltd v Edwards	
Symes (A Debtor), Re; sub nom. Kent Carpets Ltd v Symes [1996] B.C.C. 137; [1995] 2 B.C.L.C. 651	IA 258(1)

T

Case	Provision
T&D Industries Plc, Re; sub nom. T&D Automotive Ltd, Re [2000] 1 W.L.R. 646; [2000] 1 All E.R. 333	IA 17(2)
TE Brinsmead & Sons, Re [1897] 1 Ch.406	IA 122(1)

Case Table

Case	Provision
TFB Mortgages Ltd v Pimlico Capital Ltd; sub nom. Pimlico Capital Ltd, Re [2002] EWHC 878; [2002] 2 B.C.L.C. 544...	IA 124(2), (3)
TSB Bank Plc v Platts (No.1) [1997] B.P.I.R. 151	IA 266(3), (4)
TSB Bank Plc v Platts (No.2); sub nom. Platts v Trustee Savings Bank Plc [1998] Lloyd's Rep. Bank. 163; [1998] 2 B.C.L.C. 1; [1998] B.P.I.R. 284	IA 267(1), (2),(4),(5)
Tack, Re [2000] B.P.I.R. 164 ...	IA 276(1)
Tager v Westpac Banking Corp [1998] B.C.C. 73; [1997] 1 B.C.L.C. 313...............	IA 262(1)–(3),(8), 376
Tajik Air Ltd, Re [1996] B.C.C. 368; [1996] 1 B.C.L.C. 317...	IA 9(4),(5)
Talbot v Grundy; Leyland DAF Ltd. *See* Powdrill v Watson	
Tasbian Ltd (No.2), Re [1990] B.C.C. 322; [1991] B.C.L.C. 59	IR 7.47
Tasbian Ltd (No.3), Re; sub nom. Official Receiver v Nixon [1992] B.C.C. 358; affirming [1991] B.C.C. 435; [1991] B.C.L.C. 792...............	IA 251, IR 7.47
Tay Bok Choon v Tahansan Sdn Bhd [1987] 1 W.L.R. 413; [1987] B.C.L.C. 472; (1987) 3 B.C.C. 132...............	IA 122(1)
Taylor v Pace Developments [1991] B.C.C. 406	IA 9(4),(5)
Taylor, Noter [1992] B.C.C. 440	IA Sch.4, paras 2,3
Taylor Sinclair (Capital) Ltd (In Liquidation), Re. *See* Knights v Seymour Pierce Ellis Ltd (formerly Ellis & Partners Ltd)	
Taylor's Industrial Flooring Ltd, Re [1990] B.C.C. 44.........	IA 123
Television Parlour plc, Re (1988) 4 B.C.C. 95	IA 124, 125(1)
Television Trade Rentals Ltd, Re [2002] EWHC 211; [2002] B.C.C. 807.................	IA Pt I, 426(4),(5),(11), 442
Theophile v Solicitor General; sub nom. Debtor (No.355 of 1947), Re [1950] A.C. 186; [1950] 1 All E.R. 405........	IA 265
Therm-a-Stor Ltd (In Administrative Receivership), Re; sub nom. Morris v Lewis [1996] 1 W.L.R. 1338; [1996] 3 All E.R. 228; [1997] B.C.C. 301	IA 35(1)
Thirty-Eight Building Ltd (No.1), Re [1999] B.C.C. 260; [1999] 1 B.C.L.C. 416...............	IA 239(4)
Thirty-Eight Building Ltd (No.2), Re; sub nom. Simms v Saunders [2000] B.C.C. 422; [2000] 1 B.C.L.C. 201; [2000] B.P.I.R. 158................	IR 7.47
Thoars (Deceased), Re; Reid v Ramlot Ltd. *See* Reid v Ramlort Ltd	
Thorne v Silverleaf [1994] B.C.C. 109; [1994] 2 B.C.L.C. 637...	IA 216, 217
Thulin, Re [1995] 1 W.L.R. 165; (1995) 92(2) L.S.G. 35.......	IA 265
Times Newspapers Ltd v Chohan (Limitation Periods); sub nom. Chohan v Times Newspapers Ltd (Limitation Periods) [2001] EWCA Civ 964; [2001] 1 W.L.R. 1859; [2001] B.P.I.R. 943	IA 267(1), (2)
Titan International Inc, Re [1998] 1 B.C.L.C. 102	IA 124A
Todd (Swanscombe), Re; sub nom. L Todd, Re [1990] B.C.C. 125; [1990] B.C.L.C. 454	IA 213(1)
Toleman Ex p. Bramble, Re; sub nom. Toleman & England Ex p. Bramble, Re; Toleman and England, Re v Ex p. Bramble (1879–80) L.R. 13 Ch. D. 885	IA 236(4)–(6)
Tony Rowse NMC Ltd, Re [1996] B.C.C. 196; [1996] 2 B.C.L.C. 225	IR 4.127–4.131, 4.218–4.220
Top Creative Ltd v St Albans District Council [1999] B.C.C. 999; [2000] 2 B.C.L.C. 379...	IA Pt IV

Case Table

	Provision		Provision
Toshoku Finance UK Plc (In Liquidation), Re; sub nom. Inland Revenue Commissioners v Kahn; Kahn v Inland Revenue Commissioners; Kahn v Inland Revenue Commissioners [2002] UKHL 6; [2002] 1 W.L.R. 671; [2002] B.C.C. 110	IA 115, IR 4.218–4.220, 13.12	Tudor Grange Holdings Ltd v Citibank NA [1992] Ch. 53; [1991] 3 W.L.R. 750	IA Pt III
		Turner v Royal Bank of Scotland Plc (Relitigation) [2000] B.P.I.R. 683	IR 6.5
		Turner, Petitioner [1993] B.C.C. 299	IA 59(1),(2)
		Turner, Re [1974] 1 W.L.R. 1556	IA 336(3)–(5)
Tottenham Hotspur Plc v Edennote Plc [1994] B.C.C. 681; [1995] 1 B.C.L.C. 65	IR 13.12	Twinsectra Ltd v Yardley [2002] UKHL 12; [2002] 2 A.C. 164	IA 107
		Tyman's Ltd v Craven [1952] 2 Q.B. 100	IA Pt IV
Trading Partners Ltd, Re. See Akers v Lomas		**U**	
Tramway Building & Construction Co Ltd, Re [1988] Ch. 293; [1988] 2 W.L.R. 640; (1987) 3 B.C.C. 443	IA 127	UCT (UK) Ltd (In Administration), Re; sub nom. UCT (UK) Ltd v Dargan [2001] 1 W.L.R. 436; [2001] 2 All E.R. 186; [2001] B.C.C. 734	IA 18(2)
TransTec Automotive (Campsie) Ltd, Re. See Ford AG-Werke AG v Transtec Automotive (Campsie) Ltd		UOC Corp, Alipour v Ary. See Alipour v Ary	
Transworld Trading, Re [1999] B.P.I.R. 628	IA 239(6)	UOC Corp (No.2), Re. See Alipour v UOC Corp (No.2)	
Trinity Insurance, Re [1990] B.C.C. 235	IA 123	Unit 2 Windows Ltd (In Liquidation), Re [1985] 1 W.L.R. 1383; [1985] 3 All E.R. 647; (1985) 1 B.C.C. 99,489	IA 59(1),(2)
Trow v Ind Coope (West Midlands) Ltd [1967] 2 Q.B. 899; [1967] 3 W.L.R. 633	IA 86	Upton v Taylor [1999] B.P.I.R. 168	IR 6.138
Trowbridge v Trowbridge [2003] B.P.I.R. 258	IA 423(1)–(3)	**V**	
Trustee in Bankruptcy of Bukhari v Bukhari [1999] B.P.I.R. 157	IA 305(2)	Vedmay, Re [1994] 1 B.C.L.C. 676; (1994) 26 H.L.R. 70	IA 181(1)–(3), 182(4)
Trustee of the Estate of Bowe (A Bankrupt) v Bowe [1998] 2 F.L.R. 439; [1997] B.P.I.R. 747	IA 336(3)–(5)	Victoria Society, Knottingley, Re [1913] 1 Ch. 167	IA Pt IV
		Vocalion (Foreign) Ltd, Re [1932] 2 Ch. 196	IA 183
Trustee of the Property of FC Jones & Sons (A Firm) v Jones [1997] Ch. 159; [1996] 3 W.L.R. 703; [1996] B.P.I.R. 644	IA 251	**W**	
		W & A Glaser, Re [1994] B.C.C. 199	IR 4.152–4.155, 4.156–4.159, 4.172A, 7.47
Tucker (a Bankrupt), Re Tucker Ex p [1990] Ch.148	IA 366(1), IR 12.12		

xlix

Case Table

Case	Provision
WBSL Realisations 1992 Ltd, Re; sub nom. Ward Group Plc, Re [1995] B.C.C. 1118; [1995] 2 B.C.L.C. 576	IA 11(5), Sch.1
WF Fearman, Re (1988) 4 B.C.C. 139	IR 2.1–2.3
WF Fearman, Re (No.2) (1988) 4 B.C.C. 141	IA 9(4),(5), 115, 135, 177, IR 4.218–4.220
WH Smith v Wyndham Investments [1994] B.C.C. 699; [1994] 2 B.C.L.C. 571	IR 4.187–4.194
Walker Morris (A Firm) v Khalastchi [2001] 1 B.C.L.C. 1	IA 234(1),(2)
Wallace v Shoa Leasing (Singapore) PTE Ltd; sub nom. Japan Leasing (Europe) Plc, Re [1999] B.P.I.R. 911; [2000] W.T.L.R. 301	IA 107
Wallace Smith Trust Co, Re [1992] B.C.C. 707	IA 131, 221, 235
Walter L Jacob & Co Ltd, Re (1989) 5 B.C.C. 244; [1989] B.C.L.C. 345	IA 124A, IR 4.25–4.31
Wavern Engineering Co Ltd (1987) 3 B.C.C. 3	IA 124(1)
Webb Distributors (Aust) Pty Ltd v Victoria (1993) 11 A.C.S.R. 731	IA 74(2)(f)
Webb Electrical, Re [1989] P.C.C. 379; [1988] P.C.C. 230	IA 127
Weddell v JA Pearce & Major (A Firm) [1988] Ch. 26; [1987] 3 W.L.R. 592	IA Sch.5
Wehmeyer v Wehmeyer [2001] 2 F.L.R. 84; [2001] B.P.I.R. 548	IA 270, 382(3),(4), IR 12.3
Weisgard v Pilkington [1995] B.C.C. 1108	IA 239(6)
Welburn v Dibb Lupton Broomhead [2002] EWCA Civ 1601; [2003] B.P.I.R. 768	IA 260(1),(2),(2A)
Wellworth Cash & Carry (North Shields) Ltd v North Eastern Electricity Board (1986) 2 B.C.C. 99,265	IA 233
Welsby v Brelec Installations Ltd (In Liquidation); sub nom. Brelec Installations Ltd, Re [2001] B.C.C. 421; [2000] 2 B.C.L.C. 576	IA 7(4)
Welsh Development Agency v Export Finance Co [1992] B.C.C. 270; [1992] B.C.L.C. 148	IA 234(3),(4)
Wessex Computer Stationers, Re [1992] B.C.L.C. 366	IA 124(2),(3)
West Bromwich Building Society v Crammer [2002] EWHC 2618; [2003] B.P.I.R. 783	IA 267(1),(2)
West Park Golf & Country Club, Re [1997] 1 B.C.L.C. 20	IR 2.1–2.3
Western Counties Construction v Witney Town Football and Social Club [1993] B.C.C. 874; [1994] 2 B.C.L.C. 487	IA 220(1)
Western Intelligence Ltd v KDO Label Printing Machines Ltd (In Administrative Receivership) [1998] B.C.C. 472	IA 216
Westlowe Storage & Distribution Ltd (In Liquidation), Re [2000] B.C.C. 851; [2000] 2 B.C.L.C. 590	IA 212(1)
Westmead Consultants Ltd (In Liquidation), Re; sub nom. Ward v Evans [2002] 1 B.C.L.C. 384	IA 236
Westminster City Council v Parkin [2001] B.P.I.R. 1156	IA 266(3),(4)
Westminster Property Management Ltd (No.2), Re; sub nom. Official Receiver v Stern (No.2) [2001] EWCA Civ 111; [2002] B.C.C. 937 affirming [2001] B.C.C. 305	IA 220, 235
Wheatley v Wheatley [1999] 2 F.L.R. 205; [1999] B.P.I.R. 431	IA 264
Whitehead v Household Mortgage Corp Plc. *See* Household Mortgage Corp Plc v Whitehead	
Whitehouse & Co, Re (1878) L.R. 9 Ch. D. 595	IA 149(1)

Case Table

Case	Provision
Wilkinson v Inland Revenue Commissioners; sub nom. Debtor v Inland Revenue Commissioners [1998] B.P.I.R. 418; 68 T.C. 157	IA 265
William Thorpe & Son, Re (1989) 5 B.C.C. 156	IA 195
Wills v Corfe Joinery Ltd (In Liquidation); sub nom. Corfe Joinery Ltd (In Liquidation), Re [1997] B.C.C. 511; [1998] 2 B.C.L.C. 75	IA 239(6)
Wilmott Trading Ltd (No.2), Re; sub nom. Henry v Environment Agency (No.2) [2000] B.C.C. 321; [1999] 2 B.C.L.C. 541 ...	IA 106, Pt IV
Wisepark Ltd, Re [1994] B.C.C. 221	IA 260(1), (2),(2A), 382(3),(4)
Wolsey Theatre Co Ltd, Re [2001] B.C.C. 486	IA 18(2)
Wood, Re [1994] 1 C.L. 257	IA 267(1),(2)
Woodland-Ferrari v UCL Group Retirement Benefits Scheme [2002] EWHC 1354; [2003] Ch. 115; [2002] B.P.I.R. 1270	IA 281(2)–(6),(8)
Woodley v Woodley (Committal Order) (No.2) [1994] 1 W.L.R. 1167; [1993] 4 All E.R. 1010 .	IA 251, 272, 284(1)–(3),(6), 354(2), 382(3),(4), 413(1), Sch.9, IR 12.3
Woodroffes (Musical Instruments) Ltd, Re [1986] Ch. 366; [1985] 3 W.L.R. 543.	IA 175(2)(b)
Wordsworth v Dixon; sub nom. Dixon v Wordsworth [1997] B.P.I.R. 337...............	IA 306
Worwood v Leisure Merchandising Services Ltd [2002] 1 B.C.L.C. 249	IA Pt III
Wright v Official Receiver [2001] B.P.I.R. 196...............	IA 253(1)–(3), 281(1)

X

Case	Provision
X, Re [1996] B.P.I.R. 494	IA 285(3),(4), 310
Xyllyx (No.1), Re [1992] B.C.L.C. 376...............	IA 124A
Xyllyx (No.2), Re [1992] B.C.L.C. 378...............	IR 4.25–4.31

Y

Case	Provision
Yagerphone Ltd, Re [1935] Ch. 392......................	IA 238
Yenidje Tobacco Co Ltd, Re [1916] 2 Ch. 426............	IA 122(1)

Z

Case	Provision
Zandfarid v Bank of Credit and Commerce International SA (In Liquidation); sub nom. Zandfarid, Re [1996] 1 W.L.R. 1420; [1997] 1 F.L.R. 274; [1996] B.P.I.R. 501	IA 269, 336(3)–(5)
Zinotty Properties Ltd, Re [1984] 1 W.L.R. 1249; [1984] 3 All E.R. 754; (1984) 1 B.C.C. 99,139	IA 122(1)

Statutes Table

This table enables the user to locate references to legislative provisions other than the Insolvency Acts 1986 and 2000, the Insolvency Rules 1986, the EC Regulation on Insolvency Proceedings 2000 and the Enterprise Act 2002 in the provisions of those Acts, Rules and Regulations and their notes.

Abbreviations in the provision column are to the Insolvency Act 1986 (IA), the Insolvency Act 2000 (IA 2000), the Insolvency Rules 1986 (IR), the EC Regulation on Insolvency Proceedings 2000 (ER) and the Enterprise Act 2002(EA).

	Provision		Provision
Access to Justice Act 1999		51	IA 310
56(1)	EA 268(15)	54(1)	IA 315(1),(2)
Adults with Incapacity (Scotland) Act 2000	IA 390(4)	54(3)	IA 317
		54(4)	IA 316
Banking Act 1979	IA 8(5), Sch.B1, para.9(1), IR 13.12A(2)	55	IA 314(1),(2),(6)
		56	IA 314(1),(2),(6)
Banking Act 1987	IA 8(5), 251, Sch.B1, para.9(1), IR 4.10(4), 4.72, 13.12A(2)	57	IA 314(1),(2),(6)
		61	IA 304(3)
92	IA 124	66	IA 244, 322(2), 343
Banking and Financial Dealings Act 1971	IR 13.13(1)	68	IA 325(2)
		70	IA 399(2)
Bankruptcy Act 1914	IA Pt IX, IR 6.36(1)	71	IA 401(1)
1(2)	IA 265	76	IA 305(4)
5(7)	IA 266(2)	77	IA 292(3)
6(2)	IA 266(2)	79(1)	IA 301(1)
10	IA 287(1),(2),(5)	79(2)	IA 314(7)
14	IA 288(1),(3)	110	IA 271(5)
15	IA 290	111	IA 271(5)
16	IA Pt VIII, 262	113	IA 266(3),(4)
16(2)	IA 258(1)	118	IA 345(4)
16(13)	IA 260(1),(2),(2A)	129	IA 275(1),(2)
16(19)	IA 258(2)–(5)	147(1)	IR 7.55
17	IA Pt VIII	154(1)	IA 356(2)
21	IA Pt VIII	154(6)	IA 356(1)
21(1)	IA 258(1)	154(7)	IA 356(2)
28	IA 281(2)–(6),(8)	154(12)	IA 356(2)
28(a)	IA 307(1)	154(16)	IA 356(2)
29(3)	IA 282(1),(3)	156	IA 357(1),(3)
33(4)	IA 328	159	IA 358
33(6)	IA 328	Sch.1	IA 293(2),(3)
34	IA 348(5),(6)	**Bankruptcy and Insolvency Act (Canada) 1992**	
36	IA 329		
42	IA 238	247	IA Pt III
43	IA 344(1),(2)	**Bankruptcy (Scotland) Act 1985**	IA 185(1), 242(3), 251, 388(4),(5), 389(2)
44	IA 238		
44(1)	IA 239(5)	31	IA 82(1),(2)
47	IA 307(4)	34	IA 242, 242(2),(3)

liii

Statutes Table

Provision

38	IA 169(2)
38(4)	IA 246
57	IA 193, 193(3)
58	IA 193(3)
73(1)	IA 193(2)
74	IA 242(2),(3)

Bankruptcy (Scotland) Act 1993 .... IA 251
Bills of Sale Act 1878 .... IA 344(1),(2)
Broadcasting Act 1990
Pt II .... IA 233(5), 372(5)
Building Societies Act 1986 ...... IA 388(4)
Pt X .... IA Pt IV
90 .... IA Pt IV, 212
90A .... IA Pt I, 8
Sch.15 .... IA Pt IV, 8
Building Societies Act 1997
39 ... IA Pt I, 8, 28, 38(3),(4), 39(1), 40(1),(2)
111 .... IA 40(1),(2)
Sch.6 ...... IA 28, 38(3),(4), 39(1), 40(1),(2)
Channel Tunnel Rail Link Act 1996
19 .... IA 72GA, EA 249(1)
Charging Orders Act 1979
1 .... IA 183(3), 346(5)
3(1) .... IR 6.237(6), 6.237D(6)
3(2) .... IR 6.237(7), 6.237D(7)
Charities Act 1960 .... IA 241(4)
Charities Act 1993
63 .... IA 124
65 .... IA 241(4)
Child Support Act 1991 .... IR 12.3(2)
Children Act 1989 .... IA 281(2)–(6),(8)
Civil Aviation Act 1982
88 .... IA 11(3), 248
Civil Jurisdiction and Judgments Act 1982 .... IA 220
Coal Industry Act 1994 ... EA Sch.17, paras 48(1),(2),(3)
36 .... ER Sch.17, para.48(1)
Companies Act 1862 .... CA 735(1)
Companies Act 1928
91 .... IA 225
Companies Act 1929 .... CA 735(1)
Companies Act 1948 .... CA 735(1), IA 101
206–208 .... IA Pt I
216 .... IA 82(1),(2)
287 .... IA Pt I
306 .... IA Pt I
Companies Act 1967
43 .... IA 78(1)
44 .... IA 77(1)
Companies Act 1980
5 .... IA 77(1)
63 .... IA 251
74 .... IA 187

Provision

Companies Act 1985 ..... IA 71, EA Sch.17, paras 3,4,5,6,7,8
Pt XI .... IA 92(3)
Pt XII .... IA Sch.B1, para.21
Pt XXI .... IA 220
14 .... IA 74(2)(f)
22 .... IA 250
35(1) .... IA 241(4)
35A .... IA 42(3)
35B .... IA 42(3)
42 .... IA 130(1)
42(1)(a) .... IA 109(1)
49 .... IA 78, 78(1)
111A .... IA 74(2)(f)
151 .... IA Pt I, 241(4)
153(3)(g) .... IA Pt I
171ff .... IA 76
179 .... IA 79(3)
s.196 .... IA 176A
238–240 .... IA Sch.B1, para.39
285 .... IA 232
306 .... IA 75
319(7) .... IA 176(3)
320 .... IA 42(1)
359 .... IA 148(1)
368 .... IA 17(3)
370(3) .... IA 17(3)
375 .... IR 2.51(2)
378 .... IA 84(1)
378(3) .... IA 84(1)
380 .... IA 84(3)
380(4)(a),(b),(j) .... IA 84(3)
380(7) .... IA 84(3)
381 .... IA 194
381A .... IA Sch.B1, para.22(1)
381A–381C .... IA 84(1)
405 .... IA 53(1),(2),(5)
405(1) .... IA 39(1)
405(2) .... IA 45(4),(5), IR 3.35
408 .... IA Sch.B1, para.15
409 .... IA 95(6), 431(1),(2),(4)
409(2) .... IR 3.35
425 .... IA 4(4), 8(3), 135, IA 176A, Sch.B1, para.72(2)(c), ER Arts 34,35, EA 255(2)
425(2) .... IA 27(3)(a)
425–427 .... IA Pt I, 9(2), 22, 27(3)(a)
431 .... IA 7A(3), 155(2), 218(5)
432 .... IA 7A(3), 218(5), 236
458 .... IA 213, 213(2)
459 IA 6, 27(1), 122(1), 125(2), Sch.B1, para.74 (1),(5)(a)
461(2) .... IA 27(4)
462–466 .... IA 50
464(4)(b) .... IA Sch.B1, para.96(4)
474 .... IA 58(2),(3)

liv

Statutes Table

Provision		Provision	
518(1)(e)	IA 123	735(1)	IA 73
528(6)	IA 131(5)	735(3)	IA 73
539(1),(2)	IA Sch.4	740	IA 432(1)–(3)
545	IA 146	741	IA 251
551	IA 234(1),(2)	744	IA 22(1)–(5), 117, 131(3), 206(3), Sch.B1, para.47(3),(4)
556	IA 177		
561	IA 133	Sch.24	IA 430(2)–(4)
579	IA 90	**Companies Act 1989**	72B(1),(2), EA Sch.17, paras 43,44,45,46,47(1),(2),(3),(4)
581(3)	IA 92(3)		
582	IA Pt I		
582(2)	110(3)	Pt VII	IA 107, Art.9, EA 249(6)
587	IA 90	108	IA 187, 241(4)
588(4)	IR 4.50–4.71	111	IA 241(4)
593	IA 110(3)	130(7)	IA 53(3)
596	IA 90	141(4)	IA Pt IV
598(1),(2)	IA Sch.4	141(5)	IA Pt IV
599(2)	IA 171	159	IA 107
601	IA Pt I	161(4)	IA 10(1), 11(2), 126, 128, 130, 185, 285
611–613	IA Pt IV		
612	IA 244	163(4)	IA 127
615	IA 238, 239	164(1)	IA 178, 186, 315, 345
615(2)	IA Pt I	165	IA 238, 239, 242, 340
617	IA 245(2), 245(3)–(5)	173	IA 10(1), 11(2),(3), 15, 43, 61(1),(2), 72F
618	IA 178		
618(1)	IA 178(3)	175	IA 10(1), 11(2),(3), 15, 43, 61(1),(2)
618(3)	IA 178(2)	175(3)–(5)	IA 127
619	IA 178	211	IA 212
619(2)	IA 178(5)	211(1),(2)	IA Pt IV
619(8)	IA 178(6)	211(2)(a),(b)	IA Pt IV, 388(4)
629	IA 178	212	IA Pt IV
630	IA 213	Sch.16	IA 45(4),(5), 53(1),(2),(5), 54(3),(4), 62(5)
651	IA Pt IV		
651(4)	IA Pt IV	Sch.17, para.10	IA 53(3)
651(5)–(7)	IA Pt IV	Sch.24	IA 45(4),(5), 53(1),(2),(5), 54(3),(4), 62(5), Pt IV, Pt IV, 212
652	IA Pt IV		
653	IA Pt IV		
654	IA 181(1)–(3)	**Companies Clauses Consolidation Act 1845**	IA 111(4)
656	IA 181(1)–(3)		
657(2)	IA 181(1)–(3)	**Companies Clauses Consolidation (Scotland) Act 1845**	IA 111(4)
665	IA 220		
680	IA 83, 83(1), 126(2), 130(3)	**Companies (Consolidation) Act 1908**	CA 735(1)
691	IA 95(6)		
711(1)(p)	IA 130(1)	**Companies (Floating Charges) (Scotland) Act 1961**	
711(2)(b)	IA 109(1)		
713	IA 170	4	IA 122(1)
719	IA 187, 187(1)	**Companies (Floating Charges and Receivers) (Scotland) Act 1972**	
719(1),(2)	IA 187(4),(5)		
719(3)	IA 187(1), 187(2)	15	IA Sch.1
719(3)(b)	IA 187(2)	**Companies (Winding-up) Rules 1949**	IA Sch.8
719(4)	IA 187(1)		
727	IA 206(3), 214	**Company Directors Disqualification Act 1986**	IA 216(3), 389A(3)
730(5)	IA 430(5)		
733	IA 432(1)–(3)	1(1)(d)	IA 206(3)
735	IA 8(1),(2),(4)–(6), Pt IV, 73(1), 110(1)	2	IA 206(3)
		4	IA 213(2)

Provision		Provision
6(2) .... IA Pt VI		**Criminal Procedure (Scotland) Act 1975**
6(2)(b) .... IA 9(4),(5)		289B .... IA Sch.10
7 .... IA 214		**Damages (Scotland) Act 1976** ..... IA Pt IV
7(2) .... IA 9(4),(5)		**Debtors Act 1869** .... IA 251
7(3) .... IA Sch.8, para.26		5 .... IA 251
7(4) .... IA 236, Sch.8, para.29		85 .... IA 371(1)
8(1) .... IA 236		**Debtors Relief Act 1729** .... IA 251
10 .... IA 213(2), 214(1)		**Deeds of Arrangement Act 1914** ... IA 251,
10(1)(aa) .... IA 2000 9		Pt VIII, 260(3), 260(3), 263D(6), 379, Sch.9,
11 .... IA 206(3), IR 6.203–6.205,		para.24
6.203(1), 6.205(1)		**Drug Trafficking Offences Act 1986**
11(3)(ba) .... IA 2000 9		1 .... IR 6.223, 12.3(2)
12 .... IA 429(2)		8 .... IA 252(2)
15 .... IA 217		**Electricity Act 1989** .... IA 372(4),(5)
15(1) .... IA 206(3)		Pt I .... IA 233(3), 372(4)
15(4) .... IA 206(3)		6 .... IA Sch.2A, para.10(1)
22(5) .... IA 251		**Employment Rights Act 1996** ... EA Sch.17,
Competition Act 1998 .... IA 428		paras 49(1),(2),(3),(4)
Consumer Credit Act 1974 ... IA 10(4), 436		Pt III .... IA Sch.6, para.13(2)
137–140 .... IA 244		Pt VII .... IA Sch.6, para.13(2)
139 .... IA 343(3),(6)		183 .... IA Pt VI
139(1)(a) .... IA 343(6)		**Enterprise Act 2002** .. IA 8, 20(2),(3), Pt III,
192(3) .... ia 283		251, Pt VIII, 5.1, 5.7, 5.34, IR 6.193C,
Sch.4, para.6 .... IA 283		13.11
Consumer Protection Act 1987		Pt 10 .... IA Pt II, Pt IX
Pt I .... IA 281(2)–(6),(8)		212 .... IA B1, para.75
Conveyancing and Feudal Reform		212(1)(b) .... IA Sch.B1, para.75
(Scotland) Act 1970 .... IA 70(1)		248 ...... IA 1, 5(3), 5(4), 6, 51(2A), IR Pt 2
County Courts Act 1984 .... IA 251		248(3) .... IA 230(1)
Pt VI .... IA 429(1)		249 .... IA Pt II, 212(1), 230
102 .... IA 347(6)		249(1)(a)–(d) .... IR Pt 2
116 .... IA 347(1),(2),(5),(9)		249(2) .... IA Sch.B1, para.10
128 .... IR 12.15		250 ..... IA 72A, Sch.B1, paras 14, 14(2),(3)
Courts and Legal Services Act 1990		250(2) .... IA 72A, Sch.2A, para.11
13 .... IA 429(1)		251 .... IA 40(1),(2), 175, Sch.6
71 .... IA Sch.7, para.1(1)		252 .... IA 40(1),(2)
Criminal Evidence Act 1999		256 .... IA Pt IX, 279
55 .... IA 219		257 .... IA 281(2)–(6),(8),
Sch.3 .... IA 219		350(3A), 360(5),(6), Sch.4A
Criminal Justice Act 1988		258 .... IA Pt IX
71 .... IR 6.223, 12.3(2)		260 .... IA 313(5)
101 .... IA 277		261 .... IA 283, 307(2),(5)
170(2)IA 264, 266(3),(4), 267(3), 277, 282(2),		261(4) .... IA 384
293(1), 327, 341(4),(5), 402(4)		261(6) .... IA 418(1)
Sch.16IA 264, 266(3),(4), 277, 282(2), 293(1),		261(8) .... IR 6.237A(2),(3), 6.237B(1)
341(4),(5), 402(4)		262 .... IA Sch.5, IR 6.224
Criminal Justice (Scotland) Act 1987		263 .... IA Pt IX, 361
1 .... IR 6.216–6.223, 12.3(2)		264 .... IA 261, 263G
Criminal Law Act 1977		265 .... IA Pt IX, 426C
38 .... IA 426(7)		266 .... IA 426C
Criminal Law (Consolidation) (Scotland)		266(2) .... IA 427(1),(2)
Act 1995		267 .... IA 426C
44(1) .... IA 7A(7), 433(3)		268 .... IA 426C
44(2) .... IA 7A(7), 433(3)		269 .... IA 282(5), 291(4),(5),
		292(1), 293(1), 294(1),(2), 297(1),(2), 298(3),
		300(5), 354(3)

lvi

Statutes Table

Provision	
270	IA 415A
270(3)	IA 392(9)
270(4)	IA 440
271	IA Sch.8
272	IA 405
272(1)	IA 408(1)
272(2)	IA 408
278	IA Sch.B1, para.75, EA Sch.26
278(2)	IA 230(1)
Sch.1, para.29	IA Sch.7
Sch.5, para.2A	IR 6.224
Sch.16	IA 212(1), 230
Sch.17	IA 1, 5(3), 5(4), 6, 51(2A), 387, Sch.8
Sch.17, para.2	IA 234(1),(2)
Sch.17, para.9	IA 230(1)
Sch.17, para.18	IA 212(1)
Sch.17, para.19	IA 230, 230(1)
Sch.17, para.20	IA 231
Sch.17, para.21	IA 232
Sch.17, para.22	IA 233
Sch.17, para.24	IA 235(4)
Sch.17, para.25	IA 238(1)
Sch.17, para.26	IA 240(1),(3), 241
Sch.17, para.28	IA 242
Sch.17, para.30	IA 244
Sch.17, para.31	IA 245
Sch.17, para.32	IA 246
Sch.17, para.33(2)	IA 247(1)
Sch.17, para.33(3)	IA 247(3)
Sch.17, para.47	IA Sch.B1, paras.70,71,72
Sch.18	IA 72A
Sch.19	IA Pt IX, 279
Sch.20	IA Sch.4A
Sch.21	IA 31, 350(3A), 360(5),(6), 390(5)
Sch.22	IA 261, 263G
Sch.23	IA 282(5), 291(4),(5), 292(1), 293(1), 294(1),(2), 297(1),(2), 298(3), 300(5), 354(3), 429(2)–(4)
Sch.24	IA 399(1)
Sch.26	IA 230(1)
Environmental Protection Act 1990	IA 178
European Communities Act 1972	
2(2)	IA Sch.6
Sch.2	IA 411(2B)
Explosives Act 1875	
23	IA 57(1)
Family Law Act 1996	IA 335A, 336(1), 337(1),(2),(3)
Pt IV	IA 336(1)
33	IA 336(2),(4)
Sch.8, para.8	IA 337(1)
Sch.8, para.50	IA 337(4)–(6)

Provision	
Sch.8, para.58	IA 337(1),(2),(3)
Fatal Accidents Act 1976	IA Pt IV
Finance Act 1985	
32	IR 2.56
Finance Act 1991	
Sch.2, para.21A	IA 386
Finance Act 1993	
36(1)	IA 386
Finance Act 1994	
Sch.7, para.7(2)	IA 386
Finance Act 2000	
30(2)	IA 386
Sch.7, para.3(1)(a)	IA 386
Financial Services and Markets Act 2000	IA Pt II, 123, 212(1), 230, EA Sch.17, paras 53, 54(1),(2),(3), 55, 56, 57, 58, 59, IR Pt 2
Pt 4	IA 8(1B), 8(5), IR 13.12A(1)
19	IA 9(1), Sch.A1
22	IA 8(IB), Sch.A1, IR 13.12A(3)
31	IA Sch.A1
39	IA Sch.A1
67(2)	IA Sch.2A, para.2(3
103(1)	IA Sch.2A, para.2(2)
212(1)	IR 4.72(2)
215(4)	IR 4.152(7)
285	IA Sch.2, para.2(3)
356	IA 6(2)
357(1)	IA 253(1)–(3)
357(3)	IA 257(2),(3)
357(5)	IA 262(1)–(3),(8)
357(6)	IA 262(1)–(3),(8)
359	IA 9(1)
359(3)	IA 9(1)
362	IA 9(1)
363(2)	IA 35(1), 63(1)
363(3)	IA 41(2), 69(2)
363(4)	IA 48(1),(4),(7), 67(1),(5),(6)
363(5)	IA 49(1), 68(1)
364	IA 48(1),(4),(7)
365	IA 112(1),(2)
367	IA 124, Sch.B1, paras 40(2), 42(4), 82(1)
371(4)(b)	IR 4.152(7)
372	IA 264
372(4)(a)	IR 6.1, 6.2, 6.3, 6.4, 6.5, 6.9, 6.25
373	IA 305(2)
374(2)	IA 264
374(3)	IA 274(1),(2)
374(4)	IA 301(1)
382(1)(a)	IR 12.3(2A)
382(1)(b)	IR 12.3(2A)
Sch.2	IA 8(1B), IR 13.12A(3)

Statutes Table

	Provision		Provision
Friendly Societies Act 1974		1	IR 1.1
7(1)(b),(c),(d),(e),(f)	EA 255(1)	1–7	IR 1
Gas Act 1986		2	IR 1.1, 1.2–1.6
Pt I	IA 233(3), 372(4)	5(2)(a)	ER Art.2(d),(e), IR 1.22–1.29
7	IA Sch.2A, para.10(1)	6	IR 1.7
7A	IA Sch.2A, para.10(1)	7(4)	IR 4.16–4.21A
Gas Act 1995		7(4)(b)	IR 4.7–4.14
16(1)	IA 233(5)(a),(b)	9	EA Sch.17, paras 2, 54(2)
Sch.4, para.14(1)	IA 233(5)(a),(b)	9(1)	IR 2.4–2.8
Greater London Authority Act 1999		9(4),(5)	ER Art.38
210	EA 249(1)	10(1)	ER Art.38
Housing Act 1985	IA 306	11(3)	IR 2.4–2.8
Housing Act 1988		17(3)(b)	IR 2.18–2.29
Pt I	IA 283(3A)	23(2)	IR 2.17
117(1)	IA 283(3A)	23(2)(b)	IR 2.17
117(3)	IA 309, 315(4)	26	IR 2.32–2.46A
Sch.17, para.73	IA 308(1),(4)	38	IR 3.32
Housing Act 1996	EA Sch.17, paras 50,51,52	43(1)	IR 3.31
		45	IR 3.33, 3.35
Pt I	IA 72G, EA 255(3)	46	IR 3.2
Housing (Scotland) Act 2001		47	IR 3.3, 3.4, 3.8(3), 7.20(1),(2)
Pt 3	IA 72G, EA 255(3)	47(5)	IR 3.6, 3.6(1)
Human Rights Act 1998	IA 235, 236, Sch.14	48	IR 3.8
Industrial and Provident Societies Act 1965	IA, IA 8, EA 255(1)	48(1)	IR 3.8(3),(5)
		48(2)	IR 3.8(1),(2), 3.9
55(a)	IA Pt IV	48(6)	IR 3.5, 12.13
Insolvency Act 1976		49	IR 3.18
10	IA 413(1)	49(2)	IR 3.28
Insolvency Act 1985	IA Pt III, 28, 35(1), 40(1),(2), 50, 124(1), 207, 212(1), 216, Pt IX, 434	s.72A	IA 176A
		86	ER Art.2(f)
		s.92	IA 415A
		s.93	IA 415A
Pt III	IA 251	112	IR 4.40–CVL, 4.41–CVL
1–11	IA Pt XIII	122	IR 4.2
15	IA 214(2)	122(1)	IR 4.2
18	IA 217	123	IR 4.4–4.6, 4.151
20–26	IA Pt I	123(1)(a)	IR 4.4–4.6
83(7)	IA 96	124	EA Sch.17, para.2, IR 4.2
85	IA 98	124(1)	IR 4.7–4.14
101	IA 240(2)	127	ER Art.24
101(11)	IA 240(2)	129	ER Art.2(f)
109	IA Pt IV	131	IR 7.20(1), 7.20(2)
222	IA 399(7)	133	IR 4.211–4.217, 7.16(2), 9.1–9.6, 10.2(1)
235(3)	IA 73	134	IR 7.22, 9.1–9.6
Sch.6, para.5	IA 79	134(2)	IR 7.21(2)
Sch.6, para.45	IA Pt IV	135	IR 4.25–4.31
Sch.10, Pt II	IA Pt I, 73, 124(1), 220	136	IR 4.52(1)
Insolvency Act 1986		136(5)(b)	IR 4.50(6), 4.74(2)
Pt I	IA 2000 1, 2, EA 255(2), IR 13.9(3)	136(5)(c)	IR 4.50(6)
		141(4)	IR 4.172
Pt II	EA 255(2), IR Pt 2, 2.1	143(1)	IR 4.221–4.222
Pt III	EA 250	143(2)	IR 7.20(1),(2)
Pt VIII	IA 2000 3, IR 5.6(1), 13.9(3)	148	IR 4.196(2)
Pt XII	IR 11.12	148(1)	IR 4.179
Pt XIII	IR 6.82, 6.144	150	IR 4.202–4.205
		154	IR 4.221–4.222

Statutes Table

Provision		Provision	
160(1)(b)	IR 4.179, 4.196(2), 4.221–4.222	256A(2)	IR 5.14(1)
160(1)(c)	IR 4.185	256A(4)(a)	IR 5.16(2)
160(1)(d)	IR 4.202–4.205	256A(4)(b)	IR 5.16(2),(3)
160(2)	IR 4.197–4.201, 4.221–4.222	257	IR 5.14(3)
167(1)(a)	IR 4.184	258(7)	IR 5.37(2)
168(2)	IR 4.50–4.71	259	IR 5.22(6)
172(6)	IR 4.109(4)	259(1)	IR 5.27(4)
175	IA, Sch, B1, para. 65(3), IR 4.73–4.85, 4.90	260(2)(a)	ER Art.2(d),(e)
176A	IA, Sch, B1, para., 78(1)–(3), EA 252, IR 1.10, 2.47(2), 3.8, 4.124(2A), 7.3A, 12.2, 12.22	261	EA Sch.22, IR 6.206–6.215
		261(2)(a)	IR 5.51, 5.52(1), 5.60(1), 5.61(1), 6A.5
176A(2)(a)	IR 3.40, 13.13(15)	261(2)(b)	IR 5.54, 5.55(1), 5.55(2), 5.60(1), 5.61(1), 6A.5
176A(3)	IR 2.33(2), 3.8(5), 3.39(2), 4.43(1A), 4.49–CVL(2)	262(1)	IR 5.52(2), 5.55(2)
176A(5)	IR 2.33(2), 2.95(2), 2.98(2), 3.8(5), 3.8(7), 3.39(2), 4.43(1A), 4.49–CVL(2), 7.3A(1), 7.4A, 12.22	262(3)(a)	IR 5.52(2), 5.55(2)
		262(4)(b)	IR 5.30(3)
		262A	IR 5.37(1)
177	IR 4.206–4.210	263A	EA 264(2), IR 5.36, 6.83, 6A.2(1)
178–182	IR 4.187–4.194	263A–263G	EA Sch.22
184	IR 12.19	263B	IR 5.35
184(2),(3)	IR 7.36(1)	263B–263G	EA 264(2)
189	IR 4.93	263B(1)	IR 5.37(1)
192	IR 4.223–CVL	263B(2)	IR 5.39(1)
202	IR 4.224–4.225	263C	IR 5.39(1), 5.58(4), 6.9(4A), 6.40(3A)
203	IR 4.224		
203(4)	IR 4.225	263D(2)(c)	IR 5.37(2)
205	IR 4.224	263D(3)	IR 5.57, 5.58(1),(2), 5.60(1), 5.61(1), 6A.5
205(4)	IR 4.225		
216	IR 4.226, 4.227	263D(4)	IR 5.58(2)
216(3)	IR 4.226, 4.227	263F	IR 5.39(1), 5.46(1), 5.58(3)
218	IA 2000 10	263F(1)	IR 5.39(1)
219	IA 2000 10	264(1)(d)	EA Sch.19, para.6, IR 6.229(1)
219(2A)	IA 2000 11	265(1)(c)	ER Art.3(1)
222(1)	IR 4.4–4.6	265(3)	IR 5.12
230	IR 4.151	268	IR 6.1, 6.1(1), 6.11(1)
234	IR 4.185	268(1)	IR 6.1(2),(3)
234(1)	IR 9.1–9.6	268(1)(a)	IR 6.1, 6.2
235	IR 7.20(1),(2)	268(1)(b)	IR 6.7, 6.8, 6.9(1)
236	IR 4.211–4.217, 7.16(2), 7.23(1), 9.1–9.6, 10.2(1), Sch.4	268(2)	IR 6.1(2),(3), 6.17
		268(2)(a)	IR 6.1, 6.2
236(1)	IR 9.1–9.6	269	IR 6.109
236(5)	IR 7.21(2)	271	IR 6.25, 6.26
237	IR 9.1–9.6	271(5)	IR 6.22
240(3)	IR 2.59–2.61	272	IR 6.37–6.39
247	IR 4.73–4.85, 4.151	272(2)	IR 6.41
247(2)	IR 4.91	273(2)	IR 6.42(3), 6.44, 7.9(1)
247(3)	IR 2.59–2.61	274	IR 6.44
247–251	IR Pt 13	275	IR 6.48–6.50
248(2)	EA Sch.17, para.1	275(3)	IR 6.48–6.50, 6.223(B)(5)
249	IR 1.13–1.21, 2.18–2.29	277	IR 6.229–6.234
252	IR 1, 5.14(2)	279	EA 256, Sch.19, paras 2,3, IR 6A.4(3)
256	EA Sch.19, paras 2,4(3),5(5), 6.9(4A), 6.40(3A)	279–281	IR 6.216–6.223
256(3)	IR 5.12(1)	279(1)	IR 6A.4(6)
256A	IR 5.14(1), 5.14(8), 5.15, 5.15(1), 6.9(4A), 6.40(3A)	279(1)(a)	IR 6.223(B)(5)

Statutes Table

Provision		Provision	
279(1)(b)	EA Sch.19, para.4(1), IR 6.223(B)(5)	298(6)	IR 6.144
279(2)	IR 6.214A, 6A.4(6)	298(7)	IR 6.126
279(3)	EA Sch.19, para.4(2), IR 6.176(4), IR 6.223(B)(5), 6A.4(5)	299	IR 6.136
		299(2)	IR 6.136(3)
279(3)–(5)	EA Sch.19, paras 4(3),5(5)	300	IR 6.122
280	EA Sch.19, paras 5(4),(6), IR 6.217(1), 6.218(1), 6.216–6.223	301	IR 6.150
		302	IR 6.166
280(2)(b),(c)	EA Sch.19, paras 5(3),(4)	305(3)	IR 6.149
280(3)	EA Sch.19, para.5(3)	306	IR 6.125
281(4)	IR 6.216–6.223	307	IR 6.200–6.202
281A	EA 257	308	IR 6.187, 6.188
282	EA Sch.19, para.5(6), IR 6.206–6.215	310	EA 259, IR 6.189(1), 6.189–6.193
282(1)	IR 6.206(1), 6.234(3)	310(3)(a)	IR 6.191(1)
282(1)(a)	IR 6A.5	310(3)(b)	IR 6.190(2), 6.191(4), 6.192(3), 6.189–6.193
282(1)(b)	IR 6.209, 6.211, 6.206–6.215, 6A.5		
		310A	EA 260, IR 13.11
282(2)	IR 6.234(3)	310A(1)	IR 6.193A(2)
283A	EA 261, IR 6.237	310A(1)(a)	IR 6.193C(5)
283A(1)	IR 6.237(1)	310A(1)(b)	IR 6.193B(3), 6.193C(5)
283A(1)(b)	IR 6.237(1)	310A(6)(b)	IR 6.193C(2),(3)
283A(1)(c)	IR 6.237(1)	313	EA 261, IR 6.237(1), 6.237(6), 6.237D(1),(6)
283A(2)	EA 261(10), IR 6.237(3), 6.237A(2),(3), 6.237B(1), 6.237C		
		313(2)	IR 6.237(5), 6.237D(5)
283A(3)	EA 261(9)	313A	EA 261
283A(4)	IR 6.237A(2),(3), 6.237B(1)	315	IR 6.178(1),(4)
283A(4)–(9)	EA 261(10)	315–319	IR 6.185
283A(5)	EA 261(10)	315–321	IR 6.178–6.186
286	IR 6.51–6.57	315(4)	IR 6.178–6.186, 6.182(1),(4)
286(2)	IR 6.54(1)	316	IR 6.178–6.186, 6.183
286(7)	IR 6.51–6.57	316(1)	IR 6.183(3)
287	IR 6.125	317	IR 6.186(7)
288	IR 6.58, 6.59, 6.75	318	IR 6.186(7)
288(1)	IR 6.58	320	IR 6.182(4), 6.186, 6.186(3), 6.186(7)
288(2)(b)	IR 6.64–6.66	322	IR 6.96, 12.3
288(3)	IR 6.62, 6.62(1)	322(3)	IR 6.100(2)
288(3)(a)	IR 6.76	323	IR 4.90
289	EA 258	324	IR 6.104, Pt 11, 11.5
290	IR 6.172(1), 6.172–6.177, 7.16(2), 9.1–9.6, 10.2(1)	328	IR 6.224
		328(4),(5)	IR 6.113
290(2)	IR 6.173(1),(3),(5)	330	IR Pt 11
293	IR 6.79, 6.120	331	IR 6.137, 6.137(1)
293(1)	IR 6.79(1)	334	IR 6.225–6.228
293(2)	IR 6.79(6), 6.97(2)	335(1)	IR 6.228
294	IR 6.79, 6.80(1), 6.83	339	IR 5.37(2)
295	IR 6.122	343	IR 5.37(2)
296	IR 6.122	346	IR 12.19
296(4)	IR 6.124(2)	346(2),(3)	IR 7.36(1)
297(3),(4)	IR 6.121	361	EA 263
297(5)	IR 6.10(6), 6.42(7), 6.121	362	EA 263
297(7)	IR 6.124(2)	364	IR 7.22
298	IR 6.146	364(1)	IR 7.21(2)
298(1)	IR 6.129, 6.131, 6.132	365(2)	IR 7.25(2)
298(5)	IR 6.133	365(3)	IR 7.21(2), 7.25(1),(2)
		366	IR 7.16(2), 7.23(1), 9.1–9.6, 10.2(1), Sch.4

lx

Statutes Table

Provision		Provision	
366(3)	IR 7.21(2)	Sch.B1, para.11	IR 2.1
367	IR 9.1–9.6	Sch.B1, para.12	EA Sch.17, paras 2, 47(4)
369	IR 6.194(1), 6.196	Sch.B1, paras 14, 22	ER Art.2(d),(e), EA Sch.17, paras 47(4), 52, 54(3), 57
369(2)	IR 6.196		
370	IR 6.167(1), 6.167–6.171	Sch.B1, paras 18, 29	ER Art.2(e),(f)
375	IR 6.223(B)(5), 6A.5, 7.47, 12.4A(3)	Sch.B1, para. 22	EA Sch.17, para.58
377	IR 3.30A	Sch.B1, para.26	IA Sch.B1, para.27
380–385	IR Pt 13	Sch.B1, para.26(2)	IA Sch.B1, para.30, para.44(7)
382	IR 12.3, 13.12		
383	IR 6.1	Sch.B1, para.26(3)	IA Sch.B1, para.27
383(2)	IR 6.109	Sch.B1, paras 27,29	EA Sch.17, para.58
385(1)	IR 6.1	Sch.B1, para.27(1)	IA Sch.B1, para.30
386	IR 4.75(1), 4.180–4.183, 6.98(1)	Sch.B1, para.28	IA Sch.B1, para.30
387(3)	IR 2.59–2.61	Sch.B1, para.28(2)	IA Sch.B1, para.30
388–389	IA 2000 4	Sch.B1, para.47	IR 7.20(1),(2)
389A	IR 13.9(3)	Sch.B1, para.52(1)(b)	IA Sch.B1, para.65(3)
389B	EA Sch.22	Sch.B1, para.57	EA Sch.17, para.57
390(3)	IR 12.8	Sch.B1, para.65	IA Sch.B1, para.99(6)
392	IA, 415A, EA 270(2)	Sch.B1, para.65(3)	IA 176A
399–401	IR Pt 10	Sch.B1, para.70	IA Sch.B1, para.65(3)
399(6)(a)	IR 7.14(4)	Sch.B1, para.74	EA Sch.17, para.57
401	IR 10.2	Sch.B1, para. 84(1)	EA Sch.17, para.48(2)
402	IR 6.229–6.234	Sch.B1, para.99(3)(b)	IA Sch.B1, para.65(3)
405	EA 272	Sch.B1, para.99(4)	IA Sch.B1, para.65(3)
406	IA 2000 13	Sch.B1, para.99(5)	IA Sch.B1, para.65(3)
408	EA 272	**Insolvency Act 1994**	IA 60(1)
412	EA 261(10)	1(1)	IA 19, 241
415A	EA 270, IR 6.221	1(2)	IA 19
421(1)	IA 2000 12	1(3)	IA 19
421A	IA 2000 12	1(4)	IA 19
423	IR 13.7	1(6)	IA 19
426	IA 2000 14(2), ER Art.44, EA 254(1)	1(7)	IA 19
426(10)(a)	IA 2000 14(4)	2	IA 29(2), 37(1),(2)
426(10)(b)	IA 2000 14(4)	2(1)	IA 44(1),(2), 342(2)
426A-C	EA 266	2(2)	IA 342(2A)
426A–426B	EA 266(3)	2(3)	IA 44(1),(2), 342(6)
427	EA 266	2(4)	IA 44(1),(2)
431	IR 12.21	3(1)	IA 57(1A),(2A),(2D), 57(2),(4),(5)
435	IR 4.149, 4.170, 6.147, 8.1–8.6	3(2)	IA 57(1A),(2A),(2D)
435–436	IR Pt 13	3(3)	IA 57(2),(4),(5)
440	EA 270(2)	3(4)	IA 57(1A),(2A),(2D)
443	IR 6.36	3(5)	IA 57(1A),(2A),(2D), 57(2),(4),(5)
Sch.4	EA 253, 257(2)	5	IA 19
Sch.4A	EA 257(2),(3), 268(10)	6	IA 241
Sch.4A, para.9	IR 6.249	Sch 2	IA 19
Sch.4A, para.9(3)	IR 6.251	**Insolvency Act 2000**	IA 72A, 251, Pt VIII, Sch.14, IR 1, 1.29, 1.54, 5.34, 6.249
Sch.4A, para.12	IR 6A.1(2)		
Sch.5	EA 262, IR 3.32	1	IA Pt I, 122(1), 233(1)
Sch.6	EA 251, IR 4.75(1), 4.180–4.183, 6.98(1)	2	IA Pt I, 1, 2, 4(2), 4A, 5(1), 5(2)(b), 5(2A), 6, 6A, 7(1),(2),(5), 7A
Sch.8	EA 271		
Sch.8, para.12	IR 13.12, IR 13.12(2)	3	IA Pt VIII, 252(2), 253, 254, 255(1),(2), 256(1), 256(3),(3A), 256A, 257(1), 258(2)–(5), 260(1),(2),(2A), 262, 262C. 263
Sch.8, para.14	IR 13.12		
Sch.9	EA 271		
Sch.9, para.17	IR 12.3		
Sch.9, para.21	IA 2000 13		
Sch.B1	EA 248, Sch.16, Sch.17, paras 1, 54(2), 57, IR 2.1		

Provision	Provision
4............IA 388(1),(2), 389(1A), 389B	**Law of Property Act 1925**........ IA 29(1)
5(3)(b).......................IA 5(3), 5(4)	30.........................IA 336(3)–(5)
5–13 ....IA Sch.14	109(8)(i)...........................IR 13.12
8.............................IA 390(4)	**Law Reform (Miscellaneous Provisions)**
9 ....IA 10(1), 248	**(Scotland) Act 1990**
10..............................IA 218	74.............................IA 53(3)
10(7) ....IA 219	Sch.8, para.35 ....IA 53(3)
11..............................IA 219	Sch.9............................IA 53(3)
13(1)..........................IA Sch.9	**Limitation Act 1980**...........IA 129, 238
13(2) ....IA 406	8(1)..............................IA 238
15(1) ....IA 5(2)	9(1)..............................IA 214
15(2) ....IA 6(2)	21(1)(b).......................IA 212(1)
Sch.1 ..... IA Pt I, 122(1), 233(1), 387, 417A	**Local Government Act 1972**
Sch.2..........IA Pt I, 1, 2, 4(2), 4A, 5(1),	80 ....IA 427(1),(2)
5(2)(b), 5(2A), 6, 6A, 7(1),(2),(5), 7A	80(1)(b)......................EA 267(1)
Sch.3.........IA Pt VIII, 252(2), 253, 254,	**Magistrates' Courts Act 1980**.. EA Sch.17,
255(1),(2), 256(1), 256(3),(3A), 256A,	para.2, IR 12.3(2)
257(1), 258(2)–(5), 260(1),(2),(2A), 262,	32 ....IA Sch.10
262C, 263, 347(1),(2),(5),(8),(9)	87A ....IA 9(1), 124(1)
Sch.4...........................IA Sch.14	87A(1)................... Sch.17, para.2
Sch.4, para.16(2).................IA 390(4)	**Matrimonial and Family Proceedings Act**
Sch.4, para.16(3) ....IA 426	**1984**......................IR 12.3(2)
Sch.5 ....IA 5(2), 255(1),(2)	**Matrimonial Causes Act 1973**
Insurance Companies Act 1982.....IA Pt I	24......................IA 284(1)–(3),(6)
Interception of Communications Act	37.................IA 272, 284(1)–(3),(6)
1985.....................IA 371(1)	**Matrimonial Homes Act 1967**.....IA 335A
Interpretation Act 1978	**Matrimonial Homes Act 1983** ....IA 335A,
6............... IA 7(6), Sch.B1, para.100	IR 7.43(1)
6(c)............................IA 231	1(7)..............................IA 338
Irish Companies Act 1963	**Mental Health Act 1983**....... IR 4.214(3)
311A ....IA Pt III	Pt VII ....IA 389A(3), 390(4)
Joint Stock Companies Act	**Mental Health (Scotland) Act 1984**
1844.....................CA 735(3)	125(1)................IA 389A(3), 390(4)
Joint Stock Companies Act	**Moneylenders Act 1927**
1856.....................CA 735(3)	9(2) ....IR 6.20, 6.102
Joint Stock Companies Act	**New Zealand Receiverships Act 1993**
1857.....................CA 735(3)	19..............................IA Pt III
Joint Stock Banking Companies Act	**Pensions Act 1995**...........IA 283(2),(3)
1857.....................CA 735(3)	91 ....IA 342C(2), 342F(5)
Judgments Act 1838	95 ....IA 342A
17 . IA 189(4),(5), 325(2), 328(5), IR 1.23(2),	**Pensions and Welfare Reform Act**
2.70(3), 2.88(6), 4.182(3), 5.26(2),	**1999**..................IA 283(2),(3)
6.113(5), 6.237(5), 6.237D(5), 7.34(3)	**Pension Schemes Act 1993**.. IA 306, 310(9)
Justices of the Peace Act 1997	159 ....IA 342C(2), 342F(5)
65 ....EA 265	190 ....IA 386(3)
Land Charges Act 1972...... IR 6.237D(8)	Sch.4............................IA 386(3)
6(1)(a).....................IR 6.237D(9)	Sch.8, para.18 ...... IA 386(3), Sch.6, para.8
Land Registration Act 2002.. IR 6.237D(8),	**Perjury Act 1911**
(9)	1.............................IA 433(3)
132(1) ....IR 6.237E(1)	2 ....IA 7A(7), 433(3)
Landlord and Tenant Act 1709	5 .....IA 7A(7), 433(3), Sch.B1, para.18(7)
1..............................IA 347(6)	**Postal Services Act 2000**........ IA 371(1)
Landlord and Tenant Act 1954... IA 11(3),	4(3)................. IA Sch.2A, para.10(1)
306	4(4)................. IA Sch.2A, para.10(1)

Provision	Provision
127(4) .... IA 371(1)	7 .... IA Sch.2A, para.10(1)
Sch.8, para.20 .... IA 371(1)	**Trade Union and Labour Relations**
Powers of the Criminal Courts Act	**(Consolidation) Act 1992**
1973......................... IA 251	169 .... IA Sch.6, para.13(2)
Pts 2,3,4 .... IR 6.223	189 .... IA Sch.6, para.13(2)
39............................ IA 277	**Transport Act 2000**
39(1) .... IA 385(1), 402(5)	26................... IA 72GA, EA 249(1)
39(3)(b)..................... IA 264(1)	**Tribunals and Inquiries Act 1992**
39(3)(c)...................... IA 382(1)	7................. IA Sch.7, para.1(2)
40 .... IA 277	**Trusts of Land and Appointment of**
40(5) .... IA 277(3)	**Trustees Act 1996**
Proceeds of Crime Act 2002	14............ IA 335A(1), 336(3)–(5)
Pts 2,3,4...................... IR 12.3(2)	25(1) .... IA 335A
417 .... IA 306A	25(2) .... IA 336(3)
417(2)(a)............. IA 306A(1), 306C(1)	27 .... IA 336(3)
417(2)(b),(c),(d) .... IA 306B(1), 306C(1)	Sch.4........................... IA 336(3)
419 .... IA 342(1)	Sch.3, para.23 .... IA 335A
Sch.11........................ IA 306A	**Trustee Act 1925**
Railways Act 1993..... IA 11(3), 72D(1),(2)	41(2) .... IA 263(5)
8 .... IA Sch.2A, para.10(1)	**Trustee Investments Act 1961**
59................... IA 72GA, EA 249(1)	Sch.1 .... IA 404
59–65 .... IA 413(2)	**Trustee Savings Bank Act 1985**
62(7) .... IA 39(1)	4(3) .... IA 221(6)
81(2) .... IA Sch.2A, para.10(1)	**Utilities Act 2000**
Sch.6.......................... IA 413(2)	108 .... IA 233(5)(a),(b)
Sch.7........................... IA 413(2)	Sch.6, para.47(1),(2)(a) ..... IA 233(5)(a),(b)
Rent Act 1977	**Value Added Tax Act 1983**........ IR 2.56
127(5) .... IA 283(3A)	22(3) .... IR 2.56(1), 3.36(1)
Requirements of Writing (Scotland) Act	22(3)(b).......... IA Sch.8, para.23, 3.36(3)
1995.................... IA 53(1)	**Value Added Tax Act 1994**
14(1) .... IA 53(1),(2),(4),(5)	36(4A)......................... IR 2.56
Sch.4, para.58(a) .... IA 53(1),(2),(4),(5)	81(4)–(5)...................... IR 4.90
Reserve Forces (Safeguard of	**Water Act 1989**............. IA 372(4),(5)
Employment) Act 1985...... IA Sch.6,	**Water Industry Act 1991**
para.12	Pt II................... IA 72GA, EA 249(1
Restrictive Trade Practices Act	23–26 .... IA 413(2)
1976......................... IA 428	Sch.3 .... IA 413(2)
Sale of Goods Act 1979.......... IA 183(4)	**Water (Scotland) Act 1980**...... IA 233(5)
61(4) .... IA Pt VI	**Welfare Reform and Pensions Act**
Scotland Act 1998	1999....................... 342C(2)
125(1) .... IA 53(1),(2),(5),	11............................ IA 306, 342A(8)
54(3),(4), 61(6),(7), 62(5), 67(1),(5),(6)	12............................ IA 306, 342A(7)
Sch.8, para.23(1)–(3) .... IA 54(3),(4),	14 .... IA 306, 342A
61(6),(7), 62(5), 67(1),(5),(6)	15 .... IA 342A, 342B, 342C
Social Security Pensions Act 1975	16 .... IA 342A
Sch.3 .... IA 386, IR 4.75(1), 6.98(1)	28(1)........................ IA 342B(3)
Solicitors Act 1974	29(1)(a) .... IA 342A(3)
69........................... IA 268	Sch.12, para.71 ... IA 342D, 342E, 342F, 384
Statutory Declarations Act	**Youth Justice and Criminal Evidence Act**
1835............ IA Sch.B1, Para.47(5)	**1999**
Supreme Court Act 1981	59 .... IA 236, 433
18(1)(f) .... IA 9(4),(5)	68(3) .... IA 433
39(1)......................... IA 33191),(3)	Sch.3 .... IA 236
130 .... IR 12.15	Sch.3, para.7(2) .... IA 433
Telecommunications Act 1984... IA 233(5),	Sch.3, para.7(3) .... IA 433
372(5)	

Statutory Instrument Table

This table enables the user to locate references to legislative provisions other than the Insolvency Acts 1986 and 2000, the Insolvency Rules 1986, the EC Regulation on Insolvency Proceedings 2000 and the Enterprise Act 2002 in the provisions of those Acts, Rules and Regulations and their notes.

Abbreviations in the provision column are to the Insolvency Act 1986 (IA), the Insolvency Act 2000 (IA 2000), the Insolvency Rules 1986 (IR), the EC Regulation on Insolvency 2000 (ER) and the Enterprise Act 2002(EA).

	Provision
Act of Sederunt (Rules of the Court of Session Amendment No.5) (Insolvency Proceedings) (SI 2003/385)	IR 0.1
Act of Sederunt (Sheriff Court Company Insolvency Rules 1986) (Amendment) (SI 2003/388)	IR 0.1
Administration of Insolvent Estates of Deceased Persons Order (SI 1986/1999)	IA 421A(1), IR 0.1
Sch.1, para.12	ER Art.2(f)
Administration of Insolvent Estates of Deceased Persons (Amendment) Order (SI 2002/1309)	IA 421(1),(1A), (1B),(2), ER, IR 0.1
Adults with Incapacity (Scotland) Act 2000 (Commencement No.1) Order (SI 2000/81)	
Art.3	IA 390(4)
Sch.2	IA 390(4)
Bankruptcy Rules 1952	
rr.188–196	IA 290
r.242	IR 12.16
Bankruptcy (Financial Services and Markets Act 2000) Rules (SI 2001/3634)	
rr.1,3	IR 6.1, 6.2, 6.4, 6.9, 6.25
rr.4,5	IR 6.1, 6.2, 6.4
r.6(1)	IR 6.3, 6.5, 6.25
r.7	IR 6.4
8	IR 6.9
Bankruptcy and Companies (Department of Trade and Industry) Fees (Amendment) Order (SI 1990/599)	IR 0.1
Banks (Administration Proceedings) Order (SI 1989/1276)	IA 8(4)–(6), Sch.B1, para.9

	Provision
Civil Courts (Amendment) Order (SI 1998/1880)	IA 374(1),(4)
Civil Courts (Amendment) (No.2) Order (SI 1998/2910)	IA 374(1),(4)
Civil Courts (Amendment No.3) Order (SI 1992/1810)	IA 374(1),(4)
Civil Procedure Rules (SI 1998/3132)	IR 0.2(1)
Pt 4	IR 13.13(7)
Pt 6	IR 12.11, 13.13(7)
Pt 29	IR 7.51(2)
Pt 31	IR 2.30(10)
r.2.3(1)	IR 7.1–7.18
r.2.8	IR 12.9(1)
r.3.1(2)(a)	IR 12.9(2)
r.3.4	IR 7.1–7.18
Pt 43	IR 7.33
Pt 44	IR 7.33
r.44.4	IR 7.34(5)
Pt 45	IR 7.33
Pt 47	IR 7.33, 7.34(1),(2)
Pt 48	IR 7.33
Companies Act 1985 (Accounts of Small and Medium-Sized Enterprises and Audit Exemption)(Amendment) Regulations (SI 2004/16)	IA Sch.A1 para.45(5)
Companies (Disqualification Orders) Regulations (SI 2001/967)	IR 0.1
Companies (Forms) (Amendment) Regulations (SI 1987/752)	
Sch.2	IA 109(1)
Companies (Northern Ireland) Order (SI 1986/1032)	IA Pt IV, 441
Companies (Northern Ireland) Order (SI 1989/2404)	IA 441
Companies (Single Member Private Limited Companies) Regulations (SI 1992/1699)	IR 0.1
reg.1	IA 122(1)

Provision	Provision
Sch., para.8. IA 122(1)	**Financial Markets and Insolvency (ECU Contracts) Regulations (SI 1998/27)**. . . . IA 43, 61(1),(2), IR 0.1
Companies (Unfair Prejudice Applications) Rules (SI 1986/2000). . . . . IR 0.1	
Companies (Winding-Up) Rules (SI 1949/1065). IA Pt IV	**Financial Markets and Insolvency (Money Markets) Regulations (SI 1995/2049)**. . . . . IA 61(1),(2)
Companies Act 1989 (Commencement No.4 and Transitional and Saving Provisions) Order (SI 1990/355)	**Financial Markets and Insolvency Regulations (SI 1991/880)** IA 10(1), 11(2),(3), 15, 43, 61(1),(2), IR 0.1
Art.5(1)(c). . . . . IA Pt IV	
Companies Act (1989 Order) (Commencement No.2) Order (Northern Ireland) (SR 1991/410). . . . . IA 441	**Financial Markets and Insolvency Regulations (SI 1996/1469)**. . . . . IA 72F, IR 0.1
Companies (Tables A to F) Regulations (SI 1985/805). . . . . IR 12.16	**Financial Markets and Insolvency Regulations (SI 1998/1748)**. . . . . IR 0.1
Co-operation of Insolvency Courts (Designation of Relevant Countries and Territories) Order (SI 1986/2123). . . . . IA 426, IR 0.1	**Financial Markets and Insolvency Regulations (Northern Ireland) (SR 1991/443)**. . . . . IA 441
Co-operation of Insolvency Courts (Designation of Relevant Countries) Order (SI 1996/253). . . . . IR 0.1	**Financial Markets and Insolvency (Settlement Finality) Regulations (SI 1999/2979)**. . . . . IA 72F, IR 0.1
County Court Fees Order (SI 1999/689). IA 414(1),(2), 415(1)–(3)	reg.2(1) . . . . IA 19(3)–(6)
	reg.14(5) . . . . IA 19(3)–(6), 115, 156, 175
County Court Fees (Amendment) Order (SI 2003/648). . . . . IA 264	reg.14(6) . . . . IA 19(3)–(6), 115, 156, 175
	reg.16(1). . . . . IA 127, 178, 186
Co-operation of Insolvency Courts (Designation of Relevant Country) Order (SI 1998/2766). . . . . IR 0.1	reg.17. . . . . IA 238, 239, 240, 242, 243
	reg.19 . . . . IA 10(1), 11(2),(3), 15
	reg.19(3) . . . . IA 127
Department of Trade and Industry (Fees) Order (SI 1988/93). . . . . IA 415(1)–(3), IR 0.1	**Financial Services and Markets Act 2000 (Administration Orders Relating to Insurers) Order (SI 2002/1242)**. . . . . . IA Pt II, 8(4)–(6), 212(1), 230, Sch.B1, para.9, IR 0.1
Enterprise Act 2002 (Commencement No.5 and Amendment) Order (SI 2003/3340, C.132). . . . . EA 270, 271	
Enterprise Act 2002 (Commencement No.4 and Transitional Provisions and Savings) Order (SI 2003/2093). . . IA Pt III, IA 20(2),(3), Sch.B1, para.1, EA Sch.19, IR 0.1	Sch., para.6 . . . . IA Sch.1
	Financial Services and Markets Act 2000 (Consequential Amendments) Order (SI 2002/1555)
Art.2(1). . . . . IA Pt II	Art.1. IA 168(5A)–(5C)
Art.3 . . . . IA 20(2),(3), 212(1), 230, 231, 232, 240(1),(3), 243, 245	Art.15. . . . . IA 168(5A)–(5C)
	Financial Services and Markets Act 2000 (Consequential Amendments and Repeals) Order (SI 2001/3649). . . IA 8, 124A, 168(5A)–(5C), IR 0.1, 2.4–2.8, 4.1, 4.7–4.14, 4.50–4.71, 4.72, 4.152–4.155, 12.3, 13.12A
Art.3(2). . . . . IA Pt II	
Sch.1. . . . . IA Pt II	
Enterprise Act 2002 (Insolvency) Order (SI 2003/2096). . . IA 62(6), 422(1),(1A), EA Sch.19, IR 0.1	
Enterprise Act 2002 (Prescribed Part) Order (SI 2003/2097). . . . . IR 0.1	
Enterprise Act 2002 (Consequential Amendments) (Prescribed Part) (Scotland) Order (SI 2003/2108). . . . . IR 0.1	**Financial Services and Markets Act 2000 (Financial Promotion) Order (SI 2001/1335)**
	Art.19(5). . . . . IA Sch.2A, paras 3(1),(3)
	Art.48(2) . . . . IA Sch.2A, para.3(1)
Financial Markets and Insolvency (Amendment) Regulations (SI 1992/716). . . . . IR 0.1	Art.49(2) . . . . IA Sch.2A, para.3(1)
	Art.50(1) . . . . IA Sch.2A, para.3(1)
	Art.67(2) . . . . IA Sch.2A, para.2(3)

Statutory Instrument Table

Financial Services and Markets Act 2000 (Regulated Activities) Order (SI 2001/544)
Art.77......... IA Sch.2A, paras 1(1), 3(2)
Arts 83–85............ IA Sch.2A, para.1(1)
Income and Corporation Taxes Act 1988
Sch.29......................... IA Sch.6
Insolvency Act 1986 (Amendment) (Administrative Receivership and Urban Regeneration, etc) Order (SI 2003/1832).. IA 72A, 72A(5),(6), 72DA (1)–(3), 72GA
Insolvency Act 1986 (Amendment) (Administrative Receivership and Capital Market Arrangements) Order (SI 2003/1468).... IA 72A, 72H(2)–(5), Sch.2A, para.11
Insolvency Act 1986 (Amendment) Regulations (SI 2002/1037). IA 421(1), (1A),(1B),(2), ER, IR 0.1, 4.73–4.85
reg.3....... IA 411(1),(2),(2A),(2B), 420(1)
reg.4.............................. IA 436
Insolvency Act 1986 (Amendment) (No.2) Regulations (SI 2002/1240).. IA 8, 117 (7), 225(2), 240(1),(3), 247(3), ER, IR 0.1
reg.4 .... IA 1(4)
reg.15 .... IA 330(6)
reg.16........................... IA 387
reg.17 .... IA 388(6)
reg.18 .... IA 436A
Insolvency Act 1986 (Amendment) (No.3) Regulations 2002 (SI 2002/1990). IA Pt I, IR 0.1
Insolvency Act 1986, Section 72A (Appointed Day) Order 2003 (SI 2003/2095)................... IA 72A(4)
Insolvency Act 1986 (Guernsey) Order (SI 1989/2409)........ IA 426, 442, IR 0.1
Insolvency Act 1986 (Prescribed Part) Order (SI 2003/2097)........ IA 176A
... r.2 ....IA 176A
... r.3.39 ....IA 176A
... r.3.39(1)(a) ....IA 176A
... rr.3.39–3.40 ....IA 176A
... r.4.43 ....IA 176A
... r.4.49 ....IA 176A
... rr4.124–4.126 ....IA 176A
... r.7.3A ....IA 176A
... r.7.4A ....IA 176A
... r.12.2(2) ....IA 176A
... r.12.22 ....IA 176A
Insolvency Act 2000 (Commencement No.1 and Transitional Provisions) Order (SI 2001/766)
Art.1..................... IA 390(4), 406
Art.2(1)(a) .... IA 390(4
Art.2(1)(b)...................... IA 406
Art.3(4) .... IA 218
Insolvency Act 2000 (Commencement No.3 and Transitional Provisions) Order 2002 (SI 2002/2711)..... IA Pt I, IR 0.1

Insolvency (Amendment) Regulations (SI 1987/1959).................... IR 0.1
Insolvency (Amendment) Regulations (SI 1988/1739).................... IR 0.1
Insolvency (Amendment) Regulations (SI 1991/380)..................... IR 0.1
Insolvency (Amendment) Regulations (SI 2000/485)..................... IR 0.1
Insolvency (Amendment) Regulations (SI 2001/762)..................... IR 0.1
Insolvency (Amendment) Rules (SI 1987/1919)........... IR 6.42, 6.229–6.234
r.3(1)...... IR 3.13, 4.31(3), 4.66, 6.13, 6.19, 6.44(4), 6.57(3), 6.92, 6.113
Sch.Pt.1, para.26 .... IR 3.13
Sch.Pt.1, para.44................ IR 4.31(3)
Sch.Pt.1, para.56 .... IR 4.66
Sch.Pt.1, para.97 .... IR 6.19
Sch.Pt.1, para.101(2) .... IR 6.44(4)
Sch.Pt.1, para.104............... IR 6.57(3)
Sch.Pt.1, para.109 .... IR 6.92
Sch.Pt.1, para.112(2)............. IR 6.113
Sch.Pt.5......................... IR 6.13
Insolvency (Amendment) Rules (SI 1991/495)... IR 6.35(2), 6.46, 6.47(2), 6.206–6.215
Insolvency (Amendment) Rules (SI 1993/602)
r.3............................. IR Sch.3
Sch., para.4..................... IR Sch.3
Insolvency (Amendment) Rules (SI 1999/359)...... IR 0.1, 6.34(3), 6.46, 6.223A
r.1 .... IR 6.216
Sch., para.7..................... IR 6.216
Insolvency (Amendment) Rules (SI 2001/763)........................ IR 0.1
Insolvency (Amendment) Rules 2002 (SI 2002/1307)... ER, IR 0.1, 1.1, 1.3, 1.24, 1.33, 2.1–2.3, 2.4–2.8, 2.9, 2.17, 2.18–2.29, 2.31, 2.59–2.61, 2.62, 4.7–4.14, 4.19, 4.16–4.21A, 4.22–4.24, 4.25–4.31, 4.50–4.71, 4.95–4.99, 4.231, 6.7, 6.8, 6.14, 6.30, 6.51, 6.93, 6.116, 6.198, 6.239, 7.63, 8.8, 11.1, 11.2, 11.3, 11.6, 12.12, 12.17, 13.14, Sch.4
Insolvency (Amendment) Rules 2003 (SI 2003/1730)..... EA, EA 0.3, IR 0.1, 1.1, 1.3, 1.10, 1.13, 1.17A, 1.23, 1.29, 3.8, 4.7–4.14, 4.43–4.49A, 5.1, 5.7, 5.28, 5.34, 5.35, 5.51, 5.54, 5.57, 5.60, 5.62, 6.9, 6.40, 6.48–6.50, 6.83, 6.111, 6.121, 6.193C, 6.202A, 6.203–6.205, 6.206, 6.206–6.215, 6.214A, 6.212A, 6.216–6.223, 6.223A, 6.237, 6.240, 6.245, 6.249, 6A, 7.3A, 7.4A, 7.19–7.25, 7.50, 7.57, 7.62, 12.2, 12.22, 13.11, 13.12, 13.14

Provision	
r.5(2)–(4)	IA Pt II
Sch.1, para.12	IR 4.1
Sch.1, paras 15,16	IR 4.43–4.49A
Sch.1, para.18	IR 4.73–4.85
Sch.1, para.19	IR 4.90
Sch.1, paras 21–23	IR 4.124–4.126
Sch.1, paras 24–26	IR 4.173–4.178

Insolvency (Amendment) Rules (SI 2004/584) IR 3.21(6), 3.23(2), 4.7–4.14, 4.73–4.85, 4.126, 4.127–4.131, 4.132–4.138, 4.139–4.148A, 4.156–4.159, 5.35, 5.60, 6.10–6.12, 6.97, 6.98, 6.136, 6.137, 6.137A, 6.138, 6.138A, 6.139, 6.146, 6.156(7), 6.158(2), 6.213(5), 6.214A(5), 6.224, 6.237CA, 6.237D, 6A.4, 6A.6

...r.3	IR 4.127–4.131
...r.28	IR 6.98

Insolvency (Amendment) (No.2) Rules (SI 1999/1022)... EA 0.2, IR 0.1, Pt 7, 7.49, 7.51, 9.1–9.6, 13.14

r.3	IR 6.197, 7.33–7.42, 7.59, 7.60, 9.2(4), 12.9, 12.11
Sch., para.2	IR 6.197(4)
Sch., para.7	IR 7.59
Sch., para.8	IR 7.60
Sch., para.9	IR 9.2(4)
Sch., para.11	IR 12.9
Sch., para.12	IR 12.11

Insolvency (Amendment) (No.2) Rules (SI 2002/2712)... IR 1.1, 1.3, 1.7, 1.8, 1.13, 1.14, 1.17A, 1.19, 1.21, 1.22, 1.22A, 1.23, 1.24, 1.27, 1.28, 1.29, 1.30, 1.54, 5.34, 6.224, 9.4, Sch.4

r.1.4(1)	IR 4.2
r.4(2)	IA 115
Sch. Pt 2, para.22	IR 4.2

Insolvency (Amendment No.2) Rules (SI 2004/1070)

...r.2	IR 6.98

Insolvency (Amendment of Subordinate Legislation) Order (SI 1986/2001) ... IR 0.1

Insolvency (Amendment of Subordinate Legislation) Order SI 1987/1398 IR 0.1

Insolvency (Northern Ireland) Order (SI 1989/2405)

... arts 40–59	IA Pt III

Insolvency (ECSC Levy Debts) Regulations (SI 1987/2093)... IA 386, Sch.6, IR 0.1

Insolvency Fees Order (SI 1986/2030)... IA 414(1),(2), IR 0.1

Insolvency Fees (Amendment) Order (SI 1988/95) ... IR 0.1

Insolvency Fees (Amendment) Order (SI 1990/560) ... IR 0.1

Insolvency Fees (Amendment) Order (SI 1991/496) ... IR 0.1

Insolvency Fees (Amendment) Order (SI 1992/34) ... IR 0.1

Provision	

Insolvency Fees (Amendment) Order (SI 1994/2541) ... IA 293(1), IR 0.1

Insolvency Fees (Amendment) Order (SI 2001/761) ... IR 0.1

Insolvency (Northern Ireland) Order (SI 1989/2405) ... IA 441

Insolvency (1989 Order) (Commencement No.4) Order (Northern Ireland) (SR 1991/411) ... IA 441

Insolvency Practitioners (Amendment) Regulations (SI 1993/221) ... IR 0.1

Insolvency Practitioners (Amendment) Regulations (SI 2002/2710) ... IR 0.1

Insolvency Practitioners (Amendment) Regulations (SI 2004/473)... IA 419(1), (2)

Insolvency Practitioners and Insolvency Services Account (Fees) Order (SI 2003/3363).. IA 391, 392(1), 393, 415A

Insolvency Practitioners Order (Northern Ireland) (SR 1995/225) ... IA 441

Insolvency Practitioners (Recognised Practitioners Regulations (Northern Ireland)) (SR 1991/3020 ... IA 441

Insolvency Practitioners Regulations (SI 1990/439) ... IA Pt XIII, 390, 393, 419(1),(2), IR 0.1

reg.4	IA 393(2)
reg.5	IA 393(2)
reg.5(2)	IA 393(2)
reg.8	IA 393(2)
reg.9	IA 392(3)–(7)
Sch.2	IA 390(3)

Insolvency Practitioners Regulations (SI 1986/1995).. IA Pt XIII, 393, IR 0.1

Insolvency Practitioners Regulations (SI 1990/439) ... IR 0.1

Insolvency Practitioners (Amendment) (No.2) Regulations (SI 2002/2748) ... IR 0.1

Insolvency Practitioners (Recognised Professional Bodies) Order (SI 1986/1764) ... IA 391(1)

Insolvency Practitioners Tribunal (Conduct of Investigations) Rules (SI 1986/952) ... IA 396(1)

Insolvency Proceedings (Fees) Order (SI 2004/593).. IA 263B(1), 274(1), (2), 415 (1)–(3), 415A

... art.6(1)(a)	IR 4.7–4.14

Insolvency Proceedings (Monetary Limits) Order (SI 1986/1996) ... IR 0.1

... art.4	IA Sch.6

Insolvency Proceedings (Monetary Limits) (Amendment) Order (SI 2004/547). IA 273(1), 313A(2), 346(3), (4), 354(1), 358, 360(1), 364(2), 418(1)

... art.3	IA 313A(2)

Statutory Instrument Table

Provision		Provision	
... art.6(1)(a)	IR 4.7–4.14	r.2.7(1)	IA 9(3)
Insolvency Regulations (SI 1986/1994)	IA 412(3),(4), Sch.9, IR 0.1	r.2.9	IA 9(3)
		r.2.9(1)(g)	IA 9(1)
Insolvency Regulations (SI 1994/2507)	IA 403(2),(3), 411(4),(5), Sch.8, para.27, Sch.9, IR 0.1, 4.127–4.131, 4.139–4.148A	r.2.10	IA 21(1),(2)
		r.2.10(2)	IA 21(1),(2)
		r.2.10(3)	IA 21(1),(2)
		r.2.11	IA 22
reg.23	IA 324(1)–(3)	r.2.16(2)	IA 18(2)
reg.30	IA 349(2)	r.2.17	IA 23(2)
reg.33	IA 399(2)	r.2.18	IA 23(1), 24(3)
Insolvency Regulations (Northern Ireland) (SR 1991/388)	IA 441	r.2.21	IA 17(3)
		r.2.28(1A)	IA 24(3)
Insolvency Rules 1986 (SI 1986/1925)	IA 411(1),(2),(2A),(2B), 412(1),(2),(2A),(2B), Sch.9	r.2.30	IA 24(4)
		r.2.32	IA 26
		r.2.53	IA 19(1)
rr.1.2–1.9	IA 2(4)	r.2.54	IA 19(1), 20(1)
r.1.3(2)(p)	IA 2(2)	rr.2.59–2.61	IA 247(3), ER Arts 36,37
r.1.4(3)	IA 2(2), 2(3)	r.2.113(4)	IA Sch.B1, para.80(1)–(5)
r.1.5(1)	IA 2(3)	r.2.123	IA Sch.B1, para.89
r.1.7(2)	IA 2(2)	r.2.125	IA Sch.B1, para.95
r.1.9	IA 3	r.2.126	IA Sch.B1, paras 92, 93, 95, 96, 97
r.1.10	IA 1(3), 3(2)	r.2.129	IA Sch.B1, paras 92, 93, 95, 96, 97
r.1.11	IA 3(2)	rr.2.130–2.132	ER Arts 36,37
r.1.11(2)	IA 3(2)	r.2.133	ER Arts 18,19,32
r.1.13	IA 3, 4(5)	r.3.1	IA 33(1),(2)
r.1.13(3)	IA 5	r.3.2	IA 46(2),(3)
r.1.14	IA 4(6)	rr.3.3–3.7	IA 47(3),(5),(6)
rr.1.17–1.20	IA 5(2)	rr.3.8–3.15	IA 48(8)
r.1.17	IA 6(2)	rr.3.16–3.30	IA 49(2)
r.1.17(1)	IA 5(2)	r.3.31	IA 43(1),(2)
r.1.17(2)	IA 5(2)	r.3.32	IA 38(5)
r.1.17(3)	IA 1, 5(2)	rr.3.33–3.35	IA 45(4),(5)
r.1.17(7)	IA 6A	rr.3.39–3.40	IA 40(1),(2)
r.1.18(2)	IA 5(2), 6(2)	r.4.4	IA 123
r.1.19(3)	IA 5(2), 6(2)	r.4.5	IA 222(1)(a)
r.1.21	IA 3	r.4.7	IA 124
r.1.21(1)	IA 5, 5(1)	r.4.7(7)(a)	IA 7(4), 124
r.1.21(4)	IA 5, 5(1)	r.4.7(9)	IA 7(4)
rr.1.22–1.23	IA 7(1), (2)	r.4.11(1)	IA 124A
r.1.22(1)	IA 7(6)	r.4.20	IA 125(1)
r.1.24	IA 4(6)	r.4.21	IA 130(1)
r.1.24(3)	IA 4(6)	r.4.25	IA 135
r.1.24(5)	IA Pt I, 4(6)	r.4.30	IA 135
r.1.25	IA 6	r.4.32	IA 131
r.1.26	IA 7(1), (2)	r.4.34	IA 95(3),(4), 99
r.1.26(1)	IA 1(2)	r.4.39	IA 235
r.1.26(2)(b)	IA Pt I	r.4.43	IA 136(4),(5)
r.1.29(3)	IA Pt I	r.4.48	IA 147(3)
rr.1.31–1.33	IA 247(3), ER Arts 36,37	r.4.49	IA 95(3),(4), 98
r.2.1(4)	IA 7(4)	r.4.49A	IA 140
r.2.2	IA 8, 8(1),(2), 9(4),(5), 19(3)–(6)	r.4.50	IA 136(4),(5)
r.2.3	IA 8(1),(2)	r.4.53	IA 98
r.2.6	IA 8(1),(2), 9(2)	r.4.54	IA 160, 168, 195
r.2.6(2)(a)	IA 9(3)	r.4.62	IA 98
r.2.6A	IA 10(1)		

lxix

Statutory Instrument Table

Provision		Provision	
r.4.73	IA 107, Pt IV	r.4.171(4)	IA 141
r.4.84	ER Art.32	r.4.172	IA 141(4),(5)
r.4.86	IA Pt IV	r.4.180	IA 107
r.4.90	IA Pt IV, Sch.4, para.6	r.4.181	IA 107
r.4.93	IA 189, 189(1)	r.4.182(2)	IA 153
r.4.93(5)	IA 189(4)	r.4.182A	IA 107
r.4.93(6)	IA 189(4)	r.4.184	IA 167(1)
r.4.100	IA 139, 140	r.4.185	IA 234(1),(2)
r.4.101	IA 100	r.4.187	IA 178(2)
r.4.102	IA 139, 140	r.4.191	IA 178(5)
r.4.103	IA 108, 109(1)	r.4.194	IA 181(1)–(3)
r.4.104	IA 137	r.4.195	IA 148(1), 150(1), 160
r.4.106	IA 109(1)	r.4.196	IA 160
r.4.107	IA 136(4),(5), 137	r.4.202	IA 150(1), 160
rr.4.108–4.110	IA 19(1)	r.4.203	IA 150(1)
r.4.108(1)	IA 171(5)	r.4.206	IA 177(5)
r.4.108(4)	IA 171(5), 172(6)	r.4.211	IA 133, 134
r.4.110(2)	IA 171(5)	r.4.213	IA 133(2),(3)
r.4.111	IA 171(5)	r.4.213(5)	IA 133(2),(3)
r.4.111(2)	IA 173(2),(3)	r.4.215	IA 133(4)
r.4.113	IA 172(1),(2), 174(4)	r.4.215(1)	IA 133
r.4.114	IA 171(1),(2),(3)	r.4.218	IA 115, 135, 156, 175(2)(a), 238, Sch.4, para.3A
r.4.114(2)	IA 173(2),(3)		
r.4.120	IA 171(1),(2)	r.4.220	IA 115, 156
rr.4.121–4.125	IA 174(4)	r.4.221	IA 154
r.4.122	IA 171(4), 173(2),(3)	r.4.223	IA 192(1)
r.4.123	IA 172(4)	r.4.224	IA 203(4), 205(3)–(4), 205(6),(7)
r.4.124	IA 174(2),(3)	r.4.225	IA 203(4), 205(3)–(4)
r.4.125	IA 146(1)	r.4.226	IA 216(3)
r.4.126	IA 106, 173(2),(3)	r.4.227	IA 216(3)
r.4.127	IA 100	r.4.228	IA 216(3)
rr.4.127–4.131	IA 144(1)	r.4.229	IA 216(3)
r.4.134	IA 172(5)	r.4.230	IA 216(3)
r.4.135	IA 171(4)	rr.5.1–5.65	IA Pt VIII
r.4.138(1)	IA 172(5)	rr.5.2–5.4	IA 253(1)–(3)
r.4.138(3)	IA 172(8)	r.5.7(4)	IA 253(4)
r.4.142(3)	IA 171(5)	r.5.8	IA 256(2)
r.4.144	IA 173(2),(3)	r.5.9	IA 256(2)
r.4.147	IA 173(2),(3)	rr.5.9–5.50	IA 255(6)
r.4.151	IA Pt VI	r.5.10	IA 256(5)
r.4.173(2)	IA Pt VI	r.5.11	IA 256(3),(3A)
r.4.179	IA 160	r.5.12	IA 256(5)
r.4.185	IA 160	rr.5.17–5.24	IA 257(2),(3), 258(6)
rr.4.218–4.220	IA 148(1)	r.5.18	IA 258(1)
r.4.136	IA 136(2)	rr.5.19–5.24	IA 259
r.4.138	IA 171	r.5.21	IA 263(5),(6)
r.4.139	IA 91(1), 92(3), 109(1)	rr.5.26–5.29	IA 263(5),(6)
r.4.140	IA 108, 109(1)	r.5.30	IA 262
r.4.141	IA 91(1)	rr.5.31–5.33	ER Arts 36,37
r.4.142(1)	IA 171(5)	rr.6.37–6.50	IA 271
r.4.147	IA 136(2)	r.6.38	IA 272(2)
r.4.148	IA 171	r.6.39	IA 272(2)
r.4.151	IA 101(1), 141(4),(5)	r.6.40(3)	IA 374(2),(3)
r.4.152	IA 141	rr.6.48–6.50	IA 273(2)

Statutory Instrument Table

Provision	Provision
rr.6.51–6.57 . . . . IA 286(1),(2)	r.7.62 . . . . ER Arts 2(d),(e), 16,17
rr.6.58–6.66 . . . . IA 288(2)	rr.7.62–7.63 . . . . IA 97(1)
r.6.62 . . . . IA 288(1),(3)	r.7.64 . . . . ER Art.32
r.6.76 . . . . IA 288(1),(3)	r.9.1 . . . . IA 236
rr.6.79–6.95 . . . . IA 293(2),(3)	rr.9.1–9.6 . . . . IA 366(1)
r.6.83 . . . . IA 294(3)	r.9.2(1) . . . . IA 236
rr.6.96–6.114 . . . . IA 322(1)	r.9.4(2) . . . . IA 236
r.6.106 . . . . ER Art.32	r.9.5(2) . . . . IA 236
rr.6.120–6.125 . . . . IA 292(1)	r.11.2 . . . . IA 153
r.6.121 . . . . IA 297(4),(5)	r.11.2(2) . . . . IA 153
r.6.122 . . . . . IA 295(4), 296(1)–(3), 300(3),(4)	r.11.5(2) . . . . IA 324(4)
r.6.124 . . . . IA 292(4), 296(4),(5)	r.11.8 . . . . IA 325(2)
rr.6.126–6.135 . . . . IA 298(9)	r.11.13 . . . . IA 189(2)
r.6.136 . . . . IA 299(1),(2)	r.12.1(1),(2) . . . . IA 287(1),(2),(5)
r.6.137 . . . . IA 299(1),(2)	r.12.1(1)(c) . . . . IA 349(2)
r.6.141 . . . . IA 363(1)	r.12.3 . . . . IA 1(1), Pt IV, 322(1)
rr.6.150–6.166 . . . . IA 301(1)	r.12.12 . . . . IA 238
rr.6.167–6.171 . . . . IA 370(1),(2)	r.12.19 . . . . IA 184
rr.6.172–6.177 . . . . IA 290	r.12.21 . . . . IA 430(1)
r.6.178 . . . . IA 315(1),(2),(4)	r.13.12 . . . . IA 1(1), 123, Pt IV
rr.6.178–6.186 . . . . . . IA 315(4), 316, 317	r.13.13(1) . . . . IA 251
r.6.182 . . . . IA 315(4)	r.17(5) . . . . IA 6
r.6.183 . . . . IA 316	Sch.2 . . . . IA 374(2),(3)
r.6.184 . . . . IA 316	Sch.6 . . . . IR 6.138A, 6.139(1)
r.6.185 . . . . IA 315	**Insolvency Rules (Northern Ireland)**
r.6.186 . . . . IA 320(1)–(4),(5),(6)	(SR 1991/364) . . . . IA 441, EA 0.3
r.6.187 . . . . IA 308, 308(1),(3)	**Insolvency (Northern Ireland) Order**
r.6.188 . . . . IA 308, 308(1),(4)	(SI 1989/2045) . . . . IA 426(10),(11),(12)
rr.6.194–6.196 . . . . IA 369(7)	**Insolvency (Scotland) Regulations**
r.6.201 . . . . IA 307(4)	(SI 2003/2109) . . . . IR 0.1
rr.6.200–6.202 . . . . IA 307(1)	**Insolvency (Scotland) Rules**
r.6.200(1) . . . . IA 307(1)	(SI 1986/1915) . . . . IR 0.1
r.6.201 . . . . IA 307(4)	r.4.22(1) . . . . IA 246
rr.6.206–6.214 . . . . IA 282(1),(3)	r.4.66(2)(b) . . . . IA 189(5)
r.6.212 . . . . IA 282(1),(3)	r.4.68 . . . . IA 169(2)
r.6.224 . . . . IA 328	**Insolvency (Scotland) Amendment Rules**
rr.6.225–6.228 . . . . IA 334(3), 335(5),(6)	(SI 1987/1921) . . . . EA, IR 0.1
r.6.230 . . . . IA 402(4)	**Insolvency (Scotland) Amendment Rules**
r.6A.2 . . . . IA 260(3)	(SI 2002/2709) . . . . IR 0.1
r.7.1 . . . . IA 168	**Insolvency (Deposits) Order (Northern**
rr.7.11–7.15 . . . . IA 373(4)	**Ireland) (SR 1991/3840** . . . . IA 441
r.7.20 . . . . IA 22, IA 47(3),(5),(6),	**Insolvency (Monetary Limits) Order**
131, 143(2), 235(5)	**(Northern Ireland)**
r.7.21 . . . . IA 365(3),(4), 366(2)–(4)	(SR 1991/386) . . . . IA 441
r.7.22 . . . . IA 134	**Insolvency (Fees) Order (Northern Ireland)**
r.7.23 . . . . IA 236(2), 366(2)–(4)	(SR 1991/385) . . . . IA 441
r.7.24 . . . . IA 236(2)	**Insolvent Companies (Disqualification of**
r.7.25 . . . . IA 365(3),(4)	**Unfit Directors) Proceedings**
r.7.36 . . . . IA 184	**(Amendment) Rules**
r.7.47 . . . . IA 18(2), 27(1), 130(1), 133	(SI 2001/765) . . . . IR 0.1
r.7.47(1) . . . . IA 147(1)	**Insolvent Partnerships Order 1986**
r.7.52 . . . . IA 399	(SI 1986/2142) . . . . . . IA 420(1), IR 0.1

Statutory Instrument Table

Insolvent Partnerships Order 1994 (SI 1994/2421) ...... IA Pt IV, 168(5A), 420(1), Sch.B1, para.10, IR 0.1
Art.1 .... IA 168(5A)–(5C)
Art.5 .... IA Pt I
Art.6 .... IA 8
Art.10 .... IA Pt XII, XIII, 435
Art.11 .... IA Pt XII, XIII, 435
Art.14(1) .... IA 168(5A)–(5C)
Art.15 .... IA 388(2A)
Sch.1 .... IA Pt I
Sch.2 .... IA 8
Sch.7 .... IA Pt XII, XIII, 435

Insolvent Partnerships (Amendment) Order 1996 (SI 1996/1308) .... IA 420(1), IR 0.1

Insolvent Partnerships (Amendment) Order 2001 (SI 2001/767) .... IA 420(1), IR 0.1

Insolvency (Northern Ireland) Order (SI 2002/1308) ... IA 420(1), ER, IR 0.1

Insolvent Partnerships (Amendment) (No.2) Order (SI 2002/2708) .... IR 0.1

Insurance Companies (Winding-up) (Amendment) Rules (SI 1986/20020 .... IR 0.1

Insurance Companies (Winding-up) (Scotland) Rules (SI 1986/1918) .... IR 0.1

Insurers (Reorganisation and Winding up) Regulations (SI 2004/353) .... IA 8, ER
... reg.52 .... IA Sch.B1, Sch.B1, 9(5)

Limited Liability Partnerships (Scotland) Regulations (SSI 2001/128) ..... IR 0.1
reg.4 .... IA 50
reg.4(1),(2) .... IA 416(1),(3),(4)
Sch.2 .... IA 50, 416(1),(3),(4)

Limited Liability Partnerships Regulations (SI 2001/1090) .... IA 110, IR 0.1
reg.5(1)(a) .... IA 8, Pt III, Pt IV
reg.5(1)(b) ...... IA Pt XII, Pt XIII, 426, 435
reg.5(2) .... IA Pt III, Pt IV, 435
reg.5(3) .... IA Pt III, Pt IV, 435

Occupational and Personal Pension Schemes (Bankruptcy) Regulations (SI 2002/427) .... IA 306

Occupational and Personal Pension Schemes (Bankruptcy) (No.2) Regulations (SI 2002/836) .... IA 342C(4),(5),(8),(9)

Postal Services Act 2000 (Commencement No.1 and Transitional Provisions) Order (SI 2000/2957)
Art.2(3) .... IA 371(1)
Sch.3 .... IA 371(1)

Receivers (Scotland) Regulations (SI 1986/1917) .. IA 53(1),(2),(5),(6),(7), 54(3),(4), 62(1)–(3), 62(5), 65(1),(2),(4), 66(1),(2), 67(2)–(4), 71(1), IR 0.1

Rules of the Supreme Court (SI 1965/1776)
Ord.11 .... IR 12.12(1)
Ord.18, r.19 .... IR 7.1–7.18

Scotland Act 1998 (Commencement) Order (SI 1998/3178)
Art.2 ... IA 53(1),(2),(5), 54(3),(4), 61(6),(7), 62(5), 67(1),(5),(6)

Scotland Act 1998 (Consequential Modifications) Order 1999 (SI 1999/1820)
Art.1(2) .... IA 155(2)
Art.4 .... IA 155(2)
Sch.2, Pt 1, para.85 .... IA 155(2)

Supreme Court Fees Order (SI 1999/687) .... IA 414(1),(2), 415(1)–(3)

Supreme Court Fees (Amendment) Order (SI 2003/646) .... IA 264

Value Added Tax (Buildings and Land) Order (SI 1991/2569)
Art.4(a) .... IA 241(4)
Art.7 .... IA 241(4)

Welfare Reform and Pensions Act 1999 (Commencement No.7) Order (SI 2000/1382) .... IA 310(7), 342A
(SR 2003/545) .... IA 441
(SR 2003/546) .... IA 441
(SR 2003/547) .... IA 441
(SR 2003/549) .... IA 441
(SI 2004/472) ..... IA 40.(2), (3), 412(3), (4), Sch.8, para.27
(SI 2004/476) .... IA 391, 392(1), 393, 415A

Introduction

The insolvency legislation of 1985 and 1986

The Insolvency Act 1985 was a major piece of new legislation, implementing the most comprehensive review of the subjects of bankruptcy and corporate insolvency for over a century. Its provisions were based largely on the recommendations contained in the Cork Report (see below), after publication of a White Paper entitled *A Revised Framework for Insolvency Law* (Cmnd 9175, February 1984). Although it received the Royal Assent and became law on October 30, 1985, the Government decided to delay implementation of all but a few of its provisions and to draw up a new Act, consolidating its provisions with those parts of the Companies Act 1985 dealing with receivership and winding up. This became the Insolvency Act 1986. At the same time a separate Bill was prepared to consolidate the law relating to the disqualification of company directors, which became the Company Directors Disqualification Act 1986. The two consolidating Acts received Royal Assent on July 25, 1986 and were brought into force together on December 29, 1986. On the same date the Insolvency Rules 1986 became operative, replacing the Companies (Winding up) Rules 1949 and the Bankruptcy Rules 1952.

The Cork Report

The main inspiration for the reforms made by the Insolvency Act 1985 was the *Report of the Review Committee on Insolvency Law and Practice*, the chairman of which was the late Sir Kenneth Cork ("the Cork Report", Cmnd 8558, 1982). This committee was appointed in January 1977 with a wide-ranging brief, and its Report, published in June 1982, made proposals for extensive and radical changes in the law and practice of bankruptcy and corporate insolvency, amounting virtually to the introduction of a completely new code.

Nature and construction of consolidating legislation

It is a fundamental principle that a consolidating Act should make no change in the substance of the law; and for this reason it is allowed an accelerated procedure in Parliament. There is a presumption on construing such a statute that no alteration of the previous law was intended, so that it is permissible to look at the superseded legislation and judicial decisions relating to it in order to determine the meaning of the new Act. This presumption applies even if the language of the two Acts is not identical. However the court will normally regard the consolidating statute as standing on its own feet, and will have recourse to the antecedent law only if the wording of the new Act is not clear.

This approach to the construction of the two Acts will be appropriate, in the main, only to those provisions of the consolidation which were formerly contained in the Companies Act 1985 and other earlier legislation. In contrast, those sections of the 1986 Act which are derived from the Insolvency Act 1985 should be construed and on the basis that that legislation was intended to make a fresh start – a view emphatically put by Millett J. in *Re M C Bacon Ltd* [1990] B.C.C. 78 at p. 87. See further the general note on Pt IX (p. 294), preceding s. 264, below.

Later legislation

There have been a number of changes made to the Act of 1986 since it came into force. Among these may be noted the following.

Introduction

Extension to building societies

The Building Societies Act 1986 was amended in 1989 so as to provide that where a building society is being wound up, the Insolvency Act 1986 (and the corresponding legislation for Northern Ireland) are to apply: see below, p. 115.

Disapplication of insolvency legislation to "market contracts" and "market charges"

The Companies Act 1989, Pt. VII has modified the application of insolvency law and the enforcement of certain rights and remedies in relation to certain contracts on the financial markets. These are contracts connected with "recognised investment exchanges" and "recognised clearing houses" (CA 1989, s. 155), with certain overseas investment exchanges and clearing houses (s. 170), with certain money market institutions (s. 171) and with settlement arrangements provided by the Bank of England (s. 172). Part VII has effect in three principal ways: (1) it gives effect to contractual settlement procedures in the various financial markets, displacing the normal rules of insolvency law, where one of the contracting parties becomes insolvent (see the notes to ss. 107 and 328, below); (2) it preserves (and, in some cases, enhances) the priority of a chargee where a charge has been taken to secure obligations and liabilities arising under a market contract (see the notes to ss. 10(1), 11(2), 11(3), 15(1), 15(2), 43, 61, 127 and 284, below); and (3) it safeguards rights and remedies in relation to property provided as cover for margin in relation to market contracts and market charges (see CA 1989, ss. 177–181, and note in particular s. 180(2), which provides that an investment exchange, clearing house or chargee may authorise the commencement or continuation of enforcement proceedings by an unsecured creditor against property held as margin "notwithstanding any provision of IA 1986"). The order-making powers of Pt. VII were brought into force on March 25, 1991 and the remaining provisions (except ss. 169(4), 170–172, 176, 178 and 181) became operative on April 25, 1991. The Financial Markets and Insolvency Regulations 1991 (SI 1991/880), which contain important modifications to the provisions of Pt. VII, also came into force on the latter date. A number of statutory instruments have since amended or extended this legislation: see, in particular, the Transfer of Functions (Financial Services) Order 1992 (SI 1992/1315) which provides for the order-making powers formerly exercisable by the Secretary of State to be now exercisable jointly with the Treasury; the Financial Markets and Insolvency (Money Markets) Regulations 1995 (SI 1995/2049, now superseded by SI 2001/3649), applying Pt. VII (with modifications) to settlement arrangements with regard to money markets under the supervision of the Bank of England; and the Financial Markets and Insolvency (Ecu Contracts) Regulations 1998 (SI 1998/27) extending the definitions of money market contracts to include settlements determined by reference to the ecu (euro), and the Financial Markets and Insolvency Regulations 1998 (SI 1998/1748), amending the definition of "market contract" in CA 1989 so as to include contracts effected off a recognised investment exchange. Other amendments of a minor nature have been made by SIs 1992/716, 1995/586, 1995/3275, 1996/1469, 1998/1120, 1998/1129, 1999/1209 and 2001/3649.

Amendments to CA 1989 have been made by EA 2002, Sch. 17, paras 43–47 to extend the above disapplication provisions to companies entering into administration under the new administration regime established by IA 1986, Sch. B1.

The insolvency legislation is similarly disapplied in relation to payment and securities settlement systems by the Financial Markets and Insolvency (Settlement Finality) Regulations 1999 (SI 1999/2979), discussed below.

Insolvency Act 1994

The ruling of the Court of Appeal in *Powdrill v Watson, Re Paramount Airways Ltd (No. 3)* [1994] B.C.C. 172 (see below, pp. 64 and 87) caused immediate concern amongst insolvency practitioners because of their possible exposure to personal liability in claims brought by former employees of companies which were, or had been, in administration or administrative receivership. The Insolvency Act 1994 was passed to clarify the question of the liability of office-holders in such circumstances, with effect from March 15, 1994 (but not retrospectively). See the notes to ss. 19 and 44, below.

Introduction

Insolvency (No. 2) Act 1994
This short Act amending the Insolvency Act 1986 was also passed in 1994, on the initiative of the Law Society, primarily to remove doubts about the position of a person who purchases unregistered land in a transaction which is challenged as a transaction at an undervalue or a preference under IA 1986, ss. 238–241 or 339–342 (or the corresponding provisions in the Northern Ireland insolvency legislation). See the notes to ss. 241 and 342, below.

The Human Rights Act 1998
The United Kingdom has been a party to the European Convention for the Protection of Human Rights and Fundamental Freedoms since its inception in 1950, but the Convention was only given force in UK domestic law by the Human Rights Act 1998, which became fully operative on October 2, 2000. In consequence, issues of human rights may now be raised before our own courts, rather than having to be litigated before the European Court of Human Rights in Strasbourg.

While the Act does not directly amend the insolvency legislation in any way, it is of significance because (a) the courts are directed to have regard to the established case-law of the European Court and opinions and decisions of the European Commission of Human Rights and the Committee of Ministers (s. 2); (b) domestic legislation must, so far as possible, be construed in a way which is compatible with Convention rights (s. 3); (c) it is unlawful for a public authority (*e.g.* the Secretary of State or the Insolvency Service) to act in a way which is incompatible with a Convention right (s. 6); and (d) in the preparation of new legislation, the draftsman is necessarily concerned to ensure that it is compatible with Convention rights. There will therefore be occasion to refer to the Convention and the Act of 1998 at various times in the discussion which follows.

The Civil Procedure Rules 1998
These Rules (commonly known as the CPR) came into force on April 26, 1999. On the same date amendments to the Insolvency Rules 1986 were brought into effect, so as to apply all those provisions of the CPR and such practice of the High Court and County Court as is not inconsistent with IR 1986 to insolvency proceedings, and to bring the terminology used in the Rules into line with the CPR.

Disapplication of insolvency legislation to payment and securities settlement systems
The Financial Markets and Insolvency (Settlement Finality) Regulations 1999 (SI 1999/2979) (the "Finality Regulations"), which became operative on December 11, 1999, were enacted in order to implement Directive 98/26/EC of the European Community (OJ L166/45, May 19, 1998) into the law of the United Kingdom. The object of the Directive is to reduce the risks associated with participation in payment and securities settlement systems by minimising the disruption caused by insolvency proceedings brought against a participant in such a system. For this purpose, a settlement system must be specifically designated by the Financial Services Authority or the Bank of England, and "insolvency proceedings" refers to a court order for bankruptcy, sequestration (in Scotland), administration or winding up, or a resolution for a creditors' voluntary winding up.

Regulations 13 to 19 modify the law of insolvency so far as it applies to transfer orders effected through a designated system and to collateral security provided in connection with participation in such a system. But the normal rules of insolvency apply to a transfer order which is entered into a designated system *after* the making of the court order or passing of a winding-up resolution, unless the transfer order is carried out on the same day as the court order or resolution and the relevant person (*e.g.* the settlement agent or clearing house) does not have notice of the insolvency at the time of settlement (reg. 20).

Where a transaction is both a market contract or market charge (as defined for the purposes of Pt. VII of the Companies Act 1989 (see above)) and a transfer order or a collateral security charge under the Finality Regulations, certain provisions of the 1989 Act are disapplied, so that the Regulations govern the situation (reg. 21).

Minor amendments were made to the Regulations by the Banking Consolidation Directive (Consequential Amendments) Regulations 2000 (SI 2000/2952), effective November 22, 2000.

Introduction

The Insolvency Act 2000
A Bill introduced into the House of Lords on February 3, 2000 passed through all stages of the parliamentary process in the course of that year and duly became the Insolvency Act 2000 on receiving the Royal Assent on November 30, 2000.

The Act contains only 18 sections and five schedules, but this apparently modest measure is deceptive, in that the schedules introduce some 50 new sections into IA 1986 and also amend over half of the sections of CDDA 1986. Moreover, the changes which it introduces have required significant amendments to be made to the existing Insolvency Rules and Regulations. The two principal reforms are (a) provision for a moratorium in voluntary arrangements for small companies (s. 1 and Sch. 1), and (b) the introduction of a formal scheme of disqualification undertakings entered into under an administrative procedure in lieu of disqualification orders made by a court (ss. 5–8). Other amendments include: improvements to the procedure for an individual voluntary arrangement (s. 3 and Sch. 3), new rules relating to the prosecution of delinquent officers and members of a company in a compulsory winding up, designed to bring the law into conformity with the Human Rights Act 1998 (s. 11), and a power conferred on the Secretary of State (by s. 14) to give effect to the UNCITRAL Model Law on Cross-Border Insolvency (discussed below, p. 598).

Section 14 (the enabling provision relating to the Model Law) came into operation with the passing of the Act. Other parts of the Act have been brought into force in stages, implementation being finally completed on January 1, 2003.

Extension to limited liability partnerships
The *Limited Liability Partnerships Act* 2000 introduced a new form of incorporated body, the limited liability partnership (LLP), into the law of Great Britain, and provided for the recognition of similar bodies incorporated or established outside the jurisdiction, which are referred to in the Act as "oversea limited liability partnerships". Section 14 of this Act authorises provision to be made by regulation about the insolvency and winding up of LLPs and oversea LLPs by applying or incorporating, with such modifications as appear appropriate, Parts I to IV, VI and VII of IA 1986. This has been done by the Limited Liability Partnership Regulations 2001 (SI 2001/1090). The Act and Regulations came into force on April 6, 2001. The modifications made to IA 1986 by the Regulations are extensive and in places quite complex: so much so that it has not been possible to include references to them in the present work.

The EC Regulation on Insolvency Proceedings 2000
This Regulation (EC Regulation 1346/2000, OJ 2000 L160/1, June 30, 2000) sets out common rules on cross-border insolvency proceedings within the European Union. It came into force on May 31, 2002. As a Regulation, it has direct applicability (*i.e.* it does not need to be implemented by domestic legislation).

The background to this legislation is set out below at p. 602, where the full text of the Regulation is reproduced with an accompanying commentary.

The Financial Services and Markets Act 2000
This major enactment has brought into being a thoroughly revised system of regulation for the financial markets in this country, replacing the Financial Services Act 1986. Although the Act does not make any substantial changes in the field of insolvency law, many amendments on points of detail have been made to the insolvency legislation and the Rules by subordinate legislation, and in particular by the Financial Services and Markets Act 2000 (Consequential Amendments and Repeals) Order 2001 (SI 2001/3649, effective December 1, 2001). These amendments have been incorporated into the text which follows.

Extension of administration procedure to insurance companies
The administration procedure was not available to insurance companies under IA 1986, as originally enacted. However, by the Financial Services and Markets Act 2000 (Administration Orders Relating to

Introduction

Insurers) Order 2002 (SI 2002/1242), which came into force on May 31, 2002, this has now become possible.

The Enterprise Act 2002
On February 2, 1999 the Secretary of State for Trade and Industry announced the setting up of a review team led jointly by the DTI and the Treasury to consider various aspects of corporate rescue law and practice, with particular focus on (a) the further development of the rescue culture, (b) a reassessment of the relative rights and remedies of secured and unsecured creditors in insolvencies, including the position of the Crown as a preferential creditor, and (c) the duties of directors of companies experiencing financial difficulties. On the same day, the Secretary of State announced that he had set up a working group to consider how insolvency and bankruptcy law could be made more enterprise-friendly, so that a proper distinction would be made between responsible risk-taking and unacceptable misconduct.

The review group published an interim report on September 20, 1999 and a final report on November 2, 2000. Among its recommendations it proposed (a) that floating charge holders should lose the right to veto the making of an administration order (IA 1986, s. 9(3)) and (b) that (pending what would necessarily be a political decision whether the Crown's preference in insolvency should be abolished) the Crown should adopt a more commercial and purposive approach to CVAs.

Meantime, the DTI had on April 7 published a consultation paper entitled *Bankruptcy – a Fresh Start*. The principal proposal put forward by this paper was that there should be a move away from a "one size fits all" approach to bankruptcies and that there should instead be greater concern to make a distinction between bankrupts on the basis of culpability, so as to reduce the impact of financial failure on the less blameworthy and to give them a fresh start, free from debt.

A White Paper, incorporating proposals from each of these documents, was published on February 13, 2000, with the arresting title *Opportunity for All in a World of Change – A White Paper on Enterprise, Skills and Innovation*. It announced the intention, *inter alia*, of introducing reforms to cut the period for discharge from bankruptcy from three years to 12 months, while imposing restrictions for up to 15 years for those whose failure is irresponsible, negligent or dishonest.

A further White Paper, presaged in the Queen's Speech a month previously (and the contemporaneous issue of yet another Treasury/DTI publication, *Productivity in the UK: Enterprise and the Productivity Challenge*), was published by the Insolvency Service on July 31, 2001. It was entitled *Productivity and Enterprise: Insolvency – A Second Chance*. Its main proposals concerning corporate insolvency were (a) that the right to appoint an administrative receiver be restricted to holders of floating charges granted in connection with transactions in the capital markets; (b) that the Crown's standing as a preferential creditor be abolished; (c) that the administration procedure be streamlined by reducing some of the present formalities, and in particular that the holder of a floating charge should be entitled to petition the court for an administration order where the chargor company is in default, in cases of urgency on a without-notice basis; and (d) to simplify the transition from an administration to a winding up where there are likely to be funds available for distribution to unsecured creditors. In regard to bankruptcy law, the reforms outlined in the White Paper of February 13, 2000 would be introduced, together with the abolition of Crown preference in personal insolvencies, and a system of "bankruptcy restriction orders", on analogy with director disqualification orders, be instituted for the more culpable debtors. It was also proposed to extend the director disqualification regime by adding the disqualification of directors as an additional sanction for breaches of the competition laws.

A Bill based on these proposals (and also involving major changes to the law relating to mergers and competition), the Enterprise Bill, was introduced into the House of Commons on March 26, 2002, and passed through all stages of the legislative process in the course of that year, receiving Royal Assent as the Enterprise Act 2002 on November 7, 2002. In some respects, the Act goes further than the proposals in the White Paper – *e.g.* in empowering a company or its directors, or the holder of a general floating charge, to appoint an administrator without the need to apply for a court order. The provisions of this Act relating to corporate insolvency and the abolition of the Crown's preferential status, together with supporting statutory instruments (principally the Insolvency (Amendment) Rules 2003 (SI 2003/1730)), were brought into force on September 15, 2003, and are fully incorporated in the statutory text and commentary which follows. The

Introduction

remaining sections dealing with the bankruptcy of individuals, however, are not to become effective until April 1, 2004. However, it has been possible to include an annotation of these amendments, so far as the relevant legislative material is available at the time when this edition goes to press. It is to be found below, at pp. 639ff.

The Proceeds of Crime Act 2002
This Act provides for the confiscation of assets of persons convicted of criminal offences, replacing parts of the Drug Trafficking Act 1994, the Criminal Justice Act 1988 and the corresponding legislation in Scotland and Northern Ireland. Part 9 of the Act, which became operative on March 24, 2003, deals with the potential conflicts which may arise between the criminal law confiscation rules and the insolvency regimes of bankruptcy, sequestration (in Scotland), winding up and receivership. It also applies in the insolvency of limited liability partnerships. The impact of this legislation is discussed at appropriate places in the text which follows.

The Debt Arrangement and Attachment (Scotland) Act 2002
This Act, passed by the Scottish Parliament in 2002, effects significant reforms to the law relating to diligence (*i.e.* execution) over moveable property, and in that respect has been in force since the beginning of 2003. Part 1 of the Act, in contrast, is not to become operative until 2004. This will introduce a debt payment and moratorium scheme for private individuals, comparable in some respects to the IVA procedure which applies in England and Wales under IA 1986, Pt VIII.

Insolvency Act 1986

On its enactment, the Insolvency Act 1986 brought into one composite Act the whole of the provisions of the Insolvency Act 1985 (except for ss. 12–14, 16, 18 and Sch. 2, which were separately consolidated into CDDA 1986) and ss. 467–650 and 659–674 of CA 1985, together with certain parts of other ancillary legislation. It deals with both corporate insolvency and the bankruptcy of individuals, but in this context "corporate insolvency" has to be understood in a much wider sense than normal, for the Act is concerned with the winding up and receivership of all companies, whether "solvent" (meaning financially viable) or not, and also with voluntary arrangements, administration orders and associated matters. Insolvent partnerships are also dealt with by subordinate legislation made under s. 420 of the Act, and limited liability partnerships by the Limited Liability Partnerships Regulations 2001 (SI 2001/1090). The Act applies also, with modifications where necessary, in the insolvency of other bodies such as building societies, friendly societies and industrial and provident societies, either by virtue of the particular legislation governing them or because they are treated as "unregistered companies" under IA 1986, Pt. V. The Act applies to England and Wales and to Scotland in relation to corporate insolvency, but only to England and Wales in regard to the bankruptcy of individuals. The corresponding bankruptcy provisions for Scotland were revised separately by the Bankruptcy (Scotland) Act 1985. Only a few sections of IA 1986 apply to Northern Ireland. (See the note to s. 441.) The corresponding law for that jurisdiction is to be found in the separate legislation which is listed in the note to s. 441, below. However the law in Northern Ireland so closely mirrors that of Great Britain that this annotation should be of assistance to practitioners in Northern Ireland when grappling with the interpretation and application of their own insolvency legislative system.

Most Acts of Parliament, or at least the larger ones, are divided into Parts, and the Parts subdivided into Chapters, with yet further subdivisions marked by italic subheadings. The present Act has one further tier in this hierarchy: the Parts are collected into three "Groups of Parts". The "First Group of Parts" comprises "Company Insolvency" and "Companies Winding Up" – once again, we notice the ambivalence in the use of the word "insolvency" – and is broken into Pts. I–VII; the Group has its own definition sections in Pt. VII. The Second Group deals with "Insolvency of Individuals" and "Bankruptcy" and contains four Parts, continuing in numerical sequence from VIII to XI, again with separate interpretation provisions. The Third Group, which comprises Pts. XII–XIX, is concerned with the administration of the Act and miscellaneous matters affecting all types of insolvency.

The Act has been amended in minor respects by later legislation, and more substantially by IA 2000, which came into force on various dates between November 30, 2000 and January 1, 2003, and the Enterprise Act 2002, which became operative as regards corporate insolvency and the abolition of Crown preference on September 15, 2003 but is not to be implemented in relation to the bankruptcy of individuals until April 1, 2004. Those amendments which have already come into effect have been incorporated into the text of the Act as set out in this work. Those which have not are discussed in the annotation to EA 2002 at pp. 639ff.

Of the subordinate legislation promulgated under IA 1986, the Insolvency Rules 1986 (see p. 654ff.) are by far the most significant. These Rules replaced the Winding-up Rules and the former Bankruptcy Rules and, like the Acts themselves, became operative on December 29, 1986. Detailed amendments to IR 1986 were made by I(A)R 1987, which came into force on January 11, 1988, I(A)R 2003 (effective from September 15, 2003), and by various minor amendments by the measures which are listed on pp. 654, 674ff. These amendments, too, have been incorporated into the text of the principal Rules.

The IA 1985, apart from a few sections which had already become operative, was brought into force immediately before the consolidating legislation, and was then at once repealed by the latter Acts (see SI 1986/1924 (C 71)). This brief moment of existence was sufficient to activate repeals which swept away many special features of insolvency law that had been familiar for over a century: the doctrine of relation back, acts of bankruptcy, winding up subject to the supervision of the court, and many more. Attention has been drawn to these changes at appropriate points in the discussion which follows.

Insolvency Act 1986

The IA 1985 and the consolidating Acts introduced a good deal of special terminology: "administration", "administrative receivers", the "liquidation committee", and so on. It is not practicable to give a repeated explanation of these terms every time that they occur in the text, and so they have been listed in Appendix I which refers the reader to the appropriate provision of the Act, where the relevant commentary also appears. In Appendix II there is a similar list for expressions used in the Insolvency Rules.

Insolvency Act 1986

(1986 Chapter 45)

ARRANGEMENT OF SECTIONS

THE FIRST GROUP OF PARTS
COMPANY INSOLVENCY;
COMPANIES WINDING UP

PART I

COMPANY VOLUNTARY ARRANGEMENTS

The proposal

1. Those who may propose an arrangement
1A. Moratorium
2. Procedure where nominee is not the liquidator or administrator
3. Summoning of meetings

Consideration and implementation of proposal

4. Decisions of meetings
4A. Approval of arrangement
5. Effect of approval
6. Challenge of decisions
6A. False representations, etc.
7. Implementation of proposal
7A. Prosecution of delinquent officers of company
7B. Arrangements coming to an end prematurely

PART II

ADMINISTRATION ORDERS

Making, etc. of administration order

8. Power of court to make order
9. Application for order
10. Effect of application
11. Effect of order
12. Notification of order

Administrators

13. Appointment of administrator
14. General powers
15. Power to deal with charged property, etc.
16. Operation of s. 15 in Scotland
17. General duties
18. Discharge or variation of administration order
19. Vacation of office
20. Release of administrator

Ascertainment and investigation of company's affairs

21. Information to be given by administrator
22. Statement of affairs to be submitted to administrator

Administrator's proposals

23. Statement of proposals
24. Consideration of proposals by creditors' meeting
25. Approval of substantial revisions

Miscellaneous

26. Creditors' committee
27. Protection of interests of creditors and members

PART III

RECEIVERSHIP

CHAPTER I

RECEIVERS AND MANAGERS (ENGLAND AND WALES)

Preliminary and general provisions

28. Extent of this Chapter
29. Definitions
30. Disqualification of body corporate from acting as receiver
31. Disqualification of bankrupt
32. Power for court to appoint official receiver

Receivers and managers appointed out of court

33. Time from which appointment is effective
34. Liability for invalid appointment
35. Application to court for directions
36. Court's power to fix remuneration
37. Liability for contracts, etc.
38. Receivership accounts to be delivered to registrar

Provisions applicable to every receivership

39. Notification that receiver or manager appointed
40. Payment of debts out of assets subject to floating charge
41. Enforcement of duty to make returns

Administrative receivers: general

42. General powers
43. Power to dispose of charged property, etc.
44. Agency and liability for contracts
45. Vacation of office

Administrative receivers: ascertainment and investigation of company's affairs

46. Information to be given by administrative receiver
47. Statement of affairs to be submitted
48. Report by administrative receiver
49. Committee of creditors

CHAPTER II

RECEIVERS (SCOTLAND)

50. Extent of this Chapter
51. Power to appoint receiver
52. Circumstances justifying appointment
53. Mode of appointment by holder of charge
54. Appointment by court
55. Powers of receiver
56. Precedence among receivers
57. Agency and liability of receiver for contracts
58. Remuneration of receiver
59. Priority of debts
60. Distribution of moneys
61. Disposal of interest in property
62. Cessation of appointment of receiver
63. Powers of court
64. Notification that receiver appointed
65. Information to be given by receiver
66. Company's statement of affairs
67. Report by receiver
68. Committee of creditors
69. Enforcement of receiver's duty to make returns, etc.
70. Interpretation for Chapter II
71. Prescription of forms, etc.; regulations

CHAPTER III

RECEIVERS' POWERS IN GREAT BRITAIN AS A WHOLE

72. Cross-border operation of receivership provisions

CHAPTER IV

PROHIBITION ON APPOINTMENT OF ADMINISTRATIVE RECEIVER

72A. Floating charge holder not to appoint administrative receiver
72B. First exception: capital market
72C. Second exception: public-private partnership
72D. Third exception: utilities
72DA. Exception in respect of urban regeneration projects
72E. Fourth exception: project finance
72F. Fifth exception: financial market
72G. Sixth exception: registered social landlord
72GA. Exception in relation to protected railway companies etc.
72H. Sections 72A–72G: supplementary

PART IV

WINDING UP OF COMPANIES REGISTERED UNDER THE COMPANIES ACTS

CHAPTER I

PRELIMINARY

Modes of winding up

73. Alternative modes of winding up

Contributories

74. Liability as contributories of present and past members
75. Directors, etc. with unlimited liability
76. Liability of past directors and shareholders
77. Limited company formerly unlimited
78. Unlimited company formerly limited
79. Meaning of "contributory"
80. Nature of contributory's liability
81. Contributories in case of death of a member
82. Effect of contributory's bankruptcy
83. Companies registered under Companies Act, Part XXII, Chapter II

Insolvency Act 1986

Chapter II

Voluntary Winding Up (Introductory and General)

Resolution for, and commencement of, voluntary winding up

84. Circumstances in which company may be wound up voluntarily
85. Notice of resolution to wind up
86. Commencement of winding up

Consequences of resolution to wind up

87. Effect on business and status of company
88. Avoidance of share transfers, etc. after winding-up resolution

Declaration of solvency

89. Statutory declaration of solvency
90. Distinction between "members'" and "creditors'" voluntary winding up

Chapter III

Members' Voluntary Winding Up

91. Appointment of liquidator
92. Power to fill vacancy in office of liquidator
93. General company meeting at each year's end
94. Final meeting prior to dissolution
95. Effect of company's insolvency
96. Conversion to creditors' voluntary winding up

Chapter IV

Creditors' Voluntary Winding Up

97. Application of this Chapter
98. Meeting of creditors
99. Directors to lay statement of affairs before creditors
100. Appointment of liquidator
101. Appointment of liquidation committee
102. Creditors' meeting where winding up converted under s. 96.
103. Cesser of directors' powers
104. Vacancy in office of liquidator
105. Meetings of company and creditors at each year's end
106. Final meeting prior to dissolution

Chapter V

Provisions Applying to Both Kinds of Voluntary Winding Up

107. Distribution of company's property
108. Appointment or removal of liquidator by the court
109. Notice by liquidator of his appointment
110. Acceptance of shares, etc., as consideration for sale of company property
111. Dissent from arrangement under s. 110.
112. Reference of questions to court
113. Court's power to control proceedings (Scotland)
114. No liquidator appointed or nominated by company
115. Expenses of voluntary winding up
116. Saving for certain rights

Chapter VI

Winding up by the Court

Jurisdiction (England and Wales)

117. High Court and county court jurisdiction
118. Proceedings taken in wrong court
119. Proceedings in county court; case stated for High Court

Jurisdiction (Scotland)

120. Court of Session and sheriff court jurisdiction
121. Power to remit winding up to Lord Ordinary

Grounds and effect of winding-up petition

122. Circumstances in which company may be wound up by the court
123. Definition of inability to pay debts
124. Application for winding up
124A. Petition for winding up on grounds of public interest
125. Powers of court on hearing of petition
126. Power to stay or restrain proceedings against company
127. Avoidance of property dispositions, etc.
128. Avoidance of attachments, etc.

Commencement of winding up

129. Commencement of winding up by the court
130. Consequences of winding-up order

Investigation procedures

131. Company's statement of affairs
132. Investigation by official receiver
133. Public examination of officers
134. Enforcement of s. 133.

Appointment of liquidator

135. Appointment and powers of provisional liquidator
136. Functions of official receiver in relation to office of liquidator
137. Appointment by Secretary of State
138. Appointment of liquidator in Scotland
139. Choice of liquidator at meetings of creditors and contributories
140. Appointment by the court following administration or voluntary arrangement

Liquidation committees

141. Liquidation committee (England and Wales)
142. Liquidation committee (Scotland)

The liquidator's functions

143. General functions in winding up by the court
144. Custody of company's property
145. Vesting of company property in liquidator
146. Duty to summon final meeting

General powers of court

147. Power to stay or sist winding up
148. Settlement of list of contributories and application of assets
149. Debts due from contributory to company
150. Power to make calls
151. Payment into bank of money due to company
152. Order on contributory to be conclusive evidence
153. Power to exclude creditors not proving in time
154. Adjustment of rights of contributories
155. Inspection of books by creditors, etc.
156. Payment of expenses of winding up
157. Attendance at company meetings (Scotland)
158. Power to arrest absconding contributory
159. Powers of court to be cumulative
160. Delegation of powers to liquidator (England and Wales)

Enforcement of, and appeal from, orders

161. Orders for calls on contributories (Scotland)
162. Appeals from orders in Scotland

CHAPTER VII

LIQUIDATORS

Preliminary

163. Style and title of liquidators
164. Corrupt inducement affecting appointment

Liquidator's powers and duties

165. Voluntary winding up
166. Creditors' voluntary winding up
167. Winding up by the court
168. Supplementary powers (England and Wales)
169. Supplementary powers (Scotland)
170. Enforcement of liquidator's duty to make returns, etc.

Removal; vacation of office

171. Removal, etc. (voluntary winding up)
172. Removal, etc. (winding up by the court)

Release of liquidator

173. Release (voluntary winding up)
174. Release (winding up by the court)

CHAPTER VIII

PROVISIONS OF GENERAL APPLICATION IN WINDING UP

Preferential debts

175. Preferential debts (general provision)
176. Preferential charge on goods distrained

Property subject to floating charge

176A. Share of assets for unsecured creditors

Special managers

177. Power to appoint special manager

Disclaimer (England and Wales only)

178. Power to disclaim onerous property
179. Disclaimer of leaseholds
180. Land subject to rentcharge
181. Powers of court (general)
182. Powers of court (leaseholds)

Execution, attachment and the Scottish equivalents

183. Effect of execution or attachment (England and Wales)
184. Duties of sheriff (England and Wales)
185. Effect of diligence (Scotland)

Miscellaneous matters

186. Rescission of contracts by the court
187. Power to make over assets to employees
188. Notification that company is in liquidation
189. Interest on debts
190. Documents exempt from stamp duty
191. Company's books to be evidence
192. Information as to pending liquidations
193. Unclaimed dividends (Scotland)
194. Resolutions passed at adjourned meetings
195. Meetings to ascertain wishes of creditors or contributories
196. Judicial notice of court documents
197. Commission for receiving evidence
198. Court order for examination of persons in Scotland
199. Costs of application for leave to proceed (Scottish companies)
200. Affidavits etc. in United Kingdom and overseas

CHAPTER IX

DISSOLUTION OF COMPANIES AFTER WINDING UP

201. Dissolution (voluntary winding up)
202. Early dissolution (England and Wales)
203. Consequence of notice under s. 202
204. Early dissolution (Scotland)
205. Dissolution otherwise than under s. 202–204

CHAPTER X

MALPRACTICE BEFORE AND DURING LIQUIDATION; PENALISATION OF COMPANIES AND COMPANY OFFICERS; INVESTIGATIONS AND PROSECUTIONS

Offences of fraud, deception, etc.

206. Fraud, etc. in anticipation of winding up
207. Transactions in fraud of creditors
208. Misconduct in course of winding up
209. Falsification of company's books
210. Material omissions from statement relating to company's affairs
211. False representations to creditors

Penalisation of directors and officers

212. Summary remedy against delinquent directors, liquidators, etc.
213. Fraudulent trading
214. Wrongful trading
215. Proceedings under s. 213, 214
216. Restriction on re-use of company names
217. Personal liability for debts, following contravention of s. 216

Investigation and prosecution of malpractice

218. Prosecution of delinquent officers and members of company
219. Obligations arising under s. 218

PART V

WINDING UP OF UNREGISTERED COMPANIES

220. Meaning of "unregistered company"
221. Winding up of unregistered companies
222. Inability to pay debts: unpaid creditor for £750 or more
223. Inability to pay debts: debt remaining unsatisfied after action brought
224. Inability to pay debts: other cases
225. Oversea company may be wound up though dissolved
226. Contributories in winding up of unregistered company
227. Power of court to stay, sist or restrain proceedings
228. Actions stayed on winding-up order
229. Provisions of this Part to be cumulative

PART VI

MISCELLANEOUS PROVISIONS APPLYING TO COMPANIES WHICH ARE INSOLVENT OR IN LIQUIDATION

Office-holders

230. Holders of office to be qualified insolvency practitioners
231. Appointment to office of two or more persons
232. Validity of office-holder's acts

Management by administrators, liquidators, etc.

233. Supplies of gas, water, electricity, etc.
234. Getting in the company's property
235. Duty to co-operate with office-holder
236. Inquiry into company's dealings, etc.
237. Court's enforcement powers under s. 236

Adjustment of prior transactions (administration and liquidation)

238. Transactions at an undervalue (England and Wales)
239. Preferences (England and Wales)
240. "Relevant time" under ss. 238, 239
241. Orders under ss. 238, 239
242. Gratuitous alienations (Scotland)
243. Unfair preferences (Scotland)
244. Extortionate credit transactions
245. Avoidance of certain floating charges
246. Unenforceability of liens on books, etc.

PART VII

INTERPRETATION FOR FIRST GROUP OF PARTS

247. "Insolvency" and "go into liquidation"
248. "Secured creditor", etc.
249. "Connected" with a company
250. "Member" of a company
251. Expressions used generally

THE SECOND GROUP OF PARTS: INSOLVENCY OF INDIVIDUALS; BANKRUPTCY

PART VIII

INDIVIDUAL VOLUNTARY ARRANGEMENTS

Moratorium for insolvent debtor

252. Interim order of court
253. Application for interim order
254. Effect of application
255. Cases in which interim order can be made
256. Nominee's report on debtor's proposal

Procedure where no interim order made

256A. Debtor's proposal and nominee's report
257. Summoning of creditors' meeting

Consideration and implementation of debtor's proposal

258. Decisions of creditors' meeting
259. Report of decisions to court
260. Effect of approval
261. Additional effect on undischarged bankrupt
262. Challenge of meeting's decision
262A. False representations, etc.
262B. Prosecution of delinquent debtors
262C. Arrangements coming to an end prematurely
263. Implementation and supervision of approved voluntary arrangement

"Fast-track voluntary arrangement"

263A. Availability
263B. Decision
263C. Result
263D. Approval of voluntary arrangement
263E. Implementation
263F. Revocation
263G. Offences

PART IX

BANKRUPTCY

CHAPTER I

BANKRUPTCY PETITIONS; BANKRUPTCY ORDERS

Preliminary

264. Who may present a bankruptcy petition
265. Conditions to be satisfied in respect of debtor
266. Other preliminary conditions

Creditor's petition

267. Grounds of creditor's petition
268. Definition of "inability to pay", etc.; the statutory demand
269. Creditor with security
270. Expedited petition
271. Proceedings on creditor's petition

Debtor's petition

272. Grounds of debtor's petition
273. Appointment of insolvency practitioner by the court
274. Action on report of insolvency practitioner
275. [Repealed]

Other cases for special consideration

276. Default in connection with voluntary arrangement
277. Petition based on criminal bankruptcy order

Commencement and duration of bankruptcy; discharge

278. Commencement and continuance
279. Duration
280. Discharge by order of the court
281. Effect of discharge
281A. Post-discharge restrictions
282. Court's power to annul bankruptcy order

CHAPTER II

PROTECTION OF BANKRUPT'S ESTATE AND INVESTIGATION OF HIS AFFAIRS

283. Definition of bankrupt's estate
283A. Bankrupt's home ceasing to form part of estate
284. Restrictions on dispositions of property
285. Restriction on proceedings and remedies
286. Power to appoint interim receiver
287. Receivership pending appointment of trustee
288. Statement of affairs
289. Investigatory duties of official receiver
290. Public examination of bankrupt
291. Duties of bankrupt in relation to official receiver

CHAPTER III

TRUSTEES IN BANKRUPTCY

Tenure of office as trustee

292. Power to make appointments
293. Summoning of meeting to appoint first trustee
294. Power of creditors to requisition meeting
295. Failure of meeting to appoint trustee
296. Appointment of trustee by Secretary of State
297. Special cases
298. Removal of trustee; vacation of office
299. Release of trustee
300. Vacancy in office of trustee

Control of trustee

301. Creditors' committee
302. Exercise by Secretary of State of functions of creditors' committee
303. General control of trustee by the court
304. Liability of trustee

CHAPTER IV

ADMINISTRATION BY TRUSTEE

Preliminary

305. General functions of trustee

Acquisition, control and realisation of bankrupt's estate

306. Vesting of bankrupt's estate in trustee
306A. Property subject to restraint order
306B. Property in respect of which receivership or administration order made
306C. Property subject to certain orders where confiscation order discharged or quashed
307. After-acquired property
308. Vesting in trustee of certain items of excess value
308A. Vesting in trustee of certain tenancies
309. Time-limit for notice under s. 307 or 308
310. Income payments orders
310A. Income payments agreement
311. Acquisition by trustee of control
312. Obligation to surrender control to trustee
313. Charge on bankrupt's home
313A. Low value home: application for sale, possession or charge
314. Powers of trustee

Disclaimer of onerous property

315. Disclaimer (general power)
316. Notice requiring trustee's decision
317. Disclaimer of leaseholds
318. Disclaimer of dwelling house
319. Disclaimer of land subject to rentcharge
320. Court order vesting disclaimed property
321. Order under s. 320 in respect of leaseholds

Distribution of bankrupt's estate

322. Proof of debts
323. Mutual credit and set-off
324. Distribution by means of dividend
325. Claims by unsatisfied creditors
326. Distribution of property in specie
327. Distribution in criminal bankruptcy
328. Priority of debts
329. Debts to spouse
330. Final distribution
331. Final meeting
332. Saving for bankrupt's home

Supplemental

333. Duties of bankrupt in relation to trustee
334. Stay of distribution in case of second bankruptcy
335. Adjustment between earlier and later bankruptcy estates

Chapter V

Effect of Bankruptcy on Certain Rights, Transactions, etc.

Rights under trusts of land

335A. Rights under trusts of land

Rights of occupation

336. Rights of occupation, etc. of bankrupt's spouse
337. Rights of occupation of bankrupt
338. Payments in respect of premises occupied by bankrupt

Adjustment of prior transactions, etc.

339. Transactions at an undervalue
340. Preferences
341. "Relevant time" under ss. 339, 340
342. Orders under ss. 339, 340
342A. Recovery of excessive pension contributions
342B. Orders made under s. 342A
342C. Orders made under s. 342A: supplementary
342D. Recovery of excessive contributions in pension-sharing cases
342E. Orders under ss. 339 or 340 in respect of pension-sharing transactions
342F. Orders under ss. 339 or 340 in pension-sharing cases: supplementary
343. Extortionate credit transactions
344. Avoidance of general assignment of book debts
345. Contracts to which bankrupt is a party
346. Enforcement procedures
347. Distress, etc.
348. Apprenticeships, etc.
349. Unenforceability of liens on books, etc.

Chapter VI

Bankruptcy Offences

Preliminary

350. Scheme of this Chapter
351. Definitions
352. Defence of innocent intention

Wrongdoing by the bankrupt before and after bankruptcy

353. Non-disclosure
354. Concealment of property
355. Concealment of books and papers; falsification
356. False statements
357. Fraudulent disposal of property
358. Absconding
359. Fraudulent dealing with property obtained on credit
360. Obtaining credit; engaging in business
361. [Repealed]
362. [Repealed from April 1, 2004]

Chapter VII

Powers of Court in Bankruptcy

363. General control of court
364. Power of arrest
365. Seizure of bankrupt's property
366. Inquiry into bankrupt's dealings and property
367. Court's enforcement powers under s. 366
368. Provision corresponding to s. 366, where interim receiver appointed
369. Order for production of documents by inland revenue
370. Power to appoint special manager
371. Re-direction of bankrupt's letters, etc.

Part X

Individual Insolvency: General Provisions

372. Supplies of gas, water, electricity, etc.
373. Jurisdiction in relation to insolvent individuals
374. Insolvency districts
375. Appeals, etc. from courts exercising insolvency jurisdiction
376. Time-limits
377. Formal defects
378. Exemption from stamp duty
379. Annual report

Part XI

Interpretation for Second Group of Parts

380. Introductory
381. "Bankrupt" and associated terminology
382. "Bankruptcy debt", etc.
383. "Creditor", "security", etc.
384. "Prescribed" and "the rules"
385. Miscellaneous definitions

The Third Group of Parts: Miscellaneous Matters Bearing on Both Company and Individual Insolvency; General Interpretation; Final Provisions

Part XII

Preferential Debts in Company and Individual Insolvency

386. Categories of preferential debts
387. "The relevant date"

Part XIII

Insolvency Practitioners and Their Qualification

Restrictions on unqualified persons acting as liquidator, trustee in bankruptcy, etc.

388. Meaning of "act as insolvency practitioner"
389. Acting without qualification an offence
389A. Authorisation of nominees and supervisors
389B. Official receiver as nominee or supervisor

The requisite qualification, and the means of obtaining it

390. Persons not qualified to act as insolvency practitioners
391. Recognised professional bodies
392. Authorisation by competent authority
393. Grant, refusal and withdrawal of authorisation
394. Notices
395. Right to make representations
396. Reference to Tribunal
397. Action of Tribunal on reference
398. Refusal or withdrawal without reference to Tribunal

Part XIV

Public Administration (England and Wales)

Official receivers

399. Appointment, etc. of official receivers
400. Functions and status of official receivers
401. Deputy official receivers and staff

The Official Petitioner

402. Official Petitioner

Insolvency Service finance, accounting and investment

403. Insolvency Services Account
404. Investment Account
405. [Repealed from April 1, 2004]
406. Interest on money received by liquidators or trustees in bankruptcy and invested
407. Unclaimed dividends and undistributed balances
408. Recourse to Consolidated Fund
409. Annual financial statement and audit

Supplementary

410. Extent of this Part

Part XV

Subordinate Legislation

General insolvency rules

411. Company insolvency rules
412. Individual insolvency rules (England and Wales)
413. Insolvency Rules Committee

Fees orders

414. Fees orders (company insolvency proceedings)
415. Fees orders (individual insolvency proceedings in England and Wales)
415A. Fees orders (general)

Specification, increase and reduction of money sums relevant in the operation of this Act

416. Monetary limits (companies winding up)
417. Money sum in s. 222
417A. Money sums (company moratorium)
418. Monetary limits (bankruptcy)

Insolvency practice

419. Regulations for purposes of Pt. XIII

Other order-making powers

420. Insolvent partnerships
421. Insolvent estates of deceased persons
421A. Insolvent estates: joint tenancies
422. Formerly authorised banks, etc.

Part XVI

Provisions Against Debt Avoidance (England and Wales Only)

423. Transactions defrauding creditors
424. Those who may apply for an order under s. 423
425. Provision which may be made by order under s. 423

Part XVII

Miscellaneous and General

426. Co-operation between courts exercising jurisdiction in relation to insolvency
426A. Disqualification from Parliament (England and Wales)
426B. Devolution
426C. Irrelevance of privilege
427. Parliamentary disqualification
428. Exemptions from Restrictive Trade Practices Act (repealed)
429. Disabilities on revocation of administration order against an individual
430. Provision introducing Schedule of punishments
431. Summary proceedings
432. Offences by bodies corporate
433. Admissibility in evidence of statements of affairs, etc.
434. Crown application

Part XVIII

Interpretation

435. Meaning of "associate"
436. Expressions used generally
436A. Proceedings under EC Regulation: Modified definition of property

Part XIX

Final Provisions

437. Transitional provisions and savings
438. Repeals
439. Amendment of enactments
440. Extent (Scotland)
441. Extent (Northern Ireland)
442. Extent (other territories)
443. Commencement
444. Citation

Schedules

1. Powers of administrator or administrative receiver
A1. Moratorium where directors propose voluntary arrangement
B1. Administration
2. Powers of a Scottish receiver (additional to those conferred on him by the instrument of charge)
2A. Exceptions to prohibition on appointment of administrative receiver: supplementary provisions
3. Orders in course of winding up pronounced in vacation (Scotland)
4. Powers of liquidator in a winding up
4A. Bankruptcy restrictions order and undertaking
5. Powers of trustee in bankruptcy
6. The categories of preferential debts
7. Insolvency Practitioners Tribunal
8. Provisions capable of inclusion in company insolvency rules
9. Provisions capable of inclusion in individual insolvency rules
10. Punishment of offences under this Act
11. Transitional provisions and savings
12. Enactments repealed
13. Consequential amendments of Companies Act 1985
14. Consequential amendments of other enactments

Insolvency Act 1986

(1986 Chapter 45)

An Act to consolidate the enactments relating to company insolvency and winding up (including the winding up of companies that are not insolvent, and of unregistered companies); enactments relating to the insolvency and bankruptcy of individuals; and other enactments bearing on those two subject matters, including the functions and qualification of insolvency practitioners, the public administration of insolvency, the penalisation and redress of malpractice and wrongdoing, and the avoidance of certain transactions at an undervalue.

[*25th July 1986*]

THE FIRST GROUP OF PARTS: COMPANY INSOLVENCY; COMPANIES WINDING UP

General comment on the First Group of Parts
The First Group of Parts deals with insolvency procedures in relation to companies (including the winding up of solvent companies), in contrast with the Second Group, which is concerned with the bankruptcy of individuals. "Company" is defined for this purpose by CA 1985, s. 735(1) and (3), incorporated into the present Act by IA 1986, s. 251. (For the text of s. 735(1), (3), see the note to s. 73, below.) Some Parts of the Act (and, in particular, Pt. IV, dealing with winding up) are extended so as to apply to bodies and associations other than "companies", including partnerships: see the general comment preceding s. 73, below. However, in the absence of any provision to this effect, the First Group of Parts apply only to companies within the statutory definition. Accordingly, where a society incorporated under the Industrial and Provident Societies Act 1965 is in receivership, the creditors who would be entitled to preferential payment in the case of a company have no priority: *Re Devon & Somerset Farmers Ltd* [1994] Ch. 57; [1993] B.C.C. 410. Exceptionally, the European Regulation on Insolvency Proceedings 2000 may confer jurisdiction under IA 1986 where the body concerned has its centre of main interests within the UK, even though it does not fall within the statutory definition: see the note to Art. 3 of the Regulation.

PART I

COMPANY VOLUNTARY ARRANGEMENTS

General comment on Pt. I
Part I of IA 1986, which replaces IA 1985, ss. 20–26, introduced an entirely new procedure into UK company law, the "Company Voluntary Arrangement" – a term which is commonly abbreviated to "CVA".

The original CVA regime as contained in Part I of the Insolvency Act 1986 has been the subject of major statutory elaboration through the mechanism of ss. 1, 2 of, and Schs. 1, 2 to, the Insolvency Act 2000. The effect of these changes has been to introduce a new optional CVA model with moratorium for small eligible companies. (For further guidance on eligibility see the Insolvency Act 1986 (Amendment) (No. 3) Regulations 2002 SI 2002/1990.) There are also amendments to the general CVA model.

The Cork Committee (*Report*, paras 400–403) considered it a weakness of the former company law that a company, unlike an individual, could not enter into a binding arrangement with its creditors for the composition of its indebtedness by some relatively simple procedure. Unless it could obtain the separate consent of every creditor, the only options previously available to a company were the formal statutory procedures of:

(1) a scheme of liquidation and reconstruction under CA 1985, s. 582 (formerly CA 1948, s. 287);

(2) a scheme of compromise or arrangement under CA 1985, ss. 425–427 (CA 1948, ss. 206–208); and

(3) the little-used "binding arrangement" under CA 1985, s. 601 (CA 1948, s. 306).

Each of these methods was too slow, cumbersome and costly to be at all useful in practice.

The present sections introduce a simpler scheme, more or less along the lines recommended by the Cork Committee. The CVA has proved to be of limited utility in practice, however, for two reasons. First, it cannot be made binding upon a secured or preferential creditor without his consent, and secondly, until the enactment of s. 1A there was no provision in the Act for obtaining a moratorium while the proposal for an arrangement is being drawn up and considered (contrast the "interim order" available in the case of an insolvent individual: see ss. 252–254). However, a moratorium could be achieved if a proposal for a voluntary arrangement is combined with an application to the court for the appointment of an administrator under Pt. II: this is, of course, a more elaborate and costly procedure.

In view of these considerations, it is not surprising that the CVA procedure has been relatively little used (especially when compared with the much larger number of individual voluntary arrangements). In the first few years after the 1986 Act, the average number was under 100 per year, and although the figure has now crept up somewhat, the overall picture has been disappointing. In the light of this experience the Government suggested modifications to the CVA procedure in order to improve its effectiveness (and appeal). In particular it favoured the introduction of an optional moratorium facility for CVAs involving small eligible companies. This reform was enacted by the Insolvency Act, 2000 s. 1 with detailed provision being made in the accompanying Schedule A1. Unfortunately, there was a delay in bringing this reform into effect; this delay was apparently caused by concerns in the City over the impact of the new CVA moratorium on certain specialised corporate financing schemes. The new model came into force only on January 1, 2003 – see the Insolvency Act 2000 (Commencement No. 3 and Transitional Provisions) Order 2002 (SI 2002/2711, c. 83).

Since December 1, 1994, a voluntary arrangement procedure modelled upon the CVA has been available for an insolvent partnership: see the Insolvent Partnerships Order 1994 (SI 1994/2421), art. 5 and Sch. 1. It is a prerequisite that the partnership be unable to pay its debts. As with a CVA, there is no provision for an interim order during which a stay of proceedings operates, although this can be achieved by applying at the same time for an administration order. Alternatively, if the partners are individuals, they may enter into individual voluntary arrangements, which will have much the same effect.

The CVA procedure has been extended to building societies by s. 90A of the Building Societies Act 1986 (inserted by Building Societies Act 1997, s. 39, effective December 1, 1997). A foreign company may be permitted to use a CVA by exploiting the facility of s. 426, IA 1986 – *Re Television Trade Rentals Ltd* [2002] EWHC 211 (Ch).

The initiative in setting up a CVA is taken by the directors or, if the company is being wound up or is subject to an administration order, by the liquidator or administrator as the case may be. A "proposal" is formulated for consideration by meetings of the company's members and creditors: if the proposal is accepted at the respective meetings, the scheme becomes operative and binding upon the company and all of its creditors – even those who did not support the proposal. Thereafter, it is administered by a "supervisor" who must be qualified to act as an insolvency practitioner in relation to the company. The arrangement is conducted throughout under the aegis of the court, but the court itself is not involved in a judicial capacity unless there is some difficulty or disagreement.

It is not a prerequisite for the application of this Part of the Act that the company should be "insolvent" or "unable to pay its debts" within the statutory definitions of those terms.

Because a scheme of voluntary arrangement does not, on its own, give the company concerned any immediate protection from its creditors (except where s. 1A applies), the procedure was commonly invoked in conjunction with an administration order made under IA 1986, s. 8ff. The purposes for which an administration order may be made specifically include "the approval of a voluntary arrangement under Part I" (s. 8(3)(b)). It is also possible to give additional flexibility to an administration order which has been sought primarily for other reasons, by extending the purposes of the order to include a voluntary arrangement. For example, in *Re St Ives Windings Ltd* (1987) 3 B.C.C. 634, an administrator had succeeded in obtaining an advantageous realisation of the company's assets under an order which specified that purpose, but was unable to implement proposals for the distribution of the proceeds among the creditors. However, this became possible when the court, on his application, granted a variation of the order by adding as a further purpose the approval of a voluntary arrangement; the proposed distribution could then be sanctioned by the creditors in the ordinary way.

It is the most practicable course, in any case where an administration and a voluntary scheme of arrangement are to be instituted in combination, for the administration order to be made first, and for the administrator himself to act as "nominee" and ultimately as the "supervisor" of the scheme. The administration order can be discharged as soon as the voluntary arrangement is approved.

It would probably be thought improper to present a petition for an administration order merely to gain a moratorium, with no intention of pursuing the application; in any case it would certainly be unwise to do so, since a petition cannot be withdrawn without the leave of the court.

A related reform effected by IA 1985 (see Sch. 10, Pt II) was the repeal of CA 1985, s. 615(2), a provision of ancient origin which stated that any general assignment by a company of its property for the benefit of its creditors was "void to all intents".

The provision which prohibits a company from giving financial assistance in the acquisition of its own shares (CA 1985, s. 151) does not apply to anything done under a voluntary arrangement: see CA 1985, s. 153(3)(g) (as amended).

For the corresponding provisions relating to voluntary arrangements for insolvent individuals, see ss. 252–263. There is a close parallel between the two sets of provisions, and so cases decided under the individual voluntary arrangement sections may well be relevant in CVA proceedings, and vice versa.

The Act contemplates that a system will be set up by subordinate legislation for the registration of voluntary arrangements in a register open to public inspection: see Sch. 8, para. 6. The rules make provision for registration with the registrar of companies: IR 1986, rr. 1.24(5), 1.26(2)(b), 1.29(3).

For the rules relating to CVAs, see IR 1986, Pt 1.

The proposal

1 Those who may propose an arrangement

1(1) [Directors] The directors of a company (other than one which is in administration or being wound up) may make a proposal under this Part to the company and to its creditors for a composition in satisfaction of its debts or a scheme of arrangement of its affairs (from here on referred to, in either case, as a "voluntary arrangement").

1(2) [Interpretation] A proposal under this part is one which provides for some person ("the nominee") to act in relation to the voluntary arrangement either as trustee or otherwise for the purpose of supervising its implementation; and the nominee must be a person who is qualified to act as an insolvency practitioner or authorised to act as nominee, in relation to the voluntary arrangement.

1(3) [Administrator, liquidator] Such a proposal may also be made–

(a) where the company is in administration, by the administrator, and

(b) where the company is being wound up, by the liquidator.

1(4) [Applicability of EC Regulation] In this Part a reference to a company includes a reference to a company in relation to which a proposal for a voluntary arrangement may be made by virtue of Article 3 of the EC Regulation.

GENERAL NOTE

In any case where the company is not subject to an administration order or being wound up, the initiative in proposing a voluntary arrangement is taken by the directors, and the more elaborate procedure laid down by s. 2 applies. An insolvency practitioner who is "qualified" to act in relation to the company must be brought in as "nominee" to report on the directors' proposals and to organise the meetings, etc. by which the scheme is to be implemented. (In practice, the directors will in most cases have consulted the proposed nominee in advance and invoked his help in drawing up the proposal). Where, however, there is an administrator or liquidator already in office, he will normally himself act as the nominee and may then proceed directly to summon meetings of the company and its creditors under s. 3.

Neither creditors nor members of a company have standing to propose a voluntary arrangement. Section 1(2) was modified by s. 2 and Sch. 2 of IA 2000 to recognise the fact that, under IA 2000, turnaround specialists may act as nominees or supervisors. The language of s. 1(1) and 1(3) was recast by s. 248 and Sch. 17 of EA 2002 to reflect the fact that it is no longer strictly accurate to refer to administration *orders*.

S. 1(1)

The directors have power to act only when the company is not in liquidation or subject to administration.

There is no statutory definition of "creditor" for the purposes of this Part of the Act. It would be normal to give the word its dictionary meaning, "one to whom a debt is owing" – a phrase which would exclude a prospective or contingent creditor and a person whose claim was for unliquidated damages (see R M Goode, *Principles of Corporate Insolvency Law* (2nd edn, 1997), pp. 47–48). This view is reinforced by the fact that the concepts of "debt" and "provable debt" are extended to include these wider categories of claim by IR 1986, rr. 13.12, 12.3; but this provision is confined to the winding up of companies. It is also noteworthy that although contingent and prospective creditors are expressly given the same rights as creditors elsewhere in the Act (see, *e.g.* ss. 9, 124 (standing to present petition for administration or winding-up order)), there is no similar provision here in Pt. I. It would therefore be reasonable to assume that the term "creditor" does not have the wider meaning in this section. However, r. 1.17(3) indicates the contrary by referring (in the context of voluntary arrangements) to "a debt for an unliquidated amount" and a "debt whose value is not ascertained". Fortunately, any doubts that there might have been on this question have now been resolved. In *Doorbar v Alltime Securities Ltd* [1996] 1 W.L.R. 456; [1995] B.C.C. 1,149 the Court of Appeal (affirming Knox J., [1994] B.C.C. 994) held that rent under a lease becoming due in the future was capable of being included in an individual voluntary arrangement under s. 258 of the Act, and this ruling has since been applied in the context of a CVA in *Re Cancol Ltd* [1996] 1 All E.R. 37; [1995] B.C.C. 1,133 and *Re Sweatfield Ltd* [1997] B.C.C. 744; and in *Beverley Group plc v McClue* [1995] B.C.C. 751 a person with a claim for an unliquidated amount was held entitled to vote as a creditor. Of course, it is possible that the terms of a scheme of voluntary arrangement should be so drawn up as to exclude future or contingent creditors from its operation. This was the case in *Burford Midland Properties Ltd v Marley Extrusions Ltd* [1994] B.C.C. 604 (a case which contains a useful discussion of the terms "future", "contingent" and "prospective" liabilities).

In *Re FMS Financial Management Services Ltd* (1989) 5 B.C.C. 191, former clients of the company who appeared to have good claims against it for damages for misrepresentation were not treated as creditors for the purposes of a CVA; but an order was made by the court, after the scheme had been approved, directing that they should be admitted to prove on the same terms as the company's creditors.

The terms "composition" and "scheme of arrangement" are not synonymous. The latter involves something less than the release or discharge of a creditor's debts – *e.g.* a moratorium. Thus, in *IRC v Adam & Partners Ltd* [2000] B.P.I.R. 986 a proposed moratorium which offered nothing to creditors was not sufficient to constitute a "composition" but could amount to a "scheme of arrangement". See also the discussion in *March Estates plc v Gunmark Ltd* [1996] 2 B.C.L.C. 1.

S. 1(2)

The Act obviously contemplates that in most cases the "nominee" himself will in due course administer the scheme (*e.g.* by acting as a trustee for the benefit of the company's creditors), although it is possible in certain circumstances for someone other than the original nominee to be appointed instead (see ss. 2(4), 4(2)). When it is finally settled who it is that is to have charge of the scheme, the Act (by s. 7(2)) designates him "the supervisor". This tends to obscure the fact that in the great majority of situations "the supervisor" will be the same person as "the nominee" and, where the company is the subject of an administration order or is being wound up, also the same person as the administrator or liquidator. By whatever means he is chosen, however, the "supervisor" must be a person who is qualified to act as an insolvency practitioner in relation to the company; and in this way the legislation ensures that no voluntary scheme can be implemented without independent professional approval and supervision.

The criteria by which a person is deemed to be "qualified" to act as an insolvency practitioner "in relation to" a particular company are laid down in ss. 388–398 and 419, below.

The section provides for the nominee or supervisor to act "as trustee or otherwise". In *Re Leisure Study Group Ltd* [1994] 2 B.C.L.C. 65, Harman J. held that funds in the hands of a supervisor were held on trust for the company's unsecured creditors, and had been put out of reach of the security conferred by a floating charge; see the note on s. 7(4).

Nothing in this Part of the Act gives the supervisor, as such, power to perform any act in the name of the company or makes him an officer of the company: whatever authority he has must come from the terms of the voluntary arrangement itself, or from the fact that he is also the company's administrator or liquidator. It has been assumed by the draftsman that a decision of the company in general meeting under s. 4(1) will be competent, as a matter of company law, to give wide powers of management to a supervisor regardless of the terms of the company's articles. We must probably infer from the general tenor of the Act that the terms of a voluntary arrangement are capable of overriding the articles if necessary. The position would have been less uncertain if the supervisor had been given certain statutory powers and a more clearly defined authority. On the question of authority, compare IR 1986, r. 1.26(1).

The nominee (and, later, the supervisor) is referred to throughout in the singular. There is nothing to prevent the appointment of joint nominees or supervisors, however: see the note to s. 7(6) below.

S. 1(3)

In the two situations referred to in this subsection, the proposal not only may but (by virtue of the bracketed words in s. 1(1)) must be made by the administrator or liquidator. In this case, the administrator or liquidator may appoint himself to be the nominee and proceed immediately to summon meetings under s. 3. If for any reason he appoints someone else, the more elaborate procedure under s. 2 must be followed.

For the rules which apply when the application is made under this subsection, see IR 1986, rr. 1.10ff.

S. 1(4)
This was inserted by Insolvency Act 1986 (Amendment) (No. 2) Regulations 2002 (SI 2002/1240) reg. 4 with effect from May 31, 2002. See pp. 602ff.

For an early application of s. 1(4) see *Re The Salvage Association* [2003] EWHC 1028 Ch., [2003] B.C.C. 504.

1A   Moratorium

1A(1)   [Directors] [Where the directors of an eligible company intend to make a proposal for a voluntary arrangement, they may take steps to obtain a moratorium for the company.]

1A(2)   [Applicability of Sch. A1] The provisions of Schedule A1 to this Act have effect with respect to—

(a)   companies eligible for a moratorium under this section,

(b)   the procedure for obtaining such a moratorium,

(c)   the effects of such a moratorium, and

(d)   the procedure applicable (in place of sections 2 to 6 and 7) in relation to the approval and implementation of a voluntary arrangement where such a moratorium is or has been in force.

GENERAL NOTE

This introduces the new Sch. A1 which offers a moratorium facility for the CVA in circumstances where the company is classed as "small" and "eligible". The criteria governing eligibility were added to by Insolvency (Amendment) Regulations 2002 (SI 2002/1990 – inserting additional paras 4A–4K into Sch. A1. See further the discussion under Sch. A1. Note in particular that a company cannot be regarded as eligible if it has incurred a liability of £10 million or more under an agreement which is part of a capital market arrangement (Sch. A1, para. 4C). The new CVA model came into operation on January 1, 2003 – see Insolvency Act 2000 (Commencement No. 3) and Transitional Provisions) Order 2002 (SI 2002/2711).

Full discussion of this CVA variant is to be found at Sch. A1. Early indications suggest that it is not being used extensively and, with the advent of the out of court administration entry model, that pattern is likely to persist.

2   Procedure where nominee is not the liquidator or administrator

2(1)   [Application] This section applies where the nominee under section 1 is not the liquidator or administrator of the company and the directors do not propose to take steps to obtain a moratorium under s. 1A for the company.

2(2)   [Report to court] The nominee shall, within 28 days (or such longer period as the court may allow) after he is given notice of the proposal for a voluntary arrangement, submit a report to the court stating–

(a)   whether, in his opinion, the proposed voluntary arrangement has a reasonable prospect of being approved and implemented,

(aa) whether, in his opinion, meetings of the company and of its creditors should be summoned to consider the proposal, and

(b)   if in his opinion such meetings should be summoned, the date on which, and time and place at which, he proposes the meetings should be held.

2(3)   [Information to nominee] For the purposes of enabling the nominee to prepare his report, the person intending to make the proposal shall submit to the nominee–

(a)   a document setting out the terms of the proposed voluntary arrangement, and

(b)   a statement of the company's affairs containing–

   (i)   such particulars of its creditors and of its debts and other liabilities and of its assets as may be prescribed, and
   (ii) such other information as may be prescribed.

Section 2 *Insolvency Act 1986*

2(4) [Replacement of nominee by court] The court may–

(a) on an application made by the person intending to make the proposal, in a case where the nominee has failed to submit the report required by this section or has died, or

(b) on an application made by that person or the nominee, in a case where it is impracticable or inappropriate for the nominee to continue to act as such,

direct that the nominee be replaced as such by another person qualified to act as an insolvency practitioner, or authorised to act as nominee, in relation to the voluntary arrangement.

GENERAL NOTE

The wording of s. 2(1) and (2) was modified by IA 2000 s. 2 and Sch. 2. Section 2(4) was also substituted by those provisions.

S. 2(1)
Section 2 will necessarily apply where the proposal is made by the directors under s. 1(1); and it will also apply when an administrator or liquidator designates someone other than himself as nominee.

S. 2(2)
No step towards implementing the proposal can be taken under this section until a report has first been submitted by the nominee to the court. The court's role is, however, primarily an administrative one, and it will not be involved judicially except when there is some dispute or difficulty. The procedure which the section envisages is as follows:

(1) The directors decide to propose an arrangement, and themselves find an insolvency practitioner who is qualified to act as nominee and who is willing, at least in principle, to do so (see IR 1986, r. 1.3(2)(p)). As has been mentioned above, it is likely in most cases that the directors will seek the intended nominee's professional assistance in preparing the proposal in advance. The routine contemplated by the Act will then be largely a formality.

(2) The directors give notice of the proposal for a voluntary arrangement to the nominee, and submit to him a document setting out the terms of the proposed arrangement and a statement of the company's affairs (s. 2(3)(a), (b)). (It is not clear from the section itself whether the "notice" referred to in s. 2(2) is constituted by the formal submission of the document and statement of affairs specified in s. 2(3) or is some separate and earlier notification. The former interpretation is plainly the one intended, since the 28-day period referred to in s. 2(2) only starts to run from the receipt of the document: see IR 1986, r. 1.4(3).)

(3) The nominee has 28 days (or longer, if the court allows) to prepare and submit a report to the court. This will ensure that a scheme always has the benefit of a preliminary opinion from a professional insolvency practitioner.

(4) If the nominee forms the view that the proposed scheme should go ahead, he reports to the court his opinion that meetings of the company and its creditors should be summoned, and he must himself fix their date, time and place. (On the formalities for summoning meetings, see the comment to s. 3(1) and (2), below.)

(5) Under s. 3(1), it will normally then be the nominee's role to summon the meetings.

(6) If the nominee considers that the proposed scheme should not be taken further, s. 2(2) appears to suggest that he should submit a negative report to the court, and this is confirmed by IR 1986, r. 1.7(2). However, nothing is made to depend on the filing of such a report, and the company is not barred from seeking a second opinion from another nominee.

(7) Where the initiative is not taken by the directors but by an administrator or liquidator who elects not to nominate himself, the responsibility for selecting the intended nominee and preparing the documentation specified in s. 2(3) falls upon that person and not on the directors.

Necessarily, the nominee is heavily reliant on the information provided by the debtor company and there is therefore a consequential need for complete candour on the part of the latter. Where the nominee has doubts about the accuracy and

S. 2(3)

This subsection gives details of the two documents on which the nominee is to base his report to the court.

It is made clear by the rules (IR 1986, r. 1.4(3)) (as noted above (s. 2(2)) that a nominee is not to be considered as having been "given notice" of a proposal until he has received the document referred to in para. (a) of this subsection. The "statement of the company's affairs" may be delivered to him up to seven days later, or after a longer period if the nominee agrees: IR 1986, r. 1.5(1).

The "statement of the company's affairs" referred to is similar to the statement which must be submitted to an administrator (s. 22), an administrative receiver (ss. 47, 66) and a liquidator (ss. 99, 131). On this topic, see the note to s. 131.

S. 2(4)

If, after the expiration of the 28 days or longer period provided for by s. 2(2), the nominee has not submitted a report either in favour of or against proceeding with the proposal, this subsection allows the directors (or the administrator or liquidator, where appropriate) to invoke the court's help and have an alternative nominee appointed. However, there appears to be no reason why an intended proposal should not be aborted without the court's involvement, for at this stage no creditor will have been affected by the scheme or even have been made aware of it, and the court itself will not yet be in the picture. This course should certainly be permissible if the first intended nominee consents; if he does not, however, a professional code of conduct might possibly inhibit a colleague from replacing him against his wishes, and in that case the court's aid would be necessary.

For details of the procedure prescribed for the purpose of this section, see IR 1986, rr. 1.2–1.9.

3 Summoning of meetings

3(1) [Meetings in accordance with report] Where the nominee under section 1 is not the liquidator or administrator, and it has been reported to the court that such meetings as are mentioned in section 2(2) should be summoned, the person making the report shall (unless the court otherwise directs) summon those meetings for the time, date and place proposed in the report.

3(2) [Where nominee liquidator or administrator] Where the nominee is the liquidator or administrator, he shall summon meetings of the company and of its creditors to consider the proposal for such a time, date and place as he thinks fit.

3(3) [Persons summoned] The persons to be summoned to a creditors' meeting under this section are every creditor of the company of whose claim and address the person summoning the meeting is aware.

GENERAL NOTE

A voluntary arrangement comes into effect under s. 5 when the proposal has been approved by both a meeting of the company and a meeting of its creditors (unless s. 4A(2)b applies).

Both s. 2(2)(b) and s. 3(2) appear to leave it to the nominee's discretion to fix such matters as the time and date of the meetings, the length of notice which is to be given and the order in which the two meetings are to be held. However such discretion as is given to the nominee by ss. 2(2)(b) and 3(2) is exercisable only within the constraints imposed by the rules: see IR 1986, rr. 1.9, 1.13, 1.21.

S. 3(1)

Where the nominee is not the liquidator or administrator, no step can be taken to summon meetings until he has made a favourable report to the court under s. 2(2). Once he has done so, it becomes his duty to summon the meetings (without any court order or other formality) in accordance with his own proposals.

No guidance is given by the section as to the basis on which the court might "otherwise direct", or as to who (apart from the nominee himself) might have standing to apply for such a direction.

S. 3(2)

Where the nominee is the liquidator or administrator, the procedure outlined in s. 2 is bypassed. He himself proceeds straight to the summoning of the meetings, and at this stage nothing is notified or reported to the court. There appears to be no power under this subsection for the court to "direct otherwise".

Section 4 *Insolvency Act 1986*

A nominee who is himself the liquidator or administrator will have received, or be entitled to receive, a "statement of affairs" under ss. 22, 99 or 131. This document, or a summary of it, must be sent, with a list of the company's creditors and the amounts of their debts, with the notices summoning the meetings: see IR 1986, r. 1.11(2).

For the appropriate rules, see IR 1986, rr. 1.10, 1.11.

S. 3(3)

A nominee who has prepared a report under s. 2(2) will have been given particulars of the company's creditors under s. 2(3)(b). A liquidator or administrator who has appointed himself as nominee will receive this information with the "statement of affairs".

Consideration and implementation of proposal

4 Decisions of meetings

4(1) [Decision] The meetings summoned under section 3 shall decide whether to approve the proposed voluntary arrangement (with or without modifications).

4(2) [Modifications] The modifications may include one conferring the functions proposed to be conferred on the nominee on another person qualified to act as an insolvency practitioner or authorised to act as nominee, in relation to the voluntary arrangement.

But they shall not include any modification by virtue of which the proposal ceases to be a proposal such as is mentioned in section 1.

4(3) [Limitation on approval] A meeting so summoned shall not approve any proposal or modification which affects the right of a secured creditor of the company to enforce his security, except with the concurrence of the creditor concerned.

4(4) [Further limitation] Subject as follows, a meeting so summoned shall not approve any proposal or modification under which–

(a) any preferential debt of the company is to be paid otherwise than in priority to such of its debts as are not preferential debts, or

(b) a preferential creditor of the company is to be paid an amount in respect of a preferential debt that bears to that debt a smaller proportion than is borne to another preferential debt by the amount that is to be paid in respect of that other debt.

However, the meeting may approve such a proposal or modification with the concurrence of the preferential creditor concerned.

4(5) [Meeting in accordance with rules] Subject as above, each of the meetings shall be conducted in accordance with the rules.

4(6) [Report to court, notice] After the conclusion of either meeting in accordance with the rules, the chairman of the meeting shall report the result of the meeting to the court, and, immediately after reporting to the court, shall give notice of the result of the meeting to such persons as may be prescribed.

4(7) [Interpretation] References in this section to preferential debts and preferential creditors are to be read in accordance with section 386 in Part XII of this Act.

GENERAL NOTE

The terms of the scheme, when approved by the meetings, bind every member and creditor (see s. 5(2)).

No provision appears to be made for any subsequent modification of the scheme unless that modification is put forward by the person who made the original proposal (see s. 6(4)). The only opportunity, therefore, for any of the company's members or creditors to seek to have the proposal modified will be at the meetings themselves.

S. 4(1)

The scheme can only go ahead in a modified form if both of the meetings approve the same modifications (but see the qualification in s. 4A).

S. 4(2)
The modifications may include the substitution of a different nominee to administer the scheme; but no modification may take the proceedings outside the scope of s. 1 altogether (*i.e.* amount to a wholly different course of action, such as putting the company into liquidation). Note that s. 4(2) was modified by IA 2000, s. 2 and Sch. 2 to reflect the fact that a wider group of professionals can now act as nominees/supervisors.

S. 4(3)
No voluntary arrangement can affect the rights of a secured creditor without his consent. In *March Estates plc v Gunmark Ltd* [1996] 2 B.C.L.C. 1 Lightman J. held that a landlord's right of forfeiture was to be treated as a security for this purpose, but in the latter case of *Razzaq v Pala* [1998] B.C.C. 66 at p. 71 the same judge said that this ruling had been given without full argument and that, on reconsideration, he should have held otherwise.

S. 4(4)
The rights of preferential creditors (as defined in s. 4(7)) are similarly protected, as regards both their priority *vis-à-vis* all other debts and their right to rank equally with each other. There is no provision which obliges the preferential creditors to accept a decision made by a majority of them, even if it is passed at a separate class meeting (contrast CA 1985, s. 425).

Apart from this and the preceding subsection, there is nothing in the Act which restricts the arrangements which a proposal may make, or requires creditors to be given equal treatment. It is thus permissible, *e.g.* for small creditors to be given more favourable treatment than larger ones.

S. 4(5)
Although this subsection refers in terms only to the conduct of the meetings (and not, *e.g.* to their summoning) it is plain that the rules apply to all aspects of such meetings: see the note to s. 3 above.

For the appropriate rules, see IR 1986, r. 1.13ff.

S. 4(6)
The chairman of the meetings will be appointed or selected in accordance with the rules (see IR 1986, r. 1.14). The rules contemplate that the same person will be chairman of both meetings. It is perhaps odd that it is the chairman, rather than the nominee, who is required to report to the court, but the report must be filed in court very quickly (within four days: see IR 1986, r. 124(3)), and difficulties could arise, if, *e.g.* the nominee was abroad. The subsection implies that separate reports of the result of each meeting are to be prepared, but the rules are less clear: see IR 1986, r. 1.24 and Form 1.1. IR 1986, r. 1.24(5) provides that if the voluntary arrangement is approved by the meetings, the supervisor must send a copy of the chairman's report to the registrar of companies.

The making of the chairman's report to the court and the giving of the prescribed notices have no direct legal consequences (although time is made to run for various purposes, *e.g.* the stay of a winding-up order, from the date that the report is made to the court). The voluntary arrangement itself takes effect as a reuslt of the meetings alone, and the court plays no active part in the proceedings at any stage.

S. 4(7)
"Preferential debts" and "preferential creditors" are defined for the purpose of this Part of the Act by s. 386 and Sch. 6, below. The list of preferential creditors is settled by reference to a "relevant date", which determines both the existence and the amount of a preferential debt. To ascertain the "relevant date" for the purpose of the present section, see s. 387(3A).

The section makes no reference to the possibility that a voluntary arrangement and a receivership might co-exist. In such a case, there would also be a list of preferential creditors who were entitled to rank in priority to the charge-holder in the receivership. There would then be two lists of preferential debts defined by reference to different "relevant dates"; but those relating to the receivership would have no significance for the purposes of this Part of the Act.

4A Approval of arrangement

4A(1) [Application] This section applies to a decision, under section 4, with respect to the approval of a proposed voluntary arrangement.

4A(2) [Decision to be in accordance with rules] The decision has effect if, in accordance with the rules–

(a) it has been taken by both meetings summoned under section 3, or

(b) (subject to any order made under subsection (4)) it has been taken by the creditors' meeting summoned under that section.

Section 5   *Insolvency Act 1986*

4A(3) **[Application to court]** If the decision taken by the creditors' meeting differs from that taken by the company meeting, a member of the company may apply to the court.

4A(4) **[Application under s. 4A(3)]** An application under subsection (3) shall not be made after the end of the period of 28 days beginning with–

(a) the day on which the decision was taken by the creditors' meeting, or

(b) where the decision of the company meeting was taken on a later day, that day.

4A(5) **[Regulated companies]** Where a member of a regulated company, within the meaning given by paragraph 44 of Schedule A1, applies to the court under subsection (3), the Financial Services Authority is entitled to be heard on the application.

4A(6) **[Court powers]** On an application under subsection (3), the court may–

(a) order the decision of the company meeting to have effect instead of the decision of the creditors' meeting, or

(b) make such other order as it thinks fit.

GENERAL NOTE

This new section was introduced by s. 2 of, and Sch. 2 to, the Insolvency Act 2000 with effect from January 1, 2003. It seeks to provide more detailed guidance on the effect of a CVA being approved.

S. 4A(1)
This identifies the applicability of s. 4A.

S. 4A(2), (3), (4), (6)
The main point to grasp from these subsections is that, if there is a mismatch between the decisions taken at the creditors' and members' meetings, the former decision will prevail. In such circumstances a member can apply to the court within 28 days to challenge this effect. On such an application the court enjoys wide powers under subs. (6).

S. 4A(5)
This provision is not of general application.

5 Effect of approval

5(1) **[Operation]** (1) This section applies where a decision approving a voluntary arrangement has effect under section 4A.

5(2) **[Effect of composition or scheme]** The voluntary arrangement–

(a) takes effect as if made by the company at the creditors' meeting, and

(b) binds every person who in accordance with the rules–

  (i) was entitled to vote at that meeting (whether or not he was present or represented at it), or
  (ii) would have been so entitled if he had had notice of it,

as if he were a party to the voluntary arrangement.

5(2A) **[Amounts payable upon cessation]** If–

(a) when the arrangement ceases to have effect any amount payable under the arrangement to a person bound by virtue of subsection (2)(b)(ii) has not been paid, and

(b) the arrangement did not come to an end prematurely,

the company shall at that time become liable to pay to that person the amount payable under the arrangement.

5(3) **[Court powers]** Subject as follows, if the company is being wound up or is in administration, the court may do one or both of the following, namely–

- (a) by order stay or sist all proceedings in the winding up or provide for the appointment of the administrator to cease to have effect;

- (b) give such directions with respect to the conduct of the winding up or the administration as it thinks appropriate for facilitating the implementation of the voluntary arrangement.

5(4) **[Limit on s. 5(3)(a)]** The court shall not make an order under subsection (3)(a)–

- (a) at any time before the end of the period of 28 days beginning with the first day on which each of the reports required by section 4(6) has been made to the court, or

- (b) at any time when an application under the next section or an appeal in respect of such an application is pending, or at any time in the period within which such an appeal may be brought.

GENERAL NOTE

The former regime under which both meetings had to approve the proposal has been mitigated by s. 4A(2). Section 5(2), however, quite clearly makes the time of the creditors' meeting the critical time for the scheme to take effect, and not that of the later of the two meetings. The rules in fact require both meetings to be held on the same day and in the same place, with the creditors' meeting fixed for an earlier time: see IR 1986, rr. 1.13(3), 1.21(4). Alternatively, they may be held together (r. 1.21(1)).

It appears that the scheme takes effect at once and continues to be effective even though a challenge is mounted under s. 6; but this is subject to any directions which may be given by the court under s. 6(6).

S. 5(2)

The word "approved" was deleted by Sch. 5 of IA 2000 by authority of s. 15(1).

For the rules relating to the right to vote and the requisite majorities at the meeting of creditors and members, see IR 1986, rr. 1.17–1.20.

This subsection appears to make the scheme binding on all the company's creditors, including absentees and dissentients.

"Notice" in the context of s. 5(2)(b) was given a broad interpretation in *Beverley Group plc v McClue* [1995] B.C.C. 751: a formal notice which had been sent had not been received by the creditor, but he had learned of the creditors' meeting indirectly and had also attended the members' meeting.

A voluntary arrangement does not bind a person who was not entitled to vote at the creditors' meeting, and such a person cannot take advantage of the arrangement: *R A Securities Ltd v Mercantile Credit Co. Ltd* [1994] B.C.C. 598. However where a creditor who was entitled to vote assigns the benefit of his contract with the company, the assignee takes that benefit as modified by the arrangement; and where land is leased to the debtor company and the reversion is assigned, the assignee is bound by the arrangement as a matter of property law: *Burford Midland Properties Ltd v Marley Extrusions Ltd* [1994] B.C.C. 604. Claims not brought within the arrangement can still be pursued by a participating creditor – *Alman v Approach Housing Ltd* [2001] B.P.I.R. 203.

On the position of creditors whose claims are future or contingent or for an unliquidated amount, see the note to IR 1986, r. 1.17(3).

The release of the debtor company from liability under a voluntary arrangement does not also release a solvent co-debtor who is not a party to the arrangement: *March Estates plc v Gunmark Ltd* [1996] 2 B.C.L.C. 1; *Johnson v Davies* [1998] 2 B.C.L.C. 252, although in the latter case the Court of Appeal stated that in principle there is no reason why a term in an agreement could not have the effect of releasing a co-debtor depending on the construction of the agreement, the surrounding circumstances and any terms that could be implied.

Note that the approval of a scheme brings into operation the provisions of s. 233, which prevent the suppliers of gas, electricity, etc. from imposing certain terms as to payment as a condition of making a supply available: see s. 233(1)(c).

S. 5(2)(b)

This was substituted by s. 2 and Sch. 2 of IA 2000. It binds in unknown creditors.

S. 5(2A)

This was inserted by s. 2 and Sch. 2 of IA 2000.

Section 6   *Insolvency Act 1986*

S. 5(3), (4)
The word "approved" was removed from s. 5(3)(b) by Sch. 5 of IA 2000 on the authority of s. 15(1). The phraseology used here was modified by s. 248 and Sch. 17 of EA 2002 to cater for the change in nature of the administration regime.

If the company is being wound up or is in administration, the court is empowered to stay (or in Scotland, sist) the winding-up order or to terminate the administration, or to give directions short of taking either of these steps which will facilitate the implementation of the scheme; but it may not make an order under s. 5(3)(a) until 28 days after the later of the chairman's reports has been made to the court under s. 4(6), nor while a hearing or an appeal from a ruling under s. 6 is pending.

6   Challenge of decisions

6(1)   [Application to court] Subject to this section, an application to the court may be made, by any of the persons specified below, on one or both of the following grounds, namely–

(a)   that a voluntary arrangement which has effect under section 4A unfairly prejudices the interests of a creditor, member or contributory of the company;

(b)   that there has been some material irregularity at or in relation to either of the meetings.

6(2)   [Applicants] The persons who may apply under this section are–

(a)   a person entitled, in accordance with the rules, to vote at either of the meetings;

(aa)   a person who would have been entitled, in accordance with the rules, to vote at the creditors' meeting if he had had notice of it.

(b)   the nominee or any person who has replaced him under section 2(4) or 4(2); and

(c)   if the company is being wound up or is in administration, the liquidator or administrator.

6(3)   [Time for application] An application under this section shall not be made–

(a)   after the end of the period of 28 days beginning with the first day on which each of the reports required by section 4(6) has been made to the court; or

(b)   in the case of a person who was not given notice of the creditors' meeting, after the end of the period of 28 days beginning with the day on which he became aware that the meeting had taken place,

but (subject to that) an application made by a person within subsection (2)(aa) on the ground that the voluntary arrangement prejudices his interests may be made after the arrangement has ceased to have effect, unless it came to an end prematurely.

6(4)   [Powers of court] Where on such an application the court is satisfied as to either of the grounds mentioned in subsection (1), it may do one or both of the following, namely–

(a)   revoke or suspend any decision approving the voluntary arrangement which has effect under section 4A or, in a case falling within subsection (1)(b), any decision taken by the meeting in question which has effect under that section;

(b)   give a direction to any person for the summoning of further meetings to consider any revised proposal the person who made the original proposal may make or, in a case falling within subsection (1)(b), a further company or (as the case may be) creditors' meeting to reconsider the original proposal.

6(5)   [Revocation or suspension of approval] Where at any time after giving a direction under subsection (4)(b) for the summoning of meetings to consider a revised proposal the court is satisfied that the person who made the original proposal does not intend to submit a revised proposal, the court shall revoke the direction and revoke or suspend any decision approving the voluntary arrangement which has effect under section 4A.

6(6) [Supplemental directions] In a case where the court, on an application under this section with respect to any meeting–

(a) gives a direction under subsection (4)(b), or

(b) revokes or suspends an approval under subsection (4)(a) or (5),

the court may give such supplemental directions as it thinks fit and, in particular, directions with respect to things done under the voluntary arrangement since it took effect.

6(7) [Effect of irregularity] Except in pursuance of the preceding provisions of this section, a decision taken at a meeting summoned under section 3 is not invalidated by any irregularity at or in relation to the meeting.

GENERAL NOTE

Section 6 lays down a procedure whereby the various interested persons who are listed in s. 6(2) may apply to the court to challenge the fairness or regularity of a voluntary arrangement which has been approved under the preceding sections and also, it would seem (under s. 6(1)(b)), the regularity of a creditors' or members' meeting in the case where such approval was not forthcoming. If a person does not come within any of the categories of applicants listed in s. 6(2) (*e.g.* because he or she was not "a person entitled to vote"), there may be available the alternative possibility of an appeal under IR 1986, r. 1.17A(3) see *Re Cranley Mansions Ltd, Saigol v Goldstein* [1994] 1 W.L.R. 1610; [1994] B.C.C. 576. By implication, and in part by the express words of s. 6(3) and (7), a scheme of voluntary arrangement, once approved, is probably not open to challenge by any other procedure or on any other grounds than are set out here.

The section is obviously modelled on CA 1985, s. 459, a provision which allows the court to grant a remedy to a member of a company who establishes that the company's affairs are being or have been conducted in a manner which is unfairly prejudicial to the interests of some or all of the members or that some act or omission of the company is or would be so prejudicial. Similar language is used also in IA 1986, s. 27. Decisions under these related provisions may be helpful in the interpretation of s. 6.

Section 6 is concerned only with the events leading up to the implementation of an arrangement and not with complaints about the conduct of the scheme of voluntary arrangement by the supervisor: this is dealt with by a different procedure under s. 7(3).

For the procedure on the making of an order under s. 6, see IR 1986, r. 1.25.

Note that it is an offence for an officer or former officer of a company to make a false representation or commit any other fraud for the purpose of obtaining the approval of the members or creditors to a proposal: IA 1986, s. 6A. An officer would also, in principle, be civilly liable to the company or any other person who could prove damage resulting from such a fraud.

The text of s. 6 was substantially amended by s. 2 of, and Sch. 2 to, IA 2000 to cater for changes brought in by that legislation. Minor linguistic changes were made to s. 6(2)(c) by s. 248 of, and Sch. 17 to, EA 2002 to acknowledge the fact that it is no longer accurate to speak of administration *orders*.

For an unsuccessful attempt to invoke s. 6 see *Swindon Town Properties v Swindon Town FC* [2003] B.P.I.R. 253.

S. 6(1)

Although the word "may" appears to be permissive, it would probably be construed by a court in the sense "may and may only be" so as to make this the only procedure for challenging a scheme once it has been approved.

It may not be unfairly prejudicial to make a differentiation in the treatment of members of the same class (*Re Cancol Ltd* [1996] 1 All E.R. 37; [1995] B.C.C. 1,133). On the question of "material irregularity" (a phrase which is used also in IR 1986, r. 1.17(7)), see the same case and also *Re Cranley Mansions Ltd, Saigol v Goldstein* [1994] 1 W.L.R. 1610; [1994] B.C.C. 576 and *Re Sweatfield Ltd* [1997] B.C.C. 744.

S. 6(2)

For the meaning of the phrase "a person entitled, in accordance with the rules, to vote" see the notes to s. 5(2) and IR 1986, r. 1.17. The FSA can apply or be heard on an application under s. 6 – Financial Services and Markets Act 2000, s. 356 as amended by s. 15(2) of the Insolvency Act 2000.

S. 6(3)

The time limit here specified is the same as that stipulated in s. 5(4). On the calculation of this time, see the note to that subsection and *Re Bournemouth and Boscombe AFC Co. Ltd* [1998] B.P.I.R. 183 which confirms that this 28-day limit cannot be extended.

S. 6(4)

The court may revoke or suspend the approvals given by the meetings, or one of the meetings, with or without giving directions as to the summoning of further meetings. If it decides to revoke but gives no such directions, it is of course always open to any of the persons mentioned in s. 1(1) or (3) to put forward a fresh scheme. However, there is probably no power to reopen the original proposal (with or without modifications) otherwise than by direction of the court under s. 6(4)(b).

Under s. 6(4)(b), the court may direct "any person" (not necessarily the nominee) to summon the further meetings. However, only the person who made the original proposal may draw up a revised one: this will be the liquidator or administrator of the company if s. 1(3) applies, and the directors if it does not. (If this person declines to co-operate, s. 6(5) applies and the arrangement falls through.)

The court seems to have no power to make any decision other than those set out in this subsection: it cannot, *e.g.* approve a proposal subject to modifications of its own devising, or even remit a proposal with such modifications to the meetings for reconsideration. (See, however, the note to s. 7(4), below.)

S. 6(5)

If it appears that the directors, the liquidator or the administrator, as the case may be (see s. 6(4)), do not intend to submit a revised scheme, the matter can proceed no further.

S. 6(6)

An arrangement is effective as soon as the two meetings have given their approval (s. 5). It is not suspended while an application under s. 6 is pending. This subsection empowers the court, in the event of a successful challenge, to give supplemental directions to cover acts done under an arrangement before the court gave its ruling.

S. 6(7)

An approval given at a meeting is not open to challenge as irregular otherwise than by proceeding under s. 6 itself. Once the 28 days laid down by s. 6(3) have elapsed, therefore, the approval is irrebuttably deemed valid for all purposes.

6A False representations, etc.

6A(1) **[Offence]** If, for the purpose of obtaining the approval of the members or creditors of a company to a proposal for a voluntary arrangement, a person who is an officer of the company–

(a) makes any false representation, or

(b) fraudulently does, or omits to do, anything,

he commits an offence.

6A(2) **[Application of s. 6A(1)]** Subsection (1) applies even if the proposal is not approved.

6A(3) **["Officer"]** For purposes of this section "officer" includes a shadow director.

6A(4) **[Penalties]** A person guilty of an offence under this section is liable to imprisonment or a fine, or both.

GENERAL NOTE

This addition was introduced via s. 2 of, and Sch. 2 to, the IA 2000 with effect from January 1, 2003. It seeks to prevent abuse of the CVA mechanism by instilling a degree of integrity reinforced by the criminal law.

S. 6A(1)

The bare bones of the offence of seeking to obtain the approval of a CVA by false misrepresentations are outlined.

S. 6A(2)

It is no defence that the CVA was voted down by creditors.

S. 6A(3)

The offence applies to officers and shadow directors – see the note to s. 206(3).

S. 6A(4)

This specifies the sanction, though the details are to be found in Sch. 10.

7 Implementation of proposal

7(1) [Application] This section applies where a voluntary arrangement has effect under section 4A.

7(2) [Supervisor of composition or scheme] The person who is for the time being carrying out in relation to the voluntary arrangement the functions conferred–

(a) on the nominee by virtue of the approval given at one or both of the meetings summoned under section 3, or

(b) by virtue of section 2(4) or 4(2) on a person other than the nominee,

shall be known as the supervisor of the voluntary arrangement.

7(3) [Application to court] If any of the company's creditors or any other person is dissatisfied by any act, omission or decision of the supervisor, he may apply to the court; and on the application the court may–

(a) confirm, reverse or modify any act or decision of the supervisor,

(b) give him directions, or

(c) make such other order as it thinks fit.

7(4) [Application for directions by supervisor] The supervisor–

(a) may apply to the court for directions in relation to any particular matter arising under the voluntary arrangement, and

(b) is included among the persons who may apply to the court for the winding up of the company or for an administration order to be made in relation to it.

7(5) [Court appointment powers] The court may, whenever–

(a) it is expedient to appoint a person to carry out the functions of the supervisor, and

(b) it is inexpedient, difficult or impracticable for an appointment to be made without the assistance of the court,

make an order appointing a person who is qualified to act as an insolvency practitioner or authorised to act as supervisor, in relation to the voluntary arrangement, either in substitution for the existing supervisor or to fill a vacancy.

7(6) [Limit on s. 7(5) power] The power conferred by subsection (5) is exercisable so as to increase the number of persons exercising the functions of supervisor or, where there is more than one person exercising those functions, so as to replace one or more of those persons.

S. 7(1), (2)
The wording of these subsections was modified by IA 2000, s. 2 and Sch. 2. As soon as a scheme of voluntary arrangement takes effect, the nominee (or his replacement appointed under s. 2(4) or 4(2)) is redesignated the "supervisor". The supervisor holds funds collected by him on trust for the creditors entitled under the arrangement. These funds cannot be seized by a subsequently appointed receiver: *Re Leisure Study Group Ltd* [1994] 2 B.C.L.C. 65.
    For the rules relating to the implementation of the arrangement and the duties of the supervisor, see IR 1986, rr. 1.22–1.23, 1.26ff.

Section 7   Insolvency Act 1986

S. 7(3)
The court is given wide – indeed, unlimited – powers to oversee the conduct of the arrangement by the supervisor; and anyone at all (subject, no doubt, to his being able to show that he has some interest in the matter) may invoke the jurisdiction under this section. As to whether a creditor can apply under s. 7(3) where the company is also undergoing administration see *Holdenhurst Securities plc v Cohen* [2001] 1 B.C.L.C. 460. The right of application under s. 7(3) does not exclude a direct action by a creditor unless the terms of the CVA preclude this – *Alman v Approach Housing Ltd* [2001] 1 B.C.L.C. 530. For an application by the company under s. 7(3) see *County Bookshops Ltd v Grove* [2002] EWHC 1160, [2002] B.P.I.R. 772.

S. 7(4)
The supervisor (like a liquidator, administrator, trustee, and others discharging comparable functions) may apply to the court for directions. Although the Act nowhere states explicitly that the court may give directions which modify the scheme or extend it to include persons who have not taken part in the meetings, this was in fact done in *Re FMS Financial Management Services Ltd* (1989) 5 B.C.C. 191. Here a voluntary arrangement had been agreed to by both the members and various groups of creditors, but not by another group composed of former clients of the company who appeared to have good claims against the company for damages for misrepresentation. Hoffmann J. directed that they should be treated as creditors and be given the benefit of the scheme, with the consequence that the other creditors received a substantially smaller dividend. The power to seek directions does not enable the court to modify the terms of a CVA – *Re Alpa Lighting Ltd* [1997] B.P.I.R. 341.

The supervisor may also apply for an administration order or a winding-up order (para. (b)), but is not listed in either s. 9 or s. 124 among the categories of persons who are entitled to petition for those orders. This difficulty has to be overcome by having the supervisor petition in the name of the company, on analogy with IR 1986, r. 4.7(7)(a). In the case of a petition for an administration order, this would be consistent with r. 2.1(4) (which states that the petition is to be treated as if it were the petition of the company); but it is less appropriate in relation to a winding-up petition, for r. 4.7(9) declares that this shall be treated as if it were a petition filed by contributories. On winding-up petitions presented by supervisors, see *Re Leisure Study Group Ltd* [1994] 2 B.C.L.C. 65.

A supervisor may apply for a winding-up order under s. 7(4)(b) even though he is no longer "carrying out the functions" under the CVA: this wording (in s. 7(2)) is descriptive only and not restrictive: *Re Arthur Rathbone Kitchens Ltd* [1998] B.C.C. 450.

Difficult issues arise where a company undergoing the CVA procedure then goes into liquidation. What is the effect of the liquidation on the CVA and what happens to the funds collected by the CVA supervisor? In spite of the relative scarcity of CVAs on the ground we now have a substantial body of case law to grapple with: *Re Halson Packaging Ltd* [1997] B.P.I.R. 194 (HHJ Maddocks); *Re Arthur Rathbone Kitchens Ltd* [1997] 2 B.C.L.C. 280 (Roger Kaye Q.C.); *Re Excalibur Airways Ltd* [1998] 1 B.C.L.C. 436 (Jonathan Parker J.); *Re Maple Environmental Services Ltd* [2000] B.C.C. 93 (HHJ Boggis); *Welsby v Brelec Installations* [2000] 2 B.C.L.C. 576 (Blackburne J.) and *Re Kudos Glass Ltd* [2000] 1 B.C.L.C. 390 (Richard McCombe Q.C.). This confusing corpus of first-instance case law arguably establishes certain propositions: a CVA can survive subsequent liquidation and the funds collected may be insulated from the residual assets of the company now undergoing the distributional process of winding up. However, whether these twin consequences will apply in an individual case depends to some extent upon the language of the CVA and also upon the circumstances under which the liquidation was commenced. The leading authority now is *Re NT Gallagher & Son Ltd* [2002] EWCA Civ 404, [2002] 1 W.L.R. 2380. Here a civil engineering company had fallen into financial difficulties in 1995 partly because of a substantial contractual dispute which was the subject of litigation initiated by the company ("the Mercury claim"). The CVA was designed to allow the company to continue trading pending the resolution of this substantial claim. Post-CVA creditors were to be paid out of cash flow. Under the CVA monthly payments were to be made by the company to the supervisors for the benefit of participating creditors; the language of "trust" was not used in relation to these payments. As is normal practice the supervisors were *required* to petition for the winding up of the company in the event of failure to comply with the terms of the CVA. By March 1997 the company had failed to keep up with the schedule of payments under the arrangement but the supervisors, after consulting the creditors, decided not to petition for winding up. In so deciding they concluded that they were not subject to an obligation to seek the winding up but were merely vested with a discretionary power; a conclusion, although not contested in the litigation, the correctness of which was viewed as "dubious" by the Court of Appeal (para. 20). In any event, the problems of the company grew and in 1997 it was eventually placed into creditors' voluntary winding up with the agreement of the directors and supervisors. The Mercury claim had not been resolved by this date. The mathematics of the insolvency were interesting; the supervisors retained a sum of in excess of £500,000, but the post-CVA liabilities amounted to approximately £2.5 million. Total liabilities exceeded £5 million. The residual assets of the company amounted to £98,000 plus two causes of action (the Mercury claim and one other claim). At first instance (see [2001] B.P.I.R. 1088) HHJ Howarth held that both the sums retained by the supervisors and the Mercury claim were held on trust for the CVA creditors and further concluded that those trusts were not terminated by the subsequent liquidation. The CVA creditors could prove in the liquidation of the company provided they surrendered their "security" in respect of the Mercury claim. The liquidators appealed but the Court of Appeal dismissed this appeal, though it varied part of the order of HHJ Howarth by allowing the CVA creditors to prove in the liquidation after giving credit for any dividends received from the supervisors. Thus, the analogy used by the trial judge under which the Mercury claim was treated as tantamount to a security (which could be surrendered) did not find favour in the Court of Appeal.

In reaching these conclusions, the Court of Appeal, through Peter Gibson L.J., recognised the unsatisfactory nature of the present law, resting as it does on fine distinctions: "It makes little sense for the form of the liquidation to affect the question of the effect of liquidation on trusts created by a CVA" (para. 43). Again, Peter Gibson L.J. stated:

"We would question whether the mere fact that a supervisor presents a petition entails that the CVA or IVA creditors have elected to terminate the CVA or IVA trust in their favour. Even if there is evidence that all the CVA or IVA creditors supported the presentation of a petition, it does not follow that they were thereby evincing an intention that the trust should come to an end and that the trust assets should revert to the company or debtor". (para. 43).

The real significance of this ruling from the Court of Appeal lies in the guidelines for future cases. The following principles have now been established (see para. 54). These general rules apply equally to cases of voluntary and compulsory liquidation. Moreover, the question of whether the petitioner is the supervisor or not is immaterial; what mattered is the solution specified in the arrangement.

The governing principles are:

1. Funds collected by the supervisor would, provided the terms of the arrangement made this clear, be held on trust exclusively for the benefit of the CVA participants. The fact that the language of "trust" is not employed in the CVA proposal is immaterial (see para. 29).

2. The fate of the CVA trust depends upon the terms under which that arrangement was entered into.

3. The stated effect of liquidation on the CVA should be respected. The contractual foundation of voluntary arrangements is thus reiterated.

4. It is perfectly possible for a CVA to come to an end but for the underlying trust to survive. In this context Peter Gibson L.J. declared: "We do not therefore accept that to treat a trust created by a CVA as continuing notwithstanding the liquidation of the company is productive of such unfairness that the court should conclude that liquidation brings the trust to an end". (para. 49). In the absence of express provision the following default rule will, according to Peter Gibson L.J., operate:

"Further, as a matter of policy, in the absence of any provision in the CVA as to what should happen to trust assets on liquidation of the company, the court should prefer a default rule which furthers rather than hinders what might be taken to be the statutory purpose of Part I of the Act. Parliament plainly intended to encourage companies and creditors to enter into CVAs so as to provide creditors with a means of recovering what they are owed without recourse to the more expensive means provided by winding up or administration, thereby giving many companies the opportunity to continue to trade". (para. 50).

5. CVA creditors who have not been fully reimbursed by the trust moneys can prove for the balance in the liquidation.

It is clear from the approach taken by the Court of Appeal in *Gallagher* that the contractual basis of the CVA is now the dominant perspective and thus CVA documentation should be reviewed. This ruling will prove a considerable boost to company voluntary arrangements by offering strong protection (with a commensurate incentive) to those creditors who choose to participate in the CVA as a way of recovering their debts, albeit over a more protracted timeframe than their original contractual rights provided for. The Court of Appeal has confirmed that at heart CVAs are a matter of contract and that this contract can have a negative impact upon the general creditors outside the scheme by establishing a resilient trust of corporate funds. From the perspective of those counterparties who continue to deal with a company undergoing a CVA the dangers of dealing with such a business are exacerbated; not surprisingly, the extension of credit to such a company will be a matter of some considerable risk requiring prudent countermeasures. At the very least some inquiries as to the financial status of the company would be wise (see here para. 49). The problem here is that it is quite possible to deal with a company already undergoing the CVA process without realising it (see paras 45 and 49). The end result, therefore, of *Gallagher* is that it may indeed encourage the setting of a CVA, but may have a negative impact upon the day-to-day operation of such arrangements by obstructing the flow of new credit.

S. 7(5)
This is a rather puzzling provision, for none of the preceding sections appears to give the meetings of shareholders and creditors, acting either together or independently, a power to fill a vacancy in the office of supervisor or to replace a supervisor once appointed: it seems that once the meetings have approved a proposal under s. 4A, they have no further role. So the reference in para. (b) to appointing a substitute supervisor "without the assistance of the court" is strange. Since no power appears to be conferred on the meetings by the rules, it seems that the only way in which a vacancy can be filled or a replacement supervisor appointed is by invoking the jurisdiction of the court under this subsection. See *Clements v Udal* [2001] B.P.I.R. 454. The wording of s. 7(5) was modified by IA 2000, s. 2 and Sch. 2.

S. 7(6)
This is the only reference in the Act to the possibility of appointing several persons as joint supervisors (or as joint nominees), although other "office-holders" are specifically covered by s. 231. It appears, however, that the general statutory assumption applies, so that words in the singular include the plural (*Interpretation Act* 1978, s. 6); and this construction may be applied throughout this Part of the Act. The rules deal with the appointment of joint supervisors in IR 1986, r. 1.22(1).

7A Prosecution of delinquent officers of company

7A(1) [Application] This section applies where a moratorium under section 1A has been obtained for a company or the approval of a voluntary arrangement in relation to a company has taken effect under section 4A or paragraph 36 of Schedule A1.

7A(2) [Procedure for reporting offence to "the appropriate authority"] If it appears to the nominee or supervisor that any past or present officer of the company has been guilty of any offence in connection with the moratorium or, as the case may be, voluntary arrangement for which he is criminally liable, the nominee or supervisor shall forthwith–

(a)   report the matter to the appropriate authority, and

(b)   provide the appropriate authority with such information and give the authority such access to and facilities for inspecting and taking copies of documents (being information or documents in the possession or under the control of the nominee or supervisor and relating to the matter in question) as the authority requires.

In this subsection, "the appropriate authority" means–

(i)   in the case of a company registered in England and Wales, the Secretary of State, and

(ii) in the case of a company registered in Scotland, the Lord Advocate.

7A(3) [Powers exercisable by Secretary of State] Where a report is made to the Secretary of State under subsection (2), he may, for the purpose of investigating the matter reported to him and such other matters relating to the affairs of the company as appear to him to require investigation, exercise any of the powers which are exercisable by inspectors appointed under section 431 or 432 of the Companies Act to investigate a company's affairs.

7A(4) [Obligations to assist Secretary of State] For the purpose of such an investigation any obligation imposed on a person by any provision of the Companies Act to produce documents or give information to, or otherwise to assist, inspectors so appointed is to be regarded as an obligation similarly to assist the Secretary of State in his investigation.

7A(5) [Answers as evidence in investigation] An answer given by a person to a question put to him in exercise of the powers conferred by subsection (3) may be used in evidence against him.

7A(6) [Answers as evidence in criminal proceedings] However, in criminal proceedings in which that person is charged with an offence to which this subsection applies–

(a)   no evidence relating to the answer may be adduced, and

(b)   no question relating to it may be asked,

by or on behalf of the prosecution, unless evidence relating to it is adduced, or a question relating to it is asked, in the proceedings by or on behalf of that person.

7A(7) [Offences under s. 7A(6)] Subsection (6) applies to any offence other than–

(a) an offence under section 2 or 5 of the Perjury Act 1911 (false statements made on oath otherwise than in judicial proceedings or made otherwise than on oath), or

(b) an offence under section 44(1) or (2) of the Criminal Law (Consolidation) (Scotland) Act 1995 (false statements made on oath or otherwise than on oath).

7A(8) [Assistance to be given to prosecuting authority] Where a prosecuting authority institutes criminal proceedings following any report under subsection (2), the nominee or supervisor, and every officer and agent of the company past and present (other than the defendant or defender), shall give the authority all assistance in connection with the prosecution which he is reasonably able to give.

For this purpose–

"agent" includes any banker or solicitor of the company and any person employed by the company as auditor, whether that person is or is not an officer of the company,

"prosecuting authority" means the Director of Public Prosecutions, the Lord Advocate or the Secretary of State.

7A(9) [Court directions under s. 7A(8)] The court may, on the application of the prosecuting authority, direct any person referred to in subsection (8) to comply with that subsection if he has failed to do so.

GENERAL NOTE

Introduced by s. 2 of, and Sch. 2 to, the Insolvency Act 2000 with effect from January 1, 2003.

S. 7A(1)
This defines the circumstances under which s. 7A applies – *i.e.* to both types of CVA.

S. 7A(2)
Here we have a formal "whistleblowing" obligation imposed on the nominee/supervisor. This is a significant departure from the previous position with regard to CVAs where insolvency practitioners were not expected to discharge such a public service duty. The absence of such a duty may well have been one of the attractions in the CVA model for company directors.

S. 7A(3), (4), (5)
This explains the powers available to the Secretary of State to follow up any report made under subs. (3). The power of investigation is bolstered by the provisions of subss. (4) and (5).

S. 7A(6)
This qualifies subs. (5), though in turn this qualification is limited by subs. (7).

S. 7A(8), (9)
These deal with follow up matters resulting from a prosecution instituted as a result of a report made under subs. (2).

7B Arrangements coming to an end prematurely

7B For the purposes of this Part, a voluntary arrangement the approval of which has taken effect under section 4A or paragraph 36 of Schedule A1 comes to an end prematurely if, when it ceases to have effect, it has not been fully implemented in respect of all persons bound by the arrangement by virtue of section 5(2)(b)(i) or, as the case may be, paragraph 37(2)(b)(i) of Schedule A1.

GENERAL NOTE

S. 7B
This is a curious definitional provision which seeks to identify when a CVA comes to an end prematurely. It needs to be read in the light of ss. 5(2A)(a) and 6(3).

ADMINISTRATION

IMPORTANT

There are now two administration regimes, each governed by what is referred to in the legislation as "Part II" of IA 1986. The "original" Pt II is set out, with annotations, below. The "new" Pt II is to be found in Sch. B1 to the Act, below at pp. 489ff. In order to distinguish between the original and the new Parts, the statutory text of the former has been set in italics, and the same distinction is made in the corresponding Rules.

8 Administration

Schedule B1 to this Act (which makes provision about the administration of companies) shall have effect.

General comment on the new Pt II
Part 10 of the EA 2002, the relevant provisions of which were brought into effect from September 15, 2003 by the Enterprise Act 2002 (Commencement No. 4 and Transitional Provisions and Savings) Order 2003 (SI 2003/2093 (C.85)), art. 2(1) and Sch. 1, has introduced a wholly new administration regime for companies. This it does by declaring (in s. 248) that a new Pt II, now to be found set out in Sch. B1 to IA 1986, is to be "substituted" for that contained in IA 1986 as originally drafted and since amended. The side-note to s. 248 refers to the "replacement" of Pt II. So the natural inference which the reader would draw is that the former Pt II has been consigned to oblivion, subject only to whatever transitional provisions might be needed to deal with companies which were in administration when s. 248 was brought into force. But this is not so. In the immediately following section (s. 249) it is provided that s. 248 "shall have no effect" in relation to a number of categories of public-utility company, and to building societies. So, so far as concerns these bodies, the former Pt II survives. It survives also where a petition for an administration order was presented to the court before September 15, 2003 (SI 2003/2093, art. 3(2)).

In consequence, we now have two versions of Pt II, one in ss. 8–27 and another in Sch.B1; and as if that were not confusing enough, we have two different sections each numbered s. 8! Section 8 of the "new" Pt II is set out above.

Because our readers will need to have access to the original ss. 8–27 in relation to both companies currently in administration and the other bodies listed above, we have decided to include both versions of Pt II in the present edition. We shall refer to the one as "the original" administration regime, or "Pt II as originally enacted" and the other as "the new" regime and "the new" Pt II. Necessarily, there will be some repetition and much cross-referencing between the two commentaries. However, the cross-references should be read with caution, since the language and some of the statutory definitions in the two Parts are not always the same.

The draftsman has endeavoured to make Sch. B1 largely self-standing, and in doing so has removed references to administration and administrators from many sections in other parts of the Act (*e.g.* in s. 212, the well-known "misfeasance" section). In order to cope with situations involving administrators appointed under the original regime, the former references are reinstated by the Enterprise Act 2002 (Commencement No. 4 and Transitional Provisions and Savings) Order 2003 (SI 2003/2093 (C.85)), arts 3(2), (3). This saving provision applies in cases where a petition for an administration order was presented before September 15, 2003, and also in the administration of insolvent partnerships, limited liability partnerships and certain bodies which are insurers under FSMA 2002 and SI 2002/1242. In the case of building societies and the utility companies mentioned in s. 249, the original wording of the Act is preserved because the new s. 8(3) disapplies Sch. 17 in regard to these bodies.

The Insolvency (Amendment) Rules 2003 (SI 2003/1730), which also came into force on September 15, 2003, supplement the new legislation by providing a new set of Rules which are to govern administrations under the new regime. But the rules in force prior to September 15, 2003 will continue to apply to administrations under the original Pt II: see the new r. 5(2)–(4):

Insolvency Act 1986   *Section 8*

Confusingly, both sets of rules are referred to as "Pt 2" of the Rules, and these use similar but not corresponding numbering. Accordingly, it has been necessary to include both versions of Pt 2 in this edition, which are to be found at pp. 706 (the original rules) and 733 (the new rules). References from the annotations to the original Pt II will be to Pt 2 of the original rules, and from the new Pt II to Pt 2 of the new rules (except where there is risk of confusion, when the appropriate label will be added). To aid in distinguishing between the two, the text of the original rules has been set in italics.

PART II

ADMINISTRATION ORDERS

General comment on the original Pt II
The company administration procedure was introduced for the first time by the legislation of 1985–86. Since then it has come to play an important, but as yet relatively small, role in the overall pattern of corporate insolvency regimes, sometimes providing a breathing space for an ailing company during which an attempt can be made to rescue the business or, at least, salvage it in part, and at other times giving an opportunity to realise its assets more advantageously than would be likely in a liquidation. There can be little doubt that the changes made by EA 2002 will see a much greater use of this procedure from now on.

When administration was first introduced, it was something of a novelty in English law. There was, however, a parallel with the appointment of a "judicial manager", which had been a feature of the company law of South Africa since 1926, and some similarity to the Australian "official management" which was introduced into jurisdictions in that country in 1961, but was little used in practice and has now been superseded. The reorganisation procedure prescribed under Ch. 11 of the United States Federal Bankruptcy Code is a less close equivalent. Legislation on the UK model has been introduced in Singapore and (with some significant differences) in the Republic of Ireland.

The provisions in the Act were based on the recommendations of the Cork Committee (*Report*, Ch. 9). The Committee thought that there was a need for a new procedure, similar to a receivership, to meet the case where a company was in difficulties but it was not possible to mount a rescue operation by having a receiver appointed because it had not given any creditor a floating charge over its undertaking. Ironically, the wheel has now come full circle. One of the principal aims of EA 2002 is to disallow the use of administrative receivership in the great majority of cases and oblige floating charge holders to place the company into administration instead. In consequence of this change, there will be a shift of emphasis: whereas the primary concern of a receiver is to protect the interest of the charge holder (in most cases by realising sufficient of the company's assets to pay off the secured debt), and he has only very limited duties *vis-à-vis* other stakeholders in the company, an administrator is bound to have regard to the interests of *all* the company's creditors and members. The rights of the secured creditor will no longer be paramount. And although receivership can sometimes result in the survival of some or all of the company's business as a going concern (either because a buyer is found to take it over, in whole or in part, or because the company is allowed to continue to trade until its financial difficulties are resolved), administration is more naturally envisaged as a "rescue" procedure and it is this purpose which ranks foremost among the objectives for which, under EA 2002, an administrator is obliged to perform his functions.

It should be borne in mind that both the Cork Committee and the Government in its White Paper thought it important that a board of directors which found that its company was in financial difficulties should seek outside help promptly and, if appropriate, hand over control of the company to experienced professional hands. (See the note to s. 214 ("wrongful trading").) An administration was plainly thought to be a proper step which a board might take in such a situation.

The timetable envisaged by the Act was leisurely (a matter of several months), and the procedure was costly, elaborate and formal. This was undoubtedly one of the reasons why administration was not as successful in practice as had been expected. It was necessary to obtain an order for the appointment of an administrator from the court, which had to be satisfied by evidence that the statutory grounds for an appointment existed, usually on the basis of a detailed report under IR 1986, r. 2.2 compiled by an independent person confirming that the appointment of an administrator was expedient. A statement of the company's affairs had then to be prepared by the directors, on the basis of which the administrator formulated "proposals" to be put before a meeting of the company's creditors some weeks later. Only after the proposals had been approved by the meeting was the administrator able to proceed to administer the company's affairs with a view to achieving the anticipated purpose.

The relative unpopularity of the procedure can be gauged from the fact that only 643 administration orders were made in the year 2002, compared with some 16,000 insolvent liquidations and 1,541 receiverships.

These considerations of delay and expense were not the only reason why the number of administrations was relatively low. Where the company had given a floating charge to its bank or some other creditor over all or substantially all of its assets, the charge-holder was given a statutory right to veto the appointment of an administrator and install an administrative receiver himself instead. Since a receiver could act more speedily, flexibly and cheaply, and was bound by law to give precedence to the interests of the secured creditor who had appointed him, it was not surprising that more often than not a charge-holder availed himself of this statutory right.

The EA 2002 has (except in a limited number of special cases) abrogated the power of a secured creditor to appoint an administrative receiver, although not with retrospective effect so as to affect the holders of floating charges created prior to September 15, 2003 (IA 1986, ss. 72Aff). Administration will henceforth be the standard procedure for the enforcement of a floating charge as well as for an attempt to achieve the rescue of a company's business where it is insolvent or nearly so – except in the case of an eligible small company, where a CVA may be preferred. The charge-holder's position has, however, been alleviated to some extent (a) by allowing such a creditor to appoint an administrator directly, by-passing the need for a court order (IA 1986, Sch. B1, para. 14), (b) by giving him the right to intervene and have an insolvency practitioner of his own choice appointed where an administration is proposed by some other person (para. 36), and (c) by specifying as one of the objectives for which an administration order can be made "realising property in order to make a distribution to one or more secured or preferential creditors" (para. 3(1)(c)). Even so, this latter objective is subordinated to the primary aim of rescuing the company as a going concern, where the administrator thinks that this is practicable.

Since December 1, 1994, the administration procedure has been available for use in the case of an insolvent partnership: see the Insolvent Partnerships Order 1994 (SI 1994/2421), art. 6 and Sch. 2. In contrast with the position as regards companies, a partnership must actually be unable to pay its debts and not merely likely to become insolvent. The purposes for which an order may be sought closely parallel those which apply in the case of a company (except that there is no counterpart to s. 8(3)(c)).

The administration procedure is also applicable to building societies: see Building Societies Act 1986, s. 90A (inserted by Building Societies Act 1997, s. 39, effective December 1, 1997), and to LLPs: see LLPR 2001, reg. 5(1)(a).

The administration regime applies with special modifications to various types of company governed by separate legislation, *e.g.* energy companies and railway companies – the main object being to ensure that supplies and services are not interrupted. A special regime also applies to insurance undertakings based in the UK (except Lloyd's): see the Insurers (Reorganisation and Winding up) Regulations 2004 (SI 2004/353), (replacing SI 2003/1102, effective February 18, 2004), implementing EC Directive 2001/17/EC. Detailed discussion of these special cases is beyond the scope of this work.

The statutory text (with annotations) which follows is that of the original IA 1986, Pt II. For the new Pt II, see Sch. B1, below, pp. 489ff.

Making, etc. of administration order

8 Power of court to make order

8(1) *[Administration order]* *Subject to this section, if the court–*

(a) *is satisfied that a company is or is likely to become unable to pay its debts (within the meaning given to that expression by section 123 of this Act), and*

(b) *considers that the making of an order under this section would be likely to achieve one or more of the purposes mentioned below,*

the court may make an administration order in relation to the company.

8(1A) *[In petition by FSA]* *For the purposes of a petition presented by the Financial Services Authority alone or together with any other party, an authorised deposit taker who defaults in an obligation to pay any*

Insolvency Act 1986 — Section 8

sum due and payable in respect of a relevant deposit is deemed to be unable to pay its debts as mentioned in subsection (1).

8(1B) *[Definitions for s. 8(1A)]* In subsection (1A)–

(a) **"authorised deposit taker"** means a person who has permission under Part 4 of the Financial Services and Markets Act 2000 to accept deposits, but excludes a person who has such permission only for the purpose of carrying on another regulated activity in accordance with that permission; and

(b) **"relevant deposit"** must be read with–

  (i) section 22 of the Financial Services and Markets Act 2000,

  (ii) any relevant order under that section, and

  (iii) Schedule 2 to that Act,

but any restriction on the meaning of deposit which arises from the identity of the person making it is to be disregarded.

8(2) *[Definition]* An administration order is an order directing that, during the period for which the order is in force, the affairs, business and property of the company shall be managed by a person ("the administrator") appointed for the purpose by the court.

8(3) *[Purposes for order]* The purposes for whose achievement an administration order may be made are–

(a) the survival of the company, and the whole or any part of its undertaking, as a going concern;

(b) the approval of a voluntary arrangement under Part I;

(c) the sanctioning under section 425 of the Companies Act of a compromise or arrangement between the company and any such persons as are mentioned in that section; and

(d) a more advantageous realisation of the company's assets than would be effected on a winding up;

and the order shall specify the purpose or purposes for which it is made.

8(4) *[No order if company in liquidation]* An administration order shall not be made in relation to a company after it has gone into liquidation.

8(5) *[Further situations where no order]* An administration order shall not be made against a company if–

(a) it has permission under Part 4 of the Financial Services and Markets Act 2000 to effect or carry out contracts of insurance in the United Kingdom;

(b) it continues to have a liability in respect of a deposit which was held by it in accordance with the Banking Act 1979 or the Banking Act 1987.

8(6) *[Provisions s. 8(5)(a) to be read with]* Subsection (5)(a) must be read with–

(a) section 22 of the Financial Services and Markets Act 2000;

(b) any relevant order under that section; and

(c) Schedule 2 to that Act.

8(7) *[Applicability of EC Regulation]* In this Part a reference to a company includes a reference to a company in relation to which an administration order may be made by virtue of Article 3 of the EC Regulation.

GENERAL NOTE

Section 8(1A), (1B), (5) and (6) were inserted, and s. 8(4)–(6) substituted, by the Financial Services and Markets Act 2000 (Consequential Amendments and Repeals) Order 2001 (SI 2001/3649) as from December 1, 2001. Section 8(7) was inserted by the Insolvency Act 1986 (Amendment) (No. 2) Regulations 2002 (SI 2002/1240) as from May 31, 2002.

S. 8(1), (2)

An administration order is defined by s. 8(2), as is the "administrator" who may be appointed to manage the affairs, etc. of a company under this section. For the meaning of "affairs" see *Polly Peck International plc v Henry* [1999] 1 B.C.L.C. 407.

The term "company" is not specifically defined for the purposes of this Part, and so reference must be made to the general definition contained in CA 1985, s. 735, which applies by virtue of s. 251. Accordingly, "company" means a company formed and registered under CA 1985 or an earlier Companies Act. It follows from this definition that an administration order cannot be made in respect of a foreign company (compare *Felixstowe Dock & Railway Co v US Lines Inc* [1989] Q.B. 360). This will be the case also (in the absence of special statutory provision) in relation to bodies other than companies, such as a society incorporated under the Industrial and Provident Societies Act 1965: see the general note to the First Group of Parts preceding s. 1. However, in the case of a foreign company, the position is different when a letter of request has been received by an English court from a court in that company's country of incorporation, for s. 426, and in particular s. 426(5), confers upon the court a jurisdiction wider than it would otherwise have: *Re Dallhold Estates (UK) Pty Ltd* [1992] B.C.C. 394.

Moreover, there has been some relaxation of the territorial limitation described above by virtue of the enactment of s. 8(7). Article 3 of the EC Regulation gives jurisdiction to a Member State of the EU to open insolvency proceedings "within the territory of which the centre of the debtor's main interests is situated" (in the case of "main" proceedings) and – subject to certain limitations – "if he possesses an establishment within the territory of that ... Member State" (in the case of "territorial" proceedings). (See the note to art. 3). Recent decisions have given a broad interpretation to this provision. In *Re BRAC Rent-A-Car International Inc.* [2003] B.C.C. 248 it was held that administration proceedings could be opened in the UK (as "main" proceedings) in respect of a company incorporated in Delaware which had conducted its operations almost entirely in the UK (and so had its "centre of main interests" within this jurisdiction): the scope of the Regulation was not restricted to companies incorporated elsewhere in the EU. In *Re The Salvage Association* [2003] B.C.C. 504, on the authority of this ruling, Blackburne J. held that the court had jurisdiction to make an administration order (and that a CVA could be implemented) in the case of a body incorporated by Royal Charter whose centre of main interests was within the UK, even though it was not a "company" for the purposes of IA 1986. It follows that the authority of cases such as *Felixstowe Dock* is likely to be restricted to bodies which do not have their centre of main interests within the UK or, arguably, an "establishment" within the UK and the centre of main interests elsewhere in the EU.

Questions of jurisdiction to petition for an administration order normally need to be resolved before an order is made; but the Act has to be interpreted realistically and, since administration orders often have to be made urgently, it may sometimes be necessary to make an order without settling (at least finally) a dispute as to locus standi or jurisdiction: *Re MTI Trading Systems Ltd* [1997] B.C.C. 703 (the Court of Appeal refused leave to appeal against this decision [1998] B.C.C. 400).

The prerequisites for the operation of the court's jurisdiction are set out in s. 8(1). The court must (1) be "satisfied" (on a balance of probabilities: *Re Colt Telecom Group plc (No. 2)* [2002] EWHC 2815 (Ch.); [2003] B.P.I.R. 324) that the company is, or is likely to become, "unable to pay its debts" (in the statutory sense of this expression, as defined by s. 123), and (2) consider that an administration order would be likely to achieve one or more of the purposes specified in s. 8(3). The Act gives no guidance as to the nature of the evidence on which a ruling on the second of these issues is to be made; and the matter was at first the subject of some judicial controversy. In *Re Consumer & Industrial Press Ltd* (1988) 4 B.C.C. 68, Peter Gibson J. was of the opinion that "likely to be achieved" meant "likely, on a balance of probabilities, to be achieved", so that the court needed to be satisfied on the evidence put before it that at least one of the purposes in s. 8(3) was likely, in the sense of "more probably than not", to be achieved. However in *Re Harris Simons Construction Ltd* [1989] 1 W.L.R. 368; (1989) 5 B.C.C. 11, Hoffmann J. took a broader view and declined to follow this ruling. He held that the requirements of s. 8(3) would be satisfied if the court considered that there was "a real prospect" that one or more of the statutory purposes might be achieved. He thought it "not unlikely that the legislature intended to set a modest threshold of probability to found jurisdiction and to rely on the court's discretion not to make orders in cases in which, weighing all the circumstances, it seemed inappropriate to do so". Since then the unanimous view of all the judges who have considered the matter (including Peter Gibson J. himself) has been that the "real prospect" test is to be preferred: in *Re Lomax Leisure Ltd* [2000] B.C.C. 352, at p. 363 he said that this approach was "now well established".

The order must specify the purpose or purposes for which it is made (s. 8(3)). Accordingly, the court must consider separately, in relation to each proposed purpose, whether the test of likelihood has been satisfied: see *Re S C L Building Services Ltd* (1989) 5 B.C.C. 746 at p. 747.

In part, the evidence on which the court bases its decision will be supplied by the affidavit filed in support of the petition under IR 1986, r. 2.3. In addition, the rules contemplate that a report by an independent person (*i.e.* someone not already connected with the company as a director, etc.) will be prepared for the assistance of the court (r. 2.2). This is not obligatory, but if a report has not been prepared, the court must be given an explanation (r. 2(3), (6)). (On the content of the report and the recommended practice in relation to such reports, see the discussion of the Practice Note of 1994 in the notes to r. 2.2, below.) It is obviously appropriate to have the report prepared by the insolvency practitioner whose appointment as administrator is being proposed, and in the great majority of cases this will be the best way of providing the court with the evidence on which it can act. Where the petitioner is a creditor, however, it is unlikely that he will have access to as much evidence as the court would like to have, and this may give rise to difficulties. Another situation which may pose problems is where there are simultaneous applications by a creditor for a winding up and by the company for an administration order which seeks the rehabilitation of the company and the survival of its undertaking as a going concern. The court may well in such a case require compelling evidence before making an administration order which would keep the creditor out of his money. On the other hand, where the object of the administration is a more advantageous realisation of assets or the furtherance of a scheme of arrangement, it would be reasonable for the court to act on rather less evidence, since the order is not likely to be any less beneficial to the general creditors than a winding up.

Insolvency, for the purposes of s. 8(1)(a), is at least primarily to be determined on a liquidity or "cash flow" basis (that is, on the company's ability to pay its current debts) rather than on a "balance sheet" basis (*i.e.* whether it is likely to have a surplus after a realisation of all its assets); but since, for this purpose, the provisions of s. 123 are relevant, the latter test is made a legitimate alternative by s. 123(2), and such a test was applied in *Re Dianoor Jewels Ltd* [2001] 1 B.C.L.C. 450. In *Re Imperial Motors (UK) Ltd* (1989) 5 B.C.C. 214 the court was prepared to find that the company was unable to pay its debts even though it appeared to be solvent on a balance-sheet basis. This was also the case in *Re Business Properties Ltd* (1988) 4 B.C.C. 684. However, Harman J. there expressed the view that in such a situation the court will not normally exercise its discretion to appoint an administrator when the essential ground for seeking relief is deadlock and a breakdown of trust and confidence between the members of the company: the more appropriate remedy is winding up. An administrator, he said, has wide powers for a "short-term, intensive-care" operation, but cannot achieve the realisation and distribution required to conclude the company's affairs.

If the conditions in s. 8(1)(a) and (b) are satisfied, the court then has a discretion whether to make an administration order. As Peter Gibson J. observed in *Re Consumer & Industrial Press Ltd* (above), this is a complete discretion, in which account must be taken of all material circumstances, and is not limited by the wording of s. 8(1)(a) and (b). The judge's task may not be at all an easy one, for his decision may benefit some creditors at the expense of others. For example, if an administration is preferred to a winding up, debts which would rank as preferential in a liquidation have no preferential status under the original Pt II. Another factor which weighed with the judge in that case, but was not held to be decisive, was that a liquidator has wider powers to investigate the conduct of directors (*e.g.* in regard to fraudulent and wrongful trading) than an administrator.

The court has, on occasion, exercised its discretion to make an administration order despite the opposition of a majority creditor which has stated its determination to oppose any proposals: see, *e.g. Re Structures & Computers Ltd* [1998] B.C.C. 348. In this case the majority creditor was allowed its costs as part of the administration.

Re Imperial Motors (UK) Ltd (above) is a further illustration of the exercise of the court's discretion. Here, the court took the view that the interests of the company's secured creditors should weigh more lightly in the scales than those of its unsecured creditors, because they did not stand to lose so much. In *Re Arrows Ltd (No. 3)* [1992] B.C.C. 131 a majority of the creditors opposed the making of an order. Hoffmann J. held that, while the court had a discretion to make an order in spite of such opposition, the fact that the proposals were unlikely to be approved by a creditors' meeting if an order were made would weigh strongly against making an order.

The fact that the genuine claims of a third party may be thwarted by putting the company into administration is not a reason for refusing an order: indeed, where the company is insolvent, an order ensures that the interests and claims of the company's creditors are not prejudiced by the outsider's claim: *Re Dianoor Jewels Ltd* [2001] 1 B.C.L.C. 450.

Section 8(2) refers to "the period for which the order is in force". Although it would not appear to follow necessarily from this that an order should be expressed to be made for a fixed period, the courts have so interpreted the provision, and a period of three months has become the standard. (This, of course, ties in with the obligation to report to creditors under IA 1986, s. 23, within the same period.) In *Re Newport County Association Football Club Ltd* (1987) 3 B.C.C. 635, Harman J. held that the company had standing to apply for an extension of this period, but expressed the view that such an application would be better made by the administrator.

On the making of a winding-up order, time ceases to run for the purposes of the statutes of limitation against the company's creditors (other than a petitioning creditor): *Re Cases of Taff's Well Ltd* [1992] Ch. 179; [1991] B.C.C. 582. However in the same case (at pp. 195; 589) the judge was of the view (but without expressing a concluded opinion) that the making of an administration order would not prevent time from running.

S. 8(3)

If the court makes an administration order, it must specify which of the purposes mentioned in s. 8(3) the order seeks to achieve. This requirement clearly limits the functions and powers of the administrator to acts which are consistent with the purpose or purposes stated. However, there is power under s. 18(1) to have the order varied so that it states an additional purpose.

Section 8(3) sets out under four headings the purposes which, separately or in combination, an administration order may seek to achieve. Headings (a) and (d) may not be altogether compatible with each other, although in practice they are commonly combined in the same petition or order. (In consequence, the decisive say as to the course which the administration should pursue is then left to the creditors at their meeting). In *Re Rowbotham Baxter Ltd* [1990] B.C.C. 113 at p. 115, Harman J. stated that a proposal involving the sale of a "hived-down" company formed to take over part of the company's business could not be brought within para. (a) ("the survival of the company and part of its undertaking as a going concern"); but it is submitted that it could plainly come within para. (d). In *Re Maxwell Communications Corporation plc* [1992] B.C.C. 372, Hoffmann J. held that the fact that Ch. 11 proceedings, affecting a substantial proportion of the company's assets, were pending in the US was relevant to the chances of the survival of the company and all or part of its business. Although in a normal case administration in itself is not an appropriate procedure for making a distribution to the company's unsecured creditors (*Rolph v A Y Bank Ltd* [2002] B.P.I.R. 1231), heading (b) may conveniently be invoked where it is proposed to make a distribution to creditors involving some modification of their rights, in a way which binds dissentients (see *Re St Ives Windings Ltd* [1987] 3 B.C.C. 634), or where a moratorium is sought and the company is not eligible for one under Sch. A1, and heading (c) gives the opportunity to combine an administration with a scheme of arrangement, so establishing a moratorium which prevents individual creditors from enforcing their rights while the necessary formalities are completed.

S. 8(4)–(6)

The administration procedure was formerly not available to insurance companies. However, by the Financial Services and Markets Act 2000 (Administration Orders Relating to Insurers) Order 2002 (SI 2002/1242), which came into force on May 31, 2002, this is now possible. The Schedule to this statutory instrument lists a series of modifications to IA 1986 in the application of that Act to insurers. The provisions of FSMA 2000 referred to in s. 8(6) define the concept of "regulated activity" for the purposes of that Act. For the same reason, banks and other "authorised institutions" under the banking legislation were excluded by the Act as originally drafted – and, indeed, by the present subsection as it now appears. However, by the Banks (Administration Proceedings) Order 1989 (SI 1989/1276), effective from August 23, 1989, Pt. II of the Act has been extended to apply in relation to banks and the other bodies mentioned in s. 8(5)(b) which are companies within the meaning of CA 1985, s. 735; and in relation to those institutions the Order (as amended) provides that certain modifications to the present Act shall be made, including the "omission" of para. (b) of the present subsection. Other modifications give standing to the Financial Services Authority for various purposes, such as presenting a petition for an administration order, and add as a ground of deemed insolvency a default by the institution in an obligation to pay any sum due in respect of a deposit.

The administration procedure may not be used if the company is already in liquidation. (For a general discussion of the relationship between winding up and administration orders, see the note to s. 10).

S. 8(7)

See the notes to s. 8(1), (2) above and to the EC Regulation, Art. 3.

9 Application for order

9(1) ***[Application to court]*** *An application to the court for an administration order shall be by petition presented either by the company or the directors, or by a creditor or creditors (including any contingent or prospective creditor or creditors), or by the clerk of a magistrates' court in the exercise of the power conferred by section 87A of the Magistrates' Courts Act 1980 (enforcement of fines imposed on companies) or by all or any of those parties, together or separately.*

9(2) ***[On presentation of petition to court]*** *Where a petition is presented to the court–*

(a) *notice of the petition shall be given forthwith to any person who has appointed, or is or may be entitled to appoint, an administrative receiver of the company, and to such other persons as may be prescribed, and*

(b) *the petition shall not be withdrawn except with the leave of the court.*

Insolvency Act 1986   Section 9

9(3) *[Duties of court]* Where the court is satisfied that there is an administrative receiver of the company, the court shall dismiss the petition unless it is also satisfied either–

(a)   that the person by whom or on whose behalf the receiver was appointed has consented to the making of the order, or

(b)   that, if an administration order were made, any security by virtue of which the receiver was appointed would–

     (i)   be liable to be released or discharged under sections 238 to 240 in Part VI (transactions at an undervalue and preferences),

     (ii)   be avoided under section 245 in that Part (avoidance of floating charges), or

     (iii)   be challengeable under section 242 (gratuitous alienations) or 243 (unfair preferences) in that Part, or under any rule of law in Scotland.

9(4) *[Court powers on hearing petition]* Subject to subsection (3), on hearing a petition the court may dismiss it, or adjourn the hearing conditionally or unconditionally, or make an interim order or any other order that it thinks fit.

9(5) *[Extent of interim order]* Without prejudice to the generality of subsection (4), an interim order under that subsection may restrict the exercise of any powers of the directors or of the company (whether by reference to the consent of the court or of a person qualified to act as an insolvency practitioner in relation to the company, or otherwise).

GENERAL NOTE

An administration order can be made only in consequence of an application made by petition under this section.
     For details of the procedure for making an application, see IR 1986, Pt. 2.

S. 9(1)
This list of persons who are eligible to apply for an administration order should be compared with those who may petition for a winding up under s. 124(1): see the comment to that subsection. The significant difference between the two is that the right of a member or members to seek an administration order is excluded. (This is in keeping with the rule in regard to winding up, laid down in *Re Rica Gold Washing Co.* (1879) 11 Ch.D. 36, that a member has no standing to present a winding-up petition where the company is insolvent. Applying this principle, Harman J. in *Re Chelmsford City Football Club (1980) Ltd* [1991] B.C.C. 133 ruled that members should not be given leave under IR 1986, r. 2.9(1)(g) to oppose an application for an administration order.) There is also no counterpart to ss. 124(4) and 124A, or to s. 124(5), which respectively empower the Secretary of State, in specified circumstances, and the official receiver to petition for a winding up. Note also that under s. 7(4)(b) the supervisor of a voluntary arrangement is included among the persons who may apply to the court for an administration order.
     Where the purpose of an administration order is the approval of a voluntary arrangement under Pt. I (see s. 8(3)(a)), it will be necessary for the directors to take steps to initiate the voluntary arrangement proceedings at the same time as the petition is presented under s. 9 (unless the voluntary arrangement is already in being), since they alone will be competent to do so.
     Contingent and prospective creditors are given standing to petition under s. 9(1), as they are for a winding-up order (see s. 124(1)). This contrasts with the position in regard to voluntary arrangements: see the note to s. 1(1).
     Where a company (or an insolvent partnership) is, or has been, an "authorised person" or "authorised representative" under FSMA 2000, or is or has been carrying on a "regulated activity" (*e.g.* an investment business) in contravention of s. 19 of that Act, the Financial Services Authority may present a petition under this section: FSMA 2000, s. 359. For this purpose, there is a special provision in s. 359(3) setting out circumstances (presumably, in addition to those contained in IA 1986, s. 123) in which such a body is to be deemed unable to pay its debts. If any other person is the petitioner, the authority is empowered to participate in the proceedings (s. 362).
     An application by the directors must be made by all the directors (*Re Instrumentation Electrical Services Ltd* (1988) 4 B.C.C. 301). This could, it is submitted, be done by all the directors acting informally (even where there is not an enabling article along the lines of Table A, art. 93): see *Charterhouse Investment Trust Ltd v Tempest Diesels Ltd* (1985) 1 B.C.C. 99,544 at p. 99,551; *Runciman v Walter Runciman plc* [1993] B.C.C. 223 at p. 230. An application can also be made in the name of all the directors once a proper resolution of the board of directors has been passed, for it then becomes the duty of all the directors, including those who took no part in the deliberations of the board and even those

Section 9 *Insolvency Act 1986*

who voted against the resolution, to implement it: see *Re Equiticorp International plc* [1989] 1 W.L.R. 1010; (1989) 5 B.C.C. 599. (Paragraph 105 of Sch. B1, which allows the directors to act informally by a majority, applies only to the new administration regime.)

A petition presented by the supervisor of a voluntary arrangement, or by the directors, is to be treated for all purposes as the petition of the company (IR 1986, rr. 2.1(4), 2.4(3)). A supervisor should petition in the name of the company: see the note to s. 7(4).

Although s. 9(2) requires notice of the petition to be given to a charge-holder, and the rules contemplate that copies of the petition shall be served on specified persons and that they and others may appear and be represented at the hearing of the petition (IR 1986, rr. 2.6, 2.9), the court has on occasion been prepared to make an administration order without notice and even, in cases of extreme urgency, to do so against an undertaking by counsel that a petition will be presented in the immediate future. Initially, Harman J. in *Re Rowbotham Baxter Ltd* [1990] B.C.C. 113 at p. 114 expressed the view that this was "an undesirable practice which should not continue". He said: "The danger is that the court hears one side only, the court has not the advantage of adversarial argument to draw its attention to points which may weigh one way or the other; and this leads ... to a serious risk of injustice being done". However, the same judge in the later case of *Re Cavco Floors Ltd* [1990] B.C.C. 589 qualified his earlier remarks by saying that, although it is undesirable for the court to act before presentation of the petition, it is a procedure which may need to be adopted in some cases; and in that case he did make an immediate order. See also *Re Shearing & Loader Ltd* [1991] B.C.C. 232 and *Re Gallidoro Trawlers Ltd* [1991] B.C.C. 691. Again, in *Re Chancery plc* [1991] B.C.C. 171, an administration order was made *ex parte* in the case of a banking company, where the judge also took the unusual course of hearing the application in camera.

There is no provision in the Act or the rules for a petition for an administration order to be advertised.

In many applications for an administration order, and in all applications made without notice, the only evidence before the court will be that submitted by the applicant company and its officers, and the insolvency practitioner's report under IR 1986, r. 2.2, which will be based on the same information. In *Re Sharps of Truro Ltd* [1990] B.C.C. 94 and also in *Astor Chemical Ltd v Synthetic Technology Ltd* [1990] B.C.C. 97 at pp. 107–108, the court laid stress on the importance of ensuring that all relevant information was put before the court. "All facts relevant to the exercise of the discretion to appoint an administrator must be revealed, even though to do so may be embarrassing to the applicant" (*ibid*). If some material fact emerges after the making of the order, it is the duty of those who learn of it to explain it to the administrator and to put it before the court; and it is proper in such circumstances for the administrator to apply to the court for the discharge of the order, or to seek directions whether he should apply for a discharge.

The hearing of an application for an administration order is normally conducted on the basis of written evidence, and an order for disclosure of documents or the cross-examination of witnesses will be made only in exceptional circumstances: *Re Colt Telecom Group plc (No. 1)* [2002] EWHC 2503 (Ch.); [2003] B.P.I.R. 311.

S. 9(2)
The holder of a floating charge who has power to appoint a receiver of the whole or substantially the whole of the company's property has the power (provided that his security is not successfully challenged under s. 9(3)(b)) to block the making of an administration order by putting the company into receivership (s. 9(3)). The notice required to be given to him by the present subsection will enable him to take this step if he wishes or, alternatively, to give his consent under s. 9(3)(a). In order to ensure that a debenture holder has the power to put in a receiver in these circumstances, it is necessary that express provision should be made in any floating charge drawn up after the Act came into force. In relation to instruments created before the commencement of the Act, there is a transitional measure in Sch. 11, para. 1, which deems such a provision to be included.

For the "other persons" prescribed by the rules as being entitled to notice of a petition, see IR 1986, r. 2.6.

The term "forthwith" has no precise meaning: "it must be done as soon as possible in the circumstances, the nature of the act to be done being taken into account" (Halsbury's *Laws of England*, 4th edn, Vol. 45, para. 1148). In the present context, it would probably be construed as "as soon as practicable" (*Sameen v Abeyewickrema* [1963] A.C. 597) or "as soon as reasonably practicable" (*Re Seagull Manufacturing Co. Ltd (in liquidation)* [1993] Ch. 345, at p. 359; [1993] B.C.C. 241, at p. 249) rather than the peremptory "at once" (*Re Muscovitch* [1939] Ch. 694) or the lax "at any reasonable time thereafter" (*Hillingdon London Borough Council v Cutler* [1968] 1 Q.B. 124).

The stipulation that a petition for an administration order shall not be withdrawn except with the leave of the court will naturally discourage irresponsible applications, and in particular the use of the procedure by a creditor for the purpose of putting pressure on a debtor company. On the other hand, it is clearly not improper for a petition to be presented under this section in order to secure a moratorium in connection with a voluntary arrangement under s. 1–7 (where this is not available under Sch. A1) or a formal scheme of arrangement under CA 1985, s. 425–427: see the note to s. 8(3).

S. 9(3)

This is the first occasion in the Act where the term "administrative receiver" is used. In broad terms, it may be taken as meaning "a receiver or manager of the whole (or substantially the whole) of a company's property". The full statutory definition appears in ss. 29(2) and 251.

Although company law generally is able to accommodate the notion that more than one receivership can operate at the same time, or a receivership co-exist with a liquidation, the legislation rules out the idea that there can be an administrator and an administrative receiver in office at the same time. To resolve the matter, the security-holder who has appointed, or has power to appoint, an administrative receiver is given the decisive say. If he has already appointed a receiver when the petition for an administration order is presented, the petition must be dismissed unless the charge-holder consents to the making of an order (s. 9(3)) and the consequent vacation of the receivership (s. 11(1)(b)). If he has not then appointed a receiver, he may do so before the application is heard (s. 10(2)(b)), and so bring about the dismissal of the petition under the present subsection. In order to enable the charge-holder to assess the position, the rules provide for him to be given five clear days' notice of the date fixed for the hearing of the application (IR 1986, rr. 2.6(2)(a), 2.7(1)). The court has power to abridge this period of notice in an appropriate case (*Re a Company No. 00175 of 1987* (1987) 3 B.C.C. 124).

In the same case, the company urged the court to grant an adjournment of the application in order that the company could arrange to pay off the charge. This would have led to the termination of the receivership and so (it was argued) have enabled an administration order to be made without violation of s. 9(3). However, Vinelott J. held that he had no jurisdiction to take this course: the wording of s. 9(3) was mandatory and he had no alternative but to dismiss the application.

The superior claims of the charge-holder will not survive if an attack is successfully mounted upon the validity of the security on any of the grounds listed under para. (b) – *i.e.* that it is a transaction at an undervalue or preference within the scope of ss. 238–240, or a floating charge that is liable to be avoided under s. 245, or is challengeable under the equivalent Scottish provisions (ss. 242, 243). It has also been suggested that a creditor taking security might seek to clothe what is essentially a fixed charge with the appearance of a floating charge, or to combine it with a meaningless floating charge, in order to obtain the power under s. 9(3) to block an administration order by the purported appointment of an administrative receiver. An argument challenging the genuineness of a floating charge along these lines failed in *Re Croftbell Ltd* [1990] B.C.C. 781: the court held that a charge which was expressed to extend to future assets was to be treated as a floating charge even though at the time of its creation the company had no assets of the class in question.

Paragraph (b) of the subsection is likely to raise procedural and evidentiary difficulties. The terms of the section make it clear that the validity or invalidity of the security may be settled in the course of the hearing of the application for an order, rather than in separate proceedings. It is plain also that the onus of satisfying the court is on the petitioner. Yet he is unlikely to have at his disposal all the evidence that an administrator or liquidator would later have when proceeding under ss. 238–240 or s. 245. Fairly obviously, the matter cannot be determined without the security-holder as well as the company being made a party (for which, indeed provision is made by IR 1986, r. 2.9). However, there are still difficult questions which the legislation does not address: is there any guarantee that the case will be properly put for the company (which, in the case of a creditor's petition, may well be opposed to the application)? There will not yet be anyone in office equivalent to the "office-holder" whose role it is to prosecute the proceedings under ss. 238–239. Suppose that a decision under the present subsection is reached in favour of the security-holder: will the matter be res judicata if a winding-up order or an unrelated administration order is later made?

There is a further difficulty which may arise under s. 9(3)(b), in reckoning the statutory period during which the security must have been created if it is to be avoided. There will be no problem in the case of ss. 238–240 and 245, since the "relevant time" will be calculated from the date when the petition for an administration order was *presented* (see ss. 240(3)(a), 245(5)(a)); but the significant date for ss. 242, 243 is the date of the making of the administration *order*, and this will set the court the impossible task of ascribing a real date to a hypothetical order.

A receiver who is not an administrative receiver (*e.g.* a receiver of part only of the company's property, or (probably) a receiver appointed by the court) is not obliged to vacate office unless required to do so by the administrator: s. 11(2).

S. 9(4), (5)

The powers of the court, especially to make interim orders, are expressed in the widest terms, and include power to subject the decision-making powers of the corporate organs to its own supervision, or to delegate that function to a qualified insolvency practitioner. It is submitted, however, that orders made under this section can affect only the company and, presumably, such creditors as have been made parties to the application. The position as regards other creditors is dealt with in s. 10, below. One question which is not at all clear is whether an interim order under s. 9(4) and (5) could restrict the exercise of powers by a security-holder or an administrative receiver pending the determination of a question as to the validity of the security under s. 9(3)(b): compare s. 10(2)(b), (c).

Section 10 Insolvency Act 1986

An interim order under s. 9(4) is not an administration order for the purposes of CDDA 1986, s. 6(2)(b), so that time does not begin to run for the purposes of the two-year limitation prescribed by CDDA 1986, s. 7(2) until an administration order under s. 8(3) is made: *Secretary of State for Trade and Industry v Palmer* [1994] B.C.C. 990.

There is no power under the Act for the court to appoint an interim administrator; but in an appropriate case (*e.g.* where the company's property is in jeopardy) it can appoint the intended administrator or another appropriate person to take control of the property and manage the company's affairs pending the final determination of the hearing: *Re a Company No. 00175 of 1987* (1987) 3 B.C.C. 124. Such an appointment would be analogous to the appointment of a receiver of disputed property or of property which is in jeopardy. In *Re Gallidoro Trawlers Ltd* [1991] B.C.C. 691 the court, instead of appointing an interim manager, made an order restricting the powers of the company's directors prior to the hearing of the petition.

Where a petition for an administration order is not proceeded with and a winding-up order is made, the court may in a proper case allow the costs of the petition to be treated as costs in the winding up: *Re Gosscott (Groundworks) Ltd* (1988) 4 B.C.C. 372; but there have been other cases where it has been ordered that costs should be borne by the directors personally: see *Re W F Fearman Ltd (No. 2)* (1988) 4 B.C.C. 1411; *Taylor v Pace Developments Ltd* [1991] B.C.C. 406; and *Re Stallton Distribution Ltd* [2002] B.C.C. 486. In *Re Land & Property Trust Co. plc; Re Andromache Properties Ltd* [1991] B.C.C. 446, Harman J at first instance made a similar order, but his ruling was reversed on appeal (*Re Land & Property Trust Co. plc (No. 2)* [1993] B.C.C. 462), after the Court of Appeal had ruled (*Re Land & Property Trust Co. plc* [1991] 1 W.L.R. 601; [1991] B.C.C. 459) that the directors' right of appeal was not barred by s. 18(1)(f) of the *Supreme Court Act* 1981. In *Re Tajik Air Ltd* [1996] B.C.C. 368 the court declared that directors would not usually be ordered to pay costs in these circumstances unless it could be established summarily that they had acted for an improper purpose, such as concealing their own wrongdoings. It was to be assumed that a report under IR 1986, r. 2.2 (if one had been obtained) was a serious and objective assessment of the company's prospects of satisfying one of the statutory purposes, and that the directors were justified in acting in reliance on it, as they would be on legal advice – even if such advice was unrealistic, or wrong.

10 *Effect of application*

10(1) *[Limitations] During the period beginning with the presentation of a petition for an administration order and ending with the making of such an order or the dismissal of the petition–*

    (a) *no resolution may be passed or order made for the winding up of the company;*

    (aa) *no landlord or other person to whom rent is payable may exercise any right of forfeiture by peaceable re-entry in relation to premises let to the company in respect of a failure by the company to comply with any term or condition of its tenancy of such premises, except with the leave of the court and subject to such terms as the court may impose.*

    (b) *no steps may be taken to enforce any security over the company's property, or to repossess goods in the company's possession under any hire-purchase agreement, except with the leave of the court and subject to such terms as the court may impose; and*

    (c) *no other proceedings and no execution or other legal process may be commenced or continued, and no distress may be levied, against the company or its property except with the leave of the court and subject to such terms as aforesaid.*

10(2) *[Where leave not required] Nothing in subsection (1) requires the leave of the court–*

    (a) *for the presentation of a petition for the winding up of the company,*

    (b) *for the appointment of an administrative receiver of the company, or*

    (c) *for the carrying out by such a receiver (whenever appointed) of any of his functions.*

10(3) *[Period in s. 10(1)] Where–*

    (a) *a petition for an administration order is presented at a time when there is an administrative receiver of the company, and*

    (b) *the person by or on whose behalf the receiver was appointed has not consented to the making of the order,*

Insolvency Act 1986   Section 10

the period mentioned in subsection (1) is deemed not to begin unless and until that person so consents.

10(4) **[Hire-purchase agreements]** *References in this section and the next to hire-purchase agreements include conditional sale agreements, chattel leasing agreements and retention of title agreements.*

10(5) **[Scotland]** *In the application of this section and the next to Scotland, references to execution being commenced or continued include references to diligence being carried out or continued, and references to distress being levied shall be omitted.*

S. 10(1)
Unless the company is already in the hands of an administrative receiver (in which case s. 10(3) applies), the presentation of a petition for an administration order imposes an automatic moratorium, which prevents certain legal acts and processes from being performed or continued until the application is finally disposed of. The company cannot be put into voluntary liquidation, nor can a winding-up order be made (although a winding-up petition may be *presented*: s. 10(2)(a)); and unless the court gives leave, the enforcement of a security, the repossession of goods held under hire-purchase and similar agreements, and the commencement and prosecution of legal proceedings, etc., may not be proceeded with. (Some exceptions are listed in s. 10(2), discussed below.) The court's discretion in granting leave under para. (b) and (c) appears to be unrestricted.

Subparagraph 10(1)(aa) was inserted by IA 2000, s. 9 with effect from 2 April 2001 to resolve doubts on the question whether the leave of the court was required where a landlord sought to exercise his right of re-entry for non-payment of rent or breach of any other covenant. On this, and more generally on the meaning of the term "security" in this context, see the note to s. 11(3)(c).

In *Re a Company No. 001448 of 1989* (1989) 5 B.C.C. 706 Millett J. held that, even though s. 10(1)(c) cannot be invoked until a petition for an administration order has been presented, the court has power under its quia timet jurisdiction to restrain the advertisement of a winding-up petition if counsel for the company has given an undertaking that a petition will be presented.

The rules provide that notice of the presentation of a petition for an administration order be given to anyone known to be issuing execution or other legal process or distraining against the company (IR 1986, r. 2.6A), in order to avoid the risk of inadvertent contraventions of s. 10(1)(c).

Section 10(1)(b) does not apply in relation to the enforcement of "market charges" (as defined by CA 1989, s. 173): see s. 175 of that Act (as qualified by the Financial Markets and Insolvency Regulations 1991 (SI 1991/880)). It is also disapplied in relation to payment and securities settlement systems by the Finality Regulations, reg. 19. (See the introductory notes at pp. 2–3 above.)

In relation to the financial markets, nothing in s. 10(1)(c) affects any action taken by an exchange or clearing house for the purpose of its default proceedings: CA 1989, s. 161(4).

S. 10(2)
Although no winding-up order may be *made* while the hearing of an application for an administration order is pending, a petition for winding up may be *presented*. It may well be the case that a creditor will wish to oppose an application for an administration order and argue instead that the company should be put into liquidation. If he has not already presented a winding-up petition, s. 10(2)(a) confirms that he is free to do so; and in any case it is open to the court to combine the hearing of the two applications – an obviously convenient course. The leave of the court under s. 10(1)(c) may, however, be necessary for such a joinder of proceedings; and if liquidation is in due course to be ordered the application for an administration order must first be dismissed (s. 10(1)(a)), and vice versa (s. 11(1)(a)).

In *Re a Company No. 001992 of 1988* (1988) 4 B.C.C. 451 the court ruled that it was proper not to proceed to advertise a winding-up petition until after determination of the application for an administration order; but in later proceedings (reported as *Re Manlon Trading Ltd* (1988) 4 B.C.C. 455) Harman J. ruled that this course should only be taken when a petition for an administration order had actually been presented or an undertaking given to the court to present one: it was not sufficient to act on affidavit evidence that administration was being contemplated.

The Act is silent on the question whether it is possible, at least without leave, to present a second administration petition specifying a different purpose (*e.g.* a realisation of assets rather than a voluntary arrangement, or vice versa). Gordon Stewart, *Administrative Receivers and Administrators* (CCH, 1987), p. 170, argues that the wording of s. 9(1) recognises such a right.

S. 10(3)
If an administrative receiver is already in office when a petition for an administration order is presented, the earlier "moratorium" provisions of this section do not apply, unless and until the debenture holder gives his consent to the

Section 11 Insolvency Act 1986

making of an administration order (thereby signalling his willingness to vacate the receivership in favour of the proposed administratorship). There is no corresponding provision dealing with the case where the holder of the charge puts in an administrative receiver *after* the petition for an administration order is presented: the moratorium which will already be in force as regards all the company's other creditors apparently continues until the petition is disposed of in one way or another.

S. 10(4)

Of the four categories of agreement mentioned in this section, "hire-purchase agreement" and "conditional sale agreement" are defined (by reference to the Consumer Credit Act 1974) in s. 436 and "chattel leasing agreement" and "retention of title agreement" in s. 251. In each of these transactions the ownership of the goods concerned remains vested in the bailor or seller, and they do not become the company's property; but the Act for many purposes treats them as if the company has become the owner and the other party has retained only a security interest. See further the notes to ss. 15 and 43.

S. 10(5)

This provision assimilates the rules contained in the subsections above to the position under Scots law.

11 Effect of order

11(1) *[On making of administration order]* On the making of an administration order–

(a) any petition for the winding up of the company shall be dismissed, and

(b) any administrative receiver of the company shall vacate office.

11(2) *[Vacation of office by receiver]* Where an administration order has been made, any receiver of part of the company's property shall vacate office on being required to do so by the administrator.

11(3) *[Limitations]* During the period for which an administration order is in force–

(a) no resolution may be passed or order made for the winding up of the company;

(b) no administrative receiver of the company may be appointed;

(ba) no landlord or other person to whom rent is payable may exercise any right of forfeiture by peaceable re-entry in relation to premises let to the company in respect of a failure by the company to comply with any term or condition of its tenancy of such premises, except with the consent of the administrator or the leave of the court and subject (where the court gives leave) to such terms as the court may impose.

(c) no other steps may be taken to enforce any security over the company's property, or to repossess goods in the company's possession under any hire-purchase agreement, except with the consent of the administrator or the leave of the court and subject (where the court gives leave) to such terms as the court may impose; and

(d) no other proceedings and no execution or other legal process may be commenced or continued, and no distress may be levied, against the company or its property except with the consent of the administrator or the leave of the court and subject (where the court gives leave) to such terms as aforesaid.

11(4) *[Where vacation of office under s. 11(1)(b), (2)]* Where at any time an administrative receiver of the company has vacated office under subsection (1)(b), or a receiver of part of the company's property has vacated office under subsection (2)–

(a) his remuneration and any expenses properly incurred by him, and

(b) any indemnity to which he is entitled out of the assets of the company, *shall be charged on and (subject to subsection (3) above) paid out of any property of the company which was in his custody or under his control at that time in priority to any security held by the person by or on whose behalf he was appointed.*

11(5) *[S. 40, 59] Neither an administrative receiver who vacates office under subsection (1)(b) nor a receiver who vacates office under subsection (2) is required on or after so vacating office to take any steps for the purpose of complying with any duty imposed on him by section 40 or 59 of this Act (duty to pay preferential creditors).*

GENERAL NOTE

On the making of an administration order, the suspension of the rights of creditors and security-holders imposed by s. 10 becomes a total ban, and the administrative receiver, if there has been one in office, must give way to the administrator.

S. 11(1)

If a petition for winding up has been presented, whether before or after the presentation of the petition for an administration order, the petitioner should take all possible steps to ensure that his case is heard before, or simultaneously with, the winding-up application: see the note to s. 10(2).

An administrative receiver will be required to vacate office under this provision only if his appointor has consented to the making of the administration order or if his security is found liable to be invalidated under s. 9(3)(b). On the effects of his vacating office, see the note to s. 11(2).

S. 11(2)

A receiver of part (*i.e.* not "substantially the whole") of the company's property is not an administrative receiver: see s. 29(2). He is not required automatically to vacate office – the administrator has a discretion; but any steps that he may take to enforce the security will need the consent of the administrator or the leave of the court under s. 11(3)(c).

The full implications of the vacation of office by a receiver under this section are not clearly spelt out in the Act. The appointment of the receiver, when it was made, will have crystallised the charge, in so far as it was a floating charge, so that the assets affected will have been subject to a fixed charge throughout the subsistence of the receivership. Section 11(4) grants the receiver a charge on the assets for his fees, etc., and in some circumstances the right to have them paid, and both this subsection and s. 15(1) confirm that the debenture-holder's security continues in force during the period when the administrator is in office. Presumably it does so as a fixed charge and is not decrystallised, for otherwise s. 15(4) would make little sense. This is not likely to be a point of great significance, however, for under the statutory definition it will be treated for all the purposes of the Act as if it were still a floating charge: see s. 251 and the notes to ss. 175(2)(b) and 245. The creditors entitled to preference in the receivership will lose all claims against the discharged receiver (s. 11(5)) and will have no claim against the administrator (s. 15(1)). However, presumably it is intended that they will retain some form of priority over the debenture holder himself by virtue of s. 15(4). This is by no means a foregone conclusion, however, for (1) if the administration order is discharged without a winding up, the debenture holder will have to appoint a receiver afresh in order to enforce his security, and this will mean a new "relevant date" for the purposes of s. 387 and different "assets coming to the hands of the receiver" for the purposes of s. 40(2) or s. 59(1); while (2) if the company is put into liquidation immediately upon the discharge of the administration order, s. 175 may apply to the exclusion of s. 40 or s. 59, and under s. 387(3)(a) a quite different list of preferential debts would need to be drawn up.

Section 11(2) does not apply in relation to a receiver appointed to enforce a "market charge" (as defined by CA 1989, s. 173): see s. 175 of that Act (as qualified by the Financial Markets and Insolvency Regulations 1991 (SI 1991/880)). It is also disapplied in relation to payment and securities settlement systems by the Finality Regulations, reg. 19. (See the introductory notes at pp. 2–3 above.)

In relation to the financial markets, nothing in s. 11(3) affects any action taken by an exchange or clearing house for the purpose of its default proceedings: CA 1989, s. 161(4).

S. 11(3)

This subsection spells out the full details of the restrictions on the enforcement of claims and securities against the company which apply once the administration order becomes operative. In one respect, the ban is strengthened: it is no longer possible to appoint an administrative receiver. In another respect, it is slightly relaxed: the acts mentioned in para. (c) and (d) may now be authorised by the administrator as an alternative to seeking the leave of the court.

In *Air Ecosse Ltd v Civil Aviation Authority* (1987) 3 B.C.C. 492, the Court of Session ruled that the term "proceedings" in s. 11(3) was confined in its scope to the activities of the company's creditors in seeking to enforce their debts, and did not extend to quasi-judicial and extra-judicial proceedings such as an application made by a competitor of the company for the revocation of an aviation licence. But this view has been much criticised, and cannot now be regarded as a correct statement of the law. It has since been held that leave is required for an application by an employee to an industrial tribunal complaining that he had been unfairly selected for redundancy (*Carr v British International Helicopters Ltd* [1993] B.C.C. 855); for an application for the revocation of a patent (*Re Axis Genetics Ltd* [2000] B.C.C. 943); and even for the bringing of criminal proceedings against the company (*Re Rhondda Waste Disposal Ltd, Environment Agency v Clark (Administrator of Rhondda Waste Disposal Ltd)* [2001] Ch. 51; [2000] B.C.C. 653). In *A Straume (UK) Ltd v Bradlor Developments Ltd* [2000] B.C.C. 333 the reference of a dispute arising under a building contract to a statutory adjudication procedure was held to be a quasi-legal proceeding akin to arbitration which required leave, even though further proceedings would be needed to enforce any award that might be made. In contrast with these decisions, the Court of Appeal has ruled in *Re Railtrack plc* [2002] 2 B.C.L.C. 755 that the determination by the Rail Regulator of an application by a train operator under the Railways Act 1993 for permission to use the railway network was not "proceedings" or a "legal process" within s.11.

The phrases "any security over the company's property" and "execution or other legal process" contained in para. (c) and (d) have also been the subject of judicial rulings in a number of contexts. In *Bristol Airport plc v Powdrill* [1990] Ch. 744 (reported as *Re Paramount Airways Ltd* [1990] B.C.C. 130) the Court of Appeal, affirming Harman J., held that for the purposes of s. 11(3)(c) and (d): (i) aircraft held by the company on lease was "property" of the company and (ii) the statutory right of an airport to detain aircraft pursuant to s. 88 of the Civil Aviation Act 1982 for failure to pay outstanding airport charges was a "lien or other security" (within the extended definition of "security" contained in IA 1986, s. 248) which could not be exercised without the leave of the court.

However, the insertion of para. (ba) into s. 11(3) (and correspondingly of para. (aa) into s. 10(1)) with effect from April 2, 2001 has laid to rest an issue on which there had been much controversy and conflicting judicial opinion, namely whether a landlord's right of re-entry for non-payment of rent or the breach of any other covenant in the lease constituted a "security" or "the commencement of a legal process" which fell within s. 11(c) or (d). The differing judicial views are collected and analysed in the latest of the reported cases, *Re Lomax Leisure Ltd* [2000] B.C.C. 352, in which Neuberger J. concluded that the balance of opinion was in favour of the view that leave was not required, and that this was indirectly supported by observations of the House of Lords in *Re Park Air Services plc* [2000] 2 A.C. 172; [1999] B.C.C. 135. The legislative amendments have therefore reversed this position. However, the views expressed in some of these cases will continue to be relevant in situations analogous to the landlord's right of re-entry which are not covered by the new subsections. In *Re Olympia & York Canary Wharf Ltd, American Express Europe Ltd v Adamson* [1993] B.C.C. 154 Millett J. said that "legal process" means a process which requires the assistance of the court, and that it does not include such steps as the serving of a notice by a party to a contract making time of the essence, or the acceptance by such a party of a repudiatory breach of contract. Similarly, in *Bristol Airport plc v Powdrill* (above) at pp. 766; 153 Browne-Wilkinson V.-C. plainly doubted whether the serving of a counter-notice claiming a new tenancy under the Landlord and Tenant Act 1954 could be regarded as a "proceeding".

An application for an extension of time for the registration of a charge cannot be described as "proceedings against a company or its property" within s. 11(3)(d): *Re Barrow Borough Transport Ltd* [1990] Ch. 227; (1989) 5 B.C.C. 646. However, once an administration order has been made and it has become clear that administration will result in the insolvent liquidation of the company, the court's discretion should be exercised against granting an extension of time for registration (*ibid*).

Section 11 does not affect the substantive rights of the parties: it is concerned merely with procedure. It imposes a moratorium on the enforcement of creditors' rights, but does not destroy those rights. The legal right of a security-holder to enforce his security, and that of an owner of goods to immediate possession of his goods, and the causes of action based on such rights, remain vested in that party. If he seeks and obtains the leave of the court to enforce his rights, the grant of leave does not alter the parties' legal rights, but merely grants the applicant liberty to enforce his rights: *Barclays Mercantile Business Finance Ltd v Sibec Developments Ltd (Re Sibec Developments Ltd)* [1992] 1 W.L.R. 1253; [1993] B.C.C. 148.

A proceeding (such as an application to an industrial tribunal) commenced without leave is not a nullity: it is in order for the proceeding to be adjourned while consent or leave is sought: *Carr v British International Helicopters Ltd* (above). This ruling means that difficulties over a possible time-bar for such applications are less likely to arise.

Section 11(3)(c) does not apply in relation to the enforcement of "market charges" (as defined by CA 1989, s. 173): see s. 175 of that Act (as qualified by the Financial Markets and Insolvency Regulations 1991 (SI 1991/880)). It is also disapplied in relation to payment and securities settlement systems by the Finality Regulations, reg. 19. (See the introductory notes at pp. 2–3 above.)

Section 11(3)(d) is similar to s. 130(2), which applies in a winding up, and decisions under that section may give guidance as to how the discretion under s. 11(3)(d) will be exercised.

Note that the reference to "any hire-purchase agreement" in para. (c) includes also conditional sale agreements, chattel leasing agreements and retention of title agreements: see s. 10(4). Section 11(3)(c) extends to goods which are the subject of a hire-purchase or similar agreement even where the agreement has been terminated before the presentation of the petition for an administration order, provided that the goods remain in the company's possession: *Re David Meek Plant Ltd; Re David Meek Access Ltd* [1993] B.C.C. 175. The landmark decision of the Court of Appeal in *Re Atlantic Computer Systems plc* [1992] Ch. 505; [1990] B.C.C. 859 contains a number of important rulings on the jurisdiction conferred by s. 11, and guidance on the principles governing the exercise of the court's discretion under the section. The company's business was leasing computers, a substantial number of which it held on hire-purchase or long lease from banks and other financial institutions (referred to in the judgment as "the funders"). Two funders applied to the court contending that the administrators, having received payments from the sub-lessees, were obliged to pay the rentals due under the head leases. Alternatively, the funders sought leave under s. 11 to repossess the computer equipment. The trial judge, applying an analogy from winding-up law, held that where leased property was used for the purposes of an administration, the rent or hire charges due to the lessor should rank as an expense of the administration and as such be payable in priority to the company's other creditors; but the Court of Appeal considered that a more appropriate analogy was with administrative receivership, where such charges would not have the same priority. The court expressed the view that, in any case, the discretionary jurisdiction conferred by s. 11 should be exercised on the broadest basis and should not be allowed to become fettered by rigid rules of automatic application. However, it went on to hold that the computers remained "goods in the company's possession", notwithstanding the sub-leases, so that the discretionary powers conferred by s. 11(3)(c) could be invoked; that lessors and other owners of property in the position of the funders should not be compelled to leave it in the company's hands against their will but should ordinarily be allowed to repossess it; and that this should normally be a matter where the administrator would be expected to give his consent, thus obviating the need to make application to the court for leave.

The judgment concludes with a statement giving guidance on the principles to be applied on applications for the grant of leave under s. 11. These principles, which are set out at length (see [1992] Ch. 505 at pp. 542–544; [1990] B.C.C. 859 at pp. 879–882), also serve as guidelines to an administrator in determining whether to grant consent, and may be summarised as follows:

(1) The person seeking leave has always to make out a case.

(2) If granting leave to an owner of land or goods to exercise his proprietary rights as lessor and repossess his land or goods is unlikely to impede the achievement of the purpose of the administration, leave should normally be given.

(3) In other cases where a lessor seeks possession, the court has to carry out a balancing exercise, weighing the legitimate interests of the lessor against those of the company's other creditors.

(4) In carrying out the balancing exercise, great importance is normally to be given to the lessor's proprietary interests: an administration for the benefit of unsecured creditors should not be conducted at the expense of those who have proprietary rights.

(5) It will normally be a sufficient ground for the grant of leave that significant loss would be caused to the lessor by a refusal. However if substantially greater loss would be caused to others by the grant of leave, that may outweigh the loss to the lessor caused by a refusal.

(6)–(8) These paragraphs list the various factors to which the court will have regard in assessing the respective losses under heading (5). These include: the financial position of the company, its ability to pay the interest, rentals or other charges (both arrears and continuing charges), the administrator's proposals and the end result sought to be achieved by the administration, the period for which the administration has already been in force and that for which it is expected to continue, the prospects of success of the administration, the likely loss to the applicant if leave is refused, and the conduct of the parties.

(9) The above considerations may be relevant not only to the decision whether or not to grant leave, but also to a decision to impose terms if leave is granted.

(10) The court may, in effect, impose conditions if leave is refused (for instance, by giving directions to the administrator), in which case the above considerations will also be applicable.

(11) A broadly similar approach will apply in many applications for leave to enforce a security.

(12) The court will not, on a leave application, seek to adjudicate upon a dispute over the existence, validity or nature of a security unless the issue raises a short point of law which it is convenient to determine without further ado.

Section 12 *Insolvency Act 1986*

See also the judgment of Peter Gibson J. in *Re Meesan Investments Ltd* (1988) 4 B.C.C. 788, where it was observed that the fact that enforcement of the security independently of the administration would increase costs was a factor that the court might take into account in refusing leave.

Although the statement above was directed primarily to the question of giving leave to enforce a security under s. 11(3)(c), parts of it may give some guidance to the court in exercising its jurisdiction to grant leave to commence proceedings under para. (d): see *Re Polly Peck International plc (in administration) (No. 4)* [1997] 2 B.C.L.C. 630.

In *Euro Commercial Leasing Ltd v Cartwright & Lewis* [1995] B.C.C. 830 it was accepted on all sides that the remedy for a breach of s. 11(3)(c) should be a claim in damages. However, in the case itself, which concerned a solicitors' lien, no damage had resulted from the breach.

Other cases concerning the grant of leave under s. 11 include *Re Carter Commercial Developments Ltd* [2002] B.C.C. 803 (enforcement of solicitors' lien), *Re City Logistics Ltd* [2002] 2 B.C.L.C. 103 (costs) and *London Flight Centre (Stanstead) Ltd v Osprey Aviation Ltd* [2002] B.P.I.R. 1115.

S. 11(4)
An administrative receiver automatically vacates office when an order is made (s. 11(1)(b)), and any other receiver may be required by the administrator to do so (s. 11(2)). This subsection seeks to secure the receiver's right to remuneration, and any entitlement to an indemnity that he may have, ahead of the claims of the security-holder who appointed him. However, (like every other creditor) he cannot receive actual payment of this claim or take steps to enforce it except with the administrator's consent or the court's leave under s. 11(3).

S. 11(5)
Under the sections mentioned, it is the duty of a receiver who is appointed to enforce a floating charge to pay the company's preferential debts "out of the assets coming into his hands". This subsection makes it clear that the assets must be surrendered to the administrator by the receiver when he vacates office, without regard to this obligation, and also that he is thereafter discharged from that duty.

On "preferential debts", see the notes to ss. 386 and 387; and see also the discussion at s. 11(2) above.

Note that there is no provision in the original Pt II giving priority to preferential debts in a company administration, unless either a winding up follows immediately on the discharge of the administration order (s. 387(3)(a)) or the administration coincides with a voluntary arrangement (s. 387(2)(a)). However in appropriate circumstances the court may make an order which reflects the rights which such creditors would have in a winding up – or even puts them in a better position: see *Re WBSL Realisations 1992 Ltd* [1995] B.C.C. 1,118 and the note to s. 18(2).

12 Notification of order

12(1) *[Information in invoices etc.]* *Every invoice, order for goods or business letter which, at a time when an administration order is in force in relation to a company, is issued by or on behalf of the company or the administrator, being a document on or in which the company's name appears, shall also contain the administrator's name and a statement that the affairs, business and property of the company are being managed by the administrator.*

12(2) *[Penalty on default]* *If default is made in complying with this section, the company and any of the following persons who without reasonable excuse authorises or permits the default, namely, the administrator and any officer of the company, is liable to a fine.*

S. 12(1)
This is a parallel provision to those requiring notification of the appointment of a receiver (s. 39, 64) and notification that a company is in liquidation (s. 188).

S. 12(2)
The policy reasons for making the company itself liable for this offence are not obvious. Note that the *company* is strictly liable, while any of the other persons named is liable only if he "without reasonable excuse authorises or permits the default". This language may be contrasted with that of ss. 39, 64 and 188: "who knowingly and wilfully authorises or permits the default".

On penalties, see s. 430 and Sch. 10.

13 Appointment of administrator

13(1) *[Appointment]* The administrator of a company shall be appointed either by the administration order or by an order under the next subsection.

13(2) *[Court may fill vacancy]* If a vacancy occurs by death, resignation or otherwise in the office of the administrator, the court may by order fill the vacancy.

13(3) *[Application for s. 13(2) order]* An application for an order under subsection (2) may be made–

(a) by any continuing administrator of the company; or

(b) where there is no such administrator, by a creditors' committee established under section 26 below; or

(c) where there is no such administrator and no such committee, by the company or the directors or by any creditor or creditors of the company.

GENERAL NOTE

These provisions deal with the appointment of an administrator and with vacancies in the office of administrator.
   It is apparent from s. 13(3)(a) and s. 231 that two or more persons may be appointed joint administrators.
   There is no power under this or any other provision for the court to appoint an interim administrator: see the note to s. 9(4).
   An administrator must be an insolvency practitioner and qualified to act in relation to the particular company: see s. 230(1).

S. 13(3)
On "the company" and "the directors", see the note to s. 124(1).

14 General powers

14(1) *[Powers of administrator]* The administrator of a company–

(a) may do all such things as may be necessary for the management of the affairs, business and property of the company, and

(b) without prejudice to the generality of paragraph (a), has the powers specified in Schedule 1 to this Act;

and in the application of that Schedule to the administrator of a company the words "he" and "him" refer to the administrator.

14(2) *[Extra powers]* The administrator also has power–

(a) to remove any director of the company and to appoint any person to be a director of it, whether to fill a vacancy or otherwise, and

(b) to call any meeting of the members or creditors of the company.

14(3) *[Application for directions]* The administrator may apply to the court for directions in relation to any particular matter arising in connection with the carrying out of his functions.

14(4) *[Conflict with other powers]* Any power conferred on the company or its officers, whether by this Act or the Companies Act or by the memorandum or articles of association, which could be exercised in such a way as to interfere with the exercise by the administrator of his powers is not exercisable except with the consent of the administrator, which may be given either generally or in relation to particular cases.

14(5) *[Administrator agent]* In exercising his powers the administrator is deemed to act as the company's agent.

Section 14   Insolvency Act 1986

14(6) *[Third party]* *A person dealing with the administrator in good faith and for value is not concerned to inquire whether the administrator is acting within his powers.*

S. 14(1)
The powers of an administrator are stated in the broadest terms in para. (a), and extend to anything which was within the powers of the directors before the administration order was made – *e.g.* appointing a trustee to an employees' pension scheme (*Denny v Yeldon* [1995] 1 B.C.L.C. 560 and *Polly Peck International plc v Henry* [1999] 1 B.C.L.C. 407). In addition, some specific powers, common to both administrators and administrative receivers, are set out in more detail in Sch. 1. These powers are not restricted to the management of the company's business (as is normally the case with the board of directors). This is indicated by the use of the word "affairs" and appears also from some of the particular matters mentioned in this section and the schedule, *e.g.* the power to remove directors (s. 14(2)).

Although the powers of an administrator are similar in many respects to those of an administrative receiver, there are also important differences, and the analogy cannot be pressed too far. An administrator is appointed to manage the affairs of the company; an administrative receiver's role is to realise the company's assets primarily for the benefit of a particular creditor: *Astor Chemical Ltd v Synthetic Technology Ltd* [1990] B.C.C. 97 at pp. 105–106. A receiver may decline to perform certain contracts which an administrator has no power to disown (*ibid*). And, unlike a liquidator, an administrator has no statutory power of disclaimer (*Re P & C and R & T (Stockport) Ltd* [1991] B.C.C. 98 at p. 104).

The powers of an administrator do not extend to acts which the company itself is not competent to perform: *Re Home Treat Ltd* [1991] B.C.C. 165. In this case, the company's objects as stated in its memorandum did not extend to the running of a nursing home (the company's actual business which the administrators wished to continue pending a sale). The court managed to circumvent this difficulty by a somewhat indulgent ruling that there had been a *de facto* alteration of the objects clause by an informal resolution of the shareholders at an earlier stage.

For the administrator's special power to deal with charged property, see s. 15.

S. 14(2)
The power given to an administrator to appoint and remove directors has no parallel elsewhere in company law, apart of course from the statutory power conferred upon the company in general meeting. (During the currency of an administration order, these powers of the general meeting will not be exercisable without the consent of the administrator: see s. 14(4).)

If the removal of a director amounts to a breach of his service contract, the company will be liable in damages, even though the removal was in exercise of a statutory power: *Southern Foundries (1926) Ltd v Shirlaw* [1940] A.C. 701; *Shindler v Northern Raincoat Co. Ltd* [1960] 1 W.L.R. 1038.

Section 14(2) does not empower the administrator to dispense with the board of directors entirely: CA 1985, s. 282 (which prescribes a minimum of two directors for every public company, and one for a private company) will still apply to a company that is subject to an administration order. See further the note to s. 14(4), below.

S. 14(3)
A similar provision applies to the supervisor of a voluntary scheme (s. 7(4)) and the liquidator in a winding up by the court (s. 168(3)).

The powers of an administrator under ss. 14(1)(a) and 17(2) to "manage the affairs, business and property of the company" are wide enough to make it unnecessary in many cases for an administrator to seek directions from the court, so that he may, *e.g.* sell a substantial asset in a proper case even before the creditors' meeting has been held: see, however, the note to s. 17(2). For examples of applications for directions under s. 14(3), see *Re British & Commonwealth Holdings plc (No. 3)* [1992] 1 W.L.R. 672; [1992] B.C.C. 58 and *Re Maxwell Communications Corporation plc (No. 3)* [1993] 1 W.L.R. 1402; [1993] B.C.C. 369 – cases which contain important rulings on the effectiveness of debt subordination arrangements created (respectively) by trust deed and by contract; and *Re Lewis's of Leicester Ltd* [1995] B.C.C. 514, where the court was asked to rule whether moneys which had been paid to the company by concession-holders and held in segregated accounts were the subject of a trust or, alternatively, whether the arrangements were open to challenge as preferences or transactions at an undervalue. The court will not normally interfere with a commercial decision of an administrator, and will do so only if what is proposed is wrong in law or is conspicuously unfair to a particular creditor or person dealing with the company: *Re CE King Ltd* [2000] 2 B.C.L.C. 297.

S. 14(4)
On the appointment of an administrator, the directors remain in office, and both the board of directors and the shareholders in general meeting retain their roles as organs of the company under the articles of association and the Companies Act – although their powers will, of course, be severely restricted by the provisions of this section. The

directors' statutory and common-law duties will continue to apply to them – including the duty to hold annual meetings, prepare accounts and make returns to the registrar.

S. 14(5)

This provision in part echoes the terms on which a receiver is customarily appointed to enforce a debenture holder's security – terms which are now given statutory expression in s. 44(1) of this Act. However, the subsection has only a limited effect: it does not make the administrator the company's agent in any full sense, nor even say (as does s. 44(1)) that he shall be deemed to *be* the agent of the company; only deemed to be *acting* as its agent in exercising his powers, although the difference in wording may not be material. He is not, like a normal agent, subject to control and direction by the company as his principal (see s. 14(4)); his actual authority is virtually unlimited (see s. 14(1)), and his ostensible authority completely so (see s. 14(6)).

The main object of this provision is to try to ensure that the administrator, at least in the normal case, incurs no personal liability on any contract or other obligation that he may enter into on the company's behalf. (Contrast the position of an administrative receiver (s. 44(1)).

Like an agent, the administrator will also owe the usual fiduciary duties to the company, and will be entitled to be indemnified out of its assets for obligations that he incurs.

S. 14(6)

This provision is probably inserted out of caution only, since such a third party would almost certainly be protected by the ordinary rules of agency.

15 Power to deal with charged property, etc.

15(1) *[Power of disposal etc.]* The administrator of a company may dispose of or otherwise exercise his powers in relation to any property of the company which is subject to a security to which this subsection applies as if the property were not subject to the security.

15(2) *[Court orders, on application by administrator]* Where, on an application by the administrator, the court is satisfied that the disposal (with or without other assets) of–

(a) any property of the company subject to a security to which this subsection applies, or

(b) any goods in the possession of the company under a hire-purchase agreement,

would be likely to promote the purpose or one or more of the purposes specified in the administration order, the court may by order authorise the administrator to dispose of the property as if it were not subject to the security or to dispose of the goods as if all rights of the owner under the hire-purchase agreement were vested in the company.

15(3) *[Application of s. 15(1), (2)]* Subsection (1) applies to any security which, as created, was a floating charge; and subsection (2) applies to any other security.

15(4) *[Effect of security where property disposed of]* Where property is disposed of under subsection (1), the holder of the security has the same priority in respect of any property of the company directly or indirectly representing the property disposed of as he would have had in respect of the property subject to the security.

15(5) *[Conditions for s. 15(2) order]* It shall be a condition of an order under subsection (2) that–

(a) the net proceeds of the disposal, and

(b) where those proceeds are less than such amount as may be determined by the court to be the net amount which would be realised on a sale of the property or goods in the open market by a willing vendor, such sums as may be required to make good the deficiency,

shall be applied towards discharging the sums secured by the security or payable under the hire-purchase agreement.

15(6) *[Where s. 15(5) condition re two or more securities]* Where a condition imposed in pursuance of subsection (5) relates to two or more securities, that condition requires the net proceeds of the disposal and, where paragraph (b) of that subsection applies, the sums mentioned in that paragraph to be applied towards discharging the sums secured by those securities in the order of their priorities.

Section 15 Insolvency Act 1986

15(7) *[Copy of s. 15(2) order to registrar] An office copy of an order under subsection (2) shall, within 14 days after the making of the order, be sent by the administrator to the registrar of companies.*

15(8) *[Non-compliance with s. 15(7)] If the administrator without reasonable excuse fails to comply with subsection (7), he is liable to a fine and, for continued contravention, to a daily default fine.*

15(9) *[Interpretation] References in this section to hire-purchase agreements include conditional sale agreements, chattel leasing agreements and retention of title agreements.*

GENERAL NOTE

This section gives to the administrator unique powers to override the rights of the holder of a security over the company's property or the owner of property held by the company under a hire-purchase or similar agreement, and to dispose of the property in question as if it were owned by the company itself unencumbered. This he may do without the consent of the chargee or owner of the property, but the authorisation of the court will be needed unless the security is (or was originally) a floating charge. The section includes provisions designed to ensure that rights roughly analogous to those previously enjoyed by the charge-holder or owner are preserved.

The power conferred by this section will be of particular value when an administrator wishes to dispose of the business of the company, or some part of it, as a going concern, and a security-holder or property-owner is not willing to co-operate. A similar power is given to an administrative receiver by s. 43.

Some guidance as to the operation of the section is given by the judgment in *Re A R V Aviation Ltd* (1988) 4 B.C.C. 708, where the holder of a charge over land owned by the company opposed the administrators' application to be authorised to dispose of it. The charge-holder contended, *inter alia*, that the administrators were basing their application on an over-optimistic valuation of the land in question. The court ruled that a *bona fide* dispute as to value would clearly call into operation the discretion of the court under s. 15(2), and stated that in principle it was desirable for the court to have proper valuation evidence before being asked to exercise that jurisdiction. It also ruled: (i) that "the sums secured by the security" in s. 15(5) covered interest and (subject to the court's overriding discretion) the charge-holder's costs, as well as the principal sum secured; and (ii) that it was not necessary at the time of making an order for disposal under s. 15(2) to assess the amount of the deficiency to which the secured creditor might be entitled under s. 15(5): this could be determined at a later hearing.

Note that nothing in this section or s. 16 is to be taken as prejudicing the right of a creditor or member to apply to the court for relief under s. 27: see s. 27(5).

Section 15(1) and (2) do not apply in relation to the enforcement of "market charges" (as defined by CA 1989, s. 173): see s. 175 of that Act (as qualified by the Financial Markets and Insolvency Regulations 1991 (SI 1991/880)). It is also disapplied in relation to payment and securities settlement systems by the Finality Regulations, reg. 19. (See the introductory notes at pp. 2–3 above.)

S. 15(1), (3), (4)

These subsections, taken together, deal with the case where property of the company is subject to a floating charge. The administrator is empowered to dispose of or deal with the property without the consent of the chargee and without seeking a court order. This is so even though the charge may have crystallised on or before the making of the administration order (s. 15(3), and see the note to s. 11(2)); but where the same obligation is secured by both a fixed and a floating charge, s. 15(2) will apply to such assets as are covered by the fixed charge.

The meaning of s. 15(4) is obscure. It seems to be intended to ensure that any dealing by the administrator with the property of the company will not prejudice the chargee's security rights. However, instead of providing that the *security* shall extend to the price or other property acquired by the company in substitution for the asset disposed of, it speaks merely of "priority". This could give rise to many difficult questions. For example, will the charge-holder be entitled to claim security over such substituted property if the administration is brought to a successful conclusion and the order discharged? Suppose that the company trades its way back into a sound financial position, though still with a modest overdraft, and control is handed back to the directors: what security will the bank have?

It is also far from clear whether the "priority" referred to means priority in the ranking of one charge *vis-à-vis* another, or priority in the order that the company's various debts are paid, or priority in some other sense. The uncertainty as to the position of those creditors whose debts would have been entitled to preferential payment in a receivership has been discussed elsewhere (see the note to s. 11(2)).

S. 15(2), (5), (6)

Property which is subject to a fixed charge (excluding a charge which was originally a floating charge but has since become fixed: see s. 15(3)) may be disposed of by the administrator under these subsections without the consent of the charge-holder, but only (1) with the authorisation of the court and (2) on terms that the whole of the net proceeds of the sale (or the open market value of the property if it is sold for less) is applied in discharge of the amount secured – not necessarily, of course, the whole of the company's indebtedness to the particular creditor. These provisions extend also to goods in the possession of the company under a hire-purchase agreement (or a conditional sale agreement, chattel leasing agreement or retention of title agreement: see s. 15(9)): the administrator may sell the goods without the owner's consent, but must apply the realised amount (or open market value) towards discharging the sums payable to the owner under the agreement.

The phrase "payable under the agreement" (s. 15(5)) may cause some difficulty, since not all of the agreements listed in s. 15(9) will contain an express provision making the company accountable to the owner for the value of the property or the proceeds of sale in the event of a (possibly wrongful) sale to a third party. If, for instance, in regard to a chattel leasing agreement, the administrator sells the chattel unencumbered to a third party under s. 15(2) at a time when only one month's rental is outstanding, it would appear to be only the latter sum, and not the full value of the lessor's interest in the property, that must be accounted for under s. 15(5). If this is so, the lessor may have only an unsecured claim for money had and received against the company in respect of the balance of the proceeds of sale, or a right to seek relief under s. 27. No claim in tort (*e.g.* for wrongful interference with goods) would appear to lie against either the administrator or the company for action taken under s. 15(2); and it must be a matter of doubt whether the court can make an order subject to conditions other than that specified in s. 15(5).

If more is realised on the sale than is needed to discharge the sums in question, the balance will go into the general company funds held by the administrator (subject to what is said above). If less, the shortfall will remain due to the chargee or owner as an unsecured debt, unless the sale has been at below the market value and s. 15(5)(b) applies.

The administrator must satisfy the court as to the need for the sale, in the terms of s. 15(2); and the court is also charged by s. 15(5)(b) with the task of settling the open market value of the property, where that provision applies.

If the administrator and the chargee or owner of the property are willing to collaborate, of course, the property may be disposed of much more simply and cheaply under s. 11(3)(c).

In *Re Consumer & Industrial Press Ltd (No. 2)* (1988) 4 B.C.C. 72 it was held that the court would not, except in "quite exceptional circumstances", authorise an administrator under s. 15(2) to dispose of assets before the administrator's proposals had been considered by a creditors' meeting. However, it is now well established that in cases of urgency an administrator may be justified in proceeding with such a sale – even a sale of the company's entire undertaking – without waiting for a creditors' meeting, and that he may do so without seeking the leave of the court: see the note to s. 17(2), below. In any event, in an appropriate case, he could enter into an agreement with an intended purchaser conditionally upon the approval of the creditors or the leave of the court.

The administrators in *Re Newman Shopfitters (Cleveland) Ltd* [1991] B.C.L.C. 407 sought the court's authority to retain the proceeds of the sale of mortgaged property in a special bank account until they had reached a decision whether to challenge the validity of the mortgage. However the court held that it had no such power under s. 15. If, on the other hand, proceedings to challenge the mortgage had been commenced, appropriate interim relief could have been sought in that action.

S. 15(6)
This deals with the application of s. 15(5) to the case where an item of property is subject to more than one charge: the normal priorities are preserved.

S. 15(7), (8)
The purpose of these provisions is, no doubt, to ensure that the register of charges kept by the registrar under CA 1985, s. 395 is kept up to date, for the benefit of people searching. However, the subsections affect all forms of security, and not merely registrable charges, and extend to hire-purchase agreements, etc., which are not charges at all.

Where charges are recorded in a register other than the Companies Registry (*e.g.* land, ships), it will no doubt be necessary to file a copy of the order in that register also in order to confirm that the transferee will take an unencumbered title.

S. 15(9)
See the note to s. 10(4).

16 Operation of s. 15 in Scotland

16(1) [*Administrator's duty*] *Where property is disposed of under section 15 in its application to Scotland, the administrator shall grant to the disponee an appropriate document of transfer or conveyance of the property, and–*

(a) *that document, or*

(b) *where any recording, intimation or registration of the document is a legal requirement for completion of title to the property, that recording, intimation or registration,*

Section 17   Insolvency Act 1986

has the effect of disencumbering the property of or, as the case may be, freeing the property from the security.

16(2)   [Disposal of goods on hire-purchase etc.] *Where goods in the possession of the company under a hire-purchase agreement, conditional sale agreement, chattel leasing agreement or retention of title agreement are disposed of under section 15 in its application to Scotland, the disposal has the effect of extinguishing, as against the disponee, all rights of the owner of the goods under the agreement.*

GENERAL NOTE

This section provides for the disponee who takes property under s. 15 to have such evidence as may be required under Scots law to effect or confirm the disencumbering of the property and to extinguish any claim of the previous owner of goods held under hire-purchase and similar agreements.

17   General duties

17(1)   [Control of company property] *The administrator of a company shall, on his appointment, take into his custody or under his control all the property to which the company is or appears to be entitled.*

17(2)   [Management of affairs etc.] *The administrator shall manage the affairs, business and property of the company–*

(a)   *at any time before proposals have been approved (with or without modifications) under section 24 below, in accordance with any directions given by the court, and*

(b)   *at any time after proposals have been so approved, in accordance with those proposals as from time to time revised, whether by him or a predecessor of his.*

17(3)   [Summoning of creditors' meeting] *The administrator shall summon a meeting of the company's creditors if–*

(a)   *he is requested, in accordance with the rules, to do so by one-tenth, in value, of the company's creditors, or*

(b)   *he is directed to do so by the court.*

GENERAL NOTE

The position of an administrator is in many ways broadly comparable with that of an administrative receiver, as is confirmed by the fact that by Sch. 1 they are given identical statutory powers; but there is an important difference in their roles. A receiver, representing a single secured creditor, is entitled to give priority to the interests of that creditor. An administrator, in contrast, like a liquidator, has no particular interest to which he should give priority. In the context of a sale of company property, a receiver acting in good faith may effect an immediate sale whether or not that is calculated to realise the best price, though he must take reasonable care to obtain a proper price for the property at the moment he chooses to sell it. However an administrator is under a duty to take reasonable care to obtain the best price that the circumstances (as he reasonably perceives them to be) permit, and this means that he must take reasonable care in choosing the time at which to sell the property. The conduct of an administrator is to be judged by the standards of a professional insolvency practitioner of ordinary skill. (See *Re Charnley Davies Ltd* [1990] B.C.C. 605 at p. 618.)

S. 17(1)

This will include property that is encumbered and property owned by another person but in the possession of the company under a hire-purchase or similar agreement: see s. 11 and 15. An administrative receiver will have vacated office under s. 11(1)(b). Exceptionally, a receiver of *part* of the company's property may be allowed by the administrator to remain in office, but he may not deal with the property in question without the consent of the administrator or the leave of the court (s. 11(2), (3)(d)).

S. 17(2)

The administrator's role is to seek to secure the financial rehabilitation of the company or one of the other purposes specified in s. 8(3); but the Act does not leave him entirely free to set about his task at once, or to do so on his own initiative. He must call for a statement of affairs (s. 22), formulate a set of proposals to define (and, by implication, to limit) the strategy he is to adopt (s. 23), and put these proposals before a specially summoned creditors' meeting for approval. This process may take a period of three months or so; hence the need to give him interim powers to act under s. 17(2)(a), subject to any directions that he may be given by the court.

These directions may be sought by the administrator himself or may be part of the relief granted on the application of a creditor or member under s. 27.

In an unreported hearing involving the company Charnley Davies Ltd in January 1987, Vinelott J. confirmed advice given to its administrator by counsel that this section is wide enough to empower an administrator to sell the entire undertaking of the company in advance of the creditors' meeting if he considers that such a course is in the best interests of the company and its creditors, and that the administrator does not need the sanction of the court to do so. He ruled that the words "any directions" in s. 17(2)(a) mean "the directions, if any". (See *Re Charnley Davies Ltd* [1990] B.C.C. 605 at pp. 610–611.) In *Re N S Distribution Ltd* [1990] B.C.L.C. 169 Harman J. took a similar view, in relation to the sale of a single asset. However these rulings, which might have encouraged administrators to act on their own initiative in such a situation, were tempered by the strongly expressed opinion of Peter Gibson J. in *Re Consumer & Industrial Press Ltd (No. 2)* (1988) 4 B.C.C. 72 that to take such action without giving the creditors the opportunity to consider the administrator's proposals would frustrate the purposes of the Act. In consequence, it was thought prudent for administrators to seek the leave of the court in cases of doubt. But in more recent cases, culminating with the fully-reasoned judgment of Neuberger J. in *Re T & D Industries plc* [2000] 1 W.L.R. 646; [2000] B.C.C. 956, the view originally put by Vinelott J. has been confirmed, and administrators should now have cause to feel less inhibited by Peter Gibson J.'s qualms, and feel free to back their own judgment in cases of urgency. An alternative course, adverted to by Neuberger J. and acceded to by Rattee J. in *Re Harris Bus Co. Ltd* [2000] B.C.C. 1,151, is for the administrator to ask the court to direct the summoning of a meeting of the creditors at short notice under s. 17(3) in order to seek their approval.

Paragraph (b) makes it plain that, after the creditors' meeting, the administrator's freedom to act is limited by the terms of the "proposals" approved by the creditors under ss. 24 or 25. However, in exceptional circumstances (*e.g.* where the delay involved in summoning a creditors' meeting to consider a revised scheme could cause substantial loss) the court has a residual jurisdiction under s. 14(3) to authorise an administrator to depart from an approved scheme: *Re Smallman Construction Ltd* (1988) 4 B.C.C. 784.

S. 17(3)

This provision corresponds to s. 168(2), which relates to a liquidator in a compulsory winding up. It is not necessary for the Act to provide in similar terms for the requisitioning of a shareholders' meeting, since the members' rights to do so under CA 1985, ss. 368 and 370(3) will not be affected by an administration order.

For the rules relating to this section, see IR 1986, rr. 2.21ff.

18 Discharge or variation of administration order

18(1) *[Application to court by administrator]* The administrator of a company may at any time apply to the court for the administration order to be discharged, or to be varied so as to specify an additional purpose.

18(2) *[Duty to make application]* The administrator shall make an application under this section if–

(a) it appears to him that the purpose or each of the purposes specified in the order either has been achieved or is incapable of achievement, or

(b) he is required to do so by a meeting of the company's creditors summoned for the purpose in accordance with the rules.

18(3) *[Court order]* On the hearing of an application under this section, the court may by order discharge or vary the administration order and make such consequential provision as it thinks fit, or adjourn the hearing conditionally or unconditionally, or make an interim order or any other order it thinks fit.

18(4) *[Copy of order to registrar]* Where the administration order is discharged or varied the administrator shall, within 14 days after the making of the order effecting the discharge or variation, send an office copy of that order to the registrar of companies.

18(5) *[Non-compliance with s. 18(4)]* If the administrator without reasonable excuse fails to comply with subsection (4), he is liable to a fine and, for continued contravention, to a daily default fine.

S. 18(1), (2)

Where the purpose of an administration order is the rehabilitation of the company, an administrator will seek to have an order discharged in two contrasting situations – triumph and disaster. If the company's survival has been ensured, his discharge will enable control of the company's affairs to be restored to its directors and shareholders. If the administrator (or a meeting of the creditors) decides that the purpose is unobtainable, the administration order may be discharged and a winding-up order may then be made (very likely on the administrator's own application) if this is appropriate.

The court has no jurisdiction to make a winding-up order otherwise than on a petition lodged under s. 124 – although Sch. B1, para. 13(1)(e) now makes an exception. Accordingly, it is not possible for a winding-up order to be made on an application for the discharge of an administration order under the present section: *Re Brooke Marine Ltd* [1988] BCLC 546.

This Part of the Act (in contrast with the new Pt II) does not make provision for a company to go into voluntary liquidation following the discharge of an administration order – a choice which may commend itself on the grounds of cost – although it is no doubt within the powers of the court to sanction such a course. Particular difficulties which have to be overcome if this method is chosen include (i) s. 11(3)(a), which forbids the passing of the necessary winding-up resolution while an administration order is in force and (ii) the fact that some creditors entitled to preferential payment may be disadvantaged because a different "relevant date" will apply: see s. 387(3)(a), (c). In practice, the first of these difficulties is overcome by making the order for discharge conditional on the passing of the winding-up resolution (or resolutions), or alternatively by directing that the orders for discharge shall not be drawn up until copies of the resolutions have been lodged in the court office: see *Re Powerstore (Trading) Ltd* [1998] B.C.C. 305 at p 307. An alternative procedure, which was adopted in *Powerstore* and also in *Re Mark One (Oxford Street) plc* [1998] B.C.C. 984, was for the company to pass a conditional resolution for winding up which remained inchoate until the court had made an order discharging the administration order. But this course is not to be recommended, since in *Re Norditrak (UK) Ltd* [2000] 1 W.L.R. 343; [2000] B.C.C. 441 Arden J. ruled that, in the light of established authority, it was not competent for a company to pass such a conditional resolution. The second difficulty was, until the *Powerstore* case, commonly met by an order under s. 18(3), directing the liquidator in the future liquidation to make payments to the creditors in question as if they were preferential creditors. However, in that case Lightman J. ruled that s. 18(3) gave the court no such power. In *Re Philip Alexander Securities and Futures Ltd* [1998] B.C.C. 819, confronted by the ruling in *Powerstore*, Neuberger J. got around the problem by proposing that if the non-preferential creditors wished to have the benefit of a creditors' voluntary liquidation as opposed to a compulsory liquidation, they would have to accept a condition that the preferential creditors would receive the same amount as if the administration were followed by a compulsory liquidation. Happily the inconvenient ruling in *Powerstore* has been superseded by the decision of Jacob J. in *Re Mark One (Oxford Street) plc* [1998] B.C.C. 984. Jacob J., after commenting that Lightman J.'s decision had "caused something of a stir in the world of insolvency", held that the court has power (derived from ss. 14(3), 18(3) and its own inherent power to control an administrator as an officer of the court) to order an administrator to pay the preferential creditors on the same basis as if the winding up was a compulsory winding up or, alternatively, to set up a trust for the benefit of such creditors which will be binding on a future liquidator. He agreed with Lightman J., however, that these powers do not extend to giving any directions to such a liquidator. *Re Mark One (Oxford Street) Ltd* has since been approved and followed in *Re Wolsey Theatre Co. Ltd* [2001] B.C.C. 486 and *Re UCT (UK) Ltd* [2001] Ch. 436; [2001] B.C.C. 734. See also *Re Oakhouse Property Holdings Ltd* [2003] B.P.I.R. 469.

In *Re Polly Peck International plc* (unreported, February 8, 1999, noted by Brier, (1999) 15 *Insolvency Law and Practice* 44) the administrators had largely completed a realisation of the company's assets and a scheme of arrangement had been approved which allowed the scheme supervisors to make distributions to creditors. Although it might have been thought appropriate for the administration to give way to a winding up, the court ordered that the company should continue under administration: it was impracticable to put the company into voluntary liquidation because the shareholders were numerous and widely scattered, and if a compulsory winding-up order were made all future realisations would have to be paid into the Insolvency Services Account where they would earn a poor rate of interest. This justified the continuation of the administration.

If the purpose of an administration order is simply the approval of a voluntary arrangement under Pt. I of the Act (see s. 8(3)(b)), the functions of the administrator will be completed and he will be entitled to a discharge as soon as the proposal for the arrangement has been approved. It is the supervisor, and not the administrator, who will administer the voluntary arrangement (though these may well be the same person). Similar considerations will apply where an administration order is made in conjunction with a statutory scheme of compromise or arrangement under CA 1985, ss. 425–427 (see s. 8(3)(c)).

The fourth of the "purposes" specified in s. 8(3) is "a more advantageous realisation of the company's assets than would be effected on a winding up". When the administrator has achieved this object, it would seem that a liquidation is bound to follow if at the end of the exercise the company is insolvent. However, if there is a surplus, there is no reason why control should not be handed back to the company's own organs, so that they may make their own decision about its future.

An administrator who intends to apply for an administration order to be discharged before he has sent a statement of his proposals to the company's creditors under s. 23(1) must comply with IR 1986, r. 2.16(2). It appears from *Re Consumer & Industrial Press Ltd (No. 2)* (1988) 4 B.C.C. 72 that the court will be reluctant to grant a discharge before the creditors have had an opportunity to consider the proposals. See, however, *Re Charnley Davies Business Services Ltd* (1987) 3 B.C.C. 408, and the note to s. 23(1).

The court is also empowered under this section to vary the original order by specifying an additional purpose (but not, apparently, a *substituted* purpose), from among those listed in s. 8(3).

In *Re St Ives Windings Ltd* (1987) 3 B.C.C. 634 an administrator who had achieved an advantageous realisation of assets applied under this section to have the administration order varied by specifying the approval of a voluntary arrangement as an additional purpose. It was then possible for the creditors to sanction proposals for the distribution of the proceeds in a way which was binding on a dissenting minority.

In *Re Sharps of Truro Ltd* [1990] B.C.C. 94 at p. 95 the view was expressed (*obiter*) that the only person who can apply to set aside an administration order is the administrator himself. While it may be true that the only person competent to apply to the court under the present section is the administrator, the Court of Appeal held in *Cornhill Insurance plc v Cornhill Finance Services Ltd* [1992] B.C.C. 818 that a creditor aggrieved by an administration order could apply to the court under IR 1986, r. 7.47 to have the order rescinded on the ground that it was an order that ought not to have been made.

On the discharge of an administration order, the administrator vacates office: s.19(2)(b).

S. 18(3)
Consequential directions may well be needed if the affairs of the company are to be handed back to its shareholders and directors, since the Act gives no detailed guidance on this. The position of some secured creditors may need to be redefined: see the note to s. 15(4).

S. 18(4)
Notice of the making of the administration order will have been sent to the registrar under s. 21(2).

S. 18(5)
On penalties, see s. 430 and Sch. 10.

19 Vacation of office

19(1) *[Removal or resignation]* The administrator of a company may at any time be removed from office by order of the court and may, in the prescribed circumstances, resign his office by giving notice of his resignation to the court.

19(2) *[Vacation of office etc.]* The administrator shall vacate office if–

(a) he ceases to be qualified to act as an insolvency practitioner in relation to the company, or

(b) the administration order is discharged.

19(3) *[Ceasing to be administrator]* Where at any time a person ceases to be administrator, the following subsections apply.

19(4) *[Remuneration and expenses]* His remuneration and any expenses properly incurred by him shall be charged on and paid out of any property of the company which is in his custody or under his control at that time in priority to any security to which section 15(1) then applies.

19(5) *[Debts or liabilities re contracts entered into]* Any sums payable in respect of debts or liabilities incurred, while he was administrator, under contracts entered into by him or a predecessor of his in the carrying out of his or the predecessor's functions shall be charged on and paid out of any such property as is mentioned in subsection (4) in priority to any charge arising under that subsection.

19(6) *[Debts or liabilities re contracts of employment adopted]* Any sums payable in respect of liabilities incurred, while he was administrator, under contracts of employment adopted by him or a predecessor of his in the carrying out of his or the predecessor's functions shall, to the extent that the liabilities are qualifying liabilities, be charged on and paid out of any such property as is mentioned in subsection (4) and enjoy the same priority as any sums to which subsection (5) applies.

Section 19   Insolvency Act 1986

For this purpose, the administrator is not to be taken to have adopted a contract of employment by reason of anything done or omitted to be done within 14 days after his appointment.

19(7) *[Interpretation of s. 19(6)] For the purposes of subsection (6), a liability under a contract of employment is a qualifying liability if–*

(a) *it is a liability to pay a sum by way of wages or salary or contribution to an occupational pension scheme, and*

(b) *it is in respect of services rendered wholly or partly after the adoption of the contract.*

19(8) *[Liability disregarded for s. 19(6)] There shall be disregarded for the purposes of subsection (6) so much of any qualifying liability as represents payment in respect of services rendered before the adoption of the contract.*

19(9) *[Interpretation of s. 19(7), (8)] For the purposes of subsections (7) and (8)–*

(a) *wages or salary payable in respect of a period of holiday or absence from work through sickness or other good cause are deemed to be wages or (as the case may be) salary in respect of services rendered in that period, and*

(b) *a sum payable in lieu of holiday is deemed to be wages or (as the case may be) salary in respect of services rendered in the period by reference to which the holiday entitlement arose.*

19(10) *[Interpretation of s. 19(9)(a)] In subsection (9)(a), the reference to wages or salary payable in respect of a period of holiday includes any sums which, if they had been paid, would have been treated for the purposes of the enactments relating to social security as earnings in respect of that period.*

GENERAL NOTE

This section was extensively amended by IA 1994, which received Royal Assent on March 25, 1994, (but not retrospectively so as to affect contracts of employment adopted by an administrator before March 15, 1994). The Act also affects the position of administrative receivers: see the notes to ss. 44 and 57, below.

The reform was enacted in order to allay doubts and fears following the decision of the Court of Appeal in *Powdrill v Watson; Re Paramount Airways Ltd (No. 3)* [1994] 2 All E.R. 513; [1994] B.C.C. 172 (which was later varied by the House of Lords on appeal: see *Powdrill v Watson* [1995] 2 A.C. 394; [1995] B.C.C. 319, discussed below). The effect of the Court of Appeal's interpretation of s. 19(5), as it was formerly worded, was to subordinate the administrator's claim to remuneration and the reimbursement of his expenses to a wide range of possible claims by employees and former employees of the company, as explained below. The Act of 1994 amends s. 19(3) and (5) and (by IA 1994, s. 1(1), (4), (6), (7)) inserts new s. 19(6)–(10).

In s. 19(3), the word "following" was substituted for the words "next two" by IA 1994, s. 1(1), (2), (7).

In s. 19(5), the words "or contracts of employment adopted", formerly appearing after the words "under contracts entered into" were omitted, and what was formerly the final paragraph of s. 19(5) was moved to become the second paragraph of s. 19(6), by IA 1994, ss. 1(1), (3), (7), 5 and Sch. 2.

The statutory reforms of 1994 were enacted before the appeal to the House of Lords in *Powdrill v Watson* had been heard and, despite powerful arguments by pressure groups, the amendments were not made retrospective (as noted above). It follows that contracts of employment adopted by an administrator before March 15, 1994 are governed by the unamended law, as interpreted by the House of Lords. This is also the case with administrative receiverships, since the House of Lords' ruling in *Powdrill v Watson* dealt also with an appeal in the *Leyland Daf* case (reported as *Talbot v Cadge*, also at [1995] 2 A.C. 395; [1995] B.C.C. 319): the former law applies to contracts of employment adopted by administrative receivers before March 15, 1994 (see the note to s. 44). Non-administrative receiverships were not included in the amending legislation of 1994 and accordingly the House of Lords' decision is applicable to all contracts of employment in such receiverships, whether adopted before or after that date (see the note to s. 37).

S. 19(1)

The circumstances in which an administrator may resign his office are prescribed by IR 1986, r. 2.53. Whether a resignation is effective as soon as notice is given to the court is not made clear by the rules. The usual understanding is that it will be so effective and that, once given, it cannot be unilaterally withdrawn (see *Glossop v Glossop* [1907] 2 Ch. 370). The present position may be contrasted with that applicable to a liquidator (s. 171(5)), where a resignation is not effective unless it has been accepted: see IR 1986, rr. 4.108–4.110.

The death of an administrator should also be notified to the court: see s. 20(1)(a), and IR 1986, r. 2.54.

S. 19(2)

An administrator will cease to be "qualified to act" as an insolvency practitioner "in relation to the company" if he fails to meet any of the criteria set out in s. 390.

On the discharge of an administration order, see s. 18.

S. 19(3)–(6)

These subsections rather oddly address the question of debts and expenses incurred by an administrator only in the context of the position when he ceases to hold office. However, in the *Paramount Airways* case (above), Dillon L.J. said ([1994] 2 All E.R. 513, at p. 522; [1994] B.C.C. 172, at p. 180):

> "Although strictly sums payable are, under s. 19(5), only payable when the administrator vacates office, it is well understood that administrators will, in the ordinary way, pay expenses of the administration including the salaries and other payments to employees as they arise during the continuance of the administration. There is no need to wait until the end, and it would be impossible as a practical matter to do that. What is picked up at the end are those matters which fall within the phrase, but have not been paid". (See also *Re Salmet International Ltd* [2001] B.C.C. 796.)

The subsections provide that the administrator's remuneration and expenses and all the contractual debts and liabilities that have been incurred while he was in office are to be paid in priority to the claims of any creditor whose debt is secured by a *floating* charge (including a charge which, as created, was a floating charge but has since become fixed: see s. 15(1) and (3)). The payments under s. 19(5) and 19(6) rank in priority to those under s. 19(4). There is no mention of the preferential creditors whose claims would have ranked ahead of the holder of the floating charge in a receivership. (On the question whether these preferential claims survive the appointment of an administrator, see the comment to s. 15(4).) If a liquidation follows the administration, the administrator's costs will have priority by virtue of s. 19(4) over all claims in the winding up other than those mentioned in s. 19(5): *Re Sheridan Securities Ltd* (1988) 4 B.C.C. 200. Where land or goods in the company's possession under a lease or hire-purchase agreement, existing at the commencement of an administration, are used for the purposes of the administration, the rent or hire charges do not rank as "expenses of the administration" within s. 19(4): *Re Atlantic Computer Systems plc* [1990] B.C.C. 859; *Re Salmet (International) Ltd* (above).

Section 19(4) says nothing about priority as between the administrator's remuneration and administration expenses (apart from those dealt with in s. 19(5)): it is up to the administrator to decide how and in what order he should discharge the obligations arising in the course of managing the company's business, including any liabilities arising under pre-administration contracts (*Re Salmet International Ltd* (above)).

In relation to payment and securities settlement systems, where "collateral security" (as defined in the Finality Regulations, reg. 2(1)) has been provided by a company to which those regulations apply, the claim of a participant or central bank to such security must be paid in priority to the administrator's expenses and remuneration, unless the terms on which the security was provided expressly state that the expenses and remuneration shall have priority (Finality Regulations, reg. 14(5), (6)). (See the introductory note at p. 3, above.)

Section 19(5) is confined to *contractual* debts and liabilities. This would include damages claims arising out of contracts entered into by the company while the administrator was in office, but not, *e.g.* any liabilities of the company in tort.

The costs of an administration petition and of the accompanying report under IR 1986, r. 2.2, although commonly ordered by the court in its discretion to be costs in the administration, are not "expenses properly incurred by the administrator" so as to attract the priority conferred by s. 19(4) or (5): *Re a Company No. 005174 of 1999* [2000] B.C.C. 698.

S. 19(5)–(10)

Section 19(5) gives priority over the administrator's remuneration and expenses to claims in respect of debts and liabilities under contracts entered into by him (or a predecessor) in the carrying out of his functions. Section 19(6) gives the same priority to "qualifying liabilities" (for definition, see below) under contracts of employment "adopted" by him (or a predecessor). However nothing done by the administrator within the first 14 days following his appointment is to be taken as "adopting" a contract of employment.

The making of an administration order does not terminate the company's existing contracts of employment or, for that matter, any other contract of a continuing nature; and so, strictly speaking, no affirmative act on the part of the administrator is needed to keep any such contract in being. This formerly led to much speculation and to differences of judicial opinion as to the meaning of the word "adopt", in relation to a contract of employment, as it appears in this section (and also in ss. 37 and 44, in relation to non-administrative and administrative receivers). In *Powdrill v Watson* (above), a definitive ruling was given on the construction of the term for the purposes of these provisions. It was held:

(i) that a contract of employment is either adopted as a whole or not; it is not open to an administrator or receiver to "cherry-pick", *i.e.* choose to accept some liabilities under the contract and not others; and (ii) that a contract of employment "is inevitably adopted if the administrator or receiver causes the company to continue the employment for more than 14 days after his employment" ([1995] 2 A.C. 394 at p. 450; [1995] B.C.C. 319 at p. 335). In the case itself, the administrators (following a practice which was widely employed at the time) had written to the employees within the first 14 days after their appointment stating that they "did not and would not at any future time adopt or assume personal liability" in respect of the contracts of employment. The Court of Appeal and House of Lords held that such a disclaimer had no effect: "adoption is a matter not merely of words but of fact" (*per* Dillon L.J. [1994] 2 All E.R. 513 at p. 521; [1994] B.C.C. 172 at p. 180). Earlier judicial views as to the meaning of "adopted" (*e.g.* that of Evans-Lombe J. at first instance in *Powdrill v Watson* [1993] B.C.C. 662, at p. 671, "procured the company to continue to carry out", and that of McPherson J. in *Re Diesels & Components Pty Ltd* (1985) 2 A.C.L.C. 555, at p. 557, "refrained from repudiating") are accordingly no longer authoritative.

In *Powdrill v Watson*, the joint administrators were held to have impliedly "adopted" the contracts of employment of two airline pilots when they had continued, after the 14-day period, to employ them and pay them in accordance with their previous contracts. Their pilots were later dismissed, and in this action successfully claimed various sums, including pay in lieu of notice, unpaid holiday pay, and pension contributions. (Certain so-called "loyalty bonuses", which had been separately agreed with the administrators, were held to be outside the contracts of employment and not recoverable.) It followed that, under the unamended s. 19(4), the employees' claims were entitled to priority over the administrators' own remuneration and expenses.

The potential consequences of the Court of Appeal's ruling in *Paramount Airways* were far-reaching, for the decision could have led to the reopening of many administrations stretching back to the commencement of the Act in 1986, and the possibility that administrators would be obliged to make restitution of their fees and remuneration in order to meet the claims of former employees, including perhaps claims for substantial "golden handshakes" by senior executives. However, happily for administrators, the House of Lords was able to find a "middle way", which reduced their risk of exposure to such very large claims. It was held that the priority under the section was restricted to liabilities under the adopted contracts incurred by the administrators during their tenure of office, and did not extend to liabilities which had accrued prior to that time. The liabilities in the former category were not limited to those incurred for services actually rendered for the benefit of the administration, but included liability for wages accruing during the contractual period of notice (or damages for failure to give such notice) and pension contributions in respect of the notice period. On the other hand, holiday pay entitlements referable to periods of service expiring before the appointment of the administrators fell into the latter category and did not attract the statutory priority. This ruling governs all contracts of employment adopted by administrators prior to March 15, 1994.

In regard to contracts of employment adopted on or after March 15, 1994, the Act (as amended) makes it plain that the liability of an administrator who (or whose predecessor) has adopted a contract of employment is to be limited to "qualifying liabilities". These are defined in s. 19(7)–(10), and are restricted to wages, salaries and occupational pension contributions (including holiday and sickness payments as set out in s. 19(9), (10)), but only in respect of services rendered wholly or partly *after* the adoption of the contract (s. 19(7)(b)) and, in the case where services are rendered partly after the adoption of the contract, so much of the qualifying liability as represents payment in respect of services rendered before the adoption are to be disregarded (s. 19(8)). An administrator can therefore now continue to retain the services of the company's employees in the knowledge that the commitment to them is only in respect of current liabilities.

The priority accorded to "sums payable in respect of liabilities incurred . . . under contracts of employment and "a liability to pay a sum by way of wages or salary" by subss. (6) and (7) include sums payable in respect of PAYE and NIC contributions related to the employment in question: *IRC v Lawrence & Anor* [2001] B.C.C. 663. Payments of salary to teachers during the school vacations were construed as being "in respect of services rendered" during the immediately preceding term under s. 19(7)(b), and also "in respect of a period of holiday" within s. 19(9)(a), in *Re a Company No. 005174 of 1999* [2000] 1 W.L.R. 502; [2000] B.C.C. 698.

Although the making of an administration order does not stop time running for the purposes of the Limitation Acts, the claims of employees under s. 19(5) and (6) arise only at the end of the administration (unless, of course, they have been met during that period). In consequence, the cause of action under s. 19(5) is subject to a limitation period of six years from that date, and the charge created by s. 19(5) to a limitation period of 12 years: *Re Maxwell Fleet & Facilities Management Ltd* [1999] 2 B.C.L.C. 721.

The administrators in *Powdrill v Watson* in their letter to the employees also stated that they disclaimed any personal liability in respect of the contracts of employment. This would appear to have been superfluous, since in the House of Lords Lord Browne-Wilkinson said ([1995] 2 A.C. 394 at p. 448; [1995] B.C.C. 319 at p. 333) that there was no question that an administrator accepted personal liability under s. 19.

The question whether an administrator, in negotiating a fresh contract with an employee (as distinct from adopting the existing one) could contract out of the statutory rules of priority laid down by s. 19(5) was expressly left open by the Court of Appeal, and was not referred to in the House of Lords.

In *Powdrill v Watson*, interest on the sums due to the employees was also awarded.

20 Release of administrator

20(1) *[Time of release]* A person who has ceased to be the administrator of a company has his release with effect from the following time, that is to say–

(a) in the case of a person who has died, the time at which notice is given to the court in accordance with the rules that he has ceased to hold office;

(b) in any other case, such time as the court may determine.

20(2) *[Discharge from liability, etc.]* Where a person has his release under this section, he is, with effect from the time specified above, discharged from all liability both in respect of acts or omissions of his in the administration and otherwise in relation to his conduct as administrator.

20(3) *[S. 212]* However, nothing in this section prevents the exercise, in relation to a person who has had his release as above, of the court's powers under section 212 in Chapter X of Part IV (summary remedy against delinquent directors, liquidators, etc.).

S. 20(1)
Except in the case of the death of an administrator, for which specific provision is made in para. (a), an administrator is to have his release only from such time as the court determines. The relevant rule for the purpose of para. (a) is IR 1986, r. 2.54.

In *Re Sibec Developments Ltd; Barclays Mercantile Finance Ltd v Sibec Developments Ltd* [1992] 1 W.L.R. 1253; [1993] B.C.C. 148, Millett J. held that the administrators should not be released (and, indeed, that an administration order should not have been discharged) while there was a proper claim against them outstanding which ought to be tried. For a case where the court postponed the administrator's release because his conduct appeared to call for investigation, see *Re Sheridan Securities Ltd* (1988) 4 B.C.C. 200. See also *Re Exchange Travel (Holdings) Ltd* [1992] B.C.C. 954, where the order for release was made to take effect after three months, to give an opportunity for steps to be taken to have the past conduct of the administrators investigated.

S. 20(2), (3)
The release of an administrator discharges him from all liability, except that s. 20(3) preserves his liability to account to the company under the "misfeasance" provisions of s. 212. Although all references to administrators have now been deleted from s. 212 by EA 2002, the former wording survives for administrations conducted under the original Pt II (see the Enterprise Act 2002 (Commencement No. 4 and Transitional Provisions and Savings Order 2003 (SI 2003/2093, effective September 15, 2003), art. 3). This section applies only in a winding up. There is something of a paradox here: the section appears to grant the office-holder a discharge, as a matter of substance, from all possible liabilities in the most comprehensive terms, and yet at the same to preserve the court's powers under s. 212 – a section which has always been understood to be purely procedural in nature.

Ascertainment and investigation of company's affairs

21 Information to be given by administrator

21(1) *[Duties of administrator]* Where an administration order has been made, the administrator shall–

(a) forthwith send to the company and publish in the prescribed manner a notice of the order, and

(b) within 28 days after the making of the order, unless the court otherwise directs, send such a notice to all creditors of the company (so far as he is aware of their addresses).

21(2) *[Copy of order to registrar]* Where an administration order has been made, the administrator shall also, within 14 days after the making of the order, send an office copy of the order to the registrar of companies and to such other persons as may be prescribed.

21(3) [Penalty for non-compliance] If the administrator without reasonable excuse fails to comply with this section, he is liable to a fine and, for continued contravention, to a daily default fine.

S. 21(1), (2)
It is the administrator's duty to see that the making of the administration order is:

- notified to the company;
- published (*i.e.* advertised, both in the *Gazette* and an appropriate newspaper (IR 1986, r. 2.10(2));
- notified to all known creditors; and
- registered with the registrar of companies.

Notice must also be given to any person who has appointed an administrative receiver of the company, or is entitled to do so, to any administrative receiver who has been appointed, to the petitioner under any pending winding-up petition, and to any provisional liquidator (IR 1986, r. 2.10(3)). The section fixes various time limits. On the meaning of the term "forthwith", see the note to s. 9(2).

For the relevant rules and forms prescribed for the purposes of this section, see IR 1986, r. 2.10.

S. 21(3)
On penalties, see s. 430 and Sch. 10.

22 Statement of affairs to be submitted to administrator

22(1) [Duty of administrator] Where an administration order has been made, the administrator shall forthwith require some or all of the persons mentioned below to make out and submit to him a statement in the prescribed form as to the affairs of the company.

22(2) [Contents of statement] The statement shall be verified by affidavit by the persons required to submit it and shall show–

(a) *particulars of the company's assets, debts and liabilities;*

(b) *the names and addresses of its creditors;*

(c) *the securities held by them respectively;*

(d) *the dates when the securities were respectively given; and*

(e) *such further or other information as may be prescribed.*

22(3) [Persons in s. 22(1)] The persons referred to in subsection (1) are–

(a) *those who are or have been officers of the company;*

(b) *those who have taken part in the company's formation at any time within one year before the date of the administration order;*

(c) *those who are in the company's employment or have been in its employment within that year, and are in the administrator's opinion capable of giving the information required;*

(d) *those who are or have been within that year officers of or in the employment of a company which is, or within that year was, an officer of the company.*

In this subsection **"employment"** *includes employment under a contract for services.*

22(4) [Time for submitting statement] Where any persons are required under this section to submit a statement of affairs to the administrator, they shall do so (subject to the next subsection) before the end of the period of 21 days beginning with the day after that on which the prescribed notice of the requirement is given to them by the administrator.

22(5) [Powers re release, extension of time] The administrator, if he thinks fit, may–

(a) *at any time release a person from an obligation imposed on him under subsection (1) or (2), or*

(b) *either when giving notice under subsection (4) or subsequently, extend the period so mentioned;*

and where the administrator has refused to exercise a power conferred by this subsection, the court, if it thinks fit, may exercise it.

***22(6)** [Penalty for non-compliance] If a person without reasonable excuse fails to comply with any obligation imposed under this section, he is liable to a fine and, for continued contravention, to a daily default fine.*

GENERAL NOTE

In this and the following sections there is set out the procedure to be followed once the administrator has been appointed. While this lengthy and formal routine may be desirable if the purpose of the administration order is to secure the rehabilitation of the company, it seems less appropriate when the object of the administration is simply to smooth the path for the approval of a voluntary arrangement or the sanctioning of a statutory scheme under CA 1985, ss. 425–427 (see s. 8(3)(b), (c)). However, the Act seems to offer no alternative, unless possibly the court is empowered to dispense with the statutory requirements under the broad wording of s. 9(4).

The "statement of affairs" has long been a feature of the liquidation procedure in a compulsory winding up (see s. 131). Its use is extended by this Act to this and a number of other analogous situations. For further comment, see the notes to s. 131.

For the relevant rules and forms prescribed for the purpose of this section, see IR 1986, rr. 2.11ff. and, on enforcement, rr. 7.20.

S. 22(1)–(5)
On the meaning of the term "forthwith", see the note to s. 9(2).

The expression "officer", in relation to a company, includes a director, manager or secretary (CA 1985, s. 744) and at least in some contexts may extend to the holders of other offices: see the note to s. 206(3). The wide definition of "employment" used here could include professionals such as the company's auditors and bankers.

S. 22(6)
On penalties, see s. 430 and Sch. 10.

Administrator's proposals

23 Statement of proposals

***23(1)** [Duties of administrator] Where an administration order has been made, the administrator shall, within 3 months (or such longer period as the court may allow) after the making of the order–*

(a) send to the registrar of companies and (so far as he is aware of their addresses) to all creditors a statement of his proposals for achieving the purpose or purposes specified in the order, and

(b) lay a copy of the statement before a meeting of the company's creditors summoned for the purpose on not less than 14 days' notice.

***23(2)** [Copies of statement] The administrator shall also, within 3 months (or such longer period as the court may allow) after the making of the order, either–*

(a) send a copy of the statement (so far as he is aware of their addresses) to all members of the company, or

(b) publish in the prescribed manner a notice stating an address to which members of the company should write for copies of the statement to be sent to them free of charge.

***23(3)** [Penalty for non-compliance] If the administrator without reasonable excuse fails to comply with this section, he is liable to a fine and, for continued contravention, to a daily default fine.*

S. 23(1)
In the light of the information given to him in the statement of affairs which he has requisitioned under s. 22, the administrator must draw up his "proposals" – his strategy for achieving the purpose or purposes specified in the

Section 24   Insolvency Act 1986

administration order – and summon a meeting of the company's creditors to consider them. A copy of the proposals must be sent to the registrar of companies for registration, and also to every known creditor. (The "statement" referred to in this section is the administrator's statement of his proposals, not the statement of the company's affairs.)

A careful reading of para. (b) reveals that the creditors' meeting must be *held*, and not merely summoned, within the specified period of three months.

A meeting under this section cannot be held for purposes other than the consideration of the administrator's proposals, *e.g.* to consider whether the company should petition for its own winding up: *Re Charnley Davies Business Services Ltd* (1987) 3 B.C.C. 408. In this case, exceptionally, Harman J. discharged the administration order before a s. 23 meeting had been held because action already taken by the administrator on his own initiative had left the meeting with nothing that it could usefully do. On the question of discharge, see further the note to s. 18(1), (2).

For the procedure for summoning the creditors' meeting, see IR 1986, rr. 2.18ff.

S. 23(2)
A copy of the statement of proposals must either be sent to all members of the company individually, or advertised as being available to members free on request. This must be done within (and not at the end of) three months: (*Re Charnley Davies Business Services Ltd*, above) although the court may grant an extension of time. (The members have little say in, or control over, the conduct of the administration – see s. 14(4); but if a member is "unfairly prejudiced" by it, he is given a statutory remedy under s. 27, and so there is a need that members should be kept broadly in the picture.)

The rules prescribed for the purpose of s. 23(2)(b) require the notice to be gazetted: see IR 1986, r. 2.17.

S. 23(3)
On penalties, see s. 430 and Sch. 10.

24   Consideration of proposals by creditors' meeting

24(1)   [Creditors' meeting to decide] *A meeting of creditors summoned under section 23 shall decide whether to approve the administrator's proposals.*

24(2)   [Approval, modifications] *The meeting may approve the proposals with modifications, but shall not do so unless the administrator consents to each modification.*

24(3)   [Meeting in accordance with rules] *Subject as above, the meeting shall be conducted in accordance with the rules.*

24(4)   [Report and notice by administrator] *After the conclusion of the meeting in accordance with the rules, the administrator shall report the result of the meeting to the court and shall give notice of that result to the registrar of companies and to such persons as may be prescribed.*

24(5)   [If meeting does not approve] *If a report is given to the court under subsection (4) that the meeting has declined to approve the administrator's proposals (with or without modifications), the court may by order discharge the administration order and make such consequential provision as it thinks fit, or adjourn the hearing conditionally or unconditionally, or make an interim order or any other order that it thinks fit.*

24(6)   [Where administration order discharged] *Where the administration order is discharged, the administrator shall, within 14 days after the making of the order effecting the discharge, send an office copy of that order to the registrar of companies.*

24(7)   [Penalty for non-compliance] *If the administrator without reasonable excuse fails to comply with subsection (6), he is liable to a fine and, for continued contravention, to a daily default fine.*

S. 24(1), (2)
The administrator's freedom to act in the exercise of his functions is limited by the scope of the proposals, once approved (see s. 17(2)(b)) – apart from "insubstantial" deviations (s. 25(1)(b)); and so it is important, from his point of view, that they should not be too restrictively drawn – indeed, in *Re Dana (UK) Ltd* [1999] 2 B.C.L.C. 239 Neuberger J. thought that it would make good sense for the proposals put before a s. 23 meeting to include a mechanism empowering the largest and/or representative creditors to approve future decisions or variations of decisions of the administrator. In any event, the court may, in exceptional circumstances, authorise the administrator to depart from the scheme, *e.g.*

where there is insufficient time to convene a meeting of the creditors under s. 25 to approve a revision of the scheme: see the note to s. 25(1), below.

S. 24(3)
For the rules governing the conduct of the meeting, see IR 1986, rr. 2.18ff. The rules invalidate any resolution of the creditors which is opposed by a majority of the creditors who are not "connected with" the company: see IR 1986, r. 2.28(1A) and, on the meaning of "connected with", see s. 249.

S. 24(4)
The administrator is required to report the result of the meeting to the court and to notify the persons specified. If the meeting has approved the proposals, the report to the court seems to be a purely administrative matter: the administrator may, without more formality, get on with his duties under s. 17(2)(b).

For the persons prescribed for the purposes of this subsection, see IR 1986, r. 2.30.

S. 24(5)
If the meeting does not approve the proposals, the initiative reverts to the court, acting in its judicial capacity. The administration meantime continues provisionally under s. 17(2)(a).

S. 24(6), (7)
These subsections repeat the corresponding provisions in s. 18(4), (5).

On penalties, see s. 430 and Sch. 10.

25 Approval of substantial revisions

25(1) *[Application] This section applies where–*

(a) *proposals have been approved (with or without modifications) under section 24, and*

(b) *the administrator proposes to make revisions of those proposals which appear to him substantial.*

25(2) *[Duties of administrator] The administrator shall–*

(a) *send to all creditors of the company (so far as he is aware of their addresses) a statement in the prescribed form of his proposed revisions, and*

(b) *lay a copy of the statement before a meeting of the company's creditors summoned for the purpose on not less than 14 days' notice;*

and he shall not make the proposed revisions unless they are approved by the meeting.

25(3) *[Copies of statement] The administrator shall also either–*

(a) *send a copy of the statement (so far as he is aware of their addresses) to all members of the company, or*

(b) *publish in the prescribed manner a notice stating an address to which members of the company should write for copies of the statement to be sent to them free of charge.*

25(4) *[Approval, modifications] The meeting of creditors may approve the proposed revisions with modifications, but shall not do so unless the administrator consents to each modification.*

25(5) *[Meeting in accordance with rules] Subject as above, the meeting shall be conducted in accordance with the rules.*

25(6) *[Notification to registrar, et al.] After the conclusion of the meeting in accordance with the rules, the administrator shall give notice of the result of the meeting to the registrar of companies and to such persons as may be prescribed.*

S. 25(1)
Once his proposals have been approved, the administrator is bound to adhere to the course of action that they prescribe (except that he may, apparently, make "insubstantial" deviations: see para. (b)). If he wishes to work to a different strategy, he must go back to the creditors for approval of revised proposals. However, in exceptional circumstances (*e.g.* where the delay involved in summoning a creditors' meeting to consider a revised scheme could cause substantial loss)

Section 26   Insolvency Act 1986

the court has a residual jurisdiction under s. 14(3) to authorise an administrator to depart from an approved scheme: see *Re Smallman Construction Ltd* (1988) 4 B.C.C. 784 and *Re Dana (UK) Ltd* [1999] 2 B.C.L.C. 239.

S. 25(2)–(5)
These provisions are effectively the same as ss. 23(1), (2) and 24(2), (3), except that there is no time limit prescribed and no obligation to send a copy of the statement of revised proposals to the registrar of companies.

S. 25(6)
This subsection echoes s. 24(4), except that under that provision it is necessary also to report the result of the meeting to the court.

If the meeting declines to approve the revised proposals, it would appear that the administrator has the following options:

- to continue to act under the old proposals;
- to draw up a new set of revised proposals and summon a further creditors' meeting under this section;
- to apply to the court under s. 18(1) to have the purpose specified in the administration order varied; or
- to apply to the court for a discharge of the order under s. 18(2), on the ground that the purpose of the order is incapable of achievement.

For more detailed comment, see the various sections refered to.

Miscellaneous

26 Creditors' committee

26(1) [Meeting may establish committee] Where a meeting of creditors summoned under section 23 has approved the administrator's proposals (with or without modifications), the meeting may, if it thinks fit, establish a committee *("the creditors' committee")* to exercise the functions conferred on it by or under this Act.

26(2) [Committee may summon administrator] If such a committee is established, the committee may, on giving not less than 7 days' notice, require the administrator to attend before it at any reasonable time and furnish it with such information relating to the carrying out of his functions as it may reasonably require.

GENERAL NOTE

Once the meeting of creditors has approved a statement of proposals, so that the administrator is empowered to act under s. 17(2)(b), it may appoint a committee of creditors under this section. Corresponding provisions are made in the case of an administrative receivership (see ss. 49 and 68) and in a winding up (where the committee was formerly called the "committee of inspection" and is now termed the "liquidation committee": see ss. 101, 141 and 142).

It is submitted that the phrase "conferred on it" in s. 26(1) means "conferred on the committee" and not "conferred on the meeting of creditors", as might appear on a first reading.

For the rules relating to the creditors' committee and its functions, see IR 1986, rr. 2.32ff.

27 Protection of interests of creditors and members

27(1) [Application by creditor or member] At any time when an administration order is in force, a creditor or member of the company may apply to the court by petition for an order under this section on the ground–

(a) that the company's affairs, business and property are being or have been managed by the administrator in a manner which is unfairly prejudicial to the interests of its creditors or members generally, or of some part of its creditors or members (including at least himself), or

(b) that any actual or proposed act or omission of the administrator is or would be so prejudicial.

27(2) [Court order] On an application for an order under this section the court may, subject as follows, make such order as it thinks fit for giving relief in respect of the matters complained of, or adjourn the hearing conditionally or unconditionally, or make an interim order or any other order that it thinks fit.

27(3) *[Limits of order]* An order under this section shall not prejudice or prevent–

(a) the implementation of a voluntary arrangement approved under section 4 in Part I, or any compromise or arrangement sanctioned under section 425 of the Companies Act; or

(b) where the application for the order was made more than 28 days after the approval of any proposals or revised proposals under section 24 or 25, the implementation of those proposals or revised proposals.

27(4) *[Contents of order]* Subject as above, an order under this section may in particular–

(a) regulate the future management by the administrator of the company's affairs, business and property;

(b) require the administrator to refrain from doing or continuing an act complained of by the petitioner, or to do an act which the petitioner has complained he has omitted to do;

(c) require the summoning of a meeting of creditors or members for the purpose of considering such matters as the court may direct;

(d) discharge the administration order and make such consequential provision as the court thinks fit.

27(5) *[S. 15, 16]* Nothing in sections 15 or 16 is to be taken as prejudicing applications to the court under this section.

27(6) *[Copy of discharge order to registrar]* Where the administration order is discharged, the administrator shall, within 14 days after the making of the order effecting the discharge, send an office copy of that order to the registrar of companies; and if without reasonable excuse he fails to comply with this subsection, he is liable to a fine and, for continued contravention, to a daily default fine.

S. 27(1)
This section, like s. 6, is based broadly on the provisions of CA 1985, s. 459. As with s. 6, it is arguable that a court might rule that a member's or creditor's *only* judicial remedy if he has any complaint against the administrator is to have recourse to the procedure under this section: this would be consistent with the apparent purpose of s. 27(3)(b). (This would not, of course, rule out proceedings brought by the company itself, or its liquidator.) However, in *Cornhill Insurance plc v Cornhill Financial Services Ltd* [1992] B.C.C. 818 the Court of Appeal held that a creditor who was aggrieved by an administration order which was unfairly prejudicial to it and accordingly ought not to have been made could invoke the jurisdiction of the court under IR 1986, r. 7.47 to have the order rescinded. The present provision differs from s. 6 in an important respect: it is concerned with the actual management of the company's affairs, etc., by the administrator, whereas s. 6 deals only with events prior to the time when the supervisor of an arrangement takes office. It may also be contrasted with CA 1985, s. 459 in that a creditor as well as a member may petition.

The scope of s. 27 is discussed in detail in the case of *Re Charnley Davies Ltd* [1990] B.C.C. 605, where it was held that a negligent sale by an administrator of a company's assets at an undervalue would be insufficient without more to establish a claim for relief under the section. The appropriate procedure in such a situation is to have the administration order discharged, the company put into compulsory liquidation, an insolvency practitioner other than the administrator appointed liquidator, and a claim brought by the liquidator against the administrator under IA 1986, s. 212. The court in *Re Charnley Davies Ltd* declined to endorse suggestions proffered by counsel as to the meaning of the words "unfairly prejudicial": "it would be wrong to substitute different language for that chosen by Parliament, if the substituted language means the same it is not helpful, and if it means something different it distorts the intention of Parliament" ([1990] B.C.C. 605 at p. 624). "An allegation that the acts complained of are unlawful or infringe the petitioner's legal rights is not a necessary averment in a s. 27 petition. [It] is not a sufficient averment either. The petitioner must allege and prove that they are evidence or instances of the management of the company's affairs by the administrator in a manner which is unfairly prejudicial to the petitioner's interests" (*ibid*, at pp. 624–625). Where the complaint may be adequately redressed by the remedy provided by law, it is unnecessary to assume the additional burden of proving unfairly prejudicial conduct. However, that burden must be assumed – but not necessarily that of proving unlawful conduct as well – if a wider remedy under s. 27 is sought.

An administrator, save in exceptional cases, does not owe duties to an individual creditor on the basis of which a claim in negligence will lie, either under this provision or at common law. If the complaint is based on a breach of duty

Section 27 *Insolvency Act 1986*

in the conduct of the administration and the company has gone into liquidation, a claim (in the nature of a class action) may be brought under s. 212, and if the administrator has had his release, the leave of the court is required under s. 20(2): *Kyrris v Oldham* [2003] 1 B.C.L.C. 35.

The courts are in principle unwilling to review commercial decisions, and discourage the use of the procedure under s. 27 for this purpose: *MTI Trading Systems Ltd v Winter* [1998] B.C.C. 591.

S. 27(3)(a)
An application for an administration order may be made in conjunction with a proposed voluntary arrangement under Pt. I of this Act or a scheme of compromise or arrangement under CA 1985, ss. 425–427. A member or creditor who objects to a scheme under either of these procedures has his separate remedies under s. 6 and 7(3) above and a right of objection under CA 1985, s. 425(2), and if he has not availed himself of these rights or has done so unsuccessfully, it is reasonable that the arrangement or scheme should stand.

S. 27(3)(b)
Under this provision, the court may upset the administration scheme itself only if an application is made within the 28-day period. After that, it may still grant the applicant other forms of relief, but the scheme itself will no longer be open to challenge.

S. 27(4)
This is modelled on CA 1985, s. 461(2); but paras (c) and (d) have no counterpart in that section.

S. 27(5)
The two sections referred to empower the administrator to deal with charged property, in some circumstances with the authorisation of the court. The fact that an act of the administrator has the backing of a court order should not prejudice an application under the present section, since members and creditors will generally have had no standing to be heard when the order was made.

S.27(6)
This is equivalent to s. 18(4), (5) and also to s. 24(6), (7).

Part III

Receivership

General comment on Pt. III
The Companies Acts have not previously contained many provisions dealing with receivership, at least in relation to England and Wales; matters were left to the general law and the terms of the instrument under or by which the receiver was appointed. The Cork Committee (*Report*, Ch. 8) recommended that the law should be amended so that in many respects it was placed on a statutory basis. The recommendations were broadly followed by IA 1985, Ch. IV, which is now consolidated along with a few sections of CA 1985 into the present Act.

Among the principal changes made are the introduction of the new concept of "administrative receiver" (s. 29(2)), and the requirement that an administrative receiver be a qualified insolvency practitioner. The date on which a receiver takes office and the extent to which agency rules apply have been clarified, and new provisions ensure that other creditors are kept in the picture regarding the progress of the receivership. The administrative receiver is given the statutory powers set out in Sch. 1, and other specific powers including power to dispose of encumbered property (s. 43). In many other respects an administrative receivership is placed on a similar footing to a liquidation – *e.g.* in regard to a statement of affairs, the appointment of a committee of creditors, and the removal of the receiver.

To all intents and purposes these days appointments of receivers to enforce security are effected out of court in pursuance of a contractual power vested in the debenture holder to make such an appointment. The advantage in this course of action is speed and lack of cost. There is, however, always the facility of applying to the court for such an appointment, but this is rare because of the cost and the delay – for an unusual example see *Bank of Credit and Commerce International SA v BRS Kumar Bros Ltd* [1994] B.C.L.C. 211.

It must be remembered that a receiver appointed to enforce a fixed charge may be subject to the old established provisions of LPA 1925. For consideration of this statutory code see *Phoenix Properties v Wimpole Street Nominees Ltd* [1992] 1 B.C.L.C. 737 and *Sargent v C & E Commrs* [1995] 2 B.C.L.C. 34. Specialised statutory regimes also exist for certain types of receivership involving (for example) companies incorporated by statute or as part of statutory insolvency regimes, but these are not our concern in this work.

The institution of receivership was unknown in Scotland until the enactment of CFCSA 1972. In the present Act the provisions of that legislation are consolidated, incorporating certain modifications made by IA 1985. Comparable provisions dealing with receivers and administrative receivers in Northern Ireland are to be found in the Insolvency (Northern Ireland) Order 1989 (SI 1989/2405) (NI 19), art. 40–59.

Although the following provisions provide some statutory framework for the mechanism of an administrative receivership there is still a substantial body of rules derived from decisions of the courts. These court-derived principles continue to be important.

Pt III applies to limited liability partnerships by virtue of the Limited Liability Partnerships Regulations 2001 (SI 2001/1090), reg. 5(1)(a) as from April 6, 2001 subject to reg. 5(2) and (3).

Many key issues are not addressed by the legislation. For example, what is the effect of the appointment of a receiver on the power of the directors to litigate on behalf of the company? Compare here *Newhart Developments v Cooperative Commercial Bank* [1978] Q.B. 814 with *Tudor Grange Holdings v Citibank* [1992] Ch. 53; the Irish High Court case of *Lascomme Ltd v United Dominions Trust (Ireland)* [1994] I.L.R.M. 227 and *Independent Pension Trustee v LAW Construction, The Times* Scots Law Report, November 1, 1996. For discussion see Doyle (1996) 17 Co Law 131.

The question of whether a receiver owes a duty of care to the company (and those claiming through it) when managing and realising the assets has also been left for the courts to grapple with. For a generous treatment of receivers' duties by the Privy Council in this scenario see *Downsview Nominees v First City Corporation Ltd* [1993] A.C. 295; [1993] B.C.C. 46. Here it was held that the responsibilities of receivers are essentially equitable in nature and there was no room for superimposing common law duties of care in negligence. This case is difficult to reconcile with earlier authorities such as *Standard Chartered Bank v Walker* [1982] 1 W.L.R. 1410 and *Knight v Lawrence* [1991] B.C.C. 411 and is best viewed as part of a general retreat on the part of the courts in the areas of economic loss and professional liability. See generally Berg [1993] J.B.L. 213 and Fealy [1994] 45 N.I.L.Q. 61. Most commentators have been critical of the approach of the Privy Council but for rare support see Rajak (1997) 21 Insolvency Lawyer 7. Those commentators who have been critical of the aforementioned Privy Council ruling will have welcomed the subsequent clarification of the law by the Court of Appeal in *Medforth v Blake* [2000] Ch. 86; [1999] B.C.C. 711. In this case it was held that a receiver taking control of a farming business had no obligation to continue to operate the farm, but if that course of action was taken, the receiver should take reasonable steps to ensure that the business was conducted as profitably as possible and, in particular, that the customary discounts on bulk purchase of livestock feed be obtained. The Court of Appeal felt able to reconcile *Downsview* by indicating that this duty to take reasonable care could be seen as part of the obligation to act in good faith. This decision is far more in tune with prevailing professional standards. For comment see *Frisby* (2000) 63 M.L.R. 413. The issue of the duties owed by receivers (or mortgagees) when managing, selling or considering the sale of charged property have continued to trouble the courts over the past two years – see for example *Hadjipanayi v Yeldon* [2001] B.P.I.R. 487, *Worwood v Leisure Merchandising* [2002] 1 B.C.L.C. 249, *Cohen v TSB Bank* [2002] 2 B.C.L.C. 32 and *Silven Properties Ltd v Royal Bank of Scotland* [2003] EWCA Civ 764. At the end of the day each case does turn on its own peculiar facts and most claims alleging breach of duty tend to fail. Another vexed issue concerns both the timing of a sale and the selection of a purchaser where the mortgagor wishes to buy the property. In *Lloyds Bank v Cassidy* [2002] EWCA Civ 1427, [2003] B.P.I.R. 425 the Court of Appeal felt that these were issues in need of clarification. If a duty of care is owed by selling receivers that duty is owed to any party having an interest in the equity of redemption – *Raja v Austin Gray (a firm)* [2002] EWCA Civ 1965, [2003] B.P.I.R. 725.

Other jurisdictions have had the foresight to address this issue through legislation – see Irish Companies Act 1963, s. 311A (introduced in 1990) and the New Zealand Receiverships Act 1993, s. 19. In both cases a statutory duty of care when selling company assets has been imposed. In Canada s. 247 of the Bankruptcy and Insolvency Act 1992 requires receivers to deal with the security in a commercially reasonable manner.

The rules on set-off on receivership are also within the province of common law: *John Dee Group Ltd v W M H (21) Ltd* [1998] B.C.C. 972.

The relationship between the various corporate insolvency regimes is interesting. It has been clear from the earliest of days that the right of a secured creditor to have a receiver appointed would be protected by the law. Thus, although receivership and liquidation can run concurrently, in practice the liquidator must wait in the wings, at least so far as concerns the property covered by the charge, until the receiver has fulfilled his functions. This is so even though the agency character of the receiver's role changes: *Sowman v David Samuel Trust Ltd* [1978] 1 W.L.R. 22 or even if liquidation precedes receivership: *Re First Express Ltd* [1991] B.C.C. 782. The advent of the administration order regime posed little threat to the rights of the secured creditor in that a right of veto was created by IA 1986, s. 9 in favour of a person having the power to appoint an administrative receiver (*i.e.* a creditor whose security includes a general floating charge) see *Re Croftbell Ltd* [1990] B.C.C. 781. However, if this veto is not exercised, the administrator did enjoy the power to interfere with the rights of the secured creditor (see IA 1986, s. 15). The new administration regime under EA 2002 offers good protection to the qualifying floating charge holder. A secured creditor who waits for a CVA to be put in place before appointing a receiver may also be in difficulties: *Re Leisure Study Group Ltd* [1994] 2 B.C.L.C. 65.

Note the limitations imposed upon a receiver's power of realisation where s. 430 of POCA 2002 applies.

As an institution the future of receivership is likely to be a diminished one. This is a result of the changes introduced by EA 2002 limiting the option of administrative receivership to pre-commencement floating charges and to other specialised corporate financing situations – see the note to ss. 72A ff. The relevant provisions barring administrative receivership do not apply to floating charges created before September 15, 2003 – see the Enterprise Act 2002 (Commencement No. 4 and Transitional Provisions and Savings) Order 2003 (SI 2003/2093, C. 85).

CHAPTER I

RECEIVERS AND MANAGERS (ENGLAND AND WALES)

Preliminary and general provisions

28 Extent of this Chapter

28 This Chapter does not apply to receivers appointed under Chapter II of this Part (Scotland).

GENERAL NOTE

This emphasises that ss. 28–49 only apply to receivers and managers appointed under English law. The Scots have their own rules: see ss. 50–71. However, Ch. 1 applies to building societies subject to certain modifications: see Sch. 15A as inserted by Sch. 6 and s. 39 of the Building Societies Act 1997.

The changes made to the law relating to receivers and managers by IA 1985 and IA 1986 are not retrospective: see Sch. 11, para. 2(2).

29 Definitions

29(1) [Interpretation] It is hereby declared that, except where the context otherwise requires–

(a) any reference in the Companies Act or this Act to a receiver or manager of the property of a company, or to a receiver of it, includes a receiver or manager, or (as the case may be) a receiver of part only of that property and a receiver only of the income arising from the property or from part of it; and

(b) any reference in the Companies Act or this Act to the appointment of a receiver or manager under powers contained in an instrument includes an appointment made under powers which, by virtue of any enactment, are implied in and have effect as if contained in an instrument.

29(2) ["Administrative receiver"] In this Chapter **"administrative receiver"** means–

(a) a receiver or manager of the whole (or substantially the whole) of a company's property appointed by or on behalf of the holders of any debentures of the company secured by a charge which, as created, was a floating charge, or by such a charge and one or more other securities; or

(b) a person who would be such a receiver or manager but for the appointment of some other person as the receiver of part of the company's property.

S. 29(1)

This section defines "receiver and manager" in such a way as to include partial receiverships. Receivers of income appointed under LPA 1925 (see above) are included under the term "receiver".

S. 29(2)
This seeks to cast light upon the unhappy term "administrative receiver", a label first introduced in 1985. It is important to distinguish an administrative receiver from his untitled fellows because, *inter alia*, ss. 42–49, the rules on office-holders and the mitigating provisions in s. 2 of IA 1994 only apply to administrative receivers. Moreover, it is only a person having the right to appoint an administrative receiver who can veto the appointment of an administrator (see IA 1986, s. 9 and *Re Croftbell Ltd* [1990] B.C.C. 781).

In view of the importance attached to the status of being an administrative receiver it is unfortunate that this provision was not drafted in clearer terms. A number of uncertainties exist:

(1) Can there be multiple concurrent administrative receivers? The better view here would appear to be "no": see Oditah [1991] J.B.L. 49.

(2) Can a court-appointed receiver enjoy this status? The consensus here appears to deny this: see Gordon Stewart, *Administrative Receivers and Administrators* (CCH 1987), p. 13 but compare Schumacher (1993) 9 I.L. & P. 43 for an interesting counter-argument. In *Re A & C Supplies Ltd* [1998] B.C.C. 708 Blackburne J. indicated that the court did not enjoy the power to appoint an administrative receiver.

(3) Can an administrative receiver be appointed over the assets of a foreign company? The general rule of interpretation of companies legislation is that the word "company" does not encompass foreign companies; however, this rule can be displaced by the context. Such a displacement was accepted in the context of s. 29(2) by Mummery J. in *Re International Bulk Commodities Ltd* [1993] Ch. 77; [1992] B.C.C. 463. This ruling has not escaped criticism and the later judgment in *Re Devon and Somerset Farmers Ltd* [1994] Ch. 57; [1993] B.C.C. 410 to the effect that an industrial and provident society cannot go into administrative receivership (because it is not a "company") sits uneasily alongside it.

(4) Can an administrative receiver be appointed by a fixed chargee? The answer to this is also negative. Moreover, even if the chargee enjoys a hybrid security comprising fixed and floating charges, the appointment must be made under the floating charge element in order for an administrative receivership to result: *Meadrealm Ltd v Transcontinental Golf Construction* (1991) (Vinelott J, unreported) noted by Marks in (1993) 6 Insolvency Intelligence 41. See also Marks and Emmett [1994] J.B.L. 1.

30 Disqualification of body corporate from acting as receiver

30 A body corporate is not qualified for appointment as receiver of the property of a company, and any body corporate which acts as such a receiver is liable to a fine.

GENERAL NOTE

This provision continues the rather curious bar on corporate receivers. If a corporate receiver is appointed, a fine will be incurred and the appointment is also invalid. On penalties, see s. 430 and Sch. 10. Corporations are also barred from being qualified to act as insolvency practitioners: see s. 390(1).

31 Disqualification of bankrupt

31(1) [Offence] A person commits an offence if he acts as receiver or manager of the property of a company on behalf of debenture holders while—

(a) he is an undischarged bankrupt, or

(b) a bankruptcy restrictions order is in force in respect of him.

31(2) [Sanction] A person guilty of an offence under subsection (1) shall be liable to imprisonment, a fine or both.

31(3) [Non-application to court appointee] This section does not apply to a receiver or manager acting under an appointment made by the court.

GENERAL NOTE

Schedule 21 of EA 2002 substitutes a new s. 31 into IA 1986 to cater for the advent of bankruptcy restrictions orders. This provision will take effect when the bankruptcy reforms come into force in April 2004. In the meantime the original s. 31 (reproduced below) with its bar on undischarged bankrupts, will continue to operate.

S. 31(1), (3)
Undischarged bankrupts or persons subject to a BRO (or BRU) are prohibited from acting as receivers and managers unless the court makes the appointment – hardly likely!

S. 31(2)
This indicates the sanction, full details of which are to be found in Sch. 10.

31 Disqualification of undischarged bankrupt [to be repealed]

31 If a person being an undischarged bankrupt acts as receiver or manager of the property or a company on behalf of debenture holders he is liable to imprisonment or a fine or both.

This does not apply to a receiver or manager acting under an appointment made by the court.

32 Power for court to appoint official receiver

32 Where application is made to the court to appoint a receiver on behalf of the debenture holders or other creditors of a company which is being wound up by the court, the official receiver may be appointed.

GENERAL NOTE

If a company is in liquidation, the court, in those rare cases where debenture holders apply to it to have a receiver appointed, may appoint the official receiver. For further details see ss. 399–401.

Receivers and managers appointed out of court

33 Time from which appointment is effective

33(1) **[Effect of appointment]** The appointment of a person as a receiver or manager of a company's property under powers contained in an instrument–

(a) is of no effect unless it is accepted by that person before the end of the business day next following that on which the instrument of appointment is received by him or on his behalf, and

(b) subject to this, is deemed to be made at the time at which the instrument of appointment is so received.

33(2) **[Joint receivers or managers]** This section applies to the appointment of two or more persons as joint receivers or managers of a company's property under powers contained in an instrument, subject to such modifications as may be prescribed by the rules.

S. 33(1)
The appointment of a receiver and manager out of court takes effect when he receives the letter of appointment, provided that he accepts the office before the end of the next business day. For administrative receivers see also IR 1986, r. 3.1.

S. 33(2)
The above rule applies to joint receivers, subject to the modifications made by the rules: see also IR 1986, r. 3.1.

34 Liability for invalid appointment

34 Where the appointment of a person as the receiver or manager of a company's property under powers contained in an instrument is discovered to be invalid (whether by virtue of the invalidity of the instrument or otherwise), the court may order the person by whom or on whose behalf the appointment was made to indemnify the person appointed against any liability which arises solely by reason of the invalidity of the appointment.

GENERAL NOTE

This permits the court to order that the appointor of a receiver indemnify the latter against liability in trespass, where the appointment turns out to be invalid. Invalidity may be the result of the debenture charge being unregistered or being avoided under IA 1986 s. 245. This provision will prove useful because challenges to appointments are becoming more common: see, *e.g. Shamji v Johnson Matthey Bankers Ltd* (1986) 2 B.C.C. 98,910 where the challenge proved unsuccessful. Short notice appointments are permitted under "on demand" debentures: *Sheppard and Cooper Ltd v TSB Bank (No. 2)* [1996] B.C.C. 965. The courts will refuse to hear belated complaints about the initiation of the receivership: see *Secretary of State v Jabble* [1998] B.C.C. 39 for an optimistic attempt to challenge the propriety of the receivership in consequential director disqualification proceedings! In *Re Asset Visions Ltd* [2003] B.P.I.R. 305 an attempt to challenge an appointment of a receiver on the grounds that the terms of the debenture governing the appointment were allegedly qualified by a verbal agreement did not appeal to the court.

35 Application to court for directions

35(1) [Application] A receiver or manager of the property of a company appointed under powers contained in an instrument, or the persons by whom or on whose behalf a receiver or manager has been so appointed, may apply to the court for directions in relation to any particular matter arising in connection with the performance of the functions of the receiver or manager.

35(2) [Order, directions by court] On such an application, the court may give such directions, or may make such order declaring the rights of persons before the court or otherwise, as it thinks just.

S. 35(1)
This allows a receiver, or his appointor, to apply to the court for directions in the event of legal uncertainty arising. The latter was only given this facility by IA 1985, as a result of the recommendations of the Cork Committee (*Report*, para. 828). This provision is to be widely interpreted and enables guidance to be sought on remuneration: *Re Therm-a-Stor Ltd* [1997] B.C.C. 301 and *Munns v Perkins* [2002] B.P.I.R. 120. Such guidance may be welcome in the light of the more stringent regime ushered in by Ferris J. in *Mirror Group Newspapers v Maxwell* [1998] B.C.C. 324.

The FSA may, in an appropriate case, be heard on such an application – FSMA 2000, s. 363(2).

S. 35(2)
The court enjoys general discretion as to any declaration it may make on such an application.

36 Court's power to fix remuneration

36(1) [Remuneration] The court may, on an application made by the liquidator of a company, by order fix the amount to be paid by way of remuneration to a person who, under powers contained in an instrument, has been appointed receiver or manager of the company's property.

36(2) [Extent of court's power] The court's power under subsection (1), where no previous order has been made with respect thereto under the subsection–

(a) extends to fixing the remuneration for any period before the making of the order or the application for it,

(b) is exercisable notwithstanding that the receiver or manager has died or ceased to act before the making of the order or the application, and

(c) where the receiver or manager has been paid or has retained for his remuneration for any period before the making of the order any amount in excess of that so fixed for that period, extends to requiring him or his personal representatives to account for the excess or such part of it as may be specified in the order.

But the power conferred by paragraph (c) shall not be exercised as respects any period before the making of the application for the order under this section, unless in the court's opinion there are special circumstances making it proper for the power to be exercised.

36(3) [Variation, amendment of order] The court may from time to time on an application made either by the liquidator or by the receiver or manager, vary or amend an order made under subsection (1).

S. 36(1)
This allows the court to determine the remuneration of a receiver and manager appointed out of court where the liquidator of the company asks for this to be done. Such applications in the past have been rare, if only because of the courtesy that exists between fellow insolvency practitioners. For a recent but unsuccessful application, see *Re Potters*

Section 37 *Insolvency Act 1986*

Oils Ltd (No. 2) [1986] 1 W.L.R. 201; (1985) 1 B.C.C. 99,593. With a more questioning era looming with regard to professional remuneration levels applications under this provision may become more commonplace. In *Munns v Perkins* [2002] B.P.I.R. 120 a fee amounting to 4.2 per cent of the value of assets realised was deemed reasonable.

S. 36(2)
This provides further details of the powers of the court where an application has been made to it under s. 36(1).

S. 36(3)
The court can vary any order it makes fixing remuneration.

37 Liability for contracts, etc.

37(1) [Personal liability, indemnity] A receiver or manager appointed under powers contained in an instrument (other than an administrative receiver) is, to the same extent as if he had been appointed by order of the court–

(a) personally liable on any contract entered into by him in the performance of his functions (except in so far as the contract otherwise provides) and on any contract of employment adopted by him in the performance of those functions, and

(b) entitled in respect of that liability to indemnity out of the assets.

37(2) [Interpretation of s. 37(1)(a)] For the purposes of subsection (1)(a), the receiver or manager is not to be taken to have adopted a contract of employment by reason of anything done or omitted to be done within 14 days after his appointment.

37(3) [Extent of s. 37(1)] Subsection (1) does not limit any right to indemnity which the receiver or manager would have apart from it, nor limit his liability on contracts entered into without authority, nor confer any right to indemnity in respect of that liability.

37(4) [Vacation of office] Where at any time the receiver or manager so appointed vacates office–

(a) his remuneration and any expenses properly incurred by him, and

(b) any indemnity to which he is entitled out of the assets of the company,

shall be charged on and paid out of any property of the company which is in his custody or under his control at that time in priority to any charge or other security held by the person by or on whose behalf he was appointed.

S. 37(1), (2)
Receivers appointed out of court are personally liable on contracts entered into by them (unless they have contracted out), and existing contracts of employment adopted by them, although they have 14 days' grace to decide whether to adopt or not. This latter provision is designed to cope with the problems thrown up by *Nicoll v Cutts* (1985) 1 B.C.C. 99,427. Where a receiver adopts a contract of employment under s. 37(1)(a) the case will be caught by the rule in *Re Paramount Airways Ltd (No. 3)* [1994] B.C.C. 172 (*Powdrill v Watson* [1995] 2 AC 394) and this adoption will impose all accrued employment liabilities on the receiver. (See the notes to ss. 19 and 44.) The relief extended by s. 2 of IA 1994 to mitigate this rule has (for unconvincing reasons) deliberately not been extended to non-administrative receivers, though the Government was supposed to be reconsidering this matter: see DTI Press Notice P/94/319. Such receivers may have to adopt contracts of employment if they are enforcing a fixed charge over, say, a hotel and they wish to retain staff pending a sale of the hotel as a going concern. It is implicit in s. 37(1)(a) that a receiver is entitled not to adopt existing contracts of the company. Where he chooses this option as a rule no injunction will lie against him to enforce observance of the contract: see *Airlines Airspares Ltd v Handley Page Ltd* [1970] Ch. 193. However, in some cases the contract may be enforced: see *Freevale Ltd v Metrostore (Holdings) Ltd* [1984] Ch. 199; *Amec Properties v Planning Research and Systems* [1992] 13 E.G. 109, the discussion in *Astor Chemical Ltd v Synthetic Technology Ltd* [1990] B.C.C. 97 and *Ash & Newman v Creative Devices Research Ltd* [1991] B.C.L.C. 403. The uncertainties in this area have continued through cases like *Transtec Automotive (Campsie) Ltd* [2001] B.C.C. 403 and *Land Rover Group v UPF (UK) Ltd* [2002] EWHC 3183 (QB); [2003] 2 B.C.L.C. 222.

S. 37(3)
The receiver's statutory indemnity in respect of contractual liability under s. 37(1)(b) is not exhaustive. On the other hand, it does not apply to contracts entered into by him without authority.

S. 37(4)
This accords high priority status to the receiver's right to remuneration and indemnity. However it is important to remember that this priority only extends to the proceeds of assets caught by the security. The right to remuneration cannot be charged against assets encompassed by a prior security: *Choudri v Palta* [1992] B.C.C. 787. Furthermore, in cases where the receiver has realised sufficient funds to repay the debenture holder and also (arguably) to satisfy his own claim to remuneration, etc. the court might intervene and offer interlocutory relief to prevent further sales until the quantum of remuneration has been settled: *Rottenberg v Monjack* [1992] B.C.C. 688.

38 Receivership accounts to be delivered to registrar

38(1) **[Where appointment under powers in instrument]** Except in the case of an administrative receiver, every receiver or manager of a company's property who has been appointed under powers contained in an instrument shall deliver to the registrar of companies for registration the requisite accounts of his receipts and payments.

38(2) **[Time for delivering accounts]** The accounts shall be delivered within one month (or such longer period as the registrar may allow) after the expiration of 12 months from the date of his appointment and of every subsequent period of 6 months, and also within one month after he ceases to act as receiver or manager.

38(3) **[Form of accounts]** The requisite accounts shall be an abstract in the prescribed form showing—

(a) receipts and payments during the relevant period of 12 or 6 months, or

(b) where the receiver or manager ceases to act, receipts and payments during the period from the end of the period of 12 or 6 months to which the last preceding abstract related (or, if no preceding abstract has been delivered under this section, from the date of his appointment) up to the date of his so ceasing, and the aggregate amount of receipts and payments during all preceding periods since his appointment.

38(4) **["Prescribed"]** In this section **"prescribed"** means prescribed by regulations made by statutory instrument by the Secretary of State.

38(5) **[Penalty on default]** A receiver or manager who makes default in complying with this section is liable to a fine and, for continued contravention, to a daily default fine.

S. 38(1), (2)
Receivers or managers other than administrative receivers must periodically submit accounts to Cardiff.

S. 38(3), (4)
These regulate the form of the accounts. For building societies see para. 25 to Sch. 15A as inserted by s. 39 and Sch. 6 to the Building Societies Act 1997.

S. 38(5)
Criminal sanctions are imposed on the receiver in the event of default. On penalties, see s. 430 and Sch. 10. Note also the enforcement procedures laid down in s. 41.
For administrative receivers, see IR 1986, r. 3.32.

Provisions applicable to every receivership

39 Notification that receiver or manager appointed

39(1) **[Statement in invoices etc.]** When a receiver or manager of the property of a company has been appointed, every invoice, order for goods or business letter issued by or on behalf of the company or the

Section 40   Insolvency Act 1986

receiver or manager or the liquidator of the company, being a document on or in which the company's name appears, shall contain a statement that a receiver or manager has been appointed.

39(2) [**Penalty on default**] If default is made in complying with this section, the company and any of the following persons, who knowingly and wilfully authorises or permits the default, namely, any officer of the company, any liquidator of the company and any receiver or manager, is liable to a fine.

S. 39(1)
Invoices, business letters, etc., must disclose the fact that a receiver and manager has been appointed. Note also that under CA 1985, s. 405(1) the fact of the appointment must be notified to Cardiff, and by virtue of IA 1986, s. 46, notice must be given to creditors. Where a secured creditor intends to enforce security in the case of a railway company special advance notification requirements have been imposed by s. 62(7) of the Railways Act 1993. For building societies see para. 26 of Sch. 15A as inserted by s. 39 and Sch. 6 to the Building Societies Act 1997.

S. 39(2)
Criminal sanctions may be imposed on various named persons in the event of a breach of s. 39(1). On penalties, see s. 430 and Sch. 10.

40 Payment of debts out of assets subject to floating charge

40(1) [**Application**] The following applies, in the case of a company, where a receiver is appointed on behalf of the holders of any debentures of the company secured by a charge which, as created, was a floating charge.

40(2) [**Payment of preferential debts**] If the company is not at the time in course of being wound up, its preferential debts (within the meaning given to that expression by section 386 in Part XII) shall be paid out of the assets coming to the hands of the receiver in priority to any claims for principal or interest in respect of the debentures.

40(3) [**Recoupment of payments**] Payments made under this section shall be recouped, as far as may be, out of the assets of the company available for payment of general creditors.

S. 40(1), (2)
These subsections impose an obligation on every receiver appointed to enforce a floating charge to pay preferential claims (see s. 386 and Sch. 6). However, this obligation does not extend to receivers of industrial and provident societies: *Re Devon and Somerset Farmers Ltd* [1994] Ch. 57; [1993] B.C.C. 410. This is a positive obligation (*IR Commrs v Goldblatt* [1972] Ch. 498) and a continuing responsibility that is not discharged simply because the debenture holder has been repaid: *Re Pearl Maintenance Services Ltd* [1995] B.C.C. 657. Note that the fact that the charge may have crystallised prior to the appointment of the receiver does not take the case outside the scope of s. 40. This follows from the revised definition of "floating charge" which was introduced by IA 1985 (see now IA 1986, s. 251), and which is incorporated into the wording of s. 40(1). For the significance of this change in the law see *Re Brightlife Ltd* [1987] Ch. 200; (1986) 2 B.C.C. 99,359. The duty imposed by s. 40 is limited by s. 11(5) but the fact that the company may go into liquidation during the currency of the receivership does not relieve the receiver of his obligation to pay preferential claims: *Re Eisc Teo Ltd* [1991] I.L.R.M. 760. The determination of whether a charge is floating or fixed is clearly of considerable importance for the purposes of s. 40 – see here *Chalk v Kahn* [2000] 2 B.C.L.C. 361. All authorities on this vexed issue of security characterisation must be read in the light of the advice of the Privy Council in *Agnew v CIR (Re Brumark Investments Ltd)* [2001] UKPC 28, [2001] 2 A.C. 710. For comment see Sealy [2001] 76 Company Law Newsletter 1. This latter ruling upset established receivership practice and created real worries for practitioners who may have made distributions on the basis of a misinterpretation of the law (relying on the discredited authority of *Re New Bullas Trading Ltd* [1994] 1 B.C.L.C. 485). These concerns were somewhat alleviated by a Crown Departments Statement offering in effect an amnesty for erroneous distributions made prior to June 5, 2001 (*i.e.* the date when the Privy Council handed down its judgment). For comment see Milman [2002] Insolvency Lawyer 77. Further confirmation of the vulnerability of "fixed charges" to judicial recharacterisation is provided by the ruling of Sir Andrew Morritt V-C in *Re Spectrum Plus Ltd* [2004] EWHC 9 (Ch), [2004] B.C.C. 51 where a standard debenture fixed charge modelled upon that upheld by Slade J in *Siebe Gorman & Co Ltd v Barclays Bank* [1979] 2 Lloyds Rep 142 was in fact held only to create a floating charge. This decision is under appeal. For a further judicial authority in this field see *Re BHT (UK) Ltd* [2004] EWHC 201 Ch. where an attempt to unwind pre-June 5, 2001 distributions under a now "suspect" fixed charge failed.

For the difficult questions of interpretation posed by s. 40 see *Re H & K Medway Ltd* [1997] 1 W.L.R. 1422; [1997] B.C.C. 853, not following *Griffiths v Yorkshire Bank* [1994] 1 W.L.R. 1427 (discussed by Cooke in (1995) 11 I.L. & P. 163). In the former case Neuberger J. explains the relationship between s. 40 and 196. See also Waller [1997–98] 3 R.A.L.Q. 131.

The receiver's obligation to cater for preferential claims will be mitigated when the full consequences of the abolition of Crown preferential debt (introduced via EA 2002, s. 251) are felt. However, not all preferential debts will disappear. Moreover, receivers will in future have to take account of the special reserve fund for unsecured creditors, which was introduced by EA 2002, s. 252 (see IA 1986, s. 176A and IR 1986, rr. 3.39–3.40). This does not apply to floating charges created before September 15, 2003. Holders of floating charges created before this date thus gain from this package of reforms.

These provisions are inapplicable to building society receiverships as the floating charge is not permitted: see para. 27 of Sch. 15A as inserted by s. 39 and Sch. 6 to the Building Societies Act 1997. Note also s. 111 of the Building Societies Act 1997.

S. 40(3)
This makes it clear that the real burden of meeting the claims of preferential creditors falls on the unsecured creditors.

41 Enforcement of duty to make returns

41(1) **[Court order re defaults]** If a receiver or manager of a company's property–

(a) having made default in filing, delivering or making any return, account or other document, or in giving any notice, which a receiver or manager is by law required to file, deliver, make or give, fails to make good the default within 14 days after the service on him of a notice requiring him to do so, or

(b) having been appointed under powers contained in an instrument, has, after being required at any time by the liquidator of the company to do so, failed to render proper accounts of his receipts and payments and to vouch them and pay over to the liquidator the amount properly payable to him,

the court may, on an application made for the purpose, make an order directing the receiver or manager (as the case may be) to make good the default within such time as may be specified in the order.

41(2) **[Application for order]** In the case of the default mentioned in subsection (1)(a), application to the court may be made by any member or creditor of the company or by the registrar of companies; and in the case of the default mentioned in subsection (1)(b), the application shall be made by the liquidator.

In either case the court's order may provide that all costs of and incidental to the application shall be borne by the receiver or manager, as the case may be.

41(3) **[Other enactments]** Nothing in this section prejudices the operation of any enactment imposing penalties on receivers in respect of any such default as is mentioned in subsection (1).

S. 41(1)
This subsection sets out an enforcement procedure to deal with receivers who fail to submit accounts, returns, etc.

S. 41(2)
Applicants to the court for an enforcement order are identified. Applicants may be indemnified against costs thereby arising. The FSA may apply where appropriate – FSMA 2000, s. 363(3).

S. 41(3)
Sanctions imposed by individual sections creating obligations to file returns, etc. are not prejudiced by s. 41.

Administrative receivers: general

42 General powers

42(1) **[Powers in Sch. 1]** The powers conferred on the administrative receiver of a company by the debentures by virtue of which he was appointed are deemed to include (except in so far as they are inconsistent with any of the provisions of those debentures) the powers specified in Schedule 1 to this Act.

42(2) [Interpretation of Sch. 1] In the application of Schedule 1 to the administrative receiver of a company–

(a) the words "he" and "him" refer to the administrative receiver, and

(b) references to the property of the company are to the property of which he is or, but for the appointment of some other person as the receiver of part of the company's property, would be the receiver or manager.

42(3) [Deemed capacity] A person dealing with the administrative receiver in good faith and for value is not concerned to inquire whether the receiver is acting within his powers.

S. 42(1)
A model list of 23 implied powers for an administrative receiver (for the definition of this term, see s. 29(2)) is set out by Sch. 1 to this Act. These are commonly found in most standard commercial debentures. These 23 implied powers would appear to cover almost every eventuality, particularly when one bears in mind the general nature of power number 23. The implied powers are the same as those accorded to an administrator by s. 14. The exercise of these powers may be subject to constraints imposed by companies legislation: see for example *Demite Ltd v Protec Health Ltd* [1998] B.C.C. 638 where the power to sell was subjected to the restrictions imposed by s. 320 of CA 1985. It is clear from the extent of these powers that once a company goes into administrative receivership the control of its management passes from the directors to the receiver. For the implications of this see *Re Joshua Shaw & Sons Ltd* (1989) 5 B.C.C. 188.

S. 42(2)
This is an interpretation provision designed to smooth out any difficulties in the application of Sch. 1.

S. 42(3)
This statutory provision is an extension of the basic company law philosophy contained in *Royal British Bank v Turquand* (1856) 6 E. & B. 327 and in CA 1985, ss. 35A and 35B.

43 Power to dispose of charged property, etc.

43(1) [Application to court] Where, on an application by the administrative receiver, the court is satisfied that the disposal (with or without other assets) of any relevant property which is subject to a security would be likely to promote a more advantageous realisation of the company's assets than would otherwise be effected, the court may by order authorise the administrative receiver to dispose of the property as if it were not subject to the security.

43(2) [Application of s. 43(1)] Subsection (1) does not apply in the case of any security held by the person by or on whose behalf the administrative receiver was appointed, or of any security to which a security so held has priority.

43(3) [Conditions for order] It shall be a condition of an order under this section that–

(a) the net proceeds of the disposal, and

(b) where those proceeds are less than such amount as may be determined by the court to be the net amount which would be realised on the sale of the property in the open market by a willing vendor, such sums as may be required to make good the deficiency,

shall be applied towards discharging the sums secured by the security.

43(4) [Where two or more securities] Where a condition imposed in pursuance of subsection (3) relates to two or more securities, that condition shall require the net proceeds of the disposal and, where paragraph (b) of that subsection applies, the sums mentioned in that paragraph to be applied towards discharging the sums secured by those securities in the order of their priorities.

43(5) [Copy of order to registrar] An office copy of an order under this section shall, within 14 days of the making of the order, be sent by the administrative receiver to the registrar of companies.

43(6) [Penalty for non-compliance] If the administrative receiver without reasonable excuse fails to comply with subsection (5), he is liable to a fine and, for continued contravention, to a daily default fine.

43(7) **["Relevant property"]** In this section **"relevant property"**, in relation to the administrative receiver, means the property of which he is or, but for the appointment of some other person as the receiver of part of the company's property, would be the receiver or manager.

GENERAL NOTE

This section applies to England and Wales only (see s. 440(2)(a)).

Section 43 does not apply in relation to the enforcement of "market charges" (as defined by CA 1989, s. 173): see s. 175 of that Act (as qualified by the Financial Markets and Insolvency Regulations 1991 (SI 1991/880, amended by SI 1995/586 and SI 1998/27)), and the introductory note at p. 2, above.

S. 43(1), (2)

These provisions create a novel facility for administrative receivers by allowing them to apply to the court for the disposal of property that is subject to a prior charge (normally a fixed charge). The court must be satisfied that such disposal would promote a more advantageous realisation of the company's assets. The word "likely" in this context would probably be construed by the courts as meaning "a reasonable prospect": see *Re Harris Simons Construction Ltd* [1989] 1 W.L.R. 368; (1989) 5 B.C.C. 11. A similar power is given to an administrator by s. 15, but the power under s. 15 is wider in that it covers property subject to title retention.

"Relevant property" is defined in s. 43(7).

For further details, see IR 1986, r. 3.31.

S. 43(3), (4)

If the court orders a disposal, the net proceeds are to be paid to discharge the prior security or securities (see s. 43(4)). If the court decides that the sale was at an undervalue, the deficiency must be made good.

S. 43(5), (6)

A copy of the disposal order must be registered at Cardiff within 14 days or else the administrative receiver may incur criminal sanctions.

On penalties, see s. 430 and Sch. 10.

S. 43(7)

This is an interpretation provision and is best understood in relation to s. 29(2)(b).

44 Agency and liability for contracts

44(1) **[Position of administrative receiver]** The administrative receiver of a company–

(a) is deemed to be the company's agent, unless and until the company goes into liquidation;

(b) is personally liable on any contract entered into by him in the carrying out of his functions (except in so far as the contract otherwise provides) and, to the extent of any qualifying liability, on any contract of employment adopted by him in the carrying out of those functions; and

(c) is entitled in respect of that liability to an indemnity out of the assets of the company.

44(2) **[Interpretation]** For the purposes of subsection (1)(b) the administrative receiver is not to be taken to have adopted a contract of employment by reason of anything done or omitted to be done within 14 days after his appointment.

44(2A) **[Interpretation of s. 44(1)(b)]** For the purposes of subsection (1)(b), a liability under a contract of employment is a qualifying liability if–

(a) it is a liability to pay a sum by way of wages or salary or contribution to an occupational pension scheme,

(b) it is incurred while the administrative receiver is in office, and

(c) it is in respect of services rendered wholly or partly after the adoption of the contract.

44(2B) **[Further interpretation of s. 44(1)(b)]** Where a sum payable in respect of a liability which is a qualifying liability for the purposes of subsection (1)(b) is payable in respect of services rendered partly before and partly after the adoption of the contract, liability under subsection (1)(b) shall only extend to so much of the sum as is payable in respect of services rendered after the adoption of the contract.

44(2C) **[Interpretation of s. 44(2A), (2B)]** For the purposes of subsections (2A) and (2B)–

(a) wages or salary payable in respect of a period of holiday or absence from work through sickness or other good cause are deemed to be wages or (as the case may be) salary in respect of services rendered in that period, and

(b) a sum payable in lieu of holiday is deemed to be wages or (as the case may be) salary in respect of services rendered in the period by reference to which the holiday entitlement arose.

44(2D) **[Interpretation of s. 44(2C)(a)]** In subsection (2C)(a), the reference to wages or salary payable in respect of a period of holiday includes any sums which, if they had been paid, would have been treated for the purposes of the enactments relating to social security as earnings in respect of that period.

44(3) **[Effect on other rights]** This section does not limit any right to indemnity which the administrative receiver would have apart from it, nor limit his liability on contracts entered into or adopted without authority, nor confer any right to indemnity in respect of that liability.

S. 44(1), (2)
By virtue of s. 44(1)(a), an administrative receiver is deemed to be the company's agent, provided that the company has not gone into liquidation, whereupon the agency relationship terminates. This is merely a statutory declaration of the standard agency provision found in most commercial debentures. For the position on winding up, see *Gosling v Gaskell and Grocott* [1897] A.C. 575 and the article by Turing in (1994) 9 I.L. & P. 163. One implication of the agency relationship was illustrated in *Brown v City of London Corporation* [1996] 1 W.L.R. 1070 (also reported as *Re Sobam BV* [1996] B.C.C. 351) where it was held that a receiver was not liable for rates during his period of occupation. The termination of this agency relationship does not result in a change of occupation for rating purposes – *Re Beck Foods Ltd* [2001] EWCA Civ 1934, [2002] B.C.C. 495. These developments represent a further blow for local authorities which no longer enjoy preferential status with respect to unpaid rates and who additionally have difficulty in protecting their interests through distress, as was confirmed by *Re ELS Ltd* [1994] B.C.C. 449.

An agent is not normally liable personally on a contract which he makes for his principal, and in the light of this, para. (b) may seem somewhat surprising – especially when it is contrasted with s. 14(5), which deems an administrator to be the company's agent without a similar qualification. The explanation is that a receiver is entitled to stipulate for an indemnity from the charge-holder as a term of his accepting office, contracting out of this liability. For a case where such contracting out would have found favour with the courts see *Amec Properties v Planning Research and Systems* [1992] 13 E.G. 109. For the practical significance of this indemnity see *Lipe Ltd v Leyland DAF Ltd* [1993] B.C.C. 385.

Sections 44(1)(a) and 44(2) now need to be read in the light of amendments made by IA 1994. The background to these amendments can be traced back ultimately to the case of *Nicoll v Cutts* (1985) 1 B.C.C. 99,427 where it was held that a receiver who continued to retain the services of company employees during the receivership did not thereby adopt their contracts of employment. This decision was immediately counteracted by an express statutory provision extending the personal contractual liability of administrative receivers to cases of adopted contracts of employment. Insolvency practitioners sought to neutralise this statutory intervention by sending all employees whose services were being retained a letter to the effect that their contracts of employment were not being adopted nor was the administrative receiver undertaking personal liability thereon. This practice drew its support from the unreported ruling of Harman J. in *Re Specialised Mouldings Ltd* (February 13, 1987). The ability of insolvency practitioners to avoid the effect of the statutory rules imposing liablity in cases of adoption was reviewed by the Court of Appeal in *Re Paramount Airways Ltd (No. 3)* [1994] B.C.C. 172 (see the note to s. 19 above). Here the Court of Appeal held (confirming the first instance ruling of Evans-Lombe J.) that adoption could occur simply by retaining staff without changing the terms of their employment. A transparent ploy such as sending a "*Specialised Mouldings*" letter was of no effect. As a result of this pronouncement from the Court of Appeal administrative receivers who retained staff after the initial 14-day period for reflection did so on the basis that they became personally liable for all accrued and current rights arising under the relevant contracts of employment. Not surprisingly, administrative receivers were reluctant to assume such personal risk, even though it would be covered by their indemnity. Debenture holders would be less willing to wait for their money by allowing the receiver to generate it through a corporate rescue but would instead insist on an immediate sale.

The economic and political consequences of abandoning a corporate rescue strategy were so great that the government was persuaded to legislate immediately. This legislation takes the form of IA 1994 which applies to contracts of employment adopted on or after March 15, 1994 (this legislation is to this extent retrospective as Royal Assent was only given on March 24, 1994). Under s. 2 of this Act where a contract of employment is adopted by an administrative receiver he will only become personally responsible for "qualifying liabilities". These are defined in the new ss. 44(2A)–(2D) (inserted by IA 1994, s. 2(1), (3), (4)) as certain liabilities accruing only after the date when the contract was adopted. The government has indicated that it will not be persuaded to extend the retrospective effect of this legislation beyond March 15, 1994: see DTI Press Notice P/95/282.

The issue was revisited when *Paramount* (and the direct appeals in *Re Leyland DAF* and *Re Ferranti International* [1994] B.C.C. 654) reached the House of Lords (reported *sub nomine Powdrill v Watson* [1995] 2 A.C. 394; [1995] B.C.C. 319). Their Lordships were of course concerned to clarify the law pre-March 15, 1994 and in essence they approved of the approach of the Court of Appeal with regard to adoption. However they took a more restrictive view of the extent of liabilities incurred in cases of adoption. For a review of the whole saga see Mudd (1994) 10 I.L. & P. 38 and (1995) 11 I.L. & P. 78. Pre-1994 claims still continue to trouble receivers, as is clear from the Scottish case of *Jamieson, Petitioners* 1997 S.C. 195, [1997] B.C.C. 682. On whether adoption can occur by error, see *Re Antal International Ltd* [2003] EWHC 1339 (Ch), a case on administration.

In s. 44(1)(b) the words ", to the extent of any qualifying liability," were inserted after "provides) and" by IA 1994, s. 2(1), (2), (4).

S. 44(3)
This, in effect, merely extends s. 37(3) to administrative receivers.

45 Vacation of office

45(1) [Removal by court, resignation] An administrative receiver of a company may at any time be removed from office by order of the court (but not otherwise) and may resign his office by giving notice of his resignation in the prescribed manner to such persons as may be prescribed.

45(2) [Vacation of office] An administrative receiver shall vacate office if he ceases to be qualified to act as an insolvency practitioner in relation to the company.

45(3) [Effect of vacation of office] Where at any time an administrative receiver vacates office–

(a)   his remuneration and any expenses properly incurred by him, and

(b)   any indemnity to which he is entitled out of the assets of the company,

shall be charged on and paid out of any property of the company which is in his custody or under his control at that time in priority to any security held by the person by or on whose behalf he was appointed.

45(4) [Notice to registrar] Where an administrative receiver vacates office otherwise than by death, he shall, within 14 days after his vacation of office, send a notice to that effect to the registrar of companies.

45(5) [Penalty for non-compliance] If an administrative receiver without reasonable excuse fails to comply with subsection (4), he is liable to a fine and, for continued contravention, to a daily default fine.

S. 45(1), (2)
These subsections outline the situations where the tenure of an administrative receiver comes to an end. Note that (as a result of a change in the law made by IA 1985) he can only be removed by debenture holders if they successfully apply to the court. This will make it clear that he is not entirely the minion of the debenture holders who appointed him. If he loses his qualification as an insolvency practitioner (see Pt XIII) he must also vacate office. Although the court has the power to remove an administrative receiver it does not enjoy the consequential power of appointing a replacement: *Re A & C Supplies Ltd* [1998] B.C.C. 708. Such a replacement can only be effected by a debenture holder enjoying a floating charge.

S. 45(3)
This subsection protects the priority status of the administrative receiver's right to remuneration and indemnity.

S. 45(4), (5)
On vacating office the administrative receiver must notify Cardiff within 14 days or incur a fine. A similar obligation is imposed by CA 1985, s. 405(2). Note prospective amendment in s. 45(5): the words "and, for continued contravention, to a daily default fine" are to be repealed by CA 1989, Sch. 16 and 24 from a day to be appointed.

On penalties, see s. 430 and Sch. 10.
For further information, see IR 1986, rr. 3.33–3.35.

Section 46 *Insolvency Act 1986*

Administrative receivers: ascertainment and investigation of company's affairs

46 Information to be given by administrative receiver

46(1) **[Notices]** Where an administrative receiver is appointed, he shall–

(a) forthwith send to the company and publish in the prescribed manner a notice of his appointment, and

(b) within 28 days after his appointment, unless the court otherwise directs, send such a notice to all the creditors of the company (so far as he is aware of their addresses).

46(2) **[Non-application]** This section and the next do not apply in relation to the appointment of an administrative receiver to act–

(a) with an existing administrative receiver, or

(b) in place of an administrative receiver dying or ceasing to act,

except that, where they apply to an administrative receiver who dies or ceases to act before they have been fully complied with, the references in this section and the next to the administrative receiver include (subject to the next subsection) his successor and any continuing administrative receiver.

46(3) **[Where company being wound up]** If the company is being wound up, this section and the next apply notwithstanding that the administrative receiver and the liquidator are the same person, but with any necessary modifications arising from that fact.

46(4) **[Penalty for non-compliance]** If the administrative receiver without reasonable excuse fails to comply with this section, he is liable to a fine and, for continued contravention, to a daily default fine.

S. 46(1), (4)
These provisions impose obligations on the administrative receiver to give notice of his appointment to various named parties. Criminal sanctions are imposed in the event of default (on penalties, see s. 430 and Sch. 10). Note also s. 39, and CA 1985, s. 405(1) (entry of appointment in register of charges).

S. 46(2), (3)
Qualifications to the above obligations are imposed. Compliance with s. 46(1) is a once and for all requirement. Provision is made for the case where the company is in liquidation and the administrative receiver is also the liquidator.
   For further details, see IR 1986, r. 3.2.

47 Statement of affairs to be submitted

47(1) **[Duty of administrative receiver]** Where an administrative receiver is appointed, he shall forthwith require some or all of the persons mentioned below to make out and submit to him a statement in the prescribed form as to the affairs of the company.

47(2) **[Contents of statement]** A statement submitted under this section shall be verified by affidavit by the persons required to submit it and shall show–

(a) particulars of the company's assets, debts and liabilities;

(b) the names and addresses of its creditors;

(c) the securities held by them respectively;

(d) the dates when the securities were respectively given; and

(e) such further or other information as may be prescribed.

47(3)   [Persons in s. 47(1)] The persons referred to in subsection (1) are–

(a)   those who are or have been officers of the company;

(b)   those who have taken part in the company's formation at any time within one year before the date of the appointment of the administrative receiver;

(c)   those who are in the company's employment, or have been in its employment within that year, and are in the administrative receiver's opinion capable of giving the information required;

(d)   those who are or have been within that year officers of or in the employment of a company which is, or within that year was, an officer of the company.

In this subsection **"employment"** includes employment under a contract for services.

47(4)   [Time for statement] Where any persons are required under this section to submit a statement of affairs to the administrative receiver, they shall do so (subject to the next subsection) before the end of the period of 21 days beginning with the day after that on which the prescribed notice of the requirement is given to them by the administrative receiver.

47(5)   [Release, extension of time] The administrative receiver, if he thinks fit, may–

(a)   at any time release a person from an obligation imposed on him under subsection (1) or (2), or

(b)   either when giving notice under subsection (4) or subsequently, extend the period so mentioned;

and where the administrative receiver has refused to exercise a power conferred by this subsection, the court, if it thinks fit, may exercise it.

47(6)   [Penalty for non-compliance] If a person without reasonable excuse fails to comply with any obligation imposed under this section, he is liable to a fine and, for continued contravention, to a daily default fine.

S. 47(1), (2), (4)
A statement of affairs containing the information outlined in s. 47(2) and the rules must be submitted to the administrative receiver within 21 days of his requiring it (or longer, if s. 47(5) is activated).

S. 47(3), (5), (6)
The persons who may be required by the administrative receiver to participate in the submission of the statement of affairs are identified by s. 47(3), although they may be excused either by the administrative receiver or the courts. Criminal sanctions are imposed on defaulters. On penalties, see s. 430 and Sch. 10.
   For further information, see IR 1986, rr. 3.3–3.7. For enforcement by the administrative receiver, see IR 1986, r. 7.20.

48   Report by administrative receiver

48(1)   [Duty of administrative receiver] Where an administrative receiver is appointed, he shall, within 3 months (or such longer period as the court may allow) after his appointment, send to the registrar of companies, to any trustees for secured creditors of the company and (so far as he is aware of their addresses) to all such creditors a report as to the following matters, namely–

(a)   the events leading up to his appointment, so far as he is aware of them;

(b)   the disposal or proposed disposal by him of any property of the company and the carrying on or proposed carrying on by him of any business of the company;

(c)   the amounts of principal and interest payable to the debenture holders by whom or on whose behalf he was appointed and the amounts payable to preferential creditors; and

(d)   the amount (if any) likely to be available for the payment of other creditors.

Section 48 Insolvency Act 1986

48(2) [Copies of report] The administrative receiver shall also, within 3 months (or such longer period as the court may allow) after his appointment, either–

(a) send a copy of the report (so far as he is aware of their addresses) to all unsecured creditors of the company; or

(b) publish in the prescribed manner a notice stating an address to which unsecured creditors of the company should write for copies of the report to be sent to them free of charge,

and (in either case), unless the court otherwise directs, lay a copy of the report before a meeting of the company's unsecured creditors summoned for the purpose on not less than 14 days' notice.

48(3) [Conditions for s. 48(2) direction] The court shall not give a direction under subsection (2) unless–

(a) the report states the intention of the administrative receiver to apply for the direction, and

(b) a copy of the report is sent to the persons mentioned in paragraph (a) of that subsection, or a notice is published as mentioned in paragraph (b) of that subsection, not less than 14 days before the hearing of the application.

48(4) [Where company in liquidation] Where the company has gone or goes into liquidation, the administrative receiver–

(a) shall, within 7 days after his compliance with subsection (1) or, if later, the nomination or appointment of the liquidator, send a copy of the report to the liquidator, and

(b) where he does so within the time limited for compliance with subsection (2), is not required to comply with that subsection.

48(5) [Report to include summary of statement] A report under this section shall include a summary of the statement of affairs made out and submitted to the administrative receiver under section 47 and of his comments (if any) upon it.

48(6) [Limit on report only] Nothing in this section is to be taken as requiring any such report to include any information the disclosure of which would seriously prejudice the carrying out by the administrative receiver of his functions.

48(7) [Application of s. 46(2)] Section 46(2) applies for the purposes of this section also.

48(8) [Penalty for non-compliance] If the administrative receiver without reasonable excuse fails to comply with this section, he is liable to a fine and, for continued contravention, to a daily default fine.

S. 48(1), (4), (7)
These subsections require an administrative receiver to submit a report (normally within 3 months of his appointment) to various named parties, including the liquidator (see s. 48(4)) and the FSA where appropriate – FSMA 2000 s. 363 (4). The contents of the report are also detailed. It is clear from s. 48(7) that this obligation does not apply to an administrative receiver succeeding another or assisting an incumbent administrative receiver.
   Note also the whistleblowing duty imposed by FSMA 2000 s. 364.

S. 48(2), (3)
More widespread publication of the report is required by s. 48(2). Unsecured creditors, in particular, are to be given access to this report. A meeting of unsecured creditors must also be called at which this report is presented. The court can relieve an administrative receiver from this latter obligation, provided that the conditions in s. 48(3) are satisfied.

S. 48(5), (6)
These provisions go into further detail on the administrative receiver's report. It should contain a summary of the statement of affairs submitted to him, but need not include "any information, the disclosure of which would seriously

prejudice the carrying out by the administrative receiver of his functions". It is not clear whether the test to be applied here is subjective or objective. See also *Gomba Holdings UK Ltd v Homan & Bird* [1986] 1 W.L.R. 1301; (1986) 2 B.C.C. 99,102.

S. 48(8)
Again, criminal sanctions are imposed on a defaulting administrative receiver. On penalties, see s. 430 and Sch. 10.
Section 48 is amplified by IR 1986, r. 3.8–3.15.

49 Committee of creditors

49(1) **[Meeting may establish committee]** Where a meeting of creditors is summoned under section 48, the meeting may, if it thinks fit, establish a committee (**"the creditors' committee"**) to exercise the functions conferred on it by or under this Act.

49(2) **[Committee may summon administrative receiver]** If such a committee is established, the committee may, on giving not less than 7 days' notice, require the administrative receiver to attend before it at any reasonable time and furnish it with such information relating to the carrying out by him of his functions as it may reasonably require.

S. 49(1)
This empowers the unsecured creditors in their meeting called under s. 48(2) to set up a committee. An FSA representative may attend where appropriate – FSMA 2000 s. 363(5).

S. 49(2)
The committee of creditors can request information from the administrative receiver. The test of reasonableness is presumably designed to protect information of the type envisaged by s. 48(6).
Further details on the constitution, role and working of this committee are provided by IR 1986, r. 3.16–3.30A.

CHAPTER II

RECEIVERS (SCOTLAND)

50 Extent of this Chapter

50 This Chapter extends to Scotland only.

GENERAL NOTE

Scottish debenture holders were only given the remedy of receivership in 1972 and, since that date, their law of receivership has developed separately from the English counterpart, although on similar lines. There have been problems in fitting this new remedy into the general system of Scottish corporate insolvency law, and problems of statutory interpretation have troubled the Scottish courts on a number of occasions. For the floating charge in Scotland, see CA 1985, ss. 462–466 and the recent discussion in the House of Lords in *Sharp v Woolwich Building Society* [1988] B.C.C. 115. Reference should also be made to the Receivers (Scotland) Regulations 1986 (SI 1986/1917 (S 141)).

The changes made in this area of the law by IA 1985 and IA 1986 do not operate retrospectively; see Sch. 11, para. 3(2).

Sections 50–71 apply to LLPs with suitable modifications – see Limited Liability Partnerships (Scotland) Regulations 2001 (SI 2001/128) reg. 4, Sch. 2.

51 Power to appoint receiver

51(1) **[Floating charge holder may appoint receiver]** It is competent under the law of Scotland for the holder of a floating charge over all or any part of the property (including uncalled capital), which may from time to time be comprised in the property and undertaking of an incorporated company (whether a company within the meaning of the Companies Act or not) which the Court of Session has jurisdiction to wind up, to appoint a receiver of such part of the property of the company as is subject to the charge.

51(2) **[Appointment by court on application]** It is competent under the law of Scotland for the court, on the application of the holder of such a floating charge, to appoint a receiver of such part of the property of the company as is subject to the charge.

51(2A) Subsections (1) and (2) are subject to section 72A.

51(3) **[Those disqualified]** The following are disqualified from being appointed as receiver–

(a) a body corporate;

(b) an undischarged bankrupt; and

(c) a firm according to the law of Scotland.

51(4) **[Scottish firm]** A body corporate or a firm according to the law of Scotland which acts as a receiver is liable to a fine.

51(5) **[Undischarged bankrupt]** An undischarged bankrupt who so acts is liable to imprisonment or a fine, or both.

51(6) **["Receiver"]** In this section, **"receiver"** includes joint receivers.

S. 51(1), (2)
These provisions authorise the holder of a floating charge in Scotland (for the meaning of this term, see IA 1986, s. 70) to appoint a receiver out of court or to apply to the court for such an appointment. For the meaning of "property" within subs. (1) see *Hawking v Hafton House Ltd* 1990 SLT 496.

S. 51(2A)
This was inserted by s. 248 and Sch. 17 of EA 2002 to reflect the new restrictive approach towards administrative receivership (or receivership in Scotland). See the commentary on s. 72A.

S. 51(3)–(5)
These subsections deal with the question of disqualification and mirror the English provisions to a large extent. However, note that Scottish partnerships, which possess legal personality, are also disqualified. A Scottish receiver will have to be a qualified insolvency practitioner within the meaning of IA 1986, Pt XIII, if he is an administrative receiver, as will commonly be the case (see IA 1986, s. 251). On penalties, see s. 430 and Sch. 10.

S. 51(6)
Joint receivers are permissible under Scottish law.

52 Circumstances justifying appointment

52(1) **[Events for s. 51(1) appointment]** A receiver may be appointed under section 51(1) by the holder of the floating charge on the occurrence of any event which, by the provisions of the instrument creating the charge, entitles the holder of the charge to make that appointment and, in so far as not otherwise provided for by the instrument, on the occurrence of any of the following events, namely–

(a) the expiry of a period of 21 days after the making of a demand for payment of the whole or any part of the principal sum secured by the charge, without payment having been made;

(b) the expiry of a period of 2 months during the whole of which interest due and payable under the charge has been in arrears;

(c) the making of an order or the passing of a resolution to wind up the company;

(d) the appointment of a receiver by virtue of any other floating charge created by the company.

52(2) **[Events for s. 51(2) appointment]** A receiver may be appointed by the court under section 51(2) on the occurrence of any event which, by the provisions of the instrument creating the floating charge, entitles the holder of the charge to make that appointment and, in so far as not otherwise provided for by the instrument, on the occurrence of any of the following events, namely–

(a) where the court, on the application of the holder of the charge, pronounces itself satisfied that the position of the holder of the charge is likely to be prejudiced if no such appointment is made;

(b) any of the events referred to in paragraphs (a) to (c) of subsection (1).

S. 52(1)
This subsection provides a model list of grounds (which can be varied by the debenture) under which a Scots receiver can be appointed out of court by a holder of a floating charge.

S. 52(2)
A receiver can be appointed by the court on the occurrence of any of the events specified in s. 52(1) or on grounds of prejudice (a Scottish synonym for "jeopardy").

53 Mode of appointment by holder of charge

53(1) [Instrument of appointment] The appointment of a receiver by the holder of the floating charge under section 51(1) shall be by means of an instrument subscribed in accordance with the Requirements of Writing (Scotland) Act 1995 (**"the instrument of appointment"**), a copy (certified in the prescribed manner to be a correct copy) whereof shall be delivered by or on behalf of the person making the appointment to the registrar of companies for registration within 7 days of its execution and shall be accompanied by a notice in the prescribed form.

53(2) [Penalty on default] If any person without reasonable excuse makes default in complying with the requirements of subsection (1), he is liable to a fine and, for continued contravention, to a daily default fine.

53(3) (Ceased to have effect and repealed by Law Reform (Miscellaneous Provisions) (Scotland) Act 1990, s. 74, Sch. 8, para. 35 and Sch. 9 as from 1 December 1990.)

53(4) [Execution on behalf of floating charge holders] If the receiver is to be appointed by the holders of a series of secured debentures, the instrument of appointment may be executed on behalf of the holders of the floating charge by any person authorised by resolution of the debenture-holders to execute the instrument.

53(5) [Entry on register] On receipt of the certified copy of the instrument of appointment in accordance with subsection (1), the registrar shall, on payment of the prescribed fee, enter the particulars of the appointment in the register of charges.

53(6) [Effect of appointment] The appointment of a person as a receiver by an instrument of appointment in accordance with subsection (1)–

(a) is of no effect unless it is accepted by that person before the end of the business day next following that on which the instrument of appointment is received by him or on his behalf, and

(b) subject to paragraph (a), is deemed to be made on the day on and at the time at which the instrument of appointment is so received, as evidenced by a written docquet by that person or on his behalf;

and this subsection applies to the appointment of joint receivers subject to such modifications as may be prescribed.

53(7) [Attachment of charge] On the appointment of a receiver under this section, the floating charge by virtue of which he was appointed attaches to the property then subject to the charge; and such attachment has effect as if the charge was a fixed security over the property to which it has attached.

S. 53(1), (2), (5)
Section 53(1) specifies the exclusive method by which a receiver can be appointed out of court. Note that, as in English law (CA 1985, s. 405), a notice in proper form of the appointment must be delivered for registration to the Scottish Companies Registry in Edinburgh, whereupon the registrar must register it: see s. 53(1). Criminal sanctions are imposed for default. A textual amendment to subs. (1) was made by the Requirements of Writing (Scotland) Act 1995,

s. 14(1) and Sch. 4, para. 58(a). Section 53(1) was modified by the Scotland Act 1998, s. 125(1) and Sch. 8, para. 23(1)–(3) so that anything done by the registrar of companies in Scotland or the assistant registrar of friendly societies for Scotland by virtue of s. 53(1) as applied in relation to friendly societies, industrial and provident societies or building societies may be done to or by the Accountant in Bankruptcy as from July 1, 1999 (see SI 1998/3178 (C. 79), art. 2). Note prospective amendment in s. 53(2): the words "and, for continued contravention, to a daily default fine" are to be repealed by CA 1989, Sch. 16 and 24 from a day to be appointed. On penalties, see s. 430 and Sch. 10. For the prescribed form under s. 53(1), see the Receivers (Scotland) Regulations 1986 (SI 1986/1917 (S 141)) Form 1 (Scot).

S. 53(3)
This subsection was repealed by the Law Reform (Miscellaneous Provisions) (Scotland) Act 1990, s. 74 and Sch. 9: see SI 1990/2328 (C. 60), art. 3.

The reference to s. 36B was substituted by CA 1989, s. 130(7) and Sch. 17, para. 10.

S. 53(4)
This subsection, which was substituted by s. 14(1) and Sch. 4, para. 58(b) to the Requirements of Writing (Scotland) Act 1995, deals with the way in which the instrument of appointment is executed. For the meaning of "holder of the floating charge" and "series of secured debentures" in s. 53(4), see s. 70.

S. 53(6), (7)
The time of the appointment is fixed (for the English position, see IA 1986, s. 33(1)). The appointment of the receiver causes crystallisation by converting the charge into a fixed security, but this does not render it immune from attack under IA 1986, s. 245, nor from the preferential claims regime. See the Receivers (Scotland) Regulations 1986 (SI 1986/1917 (S 141)). On s. 53(7) see *Myles J. Callaghan Ltd (in receivership) v City of Glasgow Direct Council* (1987) 3 B.C.C. 337; *Scottish and Newcastle plc, Petitioners* [1993] B.C.C. 634 and *Sharp v Woolwich Building Society* [1998] B.C.C. 115.

54 Appointment by court

54(1) [Petition to court] Application for the appointment of a receiver by the court under section 51(2) shall be by petition to the court, which shall be served on the company.

54(2) [Issue of interlocutor] On such an application, the court shall, if it thinks fit, issue an interlocutor making the appointment of the receiver.

54(3) [Copy of interlocutor to registrar, penalty on default] A copy (certified by the clerk of the court to be a correct copy) of the court's interlocutor making the appointment shall be delivered by or on behalf of the petitioner to the registrar of companies for registration, accompanied by a notice in the prescribed form, within 7 days of the date of the interlocutor or such longer period as the court may allow.

If any person without reasonable excuse makes default in complying with the requirements of this subsection, he is liable to a fine and, for continued contravention, to a daily default fine.

54(4) [Entry on register] On receipt of the certified copy interlocutor in accordance with subsection (3), the registrar shall, on payment of the prescribed fee, enter the particulars of the appointment in the register of charges.

54(5) [Date of appointment] The receiver is to be regarded as having been appointed on the date of his being appointed by the court.

54(6) [Attachment of charge] On the appointment of a receiver under this section, the floating charge by virtue of which he was appointed attaches to the property then subject to the charge; and such attachment has effect as if the charge were a fixed security over the property to which it has attached.

54(7) [Rules of court re urgent cases] In making rules of court for the purposes of this section, the Court of Session shall have regard to the need for special provision for cases which appear to the court to require to be dealt with as a matter of urgency.

S. 54(1), (2)
These provisions outline the procedure by which a receiver can be appointed by the court in Scotland.

S. 54(3), (4)
The court's order (interlocutor) is to be registered at Edinburgh, normally within seven days. Criminal sanctions are imposed for failure to submit the order for registration. Section 54(3) modified by Scotland Act 1998, s. 125(1) and Sch. 8, para. 23(1)–(3) so that anything done by the registrar of companies in Scotland or the assistant registrar of friendly societies for Scotland by virtue of s. 54(3) as applied in relation to friendly societies, industrial and provident societies or building societies may be done to or by the Accountant in Bankruptcy as from July 1, 1999 (see SI 1998/3178 (C. 79), art. 2). Note prospective amendment in s. 54(3): the words "and, for continued contravention, to a daily default fine" are to be repealed by CA 1989, Schs 16 and 24 from a day to be appointed. On penalties, see s. 430 and Sch. 10. For the notice in prescribed form under s. 54(3), see Form 2 (Scot) in the Receivers (Scotland) Regulations 1986 (SI 1986/1917 (SS 141)).

S. 54(5), (6)
These subsections regulate the timing and the effect of the appointment.

S. 54(7)
Special rules of court may be devised to expedite urgent cases.

55 Powers of receiver

55(1) **[Powers in instrument]** Subject to the next subsection, a receiver has in relation to such part of the property of the company as is attached by the floating charge by virtue of which he was appointed, the powers, if any, given to him by the instrument creating that charge.

55(2) **[Powers in Sch. 2]** In addition, the receiver has under this Chapter the powers as respects that property (in so far as these are not inconsistent with any provision contained in that instrument) which are specified in Schedule 2 to this Act.

55(3) **[Restriction on powers]** Subsections (1) and (2) apply–

(a) subject to the rights of any person who has effectually executed diligence on all or any part of the property of the company prior to the appointment of the receiver, and

(b) subject to the rights of any person who holds over all or any part of the property of the company a fixed security or floating charge having priority over, or ranking pari passu with, the floating charge by virtue of which the receiver was appointed.

55(4) **[Enquiry as to authority not necessary]** A person dealing with a receiver in good faith and for value is not concerned to enquire whether the receiver is acting within his powers.

S. 55(1), (2)
Scottish receivers enjoy the 23 implied powers listed in Sch. 2 to the Act. These can be added to by the debenture. For the English position, see s. 42 and Sch. 1. For a recent authority here, see *Myles J. Callaghan Ltd (in receivership) v City of Glasgow District Council* (1987) 3 B.C.C. 337. The powers of the receiver do not extend to assets which cannot be regarded as the "property" of the company: see *Hawking v Hafton House Ltd* 1990 S.L.T. 496.

S. 55(3), (4)
The rights of third parties, such as holders of a fixed security (for definition, see s. 70) and execution creditors, vis-à-vis the receiver in the exercise of his powers are regulated. Third parties need not check to see that the receiver is acting within his powers. See *Iona Hotels Ltd, Petitioners* 1991 S.L.T. 11.

56 Precedence among receivers

56(1) **[Order of precedence]** Where there are two or more floating charges subsisting over all or any part of the property of the company, a receiver may be appointed under this Chapter by virtue of each such charge; but a receiver appointed by, or on the application of, the holder of a floating charge having priority of ranking over any other floating charge by virtue of which a receiver has been appointed has the powers given to a receiver by section 55 and Schedule 2 to the exclusion of any other receiver.

56(2) **[Where floating charges rank equally]** Where two or more floating charges rank with one another equally, and two or more receivers have been appointed by virtue of such charges, the receivers so appointed are deemed to have been appointed as joint receivers.

56(3) [Receivers to act jointly] Receivers appointed, or deemed to have been appointed, as joint receivers shall act jointly unless the instrument of appointment or respective instruments of appointment otherwise provide.

56(4) [Suspension of receiver's powers] Subject to subsection (5) below, the powers of a receiver appointed by, or on the application of, the holder of a floating charge are suspended by, and as from the date of, the appointment of a receiver by, or on the application of, the holder of a floating charge having priority of ranking over that charge to such extent as may be necessary to enable the receiver second mentioned to exercise his powers under section 55 and Schedule 2; and any powers so suspended take effect again when the floating charge having priority of ranking ceases to attach to the property then subject to the charge, whether such cessation is by virtue of section 62(6) or otherwise.

56(5) [Effect of suspension] The suspension of the powers of a receiver under sub-section (4) does not have the effect of requiring him to release any part of the property (including any letters or documents) of the company from his control until he receives from the receiver superseding him a valid indemnity (subject to the limit of the value of such part of the property of the company as is subject to the charge by virtue of which he was appointed) in respect of any expenses, charges and liabilities he may have incurred in the performance of his functions as receiver.

56(6) [Floating charge remains attached] The suspension of the powers of a receiver under subsection (4) does not cause the floating charge by virtue of which he was appointed to cease to attach to the property to which it attached by virtue of section 53(7) or 54(6).

56(7) [Same receiver by several charges] Nothing in this section prevents the same receiver being appointed by virtue of two or more floating charges.

S. 56(1), (2), (3)
Two competing receivers may be appointed over the same company's assets, but only the one with priority can exercise the statutory powers conferred on receivers. In the event of a "tie" they are deemed to have been appointed as joint receivers, and must act jointly.

S. 56(4), (5), (6)
These subsections deal with the situation where the receiver who was appointed first has to give way to a receiver appointed subsequently, but enjoying priority. This is a matter not dealt with by any English statutory provision. The first receiver's powers are suspended until the latter has fulfilled his role. However, he should not hand over property to the latter until he has received an indemnity from him. Furthermore, the mere fact that a receiver's powers have been suspended does not cause the floating charge under which he was appointed to refloat.

S. 56(7)
To make matters easier, the same receiver can act for competing chargees, although this may produce conflicts of interest.

57 Agency and liability of receiver for contracts

57(1) [Receiver deemed agent] A receiver is deemed to be the agent of the company in relation to such property of the company as is attached by the floating charge by virtue of which he was appointed.

57(1A) [Further qualification re receiver as agent] Without prejudice to subsection (1), a receiver is deemed to be the agent of the company in relation to any contract of employment adopted by him in the carrying out of his functions.

57(2) [Personal liability] A receiver (including a receiver whose powers are subsequently suspended under section 56) is personally liable on any contract entered into by him in the performance of his functions, except in so far as the contract otherwise provides, and, to the extent of any qualifying liability, on any contract of employment adopted by him in the carrying out of those functions.

57(2A) **[Interpretation of s. 57(2)]** For the purposes of subsection (2), a liability under a contract of employment is a qualifying liability if–

(a) it is a liability to pay a sum by way of wages or salary or contribution to an occupational pension scheme,

(b) it is incurred while the receiver is in office, and

(c) it is in respect of services rendered wholly or partly after the adoption of the contract.

57(2B) **[Further interpretation of s. 57(2)]** Where a sum payable in respect of a liability which is a qualifying liability for the purposes of subsection (2) is payable in respect of services rendered partly before and partly after the adoption of the contract, liability under that subsection shall only extend to so much of the sum as is payable in respect of services rendered after the adoption of the contract.

57(2C) **[Interpretation of s. 57(2A), (2B)]** For the purposes of subsections (2A) and (2B)–

(a) wages or salary payable in respect of a period of holiday or absence from work through sickness or other good cause are deemed to be wages or (as the case may be) salary in respect of services rendered in that period, and

(b) a sum payable in lieu of holiday is deemed to be wages or (as the case may be) salary in respect of services rendered in the period by reference to which the holiday entitlement arose.

57(2D) **[Interpretation of s. 57(2C)(a)]** In subsection (2C)(a), the reference to wages or salary payable in respect of a period of holiday includes any sums which, if they had been paid, would have been treated for the purposes of the enactments relating to social security as earnings in respect of that period.

57(3) **[Indemnity]** A receiver who is personally liable by virtue of subsection (2) is entitled to be indemnified out of the property in respect of which he was appointed.

57(4) **[Contracts before appointment]** Any contract entered into by or on behalf of the company prior to the appointment of a receiver continues in force (subject to its terms) notwithstanding that appointment, but the receiver does not by virtue only of his appointment incur any personal liability on any such contract.

57(5) **[Interpretation of s. 57(2)]** For the purposes of subsection (2), a receiver is not to be taken to have adopted a contract of employment by reason of anything done or omitted to be done within 14 days after his appointment.

57(6) **[Effect]** This section does not limit any right to indemnity which the receiver would have apart from it, nor limit his liability on contracts entered into or adopted without authority, nor confer any right to indemnity in respect of that liability.

57(7) **[Continuation of contract]** Any contract entered into by a receiver in the performance of his functions continues in force (subject to its terms) although the powers of the receiver are subsequently suspended under section 56.

S. 57(1)
As in English law, this subsection makes the receiver the company's agent. Indeed, it goes further, because it would appear to confer such status on court-appointed receivers. In view of this agency relationship there is no change of occupation when a receiver takes possession of the company's premises, and the receiver does not become personally liable for rates accruing on such premises: *McKillop and Watters, Petitioners* [1994] B.C.C. 677. Having said that, it may well be in the case of certain statutory provisions that the court might find a receiver to be in joint occupation. Such a conclusion was arrived at in *Lord Advocate v Aero Technologies Ltd*, 1991 S.L.T. 134 in the context of s. 23 of the Explosives Act 1875.

S. 57(1A), (2A)–(2D)
These were inserted by IA 1994 (s. 3(1), (2), (4), (5)) to counteract the problems posed for Scottish receivers by the ruling of the Court of Appeal in *Re Paramount Airways Ltd (No. 3)* [1994] B.C.C. 172; see the discussions on ss. 19, 37 and 44 above. A receiver's personal liability under s. 57(2) on adoption was distinct from the company's liability under s. 60 – *Lindop v Stewart Noble & Sons Ltd* [1999] S.C.L.R. 889 which is discussed by Lewis [1999] Insolvency Lawyer 303.

Section 58 *Insolvency Act 1986*

S. 57(2), (4), (5)

These provisions reproduce the position in English law by making the receiver personally liable on contracts entered into by him and on existing contracts of employment adopted by him, although the circumstances where adoption will occur are limited by s. 57(5). Apart from contracts of employment adopted by the receiver, he is not personally liable on the company's existing contracts. For discussion of s. 57(2) see *Hill Samuel & Co. Ltd v Laing* [1991] B.C.C. 665. In s. 57(2) the words ", to the extent of any qualifying liability," inserted after the words "provides, and" by IA 1994, s. 3(1), (3), (5) in relation to contracts of employment adopted on or after March 15, 1994. For judicial support for the policy behind IA 1994 reforms in this area see *Lindop v Stuart Noble & Sons Ltd* [1999] S.C.L.R. 889.

S. 57(3), (6)

These subsections deal with the receiver's indemnity against personal liability, and make it clear that it does not extend to unauthorised contracts.

S. 57(7)

If a receiver's powers are suspended under s. 56, contracts entered into by the receiver will normally remain in force.

58 Remuneration of receiver

58(1) [Remuneration by agreement] The remuneration to be paid to a receiver is to be determined by agreement between the receiver and the holder of the floating charge by virtue of which he was appointed.

58(2) [Where remuneration not specified or disputed] Where the remuneration to be paid to the receiver has not been determined under subsection (1), or where it has been so determined but is disputed by any of the persons mentioned in paragraphs (a) to (d) below, it may be fixed instead by the Auditor of the Court of Session on application made to him by–

(a) the receiver;

(b) the holder of any floating charge or fixed security over all or any part of the property of the company;

(c) the company; or

(d) the liquidator of the company.

58(3) [Accounting for excess] Where the receiver has been paid or has retained for his remuneration for any period before the remuneration has been fixed by the Auditor of the Court of Session under subsection (2) any amount in excess of the remuneration so fixed for that period, the receiver or his personal representatives shall account for the excess.

S. 58(1)

This subsection states the general rule that the receiver's remuneration is to be fixed by agreement with the debenture holder who appointed him.

S. 58(2), (3)

This is a fall-back provision, permitting the Auditor of the Court of Session, on the application of any of various named parties, to fix remuneration in cases where there is no agreement within the meaning of s. 58(1), or where there is a dispute as to the level of remuneration. It is interesting to note that CA 1985, s. 474 fixed a time-limit for such an application and also specified the correct procedure to be followed – this has been omitted in s. 58. Presumably this could be dealt with in the rules: see Sch. 8, para. 15. Section 58(3) deals with the position when a receiver has received remuneration which turns out to be excessive: surplus amounts have to be repaid.

59 Priority of debts

59(1) [Certain debts to be paid in priority out of assets] Where a receiver is appointed and the company is not at the time of the appointment in course of being wound up, the debts which fall under subsection (2) of this section shall be paid out of any assets coming to the hands of the receiver in priority to any claim for principal or interest by the holder of the floating charge by virtue of which the receiver was appointed.

59(2) [Preferential debts] Debts falling under this subsection are preferential debts (within the meaning given by section 386 in Part XII) which, by the end of a period of 6 months after advertisement by the receiver for claims in the *Edinburgh Gazette* and in a newspaper circulating in the district where the company carries on business either–

(i) have been intimated to him, or

(ii) have become known to him.

59(3) **[Recoupment of payments]** Any payments made under this section shall be recouped as far as may be out of the assets of the company available for payment of ordinary creditors.

S. 59(1), (2)
These subsections impose a positive obligation on the receiver to meet the preferential claims listed in Sch. 6 to the Act. The position in Scottish law differs from its English counterpart in that claims must be submitted to the receiver within six months of an advertisement being placed in the *Gazette*. A further difference exists between English and Scottish law with regard to preferential debts on receivership. Where the Crown wishes to exercise a set-off and has total debts owed to it which have both unsecured and preferential elements, it can exercise the set-off with respect to the unsecured debts without rateably setting off preferential debts. The effect of this is to enhance its overall priority position by preserving its preferential status: see *Turner, Petitioner* [1993] B.C.C. 299. For the approach in English law see *Re Unit 2 Windows Ltd* (1985) 1 B.C.C. 99,489. Note the limitation upon this duty imposed by s. 11(5).

S. 59(3)
As with s. 40(3), this makes it clear that the burden of meeting the preferential claims will ultimately fall on the unsecured creditors.

60 Distribution of moneys

60(1) **[Payment of moneys by receiver]** Subject to the next section, and to the rights of any of the following categories of persons (which rights shall, except to the extent otherwise provided in any instrument, have the following order of priority), namely–

(a) the holder of any fixed security which is over property subject to the floating charge and which ranks prior to, or pari passu with, the floating charge;

(b) all persons who have effectually executed diligence on any part of the property of the company which is subject to the charge by virtue of which the receiver was appointed;

(c) creditors in respect of all liabilities, charges and expenses incurred by or on behalf of the receiver;

(d) the receiver in respect of his liabilities, expenses and remuneration, and any indemnity to which he is entitled out of the property of the company; and

(e) the preferential creditors entitled to payment under section 59,

the receiver shall pay moneys received by him to the holder of the floating charge by virtue of which the receiver was appointed in or towards satisfaction of the debt secured by the floating charge.

60(2) **[Balance of moneys]** Any balance of moneys remaining after the provisions of subsection (1) and section 61 below have been satisfied shall be paid in accordance with their respective rights and interests to the following persons, as the case may require–

(a) any other receiver;

(b) the holder of a fixed security which is over property subject to the floating charge;

(c) the company or its liquidator, as the case may be.

60(3) **[Doubt as to person entitled]** Where any question arises as to the person entitled to a payment under this section, or where a receipt or a discharge of a security cannot be obtained in respect of any such payment, the receiver shall consign the amount of such payment in any joint stock bank of issue in Scotland in name of the Accountant of Court for behoof of the person or persons entitled thereto.

S. 60(1)
This subsection outlines a priority ranking for claims against the assets of a company which is in receivership. There is no parallel provision in English law. When presented in this way it is not surprising that banks have become uneasy

Section 61 *Insolvency Act 1986*

about the protection offered by the floating charge. However, EA 2002 does offer them some comfort in that it radically reduces the categories of preferential claim. For the meaning of "fixed security" in subs. (1)(a), see s. 70. The position under subs. (1)(c) was considered by the Court of Session (Inner House) in *Lindop v. Stuart Noble & Sons Ltd* [1999] S.C.L.R. 889 in the context of an employee whose contract of employment had initially been adopted by the receiver and then who had subsequently been dismissed. The claim based upon s. 60(1)(c) for preferential treatment in respect of salary in lieu of notice was rejected; only new contracts made by receivers were covered by s. 60(1)(c). In rejecting this claim the court was mindful not to allow the policy of IA 1994 limiting a receiver's liabilities to "qualifying liabilities" to be circumvented. See also *Scottish and Newcastle plc, Petitioners* [1993] B.C.C. 634 for further guidance on the operation of s. 60.

S. 60(2)
This provision maps out the fate of any surplus moneys in the hands of the receiver, after the claims listed in s. 60(1) have been met.

S. 60(3)
In the event of a dispute over whether a claim should be met or not, the receiver should pay an appropriate sum of money into a recognised Scottish bank in the name of the Accountant of Court, pending the resolution of the dispute.

61 Disposal of interest in property

61(1) [Application to court] Where the receiver sells or disposes, or is desirous of selling or disposing, of any property or interest in property of the company which is subject to the floating charge by virtue of which the receiver was appointed and which is–

(a) subject to any security or interest of, or burden or encumbrance in favour of, a creditor the ranking of which is prior to, or pari passu with, or postponed to the floating charge, or

(b) property or an interest in property affected or attached by effectual diligence executed by any person,

and the receiver is unable to obtain the consent of such creditor or, as the case may be, such person to such a sale or disposal, the receiver may apply to the court for authority to sell or dispose of the property or interest in property free of such security, interest, burden, encumbrance or diligence.

61(2) [Authorisation by court] Subject to the next subsection, on such an application the court may, if it thinks fit, authorise the sale or disposal of the property or interest in question free of such security, interest, burden, encumbrance or diligence, and such authorisation may be on such terms or conditions as the court thinks fit.

61(3) [Condition for authorisation] In the case of an application where a fixed security over the property or interest in question which ranks prior to the floating charge has not been met or provided for in full, the court shall not authorise the sale or disposal of the property or interest in question unless it is satisifed that the sale or disposal would be likely to provide a more advantageous realisation of the company's assets than would otherwise be effected.

61(4) [Condition for s. 61(3)] It shall be a condition of an authorisation to which subsection (3) applies that–

(a) the net proceeds of the disposal, and

(b) where those proceeds are less than such amount as may be determined by the court to be the net amount which would be realised on a sale of the property or interest in the open market by a willing seller, such sums as may be required to make good the deficiency,

shall be applied towards discharging the sums secured by the fixed security.

61(5) [Where s. 61(4) condition re several securities] Where a condition imposed in pursuance of subsection (4) relates to two or more such fixed securities, that condition shall require the net proceeds of the disposal and, where paragraph (b) of that subsection applies, the sums mentioned in that paragraph to be applied towards discharging the sums secured by those fixed securities in the order of their priorities.

61(6) **[Copy of authorisation to registrar]** A copy of an authorisation under subsection (2) certified by the clerk of court shall, within 14 days of the granting of the authorisation, be sent by the receiver to the registrar of companies.

61(7) **[Penalty for non-compliance]** If the receiver without reasonable excuse fails to comply with subsection (6), he is liable to a fine and, for continued contravention, to a daily default fine.

61(8) **[Receiver to give document to disponee]** Where any sale or disposal is effected in accordance with the authorisation of the court under subsection (2), the receiver shall grant to the purchaser or disponee an appropriate document of transfer or conveyance of the property or interest in question, and that document has the effect, or, where recording, intimation or registration of that document is a legal requirement for completion of title to the property or interest, then that recording, intimation or registration (as the case may be) has the effect, of–

    (a)   disencumbering the property or interest of the security, interest, burden or encumbrance affecting it, and

    (b)   freeing the property or interest from the diligence executed upon it.

61(9) **[Ranking of creditor in winding up]** Nothing in this section prejudices the right of any creditor of the company to rank for his debt in the winding up of the company.

S. 61(1), (2)
These subsections allow a receiver to apply to the court for the sale of property subject to a fixed charge, or over which diligence has been effectually executed.

    Section 61 does not apply in relation to the enforcement of "market charges" (as defined by CA 1989, s. 173): see s. 175 of that Act (as qualified by the Financial Markets and Insolvency Regulations 1991 (SI 1991/880)) (as amended by SI 1995/2049 and SI 1998/27), and the introductory note at p. 2, above.

S. 61(3), (4), (5)
If the receiver has not set aside a sufficient sum to meet the claim of the holder of the "fixed security" (for the meaning of this term, see s. 70), the court should only assent to the sale if it would promote a more effective realisation of the company's assets. Even where assent is given, the actual net proceeds (or a reasonable amount, if the sale was at an undervalue) must be set aside for the fixed chargee (or chargees).

S. 61(6), (7)
If the court permits the sale to go ahead, the receiver must register the fact at Edinburgh, or incur a default fine. On penalties, see s. 430 and Sch. 10. Section 61(6) modified by Scotland Act 1998, s. 125(1) and Sch. 8, para. 23(1)–(3) so that anything done by the registrar of companies in Scotland or the assistant registrar of friendly societies for Scotland by virtue of s. 61(6) as applied in relation to friendly societies, industrial and provident societies or building societies may be done to or by the Accountant in Bankruptcy as from July 1, 1999 (see SI 1998/3178 (C. 79), art. 2).

S. 61(8)
This subsection provides a mechanism for assuring the purchaser under the forced sale that he can acquire an effective title from the receiver.

S. 61(9)
This is a saving provision allowing a person who has been deprived of his claim against specific property to rank instead as a creditor of the company on winding up.

62   Cessation of appointment of receiver

62(1) **[Removal, resignation]** A receiver may be removed from office by the court under subsection (3) below and may resign his office by giving notice of his resignation in the prescribed manner to such persons as may be prescribed.

62(2) **[Cessation of qualification]** A receiver shall vacate office if he ceases to be qualified to act as an insolvency practitioner in relation to the company.

62(3) **[Removal on application]** Subject to the next subsection, a receiver may, on application to the court by the holder of the floating charge by virtue of which he was appointed, be removed by the court on cause shown.

62(4) [On vacation of office] Where at any time a receiver vacates office–

(a) his remuneration and any expenses properly incurred by him, and

(b) any indemnity to which he is entitled out of the property of the company,

shall be paid out of the property of the company which is subject to the floating charge and shall have priority as provided for in section 60(1).

62(5) [Notice of cessation to registrar, penalty on default] When a receiver ceases to act as such otherwise than by death he shall, and, when a receiver is removed by the court, the holder of the floating charge by virtue of which he was appointed shall, within 14 days of the cessation or removal (as the case may be) give the registrar of companies notice to that effect, and the registrar shall enter the notice in the register of charges.

If the receiver or the holder of the floating charge (as the case may require) makes default in complying with the requirements of this subsection, he is liable to a fine and, for continued contravention, to a daily default fine.

62(6) [Cessation of attachment of charge] If by the expiry of a period of one month following upon the removal of the receiver or his ceasing to act as such no other receiver has been appointed, the floating charge by virtue of which the receiver was appointed–

(a) thereupon ceases to attach to the property then subject to the charge, and

(b) again subsists as a floating charge;

and for the purposes of calculating the period of one month under this subsection no account shall be taken of any period during which the company is in administration under Part II of this Act.

S. 62(1)–(3)
These subsections deal with the situations where a receiver will vacate office. Note that he can only be removed by the court on the application of the holder of the floating charge (for the meaning of this term, see s. 70), and not out of court by the holder of the floating charge who appointed him. As to the qualification as an insolvency practitioner, see Pt XIII. For the relevant notice of resignation under s. 62(1), see the Receivers (Scotland) Regulations 1986 (SI 1986/1917 (S 141)).

S. 62(4)
This protects the priority of the receiver's right to indemity and remuneration.

S. 62(5)
Notification must be given to Edinburgh of the receiver leaving office: see Form 3 (Scot) under the Receivers (Scotland) Regulations 1986 (SI 1986/1917 (S 141)). The person responsible for giving notice will incur criminal sanctions in the event of default. On penalties, see s. 430 and Sch. 10. Section 62(5) was modified by the Scotland Act 1998, s. 125(1) and Sch. 8, para. 23(1)–(3) so that anything done by the registrar of companies in Scotland or the assistant registrar of friendly societies for Scotland by virtue of s. 62(5) as applied in relation to friendly societies, industrial and provident societies or building societies may be done to or by the Accountant in Bankruptcy as from July 1, 1999 (see SI 1998/3178 (C. 79), art. 2). Note prospective amendment: the words "and, for continued contravention, to a daily default fine" are to be repealed by CA 1989, Schs 16 and 24 from a day to be appointed.

S. 62(6)
This provides for the "refloating" of the floating charge on the expiry of one month after the receiver leaves office. Note the semantic change made by the Enterprise Act 2002 (Insolvency) Order 2003 (SI 2003/2096).

63 Powers of court

63(1) [Directions, on application] The court on the application of–

(a) the holder of a floating charge by virtue of which a receiver was appointed, or

(b) a receiver appointed under section 51,

may give directions to the receiver in respect of any matter arising in connection with the performance by him of his functions.

63(2) [Where receiver's appointment invalid] Where the appointment of a person as a receiver by the holder of a floating charge is discovered to be invalid (whether by virtue of the invalidity of the instrument or otherwise), the court may order the holder of the floating charge to indemnify the person appointed against any liability which arises solely by reason of the invalidity of the appointment.

S. 63(1)
This provision, like its English counterpart (IA 1986, s. 35), allows both the receiver or the holder of the floating charge (for definition, see s. 70) under which he was appointed to apply to the court for guidance. Such an application was the basis for the litigation in *McKillop and Watters, Petitioners* [1994] B.C.C. 677. Prior to IA 1985, only the appointor (and not the receiver) could make such an application. The power of the Scottish courts to give directions is more limited than the power of their English counterparts under s. 35: see here *Jamieson, Petitioners* 1997 S.C. 195; [1997] B.C.C. 682.

The FSA may in an appropriate case be heard on a s. 63 application – FSMA 2000, s. 363(2).

S. 63(2)
This allows the court to excuse a receiver from trespass liability arising out of an invalid appointment, and instead to impose that liability on his appointor. For the English counterpart, see s. 34.

64 Notification that receiver appointed

64(1) [Statement in invoices etc.] Where a receiver has been appointed, every invoice, order for goods or business letter issued by or on behalf of the company or the receiver or the liquidator of the company, being a document on or in which the name of the company appears, shall contain a statement that a receiver has been appointed.

64(2) [Penalty on default] If default is made in complying with the requirements of this section, the company and any of the following persons who knowingly and wilfully authorises or permits the default, namely any officer of the company, any liquidator of the company and any receiver, is liable to a fine.

S. 64(1)
Invoices, business letters, etc., must disclose the fact that a receiver has been appointed. The English equivalent is to be found in s. 39.

S. 64(2)
Criminal sanctions are imposed on various named parties for breach of s. 64(1). On penalties, see s. 430 and Sch. 10.

65 Information to be given by receiver

65(1) [Notification of appointment] Where a receiver is appointed, he shall–

(a) forthwith send to the company and publish notice of his appointment, and

(b) within 28 days after his appointment, unless the court otherwise directs, send such notice to all the creditors of the company (so far as he is aware of their addresses).

65(2) [Restriction] This section and the next do not apply in relation to the appointment of a receiver to act–

(a) with an existing receiver, or

(b) in place of a receiver who has died or ceased to act,

except that, where they apply to a receiver who dies or ceases to act before they have been fully complied with, the references in this section and the next to the receiver include (subject to subsection (3) of this section) his successor and any continuing receiver.

65(3) [If company being wound up] If the company is being wound up, this section and the next apply notwithstanding that the receiver and the liquidator are the same person, but with any necessary modifications arising from that fact.

65(4) [Penalty for non-compliance] If a person without reasonable excuse fails to comply with this section, he is liable to a fine and, for continued contravention, to a daily default fine.

Section 66 *Insolvency Act 1986*

S. 65(1), (2), (4)
These subsections provide for a receiver on taking up his appointment to give notice to the company and its creditors. See note to s. 62(5). This obligation, once complied with, does not have to be fulfilled by successor receivers, or a later appointed joint receiver. Criminal sanctions are imposed in the event of default. On penalties, see s. 430 and Sch. 10. For the notice under s. 65(1)(a) see Form 4 (Scot) in the Receivers (Scotland) Regulations 1986 (S.I. 1986/1917 (S 141)).

S. 65(3)
This caters for the situation where the receiver and liquidator are the same person. It also applies to s. 66.

66 Company's statement of affairs

66(1) **[Duty of receiver]** Where a receiver of a company is appointed, the receiver shall forthwith require some or all of the persons mentioned in subsection (3) below to make out and submit to him a statement in the prescribed form as to the affairs of the company.

66(2) **[Contents of statement]** A statement submitted under this section shall be verified by affidavit by the persons required to submit it and shall show–

(a) particulars of the company's assets, debts and liabilities;

(b) the names and addresses of its creditors;

(c) the securities held by them respectively;

(d) the dates when the securities were respectively given; and

(e) such further or other information as may be prescribed.

66(3) **[Persons in s. 66(1)]** The persons referred to in subsection (1) are–

(a) those who are or have been officers of the company;

(b) those who have taken part in the company's formation at any time within one year before the date of the appointment of the receiver;

(c) those who are in the company's employment or have been in its employment within that year, and are in the receiver's opinion capable of giving the information required;

(d) those who are or have been within that year officers of or in the employment of a company which is, or within that year was, an officer of the company.

In this subsection **"employment"** includes employment under a contract for services.

66(4) **[Time for statement]** Where any persons are required under this section to submit a statement of affairs to the receiver they shall do so (subject to the next subsection) before the end of the period of 21 days beginning with the day after that on which the prescribed notice of the requirement is given to them by the receiver.

66(5) **[Release, extension re statement]** The receiver, if he thinks fit, may–

(a) at any time release a person from an obligation imposed on him under subsection (1) or (2), or

(b) either when giving the notice mentioned in subsection (4) or subsequently extend the period so mentioned,

and where the receiver has refused to exercise a power conferred by this subsection, the court, if it thinks fit, may exercise it.

66(6) [Penalty for non-compliance] If a person without reasonable excuse fails to comply with any obligation imposed under this section, he is liable to a fine and, for continued contravention, to a daily default fine.

S. 66(1), (2)
These provisions require the receiver to ask persons listed in s. 66(3) for a statement of the company's affairs in the prescribed form (see s. 70), containing details specified in s. 66(2). For the relevant form of the statement, see Form 5 (Scot) in the Receivers (Scotland) Regulations 1986 (SI 1986/1917 (S 141)).

S. 66(3)–(6)
Section 66(3) identifies the persons who may be required to contribute towards the submission of the statement of affairs, which must normally be submitted within 21 days of a request for it. Criminal sanctions are imposed to deal with defaults. On penalties, see s. 430 and Sch. 10.

The receiver enjoys discretion under s. 66(5) to release certain persons from their obligations in respect of the statement of affairs or to extend the deadline for submission.

67 Report by receiver

67(1) [Duty of receiver] Where a receiver is appointed under section 51, he shall within 3 months (or such longer period as the court may allow) after his appointment, send to the registrar of companies, to the holder of the floating charge by virtue of which he was appointed and to any trustees for secured creditors of the company and (so far as he is aware of their addresses) to all such creditors a report as to the following matters, namely–

(a) the events leading up to his appointment, so far as he is aware of them;

(b) the disposal or proposed disposal by him of any property of the company and the carrying on or proposed carrying on by him of any business of the company;

(c) the amounts of principal and interest payable to the holder of the floating charge by virtue of which he was appointed and the amounts payable to preferential creditors; and

(d) the amount (if any) likely to be available for the payment of other creditors.

67(2) [Copies of report] The receiver shall also, within 3 months (or such longer period as the court may allow) after his appointment, either–

(a) send a copy of the report (so far as he is aware of their addresses) to all unsecured creditors of the company, or

(b) publish in the prescribed manner a notice stating an address to which unsecured creditors of the company should write for copies of the report to be sent to them free of charge,

and (in either case), unless the court otherwise directs, lay a copy of the report before a meeting of the company's unsecured creditors summoned for the purpose on not less than 14 days' notice.

67(3) [Condition for court direction in s. 67(2)] The court shall not give a direction under subsection (2) unless–

(a) the report states the intention of the receiver to apply for the direction, and

(b) a copy of the report is sent to the persons mentioned in paragraph (a) of that subsection, or a notice is published as mentioned in paragraph (b) of that subsection, not less than 14 days before the hearing of the application.

67(4) [Where company in liquidation] Where the company has gone or goes into liquidation, the receiver–

(a) shall, within 7 days after his compliance with subsection (1) or, if later, the nomination or appointment of the liquidator, send a copy of the report to the liquidator, and

(b) where he does so within the time limited for compliance with subsection (2), is not required to comply with that subsection.

67(5) **[Report to involve summary of statement of affairs]** A report under this section shall include a summary of the statement of affairs made out and submitted under section 66 and of his comments (if any) on it.

67(6) **[Information not to be disclosed]** Nothing in this section shall be taken as requiring any such report to include any information the disclosure of which would seriously prejudice the carrying out by the receiver of his functions.

67(7) **[S. 65(2)]** Section 65(2) applies for the purposes of this section also.

67(8) **[Penalty for non-compliance]** If a person without reasonable excuse fails to comply with this section, he is liable to a fine and, for continued contravention, to a daily default fine.

67(9) **["Secured creditor"]** In this section **"secured creditor"**, in relation to a company, means a creditor who holds in respect of his debt a security over property of the company, and **"unsecured creditor"** shall be construed accordingly.

S. 67(1), (5), (6)
These subsections require the receiver to prepare a report which must be submitted to various named parties (including the FSA in an appropriate case – FSMA 2000, s. 363(4)). The report should include certain specified details but need not disclose "prejudicial" information (see s. 67(6)). It should also include a summary of the statement of affairs submitted to him under s. 66, plus any comments he wishes to make. Section 67(1) was modified by the Scotland Act 1998, s. 125(1) and Sch. 8, para. 23(1)–(3) so that anything done by the registrar of companies in Scotland or the assistant registrar of friendly societies for Scotland by virtue of s. 67(1) as applied in relation to friendly societies, industrial and provident societies or building societies may be done to or by the Accountant in Bankruptcy as from July 1, 1999 (see SI 1998/3178 (C. 79), art. 2).

S. 67(2)–(4)
These provisions relate to the dissemination of the receiver's report to creditors and liquidator (if applicable). The report is to be submitted to a meeting of the company's creditors, unless the court rules to the contrary. With regards to s. 67(2) see the Receivers (Scotland) Regulations 1986 (SI 1986/1917 (S 141)).

S. 67(7), (9)
These are merely interpretation provisions. Section 65(2) dispenses with the need for a report when an additional receiver is appointed to act with an existing receiver, or a new receiver to replace one who has ceased to act.

S. 67(8)
The receiver will incur criminal sanctions for failure to fulfil any of the stated obligations. On penalties, see s. 430 and Sch. 10.

68 Committee of creditors

68(1) **[Creditors' meeting may establish committee]** Where a meeting of creditors is summoned under section 67, the meeting may, if it thinks fit, establish a committee (**"the creditors' committee"**) to exercise the functions conferred on it by or under this Act.

68(2) **[Powers of committee]** If such a committee is established, the committee may on giving not less than 7 days' notice require the receiver to attend before it at any reasonable time and furnish it with such information relating to the carrying out by him of his functions as it may reasonably require.

S. 68(1)
A meeting of creditors summoned under s. 67(2) may set up a committee of creditors. In an appropriate case an FSA representative can attend – FSMA 2000, s. 363(5).

S. 68(2)
This committee can make reasonable requests for information from the receiver. It may be unreasonable to request information covered by s. 67(6).

69 Enforcement of receiver's duty to make returns, etc.

69(1) **[Court order re receiver's default]** If any receiver–

(a) having made default in filing, delivering or making any return, account or other document, or in giving any notice, which a receiver is by law required to file, deliver, make or give, fails to make good the default within 14 days after the service on him of a notice requiring him to do so; or

(b) has, after being required at any time by the liquidator of the company so to do, failed to render proper accounts of his receipts and payments and to vouch the same and to pay over to the liquidator the amount properly payable to him,

the court may, on an application made for the purpose, make an order directing the receiver to make good the default within such time as may be specified in the order.

69(2) **[Application to court]** In the case of any such default as is mentioned in subsection (1)(a), an application for the purposes of this section may be made by any member or creditor of the company or by the registrar of companies; and, in the case of any such default as is mentioned in subsection (1)(b), the application shall be made by the liquidator; and, in either case, the order may provide that all expenses of and incidental to the application shall be borne by the receiver.

69(3) **[Other enactments]** Nothing in this section prejudices the operation of any enactments imposing penalties on receivers in respect of any such default as is mentioned in subsection (1).

S. 69(1)
The court can compel a receiver to submit returns, etc., if he fails to comply with a notice to do so. For the English counterpart, see s. 41.

S. 69(2)
This subsection identifies the applicants for an enforcement order under s. 69(1). The FSA may apply in an appropriate case – FSMA 2000, s. 363(3).

S. 69(3)
This enforcement mechanism is in addition to any criminal sanctions that may be imposed by individual provisions.

70 Interpretation for Chapter II

70(1) **[Definitions]** In this Chapter, unless the contrary intention appears, the following expressions have the following meanings respectively assigned to them–

"**company**" means an incorporated company (whether or not a company within the meaning of the Companies Act) which the Court of Session has jurisdiction to wind up;

"**fixed security**", in relation to any property of a company, means any security, other than a floating charge or a charge having the nature of a floating charge, which on the winding up of the company in Scotland would be treated as an effective security over that property, and (without prejudice to that generality) includes a security over that property, being a heritable security within the meaning of the Conveyancing and Feudal Reform (Scotland) Act 1970;

"**instrument of appointment**" has the meaning given by section 53(1);

"**prescribed**" means prescribed by regulations made under this Chapter by the Secretary of State;

"**receiver**" means a receiver of such part of the property of the company as is subject to the floating charge by virtue of which he has been appointed under section 51;

"**register of charges**" means the register kept by the registrar of companies for the purposes of Chapter II of Part XII of the Companies Act;

"**secured debenture**" means a bond, debenture, debenture stock or other security which, either itself or by reference to any other instrument, creates a floating charge over all or any part of the property of the company, but does not include a security which creates no charge other than a fixed security; and "**series of secured debentures**" means two or more secured debentures created as a series by the company in such a manner that the holders thereof are entitled pari passu to the benefit of the floating charge.

70(2) **[Reference to holder of floating charge]** Where a floating charge, secured debenture or series of secured debentures has been created by the company, then, except where the context otherwise requires, any reference in this Chapter to the holder of the floating charge shall–

(a) where the floating charge, secured debenture or series of secured debentures provides for a receiver to be appointed by any person or body, be construed as a reference to that person or body;

(b) where, in the case of a series of secured debentures, no such provision has been made therein but–

   (i) there are trustees acting for the debenture-holders under and in accordance with a trust deed, be construed as a reference to those trustees, and
   (ii) where no such trustees are acting, be construed as a reference to –

      (aa) a majority in nominal value of those present or represented by proxy and voting at a meeting of debenture-holders at which the holders of at least one-third in nominal value of the outstanding debentures of the series are present or so represented, or

      (bb) where no such meeting is held, the holders of at least one-half in nominal value of the outstanding debentures of the series.

70(3) **[Reference to floating charge etc.]** Any reference in this Chapter to a floating charge, secured debenture, series of secured debentures or instrument creating a charge includes, except where the context otherwise requires, a reference to that floating charge, debenture, series of debentures or instrument as varied by any instrument.

70(4) **[Reference to instrument]** References in this Chapter to the instrument by which a floating charge was created are, in the case of a floating charge created by words in a bond or other written acknowledgement, references to the bond or, as the case may be, the other written acknowledgement.

GENERAL NOTE

These are general interpretation provisions for the purposes of ss. 50–71 and their main aim is to link these provisions dealing with Scottish receiverships with the sections in CA 1985 regulating the floating charge in Scotland, and also with the general rules of Scots law.

71 Prescription of forms, etc.; regulations

71(1) **[Prescribed forms]** The notice referred to in section 62(5), and the notice referred to in section 65(1)(a) shall be in such form as may be prescribed.

71(2) **[Regulations]** Any power conferred by this Chapter on the Secretary of State to make regulations is exercisable by statutory instrument; and a statutory instrument made in the exercise of the power so conferred to prescribe a fee is subject to annulment in pursuance of a resolution of either House of Parliament.

S. 71(1)
The notice of a receiver taking office or ceasing to act is in a form prescribed by the Receivers (Scotland) Regulations 1986 (SI 1986/1917 (S 141)). See note to ss. 62, 65.

S. 71(2)
The Secretary of State may make regulations, but where the power involves the prescribing of a fee it is subject to annulment by either the House of Lords or the Commons. See the regulations referred to above.

Insolvency Act 1986 *Section 72*

CHAPTER III

RECEIVERS' POWERS IN GREAT BRITAIN AS A WHOLE

72 Cross-border operation of receivership provisions

72(1) [Receivers' powers] A receiver appointed under the law of either part of Great Britain in respect of the whole or any part of any property or undertaking of a company and in consequence of the company having created a charge which, as created, was a floating charge may exercise his powers in the other part of Great Britain so far as their exercise is not inconsistent with the law applicable there.

72(2) ["Receiver"] In subsection (1) **"receiver"** includes a manager and a person who is appointed both receiver and manager.

GENERAL NOTE

This section allows a receiver appointed in England to act in Scotland, and vice versa, in so far as this is not inconsistent with local law. This provision, which can be traced back to 1970, is less important now that the Scots have a system of receivership running along similar lines to the English regime. For the utility of s. 72 see *Norfolk House v Repsol Petroleum* 1992 SLT 235.

CHAPTER IV

PROHIBITION OF APPOINTMENT OF ADMINISTRATIVE RECEIVER

72A Floating charge holder not to appoint administrative receiver

72A(1) [Prohibition] The holder of a qualifying floating charge in respect of a company's property may not appoint an administrative receiver of the company.

72A(2) [Scotland] In Scotland, the holder of a qualifying floating charge in respect of a company's property may not appoint or apply to the court for the appointment of a receiver who on appointment would be an administrative receiver of property of the company.

72A(3) [Meanings in s. 72A(1), (2)] In subsections (1) and (2)—

"holder of a qualifying floating charge in respect of a company's property" has the same meaning as in paragraph 14 of Schedule B1 to this Act, and

"administrative receiver" has the meaning given by section 251.

72A(4) [Application of section] This section applies—

(a) to a floating charge created on or after a date appointed by the Secretary of State by order made by statutory instrument, and

(b) in spite of any provision of an agreement or instrument which purports to empower a person to appoint an administrative receiver (by whatever name).

72A(5) [Provision in order] An order under subsection (4)(a) may—

(a) make provision which applies generally or only for a specified purpose;

(b) make different provision for different purposes;

(c) make transitional provision.

72A(6) [Exceptions] This section is subject to the exceptions specified in sections 72B to 72GA.

GENERAL NOTE

S. 72A
This new section, and those following, were added by s. 250 of EA 2002. That provision was modified by the Insolvency Act 1986 (Amendment) (Administrative Receivership and Urban Regeneration etc.) Order 2003 (SI 2003/1832) to take effect immediately on the coming into force of s. 72A on September 15, 2003. Note also the insertion by s. 250(2) and Sch. 18 of Sch. 2A into the 1986 Act to further bolster these provisions. Schedule 2A was also modified by the Insolvency Act 1986 (Amendment) (Administrative Receivership and Capital Market Arrangements) Order 2003 (SI 2003/1468).

Perhaps the most high profile of all of the changes introduced by EA 2002 was the curtailing of the floating charge-holder's entitlement to enforce security through the appointment of an "administrative receiver" (see IA 1986, s. 29). After some debate the Government was convinced by the argument that administrative receivership was not a rescue procedure in keeping with the spirit of collectivism but rather a selfish and largely unaccountable recovery mechanism. It therefore decided to curtail its usage, though as a concession to the banking community it offered the option of appointing an administrator out of court.

This change was not retrospective – *i.e.* it does not deprive this option of installing an administrative receiver from those creditors covered by a floating charge created before the operational date. This point was conceded early on in the gestation of the Enterprise Bill – DTI Press Notice P/2001/629). The Government may have been concerned to head off challenges by banks alleging infringement of their property rights under Art. 1 of the First Protocol of the ECHR. Moreover, administrative receivership is to survive for certain specialised financing arrangements; these mirror the exceptions to the CVA *cum moratorium* procedure in IA 2000.

S. 72A(1)(3)
This outlines the basic prohibition – note again that the wording (albeit obtusely) allows existing floating charges to retain this traditional enforcement mode.

S. 72A(2)(3)
Administrative receivership is not a term recognised in Scotland; the institution in that jurisdiction uses the clearer denomination of receivership. Hence the need for separate legislative treatment.

S. 72A(4)
This reinforces the prospective-only nature of the reform. However, its restrictive effect cannot be overridden by provision in any debenture. The date appointed under s. 72A(4)(a) is September 15, 2003 – see the Insolvency Act 1986, Section 72A (Appointed Day) Order 2003 (SI 2003/2095).

S. 72A(5)(6)
These rules may be modified by secondary legislation and are qualified by later statutory provisions. Note subs. (6) was modified slightly by the Insolvency Act 1986 (Amendment) (Administrative Receivership and Urban Regeneration etc.) Order 2003 (SI 2003/1832).

72B First exception: capital market

72B(1) [**Conditions for capital market arrangement**] Section 72A does not prevent the appointment of an administrative receiver in pursuance of an agreement which is or forms part of a capital market arrangement if—

(a) a party incurs or, when the agreement was entered into was expected to incur, a debt of at least £50 million under the arrangement, and

(b) the arrangement involves the issue of a capital market investment.

72B(2) [**"Capital market arrangement", "capital market investment"**] In subsection (1)—

"capital market arrangement" means an arrangement of a kind described in paragraph 1 of Schedule 2A, and

"capital market investment" means an investment of a kind described in paragraph 2 or 3 of that Schedule.

S. 72B(1)(2)
This exception relates to capital market agreements. The exclusion of general insolvency principles from this area of commerce has precedents – witness Companies Act 1989.

72C Second exception: public-private partnership

72C(1) **[Requirement of step-in rights]** Section 72A does not prevent the appointment of an administrative receiver of a project company of a project which—

(a) is a public-private partnership project, and

(b) includes step-in rights.

72C(2) **["Public-private partnership project"]** In this section "public-private partnership project" means a project—

(a) the resources for which are provided partly by one or more public bodies and partly by one or more private persons, or

(b) which is designed wholly or mainly for the purpose of assisting a public body to discharge a function.

72C(3) **["Step-in rights", "project company"]** In this section—

"step-in rights" has the meaning given by paragraph 6 of Schedule 2A, and

"project company" has the meaning given by paragraph 7 of that Schedule.

S. 72C(1), (2), (3)
These provide the continuance of administrative receivership for certain public finance initiative agreements containing "step in" rights as defined by subs. (3).

72D Third exception: utilities

72D(1) **[Requirement of step-in rights]** Section 72A does not prevent the appointment of an administrative receiver of a project company of a project which—

(a) is a utility project, and

(b) includes step-in rights.

72D(2) **["Utility project", "regulated business", "Step-in rights", "project company"]** In this section—

(a) "utility project" means a project designed wholly or mainly for the purpose of a regulated business,

(b) "regulated business" means a business of a kind listed in paragraph 10 of Schedule 2A,

(c) "step-in rights" has the meaning given by paragraph 6 of that Schedule, and

(d) "project company" has the meaning given by paragraph 7 of that Schedule.

S. 72D(1), (2)
The creation of discrete insolvency regimes for utilities is now well established – witness the special administration regime under the Railways Act 1993.

Section 72   *Insolvency Act 1986*

72DA   Exception in respect of urban regeneration projects

72DA(1)   **[Administrative receiver of project company]** Section 72A does not prevent the appointment of an administrative receiver of a project company of a project which—

(a)   is designed wholly or mainly to develop land which at the commencement of the project is wholly or partly in a designated disadvantaged area outside Northern Ireland, and

(b)   includes step-in rights.

72DA(2)   **["Develop"]** In subsection (1) "develop" means to carry out—

(a)   building operations,

(b)   any operation for the removal of substances or waste from land and the levelling of the surface of the land, or

(c)   engineering operations in connection with the activities mentioned in paragraph (a) or (b).

72DA(3)   **[Meanings]** In this section—

"building" includes any structure or erection, and any part of a building as so defined, but does not include plant and machinery comprised in a building,

"building operations" includes—

(a)   demolition of buildings,

(b)   filling in of trenches,

(c)   rebuilding,

(d)   structural alterations of, or additions to, buildings and

(e)   other operations normally undertaken by a person carrying on business as a builder,

"designated disadvantaged area" means an area designated as a disadvantaged area under section 92 of the Finance Act 2001,

"engineering operations" includes the formation and laying out of means of access to highways,

"project company" has the meaning given by paragraph 7 of Schedule 2A,

"step-in rights" has the meaning given by paragraph 6 of that Schedule,

"substance" means any natural or artificial substance whether in solid or liquid form or in the form of a gas or vapour, and

"waste" includes any waste materials, spoil, refuse or other matter deposited on land.

S. 72DA(1)–(3)
This additional exception was created by the Insolvency Act 1986 (Amendment) (Administrative Receivership and Urban Regeneration etc.) Order 2003 (SI 2003/1832) for reasons of social policy.

72E Fourth exception: project finance

72E(1) [Requirement of step-in rights] Section 72A does not prevent the appointment of an administrative receiver of a project company of a project which—

(a) is a financed project, and

(b) includes step-in rights.

72E(2) ["Financed", "project company", "step-in rights"] In this section—

(a) a project is "financed" if under an agreement relating to the project a project company incurs, or when the agreement *is* entered into is expected to incur, a debt of at least £50 million for the purposes of carrying out the project,

(b) "project company" has the meaning given by paragraph 7 of Schedule 2A, and

(c) "step-in rights" has the meaning given by paragraph 6 of that Schedule.

S. 72E(1), (2)
This fourth exception deals with certain project finance agreements containing "step in" rights.

72F Fifth exception: financial market

72F Section 72A does not prevent the appointment of an administrative receiver of a company by virtue of—

(a) a market charge within the meaning of section 173 of the Companies Act 1989 (c. 40),

(b) a system-charge within the meaning of the Financial Markets and Insolvency Regulations 1996 (S.I. 1996/1469),

(c) a collateral security charge within the meaning of the Financial Markets and Insolvency (Settlement Finality) Regulations 1999 (S.I. 1999/2979).

S. 72F
This section deals specifically with the financial markets.

72G Sixth exception: registered social landlord

72G Section 72A does not prevent the appointment of an administrative receiver of a company which is registered as a social landlord under Part I of the Housing Act 1996 (c. 52) or under Part 3 of the Housing (Scotland) Act 2001 (asp 10).

S. 72G
This section deals with the possibility of administrative receivership in the case of a registered social landlord.

72GA Exception in relation to protected railway companies etc.

72GA Section 72A does not prevent the appointment of an administrative receiver of—

(a) a company holding an appointment under Chapter I of Part II of the Water Industry Act 1991,

(b) a protected railway company within the meaning of section 59 of the Railways Act 1993 (including that section as it has effect by virtue of section 19 of the Channel Tunnel Rail Link Act 1996, or

(c) a licence company within the meaning of section 26 of the Transport Act 2000.

Section 72   *Insolvency Act 1986*

S. 72GA
This further exception relating to "protected companies" was created by the Insolvency Act 1986 (Amendment) (Administrative Receivership and Urban Regeneration etc.) Order 2003 (SI 2003/1832).

72H   Sections 72A to 72G: supplementary

72H(1)   **[Conditions for capital market arrangement]** Schedule 2A (which supplements sections 72B to 72G) shall have effect.

72H(2)   **[Order-making power]** The Secretary of State may by order—

(a)   insert into this Act provision creating an additional exception to section 72A(1) or (2);

(b)   provide for a provision of this Act which creates an exception to section 72A(1) or (2) to cease to have effect;

(c)   amend section 72A in consequence of provision made under paragraph (a) or (b);

(d)   amend any of sections 72B to 72G;

(e)   amend Schedule 2A.

72H(3)   **[Statutory instrument]** An order under subsection (2) must be made by statutory instrument.

72H(4)   **[Provision in order]** An order under subsection (2) may make—

(a)   provision which applies generally or only for a specified purpose;

(b)   different provision for different purposes;

(c)   consequential or supplementary provision;

(d)   transitional provision.

72H(5)   **[Procedure for order]** An order under subsection (2)—

(a)   in the case of an order under subsection (2)(e), shall be subject to annulment in pursuance of a resolution of either House of Parliament,

(b)   in the case of an order under subsection (2)(d) varying the sum specified in section 72B(1)(a) or 72E(2)(a) (whether or not the order also makes consequential or transitional provision), shall be subject to annulment in pursuance of a resolution of either House of Parliament, and

(c)   in the case of any other order under subsection (2)(a) to (d), may not be made unless a draft has been laid before and approved by resolution of each House of Parliament.

S. 72H(1)
This directs us to Sch. 2A.

S. 72H(2)–(5)
Subsection (2) creates a power to make delegated rules. This order making power lead to the Insolvency Act 1986 (Amendment) (Administrative Receivership and Capital Market Arrangements) Order 2003 (SI 2003/1468) and the

Insolvency Act 1986   Section 73

Insolvency Act 1986 (Amendment) (Administrative Receivership and Urban Regeneration) Order 2003 (SI 2003/1832), both of which modify primary provisions inserted by EA 2000 – see Sch. 2A. For legal aspects of such delegated rules the position is outlined by subss. (3)–(5).

Part IV

Winding Up of Companies Registered Under the Companies Acts

General comment on Pt IV
This Part of the Act deals with the winding up of all registered companies, whether solvent or insolvent. For this purpose, the term "company" (or "registered company") is defined by CA 1985, s. 735 (see the note to s. 73(1) below). The winding up provisions are extended to unregistered companies by Pt V of the Act: for the definition of "unregistered company", see s. 220. Insolvent partnerships may also be wound up under Pt V of the Act as unregistered companies by virtue of the Insolvent Partnerships Order 1994 (SI 1994/2421): see the note to s. 420. Part V also governs the winding up of limited liability partnerships by virtue of LLPR 2001, reg. 5(1)(a), as modified by reg. 5(2) and (3).

Part IV applies generally to Scotland as well as to England and Wales, apart from particular sections which are noted as they occur.

The former Companies (Winding Up) Rules 1949 have been replaced by IR 1986, Pt 4.

The changes made to the law by IA 1985 and IA 1986 do not generally apply retrospectively, so as to affect liquidations which were already in progress when these Acts came into force: Sch. 11, para. 4. The few exceptions to this (Sch. 11, paras 5–9) are noted at the appropriate places in the text which follows.

Where a building society is being wound up under Pt X of the Building Societies Act 1986, Pts IV, VI, VII, XII and XIII of the present Act (and, for Northern Ireland, Pt XX of the Companies (Northern Ireland) Order 1986) apply, subject to the modifications made by Sch. 15 to that Act: see Building Societies Act 1986, s. 90 and Sch. 15, as amended by CA 1989, s. 211(1), (2) and Sch. 24. Note that the amendments made by CA 1989: (i) require the liquidator of a building society to be a qualified insolvency practitioner under Pt XIII of IA 1986 (s. 211(2)(a)); and (ii) extend the concept of "shadow director" to building societies (s. 211(2)(b)). Transitional provisions contained in SI 1990/1392 (C 41), art. 7, protect the position of liquidators appointed prior to the commencement of CA 1989, s. 211(2)(a), *i.e.* July 31, 1990.

The provisions of IA 1986 are made to apply to the winding up of an industrial and provident society (such as a co-operative) by the Industrial and Provident Societies Act 1965, s. 55(a) (as amended by IA 1986, s. 439(2) and Sch. 14), subject to the modifications which are set out in that Act. Other bodies, such as friendly societies, which are not provided for by specific legislation, may be wound up as unregistered companies under Pt V of IA 1986: see *Re Victoria Society, Knottingley* [1913] 1 Ch. 167.

The winding up of insurance undertakings based in the UK (except Lloyd's) is the subject of a special regime: see the Insurers (Reorganisation and Winding up) Regulations 2003 (SI 2003/1102, effective April 20, 2003), implementing EC Directive 2001/17/EC.

Chapter I

Preliminary

Modes of winding up

73 Alternative modes of winding up

73(1) [Voluntary, by court] The winding up of a company, within the meaning given to that expression by section 735 of the Companies Act, may be either voluntary (Chapters II, III, IV and V in this Part) or by the court (Chapter VI).

73(2) [Application of Ch. I, VII–X] This Chapter, and Chapters VII to X, relate to winding up generally, except where otherwise stated.

GENERAL NOTE

Prior to the coming into force of this Act, there were three modes of winding up: (1) voluntary; (2) by the court; and (3) subject to the supervision of the court. The last of these methods was little used, and was abolished by IA 1985, s. 235(3) and Sch. 10, Pt II. A voluntary winding up is commenced by the passing of a resolution (usually a special or extraordinary resolution) by the company in general meeting (see s. 84): it may be either a "members' voluntary winding up", conducted under the control of the members, if the directors are able to make a declaration of solvency under ss. 89, or a "creditors' voluntary winding up", if the directors cannot make such a declaration, in which case the creditors have control (see ss. 89, 90). A winding up by the court (or "compulsory winding up"), as the name suggests, follows from the making of a court order (see ss. 122ff.).

"Company", for the purposes of this section, is defined by CA 1985, s. 735(1) and (3) as follows:

"**S. 735 'Company', etc.**

735(1) In this Act–

  (a) '**company**' means a company formed and registered under this Act, or an existing company;
  (b) '**existing company**' means a company formed and registered under the former Companies Acts, but does not include a company registered under the Joint Stock Companies Acts, the Companies Act 1862 or the Companies (Consolidation) Act 1908 in what was then Ireland;
  (c) '**the former Companies Acts**' means the Joint Stock Companies Acts, the Companies Act 1862, the Companies (Consolidation) Act 1908, the Companies Act 1929 and the Companies Acts 1948 to 1983.

...

735(3) 'The Joint Stock Companies Acts' means the Joint Stock Companies Act 1856, the Joint Stock Companies Acts 1856, 1857, the Joint Stock Banking Companies Act 1857 and the Act to enable Joint Stock Banking Companies to be formed on the principle of limited liability, or any one or more of those Acts (as the case may require), but does not include the Joint Stock Companies Act 1844."

Contributories

74 Liability as contributories of present and past members

74(1) [Liability to contribute] When a company is wound up, every present and past member is liable to contribute to its assets to any amount sufficient for payment of its debts and liabilities, and the expenses of the winding up, and for the adjustment of the rights of the contributories among themselves.

74(2) [Qualifications to liability] This is subject as follows–

  (a) a past member is not liable to contribute if he has ceased to be a member for one year or more before the commencement of the winding up;
  (b) a past member is not liable to contribute in respect of any debt or liability of the company contracted after he ceased to be a member;
  (c) a past member is not liable to contribute, unless it appears to the court that the existing members are unable to satisfy the contributions required to be made by them in pursuance of the Companies Act and this Act;
  (d) in the case of a company limited by shares, no contribution is required from any member exceeding the amount (if any) unpaid on the shares in respect of which he is liable as a present or past member;
  (e) nothing in the Companies Act or this Act invalidates any provision contained in a policy of insurance or other contract whereby the liability of individual members on the policy or contract is

restricted, or whereby the funds of the company are alone made liable in respect of the policy or contract;

(f) a sum due to any member of the company (in his character of a member) by way of dividends, profits or otherwise is not deemed to be a debt of the company, payable to that member in a case of competition between himself and any other creditor not a member of the company, but any such sum may be taken into account for the purpose of the final adjustment of the rights of the contributories among themselves.

74(3) **[Company limited by guarantee]** In the case of a company limited by guarantee, no contribution is required from any member exceeding the amount undertaken to be contributed by him to the company's assets in the event of its being wound up; but if it is a company with a share capital, every member of it is liable (in addition to the amount so undertaken to be contributed to the assets), to contribute to the extent of any sums unpaid on shares held by him.

S. 74(1)
A "contributory" is a member or past member of the company who is liable to contribute to the assets of the company in a winding up (s. 79). This includes a member whose shares are fully paid: *Re Anglesea Colliery Company* (1866) L.R. 1 Ch. 555, and a former member: *Re Consolidated Goldfields of New Zealand Ltd* [1953] Ch. 689. However the court has power to order the rectification of the register of members with retrospective effect, where it is satisfied that a person has never been a member: see *Barbor v Middleton* (1988) 4 B.C.C. 681.

S. 74(2)
This provision defines the extent to which both present and past members are liable to contribute to the assets. The principle of limited liability will, where appropriate, apply so as to restrict the amount payable (para. (d)). A past member is liable only in the circumstances listed in paras (a)–(c).

Paragraph (f) subordinates any sums payable by the company to any member qua member (*e.g.* a dividend declared but not paid) to the company's obligations to its general creditors. The member cannot set off these sums directly against his own contribution.

S. 74(2)(f)
In *Soden v British & Commonwealth Holdings plc (in administration)* [1998] A.C. 298; [1997] B.C.C. 952 the House of Lords held that sums due to a member "in his character of a member" were only those sums the right to which was based on a cause of action on the statutory contract contained in s. 14 of CA 1985 and other rights imposed by the Companies Acts. The expression did not include damages awarded to a person who had acquired shares in the company by purchase from an existing member in reliance on a misrepresentation by the company. In contrast, damages for misrepresentation or breach of warranty awarded to a person who had obtained the shares by subscription from the company have been held to be within the section (*Re Addlestone Linoleum Co.* (1887) 37 Ch.D. 191; *Webb Distributors (Australia) Pty Ltd v State of Victoria* (1993) 11 A.C.L.C. 1178). The question may, however, be open to reargument following the enactment of CA 1985, s. 111A, which overrides part of the *ratio decidendi* of the *Addlestone Linoleum* case.

S. 74(3)
This states the limit of the liability of a contributory where a company is limited by guarantee.

75 Directors, etc. with unlimited liability

75(1) **[Liability in winding up]** In the winding up of a limited company, any director or manager (whether past or present) whose liability is under the Companies Act unlimited is liable, in addition to his liability (if any) to contribute as an ordinary member, to make a further contribution as if he were at the commencement of the winding up a member of an unlimited company.

75(2) **[Qualifications to liability]** However–

(a) a past director or manager is not liable to make such further contribution if he has ceased to hold office for a year or more before the commencement of the winding up;

(b) a past director or manager is not liable to make such further contribution in respect of any debt or liability of the company contracted after he ceased to hold office;

Section 76   Insolvency Act 1986

(c)   subject to the company's articles, a director or manager is not liable to make such further contribution unless the court deems it necessary to require that contribution in order to satisfy the company's debts and liabilities, and the expenses of the winding up.

GENERAL NOTE

CA 1985, s. 306, which is virtually never used in practice, enables a limited company to provide by its memorandum for its directors and managers to have unlimited liability. This section deals with the winding up of such companies.

76 Liability of past directors and shareholders

76(1) **[Application]** This section applies where a company is being wound up and–

(a)   it has under Chapter VII of Part V of the Companies Act (redeemable shares; purchase by a company of its own shares) made a payment out of capital in respect of the redemption or purchase of any of its own shares (the payment being referred to below as "the relevant payment"), and

(b)   the aggregate amount of the company's assets and the amounts paid by way of contribution to its assets (apart from this section) is not sufficient for payment of its debts and liabilities, and the expenses of the winding up.

76(2) **[Contribution of past shareholders, directors]** If the winding up commenced within one year of the date on which the relevant payment was made, then–

(a)   the person from whom the shares were redeemed or purchased, and

(b)   the directors who signed the statutory declaration made in accordance with section 173(3) of the Companies Act for purposes of the redemption or purchase (except a director who shows that he had reasonable grounds for forming the opinion set out in the declaration),

are, so as to enable that insufficiency to be met, liable to contribute to the following extent to the company's assets.

76(3) **[Amount payable]** A person from whom any of the shares were redeemed or purchased is liable to contribute an amount not exceeding so much of the relevant payment as was made by the company in respect of his shares; and the directors are jointly and severally liable with that person to contribute that amount.

76(4) **[Application to court]** A person who has contributed any amount to the assets in pursuance of this section may apply to the court for an order directing any other person jointly and severally liable in respect of that amount to pay him such amount as the court thinks just and equitable.

76(5) **[Non-application of s. 74, 75]** Sections 74 and 75 do not apply in relation to liability accruing by virtue of this section.

76(6) **[Regulations]** This section is deemed included in Chapter VII of Part V of the Companies Act for the purposes of the Secretary of State's power to make regulations under section 179 of that Act.

GENERAL NOTE

When a payment has been made out of capital by a private company in connection with a redemption or repurchase of shares under CA 1985, ss. 171ff., and the company is wound up insolvent within one year of the payment, this section applies so as to make the recipient of the payment liable to refund it in whole or part and, in some circumstances also, the directors jointly and severally liable with him.
  Note that although the persons liable under this section fall within the definition of "contributory" for the purposes of this Act, they will not normally be regarded as "contributories" when construing a company's articles (see s. 79(3)).

77 Limited company formerly unlimited

77(1) [Application] This section applies in the case of a company being wound up which was at some former time registered as unlimited but has re-registered–

(a) as a public company under section 43 of the Companies Act (or the former corresponding provision, section 5 of the Companies Act 1980), or

(b) as a limited company under section 51 of the Companies Act (or the former corresponding provision, section 44 of the Companies Act 1967).

77(2) [Contribution by past members] Notwithstanding section 74(2)(a) above, a past member of the company who was a member of it at the time of re-registration, if the winding up commences within the period of 3 years beginning with the day on which the company was re-registered, is liable to contribute to the assets of the company in respect of debts and liabilities contracted before that time.

77(3) [If no past members existing members] If no persons who were members of the company at that time are existing members of it, a person who at that time was a present or past member is liable to contribute as above notwithstanding that the existing members have satisfied the contributions required to be made by them under the Companies Act and this Act.

This applies subject to section 74(2)(a) above and to subsection (2) of this section, but notwithstanding section 74(2)(c).

77(4) [No limitation on contribution] Notwithstanding section 74(2)(d) and (3), there is no limit on the amount which a person who, at that time, was a past or present member of the company is liable to contribute as above.

GENERAL NOTE

The provisions of the Companies Acts mentioned in s. 77(1) enable an unlimited company to reregister as limited, but the unlimited liability of both present and past members continues if a winding up ensues within three years of the date of reregistration. The present section deals with the liability of these persons as contributories.

78 Unlimited company formerly limited

78(1) [Application] This section applies in the case of a company being wound up which was at some former time registered as limited but has been re-registered as unlimited under section 49 of the Companies Act (or the former corresponding provision, section 43 of the Companies Act 1967).

78(2) [Limitation on contribution] A person who, at the time when the application for the company to be re-registered was lodged, was a past member of the company and did not after that again become a member of it is not liable to contribute to the assets of the company more than he would have been liable to contribute had the company not been re-registered.

GENERAL NOTE

When a limited company is converted to an unlimited company under CA 1985, s. 49, the limited liability of past members is preserved by this provision.

79 Meaning of "contributory"

79(1) ["Contributory"] In this Act and the Companies Act the expression **"contributory"** means every person liable to contribute to the assets of a company in the event of its being wound up, and for the purposes of all proceedings for determining, and all proceedings prior to the final determination of, the persons who are to be deemed contributories, includes any person alleged to be a contributory.

79(2) [Qualification] The reference in subsection (1) to persons liable to contribute to the assets does not include a person so liable by virtue of a declaration by the court under section 213 (imputed responsibility for company's fraudulent trading) or section 214 (wrongful trading) in Chapter X of this Part.

79(3) [Reference in articles] A reference in a company's articles to a contributory does not (unless the context requires) include a person who is a contributory only by virtue of section 76.

This subsection is deemed included in Chapter VII of Part V of the Companies Act for the purposes of the Secretary of State's power to make regulations under section 179 of that Act.

GENERAL NOTE

This section defines the term "contributory" for the purposes of both the present Act and CA 1985. It incorporates (by s. 79(2)) an amendment made by IA 1985, Sch. 6, para. 5 which makes it plain that a person is not deemed a contributory merely because he has been ordered by the court to contribute to the company's assets following a finding of fraudulent or wrongful trading under ss. 213, 214.

See also the note to s. 74(1).

80 Nature of contributory's liability

80 The liability of a contributory creates a debt (in England and Wales in the nature of a speciality) accruing due from him at the time when his liability commenced, but payable at the times when calls are made for enforcing the liability.

GENERAL NOTE

"Due" in this section is equivalent to "owing", or "constituting a debt", in contrast with "payable", which is the relevant date for the purposes of the Statutes of Limitation. The period of limitation applicable to a speciality debt is 12 years, instead of the normal six.

81 Contributories in case of death of a member

81(1) [Personal representative liable] If a contributory dies either before or after he has been placed on the list of contributories, his personal representatives, and the heirs and legatees of heritage of his heritable estate in Scotland, are liable in a due course of administration to contribute to the assets of the company in discharge of his liability and are contributories accordingly.

81(2) [Where personal representatives on list of contributories] Where the personal representatives are placed on the list of contributories, the heirs or legatees of heritage need not be added, but they may be added as and when the court thinks fit.

81(3) [Where default in payment] If in England and Wales the personal representatives make default in paying any money ordered to be paid by them, proceedings may be taken for administering the estate of the deceased contributory and for compelling payment out of it of the money due.

GENERAL NOTE

This section provides that on the death of a contributory, his personal representatives (or their Scottish counterparts) are substituted for him as contributories.

82 Effect of contributory's bankruptcy

82(1) [Application] The following applies if a contributory becomes bankrupt, either before or after he has been placed on the list of contributories.

82(2) [Trustee in bankruptcy a contributory] His trustee in bankruptcy represents him for all purposes of the winding up, and is a contributory accordingly.

82(3) [Trustee called on to admit to proof] The trustee may be called on to admit to proof against the bankrupt's estate, or otherwise allow to be paid out of the bankrupt's assets in due course of law, any money due from the bankrupt in respect of his liability to contribute to the company's assets.

82(4) **[Estimated value of liability to future calls]** There may be proved against the bankrupt's estate the estimated value of his liability to future calls as well as calls already made.

S. 82(1), (2)
The trustee in bankruptcy is deemed a contributory and represents the bankrupt for all purposes of the winding up. It was held under the virtually identical wording of CA 1948, s. 216 that this section does not empower a contributory's trustee in bankruptcy to present a winding-up petition (unless the trustee has been registered as a member), since its provisions only become effective once a winding up is in place: *Re H L Bolton (Engineering) Co. Ltd* [1956] Ch. 577 at pp. 582–583. In Scotland, however, the wording of the Bankruptcy (Scotland) Act 1985, s. 31 is sufficiently wide to empower a trustee to petition: *Taylor, Petitioner; Cumming's Trustee v Glenrinnes Farms Ltd* [1993] B.C.C. 829.

S. 82(3), (4)
These subsections deal with the proof against the bankrupt's estate of his liability to the company as a contributory.

83 Companies registered under Companies Act, Part XXII, Chapter II

83(1) **[Application]** The following applies in the event of a company being wound up which has been registered under section 680 of the Companies Act (or previous corresponding provisions in the Companies Act 1948 or earlier Acts).

83(2) **[Contributories re debts and liabilities before registration]** Every person is a contributory, in respect of the company's debts and liabilities contracted before registration, who is liable–

(a) to pay, or contribute to the payment of, any debt or liability so contracted, or

(b) to pay, or contribute to the payment of, any sum for the adjustment of the rights of the members among themselves in respect of any such debt or liability, or

(c) to pay, or contribute to the amount of, the expenses of winding up the company, so far as relates to the debts or liabilities above-mentioned.

83(3) **[Amounts liable to be contributed]** Every contributory is liable to contribute to the assets of the company, in the course of the winding up, all sums due from him in respect of any such liability.

83(4) **[Death etc. of contributory]** In the event of the death, bankruptcy or insolvency of any contributory, provisions of this Act, with respect to the personal representatives, to the heirs and legatees of the heritage of the heritable estate in Scotland of deceased contributories and to the trustees of bankrupt or insolvent contributories respectively, apply.

GENERAL NOTE

The companies referred to are those not formed under the Companies Acts but authorised to register under CA 1985, s. 680 or its predecessors – *e.g.* a company incorporated by a private Act of Parliament.

CHAPTER II

VOLUNTARY WINDING UP (INTRODUCTORY AND GENERAL)

Resolutions for, and commencement of, voluntary winding up

84 Circumstances in which company may be wound up voluntarily

84(1) **[Circumstances]** A company may be wound up voluntarily–

(a) when the period (if any) fixed for the duration of the company by the articles expires, or the event (if any) occurs, on the occurence of which the articles provide that the company is to be dissolved, and the company in general meeting has passed a resolution requiring it to be wound up voluntarily;

(b) if the company resolves by special resolution that it be wound up voluntarily;

(c) if the company resolves by extraordinary resolution to the effect that it cannot by reason of its liabilities continue its business, and that it is advisable to wind up.

84(2) **[Definition]** In this Act the expression **"a resolution for voluntary winding up"** means a resolution passed under any of the paragraphs of subsection (1).

84(2A) **[Written notice to holder of qualifying floating charge]** Before a company passes a resolution for voluntary winding up it must give written notice of the resolution to the holder of any qualifying floating charge to which section 72A applies.

84(2B) **[Where written notice given]** Where notice is given under subsection (2A) a resolution for voluntary winding up may be passed only –

(a) after the end of the period of five business days beginning with the day on which the notice was given, or

(b) if the person to whom the notice was given has consented in writing to the passing of the resolution.

84(3) **[Copy of resolution to registrar]** A resolution passed under paragraph (a) of subsection (1), as well as a special resolution under paragraph (b) and an extraordinary resolution under paragraph (c), is subject to section 380 of the Companies Act (copy of resolution to be forwarded to registrar of companies within 15 days).

S. 84(1)
Paragraph (a) calls for a "resolution" (*i.e.* an *ordinary* resolution), para. (b) for a *special* resolution and para. (c) for an *extraordinary* resolution.

S. 84(2A), (2B)
These provisions (inserted by SI 2003/2096 from September 15, 2003) give the charge-holder a brief opportunity to appoint an administrator, failing which his right to do so will be lost.
 A resolution for voluntary winding up cannot be passed conditionally upon the happening of some other event, *e.g.* the discharge of an administration order: *Re Norditrak (UK) Ltd* [2000] B.C.C. 441.

S. 84(3)
The obligation to register these resolutions is laid down also by CA 1985, s. 380(4)(a), (b) and (j). The liquidator, for the purposes of these provisions, is deemed to be an officer of the company and liable accordingly to penal sanctions for non-compliance (CA 1985, s. 380(7)).

85 Notice of resolution to wind up

85(1) **[Notice in Gazette]** When a company has passed a resolution for voluntary winding up, it shall, within 14 days after the passing of the resolution, give notice of the resolution by advertisement in the Gazette.

85(2) **[Penalty on default]** If default is made in complying with this section, the company and every officer of it who is in default is liable to a fine and, for continued contravention, to a daily default fine.
 For purposes of this subsection the liquidator is deemed an officer of the company.

GENERAL NOTE

It is the responsibility of the company and its officers (including the liquidator: s. 85(2)) to see that notice of the resolution to wind up is gazetted. The liquidator, when appointed, is under a separate obligation to publish notice of his appointment in the *Gazette*: see s. 109.

S. 85(2)
On penalties, see s. 430 and Sch. 10.

86 Commencement of winding up

86 A voluntary winding up is deemed to commence at the time of the passing of the resolution for voluntary winding up.

GENERAL NOTE

The "commencement" of a winding up is significant for many purposes under this Act and, previously, the Companies Acts. For the corresponding provision in relation to a winding up by the court, see s. 129.

It should be noted that this section refers to the "time" of commencement, as does s. 129. In contrast, s. 278, the corresponding provision in bankruptcy, states that a bankruptcy "commences *with the day* on which the order is made" – an expression which clearly relates back to the preceding midnight – while other sections of the Act and provisions in the rules refer to the "date" of an event (see, *e.g.* s. 183(2)(a): "date on which he had notice"; "date of commencement of the winding up"; s. 240(3): "date of the commencement of the winding up"; and r. 4.91(1): "date when the company went into liquidation"). It must be inferred that the draftsmen used these different wordings deliberately, so that where the word "time" is used the normal convention that "the law takes no account of part of a day" (*Trow v Ind Coope (West Midlands) Ltd* [1967] 2 Q.B. 899) is ousted, and an event is to be pinpointed to the precise time of the day when it occurred. This could be an important consideration in some areas of commerce (*e.g.* financial dealing rooms), where even seconds can count.

The EC Regulation refers to the "time of the opening" of insolvency proceedings. In the case of a creditors' voluntary winding up, this will be the time of the passing of the shareholders' resolution. See the note to the Regulation, Art. 2(f).

Consequences of resolution to wind up

87 Effect on business and status of company

87(1) **[Cessation of business]** In case of a voluntary winding up, the company shall from the commencement of the winding up cease to carry on its business, except so far as may be required for its beneficial winding up.

87(2) **[Continuation of corporate state etc.]** However, the corporate state and corporate powers of the company, notwithstanding anything to the contrary in its articles, continue until the company is dissolved.

S. 87(1)

In the case of a compulsory winding up, the liquidator may carry on the company's business, "so far as may be necessary for its beneficial winding up" (see s. 167(1)(a) and Sch. IV, para. 5 and, in Scotland, s. 169), but normally only with the sanction of the court or the liquidation committee. In a voluntary winding up the question whether it is beneficial to continue the business is a matter for the liquidator's own bona fide judgment.

S. 87(2)

The corporate personality of the company in a compulsory winding up also continues until dissolution, although this is not expressly stated in the Act. It follows that acts must be done by the liquidator in the name of the company, and not in his own name.

88 Avoidance of share transfers, etc. after winding-up resolution

88 Any transfer of shares, not being a transfer made to or with the sanction of the liquidator, and any alteration in the status of the company's members, made after the commencement of a voluntary winding up, is void.

GENERAL NOTE

In a compulsory winding up, a transfer of shares made after the commencement of the winding up is similarly void, but can be validated only by order of the court: see s. 127.

Declaration of solvency

89 Statutory declaration of solvency

89(1) **[Declaration by directors]** Where it is proposed to wind up a company voluntarily, the directors (or, in the case of a company having more than two directors, the majority of them) may at a directors' meeting make a statutory declaration to the effect that they have made a full inquiry into the company's affairs and that, having done so, they have formed the opinion that the company will be able to pay its debts in full, together with interest at the official rate (as defined in section 251), within such period, not exceeding 12 months from the commencement of the winding up, as may be specified in the declaration.

89(2) [Requirements for declaration] Such a declaration by the directors has no effect for purposes of this Act unless–

(a) it is made within the 5 weeks immediately preceding the date of the passing of the resolution for winding up, or on that date but before the passing of the resolution, and

(b) it embodies a statement of the company's assets and liabilities as at the latest practicable date before the making of the declaration.

89(3) [Declaration to registrar] The declaration shall be delivered to the registrar of companies before the expiration of 15 days immediately following the date on which the resolution for winding up is passed.

89(4) [Offence, penalty] A director making a declaration under this section without having reasonable grounds for the opinion that the company will be able to pay its debts in full, together with interest at the official rate, within the period specified is liable to imprisonment or a fine, or both.

89(5) [Presumption] If the company is wound up in pursuance of a resolution passed within 5 weeks after the making of the declaration, and its debts (together with interest at the official rate) are not paid or provided for in full within the period specified, it is to be presumed (unless the contrary is shown) that the director did not have reasonable grounds for his opinion.

89(6) [Penalty for non-compliance with s. 89(3)] If a declaration required by subsection (3) to be delivered to the registrar is not so delivered within the time prescribed by that subsection, the company and every officer in default is liable to a fine and, for continued contravention, to a daily default fine.

GENERAL NOTE

The category of a voluntary winding up (members' or creditors': see s. 90), and the legal rules which apply to it in consequence, depend on whether a statutory declaration of solvency has been made under this section. The responsibility for assessing the likely solvency of the company is placed squarely on the directors (or a majority of them): if they make the declaration, the matter proceeds as a members' voluntary winding up under the control of the members; if they do not, the creditors take over. The severe penalties and reversed onus of proof prescribed by s. 89(4) and (5) provide directors with a strong deterrent against making a declaration of solvency irresponsibly.

There is no obligation upon the directors to make a statutory declaration when the company is insolvent or not believed to be solvent: the matter simply proceeds as a creditors' voluntary winding up.

S. 89(1)
A statutory declaration is a formal declaration made before a justice of the peace or commissioner for oaths, and is equivalent to an oath for most legal purposes, including the law of perjury. The declaration here required must be made at a directors' meeting, held before the shareholders' meeting at which the resolution for winding up is to be passed, and within the time specified in s. 89(2).

The directors must themselves fix the period, not exceeding 12 months from the commencement of the winding up, within which they predict that the company will be able to pay its debts in full. Since the directors' declaration must be made with reference to a future date, they should plainly take into account any prospective and contingent liabilities of which they are aware. On the other hand, it should be noted that they are not required to assert that the company itself is, or will be, "solvent": if the directors have a firm commitment from a third party (such as parent company) that it will meet any liabilities that the company cannot discharge from its own resources, they may well be justified in making a declaration and allowing the liquidation to proceed as a members' voluntary winding up.

S. 89(2)
The five-week period is reckoned back from the date of the winding-up resolution, and the declaration must be based on a financial statement which is as up-to-date as practicable.

S. 89(3)
Form 4.70 should be used.

S. 89(4)–(6)

The penalties under s. 89(4) are stringent – up to two years' imprisonment and an unlimited fine, if the proceedings are on indictment (see Sch. 10). If a director's prediction of solvency turns out in the event to be wrong, s. 89(5) reverses the normal burden of proof and requires him to show that in fact he had reasonable grounds for making it.

On penalties, see s. 430 and Sch. 10.

90 Distinction between "members' " and "creditors' " voluntary winding up

90 A winding up in the case of which a directors' statutory declaration under section 89 has been made is a "members' voluntary winding up"; and a winding up in the case of which such a declaration has not been made is a "creditors' voluntary winding up".

GENERAL NOTE

In the sections of the Act which follow, Ch. III (ss. 91–96) applies only to a members' voluntary winding up and Ch. IV (ss. 97–106) only to a creditors' voluntary winding up, while Ch. V (ss. 107–116) applies to a voluntary winding up of either kind. This was formerly made clear in the Companies Acts by introductory sections in each case (*e.g.* CA 1985, ss. 579, 587, 596); in the present Act it is left (with the exception of Ch. IV) to be inferred from the title to the chapter in question. (On the relevance of chapter titles in the construction of statutes, see the comment preceding s. 230.)

CHAPTER III

MEMBERS' VOLUNTARY WINDING UP

91 Appointment of liquidator

91(1) [**Appointment by general meeting**] In a members' voluntary winding up, the company in general meeting shall appoint one or more liquidators for the purpose of winding up the company's affairs and distributing its assets.

91(2) [**Cessation of directors' powers**] On the appointment of a liquidator all the powers of the directors cease, except so far as the company in general meeting or the liquidator sanctions their continuance.

S. 91(1)

For the relevant rules, see IR 1986, rr. 4.139, 4.141.

S. 91(2)

On the making of a winding-up order *by the court* the appointments of all the directors are terminated automatically: *Measures Brothers Ltd v Measures* [1910] 2 Ch. 248. It appears from this subsection that a resolution for voluntary winding up does not of itself operate to remove the directors from office, for if this were the case it would not be possible to sanction the continuance of their powers. This view is, perhaps, confirmed by some reported cases concerning employees, *e.g. Midland Counties District Bank Ltd v Attwood* [1905] 1 Ch. 357, although there are dicta in other cases to the contrary (*e.g. Reigate v Union Manufacturing Co. (Ramsbottom) Ltd* [1918] 1 K.B. 592 at p. 606). It is also endorsed by s. 114(2), (3).

92 Power to fill vacancy in office of liquidator

92(1) [**Filling of vacancy**] If a vacancy occurs by death, resignation or otherwise in the office of liquidator appointed by the company, the company in general meeting may, subject to any arrangement with its creditors, fill the vacancy.

92(2) [**Convening of general meeting**] For that purpose a general meeting may be convened by any contributory or, if there were more liquidators than one, by the continuing liquidators.

92(3) [**Manner of holding meeting**] The meeting shall be held in manner provided by this Act or by the articles, or in such manner as may, on application by any contributory or by the continuing liquidators, be determined by the court.

S. 92(3)
The reference to "this Act" is probably a slip: fairly obviously, it should have been to CA 1985, as was the case in the pre-consolidation provision (CA 1985, s. 581(3)). The present Act contains no provisions regulating the holding of meetings in a members' voluntary winding up (apart from s. 194, which deals with resolutions passed at adjourned meetings). The subject is not dealt with in the rules apart from IR 1986, r. 4.139, concerning the appointment of the liquidator. In all other respects, the procedure will be the normal one for company meetings laid down by the company's articles and CA 1985, Pt XI, Ch. IV.

93 General company meeting at each year's end

93(1) [If winding up for more than one year] Subject to sections 96 and 102, in the event of the winding up continuing for more than one year, the liquidator shall summon a general meeting of the company at the end of the first year from the commencement of the winding up, and of each succeeding year, or at the first convenient date within 3 months from the end of the year or such longer period as the Secretary of State may allow.

93(2) [Account by liquidator] The liquidator shall lay before the meeting an account of his acts and dealings, and of the conduct of the winding up, during the preceding year.

93(3) [Penalty for non-compliance] If the liquidator fails to comply with this section, he is liable to a fine.

GENERAL NOTE
On the holding of meetings during a winding up, see the note to s. 92(3).

S. 93(3)
On penalties, see s. 430 and Sch. 10.

94 Final meeting prior to dissolution

94(1) [Account of winding up, final meeting] As soon as the company's affairs are fully wound up, the liquidator shall make up an account of the winding up showing how it has been conducted and the company's property has been disposed of, and thereupon shall call a general meeting of the company for the purpose of laying before it the account and giving an explanation of it.

94(2) [Advertisement in Gazette] The meeting shall be called by advertisement in the Gazette, specifying its time, place and object and published at least one month before the meeting.

94(3) [Copy of account etc. to registrar] Within one week after the meeting, the liquidator shall send to the registrar of companies a copy of the account, and shall make a return to him of the holding of the meeting and of its date.

94(4) [Penalty on default] If the copy is not sent or the return is not made in accordance with subsection (3), the liquidator is liable to a fine and, for continued contravention, to a daily default fine.

94(5) [If no quorum at meeting] If a quorum is not present at the meeting, the liquidator shall, in lieu of the return mentioned above, make a return that the meeting was duly summoned and that no quorum was present; and upon such a return being made, the provisions of subsection (3) as to the making of the return are deemed complied with.

94(6) [Penalty if no general meeting called] If the liquidator fails to call a general meeting of the company as required by subsection (1), he is liable to a fine.

GENERAL NOTE
When the liquidator has sent to the registrar his final account and return under this section, dissolution of the company follows automatically three months after the return is registered, unless the court makes an order deferring the date: see s. 201(2), (3).

S. 94(4), (6)
On penalties, see s. 430 and Sch. 10.

S. 94(5)
This provision enables the liquidator to cut short the statutory formalities if the meeting, when summoned, is inquorate.

95 Effect of company's insolvency

95(1) [Application] This section applies where the liquidator is of the opinion that the company will be unable to pay its debts in full (together with interest at the official rate) within the period stated in the directors' declaration under section 89.

95(2) [Duties of liquidator] The liquidator shall–

(a) summon a meeting of creditors for a day not later than the 28th day after the day on which he formed that opinion;

(b) send notices of the creditors' meeting to the creditors by post not less than 7 days before the day on which that meeting is to be held;

(c) cause notice of the creditors' meeting to be advertised once in the Gazette and once at least in 2 newspapers circulating in the relevant locality (that is to say the locality in which the company's principal place of business in Great Britain was situated during the relevant period); and

(d) during the period before the day on which the creditors' meeting is to be held, furnish creditors free of charge with such information concerning the affairs of the company as they may reasonably require;

and the notice of the creditors' meeting shall state the duty imposed by paragraph (d) above.

95(3) [Duties of liquidator re statement of affairs] The liquidator shall also–

(a) make out a statement in the prescribed form as to the affairs of the company;

(b) lay that statement before the creditors' meeting; and

(c) attend and preside at that meeting.

95(4) [Contents of statement of affairs] The statement as to the affairs of the company shall be verified by affidavit by the liquidator and shall show–

(a) particulars of the company's assets, debts and liabilities;

(b) the names and addresses of the company's creditors;

(c) the securities held by them respectively;

(d) the dates when the securities were respectively given; and

(e) such further or other information as may be prescribed.

95(5) [Where principal place of business in different places] Where the company's principal place of business in Great Britain was situated in different localities at different times during the relevant period, the duty imposed by subsection (2)(c) applies separately in relation to each of those localities.

95(6) [Where no place of business in Great Britain] Where the company had no place of business in Great Britain during the relevant period, references in subsections (2)(c) and (5) to the company's principal place of business in Great Britain are replaced by references to its registered office.

95(7) ["The relevant period"] In this section **"the relevant period"** means the period of 6 months immediately preceding the day on which were sent the notices summoning the company meeting at which it was resolved that the company be wound up voluntarily.

95(8) [Penalty for non-compliance] If the liquidator without reasonable excuse fails to comply with this section, he is liable to a fine.

Section 96 *Insolvency Act 1986*

GENERAL NOTE

The earlier law had for a long time been criticised as unsatisfactory (see, *e.g.* the Cork Committee's *Report*, paras 674–676). The repealed section in the Companies Act required the liquidator in a members' voluntary winding up, if he formed the opinion that the company was insolvent, to summon a meeting of the creditors and inform them of the position. However, the Act made no further provision, and so all that the creditors could then do was petition the court for a compulsory winding-up order to replace the voluntary liquidation. The new section empowers the creditors, without applying to the court, to convert the liquidation into a creditors' voluntary winding up and, if they wish, to substitute a liquidator of their own choice.

S. 95(1)
The reference is to the directors' statutory declaration of solvency by virtue of which the liquidation proceeded initially as a members' voluntary winding up: see s. 89(1).

S. 95(2)(c)
Where the company's principal place of business was situated in different localities at different times within the relevant period, s. 95(5) applies; and where the company had no place of business in Great Britain during the relevant period, s. 95(6) applies. For the meaning of "the relevant period", see s. 95(7).

S. 95(3), (4)
The "statement of affairs" provision is parallel to that which applies in a creditors' voluntary winding up (see the comments to s. 99 and s. 131), except that in the present situation the responsibilities in connection with the statement are imposed on the liquidator and not the directors.
    For the rules and forms prescribed for the purposes of this section, see IR 1986, rr. 4.34ff., 4.49.

S. 95(6)
The question whether a company has established a place of business within the jurisdiction normally arises in relation to the registration requirements of CA 1985, s. 409 and 691. The meaning of the phrase "established a place of business" has been the subject of judicial determination in a number of cases, *e.g. South India Shipping Corporation Ltd v The Export-Import Bank of Korea* [1985] 1 W.L.R. 585; (1985) 1 B.C.C. 99,350; *Re Oriel Ltd* [1986] 1 W.L.R. 180; (1985) 1 B.C.C. 99,444; *Cleveland Museum of Art v Capricorn Art International SA* (1989) 5 B.C.C. 860.

S. 95(8)
On penalties, see s. 430 and Sch. 10.

96 Conversion to creditors' voluntary winding up

96 As from the day on which the creditors' meeting is held under section 95, this Act has effect as if—

(a) the directors' declaration under section 89 had not been made; and

(b) the creditors' meeting and the company meeting at which it was resolved that the company be wound up voluntarily were the meetings mentioned in section 98 in the next Chapter;

and accordingly the winding up becomes a creditors' voluntary winding up.

GENERAL NOTE

This section reproduces part of IA 1985, s. 83(7), omitting some final words ("and any appointment made or committee established by the creditors' meeting shall be deemed to have been made or established by the creditors' meeting so mentioned"), which were probably discarded as superfluous.
    It will, of course, be competent for the creditors at their meeting to appoint a liquidator of their own choosing and to establish a liquidation committee under ss. 100 and 101, respectively, by virtue of the general provisions of the present section.
    Section 97(2) makes it clear that the meeting of creditors held under s. 95(2)–(3) and the statement of affairs prepared under s. 95(4) are deemed equivalent to the meeting and statement required respectively by ss. 98 and 99, so that there is no need to duplicate either of these exercises. This is also confirmed by s. 102.

Insolvency Act 1986   Section 98

CHAPTER IV

CREDITORS' VOLUNTARY WINDING UP

97 Application of this Chapter

97(1) [Application] Subject as follows, this Chapter applies in relation to a creditors' voluntary winding up.

97(2) [Non-application of s. 98, 99] Sections 98 and 99 do not apply where, under section 96 in Chapter III, a members' voluntary winding up has become a creditors' voluntary winding up.

S. 97(1)
Chapter IV applies in every voluntary winding up where the directors do not make a statutory declaration of solvency under s. 89(1).

A creditors' voluntary winding up is a "collective insolvency proceeding" within the scope of the EC Regulation: see the note to the Regulation, Art. 1(1). In order to secure recognition of the winding up in other EU Member States, a certificate of confirmation must be obtained from the court: see Annex A of the Regulation and IR 1986, rr. 7.62–7.63.

S. 97(2)
See the note to s. 96, above.

98 Meeting of creditors

98(1) [Duty of company] The company shall–

(a) cause a meeting of its creditors to be summoned for a day not later than the 14th day after the day on which there is to be held the company meeting at which the resolution for voluntary winding up is to be proposed;

(b) cause the notices of the creditors' meeting to be sent by post to the creditors not less than 7 days before the day on which that meeting is to be held; and

(c) cause notice of the creditors' meeting to be advertised once in the Gazette and once at least in two newspapers circulating in the relevant locality (that is to say the locality in which the company's principal place of business in Great Britain was situated during the relevant period).

98(2) [Contents of notice of meeting] The notice of the creditors' meeting shall state either–

(a) the name and address of a person qualified to act as an insolvency practitioner in relation to the company who, during the period before the day on which that meeting is to be held, will furnish creditors free of charge with such information concerning the company's affairs as they may reasonably require; or

(b) a place in the relevant locality where, on the two business days falling next before the day on which that meeting is to be held, a list of the names and addresses of the company's creditors will be available for inspection free of charge.

98(3) [Where principal place of business in different places, etc.] Where the company's principal place of business in Great Britain was situated in different localities at different times during the relevant period, the duties imposed by subsections (1)(c) and (2)(b) above apply separately in relation to each of those localities.

98(4) [Where no place of business in Great Britain] Where the company had no place of business in Great Britain during the relevant period, references in subsections (1)(c) and (3) to the company's principal place of business in Great Britain are replaced by references to its registered office.

Section 99   *Insolvency Act 1986*

98(5) **["The relevant period"]** In this section **"the relevant period"** means the period of 6 months immediately preceding the day on which were sent the notices summoning the company meeting at which it was resolved that the company be wound up voluntarily.

98(6) **[Penalty for non-compliance]** If the company without reasonable excuse fails to comply with subsection (1) or (2), it is guilty of an offence and liable to a fine.

GENERAL NOTE

The provisions governing the covening of a creditors' meeting, after the passing by the members of the resolution for voluntary winding up, were extensively redrafted by IA 1985, s. 85, which is consolidated in this and the next section. Under the former law, the creditors' meeting was required to be held on the same day as the members' meeting or the day after, and this meant that it had to be summoned before the shareholders' meeting had been held, with little time to prepare information which would put the creditors properly in the picture. Furthermore, by the device known as "centrebinding" (see the note to s. 166), the directors were sometimes able to contrive to dispose of the company's assets, or a substantial part of them, before the creditors had a chance to consider their position at all. The present law is designed to ensure that the decisive say in a creditors' voluntary winding up really does lie with the creditors' meeting, that they have proper information on which to base their decisions, and that no action which could be adverse to their interests can be taken before their meeting is held, except to a restricted extent through the agency of a qualified insolvency practitioner (see s. 166(3), and also s. 114(3)).

For the rules relating to this section, see IR 1986, rr. 4.49, 4.53ff., 4.62.

S. 98(1)

The 14-day period replaces the former requirement that the creditors' meeting be held on the same day as the company meeting or the next day. This longer interval enables the directors to prepare properly the information which must be laid before the creditors' meeting under s. 99. The directors have very restricted powers to act in relation to the company's property during the period between the two meetings (see s. 114) and so it will normally be necessary for the members to appoint an insolvency practitioner to act as liquidator on a provisional basis. He will be empowered to act within the limits prescribed by s. 166, and will be able also to make available to creditors the information referred to in s. 98(2)(a).

Where the company has had more than one "principal place of business" in Great Britain during the "relevant period", s. 98(3) will apply; and if it had no place of business in this country, s. 98(4) applies instead. The "relevant period" is defined in s. 98(5).

S. 98(2)

The directors are, in effect, given a choice. They may either hand over the task of furnishing the creditors with such information as they may require to a person qualified to act as an insolvency practitioner (for the meaning of this expression, see ss. 388ff.), or they must arrange for a list of all the company's creditors to be kept available for inspection. It is not necessary that this insolvency practitioner should be the liquidator, if a liquidator has been appointed by the members on a provisional basis under s. 166; but it will obviously be convenient that he should be, and the requirements of this section will be something of an inducement to appoint a liquidator.

S. 98(3)–(5)
See the note to the corresponding s. 95(5)–(7).

S. 98(6)
On penalties, see s. 430 and Sch. 10.

99 Directors to lay statement of affairs before creditors

99(1) **[Duty of directors]** The directors of the company shall–

    (a)   make out a statement in the prescribed form as to the affairs of the company;

    (b)   cause that statement to be laid before the creditors' meeting under section 98; and

    (c)   appoint one of their number to preside at that meeting;

and it is the duty of the director so appointed to attend the meeting and preside over it.

99(2) **[Contents of statement]** The statement as to the affairs of the company shall be verified by affidavit by some or all of the directors and shall show—

(a) particulars of the company's assets, debts and liabilities;

(b) the names and addresses of the company's creditors;

(c) the securities held by them respectively;

(d) the dates when the securities were respectively given; and

(e) such further or other information as may be prescribed.

99(3) **[Penalty for non-compliance]** If—

(a) the directors without reasonable excuse fail to comply with subsection (1) or (2); or

(b) any director without reasonable excuse fails to comply with subsection (1), so far as requiring him to attend and preside at the creditors' meeting,

the directors are or (as the case may be) the director is guilty of an offence and liable to a fine.

GENERAL NOTE

By this provision the Act imposes an obligation on those who have had control of an insolvent company to make full disclosure of its affairs in a creditors' voluntary winding up. The "statement of affairs" is called for in other situations: for detailed discussion, see the note to s. 131.

For the rules and forms prescribed for the purposes of this section, see IR 1986, rr. 4.34ff.

If a liquidator has been nominated by the shareholders at their meeting, he is required by s. 166(4) to attend the creditors' meeting and report to it on any exercise of his powers during the period between the two meetings.

S. 99(1)

If the designated director fails to attend the creditors' meeting, it is open to the creditors to appoint someone else to preside, and a meeting so conducted will be valid: *Re Salcombe Hotel Development Co. Ltd* (1989) 5 B.C.C. 807.

S. 99(3)

On penalties, see s. 430 and Sch. 10.

100 Appointment of liquidator

100(1) **[Nomination of liquidator at meetings]** The creditors and the company at their respective meetings mentioned in section 98 may nominate a person to be liquidator for the purpose of winding up the company's affairs and distributing its assets.

100(2) **[Person who is liquidator]** The liquidator shall be the person nominated by the creditors or, where no person has been so nominated, the person (if any) nominated by the company.

100(3) **[Where different persons nominated]** In the case of different persons being nominated, any director, member or creditor of the company may, within 7 days after the date on which the nomination was made by the creditors, apply to the court for an order either—

(a) directing that the person nominated as liquidator by the company shall be liquidator instead of or jointly with the person nominated by the creditors, or

(b) appointing some other person to be liquidator instead of the person nominated by the creditors.

GENERAL NOTE

Although the section uses the word "nominate" rather than "appoint", the nomination is immediately effective in that nothing more is needed to empower the person so chosen to act. This is confirmed by s. 166, which deals with the exercise by the members' nominee of his powers as liquidator during the interval between the two meetings.

The person nominated must be qualified to act in relation to the company as an insolvency practitioner: see ss. 388, 389. A liquidator appointed under this section is not an officer of the court: *Re T H Knitwear (Wholesale) Ltd* [1988] Ch. 275; (1988) 4 B.C.C. 102.

For the relevant rules, see IR 1986, rr. 4.101ff.; and in regard to the liquidator's remuneration, rr. 4.127ff.

Note prospective insertion of new s. 100(4) by EA 2002, s. 248 and Sch. 17, para. 14. The holder of a "qualifying" floating charge (for definition, see Sch. B1, para. 14(2)–(3)) is to be given the power to select the liquidator unless the court thinks the circumstances exceptional.

101 Appointment of liquidation committee

101(1) [**Creditors may appoint committee**] The creditors at the meeting to be held under section 98 or at any subsequent meeting may, if they think fit, appoint a committee (" the liquidation committee") of not more than 5 persons to exercise the functions conferred on it by or under this Act.

101(2) [**Members appointed by company**] If such a committee is appointed, the company may, either at the meeting at which the resolution for voluntary winding up is passed or at any time subsequently in general meeting, appoint such number of persons as they think fit to act as members of the committee, not exceeding 5.

101(3) [**Creditors may object to members appointed by company**] However, the creditors may, if they think fit, resolve that all or any of the persons so appointed by the company ought not to be members of the liquidation committee; and if the creditors so resolve–

(a) the persons mentioned in the resolution are not then, unless the court otherwise directs, qualified to act as members of the committee; and

(b) on any application to the court under this provision the court may, if it thinks fit, appoint other persons to act as such members in place of the persons mentioned in the resolution.

101(4) [**Scotland**] In Scotland, the liquidation committee has, in addition to the powers and duties conferred and imposed on it by this Act, such of the powers and duties of commissioners on a bankrupt estate as may be conferred and imposed on liquidation committees by the rules.

GENERAL NOTE

The designation of the committee as the "liquidation committee" is a novelty introduced by the draftsman of the consolidating legislation. Under CA 1948, such a committee was given the traditional name, "committee of inspection"; the new name is to reflect the fact that "inspection" of the company's affairs is no longer the primary function of such a committee.

Provision is made for comparable committees by s. 26 (administration), ss. 49, 68 (administrative receivership) and ss. 141, 142 (winding up by the court).

S. 101(1)
In addition to the functions conferred on the liquidation committee by the Act itself (see, *e.g.* s. 103), further provisions about its functions, membership and proceedings are contained in the rules: see IR 1986, rr. 4.151ff.

102 Creditors' meeting where winding up converted under s. 96

102 Where, in the case of a winding up which was, under section 96 in Chapter III, converted to a creditors' voluntary winding up, a creditors' meeting is held in accordance with section 95, any appointment made or committee established by that meeting is deemed to have been made or established by a meeting held in accordance with section 98 in this Chapter.

GENERAL NOTE

This section applies when the company in a members' voluntary winding up proves to be insolvent and the liquidation has been converted into a creditors' voluntary winding up under ss. 95, 96. Its purpose is to remove any doubts that might otherwise arise about the standing and functions of a liquidator appointed or a liquidation committee established in such a case.

103 Cesser of directors' powers

103 On the appointment of a liquidator, all the powers of the directors cease, except so far as the liquidation committee (or, if there is no such committee, the creditors) sanction their continuance.

GENERAL NOTE

The appointment of a liquidator does not operate of itself to remove the directors from office: see the note to s. 91(2).

104 Vacancy in office of liquidator

104 If a vacancy occurs, by death, resignation or otherwise, in the office of a liquidator (other than a liquidator appointed by, or by the direction of, the court), the creditors may fill the vacancy.

GENERAL NOTE

Where the appointment of the previous liquidator was made by or under a court order (see s. 100(3)), it appears that a further application to the court is required to fill the vacancy.

105 Meetings of company and creditors at each year's end

105(1) [Liquidator to summon meetings] If the winding up continues for more than one year, the liquidator shall summon a general meeting of the company and a meeting of the creditors at the end of the first year from the commencement of the winding up, and of each succeeding year, or at the first convenient date within 3 months from the end of the year or such longer period as the Secretary of State may allow.

105(2) [Liquidator to lay account] The liquidator shall lay before each of the meetings an account of his acts and dealings and of the conduct of the winding up during the preceding year.

105(3) [Penalty for non-compliance] If the liquidator fails to comply with this section, he is liable to a fine.

105(4) [Qualification to requirement] Where under section 96 a members' voluntary winding up has become a creditors' voluntary winding up, and the creditors' meeting under section 95 is held 3 months or less before the end of the first year from the commencement of the winding up, the liquidator is not required by this section to summon a meeting of creditors at the end of that year.

S. 105(1)
The corresponding provision in the case of a members' voluntary winding up is s. 93; under that section, however, the liquidator is required to report only to the members.

S. 105(3)
On penalties, see s. 430 and Sch. 10.

S. 105(4)
This subsection is linked with the procedure prescribed by ss. 95, 96 for the situation when a company in a members' voluntary winding up proves to be insolvent. In that case, a creditors' meeting will have been held quite recently, under s. 95(2), and there would be little point in summoning a second one so soon afterwards. A general meeting of the company under s. 105(1) must, however, still be convened.

106 Final meeting prior to dissolution

106(1) [Account of winding up, meetings] As soon as the company's affairs are fully wound up, the liquidator shall make up an account of the winding up, showing how it has been conducted and the company's property has been disposed of, and thereupon shall call a general meeting of the company and a meeting of the creditors for the purpose of laying the account before the meetings and giving an explanation of it.

Section 107 Insolvency Act 1986

106(2) [**Advertisement in Gazette**] Each such meeting shall be called by advertisement in the Gazette specifying the time, place and object of the meeting, and published at least one month before it.

106(3) [**Copy of account, return to registrar**] Within one week after the date of the meetings (or, if they are not held on the same date, after the date of the later one) the liquidator shall send to the registrar of companies a copy of the account, and shall make a return to him of the holding of the meetings and of their dates.

106(4) [**Penalty on default re s. 106(3)**] If the copy is not sent or the return is not made in accordance with subsection (3), the liquidator is liable to a fine and, for continued contravention, to a daily default fine.

106(5) [**If quorum not present at either meeting**] However, if a quorum is not present at either such meeting, the liquidator shall, in lieu of the return required by subsection (3), make a return that the meeting was duly summoned and that no quorum was present; and upon such return being made the provisions of that subsection as to the making of the return are, in respect of that meeting, deemed complied with.

106(6) [**Penalty if no meetings called**] If the liquidator fails to call a general meeting of the company or a meeting of the creditors as required by this section, he is liable to a fine.

GENERAL NOTE

This section corresponds with s. 94, which deals with a members' voluntary winding up; but in that case no meeting of the creditors is required.

The affairs of a company may be "fully wound up" even though the company continues to hold property, if the liquidator has done all that he can do to wind up the company: *Re Wilmott Trading Ltd* [2000] B.C.C. 321. The property in that case was a waste management licence. Neuberger J. held that on the subsequent dissolution of the company the licence would cease to exist.

See generally the notes to s. 94.

For the relevant rules, see IR 1986, r. 4.126.

On penalties, see s. 430 and Sch. 10.

CHAPTER V

PROVISIONS APPLYING TO BOTH KINDS OF VOLUNTARY WINDING UP

107 Distribution of company's property

107 Subject to the provisions of this Act as to preferential payments, the company's property in a voluntary winding up shall on the winding up be applied in satisfaction of the company's liabilities pari passu and, subject to that application, shall (unless the articles otherwise provide) be distributed among the members according to their rights and interests in the company.

GENERAL NOTE

This section refers to "preferential payments", and not merely to "preferential debts", and thus includes, *e.g.* the expenses of the winding up (including the liquidator's remuneration) which are given priority by s. 115, as well as the preferential debts defined by ss. 386, 387.

The company's "property" or "assets" which it is the liquidator's duty to get in and apply under this section is property which is beneficially owned by the company (although where the company holds property on trust, it may also be the duty of the liquidator to see to the due administration of the trust). Property which the company does not own beneficially does not form part of the insolvent estate (and similarly is not caught by a floating charge in a receivership). In a number of cases (of which the best known are perhaps *Barclays Bank Ltd v Quistclose Investments Ltd* [1970] A.C. 567, *Re Kayford Ltd* [1975] 1 W.L.R. 279, *Chase Manhattan Bank NA v Israel–British Bank (London) Ltd* [1979] 3 All E.R. 1025 and *Carreras Rothmans Ltd v Freeman Matthews Treasure Ltd* [1985] 1 All E.R. 155), sums which might have been thought to be recoverable from the company as a debt or in other common-law proceedings have been held to be subject to a trust in the company's hands, with the consequence that the party beneficially entitled could claim the sum in full rather than be obliged to prove as a creditor. Recent cases applying these precedents include *Re Japan Leasing (Europe) plc* [1999] B.P.I.R. 911, *Re Niagara Mechanical Services International Ltd* [2001] B.C.C. 393 and *Twinsectra Ltd v Yardley* [2002] UKHL 12; [2002] 2 A.C. 164.

The order of application of the assets in the hands of the liquidator will therefore be:

(1)   the expenses of the winding up, including the liquidator's remuneration (s. 115);

(2)   the preferential debts, as defined by ss. 386, 387 and Sch. 6 (s. 175);

(3)   any preferential charge on goods distrained that arises under s. 176(3);

(4)   the company's general creditors;

(5)   any debts or other sums due from the company to its members qua members (s. 74(2)(f));

(6)   the members generally, in accordance with their respective rights and interests (s. 107).

Secured creditors will, in principle, be entitled to be paid out of the proceeds of their security (so far as it extends) ahead of all other claims. However, where the security is by way of floating charge, the debts which are preferential debts in the liquidation must be paid first (s. 175(2)(b)). The ruling in *Re Barleycorn Enterprises Ltd* [1970] Ch. 465 (which was followed in a number of cases including *Re Portbase Clothing Ltd, Mond v Taylor* [1993] Ch. 388, [1993] B.C.C. 96) that for the purposes of s. 107, "the company's property" includes assets covered by a floating charge, has been overruled by the House of Lords in *Re Leyland Daf Ltd, Buchler v Talbot* [2004] UKHL 9; B.C.C. 214. It follows that the liquidator is not entitled to claim his expenses in priority to the rights of the holder of a floating charge (except the costs of preserving and realising the assets covered by the charge, in so far as he has incurred them). It is immaterial whether or not the charge crystallised before the commencement of the liquidation.

The statutory order for the application of assets may not be varied by contractual arrangements between the parties concerned, such as a pooling or clearing-house arrangement: *British Eagle International Air Lines Ltd v Cie Nationale Air France* [1975] 1 W.L.R. 758. However there is a statutory exception for such arrangements in the financial markets and payment and securities settlement systems: see CA 1989, s. 159 and the Finality Regulations: see the notes on pp. 2, 3.

The rule in the *British Eagle* case is part of a wider principle, which declares it to be against public policy to displace the insolvency laws by any provision in a contract or other transaction inter partes, *e.g.* by a term that in the event of one party's bankruptcy a specified asset should become the property of the other (*Ex parte Mackay* (1873) L.R. 8 Ch. App. 643). But in *Money Markets International Stockbrokers Ltd v London Stock Exchange Ltd* [2001] 2 B.C.L.C. 347 it was held that this principle was not infringed where the rules of a mutual company provided that a member's share should be transferred to a trustee without consideration on his ceasing to be a member, and the member's insolvency was an event leading to the termination of his membership. The share in these circumstances was not a free-standing asset but merely something incidental to his membership rights.

Moreover, it should be noted that both CA 1989, Pt VII and the Finality Regulations remove various arrangements and transactions altogether from the scope of the insolvency legislation, and specifically disapply particular provisions of the latter legislation in relation to market transactions or payment or settlement systems which come within their ambit. (See also the general reversal of the *British Eagle* principle in the Finality Regulations, reg. 14.) The impact of these provisions is noted at the relevant places in this *Guide*.

Property subject to a restraint order or other order under POCA 2002 is also excluded from the assets available for distribution by the liquidator: see s. 426 of that Act. But once the company is in liquidation, the powers under the 2002 Act may not be exercised in relation to property which belonged to the company at the time when it went into liquidation (see s. 426(4)–(6), (9)).

A creditor or contributory has no legal or equitable interest in the property of the company held by the liquidator, but only a right to have the assets duly administered by him: *Banque Nationelle de Paris plc v Montman Ltd* [2000] 1 B.C.L.C. 576.

Section 108   Insolvency Act 1986

Provision is made for the proof and payment of debts in a members' voluntary winding up by IR 1986, r. 4.182A, and in a creditors' voluntary winding up by rr. 4.73ff., 4.180.

For the application of assets in a winding up by the court, see s. 148 and IR 1986, r. 4.181.

108 Appointment or removal of liquidator by the court

108(1) [**If no liquidator acting**] If from any cause whatever there is no liquidator acting, the court may appoint a liquidator.

108(2) [**Removal, replacement**] The court may, on cause shown, remove a liquidator and appoint another.

GENERAL NOTE

The power of the court supplements the power of the members under s. 92 (members' voluntary winding up) and that of the creditors under s. 104 (creditors' voluntary winding up) to fill any such vacancy themselves. A liquidator once appointed, however, may be removed only by the court "on cause shown" under s. 108(2). The case of *Re Keypak Homecare Ltd* (1987) 3 B.C.C. 558 contains a useful review of the principles upon which the court will act in exercising its power to remove a liquidator under s. 108(2). In *Re Bridgend Goldsmiths Ltd* [1995] B.C.C. 226 the court exercised its powers under s. 108(1) to appoint a new liquidator when the previous liquidator had ceased to be qualified to act as an insolvency practitioner. An application to remove liquidators was refused in *AMP Music Box Enterprises Ltd v Hoffman* [2002] B.C.C. 996, where their conduct had, in the past, been open to the criticism that they had not pursued certain claims very actively but the court considered that they had more recently given the matter more attention.

In *Re Sankey Furniture Ltd Ex p. Harding* [1995] 2 B.C.L.C. 594 the court declined to use its power under s. 108(2) to remove a liquidator (who wished to resign) where this would by-pass the statutory requirement that a meeting of creditors be called to consider whether or not to accept the resignation: the fact that this would save the expense of a meeting was not sufficient to justify the court intervening in a matter which was for the creditors to decide. However, in a number of cases where an insolvency practitioner has sought to resign from multiple offices and be replaced (usually by other members of the same firm), the court has been willing to make orders without the statutory formalities: see the note to s. 172(1), (2).

An application may be made under s. 108 by anyone whom the court considers proper, *e.g.* a former liquidator who has ceased to be qualified to act in relation to the company (*Re A J Adams (Builders) Ltd* [1991] B.C.C. 62) or the recognised professional body of which such a person was once a member. (*Re Stella Metals Ltd (in liq.)* [1997] B.C.C. 626.) But the court will not remove the liquidator of an insolvent company on the application of a contributory: *Deloitte & Touche AG v Johnson* [1999] B.C.C. 992.

Save in very exceptional cases, notice of the application should be given to the liquidator whom it is sought to remove, in order to give him an opportunity to be heard: *Clemens v Udal* [2001] B.C.C. 658.

For the relevant rules, see IR 1986, rr. 4.103, 4.140.

109 Notice by liquidator of his appointment

109(1) [**Notice in Gazette and to registrar**] The liquidator shall, within 14 days after his appointment, publish in the Gazette and deliver to the registrar of companies for registration a notice of his appointment in the form prescribed by statutory instrument made by the Secretary of State.

109(2) [**Penalty on default**] If the liquidator fails to comply with this section, he is liable to a fine and, for continued contravention, to a daily default fine.

S. 109(1)

The duty of the liquidator to give notice of his appointment under this section is additional to his duty to notify creditors under IR 1986, rr. 4.103, 4.139 and 4.140 and also to the obligation imposed by s. 85 on the company and its officers (including the liquidator) to notify the passing of the resolution for voluntary winding up by advertisement in the *Gazette*. Further advertising and registration requirements are imposed by r. 4.106.

The gazetting of the liquidator's appointment under this section constitutes an "official notification" of the event for the purposes of CA 1985, s. 42(1)(a): see CA 1985, s. 711(2)(b). If there has not been an official notification, or (in some circumstances) if the official notification is less than 15 days old, s. 42 provides that the company "is not entitled to rely against other persons on the happening" of the appointment of the liquidator. This provision has its origin in the EC First Company Law Directive; its meaning and effect (so far as English law is concerned) is obscure. What matters under the Act is the fact that the company has gone into liquidation: nothing turns on the appointment of the liquidator, as such.

The relevant forms are Forms 600 and 600a set out in Sch. 2, Pt II to the Companies (Forms) (Amendment) Regulations 1987 (SI 1987/752).

S. 109(2)
On penalties, see s. 430 and Sch. 10.

110 Acceptance of shares, etc., as consideration for sale of company property

110(1) **[Application]** This section applies, in the case of a company proposed to be, or being, wound up voluntarily, where the whole or part of the company's business or property is proposed to be transferred or sold–

(a) to another company ("the transferee company"), whether or not the latter is a company within the meaning of the Companies Act, or

(b) to a limited liability partnership (the "transferee limited liability partnership").

110(2) **[Shares etc. in compensation for transfer]** With the requisite sanction, the liquidator of the company being, or proposed to be, wound up ("the transferor company") may receive, in compensation or part compensation for the transfer or sale–

(a) in the case of the transferee company, shares, policies or other like interests in the transferee company for distribution among the members of the transferor company, or

(b) in the case of the transferee limited liability partnership, membership in the transferee limited liability partnership for distribution among the members of the transferor company.

110(3) **[Sanction for s. 110(2)]** The sanction requisite under subsection (2) is–

(a) in the case of a members' voluntary winding up, that of a special resolution of the company, conferring either a general authority on the liquidator or an authority in respect of any particular arrangement, and

(b) in the case of a creditors' voluntary winding up, that of either the court or the liquidation committee.

110(4) **[Alternative to s. 110(2)]** Alternatively to subsection (2), the liquidator may (with that sanction) enter into any other arrangement whereby the members of the transferor company may–

(a) in the case of the transferee company, in lieu of receiving cash, shares, policies or other like interests (or in addition thereto) participate in the profits of, or receive any other benefit from, the transferee company, or

(b) in the case of the transferee limited liability partnership, in lieu of receiving cash or membership (or in addition thereto), participate in some other way in the profits of, or receive any other benefit from, the transferee limited liability partnership.

110(5) **[Sale binding on transferors]** A sale or arrangement in pursuance of this section is binding on members of the transferor company.

110(6) **[Special resolution]** A special resolution is not invalid for purposes of this section by reason that it is passed before or concurrently with a resolution for voluntary winding up or for appointing liquidators;

Section 111 *Insolvency Act 1986*

but, if an order is made within a year for winding up the company by the court, the special resolution is not valid unless sanctioned by the court.

GENERAL NOTE

This section deals with a corporate "reconstruction", under which the whole or part of the business of a company in liquidation is sold by the liquidator to another company or limited liability partnership and the members of the first company agree to accept shares or other securities in the purchasing company instead of the cash distribution to which they would normally be entitled. Provided that the sanction referred to in s. 110(3) is obtained, the scheme is binding on all the members except those who dissent in writing under s. 111(1).

Subsections (1), (2) and (4) were amended by the Limited Liability Partnerships Regulations 2001 (SI 2001/1090, effective April 6, 2001) to make possible the use of a limited liability partnership as the transferee.

S. 110(1)
For the definition of "company" referred to, see CA 1985, s. 735, and the note to s. 73 above. The "transferee company" may be a company outside this definition – *e.g.* a company incorporated overseas.

S. 110(2), (4)
The consideration which the members agree to accept normally consists of or includes shares in the transferee company, or corresponding interests in an LLP, but it may take other forms.

S. 110(3)
The consolidation has introduced an ambiguity into the section by running together two provisions which were formerly stated separately in CA 1985, s. 582(2) and s. 593. As it stands, para. (b) of the new subsection appears to read as an *alternative* to para. (a), but it should be an *additional* requirement; *i.e.* in a members' voluntary winding up, only the sanction in para. (a) is needed, but in a creditors' winding up, *both* para. (a) and para. (b) apply. If this were not so, the members could be obliged to accept shares without their consent, and s. 111 would not apply at all!

S. 110(5)
This should be read subject to the right of a member to dissent under s. 111. In fact, although the arrangement may be "binding" under this provision, in the sense that a dissenting member cannot prevent the deal from going ahead, nothing can oblige him to become a member of the transferee company without his consent. It is necessary in practice therefore for a scheme of reconstruction to make express provision for recalcitrant but inactive shareholders, *e.g.* by creating a trust to hold the new shares on their behalf.

S. 110(6)
The sanction of the court is not required before the liquidator puts a scheme of reconstruction into effect.

111 Dissent from arrangement under s. 110

111(1) [Application] This section applies in the case of a voluntary winding up where, for the purposes of section 110(2) or (4), there has been passed a special resolution of the transferor company providing the sanction requisite for the liquidator under that section.

111(2) [Objections by members of transferor company] If a member of the transferor company who did not vote in favour of the special resolution expresses his dissent from it in writing, addressed to the liquidator and left at the company's registered office within 7 days after the passing of the resolution, he may require the liquidator either to abstain from carrying the resolution into effect or to purchase his interest at a price to be determined by agreement or by arbitration under this section.

111(3) [Where liquidator purchases member's interest] If the liquidator elects to purchase the member's interest, the purchase money must be paid before the company is dissolved and be raised by the liquidator in such manner as may be determined by special resolution.

111(4) [Arbitration] For purposes of an arbitration under this section, the provisions of the Companies Clauses Consolidation Act 1845 or, in the case of a winding up in Scotland, the Companies Clauses

Consolidation (Scotland) Act 1845 with respect to the settlement of disputes by arbitration are incorporated with this Act, and–

(a) in the construction of those provisions this Act is deemed the special Act and **"the company"** means the transferor company, and

(b) any appointment by the incorporated provisions directed to be made under the hand of the secretary or any two of the directors may be made in writing by the liquidator (or, if there is more than one liquidator, then any two or more of them).

GENERAL NOTE

This section confers on a dissenting member the right to have his shareholding in the company bought out in cash, provided that he takes the prompt action prescribed by s. 111(2).

112 Reference of questions to court

112(1) [Application to court] The liquidator or any contributory or creditor may apply to the court to determine any question arising in the winding up of a company, or to exercise, as respects the enforcing of calls or any other matter, all or any of the powers which the court might exercise if the company were being wound up by the court.

112(2) [Court order] The court, if satisfied that the determination of the question or the required exercise of power will be just and beneficial, may accede wholly or partially to the application on such terms and conditions as it thinks fit, or may make such other order on the application as it thinks just.

112(3) [Copy of order to registrar] A copy of an order made by virtue of this section staying the proceedings in the winding up shall forthwith be forwarded by the company, or otherwise as may be prescribed, to the registrar of companies, who shall enter it in his records relating to the company.

S. 112(1), (2)
The powers of the court in a winding up by the court are contained in Ch. VI of the Act, and more specifically in ss. 147ff.

Where a company is an "authorised person" under FSMA 2000, the Financial Services Authority may apply to the court or participate in the proceedings: FSMA 2000, s. 365.

S. 112(2)
The court's powers are discretionary. It may refuse to permit proceedings under this provision where some other procedure is more appropriate: *Re Stetzel Thomson & Co. Ltd* (1988) 4 B.C.C. 74, or when the applicant would not have standing to invoke some other, more appropriate, procedure: *Re James McHale Automobiles Ltd* [1997] B.C.C. 202. It is not a complete bar to the exercise of discretion that the applicant is using the procedure to obtain a collateral advantage: *Re Movitex Ltd* [1992] B.C.C. 101.

S. 112(3)
No rules appear to have been prescribed for the purposes of this section.

113 Court's power to control proceedings (Scotland)

113 If the court, on the application of the liquidator in the winding up of a company registered in Scotland, so directs, no action or proceeding shall be proceeded with or commenced against the company except by leave of the court and subject to such terms as the court may impose.

114 No liquidator appointed or nominated by company

114(1) [Application] This section applies where, in the case of a voluntary winding up, no liquidator has been appointed or nominated by the company.

114(2) [Limit on exercise of directors' powers] The powers of the directors shall not be exercised, except with the sanction of the court or (in the case of a creditors' voluntary winding up) so far as may be necessary to secure compliance with sections 98 (creditors' meeting) and 99 (statement of affairs), during the period before the appointment or nomination of a liquidator of the company.

114(3) **[Non-application of s. 114(2)]** Subsection (2) does not apply in relation to the powers of the directors–

(a) to dispose of perishable goods and other goods the value of which is likely to diminish if they are not immediately disposed of, and

(b) to do all such other things as may be necessary for the protection of the company's assets.

114(4) **[Penalty for non-compliance]** If the directors of the company without reasonable excuse fail to comply with this section, they are liable to a fine.

General Note

This section is designed as a counter to the practice of "centrebinding" which was condemned as unsatisfactory by the Cork Committee (*Report*, paras 666ff.), and should be read in conjunction with the notes to s. 166 below. The Committee drew attention to the fact that there was in every voluntary liquidation a period of time during which the directors remained in control of the company but, until the necessary meetings had been convened and a liquidator appointed, the company's assets and the interests of creditors were most inadequately protected. This period could be extended if the appointment of the liquidator was not made at the same time as the passing of the resolution for winding up but deferred until a later occasion. The Committee's recommendation was that a voluntary liquidation should commence as soon as the *directors* had decided that, because of its liabilities, the company could not carry on business, and that they should be obliged immediately to appoint a provisional liquidator who would assume effective control and safeguard the position until the appropriate meeting had made a permanent appointment.

The legislature did not accept this recommendation of the Committee, and so it remains the law that a voluntary winding up commences when the company's special resolution is passed. This section does, however, in part curb the abuse to which the report drew attention, by providing that the directors should have only very limited powers, restricted to the preservation of the company's assets, until a liquidator has been appointed. The weakness of the section is, however, that it operates only *after* the voluntary winding up has commenced: the directors will still be in full control during the period which must elapse while the meeting of the company is being convened.

S. 114(1), (2)
In a members' voluntary winding up, the liquidator is appointed by the company in general meeting under s. 91. These new provisions should ensure that an appointment is made promptly, whereupon the powers of the directors will normally cease (see s. 91(2)). Section 114(2) should also encourage the members to nominate a liquidator promptly in the case of a creditors' voluntary winding up. In this event, it may be inferred from the wording of s. 166 that, once the company has nominated a liquidator, he automatically takes office and is vested with the powers and duties set out in that section.

S. 114(3)
The very limited powers which the directors retain are confined to the disposal of perishable goods and the protection of assets. They will not extend to continuing to manage the business in any general sense. (Note that para. (a) is confined in its scope to *goods*. Other property which may be likely to diminish in value (*e.g.* shares in a bear market) is not covered by this paragraph, although some actions of the directors in relation to such property may be justified under para. (b).)

S. 114(4)
A contract entered into in breach of s. 114 would, at least prima facie, be illegal and void. However it is possible that a third party who has dealt with the directors in good faith and without knowledge of the resolution could enforce the transaction on the basis of the directors' ostensible authority: *Re a Company (No. 006341 of 1992), ex parte B Ltd* [1994] 1 B.C.L.C. 225.

On penalties, see s. 430 and Sch. 10.

115 Expenses of voluntary winding up

115 All expenses properly incurred in the winding up, including the remuneration of the liquidator, are payable out of the company's assets in priority to all other claims.

GENERAL NOTE

The expenses of the winding up rank ahead of the claims of the preferential creditors who are given priority by ss. 175, 176.

In the case of a creditors' voluntary winding up (including one which has commenced as a members' winding up but later proves to be insolvent), the order of priority as between the different categories of expenses is set out in IR 1986, r. 4.218, but the court has power to vary these general rules by virtue of ss. 112(1) and 156 and r. 4.220.

The ruling in *Re Barleycorn Enterprises Ltd* [1970] Ch. 465 (which was followed in a number of cases including *Re Portbase Clothing Ltd, Mond v Taylor* [1993] Ch. 388, [1993] B.C.C. 96) that for the purposes of s. 115, the company's "assets" include assets covered by a floating charge, has been overruled by the House of Lords in *Re Leyland Daf Ltd, Buchler v Talbot* [2004] UKHL 9; [2004] B.C.C. 214: see the note to s. 107, above.

This section does not declare that all expenses properly incurred by a liquidator are payable out of the company's assets, but only that expenses which *are* so payable should have priority to other claims.

In a number of cases, *e.g. Re MC Bacon Ltd (No.2)* [1991] Ch. 127, [1990] B.C.C. 430; *Re RS & M Engineering Co. Ltd, Mond v Hammond Suddards (a firm)* [2000] Ch. 40, [2000] B.C.C. 445 and *Re Floor Fourteen Ltd, Lewis v Inland Revenue Commr* [2001] 3 All E.R. 449, [2002] B.C.C. 198, it was held that a liquidator's costs in pursuing claims under ss. 238 (transaction at an undervalue), 239 (preference), or 214 (wrongful trading), however properly the litigation may have been brought, were not payable out of the company's assets. However, the effect of these rulings has been reversed by an amendment made to IR 1986, r. 4.218 by the Insolvency (Amendment) (No. 2) Rules 2002 (SI 2002/2712, effective January 1, 2003, subject to transitional provisions contained in r. 4(2)). Rule 4.218 now specifies as expenses of the liquidation expenses or costs which are properly chargeable or incurred by the official receiver or liquidator "relating to the conduct of any legal proceedings which he has power to bring or defend whether in his own name or the name of the company". This puts beyond doubt any contention that such expenses do not fall within s. 115.

Pre-liquidation expenses, other than those specifically incurred for the purpose of enabling the company to pass the winding-up resolution and take other steps required by statute, cannot ordinarily be claimed under this section: *Re A V Sorge & Co. Ltd* (1986) 2 B.C.C. 99,306; *Re Sandwell Copiers Ltd* (1988) 4 B.C.C. 227; *Re W F Fearman Ltd (No. 2)* (1988) 4 B.C.C. 141.

Corporation tax on post-liquidation profits is payable in priority as a liquidation expense, even if the income in question has not been, and never will be, received: *Kahn v Commrs of Inland Revenue, Re Toshoku Finance (UK) plc* [2002] UKHL 6; [2002] 1 W.L.R. 671; [2002] B.C.C. 110. In the same case it was also held that rates and similar local taxes will also come within the definition of liquidation expenses (at paras 34, 40–41, overruling *Re Kentish Homes Ltd* [1993] B.C.C. 212).

In *Re Berkeley Applegate (Investment Consultants) Ltd (No. 2)* (1988) 4 B.C.C. 279, a liquidator had done substantial work in relation to assets in which, after investigation, the company proved to have no beneficial interest. It was held, in the circumstances, that he was entitled to be paid his proper expenses and remuneration as a charge on those assets, even though they were not "the company's assets" within s. 115. (See further *Re Berkeley Applegate (Investment Consultants) Ltd (No. 3)* (1989) 5 B.C.C. 803, and compare *Re Eastern Capital Futures Ltd* (1989) 5 B.C.C. 223.)

In relation to the financial markets and securities settlement systems, s. 175 has effect subject to the priority accorded to the claim of a participant or central bank to collateral security by the Finality Regulations, reg. 14(5), (6), unless the terms on which the collateral security was provided expressly state that the expenses, remuneration or preferential debts are to have priority: see the note on p. 3.

On the general rules regarding the distribution of assets in a voluntary winding up, see the note to s. 107.

116 Saving for certain rights

116 The voluntary winding up of a company does not bar the right of any creditor or contributory to have it wound up by the court; but in the case of an application by a contributory the court must be satisfied that the rights of the contributories will be prejudiced by a voluntary winding up.

GENERAL NOTE

The court has, in any case, a discretion under s. 125 to refuse a winding-up order, even where the application is made by a creditor. The wishes of a majority of the company's creditors will be taken into account, but will not be regarded as decisive: see *Re Home Remedies Ltd* [1943] Ch. 1; *Re Southard & Co. Ltd* [1979] 1 W.L.R. 1198; *Re Medisco Equipment Ltd* (1983) 1 B.C.C. 98,944.

CHAPTER VI

WINDING UP BY THE COURT

Jurisdiction (England and Wales)

117 High Court and county court jurisdiction

117(1) **[High Court]** The High Court has jurisdiction to wind up any company registered in England and Wales.

117(2) **[County court]** Where the amount of a company's share capital paid up or credited as paid up does not exceed £120,000, then (subject to this section) the county court of the district in which the company's registered office is situated has concurrent jurisdiction with the High Court to wind up the company.

117(3) **[Increase, reduction of s. 117(2) sum]** The money sum for the time being specified in subsection (2) is subject to increase or reduction by order under section 416 in Part XV.

117(4) **[Exclusion of jurisdiction for county court]** The Lord Chancellor may by order in a statutory instrument exclude a county court from having winding-up jurisdiction, and for the purposes of that jurisdiction may attach its district, or any part thereof, to any other county court, and may by statutory instrument revoke or vary any such order.

In exercising the powers of this section, the Lord Chancellor shall provide that a county court is not to have winding-up jurisdiction unless it has for the time being jurisdiction for the purposes of Parts VIII to XI of this Act (individual insolvency).

117(5) **[Extent of winding-up jurisdiction]** Every court in England and Wales having winding-up jurisdiction has for the purposes of that jurisdiction all the powers of the High Court; and every prescribed officer of the court shall perform any duties which an officer of the High Court may discharge by order of a judge of that court or otherwise in relation to winding up.

117(6) **["Registered office"]** For the purposes of this section, a company's **"registered office"** is the place which has longest been its registered office during the 6 months immediately preceding the presentation of the petition for winding up.

117(7) **[Applicability of EC Regulation]** This section is subject to Article 3 of the EC Regulation (jurisdiction under EC Regulation).

GENERAL NOTE

For the corresponding provisions relating to Scotland, see ss. 120, 121.

In CA 1985 and in the present Act, the word "court", when used in relation to a company, means the court having jurisdiction to wind up the company: see CA 1985, s. 744 and IA 1986, s. 251. This will be the appropriate court as defined by this section. The relevant date for determining the question of jurisdiction is that when the proceedings in question are commenced (which in some contexts may be a date later than that on which the company in fact went into liquidation): *Re Lichfield Freight Terminal Ltd* [1997] B.C.C. 11.

Where a matter is already the subject of proceedings in a county court, application should be made to that court and not to the High Court. The latter may, however, allow such an application to continue under IR 1986, r. 7.12: *Re Sankey Furniture Ltd Ex p.Harding* [1995] 2 B.C.L.C. 594.

Winding-up proceedings are a form of "suit and legal process", but are not a method of "enforcing a judgment or arbitration award": *Re International Tin Council* [1989] Ch. 309; (1988) 4 B.C.C. 653 (CA), affirming [1987] Ch. 419; (1987) 3 B.C.C. 103.

S. 117(7)
Article 3 of the EC Regulation, which is supplemented by the Insolvency Act 1986 (Amendment) (No. 2) Regulations 2002 (SI 2002/1240, effective May 31, 2002), empowers the courts of a Member State to open insolvency proceedings only if the centre of the debtor's main interests is situated within its territory (in the case of "main" proceedings) or – subject to certain limitations – if it possesses an establishment within that territory (in the case of "secondary" or "territorial" proceedings). (See the note to the Regulation, Art. 3.) Although there is a presumption that a company's centre of main interests is the place of its registered office, there will be some exceptional cases where a company incorporated in England and Wales and having its registered office here has its "centre of main interests" in another Member State. In that event, our courts will have no jurisdiction at all to open main proceedings and will be able to open secondary or territorial proceedings only if the company possesses an establishment here. These questions of jurisdiction are discussed more fully in the note to Art. 3 referred to above.

118 Proceedings taken in wrong court

118(1) [**Wrong court**] Nothing in section 117 invalidates a proceeding by reason of its being taken in the wrong court.

118(2) [**Continuation**] The winding up of a company by the court in England and Wales, or any proceedings in the winding up, may be retained in the court in which the proceedings were commenced, although it may not be the court in which they ought to have been commenced.

GENERAL NOTE

It would appear that this provision may be invoked to validate proceedings which have been mistakenly brought in a court which has no insolvency jurisdiction at all: *Re Pleatfine Ltd* (1983) 1 B.C.C. 98,942.

119 Proceedings in county court; case stated for High Court

119(1) [**Special case**] If any question arises in any winding-up proceedings in a county court which all the parties to the proceedings, or which one of them and the judge of the court, desire to have determined in the first instance in the High Court, the judge shall state the facts in the form of a special case for the opinion of the High Court.

119(2) [**Transmission**] Thereupon the special case and the proceedings (or such of them as may be required) shall be transmitted to the High Court for the purposes of the determination.

Jurisdiction (Scotland)

120 Court of Session and sheriff court jurisdiction

120(1) [**Court of Session**] The Court of Session has jurisdiction to wind up any company registered in Scotland.

120(2) [**Vacation judge**] When the Court of Session is in vacation, the jurisdiction conferred on that court by this section may (subject to the provisions of this Part) be exercised by the judge acting as vacation judge.

120(3) [**Concurrent jurisdiction of sheriff court**] Where the amount of a company's share capital paid up or credited as paid up does not exceed £120,000, the sheriff court of the sheriffdom in which the

Section 121   *Insolvency Act 1986*

company's registered office is situated has concurrent jurisdiction with the Court of Session to wind up the company; but–

- (a) the Court of Session may, if it thinks expedient having regard to the amount of the company's assets to do so–
  - (i) remit to a sheriff court any petition presented to the Court of Session for winding up such a company, or
  - (ii) require such a petition presented to a sheriff court to be remitted to the Court of Session; and
- (b) the Court of Session may require any such petition as above-mentioned presented to one sheriff court to be remitted to another sheriff court; and
- (c) in a winding up in the sheriff court the sheriff may submit a stated case for the opinion of the Court of Session on any question of law arising in that winding up.

120(4) **["Registered office"]** For the purposes of this section, the expression **"registered office"** means the place which has longest been the company's registered office during the 6 months immediately preceding the presentation of the petition for winding up.

120(5) **[Increase, reduction of s. 120(3) sum]** The money sum for the time being specified in subsection (3) is subject to increase or reduction by order under section 416 in Part XV.

120(6) **[Applicability of EC Regulation]** This section is subject to Article 3 of the EC Regulation (jurisdiction under EC Regulation).

GENERAL NOTE

This section lays down provisions for Scotland which correspond generally with those made for England and Wales by s. 117. There are, however, no Scottish counterparts to ss. 118 and 119.

The new s. 120(6) is the counterpart for Scotland of s. 117(7): see the note to that subsection.

121 Power to remit winding up to Lord Ordinary

121(1) **[Remission to Lord Ordinary]** The Court of Session may, by Act of Sederunt, make provision for the taking of proceedings in a winding up before one of the Lords Ordinary; and, where provision is so made, the Lord Ordinary has, for the purposes of the winding up, all the powers and jurisdiction of the court.

121(2) **[Report by Lord Ordinary]** However, the Lord Ordinary may report to the Inner House any matter which may arise in the course of a winding up.

Grounds and effect of winding-up petition

122 Circumstances in which company may be wound up by the court

122(1) **[Circumstances]** A company may be wound up by the court if–

- (a) the company has by special resolution resolved that the company be wound up by the court,
- (b) being a public company which was registered as such on its original incorporation, the company has not been issued with a certificate under section 117 of the Companies Act (public company share capital requirements) and more than a year has expired since it was so registered,
- (c) it is an old public company, within the meaning of the Consequential Provisions Act,
- (d) the company does not commence its business within a year from its incorporation or suspends its business for a whole year,
- (e) except in the case of a private company limited by shares or by guarantee, the number of members is reduced below 2,

Insolvency Act 1986 *Section 122*

(f) the company is unable to pay its debts,

(fa) at the time at which a moratorium for the company under section 1A comes to an end, no voluntary arrangement approved under Part I has effect in relation to the company,

(g) the court is of the opinion that it is just and equitable that the company should be wound up.

122(2) **[Scotland]** In Scotland, a company which the Court of Session has jurisdiction to wind up may be wound up by the Court if there is subsisting a floating charge over property comprised in the the company's property and undertaking, and the court is satisfied that the security of the creditor entitled to the benefit of the floating charge is in jeopardy.

For this purpose a creditor's security is deemed to be in jeopardy if the Court is satisfied that events have occurred or are about to occur which render it unreasonable in the creditor's interests that the company should retain power to dispose of the property which is subject to the floating charge.

S. 122(1)
The court has in all cases a discretion whether to make a winding-up order or not. This is implicit in the opening words of the section, and is confirmed by s. 125. Thus, it may decide that another jurisdiction is a more appropriate forum: *Re Harrods (Buenos Aires) Ltd* [1992] Ch. 72; [1991] B.C.C. 249.

Paragraphs (b) and (c) were introduced in conjunction with the redefinition of the public company and the enactment of new statutory rules applicable to such companies by CA 1980. The remaining paragraphs of this subsection are of long standing, except that the minimum number of members for a public company was seven until 1980.

In s. 122(1)(e) the words "except in the case of a private company limited by shares or by guarantee" were inserted by the Companies (Single Member Private Limited Companies) Regulations 1992 (SI 1992/1699), reg. 1 and Sch., para. 8, as from July 15, 1992. These regulations implemented the EC Twelfth Company Law Directive.

Paragraph (f) is elaborated by the presumptions set out in s. 123. If a creditor establishes that a company is unable to pay its debts, he is normally entitled to have a winding-up order made as of course, unless the court considers that there is some special reason why it should not do so. One consideration which would incline the court to refuse an order would be that a majority of the company's creditors were opposed to the making of an order; but if the opposing creditors are not independent outsiders but are associated with the directors their views are likely to be discounted: *Re Lummus Agricultural Services Ltd* [1999] B.C.C. 953.

Paragraph (fa) was inserted by the Insolvency Act 2000, s. 1, Sch.1, paras 1, 6 with effect from January 1, 2003. The addition of this ground will obviate the need to prove insolvency under s. 123. But in most cases the alternative of a creditors' voluntary winding up will be preferred. A petition on this ground may be presented only by one or more creditors: s. 124(3A)).

Paragraph (g) has been the subject of interpretation in a considerable number of cases, among the best known of which are *Re German Date Coffee Company* (1882) 20 Ch.D. 169 (failure of object); *Re T E Brinsmead & Sons* [1897] 1 Ch. 406 (fraud); *Re Yenidje Tobacco Co. Ltd* [1916] 2 Ch. 426 (deadlock); *Loch v John Blackwood Ltd* [1924] A.C. 783 (impropriety), and *Ebrahimi v Westbourne Galleries Ltd* [1973] A.C. 360 (breakdown of confidence). The last-mentioned case established that in the exercise of its jurisdiction on the "just and equitable" ground the court is not restricted by the rights and wrongs of the position as a matter of law but may have regard to wider considerations, such as the expectation of a member of a small "quasi-partnership" company that he will have a say in matters of management. For further illustrations on this point, see *Re Zinotty Properties Ltd* [1984] 1 W.L.R. 1249; (1984) 1 B.C.C. 99,139; *Tay Bok Choon v Tahansan Snd Bhd* [1987] 1 W.L.R. 413; (1987) 3 B.C.C. 132. Failure on the part of the directors to pay reasonable dividends is conduct conceptually capable of supporting a winding-up petition on the "just and equitable" ground, although such a case would be extremely difficult to prove: *Re a Company No. 00370 of 1987* [1988] 1 W.L.R. 1068; (1988) 4 B.C.C. 506.

The jurisdiction under s. 122(1)(g) may not be invoked to protect interests of the petitioner other than his interests as a member: *Re J E Cade & Son Ltd* [1991] B.C.C. 360 (petitioner seeking to assert rights as freeholder of land in occupation of company).

There is in practice a considerable overlap between the jurisdiction to grant a winding-up order under s. 122(1)(g) and that for relief on the ground of unfairly prejudicial conduct under CA 1985, s. 459, and it has been common for a petition to seek orders under each of these provisions in the alternative. In *Practice Direction: Applications under the Companies Act 1985 and the Insurance Companies Act 1982* [1999] B.C.C. 741 at p. 744 (reproduced in Appendix V to this *Guide*), attention is drawn to the undesirability of asking as a matter of course for a winding-up order unless that is the relief which the petitioner would prefer or may be the only relief to which he may be entitled. The Practice Direction

Section 123 *Insolvency Act 1986*

also requires a person presenting a petition under s. 122(1)(g) to state whether he consents to an order under IA 1986, s. 127: see the note to that section.

In *Re Guidezone Ltd* [2001] B.C.C. 692 Jonathan Parker J. stated that the jurisdiction under s. 122(1)(g) was no wider than that under s. 459: in other words, that if conduct was not unfair for the purposes of the latter provision it could not found a case for a winding-up order.

Where the dispute in a petition for winding up under s. 122(1)(g) is essentially one which involves only rival factions of shareholders, it is a misfeasance for those in control of the company to spend its money in the proceedings, except in relation to matters in which the company, as such, is concerned, *e.g.* in making discovery of documents in the possession of the company, or in connection with an application under s. 127 (below) to validate a disposition of the company's property or sanction the continuance of its business pending the hearing of the petition: *Re Milgate Developments Ltd* [1991] B.C.C. 24; *Re a Company No. 004502 of 1988 Ex p. Johnson* [1991] B.C.C. 234.

It is an abuse of the process of the court to present a winding-up petition for an improper purpose, *e.g.* to bring pressure on the directors to register share transfers (*Charles Forte Investments Ltd v Amanda* [1964] Ch. 240), but this will not necessarily be the case where the complainant has no other remedy: *CVC/Opportunity Equity Partners Ltd v Demarco Almeida* [2002] UKPC 16; [2002] B.C.C. 684.

S. 122(2)

This provision can be traced back to s. 4 of the Companies (Floating Charges) (Scotland) Act 1961, the Act which first introduced the floating charge to Scotland, where it was unknown at common law. At that time, however, it was not possible in Scotland to enforce a floating charge by the appointment of a receiver, and so winding up was the only remedy which the law could provide for in a case when the security was in jeopardy. The present subsection is arguably no longer required, now that receivership is available: see s. 52(2) above.

123 Definition of inability to pay debts

123(1) **[Inability to pay debts]** A company is deemed unable to pay its debts–

(a) if a creditor (by assignment or otherwise) to whom the company is indebted in a sum exceeding £750 then due has served on the company, by leaving it at the company's registered office, a written demand (in the prescribed form) requiring the company to pay the sum so due and the company has for 3 weeks thereafter neglected to pay the sum or to secure or compound for it to the reasonable satisfaction of the creditor, or

(b) if, in England and Wales, execution or other process issued on a judgment, decree or order of any court in favour of a creditor of the company is returned unsatisfied in whole or in part, or

(c) if, in Scotland, the induciae of a charge for payment on an extract decree, or an extract registered bond, or an extract registered protest, have expired without payment being made, or

(d) if, in Northern Ireland, a certificate of unenforceability has been granted in respect of a judgment against the company, or

(e) if it is proved to the satisfaction of the court that the company is unable to pay its debts as they fall due.

123(2) **[Proof that assets less than liabilities]** A company is also deemed unable to pay its debts if it is proved to the satisfaction of the court that the value of the company's assets is less than the amount of its liabilities, taking into account its contingent and prospective liabilities.

123(3) **[Increase, reduction of sum in s. 123(1)(a)]** The money sum for the time being specified in subsection (1)(a) is subject to increase or reduction by order under section 416 in Part XV.

GENERAL NOTE

The question of a company's inability to pay its debts may be determined by the court as a matter of fact (s. 123(1)(e)) or settled by the application of a number of presumptions, four of which (s. 123(1)(a)–(d)) turn purely on the evidence, while the fifth (s. 123(2)) involves a judicial assessment of the position.

On the meaning of the term "debt" in the present context, see IR 1986, r. 13.12. See also the discussion of the related term "creditor" in the note to s. 1(1). It is sufficient to give a creditor standing to petition that he should have a legal title to the debt, even though the beneficial interest may be in another person: *Bell Group Finance (Pty) Ltd (in liq.) v Bell Group (UK) Holdings Ltd* [1996] B.C.C. 505.

A winding-up order will not be made on the basis of a debt which is genuinely disputed: *Re LHF Wools Ltd* [1970] Ch. 27; *Re Trinity Assurance Co. Ltd* [1990] B.C.C. 235; *Re Janeash Ltd* [1990] B.C.C. 250; *Re a Company (No. 0010656 of 1990)* [1991] B.C.L.C. 464; *Re Richbell Strategic Holdings Ltd* [1997] 2 B.C.L.C. 429; *Re a company (No. 2634 of 2002)* [2002] EWHC 944 (Ch), [2002] 2 B.C.L.C. 591; *Re MCI WorldCom Ltd* [2002] EWHC 2436 (Ch), [2003] 1 B.C.L.C. 330. This is also the case where the company has a genuine and serious cross-claim for an amount which exceeds the petition debt (or which, if successful, would reduce the company's net indebtedness below the statutory minimum of £750): *Re Bayoil SA* [1998] B.C.C. 988: *Richbell Information Services Inc v Atlantic General Investments Trust Ltd* [1999] B.C.C. 871; *Re Latreefers Inc* [1999] 1 B.C.L.C. 271; *Greenacre Publishing Group v The Manson Group* [2000] B.C.C. 11; *Orion Media Marketing Ltd v Media Brook Ltd* [2002] 1 B.C.L.C. 184; *Re Ringinfo Ltd* [2002] 1 B.C.L.C. 210; *Montgomery v Wanda Modes Ltd* [2002] 1 B.C.L.C. 289. However a petition will not be struck out or dismissed merely because the company alleges that the debt is disputed; the court must be satisfied that there is a genuine dispute founded on substantial grounds: *Re a Company No. 006685 of 1996* [1997] B.C.C. 830; compare *Re a Company (No. 001946 of 1991) Ex p. Fin Soft Holding SA* [1991] B.C.L.C. 737. If the debt is disputed, the court will normally strike out the petition, leaving the question of its validity to be determined in other proceedings. However this is a rule of practice and not of law, and so may be departed from in an appropriate case – *e.g.* where, in the case of a foreign company, the petitioner would otherwise be without a remedy; *Re Russian & English Bank* [1932] Ch. 663; *Re Claybridge Shipping Co. SA* [1981] Com LR 107n; *cf. Re UOC Corp., Alipour v Ary* [1997] 1 W.L.R. 534; [1997] B.C.C. 377. Where the company is solvent, it is an abuse of the process of the court to present a petition for winding up based on a disputed debt, which the court will restrain by injunction and may penalise in costs: *Re a Company (No. 0012209 of 1991)* [1991] 1 W.L.R. 351. In the case of a prospective debt which has not yet fallen due, the court may take the view that the matter should be resolved when the petition is heard rather than on an application to strike out: *Securum Finance Ltd v Camswell Ltd* [1994] B.C.C. 434. (On petitions by a prospective or contingent creditor, see further *Re a Company No. 003028 of 1987* (1987) 3 B.C.C. 575 at p. 585 and *JSF Finance & Currency Exchange Co. Ltd v Akma Solutions Inc* [2001] 2 B.C.L.C. 307.)

Where the company has a cross-claim against the petitioner pending in another court, the court has a discretion whether to make a winding-up order or to dismiss the petition: *Re FSA Business Software Ltd* [1990] B.C.C. 465.

A dispute as to the genuineness of a debt may also be relevant to determine the standing of a person claiming to be a creditor who seeks a winding-up order on grounds other than the company's insolvency. In this case the question is necessarily one for the court to determine: *Morrice (or Rocks) v Brae Hotel (Shetland) Ltd* [1997] B.C.C. 670.

A petition may not be presented based on a statute-barred debt: *Re Karnos Property Co. Ltd* (1989) 5 B.C.C. 14.

Where a company or other body is, or has been, an "authorised person" or "authorised representative" under FSMA 2000, or is or has been carrying on a "regulated activity" in contravention of s. 19 of that Act, there is a special provision in s. 367(4) of that Act setting out (presumably, additional) circumstances in which such a body is to be deemed unable to pay its debts.

Under the EC Regulation, art. 27, where "main" insolvency proceedings have been opened in the Member State where the debtor has his centre of main interests, his insolvency is to be taken as conclusively established for the purposes of any secondary proceedings. In such a situation it would not be necessary or, indeed, relevant to invoke the provisions of the present section.

S. 123(1)

Paragraphs (a) to (d) correspond with events which would, in the case of an individual, have been acts of bankruptcy prior to the passing of the present Act, and survive as grounds for the making of a bankruptcy order (ss. 267, 268). Paragraph (a) was modified by IA 1985 by the addition of the words "in the prescribed form", so that an informal demand will now no longer be sufficient for the purpose of this provision.

In *Re a debtor (No. 544/SD/98)* [2000] 1 B.C.L.C. 103 at p. 116, Robert Walker L.J. drew attention to a significant difference between the function of the statutory demand in the individual and corporate insolvency regimes respectively. In the former, it merely provides one means of establishing a company's inability to pay its debts, but in bankruptcy it is not the debtor's general inability to pay his debts that is crucial but his apparent inability to pay the debt which is the subject of the statutory demand.

Section 123(1)(a) specifies only one method for the service of a statutory demand, viz. by leaving it at the company's registered office. In *Re a Company* [1985] B.C.L.C. 37 Nourse J. held that a demand sent by telex was not a good statutory demand; but when Morritt J. in *Re a Company No. 008790 of 1990* [1992] B.C.C. 11 was asked to follow this ruling in relation to a demand which had been sent by registered post, he held that, once it was admitted that the demand had been received at the office (albeit through the post), it had been "left at" the office and therefore properly served. Proof of posting alone, however, would not have been sufficient. It is not clear whether a similar interpretation could be applied to the case of a demand sent by telex, fax or electronic means which had admittedly been received.

Under the previous legislation an inaccuracy in the statutory demand, such as an overstatement of the sum due, was normally regarded as fatal, but there have now been several rulings under s. 268 of the present Act which mark a departure from the earlier law, and have not treated a defective statutory demand as invalid: see the notes to that section. It is likely that a similar approach will be taken in regard to a statutory demand under s. 123.

For the form and rules relating to the statutory demand, see IR 1986, rr. 4.4ff.

Paragraph (e) (as CA 1985, s. 518(1)(e)) formerly read: "if it is proved to the satisfaction of the court that the company is unable to pay its debts (and, in determining that question, the court shall take into account the company's contingent and prospective liabilities)". This formula was unhelpful in that it ran together two issues: (1) the question whether current debts could be met as they fell due, *i.e.* "commercial" solvency; and (2) the question whether the company would ultimately prove solvent if its future as well as its present liabilities were brought into the reckoning. The confusion was resolved by the amendment made by IA 1985: contingent and prospective liabilities are no longer to be taken into account for the purposes of para. (e), while insolvency calculated on a balance-sheet basis becomes a separate test under s. 123(2).

It has been held that failure to pay a debt which is due and not disputed is of itself evidence of insolvency under s. 123(1)(e), even though there is other evidence showing a substantial surplus of assets over liabilities (*Cornhill Insurance plc v Improvement Services Ltd* [1986] 1 W.L.R. 114; (1986) 2 B.C.C. 98,942), and even though a statutory demand has not been served under s. 123(1)(e) (*Re Taylor's Industrial Flooring Ltd* [1990] B.C.C. 44).

S. 123(2)
It is not clear from the language of this provision whether the presumption implied by the word "deemed" may be rebutted by proof that the company is in fact able to meet all its current debts. The issue might in any case be resolved by the court deciding in its discretion (see ss. 122, 125) not to make a winding-up order.

124 Application for winding up

124(1) **[Application to court]** Subject to the provisions of this section, an application to the court for the winding up of a company shall be by petition presented either by the company, or the directors, or by any creditor or creditors (including any contingent or prospective creditor or creditors), contributory or contributories, or by a liquidator (within the meaning of Article 2(b) of the EC Regulation) appointed in proceedings by virtue of Article 3(1) of the EC Regulation or a temporary administrator (within the meaning of Article 38 of the EC Regulation) or by the clerk of a magistrates' court in the exercise of the power conferred by section 87A of the Magistrates' Courts Act 1980 (enforcement of fines imposed on companies), or by all or any of those parties, together or separately.

124(2) **[Conditions for contributory to present winding-up petition]** Except as mentioned below, a contributory is not entitled to present a winding-up petition unless either–

(a) the number of members is reduced below 2, or

(b) the shares in respect of which he is a contributory, or some of them, either were originally allotted to him, or have been held by him, and registered in his name, for at least 6 months during the 18 months before the commencement of the winding up, or have devolved on him through the death of a former holder.

124(3) **[Non-application of s. 124(2)]** A person who is liable under section 76 to contribute to a company's assets in the event of its being wound up may petition on either of the grounds set out in section 122(1)(f) and (g), and subsection (2) above does not then apply; but unless the person is a contributory otherwise than under section 76, he may not in his character as contributory petition on any other ground.

This subsection is deemed included in Chapter VII of Part V of the Companies Act (redeemable shares; purchase by a company of its own shares) for the purposes of the Secretary of State's power to make regulations under section 179 of that Act.

124(3A) **[Petition on s. 122(1)(fa) ground]** A winding-up petition on the ground set out in section 122(1)(fa) may only be presented by one or more creditors.

124(4) **[Petition by Secretary of State]** A winding-up petition may be presented by the Secretary of State–

(a)   if the ground of the petition is that in section 122(1)(b) or (c), or

(b)   in a case falling within section 124A below.

124(5) **[Petition by official receiver]** Where a company is being wound up voluntarily in England and Wales, a winding-up petition may be presented by the official receiver attached to the court as well as by any other person authorised in that behalf under the other provisions of this section; but the court shall not make a winding-up order on the petition unless it is satisfied that the voluntary winding up cannot be continued with due regard to the interests of the creditors or contributories.

GENERAL NOTE

This section lists the persons who have standing to present a winding-up petition; but it is not exhaustive, for the Bank of England is empowered to do so by the Banking Act 1987, s. 92, the Attorney-General may petition in the case of a charitable company (Charities Act 1993, s. 63) and the Financial Services Authority may do so in the case of various bodies carrying on investment business: FSMA 2000, s. 367.

The Act empowers the supervisor of a voluntary scheme (s. 7(4)(b)) to apply to the court for a winding-up order and by Sch. 1, para. 21, states that an administrator and an administrative receiver may present a petition for winding up; but (no doubt as a result of a drafting slip) no mention is made of these office-holders in s. 124(1). A partial attempt has been made to overcome this difficulty without amendment of s. 124(1) by an alteration made to the rules in 1987: r. 4.7(7)(a) declares that an administrator's petition shall be expressed to be "the petition of the company by its administrator". There is no corresponding provision for an administrative receiver, but it appears that the court is prepared to accept a similar practice in this case, *i.e.* a petition presented by the receiver as the company's agent and in its name: see *Re Television Parlour plc* (1988) 4 B.C.C. 95 at p. 98, and for a case before the present Act (which could well still govern the situation where the receiver is not an administrative receiver) *Re Emmadart Ltd* [1979] Ch. 540. The supervisor of a voluntary arrangement should probably also petition in the name of the company, although this is nowhere spelt out in the legislation: see the note to s. 7(4)(b).

The terms "liquidator" and "temporary administrator" have special meanings for the purposes of the EC Regulation: see the notes to the Regulation, art. 2(b) and 38. In particular, "liquidator" extends to the office-holder in most forms of insolvency proceeding (apart from receivership). A "liquidator" appointed under art. 3(1) will have been appointed in "main" proceedings in a Member State other than the UK and, as such, is empowered by art. 29(a) to request the opening of secondary proceedings (*i.e.* apply for a winding-up order) in this jurisdiction if the debtor possesses an establishment here. See generally the notes to the articles referred to.

As a general rule, a winding-up order may only be made on the basis of a petition presented under this section: *Re Brooke Marine Ltd* [1988] B.C.L.C. 546. However, the court may in a proper case make an order of its own motion (*Lancefield v Lancefield* [2002] B.P.I.R. 1108), and an exception has now also been made by Sch. B1, para. 13(1)(e): on an application for an administration order made under para. 12 of that Schedule, the court may treat the application as a winding-up petition and make any order which the court could make under s. 125.

For the procedure on an application for winding up, see IR 1986, rr. 4.7ff.

An application to restrain the presentation or advertisement of a winding-up petition should be made direct to the judge by the issue of an originating application: see the *Practice Direction: Insolvency Proceedings* [2000] B.C.C. 927 (reproduced in Appendix IV of this *Guide*), para. 5.1(3), 8.1.

S. 124(1)

The directors are empowered to present a petition for the winding up of their company, as a result of a change made by IA 1985. This has overcome a difficulty revealed in *Re Emmadart Ltd* [1979] Ch. 540, in which the court ruled that the practice of allowing a company to present a petition on the strength of a resolution of the directors, which had been tolerated for many years, was irregular (at least in the absence of an enabling provision in the company's articles). The amendments make it possible in cases of urgency for a petition to be presented without the delay necessarily involved in summoning a general meeting of the company. Where the petition is presented by the directors, they petition in their own names, rather than that of the company; and – at least in the absence of a formal board resolution – they must act unanimously: *Re Instrumentation Electrical Services Ltd* (1988) 4 B.C.C. 301. However, where a proper resolution has been passed by a majority of the directors at a board meeting, it becomes the duty of all its directors, including those who took no part in the meeting and those who voted against the resolution, to implement it; and thereafter any director has authority to present a petition on behalf of all of them: *Re Equiticorp International plc* [1989] 1 W.L.R. 1010; (1989) 5 B.C.C. 599 (a case decided on the similar wording of IA 1986, s. 9(1)).

Section 124 *Insolvency Act 1986*

Under the former law, a contingent or prospective creditor could not be heard on a petition until he had given security for costs and had established that he had a prima facie case. This requirement was repealed by IA 1985, Sch. 10, Pt II. A contingent creditor may present a petition on the "just and equitable" ground (s. 122(1)(g)): *Re a Company No. 003028 of 1987* (1987) 3 B.C.C. 575; compare *Re Dollar Land Holdings plc* [1993] B.C.C. 823.

On the standing of a person claiming to be a creditor where his debt is disputed by the company, see the note to s. 123.

Where a person has been compelled to pay a debt owed by a company to a third party, the company is under an obligation at common law to reimburse the person who made the payment, and the latter is a prospective creditor of the company with standing to present a petition for its winding up: *Re Healing Research Trustee Co. Ltd* [1991] B.C.L.C. 716.

Where a creditor seeks to withdraw a petition, another creditor may apply to be substituted as petitioner. In *Re Wavern Engineering Co. Ltd* (1987) 3 B.C.C. 3 leave was given by the court to a creditor to withdraw a petition in the mistaken belief that no other creditor was willing to support the petition. The court rescinded the leave to withdraw and made an order substituting another creditor as petitioner.

A person who has agreed to take a transfer of shares but whose name has not been entered on the register of members has no standing as a "contributory" to present a winding-up petition: *Re a Company No. 003160 of 1986* (1986) 2 B.C.C. 99, 276; *Re Quickdome Ltd* (1988) 4 B.C.C. 296. As regards the trustee in bankruptcy of a member, see the note to s. 82, above.

Where the petitioner's status as a contributory is in dispute, it was formerly the practice that his standing to petition should be established in separate proceedings: *Re J N 2 Ltd* [1978] 1 W.L.R. 183; but it is now accepted that this is not an inflexible rule and that it may be departed from in the interests of justice: *Re UOC Corp. Ltd, Alipour v Ary* [1997] 1 W.L.R. 534; [1997] B.C.C. 377; further proceedings [2002] EWHC 937 (Ch), [2002] 2 B.C.L.C. 770.

S. 124(2), (3)

These provisions restrict the circumstances in which winding-up proceedings may be instituted by a contributory: generally speaking, he must have been a member of at least six months' standing. Supplementing this statutory rule is the principle, long settled at common law, under which the court will dismiss a petition brought by a contributory unless he shows that he will have a financial interest in the outcome of the liquidation, so that, *e.g.*, the holder of fully paid shares may not seek an order for the winding up of a wholly insolvent company (*Re Rica Gold Washing Company* (1879) 11 Ch. D. 36; *Re Chesterfield Catering Co. Ltd* [1977] Ch. 373; *Re Martin-Coulter Enterprises Ltd* (1988) 4 B.C.C. 210). Exceptionally, where the petition (on the "just and equitable" ground) is based on or alleges a failure to supply accounts, and by reason of the company's default insufficient accounts are available to tell whether there will in fact be a surplus for contributories, the petitioner is not required to prove that he has a tangible interest in the outcome: *Re Wessex Computer Stationers Ltd* [1992] B.C.L.C. 366; *Re a Company No. 007936 of 1994* [1995] B.C.C. 705. The persons liable under s. 76 are (1) former shareholders whose shares have been redeemed or repurchased out of capital by a company which is subsequently wound up insolvent within a year of the transaction, and (2) directors made jointly and severally liable with such former shareholders.

Section 124(2)(a) does not apply where the company has always had only one shareholder (*Re Pimlico Capital Ltd* [2002] EWHC 878 (Ch), [2002] 2 B.C.L.C. 544); indeed, it is arguable that it applies only where the ground on which the petition is based is s. 122(1)(e).

Section 124(3A) was inserted by IA 2000, s. 1, Sch. 1, paras 1, 6 with effect from January 1, 2003, when the new ground of winding up under s. 122(1)(fa) was also introduced.

S. 124(5)

An example of this jurisdiction occurred in May 1988 when the official receiver obtained High Court orders appointing him provisional liquidator of some 53 companies in the Manchester area, replacing three named accountants in whose hands the liquidations had been progressing. The official receiver was directed to take possession of papers relating to 200 companies being administered by the accountants, with a view to bringing proceedings on the ground that the voluntary liquidations could not be continued with due regard to the interests of creditors and shareholders as required by s. 124(5).

In the exercise of its discretion under this provision the court will normally have regard to the wishes of a majority in value of the company's creditors, where the company is insolvent, but will not necessarily be bound by this: *Re Southard & Co. Ltd* [1979] 1 W.L.R. 1198; *Re Medisco Equipment Ltd* (1983) 1 B.C.C. 98,944; *Re Falcon R J Developments Ltd* (1987) 3 B.C.C. 146; *Re M C H Services Ltd* (1987) 3 B.C.C. 179; *Re Hewitt Brannan (Tools) Co. Ltd* [1990] B.C.C. 354. The case for a court order will be stronger where there is a suspicion of sharp practice calling for an impartial investigation of the company's affairs: *Re Gordon & Breach Science Publishers Ltd* [1995] B.C.C. 261.

124A Petition for winding up on grounds of public interest

124A(1) **[Power of Secretary of State]** Where it appears to the Secretary of State from–

(a) any report made or information obtained under Part XIV of the Companies Act 1985 (company investigations, etc.),

(b) any report made by inspectors under–

    (i) section 167, 168, 169 or 284 of the Financial Services and Markets Act 2000, or
    (ii) where the company is an open-ended investment company (within the meaning of that Act), regulations made as a result of section 262(2)(k) of that Act;

(bb) any information or documents obtained under section 165, 171, 172, 173 or 175 of that Act,

(c) any information obtained under section 2 of the Criminal Justice Act 1987 or section 52 of the Criminal Justice (Scotland) Act 1987 (fraud investigations), or

(d) any information obtained under section 83 of the Companies Act 1989 (powers exercisable for purpose of assisting overseas regulatory authorities),

that it is expedient in the public interest that a company should be wound up, he may present a petition for it to be wound up if the court thinks it just and equitable for it to be so.

124A(2) **[Non-application]** This section does not apply if the company is already being wound up by the court.

GENERAL NOTE

For examples of the exercise of this jurisdiction, see *Re Walter L Jacob & Co. Ltd* (1989) 5 B.C.C. 244; *Re Market Wizard Systems (UK) Ltd* [1998] 2 B.C.L.C. 282; *Secretary of State for Trade & Industry v Leyton Housing Trustees Ltd* [2000] 2 B.C.L.C. 808; *Re Equity & Provident Ltd* [2002] EWHC 188 (Ch), [2002] 2 B.C.L.C. 78; and *Re Delfin International (SA) Ltd* [2000] 1 B.C.L.C. 71 (where a foreign company was ordered to be wound up under the section); and of a refusal to exercise it, *Re Secure & Provide plc* [1992] B.C.C. 405; *Re Forrester & Lamego Ltd* [1997] 2 B.C.L.C. 155 and *Secretary of State for Trade & Industry v Travel Time (UK) Ltd* [2000] B.C.C. 792. See also *Re ForceSun Ltd* [2002] EWHC 443 (Ch), [2002] 2 B.C.L.C. 302 and *Re Alpha Club (UK) Ltd* [2002] EWHC 884 (Ch), [2002] 2 B.C.L.C. 612, where the court ruled it appropriate to make a winding-up order under s. 124A even though the company was already in voluntary liquidation. In *Re a Company (No. 007816 of 1994)* [1997] 2 B.C.L.C. 685 and *Re Titan International Inc.* [1998] 1 B.C.L.C. 102 the court declined to order the winding up of foreign companies on public interest grounds for want of evidence of a sufficient connection with the jurisdiction or of prejudice to the public interest in this country.

Note that proceedings under s. 124A do not fall within the scope of the EC Regulation, even where the company in question is insolvent: *Re Marann Brooks CSV Ltd* [2003] B.C.C. 239, or the Brussels Convention on Jurisdiction and Enforcement of Judgments: *Re Senator Hanseatische Verwaltungsgesellschaft mbH* [1997] B.C.C. 112.

It may be expedient to order that a company should be wound up in the public interest even though it has not acted unlawfully: *Re S H V Senator Hanseatische Verwaltungs Gesellschaft mbH* [1997] 1 W.L.R. 515; [1997] B.C.C. 112.

Where the Secretary of State decided not to pursue a petition on public interest grounds under s. 124A, Harman J. declined an application by contributories of the company to be substituted as petitioners: the existing evidence, he said, would not be material to the revised petition, which would be on different grounds (*Re Xyllyx plc (No. 1)* [1992] B.C.L.C. 376).

A petition presented under this section on public interest grounds is required to be advertised in the same way as a creditor's petition, unless the court directs otherwise under IR 1986, r. 4.11(1). For a discussion of the considerations affecting the exercise of the court's discretion in this respect, see *Re a Company No. 007923 of 1994, Re a Company No. 007924 of 1994* [1995] B.C.C. 634 and 641.

In *Secretary of State for Trade and Industry v Aurum Marketing Ltd* [2002] B.C.C. 31, where a company which had operated a swindle was ordered to be wound up on public interest grounds, its sole director was ordered to pay both the applicant's and the company's costs personally. Costs were also awarded against directors personally in *Re North West Holdings plc* [2001] EWCA Civ 67, [2002] B.C.C. 441, where the Court of Appeal held that, although it was the normal rule that directors should not be ordered to pay their company's costs, an exception should be made where the directors had no *bona fide* belief that the company had an arguable defence and that it was in the interests of the public to advance that defence. A similar order was made against a majority shareholder in *Secretary of State for Trade and Industry v Liquid Acquisitions Ltd* [2002] EWHC 180 (Ch), [2003] 1 B.C.L.C. 375.

Section 124A(1)(b) was substituted and s. 124A(1)(bb) inserted by the *Financial Services and Markets Act 2000 (Consequential Amendments and Repeals) Order* 2001 (SI 2001/3649) as from December 1, 2001.

Generally on s. 124A, see Keay, (1999) 20 *Company Lawyer* 296.

125 Powers of court on hearing of petition

125(1) **[Extent of powers]** On hearing a winding-up petition the court may dismiss it, or adjourn the hearing conditionally or unconditionally, or make an interim order, or any other order that it thinks fit; but the court shall not refuse to make a winding-up order on the ground only that the company's assets have been mortgaged to an amount equal to or in excess of those assets, or that the company has no assets.

125(2) **[Just and equitable winding up]** If the petition is presented by members of the company as contributories on the ground that it is just and equitable that the company should be wound up, the court, if it is of opinion–

(a) that the petitioners are entitled to relief either by winding up the company or by some other means, and

(b) that in the absence of any other remedy it would be just and equitable that the company should be wound up,

shall make a winding-up order; but this does not apply if the court is also of the opinion both that some other remedy is available to the petitioners and that they are acting unreasonably in seeking to have the company wound up instead of pursuing that other remedy.

S. 125(1)
This provision gives the court the widest discretion.

There is no established rule, comparable with that applicable in the case of a contributory petitioner (see the note to s. 124(2) above), that a creditor's petition will be dismissed unless he can show that he will have a tangible benefit from the liquidation (*Re Crigglestone Coal Co. Ltd* [1906] 2 Ch. 327), but the court's discretion is none the less unfettered, except by the concluding words of the subsection. For recent cases in which the court reviewed the authorities and discussed the basis on which the discretion will be exercised, where a petition is opposed by some creditors, see *Re Television Parlour plc* (1988) 4 B.C.C. 95; *Re H J Tomkins & Son Ltd* [1990] B.C.L.C. 76; *Re Leigh Estates (UK) Ltd* [1994] B.C.C. 292; *Re Lummus Agricultural Services Ltd* [1999] B.C.C. 953 and *Re Demaglass Holdings Ltd* [2001] 2 B.C.L.C. 633. In *Bell Group Finance (Pty) Ltd v Bell Group (UK) Holdings Ltd* [1996] B.C.C. 505 it was held to be a good reason for the making of a winding-up order that it would allow an investigation to take place into the affairs of a hopelessly insolvent company. An argument that the only proper procedure in such a case was the Secretary of State petitioning on the grounds of public interest, and not a creditor petitioning on the grounds of insolvency, was rejected by the court.

One basis for the exercise of the court's discretion to dismiss a winding-up petition (or to grant a stay of the winding-up proceedings under s. 147) is that of *forum non conveniens, i.e.* that it is more appropriate that the matter be dealt with by a court in some other jurisdiction. In *Re Harrods (Buenos Aires) Ltd* [1992] Ch. 72; [1991] B.C.C. 249, a petition was presented for the winding up of an English-registered company which carried on business exclusively in Argentina. The Court of Appeal ruled that the courts of Argentina were the appropriate forum, and ordered a stay of the English proceedings.

For the procedure on the making of a winding-up order, see IR 1986, rr. 4.20ff.

It is the usual practice, where a creditor's petition is dismissed because the debt on which it is based has been paid in full, for the court in its discretion to order the company to pay the petitioner's costs, whether or not the company appears at the hearing. See this matter discussed fully in *Re Nowmost Co. Ltd* [1997] B.C.C. 105.

The jurisdiction conferred by s. 125 is confined to the disposal of the petition. The section does not confer on the court jurisdiction to deal with other matters, such as a claim for damages in tort for the malicious institution of proceedings: *Partizan Ltd v O J Kilkenny & Co. Ltd* [1998] B.C.C. 912.

S. 125(2)
It is not sufficient for the purposes of this provision simply to show that the petitioner has alternative remedies open to him; he must also be acting unreasonably in not pursuing them.

In *Re a Company No. 002567 of 1982* [1983] 1 W.L.R. 927, this subsection was relied on to refuse relief to a petitioner who had agreed to sell his shares to the majority shareholders at an independent valuation and had then reneged on this arrangement. A similar ruling was given in *Fuller v Cyracuse Ltd* [2001] B.C.C. 806, where the petitioner had refused to accept an offer by the company to buy his shares at an independent valuation. In contrast, it was held not unreasonable to refuse a similar offer in *Re Data Online Transactions (UK) Ltd, Apcar v Aftab* [2003] B.C.C. 510.

This was a minority shareholder's petition on the "just and equitable" ground, where it is common to seek in the alternative an order under CA 1985, s. 459, on the grounds of "unfair prejudice". In this situation the court is frequently asked to exercise its discretion under s. 125(2) on the ground that the petitioner is unreasonably refusing to pursue some other form of relief or to accept some other remedy. See also *CVC/Opportunity Equity Partners Ltd v Demarco Almeida* [2002] UKPC 16, [2002] 2 B.C.L.C. 108. On the exercise of the court's discretion, see, *e.g. Re a Company No. 003028 of 1987* (1987) 3 B.C.C. 575; *Re a Company No. 003843 of 1986* (1987) 3 B.C.C. 624; *Re a Company No. 003096 of 1987* (1988) 4 B.C.C. 80; *Re a Company No. 001363 of 1988* (1989) 5 B.C.C. 18; *Vujnovich v Vujnovich* (1989) 5 B.C.C. 740; *Re Abbey Leisure Ltd* [1990] B.C.C. 60; *Re a Company No. 00330 of 1991 Ex p. Holden* [1991] B.C.C. 241; *Re Copeland & Craddock Ltd* [1997] B.C.C. 294; *Re a Company (No. 004415 of 1996)* [1997] 1 B.C.L.C. 479.

In a Practice Direction (see *Practice Direction: Applications under the Companies Act 1985 and the Insurance Companies Act 1982* [1999] B.C.C. 741 (reproduced as Appendix V to this *Guide*)) the attention of practitioners is drawn to the undesirability of including "as a matter of course" a prayer for winding up as an alternative to a s. 459 order. It should be included only if that is the relief which the petitioner prefers or if it is considered that it may be the only relief to which he is entitled. This may be seen as an attempt to discourage the use of an alternative prayer for winding up as a tactical device to put pressure on the company and its controllers. (See further the notes to s. 127 below.)

126 Power to stay or restrain proceedings against company

126(1) [Exercise of power] At any time after the presentation of a winding-up petition, and before a winding-up order has been made, the company, or any creditor or contributory, may–

(a) where any action or proceeding against the company is pending in the High Court or Court of Appeal in England and Wales or Northern Ireland, apply to the court in which the action or proceeding is pending for a stay of proceedings therein, and

(b) where any other action or proceeding is pending against the company, apply to the court having jurisdiction to wind up the company to restrain further proceedings in the action or proceeding;

and the court to which application is so made may (as the case may be) stay, sist or restrain the proceedings accordingly on such terms as it thinks fit.

126(2) [Where company registered under CA 1985, s. 680] In the case of a company registered under section 680 of the Companies Act (pre-1862 companies; companies formed under legislation other than the Companies Acts) or the previous corresponding legislation, where the application to stay, sist or restrain is by a creditor, this section extends to actions and proceedings against any contributory of the company.

GENERAL NOTE

The making of a winding-up order operates automatically to stay all actions and proceedings against the company, as does also the appointment of a provisional liquidator, unless the court directs otherwise (see s. 130(2)). This section empowers the court to make interim orders during the period when the hearing of a winding-up application is pending.

In relation to the financial markets, nothing in s. 126 affects any action taken by an exchange or clearing house for the purpose of its default proceedings: CA 1989, s. 161(4).

127 Avoidance of property dispositions, etc.

127(1) [Dispositions etc. void after commencement of winding up] In a winding up by the court, any disposition of the company's property, and any transfer of shares, or alteration in the status of the company's members, made after the commencement of the winding up is, unless the court otherwise orders, void.

127(2) [No effect on administrator while petition suspended] This section has no effect in respect of anything done by an administrator of a company while a winding-up petition is suspended under paragraph 40 of Schedule B1.

Section 127 *Insolvency Act 1986*

GENERAL NOTE

When an order is made for the winding up of a company by the court, it is deemed to have commenced from the time of the presentation of the petition or an even earlier time: see s. 129. This section accordingly operates with retrospective effect to avoid the property dispositions and other legal events mentioned, unless the court orders otherwise. It is not necessary that the company should be insolvent.

An application may be made to the court under this section for the prospective validation of a transaction before a winding-up order has been made: see, *e.g. Re A I Levy (Holdings) Ltd* [1964] Ch. 19.

Application may be made to the court by the company itself or by any interested person, such as the disponee of the property: *Re Argentum Reductions (UK) Ltd* [1975] 1 W.L.R. 186. The principles upon which the court will act in exercising its discretion under this section are well settled. The leading case is *Re Gray's Inn Construction Co. Ltd* [1980] 1 W.L.R. 711. Where the company is insolvent, the primary purpose of the section is to ensure that all creditors are paid *pari passu*. A transaction which has, or is likely to have, the effect of reducing the assets available to creditors will not be validated; but if there is no serious risk to creditors or if the company is likely to improve the position of its creditors by trading profitably pending the hearing of the petition, the discretion may be exercised. Payments into or out of the company's bank account were held (or in some respects conceded) to be "dispositions of the company's property" for the purposes of this section, both when the account was in credit and when it was overdrawn, in *Re Gray's Inn Construction Co. Ltd* (above) and in *Re McGuinness Bros (UK) Ltd* (1987) 3 B.C.C. 571 at p. 574. But later cases suggest that this view is too wide. In *Re Barn Crown Ltd* [1994] 1 W.L.R. 147; [1994] B.C.C. 381 payments into an account which was in credit were held not to be within the section – a ruling which has been criticised by Professor Goode, *Principles of Corporate Insolvency Law* (2nd edn, 1997), pp. 427–428. Professor Goode (*ibid*, pp. 429–432) also considers that *Re Gray's Inn Construction Co. Ltd* is wrong (save in certain exceptional cases) in so far as it supports the view that payments out of an account which is overdrawn involve a disposition of the company's property. And in *Bank of Ireland v Hollicourt (Contractors) Ltd* [2001] Ch. 555; [2000] B.C.C. 1210 the Court of Appeal, endorsing the ruling of Lightman J. in *Coutts & Co. v Stock* [2000] 1 W.L.R. 906; [2000] B.C.C. 247, held that payments made by cheque out of a company's bank account to a third party involve no disposition of the company's property to the bank – which merely acts as the company's agent in making a disposition in favour of the third party – and that this is so whether the account is in credit or overdrawn. For other decisions under the section, see *Re a Company No. 007523 of 1986* (1987) 3 B.C.C. 57 (order refused – company currently trading at a loss); *Re Sugar Properties (Derisley Wood) Ltd* (1987) 3 B.C.C. 88 (order granted authorising sale of shares in racehorses); *Re French's Wine Bar Ltd* (1987) 3 B.C.C. 173 (completion of agreement to sell leasehold property sanctioned); *Re Tramway Building & Construction Co. Ltd* [1988] Ch. 293; (1987) 3 B.C.C. 443 (transfer of land validated: no reduction of assets); *Re Webb Electrical Ltd* (1988) 4 B.C.C. 230 (repayment of advance made by director to company not validated: no benefit to company); *Re Fairway Graphics Ltd* [1991] B.C.L.C. 468 (order refused: benefit to creditors not shown); *Re Rafidain Bank* [1992] B.C.C. 376 (order sought for benefit of one creditor only: refused); *Re S A & D Wright Ltd, Denney v John Hudson & Co. Ltd* [1992] B.C.C. 503 (fuel oil supplied to company which enabled it to continue its business; seller's requirement in usual course of trading that payment for previous supplies be made as a condition for delivery of new supplies: held not a preference, and order made validating such payments); *Richbell Information Services Inc. v Atlantic General Investments Ltd* [1999] B.C.C. 971 (a funding arrangement to enable litigation to be conducted to pursue a claim to recover assets claimed by the company, which would ultimately involve a disposition of proceeds of the litigation: validating order made); and *Rose v AIB Group (UK) plc* (June 9, 2003, Sweet & Maxwell's *British Company Law and Practice, New Developments*, para. 96–728) (payments into company's bank accounts not validated, even though made in good faith, up to an amount sufficient to pay off bank's overdraft; defence of change of position in principle held to be available but failed on the evidence; later payments into account validated).

Where the company is solvent, the same considerations do not arise. The court will be concerned to avoid paralysing the company's business, and will normally give leave for it to continue trading, the onus being on the person opposing the grant of leave to justify refusal (*Re Burton & Deakin Ltd* [1977] 1 W.L.R. 390). But the fact that the company is solvent is not determinative: in *Re a company (No. 007130 of 1988)* [2000] 1 B.C.L.C. 582 the court refused to authorise payments out of the bank account of a solvent company which was the subject of a petition to wind it up on public interest grounds, there being evidence of irregularities in the conduct of the company's management.

"The company's property", in s. 127, means property beneficially owned by the company: *Re Margart Pty Ltd, Hamilton v Westpac Banking Corp.* (1984) 2 A.C.L.C. 709; *Re Branston & Gothard Ltd* [1999] B.P.I.R. 466. Where a company has entered into a binding and unconditional contract for the sale of an interest in land (or, probably, any other specifically enforceable contract to alienate property) before the presentation of a winding-up petition against it, it will in most cases already have disposed of the beneficial interest in the property concerned, and so, strictly speaking, the completion of the transaction by the conveyance of the legal title after the presentation of the petition is not a "disposition" within s. 127. However, in practice it may be prudent to seek an order from the court that, in so far as the completion may involve any disposition of the property of the company, it should be treated as valid and effective: *Re French's Wine Bar Ltd* (above).

Where property is recovered by a liquidator under s. 127 and the company's assets are subject to a floating charge, the charge attaches to the property, which is deemed to have remained all along the property of the company: *Re R S & M Engineering Co. Ltd, Mond v Hammond Suddards* [2000] Ch. 40 at p. 50; [2000] B.C.C. 445 at p. 451. However the liquidator cannot assign to a third party the right to bring proceedings to have a disposition declared void under s. 127 and to recover the property from the recipient: *Re Ayala Holdings Ltd (No. 2)* [1996] 1 B.C.L.C. 467. (However, this ruling may be open to question (although no doubt correct on the facts of the case itself), for no right to bring proceedings is specifically conferred on the liquidator. It is hard to see why an assignment in favour of a person having a charge over the company's assets should not be effective – or, for that matter, why such a chargee could not institute proceedings in his own right.)

Expenditure of the company's money on litigating the disputes of an individual member will not be condoned by the court: *Re Crossmore Electrical and Civil Engineering Ltd* (1989) 5 B.C.C. 37; *Re a Company No. 005685 of 1988* (1989) 5 B.C.C. 79.

The section applies in the winding up of a foreign company: *Re Sugar Properties (Derisley Wood) Ltd* (above).

It has been common practice for a shareholder petitioning for relief on the grounds of unfair prejudice (CA 1985, s. 459) to add an alternative prayer for the winding up of the company. This automatically brings into operation the provisions of s. 127 so that, unless the court gives leave, the company's business will be paralysed, usually to the prejudice of all concerned. Accordingly, in a Practice Direction (*Practice Direction: Applications under the Companies Act 1985 and the Insurance Companies Act 1982* [1999] B.C.C. 741, para. 9, replacing *Practice Direction No. 1 of 1990* [1990] 1 W.L.R. 490; [1990] B.C.C. 292), attention is drawn to the undesirability of asking as a matter of course for a winding-up order as an alternative to relief under s. 459; and whenever a winding-up order is asked for in any petition by a contributory the petitioner is required to state in advance whether he consents or objects to a s. 127 order in the standard form which is appended to the Practice Direction. If he is prepared to consent, the registrar will normally make an order without further inquiry. The relevant part of the Practice Direction (including the standard form of order) is reproduced at Appendix V of this *Guide*.

The court's discretion can extend to validating a transaction to which the company is not a party, but only in special circumstances. In *Re Dewrun Ltd* [2002] B.C.C. 57 the company had transferred freehold property to another company which had given a charge to its bank. An order was made validating the transaction to the limited extent of confirming the bank's charge.

A provision similar to s. 127 is made in relation to a voluntary winding up by s. 88, except that it applies only to transfers of shares and alterations in the status of the company's members; and in this case the sanction of the liquidator and not the leave of the court is needed to validate the transaction.

In the context of the financial markets, s. 127 does not apply to a market contract or any disposition of property in pursuance of such a contract, the provision of margin in relation to market contracts, a market charge, and certain other transactions: see CA 1989, ss. 163(4), 175(3)–(5). A similar dispensation applies in relation to financial and securities settlement systems: s. 127 does not apply to a disposition of property as a result of which the property becomes subject to a collateral security charge, or any transactions pursuant to which that transaction is made: Finality Regulations, reg. 19(3). Section 127 is also disapplied in relation to a transfer order or a contract for the purpose of realising security in such systems: reg. 16(1). See the notes on pp. 2–3.

Note that there is no scope for the application of s. 127 in the case where the court exercises the new power (conferred by Sch. B1, para. 13(1)(e)) to order a winding up instead of making an administration order, since in that case the winding up is deemed to commence on the making of the order: see s. 129(1A).

S. 127(2)

This new provision was inserted (and the former s. 127 renumbered as s. 127(1)) by EA 2002, s. 248 and Sch. 17, para. 15, with effect from September 15, 2003. See further the notes to Sch. B1, para. 40.

128   Avoidance of attachments, etc.

128(1)   [Attachments etc. void] Where a company registered in England and Wales is being wound up by the court, any attachment, sequestration, distress or execution put in force against the estate or effects of the company after the commencement of the winding up is void.

128(2) **[Application to Scotland]** This section, so far as relates to any estate or effects of the company situated in England and Wales, applies in the case of a company registered in Scotland as it applies in the case of a company registered in England and Wales.

GENERAL NOTE

In spite of the apparently unqualified wording of s. 128, it has been held that the court may override the effect of the section by an order made under s. 126(1) or s. 130(2): see, *e.g. The Constellation* [1966] 1 W.L.R. 272.

There is no provision in the Act which avoids attachments, etc. in a similar way in a voluntary winding up; but the liquidator may apply to the court under either s. 126(1) or s. 130(2) to have such a process stayed or set aside, by virtue of the powers conferred on the court by s. 112(1).

Further sections of the Act deal with the question of executions, etc. which have been begun but not completed at the time when the winding up of the company is deemed to commence: see ss. 183, 184.

Section 176 of the Act is expressed to be without prejudice to this section. Section 176 imposes a charge on goods which have been distrained in the three months before a winding-up order (or their proceeds, if they have been sold) for the benefit of the company's preferential creditors.

In relation to the financial markets, nothing in s. 128 affects any action taken by an exchange or clearing house for the purpose of its default proceedings: CA 1989, s. 161(4).

Commencement of winding up

129 Commencement of winding up by the court

129(1) **[Time of passing of resolution]** If, before the presentation of a petition for the winding up of a company by the court, a resolution has been passed by the company for voluntary winding up, the winding up of the company is deemed to have commenced at the time of the passing of the resolution; and unless the court, on proof of fraud or mistake, directs otherwise, all proceedings taken in the voluntary winding up are deemed to have been validly taken.

129(1A) **[Winding-up order on administration application]** Where the court makes a winding-up order by virtue of paragraph 13(1)(e) of Schedule B1, the winding up is deemed to commence on the making of the order.

129(2) **[Time of presentation of petition]** In any other case, the winding up of a company by the court is deemed to commence at the time of the presentation of the petition for winding up.

GENERAL NOTE

The effect of the section is to backdate the operation of the winding-up order to the time when the petition for winding up was presented (or, if the company was then already in voluntary liquidation, to the time when the resolution for voluntary winding up was passed).

On the significance of the word "time", see the note to s. 86.

In the former bankruptcy law, the "doctrine of relation back" applied with similar retrospectivity, so that for many purposes the bankruptcy was deemed to commence from an earlier "available act of bankruptcy". Both the concept of "act of bankruptcy" and the doctrine of relation back were abolished by IA 1985, so that a bankruptcy order is no longer backdated in this way; but no corresponding change has been made in the case of corporate insolvency.

A voluntary liquidation commences at the time of the passing of the resolution for voluntary winding up: see s. 86.

The term "commencement of the winding up" is defined differently for the purposes of s. 185 (effect of diligence in Scotland): see s. 185(3).

Subsection (1A) was inserted by EA 2002, s. 248 and Sch. 17, para. 16, with effect from September 15, 2003. Under Sch. B1, para. 13(1)(e) the court is empowered, in hearing an application for an administration order, to treat the application as a winding-up petition and order the company to be wound up. In this case, the commencement of the winding up is not back-dated.

For the purposes of the EC Regulation, the critical point is the "time of the opening of proceedings", which is defined by art. 2(f) as "the time at which the judgment opening proceedings becomes effective, whether it is a final judgment or not". This must refer to the time when the court pronounces its order, except in the case where the company is already in creditors' voluntary liquidation, when it would be the time of the passing of the shareholders' resolution.

It has been held that the periods of limitation prescribed by the Limitation Act 1980 cease to run on the making of a winding-up order, and not (except as against the petitioning creditor) at the time when the winding-up petition is presented: *Re Cases of Taff's Well Ltd* [1992] Ch. 179; [1991] B.C.C. 582. Accordingly, in the case of a six-year period of limitation, the liquidator in a winding up by the court is at liberty to distribute the assets of the company without regard to the claims of creditors which accrued more than six years before the making of the winding-up order. In the same case the judge expressed the view, *obiter*, that an administration order would not prevent time running against a creditor of the company.

130 Consequences of winding-up order

130(1) **[Copy of order to registrar]** On the making of a winding-up order, a copy of the order must forthwith be forwarded by the company (or otherwise as may be prescribed) to the registrar of companies, who shall enter it in his records relating to the company.

130(2) **[Actions stayed on winding-up order]** When a winding-up order has been made or a provisional liquidator has been appointed, no action or proceeding shall be proceeded with or commenced against the company or its property, except by leave of the court and subject to such terms as the court may impose.

130(3) **[Actions stayed re companies registered under CA 1985, s. 680]** When an order has been made for winding up a company registered under section 680 of the Companies Act, no action or proceeding shall be commenced or proceeded with against the company or its property or any contibutory of the company, in respect of any debt of the company, except by leave of the court, and subject to such terms as the court may impose.

130(4) **[Effect of order]** An order for winding up a company operates in favour of all the creditors and of all contributories of the company as if made on the joint petition of a creditor and of a contributory.

GENERAL NOTE

In relation to the financial markets, nothing in s. 130 affects any action taken by an exchange or clearing house for the purpose of its default proceedings: CA 1989, s. 161(4).

S. 130(1)
Under the rules prescribed for the purposes of this provision the court is required to send three copies of the order to the official receiver, who is then charged with the responsibility for serving the company and the registrar and for gazetting and advertising the order: see IR 1986, r. 4.21.

Neither the registration of a winding-up order in the Companies Registry nor the gazetting of the fact that a company is in liquidation or of the appointment of a liquidator operates as notice to the world that the company is in liquidation: *Ewart v Fryer* [1901] 1 Ch. 499 (but see more particularly the report in (1900) 82 L.T. 415), affirmed *sub nom. Fryer v Ewart* [1902] A.C. 187; *Official Custodian for Charities v Parway Estates Developments Ltd (in liquidation)* [1985] Ch. 151 at p. 160.

The registrar is required to publish in the *Gazette* notice of the receipt by him of the copy of the winding-up order (CA 1985, s. 711(1)(p)); and this amounts to "official notification" of the making of the winding-up order for the purposes of CA 1985, s. 42. On the effect of "official notification", see the note to s. 109, above. It is not easy, however, to reconcile s. 42(1)(a) with the provisions contained in ss. 127–129 above which give a winding-up order retrospective effect: this is a difficult question which awaits judicial determination.

In *Re Calmex Ltd* [1989] 1 All E.R. 485; (1988) 4 B.C.C. 761, a winding-up order had been made against the company in error, and the court exercised its jurisdiction under IR 1986, r. 7.47 to rescind it. The registrar of companies took the view that the winding-up order which had been recorded under s. 130(1) should remain on his files, but the court ordered it to be removed on the ground that the rescinding order had rendered it a nullity.

S. 130(2)
The power conferred on the court by this subsection complements that provided for in s. 126(1), and has been held to qualify the apparently categorical wording of s. 128: see the note to that section.

Section 131   Insolvency Act 1986

Where the court is asked to give leave to bring an action against a company which is in liquidation, it will seek to do what is right and fair in all the circumstances. In *New Cap Reinsurance Corp. Ltd v HIH Casualty & General Insurance Ltd* [2002] EWCA Civ 300, [2002] 2 B.C.L.C. 228 there were issues common to the claim pending against the company and an action between the claimants and third parties, and the hearing of the latter was imminent. The judge's decision to allow the action to proceed was upheld by the Court of Appeal. Leave will be refused if the proposed action raises issues which can with equal convenience and less delay and expense be decided in the liquidation proceedings: *Re Exchange Securities & Commodities Ltd* [1983] B.C.L.C. 186. The court will not undertake any investigation into the merits of the proposed claim or consider the background material to the s. 130 application (*Re Bank of Credit and Commerce International SA (No. 4)* [1994] 1 B.C.L.C. 419); and accordingly in that case the court declined to make an order for specific discovery of certain documents in favour of the liquidators.

In *Re National Employers' Mutual General Insurance Association* [1995] B.C.C. 774 Rattee J. held that the court could not give leave under this section retrospectively; but in the later case of *Re Saunders (a Bankrupt), Bristol & West Building Society v Saunders* [1997] Ch. 60; [1997] B.C.C. 83 Lindsay J. (after an exhaustive examination of authorities which had not been cited to Rattee J. in the previous case) ruled that this was not so, and that the lack of prior consent was not an absolute bar to the commencement of an action or proceeding. This decision was followed in *Re Linkrealm Ltd* [1998] B.C.C. 478.

Leave is not needed where the applicants are not proceeding against either the company or the company's property: *Re Lineas Navieras Bolivianas SAM* [1995] B.C.C. 666 (a case where the Admiralty Court had made an order for the sale of a ship belonging to the company: the effect of this order was to convert the company's interest in the ship into a right on the part of the applicants to have their claims met from the proceeds of sale).

In *Re Swissair Schweizerische Luftverkehr-Aktiengesellschaft, Flightline Ltd v Edwards* [2003] EWCA (Civ) 63, [2003] B.C.C. 361 an action had been begun against the company and the claimant had obtained a freezing order over assets up to the amount being claimed. The freezing order was later discharged when an equivalent sum was paid into an account in the joint names of the parties' solicitors. Neuberger J., at first instance, took the view that the arrangement gave the claimant a security interest in the funds so held, and in the light of that ruling granted leave for the action to continue. The Court of Appeal decided that no security interest had been created and accordingly that leave should be refused.

A criminal prosecution against a company is a "proceeding" within the meaning of this subsection. Accordingly, the leave of the court is required before any prosecution may be brought: *R v Dickson* [1991] B.C.C. 719.

S. 130(3)
The companies referred to are those described in s. 126(2) as "pre-1862 companies" and "companies formed under legislation other than the Companies Acts".

Investigation procedures

131 Company's statement of affairs

131(1) [Powers of official receiver] Where the court has made a winding-up order or appointed a provisional liquidator, the official receiver may require some or all of the persons mentioned in subsection (3) below to make out and submit to him a statement in the prescribed form as to the affairs of the company.

131(2) [Contents of statement] The statement shall be verified by affidavit by the persons required to submit it and shall show–

- (a) particulars of the company's assets, debts and liabilities;
- (b) the names and addresses of the company's creditors;
- (c) the securities held by them respectively;
- (d) the dates when the securities were respectively given; and
- (e) such further or other information as may be prescribed or as the official receiver may require.

131(3) **[Persons in s. 131(1)]** The persons referred to in subsection (1) are–

(a) those who are or have been officers of the company;

(b) those who have taken part in the formation of the company at any time within one year before the relevant date;

(c) those who are in the company's employment, or have been in its employment within that year, and are in the official receiver's opinion capable of giving the information required;

(d) those who are or have been within that year officers of, or in the employment of, a company which is, or within that year was, an officer of the company.

131(4) **[Time for submitting statement]** Where any persons are required under this section to submit a statement of affairs to the official receiver, they shall do so (subject to the next subsection) before the end of the period of 21 days beginning with the day after that on which the prescribed notice of the requirement is given to them by the official receiver.

131(5) **[Release, extension of time]** The official receiver, if he thinks fit, may–

(a) at any time release a person from an obligation imposed on him under subsection (1) or (2) above; or

(b) either when giving the notice mentioned in subsection (4) or subsequently, extend the period so mentioned;

and where the official receiver has refused to exercise a power conferred by this subsection, the court, if it thinks fit, may exercise it.

131(6) **[Definitions]** In this section–

"**employment**" includes employment under a contract for services; and

"**the relevant date**" means–

(a) in a case where a provisional liquidator is appointed, the date of his appointment; and

(b) in a case where no such appointment is made, the date of the winding-up order.

131(7) **[Penalty on default]** If a person without reasonable excuse fails to comply with any obligation imposed under this section, he is liable to a fine and, for continued contravention, to a daily default fine.

131(8) **[Scotland]** In the application of this section to Scotland references to the official receiver are to the liquidator or, in a case where a provisional liquidator is appointed, the provisional liquidator.

GENERAL NOTE

On the making of a winding-up order, the official receiver (in England and Wales) normally becomes liquidator of the company, at least on an interim basis until a liquidator is chosen by the meetings of creditors and contributories under s. 139. (The one exception is where the company is already under the control of an administrator or of the supervisor of a voluntary arrangement: see s. 140). In order to put the official receiver in possession of information about the company so that he may make the decisions and discharge the duties which rest upon him under the provisions of the Act which follow, the officers and employees of the company and others specified are required to complete and submit to him a "statement of affairs" under this section. This has long been a feature of a winding up by the court, and it is not simply continued in the present Act but extended to the analogous cases of a voluntary arrangement (s. 2(3)(b)), an administration (s. 22 and Sch. B1, para. 47), an administrative receivership (ss. 47, 66) and a creditors' voluntary winding up, whether originally so constituted (s. 99) or converted from a members' voluntary winding up when the company turns out to be insolvent (s. 95(3)(a)). Failure by the officers and others concerned to comply with this requirement is sanctioned by criminal penalties (s. 131(7)), and untruthfulness in the answers given is punishable as perjury, since s. 131(2) stipulates that the statement shall be verified by affidavit.

In *Re Wallace Smith Trust Co. Ltd* [1992] B.C.C. 707, the respondent director had failed to submit a statement of affairs after being required by the official receiver to do so; and the official receiver had then sought and obtained an

Section 132   Insolvency Act 1986

order *ex parte* for his public examination in order to obtain the information which ought to have been furnished in the statement of affairs. Ferris J. held that, while this course was not an abuse of the process of the court, it would have been more appropriate for a specific order or orders to have been sought under IR 1986, r.7.20 requiring the director to complete and submit the statement of affairs, and possibly also seeking the order for public examination as an alternative in case the court refused to make the specific orders.

The information given by a person in a statement of affairs may (subject to certain safeguards) be used in evidence in subsequent proceedings against him, and also against any other person who concurs in the making of the statement: see s. 433.

Where a provisional liquidator has been appointed by the court under s. 135 before a winding-up order has been made, the section also comes into operation and the official receiver may proceed to requisition a statement of affairs in anticipation of the making of a winding-up order which may in due course be made.

The provisions of this and the succeeding sections apply whether or not the company is insolvent.

On the office of official receiver, see ss. 399ff., below.

In Scotland, where there is no official receiver, the functions of the official receiver under this section are conferred by s. 131(8) on the liquidator, who is appointed by the court when the winding-up order is made (s. 138(1)).

For the rules and forms prescribed for the purposes of this section, see IR 1986, rr. 4.32ff. and on enforcement, r. 7.20.

S. 131(1)

The Act gives the official receiver a discretion, so that he may dispense with the procedure in any case he considers appropriate. One situation where this would be so is where the winding-up order follows the discharge of an administration order (s. 140), and the administrator is appointed liquidator by the court. (No similar discretion is given to the supervisor, administrator, etc. in the analogous cases established by s. 2(3)(b), 22, etc. that are referred to in the general note to this section.)

S. 131(2)

The information listed here will be required by the official receiver in order that he may make his report to the court under s. 132, and may be relevant to the question whether an application to the court under s. 133 should be made or granted. Details of the creditors will be needed if a meeting of creditors is to be summoned under s. 136(5).

S. 131(3)

The terms "employment" and "the relevant date" are defined in s. 131(6), below. "Officer" includes a director, manager or secretary: see CA 1985, s. 744 and the note to s. 206(3).

S. 131(5)

The discretion here given to the official receiver supplements the general discretionary terms of s. 131(1).

S. 131(6)

The inclusion of a person employed under a contract for services gives the section potentially a very wide scope, extending (for example) to an accountant or auditor.

S. 131(7)

On penalties, see s. 430 and Sch. 10.

S. 131(8)

As noted above, there is no official receiver in Scotland and so the liquidator or provisional liquidator is empowered to act instead. A liquidator or provisional liquidator will have the full range of discretionary powers conferred by this section on the official receiver.

132 Investigation by official receiver

132(1) [Duty of official receiver] Where a winding-up order is made by the court in England and Wales, it is the duty of the official receiver to investigate–

(a)   if the company has failed, the causes of the failure; and

(b)   generally, the promotion, formation, business, dealings and affairs of the company,

and to make such report (if any) to the court as he thinks fit.

132(2) [Report prima facie evidence] The report is, in any proceedings, prima facie evidence of the facts stated in it.

S. 132(1)
The official receiver has a discretion to decide whether a report to the court is called for, but has a statutory duty to investigate the matters listed in paras (a) and (b), which applies whether or not he is also the liquidator.

The officers of the company (and its employees and other persons who are specified in s. 235(3)) are under a duty to co-operate with the official receiver: see s. 235, below.

S. 132(2)
The evidentiary presumption applies not only for the purpose of any immediate court hearing, but "in any proceedings".

133 Public examination of officers

133(1) [Application to court] Where a company is being wound up by the court, the official receiver or, in Scotland, the liquidator may at any time before the dissolution of the company apply to the court for the public examination of any person who–

(a) is or has been an officer of the company; or

(b) has acted as liquidator or administrator of the company or as receiver or manager or, in Scotland, receiver of its property; or

(c) not being a person falling within paragraph (a) or (b), is or has been concerned, or has taken part, in the promotion, formation or management of the company.

133(2) [Request to make application] Unless the court otherwise orders, the official receiver or, in Scotland, the liquidator shall make an application under subsection (1) if he is requested in accordance with the rules to do so by–

(a) one-half, in value, of the company's creditors; or

(b) three-quarters, in value, of the company's contributories.

133(3) [Court's duties] On an application under subsection (1), the court shall direct that a public examination of the person to whom the application relates shall be held on a day appointed by the court; and that person shall attend on that day and be publicly examined as to the promotion, formation or management of the company or as to the conduct of its business and affairs, or his conduct or dealings in relation to the company.

133(4) [Persons taking part] The following may take part in the public examination of a person under this section and may question that person concerning the matters mentioned in subsection (3), namely–

(a) the official receiver;

(b) the liquidator of the company;

(c) any person who has been appointed as special manager of the company's property or business;

(d) any creditor of the company who has tendered a proof or, in Scotland, submitted a claim in the winding up;

(e) any contributory of the company.

GENERAL NOTE

The Act makes provision for both a public examination under this section and a private examination under s. 236.

The power conferred on the court by CA 1985, s. 561 to summon a somewhat wider range of persons to appear before it for private examination is to be found in ss. 236, 237, below.

Although s. 133 is by its terms expressed to apply only in a winding up by the court, s. 112 can be invoked to make it apply also in a voluntary liquidation: see *Re Campbell Coverings Ltd (No. 2)* [1954] Ch. 225, and *Bishopsgate Investment Management Ltd (in provisional liquidation) v Maxwell, Mirror Group Newspapers plc v Maxwell* [1993] Ch. 1 at pp. 24, 46; [1992] B.C.C. 222 at pp. 232, 249; *Re Pantmaenog Timber Co. Ltd, Official Receiver v Wadge, Rapps & Hunt (a firm)* [2003] UKHL 49; [2003] B.C.C. 659, at para. 56.

Under the present section, the court has power to direct the public examination of an officer of a company in compulsory liquidation who is outside the jurisdiction, and to order service of the order of the court or other relevant document to be effected on him outside the jurisdiction: *Re Seagull Manufacturing Co. Ltd (in liq.)* [1993] Ch. 345; [1993] B.C.C. 241; *Re Casterbridge Properties Ltd* [2002] B.C.C. 453. (For the position in a private examination, see the notes to ss. 236, below).

An application under s. 133 is normally brought without notice, and under s. 133(3) the court is bound to make an order. But a person against whom an order has been made may apply to the court under IR 1986, r. 7.47 to have it discharged, and the court is not then obliged to continue or uphold the order: the onus being on the person concerned to show why the mandatory order under s. 133 should not stand: *Re Casterbridge Properties Ltd* (above).

A person who is subject to examination under s. 133 is not entitled to refuse to answer questions on the ground that in doing so he may incriminate himself: this follows by analogy with the cases decided under ss. 236, 290 and 366; see *Bishopsgate Investment Management Ltd (in provisional liquidation) v Maxwell* [1993] Ch. 1 at pp. 24, 46, 62; [1992] B.C.C. 222 at pp. 233, 249, 262, and the notes to those sections.

The use of statements made under compulsion as evidence in subsequent criminal proceedings is now restricted by statute: see the notes to ss. 236 and 433.

For the rules regarding the procedure for obtaining an order for examination, and the conduct of the examination, see IR 1986, rr. 4.211ff. The examination is on oath: r. 4.215(1). Questions as to the admissibility or otherwise of questions at the examination are a matter for the presiding judge or registrar at the hearing, although the court does have power when ordering the examination to control the form of the examination (as distinct from giving directions as to the conduct of the hearing itself): *Re Richbell Strategic Holdings Ltd* [2001] B.C.C. 409. For the sanctions for non-attendance, see s. 134, below.

S. 133(1)

The public examination provisions apply also to Scotland (unlike s. 132). They maybe invoked whether the company is solvent or insolvent.

On the meaning of the term "officer", see the note to s. 206(3).

S. 133(2), (3)

The role of the court is curiously stated, in that is given no discretion by s. 133(3) to refuse an order once an application has been made; but under s. 133(2) it is empowered to intervene in order to *prevent* an application from being made to it by the official receiver following a request by the creditors or contributories. The grounds on which the court may make such an order are not stated in the present section, but IR 1986, r. 4.213(5) indicates that the official receiver may object that the creditors' request is an unreasonable one. It does, however, appear to be plain from the two subsections, read together, that any other objectors will be out of court if they do not take action before the official receiver does.

For the procedure, see IR 1986, rr. 4.213ff.

S. 133(4)

It appears that an officer or past officer of the company, though liable himself to be examined under the section, has no right to question those of his colleagues being examined with him unless he falls coincidentally within one of the categories (a)–(e). See further IR 1986, r. 4.215.

134 Enforcement of s. 133

134(1) [**Non-attendance**] If a person without reasonable excuse fails at any time to attend his public examination under section 133, he is guilty of a contempt of court and liable to be punished accordingly.

134(2) [**Warrant etc. re non-attendance**] In a case where a person without reasonable excuse fails at any time to attend his examination under section 133 or there are reasonable grounds for believing that a person has absconded, or is about to abscond, with a view to avoiding or delaying his examination under that section, the court may cause a warrant to be issued to a constable or prescribed officer of the court–

(a) for the arrest of that person; and

(b) for the seizure of any books, papers, records, money or goods in that person's possession.

134(3) [**Consequences of warrant**] In such a case the court may authorise the person arrested under the warrant to be kept in custody, and anything seized under such a warrant to be held, in accordance with the rules, until such time as the court may order.

General Note

This provision deals with the enforcement of s. 133. Other details relating to the conduct of the examination and summoning of those required to attend are dealt with in the rules: see IR 1986, rr. 4.211ff., 7.22.

S. 134(2)
A person who appeals unsuccessfully against an order for his arrest under s. 134(2)(a) is "singularly close" to being in contempt of court, and may be ordered to pay the official receiver's costs on an indemnity basis: *Re Avatar Communications Ltd* (1988) 4 B.C.C. 473.

Appointment of liquidator

135 Appointment and powers of provisional liquidator

135(1) **[Time of appointment]** Subject to the provisions of this section, the court may, at any time after the presentation of a winding-up petition, appoint a liquidator provisionally.

135(2) **[Appointment in England, Wales]** In England and Wales, the appointment of a provisional liquidator may be made at any time before the making of a winding-up order; and either the official receiver or any other fit person may be appointed.

135(3) **[Appointment in Scotland]** In Scotland, such an appointment may be made at any time before the first appointment of liquidators.

135(4) **[Provisional liquidator]** The provisional liquidator shall carry out such functions as the court may confer on him.

135(5) **[Powers of provisional liquidator]** When a liquidator is provisionally appointed by the court, his powers may be limited by the order appointing him.

GENERAL NOTE

The primary reason for appointing a provisional liquidator is normally to ensure the preservation of the company's assets pending the hearing of the winding-up petition. Since an appointment in such circumstances anticipates the eventual making of a winding-up order virtually as a foregone conclusion, it is usually made only with the consent of the company itself or in a clear case of insolvency. But provisional liquidators are also appointed in other situations – as formerly, in the case of an insurance company, when the alternative of administration was not available, as a step towards putting in place a scheme of arrangement under CA 1985, s. 425 (*Smith v UIC Insurance Co. Ltd* [2001] B.C.C. 11, at pp. 20–21); or in order to investigate whether there might be possible claims for fraudulent or wrongful trading under IA 1986, ss. 213 or 214 (*Re Latreefers Inc.* [2001] B.C.C. 174, at pp. 184–185).

An application for the appointment of a provisional liquidator must be made to a Companies Court judge and, unless otherwise ordered, is held in public. (See *Practice Direction: Insolvency Proceedings* [1999] B.C.C. 927, para. 5.1(4) (reproduced as Appendix IV to this *Guide*).)

A provisional liquidator must be qualified to act as an insolvency practitioner in relation to the company in question: see s. 388(1)(a). In *Re W F Fearman Ltd (No. 2)* (1988) 4 B.C.C. 141 it was held to be inappropriate for the court to make an order directly appointing the provisional liquidators, who were already in office, to be the liquidators of the company when the winding-up order was subsequently made, since to do so would deprive the creditors of their say in the selection of a liquidator under s. 136. However, a practical solution was found by giving leave to the official receiver to continue to use the services of the former provisional liquidators as special managers.

The appointment of a provisional liquidator automatically revokes the authority of an agent appointed to act on behalf of the company by or on behalf of the directors: *Pacific & General Insurance Ltd (in liq.) v Home & Overseas Insurance Co. Ltd* [1997] B.C.C. 400.

For further examples of the exercise of the jurisdiction under this section see *Re Pinstripe Farming Co. Ltd* [1996] B.C.C. 913, *Re UOC Corp., Alipour v Ary* [1997] B.C.C. 377, *Re Goodwill Merchant Financial Services Ltd* [2001] 1 B.C.L.C. 259 and *Re Namco UK Ltd* [2003] EWHC 989 (Ch), [2003] 2 B.C.L.C. 78. The last-mentioned case also contains a discussion of the powers under s. 135(5) which it is appropriate to include in the form of the court's order.

On the remuneration and expenses of a provisional liquidator, see the notes to rr. 4.30 and 4.218.

For the relevant rules, see IR 1986, rr. 4.25ff.

136 Functions of official receiver in relation to office of liquidator

136(1) **[Application]** The following provisions of this section have effect, subject to section 140 below, on a winding-up order being made by the court in England and Wales.

Section 136   Insolvency Act 1986

136(2) **[Official receiver liquidator]** The official receiver, by virtue of his office, becomes the liquidator of the company and continues in office until another person becomes liquidator under the provisions of this Part.

136(3) **[Vacancy]** The official receiver is, by virtue of his office, the liquidator during any vacancy.

136(4) **[Powers of official receiver when liquidator]** At any time when he is the liquidator of the company, the official receiver may summon separate meetings of the company's creditors and contributories for the purpose of choosing a person to be liquidator of the company in place of the official receiver.

136(5) **[Duty of official receiver]** It is the duty of the official receiver–

(a)   as soon as practicable in the period of 12 weeks beginning with the day on which the winding-up order was made, to decide whether to exercise his power under subsection (4) to summon meetings, and

(b)   if in pursuance of paragraph (a) he decides not to exercise that power, to give notice of his decision, before the end of that period, to the court and to the company's creditors and contributories, and

(c)   (whether or not he has decided to exercise that power) to exercise his power to summon meetings under subsection (4) if he is at any time requested, in accordance with the rules, to do so by one-quarter, in value, of the company's creditors;

and accordingly, where the duty imposed by paragraph (c) arises before the official receiver has performed a duty imposed by paragraph (a) or (b), he is not required to perform the latter duty.

136(6) **[Contents of s. 136(5)(b) notice]** A notice given under subsection (5)(b) to the company's creditors shall contain an explanation of the creditors' power under subsection (5)(c) to require the official receiver to summon meetings of the company's creditors and contributories.

GENERAL NOTE

The official receiver has a discretion to decide whether or not to convene the meetings. He has 12 weeks in which to reach a decision, but the creditors may in any case require him to summon the meetings.
   If no meetings are convened, the official receiver continues in office as liquidator. His decision not to convene meetings is therefore, in effect, a decision to keep the liquidation in his own hands.
   Section 136 should be read in conjunction with s. 137, which alternatively gives the Secretary of State power to appoint a liquidator other than the official receiver.

S. 136(1)
Section 140 applies when the company is already subject to administration or a voluntary arrangement. The court is then empowered to make an immediate appointment of the insolvency practitioner who has been the administrator or supervisor to be the liquidator in the winding up.

S. 136(2)
If the company is already in voluntary liquidation when a winding-up order is made, the existing liquidator is displaced: see IR 1986, rr. 4.136 and 4.147.

S. 136(4), (5)
The official receiver must make an initial decision, within the first 12 weeks after the making of the winding-up order, whether to summon meetings or not; and if he decides not to, he must give the notices specified by s. 136(5)(b). However, he is free to convene the meetings even after this 12-week period has expired, and the creditors' power to requisition him to call the meetings also continues. This is made clear by the use of the phrase "at any time" in s. 136(4) and (5)(c).
   For the rules dealing with the summoning of meetings under this section, see IR 1986, rr. 4.50ff.; and for the official receiver's reporting obligations, see rr. 4.43ff.: see also r. 4.107 (hand-over of assets).

137 Appointment by Secretary of State

137(1) [**Application by official receiver**] In a winding up by the court in England and Wales the official receiver may, at any time when he is the liquidator of the company, apply to the Secretary of State for the appointment of a person as liquidator in his place.

137(2) [**Decision by official receiver**] If meetings are held in pursuance of a decision under section 136(5)(a), but no person is chosen to be liquidator as a result of those meetings, it is the duty of the official receiver to decide whether to refer the need for an appointment to the Secretary of State.

137(3) [**Duty of Secretary of State**] On an application under subsection (1), or a reference made in pursuance of a decision under subsection (2), the Secretary of State shall either make an appointment or decline to make one.

137(4) [**Notice of appointment by liquidator**] Where a liquidator has been appointed by the Secretary of State under subsection (3), the liquidator shall give notice of his appointment to the company's creditors or, if the court so allows, shall advertise his appointment in accordance with the directions of the court.

137(5) [**Contents of notice or advertisement**] In that notice or advertisement the liquidator shall–

(a) state whether he proposes to summon a general meeting of the company's creditors under section 141 below for the purpose of determining (together with any meeting of contributories) whether a liquidation committee should be established under that section, and

(b) if he does not propose to summon such a meeting, set out the power of the company's creditors under that section to require him to summon one.

GENERAL NOTE

If the official receiver forms the opinion that the conduct of the winding up may be handed over to a private liquidator, he may either invite the creditors and contributories to choose an insolvency practitioner at meetings convened under s. 136, or apply under the present section to the Secretary of State to make an appointment. The Secretary of State may decline to do so (s. 137(3)), in which case the official receiver is, in effect, directed to continue in office.

There is no provision corresponding to s. 136(5)(c) empowering the creditors to require the official receiver to make an application to the Secretary of State under this section, or to apply to him directly themselves.

For the relevant rules, see IR 1986, rr. 4.104, 4.107.

S. 137(1)
The official receiver may make an application under this section "at any time", and may plainly do so as an alternative to summoning meetings under s. 136(4). Once he has called the meetings, however, he is probably bound to go through with that procedure, and could have recourse to his powers under the present section only if the meetings fail to choose a liquidator.

S. 137(2)
If the meetings do not choose a liquidator, it is the duty of the official liquidator to make a *decision* under this subsection, but he is under no duty to make a *reference*: he may perfectly well decide to stay in office as liquidator himself.

S. 137(3)
As has already been observed, a negative decision by the Secretary of State is effectively a direction to the official receiver that he should continue in office himself.

S. 137(4), (5)
The court may allow the liquidator to advertise the fact of his appointment rather than notify creditors individually. No guidance is given as to the basis on which the court should exercise this discretion, but fairly obviously it might be used to avoid unjustified expense where there are many creditors, bearing in mind that the only purpose for which the meeting is to be summoned is to decide whether to appoint a liquidation committee.

138 Appointment of liquidator in Scotland

138(1) [**Appointment**] Where a winding-up order is made by the court in Scotland, a liquidator shall be appointed by the court at the time when the order is made.

138(2) **[Period of office of interim liquidator]** The liquidator so appointed (here referred to as "the interim liquidator") continues in office until another person becomes liquidator in his place under this section or the next.

138(3) **[Meetings to be summoned]** The interim liquidator shall (subject to the next subsection) as soon as practicable in the period of 28 days beginning with the day on which the winding-up order was made or such longer period as the court may allow, summon separate meetings of the company's creditors and contributories for the purpose of choosing a person (who may be the person who is the interim liquidator) to be liquidator of the company in place of the interim liquidator.

138(4) **[Qualification to s. 138(3)]** If it appears to the interim liquidator, in any case where a company is being wound up on grounds including its inability to pay its debts, that it would be inappropriate to summon under subsection (3) a meeting of the company's contributories, he may summon only a meeting of the company's creditors for the purpose mentioned in that subsection.

138(5) **[If no person appointed at meetings]** If one or more meetings are held in pursuance of this section but no person is appointed or nominated by the meeting or meetings, the interim liquidator shall make a report to the court which shall appoint either the interim liquidator or some other person to be liquidator of the company.

138(6) **[Notification]** A person who becomes liquidator of the company in place of the interim liquidator shall, unless he is appointed by the court, forthwith notify the court of that fact.

GENERAL NOTE

There is no official receiver in Scotland, or any equivalent public officer, and so the liquidator in a Scottish winding up is invariably a private insolvency practitioner. This section provides for the appointment of an "interim liquidator", whose duty it is to take custody of the company's property and to summon meetings, etc., as in a winding up in England or Wales, but he does not enjoy the discretionary powers entrusted to the official receiver under ss. 136, 137, and the court is more closely involved throughout the proceedings. The Secretary of State's powers under s. 137 do not apply in Scotland.

S. 138(5)
In contrast with the position in England and Wales (s. 137(2)), the interim liquidator's obligation is mandatory and not discretionary, and the residual power of appointment lies with the court rather than the Secretary of State.

139 Choice of liquidator at meetings of creditors and contributories

139(1) **[Application]** This section applies where a company is being wound up by the court and separate meetings of the company's creditors and contributories are summoned for the purpose of choosing a person to be liquidator of the company.

139(2) **[Nomination of liquidator]** The creditors and the contributories at their respective meetings may nominate a person to be liquidator.

139(3) **[Liquidator]** The liquidator shall be the person nominated by the creditors or, where no person has been so nominated, the person (if any) nominated by the contributories.

139(4) **[Where different persons nominated]** In the case of different persons being nominated, any contributory or creditor may, within 7 days after the date on which the nomination was made by the creditors, apply to the court for an order either–

  (a) appointing the person nominated as liquidator by the contributories to be a liquidator instead of, or jointly with, the person nominated by the creditors; or

  (b) appointing some other person to be liquidator instead of the person nominated by the creditors.

GENERAL NOTE

This section lays down the rules and procedure for the appointment of a liquidator when meetings of the creditors and contributories are convened for the purpose. It is very similar in terms to s. 100, which governs a creditors' voluntary winding up. Unlike ss. 136, 137, it applies in Scotland as well as England and Wales.

The word "nominate" is used in a sense equivalent to "appoint": see the notes to s. 100.

For the relevant rules, see IR 1986, rr. 4.100, 4.102.

140 Appointment by the court following administration or voluntary arrangement

140(1) [**Appointment of administrator**] Where a winding-up order is made immediately upon the appointment of an administrator ceasing to have effect, the court may appoint as liquidator of the company the person whose appointment as administrator has ceased to have effect.

140(2) [**Appointment of supervisor**] Where a winding-up order is made at a time when there is a supervisor of a voluntary arrangement approved in relation to the company under Part I, the court may appoint as liquidator of the company the person who is the supervisor at the time when the winding-up order is made.

140(3) [**Position of official receiver**] Where the court makes an appointment under this section, the official receiver does not become the liquidator as otherwise provided by section 136(2), and he has no duty under section 136(5)(a) or (b) in respect of the summoning of creditors' or contributories' meetings.

GENERAL NOTE

This section links in with the procedures for the appointment of an administrator (IA 1986, ss. 8ff. and Sch. B1) and for instituting a scheme of voluntary arrangement (IA 1986, ss. 1ff.). If a compulsory winding up follows immediately upon the termination of an administration or a voluntary arrangement, an insolvency practitioner who is fully aware of the company's circumstances will already be in office as the administrator or supervisor of the scheme, and it may make good sense to appoint him to the post of liquidator at the time when the winding-up order is made, so that he can get on with the conduct of the liquidation straightaway. Many of the formalities which are necessary in the case of a normal winding-up order can be by-passed in such a case. In *Re Charnley Davies Business Services Ltd* (1987) 3 B.C.C. 408, the court (with some reluctance) appointed the former administrator as liquidator even though litigation was pending in which his conduct while administrator was to be challenged as irregular.

Subsection (1) was reworded by EA 2002, s. 248 and Sch. B1, para. 17, to reflect the fact that a company may now be put into administration without a court order. The expression "the appointment of an administrator ceases to have effect" means "the administration is terminated": see Sch. B1, para. 1(2)(c), (d).

For the relevant rules, see IR 1986, rr. 4.49A, 4.102. Rule 4.49A, inserted by I(A)R 1987, deals with the situation where the existence of further creditors becomes known to the insolvency practitioner who becomes liquidator.

S. 140(1), (2)

Section 140 does not empower the court to appoint as liquidator a person who has not previously occupied the position of administrator or supervisor, whether alone or as an additional liquidator (*Re Exchange Travel (Holdings) Ltd* [1992] B.C.C. 954). If an appointment is not made under this section, the normal procedure under ss. 136 and 139 must be followed.

Liquidation committees

141 Liquidation committee (England and Wales)

141(1) [**Meetings may establish committee**] Where a winding-up order has been made by the court in England and Wales and separate meetings of creditors and contributories have been summoned for the purpose of choosing a person to be liquidator, those meetings may establish a committee ("the liquidation committee") to exercise the functions conferred on it by or under this Act.

141(2) [**Separate meetings may be summoned**] The liquidator (not being the official receiver) may at any time, if he thinks fit, summon separate general meetings of the company's creditors and contributories for the purpose of determining whether such a committee should be established and, if it is so determined, of establishing it.

The liquidator (not being the official receiver) shall summon such a meeting if he is requested, in accordance with the rules, to do so by one-tenth, in value, of the company's creditors.

141(3) **[Where meetings disagree]** Where meetings are summoned under this section, or for the purpose of choosing a person to be liquidator, and either the meeting of creditors or the meeting of contributories decides that a liquidation committee should be established, but the other meeting does not so decide or decides that a committee should not be established, the committee shall be established in accordance with the rules, unless the court otherwise orders.

141(4) **[Committee not to function where official receiver liquidator]** The liquidation committee is not to be able or required to carry out its functions at any time when the official receiver is liquidator; but at any such time its functions are vested in the Secretary of State except to the extent that the rules otherwise provide.

141(5) **[Where no committee etc.]** Where there is for the time being no liquidation committee, and the liquidator is a person other than the official receiver, the functions of such a committee are vested in the Secretary of State except to the extent that the rules otherwise provide.

GENERAL NOTE

Prior to the reforms effected by IA 1985, 1986, the "committee of inspection" had been a feature of the law of bankruptcy and company liquidation for over a century. The title (said to be of Scottish origin) had become a misnomer, as the Cork Committee (*Report*, para. 930) observed, for "inspection" (presumably, of the company's books) has not been part of the role of such a committee in recent practice. The Cork Committee recommended that the committee should be retained, to receive regular reports on the progress of the liquidation, to refer any grievances that they might have to the court, and also to discharge the traditional statutory function of giving consent on behalf of the creditors generally to certain courses of action by the liquidator. It was further recommended that similar committees should be established for other insolvency procedures, such as administration and administrative receivership; and finally that the name "committee of inspection" should be abandoned.

In the present Act, the title "liquidation committee" has been substituted, both here and in relation to a creditors' voluntary winding up (s. 101), while for the purposes of an administration (s. 26) and an administrative receivership (ss. 49, 68), where it is composed entirely of creditors, it is called the "creditors' committee" or "committee of creditors".

In marked contrast to the detailed provisions of s. 101, the present section has nothing to say about the composition of the committee, but this is clarified by the rules. It is stated in IR 1986, r. 4.152 that the committee shall consist of between three and five creditors and also (if the company is solvent) up to three contributories. Once the creditors have all been paid in full, the creditor members of the committee cease to be members: r. 4.171(4).

S. 141(1), (2)
The liquidation committee has no role to play while the official receiver is liquidator, as is confirmed by later subsections, and so the machinery for establishing a committee comes into operation only when there is a private liquidator, or when the appointment of a private liquidator is contemplated. The present provisions should be read in conjunction with ss. 136(4), 137(5), 139 and 140(3).

Where a liquidator has been appointed by court order under s. 140, following upon an administration or voluntary arrangement, s. 141(2) will apply, so that he or the creditors may take steps to establish a liquidation committee even though the official receiver is released from his duties in this regard by s. 140(3).

S. 141(4), (5)
A number of provisions in the Act empower the liquidator to act "with the consent of the liquidation committee" (see, *e.g.* s. 167(1)(a)), while others require him to give notice to the committee of what he has done (see, *e.g.* s. 167(2)). By substituting the Secretary of State for the committee in the circumstances set out, the present subsections enable the liquidator to exercise such powers when there is no committee or none competent to act.

The rules which have been made for the purposes of this section are IR 1986, rr. 4.151ff. and, for s. 141(4), (5), r. 4.172. For further guidance, see [2001] Insolvency Intelligence, p. 61.

142 Liquidation committee (Scotland)

142(1) **[Establishing committees in Scotland]** Where a winding-up order has been made by the court in Scotland and separate meetings of creditors and contributories have been summoned for the purpose of choosing a person to be liquidator or, under section 138(4), only a meeting of creditors has been summoned for that purpose, those meetings or (as the case may be) that meeting may establish a committee ("the liquidation committee") to exercise the functions conferred on it by or under this Act.

142(2) **[Separate meetings may be summoned]** The liquidator may at any time, if he thinks fit, summon separate general meetings of the company's creditors and contributories for the purpose of determining whether such a committee should be established and, if it is so determined, of establishing it.

142(3) **[Meetings to be summoned on request]** The liquidator, if appointed by the court otherwise than under section 139(4)(a), is required to summon meetings under subsection (2) if he is requested, in accordance with the rules, to do so by one-tenth, in value, of the company's creditors.

142(4) **[Where meetings disagree]** Where meetings are summoned under this section, or for the purpose of choosing a person to be liquidator, and either the meeting of creditors or the meeting of contributories decides that a liquidation committee should be established, but the other meeting does not so decide or decides that a committee should not be established, the committee shall be established in accordance with the rules, unless the court otherwise orders.

142(5) **[Where no committee etc.]** Where in the case of any winding up there is for the time being no liquidation committee, the functions of such a committee are vested in the court except to the extent that the rules otherwise provide.

142(6) **[Powers and duties of committee]** In addition to the powers and duties conferred and imposed on it by this Act, a liquidation committee has such of the powers and duties of commissioners in a sequestration as may be conferred and imposed on such committees by the rules.

GENERAL NOTE

This section contains provisions for Scotland similar to those laid down for England and Wales by s. 141, and the notes to that section generally apply here also, apart from the references to the official receiver, who of course has no Scottish counterpart.

The liquidator's functions

143 General functions in winding up by the court

143(1) **[Functions]** The functions of the liquidator of a company which is being wound up by the court are to secure that the assets of the company are got in, realised and distributed to the company's creditors and, if there is a surplus, to the persons entitled to it.

143(2) **[Duty of liquidator not official receiver]** It is the duty of the liquidator of a company which is being wound up by the court in England and Wales, if he is not the official receiver–

(a) to furnish the official receiver with such information,

(b) to produce to the official receiver, and permit inspection by the official receiver of, such books, papers and other records, and

(c) to give the official receiver such other assistance,

as the official receiver may reasonably require for the purposes of carrying out his functions in relation to the winding up.

S. 143(1)
The functions of a liquidator in a compulsory winding up are expressed in this subsection rather differently from those of a liquidator in a voluntary liquidation, set out in s. 107; but in substance their duties are broadly the same; and similar rules apply regarding the application of assets: see the notes to s. 107.

S. 143(2)
On the liquidator's duties of care, etc, see the note to s. 212; and on enforcement of the liquidator's obligations, see IR 1986, r. 7.20.

144 Custody of company's property

144(1) [**Liquidator to take property into custody**] When a winding-up order has been made, or where a provisional liquidator has been appointed, the liquidator or the provisional liquidator (as the case may be) shall take into his custody or under his control all the property and things in action to which the company is or appears to be entitled.

144(2) [**In Scotland where no liquidator**] In a winding up by the court in Scotland, if and so long as there is no liquidator, all the property of the company is deemed to be in the custody of the court.

S. 144(1)
The term "property" has a very comprehensive definition for the purposes of the present Act: see s. 436.
It is also the duty of the liquidator to take control of assets held by the company on trust, although such assets are not available for distribution under the winding up. On the question of the liquidator's right to remuneration and his costs and expenses incurred in performing the company's functions as trustee, see the note to rr. 4.127–4.131.

S. 144(2)
There is no equivalent to this provision for England and Wales in view of s. 136(2), (3), which ensures that the official receiver holds the office of liquidator if there is any vacancy.

145 Vesting of company property in liquidator

145(1) [**Court order**] When a company is being wound up by the court, the court may on the application of the liquidator by order direct that all or any part of the property of whatsoever description belonging to the company or held by trustees on its behalf shall vest in the liquidator by his official name; and thereupon the property to which the order relates vests accordingly.

145(2) [**Action re property by liquidator**] The liquidator may, after giving such indemnity (if any) as the court may direct, bring or defend in his official name any action or other legal proceeding which relates to that property or which it is necessary to bring or defend for the purpose of effectually winding up the company and recovering its property.

GENERAL NOTE

The estate of a bankrupt individual vests automatically in his trustee by operation of law: see s. 306. In contrast, the property of a company which is in liquidation remains vested in it unless an order is sought under the present section.

S. 145(1)
It is normally unnecessary to have a vesting order made, in view of the wide powers conferred on the liquidator to act in the company's name (see Sch. 4). However, an order may be needed in special circumstances: *e.g.* where the company is a foreign company which has already been wound up or dissolved in its home jurisdiction; or where the body is unincorporated and is being wound up as an "unregistered company" under ss. 220ff.

S. 145(2)
The liquidator would normally bring and defend actions in the name of the company: see Sch. 4, para. 4.

146 Duty to summon final meeting

146(1) [**Summoning final meeting**] Subject to the next subsection, if it appears to the liquidator of a company which is being wound up by the court that the winding up of the company is for practical purposes complete and the liquidator is not the official receiver, the liquidator shall summon a final general meeting of the company's creditors which–

(a) shall receive the liquidator's report of the winding up, and

(b) shall determine whether the liquidator should have his release under section 174 in Chapter VII of this Part.

146(2) **[Time for notice]** The liquidator may, if he thinks fit, give the notice summoning the final general meeting at the same time as giving notice of any final distribution of the company's property but, if summoned for an earlier date, that meeting shall be adjourned (and, if necessary, further adjourned) until a date on which the liquidator is able to report to the meeting that the winding up of the company is for practical purposes complete.

146(3) **[Retention of sums]** In the carrying out of his functions in the winding up it is the duty of the liquidator to retain sufficient sums from the company's property to cover the expenses of summoning and holding the meeting required by this section.

GENERAL NOTE

This section applies only where a company is being wound up by the court and the liquidator is not the official receiver. It introduces a marked change from the former procedure under CA 1985, s. 545, by which the liquidator obtained his release. Previously, the liquidator had to apply for a release to the Secretary of State. He is now required instead to report to the meeting of creditors on the completion of the liquidation and it is left to that meeting to determine whether he should have his release. The creditors are thus kept in the picture throughout the winding up and the liquidator made accountable to them, and at the same time the Secretary of State is relieved from the burden of examining the liquidator's accounts, etc., in order to determine whether he is entitled to his release. The present provision complements, and in part runs parallel to, ss. 94 and 106 which apply respectively in a members' and creditors' voluntary winding up.

S. 146(1)
Where the official receiver is the liquidator, the question of his release is for the Secretary of State to determine: see s. 174(3). The procedure governing the summoning and conduct of the meeting is in IR 1986, r. 4.125.

S. 146(2), (3)
It is clear that the winding up must in fact be completed and the company's property finally distributed (apart from what needs to be retained under s. 146(3)): the meeting cannot grant the liquidator a prospective or conditional release.

The liquidator must give notice to the court and the registrar of companies that the meeting has been held and report what decisions were made: see s. 172(8).

General powers of court

147 Power to stay or sist winding up

147(1) **[Court may order stay on application]** The court may at any time after an order for winding up, on the application either of the liquidator or the official receiver or any creditor or contributory, and on proof to the satisfaction of the court that all proceedings in the winding up ought to be stayed or sisted, make an order staying or sisting the proceedings, either altogether or for a limited time, on such terms and conditions as the court thinks fit.

147(2) **[Report by official receiver]** The court may, before making an order, require the official receiver to furnish to it a report with respect to any facts or matters which are in his opinion relevant to the application.

147(3) **[Copy of order to registrar]** A copy of every order made under this section shall forthwith be forwarded by the company, or otherwise as may be prescribed, to the registrar of companies, who shall enter it in his records relating to the company.

S. 147(1)
An order for the stay (or, in Scotland, sist) of the winding-up proceedings may be made either for a limited time, or "altogether". In the latter case, the order for liquidation is, in effect, terminated; the liquidator will then be entitled to a discharge and the directors reinstated in control. For the principles on which the court will grant or refuse a stay, see *Re Lowston Ltd* [1991] B.C.L.C. 570.

Prior to the 1986 legislation, it was not possible to rescind a winding-up order altogether: the nearest possible thing was the grant of a permanent stay. The consequence was that, technically, the company remained subject to the order, although its operation was suspended. In this situation, a copy of the winding-up order remains on the file at Companies House (see IA 1986, s. 130(1)), where it can be the source of misunderstanding (*e.g.* in relation to credit references). It is now possible, however, for the court to rescind a winding-up order under IR 1986, r. 7.47(1) (*e.g.* on the ground of mistake), and declare it to have been a nullity. The registrar is then bound to remove the order from his files: *Re Calmex Ltd* [1989] 1 All E.R. 485; (1988) 4 B.C.C. 761. However, the jurisdiction to rescind is to be exercised very cautiously, and only to correct an obvious injustice (*Leicester v Stevenson* [2003] 2 B.C.L.C. 97).

A stay may be granted on the ground of forum non conveniens, *i.e.* that the courts of another jurisdiction are more appropriately placed to deal with the proceedings: see the note to s. 125(1).

S. 147(2)
The officers of the company and its employees and others specified are under a duty to co-operate with the official receiver: see s. 235.

S. 147(3)
No regulations appear to have been prescribed for the purposes of this section; but IR 1986, r. 4.48 empowers the court to impose requirements as to notification.

148 Settlement of list of contributories and application of assets

148(1) [**Court's duties**] As soon as may be after making a winding-up order, the court shall settle a list of contributories, with power to rectify the register of members in all cases where rectification is required in pursuance of the Companies Act or this Act, and shall cause the company's assets to be collected, and applied in discharge of its liabilities.

148(2) [**Court may dispense with list**] If it appears to the court that it will not be necessary to make calls on or adjust the rights of contributories, the court may dispense with the settlement of a list of contributories.

148(3) [**Distinction between types of contributories**] In settling the list, the court shall distinguish between persons who are contributories in their own right and persons who are contributories as being representatives of or liable for the debts of others.

S. 148(1)
On the meaning of contributories, and their liability, see the note to s. 74 above.

The powers conferred by this section have been delegated to the liquidator by rules made under s. 160, below; but the power to rectify the register of members may be exercised by the liquidator only with the special leave of the court: s. 160(2). For the relevant rules, see IR 1986, rr. 4.195ff.

The general power of the court to rectify the register of members (*e.g.* in the case of omission or mistake) is contained in CA 1985, s. 359.

The principles governing the application of assets in a voluntary winding up (s. 107) and in a winding up by the court under this section are substantially equivalent. See further the note to that section.

On the order of priority of the expenses of a liquidation *inter se*, see IR 1986, rr. 4.218–4.220, and the note to s. 156.

S. 148(2)
This would apply, in particular, where the shares are fully paid.

S. 148(3)
The categories of contributories are known as the "A List" and "B List" contributories. The circumstances in which the latter are liable to contribute are set out in in s. 74(2); see also ss. 75, 76.

149 Debts due from contributory to company

149(1) [**Court may order payment from contributory**] The court may, at any time after making a winding-up order, make an order on any contributory for the time being on the list of contributories to pay, in manner directed by the order, any money due from him (or from the estate of the person whom he represents) to the company, exclusive of any money payable by him or the estate by virtue of any call in pursuance of the Companies Act or this Act.

149(2) [**Allowances and set-offs**] The court in making such an order may–

(a) in the case of an unlimited company, allow to the contributory by way of set-off any money due to him or the estate which he represents from the company on any independent dealing or contract with the company, but not any money due to him as a member of the company in respect of any dividend or profit, and

(b) in the case of a limited company, make to any director or manager whose liability is unlimited or to his estate the like allowance.

149(3) [**Money due to contributory may be allowed when creditors paid**] In the case of any company, whether limited or unlimited, when all the creditors are paid in full (together with interest at the official rate), any money due on any account whatever to a contributory from the company may be allowed to him by way of set-off against any subsequent call.

S. 149(1)
This provision allows the liquidator to recover in a summary way moneys (other than calls, which are dealt with in s. 150) due by a member to the company, thus avoiding the formality of a conventional action. However, it is confined to sums owed by the member *qua* member, *e.g.* dividends improperly paid to him, and may not be used to claim an ordinary debt: *Re Marlborough Club Co.* (1868) L.R. 5 Eq. 365. One consequence of this is that the contributory loses his normal right as a debtor to set off against such a claim any sums due from the company to him (*Re Whitehouse & Co.* (1878) 9 Ch.D. 595), apart from the special case where a contributory's liability is unlimited, which is dealt with in s. 149(2).

S. 149(2)
The right of set-off in the two situations of unlimited liability referred to is not automatic, but rests in the discretion of the court. No set-off lies in any case in regard to dividends or profits payable to the member, in keeping with the principle expressed in s. 74(2)(f).

On the question of set-off generally, see the general comment preceding s. 175.

S. 149(3)
The restrictions as to set-off described in the notes to s. 149(1) and (2) no longer apply once the claims of the general creditors have been fully satisfied.

On the entitlement of a creditor to interest, see the note to s. 189.

150 Power to make calls

150(1) [**Court may make calls to satisfy debts**] The court may, at any time after making a winding-up order, and either before or after it has ascertained the sufficiency of the company's assets, make calls on all or any of the contributories for the time being settled on the list of the contributories to the extent of their liability, for payment of any money which the court considers necessary to satisfy the company's debts and liabilities, and the expenses of winding up, and for the adjustment of the rights of the contributories among themselves, and make an order for payment of any calls so made.

150(2) [**Matters to be considered**] In making a call the court may take into consideration the probability that some of the contributories may partly or wholly fail to pay it.

S. 150(1)
This provision authorises the court to settle the liability of contributories to pay calls, and to enforce this liability in a summary way. The powers of the court have been delegated to the liquidator by regulations made under s. 160(1): see IR 1986, rr. 4.195, 4.202ff. In regard to the making of calls, the rules provide for the liquidator to act with the alternative sanction of the liquidation committee: r. 4.203. The liquidator may not act without authorisation unless the court gives special leave: s. 160(2).

S. 150(2)
The court may take into account the likelihood that some contributories may default, so saving the need for a further call on the remainder. If the amount thus raised is surplus to the liquidator's needs, it is of course returnable under s. 154.

151 Payment into bank of money due to company

151(1) [**Court may order payment into Bank of England**] The court may order any contributory, purchaser or other person from whom money is due to the company to pay the amount due into the Bank of England (or any branch of it) to the account of the liquidator instead of to the liquidator, and such an order may be enforced in the same manner as if it had directed payment to the liquidator.

151(2) [**Moneys in Bank subject to court orders**] All money and securities paid or delivered into the Bank of England (or branch) in the event of a winding up by the court are subject in all respects to the orders of the court.

GENERAL NOTE

The power to order payment to be made direct to the Bank of England is not confined to calls and other sums due from contributories, but may be invoked in relation to any debtor.

152 Order on contributory to be conclusive evidence

152(1) [**Order evidence that money due**] An order made by the court on a contributory is conclusive evidence that the money (if any) thereby appearing to be due or ordered to be paid is due, but subject to any right of appeal.

152(2) [**Other matters stated in order**] All other pertinent matters stated in the order are to be taken as truly stated as against all persons and in all proceedings except proceedings in Scotland against the heritable estate of a deceased contributory; and in that case the order is only prima facie evidence for the purpose of charging his heritable estate, unless his heirs or legatees of heritage were on the list of contributories at the time of the order being made.

GENERAL NOTE

This section applies only to orders against contributories, but it is not confined to orders for the payment of calls.

153 Power to exclude creditors not proving in time

153 The court may fix a time or times within which creditors are to prove their debts or claims or to be excluded from the benefit of any distribution made before those debts are proved.

GENERAL NOTE

A creditor who does not prove his debt within the time fixed by the court is excluded from participating in any distribution made before he proves, but his right to prove is not itself affected, and he may be paid out of such assets as remain or later become available. See further IR 1986, rr. 4.182(2) and 11.2(2).

The power of the court under this section may be delegated by rules to the liquidator: see s. 160(1). There does not appear to have been any specific exercise of this power in IR 1986, but the same result is achieved, in effect, by r. 11.2.

A creditor may, of course, be barred from claiming by the operation of the statutes of limitation. In *Re Joshua Shaw & Sons Ltd* (1989) 5 B.C.C. 188 the debts of all the company's unsecured creditors, apart from the Crown, became statute-barred during the course of a long-running receivership. The ironic consequence was that the surplus which was found to exist at the conclusion of the receivership went to the company's shareholders.

154 Adjustment of rights of contributories

154 The court shall adjust the rights of the contributories among themselves and distribute any surplus among the persons entitled to it.

GENERAL NOTE

For the corresponding provision in a voluntary winding up, see s. 107.
 For the relevant rules, see IR 1986, rr. 4.221ff.

155 Inspection of books by creditors, etc.

155(1) [**Court may make order for inspection**] The court may, at any time after making a winding-up order, make such order for inspection of the company's books and papers by creditors and contributories as the court thinks just; and any books and papers in the company's possession may be inspected by creditors and contributories accordingly, but not further or otherwise.

155(2) [**Statutory rights of government department**] Nothing in this section excludes or restricts any statutory rights of a government department or person acting under the authority of a government department.

155(3) [**Government department includes Scottish Administration**] For the purposes of sub-section (2) above, references to a government department shall be construed as including references to any part of the Scottish Administration.

S. 155(1)
The company's books and papers are not ordinarily accessible even to members while the company is a going concern; and although this section does confer such a right on creditors and contributories in a winding up, subject to the leave of the court, there are dicta which state that the court's leave will in practice be granted only for purposes directly connected with the liquidation: *Re North Brazilian Sugar Factories* (1887) 37 Ch.D. 83; *Re D P R Futures Ltd* [1989] 1 W.L.R. 778; (1989) 5 B.C.C. 603. However, it is understood that the court will in fact grant leave in a suitable case, *e.g.* where a creditor needs to obtain information to defend a claim under a guarantee, or an insurance company to defend a claim made against it, even though the claim in question may not be so connected. The same cases also held that the court's jurisdiction under s. 155 extends only to books and papers in the possession of the company: it cannot, for instance, extend to documents formerly in the custody of the company which have been seized by the Serious Fraud Office.

S. 155(2)
The statutory rights most obviously referred to here are those of the Secretary of State, and inspectors appointed by him, under CA 1985, ss. 431ff.

S. 155(3)
This subsection was inserted by the Scotland Act 1998 (Consequential Modifications) Order 1999 (SI 1999/1820), arts 1(2), 4 and Sch. 2, Pt 1, para. 85, effective July 1, 1999.

156 Payment of expenses of winding up

156 The court may, in the event of the assets being insufficient to satisfy the liabilities, make an order as to the payment out of the assets of the expenses incurred in the winding up in such order of priority as the court thinks just.

GENERAL NOTE

On the meaning of "assets" in the context of the present section, see the note to s. 115.

The rules contain provisions dealing with the payment of expenses of a winding up in the normal case, but subject to any order of the court: IR 1986, rr. 4.218, 4.220. The present section gives the court the power to make such an order where it is appropriate, but the power is limited to varying the order of priority and does not extend to making an order giving priority to costs that are not so entitled: *Re R S & M Engineering Co. Ltd* [2000] Ch. 40; [2000] B.C.C. 445. The court will only in exceptional circumstances exercise its jurisdiction under this section to confer on the liquidator's remuneration, or any part of it, priority over liquidation expenses which would normally rank before it: *Re Linda Marie Ltd (in liquidation)* (1988) 4 B.C.C. 463.

In relation to the financial markets and securities settlement systems, s. 156 has effect subject to the priority accorded to the claim of a participant or central bank to collateral security by the Finality Regulations, reg. 14(5), (6), unless the terms on which the collateral security was provided expressly state that the expenses, remuneration or preferential debts are to have priority: see the note on p. 3.

157 Attendance at company meetings (Scotland)

157 In the winding up by the court of a company registered in Scotland, the court has power to require the attendance of any officer of the company at any meeting of creditors or of contributories, or of a liquidation committee, for the purpose of giving information as to the trade, dealings, affairs or property of the company.

GENERAL NOTE

There is no direct counterpart of this provision for England and Wales.

158 Power to arrest absconding contributory

158 The court, at any time either before or after making a winding-up order, on proof of probable cause for believing that a contributory is about to quit the United Kingdom or otherwise to abscond or to remove or conceal any of his property for the purpose of evading payment of calls, may cause the contributory to be arrested and his books and papers and movable personal property to be seized and him and them to be kept safely until such time as the court may order.

GENERAL NOTE

The former legislation, after the phrase "for the purpose of evading calls" contained the additional words "or of avoiding examination respecting the company's affairs". These words have been deleted; the point is amply covered elsewhere in the Act: see s. 236(5).

159 Powers of court to be cumulative

159 Powers conferred by this Act and the Companies Act on the court are in addition to, and not in restriction of, any existing powers of instituting proceedings against a contributory or debtor of the company, or the estate of any contributory or debtor, for the recovery of any call or other sums.

160 Delegation of powers to liquidator (England and Wales)

160(1) [Delegation by rules] Provision may be made by rules for enabling or requiring all or any of the powers and duties conferred and imposed on the court in England and Wales by the Companies Act and this Act in respect of the following matters–

(a) the holding and conducting of meetings to ascertain the wishes of creditors and contributories,

(b) the settling of lists of contributories and the rectifying of the register of members where required, and the collection and application of the assets,

(c) the payment, delivery, conveyance, surrender or transfer of money, property, books or papers to the liquidator,

(d) the making of calls,

(e) the fixing of a time within which debts and claims must be proved,

to be exercised or performed by the liquidator as an officer of the court, and subject to the court's control.

160(2) [No rectification etc. without special leave] But the liquidator shall not, without the special leave of the court, rectify the register of members, and shall not make any call without either that special leave or the sanction of the liquidation committee.

GENERAL NOTE

For the relevant rules, see IR 1986, rr. 4.54ff. (meetings); 4.179ff. (assets); 4.185 (surrender of books, etc.); 4.195ff. (list of contributories); 4.196 (rectifying register); 4.202ff. (calls), and see the note to s. 153 (time for proving).

161 Orders for calls on contributories (Scotland)

161(1) [Court may order calls on contributories on receipt of list] In Scotland, where an order, interlocutor or decree has been made for winding up a company by the court, it is competent to the court, on production by the liquidators of a list certified by them of the names of the contributories liable in payment of any calls, and of the amount due by each contributory, and of the date when that amount became due, to pronounce forthwith a decree against those contributories for payment of the sums so certified to be due, with interest from that date until payment (at 5 per cent per annum) in the same way and to the same effect as if they had severally consented to registration for execution, on a charge of 6 days, of a legal obligation to pay those calls and interest.

161(2) [Extraction of decree] The decree may be extracted immediately, and no suspension of it is competent, except on caution or consignation, unless with special leave of the court.

GENERAL NOTE

The procedure for making calls on contributories in a winding up by the court in England and Wales is prescribed in rather different terms by s. 160(1)(d) and the rules made thereunder.

162 Appeals from orders in Scotland

162(1) [Appeal from order on winding up] Subject to the provisions of this section and to rules of court, an appeal from any order or decision made or given in the winding up of a company by the court in Scotland under this Act lies in the same manner and subject to the same conditions as an appeal from an order or decision of the court in cases within its ordinary jurisdiction.

162(2) [Orders by judge acting as vacation judge] In regard to orders or judgments pronounced by the judge acting as vacation judge–

(a) none of the orders specified in Part I of Schedule 3 to this Act are subject to review, reduction, suspension or stay of execution, and

(b) every other order or judgment (except as mentioned below) may be submitted to review by the Inner House by reclaiming motion enrolled within 14 days from the date of the order or judgment.

162(3) [Order in Sch. 3, Pt II] However, an order being one of those specified in Part II of that Schedule shall, from the date of the order and notwithstanding that it has been submitted to review as above, be carried out and receive effect until the Inner House have disposed of the matter.

162(4) [Orders by Lord Ordinary] In regard to orders of judgments pronounced in Scotland by a Lord Ordinary before whom proceedings in a winding up are being taken, any such order or judgment may be submitted to review by the Inner House by reclaiming motion enrolled within 14 days from its date; but should it not be so submitted to review during session, the provisions of this section in regard to orders or judgments pronounced by the judge acting as vacation judge apply.

162(5) [Decrees for payment of calls in winding up] Nothing in this section affects provisions of the Companies Act or this Act in reference to decrees in Scotland for payment of calls in the winding up of companies, whether voluntary or by the court.

GENERAL NOTE

This section deals with a number of special points of Scottish procedure. It should be read in conjunction with Sch. 3, below, which makes more detailed provisions for the purposes of s. 162(2) and (3).

Section 163　　　　　　　　　　　*Insolvency Act 1986*

CHAPTER VII

LIQUIDATORS

Preliminary

163　Style and title of liquidators

163　The liquidator of a company shall be described–

(a) where a person other than the official receiver is liquidator, by the style of "the liquidator" of the particular company, or

(b) where the official receiver is liquidator, by the style of "the official receiver and liquidator" of the particular company;

and in neither case shall he be described by an individual name.

164　Corrupt inducement affecting appointment

164　A person who gives, or agrees or offers to give, to any member or creditor of a company any valuable consideration with a view to securing his own appointment or nomination, or to securing or preventing the appointment or nomination of some person other than himself, as the company's liquidator is liable to a fine.

GENERAL NOTE

It is perhaps surprising that this old provision has survived the reforms made by IA 1985, including the requirement that a liquidator must now be a professional insolvency practitioner.
　On penalties, see s. 430 and Sch. 10.

Liquidator's powers and duties

165　Voluntary winding up

165(1)　**[Application]** This section has effect where a company is being wound up voluntarily, but subject to section 166 below in the case of a creditors' voluntary winding up.

165(2)　**[Powers in Sch. 4, Pt. I]** The liquidator may–

(a) in the case of a members' voluntary winding up, with the sanction of an extraordinary resolution of the company, and

(b) in the case of a creditors' voluntary winding up, with the sanction of the court or the liquidation committee (or, if there is no such committee, a meeting of the company's creditors),

exercise any of the powers specified in Part I of Schedule 4 to this Act (payment of debts, compromise of claims, etc.).

165(3)　**[Powers in Sch. 4, Pt. II, III]** The liquidator may, without sanction, exercise either of the powers specified in Part II of that Schedule (institution and defence of proceedings; carrying on the business of the company) and any of the general powers specified in Part III of that Schedule.

165(4) [Other powers] The liquidator may–

(a) exercise the court's power of settling a list of contributories (which list is prima facie evidence of the liability of the persons named in it to be contributories),

(b) exercise the court's power of making calls,

(c) summon general meetings of the company for the purpose of obtaining its sanction by special or extraordinary resolution or for any other purpose he may think fit.

165(5) [Duty re payment of debts] The liquidator shall pay the company's debts and adjust the rights of the contributories among themselves.

165(6) [Notice to committee re exercise of powers] Where the liquidator in exercise of the powers conferred on him by this Act disposes of any property of the company to a person who is connected with the company (within the meaning of section 249 in Part VII), he shall, if there is for the time being a liquidation committee, give notice to the committee of that exercise of his powers.

GENERAL NOTE

This section deals with the powers and duties of the liquidator in a voluntary winding up. It is to be read in conjunction with Sch. 4, in which some powers are set out in detail. Note the limitation on powers with regard to property covered by s. 426 of the POCA 2002.

S. 165(1)
The relationship between ss. 165 and 166 is a little confusing. Section 165 applies to every voluntary winding up, *including* a creditors' voluntary winding up where the liquidator has been nominated by the company; but s. 166 supplements s. 165 in the latter case (1) by imposing restrictions on the powers exercisable by the liquidator pending the holding of the creditors' meeting, and (2) by imposing on the liquidator the duty of attending the creditors' meeting (see s. 166(4)).

S. 165(2)
Schedule 4 is divided into three Parts, listing respectively:

Pt. I: powers exercisable with sanction;

Pt. II: powers exercisable without sanction in a voluntary winding up, but with sanction in a winding up by the court; and

Pt. III: powers exercisable without sanction in any winding up.

The present subsection relates to Pt I of the Schedule and specifies the appropriate sanctioning body in each case.

S. 165(3)
In the case of a voluntary winding up, no distinction is made between the powers listed in Pt II and those in Pt III of the Schedule. No sanction is required for the exercise of any of these powers.

S. 165(4)
These are matters for which, in the case of a winding up by the court, power is in the first instance conferred by the Act upon the court itself, but then normally delegated to the liquidator by rules made under s. 160. Note, however, that under the present section the liquidator in a voluntary winding up may make calls without any sanction (para. (b)), in contrast with s. 160(2) which stipulates that in a compulsory winding up he may do so only with the special leave of the court.

Reference should be made also to s. 112, which empowers the court to determine questions and exercise powers in a voluntary winding up as if the company were being wound up by the court.

S. 165(5)
There is some overlap between this provision and s. 107. On the application of assets generally, see the note to that section.

Section 166   Insolvency Act 1986

S. 165(6)
This provision, first introduced by IA 1985, is designed to ensure that, at least in any voluntary winding up where there is a liquidation committee, no property of the company shall be disposed of to someone "connected with" the company unless it is done with the modest amount of disclosure specified. (The legislators have not gone so far as to stipulate for the *sanction* of the committee.) No doubt this requirement is part of the general package of measures aimed at the abuse known as the "phoenix syndrome" (see the note to s. 216, below). If there is no liquidation committee, s. 141(5) applies, vesting the relevant powers in the Secretary of State.

The category of persons "connected with" a company is very widely defined, and includes a director, employee or controlling shareholder, a close relative of any of these persons, and a company in the same group. See the notes to ss. 249 and 435, below.

166   Creditors' voluntary winding up

166(1)   [Application] This section applies where, in the case of a creditors' voluntary winding up, a liquidator has been nominated by the company.

166(2)   [Non-exercise of s. 165 powers] The powers conferred on the liquidator by section 165 shall not be exercised, except with the sanction of the court, during the period before the holding of the creditors' meeting under section 98 in Chapter IV.

166(3)   [Non-application of s. 166(2)] Subsection (2) does not apply in relation to the power of the liquidator–

(a)   to take into his custody or under his control all the property to which the company is or appears to be entitled;

(b)   to dispose of perishable goods and other goods the value of which is likely to diminish if they are not immediately disposed of; and

(c)   to do all such other things as may be necessary for the protection of the company's assets.

166(4)   [Liquidator to attend s. 98 meeting] The liquidator shall attend the creditors' meeting held under section 98 and shall report to the meeting on any exercise by him of his powers (whether or not under this section or under section 112 or 165).

166(5)   [Where default re s. 98, 99] If default is made–

(a)   by the company in complying with subsection (1) or (2) of section 98, or

(b)   by the directors in complying with subsection (1) or (2) of section 99,

the liquidator shall, within 7 days of the relevant day, apply to the court for directions as to the manner in which that default is to be remedied.

166(6)   ["The relevant day"] "The relevant day" means the day on which the liquidator was nominated by the company or the day on which he first became aware of the default, whichever is the later.

166(7)   [Penalty for non-compliance] If the liquidator without reasonable excuse fails to comply with this section, he is liable to a fine.

GENERAL NOTE

This section should be read in conjunction with ss. 98 and 114, above. Taken together, they should ensure (as is undoubtedly intended) that the practice which had become notorious under the name of "centrebinding" is totally stamped out. The abuse takes it name from the case of *Re Centrebind Ltd* [1967] 1 W.L.R. 377, where the members of an insolvent company resolved to go into voluntary liquidation and appointed their own liquidator who, before any creditors' meeting had been held, took immediate steps to restrain the Inland Revenue from proceeding with a distress on the company's assets. Plowman J. held that the liquidator had power to act until the creditors' meeting had been held.

Although the acts of the company and its liquidator in the *Centrebind* case itself were done entirely in good faith, it was not long before the practice developed of calling only a shareholders' meeting in the first instance to pass a winding-up resolution and, although the company was known to be insolvent, deliberately putting off for some time, or perhaps indefinitely, the holding of the creditors' meeting. This, of course, involved a technical breach of the Companies Act (CA 1985, s. 588(2)), which required the latter meeting to be held on the same day as the members' meeting or the very next day and, indeed, was a criminal offence. However, it meant that the controllers of a company, with the aid of an unscrupulous liquidator nominated by them, could effectively sell the assets off at a knock-down price to a purchaser closely connected with themselves (*e.g.* a new company controlled by them), and the creditors were powerless to prevent it.

The introduction by IA 1985 of a mandatory requirement that liquidators shall be of professional standing is probably in itself sufficient to ensure that "centrebinding" will no longer be part of insolvency practice; but the legislature has made doubly sure of this by provisions such as the present.

S. 166(1)
Where no liquidator has been nominated by the company the directors will remain in control of the company's property, but their powers will be limited to protecting the assets and disposing of perishable goods, unless they obtain the sanction of the court (see s. 114).

S. 166(2)
The provisions of s. 166 operate to qualify s. 165 only during the interval between the nomination of a liquidator by the company and the holding of the creditors' meeting – a period which ought not to exceed 14 days (see s. 98(1)(a)).

S. 166(3)
The restricted powers given to the liquidator (unless he has the sanction of the court under s. 166(2)) are, as regards paras (b) and (c), the same as those allowed to directors by s. 114(3). In addition he has, by para. (a), the power to take over custody and control of the company's property from the directors. The term "property" is widely defined: see s. 436.

S. 166(4), (5)
The obligations imposed on the company by s. 98 are to convene a creditor's meeting within 14 days of the company's own meeting and to give the appropriate notices; while under s. 99 the directors are required to make out a statement of affairs to be laid before the creditors' meeting and to depute one of their number to attend the meeting. The "relevant day" is defined in s. 166(6).

The language of s. 166(5) is permissive rather than mandatory. There is no obligation on the liquidator to apply for directions where there is no need for them: *Re Salcombe Hotel Development Co. Ltd* (1989) 5 B.C.C. 807.

S. 166(7)
On penalties, see s. 430 and Sch. 10.

167 Winding up by the court

167(1) **[Powers of liquidator]** Where a company is being wound up by the court, the liquidator may–

(a) with the sanction of the court or the liquidation committee, exercise any of the powers specified in Parts I and II of Schedule 4 to this Act (payment of debts; compromise of claims, etc.; institution and defence of proceedings; carrying on of the business of the company), and

(b) with or without that sanction, exercise any of the general powers specified in Part III of that Schedule.

167(2) **[Duty of liquidator]** Where the liquidator (not being the official receiver), in exercise of the powers conferred on him by this Act–

(a) disposes of any property of the company to a person who is connected with the company (within the meaning of section 249 in Part VII), or

(b) employs a solicitor to assist him in the carrying out of his functions,

he shall, if there is for the time being a liquidation committee, give notice to the committee of that exercise of his powers.

167(3) **[Control of court]** The exercise by the liquidator in a winding up by the court of the powers conferred by this section is subject to the control of the court, and any creditor or contributory may apply to the court with respect to any exercise or proposed exercise of any of those powers.

Section 168　　　　　　　　　　　　　Insolvency Act 1986

GENERAL NOTE

The liquidator, in a winding up by the court, is given specific powers and duties by various other sections of the Act. In addition, the present provision confers on him general powers by reference to Sch 4. Note the limitation on powers with regard to property covered by s. 426 of the POCA 2002.

S. 167(1)

Although every liquidator has all the powers listed in Sch. 4, those of a liquidator in a winding up by the court are more restricted, in that the powers specified in Pt II of the Schedule (instituting and defending proceedings, and carrying on the company's business) are exercisable only with the sanctions specified in para. (a). The rules state that any permission given under this section shall be given in the particular case, and not generally: see IR 1986, r. 4.184.

In exercising its powers under s. 167(1)(a) the court may have regard to the wishes of creditors and contributories (see s. 175), and a creditor or contributory is entitled to be heard on an application by the liquidator: *Re Greenhaven Motors Ltd* [1999] B.C.C. 463. However, the views of those who have no realistic prospect of participating in the ultimate distribution of assets will be disregarded: *Re Barings plc (No. 7)* [2002] 1 B.C.L.C. 401. The court will attach considerable weight to the views of the liquidator: *Re Edennote Ltd (No. 2)* [1997] 2 B.C.L.C. 89 at p. 92. But the court is exercising its own discretion and not reviewing a decision of the liquidator (where the basis on which the court will interfere is restricted): see *Re Greenhaven Motors Ltd* (above) and the notes to ss. 167(3) and 168(5).

S. 167(2)

This subsection, apart from para. (b) relating to the employment of a solicitor, is parallel to s. 165(6) which applies in a voluntary winding up. (Note that it does not apply where the official receiver is the liquidator.)

A transitional provision extends this power to liquidations existing at the commencement of the Act: see Sch. 11, para. 6(5).

S. 167(3)

There is no provision in the Act directly corresponding to this subsection which applies in a voluntary winding up, but the supervisory powers of the court may be invoked in such a case by an application made under s. 112.

The court is traditionally reluctant to interfere in the exercise of discretion by a liquidator, and will not do so where it has been exercised in good faith: see the note to s. 168(5), below. This is to be contrasted with the situation where the court is exercising its own discretion, as under s. 167(1)(a), above. In *Re Greenhaven Motors Ltd* [1997] B.C.C. 547 at first instance, Harman J. thought that a contributory should not be entitled to make an application under this subsection unless there was a real prospect that there would be assets available to yield him a substantial return, but on appeal ([1999] B.C.C. 463 at p. 466) this point was left open.

168　Supplementary powers (England and Wales)

168(1)　[Application] This section applies in the case of a company which is being wound up by the court in England and Wales.

168(2)　[Liquidator may summon general meetings] The liquidator may summon general meetings of the creditors or contributories for the purpose of ascertaining their wishes; and it is his duty to summon meetings at such times as the creditors or contributories by resolution (either at the meeting appointing the liquidator or otherwise) may direct, or whenever requested in writing to do so by one-tenth in value of the creditors or contributories (as the case may be).

168(3)　[Liquidator may apply to court for directions] The liquidator may apply to the court (in the prescribed manner) for directions in relation to any particular matter arising in the winding up.

168(4)　[Liquidator to use own discretion] Subject to the provisions of this Act, the liquidator shall use his own discretion in the management of the assets and their distribution among the creditors.

168(5)　[Application to court re acts of liquidator] If any person is aggrieved by an act or decision of the liquidator, that person may apply to the court; and the court may confirm, reverse or modify the act or decision complained of, and make such order in the case as it thinks just.

168(5A)　[Court order re insolvent partnerships] Where at any time after a winding-up petition has been presented to the court against any person (including an insolvent partnership or other body which may be wound up under Part V of the Act as an unregistered company), whether by virtue of the provisions of the Insolvent Partnerships Order 1994 or not, the attention of the court is drawn to the fact that the person in question is a member of an insolvent partnership, the court may make an order as to the future conduct of the insolvency proceedings and any such order may apply any provisions of that Order with any necessary modifications.

168(5B) [Order or directions under s. 168(5A)] Any order or directions under subsection (5A) may be made or given on the application of the official receiver, any responsible insolvency practitioner, the trustee of the partnership or any other interested person and may include provisions as to the administration of the joint estate of the partnership, and in particular how it and the separate estate of any member are to be administered.

168(5C) [Sections under which court order made re insolvent partnerships] Where the court makes an order for the winding up of an insolvent partnership under–

(a) section 72(1)(a) of the Financial Services Act 1986;

(b) section 92(1)(a) of the Banking Act 1987; or

(c) section 367(3)(a) of the Financial Services and Markets Act 2000,

the court may make an order as to the future conduct of the winding up proceedings, and any such order may apply any provisions of the Insolvent Partnerships Order 1994 with any necessary modifications.

GENERAL NOTE

This section provides in general terms for consultation between the liquidator and the meetings of creditors and contributories, either on his initiative or on requisition by one-tenth in value of those concerned, and also for the court to give directions and to supervise and control the acts and decisions of the liquidator.

For the rules relating to the summoning of meetings, see IR 1986, rr. 4.54ff., and as regard applications to the court, rr. 7.1ff.

S. 168(2)

Although this subsection imposes a duty on the liquidator who has received a requisition to summon a meeting, the court has jurisdiction to override that duty by directing him not to comply with it: *Re Barings plc, Hamilton v Law Debenture Trustees Ltd* [2001] 2 B.C.L.C. 159.

S. 168(5)

Notwithstanding the width of the words "may ... make such order in the case as it thinks just", the court will not normally review the exercise by the liquidator of his powers and discretions in the management and realisation of the corporate property. The court will only interfere with a decision of a liquidator if it was taken in bad faith or if it was so perverse as to demonstrate that no liquidator properly advised could have taken it: *Re a Debtor* [1949] Ch. 236 at p. 241; *Re Hans Place Ltd* [1992] B.C.C. 737 at pp. 745–746; *Leon v York-o-Matic Ltd* [1966] 1 W.L.R. 1450; *Re Greenhaven Motors Ltd* [1997] B.C.C. 547; *Re Edennote Ltd, Tottenham Hotspur v Ryman* [1996] B.C.C. 718; *Hamilton v Official Receiver* [1998] B.P.I.R. 602.

On the meaning of "person aggrieved", see the remarks of Warner J. (*obiter*) in *Re ACLI Metals (London) Ltd (AML Holdings Inc. v Auger)* (1989) 5 B.C.C. 749 at p. 754 and *Re Edennote Ltd* (above) at pp. 721–722. Apart from creditors and contributories, those who may apply are not "any outsider" who is dissatisfied with some act or decision of a liquidator, but rather persons directly affected by a power given specifically to a liquidator, such as a landlord following the disclaimer of a lease: *Mahomed v Morris* [2001] B.C.C. 233.

S.168(5A)–(5C)

These subsections were inserted by the Insolvent Partnerships Order 1994 (SI 1994/2421), arts. 1, 14(1) with effect from December 1, 1994. Subsection (5C) was briefly repealed by SI 2001/3649, arts. 1, 306 as from December 1, 2001 and then reinstated in revised form by SI 2002/1555, arts. 1, 15 as from July 3, 2002. They empower the court to make appropriate orders when a winding-up petition has been presented against any person (including a company, partnership or other body) and it appears that that person is a member of an insolvent partnership. Similar provisions apply in regard to bankruptcy petitions: see s. 303(2A)–(2C).

169 Supplementary powers (Scotland)

169(1) [Where no liquidation committee] In the case of a winding up in Scotland, the court may provide by order that the liquidator may, where there is no liquidation committee, exercise any of the following powers, namely–

Section 170   Insolvency Act 1986

(a) to bring or defend any action or other legal proceeding in the name and on behalf of the company, or

(b) to carry on the business of the company so far as may be necessary for its beneficial winding up,

without the sanction or intervention of the court.

169(2) **[Liquidator's powers]** In a winding up by the court in Scotland, the liquidator has (subject to the rules) the same powers as a trustee on a bankrupt estate.

S. 169(1)

This provision rather oddly allows the court to dispense with its own sanction where there is no liquidation committee. Where there is such a committee, one or other of the sanctions specified in s. 167(1)(a) must be obtained.

S. 169(2)

For the powers of the trustee on a bankrupt estate in Scotland, see the Bankruptcy (Scotland) Act 1985, especially ss. 38ff. For the relevant rules see the Insolvency (Scotland) Rules 1986 (SI 1986/1915 (S 139)), r. 4.68.

170 Enforcement of liquidator's duty to make returns, etc.

170(1) **[Powers of court if liquidator fails to file returns, etc.]** If a liquidator who has made any default–

(a) in filing, delivering or making any return, account or other document, or

(b) in giving any notice which he is by law required to file, deliver, make or give,

fails to make good the default within 14 days after the service on him of a notice requiring him to do so, the court has the following powers.

170(2) **[On application court may order to make good default]** On an application made by any creditor or contributory of the company, or by the registrar of companies, the court may make an order directing the liquidator to make good the default within such time as may be specified in the order.

170(3) **[Costs]** The court's order may provide that all costs of and incidental to the application shall be borne by the liquidator.

170(4) **[Penalties]** Nothing in this section prejudices the operation of any enactment imposing penalties on a liquidator in respect of any such default as is mentioned above.

GENERAL NOTE

This section contains provisions parallel to those in CA 1985, s. 713, which deal with the enforcement of such defaults against the company itself and its officers and are, of course, not confined to a winding up. A liquidator is not normally an "officer" for the purposes of the Companies Acts: see the note to s. 206(3).

Removal; vacation of office

171 Removal, etc. (voluntary winding up)

171(1) **[Application]** This section applies with respect to the removal from office and vacation of office of the liquidator of a company which is being wound up voluntarily.

171(2) **[Removal from office]** Subject to the next subsection, the liquidator may be removed from office only by an order of the court or–

(a) in the case of a members' voluntary winding up, by a general meeting of the company summoned specially for that purpose, or

(b) in the case of a creditors' voluntary winding up, by a general meeting of the company's creditors summoned specially for that purpose in accordance with the rules.

171(3) **[Where liquidator appointed by court under s. 108]** Where the liquidator was appointed by the court under section 108 in Chapter V, a meeting such as is mentioned in subsection (2) above shall be summoned for the purpose of replacing him only if he thinks fit or the court so directs or the meeting is requested, in accordance with the rules–

(a) in the case of a members' voluntary winding up, by members representing not less than one-half of the total voting rights of all the members having at the date of the request a right to vote at the meeting, or

(b) in the case of a creditors' voluntary winding up, by not less than one-half, in value, of the company's creditors.

171(4) **[Vacation of office]** A liquidator shall vacate office if he ceases to be a person who is qualified to act as an insolvency practitioner in relation to the company.

171(5) **[Resignation]** A liquidator may, in the prescribed circumstances, resign his office by giving notice of his resignation to the registrar of companies.

171(6) **[Where final meetings held]** Where–

(a) in the case of a members' voluntary winding up, a final meeting of the company has been held under section 94 in Chapter III, or

(b) in the case of a creditors' voluntary winding up, final meetings of the company and of the creditors have been held under section 106 in Chapter IV,

the liquidator whose report was considered at the meeting or meetings shall vacate office as soon as he has complied with subsection (3) of that section and has given notice to the registrar of companies that the meeting or meetings have been held and of the decisions (if any) of the meeting or meetings.

GENERAL NOTE

This section sets out in detail the manner by which a liquidator in a voluntary winding up may be removed or resign from his office, and the circumstances in which he must vacate it. It complements s. 172, which applies in a winding up by the court. Together, the two sections set out the legal position comprehensively and in some detail, in sharp contrast to the situation prior to IA 1985, where the legislation said virtually nothing about the matter (apart from CA 1985, s. 599(2), now IA 1986, s. 108(2), empowering the court to remove a liquidator "on cause shown"). An important consequence of this change is that the power of the company or of the contributories in general meeting to remove the liquidator in a creditors' voluntary winding up – even a liquidator whom they have themselves appointed – is no longer recognised.

For the liquidator's duties on vacating office, see IR 1986, rr. 4.138, 4.148. A liquidator who ought to have resigned but instead resists an application for his removal may be ordered to pay costs on an indemnity basis: *Shepheard v Lamey* [2001] B.P.I.R. 939.

On a petition for the compulsory winding up of a company which is already in voluntary liquidation, the court may decline to make an order where a more appropriate course would be to allow the voluntary winding up to continue and apply to the court to have the liquidator removed and replaced: see *Re Inside Sports Ltd* [2000] B.C.C. 40, at p. 43 (where on the special facts of the case a winding-up order was considered more appropriate).

S. 171(1), (2)

The members may remove a liquidator only in a members' voluntary winding up. The creditors alone have this power in a creditors' winding up, even where the liquidator was originally appointed by the members under s. 100(2).

For the rules prescribed for the purposes of s. 171(2)(b), see IR 1986, rr. 4.114, 4.120.

S. 171(3)

Section 108 empowers the court to appoint a liquidator in a voluntary winding up in the circumstances there set out. A liquidator so appointed may be removed:

(1) "on cause shown", by order of the court (s. 108(2));

(2) by the members or the creditors under s. 171(2), if the liquidator himself thinks it "fit" to summon a meeting for the purpose (s. 171(3));

(3) by the members or the creditors under s. 171(2) if the court so directs (s. 171(3)); or

(4) by the members or the creditors under s. 171(2), if the meeting is requested by members or creditors, as the case may be, having the necessary 50 per cent-plus majority stipulated for by s. 171(3)(a) or (b).

For the relevant rules, see IR 1986, r. 4.114.

Section 172   *Insolvency Act 1986*

S. 171(4)
The terms "act as an insolvency practitioner in relation to" a particular company, and "qualified to act as an insolvency practitioner" are defined respectively in s. 388(1) and s. 390.
 When a liquidator ceases to be qualified to act as an insolvency practitioner in relation to a company, he vacates office ipso facto and automatically, and does not continue in office until he has complied with his obligations under the rules to notify the registrar, etc. However, the former liquidator in a voluntary liquidation who has vacated office on the ground of disqualification is a proper person to make application to the court under s. 108 to have another liquidator appointed in his place (*Re A J. Adams (Builders) Ltd* [1991] B.C.C. 62).
 For the relevant rules, see IR 1986, rr. 4.135, 4.122.

S. 171(5)
The circumstances in which a liquidator may resign are defined in IR 1986, rr. 4.108(4), 4.142(3). Before resigning his office, the liquidator must summon a meeting of the company or the creditors (depending upon the category of winding up) for the purpose of receiving his resignation (rr. 4.108(1), 4.142(1)). (However, the court has an overriding power to make an order dispensing with this requirement: see the note to s. 172(1), (2).) The notice to the registrar must be given by the liquidator "forthwith after the meeting" (r. 4.110(2)). The meeting may decline to accept the resignation, in which event the liquidator may apply to the court for leave to resign (r. 4.111).

S. 171(6)
If the meeting in question was inquorate, so that the liquidator's report could not be considered, s. 94(5) and s. 106(5) respectively state that the liquidator shall be deemed to have complied with the requirements of the section in question. It would seem therefore that the words "whose report was considered at the meeting" in the present subsection should be taken to include such cases of deemed compliance.

172 Removal, etc. (winding up by the court)

172(1) **[Application]** This section applies with respect to the removal from office and vacation of office of the liquidator of a company which is being wound up by the court, or of a provisional liquidator.

172(2) **[Removal from office]** Subject as follows, the liquidator may be removed from office only by an order of the court or by a general meeting of the company's creditors summoned specially for that purpose in accordance with the rules; and a provisional liquidator may be removed from office only by an order of the court.

172(3) **[Replacing certain types of liquidator]** Where–

 (a) the official receiver is liquidator otherwise than in succession under section 136(3) to a person who held office as a result of a nomination by a meeting of the company's creditors or contributories, or

 (b) the liquidator was appointed by the court otherwise than under section 139(4)(a) or 140(1), or was appointed by the Secretary of State,

a general meeting of the company's creditors shall be summoned for the purpose of replacing him only if he thinks fit, or the court so directs, or the meeting is requested, in accordance with the rules, by not less than one-quarter, in value, of the creditors.

172(4) **[If liquidator appointed by Secretary of State]** If appointed by the Secretary of State, the liquidator may be removed from office by a direction of the Secretary of State.

172(5) **[Vacation of office]** A liquidator or provisional liquidator, not being the official receiver, shall vacate office if he ceases to be a person who is qualified to act as an insolvency practitioner in relation to the company.

172(6) **[Resignation]** A liquidator may, in the prescribed circumstances, resign his office by giving notice of his resignation to the court.

172(7) **[Where s. 204 order]** Where an order is made under section 204 (early dissolution in Scotland) for the dissolution of the company, the liquidator shall vacate office when the dissolution of the company takes effect in accordance with that section.

172(8) [Where final meeting under s. 146] Where a final meeting has been held under section 146 (liquidator's report on completion of winding up), the liquidator whose report was considered at the meeting shall vacate office as soon as he has given notice to the court and the registrar of companies that the meeting has been held and of the decisions (if any) of the meeting.

GENERAL NOTE

This section contains provisions, complementary to those in s. 171, which apply in a compulsory winding up. The notes to s. 171 apply generally to the present section also, subject to the additional points below.

S. 172(1), (2)
A provisional liquidator may be removed only by court order.

There is nothing in the present section which empowers the shareholders or contributories in general meeting to remove a liquidator, even in cases where the company is demonstrably solvent, and even where the original liquidator was the members' appointee.

Where a liquidator who has been appointed by the creditors wishes to vacate office, the creditors have the right to decide whether to accept his resignation and the court will not exercise its own power to do so without good reason: see *Re Sankey Furniture Ltd Ex p. Harding* [1995] 2 B.C.L.C. 594.

Although r. 4.108(1) states that it is mandatory for the liquidator to call a meeting of creditors before resigning his office, the court has an overriding power to by-pass this procedure and make orders for his removal and replacement without the statutory formalities. This course may be particularly appropriate where the insolvency practitioner concerned wishes to be relieved from multiple offices by making a single application. The terms on which such orders have been made in the past were examined by Neuberger J. in *Re Equity Nominees Ltd* [2000] B.C.C. 84 and a new form of order settled, dealing with the information to be given to creditors and the manner in which the outgoing liquidator should deal with the accounts of his administration. The Practice Direction: Insolvency Proceedings [2000] B.C.C. 927 (reproduced as Appendix IV of this *Guide*) has been amended to give guidance on the procedure. See also *Re Alt Landscapes Ltd* [1999] B.P.I.R. 459; *Re A & C Supplies Ltd* [1998] B.C.C. 708 and *Clements v Udal* [2002] 2 B.C.L.C. 606.

A contributory holding fully-paid shares in an insolvent company has no standing to apply to the court for an order removing a liquidator, on the analogy of *Re Rica Gold Washing Co.* (1879) 11 Ch.D. 36 (see the note to s. 124(2), (3) above): *Re Corbenstoke Ltd (No. 2)* (1989) 5 B.C.C. 767.

For the rules prescribed for the purposes of s. 172, see IR 1986, rr. 4.113ff.

S. 172(3)
The liquidator may be removed by a general meeting of the creditors without any special formality under s. 172(2) above only where:

(1) he was originally appointed by a meeting of the company's creditors or contributories (s. 172(2));

(2) the official receiver is liquidator in succession to a person who was appointed as in (1) (s. 172(3)(a));

(3) the liquidator was a nominee of the contributories whom the court appointed liquidator either jointly with, or instead of, a nominee of the creditors (ss. 139(4)(a), 172(3)(b)); or

(4) the liquidator was formerly the administrator of the company who was appointed by the court when the winding-up order was made immediately upon the termination of the administration (ss. 140(1), 172(3)(b)).

The special preconditions to the summoning of the creditors' general meeting will apply, however, where the official receiver is liquidator otherwise than in (2) above, where the liquidator was appointed by the Secretary of State, or where the liquidator was appointed by the court otherwise than in (3) or (4) above. (Note that this will include, first, a "neutral" liquidator who is appointed on the court's own nomination under s. 139(4)(b), following a disagreement between the creditors' and the contributories' meetings, and, secondly, a liquidator appointed by the court under s. 140(2), who was formerly the supervisor of a CVA.) In contrast with s. 171(3), the percentage of creditors necessary to request a meeting under s. 172(2) is one-quarter, rather than "not less than one-half".

S. 172(4)
This power is additional to that of the court under s. 172(2) and that of the creditors under s. 172(3)(b). For the relevant rules, see IR 1986, r. 4.123.

S. 172(5)
For the relevant rules, see IR 1986, rr. 4.134, 4.138(1).

Section 173 *Insolvency Act 1986*

S. 172(6)
The relevant circumstances are prescribed by IR 1986, r. 4.108(4).

S. 172(8)
When the liquidator vacates office pursuant to this provision, he must deliver up the company's books and records to the official receiver: see IR 1986, r. 4.138(3).

Release of liquidator

173 Release (voluntary winding up)

173(1) [Application] This section applies with respect to the release of the liquidator of a company which is being wound up voluntarily.

173(2) [Time of release] A person who has ceased to be a liquidator shall have his release with effect from the following time, that is to say–

(a) in the case of a person who has been removed from office by a general meeting of the company or by a general meeting of the company's creditors that has not resolved against his release or who has died, the time at which notice is given to the registrar of companies in accordance with the rules that that person has ceased to hold office;

(b) in the case of a person who has been removed from office by a general meeting of the company's creditors that has resolved against his release, or by the court, or who has vacated office under section 171(4) above, such time as the Secretary of State may, on the application of that person, determine;

(c) in the case of a person who has resigned, such time as may be prescribed;

(d) in the case of a person who has vacated office under subsection (6)(a) of section 171, the time at which he vacated office;

(e) in the case of a person who has vacated office under subsection (6)(b) of that section–

   (i) if the final meeting of the creditors referred to in that subsection has resolved against that person's release, such time as the Secretary of State may, on an application by that person, determine, and

   (ii) if that meeting has not resolved against that person's release, the time at which he vacated office.

173(3) [Application to Scotland] In the application of subsection (2) to the winding up of a company registered in Scotland, the references to a determination by the Secretary of State as to the time from which a person who has ceased to be liquidator shall have his release are to be read as references to such a determination by the Accountant of Court.

173(4) [Effect of release] Where a liquidator has his release under subsection (2), he is, with effect from the time specified in that subsection, discharged from all liability both in respect of acts or omissions of his in the winding up and otherwise in relation to his conduct as liquidator.

But nothing in this section prevents the exercise, in relation to a person who has had his release under subsection (2), of the court's powers under section 212 of this Act (summary remedy against delinquent directors, liquidators, etc.).

S. 173(1)
For the corresponding provisions relating to a winding up by the court, see s. 174. The effect of a release is stated in s. 173(4).

S. 173(2), (3)
The times at which the release of a liquidator becomes effective in different circumstances are set out in the various paragraphs of this subsection. For the relevant rules, see IR 1986, rr. 4.111(2), 4.114(2), 4.122 and 4.126 (creditors' voluntary winding up) and rr. 4.144 and 4.147 (members' voluntary winding up).

It is open to the members' or creditors' meeting to resolve against the release of a liquidator in the cases mentioned in paras (b) and (e)(i). The question of a release is then a matter for the Secretary of State (or, in Scotland, the Accountant of Court) to determine.

S. 173(4)
The terms of this subsection are in all material respects the same as those of s. 20(2), (3), relating to the release of an administrator: see, further, the notes to that section.

174 Release (winding up by the court)

174(1) [Application] This section applies with respect to the release of the liquidator of a company which is being wound up by the court, or of a provisional liquidator.

174(2) [Where official receiver ceases to be liquidator] Where the official receiver has ceased to be liquidator and a person becomes liquidator in his stead, the official receiver has his release with effect from the following time, that is to say–

(a) in a case where that person was nominated by a general meeting of creditors or contributories, or was appointed by the Secretary of State, the time at which the official receiver gives notice to the court that he has been replaced;

(b) in a case where that person is appointed by the court, such time as the court may determine.

174(3) [Where official receiver gives notice to Secretary of State] If the official receiver while he is a liquidator gives notice to the Secretary of State that the winding up is for practical purposes complete, he has his release with effect from such time as the Secretary of State may determine.

174(4) [Person other than official receiver] A person other than the official receiver who has ceased to be a liquidator has his release with effect from the following time, that is to say–

(a) in the case of a person who has been removed from office by a general meeting of creditors that has not resolved against his release or who has died, the time at which notice is given to the court in accordance with the rules that that person has ceased to hold office;

(b) in the case of a person who has been removed from office by a general meeting of creditors that has resolved against his release, or by the court or the Secretary of State, or who has vacated office under section 172(5) or (7), such time as the Secretary of State may, on an application by that person, determine;

(c) in the case of a person who has resigned, such time as may be prescribed;

(d) in the case of a person who has vacated office under section 172(8)–

　　(i) if the final meeting referred to in that subsection has resolved against that person's release, such time as the Secretary of State may, on an application by that person, determine, and

　　(ii) if that meeting has not so resolved, the time at which that person vacated office.

174(5) [Provisional liquidator] A person who has ceased to hold office as a provisional liquidator has his release with effect from such time as the court may, on an application by him, determine.

174(6) [Effect of release] Where the official receiver or a liquidator or provisional liquidator has his release under this section, he is, with effect from the time specified in the preceding provisions of this section, discharged from all liability both in respect of acts or omissions of his in the winding up and otherwise in relation to his conduct as liquidator or provisional liquidator.

But nothing in this section prevents the exercise, in relation to a person who has had his release under this section, of the court's powers under section 212 (summary remedy against delinquent directors, liquidators, etc.).

174(7) **[Application to Scotland]** In the application of this section to a case where the order for winding up has been made by the court in Scotland, the references to a determination by the Secretary of State as to the time from which a person who has ceased to be liquidator has his release are to such a determination by the Accountant of Court.

S. 174(1)
Section 173 deals with the corresponding questions in a voluntary liquidation.

S. 174(2), (3)
These two subsections govern the release of the official receiver as liquidator. Necessarily, of course, they apply only in England and Wales.
For the relevant rules, see IR 1986, r. 4.124.

S. 174(4)
The provisions of this subsection are broadly parallel to those of s. 173(2). For the rules prescribed for the purposes of s. 174, see IR 1986, rr. 4.113, 4.121–4.125.

S. 174(6)
See the corresponding provisions relating to an administrator (s. 20(2), (3)) and a liquidator in a voluntary winding up (s. 173(4)).

CHAPTER VIII

PROVISIONS OF GENERAL APPLICATION IN WINDING UP

General comment on Pt IV, Ch. VIII
Those familiar with the former law relating to company liquidations, as contained in CA 1985 and its predecessors, would naturally expect to find at about this point in the present Act provisions corresponding to CA 1985, ss. 611–613. The first of these sections dealt with the question of debts provable in a liquidation, set-off, and related questions. The debts provable in a liquidation are now dealt with in IR 1986, Ch. 9 (rr. 4.73ff., and especially r. 4.86), and rr. 12.3 and 13.12, while the questions of mutual credit and set-off are provided for by r. 4.90. The corresponding provisions for bankruptcy continue to be set out in primary legislation and are to be found in ss. 382 and 323, respectively.

Preferential debts

175 Preferential debts (general provision)

175(1) **[Payment in priority]** In a winding up the company's preferential debts (within the meaning given by section 386 in Part XII) shall be paid in priority to all other debts.

175(2) **[Ranking and priority]** Preferential debts–

(a) rank equally among themselves after the expenses of the winding up and shall be paid in full, unless the assets are insufficient to meet them, in which case they abate in equal proportions; and

(b) so far as the assets of the company available for payment of general creditors are insufficient to meet them, have priority over the claims of holders of debentures secured by, or holders of, any floating charge created by the company, and shall be paid accordingly out of any property comprised in or subject to that charge.

GENERAL NOTE

Rules giving certain categories of unsecured debt priority in a bankruptcy or winding up have been a feature of the legislation for over a century. However, the impact of this provision (and the corresponding section in bankruptcy, s. 328) will now be significantly reduced following the abolition of the Crown's priority in regard to PAYE, NIC contributions and VAT, effected by EA 2002, s. 251.

It is not only the preferential debts which are given priority by this section, but also the expenses of the winding up, which rank before both the preferential creditors and the floating charge-holder.

Where a company is in receivership and was not, at the time when the receiver was appointed, in course of being wound up, s. 40 applies (and not the present section), to give similar priority to preferential debts. However in that situation the list of preferential creditors is settled by reference to a different "relevant date" (see s. 387(4)). The fact that a winding up later supervenes leads to the consequence that s. 175 displaces s. 40. This was settled by the ruling in *Re Leyland Daf Ltd* [2001] 1 B.C.L.C. 419, although there remains some doubt whether (and if so, to what extent) this displacement may have retrospective effect. In the *Leyland Daf* case the receivers still had assets in their hands at the beginning of the liquidation, and Rimer J. ruled that the present section applied to give the liquidation expenses priority in so far as the receivers still held assets subject to the charge. But no claim was made in that case for the liquidator to have recourse to any of the assets that had already been distributed, or to make the receivers accountable for such assets. See further the notes to s. 107 and 115. The decision of Rimer J. has since been upheld by the Court of Appeal [2002] EWCA Civ 228; [2002] 1 B.C.L.C. 571. An appeal to the House of Lords is pending.

A further change made by the insolvency legislation of 1985 was to bring into line, not only the law of company insolvency and individual bankruptcy, but also that of CVAs, receiverships and individual voluntary arrangements, so that the same rules set out in Sch. 6 apply to them all.

Note that there was no provision for preferential debts in a company administration under the original IA 1986, Pt II, except where the administration was linked with a voluntary arrangement (s. 387(2)) or where a winding-up order immediately followed upon the discharge of the administration order (s. 387(3)(a)). However, a new subsection (3A) has been added to s. 387, which will apply to all administrations from September 15, 2003, bringing administrations into line with other insolvency procedures in this respect. See the notes to that provision.

In relation to payment and securities settlement systems, where "collateral security" (as defined in the Finality Regulations, reg. 2(1)) has been provided by a company to which those regulations apply, the claim of a participant or central bank to such security must be paid in priority to the expenses of the winding up, remuneration and preferential debts, unless the terms on which the security was provided expressly state that the expenses, remuneration and preferential debts shall have priority (Finality Regulations, reg. 14(5), (6)). (See the introductory note at p. 3, above.)

S. 175(2)(a)
Expenses incurred by a liquidator in pursuing claims under ss. 127 (post-petition dispositions), 214 (wrongful trading), 238 (transactions at an undervalue) and 239 (preferences) were held not to be "expenses of the liquidation" in a number of cases, culminating with *Re Floor Fourteen Ltd, Lewis v IRC* [2001] 3 All E.R. 499, [2002] B.C.C. 198. But an amendment to IR 1986, r. 4.218 has reversed these rulings: see the note to that rule.

S. 175(2)(b)
This important provision continues the rule, laid down in successive Companies Acts, which subordinates the claims of a secured creditor holding a floating charge (but not a fixed charge) to those of the preferential creditors. A similar rule applies in a receivership (ss. 40, 59).

However, the application of the rule is now different because the statutory definition of a floating charge has been reworded, so that it includes any charge which, *as created*, was a floating charge (see s. 251). In consequence, any charge which was originally a floating charge but has become a fixed charge (*e.g.* by crystallisation, or by a notice of conversion) before the "relevant date" defined by s. 387 will now by subordinated to the preferential debts under the present section. The decisions in *Re Woodroffes (Musical Instruments) Ltd* [1986] Ch. 366; *Re Brightlife Ltd* [1987] Ch. 200; (1986) 2 B.C.C. 99,359; *Stein v Saywell* (1969) 121 C.L.R. 529 and *Re Griffin Hotel Co. Ltd* [1941] Ch. 129, which were previously authorities to the contrary, are accordingly no longer good law.

176 Preferential charge on goods distrained

176(1) [Application] This section applies where a company is being wound up by the court in England and Wales, and is without prejudice to section 128 (avoidance of attachments, etc.).

Section 176 *Insolvency Act 1986*

176(2) [Where distraining in previous 3 months] Where any person (whether or not a landlord or person entitled to rent) has distrained upon the goods or effects of the company in the period of 3 months ending with the date of the winding-up order, those goods or effects, or the proceeds of their sale, shall be charged for the benefit of the company with the preferential debts of the company to the extent that the company's property is for the time being insufficient for meeting them.

176(3) [Surrender of goods under s. 176(2)] Where by virtue of a charge under subsection (2) any person surrenders any goods or effects to a company or makes a payment to a company, that person ranks, in respect of the amount of the proceeds of sale of those goods or effects by the liquidator or (as the case may be) the amount of the payment, as a preferential creditor of the company, except as against so much of the company's property as is available for the payment of preferential creditors by virtue of the surrender or payment.

S. 176(1)
The present section does not apply in the case of a voluntary liquidation; and it will apply only if the distress is not void, under the provisions of s. 128, as having been put in force after the commencement of the winding up.

S. 176(2)
The effect of the subsection is to make the claims of the preferential creditors a first charge on the goods distrained or their proceeds. Note that the significant date for reckoning the three-month period is that of the winding-up *order*, and not (as in s. 128) the date of commencement of the winding up, which will be earlier (see s. 129).

S. 176(3)
The effect of subsections (2) and (3), taken together, is as follows:

(1)   To the extent that there is property of the company (independently of the proceeds of sale or payment) available for payment of the preferential debts, the preferential creditors participate pari passu.

(2)   In regard to the proceeds of sale or payment, the person who has surrendered the goods or made the payment and the preferential creditors together rank *pari passu*.

Accordingly, that person is not a "postponed" preferential creditor except as regards the property referred to in para. (1) above: *Re Memco Engineering Ltd* [1986] Ch. 86; (1985) 1 B.C.C. 99,460 (a case on the repealed CA 1985, s. 319(7)).

Property subject to floating charge

176A   Share of assets for unsecured creditors

176A(1) [Application of section] This section applies where a floating charge relates to property of a company –

(a)   which has gone into liquidation,

(b)   which is in administration,

(c)   of which there is a provisional liquidator, or

(d)   of which there is a receiver.

176A(2) [Prescribed part for unsecured debts] The liquidator, administrator or receiver –

(a)   shall make a prescribed part of the company's net property available for the satisfaction of unsecured debts, and

(b)   shall not distribute that part to the proprietor of a floating charge except in so far as it exceeds the amount required for the satisfaction of unsecured debts.

176A(3) **[Non-application of s. 176A(2)]** Subsection (2) shall not apply to a company if –

(a) the company's net property is less than the prescribed minimum, and

(b) the liquidator, administrator or receiver thinks that the cost of making a distribution to unsecured creditors would be disproportionate to the benefits.

176A(4) **[Disapplication of s. 176A(2)]** Subsection (2) shall also not apply to a company if or in so far as it is disapplied by –

(a) a voluntary arrangement in respect of the company, or

(b) a compromise or arrangement agreed under section 425 of the Companies Act (compromise with creditors and members).

176A(5) **[Non-application by court order]** Subsection (2) shall also not apply to a company if –

(a) the liquidator, administrator or receiver applies to the court for an order under this subsection on the ground that the cost of making a distribution to unsecured creditors would be disproportionate to the benefits, and

(b) the court orders that subsection (2) shall not apply.

176A(6) **[Net property in s. 176A(2), (3)]** In subsections (2) and (3) a company's net property is the amount of its property which would, but for this section, be available for satisfaction of claims of holders of debentures secured by, or holders of, any floating charge created by the company.

176A(7) **[Provision in order]** An order under subsection (2) prescribing part of a company's net property may, in particular, provide for its calculation –

(a) as a percentage of the company's net property, or

(b) as an aggregate of different percentages of different parts of the company's net property.

176A(8) **[Procedure for order]** An order under this section –

(a) must be made by statutory instrument, and

(b) shall be subject to annulment pursuant to a resolution of either House of Parliament.

176A(9) **["Floating charge", "prescribed"]** In this section – **"floating charge"** means a charge which is a floating charge on its creation and which is created after the first order under subsection (2)(a) comes into force, and **"prescribed"** means prescribed by order by the Secretary of State.

176A(10) **[Transitional or incidental provision]** An order under this section may include transitional or incidental provision.

GENERAL NOTE

This section, introduced by EA 2002, s. 252 with effect from September 15, 2003, is one of the major innovations made by the 2002 Act. The measure has its origins in a recommendation of the Cork Committee (Cmnd 8558, 1982, at para. 1538) that a "10 per cent fund" should be set aside out of the net realisations of property subject to a floating charge and that this fund be made available to unsecured creditors upon the insolvency of the company. This is seen by some as a *quid pro quo* for the abolition of the major part of the Crown's preferential status as a creditor: without such a provision, there would simply be a windfall for the charge holder. The "prescribed part" (also referred to as the "special reserved fund" or "ring-fenced sum" for the unsecured creditors) is calculated on the net realisations of property subject

Section 177 Insolvency Act 1986

to any floating (but not fixed) charge, and will be payable to the charge holder only in so far as anything remains after the unsecured creditors have been paid in full.

The amount of the prescribed part has been fixed as follows:

Where the net property is less than £10,000: 50% of that property

Where the net property is at least £10,000: 50% of the first £10,000, plus 20% of the property which exceeds £10,000, up to a maximum prescribed part of £600,000.

(See the Insolvency Act 1986 (Prescribed Part) Order 2003 (SI 2003/2097), effective September 15, 2003.)

Subsections (3)–(5) set out various situations in which the obligation to set aside a prescribed part does not apply.

Rule 12.2(2) states that the costs associated with the prescribed part shall be paid out of that part. For other relevant rules, see rr. 3.39–3.40, 4.43, 4.49, 4.124–4.126, 7.3A, 7.4A, and 12.22.

S. 176A(1)

The section only applies where there is a floating charge. Paragraph (d) would therefore not apply to a fixed-charge receivership, but it would apply to any other kind of receivership, including an administrative receivership and a court-appointed receivership (for confirmation, see r.3.39). An administrative receiver is excluded from r. 3.39(1)(a) only because he already has reporting obligations under s. 48.

There is no obligation to set aside a prescribed part where a charge-holder, instead of appointing a receiver, enters into possession (personally or through an agent) under CA 1985, s. 196.

S. 176A(2), (6)

The office-holder is required by s. 176A only to set the prescribed part aside: this section does not authorise him to make a distribution (for which the consent of the court may be required: see, e.g. Sch. B1, para. 65(3)). Where there are preferential creditors, the prescribed part is reckoned by reference to net property remaining after their claims have been satisfied, i.e. out of the property which is available to be paid to the floating charge holder.

S. 176A(3)–(5)

These provisions can be invoked in order to excuse the office-holder from his obligation to set aside the prescribed part in the following situations:

- where the net property is less than the prescribed minimum (fixed by SI 2003/2097, para. 2 at £10,000) and he thinks that the cost of making a distribution to the unsecured creditors would be disproportionate to the benefits;

- where the net property is £10,000 or more and the office-holder applies to the court for an order disapplying subsection (2) on the same ground; or

- where it is disapplied by the terms of a CVA or scheme of compromise or arrangement under CA 1985, s. 425. Rules 7.3A, 7.4A and 12.22 deal with the procedure where applicaion is made to the court under s. 176A(5).

S. 176A(9)

This section applies only in relation to floating charges that are *created* after the section is brought into force (i.e. on or after September 15, 2003). Where the relevant insolvency proceedings are instituted on or after that date but the charge was created on an earlier date, the charge-holder will get the best of both worlds, enjoying the benefit of the abolition of the Crown's preference but not being subject to the deduction of the prescribed part.

Special managers

177 Power to appoint special manager

177(1) [Power of court] Where a company has gone into liquidation or a provisional liquidator has been appointed, the court may, on an application under this section, appoint any person to be the special manager of the business or property of the company.

177(2) [Application to court] The application may be made by the liquidator or provisional liquidator in any case where it appears to him that the nature of the business or property of the company, or the interests of the company's creditors or contributories or members generally, require the appointment of another person to manage the company's business or property.

177(3) **[Powers of special manager]** The special manager has such powers as may be entrusted to him by the court.

177(4) **[Extent of s. 177(3) powers]** The court's power to entrust powers to the special manager includes power to direct that any provision of this Act that has effect in relation to the provisional liquidator or liquidator of a company shall have the like effect in relation to the special manager for the purposes of the carrying out by him of any of the functions of the provisional liquidator or liquidator.

177(5) **[Duties of special manager]** The special manager shall–

(a) give such security or, in Scotland, caution as may be prescribed;

(b) prepare and keep such accounts as may be prescribed; and

(c) produce those accounts in accordance with the rules to the Secretary of State or to such other persons as may be prescribed.

GENERAL NOTE

The former CA 1985, s. 556 provided for the appointment of a special manager when the official receiver became the liquidator or provisional liquidator of a company. The present section extends this facility to all liquidators, and now applies also to Scotland. The appointment of a special manager allows a liquidator to have assistance from someone with particular managerial or commercial expertise that he may not have himself.

A special manager is not required to be qualified to act as an insolvency practitioner: indeed, there may be a particular need to invoke the present section when the skills in question are those which an insolvency practitioner does not normally have. (There is no longer the option of bringing in such an expert in the role of liquidator, or joint liquidator, unless by chance he is also qualified under this Act for appointment.)

In *Re W F Fearman Ltd (No. 2)* (1988) 4 B.C.C. 141 the court gave leave to the official receiver to use the services of the outgoing provisional liquidators as special managers, in order to maintain continuity in the administration of the insolvency pending the choice by a creditors' meeting of liquidators on a permanent basis.

S. 177(1), (2)
The appointment must in all cases be made by the court, on the application of the liquidator or provisional liquidator himself.

S. 177(3), (4)
The powers of a special manager are determined in each case by the court, and they may be made subject to any statutory provision that applies to a liquidator – *e.g.* an obligation to obtain the consent of the liquidation committee on particular matters.

S. 177(5)
The rules prescribed for the purposes of this section are to be found in IR 1986, Ch. 18 (rr. 4.206ff.).

Disclaimer (England and Wales only)

178 Power to disclaim onerous property

178(1) **[Application]** This and the next two sections apply to a company that is being wound up in England and Wales.

178(2) **[Disclaimer by liquidator]** Subject as follows, the liquidator may, by the giving of the prescribed notice, disclaim any onerous property and may do so notwithstanding that he has taken possession of it, endeavoured to sell it, or otherwise exercised rights of ownership in relation to it.

178(3) **[Onerous property]** The following is onerous property for the purposes of this section–

(a) any unprofitable contract, and

(b) any other property of the company which is unsaleable or not readily saleable or is such that it may give rise to a liability to pay money or perform any other onerous act.

178(4) **[Effect of disclaimer]** A disclaimer under this section—

(a) operates so as to determine, as from the date of the disclaimer, the rights, interests and liabilities of the company in or in respect of the property disclaimed; but

(b) does not, except so far as is necessary for the purpose of releasing the company from any liability, affect the rights or liabilities of any other person.

178(5) **[Where notice of disclaimer not to be given]** A notice of disclaimer shall not be given under this section in respect of any property if—

(a) a person interested in the property has applied in writing to the liquidator or one of his predecessors as liquidator requiring the liquidator or that predecessor to decide whether he will disclaim or not, and

(b) the period of 28 days begining with the day on which that application was made, or such longer period as the court may allow, has expired without a notice of disclaimer having been given under this section in respect of that property.

178(6) **[Persons sustaining loss etc.]** Any person sustaining loss or damage in consequence of the operation of a disclaimer under this section is deemed a creditor of the company to the extent of the loss or damage and accordingly may prove for the loss or damage in the winding up.

GENERAL NOTE

Sections 178–182 enlarge and, in some respects, modify the law regarding disclaimer which was formerly contained in CA 1985, ss. 618, 619 and 629. These provisions apply only in England and Wales. They correspond to the bankruptcy rules set out in ss. 315ff., below.

In the context of the financial markets, s. 178 does not apply in relation to a market contract or a contract effected by an exchange or clearing house for the purpose of realising property provided as margin in relation to market contracts: see CA 1989, s. 164(1). The section is also disapplied by the Finality Regulations, reg. 16(1) in relation to a transfer order or a contract for the purpose of realising security in payment and securities settlement systems. (See the notes on pp. 2–3 above.)

A waste management licence is "property", or alternatively an interest incidental to property, which may be disclaimed under the section: *Celtic Extraction Ltd & Bluestone Chemicals Ltd v Environment Agency* [2001] Ch. 475; [2000] B.C.C. 487 (overruling *Re Mineral Resources Ltd* [1999] B.C.C. 422, in which Neuberger J. had held that a licence could not be disclaimed because that would be inconsistent with the Environmental Protection Act 1990).

S. 178(2)

Under the former law as contained in CA 1985, only the official receiver was empowered to disclaim property on his own authority; any other liquidator was required to obtain the leave of the court. Every liquidator may now exercise the power to disclaim without leave. It is left to the person affected by the proposed disclaimer to take his objection to the court, if he has one. However, the effect of the change in the law removing the requirement of leave is to make the liquidator's decision to disclaim primarily a matter for his discretion, similar to his other powers in the management and realisation of the company's property, which will normally be reviewed by the court only if it has been exercised *mala fide* or perversely. Cases relating to the granting of leave under the former law are now irrelevant (*Re Hans Place Ltd* [1992] B.C.C. 737).

A notice of disclaimer must now be "in the prescribed form": see IR 1986, rr. 4.187, and Form 4.53. For the rules regulating the procedure generally, see IR 1986, Ch. 15 (rr. 4.187ff.).

The 12-month time limit which was formerly imposed by CA 1985, s. 618(3) has been abolished.

S. 178(3)

This is a new and wider definition of "onerous property". The previous specific references in CA 1985, s. 618(1) to "land (of any tenure) burdened with onerous covenants" and "shares or stock in companies" have been dropped – though such items are clearly within the wider terms of the new definition – and the former requirement that, to be "onerous", property had to be "unsaleable, or not readily saleable, by reason of its binding its possessor to the performance of any onerous act or to the payment of any sum of money" has now been replaced by s. 178(3)(b), in which these attributes are expressed as alternatives.

The term "property" is itself widely defined for the purposes of the present Act by s. 436, below.

S. 178(4)
The effect of a disclaimer is, apart from the operation of any vesting order made by the court under the succeeding sections, that the disclaimed property vests in the Crown as *bona vacantia* (or, in the case of land held in fee simple, by escheat). In *Scmlla Properties Ltd v Gesso Properties (BVI) Ltd* [1995] B.C.C. 793 it was held that a legal charge over a freehold interest in land, and the leases of tenants created out of the freehold, survived a disclaimer of the freehold interest.

A disclaimer should be construed so as to interfere with the rights of third parties as little as possible: thus, although the effect of the disclaimer of a contract is to release the company from its obligations, it does not undo the contract in so far as it has been performed and other parties have acquired rights and interests under it: *Capital Prime Properties plc v Worthgate Ltd* [2000] B.C.C. 525.

S. 178(5)
This corresponds with the repealed CA 1985, s. 619(2), with the necessary modification that in para. (b) the liquidator must now give an actual notice of disclaimer within the 28-day period, instead of a notice that he intends to apply to the court for leave to disclaim. For the procedure under this subsection, see IR 1986, r. 4.191.

S. 178(6)
This is the same as the former CA 1985, s. 619(8), with the substitution of the words "sustaining loss or damage" for the less precise term "injured". *Re Park Air Services plc* [2000] 2 A.C. 172; [1999] B.C.C. 135 gives guidance on the method of calculating the loss or damage suffered by a landlord in consequence of the disclaimer of a lease. The company in this case was solvent. The House of Lords held that, following disclaimer, the landlord could not prove in the winding up for future rent but instead had a statutory right to compensation, to be reckoned on the same basis as if he were claiming damages for breach of a contract that had been wrongfully terminated (with an allowance or discount for the accelerated receipt of sums falling due in the future). Interest under s. 189 was also allowed.

179 Disclaimer of leaseholds

179(1) [Requirement for disclaimer to take effect] The disclaimer under section 178 of any property of a leasehold nature does not take effect unless a copy of the disclaimer has been served (so far as the liquidator is aware of their addresses) on every person claiming under the company as underlessee or mortgagee and either–

(a) no application under section 181 below is made with respect to that property before the end of the period of 14 days beginning with the day on which the last notice served under this subsection was served; or

(b) where such an application has been made, the court directs that the disclaimer shall take effect.

179(2) [Court's directions or orders] Where the court gives a direction under subsection (1)(b) it may also, instead of or in addition to any order it makes under section 181, make such orders with respect to fixtures, tenant's improvements and other matters arising out of the lease as it thinks fit.

GENERAL NOTE

Under the former law, when leave to disclaim had to be sought in every case, the court could require such notices to be given to persons interested as it thought appropriate. The present section, now that the court is no longer involved, makes express provision for notice to be given to underlessees and mortgagees of leasehold property, at least 14 days before the disclaimer can take effect.

The disclaimer of a lease has the effect of destroying any underlease; but the underlessee has the right, if he chooses, to remain in occupation for the term of the underlease, paying the rent reserved by the lease and performing the covenants contained in it: *Re A E Realisations (1985) Ltd* [1988] 1 W.L.R. 200; (1987) 3 B.C.C. 136.

There is no jurisdiction to make a vesting order in favour of a landlord on terms that it shall be subject to and with the benefit of existing subleases: *Re I T M Corp. Ltd (in liq.)* [1997] B.C.C. 554.

S. 179(1)
An underlessee or mortgagee has 14 days after receiving notice of the proposed disclaimer in which to apply to the court to have a vesting order made in his favour, or such other relief as the court thinks fit.

S. 179(2)
This provision confers on the court additional powers to those prescribed by ss. 181, 182.

180 Land subject to rentcharge

180(1) [Application] The following applies where, in consequence of the disclaimer under section 178 of any land subject to a rentcharge, that land vests by operation of law in the Crown or any other person (referred to in the next subsection as "the proprietor").

180(2) [Liability of proprietor et al.] The proprietor and the successors in title of the proprietor are not subject to any personal liability in repect of any sums becoming due under the rentcharge except sums becoming due after the proprietor, or some person claiming under or through the proprietor, has taken possession or control of the land or has entered into occupation of it.

GENERAL NOTE

The purpose of this section is to ensure that the Crown or any other person in whom land vests as a result of a disclaimer (see the note to s. 178(4)) is not made personally liable in respect of the rentcharge unless it (or he) takes possession or control of the land.

181 Powers of court (general)

181(1) [Application] This section and the next apply where the liquidator has disclaimed property under section 178.

181(2) [Application to court] An application under this section may be made to the court by–

(a) any person who claims an interest in the disclaimed property, or

(b) any person who is under any liability in respect of the disclaimed property, not being a liability discharged by the disclaimer.

181(3) [Powers of court] Subject as follows, the court may on the application make an order, on such terms as it thinks fit, for the vesting of the disclaimed property in, or for its delivery to–

(a) a person entitled to it or a trustee for such a person, or

(b) a person subject to such a liability as is mentioned in subsection (2)(b) or a trustee for such a person.

181(4) [Limit on court's powers] The court shall not make an order under subsection (3)(b) except where it appears to the court that it would be just to do so for the purpose of compensating the person subject to the liability in respect of the disclaimer.

181(5) [Relationship with s. 178(6)] The effect of any order under this section shall be taken into account in assessing for the purpose of section 178(6) the extent of any loss or damage sustained by any person in consequence of the disclaimer.

181(6) [Effect of vesting order] An order under this section vesting property in any person need not be completed by conveyance, assignment or transfer.

S. 181(1)–(3)

As has been explained above, the liquidator's power to disclaim no longer requires the leave of the court, and so the court becomes involved only if an application is made to it by a person who is interested in the property or otherwise affected by the disclaimer. These subsections deal with the right to make such an application, and set out the general powers of the court in such proceedings. The relevant procedure is laid down by IR 1986, r. 4.194. (In regard to vesting orders affecting leasehold property, the provisions of s. 182 apply in addition.)

In *Re Vedmay Ltd* [1994] 1 B.C.L.C. 676 it was held that the term "interest" in s. 181(2) is not confined to a proprietary interest, and that a subtenant of premises who was in occupation as a statutory tenant had no proprietary interest in the premises, but merely a "status of irremovability"; but even so, since he had a financial interest in the subsistence of the head-lease, he had a sufficient interest for the purpose of s. 181. However in *Lloyds Bank SF Nominees v Aladdin Ltd (in liq.)* [1996] 1 B.C.L.C. 720 it was held that a proprietary interest of some kind was essential, so that, if the *Vedmay* decision is to stand, it must be because of the finding that the tenant had a "status of irremovability". The guarantor of a debt secured by a charge over a company's assets similarly has only a financial and not a proprietary interest in those assets: *Re Spirit Motorsport Ltd (in liq.)* [1996] 1 B.C.L.C. 684.

In *Stacey v Hill* [1991] 1 K.B. 660 it was held that the disclaimer of a lease brought to an end the obligations of a guarantor or surety in respect of future liabilities under the lease. This ruling was in stark contrast with *Hill v East & West India Dock Co.* (1884) 9 App. Cas. 448, in which the House of Lords had held that the disclaimer of a lease which has been assigned does not determine the continuing liability of the original lessee on the covenants in the lease, or the liability of any surety for the original lessee. The anomaly has now been rectified. In *Hindcastle Ltd v Barbara Attenborough Associates Ltd* [1997] A.C. 70; [1996] B.C.C. 636 the House of Lords decided that the two could not stand together and that *Stacey v Hill* should be overruled. It follows that both a guarantor of a lease and an original or former lessee of a lease which has been assigned are "persons under a liability in respect of the disclaimed property, not being a liability discharged by the disclaimer" under s. 181(2)(b), and that accordingly they have standing to apply for a vesting order under the present section.

The terms of a guarantee sometimes provide that in the event of the lease being disclaimed the guarantor will take a new lease from the landlord for the residue of the term at the same rent. In *Re A E Realisations (1985) Ltd* [1988] 1 W.L.R. 200; (1987) 3 B.C.C. 136, the court declined to make a vesting order in favour of a guarantor because it would have achieved nothing that would not be brought about by the grant of a new lease under the agreement.

Section 654 of CA 1985 provides that the property of a defunct company which has been struck off the register vests in the Crown as bona vacantia, subject to the Crown's right to disclaim the property under s. 656; and s. 657(2) states that, as regards property in England and Wales, ss. 178(4) and 179–182 of IA 1986 shall apply to such property as if it had been disclaimed by a liquidator.

S. 181(4)

If a vesting order is made under s. 181(3)(b), the beneficiary will not be someone "entitled" to the property in question (compare s. 181(3)(a)), but someone who is under a liability in respect of it. A vesting order allows the court to do rough justice by allowing the applicant to take over the property in exchange for the extinction of his liability, provided that the condition in this subsection is met.

S. 181(5)

The beneficiary under a vesting order proves in the winding up under s. 178(6) for any loss or damage which he may have sustained overall, after bringing into account the effect of the order, which may in itself have left him better or worse off.

S. 181(6)

The vesting order operates itself as a conveyance of the property without the need for any other legal act.

182 Powers of court (leaseholds)

182(1) **[Limit on court's power]** The court shall not make an order under section 181 vesting property of a leasehold nature in any person claiming under the company as underlessee or mortgagee except on terms making that person–

(a) subject to the same liabilities and obligations as the company was subject to under the lease at the commencement of the winding up, or

(b) if the court thinks fit, subject to the same liabilities and obligations as that person would be subject to if the lease had been assigned to him at the commencement of the winding up.

182(2) **[Where order re part of property in lease]** For the purposes of an order under section 181 relating to only part of any property comprised in a lease, the requirements of subsection (1) apply as if the lease comprised only the property to which the order relates.

182(3) **[Court may vest estate in someone else]** Where subsection (1) applies and no person claiming under the company as underlessee or mortagee is willing to accept an order under section 181 on the terms required by virtue of that subsection, the court may, by order under that section, vest the company's estate or interest in the property in any person who is liable (whether personally or in a representative capacity, and whether alone or jointly with the company) to perform the lessee's covenants in the lease.

The court may vest that estate and interest in such a person freed and discharged from all estates, incumbrances and interests created by the company.

182(4) **[Where s. 182(1) applies]** Where subsection (1) applies and a person claiming under the company as underlessee or mortgagee declines to accept an order under section 181, that person is excluded from all interest in the property.

Section 183 *Insolvency Act 1986*

GENERAL NOTE

This provision is designed to ensure that persons who have a subordinate interest in leasehold property owned by the company have an opportunity to take over the property itself on the same terms, in effect, as those upon which the company formerly held it.

In *Re I T M Corp. Ltd (in liq.)* [1997] B.C.C. 554, a vesting order had been made in favour of a landlord on terms that it should be subject to and with the benefit of existing subleases. On appeal, it was held (1) that the court had no jurisdiction to make an order in favour of a landlord until the interests of all the other relevant parties who could obtain an interest in the property under the statutory mechanism had been cleared away, and (2) that a vesting order in favour of a landlord could only be made freed of the sublessees' interests.

S. 182(4)

This provision is limited in its application to persons who have a proprietary interest in the property. It cannot be invoked to determine a statutory tenancy: *Re Vedmay Ltd* [1994] 1 B.C.L.C. 676.

Execution, attachment and the Scottish equivalents

183 Effect of execution or attachment (England and Wales)

183(1) **[Where creditor seeking benefit of execution or attachment]** Where a creditor has issued execution against the goods or land of a company or has attached any debt due to it, and the company is subsequently wound up, he is not entitled to retain the benefit of the execution or attachment against the liquidator unless he has completed the execution or attachment before the commencement of the winding up.

183(2) **[Qualifications]** However–

(a) if a creditor has had notice of a meeting having been called at which a resolution for voluntary winding up is to be proposed, the date on which he had notice is substituted, for the purpose of subsection (1), for the date of commencement of the winding up;

(b) a person who purchases in good faith under a sale by the sheriff any goods of a company on which execution has been levied in all cases acquires a good title to them against the liquidator; and

(c) the rights conferred by subsection (1) on the liquidator may be set aside by the court in favour of the creditor to such extent and subject to such terms as the court thinks fit.

183(3) **[Execution, attachment]** For the purposes of this Act–

(a) an execution against goods is completed by seizure and sale, or by the making of a charging order under section 1 of the Charging Orders Act 1979;

(b) an attachment of a debt is completed by receipt of the debt; and

(c) an execution against land is completed by seizure, by the appointment of a receiver, or by the making of a charging order under section 1 of the Act above mentioned.

183(4) **[Definitions]** In this section **"goods"** includes all chattels personal; and **"the sheriff"** includes any officer charged with the execution of a writ or other process.

183(5) **[Scotland]** This section does not apply in the case of a winding up in Scotland.

GENERAL NOTE

Section 183 does not have extra-territorial effect, so as to deprive a creditor who has completed an execution process abroad of the assets which he has successfully seized. However the court has a discretion (at least where the creditor in question is amenable to the jurisdiction) to restrain a creditor from bringing or continuing a foreign execution process (*Re Oriental Inland Steam Co. Ex p. Scinde Railway Co.* (1874) 9 Ch. App. 557; *Re North Carolina Estate Co.* (1889) 5 T.L.R. 328; *Re Vocalion (Foreign) Ltd* [1932] 2 Ch. 196); and it also has authority to direct a liquidator to intervene in foreign garnishment proceedings, or to direct him not to do so: *Mitchell v Carter* [1997] B.C.C. 907. Accordingly, it has jurisdiction to decide whether a creditor may retain the fruits of a current or future foreign execution process. (However, in later proceedings (reported as *Re Buckingham International plc (No. 2)* [1998] B.C.C. 943) the court declined to make such an order, holding that the circumstances did not justify disturbing the statutory *pari passu* principle.)

S. 183(1)

This section deals with the situation where a creditor has levied execution against the property of a company which then goes into liquidation. Its effect is to deprive him of the benefit of the execution unless it has been "completed" (as that term is defined in s. 183(3)) before the commencement of the winding up. Since a winding up may commence at a time earlier than the date of a winding-up order, an execution which has in fact then been completed may be avoided retrospectively.

On the "commencement" of a winding up, see ss. 86 and 129. The section may operate even earlier than this time: see s. 182(3)(a).

The present provisions are complementary to s. 128, which avoids all executions and attachments put in force *after* the commencement of a winding up, but whereas s. 128 is restricted to a winding up by the court, s. 183 applies to all categories of winding up.

S. 183(2)

Notice of the summoning of a meeting is here, in effect, treated as equivalent to the now discarded "notice of an act of bankruptcy" formerly applicable in the case of an insolvent individual.

The present provision causes the execution creditor to lose the benefit of his execution, but a bona fide purchaser of goods from the sheriff is protected by para. (b).

On the significance of the word "date", see the note to s. 86.

The court has an overriding jurisdiction: see para. (c).

S. 183(3)

These provisions define with precision the point at which an execution or attachment is "completed".

S. 183(4)

The definition of "goods" is much wider than, *e.g.* that in the *Sale of Goods Act* 1979, and extends to intangible property such as choses in action.

S. 183(5)

For the position governing the winding up of a company in Scotland, see s. 185. Note, however, that where a company registered in England or Wales has assets in Scotland, the provisions of s. 185 will apply, presumably to the exclusion of the present section: see s. 185(4).

184 Duties of sheriff (England and Wales)

184(1) [Application] The following applies where a company's goods are taken in execution and, before their sale or the completion of the execution (by the receipt or recovery of the full amount of the levy), notice is served on the sheriff that a provisional liquidator has been appointed or that a winding-up order has been made, or that a resolution for voluntary winding up has been passed.

184(2) [Sheriff to deliver goods and money to liquidator] The sheriff shall, on being so required, deliver the goods and any money seized or received in part satisfaction of the execution to the liquidator; but the costs of execution are a first charge on the goods or money so delivered, and the liquidator may sell the goods, or a sufficient part of them, for the purpose of satisfying the charge.

184(3) [Costs where goods sold etc.] If under an execution in respect of a judgment for a sum exceeding £500 a company's goods are sold or money is paid in order to avoid sale, the sheriff shall deduct the costs of the execution from the proceeds of sale or the money paid and retain the balance for 14 days.

184(4) [If within time notice is served] If within that time notice is served on the sheriff of a petition for the winding up of the company having been presented, or of a meeting having been called at which there is to be proposed a resolution for voluntary winding up, and an order is made or a resolution passed (as the case may be), the sheriff shall pay the balance to the liquidator who is entitled to retain it as against the execution creditor.

184(5) [Liquidator's rights may be set aside by court] The rights conferred by this section on the liquidator may be set aside by the court in favour of the creditor to such extent and subject to such terms as the court thinks fit.

184(6) [Definitions] In this section, **"goods"** includes all chattels personal; and **"the sheriff"** includes any officer charged with the execution of a writ or other process.

Section 185   Insolvency Act 1986

184(7) [**Increase, reduction of s. 184(3) sum**] The money sum for the time being specified in subsection (3) is subject to increase or reduction by order under section 416 in Part XV.

184(8) [**Scotland**] This section does not apply in the case of a winding up in Scotland.

GENERAL NOTE

This section defines the obligations of a sheriff where a company's goods are taken in execution, thus facilitating the operation of s. 184. For the rules relating to this section, see IR 1986, r. 12.19 and, as regards costs, r. 7.36.

S. 184(1), (2)
These subsections apply where a notice is served on the sheriff that the company in question is either actually in liquidation or in the hands of a provisional liquidator. The benefit of the execution must be surrendered to the liquidator, subject to payment of the sheriff's costs.

S. 184(3)–(5)
These provisions deal with the duties of a sheriff enforcing a judgment debt of over £500. He is required to retain in his hands the net proceeds of the sale, or any money paid to him in order to avoid sale, for 14 days; and if within that time he receives notice that a winding-up petition has been presented or a meeting called to consider a resolution for voluntary winding up, he must continue to hold the money until he learns whether a liquidation has in fact resulted and, if so, hand it to the liquidator (unless the court orders otherwise under s. 184(5)).

S. 184(6)
The definitions are identical with those in s. 183(4).

185   Effect of diligence (Scotland)

185(1) [**Application of Bankruptcy (Scotland) Act**] In the winding up of a company registered in Scotland, the following provisions of the Bankruptcy (Scotland) Act 1985–

(a)   subsections (1) to (6) of section 37 (effect of sequestration on diligence); and

(b)   subsections (3), (4), (7) and (8) of section 39 (realisation of estate),

apply, so far as consistent with this Act, in like manner as they apply in the sequestration of a debtor's estate, with the substitutions specified below and with any other necessary modifications.

185(2) [**Substitutions**] The substitutions to be made in those sections of the Act of 1985 are as follows–

(a)   for references to the debtor, substitute references to the company;

(b)   for references to the sequestration, substitute references to the winding up;

(c)   for references to the date of sequestration, substitute references to the commencement of the winding up of the company; and

(d)   for references to the permanent trustee, substitute references to the liquidator.

185(3) [**Definition**] In this section, **"the commencement of the winding up of the company"** means, where it is being wound up by the court, the day on which the winding-up order is made.

185(4) [**English company with estate in Scotland**] This section, so far as relating to any estate or effects of the company situated in Scotland, applies in the case of a company registered in England and Wales as in the case of one registered in Scotland.

GENERAL NOTE

In relation to the financial markets, nothing in s. 185 affects any action taken by an exchange or clearing house for the purpose of its default proceedings: see the note on p. 2, and CA 1989, s. 161(4).

S. 185(1)–(3)
These provisions apply to the winding up of a company in Scotland the rules relating to diligence, etc. (the Scottish equivalent of execution and attachment) in the bankruptcy of an individual. (Note, particularly, the special definition of the term "the commencement of the winding up" for this purpose.)

S. 185(4)
It is plain from ss. 183(5) and 184(8) that the converse to s. 185(4) does not apply: *i.e.* a company registered in Scotland which has assets in England and Wales will be governed in relation to such property by s. 185, and not by those sections.

186 Rescission of contracts by the court

186(1) [Power of court] The court may, on the application of a person who is, as against the liquidator, entitled to the benefit or subject to the burden of a contract made with the company, make an order rescinding the contract on such terms as to payment by or to either party of damages for the non-performance of the contract, or otherwise as the court thinks just.

186(2) [Damages] Any damages payable under the order to such a person may be proved by him as a debt in the winding up.

GENERAL NOTE

This provision was formerly included in the section of the Companies Act dealing with the disclaimer of onerous property. It is now more fittingly treated separately. The intervention of the court remains necessary in all cases.

In the context of the financial markets, s. 186 does not apply in relation to a market contract or a contract effected by an exchange or clearing house for the purpose of realising property provided as margin in relation to market contracts: see CA 1989, s. 164(1). The section is also disapplied by the Finality Regulations, reg. 16(1) in relation to a transfer order or a contract for the purpose of realising security in payment and securities settlement systems. (See the notes on pp. 2–3 above.)

187 Power to make over assets to employees

187(1) [CA 1985, s. 719 payment on winding up] On the winding up of a company (whether by the court or voluntarily), the liquidator may, subject to the following provisions of this section, make any payment which the company has, before the commencement of the winding up, decided to make under section 719 of the Companies Act (power to provide for employees or former employees on cessation or transfer of business).

187(2) [Power exercisable by liquidator] The power which a company may exercise by virtue only of that section may be exercised by the liquidator after the winding up has commenced if, after the company's liabilities have been fully satisfied and provision has been made for the expenses of the winding up, the exercise of that power has been sanctioned by such a resolution of the company as would be required of the company itself by section 719(3) before that commencement, if paragraph (b) of that subsection were omitted and any other requirement applicable to its exercise by the company had been met.

187(3) [Source of payment] Any payment which may be made by a company under this section (that is, a payment after the commencement of its winding up) may be made out of the company's assets which are available to the members on the winding up.

187(4) [Control by court] On a winding up by the court, the exercise by the liquidator of his powers under this section is subject to the court's control, and any creditor or contributory may apply to the court with respect to any exercise or proposed exercise of the power.

187(5) [Effect] Subsections (1) and (2) above have effect notwithstanding anything in any rule of law or in section 107 of this Act (property of company after satisfaction of liabilities to be distributed among members).

GENERAL NOTE

The provisions of this section and of CA 1985, s. 719 were first introduced (as CA 1980, s. 74) to negate the common law ruling in *Parke v Daily News Ltd* [1962] Ch. 927. Section 719 applies when the company is a going concern, and the present section when it is being wound up. In *Parke's* case, it was held to be ultra vires for a company which had sold its business to a third party to make substantial ex gratia payments to the employees who were thereby made redundant. Both s. 719 and the present section are framed in wide terms, so as not merely to negative any question of ultra vires (abolished by CA 1989, s. 108 from February 4, 1991), but to ensure that such payments will not be invalidated on any other grounds.

S. 187(1)
This subsection applies where the company has already resolved under CA 1985, s. 719(3), before the commencement of the winding up, to make a payment to the employees: the liquidator is authorised to implement the resolution and make that payment. This may be made only out of profits of the company which are available for dividend (s. 719(4)).

S. 187(2)
Once the winding up has commenced, it is still permissible for a company's shareholders to agree to make over assets to the employees, but the restriction to profits available for dividend no longer applies, and instead the payment must be made out of the surplus in the hands of the liquidator after all the company's debts and the costs of the winding up have been met. An ordinary resolution of the shareholders is required or, if the company's memorandum or articles so stipulate, a resolution passed by a larger majority. However, a payment cannot be made on the basis of a decision of the directors alone, even if the memorandum or articles authorise this course, since CA 1985, s. 719(3)(b), which permits this prior to the commencement of winding up, is nullified by the present provision.

S. 187(3)
This provision is not permissive (as it appears to be), but mandatory: the payment cannot be made out of any assets other than those available to the members.

S. 187(4), (5)
The grounds on which the court might interfere to set aside a resolution of the members are not set out. It may be assumed that a plea of *ultra vires* would not succeed, or an objection that the exercise of power by the majority was not in the best interests of the company (see CA 1985, s. 719(1), (2)). However, there are clearly circumstances where a minority shareholder might claim that the majority was acting oppressively or *mala fide* or in a discriminatory way – *e.g.* perhaps if the majority shareholders were themselves the employees who stood to benefit.

188 Notification that company is in liquidation

188(1) [Statement in invoices etc.] When a company is being wound up, whether by the court or voluntarily, every invoice, order for goods or business letter issued by or on behalf of the company, or a liquidator of the company, or a receiver or manager of the company's property, being a document on or in which the name of the company appears, shall contain a statement that the company is being wound up.

188(2) [Penalty on default] If default is made in complying with this section, the company and any of the following persons who knowingly and wilfully authorises or permits the default, namely, any officer of the company, any liquidator of the company and any receiver or manager, is liable to a fine.

GENERAL NOTE

This section has its counterpart in the provisions relating to administration (s. 12) and receivership (ss. 39, 64).

S. 188(2)
On penalties, see s. 430 and Sch. 10.

189 Interest on debts

189(1) [Payment of interest] In a winding up interest is payable in accordance with this section on any debt proved in the winding up, including so much of any such debt as represents interest on the remainder.

189(2) [Surplus after payment of debts] Any surplus remaining after the payment of the debts proved in a winding up shall, before being applied for any other purpose, be applied in paying interest on those debts in respect of the periods during which they have been outstanding since the company went into liquidation.

189(3) [Ranking of interest] All interest under this section ranks equally, whether or not the debts on which it is payable rank equally.

189(4) [Rate of interest] The rate of interest payable under this section in respect of any debt ("the official rate" for the purposes of any provision of this Act in which that expression is used) is whichever is the greater of–

(a) the rate specified in section 17 of the Judgments Act 1838 on the day on which the company went into liquidation, and

(b) the rate applicable to that debt apart from the winding up.

189(5) **[Scotland]** In the application of this section to Scotland–

(a) references to a debt proved in a winding up have effect as references to a claim accepted in a winding up, and

(b) the reference to section 17 of the Judgments Act 1838 has effect as a reference to the rules.

GENERAL NOTE

Before the reform of insolvency legislation in 1985, the legal rules governing the entitlement to interest on debts in a winding up were confused and unsatisfactory (see the Cork Committee's *Report*, Ch. 31). On the recommendation of the Committee, all these old rules and the associated anomalies have been done away with and replaced by new provisions. Note that the new law applies in both solvent and insolvent liquidations.

In *Re Empire Paper Ltd* [1999] B.C.C. 406 X Ltd had guaranteed the debt of E Ltd. Both companies were in liquidation. X Ltd had been called upon to pay the debt and, since it was solvent, the debt had been paid with statutory interest under s. 189. E Ltd, however, was insolvent, and it was held that this fact prevented X Ltd from proving in the liquidation for the sum which it had paid as interest.

For the relevant rules, see IR 1986, r. 4.93.

S. 189(1)
Interest at the "official rate" (see s. 189(4)) runs on all debts and liabilities proved in the winding up, including any debts representing interest due up to the effective date of proof, and it runs from that date until a final dividend is declared or all the proved debts have been paid in full. The date will be, in a compulsory winding up, that of the winding-up order, and in a voluntary winding up, that of the winding-up resolution: *Re Lines Bros Ltd* [1983] Ch. 1, and compare s. 247(2) and IR 1986, r. 4.93. Where a creditor proves for loss or damage following a disclaimer by the liquidator, interest runs from the date of the disclaimer: *Re Park Air Services plc* [2000] 2 A.C. 172; [1999] B.C.C. 135.

S. 189(2)
Where all the debts have been paid in full, the interest allowed for by this section is payable before any money is returned to shareholders.

In regard to debts payable at a future time, see IR 1986, r. 11.13.

S. 189(3)
The preferential and non-preferential debts rank equally as regards their right to interest. To give true effect to this provision, it is submitted that no interest should be payable on the preferential debts until the preferential and non-preferential debts have both been paid in full, without interest. Any other construction of the section (*e.g.* to treat the interest on a preferential debt as being itself simply a non-preferential debt – whether or not the other non-preferential debts are reckoned with interest) would be, in effect, to give the preferential creditors an additional preference in regard to interest.

S. 189(4)
The rate of interest payable under the Judgments Act 1838, s. 17, is currently 8 per cent (SI 1993/564). If the debt itself carries interest at a higher rate, the latter is payable; but a creditor cannot merely by giving notice impose an obligation to pay interest at a rate higher than that specified in s. 189(4)(a): see IR 1986, r. 4.93(5), (6) (as amended).

S. 189(5)
A rate of 15 per cent is specified in the Insolvency (Scotland) Rules 1986 (SI 1986/1915 (S 139)), r. 4.66(2)(b).

190 Documents exempt from stamp duty

190(1) **[Application]** In the case of a winding up by the court, or of a creditors' voluntary winding up, the following has effect as regards exemption from duties chargeable under the enactments relating to stamp duties.

190(2) [Exempt documents of company registered in England and Wales] If the company is registered in England and Wales, the following documents are exempt from stamp duty–

- (a) every assurance relating solely to freehold or leasehold property, or to any estate, right or interest in, any real or personal property, which forms part of the company's assets and which, after the execution of the assurance, either at law or in equity, is or remains part of those assets, and

- (b) every writ, order, certificate, or other instrument or writing relating solely to the property of any company which is being wound up as mentioned in subsection (1), or to any proceeding under such a winding up.

"**Assurance**" here includes deed, conveyance, assignment and surrender.

190(3) [Exempt document of company registered in Scotland] If the company is registered in Scotland, the following documents are exempt from stamp duty–

- (a) every conveyance relating solely to property, which forms part of the company's assets and which, after the execution of the conveyance, is or remains the company's property for the benefit of its creditors,

- (b) any articles of roup or sale, submission and every other instrument and writing whatsoever relating solely to the company's property, and

- (c) every deed or writing forming part of the proceedings in the winding up.

"**Conveyance**" here includes assignation, instrument, discharge, writing and deed.

GENERAL NOTE

This section applies only in the case of a winding up by the court or a creditors' voluntary winding up. It exempts from stamp duty all conveyances, etc. which are made to facilitate the winding up and which do not beneficially transfer assets out the hands of the liquidator.

191   Company's books to be evidence

191   Where a company is being wound up, all books and papers of the company and of the liquidators are, as between the contributories of the company, prima facie evidence of the truth of all matters purporting to be recorded in them.

GENERAL NOTE

The presumption which this provision creates applies only "as between the contributories of the company", and is rebuttable.

192   Information as to pending liquidations

192(1) [Statement to registrar] If the winding up of a company is not concluded within one year after its commencement, the liquidator shall, at such intervals as may be prescribed, until the winding up is concluded, send to the registrar of companies a statement in the prescribed form and containing the prescribed particulars with respect to the proceedings in, and position of, the liquidation.

192(2) [Penalty on default] If a liquidator fails to comply with this section, he is liable to a fine and, for continued contravention, to a daily default fine.

S. 192(1)
The rules prescribed for the purposes of this provision are to be found in IR 1986, r. 4.223, which appears to apply only in a voluntary winding up; the "intervals prescribed" are every six months, after the initial year of the liquidation.

S. 192(2)
On penalties, see s. 430 and Sch. 10.
 The liquidator's obligations may also be enforced by seeking an order for compliance under s. 170. If a liquidator fails to comply with such an order, he will be in contempt of court and liable to imprisonment: *Re S & A Conversions Ltd* (1988) 4 B.C.C. 384; *Re Allan Ellis (Transport & Packing) Services Ltd* (1989) 5 B.C.C. 835.

193 Unclaimed dividends (Scotland)

193(1) **[Application]** The following applies where a company registered in Scotland has been wound up, and is about to be dissolved.

193(2) **[Liquidator to lodge unclaimed money in bank]** The liquidator shall lodge in an appropriate bank or institution as defined in section 73(1) of the Bankruptcy (Scotland) Act 1985 (not being a bank or institution in or of which the liquidator is an acting partner, manager, agent or cashier) in the name of the Accountant of Court the whole unclaimed dividends and unapplied or undistributable balances, and the deposit receipts shall be transmitted to the Accountant of Court.

193(3) **[Application of Bankruptcy (Scotland) Act]** The provisions of section 58 of the Bankruptcy (Scotland) Act 1985 (so far as consistent with this Act and the Companies Act) apply with any necessary modifications to sums lodged in a bank or institution under this section as they apply to sums deposited under section 57 of the Act first mentioned.

GENERAL NOTE

Section 57 of the Bankruptcy (Scotland) Act 1985 (as amended) provides that unclaimed dividends in an individual bankruptcy shall be held in a bank in the name of the Accountant in Bankruptcy for a period of seven years, during which they may be claimed by those entitled. After the seven years, the money passes to the Secretary of State who may thereafter pay undisputed claims in his discretion.
 The present section applies the same rules to a company liquidation in Scotland.

194 Resolutions passed at adjourned meetings

194 Where a resolution is passed at an adjourned meeting of a company's creditors or contributories, the resolution is treated for all purposes as having been passed on the date on which it was in fact passed, and not as having been passed on any earlier date.

GENERAL NOTE

This provision is confirmed in its application to meetings held in connection with a winding up. For other meetings, CA 1985, s. 381 lays down a similar rule, reversing the decision at common law in *Neuschild v British Equitorial Oil Co. Ltd* [1925] Ch. 346.

195 Meetings to ascertain wishes of creditors or contributories

195(1) **[Power of court]** The court may–

(a) as to all matters relating to the winding up of a company, have regard to the wishes of the creditors or contributories (as proved to it by any sufficient evidence), and

(b) if it thinks fit, for the purpose of ascertaining those wishes, direct meetings of the creditors or contributories to be called, held and conducted in such manner as the court directs, and appoint a person to act as chairman of any such meeting and report the result of it to the court.

195(2) **[Creditors]** In the case of creditors, regard shall be had to the value of each creditor's debt.

195(3) **[Contributories]** In the case of contributories, regard shall be had to the number of votes conferred on each contributory by the Companies Act or the articles.

GENERAL NOTE

The use of "may", rather than "shall", in the opening words of the section gives the court a residuary discretion to act without having regard to the wishes of the creditors (or contributories) where there are "special circumstances" – *e.g.* where it is not practicable to hold meetings because of the complexities of the case and the difficulty of identifying who the creditors are: *Re Bank of Credit & Commerce International SA (No. 2)* [1992] B.C.C. 715. However, the court will not lightly disregard or overrule the views of the majority creditors whose interests are at stake: *Re Falcon R J. Developments Ltd* (1987) 3 B.C.C. 146: *Re William Thorpe & Son Ltd* (1989) 5 B.C.C. 156. See also the note to s. 125(1), above.

The conduct of any meetings directed by the court to be called is dealt with by the rules, as well as being covered in part by the terms of the section itself. For the relevant rules, see IR 1986, rr. 4.54ff.

196 Judicial notice of court documents

196 In all proceedings under this Part, all courts, judges and persons judicially acting, and all officers, judicial or ministerial, of any court, or employed in enforcing the process of any court shall take judicial notice–

(a) of the signature of any officer of the High Court or of a county court in England and Wales, or of the Court of Session or a sheriff court in Scotland, or of the High Court in Northern Ireland, and also

(b) of the official seal or stamp of the several offices of the High Court in England and Wales or Northern Ireland, or of the Court of Session, appended to or impressed on any document made, issued or signed under the provisions of this Act or the Companies Act, or any official copy of such a document.

197 Commission for receiving evidence

197(1) [**Courts for examination of witnesses**] When a company is wound up in England and Wales or in Scotland, the court may refer the whole or any part of the examination of witnesses–

(a) to a specified county court in England and Wales, or

(b) to the sheriff principal for a specified sheriffdom in Scotland, or

(c) to the High Court in Northern Ireland or a specified Northern Ireland County Court,

(**"specified"** meaning specified in the order of the winding-up court).

197(2) [**Commissioners for taking evidence**] Any person exercising jurisdiction as a judge of the court to which the reference is made (or, in Scotland, the sheriff principal to whom it is made) shall then, by virtue of this section, be a commissioner for the purpose of taking the evidence of those witnesses.

197(3) [**Power of judge or sheriff principal**] The judge or sheriff principal has in the matter referred the same power of summoning and examining witnesses, of requiring the production and delivery of documents, of punishing defaults by witnesses, and of allowing costs and expenses to witnesses, as the court which made the winding-up order.

These powers are in addition to any which the judge or sheriff principal might lawfully exercise apart from this section.

197(4) [**Return or report re examination**] The examination so taken shall be returned or reported to the court which made the order in such manner as that court requests.

197(5) [**Northern Ireland**] This section extends to Northern Ireland.

198 Court order for examination of persons in Scotland

198(1) [**Examination of any person on affairs of company**] The court may direct the examination in Scotland of any person for the time being in Scotland (whether a contributory of the company or not), in regard to the trade, dealings, affairs or property of any company in the course of being wound up, or of any person being a contributory of the company, so far as the company may be interested by reason of his being a contributory.

198(2) **[Directions to take examination]** The order or commission to take the examination shall be directed to the sheriff principal of the sheriffdom in which the person to be examined is residing or happens to be for the time; and the sheriff principal shall summon the person to appear before him at a time and place to be specified in the summons for examination on oath as a witness or as a haver, and to produce any books or papers called for which are in his possession or power.

198(3) **[Duties of sheriff principal re examination]** The sheriff principal may take the examination either orally or on written interrogatories, and shall report the same in writing in the usual form to the court, and shall transmit with the report the books and papers produced, if the originals are required and specified by the order or commission, or otherwise copies or extracts authenticated by the sheriff.

198(4) **[Where person fails to appear for examination]** If a person so summoned fails to appear at the time and place specified, or refuses to be examined or to make the production required, the sheriff principal shall proceed against him as a witness or haver duly cited; and failing to appear or refusing to give evidence or make production may be proceeded against by the law of Scotland.

198(5) **[Fees and allowances]** The sheriff principal is entitled to such fees, and the witness is entitled to such allowances, as sheriffs principal when acting as commissioners under appointment from the Court of Session and as witnesses and havers are entitled to in the like cases according to the law and practice of Scotland.

198(6) **[Objection by witness]** If any objection is stated to the sheriff principal by the witness, either on the ground of his incompetency as a witness, or as to the production required, or on any other ground, the sheriff principal may, if he thinks fit, report the objection to the court, and suspend the examination of the witness until it has been disposed of by the court.

GENERAL NOTE

This section applies in Scotland in addition to ss. 133 and 236, which also provide for the judicial examination of persons who have been connected with a company that is in liquidation. There appears to be a considerable degree of overlap.

199 Costs of application for leave to proceed (Scottish companies)

199 Where a petition or application for leave to proceed with an action or proceeding against a company which is being wound up in Scotland is unopposed and is granted by the court, the costs of the petition or application shall, unless the court otherwise directs, be added to the amount of the petitioner's or applicant's claim against the company.

200 Affidavits etc. in United Kingdom and overseas

200(1) **[Swearing of affidavit]** An affidavit required to be sworn under or for the purposes of this Part may be sworn in the United Kingdom, or elsewhere in Her Majesty's dominions, before any court, judge or person lawfully authorised to take and receive affidavits, or before any of Her Majesty's consuls or vice-consuls in any place outside Her dominions.

200(2) **[Judicial notice of signatures etc.]** All courts, judges, justices, commissioners and persons acting judicially shall take judicial notice of the seal or stamp or signature (as the case may be) of any such court, judge, person, consul or vice-consul attached, appended or subscribed to any such affidavit, or to any other document to be used for the purposes of this Part.

GENERAL NOTE

This provision is designed to simplify the normal requirements for the taking of evidence abroad, for use in winding-up proceedings.

CHAPTER IX

DISSOLUTION OF COMPANIES AFTER WINDING UP

General comment on Pt IV, Ch. IX
The dissolution of a company extinguishes its legal personality, so that it goes out of existence for all purposes. Any property and rights formerly vested in it are deemed to belong to the Crown, as *bona vacantia*. (Note, however, that in *Re Wilmott Trading Ltd* [2000] B.C.C. 321 Neuberger J. held that the particular "property" in that case – a waste management licence – did not revert to the Crown on the dissolution of the company, but ceased to exist.)

The court is, however, given power by CA 1985, s. 651, to declare the dissolution of a company void, so that it is reinstated. An application for reinstatement under this section must normally be made within two years from the date of dissolution (s. 651(4)) but special provisions (effective from November 16, 1989: see SI 1990/1392 (C. 41)) declare that this limitation shall not apply where the application is made for the purpose of bringing actions for personal injuries or claims under the Fatal Accidents Act 1976 or the Damages (Scotland) Act 1976 (see s. 651(5)–(7) and, for transitional provisions, CA 1989, s. 141(4), (5)). (Note that the proposed extension from two to 12 years contemplated by IA 1985, s. 109 and Sch. 6, para. 45 was never brought into effect and has now been repealed: see CA 1989, s. 212 and Sch. 24, and SI 1990/355 (C. 13), art. 5(1)(c).)

Applications under s. 651 may be made by "any person appearing to the court to be interested" – a phrase which has been construed as extending to the Secretary of State, who sought reinstatement for the purpose of instituting director disqualification proceedings and investigating the company's affairs (*Re a Company No. 002081 of 1994, Re a Company No. 002082 of 1994* [1994] B.C.C. 933). If an order for reinstatement would affect the rights of a third party, that person is entitled to be joined in the application: *Re Forte's (Manufacturing) Ltd, Stanhope Pension Trust Ltd v Registrar of Companies* [1994] B.C.C. 84.

Under the former provisions of the Companies Acts, different rules regarding dissolution applied in a compulsory winding up and a voluntary winding up, a court order being always required in the former case. The reforms in the law of insolvency introduced by IA 1985 have dispensed with this need for a court order and so brought the various types of winding up into line. A further innovation is the provision for early dissolution now contained in s. 202 below. This enables the official receiver, in a winding up by the court, to apply to the registrar of companies to have the company dissolved at an early stage in the liquidation, when the company is so hopelessly insolvent that it is pointless to proceed further. In Scotland, the liquidator is empowered to make a similar application to the court (s. 204).

In addition to these procedures, a company may be dissolved by having its name struck off the register under CA 1985, s. 652, on the ground that it has ceased to carry on business. The court has power to restore to the register the name of a company so struck off if application is made to it by the company, a member or a creditor within 20 years (CA 1985, s. 653). Restoration under s. 653, unlike reinstatement under s. 651, is retrospective in its effect, so that everything that has been done in the company's name during the period when it was struck off is automatically validated: compare *Morris v Harris* [1927] A.C. 252 and *Tyman's Ltd v Craven* [1952] 2 Q.B. 100; and see *Top Creative Ltd v St Albans DC* [1999] B.C.C. 999.

For cases on the exercise of the jurisdiction under s. 653, see *Shire Court Residents Ltd v Registrar of Companies* [1995] B.C.C. 821; *Re Jayham Ltd* [1996] B.C.C. 224; *Re Priceland Ltd* [1997] B.C.C. 207; *City of Westminster Assurance Co. Ltd v Registrar of Companies* [1997] B.C.C. 960.

201 Dissolution (voluntary winding up)

201(1) **[Application]** This section applies, in the case of a company wound up voluntarily, where the liquidator has sent to the registrar of companies his final account and return under section 94 (members' voluntary) or section 106 (creditors' voluntary).

201(2) **[Duty of registrar]** The registrar on receiving the account and return shall forthwith register them; and on the expiration of 3 months from the registration of the return the company is deemed to be dissolved.

201(3) **[Power of court re deferring date]** However, the court may, on the application of the liquidator or any other person who appears to the court to be interested, make an order deferring the date at which the dissolution of the company is to take effect for such time as the court thinks fit.

201(4) **[Copy of order to registrar]** It is the duty of the person on whose application an order of the court under this section is made within 7 days after the making of the order to deliver to the registrar an office copy of the order for registration; and if that person fails to do so he is liable to a fine and, for continued contravention, to a daily default fine.

GENERAL NOTE

The company is automatically dissolved under this section on the expiration of three months from the filing of the liquidator's final return: no further formality is needed.

S. 201(3), (4)
The power of the court under subsection (3) is limited to extending the three-month period.
   On penalties, see s. 430 and Sch. 10.

202 Early dissolution (England and Wales)

202(1) **[Application]** This section applies where an order for the winding up of a company has been made by the court in England and Wales.

202(2) **[Official receiver may apply for dissolution]** The official receiver, if–

(a)   he is the liquidator of the company, and

(b)   it appears to him–

> (i) that the realisable assets of the company are insufficient to cover the expenses of the winding up, and
> (ii) that the affairs of the company do not require any further investigation,

may at any time apply to the registrar of companies for the early dissolution of the company.

202(3) **[Notice by official receiver]** Before making that application, the official receiver shall give not less than 28 days' notice of his intention to do so to the company's creditors and contributories and, if there is an administrative receiver of the company, to that receiver.

202(4) **[Effect of notice on official receiver]** With the giving of that notice the official receiver ceases (subject to any directions under the next section) to be required to perform any duties imposed on him in relation to the company, its creditors or contributories by virtue of any provision of this Act, apart from a duty to make an application under subsection (2) of this section.

202(5) **[Duty of registrar]** On the receipt of the official receiver's application under subsection (2) the registrar shall forthwith register it and, at the end of the period of 3 months beginning with the day of the registration of the application, the company shall be dissolved.

   However, the Secretary of State may, on the application of the official receiver or any other person who appears to the Secretary of State to be interested, give directions under section 203 at any time before the end of that period.

GENERAL NOTE

The Cork Committee (*Report*, paras 649–651) recommended that a procedure should be introduced to enable the official receiver to apply to the court for the early dissolution of a company which was in compulsory liquidation and hopelessly insolvent. The legislature has gone one better and dispensed with the need for a court order: the official receiver's application is sent to the registrar of companies and takes effect automatically after three months, unless the Secretary of State intervenes in the meantime. The official receiver (and the taxpayer) is thus spared the pointless expense of completing the winding up. A similar procedure is now available where a company in administration is hopelessly insolvent: see Sch. B1, para. 84.

S. 202(1)
For the corresponding provision for Scotland, see s. 204.

S. 202(2)

The powers under this section may be exercised only by the official receiver, and only if he is the liquidator.

Paragraph (2)(b)(ii) leaves it to the judgment of the official receiver to decide that the circumstances of the insolvency do not create any suspicion of impropriety, and perhaps even to consider such policy questions as whether the circumstances, though dubious, really justify the expenditure of public money which would be involved in investigating the company's affairs further.

S. 202(3), (4)

The official receiver's duties (as liquidator or otherwise) cease as soon as he gives the notice, *i.e.* even while the 28-day period referred to in s. 202(3) and the three-month period in s. 202(5) are running, he has no obligation to take further steps in the liquidation.

It seems that the liquidator comes under a *duty* to apply for a dissolution once he has given a notice under s. 202(3): if he starts the dissolution process, he must go through with it, and if he has second thoughts he must invoke the powers of the Secretary of State under s. 203.

S. 202(5)

The dissolution takes effect automatically on the expiry of the three-month period, unless the Secretary of State has directed that a longer period than three months be substituted.

203   Consequence of notice under s. 202

203(1)   [Application for directions] Where a notice has been given under section 202(3), the official receiver or any creditor or contributory of the company, or the administrative receiver of the company (if there is one) may apply to the Secretary of State for directions under this section.

203(2)   [Grounds for application] The grounds on which that application may be made are–

(a)   that the realisable assets of the company are sufficient to cover the expenses of the winding up;

(b)   that the affairs of the company do require further investigation; or

(c)   that for any other reason the early dissolution of the company is inappropriate.

203(3)   [Scope of directions] Directions under this section–

(a)   are directions making such provision as the Secretary of State thinks fit for enabling the winding up of the company to proceed as if no notice had been given under section 202(3), and

(b)   may, in the case of an application under section 202(5), include a direction deferring the date at which the dissolution of the company is to take effect for such period as the Secretary of State thinks fit.

203(4)   [Appeal to court] An appeal to the court lies from any decision of the Secretary of State on an application for directions under this section.

203(5)   [Copy of directions etc. to registrar] It is the duty of the person on whose application any directions are given under this section, or in whose favour an appeal with respect to an application for such directions is determined, within 7 days after the giving of the directions or the determination of the appeal, to deliver to the registrar of companies for registration such a copy of the directions or determination as is prescribed.

203(6)   [Penalty on default re s. 203(5)] If a person without reasonable excuse fails to deliver a copy as required by subsection (5), he is liable to a fine and, for continued contravention, to a daily default fine.

S. 203(1)–(3)

The Secretary of State is empowered by this section to override the official receiver's notice under s. 202(3) which initiated the dissolution process, so that the winding up proceeds as before. It also appears from s. 203(3)(b) that the Secretary of State may confirm the effect of the notice but delay the dissolution by substituting a longer period than three months for the operation of s. 202(5).

S. 203(4)

The use of the term "appeal" is significant, since it makes it clear that the court may substitute its own decision on the merits of the case for that of the Secretary of State. For the relevant procedure, see IR 1986, rr. 4.224, 4.225.

S. 203(5)
The seven-day period is extremely short, especially since it runs from the date of the giving of the directions or determination of the appeal, and not from the day when the applicant is notified of the outcome of his application.

It does not appear that there is any obligation to register a decision on the part of the Secretary of State to give no "directions". (However, there is equally no machinery provided to warn the registrar that an application to the Secretary of State has been made: time will continue to run for the purposes of s. 202(5) while such an application is under consideration.)

S. 203(6)
On penalties, see s. 430 and Sch. 10.

204 Early dissolution (Scotland)

204(1) [Application] This section applies where a winding-up order has been made by the court in Scotland.

204(2) [Application by liquidator] If after a meeting or meetings under section 138 (appointment of liquidator in Scotland) it appears to the liquidator that the realisable assets of the company are insufficient to cover the expenses of the winding up, he may apply to the court for an order that the company be dissolved.

204(3) [Court order] Where the liquidator makes that application, if the court is satisfied that the realisable assets of the company are insufficient to cover the expenses of the winding up and it appears to the court appropriate to do so, the court shall make an order that the company be dissolved in accordance with this section.

204(4) [Copy of order to registrar etc.] A copy of the order shall within 14 days from its date be forwarded by the liquidator to the registrar of companies, who shall forthwith register it; and, at the end of the period of 3 months beginning with the day of the registration of the order, the company shall be dissolved.

204(5) [Court may defer dissolution] The court may, on an application by any person who appears to the court to have an interest, order that the date at which the dissolution of the company is to take effect shall be deferred for such period as the court thinks fit.

204(6) [Copy of s. 204(5) order to registrar] It is the duty of the person on whose application an order is made under subsection (5), within 7 days after the making of the order, to deliver to the registrar of companies such a copy of the order as is prescribed.

204(7) [Penalty for non-compliance with s. 204(4)] If the liquidator without reasonable excuse fails to comply with the requirements of subsection (4), he is liable to a fine and, for continued contravention, to a daily default fine.

204(8) [Penalty for non-compliance with s. 204(6)] If a person without reasonable excuse fails to deliver a copy as required by subsection (6), he is liable to a fine and, for continued contravention, to a daily default fine.

GENERAL NOTE

There is no official receiver in Scotland, so that a private liquidator will be in office in every winding up by the court. In the absence of a public officer comparable with the official receiver, it is necessary in Scotland to refer to the court for decision the question whether an early dissolution of the company is justified. This section accordingly modifies the procedure of ss. 202, 203 to meet the different circumstances in Scotland.

S. 204(2)
There is no obligation in Scotland to give the company's creditors and contributories the 28-day notice required in England and Wales by s. 202(3). In Scotland, on the other hand, the liquidator cannot set any steps in motion to bring

Section 205   Insolvency Act 1986

about an early dissolution until after the meetings of creditors and contributories have been held. It is reasonable to assume that they will have been made aware of the company's hopeless insolvency at the statutory meetings.

S. 204(3)–(8)
The whole of the proceedings in an application for early dissolution in Scotland are dealt with by the court. There is no involvement of the Secretary of State at any stage. Apart from this, the comments to ss. 202, 203 apply to the present section.
On penalties, see s. 430 and Sch. 10.

205   Dissolution otherwise than under ss. 202–204

205(1)   [Application] This section applies where the registrar of companies receives–

(a)   a notice served for the purposes of section 172(8) (final meeting of creditors and vacation of office by liquidator), or

(b)   a notice from the official receiver that the winding up of a company by the court is complete.

205(2)   [Duty of registrar etc.] The registrar shall, on receipt of the notice, forthwith register it; and, subject as follows, at the end of the period of 3 months beginning with the day of the registration of the notice, the company shall be dissolved.

205(3)   [Deferral by Secretary of State] The Secretary of State may, on the application of the official receiver or any other person who appears to the Secretary of State to be interested, give a direction deferring the date at which the dissolution of the company is to take effect for such period as the Secretary of State thinks fit.

205(4)   [Appeal to court] An appeal to the court lies from any decision of the Secretary of State on an application for a direction under subsection (3).

205(5)   [Non-application of s. 205(3) in Scotland] Subsection (3) does not apply in a case where the winding-up order was made by the court in Scotland, but in such a case the court may, on an application by any person appearing to the court to have an interest, order that the date at which the dissolution of the company is to take effect shall be deferred for such period as the court thinks fit.

205(6)   [Copy of direction etc. to registrar] It is the duty of the person–

(a)   on whose application a direction is given under subsection (3);

(b)   in whose favour an appeal with respect to an application for such a direction is determined; or

(c)   on whose application an order is made under subsection (5),

within 7 days after the giving of the direction, the determination of the appeal or the making of the order, to deliver to the registrar for registration such a copy of the direction, determination or order as is prescribed.

205(7)   [Penalty for non-compliance with s. 205(6)] If a person without reasonable excuse fails to deliver a copy as required by subsection (6), he is liable to a fine and, for continued contravention, to a daily default fine.

S. 205(1), (2)
Dissolution takes place automatically three months after the registrar has been given the notification by the liquidator or the official receiver required by this section: no court order is required.

S. 205(3)–(4)
The Secretary of State, in England and Wales, and the court are given roles under the present section comparable with those which they discharge in relation to the early liquidation procedure under ss. 202(5), 203(3)(b) and 203(4): see, further, the notes to those provisions, and for the relevant procedure, see IR 1986, rr. 4.224, 4.225.

S. 205(5)
Compare s. 204(5), and see the notes to that subsection.

S. 205(6), (7)
Compare ss. 203(5), (6) and 204(6), (8), and for the relevant rule, see IR 1986, r. 4.224.
On penalties, see s. 430 and Sch. 10.

CHAPTER X

MALPRACTICE BEFORE AND DURING LIQUIDATION; PENALISATION OF COMPANIES AND COMPANY OFFICERS; INVESTIGATIONS AND PROSECUTIONS

Offences of fraud, deception, etc.

206 Fraud, etc. in anticipation of winding up

206(1) **[Offences by officers]** When a company is ordered to be wound up by the court, or passes a resolution for voluntary winding up, any person, being a past or present officer of the company, is deemed to have committed an offence if, within the 12 months immediately preceding the commencement of the winding up, he has–

(a) concealed any part of the company's property to the value of £500 or more, or concealed any debt due to or from the company, or

(b) fraudulently removed any part of the company's property to the value of £500 or more, or

(c) concealed, destroyed, mutilated or falsified any book or paper affecting or relating to the company's property or affairs, or

(d) made any false entry in any book or paper affecting or relating to the company's property or affairs, or

(e) fraudulently parted with, altered or made any omission in any document affecting or relating to the company's property or affairs, or

(f) pawned, pledged or disposed of any property of the company which has been obtained on credit and has not been paid for (unless the pawning, pledging or disposal was in the ordinary way of the company's business).

206(2) **[Further offences]** Such a person is deemed to have committed an offence if within the period above mentioned he has been privy to the doing by others of any of the things mentioned in paragraphs (c), (d) and (e) of subsection (1); and he commits an offence if, at any time after the commencement of the winding up, he does any of the things mentioned in paragraphs (a) to (f) of that subsection, or is privy to the doing by others of any of the things mentioned in paragraphs (c) to (e) of it.

206(3) **["Officer"]** For purposes of this section, **"officer"** includes a shadow director.

206(4) **[Defences]** It is a defence–

(a) for a person charged under paragraph (a) or (f) of subsection (1) (or under subsection (2) in respect of the things mentioned in either of those two paragraphs) to prove that he had no intent to defraud, and

(b) for a person charged under paragraph (c) or (d) of subsection (1) (or under subsection (2) in respect of the things mentioned in either of those two paragraphs) to prove that he had no intent to conceal the state of affairs of the company or to defeat the law.

206(5) **[Offence re person pawning property etc. as in s. 206(1)(f)]** Where a person pawns, pledges or disposes of any property in circumstances which amount to an offence under subsection (1)(f), every person who takes in pawn or pledge, or otherwise receives, the property knowing it to be pawned, pledged or disposed of in such circumstances, is guilty of an offence.

206(6) **[Penalty]** A person guilty of an offence under this section is liable to imprisonment or a fine, or both.

206(7) **[Increase, reduction of sums in s. 206(1)(a), (b)]** The money sums specified in paragraphs (a) and (b) of subsection (1) are subject to increase or reduction by order under section 416 in Part XV.

S. 206(1), (2)
This section makes it an offence for an officer of a company to conceal or remove property, falsify entries in the company's books or perpetrate other similar acts after the commencement of a winding up (s. 206(2)), and "deems" an officer or past officer to have committed an offence if he has been guilty of any of these acts and a winding up ensues within the next 12 months (s. 206(1)).

The diversion of a debt due to a company into the account of the accused or a third party is equivalent to the "removal" of property for the purposes of s. 206(1)(b): *R. v Robinson* [1990] B.C.C. 656.

It may be a defence to a charge under s. 206(1) that the liquidator has abandoned the property in question, but this will not be established without proof that the liquidator is aware of its existence – which it will be the duty of the officers of the company (in most cases, the defendants themselves) to declare and deliver up under s. 208: *R. v McCredie* [2000] B.C.C. 617.

S. 206(3)
The term "officer" is not defined with precision: the definition in CA 1985, s. 744 (which is incorporated into the present Act by the concluding words of s. 251) merely states that "officer, in relation to a body corporate, *includes* a director, manager or secretary". A director "includes any person occupying the position of director, by whatever name called" (s. 251). A director (in this extended sense) and a secretary plainly will always be "officers". Shadow directors (for definition, see s. 251) are frequently declared to be officers for the purposes of a particular provision, as in the present subsection, and so it might be reasonable to infer that where there is no such statement (*e.g.* as in s. 207) the opposite is the case. The same argument would apply in the case of a liquidator: the fact that he is declared to be an officer for the purposes of s. 85(2), for example, suggests that he is ordinarily not to be deemed one. This is confirmed by the distinction that appears to be drawn between "officers" on the one hand and liquidators, administrators and receivers on the other (*e.g.* by ss. 133(1) and 212(1), and compare also s. 219(3)).

The word "manager", used in CA 1985, s. 744, could well be a source of difficulty. It is not clear whether a person would need to have been appointed to a post carrying managerial responsibilities to come within this concept, or whether it is sufficient that he has taken some part in the management of the company's business, even at a relatively humble level. In *Re a Company No. 00996 of 1979* [1980] Ch. 138 at p. 144, Shaw L.J. said:

> "The expression 'manager' should not be too narrowly construed. It is not to be equated with a managing or other director or a general manager. . . . [Any] person who in the affairs of the company exercises a supervisory control which reflects the general policy of the company for the time being or which is related to the general administration of the company is in the sphere of management. He need not be a member of the board of directors. He need not be subject to specific instructions from the board".

A number of provisions in the legislation (*e.g.* IA 1986, ss. 212(1)(c), 216(3), 217(4) and CDDA 1986, ss. 1(1)(d), 11, 15(4)) refer to a person "taking part in the management" of a company (and compare "involved in the management": IA 1986, s. 217(1), CDDA 1986, ss. 2, 15(1)). It would not necessarily follow that a person coming within such a formula was a "manager" for the purposes of the present section, but cases decided under these provisions may be of some relevance: see, *e.g. CCA v Brecht* (1987) 7 A.C.L.C. 40; *Re Clasper Group Services Ltd* (1988) 4 B.C.C. 673; *Drew v Lord Advocate* 1996 S.L.T. 1062; *Re a Company* [1980] Ch. 138; *Re Market Wizard Systems (UK) Ltd* [1998] 2 B.C.L.C. 282; and *R. v Doring* [2002] EWCA Crim 1695, [2002] B.C.C. 838.

Both an administrator and a receiver and manager (including an administrative receiver) discharge functions which can only be described as managerial, but in the leading case of *Re B Johnson & Co. (Builders) Ltd* [1955] Ch. 634 a receiver and manager appointed by a debenture-holder was held not to be an "officer" for the purposes of what is now s. 212. (The point is now covered by s. 212(1)(b)). An administrator has been held to be an "officer" who may be granted relief under the court's discretionary jurisdiction conferred by CA 1985, s. 727: *Re Home Treat Ltd* [1991] B.C.C. 165.

An auditor has been held to be an officer for the purposes of s. 212 in a number of cases, *e.g. Re London and General Bank* [1895] 2 Ch. 166; *Re Thomas Gerrard & Son Ltd* [1968] Ch. 455 at p. 473; and also under other statutory provisions similar to s. 206: *R v Shacter* [1960] 2 Q.B. 252; but the question is not free from doubt: compare CA 1985, s. 727 ("whether or not he is an officer of the company").

Bankers and solicitors and other professional advisers are not, as such, "officers" of the company (*Re Imperial Land Co. of Marseilles, Re National Bank* (1870) L.R. 10 Eq. 298), as appears to be confirmed by s. 219(3).

S. 206(4)

The onus of proof with respect to *mens rea* is, unusually, put on the defendant. In such a case, the burden of proof on the accused is less than that required at the hands of the prosecution, which must prove the case "beyond reasonable doubt": instead, the burden may be discharged by evidence which satisfies the court on a balance of probabilities: *R. v Carr-Briant* [1943] K.B. 607; *Morton v Confer* [1963] 1 W.L.R. 763; [1963] 2 All E.R. 765. This, at least, was the position before the enactment of the Human Rights Act 1986. In *R. v Carass* [2001] EWCA Civ. 2845, [2002] 1 W.L.R. 1714, the Court of Appeal preferred to state the present law as follows: "It is a defence for a person charged ... to adduce evidence sufficient to raise an issue that he had no intent to defraud unless, if he does so, the prosecution proves the contrary beyond reasonable doubt".

S. 206(5)

In regard to the offence created by this provision, the normal rule as to onus of proof will apply.

S. 206(6)

The sanctions fixed by Sch. 10 for these offences and the other offences involving dishonesty defined in the following sections are severe: up to seven years' imprisonment.

On penalties, see s. 430 and Sch. 10.

S. 206(7)

See the note to s. 206(1), (2) above.

207 Transactions in fraud of creditors

207(1) [Offences by officers] When a company is ordered to be wound up by the court or passes a resolution for voluntary winding up, a person is deemed to have committed an offence if he, being at the time an officer of the company–

(a) has made or caused to be made any gift or transfer of, or charge on, or has caused or connived at the levying of any execution against, the company's property, or

(b) has concealed or removed any part of the company's property since, or within 2 months before, the date of any unsatisfied judgment or order for the payment of money obtained against the company.

207(2) [Exception] A person is not guilty of an offence under this section–

(a) by reason of conduct constituting an offence under subsection (1)(a) which occurred more than 5 years before the commencement of the winding up, or

(b) if he proves that, at the time of the conduct constituting the offence, he had no intent to defraud the company's creditors.

207(3) [Penalty] A person guilty of an offence under this section is liable to imprisonment or a fine, or both.

GENERAL NOTE

The offences defined by this section are brought forward from earlier Companies Acts. However, a modification made by IA 1985 has had the effect of reversing the onus of proof of *mens rea*: the words "with intent to defraud creditors of the company" have been removed from the substantive definition of the crime, and s. 207(2)(b) (matching s. 206(4) above) has been added.

Section 208 *Insolvency Act 1986*

S. 207(1)
There is no definition of "officer", corresponding to ss. 206(3) and 208(3), extending the term to include a shadow director for the purposes of this section.

S. 207(3)
On penalties, see s. 430 and Sch. 10.

208 Misconduct in course of winding up

208(1) [Offences by officers] When a company is being wound up, whether by the court or voluntarily, any person, being a past or present officer of the company, commits an offence if he–

(a) does not to the best of his knowledge and belief fully and truly discover to the liquidator all the company's property, and how and to whom and for what consideration and when the company disposed of any part of that property (except such part as has been disposed of in the ordinary way of the company's business), or

(b) does not deliver up to the liquidator (or as he directs) all such part of the company's property as is in his custody or under his control, and which he is required by law to deliver up, or

(c) does not deliver up to the liquidator (or as he directs) all books and papers in his custody or under his control belonging to the company and which he is required by law to deliver up, or

(d) knowing or believing that a false debt has been proved by any person in the winding up, fails to inform the liquidator as soon as practicable, or

(e) after the commencement of the winding up, prevents the production of any book or paper affecting or relating to the company's property or affairs.

208(2) [Further offences] Such a person commits an offence if after the commencement of the winding up he attempts to account for any part of the company's property by fictitious losses or expenses; and he is deemed to have committed that offence if he has so attempted at any meeting of the company's creditors within the 12 months immediately preceding the commencement of the winding up.

208(3) ["Officer"] For purposes of this section, **"officer"** includes a shadow director.

208(4) [Defences] It is a defence–

(a) for a person charged under paragraph (a), (b) or (c) of subsection (1) to prove that he had no intent to defraud, and

(b) for a person charged under paragraph (e) of that subsection to prove that he had no intent to conceal the state of affairs of the company or to defeat the law.

208(5) [Penalty] A person guilty of an offence under this section is liable to imprisonment or a fine, or both.

GENERAL NOTE

The notes to s. 206 apply generally to the present section.

S. 208(4)
See the note to s. 206(4).

209 Falsification of company's books

209(1) [Offence by officer or contributory] When a company is being wound up, an officer or contributory of the company commits an offence if he destroys, mutilates, alters or falsifies any books, papers or securities, or makes or is privy to the making of any false or fraudulent entry in any register, book of account or document belonging to the company with intent to defraud or deceive any person.

209(2) [Penalty] A person guilty of an offence under this section is liable to imprisonment or a fine, or both.

GENERAL NOTE

The offences which this section defines largely duplicate those specified in s. 206(1)(c)–(e), which apply in a winding up by virtue of s. 206(2); but those potentially liable include contributories (though not, at least in specific terms, "shadow directors"), and the element of *mens rea* is expressed differently: compare s. 206(4)(b).

210 Material omissions from statement relating to company's affairs

210(1) **[Offence by past or present officer]** When a company is being wound up, whether by the court or voluntarily, any person, being a past or present officer of the company, commits an offence if he makes any material omission in any statement relating to the company's affairs.

210(2) **[Offence prior to winding up]** When a company has been ordered to be wound up by the court, or has passed a resolution for voluntary winding up, any such person is deemed to have committed that offence if, prior to the winding up, he has made any material omission in any such statement.

210(3) **["Officer"]** For purposes of this section, **"officer"** includes a shadow director.

210(4) **[Defence]** It is a defence for a person charged under this section to prove that he had no intent to defraud.

210(5) **[Penalty]** A person guilty of an offence under this section is liable to imprisonment or a fine, or both.

GENERAL NOTE

The "statement of affairs", which under the Companies Acts was part of the standard procedure in a winding up by the court, has now become a feature of many other forms of insolvency procedure, *e.g.* administration and receivership (see the note to s. 131). The present section is not confined in its scope to the statutory "statement of affairs" so defined, but applies to "any statement in relation to the company's affairs". It is, however, limited to statements made when a company is being wound up, or prior to a winding up; and it is concerned only with omissions. *Positive* misstatements relating to a company's affairs in a winding up will almost certainly amount to one or other of the offences defined in ss. 206–209; but similar wrongdoing in other insolvency proceedings may be sanctioned only by the less draconian provisions of s. 235, unless of course they are criminal offences apart from the present Act.

Liability under the section is limited to past and present officers of the company (including shadow directors: s. 210(3)). On this point and generally, see the notes to s. 206.

S. 210(4)
See the note to s. 206(4).

211 False representations to creditors

211(1) **[Offences by past or present officer]** When a company is being wound up, whether by the court or voluntarily, any person, being a past or present officer of the company–

(a) commits an offence if he makes any false representation or commits any other fraud for the purpose of obtaining the consent of the company's creditors or any of them to an agreement with reference to the company's affairs or to the winding up, and

(b) is deemed to have committed that offence if, prior to the winding up, he has made any false representation, or committed any other fraud, for that purpose.

211(2) **["Officer"]** For purposes of this section, **"officer"** includes a shadow director.

211(3) **[Penalty]** A person guilty of an offence under this section is liable to imprisonment or a fine, or both.

GENERAL NOTE

This section applies only to past and present officers (including shadow directors). The notes to s. 206 apply generally to s. 211; but the onus of establishing fraud is here placed on the prosecution.

212 Summary remedy against delinquent directors, liquidators, etc.

212(1) [**Application**] This section applies if in the course of the winding up of a company it appears that a person who–

(a) is or has been an officer of the company,

(b) has acted as liquidator or administrative receiver of the company, or

(c) not being a person falling within paragraph (a) or (b), is or has been concerned, or has taken part, in the promotion, formation or management of the company,

has misapplied or retained, or become accountable for, any money or other property of the company, or been guilty of any misfeasance or breach of any fiduciary or other duty in relation to the company.

212(2) [**Interpretation**] The reference in subsection (1) to any misfeasance or breach of any fiduciary or other duty in relation to the company includes, in the case of a person who has acted as liquidator of the company, any misfeasance or breach of any fiduciary or other duty in connection with the carrying out of his functions as liquidator of the company.

212(3) [**Examination, orders**] The court may, on the application of the official receiver or the liquidator, or of any creditor or contributory, examine into the conduct of the person falling within subsection (1) and compel him–

(a) to repay, restore or account for the money or property or any part of it, with interest at such rate as the court thinks just, or

(b) to contribute such sum to the company's assets by way of compensation in respect of the misfeasance or breach of fiduciary or other duty as the court thinks just.

212(4) [**Limit on s. 212(3) application**] The power to make an application under subsection (3) in relation to a person who has acted as liquidator of the company is not exercisable, except with the leave of the court, after he has had his release.

212(5) [**Exercise of s. 212(3) power**] The power of a contributory to make an application under subsection (3) is not exercisable except with the leave of the court, but is exercisable notwithstanding that he will not benefit from any order the court may make on the application.

S. 212(1)

This re-enacts, with some amendments introduced by IA 1985, the traditional "misfeasance" section of successive Companies Acts, providing a summary remedy in the liquidation of a company for the assessment of compensation or damages for breach of duty against its former officers and others. (On the meaning of the term "officer", see the note to s. 206(3).)

As originally enacted, the section applied to administrators as well as those listed, but all references to administrators were removed by EA 2002, Sch. 17, para. 18, which came into effect on September 15, 2003. At the same time a separate provision dealing with misfeasance by administrators was enacted in EA 2002, Sch. 16, which is now to be found in IA 1986, Sch. B1, para. 75, and a saving provision, reinstating s. 212 as formerly worded, came into effect under the Enterprise Act 2002 (Commencement No. 4 and Transitional Provisions and Savings) Order 2003 (SI 2003/2093 (C. 85)), art. 3. This saving provision applies in cases where a petition for an administration order was presented before September 15, 2003, and also in the administration of insolvent partnerships, limited liability partnerships and bodies which are insurers under FSMA 2002 and SI 2002/1242. There is no mention in the Order of building societies and the public utility companies listed in EA 2002, s. 249, but in these cases the original s. 212 will continue to apply because s. 249 disapplies the new s. 8(3) in regard to such bodies. There is no mention of the supervisor of a CVA, but subs. (2)(c) could no doubt be invoked. The words "breach of trust" in CA 1985 have been replaced by "breach of any fiduciary or other duty", and this also has the effect of extending the coverage of the remedy, for although "breach of trust" and "breach of fiduciary duty" may be regarded as synonymous, it had been held that the former wording did not include claims based on negligence (*Re B Johnson & Co. (Builders) Ltd* [1955] Ch. 634).

However in *Re D'Jan of London Ltd* [1993] B.C.C. 646 Hoffmann L.J. clearly accepted that the section now covers "breaches of any duty including the duty of care", and applied it in a straightforward case of negligence brought against a director. See also *Re Centralcrest Engineering Ltd* [2000] B.C.C. 727 (where a liquidator was held liable), *Re Westlowe Storage & Distribution Ltd* [2000] B.C.C. 851, *Re Pantone 485 Ltd* (below) and *Re Continental Assurance Co. of London plc* [2001] B.P.I.R. 733 (a lengthy judgment in which it was held that the case in misfeasance against both the executive and the non-executive directors of the company had not been made out).

It is well settled that the section creates no new liabilities, but only provides a simpler procedure for the recovery of property or compensation in a winding up. Even here, there are limitations on its use – e.g. it is not available to enforce a contractual debt (*Re Etic Ltd* [1928] Ch. 861), and in *Re Continental Assurance Co. of London plc* (above), at p. 855 it was said to be improper to use it to circumvent the difficulties of establishing a preference claim. Note, however, that the fact that s. 212 provides a statutory remedy against a company officer does not in any way exclude the pursuit of common-law remedies in contract and tort against the same person: *A & J. Fabrications (Batley) Ltd v Grant Thornton* [1999] B.C.C. 807).

The question whether a claim under s. 212 is statute-barred is determined on the same basis as for other claims. So, in *Re Pantone 485 Ltd* [2002] 1 B.C.L.C. 266,where a director used the company's money for his own benefit in a way which rendered him accountable to it as trustee, the claim was held to be within s. 21(1)(b) of the Limitation Act 1980 and accordingly not statute-barred.

Sums or property recovered under this section are the product of a chose in action vested in the company prior to the liquidation and are accordingly "assets of the company" which are capable of being made the subject of a charge (*Re Anglo-Austrian Printing & Publishing Union* [1895] 2 Ch. 891), or of being assigned by it or the liquidator: *Re Oasis Merchandising Services Ltd* [1998] Ch. 170; [1997] B.C.C. 282.

Where directors make payments in breach of duty to one or more of their number, there may be concurrent liability under this section and under such other provisions as s. 214 (wrongful trading) and s. 239 (preference). In one such case, *Re DKG Contractors Ltd* [1990] B.C.C. 903, it was ordered that liability under the various heads should not be cumulative but that payments made under s. 212 and 239 should go to satisfy the liability under s. 214. However, in a later case, *Re Purpoint Ltd* [1991] B.C.C. 121, Vinelott J. made orders against the respondent for the payment of separate sums under s. 212 and 214, being satisfied that there was no injustice in the nature of overlap or "double counting" in making the orders cumulative. For a comprehensive discussion of this and related questions, see R M Goode, *Principles of Corporate Insolvency Law* (2nd edn, 1997), pp. 461–464.

A sum awarded against a misfeasant officer under s. 212 cannot be set off against a debt due to him from the company: *Re Anglo-French Co-operative Society Ex p. Pelly* (1882) 21 Ch.D. 492; *Manson v Smith (liquidator of Thomas Christy Ltd)* [1997] 2 B.C.L.C. 161.

The provisions of s. 212 apply to directors (including shadow directors) of building societies: see Building Societies Act 1986, s. 90 and Sch. 15, as amended by CA 1989, s. 211 and Sch. 24.

S. 212(2)
This provision is probably intended to remove any doubts on the question whether all the duties of a liquidator or administrator are owed to the company. It is curious, but at the same time it may well be significant, that there is no mention of an administrative receiver in this subsection, even though he is mentioned in s. 212(1)(b). *Johnson's* case (above) held that a receiver and manager at common law was not concerned to manage the business for the benefit of the company, but only to realise his creditor's security, and that he was under no duty to the company or its contributories to preserve the goodwill and business of the company. This view was confirmed by the Privy Council in *Downsview Nominees Ltd v First City Corporation Ltd* [1993] A.C. 295; [1993] B.C.C. 46, where it was held that a receiver and manager owes no general duty in negligence to, *inter alia*, the debtor company to use reasonable care in the exercise of his powers. However, it was also stated in the latter case that equity imposes specific duties on such a receiver, including a duty to exercise his powers in good faith; and that, if a receiver decides to sell the charged property, he must take reasonable care to obtain a proper price. (See also *Medforth v Blake* [2000] Ch. 86; [1999] B.C.C. 771, and the general comment to Pt III.) There is thus potentially scope (albeit of a limited nature) for s. 212 to be invoked against an administrative receiver or a receiver and manager.

S. 212(3)
A contributory's right to make an application is qualified by s. 212(5).

The court has a discretion under para. (a) to order the respondent to make restitution in whole or in part, and under para. (b) to order payment of "such sum ... as the court thinks just". Clearly, in relation to para. (b), the question of quantum is a matter for the discretion of the court (but even so, it does not extend to enabling the court to disregard the need to establish causation: *Re Simmon Box (Diamonds) Ltd, Cohen v Selby* [2002] B.C.C. 82). In *Re D'Jan of London Ltd* (above) the respondent was ordered to pay a sum which was less than the company's actual loss. However under

Section 213   Insolvency Act 1986

para. (a) the court (although empowered to order restoration of "all or any part" of the misapplied money or property) does not have a discretion which is similarly unfettered: in particular, it will not reopen a decision as to quantum which has already been settled in the course of the liquidation or in other proceedings: *Re AMF International Ltd* [1996] B.C.C. 335.

S. 212(4)

For the release of a liquidator, see ss. 173, 174, and an administrator, s. 20 and Sch. B1, para. 98.

S. 212(5)

Formerly, a contributory had standing to apply without the leave of the court, but only when he could show that he had an interest in the outcome of the proceedings. The subsection in its present form runs counter to the approach reflected in such decisions as *Re Rica Gold Washing Co.* (1879) 11 Ch.D. 36: see the notes to ss. 124(2), (3), 172(1), (2) above.

213 Fraudulent trading

213(1) [Application] If in the course of the winding up of a company it appears that any business of the company has been carried on with intent to defraud creditors of the company or creditors of any other person, or for any fraudulent purpose, the following has effect.

213(2) [Court may hold persons liable] The court, on the application of the liquidator may declare that any persons who were knowingly parties to the carrying on of the business in the manner above-mentioned are to be liable to make such contributions (if any) to the company's assets as the court thinks proper.

GENERAL NOTE

The Companies Acts have for a long time contained provisions dealing with "fraudulent trading", making it both a criminal offence (CA 1985, s. 458) and a ground for imposing personal liability upon those concerned (CA 1985, s. 630, now replaced by the present section). Originally, both the criminal and the civil sanctions could be invoked only in a winding up, but the criminal provision (s. 458) has for some years applied without this limitation.

The Cork Committee (*Report*, Ch. 44) considered that the previous law in this area was inadequate to deal with irresponsible trading, mainly because the courts have always insisted on the very strict standards of pleading and proof which are invariably applied in cases of fraud. It is not enough, for "fraudulent trading", to show that the company continued to run up debts when the directors knew that it was insolvent; there has to be "actual dishonesty, involving real moral blame" (*Re Patrick and Lyon Ltd* [1933] Ch. 786). (See also *Aktieselskabet Dansk Skibsfinansiering v Brothers* [2001] 2 B.C.L.C. 324 and *Bernasconi v Nicholas Bennett & Co.* [2000] B.C.C. 921.)

The Committee recommended that while this should continue to be the approach in criminal proceedings for fraudulent trading, civil liability to pay compensation could arise where loss was suffered as a result of "unreasonable" conduct, which they proposed should be termed "wrongful trading", and that for this purpose the more relaxed standard of proof appropriate to civil proceedings should apply. The former provision creating civil liability for fraudulent trading (CA 1985, s. 630) could be subsumed into the new law of wrongful trading.

In the event, the legislators have adopted the Committee's recommendations on wrongful trading in broad terms, but they have done so by creating an *additional* new provision (s. 214, below) and left the former law on fraudulent trading intact, with one or two minor amendments (the present section). There will, however, be less reason for liquidators to invoke it, since the concept of wrongful trading, with its less onerous standard of proof, is wide enough to include all cases of fraudulent trading perpetrated by directors, and for all practical purposes the consequences will be the same. However, s. 213 will continue to have a role to play where allegations of fraudulent trading are made against other parties, as is dramatically illustrated by the number of cases currently being brought by the liquidators of BCCI: see *Re BCCI, Morris v State Bank of India* [1999] B.C.C. 943; *Morris v Bank of America National Trust* [2000] B.C.C. 1076, *Re BCCI, Banque Arabe Internationale d'Investissement SA v Morris* [2002] B.C.C. 407.

S. 213(1)

The section, unlike the equivalent criminal provision (see above), applies only in a winding up.

The words "or for any fraudulent purpose" could not be wider, and should not be construed in any limiting way. The wording is certainly wide enough to include frauds committed against potential creditors: see *R. v Kemp* [1988] Q.B. 645; (1988) 4 B.C.C. 203. See also *Re L Todd (Swanscombe) Ltd* [1990] B.C.C. 125 (fraudulent evasion of value added tax). However, in *Morphitis v Bernasconi* [2002] EWCA Civ 289; [2003] 2 W.L.R. 1521; [2003] B.C.C. 540 the Court of Appeal ruled that, although a business may be found to have been carried on with intent to defraud creditors even where only one creditor is shown to have been defrauded, it does not necessarily follow that this is the case whenever a fraud on a creditor has been perpetrated. In such a situation the appropriate remedy may be for the creditor to pursue his own remedy under the general law, and not for the liquidator to seek a contribution to the general assets of the company in the winding up.

S. 213(2)
Two changes are made from the former law.

First, it is only the liquidator who has standing to apply for relief under this section. Previously, an individual creditor or contributory could also apply, but this was thought undesirable because it might encourage a creditor to put improper pressure upon directors to settle his claim personally.

Secondly, the order which the court may make declares the wrongdoers "liable to make such contributions (if any) to the company's assets as the court thinks proper". This makes it clear that any sums ordered to be paid must go into the general funds in the hands of the liquidator and be held for the benefit of the whole body of creditors. Under the previous wording, the court had power to order that a defendant should directly reimburse a particular creditor (*Re Cyona Distributors Ltd* [1967] Ch. 889; *Re Gerald Cooper Chemicals Ltd (in liq.)* [1978] Ch. 262).

In other respects, the law remains the same. Thus, those who may be made liable are "any persons who were knowingly parties" to the fraudulent trading (who need not have any connection with the company itself: *Re BCCI, Banque Arabe Internationale d'Investissement SA v Morris* (above)). This may be contrasted with the new wrongful trading provision (s. 214) which is limited in its scope to directors and former directors, but pointedly avoids the words "parties to" (and, indeed, "business" or "trading").

In certain cases under the former law it was held appropriate to include a punitive as well as a compensatory element in the court's order, but in *Morphitis v Bernasconi* (above) the Court of Appeal has denied that there is any such power: to make such an award would be foreign to the principle underlying s. 213.

Further provisions relating to proceedings for fraudulent trading are contained in s. 215, below.

In addition to the civil liability to pay compensation under this section and the criminal sanctions of CA 1985, s. 458, a person who is guilty of fraudulent trading may be made the subject of a disqualification order: see CDDA 1986, ss. 4, 10.

214 Wrongful trading

214(1) [Declaration by court, on application] Subject to subsection (3) below, if in the course of the winding up of a company it appears that subsection (2) of this section applies in relation to a person who is or has been a director of the company, the court, on the application of the liquidator, may declare that that person is to be liable to make such contribution (if any) to the company's assets as the court thinks proper.

214(2) [Application] This subsection applies in relation to a person if–

(a) the company has gone into insolvent liquidation,

(b) at some time before the commencement of the winding up of the company, that person knew or ought to have concluded that there was no reasonable prospect that the company would avoid going into insolvent liquidation, and

(c) that person was a director of the company at that time;

but the court shall not make a declaration under this section in any case where the time mentioned in paragraph (b) above was before 28th April 1986.

214(3) [Limit on declaration] The court shall not make a declaration under this section with respect to any person if it is satisfied that after the condition specified in subsection (2)(b) was first satisfied in relation to him that person took every step with a view to minimising the potential loss to the company's creditors as (assuming him to have known that there was no reasonable prospect that the company would avoid going into insolvent liquidation) he ought to have taken.

Section 214 *Insolvency Act 1986*

214(4) **[Interpretation of s. 214(2), (3)]** For the purposes of subsections (2) and (3), the facts which a director of a company ought to know or ascertain, the conclusions which he ought to reach and the steps which he ought to take are those which would be known or ascertained, or reached or taken, by a reasonably diligent person having both–

(a)   the general knowledge, skill and experience that may reasonably be expected of a person carrying out the same functions as are carried out by that director in relation to the company, and

(b)   the general knowledge, skill and experience that that director has.

214(5) **[Interpretation of s. 214(4)]** The reference in subsection (4) to the functions carried out in relation to a company by a director of the company includes any functions which he does not carry out but which have been entrusted to him.

214(6) **[Interpretation re insolvent liquidation]** For the purposes of this section a company goes into insolvent liquidation if it goes into liquidation at a time when its assets are insufficient for the payment of its debts and other liabilities and the expenses of the winding up.

214(7) **["Director"]** In this section **"director"** includes a shadow director.

214(8) **[S. 213]** This section is without prejudice to section 213.

GENERAL NOTE

For the background to this provision, see the note to s. 213 above.

The section, according to the marginal note, is concerned with "wrongful trading"; but it is notable that the word "trading" is not used in the text of the Act. (The marginal note may not be used as an aid for the construction of the text: *Chandler v Director of Public Prosecutions* [1964] A.C. 763). The section itself is singularly imprecise in defining just what conduct on the part of a director will bring him within its scope.

The Cork Committee (*Report*, para. 1806) did put forward its own draft definition of "wrongful trading", the essential part of which read: " ... at any time when the company is insolvent or unable to pay its debts as they fall due it incurs further debts or other liabilities to other persons without a reasonable prospect of meeting them in full". However, this definition was explicitly rejected by Parliament when an attempt was made to introduce it as an amendment to the Insolvency Bill 1985, and so it would be wrong to refer to it for guidance on the meaning of the present section. In particular, there may be wrongful trading under s. 214 even though the company does not incur further debts: one example mentioned during the parliamentary debate was the case where a company allows its assets to be depleted, *e.g.* by the payment of excessive directors' fees. It was, presumably, a concern to ensure that this kind of conduct was caught that led the draftsman to omit the word "trading" from his formulation.

The amount of contribution to be ordered is left entirely to the court's discretion, and is not related by the terms of the Act either to any particular period of trading or to the loss suffered by the company or creditors. However, in *Re Produce Marketing Consortium Ltd* (1989) 5 B.C.C. 569 at p. 597, Knox J. said:

"In my judgment the jurisdiction under sec. 214 is primarily compensatory rather than penal. Prime facie the appropriate amount that a director is declared to be liable to contribute is the amount by which the company's assets can be discerned to have been depleted by the director's conduct which caused the discretion under sec. 214(1) to arise. However Parliament has indeed chosen very wide words of discretion and it would be undesirable to seek to spell out limits on that discretion ... The fact that there was no fraudulent intent is not of itself a reason for fixing the amount at a nominal or low figure, for that would amount to frustrating what I discern as Parliament's intention in adding sec. 214 to sec. 213 in the *Insolvency Act* 1986, but I am not persuaded that it is right to ignore that fact totally".

In the light of the ruling of the Court of Appeal in *Morphitis v Bernasconi* [2002] EWCA Civ 289, [2003] 2 W.L.R. 1521; [2003] B.C.C. 540, it will not be appropriate to include a punitive element in the amount of contribution awarded: see the note to s. 213(2), above.

Where a claim under s. 214 is brought against a number of directors, liability is several and not joint and several, that is to say that the position of each individual has to be separately assessed, and payment by one does not discharge the liability of any other: *Re Continental Assurance Co. of London plc* [2001] B.P.I.R. 733 at pp. 846–848. However, it was also said in this case that the court may, in its discretion, order that the liability of any two or more directors should be joint and several for the whole or part of the sum which the court has assessed for contribution to the company's assets.

In an appropriate case, an application may be made under s. 214 against the foreign directors of a foreign company which is being wound up in this jurisdiction as an unregistered company: *Re Howard Holdings Ltd* [1998] B.C.C. 549.

There will plainly be cases in which claims will be made against the former director of a company both under this section and under some other provisions of the Act, *e.g.* s. 212 (misfeasance) or s. 239 (preference). In such a case there may be no injustice in making orders which impose cumulative liability on the defendant: *Re Purpoint Ltd* [1991] B.C.C. 121. However, in *Re DKG Contractors Ltd* [1990] B.C.C. 903 the court ruled that payments made under ss. 212 and 239 should go to satisfy the liability under s. 214, and that enforcement should be limited to what was necessary to pay the company's creditors and the costs and expenses of the liquidation. On this and related questions, see the note to s. 212(1).

It has been ruled that, as a matter of law, CA 1985, s. 727 (which empowers the court to relieve a director from liability for breach of duty where he has acted honestly and reasonably and ought fairly to be excused) is not available to a director in s. 214 proceedings: *Re Produce Marketing Consortium Ltd (Halls v David)* [1989] 1 W.L.R. 745; (1989) 5 B.C.C. 399.

A claim under s. 214 (and, similarly, a claim under s. 213) is a "claim for the recovery of a sum recoverable under any enactment" within s. 9(1) of the Limitation Act 1980, and the appropriate limitation period is six years, reckoned from the date when the company went into insolvent liquidation: *Re Farmizer (Products) Ltd, Moore v Gadd* [1997] B.C.C. 655. However even if proceedings are commenced within the limitation period, unreasonable delay in prosecuting the claim may justify a striking-out order (*ibid*).

The provisions of ss. 214–217 apply to the directors of building societies: see the note to CDDA 1986, s. 7.

S. 214(1)
Four points may be noted:

(1) The section applies only to present and past directors (including shadow directors: s. 214(7)). In *Re a Company No. 005009 of 1987* (1988) 4 B.C.C. 424 (interlocutory proceedings in the saga of *Re M C Bacon Ltd*: see [1990] B.C.C. 78 at p. 79G) Knox J. ruled that a company's bank which, on becoming apprised of the fact that its client company is in financial difficulties, makes recommendations to its directors as to the future conduct of its business could, in principle, incur liability under the section as a "shadow director" – or, at least, that on the evidence before him the case was not so obviously unsustainable that an allegation to that effect should be struck out without proceeding to trial. A bank would not, however (it is submitted), risk liability as a shadow director if its requirements were expressed as conditions of extending loan facilities to the company rather than as instructions. (Compare the views expressed in *Re PFTZM Ltd (in liq.)* [1995] B.C.C. 280.) In *Re Hydrodan (Corby) Ltd* [1994] B.C.C. 161, Millett J. accepted as correct a concession by counsel that s. 214 applies also to *de facto* directors. (See further on this point the notes to s. 251, below.) Proceedings may be brought against the estate of a deceased director: *Re Sherborne Associates Ltd* [1995] B.C.C. 40.

(2) Section 214 applies only in a winding up.

(3) Only the liquidator has standing to bring proceedings.

(4) Any sum paid by a defendant goes into the general assets in the hands of the liquidator. Accordingly, it will not be caught by a charge over the assets of the company (despite the assumption to the contrary made by Knox J. in *Re Produce Marketing Consortium Ltd* (1989) 5 B.C.C. 569 at p. 598); and it is incapable of assignment (*Re Oasis Merchandising Services Ltd* [1998] Ch. 170; [1997] B.C.C. 282. See the note to Sch. 4, paras 6, 13.

The comments to s. 213 on these points are also relevant for this subsection.

A person held liable under this section may also have a disqualification order made against him: see CDDA 1986, s. 10, although the power appears to be used sparingly (see *Re Brian D Pierson (Contractors) Ltd* [1999] B.C.C. 26). Alternatively, an application under this section may be consolidated with proceedings for a disqualification order, as was done in *Official Receiver v Doshi* [2001] 2 B.C.L.C. 235.

Section 214   Insolvency Act 1986

S. 214(2)

On the meaning of "has gone into insolvent liquidation" see s. 214(6); and for "the commencement of the winding up" see s. 86 and 129.

April 28, 1986 was the date when this provision (as IA 1985, s. 15) was first brought into force (SI 1986/463).

The words "knew or ought to have concluded" are to be read in conjunction with s. 214(4). See the note to that provision, below.

Where the liquidator alleges that a respondent knew or ought to have concluded that there was no reasonable prospect of avoiding insolvent liquidation by reference to specific dates, but fails to make out his case as to the dates pleaded, he is not entitled to substitute later dates: *Re Sherborne Associates Ltd* [1995] B.C.C. 40.

S. 214(3)

The section, as has been noted, pointedly avoids giving any concrete meaning to the concept of "wrongful trading" or any positive guidance as to the types of conduct which will lead to liability. There is thus a major gap in the law, as framed, which is having to be filled by decisions of the courts in test cases. The only objective facts that need to be established are those relating to the winding up of the company, its insolvency, and that the director held office at the material time (s. 214(2)); beyond that, liability turns on his knowledge or imputed knowledge (s. 214(2)(b)) and his failure to take "every step with a view to minimising the potential loss to the company's creditors as . . . he ought to have taken". What a director knows, or must be taken to know, for these purposes is assessed by a mixture of subjective and objective tests (see the note to s. 214(4) below).

The phrases "took *every* step" and "*minimising* the potential loss to creditors" seem, at first sight, rather overstated. However, there is no doubt that the use of "every step" was deliberate: a proposed amendment to "every reasonable step" was expressly rejected in Parliament; and on similar reasoning, we must assume that "minimise" was fully intended, rather than, say, "reduce" or "avert".

The bracketed words in the subsection credit a director, for the purpose of determining what he "ought" to have done, with an awareness of the company's financial position and (by virtue of s. 214(4)) with a degree of general knowledge, skill and experience which in reality he may not have had. These fictitious assumptions as to the directors' state of mind were invoked against the defendants in *Re Produce Marketing Consortium Ltd* (1989) 5 B.C.C. 569. The company had kept inadequate accounting records, and in consequence the directors were in breach of their statutory duty to prepare accounts for the financial year ending September 30, 1985, which should have been laid before the shareholders and delivered to the registrar of companies by the end of July 1986. Knox J. held that he should assume, for the purposes of s. 214, that these financial results were known to the directors at the latter date, at least to the extent of the size of the deficiency of assets over liabilities.

The Act gives no affirmative guidance as to the steps which a director "ought" to take when insolvency is threatening. It was plainly assumed in the Government's White Paper (Cmnd 9175, para. 12) that a conscientious director would seek to have the company put into receivership, administration, or voluntary liquidation as soon as possible. There is a clear risk that this may seem the safest course for directors, faced as they are with the threat of personal liability and possible disqualification, even when in their own business judgment there is a good case for carrying on. It is clear that any decision to do so ought to be fully reasoned and documented and, where necessary, made with the benefit of outside professional advice, in order that the requirements of the present subsection can be met if a charge of wrongful trading is brought. It is significant that in *Re Continental Assurance Co. of London plc* [2001] B.P.I.R. 733, in which all of the directors concerned were held not to be liable for wrongful trading, management accounts had been prepared (albeit that they may not have been wholly accurate) and two licensed insolvency practitioners were advising the company at the material time.

On principle and, it is submitted, on the language of the section, the onus of proof to show that a director has failed to take every step that he ought to have taken should be on the liquidator. In *Re Sherborne Associates Ltd* (above) it was emphasised that the court should be aware of the danger of making assumptions with the benefit of hindsight, and in the case of a claim against the estate of a deceased director should be particularly astute to recognise the possibility of explanations for his conduct which he might have been able to give had he lived.

S. 214(4)

The tests to be applied under this subsection combine both subjective and objective criteria. The director is thus to be judged by the standards of the "reasonable" director, even though he himself is lacking or below average in knowledge, skill or experience, but by his own higher standards if these are above average. In *Re DKG Contractors Ltd* [1990] B.C.C. 903 it was observed: "Patently, [the directors'] own knowledge, skill and experience were hopelessly inadequate for the task they undertook. That is not sufficient to protect them". However, it should be noted that in the *Produce Marketing* case (above), Knox J. accepted a submission that the objective standards fixed by the section do require the court to have regard to the particular company and its business, so that the general knowledge, skill and experience postulated will be much less extensive in a small company in a modest way of business, with simple accounting procedures and equipment, than it will be in a large company with sophisticated procedures. This approach could also give scope for the courts to make some allowances in the case of non-executive and part-time directors. (*Re Continental Assurance Co. of London plc* (above) contains an important analysis of the position of non-executive directors in this context.)

In applying objective standards to the conduct of company directors in this way, the Act breaks new ground, for the case law has traditionally emphasised the need for honesty and conscientiousness but not demanded that directors should exercise any particular degree of competence or diligence or skill. (However, in *Re D'Jan of London Ltd* [1993] B.C.C. 646, Hoffmann L.J. expressed the view that "the duty of care owed by a director at common law is accurately stated in s. 214 of the Insolvency Act 1986".)

S. 214(5)
The remarks made in the preceding paragraph are underlined by the present subsection, which puts sins of omission into the same category as sins of commission. This, too, is a departure from the common law, which has never had effective sanctions to penalise passive defaults such as non-attendance at board meetings.

S. 214(6)
Section 214 applies only in a liquidation; but it is immaterial whether this is a compulsory or voluntary liquidation. The phrase "goes into liquidation" is defined in s. 247(2). The test of insolvency applied by s. 214(6) is on a "balance sheet" rather than a "liquidity" or "commercial" basis. (The recommendation of the Cork Committee was that *either* should be sufficient.) The definition of "inability to pay debts" in s. 123(1)(e) and (2) may be contrasted.

The Act gives no indication whether the company's assets are to be valued for the purpose of s. 214 on a "going concern" rather than a "break-up" basis, or whether contingent and future liabilities are to be brought into the reckoning. It is submitted that it would be wrong to judge these matters with the wisdom of hindsight, if it does happen that, *e.g.*, the assets have had to be sold up piecemeal in the winding up which has resulted. The reference to "going into insolvent liquidation" in relation to the making of business judgments in s. 214(2)(b) surely indicates that the question of solvency is to be assessed on the basis of going-concern assumptions for all the purposes of the present section.

On the problems of valuation for the purposes of determining "insolvency" under the present section, see the comments of Professor R M Goode, *Principles of Corporate Insolvency Law* (2nd edn, 1997), pp. 83–100.

S. 214(7)
For the definition of these terms, see the note to s. 206.

S. 214(8)
In view of the heavier onus of proof required by s. 213, it is unlikely that that section will be invoked in future where a liquidator has a choice of proceeding under either section. The one respect in which the two sections do not overlap, however, is that s. 213 applies to persons other than directors and shadow directors, provided that they are knowingly parties to the fraudulent trading.

215 Proceedings under s. 213, 214

215(1) **[Evidence by liquidator]** On the hearing of an application under section 213 or 214, the liquidator may himself give evidence or call witnesses.

215(2) **[Further court directions]** Where under either section the court makes a declaration, it may give such further directions as it thinks proper for giving effect to the declaration; and in particular, the court may–

(a) provide for the liability of any person under the declaration to be a charge on any debt or obligation due from the company to him, or on any mortgage or charge or any interest in a mortgage or charge on assets of the company held by or vested in him, or any person on his behalf, or any person claiming as assignee from or through the person liable or any person acting on his behalf, and

(b) from time to time make such further order as may be necessary for enforcing any charge imposed under this subsection.

215(3) **["Assignee"]** For the purposes of subsection (2), **"assignee"** –

(a) includes a person to whom or in whose favour, by the directions of the person made liable, the debt, obligation, mortgage or charge was created, issued or transferred or the interest created, but

(b) does not include an assignee for valuable consideration (not including consideration by way of marriage) given in good faith and without notice of any of the matters on the ground of which the declaration is made.

215(4) **[Directions re priority of debts]** Where the court makes a declaration under either section in relation to a person who is a creditor of the company, it may direct that the whole or any part of any debt owed by the company to that person and any interest thereon shall rank in priority after all other debts owed by the company and after any interest on those debts.

215(5) **[Ss. 213, 214]** Sections 213 and 214 have effect notwithstanding that the person concerned may be criminally liable in respect of matters on the ground of which the declaration under the section is to be made.

S. 215(4)
The court is empowered to make a declaration, ancillary to an order for contribution, subordinating any debt owed by the company to a respondent so that it ranks after the company's other debts. Such a declaration was made in *Re Purpoint Ltd* [1991] B.C.C. 121.

216 Restriction on re-use of company names

216(1) **[Application]** This section applies to a person where a company ("the liquidating company") has gone into insolvent liquidation on or after the appointed day and he was a director or shadow director of the company at any time in the period of 12 months ending with the day before it went into liquidation.

216(2) **[Prohibited name]** For the purposes of this section, a name is a prohibited name in relation to such a person if–

(a) it is a name by which the liquidating company was known at any time in that period of 12 months, or

(b) it is a name which is so similar to a name falling within paragraph (a) as to suggest an association with that company.

216(3) **[Restriction]** Except with leave of the court or in such circumstances as may be prescribed, a person to whom this section applies shall not at any time in the period of 5 years beginning with the day on which the liquidating company went into liquidation–

(a) be a director of any other company that is known by a prohibited name, or

(b) in any way, whether directly or indirectly, be concerned or take part in the promotion, formation or management of any such company, or

(c) in any way, whether directly or indirectly, be concerned or take part in the carrying on of a business carried on (otherwise than by a company) under a prohibited name.

216(4) **[Penalty]** If a person acts in contravention of this section, he is liable to imprisonment or a fine, or both.

216(5) **["The court"]** In subsection (3) **"the court"** means any court having jurisdiction to wind up companies; and on an application for leave under that subsection, the Secretary of State or the official receiver may appear and call the attention of the court to any matters which seem to him to be relevant.

216(6) **[Interpretation re name]** References in this section, in relation to any time, to a name by which a company is known are to the name of the company at that time or to any name under which the company carries on business at that time.

216(7) **[Interpretation re insolvent liquidation]** For the purposes of this section a company goes into insolvent liquidation if it goes into liquidation at a time when its assets are insufficient for the payment of its debts and other liabilities and the expenses of the winding up.

216(8) **["Company"]** In this section **"company"** includes a company which may be wound up under Part V of this Act.

GENERAL NOTE

This is one of a number of innovations made by IA 1985 which together form a package designed to strike down the "phoenix" phenomenon. This term was used to describe an abuse of the privilege of limited liability which, perhaps more than anything else, showed the inadequacies of the former insolvency law in the corporate sector. A company would be put into receivership (or voluntary liquidation) at a time when it owed large sums to its unsecured creditors. Frequently, the receiver was appointed by a controlling shareholder who had himself taken a floating charge over the whole of the company's undertaking, and there was nothing to stop him from appointing a receiver with whom he could act in collusion. The receiver would sell the entire business as a going concern at a knock-down price to a new company incorporated by the former controllers of the defunct company. As a result, what was essentially the same business would be carried on by the same people in disregard of the claims of the creditors of the first company, who in effect subsidised the launch of the new company debt-free. It was not unknown for the procedure to be repeated several times. The use of nominees or "front men" could add to the confusion and help to deceive future creditors: on the other hand, advantage could sometimes be gained from using a new company name similar to that of the old company, and cashing in on what was left of its goodwill. (On phoenix companies, see the comments of Jacob J. in *Western Intelligence Ltd v KDO Label Printing Machines Ltd* [1998] B.C.C. 472.) The present section is aimed to counter both of these latter aspects of the "phoenix syndrome". It is not based on any of the Cork Committee's recommendations, and was introduced at a late stage during the passage of the Insolvency Bill through Parliament in 1985. It simply makes the re-use of the name of a company which has been wound up insolvent a criminal offence in the circumstances defined; but it is not based on any requirement that there should be an attempt to exploit the goodwill of the previous company (see the comments of Peter Gibson L.J. in *Thorne v Silverleaf* [1994] B.C.C. 113). It is rather surprisingly confined in its scope to directors and shadow directors of the extinct company, but it is not necessary that the person concerned should hold such a position in the new company (*R. v Doring* [2002] EWCA Crim 1695, [2002] B.C.C. 838). In addition, any such person and any nominee or "front man" through whom he conducts the second business may incur personal liability, without limitation, under s. 217.

S. 216(1)

Many phrases in this subsection have special meanings. "Company" and "gone into insolvent liquidation" are defined in s. 216(8) and 216(7) respectively; the "appointed day" is the day on which the present Act came into force (December 29, 1986: see ss. 436, 443); "director" and "shadow director" have the meanings ascribed to them by s. 251.

The prohibition applies to anyone who has been a director or shadow director of the old company within the 12 months prior to its liquidation, and lasts for the period of five years that follows that event (s. 216(3)).

S. 216(2)

The ban applies to the use of the same name or a similar name: see, further, the note to s. 216(6).

It should be emphasised that the present section is not directed against the reuse of an insolvent company's name in itself: there will be no ban on this practice provided that no director of the former company is associated with the second business. It is only directors who can contravene the section, and only directors who are liable to punishment. This explains the phrase "a prohibited name *in relation* to such a person".

S. 216(3)

The ban is not restricted to the use of a prohibited name by a newly formed company: an established company (perhaps a member of the same group as the defunct company) may well have a "similar" name already, or may change its name to a "prohibited" name, with the result that its directors may be caught by this section. (Note that IR 1986, r. 4.230, may give a director an exemption in the former of these cases.) Leave may be granted in respect of "dormant" companies, provided that they are specified; but the court will not give a blanket permission to use the prohibited name in respect of any company to be formed in the future: *Re Lightning Electrical Contractors Ltd* [1996] B.C.C. 950.

The court is given power to grant dispensations from the prohibition imposed by this section, which it is likely to do when the insolvency is not linked with any blameworthy conduct on the part of the director concerned. *Re Bonus Breaks Ltd* [1991] B.C.C. 546 is an illustration of such a case. There, the applicant had been a director of a company which had gone into insolvent liquidation, but she had not behaved culpably and had lost substantial sums of her own money. A new company was set up with a capital of £50,000, including £49,000 in redeemable shares. Morritt J. gave leave for her to be a director of the new company against undertakings offered by the applicant that its capital base would be maintained and that it would not redeem any redeemable shares nor purchase its own shares out of distributable profits for a period of two years, unless such action was approved by a director independent of the company's founders. However, in *Penrose v Official Receiver* [1996] 1 W.L.R. 482; [1996] B.C.C. 311, Chadwick J. held that neither the fact that the new company was undercapitalised nor that the applicant was inexperienced and lacked management skills were relevant factors: the object of the section is to prevent abuses of the "phoenix" variety, and therefore the appropriate questions are whether there is any risk to the creditors of the new company beyond that permitted under the law relating to the incorporation of limited liability companies, or any substantial risk that people would be confused by the similarity of names. (See also *Re Lightning Electrical Contractors Ltd* [1996] B.C.C. 950.) In this case it was also held that it is wrong in principle to treat an applicant for leave under s. 216 as if he were a person who has been disqualified on the grounds of unfitness from acting as a director under CDDA 1986 – at least without evidence of misconduct. (However, a contravention of s. 216 may be evidence of "unfitness" justifying disqualification: *Re Migration Services International Ltd* [2000] B.C.C. 1095.)

The rules also specify three sets of circumstances where the section will not apply: see IR 1986, rr. 4.228ff. These are (1) where the whole, or substantially the whole, of the business of an insolvent company is acquired by a successor company and the liquidator (or equivalent office-holder) of the insolvent company gives notice to its creditors under r. 4.228; (2) for an interim period, where an application is made to the court within seven days of the liquidation and the court grants leave not later than six weeks from that date (r. 4.229); and (3) where the second company has been known by the name in question for at least 12 months prior to the liquidation and has not been a dormant company (r. 4.230). All other cases will have to go to the court for authorisation: the relevant rules are rr. 4.226, 4.227.

Paragraphs (b) and (c), by the use of the term "indirectly", will be effective to stop a person from controlling another company or carrying on a new business through others as "front" men. In addition, para. (c) makes it clear that it will be an offence to use a prohibited name even where no second company is involved, but in this case the civil consequences prescribed by s. 217 will not be applicable.

The phrase "concerned or take part in the management of a company" is not defined, but the note to s. 217 is relevant in this context.

S. 216(4)

Note that it is only a person who was a director or shadow director of the liquidating company who can be convicted of an offence under this section. In contrast, the civil liability imposed by s. 217 extends also to persons who act on the instructions of such ex-directors.

The offence under this section is one of strict liability: *mens rea* need not be shown; *R. v Cole, Lees & Birch* [1998] B.C.C. 87. In the same case it was held that a sentence of community service is not inappropriate in this context. (See also *R. v McCredie* [2000] B.C.C. 617 and *R. v Doring* (above).)

On penalties, see s. 430 and Sch. 10.

S. 216(5)

For the courts having jurisdiction to wind up companies, see s. 117 and 120. It is clear that "the court" need not be the same court as that which may have been involved in the liquidation of the old company.

S. 216(6)

This provision should be read with s. 216(2) above. In addition to forbidding the use of an identical name, the section bans a name "so similar as to suggest an association with" the former company. It is likely that this will catch the common and, in many ways, convenient practice of calling a new company by a name such as "John Smith (2002) Ltd", after the original John Smith Ltd has gone out of business. (There will, of course, be no objection to this so long as the first company was wound up solvent.)

The offence is not confined to the use of a prohibited name by a company: an unincorporated business is caught as well (s. 216(3)(c)). Further, the prohibition is not confined to a company's registered name. A company may carry on business under another name. Thus, for example, John Smith Ltd, before it went into solvent liquidation, may have used the trade name of "City Autos". It will be an offence for a former director of the company to take part in the management of any business using the name "John Smith", or "City Autos", or any name similar to either. It will also be an offence for him to be a director of any company having the registered name "John Smith Ltd" or "City Autos Ltd" and also of any other company, X Ltd, if it trades under the name "John Smith" or "City Autos" – or a similar name in each case.

It is the last of these possibilities that it is most likely to mislead creditors and members of the public generally, *i.e.* the use of the same trade name by a succession of limited companies.

S. 216(7)

This subsection defines "goes into insolvent liquidation" in terms identical to s. 214(6). See the note to that provision and, for the meaning of "goes into liquidation", s. 247(2).

S. 216(8)
The effect of this provision is to include "unregistered" as well as registered companies within the section. See the note to s. 220.

217 Personal liability for debts, following contravention of s. 216

217(1) [Personal liability] A person is personally responsible for all the relevant debts of a company if at any time–

(a) in a contravention of section 216, he is involved in the management of the company, or

(b) as a person who is involved in the management of the company, he acts or is willing to act on instructions given (without the leave of the court) by a person whom he knows at that time to be in contravention in relation to the company of section 216.

217(2) [Joint and several liability] Where a person is personally responsible under this section for the relevant debts of a company, he is jointly and severally liable in respect of those debts with the company and any other person who, whether under this section or otherwise, is so liable.

217(3) [Relevant debts of company] For the purposes of this section the relevant debts of a company are–

(a) in relation to a person who is personally responsible under paragraph (a) of subsection (1), such debts and other liabilities of the company as are incurred at a time when that person was involved in the management of the company, and

(b) in relation to a person who is personally responsible under paragraph (b) of that subsection, such debts and other liabilities of the company as are incurred at a time when that person was acting or was willing to act on instructions given as mentioned in that paragraph.

217(4) [Person involved in management] For the purposes of this section, a person is involved in the management of a company if he is a director of the company or if he is concerned, whether directly or indirectly, or takes part, in the management of the company.

217(5) [Interpretation] For the purposes of this section a person who, as a person involved in the management of a company, has at any time acted on instructions given (without the leave of the court) by a person whom he knew at that time to be in contravention in relation to the company of section 216 is presumed, unless the contrary is shown, to have been willing at any time thereafter to act on any instructions given by that person.

217(6) ["Company"] In this section **"company"** includes a company which may be wound up under Part V.

GENERAL NOTE

This section imposes personal liability on a person who contravenes s. 216 by reusing a prohibited company name. In addition, it makes similarly liable anyone who allows himself to be used as a "front" man or nominee in breach of that section. Since the criminal liability prescribed by s. 216 affects only directors and shadow directors, the category of those who are potentially liable on a civil basis is wider than those who may be convicted of the statutory offence.

In *Thorne v Silverleaf* [1994] B.C.C. 109, summary judgment was given in favour of the plaintiff against a director who had infringed s. 216. The Court of Appeal held that it was irrelevant that the plaintiff had allegedly aided and abetted the director in the commission of this offence. It was immaterial that he was aware of the facts, and even that he was aware both of the facts and that they constituted a contravention of s. 216. It was also held on the evidence that the plaintiff had not waived his right to seek recovery against the director under s. 217.

I.R.C. v Nash [2003] EWHC 686 (Ch) and *Archer Structures Ltd v Griffiths* [2003] EWHC 957 (Ch) suggest that increasing use is being made of this remedy.

S. 217(1)
Many of the terms used in this provision are defined or explained in the following subsections, and in particular "relevant debts", "involved in the management of a company", "is willing to act" and "company".

For a person to be made liable under para. (b), it will be necessary to show that he knew all the facts which are relevant to a contravention of s. 216.

Section 218 Insolvency Act 1986

Liability under the section is automatic, not requiring a special application to the court or court order of any sort and, for a case coming within para. (a), not requiring a prior conviction of the director concerned.

S. 217(2)
A person liable under this section is primarily liable, jointly and severally with the company and others concerned, and not in any secondary way.

S. 217(3)
Liability extends not only to debts in the narrow sense but also to all other obligations, such as claims for damages; and it applies to all debts and obligations arising during the relevant time and not merely those incurred *by* the acts of the person in question.

The phrase "willing to act" is explained in s. 217(5).

S. 217(4)
A director is irrebuttably presumed to be "involved in the management" of the company.

In regard to other persons, the best guide to the meaning of the phrase may be found in cases where the courts have construed closely similar, but not identical, provisions such as "take part in" or "be concerned in" the management of a company. For a full discussion, see the note to s. 206(3).

S. 217(5)
This provision creates a presumption against a person who is proved at any one time to have acted on the instructions of another whom he then knew to be contravening s. 216. Once this is shown, he is rebuttably presumed to have been "willing to act" on the other's instructions at any time afterwards.

S. 217(6)
"Unregistered" companies are included by this formula. See the note to s. 220.

Investigation and prosecution of malpractice

218 Prosecution of delinquent officers and members of company

218(1) **[Court may direct matter to be referred for prosecution]** If it appears to the court in the course of a winding up by the court that any past or present officer, or any member, of the company has been guilty of any offence in relation to the company for which he is criminally liable, the court may (either on the application of a person interested in the winding up or of its own motion) direct the liquidator to refer the matter–

(a) in the case of a winding up in England and Wales, to the Secretary of State, and

(b) in the case of a winding up in Scotland, to the Lord Advocate.

218(2) **[Deleted]**

218(3) **[Report – winding up by court]** If in the case of a winding up by the court in England and Wales it appears to the liquidator, not being the official receiver, that any past or present officer of the company, or any member of it, has been guilty of an offence in relation to the company for which he is criminally liable, the liquidator shall report the matter to the official receiver.

218(4) **[Report – voluntary winding up]** If it appears to the liquidator in the course of a voluntary winding up that any past or present officer of the company, or any member of it, has been guilty of an offence in relation to the company for which he is criminally liable, he shall forthwith report the matter–

(a) in the case of a winding up in England and Wales, to the Secretary of State, and

(b) in the case of a winding up in Scotland, to the Lord Advocate,

and shall furnish to the Secretary of State or (as the case may be) the Lord Advocate, such information and give to him such access to and facilities for inspecting and taking copies of documents (being information or documents in the possession or under the control of the liquidator and relating to the matter in question) as the Secretary of State or (as the case may be) the Lord Advocate requires.

218(5) **[Reference to Secretary of State]** Where a report is made to the Secretary of State under subsection (4) he may, for the purpose of investigating the matter reported to him and such other matters relating to the affairs of the company as appear to him to require investigation, exercise any of the powers which are exercisable by inspectors appointed under section 431 or 432 of the Companies Act to investigate a company's affairs.

218(6) **[Court may direct liquidator to make report]** If it appears to the court in the course of a voluntary winding up that–

(a) any past or present officer of the company, or any member of it, has been guilty as above-mentioned, and

(b) no report with respect to the matter has been made by the liquidator under subsection (4),

the court may (on the application of any person interested in the winding up or of its own motion) direct the liquidator to make such a report.

On a report being made accordingly, this section has effect as though the report had been made in pursuance of subsection (4).

GENERAL NOTE

This provision establishes a reporting chain through which suspected criminal offences uncovered in the course of a winding up may be referred to the appropriate persons for investigation and, where appropriate, prosecution. This section and s. 219 were amended by IA 2000, s. 10 as from April 2, 2001 as a streamlining measure. Reports in England and Wales now go directly to the Secretary of State and not as previously in the first instance to the Director of Public Prosecutions. (For transitional provisions, see the Insolvency Act 2000 (Commencement No. 1 and Transitional Provisions) Order 2001 (SI 2001/766), art. 3(4).) The former s. 218(2) became redundant and was accordingly repealed.

S. 218(1)
In a winding up by the court, the court is empowered to take the initial step when an offence is suspected, by directing the liquidator to refer the matter to the Secretary of State or the Lord Advocate. The court may act of its own motion or on the application of "a person interested in the winding up". In England and Wales, if the liquidator (not being the official receiver) himself suspects wrongdoing, he is obliged to report the matter to the official receiver (s. 218(3)); but it is unclear whether that provision by implication debars him from making an application to the court on his own initiative under s. 218(1). In Scotland, where s. 218(3) does not apply, it would seem to be clear that the liquidator should make application to the court in all cases.

On the meaning of "officer", see the note to s. 206(3).

S. 218(3)
The section is oddly silent as to what the official receiver should do, both in the case when he is not the liquidator and receives a report of a suspected offence, and in the case where, as liquidator, he suspects an offence himself. It must be intended that he shall (either with or without conducting his own investigation into the matter) refer the case to the prosecuting authority without the need for any intervention by the court. However, the rules are silent on this point.

S. 218(4), (6)
In a voluntary winding up, the liquidator's duty is to report the matter himself directly to the Secretary of State or the Lord Advocate, and thereafter to co-operate with the authority as described, and also give the further assistance referred to in s. 219(3). The court has, under s. 218(6), a further power to give the liquidator directions to this effect.

S. 218(5)
The Secretary of State's powers of investigation under CA 1985, ss. 431, 432, are far-reaching, and under those sections are not restricted to pursuing inquiries in connection with suspected criminal offences. Additional provisions governing an investigation by the Secretary of State under the present subsection are laid down by s. 219 below.

219 Obligations arising under s. 218

219(1) **[Assistance to investigation by Secretary of State]** For the purpose of an investigation by the Secretary of State in consequence of a report made to him under section 218(4), any obligation imposed on a

Section 219 Insolvency Act 1986

person by any provision of the Companies Act to produce documents or give information to, or otherwise to assist, inspectors appointed as mentioned in section 218(5) is to be regarded as an obligation similarly to assist the Secretary of State in his investigation.

219(2) **[Answer may be used as evidence]** An answer given by a person to a question put to him in exercise of the powers conferred by section 218(5) may be used in evidence against him.

219(2A) **[Use of evidence in criminal proceedings]** However, in criminal proceedings in which that person is charged with an offence to which this subsection applies–

(a) no evidence relating to the answer may be adduced, and

(b) no question relating to it may be asked,

by or on behalf of the prosecution, unless evidence relating to it is adduced, or a question relating to it is asked, in the proceedings by or on behalf of that person.

219(2B) **[Offences to which s. 219(2A) not applicable]** Subsection (2A) applies to any offence other than–

(a) an offence under section 2 or 5 of the Perjury Act 1911 (false statements made on oath otherwise than in judicial proceedings or made otherwise than on oath), or

(b) an offence under section 44(1) or (2) of the Criminal Law (Consolidation) (Scotland) Act 1995 (false statements made on oath or otherwise than on oath).

219(3) **[Liquidator and officer to assist, where criminal proceedings instituted]** Where criminal proceedings are instituted by the Director of Public Prosecutions, the Lord Advocate or the Secretary of State following any report or reference under section 218, it is the duty of the liquidator and every officer and agent of the company past and present (other than the defendant or defender) to give to the Director of Public Prosecutions, the Lord Advocate or the Secretary of State (as the case may be) all assistance in connection with the prosecution which he is reasonably able to give.

For this purpose **"agent"** includes any banker or solicitor of the company and any person employed by the company as auditor, whether that person is or is not an officer of the company.

219(4) **[Direction by court re assistance]** If a person fails or neglects to give assistance in the manner required by subsection (3), the court may, on the application of the Director of Public Prosecutions, the Lord Advocate or the Secretary of State (as the case may be) direct the person to comply with that subsection; and if the application is made with respect to a liquidator, the court may (unless it appears that the failure or neglect to comply was due to the liquidator not having in his hands sufficient assets of the company to enable him to do so) direct that the costs shall be borne by the liquidator personally.

GENERAL NOTE

The provisions of this section are designed to facilitate the investigations which may be made by the various officials and authorities when a suspected criminal offence is reported to them under the preceding section. The company's bankers, solicitors and auditors are specifically included among those obliged to assist (s. 219(3)).

Changes were made to the wording of s. 219(1), (3) and (4) by IA 2000, s. 10(7) with effect from April 2, 2001 consequentially upon the reform of s. 218: see the note to that section.

Section 11 of the same Act inserted the new subss. (2A) and (2B) as from the same date. These provisions limit the use of evidence obtained under compulsion in subsequent criminal prosecutions. A similar reform was made by the Youth Justice and Criminal Evidence Act 1999, s. 55 and Sch. 3, covering most of the provisions in the companies and insolvency legislation dealing with the use of such evidence, but this provision did not include s. 219. See further the notes to ss. 236 and 433.

Part V

Winding Up of Unregistered Companies

220 Meaning of "unregistered company"

220(1) **["Unregistered company"]** For the purposes of this Part, the expression **"unregistered company"** includes any association and any company, with the following exceptions–

(a) [Repealed]

(b) a company registered in any part of the United Kingdom under the Joint Stock Companies Acts or under the legislation (past or present) relating to companies in Great Britain.

220(2) **[Former references to trustee savings banks, now repealed.]**

General Note

The earliest companies legislation that enabled companies to acquire corporate status by registration was accompanied by Winding-up Acts which provided machinery for the winding up of companies which had not registered. Part V of the present Act, which consolidates CA 1985, Pt XXI, is what survives today of that legislation. There are almost certainly, however, no "unregistered companies" in the old sense still around; and for practical purposes it is probably true to say that Pt V will be applied to two or three other types of "unregistered" company – (1) statutory companies incorporated by private Act of Parliament, (2) foreign companies which have been carrying on business in Great Britain or have some other relevant connection with this jurisdiction, and (3) other bodies, such as unregistered friendly societies, for which provision for winding up is not made by specific legislation. Obsolete references to partnerships and limited partnerships contained in CA 1985, s. 665, were repealed by IA 1985, Sch. 10, Pt II; but paradoxically this Part of the Act is now made to apply to the winding up of insolvent partnerships: see the note to s. 420. (Limited liability partnerships, in contrast, are wound up under Pt IV.)

English courts have exercised jurisdiction to wind up foreign companies under the present section or its predecessors for a very long period: s. 225, which expressly refers to companies incorporated outside Great Britain but applies in limited circumstances only, is a relative newcomer which has rarely, if ever, been invoked.

Sections 220 and 221 give no guidance as to the criteria which will justify an English court in assuming jurisdiction. The matter has been left to the discretion of the courts. In practice, it is normally considered a sufficient nexus for the company to have, or have had, a place of business or branch office within the jurisdiction, or to have assets here (*Banque des Marchands de Moscou (Koupetschesky) v Kindersley* [1951] Ch. 112; [1950] 2 All E.R. 549), but other factors may also be regarded as relevant, *e.g.* the fact that a claim may be brought by the company against an insurer in England (*Re Compania Merabello San Nicholas SA* [1973] Ch. 75; [1972] 3 All E.R. 448), that a winding-up order will entitle former employees of the company to claim statutory redundancy payments (*Re Eloc Electro-Optieck and Communicatie BV* [1982] Ch. 43; [1981] 2 All E.R. 1111), or that the debt upon which the petition is founded was incurred here (*Re a Company No. 00359 of 1987* [1988] Ch. 210; (1987) 3 B.C.C. 160 (also known as *Re Okeanos Maritime Corp.*)). It is not necessary that the company should have assets within the jurisdiction: *Re a Company (No. 003102 of 1991) Ex p. Nyckeln Finance Co. Ltd* [1991] B.C.L.C. 539. However the court must be satisfied that there is a reasonable possibility that the winding-up order will benefit those applying for it, and the court must be able to exercise jurisdiction over one or more persons interested in the distribution of the company's assets: *Re Real Estate Development Co.* [1991] B.C.L.C. 210; *Atlantic & General Investment Trust Ltd v Richbell Information Services Inc.* [2000] B.C.C. 111; *Re Latreefers Inc.* [2001] B.C.C. 174; *Re Westminster Property Management Ltd, Official Receiver v Stern (No. 2)* [2001] B.C.C. 305. These cases may be contrasted with *Banco Nacional de Cuba v Cosmos Trading Corp.* [2000] B.C.C. 910, where an order was refused because the connection with the UK was minimal and no benefit to the creditors could realistically be expected.

Everything in the preceding paragraph must now be reconsidered in the light of the EC Regulation, which became effective on May 31, 2002, so far as concerns companies which have their "centre of main interests" in another EU Member State. The Regulation confers exclusive jurisdiction to open "main" insolvency proceedings upon the State where the "centre" is situated – which is rebuttably presumed to be the place of its registered office (art. 3(1)). In regard to "secondary" and "territorial" proceedings – where the "centre" is in another Member State – art. 3(2) stipulates that the local courts have jurisdiction only if the debtor "possesses an establishment" within the territory of the latter. The effect of secondary or territorial proceedings is restricted to the assets of the debtor situated in that territory. If main proceedings have already been opened, the ancillary proceedings are termed "secondary", and they must be winding-up proceedings. If main proceedings have not yet been opened, the proceedings are "territorial", and another Member State has jurisdiction in only two cases: (a) where main proceedings cannot be opened because of conditions laid down by the law of the "main" State, or (b) where the opening of territorial proceedings is requested by a creditor who has his domicile, habitual residence or registered office within the territory in question, or whose claim arises from the operation of that establishment. These questions of jurisdiction are discussed more fully in the note to the EC Regulation, art. 3; but it will be apparent that where the Regulation applies, the UK courts' jurisdiction under s. 220 is more limited than that described above.

The court, having exercised its discretion to hold that it has jurisdiction in respect of the particular company, has a further discretion whether or not to make an order, and if so upon what terms: see the notes to s. 221.

The object of s. 220(1)(b) appears fairly plainly to be to ensure that a company registered in one part of the UK may be wound up only in that jurisdiction, *e.g.* a company registered in England and Wales may only be wound up by the High Court or the county court (s. 117), and a company registered in Scotland only by the Court of Session or a sheriff court (s. 120). However this is not the case so far as concerns a company registered in Northern Ireland. In *Re Normandy Marketing Ltd* [1993] B.C.C. 879 Morritt J. held that by virtue of s. 220 and s. 441, read together, the court in England had jurisdiction to wind up a company registered in Northern Ireland, on the petition of the Secretary of State under s. 124A, provided that it had a principal place of business in England or Wales. In an appropriate case, s. 225 could also be invoked to give a court in Great Britain jurisdiction over a Northern Ireland company.

The allocation of jurisdiction over a foreign company as between the different parts of the UK is dealt with by s. 221(2), (3).

The Civil Jurisdiction and Judgments Act 1982, which gives effect to the Brussels Convention of 1968, does not apply at all to the winding up of insolvent companies (art. 1(2)). In regard to solvent foreign companies, art. 16(2) has the effect of denying a British court jurisdiction where the company has its "seat" (as defined by s. 43 of the Act) in a Contracting State other than the UK. However, conversely, a solvent company which is incorporated abroad in a contracting state will be subject to jurisdiction here under Pt V of IA 1986 if it has its "seat" in this country.

An unregistered company can be wound up only by order of the court: s. 221(4) – except where the European Regulation applies: see the note to s. 221(4).

S. 220(1)

The term "association" has been held to mean only an association formed for gain or profit: *Re St James's Club* (1852) 2 De G.M. & G. 383; *Re The Bristol Athenaeum* (1889) 43 Ch.D. 236. These decisions may have turned, in part, upon the special wording of the earlier legislation; but the ruling in the former case was given renewed authority when it was endorsed by the Court of Appeal in *Re International Tin Council* [1989] Ch. 309; (1988) 4 B.C.C. 653. The Council was an organisation formed by international treaty with the legal character, status and capacities of a corporate body. In holding that it was not within CA 1985, s. 665 (the precursor of the present section), the court adopted the broad test laid down in *Re St James's Club* (above): was the association one which Parliament could reasonably have intended should be subject to the winding-up process? If any state, whether a member of the Council or not, could subject that enterprise to its own domestic law, the independence and international character of the organisation would be fragmented and destroyed. Accordingly, an English court would not assume jurisdiction under s. 665. The ruling in *Re St James's Club* was applied to a professional football club in *Re Witney Town Football and Social Club* [1993] B.C.C. 874.

221 Winding up of unregistered companies

221(1) **[Application of winding-up provisions]** Subject to the provisions of this Part, any unregistered company may be wound up under this Act; and all the provisions of this Act and the Companies Act about winding up apply to an unregistered company with the exceptions and additions mentioned in the following subsections.

221(2) **[Principal place of business in Northern Ireland]** If an unregistered company has a principal place of business situated in Northern Ireland, it shall not be wound up under this Part unless it has a principal place of business situated in England and Wales or Scotland, or in both England and Wales and Scotland.

221(3) **[Deemed registration, registered office]** For the purpose of determining a court's winding-up jurisdiction, an unregistered company is deemed–

(a) to be registered in England and Wales or Scotland, according as its principal place of business is situated in England and Wales or Scotland, or

(b) if it has a principal place of business situated in both countries, to be registered in both countries;

and the principal place of business situated in that part of Great Britain in which proceedings are being instituted is, for all purposes of the winding up, deemed to be the registered office of the company.

221(4) **[No voluntary winding up]** No unregistered company shall be wound up under this Act voluntarily, except in accordance with the EC Regulation.

221(5) **[Circumstances for winding up]** The circumstances in which an unregistered company may be wound up are as follows–

(a) if the company is dissolved, or has ceased to carry on business, or is carrying on business only for the purpose of winding up its affairs;

(b) if the company is unable to pay its debts;

(c) if the court is of opinion that it is just and equitable that the company should be wound up.

221(6) (Repealed as from 21 July 1986 – Trustee Savings Bank Act 1985, s. 4(3) and SI 1986/1223 (C 36).)

221(7) **[Scotland]** In Scotland, an unregistered company which the Court of Session has jurisdiction to wind up may be wound up by the court if there is subsisting a floating charge over property comprised in the company's property and undertaking, and the court is satisfied that the security of the creditor entitled to the benefit of the floating charge is in jeopardy.

For this purpose a creditor's security is deemed to be in jeopardy if the court is satisfied that events have occurred or are about to occur which render it unreasonable in the creditor's interest that the company should retain power to dispose of the property which is subject to the floating charge.

GENERAL NOTE

On the question when the court will exercise jurisdiction to wind up a foreign company, see the note to s. 220.

The court has an unrestricted discretion to make or refuse an order, or to make an order subject to conditions. Thus, in the case of an oversea company, it may decline to order a winding up, or grant a stay of proceedings here, on the ground that the courts of another country would provide a more appropriate forum (see *Re Harrods (Buenos Aires) Ltd* [1992] Ch. 72; [1991] B.C.C. 249; *Re Wallace Smith & Co. Ltd* [1992] B.C.L.C. 970); or that insolvency proceedings already instituted in another jurisdiction are capable of dealing with the matter (*New Hampshire Insurance Co. v Rush & Tompkins Group plc* [1998] 2 B.C.L.C. 417). Alternatively, it may direct that the local winding up be conducted on a basis ancillary to a principal liquidation elsewhere (see *Re Commercial Bank of South Australia* (1886) 33 Ch.D. 174; *Re Hibernian Merchants Ltd* [1958] Ch. 76). In *Lancefield v Lancefield* [2002] B.P.I.R. 1108 it was held that the court could of its own motion make a winding-up order under s. 220 even though no petition had been presented.

S. 221(4)
The words "except in accordance with the EC Regulation" were added by the Insolvency Act 1986 (Amendment) (No. 2) Regulations 2002 (SI 2002/1240, effective May 31, 2002). It will thus now be possible for (say) a company incorporated in Ireland which has its centre of main interests in England to be wound up in England under a creditors' voluntary winding up. The administration of such a liquidation will presumably be governed by English law.

S. 221(5)
The grounds for the winding up of an unregistered company which are set out in this subsection are more restricted than those for registered companies: see s. 122.

The court has jurisdiction to wind up a foreign company under this subsection even though it has no assets here, provided that a sufficiently close connection can be shown, *e.g.* that the debt upon which the petition is founded was incurred here: *Re a Company No. 00359 of 1987* [1988] Ch. 210; (1987) 3 B.C.C. 160. However, this will not be the case where the EC Regulation applies.

S. 221(6)
This was repealed as from July 21, 1986 – Trustee Savings Bank Act 1985, s. 4(3) and SI 1986/1223 (C 36).

S. 221(7)
See the note to s. 122(2).

222 Inability to pay debts: unpaid creditor for £750 or more

222(1) **[Deemed inability to pay debts]** An unregistered company is deemed (for the purposes of section 221) unable to pay its debts if there is a creditor, by assignment or otherwise, to whom the company is indebted in a sum exceeding £750 then due and–

(a) the creditor has served on the company, by leaving at its principal place of business, or by delivering to the secretary or some director, manager or principal officer of the company, or by otherwise serving in such manner as the court may approve or direct, a written demand in the prescribed form requiring the company to pay the sum due, and

(b) the company has for 3 weeks after the service of the demand neglected to pay the sum or to secure or compound for it to the creditor's satisfaction.

222(2) **[Increase or reduction of s. 222(1) sum]** The money sum for the time being specified in subsection (1) is subject to increase or reduction by regulations under section 417 in Part XV; but no increase in the sum so specified affects any case in which the winding-up petition was presented before the coming into force of the increase.

GENERAL NOTE

This provision modifies the definition of "inability to pay debts" contained in s. 123(1)(a) above to meet the case of an unregistered company. See further the notes to that section.

S. 222(1)(a)
The demand must be "in the prescribed form". For details, see IR 1986, rr. 4.5ff. and Form 4.1.

223 Inability to pay debts: debt remaining unsatisfied after action brought

223 An unregistered company is deemed (for the purposes of section 221) unable to pay its debts if an action or other proceeding has been instituted against any member for any debt or demand due, or claimed to be due, from the company, or from him in his character of member, and–

(a) notice in writing of the institution of the action or proceeding has been served on the company by leaving it at the company's principal place of business (or by delivering it to the secretary, or some director, manager or principal officer of the company, or by otherwise serving it in such manner as the court may approve or direct), and

(b) the company has not within 3 weeks after service of the notice paid, secured or compounded for the debt or demand, or procured the action or proceeding to be stayed or sisted, or indemnified the defendant or defender to his reasonable satisfaction against the action or proceeding, and against all costs, damages and expenses to be incurred by him because of it.

GENERAL NOTE

There is no provision corresponding directly to this section in the case of a registered company.

224 Inability to pay debts: other cases

224(1) [Deemed inability to pay debts] An unregistered company is deemed (for purposes of section 221) unable to pay its debts–

(a) if in England and Wales execution or other process issued on a judgment, decree or order obtained in any court in favour of a creditor against the company, or any member of it as such, or any person authorised to be sued as nominal defendant on behalf of the company, is returned unsatisfied;

(b) if in Scotland the induciae of a charge for payment on an extract decree, or an extract registered bond, or an extract registered protest, have expired without payment being made;

(c) if in Northern Ireland a certificate of unenforceability has been granted in respect of any judgment, decree or order obtained as mentioned in paragraph (a);

(d) it is otherwise proved to the satisfaction of the court that the company is unable to pay its debts as they fall due.

224(2) [Deemed inability – another situation] An unregistered company is also deemed unable to pay its debts if it is proved to the satisfaction of the court that the value of the company's assets is less than the amount of its liabilities, taking into account its contingent and prospective liabilities.

GENERAL NOTE

The provisions of this section correspond with those of s. 123(1)(b)–(e), (2): see the notes to that section.

225 Oversea company may be wound up though dissolved

225(1) [Extent] Where a company incorporated outside Great Britain which has been carrying on business in Great Britain ceases to carry on business in Great Britain, it may be wound up as an unregistered company under this Act, notwithstanding that it has been dissolved or otherwise ceased to exist as a company under or by virtue of the laws of the country under which it was incorporated.

225(2) [Applicability EC Regulation] This section is subject to the EC Regulation.

GENERAL NOTE

The jurisdiction of the court to wind up a foreign company is not, of course, limited to the circumstances set out in this section. In practice, the more widely drawn provisions of s. 221 are normally relied on: s. 225 derives originally from CA 1928, s. 91, which was enacted to remove a doubt as to the court's jurisdiction which arose in connection with the dissolution of Russian banks following the revolution of 1917; it did not confer any new power to wind up companies (*per* Megarry J. in *Re Compania Merabello San Nicholas SA* [1973] Ch. 75 at pp. 85, 86; and *per* Morritt J. in *Re Normandy Marketing Ltd* [1993] B.C.C. 879 at p. 883).

S. 225(2)
This subsection was added by the Insolvency Act 1986 (Amendment) (No. 2) Regulations 2002 (SI 2002/1240, effective May 31, 2002), in parallel with the amendment to s. 221(4). See the note to that section.

226 Contributories in winding up of unregistered company

226(1) [Deemed contributory] In the event of an unregistered company being wound up, every person is deemed a contributory who is liable to pay or contribute to the payment of any debt or liability of the company, or to pay or contribute to the payment of any sum for the adjustment of the rights of members among themselves, or to pay or contribute to the payment of the expenses of winding up the company.

226(2) [Liability for contribution] Every contributory is liable to contribute to the company's assets all sums due from him in respect of any such liability as is mentioned above.

226(3) [Unregistered company re mines in stannaries] In the case of an unregistered company engaged in or formed for working mines within the stannaries, a past member is not liable to contribute to the assets if he has ceased to be a member for 2 years or more either before the mine ceased to be worked or before the date of the winding-up order.

226(4) [Death, bankruptcy, insolvency of contributory] In the event of the death, bankruptcy or insolvency of any contributory, the provisions of this Act with respect to the personal representatives, to the heirs and legatees of heritage of the heritable estate in Scotland of deceased contributories, and to the trustees of bankrupt or insolvent contributories, respectively apply.

GENERAL NOTE

The reference in s. 226(3) to "the stannaries" is to certain Cornish tin-mining companies, which were formerly governed by separate legislation.

227 Power of court to stay, sist or restrain proceedings

227 The provisions of this Part with respect to staying, sisting or restraining actions and proceedings against a company at any time after the presentation of a petition for winding up and before the making of a winding-up order extend, in the case of an unregistered company, where the application to stay, sist or restrain is presented by a creditor, to actions and proceedings against any contributory of the company.

228 Actions stayed on winding-up order

228 Where an order has been made for winding up an unregistered company, no action or proceeding shall be proceeded with or commenced against any contributory of the company in respect of any debt of the company, except by leave of the court, and subject to such terms as the court may impose.

229 Provisions of this Part to be cumulative

229(1) [Pt. V in addition to Pt. IV] The provisions of this Part with respect to unregistered companies are in addition to and not in restriction of any provisions in Part IV with respect to winding up companies by the court; and the court or liquidator may exercise any powers or do any act in the case of unregistered companies which might be exercised or done by it or him in winding up companies formed and registered under the Companies Act.

229(2) [Unregistered company not usually company under Companies Act] However, an unregistered company is not, except in the event of its being wound up, deemed to be a company under the Companies Act, and then only to the extent provided by this Part of this Act.

PART VI

MISCELLANEOUS PROVISIONS APPLYING TO COMPANIES WHICH ARE INSOLVENT OR IN LIQUIDATION

General comment on Pt VI
The heading to this Part is likely to give rise to confusion, because of the phrase "companies which are insolvent". The natural inference to be drawn from this would be that nothing in ss. 230–246 applies to a company which is solvent (in a financial sense) so that, for instance, an officer of a company is not under a duty to co-operate with an administrative receiver if the company in question is in fact solvent. The possible confusion is made worse by the absence of any statutory definition of "insolvent" company, though there is a definition of "insolvency" in s. 247(1) (and of "onset of insolvency" in ss. 240(3) and 245(5), of "goes into insolvent liquidation" in ss. 214(6) and 216(7), and of "becomes insolvent" in CDDA 1986, s. 6(2)). "Insolvency" in ss. 247(1), 240(3) and 245(5) plainly refers to the various types of insolvency *proceedings* (liquidation, administration, administrative receivership, etc.), while "insolvent" in ss. 214(6), 214(7) and CDDA 1986, s. 6(2) is concerned with the company's financial state. (To add to the confusion, "insolvent" is given yet another special meaning in two chapters of the rules: see IR 1986, rr. 4.151, 4.173(2).)

In the heading to this Part, the words "which are insolvent" should probably be taken as meaning "which are the subject of insolvency proceedings"; and "insolvency" could then be construed in accordance with the definition in s. 247(1). This may violate to a degree the more natural connotation of the word "insolvent"; but it does mean that the whole of Pt VI can be applied without qualification. The alternative is to take "insolvent" as meaning "not financially viable", which raises serious problems because (1) no definition of "insolvent" is given in the body of this Part, and the word admits of many interpretations (see the note to s. 123); and (2) the whole of Pt VI would be subject to limitations which the text of the Act does not specify.

It is generally understood that headings within a statute (in contrast to marginal notes) may be looked at to resolve an ambiguity in the sections that are grouped under them (Halsbury, *Laws of England*, 4th edn, Vol. 44, para. 818); but it would be unusual to import into the text of an Act qualifications (and ambiguities) which appear only from the words of a heading.

It is therefore submitted that Pt VI applies to *all* companies, whether financially "solvent" or "insolvent", and that "insolvent" must be read analogously with the definition of "insolvency" in s. 247(1) – that is, as meaning "which are the subject of insolvency proceedings".

On the scope of the EC Regulation on Insolvency Proceedings 2000, see the general note to the Regulation on pp. 602ff.

Various definitions of insolvency are found in other legislation: see, *e.g.* Sale of Goods Act 1979, s. 61(4); Employment Rights Act 1996, s. 183.

Office-holders

230 Holders of office to be qualified insolvency practitioners

230(1) (S. 230(1) ceased to have effect and repealed by the Enterprise Act 2002, s. 248(3), Sch. 17, para. 9, 19 and s. 278(2), Sch. 26 as from September 15, 2003.)

230(2) **[Administrative receiver]** Where an administrative receiver of a company is appointed, he must be a person who is so qualified.

230(3) **[Liquidator]** Where a company goes into liquidation, the liquidator must be a person who is so qualified.

230(4) **[Provisional liquidator]** Where a provisional liquidator is appointed, he must be a person who is so qualified.

230(5) **[Official receiver]** Subsections (3) and (4) are without prejudice to any enactment under which the official receiver is to be, or may be, liquidator or provisional liquidator.

GENERAL NOTE

This section requires that a person appointed to any of the various offices mentioned shall be qualified to act as an insolvency practitioner in relation to the company in question. The term "act as an insolvency practitioner" (in relation to a company) is defined by s. 388(1), and "qualified" and "qualified ... in relation to" by s. 390(2) and s. 390(3) respectively. It is an offence under s. 389 for a person to act as an insolvency practitioner in relation to a company at a time when he is not qualified to do so.

Section 230(1), which required an administrator to be qualified to act as an insolvency practitioner in relation to the company, was repealed by EA 2002, Sch. 17, para. 19 with effect from September 15, 2003. The point, so far as concerns administrators appointed under IA 1986, Sch. B1, is now covered by para. 6 of the latter Schedule. At the same time a separate provision dealing with this category of administrators was enacted in EA 2002, Sch. 16, which is now to be found in IA 1986, Sch. B1, para. 75, and a saving provision, reinstating s. 230(1), came into effect under the Enterprise Act 2002 (Commencement No. 4 and Transitional Provisions and Savings) Order 2003 (SI 2003/2093 (C. 85)), art. 3. This saving provision applies in cases where a petition for an administration order was presented before September 15, 2003, and also in the administration of insolvent partnerships, limited liability partnerships and bodies which are insurers under FSMA 2002 and SI 2002/1242. There is no mention in the Order of building societies and the public utility companies listed in EA 2002, s. 249 but in these cases the original s. 230 will continue to apply because s. 249 disapplies the new s. 8(3) in regard to such bodies.

See also the note to s. 212(1).

There is no reference in s. 230 to the nominee or the supervisor of a voluntary arrangement under Pt I of the Act, which is a little odd since each of these is required also to be a "qualified" insolvency practitioner (see ss. 1(2), 2(4), 4(2), 7(5)).

A receiver who is not an administrative receiver is not required to be a qualified insolvency practitioner, but there are specific prohibitions in ss. 30, 31, 51(3) on the appointment of corporate bodies and undischarged bankrupts as receivers.

S. 230(5)

The official receiver is an officer of the court and is responsible directly to it and to the Secretary of State (see s. 400(2)). He is not subject to the regulatory regime introduced by this Act for private insolvency practitioners.

231 Appointment to office of two or more persons

231(1) [Application] This section applies if an appointment or nomination of any person to the office of administrative receiver, liquidator or provisional liquidator–

(a) relates to more than one person, or

(b) has the effect that the office is to be held by more than one person.

231(2) [Declaration in appointment or nomination] The appointment or nomination shall declare whether any act required or authorised under any enactment to be done by the administrative receiver, liquidator or provisional liquidator is to be done by all or any one or more of the persons for the time being holding the office in question.

GENERAL NOTE

There are very few references in the present Act to joint appointments, but under the normal rules of statutory interpretation words in the singular may be taken to include the plural (Interpretation Act 1978, s. 6(c)), and (if it were needed) this section adds further confirmation.

Section 231 makes no reference to the possibility of making a joint appointment to the post of nominee or supervisor of a voluntary arrangement, but it appears from s. 7(6) that this, too, is contemplated by the Act: see the note to that provision.

The word "administrator" has been omitted from subss. (1) and (2) by EA 2002, Sch. 17, para. 20. The point is now covered by IA 1986, Sch. B1, paras 100ff. for administrators appointed under that Schedule, and in other cases by s. 249 and the Enterprise Act 2002 (Commencement No. 4 and Transitional Provisions and Savings) Order 2003 (SI 2003/2093 (C. 85)), art. 3. See the notes to ss. 212(1) and 230.

232 Validity of office-holder's acts

232 The acts of an individual as administrative receiver, liquidator or provisional liquidator of a company are valid notwithstanding any defect in his appointment, nomination or qualifications.

GENERAL NOTE

This is a standard-form provision, similar to that applicable to directors (CA 1985, s. 285). It could not operate, however, to protect acts done where there was no power to appoint at all – *e.g.* where an administrative receiver is purportedly appointed under an invalid instrument. (See, on this latter point, s. 34 above, and on void appointments generally, *Morris v Kanssen* [1946] A.C. 459; *Rolled Steel Products (Holdings) Ltd v British Steel Corporation* [1986] Ch. 246; (1984) 1 B.C.C. 99,158.)

The protection conferred by s. 232 is confined to acts done by an *individual*. A body corporate is not qualified to act as an insolvency practitioner (s. 390(1)), and it is extremely unlikely that in future there would ever be an attempt to appoint one to hold any of the offices listed in s. 232. It is probably correct to infer from the express limitation of s. 232 to individuals that any act done by such a corporate appointee would be wholly void. In the case of a receiver (not necessarily an administrative receiver), s. 30 adds a further statutory ban on corporate appointments, and it is established that acts done by a receiver appointed in breach of this provision are totally ineffective: see *Portman Building Society v Gallwey* [1955] 1 W.L.R. 96.

Insolvency Act 1986 Section 233

The word "administrator" has been omitted from s. 232 by EA 2002, Sch. 17, para. 21. The point is now covered by IA 1986, Sch. B1, para. 104 for administrators appointed under that Schedule, and in other cases by EA 2002, s. 249 and the Enterprise Act 2002 (Commencement No. 4 and Transitional Provisions and Savings) Order 2003 (SI 2003/2093 (C. 85)), art. 3. See the notes to ss. 212(1) and 230.

There is again no reference in this section to the acts of a person as the nominee or supervisor of a voluntary arrangement. The explanation must be that such a person's role and functions are not statutory, but depend in each case upon the terms of the arrangement.

Management by administrators, liquidators, etc.

233 Supplies of gas, water, electricity, etc.

233(1) [Application] This section applies in the case of a company where–

(a) the company enters administration, or

(b) an administrative receiver is appointed, or

(ba) a moratorium under section 1A is in force, or

(c) a voluntary arrangement approved under Part I, has taken effect, or

(d) the company goes into liquidation, or

(e) a provisional liquidator is appointed;

and **"the office-holder"** means the administrator, the administrative receiver, the nominee, the supervisor of the voluntary arrangement, the liquidator or the provisional liquidator, as the case may be.

233(2) [If request by office-holder] If a request is made by or with the concurrence of the office-holder for the giving, after the effective date, of any of the supplies mentioned in the next subsection, the supplier–

(a) may make it a condition of the giving of the supply that the office-holder personally guarantees the payment of any charges in respect of the supply, but

(b) shall not make it a condition of the giving of the supply, or do anything which has the effect of making it a condition of the giving of the supply, that any outstanding charges in respect of a supply given to the company before the effective date are paid.

233(3) [Supplies in s. 233(2)] The supplies referred to in subsection (2) are–

(a) a supply of gas by a gas supplier within the meaning of Part I of the Gas Act 1986,

(b) a supply of electricity by an electricity supplier within the meaning of Part I of the Electricity Act 1989,

(c) a supply of water by a water undertaker or, in Scotland, a water authority,

(d) a supply of communications services by a provider of a public electronic communications service.

233(4) [Effective date] "The effective date" for the purposes of this section is whichever is applicable of the following dates–

(a) the date on which the company entered administration,

(b) the date on which the administrative receiver was appointed (or, if he was appointed in succession to another administrative receiver, the date on which the first of his predecessors was appointed),

(ba) the date on which the moratorium came into force,

(c) the date on which the voluntary arrangement took effect,

(d) the date on which the company went into liquidation,

(e) the date on which the provisional liquidator was appointed.

233(5) [Definitions] The following applies to expressions used in subsection (3)–

(a) **[Repealed]**

(b) **[Repealed]**

(c) **"water authority"** means the same as in the Water (Scotland) Act 1980, and

(d) **"communications services"** do not include electronic communications services to the extent that they are used to broadcast or otherwise transmit programme services (within the meaning of the Communications Act 2003).

GENERAL NOTE

This section (and its counterpart in bankruptcy, s. 372 below) implements a recommendation of the Cork Committee (*Report*, para. 1462). Prior to the present Act, a supplier of goods like gas or water or services such as the telephone was able, by virtue of its monopoly position, to compel the payment of an account incurred before the commencement of a liquidation or receivership by threatening to cut off the connection unless the arrears were paid in full or payment was personally guaranteed by the liquidator or receiver. If the supply was essential for the preservation of the company's assets (*e.g.* livestock or frozen food), there was little choice but to pay, and so the supplier could have its debt paid in priority even to the statutory preferential creditors. The legality of this practice was upheld in *Wellworth Cash & Carry (North Shields) Ltd v North Eastern Electricity Board* (1986) 2 B.C.C. 99,265. This section prohibits further resort to this practice. The supplier may require the "office-holder" to undertake personal responsibility for payment for any new supply, but may not make the provision of a new supply conditional upon receiving payment or security for the old.

In subss. (1)(a) and (4)(a) the reference was formerly to the making of an administration order. The new wording was substituted by EA 2002, Sch. 17, para. 22, with effect from September 15, 2003, to take account of appointments made out of court.

S. 233(1)
The section extends to a voluntary arrangement under Pt I, provided that it has taken effect, as well as to the other situations listed, and "office-holder" is accordingly defined to include the supervisor of such a scheme. Formerly, there was no equivalent protection during the period prior to the holding of the statutory meetings, but amendments made by IA 2000, s. 1 and Sch. 1, paras 1, 8(1), (2) as from January 1, 2003 (by the insertion of para. (ba) into subss. (1) and (4)) now meet that need for companies which are eligible for a moratorium. Other companies may be well advised to consider the alternative of administration.

S. 233(2)
The "effective date" is defined by s. 233(4).

S. 233(3)
Some of the terms used in this subsection are explained in s. 233(5). The scope of the section is confined to statutory undertakers and similar bodies which are under a legal obligation to provide a service to the public: a private supplier of, *e.g.* gas or water is not affected.

S. 233(4)
The phrase "go into liquidation" is defined in s. 247(2): see the note to that subsection.

Insolvency Act 1986 — Section 234

S. 233(5)(a), (b)
The definitions formerly set out here became redundant when s. 233(3)(a), (b) were reworded by the Gas Act 1995, s. 16(1) and Sch. 4, para. 14(1), as from March 1, 1996 and the Utilities Act 2000, s. 108 and Sch. 6, para. 47(1), (2)(a) as from October 1, 2001, respectively. The substance of s. 233 is unchanged.

234 Getting in the company's property

234(1) [Application] This section applies in the case of a company where–

(a) the company enters administration, or

(b) an administrative receiver is appointed, or

(c) the company goes into liquidation, or

(d) a provisional liquidator is appointed;

and **"the office-holder"** means the administrator, the administrative receiver, the liquidator or the provisional liquidator, as the case may be.

234(2) [Court's powers] Where any person has in his possession or control any property, books, papers or records to which the company appears to be entitled, the court may require that person forthwith (or within such period as the court may direct) to pay, deliver, convey, surrender or transfer the property, books, papers or records to the office-holder.

234(3) [Application of s. 234(4)] Where the office-holder–

(a) seizes or disposes of any property which is not property of the company, and

(b) at the time of seizure or disposal believes, and has reasonable grounds for believing, that he is entitled (whether in pursuance of an order of the court or otherwise) to seize or dispose of that property,

the next subsection has effect.

234(4) [Liability of office-holder] In that case the office-holder–

(a) is not liable to any person in respect of any loss or damage resulting from the seizure or disposal except in so far as that loss or damage is caused by the office-holder's own negligence, and

(b) has a lien on the property, or the proceeds of its sale, for such expenses as were incurred in connection with the seizure or disposal.

S. 234(1), (2)
The present section replaces CA 1985, s. 551, which applied only to a winding up by the court, and extends its provisions to every kind of winding up and to all other "insolvency" procedures except a voluntary arrangement. The office-holder may invoke the assistance of the court to get possession of the company's property and records.

An order under s. 234 should not be sought *ex parte*, except perhaps in very exceptional circumstances: *Re First Express Ltd* [1991] B.C.C. 782. The application should be brought in the name of the office-holder, rather than that of the company: *Re Cosslett (Contractors) Ltd (No. 2), Smith v Bridgend County Borough Council* [2001] UKHL 58; [2002] 1 A.C. 336; [2001] B.C.C. 740 at [32].

Under earlier provisions corresponding to the present section, the courts had held that its procedure was not appropriate to determine questions of disputed ownership, but in *Re London Iron & Steel Co. Ltd* [1990] B.C.C. 159 Warner J. held that the words "to which the company appears to be entitled", coupled with the comprehensive rules laid down in Pt 7 of IR 1986, are of sufficient scope to enable the court to settle such matters; and it now seems that the courts entertain such questions as a matter of course: see *Euro Commercial Leasing Ltd v Cartwright & Lewis* [1995] B.C.C. 830 (solicitor's lien); *Re Cosslett (Contractors) Ltd* [1998] Ch. 495; [1997] B.C.C. 724 (plant on construction site). However the court has no such power where the question of ownership falls to be determined by a foreign court: *Re Leyland DAF Ltd, Talbot v Edcrest Ltd* [1994] B.C.C. 166.

In *Walker Morris v Khalastchi* [2001] 1 B.C.L.C. 1 the applicants, who had been requested by the liquidator to hand over files of documents relating to the company, wished to impose conditions that the liquidator should not release any

Section 235 Insolvency Act 1986

of the documents or disclose their contents to the Revenue without an order of the court, but it was ruled that, since the files were the property of the company, the liquidator was entitled to possession of them and that it was for the liquidator to decide whether to make voluntary disclosure of the documents.

In a winding up by the court, the powers conferred on the court by this section are exercisable by the liquidator or provisional liquidator: see IR 1986, r. 4.185. The liquidator is thus empowered to impose the requirement on his own authority.

No sanction is spelt out either in the Act or in the rules for a failure to comply with a requirement imposed under this subsection. No doubt such a failure could be dealt with under the inherent powers of the court, even in the case where the requirement is imposed by a liquidator.

In subs. (1)(a) the reference was formerly to the making of an administration order. The new wording was substituted by EA 2002, Sch. 17, para. 23, with effect from September 15, 2003, to take account of appointments made out of court.

S. 234(3), (4)

These provisions give an immunity to the office-holder (and a lien for his expenses) where he mistakenly but bona fide seizes or disposes of property which does not belong to the company. The protection is given whether or not he has acted in pursuance of a court order granted under s. 234(2) – although such an order would go a long way towards establishing his good faith.

The immunity is "in respect of any loss or damage resulting from the seizure or sale" (negligence apart). It does not appear to extend to liability for the wrongful interference *per se*, and so the owner would not be prevented from suing to establish his right to the return of the property itself or the proceeds of its sale.

It was held in *Welsh Development Agency Ltd v Export Finance Co.* [1992] B.C.C. 270 that (notwithstanding the wide definition of "property" in s. 436) the protection given to office-holders by these subsections extends only to the seizure and disposal of tangible property, and that they do not apply to wrongful dealings with choses in action.

235 Duty to co-operate with office-holder

235(1) [Application] This section applies as does section 234; and it also applies, in the case of a company in respect of which a winding-up order has been made by the court in England and Wales, as if references to the office-holder included the official receiver, whether or not he is the liquidator.

235(2) [Duty to give information etc.] Each of the persons mentioned in the next subsection shall–

(a) give to the office-holder such information concerning the company and its promotion, formation, business, dealings, affairs or property as the office-holder may at any time after the effective date reasonably require, and

(b) attend on the office-holder at such times as the latter may reasonably require.

235(3) [Persons in s. 235(2)] The persons referred to above are–

(a) those who are or have at any time been officers of the company,

(b) those who have taken part in the formation of the company at any time within one year before the effective date,

(c) those who are in the employment of the company, or have been in its employment (including employment under a contract for services) within that year, and are in the office-holder's opinion capable of giving information which he requires,

(d) those who are, or have within that year been, officers of, or in the employment (including employment under a contract for services) of, another company which is, or within that year was, an officer of the company in question, and

(e) in the case of a company being wound up by the court, any person who has acted as administrator, administrative receiver or liquidator of the company.

235(4) **["The effective date"]** For the purposes of subsections (2) and (3), **"the effective date"** is whichever is applicable of the following dates–

(a) the date on which the company entered administration,

(b) the date on which the administrative receiver was appointed or, if he was appointed in succession to another administrative receiver, the date on which the first of his predecessors was appointed,

(c) the date on which the provisional liquidator was appointed, and

(d) the date on which the company went into liquidation.

235(5) **[Penalty for non-compliance]** If a person without reasonable excuse fails to comply with any obligation imposed by this section, he is liable to a fine and, for continued contravention, to a daily default fine.

GENERAL NOTE

In imposing on the former officers and employees of the company, and others, a statutory duty to "co-operate" with the liquidator or other office-holder by giving him such information as he may reasonably require (and to attend for this purpose on the office-holder), this section supplements the traditional powers to have such persons examined either publicly (s. 133) or privately (s. 236) before the court. No court order is required under the present provisions.

Information and documents obtained by the office-holder pursuant to this section may properly be disclosed to the Secretary of State so that he may determine whether director disqualification proceedings should be brought. This is so even though the office-holder has given an assurance that the information or documents will be used only for the purposes of the administration, since such disclosure is within "the purposes of the administration" (*Re Polly Peck International plc Ex p. the joint administrators* [1994] B.C.C. 15). The use of statements obtained under s. 235 in disqualification proceedings does not in itself involve a breach of the European Convention on Human Rights (or, by inference, of the Human Rights Act 1998): *Re Westminster Property Management Ltd, Official Receiver v Stern* [2000] 1 W.L.R. 2230; [2001] B.C.C. 121. The question whether the use of such statements is unfair is to be determined by the trial judge.

S. 235(1)
The situations to which the section applies, and the consequent definition of "office-holder", are the same as are described in s. 234(1). A voluntary arrangement is excluded. Where the liquidator in a winding up by the court in England and Wales is not the official receiver, the official receiver as well as the private liquidator has the powers conferred by the section.

S. 235(2), (3)
The "effective date" is defined in s. 235(4) below.
For the meaning of the term "officer", see the note to s. 206(3).
The extension of "employment" to include employment under a contract for services is wide enough to include accountants and others who have rendered professional services to the company.
The phrases "as the office-holder may reasonably require" and "in the office-holder's opinion" are matters left by the statute to the office-holder's discretion, but would no doubt be subject to the general powers of the court to control an office-holder if he were acting unreasonably; and in any event the question of reasonableness could be raised as a defence if a prosecution were brought.

S. 235(4)
In subs. (4)(a) the reference was formerly to the making of an administration order. The new wording was substituted by EA 2002, Sch. 17, para. 24, with effect from September 15, 2003, to take account of appointments made out of court.
A company "goes into liquidation" at the times described in s. 247(2): see the note to that subsection.

S. 235(5)
On penalties, see s. 430 and Sch. 10.
The duty imposed by this section may also be enforced by court order – *e.g.* where a director has failed to submit a statement of affairs when required by an office-holder to do so: see IR 1986, r. 7.20, and *Re Wallace Smith Trust Co. Ltd* [1992] B.C.C. 707. For other relevant rules, see rr. 4.39ff.

236 Inquiry into company's dealings, etc.

236(1) [Application] This section applies as does section 234; and it also applies in the case of a company in respect of which a winding-up order has been made by the court in England and Wales as if references to the office-holder included the official receiver, whether or not he is the liquidator.

236(2) [Court's powers] The court may, on the application of the office-holder, summon to appear before it–

(a) any officer of the company,

(b) any person known or suspected to have in his possession any property of the company or supposed to be indebted to the company, or

(c) any person whom the court thinks capable of giving information concerning the promotion, formation, business, dealings, affairs or property of the company.

236(3) [Powers re account, production] The court may require any such person as is mentioned in subsection (2)(a) to (c) to submit an affidavit to the court containing an account of his dealings with the company or to produce any books, papers or other records in his possession or under his control relating to the company or the matters mentioned in paragraph (c) of the subsection.

236(4) [Application of s. 236(5)] The following applies in a case where–

(a) a person without reasonable excuse fails to appear before the court when he is summoned to do so under this section, or

(b) there are reasonable grounds for believing that a person has absconded, or is about to abscond, with a view to avoiding his appearance before the court under this section.

236(5) [Court's power re warrant] The court may, for the purpose of bringing that person and anything in his possession before the court, cause a warrant to be issued to a constable or prescribed officer of the court–

(a) for the arrest of that person, and

(b) for the seizure of any books, papers, records, money or goods in that person's possession.

236(6) [Court authorisation re custody] The court may authorise a person arrested under such a warrant to be kept in custody, and anything seized under such a warrant to be held, in accordance with the rules, until that person is brought before the court under the warrant or until such other time as the court may order.

GENERAL NOTE

This power of the court to summon persons to appear before it for examination was formerly provided for by CA 1985, s. 561, but that section was confined in its scope to a winding up by the court. It is now extended to other forms of corporate "insolvency" proceedings, although not to a voluntary arrangement. An examination conducted under this section is private, in contrast to the public examination of officers and others which may be ordered under s. 133.

The court's discretion under this section is unfettered, although it is generally exercised along fairly well-settled lines. There are overriding requirements that the examination should be necessary in the interests of the winding up, and that it should not be oppressive or unfair to the respondent (*Re Embassy Art Products Ltd* (1987) 3 B.C.C. 292; *Re Adlards Motor Group Holding Ltd* [1990] B.C.L.C. 68, and see also *British & Commonwealth Holdings plc (Joint Administrators) v Spicer & Oppenheim, Re British & Commonwealth Holdings plc (No. 2)* [1993] A.C. 426; [1992] B.C.C. 977). The onus of establishing a case is on the office-holder, but the views of office-holders that an examination should be ordered "are normally entitled to a good deal of weight" (*Joint Liquidators of Sasea Finance Ltd v KPMG* [1998] B.C.C. 216 at p. 220). The section is not to be used just to give the office-holder special advantages in ordinary litigation: *Re Atlantic Computers plc* [1998] B.C.C. 200; *Re Sasea Finance Ltd* [1999] B.C.C. 103. As a general (but not invariable) rule, an office-holder may not apply for examination if he has made a firm decision to commence proceedings against the respondent (*Re Castle New Homes Ltd* [1979] 1 W.L.R. 1075; [1979] 2 All E.R. 775, as explained in *Cloverbay Ltd (Joint Administrators) v Bank of Credit and Commerce International SA (Re Cloverbay Ltd (No. 2))* [1991] Ch. 90; [1990] B.C.C. 414; and see *Re RBG Resources plc* [2002] EWCA Civ 1624, [2002] B.C.C.

1005. However even the fact that criminal charges have already been brought against the respondent does not constitute an absolute bar to the making of an order (*Re Arrows Ltd (No. 2)* [1992] B.C.C. 446). The court has to balance the importance to the office-holder of obtaining the information against the degree of oppression to the person sought to be examined, bearing in mind that the office-holder's views should be afforded great weight but are not determinative. The case for making an order against an officer or former officer of the company will usually be stronger than it would be against a third party (see *Re Westmead Consultants Ltd* [2002] 1 B.C.L.C. 384); and an order for oral examination is much more likely to be oppressive than an order for the production of documents (*Cloverbay Ltd*, above). However (even in the case of a third party) an application is not necessarily unreasonable because it is inconvenient for the respondent or may cause him considerable work, or may make him vulnerable to future claims (*British & Commonwealth Holdings*, above). In *Re Trading Partners Ltd* [2002] 1 B.C.L.C. 655 an order was made in favour of liquidators against receivers for the production of material which had been collected by the receivers at their debenture-holders' expense, despite objections based on a possible conflict of interest, the only restriction placed by the court being on documents which might disclose the strategy proposed to be adopted for the receivership. It may be oppressive to seek an order for examination without prior notice to the respondents or without first having asked for the information by letter or some similar means, although such a course of action would be justified in some exceptional cases (*Re Embassy Art Products Ltd*, above). In *Re an Inquiry into Mirror Group Newspapers plc* [2000] B.C.C. 217 inspectors appointed under CA 1985, s. 432 and 442 wished to put extensive questions to the respondent on matters on which he had already been questioned at length under (*inter alia*) s. 236, and had been questioned in cross-examination in a criminal trial: in all, he had undergone interrogations over a total of 61 days. The court directed the inspectors to do their best to avoid questioning him on topics on which he had been questioned before, and so far as possible to rely on the answers which he had already given in the course of the earlier procedures.

In *Re Bank of Credit & Commerce International SA* [1997] B.C.C. 561, where the office-holders in the BCCI liquidation applied to have the production by members of the Bank of America Group of an extensive list of books and documents set out under 12 heads, the court ordered disclosure subject to staging periods spread out between 14 and 84 days, and expressed the tentative view that the costs of compliance with the order (involving, *inter alia*, air freighting 100 boxes of documents from San Francisco to London) should be costs in the liquidation.

Any doubts which there might have been on the question whether a respondent could be excused from complying with an order under s. 236 on the ground of self-incrimination were set at rest by a series of cases in 1992 – at least in the case where he is an officer or former officer of the insolvent company. The relevant cases are: *Re Jeffrey S Levitt Ltd* [1992] Ch. 457; [1992] B.C.C. 137, not following *Re Barlow Clowes (Gilt Managers) Ltd (No. 2)* (Ferris J, unreported, July 31, 1990); *Re A E Farr Ltd* [1992] B.C.C. 150 (where Ferris J. decided not to follow his earlier judgment) and *Bishopsgate Investment Management Ltd (in provisional liquidation) v Maxwell (Re Bishopsgate Investment Management Ltd, Mirror Group Newspapers plc v Maxwell and Ors)* [1993] Ch. 1; [1992] B.C.C. 222. However, the fact that the privilege against self-incrimination has been impliedly abrogated by statute is a factor which can be taken into account when the court exercises its discretion whether or not to make an order ([1993] Ch. 1 at p. 63; [1992] B.C.C. 222 at p. 262). Where the person concerned is not an officer or former officer, the plea of self-incrimination may be available (see the Australian case *O'Toole v Mitcham* (1978) C.L.C. para. 40–429). However, it should be noted that these cases were decided before the ruling, discussed below, in *Saunders v United Kingdom* [1997] E.H.R.R. 313; [1997] B.C.C. 872 in which it was held that the *use* in later criminal proceedings of statements obtained under compulsion was contrary to the European Convention on Human Rights, and in practice the use of such statements was discontinued and is now banned by law. This development would suggest that an objection on the ground of self-incrimination is now even less likely to be upheld. For further proceedings, see *R. v Lyons* [2002] UKHL 44; [2003] 1 A.C. 976; [2002] B.C.C. 968.

In *Re Pantmaenog Timber Co. Ltd, Official Receiver v Wadge Rapps & Hunt (a firm)* [2003] UKHL 49, [2003] 3 W.L.R. 767, [2003] B.C.C. 659 the House of Lords, reversing the Court of Appeal, ruled that the Official Receiver could make an application under s. 236 even when his sole purpose was to obtain information for the purposes of instituting disqualification proceedings against a director on the ground of unfitness under CDDA 1986, s. 6. The Court of Appeal had held that the Official Receiver's powers in this regard were limited to those conferred by CDDA 1986, s. 7(4), but the House of Lords said that the two provisions should be seen as complementary to each other. It was also open to an office-holder, such as a liquidator, to invoke s. 236 for the same purpose – his functions were not confined to the administration of the insolvent company's estate – and the Official Receiver could do so whether or not he was the company's liquidator.

In *Bellmex International Ltd v Green* [2001] B.C.C. 253 it was said that the s. 236 power should not normally be used to deal with factual issues arising on a proof of debt.

In *Re Brook Martin & Co. (Nominees) Ltd* [1993] B.C.L.C. 328, the directors of the company against whom a s. 236 order was sought were also the company's solicitors, and they raised a plea of professional privilege. Vinelott J. held that no privilege could be asserted in respect of documents which belonged to the company itself. In regard to

Section 236   Insolvency Act 1986

documents where the privilege arose through acts done on behalf of other clients, he left open the question whether it could, in exceptional circumstances, be overridden by an order under s. 236. In *Re Galileo Group Ltd* [1998] B.C.C. 228 an order was refused where the information which was being sought had been given in confidence.

The transcripts of the examination of a person under this section attract legal professional privilege (*Dubai Bank Ltd v Galadari* (1989) 5 B.C.C. 722), but this is subject to the powers of the court to allow inspection under r. 9.5(2).

The object of an order under s. 236 was said by Browne-Wilkinson V.-C. in the *Cloverbay Ltd* case ([1991] Ch. 90 at p. 102; [1990] B.C.C. 415 at pp. 419–420) to be limited to enabling the office-holder "to get sufficient information to reconstitute the state of knowledge that the company should possess. In my judgment its purpose is not to put the company in a better position than it would have enjoyed if liquidation or administration had not supervened." However, in *British & Commonwealth Holdings plc (Joint Administrators) v Spicer & Oppenheim (Re British & Commonwealth Holdings plc (No. 2)* [1993] A.C. 426; [1992] B.C.C. 977, the House of Lords rejected this narrow approach, holding that an order could properly be made extending to all documents (and, it would appear, all information) which the office-holder reasonably required to have to carry out his functions.

In some early cases decided under the section, an order was made on terms that the record should not be used in subsequent criminal proceedings, or disclosed to the Serious Fraud Office (*e.g. Re Arrows Ltd (No. 2))* [1992] B.C.C. 125 and *Re Arrows Ltd (No. 4)* (at first instance) [1992] B.C.C. 987). However, in the light of the rulings in *Rank Film Distributors Ltd v Video Information Centre* [1982] A.C. 380 and *AT & T Istel Ltd v Tully* [1992] Q.B. 315 (cases decided on analogous statutory provisions), it was later accepted that the civil courts have no jurisdiction to impose a condition on the use by prosecuting authorities in criminal proceedings of evidence given in the civil proceedings, such as a condition of the kind described: see the *Bishopsgate Investment Management Ltd* case [1992] Ch. 1 at p. 19; [1992] B.C.C. 222 at p. 228 and *Re Arrows Ltd (No. 4); Hamilton v Naviede* in the House of Lords [1995] 2 A.C. 75; [1994] B.C.C. 641. However, these rulings must now be reconsidered in the light of the decision of the European Court of Human Rights in *Saunders v United Kingdom* [1997] E.H.R.R. 313; [1997] B.C.C. 872, which held that the use of self-incriminating statements obtained under compulsion (in that case, by DTI inspectors acting under CA 1985, s. 432) in subsequent criminal proceedings was unfair and a breach of Art. 6(1) of the European Convention on Human Rights. In the light of this ruling, the practice of using such statements in criminal proceedings was discontinued, and the Youth Justice and Criminal Evidence Act 1999, s. 59 and Sch. 3 now forbids prosecutors from doing so by statute. (But such statements may be used in disqualification proceedings: *R. v Secretary of State for Trade and Industry, ex parte McCormick* [1998] B.C.C. 379.) Moreover, the Convention has since been incorporated into the domestic law of the United Kingdom by the Human Rights Act 1998.

In *R v Faryab* [1999] B.P.I.R. 569 the Court of Appeal warned against using answers given in a s. 236 examination in a subsequent criminal trial of the examinee without an appropriate direction being given to the jury as to their possible unreliability.

In *Re Headington Investments Ltd Ex p. Maxwell* [1993] B.C.C. 500, the Court of Appeal held that there was no public interest immunity to prevent the disclosure of s. 236 transcripts to the prosecution or regulatory authorities and that, if such disclosure is made, a person facing actual or potential prosecution was not entitled to have simultaneous disclosure made to him: the material would in due course be made available to him in the criminal proceedings, and any question of unfairness or prejudice was a matter for the judge at trial.

For the rules and procedure governing the examinations, see IR 1986, rr. 9.1ff. Application is made to the court by the office-holder. Although in many, if not most, cases it may be appropriate for the application to be made *ex parte*, Vinelott J. in *Re Maxwell Communications Corporation plc, Homan v Vogel* [1994] B.C.C. 741 said that some good reason must be shown to justify this course: if the person affected is given notice it may enable the scope of the order to be clarified and in this and in other ways save time and expense. See also on this issue *Re Embassy Art Products Ltd* (1987) 3 B.C.C. 292 and *Re PFTZM Ltd (in liq.)* [1995] B.C.C. 280 (where an order obtained *ex parte* was set aside on the ground that it was oppressive). In *Miller v Bain* [2002] B.C.C. 899 the respondent director had failed to co-operate with the liquidator by attending for interview and proposed to absent himself for over a year. The liquidator applied *ex parte* for an order requiring him to attend for a private examination, and was awarded costs of the *ex parte* application in view of the respondent's recalcitrant attitude.

The applicant submits to the court an unsworn statement of the grounds on which the application is being made (r. 9.2(1)). The statement is confidential, and may not be inspected by anyone, without an order of the court, other than the persons mentioned in r. 9.5(2). It had been the invariable practice since *Re Gold Co.* (1879) 12 Ch.D. 77 that this statement should not be disclosed to the person against whom the order was sought – *i.e.* that the court would never exercise its discretion to allow inspection by such a person. However, in *Re British & Commonwealth Holdings plc (No. 1)* [1992] Ch. 342; [1992] B.C.C. 165, the Court of Appeal decided to depart from this practice, and ruled instead that where an application has been made to have the order set aside, inspection of the statement should prima facie be allowed if the court is of the opinion that otherwise it might be unable fairly or properly to dispose of the application. It is for the office-holder to satisfy the court that confidentiality in whole or in part would nevertheless be appropriate. See further on this question *Re Bishopsgate Investment Management Ltd (No. 2)* [1994] B.C.C. 732.

In *Re Seagull Manufacturing Co. Ltd (in liquidation)* [1993] Ch. 345; [1993] B.C.C. 241 the Court of Appeal, affirming Mummery J. [1992] Ch. 128; [1991] B.C.C. 550, held that the public examination provisions of s. 133 have extra-territorial effect, and Mummery J. in particular contrasted s. 133 with the powers under s. 236, 237 which, he said, did not extend beyond the jurisdiction. However, the Court of Session in *McIsaac, Petitioners; Joint Liquidators of First Tokyo Index Trust Ltd* [1994] B.C.C. 410, rejected a submission that a s. 236 order could not be made against a person resident in New York. The issue is examined in detail by Burton J. in *Re Casterbridge Properties Ltd* [2002] B.C.C. 453, at pp. 475ff. Here, it was held that while s. 236 undoubtedly has extra-territorial effect to the extent that the court may order the private examination of a person based in a foreign country if the examination is to be held abroad, the question whether an order may be made for such a person to be examined within the UK remains unresolved. In *Re Anglo American Insurance Co. Ltd* [2002] B.C.C. 715 the alternative course was adopted of applying for letters of request to courts in Bermuda and the United States, and Neuberger J. held that for this purpose the rules governing the exercise of the s. 236 jurisdiction, set out in IR 1986, Pt 9, reflected the way in which the court would exercise its inherent jurisdiction where an application is made for letters of request. In *Re Mid East Trading Ltd, Phillips v Lehman Brothers* [1998] B.C.C. 726, the Court of Appeal held that an order could be made under s. 236 in respect of documents situated abroad, where the company in question was being wound up as an unregistered company under IA 1986, Pt V. However, it was emphasised in that case that the court's power extended only to order the production of documents relating to the particular company which was in liquidation. In *Re a Company No. 003318 of 1987 (Oriental Credit Ltd)* [1988] Ch. 204; (1987) 3 B.C.C. 564 it was held that the court has the power to grant an order restraining a person from leaving the jurisdiction pending the holding of an examination under this section.

It has been held that where a foreign court seeks the co-operation of a court in the United Kingdom to have a person who is resident here examined for the purposes of an insolvency proceeding in the foreign jurisdiction, the considerations which might inhibit an English court from making an order under ss. 236 should not be taken into account: see the notes to s. 426, below.

In *Re Barlow Clowes Gilt Managers Ltd* [1992] Ch. 208; [1991] B.C.C. 608, statements had been given voluntarily by various persons to a representative of the liquidators of a company under the threat, express or implicit, that if they did not do so voluntarily the liquidators would have recourse to their powers under ss. 236, 237. Other persons, who had been charged with criminal offences in connection with the affairs of the company, sought to have access to the transcripts of these interviews; but Millett J. held that the information contained in the transcripts could be used only for purposes connected with the liquidation. The liquidators had, in this instance, given the interviewees assurances of confidentiality which would not have been needed had the information been obtained under s. 236; but even so, information obtained in a private examination under the statute could also have been disclosed only to the extent that it was for the benefit of the liquidation. (On the giving of undertakings by office-holders, see further *McIsaac, Petitioners* [1994] B.C.C. 410.)

Information or documents obtained by an office-holder pursuant to s. 236 are subject to an obligation of confidentiality, but this may in an appropriate case be waived by the court: *Re a Company No. 005374 of 1993* [1993] B.C.C. 734. In that case administrative receivers were allowed to disclose information to the bank which had appointed them. Information may also be disclosed to the Secretary of State for the purpose of considering whether to bring disqualification proceedings: see the notes to s. 235, above.

The court has no jurisdiction to authorise anyone other than the applicant (or a solicitor or counsel instructed by him) to examine the witness, except in the rare case where there are two office-holders and IR 1986, r. 9.4(2) applies: *Re Maxwell Communications Corporation plc, Homan v Vogel* [1994] B.C.C. 741.

An order under s. 236 becomes inoperative if the office-holder in whose favour it has been granted ceases to hold office: *Re Kingscroft Insurance Co. Ltd* [1994] B.C.C. 343.

In *Re Galileo Group Ltd* [1998] B.C.C. 228, Lightman J. expressed the view that s. 236 was, at least primarily, designed to protect the interests of creditors in an insolvent liquidation: it was not intended to gain a windfall for shareholders in a solvent liquidation. This was a factor that the court might take into account in deciding whether, in its discretion, to grant an order under s. 236.

Section 236 binds the Crown, so that it may be ordered to disclose information obtained in the form of transcripts of evidence under the powers of investigation conferred by CA 1985, s. 432, subject to prior disclosure to the witnesses whose evidence was covered by the order and subject also to any application by them to have the order set aside: *Soden v Burns* [1996] 1 W.L.R. 1512; [1997] B.C.C. 308.

S. 236(1)
This provision is identical with s. 235(1): see the note to that subsection.

S. 236(2)

Only the office-holder has standing to make application to the court: *Re James McHale Automobiles Ltd* [1997] B.C.C. 202. The former legislation was not so restricted and other persons, such as contributories, were commonly allowed to apply.

The list of persons who may be summoned is shorter than that in s. 235(2), but it is potentially of wider scope in view of the discretion given to the court by para. (c). In *Joint Liquidators of Sasea Finance Ltd v KPMG* [1998] B.C.C. 216 at p. 222 it was said that a company's auditors were "most probably" office-holders within s. 236(2)(a). In *Re Trading Partners Ltd, Akers v Lomas* [2002] 1 B.C.L.C. 655 an order was made for the inspection of working papers and litigation documents held by the administrative receivers of companies related to the company in liquidation.

S. 236(3)

The requirement as to an affidavit should significantly shorten the proceedings in many cases.

S. 236(4)–(6)

These provisions, especially when read in conjunction with s. 237, are more extensive and detailed than the former CA 1985, s. 561(4), which was confined to the apprehension of the person summoned, and also stipulated that he had to be tendered a reasonable sum for his expenses. The repealed section also stated (s. 561(3)) that if a person (*e.g.* a solicitor) who was ordered to produce a document relating to the company claimed a lien on it, such production should be without prejudice to the lien. The present section does not reproduce this provision. In many cases the lien will now be unenforceable by virtue of s. 246, which will allow the office-holder to demand possession of the document and so make the need for an order for its production superfluous. However even in those cases where s. 246 does not apply (*e.g.* where the office-holder is an administrative receiver, or where the document gives a title to property and is held as such (s. 246(3)), an order for production under s. 236 will not affect the lien: *Ex parte Bramble* (1880) 13 Ch.D. 885; *Re Aveling Barford Ltd* [1989] 1 W.L.R. 360; (1988) 4 B.C.C. 548).

In *Re Bank of Credit & Commerce International (No. 7)* [1994] 1 B.C.L.C. 455 an order made under s. 236 against a person domiciled abroad was buttressed by a requirement that he should give security in the sum of £500,000 as a condition of being allowed to leave the country.

For relevant rules, see IR 1986, rr. 7.23, 7.24.

237 Court's enforcement powers under s. 236

237(1) **[Order to deliver property]** If it appears to the court, on consideration of any evidence obtained under section 236 or this section, that any person has in his possession any property of the company, the court may, on the application of the office-holder, order that person to deliver the whole or any part of the property to the officer-holder at such time, in such manner and on such terms as the court thinks fit.

237(2) **[Order to pay money due]** If it appears to the court, on consideration of any evidence so obtained, that any person is indebted to the company, the court may, on the application of the office-holder, order that person to pay to the office-holder, at such time and in such manner as the court may direct, the whole or any part of the amount due, whether in full discharge of the debt or otherwise, as the court thinks fit.

237(3) **[Order re examination of persons]** The court may, if it thinks fit, order that any person who if within the jurisdiction of the court would be liable to be summoned to appear before it under section 236 or this section shall be examined in any part of the United Kingdom where he may for the time being be, or in a place outside the United Kingdom.

237(4) **[Examination on oath etc.]** Any person who appears or is brought before the court under section 236 or this section may be examined on oath, either orally or (except in Scotland) by interrogatories, concerning the company or the matters mentioned in section 236(2)(c).

GENERAL NOTE

Most of these detailed provisions supplementing s. 236 had no counterpart in earlier legislation. There is some overlap with s. 234.

Adjustment of prior transactions (administration and liquidation)

238 Transactions at an undervalue (England and Wales)

238(1) [Application] This section applies in the case of a company where–

(a) the company enters administration, or

(b) the company goes into liquidation;

and **"the office-holder"** means the administrator or the liquidator, as the case may be.

238(2) [Application to court by office-holder] Where the company has at a relevant time (defined in section 240) entered into a transaction with any person at an undervalue, the office-holder may apply to the court for an order under this section.

238(3) [Court order] Subject as follows, the court shall, on such an application, make such order as it thinks fit for restoring the position to what it would have been if the company had not entered into that transaction.

238(4) [Interpretation] For the purposes of this section and section 241, a company enters into a transaction with a person at an undervalue if–

(a) the company makes a gift to that person or otherwise enters into a transaction with that person on terms that provide for the company to receive no consideration, or

(b) the company enters into a transaction with that person for a consideration the value of which, in money or money's worth, is significantly less than the value, in money or money's worth, of the consideration provided by the company.

238(5) [Restriction on court order] The court shall not make an order under this section in respect of a transaction at an undervalue if it is satisfied–

(a) that the company which entered into the transaction did so in good faith and for the purpose of carrying on its business, and

(b) that at the time it did so there were reasonable grounds for believing that the transaction would benefit the company.

GENERAL NOTE

To put the present section into context, it is necessary to discuss briefly the reforms made by IA 1985 in response to the recommendations made in Ch. 28 of the Cork Committee's *Report*, which appear in the present Act under the headings "transactions at an undervalue"; "preferences"; and "provisions against debt avoidance" (see respectively ss. 238 and 339; ss. 239 and 340; and s. 423ff.). The concern of the Committee was to state the law more logically and accurately and remove doubts as to its scope, to make the law relating to corporate insolvency and individual bankruptcy broadly the same, and to remove the former emphasis on fraud which was implicit in the traditional terms "fraudulent conveyance" and "fraudulent preference".

The new concept of "transactions at an undervalue" is based on the former BA 1914, s. 42, which declared void against the trustee in bankruptcy settlements of property made by a person who became bankrupt within a stated period thereafter. This section has been replaced, in the case of an individual bankrupt, by the broader provisions of IA 1986, s. 339, and (in accordance with the recommendations of the Cork Committee (*Report*, para. 1237)) applied to corporate insolvency as well as bankruptcy by the present section.

The former rules relating to "fraudulent preferences" (BA 1914, s. 44; CA 1985, s. 615) are redefined (under the neutral title of "preferences") by IA 1986, s. 239 for company insolvencies and s. 340 for bankruptcies. As is indicated by the new designation, the law has been changed so that it is no longer necessary to show a dominant and improper intention to give the creditor in question a preference over creditors generally.

Finally, the law governing "fraudulent conveyances", which can be traced back to a statute of Elizabeth I, has been brought up to date and appears in IA 1986 as ss. 423ff., which apply to both companies and individuals. Once again, the word "fraudulent" has been pointedly dropped from the present statutory provision.

There is a considerable overlap between the three topics here discussed, and particularly, as regards transactions at an undervalue, between ss. 238 and 423ff. The distinguishing features of the latter sections are: (1) they are not confined to situations where a company is in liquidation or subject to an administration order, or an individual is bankrupt, (2) there is no time limit, and (3) application may be made to the court by any "victim" of the transaction, and not merely the "office-holder" or trustee in bankruptcy; but (4) the requisite intention to put assets out of reach of creditors or prejudice their interests must be shown.

Sections 238–241 deal with transactions at an undervalue and preferences involving companies incorporated in England and Wales: see s. 440(2)(a). Equivalent provision is made for Scotland, with the distinctive labels "gratuitous alienations" and "unfair preferences", by ss. 242, 243; but these sections follow in detail the rather different bankruptcy law of Scotland.

The provisions of ss. 238–243 do not operate retrospectively so as to invalidate a transaction which occurred before the present Act came into force, unless it could have been invalidated under the corresponding provisions of the former law: see Sch. 11, para. 9.

For the purposes of the Limitation Act 1980, applications to set aside transactions under ss. 238–241 are generally actions on a speciality within s. 8(1) of that Act, to which a 12-year period of limitation applies, but where the substance of the claim is not to set aside a transaction but to recover a sum by virtue of these sections the period is six years: *Re Priory Garage (Walthamstow) Ltd* [2001] B.P.I.R. 144.

Sections 238 and 239 (and also ss. 423ff.) are to be construed as having extraterritorial effect, so that an order may be made against a person who is outside the jurisdiction: *Re Paramount Airways Ltd (in administration)* [1993] Ch. 223; [1992] B.C.C. 416. There are, however, two safeguards: first, the court has a discretion under the sections as to the order which it may make. If a foreign element is involved, it will have to be satisfied that, in respect of the relief sought against him, the respondent is a person sufficiently connected with this jurisdiction for it to be just and proper to make the order. Secondly, a person who wishes to serve the proceedings has to obtain the leave of the court to do so under IR 1986, r. 12.12.

The right of a liquidator to institute proceedings to set aside a transaction at an undervalue or a preference under ss. 238 and 239 does not form part of the company's property at the commencement of the liquidation so as to be capable of being charged by the company before the winding up or of being sold by the liquidator afterwards: *Re Yagerphone Ltd* [1935] Ch. 392; *Re Oasis Merchandising Services Ltd* [1998] Ch. 170; [1997] B.C.C. 282: see the note to s. 214(1). It has also been held that the liquidator cannot recoup the costs of such litigation out of the general assets in the liquidation: *Re Floor Fourteen Ltd, Lewis v IRC* [2001] 3 All E.R. 499; [2002] B.C.C. 198, but this ruling has been nullified as a result of changes made to IR 1986, r. 4.218: see the note to s. 115.

In the context of the financial markets, no order may be made under s. 238 in relation to a market contract to which a recognised investment exchange or clearing house is a party or which is entered into under its default rules, or a disposition of property in pursuance of such a market contract: see CA 1989, s. 165. It is also disapplied in relation to payment and securities settlement systems by the Finality Regulations 1999, reg. 17. (See the introductory notes at pp. 2–3 above.)

A transaction may be the subject of a challenge under ss. 238–243 and at the same time open to objection as a "tainted gift" under POCA 2002. In that case, s. 427 of the latter Act provides that no order or decree may be made under s. 238, 239, 242, 243 or 423 at a time when the recipient of the tainted gift is the subject of a restraint order or confiscation order under the 2002 Act, and any order or decree made under the above sections after the POCA order is discharged shall take into account any realisation made of property held by the recipient.

S. 238(1)

This and the next three sections apply in a narrower range of situations than do earlier sections in this Part, *i.e.* only to company administrations and liquidations, and "office-holder" means the administrator or liquidator. It does not appear that the official receiver, where he is not the liquidator, is given standing also, as he is by s. 235.

In subs. (1)(a) the reference was formerly to the making of an administration order. The new wording was substituted by EA 2002, Sch. 17, para. 25, with effect from September 15, 2003, to take account of appointments made out of court.

For the meaning of "goes into liquidation", see s. 247(2).

S. 238(2)

Only the office-holder, as defined in s. 238(1), may make application. This may be contrasted with the wider category permitted to apply for an order under s. 423: see s. 424(1).

A "relevant time" for the purposes of this section is defined by reference not only to the calendar but also to the company's solvency: see s. 240.

S. 238(3)

This subsection (and the corresponding s. 239(3) relating to preferences) is curiously worded. On the face of it, the use of the word "shall" and the concluding phrase "for restoring the position to what it would have been if the company had not entered into that transaction" would appear to tie the court's hands, so that (subject only to s. 238(5)) it *must* make an order, and then only an order which restores the status quo. However the words "as it thinks fit" and the many and varied examples of possible orders (set out in s. 241) which it is open to the court to make clearly indicate that the applicant is not entitled to demand any particular form of order as of right, and this consideration, coupled with the fact that the court's jurisdiction in this sphere is equitable in origin, must lead to the conclusion that the court may in its discretion decline to make any order at all. In *Re Paramount Airways Ltd (in administration)* [1993] Ch. 223 at p. 239; [1992] B.C.C. 416 at p. 425, Nicholls V.-C. endorsed this view.

S. 238(4)

A "transaction at an undervalue" may include an outright gift (para. (a)), but otherwise must involve some form of dealing between the parties (*Re Taylor Sinclair (Capital) Ltd* [2001] 2 B.C.L.C. 176), and where consideration is given, the discrepancy in value must be "significant" (para. (b)).

In the leading case of *Re M C Bacon Ltd* [1990] B.C.C. 78 Millett J. held that the creation of security over a company's assets was not a transaction at an undervalue. Section 238(4)(b), he said, requires a comparison to be made between the value obtained by the company for the transaction and the value of the consideration provided by the company. Both values have to be measurable in money or money's worth and have to be considered from the company's point of view. The mere creation of security over the company's assets does not deplete them or diminish their value. Loss by the company of the ability to apply the proceeds of the assets otherwise than in satisfaction of the secured debt is not capable of valuation in money terms, nor is the consideration received by the company in return. The ruling in *Re Mistral Finance Ltd* [2001] B.C.C. 27 is to the same effect.

Similar reasoning would very possibly be applicable to a guarantee given by a company of another's indebtedness.

In *Phillips v Brewin Dolphin Bell Lawrie Ltd* [2001] 1 W.L.R. 143; [2001] B.C.C. 864 the House of Lords was concerned with a complex series of linked transactions, in one of which the company had sold its business, worth £1.05m., to B Ltd for a nominal consideration of £1 and the assumption by B Ltd of redundancy costs of £325,000, and by a contract executed contemporaneously B Ltd's parent company had agreed to lease computers from the company for four quarterly payments of £312,500. The Court of Appeal had considered that the only "transaction" to be considered under s. 238 was that for the sale of the business and that no account should be taken of the related contracts; but the House of Lords held that there was no reason why the consideration for a transaction should not be provided by a third party and that, on the facts, the agreement for the sale of the business had been entered into for a consideration which included the benefit of the leasing agreement. The leasing agreement turned out to be worthless but one payment of £312,500 had been made in advance. It followed that credit ought to be given both for this sum and for the £325,000 in determining the amount which the court should order to be repaid to the company's liquidator under s. 238.

In *Re Lewis's of Leicester Ltd* [1995] B.C.C. 514 a company trading as a department store, in anticipation of closing down its operations, had segregated moneys received from several of its concessionaires and placed them in separate bank accounts in circumstances which, the court held, established a trust in their favour. It was further held that the creation of a trust in this way was not a transaction at an undervalue, since the company's assets were not diminished by what was in substance an arrangement for accelerated payment of sums which would in any event become due to the concessionaires in the future.

See also *Re Barton Manufacturing Co. Ltd* [1998] B.C.C. 827 (alleged loans to directors held to be gratuitous payments), *Re Shapland Inc.* [2000] B.C.C. 106 (retrospective conversion of interest-free loan to interest-bearing loan) and *Re Thoars (decd)* [2002] EWHC 2416 (Ch), [2003] 1 B.C.L.C. 499 (possibility of taking into account events after the transaction in assessing the value of property or consideration).

S. 238(5)

These provisions bear a distinct resemblance to the "three-fold test" of Eve J. in *Re Lee, Behrens and Co. Ltd* [1932] 2 Ch. 46, which had a chequered history in the context of the doctrine of ultra vires (and, in that context, was later declared to be largely inappropriate: see *Rolled Steel Products (Holdings) Ltd v British Steel Corporation* [1986] Ch. 246; (1984) 1 B.C.C. 99,158). It may well be that s. 238(5) will prove most difficult to apply in relation to the very types of transaction illustrated by the facts of the two cases mentioned: the payment of gratuities and pensions to employees and their dependants, and the giving of guarantees (especially within corporate groups). There may be problems, too, with regard to the "genuineness" of directors' remuneration (compare *Re Halt Garage (1964) Ltd* [1982] 3 All E.R. 1016), but it is very likely that the present section will make it easier to impeach such transactions.

239 Preferences (England and Wales)

239(1) [Application] This section applies as does section 238.

239(2) [Application to court by office-holder] Where the company has at a relevant time (defined in the next section) given a preference to any person, the office-holder may apply to the court for an order under this section.

239(3) [Court order] Subject as follows, the court shall, on such an application, make such order as it thinks fit for restoring the position to what it would have been if the company had not given that preference.

239(4) [Interpretation] For the purposes of this section and section 241, a company gives a preference to a person if—

(a) that person is one of the company's creditors or a surety or guarantor for any of the company's debts or other liabilities, and

(b) the company does anything or suffers anything to be done which (in either case) has the effect of putting that person into a position which, in the event of the company going into insolvent liquidation, will be better than the position he would have been in if that thing had not been done.

239(5) [Restriction on court order] The court shall not make an order under this section in respect of a preference given to any person unless the company which gave the preference was influenced in deciding to give it by a desire to produce in relation to that person the effect mentioned in subsection (4)(b).

239(6) [Presumption] A company which has given a preference to a person connected with the company (otherwise than by reason only of being its employee) at the time the preference was given is presumed, unless the contrary is shown, to have been influenced in deciding to give it by such a desire as is mentioned in subsection (5).

239(7) [Interpretation re preference] The fact that something has been done in pursuance of the order of a court does not, without more, prevent the doing or suffering of that thing from constituting the giving of a preference.

GENERAL NOTE

The former law relating to "fraudulent preferences", as contained in CA 1985, s. 615 and earlier Companies Acts, had long been thought unsatisfactory and, in particular, as the Cork Committee pointed out (*Report*, para. 1244), the word "fraudulent" was both inaccurate and misleading. The Committee recommended that the term "fraudulent preference" should be replaced by "voidable preference". The draftsman, however, has rejected this suggestion (and the expression "undue preference", which is common in Australia) in favour of simply "preference", except in Scotland, for which "unfair preference" has been chosen. These differences over terminology are unimportant. The object of the change, at least in regard to England and Wales, is to remove the implication that an improper motive approaching fraud must be shown (and proved to the high standard which that charge requires), and to reflect the fact that under the redefined law it is not necessary for the liquidator even to show that the *dominant* intention of the company was to give the one creditor a preference. It need now only be established that the company was "influenced by a desire" to bring about a preference, and in some cases the burden of proof on this point is reversed (see s. 239(5), (6)).

In the first reported case under the new section, *Re M C Bacon Ltd* [1990] B.C.C. 78, Millett J. "emphatically protested" against the citation of cases decided under the old law: these, he said, could not be of any assistance in construing the language of the new statute, which had been so completely and deliberately changed.

On the question whether the right of a liquidator to institute proceedings under s. 239 is capable of being charged or assigned, and whether the costs of litigation under the section may be recouped from the general assets in the liquidation, see the general note to s. 238.

In the context of the financial markets, no order may be made under s. 239 in relation to a market contract to which a recognised investment exchange or clearing house is a party or which is entered into under its default rules, or a disposition of property in pursuance of such a market contract: see CA 1989, s. 165. It is also disapplied in relation to payment and securities settlement systems by the Finality Regulations 1999, reg. 17. (See the introductory notes at pp. 2–3 above.) Note again the potential impact of s. 427 of the POCA 2002.

For the corresponding provisions in bankruptcy, see s. 340; and for the position in Scotland, see s. 243.

S. 239(1)

Section 238, which is referred to, restricts the jurisdiction to cases where a company is in administration or liquidation, and defines "office-holder" accordingly.

S. 239(2)

"Relevant time" refers both to the period within which the preference is given and to the company's solvency: see s. 240(2). This is the time when the decision to enter into the transaction is taken, and not the time when the transaction is effected (see *Re M C Bacon Ltd* (above) at p. 88). The terms "preference" and "any person" are explained in s. 239(4).

S. 239(3)

The court's powers are similar to those conferred by s. 238(3) and include the power to decline to make any order: see the note to that subsection. In *Re Kayford Ltd* [1975] 1 W.L.R. 279 a mail-order company in anticipation of possible insolvency had placed money sent as prepayments by its customers into a special bank account, and it was held that these sums were impressed with a trust which took them out of the insolvent estate when the company was later wound up. Under the law as it then stood, no question of fraudulent preference arose, but such an arrangement could now fall within s. 239. If this were so, the circumstances might well justify the court in refusing to make an order. In *Re Lewis's of Leicester Ltd* [1995] B.C.C. 514 a somewhat similar arrangement in favour of certain concessionaires was made by a department store in anticipation of closing down its trading operations; but the court held that the company's desire was not to give the concessionaires a preference but to prevent the store from looking "more like a morgue than a market during its final weeks of trading".

S. 239(4)

Examples of a preference given by the Cork Committee in its *Report* (para. 1208) were: paying the whole or part of a debt, providing security or further security for an existing debt, and returning goods which have been delivered but not paid for. In *Re Mistral Finance Ltd* [2001] B.C.C. 27 the giving of security to secure an existing debt was struck down as a preference, but a clause which accelerated the obligations of both parties in the event of a liquidation, in consequence of which the creditor acquired a right of set-off, was held not to be open to challenge.

The phrase "going into insolvent liquidation" is not expressly defined for the purposes of the present section as it is for ss. 214 and 216. That may, however, be a more helpful definition than anything that can be inferred from ss. 240 and 247.

In *Re Thirty-Eight Building Ltd* [1999] B.C.C. 260 the transaction which was challenged was a transfer of the beneficial interest in certain assets to the trustees of a pension fund. It was held that the "creditor" who had to be identified under s. 239(4) was the person who was the transferee in law (in this case the trustees and not the beneficiaries under the trust), and it was that person who had to receive a preference. The question was left open whether different considerations would apply where the trustees and the beneficiaries were the same individuals.

A transfer of funds held by the company on trust does not amount to a preference: *Re Branston & Gothard Ltd* [1999] B.P.I.R. 466.

In *Re Shapland Inc.* [2000] B.C.C. 106 it was argued that even if the transaction in question was a preference, no order should be made because it would result in advantage to a secured creditor, rather than the company's unsecured creditors whose interests it was understood the legislation was intended to benefit. The court, although holding that the submission was not borne out by the facts of the case, thought it very doubtful that it was correct.

S. 239(5)

The phrase "was influenced ... by a desire to produce" replaces language contained in BA 1914, s. 44(1) which had been construed as requiring the person who sought to have the payment or other transaction avoided to show that it had been made "with the dominant intention to prefer" the particular creditor. The Cork Committee (*Report*, paras 1248–1258), by a majority, took the view that the requirement of an intention (or dominant intention) to prefer should be retained, and rejected the alternative (established in Australia and the US and adopted in Scotland: see s. 243) that it should be sufficient that the conduct in question had the *effect* of giving a preference.

In *Re M C Bacon Ltd* [1990] B.C.C. 78 at p. 87, Millett J. held that it is no longer necessary to establish a dominant intention to prefer, nor is it sufficient to establish an *intention*: there must be a desire to produce the effect mentioned in the section. "Intention is objective, desire is subjective. A man can choose the lesser of two evils without desiring either ... A man is not to be taken as *desiring* all the necessary consequences of his actions ... It will still be possible to provide assistance to a company in financial difficulties provided that the company is actuated only by proper commercial considerations. Under the new regime a transaction will not be set aside as a voidable preference unless the company positively wished to improve the creditor's position in the event of its own insolvent liquidation." Accordingly, in that case, it was held that a decision by a company to give its bank a charge to secure existing borrowings (when the only alternative, if the bank withdrew its support, was liquidation) was not voidable as a preference under the present section.

Section 240   Insolvency Act 1986

The Cork Committee (*Report*, para. 1256) took the view that pressure for payment by the creditor should continue, as under the former law, to afford a defence to a claim for the avoidance of a preference. The decision in *Re M C Bacon Ltd* (above) suggests that the new section will be so interpreted "unless the company positively wished to improve the creditor's position in the event of its own insolvency".

S. 239(6)
This important change, introduced on the recommendation of the Cork Committee, reverses the burden of proof in regard to intention when the beneficiary of the preference is a person "connected with" the company. This phrase is defined by s. 249 and is fully discussed in the note to that section (but the special exception of employees in the present provision should be noted). The effect of s. 239(6) – not least when s. 240(2) is also taken into account – will make it very difficult for directors and controlling shareholders and their relatives, and other companies in the same group (all of which are "connected persons"), to retain the benefit of a preferential payment under the new legislation. For cases where the statutory presumption against connected persons was held to have been rebutted on the evidence, see *Re Beacon Leisure Ltd* [1991] B.C.C. 213 and *Re Fairway Magazines Ltd* [1992] B.C.C. 924. These may be contrasted with *Re DKG Contractors Ltd* [1990] B.C.C. 903; *Weisgard v Pilkington* [1995] B.C.C. 1,108; *Re Brian D Pierson (Contractors) Ltd* [1999] B.C.C. 26; *Wills v Corfe Joinery Ltd (in liq.)* [1997] B.C.C. 511; *Re Transworld Trading Ltd* [1999] B.P.I.R. 628; *Katz v McNally* [1999] B.C.C. 291 and *Re Shapland Inc.* [2000] B.C.C. 106, where the presumption was applied.

240   "Relevant time" under s. 238, 239

240(1)   [Relevant time] Subject to the next subsection, the time at which a company enters into a transaction at an undervalue or gives a preference is a relevant time if the transaction is entered into, or the preference given–

(a)   in the case of a transaction at an undervalue or of a preference which is given to a person who is connected with the company (otherwise than by reason only of being its employee), at a time in the period of 2 years ending with the onset of insolvency (which expression is defined below),

(b)   in the case of a preference which is not such a transaction and is not so given, at a time in the period of 6 months ending with the onset of insolvency,

(c)   in either case, at a time between the making of an administration application in respect of the company and the making of an administration order on that application, and

(d)   in either case, at a time between the filing with the court of a copy of notice of intention to appoint an administrator under paragraph 14 or 22 of Schedule B1 and the making of an appointment under that paragraph.

240(2)   [Where not relevant time] Where a company enters into a transaction at an undervalue or gives a preference at a time mentioned in subsection (1)(a) or (b), that time is not a relevant time for the purposes of section 238 or 239 unless the company–

(a)   is at that time unable to pay its debts within the meaning of section 123 in Chapter VI of Part IV, or

(b)   becomes unable to pay its debts within the meaning of that section in consequence of the transaction or preference;

but the requirements of this subsection are presumed to be satisfied, unless the contrary is shown, in relation to any transaction at an undervalue which is entered into by a company with a person who is connected with the company.

240(3) **[Onset of insolvency]** For the purposes of subsection (1), the onset of insolvency is–

(a) in a case where section 238 or 239 applies by reason of an administrator of a company being appointed by administration order, the date on which the administration application is made,

(b) in a case where section 238 or 239 applies by reason of an administrator of a company being appointed under paragraph 14 or 22 of Schedule B1 following filing with the court of a copy of a notice of intention to appoint under that paragraph, the date on which the copy of the notice is filed,

(c) in a case where section 238 or 239 applies by reason of an administrator of a company being appointed otherwise than as mentioned in paragraph (a) or (b), the date on which the appointment takes effect,

(d) in a case where section 238 or 239 applies by reason of a company going into liquidation either following conversion of administration into winding up by virtue of Article 37 of the EC Regulation or at the time when the appointment of an administrator ceases to have effect, the date on which the company entered administration (or, if relevant, the date on which the application for the administration order was made or a copy of the notice of intention to appoint was filed), and

(e) in a case where section 238 or 239 applies by reason of a company going into liquidation at any other time, the date of the commencement of the winding up.

GENERAL NOTE

Both ss. 238 and 239 apply only to a transaction or preference which takes place at a "relevant time". This section explains that term. Two factors may be in issue in determining the question whether a time is a "relevant time": (1) whether the transaction takes place within one of the four periods set out in s. 240(1); and (2) whether the company is, at that time, insolvent, or becomes insolvent as a result of the transaction.

Once again, as with s. 239(6), the burden of proof (this time, of "insolvency") varies with the position of the other party to the transaction: it is on the liquidator or administrator in the normal case, but on that other party if he is a person "connected with" the company (s. 240(2)). Moreover, in the case of a preference, the period by reference to which a "relevant time" is reckoned is increased from six months to two years if the other party is a "connected person" (s. 240(1)(a), (b)). In regard to a transaction at an undervalue, the period is two years in all cases (s. 240(1)(a).)

It is, in principle, possible for a company's bank to come within the definition of a "connected person" for the purposes of the present group of sections, if its involvement in the company's affairs is such as to make it a "shadow director": see *Re a Company No. 005009 of 1987* (1988) 4 B.C.C. 424 and s. 249(a), 251. However where a bank or other creditor of a company simply makes terms for the continuation of credit in the light of threatened default, the court will not infer that its directors are accustomed to act in accordance with its directions so as to make it a shadow director: *Re PFTZM Ltd (in liq.)* [1995] B.C.C. 280.

Section 240 is disapplied in relation to payment and securities settlement systems by the Finality regulations, reg. 17. (See the introductory note at p. 3 above.)

S. 240(1), (3)

The periods for the purposes of ss. 238, 239 are determined by reference to a date which is defined by s. 240(3) and is very misleadingly called "the onset of insolvency". This has nothing whatever to do with the company's inability to pay its debts (although, to add to the confusion, that issue does matter for the wholly unrelated questions raised by s. 240(2)). The "onset of insolvency" is to be determined by reference to the various dates set out in s. 240(3).

(On the "commencement" of a winding up, see the notes to ss. 86 and 129, where the reference is, more precisely, to the "time" rather than the "date" of commencement. It must be assumed that this variation in language is deliberate: see the note to s. 86.)

The requirement that the company should go into liquidation *immediately* upon the discharge of an administration order for s. 240(3)(a) to apply calls for a measure of procedural ingenuity if it is proposed that the winding up should be a voluntary winding up, where the order was made under the original Pt II. See *Re Norditrack (UK) Ltd* [2000] 1 W.L.R. 343; [2000] B.C.C. 441, and the notes to s. 18.

Subsection (1)(c) was reworded and subs. (1)(d) added, and subs. (3)(a)–(e) substituted for the former subsection (3)(a)–(b) by EA 2002, Sch. 17, para. 26, with effect from September 15, 2003, to take account of the fact that applications for an administration order under IA 1986, Sch. B1 are not made by petition and that appointments may also be made out of court. However, the former wording (which referred to the time or date of the presentation of a petition for an administration order), has been reinstated for cases not coming within Sch. B1 by EA 2002, s. 249 and the Enterprise Act 2002 (Commencement No. 4 and Transitional Provisions and Savings) Order 2003 (SI 2003/2093 (C. 85)), art. 3. See the notes to ss. 212 and 230(1).

Section 240(3)(d) (as the former s. 240(3)(aa)) was inserted by the Insolvency Act 1986 (Amendment) (No. 2) Regulations 2002 (SI 2002/1240, effective May 31, 2002). Article 37 of the EC Regulation empowers the "liquidator" in "main" insolvency proceedings in one Member State to apply to have an administration in another Member State (which will be "secondary" or "territorial" proceedings) converted into a winding up. For the meaning of these technical terms, see the notes to the Regulation, Arts 2, 3.

The "relevant time" is a time within the six-month or two-year period ending with the "onset of insolvency" as defined in s. 240(3). The period will be two years for all undervalue-transactions (s. 240(1)(a)); in the case of a preference, it will be two years if the recipient of the preference is a "connected person", and six months if he is not; but employees are again not treated as "connected persons" for this purpose (s. 240(1)(a), (b)). (For the meaning of "connected person", see the note to s. 249.)

S. 240(2)

Section 240(1) and (3) are concerned only with the calculation of time, in the ordinary sense. However, s. 240(2) introduces a further factor: a "time" will not be a "relevant" time (and therefore a transaction at an undervalue or a preference will not be liable to be set aside) unless the company is then unable to pay its debts, or becomes unable to pay its debts as a result of the impugned transaction. In other words, a company may enter into any transaction at an undervalue that it chooses or give any creditor a preference without violating ss. 238 or 239, so long as it is solvent or so long as the event takes place outside the period leading up to its being put into administration or liquidation that is specified in s. 240(1): only if both these conditions are satisfied will the transaction have occurred at a "relevant time" so as to bring those sections into play. (Note, however, that s. 423 may be applicable if the necessary intent can be proved.)

The definition of "unable to pay its debts", for the purpose of s. 240(2), is the same as in s. 123, that is, either (1) deemed unable to pay because of an unpaid statutory demand for over £750 or an unsatisfied execution, or (2) proved unable in either a "commercial" or a "balance-sheet" sense. Inability may also be inferred from the fact that the company has invoices which it has not paid: *Re DKG Contractors Ltd* [1990] B.C.C. 903. For further discussion, see the note to s. 123.

Finally, as regards inability to pay debts, there is the question of the burden of proof. This, in relation to a transaction at an undervalue, lies on the liquidator or administrator when the other party is not a "connected person", but on that other party if he is. (There is no similar provision in relation to a preference, but the question of the company's solvency will be relevant, at least indirectly, to the question of intention for which s. 239(6) places the burden of proof on the "connected person"). On the meaning of "connected person", see the note to s. 249; but note that s. 240(2) rather oddly does not repeat the exception for employees which appears in s. 239(6) and 240(1)(a). (This may be a drafting error, in that the former provision corresponding to ss. 238–240, IA 1985, s. 101, applied the employee exception to all connected persons in the provision: see IA 1985, s. 101(11).)

241 Orders under s. 238, 239

241(1) **[Extent of orders]** Without prejudice to the generality of sections 238(3) and 239(3), an order under either of those sections with respect to a transaction or preference entered into or given by a company may (subject to the next subsection)–

- (a) require any property transferred as part of the transaction, or in connection with the giving of the preference, to be vested in the company,

- (b) require any property to be so vested if it represents in any person's hands the application either of the proceeds of sale of property so transferred or of money so transferred,

- (c) release or discharge (in whole or in part) any security given by the company,

- (d) require any person to pay, in respect of benefits received by him from the company, such sums to the office-holder as the court may direct,

(e) provide for any surety or guarantor whose obligations to any person were released or discharged (in whole or in part) under the transaction, or by the giving of the preference, to be under such new or revived obligations to that person as the court thinks appropriate,

(f) provide for security to be provided for the discharge of any obligation imposed by or arising under the order, for such an obligation to be charged on any property and for the security or charge to have the same priority as a security or charge released or discharged (in whole or in part) under the transaction or by the giving of the preference, and

(g) provide for the extent to which any person whose property is vested by the order in the company, or on whom obligations are imposed by the order, is to be able to prove in the winding up of the company for debts or other liabilities which arose from, or were released or discharged (in whole or in part) under or by, the transaction or the giving of the preference.

241(2) **[Restriction on orders]** An order under section 238 or 239 may affect the property of, or impose any obligation on, any person whether or not he is the person with whom the company in question entered into the transaction or (as the case may be) the person to whom the preference was given; but such an order–

(a) shall not prejudice any interest in property which was acquired from a person other than the company and was acquired in good faith and for value, or prejudice any interest deriving from such an interest, and

(b) shall not require a person who received a benefit from the transaction or preference in good faith and for value to pay a sum to the office-holder, except where that person was a party to the transaction or the payment is to be in respect of a preference given to that person at a time when he was a creditor of the company.

241(2A) **[Presumption re good faith in s. 241(2)]** Where a person has acquired an interest in property from a person other than the company in question, or has received a benefit from the transaction or preference, and at the time of that acquisition or receipt–

(a) he had notice of the relevant surrounding circumstances and of the relevant proceedings, or

(b) he was connected with, or was an associate of, either the company in question or the person with whom that company entered into the transaction or to whom that company gave the preference,

then, unless the contrary is shown, it shall be presumed for the purposes of paragraph (a) or (as the case may be) paragraph (b) of subsection (2) that the interest was acquired or the benefit was received otherwise than in good faith.

241(3) **[Relevant surrounding circumstances in s. 241(2A)(a)]** For the purposes of subsection (2A)(a), the relevant surrounding circumstances are (as the case may require)–

(a) the fact that the company in question entered into the transaction at an undervalue; or

(b) the circumstances which amounted to the giving of the preference by the company in question;

and subsections (3A) to (3C) have effect to determine whether, for those purposes, a person has notice of the relevant proceedings.

241(3A) **[Notice of administration proceedings]** Where section 238 or 239 applies by reason of a company's entering administration, a person has notice of the relevant proceedings if he has notice that–

(a) an administration application has been made,

(b) an administration order has been made,

(c) a copy of a notice of intention to appoint an administrator under paragraph 14 or 22 of Schedule B1 has been filed, or

(d) notice of the appointment of an administrator has been filed under paragraph 18 or 29 of that Schedule.

241(3B) **[Notice of liquidation following administration]** Where section 238 or 239 applies by reason of a company's going into liquidation at the time when the appointment of an administrator of the company ceases to have effect, a person has notice of the relevant proceedings if he has notice that–

(a)   an administration application has been made,

(b)   an administration order has been made,

(c)   a copy of a notice of intention to appoint an administrator under paragraph 14 or 22 of Schedule B1 has been filed,

(d)   notice of the appointment of an administrator has been filed under paragraph 18 or 29 of that Schedule, or

(e)   the company has gone into liquidation.

241(3C) **[Notice where liquidation at other times]** In a case where section 238 or 239 applies by reason of the company in question going into liquidation at any other time, a person has notice of the relevant proceedings if he has notice–

(a)   where the company goes into liquidation on the making of a winding-up order, of the fact that the petition on which the winding-up order is made has been presented or of the fact that the company has gone into liquidation;

(b)   in any other case, of the fact that the company has gone into liquidation.

241(4) **[Application of ss. 238–241]** The provisions of sections 238 to 241 apply without prejudice to the availability of any other remedy, even in relation to a transaction or preference which the company had no power to enter into or give.

GENERAL NOTE

The present section sets out in detail various orders which the court is empowered to make when avoiding a preference or a transaction at an undervalue under ss. 238, 239, although it is not intended to limit the general powers of the court. It is designed in part to meet defects in the former law which the Cork Committee (*Report*, paras 1270–1276) identified as likely to arise when a company's obligation is backed by a surety or guarantor. For example, a payment may have been made to a creditor with a view to releasing the surety or guarantor rather than preferring the creditor, and the creditor may have released the guarantee and returned any security given before the payment is struck down as a preference. The creditor would then in all probability have had no remedy against the guarantor.

Section 241 was amended by the Insolvency (No. 2) Act 1994, ss. 1(1) and 6, with effect from July 26, 1994, as follows:

(1)   in s. 241(2), in both para. (a) and para. (b), the words "in good faith and for value" were substituted for the former wording, "in good faith, for value and without notice of the relevant circumstances";

(2)   new subs. (2A) was inserted, and

(3)   new subs. (3), (3A), (3B) and (3C) were substituted for the former subs. (3).

The repealed s. 241(3) read as follows:

"For the purposes of this section the relevant circumstances, in relation to a transaction or preference, are–

(a)   the circumstances by virtue of which an order under section 238 or (as the case may be) 239 could be made in respect of the transaction or preference if the company were to go into liquidation, or an administration order were made in relation to the company, within a particular period after the transaction is entered into or the preference given, and

(b)   if that period has expired, the fact that the company has gone into liquidation or that such an order has been made."

The amendments have effect only in relation to interests acquired and benefits received after the 1994 Act came into force (s. 6(3)). For the corresponding provisions in relation to bankruptcy, see s. 342 below (as amended).

The amendment, which stems from a recommendation of the Law Society, was designed to get over a perceived difficulty in relation to unregistered land, where a *bona fide* purchaser might have been taken to have had notice of a transaction that was liable to be set aside under either ss. 238 or 239 in the event of a later insolvency. By removing the references to notice from s. 241(2), a buyer of unregistered land is put into the same position as a buyer of registered land.

In subss. (3A) and (3B) the reference was formerly to the making of an administration order. The new wording was substituted by EA 2002, Sch. 17, para. 26, with effect from September 15, 2003, to take account of the fact that applications are no longer made by petition, and that appointments may also be made out of court. However, orders under the original IA 1986, Pt II are made on a petition, and where that regime continues to apply the original wording of the two subsections remains effective.

S. 241(1)
Section 241(1) is "subject to the next subsection", which protects *bona fide* purchasers for value.

The court's discretion extends to refusing to make any order: see the note to s. 238(3). In an appropriate case it may appoint a receiver and manager pending trial: *Walker v WA Personnel Ltd* [2002] B.P.I.R. 621. On the question whether the discretion may be exercised so as to benefit the holder of a security, rather than the company's unsecured creditors, see the remarks of Neuberger J., *obiter*, in *Ciro Citterio Menswear plc v Thakrar* (July 10, 2002, referred to by P. Fleming in [2003] *Insolvency Intelligence* 33, at p. 34).

Paragraphs (e) and (f) will empower the court to impose revived or new obligations on a guarantor or surety if his former obligations were released or discharged by the transaction which is later impugned, and to reinstate a security with the same priority as a former security or charge.

S. 241(2)
This subsection allows third parties to be brought into the proceedings and orders to be made against them or their property instead of, or as well as, against the party with whom the company has dealt in the transaction under challenge. In particular, it will enable an order for repayment to be made directly against a surety or guarantor when the real object of a payment made by the company to a particular creditor was to release the guarantee rather than prefer the creditor. *Bona fide* third parties acquiring property or benefits for value will, however, be protected. Nevertheless, the concluding words of para. (b) indicate that the person who was the actual counterparty to a transaction at an undervalue or who himself, as a creditor, received the benefit of a preference will not be protected merely because he acted in good faith and for value. (This is in keeping with the traditional view taken in relation to fraudulent preferences, that it is the intention of the company to give an improper preference which is crucial, and that the state of mind of the creditor himself is immaterial.)

S. 241(2A)–(3C)
These subsections, which were substituted for the former s. 241(3) as described above, relate to two categories of person who have acquired an interest in property otherwise than from the company itself: (1) one who had notice of the "relevant surrounding circumstances" *and* of the "relevant proceedings" at the material time; and (2) one who was "connected with" or an "associate" of the company or the counterparty to the transaction. (For the meaning of the terms "connected with" and "associate", see ss. 249 and 435, below.) As against such a person, there is a (rebuttable) statutory presumption of a lack of good faith, thereby depriving him of the protection of s. 241(2). The requirement in s. 241(2A)(a) that the person (if not a "connected person" or "associate") should have notice of the insolvency proceedings as well as of the relevant surrounding circumstances is the major change effected by the 1994 reform.

Sections 241(3)–(3C) clarify the meaning of the terms "the relevant surrounding circumstances" and "notice of the relevant proceedings" used in s. 241(2A).

S. 241(4)
The phrase "a transaction which the company had no power to enter into or give" is, no doubt, a reference to the common-law doctrine of *ultra vires*, which was abolished for almost all purposes by CA 1989, s. 108 (which inserted a revised s. 35(1) into CA 1985 with effect from February 4, 1991 (see SI 1991/2569 (C 68), art. 4(a), 7)). However, the question of corporate capacity still has some relevance in relation to charitable companies (see CA 1989, s. 111, amending Charities Act 1960 by the insertion of a new s. 30B, effective from the same date, now replaced by Charities Act 1993, s. 65), and so the doctrine of *ultra vires* could apply in this restricted area. It is possible also that s. 241(1) could be construed as extending to illegal transactions, *e.g.* those in contravention of the "financial assistance" provisions contained in CA 1985, ss. 151ff. This subsection will allow the court to override the general law by, *e.g.* ordering the recipient of an *ultra vires* loan or gift to give security for its due repayment (s. 241(1)(f)).

242 Gratuitous alienations (Scotland)

242(1) [Challenge to alienations] Where this subsection applies and—

(a) the winding up of a company has commenced, an alienation by the company is challengeable by—

(i) any creditor who is a creditor by virtue of a debt incurred on or before the date of such commencement, or
(ii) the liquidator;

(b) a company enters administration, an alienation by the company is challengeable by the administrator.

242(2) [Application of s. 242(1)] Subsection (1) applies where—

(a) by the alienation, whether before or after April 1, 1986 (the coming into force of section 75 of the Bankruptcy (Scotland) Act 1985), any part of the company's property is transferred or any claim or right of the company is discharged or renounced, and

(b) the alienation takes place on a relevant day.

242(3) [Interpretation of s. 242(2)(b)] For the purposes of subsection (2)(b), the day on which an alienation takes place is the day on which it becomes completely effectual; and in that subsection **"relevant day"** means, if the alienation has the effect of favouring—

(a) a person who is an associate (within the meaning of the Bankruptcy (Scotland) Act 1985) of the company, a day not earlier than 5 years before the date on which—

(i) the winding up of the company commences, or
(ii) as the case may be, the company enters administration; or

(b) any other person, a day not earlier than 2 years before that date.

242(4) [Duties of court on challenge under s. 242(1)] On a challenge being brought under subsection (1), the court shall grant decree of reduction or for such restoration of property to the company's assets or other redress as may be appropriate; but the court shall not grant such a decree if the person seeking to uphold the alienation establishes—

(a) that immediately, or at any other time, after the alienation the company's assets were greater than its liabilities, or

(b) that the alienation was made for adequate consideration, or

(c) that the alienation—

(i) was a birthday, Christmas or other conventional gift, or
(ii) was a gift made, for a charitable purpose, to a person who is not an associate of the company,

which, having regard to all the circumstances, it was reasonable for the company to make:

Provided that this subsection is without prejudice to any right or interest acquired in good faith and for value from or through the transferee in the alienation.

242(5) ["Charitable purpose" in s. 242(4)] In subsection (4) above, **"charitable purpose"** means any charitable, benevolent or philanthropic purpose, whether or not it is charitable within the meaning of any rule of law.

242(6) [Interpretation] For the purposes of the foregoing provisions of this section, an alienation in implementation of a prior obligation is deemed to be one for which there was no consideration or no adequate consideration to the extent that the prior obligation was undertaken for no consideration or no adequate consideration.

242(7) [Rights of challenge] A liquidator and an administrator have the same right as a creditor has under any rule of law to challenge an alienation of a company made for no consideration or no adequate consideration.

242(8) [Scotland only] This section applies to Scotland only.

GENERAL NOTE

This section deals with the setting aside of transactions at an undervalue (or the granting of "other redress": s. 242(4)) in Scotland. It differs on a number of points of substance from s. 238, following in these respects the Bankruptcy (Scotland) Act 1985, s. 34.

The rights of creditors under Scots common law, including the right to challenge a debtor's action as a gratuitous alienation, survive the present legislation: see *Bank of Scotland v Pacific Shelf (Sixty Two) Ltd* (1988) 4 B.C.C. 457.

In subss. (1)(b) and (3)(a)(ii) the reference was formerly to the making of an administration order. The new wording was substituted by EA 2002, Sch. 17, para. 28, with effect from September 15, 2003, to take account of the fact that applications are no longer made by petition, and that appointments may also be made out of court. However, orders under the original IA 1986, Pt II are made on a petition, and where that regime continues to apply the original wording of the two subsections remains effective.

In the context of the financial markets, no decree may be granted under s. 242 in relation to a market contract to which a recognised investment exchange or clearing house is a party or which is entered into under its default rules, or a disposition of property in pursuance of such a market contract: see CA 1989, s. 165. Section 242 is also disapplied in relation to payment and securities settlement systems by the Finality Regulations, reg. 17. (See the introductory notes at pp. 2–3 above.)

S. 242(1)

In the case of a liquidation, a creditor is given standing to challenge under para. (a)(i), in contrast with s. 238(2), which restricts the right to the "office-holder". A liquidator does not require sanction under s. 167 to commence s. 242 proceedings – see *Dyer v Hyslop* 1994 S.C.L.R. 171. Such proceedings are not taken on behalf of or in the name of the company.

S. 242(2), (3)

The periods of five years and two years fixed by s. 242(3) are different from those prescribed for England and Wales by s. 240(1), but correspond with those that apply in the bankruptcy of an individual in Scotland: see the Bankruptcy (Scotland) Act 1985, s. 34. The meaning of "associate" under the Bankruptcy (Scotland) Act 1985, s. 74, is similar to, but not co-extensive with, that of "associate" as defined for the purposes of this Act: see s. 435 and the note to that section. For England and Wales, the term used by s. 240(1) is "connected person", which is slightly wider in scope: see s. 249.

S. 242(4)

"Gratuitous alienation" includes a transaction for consideration at an undervalue (para. (b)); "reasonable" gifts and charitable donations may be justified (para. (c)). The requirement as to solvency is here more logically placed with the substantive aspects of the statutory provision, rather than linked to the definition of "relevant day": contrast s. 240(2). See *McLuckie Bros Ltd v Newhouse Contracts Ltd* 1993 S.L.T. 641.

243 Unfair preferences (Scotland)

243(1) [Application of s. 243(4)] Subject to subsection (2) below, subsection (4) below applies to a transaction entered into by a company, whether before or after 1st April 1986, which has the effect of creating a preference in favour of a creditor to the prejudice of the general body of creditors, being a preference created not earlier than 6 months before the commencement of the winding up of the company or the company enters administration.

Section 243   Insolvency Act 1986

243(2) [Non-application of s. 243(4)] Subsection (4) below does not apply to any of the following transactions–

(a)   a transaction in the ordinary course of trade or business;

(b)   a payment in cash for a debt which when it was paid had become payable, unless the transaction was collusive with the purpose of prejudicing the general body of creditors;

(c)   a transaction whereby the parties to it undertake reciprocal obligations (whether the performance by the parties of their respective obligations occurs at the same time or at different times) unless the transaction was collusive as aforesaid;

(d)   the granting of a mandate by a company authorising an arrestee to pay over the arrested funds or part thereof to the arrester where–

   (i) there has been a decree for payment or a warrant for summary diligence, and
   (ii) the decree or warrant has been preceded by an arrestment on the dependence of the action or followed by an arrestment in execution.

243(3) [Interpretation of s. 243(1)] For the purposes of subsection (1) above, the day on which a preference was created is the day on which the preference became completely effectual.

243(4) [Persons who may challenge] A transaction to which this subsection applies is challengeable by–

(a)   in the case of a winding up–

   (i) any creditor who is a creditor by virtue of a debt incurred on or before the date of commencement of the winding up, or
   (ii) the liquidator; and

(b)   where the company has entered administration, the administrator.

243(5) [Duties of court on s. 243(4) challenge] On a challenge being brought under subsection (4) above, the court, if satisfied that the transaction challenged is a transaction to which this section applies, shall grant decree of reduction or for such restoration of property to the company's assets or other redress as may be appropriate:

Provided that this subsection is without prejudice to any right or interest acquired in good faith and for value from or through the creditor in whose favour the preference was created.

243(6) [Rights of challenge] A liquidator and an administrator have the same right as a creditor has under any rule of law to challenge a preference created by a debtor.

243(7) [Scotland only] This section applies to Scotland only.

GENERAL NOTE

The law relating to unfair preferences in the bankruptcy of individuals is contained in the Bankruptcy (Scotland) Act 1985, s. 36. The present section substantially follows that provision and differs in material respects from s. 239 – most notably in not requiring any proof of a desire to prefer. For the survival of the common law, see *Bank of Scotland v Pacific Shelf (Sixty Two) Ltd* (1988) 4 B.C.C. 457.

In subss. (1) and (4)(b) the reference was formerly to the making of an administration order. The new wording was substituted by EA 2002, Sch. 17, para. 29, with effect from September 15, 2003, to take account of the fact that applications are no longer made by petition, and that appointments may also be made out of court. However, the former wording has been reinstated for cases not coming within Sch. B1 by EA 2002, s. 249 and by the Enterprise Act 2002 (Commencement No. 4 and Transitional Provisions and Savings) Order 2003 (SI 2003/2093 (C. 85)), art. 3. See the notes to ss. 212 and 230(1).

A payment made by a company is not within the section unless it has completely divested itself of the funds within the relevant period: *Craiglaw Developments Ltd v Wilson* [1998] B.C.C. 530.

In the context of the financial markets, no decree may be granted under s. 243 in relation to a market contract to which a recognised investment exchange or clearing house is a party or which is entered into under its default rules, or a disposition of property in pursuance of such a market contract. Section 243 is also disapplied in relation to payment and securities settlement systems by the Finality Regulations, reg. 17. (See the introductory notes at pp. 2–3 above.)

S. 243(1), (2)
The vital factor, in contrast with the subjective requirement regarding intent in s. 239(1), (5), is whether the transaction has the effect of creating a preference: the intention of the parties is not relevant, unless there is collusion (s. 243(2)(b), (c)). For the purposes of s. 243(2)(c) there must be a strict equivalence of reciprocal obligations: *Nicoll v Steelpress (Supplies) Ltd* 1993 S.L.T. 533.

S. 243(4)
As with s. 242, a creditor has standing to bring proceedings in the case of a winding up.

244 Extortionate credit transactions

244(1) [Application] This section applies as does section 238, and where the company is, or has been, a party to a transaction for, or involving, the provision of credit to the company.

244(2) [Court order re extortionate transaction] The court may, on the application of the office-holder, make an order with respect to the transaction if the transaction is or was extortionate and was entered into in the period of 3 years ending with the day on which the company entered administration or went into liquidation.

244(3) [Extortionate transaction – interpretation] For the purposes of this section a transaction is extortionate if, having regard to the risk accepted by the person providing the credit–

(a) the terms of it are or were such as to require grossly exorbitant payments to be made (whether unconditionally or in certain contingencies) in respect of the provision of the credit, or

(b) it otherwise grossly contravened ordinary principles of fair dealing;

and it shall be presumed, unless the contrary is proved, that a transaction with respect to which an application is made under this section is or, as the case may be, was extortionate.

244(4) [Extent of court order] An order under this section with respect to any transaction may contain such one or more of the following as the court thinks fit, that is to say–

(a) provision setting aside the whole or part of any obligation created by the transaction,

(b) provision otherwise varying the terms of the transaction or varying the terms on which any security for the purposes of the transaction is held,

(c) provision requiring any person who is or was a party to the transaction to pay to the office-holder any sums paid to that person, by virtue of the transaction, by the company,

(d) provision requiring any person to surrender to the office-holder any property held by him as security for the purposes of the transaction,

(e) provision directing accounts to be taken between any persons.

244(5) [Exercise of powers] The powers conferred by this section are exercisable in relation to any transaction concurrently with any powers exercisable in relation to that transaction as a transaction at an undervalue or under section 242 (gratuitous alienations in Scotland).

GENERAL NOTE

Section 66 of BA 1914, which was formerly applied in the winding up of insolvent companies by CA 1985, s. 612, restricted the rate of interest that could be proved for in a liquidation, in the case of a debt carrying interest, to five per cent p.a. In keeping with the recommendations of the Cork Committee (Report, para. 1380), s. 66 has now been repealed (see the note to s. 189). The removal of s. 66, without more, would allow proofs in a winding up to include sums representing exorbitant rates of interest; and accordingly the court is given power by this section to reopen credit agreements on the application of a liquidator or administrator. This is in keeping with a recommendation of the Cork Committee (*Report*, para. 1381). The section is modelled on ss. 137–140 of the Consumer Credit Act 1974.

Section 245 *Insolvency Act 1986*

For the corresponding provision in bankruptcy, see s. 343.

In subs. (2) the reference was formerly to the making of an administration order. The new wording was substituted by EA 2002, Sch. 17, para. 30, with effect from September 15, 2003, to take account of the fact that appointments may also be made out of court.

S. 244(1)
Section 238 applies to companies that are in liquidation or administration. Although s. 238 is confined to England and Wales, it is submitted that the present section extends also to Scotland, for otherwise the reference to Scotland in s. 244(5) would be pointless. This means that the word "applies" in s. 244(1) must be construed with reference only to the different forms of insolvency proceedings and not to questions of geography or jurisdiction (even though the wording of s. 245(1) would suggest the contrary). This interpretation is supported by s. 440(2).

"Credit" is not defined.

S. 244(2)
There is a three-year time limit for the retrospective re-opening of transactions under this section. (Note, however, that the time is reckoned from the date when the company "went into liquidation", in the case of a liquidation, and not from the "commencement of the winding up".)

S. 244(3)
The onus of proof that a transaction was not extortionate is put in every case on to the person who gave the credit.

S. 244(4)
The orders which the court is empowered to make include orders affecting third parties, *e.g.* sureties.

S. 244(5)
On transactions at an undervalue, see ss. 238, 240, 241.

245 Avoidance of certain floating charges

245(1) **[Application]** This section applies as does section 238, but applies to Scotland as well as to England and Wales.

245(2) **[Invalidity of floating charge]** Subject as follows, a floating charge on the company's undertaking or property created at a relevant time is invalid except to the extent of the aggregate of–

- (a) the value of so much of the consideration for the creation of the charge as consists of money paid, or goods or services supplied, to the company at the same time as, or after, the creation of the charge,

- (b) the value of so much of that consideration as consists of the discharge or reduction, at the same time as, or after, the creation of the charge, of any debt of the company, and

- (c) the amount of such interest (if any) as is payable on the amount falling within paragraph (a) or (b) in pursuance of any agreement under which the money was so paid, the goods or services were so supplied or the debt was so discharged or reduced.

245(3) **[Relevant time]** Subject to the next subsection, the time at which a floating charge is created by a company is a relevant time for the purposes of this section if the charge is created–

- (a) in the case of a charge which is created in favour of a person who is connected with the company, at a time in the period of 2 years ending with the onset of insolvency,

- (b) in the case of a charge which is created in favour of any other person, at a time in the period of 12 months ending with the onset of insolvency,

- (c) in either case, at a time between the making of an administration application in respect of the company and the making of an administration order on that application, or

- (d) in either case, at a time between the filing with the court of a copy of notice of intention to appoint an administrator under paragraph 14 or 22 of Schedule B1 and the making of an appointment under that paragraph.

245(4) **[Qualification to s. 245(3)(b)]** Where a company creates a floating charge at a time mentioned in subsection (3)(b) and the person in favour of whom the charge is created is not connected with the company, that time is not a relevant time for the purposes of this section unless the company–

(a) is at that time unable to pay its debts within the meaning of section 123 in Chapter VI of Part IV, or

(b) becomes unable to pay its debts within the meaning of that section in consequence of the transaction under which the charge is created.

245(5) **[Onset of insolvency in s. 245(3)]** For the purposes of subsection (3), the onset of insolvency is–

(a) in a case where this section applies by reason of an administrator of a company being appointed by administration order, the date on which the administration application is made,

(b) in a case where this section applies by reason of an administrator of a company being appointed under paragraph 14 or 22 of Schedule B1 following filing with the court of a copy of notice of intention to appoint under that paragraph, the date on which the copy of the notice is filed,

(c) in a case where this section applies by reason of an administrator of a company being appointed otherwise than as mentioned in paragraph (a) or (b), the date on which the appointment takes effect, and

(d) in a case where this section applies by reason of a company going into liquidation, the date of the commencement of the winding up.

245(6) **[Value of goods, services etc. in s. 245(2)(a)]** For the purposes of subsection (2)(a) the value of any goods or services supplied by way of consideration for a floating charge is the amount in money which at the time they were supplied could reasonably have been expected to be obtained for supplying the goods or services in the ordinary course of business and on the same terms (apart from the consideration) as those on which they were supplied to the company.

General Note

Under CA 1985, s. 617, which this section replaces, a floating charge was declared invalid if it was created within 12 months of the commencement of a winding up (unless it could be proved that the company, immediately after the creation of the charge, was solvent), except to the amount of any cash paid to the company at the time of, or subsequently to the creation of, and in consideration for, the charge. In other words, a floating charge could not be created within that time to secure past indebtedness, but only an advance of "new money".

The present Act not only formulates more elaborate provisions to apply in such circumstances, but introduces several major changes:

(1) "floating charge" is redefined so as to include any charge which was originally created as a floating charge but has since become a fixed charge (s. 251);

(2) the provisions apply in an administration as well as a liquidation;

(3) the section expressly covers some benefits conferred on the company otherwise than by the payment of "cash";

(4) the 12-month period is extended to two years if the chargee is a person "connected with" the company; and

(5) the exception where the company is proved at the material time to have been solvent will not be available to a chargee who is a person "connected with" the company.

The provisions of s. 245 do not apply to invalidate a charge created before the Act came into force, except to the extent that it could have been invalidated under the previous law: see Sch. 11, para. 9.

In subss. (3). and (5) the references were formerly to the presentation of a petition for an administration order and the making of such an order. The new wording was substituted by EA 2002, Sch. 17, para. 31, with effect from September 15, 2003, to take account of the fact that the procedure is now by application and appointments may be made out of court. However, the former wording has been reinstated for cases not coming within Sch. B1 by EA 2002, s. 249

and the Enterprise Act 2002 (Commencement No. 4 and Transitional Provisions and Savings) Order 2003 (SI 2003/2093 (C. 85)), art. 3. See the notes to ss. 212 and 230(1).

S. 245(1)
The section applies where a company is in liquidation or is in administration.

S. 245(2)
A charge will not be invalidated by this section to the extent that the chargee has increased the company's assets in any of the ways described. The extended wording removes doubts about the scope of the former phrase "cash paid to the company" by stipulating that goods or services supplied to the company or the release of a debt in whole or part will be as good as "new money". Whether para. (a) and (b) will themselves be open to a restrictive interpretation is unclear: it is hard to see why other forms of valuable consideration (*e.g.* the transfer of land or shares) were not included within the reform that was made.

The question whether the payment of money or the supply of goods or services is made "at the same time as" the execution of a charge is one of fact and degree: – *Re Shoe Lace Ltd, Power v Sharp Investments Ltd* [1993] B.C.C. 609. In that case, money was advanced in four payments on different dates in April, May, June and on July 16, following a resolution of the company's directors to grant the debenture in March; but the debenture was not executed until July 24. The Court of Appeal, affirming Hoffmann J. [1992] B.C.C. 367, held that the payments could not be said to have been made at the same time as the execution of the debenture. Sir Christopher Slade, giving the leading judgment, said (at p. 620):

> "In a case where no presently existing charge has been created by any agreement or company resolution preceding the execution of the formal debenture, then ... no moneys paid before the execution of the debenture will qualify for exemption under the subsection, unless the interval between payment and execution is so short that it can be regarded as minimal and payment and execution can be regarded as contemporaneous".

However, where a promise to execute a debenture creates a present equitable right to a security, and moneys are advanced in reliance on it, any delay between the advances and the execution of the formal instrument of charge is immaterial: the charge has already been "created" and is immediately registrable, so that other creditors of the company will have had the opportunity to learn of its existence (*ibid* at p. 619).

In *Re Fairway Magazines Ltd* [1992] B.C.C. 924 it was held, following *Re Orleans Motor Co. Ltd* [1911] 2 Ch. 41, that payments made by the lender directly to the company's bank which reduced its overdraft (and consequently the lender's liability under a personal guarantee) were not payments made "to the company" within the meaning of the section: the money never became available to the company to be used as it liked.

Interest was allowable under the repealed CA 1985, s. 617, as it is under para. (c).

S. 245(3)–(5)
These provisions are similar to s. 240, both in their effect and in the very confusing language which is used. For more detailed comment, see the notes to that section: it is necessary to give the reminder that the phrase "the onset of insolvency" is not used with reference to the company's financial state but only with the question whether an administration or liquidation is deemed to have "commenced"; the issue of its financial well-being (or otherwise) is separately dealt with in s. 245(4) in language which avoids the words "solvent" and "insolvent".

To sum up these provisions:

- a floating charge can be retrospectively invalidated within a two-year period for a "connected" chargee, and a 12-month period in other cases; further, if there is, or has been, an administration order in force, the period is extended to include the time between the making of an application for an administration order and the administration order, or the filing of a notice of intention to appoint an administrator and the making of an appointment under Sch. B1, paras 14 or 22;

- the "new consideration" exception applies whether the chargee is a connected person or not; and

- the "solvency" exception will now apply only where the chargee is not a connected person (using the term "solvency" in its everyday sense). The burden of establishing "solvency" under CA 1985, s. 617, was put on the person seeking to uphold the charge. This is presumably still the case, although the section does not make the point clear.

The various technical expressions which appear in these provisions are discussed in more detail in the note to s. 240.

It is, in principle, possible for a company's bank to come within the definition of a "connected person" for the purposes of the present section, if its involvement in the company's affairs is such as to make it a "shadow director": see *Re a Company No. 005009 of 1987* (1988) 4 B.C.C. 424 and ss. 249(a), 251.

All the references to time in s. 245(2) are to the time of creation of the charge. So it would seem that a floating charge created in favour of A will attract all the disadvantages associated with "connected" chargees if A was a "connected person" at that time, and it will be immaterial that he has since ceased to be so connected. Conversely, if A was not a connected person at the time of creation, but becomes "connected" within the two-year period, his charge will have the more favourable treatment accorded by s. 245(3)(b) and (4). Again, if a floating charge is created in favour of A and is later assigned to B, the only relevant question will be whether A was, at the time of creation, a "connected person": it will not matter whether B was then, or was at the time of the assignment, or has since become, a "connected person". There are clearly advantages, if one is a "connected person", of taking a charge by assignment rather than directly and, if one is not, of re-financing with a new charge rather than taking an assignment of a charge from a "connected" chargee – unless in either case the whole arrangement could be challenged as evasive.

S. 245(6)

This subsection deals with the position where goods or services, rather than "new money", is the consideration provided for a charge. It is made clear that it is the true value of the goods or services that counts, and not the price or valuation that the parties themselves have agreed on as the consideration for the supply. The chargee cannot defeat the object of the Act by having the company credit him with an unrealistic sum.

246 Unenforceability of liens on books, etc.

246(1) [Application] This section applies in the case of a company where–

(a) the company enters administration, or

(b) the company goes into liquidation, or

(c) a provisional liquidator is appointed;

and **"the office-holder"** means the administrator, the liquidator or the provisional liquidator, as the case may be.

246(2) [Lien etc. unenforceable] Subject as follows, a lien or other right to retain possession of any of the books, papers or other records of the company is unenforceable to the extent that its enforcement would deny possession of any books, papers or other records to the office-holder.

246(3) [Non-application] This does not apply to a lien on documents which give a title to property and are held as such.

GENERAL NOTE

This section ensures that a liquidator or administrator is not prevented from taking possession of any of the company's books, etc., because a lien is claimed over them (*e.g.* by a solicitor or accountant for outstanding fees). It relates only to liens on "books, papers and other records" and not to liens on other categories of goods, and operates to extinguish the lien (or, at the least, to render it unenforceable to the extent specified in s. 246(2)). Liens not caught by the section remain valid, but in the case of an administration will not be enforceable without the leave of the court under s. 11(3): *Bristol Airport plc v Powdrill* [1990] Ch. 744 at p. 762 (reported as *Re Paramount Airways Ltd* [1990] B.C.C. 130 at p. 150).

In subs. (1)(a) the reference was formerly to the making of an administration order. The new wording was substituted by EA 2002, Sch. 17, para. 32, with effect from September 15, 2003, to take account of appointments made out of court.

Note that s. 246 does not apply in favour of an administrative receiver or the supervisor of a voluntary arrangement.

Section 246 does not apply to Scotland (see s. 440(2)(a)); but the corresponding provisions of the Bankruptcy (Scotland) Act 1985, s. 38(4), which are more limited in scope, have been extended to company liquidations by the rules: see the Insolvency (Scotland) Rules 1986 (SI 1986/1915 (S. 139)), r. 4.22(1).

S. 246(3)

The exception created by s. 246(3) is not limited to the case where the person claiming the lien does so by reason of the fact that the documents in question confer "a title to property" upon him. The words "as such" mean "in circumstances which are such as to give rise to a lien". In other words, it is sufficient that the person has a lien over the documents, and the documents are of a kind which give a title to property to somebody: *Re SEIL Trade Finance Ltd* [1992] B.C.C. 538. See also the case of *Carter*, noted by S. Unwin in [2003] *Insolvency Intelligence* 4.

Section 247 *Insolvency Act 1986*

Part VII

Interpretation for First Group of Parts

247 "Insolvency" and "go into liquidation"

247(1) **["Insolvency"]** In this Group of Parts, except in so far as the context otherwise requires, **"insolvency"**, in relation to a company, includes the approval of a voluntary arrangement under Part I, or the appointment of an administrator or administrative receiver.

247(2) **[Company in liquidation]** For the purposes of any provision in this Group of Parts, a company goes into liquidation if it passes a resolution for voluntary winding up or an order for its winding up is made by the court at a time when it has not already gone into liquidation by passing such a resolution.

247(3) **[Resolution following administration or voluntary arrangement]** The reference to a resolution for voluntary winding up in subsection (2) includes a reference to a resolution which is deemed to occur by virtue of–

(a) paragraph 83(6)(b) of Schedule B1, or

(b) an order made following conversion of administration or a voluntary arrangement into winding up by virtue of Article 37 of the EC Regulation.

S. 247(1)
This meaning of "insolvency" is discussed in the general comment on Pt VI, preceding s. 230, above, where attention is drawn to the fact that the Act uses the term to describe the various *proceedings*, such as winding up, administration and receivership, which are the subject of the present Act, and not to describe a company's adverse financial situation. The related word "insolvent" is not defined by this section, and at times it appears to be used in the Act in the everyday sense (*e.g.* "goes into insolvent liquidation": s. 214(6)) rather than analogously with the definition of "insolvency" in the present section.
  In subs. (1) the reference was formerly to the making of an administration order. The new wording was substituted by EA 2002, Sch. 17, para. 33(2), with effect from September 15, 2003, to take account of appointments made out of court.

S. 247(2)
The time when a company "goes into liquidation" is to be distinguished from the time when its winding up *commences*: see the notes to ss. 86 and 129. The phrase was the subject of judicial consideration (in connection with the construction of a trust deed) in *Mettoy Pension Trustees Ltd v Evans* [1991] 2 All E.R. 513, where a meaning in conformity with the definition in the present subsection was approved.

S. 247(3)
This subsection was amended by EA 2002, Sch. 17, para. 33(3), with effect from September 15, 2003, by the insertion of the reference to para. 83(6)(b).
  Section 247(3), in its original form, was inserted by the Insolvency Act 1986 (Amendment) (No. 2) Regulations 2002 (SI 2002/1240, effective May 31, 2002). Where "main" insolvency proceedings have been opened in the Member State where the company in question has its centre of main interests, and the company is already subject to a CVA or administration in "territorial" proceedings in this country, art. 37 empowers its "liquidator" to apply to a UK court to have these proceedings converted to a winding up. (For the meaning of these technical terms, see the notes to the EC Regulation, Arts 2, 3.) The intention behind s. 247(3) might have been thought to be to back-date the time of "going into liquidation" to that when the CVA or administration took effect, but even so the reference to a "resolution" which is "deemed to occur" is, at first sight, baffling, particularly as regards a company in administration. For elucidation, we must look to the new IA 1986, rr. 1.31–1.33 and rr. 2.59–2.61. This rules out any question of back-dating. The court making an order for conversion under these rules may (inter alia) order that the company be wound up "as if a resolution for a voluntary winding up under s. 184 were passed on the day on which the order was made". Unless, therefore, the court were to assume jurisdiction to make an order to the contrary, the time of "going into liquidation" will not be retrospective.

248 "Secured creditor", etc.

248 In this Group of Parts, except in so far as the context otherwise requires–

(a) **"secured creditor"**, in relation to a company, means a creditor of the company who holds in respect of his debt a security over property of the company, and **"unsecured creditor"** is to be read accordingly; and

(b) **"security"** means–

(i) in relation to England and Wales, any mortgage, charge, lien or other security, and
(ii) in relation to Scotland, any security (whether heritable or moveable), any floating charge and any right of lien or preference and any right of retention (other than a right of compensation or set off).

GENERAL NOTE

The term "security" as here defined does not include the owner's rights under a hire-purchase, conditional sale, chattel leasing or retention of title agreement, although for some purposes (*e.g.* s. 15(2)) these rights are treated analogously with security interests.

In *Bristol Airport plc v Powdrill* [1990] Ch. 744 (reported as *Re Paramount Airways Ltd* [1990] B.C.C. 130) it was held that the statutory right of an airport under the Civil Aviation Act 1982, s. 88, to detain an aircraft for failure to pay outstanding aircraft charges was a "lien or other security" within s. 248(b)(i). In *Exchange Travel Agency Ltd v Triton Property Trust plc* [1991] B.C.C. 341 a landlord's right of re-entry on non-payment of rent was held to be a "security", and this ruling was followed by Lightman J. in *March Estates plc v Gunmark Ltd* [1996] 2 B.C.L.C. 1; but in *Razzaq v Pala* [1998] B.C.C. 66 the same judge, after hearing full argument, said that he had been wrong to do so. Later cases (notably *Re Lomax Leisure Ltd* [2000] B.C.C. 352) have endorsed the latter ruling. The position thus appears to be settled as a matter of law, but for practical purposes the agreed view has been reversed as regards IA 1986, ss. 10 and 11 by the amendments made to those sections by IA 2000, s. 9. See the detailed discussion in the notes to ss. 10(1) and 11(3). Corresponding provisions now also apply in CVAs (see Sch. A1, para. 12(1)(f)), administrations under the new Pt II (Sch. B1, paras 43(4), 44(5)) and IVAs (s. 252(2)(aa)).

249 "Connected" with a company

249 For the purposes of any provision in this Group of Parts, a person is connected with a company if–

(a) he is a director or shadow director of the company or an associate of such a director or shadow director, or

(b) he is an associate of the company;

and **"associate"** has the meaning given by section 435 in Part XVIII of this Act.

GENERAL NOTE

The meaning of "associate" (a term which the Act applies in the bankruptcy of individuals as well as in the winding up, etc. of companies) is defined at length in s. 435. The phrase "connected with" a company is used largely to put it beyond doubt that a director or shadow director is always included for the purposes of the statutory provision in question. So, also, will be the "associates" of such a director or shadow director.

It is, in principle, possible for a company's bank to come within the definition of a "connected person", if its involvement in the company's affairs is such as to make it a "shadow director": see *Re a Company No. 005009 of 1987* (1988) 4 B.C.C. 424.

For the meaning of "associate", see the note to s. 435; and for "director" and "shadow director", see s. 251.

250 "Member" of a company

250 For the purposes of any provision in this Group of Parts, a person who is not a member of a company but to whom shares in the company have been transferred, or transmitted by operation of law, is to be regarded as a member of the company, and references to a member or members are to be read accordingly.

Section 251 *Insolvency Act 1986*

GENERAL NOTE

"Member" is defined for the purposes of the Companies Acts by CA 1985, s. 22, and under that definition the term is confined to (1) the subscribers to the memorandum, and (2) those who have agreed to become members and whose names are entered in the register of members. The present provision is designed to include the transferees of shares under unregistered transfers, and the personal representatives of deceased members and others to whom shares have been transmitted by operation of law. It is wide enough, however, to include other categories of person, *e.g.* holders of share warrants to bearer.

This section was no doubt inserted with the benign intention of ensuring that an unregistered transferee of shares should enjoy the same rights as a member – for instance, to petition for a winding-up order and to vote at meetings of contributories. It appears to be wide enough, however, to impose burdens upon an unregistered transferee as well – for instance, if the shares are not fully paid, to render him directly liable to the company as a contributory for calls on the shares under s. 74. Whether the legislators intended to effect such a radical change in the law by a side-wind must be open to question.

251 Expressions used generally

251 In this Group of Parts, except in so far as the context otherwise requires–

"administrative receiver" means–

(a) an administrative receiver as defined by section 29(2) in Chapter I of Part III, or

(b) a receiver appointed under section 51 in Chapter II of that Part in a case where the whole (or substantially the whole) of the company's property is attached by the floating charge;

"business day" means any day other than a Saturday, a Sunday, Christmas Day, Good Friday or a day which is a bank holiday in any part of Great Britain;

"chattel leasing agreement" means an agreement for the bailment or, in Scotland, the hiring of goods which is capable of subsisting for more than 3 months;

"contributory" has the meaning given by section 79;

"director" includes any person occupying the position of director, by whatever name called;

"floating charge" means a charge which, as created, was a floating charge and includes a floating charge within section 462 of the Companies Act (Scottish floating charges);

"office copy", in relation to Scotland, means a copy certified by the clerk of court;

"the official rate", in relation to interest, means the rate payable under section 189(4);

"prescribed" means prescribed by the rules;

"receiver", in the expression **"receiver or manager"**, does not include a receiver appointed under section 51 in Chapter II of Part III;

"retention of title agreement" means an agreement for the sale of goods to a company, being an agreement–

(a) which does not constitute a charge on the goods, but

(b) under which, if the seller is not paid and the company is wound up, the seller will have priority over all other creditors of the company as respects the goods or any property representing the goods;

"the rules" means rules under section 411 in Part XV; and

"shadow director", in relation to a company, means a person in accordance with whose directions or instructions the directors of the company are accustomed to act (but so that a person is not deemed a shadow director by reason only that the directors act on advice given by him in a professional capacity);

and any expression for whose interpretation provision is made by Part XXVI of the Companies Act, other than an expression defined above in this section, is to be construed in accordance with that provision.

GENERAL NOTE

Most of the definitions listed here are self-explanatory. For a discussion of terms defined by reference to other sections, see the notes to those sections.

The term "administrative receiver" may include a receiver of the property of a foreign company: see *Re International Bulk Commodities Ltd* [1993] Ch. 77; [1992] B.C.C. 463 and the notes to s. 29(2), above.

The definition of "business day" in the Act differs from that in the rules, at least in some contexts. See the note to IR 1986, r. 13.13(1).

The definition of "floating charge" was introduced by the 1986 Act. The change is discussed in the notes to ss. 175(2)(b) and 245.

The definitions of "director" and "shadow director" have been incorporated from CA 1985, s. 741. The *concept* of a shadow director has been a feature of Companies Acts for many decades; the name itself was first introduced by CA 1980, s. 63. In *Re a Company No. 005009 of 1987* (1988) 4 B.C.C. 424 it was recognised that the conduct of a company's bank in relation to its affairs might make it a shadow director.

A shadow director is to be distinguished from a *de facto* director: the terms do not overlap, but are alternatives, and in most if not all cases are mutually exclusive. A de facto director is a person who assumes to act as a director and is held out as such by the company, and who claims and purports to be a director, although never actually or validly appointed as such. A shadow director, in contrast, claims not to be a director but claims that others are the directors to the exclusion of himself. An allegation that a person has acted as a *de facto* or shadow director, without distinguishing between the two, is embarrassing: *Re Hydrodan (Corby) Ltd* [1994] B.C.C. 161.

If a parent company is a shadow director of its subsidiary, it does not follow that the directors of the parent company are also, without more, its shadow directors. However where the director of a company is a body corporate, there must be an inference that it is accustomed to act on the directions of others, who will be shadow directors (*Re Hydrodan (Corby) Ltd*, above). There is no assumption that a director who is the nominee of a particular shareholder or creditor is the agent of his appointor or acts under his directions or instructions (*Kuwait Asia Bank EC v National Mutual Life Nominees Ltd* [1991] 1 A.C. 187; [1990] B.C.C. 567).

In *Re Tasbian Ltd (No. 3)* [1992] B.C.C. 358 there was held to be an arguable case that a person appointed as a consultant to a company by an outside investor was a shadow director. The dividing line between the position of a watchdog or adviser and a shadow director was difficult to draw, but there was a serious question to be tried whether the respondent might have crossed over it.

THE SECOND GROUP OF PARTS INSOLVENCY OF INDIVIDUALS; BANKRUPTCY

Introduction to the Second Group of Parts
Bankruptcy legislation in England can be traced back to 1542, and the system with which practitioners will be familiar was contained in BA 1914 (as amended in 1926 and 1976). This system was the product of the 1883 reforms pushed through by Gladstone and Joseph Chamberlain. For a superb historical review outlining the violent policy swings in the 19th century see Lester, *Victorian Insolvency* (1995). In view of the changed social conditions and altered political economy in the 20th century it is not surprising that both the Blagden Committee (Cmnd 221) in 1957 and the Cork Committee (Cmnd 8558) in 1982 felt that major revision was long overdue. Part III of IA 1985 did put the law on a modern footing, although its changes were less radical than the Cork Committee had hoped for. IA 1986, ss. 252–385 remodels the 1985 legislation mainly by fragmenting its more cumbersome provisions into several sections. Most of the provisions in the 1985 Act relating to bankruptcy never came into force. Cases under the 1914 Act still came before the courts for many years after 1986 – see for example *Re Dent* [1994] 1 W.L.R. 956; *Re Dennis* [1996] Ch. 80, discussed by Tee in (1996) 55 C.L.J. 21; *Trustee of F C Jones v Jones* [1996] B.P.I.R. 644; *Re Ross* [1997] B.C.C. 29.

What are the most obvious reforms introduced by the 1985 Act and now found in the 1986 Act? The bankruptcy procedure was greatly simplified, with the abolition of the concept of the act of bankruptcy and the intermediate stage of the receiving order. An attempt was made wherever possible to harmonise bankruptcy procedures with those of company liquidations, although unlike many jurisdictions there is still a distinction between corporate and personal insolvency law. Another reform which is more symbolic than significant in practice was the abolition of the concept of reputed ownership in bankruptcy law (it did not operate on corporate insolvency). Other changes worthy of mention were the rules giving increased protection to the family home (see s. 336–338), the attempt to produce a viable alternative to bankruptcy via voluntary arrangements (s. 252–263), plus a host of minor measures designed to streamline and improve the effectiveness of bankruptcy procedures. The liberalising trend dating back to the Justice Report of 1975 and IA 1976 is again apparent, particularly with the provisions on discharge (ss. 279 and 280). This trend has continued with EA 2002.

Criticisms can be made of the 1986 Act. It was heavily dependent on IR 1986. On the other hand it must be conceded that the 1914 Act was considerably supplemented by BR 1952. The drafting of the provisions of Pt III of the 1985 Act left much to be desired, and Muir Hunter QC, a leading commentator on bankruptcy law, predicted that this deficiency would lead to an increase in litigation. The drafting of the 1986 Act was much improved. In its 1994 Report entitled *Insolvency Law: An Agenda for Reform* Justice identified a number of weaknesses with the post-1986 bankruptcy regime. Concerns were expressed about the increasing use of bankruptcy to recover small debts and the considerable amount of litigation surrounding the use of statutory demands. Many of these problems could be traced back to the failure of government to implement the changes to the county court administration order procedure which were enacted in 1990.

Finally, it should be noted that ss. 252–385 of IA 1986 are not the sole source of law on debt and personal insolvency. Parts XII and XIX of the Act also contain provisions that will be important in practice. Criminal bankruptcy (so far as concerns orders which are still in force: see the notes to ss. 264 and 277) is dealt with by the Powers of the Criminal Courts Act 1973. The Deeds of Arrangement Act 1914 survives largely intact, though the number of deeds entered into each year is miniscule. Administration orders against judgment debtors remain governed by the County Courts Act 1984 (as amended). Indeed there are still provisions of the Debtors Act 1869 which may return to haunt debtors – see for example s. 13 (offence to make a gift to defeat creditors). Thus in *Woodley v Woodley (No. 2)* [1994] 1 W.L.R. 1167 a debtor (who subsequently became bankrupt on his own petition) was threatened with imprisonment by a judge under s. 5 of the 1869 Act for wilfully refusing to pay a judgment debt where he had the means to do so prior to his bankruptcy. On appeal, the committal order was quashed by the Court of Appeal because there was a sufficient degree of doubt as to whether he was deliberately defying the law or had been confused as to his obligations. For a more recent case involving s. 5 of the Debtors Act 1869 see *L v L* [1997] 2 F.L.R. 252. Note also Insolvent Debtors Relief Act 1729 as discussed in *Aectra Refining v Exmar, The Times* August 15, 1994.

The personal insolvency provisions in the 1986 legislation have been amended considerably by IA 2000 and EA 2002 (see below).

The law on personal insolvency in Scotland (or sequestration, as it is termed) is to be found in the Bankruptcy (Scotland) Act 1985 (as amended by the Bankruptcy (Scotland) Act 1993) and associated delegated legislation. In 1997 there were 2,502 sequestrations in Scotland. Comparable provisions dealing with personal insolvency in Northern Ireland are now contained in the Insolvency (Northern Ireland) Order 1989 (SI 1989/2405) (NI 19), arts 226–345 in particular.

Part VIII

Individual Voluntary Arrangements

General comment on Pt VIII
The provisions of Pt VIII deal with voluntary arrangements entered into by debtors as an alternative to bankruptcy. A debtor can select a "nominee" to put his proposals into effect. Prior to 1985, a debtor who wished to make an arrangement with his creditors to avoid the consequences of bankruptcy could use the Deeds of Arrangement Act 1914, much of which has survived IA 1986. The problem with a deed of arrangement made under this 1914 legislation was that it could easily be frustrated by a dissenting creditor petitioning for bankruptcy, especially as the mere execution of a deed of arrangement was construed as an act of bankruptcy. Consequently, such deeds of arrangement came to be increasingly under-employed (there were only 51 in 1984). Deeds of arrangement have not been abolished, but rather have been left to wither on the vine. Deeds of arrangement and individual voluntary arrangements are mutually exclusive: see s. 260(3) below. There were two deeds of arrangement entered into in 1992, though this figure had leaped to four for 1997. The annual report of the Secretary of State made under s. 379 must disclose statistics concerning the Deeds of Arrangement Act 1914. Under BA 1914, s. 16, 17, and 21 there was provision for schemes of composition or arrangement once bankruptcy proceedings had started (and even after adjudication). These provisions were little used and have now been supplanted by the more flexible system of voluntary arrangements established by the 1985 Act, and now to be found in the 1986 legislation. The Cork Committee (*Report*, para. 399) called for the introduction of a more

effective system of voluntary arrangements. Although IA 1986 has not adopted the specific Cork proposal for debts arrangement orders, the general policy of the Cork Committee has been followed.

The original IVA regime as set forth in Part VIII of the Insolvency Act 1986 has been the subject of significant changes introduced through the medium of s. 3 and Sch. 3 of the Insolvency Act 2000. The IVA regime has undergone change as a result of IA 2000. Procedural modifications have been introduced, including the decoupling of the IVA institution from the interim order. An IVA can come into being without the need for an interim order in an appropriate case. These reforms took effect on January 1, 2003.

A number of further changes were also introduced into the IVA mechanism via the provisions of EA 2002. These latter reforms, which include the "fast-track IVA", will not, however, take effect until April 2004.

Individual voluntary arrangements have proved popular with debtors. For background discussion see Williams (1986) 2 I.L. & P. 11. The impact of the new system of individual voluntary arrangements is covered by Pond in (1988) 4 I.L. & P. 66, 104; (1989) 5 I.L. & P. 73; [1995] J.B.L. 118. There were 6,298 IVAs entered into in 2001 (as compared to 23,477 bankruptcies). This increasing popularity may be attributed to a number of factors. The moratorium initiated by the interim order does allow a period of calm during which a debtor can seek to come to a mutually beneficial arrangement with his creditors without fear of an impatient creditor throwing a spanner in the works by petitioning for bankruptcy. Statistics do show that creditors achieve a higher rate of return under an IVA because the administration costs are so much lower – rates of return double those found in bankruptcy cases are sometimes cited. An increasingly important advantage for the debtor is that in avoiding bankruptcy he also avoids the attendant restrictions and disqualifications – *e.g.* the bar on becoming a company director. For the impact of an IVA on a debtor's right to litigate see *Envis v Thakkar* [1997] B.P.I.R. 189. For general discussion see Mullarkey (1993) 137 S.J. 192; Oditah [1994] L.M.C.L.Q. 210 and Pond (1993) 9 *Insolvency Lawyer* 9, (1994) 10 *Insolvency Lawyer* 2.

Part VIII of the Act is supplemented by IR 1986, rr. 5.1–5.65 and by *Practice Direction (Bankruptcy: Voluntary Arrangements)* [1992] 1 W.L.R. 120. Note in particular that it is a crime fraudulently to procure a voluntary arrangement: IA 1986, s. 262A. Although IVAs are provided with a statutory framework, the fact that they are at heart contracts must not be forgotten – *Raja v Rubin* [1999] B.P.I.R. 575.

Moratorium for insolvent debtor

252 Interim order of court

252(1) **[Power of court]** In the circumstances specified below, the court may in the case of a debtor (being an individual) make an interim order under this section.

252(2) **[Effect of interim order]** An interim order has the effect that, during the period for which it is in force–

(a) no bankruptcy petition relating to the debtor may be presented or proceeded with,

(aa) no landlord or other person to whom rent is payable may exercise any right of forfeiture by peaceable re-entry in relation to premises let to the debtor in respect of a failure by the debtor to comply with any term or condition of his tenancy of such premises, except with the leave of the court, and

(b) no other proceedings, and no execution or other legal process, may be commenced or continued and no distress may be levied against the debtor or his property except with the leave of the court.

S. 252(1)
In effect, this section allows for an application for an interim order in circumstances described in s. 253. On the exercise of discretion see s. 255. Prior to the coming into force of the Insolvency Act 2000 the making of an interim order was an essential prerequisite to any valid IVA – *Fletcher v Vooght* [2000] B.P.I.R. 435.

S. 252(2)
The effect of an interim order is to impose a moratorium on proceedings *against* an insolvent debtor (see *Frost v Unity Trust Bank* [1998] B.P.I.R. 459). The aim of this provision is to prevent a viable proposal being destroyed by a selfish creditor. For an early illustration of an interim order being used to prevent a sheriff acting on behalf of judgment creditors from completing the execution process, see *Re Peake* [1987] C.L.Y. 215 (Blackburn County Court). An

attempt to use an interim order to continually block bankruptcy proceedings proved unsuccessful before Scott J. in *Re a Debtor (No. 83 of 1988)* [1990] 1 W.L.R. 708 (this case is reported as *Re Cove (a debtor)* in [1990] 1 All E.R. 949).

In *Re M (Restraint Order)* [1992] 2 W.L.R. 340 Otton J. held that the making of an interim order under s. 252 did not affect the right of the prosecution to make an application for a receiver of realisable property of a person against whom a restraint order had already been made under s. 8 of the Drug Trafficking Offences Act 1986. The effect of the interim order was only to protect assets not already covered by the restraint order. Assets covered by the restraint order could no longer be considered as part of the debtor's estate until the defendant was either acquitted, in which case the restraint order would be discharged, or convicted whereupon the restraint order would be converted into a confiscation order. See also *R. v Barnet Justices Ex p. Phillippou* [1997] B.P.I.R. 134, where the court concluded that an interim order did not offer protection against the enforcement of a criminal compensation order which was viewed as being akin to a fine.

The wording of s. 252(2) was modified by s. 3 and Sch. 3 of IA 2000 to strengthen the moratorium by the amendment of subs. (2)(b). Note the addition of sub-para. 2(2)(aa) covering forfeiture by a landlord and the inclusion of distress within the moratorium. Thus *Re A Debtor (No. 13A IO and 14A IO of 1994)* [1995] 1 W.L.R. 1127, [1996] B.C.C. 57 is no longer representative of the law. The latter amendment of subs. (2)(b) counteracts *McMullen & Sons v Cerrone* [1994] B.C.C. 25.

For the consequences of non-compliance with s. 252(2) see *Clarke v Coutts & Co. (a firm)* [2002] EWCA Civ 943, [2002] B.P.I.R. 916.

253 Application for interim order

253(1) **[Where application made]** Application to the court for an interim order may be made where the debtor intends to make a proposal under this Part, that is, a proposal to his creditors for a composition in satisfaction of his debts or a scheme of arrangement of his affairs (from here on referred to, in either case, as a "voluntary arrangement").

253(2) **[Nominee]** The proposal must provide for some person ("the nominee") to act in relation to the voluntary arrangement either as trustee or otherwise for the purpose of supervising its implementation and the nominee must be a person who is qualified to act as an insolvency practitioner, or authorised to act as nominee, in relation to the voluntary arrangement.

253(3) **[Applicants]** Subject as follows, the application may be made–

(a) if the debtor is an undischarged bankrupt, by the debtor, the trustee of his estate, or the official receiver, and

(b) in any other case, by the debtor.

253(4) **[Notice for s. 253(3)(a)]** An application shall not be made under subsection (3)(a) unless the debtor has given notice of the proposal to the official receiver and, if there is one, the trustee of his estate.

253(5) **[When application not to be made]** An application shall not be made while a bankruptcy petition presented by the debtor is pending, if the court has, under section 273 below, appointed an insolvency practitioner to inquire into the debtor's affairs and report.

GENERAL NOTE

A number of relatively minor textual amendments were made to s. 253(1), (2) and (4) by s. 3 and Sch. 3 of IA 2000. The amendment to subs. (2) reflects the fact that in future a wider category of professionals may be permitted to act as nominees/supervisors of voluntary arrangements.

S. 253(1)–(3)
These provisions define the essence of the proposal for a voluntary arrangement, to implement which the interim order is sought, and they identify who may apply for an interim order. In an appropriate case the FSA may be heard on such an application – FSMA 2000, s. 357(1). For further details, see IR 1986, rr. 5.2–5.6. It seems that an interim order may be sought in respect of partnership debts: *Re Cupit (Note)* [1996] B.P.I.R. 560. A discharged bankrupt cannot access the IVA procedure by seeking an interim order – *Wright v Official Receiver* [2001] B.P.I.R. 196.

S. 253(4)
Where the debtor is an undischarged bankrupt two days' notice is required: see IR 1986, r. 5.7(4).

S. 253(5)
This provision restricts an application for an interim order where a bankruptcy petition is pending and the affairs of the debtor are being investigated under s. 273. This is because the court can on its own initiative, in such circumstances, grant an interim order.

254 Effect of application

254(1) **[Stay pending interim order]** At any time when an application under section 253 for an interim order is pending–

(a) no landlord or other person to whom rent is payable may exercise any right of forfeiture by peaceable re-entry in relation to premises let to the debtor in respect of a failure by the debtor to comply with any term or condition of his tenancy of such premises, except with the leave of the court, and

(b) the court may forbid the levying of any distress on the debtor's property or its subsequent sale, or both, and stay any action, execution or other legal process against the property or person of the debtor.

254(2) **[Stay or continuance]** Any court in which proceedings are pending against an individual may, on proof that an application under that section has been made in respect of that individual, either stay the proceedings or allow them to continue on such terms as it thinks fit.

GENERAL NOTE

Where an application for an interim order is pending, the court can take immediate steps to protect the debtor and his assets from legal action. (For the meaning of "the court", see s. 385(1).) Indeed, any court in which proceedings are pending can also take such protective steps. The effect of the application has been broadened by s. 3 and Sch. 3 of IA 2000 to enable the court to place restrictions on forfeiture and distress.

255 Cases in which interim order can be made

255(1) **[Conditions for order]** The court shall not make an interim order on an application under section 253 unless it is satisfied–

(a) that the debtor intends to make a proposal under this Part;

(b) that on the day of the making of the application the debtor was an undischarged bankrupt or was able to petition for his own bankruptcy;

(c) that no previous application has been made by the debtor for an interim order in the period of 12 months ending with that day; and

(d) that the nominee under the debtor's proposal is willing to act in relation to the proposal.

255(2) **[Order to facilitate consideration and implementation of proposal]** The court may make an order if it thinks that it would be appropriate to do so for the purpose of facilitating the consideration and implementation of the debtor's proposal.

255(3) **[Where debtor is undischarged bankrupt]** Where the debtor is an undischarged bankrupt, the interim order may contain provision as to the conduct of the bankruptcy, and the administration of the bankrupt's estate, during the period for which the order is in force.

255(4) **[Extent of s. 255(3) provision]** Subject as follows, the provision contained in an interim order by virtue of subsection (3) may include provision staying proceedings in the bankruptcy or modifying any provision in this Group of Parts, and any provision of the rules in their application to the debtor's bankruptcy.

255(5) **[Limit to interim order]** An interim order shall not, in relation to a bankrupt, make provision relaxing or removing any of the requirements of provisions in this Group of Parts, or of the rules, unless the court is satisfied that that provision is unlikely to result in any significant diminution in, or in the value of, the debtor's estate for the purposes of the bankruptcy.

255(6) **[When order ceases to have effect]** Subject to the following provisions of this Part, an interim order made on an application under section 253 ceases to have effect at the end of the period of 14 days beginning with the day after the making of the order.

S. 255(1), (2)
These subsections deal with the circumstances under which the court may make an interim order. Note the minor textual change to subs. (1) by IA 2000, s. 3 and Sch. 3. Section 255(2) gives general discretion provided the order would facilitate the consideration and implementation of the proposals. Section 255(1) cuts down this discretion by establishing a series of pre-conditions. The reference in s. 255(1)(d) to the nominee being qualified was removed by Sch. 5 to IA 2000 on the authority of s. 15(1). The debtor must not have applied for a similar order within the previous 12 months. This restriction cannot be circumvented by an application under s. 375 – *Hurst v Bennett (No. 2)* [2002] B.P.I.R. 102.

The proposal must be viable: *Cooper v Fearnley* [1997] B.P.I.R. 20; *Hook v Jewson Ltd* [1997] B.C.C. 752; *Knowles v Coutts & Co.* [1998] B.P.I.R. 96. It appears that this "viability" requirement permits the court to review the proposed fee for the nominee – *Re Julie O'Sullivan* [2001] B.P.I.R. 534.

S. 255(3)–(5)
These provisions deal with supplementary matters that may be included in the interim order where the applicant is an undischarged bankrupt – but such a provision in an interim order must not reduce the value of the debtor's estate.

S. 255(6)
The interim order will normally expire within 14 days of the order.

256 Nominee's report on debtor's proposal

256(1) **[Report to court]** Where an interim order has been made on an application under section 253, the nominee shall, before the order ceases to have effect, submit a report to the court stating–

(a) whether, in his opinion, the voluntary arrangement which the debtor is proposing has a reasonable prospect of being approved and implemented,

(aa) whether, in his opinion, a meeting of the debtor's creditors should be summoned to consider the debtor's proposal, and

(b) if in his opinion such a meeting should be summoned, the date on which, and time and place at which, he proposes the meeting should be held.

256(2) **[Information to nominee]** For the purpose of enabling a nominee to prepare his report the debtor shall submit to the nominee–

(a) a document setting out the terms of the voluntary arrangement which the debtor is proposing, and

(b) a statement of his affairs containing–

   (i) such particulars of his creditors and of his debts and other liabilities and of his assets as may be prescribed, and
   (ii) such other information as may be prescribed.

256(3) **[Directions by court]** The court may–

(a) on an application made by the debtor in a case where the nominee has failed to submit the report required by this section or has died, or

(b) on an application made by the debtor or the nominee in a case where it is impracticable or inappropriate for the nominee to continue to act as such, direct that the nominee shall be replaced as such by another person qualified to act as an insolvency practitioner, or authorised to act as nominee, in relation to the voluntary arrangement.

256(3A) The court may, on an application made by the debtor in a case where the nominee has failed to submit the report required by this section, direct that the interim order shall continue, or (if it has ceased to have effect) be renewed, for such further period as the court may specify in the direction.

256(4) **[Extension of period of interim order]** The court may, on the application of the nominee, extend the period for which the interim order has effect so as to enable the nominee to have more time to prepare his report.

256(5) **[Extension for consideration by creditors]** If the court is satisfied on receiving the nominee's report that a meeting of the debtor's creditors should be summoned to consider the debtor's proposal, the court shall direct that the period for which the interim order has effect shall be extended, for such further period as it may specify in the direction, for the purpose of enabling the debtor's proposal to be considered by his creditors in accordance with the following provisions of this Part.

256(6) **[Discharge of interim order]** The court may discharge the interim order if it is satisfied, on the application of the nominee–

(a) that the debtor has failed to comply with his obligations under subsection (2), or

(b) that for any other reason it would be inappropriate for a meeting of the debtor's creditors to be summoned to consider the debtor's proposal.

S. 256(1)
The nominee of the debtor must, before the interim order has expired (see s. 255(6)), report to the court whether in his opinion it is worth calling a creditors' meeting to consider the debtor's proposal. For the nominee's responsibilities when evaluating the proposal see *Greystoke v Hamilton-Smith* [1997] B.P.I.R. 24 and *Shah v Cooper* [2003] B.P.I.R. 1018. The wording of subs (1) was subsequently amended by IA 2000, s. 3 and Sch. 3 by the insertion of a new sub-para. (a) requiring the nominee to attest to the viability of the proposal, thus reflecting the standards previously developed at common law. For general discussion of the responsibilities of nominees, see *Prosser v Castle Sanderson (a firm)* [2002] EWCA Civ 1140, [2003] B.C.C. 440.

S. 256(2)
To facilitate the nominee making his report, the debtor must submit to him details of his proposal and statement of affairs. See IR 1986, rr. 5.5, 5.6.

S. 256(3), (3A)
Subsection (3) has been replaced and subs. (3A) inserted by s. 3 of and Sch. 3 to IA 2000. If the nominee fails to submit a report the debtor can apply to the court to have him replaced, and the interim order may be extended in such a situation. See IR 1986, r. 5.12.

S. 256(4)
This also allows for the extension of the order where the nominee requires more time to prepare his report.

S. 256(5)
If, after receiving the nominee's report, the court is satisfied that a meeting of creditors should be summoned, the court can again extend the interim order. Note also IR 1986, rr. 5.10, 5.12. Several such extensions can be granted but the patience of the court is not limitless: *Re a Debtor (No. 83 of 1988)* [1990] 1 W.L.R. 708.

S. 256(6)
The interim order can be discharged by the court if the debtor has failed to play his part or if it would be inappropriate to call a creditors' meeting.

Procedure where no interim order made

256A Debtor's proposal and nominee's report

256A(1) [**Application**] This section applies where a debtor (being an individual)–

(a) intends to make a proposal under this Part (but an interim order has not been made in relation to the proposal and no application for such an order is pending), and

(b) if he is an undischarged bankrupt, has given notice of the proposal to the official receiver and, if there is one, the trustee of his estate,

unless a bankruptcy petition presented by the debtor is pending and the court has, under section 273, appointed an insolvency practitioner to inquire into the debtor's affairs and report.

256A(2) [**Duty of debtor**] For the purpose of enabling the nominee to prepare a report to the court, the debtor shall submit to the nominee–

(a) a document setting out the terms of the voluntary arrangement which the debtor is proposing, and

(b) a statement of his affairs containing–

(i) such particulars of his creditors and of his debts and other liabilities and of his assets as may be prescribed, and

(ii) such other information as may be prescribed.

256A(3) [**Report of nominee**] If the nominee is of the opinion that the debtor is an undischarged bankrupt, or is able to petition for his own bankruptcy, the nominee shall, within 14 days (or such longer period as the court may allow) after receiving the document and statement mentioned in subsection (2), submit a report to the court stating–

(a) whether, in his opinion, the voluntary arrangement which the debtor is proposing has a reasonable prospect of being approved and implemented,

(b) whether, in his opinion, a meeting of the debtor's creditors should be summoned to consider the debtor's proposal, and

(c) if in his opinion such a meeting should be summoned, the date on which, and time and place at which, he proposes the meeting should be held.

256A(4) [**Court response**] The court may–

(a) on an application made by the debtor in a case where the nominee has failed to submit the report required by this section or has died, or

(b) on an application made by the debtor or the nominee in a case where it is impracticable or inappropriate for the nominee to continue to act as such,

direct that the nominee shall be replaced as such by another person qualified to act as an insolvency practitioner, or authorised to act as nominee, in relation to the voluntary arrangement.

256A(5) [**Time limit extended**] The court may, on an application made by the nominee, extend the period within which the nominee is to submit his report.

GENERAL NOTE

This new provision was introduced by IA 2000, s. 3 and Sch. 3 with effect from January 1, 2003. It is designed to decouple the IVA procedure from the need to have an interim order. Under the original model a purported IVA constructed without an interim order was a nullity – *Fletcher v Vooght* [2000] B.P.I.R. 435.

S. 256A(1)
This defines where s. 256A applies.

S. 256A(2)
This indicates the information required of the debtor.

Insolvency Act 1986 Section 258

S. 256A(3), (5)
Where the nominee reaches certain conclusions on the documentation furnished to him he makes a report to the court on whether an IVA is suitable. The 14-day period may be extended – subs. (5).

S. 256A(4)
This provides a protective mechanism for the debtor where the nominee has failed to act in accordance with subs. (4).

S. 256A(5)
The court can extend the time-limit specified in subs. (3).

257 Summoning of creditors' meeting

257(1) **[Meeting to be summoned]** Where it has been reported to the court under section 256 or 256A that a meeting of the debtor's creditors should be summoned, the nominee (or his replacement under section 256(3) or 256A(4)) shall, unless the court otherwise directs, summon that meeting for the time, date and place proposed in his report.

257(2) **[Persons summoned to meeting]** The persons to be summoned to the meeting are every creditor of the debtor of whose claim and address the person summoning the meeting is aware.

257(3) **[Creditors of debtor]** For this purpose the creditors of a debtor who is an undischarged bankrupt include–

(a) every person who is a creditor of the bankrupt in respect of a bankruptcy debt, and

(b) every person who would be such a creditor if the bankruptcy had commenced on the day on which notice of the meeting is given.

S. 257(1)
This provision requires the nominee to summon the meeting of creditors in accordance with his report, unless the court has directed otherwise. In *Re a Debtor (No. 83 of 1988)* [1990] 1 W.L.R. 708, Scott J. held that this provision (in appropriate circumstances) enables the court to discharge any previous order directing that a creditors' meeting be convened. In order for the approval of the IVA to be binding the meeting must be summoned strictly in accordance with the report to the court – *Re N (a debtor)* [2002] B.P.I.R. 1024. Minor textual changes were made by IA 2000 s. 3 and Sch. 3 to cater for the advent of s. 256A.

S. 257(2), (3)
These subsections identify which creditors are to be summoned to the meeting – this will depend on whether the debtor is an undischarged bankrupt or not. An FSA representative may attend in an appropriate case – FSMA 2000 s. 357(3).
  For further information, reference should be made to IR 1986, rr. 5.17–5.24.

Consideration and implementation of debtor's proposal

258 Decisions of creditors' meeting

258(1) **[Decision re approval]** A creditors' meeting summoned under section 257 shall decide whether to approve the proposed voluntary arrangement.

258(2) **[Approval with modifications]** The meeting may approve the proposed voluntary arrangement with modifications, but shall not do so unless the debtor consents to each modification.

258(3) **[Extent of modifications]** The modifications subject to which the proposed voluntary arrangement may be approved may include one conferring the functions proposed to be conferred on the nominee on another person qualified to act as an insolvency practitioner or authorised to act as nominee, in relation to the voluntary arrangement

  But they shall not include any modification by virtue of which the proposal ceases to be a proposal under this Part.

258(4) **[Certain modifications not to be approved]** The meeting shall not approve any proposal or modification which affects the right of a secured creditor of the debtor to enforce his security, except with the concurrence of the creditor concerned.

258(5) **[Other modifications not to be approved]** Subject as follows, the meeting shall not approve any proposal or modification under which–

(a) any preferential debt of the debtor is to be paid otherwise than in priority to such of his debts as are not preferential debts, or

(b) a preferential creditor of the debtor is to be paid an amount in respect of a preferential debt that bears to that debt a smaller proportion than is borne to another preferential debt by the amount that is to be paid in respect of that other debt.

However, the meeting may approve such a proposal or modification with the concurrence of the preferential creditor concerned.

258(6) **[Meeting in accordance with rules]** Subject as above, the meeting shall be conducted in accordance with the rules.

258(7) **[Definitions]** In this section **"preferential debt"** has the meaning given by section 386 in Part XII; and **"preferential creditor"** is to be construed accordingly.

S. 258(1)
The meeting of creditors can either approve or reject the composition which is being put to them. No mention is made of any required majority – under BA 1914, ss. 16(2) and 21(1) it was three-fourths in value of the debtor's creditors: IR 1986, r. 5.23 essentially retains the position, although it actually specifies a majority *in excess of* three-quarters. The decision of the meeting is final: *Kent Carpets Ltd v Symes* [1996] B.C.C. 137.

S. 258(2)–(5)
These provisions deal with modifications to the proposed scheme. Textual changes were made to subs. (3) by s. 3 of, and Sch. 3 to, IA 2000. The debtor must assent to any modification and the modification may involve a change of nominee, but the basic proposal must still fall within s. 253. A modified IVA that does not have the support of the debtor is void – *Reid v Hamblin* [2001] B.P.I.R. 929. Changes affecting the rights of secured creditors are only permitted in so far as the secured creditors agree, see *Khan v Permayer* [2001] B.P.I.R. 95 where the secured creditor waived his security in favour of a dividend. On who is a secured creditor for these purposes see *Re a Debtor (No. 10 of 1992)* [1995] Ch. 525, reported as *Peck v Craighead* [1995] B.C.C. 525. Similar protection is available to consolidate the priority enjoyed by preferential creditors on bankruptcy. This confirms the position under BA 1914, s. 16(19).

S. 258(6)
The meeting must be conducted according to the rules: see IR 1986, rr. 5.17–5.24.

S. 258(7)
This defines preferential debts, etc., for the purposes of this provision.

259 Report of decisions to court

259(1) **[Report to court, notice]** After the conclusion in accordance with the rules of the meeting summoned under section 257, the chairman of the meeting shall report the result of it to the court and, immediately after so reporting, shall give notice of the result of the meeting to such persons as may be prescribed.

259(2) **[Discharge of interim order]** If the report is that the meeting has declined (with or without modifications) to approve the debtor's proposal, the court may discharge any interim order which is in force in relation to the debtor.

GENERAL NOTE

The chairman of the creditors' meeting must report its decision to the court and give notice to prescribed persons. If the creditors have completely rejected the debtor's proposals, the court may discharge any interim order.

For further obligations imposed on the chairman, see IR 1986, rr. 5.19–5.24.

260 Effect of approval

260(1) **[Effect]** This section has effect where the meeting summoned under section 257 approves the proposed voluntary arrangement (with or without modifications).

260(2) **[Effect of approved composition or scheme]** The approved arrangement–

(a) takes effect as if made by the debtor at the meeting, and

(b) binds every person who in accordance with the rules–

    (i) was entitled to vote at the meeting (whether or not he was present or represented at it), or
    (ii) would have been so entitled if he had had notice of it,

as if he were a party to the arrangement.

260(2A) If–

(a) when the arrangement ceases to have effect any amount payable under the arrangement to a person bound by virtue of subsection (2)(b)(ii) has not been paid, and

(b) the arrangement did not come to an end prematurely,

the debtor shall at that time become liable to pay to that person the amount payable under the arrangement.

260(3) **[Deeds of Arrangement Act]** The Deeds of Arrangement Act 1914 does not apply to the approved voluntary arrangement.

260(4) **[Certain interim orders to cease]** Any interim order in force in relation to the debtor immediately before the end of the period of 28 days beginning with the day on which the report with respect to the creditors' meeting was made to the court under section 259 ceases to have effect at the end of that period.

This subsection applies except to such extent as the court may direct for the purposes of any application under section 262 below.

260(5) **[Bankruptcy petition stayed by s. 260(4) interim order]** Where proceedings on a bankruptcy petition have been stayed by an interim order which ceases to have effect under subsection (4), that petition is deemed, unless the court otherwise orders, to have been dismissed.

S. 260(1), (2), (2A)
Subsection 2(b) was replaced and subs (2A) was inserted by IA 2000, s. 3 and Sch. 3. These modifications deal with the position of unknown creditors and their rights in cesser of the arrangement in circumstances where they have still not been paid. Where the creditors' meeting approves the debtor's proposal (whether modified or not), this will bind every creditor who had notice of, and was entitled to vote at, the meeting. (Compare BA 1914, s. 16(13).) "Notice" in the context of s. 260(2)(b) means actual notice. The courts will resist any attempt to introduce notions of constructive notice into this area of the law, as is attested by *Re a Debtor (No. 64 of 1992) (Bradford & Bingley Building Society v A Debtor)* [1994] B.C.C. 55. The onus is therefore on the debtor to keep accurate records of creditors' names and addresses or else an IVA proposal might flounder through inability to contact and therefore bind certain creditors to the scheme. A creditor can split a debt and be bound by the IVA only in respect of part of the sums owing: *Re Hoare* [1997] B.P.I.R. 683. The legislation does not fully bring out the contractual foundation of a voluntary arrangement. That has been illustrated by court decisions. For example, in *Welburn v Dibb Lupton Broomhead* [2002] EWCA Civ 1601, [2003] B.P.I.R. 768, the court indicated that whether a cause of action had become one of the "trust assets" was essentially a matter of contractual construction.

A secured creditor who accepts a dividend on a voluntary arrangement does not necessarily waive rights of security – *Whitehead v Household Mortgage Corporation* [2002] EWCA Civ 1657.

Note that court approval is not required to make the scheme binding, unlike under s. 16 of the 1914 Act. Notwithstanding approval of a scheme by creditors under s. 260, an aggrieved creditor may apply to the court under s. 262 if the scheme unfairly prejudices him in his capacity as a creditor: see here *Re Naeem (a Bankrupt) (No. 18 of 1988)* [1990] 1 W.L.R. 48.

For the effect of s. 260 in releasing old debts and creating new obligations see *Re Wisepark Ltd* [1994] B.C.C. 221 at p. 223. On the effect of an IVA on sureties see *Johnson v Davies* [1998] 1 B.C.L.C. 580, *Greene King plc v Stanley* [2001] EWCA Civ 1966, [2002] B.P.I.R. 491, *Lombard Natwest Factors Ltd v Koutrouzas* [2002] EWHC 1084 (QB),

[2003] B.P.I.R. 444 and *Lloyds Bank v Ellicott* [2002] EWCA Civ 1333, [2003] B.P.I.R. 632. A creditor with a non-provable matrimonial debt can be bound by an IVA – *JP v A Debtor* [1999] B.P.I.R. 206.

On whether a post-IVA creditor can become bound see *Re Goldspan Ltd* [2003] B.P.I.R. 93.

S. 260(3)

The Deeds of Arrangement Act 1914 does not apply to the approved scheme. Registration of voluntary arrangements is provided for by IR 1986, r. 6A.2.

S. 260(4), (5)

Interim orders automatically lapse within 28 days of the chairman's report to the court. One effect of this is that if the interim order has "blocked" a bankruptcy petition, the petition is now to be treated as having been dismissed.

261 Additional effect on undischarged bankrupt

261(1) [**Application of section**] This section applies where–

(a) the creditors' meeting summoned under section 257 approves the proposed voluntary arrangement (with or without modifications), and

(b) the debtor is an undischarged bankrupt.

261(2) [**Annulment of bankruptcy order**] Where this section applies the court shall annul the bankruptcy order on an application made–

(a) by the bankrupt, or

(b) where the bankrupt has not made an application within the prescribed period, by the official receiver.

261(3) [**When application for annulment not to be made**] An application under subsection (2) may not be made–

(a) during the period specified in section 262(3)(a) during which the decision of the creditors' meeting can be challenged by application under section 262,

(b) while an application under that section is pending, or

(c) while an appeal in respect of an application under that section is pending or may be brought.

261(4) [**Court to give directions**] Where this section applies the court may give such directions about the conduct of the bankruptcy and the administration of the bankrupt's estate as it thinks appropriate for facilitating the implementation of the approved voluntary arrangement.

GENERAL NOTE

This was replaced and reconstituted by EA 2002, s. 264 and Sch. 22. The former provision, which will remain in force until April 2004, is reproduced below.

261(1) *[If debtor undischarged bankrupt] Subject as follows, where the creditors' meeting summoned under section 257 approves the proposed voluntary arrangement (with or without modifications) and the debtor is an undischarged bankrupt, the court may do one or both of the following, namely–*

(a) annul the bankruptcy order by which he was adjudged bankrupt;

(b) give such directions with respect to the conduct of the bankruptcy and the administration of the bankrupt's estate as it thinks appropriate for facilitating the implementation of the approved voluntary arrangement.

261(2) *[Annulment of bankruptcy order] The court shall not annul a bankruptcy order under subsection (1) –*

(a) at any time before the end of the period of 28 days beginning with the day on which the report of the creditors' meeting was made to the court under section 259, or

(b) at any time when an application under section 262 below, or an appeal in respect of such an application, is pending or at any time in the period within which such an appeal may be brought.

S. 261(1)

This explains the ambit of this section.

S. 261(2)
If an IVA is made under this provision the court should annul the extant bankruptcy order.

S. 261(3)
This explains when an application can be made under this provision.

S. 261(4)
This outlines the wide consequential powers of the court.

262 Challenge of meeting's decision

262(1) [Application to court] Subject to this section, an application to the court may be made, by any of the persons specified below, on one or both of the following grounds, namely–

(a) that a voluntary arrangement approved by a creditors' meeting summoned under section 257 unfairly prejudices the interests of a creditor of the debtor;

(b) that there has been some material irregularity at or in relation to such a meeting.

262(2) [Applicants] The persons who may apply under this section are–

(a) the debtor;

(b) a person who–

(i) was entitled, in accordance with the rules, to vote at the creditors' meeting, or
(ii) would have been so entitled if he had had notice of it;

(c) the nominee (or his replacement under section 256(3), 256A(4) or 258(3)); and

(d) if the debtor is an undischarged bankrupt, the trustee of his estate or the official receiver.

262(3) [Time for application] An application under this section shall not be made

(a) after the end of the period of 28 days beginning with the day on which the report of the creditors' meeting was made to the court under section 259 or

(b) in the case of a person who was not given notice of the creditors' meeting, after the end of the period of 28 days beginning with the day on which he became aware that the meeting had taken place,

but (subject to that) an application made by a person within subsection (2)(b)(ii) on the ground that the arrangement prejudices his interests may be made after the arrangement has ceased to have effect, unless it has come to an end prematurely.

262(4) [Court's powers] Where on an application under this section the court is satisfied as to either of the grounds mentioned in subsection (1), it may do one or both of the following, namely–

(a) revoke or suspend any approval given by the meeting;

(b) give a direction to any person for the summoning of a further meeting of the debtor's creditors to consider any revised proposal he may make or, in a case falling within subsection (1)(b), to reconsider his original proposal.

262(5) [Revocation of direction, approval] Where at any time after giving a direction under subsection (4)(b) for the summoning of a meeting to consider a revised proposal the court is satisfied that the debtor does not intend to submit such a proposal, the court shall revoke the direction and revoke or suspend any approval given at the previous meeting.

262(6) [Further direction] Where the court gives a direction under subsection (4)(b), it may also give a direction continuing or, as the case may require, renewing, for such period as may be specified in the direction, the effect in relation to the debtor of any interim order.

262(7) **[Supplemental directions]** In any case where the court, on an application made under this section with respect to a creditors' meeting, gives a direction under subsection (4)(b) or revokes or suspends an approval under subsection (4)(a) or (5), the court may give such supplemental directions as it thinks fit, and, in particular, directions with respect to–

(a) things done since the meeting under any voluntary arrangement approved by the meeting, and

(b) such things done since the meeting as could not have been done if an interim order had been in force in relation to the debtor when they were done.

262(8) **[Effects of irregularity at meeting]** Except in pursuance of the preceding provisions of this section, an approval given at a creditors' meeting summoned under section 257 is not invalidated by any irregularity at or in relation to the meeting.

GENERAL NOTE

Modifications to s. 262 were made by IA 2000, s. 3 and Sch. 3. Of these modifications the provisions dealing with unidentified (and therefore unnotified) creditors are the most significant. Under s. 16 of BA 1914, it was the task of the court to approve the scheme, and it had to consider whether it was reasonable and for the benefit of the general creditors. Under the 1986 Act, the court's role is reduced and it will assume such a paternal posture only if the decision of the majority of creditors is challenged under s. 262. The court will consider whether the interests of some creditors have been unfairly prejudiced and will be less concerned with an overview of the scheme – it will assume that it is beneficial to the creditors if the majority support it. It is important to grasp that the remedy is only available to protect the complainant's interests as a creditor and not ulterior interests, a point confirmed in *Doorbar v Alltime Securities Ltd (No. 2)* [1995] B.C.C. 1,149. Furthermore, the court has more discretion under s. 262 to secure the revision of the scheme to meet any objections. In *Re Naeem (a Bankrupt) (No. 18 of 1988)* [1990] 1 W.L.R. 48 a landlord successfully exploited s. 262 before a registrar to block a scheme on the ground that it unfairly prejudiced his interests, but on appeal to Hoffmann J. the scheme was reinstated as no unfair prejudice to his interests as a creditor could be established. This case is also instructive on the question of who pays the costs of a s. 262 application. See also *March Estates v Gunmark* [1996] B.P.I.R. 439.

A success for s. 262 was notched up in *Re a Debtor (No. 222 of 1990) Ex p. Bank of Ireland (No. 2)* [1993] B.C.L.C. 233 where Harman J. found that as the nominee/chairman had conducted the IVA meeting in a materially irregular way by denying certain creditors a vote (see the earlier proceedings reported in [1992] B.C.L.C. 137) he should be personally liable for the costs of the IVA which had to be set aside. It is difficult not to feel some sympathy for the unfortunate insolvency practitioner here as the right to vote on an IVA in certain contentious cases is less than clear. For another s. 262 application that resulted in difficulties for the insolvency practitioner concerned, see *Re N (a Debtor)* [2002] B.P.I.R. 1024. A s. 262 application on the grounds of unfair prejudice also succeeded in *Re A Debtor (No. 1 of 1999)* [2000] B.P.I.R. 998.

By way of comparison a s. 262 application failed in *Re a Debtor (No. 259 of 1990)* [1992] 1 W.L.R. 226 where the court made the point that the alleged unfairness must emanate from the scheme itself. For another unsuccessful petition alleging unfair prejudice see *National Westminster Bank v Scher* [1998] B.P.I.R. 224.

For consequential procedural aspects of an application under s. 262, see IR 1986, r. 5.30. Note also *Re a Debtor (No. 87 of 1993) (No. 1)* [1996] B.C.C. 74 (hearsay evidence not admissible).

S. 262(1)–(3), (8)

Within 28 days of the chairman's report to the court a dissenter may apply to the court to challenge the scheme. Section 262(2) allows the debtor, creditors, nominee, trustee or official receiver to make such an application. As to who is a creditor, see *Sea Voyager Maritime Inc. v Bielecki* [1999] 1 All E.R. 628. The FSA may apply (and be heard on the application of another) in an appropriate case – FSMA 2000, s. 357(5) and (6). The grounds for the challenge are that the scheme unfairly prejudices the interests of a creditor, or that there has been some *material* irregularity in relation to the meeting. The test for material irregularity is the same under the Act and the Rules: *Re Sweatfield Ltd* [1997] B.C.C. 744. Irregularity will not be regarded as material unless it would be likely to affect the outcome of the vote: *Doorbar v Alltime Securities* [1995] B.C.C. 1,149. The irregularity need not be at the meeting as such but may occur in the preparatory documentation: *Re a Debtor (No. 87 of 1993) (No. 2)* [1996] B.C.C. 80. See also *IRC v Duce* [1999] B.P.I.R. 189. Material irregularity can arise even though no party can be said to be at blame: *Great Yarmouth BC v Alterman* (unreported county court ruling noted in *Current Law Week* April 17, 1998).

Unless there has been a successful challenge under this section, irregularities will not invalidate the scheme – see s. 262(8).

The 28-day period for challenge can be extended: *Tager v Westpac Banking Corp.* [1998] B.C.C. 73.

S. 262(4)–(7)
These provisions outline what the court may do where a scheme is challenged. It may revoke or suspend the approval or call for further meetings to be held – *i.e.* to reconsider the proposals or to consider revised proposals. If the debtor does not intend to put revised proposals the court can simply revoke or suspend its support for the scheme, although it can direct the interim relief to continue and also make supplementary directions. The court refused to give a direction under s. 262(4)(b) for a further meeting in *Re A Debtor (No. 101 of 1999) (No. 2)* [2001] B.P.I.R. 996. On directions under s. 262(7) see *IRC v Duce* [1999] B.P.I.R. 189. For the scope of the jurisdiction under s. 262(7) see *Re a Debtor (No. 83 of 1988)* [1990] 1 W.L.R. 708. On revoking see *Re Cardona* [1997] B.C.C. 697.

262A False representations etc.

262A(1) **[Offence]** If for the purpose of obtaining the approval of his creditors to a proposal for a voluntary arrangement, the debtor–

(a) makes any false representation, or

(b) fraudulently does, or omits to do, anything,

he commits an offence.

262A(2) **[Unapproved proposal]** Subsection (1) applies even if the proposal is not approved.

262A(3) **[Penalty]** A person guilty of an offence under this section is liable to imprisonment or a fine, or both.

GENERAL NOTE

Introduced by IA 2000, s. 3 and Sch. 3 with effect from January 1, 2003, this new provision seeks to introduce a new sanction for those debtors who make false representations to seek creditor approval for a voluntary arrangement.

S. 262A(1), (2)
These define the extent of the offence – the fact that the IVA is voted down by creditors is immaterial. See the note to s. 6A.

S. 262A(3)
The sanction is hereby specified, though details of this can only be discovered by reference to Sch. 10.

262B Prosecution of delinquent debtors

262B(1) **[Application]** This section applies where a voluntary arrangement approved by a creditors' meeting summoned under section 257 has taken effect.

262B(2) **[Whistleblowing obligation]** If it appears to the nominee or supervisor that the debtor has been guilty of any offence in connection with the arrangement for which he is criminally liable, he shall forthwith–

(a) report the matter to the Secretary of State, and

(b) provide the Secretary of State with such information and give the Secretary of State such access to and facilities for inspecting and taking copies of documents (being information or documents in his possession or under his control and relating to the matter in question) as the Secretary of State requires.

262B(3) **[Consequences]** Where a prosecuting authority institutes criminal proceedings following any report under subsection (2), the nominee or, as the case may be, supervisor shall give the authority all assistance in connection with the prosecution which he is reasonably able to give.

For this purpose, "prosecuting authority" means the Director of Public Prosecutions or the Secretary of State.

262B(4) **[Power of court]** The court may, on the application of the prosecuting authority, direct a nominee or supervisor to comply with subsection (3) if he has failed to do so.

S. 262B
This again reflects a desire to combat IVA abuse by imposing a "whistleblowing" obligation on the nominee/supervisor.

S. 262B(1)
This indicates the applicability of this section.

S. 262B(2)
The details of the whistleblowing obligation are specified.

S. 262B(3), (4)
These deal with consequential matters where a prosecution of a debtor is instituted in the wake of a report made under subs. (2).

262C Arrangements coming to an end prematurely

262C For the purposes of this Part, a voluntary arrangement approved by a creditors' meeting summoned under section 257 comes to an end prematurely if, when it ceases to have effect, it has not been fully implemented in respect of all persons bound by the arrangement by virtue of section 260(2)(b)(i).

S. 262C
This explains when an IVA can be said to come to an end prematurely. This new provision was inserted by IA 2000, s. 3 and Sch. 3 with effect from January 1, 2003. Its importance can be gleaned by reference to s. 260(2A).

263 Implementation and supervision of approved voluntary arrangement

263(1) [Application] This section applies where a voluntary arrangement approved by a creditors' meeting summoned under section 257 has taken effect.

263(2) [Supervisor of voluntary arrangement] The person who is for the time being carrying out, in relation to the voluntary arrangement, the functions conferred by virtue of the approval on the nominee (or his replacement under section 256(3), 256A(4) or 258(3)) shall be known as the supervisor of the voluntary arrangement.

263(3) [Application to court re actions of supervisor] If the debtor, any of his creditors or any other person is dissatisfied by any act, omission or decision of the supervisor, he may apply to the court; and on such an application the court may—

(a) confirm, reverse or modify any act or decision of the supervisor,

(b) give him directions, or

(c) make such other order as it thinks fit.

263(4) [Application for directions] The supervisor may apply to the court for directions in relation to any particular matter arising under the voluntary arrangement.

263(5) [Court may fill supervisor vacancy etc.] The court may, whenever—

(a) it is expedient to appoint a person to carry out the functions of the supervisor, and

(b) it is inexpedient, difficult or impracticable for an appointment to be made without the assistance of the court,

make an order appointing a person who is qualified to act as an insolvency practitioner or authorised to act as supervisor in relation to the voluntary arrangement, either in substitution for the existing supervisor or to fill a vacancy.

This is without prejudice to section 41(2) of the Trustee Act 1925 (power of court to appoint trustees of deeds of arrangement).

263(6) [Exercise of s. 263(5) power] The power conferred by subsection (5) is exercisable so as to increase the number of persons exercising the functions of the supervisor or, where there is more than one person exercising those functions, so as to replace one or more of those persons.

GENERAL NOTE

Minor textual amendments were made to s. 263(3) and (5) by IA 2000, s. 3 and Sch. 3. In s. 263(5) the amendment reflects the possibility of non-IPs in future acting as nominees/supervisors.

S. 263(1), (2)
Once the scheme has taken effect the "nominee" will be transformed into the "supervisor" of the composition or scheme. On the standards of competence expected of the nominee/supervisor see *Heritage Joinery v Krasner* [1999] B.P.I.R. 683 and *Pitt v Mond* [2001] B.P.I.R. 624. Compare *Harmony Carpets v Chaffin-Laird* [2000] B.P.I.R. 61.

S. 263(3)
This allows for the court to interfere with decisions of the supervisor which have been objected to. Compare IA 1986, s. 303(1). For a direction under para. (b) see *Ing Lease (UK) Ltd v Griswold* [1998] B.C.C. 905. Creditors have no private rights of action outside s. 263 to enforce a supervisor's duties – *King v Anthony* [1999] B.P.I.R. 73.

S. 263(4)
The supervisor may apply to the court for directions, as can a trustee in bankruptcy under IA 1986, s. 303(2). For an example see *Re a Debtor (No. 638 IO of 1994), The Times* December 3, 1998 and *Horrocks v Broome* [1999] B.P.I.R. 66. This power to seek directions does not authorise the court to vary the IVA – *Re Alpa Lighting Ltd* [1997] B.P.I.R. 341, *Raja v Rubin* [1999] B.P.I.R. 575.

S. 263(5), (6)
The court can fill vacancies, appoint substitutes or increase the number of supervisors. On this jurisdiction see *Re Bridgend Goldsmiths* [1995] B.C.C. 226 (a questionable authority); *Re Bullard & Taplin* [1996] B.C.C. 973; *Re Stella Metals Ltd* [1997] B.C.C. 626 (professional body can apply for replacement where original appointee ceases to be qualified), *Re Abbott* [1997] B.C.C. 666 (original appointment made by county court therefore case had to be transferred High Court to enable it to replace) and *Clements v Udal* [2001] B.P.I.R. 454.

For further provisions on the implementation of the voluntary arrangement and the role of the supervisor, see IR 1986, rr. 5.26, 5.31, 5.32 and 5.34. Note that an IVA may expire automatically by effluxion of time – *Strongmaster Ltd v Kaye* [2002] EWHC 444 (Ch), [2002] B.P.I.R. 1259.

It is disappointing that the IVA legislation does not address the scenario where an IVA established under Pt VIII of IA 1986 fails and the debtor is declared bankrupt. We are told by s. 264(1)(c) that a supervisor may present a bankruptcy petition but bankruptcy may occur in other circumstances – *e.g.* by default towards post-IVA creditors. What is the impact of bankruptcy upon the earlier IVA? More importantly, what happens to the funds collected by the IVA supervisor – are they reserved exclusively for the IVA participants or can they be claimed by the trustee in bankruptcy for the benefit of the creditors at large? The case law here is voluminous: *Re McKeen* [1995] B.C.C. 412 (Morritt J.), *Re Bradley-Hole* [1995] 1 W.L.R. 1097 (Rimer J.), *Davis v Martin-Sklan* [1995] 2 B.C.L.C. 483 (Blackburne J.), *Kings v Cleghorn* [1998] B.P.I.R. 463 (HHJ Behrens) and *Re Coath* [2000] B.P.I.R. 981 (DJ Field). A useful analysis of some of the earlier of these authorities is provided by Bailey in [1995–96] 2 R.A.L.Q. 87 and Walton [1997–98] 3 R.A.L.Q. 277. Some clarity in the law has now been introduced by the Court of Appeal ruling in *Re N.T. Gallagher & Son Ltd* [2002] EWCA Civ 404. Although this case is concerned with CVAs the principles developed in that case were expressly intended to apply *mutatis mutandis* to IVAs. In short it is clear that an IVA may survive subsequent bankruptcy and that funds collected by the supervisor may be retained and kept out of the hands of the trustee in bankruptcy. The IVA documentation will be important here. For a full discussion of these principles see pp. 34–35 above.

Fast-track voluntary arrangement

263A Availability

263A Section 263B applies where an individual debtor intends to make a proposal to his creditors for a voluntary arrangement and–

(a) the debtor is an undischarged bankrupt,

(b) the official receiver is specified in the proposal as the nominee in relation to the voluntary arrangement, and

(c) no interim order is applied for under section 253.

GENERAL NOTE

This group of provisions was added by EA 2002, s. 264 and Sch. 22 with effect from April 1, 2004. It establishes yet another IVA variant – namely the "fast-track IVA" which can be used by undischarged bankrupts and managed by the official receiver. The criteria for application are mapped out in s. 263A. One concern about this new procedure is whether it will appeal to undischarged bankrupts, who in future are going to be discharged after one year in any case. Other debtors in a position to avoid bankruptcy by proposing an IVA to creditors are clearly not going to be caught by the net because they will not enter bankruptcy in the first place.

263B Decision

263B(1) [**Documents to official receiver**] The debtor may submit to the official receiver–

(a) a document setting out the terms of the voluntary arrangement which the debtor is proposing, and

(b) a statement of his affairs containing such particulars as may be prescribed of his creditors, debts, other liabilities and assets and such other information as may be prescribed.

263B(2) [**Invitation to creditors to approve**] If the official receiver thinks that the voluntary arrangement proposed has a reasonable prospect of being approved and implemented, he may make arrangements for inviting creditors to decide whether to approve it.

263B(3) [**"Creditor"**] For the purposes of subsection (2) a person is a "creditor" only if–

(a) he is a creditor of the debtor in respect of a bankruptcy debt, and

(b) the official receiver is aware of his claim and his address.

263B(4) [**Arrangements under s. 236B**] Arrangements made under subsection (2)–

(a) must include the provision to each creditor of a copy of the proposed voluntary arrangement,

(b) must include the provision to each creditor of information about the criteria by reference to which the official receiver will determine whether the creditors approve or reject the proposed voluntary arrangement, and

(c) may not include an opportunity for modifications to the proposed voluntary arrangement to be suggested or made.

263B(5) [**When no interim order to be made**] Where a debtor submits documents to the official receiver under subsection (1) no application under section 253 for an interim order may be made in respect of the debtor until the official receiver has–

(a) made arrangements as described in subsection (2), or

(b) informed the debtor that he does not intend to make arrangements (whether because he does not think the voluntary arrangement has a reasonable prospect of being approved and implemented or because he declines to act).

S. 263B(1)
The onus is on the undischarged bankrupt to initiate this procedure. On notification a deposit of £335 is payable (Insolvency Proceedings (Fees) Order 2004 (SI 2004/593)).

S. 263B(2), (3)
The official receiver acts as facilitator. For bankruptcy debt see s. 382.

S. 263B(4), (5)
These deal with various operational issues.

263C Result

263C As soon as is reasonably practicable after the implementation of arrangements under section 263B(2) the official receiver shall report to the court whether the proposed voluntary arrangement has been approved or rejected.

S. 263C
The only role of the court up to this stage is to be notified of the creditors' decision.

263D Approval of voluntary arrangement

263D(1) [**Application of section**] This section applies where the official receiver reports to the court under section 263C that a proposed voluntary arrangement has been approved.

263D(2) [**Binding effect of arrangement**] The voluntary arrangement–

(a) takes effect,

(b) binds the debtor, and

(c) binds every person who was entitled to participate in the arrangements made under section 263B(2).

263D(3) [**Bankruptcy order to be annulled**] The court shall annul the bankruptcy order in respect of the debtor on an application made by the official receiver.

263D(4) [**When no application to annul to be made**] An application under subsection (3) may not be made–

(a) during the period specified in section 263F(3) during which the voluntary arrangement can be challenged by application under section 263F(2),

(b) while an application under that section is pending, or

(c) while an appeal in respect of an application under that section is pending or may be brought.

263D(5) [**Directions**] The court may give such directions about the conduct of the bankruptcy and the administration of the bankrupt's estate as it thinks appropriate for facilitating the implementation of the approved voluntary arrangement.

263D(6) [**Non-application of Deeds of Arrangement Act 1914**] The Deeds of Arrangement Act 1914 (c. 47) does not apply to the voluntary arrangement.

263D(7) [**Reference to voluntary arrangement**] A reference in this Act or another enactment to a voluntary arrangement approved under this Part includes a reference to a voluntary arrangement which has effect by virtue of this section.

S. 263D(1), (2)
These are the usual consequences attendant upon VA approval.

S. 263D(3)
This is more specific and requires the court to annul the bankruptcy order.

S. 263D(4)
This qualifies subs. (3).

S. 263D(5)
In spite of what was said above, the court may have a continuing role to deal with transition from bankruptcy to IVA.

S. 263D(6)
This is true of all IVAs.

S. 263D(7)
This is purely explanatory.

263E Implementation

263E Section 263 shall apply to a voluntary arrangement which has effect by virtue of section 263D(2) as it applies to a voluntary arrangement approved by a creditors' meeting.

S. 263E
This applies s. 263 to fast-track IVAs.

263F Revocation

263F(1) **[Grounds for revocation]** The court may make an order revoking a voluntary arrangement which has effect by virtue of section 263D(2) on the ground–

(a) that it unfairly prejudices the interests of a creditor of the debtor, or

(b) that a material irregularity occurred in relation to the arrangements made under section 263B(2).

263F(2) **[Applicant for revocation order]** An order under subsection (1) may be made only on the application of–

(a) the debtor,

(b) a person who was entitled to participate in the arrangements made under section 263B(2),

(c) the trustee of the bankrupt's estate, or

(d) the official receiver.

263F(3) **[Period when application may not be made]** An application under subsection (2) may not be made after the end of the period of 28 days beginning with the date on which the official receiver makes his report to the court under section 263C.

263F(4) **[Where creditor not aware of arrangement]** But a creditor who was not made aware of the arrangements under section 263B(2) at the time when they were made may make an application under subsection (2) during the period of 28 days beginning with the date on which he becomes aware of the voluntary arrangement.

S. 263F(1), (2)
This confers wide intervention powers on the court provided the applicant qualifies under subs. (2).

S. 263F(3), (4)
This is the standard 28-day time-limit subject to extension if the conditions in subs. (4) are met.

263G Offences

263G(1) **[False representations etc.]** Section 262A shall have effect in relation to obtaining approval to a proposal for a voluntary arrangement under section 263D.

263G(2) **[Prosecution of delinquent debtors]** Section 262B shall have effect in relation to a voluntary arrangement which has effect by virtue of section 263D(2) (for which purposes the words "by a creditors' meeting summoned under section 257" shall be disregarded).

S. 263G(1)
This extends the offence in s. 262A to fast-track IVAs.

S. 263G(2)
This makes provision for s. 262B to apply to fast-track IVAs.

Part IX

Bankruptcy

General comment on Pt IX
Before embarking upon the analysis of the provisions of IA 1986 with regard to bankruptcy a caveat ought to be issued with regard to usage of statutory predecessors. Where this is appropriate the legislative origins of particular provisions

are identified in the following text. However, care must be taken in handling these former provisions (which are largely from BA 1914) for it is now clear that the courts are minded to interpret the bankruptcy sections of IA 1986 in their own light and are not necessarily going to take advantage of earlier interpretations of similar provisions in the 1914 Act. Thus in *Re a Debtor (No. 1 of 1987)* [1989] 1 W.L.R. 271, a leading case on statutory demands, Nicholls L.J. declared:

"I do not think that on this the new bankruptcy code simply incorporates and adopts the same approach as the old code. The new code has made many changes in the law of bankruptcy, and the court's task, with regard to the new code, must be to construe the new statutory provisions in accordance with the ordinary canons of construction, unfettered by previous authorities." (*Ibid.*, at p. 276.)

More recently in the House of Lords' ruling in *Smith v Braintree District Council* [1990] 2 A.C. 215, which was concerned with the interpretation of IA 1986, s. 285, Lord Jauncey (at pp. 237–238) reinforced this view on the *modus operandi* of interpretation:

"... the Act of 1986, although re-enacting many provisions from earlier statutes, contains a good deal of fresh material derived from the Insolvency Act 1985. In particular, the legislation now emphasises the importance of the rehabilitation of the individual insolvent, it provides for automatic discharge from bankruptcy in many cases, and it abolishes mandatory public examinations as well as enabling a bankrupt to be discharged without public examination. Thus not only has the legislative approach to individual bankruptcy altered since the mid-19th century, but social views as to what conduct involves delinquency, as to punishment and as to the desirability of imprisonment have drastically changed ... In these circumstances, I feel justified in construing section 285 of the Act of 1986 as a piece of new legislation without regard to 19th century authorities or similar provisions of repealed Bankruptcy Acts ...".

These are important statements of principle that should be borne in mind when trying to attach meaning to the new statutory provisions in bankruptcy law. Having said that, there are instances where pre-1985 law has been important and therefore generalisations must be treated with caution.

It should also be borne in mind that there are significant principles of common law in bankruptcy which have never been embodied in legislation. For example the rule against double proof and the curious duty imposed on trustees to act honourably as devised in *Ex parte James* (1874) 9 Ch. App. 609, which for once was applied in *Patel v Jones* [2001] B.P.I.R. 919.

It should be remembered that in addition to the Act and the Rules and the underlying common law, there are a number of relevant practice directions governing bankruptcy cases. Some of these are referred to in connection with the relevant legislative provisions. Most, however, have now been overtaken by the *Practice Direction: Insolvency Proceedings* [2000] B.C.C. 927 (reproduced as Appendix IV to this *Guide*) which can also be found reported in [1999] B.P.I.R. 441 (as revised in [2000] B.P.I.R. 647). A case of general significance in bankruptcy litigation is *Hocking v Walker* [1997] B.P.I.R. 93, where the Court of Appeal held that a bankrupt may be required to give security for costs when appealing against a bankruptcy order.

The provisions in Part IX of IA 1986 have been substantially amended by Part 10 of EA 2002. Most of these changes will take effect in April 2004. Transitional provisions are contained in s. 256 and Sch. 19 EA 2002. The purpose of these amending provisions was to liberalise bankruptcy law in this country. The thinking behind this reform was that by removing some of the unpleasantness associated with business failure individuals would be more inclined to undertake entrepreneurial risk. The problem with this reasoning is that the majority of bankrupts these days are consumer debtors taking no part whatsoever in the risks associated with trade. Having said that, consumer credit is now a key feature of our economy and any government is naturally concerned with the downside of such an economic facility deemed so vital to the health of the national economy. The 2002 Act changes bankruptcy topography in a number of ways. First, automatic discharge will now be available after a maximum of one year (EA 2002, s. 256). Official receivers will no longer be subject to a statutory obligation to investigate the causes of every bankruptcy (EA 2002, s. 258). Disqualifications of bankrupts will be relaxed in a variety of ways (see EA 2002, ss. 265–268). Certain bankruptcy offences will be decriminalised (EA 2002, s. 263). The rights of bankrupts and their families over the home will be further strengthened by requiring a trustee to take firm action within 3 years or lose entitlement to this major asset (s. 261). To compensate for these changes the concept of a bankruptcy restriction order (or undertaking) is introduced to deal with those bankrupts whose conduct is not beyond reproach (s. 257 and Schs 20, 21). Other changes introduced by the 2002 Act include reforms to the income payments regime (ss. 259, 260). Each of these reforms will be considered below at the appropriate statutory point in the amended 1986 Act.

Section 264 *Insolvency Act 1986*

CHAPTER I

BANKRUPTCY PETITIONS; BANKRUPTCY ORDERS

Introductory note to Pt IX, Ch. I
The 1985 Act implemented the recommendation of the Cork Committee (*Report*, para. 529), that the obsolete concept of acts of bankruptcy should be abolished.

Preliminary

264 Who may present a bankruptcy petition

264(1) [Presentation of petition] A petition for a bankruptcy order to be made against an individual may be presented to the court in accordance with the following provisions of this Part–

(a) by one of the individual's creditors or jointly by more than one of them,

(b) by the individual himself,

(ba) by a temporary administrator (within the meaning of Article 38 of the EC Regulation),

(bb) by a liquidator (within the meaning of Article 2(b) of the EC Regulation) appointed in proceedings by virtue of Article 3(1) of the EC Regulation,

(c) by the supervisor of, or any person (other than the individual) who is for the time being bound by, a voluntary arrangement proposed by the individual and approved under Part VIII, or

(d) where a criminal bankruptcy order has been made against the individual, by the Official Petitioner or by any person specified in the order in pursuance of section 39(3)(b) of the Powers of Criminal Courts Act 1973.

264(2) [Power of court to make order] Subject to those provisions, the court may make a bankruptcy order on any such petition.

GENERAL NOTE

This section describes the persons who may present a bankruptcy petition and authorises the court to make an order on such a petition. Sub-subsections (1)(ba) and (bb) were introduced to cater for the advent of EC Council Regulation 1346/2000 with effect from May 31, 2002. For the "Official Petitioner" in s. 264(1)(d) see s. 402. The FSA may petition in an appropriate case – for the position here see s. 372 of FSMA 2000. It may also be heard on a s. 264 petition presented by any other party – see FSMA 2000, s. 374(2). Creditors with separate debts can join together and present a single bankruptcy petition: *Re Allen (Re a Debtor 367 of 1992)* [1998] B.P.I.R. 319. A creditor with a non provable bankruptcy debt is entitled to present a petition, though the court is unlikely to accede to it unless there are exceptional circumstances – *Russell v Russell* [1998] B.P.I.R. 259. Such exceptional circumstances were present in *Wheatley v Wheatley* [1999] B.P.I.R. 431. On the general issue of petitions and non-provable debts see *Levy v Legal Services Commission* [2000] B.P.I.R. 1065.

See the discussion on pp. 34–36 above for the impact of bankruptcy upon an IVA.

A default petition can be presented under s. 264(1)(c) even though the specified duration for the IVA has expired – *Harris v Gross* [2001] B.P.I.R. 586.

Note prospective amendment: s. 264(1)(d) and the word "or" immediately preceding it are to be repealed by CJA 1988, s. 170(2) and Sch. 16 as from a day to be appointed. (The power to make criminal bankruptcy orders has been abolished by s. 101 of this Act, with effect from April 3, 1989 (see SI 1989/264 (C 8)), but this and other provisions of IA 1986 and IR 1986 remain in force for the time being to govern orders already existing: see further the note to s. 277.)

The fee for a creditor's petition is now £180, with a debtor's petition costing £140: see the Supreme Court Fees (Amendment) Order 2003 (SI 2003/646) and County Court Fees (Amendment) Order 2003 (SI 2003/648). The relevant deposits for petitions presented under s. 264(1) are £370 for petitions presented under para. (a), (c) and (d) and £310 for petitions presented by debtors under para. (b) (from April 1, 2004 – see the Insolvency Proceedings (Fees) Order 2004 (SI 2004/593)).

265 Conditions to be satisfied in respect of debtor

265(1) **[Conditions for presentation of petition]** A bankruptcy petition shall not be presented to the court under section 264(1)(a) or (b) unless the debtor–

(a) is domiciled in England and Wales,

(b) is personally present in England and Wales on the day on which the petition is presented, or

(c) at any time in the period of 3 years ending with that day–

  (i) has been ordinarily resident, or has had a place of residence, in England and Wales, or
  (ii) has carried on business in England and Wales.

265(2) **[Interpretation]** The reference in subsection (1)(c) to an individual carrying on business includes–

(a) the carrying on of business by a firm or partnership of which the individual is a member, and

(b) the carrying on of business by an agent or manager for the individual or for such a firm or partnership.

265(3) **[EC Regulation]** This section is subject to Article 3 of the EC Regulation.

GENERAL NOTE

This section largely repeats provisions to the same effect in BA 1914, s. 1(2). The purpose of these provisions is to establish a geographic connection between the debtor and the English bankruptcy system. For an instructive authority here, see *Re Brauch* [1978] Ch. 316. In *Re Thulin* [1995] 1 W.L.R. 165 a non-resident Swede was bankrupted by the English courts to facilitate the international collection of his assets. For the purposes of s. 265(1)(c)(ii) a person does not cease to carry on business until arrangements have been made to settle business debts: see *Re a Debtor (No. 784 of 1991)* [1992] Ch. 554 where Hoffmann J. followed *Theophile v Solicitor General* [1950] A.C. 186. Note also *Wilkinson v IRC* [1998] B.P.I.R. 418.

Subs. (3) was inserted by Insolvency Act 1986 (Amendment) (No. 2) Regulations 2002 (SI 2002/1240) reg. 14 with effect from May 31, 2002. Art. 3 of the EC Regulation overrides s. 265(1) where the debtor has his centre of main interests in another EU Member State – our local courts enjoy only limited jurisdiction to open a local bankruptcy – see pp. 614–615. Where there is no COMI within an EU Member State, s. 265 retains its importance to found jurisdiction – *Geveran Trading Co. v Skjevesland* [2003] B.C.C. 209 (confirmed on appeal [2002] EWHC 2898 (Ch), [2003] B.C.C. 391).

266 Other preliminary conditions

266(1) **[Treatment of petition]** Where a bankruptcy petition relating to an individual is presented by a person who is entitled to present a petition under two or more paragraphs of section 264(1), the petition is to be treated for the purposes of this Part as a petition under such one of those paragraphs as may be specified in the petition.

266(2) **[Limit on withdrawal of petition]** A bankruptcy petition shall not be withdrawn without the leave of the court.

266(3) **[Power of dismissal or stay]** The court has a general power, if it appears to it appropriate to do so on the grounds that there has been a contravention of rules or for any other reason, to dismiss a bankruptcy petition or to stay proceedings on such a petition; and, where it stays proceedings on a petition, it may do so on such terms and conditions as it thinks fit.

266(4) **[Where criminal bankruptcy order]** Without prejudice to subsection (3), where a petition under section 264(1)(a), (b) or (c) in respect of an individual is pending at a time when a criminal bankruptcy order

Section 267   *Insolvency Act 1986*

is made against him, or is presented after such an order has been so made, the court may on the application of the Official Petitioner dismiss the petition if it appears to it appropriate to do so.

S. 266(1)
A person may be entitled to present a petition under two or more paragraphs of s. 264(1), but he must specify which paragraph he is relying on.

S. 266(2)
The leave of the court is required before a petition can be withdrawn. This repeats BA 1914, s. 5(7) and 6(2).

S. 266(3), (4)
The court has general discretion to stay or dismiss petitions, as was the case under BA 1914, s. 113. This discretion is to be kept flexible: *TSB Bank v Platts* [1997] B.P.I.R. 151. See also *Oxted Financial Services v Gordon* [1998] B.P.I.R. 231 and *Re Micklethwait* [2002] EWHC 1123 (Ch), [2003] B.P.I.R. 101 where the court refused to invoke s. 266(3). Compare *Re Ross (No. 2)* [2000] B.P.I.R. 636. See also *Westminster CC v Parkin* [2001] B.P.I.R. 1156, where the court refused to intervene even where the petition debt was subject to appeal because it did not believe that the appeal had a reasonable prospect of success. Note *Shepherd v LSC* [2003] B.P.I.R. 140 where a bankruptcy order was made notwithstanding the fact that it was conceded by all sides that there were no assets to realise. Section 266(4) ensures that if there is a possibility of a petition based on a criminal bankruptcy order, that should receive priority treatment. For the role of the official petitioner, see s. 402.

Note prospective amendment: s. 266(4) is to be repealed by CJA 1988, s. 170(2) and Sch. 16 as from a day to be appointed: see the note to s. 264.

Creditor's petition

267   Grounds of creditor's petition

267(1)   [Requirements] A creditor's petition must be in respect of one or more debts owed by the debtor, and the petitioning creditor or each of the petitioning creditors must be a person to whom the debt or (as the case may be) at least one of the debts is owed.

267(2)   [Conditions for presentation of petition] Subject to the next three sections, a creditor's petition may be presented to the court in respect of a debt or debts only if, at the time the petition is presented–

(a)   the amount of the debt, or the aggregate amount of the debts, is equal to or exceeds the bankruptcy level,

(b)   the debt, or each of the debts, is for a liquidated sum payable to the petitioning creditor, or one or more of the petitioning creditors, either immediately or at some certain, future time, and is unsecured,

(c)   the debt, or each of the debts, is a debt which the debtor appears either to be unable to pay or to have no reasonable prospect of being able to pay, and

(d)   there is no outstanding application to set aside a statutory demand served (under section 268 below) in respect of the debt or any of the debts.

267(3)   [Interpretation] A debt is not to be regarded for the purposes of subsection (2) as a debt for a liquidated sum by reason only that the amount of the debt is specified in a criminal bankruptcy order.

267(4)   ["The bankruptcy level"] "The bankruptcy level" is £750; but the Secretary of State may by order in a statutory instrument substitute any amount specified in the order for that amount or (as the case may be) for the amount which by virtue of such an order is for the time being the amount of the bankruptcy level.

267(5)   [Approval of order by Parliament] An order shall not be made under subsection (4) unless a draft of it has been laid before, and approved by a resolution of, each House of Parliament.

S. 267(1), (2)
These provisions explain what debts can be used as the basis of a creditor's petition. Basically, the debt must be undisputed and for a liquidated sum in excess of the bankruptcy level (see s. 267(4)). An unliquidated claim cannot provide the basis for a petition – *Hope v Premierpace (Europe) Ltd* [1999] B.P.I.R. 695. On whether a debt is unliquidated or disputed see *TSB v Platts (No. 2)* [1998] B.P.I.R. 284. The debtor must appear to be unable to pay or have no reasonable prospect of paying this debt. If an application is pending to set aside the statutory demand for payment of this debt, it falls outside the category of qualifying debts. For what constitutes an outstanding set-aside application see *Ariyo v Sovereign Leasing* [1998] B.P.I.R. 177. A statute-barred debt cannot form the basis for a statutory demand: *Jelly v All Type Roofing* [1997] B.C.C. 465, *Bruton v IRC* [2000] B.P.I.R. 946. Compare *Times Newspapers Ltd v Chohan* [2001] B.P.I.R. 943, *Global Finance Recoveries Ltd v Jones* [2000] B.P.I.R. 1029 and *West Bromwich Building Society v Crammer* [2002] EWHC 2618 (Ch); [2003] B.P.I.R. 783.

See also *Rio Properties Inc. v Al-Midani* [2003] B.P.I.R. 128 where the court held that a foreign gaming debt which had apparently been settled via an English law compromise could form the basis of a bankruptcy petition.

A sum due under an interim payments order made under CPR r. 25.6 is a "debt" for these purposes: *Maxwell v Bishopsgate Investment Management Ltd* [1993] T.L.R. 67. In so deciding Chadwick J. noted that the abolition of acts of bankruptcy had produced this change in the law – a final judgment was not necessary under the new bankruptcy code to justify a statutory demand. A taxed costs order can found a statutory demand – *Galloppa v Galloppa* [1999] B.P.I.R. 352. A debt arising under a regulated hire purchase agreement can found the basis for a statutory demand: *Mills v Grove Securities Ltd* [1997] B.P.I.R. 243. A joint debt owed by a partner also falls within s. 267(1) according to *Schooler v Customs and Excise* [1996] B.P.I.R. 207. Non-provable bankruptcy debts can provide the basis for a petition – *Levy v Legal Services Commission* [2000] B.P.I.R. 1065. On the status of unpaid community charge see *Re Wood* [1994] 1 C.L. 257 (1993, Tamworth County Court). The debt can be a sum due in a foreign currency according to Morritt J. in *Re a Debtor (51/SD/1991)* [1992] 1 W.L.R. 1294.

Presumably the rule in *Re McGreavy* [1950] Ch. 269, that an unpaid rates demand is a "debt" for the purposes of a bankruptcy petition, is preserved by s. 267. For discussion of the position with regard to unpaid community charges see *Preston BC v Riley* [1999] B.P.I.R. 284 (an authority on county court administration orders).

For guidance on preparing the petition see *Practice Note (Bankruptcy: Petition)* [1987] 1 W.L.R. 81.

Section 267(2)(d) must, in the opinion of Mummery J, be read as being subject to s. 270: see *Re a Debtor (No. 22 of 1993)* [1994] 1 W.L.R. 46 (sometimes cited as *Focus Insurance v A Debtor*).

S. 267(3)
This narrows the definition of a liquidated sum to exclude amounts of debts specified in criminal bankruptcy orders.

Note prospective amendment: s. 267(3) is to be repealed by CJA 1988, s. 170(2) and Sch. 16 as from a day to be appointed: see the note to s. 264.

S. 267(4), (5)
The current bankruptcy level is £750, although the Secretary of State can increase it. On whether this amount must still be outstanding at the date of the hearing: *Re Patel* [1986] 1 W.L.R. 221 (a case decided under the 1914 Act). Whether this case would be followed under the new regime is questionable – *Lilley v American Express (Europe) Ltd* [2000] B.P.I.R. 70. The courts are not favourably disposed to bankruptcy proceedings brought to recover debts slightly in excess of £750: *City Electrical Factors Ltd v Hardingham* [1996] B.P.I.R. 541. Where there is an undisputed debt clearly in excess of the statutory minimum but a balance that is disputed the petition can proceed: *TSB Bank v Platts (No. 2)* [1998] B.P.I.R. 284.

268 Definition of "inability to pay", etc.; the statutory demand

268(1) [**Interpretation of s. 267(2)(c)**] For the purposes of section 267(2)(c), the debtor appears to be unable to pay a debt if, but only if, the debt is payable immediately and either–

(a) the petitioning creditor to whom the debt is owed has served on the debtor a demand (known as "the statutory demand") in the prescribed form requiring him to pay the debt or to secure or compound for it to the satisfaction of the creditor, at least 3 weeks have elapsed since the demand was served and the demand has been neither complied with nor set aside in accordance with the rules, or

(b) execution or other process issued in respect of the debt on a judgment or order of any court in favour of the petitioning creditor, or one or more of the petitioning creditors to whom the debt is owed, has been returned unsatisfied in whole or in part.

268(2) **[Further interpretation]** For the purposes of section 267(2)(c) the debtor appears to have no reasonable prospect of being able to pay a debt if, but only if, the debt is not immediately payable and–

(a) the petitioning creditor to whom it is owed has served on the debtor a demand (also known as "the statutory demand") in the prescribed form requiring him to establish to the satisfaction of the creditor that there is a reasonable prospect that the debtor will be able to pay the debt when it falls due,

(b) at least 3 weeks have elapsed since the demand was served, and

(c) the demand has been neither complied with nor set aside in accordance with the rules.

GENERAL NOTE

This section defines "inability to pay" and "statutory demand", terms featuring in s. 267. A debtor will be deemed unable to pay a debt if he fails to meet a demand in the prescribed form served on him within three weeks – under the previous law the debtor was given only ten days' grace – or an execution for a judgment debt has been returned unsatisfied. In *Re a Debtor (No. 1 of 1987)* [1989] 1 W.L.R. 271 the Court of Appeal, confirming a ruling of Warner J, took a relaxed view of a statutory demand that contained errors as to the amount owed. The Court of Appeal refused to set aside this demand as no injustice had been done to the debtor. In so deciding the Court of Appeal departed from the position under the pre-1985 bankruptcy law and indicated that the new provisions had to be interpreted in their own context. This case is a watershed authority marking a fundamental change in attitude on the part of the courts to procedural errors in the bankruptcy process. Formerly, in the case of a defect in a bankruptcy notice the whole proceedings would be invalidated. Now that bankruptcy is viewed as a more user-friendly regime for the debtor the courts feel justified in adopting a more pragmatic stance. For a full discussion of this relaxation of judicial attitudes see Milman [1994] Conv 289–298. Thus if the debt mentioned in the demand is overstated this will not invalidate the demand (provided the undisputed element exceeds the minimum bankruptcy level): see here *Re a Debtor (490/SD/1991)* [1992] 1 W.L.R. 507 where Hoffmann J. disclaimed his earlier contrary view in *Re a Debtor (No. 10 of 1988)* [1989] 1 W.L.R. 405. Similar principles would appear to apply if part of the debt is disputed but there is an undisputed balance – failure to highlight the dispute may not be critical (*Re a Debtor (657/SD/1991)* [1993] B.C.L.C. 1280 *per* Ferris J.). Equally errors as to the degree of security enjoyed by the creditor might be overlooked: see *Re a Debtor (No. 106 of 1992), The Independent* April 20, 1992.

Bankruptcy proceedings cannot be used to go behind a determination of the Revenue General Commissioners – *Cullinane v IRC* [2000] B.P.I.R. 996.

An important point to note is that a statutory demand is a document issued by a creditor. Unlike the old bankruptcy notice it is not issued by the court and does not form part of court proceedings. This can have implications. Thus in *Re a Debtor (No. 190 of 1987), The Times* May 21, 1988 Vinelott J. held that the relieving jurisdiction in r. 7.55 was inapplicable – but in view of the more liberal attitude of the courts to procedural irregularities this hardly matters. Equally it was held in *Re a Debtor (No. 88 of 1991)* [1993] Ch. 286 that the presentation of a statutory demand is not an "action" within the meaning of s. 69 of the Solicitors Act 1974 and so the one month moratorium imposed on solicitors seeking to recover fees from debtor clients does not apply (though the moratorium would extend to the presentation of the petition). For discussion see Start (1992) 142 N.L.J. 1121 and Simmonds (1992) 26 Law. Soc. Gaz. 18.

On issue estoppel and failed set-aside applications note *Eberhardt & Co. v Mair* [1995] B.C.C. 845.

On what constitutes an unsatisfied execution within s. 268(1)(b) see *Re a Debtor (No. 340 of 1992)* [1996] 2 All E.R. 211 and *Skarzynski v Chalford Property Co. Ltd* [2001] B.P.I.R. 673.

For further details on the statutory demand, see IR 1986, rr. 6.1–6.5 and *Practice Note (Bankruptcy: Statutory Demand)* [1987] 1 W.L.R. 85. See also *Practice Note (Bankruptcy) No. 2 of 1987)* [1987] 1 W.L.R. 1424.

For security as to costs where s. 268(2) is relied upon see IR 1986, r. 6.17.

269 Creditor with security

269(1) **[Where debt not unsecured]** A debt which is the debt, or one of the debts, in respect of which a creditor's petition is presented need not be unsecured if either–

(a) the petition contains a statement by the person having the right to enforce the security that he is willing, in the event of a bankruptcy order being made, to give up his security for the benefit of all the bankrupt's creditors, or

(b) the petition is expressed not to be made in respect of the secured part of the debt and contains a statement by that person of the estimated value at the date of the petition of the security for the secured part of the debt.

269(2) **[Debt in s. 269(1)(b)]** In a case falling within subsection (1)(b) the secured and unsecured parts of the debt are to be treated for the purposes of sections 267 to 270 as separate debts.

GENERAL NOTE

Secured debts can form the basis of a creditor's petition, provided the creditor is willing to give up his security or if the petition is in respect of an unsecured part of the same debt. See *Zandfarid v BCCI* [1996] B.P.I.R. 501. Note also s. 383 here (definition of "secured debt", etc.).

See also IR 1986, rr. 6.115–6.119.

270 Expedited petition

270 In the case of a creditor's petition presented wholly or partly in respect of a debt which is the subject of a statutory demand under section 268, the petition may be presented before the end of the 3-week period there mentioned if there is a serious possibility that the debtor's property or the value of any of his property will be significantly diminished during that period and the petition contains a statement to that effect.

GENERAL NOTE

The three weeks' grace given to the debtor by s. 268 can be cut short and the petition presented prematurely if the petition alleges that there is a serious possibility of a significant fall in value of the debtor's assets. The power to expedite the petition under s. 270 can only be invoked if the statutory demand has been served – *Wehmeyer v Wehmeyer* [2001] B.P.I.R. 548. This procedure can still be invoked even though there is an extant set-aside application with respect to the statutory demand: see the ruling of Mummery J. in *Re a Debtor (No. 22 of 1993)* [1994] 1 W.L.R. 46 (sometimes cited as *Focus Insurance v A Debtor*). However, should the set-aside application succeed at the end of the day the creditor might be exposed to some sort of personal claim by the debtor, a point considered by Mummery J.

271 Proceedings on creditor's petition

271(1) **[Conditions for bankruptcy order]** The court shall not make a bankruptcy order on a creditor's petition unless it is satisfied that the debt, or one of the debts, in respect of which the petition was presented is either–

(a) a debt which, having been payable at the date of the petition or having since become payable, has been neither paid nor secured nor compounded for, or

(b) a debt which the debtor has no reasonable prospect of being able to pay when it falls due.

271(2) **[Where petition contains s. 270 statement]** In a case in which the petition contains such a statement as is required by section 270, the court shall not make a bankruptcy order until at least 3 weeks have elapsed since the service of any statutory demand under section 268.

271(3) **[Dismissal of petition]** The court may dismiss the petition if it is satisfied that the debtor is able to pay all his debts or is satisfied–

(a) that the debtor has made an offer to secure or compound for a debt in respect of which the petition is presented,

(b) that the acceptance of that offer would have required the dismissal of the petition, and

(c) that the offer has been unreasonably refused;

and, in determining for the purposes of this subsection whether the debtor is able to pay all his debts, the court shall take into account his contingent and prospective liabilities.

271(4) **[Interpretation]** In determining for the purposes of this section what constitutes a reasonable prospect that a debtor will be able to pay a debt when it falls due, it is to be assumed that the prospect given by the facts and other matters known to the creditor at the time he entered into the transaction resulting in the debt was a reasonable prospect.

Section 272	Insolvency Act 1986

271(5) [Powers of court to amend etc.] Nothing in sections 267 to 271 prejudices the power of the court, in accordance with the rules, to authorise a creditor's petition to be amended by the omission of any creditor sections had been done only by or in relation to the remaining creditors or debts.

GENERAL NOTE

If a petition is granted under IA 1986 it is followed by a bankruptcy order. The previous intermediate stage of a receiving order (BA 1914, s. 3) has been abolished. Note also IR 1986, rr. 6.18, 6.22 and 6.25 and 6.33.

S. 271(1), (2), (4)

The power of the court to make a bankruptcy order is qualified by these provisions. Note that in the event of a petition presented prematurely the court must wait until the three weeks have elapsed before making the order. The definition of when a debtor has a "reasonable prospect" of paying a debt certainly leaves a lot to be desired. On s. 271(1)(a) see the *Practice Direction* in [1986] 3 All E.R. 864 and *Artman v Artman* [1996] B.P.I.R. 511. On whether joint debts have been compounded see *Re a Bankrupt (No. 622 of 1995), The Times* June 27, 1996.

S. 271(3)

This provision states that the court may dismiss the petition if the debtor is able to meet his debts, or has made a proposal to the creditor to secure or compound the debt and it has been unreasonably refused. For discussion of the operation of this provision see *Re Gilmartin (a Bankrupt)* [1989] 1 W.L.R. 513 where Harman J. concluded that the registrar had been correct in deciding that an offer had not been unreasonably refused by the petitioner and the supporting creditors. In *Re a Debtor (No. 32 of 1993)* [1994] 1 W.L.R. 899; [1994] B.C.C. 438 it was held by Timothy Lloyd Q.C. (sitting as a deputy High Court judge) that a debtor can offer to secure or compound within the meaning of s. 271(3) where there is just a single creditor involved. However, in determining whether the creditor's refusal of the offer was unreasonable it must be established to the satisfaction of the court that no reasonable hypothetical creditor would have rejected the debtor's offer; the fact that some creditors might have accepted it is not conclusive. In *Inland Revenue v A Debtor* [1995] B.C.C. 971 the court could not be persuaded that the refusal of tax officers to accept security for a debt was unreasonable. On s. 271(3) generally see *Re a Debtor (No. 415/SD/1993)* [1994] 1 W.L.R. 917 and *King v IRC* [1996] B.P.I.R. 414. In *Re a Debtor (No. 2389 of 1989)* [1991] Ch. 326 Vinelott J. held that the proposal of a voluntary arrangement by the debtor under Pt VIII of the Act cannot be regarded as an "offer" for the purposes of s. 271(3) in that the decision on acceptance is not solely a matter for the petitioning creditor. The consequences of acceptance or refusal of such a proposal are dealt with exclusively by Pt VIII. For discussion, see Griffiths (1991) 135 Sol. Jo. 598.

S. 271(5)

This protects the discretion of the court to amend petitions, etc. Presumably this would permit consolidation of petitions or changes in the carriage of proceedings (compare the repealed BA 1914, ss. 110 and 111). See *Re Purvis* [1998] B.P.I.R. 153.

Debtor's petition

272 Grounds of debtor's petition

272(1) [Presentation to court] A debtor's petition may be presented to the court only on the grounds that the debtor is unable to pay his debts.

272(2) [Statement of debtor's affairs] The petition shall be accompanied by a statement of the debtor's affairs containing–

(a) such particulars of the debtor's creditors and of his debts and other liabilities and of his assets as may be prescribed, and

(b) such other information as may be prescribed.

GENERAL NOTE

This again is, in many senses, a new provision, though the break with the past is not as radical as it might appear at first sight. A debtor could file for his own bankruptcy under the old law – indeed, this was an act of bankruptcy. For further guidance on a debtor's petition see IR 1986, rr. 6.37–6.50. The fee for such a petition is £25 (SI 1995/2629). A deposit of

£250 is also payable to cover the costs of the official receiver. This deposit requirement does not deprive the debtor of a fundamental right of access to the court – *R. v Lord Chancellor Ex p. Lightfoot* [2000] B.P.I.R. 120. A debtor who petitions for his own bankruptcy does not thereby make a disposition of his property contrary to s. 37 of the *Matrimonial Causes Act* 1973: *Woodley v Woodley (No. 2)* [1994] 1 W.L.R. 1167.

S. 272(1)
This provision preserves a debtor's right to petition for his own bankruptcy. Note that no minimum debt is required here. The test for inability to pay debts here appears to be based upon current liquidity: *Re Coney* [1998] B.P.I.R. 333.

S. 272(2)
This provision details the content of the petition. The rules are important for clarification purposes here: see IR 1986, rr. 6.38, 6.39.

273 Appointment of insolvency practitioner by the court

273(1) **[Where court not to make bankruptcy order]** Subject to the next section, on the hearing of a debtor's petition the court shall not make a bankruptcy order if it appears to the court–

(a) that if a bankruptcy order were made the aggregate amount of the bankruptcy debts, so far as unsecured, would be less than the small bankruptcies level,

(b) that if a bankruptcy order were made, the value of the bankrupt's estate would be equal to or more than the minimum amount,

(c) that within the period of 5 years ending with the presentation of the petition the debtor has neither been adjudged bankrupt nor made a composition with his creditors in satisfaction of his debts or a scheme of arrangement of his affairs, and

(d) that it would be appropriate to appoint a person to prepare a report under section 274.

"The minimum amount" and **"the small bankruptcies level"** mean such amounts as may for the time being be prescribed for the purposes of this section.

273(2) **[Appointment of person to prepare report]** Where on the hearing of the petition, it appears to the court as mentioned in subsection (1), the court shall appoint a person who is qualified to act as an insolvency practitioner in relation to the debtor–

(a) to prepare a report under the next section, and

(b) subject to section 258(3) in Part VIII, to act in relation to any voluntary arrangement to which the report relates either as trustee or otherwise for the purpose of supervising its implementation.

GENERAL NOTE

This provision reflects the strategy of the Cork Committee, which was to use bankruptcy only as a last resort, especially where the amounts involved were small.

S. 273(1)
The power of the court to make a bankruptcy order on a debtor's petition is restricted. Where the court is satisfied that the debts do not exceed the "small bankruptcies level" (£40,000), the estate's value exceeds the "minimum amount" £4,000 (see the Insolvency Proceedings (Monetary Limits) (Amendment) Order 2004 (SI 2004/547)), and the debtor has not been in serious financial difficulties within the previous five years, it may feel it more appropriate to ask for a report as described below.

S. 273(2)
If the conditions in s. 273(1) are satisfied, the court can appoint a qualified insolvency practitioner to prepare a s. 274 report, and to act as supervisor of a voluntary arrangement.
    See also IR 1986, r. 6.44.

274 Action on report of insolvency practitioner

274(1) [**Report to court**] A person appointed under section 273 shall inquire into the debtor's affairs and, within such period as the court may direct, shall submit a report to the court stating whether the debtor is willing, for the purposes of Part VIII, to make a proposal for a voluntary arrangement.

274(2) [**Contents of report**] A report which states that the debtor is willing as above mentioned shall also state–

(a) whether, in the opinion of the person making the report, a meeting of the debtor's creditors should be summoned to consider the proposal, and

(b) if in that person's opinion such a meeting should be summoned, the date on which, and time and place at which, he proposes the meetings should be held.

274(3) [**Powers of court**] On considering a report under this section the court may–

(a) without any application, make an interim order under section 252, if it thinks that it is appropriate to do so for the purpose of facilitating the consideration and implementation of the debtor's proposal, or

(b) if it thinks it would be inappropriate to make such an order, make a bankruptcy order.

274(4) [**Cessation of interim order**] An interim order by virtue of this section ceases to have effect at the end of such period as the court may specify for the purpose of enabling the debtor's proposal to be considered by his creditors in accordance with the applicable provisions of Part VIII.

274(5) [**Summoning of meeting**] Where it has been reported to the court under this section that a meeting of the debtor's creditors should be summoned, the person making the report shall, unless the court otherwise directs, summon that meeting for the time, date and place proposed in his report.

The meeting is then deemed to have been summoned under section 257 in Part VIII, and subsections (2) and (3) of that section, and sections 258 to 263 apply accordingly.

S. 274(1), (2)
If the court makes a s. 273 appointment, the appointee must investigate the debtor's affairs to see whether a viable proposal for a voluntary arrangement (see ss. 252–263 above) can be constructed and, if so, whether a creditors' meeting should be held. Where the court appoints an insolvency practitioner under s. 273(2) to prepare and submit a report under s. 274 the court must, on submission of that report, pay to the practitioner a fee of £310 (which is inclusive of VAT): see the Insolvency Proceedings (Fees) Order 2004 (SI 2004/593).
A copy of an s. 274 must be sent to the FSA where appropriate – FSMA 2000, s. 374(3).

S. 274(3)
This maps out the court's options on receiving the above report – these are to make either an interim order with a view to facilitating a voluntary arrangement or a bankruptcy order.

S. 274(4)
This provision describes the duration of an interim order made under s. 274(3).

S. 274(5)
This makes provision for any meeting of creditors which has to be held to consider the voluntary arrangement.

275 Summary administration *[repealed]*

275(1) [**Issue of certificate**] *Where on the hearing of a debtor's petition the court makes a bankruptcy order and the case is as specified in the next subsection, the court shall, if it appears to it appropriate to do so, issue a certificate for the summary administration of the bankrupt's estate.*

275(2) *[Case for issue of certificate]* That case is where it appears to the court–

(a) that if a bankruptcy order were made the aggregate amount of the bankruptcy debts so far as unsecured would be less than the small bankruptcies level (within the meaning given by section 273), and

(b) that within the period of 5 years ending with the presentation of the petition the debtor has neither been adjudged bankrupt nor made a composition with his creditors in satisfaction of his debts or a scheme of arrangement of his affairs,

whether the bankruptcy order is made because it does not appear to the court as mentioned in section 273(1)(b) or (d), or it is made because the court thinks it would be inappropriate to make an interim order under section 252.

275(3) *[Revocation of certificate by court]* The court may at any time revoke a certificate issued under this section if it appears to it that, on any grounds existing at the time the certificate was issued, the certificate ought not to have been issued.

GENERAL NOTE

Editor's note – summary administration is to be repealed from April 1, 2004 – see s. 269 and Sch. 23 EA 2002.

These provisions relating to certificates for summary administration must be viewed in the light of s. 289(5) and 297. The small bankruptcies level has been fixed at £20,000: see note to s. 273. For procedural matters see IR 1986, rr. 6.48–6.50.

S. 275(1), (2)

In cases of small bankruptcy arising out of a debtor's petition, the court, if it is satisfied that the conditions in s. 275(2) are present, must issue a certificate for summary administration. This possibility was covered by BA 1914, s. 129.

S. 275(3)

Such a certificate can be revoked if it was wrongfully issued. See also IR 1986, r. 6.50 and Form 6.31 here.

Other cases for special consideration

276 Default in connection with voluntary arrangement

276(1) **[Conditions for s. 264(1)(c) bankruptcy order]** The court shall not make a bankruptcy order on a petition under section 264(1)(c) (supervisor of, or person bound by, voluntary arrangement proposed and approved) unless it is satisfied–

(a) that the debtor has failed to comply with his obligations under the voluntary arrangement, or

(b) that information which was false or misleading in any material particular or which contained material omissions–

  (i) was contained in any statement of affairs or other document supplied by the debtor under Part VIII to any person, or
  (ii) was otherwise made available by the debtor to his creditors at or in connection with a meeting summoned under that Part, or

(c) that the debtor has failed to do all such things as may for the purposes of the voluntary arrangement have been reasonably required of him by the supervisor of the arrangement.

276(2) **[Expenses]** Where a bankruptcy order is made on a petition under section 264(1)(c), any expenses properly incurred as expenses of the administration of the voluntary arrangement in question shall be a first charge on the bankrupt's estate.

S. 276(1)

This allows the court to make a bankruptcy order where a debtor has failed to fulfil his obligations under a voluntary arrangement set up by virtue of ss. 252–263. Material omissions in the proposal, etc., may also justify this course of action – *Re Tack* [2000] B.P.I.R. 164. On s. 276(1)(b) and the continuing duty of disclosure see *Somji v. Cadbury Schweppes plc* [2001] B.P.I.R. 172. The fact that the debtor is not to blame for the failure of the IVA is irrelevant: *Re Keenan* [1998] B.P.I.R. 205. Nor indeed is it a bar to a s. 276 petition that the debtor has remedied the default by the time the petition is heard – *Carter-Knight v Peat* [2000] B.P.I.R. 268. A default petition can be presented by the supervisor even though the time period specified in the IVA has expired – *Harris v Gross* [2001] B.P.I.R. 586. Where an IVA is set aside under s. 276 it is not a nullity *ab initio* – see *Cooper v Official Receiver* [2002] EWHC 1970 (Ch), [2003] B.P.I.R. 55.

S. 276(2)
Where the court takes this drastic step, the expenses already incurred in connection with the scheme become a first charge on the bankrupt's estate.

277 Petition based on criminal bankruptcy order

277(1) [Duty of court] Subject to section 266(3), the court shall make a bankruptcy order on a petition under section 264(1)(d) on production of a copy of the criminal bankruptcy order on which the petition is based.

This does not apply if it appears to the court that the criminal bankruptcy order has been rescinded on appeal.

277(2) [Effect of appeal pending] Subject to the provisions of this Part, the fact that an appeal is pending against any conviction by virtue of which a criminal bankruptcy order was made does not affect any proceedings on a petition under section 264(1)(d) based on that order.

277(3) [When appeal is pending] For the purposes of this section, an appeal against a conviction is pending–

(a) in any case, until the expiration of the period of 28 days beginning with the date of conviction;

(b) if notice of appeal to the Court of Appeal is given during that period and during that period the appellant notifies the official receiver of it, until the determination of the appeal and thereafter for so long as an appeal to the House of Lords is pending within the meaning of section 40(5) of the Powers of Criminal Courts Act 1973.

GENERAL NOTE

This section deals with petitions arising out of criminal bankruptcy orders. Criminal bankruptcy orders were first introduced in 1972, and the legislation currently in force is the Powers of the Criminal Courts Act 1973, ss. 39, 40. However, the power to make such orders was abolished by CJA 1988, s. 101, with effect from April 3, 1989 (see SI 1989/264 (C. 8)), and so it is most unlikely that there will be any occasion to invoke the provisions of s. 264(1)(d) or s. 277 in the future.

Criminal bankruptcy orders were designed to punish offenders who caused financial loss to others exceeding £15,000; but they were rarely used – there were a mere 150 in the first five years of the scheme. The Cork Committee regarded them as anomalous, and took the view that they should have no future in insolvency law (see the *Report*, Ch. 41). The Committee called for the whole system of criminal bankruptcy to be re-examined (see paras 1722–1724); and, although the ensuing review by the Hodgson Committee in 1984 recommended, with some reservations, that it should be retained, the government went ahead and abolished it in 1988.

A number of criminal bankruptcy orders remain in force, however, and will continue to do so for some time. Accordingly, although the present section, and the various other sections of IA 1986 which refer to such orders, have also been repealed by CJA 1988, s. 170(2) and Sch. 16, the repeal is prospective only and will not come into effect until a day to be appointed. (See also the note to s. 264).

Commencement and duration of bankruptcy; discharge

278 Commencement and continuance

278 The bankruptcy of an individual against whom a bankruptcy order has been made–

(a) commences with the day on which the order is made, and

(b) continues until the individual is discharged under the following provisions of this Chapter.

GENERAL NOTE

Bankruptcy commences at the date of the order (and not when the petition was presented), and lasts until discharge. See IR 1986, rr. 6.34 and 6.46.

279 Duration

279(1) **[Discharge from bankruptcy in one year]** A bankrupt is discharged from bankruptcy at the end of the period of one year beginning with the date on which the bankruptcy commences.

279(2) **[Earlier discharge on official receiver's notice]** If before the end of that period the official receiver files with the court a notice stating that investigation of the conduct and affairs of the bankrupt under section 289 is unnecessary or concluded, the bankrupt is discharged when the notice is filed.

279(3) **[Order that discharge period ceases to run]** On the application of the official receiver or the trustee of a bankrupt's estate, the court may order that the period specified in subsection (1) shall cease to run until–

(a) the end of a specified period, or

(b) the fulfilment of a specified condition.

279(4) **[When order may be made]** The court may make an order under subsection (3) only if satisfied that the bankrupt has failed or is failing to comply with an obligation under this Part.

279(5) **["Condition" in s. 279(3)(b)]** In subsection (3)(b) "condition" includes a condition requiring that the court be satisfied of something.

279(6) **[Non-application of s. 279(1)–(5)]** In the case of an individual who is adjudged bankrupt on a petition under section 264(1)(d)–

(a) subsections (1) to (5) shall not apply, and

(b) the bankrupt is discharged from bankruptcy by an order of the court under section 280.

279(7) **[Power of court to annul bankruptcy order]** This section is without prejudice to any power of the court to annul a bankruptcy order.

GENERAL NOTE

These new provisions on discharge, which were introduced by s. 256 of EA 2002, come into effect in April 2004. These provisions must be read in the light of Sch. 19 to EA 2002 which makes transitional provisions. The text of the current s. 279 which ceases to have effect in April 2004 is reproduced immediately below.

279 Duration

279(1) *[Discharge from bankruptcy] Subject as follows, a bankrupt is discharged from bankruptcy–*

(a) *in the case of an individual who was adjudged bankrupt on a petition under section 264(1)(d) or who had been an undischarged bankrupt at any time in the period of 15 years ending with the commencement of the bankruptcy, by an order of the court under the section next following, and*

(b) *in any other case, by the expiration of the relevant period under this section.*

279(2) *[Relevant period] That period is as follows–*

(a) *where a certificate for the summary administration of the bankrupt's estate has been issued and is not revoked before the bankrupt's discharge, the period of 2 years beginning with the commencement of the bankruptcy, and*

(b) *in any other case, the period of 3 years beginning with the commencement of the bankruptcy.*

279(3) *[Court order] Where the court is satisfied on the application of the official receiver that an undischarged bankrupt in relation to whom subsection (1)(b) applies has failed or is failing to comply with any of his obligations under this Part, the court may order that the relevant period under this section shall*

Section 280 *Insolvency Act 1986*

cease to run for such period, or until the fulfilment of such conditions (including a condition requiring the court to be satisfied as to any matter), as may be specified in the order.

279(4) **[Power of annulment]** *This section is without prejudice to any power of the court to annul a bankruptcy order.*

Automatic discharge, which was pioneered in 1976 is now widely accepted as a feature of bankruptcy regulation, in spite of concerns raised by the Cork Committee (Cmnd 8558, para. 607).

For further provisions on discharge see IR 1986, rr. 6.215–6.222.

S. 279(1)
This introduces the new one-year maximum period before discharge takes effect. It is a significant reduction on the existing three-year period, though not as great as the government intended when it initially proposed six months! When assessing this discharge period it must be borne in mind that discharge does not for the most part mean that the powers of the trustee *vis-à-vis* the estate have come to an end. Realisation powers and income payments matters can continue for some time thereafter.

S. 279(2)
Discharge can take place before the one year is up if the official receiver gives the green light.

S. 279(3)–(5)
These deal with the converse situation where the trustee or official receiver wish to extend the one-year period for a specified period or until a condition is satisfied. This will only happen if the bankrupt has failed to fulfil his obligations. Cases decided under the former s. 279(3) will continue to be instructive – see here *Hardy v Focus Insurance Co. Ltd* [1997] B.P.I.R. 77, *Holmes v Official Receiver* [1996] B.C.C. 246, *Jacobs v Official Receiver* [1999] 1 W.L.R. 619 and *Bagnall v Official Receiver* [2003] EWHC 1398 (Ch).

S. 279(6)
This deals with a special (and extremely rare) case involving criminal bankruptcy.

S. 279(7)
This provision governing discharge does not affect the power of the court to annul a bankruptcy order – see s. 282.

280 Discharge by order of the court

280(1) **[Application to court]** An application for an order of the court discharging an individual from bankruptcy in a case falling within section 279(6) may be made by the bankrupt at any time after the end of the period of 5 years beginning with the date on which the bankruptcy commences.

280(2) **[Powers of court]** On an application under this section the court may–

(a) refuse to discharge the bankrupt from bankruptcy,

(b) make an order discharging him absolutely, or

(c) make an order discharging him subject to such conditions with respect to any income which may subsequently become due to him, or with respect to property devolving upon him, or acquired by him, after his discharge, as may be specified in the order.

280(3) **[Commencement of effect of order]** The court may provide for an order falling within subsection (2)(b) or (c) to have immediate effect or to have its effect suspended for such period, or until the fulfilment of such conditions (including a condition requiring the court to be satisfied as to any matter), as may be specified in the order.

GENERAL NOTE

Minor textual changes were made by s. 269 and Sch. 23 EA 2002.

S. 280(1)
This provision deals with the situation where an undischarged bankrupt applies to the court for his discharge. Automatic discharge is not available where a person was made bankrupt as a result of a criminal bankruptcy order or where he had

experienced an earlier bankruptcy within the 15 years prior to the commencement of the present bankruptcy. In these cases he must wait for five years after the commencement of the bankruptcy to elapse before applying to the court for his discharge. See also IR 1986, rr. 6.215–6.223.

There is no provision in the present Act for the automatic review of cases every five years by the official receiver, as was required by IA 1976, s. 8. However, this is immaterial, as automatic discharge under s. 279 is now the general rule.

S. 280(2), (3)
On such an application the court has a variety of options open to it, including the grant of conditional or suspended discharges. The Secretary of State can appeal against a discharge order, see IR 1986, r. 7.48.

281 Effect of discharge

281(1) [Discharge qualified release] Subject as follows, where a bankrupt is discharged, the discharge releases him from all the bankruptcy debts, but has no effect–

(a) on the functions (so far as they remain to be carried out) of the trustee of his estate, or

(b) on the operation, for the purposes of the carrying out of those functions, of the provisions of this Part;

and, in particular, discharge does not affect the right of any creditor of the bankrupt to prove in the bankruptcy for any debt from which the bankrupt is released.

281(2) [Enforcement of security] Discharge does not affect the right of any secured creditor of the bankrupt to enforce his security for the payment of a debt from which the bankrupt is released.

281(3) [Fraud etc.] Discharge does not release the bankrupt from any bankruptcy debt which he incurred in respect of, or forbearance in respect of which was secured by means of, any fraud or fraudulent breach of trust to which he was a party.

281(4) [Fines, other penalties] Discharge does not release the bankrupt from any liability in respect of a fine imposed for an offence or from any liability under a recognisance except, in the case of a penalty imposed for an offence under an enactment relating to the public revenue or of a recognisance, with the consent of the Treasury.

281(4A) [Confiscation order] In subsection (4) the reference to a fine includes a reference to a confiscation order under Part 2, 3 or 4 of the Proceeds of Crime Act 2002.

281(5) [Debts re damages etc.] Discharge does not, except to such extent and on such conditions as the court may direct, release the bankrupt from any bankruptcy debt which–

(a) consists in a liability to pay damages for negligence, nuisance or breach of a statutory, contractual or other duty, or to pay damages by virtue of Part I of the Consumer Protection Act 1987, being in either case damages in respect of personal injuries to any person, or

(b) arises under any order made in family proceedings.

281(6) [Other bankruptcy debts] Discharge does not release the bankrupt from such other bankruptcy debts, not being debts provable in his bankruptcy, as are prescribed.

281(7) [Liability as surety] Discharge does not release any person other than the bankrupt from any liability (whether as partner or co-trustee of the bankrupt or otherwise) from which the bankrupt is released by the discharge, or from any liability as surety for the bankrupt or as a person in the nature of such a surety.

281(8) [Definitions] In this section–

"family proceedings" means–

(a) family proceedings within the meaning of the Magistrates Courts Act 1980 and any proceedings which would be such proceedings but for section 65(1)(ii) of that Act (proceedings for variation of order for periodical payments); and

(b) family proceedings within the meaning of Part V of the Matrimonial and Family Proceedings Act 1984.

"fine" means the same as in the Magistrates' Courts Act 1980; and

"personal injuries" includes death and any disease or other impairment of a person's physical or mental condition.

S. 281(1)

As a general rule, discharge releases the bankrupt from liability in respect of "bankruptcy debts" (see s. 382). However, any residual functions of the trustee are not to be affected, and creditors in respect of whose debts the bankrupt has been released by the discharge may still prove in the bankruptcy. See further IR 1986, r. 6.223. A discharged bankrupt cannot escape the attentions of a trustee by seeking an IVA as at this stage he is no longer a "debtor" for the purposes of s. 253 – see *Wright v Official Receiver* [2001] B.P.I.R. 196.

Note also the effect of discharge on disqualifications, see for example s. 427(2)(a).

S. 281(2)–(6), (8)

In s. 281(5)(a) the words "or to pay damages by virtue of Part I of the Consumer Protection Act 1987, being in either case" have been substituted by the Consumer Protection Act 1987. Subsection (5) has been amended by the Children Act 1989 which removed the words "or in domestic proceedings" from the original text. Subsection (8) now has a new definition of "family proceedings" provided by the Children Act 1989.

These provisions deal with the exceptions to the general release in s. 281(1). Note especially IR 1986, r. 6.223 to explain the word "prescribed" in s. 281(6). Security enforcement rights are preserved notwithstanding the release of the debt. Debts connected with fraud or breach of trust survive, as does liability in respect of a fine (see s. 281(8)) or similar penalty (note the exception for fines, etc., in respect of public revenue offences). On the meaning of "fraud" for the purposes of s. 281(3) see *Masters v Leaver* [2000] B.P.I.R. 284, *Mander v Evans* [2001] B.P.I.R. 902 and *Woodland Ferrari v UCL Group Retirement Benefits Scheme* [2002] B.P.I.R. 1270. Note here *Anglo Manx Group Ltd v Aitken* [2002] B.P.I.R. 215 where the significance of limitation periods continuing to run throughout the period of bankruptcy was emphasised. Liability to pay damages in respect of personal injuries (see s. 281(8)), or liability arising from family or domestic proceedings (see s. 281(8)) is not released unless the court so directs. There is also no release in respect of debts not provable in bankruptcy. Note that the list of exceptions in BA 1914, s. 28 has been widened. The Cork Committee recommended that there should be no release of fines on discharge, but by a majority voted against allowing claims for personal injury to survive – see the *Report*, paras 1330 and 1333 respectively. Both items, however, have been added to the list of exceptions.

Section 281(4) has effect as if the reference to a fine included a reference to a confiscation order (an extended meaning introduced by CJA 1988). Section 281(4A) was inserted by POCA 2002 Sch. 11, para. 16(2).

S. 281(7)

Although the bankrupt may be released from liability for a debt, any co-obligor (*e.g.* a partner of the bankrupt, or co-trustee, etc.) and any person liable as surety for him is not so released.

281A Post-discharge restrictions

281A Schedule 4A to this Act (bankruptcy restrictions order and bankruptcy restrictions undertaking) shall have effect.

General Note

This new provision is introduced via s. 257 of EA 2002 with effect from April 2004. It directs our attention to the new Sch. 4A. In order to reassure the public concerned about the risks posed by early discharge the government introduced a degree of balance in the form of a bankruptcy restriction order which will be applied to those bankrupts deemed not to be "honest" or, more accurately, those whose conduct falls within sub-paras (a)–(m) of para. 2(2) in Sch. 4A. We thus have a return to a former manifestation in bankruptcy law under which legal distinctions were drawn between types of bankrupt. Looking at (a)–(m) there are some predictable *indiciae* of misbehaviour – note the reappearance of now decriminalised conduct in (a) and (j). Of the other *indiciae* one can envisage a flood of litigation clarifying the ambit of these provisions – para. (k) looks a prime candidate. Sub-paragraph (e) will raise many concerns and guidance may have to be drawn from any jurisprudence under s. 342A. Serial bankrupts will fall foul of para. 2(3).

Applications for a BRO must normally be made within one year of the bankruptcy, though the court can grant an extension. The possibility of an interim order is provided for by para. 5 for extreme cases.

Where the court grants a BRO against a bankrupt a series of restrictions will be applied for a period of not less than 2 years and up to 15 years after the grant of the order (see Sch. 21 to the 2002 Act). In anticipation of a flood of cases disabling the courts the possibility of securing restrictions via an undertakings procedure is provided for by para. 7.

All BROs and BRUs should be listed in a public register – Sch. 4A, para. 12.

282 Court's power to annul bankruptcy order

282(1) **[Power of annulment]** The court may annul a bankruptcy order if it at any time appears to the court–

(a) that, on any grounds existing at the time the order was made, the order ought not to have been made, or

(b) that, to the extent required by the rules, the bankruptcy debts and the expenses of the bankruptcy have all, since the making of the order, been either paid or secured for to the satisfaction of the court.

282(2) **[Where petition under s. 264(1)(a), (b), (c)]** The court may annul a bankruptcy order made against an individual on a petition under paragraph (a), (b) or (c) of section 264(1) if it at any time appears to the court, on an application by the Official Petitioner–

(a) that the petition was pending at a time when a criminal bankruptcy order was made against the individual or was presented after such an order was so made, and

(b) no appeal is pending (within the meaning of section 277) against the individual's conviction of any offence by virtue of which the criminal bankruptcy order was made;

and the court shall annul a bankruptcy order made on a petition under section 264(1)(d) if it at any time appears to the court that the criminal bankruptcy order on which the petition was based has been rescinded in consequence of an appeal.

282(3) **[Annulment whether or not discharged]** The court may annul a bankruptcy order whether or not the bankrupt has been discharged from the bankruptcy.

282(4) **[Effect of annulment]** Where the court annuls a bankruptcy order (whether under this section or under section 261 or 263D in Part VIII)–

(a) any sale or other disposition of property, payment made or other thing duly done, under any provision in this Group of Parts, by or under the authority of the official receiver or a trustee of the bankrupt's estate or by the court is valid, but

(b) if any of the bankrupt's estate is then vested, under any such provision, in such a trustee, it shall vest in such person as the court may appoint or, in default of any such appointment, revert to the bankrupt on such terms (if any) as the court may direct;

and the court may include in its order such supplemental provisions as may be authorised by the rules.

282(5) **[Repealed from April 1, 2004]**

S. 282(1), (3)

The court can annul a bankruptcy order if it should never have been made (compare here *Re a Bankrupt (No. 622 of 1995), The Times* June 27, 1996, *Henwood v Customs and Excise* [1998] B.P.I.R. 339 and *Hope v Premierpace (Europe) Ltd* [1999] B.P.I.R. 695) and also if the bankrupt has paid all his debts and bankruptcy expenses to the extent required by the rules: see IR 1986, r. 6.211. The question of annulment rests upon the discretion of the court: *Askew v Peter Dominic Ltd* [1997] B.P.I.R. 163; *Re Coney* [1998] B.P.I.R. 333: *Skarzynski v Chalford Property Co. Ltd* [2001] B.P.I.R. 673. But the court stressed in *Royal Bank of Scotland v The Debtor* [1996] B.P.I.R. 478 that there is no inherent power of annulment beyond the statutory power. Moreover the s. 375 review jurisdiction cannot be used to circumvent the stringent conditions of s. 282 – *IRC v Robinson* [1999] B.P.I.R. 329. For the distinction between rescission and annulment see *Hoare v IRC* [2002] EWHC 755 (Ch); [2002] B.P.I.R. 986. For discussion of the role of the court under these distinct jurisdictions see *Hunt v Peasegood* [2001] B.P.I.R. 76. Annulment can be granted even though discharge has occurred. The Secretary of State can appeal against an annulment order, see IR 1986, r. 7.48. An annulment of a bankruptcy order was refused by Warner J. in *Re Robertson (a Bankrupt)* [1989] 1 W.L.R. 1139 where there had been failure to prove all debts. See also *Artman v Artman* [1996] B.P.I.R. 511 (annulment refused). The court can annul conditionally – *Engel v Peri* [2002] EWHC 799 (Ch); [2002] B.P.I.R. 961.

Harman J. considered the nature of the jurisdiction to annul in *Re a Debtor (No. 68 of 1992)* [1993] T.L.R. 69. Here the point was made that on an annulment hearing under s. 282 it was not possible for the court to consider evidence which had been unavailable to the court which had made the bankruptcy in the first place. Relevant considerations on an annulment application were discussed in *Lloyds v Waters* [2001] B.P.I.R. 698. For an unsuccessful s. 282 application see *Shamash v IRC* [2002] B.P.I.R. 189.

Bankruptcy is a class remedy and the court should not annul without a proper investigation of the facts – *Housiaux v Customs and Excise Commissioners* [2003] EWCA Civ 257; [2003] B.P.I.R. 858.

On going behind a default judgment for the purposes of s. 282(1)(a) see *Royal Bank of Scotland v Farley* [1996] B.P.I.R. 638. In *Re a Debtor (No. 169 of 1997)* (unreported but noted in *Current Law Week* August 14, 1998) a county court judge annulled a bankruptcy order under s. 282(1)(a) because the consent order upon which the petition has been based should never have been made.

There is no provision in s. 282 requiring the annulment order to be gazetted and published in a local paper, as was necessary under BA 1914, s. 29(3): now see IR 1986, r. 6.212. Formerly an application for annulment had to be supplemented with a request for rescission of the receiving order under what is now s. 375(1). With the abolition of receiving orders this is no longer necessary. For a Court of Appeal authority on rescission of receiving orders, which might have some impact on judicial practice in cases of annulment of bankruptcy orders, see *Re a Debtor (No. 707 of 1985)*, *The Times* January 21, 1988.

Under BA 1914, s. 29, the application for annulment had to be made by "any person interested". This requirement, which caused problems in *Re Beesley Ex p. Beesley v The Official Receiver* [1975] 1 All E.R. 385, has been dropped. See here *F v F* [1994] 1 F.L.R. 359 (application by wife of debtor). For discussion, see Miller (1994) 10 I.L. & P. 66. A similar change has been made with regard to s. 375.

For further provisions on annulment, see IR 1986, rr. 6.206–6.214. For an illuminating review of this jurisdiction see Briggs and Sims [2002] *Insolvency Lawyer* 2.

S. 282(2)

This provision confirms the supremacy of the system of criminal bankruptcy over ordinary bankruptcy cases. The subsection also allows the court to annul a bankruptcy order which was granted on a petition based on a criminal bankruptcy order if that latter order has been rescinded on appeal.

Note prospective amendment: s. 282(2) is to be repealed by CJA 1988, s. 170(2) and Sch. 16 as from a day to be appointed; see the note to s. 264.

S. 282(4)

This deals with the practical effects of annulment – dispositions of property, etc. carried out by a trustee are valid. On annulment, the court can order the revesting of the property in the former bankrupt or some other person. For the rules on liability for costs of the trustee where the bankruptcy is annulled see *Butterworth v Soutter* [2000] B.P.I.R. 582. For the effect of annulment on prosecutions for bankruptcy offices, see s. 350(2). On annulment a bankruptcy petition does not necessarily lapse – *Choudhury v IRC* [2000] B.P.I.R. 246. This conclusion was reached notwithstanding the terms of r. 6.213.

S. 282(5)

This provision (which dealt with the implications of annulment) was repealed by EA 2002, s. 269 and Sch. 23 with effect from April 1, 2004.

CHAPTER II

PROTECTION OF BANKRUPT'S ESTATE AND INVESTIGATION OF HIS AFFAIRS

283 Definition of bankrupt's estate

283(1) **[Bankrupt's estate]** Subject as follows, a bankrupt's estate for the purposes of any of this Group of Parts comprises–

(a) all property belonging to or vested in the bankrupt at the commencement of the bankruptcy, and

(b) any property which by virtue of any of the following provisions of this Part is comprised in that estate or is treated as falling within the preceding paragraph.

283(2) **[Non-application of s. 283(1)]** Subsection (1) does not apply to—

(a) such tools, books, vehicles and other items of equipment as are necessary to the bankrupt for use personally by him in his employment, business or vocation;

(b) such clothing, bedding, furniture, household equipment and provisions as are necessary for satisfying the basic domestic needs of the bankrupt and his family.

This subsection is subject to section 308 in Chapter IV (certain excluded property reclaimable by trustee).

283(3) **[Further non-application of s. 283(1)]** Subsection (1) does not apply to—

(a) property held by the bankrupt on trust for any other person, or

(b) the right of nomination to a vacant ecclesiastical benefice.

283(3A) **[Further non-application of s. 283(1)]** Subject to section 308A in Chapter IV, subsection (1) does not apply to—

(a) a tenancy which is an assured tenancy or an assured agricultural occupancy, within the meaning of Part I of the Housing Act 1988, and the terms of which inhibit an assignment as mentioned in section 127(5) of the Rent Act 1977, or

(b) a protected tenancy, within the meaning of the Rent Act 1977, in respect of which, by virtue of any provision of Part IX of that Act, no premium can lawfully be required as a condition of assignment, or

(c) a tenancy of a dwelling-house by virtue of which the bankrupt is, within the meaning of the Rent (Agriculture) Act 1976, a protected occupier of the dwelling-house, and the terms of which inhibit an assignment as mentioned in section 127(5) of the Rent Act 1977, or

(d) a secure tenancy, within the meaning of Part IV of the Housing Act 1985, which is not capable of being assigned, except in the cases mentioned in section 91(3) of that Act.

283(4) **[References to property]** References in any of this Group of Parts to property, in relation to a bankrupt, include references to any power exercisable by him over or in respect of property except in so far as the power is exercisable over or in respect of property not for the time being comprised in the bankrupt's estate and—

(a) is so exercisable at a time after either the official receiver has had his release in respect of that estate under section 299(2) in Chapter III or a meeting summoned by the trustee of that estate under section 331 in Chapter IV has been held, or

(b) cannot be so exercised for the benefit of the bankrupt;

and a power exercisable over or in respect of property is deemed for the purposes of any of this Group of Parts to vest in the person entitled to exercise it at the time of the transaction or event by virtue of which it is exercisable by that person (whether or not it becomes so exercisable at that time).

283(5) **[Property in bankrupt's estate]** For the purposes of any such provision in this Group of Parts, property comprised in a bankrupt's estate is so comprised subject to the rights of any person other than the bankrupt (whether as a secured creditor of the bankrupt or otherwise) in relation thereto, but disregarding—

(a) any rights in relation to which a statement such as is required by section 269(1)(a) was made in the petition on which the bankrupt was adjudged bankrupt, and

(b) any rights which have been otherwise given up in accordance with the rules.

283(6) **[Other enactments]** This section has effect subject to the provisions of any enactment not contained in this Act under which any property is to be excluded from a bankrupt's estate.

General Note

The major change effected by this provision is the abolition of the doctrine of reputed ownership. This doctrine, which could trace its origins back to 1623, stated that if the debtor appeared to be in possession of property which secretly belonged to another, that would boost his creditworthiness, and therefore his creditors should be entitled to treat that property as part of the bankrupt's estate. The rationale of this doctrine, which applied only to traders who became

Section 283 *Insolvency Act 1986*

bankrupt, was criticised by Parke B long ago in *Belcher v Bellamy* (1848) 2 Exch. 303. It did not reflect commercial practices and it appeared particularly inappropriate with the growth of hire-purchase and consumer credit in the twentieth century. Both the courts and Parliament began to curtail the scope of the doctrine: see, *e.g. Consumer Credit Act* 1974, s. 192(3) and Sch. 4, para. 6. The doctrine did not apply in Ireland and many Commonwealth jurisdictions. Accordingly, calls for abolition were made by the Cork Committee (*Report*, 1093) and the White Paper, para. 116. Incidentally, the abolition of the doctrine may throw up difficulties – the problem of title retention clauses which has troubled corporate insolvency law over the past decade might now raise its ugly head. The doctrine of reputed ownership which applied only to personal and not corporate insolvency law at least served to keep that problem at bay in the law of bankruptcy. The doctrine of "relation back" of the trustee's title to the date of the act of bankruptcy has also been abandoned in the wake of the new procedures for bankruptcy. See *Re Dennis* [1996] B.P.I.R. 106 for the significance of this change. For general discussion of the new rules on the bankrupt's estate see Milman (1988) 4 I.L. & P. 71. On the entitlement of the estate to claim windfalls see *Trustee of F C Jones v Jones* [1996] B.P.I.R. 644. Note that property subject to a restraint, etc. order under the Proceeds of Crime Act 2002 is also excluded from the estate – POCA 2002, s. 417.

S. 283(1)
This section identifies the bankrupt's estate. Note the possible impact of ss. 307–309 here and the general definition of "property" in s. 436. Notwithstanding the wide terms of s. 283(1)(a) personal correspondence of the debtor does not vest in the trustee – *Haig v Aitken* [2000] B.P.I.R. 462.

For the commencement of the bankruptcy, see s. 278(a).

S. 283(2), (3)
These provisions list those items that are excluded from the estate. Section 283(2) again reflects a change in the law. It was felt that a bankrupt ought to be allowed to keep a greater range of personal possessions than BA 1914 permitted – see the Cork *Report*, para. 1113. Thus, the £250 limit has been dropped. It had been overtaken by inflation and discriminated against debtors with capital-intensive businesses. Vehicles are now included among the exceptions, as are general items of business equipment. Thus the old restrictive authorities on "tools" such as *Re Sherman* [1916] W.N. 26 have lost much of their importance. On the other hand, such property may now be "replaced" by the trustee under s. 308. Trust property is not included in the estate: see *Re Tout & Finch Ltd* [1954] 1 W.L.R. 178 and *Re McKeown* [1974] N.I. 226. Funds held on trust for IVA creditors all come within this exception – *Re Coath* [2000] B.P.I.R. 981. See also *Abrahams v Trustee of Property of Abrahams* [1999] B.P.I.R. 637 (bankrupt holds lottery win on resulting trust for ticket purchaser). For a more complex question relating to a possible trust see *Rooney v Cardona* [1999] B.P.I.R. 291. Where the trustee in bankruptcy realises trust property with the consent of the beneficiary he may be entitled to realisation costs out of the trust fund – *Re Sobey* [1999] B.P.I.R. 1009. Section 283(3) repeats BA 1914, s. 38(b).

Certain "personal" claims may also be excluded from the estate – for discussion see *Collins v Official Receiver* [1996] B.P.I.R. 552; *Lang v McKenna* [1997] B.P.I.R. 340; *Re Bell* [1998] B.P.I.R. 26. Compare *Cork v Rawlins* [2001] B.P.I.R. 222.

Note that pensions benefits can be excluded from the estate if they have been lawfully forfeited. For the position at common law see *Aitchison and Tuivaiti v NZI Life Superannuation Nominees* [1996] B.P.I.R. 215 and *Re The Trusts of the Scientific Investment Pension Plan* [1998] B.P.I.R. 410. The position here is now governed by the Pensions Act 1995 and the Pensions and Welfare Reform Act 1999.

S. 283(3A)
Subsection (3A) was introduced into s. 283 by s. 117(1) of the Housing Act 1988. Its effect is to add assured tenancies, protected tenancies, protected occupancies of dwelling houses and secure tenancies to the list of exclusions from the bankrupt's estate. Continuation tenancies are outside this exclusion – *Rothschild v Bell* [1999] B.P.I.R. 300. This provision has to be read however in the light of the newly introduced s. 308A which enables the trustee to claim such tenancies by giving notice to the bankrupt.

S. 283(4)
This deals with rights to exercise powers over the property of others. Note *Clarkson v Clarkson* [1994] B.C.C. 921.

S. 283(5)
Third-party rights over the bankrupt's property are preserved, unless those rights have been surrendered. Rights in this context means property rights (including equitable interests) – *Mountney v Treharne* [2002] EWCA Civ 1174.

S. 283(6)
Property may be excluded from the estate by other statutes.

283A Bankrupt's home ceasing to form part of estate

283A(1) [**Application of section**] This section applies where property comprised in the bankrupt's estate consists of an interest in a dwelling-house which at the date of the bankruptcy was the sole or principal residence of–

(a) the bankrupt,

(b) the bankrupt's spouse, or

(c) a former spouse of the bankrupt.

283A(2) [**Interest to vest in bankrupt**] At the end of the period of three years beginning with the date of the bankruptcy the interest mentioned in subsection (1) shall–

(a) cease to be comprised in the bankrupt's estate, and

(b) vest in the bankrupt (without conveyance, assignment or transfer).

283A(3) [**Non-application of s. 283A(2)**] Subsection (2) shall not apply if during the period mentioned in that subsection–

(a) the trustee realises the interest mentioned in subsection (1),

(b) the trustee applies for an order for sale in respect of the dwelling-house,

(c) the trustee applies for an order for possession of the dwelling-house,

(d) the trustee applies for an order under section 313 in Chapter IV in respect of that interest, or

(e) the trustee and the bankrupt agree that the bankrupt shall incur a specified liability to his estate (with or without the addition of interest from the date of the agreement) in consideration of which the interest mentioned in subsection (1) shall cease to form part of the estate.

283A(4) [**Where application for order dismissed**] Where an application of a kind described in subsection (3)(b) to (d) is made during the period mentioned in subsection (2) and is dismissed, unless the court orders otherwise the interest to which the application relates shall on the dismissal of the application–

(a) cease to be comprised in the bankrupt's estate, and

(b) vest in the bankrupt (without conveyance, assignment or transfer).

283A(5) [**Effect of late notification of interest**] If the bankrupt does not inform the trustee or the official receiver of his interest in a property before the end of the period of three months beginning with the date of the bankruptcy, the period of three years mentioned in subsection (2)–

(a) shall not begin with the date of the bankruptcy, but

(b) shall begin with the date on which the trustee or official receiver becomes aware of the bankrupt's interest.

283A(6) [**Power of court to substitute longer period**] The court may substitute for the period of three years mentioned in subsection (2) a longer period–

(a) in prescribed circumstances, and

(b) in such other circumstances as the court thinks appropriate.

283A(7) [**Provision in rules for shorter period**] The rules may make provision for this section to have effect with the substitution of a shorter period for the period of three years mentioned in subsection (2) in specified circumstances (which may be described by reference to action to be taken by a trustee in bankruptcy).

283A(8) [**Other provision in rules**] The rules may also, in particular, make provision–

(a) requiring or enabling the trustee of a bankrupt's estate to give notice that this section applies or does not apply;

(b) about the effect of a notice under paragraph (a);

(c) requiring the trustee of a bankrupt's estate to make an application to the Chief Land Registrar.

283A(9) [Rules concerning notice of disapplication of section] Rules under subsection (8)(b) may, in particular–

(a) disapply this section;

(b) enable a court to disapply this section;

(c) make provision in consequence of a disapplication of this section;

(d) enable a court to make provision in consequence of a disapplication of this section;

(e) make provision (which may include provision conferring jurisdiction on a court or tribunal) about compensation.

GENERAL NOTE

This important reform is introduced by s. 261 of EA 2002. In the debate on the powers of a trustee in bankruptcy concerns were expressed about the practice adopted by certain trustees of not realising family homes immediately but allowing the matter to lie dormant, only acting many years after discharge where the value of the property had increased due to inflation. This was seen as unjust, a criticism accepted by the Government, which permitted a late amendment of the Bill. For judicial comment on the thinking behind the new policy here see Lawrence Collins J. in *Re Byford (decd)* [2003] EWHC 1267 (Ch). We thus move over to a regime under which the trustee in dealing with the bankrupt's home must "use it or lose it".

S. 283A(1)
This defines the type of property covered by this new restrictive provision. The interest must be in a dwelling house that is the sole or principal residence of the bankrupt, the bankrupt's spouse or former spouse. Thus the provision does not protect interests in second homes purchased for investment or recreation purposes. However, one could envisage a situation where two or even three properties were caught by this provision if for example the bankrupt was divorced and was also living apart from a second spouse. Thus, low value dwelling 1 was occupied by the bankrupt, low value dwelling 2 was occupied by current (but separated) spouse, and low value property 3 was occupied by former spouse.

S. 283A(2), (3), (4)
If the trustee fails to take the specified action within 3 years the property will revest in the bankrupt. The specified courses of action which the trustee must take are identified in subs. (3). Note the qualification dealt with by subs. (4) – early unsuccessful action by the trustee might result in the *immediate* revesting of the dwelling in the bankrupt.

S. 283A(5), (6)
The three-year period does not begin to run until the trustee has been informed of the bankrupt's interest where notification has not occurred within the initial three months. This provision suggests that if a bankrupt waits until the three months are nearly expired before notifying the interest then the trustee in effect has only two years and nine months to take action. Generally, the three-year period may be extended according to subs. (6) and one would imagine that this power might be used in cases where the bankrupt is seen as trying to exploit this potential loophole.

S. 283A(7)–(9)
These deal with the potential content of secondary rules.

284 Restrictions on dispositions of property

284(1) [Where person adjudged bankrupt] Where a person is adjudged bankrupt, any disposition of property made by that person in the period to which this section applies is void except to the extent that it is or was made with the consent of the court, or is or was subsequently ratified by the court.

284(2) [Application of s. 284(1) to payment] Subsection (1) applies to a payment (whether in cash or otherwise) as it applies to a disposition of property and, accordingly, where any payment is void by virtue of that subsection, the person paid shall hold the sum paid for the bankrupt as part of his estate.

284(3) [Relevant period] This section applies to the period beginning with the day of the presentation of the petition for the bankruptcy order and ending with the vesting, under Chapter IV of this Part, of the bankrupt's estate in a trustee.

284(4) **[Limit to effect of s. 284(1)–(3)]** The preceding provisions of this section do not give a remedy against any person–

(a) in respect of any property or payment which he received before the commencement of the bankruptcy in good faith, for value and without notice that the petition had been presented, or

(b) in respect of any interest in property which derives from an interest in respect of which there is, by virtue of this subsection, no remedy.

284(5) **[Debt after commencement of bankruptcy]** Where after the commencement of his bankruptcy the bankrupt has incurred a debt to a banker or other person by reason of the making of a payment which is void under this section, that debt is deemed for the purposes of any of this Group of Parts to have been incurred before the commencement of the bankruptcy unless–

(a) that banker or person had notice of the bankruptcy before the debt was incurred, or

(b) it is not reasonably practicable for the amount of the payment to be recovered from the person to whom it was made.

284(6) **[Property not in bankrupt's estate]** A disposition of property is void under this section notwithstanding that the property is not or, as the case may be, would not be comprised in the bankrupt's estate; but nothing in this section affects any disposition made by a person of property held by him on trust for any other person.

GENERAL NOTE

In the context of the financial markets, s. 284 does not apply to a market contract or any disposition of property in pursuance of such a contract, the provision of margin in relation to market contracts, a market charge, and certain other transactions: see CA 1989, ss. 163(4), 175(3)–(5), and the note on p. 2.

S. 284(1)–(3), (6)
Any disposition of property or payment of money by the debtor after the date of the petition will be void unless approved by the court, either at the time or subsequently. This is so even if the property would not have formed part of the bankrupt's estate under s. 283. Moreover, it would appear that a transfer of an interest in the matrimonial home pursuant to a consent order made under s. 24 of the Matrimonial Causes Act 1973 constitutes a "disposition" for these purposes and is therefore void. This startling conclusion was arrived at by Nicholas Stewart Q.C. (sitting as a deputy judge of the High Court) in *Re Flint* [1993] Ch. 319. This case once again illustrates that where a conflict occurs between rules of family law and principles of bankruptcy law the latter are often victorious. This critical view of the law is reinforced by *Woodley v Woodley (No. 2)* [1994] 1 W.L.R. 1167 where the Court of Appeal held that the presentation of a bankruptcy petition by a debtor husband is not a disposition for the purposes of s. 37 of the Matrimonial Causes Act 1973 and cannot be challenged as an attempt to avoid an order for matrimonial relief. *Re Flint* (above) is inconsistent with *Burton v Burton* [1986] 2 F.L.R. 419 and was not followed by Jonathan Parker J. in *Beer v Higham* [1997] B.P.I.R. 349. However, see *Harper v O'Reilly* [1997] B.P.I.R. 656 and *Mountney v Treharne* [2002] EWCA Civ 1174 for continuing problems of uncertainty on the interface between matrimonial law and insolvency law. *Beer v Higham* (above) is no longer good law.

This provision compensates for the abolition of the doctrine of "relation back" of title and the end of the protection offered by receiving orders.

Note that s. 284 allows the court some discretion with regard to avoidance – the provision in BA 1914 allowed no such flexibility. Leave was granted in *Rio Properties Inc. v Al-Midani* [2003] B.P.I.R. 128 to enable funds to be used as payment for legal advice. On s. 284(6) and sums akin to trust moneys see *Re Mordant* [1996] B.P.I.R. 302.

S. 284(4)
This offers protection to third parties, especially *bona fide* purchasers for value without notice of the petition.

S. 284(5)
This provision deals with payments by the bankrupt avoided under this section, thus leaving the bankrupt indebted to the payee. If the sum of money can be recovered from the payee he will be treated as a pre-bankruptcy creditor unless he had notice of the petition at the time the debt was incurred.

285 Restriction on proceedings and remedies

285(1) [Court's power to stay] At any time when proceedings on a bankruptcy petition are pending or an individual has been adjudged bankrupt the court may stay any action, execution or other legal process against the property or person of the debtor or, as the case may be, of the bankrupt.

285(2) [Where proceedings pending against individual] Any court in which proceedings are pending against any individual may, on proof that a bankruptcy petition has been presented in respect of that individual or that he is an undischarged bankrupt, either stay the proceedings or allow them to continue on such terms as it thinks fit.

285(3) [Limit on creditors' actions] After the making of a bankruptcy order no person who is a creditor of the bankrupt in respect of a debt provable in the bankruptcy shall–

(a) have any remedy against the property or person of the bankrupt in respect of that debt, or

(b) before the discharge of the bankrupt, commence any action or other legal proceedings against the bankrupt except with leave of the court and on such terms as the court may impose.

This is subject to sections 346 (enforcement procedures) and 347 (limited right to distress).

285(4) [Right of secured creditor] Subject as follows, subsection (3) does not affect the right of a secured creditor of the bankrupt to enforce his security.

285(5) [Where goods of undischarged bankrupt held by pledge etc.] Where any goods of an undischarged bankrupt are held by any person by way of pledge, pawn or other security, the official receiver may, after giving notice in writing of his intention to do so, inspect the goods.

Where such a notice has been given to any person, that person is not entitled, without leave of the court, to realise his security unless he has given the trustee of the bankrupt's estate a reasonable opportunity of inspecting the goods and of exercising the bankrupt's right of redemption.

285(6) [Interpretation] References in this section to the property or goods of the bankrupt are to any of his property or goods, whether or not comprised in his estate.

GENERAL NOTE

In relation to the financial markets, nothing in s. 285 affects any action taken by an exchange or clearing house for the purpose of its default proceedings: CA 1989, s. 161(4).

S. 285(1)
This provision authorises the court (for definition, see s. 385) to stay actions, executions etc., where a bankruptcy petition is pending or, indeed, after the grant of the order. The Blagden Committee (Cmnd 221, 1957), paras 19–20, called for the insertion of a provision *ex abundanti cautela* to the effect that High Court proceedings could be stayed under this provision. This has not been done, presumably because the existing language was deemed sufficiently wide. In *Re Smith (a Bankrupt) Ex p. Braintree District Council* [1990] 2 A.C. 215, the House of Lords held that this provision did enable it to stay proceedings for commital for non-payment of rates. There was no justification for excluding such proceedings from the scope of s. 285. See also *Lewis v Ogwr BC* [1996] Rating Appeals 124. Compare *R. v Secretary of State for Social Security Ex p. Taylor* [1997] B.P.I.R. 505 (authorities' right to deduct benefits at source not prejudiced by s. 285(3)).

S. 285(2)
Any court may exercise such staying powers on proof that a bankruptcy petition is pending. On this see *Re Eileen Davies* [1997] B.P.I.R. 619.

S. 285(3), (4)
This compels unsecured creditors of the bankrupt to look solely to bankruptcy procedures as a remedy to secure payment of their debts once the bankruptcy order has been made. This general rule is qualified by ss. 346, 347. Secured creditors do not suffer such a disability, unless s. 285(5) below applies. Matrimonial partners seeking lump sum payments (which are not provable debts) are not caught by s. 285(3): *Re X* [1996] B.P.I.R. 494. Landlords exercising powers of re-entry are also not hindered by this provision: *Razzaq v Pala* [1998] B.C.C. 66.

Section 285(3) is to be interpreted in a purposive manner: *Bristol and West Building Society v Saunders* [1997] Ch. 60; [1997] B.C.C. 83 and leave can therefore be granted retrospectively. For factors relevant to the grant of leave *nunc pro tunc* see *Bristol and West Building Society v Back and Melinek* [1997] B.P.I.R. 358.

S. 285(5)
This allows the official receiver to inspect any of the bankrupt's goods which have been used as security and to redeem them if necessary. The person holding the goods cannot enforce his security without the leave of the court.

S. 285(6)
This gives the words "property" and "goods" a meaning that is not restricted by s. 283.

286 Power to appoint interim receiver

286(1) [Court's power] The court may, if it is shown to be necessary for the protection of the debtor's property, at any time after the presentation of a bankruptcy petition and before making a bankruptcy order, appoint the official receiver to be interim receiver of the debtor's property.

286(2) [Appointment of person instead of official receiver] Where the court has, on a debtor's petition, appointed an insolvency practitioner under section 273 and it is shown to the court as mentioned in subsection (1) of this section, the court may, without making a bankruptcy order, appoint that practitioner, instead of the official receiver, to be interim receiver of the debtor's property.

286(3) [Rights, powers etc. of interim receiver] The court may by an order appointing any person to be an interim receiver direct that his powers shall be limited or restricted in any respect; but, save as so directed, an interim receiver has, in relation to the debtor's property, all the rights, powers, duties and immunities of a receiver and manager under the next section.

286(4) [Contents of court order] An order of the court appointing any person to be an interim receiver shall require that person to take immediate possession of the debtor's property or, as the case may be, the part of it to which his powers as interim receiver are limited.

286(5) [Duties of debtor] Where an interim receiver has been appointed, the debtor shall give him such inventory of his property and such other information, and shall attend on the interim receiver at such times, as the latter may for the purpose of carrying out his functions under this section reasonably require.

286(6) [Application of s. 285(3)] Where an interim receiver is appointed, section 285(3) applies for the period between the appointment and the making of a bankruptcy order on the petition, or the dismissal of the petition, as if the appointment were the making of such an order.

286(7) [Ceasing to be interim receiver] A person ceases to be interim receiver of a debtor's property if the bankruptcy petition relating to the debtor is dismissed, if a bankruptcy order is made on the petition or if the court by order otherwise terminates the appointment.

286(8) [Interpretation] References in this section to the debtor's property are to all his property, whether or not it would be comprised in his estate if he were adjudged bankrupt.

S. 286(1), (2)
The court may appoint the official receiver as an interim receiver after the presentation of the bankruptcy petition if such an appointment is necessary to protect the debtor's property. The interim receiver has a company law counterpart in the provisional liquidator (IA 1986, s. 135). As an alternative to the official receiver, the person appointed on a debtor's petition under s. 273(2) to make a report on the possibility of a rescue plan can be given the role of interim receiver. For the powers and role of an interim receiver *vis-à-vis* the debtor see *Re Baars* [2002] EWHC 2159 (Ch); [2003] B.P.I.R. 523.

The law on interim receivers can be expanded by the rules – see Sch. 9, paras 9, 30. The key provisions are IR 1986, rr. 6.51–6.57.

S. 286(3)
This describes the role of such an interim receiver – note the degree of control over him exercised by the court.

S. 286(4), (8)
The interim receiver should normally take immediate possession of the debtor's assets – even those assets which would not subsequently form part of the bankrupt's estate.

Section 287　　　　　　　　　　　　　　　　　　Insolvency Act 1986

S. 286(5)
This requires the debtor to accede to the interim receiver's demands for assistance.

S. 286(6)
During this interim receivership the debtor's assets enjoy the same protection as if a bankruptcy order had been made.

S. 286(7)
This deals with termination of the interim receivership.

287　Receivership pending appointment of trustee

287(1)　[Official receiver, receiver and manager] Between the making of a bankruptcy order and the time at which the bankrupt's estate vests in a trustee under Chapter IV of this Part, the official receiver is the receiver and (subject to section 370 (special manager)) the manager of the bankrupt's estate and is under a duty to act as such.

287(2)　[Function and powers of official receiver] The function of the official receiver while acting as receiver or manager of the bankrupt's estate under this section is to protect the estate; and for this purpose–

(a)　he has the same powers as if he were a receiver or manager appointed by the High Court, and

(b)　he is entitled to sell or otherwise dispose of any perishable goods comprised in the estate and any other goods so comprised the value of which is likely to diminish if they are not disposed of.

287(3)　[Steps re protecting property] The official receiver while acting as receiver or manager of the estate under this section–

(a)　shall take all such steps as he thinks fit for protecting any property which may be claimed for the estate by the trustee of that estate,

(b)　is not, except in pursuance of directions given by the Secretary of State, required to do anything that involves his incurring expenditure,

(c)　may, if he thinks fit (and shall, if so directed by the court) at any time summon a general meeting of the bankrupt's creditors.

287(4)　[Liability of official receiver] Where–

(a)　the official receiver acting as receiver or manager of the estate under this section seizes or disposes of any property which is not comprised in the estate, and

(b)　at the time of the seizure or disposal the official receiver believes, and has reasonable grounds for believing, that he is entitled (whether in pursuance of an order of the court or otherwise) to seize or dispose of that property,

the official receiver is not liable to any person in respect of any loss or damage resulting from the seizure or disposal except in so far as that loss or damage is caused by his negligence; and he has a lien on the property, or the proceeds of its sale, for such of the expenses of the bankruptcy as were incurred in connection with the seizure or disposal.

287(5)　[Non-application] This section does not apply where by virtue of section 297 (appointment of trustee; special cases) the bankrupt's estate vests in a trustee immediately on the making of the bankruptcy order.

S. 287(1), (2), (5)
The official receiver is to act as receiver and manager of the bankrupt's estate between the date of the bankruptcy order and when the trustee takes control. If the estate has vested immediately in the trustee by virtue of s. 297, then s. 287 does not apply. His role is of a caretaker nature (like a court-appointed receiver and manager), although he may sell perishables, etc.

　　Under BA 1914, s. 10, the official receiver could, in the period before the receiving order and the trustee taking over, appoint a manager – under s. 287 it seems that the official receiver must fulfil this role himself. The court can, however, appoint a special manager under s. 370 instead of the official receiver.

Insolvency Act 1986   Section 288

Further details on the role of the official receiver as receiver and manager may be provided by regulations which may be made by the Secretary of State under the rules: see Sch. 9, para. 10, 30 and IR 1986, r. 12.1(1), (2).

S. 287(3)
These paragraphs detail further the obligations of the official receiver while acting as receiver and manager. His duty to protect the assets is stressed, although he cannot incur expenditure unless directed to do so by the Secretary of State. He may, and, if directed by the court, must, call meetings of creditors.

S. 287(4)
This offers protection from liability for wrongful seizure of assets where the official receiver has acted reasonably and without negligence. Moreover, he has a lien over any proceeds of the wrongful sale to cover his expenses.

288 Statement of affairs

288(1) **[Submission of statement to official receiver]** Where a bankruptcy order has been made otherwise than on a debtor's petition, the bankrupt shall submit a statement of his affairs to the official receiver before the end of the period of 21 days beginning with the commencement of the bankruptcy.

288(2) **[Contents of statement]** The statement of affairs shall contain–

(a) such particulars of the bankrupt's creditors and of his debts and other liabilities and of his assets as may be prescribed, and

(b) such other information as may be prescribed.

288(3) **[Powers of official receiver]** The official receiver may, if he thinks fit–

(a) release the bankrupt from his duty under subsection (1), or

(b) extend the period specified in that subsection;

and where the official receiver has refused to exercise a power conferred by this section, the court, if it thinks fit, may exercise it.

288(4) **[Penalty for non-compliance]** A bankrupt who–

(a) without reasonable excuse fails to comply with the obligation imposed by this section, or

(b) without reasonable excuse submits a statement of affairs that does not comply with the prescribed requirements,

is guilty of a contempt of court and liable to be punished accordingly (in addition to any other punishment to which he may be subject).

S. 288(1), (3)
Where a bankruptcy order has been made on the initiative of a creditor, the bankrupt normally has 21 days to submit a statement of affairs to the official receiver. A bankrupt may be released from this obligation by the official receiver (see IR 1986, r. 6.62 and r. 6.76), who may also extend the 21-day period. If the official receiver refuses to exercise his discretion the court may intervene. This provision differs from its predecessor in a number of respects. The time period mentioned in BA 1914, s. 14 was seven days. Furthermore, under the 1914 Act a statement of affairs was required within three days where the debtor had petitioned for his own bankruptcy: the position now is governed by s. 272(2).

S. 288(2)
This specifies the contents of the statement of affairs. The rules amplify these requirements: see IR 1986, r. 6.58–6.66. For the evidential status of such a statement, see s. 433.

S. 288(4)
Non-compliance can result in liability for contempt of court.

289 Investigatory duties of official receiver

289(1) **[Investigation and report]** The official receiver shall–

(a) investigate the conduct and affairs of each bankrupt (including his conduct and affairs before the making of the bankruptcy order), and

(b) make such report (if any) to the court as the official receiver thinks fit.

289(2) **[Non-application of s. 289(1)]** Subsection (1) shall not apply to a case in which the official receiver thinks an investigation under that subsection unnecessary.

289(3) **[Where application for discharge]** Where a bankrupt makes an application for discharge under section 280 –

(a) the official receiver shall make a report to the court about such matters as may be prescribed, and

(b) the court shall consider the report before determining the application.

289(4) **[Report prima facie evidence of facts]** A report by the official receiver under this section shall in any proceedings be prima facie evidence of the facts stated in it.

GENERAL NOTE

This substituted provision was introduced by s. 258 of EA 2002 with effect from April 2004. The former provision is reproduced below in italics.

S. 289(1)
This in effect repeats the current position suggesting that all bankrupts should be investigated by the OR.

S. 289(2)
This is the key change, removing the mandatory obligation to investigate in circumstances where the OR deems this "unnecessary". No criteria are given for the making of this judgment, but reference to the grounds for the making of a BRO in Sch. 4A might provide a useful pointer. One would imagine that the Insolvency Service would produce its own internal guidelines for official receivers. One effect of not having an investigation would be the reduction in bankruptcy administration costs.

S. 289(3)
This deals with reports to the court where the bankrupt makes a discharge application under s. 280.

S. 289(4)
This outlines the evidential status of any report made by the OR.

289 Investigatory duties of official receiver

289(1) *[Investigation and report] Subject to subsection (5) below, it is the duty of the official receiver to investigate the conduct and affairs of every bankrupt and to make such report (if any) to the court as he thinks fit.*

289(2) *[Where application under s. 280] Where an application is made by the bankrupt under section 280 for his discharge from bankruptcy, it is the duty of the official receiver to make a report to the court with respect to the prescribed matters; and the court shall consider that report before determining what order (if any) to make under that section.*

289(3) *[Report prima facie evidence] A report by the official receiver under this section shall, in any proceedings, be prima facie evidence of the facts stated in it.*

289(4) *[Interpretation of s. 289(1)] In subsection (1) the reference to the conduct and affairs of a bankrupt includes his conduct and affairs before the making of the order by which he was adjudged bankrupt.*

289(5) *[Where certificate for administration] Where a certificate for the summary administration of the bankrupt's estate is for the time being in force, the official receiver shall carry out an investigation under subsection (1) only if he thinks fit.*

290 Public examination of bankrupt

290(1) **[Application to court]** Where a bankruptcy order has been made, the official receiver may at any time before the discharge of the bankrupt apply to the court for the public examination of the bankrupt.

290(2) **[Duty of official receiver to make application]** Unless the court otherwise orders, the official receiver shall make an application under subsection (1) if notice requiring him to do so is given to him, in accordance with the rules, by one of the bankrupt's creditors with the concurrence of not less than one-half, in value, of those creditors (including the creditor giving notice).

290(3) **[Direction re public examination]** On an application under subsection (1), the court shall direct that a public examination of the bankrupt shall be held on a day appointed by the court; and the bankrupt shall attend on that day and be publicly examined as to his affairs, dealings and property.

290(4) **[Persons taking part in examination]** The following may take part in the public examination of the bankrupt and may question him concerning his affairs, dealings and property and the causes of his failure, namely–

(a) the official receiver and, in the case of an individual adjudged bankrupt on a petition under section 264(1)(d), the Official Petitioner,

(b) the trustee of the bankrupt's estate, if his appointment has taken effect,

(c) any person who has been appointed as special manager of the bankrupt's estate or business,

(d) any creditor of the bankrupt who has tendered a proof in the bankruptcy.

290(5) **[Penalty re non-attendance]** If a bankrupt without reasonable excuse fails at any time to attend his public examination under this section he is guilty of a contempt of court and liable to be punished accordingly (in addition to any other punishment to which he may be subject).

GENERAL NOTE

Under BA 1914, s. 15, a public examination was required in every case of bankruptcy. This was unfortunate because it seemed unnecessary to ask every bankrupt to undergo such an ordeal and, in some cases, public examinations caused embarrassment to third parties not directly concerned with the bankruptcy. The most notorious example of this was provided by the public examination of John Poulson in 1972. Accordingly, IA 1976, s. 6 permitted the official receiver to ask the court to relieve certain bankrupts of this onerous procedure.

The Bankruptcy Rules 1952, rr. 188–196 contained additional material on public examinations and the relevant provisions are now IR 1986, rr. 6.172–6.177.

S. 290(1), (2)
The position now is that a public examination will only be held where the official receiver asks for one. However, his hand can be forced by a majority of the bankrupt's creditors. It was held by the Court of Appeal in *Re Seagull Manufacturing Co. Ltd* [1993] Ch. 345; [1993] B.C.C. 241 that the court has jurisdiction in the case of a public examination under s. 133 to order a person resident outside the jurisdiction to attend for examination. (For the position in a private examination, see the notes to s. 236, above.)

S. 290(3), (5)
The court fixes the date of the public examination and the bankrupt must attend or face liability for contempt. Self-incrimination is no excuse for refusal to answer questions (*Re Paget* [1927] 2 Ch. 85).

S. 290(4)
This determines who may attend and participate in the public examination. This means that the authority of *Re Stern (a Bankrupt)* [1982] 1 W.L.R. 860 has been superseded.

291 Duties of bankrupt in relation to official receiver

291(1) [Duties where bankruptcy order made] Where a bankruptcy order has been made, the bankrupt is under a duty–

(a) to deliver possession of his estate to the official receiver, and

(b) to deliver up to the official receiver all books, papers and other records of which he has possession or control and which relate to his estate and affairs (including any which would be privileged from disclosure in any proceedings).

291(2) [Property not capable of delivery to official receiver] In the case of any part of the bankrupt's estate which consists of things possession of which cannot be delivered to the official receiver, and in the case of any property that may be claimed for the bankrupt's estate by the trustee, it is the bankrupt's duty to do all things as may reasonably be required by the official receiver for the protection of those things or that property.

291(3) [Non-application of s. 291(1), (2)] Subsections (1) and (2) do not apply where by virtue of section 297 below the bankrupt's estate vests in a trustee immediately on the making of the bankruptcy order.

291(4) [Bankrupt to give information] The bankrupt shall give the official receiver such inventory of his estate and such other information, and shall attend on the official receiver at such times, as the official receiver may reasonably require–

(a) for a purpose of this Chapter, or

(b) in connection with the making of a bankruptcy restrictions order.

291(5) [Application of s. 291(4)] Subsection (4) applies to a bankrupt after his discharge.

291(6) [Penalty for non-compliance] If the bankrupt without reasonable excuse fails to comply with any obligation imposed by this section, he is guilty of a contempt of court and liable to be punished accordingly (in addition to any other punishment to which he may be subject).

S. 291(1)–(3)
This lists some of the obligations of the bankrupt towards the official receiver – this includes handing over property in his possession, assisting the recovery of other items and delivering up all relevant books and records. These obligations do not apply to the special cases covered by s. 297.

S. 291(4), (5)
Subsection (4) was reconstituted by EA 2002, s. 269 and Sch. 23 with effect from April 1, 2004. This imposes an additional obligation on the bankrupt to provide information and be prepared to assist the official receiver where this is reasonably requested. The obligation continues to apply after discharge.

S. 291(6)
Failure to comply with the above obligations results in liability for contempt of court.

CHAPTER III

TRUSTEES IN BANKRUPTCY

Tenure of office as trustee

292 Power to make appointments

292(1) [Exercise of power] The power to appoint a person as trustee of a bankrupt's estate (whether the first such trustee or a trustee appointed to fill any vacancy) is exercisable–

(a) by a general meeting of the bankrupt's creditors;

(b) under section 295(2), 296(2) or 300(6) below in this Chapter, by the Secretary of State; or

(c) under section 297, by the court.

292(2) [Qualification for trustee] No person may be appointed as trustee of a bankrupt's estate unless he is, at the time of the appointment, qualified to act as an insolvency practitioner in relation to the bankrupt.

292(3) [Joint trustees] Any power to appoint a person as trustee of a bankrupt's estate includes power to appoint two or more persons as joint trustees; but such an appointment must make provision as to the circumstances in which the trustees must act together and the circumstances in which one or more of them may act for the others.

292(4) [Requirement of acceptance of appointment] The appointment of any person as trustee takes effect only if that person accepts the appointment in accordance with the rules. Subject to this, the appointment of any person as trustee takes effect at the time specified in his certificate of appointment.

292(5) [Effect] This section is without prejudice to the provisions of this Chapter under which the official receiver is, in certain circumstances, to be trustee of the estate.

S. 292(1)
This determines who may appoint a trustee in bankruptcy. Normally it will be a decision for the creditors, although there are situations whether the Secretary of State, or the court, may assume responsibility for the appointment. A reference to summary administration was deleted by EA 2002, s. 269 and Sch. 23 with effect from April 1, 2004. See generally IR 1986, rr. 6.120–6.125.

S. 292(2)
Under BA 1914, s. 19 the trustee had to be a "fit person" – now he must be properly qualified under Pt XIII.

S. 292(3)
This restates BA 1914, s. 77 which permitted the appointment of joint trustees.

S. 292(4)
For the appointment to take effect the trustee must accept the post in accordance with the rules (see IR 1986, r. 6.124). The date of the appointment is specified in the certificate of appointment.

S. 292(5)
The aforementioned provisions do not apply where the official receiver acts as trustee: see ss. 293(3), 295(4), 297 and 300(2).

293 Summoning of meeting to appoint first trustee

293(1) [Duty of official receiver] Where a bankruptcy order has been made, it is the duty of the official receiver, as soon as practicable in the period of 12 weeks beginning with the day on which the order was made, to decide whether to summon a general meeting of the bankrupt's creditors for the purpose of appointing a trustee of the bankrupt's estate.

This section does not apply where the bankruptcy order was made on a petition under section 264(1)(d) (criminal bankruptcy); and it is subject to the provision made in sections 294(3) and 297(6) below.

293(2) [Duty if no meeting summoned] Subject to the next section, if the official receiver decides not to summon such a meeting, he shall, before the end of the period of 12 weeks above mentioned, give notice of his decision to the court and to every creditor of the bankrupt who is known to the official receiver or is identified in the bankrupt's statement of affairs.

293(3) [Official receiver trustee from s. 293(2) notice] As from the giving to the court of a notice under subsection (2), the official receiver is the trustee of the bankrupt's estate.

S. 293(1)
The official receiver must within 12 weeks of the bankruptcy order decide whether to call a general meeting of the bankrupt's creditors in order to appoint a trustee. The reference to summary administration in subs. (1) was deleted with effect from April 1, 2004 by EA 2002, s. 269 and Sch. 23.

Section 294 *Insolvency Act 1986*

Note prospective amendment: in s. 293(1) the words "does not apply where the bankruptcy order was made on a petition under section 264(1)(d) (criminal bankruptcy) and it" are to be repealed by CJA 1988, s. 170(2) and Sch. 16 as from a day to be appointed. See the note to s. 264.

S. 293(2), (3)
If he decides not to summon such a meeting he must inform the court and every known creditor of his decision. He thereupon becomes a trustee of the estate.

The BA 1914, Sch. 1 contained details of creditors' meetings; such matters are now dealt with by the rules (Sch. 9, para. 12): see IR 1986, r. 6.79–6.95.

294 Power of creditors to requisition meeting

294(1) **[Request to official receiver]** Where in the case of any bankruptcy the official receiver has not yet summoned, or has decided not to summon, a general meeting of the bankrupt's creditors for the purpose of appointing the trustee any creditor of the bankrupt may request the official receiver to summon such a meeting for that purpose.

294(2) **[Duty to summon meeting on request]** If such a request appears to the official receiver to be made with the concurrence of not less than one-quarter, in value, of the bankrupt's creditors (including the creditor making the request), it is the duty of the official receiver to summon the requested meeting.

294(3) **[Where s. 294(2) duty has arisen]** Accordingly, where the duty imposed by subsection (2) has arisen, the official receiver is required neither to reach a decision for the purposes of section 293(1) nor (if he has reached one) to serve any notice under section 293(2).

S. 294(1), (2)
In a normal bankruptcy case a creditor can ask the official receiver to call a creditors' meeting, with a view to appointing a trustee. Indeed, he *must* summon such a meeting if the request is backed by creditors owed 25 per cent of the bankrupt's debts. (This percentage was reduced from the original figure of 50 per cent at the Report Stage of the 1985 Bill.) The reference to summary administration in subs. (1)(b) was deleted with effect from April 1, 2004 by s. 269 and Sch. 23 EA 2002.

S. 294(3)
Where the creditors have forced the official receiver's hand in this way, he is excused his obligations under s. 293.
See also IR 1986, r. 6.83.

295 Failure of meeting to appoint trustee

295(1) **[Duty of official receiver]** If a meeting summoned under section 293 or 294 is held but no appointment of a person as trustee is made, it is the duty of the official receiver to decide whether to refer the need for an appointment to the Secretary of State.

295(2) **[Duty of Secretary of State]** On a reference made in pursuance of that decision, the Secretary of State shall either make an appointment or decline to make one.

295(3) **[Notice to court]** If–

(a) the official receiver decides not to refer the need for an appointment to the Secretary of State, or

(b) on such a reference the Secretary of State declines to make an appointment,

the official receiver shall give notice of his decision or, as the case may be, of the Secretary of State's decision to the court.

295(4) **[As from notice official receiver trustee]** As from the giving of notice under subsection (3) in a case in which no notice has been given under section 293(2), the official receiver shall be trustee of the bankrupt's estate.

S. 295(1), (2)
Where the creditors in meeting fail to appoint a trustee, the official receiver must decide whether to refer the matter to the Secretary of State, who has discretion whether to appoint a trustee or not. The value of the bankrupt's estate will clearly be relevant in such cases even if the small bankruptcies level (see s. 273) has been exceeded.

S. 295(3)
If the official receiver has decided not to refer the matter to the Secretary of State, or the Secretary of State has decided not to make an appointment, the official receiver must notify the court.

S. 295(4)
Where the official receiver has decided not to call on the assistance of the Secretary of State or the latter has failed to make an appointment, the official receiver will become the trustee.

See also IR 1986, r. 6.122.

296 Appointment of trustee by Secretary of State

296(1) [**Application for appointment instead of official receiver**] At any time when the official receiver is the trustee of a bankrupt's estate by virtue of any provision of this Chapter (other than section 297(1) below) he may apply to the Secretary of State for the appointment of a person as trustee instead of the official receiver.

296(2) [**Duty of Secretary of State**] On an application under subsection (1) the Secretary of State shall either make an appointment or decline to make one.

296(3) [**Making of application**] Such an application may be made notwithstanding that the Secretary of State has declined to make an appointment either on a previous application under subsection (1) or on a reference under section 295 or under section 300(4) below.

296(4) [**Notice etc., re appointment**] Where the trustee of a bankrupt's estate has been appointed by the Secretary of State (whether under this section or otherwise), the trustee shall give notice to the bankrupt's creditors of his appointment or, if the court so allows, shall advertise his appointment in accordance with the court's directions.

296(5) [**Contents of notice**] In that notice or advertisement the trustee shall–

(a) state whether he proposes to summon a general meeting of the bankrupt's creditors for the purpose of establishing a creditors' committee under section 301, and

(b) if he does not propose to summon such a meeting, set out the power of the creditors under this Part to require him to summon one.

S. 296(1)–(3)
This permits the official receiver when acting as a trustee to seek another appointment in his stead. He cannot do this where he is acting as a trustee in case of summary administration or a bankruptcy initiated as the result of a criminal bankruptcy order. On the other hand, he is not precluded from making such an application by the fact that he has previously made unsuccessful applications under s. 295, 296(1) or 300(4). On an application by the official receiver the Secretary of State has discretion whether to appoint a trustee or not. See also IR 1986, r. 6.122.

S. 296(4), (5)
Any appointment of a trustee by the Secretary of State must be notified to the creditors by the trustee or, if the court permits, be advertised with a view to informing the creditors whether a committee should be set up under s. 301. See also IR 1986, r. 6.124 for the advertisement of the appointment.

297 Special cases

297(1) [**Where s. 264(1)(d) bankruptcy order**] Where a bankruptcy order is made on a petition under section 264(1)(d) (criminal bankruptcy), the official receiver shall be trustee of the bankrupt's estate.

297(2) [Repealed]

297(3) [Repealed]

297(4) [**Where no certificate for summary administration**] Where a bankruptcy order is made in a case in which an insolvency practitioner's report has been submitted to the court under section 274 but no certificate for the summary administration of the estate is issued, the court, if it thinks fit, may on making the order appoint the person who made the report as trustee.

Section 298 *Insolvency Act 1986*

297(5) **[Where there is supervisor]** Where a bankruptcy order is made (whether or not on a petition under section 264(1)(c)) at a time when there is a supervisor of a voluntary arrangement approved in relation to the bankrupt under Part VIII, the court, if it thinks fit, may on making the order appoint the supervisor of the arrangement as trustee.

297(6) **[Exception re s. 293(1) duty]** Where an appointment is made under subsection (4) or (5) of this section, the official receiver is not under the duty imposed by section 293(1) (to decide whether or not to summon a meeting of creditors).

297(7) **[Notice where trustee appointed by court]** Where the trustee of a bankrupt's estate has been appointed by the court, the trustee shall give notice to the bankrupt's creditors of his appointment or, if the court so allows, shall advertise his appointment in accordance with the directions of the court.

297(8) **[Contents of notice]** In that notice or advertisement he shall–

(a) state whether he proposes to summon a general meeting of the bankrupt's creditors for the purpose of establishing a creditors' committee under section 301 below, and

(b) if he does not propose to summon such a meeting, set out the power of the creditors under this Part to require him to summon one.

S. 297(1)
These provisions deal with cases where the official receiver is to act as trustee: *e.g.* on bankruptcy initiated as the result of a criminal bankruptcy order. These are not the only instances where the official receiver acts as trustee: see ss. 293(3) and 295(4).

Note prospective amendment: s. 297(1) is to be repealed by CJA 1988, s. 170(2) and Sch. 16 as from a day to be appointed; see the note to s. 264.

S. 297(2), (3)
These subsections were deleted by s. 269 and Sch. 23 EA 2002 with effect from April 1, 2004. They dealt with summary administration.

S. 297(4)
This deals with another special case. Where in a small bankruptcy case the court can select the person who made the crucial report to it under s. 274(1) as trustee. See also IR 1986, r. 6.121.

S. 297(5)
If bankruptcy has been initiated notwithstanding the existence of a composition or scheme (see ss. 252–263) the court may appoint the supervisor as trustee. See also IR 1986, r. 6.121.

S. 297(6)
In cases covered by s. 297(4) and (5) the official receiver is not under a duty to decide whether to call a general meeting of creditors for the purpose of appointing a trustee.

S. 297(7), (8)
This mirrors s. 296(4) and (5), although the appointor here is the court and not the Secretary of State.

298 Removal of trustee; vacation of office

298(1) **[Removal by court order or creditors' meeting]** Subject as follows, the trustee of a bankrupt's estate may be removed from office only by an order of the court or by a general meeting of the bankrupt's creditors summoned specially for that purpose in accordance with the rules.

298(2) **[Where official receiver trustee under s. 297(1)]** Where the official receiver is trustee by virtue of section 297(1), he shall not be removed from office under this section.

298(3) **[Deleted]**

298(4) **[Where official receiver trustee under s. 293(3), 295(4)]** Where the official receiver is trustee by virtue of section 293(3) or 295(4) or a trustee is appointed by the Secretary of State or (otherwise than under section 297(5)) by the court, a general meeting of the bankrupt's creditors shall be summoned for the purpose of replacing the trustee only if–

(a) the trustee thinks fit, or

(b) the court so directs, or

(c) the meeting is requested by one of the bankrupt's creditors with the concurrence of not less than one-quarter, in value, of the creditors (including the creditor making the request).

298(5) **[Where trustee appointed by Secretary of State]** If the trustee was appointed by the Secretary of State, he may be removed by a direction of the Secretary of State.

298(6) **[Vacation of office]** The trustee (not being the official receiver) shall vacate office if he ceases to be a person who is for the time being qualified to act as an insolvency practitioner in relation to the bankrupt.

298(7) **[Resignation]** The trustee may, in the prescribed circumstances, resign his office by giving notice of his resignation to the court.

298(8) **[Vacation on s. 331 notice]** The trustee shall vacate office on giving notice to the court that a final meeting has been held under section 331 in Chapter IV and of the decision (if any) of that meeting.

298(9) **[When bankruptcy order annulled]** The trustee shall vacate office if the bankruptcy order is annulled.

S. 298(1), (2)
Trustees may as a general rule only be removed by the court or the general meeting of creditors. However, this does not apply where the official receiver is trustee.

S. 298(3)
This was deleted by s. 269 and Sch. 23 EA 2002 as from April 1, 2004. It covered summary administration.

S. 298(4)
The drafting of this provision is complex. It covers the official receiver acting as trustee by virtue of ss. 293(3) or 295(4), and trustees appointed by the Secretary of State, or by the court (but not under s. 297(5)). This allows a meeting to be called to dismiss the trustee – either the trustee himself, the court or creditors owed 25 per cent of the bankrupt's debts can call for this. This was reduced from 50 per cent in the original 1985 Bill.

S. 298(5)
The Secretary of State can remove his own appointees.

S. 298(6)
A trustee must vacate office if he ceases to be qualified to act: see Pt XIII and r. 6.144(1).

S. 298(7)
Resignation in the circumstances prescribed is permitted.

S. 298(8)
The trustee shall vacate office after giving notice to the court of the outcome of the final meeting of creditors (see s. 331).

S. 298(9)
Annulment of the bankruptcy order will cause the trustee to vacate office.

For further details on removal and vacation of office, see IR 1986, rr. 6.126–6.135.

299 Release of trustee

299(1) **[Time of release for official receiver]** Where the official receiver has ceased to be the trustee of a bankrupt's estate and a person is appointed in his stead, the official receiver shall have his release with effect from the following time, that is to say–

(a) where that person is appointed by a general meeting of the bankrupt's creditors or by the Secretary of State, the time at which the official receiver gives notice to the court that he has been replaced, and

(b) where that person is appointed by the court, such time as the court may determine.

299(2) [**Time of release if notice given by official receiver**] If the official receiver while he is the trustee gives notice to the Secretary of State that the administration of the bankrupt's estate in accordance with Chapter IV of this Part is for practical purposes complete, he shall have his release with effect from such time as the Secretary of State may determine.

299(3) [**Time of release for person not official receiver**] A person other than the official receiver who has ceased to be the trustee shall have his release with effect from the following time, that is to say—

(a) in the case of a person who has been removed from office by a general meeting of the bankrupt's creditors that has not resolved against his release or who has died, the time at which notice is given to the court in accordance with the rules that that person has ceased to hold office;

(b) in the case of a person who has been removed from office by a general meeting of the bankrupt's creditors that has resolved against his release, or by the court, or by the Secretary of State, or who has vacated office under section 298(6), such time as the Secretary of State may, on an application by that person, determine;

(c) in the case of a person who has resigned, such time as may be prescribed;

(d) in the case of a person who has vacated office under section 298(8)—

   (i) if the final meeting referred to in that subsection has resolved against that person's release, such time as the Secretary of State may, on an application by that person, determine; and

   (ii) if that meeting has not so resolved, the time at which the person vacated office.

299(4) [**Time of release where bankruptcy order annulled**] Where a bankruptcy order is annulled, the trustee at the time of the annulment has his release with effect from such time as the court may determine.

299(5) [**Effect of release**] Where the official receiver or the trustee has his release under this section, he shall, with effect from the time specified in the preceding provisions of this section, be discharged from all liability both in respect of acts or omissions of his in the administration of the estate and otherwise in relation to his conduct as trustee.

But nothing in this section prevents the exercise, in relation to a person who has had his release under this section, of the court's powers under section 304.

S. 299(1), (2)

These provisions deal with the release of an official receiver who has been acting as trustee. The procedure to be followed depends on whether he is being replaced or whether he has simply completed the administration of the estate.

For the equivalent provision for the release of liquidators, see s. 174. As to the possibility of a release being set aside, see *Re Munro Ex p. Singer v Trustee in Bankruptcy* [1981] 1 W.L.R. 1358. Release is also dealt with by IR 1986, rr. 6.136, 6.137.

S. 299(3)

This fixes the date of release for trustees other than the official receiver. Again, the date will vary according to the circumstances of the case – a comprehensive list of possibilities is provided for.

S. 299(4)

Where release is the result of the annulment of the bankruptcy order the court will fix the date of release.

S. 299(5)

This is a general provision dealing with the *effect* of a release: it serves as a discharge of liabilities, unless an action is subsequently brought under s. 304.

300 Vacancy in office of trustee

300(1) [**Application**] This section applies where the appointment of any person as trustee of a bankrupt's estate fails to take effect or, such an appointment having taken effect, there is otherwise a vacancy in the office of trustee.

300(2) [**Official receiver trustee**] The official receiver shall be trustee until the vacancy is filled.

300(3) [**Summoning creditors' meeting**] The official receiver may summon a general meeting of the bankrupt's creditors for the purpose of filling the vacancy and shall summon such a meeting if required to do so in pursuance of section 314(7) (creditors' requisition).

300(4) [**If no meeting summoned within 28 days**] If at the end of the period of 28 days beginning with the day on which the vacancy first came to the official receiver's attention he has not summoned, and is not proposing to summon, a general meeting of creditors for the purpose of filling the vacancy, he shall refer the need for an appointment to the Secretary of State.

300(5) [**Deleted**]

300(6) [**Duty of Secretary of State re s. 300(4), (5)**] On a reference to the Secretary of State under subsection (4) the Secretary of State shall either make an appointment or decline to make one.

300(7) [**If no appointment on s. 300(4), (5) reference**] If on a reference under subsection (4) no appointment is made, the official receiver shall continue to be trustee of the bankrupt's estate, but without prejudice to his power to make a further reference.

300(8) [**Interpretation**] References in this section to a vacancy include a case where it is necessary, in relation to any property which is or may be comprised in a bankrupt's estate, to revive the trusteeship of that estate after holding of a final meeting summoned under section 331 or the giving by the official receiver of notice under section 299(2).

S. 300(1), (2)
Where the appointment of a trustee fails to take effect (*e.g.* because he refuses the appointment) or a casual vacancy occurs, the official receiver must act as trustee during the interregnum.

S. 300(3), (4)
The official receiver may (and, in cases under s. 314(7), must) call a general meeting to fill this vacancy. If he fails to act within 28 days he must refer the matter to the Secretary of State. See IR 1986, r. 6.122.

S. 300(5)
This was deleted by s. 269 and Sch. 23 EA 2002 with effect from April 1, 2004. It dealt with summary administration.

S. 300(6), (7)
Where a casual vacancy has been referred to the Secretary of State he has discretion whether to fill it or not. If the vacancy is not filled the official receiver must act as trustee pending the resolution of the matter.

S. 300(8)
This defines what is meant by a "vacancy" for the purposes of the present section.

Control of trustee

301 Creditors' committee

301(1) [**Meeting may establish committee**] Subject as follows, a general meeting of a bankrupt's creditors (whether summoned under the preceding provisions of this Chapter or otherwise) may, in accordance with the rules, establish a committee (known as "the creditors' committee") to exercise the functions conferred on it by or under this Act.

301(2) [**Exception**] A general meeting of the bankrupt's creditors shall not establish such a committee, or confer any functions on such a committee, at any time when the official receiver is the trustee of the bankrupt's estate, except in connection with an appointment made by that meeting of a person to be trustee instead of the official receiver.

S. 301(1)
This enables the general meeting of creditors to establish a committee to supervise the trustee. Under the 1914 Act this committee was known as a "committee of inspection" but this title has now been dropped on the recommendation of the

Cork Committee (*Report*, para. 932). The role and general position of the committee is now governed by the Rules – see now IR 1986, rr. 6.150–6.166. Under BA 1914 many of these details were spelled out in the provisions of the Act itself. Under BA 1914, s. 79(1) the committee had general power to give directions to the trustee. This power was not re-enacted in the 1986 Act and therefore the role of the committee is more limited. Members of this committee occupy a fiduciary position *vis-à-vis* the bankrupt's estate: *Re Bulmer, Ex p. Greaves* [1937] Ch. 499.

An FSA representative can attend where appropriate – FSMA 2000 s. 374(4).

S. 301(2)
The committee has no role where the official receiver is trustee – he is supervised by the Secretary of State under s. 302. This could apply to cases of criminal bankruptcy.

302 Exercise by Secretary of State of functions of creditors' committee

302(1) [**Where official receiver trustee**] The creditors' committee is not to be able or required to carry out its functions at any time when the official receiver is trustee of the bankrupt's estate; but at any such time the functions of the committee under this Act shall be vested in the Secretary of State, except to the extent that the rules otherwise provide.

302(2) [**Where no committee**] Where in the case of any bankruptcy there is for the time being no creditors' committee and the trustee of the bankrupt's estate is a person other than the official receiver, the functions of such a committee shall be vested in the Secretary of State, except to the extent that the rules otherwise provide.

S. 302(1)
This reiterates that the committee established under s. 301 cannot exercise any control functions when the official receiver is acting as trustee. Instead, control in such cases must be exercised by the Secretary of State. See IR 1986, r. 6.166.

S. 302(2)
For the relevant rules, see IR 1986, r. 6.166.

303 General control of trustee by the court

303(1) [**Application to court**] If a bankrupt or any of his creditors or any other person is dissatisfied by any act, omission or decision of a trustee of the bankrupt's estate, he may apply to the court; and on such an application the court may confirm, reverse or modify any act or decision of the trustee, may give him directions or may make such other order as it thinks fit.

303(2) [**Application by trustee for directions**] The trustee of a bankrupt's estate may apply to the court for directions in relation to any particular matter arising under the bankruptcy.

S. 303(1)
This permits any person (including a discharged bankrupt – *Osborn v Cole* [1999] B.P.I.R. 251 or a person whose bankruptcy has been annulled – *Engel v Peri* [2002] EWHC 799 (Ch); [2002] B.P.I.R. 961.) who is dissatisfied with a decision of a trustee in bankruptcy to apply to the court for relief. On such an application the court enjoys general discretion to deal with the matter. This is a useful reserve control power, but in practice, as the Cork Committee observed (*Report*, para. 779), such applications rarely succeed: see, for an example of an unsuccessful application, *Re a Debtor, ex parte The Debtor v Dodwell (The Trustee)* [1949] Ch. 236. In *Osborn v Cole* (above) this difficulty was exemplified by requiring proof that the trustee was acting in a manner in which no reasonable trustee would act. Certainly this provision cannot be used to challenge the exercise of public law functions by an official receiver: *Hardy v Focus Insurance Co. Ltd* [1997] B.P.I.R. 77.

It is uncertain whether the change from "aggrieved" in BA 1914 to "dissatisfied" will produce any practical differences. In *Osborn v Cole* (above) the old law was found to be of some value. Note also IR 1986, Pt 7. Section 303 is not an appropriate tool to use to fix the trustee's remuneration – *Engel v Peri* [2002] EWHC 799 (Ch); [2002] B.P.I.R. 961.

Those lawyers looking for a more liberal use of this control facility will have been disappointed by the comments of Harman J. in *Port v Auger* [1994] 1 W.L.R. 862 at pp. 873–874. Although Harman J. appeared to accept that the change in terminology from "aggrieved" to "dissatisfied" may have indicated an intention on the part of the legislature to widen access to the court he expressed the view that the applicant must have some substantial interest that has been adversely affected and then went on to suggest that the s. 303 jurisdiction should not be invoked lightly by the court for fear of inflicting unnecessary expense on the insolvent estate. For a case which pushed the s. 303 jurisdiction to the limit see *Re Cook* [1999] B.P.I.R. 881.

In *Heath v Tang* [1993] 1 W.L.R. 1421 it was suggested by the court that this provision might prove useful if the trustee refuses to pursue a claim of action belonging to the debtor but now vested in the estate. On this see also the notes on ss. 285(3) and 306.

On the interface between s. 303 and s. 304 see *Brown v Beat* [2002] B.P.I.R. 421.

S. 303(2)

This is a useful facility in that it allows a trustee in bankruptcy to apply to the court for guidance on a difficult matter. For an illustration of the court giving such directions see *Re a Debtor (No. 26A of 1975)* [1985] 1 W.L.R. 6. Other interested parties may also apply – *Supperstone v Auger* [1999] B.P.I.R. 152.

304 Liability of trustee

304(1) [Powers of court on application] Where on an application under this section the court is satisfied–

(a) that the trustee of a bankrupt's estate has misapplied or retained, or become accountable for, any money or other property comprised in the bankrupt's estate, or

(b) that a bankrupt's estate has suffered any loss in consequence of any misfeasance or breach of fiduciary or other duty by a trustee of the estate in the carrying out of his functions,

the court may order the trustee, for the benefit of the estate, to repay, restore or account for money or other property (together with interest at such rate as the court thinks just) or, as the case may require, to pay such sum by way of compensation in respect of the misfeasance or breach of fiduciary or other duty as the court thinks just.

This is without prejudice to any liability arising apart from this section.

304(2) [Applicants] An application under this section may be made by the official receiver, the Secretary of State, a creditor of the bankrupt or (whether or not there is, or is likely to be, a surplus for the purposes of section 330(5) (final distribution)) the bankrupt himself.

But the leave of the court is required for the making of an application if it is to be made by the bankrupt or if it is to be made after the trustee has had his release under section 299.

304(3) [Limit on liability] Where–

(a) the trustee seizes or disposes of any property which is not comprised in the bankrupt's estate, and

(b) at the time of the seizure or disposal the trustee believes, and has reasonable grounds for believing, that he is entitled (whether in pursuance of an order of the court or otherwise) to seize or dispose of that property,

the trustee is not liable to any person (whether under this section or otherwise) in respect of any loss or damage resulting from the seizure or disposal except in so far as that loss or damage is caused by the negligence of the trustee; and he has a lien on the property, or the proceeds of its sale, for such of the expenses of the bankruptcy as were incurred in connection with the seizure or disposal.

GENERAL NOTE

The Cork Committee (*Report*, paras 777–788) called for the introduction of a statutory duty of care imposed on trustees. This section goes some way towards this, and towards rationalising the law on the liability of trustees.

S. 304(1)

This allows the court to impose liability on the trustee for misfeasance or misapplication of money belonging to the estate, etc. The remedy is at the discretion of the court, and it is worth noting that interest can be awarded against the trustee. The comparable provision in company law is to be found in s. 212. See *Green v Satsangi* [1998] B.P.I.R. 55 where an order made against a trustee under s. 304 was quashed on appeal.

Section 305 *Insolvency Act 1986*

S. 304(2)
This determines who can apply for relief under s. 304(1). Note that if the bankrupt applies, or the application is made after the date of the trustee's release, the leave of the court must first be obtained. See here *Brown v Beat* [2002] B.P.I.R. 421.

S. 304(3)
This is not a new provision, but rather a reformulation of BA 1914, s. 61. It is designed to protect a trustee who innocently seizes or disposes of property belonging to a third party. Note that this protection is lost if he acts negligently. The problem of a trustee seizing property which does not belong to the bankrupt may arise more frequently in the future with the abolition of the concept of reputed ownership.

CHAPTER IV

ADMINISTRATION BY TRUSTEE

Preliminary

305 General functions of trustee

305(1) [Application of Ch. IV] This Chapter applies in relation to any bankruptcy where either–

(a) the appointment of a person as trustee of a bankrupt's estate takes effect, or

(b) the official receiver becomes trustee of a bankrupt's estate.

305(2) [Function of trustee] The function of the trustee is to get in, realise and distribute the bankrupt's estate in accordance with the following provisions of this Chapter; and in the carrying out of that function and in the management of the bankrupt's estate the trustee is entitled, subject to those provisions, to use his own discretion.

305(3) [Duties of trustee] It is the duty of the trustee, if he is not the official receiver–

(a) to furnish the official receiver with such information,

(b) to produce to the official receiver, and permit inspection by the official receiver of, such books, papers and other records, and

(c) to give the official receiver such other assistance,

as the official receiver may reasonably require for the purpose of enabling him to carry out his functions in relation to the bankruptcy.

305(4) [Official name of trustee] The official name of the trustee shall be "the trustee of the estate of . . . ., a bankrupt" (inserting the name of the bankrupt); but he may be referred to as "the trustee in bankruptcy" of the particular bankrupt.

S. 305(1)
Sections 305–335 apply to cases where the trustee's appointment is effective or where the official receiver is acting as trustee.

S. 305(2)
This describes the general role of the trustee and confers considerable residual discretion upon him. The courts are minded to maximise his room for manouevre: *Judd v Brown* [1997] B.P.I.R. 470 at pp. 476–477. It is important that the trustee retains professional independence and is not seen to be acting as a hired gun for a major creditor – *Re Ng* [1997] B.C.C. 507 *per* Lightman J., a comment which was approved by the Court of Appeal in *Trustee in Bankruptcy of Bukhari v Bukhari* [1999] B.P.I.R. 157.

Note the new whistleblowing duty imposed in appropriate cases by s. 373 of FSMA 2000.

S. 305(3)
This provision makes the trustee subordinate to the official receiver. Further details of the relationship can be seen in IR 1986, r. 6.149.

S. 305(4)
This describes the official name of the trustee and repeats BA 1914, s. 76, although his powers are not mentioned in the new provision.

Acquisition, control and realisation of bankrupt's estate

306 Vesting of bankrupt's estate in trustee

306(1) **[Time of vesting]** The bankrupt's estate shall vest in the trustee immediately on his appointment taking effect or, in the case of the official receiver, on his becoming trustee.

306(2) **[Mode of vesting]** Where any property which is, or is to be, comprised in the bankrupt's estate vests in the trustee (whether under this section or under any other provision of this Part), it shall so vest without any conveyance, assignment or transfer.

GENERAL NOTE

This section provides that the bankrupt's property shall vest in the trustee, on his appointment taking effect, or in the official receiver where he becomes trustee. No conveyance, etc., is required.

This automatic vesting is to be compared with the position under s. 145 where the court may direct that some or all of the company's property shall vest in the liquidator in a compulsory liquidation.

The property does not have to be located within the jurisdiction to vest: *Singh v Official Receiver* [1997] B.P.I.R. 530, *Pollard v Ashurst* [2001] B.P.I.R. 131.

For the meaning of "property" within s. 306(2) see *London City Corp. v Bown*, *The Times* October 11, 1989, where it was held by the Court of Appeal that a non-assignable secure periodic tenancy within the meaning of the Housing Act 1985 confers only personal rights and therefore could not be regarded as "property" for these purposes. Similarly in *Re Rae* [1995] B.C.C. 102 and *Griffiths v Civil Aviation Authority* [1997] B.P.I.R. 50 personal and non-transferable rights to hold a licence did not vest in the trustee. Compare *Cork v Rawlins* [2001] B.P.I.R. 222 (insurance policies). Transferable licences of value may on the other hand be regarded as property: *Environment Agency v Stout* [1998] B.P.I.R. 576. Personal injury compensation also cannot be claimed by the trustee for the estate: *Lang v McKenna* [1996] B.P.I.R. 419 and [1997] B.P.I.R. 340 and *Rahall v McLennan* [2000] B.P.I.R. 140. The generality of this latter statement was questioned in *Re Bell* [1998] B.P.I.R. 26 where it was held that compensation for personal injury leading to damage to assets of economic value might form part of the estate, see also *Davis v Trustee in Bankruptcy of Davis* [1998] B.P.I.R. 572. If the claim is hybrid (*i.e.* contains an element relating to an allegation of damage to assets of the bankrupt coupled with a personal claim) the claim vests in the trustee, but any proceeds of action relating to the personal element are held on trust for the bankrupt – see here *Ord v Upton* [2000] 2 W.L.R. 755. The difficulty in distinguishing these issues was reflected by *Mulkerrins v PricewaterhouseCoopers* [2003] UKHL 41; [2003] 1 W.L.R. 1937. In *Grady v Prison Service* [2003] EWCA Civ 527 a claim for unfair dismissal was held to be "personal" and therefore did not vest within the estate. Ironically, the court indicated that the proceeds of such a claim might be treated as being encompassed within that estate. By way of contrast in *Saini v Petroform Ltd* [1997] B.P.I.R. 515 the right to seek a new business tenancy under the Landlord and Tenant Act 1954 was held to be property. Again in *Performing Rights Society v Rowland* [1998] B.P.I.R. 128 the personal right to receive royalties from the PRS vested in the trustee as property as did the right of a lawyer to receive professional fees under a contingency fee agreement in *Royal Bank of Canada and Burlingham Associates v Chetty* [1997] B.P.I.R. 137. One can only conclude that the dividing line between personal rights which are outside the estate and property rights which the trustee can lay claim to is unclear. On current trends the courts are inclined to treat assets of value as being proprietorial and therefore caught by s. 306.

The rights of action possessed by the debtor at the time of his bankruptcy form part of the estate under the control of the trustee: see *Heath v Tang* [1993] 1 W.L.R. 1421; *Nelson v Nelson* [1997] B.P.I.R. 702. The issue of whether rights of appeal pass to the trustee or are retained by the bankrupt has generated much controversy but again the courts are inclined to treat these as forming part of the estate: *Wordsworth v Dixon* [1997] B.P.I.R. 337; *Church of Scientology v*

Section 306A *Insolvency Act 1986*

Scott [1997] B.P.I.R. 418; and *Cummings and Fuller v Claremont Petroleum* [1998] B.P.I.R. 187. See also *Seven Eight Six Properties Ltd v Ghafoor* B.P.I.R. 519 (right to resist possession proceedings forms part of estate), *Hunt v Peasegood* [2001] B.P.I.R. 76.

The position with regard to pension benefits has undergone considerable change in recent years. For bankruptcies commencing prior to May 29, 2000 personal and occupational pension benefits automatically vest in the estate – *Re Landau* [1998] Ch. 223, *Krasner v Dennison* [2001] Ch. 76, *Patel v Jones* [2001] B.P.I.R. 919 and *Rowe v Sanders* [2002] EWCA Civ 242, [2002] B.P.I.R. 847. In the latter case the Court of Appeal has confirmed that there is no infringement of fundamental rights expectations as a result of this automatic vesting. Moreover, in view of this vesting there is no need to seek an income payments order in respect of pension benefits. For bankruptcies commencing after 29 May 2000 the position is governed by ss. 11 and 12 of the Welfare Reform and Pensions Act 1999 which seeks to exclude certain specified pensions from the estate, subject to the clawback provisions in ss. 342A–342C of the 1986 Act. More detailed legislative provision on the new scheme is found in The Occupational and Personal Pension Schemes (Bankruptcy) Regulations 2002 (SI 2002/427). This establishes machinery to enable a bankrupt to seek a court order to exclude pension benefits from his estate or to facilitate agreements between the trustee and the bankrupt as to pension rights.

Provisions seeking to forfeit personal pension rights on bankruptcy (and thereby to circumvent bankruptcy law) are ineffective – Welfare Reform and Pensions Act 1999 s. 14 (which inserts a new section 159A into the Pensions Schemes Act 1993).

Income-related social security benefits do not form part of the estate: *Mulvey v Secretary of State for Social Security* [1997] B.P.I.R. 696.

306A Property subject to restraint order

306A(1) **[Application]** This section applies where–

(a) property is excluded from the bankrupt's estate by virtue of section 417(2)(a) of the Proceeds of Crime Act 2002 (property subject to a restraint order),

(b) an order under section 50, 52, 128, 198 or 200 of that Act has not been made in respect of the property, and

(c) the restraint order is discharged.

306A(2) **[Vesting]** On the discharge of the restraint order the property vests in the trustee as part of the bankrupt's estate.

306A(3) **[Non-application of s. 306A(2)]** But subsection (2) does not apply to the proceeds of property realised by a management receiver under section 49(2)(d) or 197(2)(d) of that Act (realisation of property to meet receiver's remuneration and expenses).

306B Property in respect of which receivership or administration order made

306B(1) **[Application]** This section applies where–

(a) property is excluded from the bankrupt's estate by virtue of section 417(2)(b), (c) or (d) of the Proceeds of Crime Act 2002 (property in respect of which an order for the appointment of a receiver or administrator under certain provisions of that Act is in force),

(b) a confiscation order is made under section 6, 92 or 156 of that Act,

(c) the amount payable under the confiscation order is fully paid, and

(d) any of the property remains in the hands of the receiver or administrator (as the case may be).

306B(2) **[Vesting]** The property vests in the trustee as part of the bankrupt's estate.

306C Property subject to certain orders where confiscation order discharged or quashed

306C(1) [Application] This section applies where–

(a) property is excluded from the bankrupt's estate by virtue of section 417(2)(a), (b), (c) or (d) of the Proceeds of Crime Act 2002 (property in respect of which a restraint order or an order for the appointment of a receiver or administrator under that Act is in force),

(b) a confiscation order is made under section 6, 92 or 156 of that Act, and

(c) the confiscation order is discharged under section 30, 114 or 180 of that Act (as the case may be) or quashed under that Act or in pursuance of any enactment relating to appeals against conviction or sentence.

306C(2) [Vesting] Any such property in the hands of a receiver appointed under Part 2 or 4 of that Act or an administrator appointed under Part 3 of that Act vests in the trustee as part of the bankrupt's estate.

306C(3) [Non-application of s. 306C] But subsection (2) does not apply to the proceeds of property realised by a management receiver under section 49(2)(d) or 197(2)(d) of that Act (realisation of property to meet receiver's remuneration and expenses).

GENERAL NOTE

S. 306A–C
Note insertion of ss. 306A, 306B and 306C by Sch. 11 to the Proceeds of Crime Act 2002. The 2002 Act deals with the interface between insolvency law and criminal proceeds recovery proceedings. Generally speaking, a bankrupt's estate will not include assets which are the subject of a criminal recovery action (s. 417 of the 2002 Act) but the three new prospective sections deal with the return to the estate of such assets if the relevant criminal proceedings order is discharged, or liability extinguished through the confiscation process or the order quashed. In such circumstances the excluded assets are returned to the estate.

307 After-acquired property

307(1) [Power of trustee] Subject to this section and section 309, the trustee may by notice in writing claim for the bankrupt's estate any property which has been acquired by, or has devolved upon, the bankrupt since the commencement of the bankruptcy.

307(2) [Limit on s. 307(1) notice] A notice under this section shall not be served in respect of–

(a) any property falling within subsection (2) or (3) of section 283 in Chapter II,

(aa) any property vesting in the bankrupt by virtue of section 283A in Chapter II,

(b) any property which by virtue of any other enactment is excluded from the bankrupt's estate, or

(c) without prejudice to section 280(2)(c) (order of court on application for discharge), any property which is acquired by, or devolves upon, the bankrupt after his discharge.

307(3) [Vesting on service of notice] Subject to the next subsection, upon the service on the bankrupt of a notice under this section the property to which the notice relates shall vest in the trustee as part of the bankrupt's estate; and the trustee's title to that property has relation back to the time at which the property was acquired by, or devolved upon, the bankrupt.

307(4) [Outsiders] Where, whether before or after service of a notice under this section–

(a) a person acquires property in good faith, for value and without notice of the bankruptcy, or

(b) a banker enters into a transaction in good faith and without such notice,

the trustee is not in respect of that property or transaction entitled by virtue of this section to any remedy against that person or banker, or any person whose title to any property derives from that person or banker.

307(5) [Interpretation] References in this section to property do not include any property which, as part of the bankrupt's income, may be the subject of an income payments order under section 310.

S. 307(1)
This enables the trustee to take the initiative and claim property vesting in the bankrupt after the commencement of the bankruptcy (as defined in s. 278(a)). Under BA 1914, s. 28(a) such property *automatically* vested in the trustee: see

Re Pascoe [1944] Ch. 219. Prior to 1944 it was generally believed that positive intervention by the trustee was required. The Cork Committee (*Report*, para. 1152) felt that it would be more flexible if the trustee could be allowed to choose whether the estate wanted such property. The advantage in such a change is highlighted by the White Paper, para. 112 – it saves the trustee from wasting his time in having to disclaim onerous after-acquired property. See also IR 1986, rr. 6.200–6.202. The operation of this provision does depend on the bankrupt being honest with his trustee, as he is required to be by ss. 333(2) and 353. The bankrupt must tell the trustee within 21 days of the acquisition of the property: see IR 1986, r. 6.200(1).

For illustrations of s. 307 at work see *Pike v Cork Gully* [1997] B.P.I.R. 723 and *Re Mathew* (unreported, but noted in *Current Law Week*, September 20, 1996). This latter case involved a trustee laying claim to a legacy where the bankrupt had not kept the trustee fully informed.

S. 307(2), (5)
Certain after-acquired property cannot be claimed by the trustee: property which would not be included in the estate in any case, and property acquired after the date of discharge. Section 307(2)(aa) was inserted by s. 261 EA 2002 with effect from April 1, 2004. Note also that income which may be caught by s. 310 cannot fall under s. 307. See *Supperstone v Lloyds Names Working Party* [1999] B.P.I.R. 832.

S. 307(3)
On service of the trustee's notice the property in question vests in the trustee. The trustee has 42 days to claim the property after receiving notice of it from the bankrupt, see IA 1986, s. 309(1)(a), or else it can be disposed of by the bankrupt.

S. 307(4)
This protects *bona fide* purchasers (for value, without notice . . .) of after-acquired property from the bankrupt. It is based on BA 1914, s. 47 which, in turn, confirmed the rule in *Cohen v Mitchell* (1890) 25 QBD 262. For a comparable Australian authority see *Rimar Pty Ltd v Pappas* (1986) 60 ALJR 309. However, the third party loses his protection if he has notice of the bankruptcy order: thus, *Hunt v Fripp* [1898] 1 Ch. 675 is reversed. If the disponee is not protected the trustee can recover the property under IR 1986, r. 6.201.

308 Vesting in trustee of certain items of excess value

308(1) [**Claim by trustee in writing**] Subject to section 309, where–

(a) property is excluded by virtue of section 283(2) (tools of trade, household effects, etc.) from the bankrupt's estate, and

(b) it appears to the trustee that the realisable value of the whole or any part of that property exceeds the cost of a reasonable replacement for that property or that part of it,

the trustee may by notice in writing claim that property or, as the case may be, that part of it for the bankrupt's estate.

308(2) [**Vesting on service of s. 308(1) notice**] Upon the service on the bankrupt of a notice under this section, the property to which the notice relates vests in the trustee as part of the bankrupt's estate; and, except against a purchaser in good faith, for value and without notice of the bankruptcy, the trustee's title to that property has relation back to the commencement of the bankruptcy.

308(3) [**Application of funds by trustee**] The trustee shall apply funds comprised in the estate to the purchase by or on behalf of the bankrupt of a reasonable replacement for any property vested in the trustee under this section; and the duty imposed by this subsection has priority over the obligation of the trustee to distribute the estate.

308(4) [**Reasonable replacement**] For the purposes of this section property is a reasonable replacement for other property if it is reasonably adequate for meeting the needs met by the other property.

GENERAL NOTE

This is a new provision which implements the recommendations of the Cork Committee (*Report*, para. 1101). This section is supplemented by IR 1986, rr. 6.187, 6.188.

S. 308(1), (4)
The trustee is allowed to claim certain property, which would normally not be included in the bankrupt's estate by virtue of s. 283(2), if that property can be reasonably replaced (as defined in s. 308(4), producing a surplus for the estate. See

Pike v Cork Gully [1997] B.P.I.R. 723. Note the 42-day limit in s. 309. The provision is designed to prevent bankrupts with large debts from continuing to live a life of luxury surrounded by expensive cars and consumer durables. A bankrupt who objects to replacement can complain to the court under s. 303. A third party can pay off the trustee to avert replacement: IR 1986, r. 6.188. A minor change has been made to subs. (1) to accomodate the insertion of s. 308A: see Housing Act 1988, Sch. 17, para. 73.

S. 308(2)
Once the trustee has given notice, the property in question will vest in the trustee, subject to the rights of any *bona fide* purchaser.

S. 308(3)
The cost of the replacement is to be met out of the estate funds and the defrayment of this cost takes priority over the trustee's obligation to distribute. The replacement may occur before or after the sale of the original item, see IR 1986, r. 6.187.

S. 308(4)
It would appear from the link with subs. (1) that the test as to what is "reasonable" is likely to be applied subjectively, *i.e.* does the trustee believe it is reasonable? Provided his decision is not totally erratic, the court would not intervene.

308A Vesting in trustee of certain tenancies

308A Upon the service on the bankrupt by the trustee of a notice in writing under this section, any tenancy–

(a) which is excluded by virtue of section 283(3A) from the bankrupt's estate, and

(b) to which the notice relates,

vests in the trustee as part of the bankrupt's estate; and, except against a purchaser in good faith, for value and without notice of the bankruptcy, the trustee's title to that tenancy has relation back to the commencement of the bankruptcy.

309 Time-limit for notice under s. 307 or 308

309(1) [Timing of notice] Except with the leave of the court, a notice shall not be served–

(a) under section 307, after the end of the period of 42 days beginning with the day on which it first came to the knowledge of the trustee that the property in question had been acquired by, or had devolved upon, the bankrupt;

(b) under section 308 or section 308A, after the end of the period of 42 days beginning with the day on which the property or tenancy in question first came to the knowledge of the trustee.

309(2) [Deemed knowledge] For the purposes of this section–

(a) anything which comes to the knowledge of the trustee is deemed in relation to any successor of his as trustee to have come to the knowledge of the successor at the same time; and

(b) anything which comes (otherwise than under paragraph (a)) to the knowledge of a person before he is the trustee is deemed to come to his knowledge on his appointment taking effect or, in the case of the official receiver, on his becoming trustee.

GENERAL NOTE

The trustee must claim the property or seek replacement (under s. 307, 308 or 308A) within 42 days after it has come to his notice, as defined by s. 309(2). The court refused to permit a s. 307 notice to be served out of time in *Solomons v Williams* [2001] B.P.I.R. 1123. Note the minor changes made to subs. 1(b) by s. 117(3) of the Housing Act 1988.

310 Income payments orders

310(1) [Order by court] The court may, make an order ("an income payments order") claiming for the bankrupt's estate so much of the income of the bankrupt during the period for which the order is in force as may be specified in the order.

310(1A) **[Applicant for order]** An income payments order may be made only on an application instituted–

(a) by the trustee, and

(b) before the discharge of the bankrupt.

310(2) **[Limit on order]** The court shall not make an income payments order the effect of which would be to reduce the income of the bankrupt when taken together with any payments to which subsection (8) applies below what appears to the court to be necessary for meeting the reasonable domestic needs of the bankrupt and his family.

310(3) **[Extent of order]** An income payments order shall, in respect of any payment of income to which it is to apply, either–

(a) require the bankrupt to pay the trustee an amount equal to so much of that payment as is claimed by the order, or

(b) require the person making the payment to pay so much of it as is so claimed to the trustee, instead of to the bankrupt.

310(4) **[Power to discharge or vary attachment of earnings]** Where the court makes an income payments order it may, if it thinks fit, discharge or vary any attachment of earnings order that is for the time being in force to secure payments by the bankrupt.

310(5) **[Sums part of estate]** Sums received by the trustee under an income payments order form part of the bankrupt's estate.

310(6) **[Period of order]** An income payments order must specify the period during which it is to have effect; and that period–

(a) may end after the discharge of the bankrupt, but

(b) may not end after the period of three years beginning with the date on which the order is made.

310(6A) **[Variation of order]** An income payments order may (subject to subsection (6)(b)) be varied on the application of the trustee or the bankrupt (whether before or after discharge).

310(7) **[Income of the bankrupt]** For the purposes of this section the income of the bankrupt comprises every payment in the nature of income which is from time to time made to him or to which he from time to time becomes entitled, including any payment in respect of the carrying on of any business or in respect of any office or employment and (despite anything in section 11 or 12 of the Welfare Reform and Pensions Act 1999) any payment under a pension scheme but excluding any payment to which subsection (8) applies.

310(8) **[Application]** This subsection applies to–

(a) payments by way of guaranteed minimum pension; and

(b) payments giving effect to the bankrupt's protected rights as a member of a pension scheme.

310(9) **[Definitions]** In this section, **"guaranteed minimum pension"** and **"protected rights"** have the same meaning as in the Pension Schemes Act 1993.

GENERAL NOTE

One of the defects in BA 1914 was that it did not have an effective mechanism to enable the trustee to appropriate the income of the bankrupt for the benefit of the estate. BA 1914, s. 51 was largely ineffective, especially where the bankrupt was self-employed. The Cork Committee (*Report*, paras 591–598) recommended a change in the law which would enable creditors to be paid off out of future income rather than the proceeds of a forced sale. Although s. 310 introduces such a mechanism the evidence is that income payment orders have not been widely used: see Justice, *Insolvency Law: An Agenda for Reform* (1994) at para. 4.30.

For the relationship with s. 306 see *Re Landau* [1998] Ch. 223, a case of major significance on pension rights and the unreported 1994 county court case of *Carman v Baron*, which is noted by Greenstreet in (1996) 12 I.L. & P. 60. Section 310 does not apply to a pension which has automatically vested in the trustee – *Lesser v Lawrence* [2000] B.P.I.R. 410

and *Rowe v Sanders* [2002] EWCA Civ 242, [2002] B.P.I.R. 847. In the context of income payments orders and pensions note also s. 91 of the Pensions Act 1995 and the amendments effected by Sch. 3, para. 15. On the role of s. 310 in matrimonial proceedings note *Albert v Albert* [1996] B.P.I.R. 232 and *Re X* [1996] B.P.I.R. 494.

S. 310(1), (1A), (2)
In subs. (1) the phrase "on the application of the trustee" was deleted by EA 2002, s. 259 with effect from April 2004. Subsection (1A) was added by that same provision. S. 310 permits an application to court for an income payments order, but the court cannot appropriate so great a proportion of the bankrupt's income as to reduce him and his family to penury. This restriction existed at common law: *Re Roberts* [1900] 1 Q.B. 122. Note the amendment introduced into subs. (2) by Sch. 3, para. 15 to the Pensions Act 1995. The bankrupt must be given 28 days' notice of the application, see IR 1986, r. 6.189. Reasonable domestic need is to be determined by reference to the circumstances of each case and may include private school fees where removal from a school might be detrimental to the children: *Re Rayatt* [1998] B.P.I.R. 495. In *Scott v Davis* [2003] B.P.I.R. 1009 the issue of private school fees was revisited and the court stressed the importance of there being evidence that on the facts of the particular case that they were a reasonable domestic need. For further discussion of this subsection see *Kilvert v Flackett* [1998] B.P.I.R. 721 and *Malcolm v Official Receiver* [1999] B.P.I.R. 97.

S. 310(3)–(5)
These provisions deal with the effect of an income payments order. Either the bankrupt or some third party can be directed to make payments to the trustee, the sums thereby received forming part of the estate. On making such an order the court can modify any attachment of earnings order relating to the bankrupt's income. Note that s. 310(3) is amplified by the rules: see Sch. 9, para. 15 and IR 1986, rr. 6.189–6.193. The order may be reviewed on the application of either party or varied on the application of the trustee. The latter might occur where the bankrupt's income increases. Note here the obligation to notify the trustee within 21 days (s. 332(2) and r. 6.200(1)).

S. 310(6), (6A)
Subsection (6) was reconstituted by s. 259 of EA 2002 with effect from April 2004. It read as follows:

310(6) *[After discharge of bankrupt] An income payments order shall not be made after the discharge of the bankrupt, and if made before, shall not have effect after his discharge except–*

(a) *in the case of a discharge under section 279(1)(a) (order of court), by virtue of a condition imposed by the court under section 280(2)(c) (income, etc. after discharge), or*

(b) *in the case of a discharge under section 279(1)(b) (expiration of relevant period), by virtue of a provision of the order requiring it to continue in force for a period ending after the discharge but no later than 3 years after the making of the order.*

Subsection (6A), which deals with variation of IPOs, was inserted by s. 259 of EA 2002 with effect from April 2004.

S. 310(7)
This defines "income" in wide terms and emphasises that it covers the income of a self-employed person. Presumably payments in the nature of capital are not covered by s. 310 unless such payments could be treated as a single surge of income, as was the subject of discussion in the case of *Kilvert v Flackett* (above). See also *Supperstone v Lloyds Names Working Party* [1999] B.P.I.R. 832. Again the text of this subsection has been supplemented by Sch. 3, para. 15 to the Pensions Act 1995 and s. 18 coupled with Sch. 2 of the Welfare Reform and Pensions Act 1999 with effect from May 29, 2000 (see Welfare Reform and Pensions Act 1999 Commencement No. 7 Order 2000 (SI 2000/1382 C. 41)).

S. 310(8), (9)
These completely new subsections were introduced by the Pensions Act 1995 (Sch. 3, para. 15).

310A   Income payments agreement

310A(1)   ["Income payments agreement"] In this section "income payments agreement" means a written agreement between a bankrupt and his trustee or between a bankrupt and the official receiver which provides–

(a) that the bankrupt is to pay to the trustee or the official receiver an amount equal to a specified part or proportion of the bankrupt's income for a specified period, or

(b) that a third person is to pay to the trustee or the official receiver a specified proportion of money due to the bankrupt by way of income for a specified period.

310A(2) [Enforceability of agreement] A provision of an income payments agreement of a kind specified in subsection (1)(a) or (b) may be enforced as if it were a provision of an income payments order.

310A(3) [Discharge or variation of attachment of earnings order] While an income payments agreement is in force the court may, on the application of the bankrupt, his trustee or the official receiver, discharge or vary an attachment of earnings order that is for the time being in force to secure payments by the bankrupt.

310A(4) [Application of s. 310(5), (7)–(9)] The following provisions of section 310 shall apply to an income payments agreement as they apply to an income payments order–

(a) subsection (5) (receipts to form part of estate), and

(b) subsections (7) to (9) (meaning of income).

310A(5) [Period of agreement] An income payments agreement must specify the period during which it is to have effect; and that period–

(a) may end after the discharge of the bankrupt, but

(b) may not end after the period of three years beginning with the date on which the agreement is made.

310A(6) [Variation of agreement] An income payments agreement may (subject to subsection (5)(b)) be varied–

(a) by written agreement between the parties, or

(b) by the court on an application made by the bankrupt, the trustee or the official receiver.

310A(7) [Power to vary] The court–

(a) may not vary an income payments agreement so as to include provision of a kind which could not be included in an income payments order, and

(b) shall grant an application to vary an income payments agreement if and to the extent that the court thinks variation necessary to avoid the effect mentioned in section 310(2).

GENERAL NOTE

This innovation (which takes effect in April 2004) came about as a result of the enactment of s. 260 of EA 2002. The aim is to put in place a legally binding income payments scheme without the need for a formal court order. Once again the underlying policy goal is to reduce administration costs, a particularly important consideration bearing in mind the inefficiencies involved in the IPO procedure. Further provision for IPAs is to be found in IR 1986, rr. 6.193A–C.

S. 310A(1)
This defines what is meant by an income payments agreement (IPA). The agreement must be in writing. IPAs can be used to divert sums due to the bankrupt from a third party.

S. 310(2), (4)
The effect of an IPA is equivalent to that of an IPO. This is reinforced by subs. (4).

S. 310(3), (6), (7)
Variation and discharge of IPAs is hereby provided for. Note also the variation possibilities covered by subs. (6), including variation by agreement in writing and the limitations on the court imposed by subs. (7).

S. 310(5)
This regulates the duration of an IPA. It can last beyond the date of discharge but cannot persist for more than three years after the agreement date.

311 Acquisition by trustee of control

311(1) [Trustee to take possession] The trustee shall take possession of all books, papers and other records which relate to the bankrupt's estate or affairs and which belong to him or are in his possession or under his control (including any which would be privileged from disclosure in any proceedings).

311(2) **[Trustee like receiver]** In relation to, and for the purpose of acquiring or retaining possession of, the bankrupt's estate, the trustee is in the same position as if he were a receiver of property appointed by the High Court; and the court may, on his application, enforce such acquisition or retention accordingly.

311(3) **[Where estate includes transferable property]** Where any part of the bankrupt's estate consists of stock or shares in a company, shares in a ship or any other property transferable in the books of a company, office or person, the trustee may exercise the right to transfer the property to the same extent as the bankrupt might have exercised it if he had not become bankrupt.

311(4) **[Where estate includes things in action]** Where any part of the estate consists of things in action, they are deemed to have been assigned to the trustee; but notice of the deemed assignment need not be given except in so far as it is necessary, in a case where the deemed assignment is from the bankrupt himself, for protecting the priority of the trustee.

311(5) **[Where goods held by pledge]** Where any goods comprised in the estate are held by any person by way of pledge, pawn or other security and no notice has been served in respect of those goods by the official receiver under subsection (5) of section 285 (restriction on realising security), the trustee may serve such a notice in respect of the goods; and whether or not a notice has been served under this subsection or that subsection, the trustee may, if he thinks fit, exercise the bankrupt's right of redemption in respect of any such goods.

311(6) **[Effect of s. 311(5) notice]** A notice served by the trustee under subsection (5) has the same effect as a notice served by the official receiver under section 285(5).

S. 311(1)
This describes the most basic duty of a trustee, which is to collect the bankrupt's property together. For the impact of this provision on privileged documents see *Re Konigsberg (a Bankrupt)* [1989] 1 W.L.R. 1257. The right to take papers is limited to business or financial records and does not include personal correspondence even if it has an economic value – see *Haig v Aitken* [2000] B.P.I.R. 462 where the possibility that seizure of such documents might infringe Art. 8 ECHR (right of privacy) was also considered by the court.

S. 311(2)
While carrying out the above function the trustee will be treated as if he were a court-appointed receiver and will, for example, enjoy the protection of the law of contempt.

S. 311(3), (4)
These provisions deal with the trustee's rights in respect of certain intangible forms of property, such as shares or choses in action.

S. 311(5), (6)
These provisions, based on BA 1914, s. 59 deal with the situation where the bankrupt's goods have been given as security to some other person. The trustee may (if the official receiver has not already done so) serve a notice on the third party in order to redeem the goods. Such a notice has the same effect as a notice served by the official receiver under s. 285(5).

312 Obligation to surrender control to trustee

312(1) **[Bankrupt to surrender property]** The bankrupt shall deliver up to the trustee possession of any property, books, papers or other records of which he has possession or control and of which the trustee is required to take possession.

This is without prejudice to the general duties of the bankrupt under section 333 in this Chapter.

312(2) **[Other persons in possession]** If any of the following is in possession of any property, books, papers or other records of which the trustee is required to take possession, namely–

(a) the official receiver,

(b) a person who has ceased to be trustee of the bankrupt's estate, or

(c) a person who has been the supervisor of a voluntary arrangement approved in relation to the bankrupt under Part VIII, the official receiver or, as the case may be, that person shall deliver up possession of the property, books, papers or records to the trustee.

312(3) **[Bankers, agents et al. of bankrupt]** Any banker or agent of the bankrupt or any other person who holds any property to the account of, or for, the bankrupt shall pay or deliver to the trustee all property in his possession or under his control which forms part of the bankrupt's estate and which he is not by law entitled to retain as against the bankrupt or trustee.

312(4) **[Penalty for non-compliance]** If any person without reasonable excuse fails to comply with any obligation imposed by this section, he is guilty of a contempt of court and liable to be punished accordingly (in addition to any other punishment to which he may be subject).

S. 312(1)
This provision obliges the bankrupt, in addition to his general duty to assist the trustee, to hand over possession of his property, books, etc., to the trustee.

S. 312(2), (3)
This obligation extends to official receivers, former trustees, supervisors of a voluntary arrangement, bankers and agents of the bankrupt, although the latter two groups may have certain rights of retention as against the trustee.

S. 312(4)
The above obligations are reinforced by the law of contempt.

313 Charge on bankrupt's home

313(1) **[Application to court by trustee]** Where any property consisting of an interest in a dwelling house which is occupied by the bankrupt or by his spouse or former spouse is comprised in the bankrupt's estate and the trustee is, for any reason, unable for the time being to realise that property, the trustee may apply to the court for an order imposing a charge on the property for the benefit of the bankrupt's estate.

313(2) **[Benefit of charge]** If on an application under this section the court imposes a charge on any property, the benefit of that charge shall be comprised in the bankrupt's estate and is enforceable, up to the charged value from time to time, for the payment of any amount which is payable otherwise than to the bankrupt out of the estate and of interest on that amount at the prescribed rate.

313(2A) **[Meaning of charged value in s. 313(2)]** In subsection (2) the charged value means–

(a) the amount specified in the charging order as the value of the bankrupt's interest in the property at the date of the order, plus

(b) interest on that amount from the date of the charging order at the prescribed rate.

313(2B) **[Court's duty in valuing interest]** In determining the value of an interest for the purposes of this section the court shall disregard any matter which it is required to disregard by the rules.

313(3) **[Provision in order]** An order under this section made in respect of property vested in the trustee shall provide, in accordance with the rules, for the property to cease to be comprised in the bankrupt's estate and, subject to the charge (and any prior charge), to vest in the bankrupt.

313(4) **[Effect of Charging Orders Act]** Subsections (1) and (2) and (4) to (6) of section 3 of the Charging Orders Act 1979 (supplemental provisions with respect to charging orders) have effect in relation to orders under this section as in relation to charging orders under that Act.

313(5) **[No power to vary a charged value]** But an order under section 3(5) of that Act may not vary a charged value.

GENERAL NOTE

This is a new provision which would probably be better located next to ss. 336–338, which also deal with the matrimonial home. This new package of provisions, which was recommended by the Cork Committee (*Report*, paras 1114–1131), is designed to tilt the balance more in favour of the bankrupt and his family when it comes to selling the family home. This provision, unlike the others dealing with the matrimonial home, was included in the original Insolvency Bill of 1895. For a general view of the operation of s. 313 in practice see Hill (1990) 6 I.L. & P. 12. Section 313 is amended with effect from April 1, 2004 by s. 260 of EA 2002. The effect is to improve the rights of bankrupts where orders under s. 313 are utilised.

S. 313(1)
If the trustee cannot sell the bankrupt's interest in the "dwelling house" (for the definition, see s. 385) occupied by him or his family he may apply to a court for a charging order on that interest.

S. 313(2)–(4)
These provisions deal with the effect of the court granting such a charging order. It attaches to the property in question until enforced, although the property ceases to vest in the trustee and will revert to the bankrupt (subject to the charge). Certain parts of s. 3 of the Charging Orders Act 1979 will apply to such an order made by the court under s. 313(1).

Amendments to ss. 313(2), 313(2A) and 313(2B) here are designed to ensure that where the value of the charged property increases over time the benefit accrues to the bankrupt and not to the estate. This in effect is achieved by providing for the value of the bankrupt's interest in the charged property to be identified on application; that charged value then gets the benefit of any inflationary uplift.

The rules provide more details of the conditions which may be attached to such a charge: see IR 1986, r. 6.237.

S. 313(5)
Inserted by s. 260 of EA 2002 with effect from April 1, 2004 this prevents a charging order from undermining the protective effect of s. 313(2A).

313A Low value home: application for sale, possession or charge

313A(1) [Application of section] This section applies where–

(a) property comprised in the bankrupt's estate consists of an interest in a dwelling-house which at the date of the bankruptcy was the sole or principal residence of–

    (i) the bankrupt,
    (ii) the bankrupt's spouse, or
    (iii) a former spouse of the bankrupt, and

(b) the trustee applies for an order for the sale of the property, for an order for possession of the property or for an order under section 313 in respect of the property.

313A(2) [Court's duty to dismiss application] The court shall dismiss the application if the value of the interest is below the amount prescribed for the purposes of this subsection.

313A(3) [Court's duty to disregard matters prescribed by order] In determining the value of an interest for the purposes of this section the court shall disregard any matter which it is required to disregard by the order which prescribes the amount for the purposes of subsection (2).

GENERAL NOTE

Again introduced by s. 261(3) of EA 2002 this deals with the realisation of low value properties. The feeling is that the marginal benefit to creditors from realising such an asset is outweighed by the disproportionate suffering imposed upon the bankrupt by the loss of his home. This provision comes into effect on April 1, 2004.

S. 313A(1)
This seeks to identify what is meant by an interest in a low value home for the purposes of this section. The problem of multiple low value homes might have to be addressed – see the comments on s. 283A.

S. 313A(2)
The trustee is hereby in effect debarred from taking specified realisation action in respect of an interest in a dwelling covered by subs. (1). The minimum amount prescribed is £1,000 (Insolvency Proceedings (Monetary Limits) (Amendment) Order 2004 (SI 2004/547)), though that valuation figure is then qualified by Art. 3 of that Order.

S. 313(A)(3)
This deals further with the question of valuation and inclusion within this restrictive mechanism.

Section 314   Insolvency Act 1986

314 Powers of trustee

314(1) [**Powers in Sch. 5, Pt. I and II**] The trustee may–

(a) with the permission of the creditors' committee or the court, exercise any of the powers specified in Part I of Schedule 5 to this Act, and

(b) without that permission, exercise any of the general powers specified in Part II of that Schedule.

314(2) [**Powers of appointment re bankrupt**] With the permission of the creditors' committee or the court, the trustee may appoint the bankrupt–

(a) to superintend the management of his estate or any part of it,

(b) to carry on his business (if any) for the benefit of his creditors, or

(c) in any other respect to assist in administering the estate in such manner and on such terms as the trustee may direct.

314(3) [**Permission in s. 314(1)(a), (2)**] A permission given for the purposes of subsection (1)(a) or (2) shall not be a general permission but shall relate to a particular proposed exercise of the power in question; and a person dealing with the trustee in good faith and for value is not to be concerned to enquire whether any permission required in either case has been given.

314(4) [**Where no permission under s. 314(1)(a), (2)**] Where the trustee has done anything without the permission required by subsection (1)(a) or (2), the court or the creditors' committee may, for the purpose of enabling him to meet his expenses out of the bankrupt's estate, ratify what the trustee has done.

But the committee shall not do so unless it is satisfied that the trustee has acted in a case of urgency and has sought its ratification without undue delay.

314(5) [**Powers in Sch. 5, Pt. III**] Part III of Schedule 5 to this Act has effect with respect to the things which the trustee is able to do for the purposes of, or in connection with, the exercise of any of his powers under any of this Group of Parts.

314(6) [**Notice to committee**] Where the trustee (not being the official receiver) in exercise of the powers conferred on him by any provision in this Group of Parts–

(a) disposes of any property comprised in the bankrupt's estate to an associate of the bankrupt, or

(b) employs a solicitor,

he shall, if there is for the time being a creditors' committee, give notice to the committee of that exercise of his powers.

314(7) [**Power to summon general meeting of creditors**] Without prejudice to the generality of subsection (5) and Part III of Schedule 5, the trustee may, if he thinks fit, at any time summon a general meeting of the bankrupt's creditors.

Subject to the preceding provisions in this Group of Parts, he shall summon such a meeting if he is requested to do so by a creditor of the bankrupt and the request is made with the concurrence of not less than one-tenth, in value, of the bankrupt's creditors (including the creditor making the request).

314(8) [**Capacity of trustee**] Nothing in this Act is to be construed as restricting the capacity of the trustee to exercise any of his powers outside England and Wales.

S. 314(1), (2), (6)
A trustee may exercise the powers listed in Pt II of Sch. 5 without obtaining permission of the committee of creditors (see s. 301). This list of powers is derived from BA 1914, s. 55. No major changes have been made to these basic

powers. Note, however, that if property is disposed of to an "associate" of the bankrupt (for the meaning of this term see s. 435), the committee of creditors must be told. Section 314(2) refers to Pt I of Sch. 5, which describes powers which the trustee may exercise only with the consent of the committee of creditors. These powers are based on BA 1914, s. 56, 57. The sanction requirement is to protect the bankrupt's estate, see *Re a Debtor (No. 26A of 1975)* [1985] 1 W.L.R. 6. The requirement that the trustee should obtain permission before employing a solicitor or agent, contained formerly in s. 56(3), has been dropped – but if he does this he must now give notice to the committee according to s. 314(6)(b).

S. 314(3), (4)

These provisions deal with the question of permission as required by s. 314(2) and (7) above. It must be specific. *Bona fide* purchasers for value dealing with the trustee need not investigate to see that it has been given: this is in line with the general policy of s. 377 validating the acts of the trustee.

S. 314(5)

This provision refers to Pt III of Sch. 5, which gives a general account of the trustee's powers (*e.g.* to hold property and make contracts) that may be exercised in his "official name" (see s. 305(4)).

S. 314(7)

This deals with the calling of a general meeting of creditors by the trustee. Note that he must call such a meeting if asked to do so by creditors owed one-tenth of the bankrupt's total debts. The figure fixed by BA 1914, s. 79(2) was one-sixth in value of the total debts.

S. 314(8)

The trustee may exercise his powers outside England and Wales. This is increasingly important as the problems of cross-border insolvency increase. See here *Re Hayward* [1997] Ch. 45 where the trustee was required by virtue of the European Convention on Jurisdiction and Enforcement of Judgments in Civil Matters to pursue a claim to Spanish real estate in Spain and not in England. Rattee J. concluded that the claim was not primarily concerned with insolvency, but with title to immoveable property, and therefore the Spanish courts enjoyed exclusive jurisdiction under the Convention. See also *Pollard v Ashurst* [2001] B.P.I.R. 131. The entry into effect of the EC Regulation on Insolvency Proceedings (discussed below at pp. 602) will improve matters considerably.

Disclaimer of onerous property

315 Disclaimer (general power)

315(1) [Power of trustee to disclaim] Subject as follows, the trustee may, by the giving of the prescribed notice, disclaim any onerous property and may do so notwithstanding that he has taken possession of it, endeavoured to sell it or otherwise exercised rights of ownership in relation to it.

315(2) [Onerous property] The following is onerous property for the purposes of this section, that is to say–

(a) any unprofitable contract, and

(b) any other property comprised in the bankrupt's estate which is unsaleable or not readily saleable, or is such that it may give rise to a liability to pay money or perform any other onerous act.

315(3) [Effect of disclaimer] A disclaimer under this section–

(a) operates so as to determine, as from the date of the disclaimer, the rights, interests and liabilities of the bankrupt and his estate in or in respect of the property disclaimed, and

(b) discharges the trustee from all personal liability in respect of that property as from the commencement of his trusteeship,

but does not, except so far as is necessary for the purpose of releasing the bankrupt, the bankrupt's estate and the trustee from any liability, affect the rights or liabilities of any other person.

315(4) [Where notice of disclaimer not to be given] A notice of disclaimer shall not be given under this section in respect of any property that has been claimed for the estate under section 307 (after-acquired property) or 308 (personal property of bankrupt exceeding reasonable replacement value) or 308A, except with the leave of the court.

315(5) **[Persons sustaining loss or damage]** Any person sustaining loss or damage in consequence of the operation of a disclaimer under this section is deemed to be a creditor of the bankrupt to the extent of the loss or damage and accordingly may prove for the loss or damage as a bankruptcy debt.

GENERAL NOTE

This section, and the ones immediately following it, deal with the power of the trustee to disclaim onerous property, and the role of the court in the event of disclaimer. The Cork Committee (*Report*, paras 1182–1199) felt that this power, which has existed since 1869, should be modified to enable the trustee to utilise it more effectively. The comparable provisions relating to disclaimers by liquidators are to be found in ss. 178–182. A disclaimer is deemed to have been validly exercised unless the contrary is established: see IR 1986, r. 6.185. For historical background see *Hindcastle v Barbara Attenborough Associates* [1997] A.C. 70; [1996] B.C.C. 636.

In the context of the financial markets, s. 315 does not apply in relation to a market contract or a contract effected by an exchange or clearing house for the purpose of realising property provided as margin in relation to market contracts: see CA 1989, s. 164(1), and the note on p. 2.

S. 315(1), (2)
This authorises disclaimer of onerous property even though the trustee may have already tried to sell it. For the form of the notice see IR 1986, r. 6.178 and Form 6.61. Communication of this notice is covered by rr. 6.179–6.181. Property which may be so disclaimed is defined in s. 315(2). For the meaning of "property" here see *London City Corporation v Bown, The Times* October 11, 1989 where a secure periodic tenancy was not so regarded. A cause of action may be disclaimed – *Khan-Ghauri v Dunbar Bank plc* [2001] B.P.I.R. 618. Note that the 12-month cut-off period for disclaimer in BA 1914, s. 54(1) has been dropped, against the wishes of the Cork Committee (*Report*, para. 1195).

S. 315(3), (5)
The effect of disclaimer is explained here. Note that third-party rights are only to be prejudiced in so far as that is absolutely necessary, and anyone suffering losses as a result of a disclaimer can prove in the bankruptcy in respect of it (but see s. 320(5) here). On the effect of disclaimer see *MEPC plc v Scottish Amicable Life Assurance Society* [1996] B.P.I.R. 447 and *Hindcastle Barbara Attenborough Associates* [1997] A.C. 70; [1996] B.C.C. 636.

S. 315(4)
Notices of disclaimer are restricted by this provision. Leave of the court is required before the trustee may disclaim after-acquired property which has already been claimed for the estate (s. 307), or property claimed under ss. 308 or 308A (added by the Housing Act 1988, s. 117(3)) with a view to replacement. For the leave procedure, see IR 1986, r. 6.182.

These rules on disclaimer are supplemented by IR 1986, rr. 6.178–6.186.

316 Notice requiring trustee's decision

316(1) **[Where notice not to be given]** Notice of disclaimer shall not be given under section 315 in respect of any property if–

(a) a person interested in the property has applied in writing to the trustee or one of his predecessors as trustee requiring the trustee or that predecessor to decide whether he will disclaim or not, and

(b) the period of 28 days beginning with the day on which that application was made has expired without a notice of disclaimer having been given under section 315 in respect of that property.

316(2) **[Deemed adoption]** The trustee is deemed to have adopted any contract which by virtue of this section he is not entitled to disclaim.

GENERAL NOTE

If the trustee, having been required to make a choice, decides not to disclaim, he cannot later change his mind. Failure to disclaim constitutes adoption. The 28-day period during which the trustee must make his decision has been retained from BA 1914, s. 54(4). For the form of a s. 316 application see IR 1986, r. 6.183. The trustee can force a person to declare his interest in disclaimable property by using IR 1986, r. 6.184 and Form 6.63.

Note also IR 1986, rr. 6.178–6.186.

317 Disclaimer of leaseholds

317(1) **[Disclaimer of leasehold property]** The disclaimer of any property of a leasehold nature does not take effect unless a copy of the disclaimer has been served (so far as the trustee is aware of their addresses) on every person claiming under the bankrupt as underlessee or mortgagee and either–

(a) no application under section 320 below is made with respect to the property before the end of the period of 14 days beginning with the day on which the last notice served under this subsection was served, or

(b) where such an application has been made, the court directs that the disclaimer is to take effect.

317(2) **[Where court gives s. 317(1)(b) direction]** Where the court gives a direction under subsection (1)(b) it may also, instead of or in addition to any order it makes under section 320, make such orders with respect to fixtures, tenant's improvements and other matters arising out of the lease as it thinks fit.

GENERAL NOTE

These provisions deal with disclaimers in respect of onerous land. In the case of leasehold property, both underlessees and mortgagees must be served with notices of disclaimer. Note here IR 1986, rr. 6.178–6.186.

Formerly, disclaimers of leases required the consent of the court: BA 1914, S. 54(3). Now the court will only be involved if an application is made to it within 14 days under s. 320. The trustee, after serving notice, must wait for the 14 days to elapse before the disclaimer can take effect. If application to the court has been made, obviously the trustee must wait for the outcome of the application.

The court, if it permits disclaimer, can make special provision for fixtures, etc.

318 Disclaimer of dwelling house

318 Without prejudice to section 317, the disclaimer of any property in a dwelling house does not take effect unless a copy of the disclaimer has been served (so far as the trustee is aware of their addresses) on every person in occupation of or claiming a right to occupy the dwelling house and either–

(a) no application under section 320 is made with respect to the property before the end of the period of 14 days beginning with the day on which the last notice served under this section was served, or

(b) where such an application has been made, the court directs that the disclaimer is to take effect.

GENERAL NOTE

In the case of dwelling houses (for definition, see s. 385), all occupiers must be notified. This is a new provision, which substantially mirrors s. 317 in many procedural respects.

319 Disclaimer of land subject to rentcharge

319(1) **[Application]** The following applies where, in consequence of the disclaimer under section 315 of any land subject to a rentcharge, that land vests by operation of law in the Crown or any other person (referred to in the next subsection as "the proprietor").

319(2) **[Limit on liability]** The proprietor, and the successors in title of the proprietor, are not subject to any personal liability in respect of any sums becoming due under the rentcharge, except sums becoming due after the proprietor, or some person claiming under or through the proprietor, has taken possession or control of the land or has entered into occupation of it.

GENERAL NOTE

These are highly specialised provisions relating to disclaimers of land subject to a rentcharge. The person in whom the land vests subsequently is not subject to the normal rentcharge obligations.

320 Court order vesting disclaimed property

320(1) **[Application]** This section and the next apply where the trustee has disclaimed property under section 315.

320(2) **[Application to court]** An application may be made to the court under this section by–

(a) any person who claims an interest in the disclaimed property,

(b) any person who is under any liability in respect of the disclaimed property, not being a liability discharged by the disclaimer, or

(c) where the disclaimed property is property in a dwelling house, any person who at the time when the bankruptcy petition was presented was in occupation of or entitled to occupy the dwelling house.

320(3) **[Order by court]** Subject as follows in this section and the next, the court may, on an application under this section, make an order on such terms as it thinks fit for the vesting of the disclaimed property in, or for its delivery to–

(a) a person entitled to it or a trustee for such a person,

(b) a person subject to such a liability as is mentioned in subsection (2)(b) or a trustee for such a person, or

(c) where the disclaimed property is property in a dwelling house, any person who at the time when the bankruptcy petition was presented was in occupation of or entitled to occupy the dwelling house.

320(4) **[Limit to s. 320(3)(b)]** The court shall not make an order by virtue of subsection (3)(b) except where it appears to the court that it would be just to do so for the purpose of compensating the person subject to the liability in respect of the disclaimer.

320(5) **[Effect of order in s. 315(5) assessment]** The effect of any order under this section shall be taken into account in assessing for the purposes of section 315(5) the extent of any loss or damage sustained by any person in consequence of the disclaimer.

320(6) **[Mode of vesting re order]** An order under this section vesting property in any person need not be completed by any conveyance, assignment or transfer.

S. 320(1)–(4)
Where a trustee has disclaimed onerous property, certain persons have the right to apply to the court for relief. Note the three-month time limit for applications, see IR 1986, r. 6.186. Note that occupiers of dwelling houses have now been given this right. The type of relief which the court may grant is described by these provisions. Vesting and delivery orders may be made according to the general discretion of the court. See *Lee v Lee* [1999] B.P.I.R. 926 for an unusual case. On s. 320(2)(a) see *Hackney LBC v Crown Estates Commissioners* [1996] B.P.I.R. 428.

S. 320(5), (6)
Where a vesting order is made, no conveyance, etc., is required to effect it. If disclaimed property is vested in a person who has suffered loss as a result of the disclaimer, that vesting is to be taken into account when assessing compensation.
  Note here IR 1986, r. 6.186.

321 Order under s. 320 in respect of leaseholds

321(1) **[Terms of order re leasehold property]** The court shall not make an order under section 320 vesting property of a leasehold nature in any person, except on terms making that person–

(a) subject to the same liabilities and obligations as the bankrupt was subject to under the lease on the day the bankruptcy petition was presented, or

(b) if the court thinks fit, subject to the same liabilities and obligations as that person would be subject to if the lease had been assigned to him on that day.

321(2) **[Where order re part of property in lease]** For the purposes of an order under section 320 relating to only part of any property comprised in a lease, the requirements of subsection (1) apply as if the lease comprised only the property to which the order relates.

321(3) **[Where no person accepts order in s. 320 case]** Where subsection (1) applies and no person is willing to accept an order under section 320 on the terms required by that subsection, the court may (by order under section 320) vest the estate or interest of the bankrupt in the property in any person who is liable (whether personally or in a representative capacity and whether alone or jointly with the bankrupt) to perform the lessee's covenants in the lease.

The court may by virtue of this subsection vest that estate and interest in such a person freed and discharged from all estates, incumbrances and interests created by the bankrupt.

321(4) **[Exclusion from interest in property]** Where subsection (1) applies and a person declines to accept any order under section 320, that person shall be excluded from all interest in the property.

GENERAL NOTE

Section 321(1) deals with applications in respect of leasehold property – the person in whom the leasehold property is vested must assume the same obligations as the lessee was subject to prior to his bankruptcy. If only part of the leasehold property is so vested, the order must take this into account when determining the obligations to impose. Section 321(2) and (3) deal with cases where persons decline to accept orders made under s. 320 – the court may make adjustments to interests in the property concerned. This includes exclusion from all interest in the property in question (s. 321(4)).

Distribution of bankrupt's estate

322 Proof of debts

322(1) **[Proof in accordance with rules]** Subject to this section and the next, the proof of any bankruptcy debt by a secured or unsecured creditor of the bankrupt and the admission or rejection of any proof shall take place in accordance with the rules.

322(2) **[Where bankruptcy debt bears interest]** Where a bankruptcy debt bears interest, that interest is provable as part of the debt except in so far as it is payable in respect of any period after the commencement of the bankruptcy.

322(3) **[Estimation of debt]** The trustee shall estimate the value of any bankruptcy debt which, by reason of its being subject to any contingency or contingencies or for any other reason, does not bear a certain value.

322(4) **[Where estimate under s. 303, 322(3)]** Where the value of a bankruptcy debt is estimated by the trustee under subsection (3) or, by virtue of section 303 in Chapter III, by the court, the amount provable in the bankruptcy in respect of the debt is the amount of the estimate.

S. 322(1)
The procedure governing proof of "bankruptcy debts" (see s. 382) is governed by the rules: see in particular IR 1986, rr. 6.96–6.114.

For the question of proof by secured creditors see s. 383. For a case where contingent tax penalties were held provable, see *Re Hurren (a Bankrupt)* [1983] 1 W.L.R. 183. Fines were provable debts under the old law: *Re Pascoe Ex p. Trustee of the Bankrupt v Lords Commissioners of His Majesty's Treasury* [1944] Ch. 310. It is not clear from the Act itself whether the recommendation of the Cork Committee (*Report*, para. 1330), that this rule should be reversed, has been implemented. However, the fact that fines are not provable is apparent from IR 1986, r. 12.3.

S. 322(2)
Under BA 1914, s. 66 there were severe restrictions on proving in respect of interest. These restrictions, which were heavily criticised by the Cork Committee (*Report*, para. 1381), have been largely removed except with regard to interest accruing after the commencement of the bankruptcy. It should also be remembered that s. 343 may be relevant here.

S. 322(3), (4)
This allows the trustee to estimate the value of contingent or uncertain debts. For the costs of the trustee see IR 1986, r. 6.100(2). Under BA 1914, s. 30 there was a facility allowing a creditor to appeal against any estimate made by a

Section 323   *Insolvency Act 1986*

trustee. This is not specifically recreated by s. 322 but possibly a disappointed creditor could make use of s. 303. This provision for estimates will be doubly useful now that the old restriction, formerly contained in BA 1914, s. 30(1), banning proof in respect of unliquidated claims, has been abolished: see s. 382(3). The Cork Committee (*Report*, para. 1318) favoured this change partly because the restriction did not apply to a corporate insolvency: *Re Berkeley Securities (Property) Ltd* [1980] 1 W.L.R. 1589 – but this had been the subject of some uncertainty.

The change in bankruptcy law will be welcomed if it avoids such confusion.

323   Mutual credit and set-off

323(1)   **[Application]** This section applies where before the commencement of the bankruptcy there have been mutual credits, mutual debts or other mutual dealings between the bankrupt and any creditor of the bankrupt proving or claiming to prove for a bankruptcy debt.

323(2)   **[Account to be taken]** An account shall be taken of what is due from each party to the other in respect of the mutual dealings and the sums due from one party shall be set off against the sums due from the other.

323(3)   **[Qualification to s. 323(2)]** Sums due from the bankrupt to another party shall not be included in the account taken under subsection (2) if that other party had notice at the time they became due that a bankruptcy petition relating to the bankrupt was pending.

323(4)   **[Balance to trustee]** Only the balance (if any) of the account taken under subsection (2) is provable as a bankruptcy debt or, as the case may be, to be paid to the trustee as part of the bankrupt's estate.

GENERAL NOTE

There is little change here. The rules are those in BA 1914, s. 31, which in turn reflected common-law authorities such as *Foster v Wilson* (1843) 12 M. & W. 191. The only changes in s. 323 are of a terminological or consequential nature reflecting the demise of concepts such as acts of bankruptcy and receiving orders. Notwithstanding the apparent desire of the legislature to reaffirm the old rules on set-off, in *Stein v Blake* [1996] A.C. 243; [1995] B.C.C. 543 the House of Lords concluded that it was possible for a trustee in bankruptcy to assign a bankrupt's right of action to a third party and in so doing defeat any right of set-off which the defendant in the proposed action might have had against the bankrupt. This decision of the House of Lords can be seen as one of a number of recent authorities favouring an "estate maximisation" policy on the part of the judiciary. *Stein v Blake* (above) was followed in Australia in *Re Bankrupt Estate of Cirillo* [1997] B.P.I.R. 574.

It is worth noting that s. 323 does not implement the recommendation of the Cork Committee (*Report*, para. 1342) that the decision in *National Westminster Bank Ltd v Halesowen Presswork & Assemblies Ltd* [1972] A.C. 785, banning contracting out of the statutory rules, be reversed. However, there is a special exception allowing contracting out on the financial markets: see CA 1989, ss. 159, 163, and the note on p. 2, above.

For the exclusion of set-off in respect of post-insolvency VAT credits, see FA 1988, s. 21 (as amended by FA 1994, s. 47).

On s. 323(3) see *Coe v Ashurst* [1999] B.P.I.R. 662.

324   Distribution by means of dividend

324(1)   **[Duty to declare and distribute]** Whenever the trustee has sufficient funds in hand for the purpose he shall, subject to the retention of such sums as may be necessary for the expenses of the bankruptcy, declare and distribute dividends among the creditors in respect of the bankruptcy debts which they have respectively proved.

324(2)   **[Notice of intention to declare and distribute]** The trustee shall give notice of his intention to declare and distribute a dividend.

324(3)   **[Notice of dividend etc.]** Where the trustee has declared a dividend, he shall give notice of the dividend and of how it is proposed to distribute it; and a notice given under this subsection shall contain the prescribed particulars of the bankrupt's estate.

324(4) **[Calculation and distribution of dividend]** In the calculation and distribution of a dividend the trustee shall make provision–

(a) for any bankruptcy debts which appear to him to be due to persons who, by reason of the distance of their place of residence, may not have had sufficient time to tender and establish their proofs,

(b) for any bankruptcy debts which are the subject of claims which have not yet been determined, and

(c) for disputed proofs and claims.

S. 324(1)–(3)
These provide for the declaration of dividends to creditors when the trustee has sufficient funds at his disposal for that purpose, once expenses have been taken into account. Notice of the dividend must be given to creditors. Under BA 1914, s. 62(2) the trustee had, as a general rule, to declare the first dividend within four months of the first meeting of creditors; this specific deadline has been dropped.

For further details on declaration of dividends, see IR 1986, Pt 11. For the mechanics of payment, see the Insolvency Regulations 1994 (SI 1994/2507), reg. 23.

S. 324(4)
This is a good housekeeping provision. The trustee should set aside funds to cover disputed claims or claims by persons who have not yet lodged proofs.

If the trustee proposes to pay an interim dividend at a time when an application to the court to challenge the admission or rejection of a proof is outstanding, the leave of the court is required under IR 1986, r. 11.5(2).

325 Claims by unsatisfied creditors

325(1) **[Entitlements of creditors]** A creditor who has not proved his debt before the declaration of any dividend is not entitled to disturb, by reason that he has not participated in it, the distribution of that dividend or any other dividend declared before his debt was proved, but–

(a) when he has proved that debt he is entitled to be paid, out of any money for the time being available for the payment of any further dividend, any dividend or dividends which he has failed to receive; and

(b) any dividend or dividends payable under paragraph (a) shall be paid before that money is applied to the payment of any such further dividend.

325(2) **[Order re payment of dividend]** No action lies against the trustee for a dividend, but if the trustee refuses to pay a dividend the court may, if it thinks fit, order him to pay it and also to pay, out of his own money–

(a) interest on the dividend, at the rate for the time being specified in section 17 of the Judgments Act 1838, from the time it was withheld, and

(b) the costs of the proceedings in which the order to pay is made.

S. 325(1)
Late claimants cannot upset properly declared dividends, but they may make a claim on any surplus available.

S. 325(2)
This curiously worded provision is derived from BA 1914, s. 68. On the one hand, it states that no action shall lie against a trustee for a dividend, but then it permits the court to order the trustee to pay one, and, indeed, to pay interest and costs out of his own pocket.

Compare IR 1986, r. 11.8.

326 Distribution of property in specie

326(1) **[Division of unsaleable property]** Without prejudice to sections 315 to 319 (disclaimer), the trustee may, with the permission of the creditors' committee, divide in its existing form amongst the bankrupt's creditors, according to its estimated value, any property which from its peculiar nature or other special circumstances cannot be readily or advantageously sold.

326(2) **[Permission under s. 326(1)]** A permission given for the purposes of subsection (1) shall not be a general permission but shall relate to a particular proposed exercise of the power in question; and a person dealing with the trustee in good faith and for value is not to be concerned to enquire whether any permission required by subsection (1) has been given.

326(3) **[Where no permission under s. 326(1)]** Where the trustee has done anything without the permission required by subsection (1), the court or the creditors' committee may, for the purpose of enabling him to meet his expenses out of the bankrupt's estate, ratify what the trustee has done.

But the committee shall not do so unless it is satisfied that the trustee acted in a case of urgency and has sought its ratification without undue delay.

S. 326(1)
This authorises the trustee to make distributions in specie of the property which is difficult to realise. This is a new facility without precedent in the 1914 Act.

S. 326(2), (3)
The trustee must obtain specific permission to exercise his power to make an in specie distribution under s. 326(1) above. Unauthorised distributions may, in certain circumstances, be ratified by the creditors' committee.

327 Distribution in criminal bankruptcy

327 Where the bankruptcy order was made on a petition under section 264(1)(d) (criminal bankruptcy), no distribution shall be made under sections 324 to 326 so long as an appeal is pending (within the meaning of section 277) against the bankrupt's conviction of any offence by virtue of which the criminal bankruptcy order on which the petition was based was made.

GENERAL NOTE

In cases of criminal bankruptcy no distribution is to be made until the final appeal in the criminal case is heard.
Note prospective amendment: s. 327 is to be repealed by CJA 1988, s. 170(2) and Sch. 16 as from a day to be appointed; see the note to s. 264.

328 Priority of debts

328(1) **[Preferential debts to be paid first]** In the distribution of the bankrupt's estate, his preferential debts (within the meaning given by section 386 in Part XII) shall be paid in priority to other debts.

328(2) **[Ranking of preferential debts]** Preferential debts rank equally between themselves after the expenses of the bankruptcy and shall be paid in full unless the bankrupt's estate is insufficient for meeting them, in which case they abate in equal proportions between themselves.

328(3) **[Debts neither preferential nor under s. 329]** Debts which are neither preferential debts nor debts to which the next section applies also rank equally between themselves and, after the preferential debts, shall be paid in full unless the bankrupt's estate is insufficient for meeting them, in which case they abate in equal proportions between themselves.

328(4) **[Surplus after payment]** Any surplus remaining after the payment of the debts that are preferential or rank equally under subsection (3) shall be applied in paying interest on those debts in respect of the periods during which they have been outstanding since the commencement of the bankruptcy; and interest on preferential debts ranks equally with interest on debts other than preferential debts.

328(5) **[Rate of interest under s. 328(4)]** The rate of interest payable under subsection (4) in respect of any debt is whichever is the greater of the following–

(a) the rate specified in section 17 of the Judgments Act 1838 at the commencement of the bankruptcy, and

(b) the rate applicable to that debt apart from the bankruptcy.

328(6) **[Other enactments]** This section and the next are without prejudice to any provision of this Act or any other Act under which the payment of any debt or the making of any other payment is, in the event of bankruptcy, to have a particular priority or to be postponed.

GENERAL NOTE

This section has dropped what was formerly BA 1914, s. 33(6), dealing with payment of debts in the case of partnership insolvency: see s. 420 now. The provision relating to insolvent estates of deceased persons has also not been retained – see s. 421. The text of BA 1914, s. 33(4) is now included in s. 347. See also IR 1986, rr. 6.224 and 11.2 in this context.

S. 328(1), (2)
These provisions deal with preferential debts. Those debts described as preferential by ss. 386, 387 and by Sch. 6 to this Act are to be paid in priority to other debts (but not the expenses of the bankruptcy: see Sch. 9, para. 22). In the event of a shortfall they are to abate in equal proportions. Note that the list of preferential debts has been pruned radically by Sch. 6 after considerable pressure had been exerted on the government. This issue is considered fully in the note to s. 386 below.

S. 328(3)
Ordinary debts – *i.e.* those which are neither preferential nor deferred – rank equally between themselves and abate rateably in the event of a shortfall.

S. 328(4), (5)
These provisions deal with the payment of interest on debts which has accrued since the commencement of the bankruptcy (for the meaning of this phrase, see s. 278). It is to be paid only after both the preferential and ordinary creditors have been satisfied in full. Interest on preferential debts receives no special treatment. Section 328(5) specifies the maximum rate of interest allowed (currently eight per cent (see SI 1993/564)).

S. 328(6)
The general law on deferred creditors is preserved – for example, a creditor whose case falls within s. 3 of the Partnership Act 1890.

329 Debts to spouse

329(1) **[Application]** This section applies to bankruptcy debts owed in respect of credit provided by a person who (whether or not the bankrupt's spouse at the time the credit was provided) was the bankrupt's spouse at the commencement of the bankruptcy.

329(2) **[Ranking, payment]** Such debts–

(a) rank in priority after the debts and interest required to be paid in pursuance of section 328(3) and (4), and

(b) are payable with interest at the rate specified in section 328(5) in respect of the period during which they have been outstanding since the commencement of the bankruptcy;

and the interest payable under paragraph (b) has the same priority as the debts on which it is payable.

GENERAL NOTE

This section differs from its predecessor in the 1914 Act in a number of respects. For example, BA 1914, s. 36 related only to a loan in connection with a business or trade carried on by the bankrupt (where the lender was a husband), but not if it was lent by a wife.

330 Final distribution

330(1) **[Notice re dividend, etc.]** When the trustee has realised all the bankrupt's estate or so much of it as can, in the trustee's opinion, be realised without needlessly protracting the trusteeship, he shall give notice in the prescribed manner either–

(a) of his intention to declare a final dividend, or

(b) that no dividend, or further dividend, will be declared.

330(2) [Contents of notice] The notice under subsection (1) shall contain the prescribed particulars and shall require claims against the bankrupt's estate to be established by a date ("the final date") specified in the notice.

330(3) [Postponement of final date] The court may, on the application of any person, postpone the final date.

330(4) [Trustee's duties after final date] After the final date, the trustee shall–

(a) defray any outstanding expenses of the bankruptcy out of the bankrupt's estate, and

(b) if he intends to declare a final dividend, declare and distribute that dividend without regard to the claim of any person in respect of a debt not already proved in the bankruptcy.

330(5) [Where surplus] If a surplus remains after payment in full and with interest of all the bankrupt's creditors and the payment of the expenses of the bankruptcy, the bankrupt is entitled to the surplus.

330(6) [Applicability of EC Regulation] Subsection (5) is subject to Article 35 of the EC Regulation (surplus in secondary proceedings to be transferred to main proceedings).

S. 330(1)–(3)
Where the trustee has realised all that can be converted into money he should notify the creditors whether he is in a position to declare a final dividend. This notice must indicate a final date for claims. This final date can be extended by the court.

S. 330(4)
Once the final date is passed the trustee should pay his final dividend, but not before the costs of the bankruptcy (which often represent a considerable figure) have been defrayed out of the proceeds of realisation.

There appears to be no provision dealing with unclaimed dividends to replace BA 1914, s. 153. Generally see IR 1986, Pt 11.

S. 330(5)
Any surplus goes to the bankrupt.

S. 330(6)
This was inserted by Insolvency Act 1986 (Amendment) (No. 2) Regulations 2002 (SI 2002/1240) reg. 15 with effect from May 31, 2002.

331 Final meeting

331(1) [Application] Subject as follows in this section and the next, this section applies where–

(a) it appears to the trustee that the administration of the bankrupt's estate in accordance with this Chapter is for practical purposes complete, and

(b) the trustee is not the official receiver.

331(2) [Duty of trustee] The trustee shall summon a final general meeting of the bankrupt's creditors which–

(a) shall receive the trustee's report of his administration of the bankrupt's estate, and

(b) shall determine whether the trustee should have his release under section 299 in Chapter III.

331(3) [Time for notice] The trustee may, if he thinks fit, give the notice summoning the final general meeting at the same time as giving notice under section 330(1); but, if summoned for an earlier date, that meeting shall be adjourned (and, if necessary, further adjourned) until a date on which the trustee is able to report to the meeting that the administration of the bankrupt's estate is for practical purposes complete.

331(4) [Expenses] In the administration of the estate it is the trustee's duty to retain sufficient sums from the estate to cover the expenses of summoning and holding the meeting required by this section.

S. 331(1), (2)
These provisions require a trustee (but not an official receiver) to call a final meeting of creditors to report on how things went. This appears to be an innovation.

S. 331(3)
To save money, notice of the final meeting can be sent out along with notice of the final dividend, but the meeting cannot be held until the final dividend has been paid.

S. 331(4)
This is a reminder to the trustees to set aside sufficient funds to cover the cost of this final meeting.

332 Saving for bankrupt's home

332(1) [Application] This section applies where–

(a) there is comprised in the bankrupt's estate property consisting of an interest in a dwelling house which is occupied by the bankrupt or by his spouse or former spouse, and

(b) the trustee has been unable for any reason to realise that property.

332(2) [Conditions for s. 331 meeting] The trustee shall not summon a meeting under section 331 unless either–

(a) the court has made an order under section 313 imposing a charge on that property for the benefit of the bankrupt's estate, or

(b) the court has declined, on an application under that section, to make such an order, or

(c) the Secretary of State has issued a certificate to the trustee stating that it would be inappropriate or inexpedient for such an application to be made in the case in question.

GENERAL NOTE

This again is a new provision. It states that as a general rule there should be no summoning of a final meeting where the bankrupt's interest in a "dwelling house" (for definition, see s. 385) has not been realised. Exceptions to this general rule are: (1) where a s. 313 charge has been imposed on the property, (2) where the court has refused to grant a s. 313 charge, or (3) where the Secretary of State has certified that it would be inappropriate for the trustee to apply for a s. 313 charge.

Supplemental

333 Duties of bankrupt in relation to trustee

333(1) [Duties] The bankrupt shall–

(a) give to the trustee such information as to his affairs,

(b) attend on the trustee at such times, and

(c) do all such other things,

as the trustee may for the purposes of carrying out his functions under any of this Group of Parts reasonably require.

333(2) [Notice re after-acquired property] Where at any time after the commencement of the bankruptcy any property is acquired by, or devolves upon, the bankrupt or there is an increase of the bankrupt's income, the bankrupt shall, within the prescribed period, give the trustee notice of the property or, as the case may be, of the increase.

333(3) [Application of s. 333(1)] Subsection (1) applies to a bankrupt after his discharge.

333(4) [Penalty for non-compliance] If the bankrupt without reasonable excuse fails to comply with any obligation imposed by this section, he is guilty of a contempt of court and liable to be punished accordingly (in addition to any other punishment to which he may be subject).

S. 333(1), (3)
These provisions impose duties on a bankrupt, up to and after the date of his discharge, to provide information and assistance to enable the *trustee* to carry out his duties. The comparable provision describing the bankrupt's duties

towards the *official receiver* is to be found in s. 291. On the nature of the respective duties of bankrupt and trustee see *Morris v Murjani* [1996] B.P.I.R. 458. In *Re Caldwell* (unreported decision of registrar, 1998) the court felt able to bolster this duty to co-operate by exercising its powers under s. 39(1) of the Supreme Court Act 1981 and authorising the trustee to execute a power of attorney on behalf of the bankrupt in order to gain access to financial information from foreign authorities: see Archer (1998) 142 Solicitors' Journal 596.

Note also the bankrupt's more specific duties in regard to property, records, etc. under s. 312.

S. 333(2)
The obligation to provide information about the property and income is a continuing one. Such an obligation is essential for the operation of ss. 307 and 310. The prescribed period is 21 days: see IR 1986, r. 6.200(1).

S. 333(4)
A bankrupt may be held liable for contempt if he breaches any of the above obligations.

334 Stay of distribution in case of second bankruptcy

334(1) **[Application, definitions]** This section and the next apply where a bankruptcy order is made against an undischarged bankrupt; and in both sections–

(a) **"the later bankruptcy"** means the bankruptcy arising from that order,

(b) **"the earlier bankruptcy"** means the bankruptcy (or, as the case may be, most recent bankruptcy) from which the bankrupt has not been discharged at the commencement of the later bankruptcy, and

(c) **"the existing trustee"** means the trustee (if any) of the bankrupt's estate for the purposes of the earlier bankruptcy.

334(2) **[Certain distributions void]** Where the existing trustee has been given the prescribed notice of the presentation of the petition for the later bankruptcy, any distribution or other disposition by him of anything to which the next subsection applies, if made after the giving of the notice, is void except to the extent that it was made with the consent of the court or is or was subsequently ratified by the court.

This is without prejudice to section 284 (restrictions on dispositions of property following bankruptcy order).

334(3) **[Application of s. 334(2)]** This subsection applies to–

(a) any property which is vested in the existing trustee under section 307(3) (after-acquired property);

(b) any money paid to the existing trustee in pursuance of an income payments order under section 310; and

(c) any property or money which is, or in the hands of the existing trustee represents, the proceeds of sale or application of property or money falling within paragraph (a) or (b) of this subsection.

GENERAL NOTE

This provision is, of necessity, more sophisticated than its predecessor as a result of the advent of the new rules on after-acquired property and income payments orders.

S. 334(1)
Where a petition for bankruptcy is issued against an undischarged bankrupt who is already undergoing the bankruptcy process, his existing trustee, on receiving notice of the petition, must not make any further distributions or dispositions without the consent of the court. However, this only applies to property covered by s. 334(3).

S. 334(3)
Section 334(3) applies to after-acquired property or money from any income payments order, or the proceeds thereof. Note also IR 1986, rr. 6.225–6.228.

335 Adjustment between earlier and later bankruptcy estates

335(1) **[Matters in bankrupt's estate]** With effect from the commencement of the later bankruptcy anything to which section 334(3) applies which, immediately before the commencement of that bankruptcy, is comprised in the bankrupt's estate for the purposes of the earlier bankruptcy is to be treated as comprised in the bankrupt's estate for the purposes of the later bankruptcy and, until there is a trustee of that estate, is to be dealt with by the existing trustee in accordance with the rules.

335(2) **[Sums paid under s. 310]** Any sums which in pursuance of an income payments order under section 310 are payable after the commencement of the later bankruptcy to the existing trustee shall form part of the bankrupt's estate for the purposes of the later bankruptcy; and the court may give such consequential directions for the modification of the order as it thinks fit.

335(3) **[Charge re bankruptcy expenses]** Anything comprised in a bankrupt's estate by virtue of subsection (1) or (2) is so comprised subject to a first charge in favour of the existing trustee for any bankruptcy expenses incurred by him in relation thereto.

335(4) **[Property not in estate]** Except as provided above and in section 334, property which is, or by virtue of section 308 (personal property of bankrupt exceeding reasonable replacement value) or section 308A (vesting in trustee of certain tenancies) is capable of being, comprised in the bankrupt's estate for the purposes of the earlier bankruptcy, or of any bankruptcy prior to it, shall not be comprised in his estate for the purposes of the later bankruptcy.

335(5) **[Creditors of earlier bankruptcies]** The creditors of the bankrupt in the earlier bankruptcy and the creditors of the bankrupt in any bankruptcy prior to the earlier one, are not to be creditors of his in the later bankruptcy in respect of the same debts; but the existing trustee may prove in the later bankruptcy for–

(a)   the unsatisfied balance of the debts (including any debt under this subsection) provable against the bankrupt's estate in the earlier bankruptcy;

(b)   any interest payable on that balance; and

(c)   any unpaid expenses of the earlier bankruptcy.

335(6) **[Priority of amounts in s. 335(5)]** Any amount provable under subsection (5) ranks in priority after all the other debts provable in the later bankruptcy and after interest on those debts and, accordingly, shall not be paid unless those debts and that interest have first been paid in full.

S. 335(1)–(3)
Such items, on the commencement of the second bankruptcy, must be treated as part of the estate for the purpose of that second bankruptcy. The same is true of any money paid to the first trustee under an income payments order after the date of the commencement of the second bankruptcy. Indeed, the income payments order can be modified. However, the first trustee may be entitled to a charge over such property to cover any expenses incurred in relation to it.

S. 335(4)
Other property comprised in the bankrupt's estate in the first bankruptcy does not pass to the estate on the second bankruptcy. A minor insertion has been made by the Housing Act 1988, Sch. 17, para. 74.

S. 335(5), (6)
These provisions deal with the status of creditors in the first bankruptcy *vis-à-vis* the second bankruptcy: any residual claims they may have can be proved for in the second bankruptcy, but they only enjoy deferred status in this respect. This implements the recommendation of the Blagden Committee (Cmnd 221, para. 114). Note also IR 1986, rr. 6.225–6.228.

CHAPTER V

EFFECT OF BANKRUPTCY ON CERTAIN RIGHTS, TRANSACTIONS, ETC.

Rights under trusts of land

335A   Rights under trusts of land

335A(1) **[Application for order for sale of land]** Any application by a trustee of a bankrupt's estate under section 14 of the Trusts of Land and Appointment of Trustees Act 1996 (powers of court in relation to trusts of land) for an order under that section for the sale of land shall be made to the court having jurisdiction in relation to the bankruptcy.

335A(2) [Interests considered before order] On such an application the court shall make such order as it thinks just and reasonable having regard to–

(a) the interests of the bankrupt's creditors;

(b) where the application is made in respect of land which includes a dwelling house which is or has been the home of the bankrupt or the bankrupt's spouse or former spouse–

(i) the conduct of the spouse or former spouse, so far as contributing to the bankruptcy,
(ii) the needs and financial resources of the spouse or former spouse, and
(iii) the needs of any children; and

(c) all the circumstances of the case other than the needs of the bankrupt.

335A(3) [Assumption by court re interests of creditors] Where such an application is made after the end of the period of one year beginning with the first vesting under Chapter IV of this Part of the bankrupt's estate in a trustee, the court shall assume, unless the circumstances of the case are exceptional, that the interests of the bankrupt's creditors outweigh all other considerations.

335A(4) [Exercise of powers conferred on court] The powers conferred on the court by this section are exercisable on an application whether it is made before or after the commencement of this section.

GENERAL NOTE

This and the following three sections are part of a package to redress the balance of rights between the trustee, on the one hand, and the bankrupt and his family on the other hand, over what will probably represent the bankrupt's most valuable asset, his family home. This is a problem that has troubled the law for many years – witness the decision in *Bendall v McWhirter* [1952] 2 Q.B. 466, which created a "deserted wife's equity" capable of prevailing over the trustee's rights, and its rejection by the House of Lords in *National Provincial Bank Ltd v Ainsworth* [1965] A.C. 1175. This decision, in turn, was reversed by the Matrimonial Homes Act 1967, a piece of legislation consolidated by the Matrimonial Homes Act 1983 which in turn was replaced by the Family Law Act 1996. Notwithstanding this, it was felt that the family's right to a roof over its head required greater protection in the event of the breadwinner becoming bankrupt: see the Cork *Report*, paras 1114–1131. These provisions on the family home were a late insertion in the Insolvency Bill 1985. For the background to this legislation, see Miller (1986) 50 Conv. 393 and Cretney (1991) 107 L.Q.R. 177. For further discussion of this area see Creasey and Doyle (1992) 136 S.J. 920.

Section 335A was inserted by s. 25(1) and Sch. 3, para. 23 the Trusts of Land and Appointment of Trustees Act 1996 with effect from 1 January 1997. For its significance see the note to s. 336 below. Early interpretation on the meaning of s. 335A is provided by the Court of Appeal in *Judd v Brown* [1999] B.P.I.R. 517 where the point was made that it may be proper to order a sale even if the prime beneficiary would be a secured creditor. In *Re Raval* [1998] B.P.I.R. 389 Blackburne J. was faced with the question of whether exceptional circumstances existed for the purposes of s. 335A(3). Again the issue centred upon the ill-health of the wife. The registrar had decided that this did constitute an exceptional circumstance but was only prepared to delay the sale of the family home for six months to enable arrangements to be made in the light of the wife's condition. Although Blackburne J. agreed with the interpretation of the registrar on whether this was an exceptional circumstance he did not feel that appropriate weight had been given to it when making the order and therefore postponed the sale for just over one year. General principles governing the s. 335A jurisdiction were laid down by the High Court in *Harrington v Bennett* [2000] B.P.I.R. 630. Exceptional circumstances within s. 335A(3) were present in *Claughton v Charalamabous* [1998] B.P.I.R. 558.

For discussion of this area see Davey [2001] Insolvency Lawyer 2 at 12.

These provisions must be read in the light of s. 283A (inserted by EA 2002 from April 1, 2004).

Rights of occupation

336 Rights of occupation etc. of bankrupt's spouse

336(1) [Family Law Act 1996] Nothing occurring in the initial period of the bankruptcy (that is to say, the period beginning with the day of the presentation of the petition for the bankruptcy order and ending with the vesting of the bankrupt's estate in a trustee) is to be taken as having given rise to any matrimonial home rights under Part IV of the Family Law Act 1996 in relation to a dwelling house comprised in the bankrupt's estate.

336(2) **[Where spouse's rights of occupation charge on estate]** Where a spouse's matrimonial home rights under the Act of 1996 are a charge on the estate or interest of the other spouse, or of trustees for the other spouse, and the other spouse is adjudged bankrupt–

(a) the charge continues to subsist notwithstanding the bankruptcy and, subject to the provisions of that Act, binds the trustee of the bankrupt's estate and persons deriving title under that trustee, and

(b) any application for an order under section 33 of that Act shall be made to the court having jurisdiction in relation to the bankruptcy.

336(3) (Repealed by Trusts of Land and Appointment of Trustees Act 1996, Pt III, s. 25(2), 27 and Sch. 4 as from 1 January 1997.)

336(4) **[Court orders]** On such an application as is mentioned in subsection (2) the court shall make such order under section 33 of the Act of 1996 as it thinks just and reasonable having regard to–

(a) the interests of the bankrupt's creditors,

(b) the conduct of the spouse or former spouse, so far as contributing to the bankruptcy,

(c) the needs and financial resources of the spouse or former spouse,

(d) the needs of any children, and

(e) all the circumstances of the case other than the needs of the bankrupt.

336(5) **[Assumption by court re interests of creditors]** Where such an application is made after the end of the period of one year beginning with the first vesting under Chapter IV of this Part of the bankrupt's estate in a trustee, the court shall assume, unless the circumstances of the case are exceptional, that the interests of the bankrupt's creditors outweigh all other considerations.

GENERAL NOTE

For the definitions of "family" and "dwelling house", see s. 385.

S. 336(1)
This prevents a spouse's matrimonial home rights under the Family Law Act 1996 arising during the period after the date of the petition and up to the time when the property vests in the trustee.

S. 336(2)
Where the spouse of a bankrupt has acquired statutory rights of occupation representing a charge on the house owned by the bankrupt, that charge is effective as against the trustee. Any applications made under s. 33 of the Family Law Act 1996 (*i.e.* to have the spouse evicted or to enable him or her to regain possession), however, must be made to the appropriate bankruptcy court. Note that s. 336(4), commented on below, applies to such an application.

S. 336(3)–(5)
These provisions cover the situation where the spouses or former spouses are joint owners of the property, and a trust for sale has arisen. Any application under s. 30 of LPA 1925 or s. 14 of the Trusts of Land and Appointment of Trustees Act 1996 (which substantially remodelled the provision in the 1925 Act) to the court by the trustee in bankruptcy of one of the spouses or ex-spouses for an enforced sale is to be made to the relevant bankruptcy court. In the past in cases under s. 30 of the 1925 Act, the courts have normally acceded to the trustee's request for sale, although the family interests have been considered: see *Re Solomon* [1967] Ch. 573; *Re Turner* [1974] 1 W.L.R. 1556; *Re Densham* [1975] 1 W.L.R. 1519; *Re Bailey* [1977] 1 W.L.R. 278; *Re Lowrie* [1981] 3 All E.R. 353; *Re Citro (a Bankrupt)* [1991] Ch. 142; *Zandfarid v BCCI* [1996] 1 W.L.R. 1420 and *Re Ng* [1997] B.C.C. 507. A decision which went against the grain and resulted in the sale of the matrimonial home being postponed for several years until the children had finished their education was *Re Holliday* [1981] Ch. 405. A similar more "caring" approach was taken by Hoffmann J. in the poorly reported *Re Mott* [1987] C.L.Y. 212 where the sick mother of the bankrupt was allowed to postpone the sale of the house until after her death. In *Re Bremner* [1999] B.P.I.R. 185 a sale was postponed for a short period to allow a terminally ill

Section 337   *Insolvency Act 1986*

bankrupt the dignity of dying in his own home. For a comparable problem posed by novel facts see *Re Gorman (a Bankrupt)* [1990] 1 All E.R. 717.

The extent to which the case law under LPA 1925 s. 30 retains value is unclear because in future cases where an application is made under s. 14 of the Trusts of Land and Appointment of Trustees Act 1996 the factors which the court shall have regard to in non-bankruptcy cases include the intentions of the settlor, the purposes of the trust, the welfare of minors in occupation and the interests of secured creditors of the beneficiary (s. 15 of the Trusts of Land and Appointment of Trustees Act 1996). Where the application for sale is by the trustee in bankruptcy the matter is governed by IA 1986 s. 335A, which identifies relevant considerations. In spite of this statutory intrusion one suspects that the courts will be reluctant to cast aside all previous jurisprudence on this difficult subject.

Now, if such an application is made, the court has general discretion and can consider all the circumstances (including the interests of the family and creditors and the contribution of either party towards the bankruptcy); but if it is made more than one year after the vesting of the property in the trustee in bankruptcy, it will be the interests of the creditors which will prevail unless there are exceptional counterbalancing factors: see s. 335A(3).

There is some discussion of s. 336(5) in *Re Citro (a Bankrupt)* (above) where the point is made that many of the old bankruptcy cases (which are discussed above) will be relevant to its interpretation. It is also stressed that this provision will only operate within the context of a marriage (and not to cohabitees). Exceptional circumstances were found to be present in *Judd v Brown* [1997] B.P.I.R. 470 where the illness of the wife was sufficient to persuade the court to refuse an application for sale. Further discussion of s. 336(5) is to be found in *Trustee of the Estate of Bowe v Bowe* [1997] B.P.I.R. 747 where Jonathan Parker J. found that there was an absence of exceptional circumstances. The fact that the sale of the property might produce no immediate benefit for creditors because the proceeds were to be used to defray the costs of the bankruptcy was not in itself a reason to block the sale.

For similar problems of social priority encountered under s. 40 of the Bankruptcy (Scotland) Act 1985 see *Gourlay's Trustee v Gourlay* 1995 SLT (Sh Ct) 7; *Hunt's Trustee v Hunt* [1995] S.C.L.R. 969, *McMahon's Trustee*, *The Times* March 26, 1997 and *Ritchie v Burns* [2001] B.P.I.R. 666.

Note the textual amendments made to s. 336 by s. 66(1) and Sch. 8, para. 57 of the Family Law Act 1996 and the repeal in its entirety of subs. (3) and minor repeal in subs. (4) effected by Sch. 4 to the Trusts of Land and Appointment of Trustees Act 1996.

337   Rights of occupation of bankrupt

337(1)   **[Application]** This section applies where–

(a)   a person who is entitled to occupy a dwelling house by virtue of a beneficial estate or interest is adjudged bankrupt, and

(b)   any persons under the age of 18 with whom that person had at some time occupied that dwelling house had their home with that person at the time when the bankruptcy petition was presented and at the commencement of the bankruptcy.

337(2)   **[Rights of occupation, etc.]** Whether or not the bankrupt's spouse (if any) has matrimonial home rights under Part IV of the Family Law Act 1996–

(a)   the bankrupt has the following rights as against the trustee of his estate–

       (i) if in occupation, right not to be evicted or excluded from the dwelling house or any part of it, except with the leave of the court,
       (ii) if not in occupation, a right with the leave of the court to enter into and occupy the dwelling house, and

(b)   the bankrupt's rights are a charge, having the like priority as an equitable interest created immediately before the commencement of the bankruptcy, on so much of his estate or interest in the dwelling house as vests in the trustee.

337(3) **[Application of Family Law Act]** The Act of 1996 has effect, with the necessary modifications, as if–

(a) the rights conferred by paragraph (a) of subsection (2) were matrimonial home rights under that Act,

(b) any application for leave such as is mentioned in that paragraph were an application for an order under section 33 of that Act, and

(c) any charge under paragraph (b) of that subsection on the estate or interest of the trustee were a charge under that Act on the estate or interest of a spouse.

337(4) **[Application to court]** Any application for leave such as is mentioned in subsection (2)(a) or otherwise by virtue of this section for an order under section 33 of the Act of 1996 shall be made to the court having jurisdiction in relation to the bankruptcy.

337(5) **[Court order under s. 337(4)]** On such an application the court shall make such order under section 33 of the Act of 1996 as it thinks just and reasonable having regard to the interests of the creditors, to the bankrupt's financial resources, to the needs of the children and to all the circumstances of the case other than the needs of the bankrupt.

337(6) **[Assumption re interests of creditors]** Where such an application is made after the end of the period of one year beginning with the first vesting (under Chapter IV of this Part) of the bankrupt's estate in a trustee, the court shall assume, unless the circumstances of the case are exceptional, that the interest of the bankrupt's creditors outweigh all other considerations.

S. 337(1), (2)
These provisions protect the rights of occupation of the bankrupt who has dependent children living with him: he cannot be evicted from the family home without a court order and can apply to the court to regain entry if out of possession. His rights under these provisions are in the nature of an equitable interest binding on the trustee. A number of textual changes have been introduced by the Family Law Act 1996 (see Sch. 8, para. 58).

S. 337(3)
This extends certain provisions in the Family Law Act 1996 relating to matrimonial home rights to bankruptcy situations. The substitution of the original subs. (3) was effected by Sch. 8, para. 58 to the 1996 Act with effect from October 1, 1997.

S. 337(4)–(6)
Applications for leave under s. 337(2)(a) must be made to the relevant bankruptcy court. On such an application the court should adopt a similar approach to that specified in s. 336(4) and (5) above (although the criteria are different), with the creditors' interests having priority where the application is made more than a year after the property has vested in the trustee. Minor textual changes were made to subs. (4) by Sch. 8, para. 50 to the Family Law Act 1996.

338 Payments in respect of premises occupied by bankrupt

338 Where any premises comprised in a bankrupt's estate are occupied by him (whether by virtue of the preceding section or otherwise) on condition that he makes payments towards satisfying any liability arising under a mortgage of the premises or otherwise towards the outgoings of the premises, the bankrupt does not, by virtue of those payments, acquire any interest in the premises.

GENERAL NOTE

This provision clarifies the position where a bankrupt is allowed to remain in occupation of premises provided that he pays the mortgage, etc. Any such payment will not result in his acquiring an interest in the property.
Compare this provision with s. 1(7) of the Matrimonial Homes Act 1983.

Adjustment of prior transactions, etc.

339 Transactions at an undervalue

339(1) **[Application to court]** Subject as follows in this section and sections 341 and 342, where an individual is adjudged bankrupt and he has at a relevant time (defined in section 341) entered into a transaction with any person at an undervalue, the trustee of the bankrupt's estate may apply to the court for an order under this section.

339(2) **[Order by court]** The court shall, on such an application, make such order as it thinks fit for restoring the position to what it would have been if that individual had not entered into that transaction.

339(3) **[Where transaction is at undervalue]** For the purposes of this section and sections 341 and 342, an individual enters into a transaction with a person at an undervalue if–

(a) he makes a gift to that person or he otherwise enters into a transaction with that person on terms that provide for him to receive no consideration,

(b) he enters into a transaction with that person in consideration of marriage, or

(c) he enters into a transaction with that person for a consideration the value of which, in money or money's worth, is significantly less than the value, in money or money's worth, of the consideration provided by the individual.

GENERAL NOTE

Sections 339–341 are new provisions designed to rationalise and update their outmoded predecessors in BA 1914. They were substantially amended at the Report Stage of the 1985 Bill. For the views of the Cork Committee on the former law, see its *Report*, paras 1226, 1285 and 1287. Unfortunately, ss. 339–341 are of Byzantine complexity. Corresponding provisions for corporate insolvency are to be found in s. 238ff. Note also that these sections are supplemented by the more general avoidance provision in s. 423.

See further the notes to ss. 238–243.

In the context of the financial markets, no order may be made under s. 339 in relation to a market contract to which a recognised investment exchange or clearing house is a party or which is entered into under its default rules, or a disposition of property in pursuance of such a market contract: see CA 1989, s. 165, and the note on p. 2.

S. 339(1)–(3)

These provisions allow the trustee to apply to the court for relief where a person who is subsequently made bankrupt has entered into a transaction at an undervalue, at the "relevant time". The transaction must have been carried out by the debtor – *Re Brabon* [2000] B.P.I.R. 537. Section 339(3) defines what is meant by a transaction at an undervalue, *e.g.* gifts, marriage settlements, etc. The meaning of the key phrase "relevant time" is supplied by s. 341 and was considered in *Clarkson v Clarkson* [1994] B.C.C. 921. This avoidance facility was successfully invoked by the trustee in *Re Kumar* [1993] 1 W.L.R. 224 where a transfer of an interest in a matrimonial home from debtor husband to wife was set aside by Ferris J. The interest in the equity that was given to the wife far exceeded in value the size of the mortgage commitments that she had taken over from the husband. Notwithstanding this ruling Ferris J. refused to make an immediate sale order under s. 30 of LPA 1925 – separate issues had to be tried here. See also *Simms v Oakes* [2002] B.P.I.R. 1244.

For an unsuccessful s. 339 claim see *Doyle v Saville and Hardwick* [2002] B.P.I.R. 947.

The Court of Appeal is to review the question of whether a transaction carried out pursuant to an order from the Family Division could be challenged under s. 339 – *Jackson v Bell* [2001] EWCA Civ 387, [2001] B.P.I.R. 612. For general discussion of s. 339 see *Re Share* [2002] B.P.I.R. 194.

On the difficult issue of valuation of consideration where the transferee has benefited from a statutory discount made only available to the bankrupt see *Pozzuto v Iacovides* [2003] EWHC 431 (Ch), [2003] B.P.I.R. 999.

For the date to be applied when valuing consideration see *Re Thoars (decd)* [2002] EWHC 2416 (Ch), [2003] B.P.I.R. 489. For later proceedings see [2003] EWHC 1999, Ch.

A s. 339 claim must be brought within the appropriate limitation period (see *Re Priory Garage (Walthamstowe) Ltd* [2001] B.P.I.R. 144) and even then can be struck out for want of prosecution – *Hamblin v Field* [2000] B.P.I.R. 621.

340 Preferences

340(1) **[Application to court]** Subject as follows in this and the next two sections, where an individual is adjudged bankrupt and he has at a relevant time (defined in section 341) given a preference to any person, the trustee of the bankrupt's estate may apply to the court for an order under this section.

340(2) **[Order by court]** The court shall, on such an application, make such order as it thinks fit for restoring the position to what it would have been if that individual had not given that preference.

340(3) **[Where preference given]** For the purposes of this and the next two sections, an individual gives a preference to a person if–

(a) that person is one of the individual's creditors or a surety or guarantor for any of his debts or other liabilities, and

(b) the individual does anything or suffers anything to be done which (in either case) has the effect of putting that person into a position which, in the event of the individual's bankruptcy, will be better than the position he would have been in if that thing had not been done.

340(4) **[Where court not to make order]** The court shall not make an order under this section in respect of a preference given to any person unless the individual who gave the preference was influenced in deciding to give it by a desire to produce in relation to that person the effect mentioned in subsection (3)(b) above.

340(5) **[Preference to associate]** An individual who has given a preference to a person who, at the time the preference was given, was an associate of his (otherwise than by reason only of being his employee) is presumed, unless the contrary is shown, to have been influenced in deciding to give it by such a desire as is mentioned in subsection (4).

340(6) **[Things done under court order]** The fact that something has been done in pursuance of the order of a court does not, without more, prevent the doing or suffering of that thing from constituting the giving of a preference.

GENERAL NOTE

In the context of the financial markets, no order may be made under s. 340 in relation to a market contract to which a recognised investment exchange or clearing house is a party or which is entered into under its default rules, or a disposition of property in pursuance of such a market contract: see CA 1989, s. 165, and the note on p. 2.

S. 340(1), (2)
These provisions mirror s. 339(1) and (2), although of course they relate to preferences.

S. 340(3)
This defines what is meant by the term "preference". See *Re Ledingham-Smith* [1993] B.C.L.C. 635. An actual preference must be established in order for the avoidance provision to operate: see here *Lewis v Hyde* [1997] B.C.C. 976. A preference can arise where an unsecured creditor is discharged out of a fund belonging exclusively to a secured creditor – *G & M Aldridge Pty Ltd v Walsh* [2002] BPIR 482.

S. 340(4), (5)
Preferences can only be challenged if the bankrupt was influenced by a desire to achieve the effect stated in s. 340(3)(b). This would appear to be a looser test than that required under the old law, which stated that the act in question must have been done "with a view" to effecting the preference. Thus under the new law an incidental or subsidiary motive to prefer could lead to the transaction being avoided. This will be presumed where the beneficiary is an "associate" (for the meaning of this term, see s. 435, as qualified here by s. 340(5)), although it is open for this presumption to be rebutted. The Cork Committee *Report*, paras 1256–1258) favoured this overall solution. Section 340 will be interpreted in the same light as s. 239 and therefore the comments of Millett J. in *Re M C Bacon Ltd* [1990] B.C.C. 78 must be taken cognisance of. This fact is apparent from the case of *Re Ledingham-Smith* [1993] B.C.L.C. 635. Here a payment by a debtor of arrears of fees due to a firm of accountants within the susceptible period was held not to be avoidable under s. 340. In following *Re M C Bacon Ltd* (above) Morritt J. held that the debtor was not influenced by a desire to prefer but rather by a desire to retain the services of the said firm of accountants so that they would continue to advise him during his period of financial difficulties. See also *Rooney v Das* [1999] B.P.I.R. 404 where the trustee again failed at this hurdle. The Court of Appeal is to review the question of whether a transaction carried out pursuant to an order of the Family Division can be challenged under s. 340 – *Jackson v Bell* [2001] EWCA Civ 387; [2001] B.P.I.R. 612.

S. 340(6)
A preference can arise out of a court order.

341 "Relevant time" under s. 339, 340

341(1) [Where relevant time] Subject as follows, the time at which an individual enters into a transaction at an undervalue or gives a preference is a relevant time if the transaction is entered into or the preference given–

(a) in the case of a transaction at an undervalue, at a time in the period of 5 years ending with the day of the presentation of the bankruptcy petition on which the individual is adjudged bankrupt,

(b) in the case of a preference which is not a transaction at an undervalue and is given to a person who is an associate of the individual (otherwise than by reason only of being his employee), at a time in the period of 2 years ending with that day, and

(c) in any other case of a preference which is not a transaction at an undervalue, at a time in the period of 6 months ending with that day.

341(2) [Conditions for relevant time] Where an individual enters into a transaction at an undervalue or gives a preference at a time mentioned in paragraph (a), (b) or (c) of subsection (1) (not being, in the case of a transaction at an undervalue, a time less than 2 years before the end of the period mentioned in paragraph (a)), that time is not a relevant time for the purposes of sections 339 and 340 unless the individual–

(a) is insolvent at that time, or

(b) becomes insolvent in consequence of the transaction or preference;

but the requirements of this subsection are presumed to be satisfied, unless the contrary is shown, in relation to any transaction at an undervalue which is entered into by an individual with a person who is an associate of his (otherwise than by reason only of being his employee).

341(3) [Insolvent individual under s. 341(2)] For the purposes of subsection (2), an individual is insolvent if–

(a) he is unable to pay his debts as they fall due, or

(b) the value of his assets is less than the amount of his liabilities, taking into account his contingent and prospective liabilities.

341(4) [Where person later bankrupt under s. 264(1)(d)] A transaction entered into or preference given by a person who is subsequently adjudged bankrupt on a petition under section 264(1)(d) (criminal bankruptcy) is to be treated as having been entered into or given at a relevant time for the purposes of sections 339 and 340 if it was entered into or given at any time on or after the date specified for the purposes of this subsection in the criminal bankruptcy order on which the petition was based.

341(5) [Where appeal pending] No order shall be made under section 339 or 340 by virtue of subsection (4) of this section where an appeal is pending (within the meaning of section 277) against the individual's conviction of any offence by virtue of which the criminal bankruptcy order was made.

S. 341(1)

This provides a general definition of "relevant time", for the purposes of ss. 339, 340 above. In the case of transactions at an undervalue, it covers a five-year period prior to the presentation of the petition. Formerly, a ten-year period was prescribed. For preferences, it is six months (this was favoured by the Cork Committee: *Report*, para. 1260), but this period is extended to two years prior to the petition where the beneficiary is an "associate" of the bankrupt (as defined by s. 435, although note the qualification in s. 340(5)).

S. 341(2), (3)

The time periods given in s. 341(1) are qualified by the fact that in most cases (but not a transaction at an undervalue within two years of the petition), it is necessary that the person entering the transaction should either have been insolvent at the time or reduced to insolvency by the transaction. Normally the onus of proving insolvency is on the trustee, but this is not so where the beneficiary of the transaction is an "associate" (see s. 435 as qualified by s. 340(5)). Note the special definition of insolvency in s. 341(3) which now also covers balance-sheet insolvency – this was a late amendment at the Report Stage of the 1985 Bill.

S. 341(4), (5)
These provisions modify the above rules where a person was made bankrupt as a result of a petition based on a criminal bankruptcy order. Special provision is made where an appeal is pending against the criminal conviction.

Note prospective amendment: s. 341(4) and (5) are to be repealed by CJA 1988, s. 170(2) and Sch. 16 as from a day to be appointed; see the note to s. 264.

342 Orders under s. 339, 340

342(1) [Extent of order] Without prejudice to the generality of section 339(2) or 340(2), an order under either of those sections with respect to a transaction or preference entered into or given by an individual who is subsequently adjudged bankrupt may (subject as follows)–

(a) require any property transferred as part of the transaction, or in connection with the giving of the preference, to be vested in the trustee of the bankrupt's estate as part of that estate;

(b) require any property to be so vested if it represents in any person's hands the application either of the proceeds of sale of property so transferred or of money so transferred;

(c) release or discharge (in whole or in part) any security given by the individual;

(d) require any person to pay, in respect of benefits received by him from the individual, such sums to the trustee of his estate as the court may direct;

(e) provide for any surety or guarantor whose obligations to any person were released or discharged (in whole or in part) under the transaction or by the giving of the preference to be under such new or revived obligations to that person as the court thinks appropriate;

(f) provide for security to be provided for the discharge of any obligation imposed by or arising under the order, for such an obligation to be charged on any property and for the security or charge to have the same priority as a security or charge released or discharged (in whole or in part) under the transaction or by the giving of the preference; and

(g) provide for the extent to which any person whose property is vested by the order in the trustee of the bankrupt's estate, or on whom obligations are imposed by the order, is to be able to prove in the bankruptcy for debts or other liabilities which arose from, or were released or discharged (in whole or in part) under or by, the transaction or the giving of the preference.

342(2) [Effect of order] An order under section 339 or 340 may affect the property of, or impose any obligation on, any person whether or not he is the person with whom the individual in question entered into the transaction or, as the case may be, the person to whom the preference was given; but such an order–

(a) shall not prejudice any interest in property which was acquired from a person other than that individual and was acquired in good faith and for value, or prejudice any interest deriving from such an interest, and

(b) shall not require a person who received a benefit from the transaction or preference in good faith and for value to pay a sum to the trustee of the bankrupt's estate, except where he was a party to the transaction or the payment is to be in respect of a preference given to that person at a time when he was a creditor of that individual.

342(2A) [Presumption re good faith in s. 342(2)] Where a person has acquired an interest in property from a person other than the individual in question, or has received a benefit from the transaction or preference, and at the time of that acquisition or receipt–

(a) he had notice of the relevant surrounding circumstances and of the relevant proceedings, or

(b) he was an associate of, or was connected with, either the individual in question or the person with whom that individual entered into the transaction or to whom that individual gave the preference,

then, unless the contrary is shown, it shall be presumed for the purposes of paragraph (a) or (as the case may be) paragraph (b) of subsection (2) that the interest was acquired or the benefit was received otherwise than in good faith.

342(3) **[Sums to be paid to trustee]** Any sums required to be paid to the trustee in accordance with an order under section 339 or 340 shall be comprised in the bankrupt's estate.

342(4) **[Relevant surrounding circumstances in s. 342(2A)(a)]** For the purposes of subsection (2A)(a), the relevant surrounding circumstances are (as the case may require)–

(a) the fact that the individual in question entered into the transaction at an undervalue; or

(b) the circumstances which amounted to the giving of the preference by the individual in question.

342(5) **[Notice of relevant proceedings in s. 342(2A)(a)]** For the purposes of subsection (2A)(a), a person has notice of the relevant proceedings if he has notice–

(a) of the fact that the petition on which the individual in question is adjudged bankrupt has been presented; or

(b) of the fact that the individual in question has been adjudged bankrupt.

342(6) **[Application of s. 249]** Section 249 in Part VII of this Act shall apply for the purposes of subsection (2A)(b) as it applies for the purposes of the first Group of Parts.

S. 342(1)
Sections 339(2) and 340(2) confer general discretion on the court where the trustee applies for relief. However, we are here given a non-exhaustive list of the possible forms of relief which the court may grant. On how the claim for relief can affect limitation periods see *Re Priory Garage (Walthamstow) Ltd* [2001] B.P.I.R. 144. Note the limitations imposed by s. 419 of POCA 2002.

S. 342(2)
This subsection was amended by s. 2(1) of the Insolvency (No. 2) Act 1994 to clarify the degree of protection offered to third parties. Comparable changes have been made in the corporate context: see the annotations to s. 241. The Bill leading to this Act was sponsored by the Law Society which was concerned by the uncertainty created by the original verson of s. 342 in the context of property purchases of unregistered land. Later purchasers in a chain started off by an undervalue transfer might theoretically be prejudiced and therefore be reluctant to transact with that risk in mind until the five-year limitation period had expired. This was creating further problems in the already depressed domestic property market by generating delays or additional cost caused by the necessity of taking out title insurance. For general discussion see Potterton and Cullen (1994) 138 S.J. 710.

Thus the words "in good faith, for value and without notice of the relevant circumstances" have been replaced by "in good faith and for value" with the question of notice now being dealt with by a new subs. (2A). Note that these changes only apply to interests acquired and benefits received after the coming into force of the 1994 Act – *i.e.* July 26, 1994 (see s. 6 (*ibid*)). Transactions occurring before that date will be governed by the original wording of s. 342.

S. 342(2A)
This subsection was introduced by s. 2(2) of the Insolvency (No. 2) Act 1994 and seeks to provide guidance on what is "good faith" for the purposes of the amended subs. (2) above. The burden of proving good faith switches to the person acquiring an interest in the property if he knows of the relevant surrounding circumstances *and* of the relevant proceedings. A similar reversal of the onus of proof occurs where the acquirer is an associate or connected person (see subs. (6) below). Further guidance on the relevant surrounding circumstances and notice of the relevant proceedings is provided by new subss. (4) and (5), also introduced by the 1994 Act.

S. 342(3)
This is unaffected by the 1994 changes.

S. 342(4), (5)
See the note to subs. (2A) above.

S. 342(6)
This was inserted by s. 2(3) of the Insolvency (No. 2) Act 1994 and merely renders applicable the standard definitions of associates and connected persons as found in IA 1986.

342A Recovery of excessive pension contributions

342A(1) **[Trustee to apply for order]** Where an individual who is adjudged bankrupt–

(a) has rights under an approved pension arrangement, or

(b) has excluded rights under an unapproved pension arrangement,

the trustee of the bankrupt's estate may apply to the court for an order under this section.

342A(2) [Court Order] If the court is satisfied–

(a) that the rights under the arrangement are to any extent, and whether directly or indirectly, the fruits of relevant contributions, and

(b) that the making of any of the relevant contributions ("the excessive contributions") has unfairly prejudiced the individual's creditors,

the court may make such order as it thinks fit for restoring the position to what it would have been had the excessive contributions not been made.

342A(3) [Application of s. 342A(4)] Subsection (4) applies where the court is satisfied that the value of the rights under the arrangement is, as a result of rights of the individual under the arrangement or any other pension arrangement having at any time become subject to a debit under section 29(1)(a) of the Welfare Reform and Pensions Act 1999 (debits giving effect to pension-sharing), less than it would otherwise have been.

342A(4) [Extent of contributions] Where this subsection applies–

(a) any relevant contributions which were represented by the rights which became subject to the debit shall, for the purposes of subsection (2), be taken to be contributions of which the rights under the arrangement are the fruits, and

(b) where the relevant contributions represented by the rights under the arrangement (including those so represented by virtue of paragraph (a)) are not all excessive contributions, relevant contributions which are represented by the rights under the arrangement otherwise than by virtue of paragraph (a) shall be treated as excessive contributions before any which are so represented by virtue of that paragraph.

342A(5) ["Relevant contributions"] In subsections (2) to (4) "relevant contributions" means contributions to the arrangement or any other pension arrangement–

(a) which the individual has at any time made on his own behalf, or

(b) which have at any time been made on his behalf.

342A(6) [Court considerations in determination] The court shall, in determining whether it is satisfied under subsection (2)(b), consider in particular–

(a) whether any of the contributions were made for the purpose of putting assets beyond the reach of the individual's creditors or any of them, and

(b) whether the total amount of any contributions–

(i) made by or on behalf of the individual to pension arrangements, and
(ii) represented (whether directly or indirectly) by rights under approved pension arrangements or excluded rights under unapproved pension arrangements,

is an amount which is excessive in view of the individual's circumstances when those contributions were made.

342A(7) [Excluded rights] For the purposes of this section and sections 342B and 342C ("the recovery provisions"), rights of an individual under an unapproved pension arrangement are excluded rights if they are rights which are excluded from his estate by virtue of regulations under section 12 of the Welfare Reform and Pensions Act 1999.

342A(8) ["Approved pension arrangement", "unapproved pension arrangement"] In the recovery provisions – **"approved pensions arrangement"** has the same meaning as in section 11 of the Welfare Reform and Pensions Act 1999; **"unapproved pensions arrangement"** has the same meaning as in section 12 of that Act.

GENERAL NOTE

These clawback provisions originated in s. 95 of the Pensions Act 1995, which in turn sought to implement the recommendations of the Goode Committee on Pension Law Review. The 1995 Act provisions were never brought into force. In view of the criticisms generated by cases like *Re Landau* [1998] Ch. 223 and with the advent of the policy in favour of pensions sharing between spouses, Parliament took the opportunity to revisit the area of interface between pensions law and bankruptcy law (see ss. 324D–F below for the new provisions on pensions sharing). As part of an overall package ss. 342A – 342C were reformulated by s. 15 of the Welfare Reform and Pensions Act 1999. These provisions were brought into force with effect from May 29, 2000 – Welfare Reform and Pensions Act 1999 (Commencement No. 7) Order 2000 (SI 2000/1382). Comparable provisions have been made for Scotland by ss. 13 and 16 of the 1999 Act.

Sections 342A – 342C must be read in the light of other changes made by the 1999 Act, namely the reversal of *Re Landau* (above) by ss. 11 and 12 of that Act (which enables the Secretary of State to make regulations to exclude pension rights from the bankrupt's estate) and s. 14 which prevents personal pension rights being forfeited in the event of the pensioner becoming bankrupt.

S. 342A(1), (2), (5)
This enables the trustee to apply to the court to claw back for the benefit of the estate excessive contributions to pension schemes which unfairly prejudice creditors. Subsection (5) is a definition provision.

S. 342A(3), (4)
These deal with the interface between the clawback and pension-sharing arrangements introduced also by the 1999 Act.

S. 342A(6)
This is an important provision which seeks to assist the court in exercising its discretion under subs. 2 in determining whether contributions were excessive in the circumstances.

S. 342A(7), (8)
These are further definition provisions linked to ss. 342B and 342C.

342B Orders under section 342A

342B(1) **[Contents of order]** Without prejudice to the generality of section 342A(2), an order under section 342A may include provision–

(a) requiring the person responsible for the arrangement to pay an amount to the individual's trustee in bankruptcy,

(b) adjusting the liabilities of the arrangement in respect of the individual,

(c) adjusting any liabilities of the arrangement in respect of any other person that derive, directly or indirectly, from rights of the individual under the arrangement,

(d) for the recovery by the person responsible for the arrangement (whether by deduction from any amount which that person is ordered to pay or otherwise) of costs incurred by that person in complying in the bankrupt's case with any requirement under section 342C(1) or in giving effect to the order.

342B(2) **[Adjusting liabilities in s. 342B(1)]** In subsection (1), references to adjusting the liabilities of the arrangement in respect of a person include (in particular) reducing the amount of any benefit or future benefit to which that person is entitled under the arrangement.

342B(3) **[Liabilities in s. 342B(1)(c)]** In subsection (1)(c), the reference to liabilities of the arrangement does not include liabilities in respect of a person which result from giving effect to an order or provision falling within section 28(1) of the Welfare Reform and Pensions Act 1999 (pension sharing orders and agreements).

342B(4) **[Maximum amount payable]** The maximum amount which the person responsible for an arrangement may be required to pay by an order under section 342A is the lesser of–

(a) the amount of the excessive contributions, and

(b) the value of the individual's rights under the arrangement (if the arrangement is an approved pension arrangement) or of his excluded rights under the arrangement (if the arrangement is an unapproved pension arrangement).

342B(5) **[Provisions in "restoration amount"]** An order under section 342A which requires the person responsible for an arrangement to pay an amount ("the restoration amount") to the individual's trustee in bankruptcy must provide for the liabilities of the arrangement to be correspondingly reduced.

342B(6) **[Liabilities in s. 342B(5)]** For the purposes of subsection (5), liabilities are correspondingly reduced if the difference between–

(a) the amount of the liabilities immediately before the reduction, and

(b) the amount of the liabilities immediately after the reduction,

is equal to the restoration amount.

342B(7) **[Effect of s. 342A order]** An order under section 342A in respect of an arrangement–

(a) shall be binding on the person responsible for the arrangement, and

(b) overrides provisions of the arrangement to the extent that they conflict with the provisions of the order.

GENERAL NOTE

This was introduced by s. 15 of the Welfare Reform and Pensions Act 1999 with effect from May 29, 2000.

S. 342B(1)
This identifies examples of the type of order the court may make under s. 342A.

S. 342B(2), (3)
These provide further clarification on the precise effect of certain s. 342A orders.

S. 342B(4)
This caps the maximum amount of an order.

S. 342B(5)–(7)
These deal with pension-sharing arrangements.

342C Orders under section 342A: supplementary

342C(1) **[Provision of information under s. 342A]** The person responsible for–

(a) an approved pension arrangement under which a bankrupt has rights,

(b) an unapproved pension arrangement under which a bankrupt has excluded rights, or

(c) a pension arrangement under which a bankrupt has at any time had rights,

shall, on the bankrupt's trustee in bankruptcy making a written request, provide the trustee with such information about the arrangement and rights as the trustee may reasonably require for, or in connection with, the making of applications under section 342A.

342C(2) **[Non-applicable provisions]** Nothing in–

(a) any provision of section 159 of the Pension Schemes Act 1993 or section 91 of the Pensions Act 1995 (which prevent assignment and the making of orders that restrain a person from receiving anything which he is prevented from assigning),

(b) any provision of any enactment (whether passed or made before or after the passing of the Welfare Reform and Pensions Act 1999) corresponding to any of the provisions mentioned in paragraph (a), or

(c) any provision of the arrangement in question corresponding to any of those provisions,

applies to a court exercising its powers under section 342A.

342C(3) **[Bankrupt's estate]** Where any sum is required by an order under section 342A to be paid to the trustee in bankruptcy, that sum shall be comprised in the bankrupt's estate.

342C(4) **[Provisions re calculation and verification etc.]** Regulations may, for the purposes of the recovery provisions, make provision about the calculation and verification of–

(a) any such value as is mentioned in section 342B(4)(b);

(b) any such amounts as are mentioned in section 342B(6)(a) and (b).

342C(5) **[Powers conferred by s. 342A]** The power conferred by subsection (4) includes power to provide for calculation or verification–

(a) in such manner as may, in the particular case, be approved by a prescribed person; or

(b) in accordance with guidance–

    (i) from time to time prepared by a prescribed person, and
    (ii) approved by the Secretary of State.

342C(6) **[Persons responsible for pension arrangements]** References in the recovery provisions to the person responsible for a pension arrangement are to–

(a) the trustees, managers or provider of the arrangement, or

(b) the person having functions in relation to the arrangement corresponding to those of a trustee, manager or provider.

342C(7) **[Meaning in ss. 342A, 342B and 342C]** In this section and sections 342A and 342B–

"**prescribed**" means prescribed by regulations;

"**the recovery provisions**" means this section and sections 342A and 342B;

"**regulations**" means regulations made by the Secretary of State.

342C(8) **[Scope of regulations]** Regulations under the recovery provisions may–

(a) make different provision for different cases;

(b) contain such incidental, supplemental and transitional provisions as appear to the Secretary of State necessary or expedient.

342C(9) **[Making of regulations]** Regulations under the recovery provisions shall be made by statutory instrument subject to annulment in pursuance of a resolution of either House of Parliament.

GENERAL NOTE

This was introduced by s. 15 of the Welfare Reform and Pensions Act 1999 with effect from May 29, 2000.

S. 342C(1), (6)
This is an important provision enabling the trustee in bankruptcy to gain access to the full details of the bankrupt's pension arrangement. Subsection (6) clarifies who is responsible for the provision of such information.

S. 342C(2)
This is a saving provision.

S. 342C(3)
Any sums clawed back under s. 342A form part of the estate.

S. 342C(4), (5), (8), (9)
These deal with the power of the Secretary of State to make delegated legislation. See now the Occupational and Personal Pension Schemes (Bankruptcy) (No. 2) Regulations 2002 (SI 2002/836) which repealed the similarly-named SI 2002/427 and came into force on April 6, 2002.

342D Recovery of excessive contributions in pension-sharing cases

342D(1) **[Meaning of pension-sharing transaction]** For the purposes of sections 339, 341 and 342, a pension-sharing transaction shall be taken–

(a) to be a transaction, entered into by the transferor with the transferee, by which the appropriate amount is transferred by the transferor to the transferee; and

(b) to be capable of being a transaction entered into at an undervalue only so far as it is a transfer of so much of the appropriate amount as is recoverable.

342D(2) **[Further meaning]** For the purposes of sections 340 to 342, a pension-sharing transaction shall be taken–

(a) to be something (namely a transfer of the appropriate amount to the transferee) done by the transferor; and

(b) to be capable of being a preference given to the transferee only so far as it is a transfer of so much of the appropriate amount as is recoverable.

342D(3) **[Determination of recoverability]** If on an application under section 339 or 340 any question arises as to whether, or the extent to which, the appropriate amount in the case of a pension-sharing transaction is recoverable, the question shall be determined in accordance with subsections (4) to (8).

342D(4) **["Personal contributions"]** The court shall first determine the extent (if any) to which the transferor's rights under the shared arrangement at the time of the transaction appear to have been (whether directly or indirectly) the fruits of contributions ("personal contributions")–

(a) which the transferor has at any time made on his own behalf, or

(b) which have at any time been made on the transferor's behalf,

to the shared arrangement or any other pension arrangement.

342D(5) **["The unfair contributions"]** Where it appears that those rights were to any extent the fruits of personal contributions, the court shall then determine the extent (if any) to which those rights appear to have been the fruits of personal contributions whose making has unfairly prejudiced the transferor's creditors ("the unfair contributions").

342D(6) **[Circumstances where not recoverable]** If it appears to the court that the extent to which those rights were the fruits of the unfair contributions is such that the transfer of the appropriate amount could have been made out of rights under the shared arrangement which were not the fruits of the unfair contributions, then the appropriate amount is not recoverable.

342D(7) **[Circumstances where recoverable]** If it appears to the court that the transfer could not have been wholly so made, then the appropriate amount is recoverable to the extent to which it appears to the court that the transfer could not have been so made.

342D(8) **[Court considerations in determination]** In making the determination mentioned in subsection (5) the court shall consider in particular–

(a) whether any of the personal contributions were made for the purpose of putting assets beyond the reach of the transferor's creditors or any of them, and

(b) whether the total amount of any personal contributions represented, at the time the pension-sharing transaction was made, by rights under pension arrangements is an amount which is excessive in view of the transferor's circumstances when those contributions were made.

342D(9) **[Definitions]** In this section and sections 342E and 342F–

"appropriate amount", in relation to a pension-sharing transaction, means the appropriate amount in relation to that transaction for the purposes of section 29(1) of the Welfare Reform and Pensions Act 1999 (creation of pension credits and debits);

"pension-sharing transaction" means an order or provision falling within section 28(1) of the Welfare Reform and Pensions Act 1999 (orders and agreements which activate pension-sharing);

"shared arrangement", in relation to a pension-sharing transaction, means the pension arrangement to which the transaction relates;

"transferee", in relation to a pension-sharing transaction, means the person for whose benefit the transaction is made;

"transferor", in relation to a pension-sharing transaction, means the person to whose rights the transaction relates.

GENERAL NOTE

This was inserted by para. 71 of Sch. 12 to the Welfare Reform and Pensions Act 1999.

S. 342D(1) and (2)
These define a pension-sharing transaction for the purposes of ss. 339–342.

S. 342D(3)–(8)
These provisions explain what is the appropriate amount recoverable on applications under ss. 339 or 340 of the 1986 Act. Essentially the law is seeking to create some sort of balance between the rights of the parties to the pension-sharing arrangement but not at the expense of unfairness to the bankrupt transferor's creditors. The critical issue is the quantum of personal contributions by the transferor and whether the making of those contributions unfairly prejudiced his creditors.

S. 342D(9)
This is a definition provision.

342E Orders under section 339 or 340 in respect of pension-sharing transactions

342E(1) **[Application]** This section and section 342F apply if the court is making an order under section 339 or 340 in a case where–

(a) the transaction or preference is, or is any part of, a pension-sharing transaction, and

(b) the transferee has rights under a pension arrangement ("the destination arrangement", which may be the shared arrangement or any other pension arrangement) that are derived, directly or indirectly, from the pension-sharing transaction.

342E(2) **[Contents of order]** Without prejudice to the generality of section 339(2) or 340(2), or of section 342, the order may include provision–

(a) requiring the person responsible for the destination arrangement to pay an amount to the transferor's trustee in bankruptcy,

(b) adjusting the liabilities of the destination arrangement in respect of the transferee,

(c) adjusting the liabilities of the destination arrangement in respect of any other person that derive, directly or indirectly, from rights of the transferee under the destination arrangement,

(d) for the recovery by the person responsible for the destination arrangement (whether by deduction from any amount which that person is ordered to pay or otherwise) of costs incurred by that person in complying in the transferor's case with any requirement under section 342F(1) or in giving effect to the order,

(e) for the recovery, from the transferor's trustee in bankruptcy, by the person responsible for a pension arrangement, of costs incurred by that person in complying in the transferor's case with any requirement under section 342F(2) or (3).

342E(3) [Adjusting liabilities in s. 342E(2)] In subsection (2), references to adjusting the liabilities of the destination arrangement in respect of a person include (in particular) reducing the amount of any benefit or future benefit to which that person is entitled under the arrangement.

342E(4) [Maximum amount payable] The maximum amount which the person responsible for the destination arrangement may be required to pay by the order is the smallest of–

(a) so much of the appropriate amount as, in accordance with section 342D, is recoverable,

(b) so much (if any) of the amount of the unfair contributions (within the meaning given by section 342D(5)) as is not recoverable by way of an order under section 342A containing provision such as is mentioned in section 342B(1)(a), and

(c) the value of the transferee's rights under the destination arrangement so far as they are derived, directly or indirectly, from the pension-sharing transactions.

342E(5) [Provision on "restoration amount"] If the order requires the person responsible for the destination arrangement to pay an amount ("the restoration amount") to the transferor's trustee in bankruptcy it must provide for the liabilities of the arrangement to be correspondingly reduced.

342E(6) [Liabilities in s. 342E(5)] For the purposes of subsection (5), liabilities are correspondingly reduced if the difference between–

(a) the amount of the liabilities immediately before the reduction, and

(b) the amount of the liabilities immediately after the reduction,

is equal to the restoration amount.

342E(7) [Effect of order] The order–

(a) shall be binding on the person responsible for the destination arrangement, and

(b) overrides provisions of the destination arrangement to the extent that they conflict with the provisions of the order.

GENERAL NOTE

This was inserted by para. 71 of Sch. 12 to the Welfare Reform and Pensions Act 1999.

S. 342E(1) and (2)
These explain the remedial powers of the court in pension-sharing cases where ss. 339 or 340 have been successfully invoked. Subsection (1) defines the parameters of the provision. The provisions in subs. (2) are not intended to prejudice the flexibility enjoyed by the court.

S. 342E(3)–(6)
These are technical provisions explaining various mechanics involving in a remedial order where there is a pension-sharing scenario.

S. 342E(7)
This makes is clear that the provisions of any remedial court order prevail over the terms of a pension-sharing agreement.

342F Orders under section 339 or 340 in pension-sharing cases: supplementary

342F(1) [Provision of information: destination arrangement] On the transferor's trustee in bankruptcy making a written request to the person responsible for the destination arrangement, that person shall provide the trustee with such information about–

(a) the arrangement,

(b) the transferee's rights under it, and

(c) where the destination arrangement is the shared arrangement, the transferor's rights under it, as the trustee may reasonably require for, or in connection with, the making of applications under sections 339 and 340.

342F(2) **[Provision of information: no destination arrangement]** Where the shared arrangement is not the destination arrangement, the person responsible for the shared arrangement shall, on the transferor's trustee in bankruptcy making a written request to that person, provide the trustee with such information about–

(a) the arrangement, and

(b) the transferor's rights under it,

as the trustee may reasonably require for, or in connection with, the making of applications under sections 339 or 340.

342F(3) **[Provision of information: no immediate arrangement]** On the transferor's trustee in bankruptcy making a written request to the person responsible for any intermediate arrangement, that person shall provide the trustee with such information about–

(a) the arrangement, and

(b) the transferee's rights under it,

as the trustee may reasonably require for, or in connection with, the making of applications under section 339 and 340.

342F(4) **["Intermediate arrangement"]** In subsection (3) "intermediate arrangement" means a pension arrangement, other than the shared arrangement or the destination arrangement, in relation to which the following conditions are fulfilled–

(a) there was a time when the transferee had rights under the arrangement that were derived (directly or indirectly) from the pension-sharing transaction, and

(b) the transferee's rights under the destination arrangement (so far as derived from the pension-sharing transaction) are to any extent derived (directly or indirectly) from the rights mentioned in paragraph (a).

342F(5) **[Non-applicable provisions]** Nothing in–

(a) any provision of section 159 of the Pension Schemes Act 1993 or section 91 of the Pensions Act 1995 (which prevent assignment and the making of orders which restrain a person from receiving anything which he is prevented from assigning),

(b) any provision of any enactment (whether passed or made before or after the passing of the Welfare Reform and Pensions Act 1999) corresponding to any of the provisions mentioned in paragraph (a), or

(c) any provision of the destination arrangement corresponding to any of those provisions,

applies to a court exercising its powers under section 339 or 340.

342F(6) **[Provisions for calculation and verification etc.]** Regulations may, for the purposes of sections 339 to 342, sections 342D and 342E and this section, make provision about the calculation and verification of–

(a) any such value as is mentioned in section 342E(4)(c);

(c) any such amounts as are mentioned in section 342E(6)(a) and (b).

342F(7) **[Powers conferred by s. 342F(6)]** The power conferred by subsection (6) includes power to provide for calculation or verification–

(a) in such manner as may, in the particular case, be approved by a prescribed person; or

(b) in accordance with guidance–

    (i) from time to time prepared by a prescribed person, and
    (ii) approved by the Secretary of State.

342F(8) **[Persons responsible for pension arrangements]** In section 342E and this section, references to the person responsible for a pension arrangement are to–

(a) the trustees, managers or provider of the arrangement, or

(b) the person having functions in relation to the arrangement corresponding to those of a trustee, manager or provider.

342F(9) **[Meanings in s. 342F]** In this section–

"**prescribed**" means prescribed by regulations;

"**regulations**" means regulations made by the Secretary of State.

342F(10) **[Scope of regulations]** Regulations under this section may–

(a) make different provision for different cases;

(b) contain such incidental, supplemental and transitional provisions as appear to the Secretary of State necessary or expedient.

342F(11) **[Making of regulations]** Regulations under this section shall be made by statutory instrument subject to annulment in pursuance of a resolution of either House of Parliament.

GENERAL NOTE

This was inserted by para. 71 of Sch. 12 to the Welfare Reform and Pensions Act 1999.

S. 342F(1)–(3)
These provisions enable a trustee in bankruptcy to secure information about pensions where there is a pensions-sharing arrangement. This is a prelude to the exercise of avoidance powers.

S. 342F(4)
This is a technical definition provision explaining a concept central to subs. (3).

S. 342F(5)
This is a saving provision preserving the powers of the court notwithstanding an apparent conflict with other legislative provisions under pensions law.

S. 342F(6), (7), (10) and (11)
These deal with the making of secondary rules.

S. 342F(8) and (9)
These again are interpretation provisions.

343 Extortionate credit transactions

343(1) **[Application]** This section applies where a person is adjudged bankrupt who is or has been a party to a transaction for, or involving, the provision to him of credit.

343(2) **[Order by court]** The court may, on the application of the trustee of the bankrupt's estate, make an order with respect to the transaction if the transaction is or was extortionate and was not entered into more than 3 years before the commencement of the bankruptcy.

343(3) **[Extortionate transaction]** For the purposes of this section a transaction is extortionate if, having regard to the risk accepted by the person providing the credit–

(a) the terms of it are or were such as to require grossly exorbitant payments to be made (whether unconditionally or in certain contingencies) in respect of the provision of the credit, or

(b) it otherwise grossly contravened ordinary principles of fair dealing;

and it shall be presumed, unless the contrary is proved, that a transaction with respect to which an application is made under this section is or, as the case may be, was extortionate.

343(4) **[Extent of order]** An order under this section with respect to any transaction may contain such one or more of the following as the court thinks fit, that is to say–

(a) provision setting aside the whole or part of any obligation created by the transaction;

(b) provision otherwise varying the terms of the transaction or varying the terms on which any security for the purposes of the transaction is held;

(c) provision requiring any person who is or was party to the transaction to pay to the trustee any sums paid to that person, by virtue of the transaction, by the bankrupt;

(d) provision requiring any person to surrender to the trustee any property held by him as security for the purposes of the transaction;

(e) provision directing accounts to be taken between any persons.

343(5) **[Sums to trustee]** Any sums or property required to be paid or surrendered to the trustee in accordance with an order under this section shall be comprised in the bankrupt's estate.

343(6) **[Application under Consumer Credit Act]** Neither the trustee of a bankrupt's estate nor an undischarged bankrupt is entitled to make an application under section 139(1)(a) of the Consumer Credit Act 1974 (re-opening of extortionate credit agreements) for any agreement by which credit is or has been provided to the bankrupt to be re-opened.

But the powers conferred by this section are exercisable in relation to any transaction concurrently with any powers exercisable under this Act in relation to that transaction as a transaction at an undervalue.

GENERAL NOTE

This is a new provision enabling the trustee in bankruptcy to reopen a credit bargain made by a bankrupt, on the grounds that it was extortionate *vis-à-vis* the bankrupt. The Cork Committee (*Report*, para. 1381) called for such a provision, and its introduction in some senses can be viewed as a *quid pro quo* for the repeal of BA 1914, s. 66, which placed restrictions on a lender proving for interest: see the White Paper, para. 87.

A corresponding provision has been introduced for corporate insolvency: see s. 244.

S. 343(1), (2)
These permit the trustee to reopen extortionate credit bargains entered into by the bankrupt for the provision of credit to him within three years of the commencement of his bankruptcy (see s. 278).

S. 343(3)
The onus is on the other party to show that the bargain was not "extortionate" within the meaning of this subsection. Note that the meaning of "extortionate" is the same as that given by s. 139 of the Consumer Credit Act 1974.

S. 343(4)
This explains what the court may do if the bargain is extortionate – again this provision has been borrowed from the Consumer Credit Act 1974.

S. 343(5)
Any "proceeds" of such an action become part of the bankrupt's estate.

S. 343(6)
This makes it clear that applications under s. 139 of the Consumer Credit Act 1974 cannot be made by the trustee or the undischarged bankrupt but should be made under this section. It reminds us, however, that the transaction may also be challenged under s. 339.

344 Avoidance of general assignment of book debts

344(1) **[Application]** The following applies where a person engaged in any business makes a general assignment to another person of his existing or future book debts, or any class of them, and is subsequently adjudged bankrupt.

344(2) **[Certain assignments void against trustee]** The assignment is void against the trustee of the bankrupt's estate as regards book debts which were not paid before the presentation of the bankruptcy petition, unless the assignment has been registered under the Bills of Sale Act 1878.

Insolvency Act 1986 Section 345

344(3) **[Definitions]** For the purposes of subsections (1) and (2) –

(a) **"assignment"** includes an assignment by way of security or charge on book debts, and

(b) **"general assignment"** does not include–

    (i) an assignment of book debts due at the date of the assignment from specified debtors or of debts becoming due under specified contracts, or

    (ii) an assignment of book debts included either in a transfer of a business made in good faith and for value or in an assignment of assets for the benefit of creditors generally.

344(4) **[Registration under Bills of Sales Act]** For the purposes of registration under the Act of 1878 an assignment of book debts is to be treated as if it were a bill of sale given otherwise than by way of security for the payment of a sum of money; and the provisions of that Act with respect to the registration of bills of sale apply accordingly with such necessary modifications as may be made by rules under that Act.

S. 344(1), (2)

This provides that a general assignment of book debts by a trader shall be void on bankruptcy unless registered under the Bills of Sale Act 1878. Note the word "general" is now used in the text of subs. (1) – in s. 43 of the 1914 Act this word merely appeared in the marginal note. For a rare authority on the effect of s. 344(2) see *Hills v Alex Lawrie Factors* [2001] B.P.I.R. 1038.

S. 344(3)

This provision clarifies s. 344(1) by stressing that assignments by way of security are covered but not specific assignments of specific book debts, nor assignments connected with a *bona fide* transfer of a business for value, nor a general assignment of assets for the benefit of creditors generally.

S. 344(4)

This provision describes the mechanics of registration under the 1878 Act.

345 Contracts to which bankrupt is a party

345(1) **[Application]** The following applies where a contract has been made with a person who is subsequently adjudged bankrupt.

345(2) **[Court order on application]** The court may, on the application of any other party to the contract, make an order discharging obligations under the contract on such terms as to payment by the applicant or the bankrupt of damages for non-performance or otherwise as appear to the court to be equitable.

345(3) **[Damages as bankruptcy debt]** Any damages payable by the bankrupt by virtue of an order of the court under this section are provable as a bankruptcy debt.

345(4) **[Where joint contract]** Where an undischarged bankrupt is a contractor in respect of any contract jointly with any person, that person may sue or be sued in respect of the contract without the joinder of the bankrupt.

GENERAL NOTE

In the context of the financial markets, s. 345 does not apply in relation to a market contract or a contract effected by an exchange or clearing house for the purpose of realising property provided as margin in relation to market contracts: see CA 1989, s. 164(1), and the note on p. 2.

S. 345(1)–(3)

This is a new provision. At common law the general rule, as laid down in *Brooke v Hewitt* (1796) 3 Ves. 253, was that the bankruptcy of a party to a contract did not terminate that contract. Hence the need to confer on trustees a power to disclaim onerous contracts. There is no need to have recourse to s. 345 if the contract provides that bankruptcy is a terminating event – on this common provision and the consequences of bankruptcy in general see *Cadogan Estates v McMahon* [2001] BPIR 17. Section 345(2) in effect redresses the balance as far as the other contracting party is concerned. He can now apply to the court to have contractual obligations discharged. The court enjoys general discretion and can order compensation payments to be paid by either party. If the bankrupt is ordered to pay compensation, that sum constitutes a provable debt.

S. 345(4)
This repeats BA 1914, s. 118 and allows a person who has entered into a contract jointly with a bankrupt to sue the other party to the contract without the joinder of the bankrupt to the proceedings.

346 Enforcement procedures

346(1) **[Creditor's execution against bankrupt]** Subject to section 285 in Chapter II (restrictions on proceedings and remedies) and to the following provisions of this section, where the creditor of any person who is adjudged bankrupt has, before the commencement of the bankruptcy–

(a) issued execution against the goods or land of that person, or

(b) attached a debt due to that person from another person,

that creditor is not entitled, as against the official receiver or trustee of the bankrupt's estate, to retain the benefit of the execution or attachment, or any sums paid to avoid it, unless the execution or attachment was completed, or the sums were paid, before the commencement of the bankruptcy.

346(2) **[Where goods taken in execution]** Subject as follows, where any goods of a person have been taken in execution, then, if before the completion of the execution notice is given to the sheriff or other officer charged with the execution that that person has been adjudged bankrupt–

(a) the sheriff or other officer shall on request deliver to the official receiver or trustee of the bankrupt's estate the goods and any money seized or recovered in part satisfaction of the execution, but

(b) the costs of the execution are a first charge on the goods or money so delivered and the official receiver or trustee may sell the goods or a sufficient part of them for the purpose of satisfying the charge.

346(3) **[Balance of sale proceeds]** Subject to subsection (6) below, where–

(a) under an execution in respect of a judgment for a sum exceeding such sum as may be prescribed for the purposes of this subsection, the goods of any person are sold or money is paid in order to avoid a sale, and

(b) before the end of the period of 14 days beginning with the day of the sale or payment the sheriff or other officer charged with the execution is given notice that a bankruptcy petition has been presented in relation to that person, and

(c) a bankruptcy order is or has been made on that petition,

the balance of the proceeds of sale or money paid, after deducting the costs of execution, shall (in priority to the claim of the execution creditor) be comprised in the bankrupt's estate.

346(4) **[Duty of sheriff re sum in s. 346(3)]** Accordingly, in the case of an execution in respect of a judgment for a sum exceeding the sum prescribed for the purposes of subsection (3), the sheriff or other officer charged with the execution–

(a) shall not dispose of the balance mentioned in subsection (3) at any time within the period of 14 days so mentioned or while there is pending a bankruptcy petition of which he has been given notice under that subsection, and

(b) shall pay that balance, where by virtue of that subsection it is comprised in the bankrupt's estate, to the official receiver or (if there is one) to the trustee of that estate.

346(5) **[Completion of execution or attachment]** For the purposes of this section–

(a) an execution against goods is completed by seizure and sale or by the making of a charging order under section 1 of the Charging Orders Act 1979;

(b) an execution against land is completed by seizure, by the appointment of a receiver or by the making of a charging order under that section;

(c) an attachment of a debt is completed by the receipt of the debt.

346(6) **[Setting aside of s. 346(1)–(3) rights by court]** The rights conferred by subsections (1) to (3) on the official receiver or the trustee may, to such extent and on such terms as it thinks fit, be set aside by the court in favour of the creditor who has issued the execution or attached the debt.

346(7) **[Acquisition in good faith]** Nothing in this section entitles the trustee of a bankrupt's estate to claim goods from a person who has acquired them in good faith under a sale by a sheriff or other officer charged with an execution.

346(8) **[Non-application of s. 346(2), (3)]** Neither subsection (2) nor subsection (3) applies in relation to any execution against property which has been acquired by or has devolved upon the bankrupt since the commencement of the bankruptcy, unless, at the time the execution is issued or before it is completed–

(a) the property has been or is claimed for the bankrupt's estate under section 307 (after-acquired property), and

(b) a copy of the notice given under that section has been or is served on the sheriff or other officer charged with the execution.

S. 346(1), (5)
Where a creditor has begun an execution process before the commencement of the bankruptcy (see s. 278(a)), but has failed to complete before that date, he will not be allowed to proceed further and any proceeds received after the commencement of the bankruptcy must be handed over to the estate. The stages at which the various execution processes are deemed to be completed are described by s. 346(5).

Executions may also be restrained under s. 285. The court retains the power to set aside a garnishee order notwithstanding the provisions of s. 346 – *Industrial Diseases Compensation Ltd v Marrons* [2001] B.P.I.R. 600.

S. 346(2)
This deals with the position of a sheriff who has seized goods in execution. The goods must be handed over to the estate, although the sheriff's costs are a first charge on such goods. Note also IR 1986, r. 12.19. For the sheriff's costs see r. 7.36.

S. 346(3), (4)
These provisions deal with the situation where the sheriff has received the proceeds of sale of goods seized in execution of a judgment for a "prescribed amount" (see s. 418), or has been paid not to sell them. The amount is £1,000 under the Insolvency Proceedings (Monetary Limits) (Amendment) Order 2004 (SI 2004/547) operating from April 1, 2004. If, within 14 days thereafter, the sheriff is given notice of the bankruptcy petition, the balance of the proceeds after deducting costs must be paid to the estate if the petition succeeds. The sheriff is therefore under a duty to retain proceeds for the required period, just in case this obligation is activated.

On s. 346(3)(b) see IR 1986, r. 12.19.

S. 346(6)
The court has discretion to set aside the rights of the estate in favour of the execution creditor.

S. 346(7)
Bona fide purchasers from the sheriff are protected.

S. 346(8)
This provision lays down special rules for execution against property acquired by the bankrupt after the commencement of the bankruptcy.

347 Distress, etc.

347(1) **[Limit on distraining goods]** The right of any landlord or other person to whom rent is payable to distrain upon the goods and effects of an undischarged bankrupt for rent due to him from the bankrupt is available (subject to sections 252(2)(b) and 254(1) above and subsection (5) below) against goods and effects comprised in the bankrupt's estate, but only for 6 months' rent accrued due before the commencement of the bankruptcy.

347(2) **[Distraining where order later made]** Where a landlord or other person to whom rent is payable has distrained for rent upon the goods and effects of an individual to whom a bankruptcy petition relates and a bankruptcy order is subsequently made on that petition, any amount recovered by way of that distress which–

(a) is in excess of the amount which by virtue of subsection (1) would have been recoverable after the commencement of the bankruptcy, or

(b) is in respect of rent for a period or part of a period after the distress was levied,

shall be held for the bankrupt as part of his estate.

347(3) [Proceeds of sale re goods not held under s. 347(2)] Where any person (whether or not a landlord or person entitled to rent) has distrained upon the goods or effects of an individual who is adjudged bankrupt before the end of the period of 3 months beginning with the distraint, so much of those goods or effects, or of the proceeds of their sale, as is not held for the bankrupt under subsection (2) shall be charged for the benefit of the bankrupt's estate with the preferential debts of the bankrupt to the extent that the bankrupt's estate is for the time being insufficient for meeting those debts.

347(4) [Where surrender under s. 347(3)] Where by virtue of any charge under subsection (3) any person surrenders any goods or effects to the trustee of a bankrupt's estate or makes a payment to such a trustee, that person ranks, in respect of the amount of the proceeds of the sale of those goods or effects by the trustee or, as the case may be, the amount of the payment, as a preferential creditor of the bankrupt, except as against so much of the bankrupt's estate as is available for the payment of preferential creditors by virtue of the surrender or payment.

347(5) [Rights of landlord after discharge] A landlord or other person to whom rent is payable is not at any time after the discharge of a bankrupt entitled to distrain upon any goods or effects comprised in the bankrupt's estate.

347(6) [Restriction of landlord's rights] Where in the case of any execution–

(a) a landlord is (apart from this section) entitled under section 1 of the Landlord and Tenant Act 1709 or section 102 of the County Courts Act 1984 (claims for rent where goods seized in execution) to claim for an amount not exceeding one year's rent, and

(b) the person against whom the execution is levied is adjudged bankrupt before the notice of claim is served on the sheriff or other officer charged with the execution,

the right of the landlord to claim under that section is restricted to a right to claim for an amount not exceeding 6 months' rent and does not extend to any rent payable in respect of a period after the notice of claim is so served.

347(7) [Limit to s. 347(6)] Nothing in subsection (6) imposes any liability on a sheriff or other officer charged with an execution to account to the official receiver or the trustee of a bankrupt's estate for any sums paid by him to a landlord at any time before the sheriff or other officer was served with notice of the bankruptcy order in question.

But this section is without prejudice to the liability of the landlord.

347(8) [Rights to distrain other than for rent] Subject to sections 252(2)(b) and 254(1) above, nothing in this Group of Parts affects any right to distrain otherwise than for rent; and any such right is at any time exercisable without restriction against property comprised in a bankrupt's estate, even if that right is expressed by any enactment to be exercisable in like manner as a right to distrain for rent.

347(9) [Exercise of right] Any right to distrain against property comprised in a bankrupt's estate is exercisable notwithstanding that the property has vested in the trustee.

347(10) [Landlord's right to prove] The provisions of this section are without prejudice to a landlord's right in a bankruptcy to prove for any bankruptcy debt in respect of rent.

S. 347(1), (2), (5), (9)
This continues the favoured treatment of landlords. A landlord may still distrain on the goods of an undischarged bankrupt (even if they have vested in the trustee – s. 347(9)), but only for a maximum of six months' rent accruing

before the commencement of the bankruptcy. There is a similar rule where an administration order is in force: see County Courts Act 1984, s. 116. Where distress is levied after the petition but before the order, the landlord must hand over any proceeds in excess of the amount of rent referred to in s. 347(1). Distress cannot be levied after the discharge of the bankrupt. Subsection (1) was subject to minor amendment by IA 2000, Sch. 3.

S. 347(3), (4)
These make special provision out of the proceeds of a distress for the preferential creditors (see s. 328) in so far as the estate is insufficient to meet their claims. However, the landlord who loses out as a result of this provision is then subrogated to the claims of the preferential creditors against the general estate of the bankrupt.

S. 347(6), (7)
These provisions deal with special forms of distress. Although normally 12 months' rent can be claimed, this is reduced to six months' rent in the event of bankruptcy. Special protection is offered to sheriffs who inadvertently breach this provision, but the landlord himself may still incur liability.

S. 347(8)
Distress otherwise than for rent is not hampered by bankruptcy. Again, note amendment by IA 2000, Sch. 3.

S. 347(10)
As an alternative to levying distress for rent, a landlord can of course prove for the unpaid amount in the bankruptcy.

348 Apprenticeships, etc.

348(1) [Application] This section applies where–

(a) a bankruptcy order is made in respect of an individual to whom another individual was an apprentice or articled clerk at the time when the petition on which the order was made was presented, and

(b) the bankrupt or the apprentice or clerk gives notice to the trustee terminating the apprenticeship or articles.

348(2) [Discharge etc.] Subject to subsection (6) below, the indenture of apprenticeship or, as the case may be, the articles of agreement shall be discharged with effect from the commencement of the bankruptcy.

348(3) [If money paid] If any money has been paid by or on behalf of the apprentice or clerk to the bankrupt as a fee, the trustee may, on an application made by or on behalf of the apprentice or clerk pay such sum to the apprentice or clerk as the trustee thinks reasonable, having regard to–

(a) the amount of the fee,

(b) the proportion of the period in respect of which the fee was paid that has been served by the apprentice or clerk before the commencement of the bankruptcy, and

(c) the other circumstances of the case.

348(4) [Priority of s. 348(3) power] The power of the trustee to make a payment under subsection (3) has priority over his obligation to distribute the bankrupt's estate.

348(5) [Instead of s. 348(3) payment] Instead of making a payment under subsection (3), the trustee may, if it appears to him expedient to do so on an application made by or on behalf of the apprentice or clerk, transfer the indenture or articles to a person other than the bankrupt.

348(6) [Where s. 348(5) transfer] Where a transfer is made under subsection (5), subsection (2) has effect only as between the apprentice or clerk and the bankrupt.

S. 348(1)
This section applies where a principal is declared bankrupt and notice is given to terminate a contract of apprenticeship or articled clerkship. Either party can give notice to terminate.

S. 348(2)
The effect of such notice is to discharge the contract from the date of the commencement of the bankruptcy (for the meaning of this term, see s. 278(a)).

S. 348(3), (4)
The trustee can repay any fee paid by the apprentice or articled clerk in whole or in part. Factors such as the duration of the apprenticeship which is unexpired and the general circumstances of the case are relevant here. The approach will be similar to that taken with regard to premiums under s. 40 of the Partnership Act 1890. The sum of money repaid under s. 348(3) ranks as a pre-preferential debt.

S. 348(5), (6)
As an alternative, the trustee can transfer the apprenticeship, etc., to another principal if the apprentice, etc., so wishes. The continuity of the apprenticeship in such a case will not be disrupted by s. 348(2). This latter provision clarifies the former law under BA 1914, s. 34.

349 Unenforceability of liens on books, etc.

349(1) [**Unenforceability**] Subject as follows, a lien or other right to retain possession of any of the books, papers or other records of a bankrupt is unenforceable to the extent that its enforcement would deny possession of any books, papers or other records to the official receiver or the trustee of the bankrupt's estate.

349(2) [**Non-application of s. 349(1)**] Subsection (1) does not apply to a lien on documents which give a title to property and are held as such.

GENERAL NOTE

This section renders ineffective liens, etc., on the books and records of a bankrupt in so far as they would deny possession of them to the official receiver or trustee. Liens on documents of title are not affected. Here the public interest is acccorded priority over private security rights.

See also s. 333(4) for another indication of how liens on books require special treatment from the law. Regulations made by the Secretary of State pursuant to the rules may allow the trustee wide powers to deal with, and dispose of, the bankrupt's books: see IR 1986, r. 12.1(1)(c). Note also the Insolvency Regulations 1994 (SI 1994/2507), reg. 30.

S. 349(2)
On the interpretation of this provision, see the note to s. 246(3).

CHAPTER VI

BANKRUPTCY OFFENCES

Preliminary

350 Scheme of this Chapter

350(1) [**Application**] Subject to section 360(3) below, this Chapter applies where the court has made a bankruptcy order on a bankruptcy petition.

350(2) [**Effect of annulment of bankruptcy**] This Chapter applies whether or not the bankruptcy order is annulled, but proceedings for an offence under this Chapter shall not be instituted after the annulment.

350(3) [**Liability of bankrupt after discharge**] Without prejudice to his liability in respect of a subsequent bankruptcy, the bankrupt is not guilty of an offence under this Chapter in respect of anything done after his discharge; but nothing in this Group of Parts prevents the institution of proceedings against a discharged bankrupt for an offence committed before his discharge.

350(3A) [**Effect of bankruptcy restrictions order**] Subsection (3) is without prejudice to any provision of this Chapter which applies to a person in respect of whom a bankruptcy restrictions order is in force.

350(4) **[Where not defence]** It is not a defence in proceedings for an offence under this Chapter that anything relied on, in whole or in part, as constituting that offence was done outside England and Wales.

350(5) **[Institution of proceedings for offence]** Proceedings for an offence under this Chapter or under the rules shall not be instituted except by the Secretary of State or by or with the consent of the Director of Public Prosecutions.

350(6) **[Penalty]** A person guilty of any offence under this Chapter is liable to imprisonment or a fine, or both.

GENERAL NOTE

The Cork Committee (*Report*, para. 1900) called for greater use to be made of the criminal law in controlling fraud in bankruptcy. In addition, it recommended a cautious tidying up of the offences (para. 1883), and this has been to some extent implemented by the following provisions in the Act. Incidentally, the Blagden Committee (Cmnd 221, 1957, paras 206–213) also suggested that the criminal law should be applied more strictly to control fraudulent bankrupts. Note that the rules themselves create several offences, the punishments for which are prescribed by Sch. 5 to the rules. For an analysis of the new regime of bankruptcy offences see Griffiths (1986) 2 I.L. & P. 73.

S. 350(1), (2)

These are new provisions dealing with bankruptcy offences in general. In particular, s. 350(2) makes it clear that the subsequent annulment of the bankruptcy is relevant only in so far as a prosecution cannot be instituted after this date.

S. 350(3)

This repeats the provision under the 1914 Act – the bankrupt cannot be guilty for acts done after his discharge, but he can be prosecuted after his discharge for earlier misconduct.

S. 350(3A)

This was inserted by EA 2002, s. 257 and Sch. 21 with effect from April 1, 2004 to deal with the effect of BROs.

S. 350(4)

By way of contrast, it is not a defence to show that the conduct complained of was done outside England and Wales.

S. 350(5)

This is a new general provision replacing the fragmentary approach of the 1914 Act. Prosecutions now require the consent of the Director of Public Prosecutions or the Secretary of State. Formerly, the court's consent was needed for certain prosecutions.

S. 350(6)

For details of penalties, see s. 430 and Sch. 10.

351 Definitions

351 In the following provisions of this Chapter–

(a) references to property comprised in the bankrupt's estate or to property possession of which is required to be delivered up to the official receiver or the trustee of the bankrupt's estate include any property which would be such property if a notice in respect of it were given under section 307 (after-acquired property), section 308 (personal property and effects of bankrupt having more than replacement value) or section 308A (vesting in trustee of certain tenancies);

(b) **"the initial period"** means the period between the presentation of the bankruptcy petition and the commencement of the bankruptcy; and

(c) a reference to a number of months or years before petition is to that period ending with the presentation of the bankruptcy petition.

GENERAL NOTE

This section contains definitions of three concepts and phrases which recur throughout ss. 352–362:

(a) "property": see ss. 353, 354, 356, 357, 358, 359, 362;

(b) "initial period": see ss. 354, 355, 356, 358, 359, 362 (for further explanation, see s. 278(a));

(c) "before petition": see ss. 354, 355, 356, 358, 359, 361, 362.

In s. 351(a) the words relating to s. 308A inserted and consequential amendment made by the Housing Act 1988, Sch. 17, para. 75.

352 Defence of innocent intention

352 Where in the case of an offence under any provision of this Chapter it is stated that this section applies, a person is not guilty of the offence if he proves that, at the time of the conduct constituting the offence, he had no intent to defraud or to conceal the state of his affairs.

GENERAL NOTE

This is an important new general defence. If the bankrupt is charged with certain offences in ss. 353–362, he has a defence if he can prove that he had not intended to defraud or conceal his affairs. The provisions creating the offences state whether s. 352 applies. On the burden of proof see *R v Daniel* [2002] EWCA Crim 959; [2002] B.P.I.R. 1193.

Wrongdoing by the bankrupt before and after bankruptcy

353 Non-disclosure

353(1) **[Offence]** The bankrupt is guilty of an offence if–

(a) he does not to the best of his knowledge and belief disclose all the property comprised in his estate to the official receiver or the trustee, or

(b) he does not inform the official receiver or the trustee of any disposal of any property which but for the disposal would be so comprised, stating how, when, to whom and for what consideration the property was disposed of.

353(2) **[Exception to s. 353(1)(b)]** Subsection (1)(b) does not apply to any disposal in the ordinary course of a business carried on by the bankrupt or to any payment of the ordinary expenses of the bankrupt or his family.

353(3) **[Application of s. 352]** Section 352 applies to this offence.

S. 353(1), (2)
This makes it an offence for the bankrupt to fail to disclose items of "property" (for definition, see s. 351(a)) to his trustee or official receiver. Moreover, certain disposals of property which have resulted in a diminution of the estate must also be revealed. Note the positive nature of the obligations imposed here. There is a defence for *bona fide* business and domestic transactions.

For the appropriate penalty, see ss. 350, 430 and Sch. 10.

S. 353(3)
The general defence in s. 352 applies here.

354 Concealment of property

354(1) **[Offence of concealment etc.]** The bankrupt is guilty of an offence if–

(a) he does not deliver up possession to the official receiver or trustee, or as the official receiver or trustee may direct, of such part of the property comprised in his estate as is in his possession or under his control and possession of which he is required by law so to deliver up,

(b) he conceals any debt due to or from him or conceals any property the value of which is not less than the prescribed amount and possession of which he is required to deliver up to the official receiver or trustee, or

(c) in the 12 months before petition, or in the initial period, he did anything which would have been an offence under paragraph (b) above if the bankruptcy order had been made immediately before he did it.

Section 352 applies to this offence.

354(2) **[Offence re removal of property]** The bankrupt is guilty of an offence if he removes, or in the initial period removed, any property the value of which was not less than the prescribed amount and possession of which he has or would have been required to deliver up to the official receiver or the trustee.

Section 352 applies to this offence.

354(3) **[Offence re failure to account for loss]** The bankrupt is guilty of an offence if he without reasonable excuse fails, on being required to do so by the official receiver, the trustee or the court–

(a) to account for the loss of any substantial part of his property incurred in the 12 months before petition or in the initial period, or

(b) to give a satisfactory explanation of the manner in which such a loss was incurred.

S. 354(1)
This is a related offence of failing to hand over "property" (for definition, see s. 351(a)), or concealing debts or property which is not less than the "prescribed amount" (see s. 418). The amount is £1,000 under the Insolvency Proceedings (Monetary Limits) (Amendment) Order 2004 (SI 2004/547) (which operates from April 1, 2004). Note that, in the case of concealment, conduct in the "initial period" (*i.e.* between the petition and order: see s. 351(b)) and, indeed, in the 12 months "before petition" (see s. 351(c)), is covered.
The general defence in s. 352 applies. See *R. v Daniel* [2002] EWCA Crim 959; [2002] B.P.I.R. 1193.
For penalties, see s. 350, 430 and Sch. 10.

S. 354(2)
Removal of "property" from the estate after the order or in the "initial period" is unlawful where the property exceeds the "prescribed amount" (£1,000 – see the note to s. 354(1)). The general defence in s. 352 applies. Settling a non-provable debt during the period in question is an offence under s. 354: *Woodley v Woodley (No. 2)* [1994] 1 W.L.R. 1167.

S. 354(3)
Failure to provide explanations for substantial losses of "property" dating back to 12 months "before petition", or in the "initial period", is unlawful, unless there is a reasonable excuse for this. The words ", the trustee" were inserted by s. 269 and Sch. 23 EA 2002 with effect from April 1, 2004. The existence of the offence under s. 354(3)(a) does not infringe fundamental human rights expectations – *R. v Kearns (Nicholas Gary)* [2002] EWCA Crim 748. The time limit referred to in s. 354(3) is the same as that in BA 1914, in spite of recommendations from the Cork Committee (*Report*, para. 1888) that it should be extended to two years.

355 Concealment of books and papers; falsification

355(1) **[Offence re non-delivery of books etc.]** The bankrupt is guilty of an offence if he does not deliver up possession to the official receiver or the trustee, or as the official receiver or trustee may direct, of all books, papers and other records of which he has possession or control and which relate to his estate or his affairs.

Section 352 applies to this offence.

355(2) **[Offence re destruction, concealment etc.]** The bankrupt is guilty of an offence if–

(a) he prevents, or in the initial period prevented, the production of any books, papers or records relating to his estate or affairs;

(b) he conceals, destroys, mutilates or falsifies, or causes or permits the concealment, destruction, mutilation or falsification of, any books, papers or other records relating to his estate or affairs;

(c) he makes, or causes or permits the making of, any false entries in any book, document or record relating to his estate or affairs; or

(d) in the 12 months before petition, or in the initial period, he did anything which would have been an offence under paragraph (b) or (c) above if the bankruptcy order had been made before he did it.

Section 352 applies to this offence.

355(3) **[Offence re disposal, alteration etc.]** The bankrupt is guilty of an offence if–

(a) he disposes of, or alters or makes any omission in, or causes or permits the disposal, altering or making of any omission in, any book, document or record relating to his estate or affairs, or

(b) in the 12 months before petition, or in the initial period, he did anything which would have been an offence under paragraph (a) if the bankruptcy order had been made before he did it.

Section 352 applies to this offence.

355(4) **[Application of s. 355(2)(d), (3)(b)]** In their application to a trading record subsections (2)(d) and (3)(b) shall have effect as if the reference to 12 months were a reference to two years.

355(5) **["Trading record"]** In subsection (4) **"trading record"** means a book, document or record which shows or explains the transactions or financial position of a person's business, including–

(a) a periodic record of cash paid and received,

(b) a statement of periodic stock-taking, and

(c) except in the case of goods sold by way of retail trade, a record of goods sold and purchased which identifies the buyer and seller or enables them to be identified.

GENERAL NOTE

This involved provision is somewhat tautological.

For penalties, see ss. 350, 430 and Sch. 10, and for defences, see s. 352. Note that, in the case of those basic records described by s. 361(3), the 12-month periods referred to in s. 355 are extended to two years: see s. 361(4).

S. 355(1), (2)

Failure to deliver up books and records is an offence. Moreover, if one prevents such books and records being produced, or conceals, destroys or falsifies them, this will also be unlawful. Note that for concealment and falsification, the relevant period is extended to 12 months "before petition" (see s. 351(c)), plus the "initial period" (see s. 351(b)).

S. 355(3)

It is unlawful for a bankrupt to dispose of or alter books or records – this again extends to the 12 months "before petition" and the "initial period".

S. 355(4), (5)

These were added by EA 2002, s. 269 and Sch. 23 with effect from April 1, 2004. They clarify the position.

356 False statements

356(1) **[Offence re material omission]** The bankrupt is guilty of an offence if he makes or has made any material omission in any statement made under any provision in this Group of Parts and relating to his affairs.

Section 352 applies to this offence.

356(2) **[Offence re failing to inform etc.]** The bankrupt is guilty of an offence if–

(a) knowing or believing that a false debt has been proved by any person under the bankruptcy, he fails to inform the trustee as soon as practicable; or

(b) he attempts to account for any part of his property by fictitious losses or expenses; or

(c) at any meeting of his creditors in the 12 months before petition or (whether or not at such a meeting) at any time in the initial period, he did anything which would have been an offence under paragraph (b) if the bankruptcy order had been made before he did it; or

(d) he is, or at any time has been, guilty of any false representation or other fraud for the purpose of obtaining the consent of his creditors, or any of them, to an agreement with reference to his affairs or to his bankruptcy.

S. 356(1)
This is a general offence derived from BA 1914, s. 154(6), prohibiting the bankrupt from making false statements by omission. The statement must relate to his "affairs" (for definition, see s. 385(2)).

Section 356(1) (unlike s. 356(2)) does not, on its face, require any intent to cheat or defraud, but of course the general defence under s. 352 can be utilised to offer a defence to the innocent bankrupt.

S. 356(2)
This provision specifies certain prohibited forms of conduct involving falsehoods. Such behaviour was an offence under BA 1914, s. 154(1), (7), (12), and (16). For definitions of "property", "before petition" and "initial period", see the note to s. 351.

The penalties for the above offences are dealt with by ss. 350, 430 and Sch. 10.

357 Fraudulent disposal of property

357(1) **[Offence re transfer]** The bankrupt is guilty of an offence if he makes or causes to be made, or has in the period of 5 years ending with the commencement of the bankruptcy made or caused to be made, any gift or transfer of, or any charge on, his property.

Section 352 applies to this offence.

357(2) **[Interpretation]** The reference to making a transfer of or charge on any property includes causing or conniving at the levying of any execution against that property.

357(3) **[Offence re concealment or removal of property]** The bankrupt is guilty of an offence if he conceals or removes, or has at any time before the commencement of the bankruptcy concealed or removed, any part of his property after, or within 2 months before, the date on which a judgment or order for the payment of money has been obtained against him, being a judgment or order which was not satisfied before the commencement of the bankruptcy.

Section 352 applies to this offence.

S. 357(1), (3)
Based partly on BA 1914, s. 156 and partly on s. 6 of the 1926 Act, this provision prohibits fraudulent disposal by the bankrupt of any "property" (see s. 351(a)) within five years of his bankruptcy commencing (for the definition of "commencement", see s. 278(a)). It also covers attempts to defeat judgments by concealment of property. For sanctions see *R v Mungroo* [1998] B.P.I.R. 784.

S. 357(2)
This is a supplementary provision, based partly on s. 6 of the 1926 Act. It indicates that the bankrupt commits an offence under s. 357(1) if he causes or connives at the levying of execution on his "property".

A bankrupt charged with offences under this section can rely on the general defence in s. 352. The relevant penalties are specified by ss. 350, 430 and Sch. 10.

358 Absconding

358 The bankrupt is guilty of an offence if–

(a) he leaves, or attempts or makes preparations to leave, England and Wales with any property the value of which is not less than the prescribed amount and possession of which he is required to deliver up to the official receiver or the trustee, or

(b) in the 6 months before petition, or in the initial period, he did anything which would have been an offence under paragraph (a) if the bankruptcy order had been made immediately before he did it.

Section 352 applies to this offence.

GENERAL NOTE

This largely repeats BA 1914, s. 159, although the previous arbitrary figure of £250 has been dropped – unfortunately, in favour of another arbitrary figure to be fixed under s. 418. The figure from April 1, 2004 is £1,000: see the Insolvency Proceedings (Monetary Limits) (Amendment) Order 2004 (SI 2004/547). For a critique of this, see the Cork *Report*, para. 1889. Note that the offence covers absconding, etc., within the six months prior to the petition.

The s. 352 defence applies here. For penalties, see ss. 350, 430 and Sch. 10. The terms "property", "before petition" and "initial period" are all defined in s. 351.

359 Fraudulent dealing with property obtained on credit

359(1) [**Offence re disposal of property obtained on credit**] The bankrupt is guilty of an offence if, in the 12 months before petition, or in the initial period, he disposed of any property which he had obtained on credit and, at the time he disposed of it, had not paid for.

Section 352 applies to this offence.

359(2) [**Offence re knowingly dealing with bankrupt**] A person is guilty of an offence if, in the 12 months before petition or in the initial period, he acquired or received property from the bankrupt knowing or believing–

(a) that the bankrupt owed money in respect of the property, and

(b) that the bankrupt did not intend, or was unlikely to be able, to pay the money he so owed.

359(3) [**Disposals etc. in ordinary course of business**] A person is not guilty of an offence under subsection (1) or (2) if the disposal, acquisition or receipt of the property was in the ordinary course of a business carried on by the bankrupt at the time of the disposal, acquisition or receipt.

359(4) [**Ordinary course of business**] In determining for the purposes of this section whether any property is disposed of, acquired or received in the ordinary course of a business carried on by the bankrupt, regard may be had, in particular, to the price paid for the property.

359(5) [**Interpretation**] In this section references to disposing of property include pawning or pledging it; and references to acquiring or receiving property shall be read accordingly.

S. 359(1)

Based on BA 1914, s. 154(1), (15), this provision prohibits a bankrupt from disposing of "property" (for definition, see s. 351(a)) obtained on credit, where the disposal occurs within 12 months "before petition" (see s. 351(c)), or in the "initial period" (see s. 351(b)).

The s. 352 defence applies here.

On penalties for the offences in this and the following subsections, see ss. 350, 430 and Sch. 10.

S. 359(2)

Derived from s. 154(3), this penalises the knowing recipient of property obtained on credit and unlawfully disposed of under s. 359(1). Note again the definitions in s. 351.

A defence for the innocent recipient is built into this subsection.

S. 359(3), (4)

These are saving provisions for disposals and receipts of "property" in the ordinary course of business. In determining whether this saving facility can operate, the price paid for the property is clearly relevant.

S. 359(5)

This provision defines disposal of "property" so as to include pawns and pledges.

360 Obtaining credit; engaging in business

360(1) [**Offence re credit, non-disclosure of bankruptcy**] The bankrupt is guilty of an offence if–

(a) either alone or jointly with any other person, he obtains credit to the extent of the prescribed amount or more without giving the person from whom he obtains it the relevant information about his status; or

(b) he engages (whether directly or indirectly) in any business under a name other than that in which he was adjudged bankrupt without disclosing to all persons with whom he enters into any business transaction the name in which he was so adjudged.

360(2) **[Cases of bankrupt obtaining credit]** The reference to the bankrupt obtaining credit includes the following cases–

(a) where goods are bailed to him under a hire-purchase agreement, or agreed to be sold to him under a conditional sale agreement, and

(b) where he is paid in advance (whether in money or otherwise) for the supply of goods or services.

360(3) **[Scotland or Northern Ireland]** A person whose estate has been sequestrated in Scotland, or who has been adjudged bankrupt in Northern Ireland, is guilty of an offence if, before his discharge, he does anything in England and Wales which would be an offence under subsection (1) if he were an undischarged bankrupt and the sequestration of his estate or the adjudication in Northern Ireland were an adjudication under this Part.

360(4) **[Information for s. 360(1)(a)]** For the purposes of subsection (1)(a), the relevant information about the status of the person in question is the information that he is an undischarged bankrupt or, as the case may be, that his estate has been sequestrated in Scotland and that he has not been discharged.

360(5) **[Application of section]** This section applies to the bankrupt after discharge while a bankruptcy restrictions order is in force in respect of him.

360(6) **[Relevant information]** For the purposes of subsection (1)(a) as it applies by virtue of subsection (5), the relevant information about the status of the person in question is the information that a bankruptcy restrictions order is in force in respect of him.

S. 360(1)
This prevents an undischarged bankrupt from obtaining credit to the extent of the prescribed amount, either solely or jointly, without disclosing the relevant information about his status. It also prohibits him from carrying on a business under a name which was not the name by which he was declared bankrupt. Note that a person who enters into an individual voluntary arrangement is not subject to these disabilities. The figure from April 1, 2004 is £500 under the Insolvency Proceedings (Monetary Limits) (Amendment) Order 2004 (SI 2004/547) made under s. 418. The offence under s. 360(1) is one of strict liability (see *R. v Scott* [1998] B.P.I.R. 471) and the general defence under s. 352 does not apply, although the offence would not operate where credit is obtained for an independent third person: *R. v Godwin* (1980) 11 Cr. App. Rep. 97.

The sanction for breach of s. 360 is specified by ss. 350, 430 and Sch. 10.

S. 360(2)
This represents a change in the law by extending the meaning of "obtaining credit" to cover receipt of goods under a hire-purchase agreement and receiving payment in advance for goods or services. Thus, authorities such as *R. v Miller* [1977] 3 All E.R. 986 and *Fisher v Raven* [1964] A.C. 210 are no longer good law on this point.

S. 360(3)
This applies the above offence to a person whose estate is sequestrated in Scotland or who is declared bankrupt in Northern Ireland and who obtains credit in England and Wales.

S. 360(4)
This provision defines the "relevant information" for the purposes of s. 360(1).

S. 360(5), (6)
This was inserted by s. 257 and Sch. 21 EA 2002 with effect from April 1, 2004 to deal with the effect of BROs.

361 [repealed]

GENERAL NOTE

This offence was repealed by EA 2002 s. 263 with effect from April 1, 2004. However such conduct might justify a BRO. S. 361 is reproduced in italics below.

361(1) *[Offence re no proper accounting records] Where the bankrupt has been engaged in any business for any of the period of 2 years before petition, he is guilty of an offence if he–*

(a) has not kept proper accounting records throughout that period and throughout any part of the initial period in which he was so engaged, or

(b) has not preserved all the accounting records which he has kept.

361(2) *[Exception to s. 361(1)]* The bankrupt is not guilty of an offence under subsection (1)–

(a) if his unsecured liabilities at the commencement of the bankruptcy did not exceed the prescribed amount, or

(b) if he proves that in the circumstances in which he carried on business the omission was honest and excusable.

361(3) *[Interpretation]* For the purposes of this section a person is deemed not to have kept proper accounting records if he has not kept such records as are necessary to show or explain his transactions and financial position in his business, including–

(a) records containing entries from day to day, in sufficient detail, of all cash paid and received,

(b) where the business involved dealings in goods, statements of annual stock-takings, and

(c) except in the case of goods sold by way of retail trade to the actual customer, records of all goods sold and purchased showing the buyers and sellers in sufficient detail to enable the goods and the buyers and sellers to be identified.

361(4) *[Application of s. 355(2)(d), (3)(b)]* In relation to any such records as are mentioned in subsection (3), subsections (2)(d) and (3)(b) of section 355 apply with the substitution of 2 years for 12 months.

362 [repealed]

GENERAL NOTE

This offence (reproduced below) was repealed by s. 263 of EA 2002 with effect from April 2004. Such behaviour is, however, still frowned upon and may form the basis for a bankruptcy restrictions order.

362(1) *[Offence re gambling, rash and hazardous speculations]* The bankrupt is guilty of an offence if he has–

(a) in the 2 years before petition, materially contributed to, or increased the extent of, his insolvency by gambling or by rash and hazardous speculations, or

(b) in the initial period, lost any part of his property by gambling or by rash and hazardous speculations.

362(2) *[Rash and hazardous speculations]* In determining for the purposes of this section whether any speculations were rash and hazardous, the financial position of the bankrupt at the time when he entered into them shall be taken into consideration.

CHAPTER VII

POWERS OF COURT IN BANKRUPTCY

363 General control of court

363(1) **[Power of court]** Every bankruptcy is under the general control of the court and, subject to the provisions in this Group of Parts, the court has full power to decide all questions of priorities and all other questions, whether of law or fact, arising in any bankruptcy.

363(2) **[Bankrupt to do as directed]** Without prejudice to any other provision in this Group of Parts, an undischarged bankrupt or a discharged bankrupt whose estate is still being administered under Chapter IV of this Part shall do all such things as he may be directed to do by the court for the purposes of his bankruptcy or, as the case may be, the administration of that estate.

363(3) **[Application for directions]** The official receiver or the trustee of a bankrupt's estate may at any time apply to the court for a direction under subsection (2).

363(4) **[Contempt of court]** If any person without reasonable excuse fails to comply with any obligation imposed on him by subsection (2), he is guilty of a contempt of court and liable to be punished accordingly (in addition to any other punishment to which he may be subject).

S. 363(1)
This confers on "the court" (see ss. 373 and 385) the power to resolve all disputes in bankruptcy matters. See also *Engel v Peri* [2002] EWHC 799 (Ch); [2002] B.P.I.R. 961 where the point was made that the s. 363 jurisdiction is still available notwithstanding the fact that the bankruptcy may already have been annulled. In *Re Colgate* [1986] Ch. 439, the court used the predecessor of this provision to fix the remuneration of a trustee where this was in dispute. Appointment of an additional trustee might also be a suitable use of this power – *Clements v Udal* [2001] B.P.I.R. 454. The rules are also relevant here: see IR 1986, r. 6.141 and Pt 7.

S. 363(2), (4)
This places an undischarged bankrupt squarely under the thumb of the court: see *Hardy v Buchler* [1997] B.P.I.R. 643. If he unreasonably fails to obey its instructions he could be liable for contempt; see *Official Receiver v Cummings-John* [2000] B.P.I.R. 320. Form 7.16 is no longer to be used for contempt proceedings, but see now Form 7.15. This change was effected by I(A)R 1987 (SI 1987/1919), r. 3(1), Sch., Pt 2, para. 159.

S. 363(3)
The trustee or official receiver may apply to the court for a direction that the undischarged bankrupt behave in a certain way. This must not be confused with the power to apply for directions under s. 303(2).

364 Power of arrest

364(1) **[Court's power re warrant]** In the cases specified in the next subsection the court may cause a warrant to be issued to a constable or prescribed officer of the court–

(a) for the arrest of a debtor to whom a bankruptcy petition relates or of an undischarged bankrupt, or of a discharged bankrupt whose estate is still being administered under Chapter IV of this Part, and

(b) for the seizure of any books, papers, records, money or goods in the possession of a person arrested under the warrant,

and may authorise a person arrested under such a warrant to be kept in custody, and anything seized under such a warrant to be held, in accordance with the rules, until such time as the court may order.

364(2) **[Where s. 364(1) powers exercisable]** The powers conferred by subsection (1) are exercisable in relation to a debtor or undischarged bankrupt if, at any time after the presentation of the bankruptcy petition relating to him or the making of the bankruptcy order against him, it appears to the court–

(a) that there are reasonable grounds for believing that he has absconded, or is about to abscond, with a view to avoiding or delaying the payment of any of his debts or his appearance to a bankruptcy petition or to avoiding, delaying or disrupting any proceedings in bankruptcy against him or any examination of his affairs, or

(b) that he is about to remove his goods with a view to preventing or delaying possession being taken of them by the official receiver or the trustee of his estate, or

(c) that there are reasonable grounds for believing that he has concealed or destroyed, or is about to conceal or destroy, any of his goods or any books, papers or records which might be of use to his creditors in the course of his bankruptcy or in connection with the administration of his estate, or

(d) that he has, without the leave of the official receiver or the trustee of his estate, removed any goods in his possession which exceed in value such sum as may be prescribed for the purposes of this paragraph, or

(e) that he has failed, without reasonable excuse, to attend any examination ordered by the court.

S. 364(1)
This provides for the issue of warrants for the arrest of debtors or undischarged bankrupts and for seizure of their books.

S. 364(2)
The court can issue such a warrant if any of the five facts listed in (a)–(e) appear to it to be present. Under BA 1914, s. 23 there were only four paragraphs ((a)–(d)), but in substance the grounds have not been added to. The grounds are aimed at debtors who are likely to abscond, avoid public examination or hide assets. What is now para. (d) used to include an arbitrary minimum amount of £60 but this has been scrapped, as the Blagden Committee recommended; but alas in favour of another random figure fixed under s. 418. From April 1, 2004 under the Insolvency Proceedings (Monetary Limits) (Amendment) Order 2004 (SI 2004/547) the figure is £1,000.

Note also IR 1986, rr. 7.21, 7.22.

365 Seizure of bankrupt's property

365(1) **[Court's power re warrant]** At any time after a bankruptcy order has been made, the court may, on the application of the official receiver or the trustee of the bankrupt's estate, issue a warrant authorising the person to whom it is directed to seize any property comprised in the bankrupt's estate which is, or any books, papers or records relating to the bankrupt's estate or affairs which are, in the possession or under the control of the bankrupt or any other person who is required to deliver the property, books, papers or records to the official receiver or trustee.

365(2) **[Power to break open premises etc.]** Any person executing a warrant under this section may, for the purpose of seizing any property comprised in the bankrupt's estate or any books, papers or records relating to the bankrupt's estate or affairs, break open any premises where the bankrupt or anything that may be seized under the warrant is or is believed to be and any receptacle of the bankrupt which contains or is believed to contain anything that may be so seized.

365(3) **[Power of court re search]** If, after a bankruptcy order has been made, the court is satisfied that any property comprised in the bankrupt's estate is, or any books, papers or records relating to the bankrupt's estate or affairs are, concealed in any premises not belonging to him, it may issue a warrant authorising any constable or prescribed officer of the court to search those premises for the property, books, papers or records.

365(4) **[Execution of s. 365(3) warrant]** A warrant under subsection (3) shall not be executed except in the prescribed manner and in accordance with its terms.

S. 365(1), (2)
These provisions allow the court to issue a warrant for the seizure of the bankrupt's property even though it may be in the possession of a third party. Forcing entry into premises or breaking open "receptacles" is permitted when executing such a warrant.

S. 365(3), (4)
A search warrant (in the prescribed form) for a third party's premises may also be obtained under this section, although the court must be satisfied that the bankrupt's property, etc. is concealed there. Fishing expeditions will not be permitted.

Note also IR 1986, rr. 7.21, 7.25.

366 Inquiry into bankrupt's dealings and property

366(1) **[Power of court to summon bankrupt to appear]** At any time after a bankruptcy order has been made the court may, on the application of the official receiver or the trustee of the bankrupt's estate, summon to appear before it–

(a) the bankrupt or the bankrupt's spouse or former spouse,

(b) any person known or believed to have any property comprised in the bankrupt's estate in his possession or to be indebted to the bankrupt,

(c) any person appearing to the court to be able to give information concerning the bankrupt or the bankrupt's dealings, affairs or property.

The court may require any such person as is mentioned in paragraph (b) or (c) to submit an affidavit to the court containing an account of his dealings with the bankrupt or to produce any documents in his possession or under his control relating to the bankrupt or the bankrupt's dealings, affairs or property.

366(2) **[Application of s. 366(3)]** Without prejudice to section 364, the following applies in a case where–

(a) a person without reasonable excuse fails to appear before the court when he is summoned to do so under this section, or

(b) there are reasonable grounds for believing that a person has absconded, or is about to abscond, with a view to avoiding his appearance before the court under this section.

366(3) **[Issue of warrant re non-appearance]** The court may, for the purpose of bringing that person and anything in his possession before the court, cause a warrant to be issued to a constable or prescribed officer of the court–

(a) for the arrest of that person, and

(b) for the seizure of any books, papers, records, money or goods in that person's possession.

366(4) **[Power re custody etc.]** The court may authorise a person arrested under such a warrant to be kept in custody, and anything seized under such a warrant to be held, in accordance with the rules, until that person is brought before the court under the warrant or until such other time as the court may order.

S. 366(1)
This permits the trustee or official receiver to ask the court to examine the bankrupt privately (or his spouse, or former spouse, or third parties believed to be in possession of the bankrupt's property or of information about his affairs). On the meaning of "affairs", see s. 385(2). The power to direct the bankrupt to attend for examination survives discharge: *Oakes v Simms* [1997] B.P.I.R. 499.

This changes the previous law in a number of respects. The BA 1914 provision referred to the bankrupt's "wife", which made an assumption which can no longer be justified in an age of sexual equality. The new provision also allows the court to require affidavits from the persons mentioned in para. (a) and (b). This reform, which was recommended by the Cork *Report*, para. 903, reverses the rule in *Ex parte Reynolds* (1882) 21 Ch.D. 601.

On the relationship between s. 366 and professional privilege see *Re Murjani* [1996] 1 W.L.R. 1498; [1996] B.C.C. 278 and *Re Ouvaroff* [1997] B.P.I.R. 712. Where inquiries are made of a bank concerning a client's affairs, major issues of confidentiality can arise – *Christofi v Barclays Bank plc* [1999] B.P.I.R. 855.

It was held in *Re Tucker (a Bankrupt) Ex p. Tucker* [1990] Ch. 148 that the court had no jurisdiction under s. 25(6) of BA 1914 (the precursor of the present section) over British subjects resident abroad. In *Re Seagull Manufacturing Co. Ltd* [1992] Ch. 128 at p. 137; [1991] B.C.C. 550 at p. 555 Mummery J. expressed the view that there was little doubt that, on the authority of *Re Tucker*, the court would construe ss. 366 and 367 as subject to the same territorial limitation. In the Court of Appeal in the same case, [1993] Ch. 345; [1993] B.C.C. 241, no opinion was expressed on this point. Contrast the position in regard to a public examination under s. 133: see the notes to that section and to s. 236. The position may be different where s. 426 can be called into aid: *McIsaac, Petitioners* [1994] B.C.C. 410.

On s. 366 generally see *Albert v Albert* [1996] B.P.I.R. 232 and *Bird v Hadkinson* [1999] B.P.I.R. 653. Further provisions on s. 366 examinations are contained in the rules: see IR 1986, rr. 9.1–9.6.

S. 366(2)–(4)
The court can order the arrest of absconders, plus the seizure of property. Note also IR 1986, rr. 7.21, 7.23.

367 Court's enforcement powers under s. 366

367(1) **[Power to order delivery]** If it appears to the court, on consideration of any evidence obtained under section 366 or this section, that any person has in his possession any property comprised in the bankrupt's estate, the court may, on the application of the official receiver or the trustee of the bankrupt's estate, order that person to deliver the whole or any part of the property to the official receiver or the trustee at such time, in such manner and on such terms as the court thinks fit.

367(2) **[Power to order payment from bankrupt debtor]** If it appears to the court, on consideration of any evidence obtained under section 366 or this section, that any person is indebted to the bankrupt, the

Section 368   Insolvency Act 1986

court may, on the application of the official receiver or the trustee of the bankrupt's estate, order that person to pay to the official receiver or trustee, at such time and in such manner as the court may direct, the whole or part of the amount due, whether in full discharge of the debt or otherwise as the court thinks fit.

367(3) **[Place of examination]** The court may, if it thinks fit, order that any person who if within the jurisdiction of the court would be liable to be summoned to appear before it under section 366 shall be examined in any part of the United Kingdom where he may be for the time being, or in any place outside the United Kingdom.

367(4) **[Examination on oath]** Any person who appears or is brought before the court under section 366 or this section may be examined on oath, either orally or by interrogatories, concerning the bankrupt or the bankrupt's dealings, affairs and property.

S. 367(1), (2)
If, as a result of information gleaned from the examination, it appears that the bankrupt's property is in the possession of a third party, the court can order it to be handed over. Debts owing to the bankrupt can also be ordered to be paid.

S. 367(3)
Examinations under s. 366 do not have to be held in the UK. In *Re Tucker (a Bankrupt) Ex p. Tucker* [1990] Ch. 148 (decided under BA 1914, s. 25(6)), the Court of Appeal refused to exercise its discretion to allow examination of a witness in Belgium, since it was not possible to compel him to attend such examination. On the question whether ss. 366–367 extend to the examinations of witnesses abroad, see the notes to s. 366.

S. 367(4)
This deals with the form of the examination under s. 366. Note also IR 1986, rr. 9.1–9.6.

368   Provision corresponding to s. 366, where interim receiver appointed

368 Sections 366 and 367 apply where an interim receiver has been appointed under section 286 as they apply where a bankruptcy order has been made, as if–

(a)   references to the official receiver or the trustee were to the interim receiver, and

(b)   references to the bankrupt and to his estate were (respectively) to the debtor and his property.

General Note

This extends s. 366 and 367 to situations where the debtor has not yet been declared bankrupt, but an interim receiver has been appointed after presentation of the petition under s. 286.

369   Order for production of documents by inland revenue

369(1) **[Power of court]** For the purposes of an examination under section 290 (public examination of bankrupt) or proceedings under sections 366 to 368, the court may, on the application of the official receiver or the trustee of the bankrupt's estate, order an inland revenue official to produce to the court–

(a)   any return, account or accounts submitted (whether before or after the commencement of the bankruptcy) by the bankrupt to any inland revenue official,

(b)   any assessment or determination made (whether before or after the commencement of the bankruptcy) in relation to the bankrupt by any inland revenue official, or

(c)   any correspondence (whether before or after the commencement of the bankruptcy) between the bankrupt and any inland revenue official.

369(2) **[Order re disclosure of document]** Where the court has made an order under subsection (1) for the purposes of any examination or proceedings, the court may, at any time after the document to which the order relates is produced to it, by order authorise the disclosure of the document, or of any part of its contents, to the official receiver, the trustee of the bankrupt's estate or the bankrupt's creditors.

369(3) **[Condition for s. 369(1) order]** The court shall not address an order under subsection (1) to an inland revenue official unless it is satisfied that that official is dealing, or has dealt, with the affairs of the bankrupt.

369(4) **[Where s. 369(1) document not in official's possession]** Where any document to which an order under subsection (1) relates is not in the possession of the official to whom the order is addressed, it is the duty of that official to take all reasonable steps to secure possession of it and, if he fails to do so, to report the reasons for his failure to the court.

369(5) **[Where document held by another official]** Where any document to which an order under subsection (1) relates is in the possession of an inland revenue official other than the one to whom the order is addressed, it is the duty of the official in possession of the document, at the request of the official to whom the order is addressed, to deliver it to the official making the request.

369(6) **["Inland revenue official"]** In this section **"inland revenue official"** means any inspector or collector of taxes appointed by the Commissioners of Inland Revenue or any person appointed by the Commissioners to serve in any other capacity.

369(7) **[Non-application]** This section does not apply for the purposes of an examination under sections 366 and 367 which takes place by virtue of section 368 (interim receiver).

S. 369(1), (3), (6)
The court can order Inland Revenue officials (as defined by s. 369(6)) to hand over tax documents relating to the bankrupt's financial affairs to assist examinations under ss. 290 or 366. Only officials dealing with the bankrupt can be so directed.

S. 369(2)
The court can order the disclosure of any document ordered to be produced under s. 369(1) to the official receiver or the trustee.

S. 369(4), (5)
Where the court makes an order under s. 369(1), an Inland Revenue official must use his best efforts to obtain the documents in question, and this may involve securing possession of them from another Inland Revenue official.

S. 369(7)
This states that s. 369 does not apply where the debtor has not been declared bankrupt and where there is merely an examination under ss. 366, 367 at the request of his interim receiver under s. 368.
For further information, see IR 1986, rr. 6.194–6.196.

370 Power to appoint special manager

370(1) **[Power of court]** The court may, on an application under this section, appoint any person to be the special manager–

(a) of a bankrupt's estate, or

(b) of the business of an undischarged bankrupt, or

(c) of the property or business of a debtor in whose case the official receiver has been appointed interim receiver under section 286.

370(2) **[Application to court]** An application under this section may be made by the official receiver or the trustee of the bankrupt's estate in any case where it appears to the official receiver or trustee that the nature of the estate, property or business, or the interests of the creditors generally, require the appointment of another person to manage the estate, property or business.

370(3) **[Powers of special manager]** A special manager appointed under this section has such powers as may be entrusted to him by the court.

370(4) **[Powers included in s. 370(3)]** The power of the court under subsection (3) to entrust powers to a special manager include power to direct that any provision in this Group of Parts that has effect in relation to the official receiver, interim receiver or trustee shall have the like effect in relation to the special manager for the purposes of the carrying out by the special manager of any of the functions of the official receiver, interim receiver or trustee.

370(5) **[Duties of special manager]** A special manager appointed under this section shall–

(a) give such security as may be prescribed,

(b) prepare and keep such accounts as may be prescribed, and

(c) produce those accounts in accordance with the rules to the Secretary of State or to such other persons as may be prescribed.

S. 370(1), (2)
The court can appoint a special manager of the bankrupt's estate or business, or indeed of a debtor's estate or business where an interim receiver has been installed. The application may be made by the official receiver or trustee where it appears that it is in the interests of the creditors that such an appointment be made. Under s. 10 of the 1914 Act the official receiver made the appointment.
    For the question of remuneration see Sch. 9, para. 20.
    This section should be read in conjunction with s. 287 and IR 1986, rr. 6.167–6.171.

371   Re-direction of bankrupt's letters, etc.

371(1) **[Power of court]** Where a bankruptcy order has been made, the court may from time to time, on the application of the official receiver or the trustee of the bankrupt's estate, order a postal operator (within the meaning of the Postal Services Act 2000) to re-direct and send or deliver to the official receiver or trustee or otherwise any postal packet (within the meaning of that Act) which would otherwise be sent or delivered by the operator concerned to the bankrupt at such place or places as may be specified in the order.

371(2) **[Duration of court order]** An order under this section has effect for such period, not exceeding 3 months, as may be specified in the order.

S. 371(1)
This provision allows the court on an application from the official receiver or trustee to order a postal operator to redirect the bankrupt's mail after a bankruptcy order has been made. The mail can then be opened by the official receiver or trustee (see s. 365). This provision dates back to s. 85 of the Debtors Act 1869. Unfortunately there are questions as to its legality in the light of art. 8 of the European Convention on Human Rights and its relationship with the Interception of Communications Act 1985: see Jaconelli [1994] Conv. 370 on these intriguing issues. In *Foxley v UK* [2000] B.P.I.R. 1009 the European Court of Human Rights held that a s. 371 order does not per se breach Art. 8 ECHR provided its terms are strictly observed and it is not used in a disproportionate manner. Interception of communications between a bankrupt and his lawyers is not acceptable. For authoritative advice on the correct procedure to be adopted see *Singh v Official Receiver* [1997] B.P.I.R. 530.
    Note that the power to open the bankrupt's mail does not extend to outgoing mail. Moreover, a debtor who enters into an individual voluntary arrangement to settle his debts cannot have his mail opened under this provision.
    In s. 371(1) the words "a postal operator (within the meaning of the Postal Services Act 2000)" substituted for the words "the Post Office", the words "that Act" substituted for the words "the Post Office Act 1953" and the words "the operator concerned" substituted for the word "them" by the Postal Services Act 2000, s. 127(4), Sch. 8, para. 20 as from March 26, 2001 (see the Postal Services Act 2000 (Commencement No. 1 and Transitional Provisions) Order 2000 (SI 2000/2957), art. 2(3), Sch. 3).

S. 371(2)
The maximum period of interference permitted by the order is three months, as was the case previously.

PART X

INDIVIDUAL INSOLVENCY: GENERAL PROVISIONS

372 Supplies of gas, water, electricity, etc.

372(1) [Application] This section applies where on any day ("**the relevant day**")–

(a) a bankruptcy order is made against an individual or an interim receiver of an individual's property is appointed, or

(b) a voluntary arrangement proposed by an individual is approved under Part VIII, or

(c) a deed of arrangement is made for the benefit of an individual's creditors;

and in this section **"the office-holder"** means the official receiver, the trustee in bankruptcy, the interim receiver, the supervisor of the voluntary arrangement or the trustee under the deed of arrangement, as the case may be.

372(2) [Where s. 372(3) request] If a request falling within the next subsection is made for the giving after the relevant day of any of the supplies mentioned in subsection (4), the supplier–

(a) may make it a condition of the giving of the supply that the office-holder personally guarantees the payment of any charges in respect of the supply, but

(b) shall not make it a condition of the giving of the supply, or do anything which has the effect of making it a condition of the giving of the supply, that any outstanding charges in respect of a supply given to the individual before the relevant day are paid.

372(3) [Type of request] A request falls within this subsection if it is made–

(a) by or with the concurrence of the office-holder, and

(b) for the purposes of any business which is or has been carried on by the individual, by a firm or partnership of which the individual is or was a member, or by an agent or manager for the individual or for such a firm or partnership.

372(4) [Supplies in s. 372(2)] The supplies referred to in subsection (2) are–

(a) a public supply of gas by a gas supplier within the meaning of Part I of the Gas Act 1986,

(b) public supply of electricity by an electricity supplier within the meaning of Part I of the Electricity Act 1989,

(c) a supply of water by a water undertaker,

(d) a supply of communications services by a provider of an electronic public communications service.

372(5) [Definitions] The following applies to expressions used in subsection (4)–

(a) **[Repealed]**

(b) **[Repealed]**

(c) **"communications services"** do not include electronic communications services to the extent that they are used to broadcast or otherwise transmit programme services (within the meaning of the Communications Act 2003).

GENERAL NOTE

This section represents a late change of mind by the government in that it did not appear in the early forms of the 1985 Bill. It is designed to stop public utilities "blackmailing" the trustee in bankruptcy, etc. of an insolvent individual into

Section 373 Insolvency Act 1986

paying arrears in respect of public utility supplies as a precondition to receiving supplies in the future. It was not clear at common law whether a public utility could behave in such a way: see *Re Flack* [1900] 2 Q.B. 32 – but the Cork Committee (*Report*, para. 1466) favoured legislation to outlaw expressly such "priority gaining".

For the corresponding provisions in corporate insolvencies, see s. 233.

S. 372(1)–(3)
These provisions enable an office-holder (as defined by s. 372(1)) to request a supply from a public utility. The supplier, although he may require the office-holder to guarantee future payments personally, cannot require arrears to be paid as a precondition to the making of the supply.

S. 372(4), (5)
These provisions list the public utilities that are covered by this section – gas, electricity, water and telecommunications (but not cable services). Subsections (4) and (5) have been amended to cope with utility privatisation legislation. Thus the words "statutory water undertakers" which originally appeared in s. 372(4)(c) have been replaced by "a water undertaker" (see Water Act 1989). The words "a supply of electricity by an Electricity Board" have been dropped from s. 374(4)(b) and substituted with the phrase, "a public supply of electricity", which is now defined in s. 372(5)(b) (see Electricity Act 1989). Subsections (4)(d) and (5)(c) were amended by the Broadcasting Act 2003.

373 Jurisdiction in relation to insolvent individuals

373(1) [**High Court and county courts**] The High Court and the county courts have jurisdiction throughout England and Wales for the purposes of the Parts in this Group.

373(2) [**Powers of county court**] For the purposes of those Parts, a county court has, in addition to its ordinary jurisdiction, all the powers and jurisdiction of the High Court; and the orders of the court may be enforced accordingly in the prescribed manner.

373(3) [**Exercise of jurisdiction**] Jurisdiction for the purposes of those Parts is exercised–

(a) by the High Court in relation to the proceedings which, in accordance with the rules, are allocated to the London insolvency district, and

(b) by each county court in relation to the proceedings which are so allocated to the insolvency district of that court.

373(4) [**Operation of s. 373(3)**] Subsection (3) is without prejudice to the transfer of proceedings from one court to another in the manner prescribed by the rules; and nothing in that subsection invalidates any proceedings on the grounds that they were initiated or continued in the wrong court.

S. 373(1)
This vests bankruptcy jurisdiction in the High Court and the county courts in the case of England and Wales. See also Pt 7 of the rules here. For the fees in county court proceedings see the County Court Fees (Amendment No. 2) Order 1986 (SI 1986/2143).

S. 373(2)
In bankruptcy matters county courts are to have all the powers of the High Court. This was the case under BA 1914, s. 103. See here *Re a Debtor (No. 2A of 1980)* [1981] Ch. 148.

S. 373(3)
This provision allocates cases between the High Court and county courts – much will depend upon the "insolvency districts" which are described in s. 374.

S. 373(4)
The transfer of proceedings from one court to another is permitted. Note IR 1986, rr. 7.11–7.15. See also IR 1986, Sch. 2, for insolvency courts.

374 Insolvency districts

374(1) [Order by Lord Chancellor] The Lord Chancellor may by order designate the areas which are for the time being to be comprised, for the purposes of the Parts in this Group, in the London insolvency district and the insolvency district of each county court; and an order under this section may—

(a) exclude any county court from having jurisdiction for the purposes of those Parts, or

(b) confer jurisdiction for those purposes on any county court which has not previously had that jurisdiction.

374(2) [Incidental provisions etc.] An order under this section may contain such incidental, supplemental and transitional provisions as may appear to the Lord Chancellor necessary or expedient.

374(3) [Order by statutory instrument] An order under this section shall be made by statutory instrument and, after being made, shall be laid before each House of Parliament.

374(4) [Relevant districts] Subject to any order under this section—

(a) the district which, immediately before the appointed day, is the London bankruptcy district becomes, on that day, the London insolvency district;

(b) any district which immediately before that day is the bankruptcy district of a county court becomes, on that day, the insolvency district of that court, and

(c) any county court which immediately before that day is excluded from having jurisdiction in bankruptcy is excluded, on and after that day, from having jurisdiction for the purposes of the Parts in this Group.

S. 374(1), (4)
The Lord Chancellor may by order designate the insolvency districts – certain county courts can be prevented from handling bankruptcy matters, whereas others may be given this jurisdiction for the first time. See for example the Civil Courts (Amendment No. 3) Order 1992 (SI 1992/1810), the Civil Courts (Amendment) Order 1998 (SI 1998/1880) and the Civil Courts (Amendment) (No. 2) Order 1998 (SI 1998/2910). Subject to this power, existing jurisdictional patterns are to be retained. For alternative county courts see Sch. 2 to IR 1986 (as amended).

S. 374(2), (3)
These provisions permit any order by the Lord Chancellor to deal with ancillary matters and regulate the mode by which such orders are to be made.
See IR 1986, r. 6.40(3) and Sch. 2.

375 Appeals etc. from courts exercising insolvency jurisdiction

375(1) [Review, rescission etc.] Every court having jurisdiction for the purposes of the Parts in this Group may review, rescind or vary any order made by it in the exercise of that jurisdiction.

375(2) [Appeals] An appeal from a decision made in the exercise of jurisdiction for the purposes of those Parts by a county court or by a registrar in bankruptcy of the High Court lies to a single judge of the High Court; and an appeal from a decision of that judge on such an appeal lies to the Court of Appeal.

375(3) [No other appeals] A county court is not, in the exercise of its jurisdiction for the purposes of those Parts, to be subject to be restrained by the order of any other court, and no appeal lies from its decision in the exercise of that jurisdiction except as provided by this section.

S. 375(1)
This confers a general "safety valve" power on the courts to review, rescind or vary orders on bankruptcy matters. The equivalent in corporate insolvency law is r. 7.47 and broadly speaking similar principles should be applied: *Midrome Ltd v Shaw* [1993] B.C.C. 659. This review jurisdiction must be kept flexible but must not be allowed to become a gateway for late appeals or to undermine the principle of *res judicata*: *Re Debtors (No. VA7 and VA8) Ex p. Stevens* [1996] B.P.I.R. 101 and *Brillouet v Hachette Magazines* [1996] B.P.I.R. 518 or to avoid other restrictions on applications to the court – *Hurst v Bennett (No. 2)* [2002] B.P.I.R. 102. For a successful attempt to invoke the jurisdiction see *Fitch v Official Receiver* [1996] 1 W.L.R. 242, CA; [1996] B.C.C. 328.

S. 375(2)
In s. 375(2) the words ", with the leave of the judge or of the Court of Appeal," formerly appearing after the words "on such an appeal lies" repealed by Access to Justice Act 1999, ss. 106, 108(3)(f), Sch. 15, Pt III as from September 27, 1999.

This provision deals with the question of appeals, whether against a decision of the county court or High Court. Under s. 55 of the Access to Justice Act 1999 a "second appeal" to the Court of Appeal is only permitted with the leave of the Court of Appeal and on restricted grounds.

In *Re a Debtor (No. 32/SD/1991)* [1993] 1 W.L.R. 314 Millett J. indicated that in a s. 375(1) review the court can hear fresh evidence not available at the original hearing. Such a review therefore differs fundamentally from a simple appeal where this would not be permitted. By way of contrast a case brought under s. 375(2) is a true appeal: *Vadher v Weisgard* [1997] B.C.C. 219. For the inconsistencies on the admission of fresh evidence see *Purvis v Customs and Excise Commissioners* [1999] B.P.I.R. 396 at 398 *per* Hazel Williamson Q.C. Vinelott J. further considered the nature of the court's jurisdiction under s. 375 in later proceedings in *Re a Debtor (No. 32/SD/1991) (No. 2)* [1994] B.C.C. 524. According to his Lordship (at p. 528G) it was an exceptional reserve jurisdiction only to be resorted to in the most extreme of cases. It existed to prevent "miscarriages of justice" in the field of bankruptcy law where a person's reputation and freedom of action was at stake.

Note also *Practice Direction (Insolvency Appeals: Individuals) (No. 1 of 1995)* [1995] B.C.C. 1,129.

S. 375(3)
This complements s. 373(2) by conferring jurisdictional integrity on the county courts.
See further IR 1986, r. 7.48.

376 Time-limits

376 Where by any provision in this Group of Parts or by the rules the time for doing anything is limited, the court may extend the time, either before or after it has expired, on such terms, if any, as it thinks fit.

GENERAL NOTE

This provision once again emphasises the general control of the court over bankruptcy proceedings by allowing it to extend time-limits. For the primacy of s. 376 see *Tager v Westpac Banking Corporation* [1998] B.C.C. 73. Note also that under BR 1952, r. 389 the court could adjust time periods on "good cause shown" – the statutory successor makes no reference to such a precondition but see IR 1986, r. 12.9.

377 Formal defects

377 The acts of a person as the trustee of a bankrupt's estate or as a special manager, and the acts of the creditors' committee established for any bankruptcy, are valid notwithstanding any defect in the appointment, election or qualifications of the trustee or manager or, as the case may be, of any member of the committee.

GENERAL NOTE

This provision displays a liberal attitude towards procedural defects in the appointment or qualifications of the trustee, etc. Corresponding sections in the case of company officers and office-holders are s. 232 above and CA 1985, s. 285. It is necessary to instil confidence in third parties and to preclude the need to investigate that correct procedures have been followed. Note that the predecessor of s. 377 only covered situations where the trustee, etc. acted in good faith, but this is not mentioned in s. 377. Under BA 1914, s. 147(1), which is not specifically repeated in IA 1986, other defects in bankruptcy proceedings could be excused by the court unless substantial and irreparable injustice has been caused by the irregularity. Presumably such cases could now be dealt with under ss. 363(1) and 375(1). Finally it should be remembered that the question of a trustee's qualifications must be viewed in the light of the requirements of Pt XIII.

Schedule 9, para. 32 states that non-compliance with the rules may be made a criminal offence.
Compare also IR 1986, r. 7.55.

378 Exemption from stamp duty

378 Stamp duty shall not be charged on–

(a) any document, being a deed, conveyance, assignment, surrender, admission or other assurance relating solely to property which is comprised in a bankrupt's estate and which, after the execution of that document, is or remains at law or in equity the property of the bankrupt or of the trustee of that estate,

(b) any writ, order, certificate or other instrument relating solely to the property of a bankrupt or to any bankruptcy proceedings.

GENERAL NOTE

This section offers welcome relief from the operation of stamp duty on documents connected with bankruptcy matters.

379 Annual report

379 As soon as practicable after the end of 1986 and each subsequent calendar year, the Secretary of State shall prepare and lay before each House of Parliament a report about the operation during that year of so much of this Act as is comprised in this Group of Parts, and about proceedings in the course of that year under the Deeds of Arrangement Act 1914.

GENERAL NOTE

This section requires the Secretary of State to lay before Parliament an annual report on the working of IA 1986 and the Deeds of Arrangement Act 1914. This is not a new obligation. The 1984 annual report (published in November 1985) is a mine of statistical information on the working of the old bankruptcy legislation.

This provision, unlike its predecessor, makes no mention of the obligation imposed on bankruptcy officers to provide the raw statistics to the Department of Trade and Industry to facilitate the preparation of this report. However, these matters are now dealt with by the rules: see IR 1986, r. 7.29.

PART XI

INTERPRETATION FOR SECOND GROUP OF PARTS

380 Introductory

380 The next five sections have effect for the interpretation of the provisions of this Act which are comprised in this Group of Parts; and where a definition is provided for a particular expression, it applies except so far as the context otherwise requires.

GENERAL NOTE

This introduces the bankruptcy interpretation sections. Meanings attributed in ss. 381–385 can be excluded by the context. Note also Pt XVIII of the Act and IR 1986, Pt 13.

381 "Bankrupt" and associated terminology

381(1) ["**Bankrupt**"] "**Bankrupt**" means an individual who has been adjudged bankrupt and, in relation to a bankruptcy order, it means the individual adjudged bankrupt by that order.

381(2) ["**Bankruptcy order**"] "**Bankruptcy order**" means an order adjudging an individual bankrupt.

381(3) ["**Bankruptcy petition**"] "**Bankruptcy petition**" means a petition to the court for a bankruptcy order.

GENERAL NOTE

These common phrases are hereby defined.

382   "Bankruptcy debt", etc.

382(1)   ["Bankruptcy debt"] "Bankruptcy debt", in relation to a bankrupt, means (subject to the next subsection) any of the following–

(a)   any debt or liability to which he is subject at the commencement of the bankruptcy,

(b)   any debt or liability to which he may become subject after the commencement of the bankruptcy (including after his discharge from bankruptcy) by reason of any obligation incurred before the commencement of the bankruptcy,

(c)   any amount specified in pursuance of section 39(3)(c) of the Powers of Criminal Courts Act 1973 in any criminal bankruptcy order made against him before the commencement of the bankruptcy, and

(d)   any interest provable as mentioned in section 322(2) in Chapter IV of Part IX.

382(2)   [Liability in tort] In determining for the purposes of any provision in this Group of Parts whether any liability in tort is a bankruptcy debt, the bankrupt is deemed to become subject to that liability by reason of an obligation incurred at the time when the cause of action accrued.

382(3)   [References to debtor liability] For the purposes of references in this Group of Parts to a debt or liability, it is immaterial whether the debt or liability is present or future, whether it is certain or contingent or whether its amount is fixed or liquidated, or is capable of being ascertained by fixed rules or as a matter of opinion; and references in this Group of Parts to owing a debt are to be read accordingly.

382(4)   ["Liability"] In this Group of Parts, except in so far as the context otherwise requires, **"liability"** means (subject to subsection (3) above) a liability to pay money or money's worth, including any liability under an enactment, any liability for breach of trust, any liability in contract, tort or bailment and any liability arising out of an obligation to make restitution.

S. 382(1), (2)
These provisions define a bankruptcy debt.
   Note prospective amendment: s. 382(1)(c) is to be repealed by CJA 1988, s. 170(2) and Sch. 16 as from a day to be appointed; see the note to s. 264.

S. 382(3), (4)
These provisions make liability in tort a bankruptcy debt and make it clear that both contingent and unliquidated liabilities are capable of forming the basis of a bankruptcy debt. On the latter point, this is a change in the law, which the Cork Committee (*Report*, para. 1318) called for. In *Re Wisepark Ltd* [1994] B.C.C. 221 it was held that a claim for costs was not a contingent liability within s. 382 because it did not exist until the court made an order for costs. This was confirmed by the Court of Appeal in *Glenister v Rowe* [1999] B.P.I.R. 674. Therefore a person having such a claim could not vote on a voluntary arrangement but conversely was not bound by its terms and could pursue the debtor if the costs order was eventually made in his favour. A debt arising in respect of a lump sum payable under matrimonial proceedings is a bankruptcy debt (*Russell v Russell* [1998] B.P.I.R. 259) but it is not a provable debt. On the significance of this see *Woodley v Woodley (No. 2)* [1994] 1 W.L.R. 1167 and *Levy v LSC* [2000] B.P.I.R. 1065. The court will only grant a bankruptcy order on the basis of a non-provable debt if the circumstances are exceptional – *Wehmeyer v Weymeyer* [2001] B.P.I.R. 548.
   For the corresponding definitions in corporate insolvency, see the note to Sch. 8, paras 12, 14.
   Note that bankruptcy debts are not always provable: see the note to IR 1986, r. 12.3.

383   "Creditor", "security", etc.

383(1)   ["Creditor"] "Creditor" –

(a)   in relation to a bankrupt, means a person to whom any of the bankruptcy debts is owed (being, in the case of an amount falling within paragraph (c) of the definition in section 382(1) of **"bankruptcy debt"**, the person in respect of whom that amount is specified in the criminal bankruptcy order in question), and

(b)   in relation to an individual to whom a bankruptcy petition relates, means a person who would be a creditor in the bankruptcy if a bankruptcy order were made on that petition.

383(2) **[Securing of debt]** Subject to the next two subsections and any provision of the rules requiring a creditor to give up his security for the purposes of proving a debt, a debt is secured for the purposes of this Group of Parts to the extent that the person to whom the debt is owed holds any security for the debt (whether a mortgage, charge, lien or other security) over any property of the person by whom the debt is owed.

383(3) **[Where s. 269(1)(a) statement made]** Where a statement such as is mentioned in section 269(1)(a) in Chapter I of Part IX has been made by a secured creditor for the purposes of any bankruptcy petition and a bankruptcy order is subsequently made on that petition, the creditor is deemed for the purposes of the Parts in this Group to have given up the security specified in the statement.

383(4) **[Qualification to s. 383(2)]** In subsection (2) the reference to a security does not include a lien on books, papers or other records, except to the extent that they consist of documents which give a title to property and are held as such.

S. 383(1)
This defines "creditor".
  Note prospective amendment: in s. 383(1)(a) the words from "(being," to "question)" are to be repealed by CJA 1988, s. 170(2) and Sch. 16 as from a day to be appointed; see the note to s. 264.

S. 383(2)–(4)
These provisions deal with the security and secured creditors. Section 383(2) defines "security", but this must be read in the light of s. 383(4), excluding liens over books, etc. A landlord's right of re-entry is not regarded as security for these purposes: *Razzaq v Pala* [1998] B.C.C. 66. See also *Re a Debtor (No. 310 of 1988)* [1989] 1 W.L.R. 452. Section 383(3) would be better located in s. 269, to which it relates.

384 "Prescribed" and "the rules"

384(1) **[Definitions]** Subject to the next subsection and sections 342C(7) and 342F(9) in Chapter V of Part IX, **"prescribed"** means prescribed by the rules; and **"the rules"** means rules made under section 412 in Part XV.

384(2) **[Interpretation]** References in this Group of Parts to the amount prescribed for the purposes of any of the following provisions–

section 273;

section 313A;

section 346(3);

section 354(1) and (2);

section 358;

section 360(1);

section 361(2); and

section 364(2)(d),

and references in those provisions to the prescribed amount are to be read in accordance with section 418 in Part XV and orders made under that section.

GENERAL NOTE

This section defines "prescribed" and "the rules" and must be read in the light of ss. 418 and 412 respectively. A textual modification to s. 384(1) was made by para. 71 of Sch. 12 to the Welfare Reform and Pensions Act 1999. The reference to s. 313A was introduced by EA 2002, s. 261(4).

385 Miscellaneous definitions

385(1) **[Definitions]** The following definitions have effect–

"the court", in relation to any matter, means the court to which, in accordance with section 373 in Part X and the rules, proceedings with respect to that matter are allocated or transferred;

"**creditor's petition**" means a bankruptcy petition under section 264(1)(a);

"**criminal bankruptcy order**" means an order under section 39(1) of the Powers of Criminal Courts Act 1973;

"**debt**" is to be construed in accordance with section 382(3);

"**the debtor**"–

(a) in relation to a proposal for the purposes of Part VIII, means the individual making or intending to make that proposal, and

(b) in relation to a bankruptcy petition, means the individual to whom the petition relates;

"**debtor's petition**" means a bankruptcy petition presented by the debtor himself under section 264(1)(b);

"**dwelling house**" includes any building or part of a building which is occupied as a dwelling and any yard, garden, garage or outhouse belonging to the dwelling house and occupied with it;

"**estate**", in relation to a bankrupt is to be construed in accordance with section 283 in Chapter II of Part IX;

"**family**", in relation to a bankrupt, means the persons (if any) who are living with him and are dependent on him;

"**secured**" and related expressions are to be construed in accordance with section 383; and

"**the trustee**", in relation to a bankruptcy and the bankrupt, means the trustee of the bankrupt's estate.

385(2) **[Interpretation]** References in this Group of Parts to a person's affairs include his business, if any.

S. 385(1)
This provides general definitions of words commonly appearing in the Second Group of Parts. There are differences from its statutory predecessor. Thus, for example, references to resolutions passed at creditors' meetings have been omitted, as have other terms which have become obsolete. On the other hand, new terms have been included, such as "dwelling house" and "family" (note its extended meaning). Note also ss. 382 and 383, and ss. 435, 436.

Note prospective amendment: in s. 385(1) the definition of "criminal bankruptcy order" is to be repealed by CJA 1988, s. 170(2) and Sch. 16 as from a day to be appointed; see the note to s. 264.

S. 385(2)
This is inserted *ex abundanti cautela* – a person's "affairs" would cover his business.

THE THIRD GROUP OF PARTS – MISCELLANEOUS MATTERS BEARING ON BOTH COMPANY AND INDIVIDUAL INSOLVENCY; GENERAL INTERPRETATION; FINAL PROVISIONS

Introduction to the Third Group of Parts
Parts XII–XIX of IA 1986 consist of a great variety of matters. Apart from the usual "mechanical" provisions (interpretation, short title, commencement, etc.), there is a group of sections, namely ss. 386–387, which substantially reduce the significance of preferential claims in insolvency law. EA 2002, s. 251 further reduces these by removing preferential status from Crown debts. The provisions on the qualification of insolvency practitioners are to be found in Pt XIII. There is also reference to official receivers (happily retained for corporate and personal insolvencies), the official petitioner, the Insolvency Rules Committee, insolvency service finance, insolvent estates of deceased persons and insolvent partnerships. The connection of other sections within Pt XVII with insolvency law is more indirect – thus there are provisions dealing with Parliamentary disqualification and restrictive trade practices.

Scholars of legislative history should note ss. 423–425, which revamp s. 172 of LPA 1925, a provision which can trace its own ancestry back to 1571!

PART XII

PREFERENTIAL DEBTS IN COMPANY AND INDIVIDUAL INSOLVENCY

General comment on Pt. XII
Preferential claims have been a part of insolvency law for nearly a hundred years. A preferential claim is essentially an unsecured one that is given especially favourable treatment by the legislature. Although the legislature is at liberty to create new preferential claims it seems clear that the courts will not do so on their own initiative: see here *Re Rafidain Bank* [1992] B.C.C. 376. It is not surprising, therefore, that the state is the main preferential claimant. In the context of corporate insolvency law, this means that preferential claims are to be satisfied out of a company's assets subject to a floating charge in priority to the debenture holder enjoying that charge. They do not rank ahead of the claims of a debenture holder secured by a fixed charge: *Re Lewis Merthyr Consolidated Collieries Ltd* [1929] 1 Ch. 498; *Re G L Saunders Ltd* [1986] 1 W.L.R. 215. Although preferential claims enjoy no inherent priority over a fixed charge, such a priority can arise if the fixed chargee surrenders priority in respect of the charged asset to a floating chargee and fails to do so via a subrogation mechanism. A simple postponement agreement can lead to the fixed chargee inadvertently also surrendering priority to preferential claims: see *Re Portbase (Clothing) Ltd* [1993] Ch. 388; [1993] B.C.C. 96.

The proliferation of preferential claims since 1945 has worried banks enjoying the security of a floating charge and has led them to seek increased security in the form of the highly artificial fixed charge over future assets. The end result of these trends has been to make the position of unsecured creditors even more unhappy.

After reviewing the evidence, the Cork Committee (*Report*, para. 1450) called for a radical reduction in the number of preferential claims:

> "We unhesitatingly reject the argument that debts owed to the community ought to be paid in priority to debts owed to private creditors. A bad debt owed to the State is likely to be insignificant, in terms of total Government receipts; the loss of a similar sum by a private creditor may cause substantial hardship, and bring further insolvencies in its train" (para. 1410).

In the early drafts of the Insolvency Bill 1985, the Government refused to act on this proposal because of the implications for the public exchequer. Reluctantly, however, it included provisions in IA 1985 (s. 89 and Sch. 4) which did reduce its own preferential position, and it is these provisions which have found their way into IA 1986.

The continued survival of preferential claims under English law was the subject of constant debate. It is interesting to note that the Crown's preferential rights have been entirely swept away in Australia by the 1992 amendments to the Corporations Law and in Canada have been significantly reduced by the Bankruptcy and Insolvency Act 1992. In view of these developments in other jurisdictions it came as no surprise when the government indicated that it was intending to abolish Crown preferential debt. That process of abolition was completed by s. 251 of EA 2002 with effect from September 15, 2003. Thus a number of preferential items are removed from the list in Sch. 6. The underlying intention was that this sacrifice on the part of the state would compensate floating charge holders for the new burden created by the reserved fund for unsecured creditors (see s. 176A). Although this is a significant change its impact must not be overestimated; other preferential claims will continue to survive for the foreseeable future.

Part XII applies to limited liability partnerships by virtue of the Limited Liability Partnerships Regulations 2001 (SI 2001/1090), reg. 5(1)(b) as from April 6, 2001 subject to reg. 5(2) and (3). For transitional provision see SI 2003/2093 (c. 85) art. 4 and SI 2003/2332.

Re application of Pt XII to insolvent partnerships, see the Insolvent Partnerships Order 1994 (SI 1994/2421), especially art. 10, 11, Sch. 7.

386 Categories of preferential debts

386(1) [Debts listed in Sch. 6] A reference in this Act to the preferential debts of a company or an individual is to the debts listed in Schedule 6 to this Act (contributions to occupational pension schemes; remuneration etc. of employees; levies on coal and steel production); and references to preferential creditors are to be read accordingly.

Section 387   Insolvency Act 1986

386(2) **["The debtor"]** In that Schedule **"the debtor"** means the company or the individual concerned.

386(3) **[Interpretation of Sch. 6]** Schedule 6 is to be read with Schedule 4 to the Pension Schemes Act 1993 (occupational pension scheme contributions).

GENERAL NOTE

These provisions, allied to Sch. 6, reduce the number of preferential claims to a bare minimum.

S. 386(3)
The reference to Sch. 4 to the Pension Scheme Act 1993 was substituted for the former reference to Sch. 3 to the Social Security Pensions Act 1975 by s. 190 of and Sch. 8, para. 18 to the 1993 Act.

387 "The relevant date"

387(1) **[Explanation of Sch. 6]** This section explains references in Schedule 6 to the relevant date (being the date which determines the existence and amount of a preferential debt).

387(2) **[Pt. I, s. 4]** For the purposes of section 4 in Part I (meetings to consider company voluntary arrangement), the relevant date in relation to a company which is not being wound up is–

(a) if the company is in administration, the date on which it entered administration, and

(b) if the company is not in administration, the date on which the voluntary arrangement takes effect.

387(2A) **[Sch. A1, para. 31]** For the purposes of paragraph 31 of Schedule A1 (meetings to consider company voluntary arrangement where a moratorium under section 1A is in force), the relevant date in relation to a company is the date of filing.

387(3) **[Company being wound up]** In relation to a company which is being wound up, the following applies–

(a) if the winding up is by the court, and the winding-up order was made immediately upon the discharge of an administration order, the date on which the company entered administration;

(aa) if the winding up is by the court and the winding-up order was made following conversion of administration into winding up by virtue of Article 37 of the EC Regulation, the relevant date is the date on which the company entered administration;

(ab) if the company is deemed to have passed a resolution for voluntary winding up by virtue of an order following conversion of administration into winding up under Article 37 of the EC Regulation, the relevant date is the date on which the company entered administration;

(b) if the case does not fall within paragraph (a), (aa) or (ab) and the company–

    (i) is being wound up by the court, and
    (ii) had not commenced to be wound up voluntarily before the date of the making of the winding-up order,

the relevant date is the date of the appointment (or first appointment) of a provisional liquidator or, if no such appointment has been made, the date of the winding-up order;

(ba) if the case does not fall within paragraph (a), (aa), (ab) or (b) and the company is being wound up following administration pursuant to paragraph 83 of Schedule B1, the relevant date is the date on which the company entered administration;

(c) if the case does not fall within either paragraph (a), (aa), (ab), (b) or (ba), the relevant date is the date of the passing of the resolution for the winding up of the company.

387(3A) **[Company in administration]** In relation to a company which is in administration (and to which no other provision of this section applies) the relevant date is the date on which the company enters administration.

387(4) **[Company in receivership]** In relation to a company in receivership (where section 40 or, as the case may be, section 59 applies), the relevant date is–

(a) in England and Wales, the date of the appointment of the receiver by debenture-holders, and

(b) in Scotland, the date of the appointment of the receiver under section 53(6) or (as the case may be) 54(5).

387(5) **[Pt VIII, s. 258]** For the purposes of section 258 in Part VIII (individual voluntary arrangements), the relevant date is, in relation to a debtor who is not an undischarged bankrupt–

(a) where an interim order has been made under section 252 with respect to his proposal, the date of that order, and

(b) in any other case, the date on which the voluntary arrangement takes effect.

387(6) **[Bankrupt]** In relation to a bankrupt, the following applies–

(a) where at the time the bankruptcy order was made there was an interim receiver appointed under section 286, the relevant date is the date on which the interim receiver was first appointed after the presentation of the bankruptcy petition;

(b) otherwise, the relevant date is the date of the making of the bankruptcy order.

GENERAL NOTE

The purpose of these provisions is to explain the meaning of the phrase "the relevant date", used extensively in Sch. 6. The timing for assessment of preferential claims depends on the particular insolvency regime involved, and whether corporate or individual.

Paragraphs (aa) and (ab) were inserted into subs. (3) by the Insolvency Act 1986 (Amendment) (No. 2) Regulations 2002 (SI 2002/1240) reg. 16 with effect from May 31, 2002. This insertion made necessary consequential amendments in the remainder of this subsection.

Subsection (2) was replaced, subs. (3) amended and subs. (3A) inserted by Sch. 17 to EA 2002. Subsection (2A) was inserted by IA 2000, Sch. 1.

PART XIII

INSOLVENCY PRACTITIONERS AND THEIR QUALIFICATION

General comment on Pt XIII
A major recommendation of the Cork Committee (*Report*, Chs 15–17) was that every insolvency practitioner should be a member of a recognised professional body, or at least have some minimum professional qualification, and that all practitioners should be subject to compulsory bonding to secure the due performance of their obligations. This, it was hoped, would curb the abuses associated in the past with "cowboy" liquidators, often people with no practical experience or relevant qualifications, who engaged in dubious practices to the detriment of creditors, sometimes in league with the controllers of the defunct company whose irresponsibility (and perhaps fraud) had brought about its collapse.

These proposals were accepted by the government in its White Paper (paras 8–11), and the framework for the new professional regime was set up by IA 1985, ss. 1–11, now Pt XIII of the present Act. Much of its detail, however, has been left to be prescribed in the form of rules: see the Insolvency Practitioners Regulations 1990 (SI 1990/439) (as amended by SI 1993/221). The law now requires every insolvency practitioner either to be a member of a recognised professional body, or to be personally authorised to act by the Secretary of State (s. 390(2)).

The Committee accepted that some concessionary arrangements would need to be made for established practitioners with substantial experience and a good record who lacked a professional qualification. However, since April 1, 1990, (the date when the 1990 Regulations referred to above came into effect), it has been necessary for persons applying to the Secretary of State for authorisation to have passed the examination set by the Joint Insolvency Examination Board or to have a similar overseas qualification, unless they already hold a current authorisation.

Section 388   Insolvency Act 1986

The introduction of professional standards for all insolvency practitioners has allowed some relaxation of the law, *e.g.* in such matters as the need to obtain the consent of the court before action is taken; and many of the functions which were formerly entrusted only to the official receiver have now been devolved upon private insolvency practitioners.

The policy towards insisting on a compulsory professional qualification limited to insolvency practitioners took a strange turn with the enactment and implementation of s. 4 of IA 2000, which permitted other authorised persons to act as nominees or supervisors of voluntary arrangement. For background comment, see the note to s. 389A below.

When the winding-up provisions of IA 1986 were extended to apply to building societies by the Building Societies Act 1986, Pt XIII was not specifically included. This oversight has since been corrected by CA 1989, s. 211(2)(a). See the general note to Pt IV, preceding s. 73, above. Part XIII applies to limited liability partnerships by virtue of the Limited Liability Partnerships Regulations 2001 (SI 2001/1090), reg. 5(1)(b) as from April 6, 2001 subject to reg. 5(2) and (3).

On the application of Pt XIII to insolvent partnerships, see the Insolvent Partnerships Order 1994 (SI 1994/2421), especially art. 10, 11, Sch. 7.

In November 1996, the DTI Insolvency Service and the recognised professional bodies established a Working Party with terms of reference to review the state of regulation of the insolvency profession and to consider whether the regulation could be made more efficient and effective. The Working Party in December 1997 issued a consultation document inviting comments on such matters as the qualifications for entry into the profession, the scope and effectiveness of the regulatory regime, and its complaints procedures, and published its report on February 24, 1999. The report recommended the establishment of a new Insolvency Practices Council, to consist of a majority of lay members together with representatives from the professions to provide expertise and informed comment. The Council's remit includes to set professional and ethical standards and to promote efficiency, transparency and independence while at the same time assisting insolvency practice to respond to changing demands. The first chairman of the Council was appointed on December 21, 1999.

In October 2001 the Insolvency Service issued a publication giving guidance on the making of complaints about insolvency practitioners.

Some information about the Insolvency Service, and its periodical publication *Dear IP*, can be found in Appendix III.

Restrictions on Unqualified Persons Acting as Liquidator, Trustee in Bankruptcy, etc.

388   Meaning of "act as insolvency practitioner"

388(1)   [Acting as insolvency practitioner re company] A person acts as an insolvency practitioner in relation to a company by acting–

(a)   as its liquidator, provisional liquidator, administrator or administrative receiver, or

(b)   where a voluntary arrangement in relation to the company is proposed or approved under Part I, as nominee or supervisor.

388(2)   [Acting as insolvency practitioner re individual] A person acts as an insolvency practitioner in relation to an individual by acting–

(a)   as his trustee in bankruptcy or interim receiver of his property or as permanent or interim trustee in the sequestration of his estate; or

(b)   as trustee under a deed which is a deed of arrangement made for the benefit of his creditors or, in Scotland, a trust deed for his creditors; or

(c)   where a voluntary arrangement in relation to the individual is proposed or approved under Part VIII, as nominee or supervisor;

(d)   in the case of a deceased individual to the administration of whose estate this section applies by virtue of an order under section 421 (application of provisions of this Act to insolvent estates of deceased persons), as administrator of that estate.

388(2A) **[Acting as insolvency practitioner re insolvent partnership]** A person acts as an insolvency practitioner in relation to an insolvent partnership by acting–

(a) as its liquidator, provisional liquidator or administrator, or

(b) as trustee of the partnership under article 11 of the Insolvent Partnerships Order 1994, or

(c) as supervisor of a voluntary arrangement approved in relation to it under Part I of this Act.

388(2B) **[Acting as nominee re voluntary arrangement]** In relation to a voluntary arrangement proposed under Part I or VIII, a person acts as nominee if he performs any of the functions conferred on nominees under the Part in question.

388(3) **[Interpretation]** References in this section to an individual include, except in so far as the context otherwise requires, references to a partnership and to any debtor within the meaning of the Bankruptcy (Scotland) Act 1985.

388(4) **[Definitions]** In this section–

"administrative receiver" has the meaning given by section 251 in Part VII;

"company" means a company within the meaning given by section 735(1) of the Companies Act or a company which may be wound up under Part V of this Act (unregistered companies); and

"interim trustee" and **"permanent trustee"** mean the same as in the Bankruptcy (Scotland) Act 1985.

388(5) **[Application]** Nothing in this section applies to anything done by–

(a) the official receiver; or

(b) the Accountant in Bankruptcy (within the meaning of the Bankruptcy (Scotland) Act 1985).

388(6) **[Applicability of EC Regulation]** Nothing in this section applies to anything done (whether in the United Kingdom or elsewhere) in relation to insolvency proceedings under the EC Regulation in a member State other than the United Kingdom.

GENERAL NOTE

The first step in establishing the statutory requirement that every insolvency practitioner should be professionally qualified is taken in this section, which defines the phrase "acts as an insolvency practitioner". This is not a *general* definition describing the work or activities of such a practitioner in the abstract, but a *specific* definition of what amounts to acting as an insolvency practitioner *in relation to* a particular company or individual. The Act does not make it an offence to carry on an insolvency practitioner's business without the requisite qualification, but rather to act "in relation to" a company or individual when the statutory requirements are not met (s. 389).

An important point to bear in mind is that it is possible to "act as an insolvency practitioner" in relation to a person who is not insolvent – and to do so in breach of the Act will be just as much an offence as in a case of actual insolvency. Thus, the liquidator appointed by a company in a members' voluntary winding up "acts as an insolvency practitioner" even where the company has a large cash surplus and has never been in trading difficulties.

Most of the expressions used in this section are defined or explained either in the section itself or elsewhere in the Act: for reference, see Appendix I.

S. 388(1), (2)
Note the amendments by IA 2000, s. 4.

S. 388(2A)
Section 388(2A) was inserted and the words "to a partnership and" in s. 388(3) were omitted for the purposes of the Insolvent Partnerships Order 1994 (SI 1994/2421), art. 15 as from December 1, 1994.

S. 388(2B)
This was inserted by IA 2000, s. 4.

S. 388(4)
A receiver who is not an administrative receiver (i.e. a receiver of less than a "substantial" part of the company's property (ss. 29(2), 251)) is not required to be qualified to act, but certain categories of person are disqualified from acting by ss. 30, 31, 51(3).

For the meaning of "company", see further the note to s. 73(1). On "unregistered companies", see s. 220. An insolvent partnership is treated as an unregistered company for the purposes of Pt V: see subs. (2A) above and the note to s. 420.

Part XIII of IA 1986 was extended to apply to the winding up of building societies by CA 1989, s. 211(2)(a) with effect from July 31, 1990, thus remedying an omission made when building societies were first made subject to the winding-up provisions by the Building Societies Act 1986.

S. 388(5)
The official receiver, as the holder of a public office, is not required to be qualified to act as an insolvency practitioner. This will include a deputy official receiver (see s. 401).

S. 388(6)
This was added by Insolvency Act 1986 (Amendment) (No. 2) Regulations 2002 (SI 2002/1240) reg. 17 with effect from May 31, 2002.

389 Acting without qualification an offence

389(1) [Penalty] A person who acts as an insolvency practitioner in relation to a company or an individual at a time when he is not qualified to do so is liable to imprisonment or a fine, or to both.

389(1A) [Limitation] This section is subject to section 389A.

389(2) [Non-application to official receiver] This section does not apply to the official receiver or the Accountant in Bankruptcy (within the meaning of the Bankruptcy (Scotland) Act 1985).

S. 389(1)
The word "qualified" refers not simply to a professional qualification (which may or may not be required: see s. 390(2)(b)), but to a complex set of requirements, some of them specifically related to the company or individual concerned.

On penalties, see s. 430 and Sch. 10.

S. 389(1A)
Inserted by IA 2000, s. 4.

389A Authorisation of nominees and supervisors

389A(1) [Non-application of s. 389] Section 389 does not apply to a person acting, in relation to a voluntary arrangement proposed or approved under Part I or Part VIII, as nominee or supervisor if he is authorised so to act.

389A(2) [Requirements for authorisation] For the purposes of subsection (1) and those Parts, an individual to whom subsection (3) does not apply is authorised to act as nominee or supervisor in relation to such an arrangement if–

(a) he is a member of a body recognised for the purpose by the Secretary of State, and

(b) there is in force security (in Scotland, caution) for the proper performance of his functions and that security or caution meets the prescribed requirements with respect to his so acting in relation to the arrangement.

389A(3) [Bars to authorisation] This subsection applies to a person if–

(a) he has been adjudged bankrupt or sequestration of his estate has been awarded and (in either case) he has not been discharged,

(b) he is subject to a disqualification order made or a disqualification undertaking accepted under the Company Directors Disqualification Act 1986 or to a disqualification order made under Part II of the Companies (Northern Ireland) Order 1989, or

(c) he is a patient within the meaning of Part VII of the Mental Health Act 1983 or section 125(1) of the Mental Health (Scotland) Act 1984.

Insolvency Act 1986 *Section 389*

389A(4) **[Order by Secretary of State]** The Secretary of State may by order declare a body which appears to him to fall within subsection (5) to be a recognised body for the purposes of subsection (2)(a).

389A(5) **[Bodies recognised]** A body may be recognised if it maintains and enforces rules for securing that its members–

(a) are fit and proper persons to act as nominees or supervisors, and

(b) meet acceptable requirements as to education and practical training and experience.

389A(6) **[Members of a body]** For the purposes of this section, a person is a member of a body only if he is subject to its rules when acting as nominee or supervisor (whether or not he is in fact a member of the body).

389A(7) **[Revocation of s. 389A(4) order]** An order made under subsection (4) in relation to a body may be revoked by a further order if it appears to the Secretary of State that the body no longer falls within subsection (5).

389A(8) **[Effect of order]** An order of the Secretary of State under this section has effect from such date as is specified in the order; and any such order revoking a previous order may make provision for members of the body in question to continue to be treated as members of a recognised body for a specified period after the revocation takes effect.

GENERAL NOTE

This new section was added by s. 4 of IA 2000. It allows a wider range of practitioners to service voluntary arrangements, and in particular those turnaround specialists who may be authorised by the Secretary of State.

S. 389A(1)
This disapplies s. 389 in the case of voluntary arrangements.

S. 389A(2) (3)
These need to be read together.

S. 389A(4)
This authorises the Secretary of State to recognise bodies of practitioners who are not licensed insolvency practitioners – *e.g.* turnaround specialists.

S. 389A(5)
This maps out the criteria for recognition under subs. (4).

S. 389A(6)
This defines member in a regulatory fashion requiring compliance with rules of the recognised body when acting as nominee/supervisor.

S. 389A(7) (8)
These deal with the status and effect of orders made under subs. (4).

389B Official receiver as nominee or supervisor

389B(1) **[Voluntary arrangement where debtor undischarged bankrupt]** The official receiver is authorised to act as nominee or supervisor in relation to a voluntary arrangement approved under Part VIII provided that the debtor is an undischarged bankrupt when the arrangement is proposed.

389B(2) **[Power of Secretary of State]** The Secretary of State may by order repeal the proviso in subsection (1).

389B(3) **[Procedure for s. 389B(2) order]** An order under subsection (2)–

(a) must be made by statutory instrument, and

(b) shall be subject to annulment in pursuance of a resolution of either House of Parliament.

S. 389B(1)
Introduced by EA 2002, s. 264 and Sch. 22, this enables the official receiver to acts as nominee/supervisor of a "fast-track IVA" agreed under s. 263A. This is an innovation – previously the role of servicing IVAs was restricted to private insolvency practitioners.

S. 389B(2), (3)
These provide future flexibility for the Secretary of State.

The Requisite Qualification, and the Means of Obtaining it

390 Persons not qualified to act as insolvency practitioners

390(1) [Must be individual] A person who is not an individual is not qualified to act as an insolvency practitioner.

390(2) [Authorisation necessary] A person is not qualified to act as an insolvency practitioner at any time unless at that time–

(a) he is authorised so to act by virtue of membership of a professional body recognised under section 391 below, being permitted so to act by or under the rules of that body, or

(b) he holds an authorisation granted by a competent authority under section 393.

390(3) [Security as condition required] A person is not qualified to act as an insolvency practitioner in relation to another person at any time unless–

(a) there is in force at that time security or, in Scotland, caution for the proper performance of his functions, and

(b) that security or caution meets the prescribed requirements with respect to his so acting in relation to that other person.

390(4) [Disqualification] A person is not qualified to act as an insolvency practitioner at any time if at that time–

(a) he has been adjudged bankrupt or sequestration of his estate has been awarded and (in either case) he has not been discharged,

(b) he is subject to a disqualification order made or a disqualification undertaking accepted under the Company Directors Disqualification Act 1986 or to a disqualification order made under Part II of the Companies (Northern Ireland) Order 1989, or

(c) he is a patient within the meaning of Part VII of the Mental Health Act 1983 or section 125(1) of the Mental Health (Scotland) Act 1984 or has had a guardian appointed to him under the Adults with Incapacity (Scotland) Act 2000 (asp 4).

390(5) [Disqualification where bankruptcy restrictions order] A person is not qualified to act as an insolvency practitioner while a bankruptcy restrictions order is in force in respect of him.

GENERAL NOTE

As explained above, the Act uses the one term "qualified" with reference both to the general eligibility of the person to act as a practitioner and also to his specific eligibility to act *vis-à-vis* a particular company or individual. This section deals mainly with the general requirement, except for the statement in s. 390(3)(b) that the practitioner's bonding obligation must relate to the person or company whose affairs he is administering. However, the subject of "qualification" is further dealt with in subordinate legislation made under s. 419(2)(b). Reference should be made to the Insolvency Practitioners Regulations 1990 (SI 1990/439) (as amended by SI 1993/221), which consolidate and replace earlier regulations dating from 1986.

Each of the regulatory bodies (see the note to s. 391(1)), and also the Insolvency Practitioners' Association and the Association of Business Recovery Professionals publishes a guide to professional conduct and ethics, which sets out guiding principles relating to the conduct of insolvency practitioners in regard to accepting appointment as a trustee or office-holder, etc.

S. 390(1)

The disqualification of corporate bodies is an extension of the prohibition that formerly applied in the case of a liquidator (CA 1985, s. 634) and still applies to a receiver (not necessarily an administrative receiver): see s. 30 and 51(3)(a), (c). An act purportedly done by a corporate receiver has been held to be a nullity: see the note to s. 232.

On the question of joint appointments, see s. 231.

S. 390(2)

The Cork Committee recommended (*Report*, para. 758) that an insolvency practitioner should be required in all cases to be a member of an "approved" professional body and to have been in general practice for five years before being eligible to act. (Transitional arrangements would have allowed experienced individuals who were not professionally qualified to obtain direct authorisation to act from the Secretary of State.) The Government in its White Paper (para. 43) broadly endorsed this view, but in the Insolvency Bill as originally published in 1984 went further, and provided that every insolvency practitioner, whether a member of a profession or not, should be required to hold a certificate issued to him personally by the Secretary of State before he was eligible to act. The legislation in its final form, however, returns to a compromise position: those who are under the supervision of a recognised professional body are to be permitted or authorised to act by that body, and will not be directly licensed or controlled by the Secretary of State, while others may be authorised as individuals to act, either by the Secretary of State or by a "competent authority" to which this function may be delegated (s. 392). The "direct licensing" provisions of the Act do not appear, however, to have been purely a transitional arrangement as the Cork Committee envisaged.

Schedule 11, para. 21 provides that a person who was already in office (*e.g.* as a liquidator) when the Act came into force could continue to discharge the functions of that particular office, and so complete the liquidation, etc., without the need for acquiring a qualification under s. 390(2) or (3).

S. 390(3)

This subsection provides for the bonding of insolvency practitioners, which is a mandatory requirement for all office-holders. The security may be provided either generally or specially for a particular insolvency, and provides a safeguard for creditors and other interested persons who may suffer loss as a result of breach by the insolvency practitioner of the duties and obligations imposed on him by the legislation. The surety's liability is limited to a sum equivalent to the losses caused by the fraud or dishonesty of the practitioner, whether acting alone or in collusion with others; and the maximum amount for which any bond must be given is £5m: see the Insolvency Practitioners Regulations 1990 (SI 1990/439, Sch. 2).

On the question of transitional provisions for persons holding office when the Act came into force, see the note to s. 390(2) above.

S. 390(4)

In s. 390(4)(c) the words "or has had a guardian appointed to him under the Adults with Incapacity (Scotland) Act 2000 (asp 4)" inserted at the end by the Adults with Incapacity (Scotland) Act 2000, s. 88(2), Sch. 5, para. 18 as from April 1, 2002 (Adults with Incapacity (Scotland) Act 2000 (Commencement No. 1) Order 2001 (SI 2000/81 (C. 2)), art. 3, Sch. 2).

In s. 390(4)(b) the words "or a disqualification undertaking accepted" and "or to a disqualification order made under Part II of the Companies (Northern Ireland) Order 1989" inserted by the Insolvency Act 2000, s. 8, Sch. 4, para. 16(2) as from April 2, 2001 (see SI 2001/766 (C. 27), art. 1, 2(1)(a)).

If a person comes under any of the disabilities mentioned, his disqualification is automatic, and does not depend upon the withdrawal of his authorisation under s. 393. Acts done by a disqualified person may, however, be valid by virtue of s. 232: see the note to that section.

S. 390(5)

This was inserted by EA 2002, Sch. 21 to respond to the advent of BROs from April 2004.

391 Recognised professional bodies

391(1) [Order by Secretary of State] The Secretary of State may by order declare a body which appears to him to fall within subsection (2) below to be a recognised professional body for the purposes of this section.

391(2) **[Bodies recognised]** A body may be recognised if it regulates the practice of a profession and maintains and enforces rules for securing that such of its members as are permitted by or under the rules to act as insolvency practitioners–

(a) are fit and proper persons so to act, and

(b) meet acceptable requirements as to education and practical training and experience.

391(3) **[Interpretation]** References to members of a recognised professional body are to persons who, whether members of that body or not, are subject to its rules in the practice of the profession in question.

The reference in section 390(2) above to membership of a professional body recognised under this section is to be read accordingly.

391(4) **[Revocation of order]** An order made under subsection (1) in relation to a professional body may be revoked by a further order if it appears to the Secretary of State that the body no longer falls within subsection (2).

391(5) **[Effect of order]** An order of the Secretary of State under this section has effect from such date as is specified in the order; and any such order revoking a previous order may make provision whereby members of the body in question continue to be treated as authorised to act as insolvency practitioners for a specified period after the revocation takes effect.

GENERAL NOTE

This section provides the machinery for "recognising" professional bodies whose members will be authorised to act as insolvency practitioners under s. 390(2)(a), and also for the withdrawal of such recognition. For application and ongoing fees see the Insolvency Practitioners and Insolvency Services Account (Fees) Order 2003 (SI 2003 (SI 2003/3363) as amendment by SI 2004/476.

S. 391(1)

The relevant order is the Insolvency Practitioners (Recognised Professional Bodies) Order 1986 (SI 1986/1764) under which the following bodies are recognised:

- The Chartered Association of Certified Accountants,
- The Institute of Chartered Accountants in England and Wales,
- The Institute of Chartered Accountants of Scotland,
- The Institute of Chartered Accountants in Ireland,
- The Insolvency Practitioners Association,
- The Law Society of Scotland,
- The Law Society.

S. 391(2)

Membership of the professional body is not in itself sufficient (nor, in some cases, even necessary: see s. 391(3)): the person must be specifically permitted by the rules of the body to act as an insolvency practitioner. This enables the professional body to restrict eligibility to those of its members who are able to satisfy prescribed requirements as to examinations and practical experience. If the professional body withdraws a member's licence to act as an insolvency practitioner he ceases, of course, to be qualified to act. This the body may do without prior notice to the member if this is thought necessary in order to protect the public: *R. v Institute of Chartered Accountants, ex rel Eliades* [2001] B.P.I.R. 363.

S. 391(3)

Persons who are subject to the rules of a professional body without having the full status and privileges of "membership" may be authorised under this section.

S. 391(4)

The only power specifically conferred on the Secretary of State is to withdraw recognition from the body concerned. He is not given power to exercise detailed control over the activities of the professional body or to give it directions about the way it conducts its affairs. Nevertheless, the fact that the ultimate sanction of revocation is in his hands enables him to ensure that a body is kept up to the mark in such matters as, *e.g.* the enforcement of its disciplinary rules. This is important, because neither the Secretary of State nor the tribunal established under s. 396 has direct jurisdiction over an individual member of a recognised professional body, or power to revoke his authorisation.

S. 391(5)
The period of grace which the Secretary of State may allow has enabled some liquidations, etc., to be completed by the existing office-holder. It also gave the individual insolvency practitioners affected by the order time to apply for direct authorisation under s. 392, or seek to become a member of another professional body.

392 Authorisation by competent authority

392(1) [Application] Application may be made to a competent authority for authorisation to act as an insolvency practitioner.

392(2) [Competent authorities] The competent authorities for this purpose are–

(a) in relation to a case of any description specified in directions given by the Secretary of State, the body or person so specified in relation to cases of that description, and

(b) in relation to a case not falling within paragraph (a), the Secretary of State.

392(3) [Application] The application–

(a) shall be made in such manner as the competent authority may direct,

(b) shall contain or be accompanied by such information as that authority may reasonably require for the purpose of determining the application, and

(c) shall be accompanied by the prescribed fee;

and the authority may direct that notice of the making of the application shall be published in such manner as may be specified in the direction.

392(4) [Additional information] At any time after receiving the application and before determining it the authority may require the applicant to furnish additional information.

392(5) [Requirements may differ] Directions and requirements given or imposed under subsection (3) or (4) may differ as between different applications.

392(6) [Forms] Any information to be furnished to the competent authority under this section shall, if it so requires, be in such form or verified in such manner as it may specify.

392(7) [Withdrawal of application] An application may be withdrawn before it is granted or refused.

392(8) [Sums received] Any sums received under this section by a competent authority other than the Secretary of State may be retained by the authority; and any sums so received by the Secretary of State shall be paid into the Consolidated Fund.

392(9) [No fee under s. 392(3)(c) in applications to Secretary of State] Subsection (3)(c) shall not have effect in respect of an application made to the Secretary of State (but this subsection is without prejudice to section 415A).

S. 392(1)
Most insolvency practitioners become qualified to act by being members of a recognised professional body under s. 391. However, these professions do not have a monopoly over insolvency work. The present section allows any individual to obtain authorisation personally, either from the Secretary of State or from a "competent authority" which may be designated to discharge this function. A person who is a member of a recognised professional body is not excluded from seeking direct authorisation under this section rather than authorisation from that body.

For the regulations relating to applications for authorisation under these provisions: see the Insolvency Practitioners Regulations 1990 (SI 1990/439) (as amended). On fees see SI 2003/3363 as amended by SI 2004/476.

S. 392(2)
The Secretary of State is himself a "competent authority" and will always have a residuary power to deal with cases not specified under para. (a), and also during times when no alternative competent authority exists.

Section 393 *Insolvency Act 1986*

No competent authority has been specified in directions given under this section, and so for the time being the only competent authority is the Secretary of State.

S. 392(3)–(7)

"Directions" relating to applications do not take the form of legislation but are made by the competent authority itself, *i.e.* at present, the Secretary of State.

S. 392(8)

This provision enables an authority other than the Secretary of State to be wholly or partly self-funded.

S. 392(9)

This was added by EA 2002 s. 270(3) with effect from September 15, 2003.

393 Grant, refusal and withdrawal of authorisation

393(1) [Power to grant, refuse application] The competent authority may, on an application duly made in accordance with section 392 and after being furnished with all such information as it may require under that section, grant or refuse the application.

393(2) [Granting application] The authority shall grant the application if it appears to it from the information furnished by the applicant and having regard to such other information, if any, as it may have–

(a) that the applicant is a fit and proper person to act as an insolvency practitioner, and

(b) that the applicant meets the prescribed requirements with respect to education and practical training and experience.

393(3) [Duration of authorisation] An authorisation granted under this section, if not previously withdrawn, continues in force for such period not exceeding the prescribed maximum as may be specified in the authorisation.

393(4) [Withdrawal of authorisation] An authorisation so granted may be withdrawn by the competent authority if it appears to it–

(a) that the holder of the authorisation is no longer a fit and proper person to act as an insolvency practitioner, or

(b) without prejudice to paragraph (a), that the holder–

   (i) has failed to comply with any provision of this Part or of any regulations made under this Part or Part XV, or
   (ii) in purported compliance with any such provision, has furnished the competent authority with false, inaccurate or misleading information.

393(5) [Withdrawal on request] An authorisation granted under this section may be withdrawn by the competent authority at the request or with the consent of the holder of the authorisation.

GENERAL NOTE

The regulations relating to the grant and refusal of authorisation in force from April 1, 1990 are the Insolvency Practitioners Regulations 1990 (SI 1990/439) (as amended). On fees see the Insolvency Practitioners and Insolvency Services Account (Fees) Order 2003 (SI 2003/3363) as amended by SI 2004/476.

S. 393(1)

The Secretary of State is the only competent authority for the time being: see the note to s. 392(2).

S. 393(2)

The regulations referred to above set out in some detail the matters which are to be taken into account in determining whether an applicant is a fit and proper person, ranging from his personal integrity and history as a law-abiding citizen to the adequacy of the systems of control and record-keeping in his business practice: see SI 1990/439, reg. 4.

The same regulations (reg. 5) give details of educational requirements, but these apply only to applicants who were born after 15 December 1951 and do not already hold an authorisation (reg. 5(2)). Practical training and experience is demanded of all applicants: this may be reckoned in a number of ways, but a minimum of five appointments to office within the past five years or 1,000 hours of "higher insolvency work experience" within the same period is stipulated (reg. 8).

S. 393(3)
The regulations referred to fix a maximum period of three years from the date on which authorisation is granted (reg. 10).

S. 393(4)
The procedure for appeal from the withdrawal, or the refusal, of an authorisation is set out in ss. 394–398.

394 Notices

394(1) **[Notice to applicant re grant]** Where a competent authority grants an authorisation under section 393, it shall give written notice of that fact to the applicant, specifying the date on which the authorisation takes effect.

394(2) **[Notice re proposed refusal, withdrawal]** Where the authority proposes to refuse an application, or to withdraw an authorisation under section 393(4), it shall give the applicant or holder of the authorisation written notice of its intention to do so, setting out particulars of the grounds on which is proposes to act.

394(3) **[Date to be stated re withdrawal]** In the case of a proposed withdrawal the notice shall state the date on which it is proposed that the withdrawal should take effect.

394(4) **[Notice to give details re rights]** A notice under subsection (2) shall give particulars of the rights exercisable under the next two sections by a person on whom the notice is served.

S. 394(1)
Without authorisation, the person will not be "qualified" under s. 390(2)(a), and will be automatically liable to criminal prosecution under s. 389 if he acts as an insolvency practitioner; but this does not affect any appointment which he already held when the Act came into force: see Sch. 11, para. 21.

S. 394(2)–(4)
It would appear from the repeated use of the word "propose" that a decision to refuse or withdraw an authorisation does not take effect until the applicant or holder is informed of his rights to make representations under s. 395(1) and to refer the matter for consideration to the Insolvency Practitioners Tribunal under s. 396, and given an opportunity to do so. It is submitted that the word "decision" in s. 396(2)(b) must mean "provisional decision", to be consistent with this view. There is no indication in s. 394(3) whether the authority is free to specify any date it chooses as the effective date, but it would seem that, to make sense of the scheme of the Act as a whole, the date should be fixed at least 28 days ahead, and the notice should probably state in addition "or such later date as the authority may subsequently fix, if steps are taken by the holder to have the case reconsidered or reviewed under s. 395 or s. 396".

395 Right to make representations

395(1) **[Right exercisable within 14 days]** A person on whom a notice is served under section 394(2) may within 14 days after the date of service make written representations to the competent authority.

395(2) **[Representations to be considered]** The competent authority shall have regard to any representations so made in determining whether to refuse the application or withdraw the authorisation, as the case may be.

GENERAL NOTE

In addition to his right to have the case referred directly to the tribunal under s. 396, the person affected by a proposed refusal or withdrawal may ask the authority itself to reconsider its decision. This will not prevent him from seeking a review by the tribunal if he is notified that the authority's earlier decision stands; and indeed he may apparently ask for a reconsideration under the present section and then change his mind and have the matter taken to the tribunal without waiting for the authority to complete its reconsideration.

396 Reference to Tribunal

396(1) **[Application of Sch. 7]** The Insolvency Practitioners Tribunal (**"the Tribunal"**) continues in being; and the provisions of Schedule 7 apply to it.

396(2) **[Person served with notice]** Where a person is served with a notice under section 394(2), he may–

(a) at any time within 28 days after the date of service of the notice, or

(b) at any time after the making by him of representations under section 395 and before the end of the period of 28 days after the date of the service on him of a notice by the competent authority that the authority does not propose to alter its decision in consequence of the representations,

give written notice to the authority requiring the case to be referred to the Tribunal.

396(3) **[Reference]** Where a requirement is made under subsection (2), then, unless the competent authority–

(a) has decided or decides to grant the application or, as the case may be, not to withdraw the authorisation, and

(b) within 7 days after the date of the making of the requirement, gives written notice of that decision to the person by whom the requirement was made,

it shall refer the case to the Tribunal.

S. 396(1)

The Insolvency Practitioners Tribunal was established by IA 1985, s. 8(6) to discharge the functions set out in ss. 396, 397 of the present Act. For further discussion, see the note to Sch. 7 and the Insolvency Practitioners Tribunal (Conduct of Investigations) Rules 1986 (SI 1986/952) which continue in force.

S. 396(2)

The present section provides a procedure which is in part alternative to s. 395 and in part supplementary to it. A person who has been notified by an authority that it proposes to refuse his application or withdraw his authorisation may invoke the jurisdiction of the tribunal *either* (1) immediately and directly, *or* (2) after the authority's own procedure for reconsideration has run its course and the decision adverse to him is confirmed; and it appears that he may also interrupt the latter procedure and have the matter referred to the tribunal without waiting for a second decision. He must act within 28 days of being notified of the authority's provisional decision (in case (1)) or of its confirmed decision (in case (2)). The case is then referred by the authority itself to the tribunal for review.

S. 396(3)

On receipt of a notice, the authority has seven days in which to change its mind and notify the person of its revised decision; failing this, it must refer the matter to the tribunal (though not necessarily within that seven-day period).

397 Action of Tribunal on reference

397(1) **[Duties of Tribunal]** On a reference under section 396 the Tribunal shall–

(a) investigate the case, and

(b) make a report to the competent authority stating what would in their opinion be the appropriate decision in the matter and the reasons for that opinion,

and it is the duty of the competent authority to decide the matter accordingly.

397(2) **[Copy of report to applicant]** The Tribunal shall send a copy of the report to the applicant or, as the case may be, the holder of the authorisation; and the competent authority shall serve him with a written notice of the decision made by it in accordance with the report.

397(3) **[Publication of report]** The competent authority may, if he thinks fit, publish the report of the Tribunal.

GENERAL NOTE

The tribunal makes its own investigation of the case but does not itself make a decision: instead, it gives directions to the authority (which are binding), supported by its reasons.

The requirement that the tribunal should give a reasoned ruling plainly contemplates that it is open to a dissatisfied applicant to seek judicial review of a decision.

398 Refusal or withdrawal without reference to Tribunal

398 Where in the case of any proposed refusal or withdrawal of an authorisation either–

(a) the period mentioned in section 396(2)(a) has expired without the making of any requirement under that subsection or of any representations under section 395, or

(b) the competent authority has given a notice such as is mentioned in section 396(2)(b) and the period so mentioned has expired without the making of any such requirement,

the competent authority may give written notice of the refusal or withdrawal to the person concerned in accordance with the proposal in the notice given under section 394(2).

GENERAL NOTE

If a person who has been notified under s. 394(2) of a proposal to refuse his application or withdraw his authorisation does not take the appropriate action within 28 days, he cannot prevent the refusal or withdrawal from taking effect. Whether this happens automatically, or whether a written notice must be given, depends upon whether the word "may" is to be read in a permissive or a mandatory sense. The stipulation that the notice shall be written probably indicates the latter: the point will be important only in regard to a withdrawal.

PART XIV

PUBLIC ADMINISTRATION (ENGLAND AND WALES)

Official Receivers

399 Appointment, etc. of official receivers

399(1) **[Official receiver]** For the purposes of this Act the official receiver, in relation to any bankruptcy, winding up or individual voluntary arrangement, is any person who by virtue of the following provisions of this section or section 401 below is authorised to act as the official receiver in relation to that bankruptcy, winding up or individual voluntary arrangement.

399(2) **[Power of appointment by Secretary of State]** The Secretary of State may (subject to the approval of the Treasury as to numbers) appoint persons to the office of official receiver, and a person appointed to that office (whether under this section or section 70 of the Bankruptcy Act 1914)–

(a) shall be paid out of money provided by Parliament such salary as the Secretary of State may with the concurrence of the Treasury direct,

(b) shall hold office on such other terms and conditions as the Secretary of State may with the concurrence of the Treasury direct, and

(c) may be removed from office by a direction of the Secretary of State.

399(3) **[Attachment to particular court]** Where a person holds the office of official receiver, the Secretary of State shall from time to time attach him either to the High Court or to a county court having jurisdiction for the purposes of the second Group of Parts of this Act.

399(4) **[Person authorised to act as official receiver]** Subject to any directions under subsection (6) below, an official receiver attached to a particular court is the person authorised to act as the official receiver in relation to every bankruptcy, winding up or individual voluntary arrangement falling within the jurisdiction of that court.

399(5) **[Each court to have official receiver]** The Secretary of State shall ensure that there is, at all times, at least one official receiver attached to the High Court and at least one attached to each county court having jurisdiction for the purposes of the second Group of Parts; but he may attach the same official receiver to two or more different courts.

399(6) **[Directions by Secretary of State]** The Secretary of State may give directions with respect to the disposal of the business of official receivers, and such directions may, in particular–

(a) authorise an official receiver attached to one court to act as the official receiver in relation to any case or description of cases falling within the jurisdiction of another court;

(b) provide, where there is more than one official receiver authorised to act as the official receiver in relation to cases falling within the jurisdiction of any court, for the distribution of their business between or among themselves.

399(7) **[Continuation of official receiver]** A person who at the coming into force of section 222 of the Insolvency Act 1985 (replaced by this section) is an official receiver attached to a court shall continue in office after the coming into force of that section as an official receiver attached to that court under this section.

GENERAL NOTE

The government in its zeal for public expenditure economies originally wanted to remove official receivers from personal insolvency law and to hive off their functions to the private sector – see its Green Paper on Bankruptcy (Cmnd 7967, July 1980), para. 8. The outcry that this proposal attracted, not least from the Cork Committee (*Report*, para. 723), was sufficient to force a rethink. The IA 1986 retains the role of the official receivers in bankruptcy law, although their involvement is now restricted to the more serious cases. For further guidance on official receivers, see IR 1986, Pt 10 and r. 7.52 (rights of audience).

S. 399(1)
This confirms that official receivers will continue to act both in individual and corporate insolvency cases. Reference to IVAs was inserted by EA 2002, Sch. 23. A similar change was also made in subs. (4).

S. 399(2)
The question of appointment, remuneration and tenure is to be determined by the Secretary of State. For the remuneration of the official receiver, see the Insolvency Regulations 1994 (SI 1994/2507), reg. 33. The present position is reviewed by Ferris J. in *Mirror Group Newspapers v Maxwell* [1998] B.C.C. 324 at p. 337 and in the Working Party chaired by Ferris J. which reported in 1998.

S. 399(3)–(5)
It is the responsibility of the Secretary of State to attach official receivers to the various courts having insolvency jurisdiction. Every court must have at least one official receiver attached to it, although that court may not be his sole responsibility.

S. 399(6)
This provision authorises the Secretary of State to give directions to facilitate the disposal of business by official receivers.

S. 399(7)
This is a transitional provision designed to ensure continuity.

400 Functions and status of official receivers

400(1) [Functions] In addition to any functions conferred on him by this Act, a person holding the office of official receiver shall carry out such other functions as may from time to time be conferred on him by the Secretary of State.

400(2) [Status] In the exercise of the functions of his office a person holding the office of official receiver shall act under the general directions of the Secretary of State and shall also be an officer of the court in relation to which he exercises those functions.

400(3) [Death or ceasing to hold office] Any property vested in his official capacity in a person holding the office of official receiver shall, on his dying, ceasing to hold office or being otherwise succeeded in relation to the bankruptcy or winding up in question by another official receiver, vest in his successor without any conveyance, assignment or transfer.

S. 400(1)
The persons holding office as official receivers will have their functions governed either by the 1986 Act or by directions from the Secretary of State.

S. 400(2)
This provision confirms that the Secretary of State has general control over official receivers although, as was the case under BA 1914, s. 70(1), it is emphasised that they are also officers of the court. The effect of this is that any wrongful interference with them will constitute contempt of court. For the legal position relating to immunity for actions see *Mond v Hyde* [1999] Q.B. 1097.

An official receiver can be a litigant in person – *Official Receiver v Brunt* [1999] B.P.I.R. 560 where the Court of Appeal gives detailed consideration to the nature of the office.

S. 400(3)
The aim of this provision is to secure continuity of property ownership if an official receiver leaves office prematurely.

401 Deputy official receivers and staff

401(1) [Deputy official receiver] The Secretary of State may, if he thinks it expedient to do so in order to facilitate the disposal of the business of the official receiver attached to any court, appoint an officer of his department to act as deputy to that official receiver.

401(2) [Same status and functions] Subject to any directions given by the Secretary of State under section 399 or 400, a person appointed to act as deputy to an official receiver has, on such conditions and for such period as may be specified in the terms of his appointment, the same status and functions as the official receiver to whom he is appointed deputy.

Accordingly, references in this Act (except section 399(1) to (5)) to an official receiver include a person appointed to act as his deputy.

401(3) [Termination of appointment] An appointment made under subsection (1) may be terminated at any time by the Secretary of State.

401(4) [Staff] The Secretary of State may, subject to the approval of the Treasury as to numbers and remuneration and as to the other terms and conditions of the appointments, appoint officers of his department to assist official receivers in the carrying out of their functions.

S. 401(1)
To facilitate the despatch of business by official receivers, the Secretary of State may appoint deputy official receivers.

Under BA 1914, s. 71, the deputy could be appointed on application from an official receiver but only for a two-month period at most. The present Act appears to be more flexible on this matter.

S. 401(2), (3)
A deputy enjoys the same status as an official receiver, fulfils the same functions and can be dismissed in the same way by the Secretary of State. References in IA 1986 to official receivers include references to deputies.

Section 402 *Insolvency Act 1986*

S. 401(4)

The Secretary of State may also appoint civil servants from his department to assist official receivers, although the consent of the Treasury must first be obtained.

The Official Petitioner

402 Official Petitioner

402(1) **[Continuation of officer]** There continues to be an officer known as the Official Petitioner for the purpose of discharging, in relation to cases in which a criminal bankruptcy order is made, the functions assigned to him by or under this Act; and the Director of Public Prosecutions continues, by virtue of his office, to be the Official Petitioner.

402(2) **[Functions]** The functions of the Official Petitioner include the following–

(a) to consider whether, in a case in which a criminal bankruptcy order is made, it is in the public interest that he should himself present a petition under section 264(1)(d) of this Act;

(b) to present such a petition in any case where he determines that it is in the public interest for him to do so;

(c) to make payments, in such cases as he may determine, towards expenses incurred by other persons in connection with proceedings in pursuance of such a petition; and

(d) to exercise, so far as he considers it in the public interest to do so, any of the powers conferred on him by or under this Act.

402(3) **[Discharge of functions on authority]** Any functions of the Official Petitioner may be discharged on his behalf by any person acting with his authority.

402(4) **[Inability]** Neither the Official Petitioner nor any person acting with his authority is liable to any action or proceeding in respect of anything done or omitted to be done in the discharge, or purported discharge, of the functions of the Official Petitioner.

402(5) **["Criminal bankruptcy order"]** In this section **"criminal bankruptcy order"** means an order under section 39(1) of the Powers of Criminal Courts Act 1973.

S. 402(1), (3)

This section preserves the post of official petitioner which will continue to be held by the Director of Public Prosecutions. The DPP can authorise junior officials to act in his stead.

S. 402(2), (5)

These provisions describe his functions, the most obvious of which is to present a petition under s. 264(1)(d) where a criminal bankruptcy order (as defined by s. 402(5)) has been made, although he does have discretion to present petitions in the public interest in other cases.

S. 402(4)

This confers immunity on the official petitioner for acts done in the discharge of his duties.

See also IR 1986, r. 6.230.

Note prospective amendment: s. 402 is to be repealed by CJA 1988, s. 170(2) and Sch. 16 as from a day to be appointed; see the note to s. 264.

Insolvency Service Finance, Accounting and Investment

403 Insolvency Services Account

403(1) **[Payment into Account]** All money received by the Secretary of State in respect of proceedings under this Act as it applies to England and Wales shall be paid into the Insolvency Services Account kept by

424

the Secretary of State with the Bank of England; and all payments out of money standing to the credit of the Secretary of State in that account shall be made by the Bank of England in such manner as he may direct.

403(2) **[Where excess amount]** Whenever the cash balance standing to the credit of the Insolvency Services Account is in excess of the amount which in the opinion of the Secretary of State is required for the time being to answer demands in respect of bankrupts' estates or companies' estates, the Secretary of State shall–

(a) notify the excess to the National Debt Commissioners, and

(b) pay into the Insolvency Services Investment Account (**"the Investment Account"**) kept by the Commissioners with the Bank of England the whole or any part of the excess as the Commissioners may require for investment in accordance with the following provisions of this Part.

403(3) **[Where invested money required]** Whenever any part of the money so invested is, in the opinion of the Secretary of State, required to answer any demand in respect of bankrupts' estates or companies' estates, he shall notify to the National Debt Commissioners the amount so required and the Commissioners–

(a) shall thereupon repay to the Secretary of State such sum as may be required to the credit of the Insolvency Services Account, and

(b) for that purpose may direct the sale of such part of the securities in which the money has been invested as may be necessary.

S. 403(1)
Fees, etc. collected in England and Wales by the Secretary of State in respect of proceedings under this Act (see ss. 414, 415) are to be paid into the Insolvency Services Account at the Bank of England.

S. 403(2), (3)
These subsections regulate investment of surplus moneys from the above Account in the Investment Account at the Bank of England. See also the Insolvency Regulations 1994 (SI 1994/2507), as amended by SI 2004/472.

404 Investment Account

404 Any money standing to the credit of the Investment Account (including any money received by the National Debt Commissioners by way of interest on or proceeds of any investment under this section) may be invested by the Commissioners, in accordance with such directions as may be given by the Treasury, in any manner for the time being specified in Part II of Schedule 1 to the Trustee Investments Act 1961.

GENERAL NOTE

This section restricts investment of money placed in the Investment Account under s. 403(2).

405 [Repealed]

405(1) *[Payment of excess into Consolidated Fund] Where the annual account to be kept by the National Debt Commissioners under section 409 below shows that in the year for which it is made up the gross amount of the interest accrued from the securities standing to the credit of the Investment Account exceeded the aggregate of–*

(a) *a sum, to be determined by the Treasury, to provide against the depreciation in the value of the securities, and*

(b) *the sums paid into the Insolvency Services Account in pursuance of the next section together with the sums paid in pursuance of that section to the Commissioners of Inland Revenue,*

the National Debt Commissioners shall, within 3 months after the account is laid before Parliament, cause the amount of the excess to be paid out of the Investment Account into the Consolidated Fund in such manner as may from time to time be agreed between the Treasury and the Commissioners.

Section 406   Insolvency Act 1986

405(2)   [Deficiency into Investment Account] Where the said annual account shows that in the year for which it is made up the gross amount of interest accrued from the securities standing to the credit of the Investment Account was less than the aggregate mentioned in subsection (1), an amount equal to the deficiency shall, at such times as the Treasury direct, be paid out of the Consolidated Fund into the Investment Account.

405(3)   [If funds in Investment Account insufficient] If the Investment Account is insufficient to meet its liabilities the Treasury may, on being informed of the insufficiency by the National Debt Commissioners, issue the amount of the deficiency out of the Consolidated Fund and the Treasury shall certify the deficiency to Parliament.

GENERAL NOTE

These provisions provided for the transfer of sums to the Consolidated Fund from the Investment Account and vice versa, where it is appropriate to adjust balances. They were repealed by EA 2002, s. 272 with effect from April 1, 2004.

406   Interest on money received by liquidators or trustees in bankruptcy and invested

406   Where under rules made by virtue of paragraph 16 of Schedule 8 to this Act (investment of money received by company liquidators) or paragraph 21 of Schedule 9 to this Act (investment of money received by trustee in bankruptcy) a company or a bankrupt's estate has become entitled to any sum by way of interest, the Secretary of State shall certify that sum and the amount of tax payable on it to the National Debt Commissioners; and the Commissioners shall pay, out of the Investment Account–

(a)   into the Insolvency Services Account, the sum so certified less the amount of tax so certified, and

(b)   to the Commissioners of Inland Revenue, the amount of tax so certified.

GENERAL NOTE

Where a liquidator or trustee has paid sums into the Insolvency Services Account which have been invested, and these sums have earned interest, s. 406 provides a mechanism for allocating these sums between those entitled, including the Revenue in respect of tax payable on the interest. In s. 406 the words "or paragraph 21 of Schedule 9 to this Act (investment of money received by trustee in bankruptcy) a company or a bankrupt's estate" substituted for the words "a company" and the sidenote substituted for the former sidenote "Interest on money received by liquidators and invested" by IA 2000, s. 13(2) as from April 2, 2001 (see SI 2001/766 (C. 27), art. 1, 2(1)(b)). This change was part of a package to benefit estates of bankrupts, which were otherwise providing an unjustified source of income for the State – a fact deplored by the Cork Committee (Cmnd 8558, para. 857).

407   Unclaimed dividends and undistributed balances

407(1)   [Duty of Secretary of State] The Secretary of State shall from time to time pay into the Consolidated Fund out of the Insolvency Services Account so much of the sums standing to the credit of that Account as represents–

(a)   dividends which were declared before such date as the Treasury may from time to time determine and have not been claimed, and

(b)   balances ascertained before that date which are too small to be divided among the persons entitled to them.

407(2)   [Sums to credit of Insolvency Services Account] For the purposes of this section the sums standing to the credit of the Insolvency Services Account are deemed to include any sums paid out of that Account and represented by any sums or securities standing to the credit of the Investment Account.

407(3)   [Power of Secretary of State] The Secretary of State may require the National Debt Commissioners to pay out of the Investment Account into the Insolvency Services Account the whole or part of any sum which he is required to pay out of that account under subsection (1); and the Commissioners may direct the sale of such securities standing to the credit of the Investment Account as may be necessary for that purpose.

GENERAL NOTE

This section states that unclaimed dividends, etc. are to be moved periodically by the Secretary of State from the Insolvency Services Account (or the Investment Account, where appropriate) to the Consolidated Fund. Investments in securities may need to be realised to achieve this end.

408 Adjustment of balances

408(1) [Payments by Treasury out of Consolidated Fund] The Treasury may direct the payment out of the Consolidated Fund of sums into–

(a) the Insolvency Services Account;

(b) the Investment Account.

408(2) [Certification of reason for payment] The Treasury shall certify to the House of Commons the reason for any payment under subsection (1).

408(3) [Payments by Secretary of State into consolidated Fund] The Secretary of State may pay sums out of the Insolvency Services Account into the Consolidated Fund.

408(4) [Payments by National Debt Commissioners into consolidated Fund] The National Debt Commissioners may pay sums out of the Investment Account into the Consolidated Fund.

GENERAL NOTE

This provision was introduced by s. 272(2) of the Enterprise Act 2002 in substitution for the original s. 408, which is reproduced below. This substitution takes place on April 1, 2004.

S. 408(1)
This permits the Treasury to direct an adjustment of balances from the Consolidated Fund into the Insolvency Services Account and Investment Account. With regard to the Investment Account note the repeal of s. 405 by s. 272(1) of EA 2002.

S. 408(2)
Directions given under subs. (1) must be reasoned.

S. 408(3)
This permits payments out of the Insolvency Services Account into the Consolidated Fund.

S. 408(4)
Payments from the Investment Fund into the Consolidated Account are hereby authorised.

408 Recourse to Consolidated Fund [to be repealed]

408 If, after any repayment due to it from the Investment Account, the Insolvency Services Account is insufficient to meet its liabilities, the Treasury may, on being informed of it by the Secretary of State, issue the amount of the deficiency out of the Consolidated Fund, and the Treasury shall certify the deficiency to Parliament.

409 Annual financial statement and audit

409(1) [Preparation of statement] The National Debt Commissioners shall for each year ending on 31st March prepare a statement of the sums credited and debited to the Investment Account in such form and manner as the Treasury may direct and shall transmit it to the Comptroller and Auditor General before the end of November next following the year.

409(2) [Duty of Secretary of State] The Secretary of State shall for each year ending 31st March prepare a statement of the sums received or paid by him under section 403 above in such form and manner as the Treasury may direct and shall transmit each statement to the Comptroller and Auditor General before the end of November next following the year.

Section 410　　　　　　　　　　　　　　　　Insolvency Act 1986

409(3) **[Additional information]** Every such statement shall include such additional information as the Treasury may direct.

409(4) **[Examination etc. of statement]** The Comptroller and Auditor General shall examine, certify and report on every such statement and shall lay copies of it, and of his report, before Parliament.

GENERAL NOTE

This section lays down a framework for annual financial statements in respect of the Investment Account and the Insolvency Services Account, and the auditing thereof.

Supplementary

410　Extent of this Part

410　This Part of this Act extends to England and Wales only.

GENERAL NOTE

Sections 399–409 do not apply in Scotland, nor in Northern Ireland. This is confirmed by ss. 440 and 441.

PART XV

SUBORDINATE LEGISLATION

General Insolvency Rules

411　Company insolvency rules

411(1) **[Rules]** Rules may be made–

(a) in relation to England and Wales, by the Lord Chancellor with the concurrence of the Secretary of State, or

(b) in relation to Scotland, by the Secretary of State,

for the purpose of giving effect to Parts I to VII of this Act or the EC Regulation.

411(2) **[Contents of rules]** Without prejudice to the generality of subsection (1), or to any provision of those Parts by virtue of which rules under this section may be made with respect to any matter, rules under this section may contain–

(a) any such provision as is specified in Schedule 8 to this Act or corresponds to provision contained immediately before the coming into force of section 106 of the Insolvency Act 1985 in rules made, or having effect as if made, under section 663(1) or (2) of the Companies Act (old winding-up rules), and

(b) such incidental, supplemental and transitional provisions as may appear to the Lord Chancellor or, as the case may be, the Secretary of State necessary or expedient.

411(2A) **[Applicability of EC Regulation]** For the purposes of subsection (2), a reference in Schedule 8 to this Act to doing anything under or for the purposes of a provision of this Act includes a reference to doing anything under or for the purposes of the EC Regulation (in so far as the provision of this Act relates to a matter to which the EC Regulation applies).

411(2B) **[Rules not to create an offence]** Rules under this section for the purpose of giving effect to the EC Regulation may not create an offence of a kind referred to in paragraph 1(1)(d) of Schedule 2 to the European Communities Act 1972.

411(3) **[Interpretation of Sch. 8]** In Schedule 8 to this Act "liquidator" includes a provisional liquidator; and references above in this section to Parts I to VII of this Act are to be read as including the Companies Act so far as relating to, and to matters connected with or arising out of, the insolvency or winding up of companies.

411(4) **[Rules by statutory instrument etc.]** Rules under this section shall be made by statutory instrument subject to annulment in pursuance of a resolution of either House of Parliament.

411(5) **[Regulations]** Regulations made by the Secretary of State under a power conferred by rules under this section shall be made by statutory instrument and, after being made, shall be laid before each House of Parliament.

411(6) **[Rules of court]** Nothing in this section prejudices any power to make rules of court.

S. 411(1), (2), (2A), (2B)
These subsections provide for the making of company insolvency rules which may include, for example, the matters specified in Sch. 8 to this Act, or former corresponding matters. Subsection (1) was amended and subss. (2A) and (2B) added by the Insolvency Act 1986 (Amendment) Regulations 2002 (SI 2002/1037) reg. 3 with effect from May 3, 2002. The Insolvency Rules 1986 (IR 1986) (SI 1986/1925), as amended, are to be found below, commencing at p. 654. See also the other rules, regulations and orders listed in the general note to IR 1986, r. 0.1 below, p. 674.

S. 411(3)
This is an interpretation provision, amplifying terms used in Sch. 8 and s. 411(1) and (2).

S. 411(4), (5)
These provisions explain how company insolvency rules and regulations may be made. The regulations are the Insolvency Regulations 1994 (SI 1994/2507).

S. 411(6)
This is a saving provision mirrored by s. 412(5).

412 Individual insolvency rules (England and Wales)

412(1) **[Rules by Lord Chancellor]** The Lord Chancellor may, with the concurrence of the Secretary of State, make rules for the purpose of giving effect to Parts VIII to XI of this Act or the EC Regulation.

412(2) **[Contents of rules]** Without prejudice to the generality of subsection (1), or to any provision of those Parts by virtue of which rules under this section may be made with respect to any matter, rules under this section may contain–

(a) any such provision as is specified in Schedule 9 to this Act or corresponds to provision contained immediately before the appointed day in rules made under section 132 of the Bankruptcy Act 1914; and

(b) such incidental, supplemental and transitional provisions as may appear to the Lord Chancellor necessary or expedient.

412(2A) **[Applicability of EC Regulation]** For the purposes of subsection (2), a reference in Schedule 9 to this Act to doing anything under or for the purposes of a provision of this Act includes a reference to doing anything under or for the purposes of the EC Regulation (in so far as the provision of this Act relates to a matter to which the EC Regulation applies).

412(2B) **[Rules not to create an offence]** Rules under this section for the purpose of giving effect to the EC Regulation may not create an offence of a kind referred to in paragraph 1(1)(d) of Schedule 2 to the European Communities Act 1972.

412(3) **[Rules to be made by statutory instrument]** Rules under this section shall be made by statutory instrument subject to annulment in pursuance of a resolution of either House of Parliament.

Section 413   Insolvency Act 1986

412(4) **[Regulations]** Regulations made by the Secretary of State under a power conferred by rules under this section shall be made by statutory instrument and, after being made, shall be laid before each House of Parliament.

412(5) **[Rules of court]** Nothing in this section prejudices any power to make rules of court.

S. 412(1), (2), (2A), (2B)
These subsections give authority to the Lord Chancellor, with the agreement of the Secretary of State, to make new rules which replace the 1952 rules. These are the Insolvency Rules 1986 (SI 1986/1925) (see below, pp. 654). Schedule 9 to the Act provides guidelines on the matters which may be dealt with by the rules – *e.g.* role of the insolvency courts; notices; registration of voluntary arrangements; role of interim receivers and receivers and managers; meetings of creditors; other matters concerned with the administration of the bankrupt's estate; financial provisions; information and records; powers of the court; and miscellaneous and supplementary matters. Subsection (1) was amended and subss. (2A) and (2B) were added by the Insolvency Act 1986 (Amendment) Regulations 2002 (SI 2002/1037) reg. 3 with effect from May 3, 2002.

S. 412(3), (4)
These provisions govern how the Lord Chancellor may make rules under s. 412 and how the Secretary of State may exercise powers by regulations under the said rules (see the Insolvency Regulations 1994 (SI 1994/2507) October 24, 1994. See also the Insolvency (Amendment) Regulations 2004 (SI 2004/472).

S. 412(5)
The power of the court to make its own rules is not to be prejudiced by this provision.

413 Insolvency Rules Committee

413(1) **[Continuation of committee]** The committee established under section 10 of the Insolvency Act 1976 (advisory committee on bankruptcy and winding-up rules) continues to exist for the purpose of being consulted under this section.

413(2) **[Consultation by Lord Chancellor]** The Lord Chancellor shall consult the committee before making any rules under section 411 or 412 other than rules which contain a statement that the only provision made by the rules is provision applying rules made under section 411, with or without modifications, for the purposes of provision made by any of sections 23 to 26 of the Water Industry Act 1991 or Schedule 3 to that Act or by any of sections 59 to 65 of, or Schedule 6 or 7 to, the Railways Act 1993.

413(3) **[Members of committee]** Subject to the next subsection, the committee shall consist of–

(a) a judge of the High Court attached to the Chancery Division;

(b) a circuit judge;

(c) a registrar in bankruptcy of the High Court;

(d) the registrar of a county court;

(e) a practising barrister;

(f) a practising solicitor; and

(g) a practising accountant;

and the appointment of any person as a member of the committee shall be made by the Lord Chancellor.

413(4) **[Additional members]** The Lord Chancellor may appoint as additional members of the committee any persons appearing to him to have qualifications or experience that would be of value to the committee in considering any matter with which it is concerned.

S. 413(1)
This provides for the continuance of the Insolvency Rules Committee established under IA 1976, s. 10. This is not to be confused with the Insolvency Court Users' Committee set up by the Vice Chancellor, Sir Nicolas Browne-Wilkinson, in April 1987 to advise on improvements to court practices: see *The Times*, April 8, 1987. In *Woodley v Woodley (No. 2)* [1994] 1 W.L.R. 1167 Balcombe L.J. (at p. 1179D) formally invited the Insolvency Rules Committee to consider

whether lump sum payments arising out of matrimonial proceedings should be made provable debts under r. 12.3 of the Insolvency Rules and so restore the pre-1986 position. See also *Re Austintel Ltd* [1997] B.C.C. 362.

S. 413(2)
This Committee must normally be consulted before the Lord Chancellor makes any insolvency rules under s. 411 or under s. 412.

S. 413(3), (4)
These provisions regulate the composition of the Committee. Like s. 413(1) and (2) they represent no real change in the law.

Fees Orders

414 Fees orders (company insolvency proceedings)

414(1) [Fees] There shall be paid in respect of–

(a) proceedings under any of Parts I to VII of this Act, and

(b) the performance by the official receiver or the Secretary of State of functions under those Parts,

such fees as the competent authority may with the sanction of the Treasury by order direct.

414(2) [Security for fees] That authority is–

(a) in relation to England and Wales, the Lord Chancellor, and

(b) in relation to Scotland, the Secretary of State.

414(3) [Order by Treasury] The Treasury may by order direct by whom and in what manner the fees are to be collected and accounted for.

414(4) [Security for fees] The Lord Chancellor may, with the sanction of the Treasury, by order provide for sums to be deposited, by such persons, in such manner and in such circumstances as may be specified in the order, by way of security for fees payable by virtue of this section.

414(5) [Incidental matter under order] An order under this section may contain such incidental, supplemental and transitional provisions as may appear to the Lord Chancellor, the Secretary of State or (as the case may be) the Treasury necessary or expedient.

414(6) [Order by statutory instrument etc.] An order under this section shall be made by statutory instrument and, after being made, shall be laid before each House of Parliament.

414(7) [Payment into Consolidated Fund] Fees payable by virtue of this section shall be paid into the Consolidated Fund.

414(8) [Interpretation] References in subsection (1) to Parts I to VII of this Act are to be read as including the Companies Act so far as relating to, and to matters connected with or arising out of, the insolvency or winding up of companies.

414(9) [Rules of court, Scotland] Nothing in this section prejudices any power to make rules of court; and the application of this section to Scotland is without prejudice to section 2 of the Courts of Law Fees (Scotland) Act 1895.

S. 414(1), (2)
These subsections govern the fixing of company insolvency fees in England and Wales, and in Scotland. Note the role of the Treasury in such matters. See the Insolvency Fees Order 1986 (SI 1986/2030), as amended by SI 1988/95; SI 1990/560 (L 9); SI 1991/496; SI 1992/34; SI 1994/2541. See also the Department of Trade and Industry (Fees) Order 1988 (SI 1988/93); the Supreme Court Fees Order 1999 (SI 1999/687); and the County Court Fees Order 1999 (SI 1999/689). Amendments were made by the Supreme Court Fees (Amendment) Order 2003 (SI 2003/646, L. 13) and the County Court Fees (Amendment) Order 2003 (SI 2003/648; L. 15).

Section 415   *Insolvency Act 1986*

S. 414(3), (7)
These provisions deal with the manner of collection and payment into the Consolidated Fund.

S. 414(4)
Deposits by way of security may also be provided for.

S. 414(5)
This is a safety valve mechanism designed to build flexibility into the system.

S. 414(6)
This describes the parliamentary procedure to be used for orders fixing company insolvency fees.

S. 414(8), (9)
These subsections provide an interpretation facility and a saving mechanism.

415   Fees orders (individual insolvency proceedings in England and Wales)

415(1)   [Payment of fees] There shall be paid in respect of–

(a)   proceedings under Parts VIII to XI of this Act, and

(b)   the performance by the official receiver or the Secretary of State of functions under those Parts,

such fees as the Lord Chancellor may with the sanction of the Treasury by order direct.

415(2)   [Order by Treasury] The Treasury may by order direct by whom and in what manner the fees are to be collected and accounted for.

415(3)   [Security for fees] The Lord Chancellor may, with the sanction of the Treasury, by order provide for sums to be deposited, by such persons, in such manner and in such circumstances as may be specified in the order, by way of security for–

(a)   fees payable by virtue of this section, and

(b)   fees payable to any person who has prepared an insolvency practitioner's report under section 274 in Chapter I of Part IX.

415(4)   [Incidental provisions etc. of order] An order under this section may contain such incidental, supplemental and transitional provisions as may appear to the Lord Chancellor or, as the case may be, the Treasury, necessary or expedient.

415(5)   [Order by statutory instrument etc.] An order under this section shall be made by statutory instrument and, after being made, shall be laid before each House of Parliament.

415(6)   [Payment into Consolidated Fund] Fees payable by virtue of this section shall be paid into the Consolidated Fund.

415(7)   [Rules of court] Nothing in this section prejudices any power to make rules of court.

S. 415(1)–(3)
These subsections permit the Lord Chancellor, with the assent of the Treasury, to fix fees for bankruptcy proceedings and for tasks carried out by the official receiver or Secretary of State. Deposits which, *e.g.* represent advance payment of fees may also be similarly prescribed. See the Insolvency Proceedings (Fees) Order 2004 (SI 2004/593). See also the Department of Trade and Industry (Fees) Order 1988 (SI 1988/93); the Supreme Court Fees Order 1999 (SI 1999/687); and the County Court Fees Order 1999 (SI 1999/689). Amendments were made by the Supreme Court Fees (Amendment) Order 2003 (SI 2003/646, L. 13) and the County Court Fees (Amendment) Order 2003 (SI 2003/648, L. 15).

For the company law counterpart, see s. 414. For further details, see Sch. 9.

S. 415(4), (5)
These provisions deal with the procedural prerequisites of such an order from the Lord Chancellor and with supplementary matters which may be included therein.

S. 415(6)
Fees collected under this provision are paid into the Consolidated Fund.

S. 415(7)
This preserves the inherent power of the court to make rules of court.

415A Fees orders (general)

415A(1) [Fee by recognised professional bodies] The Secretary of State–

(a) may by order require a body to pay a fee in connection with the grant or maintenance of recognition of the body under section 391, and

(b) may refuse recognition, or revoke an order of recognition under section 391(1) by a further order, where a fee is not paid.

415A(2) [Fee by applicant as insolvency practitioner] The Secretary of State–

(a) may by order require a person to pay a fee in connection with the grant or maintenance of authorisation of the person under section 393, and

(b) may disregard an application or withdraw an authorisation where a fee is not paid.

415A(3) [Insolvency Services Account] The Secretary of State may by order require the payment of fees in respect of–

(a) the operation of the Insolvency Services Account;

(b) payments into and out of that Account.

415A(4) [Application of s. 414(3), (5)–(7), (9)] The following provisions of section 414 apply to fees under this section as they apply to fees under that section–

(a) subsection (3) (manner of payment),

(b) subsection (5) (additional provision),

(c) subsection (6) (statutory instrument),

(d) subsection (7) (payment into Consolidated Fund), and

(e) subsection (9) (saving for rules of court).

GENERAL NOTE

This additional provision was introduced by s. 270 of EA 2002. The Secretary of State has made the following order under s. 415A – the Insolvency Practitioners and Insolvency Services Account (Fees) Order 2003 (SI 2003/3363) as amended by SI 2004/476. This Order provides for payment of fees in connection with the authorisation of insolvency practitioners and the recognition of bodies under ss. 391, 392, 393. Payment of fees in connection with transactions with the ISA is also prescribed.

S. 415A(1), (2)
The Secretary of State may charge a fee for recognising certain bodies under s. 391 or persons under s. 393 and may remove recognition if the appropriate fee is not paid.

S. 415A(3)
Fees may be charged in respect of the operation of the Insolvency Services Account.

S. 415A(4)
This extends various provisions in s. 414 to s. 415A.

Specification, Increase and Reduction of Money Sums Relevant in the Operation of this Act

416 Monetary limits (companies winding up)

416(1) [Increase or reduction of certain provisions] The Secretary of State may by order in a statutory instrument increase or reduce any of the money sums for the time being specified in the following provisions in the first Group of Parts–

section 117(2) (amount of company's share capital determining whether county court has jurisdiction to wind it up);

section 120(3) (the equivalent as respects sheriff court jurisdiction in Scotland);

section 123(1)(a) (minimum debt for service of demand on company by unpaid creditor);

section 184(3) (minimum value of judgment, affecting sheriff's duties on levying execution);

section 206(1)(a) and (b) (minimum value of company property concealed or fraudulently removed, affecting criminal liability of company's officer).

416(2) **[Transitional provisions]** An order under this section may contain such transitional provisions as may appear to the Secretary of State necessary or expedient.

416(3) **[Approval by Parliament]** No order under this section increasing or reducing any of the money sums for the time being specified in section 117(2), 120(3) or 123(1)(a) shall be made unless a draft of the order has been laid before and approved by a resolution of each House of Parliament.

416(4) **[Annulment of statutory instrument]** A statutory instrument containing an order under this section, other than an order to which subsection (3) applies, is subject to annulment in pursuance of a resolution of either House of Parliament.

S. 416(1)
This provision allows the Secretary of State to use statutory instruments to increase or reduce various figures specified in the First Group of Parts without recourse to primary legislation.

In relation to Scotland, s. 416(1) applies (with modifications) to limited liability partnerships by virtue of the Limited Liability Partnerships (Scotland) Regulations 2001 (SI 2001/128), reg. 4(1), (2) and Sch. 2 as from April 6, 2001.

S. 416(2)
The statutory instrument may provide for transitional matters.

S. 416(3), (4)
The basic parliamentary procedure to be used is mapped out by s. 416(4), although this is qualified by s. 416(3) in respect of the variation of certain figures. In relation to Scotland, s. 416(4) applies (with modifications) to limited liability partnerships by virtue of the Limited Liability Partnerships (Scotland) Regulations 2001 (SI 2001/128), reg. 4(1), (2) and Sch. 2 as from April 6, 2001.

417 Money sum in s. 222

417 The Secretary of State may by regulations in a statutory instrument increase or reduce the money sum for the time being specified in section 222(1) (minimum debt for service of demand on unregistered company by unpaid creditor); but such regulations shall not be made unless a draft of the statutory instrument containing them has been approved by resolution of each House of Parliament.

GENERAL NOTE

This section provides a procedure for modifying the minimum debt for a statutory demand (currently £750).

417A Money sums (company moratorium)

417A(1) **[Change of sums]** The Secretary of State may by order increase or reduce any of the money sums for the time being specified in the following provisions of Schedule A1 to this Act–

paragraph 17(1) (maximum amount of credit which company may obtain without disclosure of moratorium);

paragraph 41(4) (minimum value of company property concealed or fraudulently removed, affecting criminal liability of company's officer).

417A(2) **[Transitional matters]** An order under this section may contain such transitional provisions as may appear to the Secretary of State necessary or expedient.

417A(3) **[Procedure]** An order under this section shall be made by statutory instrument subject to annulment in pursuance of a resolution of either House of Parliament.

GENERAL NOTE

This was introduced by Sch. 1 to IA 2000 with effect from January 1, 2003. It enables monetary figures mentioned in connection with the new CVA moratorium procedure to be modified by the Secretary of State.

418 Monetary limits (bankruptcy)

418(1) **[Powers of Secretary of State]** The Secretary of State may by order prescribe amounts for the purposes of the following provisions in the second Group of Parts–

section 273 (minimum value of debtor's estate determining whether immediate bankruptcy order should be made; small bankruptcies level);

section 313A (value of property below which application for sale, possession or charge to be dismissed);

section 346(3) (minimum amount of judgment, determining whether amount recovered on sale of debtor's goods is to be treated as part of his estate in bankruptcy);

section 354(1) and (2) (minimum amount of concealed debt, or value of property concealed or removed, determining criminal liability under the section);

section 358 (minimum value of property taken by a bankrupt out of England and Wales, determining his criminal liability);

section 360(1) (maximum amount of credit which bankrupt may obtain without disclosure of his status);

section 361(2) (exemption of bankrupt from criminal liability for failure to keep proper accounts, if unsecured debts not more than the prescribed minimum);

section 364(2)(d) (minimum value of goods removed by the bankrupt, determining his liability to arrest);

and references in the second Group of Parts to the amount prescribed for the purposes of any of those provisions, and references in those provisions to the prescribed amount, are to be construed accordingly.

418(2) **[Transitional provisions]** An order under this section may contain such transitional provisions as may appear to the Secretary of State necessary or expedient.

418(3) **[Order by statutory instrument etc.]** An order under this section shall be made by statutory instrument subject to annulment in pursuance of a resolution of either House of Parliament.

S. 418(1)

This provision authorises the Secretary of State to fix monetary amounts for a number of provisions in the Second Group of Parts. For example, he can determine the "minimum amount" and the "small bankruptcies level" for the purposes of s. 273, the minimum judgment for s. 364(3), property values for the purposes of s. 354, and so on. This represents a trend away from mentioning specific figures in the statutory provision itself to a more flexible regime suited to coping with inflation. The reference to s. 313A was made by EA 2002, s. 261(6). See Insolvency Proceedings (Monetary Limits) (Amendment) Order (SI 2004/547).

S. 418(2), (3)

These deal with ancillary matters and the form of any order made by the Secretary of State under s. 418(1).

Insolvency Practice

419 Regulations for purposes of Part XIII

419(1) **[Power to make regulations]** The Secretary of State may make regulations for the purpose of giving effect to Part XIII of this Act; and **"prescribed"** in that Part means prescribed by regulations made by the Secretary of State.

419(2) **[Extent of regulations]** Without prejudice to the generality of subsection (1) or to any provision of that Part by virtue of which regulations may be made with respect to any matter, regulations under this section may contain–

(a) provision as to the matters to be taken into account in determining whether a person is a fit and proper person to act as an insolvency practitioner;

(b) provision prohibiting a person from so acting in prescribed cases, being cases in which a conflict of interest will or may arise;

(c) provision imposing requirements with respect to–

   (i) the preparation and keeping by a person who acts as an insolvency practitioner of prescribed books, accounts and other records, and
   (ii) the production of those books, accounts and records to prescribed persons;

(d) provision conferring power on prescribed persons–

   (i) to require any person who acts or has acted as an insolvency practitioner to answer any inquiry in relation to a case in which he is so acting or has so acted, and
   (ii) to apply to a court to examine such a person or any other person on oath concerning such a case;

(e) provision making non-compliance with any of the regulations a criminal offence; and

(f) such incidental, supplemental and transitional provisions as may appear to the Secretary of State necessary or expedient.

419(3) **[Power exercisable by statutory instrument etc.]** Any power conferred by Part XIII or this Part to make regulations, rules or orders is exercisable by statutory instrument subject to annulment by resolution of either House of Parliament.

419(4) **[Different provisions for different cases]** Any rule or regulation under Part XIII or this Part may make different provision with respect to different cases or descriptions of cases, including different provision for different areas.

S. 419(1), (2)
This section provides for regulations to be made by the Secretary of State in order to achieve the aims of Pt XIII (qualification of insolvency practitioners). Examples of the matters which may be provided for are listed. It would perhaps have been more appropriate to include these provisions within Pt XIII itself. For the relevant regulations see the Insolvency Practitioners Regulations 1990 (SI 1990/439) which consolidate and amend earlier regulations with effect from April 1, 1990. Note also The Insolvency Practitioners (Amendment) Regulations 2004 (SI 2004/473).

S. 419(3)
This lays down the parliamentary procedure to be used for creating such regulations.

S. 419(4)
This subsection, coupled with the generality of s. 419(1), gives the Secretary of State considerable freedom for manoeuvre.

Other Order-making Powers

420 Insolvent partnerships

420(1) **[Application to insolvent partnerships]** The Lord Chancellor may, by order made with the concurrence of the Secretary of State, provide that such provisions of this Act as may be specified in the order shall apply in relation to insolvent partnerships with such modifications as may be so specified.

420(1A) **[Provision re EC Regulation]** An order under this section may make provision in relation to the EC Regulation.

420(1B) [**Provision must not create an offence**] But provision made by virtue of this section in relation to the EC Regulation may not create an offence of a kind referred to in paragraph (1)(1)(d) of Schedule 2 to the European Communities Act 1972.

420(2) [**Incidental provisions etc.**] An order under this section may make different provision for different cases and may contain such incidental, supplemental and transitional provisions as may appear to the Lord Chancellor necessary or expedient.

420(3) [**Order by statutory instrument etc.**] An order under this section shall be made by statutory instrument subject to annulment in pursuance of a resolution of either House of Parliament.

S. 420(1)

This allows the provisions of the Act to be extended (with suitable modifications) to deal with situations where insolvent partnerships are being wound up or are subject to various other insolvency regimes. Note the insertion of subss. (1A) and (1B) by the Insolvency Act 1986 (Amendment) Regulations 2002 (SI 2002/1037) reg. 3 with effect from May 3, 2002. The Lord Chancellor originally exercised his power under subs. (1) to make the Insolvent Partnerships Order 1986 (SI 1986/2142), which has been replaced by the Insolvent Partnerships Order 1994 (SI 1994/2421). The 1994 Order provides the details of the necessary procedures with the modified primary legislation being reproduced *in extenso* in the Schedules to the Order. Appropriate forms are also appended. In the case of insolvency orders made before the coming into force of the 1994 Order (December 1, 1994) the provisions of the 1986 Order will continue to apply. Transitional matters are dealt with by art. 19 of the 1994 Order. For discussion of the 1994 Order see Frith and Jones (1995) 11 I.L. & P. 14.

The 1986 Order replaced the provisions in BA 1914 which dealt with insolvent partnerships: *e.g.*, ss. 114, 116, 119 and 127, plus rr. 279–297 of BR 1952. For analysis of art. 15(3) of the original 1986 Order see *Schooler v Customs and Excise* [1996] B.P.I.R. 207. The 1986 Order in turn has been completely replaced by the 1994 Order. There were a number of factors which led to the introduction of the new Order. Amongst these were:

(1) a desire to promote rescue procedures for insolvent partnerships;

(2) the need to enhance the presentation of the relevant provisions to enable practitioners to interpret them more easily;

(3) the necessity of dealing with the problems of conflict between the Act and the 1986 Order as revealed by the case of *Re Marr* [1990] Ch. 773;

(4) the desirability of implementing the recommendations of the Cork Committee on distribution of assets of joint and several estates (see *Report*, paras 1685–1690);

(5) the attractions of streamlining unnecessary procedures in order to reduce running costs.

For a fuller insight into the motivation leading to the introduction of the 1994 Order, see the Insolvency Service's Consultation Document of November 1992.

Under the 1994 Order a partnership continues to be treated as an unregistered company and therefore the provisions of Pt V of IA 1986 are made applicable (with necessary modifications). The purpose of the new rules is to facilitate combined insolvency proceedings against both the firm and its members, where the business is insolvent. If the business is solvent, but an individual partner is in financial difficulties, then the general procedures relating to personal or corporate insolvency, as contained in the 1986 Act, must be used instead.

The 1994 Order (in force from December 1, 1994) deals with a number of distinct insolvency situations:

A voluntary arrangement in respect of the firm (a partnership voluntary arrangement or PVA) (art. 4). Full details of how Pt I of the Act is to be modified to deal with such a case are provided by Sch. 1 to the Order. For analysis of a PVA see Bacon (1994) 10 I.L. & P. 166.

A voluntary arrangement in respect of the members of an insolvent partnership (art. 5). This was already a possibility before 1994, but art. 5 clarifies the position (especially where both the firm and the partners are participating in voluntary arrangements).

An administration order in respect of the firm (art. 6). Details of the *modus operandi* here are found in Sch. 2 to the Order. See *Re Kyrris (No. 1)* [1998] B.P.I.R. 103 and *Re Kyrris (No. 2)* [1998] B.P.I.R. 111.

The winding up of the partnership firm (arts 7 and 9). Here, the partnership is treated as an unregistered company with the effect that the procedures contained in Pt V of the Act relating to the winding up of such companies are made applicable. The main ground for a winding-up petition is that the firm is unable to pay its debts. Such a petition may be presented by a creditor, or, where the firm consists of not less than eight partners by any member of the partnership. Separate provision is made for petitions presented by creditors (art. 7 and Sch. 3) and by members (art. 9 and Sch. 5).

The 1994 Order extends the availability of this winding-up procedure to the case of the winding up by creditor's petition of insolvent partnerships where the partnership has a place of business in England or Wales – it is not necessary that the principal place of business be so located. Thus certain overseas partnerships can now be brought within this regime.

Concurrent insolvency proceedings against the firm and individual partners (arts 8 and 10). Here, it is possible to present consolidated petitions against both the partnership firm and one or more partners in that firm (whether they be individuals or companies). The petitions will be presented to and heard by the same court. The petition against the firm is treated as the principal petition. A creditor can present a petition in such a case on the ground that the partnership is unable to pay its debts. The aim of this procedure is to facilitate the concurrent insolvency regimes – thus normally a single insolvency practitioner will handle the winding up of the firm and the insolvency proceedings against the individual members. A single public examination may be used to kill two birds with one stone. The partnership assets are to be used primarily to settle partnership liabilities; the old bankruptcy rule that the separate estates of the individual partners must first be utilised towards satisfying the claims of their own individual creditors has given way to a system under which creditors of the firm who have not been able to obtain satisfaction out of the firm's assets are entitled to equal treatment in any distribution of the separate estates. Thus the rule in s. 33(6) of BA 1914 is abolished and English law is brought into line with Scottish law.

The other main changes introduced by the 1994 Order in this hybrid scenario are as follows:

- this procedure can be used where only one of the members (as opposed to the previous requirement of two) is facing insolvency proceedings concurrently with the partnership;
- special amendments are made to s. 271 of the Act to reduce the difficulties encountered in *Re Marr* (above);
- procedural changes are made to cut costs (*e.g.* by removing the requirement for meetings that may be deemed to be unnecessary).

A joint bankruptcy petition covering all of the partners (art. 11). It is possible for all of the partners to petition jointly for their own bankruptcy, or alternatively for some of the partners with the concurrence of the others to do this. In such a case, the trustee acting for the insolvent partners has authority to wind up the partnership firm even though no petition has been presented against it. This form of proceedings can only be initiated by the partners themselves, on the ground that the firm is unable to meet its debts, and it cannot be used if there are corporate partners or partners who dissent from this course of action. Summary administration is now available in appropriate cases.

Winding up an unregistered company where an insolvent partnership is a member (art. 12). Here the insolvent partnership is treated as if it were a corporate member of the unregistered company.

In addition to the above procedural changes the 1994 Order also makes changes, for the purposes of the Order, to ss. 168 and 303 of the Act (supplemental powers of court) and to s. 388 (meaning of "act as insolvency practitioner"): see the notes to those sections.

A further amendment to the discrete insolvency regime for partnerships was introduced by the Insolvent Partnerships (Amendment) Order 1996 (SI 1996/1308). The main effect of this amendment was to allow the Bank of England and the Securities and Investments Board (now the FSA) to present winding up petitions in certain circumstances.

The Insolvent Partnerships (Amendment) Order 2001 (SI 2001/767) applies additional provisions inserted into CDDA 1986 to insolvent partnerships where appropriate.

The Insolvent Partnerships (Amendment) Order 2002 (SI 2002/1308) makes further changes into the legal regime governing insolvent partnerships. Essentially this Order caters for the introduction of the EC Regulation (1346/2000) by amending various procedural requirements relating to petitions and providing new forms which must be used for petitions presented after May 31, 2002. Note also SI 2002/2708.

S. 420(2), (3)

These subsections provide for flexibility of application, transitional matters and the procedure by which delegated legislation is to be made under this section.

421 Insolvent estates of deceased persons

421(1) **[Order by Lord Chancellor]** The Lord Chancellor may, by order made with the concurrence of the Secretary of State, provide that such provisions of this Act as may be specified in the order shall apply in relation to the administration of the insolvent estates of deceased persons with such modifications as may be so specified.

421(1A) **[Provision re EC Regulation]** An order under this section may make provision in relation to the EC Regulation.

421(1B) **[Provision must not create an offence]** But provision made by virtue of this section in relation to the EC Regulation may not create an offence of a kind referred to in paragraph 1(1)(d) of Schedule 2 to the European Communities Act 1972.

421(2) **[Incidental provisions etc.]** An order under this section may make different provision for different cases and may contain such incidental, supplemental and transitional provisions as may appear to the Lord Chancellor necessary or expedient.

421(3) **[Order by statutory instrument]** An order under this section shall be made by statutory instrument subject to annulment in pursuance of a resolution of either House of Parliament.

421(4) **[Interpretation]** For the purposes of this section the estate of a deceased person is insolvent if, when realised, it will be insufficient to meet in full all the debts and other liabilities to which it is subject.

S. 421(1), (1A), (1B), (2)
This authorises the Lord Chancellor, with the agreement of the Secretary of State, to extend the provisions of IA 1986 to the insolvent estates of deceased persons, subject to any modifications deemed necessary. A minor textual change was made by s. 12(2) IA 2000 with effect from April 2, 2001. See SI 2001/766, c. 27. Subsections (1A) and (1B) were inserted by the Insolvency Act 1986 (Amendment) Regulations 2002 (SI 2002/1037) with effect from May 3, 2002.

The BA 1914 laid down considerable detail on the administration of estates of deceased insolvents, whereas the present Act clearly leaves much to the rules in delegated legislation: see Sch. 9, para. 19 and the Administration of Insolvent Estates of Deceased Persons Order 1986 (SI 1986/1999).

Orders granted under s. 421 and the 1986 Order are extremely rare. The relationship between the Act, the Order and certain common law presumptions was the subject of judicial comment in *Re Palmer* [1994] Ch. 316. Here it was held by the Court of Appeal that the general legal presumption that a judicial act is deemed to have occurred at the earliest moment from the day on which it was done cannot be used to provide an interpretation of the Order that would make it inconsistent with the Act or make the Order *ultra vires* s. 421. Thus an administration order made by the court in respect of the estate of a deceased insolvent could not by using judicial fictions be deemed to have been made during the lifetime of that person. In so deciding the Court of Appeal rejected the approach adopted by Vinelott J. at first instance: see [1994] Ch. 316.

Another case where this regime was considered, albeit in a Northern Irish context, was *McAteer v Lismore (No. 1)* [2002] B.P.I.R. 804. Here Girvan J. held that the *modus operandi* of various transactional avoidance provisions which sought to avoid transactions from the date of the death rather than from the actual date of the commencement of the insolvency administration would have to be reviewed by the court in the light of the right to peaceable enjoyment of one's property as conferred by Art. 1 of the First Protocol of the European Convention on Human Rights.

The regime governing the administration of estates of deceased insolvents was modified with effect from May 31, 2002 by the *Administration of Insolvent Estates of Deceased Persons (Amendment) Order* 2002 (SI 2002/1309). This piece of delegated legislation owes its existence to EC Council Regulation 1346/2000 on Insolvency Proceedings. The effect of these changes is to facilitate cross-border insolvency administration by providing new forms (instead of those found in the 1986 Order) which are to be used where the EC Regulation applies.

S. 421(3)
This describes the *modus operandi* of such extension.

S. 421(4)
This determines when the estate of a deceased person is insolvent.

421A Insolvent estates: joint tenancies

421A(1) **[Application]** This section applies where–

(a) an insolvency administration order has been made in respect of the insolvent estate of a deceased person.

(b) the petition for the order was presented after the commencement of this section and within the period of five years beginning with the day on which he died, and

(c) immediately before his death he was beneficially entitled to an interest in any property as joint tenant.

421A(2) **[Power of court]** For the purpose of securing that debts and other liabilities to which the estate is subject are met, the court may, on an application by the trustee appointed pursuant to the insolvency administration order, make an order under this section requiring the survivor to pay to the trustee an amount not exceeding the value lost to the estate.

421A(3) **[Duty of court]** In determining whether to make an order under this section, and the terms of such an order, the court must have regard to all the circumstances of the case, including the interests of the deceased's creditors and of the survivor; but, unless the circumstances are exceptional, the court must assume that the interests of the deceased's creditors outweigh all other considerations.

421A(4) **[Terms, etc. of order]** The order may be made on such terms and conditions as the court thinks fit.

421A(5) **[Sums to be comprised in the estate]** Any sums required to be paid to the trustee in accordance with an order under this section shall be comprised in the estate.

421A(6) **[S. 421 modifications]** The modifications of this Act which may be made by an order under section 421 include any modifications which are necessary or expedient in consequence of this section.

421A(7) **["Survivor"]** In this section, "survivor" means the person who, immediately before the death, was beneficially entitled as joint tenant with the deceased or, if the person who was so entitled dies after the making of the insolvency administration order, his personal representatives.

421A(8) **[Multiple survivors]** If there is more than one survivor–

(a) an order under this section may be made against all or any of them, but

(b) no survivor shall be required to pay more than so much of the value lost to the estate as is properly attributable to him.

421A(9) **[Definitions]** In this section–

"insolvency administration order" has the same meaning as in any order under section 421 having effect for the time being,

"value lost to the estate" means the amount which, if paid to the trustee, would in the court's opinion restore the position to what it would have been if the deceased had been adjudged bankrupt immediately before his death.

GENERAL NOTE

Introduced by s. 12 IA 2000 with effect from April 2, 2001, this introduces a new section 421A whose effect is to reverse the inconvenient decision of the Court of Appeal in *Re Palmer (deceased)* [1994] Ch. 316 which cast doubt upon the effectiveness of secondary legislation made under s. 421. Here the Court of Appeal ruled that the Administration of Insolvent Estates of Deceased Persons Order 1986 (SI 1986/1999) did not have the effect that it was apparently intended to have and in particular where a joint tenant of property died insolvent his or her interest in the property passed automatically to the other joint tenant and did not form part of the insolvent estate for distribution amongst creditors. This ruling was seen to favour spouses in particular at the expense of creditors. There are admittedly very few cases where an administration of an estate of a deceased insolvent is required, but the problem was deemed sufficiently serious to require legislative correction. The original clause in the Bill had to be rewritten to counteract unintended consequences with regard to the marketability of property and the final provision arose out of the work of HC Standing Committee B (for explanation see *Hansard*, HL, Vol. 619, cols. 1345–1350).

Under s. 421A the survivor can be ordered to pay value to the estate; there is no transfer of property rights as such. The court enjoys discretion to deal with the matter, but as in insolvency generally the interests of creditors prevail unless the case is exceptional. The jurisprudence under s. 336 IA 1986 is likely to be influential here. Subsections (7) and (9) of the new s. 421A are definitional.

Concerns were raised as to whether this provision would have retrospective effect. This was eventually conceded by the government, who argued that the limited degree of retroactivity struck the right balance – see *Hansard*, HL, Vol. 619, cols. 1348–9. On closer examination of s. 421A(1) the position is that this new provision can only operate if the petition for the administration order was brought within five years of the death and after the coming into force of the section. Therefore there may be some retrospectivity at work depending on commencement dates though the danger here looks to be more theoretical than real.

422 Formerly authorised banks, etc.

422(1) **[Order by Secretary of State]** The Secretary of State may by order made with the concurrence of the Treasury and after consultation with the Financial Services Authority provide that specified provisions in the first Group of Parts shall apply with specified modifications in relation to any person who –

(a) has a liability in respect of a deposit which he accepted in accordance with the Banking Act 1979 (c. 37) or 1987 (c. 22), but

(b) does not have permission under Part IV of the Financial Services and Markets Act 2000 (c. 8) (regulated activities) to accept deposits.

422(1A) **[Where no permission under Financial Services and Markets Act 2000]** Subsection (1)(b) shall be construed in accordance with–

(a) section 22 of the Financial Services and Markets Act 2000 (classes of regulated activity and categories of investment),

(b) any relevant order under that section, and

(c) Schedule 2 to that Act (regulated activities).

422(2) **[Incidental provisions etc.]** An order under this section may make different provision for different cases and may contain such incidental, supplemental and transitional provisions as may appear to the Secretary of State necessary or expedient.

422(3) **[Order by statutory instrument etc.]** An order under this section shall be made by statutory instrument subject to annulment in pursuance of a resolution of either House of Parliament.

S. 422(1), (1A)
Subsection (1) was replaced by EA 2002, s. 248 and Sch. 17. Subsection (1A) was also inserted in this manner. It replaces an earlier version of subs.(1A) inserted by SI 2002/1555 which was then omitted by the Enterprise Act 2002 (Insolvency) Order 2003 (SI 2003/2096).

S. 422(2), (3)
These provisions regulate procedural and transitional matters.

Part XVI

Provisions Against Debt Avoidance (England and Wales Only)

423 Transactions defrauding creditors

423(1) **[Transaction at undervalue]** This section relates to transactions entered into at an undervalue; and a person enters into such a transaction with another person if–

(a) he makes a gift to the other person or he otherwise enters into a transaction with the other on terms that provide for him to receive no consideration;

(b) he enters into a transaction with the other in consideration of marriage; or

(c) he enters into a transaction with the other for a consideration the value of which, in money or money's worth, is significantly less than the value, in money or money's worth, of the consideration provided by himself.

Section 423　　　　　　　　　　　　　　　　　Insolvency Act 1986

423(2) **[Order by court]** Where a person has entered into such a transaction, the court may, if satisfied under the next subsection, make such order as it thinks fit for–

(a)　restoring the position to what it would have been if the transaction had not been entered into, and

(b)　protecting the interests of persons who are victims of the transaction.

423(3) **[Conditions for court order]** In the case of a person entering into such a transaction, an order shall only be made if the court is satisfied that it was entered into by him for the purpose–

(a)　of putting assets beyond the reach of a person who is making, or may at some time make, a claim against him, or

(b)　of otherwise prejudicing the interests of such a person in relation to the claim which he is making or may make.

423(4) **["The court"]** In this section **"the court"** means the High Court or–

(a)　if the person entering into the transaction is an individual, any other court which would have jurisdiction in relation to a bankruptcy petition relating to him;

(b)　if that person is a body capable of being wound up under Part IV or V of this Act, any other court having jurisdiction to wind it up.

423(5) **[Interpretation]** In relation to a transaction at an undervalue, references here and below to a victim of the transaction are to a person who is, or is capable of being, prejudiced by it; and in the following two sections the person entering into the transaction is referred to as **"the debtor"** .

GENERAL NOTE

The purpose of this section and those immediately following it is to revamp s. 172 of LPA 1925, which was used to avoid fraudulent conveyances. The Cork Committee wanted this provision widened, and, in particular, to cover payments of money: see the *Report*, para. 1238. This has been done. There has been a provision along these lines in English law since 1571, and ultimately it can trace its ancestry back to the Paulian action of Roman law. This provision applies to both individuals and companies alike: *Re Shilena Hosiery Co. Ltd* [1980] Ch. 219. The great utility of this provision lies in the fact that no time-limit for avoidance is fixed, in contrast with the case of ss. 238, 239 and 339, 340. However, this advantage may be more illusory than real in that the courts are reluctant to reopen transactions going back many years – *The Law Society v Southall* [2001] EWCA Civ 2001; [2002] B.P.I.R. 336. (For further points of comparison, see the note to s. 238.) See generally Milman and Parry (1997) 48 N.I.L.Q. 24 and Keay [1998] J.B.L. 515.

S. 423(1)–(3)

These provisions allow the court to set aside transactions at an undervalue designed to put assets out of reach of creditors. They explain what a transaction at an undervalue is. The definition is similar to that in ss. 238(4) and 339(3). On identification of the relevant "transaction" see *National Westminster Bank v Jones* [2001] EWCA Civ 1541; [2002] B.P.I.R. 361. The broad remedy which the court should have in mind is stated in s. 423(2), although the specifics are detailed in s. 425. Section 423(3) makes it clear that the transaction must have been intended to have a prejudicial effect.

Section 423 was the basis of a successful application by a creditor in *Arbuthnot Leasing International Ltd v Havelet Leasing Ltd (No. 2)* [1990] B.C.C. 636. In acceding to the application Scott J. held that the fact that the debtor had acted on legal advice did not exclude the debtor having the purpose specified in s. 423(3)(a). Where there is a prima facie breach of s. 423 the court may lift the veil of professional privilege to ascertain motives: *Barclays Bank v Eustice* [1995] 1 W.L.R. 1238; [1995] B.C.C. 978. See also *Re Schuppan* [1997] B.P.I.R. 271.

In *Chohan v Saggar* [1992] B.C.C. 306 (on appeal, [1994] B.C.C. 134) it was held that the requirements of subs. (3) are satisfied provided the dominant purpose of the debtor was to achieve one of the prohibited aims. This analysis sits uneasily alongside the approach the courts have taken to s. 238 (see above). Indeed, in *Royscot Spa Leasing Ltd v Lovett* [1995] B.C.C. 502 the Court of Appeal was prepared to accept a test based upon substantial (rather than dominant) purpose, though it did stress that it was important to distinguish between the purpose behind a transaction and the result of it. The dominant purpose test was favoured by Lightman J. in *Banca Carige v Banco Nacional de Cuba* [2001] B.P.I.R. 407. The opposite view was taken by the Court of Appeal in *Hashmi v IRC* [2002] EWCA Civ 981 and that now represents the accepted view – *Kubiangha v Ekpenyong* [2002] EWHC 1567 (Ch); [2002] 2 B.C.L.C. 597. The mental state of the recipient is not relevant when trying to determine the purpose of the debtor when entering into the transaction: *Moon v Franklin* [1996] B.P.I.R. 196.

In *Agricultural Mortgage Corporation plc v Woodward* [1994] B.C.C. 688 a transaction falling within s. 423(1)(c) was encountered. Here the Court of Appeal found that a grant of an agricultural tenancy by a farmer to his wife just before the mortgagee of the farm was intending to enforce the security was a transaction at an undervalue and should be set aside. Although a fair market rent had been charged by the husband, that rent did not take into account the fact that the wife as tenant could effectively hold the mortgagee to ransom by denying it vacant possession and thus preventing it enforcing its security. Looking at the transaction as a whole the arrangement was designed to defeat the interests of the mortgagee and the wife received real benefits outside the formal tenancy agreement that had not been paid for. In *Midland Bank v Wyatt* [1996] B.P.I.R. 288 a sham family trust established to protect assets in the event of business failure was avoided under s. 423. Note also *Re Schuppan* [1997] B.P.I.R. 271 where an attempt by a wife to argue that nothing of value had been transferred was unsuccessful. A successful s. 423 case was found in *Trowbridge v Trowbridge* [2003] B.P.I.R. 258. For cases falling on the other side of the line see *Menzies v National Bank of Kuwait SAK* [1994] B.C.C. 119; *Pinewood Joinery v Starelm Properties Ltd* [1994] B.C.C. 569; *Re Brabon* [2000] B.P.I.R. 537; *Re Taylor Sinclair (Capital) Ltd* [2002] B.P.I.R. 203. On s. 423 note also *Ashe v Mumford* [2001] B.P.I.R. 1.

S. 423(4), (5)
These provisions define "court" and "victim" (see ss. 423(2)(b), 424(1)(a)–(c), 424(2)). The latter term was not used in IA 1985. In *Moon v Franklin* (above) the victims were persons who were suing the debtor for professional negligence. See also *Pinewood Joinery v Starelm Properties* (above) and *Jyske Bank (Gibraltar) v Spjeldnaes (No. 2)* [1999] B.P.I.R. 525.

Section 423 can be invoked by a plaintiff in any part of the High Court provided the claim does not form part of proceedings being conducted in the Bankruptcy Court or the Companies Court: *TSB Bank plc v Katz* [1997] B.P.I.R. 147. On extraterritoriality see *Jyske Bank (Gibraltar) Ltd v Spjeldnaes (No. 2)*, (above). In *Banca Carige v Banco Nacional de Cuba* [2001] B.P.I.R. 407 Lightman J. stressed that leave is required in order to serve a s. 423 claim abroad.

424 Those who may apply for an order under s. 423

424(1) **[Conditions for s. 423 application]** An application for an order under section 423 shall not be made in relation to a transaction except–

(a) in a case where the debtor has been adjudged bankrupt or is a body corporate which is being wound up or is in administration, by the official receiver, by the trustee of the bankrupt's estate or the liquidator or administrator of the body corporate or (with the leave of the court) by a victim of the transaction;

(b) in a case where a victim of the transaction is bound by a voluntary arrangement approved under Part I or Part VIII of this Act, by the supervisor of the voluntary arrangement or by any person who (whether or not so bound) is such a victim; or

(c) in any other case, by a victim of the transaction.

424(2) **[Treatment of application]** An application made under any of the paragraphs of subsection (1) is to be treated as made on behalf of every victim of the transaction.

GENERAL NOTE

These provisions explain who may make a s. 423 application. A minor textual change to subs. (1)(a) was made by Sch. 17 to EA 2002. Note the leave requirement is s. 424(1)(a). As to whether leave can be granted retrospectively see the discussion in *Dora v Simper* [2000] 2 B.C.L.C. 561. If the person entering into the transaction was a company, then it may be challenged under this provision by the liquidator or administrator. If it was an individual, then the official receiver or trustee may bring the proceedings. Supervisors of voluntary arrangements may also apply in certain cases (most avoidance provisions are not available in the cases of a company or individual voluntary arrangement), as may "victims" (for definition see s. 423(5)), who may bring an action either individually or in a representative capacity. See *Moon v Franklin* [1996] B.P.I.R. 196 for an example of a victim making the application. A creditor of an insolvent company can be a victim: *Re Ayala Holdings Ltd* [1993] B.C.L.C. 256. See also *Pinewood Joinery v Starelm Properties Ltd* [1994] B.C.C. 569.

Note that the FSA may apply in an appropriate case – FSMA 2000, s. 375.

425 Provision which may be made by order under s. 423

425(1) [Scope of order] Without prejudice to the generality of section 423, an order made under that section with respect to a transaction may (subject as follows)–

(a) require any property transferred as part of the transaction to be vested in any person, either absolutely or for the benefit of all the persons on whose behalf the application for the order is treated as made;

(b) require any property to be so vested if it represents, in any person's hands, the application either of the proceeds of sale of property so transferred or of money so transferred;

(c) release or discharge (in whole or in part) any security given by the debtor;

(d) require any person to pay to any other person in respect of benefits received from the debtor such sums as the court may direct;

(e) provide for any surety or guarantor whose obligations to any person were released or discharged (in whole or in part) under the transaction to be under such new or revived obligations as the court thinks appropriate;

(f) provide for security to be provided for the discharge of any obligation imposed by or arising under the order, for such an obligation to be charged on any property and for such security or charge to have the same priority as a security or charge released or discharged (in whole or in part) under the transaction.

425(2) [Limit to order] An order under section 423 may affect the property of, or impose any obligation on, any person whether or not he is the person with whom the debtor entered into the transaction; but such an order–

(a) shall not prejudice any interest in property which was acquired from a person other than the debtor and was acquired in good faith, for value and without notice of the relevant circumstances, or prejudice any interest deriving from such an interest, and

(b) shall not require a person who received a benefit from the transaction in good faith, for value and without notice of the relevant circumstances to pay any sum unless he was a party to the transaction.

425(3) [Relevant circumstances] For the purposes of this section the relevant circumstances in relation to a transaction are the circumstances by virtue of which an order under section 423 may be made in respect of the transaction.

425(4) ["Security"] In this section **"security"** means any mortgage, charge, lien or other security.

S. 425(1)
This gives illustrations of the types of order the court may make under s. 423. This is similar to s. 241(1) and 342(1), but with the omission of para. (g). A declaration was the basis of the relief granted in *Moon v Franklin* [1996] B.P.I.R. 196. Interim relief may be available: *Aiglon Ltd v Gau Shan Co. Ltd* [1993] 1 Lloyd's Rep. 164. For an order given extra-territorial effect see *Jyske Bank (Gibraltar) Ltd v Spjeldnaes (No. 2)* [1999] B.P.I.R. 525. Note the limitation imposed on any relief by POCA 2002, s. 419.

S. 425(2), (3)
Although third-party rights may be affected, there is protection for bona fide purchasers, for value and without notice, who have taken without notice of the relevant circumstances, as defined by s. 425(3). The relief granted in *Arbuthnot Leasing International Ltd v Havelet Leasing Ltd (No. 2)* [1990] B.C.C. 636 (see the note to s. 423, above) took the form of an order that the assets improperly transferred should be held on trust for the transferor, but without prejudice to the claims of those who had become creditors of the transferee since the date of the transfer. In *Chohan v Saggar* [1994] B.C.C. 134 the Court of Appeal considered the aim of an order under s. 425. Although the order should seek to restore the original pre-transaction position, sometimes the need to protect third parties may prevent a complete restoration. Partial invalidation of transactions may therefore be the best answer to the problem of balancing the competing interests of creditors and bona fide third parties.

S. 425(4)
This is an interpretation provision relevant to s. 425(1)(c) and (f).

PART XVII

MISCELLANEOUS AND GENERAL

426 Co-operation between courts exercising jurisdiction in relation to insolvency

426(1) **[Enforcement in other parts of UK]** An order made by a court in any part of the United Kingdom in the exercise of jurisdiction in relation to insolvency law shall be enforced in any other part of the United Kingdom as if it were made by a court exercising the corresponding jurisdiction in that other part.

426(2) **[Limit to s. 426(1)]** However, without prejudice to the following provisions of this section, nothing in subsection (1) requires a court in any part of the United Kingdom to enforce, in relation to property situated in that part, any order made by a court in any other part of the United Kingdom.

426(3) **[Order by Secretary of State]** The Secretary of State, with the concurrence in relation to property situated in England and Wales of the Lord Chancellor, may by order make provision for securing that a trustee or assignee under the insolvency law of any part of the United Kingdom has, with such modifications as may be specified in the order, the same rights in relation to any property situated in another part of the United Kingdom as he would have in the corresponding circumstances if he were a trustee or assignee under the insolvency law of that other part.

426(4) **[Assistance between courts]** The courts having jurisdiction in relation to insolvency law in any part of the United Kingdom shall assist the courts having the corresponding jurisdiction in any other part of the United Kingdom or any relevant country or territory.

426(5) **[Request under s. 426(4)]** For the purposes of subsection (4) a request made to a court in any part of the United Kingdom by a court in any other part of the United Kingdom or in a relevant country or territory is authority for the court to which the request is made to apply, in relation to any matters specified in the request, the insolvency law which is applicable by either court in relation to comparable matters falling within its jurisdiction. In exercising its discretion under this subsection, a court shall have regard in particular to the rules of private international law.

426(6) **[Claim by trustee or assignee]** Where a person who is a trustee or assignee under the insolvency law of any part of the United Kingdom claims property situated in any other part of the United Kingdom (whether by virtue of an order under subsection (3) or otherwise), the submission of that claim to the court exercising jurisdiction in relation to insolvency law in that other part shall be treated in the same manner as a request made by a court for the purpose of subsection (4).

426(7) **[Application of Criminal Law Act]** Section 38 of the Criminal Law Act 1977 (execution of warrant of arrest throughout the United Kingdom) applies to a warrant which, in exercise of any jurisdiction in relation to insolvency law, is issued in any part of the United Kingdom for the arrest of a person as it applies to a warrant issued in that part of the United Kingdom for the arrest of a person charged with an offence.

426(8) **[Powers in subordinate legislation]** Without prejudice to any power to make rules of court, any power to make provision by subordinate legislation for the purpose of giving effect in relation to companies or individuals to the insolvency law of any part of the United Kingdom includes power to make provision for the purpose of giving effect in that part to any provision made by or under the preceding provisions of this section.

426(9) **[S. 426(3) order by statutory instrument etc.]** An order under subsection (3) shall be made by statutory instrument subject to annulment in pursuance of a resolution of either House of Parliament.

426(10) **["Insolvency law"]** In this section **"insolvency law"** means–

(a) in relation to England and Wales, provision extending to England and Wales and made by or under this Act or sections 1A, 6 to 10, 12 to 15, 19(c) and 20 (with Schedule 1) of the Company Directors Disqualification Act 1986 and sections 1 to 17 of that Act as they apply for the purposes of those provisions of that Act;

(b) in relation to Scotland, provision extending to Scotland and made by or under this Act, sections 6 to 10, 12, 15, 19(c) and 20 (with Schedule 1) of the Company Directors Disqualification Act 1986 and sections 1 to 17 of that Act as they apply for the purposes of those provisions of that Act, Part XVIII of the Companies Act or the Bankruptcy (Scotland) Act 1985;

(c) in relation to Northern Ireland, provision made by or under the Insolvency (Northern Ireland) Order 1989 or the Company Directors Disqualification (Northern Ireland) Order 2002;

(d) in relation to any relevant country or territory, so much of the law of that country or territory as corresponds to provisions falling within any of the foregoing paragraphs;

and references in this subsection to any enactment include, in relation to any time before the coming into force of that enactment the corresponding enactment in force at that time.

426(11) **["Relevant country or territory"]** In this section **"relevant country or territory"** means–

(a) any of the Channel Islands or the Isle of Man, or

(b) any country or territory designated for the purposes of this section by the Secretary of State by order made by statutory instrument.

426(12) **[Application to Northern Ireland]** In the application of this section to Northern Ireland–

(a) for any reference to the Secretary of State there is substituted a reference to the Department of Economic Development in Northern Ireland;

(b) in subsection (3) for the words "another part of the United Kingdom" and the words " that other part" there is substituted the words "Northern Ireland";

(c) for subsection (9) there is substituted the following subsection–

"(9) An order made under subsection (3) by the Department of Economic Development in Northern Ireland shall be a statutory rule for the purposes of the Statutory Rules (Northern Ireland) Order 1979 and shall be subject to negative resolution within the meaning of section 41(6) of the Interpretation Act (Northern Ireland) 1954."

GENERAL NOTE

The Cork *Report*, Ch. 49, called for the rationalisation and improvement of co-operation between the insolvency courts in the UK. This section represents a step in that direction. However there are problems of interpretation particularly concerned with the freedom of action enjoyed by the English courts and these have troubled the judiciary in a number of recent cases discussed below.

A number of countries and territories were designated for the purposes of s. 426 by the Co-operation of Insolvency Courts (Designation of Relevant Countries and Territories) Order 1986 (SI 1986/2123), effective December 29, 1986. These were: Anguilla, Australia, the Bahamas, Bermuda, Botswana, Canada, Cayman Islands, Falkland Islands, Gibraltar, Hong Kong, the Republic of Ireland, Montserrat, New Zealand, St Helena, Turks and Caicos Islands, Tuvalu and the Virgin Islands. Malaysia and South Africa were added by SI 1996/253. Brunei was included by SI 1998/2766. In consequence, the courts of these countries and territories have the right to request assistance in matters of insolvency from courts having jurisdiction in insolvency in any part of the UK.

Subsections (4), (5), (10) and (11) of s. 426 were extended to the Bailiwick of Guernsey by the Insolvency Act 1986 (Guernsey) Order 1989 (SI 1989/2409), with the modifications specified in the Schedule to that Order, as from February

1, 1990. Accordingly, a co-operative insolvency regime is now established between Guernsey (including Alderney and Sark) and the UK.

Note the modifications to s. 426(10) by para. 16(3) of Sch. 4 to the Insolvency Act 2000.

In relation to the financial markets (see the note on p. 2), the provisions of s. 426 are subject to the limitations set out in CA 1989, s. 183. Part XVII applies to limited liability partnerships by virtue of the Limited Liability Partnerships Regulations 2001 (SI 2001/1090), reg. 5(1)(b) as from April 6, 2001 subject to reg. 5(2) and (3).

In future s. 426 will have to be read alongside s. 14 IA 2000 and regulations made thereunder. Section 14 permits the Secretary of State to sign up to the UNICITRAL Model Law on Cross-Border Insolvency Proceedings and to modify existing rules (including s. 426). On an EU level judicial comity in insolvency matters is to be promoted by EC Council Regulation 1346/2000 on insolvency proceedings. See the discussion at pp. 598, 602 in this work.

S. 426(1), (2)
This allows for general enforcement of court orders throughout the UK, although there are limitations expressed with regard to enforcement of court orders against property in different parts of the UK.

S. 426(3), (9)
Assimilation of the powers of a trustee, etc. in the different UK jurisdictions is provided for here. The Secretary of State may use statutory instruments to do this.

S. 426(4), (5), (11)
The UK courts must on a matter of insolvency law co-operate with each other, and indeed with courts from the Isle of Man, Channel Isles or from any jurisdiction specified by the Secretary of State. These provisions permit the court to offer assistance to courts in other parts of the UK or in other "relevant" countries, as defined in s. 426(11). With the increased incidence of cross-border insolvency in recent years the UK courts have increasingly been faced with requests for assistance. For a review of this jurisdiction see Smart (1996) 112 L.Q.R. 397; (1998) 114 L.Q.R. 46 and Fletcher [1997] J.B.L. 470.

In spite of the apparent statutory obligation to lend assistance the Court of Appeal confirmed in *Hughes v Hannover-Rucksversicherungs AG* [1997] B.C.C. 921 that the court continues to enjoy discretion in such applications and may think it appropriate to reject the request for assistance. Indeed it chose this course of action in that particular case because the circumstances had changed materially since the date of the request. In *Re Focus Insurance Co. Ltd* [1996] B.C.C. 659 Scott V.-C. refused assistance to foreign liquidators who had successfully petitioned for the respondent to be bankrupted in England. To offer the assistance sought would involve complicating and possibly undermining the English bankruptcy which the applicants themselves had initiated. Again in *Re J N Taylor Pty Ltd* [1998] B.P.I.R. 347 the primary request for assistance was also rejected because to have acceded to it would result in company officers being subjected to examination by an Australian liquidator in circumstances where no such examination would have been permitted under English law. This decision must be of questionable authority in view of the later Court of Appeal ruling in *England v Smith (Re Southern Equities Corp.)* [2001] Ch. 419 [2000] B.P.I.R. 28. Here it was held that the policy of judicial comity was the starting point on any s. 426 request. Thus it was possible for the English courts to accede to a request to interview a party under the machinery of Australian insolvency law even though such an interview would not have been allowed had this been an entirely domestic case. Differences in the substantive law between nations on individual statutory provisions did not necessarily mean that one system was fairer than another. The whole picture required consideration. Subsequently, a similar approach was taken by Jonathan Parker J. in *Duke Group Ltd v Carver* [2001] B.P.I.R. 459 where an Australian judge was permitted to examine a witness in England pursuant to Australian law. The point was made that it would require something extraordinary to refuse a request for assistance and it was not for the English courts to water down the assistance requested. In *Re Trading Partners Ltd* [2002] B.P.I.R. 605 Patten J. acceded to a request from the courts of the British Virgin Islands to allow liquidators of a company to take advantage of s. 236 of IA 1986 in order to gain access to documents in the possession of administrative receivers of a related company. In *Re Television Trade Rentals Ltd* [2002] EWHC 211 (Ch), s. 426 was used to apply the CVA procedure to companies incorporated in the Isle of Man. A request to do this retrospectively was refused.

When considering whether to offer assistance the court has a range of options available. According to the Court of Appeal in *Hughes v Hannover-Rucksversicherungs AG* (above) the courts can apply their own inherent general jurisdiction, substantive English insolvency law or the substantive insolvency law of the foreign jurisdiction insofar as it is consistent with English law.

An order was made under s. 426(4) in the case of *Re Dallhold Estates (UK) Pty Ltd* [1992] B.C.C. 394. Here the courts of Western Australia sought help from the English courts to protect the assets of an Australian company having property in this jurisdiction. Although it seems that it is not possible for the English courts to grant an administration order in respect of a foreign company on their own initiative they can in effect do this if they receive a request under s. 426. Accordingly the administration order was granted. In *Re Bank of Credit and Commerce International SA* [1993]

B.C.C. 787 Rattee J. held that when faced with a request for assistance (in this case from the Grand Court of the Cayman Islands) the English courts were not restricted to rendering applicable procedural facilities of English law but could also declare principles of substantive English insolvency law applicable in the particular case. In *Re Business City Express Ltd* [1997] B.C.C. 826 relief was offered by Rattee J. to facilitate a rescue plan mounted by the examiner of an Irish company. Although the request involved some departure from normal distribution rules on insolvency the circumstances were such as to justify this on utilitarian grounds.

S. 426(6)
This subsection allows trustees, etc. to claim property situated in other parts of the UK by calling on the assistance of the courts where the property is situated.

S. 426(7)
This applies s. 38 of the Criminal Law Act 1977 to warrants for arrest in connection with insolvency law matters.

S. 426(8)
Delegated legislation can be used to achieve the aim of co-operation as contained in s. 426: see the Co-operation of Insolvency Courts (Designation of Relevant Countries and Territories) Order 1986 (SI 1986/2123).

S. 426(10), (11), (12)
These provisions define "insolvency law" and "relevant country or territory" for the purposes of this section and these definitions are exhaustive: see *Hughes v Hannover-Rucksversicherungs AG* [1997] B.C.C. 921 here. Provision is also made for Northern Ireland. Subsection (10) was amended and subs. (12) added by Sch. 9 to the Insolvency (Northern Ireland) Order 1989 (SI 1989/2045 (NI 19)).

426A Disqualification from Parliament (England and Wales)

426A(1) [**Bankruptcy restrictions order**] A person in respect of whom a bankruptcy restrictions order has effect shall be disqualified–

(a)   from membership of the House of Commons,

(b)   from sitting or voting in the House of Lords, and

(c)   from sitting or voting in a committee of the House of Lords or a joint committee of both Houses.

426A(2) [**MP to vacate seat**] If a member of the House of Commons becomes disqualified under this section, his seat shall be vacated.

426A(3) [**Election return void**] If a person who is disqualified under this section is returned as a member of the House of Commons, his return shall be void.

426A(4) [**No writ to member of House of Lords**] No writ of summons shall be issued to a member of the House of Lords who is disqualified under this section.

426A(5) [**Notification of Speaker of bankruptcy restrictions order**] If a court makes a bankruptcy restrictions order or interim order in respect of a member of the House of Commons or the House of Lords the court shall notify the Speaker of that House.

426A(6) [**Notification of Speaker of bankruptcy restrictions undertaking**] If the Secretary of State accepts a bankruptcy restrictions undertaking made by a member of the House of Commons or the House of Lords, the Secretary of State shall notify the Speaker of that House.

GENERAL NOTE

Sections 426A–C were introduced by s. 266 of EA 2002 as part of a policy of removing automatic restrictions from the shoulders of bankrupts. This policy has lead to the removal of the automatic bar on being a JP (see EA 2002, s. 265), a local government member (EA 2002, s. 267) and to the introduction of a general power to relax such disqualifications (EA 2002, s. 268). Section 426A addresses specifically the position of MPs and members of the House of Lords. These sections take effect in April 2004.

S. 426A(1)
Those individuals who are the subject of a BRO or BRU are disqualified from Parliament.

S. 426A(2)–(4)
These provisions amplify the consequences of disqualification.

S. 426A(5), (6)
This imposes an additional obligation on a court making a BRO or interim order or on the Secretary of State accepting a BRU. It is unlikely to be onerous in view of the rarity of the situation.

426B Devolution

426B(1) [Bankruptcy restrictions order in Scotland, Northern Ireland, Wales] If a court makes a bankruptcy restrictions order or interim order in respect of a member of the Scottish Parliament, the Northern Ireland Assembly or the National Assembly for Wales, the court shall notify the presiding officer of that body.

426B(2) [Bankruptcy restrictions undertaking in Scotland, Northern Ireland, Wales] If the Secretary of State accepts a bankruptcy restrictions undertaking made by a member of the Scottish Parliament, the Northern Ireland Assembly or the National Assembly for Wales, the Secretary of State shall notify the presiding officer of that body.

S. 426B(1), (2)
These make special provision for disqualification attendant upon a BRO or BRU or interim order granted in respect of a member of a dissolved assembly.

426C Irrelevance of privilege

426C(1) [No effect of Parliamentary privilege on insolvency enactment] An enactment about insolvency applies in relation to a member of the House of Commons or the House of Lords irrespective of any Parliamentary privilege.

426C(2) ["Enactment"] In this section "enactment" includes a provision made by or under–

(a) an Act of the Scottish Parliament, or

(b) Northern Ireland legislation.

S. 426C(1), (2)
Parliamentary privilege does not protect Members of Parliament, etc., from the consequences of insolvency prescribed by legislation.

427 Parliamentary disqualification

427(1) [Disqualification of bankrupt] Where a court in Northern Ireland adjudges an individual bankrupt or a court in Scotland awards sequestration of an individual's estate, the individual is disqualified–

(a) for sitting or voting in the House of Lords,

(b) for being elected to, or sitting or voting in, the House of Commons, and

(c) for sitting or voting in a committee of either House.

427(2) [When disqualification ceases] Where an individual is disqualified under this section, the disqualification ceases–

(a) except where the adjudication is annulled or the award recalled or reduced without the individual having been first discharged, on the discharge of the individual, and

(b) in the excepted case, on the annulment, recall or reduction, as the case may be.

427(3) [Disqualified peer] No writ of summons shall be issued to any lord of Parliament who is for the time being disqualified under this section for sitting and voting in the House of Lords.

427(4) [Disqualified MP] Where a member of the House of Commons who is disqualified under this section continues to be so disqualified until the end of the period of 6 months beginning with the day of the adjudication or award, his seat shall be vacated at the end of that period.

427(5) **[Certification of s. 427(1) award etc.]** A court which makes an adjudication or award such as is mentioned in subsection (1) in relation to any lord of Parliament or member of the House of Commons shall forthwith certify the adjudication or award to the Speaker of the House of Lords or, as the case may be, to the Speaker of the House of Commons.

427(6) **[Further certification after s. 427(5)]** Where a court has certified an adjudication or award to the Speaker of the House of Commons under subsection (5), then immediately after it becomes apparent which of the following certificates is applicable, the court shall certify to the Speaker of the House of Commons–

(a) that the period of 6 months beginning with the day of the adjudication or award has expired without the adjudication or award having been annulled, recalled or reduced, or

(b) that the adjudication or award has been annulled, recalled or reduced before the end of that period.

427(6A) **[Members of the Scottish Parliament]** Subsections (4) to (6) have effect in relation to a member of the Scottish Parliament but as if–

(a) references to the House of Commons were to the Parliament and references to the Speaker were to the Presiding Officer, and

(b) in subsection (4), for "under this section" there were substituted "under section 15(1)(b) of the Scotland Act 1998 by virtue of this section".

427(6B) **[Members of the National Assembly for Wales]** Subsections (4) to (6) have effect in relation to a member of the National Assembly for Wales but as if–

(a) references to the House of Commons were to the Assembly and references to the Speaker were to the presiding officer, and

(b) in subsection (4), for "under this section" there were substituted "under section 12(2) of the Government of Wales Act 1998 by virtue of this section".

427(6C) **[Members of the Northern Ireland Assembly]** Subsection (1), as applied to a member of the Northern Ireland Assembly by virtue of section 36(4) of the Northern Ireland Act 1998, has effect as if "or Northern Ireland" were omitted; and subsections (4) to (6) have effect in relation to such a member as if–

(a) references to the House of Commons were to the Assembly and references to the Speaker were to the Presiding Officer; and

(b) in subsection (4), for "under this section" there were substituted "under section 36(4) of the Northern Ireland Act 1998 by virtue of this section".

427(7) **[Repealed by EA 2002, s.266(2) with effect from April 1, 2004]**

S. 427(1), (2)
Where a person has been adjudged bankrupt in Scotland or Northern Ireland he is disqualified from both Houses of Parliament until he is discharged or the order is annulled. Similar provision is made for Scotland and Northern Ireland. Local government councillors face a similar bar: Local Government Act 1972, s. 80. The former reference to England and Wales was dropped by EA 2002, s. 266(2).

S. 427(3)
A writ of summons must not be issued in respect of any person so disqualified who is a member of the House of Lords.

S. 427(4)
A Member of Parliament who is so disqualified has six months to vacate his seat.

S. 427(5), (6)
Where a court makes a bankruptcy order, etc., the Speaker of the appropriate House of Parliament must be notified. Further, the court must notify the Speaker of the Commons of the elapse of the six-month period mentioned in s. 427(4) or of any annulment in the meantime.

S. 427(6A), (6B), (6C)
These subsections were inserted respectively by the Scotland Act 1998, s. 125(1) and Sch. 8, para. 23 as from November 19, 1998, the Government of Wales Act 1998, ss. 125, 158(1) and Sch. 12, para. 24 as from April 1, 1999 and the Northern Ireland Act, in order to take account of the devolution of legislative powers to the regional assemblies.

S. 427(7)
Repealed by EA 2002, s. 266(2). Its text ran as follows:

427(7) [Application of relevant law to peer or MP] Subject to the preceding provisions of this section, so much of this Act and any other enactment (whenever passed) and of any subordinate legislation (whenever made) as–

(a) makes provision for or in connection with bankruptcy in one or more parts of the United Kingdom, or

(b) makes provision conferring a power of arrest in connection with the winding up or insolvency of companies in one or more parts of the United Kingdom,

applies in relation to persons having privilege of Parliament or peerage as it applies in relation to persons not having such privilege.

428 Exemptions from Restrictive Trade Practices Act

428(1, 2) **[Repealed]**

428(3) **["Insolvency services"]** In this section **"insolvency services"** means the services of persons acting as insolvency practitioners or carrying out under the law of Northern Ireland functions corresponding to those mentioned in section 388(1) or (2) in Part XIII, in their capacity as such.

GENERAL NOTE

Formerly s. 428 sought to exclude agreements relating to fees charged for insolvency services, etc. being made subject to the Restrictive Trade Practices Act 1976, especially Pt III of that Act. Schedule 14 also adds insolvency services to the list of exempt services described in Sch. 1 to the Restrictive Trade Practices Act 1976, such as legal services, medical services, accountancy services and many other professional services. This is in accord with the general policy of the Act, and in particular Pt XIII, which requires insolvency practitioners to be professionals. The Restrictive Trade Practices Act was repealed by the Competition Act 1998 which introduced a new competition regime on the intended date of March 1, 2000.

429 Disabilities on revocation of administration order against an individual

429(1) **[Application]** The following applies where a person fails to make any payment which he is required to make by virtue of an administration order under Part VI of the County Courts Act 1984.

429(2) **[Power of court]** The court which is administering that person's estate under the order may, if it thinks fit–

(a) revoke the administration order, and

(b) make an order directing that this section and section 12 of the Company Directors Disqualification Act 1986 shall apply to the person for such period, not exceeding 1 year, as may be specified in the order.

429(3) **[Restrictions]** A person to whom this section so applies shall not–

(a) either alone or jointly with another person, obtain credit to the extent of the amount prescribed for the purposes of section 360(1)(a) or more, or

(b) enter into any transaction in the course of or for the purposes of any business in which he is directly or indirectly engaged,

without disclosing to the person from whom he obtains the credit, or (as the case may be) with whom the transaction is entered into, the fact that this section applies to him.

429(4) **[Person obtaining credit]** The reference in subsection (3) to a person obtaining credit includes–

(a) a case where goods are bailed or hired to him under a hire-purchase agreement or agreed to be sold to him under a conditional sale agreement, and

(b) a case where he is paid in advance (whether in money or otherwise) for the supply of goods or services.

429(5) **[Penalty]** A person who contravenes this section is guilty of an offence and liable to imprisonment or a fine, or both.

S. 429(1)
This section applies where a debtor has failed to comply with his obligations under an administration order granted under Pt VI of the County Courts Act 1984 (as amended by s. 13 of the Courts and Legal Services Act 1990). (Note that this type of administration order, which is granted against an individual, must be distinguished from the new regime established by Pt II of IA 1986 enabling an administration order to be made against a company which is insolvent or near-insolvent).

S. 429(2)–(4)
The court has discretion to revoke the administration order and instead apply the following restrictions for a maximum period of one year – subs. (2)(b) was changed by Sch. 23, EA 2002 by the substitution of one year for two years. Prior to IA 1985 there was a similar provision in IA 1976, s. 11, allowing for the revocation of administration orders and substitution of receiving orders. The new restrictions are more flexible.

The restrictions that may be imposed by the court where an administration order is revoked are then outlined. Thus, the debtor can be banned from acting as company director, liquidator or promoter, etc. (see CDDA 1986, s. 12(2)). Furthermore, he can be made subject to restrictions which are similar to the s. 360 curbs – *e.g.* restrictions on obtaining credit (widely defined by s. 429(4)), or, indeed, entering into business transactions without disclosing his true status. The Cork Committee (*Report*, para. 317) was in favour of such restrictions.

S. 429(5)
The sanctions for the breach of this provision are the same as for contravening s. 360: see s. 430 and Sch. 10.

430 Provision introducing Schedule of punishments

430(1) **[Sch. 10]** Schedule 10 to this Act has effect with respect to the way in which offences under this Act are punishable on conviction.

430(2) **[First, second and third columns of Schedule]** In relation to an offence under a provision of this Act specified in the first column of the Schedule (the general nature of the offence being described in the second column), the third column shows whether the offence is punishable on conviction on indictment, or on summary conviction, or either in the one way or the other.

430(3) **[Fourth column]** The fourth column of the Schedule shows, in relation to an offence, the maximum punishment by way of fine or imprisonment under this Act which may be imposed on a person convicted of the offence in the way specified in relation to it in the third column (that is to say, on indictment or summarily), a reference to a period of years or months being to a term of imprisonment of that duration.

430(4) **[Fifth column]** The fifth column shows (in relation to an offence for which there is an entry in that column) that a person convicted of the offence after continued contravention is liable to a daily default fine; that is to say, he is liable on a second or subsequent conviction of the offence to the fine specified in that column for each day on which the contravention is continued (instead of the penalty specified for the offence in the fourth column of the Schedule).

430(5) **["Officer who is in default"]** For the purpose of any enactment in this Act whereby an officer of a company who is in default is liable to a fine or penalty, the expression **"officer who is in default"** means any officer of the company who knowingly and wilfully authorises or permits the default, refusal or contravention mentioned in the enactment.

S. 430(1)
This directs the reader to Sch. 10 for a comprehensive list of punishments for offences created by the Act. For offences under the rules and their punishment see IR 1986, r. 12.21 and Sch. 5.

S. 430(2)–(4)
These subsections provide a guide to the use of Sch. 10. This schedule is similar in form to CA 1985, Sch. 24.

S. 430(5)
This defines the common phrase "officer who is in default" in the same terms as CA 1985, s. 730(5).

431 Summary proceedings

431(1) **[Taking of summary proceedings]** Summary proceedings for any offence under any of Parts I to VII of this Act may (without prejudice to any jurisdiction exercisable apart from this subsection) be taken against a body corporate at any place at which the body has a place of business, and against any other person at any place at which he is for the time being.

431(2) **[Time for laying information]** Notwithstanding anything in section 127(1) of the Magistrates' Courts Act 1980, an information relating to such an offence which is triable by a magistrates' court in England and Wales may be so tried if it is laid at any time within 3 years after the commission of the offence and within 12 months after the date on which evidence sufficient in the opinion of the Director of Public Prosecutions or the Secretary of State (as the case may be) to justify the proceedings comes to his knowledge.

431(3) **[Time for commencement of summary proceedings in Scotland]** Summary proceedings in Scotland for such an offence shall not be commenced after the expiration of 3 years from the commission of the offence. Subject to this (and notwithstanding anything in section 136 of the Criminal Procedure (Scotland) Act 1995), such proceedings may (in Scotland) be commenced at any time within 12 months after the date on which evidence sufficient in the Lord Advocate's opinion to justify the proceedings came to his knowledge or, where such evidence was reported to him by the Secretary of State, within 12 months after the date on which it came to the knowledge of the latter; and subsection (3) of that section applies for the purpose of this subsection as it applies for the purpose of that section.

431(4) **[Certificate by DPP et al. conclusive evidence]** For the purposes of this section, a certificate of the Director of Public Prosecutions, the Lord Advocate or the Secretary of State (as the case may be) as to the date on which such evidence as is referred to above came to his knowledge is conclusive evidence.

S. 431(1), (2), (4)
These subsections regulate summary proceedings under this Act in England and Wales. The phrase "a place of business" is much wider than "an established place of business", which is the formula used in CA 1985, s. 409, for example.

S. 431(3), (4)
Summary proceedings in Scotland are provided for.

432 Offences by bodies corporate

432(1) **[Application]** This section applies to offences under this Act other than those excepted by subsection (4).

432(2) **[Consent or connivance of various persons]** Where a body corporate is guilty of an offence to which this section applies and the offence is proved to have been committed with the consent or connivance of, or to be attributable to any neglect on the part of, any director, manager, secretary or other similar officer of the body corporate or any person who was purporting to act in any such capacity he, as well as the body corporate, is guilty of the offence and liable to be proceeded against and punished accordingly.

432(3) **[Where affairs managed by members]** Where the affairs of a body corporate are managed by its members, subsection (2) applies in relation to the acts and defaults of a member in connection with his functions of management as if he were a director of the body corporate.

432(4) **[Offences excepted]** The offences excepted from this section are those under sections 30, 39, 51, 53, 54, 62, 64, 66, 85, 89, 164, 188, 201, 206, 207, 208, 209, 210 and 211 and those under paragraphs 16(2), 17(3)(a), 18(3)(a), 19(3)(a), 22(1) and 23(1)(a) of Schedule A1.

S. 432(1)–(3)

Here there is a repetition of CA 1985, s. 733. Where an offence under this Act has been committed by a body corporate, any officer who was a party to or responsible for the offence is subject to criminal liability, as well as the body corporate. *De facto* officers are similarly liable. "Body corporate" is not defined for the purposes of this Part of IA 1986; the definition contained in CA 1985, s. 740 applies only to Pts I–VII (see s. 251). It is therefore likely that a Scottish firm and a foreign corporation would be within the scope of this provision, even though they are not within s. 740.

S. 432(3)

Some corporations, and in particular some incorporated by Royal Charter, have no body equivalent to a board of directors and are managed by their members. This is also true of a Scottish firm, if it is within the present provision. In such cases the members may incur personal liability under this section.

S. 432(4)

Offences under certain named sections of the Act are excluded from the operation of s. 432. Note the addition made by IA 2000, Sch. 1.

433 Admissibility in evidence of statements of affairs, etc.

433(1) [General rule on admissibility of statements] In any proceedings (whether or not under this Act)–

(a) a statement of affairs prepared for the purposes of any provision of this Act which is derived from the Insolvency Act 1985, and

(b) any other statement made in pursuance of a requirement imposed by or under any such provision or by or under rules made under this Act,

may be used in evidence against any person making or concurring in making the statement.

433(2) [Limits on use of statement in criminal proceedings] However, in criminal proceedings in which any such person is charged with an offence to which this subsection applies–

(a) no evidence relating to the statement may be adduced, and

(b) no question relating to it may be asked,

by or on behalf of the prosecution, unless evidence relating to it is adduced, or a question relating to it is asked, in the proceedings by or on behalf of that person.

433(3) [Offences to which s. 433(2) applies] Subsection (2) applies to any offence other than–

(a) an offence under section 22(6), 47(6), 48(8), 66(6), 67(8), 95(8), 98(6), 99(3)(a), 131(7), 192(2), 208(1)(a) or (d) or (2), 210, 235(5), 353(1), 354(1)(b) or (3) or 356(1) or 356(2)(a) or (b) or paragraph 4(3)(a) of Schedule 7;

(b) an offence which is–
   (i) created by rules made under this Act, and
   (ii) designated for the purposes of this subsection by such rules or by regulations made by the Secretary of State;

(c) an offence which is–
   (i) created by regulations made under any such rules, and
   (ii) designated for the purposes of this subsection by such regulations;

(d) an offence under section 1, 2 or 5 of the Perjury Act 1911 (false statements made on oath or made otherwise than on oath); or

(e) an offence under section 44(1) or (2) of the Criminal Law (Consolidation) (Scotland) Act 1995 (false statements made on oath or otherwise than on oath).

433(4) [Procedure for making regulations] Regulations under subsection (3)(b)(ii) shall be made by statutory instrument and, after being made, shall be laid before each House of Parliament.

GENERAL NOTE

Section 433 was expanded considerably by the addition of three new subss. (2)–(4) via the Youth Justice and Criminal Evidence Act 1999 (s. 59, 68(3) and Sch. 3 para. 7(2) and (3)) with effect from April 14, 2000.

S. 433(1)
This was in the original version of the 1986 Act and although renumbered it remains unamended. It declares that any statement of affairs or other statement made in pursuance of a requirement under the insolvency legislation may be used in evidence against the person making it. See *R. v Kansal* [1993] Q.B. 244; [1992] B.C.C. 615 and *Hamilton v Naviede (Re Arrows Ltd (No. 4)* [1995] 2 A.C. 75; [1994] B.C.C. 641. On the meaning of what is now s. 433(1)(b) see *R. v Sawtell* [2001] B.P.I.R. 381. This wide evidential provision became suspect in view of the ruling of the European Court of Human Rights in *Saunders v UK* (1997) 23 E.H.R.R. 313 on the oppressive usage of compelled evidence in criminal prosecutions. Hence the need for modification by the introduction of subss. (2)–(4) in the Youth Justice and Criminal Evidence Act 1999. Note also *R. v Faryab* [1999] B.P.I.R. 569. On reopening "safe" convictions see *R. v Kansal* [2001] UKHL 62, [2002] B.P.I.R. 370.

S. 433(2)–(4)
Significant limitations are placed by the new provisions introduced via the 1999 Act upon the use by the prosecution of evidence made available pursuant to subs. (1) in a whole range of prosecutions unless the offence falls within the list prescribed by subs. (3). This list may, according to subs. (4), be modified by delegated legislation. See *Attorney General's Reference (No. 7 of 2000)* [2001] EWCA Civ 888; [2001] 1 W.L.R. 1879.

434 Crown application

434 For the avoidance of doubt it is hereby declared that provisions of this Act which derive from the Insolvency Act 1985 bind the Crown so far as affecting or relating to the following matters, namely–

(a) remedies against, or against the property of, companies or individuals;

(b) priorities of debts;

(c) transactions at an undervalue or preferences;

(d) voluntary arrangements approved under Part I or Part VIII, and

(e) discharge from bankruptcy.

GENERAL NOTE

This section makes it clear that specified provisions of the Act, whether they relate to companies or individuals, bind the Crown. Indeed, certain sections are specifically designed to take away Crown privileges – *e.g.* s. 386 and Sch. 6.

PART XVIII

INTERPRETATION

435 Meaning of "associate"

435(1) [Determination of whether associate] For the purposes of this Act any question whether a person is an associate of another person is to be determined in accordance with the following provisions of this section (any provision that a person is an associate of another person being taken to mean that they are associates of each other).

435(2) [Associate of individual] A person is an associate of an individual if that person is the individual's husband or wife, or is a relative, or the husband or wife of a relative, of the individual or of the individual's husband or wife.

435(3) [Associate of partner] A person is an associate of any person with whom he is in partnership, and of the husband or wife or a relative of any individual with whom he is in partnership; and a Scottish firm is an associate of any person who is a member of the firm.

435(4) **[Associate of employee, employer]** A person is an associate of any person whom he employs or by whom he is employed.

435(5) **[Associate of trustee]** A person in his capacity as trustee of a trust other than–

(a) a trust arising under any of the second Group of Parts or the Bankruptcy (Scotland) Act 1985, or

(b) a pension scheme or an employees' share scheme (within the meaning of the Companies Act),

is an associate of another person if the beneficiaries of the trust include, or the terms of the trust confer a power that may be exercised for the benefit of, that other person or an associate of that other person.

435(6) **[Company associate of another company]** A company is an associate of another company–

(a) if the same person has control of both, or a person has control of one and persons who are his associates, or he and persons who are his associates, have control of the other, or

(b) if a group of two or more persons has control of each company, and the groups either consist of the same persons or could be regarded as consisting of the same persons by treating (in one or more cases) a member of either group as replaced by a person of whom he is an associate.

435(7) **[Company associate of another person]** A company is an associate of another person if that person has control of it or if that person and persons who are his associates together have control of it.

435(8) **[Person relative of individual]** For the purposes of this section a person is a relative of an individual if he is that individual's brother, sister, uncle, aunt, nephew, niece, lineal ancestor or lineal descendant, treating–

(a) any relationship of the half blood as a relationship of the whole blood and the stepchild or adopted child of any person as his child, and

(b) an illegitimate child as the legitimate child of his mother and reputed father;

and references in this section to a husband or wife include a former husband or wife and a reputed husband or wife.

435(9) **[Director employee]** For the purposes of this section any director or other officer of a company is to be treated as employed by that company.

435(10) **[Person with control]** For the purposes of this section a person is to be taken as having control of a company if–

(a) the directors of the company or of another company which has control of it (or any of them) are accustomed to act in accordance with his directions or instructions, or

(b) he is entitled to exercise, or control the exercise of, one third or more of the voting power at any general meeting of the company or of another company which has control of it;

and where two or more persons together satisfy either of the above conditions, they are to be taken as having control of the company.

435(11) **["Company"]** In this section **"company"** includes any body corporate (whether incorporated in Great Britain or elsewhere); and references to directors and other officers of a company and to voting power at any general meeting of a company have effect with any necessary modifications.

GENERAL NOTE

Part XVIII applies to limited liability partnerships by virtue of the Limited Liability Partnerships Regulations 2001 (SI 2001/1090), reg. 5(1)(b) as from April 6, 2001 subject to reg. 5(2) and (3).

Re application of Pt XVIII to insolvent partnerships, see the Insolvent Partnerships Order 1994 (SI 1994/2121), especially arts 10, 11, Sch. 7.

S. 435(1)
This is a new and complex provision defining the word "associate" for the purposes of the Act. It will be particularly relevant to ss. 314(6) and 340(5), and to the definition of "connected person" (s. 249), a term extensively used in Pts I–VII.

S. 435(2), (8)
Close family connections are sufficient to make one person an associate of another.

S. 435(3)
Partnership links with an individual, or his close family, are sufficient to give rise to an "associate" relationship.

S. 435(4)
Employers and employees are associates. However, see ss. 239(6), 240(1)(a), 340(5).

S. 435(5)
Certain trust relationships are caught by the net, where the insolvent or his or its associates could benefit from the trust.

S. 435(6), (7), (9)–(11)
These deal with the concept of "associate" in relation to companies (including companies incorporated outside Great Britain: see s. 435(11)). A company can become an associate if it is controlled by the person in question or by his associate. Control can be determined by reference to a third of voting power at shareholders' meetings or by whether the directors normally act in accordance with his instructions. Directors and officers are to be treated as being employed by their companies – this will be relevant in connection with s. 435(4).

436 Expressions used generally

436 In this Act, except in so far as the context otherwise requires (and subject to Parts VII and XI)–

"the appointed day" means the day on which this Act comes into force under section 443;

"associate" has the meaning given by section 435;

"business" includes a trade or profession;

"the Companies Act" means the Companies Act 1985;

"conditional sale agreement" and **"hire-purchase agreement"** have the same meanings as in the Consumer Credit Act 1974;

"the EC Regulation" means Council Regulation (EC) No. 1346/2000;

"modifications" includes additions, alterations and omissions and cognate expressions shall be construed accordingly;

"property" includes money, goods, things in action, land and every description of property wherever situated and also obligations and every description of interest, whether present or future or vested or contingent, arising out of, or incidental to, property;

"records" includes computer records and other non-documentary records;

"subordinate legislation" has the same meaning as in the Interpretation Act 1978; and

"transaction" includes a gift, agreement or arrangement, and references to entering into a transaction shall be construed accordingly.

GENERAL NOTE

This is general interpretation provision for the Act. It should be read in the light of Pts VII, XI and s. 435. Note that the general meaning given to words by s. 436 can be excluded where the context demands this.

The "appointed day" was December 29, 1986: see the note to s. 443.

The reference to the EC Regulation was inserted by the Insolvency Act 1986 (Amendment) Regulations 2002 (SI 2002/1037) reg. 4 with effect from May 3, 2002.

A company's interest as lessee under a lease of a chattel (an aircraft) was held to be "property" within the statutory definition contained in this section in *Bristol Airport plc v Powdrill; Re Paramount Airways Ltd* [1990] Ch. 744; [1990] B.C.C. 130. An expectation to receive a payment from the Criminal Injuries Compensation Board is not property: *Re a Bankrupt (No. 145 of 1995)* [1996] B.P.I.R. 238. Compare *Re Rae* [1995] B.C.C. 102 and *Performing Rights Society v Rowland* [1998] B.P.I.R. 128. In *Official Receiver v Environment Agency* [1999] B.P.I.R. 986 the Court of Appeal held that a waste management licence was property for the purposes of s. 436. In *Dear v Reeves* [2001] EWCA Civ 277, [2001] B.P.I.R. 577 a right of preemption was held to constitute "property" as were occupational benefits in *Patel v Jones* [2001] B.P.I.R. 919.

436A Proceedings under EC Regulation: modified definition of property

436A In the application of this Act to proceedings by virtue of Article 3 of the EC Regulation, a reference to property is a reference to property which may be dealt with in the proceedings.

GENERAL NOTE

Section 436A was inserted by Insolvency Act 1986 (Amendment) (No. 2) Regulations 2002 (SI 2002/1240) reg. 18 with effect from May 31, 2002. This limitation is needed to comply with the EC Regulation on Insolvency Proceedings, where the jurisdiction is sometimes restricted to local assets—see pp. 602 and 614–615 below.

PART XIX

FINAL PROVISIONS

437 Transitional provisions and savings

437 The transitional provisions and savings set out in Schedule 11 to this Act shall have effect, the Schedule comprising the following Parts–

> Part I: company insolvency and winding up (matters arising before appointed day, and continuance of proceedings in certain cases as before that day);

> Part II: individual insolvency (matters so arising, and continuance of bankruptcy proceedings in certain cases as before that day);

> Part III: transactions entered into before the appointed day and capable of being affected by orders of the court under Part XVI of this Act;

> Part IV: insolvency practitioners acting as such before the appointed day; and

> Part V: general transitional provisions and savings required consequentially on, and in connection with, the repeal and replacement by this Act and the Company Directors Disqualification Act 1986 of provisions of the Companies Act, the greater part of the Insolvency Act 1985 and other enactments.

GENERAL NOTE

This, coupled with Sch. 11, makes transitional provisions and savings.

The significant transitional provisions have been noted at the relevant places in the text.

438 Repeals

438 The enactments specified in the second column of Schedule 12 to this Act are repealed to the extent specified in the third column of that Schedule.

GENERAL NOTE

This section refers the reader to Sch. 12, which lists the provisions repealed by IA 1986. Included amongst the repeals are a large number of provisions in CA 1985, plus virtually the entirety of IA 1985. See also Sch. 4 to CDDA 1986.

439 Amendment of enactments

439(1) [Amendment of Companies Act] The Companies Act is amended as shown in Parts I and II of Schedule 13 to this Act, being amendments consequential on this Act and the Company Directors Disqualification Act 1986.

439(2) [Enactments in Sch. 14] The enactments specified in the first column of Schedule 14 to this Act (being enactments which refer, or otherwise relate, to those which are repealed and replaced by this Act or the Company Directors Disqualification Act 1986) are amended as shown in the second column of that Schedule.

439(3) [Consequential modifications of subordinate legislation] The Lord Chancellor may by order make such consequential modifications of any provision contained in any subordinate legislation made before the appointed day and such transitional provisions in connection with those modifications as appear to him necessary or expedient in respect of–

(a) any reference in that subordinate legislation to the Bankruptcy Act 1914;

(b) any reference in that subordinate legislation to any enactment repealed by Part III or IV of Schedule 10 to the Insolvency Act 1985; or

(c) any reference in that subordinate legislation to any matter provided for under the Act of 1914 or under any enactment so repealed.

439(4) [Order by statutory instrument etc.] An order under this section shall be made by statutory instrument subject to annulment in pursuance of a resolution of either House of Parliament.

S. 439(1), (2)
These subsections refer to Schs 13 and 14 which respectively make consequential amendments to CA 1985 and other legislation. Most of the consequential amendments of CA 1985 are purely minor textual changes. A new s. 196 of CA 1985 is enacted to apply the new preferential claims regime to the situation where the holder of a floating charge, instead of putting in a receiver, takes possession of the charged property. The consequential amendments effected by Sch. 14 are also of a minor nature.

440 Extent (Scotland)

440(1) [Extension to Scotland except where stated] Subject to the next subsection, provisions of this Act contained in the first Group of Parts extend to Scotland except where otherwise stated.

440(2) [Provisions not extending to Scotland] The following provisions of this Act do not extend to Scotland–

(a) in the first Groups of Parts–

section 43;

sections 238 to 241 ; and

section 246;

(b) the second Group of Parts;

(c) in the third Group of Parts–

sections 399 to 402,

sections 412, 413, 415, 415A(3), 418, 420 and 421,

sections 423 to 425, and

section 429(1) and (2); and

(d) in the Schedules–

Parts II and III of Schedule 11; and

Schedules 12 and 14 so far as they repeal or amend enactments which extend to England and Wales only.

GENERAL NOTE

This section identifies those provisions in IA 1986 which apply to Scotland. Most of the provisions on corporate insolvency apply equally to Scotland, except for certain receivership provisions (Scotland has its own receivership system in ss. 50–71), the rules on preferences and transactions at an undervalue (again the Scots have their own rules in ss. 242, 243 and also s. 246). The rules on personal insolvency do not apply to Scotland, which has its own system contained in the Bankruptcy (Scotland) Act 1985. Note also the Debt Arrangement and Attachment (Scotland) Act 2002. Bearing in mind this point, it is not surprising that certain named miscellaneous provisions in the Third Group of Parts and the Schedules do not operate north of the border. The reference to s. 415A(3) in subs. (2)(c) was added by EA 2002, s. 270(4).

441   Extent (Northern Ireland)

441(1)   [Provisions extending to Northern Ireland] The following provisions of this Act extend to Northern Ireland–

(a) sections 197, 426, 427 and 428; and

(b) so much of section 439 and Schedule 14 as relates to enactments which extend to Northern Ireland.

441(2)   [Most of provisions not extending to Northern Ireland] Subject as above, and to any provision expressly relating to companies incorporated elsewhere than in Great Britain, nothing in this Act extends to Northern Ireland or applies to or in relation to companies registered or incorporated in Northern Ireland.

GENERAL NOTE

The Act, generally speaking, does not apply to Northern Ireland, which has its own distinct systems of corporate and personal insolvency law. Certain exceptional provisions do apply in Northern Ireland, however – *e.g.* s. 426, which provides for co-operation between the various UK insolvency courts and s. 427, which deals with parliamentary disqualification.

However, legislation has since been enacted which has made the insolvency law of Northern Ireland broadly similar to that of England and Wales. New rules relating to the disqualification of company directors were introduced with effect from September 24, 1986 by the Companies (Northern Ireland) Order 1986 (SI 1986/1032 (NI 6)), and these have since been re-enacted and extended by Pt. II of the Companies (Northern Ireland) Order 1989 (SI 1989/2404 (NI 18)). In consequence, legislation equivalent to CDDA 1986 is now in place in Northern Ireland. The 1989 Order was brought into force with effect from October 1, 1991 by the Companies Act (1989 Order) (Commencement No. 2) Order (Northern Ireland) 1991 (SR 1991/410 (C 19)). The Insolvency (Northern Ireland) Order 1989 (SI 1989/2405 (NI 19)) is the counterpart for Northern Ireland of IA 1986. The object of the order is to bring the insolvency legislation, both personal and corporate, of that jurisdiction into line with that of England and Wales. This order was made on December 19, 1989, and was brought into operation in full on October 1, 1991 by the Insolvency (1989 Order) (Commencement No. 4) Order (Northern Ireland) 1991 (SR 1991/411 (C 20)). Previous Commencement Orders were of minimal impact. Note also SI 2002/3152, NI 6 (SR 2003/545 and SR 2003/546). Other provisions which have been put into force as part of the new insolvency regime in Northern Ireland include the Insolvency Practitioners (Recognised Practitioners) Regulations (Northern Ireland) 1991 (SR 1991/302 as amended by SR 2003/547); the Insolvency Rules (Northern Ireland) 1991 (SR 1991/364 as amended by SR 2000/247 and SR 2003/549), the Insolvency (Deposits) Order (Northern Ireland) 1991 (SR 1991/384), the Insolvency (Monetary Limits) Order (Northern Ireland) 1991 (SR 1991/386), the Insolvency (Fees) Order (Northern Ireland) 1991 (SR 1991/385), the Insolvency Regulations (Northern Ireland) 1991 (SR 1991/388) and the Financial Markets and Insolvency Regulations (Northern Ireland) 1991 (SR 1991/443), and the Insolvency Practitioners Order (Northern Ireland) 1995 (SR 1995/225, (as amended by SR 1996/472)). Note also Occupational and Personal Pension Schemes (Bankruptcy) Regulations (Northern Ireland) 2002 (SR 2002/127).

The IA 1994, which amended the law relating to the "adoption" of contracts of employment by administrators and administrative receivers, also amends the law applicable in Northern Ireland: see s. 4 of and Sch. 1 to that Act. There is also an Insolvent Partnerships (Northern Ireland) Order 1991 (SR 1991/366 most recently amended by SI 2003/144 and SR 2003/550) and specific regulations dealing with proceedings and reports arising out of the disqualification of directors (see SR 1991/367, 1991/368, 1991/413 and SR 2003/345–347). Administration of estates of deceased insolvents in Northern Ireland is covered by SR 1991/365. Many of these provisions have since been the subject of amending legislation: see, *e.g.* SR 1992/398, 1993/302, 1993/454, 1994/26, 1995/291, 1996/471, 1996/574–577, 1997/1072, SR 2002/334.

Section 441(2) was considered by the court in *Re Normandy Marketing Ltd* [1993] B.C.C. 879. Here it was held that s. 221 was wide enough to cover Northern Ireland companies and therefore such a company could be wound up under English law under s. 124A of IA 1986 on the grounds that it was in the public interest to do so.

For a review of insolvency litigation in the Province see Capper [2001] Ins Law 119 and [2003] Ins Law 132.

442 Extent (other territories)

442 Her Majesty may, by Order in Council, direct that such of the provisions of this Act as are specified in the Order, being provisions formerly contained in the Insolvency Act 1985, shall extend to any of the Channel Islands or any colony with such modifications as may be so specified.

GENERAL NOTE

This provides for the extension of the Act by Order in Council to any of the Channel Islands or any colony. The Isle of Man is not included. Note *Re Television Trade Rentals Ltd* [2002] EWHC 211 (Ch) where s. 426 of IA 1986 was used to extend the CVA provisions in Pt I of the Act to companies incorporated in the Isle of Man.

The Insolvency Act 1986 (Guernsey) Order 1989 (SI 1989/2409) makes provision for co-operation between the courts of the Bailiwick of Guernsey (including Alderney and Sark) and the courts of the UK: see the note to s. 426.

443 Commencement

443 This Act comes into force on the day appointed under section 236(2) of the Insolvency Act 1985 for the coming into force of Part III of that Act (individual insolvency and bankruptcy), immediately after that part of that Act comes into force for England and Wales.

GENERAL NOTE

This odd formula ties the commencement date of IA 1986 to the commencement date of Pt III of IA 1985: see SI 1986/1924 (C 71) and the general note to s. 439 above. The date was December 29, 1986. Certain other provisions in the 1985 Act, relating to corporate insolvency and the licensing of insolvency practitioners, had already been put into force (and now form part of the 1986 consolidation).

444 Citation

444 This Act may be cited as the Insolvency Act 1986.

SCHEDULE A1

MORATORIUM WHERE DIRECTORS PROPOSE VOLUNTARY ARRANGEMENT

PART I

INTRODUCTORY

Interpretation

1 In this Schedule–

"**the beginning of the moratorium**" has the meaning given by paragraph 8(1),

Schedule A1   *Insolvency Act 1986*

    "the date of filing" means the date on which the documents for the time being referred to in paragraph 7(1) are filed or lodged with the court,

    "hire-purchase agreement" includes a conditional sale agreement, a chattel leasing agreement and a retention of title agreement,

    "market contract" and **"market charge"** have the meanings given by Part VII of the Companies Act 1989,

    "money market contract" and **"money market charge"** have the meanings given by the Financial Markets and Insolvency (Money Market) Regulations 1995 (**"the 1995 regulations"**),

    "moratorium" means a moratorium under section 1A,

    "the nominee" includes any person for the time being carrying out the functions of a nominee under this Schedule,

    "related contract" has the meaning given by the 1995 regulations,

    "the settlement finality regulations" means the Financial Markets and Insolvency (Settlement Finality) Regulations 1999,

    "system-charge" has the meaning given by the Financial Markets and Insolvency Regulations 1996.

Eligible companies

2(1) A company is eligible for a moratorium if it meets the requirements of paragraph 3, unless–

    (a)   it is excluded from being eligible by virtue of paragraph 4, or

    (b)   it falls within sub-paragraph (2).

2(2) A company falls within this sub-paragraph if–

    (a)   it effects or carries out contracts of insurance, but is not exempt from the general prohibition, within the meaning of section 19 of the Financial Services and Markets Act 2000, in relation to that activity,

    (b)   it has permission under Part IV of that Act to accept deposits,

    (bb)   it has a liability in respect of a deposit which it accepted in accordance with the Banking Act 1979 (c. 37) or 1987 (c. 22),

    (c)   it is a party to a market contract or any of its property is subject to a market charge or a system-charge, or

    (d)   it is a participant (within the meaning of the settlement finality regulations) or any of its property is subject to a collateral security charge (within the meaning of those regulations).

2(3) Paragraphs (a), (b) and (bb) of sub-paragraph (2) must be read with–

    (a)   section 22 of the Financial Services and Markets Act 2000;

    (b)   any relevant order under that section; and

    (c)   Schedule 2 to that Act.

3(1) A company meets the requirements of this paragraph if the qualifying conditions are met–

    (a)   in the year ending with the date of filing, or

    (b)   in the financial year of the company which ended last before that date.

3(2) For the purposes of sub-paragraph (1)–

(a) the qualifying conditions are met by a company in a period if, in that period, it satisfies two or more of the requirements for being a small company specified for the time being in section 247(3) of the Companies Act 1985, and

(b) a company's financial year is to be determined in accordance with that Act.

3(3) Subsections (4), (5) and (6) of section 247 of that Act apply for the purposes of this paragraph as they apply for the purposes of that section.

3(4) A company does not meet the requirements of this paragraph if it is a holding company of a group of companies which does not qualify as a small group or a medium-sized group in respect of the financial year of the company which ended last before the date of filing.

3(5) For the purposes of sub-paragraph (4) "group" has the meaning given by section 262 of the Companies Act 1985 (c. 6) (definitions for Part VII) and a group qualifies as small or medium-sized if it qualifies as such under section 249 of the Companies Act 1985 (qualification of group as small or medium-sized).

4(1) A company is excluded from being eligible for a moratorium if, on the date of filing–

(a) the company is in administration,

(b) the company is being wound up,

(c) there is an administrative receiver of the company,

(d) a voluntary arrangement has effect in relation to the company,

(e) there is a provisional liquidator of the company,

(f) a moratorium has been in force for the company at any time during the period of 12 months ending with the date of filing and–

  (i) no voluntary arrangement had effect at the time at which the moratorium came to an end, or

  (ii) a voluntary arrangement which had effect at any time in that period has come to an end prematurely, or

(fa) an administrator appointed under paragraph 22 of Schedule B1 has held office in the period of 12 months ending with the date of filing,

(g) a voluntary arrangement in relation to the company which had effect in pursuance of a proposal under section 1(3) has come to an end prematurely and, during the period of 12 months ending with the date of filing, an order under section 5(3)(a) has been made.

4(2) Sub-paragraph (1)(b) does not apply to a company which, by reason of a winding-up order made after the date of filing, is treated as being wound up on that date.

Capital market arrangement

4A A company is also excluded from being eligible for a moratorium if, on the date of filing, it is a party to an agreement which is or forms part of a capital market arrangement under which –

(i) a party has incurred, or when the agreement was entered into was expected to incur, a debt of at least £10 million under the arrangement, and

(ii) the arrangement involves the issue of a capital market investment.

Schedule A1 Insolvency Act 1986

Public private partnership

4B A company is also excluded from being eligible for a moratorium if, on the date of filing, it is a project company of a project which –

(i) is a public-private partnership project, and

(ii) includes step-in rights.

Liability under an arrangement

4C(1) A company is also excluded from being eligible for a moratorium if, on the date of filing, it has incurred a liability under an agreement of £10 million or more.

4C(2) Where the liability in sub-paragraph (1) is a contingent liability under or by virtue of a guarantee or an indemnity or security provided on behalf of another person, the amount of that liability is the full amount of the liability in relation to which the guarantee, indemnity or security is provided.

4C(3) In this paragraph –

(a) the reference to "liability" includes a present or future liability whether, in either case, it is certain or contingent,

(b) the reference to "liability" includes a reference to a liability to be paid wholly or partly in foreign currency (in which case the sterling equivalent shall be calculated as at the time when the liability is incurred).

Interpretation of capital market arrangement

4D(1) For the purposes of paragraph 4A an arrangement is a capital market arrangement if–

(a) it involves a grant of security to a person holding it as trustee for a person who holds a capital market investment issued by a party to the arrangement, or

(b) at least one party guarantees the performance of obligations of another party, or

(c) at least one party provides security in respect of the performance of obligations of another party, or

(d) the arrangement involves an investment of a kind described in articles 83 to 85 of the Financial Services and Markets Act 2000 (Regulated Activities) Order 2001 (S.I. 2001/544) (options, futures and contracts for differences).

4D(2) For the purposes of sub-paragraph (1) –

(a) a reference to holding as trustee includes a reference to holding as nominee or agent,

(b) a reference to holding for a person who holds a capital market investment includes a reference to holding for a number of persons at least one of whom holds a capital market investment, and

(c) a person holds a capital market investment if he has a legal or beneficial interest in it.

4D(3) In paragraph 4A, 4C, 4J and this paragraph –

"**agreement**" includes an agreement or undertaking effected by–
(a) contract,
(b) deed, or
(c) any other instrument intended to have effect in accordance with the law of England and Wales, Scotland or another jurisdiction, and

"**party**" to an arrangement includes a party to an agreement which–
(a) forms part of the arrangement,
(b) provides for the raising of finance as part of the arrangement, or
(c) is necessary for the purposes of implementing the arrangement.

Capital market investment

4E(1) For the purposes of paragraphs 4A and 4D, an investment is a capital market investment if –

(a) it is within article 77 of the Financial Services and Markets Act 2000 (Regulated Activities) Order 2001 (S.I. 2001/544) (debt instruments) and

(b) it is rated, listed or traded or designed to be rated, listed or traded.

4E(2) In sub-paragraph (1)–

"**listed**" means admitted to the official list within the meaning given by section 103(1) of the Financial Services and Markets Act 2000 (c. 8) (interpretation),
"**rated**" means rated for the purposes of investment by an internationally recognised rating agency,
"**traded**" means admitted to trading on a market established under the rules of a recognised investment exchange or on a foreign market.

4E(3) In sub-paragraph (2)–

"**foreign market**" has the same meaning as "relevant market" in article 67(2) of the Financial Services and Markets Act 2000 (Financial Promotion) Order 2001 (S.I. 2001/1335) (foreign markets),
"**recognised investment exchange**" has the meaning given by section 285 of the Financial Services and Markets Act 2000 (recognised investment exchange).

4F(1) For the purposes of paragraphs 4A and 4D an investment is also a capital market investment if it consists of a bond or commercial paper issued to one or more of the following–

(a) an investment professional within the meaning of article 19(5) of the Financial Services and Markets Act 2000 (Financial Promotion) Order 2001,

(b) a person who is, when the agreement mentioned in paragraph 4A is entered into, a certified high net worth individual in relation to a communication within the meaning of article 48(2) of that order,

(c) a person to whom article 49(2) of that order applies (high net worth company, &c),

(d) a person who is, when the agreement mentioned in paragraph 4A is entered into, a certified sophisticated investor in relation to a communication within the meaning of article 50(1) of that order, and

(e) a person in a State other than the United Kingdom who under the law of that State is not prohibited from investing in bonds or commercial paper.

Schedule A1   Insolvency Act 1986

4F(2) For the purposes of sub-paragraph (1) –

(a) in applying article 19(5) of the Financial Services and Markets Act 2000 (Financial Promotion) Order 2001 for the purposes of sub-paragraph (1)(a) –

(i) in article 19(5)(b), ignore the words after "exempt person",

(ii) in article 19(5)(c)(i), for the words from "the controlled activity" to the end substitute "a controlled activity", and

(iii) in article 19(5)(e) ignore the words from "where the communication" to the end, and

(b) in applying article 49(2) of that order for the purposes of sub-paragraph (1)(c), ignore article 49(2)(e).

4F(3) In sub-paragraph (1) –

"bond" shall be construed in accordance with article 77 of the Financial Services and Markets Act 2000 (Regulated Activities) Order 2001 (S.I. 2001/544), and
"commercial paper" has the meaning given by article 9(3) of that order.

Debt

4G The debt of at least £10 million referred to in paragraph 4A –

(a) may be incurred at any time during the life of the capital market arrangement, and

(b) may be expressed wholly or partly in a foreign currency (in which case the sterling equivalent shall be calculated as at the time when the arrangement is entered into).

Interpretation of project company

4H(1) For the purposes of paragraph 4B a company is a "project company" of a project if–

(a) it holds property for the purpose of the project,

(b) it has sole or principal responsibility under an agreement for carrying out all or part of the project,

(c) it is one of a number of companies which together carry out the project,

(d) it has the purpose of supplying finance to enable the project to be carried out, or

(e) it is the holding company of a company within any of paragraphs (a) to (d).

4H(2) But a company is not a "project company" of a project if–

(a) it performs a function within sub-paragraph (1)(a) to (d) or is within sub-paragraph (1)(e), but

(b) it also performs a function which is not–

(i) within sub-paragraph (1)(a) to (d),

(ii) related to a function within sub-paragraph (1)(a) to (d), or

(iii) related to the project.

Insolvency Act 1986 *Schedule A1*

4H(3) For the purposes of this paragraph a company carries out all or part of a project whether or not it acts wholly or partly through agents.

Public-private partnership project

4I(1) In paragraph 4B "public-private partnership project" means a project –

(a) the resources for which are provided partly by one or more public bodies and partly by one or more private persons, or

(b) which is designed wholly or mainly for the purpose of assisting a public body to discharge a function.

4I(2) In sub-paragraph (1) "resources" includes –

(a) funds (including payment for the provision of services or facilities),

(b) assets,

(c) professional skill,

(d) the grant of a concession or franchise, and

(e) any other commercial resource.

4I(3) In sub-paragraph (1) "public body" means –

(a) a body which exercises public functions,

(b) a body specified for the purposes of this paragraph by the Secretary of State, and

(c) a body within a class specified for the purposes of this paragraph by the Secretary of State.

4I(4) A specification under sub-paragraph (3) may be -

(a) general, or

(b) for the purpose of the application of paragraph 4B to a specified case.

Step-in rights

4J(1) For the purposes of paragraph 4B a project has "step-in rights" if a person who provides finance in connection with the project has a conditional entitlement under an agreement to –

(i) assume sole or principal responsibility under an agreement for carrying out all or part of the project, or

(ii) make arrangements for carrying out all or part of the project.

4J(2) In sub-paragraph (1) a reference to the provision of finance includes a reference to the provision of an indemnity.

Person

4K For the purposes of paragraphs 4A to 4J, a reference to a person includes a reference to a partnership or another unincorporated group of persons.

Schedule A1 *Insolvency Act 1986*

5 The Secretary of State may by regulations modify the qualifications for eligibility of a company for a moratorium.

PART II

OBTAINING A MORATORIUM

Nominee's statement

6(1) Where the directors of a company wish to obtain a moratorium, they shall submit to the nominee—

(a) a document setting out the terms of the proposed voluntary arrangement,

(b) a statement of the company's affairs containing—

(i) such particulars of its creditors and of its debts and other liabilities and of its assets as may be prescribed, and

(ii) such other information as may be prescribed, and

(c) any other information necessary to enable the nominee to comply with sub-paragraph (2) which he requests from them.

6(2) The nominee shall submit to the directors a statement in the prescribed form indicating whether or not, in his opinion—

(a) the proposed voluntary arrangement has a reasonable prospect of being approved and implemented,

(b) the company is likely to have sufficient funds available to it during the proposed moratorium to enable it to carry on its business, and

(c) meetings of the company and its creditors should be summoned to consider the proposed voluntary arrangement.

6(3) In forming his opinion on the matters mentioned in sub-paragraph (2), the nominee is entitled to rely on the information submitted to him under sub-paragraph (1) unless he has reason to doubt its accuracy.

6(4) The reference in sub-paragraph (2)(b) to the company's business is to that business as the company proposes to carry it on during the moratorium.

Documents to be submitted to court

7(1) To obtain a moratorium the directors of a company must file (in Scotland, lodge) with the court—

(a) a document setting out the terms of the proposed voluntary arrangement,

(b) a statement of the company's affairs containing—

(i) such particulars of its creditors and of its debts and other liabilities and of its assets as may be prescribed, and

(ii) such other information as may be prescribed,

(c) a statement that the company is eligible for a moratorium,

(d) a statement from the nominee that he has given his consent to act, and

(e) a statement from the nominee that, in his opinion–

(i) the proposed voluntary arrangement has a reasonable prospect of being approved and implemented,
(ii) the company is likely to have sufficient funds available to it during the proposed moratorium to enable it to carry on its business, and
(iii) meetings of the company and its creditors should be summoned to consider the proposed voluntary arrangement.

7(2) Each of the statements mentioned in sub-paragraph (1)(b) to (e), except so far as it contains the particulars referred to in paragraph (b)(i), must be in the prescribed form.

7(3) The reference in sub-paragraph (1)(e)(ii) to the company's business is to that business as the company proposes to carry it on during the moratorium.

7(4) The Secretary of State may by regulations modify the requirements of this paragraph as to the documents required to be filed (in Scotland, lodged) with the court in order to obtain a moratorium.

Duration of moratorium

8(1) A moratorium comes into force when the documents for the time being referred to in paragraph 7(1) are filed or lodged with the court and references in this Schedule to "the beginning of the moratorium" shall be construed accordingly.

8(2) A moratorium ends at the end of the day on which the meetings summoned under paragraph 29(1) are first held (or, if the meetings are held on different days, the later of those days), unless it is extended under paragraph 32.

8(3) If either of those meetings has not first met before the end of the period of 28 days beginning with the day on which the moratorium comes into force, the moratorium ends at the end of the day on which those meetings were to be held (or, if those meetings were summoned to be held on different days, the later of those days), unless it is extended under paragraph 32.

8(4) If the nominee fails to summon either meeting within the period required by paragraph 29(1), the moratorium ends at the end of the last day of that period.

8(5) If the moratorium is extended (or further extended) under paragraph 32, it ends at the end of the day to which it is extended (or further extended).

8(6) Sub-paragraphs (2) to (5) do not apply if the moratorium comes to an end before the time concerned by virtue of–

(a) paragraph 25(4) (effect of withdrawal by nominee of consent to act),

(b) an order under paragraph 26(3), 27(3) or 40 (challenge of actions of nominee or directors), or

(c) a decision of one or both of the meetings summoned under paragraph 29.

8(7) If the moratorium has not previously come to an end in accordance with sub-paragraphs (2) to (6), it ends at the end of the day on which a decision under paragraph 31 to approve a voluntary arrangement takes effect under paragraph 36.

8(8) The Secretary of State may by order increase or reduce the period for the time being specified in sub-paragraph (3).

Schedule A1 *Insolvency Act 1986*

Notification of beginning of moratorium

9(1) When a moratorium comes into force, the directors shall notify the nominee of that fact forthwith.

9(2) If the directors without reasonable excuse fail to comply with sub-paragraph (1), each of them is liable to imprisonment or a fine, or both.

10(1) When a moratorium comes into force, the nominee shall, in accordance with the rules–

(a) advertise that fact forthwith, and

(b) notify the registrar of companies, the company and any petitioning creditor of the company of whose claim he is aware of that fact.

10(2) In sub-paragraph (1)(b), "petitioning creditor" means a creditor by whom a winding-up petition has been presented before the beginning of the moratorium, as long as the petition has not been dismissed or withdrawn.

10(3) If the nominee without reasonable excuse fails to comply with sub-paragraph (1)(a) or (b), he is liable to a fine.

Notification of end of moratorium

11(1) When a moratorium comes to an end, the nominee shall, in accordance with the rules–

(a) advertise that fact forthwith, and

(b) notify the court, the registrar of companies, the company and any creditor of the company of whose claim he is aware of that fact.

11(2) If the nominee without reasonable excuse fails to comply with sub-paragraph (1)(a) or (b), he is liable to a fine.

PART III

EFFECTS OF MORATORIUM

Effect on creditors, etc.

12(1) During the period for which a moratorium is in force for a company–

(a) no petition may be presented for the winding up of the company,

(b) no meeting of the company may be called or requisitioned except with the consent of the nominee or the leave of the court and subject (where the court gives leave) to such terms as the court may impose,

(c) no resolution may be passed or order made for the winding up of the company,

(d) no administration application may be made in respect of the company,

(da) no administrator of the company may be appointed under paragraph 14 or 22 of Schedule B1,

(e) no administrative receiver of the company may be appointed,

(f) no landlord or other person to whom rent is payable may exercise any right of forfeiture by peaceable re-entry in relation to premises let to the company in respect of a failure by the company to comply with any term or condition of its tenancy of such premises, except with the leave of the court and subject to such terms as the court may impose,

(g) no other steps may be taken to enforce any security over the company's property, or to repossess goods in the company's possession under any hire-purchase agreement, except with the leave of the court and subject to such terms as the court may impose, and

(h) no other proceedings and no execution or other legal process may be commenced or continued, and no distress may be levied, against the company or its property except with the leave of the court and subject to such terms as the court may impose.

12(2) Where a petition, other than an excepted petition, for the winding up of the company has been presented before the beginning of the moratorium, section 127 shall not apply in relation to any disposition of property, transfer of shares or alteration in status made during the moratorium or at a time mentioned in paragraph 37(5)(a).

12(3) In the application of sub-paragraph (1)(h) to Scotland, the reference to execution being commenced or continued includes a reference to diligence being carried out or continued, and the reference to distress being levied is omitted.

12(4) Paragraph (a) of sub-paragraph (1) does not apply to an excepted petition and, where such a petition has been presented before the beginning of the moratorium or is presented during the moratorium, paragraphs (b) and (c) of that sub-paragraph do not apply in relation to proceedings on the petition.

12(5) For the purposes of this paragraph, "excepted petition" means a petition under–

(a) section 124A of this Act,

(b) section 72 of the Financial Services Act 1986 on the ground mentioned in subsection (1)(b) of that section, or

(c) section 92 of the Banking Act 1987 on the ground mentioned in subsection (1)(b) of that section.

(d) section 367 of the Financial Services and Markets Act 2000 on the ground mentioned in subsection 3(b) of that section.

13(1) This paragraph applies where there is an uncrystallised floating charge on the property of a company for which a moratorium is in force.

13(2) If the conditions for the holder of the charge to give a notice having the effect mentioned in sub-paragraph (4) are met at any time, the notice may not be given at that time but may instead be given as soon as practicable after the moratorium has come to an end.

13(3) If any other event occurs at any time which (apart from this sub-paragraph) would have the effect mentioned in sub-paragraph (4), then–

(a) the event shall not have the effect in question at that time, but

(b) if notice of the event is given to the company by the holder of the charge as soon as is practicable after the moratorium has come to an end, the event is to be treated as if it had occurred when the notice was given.

13(4) The effect referred to in sub-paragraphs (2) and (3) is–

(a) causing the crystallisation of the floating charge, or

(b) causing the imposition, by virtue of provision in the instrument creating the charge, of any restriction on the disposal of any property of the company.

13(5) Application may not be made for leave under paragraph 12(1)(g) or (h) with a view to obtaining–

(a) the crystallisation of the floating charge, or

(b) the imposition, by virtue of provision in the instrument creating the charge, of any restriction on the disposal of any property of the company.

Schedule A1 *Insolvency Act 1986*

14 Security granted by a company at a time when a moratorium is in force in relation to the company may only be enforced if, at that time, there were reasonable grounds for believing that it would benefit the company.

Effect on company

15(1) Paragraphs 16 to 23 apply in relation to a company for which a moratorium is in force.

15(2) The fact that a company enters into a transaction in contravention of any of paragraphs 16 to 22 does not–

(a) make the transaction void, or

(b) make it to any extent unenforceable against the company.

Company invoices, etc.

16(1) Every invoice, order for goods or business letter which–

(a) is issued by or on behalf of the company, and

(b) on or in which the company's name appears,

shall also contain the nominee's name and a statement that the moratorium is in force for the company.

16(2) If default is made in complying with sub-paragraph (1), the company and (subject to sub-paragraph (3)) any officer of the company is liable to a fine.

16(3) An officer of the company is only liable under sub-paragraph (2) if, without reasonable excuse, he authorises or permits the default.

Obtaining credit during moratorium

17(1) The company may not obtain credit to the extent of £250 or more from a person who has not been informed that a moratorium is in force in relation to the company.

17(2) The reference to the company obtaining credit includes the following cases–

(a) where goods are bailed (in Scotland, hired) to the company under a hire-purchase agreement, or agreed to be sold to the company under a conditional sale agreement, and

(b) where the company is paid in advance (whether in money or otherwise) for the supply of goods or services.

17(3) Where the company obtains credit in contravention of sub-paragraph (1)–

(a) the company is liable to a fine, and

(b) if any officer of the company knowingly and wilfully authorised or permitted the contravention, he is liable to imprisonment or a fine, or both.

17(4) The money sum specified in sub-paragraph (1) is subject to increase or reduction by order under section 417A in Part XV.

Disposals and payments

18(1) Subject to sub-paragraph (2), the company may only dispose of any of its property if–

(a) there are reasonable grounds for believing that the disposal will benefit the company, and

(b) the disposal is approved by the committee established under paragraph 35(1) or, where there is no such committee, by the nominee.

18(2) Sub-paragraph (1) does not apply to a disposal made in the ordinary way of the company's business.

18(3) If the company makes a disposal in contravention of sub-paragraph (1) otherwise than in pursuance of an order of the court–

(a) the company is liable to a fine, and

(b) if any officer of the company authorised or permitted the contravention, without reasonable excuse, he is liable to imprisonment or a fine, or both.

19(1) Subject to sub-paragraph (2), the company may only make any payment in respect of any debt or other liability of the company in existence before the beginning of the moratorium if–

(a) there are reasonable grounds for believing that the payment will benefit the company, and

(b) the payment is approved by the committee established under paragraph 35(1) or, where there is no such committee, by the nominee.

19(2) Sub-paragraph (1) does not apply to a payment required by paragraph 20(6).

19(3) If the company makes a payment in contravention of sub-paragraph (1) otherwise than in pursuance of an order of the court–

(a) the company is liable to a fine, and

(b) if any officer of the company authorised or permitted the contravention, without reasonable excuse, he is liable to imprisonment or a fine, or both.

Disposal of charged property, etc.

20(1) This paragraph applies where–

(a) any property of the company is subject to a security, or

(b) any goods are in the possession of the company under a hire-purchase agreement.

20(2) If the holder of the security consents, or the court gives leave, the company may dispose of the property as if it were not subject to the security.

20(3) If the owner of the goods consents, or the court gives leave, the company may dispose of the goods as if all rights of the owner under the hire-purchase agreement were vested in the company.

20(4) Where property subject to a security which, as created, was a floating charge is disposed of under sub-paragraph (2), the holder of the security has the same priority in respect of any property of the company directly or indirectly representing the property disposed of as he would have had in respect of the property subject to the security.

20(5) Sub-paragraph (6) applies to the disposal under sub-paragraph (2) or (as the case may be) sub-paragraph (3) of–

(a) any property subject to a security other than a security which, as created, was a floating charge, or

(b) any goods in the possession of the company under a hire-purchase agreement.

20(6) It shall be a condition of any consent or leave under sub-paragraph (2) or (as the case may be) sub-paragraph (3) that–

(a) the net proceeds of the disposal, and

(b) where those proceeds are less than such amount as may be agreed, or determined by the court, to be the net amount which would be realised on a sale of the property or goods in the open market by a willing vendor, such sums as may be required to make good the deficiency, shall be applied towards discharging the sums secured by the security or payable under the hire-purchase agreement.

20(7) Where a condition imposed in pursuance of sub-paragraph (6) relates to two or more securities, that condition requires–

(a) the net proceeds of the disposal, and

(b) where paragraph (b) of sub-paragraph (6) applies, the sums mentioned in that paragraph,

to be applied towards discharging the sums secured by those securities in the order of their priorities.

20(8) Where the court gives leave for a disposal under sub-paragraph (2) or (3), the directors shall, within 14 days after leave is given, send an office copy of the order giving leave to the registrar of companies.

20(9) If the directors without reasonable excuse fail to comply with sub-paragraph (8), they are liable to a fine.

21(1) Where property is disposed of under paragraph 20 in its application to Scotland, the company shall grant to the disponee an appropriate document of transfer or conveyance of the property, and

(a) that document, or

(b) where any recording, intimation or registration of the document is a legal requirement for completion of title to the property, that recording, intimation or registration,

has the effect of disencumbering the property of, or (as the case may be) freeing the property from, the security.

21(2) Where goods in the possession of the company under a hire-purchase agreement are disposed of under paragraph 20 in its application to Scotland, the disposal has the effect of extinguishing, as against the disponee, all rights of the owner of the goods under the agreement.

22(1) If the company–

(a) without any consent or leave under paragraph 20, disposes of any of its property which is subject to a security otherwise than in accordance with the terms of the security,

(b) without any consent or leave under paragraph 20, disposes of any goods in the possession of the company under a hire-purchase agreement otherwise than in accordance with the terms of the agreement, or

(c) fails to comply with any requirement imposed by paragraph 20 or 21,

it is liable to a fine.

22(2) If any officer of the company, without reasonable excuse, authorises or permits any such disposal or failure to comply, he is liable to imprisonment or a fine, or both.

Market contracts, etc.

23(1) If the company enters into any transaction to which this paragraph applies–

(a) the company is liable to a fine, and

(b) if any officer of the company, without reasonable excuse, authorised or permitted the company to enter into the transaction, he is liable to imprisonment or a fine, or both.

23(2) A company enters into a transaction to which this paragraph applies if it–

(a) enters into a market contract, a money market contract or a related contract,

(b) gives a transfer order,

(c) grants a market charge, a money market charge or a system-charge, or

(d) provides any collateral security.

23(3) The fact that a company enters into a transaction in contravention of this paragraph does not–

(a) make the transaction void, or

(b) make it to any extent unenforceable by or against the company.

23(4) Where during the moratorium a company enters into a transaction to which this paragraph applies, nothing done by or in pursuance of the transaction is to be treated as done in contravention of paragraphs 12(1)(g), 14 or 16 to 22.

23(5) Paragraph 20 does not apply in relation to any property which is subject to a market charge, a money market charge, a system-charge or a collateral security charge.

23(6) In this paragraph, "transfer order", "collateral security" and "collateral security charge" have the same meanings as in the settlement finality regulations.

Part IV

Nominees

Monitoring of company's activities

24(1) During a moratorium, the nominee shall monitor the company's affairs for the purpose of forming an opinion as to whether–

(a) the proposed voluntary arrangement or, if he has received notice of proposed modifications under paragraph 31(7), the proposed arrangement with those modifications has a reasonable prospect of being approved and implemented, and

(b) the company is likely to have sufficient funds available to it during the remainder of the moratorium to enable it to continue to carry on its business.

24(2) The directors shall submit to the nominee any information necessary to enable him to comply with sub-paragraph (1) which he requests from them.

24(3) In forming his opinion on the matters mentioned in sub-paragraph (1), the nominee is entitled to rely on the information submitted to him under sub-paragraph (2) unless he has reason to doubt its accuracy.

24(4) The reference in sub-paragraph (1)(b) to the company's business is to that business as the company proposes to carry it on during the remainder of the moratorium.

Withdrawal of consent to act

25(1) The nominee may only withdraw his consent to act in the circumstances mentioned in this paragraph.

25(2) The nominee must withdraw his consent to act if, at any time during a moratorium–

(a) he forms the opinion that–

(i) the proposed voluntary arrangement or, if he has received notice of proposed modifications under paragraph 31(7), the proposed arrangement with those modifications no longer has a reasonable prospect of being approved or implemented, or

(ii) the company will not have sufficient funds available to it during the remainder of the moratorium to enable it to continue to carry on its business,

(b) he becomes aware that, on the date of filing, the company was not eligible for a moratorium, or

(c) the directors fail to comply with their duty under paragraph 24(2).

25(3) The reference in sub-paragraph (2)(a)(ii) to the company's business is to that business as the company proposes to carry it on during the remainder of the moratorium.

25(4) If the nominee withdraws his consent to act, the moratorium comes to an end.

25(5) If the nominee withdraws his consent to act he must, in accordance with the rules, notify the court, the registrar of companies, the company and any creditor of the company of whose claim he is aware of his withdrawal and the reason for it.

25(6) If the nominee without reasonable excuse fails to comply with sub-paragraph (5), he is liable to a fine.

Challenge of nominee's actions, etc.

26(1) If any creditor, director or member of the company, or any other person affected by a moratorium, is dissatisfied by any act, omission or decision of the nominee during the moratorium, he may apply to the court.

26(2) An application under sub-paragraph (1) may be made during the moratorium or after it has ended.

26(3) On an application under sub-paragraph (1) the court may–

(a) confirm, reverse or modify any act or decision of the nominee,

(b) give him directions, or

(c) make such other order as it thinks fit.

26(4) An order under sub-paragraph (3) may (among other things) bring the moratorium to an end and make such consequential provision as the court thinks fit.

27(1) Where there are reasonable grounds for believing that–

(a) as a result of any act, omission or decision of the nominee during the moratorium, the company has suffered loss, but

(b) the company does not intend to pursue any claim it may have against the nominee,

any creditor of the company may apply to the court.

27(2) An application under sub-paragraph (1) may be made during the moratorium or after it has ended.

27(3) On an application under sub-paragraph (1) the court may–

(a) order the company to pursue any claim against the nominee,

(b) authorise any creditor to pursue such a claim in the name of the company, or

(c) make such other order with respect to such a claim as it thinks fit, unless the court is satisfied that the act, omission or decision of the nominee was in all the circumstances reasonable.

27(4) An order under sub-paragraph (3) may (among other things)–

(a) impose conditions on any authority given to pursue a claim,

(b) direct the company to assist in the pursuit of a claim,

(c) make directions with respect to the distribution of anything received as a result of the pursuit of a claim,

(d) bring the moratorium to an end and make such consequential provision as the court thinks fit.

27(5) On an application under sub-paragraph (1) the court shall have regard to the interests of the members and creditors of the company generally.

Replacement of nominee by court

28(1) The court may–

(a) on an application made by the directors in a case where the nominee has failed to comply with any duty imposed on him under this Schedule or has died, or

(b) on an application made by the directors or the nominee in a case where it is impracticable or inappropriate for the nominee to continue to act as such,

direct that the nominee be replaced as such by another person qualified to act as an insolvency practitioner, or authorised to act as nominee, in relation to the voluntary arrangement.

28(2) A person may only be appointed as a replacement nominee under this paragraph if he submits to the court a statement indicating his consent to act.

PART V

CONSIDERATION AND IMPLEMENTATION OF VOLUNTARY ARRANGEMENT

Summoning of meetings

29(1) Where a moratorium is in force, the nominee shall summon meetings of the company and its creditors for such a time, date (within the period for the time being specified in paragraph 8(3)) and place as he thinks fit.

29(2) The persons to be summoned to a creditors' meeting under this paragraph are every creditor of the company of whose claim the nominee is aware.

Conduct of meetings

30(1) Subject to the provisions of paragraphs 31 to 35, the meetings summoned under paragraph 29 shall be conducted in accordance with the rules.

30(2) A meeting so summoned may resolve that it be adjourned (or further adjourned).

30(3) After the conclusion of either meeting in accordance with the rules, the chairman of the meeting shall report the result of the meeting to the court, and, immediately after reporting to the court, shall give notice of the result of the meeting to such persons as may be prescribed.

Approval of voluntary arrangement

31(1) The meetings summoned under paragraph 29 shall decide whether to approve the proposed voluntary arrangement (with or without modifications).

31(2) The modifications may include one conferring the functions proposed to be conferred on the nominee on another person qualified to act as an insolvency practitioner, or authorised to act as nominee, in relation to the voluntary arrangement.

31(3) The modifications shall not include one by virtue of which the proposal ceases to be a proposal such as is mentioned in section 1.

31(4) A meeting summoned under paragraph 29 shall not approve any proposal or modification which affects the right of a secured creditor of the company to enforce his security, except with the concurrence of the creditor concerned.

31(5) Subject to sub-paragraph (6), a meeting so summoned shall not approve any proposal or modification under which–

(a) any preferential debt of the company is to be paid otherwise than in priority to such of its debts as are not preferential debts, or

(b) a preferential creditor of the company is to be paid an amount in respect of a preferential debt that bears to that debt a smaller proportion than is borne to another preferential debt by the amount that is to be paid in respect of that other debt.

31(6) The meeting may approve such a proposal or modification with the concurrence of the preferential creditor concerned.

31(7) The directors of the company may, before the beginning of the period of seven days which ends with the meetings (or either of them) summoned under paragraph 29 being held, give notice to the nominee of any modifications of the proposal for which the directors intend to seek the approval of those meetings.

31(8) References in this paragraph to preferential debts and preferential creditors are to be read in accordance with section 386 in Part XII of this Act.

Extension of moratorium

32(1) Subject to sub-paragraph (2), a meeting summoned under paragraph 29 which resolves that it be adjourned (or further adjourned) may resolve that the moratorium be extended (or further extended), with or without conditions.

32(2) The moratorium may not be extended (or further extended) to a day later than the end of the period of two months which begins–

(a) where both meetings summoned under paragraph 29 are first held on the same day, with that day,

(b) in any other case, with the day on which the later of those meetings is first held.

32(3) At any meeting where it is proposed to extend (or further extend) the moratorium, before a decision is taken with respect to that proposal, the nominee shall inform the meeting–

(a) of what he has done in order to comply with his duty under paragraph 24 and the cost of his actions for the company, and

(b) of what he intends to do to continue to comply with that duty if the moratorium is extended (or further extended) and the expected cost of his actions for the company.

32(4) Where, in accordance with sub-paragraph (3)(b), the nominee informs a meeting of the expected cost of his intended actions, the meeting shall resolve whether or not to approve that expected cost.

32(5) If a decision not to approve the expected cost of the nominee's intended actions has effect under paragraph 36, the moratorium comes to an end.

32(6) A meeting may resolve that a moratorium which has been extended (or further extended) be brought to an end before the end of the period of the extension (or further extension).

32(7) The Secretary of State may by order increase or reduce the period for the time being specified in sub-paragraph (2).

33(1) The conditions which may be imposed when a moratorium is extended (or further extended) include a requirement that the nominee be replaced as such by another person qualified to act as an insolvency practitioner, or authorised to act as nominee, in relation to the voluntary arrangement.

33(2) A person may only be appointed as a replacement nominee by virtue of sub-paragraph (1) if he submits to the court a statement indicating his consent to act.

33(3) At any meeting where it is proposed to appoint a replacement nominee as a condition of extending (or further extending) the moratorium–

(a) the duty imposed by paragraph 32(3)(b) on the nominee shall instead be imposed on the person proposed as the replacement nominee, and

(b) paragraphs 32(4) and (5) and 36(1)(e) apply as if the references to the nominee were to that person.

34(1) If a decision to extend, or further extend, the moratorium takes effect under paragraph 36, the nominee shall, in accordance with the rules, notify the registrar of companies and the court.

34(2) If the moratorium is extended, or further extended, by virtue of an order under paragraph 36(5), the nominee shall, in accordance with the rules, send an office copy of the order to the registrar of companies.

34(3) If the nominee without reasonable excuse fails to comply with this paragraph, he is liable to a fine.

Moratorium committee

35(1) A meeting summoned under paragraph 29 which resolves that the moratorium be extended (or further extended) may, with the consent of the nominee, resolve that a committee be established to exercise the functions conferred on it by the meeting.

35(2) The meeting may not so resolve unless it has approved an estimate of the expenses to be incurred by the committee in the exercise of the proposed functions.

35(3) Any expenses, not exceeding the amount of the estimate, incurred by the committee in the exercise of its functions shall be reimbursed by the nominee.

Schedule A1 *Insolvency Act 1986*

35(4) The committee shall cease to exist when the moratorium comes to an end.

Effectiveness of decisions

36(1) Sub-paragraph (2) applies to references to one of the following decisions having effect, that is, a decision, under paragraph 31, 32 or 35, with respect to–

(a) the approval of a proposed voluntary arrangement,

(b) the extension (or further extension) of a moratorium,

(c) the bringing of a moratorium to an end,

(d) the establishment of a committee, or

(e) the approval of the expected cost of a nominee's intended actions.

36(2) The decision has effect if, in accordance with the rules–

(a) it has been taken by both meetings summoned under paragraph 29, or

(b) (subject to any order made under sub-paragraph (5)) it has been taken by the creditors' meeting summoned under that paragraph.

36(3) If a decision taken by the creditors' meeting under any of paragraphs 31, 32 or 35 with respect to any of the matters mentioned in sub-paragraph (1) differs from one so taken by the company meeting with respect to that matter, a member of the company may apply to the court.

36(4) An application under sub-paragraph (3) shall not be made after the end of the period of 28 days beginning with–

(a) the day on which the decision was taken by the creditors' meeting, or

(b) where the decision of the company meeting was taken on a later day, that day.

36(5) On an application under sub-paragraph (3), the court may–

(a) order the decision of the company meeting to have effect instead of the decision of the creditors' meeting, or

(b) make such other order as it thinks fit.

Effect of approval of voluntary arrangement

37(1) This paragraph applies where a decision approving a voluntary arrangement has effect under paragraph 36.

37(2) The approved voluntary arrangement–

(a) takes effect as if made by the company at the creditors' meeting, and

(b) binds every person who in accordance with the rules–

(i) was entitled to vote at that meeting (whether or not he was present or represented at it), or
(ii) would have been so entitled if he had had notice of it,

as if he were a party to the voluntary arrangement.

37(3) If–

(a) when the arrangement ceases to have effect any amount payable under the arrangement to a person bound by virtue of sub-paragraph (2)(b)(ii) has not been paid, and

(b) the arrangement did not come to an end prematurely,

the company shall at that time become liable to pay to that person the amount payable under the arrangement.

37(4) Where a petition for the winding up of the company, other than an excepted petition within the meaning of paragraph 12, was presented before the beginning of the moratorium, the court shall dismiss the petition.

37(5) The court shall not dismiss a petition under sub-paragraph (4)–

(a) at any time before the end of the period of 28 days beginning with the first day on which each of the reports of the meetings required by paragraph 30(3) has been made to the court, or

(b) at any time when an application under paragraph 38 or an appeal in respect of such an application is pending, or at any time in the period within which such an appeal may be brought.

Challenge of decisions

38(1) Subject to the following provisions of this paragraph, any of the persons mentioned in sub-paragraph (2) may apply to the court on one or both of the following grounds–

(a) that a voluntary arrangement approved at one or both of the meetings summoned under paragraph 29 and which has taken effect unfairly prejudices the interests of a creditor, member or contributory of the company,

(b) that there has been some material irregularity at or in relation to either of those meetings.

38(2) The persons who may apply under this paragraph are–

(a) a person entitled, in accordance with the rules, to vote at either of the meetings,

(b) a person who would have been entitled, in accordance with the rules, to vote at the creditors' meeting if he had had notice of it, and

(c) the nominee.

38(3) An application under this paragraph shall not be made–

(a) after the end of the period of 28 days beginning with the first day on which each of the reports required by paragraph 30(3) has been made to the court, or

(b) in the case of a person who was not given notice of the creditors' meeting, after the end of the period of 28 days beginning with the day on which he became aware that the meeting had taken place,

but (subject to that) an application made by a person within sub-paragraph (2)(b) on the ground that the arrangement prejudices his interests may be made after the arrangement has ceased to have effect, unless it came to an end prematurely.

Schedule A1 *Insolvency Act 1986*

38(4) Where on an application under this paragraph the court is satisfied as to either of the grounds mentioned in sub-paragraph (1), it may do any of the following–

(a) revoke or suspend–

 (i) any decision approving the voluntary arrangement which has effect under paragraph 36, or
 (ii) in a case falling within sub-paragraph (1)(b), any decision taken by the meeting in question which has effect under that paragraph,

(b) give a direction to any person–

 (i) for the summoning of further meetings to consider any revised proposal for a voluntary arrangement which the directors may make, or
 (ii) in a case falling within sub-paragraph (1)(b), for the summoning of a further company or (as the case may be) creditors' meeting to reconsider the original proposal.

38(5) Where at any time after giving a direction under sub-paragraph (4)(b)(i) the court is satisfied that the directors do not intend to submit a revised proposal, the court shall revoke the direction and revoke or suspend any decision approving the voluntary arrangement which has effect under paragraph 36.

38(6) Where the court gives a direction under sub-paragraph (4)(b), it may also give a direction continuing or, as the case may require, renewing, for such period as may be specified in the direction, the effect of the moratorium.

38(7) Sub-paragraph (8) applies in a case where the court, on an application under this paragraph–

(a) gives a direction under sub-paragraph (4)(b), or

(b) revokes or suspends a decision under sub-paragraph (4)(a) or (5).

38(8) In such a case, the court may give such supplemental directions as it thinks fit and, in particular, directions with respect to–

(a) things done under the voluntary arrangement since it took effect, and

(b) such things done since that time as could not have been done if a moratorium had been in force in relation to the company when they were done.

38(9) Except in pursuance of the preceding provisions of this paragraph, a decision taken at a meeting summoned under paragraph 29 is not invalidated by any irregularity at or in relation to the meeting.

Implementation of voluntary arrangement

39(1) This paragraph applies where a voluntary arrangement approved by one or both of the meetings summoned under paragraph 29 has taken effect.

39(2) The person who is for the time being carrying out in relation to the voluntary arrangement the functions conferred–

(a) by virtue of the approval of the arrangement, on the nominee, or

(b) by virtue of paragraph 31(2), on a person other than the nominee,

shall be known as the supervisor of the voluntary arrangement.

39(3) If any of the company's creditors or any other person is dissatisfied by any act, omission or decision of the supervisor, he may apply to the court.

39(4) On an application under sub-paragraph (3) the court may–

(a) confirm, reverse or modify any act or decision of the supervisor,

(b) give him directions, or

(c) make such other order as it thinks fit.

39(5) The supervisor–

(a) may apply to the court for directions in relation to any particular matter arising under the voluntary arrangement, and

(b) is included among the persons who may apply to the court for the winding up of the company or for an administration order to be made in relation to it.

39(6) The court may, whenever–

(a) it is expedient to appoint a person to carry out the functions of the supervisor, and

(b) it is inexpedient, difficult or impracticable for an appointment to be made without the assistance of the court,

make an order appointing a person who is qualified to act as an insolvency practitioner, or authorised to act as supervisor, in relation to the voluntary arrangement, either in substitution for the existing supervisor or to fill a vacancy.

39(7) The power conferred by sub-paragraph (6) is exercisable so as to increase the number of persons exercising the functions of supervisor or, where there is more than one person exercising those functions, so as to replace one or more of those persons.

PART VI

MISCELLANEOUS

Challenge of directors' actions

40(1) This paragraph applies in relation to acts or omissions of the directors of a company during a moratorium.

40(2) A creditor or member of the company may apply to the court for an order under this paragraph on the ground–

(a) that the company's affairs, business and property are being or have been managed by the directors in a manner which is unfairly prejudicial to the interests of its creditors or members generally, or of some part of its creditors or members (including at least the petitioner), or

(b) that any actual or proposed act or omission of the directors is or would be so prejudicial.

40(3) An application for an order under this paragraph may be made during or after the moratorium.

40(4) On an application for an order under this paragraph the court may–

(a) make such order as it thinks fit for giving relief in respect of the matters complained of,

(b) adjourn the hearing conditionally or unconditionally, or

(c) make an interim order or any other order that it thinks fit.

40(5) An order under this paragraph may in particular–

(a) regulate the management by the directors of the company's affairs, business and property during the remainder of the moratorium,

(b) require the directors to refrain from doing or continuing an act complained of by the petitioner, or to do an act which the petitioner has complained they have omitted to do,

(c) require the summoning of a meeting of creditors or members for the purpose of considering such matters as the court may direct,

(d) bring the moratorium to an end and make such consequential provision as the court thinks fit.

40(6) In making an order under this paragraph the court shall have regard to the need to safeguard the interests of persons who have dealt with the company in good faith and for value.

40(7) Sub-paragraph (8) applies where–

(a) the appointment of an administrator has effect in relation to the company and the appointment took effect before the moratorium came into force, or

(b) the company is being wound up in pursuance of a petition presented before the moratorium came into force.

40(8) No application for an order under this paragraph may be made by a creditor or member of the company; but such an application may be made instead by the administrator or (as the case may be) the liquidator.

Offences

41(1) This paragraph applies where a moratorium has been obtained for a company.

41(2) If, within the period of 12 months ending with the day on which the moratorium came into force, a person who was at the time an officer of the company–

(a) did any of the things mentioned in paragraphs (a) to (f) of sub-paragraph (4), or

(b) was privy to the doing by others of any of the things mentioned in paragraphs (c), (d) and (e) of that sub-paragraph,

he is to be treated as having committed an offence at that time.

41(3) If, at any time during the moratorium, a person who is an officer of the company–

(a) does any of the things mentioned in paragraphs (a) to (f) of sub-paragraph (4), or

(b) is privy to the doing by others of any of the things mentioned in paragraphs (c), (d) and (e) of that sub-paragraph,

he commits an offence.

41(4) Those things are–

(a) concealing any part of the company's property to the value of £500 or more, or concealing any debt due to or from the company, or

(b) fraudulently removing any part of the company's property to the value of £500 or more, or

(c) concealing, destroying, mutilating or falsifying any book or paper affecting or relating to the company's property or affairs, or

(d) making any false entry in any book or paper affecting or relating to the company's property or affairs, or

(e) fraudulently parting with, altering or making any omission in any document affecting or relating to the company's property or affairs, or

(f) pawning, pledging or disposing of any property of the company which has been obtained on credit and has not been paid for (unless the pawning, pledging or disposal was in the ordinary way of the company's business).

41(5) For the purposes of this paragraph, "officer" includes a shadow director.

41(6) It is a defence–

(a) for a person charged under sub-paragraph (2) or (3) in respect of the things mentioned in paragraph (a) or (f) of sub-paragraph (4) to prove that he had no intent to defraud, and

(b) for a person charged under sub-paragraph (2) or (3) in respect of the things mentioned in paragraph (c) or (d) of sub-paragraph (4) to prove that he had no intent to conceal the state of affairs of the company or to defeat the law.

41(7) Where a person pawns, pledges or disposes of any property of a company in circumstances which amount to an offence under sub-paragraph (2) or (3), every person who takes in pawn or pledge, or otherwise receives, the property knowing it to be pawned, pledged or disposed of in circumstances which–

(a) would, if a moratorium were obtained for the company within the period of 12 months beginning with the day on which the pawning, pledging or disposal took place, amount to an offence under sub-paragraph (2), or

(b) amount to an offence under sub-paragraph (3),

commits an offence.

41(8) A person guilty of an offence under this paragraph is liable to imprisonment or a fine, or both.

41(9) The money sums specified in paragraphs (a) and (b) of sub-paragraph (4) are subject to increase or reduction by order under section 417A in Part XV.

42(1) If, for the purpose of obtaining a moratorium, or an extension of a moratorium, for a company, a person who is an officer of the company–

(a) makes any false representation, or

(b) fraudulently does, or omits to do, anything,

he commits an offence.

42(2) Sub-paragraph (1) applies even if no moratorium or extension is obtained.

42(3) For the purposes of this paragraph, "officer" includes a shadow director.

42(4) A person guilty of an offence under this paragraph is liable to imprisonment or a fine, or both.

Void provisions in floating charge documents

43(1) A provision in an instrument creating a floating charge is void if it provides for–

(a) obtaining a moratorium, or

(b) anything done with a view to obtaining a moratorium (including any preliminary decision or investigation),

to be an event causing the floating charge to crystallise or causing restrictions which would not otherwise apply to be imposed on the disposal of property by the company or a ground for the appointment of a receiver.

43(2) In sub-paragraph (1), "receiver" includes a manager and a person who is appointed both receiver and manager.

Functions of the Financial Services Authority

44(1) This Schedule has effect in relation to a moratorium for a regulated company with the modifications in sub-paragraphs (2) to (16) below.

44(2) Any notice or other document required by virtue of this Schedule to be sent to a creditor of a regulated company must also be sent to the Authority.

44(3) The Authority is entitled to be heard on any application to the court for leave under paragraph 20(2) or 20(3) (disposal of charged property, etc.).

44(4) Where paragraph 26(1) (challenge of nominee's actions, etc.) applies, the persons who may apply to the court include the Authority.

44(5) If a person other than the Authority applies to the court under that paragraph, the Authority is entitled to be heard on the application.

44(6) Where paragraph 27(1) (challenge of nominee's actions, etc.) applies, the persons who may apply to the court include the Authority.

44(7) If a person other than the Authority applies to the court under that paragraph, the Authority is entitled to be heard on the application.

44(8) The persons to be summoned to a creditors' meeting under paragraph 29 include the Authority.

44(9) A person appointed for the purpose by the Authority is entitled to attend and participate in (but not to vote at)–

(a)   any creditors' meeting summoned under that paragraph,

(b)   any meeting of a committee established under paragraph 35 (moratorium committee).

44(10) The Authority is entitled to be heard on any application under paragraph 36(3) (effectiveness of decisions).

44(11) Where paragraph 38(1) (challenge of decisions) applies, the persons who may apply to the court include the Authority.

44(12) If a person other than the Authority applies to the court under that paragraph, the Authority is entitled to be heard on the application.

44(13) Where paragraph 39(3) (implementation of voluntary arrangement) applies, the persons who may apply to the court include the Authority.

44(14) If a person other than the Authority applies to the court under that paragraph, the Authority is entitled to be heard on the application.

44(15) Where paragraph 40(2) (challenge of directors' actions) applies, the persons who may apply to the court include the Authority.

44(16) If a person other than the Authority applies to the court under that paragraph, the Authority is entitled to be heard on the application.

44(17) This paragraph does not prejudice any right the Authority has (apart from this paragraph) as a creditor of a regulated company.

44(18) In this paragraph–

"**the Authority**" means the Financial Services Authority, and

"**regulated company**" means a company which–

(a) is, or has been, an authorised person within the meaning given by section 31 of the Financial Services and Markets Act 2000,

(b) is, or has been, an appointed representative within the meaning given by section 39 of that Act, or

(c) is carrying on, or has carried on, a regulated activity, within the meaning given by section 22 of that Act, in contravention of the general prohibition within the meaning given by section 19 of that Act.

Subordinate legislation

45(1) Regulations or an order made by the Secretary of State under this Schedule may make different provision for different cases.

45(2) Regulations so made may make such consequential, incidental, supplemental and transitional provision as may appear to the Secretary of State necessary or expedient.

45(3) Any power of the Secretary of State to make regulations under this Schedule may be exercised by amending or repealing any enactment contained in this Act (including one contained in this Schedule) or contained in the Company Directors Disqualification Act 1986.

45(4) Regulations (except regulations under paragraph 5) or an order made by the Secretary of State under this Schedule shall be made by statutory instrument subject to annulment in pursuance of a resolution of either House of Parliament.

45(5) Regulations under paragraph 5 of this Schedule are to be made by statutory instrument and shall only be made if a draft containing the regulations has been laid before and approved by resolution of each House of Parliament.

GENERAL NOTE

On close examination of Sch. A1, we find that this moratorium facility is restricted to "eligible" companies, *i.e.* small companies, excluding companies such as banks, insurance companies, companies involved with the performance of market contracts. A small company is defined by s. 247(3) of CA 1985 as one which fulfils two of the following three conditions:

(a) turnover less than £5.6 million;

(b) balance sheet total less than £2.8 million; and

(c) having fewer than 50 employees.

These criteria (which apply to any filing after January 30, 2004) may be changed in the future through delegated legislation. The new criteria are specified in the Companies Act 1985 (Accounts of Small and Medium-sized Enterprises and Audit Exemption) (Amendment) Regulations 2004 (SI 2004/16). Possible changes in eligibility might bring larger companies within the catchment and deal with the technical issue of "special purpose vehicle companies" for whom this reform has posed difficulties (see Livingston, (2000) 16 IL & P 189). This latter problem has been recognised by the Government (see *Hansard*, H.C. Vol. 355, cols. 163–4)—note the further exceptions introduced via paras 4A–4K (see note to s. 1A).

The new CVA with moratorium also cannot operate where the company is already undergoing administration, administrative receivership or liquidation (including provisional liquidation). The moratorium is also denied to a company currently undergoing a CVA and also to one which has already had recourse to such protection in the previous 12 months. It is estimated that some 38 per cent of all companies may access this new CVA moratorium model.

In order to obtain the CVA moratorium the directors must prepare documents and submit these to the nominee. Subsequently, these documents, accompanied by the nominee's statement, must be submitted by the directors to the court. The nominee must state whether there is a reasonable prospect of the purpose being approved and implemented. The test of "reasonable prospect" for these purposes will presumably be the same as that laid down in administration order cases in *Re Harris Simons Construction Ltd* [1989] 1 WLR 368. The nominee in promoting the proposal is entitled to rely on information provided by the directors and it is an offence for company officers to seek to obtain a moratorium by false representations (para. 42). The filing of these documents triggers an initial moratorium (para. 8) that will last 28 days or until the creditors' meeting is held. Extensions for a further two months are possible under para. 32. No court order as such is required to initiate the moratorium. The moratorium is to be advertised and any creditor who has petitioned for winding up must be personally notified.

The moratorium has the standard incidents found in corporate insolvency law of excluding most hostile actions against the company (see para. 12). Proceedings on extant winding-up petitions are stayed and the disabling effect of s. 127 of IA 1986 does not operate, though certain restrictions are imposed on the directors' freedom of action during the currency of the moratorium. However, petitions presented to wind up a company in the public interest are not to be obstructed. The effect of the moratorium upon the rights of the floating-charge holder is dealt with in some detail by para. 13. Debenture provisions allowing a floating charge to crystallise on the taking of preparatory steps to obtain a moratorium are void (para. 43). In this sense this legislation is to have retrospective effect. There is an interesting contrast with administration where the floating charge holder has a right of veto – see *Re Croftbell Ltd* [1990] BCC 781. The exclusion of traditional remedies exercised by secured creditors in the new CVA moratorium has aroused concern, but in practice banks often choose not to exercise such remedies. See Milman and Chittenden, *Corporate Rescue – CVAs and the Challenge of Small Companies*, ACCA Research Report No. 44 (1995). This abstinence has become even more noticeable since the advent of the Bankers' Code of Practice in July 1997 under which banks undertake to support business rescues. In any case, banks may still exert considerable influence because they are not obliged to offer continued funding; if the funding for the rescue is not available the nominee must terminate the moratorium (see *Hansard*, H.L. Vol. 613, CWH 13). In addition to the curbs on security enforcement, one effect of the moratorium is that security rights may be overridden with the leave of the court (see para. 20). Section 233 of IA 1986 is extended forward to prevent "blackmail" by utility suppliers during the preliminary moratorium period (this prohibition already operates once the CVA has been agreed).

The directors may provide additional security during the moratorium but this will only be enforceable if it is for the benefit of the company (e.g. it has produced rescue funding).

An interesting feature of the moratorium is that it constrains managerial actions on obtaining credit of more than £250 (unless the credit provider has been informed of the moratorium) and also when disposing of property. With regard to the obtaining of credit the case law under IA 1986, s. 360 may be relevant. There must be reasonable grounds for believing that the disposal will benefit the company and the nominee (or creditors' committee appointed under para. 35) must give approval. Where the directors exceed their limited powers during this period the transaction is not rendered unenforceable (see para. 15), though the directors may incur penalties (para. 18(3)). Certain other prejudicial conduct by directors in the 12 months prior to the moratorium may be subject to criminal sanction (para. 41). The figure of £500 in para. 41(4) has been the subject of much parliamentary debate and has been criticised for being arbitrary. Although the Government has stoutly defended its usage, it has nevertheless indicated that the figure could be revised if a problem arose (*Hansard*, H.C. Standing Committee B, 2 November, 2000, col. 75). The actions of directors may be challenged by creditors on the grounds of unfair prejudice (para. 40). These provisions are clearly designed to prevent abuse of the moratorium facility. Moreover, the nominee is expected to assume a monitoring role during this critical period (para. 24).

The actions of the nominee during the moratorium are open to challenge (para. 26 and 27). Nominees must withdraw their consent to act under certain conditions set out in para. 25. The court can also replace the nominee.

Part V deals with the consideration and implementation of the proposed CVA. These provisions mirror those found in Pt. I of IA 1986.

Schedule B1

Administration

General comment on Sch. B1

Schedule B1 was inserted into IA 1986 by EA 2002, s. 248, (1), (2), with effect from September 15, 2003 (see the Enterprise Act 2002 (Commencement No. 4 and Transitional Provisions and Savings) Order 2003 (SI 2003/2093 (C. 85)), art. 2(1) and Sch. (1), introducing a new Pt II and inaugurating a wholly new corporate administration regime – or range of regimes. Section 248 states that the new Pt II shall "be substituted" for the original Pt II, but this does not mean that the original Pt II is repealed, for s. 249, immediately following, reinstates the latter for many purposes. (See the note preceding s. 8 on p. 38.) The original Pt II, with annotations, is to be found at pp. 39ff.

The Insolvency (Amendment) Rules 2003 (SI 2003/1730, also effective September 15, 2003), para. 5 complements Sch. B1 by substituting a new Pt 2 for the original Pt 2 of IR 1986. However, as with Pt II of the Act, the original Pt 2 is preserved for those cases where a company or other body is put into administration under the original Pt II. (For a list of the bodies concerned, see I(A)R 2003, para. 5(2)–(4)). There are thus two sets of rules governing corporate administrations; and, confusingly, the rules of each Pt 2 are similarly (but not correspondingly) numbered. All references to the rules in this annotation to Sch. B1 are to the substituted rules, unless otherwise stated.

Schedule B1 applies (with modifications) to insurance companies, except that the appointment of an administrator can only be made by court order: see the Insurers (Reorganisation and Winding Up) Regulations Order 2004 (SI 2004/353), effective February 18, 2004, reg. 52.

The Insolvency Service early in 2003 issued a consultation paper proposing that the new Pt II regime should be extended to insolvent partnerships.

Nature of Administration

Administration

1(1) For the purposes of this Act "administrator" of a company means a person appointed under this Schedule to manage the company's affairs, business and property.

1(2) For the purposes of this Act–

(a) a company is "in administration" while the appointment of an administrator of the company has effect,

(b) a company "enters administration" when the appointment of an administrator takes effect,

(c) a company ceases to be in administration when the appointment of an administrator of the company ceases to have effect in accordance with this Schedule, and

(d) a company does not cease to be in administration merely because an administrator vacates office (by reason of resignation, death or otherwise) or is removed from office.

General Note

The original legislation, s. 8(2) contains definitions of "administration order" and "administrator" ("an administration order is an order directing that . . . the affairs, business and property of the company shall be managed by a person ('the administrator') appointed for the purpose by the court"). While the definition of "administrator" remains essentially the same, the new definitions introduced by sub-para. (2) are necessary because an administrator can now in many cases be appointed under the present Schedule without a court order.

These definitions are confined to administrators "appointed under this Schedule". In other cases, the original definitions of "administration order" and "administrator" will continue to apply, by virtue of EA 2002, s. 289 and the saving provisions of the Enterprise Act 2002 (Commencement No. 4 and Transitional Provisions and Savings) Order 2003 (SI 2003/2093 (C.85)). See the note preceding s. 8, on p. 38.

Para. 1(2)(c), (d)

It is particularly important to note the use of this wording in later provisions of the Schedule, since it is likely to be the source of much confusion. The draftsman has throughout chosen to avoid terms such as the "termination" of an

Schedule B1 *Insolvency Act 1986*

administration, or an administration "coming to an end", or a company "ceasing to be in administration" (except in the marginal notes). Instead, the circumlocution "the appointment of an administrator ceases to have effect" has been preferred. As is explained in sub-para. (2)(d), this does not refer to the ending of the appointment of the particular individual as administrator, but to the ending of the administration itself: the *office* of administrator continues in being, even though it may for the time being be unoccupied.

2 A person may be appointed as administrator of a company–

(a) by administration order of the court under paragraph 10,

(b) by the holder of a floating charge under paragraph 14, or

(c) by the company or its directors under paragraph 22.

GENERAL NOTE

Under the original legislation, an administrator could only be appointed by court order. The alternative of a direct appointment without application to the court under paras 14 and 22 will clearly now save time and expense and is likely to become the norm in the great majority of cases.

Para. 2(b)

The power of the holder of a floating charge to appoint an administrative receiver has generally been abrogated by IA 1986, s. 72A as from September 15, 2003 (but not with retrospective effect): see the note to that section. It is anticipated that charges created after that date will normally be enforced by the appointment of an administrator under para. 14.

Purpose of administration

3(1) The administrator of a company must perform his functions with the objective of–

(a) rescuing the company as a going concern, or

(b) achieving a better result for the company's creditors as a whole than would be likely if the company were wound up (without first being in administration), or

(c) realising property in order to make a distribution to one or more secured or preferential creditors.

3(2) Subject to sub-paragraph (4), the administrator of a company must perform his functions in the interests of the company's creditors as a whole.

3(3) The administrator must perform his functions with the objective specified in sub-paragraph (1)(a) unless he thinks either–

(a) that it is not reasonably practicable to achieve that objective, or

(b) that the objective specified in sub-paragraph (1)(b) would achieve a better result for the company's creditors as a whole.

3(4) The administrator may perform his functions with the objective specified in sub-paragraph (1)(c) only if–

(a) he thinks that it is not reasonably practicable to achieve either of the objectives specified in sub-paragraph (1)(a) and (b), and

(b) he does not unnecessarily harm the interests of the creditors of the company as a whole.

GENERAL NOTE

This paragraph contains one of the major changes introduced by the new administration regime. Under the original regime an order may specify one or more of four alternatives: (a) the survival of the company, and the whole or any part of its undertaking, as a going concern; (b) the approval of a voluntary arrangement under IA 1986, Pt I; (c) the sanctioning of a scheme of arrangement or compromise under CA 1985, s. 425; and (d) a more advantageous realisation of the company's assets than would be effected on a winding up. For the new regime this formulation has been entirely replaced, and the new wording is significant in a number of respects. First, and most importantly, there is no longer a choice of alternative purposes but a single hierarchy of objects. All administrations, whether instituted by court order or out of court, and regardless of the purpose of the person seeking or making the appointment of the administrator, are to have the same statutory objectives. The rescue of the company is made a matter of priority, and it is only if the administrator is of the opinion that this is not reasonably practicable or that a better result can be achieved for the company's creditors by pursuing some other course that he is permitted to disregard that primary objective.

Next, there is a repeated emphasis in all four sub-paragraphs on the interests of "the company's creditors as a whole". The purpose of this is not so much to make any change in the law governing administrations as to underline the contrast between administration and receivership, and particularly administrative receivership. It is well established that a receiver's duties are owed primarily to the secured creditor who has appointed him, and that all other interests are subordinated to the obligation to safeguard and enforce that security. Subject only to the statutory rights of the company's preferential creditors and a duty to act in good faith, a receiver is generally free to realise sufficient assets to pay off the secured debt without any concern for the interests of the company itself or its other creditors. Moreover, the holder of a floating charge over all, or substantially all, of the company's assets has the power under the original law to veto the appointment of an administrator and appoint an administrative receiver instead. EA 2002 no longer gives these secured creditors the whip hand: not only does it remove this power of veto (subject to certain specific exceptions and some transitional provisions: see the note to IA 1986, s. 72A), so obliging the holder of a floating charge to appoint an administrator rather than a receiver if he wishes to enforce his security, but it lumps the company's secured and preferential creditors together with all the other creditors and requires the administrator to act in the interests of them all. It is only if the requirements of sub-para. (4)(a) can be met that the administrator is permitted to realise assets in order to pay off the preferential and secured creditors (para. (1)(c)), and even then only on condition that he does not unnecessarily harm the interests of the creditors as a whole. The priority traditionally attaching to receivership is thus virtually stood on its head.

Para. 3(1), (3)
The formula "rescuing the company as a going concern" may be contrasted with the wording under the original legislation, "the survival of *the company, and* the whole or any part of its undertaking, as a going concern". The emphasis placed on the rescue or survival of the company (as distinct from its business or undertaking) is rather curious, for the Cork Committee was firmly of the view that it was only the latter that really mattered. In *Re Rowbotham Baxter Ltd* [1990] B.C.C. 113 at 115, Harman J. stated that a proposal involving the sale of a "hived down" company formed to take over part of a company's business could not be brought within the original wording, in view of the words which have been italicised above; and even more plainly it could not come within the new formulation. However, this may in fact make it easier for an administrator to conclude that it is not reasonably practicable to achieve a rescue of the company and so move on to the second statutory objective (achieving a better result for the company's creditors as a whole than would be likely under an immediate winding up).

Para. 3(2), (4)
As noted above, the administrator, unlike a receiver, is not subject to an overriding obligation to have regard to the interests of the company's secured and preferential creditors: he must have regard to the interests of the company's creditors as a whole. Once a receiver has paid off the secured charge, his functions are completed: he must hand over control of the company's property to its directors or liquidator. Apart from the statutory obligation to pay the preferential creditors, it is not his concern to see that any of the other creditors' debts are paid, and he owes them no duties either at law or in equity. An administrator, in contrast, is now by these sub-paragraphs bound to perform his functions in the interests of the company's creditors as a whole: paying off the secured creditors ranks last in the statutory objectives, and in doing so he is under a positive duty not to harm the company's other creditors. A creditor has standing to complain of a breach of this duty under para. 74.

4 The administrator of a company must perform his functions as quickly and efficiently as is reasonably practicable.

GENERAL NOTE
This provision may have been inserted to meet criticisms that, in contrast with receivership, the administration procedure (involving meetings of creditors, etc.) is relatively more slow, formal and expensive. It may be thought rather too vague to establish a positive legal duty remediable in damages: the most obvious sanction would be an application to the court to have the defaulting administrator removed and replaced, and for this purpose para. 74(2) may help to smooth the path.

Status of administrator

5 An administrator is an officer of the court (whether or not he is appointed by the court).

Schedule B1 — *Insolvency Act 1986*

GENERAL NOTE

As an officer of the court (like the liquidator in a compulsory liquidation), an administrator is bound by the rule in *Ex p. James* (1874) L.R. 9 Ch.App. 609, which imposes a rather ill-defined obligation to act honourably and fairly. He also enjoys the protection of the law of contempt of court if there is any interference with the performance of his duties.

General restrictions

6   A person may be appointed as administrator of a company only if he is qualified to act as an insolvency practitioner in relation to the company.

GENERAL NOTE

The expression "qualified to act as an insolvency practitioner in relation to the company" refers not only to the requirement that the individual concerned should have the appropriate professional qualification but also to his specific eligibility to act *vis-à-vis* the particular company. See the note to s. 390.

7   A person may not be appointed as administrator of a company which is in administration (subject to the provisions of paragraphs 90 to 97 and 100 to 103 about replacement and additional administrators).

GENERAL NOTE

There cannot be two administrations simultaneously in existence, *e.g.* one appointed on the initiative of the directors and another by the holder of a floating charge. But it is possible to have administrators representing such different interests appointed to act jointly or concurrently in the same administration: see the notes to paras 90–97 and 100–103.

8(1)   A person may not be appointed as administrator of a company which is in liquidation by virtue of–

(a)   a resolution for voluntary winding up, or

(b)   a winding-up order.

8(2)   Sub-paragraph (1)(a) is subject to paragraph 38.

8(3)   Sub-paragraph (1)(b) is subject to paragraphs 37 and 38.

GENERAL NOTE

A company which is in liquidation cannot at the same time be put into administration. But paras 37 and 38 empower the court, on the application respectively of a floating charge holder or the liquidator, to order that administration be substituted for a winding up. And in the special case where a winding-up order is made on public interest grounds in relation to a company which is already in administration, the court may order the administration to continue under para. 82. See further the notes to those paragraphs.

9(1)   A person may not be appointed as administrator of a company which–

(a)   has a liability in respect of a deposit which it accepted in accordance with the Banking Act 1979 (c. 37) or 1987 (c. 22), but

(b)   is not an authorised deposit taker.

9(2)   A person may not be appointed as administrator of a company which effects or carries out contracts of insurance.

9(3)   But sub-paragraph (2) does not apply to a company which–

(a)   is exempt from the general prohibition in relation to effecting or carrying out contracts of insurance, or

(b)   is an authorised deposit taker effecting or carrying out contracts of insurance in the course of a banking business.

9(4)   In this paragraph–

"authorised deposit taker" means a person with permission under Part IV of the Financial Services and Markets Act 2000 (c. 8) to accept deposits, and

"the general prohibition" has the meaning given by section 19 of that Act.

9(5) This paragraph shall be construed in accordance with–

(a) section 22 of the Financial Services and Markets Act 2000 (classes of regulated activity and categories of investment),

(b) any relevant order under that section, and

(c) Schedule 2 to that Act (regulated activities).

GENERAL NOTE

Under IA 1986 as originally enacted, banking and insurance companies were excluded from the administration regime. But Pt II of the Act was extended to apply (with certain modifications) to banks and the other bodies mentioned in para. 9(1)(a), if they were companies within the meaning of CA 1985, s. 735, by the Banks (Administration Proceedings) Order 1989 (SI 1989/1276) with effect from August 23, 1989; and similarly the administration procedure was made available to insurance companies by the Financial Services and Markets Act 2000 (Administration Orders Relating to Insurers) Order 2002 (SI 2002/1242) from May 31, 2002. This paragraph brings forward those provisions so that the categories of banking and insurance companies identified may be made subject to the new administration regime, (but, in regard to insurance companies, a company can only be put into administration by court order: see the Financial Services and Markets Act 2000 (Administration Orders Relating to Insurers) Order 2002 (SI 2002/1242, as amended by SI 2003/2134 and SI 2004/353, reg. 52, as from February 18, 2004)). However, the Enterprise Act 2002 (Commencement No. 4 and Transitional Provisions and Savings) Order 2003 (SI 2003/2093, effective September 15, 2003), art. 3(3) provides that the original IA 1986, Pt II will continue to apply insofar as is necessary to give effect to the above order of 2002, so that, for administrations already current, it is the provisions of the original Pt II and not the present Schedule that govern the position.

APPOINTMENT OF ADMINISTRATOR BY COURT

Administration order

10 An administration order is an order appointing a person as the administrator of a company.

GENERAL NOTE

Under the original Pt II regime, a company can be put into administration only by court order. Paras 14–34 now authorise the alternative of making an appointment extra-judicially, which is likely to be the procedure used in the great majority of cases in future because of the saving in time, formality and expense. It is only in cases where the initiative is taken by a person other than the company or its directors or the holder of a "qualifying" floating charge (see the note to para. 14(2)) that it will be obligatory to use the court procedure. (Note also that for building societies and the categories of company mentioned in EA 2002, s. 249 and the bodies mentioned in the next paragraph, the only way to have the company put into administration is by court order, but in this case it is the regime under the unamended IA 1986, Pt II which will apply.)

For court appointments under the new regime (*i.e.* where the application for an order is presented to the court on or after September 15, 2003), the relevant rules are to be found the new Pt 2 of Sch. 1 to the Rules: see I(A)R 2003, para. 5(1) and below, pp. 733ff. For appointments under the original regime (including appointments made on petitions presented before that date, and all applications under EA 2002, s. 249(2), the Insolvent Partnerships Order 1994, the Limited Liability Partnerships Regulations 2001 and the Financial Services and Markets Act 2000 (Administration Orders relating to Insurers) Order 2002 (as amended), the original Pt 2 of the rules applies: see I(A)R 2003, para. 5(2)–(4) and below, pp. 706ff.

Conditions for making order

11 The court may make an administration order in relation to a company only if satisfied–

(a) that the company is or is likely to become unable to pay its debts, and

(b) that the administration order is reasonably likely to achieve the purpose of administration.

GENERAL NOTE

As under the original IA 1986, s. 8(1), there are here two preconditions for the making of an administration order: (a) actual or likely insolvency, and (b) the likely achievement of the purpose of the administration. But under that section there was for a time considerable judicial disagreement as to the degree of probability and the appropriate standard of proof to be applied in construing such expressions as "satisfied" and "likely". The decisions under that provision are no doubt apt to give guidance in the construction of the present paragraph, but a note of caution must be expressed because the wording of the two statutory provisions is not identical.

So far as concerns the phrase "satisfied ... that the company is or is likely to become unable to pay its debts", however, the language is the same. In *Re COLT Telecom Group plc* [2002] EWCH 2815 (Ch.) Jacob J. ruled that "likely" in this context meant "more probable than not". It was not enough for the petitioner to give evidence sufficient to satisfy some lesser test, *e.g.* that there was a "real prospect" of insolvency (as had been held to be the case in regard to the same word, "likely" where it appeared later in the original subsection: see below). "Satisfied" thus means "satisfied on a balance of probabilities". The term "unable to pay its debts" has the meaning given by IA 1986, s. 123, *i.e.* insolvent on either a "cash-flow" or a "balance-sheet" basis: see para. 111(1) and the notes to s. 123.

There is a slight change in the wording used in para. 11(b): the court must now be "satisfied" that "the administration order is reasonably likely to achieve the purpose of the administration", whereas the original s. 8(1)(b) reads "considers that the making of an order under this section would be likely to achieve one or more of the purposes mentioned below". Thus "is satisfied" replaces "considers" and "likely" becomes "reasonably likely". In *Re Harris Simons Construction Ltd* [1989] 1 W.L.R. 368, (1989) 5 B.C.C. 11, Hoffmann J. held that it was sufficient that the court should consider that there was "a real prospect" that one or more of the statutory purposes might be achieved, and later cases (*e.g. Re Lomax Leisure Ltd* [2000] B.C.C. 352 at 363) have consistently applied the "real prospect" test: see the note to the original IA 1986, s. 8(1), (2). In construing the new provision, the phrase "is satisfied" may be thought to impose a more stringent standard than "considers", but this appears to be balanced by the insertion of the word "reasonably" before "likely". Overall, it seems probable that the new wording will be regarded as a restatement in different terms of Hoffmann J.'s test.

It should be noted that para. 11(a) does not apply – *i.e.* insolvency or near-insolvency is not a prerequisite – where the applicant is the holder of a "qualifying" floating charge and satisfies the court that it is in a position to appoint an administrator under para. 14 (see para. 35). This reflects the fact that there is no similar prerequisite where the charge holder makes an out-of-court appointment.

Administration application

12(1) An application to the court for an administration order in respect of a company (an "administration application") may be made only by–

(a) the company,

(b) the directors of the company,

(c) one or more creditors of the company,

(d) the justices' chief executive for a magistrates' court in the exercise of the power conferred by section 87A of the Magistrates' Courts Act 1980 (c. 43) (fine imposed on company), or

(e) a combination of persons listed in paragraphs (a) to (d).

12(2) As soon as is reasonably practicable after the making of an administration application the applicant shall notify–

(a) any person who has appointed an administrative receiver of the company,

(b) any person who is or may be entitled to appoint an administrative receiver of the company,

(c) any person who is or may be entitled to appoint an administrator of the company under paragraph 14, and

(d) such other persons as may be prescribed.

12(3) An administration application may not be withdrawn without the permission of the court.

12(4) In sub-paragraph (1) "creditor" includes a contingent creditor and a prospective creditor.

12(5) Sub-paragraph (1) is without prejudice to section 7(4)(b).

GENERAL NOTE

The former procedure, involving a petition to the court, has been replaced by an "administration application" in Form 2.1B. For the relevant rules, see IR 1986, rr. 2.2ff.

The court can only make an administration order on an application made under this provision. The recommendation of the Cork Committee (*Report,* para. 510) that an order might be made as an alternative to liquidation on the hearing of a winding-up petition was not accepted.

Para. 12(1), (4)
These sub-paragraphs cover essentially the same ground as the original s. 9(1). The notes to that section may be relevant here. It should be noted that the following, in addition to those listed in this sub-paragraph, also have standing to apply:

- the liquidator of the company (see para. 38);
- the supervisor of a CVA see para. 12(5) and s. 7(4)(b);
- the Financial Services Authority, under FSMA 2000, s. 359 (as amended by EA 2002, Sch. 17, para. 55).

An application by the supervisor of a CVA is treated as if it were an application by the company: see r. 2.2(4). The holder of a "qualifying" floating charge is also singled out for special mention in Form 2.1B as a separate category of applicant. This is no doubt a matter of administrative convenience: of course, the holder of any charge will in any case have standing as a creditor under para. 12(1)(c).

Under the original s. 9(1), there was uncertainty for a time regarding an application made by "the directors": could they act informally, and must they be unanimous? Happily, for the purposes of the present Schedule, para. 105 states that they may act by a majority and imposes no formal requirement.

Para. 12(2)
The list of persons who must be given notice has been extended by the inclusion of sub-para. (2)(c): this is now necessary because EA 2002, s. 250, inserting new ss. 72A–72H into IA 1986, means that the holder of a floating charge can no longer prevent the appointment of an administrator by putting the company into administrative receivership. But, even so, the holder of such a charge may wish to take action under para. 14 or para. 36 in order to ensure that, if the company is to be put into administration, the administrator will be a person of whom he approves. However, since s. 250 is not retrospective, and is also subject to the exceptions set out in ss. 72B–72H, it has been necessary to continue to include sub-paras. (a) and (b).

For the persons prescribed for the purposes of sub-para. (2)(d), see rr. 2.6(3), 2.7.

In cases brought under the original Pt II the court has been prepared in a situation of urgency to hear an application without observing the formalities as to notice, etc. required by the Act: see the note to s. 9(1).

Para. 12(5)
This subparagraph was inserted by the Enterprise Act 2002 (Insolvency) Order 2003 (SI 2003/2096), arts. 1, 2(1), (2), effective September 15, 2003.

Powers of court

13(1) On hearing an administration application the court may–
- (a) make the administration order sought;
- (b) dismiss the application;
- (c) adjourn the hearing conditionally or unconditionally;
- (d) make an interim order;
- (e) treat the application as a winding-up petition and make any order which the court could make under section 125;
- (f) make any other order which the court thinks appropriate.

13(2) An appointment of an administrator by administration order takes effect–
- (a) at a time appointed by the order, or
- (b) where no time is appointed by the order, when the order is made.

13(3) An interim order under sub-paragraph (1)(d) may, in particular–
- (a) restrict the exercise of a power of the directors or the company;
- (b) make provision conferring a discretion on the court or on a person qualified to act as an insolvency practitioner in relation to the company.

13(4) This paragraph is subject to paragraph 39.

Schedule B1   *Insolvency Act 1986*

GENERAL NOTE

This paragraph corresponds broadly to the original s. 9(4)–(5), with certain additions and modifications, and the notes to those provisions may be relevant here. However, the power conferred by sub-para. (1)(e) to make a winding-up order in lieu of an administration order is new: previously, in *Re Brooke Marine Ltd* [1988] B.C.L.C. 546 it was ruled that a winding-up order could only be made on a petition presented under s. 124.

For the rules and prescribed forms governing an application for an administration order and the supporting documents which must be filed with the application, see rr. 2.2ff. Among these documents is a statement by the proposed administrator (in Form 2.2B) that he consents to act, and that in his opinion the purpose of the administration is reasonably likely to be achieved.

Para. 13(1), (3)

As noted above, the power conferred on the court by sub-para. (1)(e) to make a winding-up order in lieu of an administration order had no counterpart in the former legislation.

Where the court makes an order under para. 13(1)(d) or (f), it must give directions regarding the giving of notice of the order under r. 2.14(3).

On the "commencement" of a winding up under para. 13(1)(e), see IA 1986, s. 129(1A).

Para. 13(2)

There was no counterpart to this provision in the former legislation: it makes clear that the court has power to fix a time other than that of the order for it to take effect.

Where the court fixes a time later than that of its order, the interim moratorium which will have been in place under para. 44(1)(a) is continued under para. 44(1)(b).

Para. 13(4)

Paragraph 39 preserves the position under the former law, *viz.* that an administration cannot co-exist with an administrative receivership. It follows that where the holder of a floating charge continues to have the power to appoint an administrative receiver (see the note to IA 1986, s. 72A), he can effectively veto the appointment of an administrator. See further the note to para. 39.

APPOINTMENT OF ADMINISTRATOR BY HOLDER OF FLOATING CHARGE

Power to appoint

14(1) The holder of a qualifying floating charge in respect of a company's property may appoint an administrator of the company.

14(2) For the purposes of sub-paragraph (1) a floating charge qualifies if created by an instrument which–

(a) states that this paragraph applies to the floating charge,

(b) purports to empower the holder of the floating charge to appoint an administrator of the company,

(c) purports to empower the holder of the floating charge to make an appointment which would be the appointment of an administrative receiver within the meaning given by section 29(2), or

(d) purports to empower the holder of a floating charge in Scotland to appoint a receiver who on appointment would be an administrative receiver.

14(3) For the purposes of sub-paragraph (1) a person is the holder of a qualifying floating charge in respect of a company's property if he holds one or more debentures of the company secured–

(a) by a qualifying floating charge which relates to the whole or substantially the whole of the company's property,

(b) by a number of qualifying floating charges which together relate to the whole or substantially the whole of the company's property, or

(c) by charges and other forms of security which together relate to the whole or substantially the whole of the company's property and at least one of which is a qualifying floating charge.

GENERAL NOTE

The power which the holder of a floating charge has enjoyed in the past to appoint an administrative receiver has been abrogated by EA 2002, s. 250 (although not with retrospective effect, and subject to the exceptions set out in IA 1986, ss. 72B–72H: see the notes to ss. 72A–72H, EA 2002, s. 250 and para. 39, below). The legislature now contemplates that a charge-holder will normally enforce his security by putting the company into administration, and in consequence (a) the objective of an administration now expressly includes "realising property in order to make a distribution to one or more secured or preferential creditors" (para. 3(1)(c) above), and (b) the holder of a "qualifying" floating charge, as defined in para. 14(2), is now given the power to appoint an administrator directly, without the need to apply to the court for an order. However, from the charge-holder's point of view, his position is considerably less advantageous than would be the case in a receivership: first, because the administrator not only has to act in the interests of the company's creditors as a whole (para. 3(2)), rather than primarily in the interests of the charge-holder; secondly, because satisfying the charge-holder's security ranks last in the hierarchy of objectives of an administration – even when the charge-holder has appointed the administrator under this paragraph; and thirdly because, even under the new administration regime, the procedure is more formal and elaborate than a receivership, and consequently slower and more expensive.

The holder of a floating charge may still enforce his security by appointing a non-administrative receiver (*i.e.* a receiver of less than a substantial part of the company's assets), but if the company is then put into administration on the initiative of some other party the receiver may be required to vacate office under para. 41(2).

For a charge-holder to be able to make an appointment under para. 14, it is necessary that a default or other event should have occurred which entitles him to enforce the charge (para. 16); but it is not a prerequisite that the company should be, or be likely to become, insolvent.

Where the appointment of an administrator is to be made under para. 14, there will be an interim moratorium only if the charge-holder files a notice of intention to appoint an administrator under para. 44(2), (3): see the note to those provisions.

For the relevant rules and prescribed forms, see rr. 2.15ff.

Para. 14(2), (3)

It is only if the charge is a "qualifying" floating charge that the holder has the power to appoint an administrator under this paragraph: the holder of any other charge (*e.g.* a floating charge over part only of the company's assets) will have to apply for a court order. The essential characteristics of a qualifying floating charge, elaborated in more detail in these sub-paragraphs, are: (a) that the charge must by its terms give the holder power to appoint an administrator (or an adminstrative receiver), and (b) the charge (or that and other charges taken together) must relate to the whole or substantially the whole of the company's property. So far as concerns characteristic (a), there is a variety of terminology which may be used in the charge instrument: sub-paras. (2)(a)–(d) are alternatives. In the first place, the draftsman may simply refer to para. 14 or he may expressly give the charge-holder power to appoint an administrator. Alternatively, if he has not brought his precedents up to date to take account of EA 2002, s. 250 or (more realistically) if the document was executed before that Act came into force, and the powers conferred on the charge-holder include a power to appoint a receiver who would be an administrative receiver as defined by IA 1986, s. 29(2), this also will enable the chargee to appoint an administrator directly under this provision.

Paragraph 14(3)(c) will cover the common case where a chargee takes security by way of a fixed charge over parts of a company's property and a floating charge over all or substantially all of the remainder, and this will be so whether there is one charge instrument or several. It would also seem, at least tacitly, to affirm the effectiveness of what is commonly referred to as a "lightweight" floating charge, which was upheld in *Re Croftbell Ltd* [1990] B.C.C. 781 (see the note to IA 1986, s. 9(3)): the holder of such a charge will be able to appoint an administrator directly if it is in his interests to do so. However, it may well make more sense to enforce the fixed-charge elements of the security by other means.

The position where there is more than one floating charge over a company's property is dealt with in para. 15.

Restrictions on power to appoint

15(1) A person may not appoint an administrator under paragraph 14 unless–

(a) he has given at least two business days' written notice to the holder of any prior floating charge which satisfies paragraph 14(2), or

(b) the holder of any prior floating charge which satisfies paragraph 14(2) has consented in writing to the making of the appointment.

15(2) One floating charge is prior to another for the purposes of this paragraph if–

(a) it was created first, or

(b) it is to be treated as having priority in accordance with an agreement to which the holder of each floating charge was party.

15(3) Sub-paragraph (2) shall have effect in relation to Scotland as if the following were substituted for paragraph (a)–

> "(a) it has priority of ranking in accordance with section 464(4)(b) of the Companies Act 1985 (c. 6),".

GENERAL NOTE

This paragraph deals with the position where there are two or more charges, each being or including a floating charge, over the company's property: a junior-ranking chargee who wishes to appoint an administrator must give at least two days' notice to those having priority, or alternatively secure their written consent. Priority is determined by reference to the time of creation, or any agreement between the charge-holders (para. 15(2)). Curiously, the obligation to give notice is imposed only by reference to the criteria set out in para. 14(2), and not also to those in para. 14(3): what matters is whether there is a power to appoint an administrator directly conferred on the senior chargee by his charge instrument rather than whether his charge is over the whole or substantially the whole of the company's property. From one point of view, this is unimportant, for there will effectively be no power to make an appointment unless the charge is "substantial". But from another viewpoint para. 15((1) poses a problem for a junior chargee, since it may be difficult for him to find out whether the instrument creating the senior-ranking charge contains any of the clauses referred to in para. 14(2). The particulars registered in Companies House will not include them unless the company has gratuitously volunteered to file the information, and while in theory he has a right under CA 1985, s. 408 to inspect the charge instrument itself at the company's registered office, it is a notorious fact that few companies bother to comply with these particular statutory obligations. The best advice for the holder of a junior-ranking charge is that he should give notice to his superior counterparts in any case, without concerning himself whether or not para. 14(2) applies.

Note that notice must be given to a senior chargee even if his charge is not currently enforceable.

The options available to a senior chargee who receives such a notice are limited. He would have no right to prevent the holder of the later charge from enforcing his security unless he could persuade the court to intervene on the ground that the appointment was being sought *mala fide* or for an improper purpose. Most obviously, he could take steps (either by negotiation or by making an appointment himself) to ensure that the proposed administrator was a practitioner of his own choosing, or that such a person should be appointed an additional administrator to act jointly or concurrently with the junior chargee's nominee.

Para. 15(1)
Although it is not necessary that the notice to the charge holder should be in a prescribed form, Form 2.5B must be used for filing in court in order to obtain a moratorium. This embodies a form of consent which the recipient has the option of using. In contrast with the position under paras 26–27, there is no obligation to file a copy of the notice with the court, although if this is done the charge holder will enjoy the benefit of a five-day moratorium under para. 44(2).

Para. 15(2)
Oddly, there is no mention of the case where a number of charges rank *pari passu*. Prudence would dictate that notice should be given anyway, and also to the trustee of any trust deed.

16 An administrator may not be appointed under paragraph 14 while a floating charge on which the appointment relies is not enforceable.

GENERAL NOTE

The power of a floating charge-holder to appoint an administrator out of court arises only if a default or other event has occurred which entitles him to enforce the charge. If this is not so, he would still have standing, as a creditor, to apply or to join with other creditors in applying to the court for an order under para. 12.

This paragraph can also be read as confirming the obvious point that if the charge is invalid or void (*e.g.* because the charge instrument was not properly executed or particulars of the charge have not been duly registered) it cannot confer any powers on the holder. If the holder purports to appoint an administrator without the power to do so, the administrator will be liable to the company as a trespasser but will be entitled to an indemnity under para. 21.

17 An administrator of a company may not be appointed under paragraph 14 if—

(a) a provisional liquidator of the company has been appointed under section 135, or

(b) an administrative receiver of the company is in office.

GENERAL NOTE

It would obviously create difficulties to have two office-holders in post at the same time administering the company's affairs with conflicting objectives. It would, of course, be open to the charge-holder to apply to the court under r. 4.31 to have the appointment of a provisional liquidator terminated and the company put into administration instead, *e.g.* with a view to rescuing the company as a going concern.

This paragraph may be contrasted with para. 25, which bars a company or its directors from appointing an administrator out of court while a petition for a winding-up order or an application to the court for the appointment of an administrator is pending. Neither of these limitations applies to an appointment by the holder of a floating charge under para. 14. If an appointment is made under para. 14, any petition for winding up is suspended while the company is in administration, unless it is a petition based on public interest grounds (para. 40(1)(b), (2)).

Although IA 1986, s. 72A now generally prevents a charge holder from appointing an administrative receiver, this provision is not retrospective so as to apply to charges already created before September 15, 2003, and so there will continue to be many cases where para. 17(b) will apply.

Notice of appointment

18(1) A person who appoints an administrator of a company under paragraph 14 shall file with the court—

(a) a notice of appointment, and

(b) such other documents as may be prescribed.

18(2) The notice of appointment must include a statutory declaration by or on behalf of the person who makes the appointment—

(a) that the person is the holder of a qualifying floating charge in respect of the company's property,

(b) that each floating charge relied on in making the appointment is (or was) enforceable on the date of the appointment, and

(c) that the appointment is in accordance with this Schedule.

18(3) The notice of appointment must identify the administrator and must be accompanied by a statement by the administrator—

(a) that he consents to the appointment,

(b) that in his opinion the purpose of administration is reasonably likely to be achieved, and

(c) giving such other information and opinions as may be prescribed.

18(4) For the purpose of a statement under sub-paragraph (3) an administrator may rely on information supplied by directors of the company (unless he has reason to doubt its accuracy).

18(5) The notice of appointment and any document accompanying it must be in the prescribed form.

18(6) A statutory declaration under sub-paragraph (2) must be made during the prescribed period.

18(7) A person commits an offence if in a statutory declaration under sub-paragraph (2) he makes a statement—

(a) which is false, and

(b) which he does not reasonably believe to be true.

GENERAL NOTE

The appointment of the administrator under para. 14 takes effect only when the requirements of this paragraph have been satisfied (para. 19). The completion of all the necessary formalities, even with the co-operation of everyone

Schedule B1 *Insolvency Act 1986*

concerned, is bound to take some time – a situation which may be thought disadvantageous from the viewpoint of the floating charge holder in comparison with the speed and simplicity of appointing a receiver. The legislators have taken some steps to meet concerns on this score: first, it is possible at least in some circumstances for the charge holder to secure an interim moratorium for up to five business days by filing a notice of intention to appoint with the court under para. 44(2), using Form 2.5B and, secondly, provision has been made by r. 2.19 for the appointment of an administrator under para. 14 to take effect even when the court is closed, by allowing notice of the appointment to be sent by fax: see the note to that rule.

For the relevant rules and prescribed forms, see rr. 2.15ff.

Para. 18(2), (6)
Form 2.6B is prescribed for the statutory declaration: it must be made not more than five business days before it is filed with the court (r. 2.16(3)).

Para. 18(3)
The same form (Form 2.2B) is used for the administrator's written statement in all proceedings under Schedule B1. It also requires the proposed administrator to certify that he is authorised to act, and to give details of any prior professional relationship with the company.

Para. 18(5)
Form 2.6B has been prescribed for the notice of appointment, Form 2.2B for the administrator's written statement and Form 2.6B for the statutory declaration. If notice of intention to appoint is to be given to the court under para. 44(2), the form that may be used is Form 2.5B. Further requirements are set out in rr. 2.15–2.17. Note that where a notice of appointment is to be sent by fax, Form 2.7B and not Form 2.6B is to be used.

Para. 18(7)
On penalties, see s. 430 and Sch. 10. The same penalties are prescribed by the Perjury Act 1911, s. 5.

Commencement of appointment

19 The appointment of an administrator under paragraph 14 takes effect when the requirements of paragraph 18 are satisfied.

GENERAL NOTE
This provision may be contrasted with the appointment of an administrator by the court, which takes effect from or under the court's order (para. 13(2)), and with the appointment of a receiver, where the court is not involved in any way and s. 33 applies.

At any time when the court is closed (but not otherwise), r. 2.19 allows a notice of appointment to be filed by fax, using Form 2.7B. A central fax telephone number is provided by the Court Service for this purpose, which is published on the website of The Insolvency Service and may also be obtained in writing from the latter on request. The number currently published is 020 7947 6607. In Scotland, the form should be faxed directly to the relevant court. The numbers can be found on the Scottish Courts website, *www.scotcourts.gov.uk*. The appointor must ensure that a fax transmission report detailing the time and date of the transmission and containing a copy of all or part of the first page of the document transmitted is created by the fax machine and he must take this, together with the original of the form and all the necessary supporting documents, to the court on the next day that it is open for business, and he must attach a statement providing, *inter alia*, "full reasons for the out of hours filing of the notice of appointment, including why it would have been damaging to the company and/or its creditors not to have so acted" (r. 2.19(8)). While the point, and indeed the legitimacy, of this last requirement may be questioned, it should not be too difficult to find a suitable form of words to meet the case.

On the possibility of putting an interim moratorium in place pending compliance with para. 19, see the note to para. 44(2).

20 A person who appoints an administrator under paragraph 14–

  (a) shall notify the administrator and such other persons as may be prescribed as soon as is reasonably practicable after the requirements of paragraph 18 are satisfied, and

  (b) commits an offence if he fails without reasonable excuse to comply with paragraph (a).

GENERAL NOTE
It will be in the interests of all concerned (and not least the administrator himself) for para. 18 to be complied with expeditiously, since until this is done he will have no power or authority to act. However, it is immaterial for this purpose whether he has been given the notice required by para. 20(a).

Rule 2.17(2) requires that the administrator should be sent a copy of the notice of appointment bearing the seal of the court and endorsed with the date and time of filing. It is no doubt intended that this should be the way in which the administrator should be "notified" under para. 20(a), although this is not stated in specific terms.

For the "other persons" prescribed by para. 20(a), see r. 2.18: if the charge holder appoints an administrator in reliance on para. 14 after he has received notice that an application has been made to the court for the appointment of an administrator, he must send a copy of the notice of appointment to the applicant and to the court in which the application has been made.

The administrator himself has obligations to give various notices under para. 46(2).

On penalties, see s. 430, Sch. 10 and para. 106(2).

Invalid appointment: indemnity

21(1) This paragraph applies where–

(a) a person purports to appoint an administrator under paragraph 14, and

(b) the appointment is discovered to be invalid.

21(2) The court may order the person who purported to make the appointment to indemnify the person appointed against liability which arises solely by reason of the appointment's invalidity.

GENERAL NOTE

The purported appointment of an administrator may be invalid for any number of reasons: for instance, the charge instrument may be void, *e.g.* for want of due execution or registration under CA 1985, Pt XII; the charge may not come within the definition of a "qualifying" floating charge under para. 14 above; or the conditions rendering the charge enforceable may not have been met. The court has a discretionary power under this provision to order the charge-holder (or, indeed, any person) who made the purported appointment to indemnify the appointee against any liability in trespass, etc. that he may have incurred. But there is no power conferred on the court to validate the appointment. There is a parallel with s. 34, which deals with the invalid appointment of a receiver. Of course, the parties may in any case have entered into a contract of indemnity, in which case no question of the court's discretion will arise.

APPOINTMENT OF ADMINISTRATOR BY COMPANY OR DIRECTORS

Power to appoint

22(1) A company may appoint an administrator.

22(2) The directors of a company may appoint an administrator.

GENERAL NOTE

As has been noted, under IA 1986, Pt II as originally enacted, a company could be put into administration only by order of the court. The reforms made by EA 2002 not only empower the holder of a floating charge to appoint an administrator without the involvement of the court, but confer a similar power on the company itself or its directors. These innovations will obviate the need for the involvement of the court (except as a repository of documents) in the great majority of cases.

For the relevant rules, see rr. 2.20ff.

Para. 22(1)

The company may take this step by resolution of the shareholders passed at a general meeting (or a unanimous informal agreement which is equivalent to such a resolution either at common law or under CA 1985, ss. 381Aff). An ordinary resolution appears to be sufficient.

Para. 22(2)

The directors for this purpose may act by a majority, and it does not appear to be necessary that they should do so at a formal meeting: see para. 105. This is confirmed by r. 2.22, which refers to "a copy of the *resolution* of the company", but "a record of the *decision* of the directors".

Schedule B1   *Insolvency Act 1986*
                        Restrictions on power to appoint

23(1) This paragraph applies where an administrator of a company is appointed–

(a) under paragraph 22, or

(b) on an administration application made by the company or its directors.

23(2) An administrator of the company may not be appointed under paragraph 22 during the period of 12 months beginning with the date on which the appointment referred to in sub-paragraph (1) ceases to have effect.

GENERAL NOTE

If a company has already been put into administration on the initiative of the company itself or its directors (either out of court under para. 22 or by a court order made on its or their application), this provision places a ban on the company being put into administration for a second time under para. 22 unless a 12-month period has elapsed since the first appointment "ceased to have effect" (*i.e.* the administration terminated: see para. 1(2)(c)). We may see a parallel here with the similar ban imposed upon a company from entering into a second CVA less than 12 months after it has had the benefit of a moratorium following a proposal for an earlier CVA: see Sch. A1, para. 4(1)(f), (g). Note, however, that this restriction only applies to a second appointment made under para. 22, *i.e.* out of court: there is no prohibition on the company or its directors making an application to the court for the appointment of a second administrator within the 12-month period.

24(1) If a moratorium for a company under Schedule A1 ends on a date when no voluntary arrangement is in force in respect of the company, this paragraph applies for the period of 12 months beginning with that date.

24(2) This paragraph also applies for the period of 12 months beginning with the date on which a voluntary arrangement in respect of a company ends if–

(a) the arrangement was made during a moratorium for the company under Schedule A1, and

(b) the arrangement ends prematurely (within the meaning of section 7B).

24(3) While this paragraph applies, an administrator of the company may not be appointed under paragraph 22.

GENERAL NOTE

As noted above, the legislation imposes a ban upon a company from entering into a second CVA less than 12 months after it has had the benefit of a moratorium following a proposal for an earlier CVA (Sch. A1, para. 4(1)(f), (g)). This paragraph similarly prohibits the company or its directors from appointing an administrator out of court within that period – although they are not prevented from making an application to the court for an administration order.

See further the note to Sch. A1, para. 4(1).

25 An administrator of a company may not be appointed under paragraph 22 if–

(a) a petition for the winding up of the company has been presented and is not yet disposed of,

(b) an administration application has been made and is not yet disposed of, or

(c) an administrative receiver of the company is in office.

GENERAL NOTE

These limitations are more extensive than those which apply where an out-of-court appointment is made by the holder of a floating charge under para. 14: see para. 17. Once again, the restrictions imposed by this paragraph apply only to the appointment of an administrator by a company or its directors out of court: there is nothing to prevent them from making an application to the court for an appointment, although if there is an administrative receiver in office, para. 39 will apply.

The reference in sub-para. (b) to the making of an application, taken literally, would arguably not cover proceedings instituted by petition under the original Pt II – *e.g.* a petition presented but not disposed of on September 15, 2003. But it would be within the court's powers to restrain the making of an appointment under para. 22.

Insolvency Act 1986   *Schedule B1*
Notice of intention to appoint

26(1) A person who proposes to make an appointment under paragraph 22 shall give at least five business days' written notice to–

(a)   any person who is or may be entitled to appoint an administrative receiver of the company, and

(b)   any person who is or may be entitled to appoint an administrator of the company under paragraph 14.

26(2) A person who proposes to make an appointment under paragraph 22 shall also give such notice as may be prescribed to such other persons as may be prescribed.

26(3) A notice under this paragraph must–

(a)   identify the proposed administrator, and

(b)   be in the prescribed form.

GENERAL NOTE

Regrettably, this section of the Schedule makes baffling reading because it does not draw attention to what is omitted. It does not mention all the possible situations. The logical approach is as follows. (1) If there is no secured creditor who has, or might have, the right to appoint an administrator under para. 14 or an administrative receiver, and there is also no person to whom notice of intention to appoint is required to be given under para. 26(2), the company or directors may proceed to make an appointment out of court without giving notice of intention to appoint to anyone, or being required to file such a notice with the court. Form 2.10B confirms this. In this situation there is no interim moratorium. It would be reasonable to suppose that a moratorium could be secured for a few days by filing with the court a notice of intention to appoint even though it there is no person to whom it is obligatory to give notice: see the note to para. 44(2); but para. 27(1) seems to apply only if a notice of intention has been given under para. 26, *i.e.* only if there are persons entitled to be given such notice. (2) If there is a secured creditor with a "qualifying" floating charge (whether or not it is currently enforceable), five business days' notice under para. 26(1) must be given before an appointment can be made, and a moratorium comes into force under para. 44(4) from the time when a copy of the notice is filed with the court. Any appointment must be made within ten business days after the specified documents have been filed. (3) If there is no such charge-holder but some other person is entitled to notice under para. 26(2), notice of intention must be given but the five-day period of notice does not apply; a copy of the notice must be filed, but there appears to be nothing to stop the company or directors proceeding to an immediate appointment, in which case no moratorium would be needed. (Form 2.9B would need minor modification.) Once again, any appointment must be made within ten days of the filing (para. 28(2)).

If there is no floating charge-holder with the power to appoint an administrative receiver or administrator, para. 28 does not apply and paras 27 and 29 are modified: see para. 30. And notice must still be given to any person entitled to receive it under para. 26(2) in such a case.

Para. 26(1)
This provision allows the charge-holder, if he is not content for the administration to proceed under the control of the person proposed by the company or the directors, to appoint an insolvency practitioner of his own choice as administrative receiver or administrator, or negotiate to have such a person appointed instead of or in addition to the company's or directors' nominee. The charge-holder would have time, also, to apply to the court to have the latter restrained from proceeding with their application, if he could show that this was inappropriate or for an improper purpose.

The use of the phrase "is or may be" makes it plain that notice must be given even though the charge is not currently enforceable.

Para. 26(2), (3)
Form 2.8B is to be used. Unhappily, this form has been drafted in order to serve a multiplicity of purposes, and this could be a source of confusion. Most persons reading the form will assume that all of its requirements must be completed,

Schedule B1   *Insolvency Act 1986*

including the statutory declaration and attachments, in order to give the statutory notice to those entitled under para. 26 (1) and (2), and yet it appears from para. 27(2) that it is only the copy filed in court that must be accompanied by the statutory declaration. Arguably, therefore, notice could be validly given to the persons entitled under para. 26 without any accompanying documents. However, since para. 26(3) requires that the notice should be "in the prescribed form", it is recommended that all the paragraphs on this form should be completed, so far as they are applicable, in order to avoid the risk that the effectiveness of the notice might be subsequently challenged.

For the relevant rules, see rr. 2.20ff. and rr. 2.2–2.8(6). A copy of the notice of intention to appoint must be filed with the court (para. 27), and written notice must be given also to the following persons as well as those mentioned in para. 26(1):

- any sheriff who is known to be charged with execution or other legal process against the company;
- any person who is known to have distrained against the company or its property;
- any supervisor of a CVA;
- the company, if it is not the company that is intending to make the appointment (r. 2.20(2)).

27(1) A person who gives notice of intention to appoint under paragraph 26 shall file with the court as soon as is reasonably practicable a copy of–

(a) the notice, and

(b) any document accompanying it.

27(2) The copy filed under sub-paragraph (1) must be accompanied by a statutory declaration made by or on behalf of the person who proposes to make the appointment–

(a) that the company is or is likely to become unable to pay its debts,

(b) that the company is not in liquidation, and

(c) that, so far as the person making the statement is able to ascertain, the appointment is not prevented by paragraphs 23 to 25, and

(d) to such additional effect, and giving such information, as may be prescribed.

27(3) A statutory declaration under sub-paragraph (2) must–

(a) be in the prescribed form, and

(b) be made during the prescribed period.

27(4) A person commits an offence if in a statutory declaration under sub-paragraph (2) he makes a statement–

(a) which is false, and

(b) which he does not reasonably believe to be true.

GENERAL NOTE

Where there is a "qualifying" floating charge-holder, compliance with this paragraph is a prerequisite to the making of an effective appointment, and the appointment must be made within the following ten business days: see para. 28. Filing the notice triggers an interim moratorium: see para. 44(4). Where there is no such charge-holder, whether or not there is any person entitled to notice under para. 26(2), the company or directors may proceed to an immediate appointment: see the note to para. 26.

Para. 27(1)
As well as the statutory declaration referred to in para. 27(2), the notice must be accompanied by one or other of the documents referred to in r. 2.22.

Para. 27(2), (3)

An appointment by the company or its directors may only be made if the company is insolvent, or nearly so. For the definition of "unable to pay its debts", see the notes to paras 11, 111(1) and s. 123.

As noted above, Form 2.8B is prescribed both for the purpose of giving notice to the floating charge-holder(s) (if any) and other persons under para. 26(1) and (2) and for the purpose of filing with the court under para. 27, and it incorporates the statutory declaration required by para. 27(2). The prescribed period is five business days (r. 2.21).

Para. 27(4)

See the note to para. 18(7).

28(1) An appointment may not be made under paragraph 22 unless the person who makes the appointment has complied with any requirement of paragraphs 26 and 27 and–

(a) the period of notice specified in paragraph 26(1) has expired, or

(b) each person to whom notice has been given under paragraph 26(1) has consented in writing to the making of the appointment.

28(2) An appointment may not be made under paragraph 22 after the period of ten business days beginning with the date on which the notice of intention to appoint is filed under paragraph 27(1).

GENERAL NOTE

The time-limits imposed by this provision impose a tight framework within which the necessary action must be taken. But para. 28(1) only applies where there are persons who must be given notice under para. 26(1): if not, an immediate appointment may be made.

Notice of appointment

29(1) A person who appoints an administrator of a company under paragraph 22 shall file with the court–

(a) a notice of appointment, and

(b) such other documents as may be prescribed.

29(2) The notice of appointment must include a statutory declaration by or on behalf of the person who makes the appointment–

(a) that the person is entitled to make an appointment under paragraph 22,

(b) that the appointment is in accordance with this Schedule, and

(c) that, so far as the person making the statement is able to ascertain, the statements made and information given in the statutory declaration filed with the notice of intention to appoint remain accurate.

29(3) The notice of appointment must identify the administrator and must be accompanied by a statement by the administrator–

(a) that he consents to the appointment,

(b) that in his opinion the purpose of administration is reasonably likely to be achieved, and

(c) giving such other information and opinions as may be prescribed.

29(4) For the purpose of a statement under sub-paragraph (3) an administrator may rely on information supplied by directors of the company (unless he has reason to doubt its accuracy).

29(5) The notice of appointment and any document accompanying it must be in the prescribed form.

29(6) A statutory declaration under sub-paragraph (2) must be made during the prescribed period.

29(7) A person commits an offence if in a statutory declaration under sub-paragraph (2) he makes a statement–

(a) which is false, and

(b) which he does not reasonably believe to be true.

GENERAL NOTE

The requirements of this paragraph closely parallel those of para. 18: see the note to that provision. The appointment of the administrator takes effect from the time of the filing of the notice of appointment under this provision (para. 31).

For the prescribed forms and other prescribed matter, see rr. 2.23ff.

Where notice of intention to appoint under para. 26 has been given, Form 2.9B is to be used. Where there is no charge-holder entitled to notice under para. 26(1), an immediate appointment may be made, using Form 2.10B. In that event, para. 30, which disapplies para. 29(2)(c), should be noted, and the notice must be accompanied by one or other of the documents specified in r. 2.22 (r. 2.25).

Para. 29(2), (6)

Note that this statutory declaration is additional to that required by para. 27(2) to accompany a notice of intention to appoint. The prescribed period is not more than five business days before the notice is filed with the court (r. 2.24).

Para. 29(7)

See the note to para. 18(7).

30 In a case in which no person is entitled to notice of intention to appoint under paragraph 26(1) (and paragraph 28 therefore does not apply)–

(a) the statutory declaration accompanying the notice of appointment must include the statements and information required under paragraph 27(2), and

(b) paragraph 29(2)(c) shall not apply.

GENERAL NOTE

Where there is no floating charge-holder entitled to notice of intention to appoint under para. 26(1), the various time-limits set out in paras 26–28(1) do not apply; but the statements and information which would otherwise have accompanied the notice of intention must be given with the notice of appointment, and the filing and notification obligations imposed by para. 29 (except for para. 29(2)(c)) must still be complied with. Although the words in brackets indicate that para. 28 does not apply where the only persons entitled to notice of intention to appoint fall within para. 26(2), this is contradicted by paras. 27(1) and 28(2), read together, from which it would follow that the ten-day time limit imposed by para. 28(2) applies in such a case.

Commencement of appointment

31 The appointment of an administrator under paragraph 22 takes effect when the requirements of paragraph 29 are satisfied.

GENERAL NOTE

As is the case with an out-of-court appointment by a floating charge-holder (see para. 19), the administrator cannot exercise any powers until the statutory filing and notification requirements have been complied with.

32 A person who appoints an administrator under paragraph 22–

(a) shall notify the administrator and such other persons as may be prescribed as soon as is reasonably practicable after the requirements of paragraph 29 are satisfied, and

(b) commits an offence if he fails without reasonable excuse to comply with paragraph (a).

GENERAL NOTE

A copy of the notice of appointment sealed by the court must be sent to the administrator as soon as reasonably practicable (r. 2.26(2)). No other persons appear to have been prescribed under para. 32(a).

On penalties, see s. 430, para. 106 and Sch. 10.

33 If before the requirements of paragraph 29 are satisfied the company enters administration by virtue of an administration order or an appointment under paragraph 14–

(a) the appointment under paragraph 22 shall not take effect, and

(b) paragraph 32 shall not apply.

GENERAL NOTE

An appointment by the court or an out-of-court appointment made by a floating charge-holder has preference over one made by the company or its directors, but only if the charge in either of the former categories "takes effect" first: see the definition of "enters administration" in para. 1(2). In any event, the company or directors will not have been free to proceed to an appointment if an application is before the court and has not yet been disposed of (para. 25(b)).

Invalid appointment: indemnity

34(1) This paragraph applies where–

(a) a person purports to appoint an administrator under paragraph 22, and

(b) the appointment is discovered to be invalid.

34(2) The court may order the person who purported to make the appointment to indemnify the person appointed against liability which arises solely by reason of the appointment's invalidity.

GENERAL NOTE

This paragraph is in identical terms to para. 20. See the note to that paragraph.

ADMINISTRATION APPLICATION – SPECIAL CASES

Application by holder of floating charge

35(1) This paragraph applies where an administration application in respect of a company–

(a) is made by the holder of a qualifying floating charge in respect of the company's property, and

(b) includes a statement that the application is made in reliance on this paragraph.

35(2) The court may make an administration order–

(a) whether or not satisfied that the company is or is likely to become unable to pay its debts, but

(b) only if satisfied that the applicant could appoint an administrator under paragraph 14.

GENERAL NOTE

It is generally a prerequisite for the making of an administration order that the company should be, or be likely to become, insolvent (para. 11); but an appointment may be made out of court by the holder of a qualifying floating charge even in the case of a solvent company: see the note to para. 14. The present provision makes an exception to para. 11 if the following conditions are satisfied:

- the applicant for the order must be the holder of a qualifying floating charge, as defined in para. 14(2);
- the application must expressly state that it is made in reliance on para. 35; and
- an event must have occurred or a condition been met which would entitle the charge holder to make an out-of-court appointment under para. 14.

If these conditions cannot all be met, the holder of a floating charge (whether or not a qualifying charge) may still apply to the court for an administration order, but the company must be shown to be insolvent or nearly so.

Intervention by holder of floating charge

36(1) This paragraph applies where–

(a) an administration application in respect of a company is made by a person who is not the holder of a qualifying floating charge in respect of the company's property, and

(b) the holder of a qualifying floating charge in respect of the company's property applies to the court to have a specified person appointed as administrator (and not the person specified by the administration applicant).

36(2) The court shall grant an application under sub-paragraph (1)(b) unless the court thinks it right to refuse the application because of the particular circumstances of the case.

GENERAL NOTE

This provision enables the holder of a qualifying floating charge to intervene, where an application to the court for an administration order has been made by someone else and he would prefer a different person to be appointed as administrator from the one who has been nominated. The charge-holder must produce to the court:

- the written consent of all holders of any prior qualifying floating charge;
- a statement in Form 2.2B by the proposed administrator; and
- sufficient evidence to satisfy the court that he is entitled to appoint an administrator under para. 14 (r. 2.10(1)).

This last requirement no doubt requires proof that the charge is immediately enforceable (para. 16).

The court is required to accede to the charge-holder's request unless the particular circumstances of the case dictate otherwise. Costs will normally be an expense of the administration (r. 2.10(2)).

Where it is proposed to make an out-of-court appointment of an administrator who does not have the approval of the charge-holder, he may take his own steps under para. 14: see the note to para. 26.

Application where company in liquidation

37(1) This paragraph applies where the holder of a qualifying floating charge in respect of a company's property could appoint an administrator under paragraph 14 but for paragraph 8(1)(b).

37(2) The holder of the qualifying floating charge may make an administration application.

37(3) If the court makes an administration order on hearing an application made by virtue of sub-paragraph (2)–

(a) the court shall discharge the winding-up order,

(b) the court shall make provision for such matters as may be prescribed,

(c) the court may make other consequential provision,

(d) the court shall specify which of the powers under this Schedule are to be exercisable by the administrator, and

(e) this Schedule shall have effect with such modifications as the court may specify.

GENERAL NOTE

Paragraph 8(1) imposes a general ban on the appointment of an administrator while a company is being wound up. However, the present provision empowers the court to substitute an administration for the liquidation where (a) the winding up is by court order and (b) application is made by the holder of a "qualifying" floating charge who would, but for the winding up, be in a position to appoint an administrator out of court under para. 14. Paragraph 37(3) ("If the court makes an administration order …") makes it plain that the court is not bound to accede to the application.

Rule 2.11 applies, specifying the matters which must be contained in the affidavit in support of the application.

Note the court's discretionary powers under para. 37(3)(c)–(e). The matters prescribed for the purposes of para. 37(3)(b) appear in r. 2.13.

38(1) The liquidator of a company may make an administration application.

38(2) If the court makes an administration order on hearing an application made by virtue of sub-paragraph (1)–

(a) the court shall discharge any winding-up order in respect of the company,

(b) the court shall make provision for such matters as may be prescribed,

(c) the court may make other consequential provision,

(d) the court shall specify which of the powers under this Schedule are to be exercisable by the administrator, and

(e) this Schedule shall have effect with such modifications as the court may specify.

GENERAL NOTE

Paragraph 8, which bans the appointment of the administrator of a company which is in liquidation, is made subject to this paragraph when the company is in voluntary as well as compulsory liquidation (para. 8(2), (3)). The administration can only be instituted by court order, and only the liquidator may make the application.

Para. 38(2)
This sub-paragraph is in similar terms to para. 37(3): the court has a discretion whether to make an order or not. But if it does decide to make an order, it must discharge any winding-up order. If the company is in voluntary liquidation, it would be open to the court to grant a stay of the proceedings under s. 147.

Rule 2.11 applies, specifying the matters which must be contained in the affidavit in support of the application. The matters prescribed for the purposes of para. 38(2)(b) appear in r. 2.13.

Effect of administrative receivership

39(1) Where there is an administrative receiver of a company the court must dismiss an administration application in respect of the company unless–

(a) the person by or on behalf of whom the receiver was appointed consents to the making of the administration order,

(b) the court thinks that the security by virtue of which the receiver was appointed would be liable to be released or discharged under sections 238 to 240 (transaction at undervalue and preference) if an administration order were made,

(c) the court thinks that the security by virtue of which the receiver was appointed would be avoided under section 245 (avoidance of floating charge) if an administration order were made, or

(d) the court thinks that the security by virtue of which the receiver was appointed would be challengeable under section 242 (gratuitous alienations) or 243 (unfair preferences) or under any rule of law in Scotland.

39(2) Sub-paragraph (1) applies whether the administrative receiver is appointed before or after the making of the administration application.

GENERAL NOTE

This provision is in similar terms to s. 9(3), which applies in the original administration regime. But in some respects the drafting is different: under that section the court was not to dismiss the petition unless it was "*satisfied* ... that, if an administration order were made, any security by virtue of which the receiver was appointed would be liable to be released or discharged" under CA 1985, ss. 238–240 (or be avoided under s. 245 or be challengeable under s. 242). It is open to debate whether the phrase "the court thinks" is intended to set a lower standard of proof than "satisfied". (Compare the construction put on the words "if the court ... *considers* that the making of an order under this section would be likely ..." in the original s. 8(1)(b) in *Re Harris Simons Construction Ltd* [1989] 1 W.L.R. 368; (1989) 5 B.C.C. 11: see the note to s. 8(1), (2).)

Schedule B1   Insolvency Act 1986
EFFECT OF ADMINISTRATION

Dismissal of pending winding-up petition

40(1) A petition for the winding up of a company–

(a) shall be dismissed on the making of an administration order in respect of the company, and

(b) shall be suspended while the company is in administration following an appointment under paragraph 14.

40(2) Sub-paragraph (1)(b) does not apply to a petition presented under–

(a) section 124A (public interest), or

(b) section 367 of the Financial Services and Markets Act 2000 (c. 8) (petition by Financial Services Authority).

40(3) Where an administrator becomes aware that a petition was presented under a provision referred to in sub-paragraph (2) before his appointment, he shall apply to the court for directions under paragraph 63.

Para. 40(1)
Where a petition for winding up has been made to the court but not yet heard or disposed of, it is to be dismissed if the company is put into administration by order of the court, and suspended if an administrator is appointed out of court by a floating charge holder. (An out-of-court appointment cannot be made by the company or its directors at such a time: see para. 25(a).)

Para. 40(2)
Although the Act does not generally allow a company to be in administration and in liquidation at the same time (see paras 8, 37, 38 and 42(4)), the possibility is recognised in the case of a winding up on public-interest grounds. If a winding-up order is made in respect of a company which is already in administration, para. 82(3)(b) empowers the court to direct that the administration shall continue to have effect, and to give consequential directions.

Dismissal of administrative or other receiver

41(1) When an administration order takes effect in respect of a company any administrative receiver of the company shall vacate office.

41(2) Where a company is in administration, any receiver of part of the company's property shall vacate office if the administrator requires him to.

41(3) Where an administrative receiver or receiver vacates office under sub-paragraph (1) or (2)–

(a) his remuneration shall be charged on and paid out of any property of the company which was in his custody or under his control immediately before he vacated office, and

(b) he need not take any further steps under section 40 or 59.

41(4) In the application of sub-paragraph (3)(a)–

(a) "remuneration" includes expenses properly incurred and any indemnity to which the administrative receiver or receiver is entitled out of the assets of the company,

(b) the charge imposed takes priority over security held by the person by whom or on whose behalf the administrative receiver or receiver was appointed, and

(c) the provision for payment is subject to paragraph 43.

GENERAL NOTE

This provision covers the same ground as s. 11(1), (2), (4), (5) which applies under the original administration regime and, although the drafting is in many respects different, there appears to be no change of substance. Paragraph 41(1) necessarily applies only where the company is put into administration by court order, but para. 41(2) applies in all administrations. (An out-of-court appointment cannot be made if an administrative receiver is already in office: see paras 17(b) and 25(c).)

Para. 41(4)(c)
This is the counterpart of s. 11(4) of the original legislation, which is expressly made subject to s. 11(3). Although the legislation makes special provision to secure payment of the outgoing receiver's remuneration and expenses, the moratorium imposed by para. 43 will prevent him from enforcing payment during the currency of the administration except with the consent of the administrator or the court.

Moratorium on insolvency proceedings

42(1) This paragraph applies to a company in administration.

42(2) No resolution may be passed for the winding up of the company.

42(3) No order may be made for the winding up of the company.

42(4) Sub-paragraph (3) does not apply to an order made on a petition presented under–

(a) section 124A (public interest), or

(b) section 367 of the Financial Services and Markets Act 2000 (c. 8) (petition by Financial Services Authority).

42(5) If a petition presented under a provision referred to in sub-paragraph (4) comes to the attention of the administrator, he shall apply to the court for directions under paragraph 63.

Para. 42(1)–(3)
Unless para. 42(4) applies, a company cannot be put into liquidation either voluntarily or compulsorily while it is in administration. If winding up is to supersede an administration, it is necessary for the administration to be terminated either before or simultaneously with the transition. Voluntary liquidation is likely to be preferred in most cases because it can be carried out more cheaply and quickly and with less formality. The new legislation makes express provision for this in para. 83 below, so avoiding many of the difficulties experienced under the original regime. Alternatively, the court may make an order under para. 79, bringing the administration to an end.

Para. 42(4), (5)
Once again, winding up on public interest grounds is made an exception, mirroring para. 40(2), (3). If the court is satisfied that a winding-up order should be made, it is not required that the administration should be immediately terminated. There might be a case for leaving the administrator in post for a brief period, for instance, if he was in the process of realising security for the benefit of a charge-holder. Paragraph 82(3)(b) makes provision for this to be done.

Moratorium on other legal process

43(1) This paragraph applies to a company in administration.

43(2) No step may be taken to enforce security over the company's property except–

(a) with the consent of the administrator, or

(b) with the permission of the court.

43(3) No step may be taken to repossess goods in the company's possession under a hire-purchase agreement except–

(a) with the consent of the administrator, or

(b) with the permission of the court.

43(4) A landlord may not exercise a right of forfeiture by peaceable re-entry in relation to premises let to the company except–

(a) with the consent of the administrator, or

(b) with the permission of the court.

43(5) In Scotland, a landlord may not exercise a right of irritancy in relation to premises let to the company except–

(a) with the consent of the administrator, or

(b) with the permission of the court.

43(6) No legal process (including legal proceedings, execution, distress and diligence) may be instituted or continued against the company or property of the company except–

(a) with the consent of the administrator, or

(b) with the permission of the court.

43(6A) An administrative receiver of the company may not be appointed.

43(7) Where the court gives permission for a transaction under this paragraph it may impose a condition on or a requirement in connection with the transaction.

43(8) In this paragraph **"landlord"** includes a person to whom rent is payable.

GENERAL NOTE

The provisions of the present paragraph correspond to parts of s. 11(3) of the original administration regime. They apply once the appointment of an administrator has taken effect: see para. 1(2)(a). An interim moratorium may already be in place under para. 44 below. For a detailed commentary, see the note to s. 11(3).

Para. 43(6A) was inserted by the Enterprise Act 2002 (Insolvency) Order 2003 (SI 2003/2096, arts 1, 2(1), (3)) as from September 15, 2003.

Interim moratorium

44(1) This paragraph applies where an administration application in respect of a company has been made and–

(a) the application has not yet been granted or dismissed, or

(b) the application has been granted but the administration order has not yet taken effect.

44(2) This paragraph also applies from the time when a copy of notice of intention to appoint an administrator under paragraph 14 is filed with the court until–

(a) the appointment of the administrator takes effect, or

(b) the period of five business days beginning with the date of filing expires without an administrator having been appointed.

44(3) Sub-paragraph (2) has effect in relation to a notice of intention to appoint only if it is in the prescribed form.

44(4) This paragraph also applies from the time when a copy of notice of intention to appoint an administrator is filed with the court under paragraph 27(1) until–

(a) the appointment of the administrator takes effect, or

(b) the period specified in paragraph 28(2) expires without an administrator having been appointed.

44(5) The provisions of paragraphs 42 and 43 shall apply (ignoring any reference to the consent of the administrator).

44(6) If there is an administrative receiver of the company when the administration application is made, the provisions of paragraphs 42 and 43 shall not begin to apply by virtue of this paragraph until the person by or on behalf of whom the receiver was appointed consents to the making of the administration order.

44(7) This paragraph does not prevent or require the permission of the court for–

(a) the presentation of a petition for the winding up of the company under a provision mentioned in paragraph 42(4),

(b) the appointment of an administrator under paragraph 14,

(c) the appointment of an administrative receiver of the company, or

(d) the carrying out by an administrative receiver (whenever appointed) of his functions.

GENERAL NOTE

Under the original administration regime, a company can be put into administration only by order of the court – a process which necessarily takes some time. In order to protect the company's assets during this period, provision is made by s. 10 for an automatic moratorium to operate from the time of the presentation of a petition to the court. The present provision gives corresponding protection in the case where the appointment of an administrator is sought by court order under para. 10, and also establishes a brief moratorium pending the taking effect of an out-of-court appointment.

Para. 44(1)

Under the original regime there is no provision corresponding to that in para. 13(2)(a) which expressly empowers the court to specify a time other than that of the order from which the appointment of an administrator is to take effect. Paragraph 44(1)(b) ensures that the interim moratorium continues where a time later that that of the order is fixed by the court. In an appropriate case the court has power under paras 13(1)(f) or 43(7) to modify the terms of the moratorium.

Paras 44(2)–(4)

Where the appointment of an administrator is being made out of court, it does not take effect until the filing and notice requirements of para. 18 or 26 have been complied with (see paras 19, 31). Paragraph 44(2) applies where a floating charge-holder intending to appoint an administrator files a notice of intention to appoint with the court. (The prescribed form is Form 2.5B: r. 2.15.) Paragraph 44(4) establishes a moratorium where it is the company or its directors who make an out-of-court appointment, for a period which at a maximum cannot exceed ten days (see r. 2.20 and Form 2.8B). The main difference between paras 44(2) and 44(4) is that the filing of a notice of intention to appoint is optional in the former case but obligatory in the latter—at least where there is a holder of a qualifying floating charge or other person to whom notice must be given under para. 26(1). It does not appear that a moratorium could be obtained in either case simply by filing a notice of intention to appoint in court when there is nobody who is required by the Act to be given notice: the general tenor of the Act, rules and prescribed forms (and especially the requirement that it is in every case a *copy* of the notice that is to be filed) suggests otherwise. In some circumstances the charge holder or the company or its directors may proceed to make an immediate appointment, in which case there will be no interim moratorium: see the note to paras 14 and 26. The position where an appointment is made by the company or its directors and the only persons entitled to notice of intention to appoint are those specified under para. 26(2) is unclear. If the appointment is made immediately upon the filing of the copy notice, there will be no need for a moratorium, but if there is any intervening period of delay para. 44(4) would appear to indicate that a moratorium comes into operation.

Para. 44(5)

Under paras 42 and 43 a dispensation from a restriction imposed by the (permanent) statutory moratorium may be granted by either the administrator or the court. Since the appointment of the administrator will not have taken effect when para. 44 applies, it is only the court which will have power to grant the necessary leave.

Para. 44(6)

This sub-paragraph refers to an "administration application", and so applies only where an appointment is sought by court order. Paragraph 39 gives the person who has appointed an administrative receiver a veto over a court appointment unless he is willing to consent to an order under para. 39(1(a). If an administrative receiver is in office when an application for an administration order is made to the court, the interim moratorium will not take effect unless and until the charge-holder decides to give his consent.

Para. 44(7)

This sub-paragraph applies only during an interim moratorium. Paragraph 43 will normally prevent similar action being taken against a company once a permanent moratorium has come into effect. Paragraph 44(7)(d) would allow the administrative receiver to continue to act until the court order is made, even where the charge-holder has signified his intention to consent to the order.

Publicity

45(1) While a company is in administration every business document issued by or on behalf of the company or the administrator must state–

(a) the name of the administrator, and

(b) that the affairs, business and property of the company are being managed by him.

45(2) Any of the following commits an offence if without reasonable excuse he authorises or permits a contravention of sub-paragraph (1)–

(a) the administrator,

(b) an officer of the company, and

(c) the company.

45(3) In sub-paragraph (1) **"business document"** means–

(a) an invoice,

(b) an order for goods or services, and

(c) a business letter.

GENERAL NOTE

This is a parallel provision to those requiring notification of the appointment of a receiver (ss. 39, 64) and notification that the company is in liquidation (s. 188). It restates in different wording the original s. 12. The policy reasons for making the company itself liable for this offence are not obvious.

On penalties, see s. 430 and Sch. 10.

PROCESS OF ADMINISTRATION

Announcement of administrator's appointment

46(1) This paragraph applies where a person becomes the administrator of a company.

46(2) As soon as is reasonably practicable the administrator shall–

(a) send a notice of his appointment to the company, and

(b) publish a notice of his appointment in the prescribed manner.

46(3) As soon as is reasonably practicable the administrator shall–

(a) obtain a list of the company's creditors, and

(b) send a notice of his appointment to each creditor of whose claim and address he is aware.

46(4) The administrator shall send a notice of his appointment to the registrar of companies before the end of the period of 7 days beginning with the date specified in sub-paragraph (6).

46(5) The administrator shall send a notice of his appointment to such persons as may be prescribed before the end of the prescribed period beginning with the date specified in sub-paragraph (6).

46(6) The date for the purpose of sub-paragraphs (4) and (5) is–

(a) in the case of an administrator appointed by administration order, the date of the order,

(b) in the case of an administrator appointed under paragraph 14, the date on which he receives notice under paragraph 20, and

(c) in the case of an administrator appointed under paragraph 22, the date on which he receives notice under paragraph 32.

46(7) The court may direct that sub-paragraph (3)(b) or (5)–

(a) shall not apply, or

(b) shall apply with the substitution of a different period.

46(8) A notice under this paragraph must—

(a) contain the prescribed information, and

(b) be in the prescribed form.

46(9) An administrator commits an offence if he fails without reasonable excuse to comply with a requirement of this paragraph.

GENERAL NOTE

This is an extended version of the original s. 21, adjusted to take account of cases where the administrator is appointed out of court. However, the time limits have been altered as noted below. For the relevant rules and forms prescribed for the purposes of this paragraph, see r. 2.27

Para. 46(2)
Form 2.12B is to be used where the notice of appointment is to be sent to any person, and Form 2.11B for the published notices. The latter must be published once in the *Gazette* and once in an appropriate newspaper (r. 2.27(1)). Where the appointment has been made by the company under para. 22, r. 46(2)(a) would seem superfluous, since the company will already have sent a notice to him under para. 32(a)!

Para. 46(3)
"As soon as reasonably practicable" has been substituted for "within 28 days after the making of the order" under the original regime.

Para. 46(4), (6)
The period under the original Pt II is 14 days from the making of the order. Note that sub-para. (a) refers to the date of the order, not the date when the order takes effect (so placing a duty on the administrator before his appointment is effective).

Para. 46(5)
The prescribed persons are:

- any receiver or administrative receiver;
- the petitioner under any pending winding-up petition, and any provisional liquidator;
- any sheriff charged with execution or other legal process against the company;
- any person who has distrained against the company or its property;
- the supervisor of any CVA (r. 2.27(2)).

No specific period is prescribed: r. 2.27(2) simply states that notice shall be given "as soon as reasonably practicable".

Para. 46(9)
On penalties, see s. 430, Sch. B1, para. 106(2) and Sch. 10.

Statement of company's affairs

47(1) As soon as is reasonably practicable after appointment the administrator of a company shall by notice in the prescribed form require one or more relevant persons to provide the administrator with a statement of the affairs of the company.

47(2) The statement must—

(a) be verified by a statement of truth in accordance with Civil Procedure Rules,

(b) be in the prescribed form,

(c) give particulars of the company's property, debts and liabilities,

(d) give the names and addresses of the company's creditors,

(e) specify the security held by each creditor,

(f) give the date on which each security was granted, and

(g) contain such other information as may be prescribed.

47(3) In sub-paragraph (1) **"relevant person"** means–

(a) a person who is or has been an officer of the company,

(b) a person who took part in the formation of the company during the period of one year ending with the date on which the company enters administration,

(c) a person employed by the company during that period, and

(d) a person who is or has been during that period an officer or employee of a company which is or has been during that year an officer of the company.

47(4) For the purpose of sub-paragraph (3) a reference to employment is a reference to employment through a contract of employment or a contract for services.

47(5) In Scotland, a statement of affairs under sub-paragraph (1) must be a statutory declaration made in accordance with the Statutory Declarations Act 1835 (c. 62) (and sub-paragraph (2)(a) shall not apply).

GENERAL NOTE

This paragraph corresponds to s. 22 in the original Pt II. The "statement of affairs", which had long been a feature of the liquidation procedure in a compulsory winding up (see s. 131), was made a requirement by IA 1986 in administration and a number of other insolvency proceedings. For further comment, see the notes to s. 131.

For the relevant rules, forms and other matters prescribed for the purposes of this paragraph, see rr. 2.28ff.

Para. 47(1)

"As soon as reasonably practicable" has been substituted for "forthwith" in the original Pt II. The notice is to be in Form 2.13B, and must contain the information specified in r. 2.28(3). In addition, the administrator must furnish each recipient with the forms required for the preparation of the statement of affairs (r. 2.28(4)).

Para. 47(2), (5)

The statement must be in Form 2.14B. A "statement of truth" has been substituted for the affidavit which is required by the original Pt II. The administrator may require any "relevant person" to submit a statement of concurrence (in Form 2.15B) stating that he concurs in the statement of affairs (r. 2.29(1), (2)). In this event:

- the person making the statement of affairs must be informed;
- that person must deliver a copy of the statement of affairs to the other "relevant person (or persons)";
- the latter then has five business days to submit the statement of concurrence to the administrator;
- a statement of concurrence may be qualified in certain events;
- every statement of concurrence is to be verified by a statement of truth;
- every statement of concurrence is to be filed together with the statement of affairs with the court and sent to the registrar of companies (r. 2.29).

Form 2.16B is to be used for the purposes of filing and registration. There is provision in r. 2.30 for the court to order that limited disclosure only should be made, or no disclosure at all, where the administrator thinks that disclosure would prejudice the conduct of the administration, and a right given to a creditor by r. 2.30(4) to apply to order the administrator to disclose the statement or part of it notwithstanding such an order

A person making a statement of affairs may be reimbursed expenses which he has incurred (r. 2.32).

Para. 47(3), (4)

The expression "officer", in relation to a company, includes a director, manager or secretary (CA 1985, s. 744), and at least in some contexts may extend to the holders of other offices: see the note to s. 206(3). The wide definition of "employment" used here could include professionals such as the company's auditors and bankers.

48(1) A person required to submit a statement of affairs must do so before the end of the period of 11 days beginning with the day on which he receives notice of the requirement.

48(2) The administrator may–

(a) revoke a requirement under paragraph 47(1), or

(b) extend the period specified in sub-paragraph (1) (whether before or after expiry).

48(3) If the administrator refuses a request to act under sub-paragraph (2)–

(a) the person whose request is refused may apply to the court, and

(b) the court may take action of a kind specified in sub-paragraph (2).

48(4) A person commits an offence if he fails without reasonable excuse to comply with a requirement under paragraph 47(1).

GENERAL NOTE

This paragraph corresponds to s. 22(4)–(6) of the original regime. For the relevant rules, see rr. 2.29ff.

Para. 48(1)
The period was formerly 21 days. Note that the period is 11 days, not 11 business days. Form 2.14B is to be used for the statement of affairs.

Para. 48(2), (3)
The language used in para. 48(2)(a) is rather less clear than that in s. 22(5), although the meaning is no doubt meant to be the same. Section 22(5) empowers the administrator to "release a person from an obligation imposed on him" to submit a statement of affairs, and also to extend the period, and continues: "where the administrator has refused to exercise a power conferred by this subsection, the court, if it thinks fit, may exercise it". Rule 2.31 sets out the procedure as regards both the grant of a release and an extension of time.

Para. 48(4)
On penalties, see s. 430, para. 106(2) and Sch. 10.

Administrator's proposals

49(1) The administrator of a company shall make a statement setting out proposals for achieving the purpose of administration.

49(2) A statement under sub-paragraph (1) must, in particular–

(a) deal with such matters as may be prescribed, and

(b) where applicable, explain why the administrator thinks that the objective mentioned in paragraph 3(1)(a) or (b) cannot be achieved.

49(3) Proposals under this paragraph may include–

(a) a proposal for a voluntary arrangement under Part I of this Act (although this paragraph is without prejudice to section 4(3));

(b) a proposal for a compromise or arrangement to be sanctioned under section 425 of the Companies Act (compromise with creditors or members).

49(4) The administrator shall send a copy of the statement of his proposals–

(a) to the registrar of companies,

(b) to every creditor of the company of whose claim and address he is aware, and

(c) to every member of the company of whose address he is aware.

49(5) The administrator shall comply with sub-paragraph (4)–

(a) as soon as is reasonably practicable after the company enters administration, and

(b) in any event, before the end of the period of eight weeks beginning with the day on which the company enters administration.

49(6) The administrator shall be taken to comply with sub-paragraph (4)(c) if he publishes in the prescribed manner a notice undertaking to provide a copy of the statement of proposals free of charge to any member of the company who applies in writing to a specified address.

Schedule B1 *Insolvency Act 1986*

49(7) An administrator commits an offence if he fails without reasonable excuse to comply with sub-paragraph (5).

49(8) A period specified in this paragraph may be varied in accordance with paragraph 107.

GENERAL NOTE

The equivalent provision under the original regime is s. 23. The most notable change is that the period allowed for the administrator to formulate his proposals has been shortened from three months to eight weeks. Rule 2.33 sets out in considerable detail the matters required to be dealt with (in addition to those prescribed by para.49) in the statement of proposals, which must be attached to Form 2.17B and sent as directed by para. 49(4).

Para. 49(2)
Paragraph 3 of Sch. B1 ranks the statutory objectives of an administration in a definite sequence: (1) corporate rescue, (2) a better result for the creditors as a whole than would be likely in a winding up without prior administration, and (3) satisfying the claims of preferential and secured creditors. Sub-paragraph (2)(b) is a reminder that the administrator cannot lightly disregard this hierarchy, *e.g.* by treating the administration as in effect a receivership and proceeding immediately to discharge the claims in category (3).

Para. 49(3)
These are two of the statutory purposes for which an administration order can be sought under the original regime. Although they have been given no place in the structured "objectives" of the new regime (see above), this is an indication that they have not been wholly forgotten. There will now be less occasion to have recourse to the former practice of combining an administration with a CVA in order to obtain a moratorium, in view of the enactment of Sch. A1, but of course a moratorium is available only for "eligible" companies; and in any case there may sometimes be advantages in a CVA which administration alone could not secure – *e.g.* if it is desired to involve the members as well as the creditors in the proposals.

Section 4(3) preserves the rights of secured creditors to enforce their security, unless they agree otherwise. (Note also the protection given to secured and preferential creditors by para. 73.)

There is at present no legal provision for a moratorium for the period in which a scheme of arrangement under CA 1985, s. 425 is formulated and sanctioned, but this can be achieved by putting a scheme together under the protective umbrella of an administration. Again, this may make it possible to achieve rather more than under administration alone, *e.g.* a restructuring involving more than one company of which some are not insolvent.

Para. 49(4)–(8)
As noted, the former period of three months has been shortened to eight weeks. Under para. 107, the court (or the administrator with the "consent" of the creditors, as there defined) may vary this period: see the note to that paragraph. If the court grants an extension of time, the persons referred to in para. 49(4) must be notified, using Form 2.18B (r. 2.33(4)).

Rule 2.33(4)–(8) deals with the situations where the administrator thinks that no meeting of creditors need be called (para. 52), where he thinks that the purpose of the administration has been sufficiently achieved before he has sent a statement of his proposals to creditors (para. 80) and where he chooses the alternative course of publishing a notice relating to the proposals under para. 49(6) rather than sending a statement to every member.

On penalties, see s. 430, para. 106(2) and Sch. 10.

Creditors' meeting

50(1) In this Schedule **"creditors' meeting"** means a meeting of creditors of a company summoned by the administrator–

(a) in the prescribed manner, and

(b) giving the prescribed period of notice to every creditor of the company of whose claim and address he is aware.

50(2) A period prescribed under sub-paragraph (1)(b) may be varied in accordance with paragraph 107.

50(3) A creditors' meeting shall be conducted in accordance with the rules.

GENERAL NOTE

This paragraph refers to all creditors' meetings. For the matters prescribed and the relevant rules, see rr. 2.34ff. The prescribed period of notice is 14 days (r. 2.35(4)), but this may be varied by the court in accordance with para. 107, or by the administrator with the consent of the creditors under para. 108: see the notes to those provisions. Notice of certain meetings (*i.e.* those summoned under paras 51, 52(2), 54(2), 56(1) and 62) must be in Form 2.20B (r. 2.35(1), (2)). Proxy forms (in Form 8.2) must also be sent (r. 2.35(4)(c)).

An administrator may also call a meeting of the company's members, although there is no statutory requirement that the members should be involved in an administration. Rule 2.49 applies to such meetings.

Requirement for initial creditors' meeting

51(1) Each copy of an administrator's statement of proposals sent to a creditor under paragraph 49(4)(b) must be accompanied by an invitation to a creditors' meeting (an "initial creditors' meeting").

51(2) The date set for an initial creditors' meeting must be–

(a) as soon as is reasonably practicable after the company enters administration, and

(b) in any event, within the period of ten weeks beginning with the date on which the company enters administration.

51(3) An administrator shall present a copy of his statement of proposals to an initial creditors' meeting.

51(4) A period specified in this paragraph may be varied in accordance with paragraph 107.

51(5) An administrator commits an offence if he fails without reasonable excuse to comply with a requirement of this paragraph.

GENERAL NOTE

Under the original regime, the administrator is required to summon a creditors' meeting on not less than 14 days' notice sent within the period of three months from the date of the administration order (IA 1986, s. 13(1)(b)). The ten-week limit here specified reflects the shortening of the three-month period to eight weeks (see the note to para. 49(4)–(8) above). This may be varied by the court under para. 107 or the administrator with the consent of the creditors under para. 108: see the notes to those provisions. Where the court orders an extension under para. 107, notice in Form 2.18B must be sent to all the persons listed in para. 49(4): see r. 2.34(3).

Notice of the initial creditors' meeting must normally be advertised in accordance with r. 2.34(1), and sent (in Form 2.21B) to those present and past directors and officers of the company whose presence the administrator thinks is required (r. 2.34(2)). A single adjournment for not more than 14 days is possible, subject to any direction by the court (r. 2.34(4)). For the circumstances in which a meeting need not be called, see para. 52(1).

Note also that the administrator may dispense with the need to call a meeting of creditors where he thinks that the purpose of the administration has already been sufficiently achieved (see para. 80 and r. 2.33(4)) or if he decides that the company should move from administration to dissolution under para.84.

Para. 51(5)

On penalties, see s. 430, para. 106(2) and Sch. 10.

52(1) Paragraph 51(1) shall not apply where the statement of proposals states that the administrator thinks–

(a) that the company has sufficient property to enable each creditor of the company to be paid in full,

(b) that the company has insufficient property to enable a distribution to be made to unsecured creditors other than by virtue of section 176A(2)(a), or

(c) that neither of the objectives specified in paragraph 3(1)(a) and (b) can be achieved.

52(2) But the administrator shall summon an initial creditors' meeting if it is requested–

(a) by creditors of the company whose debts amount to at least 10% of the total debts of the company,

(b) in the prescribed manner, and

(c) in the prescribed period.

52(3) A meeting requested under sub-paragraph (2) must be summoned for a date in the prescribed period.

Schedule B1 *Insolvency Act 1986*

52(4) The period prescribed under sub-paragraph (3) may be varied in accordance with paragraph 107.

GENERAL NOTE

Paragraph 52(1), which authorises the administrator to dispense with the need to summon an initial creditors' meeting, is new. In essence, it applies in circumstances where there is likely to be nothing of substance that a creditors' meeting could decide. These circumstances are:

- that there are sufficient assets to enable all the company's creditors to be paid in full;
- that there will be insufficient assets to enable anything to be paid to the unsecured creditors (apart from anything that may come to them as their "percentage share" in the realisation of assets subject to a floating charge: see the notes to s. 176A); or
- that the only objective of the administration which the administrator thinks is capable of achievement is "realising property in order to make a distribution to one or more secured or preferential creditors" (para. 3(1)(c)).

There is obviously an overlap between the latter two situations, but the third would apply and not the second where there was no floating charge or where there are only sufficient assets to make a part payment to the unsecured creditors.

Para. 52(2)–(4)
Rule 2.37 applies. The request must be in Form 2.21B. The period prescribed is 12 days from the date on which the administrator's proposals are sent out, and the meeting must be held within 28 days of the request being received by the administrator. Security must be given for the expenses of summoning and holding the meeting. Notice of the meeting must be in Form 2.20B (r. 2.35(2)). The 12-day period may be varied by the court under para. 107.

Business and result of initial creditors' meeting

53(1) An initial creditors' meeting to which an administrator's proposals are presented shall consider them and may–

(a) approve them without modification, or

(b) approve them with modification to which the administrator consents.

53(2) After the conclusion of an initial creditors' meeting the administrator shall as soon as is reasonably practicable report any decision taken to–

(a) the court,

(b) the registrar of companies, and

(c) such other persons as may be prescribed.

53(3) An administrator commits an offence if he fails without reasonable excuse to comply with sub-paragraph (2).

GENERAL NOTE

This provision has its counterpart in s. 24(2), (4) of the original regime.

The administrator's freedom to act in the exercise of his functions is limited by the scope of the proposals, once approved (see para. 68(1)) – apart from "insubstantial" deviations (para. 54(1)(c)); and so it is important, from his point of view, that they should not be too restrictively drawn. Indeed, in *Re Dana (UK) Ltd* [1999] 2 B.C.L.C. 239 Neuberger J. thought that it would make good sense for the proposals put before an initial meeting to include a mechanism empowering the largest and/or representative creditors to approve future deviations or variations of decisions of the administrator. In any event the court may, in exceptional circumstances, authorise the administrator to depart from the approved scheme: see the note to para. 54, below.

For the rules governing the conduct of the meeting, see rr. 2.36, 2.38ff. Note that the rules invalidate any resolution of the creditors which is opposed by a majority of the creditors who are not "connected with" the company: see r. 2.43(2) and, on the meaning of "connected with", s. 249.

On the persons prescribed for the purposes of para. 53(2)(c), see r. 2.46. Form 2.23B is to be used.

On penalties, see s. 430, para. 106(2) and Sch. 10.

Revision of administrator's proposals

54(1) This paragraph applies where–

(a) an administrator's proposals have been approved (with or without modification) at an initial creditors' meeting,

(b) the administrator proposes a revision to the proposals, and

(c) the administrator thinks that the proposed revision is substantial.

54(2) The administrator shall–

(a) summon a creditors' meeting,

(b) send a statement in the prescribed form of the proposed revision with the notice of the meeting sent to each creditor,

(c) send a copy of the statement, within the prescribed period, to each member of the company of whose address he is aware, and

(d) present a copy of the statement to the meeting.

54(3) The administrator shall be taken to have complied with sub-paragraph (2)(c) if he publishes a notice undertaking to provide a copy of the statement free of charge to any member of the company who applies in writing to a specified address.

54(4) A notice under sub-paragraph (3) must be published–

(a) in the prescribed manner, and

(b) within the prescribed period.

54(5) A creditors' meeting to which a proposed revision is presented shall consider it and may–

(a) approve it without modification, or

(b) approve it with modification to which the administrator consents.

54(6) After the conclusion of a creditors' meeting the administrator shall as soon as is reasonably practicable report any decision taken to–

(a) the court,

(b) the registrar of companies, and

(c) such other persons as may be prescribed.

54(7) An administrator commits an offence if he fails without reasonable excuse to comply with sub-paragraph (6).

GENERAL NOTE

This paragraph corresponds to IA 1986, s. 25, which applies under the original regime. Its wording often repeats provisions to be found in elsewhere, *e.g.* in paras 49, 51 and 53, and it may be helpful to refer to the notes to those provisions.

The administrator is bound to adhere to the course of action agreed to by the creditors at their initial meeting (except that he may, apparently, make "insubstantial" deviations: see para. 54(1)(c)). If he wishes to work to a different strategy, he must go back to the creditors for approval of revised proposals. However, in exceptional circumstances (*e.g.* where the delay involved in summoning a creditors' meeting to consider a revised scheme could cause substantial loss) the court has power under para. 68(3)(c)) to authorise an administrator to depart from an approved scheme: *cf. Re Smallman Construction Ltd* (1988) 4 B.C.C. 784 and *Re Dana (UK) Ltd* [1999] 2 B.C.L.C. 239.

Para. 54(2)–(4)

Rules 2.35ff, and more particularly r. 2.45 apply. Form 2.22B is to be used, with a statement attached setting out the proposed revisions. Members must be sent copies of the statement within five days of sending the statement to creditors, unless s. 54(3) applies, when the administrator must publish a notice in accordance with r. 2.45(4).

Schedule B1 *Insolvency Act 1986*

Para. 2.45(6)
Rule 2.45 applies, and Form 2.23B is to be used.

Para. 54(7)
On penalties, see s. 430, para. 106(2) and Sch. 10.

Failure to obtain approval of administrator's proposals

55(1) This paragraph applies where an administrator reports to the court that–

(a) an initial creditors' meeting has failed to approve the administrator's proposals presented to it, or

(b) a creditors' meeting has failed to approve a revision of the administrator's proposals presented to it.

55(2) The court may–

(a) provide that the appointment of an administrator shall cease to have effect from a specified time;

(b) adjourn the hearing conditionally or unconditionally;

(c) make an interim order;

(d) make an order on a petition for winding up suspended by virtue of paragraph 40(1)(b);

(e) make any other order (including an order making consequential provision) that the court thinks appropriate.

GENERAL NOTE

This provision gives discretionary powers to the court in the event that proposals or revised proposals are not approved at the creditors' meeting. Although the administrator is required to report the failure to gain approval to the court, it does not appear to be essential that he should seek any ruling from the court: in particular, if revised proposals are not approved, he is surely free to continue to act under the original proposals or to draw up a new set of revised proposals and summon a further creditors' meeting. But despite the wide wording of para. (2)(e), the court's powers must be of a limited nature: it could not, for example, impose on the creditors a set of proposals to which they have not agreed.

Further creditors' meetings

56(1) The administrator of a company shall summon a creditors' meeting if–

(a) it is requested in the prescribed manner by creditors of the company whose debts amount to at least 10% of the total debts of the company, or

(b) he is directed by the court to summon a creditors' meeting.

56(2) An administrator commits an offence if he fails without reasonable excuse to summon a creditors' meeting as required by this paragraph.

GENERAL NOTE

There appears to be no restriction on the circumstances in which the creditors may exercise this power to have a meeting summoned, or on their reasons or motivation, except that such a meeting probably could not be called before the initial creditors' meeting.

Para. 56(2)
On penalties, see s. 430, para. 106(2) and Sch. 10.

Insolvency Act 1986 *Schedule B1*
Creditors' committee

57(1) A creditors' meeting may establish a creditors' committee.

57(2) A creditors' committee shall carry out functions conferred on it by or under this Act.

57(3) A creditors' committee may require the administrator–

(a) to attend on the committee at any reasonable time of which he is given at least seven days' notice, and

(b) to provide the committee with information about the exercise of his functions.

GENERAL NOTE

The appointment of a creditors' or liquidation committee is a feature of most insolvency proceedings: see, *e.g.* ss. 49, 68, 101 and 141–142. For the rules relating to the creditors' committee, see rr. 2.50ff. The business of the committee may be conducted by post (r. 2.61) – or, probably, any other form of correspondence (despite the limitation suggested by the side-note to this rule).

Correspondence instead of creditors' meeting

58(1) Anything which is required or permitted by or under this Schedule to be done at a creditors' meeting may be done by correspondence between the administrator and creditors–

(a) in accordance with the rules, and

(b) subject to any prescribed condition.

58(2) A reference in this Schedule to anything done at a creditors' meeting includes a reference to anything done in the course of correspondence in reliance on sub-paragraph (1).

58(3) A requirement to hold a creditors' meeting is satisfied by conducting correspondence in accordance with this paragraph.

GENERAL NOTE

This provision is new. Plainly, it can operate only where the number of creditors is small. For the relevant rule, see r. 2.48. "Correspondence" includes correspondence by telephonic or other electronic means (para. 111(1)). A notice in Form 2.25B must be sent to every creditor entitled to notice of a creditors' meeting. If no valid Forms 2.25B are received by the administrator by the specified time he must call a creditors' meeting (r. 2.48(6)). A creditor or creditors whose debt(s) amount to at least 10 per cent of the total debts of the company may require a meeting to be summoned in the normal way; and the administrator may also call a meeting if his proposals or revised proposals are rejected by the votes cast by correspondence (r. 2.48(7), (8)).

FUNCTIONS OF ADMINISTRATOR

General powers

59(1) The administrator of a company may do anything necessary or expedient for the management of the affairs, business and property of the company.

59(2) A provision of this Schedule which expressly permits the administrator to do a specified thing is without prejudice to the generality of sub-paragraph (1).

59(3) A person who deals with the administrator of a company in good faith and for value need not inquire whether the administrator is acting within his powers.

GENERAL NOTE

The powers of an administrator under the original regime are set out in IA 1986, ss. 14–16, which correspond broadly to paras 59–72 of this Schedule.

Schedule B1 *Insolvency Act 1986*

Para. 59(1), (2)

The powers are here conferred in the widest terms. These powers are not, however, restricted to the management of the company's business (as is normally the case with the board of directors). This is indicated by the use of the word "affairs", and appears also from some of the particular matters mentioned in this Schedule and in Sch. 1, *e.g.* the power to remove a director (para. 61). The administrator may summon a meeting of shareholders: see r. 2.49.

The notes to s. 14(1) will be generally applicable, since the wording is very similar.

Para. 59(3)

This provision is probably only inserted out of caution, since a third party would almost certainly be protected by the ordinary rules of agency.

60 The administrator of a company has the powers specified in Schedule 1 to this Act.

GENERAL NOTE

The powers conferred by Sch .1, which are common to both administrators and administrative receivers, also apply under the original regime. See the notes to s. 14 and Sch. 1.

61 The administrator of a company–

(a) may remove a director of the company, and

(b) may appoint a director of the company (whether or not to fill a vacancy).

GENERAL NOTE

This provision has its counterpart in s. 14(2)(a). See the note to s. 14(2).

62 The administrator of a company may call a meeting of members or creditors of the company.

63 The administrator of a company may apply to the court for directions in connection with his functions.

GENERAL NOTE

This provision corresponds to s. 14(3) of the original regime. See the note to that provision.

64(1) A company in administration or an officer of a company in administration may not exercise a management power without the consent of the administrator.

64(2) For the purpose of sub-paragraph (1)–

(a) "management power" means a power which could be exercised so as to interfere with the exercise of the administrator's powers,

(b) it is immaterial whether the power is conferred by an enactment or an instrument, and

(c) consent may be general or specific.

GENERAL NOTE

This paragraph corresponds to IA 1986, s. 14(4), which applies under the original regime. See the note to that provision.

The definition of "management power" extends to functions which are wider than those usually associated with management – *e.g.* the appointment of directors by the company in general meeting.

It is clear that the proposals, or the administrator himself, may leave some functions in the hands of the company's directors or other officers, but not of course so as to absolve the administrator from his own responsibilities.

Distribution

65(1) The administrator of a company may make a distribution to a creditor of the company.

65(2) Section 175 shall apply in relation to a distribution under this paragraph as it applies in relation to a winding up.

65(3) A payment may not be made by way of distribution under this paragraph to a creditor of the company who is neither secured nor preferential unless the court gives permission.

GENERAL NOTE

There is no counterpart to this provision under the original regime. It is left to the proposals as approved by the creditors to determine when and how payments are to be made to those entitled.

Chapter 10 of the Rules (rr. 2.68–2.105) deals in detail with the making of distributions to creditors: with the proving of debts, quantification of claims, mutual credit and set-off, interest, proof by secured creditors, etc. These largely mirror the provisions which apply in a winding up (rr. 4.73–4.99).

Para. 65(1)

The term "distribution" is not defined for the purposes of this Schedule or for the Act as a whole, although it is used also in the context of liquidations (ss. 107, 143, 146, etc.) and personal bankruptcy (ss. 324, 330, etc.). The term necessarily relates only to pre-administration creditors. Unsecured creditors rank on a *pari passu* basis (r. 2.69). The rules regarding the declaration and payment of a dividend are rr. 2.97ff.

Para. 65(2)

Section 175 gives priority the company's preferential creditors ahead of the claims of any floating charge holder (but not the holder of a fixed charge). Note also that s. 176A now directs that a "prescribed part" of the company's net property shall be made available for the satisfaction of its unsecured debts and paid in priority to the holder of a floating charge. Under IA 1986, Pt II, as originally drafted, there was no statutory category of preferential debts in an administration, unless the administration was followed immediately by a winding up. The new regime introduced by Sch. B1, and in particular this sub-paragraph, now makes provision for preferential debts to have priority, and s. 387 has been amended so as to make the date on which the company enters into administration the relevant date to determine the existence and amount of such debts. The categories of preferential debts are the same as those in other insolvency proceedings, as defined in Sch. 6.

Section 175(2)(a) also states that the preferential debts shall rank after the expenses of the winding up. By analogy, the same priority is accorded to the expenses of the administration (including the administrator's remuneration, and those expenses (amplified by the debts referred to in para. 99(4) and (5)) will be given priority over the claim of any floating charge holder – or at least those to which para. 70 applies (see para. 99(3)(b)). However, if a receiver has been in office prior to the appointment of the administrator (and also, it would appear, if the appointment of the administrator or any other event has had the effect of crystallising the floating charge), the ruling of the House of Lords in *Re Leyland Daf Ltd, Buchler v Talbot* [2004] UKHL 9) indicates that the property subject to the charge becomes beneficially the property of the charge holder and forms no part of the fund from which the preferential creditors in the administration and the administrator's remuneration and expenses can be paid (see the note to s. 175). However, the application of *Re Leyland Daf Ltd* to the case where the company is in administration rather than in liquidation remains open to debate, since there are differences in the applicable legislation and, in particular, there is nothing in the rules governing liquidation corresponding to para. 99(3)(b).

Para. 65(3)

This provision applies even though the claims of the secured and preferential creditors have been fully met, and (it would seem) even in relation to the "prescribed part" to which unsecured creditors are entitled under s. 176A. Note, however, the special power given to the administrator by para. 66.

66 The administrator of a company may make a payment otherwise than in accordance with paragraph 65 or paragraph 13 of Schedule 1 if he thinks it likely to assist achievement of the purpose of administration.

GENERAL NOTE

This provision would, for example, allow the administrator, without reference to the court, to pay off arrears owed to a creditor who made such a payment a condition of making further essential supplies, *e.g.* of fuel or raw materials. So far as concerns para. 13 of Sch. 1, it is not easy to think of a payment "likely to assist achievement of the purpose of administration" which is not also "necessary or incidental to the performance of his functions".

General duties

67 The administrator of a company shall on his appointment take custody or control of all the property to which he thinks the company is entitled.

GENERAL NOTE

This provision corresponds to IA 1986, s. 17(1), which applies under the original regime, but the phrase "to which he thinks the company is entitled" has been substituted for "to which the company is or appears to be entitled", so making the administrator's subjective belief the critical factor.

68(1) Subject to sub-paragraph (2), the administrator of a company shall manage its affairs, business and property in accordance with–

(a) any proposals approved under paragraph 53,

(b) any revision of those proposals which is made by him and which he does not consider substantial, and

(c) any revision of those proposals approved under paragraph 54.

68(2) If the court gives directions to the administrator of a company in connection with any aspect of his management of the company's affairs, business or property, the administrator shall comply with the directions.

68(3) The court may give directions under sub-paragraph (2) only if–

(a) no proposals have been approved under paragraph 53,

(b) the directions are consistent with any proposals or revision approved under paragraph 53 or 54,

(c) the court thinks the directions are required in order to reflect a change in circumstances since the approval of proposals or a revision under paragraph 53 or 54, or

(d) the court thinks the directions are desirable because of a misunderstanding about proposals or a revision approved under paragraph 53 or 54.

GENERAL NOTE

This provision is comparable with IA 1986, s. 17(2), but is more elaborately expressed. See the note to that subsection.

Para. 68(1)
The Act gives few directions as to the functions of an administrator: it is the proposals approved by the creditors which instruct him what he is to do. He may depart from these proposals only in a respect which he does not consider substantial (sub-para. (1)(b)), and even the court's power to depart from the approved proposals appears to be strictly limited by para. 68(3).

Para. 68(2), (3)
The apparent breadth of para. 68(2) is misleading: it is severely cut down by para. 68(3).

The Act sets out an elaborate procedure which an administrator must follow before his terms of reference are eventually settled by the creditors' approval of the proposals which he has drawn up on the basis of the statement of affairs which he has obtained from the company's officers. This process will necessarily take the best part of two or three months – hence the need to give him interim powers to act under sub-para. (3)(a), under the direction of the court. But the Act does not expressly authorise him to set about his task of seeking the rehabilitation of the company at once, on his own initiative.

However the legislation, as worded for the original regime (IA 1986, s. 17(2)(a)), which has a slightly different emphasis, has been interpreted by the courts as empowering an administrator to take immediate steps, in advance of the creditors' meeting and without reference to the court, if he considers that to do so is in the best interests of the company and its creditors. (See the note to that provision.) Although the language of para. 68(2)–(3) is not the same as that of s. 17(2)(a), and arguably leaves less scope for an interpretation similar to that of Vinelott J. (discussed in the note to s. 17(2)(a)), it is understood that the intention of this paragraph is to replicate s.17(2)(a) in its effect, *i.e.* to give the same interpretation to the two provisions, so that the court's directions are to be followed only if any have been given. This was confirmed by the Minister in the Committee stage of the Bill in the House of Commons.

It may be relevant to note that r. 2.33(6) contemplates that the purposes of an administration may be achieved before a statement of proposals has been sent to creditors.

Para. 68(3)(c) and (d) expressly give the court power to act in circumstances which might have given rise to doubts under the former legislation, although in *Re Smallman Construction Ltd* (1988) 4 B.C.C. 784 and *Re Dana (UK) Ltd* [1999] 2 B.C.L.C. 239 the court considered that the general power conferred by s. 14(3) (now para. 63) was sufficiently

Administrator as agent of company

69 In exercising his functions under this Schedule the administrator of a company acts as its agent.

GENERAL NOTE

This provision corresponds with s. 14(5), which applies under the original regime. See the note to that subsection.

Charged property: floating charge

70(1) The administrator of a company may dispose of or take action relating to property which is subject to a floating charge as if it were not subject to the charge.

70(2) Where property is disposed of in reliance on sub-paragraph (1) the holder of the floating charge shall have the same priority in respect of acquired property as he had in respect of the property disposed of.

70(3) In sub-paragraph (2) **"acquired property"** means property of the company which directly or indirectly represents the property disposed of.

GENERAL NOTE

This provision is similar to s. 15(1), (3), (4), which applies under the original regime. See the note to that section. The disapplication provisions in relation to market charges, etc. there referred to now apply to administrations under Sch. B1: see EA 2002, Sch. 17, para. 47.

Charged property: non-floating charge

71(1) The court may by order enable the administrator of a company to dispose of property which is subject to a security (other than a floating charge) as if it were not subject to the security.

71(2) An order under sub-paragraph (1) may be made only–

(a) on the application of the administrator, and

(b) where the court thinks that disposal of the property would be likely to promote the purpose of administration in respect of the company.

71(3) An order under this paragraph is subject to the condition that there be applied towards discharging the sums secured by the security–

(a) the net proceeds of disposal of the property, and

(b) any additional money required to be added to the net proceeds so as to produce the amount determined by the court as the net amount which would be realised on a sale of the property at market value.

71(4) If an order under this paragraph relates to more than one security, application of money under sub-paragraph (3) shall be in the order of the priorities of the securities.

71(5) An administrator who makes a successful application for an order under this paragraph shall send a copy of the order to the registrar of companies before the end of the period of 14 days starting with the date of the order.

71(6) An administrator commits an offence if he fails to comply with sub-paragraph (5) without reasonable excuse.

GENERAL NOTE

This provision is similar to s. 15(2),(3),(5)–(8) which applies under the original regime. See the note to that section. The disapplication provisions in relation to market charges, etc. there referred to now apply to administrations under Sch. B1: see EA 2002, Sch. 17, para. 47.

Schedule B1   Insolvency Act 1986

Rule 2.66 governs the application to the court. "Hire-purchase agreement" extends to retention of title, etc. Transactions by virtue of the definition in para. 111(1), where "market value" is also defined.

Para. 71(6)
On penalties, see s. 430, para. 106(2) and Sch. 10.

Hire-purchase property

72(1) The court may by order enable the administrator of a company to dispose of goods which are in the possession of the company under a hire-purchase agreement as if all the rights of the owner under the agreement were vested in the company.

72(2) An order under sub-paragraph (1) may be made only–

(a) on the application of the administrator, and

(b) where the court thinks that disposal of the goods would be likely to promote the purpose of administration in respect of the company.

72(3) An order under this paragraph is subject to the condition that there be applied towards discharging the sums payable under the hire-purchase agreement–

(a) the net proceeds of disposal of the goods, and

(b) any additional money required to be added to the net proceeds so as to produce the amount determined by the court as the net amount which would be realised on a sale of the goods at market value.

72(4) An administrator who makes a successful application for an order under this paragraph shall send a copy of the order to the registrar of companies before the end of the period of 14 days starting with the date of the order.

72(5) An administrator commits an offence if he fails without reasonable excuse to comply with sub-paragraph (4).

GENERAL NOTE

In s. 15, which applies under the original regime, the power conferred upon an administrator, with the leave of the court, to dispose of (a) property subject to a security and (b) property in the possession of the company under a hire-purchase or similar agreement is dealt with in the same section. The two are now treated separately in paras 71 and 72. The notes to paras 70 and 71 are therefore relevant here. See also the note to s. 15. The disapplication provisions in relation to market charges, etc there referred to now apply to administrations under Sch. B1: see EA 2002, Sch. 17, para. 47.

Rule 2.66 governs the application to the court. "Hire-purchase agreement" extends to retention of title, etc. transactions by virtue of the definition in para. 111(1), where "market value" is also defined.

Para. 71(6)
On penalties, see s. 430, para. 106(2) and Sch. 10.

Protection for secured or preferential creditor

73(1) An administrator's statement of proposals under paragraph 49 may not include any action which–

(a) affects the right of a secured creditor of the company to enforce his security,

(b) would result in a preferential debt of the company being paid otherwise than in priority to its non-preferential debts, or

(c) would result in one preferential creditor of the company being paid a smaller proportion of his debt than another.

73(2) Sub-paragraph (1) does not apply to–

(a) action to which the relevant creditor consents,

(b) a proposal for a voluntary arrangement under Part I of this Act (although this sub-paragraph is without prejudice to section 4(3)), or

(c) a proposal for a compromise or arrangement to be sanctioned under section 425 of the Companies Act (compromise with creditors or members).

73(3) The reference to a statement of proposals in sub-paragraph (1) includes a reference to a statement as revised or modified.

General Note

There was no provision corresponding to this paragraph in the Pt II regime, as originally drafted. There were no preferential creditors; and any secured creditor who felt himself disadvantaged by the proposals could take his complaint to the court under s. 27. This paragraph is modelled on s. 4(3), (4) and Sch. A1, para. 31(4), (5), which apply in a CVA, and the notes to those provisions may be relevant here.

Para. 73(1)(a)
The question whether a landlord seeking to exercise rights of forfeiture, etc. for non-payment of rent is a secured creditor has been the subject of much debate: see the note to s. 11(3). Although the issue has been resolved for the purposes of that section by legislation, the cases referred to in that note remain relevant generally.

Para. 73(2)(b)
A secured creditor will in any case have similar protection under s. 4(3). It is surprising that there is no reference to the corresponding provisions in Sch. A1, para. 31(4)–(6). The intention may be to pass the consideration of all the issues that may arise to the CVA meetings.

Para. 72(2)(c)
A scheme under CA 1985, s. 425 may involve the variation or abrogation of the rights of secured and preferential creditors, and will be effective (and binding on minorities) if carried at the relevant class meetings and confirmed by the court. Paragraph 73(1) is not to affect this well-sanctioned procedure.

Challenge to administrator's conduct of company

74(1) A creditor or member of a company in administration may apply to the court claiming that–

(a) the administrator is acting or has acted so as unfairly to harm the interests of the applicant (whether alone or in common with some or all other members or creditors), or

(b) the administrator proposes to act in a way which would unfairly harm the interests of the applicant (whether alone or in common with some or all other members or creditors).

74(2) A creditor or member of a company in administration may apply to the court claiming that the administrator is not performing his functions as quickly or as efficiently as is reasonably practicable.

74(3) The court may–

(a) grant relief;

(b) dismiss the application;

(c) adjourn the hearing conditionally or unconditionally;

(d) make an interim order;

(e) make any other order it thinks appropriate.

Schedule B1 *Insolvency Act 1986*

74(4) In particular, an order under this paragraph may–
(a) regulate the administrator's exercise of his functions;
(b) require the administrator to do or not do a specified thing;
(c) require a creditors' meeting to be held for a specified purpose;
(d) provide for the appointment of an administrator to cease to have effect;
(e) make consequential provision.

74(5) An order may be made on a claim under sub-paragraph (1) whether or not the action complained of–
(a) is within the administrator's powers under this Schedule;
(b) was taken in reliance on an order under paragraph 71 or 72.

74(6) An order may not be made under this paragraph if it would impede or prevent the implementation of–
(a) a voluntary arrangement approved under Part I,
(b) a compromise or arrangement sanctioned under section 425 of the Companies Act (compromise with creditors and members), or
(c) proposals or a revision approved under paragraph 53 or 54 more than 28 days before the day on which the application for the order under this paragraph is made.

GENERAL NOTE

This provision corresponds to s. 27, which applies under the original regime. The notes to that provision may be relevant.

Para. 74(1)
Surprisingly, the draftsman has chosen to abandon the time-honoured expression "unfairly prejudicial to the interests" (familiar to company lawyers from its use in CA 1985, s. 459) in favour of "unfairly to harm the interests". It will be a matter for judicial interpretation whether any different meaning is intended.

Para. 74(2)
This provision is new, and reflects the duty to act expeditiously specifically imposed on an administrator by para. 4.

Para. 74(5)(a)
This provision has no counterpart in the original s. 27. As with s. 459, the fact that an act is lawful and within the actor's powers does not prevent the court from having regard to wider considerations of an equitable nature in determining whether it is unfairly harmful.

Para. 74(5)(b), (6)
The comments made (respectively) in the notes to ss. 27(5), 27(3) apply here.

Misfeasance

75(1) The court may examine the conduct of a person who–
(a) is or purports to be the administrator of a company, or
(b) has been or has purported to be the administrator of a company.

75(2) An examination under this paragraph may be held only on the application of–
(a) the official receiver,
(b) the administrator of the company,
(c) the liquidator of the company,
(d) a creditor of the company, or
(e) a contributory of the company.

75(3) An application under sub-paragraph (2) must allege that the administrator–

(a) has misapplied or retained money or other property of the company,

(b) has become accountable for money or other property of the company,

(c) has breached a fiduciary or other duty in relation to the company, or

(d) has been guilty of misfeasance.

75(4) On an examination under this paragraph into a person's conduct the court may order him–

(a) to repay, restore or account for money or property;

(b) to pay interest;

(c) to contribute a sum to the company's property by way of compensation for breach of duty or misfeasance.

75(5) In sub-paragraph (3) **"administrator"** includes a person who purports or has purported to be a company's administrator.

75(6) An application under sub-paragraph (2) may be made in respect of an administrator who has been discharged under paragraph 98 only with the permission of the court.

GENERAL NOTE

The "misfeasance" section applicable generally in corporate insolvency proceedings is s. 212. In the Act as originally drafted, an administrator was listed in s. 212(1)(b) as an office-holder who could be made accountable under the section. All references to an administrator have now been removed from s. 212 by EA 2002, s. 278 and Sch. 26, and the present paragraph will now apply instead to an administrator appointed under the new regime. The main difference from s. 212 is that it is not necessary that the company should be in liquidation. The only other change of significance appears to be the inclusion of a person who has purported to be an administrator. In other respects, the notes to s. 212 may be treated as applicable.

ENDING ADMINISTRATION

Automatic end of administration

76(1) The appointment of an administrator shall cease to have effect at the end of the period of one year beginning with the date on which it takes effect.

76(2) But–

(a) on the application of an administrator the court may by order extend his term of office for a specified period, and

(b) an administrator's term of office may be extended for a specified period not exceeding six months by consent.

GENERAL NOTE

Paragraphs 76–86 deal with the ending, or termination, of an administration. However, in these provisions the draftsman prefers to refer to "the appointment of an administrator ceasing to have effect", in keeping with the definition in para. 1(2).

The automatic termination of an administration after one year is a novel feature introduced by the 2002 reforms, emphasising the legislature's concern that matters should be dealt with expeditiously that is also reflected in para. 4. The administration may, however, be extended by court order or (subject to a limit of six months) by consent of the creditors in accordance with para. 78.

Rules 2.110–2.112 apply in regard to paras 76–78.

77(1) An order of the court under paragraph 76–

(a) may be made in respect of an administrator whose term of office has already been extended by order or by consent, but

(b) may not be made after the expiry of the administrator's term of office.

77(2) Where an order is made under paragraph 76 the administrator shall as soon as is reasonably practicable notify the registrar of companies.

77(3) An administrator who fails without reasonable excuse to comply with sub-paragraph (2) commits an offence.

Para. 77(1)
The maximum period for which an administration may be extended out of court is six months (para. 76(2)(b)), and there can be only one such an extension (para. 78(4)). However, the court may grant a further extension without regard to these restrictions. Even so, there can be no retrospective extension once an administrator's term of office has expired.

Para. 77(2), (3)
On penalties, see s. 430, para. 106(2) and Sch. 10.

78(1) In paragraph 76(2)(b) **"consent"** means consent of–

(a) each secured creditor of the company, and

(b) if the company has unsecured debts, creditors whose debts amount to more than 50% of the company's unsecured debts, disregarding debts of any creditor who does not respond to an invitation to give or withhold consent.

78(2) But where the administrator has made a statement under paragraph 52(1)(b) "consent" means–

(a) consent of each secured creditor of the company, or

(b) if the administrator thinks that a distribution may be made to preferential creditors, consent of–

　(i) each secured creditor of the company, and

　(ii) preferential creditors whose debts amount to more than 50% of the preferential debts of the company, disregarding debts of any creditor who does not respond to an invitation to give or withhold consent.

78(3) Consent for the purposes of paragraph 76(2)(b) may be–

(a) written, or

(b) signified at a creditors' meeting.

78(4) An administrator's term of office–

(a) may be extended by consent only once,

(b) may not be extended by consent after extension by order of the court, and

(c) may not be extended by consent after expiry.

78(5) Where an administrator's term of office is extended by consent he shall as soon as is reasonably practicable–

(a) file notice of the extension with the court, and

(b) notify the registrar of companies.

78(6) An administrator who fails without reasonable excuse to comply with sub-paragraph (5) commits an offence.

Para. 78(1)–(3)
Paragraph 78 defines "consent" in various ways for the purposes of the one-off extension of an administration which can be made out of court under para. 76(2)(b). The alternatives depend on whether the administrator has included in his proposals a statement under para. 52(1)(b) that he thinks that the company has insufficient property to enable a distribution to be made to unsecured creditors (other than what they might be entitled to under the "prescribed part" provisions of s. 176A). If he has not, and the company has unsecured creditors, the consent must be that of each secured creditor of the company and over 50 per cent in value of the company's unsecured creditors. If he has made such a statement, the consent must be *either* that of each secured creditor of the company *or*, if the administrator thinks that a distribution may be made to the company's preferential creditors, the consent of each secured creditor and over 50 per cent in value of the preferential creditors. There are thus three possible scenarios. The debts of creditors who abstain or choose not to respond are ignored. Consent may be obtained either at a creditors' meeting or in writing (which may be in electronic form: para. 111(2)) from each individual creditor.

Para. 78(4)
Note these further limitations on the power to extend an administration by consent.

Para. 78(5), (6)
On penalties, see s. 430, para. 106(2) and Sch. 10.

Court ending administration on application of administrator

79(1) On the application of the administrator of a company the court may provide for the appointment of an administrator of the company to cease to have effect from a specified time.

79(2) The administrator of a company shall make an application under this paragraph if–

(a) he thinks the purpose of administration cannot be achieved in relation to the company,

(b) he thinks the company should not have entered administration, or

(c) a creditors' meeting requires him to make an application under this paragraph.

79(3) The administrator of a company shall make an application under this paragraph if–

(a) the administration is pursuant to an administration order, and

(b) the administrator thinks that the purpose of administration has been sufficiently achieved in relation to the company.

79(4) On an application under this paragraph the court may–

(a) adjourn the hearing conditionally or unconditionally;

(b) dismiss the application;

(c) make an interim order;

(d) make any order it thinks appropriate (whether in addition to, in consequence of or instead of the order applied for).

GENERAL NOTE

This paragraph deals with the ending of the administration by order of the court. Paragraph 79(2) applies in all administrations, while para. 79(3) is applicable only where the administrator was appointed by the court.

Rules 2.114 and 2.116 apply in this case.

Para. 79(2)
The grounds on which an application can be made by the administrator appear to be limited to the four situations listed. One reason why a company might fall within para. 79(2)(b) would be if it is proved to have been solvent all along.

Para. 79(3)
If the administrator was appointed by the court, the administration can only be terminated under this paragraph. If he was appointed out of court and he thinks that the purpose of the administration has been sufficiently achieved, he may follow the alternative procedure under para. 80.

Schedule B1　　　　　　　　　　*Insolvency Act 1986*

Termination of administration where objective achieved

80(1)　This paragraph applies where an administrator of a company is appointed under paragraph 14 or 22.

80(2)　If the administrator thinks that the purpose of administration has been sufficiently achieved in relation to the company he may file a notice in the prescribed form–

(a)　with the court, and

(b)　with the registrar of companies.

80(3)　The administrator's appointment shall cease to have effect when the requirements of sub-paragraph (2) are satisfied.

80(4)　Where the administrator files a notice he shall within the prescribed period send a copy to every creditor of the company of whose claim and address he is aware.

80(5)　The rules may provide that the administrator is taken to have complied with sub-paragraph (4) if before the end of the prescribed period he publishes in the prescribed manner a notice undertaking to provide a copy of the notice under sub-paragraph (2) to any creditor of the company who applies in writing to a specified address.

80(6)　An administrator who fails without reasonable excuse to comply with sub-paragraph (4) commits an offence.

GENERAL NOTE

Where the administrator has been appointed out of court and he thinks that he has sufficiently achieved the objective of the administration, this paragraph provides a simple and informal way for him to sign off and bring the administration to an end.
　Rules 2.110 and 2.113 apply, and Form 2.32B is prescribed.

Para. 80(1)–(5)
The notice must be sent to creditors (or published under para. 80(5) within five business days (r. 2.113(4)). The obligation to notify creditors ensures that any of them who disagree with the administrator's decision may take appropriate action, but this will necessarily only happen after the administration has been terminated pursuant to para. 80(3) and it would appear that the court has no power to reinstate the administration.

Para. 80(6)
On penalties, see s. 430, para. 106(2) and Sch. 10.

Court ending administration on application of creditor

81(1)　On the application of a creditor of a company the court may provide for the appointment of an administrator of the company to cease to have effect at a specified time.

81(2)　An application under this paragraph must allege an improper motive–

(a)　in the case of an administrator appointed by administration order, on the part of the applicant for the order, or

(b)　in any other case, on the part of the person who appointed the administrator.

81(3)　On an application under this paragraph the court may–

(a)　adjourn the hearing conditionally or unconditionally;

(b)　dismiss the application;

(c)　make an interim order;

(d)　make any order it thinks appropriate (whether in addition to, in consequence of or instead of the order applied for).

GENERAL NOTE

A creditor may apply to the court to have the administration terminated, but only on the limited grounds set out in para. 81(2). Rule 2.115 applies.

Public interest winding-up

82(1) This paragraph applies where a winding-up order is made for the winding up of a company in administration on a petition presented under–

(a) section 124A (public interest), or

(b) section 367 of the Financial Services and Markets Act 2000 (c. 8) (petition by Financial Services Authority).

82(2) This paragraph also applies where a provisional liquidator of a company in administration is appointed following the presentation of a petition under any of the provisions listed in sub-paragraph (1).

82(3) The court shall order–

(a) that the appointment of the administrator shall cease to have effect, or

(b) that the appointment of the administrator shall continue to have effect.

82(4) If the court makes an order under sub-paragraph (3)(b) it may also–

(a) specify which of the powers under this Schedule are to be exercisable by the administrator, and

(b) order that this Schedule shall have effect in relation to the administrator with specified modifications.

GENERAL NOTE

It is only where a winding-up order is made, or a provisional administrator appointed, on public interest grounds under one of the provisions mentioned in para. 82(1) that an administrator can hold office concurrently with a liquidator or provisional liquidator: see para. 40(2). The court is here given power either to terminate the administration or to allow it to continue and allocate responsibilities between the two office-holders.

Moving from administration to creditors' voluntary liquidation

83(1) This paragraph applies in England and Wales where the administrator of a company thinks–

(a) that the total amount which each secured creditor of the company is likely to receive has been paid to him or set aside for him, and

(b) that a distribution will be made to unsecured creditors of the company (if there are any).

83(2) This paragraph applies in Scotland where the administrator of a company thinks–

(a) that each secured creditor of the company will receive payment in respect of his debt, and

(b) that a distribution will be made to unsecured creditors (if there are any).

83(3) The administrator may send to the registrar of companies a notice that this paragraph applies.

83(4) On receipt of a notice under sub-paragraph (3) the registrar shall register it.

83(5) If an administrator sends a notice under sub-paragraph (3) he shall as soon as is reasonably practicable–

(a) file a copy of the notice with the court, and

(b) send a copy of the notice to each creditor of whose claim and address he is aware.

Schedule B1 *Insolvency Act 1986*

83(6) On the registration of a notice under sub-paragraph (3)–

(a) the appointment of an administrator in respect of the company shall cease to have effect, and

(b) the company shall be wound up as if a resolution for voluntary winding up under section 84 were passed on the day on which the notice is registered.

83(7) The liquidator for the purposes of the winding up shall be–

(a) a person nominated by the creditors of the company in the prescribed manner and within the prescribed period, or

(b) if no person is nominated under paragraph (a), the administrator.

83(8) In the application of Part IV to a winding up by virtue of this paragraph–

(a) section 85 shall not apply,

(b) section 86 shall apply as if the reference to the time of the passing of the resolution for voluntary winding up were a reference to the beginning of the date of registration of the notice under sub-paragraph (3),

(c) section 89 does not apply,

(d) sections 98, 99 and 100 shall not apply,

(e) section 129 shall apply as if the reference to the time of the passing of the resolution for voluntary winding up were a reference to the beginning of the date of registration of the notice under sub-paragraph (3), and

(f) any creditors' committee which is in existence immediately before the company ceases to be in administration shall continue in existence after that time as if appointed as a liquidation committee under section 101.

GENERAL NOTE

Under the original Pt II of IA 1986 it is possible for a company to move more or less seamlessly from administration to compulsory winding up, but various obstacles stand in the way of a move to voluntary liquidation, which have only been overcome with some difficulty: see the note to s. 18(1),(2). In the new regime these obstacles are eliminated, and a straightforward procedure is laid down by the present provision to facilitate such a move. Paragraph 83(1), (2) lays down preconditions: first, provision must have been made to ensure that all secured creditors will be paid off and secondly, after that, there must be something remaining available for the unsecured creditors. The simple act of filing a notice with the registrar of companies is then all that is needed to transform the administration into a creditors' voluntary winding up, with an insolvency practitioner chosen by the creditors or the former administrator as liquidator (para. 83 (6)(a), (7)). Necessarily, a certain amount of "deeming" is required to take account of the fact that this creditors' voluntary liquidation has not come into being by the usual procedure.

Rule 2.117 applies.

Para. 83(7)

The appointment, if made by the creditors, follows the procedure in r. 2.33(2)(m) or r. 2.45(2)(g), and takes effect by the creditors approving the administrator's proposals or revised proposals (r. 2.117(3)).

Moving from administration to dissolution

84(1) If the administrator of a company thinks that the company has no property which might permit a distribution to its creditors, he shall send a notice to that effect to the registrar of companies.

84(2) The court may on the application of the administrator of a company disapply sub-paragraph (1) in respect of the company.

84(3) On receipt of a notice under sub-paragraph (1) the registrar shall register it.

84(4) On the registration of a notice in respect of a company under sub-paragraph (1) the appointment of an administrator of the company shall cease to have effect.

84(5) If an administrator sends a notice under sub-paragraph (1) he shall as soon as is reasonably practicable–

(a) file a copy of the notice with the court, and

(b) send a copy of the notice to each creditor of whose claim and address he is aware.

84(6) At the end of the period of three months beginning with the date of registration of a notice in respect of a company under sub-paragraph (1) the company is deemed to be dissolved.

84(7) On an application in respect of a company by the administrator or another interested person the court may–

(a) extend the period specified in sub-paragraph (6),

(b) suspend that period, or

(c) disapply sub-paragraph (6).

84(8) Where an order is made under sub-paragraph (7) in respect of a company the administrator shall as soon as is reasonably practicable notify the registrar of companies.

84(9) An administrator commits an offence if he fails without reasonable excuse to comply with sub-paragraph (5).

GENERAL NOTE

This is a new provision which has no counterpart in the original IA 1986, Pt II. It is modelled on the "early dissolution" procedure (ss. 202–204) that enables a company in compulsory liquidation to move to dissolution without further formality if it has no assets worth realising. All that is required is for the administrator to send the requisite notice to the registrar of companies and notify the court and the creditors. Unless the court orders otherwise under para. 84(7), dissolution follows automatically three months later.

Para. 84(1), (2)
It would appear from the wording of these sub-paragraphs, taken together, that once the administrator has reached a conclusion that the property is insufficient he has no discretion to do otherwise than proceed to a dissolution: only the court can determine that the administration should continue. One situation where this might be appropriate would be where there are circumstances suggesting misconduct which require investigation. Note that there is no special mention of secured creditors: if there is even a small amount available to be paid to a secured creditor, this paragraph will not apply and para. 79(3) or 80 should be followed instead.
Rule 2.117 applies, and Form 2.34B is prescribed for the notice.

Para. 84(4)
The administration comes to an end on registration. There would appear to be no power to reinstate the administration once this has been done.

Para. 84(6)
Should it be necessary to revive the company (*e.g.* if unknown assets belonging to the company come to light), CA 1985, s. 651 empowers the court to declare the dissolution void if application is made within the ensuing two years.

Para. 84(7)
The powers of the court under this sub-paragraph apply only to para. 84(6), *i.e.* to the anticipated dissolution of the company, and not to the ending of the administration under para. 84(4).

Para.84(8), (9)
Form 2.36B should be used. On penalties, see s. 430, para. 106(2) and Sch. 10.

Discharge of administration order where administration ends

85(1) This paragraph applies where–

(a) the court makes an order under this Schedule providing for the appointment of an administrator of a company to cease to have effect, and

(b) the administrator was appointed by administration order.

Schedule B1 *Insolvency Act 1986*

85(2) The court shall discharge the administration order.

GENERAL NOTE

This paragraph applies only where the administrator was appointed by court order. Under the original Pt II, it is the discharge of the order which brings the administration to an end. Under Sch. B1, the sequence is reversed.

Notice to Companies Registrar where administration ends

86(1) This paragraph applies where the court makes an order under this Schedule providing for the appointment of an administrator to cease to have effect.

86(2) The administrator shall send a copy of the order to the registrar of companies within the period of 14 days beginning with the date of the order.

86(3) An administrator who fails without reasonable excuse to comply with sub-paragraph (2) commits an offence.

GENERAL NOTE

This provision, again, is not concerned with the situation where an individual administrator ceases to hold office, but with the termination of the administration itself. In contrast with para. 85, it is not confined to the case of an administrator appointed by the court: there are other provisions (*e.g.* para. 81) empowering the court to order that an administration should come to an end.

Rule 2.116 applies, and Form 2.33B is prescribed.

Para. 86(3)
On penalties, see s. 430, para. 106(2) and Sch. 10.

REPLACING ADMINISTRATOR

Resignation of administrator

88(1) An administrator may resign only in prescribed circumstances.

87(2) Where an administrator may resign he may do so only–

(a) in the case of an administrator appointed by administration order, by notice in writing to the court,

(b) in the case of an administrator appointed under paragraph 14, by notice in writing to the holder of the floating charge by virtue of which the appointment was made,

(c) in the case of an administrator appointed under paragraph 22(1), by notice in writing to the company, or

(d) in the case of an administrator appointed under paragraph 22(2), by notice in writing to the directors of the company.

GENERAL NOTE

The circumstances in which an administrator may resign his office are prescribed by r. 2.119. Forms 2.37B and 2.38B (respectively) are to be used for the notice of intention to resign and the notice of resignation: see rr. 2.120–121, which give further details regarding the giving of notice and its filing with the court and the registrar of companies.

On the question when a notice of resignation takes effect, see the note to s. 19(1).

Removal of administrator from office

88(1) The court may by order remove an administrator from office.

Administrator ceasing to be qualified

89(1) The administrator of a company shall vacate office if he ceases to be qualified to act as an insolvency practitioner in relation to the company.

89(2) Where an administrator vacates office by virtue of sub-paragraph (1) he shall give notice in writing–

(a) in the case of an administrator appointed by administration order, to the court,

(b) in the case of an administrator appointed under paragraph 14, to the holder of the floating charge by virtue of which the appointment was made,

(c) in the case of an administrator appointed under paragraph 22(1), to the company, or

(d) in the case of an administrator appointed under paragraph 22(2), to the directors of the company.

89(3) An administrator who fails without reasonable excuse to comply with sub-paragraph (2) commits an offence.

GENERAL NOTE

An administrator will "cease to be qualified to act" in relation to the company if at any time he fails to meet the criteria set out in s. 390. "Shall vacate office" may be read as meaning either something that happens automatically or something which depends on the administrator taking action to step aside. It is probably the former that is intended, the giving of notice under para. 89(2) being merely consequential.

Notice must also be given to the registrar of companies, using Form 2.39B (r. 2.123).

Para. 89(3)
On penalties, see s. 390, para. 106(2) and Sch. 10.

Supplying vacancy in office of administrator

90 Paragraphs 91 to 95 apply where an administrator–

(a) dies,

(b) resigns,

(c) is removed from office under paragraph 88, or

(d) vacates office under paragraph 89.

GENERAL NOTE

Paragraphs 91–95 apply only if the office of administrator has become vacant. The substitution of one administrator by another is dealt with in paras 96–97, and the appointment of one or more additional administrators in paras 100–103.

Rules 2.12ff. apply in these cases.

91(1) Where the administrator was appointed by administration order, the court may replace the administrator on an application under this sub-paragraph made by–

(a) a creditors' committee of the company,

(b) the company,

(c) the directors of the company,

(d) one or more creditors of the company, or

(e) where more than one person was appointed to act jointly or concurrently as the administrator, any of those persons who remains in office.

91(2) But an application may be made in reliance on sub-paragraph (1)(b) to (d) only where–

(a) there is no creditors' committee of the company,

(b) the court is satisfied that the creditors' committee or a remaining administrator is not taking reasonable steps to make a replacement, or

(c) the court is satisfied that for another reason it is right for the application to be made.

GENERAL NOTE

This paragraph applies only where the administrator who has vacated office was appointed by the court. Where the administrator was appointed out of court, a replacement will normally be appointed out of court under paras. 92–94, but the court has back-up and, where appropriate, overriding powers in the circumstances set out in para. 95.
  Rules 2.125ff. give details of the procedure and notification requirements.

Para. 91(1)
It does not appear that the outgoing administrator may make an application under this provision. But there are situations where this would be appropriate, perhaps particularly where it is sought to replace an insolvency practitioner who holds multiple offices in a single application and appoint replacements, *e.g.* one or more members of the same firm, as in *Re Equity Nominees Ltd* [2000] B.C.C. 84. The court would no doubt allow the application to be made under some other provision, *e.g.* para. 63.

Para. 91(2)
The persons listed in sub-paras. (1)(b)–(d) must stand aside and allow the creditors' committee, if there is one, or a remaining administrator where there were joint or concurrent appointments, to have first bite at the cherry (not necessarily by applying to the court), subject to the court's discretion under para. 91(2)(c).

92 Where the administrator was appointed under paragraph 14 the holder of the floating charge by virtue of which the appointment was made may replace the administrator.

GENERAL NOTE

This provision applies only where the office of administrator has become vacant: for the replacement of an administrator currently in office, see paras 87–97. The right of the holder of the floating charge to replace his own appointee is unqualified, although no doubt this could be challenged under para. 95(b) if good reason could be shown.
  Rules 2.126, 2.129 apply.

93(1) Where the administrator was appointed under paragraph 22(1) by the company it may replace the administrator.

93(2) A replacement under this paragraph may be made only–

(a) with the consent of each person who is the holder of a qualifying floating charge in respect of the company's property, or

(b) where consent is withheld, with the permission of the court.

GENERAL NOTE

The initial appointment of an administrator by the company under para. 22(1) may be made only after giving five days' notice to the holder of a qualifying floating charge under para. 26, so enabling the latter to make his own appointment instead. The present paragraph to some extent echoes para. 26, giving the charge holder an opportunity to have some say in the choice of a replacement, but stops short of giving him an outright veto.
  Rules 2.126, 2.129 apply.

94(1) Where the administrator was appointed under paragraph 22(2) the directors of the company may replace the administrator.

94(2) A replacement under this paragraph may be made only–

(a) with the consent of each person who is the holder of a qualifying floating charge in respect of the company's property, or

(b) where consent is withheld, with the permission of the court.

GENERAL NOTE

This provision is in similar terms to para. 93. See the comment to that paragraph.

95 The court may replace an administrator on the application of a person listed in paragraph 91(1) if the court–

(a) is satisfied that a person who is entitled to replace the administrator under any of paragraphs 92 to 94 is not taking reasonable steps to make a replacement, or

(b) that for another reason it is right for the court to make the replacement.

GENERAL NOTE

This provision gives the court back-up powers to deal with situations of inertia or dispute. Only those persons listed in para. 91(1) have standing to apply. If anyone else (*e.g.* an outgoing administrator) wishes to have the court make a replacement, application would have to be made under some other provision, such as para. 63. Rule 2.125 applies to the application. See the note to para. 91(1).
Rules 2.126, 2.129 apply.

Substitution of administrator: competing floating charge-holder

96(1) This paragraph applies where an administrator of a company is appointed under paragraph 14 by the holder of a qualifying floating charge in respect of the company's property.

96(2) The holder of a prior qualifying floating charge in respect of the company's property may apply to the court for the administrator to be replaced by an administrator nominated by the holder of the prior floating charge.

96(3) One floating charge is prior to another for the purposes of this paragraph if–

(a) it was created first, or

(b) it is to be treated as having priority in accordance with an agreement to which the holder of each floating charge was party.

96(4) Sub-paragraph (3) shall have effect in relation to Scotland as if the following were substituted for paragraph (a)–

"(a) it has priority of ranking in accordance with section 464(4)(b) of the Companies Act 1985 (c. 6),".

GENERAL NOTE

In contrast with paras 87–95, this provision appears to apply whether or not there is a vacancy in the office of administrator. It deals with the situation where an administrator is or has been in office who has been appointed by the holder of a junior-ranking floating charge. When the initial appointment was made, the charge-holder making the appointment would have been required to notify or secure the consent of any senior-ranking charge-holder(s) under para. 15(1), and it is assumed that the latter took no steps at that time to block the appointment. The present provision allows the holder of a senior-ranking charge to apply to the court subsequently to request that a different person be appointed administrator in place of the junior charge-holder's appointee. No guidance is given to the court as to the basis on which it should exercise its discretion to accede to such a request, although prima facie the holder of a senior-ranking charge would expect the court to support his choice of nominee.

On the meaning of "qualifying" floating charge, see para. 14(2). The court would surely also require the senior-ranking charge to be enforceable at the time the application is made, in keeping with para. 16, although this is not stated in para. 96.

Schedule B1 *Insolvency Act 1986*

Rules 2.126, 2.129 apply.

Substitution of administrator appointed by company or directors: creditors' meeting

97(1) This paragraph applies where–

(a) an administrator of a company is appointed by a company or directors under paragraph 22, and

(b) there is no holder of a qualifying floating charge in respect of the company's property.

97(2) A creditors' meeting may replace the administrator.

97(3) A creditors' meeting may act under sub-paragraph (2) only if the new administrator's written consent to act is presented to the meeting before the replacement is made.

GENERAL NOTE

As with para. 96, this provision appears to apply whether or not there is a vacancy in the office of administrator but, in contrast with that paragraph, no application to the court is needed. If there is a vacancy, the company or the directors (as the case may be) will also have the power to appoint a replacement under paras 93 or 94, but it would make no sense for either of them to do so if there is opposition from the creditors' committee, since it could use its power under the present paragraph to override their appointment.

Rules 2.126, 2.129 apply.

Vacation of office: discharge from liability

98(1) Where a person ceases to be the administrator of a company (whether because he vacates office by reason of resignation, death or otherwise, because he is removed from office or because his appointment ceases to have effect) he is discharged from liability in respect of any action of his as administrator.

98(2) The discharge provided by sub-paragraph (1) takes effect–

(a) in the case of an administrator who dies, on the filing with the court of notice of his death,

(b) in the case of an administrator appointed under paragraph 14 or 22, at a time appointed by resolution of the creditors' committee or, if there is no committee, by resolution of the creditors, or

(c) in any case, at a time specified by the court.

98(3) For the purpose of the application of sub-paragraph (2)(b) in a case where the administrator has made a statement under paragraph 52(1)(b), a resolution shall be taken as passed if (and only if) passed with the approval of–

(a) each secured creditor of the company, or

(b) if the administrator has made a distribution to preferential creditors or thinks that a distribution may be made to preferential creditors–

   (i) each secured creditor of the company, and
   (ii) preferential creditors whose debts amount to more than 50% of the preferential debts of the company, disregarding debts of any creditor who does not respond to an invitation to give or withhold approval.

98(4) Discharge–

(a) applies to liability accrued before the discharge takes effect, and

(b) does not prevent the exercise of the court's powers under paragraph 75.

GENERAL NOTE

This provision corresponds to IA 1986, s. 20, which applies in the original regime. It uses the expression "he is discharged from liability" instead of "he has his release", but once s. 20(2) is taken into account, the net result appears to be the same. The comment to s. 20 may be helpful.

The phrase "the appointment of an administrator ceases to have effect" is used by the draftsman as equivalent to "the administration comes to an end" or "is terminated": see, e.g. paras 76, 80, 81. The present provision thus applies both in the case where an administrator is replaced and also where the administration has come to an end.

Para. 98(1)
The discharge is not automatic, but takes effect only from the time specified in sub-para.(2).

Para. 98(2)
Paragraph 98(2)(c) corresponds to s. 20(1)(b), except that the latter states "in any *other* case". It is thus conceivable that the court could fix a time other than those mentioned in sub-para. (2)(a) and (b), although the court would not normally be involved in either of these cases.

Where the administrator in question was appointed out of court under para. 14 or 22, it is left to the creditors' committee or creditors to decide when the discharge should take effect. There is some parallel with s. 173, which deals with the release of a liquidator in a voluntary winding up, but there is no provision in the present paragraph for the relevant meeting to resolve against a discharge. If the meeting is unwilling to set a date from which the discharge is to take effect, and the contention above is correct, recourse could be had to the court to resolve the matter.

Para. 98(3)
Paragraph 52(1)(b) applies where the administrator thinks that the company has insufficient property to enable a distribution to be made to the company's unsecured creditors (apart from anything the may get through the "prescribed part" provisions of s. 176A). In such circumstances it is inappropriate that the decision on the administrator's discharge should be in the hands of the creditors' committee or the creditors at large, most of whom will have no interest in the outcome of the administration: hence the need for the consents required by this sub-paragraph.

Para. 98(4)
See the note to s. 20(2), (3).

Vacation of office: charges and liabilities

99(1) This paragraph applies where a person ceases to be the administrator of a company (whether because he vacates office by reason of resignation, death or otherwise, because he is removed from office or because his appointment ceases to have effect).

99(2) In this paragraph–

"**the former administrator**" means the person referred to in sub-paragraph (1), and

"**cessation**" means the time when he ceases to be the company's administrator.

99(3) The former administrator's remuneration and expenses shall be–

(a) charged on and payable out of property of which he had custody or control immediately before cessation, and

(b) payable in priority to any security to which paragraph 70 applies.

99(4) A sum payable in respect of a debt or liability arising out of a contract entered into by the former administrator or a predecessor before cessation shall be–

(a) charged on and payable out of property of which the former administrator had custody or control immediately before cessation, and

(b) payable in priority to any charge arising under sub-paragraph (3).

99(5) Sub-paragraph (4) shall apply to a liability arising under a contract of employment which was adopted by the former administrator or a predecessor before cessation; and for that purpose–

(a) action taken within the period of 14 days after an administrator's appointment shall not be taken to amount or contribute to the adoption of a contract,

(b) no account shall be taken of a liability which arises, or in so far as it arises, by reference to anything which is done or which occurs before the adoption of the contract of employment, and

(c) no account shall be taken of a liability to make a payment other than wages or salary.

99(6) In sub-paragraph (5)(c) "wages or salary" includes–

(a) a sum payable in respect of a period of holiday (for which purpose the sum shall be treated as relating to the period by reference to which the entitlement to holiday accrued),

(b) a sum payable in respect of a period of absence through illness or other good cause,

(c) a sum payable in lieu of holiday,

(d) in respect of a period, a sum which would be treated as earnings for that period for the purposes of an enactment about social security, and

(e) a contribution to an occupational pension scheme.

GENERAL NOTE

This provision corresponds to s. 19(4)–(10), including the reforms made by IA 1994 in consequence of the ruling of the Court of Appeal in *Powdrill v Watson; Re Paramount Airways Ltd (No. 3)* [1994] 2 All E.R. 513; [1994] B.C.C. 172. Although the drafting follows a different style, it does not appear that any change is intended to be made in the law as established by s. 19(4)–(10), and so the comment to those provisions will be applicable here also. Note that although the paragraph is expressed to apply only where a person ceases to be the administrator, it is well recognised that many of the payments referred to will, in the ordinary case, be paid in the course of the administration: see the note to s. 19(3)–(6).

On the effect in this context of the ruling of the House of Lords in *Re Leyland Daf Ltd, Buchler v Talbot* [2004] UKHL 9, see the note to para. 65.

GENERAL

Joint and concurrent administrators

100(1) In this Schedule–

(a) a reference to the appointment of an administrator of a company includes a reference to the appointment of a number of persons to act jointly or concurrently as the administrator of a company, and

(b) a reference to the appointment of a person as administrator of a company includes a reference to the appointment of a person as one of a number of persons to act jointly or concurrently as the administrator of a company.

100(2) The appointment of a number of persons to act as administrator of a company must specify–

(a) which functions (if any) are to be exercised by the persons appointed acting jointly, and

(b) which functions (if any) are to be exercised by any or all of the persons appointed.

GENERAL NOTE

It is well established that expressions in the singular in legislation are to be read as including the plural (Interpretation Act 1978, s. 6), but this and the ensuing paragraphs go further, providing that where an appointment is made of more than one person as administrators, they may empowered to act either jointly or concurrently, identifying the functions which each may exercise. Note that the Act does not require the appointment, as such, to be of administrators empowered to act either jointly or concurrently in everything that they do – although these options are permitted. Rather, the appointment must name the persons as administrators and then specify which functions are to be exercised jointly and which may be exercised by any or all (or fewer than all, *e.g.* authorising cheques to be signed by any two): para. 100(2).

Rule 2.127 applies where a joint administrator is appointed.

101(1) This paragraph applies where two or more persons are appointed to act jointly as the administrator of a company.

101(2) A reference to the administrator of the company is a reference to those persons acting jointly.

101(3) But a reference to the administrator of a company in paragraphs 87 to 99 of this Schedule is a reference to any or all of the persons appointed to act jointly.

101(4) Where an offence of omission is committed by the administrator, each of the persons appointed to act jointly–

(a) commits the offence, and

(b) may be proceeded against and punished individually.

101(5) The reference in paragraph 45(1)(a) to the name of the administrator is a reference to the name of each of the persons appointed to act jointly.

101(6) Where persons are appointed to act jointly in respect of only some of the functions of the administrator of a company, this paragraph applies only in relation to those functions.

GENERAL NOTE

It would be an affront to the intelligence of the reader to add any comment to the astonishing verbosity of this paragraph.

102(1) This paragraph applies where two or more persons are appointed to act concurrently as the administrator of a company.

102(2) A reference to the administrator of a company in this Schedule is a reference to any of the persons appointed (or any combination of them).

GENERAL NOTE

For the position where administrators are appointed to act jointly, see para. 101.

103(1) Where a company is in administration, a person may be appointed to act as administrator jointly or concurrently with the person or persons acting as the administrator of the company.

103(2) Where a company entered administration by administration order, an appointment under sub-paragraph (1) must be made by the court on the application of–

(a) a person or group listed in paragraph 12(1)(a) to (e), or

(b) the person or persons acting as the administrator of the company.

103(3) Where a company entered administration by virtue of an appointment under paragraph 14, an appointment under sub-paragraph (1) must be made by–

(a) the holder of the floating charge by virtue of which the appointment was made, or

(b) the court on the application of the person or persons acting as the administrator of the company.

103(4) Where a company entered administration by virtue of an appointment under paragraph 22(1), an appointment under sub-paragraph (1) above must be made either by the court on the application of the person or persons acting as the administrator of the company or–

(a) by the company, and

(b) with the consent of each person who is the holder of a qualifying floating charge in respect of the company's property or, where consent is withheld, with the permission of the court.

103(5) Where a company entered administration by virtue of an appointment under paragraph 22(2), an appointment under sub-paragraph (1) must be made either by the court on the application of the person or persons acting as the administrator of the company or–

(a) by the directors of the company, and

(b) with the consent of each person who is the holder of a qualifying floating charge in respect of the company's property or, where consent is withheld, with the permission of the court.

103(6) An appointment under sub-paragraph (1) may be made only with the consent of the person or persons acting as the administrator of the company.

Schedule B1	*Insolvency Act 1986*

GENERAL NOTE

There may be situations in which it is thought advisable or necessary to appoint one or more additional administrators to act jointly or concurrently with the administrator(s) already in office: the task may call for more manpower than was originally envisaged, or a creditor who holds a "qualifying" floating charge may feel happier if his own appointee joins the person or persons already in office who have been appointed by somebody else. This paragraph spells out the procedure to be followed. The court has overall control but, subject to that, deference must be shown to floating chargeholders. Since the administrator currently in office may have an interest in what is proposed, he is given standing to apply to the court and also a veto on the proposed appointment.

Para.103(6)

This provision applies in each of the cases covered by para. 103(2)–(5). It ensures that anyone already in office is not to have wished on to him a newcomer that he does not feel happy to work with – even where the new appointment is made by the court.

Presumption of validity

104 An act of the administrator of a company is valid in spite of a defect in his appointment or qualification.

GENERAL NOTE

This is a standard provision, which under the original Pt II is catered for by s. 232: see the note to that section.

Majority decision of directors

105 A reference in this Schedule to something done by the directors of a company includes a reference to the same thing done by a majority of the directors of a company.

GENERAL NOTE

This is a novel and welcome provision: references in earlier legislation to an act done by the directors have been construed as requiring either that the directors should act unanimously or that a meeting be duly convened at which a decision is reached by the requisite majority: see the notes to ss. 9(1) and 124(1). Under the present provision a meeting is not required.

Penalties

106(1) A person who is guilty of an offence under this Schedule is liable to a fine (in accordance with section 430 and Schedule 10).

106(2) A person who is guilty of an offence under any of the following paragraphs of this Schedule is liable to a daily default fine (in accordance with section 430 and Schedule 10)–

- (a) paragraph 20,
- (b) paragraph 32,
- (c) paragraph 46,
- (d) paragraph 48,
- (e) paragraph 49,
- (f) paragraph 51,
- (g) paragraph 53,
- (h) paragraph 54,
- (i) paragraph 56,
- (j) paragraph 71,

(k)   paragraph 72,

(l)   paragraph 77,

(m) paragraph 78,

(n)   paragraph 80,

(o)   paragraph 84,

(p)   paragraph 86, and

(q)   paragraph 89.

GENERAL NOTE

For the amounts payable as fines for each of these offences, see Sch. 10 and comments.

Extension of time limit

107(1) Where a provision of this Schedule provides that a period may be varied in accordance with this paragraph, the period may be varied in respect of a company–

(a)   by the court, and

(b)   on the application of the administrator.

107(2) A time period may be extended in respect of a company under this paragraph–

(a)   more than once, and

(b)   after expiry.

GENERAL NOTE

The scope of this paragraph is limited by the words "varied in accordance with this paragraph". Those paragraphs which refer to para. 107 are paras 49, 50, 51, However, it is unlikely that this limitation would override the court's powers under more general provisions such as para. 55(2)(e).

Some of the statutory time periods may also be varied by the administrator with the creditors' consent under para. 108.

108(1) A period specified in paragraph 49(5), 50(1)(b) or 51(2) may be varied in respect of a company by the administrator with consent.

108(2) In sub-paragraph (1) **"consent"** means consent of–

(a)   each secured creditor of the company, and

(b)   if the company has unsecured debts, creditors whose debts amount to more than 50% of the company's unsecured debts, disregarding debts of any creditor who does not respond to an invitation to give or withhold consent.

108(3) But where the administrator has made a statement under paragraph 52(1)(b) "consent" means–

(a)   consent of each secured creditor of the company, or

(b)   if the administrator thinks that a distribution may be made to preferential creditors, consent of–

   (i) each secured creditor of the company, and
   (ii) preferential creditors whose debts amount to more than 50% of the total preferential debts of the company, disregarding debts of any creditor who does not respond to an invitation to give or withhold consent.

108(4) Consent for the purposes of sub-paragraph (1) may be–

(a)   written, or

(b)   signified at a creditors' meeting.

Schedule B1   *Insolvency Act 1986*

108(5) The power to extend under sub-paragraph (1)–

(a) may be exercised in respect of a period only once,

(b) may not be used to extend a period by more than 28 days,

(c) may not be used to extend a period which has been extended by the court, and

(d) may not be used to extend a period after expiry.

GENERAL NOTE

The time-limits prescribed by the three paragraphs referred to may be varied by the administrator without a court order if the consent of the secured and unsecured creditors is obtained in accordance with this provision. Note the limitations imposed by para. 108(5): in these cases there is no alternative but to apply to the court under para.107. Reference may be made also to the notes to paras 76–78, which are drafted in similar language.

Para. 108(4)
"Written" includes the use of electronic means: para. 111(2).

109 Where a period is extended under paragraph 107 or 108, a reference to the period shall be taken as a reference to the period as extended.

Amendment of provision about time

110(1) The Secretary of State may by order amend a provision of this Schedule which–

(a) requires anything to be done within a specified period of time,

(b) prevents anything from being done after a specified time, or

(c) requires a specified minimum period of notice to be given.

110(2) An order under this paragraph–

(a) must be made by statutory instrument, and

(b) shall be subject to annulment in pursuance of a resolution of either House of Parliament.

GENERAL NOTE

The power conferred by this paragraph will allow for adjustments to be made to time provisions specified for the new regime if they prove to be inconvenient in practice, or if it is decided as a matter of policy to set shorter time-limits in order to speed up the rescue process.

Interpretation

111(1) In this Schedule–

"**administrative receiver**" has the meaning given by section 251,

"**administrator**" has the meaning given by paragraph 1 and, where the context requires, includes a reference to a former administrator,

"**company**" includes a company which may enter administration by virtue of Article 3 of the EC Regulation,

"**correspondence**" includes correspondence by telephonic or other electronic means,

"**creditors' meeting**" has the meaning given by paragraph 50,

"**enters administration**" has the meaning given by paragraph 1,

"**floating charge**" means a charge which is a floating charge on its creation,

"**in administration**" has the meaning given by paragraph 1,

Insolvency Act 1986 *Schedule B1*

"**hire-purchase agreement**" includes a conditional sale agreement, a chattel leasing agreement and a retention of title agreement,

"**holder of a qualifying floating charge**" in respect of a company's property has the meaning given by paragraph 14,

"**market value**" means the amount which would be realised on a sale of property in the open market by a willing vendor,

"**the purpose of administration**" means an objective specified in paragraph 3, and

"**unable to pay its debts**" has the meaning given by section 123.

111(2) A reference in this Schedule to a thing in writing includes a reference to a thing in electronic form.

111(3) In this Schedule a reference to action includes a reference to inaction.

General Note

The definitions here set out apply only for the purposes of the present Schedule. This limitation may create some difficulties – for instance, the word "administrator" will have only one meaning for the purposes of the Schedule and another where the original s. 8 applies. By way of example, does the term "a former administrator" in the definition in para. 111(1) include an administrator who was appointed under s. 8?

Other definitions may be found in ss. 247ff and 435ff.

Para. 111(1)
"Company": see the notes to the original s.8 (1), (2), (7) and to the EC Regulation, art. 3.
"Correspondence": this definition is clearly intended to include communications by email, etc. in written form, but clearer language would surely be needed if it were meant to extend to oral conversations by telephone.
"Floating charge": compare the definition in IA 1986, s. 251. It is not obvious why different wording has been used.

Scotland

112 In the application of this Schedule to Scotland–

(a) a reference to filing with the court is a reference to lodging in court, and

(b) a reference to a charge is a reference to a right in security.

(See General Note after para. 116)

113 Where property in Scotland is disposed of under paragraph 70 or 71, the administrator shall grant to the disponee an appropriate document of transfer or conveyance of the property, and–

(a) that document, or

(b) recording, intimation or registration of that document (where recording, intimation or registration of the document is a legal requirement for completion of title to the property),

has the effect of disencumbering the property of or, as the case may be, freeing the property from, the security.

(See General Note after para. 116)

114 In Scotland, where goods in the possession of a company under a hire-purchase agreement are disposed of under paragraph 72, the disposal has the effect of extinguishing as against the disponee all rights of the owner of the goods under the agreement.

(See General Note after para. 116)

115(1) In Scotland, the administrator of a company may make, in or towards the satisfaction of the debt secured by the floating charge, a payment to the holder of a floating charge which has attached to the property subject to the charge.

115(2) In Scotland, where the administrator thinks that the company has insufficient property to enable a distribution to be made to unsecured creditors other than by virtue of section 176A(2)(a), he may file a notice to that effect with the registrar of companies.

Schedule 1   Insolvency Act 1986

115(3) On delivery of the notice to the registrar of companies, any floating charge granted by the company shall, unless it has already so attached, attach to the property which is subject to the charge and that attachment shall have effect as if each floating charge is a fixed security over the property to which it has attached.
(See General Note after para. 116)

116 In Scotland, the administrator in making any payment in accordance with paragraph 115 shall make such payment subject to the rights of any of the following categories of persons (which rights shall, except to the extent provided in any instrument, have the following order of priority)–

(a) the holder of any fixed security which is over property subject to the floating charge and which ranks prior to, or pari passu with, the floating charge,

(b) creditors in respect of all liabilities and expenses incurred by or on behalf of the administrator,

(c) the administrator in respect of his liabilities, expenses and remuneration and any indemnity to which he is entitled out of the property of the company,

(d) the preferential creditors entitled to payment in accordance with paragraph 65,

(e) the holder of the floating charge in accordance with the priority of that charge in relation to any other floating charge which has attached, and

(f) the holder of a fixed security, other than one referred to in paragraph (a), which is over property subject to the floating charge.

GENERAL NOTE TO PARAS 112–116

These paragraphs make minor modifications to the provisions of Sch. 16 in its application to Scotland. Some of these are purely terminological. Others reflect differences in conveyancing practice and property law, and the fact that the floating charge is based on statute rather than common law in Scots law.
Paragraphs 115–116 supplement para. 99.

SCHEDULE 1

POWERS OF ADMINISTRATOR OR ADMINISTRATIVE RECEIVER

Sections 14, 42

1 Power to take possession of, collect and get in the property of the company and, for that purpose, to take such proceedings as may seem to him expedient.

2 Power to sell or otherwise dispose of the property of the company by public auction or private auction or private contract or, in Scotland, to sell, feu, hire out or otherwise dispose of the property of the company by public roup or private bargain.

3 Power to raise or borrow money and grant security therefor over the property of the company.

4 Power to appoint a solicitor or accountant or other professionally qualified person to assist him in the performance of his functions.

5 Power to bring or defend any action or other legal proceedings in the name and on behalf of the company.

6 Power to refer to arbitration any question affecting the company.

7 Power to effect and maintain insurances in respect of the business and property of the company.

8 Power to use the company's seal.

9 Power to do all acts and to execute in the name and on behalf of the company any deed, receipt or other document.

10 Power to draw, accept, make and endorse any bill of exchange or promissory note in the name and on behalf of the company.

11 Power to appoint any agent to do any business which he is unable to do himself or which can more conveniently be done by an agent and power to employ and dismiss employees.

12 Power to do all such things (including the carrying out of works) as may be necessary for the realisation of the property of the company.

13 Power to make any payment which is necessary or incidental to the performance of his functions.

14 Power to carry on the business of the company.

15 Power to establish subsidiaries of the company.

16 Power to transfer to subsidiaries of the company the whole or any part of the business and property of the company.

17 Power to grant or accept a surrender of a lease or tenancy of any of the property of the company, and to take a lease or tenancy of any property required or convenient for the business of the company.

18 Power to make any arrangement or compromise on behalf of the company.

19 Power to call up any uncalled capital of the company.

20 Power to rank and claim in the bankruptcy, insolvency, sequestration or liquidation of any person indebted to the company and to receive dividends, and to accede to trust deeds for the creditors of any such person.

21 Power to present or defend a petition for the winding up of the company.

22 Power to change the situation of the company's registered office.

23 Power to do all other things incidental to the exercise of the foregoing powers.

GENERAL NOTE

This Schedule applies to all administrators, whether appointed under the original Pt II or under Sch. B1, and to administrative receivers.

Under CA 1985, the powers of a receiver (or receiver and manager) appointed out of court were left to be settled almost entirely by the provisions of the instrument under which he was appointed and the terms of the appointment itself. The Cork Committee (*Report*, para. 494) recommended that the general powers of a receiver should be set out in a statute, so that it would not be necessary for a person dealing with him to refer to the particular debenture to find out what powers he could exercise in the circumstances. (This was, in fact, already the case in Scotland under Companies (Floating Charges and Receivers) (Scotland) Act 1972, s. 15.) The present Schedule and IA 1986, s. 42, implement those recommendations, which apply in every *administrative* receivership, and – no doubt reflecting the fact that the administration order regime set up by s. 8ff. was modelled on the institution of receivership – the Schedule is made by s. 14 and Sch B1, para. 60 to apply to an administrator as well. An administrator has, in adition, the general statutory powers set out in s. 14(1)(a) and para. 59, and the specific powers given by s. 14(2) and 15 and paras 70–72.

On the power of an administrator to sell the business or its property prior to the holding of a creditors' meeting, see the notes to s. 17(2) and para. 68.

The powers of an administrative receiver listed in this Schedule may be overridden by the terms of the debenture under which he is appointed, but a person dealing with him in good faith and for value is not concerned to inquire whether he is acting within his powers (s. 42(3)). The Act, by s. 43, also confers special powers on an administrative receiver to dispose of charged property, etc.

A receiver who is not an administrative receiver is not affected by the provisions described above, and Sch. 1 does not apply in such a case.

The Schedule applies in Scotland in the case of an administrator, but not an administrative receiver; all Scottish receivers, however, have the powers set out in s. 55 and Sch. 2.

Schedule 2   Insolvency Act 1986

The specific powers listed in Sch. 1 do not, on the whole, call for detailed comment, apart from para. 21 (power to present or defend a winding-up petition), which has clarified doubts regarding a receiver's ability to present such a petition at common law, and removes the limitations upon such powers as he may have had: compare *Re Emmadart Ltd* [1979] Ch. 540. A petition by an administrator or administrative receiver is presented in the name of the company: see the note to s. 124. The power of a receiver to present a winding-up petition was also the subject of comment in *Re Anvil Estates Ltd* (unreported, 1993) – discussed by Pugh and Ede in (1994) 10 I.L. & P. 48. The case was actually decided on the basis of the right of the secured creditor (as opposed to the receiver) to petition but there is some useful general discussion in the judgment. The power of an administrative receiver to oppose a winding-up petition presented by another creditor was considered in *Re Leigh Estates (UK) Ltd* [1994] B.C.C. 292.

Paragraph 13 is expressed in sufficiently wide terms as to permit a distribution of assets to be made on the same basis as would have applied if the company had been put into liquidation on the date of the administration order, so giving priority to those creditors whose debts would have been preferential on a winding up: *Re WBSL Realisations 1992 Ltd* [1995] B.C.L.C. 576, and also to authorise an administrator to pay all the company's pre-administration creditors in full: *Re John Slack Ltd* [1995] B.C.C. 1,116. (See further the note to IA 1986, s. 18(2).)

As noted below (see the note to Sch. 4, para. 6) the statutory authority given to a liquidator to sell any of the company's property enables him to assign a cause of action vested in the company without infringing the common-law rule which declares transactions involving maintenance or champerty to be illegal. A similar protection is given to a trustee in bankruptcy by Sch. 6, para. 9, and to an administrator by s. 14 and para. 1 of this Schedule. However, the position as regards an administrative receiver may be different, for the power is derived from s. 42, which does not confer the power by virtue of the statute itself but instead by deeming it to have been included in the charge instrument under which the receiver has been appointed. As a mere term in a contract it would not be sufficient to displace the common-law rule.

Where an administration order is in force in relation to an insurance company, the powers of the administrator include the power to make certain payments to a creditor in advance of the holding of a meeting under IA 1986, s. 23: see the Financial Services and Markets Act 2000 (Administration Orders Relating to Insurers) Order 2002 (SI 2002/1242), Sch., para. 6.

SCHEDULE 2

POWERS OF A SCOTTISH RECEIVER (ADDITIONAL TO THOSE CONFERRED ON HIM BY THE INSTRUMENT OF CHARGE)

Section 55

1 Power to take possession of, collect and get in the property from the company or a liquidator thereof or any other person, and for that purpose, to take such proceedings as may seem to him expedient.

2 Power to sell, feu, hire out or otherwise dispose of the property by public roup or private bargain and with or without advertisement.

3 Power to raise or borrow money and grant security therefor over the property.

4 Power to appoint a solicitor or accountant or other professionally qualified person to assist him in the performance of his functions.

5 Power to bring or defend any action or other legal proceedings in the name and on behalf of the company.

6 Power to refer to arbitration all questions affecting the company.

7 Power to effect and maintain insurances in respect of the business and property of the company.

8 Power to use the company's seal.

9 Power to do all acts and to execute in the name and on behalf of the company any deed, receipt or other document.

10 Power to draw, accept, make and endorse any bill of exchange or promissory note in the name and on behalf of the company.

11 Power to appoint any agent to do any business which he is unable to do himself or which can more conveniently be done by an agent, and power to employ and dismiss employees.

12 Power to do all such things (including the carrying out of works), as may be necessary for the realisation of the property.

13 Power to make any payment which is necessary or incidental to the performance of his functions.

14 Power to carry on the business of the company or any part of it.

15 Power to grant or accept a surrender of a lease or tenancy of any of the property, and to take a lease or tenancy of any property required or covenient for the business of the company.

16 Power to make any arrangement or compromise on behalf of the company.

17 Power to call up any uncalled capital of the company.

18 Power to establish subsidiaries of the company.

19 Power to transfer to subsidiaries of the company the business of the company or any part of it and any of the property.

20 Power to rank and claim in the bankruptcy, insolvency, sequestrian or liquidation of any person or company indebted to the company and to receive dividends, and to accede to trust deeds for creditors of any such person.

21 Power to present or defend a petition for the winding up of the company.

22 Power to change the situation of the company's registered office.

23 Power to do all other things incidental to the exercise of the powers mentioned in section 55(1) of this Act or above in this Schedule.

GENERAL NOTE

This Schedule provides a model list of powers for a Scottish receiver appointed by a holder of a floating charge. The list, although modified, dates back to the introduction of receivership in Scotland in 1972. The 23 implied powers mirror those of an English administrative receiver set out in Sch. 1, with only slight changes in the order. For further comment, see s. 55.

SCHEDULE 2A

EXCEPTIONS TO PROHIBITION ON APPOINTMENT OF ADMINISTRATIVE RECEIVER: SUPPLEMENTARY PROVISIONS

1 Capital market arrangement

1(1) For the purposes of section 72B an arrangement is a capital market arrangement if–

    (a) it involves a grant of security to a person holding it as trustee for a person who holds a capital market investment issued by a party to the arrangement, or

    (aa) it involves a grant of security to–

        (i) a party to the arrangement who issues a capital market investment, or

        (ii) a person who holds the security as trustee for a party to the arrangement in connection with the issue of a capital market investment, or

Schedule 2A   *Insolvency Act 1986*

(ab)   it involves a grant of security to a person who holds the security as trustee for a party to the arrangement who agrees to provide finance to another party, or

(b)   at least one party guarantees the performance of obligations of another party, or

(c)   at least one party provides security in respect of the performance of obligations of another party, or

(d)   the arrangement involves an investment of a kind described in articles 83 to 85 of the Financial Services and Markets Act 2000 (Regulated Activities) Order 2001 (SI 2001/544) (options, futures and contracts for differences).

1(2)   For the purposes of sub-paragraph (1)–

(a)   a reference to holding as trustee includes a reference to holding as nominee or agent,

(b)   a reference to holding for a person who holds a capital market investment includes a reference to holding for a number of persons at least one of whom holds a capital market investment, and

(c)   a person holds a capital market investment if he has a legal or beneficial interest in it, and

(d)   the reference to the provision of finance includes the provision of an indemnity.

1(3)   In section 72B(1) and this paragraph "party" to an arrangement includes a party to an agreement which–

(a)   forms part of the arrangement,

(b)   provides for the raising of finance as part of the arrangement, or

(c)   is necessary for the purposes of implementing the arrangement.

2   **Capital market investment**

2(1)   For the purposes of section 72B an investment is a capital market investment if it–

(a)   is within article 77 of the Financial Services and Markets Act 2000 (Regulated Activities) Order 2001 (SI 2001/544) (debt instruments), and

(b)   is rated, listed or traded or designed to be rated, listed or traded.

2(2)   In sub-paragraph (1)–

"**rated**" means rated for the purposes of investment by an internationally recognised rating agency,

"**listed**" means admitted to the official list within the meaning given by section 103(1) of the Financial Services and Markets Act 2000 (c. 8) (interpretation), and

"**traded**" means admitted to trading on a market established under the rule of a recognised investment exchange or on a foreign market.

2(3)   In sub-paragraph (2)–

"**recognised investment exchange**" has the meaning given by section 285 of the Financial Services and Markets Act 2000 (recognised investment exchange), and

"**foreign market**" has the same meaning as "relevant market" in article 67(2) of the Financial Services and Markets Act 2000 (Financial Promotion) Order 2001 (SI 2001/1335) (foreign markets).

3(1) An investment is also a capital market investment for the purposes of section 72B if it consists of a bond or commercial paper issued to one or more of the following–

    (a)   an investment professional within the meaning of article 19(5) of the Financial Services and Markets Act 2000 (Financial Promotion) Order 2001,

    (b)   a person who is, when the agreement mentioned in section 72B(1) is entered into, a certified high net worth individual in relation to a communication within the meaning of article 48(2) of that order,

    (c)   a person to whom article 49(2) of that order applies (high net worth company, &c.),

    (d)   a person who is, when the agreement mentioned in section 72B(1) is entered into, a certified sophisticated investor in relation to a communication within the meaning of article 50(1) of that order, and

    (e)   a person in a State other than the United Kingdom who under the law of that State is not prohibited from investing in bonds or commercial paper.

3(2) In sub-paragraph (1)–

    "bond" shall be construed in accordance with article 77 of the Financial Services and Markets Act 2000 (Regulated Activities) Order 2001 (SI 2001/544), and

    "commercial paper" has the meaning given by article 9(3) of that order.

3(3) For the purposes of sub-paragraph (1)–

    (a)   in applying article 19(5) of the Financial Promotion Order for the purposes of sub-paragraph (1)(a)–

        (i)   in article 19(5)(b), ignore the words after "exempt person",

        (ii)   in article 19(5)(c)(i), for the words from "the controlled activity" to the end substitute "a controlled activity", and

        (iii)   in article 19(5)(e) ignore the words from "where the communication" to the end, and

    (b)   in applying article 49(2) of that order for the purposes of sub-paragraph (1)(c), ignore article 49(2)(e).

4 "Agreement"

4 For the purposes of sections 72B and 72E and this Schedule **"agreement"** includes an agreement or undertaking effected by–

    (a)   contract,

    (b)   deed, or

    (c)   any other instrument intended to have effect in accordance with the law of England and Wales, Scotland or another jurisdiction.

5 Debt

5 The debt of at least £50 million referred to in section 72B(1)(a) or 72E(2)(a)–

    (a)   may be incurred at any time during the life of the capital market arrangement or financed project, and

    (b)   may be expressed wholly or partly in foreign currency (in which case the sterling equivalent shall be calculated as at the time when the arrangement is entered into or the project begins).

6 Step-in rights

6(1) For the purposes of sections 72C to 72E a project has "step-in rights" if a person who provides finance in connection with the project has a conditional entitlement under an agreement to–

(a) assume sole or principal responsibility under an agreement for carrying out all or part of the project, or

(b) make arrangements for carrying out all or part of the project.

6(2) In sub-paragraph (1) a reference to the provision of finance includes a reference to the provision of an indemnity.

7 Project company

7(1) For the purposes of sections 72C to 72E a company is a "project company" of a project if–

(a) it holds property for the purpose of the project,

(b) it has sole or principal responsibility under an agreement for carrying out all or part of the project,

(c) it is one of a number of companies which together carry out the project,

(d) it has the purpose of supplying finance to enable the project to be carried out, or

(e) it is the holding company of a company within any of paragraphs (a) to (d).

7(2) But a company is not a "project company" of a project if–

(a) it performs a function within sub-paragraph (1)(a) to (d) or is within sub-paragraph (1)(e), but

(b) it also performs a function which is not–
   (i) within sub-paragraph (1)(a) to (d),
   (ii) related to a function within sub-paragraph (1)(a) to (d), or
   (iii) related to the project.

7(3) For the purposes of this paragraph a company carries out all or part of a project whether or not it acts wholly or partly through agents.

8 "Resources"

8 In section 72C **"resources"** includes–

(a) funds (including payment for the provision of services or facilities),

(b) assets,

(c) professional skill,

(d) the grant of a concession or franchise, and

(e) any other commercial resource.

9 "Public body"

9(1) In section 72C **"public body"** means–

(a) a body which exercises public functions,

(b) a body specified for the purposes of this paragraph by the Secretary of State, and

(c) a body within a class specified for the purposes of this paragraph by the Secretary of State.

9(2) A specification under sub-paragraph (1) may be–

(a) general, or

(b) for the purpose of the application of section 72C to a specified case.

10 Regulated business

10(1) For the purposes of section 72D a business is regulated if it is carried on–

(a) [repealed]

(b) in reliance on a licence under sesction 7 or 7A of the Gas Act 1986 (c. 44) (transport and supply of gas),

(c) in reliance on a licence granted by virtue of section 41C of that Act (power to prescribe additional licensable activity),

(d) in reliance on a licence under section 6 of the Electricity Act 1989 (c. 29) (supply of electricity),

(e) by a water undertaker,

(f) by a sewerage undertaker,

(g) by a universal service provider within the meaning given by section 4(3) and (4) of the Postal Services Act 2000 (c. 26),

(h) by the Post Office company within the meaning given by section 62 of that Act (transfer of property),

(i) by a relevant subsidiary of the Post Office Company within the meaning given by section 63 of that Act (government holding),

(j) in reliance on a licence under section 8 of the Railways Act 1993 (c. 43) (railway services),

(k) in reliance on a licence exemption under section 7 of that Act (subject to sub-paragraph (2) below),

(l) by the operator of a system of transport which is deemed to be a railway for a purpose of Part I of that Act by virtue of section 81(2) of that Act (tramways, &c.), or

(m) by the operator of a vehicle carried on flanged wheels along a system within paragraph (l).

10(2) Sub-paragraph (1)(k) does not apply to the operator of a railway asset on a railway unless on some part of the railway there is a permitted line speed exceeding 40 kilometres per hour.

10(2A) For the purposes of section 72D a business is also regulated to the extent that it consists in the provision of a public electronic communications network or a public electronic communications service.

11 "Person"

11 A reference to a person in this Schedule includes a reference to a partnership or another unincorporated group of persons.

GENERAL NOTE

This was inserted by EA 2002, s. 250(2) and Sch. 8 to further supplement the provisions in ss. 72A–H with particular reference to those exceptional situations where the appointment of an administrative receiver is still possible notwithstanding the general bar on that remedy. Before the provisions of Sch. 2A came into force they were then modified by the Insolvency Act 1986 (Amendment) (Administrative Receivership and Capital Market Arrangements) Order 2003 (SI 2003/1468) by the addition of paras 1(1)(aa), 1(1)(ab) and 1(2)(d). Essentially, Sch. 2A serves as a complex interpretation provision. These provisions took effect on September 15, 2003. Curiously para. 10(1)(a) was omitted and 10(2A) inserted by the Communications Act 2003 with effect from July 25, 2003.

SCHEDULE 3

ORDERS IN COURSE OF WINDING UP PRONOUNCED IN VACATION (SCOTLAND)

Section 162

PART I

ORDERS WHICH ARE TO BE FINAL

Orders under section 153, as to the time for proving debts and claims.

Orders under section 195 as to meetings for ascertaining wishes of creditors or contributories.

Orders under section 198, as to the examination of witnesses in regard to the property or affairs of a company.

PART II

ORDERS WHICH ARE TO TAKE EFFECT UNTIL MATTER DISPOSED OF BY INNER HOUSE

Orders under section 126(1), 130(2) or (3), 147, 227 or 228, restraining or permitting the commencement or the continuance of legal proceedings.

Orders under section 135(5), limiting the powers of provisional liquidators.

Orders under section 108, appointing a liquidator to fill a vacancy.

Orders under section 167 or 169, sanctioning the exercise of any powers by a liquidator, other than the powers specified in paragraphs 1, 2 and 3 of Schedule 4 to this Act.

Orders under section 158, as to the arrest and detention of an absconding contributory and his property.

SCHEDULE 4

POWERS OF LIQUIDATOR IN A WINDING UP

Sections 165, 167

PART I

POWERS EXERCISABLE WITH SANCTION

1 Power to pay any class of creditors in full.

2 Power to make any compromise or arrangement with creditors or persons claiming to be creditors, or having or alleging themselves to have any claim (present or future, certain or contingent, ascertained or sounding only in damages) against the company, or whereby the company may be rendered liable.

3 Power to compromise, on such terms as may be agreed–

(a) all calls and liabilities to calls, all debts and liabilities capable of resulting in debts, and all claims (present or future, certain or contingent, ascertained or sounding only in damages) subsisting or supposed to subsist between the company and a contributory or alleged contributory or other debtor or person apprehending liability to the company, and

(b) all questions in any way relating to or affecting the assets or the winding up of the company,

and take any security for the discharge of any such call, debt, liability or claim and give a complete discharge in respect of it.

3A Power to bring legal proceedings under section 213, 214, 238, 239, 242, 243 or 423.

PART II

POWERS EXERCISABLE WITHOUT SANCTION IN VOLUNTARY WINDING UP, WITH SANCTION IN WINDING UP BY THE COURT

4 Power to bring or defend any action or other legal proceeding in the name and on behalf of the company.

5 Power to carry on the business of the company so far as may be necessary for its beneficial winding up.

PART III

POWERS EXERCISABLE WITHOUT SANCTION IN ANY WINDING UP

6 Power to sell any of the company's property by public auction or private contract, with power to transfer the whole of it to any person or to sell the same in parcels.

Schedule 4 *Insolvency Act 1986*

7 Power to do all acts and execute, in the name and on behalf of the company, all deeds, receipts and other documents and for that purpose to use, when necessary, the company's seal.

8 Power to prove, rank and claim in the bankruptcy, insolvency or sequestration of any contributory for any balance against his estate, and to receive dividends in the bankruptcy, insolvency or sequestration in respect of that balance, as a separate debt due from the bankrupt or insolvent, and rateably with the other separate creditors.

9 Power to draw, accept, make and indorse any bill of exchange or promissory note in the name and on behalf of the company, with the same effect with respect to the company's liability as if the bill or note had been drawn, accepted, made or indorsed by or on behalf of the company in the course of its business.

10 Power to raise on the security of the assets of the company any money requisite.

11 Power to take out in his official name letters of administration to any deceased contributory, and to do in his official name any other act necessary for obtaining payment of any money due from a contributory or his estate which cannot conveniently be done in the name of the company.

In all such cases the money due is deemed, for the purpose of enabling the liquidator to take out the letters of administration or recover the money, to be due to the liquidator himself.

12 Power to appoint an agent to do any business which the liquidator is unable to do himself.

13 Power to do all such other things as may be necessary for winding up the company's affairs and distributing its assets.

General Note

The powers of a liquidator in a winding up by the court were formerly set out in CA 1985, s. 539(1), (2), and those in a voluntary winding up in CA 1985, s. 598(1), (2). Many of these powers are now conveniently collected together and arranged in tabulated form in this Schedule, which applies both in England and Wales and in Scotland.

A liquidator in a winding up by the court has also the supplementary powers listed in s. 168 (England and Wales) and s. 169 (Scotland); and further powers are given to a voluntary liquidator by ss. 165, 166.

Schedule 4 does not apply in the case of a provisional liquidator. However, the court has jurisdiction under s. 135(4) to confer powers on a provisional liquidator which may include powers corresponding to those set out in Sch. 4: *Re Hawk Insurance Co. Ltd* [2001] B.C.C. 57.

Para. 1
The Insolvency Service takes the view that the court's sanction is not required before paying the preferential creditors in full, since the liquidator has a *duty* to do so under IA 1986, s. 175: see *Dear IP*, Chap. 17(2).

Para. 2, 3
It was held in *Taylor, Noter* [1992] B.C.C. 440 that the corresponding provisions of CA 1948 empowered the liquidator of a company, with the necessary sanction, to enter into any compromise or arrangement that might have been entered into by the company itself. In that case the affairs of a number of companies controlled by the same person had been treated as one, and the liquidator had found it impossible to determine which creditors had claims against the particular companies and which had claims against the individual controller, who was now bankrupt. A scheme was agreed for a single scheme of ranking and division of all the assets and creditors. This case was followed by the Court of Appeal in England in somewhat similar circumstances in *Re Bank of Credit & Commerce International SA (No. 2)* [1992] B.C.C. 715. The compromise powers include power to depart from the general rule that creditors are entitled to participate in the estate on a *pari passu* basis (above).

Para. 3A
This paragraph was inserted by EA 2002, s. 253, with effect from September 15, 2003. It is part of the package of reforms designed to reverse the effect of decisions such as *Re Floor Fourteen Ltd, Lewis v IRC* [2001] 3 All E.R. 499; [2002] B.C.C. 198, which held that a liquidator pursuing claims under the sections referred to could not claim his costs as expenses of the liquidation. This has now been rectified by an amendment to IR 1986, r. 4.218 but, in order to ensure

that liquidators do not make such claims at the expense of the creditors without their approval (or, alternatively, the leave of the court). See further the notes to s. 115 and r. 4.218.

Para. 6
The liquidator's power to sell "any of the company's property" enables him to assign any causes of action which were vested in the company at the time of the winding up, including the right to bring misfeasance proceedings under IA 1986, s. 212. The rule of law which would normally prohibit such an assignment – at least an assignment to a third party who had no interest otherwise in the litigation – on the ground that it would be champertous and illegal is displaced by this statutory authority: *Re Park Gate Waggon Works Co.* (1881) 17 Ch.D. 234. Such a sale may be made for any consideration, including a share of any proceeds of the action if it is successful. The fact that the company (or the liquidator) is not eligible for legal aid but the assignee may be entitled to it is not a ground for the court to declare the assignment unlawful, but a matter for consideration by the Legal Aid Board (*Norglen Ltd (in liq.) v Reeds Rains Prudential Ltd* [1999] 2 A.C. 1; [1998] B.C.C. 44). This provision does not, however, empower the liquidator to assign a right of action which arises only in the event of a liquidation and is vested in him by statute, *e.g.* the right to bring proceedings to recover a preference (IA 1986, s. 239) or compensation for fraudulent or wrongful trading (s. 213, 214) or to set aside a transaction at an undervalue (s. 238) or have a disposition of the company's property after the commencement of the winding up declared void under s. 127, or a floating charge declared void under s. 245. (See *Re Oasis Merchandising Services Ltd* [1998] Ch. 170; [1997] B.C.C. 282; *Re Ayala Holdings Ltd (No. 2)* [1996] 1 B.C.L.C. 467). However, if the assignee has a genuine interest in the outcome of the litigation (*e.g.* as a creditor of the company), an assignment of the "fruits" of such litigation may not be unlawful at common law, at least if the liquidator is left free to conduct the litigation without interference by the assignee; and there is certainly no objection to such a creditor simply putting the liquidator in funds to conduct the litigation on terms that any proceeds shall go in the first instance towards reimbursing him (*Katz v McNally* [1997] B.C.C. 784). See also *Empire Resolution Ltd v MPW Insurance Brokers Ltd* [1999] B.P.I.R. 486, *Farmer v Moseley (Holdings) Ltd* [2001] 2 B.C.L.C. 572 and the analysis of the present state of the law put forward by counsel and approved by the Court of Appeal (as "a valuable aid to clarification of the position") in *ANC Ltd v Clark Goldring & Page Ltd* [2001] B.C.C. 479. The ruling of Lightman J. in *Grovewood Holdings plc v James Capel & Co. Ltd* [1995] Ch. 80; [1995] B.C.C. 760, that a sale for a consideration which included a provision for the purchaser to finance the litigation was champertous has been much criticised and is probably open to reconsideration: see the *Oasis* judgment [1998] Ch. 170 at p. 179; [1997] B.C.C. 282 at p. 288, and *Farmer v Moseley (Holdings) Ltd* [2002] B.P.I.R. 473.

A prohibition on assignment by a company of a claim arising out of a contract is binding on its liquidator: *Quadmost Ltd v Reprotech (Pebsham) Ltd* [2001] B.P.I.R. 349. The fact that the intended defendant has a cross-claim for a larger amount, which can be set off in the liquidation under IR 1986, r. 4.90, is also effectively a bar to the assignment of a cause of action by a liquidator: *Craig v Humberclyde Industrial Finance Group Ltd* [1999] B.C.C. 378.

SCHEDULE 4A

BANKRUPTCY RESTRICTIONS ORDER AND UNDERTAKING

1 Bankruptcy restrictions order

1(1) A bankruptcy restrictions order may be made by the court.

1(2) An order may be made only on the application of–

(a) the Secretary of State, or

(b) the official receiver acting on a direction of the Secretary of State.

2 Grounds for making order

2(1) The court shall grant an application for a bankruptcy restrictions order if it thinks it appropriate having regard to the conduct of the bankrupt (whether before or after the making of the bankruptcy order).

2(2) The court shall, in particular, take into account any of the following kinds of behaviour on the part of the bankrupt–

- (a) failing to keep records which account for a loss of property by the bankrupt, or by a business carried on by him, where the loss occurred in the period beginning 2 years before petition and ending with the date of the application;

- (b) failing to produce records of that kind on demand by the official receiver or the trustee;

- (c) entering into a transaction at an undervalue;

- (d) giving a preference;

- (e) making an excessive pension contribution;

- (f) a failure to supply goods or services which were wholly or partly paid for which gave rise to a claim provable in the bankruptcy;

- (g) trading at a time before commencement of the bankruptcy when the bankrupt knew or ought to have known that he was himself to be unable to pay his debts;

- (h) incurring, before commencement of the bankruptcy, a debt which the bankrupt had no reasonable expectation of being able to pay;

- (i) failing to account satisfactorily to the court, the official receiver or the trustee for a loss of property or for an insufficiency of property to meet bankruptcy debts;

- (j) carrying on any gambling, rash and hazardous speculation or unreasonable extravagance which may have materially contributed to or increased the extent of the bankruptcy or which took place between presentation of the petition and commencement of the bankruptcy;

- (k) neglect of business affairs of a kind which may have materially contributed to or increased the extent of the bankruptcy;

- (l) fraud or fraudulent breach of trust;

- (m) failing to co-operate with the official receiver or the trustee.

2(3) The court shall also, in particular, consider whether the bankrupt was an undischarged bankrupt at some time during the period of six years ending with the date of the bankruptcy to which the application relates.

2(4) For the purpose of sub-paragraph (2)–

"**before petition**" shall be construed in accordance with section 351(c),

"**excessive pension contribution**" shall be construed in accordance with section 342A,

"**preference**" shall be construed in accordance with section 340, and

"**undervalue**" shall be construed in accordance with section 339.

3 Timing of application for order

3(1) An application for a bankruptcy restrictions order in respect of a bankrupt must be made–

- (a) before the end of the period of one year beginning with the date on which the bankruptcy commences, or

- (b) with the permission of the court.

3(2) The period specified in sub-paragraph (1)(a) shall cease to run in respect of a bankrupt while the period set for his discharge is suspended under section 279(3).

4 Duration of order

4(1) A bankruptcy restrictions order–

(a) shall come into force when it is made, and

(b) shall cease to have effect at the end of a date specified in the order.

4(2) The date specified in a bankruptcy restrictions order under sub-paragraph (1)(b) must not be–

(a) before the end of the period of two years beginning with the date on which the order is made, or

(b) after the end of the period of 15 years beginning with that date.

5 Interim bankruptcy restrictions order

5(1) This paragraph applies at any time between–

(a) the institution of an application for a bankruptcy restrictions order, and

(b) the determination of the application.

5(2) The court may make an interim bankruptcy restrictions order if the court thinks that–

(a) there are prima facie grounds to suggest that the application for the bankruptcy restrictions order will be successful, and

(b) it is in the public interest to make an interim order.

5(3) An interim order may be made only on the application of–

(a) the Secretary of State, or

(b) the official receiver acting on a direction of the Secretary of State.

5(4) An interim order–

(a) shall have the same effect as a bankruptcy restrictions order, and

(b) shall come into force when it is made.

5(5) An interim order shall cease to have effect–

(a) on the determination of the application for the bankruptcy restrictions order,

(b) on the acceptance of a bankruptcy restrictions undertaking made by the bankrupt, or

(c) if the court discharges the interim order on the application of the perso who applied for it or of the bankrupt.

6(1) This paragraph applies to a case in which both an interim bankruptcy restrictions order and a bankruptcy restrictions order are made.

6(2) Paragraph 4(2) shall have effect in relation to the bankruptcy restrictions order as if a reference to the date of that order were a reference to the date of the interim order.

7 Bankruptcy restrictions undertaking

7(1) A bankrupt may offer a bankruptcy restrictions undertaking to the Secretary of State.

7(2) In determining whether to accept a bankruptcy restrictions undertaking the Secretary of State shall have regard to the matters specified in paragraph 2(2) and (3).

8 A reference in an enactment to a person in respect of whom a bankruptcy restrictions order has effect (or who is "the subject of" a bankruptcy restrictions order) includes a reference to a person in respect of whom a bankruptcy restrictions undertaking has effect.

9(1) A bankruptcy restrictions undertaking–

(a) shall come into force on being accepted by the Secretary of State, and

(b) shall cease to have effect at the end of a date specified in the undertaking.

9(2) The date specified under sub-paragraph (1)(b) must not be–

(a) before the end of the period of two years beginning with the date on which the undertaking is accepted, or

(b) after the end of the period of 15 years beginning with that date.

9(3) On an application by the bankrupt the court may–

(a) annul a bankruptcy restrictions undertaking;

(b) provide for a bankruptcy restrictions undertaking to cease to have effect before the date specified under sub-paragraph (1)(b).

10 Effect of annulment of bankruptcy order

10 Where a bankruptcy order is annulled under section 282(1)(a) or (2)–

(a) any bankruptcy restrictions order, interim order or undertaking which is in force in respect of the bankrupt shall be annulled,

(b) no new bankruptcy restrictions order or interim order may be made in respect of the bankrupt, and

(c) no new bankruptcy restrictions undertaking by the bankrupt may be accepted.

11 Where a bankruptcy order is annulled under section 261, 263D or 282(1)(b)–

(a) the annulment shall not affect any bankruptcy restrictions order, interim order or undertaking in respect of the bankrupt,

(b) the court may make a bankruptcy restrictions order in relation to the bankrupt on an application instituted before the annulment,

(c) the Secretary of State may accept a bankruptcy restrictions undertaking offered before the annulment, and

(d) an application for a bankruptcy restrictions order or interim order in respect of the bankrupt may not be instituted after the annulment.

12 Registration

12 The Secretary of State shall maintain a register of–

(a) bankruptcy restrictions orders,

(b) interim bankruptcy restrictions orders, and

(c) bankruptcy restrictions undertakings.

GENERAL NOTE

This was inserted by EA 2002, s. 257 and Sch. 20 to further supplement the rules on BROs and BRUs. See the notes to s. 281A above.

SCHEDULE 5

POWERS OF TRUSTEE IN BANKRUPTCY

Section 314

PART I

POWERS EXERCISABLE WITH SANCTION

1 Power to carry on any business of the bankrupt so far as may be necessary for winding it up beneficially and so far as the trustee is able to do so without contravening any requirement imposed by or under any enactment.

2 Power to bring, institute or defend any action or legal proceedings relating to the property comprised in the bankrupt's estate.

2A Power to bring legal proceedings under section 339, 340 or 423.

3 Power to accept as the consideration for the sale of any property comprised in the bankrupt's estate a sum of money payable at a future time subject to such stipulations as to security or otherwise as the creditors' committee or the court thinks fit.

4 Power to mortgage or pledge any part of the property comprised in the bankrupt's estate for the purpose of raising money for the payment of his debts.

5 Power, where any right, option or other power forms part of the bankrupt's estate, to make payments or incur liabilities with a view to obtaining, for the benefit of the creditors, any property which is the subject of the right, option or power.

6 Power to refer to arbitration, or compromise on such terms as may be agreed on, any debts, claims or liabilities subsisting or supposed to subsist between the bankrupt and any person who may have incurred any liability to the bankrupt.

7 Power to make such compromise or other arrangement as may be thought expedient with creditors, or persons claiming to be creditors, in respect of bankruptcy debts.

8 Power to make such compromise or other arrangement as may be thought expedient with respect to any claim arising out of or incidental to the bankrupt's estate made or capable of being made on the trustee by any person or by the trustee on any person.

Schedule 5 *Insolvency Act 1986*

PART II

GENERAL POWERS

9 Power to sell any part of the property for the time being comprised in the bankrupt's estate, including the goodwill and book debts of any business.

10 Power to give receipts for any money received by him, being receipts which effectually discharge the person paying the money from all responsibility in respect of its application.

11 Power to prove, rank, claim and draw a dividend in respect of such debts due to the bankrupt as are comprised in his estate.

12 Power to exercise in relation to any property comprised in the bankrupt's estate any powers the capacity to exercise which is vested in him under Parts VIII to XI of this Act.

13 Power to deal with any property comprised in the estate to which the bankrupt is beneficially entitled as tenant in tail in the same manner as the bankrupt might have dealt with it.

PART III

ANCILLARY POWERS

14 For the purposes of, or in connection with, the exercise of any of his powers under Parts VIII to XI of this Act, the trustee may, by his official name–

(a) hold property of every description,

(b) make contracts,

(c) sue and be sued,

(d) enter into engagements binding on himself and, in respect of the bankrupt's estate, on his successors in office,

(e) employ an agent,

(f) execute any power of attorney, deed or other instrument;

and he may do any other act which is necessary or expedient for the purposes of or in connection with the exercise of those powers.

GENERAL NOTE

This schedule, allied to s. 314, lists the powers of a trustee in bankruptcy. Like Sch. 2, it has been hived off from the mainstream of the legislation. The crucial distinguishing factor is the need to obtain the sanction of the committee of creditors (see s. 301) before the powers listed in Pt I can be exercised. Paragraph 2A was inserted by s. 262 of EA 2002 to ensure that recovery actions were properly sanctioned as the costs of such actions can now be treated as a winding-up expense, see IR 6.224.

For a recent decision on the effect of the power now contained in Sch. 5, para. 3, see *Weddell v Pearce (JA) & Major* [1988] Ch. 26. This case involved the assignment of a cause of action by the trustee for future consideration without obtaining the requisite sanction. It was held by Scott J. that notwithstanding this failure to obtain sanction, the assignment took effect in equity. This ruling is in line with the philosophy now expressed in ss. 314(3) and 377 of IA 1986. The power to assign was also reviewed by the Australian courts in *Re Cirillo* [1997] B.P.I.R. 166. On the power to employ a solicitor see *Re Schuppan* [1996] B.P.I.R. 486.

For further guidance on this Schedule see the note to s. 314.

Schedule 6

The Categories of Preferential Debts

Section 386

Category 1: Debts due to Inland Revenue

[Deleted]

Category 2: Debts due to Customs and Excise

[Deleted]

Category 3: Social Security Contributions

[Deleted]

Category 4: Contributions to Occupational Pension Schemes, etc.

8 Any sum which is owed by the debtor and is a sum to which Schedule 4 to the Pension Schemes Act 1993 applies (contributions to occupational pension schemes and state scheme premiums).

Category 5: Remuneration, etc., of Employees

9 So much of any amount which–
- (a) is owed by the debtor to a person who is or has been an employee of the debtor, and
- (b) is payable by way of remuneration in respect of the whole or any part of the period of 4 months next before the relevant date,

as does not exceed so much as may be prescribed by order made by the Secretary of State.

10 An amount owed by way of accrued holiday remuneration, in respect of any period of employment before the relevant date, to a person whose employment by the debtor has been terminated, whether before, on or after that date.

11 So much of any sum owed in respect of money advanced for the purpose as has been applied for the payment of a debt which, if it had not been paid, would have been a debt falling within paragraph 9 or 10.

12 So much of any amount which–
- (a) is ordered (whether before or after the relevant date) to be paid by the debtor under the Reserve Forces (Safeguard of Employment) Act 1985, and
- (b) is so ordered in respect of a default made by the debtor before that date in the discharge of his obligations under that Act,

as does not exceed such amount as may be prescribed by order made by the Secretary of State.

Interpretation for Category 5

13(1) For the purposes of paragraphs 9 to 12, a sum is payable by the debtor to a person by way of remuneration in respect of any period if–

(a) it is paid as wages or salary (whether payable for time or for piece work or earned wholly or partly by way of commission) in respect of services rendered to the debtor in that period, or

(b) it is an amount falling within the following sub-paragraph and is payable by the debtor in respect of that period.

13(2) An amount falls within this sub-paragraph if it is–

(a) a guarantee payment under Part III of the Employment Rights Act 1996 (employee without work to do);

(b) any payment for time off under section 53 (time off to look for work to arrange training) or section 56 (time off for ante-natal care) of that Act or under section 169 of the Trade Union and Labour Relations (Consolidation) Act 1992 (time off for carrying out trade union duties etc.);

(c) remuneration on suspension on medical grounds, or on maternity grounds, under Part VII of the Employment Rights Act 1996; or

(d) remuneration under a protective award under section 189 of the Trade Union and Labour Relations (Consolidation) Act 1992 (redundancy dismissal with compensation).

14(1) This paragraph relates to a case in which a person's employment has been terminated by or in consequence of his employer going into liquidation or being adjudged bankrupt or (his employer being a company not in liquidation) by or in consequence of–

(a) a receiver being appointed as mentioned in section 40 of this Act (debenture-holders secured by floating charge), or

(b) the appointment of a receiver under section 53(6) or 54(5) of this Act (Scottish company with property subject to floating charge), or

(c) the taking of possession by debenture-holders (so secured), as mentioned in section 196 of the Companies Act.

14(2) For the purposes of paragraphs 9 to 12, holiday remuneration is deemed to have accrued to that person in respect of any period of employment if, by virtue of his contract of employment or of any enactment, that remuneration would have accrued in respect of that period if his employment had continued until he became entitled to be allowed the holiday.

14(3) The reference in sub-paragraph (2) to any enactment includes an order or direction made under an enactment.

15 Without prejudice to paragraphs 13 and 14–

(a) any remuneration payable by the debtor to a person in respect of a period of holiday or of absence from work through sickness or other good cause is deemed to be wages or (as the case may be) salary in respect of services rendered to the debtor in that period, and

(b) references here and in those paragraphs to remuneration in respect of a period of holiday include any sums which, if they had been paid, would have been treated for the purposes of the enactments relating to social security as earnings in respect of that period.

Category 6: Levies on Coal and Steel Production

15A Any sums due at the relevant date from the debtor in respect of–

(a) the levies on the production of coal and steel referred to in Article 49 and 50 of the E.C.S.C. Treaty, or

(b) any surcharge for delay provided for in Article 50(3) of that Treaty and Article 6 of Decision 3/52 of the High Authority of the Coal and Steel Community.

Orders

16 An order under paragraph 9 or 12–

(a) may contain such transitional provisions as may appear to the Secretary of State necessary or expedient;

(b) shall be made by statutory instrument subject to annulment in pursuance of a resolution of either House of Parliament.

GENERAL NOTE

This Schedule, which is brought into play by s. 386, largely reflects the preferential claims regime as suggested by the Cork Committee (Cmnd 8558, para. 1450) and further pruned by EA 2002. Categories 1, 2 and 3 (Crown debts) were abolished by s. 251 of EA 2002 effective September 15, 2003. (For transitional provisions, see SI 2003/2093, art. 4.)

For the meaning of the phrase "the relevant date", see s. 387. For further comment, see the general note to Pt XII. The amount for para. 9 and 12 is fixed at £800: see the Insolvency Proceedings (Monetary Limits) Order 1986 (SI 1986/1996), art. 4.

Para. 8
A minor textual amendment was made here by the Pension Schemes Act 1993, Sch. 8, para. 18.

Para. 13
A new sub-para. (2) was added by para. 29 of Sch. 1 to the Employment Rights Act 1996 to facilitate the recent changes in employment legislation.

SCHEDULE 7

INSOLVENCY PRACTITIONERS TRIBUNAL

Section 396

Panels of Members

1(1) The Secretary of State shall draw up and from time to time revise–

(a) a panel of persons who

(i) have a 7 year general qualification, within the meaning of s. 71 of the Courts and Legal Services Act 1990;

(ii) are advocates or solicitors in Scotland of at least 7 years' standing, and are nominated for the purpose by the Lord Chancellor or the Lord President of the Court of Session, and

(b) a panel of persons who are experienced in insolvency matters;

and the members of the Tribunal shall be selected from those panels in accordance with this Schedule.

Schedule 7 *Insolvency Act 1986*

1(2) The power to revise the panels includes power to terminate a person's membership of either of them, and is accordingly to that extent subject to section 7 of the Tribunals and Inquiries Act 1992 (which makes it necessary to obtain the concurrence of the Lord Chancellor and the Lord President of the Court of Session to dismissals in certain cases).

Remuneration of Members

2 The Secretary of State may out of money provided by Parliament pay to members of the Tribunal such remuneration as he may with the approval of the Treasury determine; and such expenses of the Tribunal as the Secretary of State and the Treasury may approve shall be defrayed by the Secretary of State out of money so provided.

Sittings of Tribunal

3(1) For the purposes of carrying out their functions in relation to any cases referred to them, the Tribunal may sit either as a single tribunal or in two or more divisions.

3(2) The functions of the Tribunal in relation to any case referred to them shall be exercised by three members consisting of–

(a) a chairman selected by the Secretary of State from the panel drawn up under paragraph 1(1)(a) above, and

(b) two other members selected by the Secretary of State from the panel drawn up under paragraph 1(1)(b) .

Procedure of Tribunal

4(1) Any investigation by the Tribunal shall be so conducted as to afford a reasonable opportunity for representations to be made to the Tribunal by or on behalf of the person whose case is the subject of the investigation.

4(2) For the purposes of any such investigation, the Tribunal–

(a) may by summons require any person to attend, at such time and place as is specified in the summons, to give evidence or to produce any books, papers and other records in his possession or under his control which the Tribunal consider it necessary for the purposes of the investigation to examine, and

(b) may take evidence on oath, and for the purpose administer oaths, or may, instead of administering an oath, require the person examined to make and subscribe a declaration of the truth of the matter respecting which he is examined;

but no person shall be required, in obedience to such a summons, to go more than ten miles from his place of residence, unless the necessary expenses of his attendance are paid or tendered to him.

4(3) Every person who–

(a) without reasonable excuse fails to attend in obedience to a summons issued under this paragraph, or refuses to give evidence, or

(b) intentionally alters, suppresses, conceals or destroys or refuses to produce any document which he may be required to produce for the purpose of an investigation by the Tribunal,

is liable to a fine.

4(4) Subject to the provisions of this paragraph, the Secretary of State may make rules for regulating the procedure on any investigation by the Tribunal.

4(5) In their application to Scotland, sub-paragraphs (2) and (3) above have effect as if for any reference to a summons there where substituted a reference to a notice in writing.

GENERAL NOTE

The Insolvency Practitioners Tribunal, which was established under IA 1985, s. 8(6) and is confirmed by s. 396(1) of the present Act, is empowered to review the decisions of the Secretary of State (or other "competent authority") to refuse an application for authorisation or withdraw an authorisation to act as an insolvency practitioner: see the note to s. 396 and the Insolvency Practitioners Tribunal (Conduct of Investigations) Rules 1986 (SI 1986/952). It is not concerned with decisions about authorisation made by professional bodies under s. 390(2)(a) and 391, since those bodies have their own reviewing procedures.

This Schedule contains details about the membership and procedure of the tribunal, which consists, for the hearing of any case, of two insolvency experts and a legally qualified chairman. Although the power of selection, and also largely that of nomination, of members rests with the Secretary of State, the tribunal is intended to function as an independent body.

SCHEDULE 8

PROVISIONS CAPABLE OF INCLUSION IN COMPANY INSOLVENCY RULES

Section 411

Courts

1 Provision for regulating the practice and procedure of any court exercising jurisdiction for the purposes of Parts I to VII of this Act or the Companies Act so far as relating to, and to matters connected with or arising out of, the insolvency or winding up of companies, being any provision that could be made by rules of court.

2(1) Provision for regulating the practice and procedure of any court exercising jurisdiction for the purposes of Parts I to VII of this Act or the Companies Act so far as relating to, and to matters connected with or arising out of, the insolvency or winding up of companies, being any provision that could be made by rules of court.

2(2) Rules made by virtue of this paragraph about the consequence of failure to comply with practice or procedure may, in particular, include provision about the termination of administration.

Notices, etc.

3 Provision requiring notice of any proceedings in connection with or arising out of the insolvency or winding up of a company to be given or published in the manner prescribed by the rules.

4 Provision with respect to the form, manner of serving, contents and proof of any petition, application, order, notice, statement or other document required to be presented, made, given, published or prepared under any enactment or subordinate legislation relating to, or to matters connected with or arising out of, the insolvency or winding up of companies.

5 Provision specifying the persons to whom any notice is to be given.

Registration of Voluntary Arrangements

6 Provision for the registration of voluntary arrangements approved under Part I of this Act, including provision for the keeping and inspection of a register.

Schedule 8 *Insolvency Act 1986*

Provisional Liquidator

7   Provision as to the manner in which a provisional liquidator appointed under section 135 is to carry out his functions.

Conduct of Insolvency

8   Provision with respect to the certification of any person as, and as to the proof that a person is, the liquidator, administrator or administrative receiver of a company.

9   The following provision with respect to meetings of a company's creditors, contributories or members–

(a)   provision as to the manner of summoning a meeting (including provision as to how any power to require a meeting is to be exercised, provision as to the manner of determining the value of any debt or contribution for the purposes of any such power and provision making the exercise of any such power subject to the deposit of a sum sufficient to cover the expenses likely to be incurred in summoning and holding a meeting);

(b)   provision specifying the time and place at which a meeting may be held and the period of notice required for a meeting;

(c)   provision as to the procedure to be followed at a meeting (including the manner in which decisions may be reached by a meeting and the manner in which the value of any vote at a meeting is to be determined);

(d)   provision for requiring a person who is or has been an officer of the company to attend a meeting;

(e)   provision creating, in the prescribed circumstances, a presumption that a meeting has been duly summoned and held;

(f)   provision as to the manner of proving the decisions of a meeting.

10(1)   Provision as to the functions, membership and proceedings of a committee established under section 49, 68, 101, 141 or 142 of, or paragraph 57 of Schedule B1 to, this Act.

10(2)   The following provision with respect to the establishment of a committee under section 101, 141 or 142 of this Act, that is to say–

(a)   provision for resolving differences between a meeting of the company's creditors and a meeting of its contributories or members;

(b)   provision authorising the establishment of the committee without a meeting of contributories in a case where a company is being wound up on grounds including its inability to pay its debts; and

(c)   provision modifying the requirements of this Act with respect to the establishment of the committee in a case where a winding-up order has been made immediately upon the discharge of an administration order.

11   Provision as to the manner in which any requirement that may be imposed on a person under any Parts I to VII of this Act by the official receiver, the liquidator, administrator or administrative receiver of a company or a special manager appointed under section 177 is to be so imposed.

12   Provision as to the debts that may be proved in a winding up, as to the manner and conditions of proving a debt and as to the manner and expenses of establishing the value of any debt or security.

13   Provision with respect to the manner of the distribution of the property of a company that is being wound up, including provision with respect to unclaimed funds and dividends.

14 Provision which, with or without modifications, applies in relation to the winding up of companies any enactment contained in Parts VIII to XI of this Act or in the Bankruptcy (Scotland) Act 1985.

14A Provision about the application of section 176A of this Act which may include, in particular–

(a) provision enabling a receiver to institute winding-up proceedings;

(b) provision requiring a receiver to institute winding-up proceedings.

Administration

14B Provision which–

(a) applies in relation to administration, with or without modifications, a provision of Parts IV to VII of this Act, or

(b) serves a purpose in relation to administration similar to a purpose that may be served by the rules in relation to winding up by virtue of a provision of this Schedule.

Financial Provisions

15 Provision as to the amount, or manner of determining the amount, payable to the liquidator, administrator or administrative receiver of a company or a special manager appointed under section 177, by way of remuneration for the carrying out of functions in connection with or arising out of the insolvency or winding up of a company.

16 Provision with respect to the manner in which moneys received by the liquidator of a company in the course of carrying out his functions as such are to be invested or otherwise handled and with respect to the payment of interest on sums which, in pursuance of rules made by virtue of this paragraph, have been paid into the Insolvency Services Account.

16A Provision enabling the Secretary of State to set the rate of interest paid on sums which have been paid into the Insolvency Services Account.

17 Provision as to the fees, costs, charges and other expenses that may be treated as the expenses of a winding up.

18 Provisions as to the fees, costs, charges and other expenses that may be treated as properly incurred by the administrator or administrative receiver of a company.

19 Provision as to the fees, costs, charges and other expenses that may be incurred for any of the purposes of Part I of this Act or in the administration of any voluntary arrangement approved under that Part.

Information and Records

20 Provision requiring registrars and other officers of courts having jurisdiction in England and Wales in relation to, or to matters connected with or arising out of, the insolvency or winding up of companies–

(a) to keep books and other records with respect to the exercise of that jurisdiction, and

(b) to make returns to the Secretary of State of the business of those courts.

21   Provision requiring a creditor, member or contributory, or such a committee as is mentioned in paragraph 10 above, to be supplied (on payment in precribed cases of the prescribed fee) with such information and with copies of such documents as may be prescribed.

22   Provision as to the manner in which public examinations under sections 133 and 134 of this Act and proceedings under sections 236 and 237 are to be conducted, as to the circumstances in which records of such examinations or proceedings are to be made available to prescribed persons and as to the costs of such examinations and proceedings.

23   Provision imposing requirements with respect to–

(a)   the preparation and keeping by the liquidator, administrator or administrative receiver of a company, or by the supervisor of a voluntary arrangement approved under Part I of this Act, of prescribed books, accounts and other records;

(b)   the production of those books, accounts and records for inspection by prescribed persons;

(c)   the auditing of accounts kept by the liquidator, administrator or administrative receiver of a company, or the supervisor of such a voluntary arrangement; and

(d)   the issue by the administrator or administrative receiver of a company of such a certificate as is mentioned in section 22(3)(b) of the Value Added Tax Act 1983 (refund of tax in cases of bad debts) and the supply of copies of the certificate to creditors of the company.

24   Provision requiring the person who is the supervisor of a voluntary arrangement approved under Part I, when it appears to him that the voluntary arrangement has been fully implemented and nothing remains to be done by him under the arrangement–

(a)   to give notice to that fact to persons bound by the voluntary arrangement, and

(b)   to report to those persons on the carrying out of the functions conferred on the supervisor of the arrangement.

25   Provision as to the manner in which the liquidator of a company is to act in relation to the books, papers and other records of the company, including provision authorising their disposal.

26   Provision imposing requirements in connection with the carrying out of functions under section 7(3) of the Company Directors Disqualification Act 1986 (including, in particular, requirements with respect to the making of periodic returns).

General

27   Provision conferring power on the Secretary of State to make regulations with respect to so much of any matter that may be provided for in the rules as relates to the carrying out of the functions of the liquidator, administrator or administrative receiver of a company.

28   Provision conferring a discretion on the court.

29   Provision conferring power on the court to make orders for the purpose of securing compliance with obligations imposed by or under section 47, 66, 131, 143(2) or 235 of, or paragraph 47 of Schedule B1 to, this Act or section 7(4) of the Company Directors Disqualification Act 1986.

30   Provision making non-compliance with any of the rules a criminal offence.

31 Provision making different provision for different cases or descriptions of cases, including different provisions for different areas.

GENERAL NOTE

Much of the detail of the insolvency regime which IA 1985 introduced and IA 1986 consolidated was left to be spelt out in subordinate legislation by regulations made under s. 411ff. This Schedule outlines some of the matters which may be the subject of rules relating to company insolvency. The Companies (Winding-Up) Rules 1949 were superseded by IR 1986, which were brought into force contemporaneously with the commencement of the Act itself; but the Schedule is by no means confined in scope to matters which have traditionally been part of winding-up rules.

Numerous amendments to this Schedule were made by EA 2002. When compared to the former version of this Schedule, the following changes should be noted:

- Para. 1 – deleted;
- Para. 2 – renumbered para. 1 by EA 2002, Sch. 17;
- Para. 2 – inserted by EA 2002, Sch. 17;
- Para. 10 – amended by EA 2002, Sch. 17;
- Paras 14A and 14B – inserted by EA 2002, Sch. 17;
- Para. 16A – inserted by EA 2002, s. 271.
- Para. 29 – amended by EA 2002, Sch. 17.

Note that in this Schedule, "liquidator" includes a provisional liquidator (s. 411(3)). Attention should also be drawn to IR 1986, r. 12.1, which authorises the Secretary of State (pursuant to Sch. 8, para. 27 and Sch. 9, para. 30) to make regulations in regard to various matters, supplementary to the Insolvency Rules made under s. 411.

Among the items listed which cannot be regarded as purely procedural or are not self-explanatory the following may be noted.

Para. 6

There is no mention in the body of the Act of any registration procedure for a CVA, although certain matters must be reported to the court (see, *e.g.*, ss. 2(2), 4(6)). The present paragraph has been implemented by IR 1986, r. 1.24(5), which provides for registration with the registrar of companies.

Paras 12, 14

The Parts of the Act dealing with company insolvency contain no definition of "debts" and no provisions relating to proofs of debts, in marked contrast to those relating to the bankruptcy of individuals (see ss. 322, 382), and, indeed, to the repealed CA 1985, s. 611. It is only by subordinate legislation made under these paragraphs of the present Schedule that such important matters as the nature of provable debts, the quantification of such debts, allowances for mutual credit and set-off, etc., are established for company liquidations and some (but not all) analogous proceedings. This has been done by IR 1986, rr. 4.73ff., 4.86ff. and 12.3.

For further discussion of the term "debts", see the notes to s. 1(1) and IR 1986, r. 13.12.

The Companies Acts prior to the present legislation always included a substantive provision (*e.g.* CA 1985, s. 612) which incorporated specified aspects of bankruptcy law into the law governing the winding up of *insolvent* companies. Paragraph 14 of this Schedule is potentially of wider scope, since it applies to solvent liquidations as well.

See further the introductory note to Pt IV, Ch. VIII, following s. 174.

Para. 27

For the relevant regulations see the Insolvency Regulations 1994 (SI 1994/2507, operative October 24, 1994, as amended by SI 2000/485, effective March 31, 2000 and SI 2001/762, effective April 2, 2001), and SI 2004/472 (effective April 1, 2004).

Schedule 9 Insolvency Act 1986
SCHEDULE 9

PROVISIONS CAPABLE OF INCLUSION IN INDIVIDUAL INSOLVENCY RULES

Section 412

Courts

1   Provision with respect to the arrangement and disposition of the business under Parts VIII to XI of this Act of courts having jurisdiction for the purpose of those Parts, including provision for the allocation of proceedings under those Parts to particular courts and for the transfer of such proceedings from one court to another.

2   Provision for enabling a registrar in bankruptcy of the High Court or a registrar of a county court having jurisdiction for the purposes of those Parts to exercise such of the jurisdiction conferred for those purposes on the High Court or, as the case may be, that county court as may be prescribed.

3   Provision for regulating the practice and procedure of any court exercising jurisdiction for the purposes of those Parts, being any provision that could be made by rules of court.

4   Provision conferring rights of audience, in courts exercising jurisdiction for the purposes of those Parts, on the official receiver and on solicitors.

Notices etc.

5   Provision requiring notice of any proceedings under Parts VIII to XI of this Act or of any matter relating to or arising out of a proposal under Part VIII or a bankruptcy to be given or published in the prescribed manner.

6   Provision with respect to the form, manner of serving, contents and proof of any petition, application, order, notice, statement or other document required to be presented, made, given, published or prepared under any enactment contained in Parts VIII to XI or subordinate legislation under those Parts or Part XV (including provision requiring prescribed matters to be verified by affidavit).

7   Provision specifying the persons to whom any notice under Parts VIII to XI is to be given.

Registration of Voluntary Arrangements

8   Provision for the registration of voluntary arrangements approved under Part VIII of this Act, including provision for the keeping and inspection of a register.

Official Receiver Acting on Voluntary Arrangement

8A   Provision about the official receiver acting as nominee or supervisor in relation to a voluntary arrangement under Part VIII of this Act, including–

(a)   provision requiring the official receiver to act in specified circumstances;

(b)   provision about remuneration;

(c)   provision prescribing terms or conditions to be treated as forming part of a voluntary arrangement in relation to which the official receiver acts as nominee or supervisor;

(d) provision enabling those terms or conditions to be varied or excluded, in specified circumstances or subject to specified conditions, by express provision in an arrangement.

Interim Receiver

9 Provision as to the manner in which an interim receiver appointed under section 286 is to carry out his functions, including any such provision as is specified in relation to the trustee of a bankrupt's estate in paragraph 21 or 27 below.

Receiver or Manager

10 Provision as to the manner in which the official receiver is to carry out his functions as receiver or manager of a bankrupt's estate under section 287, including any such provision as is specified in relation to the trustee of a bankrupt's estate in paragraph 21 or 27 below.

Administration of Individual Insolvency

11 Provision with respect to the certification of the appointment of any person as trustee of a bankrupt's estate and as to the proof of that appointment.

12 The following provision with respect to meetings of creditors–

(a) provision as to the manner of summoning a meeting (including provision as to how any power to require a meeting is to be exercised, provision as to the manner of determining the value of any debt for the purposes of any such power and provision making the exercise of any such power subject to the deposit of a sum sufficient to cover the expenses likely to be incurred in summoning and holding a meeting);

(b) provision specifying the time and place at which a meeting may be held and the period of notice required for a meeting;

(c) provision as to the procedure to be followed at such a meeting (including the manner in which decisions may be reached by a meeting and the manner in which the value of any vote at a meeting is to be determined);

(d) provision for requiring a bankrupt or debtor to attend a meeting;

(e) provision creating, in the prescribed circumstances, a presumption that a meeting has been duly summoned and held; and

(f) provision as to the manner of proving the decisions of a meeting.

13 Provision as to the functions, membership and proceedings of a creditors' committee established under section 301.

14 Provision as to the manner in which any requirement that may be imposed on a person under Parts VIII to XI of this Act by the official receiver, the trustee of a bankrupt's estate or a special manager appointed under section 370 is to be imposed and, in the case of any requirement imposed under section 305(3) (information etc. to be given by the trustee to the official receiver), provision conferring power on the court to make orders for the purpose of securing compliance with that requirement.

15 Provision as to the manner in which any requirement imposed by virtue of section 310(3) (compliance with income payments order) is to take effect.

16 Provision as to the terms and conditions that may be included in a charge under section 313 (dwelling house forming part of bankrupt's estate).

17 Provision as to the debts that may be proved in any bankruptcy, as to the manner and conditions of proving a debt and as to the manner and expenses of establishing the value of any debt or security.

18 Provision with respect to the manner of the distribution of a bankrupt's estate, including provision with respect to unclaimed funds and dividends.

19 Provision modifying the application of Parts VIII to XI of this Act in relation to a debtor or bankrupt who has died.

Financial Provisions

20 Provision as to the amount, or manner of determining the amount, payable to an interim receiver, the trustee of a bankrupt's estate or a special manager appointed under section 370 by way of remuneration for the performance of functions in connection with or arising out of the bankruptcy of any person.

21 Provision with respect to the manner in which moneys received by the trustee of a bankrupt's estate in the course of carrying out his functions as such are to be invested or otherwise handled with respect to the payment of interest on sums which, in pursuance of rules made by virtue of this paragraph, have been paid into the Insolvency Services Account.

21A Provision enabling the Secretary of State to set the rate of interest paid on sums which have been paid into the Insolvency Services Account.

22 Provision as to the fees, costs, charges and other expenses that may be treated as the expenses of a bankruptcy.

23 Provision as to the fees, costs, charges and other expenses that may be incurred for any of the purposes of Part VIII of this Act or in the administration of any voluntary arrangement approved under that Part.

Information and Records

24 Provision requiring registrars and other officers of courts having jurisdiction for the purposes of Parts VIII to XI–

(a) to keep books and other records with respect to the exercise of that jurisdiction and of jurisdiction under the Deeds of Arrangement Act 1914, and

(b) to make returns to the Secretary of State of the business of those courts.

25 Provision requiring a creditor or a committee established under section 301 to be supplied (on payment in prescribed cases of the prescribed fee) with such information and with copies of such documents as may be prescribed.

26 Provision as to the manner in which public examinations under section 290 and proceedings under sections 366 to 368 are to be conducted, as to the circumstances in which records of such examinations and proceedings are to be made available to prescribed persons and as to the costs of such examinations and proceedings.

27 Provision imposing requirements with respect to–

  (a) the preparation and keeping by the trustee of a bankrupt's estate, or the supervisor of a voluntary arrangement approved under Part VIII, of prescribed books, accounts and other records;

  (b) the production of those books, accounts and records for inspection by prescribed persons; and

  (c) the auditing of accounts kept by the trustee of a bankrupt's estate or the supervisor of such a voluntary arrangement.

28 Provision requiring the person who is the supervisor of a voluntary arrangement approved under Part VIII, when it appears to him that the voluntary arrangement has been fully implemented and that nothing remains to be done by him under it–

  (a) to give notice of that fact to persons bound by the voluntary arrangement, and

  (b) to report to those persons on the carrying out of the functions conferred on the supervisor of it.

29 Provision as to the manner in which the trustee of a bankrupt's estate is to act in relation to the books, papers and other records of the bankrupt, including provision authorising their disposal.

Bankruptcy Restrictions Orders and Undertakings

29A Provision about bankruptcy restrictions orders, interim orders and undertakings, including–

  (a) provision about evidence;

  (b) provision enabling the amalgamation of the register mentioned in paragraph 12 of Schedule 4A with another register;

  (c) provision enabling inspection of that register by the public.

General

30 Provision conferring power on the Secretary of State to make regulations with respect to so much of any matter that may be provided for in the rules as relates to the carrying out of the functions of an interim receiver appointed under section 286, of the official receiver while acting as a receiver or manager under section 287 or of a trustee of a bankrupt's estate.

31 Provision conferring a discretion on the court.

32 Provision making non-compliance with any of the rules a criminal offence.

33 Provision making different provision for different cases, including different provision for different areas.

General Note

This provides a useful guide to the matters which may be provided for by the rules. Authority to make these rules is given by s. 412, and the note on that section should be referred to. Paragraphs 8A and 29A were inserted by EA 2002, s. 269 and Sch. 23 to deal with the advent of fast-track IVAs and BROs. The utility of para. 17 was illustrated in *Woodley v Woodley (No. 2)* [1994] 1 W.L.R. 1167. For the text of the Insolvency Rules (1986/1925) as amended see below, at pp. 654. For the regulations referred to in para. 30 see the Insolvency Regulations 1994 (SI 1994/2507), operative October 24, 1994, replacing the original Insolvency Regulations 1986 (SI 1986/1994), as amended.

In para. 21 the words "invested or otherwise handled and with respect to the payment of interest on sums which, in pursuance of rules made by virtue of this paragraph, have been paid into the Insolvency Services Account" substituted for the word "handled" by the Insolvency Act 2000 (s. 13(1) as from April 2, 2001 (see SI 2001/766 (C 27), art. 1, 2(1)(b)). See note to s. 406.

Schedule 10 *Insolvency Act 1986*

SCHEDULE 10

PUNISHMENT OF OFFENCES UNDER THIS ACT

Section 430

Note: In the fourth and fifth columns of this Schedule, **"the statutory maximum"** means–

(a) in England and Wales, the prescribed sum under section 32 of the Magistrates' Courts Act 1980 (c. 43), and

(b) in Scotland, the prescribed sum under section 289B of the Criminal Procedure (Scotland) Act 1975 (c. 21).

Insolvency Act 1986   Schedule 10

Section of Act creating offence	General nature of offence	Mode of prosecution	Punishment	Daily default fine (where applicable)
6A(1)	False representation or fraud for purpose of obtaining members' or creditors' approval of proposed voluntary arrangement.	1. On indictment. 2. Summary.	7 years or a fine, or both. 6 months or the statutory maximum, or both.	
12(2)	Company and others failing to state in correspondence etc. that administrator appointed.	Summary.	One-fifth of the statutory maximum.	
15(8)	Failure of administrator to register office copy of court order permitting disposal of charged property.	Summary.	One-fifth of the statutory maximum.	One-fiftieth of the statutory maximum.
18(5)	Failure of administrator to register office copy of court order varying or discharging administration order.	Summary.	One-fifth of the statutory maximum.	One-fiftieth of the statutory maximum.
21(3)	Administrator failing to register administration order and give notice of appointment.	Summary.	One-fifth of the statutory maximum.	One-fiftieth of the statutory maximum.
22(6)	Failure to comply with provisions relating to statement of affairs, where administrator appointed.	1. On indictment. 2. Summary.	A fine. The statutory maximum.	One-tenth of the statutory maximum.
23(3)	Administrator failing to send out, register and lay before creditors statement of his proposals.	Summary.	One-fifth of the statutory maximum.	One-fiftieth of the statutory maximum.
24(7)	Administrator failing to file court order discharging administration order under s. 24.	Summary.	One-fifth of the statutory maximum.	One-fiftieth of the statutory maximum.
27(6)	Administrator failing to file court order discharging administration order under s. 27.	Summary.	One-fifth of the statutory maximum.	One-fiftieth of the statutory maximum.
30	Body corporate acting as receiver.	1. On indictment. 2. Summary.	A fine. The statutory maximum.	
31	Bankrupt acting as receiver or manager.	1. On indictment. 2. Summary.	2 years or a fine, or both. 6 months or the statutory maximum, or both.	
38(5)	Receiver failing to deliver accounts to registrar.	Summary.	One-fifth of the statutory maximum.	One-fiftieth of the statutory maximum.
39(2)	Company and others failing to state in correspondence that receiver appointed.	Summary.	One-fifth of the statutory maximum.	

Schedule 10   *Insolvency Act 1986*

Section of Act creating offence	General nature of offence	Mode of prosecution	Punishment	Daily default fine (where applicable)
43(6)	Administrative receiver failing to file office copy of order permitting disposal of charged property.	Summary.	One-fifth of the statutory maximum.	One-fiftieth of the statutory maximum.
45(5)	Administrative receiver failing to file notice of vacation of office.	Summary.	One-fifth of the statutory maximum.	One-fiftieth of the statutory maximum.
46(4)	Administrative receiver failing to give notice of his appointment.	Summary.	One-fifth of the statutory maximum.	One-fiftieth of the statutory maximum.
47(6)	Failure to comply with provisions relating to statement of affairs where administrative receiver appointed.	1. On indictment. 2. Summary.	A fine. The statutory maximum.	One-tenth of the statutory maximum.
48(8)	Administrative receiver failing to comply with requirements as to his report.	Summary.	One-fifth of the statutory maximum.	One-fiftieth of the statutory maximum.
51(4)	Body corporate or Scottish firm acting as receiver.	1. On indictment. 2. Summary.	A fine. The statutory maximum.	
51(5)	Undischarged bankrupt acting as receiver (Scotland).	1. On indictment. 2. Summary.	2 years or a fine, or both. 6 months or the statutory maximum, or both.	
53(2)	Failing to deliver to registrar copy of instrument of appointing of receiver.	Summary.	One-fifth of the statutory maximum.	One-fiftieth of the statutory maximum.
54(3)	Failing to deliver to registrar the court's interlocutor appointing receiver.	Summary.	One-fifth of the statutory maximum.	One-fiftieth of the statutory maximum.
61(7)	Receiver failing to send registrar certified copy of court order authorising disposal of charged property.	Summary.	One-fifth of the statutory maximum.	One-fiftieth of the statutory maximum.
62(5)	Failing to give notice to registrar of cessation or removal of receiver.	Summary.	One-fifth of the statutory maximum.	One-fiftieth of the statutory maximum.
64(2)	Company and others failing to state on correspondence etc. that receiver appointed.	Summary.	One-fifth of the statutory maximum.	
65(4)	Receiver failing to send or publish notice of his appointment.	Summary.	One-fifth of the statutory maximum.	One-fiftieth of the statutory maximum.
66(6)	Failing to comply with provisions concerning statement of affairs where receiver appointed.	1. On indictment. 2. Summary.	A fine. The statutory maximum.	One-tenth of the statutory maximum.

Insolvency Act 1986   Schedule 10

Section of Act creating offence	General nature of offence	Mode of prosecution	Punishment	Daily default fine (where applicable)
67(8)	Receiver failing to comply with requirements as to his report.	Summary.	One-fifth of the statutory maximum.	One-fiftieth of the statutory maximum.
85(2)	Company failing to give notice in Gazette of resolution for voluntary winding up.	Summary.	One-fifth of the statutory maximum.	One-fiftieth of the statutory maximum.
89(4)	Director making statutory declaration of company's solvency without reasonable grounds for his opinion.	1. On indictment. 2. Summary.	2 years or a fine, or both. 6 months or the statutory maximum, or both.	
89(6)	Declaration under s. 89 not delivered to registrar within prescribed time.	Summary.	One-fifth of the statutory maximum.	One-fiftieth of the statutory maximum.
93(3)	Liquidator failing to summon general meeting of company at each year's end.	Summary.	One-fifth of the statutory maximum.	One-fiftieth of the statutory maximum.
94(4)	Liquidator failing to send to registrar a copy of account of winding up and return of final meeting.	Summary.	One-fifth of the statutory maximum.	
94(6)	Liquidator failing to call final meeting.	Summary.	One-fifth of the statutory maximum.	
95(8)	Liquidator failing to comply with s. 95, where company insolvent	Summary.	The statutory maximum.	
98(6)	Company failing to comply with s. 98 in respect of summoning and giving notice of creditors' meeting.	1. On indictment. 2. Summary.	A fine. The statutory maximum.	
99(3)	Directors failing to attend and lay statement in prescribed form before creditors' meeting.	1. On indictment. 2. Summary.	A fine. The statutory maximum.	
105(3)	Liquidator failing to summon company general meeting and creditors' meeting at each year's end.	Summary.	One-fifth of the statutory maximum.	
106(4)	Liquidator failing to send to registrar account of winding up and return of final meetings.	Summary.	One-fifth of the statutory maximum.	One-fiftieth of the statutory maximum.
106(6)	Liquidator failing to call final meeting of company or creditors.	Summary.	One-fifth of the statutory maximum.	
109(2)	Liquidator failing to publish notice of his appointment.	Summary.	One-fifth of the statutory maximum.	One-fiftieth of the statutory maximum.
114(4)	Directors exercising powers in breach of s. 114, where no liquidator.	Summary.	The statutory maximum.	

583

Schedule 10   *Insolvency Act 1986*

Section of Act creating offence	General nature of offence	Mode of prosecution	Punishment	Daily default fine (where applicable)
131(7)	Failing to comply with requirements as to statement of affairs, where liquidator appointed.	1. On indictment. 2. Summary.	A fine. The statutory maximum.	One-tenth of the statutory maximum.
164	Giving, offering etc. corrupt inducement affecting appointment of liquidator.	1. On indictment. 2. Summary.	A fine. The statutory maximum.	
166(7)	Liquidator failing to comply with requirements of s. 166 in creditors' voluntary winding up.	Summary.	The statutory maximum.	
188(2)	Default in compliance with s. 188 as to notification that company being wound up.	Summary.	One-fifth of the statutory maximum.	One-fiftieth of the statutory maximum.
192(2)	Liquidator failing to notify registrar as to progress of winding up.	Summary.	One-fifth of the statutory maximum.	One-fiftieth of the statutory maximum.
201(4)	Failing to deliver to registrar office copy of court order deferring dissolution.	Summary.	One-fifth of the statutory maximum.	One-fiftieth of the statutory maximum.
203(6)	Failing to deliver to registrar copy of directions or result of appeal under s. 203.	Summary.	One-fifth of the statutory maximum.	One-fiftieth of the statutory maximum.
204(7)	Liquidator failing to deliver to registrar copy of court order for early dissolution.	Summary.	One-fifth of the statutory maximum.	One-fiftieth of the statutory maximum.
204(8)	Failing to deliver to registrar copy of court order deferring early dissolution.	Summary.	One-fifth of the statutory maximum.	One-fiftieth of the statutory maximum.
205(7)	Failing to deliver to registrar copy of Secretary of State's directions or court order deferring dissolution.	Summary.	One-fifth of the statutory maximum.	One-fiftieth of the statutory maximum.
206(1)	Fraud etc. in anticipation of winding up.	1. On indictment. 2. Summary.	7 years or a fine, or both. 6 months or the statutory maximum, or both.	
206(2)	Privity to fraud in anticipation of winding up; fraud or privity to fraud, after commencement of winding up.	1. On indictment. 2. Summary.	7 years or a fine, or both. 6 months or the statutory maximum, or both.	
206(5)	Knowingly taking in pawn or pledge, or otherwise receiving, company property.	1. On indictment. 2. Summary.	7 years or a fine, or both. 6 months or the statutory maximum, or both.	

Section of Act creating offence	General nature of offence	Mode of prosecution	Punishment	Daily default fine (where applicable)
207	Officer of company entering into transaction in fraud of company's creditors.	1. On indictment. 2. Summary.	2 years or a fine, or both. 6 months or the statutory maximum, or both.	
208	Officer of company misconducting himself in course of winding up.	1. On indictment. 2. Summary.	7 years or a fine, or both. 6 months or the statutory maximum, or both.	
209	Officer or contributory destroying, falsifying, etc. company's books.	1. On indictment. 2. Summary.	7 years or a fine, or both. 6 months or the statutory maximum, or both.	
210	Officer of company making material omission from statement relating to company's affairs.	1. On indictment. 2. Summary.	7 years or a fine, or both. 6 months or the statutory maximum, or both.	
211	False representation or fraud for purpose of obtaining creditors' consent to an agreement in connection with winding up.	1. On indictment. 2. Summary.	7 years or a fine, or both. 6 months or the statutory maximum, or both.	
216(4)	Contravening restrictions on re-use of name of company in insolvent liquidation	1. On indictment. 2. Summary.	2 years or a fine, or both. 6 months or the statutory maximum, or both.	
235(5)	Failing to co-operate with office-holder.	1. On indictment. 2. Summary.	A fine. The statutory maximum.	One-tenth of the statutory maximum.
262A(1)	False representation or fraud for purpose of obtaining creditors' approval of proposed voluntary arrangement.	1. On indictment. 2. Summary.	7 years or a fine, or both. 6 months or the statutory maximum, or both.	
353(1)	Bankrupt failing to disclose property or disposals to official receiver or trustee.	1. On indictment. 2. Summary.	7 years or a fine, or both. 6 months or the statutory maximum, or both.	
354(1)	Bankrupt failing to deliver property to, or concealing property from, official receiver or trustee.	1. On indictment. 2. Summary.	7 years or a fine, or both. 6 months or the statutory maximum, or both.	
354(2)	Bankrupt removing property which he is required to deliver to official receiver or trustee.	1. On indictment. 2. Summary.	7 years or a fine, or both. 6 months or the statutory maximum, or both.	

Schedule 10 Insolvency Act 1986

Section of Act creating offence	General nature of offence	Mode of prosecution	Punishment	Daily default fine (where applicable)
354(3)	Bankrupt failing to account for loss of substantial part of property.	1. On indictment. 2. Summary.	2 years or a fine, or both. 6 months or the statutory maximum, or both.	
355(1)	Bankrupt failing to deliver books, papers and records to official receiver or trustee.	1. On indictment. 2. Summary.	7 years or a fine, or both. 6 months or the statutory maximum, or both.	
355(2)	Bankrupt concealing, destroying etc. books, papers or records, or making false entries in them.	1. On indictment. 2. Summary.	7 years or a fine, or both. 6 months or the statutory maximum, or both.	
355(3)	Bankrupt disposing of, or altering, books, papers or records relating to his estate or affairs.	1. On indictment. 2. Summary.	7 years or a fine, or both. 6 months or the statutory maximum, or both.	
356(1)	Bankrupt making material omission in statement relating to his affairs.	1. On indictment. 2. Summary.	7 years or a fine, or both. 6 months or the statutory maximum, or both.	
356(2)	Bankrupt making false statement, or failing to inform trustee, where false debt proved.	1. On indictment. 2. Summary.	7 years or a fine, or both. 6 months or the statutory maximum, or both.	
357	Bankrupt fraudulently disposing of property.	1. On indictment. 2. Summary.	2 years or a fine, or both. 6 months or the statutory maximum, or both.	
358	Bankrupt absconding with property he is required to deliver to official receiver or trustee.	1. On indictment. 2. Summary.	2 years or a fine, or both. 6 months or the statutory maximum, or both.	
359(1)	Bankrupt disposing of property obtained on credit and not paid for.	1. On indictment. 2. Summary.	7 years or a fine, or both. 6 months or the statutory maximum, or both.	
359(2)	Obtaining property in respect of which money is owed by a bankrupt.	1. On indictment. 2. Summary.	7 years or a fine, or both. 6 months or the statutory maximum, or both.	
360(1)	Bankrupt obtaining credit or engaging in business without disclosing his status or name in which he was made bankrupt.	1. On indictment. 2. Summary.	2 years or a fine, or both. 6 months or the statutory maximum, or both.	

Section of Act creating offence	General nature of offence	Mode of prosecution	Punishment	Daily default fine (where applicable)
360(3)	Person made bankrupt in Scotland or Northern Ireland obtaining credit, etc. in England and Wales.	1. On indictment. 2. Summary.	2 years or a fine, or both. 6 months or the statutory maximum, or both.	
389	Acting as insolvency practitioner when not qualified.	1. On indictment. 2. Summary.	2 years or a fine, or both. 6 months or the statutory maximum, or both.	
429(5)	Contravening s. 429 in respect of disabilities imposed by county court on revocation of administration order.	1. On indictment. 2. Summary.	2 years or a fine, or both. 6 months or the statutory maximum, or both.	
Sch. A1, para. 9(2)	Directors failing to notify nominee of beginning of moratorium.	1. On indictment. 2. Summary.	2 years or a fine, or both. 6 months or the statutory maximum, or both.	
Sch. A1, para. 10(3)	Nominee failing to advertise or notify beginning of moratorium.	Summary.	One-fifth of the statutory maximum.	
Sch. A1, para. 11(2)	Nominee failing to advertise or notify end of moratorium.	Summary.	One-fifth of the statutory maximum.	
Sch. A1, para. 16(2)	Company and officers failing to state in correspondence etc. that moratorium in force.	Summary.	One-fifth of the statutory maximum.	
Sch. A1, para. 17(3)(a)	Company obtaining credit without disclosing existence of moratorium.	1. On indictment. 2. Summary.	A fine. The statutory maximum.	
Sch. A1, para. 17(3)(b)	Obtaining credit for company without disclosing existence of moratorium.	1. On indictment. 2. Summary.	2 years or a fine, or both. 6 months or the statutory maximum, or both.	
Sch. A1, para. 18(3)(a)	Company disposing of property otherwise than in ordinary way of business.	1. On indictment. 2. Summary.	A fine. The statutory maximum.	
Sch. A1, para. 18(3)(b)	Authorising or permitting disposal of company property.	1. On indictment. 2. Summary.	2 years or a fine, or both. 6 months or the statutory maximum, or both.	
Sch. A1, para. 19(3)(a)	Company making payments in respect of liabilities existing before beginning of moratorium.	1. On indictment. 2. Summary.	A fine. The statutory maximum.	

Schedule 10   Insolvency Act 1986

Section of Act creating offence	General nature of offence	Mode of prosecution	Punishment	Daily default fine (where applicable)
Sch. A1, para. 19(3)(b)	Authorising or permitting such a payment.	1. On indictment. 2. Summary.	2 years or a fine, or both. 6 months or the statutory maximum, or both.	
Sch. A1, para. 20(9)	Directors failing to send to registrar office copy of court order permitting disposal of charged property.	Summary.	One-fifth of the statutory maximum.	
Sch. A1, para. 22(1)	Company disposing of charged property.	1. On indictment. 2. Summary.	A fine. The statutory maximum.	
Sch. A1, para. 22(2)	Authorising or permitting such a disposal.	1. On indictment. 2. Summary.	2 years or a fine, or both. 6 months or the statutory maximum, or both.	
Sch. A1, para. 23(1)(a)	Company entering into market contract, etc.	1. On indictment. 2. Summary.	A fine. The statutory maximum.	
Sch. A1, para. 23(1)(b)	Authorising or permitting company to do so.	1. On indictment. 2. Summary.	2 years or a fine, or both. 6 months or the statutory maximum, or both.	
Sch. A1, para. 25(6)	Nominee failing to give notice of withdrawal of consent to act.	Summary.	One-fifth of the statutory maximum.	
Sch. A1, para. 34(3)	Nominee failing to give notice of extension of moratorium.	Summary.	One-fifth of the statutory maximum.	
Sch. A1, para. 41(2)	Fraud or privity to fraud in anticipation of moratorium.	1. On indictment. 2. Summary.	7 years or a fine, or both. 6 months or the statutory maximum, or both.	
Sch. A1, para. 41(3)	Fraud or privity to fraud during moratorium.	1. On indictment. 2. Summary.	7 years or a fine, or both. 6 months or the statutory maximum, or both.	
Sch. A1, para. 41(7)	Knowingly taking in pawn or pledge, or otherwise receiving, company property.	1. On indictment. 2. Summary.	7 years or a fine, or both. 6 months or the statutory maximum, or both.	
Sch. A1, para. 42(1)	False representation or fraud for purpose of obtaining or extending moratorium.	1. On indictment. 2. Summary.	7 years or a fine, or both. 6 months or the statutory maximum, or both.	
Sch. B1, para. 18(7).	Making false statement in statutory declaration where administrator appointed by holder of floating charge.	1. On indictment. 2. Summary.	2 years, or a fine or both. 6 months, or the statutory maximum or both.	

Insolvency Act 1986   Schedule 10

Section of Act creating offence	General nature of offence	Mode of prosecution	Punishment	Daily default fine (where applicable)
Sch. B1, para. 20.	Holder of floating charge failing to notify administrator or others of commencement of appointment.	1. On indictment. 2. Summary.	2 years, or a fine or both. 6 months, or the statutory maximum or both.	One-tenth of the statutory maximum.
Sch. B1, para. 27(4).	Making false statement in statutory declaration where appointment of administrator proposed by company or directors.	1. On indictment. 2. Summary.	2 years, or a fine or both. 6 months, or the statutory maximum or both.	
Sch. B1, para. 29(7).	Making false statement in statutory declaration where administrator appointed by company or directors.	1. On indictment. 2. Summary.	2 years, or a fine or both. 6 months, or the statutory maximum or both.	
Sch. B1, para. 32.	Company or directors failing to notify administrator or others of commencement of appointment.	1. On indictment. 2. Summary.	2 years, or a fine or both. 6 months, or the statutory maximum or both.	One-tenth of the statutory maximum.
Sch. B1, para. 45(2).	Administrator, company or officer failing to state in business document that administrator appointed.	Summary.	One-fifth of the statutory maximum.	
Sch. B1, para. 46(9).	Administrator failing to give notice of his appointment.	Summary.	One-fifth of the statutory maximum.	One-fiftieth of the statutory maximum.
Sch. B1, para. 48(4).	Failing to comply with provisions about statement of affairs where administrator appointed.	1. On indictment. 2. Summary.	A fine. The statutory maximum.	One-tenth of the statutory maximum.
Sch. B1, para. 49(7).	Administrator failing to send out statement of his proposals.	Summary.	One-fifth of the statutory maximum.	One-fiftieth of the statutory maximum.
Sch. B1, para. 51(5).	Administrator failing to arrange initial creditors' meeting.	Summary.	One-fifth of the statutory maximum.	One-fiftieth of the statutory maximum.
Sch. B1, para. 53(3).	Administrator failing to report decision taken at initial creditors' meeting.	Summary.	One-fifth of the statutory maximum.	One-fiftieth of the statutory maximum.
Sch. B1, para. 54(7).	Administrator failing to report decision taken at creditors' meeting summoned to consider revised proposal.	Summary.	One-fifth of the statutory maximum.	One-fiftieth of the statutory maximum.
Sch. B1, para. 56(2).	Administrator failing to summon creditors' meeting.	Summary.	One-fifth of the statutory maximum.	One-fiftieth of the statutory maximum.
Sch. B1, para. 71(6).	Administrator failing to file court order enabling disposal of charged property.	Summary.	One-fifth of the statutory maximum.	One-fiftieth of the statutory maximum.
Sch. B1, para. 72(5).	Administrator failing to file court order enabling disposal of hire-purchase property.	Summary.	One-fifth of the statutory maximum.	One-fiftieth of the statutory maximum.

Section of Act creating offence	General nature of offence	Mode of prosecution	Punishment	Daily default fine (where applicable)
Sch. B1, para. 77(3).	Administrator failing to notify Registrar of Companies of automatic end of administration.	Summary.	One-fifth of the statutory maximum.	One-fiftieth of the statutory maximum.
Sch. B1, para. 78(6).	Administrator failing to give notice of extension by consent of term of office.	Summary.	One-fifth of the statutory maximum.	One-fiftieth of the statutory maximum.
Sch. B1, para. 80(6).	Administrator failing to give notice of termination of administration where objective achieved.	Summary.	One-fifth of the statutory maximum.	One-fiftieth of the statutory maximum.
Sch. B1, para. 84(9).	Administrator failing to comply with provisions where company moves to dissolution.	Summary.	One-fifth of the statutory maximum.	One-fiftieth of the statutory maximum.
Sch. B1, para. 86(3).	Administrator failing to notify Registrar of Companies where court terminates administration.	Summary.	One-fifth of the statutory maximum.	One-fiftieth of the statutory maximum.
Sch. B1, para. 89(3).	Administrator failing to give notice on ceasing to be qualified.	Summary.	One-fifth of the statutory maximum.	One-fiftieth of the statutory maximum.
Sch. 7, para. 4(3)	Failure to attend and give evidence to Insolvency Practitioners Tribunal; suppressing, concealing, etc. relevant documents.	Summary.	Level 3 on the standard scale within the meaning given by section 75 of the Criminal Justice Act 1982.	

GENERAL NOTE

This technique of using a Schedule of punishments is used by CA 1985, but not by IA 1985. Guidance on the use of Sch. 10 is provided by s. 430. Sections 431 and 432 are also of assistance when applying Sch. 10.

The "statutory maximum" referred to in the introductory note to the Schedule and in cols 4 and 5 is at present £5,000 (but £2,000 in respect of offences committed before October 1, 1992): see CJA 1991, s. 17 and SI 1992/333, SI 1993/2118.

Schedule 10 was substantially modified by IA 2000 and EA 2002, Sch. 17.

SCHEDULE 11

TRANSITIONAL PROVISIONS AND SAVINGS

SCHEDULE 12

ENACTMENTS REPEALED

SCHEDULE 13

CONSEQUENTIAL AMENDMENTS OF COMPANIES ACT 1985

SCHEDULE 14

CONSEQUENTIAL AMENDMENTS OF OTHER ENACTMENTS

[Schedules 11–14 have not been reproduced in the present edition of the *Guide*. The full text may be found in *British Companies Legislation*, pp. 56,652ff., or in the official version of IA 1986 published by The Stationery Office.]

Insolvency Act 2000

This Act is now fully in force. In particular, those parts dealing with director disqualification (ss. 5–13 and Sch. 4) became effective on April 2, 2001, and those dealing with voluntary arrangements on January 1, 2003. In so far as the Act amends IA 1986, the amendments have been taken into account in the text to that Act. The remaining, "free-standing" provisions (*e.g.* s. 14) are annotated in this section of the *Guide*.

Insolvency Act 2000

Insolvency Act 2000

(2000 Chapter 39)

ARRANGEMENT OF SECTIONS

SECT.
1. Moratorium where directors propose voluntary arrangement.
2. Company voluntary arrangements.
3. Individual voluntary arrangements.
4. Qualification or authorisation of nominees and supervisors.

Disqualification of company directors, etc.

5. Disqualification orders.
6. Disqualification undertakings.
7. Effect of Northern Irish disqualifications.
8. Amendments.

Miscellaneous

9. Administration orders [repealed by EA 2002].
10. Investigation and prosecution of malpractice.
11. Restriction on use of answers obtained under compulsion.
12. Insolvent estates of deceased persons.
13. Bankruptcy: interest on sums held in Insolvency Services Account.
14. Model law on cross-border insolvency.

General

15. Amendments of Financial Services and Markets Act 2000 and repeals.
16. Commencement.
17. Extent.
18. Short title.

Insolvency Act 2000

SCHEDULES:

Schedule 1 – Moratorium where directors propose voluntary arrangement.
Schedule 2 – Company voluntary arrangements.
Part I – Amendments of the Insolvency Act 1986.
Part II – Amendments of the Building Societies Act 1986.
Schedule 3 – Individual voluntary arrangements.
Schedule 4 – Minor and consequential amendments about disqualification of company directors, etc.
Part I – Amendments of the Company Directors Disqualification Act 1986.
Part II – Consequential amendments of other enactments.
Schedule 5 – Repeals.

An Act to amend the law about insolvency; to amend the Company Directors Disqualification Act 1986; and for connected purposes.

[*30th November 2000*]

INTRODUCTORY NOTE TO INSOLVENCY ACT 2000

This legislation was finally brought fully into force on January 1, 2003. As many of the provisions operate as amendments to the 1986 Act they are not reproduced below but rather at the appropriate location within the 1986 Act. However, a number of the provisions could be regarded as "free-standing" and are included below with comment where appropriate.

General comment on the Act as a whole

This chapter in the reform of insolvency law has modest aims as was immediately conceded by the Government spokesman when the Bill was given its Second Reading in the House of Lords. The Bill was famously put down by Rt Hon. Tony Benn, MP on October 23, 2000, the day before the Bill had its Second Reading in the Commons (see *Hansard*, HC Vol. 355, col. 12 and the retort from Kim Howells MP *Hansard*, HC Vol. 355, col. 160). While recognising that it may not have major constitutional implications, it does deal with significant matters in the regulation of commerce. Essentially it is intended to improve debtor rehabilitation procedures, both in personal and corporate insolvency law. Thus, there are reforms to the company voluntary arrangement procedure (CVA), (contained in Pt I of IA 1986) to permit the proposal for an arrangement to enjoy the benefit of a moratorium whilst the CVA is being constructed and approved (s. 1 and Sch. 1). Conversely, the IVA procedure (Pt VIII of IA 1986) is modified to introduce a variant which can operate without the protection of an interim order (s. 3 and Sch. 3). There are general changes to both the CVA and IVA procedures (see ss. 2 and 3) and the moratorium applying in case of company administration is extended by s. 9 to encompass a landlord's right of re-entry.

Another aim of the Act (see s. 6), is to formalise a system whereby the authorities can accept a legally binding undertaking from a director facing disqualification proceedings, rather than pursuing him (or her) at great cost through the courts under the provisions of CDDA 1986. This reform is to some extent designed to save public expenditure, but it is also intended to speed up the process of disqualification, which can take as much as three years to complete. As a result, this might have been contrary to the right of a speedy trial enshrined by Art. 6 of the European Convention on Human Rights (now incorporated by the Human Rights Act 1998 (c. 42)).

The Insolvency Act 2000 addresses other areas of concern. The prosecution and investigation of those suspected of committing offences under insolvency law, is the subject of attention in ss. 10 and 11. A technical difficulty in the law relating to the administration of estates of deceased insolvents is resolved by s. 12. The legislation permits (in s. 13) trustees in bankruptcy greater flexibility in exploiting funds paid into the Insolvency Services Account. Section 14 enables the authorities to implement the United Nations Commission on International Trade Law (UNCITRAL) Convention on Cross Border Insolvency Proceedings and to amend domestic law to promote the aim of judicial co-operation in cross-border insolvency matters. A curious reform is the introduction by s. 4 of the possibility of non-qualified insolvency practitioners acting as nominees and supervisors for voluntary arrangements. This mirrors the growth of the "turnaround specialist" but it does represent a reversal of the policy enshrined in the IA 1986 of compulsory qualification as the norm for all insolvency practitioners. This is a development that will have to be watched carefully lest it provides a Trojan horse for cowboy operators in insolvency practice.

The matters dealt with in this Act have undergone considerable discussion. The issue of improving the CVA procedure via the introduction of a moratorium was the subject of a number of Insolvency Service consultation exercises in the 1990s (see *Company Voluntary Arrangements and Administration Orders* (October 1993), Bannister, [1994] 10 Insolvency Lawyer 5; *Revised Proposals for a New Company Voluntary Arrangement Procedure* (April

1995), Campbell, Palmer's *In Company*, June 1995; *Review of Company Rescue and Business Reconstruction Mechanisms* (September 1999)).

Voluntary arrangements

1 Moratorium where directors propose voluntary arrangement

1   Schedule 1 (which–

(a) enables the directors of a company to obtain an initial moratorium for the company where they propose a voluntary arrangement under Part I of the Insolvency Act 1986,

(b) makes provision about the approval and implementation of such a voluntary arrangement where a moratorium is obtained, and

(c) makes consequential amendments),

is to have effect.

[Amends IA 1986 by inserting s. 1A and Sch. A1: see the notes to those provisions. Minor consequential amendments are made to other parts of the Act.]

2 Company voluntary arrangements

2   Schedule 2 (which–

(a) amends the provisions about company voluntary arrangements under Part I of the Insolvency Act 1986, and

(b) in consequence of Schedule 1 and those amendments, makes amendments of the Building Societies Act 1986),

is to have effect.

GENERAL NOTE

This makes applicable the general CVA reform provisions in Sch. 2. For example, the nominee is now required to state in the report to the court whether the proposal has a reasonable prospect of being approved and implemented. This addresses issues raised in cases such as *Greystoke v Hamilton-Smith* [1997] B.P.I.R. 24 where the court made it clear that the nominee should reassure himself about the viability of the proposal before promoting it. There are also technical changes in the provisions relating to the approval of CVAs. Members lose their automatic veto over an arrangement that meets with the approval of creditors, though a member may have recourse to the courts (new s. 4A). A facility under which the CVA will bind unknown creditors is introduced (new s. 5(2)(b)). Nominees are also now required to "blow the whistle" on directors suspected of committing offences during the moratorium period. This change (contained in s. 7A) will reassure those commentators who suspect that voluntary arrangements are simply being used by unscrupulous directors to buy time for a failing business. A new s. 6A also creates an offence of seeking to obtain a CVA by false representations.

Schedule 2, Pt II, makes a number of changes in the context of building societies, which can exploit the CVA option but are prevented from benefiting from the moratorium. This is consistent with the treatment of banks with regard to the moratorium variation. Some of the provisions that deal with investigations carried out by inspectors appointed by the Building Societies Commission would appear to have more in common with the reforms introduced under ss. 10 and 11.

3 Individual voluntary arrangements

3   Schedule 3 (which enables the procedure for the approval of individual voluntary arrangements under Part VIII of the Insolvency Act 1986 to be started without an initial moratorium for the insolvent debtor and makes other amendments of the provisions about individual voluntary arrangements) is to have effect.

4 Qualification or authorisation of nominees and supervisors

[Amends IA 1986, ss. 388–389 in various respects and inserts s. 389A. See the notes to those sections.]

Disqualification of company directors etc.

[Sections 5–8 make amendments to CDDA 1986, and are not reproduced in this edition.]

5 Disqualification orders

6 Disqualification undertakings

7 Effect of Northern Irish disqualifications

8 Amendments

Miscellaneous

9 Administration orders

[Inserts new s. 10(1)(aa) and 11(3)(ba) into CDDA 1986 repealed by Sch. 26 to EA 2002.]

10 Investigation and prosecution of malpractice

[Amends s. 218, 219 of IA 1986: see the notes to those sections.]

11 Restriction on use of answers obtained under compulsion

[Inserts s. 219(2A) into IA 1986: see the note to that subsection.]

12 Insolvent estates of deceased persons

[Amends s. 421(1) and inserts new s. 421A into IA 1986: see the note to those sections.]

13 Bankruptcy: interest on sums held in Insolvency Services Account

[Amends s. 406 and Sch. 9, para. 21 of IA 1986: see the note to s. 406.]

14 Model law on cross-border insolvency

14(1) [Adoption of model law] The Secretary of State may by regulations make any provision which he considers necessary or expedient for the purpose of giving effect, with or without modifications, to the model law on cross-border insolvency.

14(2) [Scope of regulations] In particular, the regulations may–

(a) apply any provision of insolvency law in relation to foreign proceedings (whether begun before or after the regulations come into force),

(b) modify the application of insolvency law (whether in relation to foreign proceedings or otherwise),

(c) amend any provision of section 426 of the Insolvency Act 1986 (co-operation between courts),

and may apply or, as the case may be, modify the application of insolvency law in relation to the Crown.

14(3) **[Special cases]** The regulations may make different provision for different purposes and may make–

(a) any supplementary, incidental or consequential provision, or

(b) any transitory, transitional or saving provision,

which the Secretary of State considers necessary or expedient.

14(4) **[Definitions]** In this section–

"**foreign proceedings**" has the same meaning as in the model law on cross-border insolvency,

"**insolvency law**" has the same meaning as in section 426(10)(a) and (b) of the Insolvency Act 1986,

"**the model law on cross-border insolvency**" means the model law contained in Annex I of the report of the 30th session of UNCITRAL.

14(5) **[Procedure]** Regulations under this section are to be made by statutory instrument and may only be made if a draft has been laid before and approved by resolution of each House of Parliament.

14(6) **[Approval]** Making regulations under this section requires the agreement–

(a) if they extend to England and Wales, of the Lord Chancellor,

(b) if they extend to Scotland, of the Scottish Ministers.

GENERAL NOTE

The problem of cross-border insolvency has become more vexed with globalised trading, ease of foreign travel and advances in communications technology. These developments have compelled national authorities to introduce tailored judicial comity mechanisms (see for example, s. 426 of IA 1986). They have also led to changes at EU level (see the EU Regulation 2000/1346 (below, pp. 602ff), which superseded the abortive Bankruptcy Convention and came into effect in May 2002). At a truly international level, UNCITRAL in 1997 sponsored a Model Law on Cross Border Insolvency and a number of leading economies have already signed up to this (USA, Canada, Australia, New Zealand, South Africa).

For a background discussion see Fletcher [2000] 13 Insolvency Intelligence 57 and 68; Dawson [2000] 4 Receivers, Administrators and Liquidators Quarterly 147; and Omar [2000] Insolvency Lawyer 211.

Section 14 came into force on November 30, 2000, the date of Royal Assent: see s. 16(2).

S. 14(1)
This permits the Secretary of State to implement the UNCITRAL Model Law on Cross Border Insolvency by Regulation. There need not be exact replication: the Secretary of State is given discretion to modify incorporation.

S. 14(2) and (3)
The Secretary of State enjoys considerable flexibility in so doing and may amend the terms of s. 426 (*e.g.* by extending the number of friendly jurisdictions covered beyond the current list of mainly Commonwealth countries).

S. 14(4)
This is a dedicated definition facility, a rarity in what is an amendment Act.

S. 14(5) and (6)
These deal with operational matters.

General

15 Amendments of Financial Services and Markets Act 2000 and repeals

[Not reproduced.]

16 Commencement

16(1) **[Commencement orders]** The preceding provisions of this Act (including the Schedules) are to come into force on such day as the Secretary of State may by order made by statutory instrument appoint.

16(2) **[S. 14]** Subsection (1) does not apply to section 14 (which accordingly comes into force on the day on which this Act is passed).

16(3) **[Special cases]** An order under this section may make different provision for different purposes and may make–

(a) any supplementary, incidental or consequential provision, and

(b) any transitory, transitional or saving provision,

which the Secretary of State considers necessary or expedient.

S. 16(1) and (2)
This clarifies commencement dates with the enabling s. 14 coming immediately into effect on Royal Assent.

S. 16(3)
Technical aspects of commencement orders are explained.

17 Extent

17 This Act, except section 15(3), Part II of Schedule 2 and paragraphs 16(3) and 22 of Schedule 4, does not extend to Northern Ireland.

GENERAL NOTE

The Act generally does not apply to Northern Ireland, which has its own distinctive system of insolvency law.

18 Short title

18 This Act may be cited as the Insolvency Act 2000.

SCHEDULES

[Schedules 1–5 are not reproduced. The amendments made to IA 1986 by these Schedules, which are all in force, have been noted at appropriate places in the text.]

SCHEDULE 1

MORATORIUM WHERE DIRECTORS PROPOSE VOLUNTARY ARRANGEMENT

SCHEDULE 2

COMPANY VOLUNTARY ARRANGEMENTS

PART I

[Not reproduced – see amendments to Part I of IA 1986.]

SCHEDULE 3

INDIVIDUAL VOLUNTARY ARRANGEMENTS

[Not reproduced – see amendments to Part VIII of IA 1986.]

Schedule 4

Minor and consequential amendments about disqualification of company directors etc.

Schedule 5

Repeals

COMPANY DIRECTORS DISQUALIFICATION ACT 1986

[Not reproduced in this edition.]

The EC Regulation on Insolvency Proceedings 2000

General comment to the Regulation

The EC Regulation on Insolvency Proceedings ("the Regulation") was adopted by the Council of the European Union on May 29, 2000. Being a Regulation (as distinct from a Convention or Directive), it had force throughout the EU (apart from Denmark, which has exercised its right to an opt-out) immediately upon its enactment, without the need for ratification or implementation by domestic legislation in the Member States. (References to the EU hereafter should not normally be taken as including Denmark.) The Regulation became operative on May 31, 2002. On the same date, a number of statutory instruments were brought into force, amending the existing insolvency legislation, Rules and prescribed forms in order to facilitate the integration of the Regulation with our own law and practice. (These changes, at least so far as concerns England and Wales, have been noted at the appropriate places in this *Guide*. To the extent that insolvency is a devolved matter, it falls to the devolved administrations to make corresponding amendments.)

The Regulation introduces an ordered regime governing the administration of the affairs of an insolvent which extend into more than one Member State of the EU. It makes major advances in such areas as ensuring the recognition without further formality throughout the Community of a court order in bankruptcy or an order or resolution for winding up, and defining the respective roles of the office-holders where more than one set of insolvency proceedings involving the same debtor have been instituted in different Member States.

The Regulation had a long and chequered history, having begun life initially in the 1960s as part of the proposals for reciprocal recognition and enforcement of foreign judgments which eventually became the Brussels Convention. But the two projects were severed at an early stage and the Draft Bankruptcy Convention (as it was then known) ran into considerable opposition, partly because its aims were over-ambitious and partly because it was over-complex and ineptly drafted. The project was quietly dropped in the 1980s. Meantime, a new initiative got under way under the aegis of the Council of Europe, which began with rather modest aims but as discussions progressed became more comprehensive and elaborate. In 1990 a final text was agreed, and the Convention was opened for signature in Istanbul in June of that year. The Istanbul Convention, as it is generally known, has been signed by a number of States (not including the UK), but has not attracted enough ratifications to come into force. So far as concerns the UK and its relationship with the rest of the EU, it is now a dead letter: art. 44(k) of the EC Regulation provides that the Regulation supersedes the Istanbul Convention in this respect.

The real significance of the Istanbul Convention is that its success in reaching the stage of a final text agreed by all participants acted as a catalyst to get the negotiations for an EC Convention restarted. A fresh working party began to work on a revived project in May 1989, and by November 1995 a finalised text had been agreed and was opened for signature and, in the next few months, signed by all the EU Member States except the UK. Regrettably, the UK failed to do so (in the wake of the "beef ban") and the entire project ran out of time and the draft convention lapsed. However, all was not lost because the text, in virtually identical form, was revived (but in the form of a Regulation, and not a Convention) and following a joint initiative by Germany and Finland in 1999 was duly adopted by the Council of Ministers in the following May.

As noted above, the Regulation has effect as primary legislation in its own right, and thus automatically repeals any existing legislation and supersedes any rule of law that is inconsistent with its provisions. The main area where this is likely to be seen is in relation to the wide jurisdiction which our courts have traditionally asserted over foreign nationals and companies to make bankruptcy and winding-up orders: from now on, in any case where the "centre of main interests" of the individual or company concerned is in another Member State, this jurisdiction will be curtailed. In contrast, in some respects our courts are given wider powers under the Regulation than they have under the domestic legislation, *e.g.* to make administration orders in respect of foreign companies and other bodies which have their centre of main interests within the UK: see the note to art. 3.

For the purposes of the Regulation, the UK is regarded as one jurisdiction, and includes Gibraltar. It applies only where the debtor's "centre of main interests" is situated in a Member State (other than Denmark). If the debtor is primarily based outside the EU, matters will continue to be governed by the existing domestic law, even as regards issues arising between EU jurisdictions inter se. And the Regulation has nothing to say about assets or creditors based outside the EU, or insolvency proceedings that have been instituted in a non-EU jurisdiction, even in a case where the debtor's centre of main interests is in a Member State. And, of course, it applies only where the individual or company concerned is insolvent.

While the Regulation aims for a substantial degree of "universality" (*i.e.* the recognition throughout the Community of proceedings that have been instituted in any Member State), it does not attempt to achieve "unity" (*i.e.* a regime which gives a single insolvency administration the sole and exclusive management of all the insolvent estate for the benefit of all the insolvent's creditors, in whatever parts of the EU it may be situated). The Regulation envisages a hierarchy of judicial competence, having one (and only one) "main" proceeding in one Member State (where the debtor's "centre of main interests" is located), with the possibility of there being any number of "secondary" or "territorial" proceedings in any other jurisdictions where there are assets. (The term "territorial proceedings" refers to ancillary proceedings instituted *before* main proceedings have been opened, and "secondary proceedings" to those instituted subsequently.) A creditor based anywhere in the EU is free to prove in the main proceedings and also in any secondary proceedings (subject to safeguards to avoid his getting more than his share), and the proceedings in each State and the authority of its office-holder are to be automatically recognised with no special formalities throughout the Community. Recognition of the competence of main proceedings brings about a moratorium on the enforcement of claims applicable in all Member States, and there is provision for communication and co-operation between the office-holders in related insolvency proceedings. In principle, assets situated outside the jurisdiction of main proceedings can be removed from there to form part of the main estate; however, there is provision for a certain degree of ring-fencing so that the claims of local creditors, and particularly those entitled to preferential treatment, can be satisfied before anything is remitted to the main jurisdiction.

The Regulation does not seek to harmonise the substantive insolvency laws of the various Member States: by and large, it enshrines the general principle that the applicable law shall be that of the State in which the particular insolvency proceedings (whether main, secondary or territorial) are being conducted. However, it does deal with certain questions in the conflict of laws, declaring that a different law shall be applicable law in specified cases (so that, for instance, set-off shall be allowed even though it is not recognised by the law of the proceedings). This is likely to reduce the occasions on which difficult issues of jurisdiction may arise in an insolvency context – as happened, for instance, in *Re Hayward* [1997] Ch. 45 and *Pollard v Ashurst* [2001] B.P.I.R. 131: see the note to IA 1986, s. 314.

The Regulation applies to both individual and corporate insolvencies. (But it should be noted that it does not apply to *solvent* liquidations: cross-border issues in these proceedings are governed by the Brussels Convention.) In its scope it is capable of including reorganisation and rehabilitation measures as well as bankruptcies and liquidations (although not in secondary proceedings). It includes creditors' voluntary liquidations (after formal confirmation by the court), but not any form of receivership. Although neither insolvent partnerships nor the estates of persons dying insolvent are specified as being within the Regulation, this has been assumed to be the case in the accompanying subordinate legislation. No special provision is made for corporate groups.

There is a specific exclusion of insolvency proceedings concerning insurance undertakings, banks and other credit institutions, and collective and other investment undertakings, since these have – or are to have – their own special legislative or regulatory regimes.

The Regulation has its own special vocabulary, which calls for some mental adjustment by an English reader. In particular, it may be necessary to issue a warning in relation to terms such as "liquidator" (a word used to describe the office-holder in any form of insolvency proceeding, even a trustee in bankruptcy), the "opening" of insolvency proceedings (see the note to art. 2(f)), and the terms "judgment" and "court", which by a mind-boggling feat are stretched so as to include the passing of a resolution for voluntary winding up by the shareholders at a general meeting!

One aspect of the Regulation which may be open to criticism is an underlying assumption that the debtor is (and continues to be) in business of some kind and that it is a creditor who will be the initiator of the insolvency proceedings. This can be seen, for instance, in art. 3(2), where secondary proceedings can be opened only in a Member State if the debtor "*possesses* an establishment" within that State (present tense); in art. 2(h), defining "establishment" as a "place of operations where the debtor *carries on* a non-transitory *economic* activity with human means and goods"; and in art. 3(4)(b), which restricts the right to open "territorial" proceedings to a creditor whose debt arises from the operation of that establishment. A non-trading individual (or a former trader who had ceased to carry on business) with an outstanding tax debt who wished to petition for his own bankruptcy in secondary or territorial proceedings could well have difficulty in surmounting the various hurdles imposed by these definitions.

Mention should also be made of the "Virgos-Schmit Report" (July 8, 1996), a commentary on the text of the Convention which preceded the Regulation. Although this report does not refer directly to the Regulation and has never been officially adopted, it contains useful background material and has already been referred to in some judgments in this country. The text is conveniently reproduced as an Appendix in Moss, Fletcher and Isaacs, *The EC Regulation on Insolvency Proceedings* (2002).

The statutory instruments enacted to make the legislation and Rules compatible with the Regulation are as follows. All except the first came into force on May 31, 2002. Attention is drawn also to the Insolvency Service's Guidance Note, referred to in the General note to arts 39–42 below.

The Insolvency Act 1986 (Amendment) Regulations 2002 (SI 2002/1037, effective May 3, 2002)

The Insolvency Act 1986 (Amendment) (No. 2) Regulations 2002 (SI 2002/1240)

The Insolvency (Amendment) Rules 2002 (SI 2002/1307)

The Insolvent Partnerships (Amendment) Order 2002 (SI 2002/1308)

The Administration of Insolvent Estates of Deceased Persons Order 2002 (SI 2002/1309)

Council Regulation (EC) No 1346/2000 of 29 May 2000 on Insolvency Proceedings

THE COUNCIL OF THE EUROPEAN UNION,

Having regard to the Treaty establishing the European Community, and in particular Articles 61(c) and 67(1) thereof,

Having regard to the initiative of the Federal Republic of Germany and the Republic of Finland,

Having regard to the opinion of the European Parliament,

Having regard to the opinion of the Economic and Social Committee,

Whereas:

(1)   The European Union has set out the aim of establishing an area of freedom, security and justice.

(2)   The proper functioning of the internal market requires that cross-border insolvency proceedings should operate efficiently and effectively and this Regulation needs to be adopted in order to achieve this objective which comes within the scope of judicial cooperation in civil matters within the meaning of Article 65 of the Treaty.

(3)   The activities of undertakings have more and more cross-border effects and are therefore increasingly being regulated by Community law. While the insolvency of such undertakings also affects the proper functioning of the internal market, there is a need for a Community act requiring coordination of the measures to be taken regarding an insolvent debtor's assets.

(4)   It is necessary for the proper functioning of the internal market to avoid incentives for the parties to transfer assets or judicial proceedings from one Member State to another, seeking to obtain a more favourable legal position (forum shopping).

(5)   These objectives cannot be achieved to a sufficient degree at national level and action at Community level is therefore justified.

(6)   In accordance with the principle of proportionality this Regulation should be confined to provisions governing jurisdiction for opening insolvency proceedings and judgments which are delivered directly on the basis of the insolvency proceedings and are closely connected with such proceedings. In addition, this Regulation should contain provisions regarding the recognition of those judgments and the applicable law which also satisfy that principle.

(7)   Insolvency proceedings relating to the winding-up of insolvent companies or other legal persons, judicial arrangements, compositions and analogous proceedings are excluded from the scope of the 1968 Brussels Convention on Jurisdiction and the Enforcement of Judgments in Civil and Commercial Matters, as amended by the Conventions on Accession to this Convention.

(8)   In order to achieve the aim of improving the efficiency and effectiveness of insolvency proceedings having cross-border effects, it is necessary, and appropriate, that the provisions on jurisdiction, recognition

and applicable law in this area should be contained in a Community law measure which is binding and directly applicable in Member States.

(9) This Regulation should apply to insolvency proceedings, whether the debtor is a natural person or a legal person, a trader or an individual. The insolvency proceedings to which this Regulation applies are listed in the Annexes. Insolvency proceedings concerning insurance undertakings, credit institutions, investment undertakings holding funds or securities for third parties and collective investment undertakings should be excluded from the scope of this Regulation. Such undertakings should not be covered by this Regulation since they are subject to special arrangements and, to some extent, the national supervisory authorities have extremely wide-ranging powers of intervention.

(10) Insolvency proceedings do not necessarily involve the intervention of a judicial authority; the expression "court" in this Regulation should be given a broad meaning and include a person or body empowered by national law to open insolvency proceedings. In order for this Regulation to apply, proceedings (comprising acts and formalities set down in law) should not only have to comply with the provisions of this Regulation, but they should also be officially recognised and legally effective in the Member State in which the insolvency proceedings are opened and should be collective insolvency proceedings which entail the partial or total divestment of the debtor and the appointment of a liquidator.

(11) This Regulation acknowledges the fact that as a result of widely differing substantive laws it is not practical to introduce insolvency proceedings with universal scope in the entire Community. The application without exception of the law of the State of opening of proceedings would, against this background, frequently lead to difficulties. This applies, for example, to the widely differing laws on security interests to be found in the Community. Furthermore, the preferential rights enjoyed by some creditors in the insolvency proceedings are, in some cases, completely different. This Regulation should take account of this in two different ways. On the one hand, provision should be made for special rules on applicable law in the case of particularly significant rights and legal relationships (*e.g.* rights in rem and contracts of employment). On the other hand, national proceedings covering only assets situated in the State of opening should also be allowed alongside main insolvency proceedings with universal scope.

(12) This Regulation enables the main insolvency proceedings to be opened in the Member State where the debtor has the centre of his main interests. These proceedings have universal scope and aim at encompassing all the debtor's assets. To protect the diversity of interests, this Regulation permits secondary proceedings to be opened to run in parallel with the main proceedings. Secondary proceedings may be opened in the Member State where the debtor has an establishment. The effects of secondary proceedings are limited to the assets located in that State. Mandatory rules of coordination with the main proceedings satisfy the need for unity in the Community.

(13) The "centre of main interests" should correspond to the place where the debtor conducts the administration of his interests on a regular basis and is therefore ascertainable by third parties.

(14) This Regulation applies only to proceedings where the centre of the debtor's main interests is located in the Community.

(15) The rules of jurisdiction set out in this Regulation establish only international jurisdiction, that is to say, they designate the Member State the courts of which may open insolvency proceedings. Territorial jurisdiction within that Member State must be established by the national law of the Member State concerned.

(16) The court having jurisdiction to open the main insolvency proceedings should be enabled to order provisional and protective measures from the time of the request to open proceedings. Preservation measures both prior to and after the commencement of the insolvency proceedings are very important to guarantee the effectiveness of the insolvency proceedings. In that connection this Regulation should afford different possibilities. On the one hand, the court competent for the main insolvency proceedings should be able also to order provisional protective measures covering assets situated in the territory of other Member States. On the other hand, a liquidator temporarily appointed prior to the opening of the main insolvency

proceedings should be able, in the Member States in which an establishment belonging to the debtor is to be found, to apply for the preservation measures which are possible under the law of those States.

(17) Prior to the opening of the main insolvency proceedings, the right to request the opening of insolvency proceedings in the Member State where the debtor has an establishment should be limited to local creditors and creditors of the local establishment or to cases where main proceedings cannot be opened under the law of the Member State where the debtor has the centre of his main interest. The reason for this restriction is that cases where territorial insolvency proceedings are requested before the main insolvency proceedings are intended to be limited to what is absolutely necessary. If the main insolvency proceedings are opened, the territorial proceedings become secondary.

(18) Following the opening of the main insolvency proceedings, the right to request the opening of insolvency proceedings in a Member State where the debtor has an establishment is not restricted by this Regulation. The liquidator in the main proceedings or any other person empowered under the national law of that Member State may request the opening of secondary insolvency proceedings.

(19) Secondary insolvency proceedings may serve different purposes, besides the protection of local interests. Cases may arise where the estate of the debtor is too complex to administer as a unit or where differences in the legal systems concerned are so great that difficulties may arise from the extension of effects deriving from the law of the State of the opening to the other States where the assets are located. For this reason the liquidator in the main proceedings may request the opening of secondary proceedings when the efficient administration of the estate so requires.

(20) Main insolvency proceedings and secondary proceedings can, however, contribute to the effective realisation of the total assets only if all the concurrent proceedings pending are coordinated. The main condition here is that the various liquidators must cooperate closely, in particular by exchanging a sufficient amount of information. In order to ensure the dominant role of the main insolvency proceedings, the liquidator in such proceedings should be given several possibilities for intervening in secondary insolvency proceedings which are pending at the same time. For example, he should be able to propose a restructuring plan or composition or apply for realisation of the assets in the secondary insolvency proceedings to be suspended.

(21) Every creditor, who has his habitual residence, domicile or registered office in the Community, should have the right to lodge his claims in each of the insolvency proceedings pending in the Community relating to the debtor's assets. This should also apply to tax authorities and social insurance institutions. However, in order to ensure equal treatment of creditors, the distribution of proceeds must be coordinated. Every creditor should be able to keep what he has received in the course of insolvency proceedings but should be entitled only to participate in the distribution of total assets in other proceedings if creditors with the same standing have obtained the same proportion of their claims.

(22) This Regulation should provide for immediate recognition of judgments concerning the opening, conduct and closure of insolvency proceedings which come within its scope and of judgments handed down in direct connection with such insolvency proceedings. Automatic recognition should therefore mean that the effects attributed to the proceedings by the law of the State in which the proceedings were opened extend to all other Member States. Recognition of judgments delivered by the courts of the Member States should be based on the principle of mutual trust. To that end, grounds for non-recognition should be reduced to the minimum necessary. This is also the basis on which any dispute should be resolved where the courts of two Member States both claim competence to open the main insolvency proceedings. The decision of the first court to open proceedings should be recognised in the other Member States without those Member States having the power to scrutinise the court's decision.

(23) This Regulation should set out, for the matters covered by it, uniform rules on conflict of laws which replace, within their scope of application, national rules of private international law. Unless otherwise stated, the law of the Member State of the opening of the proceedings should be applicable (lex concursus). This rule on conflict of laws should be valid both for the main proceedings and for local proceedings; the lex

concursus determines all the effects of the insolvency proceedings, both procedural and substantive, on the persons and legal relations concerned. It governs all the conditions for the opening, conduct and closure of the insolvency proceedings.

(24) Automatic recognition of insolvency proceedings to which the law of the opening State normally applies may interfere with the rules under which transactions are carried out in other Member States. To protect legitimate expectations and the certainty of transactions in Member States other than that in which proceedings are opened, provisions should be made for a number of exceptions to the general rule.

(25) There is a particular need for a special reference diverging from the law of the opening State in the case of rights in rem, since these are of considerable importance for the granting of credit. The basis, validity and extent of such a right in rem should therefore normally be determined according to the lex situs and not be affected by the opening of insolvency proceedings. The proprietor of the right in rem should therefore be able to continue to assert his right to segregation or separate settlement of the collateral security. Where assets are subject to rights in rem under the lex situs in one Member State but the main proceedings are being carried out in another Member State, the liquidator in the main proceedings should be able to request the opening of secondary proceedings in the jurisdiction where the rights in rem arise if the debtor has an establishment there. If a secondary proceeding is not opened, the surplus on sale of the asset covered by rights in rem must be paid to the liquidator in the main proceedings.

(26) If a set-off is not permitted under the law of the opening State, a creditor should nevertheless be entitled to the set-off if it is possible under the law applicable to the claim of the insolvent debtor. In this way, set-off will acquire a kind of guarantee function based on legal provisions on which the creditor concerned can rely at the time when the claim arises.

(27) There is also a need for special protection in the case of payment systems and financial markets. This applies for example to the position-closing agreements and netting agreements to be found in such systems as well as to the sale of securities and to the guarantees provided for such transactions as governed in particular by Directive 98/26/EC of the European Parliament and of the Council of 19 May 1998 on settlement finality in payment and securities settlement systems. For such transactions, the only law which is material should thus be that applicable to the system or market concerned. This provision is intended to prevent the possibility of mechanisms for the payment and settlement of transactions provided for in the payment and set-off systems or on the regulated financial markets of the Member States being altered in the case of insolvency of a business partner. Directive 98/26/EC contains special provisions which should take precedence over the general rules in this Regulation.

(28) In order to protect employees and jobs, the effects of insolvency proceedings on the continuation or termination of employment and on the rights and obligations of all parties to such employment must be determined by the law applicable to the agreement in accordance with the general rules on conflict of law. Any other insolvency-law questions, such as whether the employees' claims are protected by preferential rights and what status such preferential rights may have, should be determined by the law of the opening State.

(29) For business considerations, the main content of the decision opening the proceedings should be published in the other Member States at the request of the liquidator. If there is an establishment in the Member State concerned, there may be a requirement that publication is compulsory. In neither case, however, should publication be a prior condition for recognition of the foreign proceedings.

(30) It may be the case that some of the persons concerned are not in fact aware that proceedings have been opened and act in good faith in a way that conflicts with the new situation. In order to protect such persons who make a payment to the debtor because they are unaware that foreign proceedings have been opened when they should in fact have made the payment to the foreign liquidator, it should be provided that such a payment is to have a debt-discharging effect.

(31) This Regulation should include Annexes relating to the organisation of insolvency proceedings. As these Annexes relate exclusively to the legislation of Member States, there are specific and substantiated

reasons for the Council to reserve the right to amend these Annexes in order to take account of any amendments to the domestic law of the Member States.

(32) The United Kingdom and Ireland, in accordance with Article 3 of the Protocol on the position of the United Kingdom and Ireland annexed to the Treaty on European Union and the Treaty establishing the European Community, have given notice of their wish to take part in the adoption and application of this Regulation.

(33) Denmark, in accordance with Articles 1 and 2 of the Protocol on the position of Denmark annexed to the Treaty on European Union and the Treaty establishing the European Community, is not participating in the adoption of this Regulation, and is therefore not bound by it nor subject to its application,

HAS ADOPTED THIS REGULATION:

GENERAL NOTE

This lengthy preamble (typical of many pieces of EC legislation) gives rise to a number of problems, some of which are discussed by Professor Rajak in [2000] C.F.I.L.R. 180. It has been accepted by the European Court of Justice that a preamble may be referred to where the text in the body of a Regulation is unclear or imprecise (*Schweizerische Lactina Panchaud AG (Bundesamt für Ernährung und Forstwirtschaft) v Germany* (No. 346/88) [1991] 2 C.M.L.R. 283), and this approach reflects that of our own courts to recitals and similar "background" statements. But this preamble, like many of its kind, goes much further: in some parts, it does simply set out the background, context and aims of the Regulation; in others, it does no more than duplicate substantive provisions in the various articles of the substantive text; and in yet others (*e.g.* para. 15) it goes out of its way to exhort Member States to take supporting action at a domestic level. However, there are other paragraphs which plainly have legislative effect (*e.g.* para. 14: "This Regulation applies only to proceedings where the centre of the debtor's main interests is located in the Community"); and also many passages (characterised by the word "should") where it is unclear whether the intention is to go beyond the normal function of a preamble and actually to formulate substantive rules which one would expect to find in the body of the legislation itself. So, *e.g.* para. 9 states that the Regulation "should apply" to insolvency proceedings, "whether the debtor is a natural person or a legal person, a trader or an individual", without any corresponding provision in the articles which follow; and the definition of a debtor's "centre of main interests" is largely set out in para. 13 ("the 'centre of main interests' should correspond to the place where the debtor conducts the administration of his interests on a regular basis and is therefore ascertainable by third parties"), but is not repeated where one would expect to find it, in Art. 3(1).

Paras 6, 7

Insolvency matters are excluded from the scope of the Brussels Convention. (But not winding-up proceedings as such; thus, matters arising in a members' voluntary winding up are within the Convention: *Re Cover Europe Ltd* [2002] 2 B.C.L.C. 61.) However, that Convention is declared to apply to certain judgments handed down by a court in the course or "closure" of insolvency proceedings, and compositions approved by a court in such a context, by Art. 25 of the present Regulation: see the note to Art. 25, below.

"Judgment", for the purposes of the Regulation, has an extended meaning: see the note to Art. 2(e).

Para. 9

There is no counterpart to the first sentence of this paragraph in the body of the Regulation. This is of no significance so far as concerns debtors based in the UK, since our domestic legislation covers all the categories that are mentioned; but it could be material in some civil-law jurisdictions where traditionally bankruptcy has not been available to non-trading individuals.

Although it would appear both from the second sentence of this paragraph and from Art. 2(a) that the application of the Regulation is confined to those forms of proceedings listed in the Annexes, we must infer that this is not so, for this would exclude the winding up, etc. of insolvent partnerships and the administration of the estates of persons dying insolvent – each of which comes within the general rubric laid down by Art. 1, and which has been the subject of specific supporting legislation (see the Insolvent Partnerships (Amendment) Order 2002 (SI 2002/1308) and the Administration of Insolvent Estates of Deceased Persons (Amendment) Order 2002 (SI 2002/1309), both effective 31 May 2002).

The exclusion of insurance undertakings, etc. is confirmed by Art. 1(2). These bodies have their own special legislative or regulatory regimes and are the subject of separate EC Directives and domestic legislation: see EC Directives 2001/17 (insurance undertakings) and 2001/24 (credit institutions). The former has been implemented by the Insurance (Reorganisation and Winding up) Regulations 2004 (SI 2004/353, replacing SI 2003/1102, effective

February 18, 2004). The latter has been implemented by the Credit Institutions (Reorganisation and Winding up) Regulations 2004 (SI 2004/1045), effective May 5, 2004. The broad effect of the 2003 Insurance Regulations is that a UK court will not be able to make an administration or winding-up order or appoint a provisional liquidator to an insurance undertaking which is authorised in another EEA Member State, and such an insurer cannot enter into a voluntary arrangement under UK law. In the winding up of UK insurance undertakings, priority is now given to insurance claims over other debts. However, the focus of the relevant directive is primarily on direct insurance, rather than reinsurance, and the 2003 Regulations do not apply to undertakings engaged purely in reinsurance (or to Lloyds).

Para. 10
See the note to Art. 2(d) and (e): the terms "court" and "judgment" are given extended definitions so as to extend to (*e.g.*) a shareholders' meeting and the passing at such a meeting of a resolution for voluntary winding up.

Para. 11
As is explained in the introductory note on p. 602, the Regulation does not aim to harmonise the substantive insolvency laws of the Member States or to achieve an insolvency regime on the principle of "unity", in which there would be only one proceeding in which the whole of the debtor's assets situated in all the Member States would be administered for the benefit of all the creditors in the Community. Instead, its principal focus is on establishing an ordered system of administration which allows for separate proceedings to be instituted in several Member States concurrently, with appropriate provisions for mutual recognition, co-operation and co-ordination designed to ensure that they do not compete with one another. Each of the separate proceedings is primarily to be governed by its national law (Art. 4), but this is subject to certain overriding rules dealing with security interests, contracts of employment, etc. (Arts 5–15). In addition, the Regulation allows each separate jurisdiction a degree of ring-fencing, so that (for instance) the rights of creditors or particular classes of creditor in that jurisdiction are respected.

Paras 12, 13
On "main" and "secondary" proceedings, see the note to Art. 3, and for the definition of "establishment", Art. 2(h). There is no definition of a debtor's "centre of main interests" in the body of the Regulation (apart from the presumptive rule that, in the case of a company or legal person, this is to be the place of its registered office: Art. 3(1)); and so we must assume that para. 13 applies. The concluding words indicate that this is to be determined objectively. See further the note to Art. 3(1).

Para. 14
The entire focus is on the debtor's centre of main interests. There is no reference to the nationality, domicile, residence or physical presence of an individual debtor or to the place of incorporation of a company (except that this is likely to be linked with the presumption in Art. 3(1)). It is plain from this statement that the Regulation does not apply to a debtor whose centre of main interests is outside the EU: in that event, the courts of the UK may continue to assert their traditional wide jurisdiction (see the notes to IA 1986, ss. 220 and 265); and in such a case the Regulation will not apply even where there are contemporaneous insolvency proceedings in more than one Member State. On the other hand, if the centre of main interests is within the UK, the Regulation applies even where the debtor is a national of a non-EU country or a company incorporated in such a country (see *Re BRAC Rent-a-Car International Inc* [2003] EWHC (Ch) 128; [2003] B.C.C. 249, discussed in the note to Art. 3 below); while if the centre of main interests is in another Member State, any proceedings instituted in the UK can only be "territorial" or "secondary" proceedings and the jurisdiction will be limited as prescribed by Art. 3(2)–(4).

Where the debtor has interests in more than one Member State and there is doubt or a dispute as to which is the centre of main interests, para. 22 of the Preamble indicates that this should be settled on a "first seised" basis.

Para. 15
Once it is settled that the courts of a Member State have jurisdiction under the Regulation, it is still necessary to satisfy the requirements of the national law.

Para. 16
This paragraph contemplates the making of "provisional and protective measures" in rather convoluted language, which is fortunately clarified by the substantive provision in Art. 38. See the note to that Article.

Para. 17
This refers forward to the remarkably restrictive conditions laid down for the opening of insolvency proceedings, other than main proceedings, by Art. 3(2)–(4): see the note to that Article.

Paras 18, 19
These paragraphs, confirmed by Art. 29, are intended to ensure that the office-holder in "main" proceedings may himself institute secondary proceedings in any other Member State where the debtor has assets.

Article 1   *EC Regulation on Insolvency Proceedings 2000*

Para. 20
Where there are several insolvency proceedings, the office-holders are urged to co-operate, but with the proviso that whoever has charge of the main proceedings has the whip-hand. Articles 31 and 33–34 give effect to these aims.

Para. 21
See the notes to Arts 20, 32 and 39, which contain the corresponding substantive provisions.

Para. 22
The automatic recognition throughout the Community of the orders and judgments of the courts of a Member State and of the authority of the office-holder in any insolvency proceedings is one of the central principles of the Regulation. Articles 16–17, 19 and 25 carry this objective into effect.

Paras 23–28
The rules relating to the applicable law in insolvency proceedings which have a cross-border dimension within the Community are set out in Arts 4ff. The basic rule is that the law of the State under which the proceedings have been instituted is prima facie to be applied, presumably including its own conflict of laws rules (Art. 4); but Arts 5–15 contain a uniform set of rules prescribing exceptions to this general rule. A security interest (such as a mortgage), for instance, over an asset situated in another Member State is to be governed by the law of that State rather than that of the proceedings; and a debtor who is entitled to a right of set-off under the law applicable to his claim may assert that right even where such a right is not recognised by the law governing the insolvency proceedings. For more detailed comments, see the notes to Arts 5–15.

Paras 29–30
Articles 21–24 give substantive effect to requirements regarding publicity and notice contained in these paragraphs.

Paras 32–33
The UK and Ireland have opted in to the Regulation, but Denmark has opted out, at least for the time being.

Chapter I – General Provisions

Article 1

[Scope]

1(1) [Application] This Regulation shall apply to collective insolvency proceedings which entail the partial or total divestment of a debtor and the appointment of a liquidator.

1(2) [Non-application] This Regulation shall not apply to insolvency proceedings concerning insurance undertakings, credit institutions, investment undertakings which provide services involving the holding of funds or securities for third parties, or to collective investment undertakings.

General Note

The scope of the Regulation is defined by this article, as amplified by Art. 2 and Annex A. So far as concerns UK insolvency procedures, it is clear that all forms of receivership are excluded, since receivership is not a "collective" procedure administered for the benefit of all concerned, or even all creditors. There might have been some doubt whether administration and voluntary arrangements were included (since neither involves the "divestment" of the debtor, except in the sense that the debtor loses some control of his assets), but for the fact that they are listed in Annex A. The use of the word "shall" in Art. 2(a) might suggest that the list in Annex A is definitive, but that it is not appears to be confirmed by the fact that statutory instruments supplementing the Regulation have been made in relation to insolvent partnerships and the insolvent estates of deceased persons (see the note to the Preamble, para. 9).

Winding up subject to the supervision of the court has, of course, been abolished in the UK.

The Regulation throughout makes the fundamental assumption that its application is confined to "insolvency" proceedings; but there is nowhere any definition of "insolvency" or an equivalent term, and no guidance given as to how it is to be determined whether a debtor is insolvent. The area in which this issue may arise is where a company has been ordered to be wound up by the court on the "just and equitable" ground under IA 1986, s. 122(1)(g). However, if the petition is brought on public interest grounds under IA 1986, s. 124A (or a corresponding provision in other legislation), the Regulation does not apply, even if the company concerned is insolvent: *Re Marann Brooks CSV Ltd* [2003] B.C.C. 239.

The term "liquidator" is used in a wide sense, to include the insolvency practitioner who administers any of the forms of insolvency proceedings covered by the Regulation: see the note to Art. 2(b).

On the exclusion of the bodies listed in Art. 1(2), see the note to the Preamble, para. 9.

Article 2

[Definitions]

2   For the purposes of this Regulation:

(a)   "insolvency proceedings" shall mean the collective proceedings referred to in Article 1(1). These proceedings are listed in Annex A;

(b)   "liquidator" shall mean any person or body whose function is to administer or liquidate assets of which the debtor has been divested or to supervise the administration of his affairs. Those persons and bodies are listed in Annex C;

(c)   "winding-up proceedings" shall mean insolvency proceedings within the meaning of point (a) involving realising the assets of the debtor, including where the proceedings have been closed by a composition or other measure terminating the insolvency, or closed by reason of the insufficiency of the assets. Those proceedings are listed in Annex B;

(d)   "court" shall mean the judicial body or any other competent body of a Member State empowered to open insolvency proceedings or to take decisions in the course of such proceedings;

(e)   "judgment" in relation to the opening of insolvency proceedings or the appointment of a liquidator shall include the decision of any court empowered to open such proceedings or to appoint a liquidator;

(f)   "the time of the opening of proceedings" shall mean the time at which the judgment opening proceedings becomes effective, whether it is a final judgment or not;

(g)   "the Member State in which assets are situated" shall mean, in the case of:

– tangible property, the Member State within the territory of which the property is situated,
– property and rights ownership of or entitlement to which must be entered in a public register, the Member State under the authority of which the register is kept,
– claims, the Member State within the territory of which the third party required to meet them has the centre of his main interests, as determined in Article 3(1);

(h)   "establishment" shall mean any place of operations where the debtor carries out a non-transitory economic activity with human means and goods.

GENERAL NOTE

This Article contains the definitions of most of the terms that are used in a technical sense in the Regulation. Note also, however, the meaning given to the phrase "the debtor's centre of main interests" by the Preamble, para. 13.

Art. 2(a)
See the notes to the Preamble, para. 9 and Art. 1(1).

Art. 2(b)
The term "liquidator" is used in a wide sense, to include the insolvency practitioner who administers any of the forms of insolvency proceedings covered by the Regulation.

As noted in the comment to Art. 1(1), the list of persons and bodies set out in Annex C cannot be considered exhaustive, in the light of the provision made by domestic legislation for insolvent partnerships and the insolvent estates of deceased persons.

Art. 2(c)

The comments made above apply also to this definition. Some mental effort will be required to accept that the term "liquidator" extends to a trustee in bankruptcy! What is clearly intended is the exclusion of any form of rehabilitation or rescue proceedings, *e.g.* an administration, IVA or CVA.

Art. 2(d), (e)

Reference should be made to the Preamble, para. 10, which makes it plain that the expression "court" is to be given a broad meaning, reflecting the fact that insolvency proceedings do not necessarily involve the intervention of a judicial authority, and is to include "a person or body empowered by national law to open insolvency proceedings". Accordingly, a creditors' voluntary winding up is within the Regulation, and in that context "court" means the members in general meeting (for it is that body, and not the meeting of creditors, whose resolution is determinative); and "judgment" must be read as meaning the resolution.

Articles 16(1) and 19 declare that a "judgment opening insolvency proceedings" and a "liquidator's appointment" shall be accorded recognition without further formality in all other Member States. Article 16(1) unhelpfully refers to such a judgment being "handed down by a court"; but any difficulty that this phrase might create is met by the requirement in Annexes A and B that a creditors' voluntary winding up should be confirmed by the court (plainly, "court" is here to be understood in its normal sense). Provision is made for such confirmation by IR 1986, r. 7.62. But the court's confirmation serves only an evidentiary purpose; it is the members' resolution that is the "judgment opening the insolvency proceedings".

On similar reasoning, the body which is to be taken as the "court" for the purposes of a CVA or IVA is the creditor's meeting: see IA 1986, ss. 5(2)(a) and 260(2)(a), and the resolution as the "judgment": see *R v The Salvage Association* [2003] EWHL 1028 (Ch); [2003] B.C.C. 504, at 19 *et seq*. There is no mention in the Regulation of any need to have such a resolution confirmed by the court: presumably it is assumed that since the outcome of the creditors' meeting will have been reported to the court, it will be possible for a certificate sufficient to meet the purposes of the Regulation to be issued by the court without the formality of confirmation. It would have been helpful if some provision dealing with this point had been included in the Rules.

Similar comments apply to administration, where a company is put into administration by the holder of a floating charge or the company or its directors without a court order under IA 1986, Sch. B1, paras 14 or 22. The "court" will be the person or persons making the appointment, and the "judgment" will be the filing of the notice of appointment under paras 18 or 29, as the case may be: this will also determine the time of the opening of the insolvency proceedings (paras 19, 31). Again, there is no reference in the legislation to any need for confirmation by the court. Some disquiet has been expressed at the lack of clear legislative guidance on these points and in consequence it has been suggested that, in order to avoid uncertainty and misunderstanding in other EC jurisdictions (and *a fortiori* in foreign jurisdictions not covered by the Regulation), it may be prudent to have the administrator appointed by the court rather than under para.14 or 22.

Art. 2(f)

This definition throws light on the meaning of the expression "the opening of proceedings", which could well be a source of confusion. It is to be taken as referring to whatever step in the proceedings marks the effective beginning of the particular insolvency regime: liquidation, bankruptcy, administration, etc. It is not to be confused with any earlier act, such as the filing in court of a petition for winding up or a bankruptcy or administration order, or with the "commencement" of a winding up as defined by IA 1986, ss. 86, 129. It follows that the event which counts will be the court order or, in the case of a voluntary winding up, CVA or IVA, the resolution of the appropriate body. In an administration where the appointment is made out of court, it will be the time of the filing of the notice of appointment under IA 1986, Sch. B1, paras 18 or 29, as noted above. The one exceptional case would appear to be the insolvent estate of a deceased person, where the court's order is related back to the date of death (Administration of Insolvent Estates of Deceased Persons Order 1986, Sch. 1, Pt II, para. 12).

There may be some significance in the use of the word "time", rather than "date": see the note to IA 1986, s. 86.

Art. 2(g)

Although this paragraph may not cover all possible forms of property (*e.g.* some non-registrable intangibles), it should avoid many conflict of laws questions that might otherwise arise.

Art. 2(h)

This term is of paramount importance where it is sought to open insolvency proceedings in a Member State other than that in which the debtor has his centre of main interests (see Art. 3(2)–(4)). It is probably not necessary to give too literal a meaning to the word "goods": it is frequently used in EC documents in the more general sense of "assets". What is more surprising, and likely to prove an unwelcome limitation, is the stress placed on an *economic* activity carried on by the debtor. This could well create an obstacle to the opening of territorial or secondary insolvency proceedings in the case of a non-trader or a retired person who may have both assets and debts, but not his home, in a Member State but does not carry on any form of business there.

Article 3

[International jurisdiction]

3(1) [Main insolvency proceedings] The courts of the Member State within the territory of which the centre of a debtor's main interests is situated shall have jurisdiction to open insolvency proceedings. In the case of a company or legal person, the place of the registered office shall be presumed to be the centre of its main interests in the absence of proof to the contrary.

3(2) [Territorial insolvency proceedings] Where the centre of a debtor's main interests is situated within the territory of a Member State, the courts of another Member State shall have jurisdiction to open insolvency proceedings against that debtor only if he possesses an establishment within the territory of that other Member State. The effects of those proceedings shall be restricted to the assets of the debtor situated in the territory of the latter Member State.

3(3) [Secondary proceedings] Where insolvency proceedings have been opened under paragraph 1, any proceedings opened subsequently under paragraph 2 shall be secondary proceedings. These latter proceedings must be winding-up proceedings.

3(4) [Territorial proceedings prior to main proceedings] Territorial insolvency proceedings referred to in paragraph 2 may be opened prior to the opening of main insolvency proceedings in accordance with paragraph 1 only:

(a) where insolvency proceedings under paragraph 1 cannot be opened because of the conditions laid down by the law of the Member State within the territory of which the centre of the debtor's main interests is situated; or

(b) where the opening of territorial insolvency proceedings is requested by a creditor who has his domicile, habitual residence or registered office in the Member State within the territory of which the establishment is situated, or whose claim arises from the operation of that establishment.

GENERAL NOTE

The Regulation only applies where the centre of the debtor's main interests is located in the EU—although he need not be an EU national: see the Preamble, para. 14. It also applies only where the debtor has assets (and, usually, creditors) in more than one Member State. And it has nothing to say about assets situated outside the EU, or creditors resident or domiciled outside the Community. In any of the situations not covered by the Regulation, a Member State is free to apply its national law.

Article 3(1) deals with the jurisdiction to open "main" proceedings and Art. 3(2)–(4) with the jurisdiction for "secondary" and "territorial" proceedings. Non-main proceedings are "secondary" if they are opened after the opening of main proceedings, and "territorial" if they precede the opening of main proceedings. (But Arts 31–35 dealing with secondary proceedings are made to apply also to territorial proceedings by Art. 36.)

The reference in Art. 3(1) and (2) to "the courts of a Member State" could give rise to difficulties where it is sought to put a company into creditors' voluntary liquidation where the company is incorporated in one State but has its centre of main interests in another. The resolution would have to be passed by the company's shareholders in accordance with the law of the State of incorporation, but even assuming that the meeting was held in the "main" Member State it would call for some ingenuity to construe "the court of that Member State" as meaning that meeting.

Article 27 provides that the fact that main proceedings have been opened is to be taken as conclusive evidence of the debtor's insolvency in any later secondary proceedings.

Art. 3(1)
Apart from the (rebuttable) presumption set out in the second sentence, there is nothing in the substantive parts of the Regulation to help in determining the debtor's "centre of main interests"; but the Preamble, para. 13, does throw some light on the meaning of the phrase. The "centre of main interests", it is stated, "should correspond to the place where the debtor conducts the administration of his interests on a regular basis and is therefore ascertainable by third parties". Unlike the definition of "establishment" in Art. 2(h), there is here no reference to a business or "economic" activity.

The meaning of the term "centre of main interests" has been the subject of judicial consideration in a number of cases. (See the article by R. Henry in Sweet & Maxwell's *Company Law Newsletter*, issue 13/2003, July 31, 2003.) In *Skjevesland v Geveran Trading Co. Ltd* [2002] EWHC 2898 (Ch); [2003] B.C.C. 391; affirming [2003] B.C.C. 209, the debtor was a banker domiciled in Switzerland who had homes in several European countries but had last lived in England over two years ago. He divided his time for business purposes between Switzerland and Spain and, although he spent more time in Spain, about 90 per cent of his economic activities were carried out in Switzerland. It was held that his centre of main interests was in Switzerland. The judge referred to the Virgos-Schmit Report (EC Council document 6500/DRS 8 (CFC)), a commentary on the draft EC Bankruptcy Convention (the forerunner of the EC Regulation), where the importance was emphasised of jurisdiction in international insolvency matters being based "on a place known to the debtor's potential creditors". The finding that the centre of main interests was in Switzerland (and accordingly not within the EU) meant that the Regulation did not apply. A bankruptcy order could therefore be made under IA 1986, s. 265(1)(c), based on his residence here within the past three years. In *Re Daisytek-ISA Ltd* [2003] B.C.C. 562 administration orders were made in respect of the English subsidiary of a US parent company (Daisytek) and its own subsidiaries incorporated respectively in England, Germany and France. Although the foreign subsidiaries had their registered offices and conducted their business abroad, they were managed to a large extent from Daisytek's head office in Bradford. In ruling that all of the European subsidiaries had their centre of main interests in England, the court had regard to various factors: the location of banking activities and the keeping of financial records, the degree of independence in making purchases (approval by the parent was required for purchases over €5000), policy in the recruitment of senior employees, the provision of services to customers, control of corporate identity and branding, and responsibility for corporate strategy. The scale and importance of the subsidiaries' interests carried out was greater in the UK than in the subsidiaries' own countries. Again, it was stressed that the most important "third parties" concerned with identifying the centre of main interests were the various companies' potential creditors – their financiers and trade suppliers. The evidence was that a large majority of these would have looked to Bradford in this regard. The case goes some way towards encouraging the view that the Regulation is able to cater for the needs of group insolvencies. (The Court of Appeal of Versailles (September 4, 2003), in a robust judgment, has since endorsed this ruling).

Note that it is not necessary that the debtor should be domiciled (or, if a company, incorporated) within the EU. In *Re BRAC Rent-a-Car International Inc* [2003] EWHC (Ch) 128; [2003] B.C.C. 248 an administration order was made in respect of a company incorporated in Delaware, on the basis of a finding that its centre of main interests was within the UK.

The use of the present tense (*is* situated), if taken literally, would rule out the opening of insolvency proceedings in some cases where this plainly cannot have been intended – *e.g.* an insolvent deceased estate. The courts would surely give a purposive construction to the phrase in such a case (*i.e.* "the place where the debtor formerly had his centre of main interests is situated"). On the other hand, it must be understood literally where the debtor has moved his centre of main interests from one Member State to another: only the latter would have jurisdiction.

On the possibility that more than one Member State may claim the right to open main proceedings, see the note to the Preamble, para. 22.

Art. 3(2)–(3)

The prerequisites for the opening of secondary proceedings in a particular Member State are:

– main proceedings have already been opened in the State where the debtor has his centre of main interests;
– the debtor must possess an establishment within that Member State;
– there must be assets of the debtor situated within that Member State;
– the proceedings must be for winding up (and not rehabilitation or rescue).

Again, the use of the present tense is disturbing, particularly since "possesses" must necessarily refer to the current position (in contrast with "is situated", which in the context of Art. 3(1) is arguably ambiguous). It may well have been intended that if a debtor has ceased to possess an establishment in a particular jurisdiction, everything is to be administered in the main proceedings; but this would prevent any ring-fencing of the local assets for the benefit of local creditors and could cost preferential creditors their priority.

The liquidator in the main proceedings is given considerable powers to intervene in the administration of the secondary proceedings: see Arts 33ff.

Art. 3(4)

Where no main proceedings have been opened in the Member State where the debtor has his centre of main interests, "territorial" proceedings may be opened in another Member State. Unlike secondary proceedings, these need not be winding-up proceedings but could take the form of an administration or a CVA or IVA. But the jurisdiction to open territorial proceedings is restricted not only by Art. 2(2), which requires the debtor to possess an establishment within the jurisdiction and confines the effect of the proceedings to assets situated there, but also more severely by Art. 3(4) to the two situations set out in subpara. (a) and (b). Paragraph (4)(a) presupposes that the "main" Member State cannot exercise jurisdiction but that the "territorial" State can: this might be (*e.g.*) because the debtor is a non-trader or minor or foreign national who cannot be bankrupted under the law of the main State. Paragraph (4)(b) requires the applicant to be a creditor based in the territorial Member State who seeks to have the debtor put into insolvency on the basis of a trading debt incurred by the debtor in running his establishment. This limitation would not only rule out an individual from petitioning for his own bankruptcy in a State other than that of his centre of main interests, but also a resolution for the (creditors') voluntary winding up of a company incorporated here but having its centre of main interests in another Member State, or an administration initiated by such a company or its directors; and it would appear to put obstacles in the way of setting up an IVA or CVA for a debtor who is a British national or UK-registered company with a centre of main interests elsewhere in the Community.

If main proceedings are subsequently opened in the State where the centre of main interests is situated, the liquidator in those proceedings has, by virtue of Art. 36, the extensive powers of intervention set out in Arts 31–35, and also the right conferred by Art. 37 to request that the proceedings be converted into winding-up proceedings if they do not already take that form.

Article 4

[Law applicable]

4(1) ["State of the opening of proceedings"] Save as otherwise provided in this Regulation, the law applicable to insolvency proceedings and their effects shall be that of the Member State within the territory of which such proceedings are opened, hereafter referred to as the "State of the opening of proceedings".

4(2) [Conditions for the opening of proceedings] The law of the State of the opening of proceedings shall determine the conditions for the opening of those proceedings, their conduct and their closure. It shall determine in particular:

(a) against which debtors insolvency proceedings may be brought on account of their capacity;

(b) the assets which form part of the estate and the treatment of assets acquired by or devolving on the debtor after the opening of the insolvency proceedings;

(c) the respective powers of the debtor and the liquidator;

(d) the conditions under which set-offs may be invoked;

(e) the effects of insolvency proceedings on current contracts to which the debtor is party;

(f) the effects of the insolvency proceedings on proceedings brought by individual creditors, with the exception of lawsuits pending;

(g) the claims which are to be lodged against the debtor's estate and the treatment of claims arising after the opening of insolvency proceedings;

(h) the rules governing the lodging, verification and admission of claims;

(i) the rules governing the distribution of proceeds from the realisation of assets, the ranking of claims and the rights of creditors who have obtained partial satisfaction after the opening of insolvency proceedings by virtue of a right in rem or through a set-off;

(j) the conditions for and the effects of closure of insolvency proceedings, in particular by composition;

(k) creditors' rights after the closure of insolvency proceedings;

(l) who is to bear the costs and expenses incurred in the insolvency proceedings;

(m) the rules relating to the voidness, voidability or unenforceability of legal acts detrimental to all the creditors.

Article 5   *EC Regulation on Insolvency Proceedings 2000*

GENERAL NOTE

Article 4 applies to all forms of insolvency proceedings, whether main, secondary or territorial. Subject to Arts 5ff, each jurisdiction is to apply its own laws and rules of procedure. To remove doubt, many of the respects to which this basic principle is to apply are spelt out in detail in para. (2). It follows that, once it is established that the UK has jurisdiction under Art. 3, the rules of law and practice and the powers of the office-holder will be the same as those in a domestic insolvency, and these will apply subject only to any limitations specifically set out elsewhere in the Regulation.

Para. 4(2)(j), (k)

This provision would appear to put it beyond doubt that a discharge in bankruptcy or a composition which is effective under the law of any competent Member State will be recognised throughout the Community as extinguishing all the debts of the insolvent (or at least those comprehended by the composition), wherever incurred, but in territorial or secondary proceedings Art. 17(2) imposes a qualification, empowering creditors who have not consented to the discharge to pursue any assets of the debtor that are situated in another State.

Article 5

[Third parties' rights in rem]

5(1) **[Proceedings not to affect third party rights in rem]** The opening of insolvency proceedings shall not affect the rights in rem of creditors or third parties in respect of tangible or intangible, moveable or immoveable assets – both specific assets and collections of indefinite assets as a whole which change from time to time – belonging to the debtor which are situated within the territory of another Member State at the time of the opening of proceedings.

5(2) **[Rights referred to in art. 5(1)]** The rights referred to in paragraph 1 shall in particular mean:

(a) the right to dispose of assets or have them disposed of and to obtain satisfaction from the proceeds of or income from those assets, in particular by virtue of a lien or a mortgage;

(b) the exclusive right to have a claim met, in particular a right guaranteed by a lien in respect of the claim or by assignment of the claim by way of a guarantee;

(c) the right to demand the assets from, and/or to require restitution by, anyone having possession or use of them contrary to the wishes of the party so entitled;

(d) a right in rem to the beneficial use of assets.

5(3) **[Recorded rights]** The right, recorded in a public register and enforceable against third parties, under which a right in rem within the meaning of paragraph 1 may be obtained, shall be considered a right in rem.

5(4) **[Actions for voidness, voidability or unenforceability not precluded]** Paragraph 1 shall not preclude actions for voidness, voidability or unenforceability as referred to in Article 4(2)(m).

GENERAL NOTE

This is the first of the exceptions to the general rule that the administration of insolvency proceedings (whether main, secondary or territorial) in a particular Member State shall be governed by the law of those proceedings: all rights in rem (including security rights of a proprietary nature) in respect of assets situated outside the territory of that State are to be determined by reference to the law ordinarily applicable to such rights under conflict of laws rules. Lawyers in common-law jurisdictions (and Scotland) will be relieved to see that the security of a floating charge is specifically included.

Article 6

[Set-off]

6(1) **[Proceedings not to affect creditors' set-off rights]** The opening of insolvency proceedings shall not affect the right of creditors to demand the set-off of their claims against the claims of the debtor, where such a set-off is permitted by the law applicable to the insolvent debtor's claim.

6(2) **[Actions for voidness, voidability or unenforceability not precluded]** Paragraph 1 shall not preclude actions for voidness, voidability or unenforceability as referred to in Article 4(2)(m).

GENERAL NOTE

The right of set-off referred to relates to the position between the debtor and a creditor whose claim arises in a jurisdiction other than that of the Member State in which the insolvency proceedings are being administered. This, as regards a claim governed by English law, will not be a right of set-off in insolvency under IA 1986, s. 323 or IR 1986, r. 4.90 but a right arising independently of the insolvency under the rules of common law or equity. See further the note to r. 4.90.

Article 7

[Reservation of title]

7(1) **[Proceedings not to affect seller's title reservation rights]** The opening of insolvency proceedings against the purchaser of an asset shall not affect the seller's rights based on a reservation of title where at the time of the opening of proceedings the asset is situated within the territory of a Member State other than the State of opening of proceedings.

7(2) **[Insufficient grounds for rescission or termination]** The opening of insolvency proceedings against the seller of an asset, after delivery of the asset, shall not constitute grounds for rescinding or terminating the sale and shall not prevent the purchaser from acquiring title where at the time of the opening of proceedings the asset sold is situated within the territory of a Member State other than the State of the opening of proceedings.

[7(3) **Actions for voidness, voidability or unenforceability not precluded]** Paragraphs 1 and 2 shall not preclude actions for voidness, voidability or unenforceability as referred to in Article 4(2)(m).
(See General Note after Art. 15.)

Article 8

[Contracts relating to immoveable property]

8 The effects of insolvency proceedings on a contract conferring the right to acquire or make use of immoveable property shall be governed solely by the law of the Member State within the territory of which the immoveable property is situated.
(See General Note after Art. 15.)

Article 9

[Payment systems and financial markets]

9(1) [Law of Member State applicable] Without prejudice to Article 5, the effects of insolvency proceedings on the rights and obligations of the parties to a payment or settlement system or to a financial market shall be governed solely by the law of the Member State applicable to that system or market.

9(2) [Actions for voidness, voidability or unenforceability not precluded] Paragraph 1 shall not preclude any action for voidness, voidability or unenforceability which may be taken to set aside payments or transactions under the law applicable to the relevant payment system or financial market.
(See General Note after Art. 15.)

Article 10

[Contracts of employment]

10 The effects of insolvency proceedings on employment contracts and relationships shall be governed solely by the law of the Member State applicable to the contract of employment.
(See General Note after Art. 15.)

Article 11

[Effects on rights subject to registration]

11 The effects of insolvency proceedings on the rights of the debtor in immoveable property, a ship or an aircraft subject to registration in a public register shall be determined by the law of the Member State under the authority of which the register is kept.
(See General Note after Art. 15.)

Article 12

[Community patents and trade marks]

12 For the purposes of this Regulation, a Community patent, a Community trade mark or any other similar right established by Community law may be included only in the proceedings referred to in Article 3(1).
(See General Note after Art. 15.)

Article 13

[Detrimental acts]

13 Article 4(2)(m) shall not apply where the person who benefited from an act detrimental to all the creditors provides proof that:

– the said act is subject to the law of a Member State other than that of the State of the opening of proceedings, and
– that law does not allow any means of challenging that act in the relevant case.

(See General Note after Art. 15.)

Article 14

[Protection of third-party purchasers]

14 Where, by an act concluded after the opening of insolvency proceedings, the debtor disposes, for consideration, of:

– an immoveable asset, or

– a ship or an aircraft subject to registration in a public register, or

– securities whose existence presupposes registration in a register laid down by law,

the validity of that act shall be governed by the law of the State within the territory of which the immoveable asset is situated or under the authority of which the register is kept.

(See General Note after Art. 15.)

Article 15

[Effects of insolvency proceedings on lawsuits pending]

15 The effects of insolvency proceedings on a lawsuit pending concerning an asset or a right of which the debtor has been divested shall be governed solely by the law of the Member State in which that lawsuit is pending.

GENERAL NOTE TO ARTS 7–15

Here are set out the remaining situations where the law of the State in which insolvency proceedings have been opened is to give way to the rules of the local law or those of some other jurisdiction.

Art. 9
Provision is made for the disapplication of the rules of insolvency law in payment and settlement systems and transactions on the financial markets by the Finality Directive and by CA 1989, Pt VII, respectively: see the notes on pp. 2–3. This article ensures that a similar disapplication will apply where the insolvency proceedings have been opened in a Member State other than that whose law is applicable to the system or market in question.

Art. 12
The effect of this article is that Community patents and trade marks cannot be dealt with at all in secondary or territorial proceedings, even (in the latter case) where no main proceedings have been opened.

Art. 13
Article 4(2)(m) gives jurisdiction to the State of the opening of the proceedings in the application of "the rules relating to the voidness, voidability or unenforceability of legal acts detrimental to all the creditors" which would include provisions relating to preferences, transactions at an undervalue, etc. Article 13 disapplies this rule where (1) the person who benefited from the transaction in question shows that the proper law would, apart from Art. 4(2)(m), be that of another Member State, and (2) the transaction would not be open to challenge at all under that law. It would follow that the transaction cannot be avoided or held to be void or unenforceable in the court where proceedings have been opened. Where, however, the transaction would be open to challenge under its proper law but the two laws differ in any respect, art. 4(2)(m) will apply.

CHAPTER II – RECOGNITION OF INSOLVENCY PROCEEDINGS

GENERAL NOTE

"Recognition" in this chapter has two aspects: first, recognition of the "judgment" (i.e. the order of a national court or act of any other person or body which has effect as the "opening" of insolvency proceedings); and, secondly, recognition of the authority of the office-holder (the "liquidator") in such proceedings. In each case the validity of the judgment and the liquidator's authority is to be accepted without the need for a court order in the nature of an exequatur or any other formality in the other Member State. All that is needed is a certified copy of the liquidator's appointment (accompanied by a translation, where appropriate). The only additional requirement is that, in the case of a creditors' voluntary winding up, a certificate of confirmation must be obtained from a court in the host country.

Article 16

[Principle]

16(1) **[Judgment pursuant to Art. 3 recognised]** Any judgment opening insolvency proceedings handed down by a court of a Member State which has jurisdiction pursuant to Article 3 shall be recognised in all the other Member States from the time that it becomes effective in the State of the opening of proceedings.

This rule shall also apply where, on account of his capacity, insolvency proceedings cannot be brought against the debtor in other Member States.

16(2) **[Recognition not to preclude secondary proceedings]** Recognition of the proceedings referred to in Article 3(1) shall not preclude the opening of the proceedings referred to in Article 3(2) by a court in another Member State. The latter proceedings shall be secondary insolvency proceedings within the meaning of Chapter III.
(See General Note after Art. 17.)

Article 17

[Effects of recognition]

17(1) **[Judgment opening proceedings where no secondary proceedings]** The judgment opening the proceedings referred to in Article 3(1) shall, with no further formalities, produce the same effects in any other Member State as under this law of the State of the opening of proceedings, unless this Regulation provides otherwise and as long as no proceedings referred to in Article 3(2) are opened in that other Member State.

17(2) **[No challenge to secondary proceedings]** The effects of the proceedings referred to in Article 3(2) may not be challenged in other Member States. Any restriction of the creditors' rights, in particular a stay or discharge, shall produce effects vis-à-vis assets situated within the territory of another Member State only in the case of those creditors who have given their consent.

GENERAL NOTE TO ARTS 16, 17

Article 16 applies to all forms of insolvency proceedings, whether main proceedings under Art. 3(1), or secondary or territorial proceedings under Art. 3(2)–(4). "Court" and "judgment" have the wider meanings given by Art. 2(d), (e), so that (*e.g.*) "judgment" includes a resolution for creditors' voluntary winding up or the appointment of an administrator made out of court: see the notes to that article. A creditors' voluntary winding up requires to be confirmed by the court, following the procedure set out in IR 1986, r. 7.62.

The concluding sentence of Art. 16(1) ensures that an insolvency proceeding opened in a Member State which has jurisdiction will be recognised in another Member State even where the debtor could not be the subject of insolvency proceedings in the latter – *e.g.* if its bankruptcy law does not extend to a debtor who is a minor.

In Art. 17(1) "this law" appears to be an error for "the law". The effect of Art. 17(1) is that once main proceedings have been opened in the State of the debtor's centre of main interests, its insolvency law is to apply automatically throughout the rest of the Community, subject to two exceptions: (i) if territorial proceedings have already been opened, or secondary proceedings are subsequently opened, in another State, the insolvency law of the latter will apply in that State; and (ii) where special provision is made elsewhere in the Regulation (as, *e.g.* under Art. 24), and in particular where Arts 5–15 apply, the law of the insolvency proceedings in question will be displaced. Although Art. 17(2), which applies to territorial and secondary proceedings, also accords general recognition to such proceedings throughout the EU, it adds a caveat which reflects the limitation of the effects such proceedings may have on assets situated in the territory of the State concerned (Art. 3(2)). So, for instance, if territorial proceedings in the UK were to result in a compromise under which every creditor accepted a 50 per cent payment in full satisfaction of his debt, this would not prevent an individual creditor from pursuing a claim for the balance in another Member State where the debtor had assets, unless he had agreed otherwise.

Article 18

[Powers of the liquidator]

18(1) **[Extent of powers]** The liquidator appointed by a court which has jurisdiction pursuant to Article 3(1) may exercise all the powers conferred on him by the law of the State of the opening of proceedings in another Member State, as long as no other insolvency proceedings have been opened there nor any preservation measure to the contrary has been taken there further to a request for the opening of insolvency proceedings in that State. He may in particular remove the debtor's assets from the territory of the Member State in which they are situated, subject to Articles 5 and 7.

18(2) **[Power concerning moveable property]** The liquidator appointed by a court which has jurisdiction pursuant to Article 3(2) may in any other Member State claim through the courts or out of court that moveable property was removed from the territory of the State of the opening of proceedings to the territory of that other Member State after the opening of the insolvency proceedings. He may also bring any action to set aside which is in the interests of the creditors.

18(3) **[Liquidator to comply with local law]** In exercising his powers, the liquidator shall comply with the law of the Member State within the territory of which he intends to take action, in particular with regard to procedures for the realisation of assets. Those powers may not include coercive measures or the right to rule on legal proceedings or disputes.
(See General Note after Art. 19.)

Article 19

[Proof of the liquidator's appointment]

19 The liquidator's appointment shall be evidenced by a certified copy of the original decision appointing him or by any other certificate issued by the court which has jurisdiction.

A translation into the official language or one of the official languages of the Member State within the territory of which he intends to act may be required. No legalisation or other similar formality shall be required.

GENERAL NOTE TO ARTS 18, 19

Article 19 ensures that the authority of an office-holder shall be recognised throughout the Community with the minimum of formality and with no additional requirement in any Member State apart from possibly a translation into the local language.

In main proceedings, the powers of the "liquidator" are extensive and, indeed, are restricted only if territorial or secondary proceedings have been opened in another Member State or if a moratorium or similar interim measure has come into operation there in anticipation of the opening of such proceedings. But whereas the liquidator in main proceedings has a general power to gather up assets that are situated in other States (Art. 18(1)), that of a liquidator in territorial or secondary proceedings is limited to repatriating assets that have been removed abroad after those proceedings have been opened – and in this regard we must bear in mind that "opened" in a winding up by the court refers to the court order and not the petition.

The local law and procedures must in all cases be respected (Art. 18(3)).
IR 1986, r. 2.133 may apply.

Article 20

[Return and imputation]

20(1) **[Creditor to return assets obtained outside Member State]** A creditor who, after the opening of the proceedings referred to in Article 3(1) obtains by any means, in particular through enforcement, total or partial satisfaction of his claim on the assets belonging to the debtor situated within the territory of another Member State, shall return what he has obtained to the liquidator, subject to Articles 5 and 7.

20(2) [Equal distribution of dividends to creditors] In order to ensure equal treatment of creditors a creditor who has, in the course of insolvency proceedings, obtained a dividend on his claim shall share in distributions made in other proceedings only where creditors of the same ranking or category have, in those other proceedings, obtained an equivalent dividend.

GENERAL NOTE

Article 20(1) empowers the liquidator in main proceedings to require any creditor who has recovered part or all of his debt by proceeding against assets of the debtor situated in another Member State to disgorge what he has received. This would not normally be possible under UK national law unless the creditor sought to prove in the insolvency, in which case he would be required to surrender his gains under the principle of hotchpot. Article 20(2), in contrast, does not oblige a creditor who has been paid a dividend in other insolvency proceedings to part with what he has received: it is only if he chooses to prove in the second insolvency that he must bring that sum into account and participate on a *pari passu* basis.

Article 21

[Publication]

21(1) [Liquidator may request publication of appointment] The liquidator may request that notice of the judgment opening insolvency proceedings and, where appropriate, the decision appointing him, be published in any other Member State in accordance with the publication procedures provided for in that State. Such publication shall also specify the liquidator appointed and whether the jurisdiction rule applied is that pursuant to Article 3(1) or Article 3(2).

21(2) [Where publication mandatory] However, any Member State within the territory of which the debtor has an establishment may require mandatory publication. In such cases, the liquidator or any authority empowered to that effect in the Member State where the proceedings referred to in Article 3(1) are opened shall take all necessary measures to ensure such publication.
(See General Note after Art. 23.)

Article 22

[Registration in a public register]

22(1) [Registration of judgment opening proceedings] The liquidator may request that the judgment opening the proceedings referred to in Article 3(1) be registered in the land register, the trade register and any other public register kept in the other Member States.

22(2) [Where registration mandatory] However, any Member State may require mandatory registration. In such cases, the liquidator or any authority empowered to that effect in the Member State where the proceedings referred to in Article 3(1) have been opened shall take all necessary measures to ensure such registration.
(See General Note after Art. 23.)

Article 23

[Costs]

23 The costs of the publication and registration provided for in Articles 21 and 22 shall be regarded as costs and expenses incurred in the proceedings.

GENERAL NOTE TO ARTS 21–23

No legislation has been enacted in this country requiring mandatory publication or registration under Arts 21(2) or 22(2). Where this is requested by the liquidator, the ordinary procedures to be followed under IA 1986 and the Rules will be applicable. No special forms have been prescribed.

Article 24

[Honouring of an obligation to a debtor]

24(1) **[Deemed discharge of obligation]** Where an obligation has been honoured in a Member State for the benefit of a debtor who is subject to insolvency proceedings opened in another Member State, when it should have been honoured for the benefit of the liquidator in those proceedings, the person honouring the obligation shall be deemed to have discharged it if he was unaware of the opening of proceedings.

24(2) **[Effect of publication]** Where such an obligation is honoured before the publication provided for in Article 21 has been effected, the person honouring the obligation shall be presumed, in the absence of proof to the contrary, to have been unaware of the opening of insolvency proceedings; where the obligation is honoured after such publication has been effected, the person honouring the obligation shall be presumed, in the absence of proof to the contrary, to have been aware of the opening of proceedings.

GENERAL NOTE

This article gives protection to a creditor, based in a Member State other than that in which the insolvency proceedings have been opened, who has paid a debt in ignorance of the existence of the proceedings. The liquidator will thus be unable to have the payment set aside as a preference or declared void under IA 1986, s. 127, for instance. Note the different rules as to the onus of proof in Art. 24(2).

Article 25

[Recognition and enforceability of other judgments]

25(1) **[Course and closure without further formality]** Judgments handed down by a court whose judgment concerning the opening of proceedings is recognised in accordance with Article 16 and which concern the course and closure of insolvency proceedings, and compositions approved by that court shall also be recognised with no further formalities. Such judgments shall be enforced in accordance with Articles 31 to 51, with the exception of Article 34(2), of the Brussels Convention on Jurisdiction and the Enforcement of Judgments in Civil and Commercial Matters, as amended by the Conventions of Accession to this Convention.

The first subparagraph shall also apply to judgments deriving directly from the insolvency proceedings and which are closely linked with them, even if they were handed down by another court.

The first subparagraph shall also apply to judgments relating to preservation measures taken after the request for the opening of insolvency proceedings.

25(2) [Other judgments] The recognition and enforcement of judgments other than those referred to in paragraph 1 shall be governed by the Convention referred to in paragraph 1, provided that that Convention is applicable.

25(3) [Exceptions] The Member States shall not be obliged to recognise or enforce a judgment referred to in paragraph 1 which might result in a limitation of personal freedom or postal secrecy.

GENERAL NOTE

As noted in the Preamble, para. 7, insolvency proceedings are specifically excluded from the scope of the Brussels Convention. However, this Article brings back within its ambit the judgments and compositions referred to in para. (1), so as to make them enforceable in other Member States in the same way as other judgments of the courts. So, for instance, an order that a creditor return a payment on the ground that it was a preference under IA 1986, s. 239 will now be enforceable under the Convention in another Member State. The object of para. 2 is, presumably, to make it clear that nothing in the Regulation is intended to qualify or restrict the operation of the Convention.

A members' voluntary winding up, not being insolvency proceedings, is within the Brussels Convention: *Re Cover Europe Ltd* [2002] 2 B.C.L.C. 61.

Article 26

[Public policy]

26 Any Member State may refuse to recognise insolvency proceedings opened in another Member State or to enforce a judgment handed down in the context of such proceedings where the effects of such recognition or enforcement would be manifestly contrary to that State's public policy, in particular its fundamental principles or the constitutional rights and liberties of the individual.

GENERAL NOTE

No doubt the inclusion of this provision was considered an important safeguard when the representatives of the Member States agreed to the final text, but it is hard to see it being invoked without the risk of a diplomatic row!

One thing which is not spelt out is the way in which the objecting State is to declare its refusal – whether by an organ of government, a court, or an office-holder.

However, one rule of public policy has been expressly abrogated by the Regulation. This is the widely accepted principle that the courts will not enforce the fiscal laws of another State. Article 39 explicitly includes the claims of the tax and social security authorities of Member States among the debts for which proofs may be lodged. But a State's penal laws are not accorded the same concession, and so it will be open to a liquidator to reject an attempt by the authorities of another State to prove for a fine imposed by a court in the latter.

CHAPTER III – SECONDARY INSOLVENCY PROCEEDINGS

Article 27

[Opening of proceedings]

27 The opening of the proceedings referred to in Article 3(1) by a court of a Member State and which is recognised in another Member State (main proceedings) shall permit the opening in that other Member State, a court of which has jurisdiction pursuant to Article 3(2), of secondary insolvency proceedings without the debtor's insolvency being examined in that other State. These latter proceedings must be among

the proceedings listed in Annex B. Their effects shall be restricted to the assets of the debtor situated within the territory of that other Member State.
(See General Note after Art. 30.)

Article 28

[Applicable law]

28 Save as otherwise provided in this Regulation, the law applicable to secondary proceedings shall be that of the Member State within the territory of which the secondary proceedings are opened.
(See General Note after Art. 30.)

Article 29

[Right to request the opening of proceedings]

29 The opening of secondary proceedings may be requested by:

(a) the liquidator in the main proceedings;

(b) any other person or authority empowered to request the opening of insolvency proceedings under the law of the Member State within the territory of which the opening of secondary proceedings is requested.

(See General Note after Art. 30.)

Article 30

[Advance payment of costs and expenses]

30 Where the law of the Member State in which the opening of secondary proceedings is requested requires that the debtor's assets be sufficient to cover in whole or in part the costs and expenses of the proceedings, the court may, when it receives such a request, require the applicant to make an advance payment of costs or to provide appropriate security.

GENERAL NOTE TO ARTS 27–30

"Secondary" insolvency proceedings are proceedings opened *after* the opening of "main" insolvency proceedings in a Member State other than that of the debtor's centre of main interests. The corresponding term for proceedings opened *prior* to main proceedings is "territorial" proceedings (Art. 3(4)). Secondary proceedings are subject to a number of limitations. In particular:

- the debtor must possess an "establishment" within the State;
- the effects of the proceedings are limited to assets situated within the State;
- the proceedings must be "winding-up" proceedings (see Annex B), and cannot be for the rehabilitation or rescue of the debtor.

In addition, secondary proceedings are subject to the wide powers of intervention conferred on the liquidator in the main proceedings by Arts 33ff. On the other hand, once secondary proceedings have been opened in another State, the powers of the "main" liquidator and the scope of the law of the "main" jurisdiction have to yield to those of the secondary proceedings.

Article 31 *EC Regulation on Insolvency Proceedings 2000*

Art. 27
Note that the fact that main insolvency proceedings have been opened is to be taken as proof of the debtor's insolvency in any secondary proceedings.

Art. 29
Even where no secondary proceedings have been opened, it may be in the interests of the main proceedings for its liquidator to open secondary proceedings in another State, *e.g.* to take advantage of "claw-back" provisions in the law of the latter. Article 29(a) gives him *locus standi* to set such proceedings in motion. IA 1986, s. 124(1) has been amended to confirm this.

Article 31

[Duty to cooperate and communicate information]

31(1) **[Duty of liquidators to communicate]** Subject to the rules restricting the communication of information, the liquidator in the main proceedings and the liquidators in the secondary proceedings shall be duty bound to communicate information to each other. They shall immediately communicate any information which may be relevant to the other proceedings, in particular the progress made in lodging and verifying claims and all measures aimed at terminating the proceedings.

31(2) **[Duty of liquidators to cooperate]** Subject to the rules applicable to each of the proceedings, the liquidator in the main proceedings and the liquidators in the secondary proceedings shall be duty bound to cooperate with each other.

31(3) **[Duty of liquidator in secondary proceedings]** The liquidator in the secondary proceedings shall give the liquidator in the main proceedings an early opportunity of submitting proposals on the liquidation or use of the assets in the secondary proceedings.

GENERAL NOTE

This article directs the liquidators in all the proceedings in quite peremptory terms to communicate information to each other and to co-operate with each other. That it applies between the liquidators in secondary proceedings *inter se* appears from the use of "the liquidators" in the plural. The secondary liquidator's obligation to receive proposals under para. 3 is more than a matter of mere courtesy: it is backed by the extensive powers of intervention conferred on the main liquidator by Arts 33ff.

Article 32

[Exercise of creditors' rights]

32(1) **[Lodgement of claim]** Any creditor may lodge his claim in the main proceedings and in any secondary proceedings.

32(2) **[Lodgement in other proceedings]** The liquidators in the main and any secondary proceedings shall lodge in other proceedings claims which have already been lodged in the proceedings for which they were appointed, provided that the interests of creditors in the latter proceedings are served thereby, subject to the right of creditors to oppose that or to withdraw the lodgement of their claims where the law applicable so provides.

32(3) **[Liquidator's power]** The liquidator in the main or secondary proceedings shall be empowered to participate in other proceedings on the same basis as a creditor, in particular by attending creditors' meetings.

GENERAL NOTE

There is an inconsistency here with the Preamble, para. 21, which states that every creditor "who has his habitual residence, domicile or registered office in the Community" should have the right to lodge a claim in each of the insolvency proceedings pending in the Community relating to the debtor's assets – a formula which is repeated in Art. 39. It may well be that Art. 32 should be read also subject to this restriction, so that a non-EU creditor could not claim to be entitled to prove by virtue of this provision. However, the point will not arise in UK proceedings, since the domestic law has always allowed foreign creditors to prove, wherever they are based.

The right of liquidators to participate in each others' proceedings on the same basis as a creditor, and in particular to prove on behalf of their own creditors in such proceedings, has been confirmed by changes to the Rules: see IR 1986, rr. 2.133, 7.64. Rules 4.84 and 6.106 provide for the withdrawal of a proof in liquidation and bankruptcy proceedings.

Article 33

[Stay of liquidation]

33(1) [**Court to stay secondary proceedings on liquidator's request**] The court, which opened the secondary proceedings, shall stay the process of liquidation in whole or in part on receipt of a request from the liquidator in the main proceedings, provided that in that event it may require the liquidator in the main proceedings to take any suitable measure to guarantee the interests of the creditors in the secondary proceedings and of individual classes of creditors. Such a request from the liquidator may be rejected only if it is manifestly of no interest to the creditors in the main proceedings. Such a stay of the process of liquidation may be ordered for up to three months. It may be continued or renewed for similar periods.

33(2) [**Termination of stay**] The court referred to in paragraph 1 shall terminate the stay of the process of liquidation:

– at the request of the liquidator in the main proceedings,

– of its own motion, at the request of a creditor or at the request of the liquidator in the secondary proceedings if that measure no longer appears justified, in particular, by the interests of creditors in the main proceedings or in the secondary proceedings.

GENERAL NOTE

Although this article uses the word "shall", the court is in fact given a considerable amount of discretion in deciding whether or not to grant a stay, in particular to secure the position of local creditors.

Article 34

[Measures ending secondary insolvency proceedings]

34(1) [**Liquidator's power to propose closure of secondary proceedings**] Where the law applicable to secondary proceedings allows for such proceedings to be closed without liquidation by a rescue plan, a composition or a comparable measure, the liquidator in the main proceedings shall be empowered to propose such a measure himself.

Closure of the secondary proceedings by a measure referred to in the first subparagraph shall not become final without the consent of the liquidator in the main proceedings; failing his agreement, however, it may become final if the financial interests of the creditors in the main proceedings are not affected by the measure proposed.

34(2) [**Creditors' consent required to restrictions**] Any restriction of creditors' rights arising from a measure referred to in paragraph 1 which is proposed in secondary proceedings, such as a stay of payment or discharge of debt, may not have effect in respect of the debtor's assets not covered by those proceedings without the consent of all the creditors having an interest.

34(3) [**Position during stay**] During a stay of the process of liquidation ordered pursuant to Article 33, only the liquidator in the main proceedings or the debtor, with the former's consent, may propose measures

laid down in paragraph 1 of this Article in the secondary proceedings; no other proposal for such a measure shall be put to the vote or approved.
(See General Note after Art. 35.)

Article 35

[Assets remaining in the secondary proceedings]

35 If by the liquidation of assets in the secondary proceedings it is possible to meet all claims allowed under those proceedings, the liquidator appointed in those proceedings shall immediately transfer any assets remaining to the liquidator in the main proceedings.

GENERAL NOTE TO ARTS 34, 35

Although secondary proceedings may be *opened* only in the form of winding-up proceedings (a term which includes bankruptcy and sequestration: see Annex B), Art. 34 contemplates that such proceedings may be terminated by a rescue plan or composition – *e.g.* a CVA or IVA, an administration or a scheme of arrangement under CA 1985, s. 425. The liquidator in the main proceedings may himself propose such an outcome, while the concluding sentence in Art. 34 gives him a limited power of veto where it is proposed by anyone else. He alone (or the debtor with his consent) may make such a proposal if the liquidation has been stayed under Art. 33.

On Art. 34(2), see the note to Art. 17(2).

Art. 35

While secondary proceedings are operative in a Member State, the liquidator in the main proceedings is debarred from using his normal power to remove assets from that jurisdiction to his own under Art. 18(1). Article 35 does not merely reinstate that right, but directs the secondary liquidator to remit the assets to him.

Article 36

[Subsequent opening of the main proceedings]

36 Where the proceedings referred to in Article 3(1) are opened following the opening of the proceedings referred to in Article 3(2) in another Member State, Articles 31 to 35 shall apply to those opened first, in so far as the progress of those proceedings so permits.
(See General Note after Art. 37.)

Article 37

[Conversion of earlier proceedings]

37 The liquidator in the main proceedings may request that proceedings listed in Annex A previously opened in another Member State be converted into winding-up proceedings if this proves to be in the interests of the creditors in the main proceedings.

The court with jurisdiction under Article 3(2) shall order conversion into one of the proceedings listed in Annex B.

GENERAL NOTE TO ARTS 36, 37

These Articles deal with the position where main proceedings are opened in the State of the debtor's centre of main interests at a time when territorial proceedings are already under way in another State. Article 36 brings into play the provisions of Arts 31–35, subject to any necessary modifications. Article 37 is more radical, giving the main liquidator the power to apply to have the territorial proceedings converted into winding-up (or bankruptcy) proceedings, so bringing the situation into line with secondary proceedings. Although it would appear from a reading of Art. 37 that the court has no option but to accede to such a request from the main liquidator (or, at the very most, require to be satisfied that conversion will be in the interests of the creditors in the main proceedings), the amendments made to the Rules assume that the court is entitled in its discretion to take account of "all other matters" that may be considered relevant in deciding whether or not to make an order (see IR 1986, rr. 1.31–1.33, *2.59–2.61*, 2.130–2.132, 5.31–5.33).

Article 38

[Preservation measures]

38 Where the court of a Member State which has jurisdiction pursuant to Article 3(1) appoints a temporary administrator in order to ensure the preservation of the debtor's assets, that temporary administrator shall be empowered to request any measures to secure and preserve any of the debtor's assets situated in another Member State, provided for under the law of that State, for the period between the request for the opening of insolvency proceedings and the judgment opening the proceedings.

General Note

Article 38 applies only in main proceedings, and deals with the position before a moratorium would come into force automatically under Art. 17(1). The "temporary administrator" who is empowered to request a stay, etc. in other Member States would plainly include a provisional liquidator. Whether Art. 38 could be invoked to enforce the moratorium which comes into force after a petition or application for an administration order has been presented (IA 1986, s. 10(1), Sch. B1, para. 44), notice of intention to appoint an administrator has been given under Sch. B1, paras 26, 44(2), or an interim order has been made pending the approval of an IVA (s. 252) is doubtful, since neither involves the appointment of a person to act as "temporary administrator". However, if the court in such a case were to appoint an interim manager or a receiver (see the note to IA 1986, s. 9(4), (5)), this difficulty could perhaps be overcome.

Chapter IV – Provision of Information for Creditors and Lodgement of their Claims

Article 39

[Right to lodge claims]

39 Any creditor who has his habitual residence, domicile or registered office in a Member State other than the State of the opening of proceedings, including the tax authorities and social security authorities of Member States, shall have the right to lodge claims in the insolvency proceedings in writing.
(See General Note after Art. 42.)

Article 40

[Duty to inform creditors]

40(1) **[Notification of proceedings to creditors in other Member States]** As soon as insolvency proceedings are opened in a Member State, the court of that State having jurisdiction or the liquidator appointed by it shall immediately inform known creditors who have their habitual residences, domiciles or registered offices in the other Member States.

40(2) **[Content of notice]** That information, provided by an individual notice, shall in particular include time limits, the penalties laid down in regard to those time limits, the body or authority empowered to accept the lodgement of claims and the other measures laid down. Such notice shall also indicate whether creditors whose claims are preferential or secured in rem need lodge their claims.
(See General Note after Art. 42.)

Article 41

[Content of the lodgement of a claim]

41 A creditor shall send copies of supporting documents, if any, and shall indicate the nature of the claim, the date on which it arose and its amount, as well as whether he alleges preference, security in rem or a reservation of title in respect of the claim and what assets are covered by the guarantee he is invoking.
(See General Note after Art. 42.)

Article 42

[Languages]

42(1) **[Information in official language]** The information provided for in Article 40 shall be provided in the official language or one of the official languages of the State of the opening of proceedings. For that purpose a form shall be used bearing the heading "Invitation to lodge a claim. Time limits to be observed" in all the official languages of the institutions of the European Union.

42(2) **[Lodgement of claim in official language]** Any creditor who has his habitual residence, domicile or registered office in a Member State other than the State of the opening of proceedings may lodge his claim in the official language or one of the official languages of that other State. In that event, however, the lodgement of his claim shall bear the heading "Lodgement of claim" in the official language or one of the official languages of the State of the opening of proceedings. In addition, he may be required to provide a translation into the official language or one of the official languages of the State of the opening of proceedings.

GENERAL NOTE TO ARTS 39–42

These articles apply in all forms of insolvency proceedings, whether main, secondary or territorial.

Art. 39
As noted in the comment to Art. 32(1), there is some inconsistentcy between these two articles. It would appear that a creditor must be based in the Community before he can assert the right under the Regulation to prove in another Member State, but that this would not rule out the right given to any other foreign creditor to prove in an insolvency under the domestic law of the particular proceedings (see Art. 4(2)(g)). The express inclusion of the tax and social security authorities among the permitted claimants is a remarkable change from the traditional position – although some other Crown debts, such as fines, will continue to be unenforceable abroad.

Art. 40
Note the link with Art. 42(1), which requires the information to be given on a form bearing a heading in all the official languages of the institutions of the EU. See the note to Art. 42(1).

Art. 41
New forms of proof of debt for use in winding-up and bankruptcy proceedings (Forms 4.25, 6.37) have been prescribed. No forms are prescribed for use in other insolvency proceedings, but the requirements of this Article should be noted.

Art. 42
Note the requirement that the form giving the information required by Art. 40 must bear a heading in *all* the official languages of the institutions of the EU (presumably including Danish, even though Denmark is not within the Regulation). A Guidance Note issued by the Insolvency Service in March 2002 and available on its website sets out these headings (Pt I, Sch. A); the Greek script may present a challenge! Also set out in the same Guidance Note are the

phrases equivalent to "Lodgement of claim" in all of these languages, required by Art. 42(2); but in this case the heading need only be in *one* language, *viz.* an official language of the State of the opening of proceedings.

CHAPTER V – TRANSITIONAL AND FINAL PROVISIONS

Article 43

[Applicability in time]

43 The provisions of this Regulation shall apply only to insolvency proceedings opened after its entry into force. Acts done by a debtor before the entry into force of this Regulation shall continue to be governed by the law which was applicable to them at the time they were done.
(See General Note after Art. 44.)

Article 44

[Relationship to Conventions]

44(1) **[Conventions replaced]** After its entry into force, this Regulation replaces, in respect of the matters referred to therein, in the relations between Member States, the Conventions concluded between two or more Member States, in particular:

(a) the Convention between Belgium and France on Jurisdiction and the Validity and Enforcement of Judgments, Arbitration Awards and Authentic Instruments, signed at Paris on 8 July 1899;

(b) the Convention between Belgium and Austria on Bankruptcy, Winding-up, Arrangements, Compositions and Suspension of Payments (with Additional Protocol of 13 June 1973), signed at Brussels on 16 July 1969;

(c) the Convention between Belgium and the Netherlands on Territorial Jurisdiction, Bankruptcy and the Validity and Enforcement of Judgments, Arbitration Awards and Authentic Instruments, signed at Brussels on 28 March 1925;

(d) the Treaty between Germany and Austria on Bankruptcy, Winding-up, Arrangements and Compositions, signed at Vienna on 25 May 1979;

(e) the Convention between France and Austria on Jurisdiction, Recognition and Enforcement of Judgments on Bankruptcy, signed at Vienna on 27 February 1979;

(f) the Convention between France and Italy on the Enforcement of Judgments in Civil and Commercial Matters, signed at Rome on 3 June 1930;

(g) the Convention between Italy and Austria on Bankruptcy, Winding-up, Arrangements and Compositions, signed at Rome on 12 July 1977;

(h) the Convention between the Kingdom of the Netherlands and the Federal Republic of Germany on the Mutual Recognition and Enforcement of Judgments and other Enforceable Instruments in Civil and Commercial Matters, signed at The Hague on 30 August 1962;

(i) the Convention between the United Kingdom and the Kingdom of Belgium providing for the Reciprocal Enforcement of Judgments in Civil and Commercial Matters, with Protocol, signed at Brussels on 2 May 1934;

(j) the Convention between Denmark, Finland, Norway, Sweden and Iceland on Bankruptcy, signed at Copenhagen on 7 November 1933;

(k) the European Convention on Certain International Aspects of Bankruptcy, signed at Istanbul on 5 June 1990.

44(2) [Proceedings commenced prior to operation of Regulation] The Conventions referred to in paragraph 1 shall continue to have effect with regard to proceedings opened before the entry into force of this Regulation.

44(3) [Non-application] This Regulation shall not apply:

(a) in any Member State, to the extent that it is irreconcilable with the obligations arising in relation to bankruptcy from a convention concluded by that State with one or more third countries before the entry into force of this Regulation;

(b) in the United Kingdom of Great Britain and Northern Ireland, to the extent that is irreconcilable with the obligations arising in relation to bankruptcy and the winding-up of insolvent companies from any arrangements with the Commonwealth existing at the time this Regulation enters into force.

General Note to Arts 43–44

Articles 43 and 44(2) make it clear that the Regulation is not retrospective, so as to apply to proceedings opened before 31 May 2002. However, it must be borne in mind that the term "opened" refers to the time when the proceedings take effect (see the note to Art. 2(f)), and not (*e.g.*) to the time of presentation of a petition for a bankruptcy or winding-up order.

Art. 44
Few will be aware of the Convention referred to in para. 1(i): it is not referred to in leading textbooks. Anyway, it is now spent!

The UK has not signed the Istanbul Convention (para. 1(k)), which is in any event now superseded within the EU by the present Convention.

The purpose of para. 3(b) is obscure. Even if "with the Commonwealth" is to be read as "within the Commonwealth" or as "with other members of the Commonwealth", it has no obvious application, although it may perhaps to be taken as a clumsy and ill-informed allusion to the procedure under IA 1986, s. 426.

Article 45

[Amendment of the Annexes]

45 The Council, acting by qualified majority on the initiative of one of its members or on a proposal from the Commission, may amend the Annexes.

Article 46

[Reports]

46 No later than 1 June 2012, and every five years thereafter, the Commission shall present to the European Parliament, the Council and the Economic and Social Committee a report on the application of this Regulation. The report shall be accompanied if need be by a proposal for adaptation of this Regulation.

Article 47

[Entry into force]

47 This Regulation shall enter into force on 31 May 2002.

This Regulation shall be binding in its entirety and directly applicable in the Member States in accordance with the Treaty establishing the European Community.

Done at Brussels, 29 May 2000.

EC Regulation on Insolvency Proceedings 2000   *Annex A*

ANNEXES

Annex A

Insolvency proceedings referred to in Article 2(a)

BELGIË—BELGIQUE
— Het faillissement/La faillite
— Het gerechtelijk akkoord/Le concordat judiciaire
— De collectieve schuldenregeling/Le règlement collectif de dettes

DEUTSCHLAND
— Das Konkursverfahren
— Das gerichtliche Vergleichsverfahren
— Das Gesamtvollstreckungsverfahren
— Das Insolvenzverfahren

ΕΛΛΑΣ
— Πτωχευση
— Η ειδικη εκκαθαριση
— Η προσωρινη διαχειριση εταιριας. Η διοικηση και η διαχειριριση των πιστωτων
— Η υπαγη επιχειρησης υπο επιτροπο με σκοπο τη συναψη συμβιβασμου με τους πιστωτες

ESPAÑA
— Concurso de acreedores
— Quiebra
— Suspensión de pagos

FRANCE
— Liquidation judiciaire
— Redressement judiciaire avec nomination d'un administrateur

IRELAND
— Compulsory winding up by the court
— Bankruptcy
— The administration in bankruptcy of the estate of persons dying insolvent
— Winding-up in bankruptcy of partnerships
— Creditors' voluntary winding up (with confirmation of a Court)
— Arrangements under the control of the court which involve the vesting of all or part of the property of the debtor in the Official Assignee for realisation and distribution
— Company examinership

ITALIA
- Fallimento
- Concordato preventivo
- Liquidazione coatta amministrativa
- Amministrazione straordinaria
- Amministrazione controllata

LUXEMBOURG
- Faillite
- Gestion contrôlée
- Concordat préventif de faillite (par abandon d'actif)
- Régime spécial de liquidation du notariat

NEDERLAND
- Het faillissement
- De surséance van betaling
- De schuldsaneringsregeling natuurlijke personen

ÖSTERREICH
- Das Konkursverfahren
- Das Ausgleichsverfahren

PORTUGAL
- O processo de falência
- Os processos especiais de recuperação de empresa, ou seja:
  - A concordata
  - A reconstituição empresarial
  - A reestruturação financeira
  - A gestão controlada

SUOMI—FINLAND
- Konkurssi/konkurs
- Yrityssaneeraus/företagssanering

SVERIGE
- Konkurs
- Företagsrekonstruktion

UNITED KINGDOM
- Winding up by or subject to the supervision of the court
- Creditors' voluntary winding up (with confirmation by the court)
- Administration
- Voluntary arrangements under insolvency legislation
- Bankruptcy or sequestration

GENERAL NOTE

See the note to Arts 1(1) and 2(a). Although art. 2(a) suggests that the list of proceedings in Annex A is definitive, it appears that other collective proceedings (*e.g.* the administration of the insolvent estates of deceased persons, and insolvent partnerships, both of which are listed by Ireland) are not excluded.

Winding up subject to the supervision of the court has been abolished in the UK, but not in Gibraltar.

Annex B

Winding up proceedings referred to in Article 2(c)

BELGIË—BELGIQUE

— Het faillissement/La faillite

DEUTSCHLAND

— Das Konkursverfahren
— Das Gesamtvollstreckungsverfahren
— Das Insolvenzverfahren

ΕΛΛΑΣ

— Πτωχευση
— Η ειδικη εκκαθαριση

ESPAÑA

— Concurso de acreedores
— Quiebra
— Suspensión de pagos basada en la insolvencia definitiva

FRANCE

— Liquidation judiciaire

IRELAND

— Compulsory winding up
— Bankruptcy
— The administration in bankruptcy of the estate of persons dying insolvent
— Winding-up in bankruptcy of partnerships
— Creditors' voluntary winding up (with confirmation of a court)
— Arrangements under the control of the court which involve the vesting of all or part of the property of the debtor in the Official Assignee for realisation and distribution

ITALIA

— Fallimento
— Liquidazione coatta amministrativa

LUXEMBOURG

— Faillite
— Régime spécial de liquidation du notariat

NEDERLAND
- Het faillissement
- De schuldsaneringsregeling natuurlijke personen

ÖSTERREICH
- Das Konkursverfahren

PORTUGAL
- O processo de falência

SUOMI—FINLAND
- Konkurssi/konkurs

SVERIGE
- Konkurs

UNITED KINGDOM
- Winding up by or subject to the supervision of the court
- Creditors' voluntary winding up (with confirmation by the court)
- Bankruptcy or sequestration

Annex C

Liquidators referred to in Article 2(b)

BELGIË—BELGIQUE
- De curator/Le curateur
- De commissaris inzake opschorting/Le commissaire au sursis
- De schuldbemiddelaar/Le médiateur de dettes

DEUTSCHLAND
- Konkursverwalter
- Vergleichsverwalter
- Sachwalter (nach der Vergleichsordnung)
- Verwalter
- Insolvenzverwalter
- Sachwalter (nach der Insolvenzordnung)
- Treuhänder
- Vorläufiger Insolvenzverwalter

ΕΛΛΑΣ
- Ο συνδικο
- Ο προσωρινος διαχειριστης. Η διοικουσα επιτροπη των πιστωτων
- Ο ειδικος εκκαθαριστης
- Ο επιτροπος

ESPAÑA
- Depositario-administrador
- Interventor o Interventores
- Síndicos
- Comisario

FRANCE
- Représentant des créanciers
- Mandataire liquidateur
- Administrateur judiciaire
- Commissaire à l'exécution de plan

IRELAND
- Liquidator
- Official Assignee
- Trustee in bankruptcy
- Provisional Liquidator
- Examiner

ITALIA
- Curatore
- Commissario

LUXEMBOURG
- Le curateur
- Le commissaire
- Le liquidateur
- Le conseil de gérance de la section d'assainissement du notariat

NEDERLAND
- De curator in het faillissement
- De bewindvoerder in de surséance van betaling
- De bewindvoerder in de schuldsaneringsregeling natuurlijke personen

ÖSTERREICH
- Masseverwalter
- Ausgleichsverwalter
- Sachwalter
- Treuhänder
- Besondere Verwalter
- Vorläufiger Verwalter
- Konkursgericht

PORTUGAL
— Gestor judicial
— Liquidatário judicial
— Comissão de credores

SUOMI—FINLAND
— Pesänhoitaja/boförvaltare
— Selvittäjä/utredare

SVERIGE
— Förvaltare
— God man
— Rekonstruktör

UNITED KINGDOM
— Liquidator
— Supervisor of a voluntary arrangement
— Administrator
— Official Receiver
— Trustee
— Judicial factor

Enterprise Act 2002

Enterprise Act 2002

(2002 Chapter 40)

LIST OF CONTENTS

PART 10

INSOLVENCY

Companies etc.

248	Replacement of Part II of Insolvency Act 1986
249	Special administration regimes
250	Prohibition of appointment of administrative receiver
251	Abolition of Crown preference
252	Unsecured creditors
253	Liquidator's powers
254	Application of insolvency law to foreign company
255	Application of law about company arrangement or administration to non-company

Individuals

256	Duration of bankruptcy
257	Post-discharge restrictions
258	Investigation by official receiver
259	Income payments order
260	Income payments agreement
261	Bankrupt's home
262	Powers of trustee in bankruptcy
263	Repeal of certain bankruptcy offences
264	Individual voluntary arrangement
265	Disqualification from office: justice of the peace
266	Disqualification from office: Parliament
267	Disqualification from office: local government
268	Disqualification from office: general
269	Minor and consequential amendments

Money

270	Fees
271	Insolvency Services Account: interest
272	Insolvency Services Accounts

Schedule 16 — Schedule B1 to Insolvency Act 1986
Schedule 17 — Administration: minor and consequential amendments
Schedule 18 — Schedule 2A to Insolvency Act 1986
Schedule 19 — Duration of bankruptcy: transitional provisions
Schedule 20 — Schedule 4A to Insolvency Act 1986
Schedule 21 — Effect of bankruptcy restrictions order and undertaking
Schedule 22 — Individual voluntary arrangement
Schedule 23 — Individual insolvency: minor and consequential amendments
Schedule 26 — Repeals and revocations

General comment on the Enterprise Act 2002

The Enterprise Act 2002 received the Royal Assent on November 7, 2002. Part 10 of that Act clearly will have a major impact upon the operation of insolvency practice in the years to come. It could also have a significant influence on social attitudes to debt and on the appropriate legislative response to that condition.

Casual observers might find the inclusion of insolvency law under the banner of an Enterprise Act curious. It may be that the opportunity was taken to "thumb a lift" on a passing statute but a more serious study would reveal potential points of interface between "enterprise" and "insolvency". The history of this legislative change can be traced via a number of documents emanating from the Insolvency Service and the DTI. Reform of corporate rescue has been on the cards since the DTI/Treasury Review Group document *A Review of Company Rescue and Business Reconstruction Mechanisms* was published in the summer of 2000. These proposals were also heralded by the 2001 White Paper, *Productivity and Enterprise: Insolvency – A Second Chance* (Cm 5234). Equally, it has been clear beyond doubt since the White Paper, *Opportunity for All in a World of Change* (2001) (Cm 5052) that the Government intended to liberalise the law on bankruptcy. This change in the approach towards bankruptcy was also apparent in *A Second Chance* (*supra*), which gave more detail on possible reforms. The thinking was that a more liberal law of bankruptcy would encourage risk taking and hence stimulate a sense of enterprise. A more probable connection between bankruptcy reform and enterprise lies in the fact that UK commercial life is now founded upon consumer spending derived from consumer credit. An earlier indication of the shape of things to come can be found in the *Bankruptcy – A Fresh Start* Consultative Document of April 2000 – see editorial [2000] Ins. Law 147 for a full account.

The Enterprise Bill was published in March 2002 with full Explanatory Notes. It was introduced into the House of Commons on March 26, 2002. For comment on the Bill see editorial in [2002] Ins. Law 119.

For corporate recovery practitioners the most important feature of the Act will be the scaling back of administrative receivership (see s. 250 inserting new ss. 72A–H into the 1986 Act) and introduction of the new style administration regime. This new insolvency model is introduced by s. 248 and then described in detail by Sch. 16 (which will become Schedule B1 of the 1986 Act). Part II of the Insolvency Act 1986 is thus of reduced significance. This new regime marks a serious departure from the former administration mechanism both in terms of availability and operation. The advent of a dedicated fund for unsecured creditors by s. 252 (inserting s. 176A into the 1986 Act) is an enlightened move, though commentators would welcome even greater enlightenment on how the "prescribed part" will operate. More certainty is provided by s. 251 which abolishes Crown preferential debts; no quibbles about this long overdue change in the law. The curious provision in s. 253 on the need for a liquidator to obtain sanction before the commencement of certain recovery actions only makes sense in the light of the reform of IR 1986, r. 4.218 and IR 6.224 by treating costs incurred in such actions as liquidation expenses – on this see SI 2002/2712. These changes to corporate insolvency law take effect on September 15, 2003.

The reforms to personal insolvency law are in many senses more radical. Thus, we see significant modifications to the IVA scheme with the introduction of post bankruptcy IVA operated by the official receiver (s. 264 and Sch. 22), the relaxation of bankruptcy discharge procedures to permit discharge after one year (s. 256) unless the bankrupt is unfortunate enough to fall within the bankruptcy restrictions regime detailed in Schs 20–21 to the Act and introduced by s. 257. The official receiver will now have a *discretion* (rather than an obligation) to investigate bankrupts (s. 258). The procedures for the use of income to settle a bankrupt's debts have been made more flexible (ss. 259–260). Powers of trustees over the bankrupt's home are circumscribed via a late amendment of the Bill (supported by the government from June 2002) and as a result this asset will automatically cease to form part of the estate after three years unless the trustee takes action in regard to it (s. 261). Certain outmoded bankruptcy offences (such as gambling) are to be abolished by s. 263, though such behaviour may continue to be relevant for the purposes of a bankruptcy restriction order. Such reforms will certainly liberalise the bankruptcy laws in this country, though the consequences of such a change are less predictable. Will there be a future for the IVA mechanism if bankruptcy becomes too gentle? What impact will these changes have on the growing social problem of consumer debt? These are important issues that will only be capable of being assessed objectively in several years time as the bankruptcy reforms will not be implemented until April 1, 2004.

The Enterprise Act, like all modern legislation depends upon secondary legislation to supplement it. The major statutory instrument in English law was the Insolvency (Amendment) Rules 2003 (SI 2003/1730) but more focused delegated legislation was required to deal with the future of administrative receivership and the reserve fund for unsecured creditors. Scots lawyers have had to navigate equivalent masses of secondary legislation in order to make sense of the Enterprise Act – note in particular the Insolvency (Scotland) Amendment Rules 2003 (SI 2003/2111 (s. 9)). The Insolvency Service website has been an invaluable source of information on the evolution of this secondary legislation.

Part 10 of this legislation introduces major reform into the areas of corporate and personal insolvency law. For the most part these reforming provisions are cast as amendments to provisions in the IA 1986 and accordingly our commentary is located at the point of amendment in the primary legislation. However, there are a number of sections (or mere subsections) that do not take this form, but rather are viewed as free standing. These are reproduced below with appropriate annotations. For commencement of this legislation see the Enterprise Act 2002 (Commencement No. 4 and Transitional Provisions and Savings) Order 2003 (SI 2003/2093, C. 85). Generally speaking, the corporate insolvency reforms took effect on September 15, 2003, with the personal insolvency law changes being deferred to April 1, 2004.

PART 10 OF ENTERPRISE ACT 2002

248 Replacement of Part II of Insolvency Act 1986

[Not reproduced – see discussion under Sch. B1 to IA 1986]

249 Special administration regimes

249(1) [Where s. 248 not to have effect] Section 248 shall have no effect in relation to—

(a) a company holding an appointment under Chapter I of Part II of the Water Industry Act 1991 (c. 56) (water and sewerage undertakers),

(b) a protected railway company within the meaning of section 59 of the Railways Act 1993 (c. 43) (railway administration order) (including that section as it has effect by virtue of section 19 of the Channel Tunnel Rail Link Act 1996 (c. 61) (administration)),

(c) a licence company within the meaning of section 26 of the Transport Act 2000 (c. 38) (air traffic services),

(d) a public-private partnership company within the meaning of section 210 of the Greater London Authority Act 1999 (c. 29) (public-private partnership agreement), or

(e) a building society within the meaning of section 119 of the Building Societies Act 1986 (c. 53) (interpretation).

249(2) [Reference in Acts in s. 249(1) to Pt II of 1986 Act] A reference in an Act listed in subsection (1) to a provision of Part II of the Insolvency Act 1986 (or to a provision which has effect in relation to a provision of that Part of that Act) shall, in so far as it relates to a company or society listed in subsection (1), continue to have effect as if it referred to Part II as it had effect immediately before the coming into force of section 248.

249(3) [Effect of s. 249(2) modified] But the effect of subsection (2) in respect of a particular class of company or society may be modified by order of—

(a) the Treasury, in the case of building societies, or

(b) the Secretary of State, in any other case.

249(4) **[Order under s. 249(3)]** An order under subsection (3) may make consequential amendment of an enactment.

249(5) **[Procedure for order]** An order under subsection (3)—

(a) must be made by statutory instrument, and

(b) may not be made unless a draft has been laid before and approved by resolution of each House of Parliament.

249(6) **[Financial markets]** An amendment of the Insolvency Act 1986 (c. 45) made by this Act is without prejudice to any power conferred by Part VII of the Companies Act 1989 (c. 40) (financial markets) to modify the law of insolvency.

S.249(1)
This preserves special administration regimes for various utility companies, etc.

S. 249(2), (3)
These deal with modifications and transitional matters.

S.249(4), (5)
These are standard operational provisions.

S.249(6)
This is a special saving provision.

250 Prohibition of appointment of administrative receiver

[Not reproduced – see discussion under Chapter IV of Part III of IA 1986]

251 Abolition of Crown preference

[Not reproduced – see discussion under Sch. 6 to IA 1986]

252 Unsecured creditors

[Not reproduced – see discussion under IA 1986, s. 176A]

253 Liquidator's powers

[Not reproduced – see discussion under Sch. 4 to IA 1986]

254 Application of insolvency law to foreign company

254(1) **[Power to make order]** The Secretary of State may by order provide for a provision of the Insolvency Act 1986 to apply (with or without modification) in relation to a company incorporated outside Great Britain.

254(2) **[Effect of order]** An order under this section—

(a) may make provision generally or for a specified purpose only,

(b) may make different provision for different purposes, and

(c) may make transitional, consequential or incidental provision.

254(3) **[Procedure for order]** An order under this section—

(a) must be made by statutory instrument, and

(b) shall be subject to annulment in pursuance of a resolution of either House of Parliament.

S. 254(1)
This enables the Secretary of State to make orders extending provisions in the Insolvency Act 1986 to apply to foreign companies. At present such application is not possible (see *Felixstowe Dock and Rwy Co. v United States Lines Inc.*

[1989] Q.B. 360) and as a result in individual cases requests to make English law provisions apply have to be channelled through the cumbersome judicial comity procedure laid down in IA 1986, s. 426 (see, *e.g. Re Dallhold Estates (UK) Pty Ltd* [1992] B.C.C. 394).

S. 254(2), (3)
These are standard operational provisions.

255 Application of law about company arrangement or administration to non-company

255(1) **[Power to make order]** The Treasury may with the concurrence of the Secretary of State by order provide for a company arrangement or administration provision to apply (with or without modification) in relation to—

(a) a society registered under the Industrial and Provident Societies Act 1965 (c. 12),

(b) a society registered under section 7(1)(b), (c), (d), (e) or (f) of the Friendly Societies Act 1974 (c. 46),

(c) a friendly society within the meaning of the Friendly Societies Act 1992 (c. 40), or

(d) an unregistered friendly society.

255(2) **["Company arrangement or administration provision"]** In subsection (1) "company arrangement or administration provision" means—

(a) a provision of Part I of the Insolvency Act 1986 (company voluntary arrangements),

(b) a provision of Part II of that Act (administration), and

(c) section 425 of the Companies Act 1985 (c. 6) (compromise or arrangement with creditors).

255(3) **[Order not to apply to social landlord]** An order under this section may not provide for a company arrangement or administration provision to apply in relation to a society which is registered as a social landlord under Part I of the Housing Act 1996 (c. 52) or under Part 3 of the Housing (Scotland) Act 2001 (asp 10).

255(4) **[Scope of order]** An order under this section—

(a) may make provision generally or for a specified purpose only,

(b) may make different provision for different purposes, and

(c) may make transitional, consequential or incidental provision.

255(5) **[Transitional, consequential or incidental provision in order]** Provision by virtue of subsection (4)(c) may, in particular—

(a) apply an enactment (with or without modification);

(b) amend an enactment.

255(6) **[Procedure for order]** An order under this section—

(a) must be made by statutory instrument, and

(b) shall be subject to annulment in pursuance of a resolution of either House of Parliament.

S. 255(1), (2)
These enable the Treasury, with the approval of the Secretary of State, to extend provisions relating to CVAs, schemes of arrangement and administration to incorporated bodies such as industrial and provident societies and friendly societies.

S. 255(3)
Societies acting as social landlords are excluded from being subject to the aforementioned legislative power. Such activities are frequently subject to discrete insolvency regulation in view of the public interest element involved.

S. 255(4)–(6)
These are standard operational provisions governing the exercise of this power to make secondary legislation.

256 Duration of bankruptcy

[Subsection (1) is not reproduced – see IA 1986, s. 279]

256(2) [Transitional provision] Schedule 19 (which makes transitional provision in relation to this section)—

(a) shall have effect, and

(b) is without prejudice to the generality of section 276.

S. 256(2)
This refers us to Sch. 19 (see pp. 650–652 below)

257 Post-discharge restrictions

[Subsection (1) is not reproduced – see IA 1986, s. 281A]

257(2) [Insertion of Sch. 4A into 1986 Act] The Schedule 4A set out in Schedule 20 to this Act shall be inserted after Schedule 4 to the Insolvency Act 1986.

257(3) [Amendments] The amendments set out in Schedule 21 (which specify the effect of a bankruptcy restrictions order or undertaking) shall have effect.

S. 257(2), (3)
These refer us to Sch. 20 (Sch. 4A to IA 1986) and Sch. 21, which supplement the law on BROs.

258 Investigation by official receiver

[Not reproduced – see IA 1986, s. 289]

259 Income payments order

[Not reproduced – see IA 1986, s. 310]

260 Income payments agreement

[Not reproduced – see IA 1986, s. 310A]

261 Bankrupt's home

[Subsections (1)–(6) not reproduced – see IA 1986, ss. 283A, 313 and 313A]

261(7) [Definitions in s. 261(8)] In subsection (8)—

(a) "pre-commencement bankrupt" means an individual who is adjudged bankrupt on a petition presented before subsection (1) above comes into force, and

(b) "the transitional period" is the period of three years beginning with the date on which subsection (1) above comes into force.

261(8) [Interest in dwelling-house] If a pre-commencement bankrupt's estate includes an interest in a dwelling-house which at the date of the bankruptcy was the sole or principal residence of him, his spouse or a former spouse of his, at the end of the transitional period that interest shall—

(a) cease to be comprised in the estate, and

(b) vest in the bankrupt (without conveyance, assignment or transfer).

261(9) [Application of s. 261(8)] But subsection (8) shall not apply if before or during the transitional period—

(a) any of the events mentioned in section 283A(3) of the Insolvency Act 1986 (c. 45) (inserted by subsection (1) above) occurs in relation to the interest or the dwelling-house, or

(b) the trustee obtains any order of a court, or makes any agreement with the bankrupt, in respect of the interest or the dwelling-house.

261(10) [Effect of s. 283A(4)–(9) of 1986 Act] Subsections 283A(4) to (9) of that Act shall have effect, with any necessary modifications, in relation to the provision made by subsections (7) to (9) above; in particular—

(a) a reference to the period mentioned in section 283A(2) shall be construed as a reference to the transitional period,

(b) in the application of section 283A(5) a reference to the date of the bankruptcy shall be construed as a reference to the date on which subsection (1) above comes into force, and

(c) a reference to the rules is a reference to rules made under section 412 of the Insolvency Act 1986 (for which purpose this section shall be treated as forming part of Parts VIII to XI of that Act).

GENERAL NOTE

This is a curious statutory provision. The bulk of it consists of transplants into IA 1986, and in particular the new s. 283A and 313A dealing with the realisation of the family home. These provisions are dealt with at the appropriate destination. Subsections (7)–(10) however are free-standing and require comment here, though sense can only be made of these provisions by referring to s. 283A.

S. 261(7)
This is an interpretation provision.

S. 261(8)–(10)
These deal with transitional matters flowing from the significant changes in the law on the bankrupt's family home introduced by s. 261 of EA 2002.

262 Powers of trustee in bankruptcy

[Not reproduced – see Sch. 5 to IA 1986]

263 Repeal of certain bankruptcy offences

[Not reproduced – see IA 1986, ss. 361 and 362]

264 Individual voluntary arrangement

264(1) [Sch. 22 to have effect] Schedule 22 (which makes provision about individual voluntary arrangements) shall have effect.

264(2) [Power to make order] The Secretary of State may by order amend the Insolvency Act 1986 so as to extend the provisions of sections 263B to 263G (which are inserted by Schedule 22 and provide a fast-track procedure for making an individual voluntary arrangement) to some or all cases other than those specified in section 263A as inserted by Schedule 22.

264(3) [Procedure for order] An order under subsection (2)—

(a) must be made by statutory instrument, and

(b) may not be made unless a draft has been laid before and approved by each House of Parliament.

264(4) [Effect of order] An order under subsection (2) may make—

(a) consequential provision (which may include provision amending the Insolvency Act 1986 or another enactment);

(b) transitional provision.

S. 264
This introduces Sch. 22, which makes amendments to IVA law and in particular introduces the fast track IVA for undischarged bankrupts. The Secretary of State is given power by subs. (2) to extend this fast track procedure to a wider range of applications by using secondary rules.

265 Disqualification from office: justice of the peace

265 Section 65 of the Justices of the Peace Act 1997 (c. 25) (disqualification of bankrupt from appointment as justice of the peace) shall cease to have effect.

S. 265
This furthers the new policy of removing automatic restrictions from bankrupts holding certain public offices. Bankrupts will no longer automatically be disqualified from holding this minor judicial office.

266 Disqualification from office: Parliament

[Subsections (1)–(2) not reproduced – see IA 1986, ss. 426A–C and 427]

266(3) [**Power to make order**] The Secretary of State may by order—

(a) provide for section 426A or 426B of that Act (as inserted by subsection (1) above) to have effect in relation to orders made or undertakings accepted in Scotland or Northern Ireland under a system which appears to the Secretary of State to be equivalent to the system operating under Schedule 4A to that Act (as inserted by section 257 of this Act);

(b) make consequential amendment of section 426A or 426B of that Act (as inserted by subsection (1) above);

(c) make other consequential amendment of an enactment.

266(4) [**Effect of order**] An order under this section may make transitional, consequential or incidental provision.

266(5) [**Procedure for order**] An order under this section—

(a) must be made by statutory instrument, and

(b) may not be made unless a draft has been laid before and approved by resolution of each House of Parliament.

S. 266
Subsections (1) and (2) insert new provisions into IA 1986 and are dealt with in the commentary to ss. 426A, 426B and 427. Subsections (3)–(6) are however "free-standing" and permit the creation of secondary rules to extend ss. 426A and 426B of IA 1986 to Scotland or Northern Ireland.

267 Disqualification from office: local government

267(1) [**Substitution of Local Government Act 1972, s. 80(1)(b)**] The following shall be substituted for section 80(1)(b) of the Local Government Act 1972 (c. 70) (disqualification for membership of local authority: bankrupt)—

"(b) is the subject of a bankruptcy restrictions order or interim order;".

267(2) [**Cessation of Local Government Act 1972, s. 81(1), (2)**] Section 81(1) and (2) of that Act (which amplify the provision substituted by subsection (1) above) shall cease to have effect.

GENERAL NOTE

This again reflects the new "softer" approach towards bankrupts by removing another automatic disqualification from their shoulders.

S. 267(1), (2)
The disqualification from holding local government office will now only apply if a bankruptcy restrictions order or interim order has been made against the individual. Presumably the same would apply in the case of a BRU – see Sch. 4A, para. 8.

268 Disqualification from office: general

268(1) [**Power to make order**] The Secretary of State may make an order under this section in relation to a disqualification provision.

268(2) **["Disqualification provision"]** A "disqualification provision" is a provision which disqualifies (whether permanently or temporarily and whether absolutely or conditionally) a bankrupt or a class of bankrupts from—

(a) being elected or appointed to an office or position,

(b) holding an office or position, or

(c) becoming or remaining a member of a body or group.

268(3) **[Reference in s. 267(2)]** In subsection (2) the reference to a provision which disqualifies a person conditionally includes a reference to a provision which enables him to be dismissed.

268(4) **[Scope of order under s. 267(1)]** An order under subsection (1) may repeal or revoke the disqualification provision.

268(5) **[Effect of order]** An order under subsection (1) may amend, or modify the effect of, the disqualification provision—

(a) so as to reduce the class of bankrupts to whom the disqualification provision applies;

(b) so as to extend the disqualification provision to some or all individuals who are subject to a bankruptcy restrictions regime;

(c) so that the disqualification provision applies only to some or all individuals who are subject to a bankruptcy restrictions regime;

(d) so as to make the application of the disqualification provision wholly or partly subject to the discretion of a specified person, body or group.

268(6) **[Discretionary provision in order]** An order by virtue of subsection (5)(d) may provide for a discretion to be subject to—

(a) the approval of a specified person or body;

(b) appeal to a specified person or body.

268(7) **[Discretion subject to appeal]** An order by virtue of subsection (5)(d) made with the concurrence of the Lord Chancellor may provide for a discretion to be subject to appeal to a specified court or tribunal.

268(8) **[Secretary of State specified]** The Secretary of State may specify himself for the purposes of subsection (5)(d) or (6)(a) or (b).

268(9) **["Bankrupt"]** In this section "bankrupt" means an individual—

(a) who has been adjudged bankrupt by a court in England and Wales or in Northern Ireland,

(b) whose estate has been sequestrated by a court in Scotland, or

(c) who has made an agreement with creditors of his for a composition of debts, for a scheme of arrangement of affairs, for the grant of a trust deed or for some other kind of settlement or arrangement.

268(10) **["Bankruptcy restrictions regime"]** In this section "bankruptcy restrictions regime" means an order or undertaking—

(a) under Schedule 4A to the Insolvency Act 1986 (c. 45) (bankruptcy restrictions orders), or

(b) under any system operating in Scotland or Northern Ireland which appears to the Secretary of State to be equivalent to the system operating under that Schedule.

268(11) **["Body", "provision"]** In this section—
"body" includes Parliament and any other legislative body, and

"provision" means—

    (a) a provision made by an Act of Parliament passed before or in the same Session as this Act, and

    (b) a provision made, before or in the same Session as this Act, under an Act of Parliament.

268(12) **[Scope of order]** An order under this section—

(a) may make provision generally or for a specified purpose only,

(b) may make different provision for different purposes, and

(c) may make transitional, consequential or incidental provision.

268(13) **[Procedure for order]** An order under this section—

(a) must be made by statutory instrument, and

(b) may not be made unless a draft has been laid before and approved by resolution of each House of Parliament.

268(14) **[National Assembly of Wales]** A reference in this section to the Secretary of State shall be treated as a reference to the National Assembly for Wales in so far as it relates to a disqualification provision which—

(a) is made by the National Assembly for Wales, or

(b) relates to a function of the National Assembly.

268(15) **[Appeals]** Provision made by virtue of subsection (7) is subject to any order of the Lord Chancellor under section 56(1) of the Access to Justice Act 1999 (c. 22) (appeals: jurisdiction).

GENERAL NOTE

This introduces the possibility of future flexibility into the area of bankruptcy disqualification. There are at present many numerous disqualifications applied to bankrupts which are not dealt with specifically by EA 2002 and thus s. 268 provides an instrument for future reform.

S. 268(1), (2), (3), (9), (10)
These define the extent of the power of the Secretary of State to make delegated provision.

S. 268(4)–(8)
These deal with the effect of the exercise of this rule-making power.

S. 268(10), (11)
These are definitional provisions.

S. 268(12), (13)
These deal with formal legislative matters.

S. 268(14)
This deals with the legislative position in Wales.

S. 268(15)
This qualifies subs. (7).

269 Minor and consequential amendments

Schedule 23 (minor and consequential amendments relating to individual insolvency) shall have effect.

GENERAL NOTE

This refers us to Sch. 23 which makes a number of minor and consequential changes to personal insolvency law.

270 Fees

[Subsection (1) not reproduced – see IA 1986, s. 415A]

270(2) [Order made before s. 270 in force] An order made by virtue of subsection (1) may relate to the maintenance of recognition or authorisation granted before this section comes into force.

[Subsections (3) and (4) amend IA 1986 ss. 392 and 440 and are not reproduced here.]

GENERAL NOTE

On commencement see Enterprise Act 2002 (Commencement No. 5 and Amendment) Order 2003 (SI 2003/3340, C. 132).

271 Insolvency Services Account: interest

[Not reproduced – see IA 1986, Schs. 8 and 9]

GENERAL NOTE

On commencement see Enterprise Act 2002 (Commencement No. 5 and Amendment) Order 2003 (SI 2003/3340, C. 132).

272 Insolvency Services Accounts

[Not reproduced – see IA 1986, ss. 405 and 408]

SCHEDULE 16

SCHEDULE B1 TO INSOLVENCY ACT 1986

[Not reproduced – see Sch. B1 to IA 1986]

SCHEDULE 17

ADMINISTRATION: MINOR AND CONSEQUENTIAL AMENDMENTS
General

1   In any instrument made before section 248(1) to (3) of this Act comes into force—
   (a)   a reference to the making of an administration order shall be treated as including a reference to the appointment of an administrator under paragraph 14 or 22 of Schedule B1 to the Insolvency Act 1986 (c. 45) (inserted by section 248(2) of this Act), and
   (b)   a reference to making an application for an administration order by petition shall be treated as including a reference to making an administration application under that Schedule, appointing an administrator under paragraph 14 or 22 of that Schedule or giving notice under paragraph 15 or 26 of that Schedule.

[Paras 2–59 not reproduced]

SCHEDULE 18

SCHEDULE 2A TO INSOLVENCY ACT 1986

[Not reproduced – see Sch. 2A to IA 1986]

Schedule 19

Duration of bankruptcy: transitional provisions

Introduction

1 This Schedule applies to an individual who immediately before commencement—

(a) has been adjudged bankrupt, and

(b) has not been discharged from the bankruptcy.

2 In this Schedule—

"commencement" means the date appointed under section 279 for the commencement of section 256, and

"pre-commencement bankrupt" means an individual to whom this Schedule applies.

Neither old law nor new law to apply

3 Section 279 of the Insolvency Act 1986 (c. 45) (bankruptcy: discharge) shall not apply to a pre-commencement bankrupt (whether in its pre-commencement or its post-commencement form).

General rule for discharge from pre-commencement bankruptcy

4(1) A pre-commencement bankrupt is, subject to sub-paragraphs (2) and (3), discharged from bankruptcy at whichever is the earlier of—

(a) the end of the period of one year beginning with commencement, and

(b) the end of the relevant period applicable to the bankrupt under section 279(1)(b) of the Insolvency Act 1986 (duration of bankruptcy) as it had effect immediately before commencement.

4(2) An order made under section 279(3) of that Act before commencement—

(a) shall continue to have effect in respect of the pre-commencement bankrupt after commencement, and

(b) may be varied or revoked after commencement by an order under section 279(3) as substituted by section 256 of this Act.

4(3) Section 279(3) to (5) of that Act as substituted by section 256 of this Act shall have effect after commencement in relation to the period mentioned in sub-paragraph (1)(a) or (b) above.

Second-time bankruptcy

5(1) This paragraph applies to a pre-commencement bankrupt who was an undischarged bankrupt at some time during the period of 15 years ending with the day before the date on which the pre-commencement bankruptcy commenced.

5(2) The pre-commencement bankrupt shall not be discharged from bankruptcy in accordance with paragraph 4 above.

5(3) An order made before commencement under section 280(2)(b) or (c) of the Insolvency Act 1986 (c. 45) (discharge by order of the court) shall continue to have effect after commencement (including any provision made by the court by virtue of section 280(3)).

5(4) A pre-commencement bankrupt to whom this paragraph applies (and in respect of whom no order is in force under section 280(2)(b) or (c) on commencement) is discharged—

(a) at the end of the period of five years beginning with commencement, or

(b) at such earlier time as the court may order on an application under section 280 of the Insolvency Act 1986 (discharge by order) heard after commencement.

5(5) Section 279(3) to (5) of the Insolvency Act 1986 as substituted by section 256 of this Act shall have effect after commencement in relation to the period mentioned in sub-paragraph (4)(a) above.

5(6) A bankruptcy annulled under section 282 shall be ignored for the purpose of sub-paragraph (1).

Criminal bankruptcy

6 A pre-commencement bankrupt who was adjudged bankrupt on a petition under section 264(1)(d) of the Insolvency Act 1986 (criminal bankruptcy)—

(a) shall not be discharged from bankruptcy in accordance with paragraph 4 above, but

(b) may be discharged from bankruptcy by an order of the court under section 280 of that Act.

Income payments order

7(1) This paragraph applies where—

(a) a pre-commencement bankrupt is discharged by virtue of paragraph 4(1)(a), and

(b) an income payments order is in force in respect of him immediately before his discharge.

7(2) If the income payments order specifies a date after which it is not to have effect, it shall continue in force until that date (and then lapse).

7(3) But the court may on the application of the pre-commencement bankrupt—

(a) vary the income payments order;

(b) provide for the income payments order to cease to have effect before the date referred to in sub-paragraph (2).

Bankruptcy restrictions order or undertaking

8 A provision of this Schedule which provides for an individual to be discharged from bankruptcy is subject to—

(a) any bankruptcy restrictions order (or interim order) which may be made in relation to that individual, and

(b) any bankruptcy restrictions undertaking entered into by that individual.

GENERAL NOTE

This deals with important transitional matters in bankruptcy law. The reforms in EA 2002 generally speaking will not affect existing bankruptcies commenced prior to April 1, 2004, though a pre-commencement bankrupt may benefit from an earlier discharge. The major exception relates to the powers of the trustee with regard to the recovery actions (see EA 2002, s. 262) – the reforms here take effect on 15 September 2003 provided the action was commenced before that date. This point is reinforced by the Enterprise Act 2002 (Commencement No. 4 and Transitional Provisions and

Savings) Order 2003 (SI 2003/2093, C. 85). It is clear from this latter SI that conduct on the part of a person who becomes bankrupt and which occurs prior to April 1, 2004 is not relevant for the purposes of a BRO or BRU. Note the minor amendment to para. 4(1) by the Enterprise Act 2002 (Insolvency) Order 2003 (SI 2003/2096).

SCHEDULE 20

SCHEDULE 4A TO INSOLVENCY ACT 1986

[Not reproduced – see above]

SCHEDULE 21

EFFECT OF BANKRUPTCY RESTRICTIONS ORDER AND UNDERTAKING

[Not reproduced – see amendments to IA 1986]

SCHEDULE 22

INDIVIDUAL VOLUNTARY ARRANGEMENT

[Not reproduced – see IA 1986, ss. 261, 263A–G and 389B]

SCHEDULE 23

INDIVIDUAL INSOLVENCY: MINOR AND CONSEQUENTIAL AMENDMENTS

[Not reproduced – see amendments to IA 1986]

SCHEDULE 26

REPEALS AND REVOCATIONS

GENERAL NOTE

Triggered by EA 2002, s. 278, this lists statutory repeals effected by the 2002 Act. Those relating to insolvency legislation are listed below in tabular form. Other non-insolvency repeals are omitted.

Reference	Extent of repeal or revocation

Insolvency Act 1986 (c. 45)	In section 212—
	    in subsection (1)(b), the word ", administrator";
	    in subsection (2), in each place, the words "or administrator";
	    in subsection (4), the words "or administrator".
	Section 230(1).
	In section 231, in each place, the word "administrator,".
	In section 232, the word "administrator,".
	In section 240(1), the word "and" before paragraph (c).
	In section 245(3), the word "or" before paragraph (c).
	Section 275.
	Section 282(5).
	In section 292(1)(a), the words "except at a time when a certificate for the summary administration of the bankrupt's estate is in force,".
	In section 293(1), the words "and no certificate for the summary administration of the bankrupt's estate has been issued,".
	In section 294(1), paragraph (b) and the word "and" before it.
	In section 297—
	    subsections (2) and (3);
	    in subsection (4), the words "but no certificate for the summary administration of the estate is issued".
	Section 298(3).
	In section 300—
	    subsection (5);
	    in subsections (6) and (7), the words "or (5)".
	In section 310(1), the words ", on the application of the trustee,".
	Sections 361 and 362.
	Section 405.
	In section 427—
	    in subsection (1), the words "England and Wales or";
	    subsection (7).
	In Schedule 6, paragraphs 1 to 7.
	In Schedule 10—
	    the entry for section 12(2);
	    the entry for section 15(8);
	    the entry for section 18(5);
	    the entry for section 21(3);
	    the entry for section 22(6);
	    the entry for section 23(3);
	    the entry for section 24(7);
	    the entry for section 27(6);
	    in the entry for section 31, the word "Undischarged";
	    the entries for sections 361 and 362.

Insolvency Act 2000 (c. 39)	Section 9. In Schedule 4, paragraph 13(3).

The Insolvency Rules 1986

(SI 1986/1925)

Made on 10 November 1986 by the Lord Chancellor under s. 411 and 412 of the Insolvency Act 1986. Operative from 29 December 1986.

[**Note:** These Rules are amended by the Insolvency (Amendment) Rules 1987 (SI 1987/1919) as from January 11, 1988, by the Insolvency (Amendment) Rules 1989 (SI 1989/397) as from April 3, 1989, by the Insolvency (Amendment) Rules 1991 (SI 1991/495) as from April 2, 1991, by the Insolvency (Amendment) Rules 1993 (SI 1993/602) as from April 5, 1993, by the Insolvency (Amendment) Rules 1995 (SI 1995/586) as from April 1, 1995, by the Insolvency (Amendment) Rules 1999 (SI 1999/359) as from March 22, 1999, by the Insolvency (Amendment) (No. 2) Rules 1999 (SI 1999/1022) as from March 22, 1999, by the Insolvency (Amendment) Rules 2001 (SI 2001/763) as from April 2, 2001, by the Insolvency (Amendment) Rules 2002 (SI 2002/1307) as from May 31, 2002, and by the Insolvency (Amendment) Rules 2003 (SI 2003/1730), as from September 15, 2003 and April 1, 2004.

ARRANGEMENT OF RULES

INTRODUCTORY PROVISIONS

RULE
0.1 Citation and commencement
0.2 Construction and interpretation
0.3 Extent

THE FIRST GROUP OF PARTS
COMPANY INSOLVENCY; COMPANIES WINDING UP

PART 1

COMPANY VOLUNTARY ARRANGEMENTS

CHAPTER 1

PRELIMINARY

1.1 Scope of this Part; interpretation

CHAPTER 2

PROPOSAL BY DIRECTORS

1.2 Preparation of proposal
1.3 Contents of proposal
1.4 Notice to intended nominee
1.5 Statement of affairs
1.6 Additional disclosure for assistance of nominee
1.7 Nominee's report on the proposal
1.8 Replacement of nominee
1.9 Summoning of meetings under s. 3

CHAPTER 3

PROPOSAL BY ADMINISTRATOR OR LIQUIDATOR (HIMSELF THE NOMINEE)

1.10 Preparation of proposal
1.11 Summoning of meetings under s. 3

CHAPTER 4

PROPOSAL BY ADMINISTRATOR OR LIQUIDATOR (ANOTHER INSOLVENCY PRACTITIONER THE NOMINEE)

1.12 Preparation of proposal and notice to nominee

The Insolvency Rules 1986

CHAPTER 5

PROCEEDINGS ON A PROPOSAL MADE BY THE DIRECTORS, OR BY THE ADMINISTRATOR, OR BY THE LIQUIDATOR

Section A: meetings of company's creditors and members

1.13   Summoning of meetings
1.14   The chairman at meetings
1.15   The chairman as proxy-holder
1.16   Attendance by company officers

Section B: voting rights and majorities

1.17   Entitlement to vote (creditors)
1.17A   Procedure for admission of creditors' claims for voting purposes
1.18   Voting rights (members)
1.19   Requisite majorities (creditors)
1.20   Requisite majorities (members)
1.21   Proceedings to obtain agreement on the proposal

Section C: implementation of the arrangement

1.22   Resolutions to follow approval
1.22A   Notice of order made under section 4A(6)
1.23   Hand-over of property etc. to supervisor
1.24   Report of meetings
1.25   Revocation or suspension of the arrangement
1.26   Supervisor's accounts and reports
1.27   Production of accounts and records to Secretary of State
1.28   Fees, costs, charges and expenses
1.29   Completion of the arrangement

CHAPTER 6

GENERAL

1.30   [Repealed]

CHAPTER 7

EC REGULATION – CONVERSION OF VOLUNTARY ARRANGEMENT INTO WINDING UP

1.31   Application for conversion into winding up
1.32   Contents of affidavit
1.33   Power of court

CHAPTER 8

EC REGULATION – MEMBER STATE LIQUIDATOR

1.34   Interpretation of creditor and notice to member State liquidator

CHAPTER 9

OBTAINING A MORATORIUM – PROCEEDINGS DURING A MORATORIUM – NOMINEES – CONSIDERATION OF PROPOSALS WHERE MORATORIUM OBTAINED

Section A: Obtaining a Moratorium

1.35   Preparation of proposal by directors and submission to nominee
1.36   Delivery of documents to the intended nominee, etc.
1.37   Statement of affairs
1.38   The nominee's statement
1.39   Documents submitted to the court to obtain moratorium
1.40   Notice and advertisement of beginning of a moratorium
1.41   Notice of extension of moratorium
1.42   Notice and advertisement of end of moratorium

Section B: Proceedings During a Moratorium

1.43   Disposal of charged property, etc. during a moratorium

Section C: Nominees

1.44   Withdrawal of nominee's consent to act
1.45   Replacement of nominee by court
1.46   Notification of appointment of a replacement nominee
1.47   Applications to court under paragraphs 26 or 27 of Schedule A1 to the Act

Section D: Consideration of Proposals where Moratorium obtained

1.48   Summoning of meetings; procedure at meetings, etc.
1.49   Entitlement to vote (creditors)

The Insolvency Rules 1986

1.50	Procedure for admission of creditor's claims for voting		2.20	The chairman at meetings
1.51	Voting rights (members)		2.21	Meeting requisitioned by creditors
1.52	Requisite majorities (creditors)		2.22	Entitlement to vote
1.53	Requisite majorities (members) and proceedings to obtain agreement on the proposal		2.23	Admission and rejection of claims
			2.24	Secured creditors
1.54	Implementation of the arrangement		2.25	Holders of negotiable instruments
			2.26	Retention of title creditors
			2.27	Hire-purchase, conditional sale and chattel leasing agreements
			2.28	Resolutions and minutes
			2.29	Reports and notices under s. 23 and 25
			2.30	Notices to creditors

Former Part 2

Administration Procedure

Chapter 1

Application for, and Making of, the Order

2.1	Affidavit to support petition
2.2	Independent report on company's affairs
2.3	Contents of affidavit
2.4	Form of petition
2.5	Filing of petition
2.6	Service of petition
2.6A	Notice to sheriff, etc.
2.7	Manner in which service to be effected
2.8	Proof of service
2.9	The hearing
2.10	Notice and advertisement of administration order

Chapter 2

Statement of Affairs and Proposals to Creditors

2.11	Notice requiring statement of affairs
2.12	Verification and filing
2.13	Limited disclosure
2.14	Release from duty to submit statement of affairs; extension of time
2.15	Expenses of statement of affairs
2.16	Statement to be annexed to proposals
2.17	Notice to members of proposals to creditors

Chapter 3

Creditors' and Company Meetings

Section A: creditors' meetings

2.18	Meeting to consider administrator's proposals
2.19	Creditors' meetings generally

Section B: company meetings

2.31	Venue and conduct of company meeting

Chapter 4

The Creditors' Committee

2.32	Constitution of committee
2.33	Formalities of establishment
2.34	Functions and meetings of the committee
2.35	The chairman at meetings
2.36	Quorum
2.37	Committee-members' representatives
2.38	Resignation
2.39	Termination of membership
2.40	Removal
2.41	Vacancies
2.42	Procedure at meetings
2.43	Resolutions by post
2.44	Information from administrator
2.45	Expenses of members
2.46	Members' dealings with the company
2.46A	Formal defects

Chapter 5

The Administrator

2.47	Fixing of remuneration
2.48	Recourse to meeting of creditors
2.49	Recourse to the court
2.50	Creditors' claim that remuneration is excessive
2.51	Disposal of charged property, etc.
2.52	Abstract of receipts and payments
2.53	Resignation
2.54	Administrator deceased
2.55	Order filling vacancy

Chapter 6

VAT Bad Debt Relief

2.56	Issue of certificate of insolvency
2.57	Notice to creditors
2.58	Preservation of certificate with company's records

The Insolvency Rules 1986

Chapter 7

EC Regulation – Conversion of Administration into Winding up

2.59 Application for conversion into winding up
2.60 Contents of affidavit
2.61 Power of court

Chapter 8

EC Regulation – Member State Regulator

2.62 Interpretation of creditor and notice to member State liquidator

Part 2

Administration Procedure

Chapter 1

Preliminary

2.1. Introductory and interpretation

Chapter 2

Appointment of Administrator by Court

2.2 Affidavit in support of administration application
2.3 Form of application
2.4 Contents of application and affidavit in support
2.5 Filing of application
2.6 Service of application
2.7 Notice to sheriff, etc.
2.8 Manner in which service to be effected
2.9 Proof of service
2.10 Application to appoint specified person as administrator by holder of qualifying floating charge
2.11 Application where company in liquidation
2.12 The hearing
2.13 (no heading provided)
2.14 Notice of administration order

Chapter 3

Appointment of Administrator by holder of Floating Charge

2.15 Notice of intention to appoint
2.16 Notice of appointment
2.17 (no heading provided)
2.18 (no heading provided)
2.19 Appointment taking place out of court business hours

Chapter 4

Appointment of Administrator by Company of Directors

2.20 Notice of intention to appoint
2.21 (no heading provided)
2.22 (no heading provided)
2.23 Notice of appointment
2.24 (no heading provided)
2.25 (no heading provided)
2.26 (no heading provided)

Chapter 5

Process of Administration

2.27 Notification and advertisement of administrator's appointment
2.28 Notice requiring statement of affairs
2.29 Verification and filing
2.30 Limited disclosure
2.31 Release from duty to submit statement of affairs; extension of time
2.32 Expenses of statement of affairs
2.33 Administrator's proposals

Chapter 6

Meetings and Reports

Section A

Creditors' Meetings

2.34 Meetings to consider administrator's proposals
2.35 Creditors' meeting generally
2.36 The chairman at meetings
2.37 Meeting requisitioned by creditors
2.38 Entitlement to vote
2.39 Admission and rejection of claims
2.40 Secured creditors
2.41 Holders of negotiable instruments
2.42 Hire-purchase, conditional sale and chattel leasing agreements
2.43 Resolutions
2.44 Minutes
2.45 Revision of the administrator's proposals
2.46 Notice to creditors
2.47 Reports to creditors
2.48 Correspondence instead of creditors' meetings

Section B

Company Meetings

2.49 Venue and conduct of company meeting

Chapter 7

The Creditors' Committee

2.50 Constitution of committee
2.51 Formalities of establishment
2.52 Functions and meetings of the committee
2.53 The chairman at meetings
2.54 Quorum
2.55 Committee-members' representatives
2.56 Resignation
2.57 Termination of membership
2.58 Removal
2.59 Vacancies
2.60 Procedure at meetings
2.61 Resolutions of creditors' committee by post
2.62 Information from administrator
2.63 Expenses of members
2.64 Members' dealing with the company
2.65 Formal defects

Chapter 8

Disposals of Charged Property

2.66 (no heading provided)

Chapter 9

Expenses of the Administration

2.67 (no heading provided)

Chapter 10

Distributions to Creditors

Section A

Application of Chapter and General

2.68 (no heading provided)
2.69 Debts of insolvent company to rank equally
2.70 Supplementary provisions as to dividend
2.71 Division of unsold assets

Section B

Machinery of Proving a Debt

2.72 Proving a debt
2.73 Claim established by affidavit
2.74 Costs of proving
2.75 Administrator to allow inspection of proofs
2.76 New administrator appointed
2.77 Admission and rejection of proofs for dividend
2.78 Appeal against decision on proof
2.79 Withdrawal or variation of proof
2.80 Expunging of proof by the court

Section C

Quantification of Claims

2.81 Estimate of quantum
2.82 Negotiable instruments, etc.

The Insolvency Rules 1986

2.83	Secured creditors		2.121	Notice of resignation
2.84	Discounts		2.122	Application to court to remove administrator from office
2.85	Mutual credit and set-off		2.123	Notice of vacation of office when administrator ceases to be qualified to act
2.86	Debt in foreign currency			
2.87	Payments of a periodical nature		2.124	Administrator deceased
2.88	Interest		2.125	Application to replace
2.89	Debt payable at future time		2.126	Notification and advertisement of appointment of replacement administrator
2.90	Value of security			
2.91	Surrender for non-disclosure		2.127	Notification and advertisement of appointment of joint administrator
2.92	Redemption by administrator			
2.93	Test of security's value		2.128	(no heading provided)
2.94	Realisation of security by creditor		2.129	Administrator's duties on vacating office
2.95	Notice of proposed distribution			
2.96	Admission or rejection of proofs			
2.97	Declaration of dividend			
2.98	Notice of declaration of a dividend			
2.99	Payments of dividends and related matters			
2.100	Notice of no dividend, or no further dividend			
2.101	Proof altered after payment of dividend			
2.102	Secured creditors			
2.103	Disqualification from dividend			
2.104	Assignment of right to dividend			
2.105	Debt payable at future time			

Chapter 14

EC Regulation: Conversion of Administration into Winding Up

2.130	Application for conversion into winding up
2.131	Contents of affidavit
2.132	Power of court

Chapter 11

The Administrator

2.106	Fixing of remuneration
2.107	Recourse to meeting of creditors
2.108	Recourse to the court
2.109	Creditors' claim that remuneration is excessive

Chapter 15

EC Regulation: Member State Liquidator

2.133	Interpretation of creditor and notice to member State liquidator

Part 3

Administrative Receivership

Chapter 12

Ending Administration

2.110	Final progress reports
2.111	Notice of automatic end of administration
2.112	Applications for extension of administration
2.113	Notice of end of administration
2.114	Application to court by administrator
2.115	Application to court by creditor
2.116	Notification by administrator of court order
2.117	Moving from administration to creditors' voluntary liquidation
2.118	Moving from administration to dissolution

Chapter 1

Appointment of Administrative Receiver

3.1	Acceptance and confirmation of acceptance of appointment
3.2	Notice and advertisement of appointment

Chapter 2

Statement of Affairs and Report to Creditors

Chapter 13

Replacing Administrator

2.119	Grounds for resignation
2.120	Notice of intention to resign

3.3	Notice requiring statement of affairs
3.4	Verification and filing

659

3.5	Limited disclosure		3.33	Resignation
3.6	Release from duty to submit statement of affairs; extension of time		3.34	Receiver deceased
			3.35	Vacation of office
3.7	Expenses of statement of affairs			
3.8	Report to creditors			

Chapter 6

VAT Bad Debt Relief

3.36	Issue of certificate of insolvency
3.37	Notice to creditors
3.38	Preservation of certificate with company's records

Chapter 3

Creditors' Meeting

3.9	Procedure for summoning meeting under s. 48(2)
3.10	The chairman at the meeting
3.11	Voting rights
3.12	Admission and rejection of claim
3.13	Quorum
3.14	Adjournment
3.15	Resolutions and minutes

Chapter 7

Section 176A: The Prescribed Part

3.39	Report to creditors
3.40	Receiver to deal with prescribed part

Part 4

Companies Winding Up

Chapter 4

The Creditors' Committee

3.16	Constitution of committee
3.17	Formalities of establishment
3.18	Functions and meetings of the committee
3.19	The chairman at meetings
3.20	Quorum
3.21	Committee-members' representatives
3.22	Resignation
3.23	Termination of membership
3.24	Removal
3.25	Vacancies
3.26	Procedure at meetings
3.27	Resolutions by post
3.28	Information from receiver
3.29	Expenses of members
3.30	Members' dealings with the company
3.30A	Formal defects

Chapter 1

The Scheme of this Part of the Rules

4.1	Voluntary winding up; winding up by the court
4.2	Winding up by the court: the various forms of petition
4.3	Time-limits

Chapter 2

The Statutory Demand (No CVL Application)

4.4	Preliminary
4.5	Form and content of statutory demand
4.6	Information to be given in statutory demand

Chapter 5

The Administrative Receiver (Miscellaneous)

3.31	Disposal of charged property
3.32	Abstract of receipts and payments

The Insolvency Rules 1986

Chapter 3

Petition to Winding-up Order (No CVL Application)
(No Application to Petition by Contributories)

4.7	Presentation and filing of petition
4.8	Service of petition
4.9	Proof of service
4.10	Other persons to receive copies of petition
4.11	Advertisement of petition
4.12	Verification of petition
4.13	Persons entitled to copy of petition
4.14	Certificate of compliance
4.15	Leave for petitioner to withdraw
4.16	Notice of appearance
4.17	List of appearances
4.18	Affidavit in opposition
4.19	Substitution of creditor or contributory for petitioner
4.20	Notice and settling of winding-up order
4.21	Transmission and advertisement of order
4.21A	Expenses of voluntary arrangement

Chapter 4

Petition by Contributories (No CVL Application)

4.22	Presentation and service of petition
4.23	Return of petition
4.24	Application of Rules in Chapter 3

Chapter 5

Provisional Liquidator (No CVL Application)

4.25	Appointment of provisional liquidator
4.25A	Notice of appointment
4.26	Order of appointment
4.27	Deposit
4.28	Security
4.29	Failure to give or keep up security
4.30	Remuneration
4.31	Termination of appointment

Chapter 6

Statement of Affairs and Other Information

4.32	Notice requiring statement of affairs
4.33	Verification and filing
4.34-CVL	Statement of affairs
4.34A-CVL	Copy statement of affairs
4.35	Limited disclosure
4.36	Release from duty to submit statement of affairs; extension of time
4.37	Expenses of statement of affairs
4.38-CVL	Expenses of statement of affairs
4.39	Submission of accounts
4.40-CVL	Submission of accounts
4.41-CVL	Expenses of preparing accounts
4.42	Further disclosure

Chapter 7

Information to Creditors and Contributories

4.43	Reports by official receiver
4.44	Meaning of "creditors"
4.45	Report where statement of affairs lodged
4.46	Statement of affairs dispensed with
4.47	General rule as to reporting
4.48	Winding up stayed
4.49-CVL	Information to creditors and contributories
4.49A	Further information where liquidation follows administration

Chapter 8

Meetings of Creditors and Contributories

Section A: rules of general application

4.50	First meetings
4.51-CVL	First meeting of creditors
4.52	Business at first meetings in the liquidation
4.53-CVL	Business at meeting under s. 95 or 98
4.53A-CVL	Effect of adjournment of company meeting
4.53B-CVL	Report by director, etc.
4.54	General power to call meetings
4.55	The chairman at meetings

The Insolvency Rules 1986

4.56-CVL	The chairman at meetings		4.97	Redemption by liquidator
4.57	Requisitioned meetings		4.98	Test of security's value
4.58	Attendance at meetings of company's personnel		4.99	Realisation of security by creditor
4.59	Notice of meetings by advertisement only			
4.60	Venue			
4.61	Expenses of summoning meetings			
4.62-CVL	Expenses of meeting under s. 98			CHAPTER 11
4.63	Resolutions			
4.64	Chairman of meeting as proxy-holder			
4.65	Suspension and adjournment			
4.66	Quorum			THE LIQUIDATOR
4.67	Entitlement to vote (creditors)			
4.68-CVL	Chairman's discretion to allow vote			
4.69	Entitlement to vote (contributories)			
4.70	Admission and rejection of proof (creditors' meeting)			*Section A: appointment and associated formalities*
4.71	Record of proceedings			

Section B: winding up of recognised banks, etc.

			4.100	Appointment by creditors or contributories
			4.101-CVL	Appointment by creditors or by the company
4.72	Additional provisions as regards certain meetings		4.101A-CVL	Power to fill vacancy in office of liquidator
			4.102	Appointment by the court
			4.103-CVL	Appointment by the court
	CHAPTER 9		4.104	Appointment by Secretary of State
			4.105	Authentication of liquidator's appointment
			4.106	Appointment to be advertised and registered
	PROOF OF DEBTS IN A LIQUIDATION		4.107	Hand-over of assets to liquidator

Section A: procedure for proving

Section B: resignation and removal; vacation of office

4.73	Meaning of "prove"			
4.74	Supply of forms			
4.75	Contents of proof		4.108	Creditors' meeting to receive liquidator's resignation
4.76-CVL	Particulars of creditor's claim		4.109	Action following acceptance of resignation
4.77	Claim established by affidavit		4.110-CVL	Action following acceptance of resignation
4.78	Cost of proving		4.111	Leave to resign granted by the court
4.79	Liquidator to allow inspection of proofs		4.112	Advertisement of resignation
4.80	Transmission of proofs to liquidator		4.113	Meeting of creditors to remove liquidator
4.81	New liquidator appointed		4.114-CVL	Meeting of creditors to remove liquidator
4.82	Admission and rejection of proofs for dividend		4.115	Court's power to regulate meetings under Rules 4.113, 4.114–CVL
4.83	Appeal against decision on proof		4.116	Procedure on removal
4.84	Withdrawal or variation of proof		4.117-CVL	Procedure on removal
4.85	Expunging of proof by the court		4.118	Advertisement of removal
			4.119	Removal of liquidator by the court
			4.120-CVL	Removal of liquidator by the court
	Section B: quantification of claim		4.121	Release of resigning or removed liquidator
			4.122-CVL	Release of resigning or removed liquidator
4.86	Estimate of quantum		4.123	Removal of liquidator by Secretary of State
4.87	Negotiable instruments, etc.			
4.88	Secured creditors			
4.89	Discounts			
4.90	Mutual credit and set-off			*Section C: release on completion of administration*
4.91	Debt in foreign currency			
4.92	Payments of a periodical nature			
4.93	Interest		4.124	Release of official receiver
4.94	Debt payable at future time		4.125	Final meeting
			4.126-CVL	Final meeting

CHAPTER 10

Section D: remuneration

SECURED CREDITORS

4.95	Value of security		4.127	Fixing of remuneration
4.96	Surrender for non-disclosure		4.128	Other matters affecting remuneration

4.129 Recourse of liquidator to meeting of creditors
4.130 Recourse to the court
4.131 Creditors' claim that remuneration is excessive

Section E: supplementary provisions

4.132 Liquidator deceased
4.133-CVL Liquidator deceased
4.134 Loss of qualification as insolvency practitioner
4.135-CVL Loss of qualification as insolvency practitioner
4.136-CVL Vacation of office on making of winding-up order
4.137 Notice to official receiver of intention to vacate office
4.138 Liquidator's duties on vacating office

Section F: the liquidator in a members' voluntary winding up

4.139 Appointment by the company
4.140 Appointment by the court
4.141 Authentication of liquidator's appointment
4.142 Company meeting to receive liquidator's resignation
4.143 Removal of liquidator by the court
4.144 Release of resigning or removed liquidator
4.145 Liquidator deceased
4.146 Loss of qualification as insolvency practitioner
4.147 Vacation of office on making of winding-up order
4.148 Liquidator's duties on vacating office
4.148A Remuneration of liquidator in members' voluntary winding up

Section G: rules applying in every winding up, whether voluntary or by the court

4.149 Power of court to set aside certain transactions
4.150 Rule against solicitation

CHAPTER 12

THE LIQUIDATION COMMITTEE

4.151 Preliminary
4.152 Membership of committee
4.153 Formalities of establishment
4.154 Committee established by contributories
4.155 Obligations of liquidator to committee
4.156 Meetings of the committee
4.157 The chairman at meetings
4.158 Quorum
4.159 Committee-members' representatives
4.160 Resignation
4.161 Termination of membership
4.162 Removal
4.163 Vacancy (creditor members)
4.164 Vacancy (contributory members)
4.165 Voting rights and resolutions
4.166-CVL Voting rights and resolutions
4.167 Resolutions by post

4.168 Liquidator's reports
4.169 Expenses of members, etc.
4.170 Dealings by committee-members and others
4.171 Composition of committee when creditors paid in full
4.172 Committee's functions vested in Secretary of State
4.172A Formal defects

CHAPTER 13

THE LIQUIDATION COMMITTEE WHERE WINDING UP FOLLOWS IMMEDIATELY ON ADMINISTRATION (NO CVL APPLICATION)

4.173 Preliminary
4.174 Continuation of creditors' committee
4.175 Membership of committee
4.176 Liquidator's certificate
4.177 Obligations of liquidator to committee
4.178 Application of Chapter 12

CHAPTER 14

COLLECTION AND DISTRIBUTION OF COMPANY'S ASSETS BY LIQUIDATOR

4.179 General duties of liquidator
4.180 Manner of distributing assets
4.181 Debts of insolvent company to rank equally
4.182 Supplementary provisions as to dividend
4.182A Distribution in members' voluntary winding up
4.183 Division of unsold assets
4.184 General powers of liquidator
4.185 Enforced delivery up of company's property
4.186 Final distribution

CHAPTER 15

DISCLAIMER

4.187 Liquidator's notice of disclaimer
4.188 Communication of disclaimer to persons interested

4.189 Additional notices
4.190 Duty to keep court informed
4.191 Application by interested party under s. 178(5)
4.192 Interest in property to be declared on request
4.193 Disclaimer presumed valid and effective
4.194 Application for exercise of court's powers under s. 181

4.213 Order on request by creditors or contributories
4.214 Witness unfit for examination
4.215 Procedure at hearing
4.216 Adjournment
4.217 Expenses of examination

Chapter 16

Settlement of List of Contributories (No CVL Application)

4.195 Preliminary
4.196 Duty of liquidator to settle list
4.197 Form of list
4.198 Procedure for settling list
4.199 Application to court for variation of the list
4.200 Variation of, or addition to, the list
4.201 Costs not to fall on official receiver

Chapter 17

Calls (No CVL Application)

4.202 Calls by liquidator
4.203 Control by liquidation committee
4.204 Application to court for leave to make a call
4.205 Making and enforcement of the call

Chapter 18

Special Manager

4.206 Appointment and remuneration
4.207 Security
4.208 Failure to give or keep up security
4.209 Accounting
4.210 Termination of appointment

Chapter 19

Public Examination of Company Officers and Others

4.211 Order for public examination
4.212 Notice of hearing

Chapter 20

Order of Payment of Costs, etc., out of Assets

4.218 General rule as to priority
4.219 Winding up commencing as voluntary
4.220 Saving for powers of the court

Chapter 21

Miscellaneous Rules

Section A: return of capital (No CVL application)

4.221 Application to court for order authorising return
4.222 Procedure for return

Section B: conclusion of winding up

4.223-CVL   Statements to registrar of companies under s. 192

Section C: dissolution after winding up

4.224 Secretary of State's directions under s. 203, 205
4.225 Procedure following appeal under s. 203(4) or 205(4)

Chapter 22

Leave to Act as Director, etc., of Company with Prohibited Name (Section 216 of the Act)

4.226 Preliminary
4.227 Application for leave under s. 216(3)

The Insolvency Rules 1986

4.228　First excepted case
4.229　Second excepted case
4.230　Third excepted case

Chapter 23

EC Regulation – Member State Liquidator

4.231　Interpretation of creditor and notice to member State liquidator

The Second Group of Parts
Individual Insolvency; Bankruptcy

Part 5

Individual Voluntary Arrangements

Chapter 1

Preliminary

5.1　Introductory

Chapter 2

Preparation of the Debtor's Proposal

5.2　Preparation of proposal
5.3　Contents of proposal
5.4　Notice to intended nominee
5.5　Statement of Affairs
5.6　Additional disclosure for assistance of nominee

Chapter 3

Cases in which an Application for an Interim Order is Made

5.7　Application for interim order
5.8　Court in which application to be made

5.9　Hearing of the application
5.10　Action to follow making of order
5.11　Nominee's report on the proposal
5.12　Replacement of nominee
5.13　Consideration of nominee's report

Chapter 4

Cases where no Interim Order is to be Obtained

5.14　Nominee's report to the court
5.15　Filing of reports made under section 256A – appropriate court
5.16　Applications to the court

Chapter 5

Creditor's Meetings

5.17　Summary of creditor's meeting
5.18　Creditor's meeting: supplementary
5.19　The chairman at the meeting
5.20　The chairman as proxy-holder
5.21　Entitlement to vote
5.22　Procedure for admission of creditor's claims for voting
5.23　Requisite majorities
5.24　Proceedings to obtain agreement on the proposal

Chapter 6

Implementation of the Arrangement

5.25　Resolutions to follow approval
5.26　Hand-over of property, etc. to supervisor
5.27　Report of creditor's meeting
5.28　Register of voluntary arrangement
5.29　Reports to Secretary of State
5.30　Revocation or suspension of the arrangement
5.31　Supervisor's accounts and reports
5.32　Production of accounts and records to Secretary of State
5.33　Fees, costs, charges and expenses
5.34　Completion or termination of the arrangement

Chapter 7

Fast-Track Voluntary Arrangement

5.35　Application of Chapter
5.36　Interpretation

5.37	Contents of proposal			**CHAPTER 12**
5.38	Requirement for the official receiver's decision			
5.39	Arrangements for approval of fast-track voluntary arrangement			
5.40	Approval by creditors			EC REGULATION: CONVERSION OF VOLUNTARY ARRANGEMENT INTO BANKRUPTCY
5.41	Entitlement to vote			
5.42	Procedure for admission of creditor's claims for voting purposes			
5.43	Requisite majorities		5.62	Application for conversion of voluntary arrangement into bankruptcy
5.44	Notification to the court			
5.45	Notice of appointment as supervisor etc		5.63	Contents of affidavit
5.46	Revocation of the fast-track voluntary arrangement		5.64	Power of court
5.47	Supervisor's accounts and reports		5.65	Notices to be given to member State liquidator
5.48	Fees, costs and expenses in respect of the performance of the functions of the official receiver			
5.49	Employment of agents by the supervisor			
5.50	Completion or termination of the fast-track voluntary arrangement			

CHAPTER 8

APPLICATION BY A BANKRUPT TO ANNUL A BANKRUPTCY ORDER UNDER SECTION 261(2)(A)

5.51	Application of this Chapter
5.52	Application to court
5.53	Notice to creditors

CHAPTER 9

APPLICATION BY OFFICIAL RECEIVER TO ANNUL A BANKRUPTCY ORDER UNDER SECTION 261(2)(B)

5.54	Application of this Chapter
5.55	Application to court
5.56	Notice to creditors

CHAPTER 10

APPLICATION BY OFFICIAL RECEIVER TO ANNUL A BANKRUPTCY ORDER UNDER SECTION 263D(3)

5.57	Application of this Chapter
5.58	Application to court
5.59	Notice to creditors

CHAPTER 11

OTHER MATTERS ARISING ON ANNULMENTS UNDER SECTIONS 261(2)(A), 261(2)(B) OR 263D(3)

5.60	
5.61	Trustee's final account

PART 6

BANKRUPTCY

CHAPTER 1

THE STATUTORY DEMAND

6.1	Form and content of statutory demand
6.2	Information to be given in statutory demand
6.3	Requirements as to service
6.4	Application to set aside statutory demand
6.5	Hearing of application to set aside

CHAPTER 2

BANKRUPTCY PETITION (CREDITOR'S)

6.6	Preliminary
6.7	Identification of debtor
6.8	Identification of debt
6.9	Court in which petition to be presented
6.10	Procedure for presentation and filing
6.11	Proof of service of statutory demand
6.12	Verification of petition
6.13	Notice to Chief Land Registrar
6.14	Service of petition
6.15	Proof of service
6.16	Death of debtor before service
6.17	Security for costs (s. 268(2) only)
6.18	Hearing of petition
6.19	Petition against two or more debtors
6.20	Petition by moneylender
6.21	Petition opposed by debtor
6.22	Amendment of petition
6.23	Notice by persons intending to appear
6.24	List of appearances
6.25	Decision on the hearing
6.26	Non-appearance of creditor

6.27	Vacating registration on dismissal of petition	6.60	Verification and filing
6.28	Extension of time for hearing	6.61	Limited disclosure
6.29	Adjournment	6.62	Release from duty to submit statement of affairs; extension of time
6.30	Substitution of petitioner		
6.31	Change of carriage of petition	6.63	Expenses of statement of affairs
6.32	Petitioner seeking dismissal or leave to withdraw	6.64	Requirement to submit accounts
6.33	Settlement and content of bankruptcy order	6.65	Submission and filing of accounts
6.34	Action to follow making of order	6.66	Further disclosure
6.35	Amendment of title of proceedings		
6.36	Old bankruptcy notices		

Chapter 3

Bankruptcy Petition (Debtor's)

Section B: debtor's petition

		6.67	Preliminary
		6.68	Contents of statement
		6.69	Requirement to submit accounts
		6.70	Submission and filing of accounts
		6.71	Expenses of preparing accounts
		6.72	Further disclosure
6.37	Preliminary		
6.38	Identification of debtor		
6.39	Admission of insolvency		
6.40	Court in which petition to be filed		
6.41	Statement of affairs		
6.42	Procedure for presentation and filing		

Chapter 6

6.43	Notice to Chief Land Registrar
6.44	Report of insolvency practitioner
6.45	Settlement and content of bankruptcy order
6.46	Action to follow making of order
6.46A	Expenses of voluntary arrangement
6.47	Amendment of title of proceedings
6.48	Certificate of summary administration
6.49	Duty of official receiver in summary administration
6.50	Revocation of certificate of summary administration

Information to Creditors

6.73	General duty of official receiver
6.74	Those entitled to be informed
6.75	Report where statement of affairs lodged
6.76	Statement of affairs dispensed with
6.77	General rule as to reporting
6.78	Bankruptcy order annulled

Chapter 4

The Interim Receiver

Chapter 7

6.51	Application for appointment of interim receiver
6.52	Order of appointment
6.53	Deposit
6.54	Security
6.55	Failure to give or keep up security
6.56	Remuneration
6.57	Termination of appointment

Creditors' Meetings

Chapter 5

Disclosure by Bankrupt with Respect to the State of his Affairs

6.79	First meeting of creditors
6.80	Business at first meeting
6.81	General power to call meetings
6.82	The chairman at a meeting
6.83	Requisitioned meetings
6.84	Attendance at meetings of bankrupt, etc.
6.85	Notice of meetings by advertisement only
6.86	Venue of meetings
6.87	Expenses of summoning meetings
6.88	Resolutions
6.89	Chairman of meeting as proxy-holder
6.90	Suspension of meeting
6.91	Adjournment

Section A: creditor's petition

6.58	Preliminary
6.59	The statement of affairs

6.92	Quorum	6.122	Appointment by Secretary of State
6.93	Entitlement to vote	6.123	Authentication of trustee's appointment
6.94	Admission and rejection of proof	6.124	Advertisement of appointment
6.95	Record of proceedings	6.125	Hand-over of estate to trustee

Chapter 8

Proof of Bankruptcy Debts

Section B: resignation and removal; vacation of office

6.126	Creditors' meeting to receive trustee's resignation
6.127	Action following acceptance of resignation
6.128	Leave to resign granted by the court
6.129	Meeting of creditors to remove trustee
6.130	Court's power to regulate meeting under Rule 6.129
6.131	Procedure on removal
6.132	Removal of trustee by the court
6.133	Removal of trustee by Secretary of State
6.134	Advertisement of resignation or removal
6.135	Release of resigning or removed trustee

Section A: procedure for proving

6.96	Meaning of "prove"
6.97	Supply of forms
6.98	Particulars of creditor's claim
6.99	Claim established by affidavit
6.100	Cost of proving
6.101	Trustee to allow inspection of proofs
6.102	Proof of licensed moneylender
6.103	Transmissions of proofs to trustee
6.104	Admission and rejection of proofs for dividend
6.105	Appeal against decision on proof
6.106	Withdrawal or variation of proof
6.107	Expunging of proof by the court

Section C: release on completion of administration

6.136	Release of official receiver
6.137	Final meeting of creditors
6.137A	Rule as to reporting

Section D: remuneration

6.138	Fixing of remuneration
6.138A	Trustee's remuneration where it is not fixed in accordance with Rule 6.138
6.139	Other matters affecting remuneration
6.140	Recourse of trustee to meeting of creditors
6.141	Recourse to the court
6.142	Creditor's claim that remuneration is excessive

Section B: quantification of claim

6.108	Negotiable instruments, etc.
6.109	Secured creditors
6.110	Discounts
6.111	Debt in foreign currency
6.112	Payments of a periodical nature
6.113	Interest
6.114	Debt payable at future time

Section E: supplementary provisions

6.143	Trustee deceased
6.144	Loss of qualification as insolvency practitioner
6.145	Notice to official receiver of intention to vacate office
6.146	Trustee's duties on vacating office
6.147	Power of court to set aside certain transactions
6.148	Rule against solicitation
6.149	Enforcement of trustee's obligations to official receiver

Chapter 9

Secured Creditors

6.115	Value of security
6.116	Surrender for non-disclosure
6.117	Redemption by trustee
6.118	Test of security's value
6.119	Realisation of security by creditor

Chapter 11

The Creditors' Committee

Chapter 10

The Trustee in Bankruptcy

Section A: appointment and associated formalities

6.120	Appointment by creditors' meeting
6.121	Appointment by the court

6.150	Membership of creditors' committee
6.151	Formalities of establishment
6.152	Obligations of trustee to committee
6.153	Meetings of the committee
6.154	The chairman at meetings
6.155	Quorum
6.156	Committee-members' representatives

The Insolvency Rules 1986

6.157 Resignation
6.158 Termination of membership
6.159 Removal
6.160 Vacancies
6.161 Voting rights and resolutions
6.162 Resolutions by post
6.163 Trustee's reports
6.164 Expenses of members etc.
6.165 Dealings by committee-members and others
6.166 Committee's functions vested in Secretary of State

Chapter 12

Special Manager

6.167 Appointment and remuneration
6.168 Security
6.169 Failure to give or keep up security
6.170 Accounting
6.171 Termination of appointment

Chapter 13

Public Examination of Bankrupt

6.172 Order for public examination
6.173 Order on request by creditors
6.174 Bankrupt unfit for examination
6.175 Procedure at hearing
6.176 Adjournment
6.177 Expenses of examination

Chapter 14

Disclaimer

6.178 Trustee's notice of disclaimer
6.179 Communication of disclaimer to persons interested
6.180 Additional notices
6.181 Duty to keep court informed
6.182 Application for leave to disclaim
6.183 Application by interested party under s. 316
6.184 Interest in property to be declared on request
6.185 Disclaimer presumed valid and effective
6.186 Application for exercise of court's powers under s. 320

Chapter 15

Replacement of Exempt Property

6.187 Purchase of replacement property
6.188 Money provided in lieu of sale

Chapter 16

Income Payments Orders

6.189 Application for order
6.190 Action to follow making of order
6.191 Variation of order
6.192 Order to payor of income: administration
6.193 Review of order

Chapter 17

Action by Court Under Section 369; Order to Inland Revenue Official

6.194 Application for order
6.195 Making and service of the order
6.196 Custody of documents

Chapter 18

Mortgaged Property

6.197 Claim by mortgagee of land
6.198 Power of court to order sale
6.199 Proceeds of sale

Chapter 19

After-Acquired Property

6.200 Duties of bankrupt in respect of after-acquired property
6.201 Trustee's recourse to disponee of property
6.202 Expenses of getting in property for the estate

Chapter 20

Leave to Act as Director, Etc.

6.203 Application for leave
6.204 Report of official receiver
6.205 Court's order on application

Chapter 21

Annulment of Bankruptcy Order

6.206 Application for annulment
6.207 Report by trustee
6.208 Power of court to stay proceedings
6.209 Notice to creditors who have not proved
6.210 The hearing
6.211 Matters to be proved under s. 282(1)(b)
6.212 Notice to creditors
6.212A Annulment under s. 261
6.213 Other matters arising on annulment
6.214 Trustee's final account

Chapter 22

Discharge

6.215 Application for suspension of discharge
6.216 Lifting of suspension of discharge
6.217 Application by bankrupt for discharge
6.218 Report of official receiver
6.219 Order of discharge on application
6.220 Certificate of discharge
6.221 Deferment of issue of order pending appeal
6.222 Costs under this Chapter
6.223 Bankrupt's debts surviving discharge

Chapter 22A

Register of Bankruptcy Orders

6.223(A) Register of bankruptcy orders
6.223(B) Specified bankruptcy information
6.223(C) Notification of changes

Chapter 23

Order of Payment of Costs, Etc., out of Estate

6.224 General rule as to priority

Chapter 24

Second Bankruptcy

6.225 Scope of this Chapter
6.226 General duty of existing trustee
6.227 Delivery up to later trustee
6.228 Existing trustee's expenses

Chapter 25

Criminal Bankruptcy

6.229 Presentation of petition
6.230 Status and functions of Official Petitioner
6.231 Interim receivership
6.232 Proof of bankruptcy debts and notice of order
6.233 Meetings under the Rules
6.234 Trustee in bankruptcy; creditors' committee; annulment of bankruptcy order

Chapter 26

Miscellaneous Rules in Bankruptcy

6.235 Bankruptcy of solicitors
6.236 Consolidation of petitions
6.237 Bankrupt's dwelling-house and home
6.237 Bankrupt's home – notification of property falling within section 283A
6.237A Application in respect of the vesting of an interest in a dwelling-house (registered land)
6.237B Vesting of bankrupt's interest (unregistered land)
6.237C (no heading provided)
6.237CA Vesting of bankrupt's estate – substituted period
6.237D Charging order
6.237E Interpretation

Chapter 27

EC Regulation – Member State Liquidator

6.238 Interpretation of creditor and notice to member State liquidator
6.239 Interpretation of creditor and notice to member State liquidator appointed in main proceedings

The Third Group of Parts

Part 7

Court Procedure and Practice

Chapter 1

Applications

7.1 Preliminary
7.2 Interpretation

The Insolvency Rules 1986

7.3	Form and contents of application
7.3A	Application under section 176A(5) to disapply section 176A
7.4	Filing and service of application
7.4A	Notice of application under section 176A(5)
7.5	Other hearings *ex parte*
7.6	Hearing of application
7.7	Use of affidavit evidence
7.8	Filing and service of affidavits
7.9	Use of reports
7.10	Adjournment of hearing; directions

Chapter 2

Transfer of Proceedings Between Courts

7.11	General power of transfer
7.12	Proceedings commenced in wrong court
7.13	Applications for transfer
7.14	Procedure following order for transfer
7.15	Consequential transfer of other proceedings

Chapter 3

Shorthand Writers

7.16	Nomination and appointment of shorthand writers
7.17	Remuneration
7.18	Cost of shorthand note

Chapter 4

Enforcement Procedures

7.19	Enforcement of court orders
7.20	Orders enforcing compliance with the Rules
7.21	Warrants (general provisions)
7.22	Warrants under s. 134, 364
7.23	Warrants under s. 236, 366
7.24	Execution of warrants outside court's district
7.25	Warrants under s. 365

Chapter 5

Court Records and Returns

7.26	Title of proceedings
7.27	Court records
7.28	Inspection of records
7.29	Returns to Secretary of State
7.30	File of court proceedings
7.31	Right to inspect the file
7.32	Filing of Gazette notices and advertisements

Chapter 6

Costs and Detailed Assessment

7.33	Application of the CPR
7.34	Requirement to assess costs by the detailed procedure
7.35	Procedure where detailed assessment required
7.36	Costs of sheriff
7.37	Petitions presented by insolvents
7.38	Costs paid otherwise than out of the insolvent estate
7.39	Award of costs against official receiver or responsible insolvency practitioner
7.40	Application for costs
7.41	Costs and expenses of witnesses
7.42	Final costs certificate

Chapter 7

Persons Incapable of Managing Their Affairs

7.43	Introductory
7.44	Appointment of another person to act
7.45	Affidavit in support of application
7.46	Service of notices following appointment

Chapter 8

Appeals in Insolvency Proceedings

7.47	Appeals and reviews of court orders (winding up)
7.48	Appeals in bankruptcy
7.49	Procedure on appeal
7.50	Appeal against decision of Secretary of State or official receiver

Chapter 9

General

7.51	Principal court rules and practice to apply
7.52	Right of audience

7.53	Right of attendance (company insolvency)		9.4	Procedure for examination
7.54	Insolvency practitioner's solicitor		9.5	Record of examination
7.55	Formal defects		9.6	Costs of proceedings under s. 236, 366
7.56	Restriction on concurrent proceedings and remedies			
7.57	Affidavits			
7.58	Security in court			
7.59	Payment into court			PART 10
7.60	Further information and disclosure			
7.61	Office copies of documents			

CHAPTER 10

OFFICIAL RECEIVERS

10.1 Appointment of official receivers
10.2 Persons entitled to act on official receiver's behalf
10.3 Application for directions
10.4 Official receiver's expenses

EC REGULATION – CREDITORS' VOLUNTARY WINDING UP: CONFIRMATION BY THE COURT

PART 11

7.62 Application for confirmation
7.63 Notice to member State liquidator and creditors in member States

DECLARATION AND PAYMENT OF DIVIDEND (WINDING UP AND BANKRUPTCY)

CHAPTER 11

11.1 Preliminary
11.2 Notice of intended dividend
11.3 Final admission/rejection of proofs
11.4 Postponement or cancellation of dividend
11.5 Decision to declare dividend
11.6 Notice of declaration
11.7 Notice of no, or no further, dividend
11.8 Proof altered after payment of dividend
11.9 Secured creditors
11.10 Disqualification from dividend
11.11 Assignment of right to dividend
11.12 Preferential creditors
11.13 Debt payable at future time

EC REGULATION – MEMBER STATE LIQUIDATOR

7.64 Interpretation of creditor

PART 8

PART 12

PROXIES AND COMPANY REPRESENTATION

MISCELLANEOUS AND GENERAL

8.1 Definition of "proxy"
8.2 Issue and use of forms
8.3 Use of proxies at meetings
8.4 Retention of proxies
8.5 Right of inspection
8.6 Proxy-holder with financial interest
8.7 Company representation
8.8 Interpretation of creditor

12.1 Power of Secretary of State to regulate certain matters
12.2 Costs, expenses, etc.
12.3 Provable debts
12.4 Notices
12.4A Quorum at meeting of creditors or contributories
12.5 Evidence of proceedings at meetings
12.6 Documents issuing from Secretary of State
12.7 Forms for use in insolvency proceedings
12.8 Insolvency practitioner's security
12.9 Time-limits
12.10 Service by post
12.11 General provisions as to service
12.12 Service outside the jurisdiction
12.13 Confidentiality of documents
12.14 Notices sent simultaneously to the same person
12.15 Right to copy documents

PART 9

EXAMINATION OF PERSONS CONCERNED IN COMPANY AND INDIVIDUAL INSOLVENCY

9.1 Preliminary
9.2 Form and contents of application
9.3 Order for examination, etc.

The Insolvency Rules 1986

12.15A	Charge for copy documents	13.7	"Insolvency proceedings"
12.16	Non-receipt of notice of meeting	13.8	"Insolvent estate"
12.17	Right to have list of creditors	13.9	"Responsible insolvency practitioner", etc.
12.18	False claim of status as creditor, etc.	13.10	"Petitioner"
12.19	Execution overtaken by judgment debtor's insolvency	13.11	"The appropriate fee"
12.20	The Gazette	13.12	"Debt", "liability" (winding up)
12.21	Punishment of offences	13.12A	"Authorised deposit-taker and former authorised deposit-taker"
12.22	Notice of order under section 176A(5)	13.13	Expressions used generally
		13.14	Application

Part 13

Interpretation and Application

13.1	Introductory
13.2	"The court"; "the registrar"
13.3	"Give notice", etc.
13.4	Notice, etc. to solicitors
13.5	Notice to joint liquidators, joint trustees, etc.
13.6	"Venue"

Schedules

1	Scheme Manager's Voting Rights
2	Alternative Courts for Debtors' Petitions in Bankruptcy
3	Shorthand Writers' Remuneration
4	Forms
5	Punishment of Offences under the Rules
6	Determination of an Insolvency Office Holder's Remuneration

Rule 0.1   *The Insolvency Rules 1986*

The Insolvency Rules 1986

(SI 1986/1925)

GENERAL NOTE

The rules in this section are prefixed with the figure 0. The remainder of the rules are grouped into Parts, numbered 1, 2, etc., and the rules in each part begin with the same figure, *e.g.* r. 1.1, 1.2, etc. The sequence of Parts broadly follows the scheme of IA 1986.

Where a rule calls for the use of a prescribed form, the reference number of the appropriate form is shown adjacent to the rule in question.

The text incorporates amendments made to the rules by SI 1987/1919, which came into force on January 11, 1988, SI 1989/397, effective from April 3, 1989, SI 1991/495, effective from April 2, 1991, SI 1993/602, effective from April 5, 1993, SI 1995/586, effective from April 1, 1995, SI 1999/359 and SI 1999/1022 (both effective from March 22, 1999), SI 2001/763, effective from April 2, 2001, and SI 2002/1307, effective from May 31, 2002, SI 2002/2712, effective from January 1, 2002 and SI 2003/1730, effective from September 15, 2003 and April 1, 2004. For Scotland, corresponding rules were enacted by SI 1986/1915 (S 139), effective from December 29, 1986, to which amendments were made by SI 1987/1921 (S 132), effective from January 11, 1988, SI 2002/2709 (S.10), effective from January 1, 2003, and SI 2003/2111 (S.9), effective from September 15, 2003.

The Rules were drawn up at a time when procedure in the civil courts was regulated by the Rules of the Supreme Court 1986 and the County Court Rules 1981. These two sets of Rules were replaced by the Civil Procedure Rules 1998 (commonly known as the CPR) which came into force on April 26, 1999. Under rule 2.1 of the CPR, the new civil procedure does not apply to insolvency proceedings, but by the Insolvency (Amendment) (No. 2) Rules 1999 (SI 1999/1022) the Insolvency Rules 1986 are amended, with effect from April 26, 1999, so as to apply all those provisions of the CPR and such practice of the High Court and County Court as is not inconsistent with provisions made by IR 1986 to insolvency proceedings. In addition, detailed amendment is made of such of the latter Rules as use language which has been discarded by the CPR, such as "*ex parte* hearings" and the "taxation" of costs. Again, in order to achieve consistency with the CPR, the amendments bring practice in insolvency proceedings into line with the new civil procedure by permitting, for example, the use of witness statements verified by statements of truth in a number of situations where affidavit evidence was formerly obligatory.

INTRODUCTORY PROVISIONS

0.1   Citation and commencement

0.1   These Rules may be cited as the Insolvency Rules 1986 and shall come into force on 29th December 1986.

GENERAL NOTE

The day appointed for the commencement of IA 1986 and these rules was December 29, 1986. Other subordinate legislation which came into force on the same date is listed below. A number of these instruments have since been amended and/or revoked and replaced; their replacements appear in the second list below.

    The Insolvency Regulations 1986 (SI 1986/1994) amended by SI 1987/1959; SI 1988/1739 and SI 1991/380; revoked and replaced by SI 1994/2507)

    The Insolvency Fees Order 1986 (SI 1986/2030) (since amended, see second list below)

    The Insolvency Proceedings (Monetary Limits) Order 1986 (SI 1986/1996)

    The Insolvent Partnerships Order 1986 (SI 1986/2142) (revoked and replaced by SI 1994/2421)

    The Administration of Insolvent Estates of Deceased Persons Order 1986 (SI 1986/1999)

    The Companies (Unfair Prejudice Applications) Rules 1986 (SI 1986/2000)

The Insolvency Practitioners Regulations 1986 (SI 1986/1995 (amended by SI 1986/2247; SI 1989/1587 and SI 1989/2170; revoked and replaced by SI 1990/439)

The Insolvency (Amendment of Subordinate Legislation) Order 1986 (SI 1986/2001)

The Co-operation of Insolvency Courts (Designation of Relevant Countries and Territories) Order 1986 (SI 1986/2123)

The Insurance Companies (Winding-up) (Amendment) Rules 1986 (SI 1986/2002)

The Insolvency (Scotland) Rules 1986 (SI 1986/1915 (S 139))

The Receivers (Scotland) Regulations 1986 (SI 1986/1917 (S 141))

The Insurance Companies (Winding Up) (Scotland) Rules 1986 (SI 1986/1918 (S 142))

Other secondary legislation (which came into force on January 11, 1988 unless otherwise stated) to note:

The Insolvency (Amendment of Subordinate Legislation) Order 1987 (SI 1987/1398) (September 1, 1987)

The Insolvency (Scotland) Amendment Rules 1987 (SI 1987/1921 (S 132))

The Insolvency (ECSC Levy Debts) Regulations 1987 (SI 1987/2093)

The Department of Trade and Industry (Fees) Order 1988 (SI 1988/93) (January 22, 1988)

The Insolvency Fees (Amendment) Order 1988 (SI 1988/95) (February 16, 1988)

The Insolvency Act 1986 (Guernsey) Order 1989 (SI 1989/2409) (February 1, 1990)

The Insolvency Fees (Amendment) Order 1990 (SI 1990/560) (April 2, 1990)

The Insolvency Practitioners Regulations 1990 (SI 1990/439) (April 1, 1990)

The Bankruptcy and Companies (Department of Trade and Industry) Fees (Amendment) Order 1990 (SI 1990/599) (April 2, 1990)

The Insolvency Fees (Amendment) Order 1991 (SI 1991/496)

The Financial Markets and Insolvency Regulations 1991 (SI 1991/880) (April 25, 1991)

The Insolvency Fees (Amendment) Order 1992 (SI 1992/34) (January 14, 1992)

The Financial Markets and Insolvency (Amendment) Regulations 1992 (SI 1992/716) (May 1, 1992)

The Companies (Single Member Private Limited Companies) Regulations 1992 (SI 1992/1699) (July 15, 1992)

The Insolvency Practitioners (Amendment) Regulations 1993 (SI 1993/221) (April 1, 1993)

The Insolvent Partnerships Order 1994 (SI 1994/2421) (December 1, 1994).

The Insolvency Regulations 1994 (SI 1994/2507) (October 24, 1994)

The Insolvency Fees (Amendment) Order 1994 (SI 1994/2541) (October 24, 1994)

The Co-operation of Insolvency Courts (Designation of Relevant Countries) Order 1996 (SI 1996/253) (March 1, 1996)

The Insolvent Partnerships (Amendment) Order 1996 (SI 1996/1308) (June 14, 1996)

The Financial Markets and Insolvency Regulations 1996 (SI 1996/1469) (July 15, 1996)

The Financial Markets and Insolvency (Ecu Contracts) Regulations 1998 (SI 1998/27) (February 2, 1998)

The Financial Markets and Insolvency Regulations 1998 (SI 1998/1748) (August 11, 1998)

The Co-operation of Insolvency Courts (Designation of Relevant Country) Order 1998 (SI 1998/2766) (December 11, 1998)

The Insolvency (Amendment) Rules 1999 (SI 1999/359) (March 22, 1999)

The Insolvency (Amendment) (No. 2) Rules 1999 (SI 1999/1022) (March 22, 1999)

Rule 0.1 *The Insolvency Rules 1986*

The Financial Markets and Insolvency (Settlement Finality) Regulations 1999 (SI 1999/2979) (December 11, 1999)

The Insolvency (Amendment) Regulations 2000 (SI 2000/485) (March 31, 2000)

The Limited Liability Partnership (Scotland) Regulations 2001 (SI 2001/128) (April 6, 2001)

The Insolvency Fees (Amendment) Order 2001 (SI 2001/761) (April 2, 2001)

The Insolvency (Amendment) Regulations 2001 (SI 2001/762) (April 2, 2001)

The Insolvency (Amendment) Rules 2001 (SI 2001/763) (April 2, 2001)

The Insolvent Companies (Disqualification of Unfit Directors) Proceedings (Amendment) Rules 2001 (SI 2001/765) (April 2, 2001)

The Insolvent Partnerships (Amendment) Order 2001 (SI 2001/767 (April 2, 2001)

The Companies (Disqualification Orders) Regulations 2001 (SI 2001/967) (April 6, 2001)

The Limited Liability Partnerships Regulations 2001 (SI 2001/1090) (April 6, 2001)

The Financial Services and Markets Act 2000 (Consequential Amendments and Repeals) Order 2001 (SI 2001/3649) (December 1, 2001)

The Insolvency Act 1986 (Amendment) Regulations 2002 (SI 2002/1037) (May 3, 2002)

The Insolvency Act 1986 (Amendment) (No. 2) Regulations 2002 (SI 2002/1240) (May 31, 2002)

The Financial Services and Markets Act 2000 (Administration Orders Relating to Insurers) Order 2002 (SI 2002/1242) (May 31, 2002)

The Insolvency (Amendment) Rules 2002 (SI 2002/1307) (May 31, 2002)

The Insolvent Partnerships (Amendment) Order 2002 (SI 2002/1308) (May 31, 2002)

The Administration of Insolvent Estates of Deceased Persons (Amendment) Order 2002 (SI 2002/1309) (May 31, 2002)

The Insolvency Act 1986 (Amendment) (No. 3) Regulations 2002 (SI 2002/1990) (January 1, 2003)

The Insolvent Partnerships (Amendment) (No. 2) Order 2002 (SI 2002/2708) (January 1, 2003)

The Insolvency (Scotland) Amendment Rules 2002 (SI 2002/2709 (S.10)) (January 1, 2003)

The Insolvency Practitioners (Amendment) Regulations 2002 (SI 2002/2710) (January 1, 2003)

The Insolvency Act 2000 (Commencement No. 3 and Transitional Provisions) Order 2002 (SI 2002/2711 (C.83)) (January 1, 2003)

The Insolvency (Amendment) (No. 2) Rules 2002 (SI 2002/2712) (January 1, 2003)

The Insolvency Practitioners (Amendment) (No. 2) Regulations 2002 (SI 2002/2748) (January 1, 2003)

The Insolvency Act 1986 (Amendment) (Administrative Receivership and Capital Market Arrangements) Order 2003 (SI 2003/1468) (September 15, 2003)

The Insolvency (Amendment) Rules 2003 (SI 2003/1730) (September 15, 2003 and April 1, 2004)

The Enterprise Act 2002 ((Commencement No. 4 and Transitional Provisions and Savings) Order 2003 (SI 2003/2093 (C.85) (September 15, 2003 and April 1, 2004)

The Insolvency Act 1986, Section 72A (Appointed Date) Order 2003 (SI 2003/2095) (September 15, 2003)

The Enterprise Act 2002 (Insolvency) Order 2003 (SI 2003/2096) (September 15, 2003)

The Enterprise Act 2002 (Prescribed Part) Order 2003 (SI 2003/2097) (September 15, 2003)

The Enterprise Act 2002 (Consequential Amendments) (Prescribed Part) (Scotland) Order 2003 (SI 2003/2108 (S.7)) (September 15, 2003)

The Insolvency (Scotland) Regulations 2003 (SI 2003/2109 (S.8)) (September 15, 2003)

The Insolvency (Scotland) Amendment Rules 2003 (SI 2003/2111) (s. 9) (September 15, 2003)

The Act of Sederunt (Rules of the Court of Session Amendment No. 5) (Insolvency Proceedings) 2003 (Scottish SI 2003/385) (September 15, 2003)

The Act of Sederunt (Sheriff Court Company Insolvency Rules 1986) (Amendment) 2003 (Scottish SI 2003/388) (September 15, 2003)

The Enterprise Act 2002 (Transitional Provisions) (Insolvency) Order 2003 (SI 2003/2332) (September 9, 2003)

The Enterprise Act 2002 (Commencement No. 5 and Amendment) Order 2003 (SI 2003/3340, C.132) (December 18, 2003)

The Insolvency Practitioners and Insolvency Services Account (Fees) Order 2003 (SI 2003/3363) (April 1, 2004)

The Insurers (Reorganisation and Winding Up) Regulations 2004 (SI 2004/353) (February 18, 2004)

The Insolvency (Amendment) Regulations 2004 (SI 2004/472) April 1, 2004)

The Insolvency Practitioners (Amendment) Regulations 2004 (SI 2004/473) (April 1, 2004)

The Insolvency Practitioners and Insolvency Services Account (Fees) (Amendment) Order 2004 (SI 2004/476) (March 31, 2004)

The Insolvency Proceedings (Monetary Limits) (Amendment) Order 2004 (SI 2004/547) (April 1, 2004)

The Insolvency (Amendment) Rules 2004 (SI 2004/584) (April 1, 2004)

The Insolvency Proceedings (Fees) Order 2004 (SI 2004/593) (April 1, 2004)

The Insolvency (Amendment) Rules 2004 (SI 2004/584) (April 1, 2004)

The Insolvency (Amendment No. 2) Rules 2004 (SI 2004/1070) (May 3, 2004)

0.2 Construction and interpretation

0.2(1) [Definitions] In these Rules–
"**the Act**" means the Insolvency Act 1986 (any reference to a numbered section being to a section of that Act);
"**the Companies Act**" means the Companies Act 1985;
"**CPR**" means the Civil Procedure Rules 1998 and "**CPR**" followed by a Part or rule by number means the Part or rule with that number in those Rules;
"**RSC**" followed by an Order by number means the Order with that number set out in Schedule 1 to the CPR; and
"**the Rules**" means the Insolvency Rules 1986.

0.2(2) [Ex parte hearings] References in the Rules to *ex parte* hearings shall be construed as references to hearings without notice being served on any other party; references to applications made *ex parte* as references to applications made without notice being served on any other party and other references which include the expression "*ex parte*" shall be similarly construed.

0.2(3) [Part 13] Subject to paragraphs (1) and (2), Part 13 of the Rules has effect for their interpretation and application.

GENERAL NOTE

Rule 0.2 was replaced by the Insolvency (Amendment) (No. 2) Rules 1999 (SI 1999/1022) with effect from April 26, 1999 to cater for the advent of the Civil Procedure Rules.

0.3 Extent

0.3(1) [Pts 1, 2 and 4] Parts 1, 2, and 4 of the Rules, and Parts 7 to 13 as they relate to company insolvency, apply in relation to companies which the courts in England and Wales have jurisdiction to wind up.

0.3(2) [Application of rr. 3.1, 3.39, 3.40, remainder of Pt 3] Rule 3.1 applies to all receivers to whom Part III of the Act applies, Rule 3.39 and 3.40 apply to all receivers who are not administrative receivers, and the remainder of Part 3 of the Rules applies to administrative receivers appointed otherwise than under section 51 (Scottish Receivership).

0.3(3) [Pts 5 and 6] Parts 5 and 6 of the Rules, and Parts 7 to 13 as they relate to individual insolvency, extend to England and Wales only.

GENERAL NOTE

Rule 0.3(2) was replaced by the Insolvency (Amendment) Rules 2003 (SI 2003/1730).

The corresponding subordinate legislation for Scotland is to be found in the last four statutory instruments listed in the first part of the general note to r. 0.1 above (as amended).

For the position in Northern Ireland see the Insolvency Rules (Northern Ireland) 1991 (SR 1991/364), (as amended) and the note to IA 1986, s. 441.

THE FIRST GROUP OF PARTS
COMPANY INSOLVENCY; COMPANIES WINDING UP

General comment on Pt 1
The topic of CVAs to which these rules relate is dealt with in IA 1986, ss. 1–7. On voluntary arrangements for individual debtors, see IA 1986, ss. 252ff., and IR 1986, Pt. 5. The alternative model of CVA with moratorium as detailed in IA 2000 is not yet in force.

PART 1

COMPANY VOLUNTARY ARRANGEMENTS

CHAPTER 1

PRELIMINARY

1.1 Scope of this Part; interpretation

1.1(1) **[Application of Pt 1 Rules]** The Rules in this Part apply where, pursuant to Part I of the Act, it is intended to make, and there is made, a proposal to a company and its creditors for a voluntary arrangement, that is to say, a composition in satisfaction of its debts or a scheme of arrangement of its affairs.

1.1(2) **[Application of Ch. 2–8]** In this Part–

(a) Chapter 2 applies where the proposal for the voluntary arrangement is made by the directors of the company and

    (i) the company is neither in liquidation nor is the company in administration; and

    (ii) no steps have been taken to obtain a moratorium under Schedule A1 to the Act in connection with the proposal;

(b) Chapter 3 applies where the company is in liquidation or the company is in administration, and the proposal is made by the liquidator or (as the case may be) the administrator, he in either case being the nominee for the purposes of the proposal;

(c) Chapter 4 applies in the same case as Chapter 3, but where the nominee is not the liquidator or administrator;

(d) Chapter 5 applies in all the three cases mentioned in sub-paragraphs (a) to (c) above;

(e) Chapters 7 and 8 apply to all voluntary arrangements with or without a moratorium; and

(f) Chapter 9 applies where the proposal is made by the directors of an eligible company with a view to obtaining a moratorium.

1.1(3) **["The responsible insolvency practitioner" in Ch. 3–5]** In Chapters 3, 4 and 5, the liquidator or the administrator is referred to as "the responsible insolvency practitioner".

1.1(4) **["Eligible company"]** In this Part, a reference to an eligible company is to a company that is eligible for a moratorium in accordance with paragraph 2 of Schedule A1 to the Act.

GENERAL NOTE

This was amended in paras (1) and (2) by the Insolvency (Amendment) (No. 2) Rules 2002 (SI 2002/2712) with effect from January 1, 2003 to cater for the coming into operation of the new optional CVA cum moratorium model. It fully reflects the increased complexity of CVA law in the wake of the full range of changes effected by IA 2000. A new para. (4) was added as part of this overhaul.

A further textual amendment came via the Insolvency (Amendment) Rules 2003 (SI 2003/1730) in recognition of the fact that it is not always appropriate to use the phrase "administration order".

GENERAL NOTE

Different procedures must be followed in the three cases listed in r. 1.1(2)(a–c): see IA 1986, ss. 1, 2. The relevant rules are set out in Chs 2, 3 and 4 respectively. Rule 1.1(2)(d) was amended by the Insolvency (Amendment) Rules 2002 (SI 2002/1307) para. 4(1).

CHAPTER 2

PROPOSAL BY DIRECTORS

1.2 Preparation of proposal

1.2 The directors shall prepare for the intended nominee a proposal on which (with or without amendments to be made under Rule 1.3 below) to make his report to the court under section 2.

(See General Note after r. 1.6.)

1.3 Contents of proposal

1.3(1) [Explanation why voluntary arrangement desirable] The directors' proposal shall provide a short explanation why, in their opinion, a voluntary arrangement under Part I of the Act is desirable, and give reasons why the company's creditors may be expected to concur with such an arrangement.

1.3(2) [Other matters] The following matters shall be stated, or otherwise dealt with, in the directors' proposal–

(a) the following matters, so far as within the directors' immediate knowledge–

  (i) the company's assets, with an estimate of their respective values,
  (ii) the extent (if any) to which the assets are charged in favour of creditors,
  (iii) the extent (if any) to which particular assets are to be excluded from the voluntary arrangement;

(b) particulars of any property, other than assets of the company itself, which is proposed to be included in the arrangement, the source of such property and the terms on which it is to be made available for inclusion;

(c) the nature and amount of the company's liabilities (so far as within the directors' immediate knowledge), the manner in which they are proposed to be met, modified, postponed or otherwise dealt with by means of the arrangement, and (in particular)–

  (i) how it is proposed to deal with preferential creditors (defined in section 4(7)) and creditors who are, or claim to be, secured,
  (ii) how persons connected with the company (being creditors) are proposed to be treated under the arrangement, and
  (iii) whether there are, to the directors' knowledge, any circumstances giving rise to the possibility, in the event that the company should go into liquidation, of claims under–

  section 238 (transactions at an undervalue),

  section 239 (preferences),

section 244 (extortionate credit transactions), or

section 245 (floating charges invalid);

and, where any such circumstances are present, whether, and if so how, it is proposed under the voluntary arrangement to make provision for wholly or partly indemnifying the company in respect of such claims;

(ca) an estimate (to the best of the directors' knowledge and belief and subject to paragraph (4)) of–

(i) the value of the prescribed part, should the company go into liquidation if the proposal for the voluntary arrangement is not accepted, whether or not section 176A is to be disapplied; and

(ii) the value of the company's net property on the date that the estimate is made.

(d) whether any, and if so what, guarantees have been given of the company's debts by other persons, specifying which (if any) of the guarantors are persons connected with the company;

(e) the proposed duration of the voluntary arrangement;

(f) the proposed dates of distributions to creditors, with estimates of their amounts;

(fa) how it is proposed to deal with the claim of any person who is bound by the arrangement by virtue of section 5(2)(b)(ii);

(g) the amount proposed to be paid to the nominee (as such) by way of remuneration and expenses;

(h) the manner in which it is proposed that the supervisor of the arrangement should be remunerated, and his expenses defrayed;

(j) whether, for the purposes of the arrangement, any guarantees are to be offered by directors, or other persons, and whether (if so) any security is to be given or sought;

(k) the manner in which funds held for the purposes of the arrangement are to be banked, invested or otherwise dealt with pending distribution to creditors;

(l) the manner in which funds held for the purpose of payment to creditors, and not so paid on the termination of the arrangement, are to be dealt with;

(m) the manner in which the business of the company is proposed to be conducted during the course of the arrangement;

(n) details of any further credit facilities which it is intended to arrange for the company, and how the debts so arising are to be paid;

(o) the functions which are to be undertaken by the supervisor of the arrangement;

(p) the name, address and qualification of the person proposed as supervisor of the voluntary arrangement, and confirmation that he is either qualified to act as an insolvency practitioner in relation to the company or is an authorised person in relation to the company; and

(q) whether the EC Regulation will apply and, if so, whether the proceedings will be main proceedings, secondary proceedings or territorial proceedings.

1.3(3) [Amendment of proposal] With the agreement in writing of the nominee, the directors' proposal may be amended at any time up to delivery of the former's report to the court under section 2(2).

1.3(4) [Disclosure of information prejudicial] Nothing in paragraph (2)(ca) is to be taken as requiring the estimate referred to in that paragraph to include any information, the disclosure of which could seriously prejudice the commercial interests of the company. If such information is excluded from the calculation the estimate shall be accompanied by a statement to that effect.

(See General Note after r. 1.6.) Paragraph 1.3(2)(q) was inserted by the *Insolvency (Amendment) Rules* 2002 (SI 2002/1307) para. 4(2).

GENERAL NOTE

New sub-paragraph (2)(fa) and a revised (2)(p) were added by the Insolvency (Amendment) (No. 2) Rules 2002 (SI 2002/2712) with effect from January 1, 2003 to cater for reforms introduced by IA 2000 particularly with regard to unknown creditors and non-IPs acting as supervisors.

This rule was then also further amended by the Insolvency (Amendment) Rules 2003 (SI 2003/1730) to address the implications of the reserved fund for unsecured creditors, though subject to the need to protect commercial confidences.

1.4 Notice to intended nominee

1.4(1) [Written notice] The directors shall give to the intended nominee written notice of their proposal.

1.4(2) [Delivery of notice] The notice, accompanied by a copy of the proposal, shall be delivered either to the nominee himself, or to a person authorised to take delivery of documents on his behalf.

1.4(3) [Endorsement of receipt] If the intended nominee agrees to act, he shall cause a copy of the notice to be endorsed to the effect that it has been received by him on a specified date; and the period of 28 days referred to in section 2(2) then runs from that date.

1.4(4) [Return of endorsed notice] The copy of the notice so endorsed shall be returned by the nominee forthwith to the directors at an address specified by them in the notice for that purpose.

(See General Note after r. 1.6.)

1.5 Statement of affairs

1.5(1) [Delivery of statement] The directors shall, within 7 days after their proposal is delivered to the nominee, or within such longer time as he may allow, deliver to him a statement of the company's affairs.

1.5(2) [Particulars in statement] The statement shall comprise the following particulars (supplementing or amplifying, so far as is necessary for clarifying the state of the company's affairs, those already given in the directors' proposal)–

(a) a list of the company's assets, divided into such categories as are appropriate for easy identification, with estimated values assigned to each category;

(b) in the case of any property on which a claim against the company is wholly or partly secured, particulars of the claim and its amount, and of how and when the security was created;

(c) the names and addresses of the company's preferential creditors (defined in section 4(7)), with the amounts of their respective claims;

(d) the names and addresses of the company's unsecured creditors, with the amounts of their respective claims;

(e) particulars of any debts owed by or to the company to or by persons connected with it;

(f) the names and addresses of the company's members, with details of their respective shareholdings;

(g) such other particulars (if any) as the nominee may in writing require to be furnished for the purposes of making his report to the court on the directors' proposal.

1.5(3) [Relevant date] The statement of affairs shall be made up to a date not earlier than 2 weeks before the date of the notice to the nominee under Rule 1.4.

However, the nominee may allow an extension of that period to the nearest practicable date (not earlier than 2 months before the date of the notice under Rule 1.4); and if he does so, he shall give his reasons in his report to the court on the directors' proposal.

1.5(4) [Certification of statement] The statement shall be certified as correct, to the best of their knowledge and belief, by two or more directors of the company, or by the company secretary and at least one director (other than the secretary himself).

(See General Note after r. 1.6.)

1.6 Additional disclosure for assistance of nominee

1.6(1) [**Nominee may request further information**] If it appears to the nominee that he cannot properly prepare his report on the basis of information in the directors' proposal and statement of affairs, he may call on the directors to provide him with–

- (a) further and better particulars as to the circumstances in which, and the reasons why, the company is insolvent or (as the case may be) threatened with insolvency;

- (b) particulars of any previous proposals which have been made in respect of the company under Part I of the Act;

- (c) any further information with respect to the company's affairs which the nominee thinks necessary for the purposes of his report.

1.6(2) [**Information about directors etc.**] The nominee may call on the directors to inform him, with respect to any person who is, or at any time in the 2 years preceding the notice under Rule 1.4 had been, a director or officer of the company, whether and in what circumstances (in those 2 years or previously) that person–

- (a) has been concerned in the affairs of any other company (whether or not incorporated in England and Wales) which has become insolvent, or

- (b) has himself been adjudged bankrupt or entered into an arrangement with his creditors.

1.6(3) [**Access to accounts and records**] For the purpose of enabling the nominee to consider their proposal and prepare his report on it, the directors must give him access to the company's accounts and records.

GENERAL NOTE TO RR. 1.2–1.6

The proposal and the statement of affairs will be relied on both by the nominee in the preparation of his report to the court under IA 1986, s. 2 and by the meetings of the company and its creditors which are summoned in due course if the proposal goes ahead. These rules seek to ensure that the decisions will be made on a basis of adequate evidence.

There is no prescribed form for the statement of affairs which is required in a voluntary arrangement, in contrast with the position in a liquidation: see rr. 4.33, 4.34.

1.7 Nominee's report on the proposal

1.7(1) [**Accompanying documents**] With his report to the court under section 2 the nominee shall deliver–

- (a) a copy of the directors' proposal (with amendments, if any, authorised under Rule 1.3(3)); and

- (b) a copy or summary of the company's statement of affairs.

1.7(2) [**Nominee's opinion re meetings**] If the nominee makes known his opinion that the directors proposal has a reasonable prospect of being approved and implemented and that meetings of the company and its creditors should be summoned under section 3, his report shall have annexed to it his comments on the proposal.

If his opinion is otherwise, he shall give his reasons for that opinion.

1.7(3) [**Endorsement of date of filing, and right to inspect**] The court shall cause the nominee's report to be endorsed with the date on which it is filed in court. Any director, member or creditor of the company is entitled, at all reasonable times on any business day, to inspect the file.

1.7(4) [**Copy to company**] The nominee shall send a copy of his report, and of his comments (if any), to the company.

GENERAL NOTE

The court's role is purely an administrative one, unless a challenge is mounted under IA 1986, s. 6. Note the amendment of para. (2) by the insertion of the words "that the directors' proposal has a reasonable prospect of being approved and implemented and" via the Insolvency (Amendment) (No. 2) Rules 2002 (SI 2002/2712). This reflects the policy for promoting greater quality controls on CVAs as pursued by IA 2000.

1.8 Replacement of nominee

1.8(1) **[Application by person other than nominee]** Where a person other than the nominee intends to apply to the court under section 2(4) for the nominee to be replaced, (except in any case where the nominee has died) he shall give to the nominee at least 7 days' notice of his application.

1.8(2) **[Application by nominee]** Where the nominee intends to apply to the court under section 2(4) of the Act to be replaced, he shall give at least 7 days' notice of his application to the person intending to make the proposal.

1.8(3) **[Statement of replacement nominee]** No appointment of a replacement nominee shall be made by the court unless there is filed in court a statement by the replacement nominee–

(a) indicating his consent to act, and

[FORM 1.8]

(b) that he is qualified to act as an insolvency practitioner in relation to the company or is an authorised person in relation to the company.

GENERAL NOTE

The provision on replacing nominees was reconstituted in the above version by the Insolvency (Amendment) (No. 2) Rules 2002 (SI 2002/2712) with effect from January 1, 2003. It recognises the fact that, in future, nominees may be authorised persons, such as "turnaround specialists", rather than restricted to insolvency practitioners. It also requires the suggested appointee to record his or her assent.

1.9 Summoning of meetings under s. 3

1.9(1) **[Date for meetings]** If in his report the nominee states that in his opinion meetings of the company and its creditors should be summoned to consider the directors' proposal, the date on which the meetings are to be held shall be not less than 14, nor more than 28, days from that on which the nominee's report is filed in court under Rule 1.7.

1.9(2) **[Notices of meetings]** Notices calling the meetings shall be sent by the nominee, at least 14 days before the day fixed for them to be held–

(a) in the case of the creditors' meeting, to all the creditors specified in the statement of affairs, and any other creditors of the company of whom he is otherwise aware; and

(b) in the case of the meeting of members of the company, to all persons who are, to the best of the nominee's belief, members of it.

1.9(3) **[Contents etc. of notice]** Each notice sent under this Rule shall specify the court to which the nominee's report under section 2 has been delivered and shall state the effect of Rule 1.19(1), (3) and (4) (requisite majorities (creditors)); and with each notice there shall be sent–

(a) a copy of the directors' proposal;

(b) a copy of the statement of affairs or, if the nominee thinks fit, a summary of it (the summary to include a list of creditors and the amount of their debts); and

(c) the nominee's comments on the proposal.

GENERAL NOTE

The Act is largely silent about the manner of summoning meetings, but it is here made plain that a fairly strict procedure must be followed. See in addition rr. 1.13ff.

CHAPTER 3

PROPOSAL BY ADMINISTRATOR OR LIQUIDATOR (HIMSELF THE NOMINEE)

1.10 Preparation of proposal

1.10(1) **[Matters to be specified]** The responsible insolvency practitioner's proposal shall specify—

(a) all such matters as under Rule 1.3 (subject to paragraph (3) below) in Chapter 2 the directors of the company would be required to include in a proposal by them, with the addition, where the company is in administration, of the names and addresses of the company's preferential creditors (defined in section 4(7)), with the amounts of their respective claims, and

(b) such other matters (if any) as the insolvency practitioner considers appropriate for ensuring that members and creditors of the company are enabled to reach an informed decision on the proposal.

1.10(2) **[Notice to official receiver]** Where the company is being wound up by the court, the insolvency practitioner shall give notice of the proposal to the official receiver.

1.10(3) **[Statement of administrator or liquidator in place of estimate]** The administrator or liquidator shall include, in place of the estimate required by Rule 1.3(2)(ca), a statement which contains—

(a) to the best of the administrator or liquidator's knowledge and belief—

(i) an estimate of the value of the prescribed part (whether or not he proposes to make an application to court under section 176A(5) or section 176A(3) applies), and
(ii) an estimate of the value of the company's net property, and

(b) whether, and, if so, why, the administrator or liquidator proposes to make an application to court under section 176A(5).

1.10(4) **[Disclosure of information prejudicial]** Nothing in this Rule is to be taken as requiring any such estimate to include any information, the disclosure of which could seriously prejudice the commercial interests of the company. If such information is excluded from the calculation the estimate shall be accompanied by a statement to that effect.

GENERAL NOTE

This was amended by Insolvency (Amendment) Rules 2003 (SI 2003/1730) to deal both with the advent of new style administration and the implications flowing from the introduction of the special reserve fund for unsecured creditors (see comments on IA 1986, s. 176A).

1.11 Summoning of meetings under s. 3

1.11(1) **[Venues and notice of meetings]** The responsible insolvency practitioner shall fix a venue for the creditors' meeting and the company meeting, and give at least 14 days' notice of the meetings—

(a) in the case of the creditors' meeting, to all the creditors specified in the company's statement of affairs, and to any other creditors of whom the insolvency practitioner is aware; and

(b) in the case of the company meeting, to all persons who are, to the best of his belief, members of the company.

1.11(2) **[Contents etc. of notice]** Each notice sent out under this Rule shall state the effect of Rule 1.19 (1), (3) and (4) (requisite majorities (creditors)); and with it there shall be sent–

(a)   a copy of the responsible insolvency practitioner's proposal, and

(b)   a copy of the statement of affairs or, if he thinks fit, a summary of it (the summary to include a list of creditors and the amounts of their debts).

General Note to rr. 1.10, 1.11

Where the administrator or liquidator is himself to be the nominee, he may proceed directly to summon meetings in accordance with this chapter.

Chapter 4

Proposal by Administrator or Liquidator (Another Insolvency Practitioner the Nominee)

1.12 Preparation of proposal and notice to nominee

1.12(1) **[Manner of giving notice etc.]** The responsible insolvency practitioner shall give notice to the intended nominee, and prepare his proposal for a voluntary arrangement, in the same manner as is required of the directors, in the case of a proposal by them, under Chapter 2.

1.12(2) **[Application of r. 1.2 and 1.4]** Rule 1.2 applies to the responsible insolvency practitioner as it applies to the directors; and Rule 1.4 applies as regards the action to be taken by the nominee.

1.12(3) **[Content of proposal]** The content of the proposal shall be as required by Rule 1.3 (and, where relevant, Rule 1.10), reading references to the directors as referring to the responsible insolvency practitioner.

1.12(4) **[Application of r. 1.6]** Rule 1.6 applies in respect of the information to be furnished to the nominee, reading references to the directors as referring to the responsible insolvency practitioner.

1.12(5) **[Copy statement of affairs]** With the proposal the responsible insolvency practitioner shall provide a copy of the company's statement of affairs.

1.12(6) **[Copy proposal to official receiver]** Where the company is being wound up by the court, the responsible insolvency practitioner shall send a copy of the proposal to the official receiver, accompanied by the name and address of the insolvency practitioner or authorised person who has agreed to act as nominee.

1.12(7) **[Application of rr. 1.7–1.9]** Rules 1.7 to 1.9 apply as regards a proposal under this Chapter as they apply to a proposal under Chapter 2.

General Note

Where the administrator or liquidator does not propose himself as nominee, the procedure is very similar to that for a directors' proposal.

CHAPTER 5

PROCEEDINGS ON A PROPOSAL MADE BY THE DIRECTORS, OR BY THE ADMINISTRATOR, OR BY THE LIQUIDATOR

Section A: meetings of company's creditors and members

1.13 Summoning of meetings

1.13(1) [**Convener to regard convenience of creditors for venue**] Subject as follows, in fixing the venue for the creditors' meeting and the company meeting, the person summoning the meeting ("the convener") shall have regard primarily to the convenience of the creditors.

1.13(2) [**Time of meetings**] Meetings shall in each case be summoned for commencement between 10.00 and 16.00 hours on a business day.

1.13(3) [**Creditors' meeting in advance of company meeting**] The meetings may be held on the same day or on different days. If held on the same day, the meetings shall be held in the same place, but in either case the creditors' meeting shall be fixed for a time in advance of the company meeting.

1.13(4) [**Maximum seven days between meetings**] Where the meetings are not held on the same day, they shall be held within 7 days of each other.

1.13(5) [**Forms of proxy with notice**] With every notice summoning either meeting there shall be sent out forms of proxy.

GENERAL NOTE

Paragraph (3) was replaced and para. (4) added by the Insolvency (Amendment) (No. 2) Rules 2002 (SI 2002/2712). These changes reflect a need for greater clarity with regard to meetings' procedures and, while introducing some flexibility (subject to a maximum hiatus of seven days between meetings), also recognise the fact that there is no point of having a meeting of members if the creditors have voted down the proposal.

This rule was then further amended in the form of a complete reconstitution by Insolvency (Amendment) Rules 2003 (SI 2003/1730).

1.14 The chairman at meetings

1.14(1) [**Convener to be chairman**] Subject as follows, at both the creditors' meeting and the company meeting, and at any combined meeting, the convener shall be chairman.

1.14(2) [**Other nominated chairman**] If for any reason he is unable to attend, he may nominate another person to act as chairman in his place; but a person so nominated must be–

(a) a person qualified to act as an insolvency practitioner in relation to the company;

(b) an authorised person in relation to the company; or

(c) an employee of the convener or his firm who is experienced in insolvency matters.

GENERAL NOTE

A number of amendments were made by Insolvency (Amendment) (No. 2) Rules 2002 (SI 2002/2712) with effect from January 1, 2003 to allow greater flexibility as to who should chair the meeting of creditors.

1.15 The chairman as proxy-holder

1.15 The chairman shall not by virtue of any proxy held by him vote to increase or reduce the amount of the remuneration or expenses of the nominee or the supervisor of the proposed arrangement, unless the proxy specifically directs him to vote in that way.

(See General Note after r. 1.21.)

1.16 Attendance by company officers

1.16(1) **[Notice to directors and officers]** At least 14 days' notice to attend the meetings shall be given by the convener—

(a) to all directors of the company, and

(b) to any persons in whose case the convener thinks that their presence is required as being officers of the company, or as having been directors or officers of it at any time in the 2 years immediately preceding the date of the notice.

1.16(2) **[Exclusion of director etc.]** The chairman may, if he thinks fit, exclude any present or former director or officer from attendance at a meeting, either completely or for any part of it; and this applies whether or not a notice under this Rule has been sent to the person excluded.

(See General Note after r. 1.21.)

Section B: voting rights and majorities

1.17 Entitlement to vote (creditors)

1.17(1) **[Entitlement to vote]** Subject as follows, every creditor who has notice of the creditors' meeting is entitled to vote at the meeting or any adjournment of it.

1.17(2) **[Calculation of votes]** Votes are calculated according to the amount of the creditor's debt as at the date of the meeting or, where the company is being wound up or in administration, the date of its going into liquidation or (as the case may be) when the company entered administration.

1.17(3) **[Limitation on voting]** A creditor may vote in respect of a debt for an unliquidated amount or any debt whose value is not ascertained and for the purposes of voting (but not otherwise) his debt shall be valued at £1 unless the chairman agrees to put a higher value on it.

1.17A Procedure for admission of creditors' claims for voting purposes

1.17A(1) **[Procedure at creditors' meeting]** Subject as follows, at any creditors' meeting the chairman shall ascertain the entitlement of persons wishing to vote and shall admit or reject their claims accordingly.

1.17A(2) **[Chairman's discretion]** The chairman may admit or reject a claim in whole or in part.

1.17A(3) **[Appeal from chairman's decision]** The chairman's decision on any matter under this Rule or under paragraph (3) of Rule 1.17 is subject to appeal to the court by any creditor or member of the company.

1.17A(4) **[Voting subject to objection]** If the chairman is in doubt whether a claim should be admitted or rejected, he shall mark it as objected to and allow votes to be cast in respect of it, subject to such votes being subsequently declared invalid if the objection to the claim is sustained.

1.17A(5) **[Where chairman's decision reversed etc.]** If on an appeal the chairman's decision is reversed or varied, or votes are declared invalid, the court may order another meeting to be summoned, or make such order as it thinks just.

The court's power to make an order under this paragraph is exercisable only if it considers that the circumstances giving rise to the appeal give rise to unfair prejudice or material irregularity.

1.17A(6) **[Time for appeal]** An application to the court by way of appeal against the chairman's decision shall not be made after the end of the period of 28 days beginning with the first day on which the report required by section 4(6) has been made to the court.

1.17A(7) **[Costs of appeal]** The chairman is not personally liable for any costs incurred by any person in respect of an appeal under this Rule.

GENERAL NOTE TO RR. 1.17, 1.17A

R. 1.17 was replaced by Insolvency (Amendment) (No. 2) Rules 2002 (SI 2002/2712) with effect from January 1, 2003. Note the use of the £1 nominal value presumption for unliquidated/unascertained debts – this reflects practice used by insolvency practitioners.

Note the change in terminology with regard to administration introduced by Insolvency (Amendment) Rules 2003 (SI 2003/1730).

R. 1.17A
This new addition was made by Insolvency (Amendment) (No. 2) Rules 2002 (SI 2002/2712) with effect from January 1, 2003. In effect it contains a number of amended provisions which were formerly contained in the original and cumbersome r. 1.17.

1.18 Voting rights (members)

1.18(1) **[Voting rights in accordance with articles]** Subject as follows, members of the company at their meeting vote according to the rights attaching to their shares respectively in accordance with the articles.

1.18(2) **[Omitted]**

1.18(3) **[Interpretation]** References in this Rule to a person's shares include any other interest which he may have as a member of the company.

(See General Note after r. 1.21). Rule 1.18(2) was omitted by Insolvency (Amendment) (No. 2) Rules 2002 (SI 2002/2712).

1.19 Requisite majorities (creditors)

1.19(1) **[Three-quarters majority]** Subject as follows, at the creditors' meeting for any resolution to pass approving any proposal or modification there must be a majority in excess of three-quarters in value of the creditors present in person or by proxy and voting on the resolution.

1.19(2) **[One-half majority]** The same applies in respect of any other resolution proposed at the meeting, but substituting one-half for three-quarters.

1.19(3) **[Votes to be left out of account]** In the following cases there is to be left out of account a creditor's vote in respect of any claim or part of a claim–

(a) where written notice of the claim was not given, either at the meeting or before it, to the chairman or convener of the meeting;

(b) where the claim or part is secured;

(c) where the claim is in respect of a debt wholly or partly on, or secured by, a current bill of exchange or promissory note, unless the creditor is willing–

  (i) to treat the liability to him on the bill or note of every person who is liable on it antecedently to the company, and against whom a bankruptcy order has not been made (or in the case of a company, which has not gone into liquidation), as a security in his hands, and

  (ii) to estimate the value of the security and (for the purpose of entitlement to vote, but not of any distribution under the arrangement) to deduct it from his claim.

1.19(4) **[Voting rendering resolution invalid]** Any resolution is invalid if those voting against it include more than half in value of the creditors, counting in these latter only those–

(a) to whom notice of the meeting was sent;

(b) whose votes are not to be left out of account under paragraph (3); and

(c) who are not, to the best of the chairman's belief, persons connected with the company.

1.19(5) **[Chairman's powers]** It is for the chairman of the meeting to decide whether under this Rule–

(a) a vote is to be left out of account in accordance with paragraph (3), or

(b) a person is a connected person for the purposes of paragraph (4)(c);

and in relation to the second of these two cases the chairman is entitled to rely on the information provided by the company's statement of affairs or otherwise in accordance with this Part of the Rules.

1.19(6) **[Use of proxy contrary to r. 1.15]** If the chairman uses a proxy contrary to Rule 1.15, his vote with that proxy does not count towards any majority under this Rule.

1.19(7) **[Appeal from chairman's decision]** The chairman's decision on any matter under this Rule is subject to appeal to the court by any creditor or member and paragraphs (5) to (7) of Rule 1.17A apply as regards such an appeal.

GENERAL NOTE

A replacement for para. (7) was made by the Insolvency (Amendment) (No. 2) Rules 2002 (SI 2002/2712) – this was necessitated by the insertion of r. 1.17A.

1.20 Requisite majorities (members)

1.20(1) **[One-half majority]** Subject as follows, and to any express provision made in the articles, at a company meeting any resolution is to be regarded as passed if voted for by more than one-half in value of the members present in person or by proxy and voting on the resolution.

The value of members is determined by reference to the number of votes conferred on each member by the company's articles.

1.20(2) **[Omitted]**

1.20(3) **[Use of proxy contrary to r. 1.15]** If the chairman uses a proxy contrary to Rule 1.15, his vote with that proxy does not count towards any majority under this Rule.

(See General Note after r. 1.21.)

1.21 Proceedings to obtain agreement on the proposal

1.21(1) **[Meetings may be held together]** If the chairman thinks fit, the creditors' meeting and the company meeting may be held together.

1.21(2) **[Chairman may adjourn meeting]** The chairman may, and shall if it is so resolved at the meeting in question, adjourn that meeting for not more than 14 days.

1.21(3) **[Final adjournment]** If there are subsequently further adjournments, the final adjournment shall not be to a day later than 14 days after the date on which the meeting in question was originally held.

1.21(4) **[Notice of adjournment]** In the case of a proposal by the directors, if the meetings are adjourned under paragraph (2), notice of the fact shall be given by the nominee forthwith to the court.

1.21(5) **[Deemed rejection of proposal]** If following the final adjournment of the creditors' meeting the proposal (with or without modifications) has not been approved by the creditors, it is deemed rejected.

GENERAL NOTE

A new version of r. 1.21 was substituted by Insolvency (Amendment) (No. 2) Rules 2002 (SI 2002/2712) with effect from January 1, 2003 to reflect the increased flexibility introduced by permitting meetings of creditors and members to be held on different days.

GENERAL NOTE TO RR. 1.13–1.21

The detailed procedure for the summoning and conduct of meetings is here set out, and a number of points which the Insolvency Act appears to leave in doubt are settled.

Rule 1.22   *The Insolvency Rules 1986*

Although the creditors' meeting must be *fixed* for a time in advance of the company meeting (r. 1.13(3)), it need not conclude its business before the company meeting begins (r. 1.22(2)); and the meetings may be held together (r. 1.21(1)).

Rules 1.16(1)(b) and 1.16(2) allow the chairman a wide discretion, on the one hand to insist on the attendance of a director whose presence he may consider helpful and, on the other, to exclude any director who may be thought to hinder the proceedings.

Although a contingent or prospective creditor, or a person who has a claim for an unliquidated amount is not, on a strict view, a "creditor", the cases now make it reasonably clear that they should be treated as creditors for the purposes of Pt I of the Act and the Rules (see the note to s. 1(1) and the cases there cited). Any such person is therefore entitled to receive notice of the creditors' meeting under r. 1.9(2) and (subject to r. 1.17(3)) to attend and vote at it. If he has had notice of the meeting and was entitled to vote at it, he is bound by the voluntary arrangement which was approved at the meetings, whether or not he attended the creditors' meeting or voted at it.

In *Beverley Group plc v McClue* [1995] B.C.C. 751 a person who had a claim for an unliquidated amount (and was accordingly held to have been entitled to vote) had been sent formal notice of the meeting by post but this had never reached him. He had, however, learned of the meeting from another source but chose not to attend it. The court ruled that he had had notice of the meeting and was bound by the arrangement.

Rule 1.17(3) allows a creditor whose debt is for an unliquidated amount or whose value is not ascertained to vote at the meeting only if the chairman agrees to put upon the debt an estimated minimum value for the purpose of entitlement to vote. It is now settled that "agrees" does not mean "agrees with the creditor" in the sense that there must be a bilateral consent to the estimated value, but rather "expresses a willingness" to put a value: *Re Cancol Ltd* [1995] B.C.C. 1,133; *Doorbar v Alltime Securities Ltd* [1995] B.C.C. 1,149. The earlier case of *Re Cranley Mansions Ltd* [1994] B.C.C. 576, in which the applicant had refused to accept the chairman's estimate of £1 on a claim for £900,000, would not now be followed on this point (Note the use of the £1 valuation prescription). If a person declines to attend the creditors' meeting it is not open to him to object that the chairman has not put an estimated valuation on his debt: see *Beverley Group plc v McClue* (above). On voting entitlement see also *Lombard North Central plc v Brook* [1999] B.P.I.R. 701.

Rule 1.17(A(6)) states categorically that there is a 28-day time-limit for appeals against the chairman's decision, and this limitation was emphasised in *Re Bournemouth & Boscombe AFC Co. Ltd* [1998] B.P.I.R. 183 (a case decided under s. 6).

The majority required by r. 1.19 is, unusually, not simply three-quarters of those present and voting, but a majority *in excess* of three-quarters. Note in addition, however, that both this majority and the ordinary majority required by r. 1.19(2) are qualified by r. 1.19(4), which in effect nullifies the votes of any creditors "connected with" the company (and certain others) who support the proposal. (For the meaning of a "connected" person, see IA 1986, s. 249).

The rules assume that the same person will be chairman of both meetings: see r. 1.24(1).

Section C: implementation of the arrangement

1.22 Resolutions to follow approval

1.22(1) [**Resolution re supervisory acts**] If the voluntary arrangement is approved (with or without modifications) by the creditors' meeting, a resolution may be taken by the creditors, where two or more supervisors are appointed, on the question whether acts to be done in connection with the arrangement may be done by any one or more of them, or must be done by all of them.

1.22(2) [**Deleted**]

1.22(3) **[Other than nominee to be supervisor]** If at either meeting a resolution is moved for the appointment of some person other than the nominee to be supervisor of the arrangement, there must be produced to the chairman, at or before the meeting–

(a) that person's written consent to act (unless he is present and then and there signifies his consent), and

(b) his written confirmation that he is qualified to act as an insolvency practitioner in relation to the company or is an authorised person in relation to the company.

1.22A Notice of order made under section 4A(6)

1.22A(1) **[Application]** This Rule applies where the court makes an order under section 4A(6).

1.22A(2) **[Service of order]** The member of the company who applied for the order shall serve sealed copies of it on–

(a) the supervisor of the voluntary arrangement; and

(b) the directors of the company.

1.22A(3) **[Service on directors]** Service on the directors may be effected by service of a single copy on the company at its registered office.

1.22A(4) **[Notice of order]** The directors or (as the case may be) the supervisor shall forthwith after receiving a copy of the court's order, give notice of it to all persons who were sent notice of the creditors' or company meetings or who, not having been sent such notice, are affected by the order.

1.22A(5) **[Office copy to registrar of companies]** The person on whose application the order of the court was made shall, within 7 days of the order, deliver an office copy to the registrar of companies.

R. 1.22
A significant amendment was made by Insolvency (Amendment) (No. 2) Rules 2002 (SI 2002/2712) with effect from January 1, 2003 to address specifically operational issues which may arise where joint supervisors are appointed.

R. 1.22A
This was added by Insolvency (Amendment) (No. 2) Rules 2002 (SI 2002/2712) with effect from January 1, 2003. It deals with orders made under s. 4A(6) – *i.e.* orders made by the court directing that the views of members shall prevail over creditors. These are expected to be rare birds.

1.23 Hand-over of property etc. to supervisor

1.23(1) **[Putting supervisor into possession of assets]** Where the decision approving the voluntary arrangement has effect under section 4A–

(a) the directors, or

(b) where the company is in liquidation or is in administration, and a person other than the responsible insolvency practitioner is appointed as supervisor of the voluntary arrangement, the insolvency practitioner,

shall forthwith do all that is required for putting the supervisor into possession of the assets included in the arrangement.

1.23(2) **[Discharge of insolvency practitioner's remuneration etc.]** Where the company is in liquidation or is in administration, the supervisor shall on taking possession of the assets discharge any balance due to the insolvency practitioner by way of remuneration or on account of–

(a) fees, costs, charges and expenses properly incurred and payable under the Act or the Rules, and

(b) any advances made in respect of the company, together with interest on such advances at the rate specified in section 17 of the Judgments Act 1838 at the date on which the company went into liquidation or (as the case may be) entered administration.

1.23(3) **[Undertaking to discharge]** Alternatively, the supervisor must, before taking possession, give the responsible insolvency practitioner a written undertaking to discharge any such balance out of the first realisation of assets.

1.23(4) **[Charge on assets]** The insolvency practitioner has a charge on the assets included in the voluntary arrangement in respect of any sums due as above until they have been discharged, subject only to the deduction from realisations by the supervisor of the proper costs and expenses of such realisations.

1.23(5) **[Discharge of guarantees etc.]** The supervisor shall from time to time out of the realisation of assets discharge all guarantees properly given by the responsible insolvency practitioner for the benefit of the company, and shall pay all the insolvency practitioner's expenses.

1.23(6) **[Interpretation]** References in this Rule to the responsible insolvency practitioner include, where a company is being wound up by the court, the official receiver, whether or not in his capacity as liquidator; and any sums due to the official receiver take priority over those due to a liquidator.

GENERAL NOTE

A minor amendment occurred via Insolvency (Amendment) (No. 2) Rules 2002 (SI 2002/2712) to cater for the coming into effect of the Insolvency Act 2000.

A further linguistic change was necessitated by the introduction of new style administration – see Insolvency (Amendment) Rules 2003 (SI 2003/1730).

1.24 Report of meetings

1.24(1) **[Chairman to prepare report]** A report of the meetings shall be prepared by the person who was chairman of them.

1.24(2) **[Contents of report]** The report shall–

(a) state whether the proposal for a voluntary arrangement was approved by the creditors of the company alone or by both the creditors and members of the company and in either case whether such approval was with any modifications;

(b) set out the resolutions which were taken at each meeting, and the decision on each one;

(c) list the creditors and members of the company (with their respective values) who were present or represented at the meetings, and how they voted on each resolution;

(ca) state whether, in the opinion of the supervisor, (i) the EC Regulation applies to the voluntary arrangement and (ii) if so, whether the proceedings are main proceedings, secondary proceedings or territorial proceedings; and

(d) include such further information (if any) as the chairman thinks it appropriate to make known to the court.

1.24(3) **[Copy report to be filed in court]** A copy of the chairman's report shall, within 4 days of the meetings being held, be filed in court; and the court shall cause that copy to be endorsed with the date of filing.

1.24(4) **[Notice of result]** In respect of each of the meetings, the persons to whom notice of its result is to be sent by the chairman under section 4(6) are all those who were sent notice of the meeting under this Part of the Rules.

The notice shall be sent immediately after a copy of the chairman's report is filed in court under paragraph (3).

1.24(5) **[Copy report to registrar of companies]** If the decision approving the voluntary arrangement has effect under section 4A (whether or not in the form proposed), the supervisor shall forthwith send a copy of the chairman's report to the registrar of companies.

[FORM 1.1]

GENERAL NOTE

Note the amendments to paras (2) and (5) by Insolvency (Amendment) (No. 2) Rules 2002 (SI 2002/2712) with effect from January 1, 2003. These relate to the report to be submitted by the chair to the court and reflect the fact that there is now greater information that has to be reported. *(See General Note after r. 1.29.)* Paragraph (ca) was inserted by the *Insolvency (Amendment) Rules* 2002 (SI 2002/1307) para. 4(3)(b).

1.25 Revocation or suspension of the arrangement

1.25(1) **[Application of Rule]** This Rule applies where the court makes an order of revocation or suspension under section 6.

1.25(2) **[Service of copy orders]** The person who applied for the order shall serve sealed copies of it–

(a) on the supervisor of the voluntary arrangement, and

(b) on the directors of the company or the administrator or liquidator (according to who made the proposal for the arrangement).

Service on the directors may be effected by service of a single copy of the order on the company at its registered office.

1.25(3) **[Notice re further meetings]** If the order includes a direction by the court under section 6(4)(b) for any further meetings to be summoned, notice shall also be given (by the person who applied for the order) to whoever is, in accordance with the direction, required to summon the meetings.

1.25(4) **[Notice of order, and of intention re proposal]** The directors or (as the case may be) the administrator or liquidator shall–

(a) forthwith after receiving a copy of the court's order, give notice of it to all persons who were sent notice of the creditors' and company meetings or who, not having been sent that notice, appear to be affected by the order;

(b) within 7 days of their receiving a copy of the order (or within such longer period as the court may allow), give notice to the court whether it is intended to make a revised proposal to the company and its creditors, or to invite re-consideration of the original proposal.

1.25(5) **[Copy order to registrar of companies]** The person on whose application the order of revocation or suspension was made shall, within 7 days after the making of the order, deliver a copy of the order to the registrar of companies.

[FORM 1.2]

(See General Note after r. 1.29.)

1.26 Supervisor's accounts and reports

1.26(1) **[Obligation to keep accounts etc.]** Where the voluntary arrangement authorises or requires the supervisor–

(a) to carry on the business of the company or trade on its behalf or in its name, or

(b) to realise assets of the company, or

(c) otherwise to administer or dispose of any of its funds, he shall keep accounts and records of his acts and dealings in and in connection with the arrangement, including in particular records of all receipts and payments of money.

1.26(2) **[Abstract of receipts and payments]** The supervisor shall, not less often than once in every 12 months beginning with the date of his appointment, prepare an abstract of such receipts and payments, and send copies of it, accompanied by his comments on the progress and efficacy of the arrangement, to–

(a) the court,

(b) the registrar of companies,

(c) the company, [FORM 1.3]

(d) all those of the company's creditors who are bound by the arrangement,

(e) subject to paragraph (5) below, the members of the company who are so bound, and

(f) if the company is not in liquidation, the company's auditors for the time being.

If in any period of 12 months he has made no payments and had no receipts, he shall at the end of that period send a statement to that effect to all those specified in sub-paragraphs (a) to (f) above.

1.26(3) **[Abstract under r. 1.26(2)]** An abstract provided under paragraph (2) shall relate to a period beginning with the date of the supervisor's appointment or (as the case may be) the day following the end of the last period for which an abstract was prepared under this Rule; and copies of the abstract shall be sent out, as required by paragraph (2), within the 2 months following the end of the period to which the abstract relates.

1.26(4) **[If supervisor not authorised as in r. 1.26(1)]** If the supervisor is not authorised as mentioned in paragraph (1), he shall, not less often than once in every 12 months beginning with the date of his appointment, send to all those specified in paragraph (2)(a) to (f) a report on the progress and efficacy of the voluntary arrangement.

1.26(5) **[Powers of court]** The court may, on application by the supervisor–

(a) dispense with the sending under this Rule of abstracts or reports to members of the company, either altogether or on the basis that the availability of the abstract or report to members is to be advertised by the supervisor in a specified manner;

(b) vary the dates on which the obligation to send abstracts or reports arises.

(See General Note after r. 1.29.)

1.27 Production of accounts and records to Secretary of State

1.27(1) **[Powers of Secretary of State]** The Secretary of State may at any time during the course of the voluntary arrangement or after its completion or termination require the supervisor to produce for inspection–

(a) his records and accounts in respect of the arrangement, and

(b) copies of abstracts and reports prepared in compliance with Rule 1.26.

1.27(2) **[Production and duty to comply]** The Secretary of State may require production either at the premises of the supervisor or elsewhere; and it is the duty of the supervisor to comply with any requirement imposed on him under this Rule.

1.27(3) **[Audit of accounts and records]** The Secretary of State may cause any accounts and records produced to him under this Rule to be audited; and the supervisor shall give to the Secretary of State such further information and assistance as he needs for the purposes of his audit.

(See General Note after r. 1.29.)

GENERAL NOTE

Note the addition of the words "or termination" in para (1) by Insolvency (Amendment) (No. 2) Rules 2002 (SI 2002/2712) with effect from January 1, 2003. This reflects the fact that CVAs may be brought to an end in a variety of ways post-IA 2000.

1.28 Fees, costs, charges and expenses

1.28 The fees, costs, charges and expenses that may be incurred for any of the purposes of the voluntary arrangement are –

(a) any disbursements made by the nominee prior to the decision approving the arrangement taking effect under section 4A and any remuneration for his services as such agreed between himself and the company (or, as the case may be, the administrator or liquidator);

(b) any fees, costs, charges or expenses which–
  (i) are sanctioned by the terms of the arrangement, or
  (ii) would be payable, or correspond to those which would be payable, in an administration or winding up.

(See General Note after r. 1.29.)

GENERAL NOTE

An amendment to para (1a) was made by Insolvency (Amendment) (No. 2) Rules 2002 (SI 2002/2712) with effect from January 1, 2003 to reflect the consequences of s. 4A (which had been introduced by IA 2000) coming into effect.

1.29 Completion or termination of the arrangement

1.29(1) **[Supervisor to send notice]** Not more than 28 days after the final completion or termination of the voluntary arrangement, the supervisor shall send to creditors and members of the company who are bound by it a notice that the voluntary arrangement has been fully implemented or (as the case may be) has terminated.

1.29(2) **[Supervisor's report]** With the notice there shall be sent to each creditor and member a copy of a report by the supervisor summarising all receipts and payments made by him in pursuance of the arrangement, and explaining in relation to implementation of the arrangement any departure from the proposals as they originally took effect, or (in the case of termination of the arrangement) explaining the reasons why the arrangement has terminated.

[FORM 1.4]

1.29(3) **[Copy notice and report to registrar and court]** The supervisor shall, within the 28 days mentioned above, send to the registrar of companies and to the court a copy of the notice to creditors and members under paragraph (1), together with a copy of the report under paragraph (2), and the supervisor shall not vacate office until after such copies have been sent.

1.29(4) **[Report to include statement as to prescribed part]** In the report under paragraph (2), the supervisor shall include a statement as to the amount paid, if any, to unsecured creditors by virtue of the application of section 176A (prescribed part).

GENERAL NOTE TO RR. 1.22–129

The detailed procedure for the implementation of the proposals, if approved, is set out here. The scheme takes effect without further formality from the time of the creditors' meeting, even though under the rules the members' meeting must be fixed for a later time on the same day: see IA 1986, s. 5(2)(a).

A new r. 1.29 was inserted by Insolvency (Amendment) (No. 2) Rules 2002 (SI 2002/2712) with effect from January 1, 2003 to cater for the coming into force of the Insolvency Act 2000 with particular reference to the possibility of termination.

This newly substituted rule was then further amended by Insolvency (Amendment) Rules 2003 (SI 2003/1730) to provide information on any distributions made in connection with the s. 176A reserve fund.

CHAPTER 6

1.30 False representations, etc. [repealed]

GENERAL NOTE

This r. 1.30 was repealed by Insolvency (Amendment) (No. 2) Rules 2002 (SI 2002/2712). These offences are now more properly dealt with by the primary legislation (*i.e.* s. 6A).

CHAPTER 7

EC REGULATION – CONVERSION OF VOLUNTARY ARRANGEMENT INTO WINDING UP

1.31 Application for conversion into winding up

1.31(1) **[Documents]** Where a member State liquidator proposes to apply to the court for the conversion under Article 37 of the EC Regulation (conversion of earlier proceedings) of a voluntary arrangement into a winding up, an affidavit complying with Rule 1.32 must be prepared and sworn, and filed in court in support of the application.

1.31(2) **[Originating application]** An application under this Rule shall be by originating application.

1.31(3) **[Service]** The application and the affidavit required under this Rule shall be served upon–

(a) the company; and

(b) the supervisor.

1.32 Contents of affidavit

1.32(1) **[Contents]** The affidavit shall state–

(a) that main proceedings have been opened in relation to the company in a member State other than the United Kingdom;

(b) the deponent's belief that the conversion of the voluntary arrangement into a winding up would prove to be in the interests of the creditors in the main proceedings;

(c) the deponent's opinion as to whether the company ought to enter voluntary winding up or be wound up by the court; and

(d) all other matters that, in the opinion of the member State liquidator, would assist the court–

(i) in deciding whether to make such an order, and
(ii) if the court were to do so, in considering the need for any consequential provision that would be necessary or desirable.

1.32(2) **[Procedure]** An affidavit under this Rule shall be sworn by, or on behalf of, the member State liquidator.

1.33 Power of court

1.33(1) **[Powers of court]** On hearing the application for conversion into winding up the court may make such order as it thinks fit.

1.33(2) **[Consequential provisions]** If the court makes an order for conversion into winding up the order may contain all such consequential provisions as the court deems necessary or desirable.

1.33(3) **[Effect of order made under r. 1.33(1)]** Without prejudice to the generality of paragraph (1), an order under that paragraph may provide that the company be wound up as if a resolution for voluntary winding up under section 84 were passed on the day on which the order is made.

1.33(4) **[Expenses incurred]** Where the court makes an order for conversion into winding up under paragraph (1), any expenses properly incurred as expenses of the administration of the voluntary arrangement in question shall be a first charge on the company's assets.

GENERAL NOTE

Chapter 7 (comprising new r. 1.31–1.33) was introduced by the *Insolvency (Amendment) Rules* 2002 (SI 2002/1307) para. 4(4) to cater for the advent of EC Council Regulation on Insolvency Proceedings (1346/2000) with effect from 31 May 2002.

CHAPTER 8

EC REGULATION – MEMBER STATE LIQUIDATOR

1.34 Interpretation of creditor and notice to member State liquidator

1.34(1) **[Application]** This Rule applies where a member State liquidator has been appointed in relation to the company.

1.34(2) **[Notice, copies]** Where the supervisor is obliged to give notice to, or provide a copy of a document (including an order of court) to, the court, the registrar of companies or the official receiver, the supervisor shall give notice or provide copies, as appropriate, to the member State liquidator.

1.34(3) **[Duty to cooperate and communicate information]** Paragraph (2) is without prejudice to the generality of the obligations imposed by Article 31 of the EC Regulation (duty to cooperate and communicate information).

GENERAL NOTE

Chapter 8 (consisting of r. 1.34) was introduced in similar circumstances to Chapter 7.

Chapter 9

Obtaining a Moratorium

Proceedings during a Moratorium

Nominees

Consideration of Proposals where Moratorium Obtained

Section A: Obtaining a Moratorium

1.35 Preparation of proposal by directors and submission to nominee

1.35(1) **[Requirements for proposal document]** The document containing the proposal referred to in paragraph 6(1)(a) of Schedule A1 to the Act shall–

(a) be prepared by the directors;

(b) comply with the requirements of paragraphs (1) and (2) of Rule 1.3 (save that the reference to preferential creditors shall be to preferential creditors within the meaning of paragraph 31(8) of Schedule A1 to the Act); and

(c) state the address to which notice of the consent of the nominee to act and the documents referred to in Rule 1.38 shall be sent.

1.35(2) **[Amendment of proposal]** With the agreement in writing of the nominee, the directors may amend the proposal at any time before submission to them by the nominee of the statement required by paragraph 6(2) of Schedule A1 to the Act.

R. 1.35
This explains how directors are to submit their draft proposals to the nominee by itemising the contents of the documentation.

1.36 Delivery of documents to the intended nominee etc.

1.36(1) **[Delivery to nominee or authorised person]** The documents required to be delivered to the nominee pursuant to paragraph 6(1) of Schedule A1 to the Act shall be delivered to the nominee himself or to a person authorised to take delivery of documents on his behalf.

1.36(2) **[Acknowledgement of receipt]** On receipt of the documents, the nominee shall forthwith issue an acknowledgement of receipt of the documents to the directors which shall indicate the date on which the documents were received.

R. 1.36
This proceeds to describe how the proposed documents are to be delivered.

1.37 Statement of affairs

1.37(1) **[Time for delivery]** The statement of the company's affairs required to be delivered to the nominee pursuant to paragraph 6(1)(b) of Schedule A1 to the Act shall be delivered to the nominee no later than 7 days after the delivery to him of the document setting out the terms of the proposed voluntary arrangement or such longer time as he may allow.

[FORM 1.6]

1.37(2) **[Particulars in statement]** The statement of affairs shall comprise the same particulars as required by Rule 1.5(2) (supplementing or amplifying, so far as is necessary for clarifying the state of the company's affairs, those already given in the directors' proposal).

1.37(3) **[Relevant date]** The statement of affairs shall be made up to a date not earlier than 2 weeks before the date of the delivery of the document containing the proposal for the voluntary arrangement to the nominee under Rule 1.36(1).

However, the nominee may allow an extension of that period to the nearest practicable date (not earlier than 2 months before the date of delivery of the documents referred to in Rule 1.36(1)) and if he does so, he shall give a statement of his reasons in writing to the directors.

1.37(4) **[Certification of statement]** The statement of affairs shall be certified as correct, to the best of their knowledge and belief, by two or more directors of the company, or by the company secretary and at least one director (other than the secretary himself).

R. 1.37
The directors must, within seven days of delivering the proposals, produce a formal statement of affairs for the nominee.

1.38 The nominee's statement

1.38(1) **[Time for submission of statement]** The nominee shall submit to the directors the statement required by paragraph 6(2) of Schedule A1 to the Act within 28 days of the submission to him of the document setting out the terms of the proposed voluntary arrangement.

[FORM 1.5]

1.38(2) **[Nominee's comments, statement of consent]** The statement shall have annexed to it–

[FORM 1.8]

(a) the nominee's comments on the proposal, unless the statement contains an opinion in the negative on any of the matters referred to in paragraph 6(2)(a) and (b) of Schedule A1 to the Act, in which case he shall instead give his reasons for that opinion, and

(b) where he is willing to act in relation to the proposed arrangement, a statement of his consent to act.

R. 1.38
This deals with the nominee's response to the directors.

1.39 Documents submitted to the court to obtain moratorium

1.39(1) **[Required documents, time for delivery]** Where pursuant to paragraph 7 of Schedule A1 to the Act the directors file the document and statements referred to in that paragraph in court, those documents shall be delivered together with 4 copies of a schedule listing them within 3 working days of the date of the submission to them of the nominee's statement under paragraph 6(2) of Schedule A1 to the Act.

[FORMS 1.5, 1.7, 1.8 AND 1.9]

1.39(2) **[Additional documents to file]** When the directors file the document and statements referred to in paragraph (1), they shall also file–

(a) a copy of any statement of reasons made by the nominee pursuant to Rule 1.37(3); and

(b) a copy of the nominee's comments on the proposal submitted to them pursuant to Rule 1.38(2).

1.39(3) **[Endorsement of schedule copies]** The copies of the schedule shall be endorsed by the court with the date on which the documents were filed in court and 3 copies of the schedule sealed by the court shall be returned by the court to the person who filed the documents in court.

1.39(4) **[Particulars in statement]** The statement of affairs required to be filed under paragraph 7(1)(b) of Schedule A1 to the Act shall comprise the same particulars as required by Rule 1.5(2).

[FORM 1.6]

R. 1.39
The documents that need to be filed in court to obtain the moratorium are explained along with the filing procedure.

1.40 Notice and advertisement of beginning of a moratorium

1.40(1) **[Service on nominee and company]** After receiving the copies of the schedule endorsed by the court under Rule 1.39(3), the directors shall forthwith serve 2 of them on the nominee and one on the company.

1.40(2) **[Advertisement by nominee]** Forthwith after receiving the copies of the schedule pursuant to paragraph (1) the nominee shall advertise the coming into force of the moratorium once in the Gazette, and once in such newspaper as he thinks most appropriate for ensuring that its coming into force comes to the notice of the company's creditors.

[FORM 1.10]

1.40(3) **[Notice of moratorium commencement date]** The nominee shall forthwith notify the registrar of companies, the company and any petitioning creditor of the company of whose claim he is aware of the coming into force of the moratorium and such notification shall specify the date on which the moratorium came into force.

[FORM 1.11]

1.40(4) **[Further notice requirements]** The nominee shall give notice of the coming into force of the moratorium specifying the date on which it came into force to–

(a) any sheriff or other officer who, to his knowledge, is charged with an execution or other legal process against the company or its property; and

(b) any person who, to his knowledge, has distrained against the company or its property.

R. 1.40
The fact that the moratorium has started needs to be advertised. This CVA model is not as discreet as the original CVA alternative.

1.41 Notice of extension of moratorium

1.41(1) **[Notice of extension etc.]** The nominee shall forthwith notify the registrar of companies and the court of a decision taking effect pursuant to paragraph 36 of Schedule A1 to the Act to extend or further extend the moratorium and such notice shall specify the new expiry date of the moratorium.

[FORM 1.12]
[FORM 1.13]

1.41(2) **[Further notice following court order]** Where an order is made by the court extending or further extending or renewing or continuing a moratorium, the nominee shall forthwith after receiving a copy of the same give notice to the registrar of companies and with the notice shall send an office copy of the order.

[FORM 1.12]

R. 1.41
The registrar and court need to be informed if the moratorium has been extended.

1.42 Notice and advertisement of end of moratorium

1.42(1) **[Advertisement, notice]** After the moratorium comes to an end, the nominee shall forthwith advertise its coming to an end once in the Gazette, and once in such newspaper as he thinks most appropriate for ensuring that its coming to an end comes to the notice of the company's creditors, and such notice shall specify the date on which the moratorium came to an end.

[FORM 1.10]

1.42(2) **[Notice to registrar etc.]** The nominee shall forthwith give notice of the ending of the moratorium to the registrar of companies, the court, the company and any creditor of the company of whose claim he is aware and such notice shall specify the date on which the moratorium came to an end.

[FORM 1.14]
[FORM 1.15]

R. 1.42
Where the moratorium has come to an end that fact must be advertised.

Section B: Proceedings during a Moratorium

1.43 Disposal of charged property etc. during a moratorium

1.43(1) **[Application]** This Rule applies in any case where the company makes an application to the court under paragraph 20 of Schedule A1 to the Act for leave to dispose of property of the company which is subject to a security, or goods in possession of the company under an agreement to which that paragraph relates.

1.43(2) **[Venue, notice to security holder etc.]** The court shall fix a venue for the hearing of the application and the company shall forthwith give notice of the venue to the person who is the holder of the security or, as the case may be, the owner under the agreement.

1.43(3) **[Notice of order]** If an order is made, the company shall forthwith give notice of it to that person or owner.

1.43(4) **[Sealed copies of order]** The court shall send 2 sealed copies of the order to the company, who shall send one of them to that person or owner.

R. 1.43
If directors wish to obtain leave to dispose of company property during the course of the moratorium the requirements of this rule must be met.

Section C: Nominees

1.44 Withdrawal of nominee's consent to act

1.44 Where the nominee withdraws his consent to act he shall, pursuant to paragraph 25(5) of Schedule A1 to the Act, forthwith give notice of his withdrawal and the reason for withdrawing his consent to act to–

    (a)   the registrar of companies;

[FORM 1.16]

    (b)   the court;

[FORM 1.17]

    (c)   the company; and

    (d)   any creditor of the company of whose claim he is aware.

R. 1.44
This outlines formal requirements where a nominee withdraws consent to act.

1.45 Replacement of nominee by the court

1.45(1) **[Notice of directors' application]** Where the directors intend to make an application to the court under paragraph 28 of Schedule A1 to the Act for the nominee to be replaced, they shall give to the nominee at least 7 days' notice of their application.

1.45(2) **[Notice of nominee's application]** Where the nominee intends to make an application to the court under that paragraph to be replaced, he shall give to the directors at least 7 days' notice of his application.

1.45(3) **[Replacement nominee's consent]** No appointment of a replacement nominee shall be made by the court unless there is filed in court a statement by the replacement nominee indicating his consent to act.

[FORM 1.8]

R. 1.45
Procedures governing the replacement of the nominee by the court are explained.

1.46 Notification of appointment of a replacement nominee

1.46 Where a person is appointed as a replacement nominee, he shall forthwith give notice of his appointment to–

(a)   the registrar of companies;

[FORM 1.18]

[FORM 1.19]

(b)   the court (in any case where he was not appointed by the court); and

(c)   the person whom he has replaced as nominee.

R. 1.46
Where a replacement nominee is installed that fact needs to be advertised.

1.47 Applications to court under paragraphs 26 or 27 of Schedule A1 to the Act

1.47 Where any person intends to make an application to the court pursuant to paragraph 26 or 27 of Schedule A1 to the Act, he shall give to the nominee at least 7 days' notice of his application.

R. 1.47
This explains procedures on applications pursuant to paras 26 and 27 of Sch. A1 (*i.e.* applications to challenge the acts and omissions of the nominee).

SECTION D: CONSIDERATION OF PROPOSALS WHERE MORATORIUM OBTAINED

1.48 Summoning of meetings; procedure at meetings etc.

1.48(1) **[Date for meetings]** Where the nominee summons meetings of creditors and the company pursuant to paragraph 29(1) of Schedule A1 to the Act, each of those meetings shall be summoned for a date that is not more than 28 days from the date on which the moratorium came into force.

1.48(2) **[Notices of creditors' meetings]** Notices calling the creditors' meetings shall be sent by the nominee to all creditors specified in the statement of affairs and any other creditors of the company of whose address he is aware at least 14 days before the day fixed for the meeting.

1.48(3) **[Notices of company meeting]** Notices calling the company meeting shall be sent by the nominee to all persons who are, to the best of the nominee's belief, members of the company at least 14 days before the day fixed for the meeting.

1.48(4) **[Contents etc. of notice]** Each notice sent under this Rule shall specify the court in which the documents relating to the obtaining of the moratorium were filed and state the effect of paragraphs (1), (3) and (4) of Rule 1.52 (requisite majorities (creditors)) and with each notice there shall be sent–

(a)   a copy of the directors' proposal;

(b)   a copy of the statement of the company's affairs or, if the nominee thinks fit, a summary of it (the summary to include a list of creditors and the amount of their debts); and

(c)   the nominee's comments on the proposal.

1.48(5) **[Application of rr. 1.13–1.16]** The provisions of Rules 1.13 to 1.16 shall apply.

R. 1.48
This explains the rules governing the summoning of meetings where the moratorium is in place and the creditors need to vote on the proposal.

1.49 Entitlement to vote (creditors)

1.49(1) [**Entitlement**] Subject as follows, every creditor who has notice of the creditors' meeting is entitled to vote at the meeting or any adjournment of it.

1.49(2) [**Calculation of votes**] Votes are calculated according to the amount of the creditor's debt as at the beginning of the moratorium, after deducting any amounts paid in respect of that debt after that date.

1.49(3) [**Limitation on voting**] A creditor may vote in respect of a debt for an unliquidated amount or any debt whose value is not ascertained and for the purposes of voting (but not otherwise) his debt shall be valued at £1 unless the chairman agrees to put a higher value on it.

R. 1.49
This explains creditors' entitlement to vote. The rules here are standard.

1.50 Procedure for admission of creditors' claims for voting purposes

1.50(1) [**Chairman's duty**] Subject as follows, at any creditors' meeting the chairman shall ascertain the entitlement of persons wishing to vote and shall admit or reject their claims accordingly.

1.50(2) [**Chairman's discretion**] The chairman may admit or reject a claim in whole or in part.

1.50(3) [**Appeal from chairman's decision**] The chairman's decision on any matter under this Rule or under paragraph (3) of Rule 1.49 is subject to appeal to the court by any creditor or member of the company.

1.50(4) [**Voting subject to objection**] If the chairman is in doubt whether a claim should be admitted or rejected, he shall mark it as objected to and allow votes to be cast in respect of it, subject to such votes being subsequently declared invalid if the objection to the claim is sustained.

1.50(5) [**Where chairman's decision reversed etc.**] If on an appeal the chairman's decision is reversed or varied, or votes are declared invalid, the court may order another meeting to be summoned, or make such order as it thinks just.

The court's power to make an order under this paragraph is exercisable only if it considers that the circumstances giving rise to the appeal are such as give rise to unfair prejudice or material irregularity.

1.50(6) [**Time for appeal**] An application to the court by way of appeal against the chairman's decision shall not be made after the end of the period of 28 days beginning with the first day on which the report required by paragraph 30(3) of Schedule A1 to the Act has been made to the court.

1.50(7) [**Costs of appeal**] The chairman is not personally liable for any costs incurred by any person in respect of an appeal under this Rule.

R. 1.50
Admission to voting in this CVA model is governed by r. 1.50.

1.51 Voting rights (members)

1.51 Rule 1.18 shall apply.

R. 1.51
This sensibly adopts r. 1.18.

1.52 Requisite majorities (creditors)

1.52(1) [**Three-quarters majority**] Subject as follows, at the creditors' meeting for any resolution to pass approving any proposal or modification there must be a majority in excess of three-quarters in value of the creditors present in person or by proxy and voting on the resolution.

1.52(2) [**One-half majority**] The same applies in respect of any other resolution proposed at the meeting, but substituting one-half for three-quarters.

1.52(3) [Extension of moratorium, non-application of r. 1.52(4)] At a meeting of the creditors for any resolution to pass extending (or further extending) a moratorium, or to bring a moratorium to an end before the end of the period of any extension, there must be a majority in excess of three quarters in value of the creditors present in person or by proxy and voting on the resolution. For this purpose paragraph (4)(b) below shall not apply and a secured creditor is entitled to vote in respect of the amount of his claim without deducting the value of his security.

1.52(4) [Votes to be left out of account] In the following cases there is to be left out of account a creditor's vote in respect of any claim or part of a claim–

(a) where written notice of the claim was not given, either at the meeting or before it, to the chairman or convenor of the meeting;

(b) where the claim or part is secured;

(c) where the claim is in respect of a debt wholly or partly on, or secured by, a current bill of exchange or promissory note, unless the creditor is willing–

  (i) to treat the liability to him on the bill or note of every person who is liable on it antecedently to the company, and against whom a bankruptcy order has not been made (or, in the case of a company, which has not gone into liquidation), as a security in his hands, and

  (ii) to estimate the value of the security and (for the purpose of entitlement to vote, but not of any distribution under the arrangement) to deduct it from his claim.

1.52(5) [Voting rendering resolution invalid] Any resolution is invalid if those voting against it include more than half in value of the creditors, counting in these latter only those–

(a) who have notice of the meeting;

(b) whose votes are not to be left out of account under paragraph (4); and

(c) who are not, to the best of the chairman's belief, persons connected with the company.

1.52(6) [Chairman's powers] It is for the chairman of the meeting to decide whether under this Rule–

(a) a vote is to be left out of account in accordance with paragraph (4), or

(b) a person is a connected person for the purposes of paragraph (5)(c);

and in relation to the second of these two cases the chairman is entitled to rely on the information provided by the statement of the company's affairs or otherwise in accordance with this Part of the Rules.

1.52(7) [Use of proxy contrary to r. 1.15] If the chairman uses a proxy contrary to Rule 1.15 as it applies by virtue of Rule 1.48(5), his vote with that proxy does not count towards any majority under this Rule.

1.52(8) [Chairman's decision subject to appeal] The chairman's decision on any matter under this Rule is subject to appeal to the court by any creditor or member and paragraphs (5) to (7) of Rule 1.50 apply as regards such an appeal.

R. 1.52
Voting majorities for creditors are laid down with the 75 per cent majority being the key threshold.

1.53 Requisite majorities (members) and proceedings to obtain agreement on the proposal

1.53(1) [Application of r. 1.20] Rule 1.20 shall apply.

1.53(2) [Chairman's discretion to hold meetings together] If the chairman thinks fit, the creditors' meeting and the company meeting may be held together.

1.53(3) [Adjournment of meeting] The chairman may, and shall if it is so resolved at the meeting in question, adjourn that meeting, but any adjournment shall not be to a day which is more than 14 days after the date on which the moratorium (including any extension) ends.

1.53(4) **[Notice of adjournment]** If the meetings are adjourned under paragraph (3), notice of the fact shall be given by the nominee forthwith to the court.

1.53(5) **[Deemed rejection of proposal]** If following the final adjournment of the creditors' meeting the proposal (with or without modifications) has not been approved by the creditors, it is deemed rejected.

R. 1.53
This incorporates r. 1.20 with some modification.

1.54 Implementation of the arrangement

1.54(1) **[Putting supervisor in possession of assets]** Where a decision approving the arrangement has effect under paragraph 36 of Schedule A1 to the Act, the directors shall forthwith do all that is required for putting the supervisor into possession of the assets included in the arrangement.

1.54(2) **[Application of rr. 1.22, 1.22A, 1.24 and 1.29]** Subject to paragraph (3), Rules 1.22, 1.22A and 1.24 to 1.29 apply.

[FORM 1.1]

1.54(3) **[Modified provisions]** The provisions referred to in paragraph (2) are modified as follows–

[FORM 1.2]

(a) in paragraph (1) of Rule 1.22A the reference to section 4A(6) is to be read as a reference to paragraph 36(5) of Schedule A1 to the Act;

[FORM 1.3]

(b) in paragraph (4) of Rule 1.24 the reference to section 4(6) is to be read as a reference to paragraph 30(3) of Schedule A1 to the Act;

[FORM 1.4]

(c) in paragraph (5) of Rule 1.24 the reference to section 4A is to be read as a reference to paragraph 36 of Schedule A1 to the Act;

(d) in paragraph (1) of Rule 1.25 the reference to section 6 is to be read as a reference to paragraph 38 of Schedule A1 to the Act and the references in paragraphs (2) and (4) to the administrator or liquidator shall be ignored;

(e) in paragraph (3) of Rule 1.25 the reference to section 6(4)(b) is to be read as a reference to paragraph 38 (4)(b) of Schedule A1 to the Act; and

(f) in sub-paragraph (a) of paragraph (1) of Rule 1.28 the reference to section 4A is to be read as a reference to paragraph 36 of Schedule A1 to the Act.

R. 1.54
This explains the responsibilities of the directors *vis-à-vis* the supervisor to facilitate implementation of the CVA.

GENERAL NOTE TO CHAPTER 9

This major insertion of rr. 1.35–1.54 was made by the Insolvency (Amendment) (No. 2) Rules 2002 (SI 2002/2712) to cater for the coming into effect of the Insolvency Act 2000. Chapter 9 deals with the new CVA moratorium which is already heavily regulated by Sch. A1.

Rule 2.2   *The Insolvency Rules 1986*

PART 2

IMPORTANT NOTE

There are now two concurrent administration regimes. For most administrations begun from September 15, 2003 onwards, the new IA 1986, Pt II introduced by EA 2002, s. 248 (as set out above on pp. 489ff.) applies. For administrations begun before that date and for building societies, insolvent partnerships, limited liability partnerships and certain bodies which are insurers under FSMA 2000, and the types of public utility company listed in EA 2002, s. 249(1)(a)–(d), Pt II as originally enacted (see pp. 38ff.) will continue to apply. The two regimes now have separate rules, each referred to as IR 1986, Pt 2. The original Pt 2 of the rules follow immediately, and are printed in italic type in order to distinguish them from the new rules, which begin on p. 733. Note that the numbering of the two sets of rules do not correspond.

ADMINISTRATION PROCEDURE

CHAPTER 1

APPLICATION FOR, AND MAKING OF, THE ORDER

2.1 Affidavit to support petition

2.1(1) [Affidavit required] Where it is proposed to apply to the court by petition for an administration order to be made in relation to a company, an affidavit complying with Rule 2.3 below must be prepared and sworn, with a view to its being filed in court in support of the petition.

[FORM 2.1]

2.1(2) [Petition presented by company or directors] If the petition is to be presented by the company or by the directors, the affidavit must be made by one of the directors, or the secretary of the company, stating himself to make it on behalf of the company or, as the case may be, on behalf of the directors.

2.1(3) [Creditor's petition] If the petition is to be presented by creditors, the affidavit must be made by a person acting under the authority of them all, whether or not himself one of their number. In any case there must be stated in the affidavit the nature of his authority and the means of his knowledge of the matters to which the affidavit relates.

2.1(4) [Supervisor's petition] If the petition is to be presented by the supervisor of a voluntary arrangement under Part I of the Act, it is to be treated as if it were a petition by the company.

(See General Note after r. 2.3.)

2.2 Independent report on company's affairs

2.2(1) [Report that administrator's appointment expedient] There may be prepared, with a view to its being exhibited to the affidavit in support of the petition, a report by an independent person to the effect that the appointment of an administrator for the company is expedient.

2.2(2) [Who may report] The report may be by the person proposed as administrator, or by any other person having adequate knowledge of the company's affairs, not being a director, secretary, manager, member, or employee of the company.

2.2(3) *[Report to specify purpose of order]* The report shall specify the purposes which, in the opinion of the person preparing it, may be achieved for the company by the making of an administration order, being purposes particularly specified in section 8(3).

(See General Note after r. 2.3.)

2.3 Contents of affidavit

2.3(1) *[Statements in affidavit]* The affidavit shall state–

(a) the deponent's belief that the company is, or is likely to become, unable to pay its debts and the grounds of that belief

(b) which of the purposes specified in section 8(3) is expected to be achieved by the making of an administration order; and

(c) whether, in the opinion of the deponent, (i) the EC Regulation will apply and (ii) if so, whether the proceedings will be main proceedings, secondary proceedings or territorial proceedings.

2.3(2) *[Company's financial position]* There shall in the affidavit be provided a statement of the company's financial position, specifying (to the best of the deponent's knowledge and belief) assets and liabilities, including contingent and prospective liabilities.

2.3(3) *[Details of creditors' security]* Details shall be given of any security known or believed to be held by creditors of the company, and whether in any case the security is such as to confer power on the holder to appoint an administrative receiver. If an administrative receiver has been appointed, that fact shall be stated.

2.3(4) *[Details of winding-up petition]* If any petition has been presented for the winding up of the company, details of it shall be given in the affidavit, so far as within the immediate knowledge of the deponent.

2.3(5) *[Other matters]* If there are other matters which, in the opinion of those intending to present the petition for an administration order, will assist the court in deciding whether to make such an order, those matters (so far as lying within the knowledge or belief of the deponent) shall also be stated.

2.3(6) *[Rule 2.2 report]* If a report has been prepared for the company under Rule 2.2, that fact shall be stated. If not, an explanation shall be provided why not.

GENERAL NOTE TO RR. 2.1–2.3

These rules give guidance as to the evidence required in support of a petition for an administration order.

It is not obligatory to obtain the report of an independent person under r. 2.2, but the absence of such a report must be explained (r. 2.3(6)). It is customary for the report to cover such matters as: the qualifications of the independent person and the fact of his independence; how far he is relying on his own work and judgment and how far on the work and opinions of others; the company's insolvency; the factors influencing his opinion in favour of recommending the making of an order and the factors against it; which of the statutory purposes are likely to be achieved; and proposals for the provision of working capital during the administration.

The Vice-Chancellor in a Practice Note dated January 17, 1994 (*Practice Note (Administration order applications: content of independent reports*) [1994] 1 W.L.R. 160; [1994] B.C.C. 35) stressed the importance of ensuring that the primary aim of administration orders (namely, to facilitate the rescue and rehabilitation of insolvent companies) is not frustrated by expense, and urged that the costs of obtaining an administration order should not operate as a disincentive or put the process out of the reach of smaller companies.

Accordingly, the Note states that the contents of a r. 2(2) report should not be unnecessarily elaborate and detailed. While the extent of the necessary investigation and the amount of material to be provided must be a matter of judgment for the person concerned and will vary from case to case, what is ordinarily required is a concise assessment of the company's situation and of the prospects of an order achieving one or more of the statutory purposes, normally including an explanation of the availability of any finance required during administration. Where the court finds that it has insufficient material on which to base a decision, the proposed administrator, if he is in court, may offer to supplement the material by giving oral evidence, and later filing a supplemental report covering this extra information.

In suitable cases the court may appoint an administrator but require him to report back to the court within a short time so that the court can consider whether to allow the administration to continue or to discharge the order. In some cases the court may require the administrator to hold a meeting of creditors before reporting back to the court, both within a relatively short period.

The Note concludes by reminding practitioners that there may be straightforward cases in which a report is not necessary.

The *Practice Note* referred to above has been supplemented by the *Practice Statement: Administration Orders – Reports* [2002] B.C.C. 354, which deals with the right to inspect reports on the court file. See also the note to rr. 7.26–7.32.

The significance of the report was stressed by Harman J. in *Re Newport County Association Football Club Ltd* (1987) 3 B.C.C. 635 at p. 635 in the following passage: "Such a report, which is of course an objective assessment by persons with no axe to grind (using that phrase non-pejoratively), that is to say by persons not having any reason to wish a particular result or to be optimistic about a particular outcome, is one which very much influences the court, because it is prepared by experienced people who are detached from the emotions raised by failure . . . , and can make a serious and objective assessment of the chances". This may be compared with *Re W F Fearman Ltd* (1988) 4 B.C.C. 139, where the absence of a report of making an order was regarded as fatal to the application. The affidavit which has to be sworn under r. 2(3) calls for full and frank disclosure of those matters which are likely to be relevant at the hearing of the petition, and deliberate concealment of the true position may also be fatal: *Re West Park Golf & Country Club* [1997] 1 B.C.L.C. 20. In *Re Digginwell Plant & Construction Ltd* [2002] B.P.I.R. 299 some creditors had expressed the view that opinions in the report were over-optimistic. The court granted an administration order, but directed the administrators to report back to the court quickly if these fears proved to be true.

In *Re Colt Telecom Group plc (No. 2)* [2002] EWHC 2815 (Ch), [2003] B.P.I.R. 324, Jacob J. stressed the fact that an insolvency practitioner giving a r. 2.2 report did so as an expert, and as such is subject to the rules in CPR, Pt 35. He emphasised that when an administration petition was likely to be contested, the practitioner should first re-read Pt 35 and the Code of Guidance on Expert Evidence of the Working Party of the Civil Justice Council; should not propose himself as administrator; must be careful not to give or appear to give opinion evidence on matters (*e.g.* on the valuation of assets) in respect of which he is not an expert; and should not allow his opinions to be misrepresented. A solicitor advising the practitioner should ensure that he his given a copy of Pt 35. Even in an uncontested case, where the practitioner routinely offers to act as administrator, he should be particularly careful to be objective because of the slight conflict of interest involved.

The reference to "all" the creditors in r. 2.1(3) is to all the petitioning creditors (if there are more than one), and not to all the creditors of the company: compare r. 2.4(4).

Paragraph (c) was inserted into r. 2.3(1) by the Insolvency (Amendment) Rules 2002 (SI 2002/1307, effective May 31, 2002). See the notes to the EC Regulation, Art. 3.

It is customary for the court, when making an administration order, to direct that the costs of the petition and of the r. 2.2 report should be costs in the administration. In *Re a Company No. 00514 of 1999* [2000] B.C.C. 698 Neuberger J. observed that such an order could in some circumstances be unsatisfactory as it gives no guidance as to how these costs should rank. He went on to say that, although they could not be "expenses properly incurred by the administrator" or "debts or liabilities while he was administrator" so as to come within s. 19(4) or (5), the court's jurisdiction under the Act was sufficiently flexible for a judge to be able to rule where such costs should rank, and he expressed the view that they should normally fall to be paid after the fixed-charge creditors and ahead of all other liabilities.

2.4 Form of petition

2.4(1) **[Petition presented by company or directors]** *If presented by the company or by the directors, the petition shall state the name of the company and its address for service, which (in the absence of special reasons to the contrary) is that of the company's registered office.*

2.4(2) **[Single creditor's petition]** *If presented by a single creditor, the petition shall state his name and address for service.*

2.4(3) **[Director's petition]** *If the petition is presented by the directors, it shall state that it is so presented under section 9; but from and after presentation it is to be treated for all purposes as the petition of the company.*

2.4(4) **[Creditors' petition]** *If the petition is presented by two or more creditors, it shall state that it is so presented (naming them); but from and after presentation it is to be treated for all purposes as the petition of* one only of them, named in the petition as petitioning on behalf of himself and other creditors. An address for service for that one shall be specified.

2.4(5) *[Specification of proposed administrator]* The petition shall specify the name and address of the person proposed to be appointed as administrator; and it shall be stated that, to the best of the petitioner's knowledge and belief, the person is qualified to act as an insolvency practitioner in relation to the company.

2.4(6) *[Documents to be exhibited]* There shall be exhibited to the affidavit in support of the petition–

(a) a copy of the petition;

(b) a written consent by the proposed administrator to accept appointment, if an administration order is made; and

[FORM 2.2]

(c) if a report has been prepared under Rule 2.2, a copy of it.

(See General Note after r. 2.8.)

2.5 Filing of petition

2.5(1) *[Filing in court]* The petition and affidavit shall be filed in court, with a sufficient number of copies for service and use as provided by Rule 2.6.

2.5(2) *[Sealed copies]* Each of the copies delivered shall have applied to it the seal of the court and be issued to the petitioner; and on each copy there shall be endorsed the date and time of filing.

2.5(3) *[Venue for hearing]* The court shall fix a venue for the hearing of the petition and this also shall be endorsed on each copy of the petition issued under paragraph (2).

2.5(4) *[After petition filed]* After the petition is filed, it is the duty of the petitioner to notify the court in writing of any winding-up petition presented against the company, as soon as he becomes aware of it.

(See General Note after r. 2.8.)

2.6 Service of petition

2.6(1) *[Interpretation]* In the following paragraphs of this Rule, references to the petition are to a copy of the petition issued by the court under Rule 2.5(2) together with the affidavit in support of it and the documents (other than the copy petition) exhibited to the affidavit.

2.6(2) *[Persons to be served]* The petition shall be served–

(a) on any person who has appointed, or is or may be entitled to appoint, an administrative receiver for the company;

(b) if an administrative receiver has been appointed, on him;

(ba) if a member State liquidator has been appointed in main proceedings in relation to the company, on him;

(c) if there is pending a petition for the winding up of the company, on the petitioner (and also on the provisional liquidator, if any); and

(d) on the person proposed as administrator.

2.6(3) *[Creditors' petition]* If the petition for the making of an administration order is presented by creditors of the company, the petition shall be served on the company.

Rule 2.6A The Insolvency Rules 1986

(See General Note after r. 2.8.)

2.6A Notice to sheriff, etc.

2.6A The petitioner shall forthwith after filing the petition give notice of its presentation to–

(a) any sheriff or other officer who to his knowledge is charged with an execution or other legal process against the company or its property, and

(b) any person who to his knowledge has distrained against the company or its property.

(See General Note after r. 2.8.)

2.7 Manner in which service to be effected

2.7(1) [Person to effect service] Service of the petition in accordance with Rule 2.6 shall be effected by the petitioner, or his solicitor, or by a person instructed by him or his solicitor, not less than 5 days before the date fixed for the hearing.

2.7(2) [How effected] Service shall be effected as follows–

(a) on the company (subject to paragraph (3) below), by delivering the documents to its registered office;

(b) on any other person (subject to paragraph (4)), by delivering the documents to his proper address;

(c) in either case, in such other manner as the court may direct.

2.7(3) [Service to registered office not practicable] If delivery to the company's registered office is not practicable, service may be effected by delivery to its last known principal place of business in England and Wales.

2.7(4) [Proper address under r. 2.7(2)(b)] Subject to paragraph (4A), for the purposes of paragraph (2)(b), a person's proper address is any which he has previously notified as his address for service; but if he has not notified any such address, service may be effected by delivery to his usual or last known address.

2.7(4A) [Other person re rr. 2.7(2)(b), 2.7(4)] In the case of a person who–

(a) is an authorised deposit-taker or former authorised deposit-taker,

(b) has appointed, or is or may be entitled to appoint, an administrative receiver of the company, and

(c) has not notified an address for service,

the proper address is the address of an office of that person where, to the knowledge of the petitioner, the company maintains a bank account or, where no such office is known to the petitioner, the registered office of that person, or, if there is no such office, his usual or last known address.

2.7(5) [What constitutes delivery] Delivery of documents to any place or address may be made by leaving them there, or sending them by first class post.

(See General Note after r. 2.8.)

2.8 Proof of service

2.8(1) [Verifying affidavit] Service of the petition shall be verified by affidavit, specifying the date on which, and the manner in which, service was effected.

[FORM 2.3]

2.8(2) [Filing in court] The affidavit, with a sealed copy of the petition exhibited to it, shall be filed in court forthwith after service, and in any event not less than one day before the hearing of the petition.

GENERAL NOTE TO RR. 2.4–2.8

Here are set out the requirements regarding the form, filing and service of the petition. A petition by the directors (r. 2.4(1), (3)) must be presented by all the directors: see the note to IA 1986, s. 9(1).

The court has power to abridge the period of five days specified by r. 2.7(1): *Re a Company No. 00175 of 1987* (1987) 3 B.C.C. 124.

Although the rules plainly contemplate that the proceedings for an administration order shall be by way of hearing on notice to interested parties, the courts are willing in a case of urgency to make an order without notice (and indeed, before the presentation of the petition), against suitable undertakings by counsel: see the note to s. 9(1) and the cases there cited.

Paragraph (ba) was inserted into r. 2.6(2) by the Insolvency (Amendment) Rules 2002 (SI 2002/1307, effective May 31, 2002). Rule 2.7(4A)(a) was substituted by the Financial Services and Markets Act 2000 (Consequential Amendments and Repeals) Order 2001 (SI 2001/3649) as from December 1, 2001.

Rule 2.6A seeks to prevent executions, etc. from being proceeded with in innocent contravention of IA 1986, s. 11(3)(d).

Rule 2.7(4A) is intended to ensure that notice to the company's bank is given at a place where its account can most easily be traced.

It is normal practice for the court to order that the costs of the petition should be costs in the administration. On the ranking of such costs, see the note to r. 2.2.

2.9 The hearing

2.9(1) *[Appearances]* At the hearing of the petition, any of the following may appear or be represented–

(a) the petitioner;

(b) the company;

(c) any person who has appointed, or is or may be entitled to appoint, an administrative receiver of the company;

(d) if an administrative receiver has been appointed, he;

(e) any person who has presented a petition for the winding up of the company;

(f) the person proposed for appointment as administrator;

(fa) if a member State liquidator has been appointed in main proceedings in relation to the company, he;

(g) with the leave of the court, any other person who appears to have an interest justifying his appearance.

2.9(2) *[Costs]* If the court makes an administration order, the costs of the petitioner, and of any person appearing whose costs are allowed by the court, are payable as an expense of the administration.

[FORM 2.4]

GENERAL NOTE

This rule ensures that all those likely to have an interest in the outcome of the proceedings may be heard, but those not particularly specified in paras (a)–(f) of r. 2.9(1) need the leave of the court. This would include a member, a director or an unsecured creditor.

On the willingness of the courts in special cases to hear applications without notice to other parties, see the note to rr. 2.4–2.8.

The court will not normally give members of the company, *qua* members, leave to be heard under this rule, at least where the company is plainly insolvent, notwithstanding the possibility that if the administration achieves its purpose they may have some interest in the outcome: *Re Chelmsford City Football Club (1980) Ltd* [1991] B.C.C. 133. However, discretion was exercised enabling shareholders to appear in *Re Farnborough-Aircraft.com Ltd* [2002] EWHC 1224 (Ch) 641; [2002] 2 B.C.L.C. 641.

Paragraph (fa) was inserted into r. 2.9(1) by the Insolvency (Amendment) Rules 2002 (SI 2002/1307, effective May 31, 2002).

2.10 Notice and advertisement of administration order

2.10(1) *[Court to give notice]* If the court makes an administration order, it shall forthwith give notice to the person appointed as administrator.

[FORM 2.4A]

2.10(2) *[Advertisement] Forthwith after the order is made, the administrator shall advertise its making once in the Gazette, and once in such newspaper as he thinks most appropriate for ensuring that the order comes to the notice of the company's creditors.*

[FORM 2.5]

2.10(3) *[Administrator to give notice] The administrator shall also forthwith give notice of the making of the order–*

- (a) *to any person who has appointed, or is or may be entitled to appoint, an administrative receiver of the company;*
- (b) *if an administrative receiver has been appointed, to him;*
- (c) *if there is pending a petition for the winding up of the company, to the petitioner (and also to the provisional liquidator, if any); and*
- (d) *to the registrar of companies.*

[FORM 2.6]

2.10(4) *[Sealed copies] Two sealed copies of the order shall be sent by the court to the administrator, one of which shall be sent by him to the registrar of companies in accordance with section 21(2).*

[FORM 2.7]

2.10(5) *[Directions under s. 9(4)] If under section 9(4) the court makes any other order, it shall give directions as to the persons to whom, and how, notice of it is to be given.*

GENERAL NOTE

This rule dealing with the notification and publicity of the administration order is supplemented by IA 1986, s. 12, which requires notification on the company's business letters, etc.

There is no power under the Act or the rules for the court to appoint an interim administrator, although if the court is satisfied that the assets or business of a company are in jeopardy and that there exists a prima facie case for the making of an administration order, it can under its inherent jurisdiction appoint a person to take control of the property of the company and manage its affairs pending the hearing of the application. Such an appointment is analogous to the appointment of a receiver of a disputed property which is in jeopardy (*Re a Company No. 00175 of 1987* (1987) 3 B.C.C. 124). An alternative course, where a petition for winding up has also been presented, is for the court to appoint a provisional liquidator.

CHAPTER 2

STATEMENT OF AFFAIRS AND PROPOSALS TO CREDITORS

2.11 Notice requiring statement of affairs

2.11(1) *[Notice] Where the administrator determines to require a statement of the company's affairs to be made out and submitted to him in accordance with section 22, he shall send notice to each of the persons whom he considers should be made responsible under that section, requiring them to prepare and submit the statement.*

[FORM 2.8]

2.11(2) *["The deponents"] The persons to whom the notice is sent are referred to in this Chapter as "the deponents".*

2.11(3) *[Contents of notice]* The notice shall inform each of the deponents–

(a) of the names and addresses of all others (if any) to whom the same notice has been sent;

(b) of the time within which the statement must be delivered;

(c) of the effect of section 22(6) (penalty for non-compliance); and

(d) of the application to him, and to each of the other deponents, of section 235 (duty to provide information, and to attend on the administrator if required).

2.11(4) *[Instructions for preparation of statement]* The administrator shall, on request, furnish each deponent with the forms required for the preparation of the statement of affairs.

(See General Note after r. 2.15.)

2.12 Verification and filing

2.12(1) *[Form and verification]* The statement of affairs shall be in Form 2.9, shall contain all the particulars required by that form and shall be verified by affidavit by the deponents (using the same form).

[FORM 2.9]

2.12(2) *[Affidavits of concurrence]* The administrator may require any of the persons mentioned in section 22(3) to submit an affidavit of concurrence, stating that he concurs in the statement of affairs.

2.12(3) *[Affidavit may be qualified]* An affidavit of concurrence may be qualified in respect of matters dealt with in the statement of affairs, where the maker of the affidavit is not in agreement with the deponents, or he considers the statement to be erroneous or misleading, or he is without the direct knowledge necessary for concurring with it.

2.12(4) *[Delivery of statement to administrator]* The statement of affairs shall be delivered to the administrator by the deponent making the affidavit of verification (or by one of them, if more than one), together with a copy of the verified statement.

2.12(5) *[Delivery of affidavit of concurrence]* Every affidavit of concurrence shall be delivered by the person who makes it, together with a copy.

2.12(6) *[Filing in court]* The administrator shall file the verified copy of the statement, and the affidavits of concurrence (if any) in court.

(See General Note after r. 2.15.)

2.13 Limited disclosure

2.13(1) *[Administrator may apply to court]* Where the administrator thinks that it would prejudice the conduct of the administration for the whole or part of the statement of affairs to be disclosed, he may apply to the court for an order of limited disclosure in respect of the statement, or any specified part of it.

2.13(2) *[Powers of court]* The court may on the application order that the statement or, as the case may be, the specified part of it, be not filed in court, or that it is to be filed separately and not be open to inspection otherwise than with leave of the court.

2.13(3) *[Directions]* The court's order may include directions as to the delivery of documents to the registrar of companies and the disclosure of relevant information to other persons.

(See General Note after r. 2.15.)

2.14 Release from duty to submit statement of affairs; extension of time

2.14(1) *[Exercise of s. 22(5) power]* The power of the administrator under section 22(5) to give a release from the obligation imposed by that section, or to grant an extension of time, may be exercised at the administrator's own discretion, or at the request of any deponent.

2.14(2) *[Deponent may apply to court]* A deponent may, if he requests a release or extension of time and it is refused by the administrator, apply to the court for it.

2.14(3) *[Court may dismiss application etc.]* The court may, if it thinks that no sufficient cause is shown for the application, dismiss it; but it shall not do so unless the applicant has had an opportunity to attend the court for an ex parte hearing, of which he has been given at least 7 days' notice.

If the application is not dismissed under this paragraph, the court shall fix a venue for it to be heard, and give notice to the deponent accordingly.

2.14(4) *[Deponent to send notice to administrator]* The deponent shall, at least 14 days before the hearing, send to the administrator a notice stating the venue and accompanied by a copy of the application, and of any evidence which he (the deponent) intends to adduce in support of it.

2.14(5) *[Appearance etc. by administrator]* The administrator may appear and be heard on the application; and, whether or not he appears, he may file a written report of any matters which he considers ought to be drawn to the court's attention.

If such a report is filed, a copy of it shall be sent by the administrator to the deponent, not later than 5 days before the hearing.

2.14(6) *[Sealed copies of order]* Sealed copies of any order made on the application shall be sent by the court to the deponent and the administrator.

2.14(7) *[Applicant's costs]* On any application under this Rule the applicant's costs shall be paid in any event by him and, unless the court otherwise orders, no allowance towards them shall be made out of the assets.

(See General Note after r. 2.15.)

2.15 Expenses of statement of affairs

2.15(1) *[Payment of expenses]* A deponent making the statement of affairs and affidavit shall be allowed, and paid by the administrator out of his receipts, any expenses incurred by the deponent in so doing which the administrator considers reasonable.

2.15(2) *[Appeal to court]* Any decision by the administrator under this Rule is subject to appeal to the court.

2.15(3) *[Effect of Rule]* Nothing in this Rule relieves a deponent from any obligation with respect to the preparation, verification and submission of the statement of affairs, or to the provision of information to the administrator.

GENERAL NOTE TO RR. 2.11–2.15

These rules give details regarding the statement of affairs, which must in this case follow a prescribed form (r. 2.12).

2.16 Statement to be annexed to proposals

2.16(1) *[Contents of statement]* There shall be annexed to the administrator's proposals, when sent to the registrar of companies under section 23 and laid before the creditors' meeting to be summoned under that section, a statement by him showing–

- (a) details relating to his appointment as administrator, the purposes for which an administration order was applied for and made, and any subsequent variation of those purposes;

- (b) the names of the directors and secretary of the company;

- (c) an account of the circumstances giving rise to the application for an administration order;

- (d) if a statement of affairs has been submitted, a copy or summary of it, with the administrator's comments, if any;

- (e) if no statement of affairs has been submitted, details of the financial position of the company at the latest practicable date (which must, unless the court otherwise orders, be a date not earlier than that of the administration order);

- (f) the manner in which the affairs and business of the company–

    - (i) have, since the date of the administrator's appointment, been managed and financed;
    - (ii) will, if the administrator's proposals are approved, continue to be managed and financed;

- (fa) whether (i) the EC Regulation applies and (ii) if so, whether the proceedings are main proceedings, secondary proceedings or territorial proceedings; and

- (g) such other information (if any) as the administrator thinks necessary to enable creditors to decide whether or not to vote for the adoption of the proposals.

2.16(2) *[Where s. 18 application]* Where the administrator intends to apply to the court under section 18 for the administration order to be discharged at a time before he has sent a statement of his proposals to creditors in accordance with section 23(1), he shall, at least 10 days before he makes such an application, send to all creditors of the company (so far as he is aware of their addresses) a report containing the information required by paragraph (1)(a)–(f)(i) of this Rule.

2.17 Notice to members of proposals to creditors

2.17 The manner of publishing–

- (a) under section 23(2)(b), notice to members of the administrator's proposals to creditors, and

- (b) under section 25(3)(b), notice to members of substantial revisions of the proposals,

shall be by gazetting; and the notice shall also in either case be advertised once in the newspaper in which the administration order was advertised.

GENERAL NOTE

The administrator's proposals must be sent to the registrar of companies and to every known creditor individually (IA 1986, s. 23(2)). The administrator must also send copies of the statement directly to members; or alternatively, by virtue of s. 23(2)(b) and r. 2.17, he may publish in the *Gazette* an address to which members should write for copies.

Paragraph (fa) was inserted into r. 2.16(1) by the Insolvency (Amendment) Rules 2002 (SI 2002/1307, effective May 31, 2002). See the notes to the EC Regulation, Art. 3.

Rule 2.18   *The Insolvency Rules 1986*

CHAPTER 3

CREDITORS' AND COMPANY MEETINGS

Section A: creditors' meetings

2.18 Meeting to consider administrator's proposals

2.18(1) *[Notice of s. 23(1) meeting]* Notice of the creditors' meeting to be summoned under section 23(1) shall be given to all the creditors of the company who are identified in the statement of affairs, or are known to the administrator and had claims against the company at the date of the administration order.

2.18(2) *[Newspaper advertisement]* Notice of the meeting shall also (unless the court otherwise directs) be given by advertisement in the newspaper in which the administration order was advertised.

2.18(3) *[Notice to directors etc.]* Notice to attend the meeting shall be sent out at the same time to any directors or officers of the company (including persons who have been directors or officers in the past) whose presence at the meeting is, in the administrator's opinion, required.

[FORM 2.10]

2.18(4) *[Adjournment of meeting]* If at the meeting there is not the requisite majority for approval of the administrator's proposals (with modifications, if any), the chairman may, and shall if a resolution is passed to that effect, adjourn the meeting for not more than 14 days.

(See General Note after r. 2.29.)

2.19 Creditors' meetings generally

2.19(1) *[Application of Rule]* This Rule applies to creditors' meetings summoned by the administrator under–

(a)   section 14(2)(b) (general power to summon meetings of creditors);

(b)   section 17(3) (requisition by creditors; direction by the court);

(c)   section 23(1) (to consider administrator's proposals); or

(d)   section 25(2)(b) (to consider substantial revisions).

2.19(2) *[Convenience of venue]* In fixing the venue for the meeting, the administrator shall have regard to the convenience of creditors.

2.19(3) *[Time of meeting]* The meeting shall be summoned for commencement between 10.00 and 16.00 hours on a business day, unless the court otherwise directs.

2.19(4) *[Notice]* Notice of the meeting shall be given to all creditors who are known to the administrator and had claims against the company at the date of the administration order; and the notice shall specify the purpose of the meeting and contain a statement of the effect of Rule 2.22(1) (entitlement to vote).

[FORM 2.11]

[FORM 2.22]

2.19(4A) *[Period of notice]* Except in relation to a meeting summoned under section 23(1) or 25(2), at least 21 days' notice of the meeting shall be given.

2.19(5) *[Forms of proxy]* With the notice summoning the meeting there shall be sent out forms of proxy.

[FORM 8.2]

2.19(6) *[Adjournment if no chairman]* If within 30 minutes from the time fixed for commencement of the meeting there is no person present to act as chairman, the meeting stands adjourned to the same time and place in the following week or, if that is not a business day, to the business day immediately following.

2.19(7) *[Further adjournments]* The meeting may from time to time be adjourned, if the chairman thinks fit, but not for more than 14 days from the date on which it was fixed to commence.

(See General Note after r. 2.29.)

2.20 The chairman at meetings

2.20(1) *[Administrator or his nominee to be chairman]* At any meeting of creditors summoned by the administrator, either he shall be chairman, or a person nominated by him in writing to act in his place.

2.20(2) *[Nominee chairman]* A person so nominated must be either–

(a) one who is qualified to act as an insolvency practitioner in relation to the company, or

(b) an employee of the administrator or his firm who is experienced in insolvency matters.

(See General Note after r. 2.29.)

2.21 Meeting requisitioned by creditors

2.21(1) *[Documents to accompany request]* Any request by creditors to the administrator for a meeting of creditors to be summoned shall be accompanied by–

(a) a list of the creditors concurring with the request, showing the amounts of their respective claims in the administration;

(b) from each creditor concurring, written confirmation of his concurrence; and

(c) a statement of the purpose of the proposed meeting.

This paragraph does not apply if the requisitioning creditor's debt is alone sufficient, without the concurrence of other creditors.

2.21(2) *[Fixing of venue]* The administrator shall, if he considers the request to be properly made in accordance with section 17(3), fix a venue for the meeting, not more than 35 days from his receipt of the request, and give at least 21 days' notice of the meeting to creditors.

2.21(3) *[Expenses]* The expenses of summoning and holding a meeting at the instance of any person other than the administrator shall be paid by that person, who shall deposit with the administrator security for their payment.

2.21(4) *[Deposit under r. 2.21(3)]* The sum to be deposited shall be such as the administrator may determine, and he shall not act without the deposit having been made.

2.21(5) *[Resolution of meeting re expenses]* The meeting may resolve that the expenses of summoning and holding it are to be payable out of the assets of the company, as an expense of the administration.

2.21(6) *[Repayment of deposit]* To the extent that any deposit made under this Rule is not required for the payment of expenses of summoning and holding the meeting, it shall be repaid to the person who made it.

(See General Note after r. 2.29.)

2.22 Entitlement to vote

2.22(1) *[Conditions for voting]* Subject as follows, at a meeting of creditors in administration proceedings a person is entitled to vote only if–

(a) he has given to the administrator, not later than 12.00 hours on the business day before the day fixed for the meeting, details in writing of the debt which

   (i) he claims to be due to him from the company, or
   (ii) in relation to a member State liquidator, is claimed to be due to creditors in proceedings in relation to which he holds office,

and the claim has been duly admitted under the following provisions of this Rule, and

(b) there has been lodged with the administrator any proxy which he intends to be used on his behalf.

Details of the debt must include any calculation for the purposes of Rules 2.24 to 2.27.

2.22(2) *[Failure to comply with r. 2.22(1)(a)]* The chairman of the meeting may allow a creditor to vote, notwithstanding that he has failed to comply with paragraph (1)(a), if satisfied that the failure was due to circumstances beyond the creditor's control.

2.22(3) *[Production of documents]* The administrator or, if other, the chairman of the meeting may call for any document or other evidence to be produced to him, where he thinks it necessary for the purpose of substantiating the whole or any part of the claim.

2.22(4) *[Calculation of votes]* Votes are calculated according to the amount of a creditor's debt as at the date of the administration order, deducting any amounts paid in respect of the debt after that date.

2.22(5) *[Limitation on voting]* A creditor shall not vote in respect of a debt for an unliquidated amount, or any debt whose value is not ascertained, except where the chairman agrees to put upon the debt an estimated minimum value for the purpose of entitlement to vote and admits the claim for that purpose.

2.22(6) *[Further limitation]* No vote shall be cast by virtue of a claim more than once on any resolution put to the meeting.

2.22(7) *[Creditor's vote]* Where–

(a) a creditor is entitled to vote under this Rule,
(b) has lodged his claim in one or more sets of other proceedings, and
(c) votes (either in person or by proxy) on a resolution put to the meeting,

only the creditor's vote shall be counted.

2.22(8) *[Lodging of claim]* Where–

(a) a creditor has lodged his claim in more than one set of other proceedings, and
(b) more than one member State liquidator seeks to vote by virtue of that claim,

the entitlement to vote by virtue of that claim is exercisable by the member State liquidator in main proceedings, whether or not the creditor has lodged his claim in the main proceedings.

2.22(9) *[Single claim]* For the purposes of paragraph (6), the claim of a creditor and of any member State liquidator in relation to the same debt are a single claim.

2.22(10) *["Other proceedings"]* For the purposes of paragraphs (7) and (8), "other proceedings" means main proceedings, secondary proceedings or territorial proceedings in another member State.

(See General Note after r. 2.29.)

2.23 Admission and rejection of claims

2.23(1) *[Power of chairman]* At any creditors' meeting the chairman has power to admit or reject a creditor's claim for the purpose of his entitlement to vote; and the power is exercisable with respect to the whole or any part of the claim.

2.23(2) *[Appeal from chairman's decision]* The chairman's decision under this Rule, or in respect of any matter arising under Rule 2.22, is subject to appeal to the court by any creditor.

2.23(3) *[Voting subject to objection]* If the chairman is in doubt whether a claim should be admitted or rejected, he shall mark it as objected to and allow the creditor to vote, subject to his vote being subsequently declared invalid if the objection to the claim is sustained.

2.23(4) *[If chairman's decision reversed etc.]* If on an appeal the chairman's decision is reversed or varied, or a creditor's vote is declared invalid, the court may order that another meeting be summoned, or make such other order as it thinks just.

2.23(5) *[In case of s. 23 meeting]* In the case of the meeting summoned under section 23 to consider the administrator's proposals, an application to the court by way of appeal under this Rule against a decision of the chairman shall not be made later than 28 days after the delivery of the administrator's report in accordance with section 24(4).

2.23(6) *[Costs of appeal]* Neither the administrator nor any person nominated by him to be chairman is personally liable for costs incurred by any person in respect of an appeal to the court under this Rule, unless the court makes an order to that effect.

(See General Note after r. 2.29.)

2.24 Secured creditors

2.24 At a meeting of creditors a secured creditor is entitled to vote only in respect of the balance (if any) of his debt after deducting the value of his security as estimated by him.

(See General Note after r. 2.29.)

2.25 Holders of negotiable instruments

2.25 A creditor shall not vote in respect of a debt on, or secured by, a current bill of exchange or promissory note, unless he is willing–

(a) to treat the liability to him on the bill or note of every person who is liable on it antecedently to the company, and against whom a bankruptcy order has not been made (or, in the case of a company, which has not gone into liquidation), as a security in his hands, and

(b) to estimate the value of the security and, for the purpose of his entitlement to vote, to deduct it from his claim.

(See General Note after r. 2.29.)

2.26 Retention of title creditors

2.26 For the purpose of entitlement to vote at a creditors' meeting in administration proceedings, a seller of goods to the company under a retention of title agreement shall deduct from his claim the value, as estimated by him, of any rights arising under that agreement in respect of goods in possession of the company.

(See General Note after r. 2.29.)

2.27 Hire-purchase, conditional sale and chattel leasing agreements

2.27(1) *[Entitlement to vote]* Subject as follows, an owner of goods under a hire-purchase or chattel leasing agreement, or a seller of goods under a conditional sale agreement, is entitled to vote in respect of the amount of the debt due and payable to him by the company as at the date of the administration order.

2.27(2) *[Calculating amount of debt]* In calculating the amount of any debt for this purpose, no account shall be taken of any amount attributable to the exercise of any right under the relevant agreement, so far as the right has become exercisable solely by virtue of the presentation of the petition for an administration order or any matter arising in consequence of that, or of the making of the order.

(See General Note after r. 2.29.)

2.28 Resolutions and minutes

2.28(1) *[Resolution passed by majority in value]* Subject to paragraph (1A), at a creditors' meeting in administration proceedings, a resolution is passed when a majority (in value) of those present and voting, in person or by proxy, have voted in favour of it.

2.28(1A) *[Resolution invalid]* Any resolution is invalid if those voting against it include more than half in value of the creditors to whom notice of the meeting was sent and who are not, to the best of the chairman's belief, persons connected with the company.

2.28(2) *[Minute book]* The chairman of the meeting shall cause minutes of its proceedings to be entered in the company's minute book.

2.28(3) *[Contents of minutes]* The minutes shall include a list of the creditors who attended (personally or by proxy) and, if a creditors' committee has been established, the names and addresses of those elected to be members of the committee.

(See General Note after r. 2.29.)

2.29 Reports and notices under s. 23 and 25

2.29 Any report or notice by the administrator of the result of a creditors' meeting held under section 23 or 25 shall have annexed to it details of the proposals which were considered by the meeting and of the revisions and modifications to the proposals which were so considered.

GENERAL NOTE TO RR. 2.18–2.29

These are the rules governing the summoning and conduct of creditors' meetings. A meeting may be summoned either by the administrator himself or on the requisition of one-tenth in value of the creditors (IA 1986, s. 17(3)(b)). A creditor is required to prove his debt prior to the meeting (r. 2.22(1)(a)), although the chairman has a limited discretion to make exceptions (r. 2.22(2)). In contrast, a creditor is not required to lodge his proxy in advance of the meeting but may do so at any time prior to the taking of the vote: *Re Philip Alexander Securities & Futures Ltd* [1998] B.C.C. 819. The "rule against double proof" applies in this context, as it does in all insolvency situations: see *Re Polly Peck International plc* [1996] B.C.C. 486, and the notes to r. 12.3. Voting is prima facie by a simple majority in value of those creditors present and voting (including proxy votes): r. 2.28(1); but r. 2.28(1A) prevents a resolution from being carried against the wish of a majority of the non-connected creditors. On the meaning of "connected with", see IA 1986, s. 249, and compare IR 1986, r. 1.19(4).

Rule 2.22(5), like r. 1.17(3), assumes that a claimant for an unliquidated amount or for a sum whose value is not ascertained may be regarded as a "creditor" for the purposes of an administration. There is, perhaps, more support for this in the case of an administration than in a voluntary arrangement, since s. 9(1) gives contingent and prospective creditors the right to present a petition. See the notes to s. 1(1) and rr. 1.13–1.21; and contrast the position in a winding up (rr. 12.3(1), 13.12).

On the meaning of "agrees", see the note to r. 1.17(3), but note that there is here no equivalent to r. 1.49(3) fixing a sum of £1 in the absence of an agreement by the chairman to fix a higher value.

A creditor may, if he wishes, split the vote to which he is entitled so as to cast his vote as to £x in value in one way and as to £y in value in the other, provided that £x + £y does not exceed the total debt in respect of which he is qualified to vote under r. 2.22: *Re Polly Peck International plc* [1991] B.C.C. 503. Accordingly, a trustee for debenture holders can give effect to the wishes of the debenture holders where they differ among themselves, or are at variance with those of the trustee as a creditor in its own right.

Sub-paragraph (fa) was added to r. 2.16(1) by the Insolvency (Amendment) Rules 2002 (SI 2002/1307, effective May 31, 2002). The reference to "secondary proceedings" appears to be an error, since art. 3(3) of the Regulation states that such proceedings can only be winding-up proceedings.

Paragraph (1)(a) was also amended, and paras (6)–(10) inserted, into r. 2.22 by SI 2002/1307. The EC Regulation, art. 32(2) and (3) authorises the "liquidator" in both main and secondary proceedings which have been opened in other Member States to prove in secondary proceedings here in respect of claims which have already been lodged in their own proceedings, and to represent their own creditors by (*e.g.*) attending creditors' meetings. The amendments to r. 2.22 are designed to ensure that a debt which has been proved in more than one set of proceedings is treated as a single claim, and that no creditor's vote is counted twice. See the notes to the EC Regulation, Art. 32 and, on the different types of proceedings, Art. 3.

2.30 Notices to creditors

2.30(1) *[Notice of result of meeting]* Within 14 days of the conclusion of a meeting of creditors to consider the administrator's proposals or revised proposals, the administrator shall send notice of the result of the meeting (including, where appropriate, details of the proposals as approved) to every creditor who received notice of the meeting under the Rules, and to any other creditor of whom the administrator has since become aware.

[FORM 2.12]

2.30(2) *[Administrator's report]* Within 14 days of the end of every period of 6 months beginning with the date of approval of the administrator's proposals or revised proposals, the administrator shall send to all creditors of the company a report on the progress of the administration.

2.30(3) *[Administrator vacating office]* On vacating office the administrator shall send to creditors a report on the administration up to that time.

This does not apply where the administration is immediately followed by the company going into liquidation, nor when the administrator is removed from office by the court or ceases to be qualified as an insolvency practitioner.

GENERAL NOTE

The result of the meeting must be notified to all known creditors.

Section B: company meetings

2.31 Venue and conduct of company meeting

2.31(1) *[Fixing of venue]* Where the administrator summons a meeting of members of the company, he shall fix a venue for it having regard to their convenience.

2.31(2) *[Chairman]* The chairman of the meeting shall be the administrator or a person nominated by him in writing to act in his place.

2.31(3) *[Nominee chairman]* A person so nominated must be either–

(a)   one who is qualified to act as an insolvency practitioner in relation to the company, or

(b)   an employee of the administrator or his firm who is experienced in insolvency matters.

2.31(4) *[Adjournment if no chairman]* If within 30 minutes from the time fixed for commencement of the meeting there is no person present to act as chairman, the meeting stands adjourned to the same time and place in the following week or, if that is not a business day, to the business day immediately following.

2.31(5) *[Summoning and conduct of meeting]* Subject as above, the meeting shall be summoned and conducted as if it were a general meeting of the company summoned under the company's articles of association, and in accordance with the applicable provisions of the Companies Act.

2.31(5A) *[Limitation of r. 2.31(5)]* Paragraph (5) does not apply where the laws of a member State and not the laws of England and Wales apply in relation to the conduct of the meeting.

2.31(5B) *[Application of r. 2.31(5A)] Where paragraph (5A) applies, subject as above, the meeting shall be summoned and conducted in accordance with the constitution of the company and the laws of the member State referred to in that paragraph shall apply to the conduct of the meeting.*

2.31(6) *[Minutes] The chairman of the meeting shall cause minutes of its proceedings to be entered in the company's minute book.*

GENERAL NOTE

Any meeting of the shareholders held during the currency of an administration order is summoned and conducted in accordance with the articles of association, but where it is summoned by the administrator, it is he or his nominee who takes the chair.

Paragraphs (5A) and (5B) were inserted into r. 2.31 by the Insolvency (Amendment) Rules 2002 (SI 2002/1307, effective May 31, 2002). By an amendment made to IR 1986, s. 8 it is now possible for a UK court to make an administration order against a company incorporated in another Member State, if its "centre of main interests" is located within the UK. The amendments to r. 2.31 make it plain that the conduct of shareholders' meetings in such a case are to be governed by the law of incorporation. See further the notes to s. 8 and to the EC Regulation, Art. 3.

No doubt r. 2.31(5B) would be applied by analogy in a case where the company was incorporated outside the EU but has its centre of main interests within the UK, so giving a UK court jurisdiction (see *Re BRAC Rent-a-Car International Inc.* [2003] EWHC (Ch) 128; [2003] B.C.C. 248).

CHAPTER 4

THE CREDITORS' COMMITTEE

2.32 Constitution of committee

2.32(1) *[Three–five creditors] Where it is resolved by a creditors' meeting to establish a creditors' committee for the purposes of the administration, the committee shall consist of at least 3 and not more than 5 creditors of the company elected at the meeting.*

2.32(2) *[Eligibility of creditors] Any creditor of the company is eligible to be a member of the committee, so long as his claim has not been rejected for the purpose of his entitlement to vote.*

2.32(3) *[Body corporate as member] A body corporate may be a member of the committee, but it cannot act as such otherwise than by a representative appointed under Rule 2.37 below.*

(See General Note after r. 2.46A.)

2.33 Formalities of establishment

2.33(1) *[Certificate of due constitution] The creditors' committee does not come into being, and accordingly cannot act, until the administrator has issued a certificate of its due constitution.*

2.33(2) *[Agreement to act] No person may act as a member of the committee unless and until he has agreed to do so and, unless the relevant proxy or authorisation contains a statement to the contrary, such agreement may be given by his proxy-holder or representative under section 375 of the Companies Act present at the meeting establishing the committee.*

2.33(2A) *[Issue of administrator's certificate] The administrator's certificate of the committee's due constitution shall not issue unless and until at least 3 of the persons who are to be members of the committee have agreed to act.*

2.33(3) *[Amended certificate] As and when the others (if any) agree to act, the administrator shall issue an amended certificate.*

2.33(4) *[Filing of certificates]* The certificate, and any amended certificate, shall be filed in court by the administrator.

[FORM 2.13]

2.33(5) *[Change in membership]* If after the first establishment of the committee there is any change in its membership, the administrator shall report the change to the court.

[FORM 2.14]

(See General Note after r. 2.46A.)

2.34 Functions and meetings of the committee

2.34(1) *[Functions]* The creditors' committee shall assist the administrator in discharging his functions, and act in relation to him in such manner as may be agreed from time to time.

2.34(2) *[Holding of meetings]* Subject as follows, meetings of the committee shall be held when and where determined by the administrator.

2.34(3) *[First and subsequent meetings]* The administrator shall call a first meeting of the committee not later than 3 months after its first establishment; and thereafter he shall call a meeting–

(a) if so requested by a member of the committee or his representative (the meeting then to be held within 21 days of the request being received by the administrator), and

(b) for a specified date, if the committee has previously resolved that a meeting be held on that date.

2.34(4) *[Notice of venue]* The administrator shall give 7 days' written notice of the venue of any meeting to every member of the committee (or his representative designated for that purpose), unless in any case the requirement of notice has been waived by or on behalf of any member.

Waiver may be signified either at or or before the meeting.

(See General Note after r. 2.46A.)

2.35 The chairman at meetings

2.35(1) *[Administrator to be chairman]* Subject to Rule 2.44(3), the chairman at any meeting of the creditors' committee shall be the administrator or a person nominated by him in writing to act.

2.35(2) *[Other nominated chairman]* A person so nominated must be either–

(a) one who is qualified to act as an insolvency practitioner in relation to the company, or

(b) an employee of the administrator or his firm who is experienced in insolvency matters.

(See General Note after r. 2.46A.)

2.36 Quorum

2.36 A meeting of the committee is duly constituted if due notice of it has been given to all the members, and at least 2 members are present or represented.

(See General Note after r. 2.46A.)

2.37 Committee-members' representatives

2.37(1) *[Representation]* A member of the committee may, in relation to the business of the committee, be represented by another person duly authorised by him for that purpose.

2.37(2) *[Letter of authority]* A person acting as a committee-member's representative must hold a letter of authority entitling him so to act (either generally or specially) and signed by or on behalf of the committee-member, and for this purpose any proxy or any authorisation under section 375 of the Companies Act in relation to any meeting of creditors of the company shall, unless it contains a statement to the contrary, be treated as a letter of authority to act generally signed by or on behalf of the committee-member.

2.37(3) *[Production of letter of authority]* The chairman at any meeting of the committee may call on a person claiming to act as a committee-member's representative to produce his letter of authority, and may exclude him if it appears that his authority is deficient.

2.37(4) *[Who may not be a representative]* No member may be represented by a body corporate, or by a person who is an undischarged bankrupt, or is subject to a composition or arrangement with his creditors.

2.37(5) *[No dual representation]* No person shall–

(a) on the same committee, act at one and the same time as representative of more than one committee-member, or

(b) act both as a member of the committee and as representative of another member.

2.37(6) *[Signing as representative]* Where a member's representative signs any document on the member's behalf, the fact that he so signs must be stated below his signature.

(See General Note after r. 2.46A.)

2.38 Resignation

2.38 *A member of the committee may resign by notice in writing delivered to the administrator.*

(See General Note after r. 2.46A.)

2.39 Termination of membership

2.39(1) *[Automatic termination]* Membership of the creditors' committee is automatically terminated if the member–

(a) becomes bankrupt, or compounds or arranges with his creditors, or

(b) at 3 consecutive meetings of the committee is neither present nor represented (unless at the third of those meetings it is resolved that this Rule is not to apply in his case), or

(c) ceases to be, or is found never to have been, a creditor.

2.39(2) *[Termination on bankruptcy]* However, if the cause of termination is the member's bankruptcy, his trustee in bankruptcy replaces him as a member of the committee.

(See General Note after r. 2.46A.)

2.40 Removal

2.40 *A member of the committee may be removed by resolution at a meeting of creditors, at least 14 days' notice having been given of the intention to move that resolution.*

(See General Note after r. 2.46A.)

2.41 Vacancies

2.41(1) *[Application of Rule]* The following applies if there is a vacancy in the membership of the creditors' committee.

2.41(2) *[Agreement not to fill vacancy]* The vacancy need not be filled if the administrator and a majority of the remaining members of the committee so agree, provided that the total number of members does not fall below the minimum required under Rule 2.32.

2.41(3) *[Filling vacancy]* The administrator may appoint any creditor (being qualified under the Rules to be a member of the committee) to fill the vacancy, if a majority of the other members of the committee agree to the appointment, and the creditor concerned consents to act.

(See General Note after r. 2.46A.)

2.42 Procedure at meetings

2.42(1) *[Votes and passing of resolutions]* At any meeting of the creditors' committee, each member of it (whether present himself, or by his representative) has one vote; and a resolution is passed when a majority of the members present or represented have voted in favour of it.

2.42(2) *[Record of resolutions]* Every resolution passed shall be recorded in writing, either separately or as part of the minutes of the meeting.

2.42(3) *[Signing of records etc.]* A record of each resolution shall be signed by the chairman and placed in the company's minute book.

(See General Note after r. 2.46A.)

2.43 Resolutions by post

2.43(1) *[Proposed resolution sent to members]* In accordance with this Rule, the administrator may seek to obtain the agreement of members of the creditors' committee to a resolution by sending to every member (or his representative designated for the purpose) a copy of the proposed resolution.

2.43(2) *[Copy of proposed resolution]* Where the administrator makes use of the procedure allowed by this Rule, he shall send out to members of the committee or their representatives (as the case may be) a copy of any proposed resolution on which a decision is sought, which shall be set out in such a way that agreement with or dissent from each separate resolution may be indicated by the recipient on the copy so sent.

2.43(3) *[Member may require meeting]* Any member of the committee may, within 7 business days from the date of the administrator sending out a resolution, require him to summon a meeting of the committee to consider the matters raised by the resolution.

2.43(4) *[Deemed passing of resolution]* In the absence of such a request, the resolution is deemed to have been passed by the committee if and when the administrator is notified in writing by a majority of the members that they concur with it.

2.43(5) *[Copy resolution etc. in minute book]* A copy of every resolution passed under this Rule, and a note that the committee's concurrence was obtained, shall be placed in the company's minute book.

(See General Note after r. 2.46A.)

2.44 Information from administrator

2.44(1) *[Notice to administrator]* Where the committee resolves to require the attendance of the administrator under section 26(2), the notice to him shall be in writing signed by the majority of the members of the committee for the time being. A member's representative may sign for him.

2.44(2) *[Time and place of meeting]* The meeting at which the administrator's attendance is required shall be fixed by the committee for a business day, and shall be held at such time and place as he determines.

2.44(3) *[Chairman]* Where the administrator so attends, the members of the committee may elect any one of their number to be chairman of the meeting, in place of the administrator or a nominee of his.

(See General Note after r. 2.46A.)

2.45 Expenses of members

2.45(1) *[Expenses defrayed out of assets]* Subject as follows, the administrator shall out of the assets of the company defray any reasonable travelling expenses directly incurred by members of the creditors' committee or their representatives in relation to their attendance at the committee's meetings, or otherwise on the committee's business, as an expense of the administration.

2.45(2) *[Non-application of r. 2.45(1)]* Paragraph (1) does not apply to any meeting of the committee held within 3 months of a previous meeting, unless the meeting in question is summoned at the instance of the administrator.

(See General Note after r. 2.46A.)

2.46 Members' dealings with the company

2.46(1) *[Effect of membership]* Membership of the committee does not prevent a person from dealing with the company while the administration order is in force, provided that any transactions in the course of such dealings are in good faith and for value.

2.46(2) *[Court may set aside transaction]* The court may, on the application of any person interested, set aside any transaction which appears to it to be contrary to the requirements of this Rule, and may give such consequential directions as it thinks fit for compensating the company for any loss which it may have incurred in consequence of the transaction.

(See General Note after r. 2.46A.)

2.46A Formal defects

2.46A The acts of the creditors' committee established for any administration are valid notwithstanding any defect in the appointment, election or qualifications of any member of the committee or any committee-member's representative or in the formalities of its establishment.

GENERAL NOTE TO RR. 2.32–2.46A

The IA 1986, s. 26 provides for the establishment of a creditors' committee, corresponding to the liquidation committee in a liquidation. These rules deal with its constitution and functioning. Rules 2.33(2) and 2.37(2) are intended to make it easier for insolvency practitioners to convene committee meetings immediately after the creditors' meeting. Rule 2.46A (and rr. 3.30A, 4.172A and 6.156(7)) is in standard form, although one would normally expect to find such a provision in the substantive legislation rather than the rules.

Rule 2.32 envisages that the election to membership of the creditors' committee will be conducted by a single ballot, with the five creditors who attract the greatest number of votes by value being chosen to form the committee: *Re Polly Peck International plc* [1991] B.C.C. 503.

CHAPTER 5

THE ADMINISTRATOR

2.47 Fixing of remuneration

2.47(1) *[Entitlement to remuneration]* The administrator is entitled to receive remuneration for his services as such.

2.47(2) *[How fixed]* The remuneration shall be fixed either–

(a) as a percentage of the value of the property with which he has to deal, or

(b) by reference to the time properly given by the insolvency practitioner (as administrator) and his staff in attending to matters arising in the administration.

2.47(3) *[Determination under r. 2.47(2)]* It is for the creditors' committee (if there is one) to determine whether the remuneration is to be fixed under paragraph (2)(a) or (b) and, if under paragraph (2)(a), to determine any percentage to be applied as there mentioned.

2.47(4) *[Matters relevant to r. 2.47(3) determination]* In arriving at that determination, the committee shall have regard to the following matters—

 (a) the complexity (or otherwise) of the case,

 (b) any respects in which, in connection with the company's affairs, there falls on the administrator any responsibility of an exceptional kind or degree,

 (c) the effectiveness with which the administrator appears to be carrying out, or to have carried out, his duties as such, and

 (d) the value and nature of the property with which he has to deal.

2.47(5) *[If no committee or determination]* If there is no creditors' committee, or the committee does not make the requisite determination, the administrator's remuneration may be fixed (in accordance with paragraph (2)) by a resolution of a meeting of creditors; and paragraph (4) applies to them as it does to the creditors' committee.

2.47(6) *[Fixed by court]* If not fixed as above, the administrator's remuneration shall, on his application, be fixed by the court.

2.47(7) *[Where joint administrators]* Where there are joint administrators, it is for them to agree between themselves as to how the remuneration payable should be apportioned. Any dispute arising between them may be referred—

 (a) to the court, for settlement by order, or

 (b) to the creditors' committee or a meeting of creditors, for settlement by resolution.

2.47(8) *[Where administrator solicitor]* If the administrator is a solicitor and employs his own firm, or any partner in it, to act on behalf of the company, profit costs shall not be paid unless this is authorised by the creditors' committee, the creditors or the court.

(See General Note after r. 2.55.)

2.48 Recourse to meeting of creditors

2.48 If the administrator's remuneration has been fixed by the creditors' committee, and he considers the rate or amount to be insufficient, he may request that it be increased by resolution of the creditors.

(See General Note after r. 2.55.)

2.49 Recourse to the court

2.49(1) *[Administrator may apply to court]* If the administrator considers that the remuneration fixed for him by the creditors' committee, or by resolution of the creditors, is insufficient, he may apply to the court for an order increasing its amount or rate.

2.49(2) *[Notice to committee members etc.]* The administrator shall give at least 14 days' notice of his application to the members of the creditors' committee; and the committee may nominate one or more members to appear or be represented, and to be heard, on the application.

2.49(3) *[Where no committee]* If there is no creditors' committee, the administrator's notice of his application shall be sent to such one or more of the company's creditors as the court may direct, which creditors may nominate one or more of their number to appear or be represented.

2.49(4) *[Costs of application]* The court may, if it appears to be a proper case, order the costs of the administrator's application, including the costs of any member of the creditors' committee appearing or being represented on it, or any creditor so appearing or being represented, to be paid as an expense of the administration.

(See General Note after r. 2.55.)

2.50 Creditors' claim that remuneration is excessive

2.50(1) *[Creditor may apply to court]* Any creditor of the company may, with the concurrence of at least 25 per cent. in value of the creditors (including himself), apply to the court for an order that the administrator's remuneration be reduced, on the grounds that it is, in all the circumstances, excessive.

2.50(2) *[Power of court to dismiss etc.]* The court may, if it thinks that no sufficient cause is shown for a reduction, dismiss the application; but it shall not do so unless the applicant has had an opportunity to attend the court for an ex parte *hearing, of which he has been given at least 7 days' notice.*

If the application is not dismissed under this paragraph, the court shall fix a venue for it to be heard, and given notice to the applicant accordingly.

2.50(3) *[Notice to administrator]* The applicant shall, at least 14 days before the hearing, send to the administrator a notice stating the venue and accompanied by a copy of the application, and of any evidence which the applicant intends to adduce in support of it.

2.50(4) *[Court order]* If the court considers the application to be well-founded, it shall make an order fixing the remuneration at a reduced amount or rate.

2.50(5) *[Costs of application]* Unless the court orders otherwise, the costs of the application shall be paid by the applicant, and are not payable as an expense of the administration.

(See General Note after r. 2.55.)

2.51 Disposal of charged property, etc.

2.51(1) *[Application of Rule]* The following applies where the administrator applies to the court under section 15(2) for authority to dispose of property of the company which is subject to a security, or goods in the possession of the company under an agreement, to which that subsection relates.

2.51(2) *[Venue and notice]* The court shall fix a venue for the hearing of the application, and the administrator shall forthwith give notice of the venue to the person who is the holder of the security or, as the case may be, the owner under the agreement.

2.51(3) *[Notice of s. 15(2) order]* If an order is made under section 15(2), the administrator shall forthwith give notice of it to that person or owner.

2.51(4) *[Sealed copies of order]* The court shall send 2 sealed copies of the order to the administrator, who shall send one of them to that person or owner.

(See General Note after r. 2.55.)

2.52 Abstract of receipts and payments

2.52(1) *[Administrator to send accounts etc.]* The administrator shall–

(a) within 2 months after the end of 6 months from the date of his appointment, and of every subsequent period of 6 months, and

(b) within 2 months after he ceases to act as administrator,

send to the court, and to registrar of companies, and to each member of the creditors' committee, the requisite accounts of the receipts and payments of the company.

[FORM 2.15]

2.52(2) *[Extension of time]* The court may, on the administrator's application, extend the period of 2 months mentioned above.

2.52(3) *[Form of abstract]* The accounts are to be in the form of an abstract showing–

(a) receipts and payments during the relevant period of 6 months, or

(b) where the administrator has ceased to act, receipts and payments during the period from the end of the last 6-month period to the time when he so ceased (alternatively, if there has been no previous abstract, receipts and payments in the period since his appointment as administrator).

2.52(4) *[Penalty on default]* If the administrator makes default in complying with this Rule, he is liable to a fine and, for continued contravention, to a daily default fine.

(See General Note after r. 2.55.)

2.53 Resignation

2.53(1) *[Grounds for resignation]* The administrator may give notice of his resignation on grounds of ill health or because–

[FORM 2.16]

(a) he intends ceasing to be in practice as an insolvency practitioner, or

(b) there is some conflict of interest, or change of personal circumstances, which precludes or makes impracticable the further discharge by him of the duties of administrator.

2.53(2) *[Other grounds]* The administrator may, with the leave of the court, give notice of his resignation on grounds other than those specified in paragraph (1).

[FORM 2.17]

2.53(3) *[Notice to specified persons]* The administrator must give to the persons specified below at least 7 days' notice of his intention to resign, or to apply for the court's leave to do so–

(a) if there is a continuing administrator of the company, to him;

(b) if there is no such administrator, to the creditors' committee; and

(c) if there is no such administrator and no creditors' committee, to the company and its creditors.

2.53(4) *[Notice]* Where the administrator gives notice under paragraph (3), he must also give notice to a member State liquidator, if such a person has been appointed in relation to the company.

(See General Note after r. 2.55.)

2.54 Administrator deceased

2.54(1) *[Notice to court]* Subject as follows, where the administrator has died, it is the duty of his personal representatives to give notice of the fact to the court, specifying the date of the death.

This does not apply if notice has been given under any of the following paragraphs of this Rule.

2.54(2) *[Notice by partner etc.]* If the deceased administrator was a partner in a firm, notice may be given by a partner in the firm who is qualified to act as an insolvency practitioner, or is a member of any body recognised by the Secretary of State for the authorisation of insolvency practitioners.

2.54(3) *[Notice by others]* Notice of the death may be given by any person producing to the court the relevant death certificate or a copy of it.

(See General Note after r. 2.55.)

2.55 Order filling vacancy

2.55 Where the court makes an order filling a vacancy in the office of administrator, the same provisions apply in respect of giving notice of, and advertising, the order as in the case of the administration order.

GENERAL NOTE TO RR. 2.47–2.55

Here are found miscellaneous rules in regard to the administrator's remuneration, his power to deal with charged property, his duties as regards accounting, and vacancies in the office resulting from his resignation, death, etc.

CHAPTER 6

VAT BAD DEBT RELIEF

2.56 Issue of certificate of insolvency

2.56(1) *[Duty of administrator]* In accordance with this Rule, it is the duty of the administrator to issue a certificate in the terms of paragraph (b) of section 22(3) of the Value Added Tax Act 1983 (which specifies the circumstances in which a company is deemed insolvent for the purposes of that section) forthwith upon his forming the opinion described in that paragraph.

2.56(2) *[Contents of certificate]* There shall in the certificate be specified–

(a) the name of the company and its registered number;

(b) the name of the administrator and the date of his appointment;

(c) the date on which the certificate is issued.

2.56(3) *[Title of certificate]* The certificate shall be intituled "CERTIFICATE OF INSOLVENCY FOR THE PURPOSES OF SECTION 22(3)(b) OF THE VALUE ADDED TAX ACT 1983".

GENERAL NOTE

Bad debt relief was available under the Value Added Tax Act 1983 only where the debtor had become insolvent. The FA 1985, s. 32 amended that section so as to include the case where an administrator or administrative receiver is appointed. This rule and r. 3.36 provide the necessary machinery for these cases.

In February 1998 HM Customs and Excise Commissioners issued an extra-statutory concession disapplying the clawback provisions of the Value Added Tax Act 1994, s. 36(4A) (which applies to supplies made after November 26, 1996). Under this concession, subject to certain conditions, insolvency practitioners will not be required to repay input tax already claimed in respect of purchases which are subject to a bad debt claim by the supplier.

2.57 Notice to creditors

2.57(1) *[Time for giving notice]* Notice of the issue of the certificate shall be given by the administrator within 3 months of his appointment or within 2 months of issuing the certificate, whichever is the later, to all of the company's unsecured creditors of whose address he is then aware and who have, to his knowledge, made supplies to the company, with a charge to value added tax, at any time before his appointment.

2.57(2) *[Later notice]* Thereafter, he shall give the notice to any such creditor of whose address and supplies to the company he becomes aware.

2.57(3) *[No obligation re certificate]* He is not under obligation to provide any creditor with a copy of the certificate.

2.58 Preservation of certificate with company's records

2.58(1) *[Retention of certificate]* The certificate shall be retained with the company's accounting records, and section 222 of the Companies Act (where and for how long records are to be kept) shall apply to the certificate as it applies to those records.

2.58(2) *[Duty of administrator]* It is the duty of the administrator, on vacating office, to bring this Rule to the attention of the directors or (as the case may be) any successor of his as administrator.

CHAPTER 7

EC REGULATION – CONVERSION OF ADMINISTRATION INTO WINDING UP

2.59 Application for conversion into winding up

2.59(1) *[Documents]* Where a member State liquidator proposes to apply to the court for the conversion under Article 37 of the EC Regulation (conversion of earlier proceedings) of an administration into a winding up, an affidavit complying with Rule 2.60 must be prepared and sworn, and filed in court in support of the application.

2.59(2) *[Originating application]* An application under this Rule shall be by originating application.

2.59(3) *[Service]* The application and the affidavit required under this Rule shall be served upon–

(a) the company; and

(b) the administrator.

(See General Note after r. 2.61.)

2.60 Contents of affidavit

2.60(1) *[Contents]* The affidavit shall state–

(a) that main proceedings have been opened in relation to the company in a member State other than the United Kingdom;

(b) the deponent's belief that the conversion of the administration into a winding up would prove to be in the interests of the creditors in the main proceedings;

(c) the deponent's opinion as to whether the company ought to enter voluntary winding up or be wound up by the court; and

(d) all other matters that, in the opinion of the member State liquidator, would assist the court–

   (i) in deciding whether to make such an order, and
   (ii) if the court were to do so, in considering the need for any consequential provision that would be necessary or desirable.

2.60(2) *[Procedure]* An affidavit under this Rule shall be sworn by, or on behalf of, the member State liquidator.

(See General Note after r. 2.61.)

2.61 Power of court

2.61(1) *[Powers of court]* On hearing the application for conversion into winding up the court may make such order as it thinks fit.

2.61(2) *[Consequential provisions]* If the court makes an order for conversion into winding up the order may contain all such consequential provisions as the court deems necessary or desirable.

2.61(3) *[Effect of order made under r. 2.61(1)]* Without prejudice to the generality of paragraph (1), an order under that paragraph may provide that the company be wound up as if a resolution for voluntary winding up under section 84 were passed on the day on which the order is made.

GENERAL NOTE TO RR. 2.59–2.61

Rules 2.59–2.61 were added by the Insolvency (Amendment) Rules 2002 (SI 2002/1307, effective May 31, 2002). Article 37 of the EC Regulation empowers the "liquidator" in main proceedings to apply to the court to have "territorial" proceedings (not being winding-up proceedings) which have already been opened in another Member State converted into winding-up proceedings. These rules deal with the procedure and the powers of the court applicable where it is sought to have administration proceedings so converted. Although the rules confer a wide discretion on the court (including the power to decline to make an order), Art. 37 is expressed in terms which appear to give the liquidator the right to an order on request. Even so, the choice between deeming the winding up to be compulsory or voluntary rests with the court. Rule 2.61(3), being expressed in permissive terms, would not rule out the court choosing a different date – e.g. the date when the administration order was made – but this will ordinarily be of little significance because provisions such as IA 1986, ss. 240(3), 247(3) and 387(3) deal explicitly with the consequential issues which would otherwise follow. See further the notes to the EC Regulation, Arts 3 and 37.

Chapter 8

EC Regulation – Member State Liquidator

2.62 Interpretation of creditor and notice to member State liquidator

2.62(1) *[Application]* This Rule applies where a member State liquidator has been appointed in relation to the company.

2.62(2) *[Member state liquidator deemed to be creditor]* For the purposes of the Rules referred to in paragraph (3) the member State liquidator is deemed to be a creditor.

2.62(3) *[Rules referred to in r. 2.62(2)]* The Rules referred to in paragraph (2) are Rules 2.18(1) (notice of creditors' meeting), 2.19(4) (creditors' meeting), 2.21 (requisitioning of creditors' meeting), 2.22 (entitlement to vote), 2.23 (admission and rejection of claims), 2.24 (secured creditors), 2.25 (holders of negotiable instruments), 2.26 (retention of title creditors), 2.27 (hire-purchase, conditional sale and chattel leasing agreements), 2.30 (notice of result of creditors' meeting), 2.32(2) (creditors' committee), 2.39(1)(b) and (c) (termination of membership of creditors' committee), 2.41(3) (vacancies in creditors' committee), 2.49(3) (administrator's remuneration – recourse to court) and 2.50 (challenge to administrator's remuneration).

2.62(4) *[Exercise of creditor's rights]* Paragraphs (2) and (3) are without prejudice to the generality of the right to participate referred to in paragraph 3 of Article 32 of the EC Regulation (exercise of creditor's rights).

2.62(5) *[Notice, copies]* Where the administrator is obliged to give notice to, or provide a copy of a document (including an order of court) to, the court, the registrar of companies or the official receiver, the administrator shall give notice or provide copies, as the case may be, to the member State liquidator.

2.62(6) *[Duty to cooperate and communicate information]* Paragraph (5) is without prejudice to the generality of the obligations imposed by Article 31 of the EC Regulation (duty to cooperate and communicate information).

General Note

The new Chapter 8 was added to the rules by the Insolvency (Amendment) Rules 2002 (SI 2002/1307, effective May 31, 2002). Article 32(2) and (3) of the EC Regulation states that the "liquidators" in the main and any secondary proceedings may (and, indeed, subject to certain conditions, *shall*) lodge in other proceedings claims which have already been lodged in the proceedings for which they have been appointed, and that such a liquidator may participate in other proceedings on the same basis as a creditor, in particular by attending creditors' meetings. The new rule spells out the rights of such a liquidator in more detail, and (by para. 5) ensures that he will receive notice of various documents, over and above those which would come to him as a deemed creditor.

PART 2

Note: The rules which follow apply in the new administration regime (Sch. B1, introduced by EA 2002 with effect from September 15, 2003). In those cases where the original regime continues to apply, reference should be made to the original Pt 2 (pp. 706ff.).

ADMINISTRATION PROCEDURE

CHAPTER 1

PRELIMINARY

2.1   Introductory and interpretation

2.1(1)   [Application of Pt 2] In this Part–

(a) Chapter 2 applies in relation to the appointment of an administrator by the court;

(b) Chapter 3 applies in relation to the appointment of an administrator by the holder of a qualifying floating charge under paragraph 14;

(c) Chapter 4 applies in relation to the appointment of an administrator by the company or the directors under paragraph 22;

(d) The following Chapters apply in all the cases mentioned in sub-paragraphs (a)–(c) above:

— Chapter 5: Process of administration;
— Chapter 6: Meetings and reports;
— Chapter 7: The creditors' committee;
— Chapter 8: Disposal of charged property;
— Chapter 9: Expenses of the administration;
— Chapter 10: Distributions to creditors;
— Chapter 11: The administrator;
— Chapter 12: Ending administration;
— Chapter 13: Replacing administrator;
— Chapter 14: EC Regulation – conversion of administration into winding up;
— Chapter 15: EC Regulation – member State liquidator.

2.1(2)   [Reference to numbered paragraphs] In this Part of these Rules a reference to a numbered paragraph shall, unless otherwise stated, be to the paragraph so numbered in Schedule B1 to the Act.

GENERAL NOTE

The rules in this Part govern administrations where the administrator is appointed under the new IA 1986, Pt II, which is to be found in Sch. B1 to the Act. The appointment may be made by the court under para. 11 of Sch. B1, by the holder of a "qualifying" floating charge under para. 14, or by the company itself or its directors under para. 22. This rule indicates the Chapters of the rules which are to apply in each of these cases.

Rule 2.2   *The Insolvency Rules 1986*

References to paragraph numbers in the notes which follow are to paragraphs of Sch. B1, and those to section numbers are to sections of IA 1986. Cross-references to other rules, if in italics, are to the original Pt 2 of IR 1986; if in roman type, to the new Pt 2. For definitions of special terms, reference should be made to Appendices I and II.

CHAPTER 2

APPOINTMENT OF ADMINISTRATOR BY COURT

2.2 Affidavit in support of administration application

2.2(1) [**Affidavit required**] Where it is proposed to apply to the court for an administration order to be made in relation to a company, the administration application shall be in Form 2.1B and an affidavit complying with Rule 2.4 must be prepared and sworn, with a view to its being filed with the court in support of the application.

[FORM 2.1B]

2.2(2) [**Application by company or directors**] If the administration application is to be made by the company or by the directors, the affidavit shall be made by one of the directors, or the secretary of the company, stating himself to make it on behalf of the company or, as the case may be, on behalf of the directors.

2.2(3) [**Application by creditors**] If the application is to be made by creditors, the affidavit shall be made by a person acting under the authority of them all, whether or not himself one of their number. In any case there must be stated in the affidavit the nature of his authority and the means of his knowledge of the matters to which the affidavit relates.

2.2(4) [**Application by CVA supervisor**] If the application is to be made by the supervisor of a voluntary arrangement under Part I of the Act, it is to be treated as if it were an application by the company.

(See General Note after r. 2.9.)

2.3 Form of application

2.3(1) [**Application by company or directors**] If made by the company or by the directors, the application shall state the name of the company and its address for service, which (in the absence of special reasons to the contrary) is that of the company's registered office.

2.3(2) [**Application by directors**] If the application is made by the directors, it shall state that it is so made under paragraph 12(1)(b); but from and after making it is to be treated for all purposes as the application of the company.

2.3(3) [**Application by single creditor**] If made by a single creditor, the application shall state his name and address for service.

2.3(4) [**Application by two or more creditors**] If the application is made by two or more creditors, it shall state that it is so made (naming them); but from and after making it is to be treated for all purposes as the application of only one of them, named in the application as applying on behalf of himself and other creditors. An address for service for that one shall be specified.

2.3(5) **[Statement by proposed administrator]** There shall be attached to the application a written statement which shall be in Form 2.2B by each of the persons proposed to be administrator stating–

[FORM 2.2B]

- (a) that he consents to accept appointment;
- (b) details of any prior professional relationship(s) that he has had with the company to which he is to be appointed as administrator; and
- (c) his opinion that it is reasonably likely that the purpose of administration will be achieved.

(See General Note after r. 2.9.)

2.4 Contents of application and affidavit in support

2.4(1) **[Inability to pay debts]** The administration application shall contain a statement of the applicant's belief that the company is, or is likely to become, unable to pay its debts, except where the applicant is the holder of a qualifying floating charge and is making the application in reliance on paragraph 35.

2.4(2) **[Company's financial position etc.]** There shall be attached to the application an affidavit in support which shall contain–

- (a) a statement of the company's financial position, specifying (to the best of the applicant's knowledge and belief) the company's assets and liabilities, including contingent and prospective liabilities;
- (b) details of any security known or believed to be held by creditors of the company, and whether in any case the security is such as to confer power on the holder to appoint an administrative receiver or to appoint an administrator under paragraph 14. If an administrative receiver has been appointed, that fact shall be stated;
- (c) details of any insolvency proceedings in relation to the company including any petition that has been presented for the winding up of the company so far as within the immediate knowledge of the applicant;
- (d) where it is intended to appoint a number of persons as administrators, details of the matters set out in paragraph 100(2) regarding the exercise of the function of the administrators; and
- (e) any other matters which, in the opinion of those intending to make the application for an administration order, will assist the court in deciding whether to make such an order, so far as lying within the knowledge or belief of the applicant.

2.4(3) **[Application by qualifying floating charge-holder]** Where the application is made by the holder of a qualifying floating charge in reliance on paragraph 35, he shall give sufficient details in the affidavit in support to satisfy the court that he is entitled to appoint an administrator under paragraph 14.

2.4(4) **[Whether EC Insolvency Proceedings Regulation applies]** The affidavit shall state whether, in the opinion of the person making the application, (i) the EC Regulation will apply and (ii) if so, whether the proceedings will be main proceedings or territorial proceedings.

(See General Note after r. 2.9.)

2.5 Filing of application

2.5(1) **[Filing in court]** The application (and all supporting documents) shall be filed with the court, with a sufficient number of copies for service and use as provided by Rule 2.6.

2.5(2) **[Sealed copies]** Each of the copies filed shall have applied to it the seal of the court and be issued to the applicant; and on each copy there shall be endorsed the date and time of filing.

2.5(3) **[Venue for hearing endorsed on copies]** The court shall fix a venue for the hearing of the application and this also shall be endorsed on each copy of the application issued under paragraph (2).

2.5(4) [Existence of insolvency proceedings] After the application is filed, it is the duty of the applicant to notify the court in writing of the existence of any insolvency proceedings, and any insolvency proceedings under the EC Regulation, in relation to the company, as soon as he becomes aware of them.

(See General Note after r. 2.9.)

2.6 Service of application

2.6(1) [References to the application] In the following paragraphs of this Rule, references to the application are to a copy of the application issued by the court under Rule 2.5(2) together with the affidavit in support of it and the documents attached to the application.

2.6(2) [Notification by service] Notification for the purposes of paragraph 12(2) shall be by way of service in accordance with Rule 2.8, verified in accordance with Rule 2.9.

2.6(3) [Persons to be served] The application shall be served in addition to those persons referred to in paragraph 12(2)–

- (a) if an administrative receiver has been appointed, on him;
- (b) if there is pending a petition for the winding-up of the company, on the petitioner (and also on the provisional liquidator, if any);
- (c) if a member State liquidator has been appointed in main proceedings in relation to the company, on him;
- (d) on the person proposed as administrator;
- (e) on the company, if the application is made by anyone other than the company;
- (f) if a supervisor of a voluntary arrangement under Part I of the Act has been appointed, on him.

(See General Note after r. 2.9.)

2.7 Notice to sheriff, etc

2.7 The applicant shall as soon as reasonably practicable after filing the application give notice of its being made to–

- (a) any sheriff or other officer who to his knowledge is charged with an execution or other legal process against the company or its property; and
- (b) any person who to his knowledge has distrained against the company or its property.

(See General Note after r. 2.9.)

2.8 Manner in which service to be effected

2.8(1) [Service not less than five days before hearing] Service of the application in accordance with Rule 2.6 shall be effected by the applicant, or his solicitor, or by a person instructed by him or his solicitor, not less than 5 days before the date fixed for the hearing.

2.8(2) [How service effected] Service shall be effected as follows–

- (a) on the company (subject to paragraph (3) below), by delivering the documents to its registered office;
- (b) on any other person (subject to paragraph (4) below), by delivering the documents to his proper address;
- (c) in either case, in such other manner as the court may direct.

2.8(3) [Service to registered office not practicable] If delivery to a company's registered office is not practicable, service may be effected by delivery to its last known principal place of business in England and Wales.

2.8(4) **[Proper address under r. 2.8(2)(b)]** Subject to paragraph (5), for the purposes of paragraph (2)(b) above, a person's proper address is any which he has previously notified as his address for service; but if he has not notified any such address, service may be effected by delivery to his usual or last known address.

2.8(5) **[Authorised deposit-taker]** In the case of a person who–

(a) is an authorised deposit-taker or former authorised deposit-taker;

(b)   (i) has appointed, or is or may be entitled to appoint, an administrative receiver of the company, or

        (ii) is, or may be, entitled to appoint an administrator of the company under paragraph 14; and

(c) has not notified an address for service,

the proper address is the address of an office of that person where, to the knowledge of the applicant, the company maintains a bank account or, where no such office is known to the applicant, the registered office of that person, or, if there is no such office, his usual or last known address.

2.8(6) **[Delivery of documents]** Delivery of documents to any place or address may be made by leaving them there, or sending them by first class post.

(See General Note after r. 2.9.)

2.9 Proof of service

2.9(1) **[Verification by affidavit of service]** Service of the application shall be verified by an affidavit of service in Form 2.3B, specifying the date on which, and the manner in which, service was effected.

[FORM 2.3B]

2.9(2) **[Affidavit filed in court]** The affidavit of service, with a sealed copy of the application exhibited to it, shall be filed with the court as soon as reasonably practicable after service, and in any event not less than 1 day before the hearing of the application.

GENERAL NOTE TO RR. 2.2–2.9

These rules correspond to rr. *2.1–2.8* which apply in the original regime, but there are many points of difference. The procedure is by way of application rather than by petition.

R. 2.3
An application by the directors may be made by a majority, not necessarily at a formal meeting (para. 105).
   The "Rule 2.2 report" required to be made under the original regime has been replaced by the simple statement described in r. 2.3(5). No affidavit or statement of truth is required.

R. 2.4(4)
On the question whether the EC Regulation applies and the different types of proceedings, see the note to Art.3 of the Regulation.

2.10 Application to appoint specified person as administrator by holder of qualifying floating charge

2.10(1) **[Production to court]** Where the holder of a qualifying floating charge applies to the court under paragraph 36(1)(b), he shall produce to the court–

(a) the written consent of all holders of any prior qualifying floating charge;

(b) a written statement in the Form 2.2B made by the specified person proposed by him as administrator; and

(c) sufficient evidence to satisfy the court that he is entitled to appoint an administrator under paragraph 14.

2.10(2) **[Costs to be expense of administration]** If an administration order is made appointing the specified person, the costs of the person who made the administration application and the applicant under paragraph 36(1)(b) shall, unless the court otherwise orders, be paid as an expense of the administration.

GENERAL NOTE

Where another person has made an application to the court for the appointment of an administrator, para. 36 allows the holder of a qualifying floating charge to intervene and request the court to appoint a specified insolvency practitioner as administrator instead of the person nominated in the application. This rule sets out the procedural requirements for such an application.

2.11 Application where company in liquidation

2.11(1) **[Contents of affidavit in support]** Where an administration application is made under paragraph 37 or paragraph 38, the affidavit in support of the administration application shall contain–

(a) full details of the existing insolvency proceedings, the name and address of the liquidator, the date he was appointed and by whom;

(b) the reasons why it has subsequently been considered appropriate that an administration application should be made;

(c) all other matters that would, in the opinion of the applicant, assist the court in considering the need to make provisions in respect of matters arising in connection with the liquidation; and

(d) the details required in Rules 2.4(2) and (4).

2.11(2) **[Application by qualifying floating charge-holder]** Where the application is made by the holder of a qualifying floating charge he shall set out sufficient evidence in the affidavit to satisfy the court that he is entitled to appoint an administrator under paragraph 14.

GENERAL NOTE

A company which is in liquidation cannot normally be put into administration (para. 8(1)), but exceptions are made by paras 37 and 38. If an order is made, the administration supersedes the liquidation. This rule spells out some procedural requirements.

2.12 The hearing

2.12(1) **[Appearances]** At the hearing of the administration application, any of the following may appear or be represented–

(a) the applicant;

(b) the company;

(c) one or more of the directors;

(d) if an administrative receiver has been appointed, that person;

(e) any person who has presented a petition for the winding-up of the company;

(f) the person proposed for appointment as administrator;

(g) if a member State liquidator has been appointed in main proceedings in relation to the company, that person;

(h) any person that is the holder of a qualifying floating charge;

(j) any supervisor of a voluntary arrangement under Part I of the Act;

(k) with the permission of the court, any other person who appears to have an interest justifying his appearance.

2.12(2) **[Form of order]** If the court makes an administration order, it shall be in Form 2.4B.

[FORM 2.4B]

2.12(3) **[Costs]** If the court makes an administration order, the costs of the applicant, and of any person whose costs are allowed by the court, are payable as an expense of the administration.

(See General Note after r. 2.14.)

2.13 Where the court makes an administration order in relation to a company upon an application under paragraph 37 or 38, the court shall include in the order–

- (a) in the case of a liquidator appointed in a voluntary winding-up, his removal from office;
- (b) details concerning the release of the liquidator;
- (c) provision for payment of the expenses of the liquidation;
- (d) provisions regarding any indemnity given to the liquidator;
- (e) provisions regarding the handling or realisation of any of the company's assets in the hands of or under the control of the liquidator;
- (f) such provision as the court thinks fit with respect to matters arising in connection with the liquidation; and
- (g) such other provisions as the court shall think fit.

(See General Note after r. 2.14.)

2.14 Notice of administration order

2.14(1) **[Court to send two sealed copies to applicant]** If the court makes an administration order, it shall as soon as reasonably practicable send two sealed copies of the order to the person who made the application.

2.14(2) **[Applicant to send copy to administrator]** The applicant shall send a sealed copy of the order as soon as reasonably practicable to the person appointed as administrator.

2.14(3) **[Directions as notice of interim or other order]** If the court makes an order under paragraph 13(1)(d) or any other order under paragraph 13(1)(f), it shall give directions as to the persons to whom, and how, notice of that order is to be given.

GENERAL NOTE

For corresponding provisions under the original regime, see rr. *2.9–2.10*. There is, however, no counterpart to r. 2.13.

CHAPTER 3

APPOINTMENT OF ADMINISTRATOR BY HOLDER OF FLOATING CHARGE

2.15 Notice of intention to appoint

2.15(1) **[Prescribed form]** The prescribed form for the notice of intention to appoint for the purposes of paragraph 44(2) is Form 2.5B.

[FORM 2.5B]

2.15(2) **[Interim moratorium]** For the purposes of paragraph 44(2), a copy of Form 2.5B shall be filed with the court at the same time as it is sent in accordance with paragraph 15(1) to the holder of any prior qualifying floating charge.

Rule 2.16   *The Insolvency Rules 1986*

2.15(3) **[Service]** The provisions of Rule 2.8(2) to 2.8(6) shall apply to the sending of a notice under this Rule as they apply to the manner in which service of an administration application is effected under that Rule.

(See General Note after r. 2.18.)

2.16 Notice of appointment

2.16(1) **[Form]** The notice of appointment for the purposes of an appointment under paragraph 14 shall be in Form 2.6B.

[FORM 2.6B]

2.16(2) **[Copies to accompanied by]** The copies of the notice filed with the court, shall be accompanied by–

(a) the administrator's written statement in Form 2.2B; and

(b) either–

  (i) evidence that the person making the appointment has given such notice as may be required by paragraph 15(1)(a); or
  (ii) copies of the written consent of all those required to give consent in accordance with paragraph 15(1)(b); and

(c) a statement of those matters provided for in paragraph 100(2), if applicable.

2.16(3) **[Statutory declaration]** The statutory declaration on Form 2.6B shall be made not more than 5 business days before the form is filed with the court.

2.16(4) **[Form of consent by prior qualifying floating charge holder]** Written consent may be given by the holder of a prior qualifying floating charge where a notice of intention to appoint an administrator has been given and filed with the court in accordance with Rule 2.15 above, by completing the section provided on Form 2.5B and returning to the appointor a copy of the form.

2.16(5) **[Written consent by prior qualifying floating charge holder]** Where the holder of a prior qualifying floating charge does not choose to complete the section provided on Form 2.5B to indicate his consent, or no such form has been sent to him, his written consent shall include–

(a) details of the name, address of registered office and registered number of the company in respect of which the appointment is proposed to be made;

(b) details of the charge held by him including the date it was registered and, where applicable, any financial limit and any deeds of priority;

(c) his name and address;

(d) the name and address of the holder of the qualifying floating charge who is proposing to make the appointment;

(e) the date that notice of intention to appoint was given;

(f) the name of the proposed administrator;

(g) a statement of consent to the proposed appointment,

and it shall be signed and dated.

2.16(6) **[Appointment out of court business hours]** This Rule and the following Rule are subject to Rule 2.19, the provisions of which apply when an appointment is to be made out of court business hours.

(See General Note after r. 2.18.)

2.17(1) **[Three copies filed in court]** Three copies of the notice of appointment shall be filed with the court and shall have applied to them the seal of the court and be endorsed with the date and time of filing.

2.17(2) **[Court to issue two sealed copies]** The court shall issue two of the sealed copies of the notice of appointment to the person making the appointment, who shall as soon as reasonably practicable send one of the sealed copies to the administrator.

2.18 Where, after receiving notice that an administration application has been made, the holder of a qualifying floating charge appoints an administrator in reliance on paragraph 14, he shall as soon as reasonably practicable send a copy of the notice of appointment to the person making the administration application and to the court in which the application has been made.

GENERAL NOTE TO RR. 2.15–2.18

The holder of a "qualifying" floating charge (as defined in para. 14(2), (3)) may appoint an administrator out of court under para. 14. These rules set out the procedural requirements.

Where there is a prior-ranking qualifying floating charge, para. 15 will apply, and either two business days' written notice must be given to the holder or his written consent must be obtained. Paragraph 15 does not specify that the notice to the creditor should be in a prescribed form, but Form 2.5B must be used to file a copy with the court under para. 44(2) if it is desired to obtain a moratorium. (Note that filing with the court is not obligatory. On the question whether a notice of intention to appoint can be filed in other circumstances, see the note to paras 15 and 44.) Where there is no prior-ranking floating charge, the charge-holder may proceed to make an appointment immediately, without the need to give or file any notice.

R. 2.16(5)
The detailed requirements of this provision make the use of Form 2.5B considerably more attractive.

2.19 Appointment taking place out of court business hours

2.19(1) **[Form when court closed]** The holder of a qualifying floating charge may file a notice of appointment with the court, notwithstanding that the court is not open for public business. When the court is closed (and only when it is closed) a notice of appointment may be filed with the court by faxing that form in accordance with paragraph (3). The notice of appointment shall be in Form 2.7B.

[FORM 2.7B]

2.19(2) **[Notice of appointment]** The filing of a notice in accordance with this Rule shall have the same effect for all purposes as a notice of appointment filed in accordance with Rule 2.16 with the court specified in the notice as having jurisdiction in the case.

2.19(3) **[Fax details when court closed]** The notice shall be faxed to a designated telephone number which shall be provided by the Court Service for that purpose. The Secretary of State shall publish the telephone number of the relevant fax machine on The Insolvency Service website and on request to The Insolvency Service, make it available in writing.

2.19(4) **[Fax transmission report]** The appointor shall ensure that a fax transmission report detailing the time and date of the fax transmission and containing a copy of the first page (in part or in full) of the document faxed is created by the fax machine that is used to fax the form.

2.19(5) **[Appointment effective from fax transmission]** The appointment shall take effect from the date and time of that fax transmission. The appointor shall notify the administrator, as soon as reasonably practicable, that the notice has been filed.

2.19(6) **[Copy of faxed notice to court]** The copy of the faxed notice of appointment received by the Court Service fax machine shall be forwarded as soon as reasonably practicable to the court specified in the notice as the court having jurisdiction in the case, to be placed on the relevant court file.

2.19(7) **[Appointor to copy court]** The appointor shall take three copies of the notice of appointment that was faxed to the designated telephone number, together with the transmission report showing the date and time that the form was faxed to the designated telephone number and all the necessary supporting documents listed on Form 2.7B, to the court on the next day that the court is open for business.

2.19(8) **[Reasons for out of hours filing]** The appointor shall attach to the notice a statement providing full reasons for the out of hours filing of the notice of appointment, including why it would have been damaging to the company and its creditors not to have so acted.

2.19(9) **[Copies sealed by court]** The copies of the notice shall be sealed by the court and shall be endorsed with the date and time when, according to the appointor's fax transmission report, the notice was faxed and the date when the notice and accompanying documents were delivered to the court.

2.19(10) **[Cessation of appointment]** The administrator's appointment shall cease to have effect if the requirements of paragraph (7) are not completed within the time period indicated in that paragraph.

2.19(11) **[Presumption as to date and time of appointment]** Where any question arises in respect of the date and time that the notice of appointment was filed with the court it shall be a presumption capable of rebuttal that the date and time shown on the appointor's fax transmission report is the date and time at which the notice was so filed.

2.19(12) **[Court to issue two sealed copies]** The court shall issue two of the sealed copies of the notice of appointment to the person making the appointment, who shall, as soon as reasonably practicable, send one of the copies to the administrator.

GENERAL NOTE

There may be occasions when the holder of a floating charge will wish to appoint an administrator at a time when the court office is closed. Since the appointment only takes effect on the filing of a notice of appointment with the court (para. 19), it has been necessary to make special provision in this rule, providing for the filing of a notice of appointment by fax, with confirmation by the lodgement of physical documents on the next day that the court is open for business. The requirements, spelt out in this rule, are quite strict; and it should be noted that the option of filing by fax is available only when the court office is closed.

The fax number is published on the Insolvency Service's website (www.insolvency.gov.uk) and is currently 020 7947 6607. In Scotland, the form should be faxed directly to the relevant court. The numbers can be found on the Scottish Courts website, *www.scotcourts.gov.uk*. Note the requirement in r. 2.19(4) that evidence be preserved both of the fact that the notice has been faxed and at least part of the first page of the fax itself.

Rule 2.19(8) carries the implication that a floating charge-holder should not use a faxed notice, rather than wait for the court office to open on a later date, without good reason. Absurdly, it is suggested that the good reason should relate to the interests of the company and/or its creditors, rather than that of the charge-holder himself. However, it should not be beyond the wit of man to devise a formula sufficient to deter anyone minded to challenge the appointment.

CHAPTER 4

APPOINTMENT OF ADMINISTRATOR BY COMPANY OR DIRECTORS

2.20 Notice of intention to appoint

2.20(1) **[Form of notice]** The notice of intention to appoint an administrator for the purposes of paragraph 26 shall be in Form 2.8B.

[FORM 2.8B]

2.20(2) **[Copy of notice to be sent to]** A copy of the notice of intention to appoint must, in addition to the persons specified in paragraph 26, be given to–

(a) any sheriff who, to the knowledge of the person giving the notice, is charged with execution or other legal process against the company;

(b) any person who, to the knowledge of the person giving the notice, has distrained against the company or its property;

(c) any supervisor of a voluntary arrangement under Part I of the Act; and

(d) the company, if the company is not intending to make the appointment.

2.20(3) **[Application of r. 2.8(2)–(6) to notice]** The provisions of Rule 2.8(2) to 2.8(6) shall apply to the sending or giving of a notice under this Rule as they apply to the manner in which service of an administration application is effected under that Rule.

(See General Note after r. 2.26.)

2.21 The statutory declaration on Form 2.8B shall be made not more than 5 business days before the notice is filed with the court.

(See General Note after r. 2.26.)

2.22 The notice of intention to appoint shall be accompanied by either a copy of the resolution of the company to appoint an administrator (where the company intends to make the appointment) or a record of the decision of the directors (where the directors intend to make the appointment).

(See General Note after r. 2.26.)

2.23 Notice of appointment

2.23(1) **[Form of notice]** The notice of appointment for the purposes of an appointment under paragraph 22 shall be in Form 2.9B or Form 2.10B, as appropriate.

[FORM 2.9B, FORM 2.10B]

2.23(2) **[Copy of notice to be filed and accompanied by]** The copies of the notice filed with the court shall be accompanied by–

(a) the administrator's written statement in Form 2.2B;

(b) the written consent of all those persons to whom notice was given in accordance with paragraph 26(1) unless the period of notice set out in paragraph 26(1) has expired; and

(c) a statement of the matters provided for in paragraph 100(2), where applicable.

(See General Note after r. 2.26.)

2.24 The statutory declaration on Form 2.9B or Form 2.10B shall be made not more than 5 business days before the notice is filed with the court.

(See General Note after r. 2.26.)

2.25 Where a notice of intention to appoint an administrator has not been given, the notice of appointment shall be accompanied by the documents specified in Rule 2.22 above.

(See General Note after r. 2.26.)

2.26(1) **[Court to seal and endorse copies]** Three copies of the notice of appointment shall be filed with the court and shall have applied to them the seal of the court and be endorsed with the date and time of filing.

2.26(2) **[Court to issue copies to appointor]** The court shall issue two of the sealed copies of the notice of appointment to the person making the appointment who shall as soon as reasonably practicable send one of the sealed copies to the administrator.

GENERAL NOTE

These rules apply in the appointment of an administrator by a company or its directors out of court under para. 22ff.

It is not necessary that the company or directors should give notice of intention to appoint under para. 26. If there is no person to whom such a notice needs to be sent, the appointment can be made directly (in which case there will be no moratorium), and the relevant form is Form 2.10B. Whether a notice of intention to appoint can be filed (so securing a brief moratorium) when there is no person entitled to the statutory notice is open to debate: see the note to para. 26.

Form 2.8B contains material which is not relevant for the purposes of para. 26, but only for para. 27 and rr.2.21–2.22 when the copy notice is later filed in court. It is probably not necessary to complete anything other than paras 1 and 2 of the form in order to comply with para. 26, but the whole form should no doubt be filled in where possible to avoid any dispute.

A second statutory declaration on Form 2.9B, in addition to that on Form 2.8B, is required, and it too must not be more than five business days old.

CHAPTER 5

PROCESS OF ADMINISTRATION

2.27 Notification and advertisement of administrator's appointment

2.27(1) **[Form of advertisement]** The administrator shall advertise his appointment once in the Gazette, and once in such newspaper as he thinks most appropriate for ensuring that the appointment comes to the notice of the company's creditors. The advertisement shall be in Form 2.11B.

[FORM 2.11B]

2.27(2) **[To whom administrator to notify appointment]** The administrator shall, as soon as reasonably practicable after the date specified in paragraph 46(6), give notice of his appointment–

(a) if a receiver or an administrative receiver has been appointed, to him;

(b) if there is pending a petition for the winding up of the company, to the petitioner (and also to the provisional liquidator, if any);

(c) to any sheriff who, to the administrator's knowledge, is charged with execution or other legal process against the company;

(d) to any person who, to the administrator's knowledge, has distrained against the company or its property; and

(e) any supervisor of a voluntary arrangement under Part I of the Act.

2.27(3) **[Form of notice]** Where, under a provision of Schedule B1 to the Act or these Rules, the administrator is required to send a notice of his appointment to any person he shall do so in Form 2.12B.

[FORM 2.12B]

(See General Note after r. 2.32.)

2.28 Notice requiring statement of affairs

2.28(1) **["Relevant person"]** In this Chapter "relevant person" shall have the meaning given to it in paragraph 47(3).

2.28(2) **[Form of notice]** The administrator shall send notice in Form 2.13B to each relevant person whom he determines appropriate requiring him to prepare and submit a statement of the company's affairs.

[FORM 2.13B]

2.28(3) **[Content of notice]** The notice shall inform each of the relevant persons -

(a) of the names and addresses of all others (if any) to whom the same notice has been sent;

(b) of the time within which the statement must be delivered;

(c) of the effect of paragraph 48(4) (penalty for non-compliance); and

(d) of the application to him, and to each other relevant person, of section 235 (duty to provide information, and to attend on the administrator, if required).

2.28(4) **[Forms for preparation of statement of affairs]** The administrator shall furnish each relevant person to whom he has sent notice in Form 2.13B with the forms required for the preparation of the statement of affairs.

(See General Note after r. 2.32.)

2.29 Verification and filing

2.29(1) **[Form and verification]** The statement of the company's affairs shall be in Form 2.14B, contain all the particulars required by that form and be verified by a statement of truth by the relevant person.

[FORM 2.14B]

2.29(2) **[Statement of concurrence]** The administrator may require any relevant person to submit a statement of concurrence in Form 2.15B stating that he concurs in the statement of affairs. Where the administrator does so, he shall inform the person making the statement of affairs of that fact.

[FORM 2.15B]

2.29(3) **[Statement of affairs to administrator]** The statement of affairs shall be delivered by the relevant person making the statement of truth, together with a copy, to the administrator. The relevant person shall also deliver a copy of the statement of affairs to all those persons whom the administrator has required to make a statement of concurrence.

2.29(4) **[Period for delivery of statement of concurrence]** A person required to submit a statement of concurrence shall do so before the end of the period of 5 business days (or such other period as the administrator may agree) beginning with the day on which the statement of affairs being concurred with is received by him.

2.29(5) **[Qualification of statement of concurrence]** A statement of concurrence may be qualified in respect of matters dealt with in the statement of affairs, where the maker of the statement of concurrence is not in agreement with the relevant person, or he considers the statement of affairs to be erroneous or misleading, or he is without the direct knowledge necessary for concurring with it.

2.29(6) **[Verification and delivery of statement of concurrence]** Every statement of concurrence shall be verified by a statement of truth and be delivered to the administrator by the person who makes it, together with a copy of it.

2.29(7) **[Form of notice of statement of affairs]** Subject to Rule 2.30 below, the administrator shall as soon as reasonably practicable send to the registrar of companies and file with the court a Form 2.16B together with a copy of the statement of affairs and any statement of concurrence.

(See General Note after r. 2.32.)

2.30 Limited disclosure

2.30(1) [Administrator may apply to court] Where the administrator thinks that it would prejudice the conduct of the administration for the whole or part of the statement of the company's affairs to be disclosed, he may apply to the court for an order of limited disclosure in respect of the statement, or any specified part of it.

2.30(2) [Powers of court] The court may, on such application, order that the statement or, as the case may be, the specified part of it, shall not be filed with the registrar of companies.

2.30(3) [Delivery to registrar of companies] The administrator shall as soon as reasonably practicable send to the registrar of companies a Form 2.16B together with a copy of the order and the statement of affairs (to the extent provided by the order) and any statement of concurrence.

2.30(4) [Application to court by creditor for disclosure] If a creditor seeks disclosure of a statement of affairs or a specified part of it in relation to which an order has been made under this Rule, he may apply to the court for an order that the administrator disclose it or a specified part of it. The application shall be supported by written evidence in the form of an affidavit.

2.30(5) [Notice of application to administrator] The applicant shall give the administrator notice of his application at least 3 days before the hearing.

2.30(6) [Power of court to order disclosure] The court may make any order for disclosure subject to any conditions as to confidentiality, duration, the scope of the order in the event of any change of circumstances, or other matters as it sees fit.

2.30(7) [Material change in circumstances] If there is a material change in circumstances rendering the limit on disclosure or any part of it unnecessary, the administrator shall, as soon as reasonably practicable after the change, apply to the court for the order or any part of it to be rescinded.

2.30(8) [Filing notice of and statement of affairs] The administrator shall, as soon as reasonably practicable after the making of an order under paragraph (7) above, file with the registrar of companies Form 2.16B together with a copy of the statement of affairs to the extent provided by the order.

2.30(9) [Copies of statement of affairs] When the statement of affairs is filed in accordance with paragraph (8), the administrator shall, where he has sent a statement of proposals under paragraph 49, provide the creditors with a copy of the statement of affairs as filed, or a summary thereof.

2.30(10) [CPR, Pt. 31 not to apply] The provisions of Part 31 of the CPR shall not apply to an application under this Rule.

(See General Note after r. 2.32.)

2.31 Release from duty to submit statement of affairs; extension of time

2.31(1) [Exercise of powers] The power of the administrator under paragraph 48(2) to give a release from the obligation imposed by paragraph 47(1), or to grant an extension of time, may be exercised at the administrator's own discretion, or at the request of any relevant person.

2.31(2) [Application to court] A relevant person may, if he requests a release or extension of time and it is refused by the administrator, apply to the court for it.

2.31(3) [Powers of court] The court may, if it thinks that no sufficient cause is shown for the application, dismiss it without a hearing but it shall not do so without giving the relevant person at least 7 days' notice, upon receipt of which the relevant person may request the court to list the application for a without notice hearing. If the application is not dismissed the court shall fix a venue for it to be heard, and give notice to the relevant person accordingly.

The Insolvency Rules 1986   Rule 2.33

2.31(4) **[Notice of hearing to administrator]** The relevant person shall, at least 14 days before the hearing, send to the administrator a notice stating the venue and accompanied by a copy of the application and of any evidence which he (the relevant person) intends to adduce in support of it.

2.31(5) **[Appearance etc. by liquidator]** The administrator may appear and be heard on the application and, whether or not he appears, he may file a written report of any matters which he considers ought to be drawn to the court's attention.

If such a report is filed, a copy of it shall be sent by the administrator to the relevant person, not later than 5 days before the hearing.

2.31(6) **[Sealed copies of order]** Sealed copies of any order made on the application shall be sent by the court to the relevant person and the administrator.

2.31(7) **[Applicant's costs]** On any application under this Rule the relevant person's costs shall be paid in any event by him and, unless the court otherwise orders, no allowance towards them shall be made out of the assets.

(See General Note after r. 2.32.)

2.32 Expenses of statement of affairs

2.32(1) **[Payment of expenses]** A relevant person making the statement of the company's affairs or statement of concurrence shall be allowed, and paid by the administrator out of his receipts, any expenses incurred by the relevant person in so doing which the administrator considers reasonable.

2.32(2) **[Appeal to court]** Any decision by the administrator under this Rule is subject to appeal to the court.

2.32(3) **[Effect of Rule]** Nothing in this Rule relieves a relevant person from any obligation with respect to the preparation, verification and submission of the statement of affairs, or to the provision of information to the administrator.

GENERAL NOTE TO RR. 2.27–2.32

These and the succeeding rules in Pt 2 apply whether the administrator is appointed by the court or out of court. For the corresponding rules under the original regime, see rr. *2.11* ff.
   On the statement of affairs generally, see the note to para. 47.

2.33 Administrator's proposals

2.33(1) **[Statement of administrator's proposals]** The administrator shall, under paragraph 49, make a statement which he shall send to the registrar of companies attached to Form 2.17B.

[FORM 2.17B]

2.33(2) **[Contents of statement]** The statement shall include, in addition to those matters set out in paragraph 49–

   (a)   details of the court where the proceedings are and the relevant court reference number;

(b) the full name, registered address, registered number and any other trading names of the company;

(c) details relating to his appointment as administrator, including the date of appointment and the person making the application or appointment and, where there are joint administrators, details of the matters set out in paragraph 100(2);

(d) the names of the directors and secretary of the company and details of any shareholdings in the company they may have;

(e) an account of the circumstances giving rise to the appointment of the administrator;

(f) if a statement of the company's affairs has been submitted, a copy or summary of it, with the administrator's comments, if any;

(g) if an order limiting the disclosure of the statement of affairs (under Rule 2.30) has been made, a statement of that fact, as well as–

  (i) details of who provided the statement of affairs;
  (ii) the date of the order of limited disclosure; and
  (iii) the details or a summary of the details that are not subject to that order;

(h) if a full statement of affairs is not provided, the names, addresses and debts of the creditors including details of any security held;

(j) if no statement of affairs has been submitted, details of the financial position of the company at the latest practicable date (which must, unless the court otherwise orders, be a date not earlier than that on which the company entered administration), a list of the company's creditors including their names, addresses and details of their debts, including any security held, and an explanation as to why there is no statement of affairs;

(k) the basis upon which it is proposed that the administrator's remuneration should be fixed under Rule 2.106;

(l) (except where the administrator proposes a voluntary arrangement in relation to the company and subject to paragraph (3))–

  (i) to the best of the administrator's knowledge and belief–

    (aa) an estimate of the value of the prescribed part (whether or not he proposes to make an application to court under section 176A(5) or section 176A(3) applies); and
    (bb) an estimate of the value of the company's net property; and

  (ii) whether, and, if so, why, the administrator proposes to make an application to court under section 176A(5);

(m) how it is envisaged the purpose of the administration will be achieved and how it is proposed that the administration shall end. If a creditors' voluntary liquidation is proposed, details of the proposed liquidator must be provided, and a statement that, in accordance with paragraph 83(7) and Rule 2.117(3), creditors may nominate a different person as the proposed liquidator, provided that the nomination is made after the receipt of the proposals and before the proposals are approved;

(n) where the administrator has decided not to call a meeting of creditors, his reasons;

(o) the manner in which the affairs and business of the company–

    (i) have, since the date of the administrator's appointment, been managed and financed, including, where any assets have been disposed of, the reasons for such disposals and the terms upon which such disposals were made; and

    (ii) will, if the administrator's proposals are approved, continue to be managed and financed;

(p) whether–

    (i) the EC Regulation applies; and

    (ii) if so, whether the proceedings are main proceedings or territorial proceedings; and

(q) such other information (if any) as the administrator thinks necessary to enable creditors to decide whether or not to vote for the adoption of the proposals.

2.33(3) **[Non-disclosure of information prejudicial to company's interests]** Nothing in paragraph (2)(l) is to be taken as requiring any such estimate to include any information, the disclosure of which could seriously prejudice the commercial interests of the company. If such information is excluded from the calculation the estimate shall be accompanied by a statement to that effect.

2.33(4) **[Notification of extension of time for proposals]** Where the court orders, upon an application by the administrator under paragraph 107, an extension of the period of time in paragraph 49(5), the administrator shall notify in Form 2.18B all the persons set out in paragraph 49(4) as soon as reasonably practicable after the making of the order.

[FORM 2.18B]

2.33(5) **[Proposals deemed approved]** Where the administrator has made a statement under paragraph 52(1) and has not called an initial meeting of creditors, the proposals sent out under this Rule and paragraph 49 will (if no meeting has been requisitioned under paragraph 52(2) within the period set out in Rule 2.37(1)) be deemed to have been approved by the creditors.

2.33(6) **[Notice where application for administration to cease]** Where the administrator intends to apply to the court (or file a notice under paragraph 80(2)) for the administration to cease at a time before he has sent a statement of his proposals to creditors in accordance with paragraph 49, he shall, at least 10 days before he makes such an application (or files such a notice), send to all creditors of the company (so far as he is aware of their addresses) a report containing the information required by paragraphs (2)(a)–(p) of this Rule.

2.33(7) **[Advertisement of notice for copy of statement of proposals]** Where the administrator wishes to publish a notice under paragraph 49(6) he shall publish the notice once in such newspaper as he thinks most appropriate for ensuring that the notice comes to the attention of the company's members. The notice shall–

(a) state the full name of the company;

(b) state the full name and address of the administrator;

(c) give details of the administrator's appointment; and

(d) specify an address to which members can write for a copy of the statement of proposals.

2.33(8) **[Time limit for publication of notice]** This notice must be published as soon as reasonably practicable after the administrator sends his statement of proposals to the company's creditors but no later than 8 weeks (or such other period as may be agreed by the creditors or as the court may order) from the date that the company entered administration.

GENERAL NOTE

This rule applies to all administrations under Sch. B1, however initiated. The legislators have embraced the philosophy of disclosure with both hands! At least they have provided administrators with a comprehensive check-list.

Form 2.17B serves only for the purpose of attaching the administrator's statement.

R. 2.33(2)(j)

It does not appear that the administrator has any discretion not to require a statement of affairs to be submitted (see para. 47(1)), but this paragraph could apply if no statement of affairs has been submitted at the time when the proposals are sent out, and conceivably also where nobody formerly connected with the company can be traced.

R. 2.33(2)(p)

On this issue, see the note to Art. 3 of the Regulation.

R. 2.33(6)

Where the company is hopelessly insolvent or has assets which will all go to paying off its secured creditors – or, on the other hand, where it is clear that there are sufficient assets for all the creditors to be paid in full – there is little point in going through with the full statutory routine. In these circumstances, the administrator may be able to sign off at an early stage.

CHAPTER 6

MEETINGS AND REPORTS

SECTION A: CREDITORS' MEETINGS

2.34 Meetings to consider administrator's proposals

2.34(1) [**Notice of initial creditors meeting**] Notice of an initial creditors' meeting shall (unless the court otherwise directs) be given by notice in the newspaper in which the administrator's appointment was advertised and, if he considers it appropriate to do so, in such other newspaper as he thinks most appropriate for ensuring that the notice comes to the attention of the company's creditors.

2.34(2) [**Notice to directors etc.**] Notice in Form 2.19B to attend the meeting shall be sent out at the same time to any directors or officers of the company (including persons who have been directors or officers in the past) whose presence at the meeting is, in the administrator's opinion, required.

[FORM 2.19B]

2.34(3) [**Notice where period for initial meeting extended**] Where the court orders an extension to the period set out in paragraph 51(2)(b) the administrator shall send a notice in Form 2.18B to each person to whom he is required to send notice by paragraph 49(4).

2.34(4) [**Single adjournment of meeting**] If at the meeting there is not the requisite majority for approval of the administrator's proposals (with modifications, if any), the chairman may, and shall if a resolution is passed to that effect, adjourn the meeting for not more than 14 days and may only adjourn once (subject to any direction by the court).

(See General Note after r. 2.44.)

2.35 Creditors' meetings generally

2.35(1) **[Application of r. 2.35]** This Rule applies to creditors' meetings summoned by the administrator under–

(a) paragraph 51 (initial creditors' meeting);

(b) paragraph 52(2) (at the request of the creditors);

(c) paragraph 54(2) (to consider revision to the administrator's proposals);

(d) paragraph 56(1) (further creditors' meetings); and

(e) paragraph 62 (general power to summon meetings of creditors).

2.35(2) **[Form of notice]** Notice of any of the meetings set out in paragraph (1) above shall be in Form 2.20B.

[FORM 2.20B]

2.35(3) **[Convenience of venue]** In fixing the venue for the meeting, the administrator shall have regard to the convenience of creditors and the meeting shall be summoned for commencement between 10.00 and 16.00 hours on a business day, unless the court otherwise directs.

2.35(4) **[Period of notice]** Subject to paragraphs (6) and (7) below, at least 14 days' notice of the meeting shall be given to all creditors who are known to the administrator and had claims against the company at the date when the company entered administration unless that creditor has subsequently been paid in full; and the notice shall–

(a) specify the purpose of the meeting;

(b) contain a statement of the effect of Rule 2.38 (entitlement to vote); and

(c) contain the forms of proxy.

[FORM 8.2]

2.35(5) **[Adjournment where no chairman]** If within 30 minutes from the time fixed for commencement of the meeting there is no person present to act as chairman, the meeting stands adjourned to the same time and place in the following week or, if that is not a business day, to the business day immediately following.

2.35(6) **[Single adjournment]** The meeting may be adjourned once, if the chairman thinks fit, but not for more than 14 days from the date on which it was fixed to commence, subject to the direction of the court.

2.35(7) **[Notification of venue of adjourned meeting]** If a meeting is adjourned the administrator shall as soon as reasonably practicable notify the creditors of the venue of the adjourned meeting.

(See General Note after r. 2.44.)

2.36 The chairman at meetings

2.36(1) **[Administrator or his nominee to be chairman]** At any meeting of creditors summoned by the administrator, either he shall be chairman, or a person nominated by him in writing to act in his place.

2.36(2) **[Nominee chairman]** A person so nominated must be either–

(a) one who is qualified to act as an insolvency practitioner in relation to the company; or

(b) an employee of the administrator or his firm who is experienced in insolvency matters.

(See General Note after r. 2.44.)

2.37 Meeting requisitioned by creditors

2.37(1) **[Form of request]** The request for a creditors' meeting under paragraph 52(2) or 56(1) shall be in Form 2.21B. A request for an initial creditors' meeting shall be made within 12 days of the date on which the administrator's statement of proposals is sent out. A request under paragraph 52(2) or 56(1) shall include–

[FORM 2.21B]

- (a) a list of the creditors concurring with the request, showing the amounts of their respective debts in the administration;
- (b) from each creditor concurring, written confirmation of his concurrence; and
- (c) a statement of the purpose of the proposed meeting,

but sub-paragraph (a) does not apply if the requisitioning creditor's debt is alone sufficient without the concurrence of other creditors.

2.37(2) **[Period for meeting to be held]** A meeting requested under paragraph 52(2) or 56(1) shall be held within 28 days of the administrator's receipt of the notice requesting the meeting.

2.37(3) **[Expenses]** The expenses of summoning and holding a meeting at the request of a creditor shall be paid by that person, who shall deposit with the administrator security for their payment.

2.37(4) **[Deposit as security for expenses]** The sum to be deposited shall be such as the administrator may determine, and he shall not act without the deposit having been made.

2.37(5) **[Resolution of meeting re expenses]** The meeting may resolve that the expenses of summoning and holding it are to be payable out of the assets of the company as an expense of the administration.

2.37(6) **[Repayment of deposit]** To the extent that any deposit made under this Rule is not required for the payment of expenses of summoning and holding the meeting, it shall be repaid to the person who made it.

(See General Note after r. 2.44.)

2.38 Entitlement to vote

2.38(1) **[Conditions for voting]** Subject as follows, at a meeting of creditors in administration proceedings a person is entitled to vote only if–

- (a) he has given to the administrator, not later than 12.00 hours on the business day before the day fixed for the meeting, details in writing of the debt which–
    - (i) he claims to be due to him from the company; or
    - (ii) in relation to a member State liquidator, is claimed to be due to creditors in proceedings in relation to which he holds office;
- (b) the claim has been duly admitted under the following provisions of this Rule; and
- (c) there has been lodged with the administrator any proxy which he intends to be used on his behalf,

and details of the debt must include any calculation for the purposes of Rules 2.40 to 2.42.

2.38(2) **[Voting despite failure to comply with r. 2.38(1)(a)]** The chairman of the meeting may allow a creditor to vote, notwithstanding that he has failed to comply with paragraph (1)(a), if satisfied that the failure was due to circumstances beyond the creditor's control.

2.38(3) **[Call for documents to substantiate claim]** The chairman of the meeting may call for any document or other evidence to be produced to him, where he thinks it necessary for the purpose of substantiating the whole or any part of the claim.

2.38(4) [**Calculation of votes**] Votes are calculated according to the amount of a creditor's claim as at the date on which the company entered administration, less any payments that have been made to him after that date in respect of his claim and any adjustment by way of set-off in accordance with Rule 2.85 as if that Rule were applied on the date that the votes are counted.

2.38(5) [**Unliquidated debts**] A creditor shall not vote in respect of a debt for an unliquidated amount, or any debt whose value is not ascertained, except where the chairman agrees to put upon the debt an estimated minimum value for the purpose of entitlement to vote and admits the claim for that purpose.

2.38(6) [**Votes cast only once**] No vote shall be cast by virtue of a claim more than once on any resolution put to the meeting.

2.38(7) [**Creditor's vote priority over member State liquidator**] Where–

(a) a creditor is entitled to vote under this Rule;

(b) has lodged his claim in one or more sets of other proceedings; and

(c) votes (either in person or by proxy) on a resolution put to the meeting; and

(d) the member State liquidator casts a vote in respect of the same claim,

only the creditor's vote shall be counted.

2.38(8) [**Voting in more than one set of proceedings**] Where–

(a) a creditor has lodged his claim in more than one set of other proceedings; and

(b) more than one member State liquidator seeks to vote by virtue of that claim,

the entitlement to vote by virtue of that claim is exercisable by the member State liquidator in main proceedings, whether or not the creditor has lodged his claim in the main proceedings.

2.38(9) [**Creditor and member State liquidator single claim**] For the purposes of paragraph (6), the claim of a creditor and of any member State liquidator in relation to the same debt are a single claim.

2.38(10) [**"Other proceedings"**] For the purposes of paragraphs (7) and (8), "other proceedings" means main proceedings, secondary proceedings or territorial proceedings in another member State.

(See General Note after r. 2.44.)

2.39 Admission and rejection of claims

2.39(1) [**Power of chairman**] At any creditors' meeting the chairman has power to admit or reject a creditor's claim for the purpose of his entitlement to vote; and the power is exercisable with respect to the whole or any part of the claim.

2.39(2) [**Appeal from chairman's decision**] The chairman's decision under this Rule, or in respect of any matter arising under Rule 2.38, is subject to appeal to the court by any creditor.

2.39(3) [**Doubtful claim vote admitted marked objected to**] If the chairman is in doubt whether a claim should be admitted or rejected, he shall mark it as objected to and allow the creditor to vote, subject to his vote being subsequently declared invalid if the objection to the claim is sustained.

2.39(4) [**If chairman's decision reversed etc.**] If on an appeal the chairman's decision is reversed or varied, or a creditor's vote is declared invalid, the court may order that another meeting be summoned, or make such other order as it thinks fit.

2.39(5) **[Appeal after administrator's report]** In the case of the meeting summoned under paragraph 51 to consider the administrator's proposals, an application to the court by way of appeal under this Rule against a decision of the chairman shall not be made later than 14 days after the delivery of the administrator's report in accordance with paragraph 53(2).

2.39(6) **[Costs of appeal]** Neither the administrator nor any person nominated by him to be chairman is personally liable for costs incurred by any person in respect of an appeal to the court under this Rule, unless the court makes an order to that effect.

(See General Note after r. 2.44.)

2.40 Secured creditors

2.40(1) **[Voting entitlement on balance of debt]** At a meeting of creditors a secured creditor is entitled to vote only in respect of the balance (if any) of his debt after deducting the value of his security as estimated by him.

2.40(2) **[Voting entitlement for full value of debt]** However, in a case where the administrator has made a statement under paragraph 52(1)(b) and an initial creditors' meeting has been requisitioned under paragraph 52(2) then a secured creditor is entitled to vote in respect of the full value of his debt without any deduction of the value of his security.

(See General Note after r. 2.44.)

2.41 Holders of negotiable instruments

2.41 A creditor shall not vote in respect of a debt on, or secured by, a current bill of exchange or promissory note, unless he is willing–

(a) to treat the liability to him on the bill or note of every person who is liable on it antecedently to the company, and against whom a bankruptcy order has not been made (or, in the case of a company, which has not gone into liquidation), as a security in his hands; and

(b) to estimate the value of the security and, for the purpose of his entitlement to vote, to deduct it from his claim.

(See General Note after r. 2.44.)

2.42 Hire-purchase, conditional sale and chattel leasing agreements

2.42(1) **[Entitlement to vote]** Subject as follows, an owner of goods under a hire-purchase or chattel leasing agreement, or a seller of goods under a conditional sale agreement, is entitled to vote in respect of the amount of the debt due and payable to him by the company on the date that the company entered administration.

2.42(2) **[Calculating amount of debt]** In calculating the amount of any debt for this purpose, no account shall be taken of any amount attributable to the exercise of any right under the relevant agreement, so far as the right has become exercisable solely by virtue of the making of an administration application, a notice of intention to appoint an administrator or any matter arising as a consequence, or of the company entering administration.

(See General Note after r. 2.44.)

2.43 Resolutions

2.43(1) **[Resolution passed by majority in value]** Subject to paragraph (2), at a creditors' meeting in administration proceedings, a resolution is passed when a majority (in value) of those present and voting, in person or by proxy, have voted in favour of it.

2.43(2) **[Resolution invalid]** Any resolution is invalid if those voting against it include more than half in value of the creditors to whom notice of the meeting was sent and who are not, to the best of the chairman's belief, persons connected with the company.

(See General Note after r. 2.44.)

2.44 Minutes

2.44(1) **[Minute book]** The chairman of the meeting shall cause minutes of its proceedings to be entered in the company's minute book.

2.44(2) **[Contents of minutes]** The minutes shall include a list of the names and addresses of creditors who attended (personally or by proxy) and, if a creditors' committee has been established, the names and addresses of those elected to be members of the committee.

GENERAL NOTE TO RR. 2.34–2.44

The corresponding rules which apply in the original regime are rr. *2.18*ff.

R. 2.35
Although this rule refers only to meetings summoned under the five provisions referred to, para. 50 defines "creditors' meeting" for the all the purposes of Sch. B1 as a meeting of creditors summoned "in the prescribed manner" and giving "the prescribed period of notice". It would therefore be prudent to follow the procedure set out in this paragraph for any other creditors' meeting.

R. 2.37
The requisitioning creditor or creditors must have debts amounting to at least 10 per cent of the total debts of the company (para. 52(2)).

R. 2.38(5)
On the meaning of "agrees", see the note to r. 1.17(3), but note that there is here no equivalent to r. 1.17(3) fixing a sum of £1 in the absence of an agreement by the chairman to fix a higher value.

R. 2.38(7)–(10)
On voting by a Member State liquidator, see the note to r. *2.29*.

R. 2.40(2)
A secured creditor may vote for the amount of his secured debt only where there is insufficient property to enable a distribution to be made to unsecured creditors (apart from the "prescribed part"): see para. 52(1)(b).

2.45 Revision of the administrator's proposals

2.45(1) **[Statement of proposed revised proposals]** The administrator shall, under paragraph 54, make a statement setting out the proposed revisions to his proposals which he shall attach to Form 2.22B and send to all those to whom he is required to send a copy of his revised proposals.

[FORM 2.22B]

2.45(2) **[Contents of statement]** The statement of revised proposals shall include–

(a) details of the court where the proceedings are and the relevant court reference number;

(b) the full name, registered address, registered number and any other trading names of the company;

(c) details relating to his appointment as administrator, including the date of appointment and the person making the administration application or appointment;

(d) the names of the directors and secretary of the company and details of any shareholdings in the company they may have;

(e) a summary of the initial proposals and the reason(s) for proposing a revision;

(f) details of the proposed revision including details of the administrator's assessment of the likely impact of the proposed revision upon creditors generally or upon each class of creditors (as the case may be);

(g) where a proposed revision relates to the ending of the administration by a creditors' voluntary liquidation and the nomination of a person to be the proposed liquidator of the company, a statement that, in accordance with paragraph 83(7) and Rule 2.117(3), creditors may nominate a different person as the proposed liquidator, provided that the nomination is made after the receipt of the revised proposals and before those revised proposals are approved; and

(h) any other information that the administrator thinks necessary to enable creditors to decide whether or not to vote for the proposed revisions.

2.45(3) [**Copy of statement to members**] Subject to paragraph 54(3), within 5 days of sending out the statement in paragraph (1) above, the administrator shall send a copy of the statement to every member of the company.

2.45(4) [**Advertisement of notice of undertaking to provide copy**] When the administrator is acting under paragraph 54(3), the notice shall be published once in such newspaper as he thinks most appropriate for ensuring that the notice comes to the attention of the company's members. The notice shall–

(a) state the full name of the company;

(b) state the name and address of the administrator;

(c) specify an address to which members can write for a copy of the statement; and

(d) be published as soon as reasonably practicable after the administrator sends the statement to creditors.

GENERAL NOTE

See para. 54. There is no equivalent provision in the rules governing the original regime; but the notes to *s. 25* may be relevant.

2.46 Notice to creditors

2.46 As soon as reasonably practicable after the conclusion of a meeting of creditors to consider the administrator's proposals or revised proposals, the administrator shall–

(a) send notice in Form 2.23B of the result of the meeting (including details of any modifications to the proposals that were approved) to every creditor who received notice of the meeting and any other person who received a copy of the original proposals; and

[FORM 2.23B]

(b) file with the court, and send to the registrar of companies, and any creditors who did not receive notice of the meeting (of whose claim he has become subsequently aware), a copy of Form 2.23B, attaching a copy of the proposals considered at the meeting.

(See General Note after r. 2.47.)

2.47 Reports to creditors

2.47(1) [**"Progress report"**] "Progress report" means a report which includes–

(a) details of the court where the proceedings are and the relevant court reference number;

(b) full details of the company's name, address of registered office and registered number;

(c) full details of the administrator's name and address, date of appointment and name and address of appointor, including any changes in office-holder, and, in the case of joint administrators, their functions as set out in the statement made for the purposes of paragraph 100(2);

(d) details of any extensions to the initial period of appointment;

(e) details of progress during the period of the report, including a receipts and payments account (as detailed in paragraph (2) below);

(f) details of any assets that remain to be realised; and

(g) any other relevant information for the creditors.

2.47(2) **[Receipts and payments account]** A receipts and payments account shall state what assets of the company have been realised, for what value, and what payments have been made to creditors or others. The account is to be in the form of an abstract showing receipts and payments during the period of the report and where the administrator has ceased to act, the receipts and payments account shall include a statement as to the amount paid to unsecured creditors by virtue of the application of section 176A (prescribed part).

2.47(3) **[Period of progress report]** The progress report shall cover–

(a) the period of 6 months commencing on the date that the company entered administration, and every subsequent period of 6 months; and

(b) when the administrator ceases to act, any period from the date of the previous report, if any, and from the date that the company entered administration if there is no previous report, until the time that the administrator ceases to act.

2.47(4) **[Copies of progress report]** The administrator shall send a copy of the progress report, attached to Form 2.24B, within 1 month of the end of the period covered by the report, to–

[FORM 2.24B]

(a) the creditors;

(b) the court; and

(c) the registrar of companies.

2.47(5) **[Extension of period to send copies]** The court may, on the administrator's application, extend the period of 1 month mentioned in paragraph (4) above, or make such other order in respect of the content of the report as it thinks fit.

2.47(6) **[Criminal liability of administrator in default of r. 2.47]** If the administrator makes default in complying with this Rule, he is liable to a fine and, for continued contravention, to a daily default fine.

GENERAL NOTE TO RR. 2.46–2.47

The corresponding rules under the original regime are rr. *2.29–2.30*.

2.48 Correspondence instead of creditors' meetings

2.48(1) **[Form of notice for correspondence]** The administrator may seek to obtain the passing of a resolution by the creditors by sending a notice in Form 2.25B to every creditor who is entitled to be notified of a creditors' meeting under Rule 2.35(4).

[FORM 2.25B]

2.48(2) **[Conditions for voting entitlement]** In order to be counted, votes must be received by the administrator by 12.00 hours on the closing date specified on Form 2.25B and must be accompanied by the statement in writing on entitlement to vote required by Rule 2.38.

2.48(3) **[When votes to be disregarded]** If any votes are received without the statement as to entitlement, or the administrator decides that the creditor is not entitled to vote according to Rules 2.38 and 2.39, then that creditor's votes shall be disregarded.

2.48(4) **[Closing date for votes]** The closing date shall be set at the discretion of the administrator. In any event it must not be set less than 14 days from the date of issue of the Form 2.25B.

2.48(5) **[Condition for business to be transacted]** For any business to be transacted the administrator must receive at least 1 valid Form 2.25B by the closing date specified by him.

2.48(6) **[Administrator to call creditors' meeting if condition unsatisfied]** If no valid Form 2.25B is received by the closing date specified then the administrator shall call a meeting of the creditors in accordance with Rule 2.35.

2.48(7) [**Requisition of creditors' meeting**] Any single creditor, or a group of creditors, of the company whose debt(s) amount to at least 10% of the total debts of the company may, within 5 business days from the date of the administrator sending out a resolution or proposals, require him to summon a meeting of creditors to consider the matters raised therein in accordance with Rule 2.37. Any meeting called under this Rule shall be conducted in accordance with Rule 2.35.

2.48(8) [**Administrator's power to call meeting if proposals rejected**] If the administrator's proposals or revised proposals are rejected by the creditors pursuant to this Rule, the administrator may call a meeting of creditors.

2.48(9) [**Requirement for creditors' meeting to include course of correspondence**] A reference in these Rules to anything done, or required to be done, at, or in connection with, or in consequence of, a creditors' meeting includes a reference to anything done in the course of correspondence in accordance with this Rule.

GENERAL NOTE

"Correspondence" includes correspondence by telephonic or other electronic means (para. 111(1)).

Note para. 2.48(8): the administrator need not accept a "No" vote by correspondence, but may disregard it and summon a meeting in the hope that the assembled creditors will think otherwise.

SECTION B: COMPANY MEETINGS

2.49 Venue and conduct of company meeting

2.49(1) [**Convenience of venue**] Where the administrator summons a meeting of members of the company, he shall fix a venue for it having regard to their convenience.

2.49(2) [**Chairman**] The chairman of the meeting shall be the administrator or a person nominated by him in writing to act in his place.

2.49(3) [**Nominee chairman**] A person so nominated must be either–

(a) one who is qualified to act as an insolvency practitioner in relation to the company; or

(b) an employee of the administrator or his firm who is experienced in insolvency matters.

2.49(4) [**Adjournment if no chairman**] If within 30 minutes from the time fixed for commencement of the meeting there is no person present to act as chairman, the meeting stands adjourned to the same time and place in the following week or, if that is not a business day, to the business day immediately following.

2.49(5) [**Summoning and conduct of meeting**] Subject as above, the meeting shall be summoned and conducted as if it were a general meeting of the company summoned under the company's articles of association, and in accordance with the applicable provisions of the Companies Act.

2.49(6) [**Non-application of r. 2.49(5)**] Paragraph (5) does not apply where the laws of a member State and not the laws of England and Wales apply in relation to the conduct of the meeting. The meeting shall be summoned and conducted in accordance with the constitution of the company and the laws of the member State referred to in this paragraph shall apply to the conduct of the meeting.

2.49(7) [**Minutes**] The chairman of the meeting shall cause minutes of its proceedings to be entered in the company's minute book.

GENERAL NOTE

There is no obligation placed on an administrator under Sch. B1 to call a shareholders' meeting for any purpose, but he may choose to do so (*e.g.* if it is proposed to institute a CVA), in which event this rule will apply.

Chapter 7

The Creditors' Committee

2.50 Constitution of committee

2.50(1) [**Three to five creditors**] Where it is resolved by a creditors' meeting to establish a creditors' committee for the purposes of the administration, the committee shall consist of at least 3 and not more than 5 creditors of the company elected at the meeting.

2.50(2) [**Eligibility of creditors**] Any creditor of the company is eligible to be a member of the committee, so long as his claim has not been rejected for the purpose of his entitlement to vote.

2.50(3) [**Body corporate as member**] A body corporate may be a member of the committee, but it cannot act as such otherwise than by a representative appointed under Rule 2.55 below.

(See General Note after r. 2.65.)

2.51 Formalities of establishment

2.51(1) [**Certificate of due constitution**] The creditors' committee does not come into being, and accordingly cannot act, until the administrator has issued a certificate in Form 2.26B of its due constitution.

[FORM 2.26B]

2.51(2) [**Agreement to act**] No person may act as a member of the committee unless and until he has agreed to do so and, unless the relevant proxy or authorisation contains a statement to the contrary, such agreement may be given by his proxy-holder or representative under section 375 of the Companies Act present at the meeting establishing the committee.

2.51(3) [**Issue of administrator's certificate**] The administrator's certificate of the committee's due constitution shall not be issued unless and until at least 3 of the persons who are to be members of the committee have agreed to act and shall be issued as soon as reasonably practicable thereafter.

2.51(4) [**Amended certificate**] As and when the others (if any) agree to act, the administrator shall issue an amended certificate in Form 2.26B.

2.51(5) [**Filing of certificates**] The certificate, and any amended certificate, shall be filed with the court and a copy sent to the registrar of companies by the administrator, as soon as reasonably practicable.

2.51(6) [**Change in membership**] If after the first establishment of the committee there is any change in its membership, the administrator shall as soon as reasonably practicable report the change to the court and the registrar of companies in Form 2.27B.

[FORM 2.27B]

(See General Note after r. 2.65.)

2.52 Functions and meetings of the committee

2.52(1) [**Functions**] The creditors' committee shall assist the administrator in discharging his functions, and act in relation to him in such manner as may be agreed from time to time.

2.52(2) **[Holding of meetings]** Subject as follows, meetings of the committee shall be held when and where determined by the administrator.

2.52(3) **[Calling of meetings]** The administrator shall call a first meeting of the committee not later than 6 weeks after its first establishment, and thereafter he shall call a meeting–

(a) if so requested by a member of the committee or his representative (the meeting then to be held within 14 days of the request being received by the administrator); and

(b) for a specified date, if the committee has previously resolved that a meeting be held on that date.

2.52(4) **[Notice of venue]** The administrator shall give 7 days' written notice of the venue of any meeting to every member of the committee (or his representative designated for that purpose), unless in any case the requirement of notice has been waived by or on behalf of any member. Waiver may be signified either at or before the meeting.

(See General Note after r. 2.65.)

2.53 The chairman at meetings

2.53(1) **[Administrator or nominee chairman]** Subject to Rule 2.62(3), the chairman at any meeting of the creditors' committee shall be the administrator or a person nominated by him in writing to act.

2.53(2) **[Nominee]** A person so nominated must be either–

(a) one who is qualified to act as an insolvency practitioner in relation to the company; or

(b) an employee of the administrator or his firm who is experienced in insolvency matters.

(See General Note after r. 2.65.)

2.54 Quorum

2.54 A meeting of the committee is duly constituted if due notice of it has been given to all the members, and at least 2 members are present or represented.

(See General Note after r. 2.65.)

2.55 Committee-members' representatives

2.55(1) **[Representation]** A member of the committee may, in relation to the business of the committee, be represented by another person duly authorised by him for that purpose.

2.55(2) **[Letter of authority or proxy]** A person acting as a committee-member's representative must hold a letter of authority entitling him so to act (either generally or specially) and signed by or on behalf of the committee-member, and for this purpose any proxy or any authorisation under section 375 of the Companies Act in relation to any meeting of creditors of the company shall, unless it contains a statement to the contrary, be treated as a letter of authority to act generally signed by or on behalf of the committee-member.

2.55(3) **[Production of letter of authority]** The chairman at any meeting of the committee may call on a person claiming to act as a committee-member's representative to produce his letter of authority, and may exclude him if it appears that his authority is deficient.

2.55(4) **[Who may not be a representative]** No member may be represented by a body corporate, a person who is an undischarged bankrupt, or a disqualified director or a person who is subject to a bankruptcy restrictions order, bankruptcy restrictions undertaking or interim bankruptcy restrictions order.

2.55(5) **[No dual representation]** No person shall on the same committee, act at one and the same time as representative of more than one committee-member.

2.55(6) **[Signing as representative]** Where a member's representative signs any document on the member's behalf, the fact that he so signs must be stated below his signature.

(See General Note after r. 2.65.)

2.56 Resignation

2.56 A member of the committee may resign by notice in writing delivered to the administrator.

(See General Note after r. 2.65.)

2.57 Termination of membership

2.57(1) **[Automatic termination]** Membership of the creditors' committee is automatically terminated if the member–

(a) becomes bankrupt; or

(b) at 3 consecutive meetings of the committee is neither present nor represented (unless at the third of those meetings it is resolved that this Rule is not to apply in his case); or

(c) ceases to be, or is found never to have been, a creditor.

2.57(2) **[Trustee in bankruptcy as member]** However, if the cause of termination is the member's bankruptcy, his trustee in bankruptcy replaces him as a member of the committee.

(See General Note after r. 2.65.)

2.58 Removal

2.58 A member of the committee may be removed by resolution at a meeting of creditors' at least 14 days' notice having been given of the intention to move that resolution.

(See General Note after r. 2.65.)

2.59 Vacancies

2.59(1) **[Application of r. 2.59]** The following applies if there is a vacancy in the membership of the creditors' committee.

2.59(2) **[Agreement not to fill vacancy]** The vacancy need not be filled if the administrator and a majority of the remaining members of the committee so agree, provided that the total number of members does not fall below the minimum required under Rule 2.50(1).

2.59(3) **[Filling vacancy]** The administrator may appoint any creditor (being qualified under the Rules to be a member of the committee) to fill the vacancy, if a majority of the other members of the committee agree to the appointment, and the creditor concerned consents to act.

(See General Note after r. 2.65.)

2.60 Procedure at meetings

2.60(1) **[Voting and resolutions]** At any meeting of the creditors' committee, each member of it (whether present himself, or by his representative) has one vote; and a resolution is passed when a majority of the members present or represented have voted in favour of it.

2.60(2) **[Record of resolutions]** Every resolution passed shall be recorded in writing, either separately or as part of the minutes of the meeting.

2.60(3) **[Signing of records etc.]** A record of each resolution shall be signed by the chairman and placed in the company's minute book.

(See General Note after r. 2.65.)

2.61 Resolutions of creditors' committee by post

2.61(1) **[Proposed resolution sent to committee members]** In accordance with this Rule, the administrator may seek to obtain the agreement of members of the creditors' committee to a resolution by sending to every member (or his representative designated for the purpose) a copy of the proposed resolution.

2.61(2) **[Voting indicated on copy]** Where the administrator makes use of the procedure allowed by this Rule, he shall send out to members of the committee or their representatives (as the case may be) a copy of any proposed resolution on which a decision is sought, which shall be set out in such a way that agreement with or dissent from each separate resolution may be indicated by the recipient on the copy so sent.

2.61(3) **[Member may require meeting]** Any member of the committee may, within 7 business days from the date of the administrator sending out a resolution, require him to summon a meeting of the committee to consider matters raised by the resolution.

2.61(4) **[Deemed passing of resolution]** In the absence of such a request, the resolution is deemed to have been passed by the committee if and when the administrator is notified in writing by a majority of the members that they concur with it.

2.61(5) **[Copy resolution etc. in minute book]** A copy of every resolution passed under this Rule, and a note that the committee's concurrence was obtained, shall be placed in the company's minute book.

(See General Note after r. 2.65.)

2.62 Information from administrator

2.62(1) **[Notice to administrator]** Where the committee resolves to require the attendance of the administrator under paragraph 57(3)(a), the notice to him shall be in writing signed by the majority of the members of the committee for the time being. A member's representative may sign for him.

2.62(2) **[Time and place of meeting]** The meeting at which the administrator's attendance is required shall be fixed by the committee for a business day, and shall be held at such time and place as he determines.

2.62(3) **[Chairman not administrator]** Where the administrator so attends, the members of the committee may elect any one of their number to be chairman of the meeting, in place of the administrator or a nominee of his.

(See General Note after r. 2.65.)

2.63 Expenses of members

2.63(1) **[Expenses defrayed out of assets]** Subject as follows, the administrator shall, out of the assets of the company, defray any reasonable travelling expenses directly incurred by members of the creditors' committee or their representatives in relation to their attendance at the committee's meetings, or otherwise on the committee's business, as an expense of the administration.

2.63(2) **[Non-application of r. 2.63(1)]** Paragraph (1) does not apply to any meeting of the committee held within 6 weeks of a previous meeting, unless the meeting in question is summoned at the instance of the administrator.

(See General Note after r. 2.65.)

2.64 Members' dealing with the company

2.64(1) **[Dealings to be in good faith]** Membership of the committee does not prevent a person from dealing with the company while the company is in administration, provided that any transactions in the course of such dealings are in good faith and for value.

2.64(2) **[Court may set aside transaction]** The court may, on the application of any person interested, set aside any transaction which appears to it to be contrary to the requirements of this Rule, and may give such consequential directions as it thinks fit for compensating the company for any loss which it may have incurred in consequence of the transaction.

(See General Note after r. 2.65.)

2.65 Formal defects

2.65 The acts of the creditors' committee established for any administration are valid notwithstanding any defect in the appointment, election or qualifications of any member of the committee or any committee-member's representative or in the formalities of its establishment.

GENERAL NOTE TO RR. 2.50–2.65

The corresponding rules under the original regime are rr. *2.32*ff. See the note following r. *2.46A*.

CHAPTER 8

DISPOSAL OF CHARGED PROPERTY

2.66(1) **[Application of r. 2.66]** The following applies where the administrator applies to the court under paragraphs 71 or 72 for authority to dispose of property of the company which is subject to a security (other than a floating charge), or goods in the possession of the company under a hire purchase agreement.

2.66(2) **[Venue and notice]** The court shall fix a venue for the hearing of the application, and the administrator shall as soon as reasonably practicable give notice of the venue to the person who is the holder of the security or, as the case may be, the owner under the agreement.

2.66(3) **[Sealed copies of order re non-floating charge or hire-purchase property]** If an order is made under paragraphs 71 or 72 the court shall send two sealed copies to the administrator.

2.66(4) **[Copy to holder of security or owner of property]** The administrator shall send one of them to that person who is the holder of the security or owner under the agreement.

2.66(5) **[Form of notice of order to registrar of companies]** The administrator shall send a Form 2.28B to the registrar of companies with a copy of the sealed order.

[FORM 2.28B]

GENERAL NOTE

The leave of the court is not required where the administrator wishes to deal with property that is subject to a floating charge.
"Hire purchase agreement" includes a conditional sale agreement, a chattel leasing agreement and a retention of title agreement (para. 111(1)).

CHAPTER 9

EXPENSES OF THE ADMINISTRATION

2.67(1) **[Priority of expenses]** The expenses of the administration are payable in the following order of priority–

(a) expenses properly incurred by the administrator in performing his functions in the administration of the company;

(b) the cost of any security provided by the administrator in accordance with the Act or the Rules;

(c) where an administration order was made, the costs of the applicant and any person appearing on the hearing of the application and where the administrator was appointed otherwise than by order of the court, any costs and expenses of the appointor in connection with the making of the appointment and the costs and expenses incurred by any other person in giving notice of intention to appoint an administrator;

(d) any amount payable to a person employed or authorised, under Chapter 5 of this Part of the Rules, to assist in the preparation of a statement of affairs or statement of concurrence;

(e) any allowance made, by order of the court, towards costs on an application for release from the obligation to submit a statement of affairs or statement of concurrence;

(f) any necessary disbursements by the administrator in the course of the administration (including any expenses incurred by members of the creditors' committee or their representatives and allowed for by the administrator under Rule 2.63, but not including any payment of corporation tax in circumstances referred to in sub-paragraph (j) below);

(g) the remuneration or emoluments of any person who has been employed by the administrator to perform any services for the company, as required or authorised under the Act or the Rules;

(h) the remuneration of the administrator agreed under Chapter 11 of this Part of the Rules;

(j) the amount of any corporation tax on chargeable gains accruing on the realisation of any asset of the company (without regard to whether the realisation is effected by the administrator, a secured creditor, or a receiver or manager appointed to deal with a security).

2.67(2) **[Priorities where assets insufficient to satisfy liabilities]** The priorities laid down by paragraph (1) of this Rule are subject to the power of the court to make orders under paragraph (3) of this Rule where the assets are insufficient to satisfy the liabilities.

2.67(3) **[Court's power to alter order of priority]** The court may, in the event of the assets being insufficient to satisfy the liabilities, make an order as to the payment out of the assets of the expenses incurred in the administration in such order of priority as the court thinks just.

GENERAL NOTE

There is no equivalent to this rule under the original regime, but the notes to s. 156 and r. 4.218 (dealing with the expenses of a liquidation) may be helpful.

CHAPTER 10

DISTRIBUTIONS TO CREDITORS

SECTION A: APPLICATION OF CHAPTER AND GENERAL

2.68(1) **[Application of Ch. 10]** This Chapter applies where the administrator makes, or proposes to make, a distribution to any class of creditors. Where the distribution is to a particular class of creditors, references in this Chapter to creditors shall, in so far as the context requires, be a reference to that class of creditors only.

2.68(2) **[Notice of intention to declare and distribute dividend]** The administrator shall give notice to the creditors of his intention to declare and distribute a dividend in accordance with Rule 2.95.

2.68(3) **[Where sole or final dividend]** Where it is intended that the distribution is to be a sole or final dividend, the administrator shall, after the date specified in the notice referred to in paragraph (2)–

- (a) defray any outstanding expenses of a liquidation (including any of the items mentioned in Rule 4.218) or provisional liquidation that immediately preceded the administration;
- (b) defray any items payable in accordance with the provisions of paragraph 99;
- (c) defray any amounts (including any debts or liabilities and his own remuneration and expenses) which would, if the administrator were to cease to be the administrator of the company, be payable out of the property of which he had custody or control in accordance with the provisions of paragraph 99; and
- (d) declare and distribute that dividend without regard to the claim of any person in respect of a debt not already proved.

2.68(4) **[Power of court to postpone date]** The court may, on the application of any person, postpone the date specified in the notice.

(See General Note after r. 2.71.)

2.69 Debts of insolvent company to rank equally

2.69 Debts other than preferential debts rank equally between themselves in the administration and, after the preferential debts, shall be paid in full unless the assets are insufficient for meeting them, in which case they abate in equal proportions between themselves.

(See General Note after r. 2.71.)

2.70 Supplementary provisions as to dividend

2.70(1) **[What administrator to make provision for]** In the calculation and distribution of a dividend the administrator shall make provision for–

- (a) any debts which appear to him to be due to persons who, by reason of the distance of their place of residence, may not have had sufficient time to tender and establish their proofs;
- (b) any debts which are the subject of claims which have not yet been determined; and
- (c) disputed proofs and claims.

2.70(2) **[Where creditor has not proved debt]** A creditor who has not proved his debt before the declaration of any dividend is not entitled to disturb, by reason that he has not participated in it, the distribution of that dividend or any other dividend declared before his debt was proved, but–

- (a) when he has proved that debt he is entitled to be paid, out of any money for the time being available for the payment of any further dividend, any dividend or dividends which he has failed to receive; and
- (b) any dividends payable under sub-paragraph (a) shall be paid before the money is applied to the payment of any such further dividend.

2.70(3) **[No action against administrator for dividend]** No action lies against the administrator for a dividend; but if he refuses to pay a dividend the court may, if it thinks fit, order him to pay it and also to pay, out of his own money–

- (a) interest on the dividend, at the rate for the time being specified in section 17 of the Judgments Act 1838, from the time when it was withheld; and
- (b) the costs of the proceedings in which the order to pay is made.

2.71 Division of unsold assets

2.71 The administrator may, with the permission of the creditors' committee, or if there is no creditors' committee, the creditors, divide in its existing form amongst the company's creditors, according to its estimated value, any property which from its peculiar nature or other special circumstances cannot be readily or advantageously sold.

GENERAL NOTE TO RR. 2.68–2.71

A distribution to creditors is not among the purposes for which an administration order can be made under the original administration regime, and where it is sought to make a distribution the most convenient course is to specify the approval of a CVA among the purposes of the order. The statutory objectives under the new regime do include the making of a distribution (although it is still contemplated that this may be done via a CVA). Where a distribution is to be made under the administration, these rules will apply.

The notes to rr.4.179ff. (which apply in a liquidation) may be helpful.

SECTION B: MACHINERY OF PROVING A DEBT

2.72 Proving a debt

2.72(1) ["Claim in writing"] A person claiming to be a creditor of the company and wishing to recover his debt in whole or in part must (subject to any order of the court to the contrary) submit his claim in writing to the administrator.

2.72(2) ["Proving" and "proof"] A creditor who claims is referred to as "proving" for his debt and a document by which he seeks to establish his claim is his "proof".

2.72(3) [Making of proof] Subject to the next paragraph, a proof must–

(a) be made out by, or under the direction of, the creditor and signed by him or a person authorised in that behalf; and

(b) state the following matters–

   (i) the creditor's name and address;
   (ii) the total amount of his claim as at the date on which the company entered administration, less any payments that have been made to him after that date in respect of his claim and any adjustment by way of set-off in accordance with Rule 2.85;
   (iii) whether or not the claim includes outstanding uncapitalised interest;
   (iv) whether or not the claim includes value added tax;
   (v) whether the whole or any part of the debt falls within any, and if so, which categories of preferential debts under section 386;
   (vi) particulars of how and when the debt was incurred by the company;
   (vii) particulars of any security held, the date on which it was given and the value which the creditor puts on it;
   (viii) details of any reservation of title in respect of goods to which the debt refers; and
   (ix) the name, address and authority of the person signing the proof (if other than the creditor himself).

2.72(4) [Substantiating documents] There shall be specified in the proof details of any documents by reference to which the debt can be substantiated; but (subject as follows) it is not essential that such document be attached to the proof or submitted with it.

2.72(5) [Power of administrator to call for other document] The administrator may call for any document or other evidence to be produced to him, where he thinks it necessary for the purpose of substantiating the whole or any part of the claim made in the proof.

(See General Note after r. 2.80.)

2.73 Claim established by affidavit

2.73(1) [Form of verification] The administrator may, if he thinks it necessary, require a claim of debt to be verified by means of an affidavit in Form 2.29B.

[FORM 2.29B]

2.73(2) [Affidavit notwithstanding lodging of proof] An affidavit may be required notwithstanding that a proof of debt has already been lodged.

(See General Note after r. 2.80.)

2.74 Costs of proving

2.74 Unless the court otherwise orders–

(a) every creditor bears the cost of proving his own debt, including costs incurred in providing documents or evidence under Rule 2.72(5); and

(b) costs incurred by the administrator in estimating the quantum of a debt under Rule 2.81 are payable out of the assets as an expense of the administration.

(See General Note after r. 2.80.)

2.75 Administrator to allow inspection of proofs

2.75 The administrator shall, so long as proofs lodged with him are in his hands, allow them to be inspected, at all reasonable times on any business day, by any of the following persons–

(a) any creditor who has submitted a proof of debt (unless his proof has been wholly rejected for purposes of dividend or otherwise);

(b) any contributory of the company; and

(c) any person acting on behalf of either of the above.

(See General Note after r. 2.80.)

2.76 New administrator appointed

2.76(1) [Proofs and itemised list to new administrator] If a new administrator is appointed in place of another, the former administrator shall transmit to him all proofs which he has received, together with an itemised list of them.

2.76(2) [Signed list returned to former administrator] The new administrator shall sign the list by way of receipt for the proofs, and return it to his predecessor.

(See General Note after r. 2.80.)

2.77 Admission and rejection of proofs for dividend

2.77(1) [Admission for whole or part] A proof may be admitted for dividend either for the whole amount claimed by the creditor, or for part of that amount.

2.77(2) **[Written statement of reasons for rejection]** If the administrator rejects a proof in whole or in part, he shall prepare a written statement of his reasons for doing so, and send it as soon as reasonably practicable to the creditor.

(See General Note after r. 2.80.)

2.78 Appeal against decision on proof

2.78(1) **[Application to court by creditor]** If a creditor is dissatisfied with the administrator's decision with respect to his proof (including any decision on the question of preference), he may apply to the court for the decision to be reversed or varied. The application must be made within 21 days of his receiving the statement sent under Rule 2.77(2).

2.78(2) **[Application by other creditor]** Any other creditor may, if dissatisfied with the administrator's decision admitting or rejecting the whole or any part of a proof, make such an application within 21 days of becoming aware of the administrator's decision.

2.78(3) **[Court to fix venue for hearing]** Where application is made to the court under this Rule, the court shall fix a venue for the application to be heard, notice of which shall be sent by the applicant to the creditor who lodged the proof in question (if it is not himself) and the administrator.

2.78(4) **[Administrator to file proof and rejection in court]** The administrator shall, on receipt of the notice, file with the court the relevant proof, together (if appropriate) with a copy of the statement sent under Rule 2.77(2).

2.78(5) **[Court to return proof to administrator]** After the application has been heard and determined, the proof shall, unless it has been wholly disallowed, be returned by the court to the administrator.

2.78(6) **[Costs of application]** The administrator is not personally liable for costs incurred by any person in respect of an application under this Rule unless the court otherwise orders.

(See General Note after r. 2.80.)

2.79 Withdrawal or variation of proof

2.79 A creditor's proof may at any time, by agreement between himself and the administrator, be withdrawn or varied as to the amount claimed.

(See General Note after r. 2.80.)

2.80 Expunging of proof by the court

2.80(1) **[Power of court]** The court may expunge a proof or reduce the amount claimed–

(a) on the administrator's application, where he thinks that the proof has been improperly admitted, or ought to be reduced; or

(b) on the application of a creditor, if the administrator declines to interfere in the matter.

2.80(2) **[Court to fix venue for hearing]** Where application is made to the court under this Rule, the court shall fix a venue for the application to be heard, notice of which shall be sent by the applicant–

(a) in the case of an application by the administrator, to the creditor who made the proof; and

(b) in the case of an application by a creditor, to the administrator and to the creditor who made the proof (if not himself).

General Note to rr. 2.72–2.80

References to "lodging a claim" under the original regime (rr. *2.22*ff.) have been changed to "proving a debt" in the present section. The corresponding rules which apply in a liquidation (rr. 4.67ff., 4.73ff.) may be relevant.

SECTION C: QUANTIFICATION OF CLAIMS

2.81 Estimate of quantum

2.81(1) **[Administrator to estimate where value uncertain]** The administrator shall estimate the value of any debt which, by reason of its being subject to any contingency or for any other reason, does not bear a certain value; and he may revise any estimate previously made, if he thinks fit by reference to any change of circumstances or to information becoming available to him. He shall inform the creditor as to his estimate and any revision of it.

2.81(2) **[Estimate provable]** Where the value of a debt is estimated under this Rule, the amount provable in the administration in the case of that debt is that of the estimate for the time being.

(See General Note after r. 2.94.)

2.82 Negotiable instruments, etc

2.82 Unless the administrator allows, a proof in respect of money owed on a bill of exchange, promissory note, cheque or other negotiable instrument or security cannot be admitted unless there is produced the instrument or security itself or a copy of it, certified by the creditor or his authorised representative to be a true copy.

(See General Note after r. 2.94.)

2.83 Secured creditors

2.83(1) **[Proof for balance of debt if security realised]** If a secured creditor realises his security, he may prove for the balance of his debt, after deducting the amount realised.

2.83(2) **[Proof for whole of debt if security surrendered]** If a secured creditor voluntarily surrenders his security for the general benefit of creditors, he may prove for his whole debt, as if it were unsecured.

(See General Note after r. 2.94.)

2.84 Discounts

2.84 There shall in every case be deducted from the claim all trade and other discounts which would have been available to the company but for its administration except any discount for immediate, early or cash settlement.

(See General Note after r. 2.94.)

2.85 Mutual credit and set-off

2.85(1) **[Application of r. 2.85]** This Rule applies–

(a) where the administrator, being authorised to make the distribution in question, has pursuant to Rule 2.95 given notice that he proposes to make it; and

(b) only for the purposes of determining the claims to be taken into account for the purposes of calculating that distribution.

2.85(2) **["Mutual dealings"]** In this Rule "mutual dealings" means mutual credits, mutual debts or other mutual dealings between the company and any creditor of the company proving or claiming to prove for a debt in the administration.

2.85(3) **[Account of mutual dealings and set-off]** An account shall be taken as at the date of the notice referred to in paragraph (1)(a) of what is due from each party to the other in respect of the mutual dealings, and the sums due from one party shall be set off against the sums due from the other.

2.85(4) [**Sums not to be taken into account**] Sums due either to or from the company shall not be taken into account under paragraph (3) if–

(a) they became due after the company entered administration;

(b) the other party had notice at the time the sums became due that–

    (i) an application for an administration order was pending; or
    (ii) any person had given notice of intention to appoint an administrator;

(c) the administration was immediately preceded by a winding up and the sums became due during the winding up; or

(d) the administration was immediately preceded by a winding up and the other party had notice at the time the sums became due that–

    (i) a meeting of creditors had been summoned under section 98; or
    (ii) a petition for the winding up of the company was pending.

2.85(5) [**Only balance provable**] Only the balance (if any) of the account is provable in the administration. Alternatively the amount shall be paid to the administrator as part of the assets.

(See General Note after r. 2.94.)

2.86 Debt in foreign currency

2.86(1) [**Conversion into sterling**] For the purpose of proving a debt incurred or payable in a currency other than sterling, the amount of the debt shall be converted into sterling at the official exchange rate prevailing on the date when the company entered administration.

2.86(2) [**"The official exchange rate"**] "The official exchange rate" is the middle exchange rate on the London Foreign Exchange Market at the close of business, as published for the date in question. In the absence of any such published rate, it is such rate as the court determines.

(See General Note after r. 2.94.)

2.87 Payments of a periodical nature

2.87(1) [**Rent etc.**] In the case of rent and other payments of a periodical nature, the creditor may prove for any amounts due and unpaid up to the date when the company entered administration.

2.87(2) [**If accruing from day to day**] Where at that date any payment was accruing due, the creditor may prove for so much as would have fallen due at that date, if accruing from day to day.

(See General Note after r. 2.94.)

2.88 Interest

2.88(1) [**Where debt bears interest**] Where a debt proved in the administration bears interest, that interest is provable as part of the debt except in so far as it is payable in respect of any period after the company entered administration.

2.88(2) [**Where claim may include interest**] In the following circumstances the creditor's claim may include interest on the debt for periods before the company entered administration, although not previously reserved or agreed.

2.88(3) [**Debt due by written instrument**] If the debt is due by virtue of a written instrument, and payable at a certain time, interest may be claimed for the period from that time to the date when the company entered administration.

2.88(4) [**Debt due otherwise**] If the debt is due otherwise, interest may only be claimed if, before that date, a demand for payment of the debt was made in writing by or on behalf of the creditor, and notice given that interest would be payable from the date of the demand to the date of payment.

2.88(5) **[Claiming interest under r. 2.88(4)]** Interest under paragraph (4) may only be claimed for the period from the date of the demand to that of the company's entering administration and for all the purposes of the Act and the Rules shall be chargeable at a rate not exceeding that mentioned in paragraph (6).

2.88(6) **[Rate of interest under r. 2.88(3), (4)]** The rate of interest to be claimed under paragraphs (3) and (4) is the rate specified in section 17 of the Judgments Act 1838 on the date when the company entered administration.

2.88(7) **[Surplus applied for payment of interest]** Subject to Rule 2.105(3), any surplus remaining after payment of the debts proved shall, before being applied for any purpose, be applied in paying interest on those debts in respect of the periods during which they have been outstanding since the company entered administration.

2.88(8) **[Interest payable under r. 2.88(7)]** All interest payable under paragraph (7) ranks equally whether or not the debts on which it is payable rank equally.

2.88(9) **[Rate of interest under r. 2.88(7)]** The rate of interest payable under paragraph (7) is whichever is the greater of the rate specified under paragraph (6) or the rate applicable to the debt apart from the administration.

(See General Note after r. 2.94.)

2.89 Debt payable at future time

2.89 A creditor may prove for a debt of which payment was not yet due on the date when the company entered administration, subject to Rule 2.105 (adjustment of dividend where payment made before time).

(See General Note after r. 2.94.)

2.90 Value of security

2.90(1) **[Altering value]** A secured creditor may, with the agreement of the administrator or the leave of the court, at any time alter the value which he has, in his proof of debt, put upon his security.

2.90(2) **[Limitation on re-valuation]** However, if a secured creditor–

(a) being the applicant for an administration order or the appointor of the administrator, has in the application or the notice of appointment put a value on his security; or

(b) has voted in respect of the unsecured balance of his debt,

he may re-value his security only with permission of the court.

(See General Note after r. 2.94.)

2.91 Surrender for non-disclosure

2.91(1) **[Omission to disclose security]** If a secured creditor omits to disclose his security in his proof of debt, he shall surrender his security for the general benefit of creditors, unless the court, on application by him, relieves him from the effect of this Rule on the ground that the omission was inadvertent or the result of honest mistake.

2.91(2) **[Relief from effect of r. 2.91(1)]** If the court grants that relief, it may require or allow the creditor's proof of debt to be amended, on such terms as may be just.

2.91(3) **[Rights protected by Art. 5 of EC Regulation]** Nothing in this Rule or the following two Rules may affect the rights in rem of creditors or third parties protected under Article 5 of the EC Regulation (third parties' rights in rem).

(See General Note after r. 2.94.)

2.92 Redemption by administrator

2.92(1) **[Notice of proposed redemption]** The administrator may at any time give notice to a creditor whose debt is secured that he proposes, at the expiration of 28 days from the date of the notice, to redeem the security at the value put upon it in the creditor's proof.

2.92(2) **[Time for revaluation etc.]** The creditor then has 21 days (or such longer period as the administrator may allow) in which, if he so wishes, to exercise his right to revalue his security (with the permission of the court, where Rule 2.90(2) applies).

If the creditor re-values his security, the administrator may only redeem at the new value.

2.92(3) **[If administrator redeems]** If the administrator redeems the security, the cost of transferring it is payable out of the assets.

2.92(4) **[Notice to administrator to elect etc.]** A secured creditor may at any time, by a notice in writing, call on the administrator to elect whether he will or will not exercise his power to redeem the security at the value then placed on it; and the administrator then has 3 months in which to exercise the power or determine not to exercise it.

(See General Note after r. 2.94.)

2.93 Test of security's value

2.93(1) **[Offer for sale]** Subject as follows, the administrator, if he is dissatisfied with the value which a secured creditor puts on his security (whether in his proof or by way of re-valuation under Rule 2.90), may require any property comprised in the security to be offered for sale.

2.93(2) **[Terms of sale]** The terms of sale shall be such as may be agreed, or as the court may direct; and if the sale is by auction, the administrator on behalf of the company, and the creditor on his own behalf, may appear and bid.

(See General Note after r. 2.94.)

2.94 Realisation of security by creditor

2.94 If a creditor who has valued his security subsequently realises it (whether or not at the instance of the administrator)–

(a) the net amount realised shall be substituted for the value previously put by the creditor on the security; and

(b) that amount shall be treated in all respects as an amended valuation made by him.

GENERAL NOTE TO RR. 2.81–2.94

There are parallels here in the rules governing claims under the original regime (rr. *2.24*ff.) and in a liquidation (rr. 4.86ff.).

R. 2.83
The secured creditor may also prove for the balance of his debt after placing an estimate on the value of his security under rr. 2.90ff.

R. 2.85
The corresponding provision in a liquidation is r. 4.90. See the note to that rule.

R. 2.88
See the note to s. 189.

2.95 Notice of proposed distribution

2.95(1) [**Period of notice**] Where an administrator is proposing to make a distribution to creditors he shall give 28 days' notice of that fact.

2.95(2) [**Contents of notice and to whom sent**] The notice given pursuant to paragraph (1) shall–

(a) be sent to–

    (i) all creditors whose addresses are known to the administrator; and
    (ii) where a member State liquidator has been appointed in relation to the company, to the member State liquidator;

(b) state whether the distribution is to preferential creditors or preferential creditors and unsecured creditors; and

(c) where the administrator proposes to make a distribution to unsecured creditors, state the value of the prescribed part, except where the court has made an order under section 176A(5).

2.95(3) [**Public advertisement**] Subject to paragraph (5), the administrator shall not declare a dividend unless he has by public advertisement invited creditors to prove their debts.

2.95(4) [**Statement etc. in notice**] A notice pursuant to paragraphs (1) or (3) shall–

(a) state that it is the intention of the administrator to make a distribution to creditors within the period of 2 months from the last date for proving;

(b) specify whether the proposed dividend is interim or final;

(c) specify a date up to which proofs may be lodged being a date which–

    (i) is the same date for all creditors; and
    (ii) is not less than 21 days from that of the notice.

2.95(5) [**Preferential creditors**] A notice pursuant to paragraph (1) where a dividend is to be declared for preferential creditors, need only be given to those creditors in whose case he has reason to believe that their debts are preferential and public advertisement of the intended dividend need only be given if the administrator thinks fit.

(See General Note after r. 2.105.)

2.96 Admission or rejection of proofs

2.96(1) [**Duty of administrator**] Unless he has already dealt with them, within 7 days of the last date for proving, the administrator shall–

(a) admit or reject proofs submitted to him; or

(b) make such provision in respect of them as he thinks fit.

2.96(2) [**Late proofs**] The administrator is not obliged to deal with proofs lodged after the last date for proving, but he may do so, if he thinks fit.

2.96(3) [**Single payment only in respect of debt**] In the declaration of a dividend no payment shall be made more than once by virtue of the same debt.

2.96(4) [**Creditor and member State liquidator**] Subject to Rule 2.104, where–

(a) a creditor has proved; and

(b) a member State liquidator has proved in relation to the same debt,

2.97 Declaration of dividend

2.97(1) [**Duty of administrator**] Subject to paragraph (2), within the 2 month period referred to in Rule 2.95(4)(a) the administrator shall proceed to declare the dividend to one or more classes of creditor of which he gave notice.

2.97(2) [**Pending applications**] Except with the permission of the court, the administrator shall not declare a dividend so long as there is pending any application to the court to reverse or vary a decision of his on a proof, or to expunge a proof or to reduce the amount claimed.

(See General Note after r. 2.105.)

2.98 Notice of declaration of a dividend

2.98(1) [**Notice to all creditors who have proved**] Where the administrator declares a dividend he shall give notice of that fact to all creditors who have proved their debts and, where a member State liquidator has been appointed in relation to the company, to the member State liquidator.

2.98(2) [**Particulars in notice**] The notice shall include the following particulars relating to the administration–

(a) amounts raised from the sale of assets, indicating (so far as practicable) amounts raised by the sale of particular assets;

(b) payments made by the administrator when acting as such;

(c) where the administrator proposed to make a distribution to unsecured creditors, the value of the prescribed part, except where the court has made an order under section 176A(5);

(d) provision (if any) made for unsettled claims, and funds (if any) retained for particular purposes;

(e) the total amount of dividend and the rate of dividend;

(f) how he proposes to distribute the dividend; and

(g) whether, and if so when, any further dividend is expected to be declared.

(See General Note after r. 2.105.)

2.99 Payments of dividends and related matters

2.99(1) [**Simultaneous distibution**] The dividend may be distributed simultaneously with the notice declaring it.

2.99(2) [**Method of payment**] Payment of dividend may be made by post, or arrangements may be made with any creditor for it to be paid to him in another way, or held for his collection.

2.99(3) [**Endorsement on negotiable instrument**] Where a dividend is paid on a bill of exchange or other negotiable instrument, the amount of the dividend shall be endorsed on the instrument, or on a certified copy of it, if required to be produced by the holder for that purpose.

(See General Note after r. 2.105.)

2.100 Notice of no dividend, or no further dividend

2.100 If the administrator gives notice to creditors that he is unable to declare any dividend or (as the case may be) any further dividend, the notice shall contain a statement to the effect either–

(a) that no funds have been realised; or

(b) that the funds realised have already been distributed or used or allocated for defraying the expenses of administration.

(See General Note after r. 2.105.)

2.101 Proof altered after payment of dividend

2.101(1) **[If amount claimed in proof increased]** If after payment of dividend the amount claimed by a creditor in his proof is increased, the creditor is not entitled to disturb the distribution of the dividend; but he is entitled to be paid, out of any money for the time being available for the payment of any further dividend, any dividend or dividends which he has failed to receive.

2.101(2) **[Payment under r. 2.101(1)]** Any dividend or dividends payable under paragraph (1) shall be paid before the money there referred to is applied to the payment of any such further dividend.

2.101(3) **[Proof withdrawn etc.]** If, after a creditor's proof has been admitted, the proof is withdrawn or expunged, or the amount is reduced, the creditor is liable to repay to the administrator any amount overpaid by way of dividend.

(See General Note after r. 2.105.)

2.102 Secured creditors

2.102(1) **[Application of r. 2.102]** The following applies where a creditor re-values his security at a time when a dividend has been declared.

2.102(2) **[Reduction of unsecured claim]** If the revaluation results in a reduction of his unsecured claim ranking for dividend, the creditor shall forthwith repay to the administrator, for the credit of the administration, any amount received by him as dividend in excess of that to which he would be entitled having regard to the revaluation of the security.

2.102(3) **[Reduction of unsecured claim]** If the revaluation results in an increase of his unsecured claim, the creditor is entitled to receive from the administrator, out of any money for the time being available for the payment of a further dividend, before any such further dividend is paid, any dividend or dividends which he has failed to receive, having regard to the revaluation of the security.

However, the creditor is not entitled to disturb any dividend declared (whether or not distributed) before the date of the revaluation.

(See General Note after r. 2.105.)

2.103 Disqualification from dividend

2.103 If a creditor contravenes any provision of the Act or the Rules relating to the valuation of securities, the court may, on the application of the administrator, order that the creditor be wholly or partly disqualified from participation in any dividend.

(See General Note after r. 2.105.)

2.104 Assignment of right to dividend

2.104(1) **[Notice of assignment etc.]** If a person entitled to a dividend gives notice to the administrator that he wishes the dividend to be paid to another person, or that he has assigned his entitlement to another person, the administrator shall pay the dividend to that other accordingly.

2.104(2) **[Contents of notice]** A notice given under this Rule must specify the name and address of the person to whom payment is to be made.

(See General Note after r. 2.105.)

2.105 Debt payable at future time

2.105(1) **[Entitlement to dividend]** Where a creditor has proved for a debt of which payment is not due at the date of the declaration of dividend, he is entitled to dividend equally with other creditors, but subject as follows.

2.105(2) **[Calculation of amount of reduction]** For the purpose of dividend (and no other purpose), the amount of the creditor's admitted proof (or, if a distribution has previously been made to him, the amount remaining outstanding in respect of his admitted proof) shall be reduced by a percentage calculated as follows

$$\frac{I \times M}{12}$$

where I is 5 per cent and M is the number of months (expressed, if need be, as or as including, fractions of months) between the declaration of dividend and the date when payment of the creditor's debt would otherwise be due.

2.105(3) **[Other creditors' entitlement to interest]** Other creditors are not entitled to interest out of surplus funds under Rule 2.88 until any creditor to whom paragraphs (1) and (2) apply has been paid the full amount of his debt.

General Note to rr. 2.95–2.105

As noted above, the making of a distribution is not among the purposes which may be specified under the original administration regime. These rules therefore have no counterpart in Pt 2 of the original rules, but they are largely modelled on rr. 11.1ff.

An administrator may not make a distribution to unsecured, non-preferential creditors without the permission of the court (para. 65(3)).

Chapter 11

The Administrator

2.106 Fixing of remuneration

2.106(1) **[Entitlement to remuneration]** The administrator is entitled to receive remuneration for his services as such.

2.106(2) **[How remuneration fixed]** The remuneration shall be fixed either–

(a) as a percentage of the value of the property with which he has to deal; or

(b) by reference to the time properly given by the insolvency practitioner (as administrator) and his staff in attending to matters arising in the administration.

2.106(3) **[Determination under r. 2.106(2)]** It is for the creditors' committee (if there is one) to determine whether the remuneration is to be fixed under paragraph (2)(a) or (b) and, if under paragraph (2)(a), to determine any percentage to be applied as there mentioned.

2.106(4) **[Matters relevant to r. 2.106(2) determination]** In arriving at that determination, the committee shall have regard to the following matters–

(a) the complexity (or otherwise) of the case;

(b) any respects in which, in connection with the company's affairs, there falls on the administrator any responsibility of an exceptional kind or degree;

(c) the effectiveness with which the administrator appears to be carrying out, or to have carried out, his duties as such; and

(d) the value and nature of the property with which he has to deal.

2.106(5) **[If no committee or determination]** If there is no creditors' committee, or the committee does not make the requisite determination, the administrator's remuneration may be fixed (in accordance with paragraph (2)) by a resolution of a meeting of creditors; and paragraph (4) applies to them as it does to the creditors' committee.

2.106(6) **[Application to court]** If not fixed as above, the administrator's remuneration shall, on his application, be fixed by the court.

2.106(7) **[Where joint administrators]** Where there are joint administrators, it is for them to agree between themselves as to how the remuneration payable should be apportioned. Any dispute arising between them may be referred–

- (a) to the court, for settlement by order; or
- (b) to the creditors' committee or a meeting of creditors, for settlement by resolution.

2.106(8) **[Where administrator a solicitor]** If the administrator is a solicitor and employs his own firm, or any partner in it, to act on behalf of the company, profit costs shall not be paid unless this is authorised by the creditors' committee, the creditors or the court.

2.106(9) **[Position where insufficient to pay unsecured creditors]** For the purpose of this Rule and Rule 2.107, in a case where the administrator has made a statement under paragraph 52(1)(b), a resolution of the creditors shall be taken as passed if (and only if) passed with the approval of–

- (a) each secured creditor of the company; or
- (b) if the administrator has made or intends to make a distribution to preferential creditors–
  - (i) each secured creditor of the company; and
  - (ii) preferential creditors whose debts amount to more than 50% of the preferential debts of the company, disregarding debts of any creditor who does not respond to an invitation to give or withhold approval.

(See General Note after r. 2.109.)

2.107 Recourse to meeting of creditors

2.107 If the administrator's remuneration has been fixed by the creditors' committee, and he considers the rate or amount to be insufficient, he may request that it be increased by resolution of the creditors.

(See General Note after r. 2.109.)

2.108 Recourse to the court

2.108(1) **[Administrator's power to apply to court]** If the administrator considers that the remuneration fixed for him by the creditors' committee, or by resolution of the creditors, is insufficient, he may apply to the court for an order increasing its amount or rate.

2.108(2) **[Notice to creditors' committee]** The administrator shall give at least 14 days' notice of his application to the members of the creditors' committee; and the committee may nominate one or more members to appear, or be represented, and to be heard on the application.

2.108(3) **[Where no creditors' committee]** If there is no creditors' committee, the administrator's notice of his application shall be sent to such one or more of the company's creditors as the court may direct, which creditors may nominate one or more of their number to appear or be represented.

2.108(4) **[Costs of application]** The court may, if it appears to be a proper case, order the costs of the administrator's application, including the costs of any member of the creditors' committee appearing or being represented on it, or any creditor so appearing or being represented, to be paid as an expense of the administration.

(See General Note after r. 2.109.)

2.109 Creditors' claim that remuneration is excessive

2.109(1) **[Power of creditor to apply to court]** Any creditor of the company may, with the concurrence of at least 25 per cent in value of the creditors (including himself), apply to the court for an order that the administrator's remuneration be reduced, on the grounds that it is, in all the circumstances, excessive.

2.109(2) **[Power of court to dismiss etc.]** The court may, if it thinks that no sufficient cause is shown for a reduction, dismiss it without a hearing but it shall not do so without giving the applicant at least 7 days' notice, upon receipt of which the applicant may require the court to list the application for a without notice hearing. If the application is not dismissed, the court shall fix a venue for it to be heard, and give notice to the applicant accordingly.

2.109(3) **[Notice to administrator]** The applicant shall, at least 14 days before the hearing, send to the administrator a notice stating the venue and accompanied by a copy of the application, and of any evidence which the applicant intends to adduce in support of it.

2.109(4) **[Court order]** If the court considers the application to be well-founded, it shall make an order fixing the remuneration at a reduced amount or rate.

2.109(5) **[Costs of application]** Unless the court orders otherwise, the costs of the application shall be paid by the applicant, and are not payable as an expense of the administration.

GENERAL NOTE TO RR. 2.106–2.109

These rules are very similar to rr. *2.47*ff., which apply in the original regime.

CHAPTER 12

ENDING ADMINISTRATION

2.110 Final progress reports

2.110(1) **[References to progress report]** In this Chapter reference to a progress report is to a report in the form specified in Rule 2.47.

2.110(2) **[Meaning of final progress report]** The final progress report means a progress report which includes a summary of–

(a) the administrator's proposals;

(b) any major amendments to, or deviations from, those proposals;

(c) the steps taken during the administration; and

(d) the outcome.

(See General Note after r. 2.118.)

2.111 Notice of automatic end of administration

2.111(1) **[Notice where appointment ceased to have effect]** Where the appointment of an administrator has ceased to have effect, and the administrator is not required by any other Rule to give notice of that fact, he shall, as soon as reasonably practicable, and in any event within 5 business days of the date when the appointment has ceased, file a notice of automatic end of administration in Form 2.30B with the court. The notice shall be accompanied by a final progress report.

[FORM 2.30B]

2.111(2) **[Copy to registrar of companies]** A copy of the notice and accompanying document shall be sent as soon as reasonably practicable to the registrar of companies, and to all persons who received a copy of the administrator's proposals.

2.111(3) **[Default fine]** If the administrator makes default in complying with this Rule, he is liable to a fine and, for continued contravention, to a daily default fine.

(See General Note after r. 2.118.)

2.112 Applications for extension of administration

2.112(1) **[Application accompanied by further progress report]** An application to court for an extension of administration shall be accompanied by a progress report for the period since the last progress report (if any) or the date the company entered administration.

2.112(2) **[Extension request by consent of creditors]** When the administrator requests an extension of the period of the administration by consent of creditors, his request shall be accompanied by a progress report for the period since the last progress report (if any) or the date the company entered administration.

2.112(3) **[Form of notice of extension]** The administrator shall use the notice of extension of period of administration in Form 2.31B in all circumstances where he is required to give such notice.

[FORM 2.31B]

(See General Note after r. 2.118.)

2.113 Notice of end of administration

2.113(1) **[Form of notice etc.]** Where an administrator who was appointed under paragraph 14 or 22 gives notice that the purpose of administration has been sufficiently achieved he shall use Form 2.32B. The notice shall be accompanied by a final progress report.

[FORM 2.32B]

2.113(2) **[Copy to registrar of companies]** The administrator shall send a copy of the notice to the registrar of companies.

2.113(3) **[Endorsement by court]** Two copies of the notice shall be filed with the court and shall contain a statement that a copy of the notice has been sent to the registrar of companies. The court shall endorse each copy with the date and time of filing. The appointment shall cease to have effect from that date and time.

2.113(4) **[Sealed copy to administrator]** The court shall give a sealed copy of the notice to the administrator.

2.113(5) **[Duty of administrator to notify]** The administrator shall, as soon as reasonably practicable, and within 5 business days, send a copy of the notice of end of administration (and the accompanying report) to every creditor of the company of whose claim and address he is aware, to all those persons who were notified of his appointment and to the company.

2.113(6) **[Advertisement in newspaper and Gazette]** The administrator shall be taken to have complied with the requirements of paragraph 80(5) if, within 5 business days of filing the notice of end of administration with the court, he publishes once in the same newspaper as he published his notice of appointment, and in the Gazette, a notice undertaking to provide a copy of the notice of end of administration to any creditor of the company.

2.113(7) **[Contents of notice]** The notice must—

(a) state the full name of the company;

(b) state the name and address of the administrator;

(c) state the date that the administration ended; and

(d) specify an address to which the creditors can write for a copy of the notice of end of administration.

(See General Note after r. 2.118.)

2.114 Application to court by administrator

2.114(1) **[Further progress report etc.]** An application to court under paragraph 79 for an order ending an administration shall have attached to it a progress report for the period since the last progress report (if any) or the date the company entered administration and a statement indicating what the administrator thinks should be the next steps for the company (if applicable).

2.114(2) **[Application at creditors' request]** Where the administrator applies to the court because the creditors' meeting has required him to, he shall also attach a statement to the application in which he shall indicate (giving reasons) whether or not he agrees with the creditors' requirement to him to make the application.

2.114(3) **[Application other than at creditors' request]** When the administrator applies other than at the request of a creditors' meeting, he shall—

(a) give notice in writing to the applicant for the administration order under which he was appointed, or the person by whom he was appointed and the creditors of his intention to apply to court at least 7 days before the date that he intends to makes his application; and

(b) attach to his application to court a statement that he has notified the creditors, and copies of any response from creditors to that notification.

2.114(4) **[Application in conjunction with winding-up petition]** Where the administrator applies to court under paragraph 79 in conjunction with a petition under section 124 for an order to wind up the company, he shall, in addition to the requirements of paragraph (3), notify the creditors whether he intends to seek appointment as liquidator.

(See General Note after r. 2.118.)

2.115 Application to court by creditor

2.115(1) **[Service of application]** Where a creditor applies to the court to end the administration a copy of the application shall be served on the administrator and the person who either made the application for the administration order or made the appointment. Where the appointment was made under paragraph 14, a copy of the application shall be served on the holder of the floating charge by virtue of which the appointment was made.

2.115(2) **[Period for service; appearance at hearing]** Service shall be effected not less than 5 business days before the date fixed for the hearing. The administrator, applicant or appointor, or holder of the floating charge by virtue of which the appointment was made may appear at the hearing of the application.

2.115(3) **[Copy of order to amend administration]** Where the court makes an order to end the administration, the court shall send a copy of the order to the administrator.

(See General Note after r. 2.118.)

2.116 Notification by administrator of court order

2.116 Where the court makes an order to end the administration, the administrator shall notify the registrar of companies in Form 2.33B, attaching a copy of the court order and a copy of his final progress report.

[FORM 2.33B]

(See General Note after r. 2.118.)

2.117 Moving from administration to creditors' voluntary liquidation

2.117(1) **[Form of notice with final progress report]** Where for the purposes of paragraph 83(3) the administrator sends a notice of moving from administration to creditors' voluntary liquidation to the registrar of companies, he shall do so in Form 2.34B and shall attach to that notice a final progress report which must include details of the assets to be dealt with in the liquidation.

[FORM 2.34B]

2.117(2) **[Copies]** As soon as reasonably practicable the administrator shall send a copy of the notice and attached document to all those who received notice of the administrator's appointment.

2.117(3) **[Nomination of liquidator]** For the purposes of paragraph 83(7) a person shall be nominated as liquidator in accordance with the provisions of Rule 2.33(2)(m) or Rule 2.45(2)(g) and his appointment takes effect by the creditors' approval, with or without modification, of the administrator's proposals or revised proposals.

(See General Note after r. 2.118.)

2.118 Moving from administration to dissolution

2.118(1) **[Form of notice with final progress report]** Where, for the purposes of paragraph 84(1), the administrator sends a notice of moving from administration to dissolution to the registrar of companies, he shall do so in Form 2.35B and shall attach to that notice a final progress report.

[FORM 2.35B]

2.118(2) **[Copies]** As soon as reasonably practicable a copy of the notice and the attached document shall be sent to all those who received notice of the administrator's appointment.

2.118(3) **[Copy of order for extension, suspension or disapplication of dissolution]** Where a court makes an order under paragraph 84(7) it shall, where the applicant is not the administrator, give a copy of the order to the administrator.

2.118(4) **[Form of notice of order]** The administrator shall use Form 2.36B to notify the registrar of companies in accordance with paragraph 84(8) of any order made by the court under paragraph 84(7).

[FORM 2.36B]

GENERAL NOTE TO RR. 2.110–2.118

Paragraphs 76ff. of Sch. B1 deal with the various ways in which an administration can come to an end (in the words of the draftsman, "the appointment of an administrator shall cease to have effect"). These rules supplement those provisions by spelling out the procedure to be followed and the forms to be used in each case.

R. 2.111(3)
On penalties, see s. 430 and Sch. 10.

Chapter 13

Replacing the Administrator

2.119 Grounds for resignation

2.119(1) **[Notice of grounds]** The administrator may give notice of his resignation on grounds of ill health or because–

(a) he intends ceasing to be in practice as an insolvency practitioner; or

(b) there is some conflict of interest, or change of personal circumstances, which precludes or makes impracticable the further discharge by him of the duties of administrator.

2.119(2) **[Other grounds]** The administrator may, with the permission of the court, give notice of his resignation on grounds other than those specified in paragraph (1).

(See General Note after r. 2.129.)

2.120 Notice of intention to resign

2.120(1) **[Form of notice of intention to resign]** The administrator shall in all cases give at least 7 days' notice in Form 2.37B of his intention to resign, or to apply for the court's permission to do so, to the following persons–

[FORM 2.37B]

(a) if there is a continuing administrator of the company, to him; and

(b) if there is a creditors' committee to it; but

(c) if there is no such administrator and no creditors' committee, to the company and its creditors.

2.120(2) **[Notice to member State liquidator]** Where the administrator gives notice under paragraph (1), he shall also give notice to a member State liquidator, if such a person has been appointed in relation to the company.

2.120(3) **[Notice to holders of prior qualifying floating charges etc.]** Where the administrator was appointed by the holder of a qualifying floating charge under paragraph 14, the notice of intention to resign shall also be sent to all holders of prior qualifying floating charges, and to the person who appointed the administrator. A copy of the notice shall also be sent to the holder of the floating charge by virtue of which the appointment was made.

2.120(4) **[Where appointed by company or directors]** Where the administrator was appointed by the company or the directors of the company under paragraph 22, a copy of the notice of intention to resign shall also be sent to the appointor and all holders of a qualifying floating charge.

(See General Note after r. 2.129.)

2.121 Notice of resignation

2.121(1) **[Form of notice]** The notice of resignation shall be in Form 2.38B.

[FORM 2.38B]

2.121(2) **[Notice filed; copies]** Where the administrator was appointed under an administration order, the notice shall be filed with the court, and a copy sent to the registrar of companies. A copy of the notice of resignation shall be sent not more than 5 business days after it has been filed with the court to all those to whom notice of intention to resign was sent.

2.121(3) **[Copies where administrator appointed by holder of qualifying floating charge]** Where the administrator was appointed by the holder of a qualifying floating charge under paragraph 14, a copy of the notice of resignation shall be filed with the court and sent to the registrar of companies, and anyone else who received a copy of the notice of intention to resign, within 5 business days of the notice of resignation being sent to the holder of the floating charge by virtue of which the appointment was made.

2.121(4) **[Copies where administrator appointed by company or directors]** Where the administrator was appointed by the company or the directors under paragraph 22, a copy of the notice of resignation shall be filed with the court and sent to the registrar of companies and to anyone else who received notice of intention to resign within 5 business days of the notice of resignation being sent to either the company or the directors that made the appointment.

(See General Note after r. 2.129.)

2.122 Application to court to remove administrator from office

2.122(1) **[Grounds]** Any application under paragraph 88 shall state the grounds on which it is requested that the administrator should be removed from office.

2.122(2) **[Service of notice]** Service of the notice of the application shall be effected on the administrator, the person who made the application for the administration order or the person who appointed the administrator, the creditors' committee (if any), the joint administrator (if any), and where there is neither a creditors' committee or joint administrator, to the company and all the creditors, including any floating charge holders not less than 5 business days before the date fixed for the application to be heard. Where the appointment was made under paragraph 14, the notice shall be served on the holder of the floating charge by virtue of which the appointment was made.

2.122(3) **[Order]** Where a court makes an order removing the administrator it shall give a copy of the order to the applicant who as soon as reasonably practicable shall send a copy to the administrator.

2.122(4) **[Copies]** The applicant shall also within 5 business days of the order being made send a copy of the order to all those to whom notice of the application was sent.

2.122(5) **[Copy to registar of companies]** A copy of the order shall also be sent to the registrar of companies in Form 2.39B within the same time period.

[FORM 2.39B]

(See General Note after r. 2.129.)

2.123 Notice of vacation of office when administrator ceases to be qualified to act

2.123 Where the administrator who has ceased to be qualified to act as an insolvency practitioner in relation to the company gives notice in accordance with paragraph 89, he shall also give notice to the registrar of companies in Form 2.39B.

(See General Note after r. 2.129.)

2.124 Administrator deceased

2.124(1) **[Notice to court]** Subject as follows, where the administrator has died, it is the duty of his personal representatives to give notice of the fact to the court, specifying the date of the death. This does not apply if notice has been given under either paragraph (2) or (3) of this Rule.

2.124(2) **[Notice by partner etc.]** If the deceased administrator was a partner in a firm, notice may be given by a partner in the firm who is qualified to act as an insolvency practitioner, or is a member of any body recognised by the Secretary of State for the authorisation of insolvency practitioners.

2.124(3) **[Notice by others]** Notice of the death may be given by any person producing to the court the relevant death certificate or a copy of it.

2.124(4) **[Notice to registrar of companies]** Where a person gives notice to the court under this Rule, he shall also give notice to the registrar of companies in Form 2.39B.

(See General Note after r. 2.129.)

2.125 Application to replace

2.125(1) **[Written statement by proposed replacement]** Where an application is made to court under paragraphs 91(1) or 95 to appoint a replacement administrator, the application shall be accompanied by a written statement in Form 2.2B by the person proposed to be the replacement administrator.

2.125(2) **[Where administrator appointed under administration order]** Where the original administrator was appointed under an administration order, a copy of the application shall be served, in addition to those persons listed in paragraph 12(2) and Rule 2.6(3), on the person who made the application for the administration order.

2.125(3) **[Affidavit of belief]** Where the application to court is made under paragraph 95, the application shall be accompanied by an affidavit setting out the applicant's belief as to the matters set out in that paragraph.

2.125(4) **[Application of r. 2.8 to service]** Rule 2.8 shall apply to the service of an application under paragraphs 91(1) and 95 as it applies to service in accordance with Rule 2.6.

2.125(5) **[[Application of rr. 2.9, 2.10, 2.12, 2.14(1), (2)]** Rules 2.9, 2.10, 2.12 and 2.14(1) and (2) apply to an application under paragraphs 91(1) and 95.]

(See General Note after r. 2.129.)

2.126 Notification and advertisement of appointment of replacement administrator

2.126 Where a replacement administrator is appointed, the same provisions apply in respect of giving notice of, and advertising, the replacement appointment as in the case of the appointment (subject to Rule 2.128), and all statements, consents etc as are required shall also be required in the case of the appointment of a replacement. All forms and notices shall clearly identify that the appointment is of a replacement administrator.

(See General Note after r. 2.129.)

2.127 Notification and advertisement of appointment of joint administrator

2.127 Where, after an initial appointment has been made, an additional person or persons are to be appointed as joint administrator the same Rules shall apply in respect of giving notice of and advertising the appointment as in the case of the initial appointment, subject to Rule 2.128.

(See General Note after r. 2.129.)

2.128 The replacement or additional administrator shall send notice of the appointment in Form 2.40B to the registrar of companies.

[FORM 2.40B]

(See General Note after r. 2.129.)

2.129 Administrator's duties on vacating office

2.129(1) **[Delivery of assets, records, books etc.]** Where the administrator ceases to be in office as such, in consequence of removal, resignation or cesser of qualification as an insolvency practitioner, he is under obligation as soon as reasonably practicable to deliver up to the person succeeding him as administrator the assets (after deduction of any expenses properly incurred and distributions made by him) and further to deliver up to that person—

(a) the records of the administration, including correspondence, proofs and other related papers appertaining to the administration while it was within his responsibility; and

(b) the company's books, papers and other records.

2.129(2) **[Default fine]** If the administrator makes default in complying with this Rule, he is liable to a fine and, for continued contravention, to a daily default fine.

GENERAL NOTE TO RR. 2.119–2.129

Paragraphs 87ff. of Sch. B1 deal with the various circumstances in which an administrator can leave office and be replaced by another, with the appointment of one or more additional administrators and with matters consequential upon an administrator leaving office. These rules supplement those provisions by spelling out the procedure to be followed and the forms to be used in each case.

CHAPTER 14

EC REGULATION: CONVERSION OF ADMINISTRATION INTO WINDING UP

2.130 Application for conversion into winding up

2.130(1) **[Affidavit filed with court]** Where a member State liquidator proposes to apply to the court for the conversion under Article 37 of the EC Regulation (conversion of earlier proceedings) of an administration into a winding up, an affidavit complying with Rule 2.131 must be prepared and sworn, and filed with the court in support of the application.

2.130(2) **[Originating application]** An application under this Rule shall be by originating application.

2.130(3) **[On whom application to be served]** The application and the affidavit required under this Rule shall be served upon—

(a) the company; and

(b) the administrator.

(See General Note after r. 2.133.)

2.131 Contents of affidavit

2.131(1) **[Contents]** The affidavit shall state—

(a) that main proceedings have been opened in relation to the company in a member State other than the United Kingdom;

(b) the deponent's belief that the conversion of the administration into a winding up would prove to be in the interests of the creditors in the main proceedings;

(c) the deponent's opinion as to whether the company ought to enter voluntary winding up or be wound up by the court; and

(d) all other matters that, in the opinion of the member State liquidator, would assist the court—

(i) in deciding whether to make such an order; and
(ii) if the court were to do so, in considering the need for any consequential provision that would be necessary or desirable.

2.131(2) [**Member State liquidator to swear**] An affidavit under this rule shall be sworn by, or on behalf of, the member State liquidator.

(See General Note after r. 2.133.)

2.132 Power of court

2.132(1) [**Order**] On hearing the application for conversion into winding up the court may make such order as it thinks fit.

2.132(2) [**Consequential provisions**] If the court makes an order for conversion into winding up the order may contain all such consequential provisions as the court deems necessary or desirable.

2.132(3) [**Power to make order as if for voluntary winding up**] Without prejudice to the generality of paragraph (1), an order under that paragraph may provide that the company be wound up as if a resolution for voluntary winding up under section 84 were passed on the day on which the order is made.

(See General Note after r. 2.133.)

CHAPTER 15

EC REGULATION: MEMBER STATE LIQUIDATOR

2.133 Interpretation of creditor and notice to member State liquidator

2.133(1) [**Application of r. 2.133**] This Rule applies where a member State liquidator has been appointed in relation to the company.

2.133(2) [**Member State liquidator deemed creditor for certain Rules**] For the purposes of the Rules referred to in paragraph (3) the member State liquidator is deemed to be a creditor.

2.133(3) [**Rules for purpose of r. 2.133(2)**] The Rules referred to in paragraph (2) are Rules 2.34 (notice of creditors' meeting), 2.35(4) (creditors' meeting), 2.37 (requisitioning of creditors' meeting), 2.38 (entitlement to vote), 2.39 (admission and rejection of claims), 2.40 (secured creditors), 2.41 (holders of negotiable instruments), 2.42 (hire-purchase, conditional sale and chattel leasing agreements), 2.46 (notice to creditors), 2.47 (reports to creditors), 2.48 (correspondence instead of creditors' meeting), 2.50(2) (creditors' committee), 2.57(1)(b) and (c) (termination of membership of creditors' committee), 2.59(3) (vacancies in creditors' committee), 2.108(3) (administrator's remuneration - recourse to court) and 2.109 (challenge to administrator's remuneration).

2.133(4) [**R. 2.133(2), (3) subject to exercise of creditors' rights**] Paragraphs (2) and (3) are without prejudice to the generality of the right to participate referred to in paragraph 3 of Article 32 of the EC Regulation (exercise of creditor's rights).

2.133(5) [**Notice or copies to the member State liquidator**] Where the administrator is obliged to give notice to, or provide a copy of a document (including an order of court) to, the court, the registrar of companies or the official receiver, the administrator shall give notice or provide copies, as the case may be, to the member State liquidator.

2.133(6) [**R. 2.133(5) subject to co-operate and communicate**] Paragraph (5) is without prejudice to the generality of the obligations imposed by Article 31 of the EC Regulation (duty to co-operate and communicate information).

GENERAL NOTE TO RR. 2.130–2.133

These rules follow closely rr. *2.59–2.62* which apply under the original regime. See the notes to those provisions.

PART 3

ADMINISTRATIVE RECEIVERSHIP

General comment on Pt 3
These rules are new and they have no counterpart in the previous legislation. The bulk of the rules deal with the creditors' committee which was an innovation introduced by IA 1986. It should be noted that the following rules do not apply to Scottish receiverships or receivers in Northern Ireland.

CHAPTER 1

APPOINTMENT OF ADMINISTRATIVE RECEIVER

3.1 Acceptance and confirmation of acceptance of appointment

3.1(1) [**Two or more persons appointed jointly**] Where two or more persons are appointed as joint receivers or managers of a company's property under powers contained in an instrument, the acceptance of such an appointment shall be made by each of them in accordance with section 33 as if that person were a sole appointee, but the joint appointment takes effect only when all such persons have so accepted and is then deemed to have been made at the time at which the instrument of appointment was received by or on behalf of all such persons.

3.1(2) [**Sole or joint receiver**] Subject to the next paragraph, where a person is appointed as the sole or joint receiver of a company's property under powers contained in an instrument, the appointee shall, if he accepts the appointment, within 7 days confirm his acceptance in writing to the person appointing him.

3.1(3) [**Non-application of r. 3.1(2)**] Paragraph (2) does not apply where an appointment is accepted in writing.

[FORM 3.1]

3.1(4) [**Who may accept or confirm**] Any acceptance or confirmation of acceptance of appointment as a receiver or manager of a company's property, whether under the Act or the Rules, may be given by any person (including, in the case of a joint appointment, any joint appointee) duly authorised for that purpose on behalf of the receiver or manager.

3.1(5) [**Statements in confirmation**] In confirming acceptance the appointee or person authorised for that purpose shall state–

(a) the time and date of receipt of the instrument of appointment, and

(b) the time and date of acceptance.

GENERAL NOTE

This rule should be viewed in the light of s. 33. It deals with acceptance and confirmation of appointment as receiver or manager (not just an administrative receiver) despite the title of this Part and Chapter of the rules: see r. 0.3(2) as amended.

3.2 Notice and advertisement of appointment

3.2(1) [**Notice required by s. 46(1)**] This Rule relates to the notice which a person is required by section 46(1) to send and publish, when appointed as administrative receiver.

3.2(2) [**Matters to be stated in notice**] The following matters shall be stated in the notices sent to the company and the creditors–

(a) the registered name of the company, as at the date of the appointment, and its registered number;

(b) any other name with which the company has been registered in the 12 months preceding that date;

(c) any name under which the company has traded at any time in those 12 months, if substantially different from its then registered name;

(d) the name and address of the administrative receiver, and the date of his appointment;

(e) the name of the person by whom the appointment was made;

(f) the date of the instrument conferring the power under which the appointment was made, and a brief description of the instrument;

(g) a brief description of the assets of the company (if any) in respect of which the person appointed is not made the receiver.

3.2(3) [**Advertisement**] The administrative receiver shall cause notice of his appointment to be advertised once in the Gazette, and once in such newspaper as he thinks most appropriate for ensuring that it comes to the notice of the company's creditors.

[FORM 3.1A]

3.2(4) [**Contents of advertisement**] The advertisement shall state all the matters specified in sub-paragraphs (a) to (e) of paragraph (2) above.

GENERAL NOTE

Details of the notices required to be given by an administrative receiver under IA 1986, s. 46 to the company and the public at large are here provided.

CHAPTER 2

STATEMENT OF AFFAIRS AND REPORT TO CREDITORS

3.3 Notice requiring statement of affairs

3.3(1) [**Notice re s. 47 statement**] Where the administrative receiver determines to require a statement of the company's affairs to be made out and submitted to him in accordance with section 47, he shall send notice to each of the persons whom he considers should be made responsible under that section, requiring them to prepare and submit the statement.

[FORM 3.1B]

3.3(2) [**"The deponents"**] The persons to whom the notice is sent are referred to in this Chapter as "the deponents".

3.3(3) [**Contents of notice**] The notice shall inform each of the deponents–

(a) of the names and addresses of all others (if any) to whom the same notice has been sent;

(b) of the time within which the statement must be delivered;

(c) of the effect of section 47(6) (penalty for non-compliance); and

(d) of the application to him, and to each of the other deponents, of section 235 (duty to provide information, and to attend on the administrative receiver if required).

3.3(4) [Instructions for preparation of statement] The administrative receiver shall, on request, furnish each deponent with the forms required for the preparation of the statement of affairs.

GENERAL NOTE

This rule fills out the contents of any notice given by an administrative receiver under IA 1986, s. 47 to "deponents" who must submit a statement of the company's affairs to him.

The receiver *must* demand a statement from someone: his only discretion is in determining who to "require" it from (see s. 47 itself).

3.4 Verification and filing

3.4(1) [Form of statement and verification] The statement of affairs shall be in Form 3.2, shall contain all the particulars required by that form and shall be verified by affidavit by the deponents (using the same form).

[FORM 3.2]

3.4(2) [Affidavits of concurrence] The administrative receiver may require any of the persons mentioned in section 47(3) to submit an affidavit of concurrence, stating that he concurs in the statement of affairs.

3.4(3) [Affidavit may be qualified] An affidavit of concurrence may be qualified in respect of matters dealt with in the statement of affairs, where the maker of the affidavit is not in agreement with the deponents, or he considers the statement to be erroneous or misleading, or he is without the direct knowledge necessary for concurring with it.

3.4(4) [Delivery of statement to receiver] The statement of affairs shall be delivered to the receiver by the deponent making the affidavit of verification (or by one of them, if more than one), together with a copy of the verified statement.

3.4(5) [Delivery of affidavit of concurrence] Every affidavit of concurrence shall be delivered by the person who makes it, together with a copy.

3.4(6) [Retention of copy statement etc.] The administrative receiver shall retain the verified copy of the statement and the affidavits of concurrence (if any) as part of the records of the receivership.

GENERAL NOTE

This relates to the form of the statement of affairs submitted under IA 1986, s. 47.

3.5 Limited disclosure

3.5(1) [Application to court] Where the administrative receiver thinks that it would prejudice the conduct of the receivership for the whole or part of the statement of affairs to be disclosed, he may apply to the court for an order of limited disclosure in respect of the statement or a specified part of it.

3.5(2) [Powers of court] The court may on the application order that the statement, or, as the case may be, the specified part of it, be not open to inspection otherwise than with leave of the court.

3.5(3) [Directions] The court's order may include directions as to the delivery of documents to the registrar of companies and the disclosure of relevant information to other persons.

GENERAL NOTE

This allows the administrative receiver to apply to the court to censor the statement of affairs if publication would prejudice his task. Compare IA 1986, s. 48(6).

3.6 Release from duty to submit statement of affairs; extension of time

3.6(1) [**Exercise of s. 47(5) power**] The power of the administrative receiver under section 47(5) to give a release from the obligation imposed by that section, or to grant an extension of time, may be exercised at the receiver's own discretion, or at the request of any deponent.

3.6(2) [**Application to court**] A deponent may, if he requests a release or extension of time and it is refused by the receiver, apply to the court for it.

3.6(3) [**Court may dismiss application etc.**] The court may, if it thinks that no sufficient cause is shown for the application, dismiss it; but it shall not do so unless the applicant has had an opportunity to attend the court for an *ex parte* hearing, of which he has been given at least 7 days' notice.

If the application is not dismissed under this paragraph, the court shall fix a venue for it to be heard, and give notice to the deponent accordingly.

3.6(4) [**Deponent to send notice to receiver**] The deponent shall, at least 14 days before the hearing, send to the receiver a notice stating the venue and accompanied by a copy of the application, and of any evidence which he (the deponent) intends to adduce in support of it.

3.6(5) [**Appearance etc. by receiver**] The receiver may appear and be heard on the application; and, whether or not he appears, he may file a written report of any matters which he considers ought to be drawn to the court's attention.

If such a report is filed, a copy of it shall be sent by the receiver to the deponent, not later than 5 days before the hearing.

3.6(6) [**Sealed copies of order**] Sealed copies of any order made on the application shall be sent by the court to the deponent and the receiver.

3.6(7) [**Costs**] On any application under this Rule the applicant's costs shall be paid in any event by him and, unless the court otherwise orders, no allowance towards them shall be made out of the assets under the administrative receiver's control.

GENERAL NOTE

Further details of any release given by an administrative receiver under IA 1986, s. 47(5) are provided by this rule.

3.7 Expenses of statement of affairs

3.7(1) [**Payment of expenses**] A deponent making the statement of affairs and affidavit shall be allowed, and paid by the administrative receiver out of his receipts, any expenses incurred by the deponent in so doing which the receiver thinks reasonable.

3.7(2) [**Appeal to court**] Any decision by the receiver under this Rule is subject to appeal to the court.

3.7(3) [**Effect of Rule**] Nothing in this Rule relieves a deponent from any obligation with respect to the preparation, verification and submission of the statement of affairs, or to the provision of information to the receiver.

GENERAL NOTE

This allows a "deponent" (see r. 3.3(2)) to recover from the company's assets his expenses incurred in producing the statement of affairs.

3.8 Report to creditors

3.8(1) [**Notice under s. 48(2)**] If under section 48(2) the administrative receiver determines not to send a copy of his report to creditors, but to publish notice under paragraph (b) of that subsection, the notice shall be published in the newspaper in which the receiver's appointment was advertised.

3.8(2) [**No s. 48(2) meeting proposed**] If he proposes to apply to the court to dispense with the holding of the meeting of unsecured creditors (otherwise required by section 48(2)), he shall in his report to creditors or (as the case may be) in the notice published as above, state the venue fixed by the court for the hearing of the application.

3.8(3) [**Documents to be attached to report**] Subject to any order of the court under Rule 3.5, the copy of the receiver's report which under section 48(1) is to be sent to the registrar of companies shall have attached to it a copy of any statement of affairs under section 47, and copies of any affidavits of concurrence.

3.8(4) [**Late submission of documents**] If the statement of affairs or affidavits of concurrence, if any, have not been submitted to the receiver by the time he sends a copy of his report to the registrar of companies, he shall send a copy of the statement and any affidavits of concurrence as soon thereafter as he receives them.

3.8(5) [**Statement in report**] The receiver's report under section 48(1) shall state, to the best of his knowledge and belief–

(a) an estimate of the value of the prescribed part (whether or not he proposes to make an application under section 176A(5) or whether section 176A(3) applies); and

(b) an estimate of the value of the company's net property.

3.8(6) [**Non-disclosure of seriously prejudicial information**] Nothing in this Rule is to be taken as requiring any such estimate to include any information, the disclosure of which could seriously prejudice the commercial interests of the company.

If such information is excluded from the calculation the estimate shall be accompanied by a statement to that effect.

3.8(7) [**Report to state whether application to court under s. 176A(5)**] The report shall also state whether, and if so why, the receiver proposes to make an application to court under section 176A(5).

[FORM 3.3]

GENERAL NOTE

If the administrative receiver opts to inform creditors under IA 1986, s. 48(2) by a notice, then this rule will apply. This rule also deals with other actions of the administrative receiver under IA 1986, s. 48.

This reporting obligation was extended by Insolvency (Amendment) Rules 2003 (SI 2003/1730) by the addition of paras (5)–(7) which deal with the special reserve fund for unsecured creditors set up by s. 176A.

CHAPTER 3

CREDITORS' MEETING

3.9 Procedure for summoning meeting under s. 48(2)

3.9(1) [**Convenience of venue**] In fixing the venue for a meeting of creditors summoned under section 48(2), the administrative receiver shall have regard to the convenience of the persons who are invited to attend.

3.9(2) [**Time of meeting**] The meeting shall be summoned for commencement between 10.00 and 16.00 hours on a business day, unless the court otherwise directs.

3.9(3) [**Notice of venue**] At least 14 days' notice of the venue shall be given to all creditors of the company who are identified in the statement of affairs, or are known to the receiver and had claims against the company at the date of his appointment.

3.9(4) [**Forms of proxy**] With the notice summoning the meeting there shall be sent out forms of proxy.

[FORM 8.3]

3.9(5) [**Statement in notice**] The notice shall include a statement to the effect that creditors whose claims are wholly secured are not entitled to attend or be represented at the meeting.

3.9(6) [**Publication of notice**] Notice of the venue shall also be published in the newspaper in which the receiver's appointment was advertised.

3.9(7) [**R. 3.11(1) statement**] The notice to creditors and the newspaper advertisement shall contain a statement of the effect of Rule 3.11(1) below (voting rights).

GENERAL NOTE

This outlines the procedure to be followed if the administrative receiver calls a meeting of creditors under IA 1986, s. 48(2). For the definition of "venue" and "business day" see rr. 13.6 and 13.3(1).

3.10 The chairman at the meeting

3.10(1) [**Receiver or his nominee to be chairman**] The chairman at the creditors' meeting shall be the receiver, or a person nominated by him in writing to act in his place.

3.10(2) [**Nominee chairman**] A person so nominated must be either–

(a) one who is qualified to act as an insolvency practitioner in relation to the company, or

(b) an employee of the receiver or his firm who is experienced in insolvency matters.

GENERAL NOTE

Where the chairman of the meeting is not the administrative receiver, then he must also be qualified as an insolvency practitioner or have experience to satisfy r. 3.10(2)(b): see Pt XIII of the Act.

3.11 Voting rights

3.11(1) [**Entitlement to vote**] Subject as follows, at the creditors' meeting a person is entitled to vote only if–

(a) he has given to the receiver, not later than 12.00 hours on the business day before the day fixed for the meeting, details in writing of the debt that he claims to be due to him from the company, and the claim has been duly admitted under the following provisions of this Rule, and

(b) there has been lodged with the administrative receiver any proxy which the creditor intends to be used on his behalf.

3.11(2) [**Failure to comply with r. 3.11(1)(a)**] The chairman of the meeting may allow a creditor to vote, notwithstanding that he has failed to comply with paragraph (1)(a), if satisifed that the failure was due to circumstances beyond the creditor's control.

3.11(3) [**Production of documents**] The receiver or (if other) the chairman of the meeting may call for any document or other evidence to be produced to him where he thinks it necessary for the purpose of substantiating the whole or any part of the claim.

3.11(4) [**Calculation of votes**] Votes are calculated according to the amount of a creditor's debt as at the date of the appointment of the receiver, after deducting any amounts paid in respect of that debt after that date.

3.11(5) [**Limitation on voting**] A creditor shall not vote in respect of a debt for an unliquidated amount, or any debt whose value is not ascertained, except where the chairman agrees to put upon the debt an estimated minimum value for the purpose of entitlement to vote and admits the claim for that purpose.

3.11(6) [**Secured creditors**] A secured creditor is entitled to vote only in respect of the balance (if any) of his debt after deducting the value of his security as estimated by him.

3.11(7) **[Further limitation on voting]** A creditor shall not vote in respect of a debt on, or secured by, a current bill of exchange or promissory note, unless he is willing–

(a) to treat the liability to him on the bill or note of every person who is liable on it antecedently to the company, and against whom a bankruptcy order has not been made (or, in the case of a company, which has not gone into liquidation), as a security in his hands, and

(b) to estimate the value of the security and, for the purpose of his entitlement to vote, to deduct it from his claim.

GENERAL NOTE

This regulates the exercise of voting rights at the creditors' meeting. The voting is likely to favour larger creditors. Note the special rules for persons having unliquidated claims in damages, etc., against the company.

3.12 Admission and rejection of claim

3.12(1) **[Power of chairman]** At the creditors' meeting the chairman has power to admit or reject a creditor's claim for the purpose of his entitlement to vote; and the power is exercisable with respect to the whole or any part of the claim.

3.12(2) **[Appeal from chairman's decision]** The chairman's decision under this Rule, or in respect of any matter arising under Rule 3.11, is subject to appeal to the court by any creditor.

3.12(3) **[Voting subject to objection]** If the chairman is in doubt whether a claim should be admitted or rejected, he shall mark it as objected to and allow the creditor to vote, subject to his vote being subsequently declared invalid if the objection to the claim is sustained.

3.12(4) **[If chairman's decision reversed etc.]** If on an appeal the chairman's decision is reversed or varied, or a creditor's vote is declared invalid, the court may order that another meeting be summoned, or make such other order as it thinks just.

3.12(5) **[Costs of appeal]** Neither the receiver nor any person nominated by him to be chairman is personally liable for costs incurred by any person in respect of an appeal to the court under this Rule, unless the court makes an order to that effect.

GENERAL NOTE

The chairman can regulate the acceptance of claims and therefore voting rights. Appeal to the court is possible.

3.13 Quorum

3.13 (Omitted by the Insolvency (Amendment) Rules 1987 (SI 1987/1919), r. 3(1), Sch. Pt 1, para. 26 as from 11 January 1988.)

GENERAL NOTE

See now the general provision in r. 12.4A.

3.14 Adjournment

3.14(1) **[Chairman's decision]** The creditors' meeting shall not be adjourned, even if no quorum is present, unless the chairman decides that it is desirable; and in that case he shall adjourn it to such date, time and place as he thinks fit.

3.14(2) **[Application of r. 3.9]** Rule 3.9(1) and (2) applies, with necessary modifications, to any adjourned meeting.

3.14(3) **[If no quorum or adjournment]** If there is no quorum, and the meeting is not adjourned, it is deemed to have been duly summoned and held.

3.15 Resolutions and minutes

3.15(1) [**Resolution passed by majority in value**] At the creditors' meeting, a resolution is passed when a majority (in value) of those present and voting in person or by proxy have voted in favour of it.

3.15(2) [**Record of proceedings**] The chairman of the meeting shall cause a record to be made of the proceedings and kept as part of the records of the receivership.

3.15(3) [**Contents of record**] The record shall include a list of the creditors who attended (personally or by proxy) and, if a creditors' committee has been established, the names and addresses of those elected to be members of the committee.

GENERAL NOTE

Resolutions are to be passed by simple majority.

CHAPTER 4

THE CREDITORS' COMMITTEE

3.16 Constitution of committee

3.16(1) [**Three–five creditors**] Where it is resolved by the creditors' meeting to establish a creditors' committee, the committee shall consist of at least 3 and not more than 5 creditors of the company elected at the meeting.

3.16(2) [**Eligibility**] Any creditor of the company is eligible to be a member of the committee, so long as his claim has not been rejected for the purpose of his entitlement to vote.

3.16(3) [**Body corporate as member**] A body corporate may be a member of the committee, but it cannot act as such otherwise than by a representative appointed under Rule 3.21 below.

GENERAL NOTE

This details the constitution and size of any committee set up under IA 1986, s. 49.

3.17 Formalities of establishment

3.17(1) [**Certificate of due constitution**] The creditors' committee does not come into being, and accordingly cannot act, until the administrative receiver has issued a certificate of its due constitution.

3.17(2) [**Agreement to act**] No person may act as a member of the committee unless and until he has agreed to do so and, unless the relevant proxy or authorisation contains a statement to the contrary, such agreement may be given by his proxy-holder or representative under section 375 of the Companies Act present at the meeting establishing the committee.

3.17(2A) [**Issue of certificate**] The receiver's certificate of the committee's due constitution shall not issue unless and until at least 3 of the persons who are to be members of the committee have agreed to act.

3.17(3) [**Amended certificate**] As and when the others (if any) agree to act, the receiver shall issue an amended certificate.

3.17(4) [**Certificates to be sent to registrar**] The certificate, and any amended certificate, shall be sent by the receiver to the registrar of companies.

[FORM 3.4]

3.17(5) [**Change in membership**] If, after the first establishment of the committee, there is any change in its membership, the receiver shall report the change to the registrar of companies.

GENERAL NOTE

It is for the administrative receiver to certify this committee.
Rules 3.17(2) and 3.17(2A) aim to facilitate the immediate establishment of a committee after the creditors' meeting.

3.18 Functions and meetings of the committee

3.18(1) [**Functions**] The creditors' committee shall assist the administrative receiver in discharging his functions, and act in relation to him in such manner as may be agreed from time to time.

3.18(2) [**Holding of meetings**] Subject as follows, meetings of the committee shall be held when and where determined by the receiver.

3.18(3) [**First and subsequent meetings**] The receiver shall call a first meeting of the committee not later than 3 months after its establishment; and thereafter he shall call a meeting–

(a) if requested by a member of the committee or his representative (the meeting then to be held within 21 days of the request being received by the receiver), and

(b) for a specified date, if the committee has previously resolved that a meeting be held on that date.

3.18(4) [**Notice of venue**] The receiver shall give 7 days' written notice of the venue of any meeting to every member (or his representative designated for that purpose), unless in any case the requirement of notice has been waived by or on behalf of any member.

Waiver may be signified either at or before the meeting.

GENERAL NOTE

This outlines the role of the committee. The committee's functions are left vague by IA 1986, s. 49. For "venue" in r. 3.18(4) see r. 13.6.

3.19 The chairman at meetings

3.19(1) [**Chairman**] Subject to Rule 3.28(3), the chairman at any meeting of the creditors' committee shall be the administrative receiver, or a person nominated by him in writing to act.

3.19(2) [**Nominated chairman**] A person so nominated must be either–

(a) one who is qualified to act as an insolvency practitioner in relation to the company, or

(b) an employee of the receiver or his firm who is experienced in insolvency matters.

GENERAL NOTE

This is similar to r. 3.10.

3.20 Quorum

3.20 A meeting of the committee is duly constituted if due notice has been given to all the members, and at least 2 members are present or represented.

GENERAL NOTE

The committee's quorum is two.

3.21 Committee-members' representatives

3.21(1) [**Representation**] A member of the committee may, in relation to the business of the committee, be represented by another person duly authorised by him for that purpose.

3.21(2) **[Letter of authority]** A person acting as a committee-member's representative must hold a letter of authority entitling him so to act (either generally or specially) and signed by or on behalf of the committee-member, and for this purpose any proxy or any authorisation under section 375 of the Companies Act in relation to any meeting of creditors of the company shall, unless it contains a statement to the contrary, be treated as a letter of authority to act generally signed by or on behalf of the committee-member.

3.21(3) **[Production of letter of authority]** The chairman at any meeting of the committee may call on a person claiming to act as a committee-member's representative to produce his letter of authority, and may exclude him if it appears that his authority is deficient.

3.21(4) **[Who may not be a representative]** No member may be represented by a body corporate, or by a person who is an undischarged bankrupt, or a disqualified director, or is subject to a bankruptcy restrictions order, bankruptcy restrictions undertaking or interim bankruptcy restrictions order.

3.21(5) **[No dual representation]** No person shall–

(a) on the same committee, act at one and the same time as representative of more than one committee-member, or

(b) act both as a member of the committee and as representative of another member.

3.21(6) **[Signing as representative]** Where a member's representative signs any document on the member's behalf, the fact that he so signs must be stated below his signature.

GENERAL NOTE

Committee members may appoint representatives to act for them. Amendments were made to paragraph (4) by I(A)R 2004 (SI 2004/584) with effect from April 1, 2004 in order inter alia to cater for the exclusion from committee membership of persons subject to BROs, BRUs, etc., and to remove the obsolete reference to persons entering compositions with creditors.

3.22 Resignation

3.22 A member of the committee may resign by notice in writing delivered to the administrative receiver.

3.23 Termination of membership

3.23(1) **[Automatic termination]** Membership of the creditors' committee is automatically terminated if the member–

(a) becomes bankrupt, or

(b) at 3 consecutive meetings of the committee is neither present nor represented (unless at the third of those meetings it is resolved that this Rule is not to apply in his case), or

(c) ceases to be, or is found never to have been, a creditor.

3.23(2) **[Termination on bankruptcy]** However, if the cause of termination is the member's bankruptcy, his trustee in bankruptcy replaces him as a member of the committee.

GENERAL NOTE

Note the sanction against absentees. The former reference in paragraph (1)(a) to compositions and arrangements with creditors was removed by I(A)R 2004 (SI 2004/584) with effect from April 1, 2004.

3.24 Removal

3.24 A member of the committee may be removed by resolution at a meeting of creditors, at least 14 days' notice having been given of the intention to move that resolution.

GENERAL NOTE

The committee is thus controlled by the creditors' meeting.

3.25 Vacancies

3.25(1) **[Application of Rule]** The following applies if there is a vacancy in the membership of the creditors' committee.

3.25(2) **[Agreement not to fill vacancy]** The vacancy need not be filled if the administrative receiver and a majority of the remaining members of the committee so agree, provided that the total number of members does not fall below the minimum required under Rule 3.16.

3.25(3) **[Filling vacancy]** The receiver may appoint any creditor (being qualified under the Rules to be a member of the committee) to fill the vacancy, if a majority of the other members of the committee agree to the appointment and the creditor concerned consents to act.

3.26 Procedure at meetings

3.26(1) **[Votes and passing of resolutions]** At any meeting of the committee, each member of it (whether present himself or by his representative) has one vote; and a resolution is passed when a majority of the members present or represented have voted in favour of it.

3.26(2) **[Record of resolutions]** Every resolution passed shall be recorded in writing, either separately or as part of the minutes of the meeting.

3.26(3) **[Signing of records etc.]** A record of each resolution shall be signed by the chairman and kept as part of the records of the receivership.

GENERAL NOTE

Votes at the committee are passed by a simple majority. There is no weighting of votes here.

3.27 Resolutions by post

3.27(1) **[Proposed resolution sent to members]** In accordance with this Rule, the administrative receiver may seek to obtain the agreement of members of the creditors' committee to a resolution by sending to every member (or his representative designated for the purpose) a copy of the proposed resolution.

3.27(2) **[Copies of proposed resolution]** Where the receiver makes use of the procedure allowed by this Rule, he shall send out to members of the committee or their representatives (as the case may be) a copy of any proposed resolution on which a decision is sought, which shall be set out in such a way that agreement with or dissent from each separate resolution may be indicated by the recipient on the copy so sent.

3.27(3) **[Member may require meeting]** Any member of the committee may, within 7 business days from the date of the receiver sending out a resolution, require him to summon a meeting of the committee to consider the matters raised by the resolution.

3.27(4) **[Deemed passing of resolution]** In the absence of such a request, the resolution is deemed to have been passed by the committee if and when the receiver is notified in writing by a majority of the members that they concur with it.

3.27(5) **[Copy resolution etc. with records]** A copy of every resolution passed under this Rule, and a note that the committee's concurrence was obtained, shall be kept with the records of the receivership.

GENERAL NOTE

Postal voting is acceptable if no member objects.
 Rule 3.27(2) was amended in 1988 to prevent duplication of papers and so to save money. For "business days" in r. 3.27(3), see r. 13.13(1).

3.28 Information from receiver

3.28(1) **[Notice to administrative receiver]** Where the committee resolves to require the attendance of the administrative receiver under section 49(2), the notice to him shall be in writing signed by the majority of the members of the committee for the time being. A member's representative may sign for him.

3.28(2) **[Time and place of meeting]** The meeting at which the receiver's attendance is required shall be fixed by the committee for a business day, and shall be held at such time and place as he determines.

3.28(3) **[Chairman]** Where the receiver so attends, the members of the committee may elect any one of their number to be chairman of the meeting, in place of the receiver or any nominee of his.

GENERAL NOTE

This provides essential procedural guidance on the operation of IA 1986, s. 49(2). "Business day" (r. 3.28(2)) is defined in r. 13.13(1).

3.29 Expenses of members

3.29(1) **[Expenses defrayed out of assets]** Subject as follows, the administrative receiver shall out of the assets of the company defray any reasonable travelling expenses directly incurred by members of the creditors' committee or their representatives in relation to their attendance at the committee's meetings, or otherwise on the committee's business, as an expense of the receivership.

3.29(2) **[Non-application of r. 3.29(1)]** Paragraph (1) does not apply to any meeting of the committee held within 3 months of a previous meeting, unless the meeting in question is summoned at the instance of the administrative receiver.

3.30 Members' dealings with the company

3.30(1) **[Effect of membership]** Membership of the committee does not prevent a person from dealing with the company while the receiver is acting, provided that any transactions in the course of such dealings are entered into in good faith and for value.

3.30(2) **[Court may set aside transaction]** The court may, on the application of any person interested, set aside a transaction which appears to it to be contrary to the requirements of this Rule, and may give such consequential directions as it thinks fit for compensating the company for any loss which it may have incurred in consequence of the transaction.

GENERAL NOTE

This allows committee members to deal with the company in good faith and for value. The court can invalidate transactions entered into in breach of this provision. Surely this power of invalidation would have been better located within the Insolvency Act itself.

3.30A Formal defects

3.30A The acts of the creditors' committee established for any administrative receivership are valid notwithstanding any defect in the appointment, election or qualifications of any member of the committee or any committee-member's representative or in the formalities of its establishment.

GENERAL NOTE

Rule 3.30A (which was inserted in 1988) reflects a common philosophy in the new insolvency legislation: see, for example, s. 377 of the Act and rr. 6.156(7) and 7.55. The insertion of rr. 2.46A and 4.172A has a similar rationale.

CHAPTER 5

THE ADMINISTRATIVE RECEIVER (MISCELLANEOUS)

3.31 Disposal of charged property

3.31(1) **[Application of Rule]** The following applies where the administrative receiver applies to the court under section 43(1) for authority to dispose of property of the company which is subject to a security.

3.31(2) [Venue for hearing] The court shall fix a venue for the hearing of the application, and the receiver shall forthwith give notice of the venue to the person who is the holder of the security.

3.31(3) [Notice of s. 43(1) order] If an order is made under section 43(1), the receiver shall forthwith give notice of it to that person.

3.31(4) [Sealed copies of order] The court shall send 2 sealed copies of the order to the receiver, who shall send one of them to that person.

GENERAL NOTE

This clarifies the position where applications are made by the administrative receiver to the court under IA 1986, s. 43(1). For "venue" in r. 3.31(2) see r. 13.6.

3.32 Abstract of receipts and payments

3.32(1) [Administrative receiver to send accounts etc.] The administrative receiver shall–

(a) within 2 months after the end of 12 months from the date of his appointment, and of every subsequent period of 12 months, and

(b) within 2 months after he ceases to act as administrative receiver,

send to the registrar of companies, to the company and to the person by whom he was appointed, and to each member of the creditors' committee (if there is one), the requisite accounts of his receipts and payments as receiver.

[FORM 3.6]

3.32(2) [Extension of time] The court may, on the receiver's application, extend the period of 2 months referred to in paragraph (1).

3.32(3) [Form of abstract] The accounts are to be in the form of an abstract showing–

(a) receipts and payments during the relevant period of 12 months, or

(b) where the receiver has ceased to act, receipts and payments during the period from the end of the last 12-month period to the time when he so ceased (alternatively, if there has been no previous abstract, receipts and payments in the period since his appointment as administrative receiver).

3.32(4) [Effect of Rule] This Rule is without prejudice to the receiver's duty to render proper accounts required otherwise than as above.

3.32(5) [Penalty on default] If the administrative receiver makes default in complying with this Rule, he is liable to a fine and, for continued contravention, to a daily default fine.

GENERAL NOTE

This imposes accounting requirements on the administrative receiver. Compare these with the requirements of IA 1986, s. 38. Rule 3.32(4) preserves the common-law duty to account: see *Smiths Ltd v Middleton* [1979] 3 All E.R. 842. For the sanction in r. 3.32(5), see IR 1986, Sch. 5.

3.33 Resignation

3.33(1) [Notice of intention] Subject as follows, before resigning his office the administrative receiver shall give at least 7 days' notice of his intention to do so to–

(a) the person by whom he was appointed,

(b) the company or, if it is then in liquidation, its liquidator, and

(c) in any case, to the members of the creditors' committee (if any).

3.33(2) [Contents of notice] A notice given under this Rule shall specify the date on which the receiver intends his resignation to take effect.

3.33(3) **[Where no notice necessary]** No notice is necessary if the receiver resigns in consequence of the making of an administration order.

GENERAL NOTE

This expands upon the provisions of IA 1986, s. 45.

3.34 Receiver deceased

3.34 If the administrative receiver dies, the person by whom he was appointed shall, forthwith on his becoming aware of the death, give notice of it to–

(a) the registrar of companies,

[FORM 3.7]

(b) the company or, if it is in liquidation, the liquidator, and

(c) in any case, to the members of the creditors' committee (if any).

3.35 Vacation of office

3.35(1) **[Notice]** The administrative receiver, on vacating office on completion of the receivership, or in consequence of his ceasing to be qualified as an insolvency practitioner, shall forthwith give notice of his doing so–

(a) to the company or, if it is in liquidation, the liquidator, and

(b) to the members of the creditors' committee (if any).

3.35(2) **[Indorsement on notice]** Where the receiver's office is vacated, the notice to the registrar of companies which is required by section 45(4) may be given by means of an indorsement on the notice required by section 405(2) of the Companies Act (notice for the purposes of the register of charges).

GENERAL NOTE

This rule should be viewed in the light of IA 1986, s. 45. As a result of CA 1989, at some unspecified time in the future CA 1985, s. 405(2) will be renumbered as s. 409(2).

CHAPTER 6

VAT BAD DEBT RELIEF

3.36 Issue of certificate of insolvency

3.36(1) **[Duty of administrative receiver]** In accordance with this Rule, it is the duty of the administrative receiver to issue a certificate in the terms of paragraph (b) of section 22(3) of the Value Added Tax Act 1983 (which specifies the circumstances in which a company is deemed insolvent for the purposes of that section) forthwith upon his forming the opinion described in that paragraph.

3.36(2) **[Contents of certificate]** There shall in the certificate be specified–

(a) the name of the company and its registered number;

(b) the name of the administrative receiver and the date of his appointment; and

(c) the date on which the certificate is issued.

3.36(3) **[Title of certificate]** The certificate shall be intituled "CERTIFICATE OF INSOLVENCY FOR THE PURPOSES OF SECTION 22(3)(B) OF THE VALUE ADDED TAX ACT 1983".

GENERAL NOTE

This obliges the administrative receiver to issue a certificate of insolvency for the purposes of VAT bad debt relief. See the note to r. *2.56.*

3.37 Notice to creditors

3.37(1) **[Time for giving notice]** Notice of the issue of the certificate shall be given by the administrative receiver within 3 months of his appointment or within 2 months of issuing the certificate, whichever is the later, to all of the company's unsecured creditors of whose address he is then aware and who have, to his knowledge, made supplies to the company, with a charge to value added tax, at any time before his appointment.

3.37(2) **[Later notice]** Thereafter, he shall give the notice to any such creditor of whose address and supplies to the company he becomes aware.

3.37(3) **[No obligation re certificate]** He is not under obligation to provide any creditor with a copy of the certificate.

GENERAL NOTE

This provides for dissemination of the fact of the issue of the certificate under r. 3.36 to creditors and suppliers.

3.38 Preservation of certificate with company's records

3.38(1) **[Retention of certificate]** The certificate shall be retained with the company's accounting records, and section 222 of the Companies Act (where and for how long records are to be kept) shall apply to the certificate as it applies to those records.

3.38(2) **[Duty of administrative receiver]** It is the duty of the administrative receiver, on vacating office, to bring this Rule to the attention of the directors or (as the case may be) any successor of his as receiver.

CHAPTER 7

SECTION 176A: THE PRESCRIBED PART

3.39 Report to creditors

3.39(1) **[Application of r. 3.39]** This Rule applies where–

(a) a receiver (other than an administrative receiver) is appointed by the court or otherwise under a charge which as created was a floating charge; and

(b) section 176A applies.

3.39(2) **[Notice of appointment and report]**Within 3 months (or such longer period as the court may allow) of the date of his appointment the receiver shall send to creditors, details of whose names and addresses are available to him, notice of his appointment and a report which will include the following matters–

(a) to the best of the receiver's knowledge and belief–

(i) an estimate of the value of the prescribed part (whether or not he proposes to make an application to the court under section 176A(5) or section 176A(3) applies); and

(ii) an estimate of the value of company's net property;

(b) whether, and if so, why, he proposes to make an application to court under section 176A(5); and

(c) whether he proposes to present a petition for the winding up of the company.

3.39(3) **[Non-disclosure of seriously prejudicial information]**Nothing in this Rule is to be taken as requiring any such estimate to include any information, the disclosure of which could seriously prejudice the commercial interests of the company. If such information is excluded from the calculation the estimate shall be accompanied by a statement to that effect.

3.39(4) **[Notice in newspaper instead of report]**Where the receiver thinks that it is impracticable to send the report required under paragraph (2) or where full details of the unsecured creditors of the company are not available to him, he may, instead of sending a report as required by this Rule, publish a notice to the same effect in such newspaper as he thinks most appropriate for ensuring that it comes to the notice of the company's unsecured creditors.

3.40 Receiver to deal with prescribed part

3.40 Where Rule 3.39 applies–

(a) the receiver may present a petition for the winding up of the company if the ground of the petition is that in section 122(1)(f);

(b) where a liquidator or administrator has been appointed to the company, the receiver shall deliver up the sums representing the prescribed part to him;

(c) in any other case, the receiver shall apply to the court for directions as to the manner in which he is to discharge his duty under section 176A(2)(a) and shall act in accordance with such directions as are given by the court.

GENERAL NOTE TO RR. 3.39, 3.40

The Insolvency (Amendment) Rules 2003 (SI 2003/1730) inserted a new Chapter 7 to deal with the provision of the prescribed part of the fund for unsecured creditors in cases of receivership. The application of Chapter 7 is defined by rule 3.39(1).

3.39
This rule requires the receiver to keep unsecured creditors informed of the prospects for them of the reserved fund being operated. Note the option of a general newspaper advert where individual notification is not feasible.

3.40
This allows a receiver to present a winding-up petition or take other specified action in order to facilitate the operation of the reserved fund mechanism.

PART 4

COMPANIES WINDING UP

CHAPTER 1

THE SCHEME OF THIS PART OF THE RULES

4.1 Voluntary winding up; winding up by the court

4.1(1) [**Members' voluntary winding up**] In a members' voluntary winding up, the Rules in this Part do not apply, except as follows—

(a) Rule 4.3 applies in the same way as it applies in a creditors' voluntary winding up;

(b) Rule 4.72 (additional provisions concerning meetings in relation to the Financial Services Authority and the scheme manager) applies in the winding up of authorised deposit-takers or former authorised deposit-takers, whether members' or creditors' voluntary or by the court;

(c) Chapters 9 (proof of debts in a liquidation), 10 (secured creditors), 15 (disclaimer) and 18 (special manager) apply wherever, and in the same way as, they apply in a creditors' voluntary winding up;

(d) Section F of Chapter 11 (the liquidator) applies only in a members' voluntary winding up, and not otherwise;

(e) Section G of that Chapter (court's power to set aside certain transactions; rule against solicitation) applies in any winding up, whether members' or creditors' voluntary or by the court;

(f) Rule 4.182A applies only in a members' voluntary winding up, and not otherwise; and

(g) Rule 4.223-CVL (liquidator's statements) applies in the same way as it applies in a creditors' voluntary winding up.

4.1(2) [**Creditors' voluntary winding up and winding up by court**] Subject as follows, the Rules in this Part apply both in a creditors' voluntary winding up and in a winding up by the court; and for this purpose a winding up is treated as a creditors' voluntary winding up if, and from the time when, the liquidator forms the opinion that the company will be unable to pay its debts in full, and determines accordingly to summon a creditors' meeting under section 95.

4.1(3) [**Creditors' voluntary winding up**] The following Chapters, or Sections of Chapters, of this Part do not apply in a creditors' voluntary winding up—

Chapter 2 – The statutory demand;

Chapter 3 – Petition to winding-up order;

Chapter 4 – Petition by contributories;

Chapter 5 – Provisional liquidator;

Chapter 11 (Section F) – The liquidator in a members' voluntary winding up;

Chapter 13 – The liquidation committee where winding up follows immediately on administration;

Chapter 16 – Settlement of list of contributories;

Chapter 17 – Calls;

Chapter 19 – Public examination of company officers and others; and

Chapter 21 (Section A) – Return of capital;

Chapter 21 (Section C) – Dissolution after winding up.

4.1(4) **["(NO CVL APPLICATION)"]** Where at the head of any Rule, or at the end of any paragraph of a Rule, there appear the words "(NO CVL APPLICATION)", this signifies that the Rule or, as the case may be, the paragraph does not apply in a creditors' voluntary winding up.

However, this does not affect the court's power to make orders under section 112 (exercise in relation to voluntary winding up of powers available in winding up by the court).

4.1(5) **["CVL"]** Where to any Rule or paragraph there is given a number incorporating the letters "CVL", that signifies that the Rule or (as the case may be) the paragraph applies in a creditors' voluntary winding up, and not in a winding up by the court.

4.1(6) **[Provisions of Pt 4 not applicable in CVL following administration]** In a voluntary winding-up which is commenced by the registration of a notice under paragraph 83(3) of Schedule B1 to the Act, the following provisions of this Part shall not apply–

Rules 4.34, 4.38, 4.49, 4.51, 4.53, 4.62, 4.101, 4.103, 4.106, 4.152, 4.153, 4.206–4.210.

GENERAL NOTE

The rules in this Part do not apply to a members' voluntary winding up, except as stated in r. 4.1(1).
Section F of Ch. 11 (rr. 4.139–4.148) applies only in a members' voluntary winding up.
The remaining rules apply generally to both a winding up by the court *and* a creditors' voluntary winding up (including a creditors' voluntary winding up that begins as a members' winding up but later proves insolvent); but some rules or parts of rules apply only in a winding up by the court, and these are marked NO CVL APPLICATION; while others apply only in a creditors' voluntary winding up, and are marked CVL.
Rule 4.1(1)(b) was substituted by the *Financial Services and Markets Act 2000 (Consequential Amendments and Repeals) Order* 2001 (SI 2001/3649) as from 1 December 2001.
Paragraph (6) was inserted by the Insolvency (Amendment) Rules 2003 (SI 2003/1730, effective September 15, 2003), Sch. 1, para. 12. The disapplication of the rules listed is designed as a short cut to the procedure where a creditors' voluntary winding up follows directly upon an administration.

4.2 Winding up by the court: the various forms of petition

(NO CVL APPLICATION)

4.2(1) **[S. 122(1)]** Insofar as the Rules in this Part apply to winding up by the court, they apply (subject as follows) whether the petition for winding up is presented under any of the several paragraphs of section 122(1), namely–

> paragraph (a) – company special resolution for winding up by the court;
>
> paragraph (b) – public company without certificate under section 117 of the Companies Act;
>
> paragraph (c) – old public company;
>
> paragraph (d) – company not commencing business after formation, or suspending business;
>
> paragraph (e) – number of company's members reduced below 2;
>
> paragraph (f) – company unable to pay its debts;
>
> paragraph (fa) – end of moratorium without approval of voluntary arrangement;
>
> paragraph (g) – court's power under the "just and equitable" rule,

or under any enactment enabling the presentation of a winding-up petition.

4.2(2) **[Petitioners]** Except as provided by the following two paragraphs or by any particular Rule, the Rules apply whether the petition for winding up is presented by the company, the directors, one or more creditors, one or more contributories, the Secretary of State, the official receiver, or any person entitled under any enactment to present such a petition.

4.2(3) **[Application of Ch. 2]** Chapter 2 (statutory demand) has no application except in relation to an unpaid creditor of the company satisfying section 123(1)(a) (the first of the two cases specified, in relation to England and Wales, of the company being deemed unable to pay its debts within section 122(1)(f)) or section 222(1) (the equivalent provision in relation to unregistered companies).

4.2(4) **[Application of Ch. 3 and 4]** Chapter 3 (petition to winding-up order) has no application to a petition for winding up presented by one or more contributories; and in relation to a petition so presented Chapter 4 has effect.

GENERAL NOTE

Rule 4.2(1) lists all the circumstances in which a company may be wound up by the court, and r. 4.2(2) all the possible petitioners: see IA 1986, ss. 122, 124. Where a receiver or administrator or the supervisor of a voluntary arrangement petitions, he does so in the name of the company: see the note to s. 124.

The reference to para. (fa) of s. 122(1) was inserted by the Insolvency (Amendment) (No. 2) Rules 2002 (SI 2002/2712, effective January 1, 2003), r. 1.4(1) and Sch. Pt 2, para. 22.

4.3 Time-limits

4.3 Where by any provision of the Act or the Rules about winding up, the time for doing anything is limited, the court may extend the time, either before or after it has expired, on such terms, if any, as it thinks fit.

GENERAL NOTE

See *Practice Direction: Insolvency Proceedings* [2000] B.C.C. 927 (reproduced in Appendix IV of this Guide).

CHAPTER 2

THE STATUTORY DEMAND (NO CVL APPLICATION)

4.4 Preliminary

4.4(1) **[Non-application of Ch. 2]** This Chapter does not apply where a petition for the winding up of a company is presented under section 124 on or after the date on which the Rules come into force and the petition is based on failure to comply with a written demand served on the company before that date.

4.4(2) **["The statutory demand"]** A written demand served by a creditor on a company under section 123(1)(a) (registered companies) or 222(1)(a) (unregistered companies) is known in winding-up proceedings as "the statutory demand".

4.4(3) **[Must be dated and signed]** The statutory demand must be dated, and be signed either by the creditor himself or by a person stating himself to be authorised to make the demand on the creditor's behalf.

(See General Note after r. 4.6.)

4.5 Form and content of statutory demand

4.5(1) **[Form of demand]** The statutory demand must state the amount of the debt and the consideration for it (or, if there is no consideration, the way in which it arises).

[FORM 4.1]

4.5(2) **[Interest and accruing charges]** If the amount claimed in the demand includes–

(a) any charge by way of interest not previously notified to the company as included in its liability, or

(b) any other charge accruing from time to time,

the amount or rate of the charge must be separately identified, and the grounds on which payment of it is claimed must be stated.

In either case the amount claimed must be limited to that which has accrued due at the date of the demand.

(See General Note after r. 4.6.)

4.6 Information to be given in statutory demand

4.6(1) **[Explanation of demand generally]** The statutory demand must include an explanation to the company of the following matters–

(a) the purpose of the demand, and the fact that, if the demand is not complied with, proceedings may be instituted for the winding up of the company;

(b) the time within which it must be complied with, if that consequence is to be avoided; and

(c) the methods of compliance which are open to the company.

4.6(2) **[Information re named individuals]** Information must be provided for the company as to how an officer or representative of it may enter into communication with one or more named individuals, with a view to securing or compounding for the debt to the creditor's satisfaction.

In the case of any individual so named in the demand, his address and telephone number (if any) must be given.

GENERAL NOTE TO RR. 4.4–4.6

This chapter has no application except in relation to an unpaid creditor of the company satisfying IA 1986, s. 123(1)(a) or s. 222(1): see r. 4.2(3).

Under IA 1986, s. 123, a written demand for the payment of a debt must be "in the prescribed form". These rules deal with the form and content of the statutory demand.

A statutory demand may be effective despite some inaccuracy, *e.g.* in relation to the sum stated to be due: see the note to s. 123.

Chapter 3

Petition to Winding-up Order (NO CVL APPLICATION)
(No Application to Petition by Contributories)

4.7 Presentation and filing of petition

4.7(1) [**Filing with verifying affidavit**] The petition, verified by affidavit in accordance with Rule 4.12 below, shall be filed in court.

[FORM 4.2]
[FORM 4.3]

4.7(2) [**When petition not filed**] No petition shall be filed unless there is produced on presentation of the petition a receipt for the deposit payable or paragraph (2A) applies.

4.7(2A) [**Notice of alternative arrangements for payment of deposit**] This paragraph applies in any case where the Secretary of State has given written notice to the court that the petitioner has made suitable alternative arrangements for the payment of the deposit to the official receiver and such notice has not been revoked in relation to the petitioner in accordance with paragraph (2B).

4.7(2B) [**Revocation of r. 4.7(2A) notice**] A notice of the kind referred to in paragraph (2A) may be revoked in relation to the petitioner in whose favour it is given by a further notice in writing to the court stating that the earlier notice is revoked in relation to the petitioner.

4.7(3) [**Petitioner other than company**] If the petitioner is other than the company itself, there shall be delivered with the petition—

(a) one copy for service on the company, and

(b) one copy to be exhibited to the affidavit verifying service.

4.7(4) [**Accompanying documents**] There shall in any case be delivered with the petition—

(a) if the company is in course of being wound up voluntarily, and a liquidator has been appointed, one copy of the petition to be sent to him;

(b) if the company is in administration, one copy to be sent to the administrator;

(c) if an administrative receiver has been appointed in relation to the company, one copy to be sent to him;

(d) if there is in force for the company a voluntary arrangement under Part I of the Act, one copy for the supervisor of the arrangement;

(da) if a member State liquidator has been appointed in main proceedings in relation to the company, one copy to be sent to him; and

(e) if the company is an authorised deposit-taker or a former authorised deposit-taker and the petitioner is not the Financial Services Authority, one copy to be sent to the Authority.

4.7(5) [**Sealed copies issued to petitioner**] Each of the copies delivered shall have applied to it the seal of the court, and shall be issued to the petitioner.

4.7(6) [**Venue for hearing**] The court shall fix a venue for the hearing of the petition; and this shall be endorsed on any copy issued to the petitioner under paragraph (5).

4.7(7) [**Petition by administrator**] Where a petition is filed at the instance of a company's administrator the petition shall—

(a) be expressed to be the petition of the company by its administrator,

(b) state the name of the administrator, the court case number and the date that the company entered administration, and

(c) contain an application under paragraph 79(2) of Schedule B1 to the Act requesting that the appointment of the administrator shall cease to have effect.

4.7(8) **[Filing if in administration or voluntary arrangement]** Any petition filed in relation to a company in respect of which there is in force a voluntary arrangement under Part I of the Act or which is in administration shall be presented to the court to which the nominee's report under section 2 was submitted or the court having jurisdiction for the administration.

4.7(9) **[Treatment of petition of administrator or supervisor]** Any petition such as is mentioned in paragraph (7) above or presented by the supervisor of a voluntary arrangement under Part I of the Act in force for the company shall be treated as if it were a petition filed by contributories, and Chapter 4 in this Part of the Rules shall apply accordingly.

4.7(10) **[Request for appointment under s. 140]** Where a petition contains a request for the appointment of a person as liquidator in accordance with section 140 (appointment of former administrator or supervisor as liquidator) the person whose appointment is sought shall, not less than 2 days before the return day for the petition, file in court a report including particulars of–

(a) a date on which he notified creditors of the company, either in writing or at a meeting of creditors, of the intention to seek his appointment as liquidator, such date to be at least 10 days before the day on which the report under this paragraph is filed, and

(b) details of any response from creditors to that notification, including any objections to his appointment.

(See General Note after r. 4.14.)

4.8 Service of petition

4.8(1) **[Application of Rule]** The following paragraphs apply as regards service of the petition on the company (where the petitioner is other than the company itself); and references to the petition are to a copy of the petition bearing the seal of the court in which it is presented.

4.8(2) **[Service]** Subject as follows, the petition shall be served at the company's registered office, that is to say–

(a) the place which is specified, in the company's statement delivered under section 10 of the Companies Act as the intended situation of its registered office on incorporation, or

(b) if notice has been given by the company to the registrar of companies under section 287 of that Act (change of registered office), the place specified in that notice or, as the case may be, in the last such notice.

4.8(3) **[Means of service]** Service of the petition at the registered office may be effected in any of the following ways–

(a) it may be handed to a person who there and then acknowledges himself to be, or to the best of the server's knowledge, information and belief is, a director or other officer, or employee, of the company; or

(b) it may be handed to a person who there and then acknowledges himself to be authorised to accept service of documents on the company's behalf; or

(c) in the absence of any such person as is mentioned in sub-paragraph (a) or (b), it may be deposited at or about the registered office in such a way that it is likely to come to the notice of a person attending at the office.

4.8(4) **[Service at registered office not practicable etc.]** If for any reason service at the registered office is not practicable, or the company has no registered office or is an unregistered company, the petition may be served on the company by leaving it at the company's last known principal place of business in such a way that it is likely to come to the attention of a person attending there, or by delivering it to the secretary or some director, manager or principal officer of the company, wherever that person may be found.

4.8(5) **[Oversea company]** In the case of an oversea company, service may be effected in any manner provided for by section 695 of the Companies Act.

4.8(6) **[Service in another manner]** If for any reason it is impracticable to effect service as provided by paragraphs (2) to (5), the petition may be served in such other manner as the court may approve or direct.

4.8(7) **[Application under r. 4.8(6)]** Application for leave of the court under paragraph (6) may be made *ex parte*, on affidavit stating what steps have been taken to comply with paragraphs (2) to (5), and the reasons why it is impracticable to effect service as there provided.

Rule 4.8(6)
See *Practice Direction: Insolvency Proceedings* [2000] B.C.C. 927 (reproduced in Appendix IV of this Guide).

(See General Note after r. 4.14.)

4.9 Proof of service

4.9(1) **[Affidavit of service]** Service of the petition shall be proved by affidavit, specifying the manner of service.

[FORM 4.4]
[FORM 4.5]

4.9(2) **[Exhibits]** The affidavit shall have exhibited to it–

(a) a sealed copy of the petition, and

(b) if substituted service has been ordered, a sealed copy of the order;

and it shall be filed in court immediately after service.

(See General Note after r. 4.14.)

4.10 Other persons to receive copies of petition

4.10(1) **[Company being wound up voluntarily]** If to the petitioner's knowledge the company is in course of being wound up voluntarily, a copy of the petition shall be sent by him to the liquidator.

4.10(2) **[Administrative receiver appointed etc.]** If to the petitioner's knowledge an administrative receiver has been appointed in relation to the company, or the company is in administration, a copy of the petition shall be sent by him to the receiver or, as the case may be, the administrator.

4.10(3) **[Voluntary arrangement in force]** If to the petitioner's knowledge there is in force for the company a voluntary arrangement under Part I of the Act, a copy of the petition shall be sent by him to the supervisor of the voluntary arrangement.

4.10(3A) **[Member state liquidator]** If to the petitioner's knowledge, there is a member State liquidator appointed in main proceedings in relation to the company, a copy of the petition shall be sent by him to that person.

This does not apply if the petitioner referred to in this paragraph is a member State liquidator.

4.10(4) **[If company is authorised institution under Banking Act]** If the company is an authorised institution or former authorised institution within the meaning of the Banking Act 1987, a copy of the petition shall be sent by the petitioner to the Financial Services Authority.

This does not apply if the petitioner is the Financial Services Authority itself.

4.10(5) **[Time for sending copy of petition]** A copy of the petition which is required by this Rule to be sent shall be despatched on the next business day after the day on which the petition is served on the company.

(See General Note after r. 4.14.)

4.11 Advertisement of petition

4.11(1) [**Advertisement in Gazette**] Unless the court otherwise directs, the petition shall be advertised once in the Gazette.

[FORM 4.6]

4.11(2) [**Time for advertisement**] The advertisement must be made to appear–

(a) if the petitioner is the company itself, not less than 7 business days before the day appointed for the hearing, and

(b) otherwise, not less than 7 business days after service of the petition on the company, nor less than 7 business days before the day so appointed.

4.11(3) [**Newspaper instead of Gazette**] The court may, if compliance with paragraph (2) is not reasonably practicable, direct that advertisement of the petition be made to appear in a specified newspaper, instead of in the Gazette.

4.11(4) [**Contents of advertisement**] The advertisement of the petition must state–

(a) the name of the company and the address of its registered office, or–

  (i) in the case of an unregistered company, the address of its principal place of business;
  (ii) in the case of an oversea company, the address at which service of the petition was effected;

(b) the name and address of the petitioner;

(c) where the petitioner is the company itself, the address of its registered office or, in the case of an unregistered company, of its principal place of business;

(d) the date on which the petition was presented;

(e) the venue fixed for the hearing of the petition;

(f) the name and address of the petitioner's solicitor (if any); and

(g) that any person intending to appear at the hearing (whether to support or oppose the petition) must give notice of his intention in accordance with Rule 4.16.

4.11(5) [**Court may dismiss petition**] If the petition is not duly advertised in accordance with this Rule, the court may dismiss it.

(See General Note after r. 4.14.)

4.12 Verification of petition

4.12(1) [**Verifying affidavit**] The petition shall be verified by an affidavit that the statements in the petition are true, or are true to the best of the deponent's knowledge, information and belief.

[FORM 4.2]
[FORM 4.3]

4.12(2) [**Debts due to different creditors**] If the petition is in respect of debts due to different creditors, the debts to each creditor must be separately verified.

4.12(3) [**Petition to be exhibited**] The petition shall be exhibited to the affidavit verifying it.

4.12(4) **[Who shall make affidavit]** The affidavit shall be made–

(a) by the petitioner (or if there are two or more petitioners, any one of them), or

(b) by some person such as a director, company secretary or similar company officer, or a solicitor, who has been concerned in the matters giving rise to the presentation of the petition, or

(c) by some responsible person who is duly authorised to make the affidavit and has the requisite knowledge of those matters.

4.12(5) **[Where deponent not petitioner]** Where the deponent is not the petitioner himself, or one of the petitioners, he must in the affidavit identify himself and state–

(a) the capacity in which, and the authority by which, he makes it, and

(b) the means of his knowledge of the matters sworn to in the affidavit.

4.12(6) **[Affidavit as prima facie evidence]** The affidavit is prima facie evidence of the statements in the petition to which it relates.

4.12(7) **[Affidavit verifying more than one petition]** An affidavit verifying more than one petition shall include in its title the names of the companies to which it relates and shall set out, in respect of each company, the statements relied on by the petitioner; and a clear and legible photocopy of the affidavit shall be filed with each petition which it verifies.

(See General Note after r. 4.14.)

4.13 Persons entitled to copy of petition

4.13 Every director, contributory or creditor of the company is entitled to be furnished by the solicitor for the petitioner (or by the petitioner himself, if acting in person) with a copy of the petition within 2 days after requiring it, on payment of the appropriate fee.

(See General Note after r. 4.14.)

4.14 Certificate of compliance

4.14(1) **[Filing in court]** The petitioner or his solicitor shall, at least 5 days before the hearing of the petition, file in court a certificate of compliance with the Rules relating to service and advertisement.

[FORM 4.7]

4.14(2) **[Contents of certificate]** The certificate shall show–

(a) the date of presentation of the petition,

(b) the date fixed for the hearing, and

(c) the date or dates on which the petition was served and advertised in compliance with the Rules.

A copy of the advertisement of the petition shall be filed in court with the certificate.

4.14(3) **[Effect of non-compliance]** Non-compliance with this Rule is a ground on which the court may, if it thinks fit, dismiss the petition.

GENERAL NOTE TO RR. 4.7–4.14

These rules deal with the filing, service, advertisement and verification of the petition.

The deposit referred to in r.4.7(2) is fixed at £620 from April 1, 2004. See the Insolvency Proceedings (Fees) Order 2004 (SI 2004/593), art.6(1)(a).

Any director, contributory or creditor of the company is entitled to a copy of the petition on payment of the appropriate fee (r. 4.13).

Rule 4.7(4)(e) was substituted by the Financial Services and Markets Act 2000 (Consequential Amendments and Repeals) Order 2001 (SI 2001/3649) as from December 1, 2001. The draftsman seems to have overlooked the need for similar amendments to r. 4.10(4).

Paragraph (da) was inserted into r. 4.7 and para. (3A) into r. 4.10(3) by the Insolvency (Amendment) Rules 2002 (SI 2002/1307, effective May 31, 2002). Note that the exception to r. 4.10(3A) is not confined to the case where the petitioner is a liquidator appointed in "main" proceedings.

Changes were made to r. 4.7, paras (4)(b), (7)(b), (7)(c) and 8 and to r. 4.10(2) by the Insolvency (Amendment) Rules 2003 (SI 2003/1730, effective September 15, 2003), Sch. 1, paras 13, 14 to reflect the fact that administrators may now also be appointed out of court. Further changes to para. (4)(b) were made, and paras. (2A), (2B) added, by the Insolvency (Amendment) Rules 2004 (SI 2004/584), effective April 1, 2004. The latter allows alternative arrangements to be made for the payment of the deposit.

The court is given a discretion by r. 4.11(5) to dismiss the petition if it has not been duly advertised. It has been the practice of the court since the ruling in *Re Signland Ltd* [1982] 2 All E.R. 609 to strike out any petition where the petitioning creditor has not observed the provisions as to time set out in r. 4.11(2)(b), and in particular where the petition has been advertised without giving the company the prescribed seven days' notice. This is confirmed by para. 2.1 of the *Practice Direction: Insolvency Proceedings* [2000] B.C.C. 927 (reproduced as Appendix IV to this *Guide*). If the court, in its discretion, grants an adjournment instead of dismissing the petition, this will be on the condition that the petition is advertised in due time for the adjourned hearing, and no further adjournment for the purpose of advertisement will be granted.

Rule 4.14 must be complied with even if the advertisement is defective in any way or if the petitioner decides not to pursue the petition (*e.g.* on receiving payment) (*ibid.*, para. 2(2)). Paragraph 3(1) of the same practice direction extends the time laid down by r. 4.14 for filing a certificate of compliance to not later than 4.30 p.m. on the Friday preceding the day on which the petition is to be heard. Applications to file later will only be allowed if good reason is shown for the delay.

The factors which the court will take into account in considering whether to order a restraint on advertisement were examined in *Re a Company No. 007923 of 1994* [1995] 1 W.L.R. 953; [1995] B.C.C. 634. In addition to satisfying the court that there was not likely to be any significant damage to the company's creditors, contributories and current trading partners, it was held that company needed to show that advertisement might cause serious damage to its reputation and financial stability.

The word "advertised" has two meanings: (1) a paid announcement in a general publication, and (2) notifying the existence of the matter in question. Where the court has made an order restraining the advertisement of a winding-up petition, the word is to be construed in a wide sense, and any communication to an unauthorised party (*e.g.* informing the company's bank) of the fact that the petition has been presented will be a breach of the order: see the note to r. 4.23(1)(c). However in rr. 4.11 and 4.14 the word refers to publication in the *Gazette* – i.e. is used in the former sense (*S N Group plc v Barclays Bank plc* [1993] B.C.C. 506), and a notification to a third party of the existence of the petition will not in itself be a breach of r. 4.11 or 4.14. The Court of Appeal in *Secretary of State for Trade and Industry v North West Holdings plc* [1998] B.C.C. 997 approved *S N Group v Barclays Bank* and held that press notices by the Department of Trade and Industry stating that a winding-up petition had been presented and provisional liquidator appointed to a company were not in breach of r. 4.11, although Chadwick L.J. warned the DTI that if it were in any doubt whether it was appropriate to issue a press notice then directions from the court should be sought. A communication to a third party, may, however be open to condemnation as an abuse of the process of the court, if made for an improper purpose such as putting pressure on the company: if so, the petition may be struck out for this reason (*Re Bill Hennessy Associates Ltd* [1992] B.C.C. 386).

The court has a discretion under r. 4.11(1) to restrain or dispense altogether with advertising, which it may do (*e.g.*) in order to enable presentation of a petition for an administration order (*Re a Company (No. 001448 of 1989)* [1989] B.C.L.C. 715) but otherwise, unless the petition is held to constitute an abuse of the process of the court, this discretion will be exercised only in exceptional circumstances: *Applied Data Base Ltd v Secretary of State for Trade & Industry* [1995] 1 B.C.L.C. 272.

Rule 4.7(7) goes some way to meet drafting deficiencies in the Act, but it does not deal with the case of a petition instituted by an administrative receiver (as might have been expected) or meet all the problems that may arise with a supervisor's petition under IA 1986, s. 7(4)(b). See the note to s. 124(1).

The procedure on a petition presented by contributories is set out in Ch. 4 (rr. 4.22ff.).

Rule 4.8(4) enables service to be effected more easily on a company which has ceased trading.

An application to restrain the presentation of a winding-up petition should be by originating application made to the judge: see the *Practice Direction* (above) at para. 8(1).

4.15 Leave for petitioner to withdraw

4.15 If at least 5 days before the hearing the petitioner, on an *ex parte* application, satisfies the court that–

(a) the petition has not been advertised, and

(b) no notices (whether in support or in opposition) have been received by him with reference to the petition, and

(c) the company consents to an order being made under this Rule, the court may order that the petitioner has leave to withdraw the petition on such terms as to costs as the parties may agree.

[FORM 4.8]

GENERAL NOTE

The circumstances in which a petition may be withdrawn are limited to those prescribed. See *Practice Direction: Insolvency Proceedings* [2000] B.C.C. 927 (reproduced in Appendix IV to this *Guide*).

4.16 Notice of appearance

4.16(1) [**Notice of intention**] Every person who intends to appear on the hearing of the petition shall give to the petitioner notice of his intention in accordance with this Rule.

[FORM 4.9]

4.16(2) [**Contents of notice**] The notice shall specify–

(a) the name and address of the person giving it, and any telephone number and reference which may be required for communication with him or with any other person (to be also specified in the notice) authorised to speak or act on his behalf;

(b) whether his intention is to support or oppose the petition; and

(c) the amount and nature of his debt.

4.16(3) [**Address for sending notice**] The notice shall be sent to the petitioner at the address shown for him in the court records, or in the advertisement of the petition required by Rule 4.11; or it may be sent to his solicitor.

4.16(4) [**Time for sending notice**] The notice shall be sent so as to reach the addressee not later than 16.00 hours on the business day before that which is appointed for the hearing (or, where the hearing has been adjourned, for the adjourned hearing).

4.16(5) [**Effect of non-compliance**] A person failing to comply with this Rule may appear on the hearing of the petition only with the leave of the court.

(See General Note after r. 4.21A.)

4.17 List of appearances

4.17(1) [**Petitioner to prepare list**] The petitioner shall prepare for the court a list of the persons (if any) who have given notice under Rule 4.16, specifying their names and addresses and (if known to him) their respective solicitors.

[FORM 4.10]

4.17(2) [**Whether creditors support or oppose**] Against the name of each creditor in the list it shall be stated whether his intention is to support the petition, or to oppose it.

4.17(3) [**Copy of list handed to court**] On the day appointed for the hearing of the petition, a copy of the list shall be handed to the court before the commencement of the hearing.

4.17(4) [**Leave under r. 4.16(5)**] If any leave is given under Rule 4.16(5), the petitioner shall add to the list the same particulars in respect of the person to whom leave has been given.

(See General Note after r. 4.21A.)

4.18 Affidavit in opposition

4.18(1) [**Filing in court**] If the company intends to oppose the petition, its affidavit in opposition shall be filed in court not less than 7 days before the date fixed for the hearing.

4.18(2) [Copy to petitioner] A copy of the affidavit shall be sent by the company to the petitioner, forthwith after filing.

(See General Note after r. 4.21A.)

4.19 Substitution of creditor or contributory for petitioner

4.19(1) [Application of Rule] This Rule applies where a person petitions and is subsequently found not entitled to do so, or where the petitioner–

(a) fails to advertise his petition within the time prescribed by the Rules or such extended time as the court may allow, or

(b) consents to withdraw his petition, or to allow it to be dismissed, consents to an adjournment, or fails to appear in support of his petition when it is called on in court on the day originally fixed for the hearing, or on a day to which it is adjourned, or

(c) appears, but does not apply for an order in the terms of the prayer of his petition.

4.19(2) [Power of court] The court may, on such terms as it thinks just, substitute as petitioner any creditor or contributory who in its opinion would have a right to present a petition, and who is desirous of prosecuting it.

4.19(2A) [Appointment of member State liquidator] Where a member State liquidator has been appointed in main proceedings in relation to the company, without prejudice to paragraph (2), the court may, on such terms as it thinks just, substitute the member State liquidator as petitioner, where he is desirous of prosecuting the petition.

4.19(3) [Making of order] An order of the court under this Rule may, where a petitioner fails to advertise his petition within the time prescribed by these Rules, or consents to withdraw his petition, be made at any time.

GENERAL NOTE

See *Practice Direction: Insolvency Proceedings* [2000] B.C.C. 927 (reproduced in Appendix IV to this *Guide*). See also General Note after r. 4.21A.

Paragraph (2A) was inserted into r. 4.19 by the Insolvency (Amendment) Rules 2002 (SI 2002/1307, effective May 31, 2002). It will apply only where the debtor company's centre of main interests is situated in another EU Member State.

4.20 Notice and settling of winding-up order

4.20(1) [Notice to official receiver] When a winding-up order has been made, the court shall forthwith give notice of the fact to the official receiver.

[FORM 4.11]
[FORM 4.12]
[FORM 4.13]

4.20(2) [Documents to be left at court] The petitioner and every other person who has appeared on the hearing of the petition shall, not later than the business day following that on which the order is made, leave at the court all the documents required for enabling the order to be completed forthwith.

4.20(3) [Appointment of venue] It is not necessary for the court to appoint a venue for any person to attend to settle the order, unless in any particular case the special circumstances make an appointment necessary.

(See General Note after r. 4.21A.)

4.21 Transmission and advertisement of order

4.21(1) [Copy of orders to official receiver] When the winding-up order has been made, 3 copies of it, sealed with the seal of the court, shall be sent forthwith by the court to the official receiver.

The Insolvency Rules 1986   *Rule 4.22*

4.21(2) **[Service on company etc.]** The official receiver shall cause a sealed copy of the order to be served on the company by prepaid letter addressed to it at its registered office (if any) or, if there is no registered office, at its principal or last known principal place of business.

Alternatively, the order may be served on such other person or persons, or in such other manner, as the court directs.

4.21(3) **[Copy of order to registrar]** The official receiver shall forward to the registrar of companies the copy of the order which by section 130(1) is directed to be so forwarded by the company.

4.21(4) **[Advertisement]** The official receiver shall forthwith–

(a)   cause the order to be gazetted, and

(b)   advertise the order in such newspaper as the official receiver may select.

(See General Note after r. 4.21A.)

4.21A   **Expenses of voluntary arrangement**

4.21A   Where a winding-up order is made and there is at the time of the presentation of the petition in force for the company a voluntary arrangement under Part I of the Act, any expenses properly incurred as expenses of the administration of the arrangement in question shall be a first charge on the company's assets.

GENERAL NOTE TO RR. 4.16–4.21A

These rules deal with the conduct of the hearing, and the steps which are to be taken once a winding-up order has been made. This includes the registration of a copy of the winding-up order in the Companies Registry.

Where the court orders the rescission of a winding-up order under r. 7.47, the registrar of companies may be directed to remove the order from his files; but he may, if he thinks it desirable, record the fact that it has been removed in a note: *Re Calmex Ltd* (1988) 4 B.C.C. 761.

For an example of the exercise of the court's discretion under r. 4.16(5), see *Re Dollar Land (Feltham) Ltd* [1995] B.C.C. 740. (Note that "appear" in this paragraph and elsewhere in r. 4.16 means "have a right of audience": *Re Piccadilly Property Management Ltd* [2000] B.C.C. 44, at p. 50.)

A petition presented in the name of a non-existent person is a nullity, but this is to be distinguished from the case where the petitioner exists but is merely misnamed, which can be dealt with by an application to amend: *Re Goldthorpe & Lacey Ltd* (1987) 3 B.C.C. 595 – a case which also illustrates the exercise of the court's discretion to substitute a petitioner under r. 4.19(2).

Where a winding-up order is made against a company which is subject to a CVA, the funds in the hands of the supervisor will in many cases be subject to a trust in favour of the CVA creditors: see the note to IA 1986, s. 7(4). Rule 4.21A does not carry the implication that in all cases the funds in a CVA should pass to the liquidator: the rule is only designed to ensure that the supervisor will obtain his expenses if the effect of a particular winding up is to discharge the CVA and any trust thereunder (see *Re NT Gallagher & Sons Ltd* [2002] EWCA Civ 404; [2002] 1 W.L.R. 2380; [2002] B.C.C. 867).

Rule 1.33(4) (introduced by the Insolvency (Amendment) Rules 2002 (SI 2002/1307, effective May 31, 2002)) makes provision similar to r. 4.21A for the case where the court makes an order converting a CVA into a winding-up in accordance with the EC Regulation, Art. 37.

CHAPTER 4

PETITION BY CONTRIBUTORIES (NO CVL APPLICATION)

4.22   **Presentation and service of petition**

4.22(1) **[Form of petition and filing in court]** The petition shall specify the grounds on which it is presented and shall be filed in court with one copy for service under this Rule.

[FORM 4.14]

4.22(1A) **[Deposit receipt to be produced]** No petition shall be filed unless there is produced with it the receipt for the deposit payable on presentation.

4.22(2) **[Fixing return day]** The court shall fix a hearing for a day ("the return day") on which, unless the court otherwise directs, the petitioner and the company shall attend before the registrar in chambers for directions to be given in relation to the procedure on the petition.

4.22(3) **[Copy of petition for service]** On fixing the return day, the court shall return to the petitioner a sealed copy of the petition for service, endorsed with the return day and time of hearing.

4.22(4) **[Service on company]** The petitioner shall, at least 14 days before the return day, serve a sealed copy of the petition on the company.

4.22(5) **[Appointment of member State liquidator]** Where a member State liquidator has been appointed in main proceedings in relation to the company, the petitioner shall send a copy of the petition to him.

(See General Note after r. 4.24.)

4.23 Return of petition

4.23(1) **[Directions]** On the return day, or at any time after it, the court shall give such directions as it thinks appropriate with respect to the following matters–

- (a) service of the petition, whether in connection with the venue for a further hearing, or for any other purpose;
- (b) whether particulars of claim and defence are to be delivered, and generally as to the procedure on the petition;
- (c) whether, and if so by what means, the petition is to be advertised;
- (d) the manner in which any evidence is to be adduced at any hearing before the judge and in particular (but without prejudice to the generality of the above) as to–
    - (i) the taking of evidence wholly or in part by affidavit or orally;
    - (ii) the cross-examination of any deponents to affidavits;
    - (iii) the matters to be dealt with in evidence;
- (e) any other matter affecting the procedure on the petition or in connection with the hearing and disposal of the petition.

4.23(2) **[Directions under r. 4.23(1)(a)]** In giving directions under paragraph (1)(a), the court shall have regard to whether any of the persons specified in Rule 4.10 should be served with a copy of the petition.

(See General Note after r. 4.24.)

4.24 Application of Rules in Chapter 3

4.24 The following Rules in Chapter 3 apply, with the necessary modifications–

Rule 4.16 (notice of appearance);

Rule 4.17 (list of appearances);

Rule 4.20 (notice and settling of winding-up order);

Rule 4.21 (transmission and advertisement of order); and

Rule 4.21A (expenses of voluntary arrangement)

GENERAL NOTE TO RR. 4.22–4.24

The procedure to be followed on a contributory's petition is generally the same as that for other petitions, with the modifications set out here. Directions from the court regarding the service, advertisement and hearing of the petition must be sought in every case. If the petition is advertised prematurely the court may order that the petition be struck out and removed from the court file: *Re a Company (No. 007020 of 1996)* [1998] 2 B.C.L.C. 54.

The word "advertised" has two meanings: primarily, a paid announcement in a general publication, but also notifying the existence of the matter in question in any way. Where the court has made an order restraining the advertisement of a winding-up petition under r. 4.23(1)(c), the word may be construed in the latter sense, and any communication to an unauthorised party (*e.g.* informing the company's bank) of the fact that the petition has been presented will be a breach of the order (*Re a Company No. 00687 of 1991* [1991] B.C.C. 210). It may also be an abuse of the process of the court to engage in premature advertisement of a contributories' petition, *e.g.* by telling the company's bank and trading partners that a petition has been or will be presented: *Re Doreen Boards Ltd* [1996] 1 B.C.L.C. 501. (See also the note to r. 4.11, above.)

Paragraph (5) was inserted into r. 4.22 by the Insolvency (Amendment) Rules 2002 (SI 2002/1307, effective May 31, 2002). It will apply only where the debtor company's centre of main interests is situated in another EU Member State.

CHAPTER 5

PROVISIONAL LIQUIDATOR (NO CVL APPLICATION)

4.25 Appointment of provisional liquidator

4.25(1) **[Who may apply to court]** An application to the court for the appointment of a provisional liquidator under section 135 may be made by–

(a) the petitioner;

(b) a creditor of the company;

(c) a contributory;

(d) the company;

(e) the Secretary of State;

(f) a temporary administrator;

(g) a member State liquidator appointed in main proceedings; or

(h) any person who under any enactment would be entitled to present a petition for the winding up of the company.

4.25(2) **[Supporting affidavit]** The application must be supported by an affidavit stating–

(a) the grounds on which it is proposed that a provisional liquidator should be appointed;

(b) if some person other than the official receiver is proposed to be appointed, that the person has consented to act and, to the best of the applicant's belief, is qualified to act as an insolvency practitioner in relation to the company;

(c) whether or not the official receiver has been informed of the application and, if so, has been furnished with a copy of it;

(d) whether to the applicant's knowledge–

   (i) there has been proposed or is in force for the company a voluntary arrangement under Part I of the Act, or

   (ii) an administrator or administrative receiver is acting in relation to the company, or

   (iii) a liquidator has been appointed for its voluntary winding up; and

(e) the applicant's estimate of the value of the assets in respect of which the provisional liquidator is to be appointed.

4.25(3) **[Copies to official receiver etc.]** The applicant shall send copies of the application and of the affidavit in support to the official receiver, who may attend the hearing and make any representations which he thinks appropriate.

If for any reason it is not practicable to comply with this paragraph, the official receiver must be informed of the application in sufficient time for him to be able to attend.

4.25(4) **[Powers of court]** The court may on the application, if satisfied that sufficient grounds are shown for the appointment, make it on such terms as it thinks fit.

(See General Note after r. 4.31.)

4.25A Notice of appointment

4.25A(1) **[Notice to official receiver]** Where a provisional liquidator has been appointed the court shall forthwith give notice of the fact to the official receiver.

4.25A(2) **[Copy to provisional liquidator]** A copy of that notice shall at the same time be sent by the court to the provisional liquidator where he is not the official receiver.

[FORM 4.14A]

(See General Note after r. 4.31.)

4.26 Order of appointment

4.26(1) **[Form of order]** The order appointing the provisional liquidator shall specify the functions to be carried out by him in relation to the company's affairs.

[FORM 4.15]

4.26(2) **[Sealed copies]** The court shall, forthwith after the order is made, send sealed copies of the order as follows–

(a) if the official receiver is appointed, two copies to him;

(b) if a person other than the official receiver is appointed–

    (i) two copies to that person, and
    (ii) one copy to the official receiver;

(c) if there is an administrative receiver acting in relation to the company, one copy to him.

4.26(3) **[One r. 4.26(2) copy sent to company or liquidator]** Of the two copies of the order sent to the official receiver under paragraph (2)(a), or to another person under paragraph (2)(b)(i), one shall in each case be sent by the recipient to the company or, if a liquidator has been appointed for the company's voluntary winding up, to him.

(See General Note after r. 4.31.)

4.27 Deposit

4.27(1) **[Security for official receiver's remuneration etc.]** Before an order appointing the official receiver as provisional liquidator is issued, the applicant for it shall deposit with him, or otherwise secure to his satisfaction, such sum as the court directs to cover the official receiver's remuneration and expenses.

4.27(2) **[Insufficiency of deposit etc.]** If the sum deposited or secured subsequently proves to be insufficient, the court may, on application by the official receiver, order that an additional sum be deposited or secured. If the order is not complied with within 2 days after service of it on the person to whom it is directed, the court may discharge the order appointing the provisional liquidator.

4.27(3) **[Repayment of deposit etc.]** If a winding-up order is made after a provisional liquidator has been appointed, any money deposited under this Rule shall (unless it is required by reason of insufficiency of assets for payment of remuneration and expenses of the provisional liquidator) be repaid to the person depositing it (or as that person may direct) out of the assets, in the prescribed order of priority.

(See General Note after r. 4.31.)

4.28 Security

4.28(1) **[Application of Rule]** The following applies where an insolvency practitioner is appointed to be provisional liquidator under section 135.

4.28(2) **[Cost of providing security]** The cost of providing the security required under the Act shall be paid in the first instance by the provisional liquidator; but–

- (a) if a winding-up order is not made, the person so appointed is entitled to be reimbursed out of the property of the company, and the court may make an order on the company accordingly, and

- (b) if a winding-up order is made, he is entitled to be reimbursed out of the assets in the prescribed order of priority.

(See General Note after r. 4.31.)

4.29 Failure to give or keep up security

4.29(1) **[Powers of court]** If the provisional liquidator fails to give or keep up his security, the court may remove him, and make such order as it thinks fit as to costs.

4.29(2) **[Directions for replacement]** If an order is made under this Rule removing the provisional liquidator, or discharging the order appointing him, the court shall give directions as to whether any, and if so what, steps should be taken for the appointment of another person in his place.

(See General Note after r. 4.31.)

4.30 Remuneration

4.30(1) **[To be fixed by court]** The remuneration of the provisional liquidator (other than the official receiver) shall be fixed by the court from time to time on his application.

4.30(2) **[Matters to be taken into account]** In fixing his remuneration, the court shall take into account–

- (a) the time properly given by him (as provisional liquidator) and his staff in attending to the company's affairs;

- (b) the complexity (or otherwise) of the case;

- (c) any respects in which, in connection with the company's affairs, there falls on the provisional liquidator any responsibility of an exceptional kind or degree;

- (d) the effectiveness with which the provisional liquidator appears to be carrying out, or to have carried out, his duties; and

- (e) the value and nature of the property with which he has to deal.

4.30(3) **[Source of payment of remuneration etc.]** Without prejudice to any order the court may make as to costs, the provisional liquidator's remuneration (whether the official receiver or another) shall be paid to him, and the amount of any expenses incurred by him (including the remuneration and expenses of any special manager appointed under section 177) reimbursed–

- (a) if a winding-up order is not made, out of the property of the company; and

- (b) if a winding-up order is made, out of the assets, in the prescribed order of priority, or, in either case (the relevant funds being insufficient), out of the deposit under Rule 4.27.

4.30(3A) **[Power of retention]** Unless the court otherwise directs, in a case falling within paragraph (3)(a) above the provisional liquidator may retain out of the company's property such sums or property as are or may be required for meeting his remuneration and expenses.

4.30(4) **[Provisional liquidator other than official receiver]** Where a person other than the official receiver has been appointed provisional liquidator, and the official receiver has taken any steps for the purpose of obtaining a statement of affairs or has performed any other duty under the Rules, he shall pay the official receiver such sum (if any) as the court may direct.

(See General Note after r. 4.31.)

4.31 Termination of appointment

4.31(1) **[Termination by court]** The appointment of the provisional liquidator may be terminated by the court on his application, or on that of any of the persons specified in Rule 4.25(1).

4.31(2) **[Directions on termination]** If the provisional liquidator's appointment terminates, in consequence of the dismissal of the winding-up petition or otherwise, the court may give such directions as it thinks fit with respect to the accounts of his administration or any other matters which it thinks appropriate.

4.31(3) (Omitted by the Insolvency (Amendment) Rules 1987 (SI 1987/1919), r. 3(1), Sch., Pt 1, para. 44 as from 11 January 1988.)

GENERAL NOTE TO RR. 4.25–4.31

These rules set out the procedure governing an application to the court for the appointment of a provisional liquidator under IA 1986, s. 135, and the associated questions of furnishing a deposit (where the official receiver is appointed) or security (where the provisional liquidator is an insolvency practitioner), and the liquidator's remuneration.

Rule 4.25(1) was substituted by the Insolvency (Amendment) Rules 2002 (SI 2002/1307, effective May 31, 2002), so as to include the persons mentioned in sub-paras (f) and (g).

The court may in an appropriate case refer the fixing of remuneration under r. 4.30 to one or more assessors: *Re Independent Insurance Co. Ltd* [2002] EWHC 1577 (Ch); [2002] 2 B.C.L.C. 709. (For further proceedings, see *Re Independent Insurance Co. Ltd (No. 2)* [2003] EWHC 51 (Ch), [2003] 1 B.C.L.C. 640, where the principles for the fixing of remuneration and making of interim payments are discussed in detail.)

There is no provision in the rules governing the priority in which the remuneration and expenses of a provisional liquidator should be paid, either *vis-à-vis* the company's debts or in relation to each other; but in *Re Grey Marlin Ltd* [2000] B.C.C. 410 and in *Smith v UIC Insurance Co. Ltd* [2001] B.C.C. 11 the rules governing a liquidator's remuneration and expenses were applied by analogy.

The provisions in rr. 4.28 and 4.30 are directory, although subject to the overall discretion conferred by r. 4.31(2) (and formerly also by r. 4.31(3)); and so a court will not normally make an order that an unsuccessful petitioner should pay the remuneration of a provisional liquidator: *Re Walter L Jacob & Co. Ltd* (1987) 3 B.C.C. 532. (See, however, *Re Secure & Provide plc* [1992] B.C.C. 405, where such an order was made against the Secretary of State following the failure of a petition under s. 124A, and compare *Re Xyllyx plc (No. 2)* [1992] B.C.L.C. 378.)

The court has power under r. 4.31(2) to direct that a provisional liquidator who has been discharged before the hearing of the petition shall be paid remuneration out of the company's assets: *Re U O C Corporation, Alipour v U O C Corporation* [1998] B.C.C. 191.

CHAPTER 6

STATEMENT OF AFFAIRS AND OTHER INFORMATION

4.32 Notice requiring statement of affairs

(NO CVL APPLICATION)

4.32(1) [**Application of Rule**] The following applies where the official receiver determines to require a statement of the company's affairs to be made out and submitted to him in accordance with section 131.

[FORM 4.16]

4.32(2) [**Notice**] He shall send notice to each of the persons whom he considers should be made responsible under that section, requiring them to prepare and submit the statement.

4.32(3) [**"The deponents"**] The persons to whom that notice is sent are referred to in this Chapter as "the deponents".

4.32(4) [**Contents of notice**] The notice shall inform each of the deponents–

(a) of the names and addresses of all others (if any) to whom the same notice has been sent;

(b) of the time within which the statement must be delivered;

(c) of the effect of section 131(7) (penalty for non-compliance); and

(d) of the application to him, and to each of the other deponents, of section 235 (duty to provide information, and to attend on the official receiver if required).

4.32(5) [**Instructions for preparation of statement**] The official receiver shall, on request, furnish a deponent with instructions for the preparation of the statement and with the forms required for that purpose.

(See General Note after r. 4.33.)

4.33 Verification and filing

(NO CVL APPLICATION)

4.33(1) [**Form and verification**] The statement of affairs shall be in Form 4.17, shall contain all the particulars required by that form and shall be verified by affidavit by the deponents (using the same form).

[FORM 4.17]

4.33(2) [**Affidavits of concurrence**] The official receiver may require any of the persons mentioned in section 131(3) to submit an affidavit of concurrence, stating that he concurs in the statement of affairs.

4.33(3) [**Affidavit may be qualified**] An affidavit of concurrence made under paragraph (2) may be qualified in respect of matters dealt with in the statement of affairs, where the maker of the affidavit is not in agreement with the deponents, or he considers the statement to be erroneous or misleading, or he is without the direct knowledge necessary for concurring in the statement.

4.33(4) [**Delivery of statement to official receiver**] The statement of affairs shall be delivered to the official receiver by the deponent making the affidavit of verification (or by one of them, if more than one), together with a copy of the verified statement.

4.33(5) [**Delivery of affidavit of concurrence**] Every affidavit of concurrence shall be delivered to the official receiver by the person who makes it, together with a copy.

4.33(6) [**Filing in court**] The official receiver shall file the verified copy of the statement and the affidavits of concurrence (if any) in court.

4.33(7) **[Swearing of affidavit]** The affidavit may be sworn before an official receiver or a deputy official receiver, or before an officer of the Department or the court duly authorised in that behalf.

GENERAL NOTE TO RR. 4.32, 4.33

The statement of affairs referred to in these rules is that which the official receiver may require when an order for winding up or for the appointment of a provisional liquidator has been made.

4.34-CVL   Statement of affairs

4.34-CVL(1) **[Application of Rule]** This Rule applies with respect to the statement of affairs made out by the liquidator under section 95(3) or (as the case may be) by the directors under section 99(1).

[FORM 4.18]
[FORM 4.19]

4.34-CVL(2) **[Made out by liquidator]** Where it is made out by the liquidator, the statement of affairs shall be delivered by him to the registrar of companies within 7 days after the creditors' meeting summoned under section 95(2).

[FORM 4.20]

4.34-CVL(3) **[Made out by directors]** Where it is made out by the directors under section 99(1) the statement of affairs shall be delivered by them to the liquidator in office following the creditors' meeting summoned under section 98 forthwith after that meeting has been held; and he shall, within 7 days, deliver it to the registrar of companies.

[FORM 4.20]

4.34-CVL(4) **[Date where made out by directors]** A statement of affairs under section 99(1) may be made up to a date not more than 14 days before that on which the resolution for voluntary winding up is passed by the company.

(See General Note after r. 4.34A-CVL)

4.34A-CVL   Copy statement of affairs

4.34A-CVL Where a liquidator is nominated by the company at a general meeting held on a day prior to that on which the creditors' meeting summoned under section 98 is held, the directors shall forthwith after his nomination or the making of the statement of affairs, whichever is the later, deliver to him a copy of the statement of affairs.

GENERAL NOTE TO RR. 4.34-CVL, 4.34A-CVL

These rules deal with the registration of the statement of affairs made out in a creditors' voluntary winding up.

4.35   Limited disclosure

(NO CVL APPLICATION)

4.35(1) **[Official receiver may apply to court]** Where the official receiver thinks that it would prejudice the conduct of the liquidation for the whole or part of the statement of affairs to be disclosed, he may apply to the court for an order of limited disclosure in respect of the statement, or any specified part of it.

4.35(2) **[Powers of court]** The court may on the application order that the statement or, as the case may be, the specified part of it be not filed, or that it is to be filed separately and not be open to inspection otherwise than with leave of the court.

GENERAL NOTE

See *Practice Direction: Insolvency Proceedings* [2000] B.C.C. 927 (reproduced in Appendix IV to this *Guide*). See also General Note after r. 4.37.

4.36 Release from duty to submit statement of affairs; extension of time

(NO CVL APPLICATION)

4.36(1) [Exercise of s. 131(5) power] The power of the official receiver under section 131(5) to give a release from the obligation imposed by that section, or to grant an extension of time, may be exercised at the official receiver's own discretion, or at the request of any deponent.

4.36(2) [Deponent may apply to court] A deponent may, if he requests a release or extension of time and it is refused by the official receiver, apply to the court for it.

4.36(3) [Court may dismiss application etc.] The court may, if it thinks that no sufficient cause is shown for the application, dismiss it; but it shall not do so unless the applicant has had an opportunity to attend the court for an *ex parte* hearing, of which he has been given at least 7 days' notice.

If the application is not dismissed under this paragraph, the court shall fix a venue for it to be heard, and give notice to the deponent accordingly.

4.36(4) [Deponent to send notice to official receiver] The deponent shall, at least 14 days before the hearing, send to the official receiver a notice stating the venue and accompanied by a copy of the application, and of any evidence which he (the deponent) intends to adduce in support of it.

4.36(5) [Appearance etc. by official receiver] The official receiver may appear and be heard on the application; and, whether or not he appears, he may file a written report of any matters which he considers ought to be drawn to the court's attention.

If such a report is filed, a copy of it shall be sent by the official receiver to the deponent, not later than 5 days before the hearing.

4.36(6) [Sealed copies of order] Sealed copies of any order made on the application shall be sent by the court to the deponent and the official receiver.

4.36(7) [Applicant's costs] On any application under this Rule the applicant's costs shall be paid in any event by him and, unless the court otherwise orders, no allowance towards them shall be made out of the assets.

(See General Note after r. 4.37.)

4.37 Expenses of statement of affairs

(NO CVL APPLICATION)

4.37(1) [Persons assisting in preparation of statement] If any deponent cannot himself prepare a proper statement of affairs, the official receiver may, at the expense of the assets, employ some person or persons to assist in the preparation of the statement.

4.37(2) [Allowance towards expenses] At the request of any deponent, made on the grounds that he cannot himself prepare a proper statement, the official receiver may authorise an allowance, payable out of the assets, towards expenses to be incurred by the deponent in employing some person or persons to assist him in preparing it.

4.37(3) [Estimate of expenses] Any such request by the deponent shall be accompanied by an estimate of the expenses involved; and the official receiver shall only authorise the employment of a named person or a named firm, being in either case approved by him.

4.37(4) [Authorisation subject to conditions] An authorisation given by the official receiver under this Rule shall be subject to such conditions (if any) as he thinks fit to impose with respect to the manner in which any person may obtain access to relevant books and papers.

4.37(5) [Effect of Rule] Nothing in this Rule relieves a deponent from any obligation with respect to the preparation, verification and submission of the statement of affairs, or to the provision of information to the official receiver or the liquidator.

4.37(6) [Priority of payment out of assets] Any payment out of the assets under this Rule shall be made in the prescribed order of priority.

4.37(7) [Application of r. 4.37(2)–(6)] Paragraphs (2) to (6) of this Rule may be applied, on application to the official receiver by any deponent, in relation to the making of an affidavit of concurrence.

General Note to rr. 4.35–4.37

These rules are concerned with various discretionary powers conferred on the official receiver in regard to the statement of affairs: to apply to the court for an order authorising limited disclosure in the statement of affairs, to grant a release or an extension of time, and to provide a deponent with professional help.

4.38-CVL   Expenses of statement of affairs

4.38-CVL(1) [Payment out of assets] Payment may be made out of the company's assets, either before or after the commencement of the winding up, of any reasonable and necessary expenses of preparing the statement of affairs under section 99.

Any such payment is an expense of the liquidation.

4.38-CVL(2) [Payment before commencement of winding up] Where such a payment is made before the commencement of the winding up, the director presiding at the creditors' meeting held under section 98 shall inform the meeting of the amount of the payment and the identity of the person to whom it was made.

4.38-CVL(3) [Payment by liquidator] The liquidator appointed under section 100 may make such a payment (subject to the next paragraph); but if there is a liquidation committee, he must give the committee at least 7 days' notice of his intention to make it.

4.38-CVL(4) [No payment by liquidator to himself] Such a payment shall not be made by the liquidator to himself, or to any associate of his, otherwise than with the approval of the liquidation committee, the creditors, or the court.

4.38-CVL(5) [Powers of court under r. 4.219] This Rule is without prejudice to the powers of the court under Rule 4.219 (voluntary winding up superseded by winding up by the court).

General Note

In a creditors' voluntary liquidation, the expenses of preparing the statement may be met from the assets, on the authority of the various persons or bodies mentioned.

4.39   Submission of accounts

(NO CVL APPLICATION)

4.39(1) [Request to persons specified in s. 235(3)] Any of the persons specified in section 235(3) shall, at the request of the official receiver, furnish him with accounts of the company of such nature, as at such date, and for such period, as he may specify.

4.39(2) [Beginning of specified period] The period specified may begin from a date up to 3 years preceding the date of the presentation of the winding-up petition, or from an earlier date to which audited accounts of the company were last prepared.

4.39(3) [Accounts for earlier period] The court may, on the official receiver's application, require accounts for any earlier period.

4.39(4) [Application of r. 4.37] Rule 4.37 applies (with the necessary modification) in relation to accounts to be furnished under this Rule as it applies in relation to the statement of affairs.

4.39(5) [Verification and delivery] The accounts shall, if the official receiver so requires, be verified by affidavit and (whether or not so verified) delivered to him within 21 days of the request under paragraph (1), or such longer period as he may allow.

4.39(6) **[Copies to official receiver etc.]** Two copies of the accounts and (where required) the affidavit shall be delivered to the official receiver by whoever is required to furnish them; and the official receiver shall file one copy in court (with the affidavit, if any).

GENERAL NOTE

The official receiver may call for accounts for up to three years past or up to the date of the last audited accounts, or for a longer period on an order of the court.

Professional assistance may be authorised under r. 4.37. The official receiver may call for further disclosure under r. 4.42.

4.40-CVL Submission of accounts

4.40-CVL(1) **[Request to persons specified in s. 235(3)]** Any of the persons specified in section 235(3) shall, at the request of the liquidator, furnish him with accounts of the company of such nature, as at such date, and for such period, as he may specify.

4.40-CVL(2) **[Beginning of specified period]** The specified period for the accounts may begin from a date up to 3 years preceding the date of the resolution for winding up, or from an earlier date to which audited accounts of the company were last prepared.

4.40-CVL(3) **[Verification and delivery]** The accounts shall, if the liquidator so requires, be verified by affidavit and (whether or not so verified) delivered to him, with the affidavit if required, within 21 days from the request under paragraph (1), or such longer period as he may allow.

(See General Note after r. 4.41-CVL.)

4.41-CVL Expenses of preparing accounts

4.41-CVL(1) **[Persons assisting in preparation of accounts]** Where a person is required under Rule 4.40–CVL to furnish accounts, the liquidator may, with the sanction of the liquidation committee (if there is one) and at the expense of the assets, employ some person or persons to assist in the preparation of the accounts.

4.41-CVL(2) **[Allowance towards expenses]** At the request of the person subject to the requirement, the liquidator may, with that sanction, authorise an allowance, payable out of the assets, towards expenses to be incurred by that person in employing others to assist him in preparing the accounts.

4.41-CVL(3) **[Estimate of expenses]** Any such request shall be accompanied by an estimate of the expenses involved; and the liquidator shall only authorise the employment of a named person or a named firm, being in either case approved by him.

GENERAL NOTE TO RR. 4.40-CVL, 4.41-CVL

These rules make provision corresponding to r. 4.39, to apply in a creditors' voluntary liquidation. If accounts are required for a period more than three years back, the court's jurisdiction under IA 1986, s. 112 may be invoked.

4.42 Further disclosure

(NO CVL APPLICATION)

4.42(1) **[Official receiver may require further information]** The official receiver may at any time require the deponents, or any one or more of them, to submit (in writing) further information amplifying, modifying or explaining any matter contained in the statement of affairs, or in accounts submitted in pursuance of the Act or the Rules.

4.42(2) **[Verification and delivery]** The information shall, if the official receiver so directs, be verified by affidavit, and (whether or not so verified) delivered to him within 21 days of the requirement under paragraph (1), or such longer period as he may allow.

4.42(3) **[Copies to official receiver etc.]** Two copies of the documents containing the information and (where verification is directed) the affidavit shall be delivered by the deponent to the official receiver, who shall file one copy in court (with the affidavit, if any).

GENERAL NOTE

This rule should be read in conjunction with rr. 4.32ff. (statement of affairs) and rr. 4.39 (submission of accounts).

CHAPTER 7

INFORMATION TO CREDITORS AND CONTRIBUTORIES

4.43 Reports by official receiver

(NO CVL APPLICATION)

4.43(1) **[Report on winding-up proceedings and state of affairs]** The official receiver shall, at least once after the making of the winding-up order, send a report to creditors and contributories with respect to the proceedings in the winding up, and the state of the company's affairs.

4.43(1A) **[Contents of report]** The official receiver shall also include in the report under paragraph (1)–

(a) to the best of his knowledge and belief–

  (i) an estimate of the value of the prescribed part (whether or not he proposes to make an application to the court under section 176A(5) or section 176A(3) applies);
  (ii) an estimate of the value of the company's net property; and

(b) whether, and if so, why, he proposes to make an application to court under section 176A(5).

4.43(1B) **[Non-disclosure of seriously prejudicial information]** Nothing in this Rule is to be taken as requiring any such estimate to include any information, the disclosure of which could seriously prejudice the commercial interests of the company. If such information is excluded from the calculation the estimate shall be accompanied by a statement to that effect.

4.43(2) **[Copy to court]** The official receiver shall file in court a copy of any report sent under this Chapter.

(See General Note after r. 4.49A.)

4.44 Meaning of "creditors"

4.44 Any reference in this Chapter to creditors is to creditors of the company who are known to the official receiver or (as the case may be) the liquidator or, where a statement of the company's affairs has been submitted, are identified in the statement.

(See General Note after r. 4.49A.)

4.45 Report where statement of affairs lodged

(NO CVL APPLICATION)

4.45(1) **[Report to creditors and contributories]** Where a statement of affairs has been submitted and filed in court, the official receiver shall send out to creditors and contributories a report containing a summary of the statement (if he thinks fit, as amplified, modified or explained by virtue of Rule 4.42) and such observations (if any) as he thinks fit to make with respect to it, or to the affairs of the company in general.

4.45(2) **[Where no need to comply with r. 4.45(1)]** The official receiver need not comply with paragraph (1) if he has previously reported to creditors and contributories with respect to the company's affairs (so far as known to him) and he is of opinion that there are no additional matters which ought to be brought to their attention.

(See General Note after r. 4.49A.)

4.46 Statement of affairs dispensed with

(NO CVL APPLICATION)

4.46(1) **[Application of Rule]** This Rule applies where, in the company's case, release from the obligation to submit a statement of affairs has been granted by the official receiver or the court.

4.46(2) **[Report to creditors and contributories]** As soon as may be after the release has been granted, the official receiver shall send to creditors and contributories a report containing a summary of the company's affairs (so far as within his knowledge), and his observations (if any) with respect to it, or to the affairs of the company in general.

4.46(3) **[Where no need to comply with r. 4.46(2)]** The official receiver need not comply with paragraph (2) if he has previously reported to creditors and contributories with respect to the company's affairs (so far as known to him) and he is of opinion that there are no additional matters which ought to be brought to their attention.

(See General Note after r. 4.49A.)

4.47 General rule as to reporting

(NO CVL APPLICATION)

4.47(1) **[Powers of court]** The court may, on the official receiver's application, relieve him of any duty imposed on him by this Chapter, or authorise him to carry out the duty in a way other than there required.

4.47(2) **[Matters for court to consider]** In considering whether to act under this Rule, the court shall have regard to the cost of carrying out the duty, to the amount of the assets available, and to the extent of the interest of creditors or contributories, or any particular class of them.

GENERAL NOTE

See *Practice Direction: Insolvency Proceedings* [2000] B.C.C. 927 (reproduced in Appendix IV to this *Guide*). See also General Note after r. 4.49A.

4.48 Winding up stayed

(NO CVL APPLICATION)

4.48(1) **[Cessation of official receiver's duty]** If proceedings in the winding up are stayed by order of the court, any duty of the official receiver to send reports under the preceding Rules in this Chapter ceases.

4.48(2) **[Notice of stay]** Where the court grants a stay, it may include in its order such requirements on the company as it thinks fit with a view to bringing the stay to the notice of creditors and contributories.

(See General Note after r. 4.49A.)

4.49-CVL Information to creditors and contributories

4.49-CVL(1) **[Report on meeting]** The liquidator shall, within 28 days of a meeting held under section 95 or 98, send to creditors and contributories of the company–

(a) a copy or summary of the statement of affairs, and

(b) a report of the proceedings at the meeting.

Rule 4.49A

4.49-CVL(2) **[Contents of report]** The report under paragraph (1) shall also include–

(a) to the best of the liquidator's knowledge and belief–

    (i) an estimate of the value of the prescribed part (whether or not he proposes to make an application to court under section 176A(5) or section 176A(3) applies); and

    (ii) an estimate of the value of the company's net property; and

(b) whether, and if so, why, the liquidator proposes to make an application to court under section 176A(5).

4.49-CVL(3) **[Non-disclosure of seriously prejudicial information]** Nothing in this Rule is to be taken as requiring any such estimate to include any information, the disclosure of which could seriously prejudice the commercial interests of the company. If such information is excluded from the calculation the estimate shall be accompanied by a statement to that effect.

(See General Note after r. 4.49A.)

4.49A Further information where liquidation follows administration

4.49A Where under section 140 the court appoints as the company's liquidator a person who was formerly its administrator or a person is appointed as liquidator upon the registration of a notice under paragraph 83(3) of Schedule B1 to the Act and that person becomes aware of creditors not formerly known to him in his capacity as administrator, he shall send to those creditors a copy of any statement or report sent by him to creditors under Rule 2.33, so noted as to indicate that it is being sent under this Rule.

GENERAL NOTE TO R. 4.43–4.49A

These rules are designed to ensure that creditors and contributories are kept informed of the state of the company's affairs in the various situations referred to.

Paragraphs (1A) and (1B) of r. 4.43 and paras (2) and (3) of r. 4.49 were inserted by the Insolvency (Amendment) Rules 2003 (SI 2003/1730, effective September 15, 2003), Sch.1, paras 15, 16. By para. 16 of that Schedule r. 4.49A was amended, *inter alia*, by replacing the former reference to r. 2.16 to r .2.33. Here, "r. 2.16" refers to the original administration regime (which still applies in some administrations) and "r. 2.33" to the new regime.

CHAPTER 8

MEETINGS OF CREDITORS AND CONTRIBUTORIES

Section A: rules of general application

4.50 First meetings

(NO CVL APPLICATION)

4.50(1) **[Venue for meetings etc.]** If under section 136(5) the official receiver decides to summon meetings of the company's creditors and contributories for the purpose of nominating a person to be liquidator in place of himself, he shall fix a venue for each meeting, in neither case more than 4 months from the date of the winding-up order.

4.50(2) **[Notice of meetings]** When for each meeting a venue has been fixed, notice of the meetings shall be given to the court and–

(a) in the case of the creditors' meeting, to every creditor who is known to the official receiver or is identified in the company's statement of affairs; and

(b) in the case of the contributories' meeting, to every person appearing (by the company's books or otherwise) to be a contributory of the company.

4.50(3) **[Time for giving notice]** Notice to the court shall be given forthwith, and the other notices shall be given at least 21 days before the date fixed for each meeting respectively.

4.50(4) **[Contents of notice]** The notice to creditors shall specify a time and date, not more than 4 days before the date fixed for the meeting, by which they must lodge proofs and (if applicable) proxies, in order to be entitled to vote at the meeting; and the same applies in respect of contributories and their proxies.

4.50(5) **[Public advertisement]** Notice of the meetings shall also be given by public advertisement.

4.50(6) **[Request by creditors under s. 136(5)(c)]** Where the official receiver receives a request by creditors under section 136(5)(c) for meetings of creditors and contributories to be summoned, and it appears to him that the request is properly made in accordance with the Act, he shall–

(a) withdraw any notices previously given by him under section 136(5)(b) (that he has decided not to summon such meetings),

(b) fix the venue of each meeting for not more than 3 months from his receipt of the creditors' request, and

(c) act in accordance with paragraphs (2) to (5) above, as if he had decided under section 136 to summon the meetings.

[FORM 4.21]

4.50(7) **[Names of meetings]** Meetings summoned by the official receiver under this Rule are known respectively as "the first meeting of creditors" and "the first meeting of contributories", and jointly as "the first meetings in the liquidation".

4.50(8) **[Where company is authorised deposit-taker]** Where the company is an authorised deposit-taker or a former authorised deposit-taker, additional notices are required by Rule 4.72.

(See General Note after r. 4.71.)

4.51-CVL First meeting of creditors

4.51-CVL(1) **[Application of Rule]** This Rule applies in the case of a meeting of creditors summoned by the liquidator under section 95 (where, in what starts as a members' voluntary winding up, he forms the opinion that the company will be unable to pay its debts) or a meeting under section 98 (first meeting of creditors in a creditors' voluntary winding up).

4.51-CVL(2) **[Contents of notice]** The notice summoning the meeting shall specify a venue for the meeting and the time (not earlier than 12.00 hours on the business day before the day fixed for the meeting) by which, and the place at which, creditors must lodge any proxies necessary to entitle them to vote at the meeting.

4.51-CVL(3) **[Where company is authorised deposit-taker]** Where the company is an authorised deposit-taker or a former authorised deposit-taker, additional notices are required by Rule 4.72.

(See General Note after r. 4.71.)

4.52 Business at first meetings in the liquidation

(NO CVL APPLICATION)

4.52(1) [**Limitation on resolutions at first meeting of creditors**] At the first meeting of creditors, no resolutions shall be taken other than the following–

(a) a resolution to appoint a named insolvency practitioner to be liquidator, or two or more insolvency practitioners as joint liquidators;

(b) a resolution to establish a liquidation committee;

(c) (unless it has been resolved to establish a liquidation committee) a resolution specifying the terms on which the liquidator is to be remunerated, or to defer consideration of that matter;

(d) (if, and only if, two or more persons are appointed to act jointly as liquidator) a resolution specifying whether acts are to be done by both or all of them, or by only one;

(e) (where the meeting has been requisitioned under section 136), a resolution authorising payment out of the assets, as an expense of the liquidation, of the cost of summoning and holding the meeting and any meeting of contributories so requisitioned and held;

(f) a resolution to adjourn the meeting for not more than 3 weeks;

(g) any other resolution which the chairman thinks it right to allow for special reasons.

4.52(2) [**At first meeting of contributories**] The same applies as regards the first meeting of contributories, but that meeting shall not pass any resolution to the effect of paragraph (1)(c) or (e).

4.52(3) [**Limitation at either meeting**] At neither meeting shall any resolution be proposed which has for its object the appointment of the official receiver as liquidator.

(See General Note after r. 4.71.)

4.53-CVL Business at meeting under s. 95 or 98

4.53-CVL Rule 4.52(1), except sub-paragraph (e), applies to a creditors' meeting under section 95 or 98.

(See General Note after r. 4.71.)

4.53A-CVL Effect of adjournment of company meeting

4.53A-CVL Where a company meeting at which a resolution for voluntary winding up is to be proposed is adjourned, any resolution passed at a meeting under section 98 held before the holding of the adjourned company meeting only has effect on and from the passing by the company of a resolution for winding up.

(See General Note after r. 4.71.)

4.53B-CVL Report by director, etc.

4.53B-CVL(1) [**State of company's affairs**] At any meeting held under section 98 where the statement of affairs laid before the meeting does not state the company's affairs as at the date of the meeting, the directors of the company shall cause to be made to the meeting, either by the director presiding at the meeting or by another person with knowledge of the relevant matters, a report (written or oral) on any material transactions relating to the company occurring between the date of the making of the statement of affairs and that of the meeting.

4.53B-CVL(2) **[Recorded in minutes]** Any such report shall be recorded in the minutes of the meeting kept under Rule 4.71.

(See General Note after r. 4.71.)

4.54 General power to call meetings

4.54(1) **[General power, "the convener"]** The official receiver or the liquidator may at any time summon and conduct meetings of creditors or of contributories for the purpose of ascertaining their wishes in all matters relating to the liquidation; and in relation to any meeting summoned under the Act or the Rules, the person summoning it is referred to as "the convener".

4.54(2) **[Notice of venue]** When (in either case) a venue for the meeting has been fixed, notice of it shall be given by the convener–

(a) in the case of a creditors' meeting, to every creditor who is known to him or is identified in the company's statement of affairs; and

[FORM 4.22]

(b) in the case of a meeting of contributories, to every person appearing (by the company's books or otherwise) to be a contributory of the company.

[FORM 4.23]

4.54(3) **[Time for giving notice etc.]** Notice of the meeting shall be given at least 21 days before the date fixed for it, and shall specify the purpose of the meeting.

4.54(4) **[Contents of notice]** The notice shall specify a time and date, not more than 4 days before the date fixed for the meeting, by which, and the place at which, creditors must lodge proofs and proxies, in order to be entitled to vote at the meeting; and the same applies in respect of contributories and their proxies.

(NO CVL APPLICATION)

4.54(5) **[Contents of notice]** The notice shall specify a time and date, not more than 4 days before that fixed for the meeting, by which, and the place at which, creditors (if not individuals attending in person) must lodge proxies, in order to be entitled to vote at the meeting.

4.54(6) **[Additional notice by public advertisement]** Additional notice of the meeting may be given by public advertisement if the convener thinks fit, and shall be so given if the court orders.

(See General Note after r. 4.71.)

4.55 The chairman at meetings

(NO CVL APPLICATION)

4.55(1) **[Application of Rule]** This Rule applies both to a meeting of creditors and to a meeting of contributories.

4.55(2) **[Where convener official receiver]** Where the convener of the meeting is the official receiver, he, or a person nominated by him, shall be chairman.

A nomination under this paragraph shall be in writing, unless the nominee is another official receiver or a deputy official receiver.

4.55(3) **[Where convener not official receiver]** Where the convener is other than the official receiver, the chairman shall be he, or a person nominated in writing by him.

A person nominated under this paragraph must be either–

(a) one who is qualified to act as an insolvency practitioner in relation to the company, or

(b) an employee of the liquidator or his firm who is experienced in insolvency matters.

(See General Note after r. 4.71.)

4.56-CVL The chairman at meetings

4.56-CVL(1) [Application of Rule] This Rule applies both to a meeting of creditors (except a meeting under section 95 or 98) and to a meeting of contributories.

4.56-CVL(2) [Liquidator or his nominee to be chairman] The liquidator, or a person nominated by him in writing to act, shall be chairman of the meeting.

A person nominated under this paragraph must be either–

(a) one who is qualified to act as an insolvency practitioner in relation to the company, or

(b) an employee of the liquidator or his firm who is experienced in insolvency matters.

(See General Note after r. 4.71.)

4.57 Requisitioned meetings

4.57(1) [Documents to accompany creditors' request] Any request by creditors to the liquidator (whether or not the official receiver) for a meeting of creditors or contributories, or meetings of both, to be summoned shall be accompanied by–

(a) a list of the creditors concurring with the request and the amount of their respective claims in the winding up;

(b) from each creditor concurring, written confirmation of his concurrence; and

(c) a statement of the purpose of the proposed meeting.

Sub-paragraphs (a) and (b) do not apply if the requisitioning creditor's debt is alone sufficient, without the concurrence of other creditors.

[FORM 4.21]

4.57(2) [Liquidator to fix venue] The liquidator shall, if he considers the request to be properly made in accordance with the Act, fix a venue for the meeting, not more than 35 days from his receipt of the request.

4.57(3) [Notice of meeting] The liquidator shall give 21 days' notice of the meeting, and the venue for it, to creditors.

4.57(4) [Application of r. 4.57(1)–(3) to contributories' meetings] Paragraphs (1) to (3) above apply to the requisitioning by contributories of contributories' meetings, with the following modifications–

(a) for the reference in paragraph (1)(a) to the creditors' respective claims substitute the contributories' respective values (being the amounts for which they may vote at any meeting); and

(b) the persons to be given notice under paragraph (3) are those appearing (by the company's books or otherwise) to be contributories of the company.

[FORM 4.24]

(NO CVL APPLICATION)

(See General Note after r. 4.71.)

4.58 Attendance at meetings of company's personnel

4.58(1) [Application of Rule] This Rule applies to meetings of creditors and to meetings of contributories.

4.58(2) [Notice to company's personnel] Whenever a meeting is summoned, the convener shall give at least 21 days' notice to such of the company's personnel as he thinks should be told of, or be present at, the meeting.

"The company's personnel" means the persons referred to in paragraphs (a) to (d) of section 235(3) (present and past officers, employees, etc.).

4.58(3) **[Notice of adjournment]** If the meeting is adjourned, the chairman of the meeting shall, unless for any reason he thinks it unnecessary or impracticable, give notice of the adjournment to such (if any) of the company's personnel as he considers appropriate, being persons who were not themselves present at the meeting.

4.58(4) **[Notice that presence required]** The convener may, if he thinks fit, give notice to any one or more of the company's personnel that he is, or they are, required to be present at the meeting, or to be in attendance.

4.58(5) **[Admission to meetings]** In the case of any meeting, any one or more of the company's personnel, and any other persons, may be admitted, but–

(a) they must have given reasonable notice of their wish to be present, and

(b) it is a matter for the chairman's discretion whether they are to be admitted or not, and his decision is final as to what (if any) intervention may be made by any of them.

4.58(6) **[Adjournment for obtaining attendance]** If it is desired to put questions to any one of the company's personnel who is not present, the chairman may adjourn the meeting with a view to obtaining his attendance.

4.58(7) **[Chairman's discretion re questions]** Where one of the company's personnel is present at a meeting, only such questions may be put to him as the chairman may in his discretion allow.

(See General Note after r. 4.71.)

4.59 Notice of meetings by advertisement only

4.59(1) **[Power of court]** In the case of any meeting of creditors or contributories to be held under the Act or the Rules, the court may order that notice of the meeting be given by public advertisement, and not by individual notice to the persons concerned.

4.59(2) **[Matters for court to consider]** In considering whether to act under this Rule, the court shall have regard to the cost of public advertisement, to the amount of the assets available, and to the extent of the interest of creditors or of contributories, or any particular class of either of them.

GENERAL NOTE

See *Practice Direction: Insolvency Proceedings* [2000] B.C.C. 927 (reproduced in Appendix IV to this *Guide*). See also General Note after r. 4.71.

4.60 Venue

4.60(1) **[Convenience of venue]** In fixing the venue for a meeting of creditors or contributories, the convener shall have regard to the convenience of the persons (other than whoever is to be chairman) who are invited to attend.

4.60(2) **[Time of meetings]** Meetings shall in all cases be summoned for commencement between the hours of 10.00 and 16.00 hours on a business day, unless the court otherwise directs.

4.60(3) **[Forms of proxy]** With every notice summoning a meeting of creditors or contributories there shall be sent out forms of proxy.

[FORM 8.4]
or [FORM 8.5]

(See General Note after r. 4.71.)

4.61 Expenses of summoning meetings

4.61(1) **[Deposit for payment of expenses]** Subject as follows, the expenses of summoning and holding a meeting of creditors or contributories at the instance of any person other than the official receiver or the liquidator shall be paid by that person, who shall deposit with the liquidator security for their payment.

4.61(2) **[Appropriate security]** The sum to be deposited shall be such as the official receiver or liquidator (as the case may be) determines to be appropriate; and neither shall act without the deposit having been made.

4.61(3) **[Vote for expenses to be paid out of assets]** Where a meeting of creditors is so summoned, it may vote that the expenses of summoning and holding it, and of summoning and holding any meeting of contributories requisitioned at the same time, shall be payable out of the assets, as an expense of the liquidation.

4.61(4) **[Contributories' meeting]** Where a meeting of contributories is summoned on the requisition of contributories, it may vote that the expenses of summoning and holding it shall be payable out of the assets, but subject to the right of creditors to be paid in full, with interest.

4.61(5) **[Repayment of deposit]** To the extent that any deposit made under this Rule is not required for the payment of expenses of summoning and holding a meeting, it shall be repaid to the person who made it.

(See General Note after r. 4.71.)

4.62-CVL Expenses of meeting under s. 98

4.62-CVL(1) **[Payment out of assets]** Payment may be made out of the company's assets, either before or after the commencement of the winding up, of any reasonable and necessary expenses incurred in connection with the summoning, advertisement and holding of a creditors' meeting under section 98.

Any such payment is an expense of the liquidation.

4.62-CVL(2) **[Payment before commencement of winding up]** Where such payments are made before the commencement of the winding up, the director presiding at the creditors' meeting shall inform the meeting of their amount and the identity of the persons to whom they were made.

4.62-CVL(3) **[Payment by s. 100 liquidator]** The liquidator appointed under section 100 may make such a payment (subject to the next paragraph); but if there is a liquidation committee, he must give the committee at least 7 days' notice of his intention to make the payment.

4.62-CVL(4) **[No payment by liquidator to himself]** Such a payment shall not be made by the liquidator to himself, or to any associate of his, otherwise than with the approval of the liquidation committee, the creditors, or the court.

4.62-CVL(5) **[Powers of court under r. 4.219]** This Rule is without prejudice to the powers of the court under Rule 4.219 (voluntary winding up superseded by winding up by the court).

(See General Note after r. 4.71.)

4.63 Resolutions

4.63(1) **[Resolution passed by majority in value]** Subject as follows, at a meeting of creditors or contributories, a resolution is passed when a majority (in value) of those present and voting, in person or by proxy, have voted in favour of the resolution.

The value of contributories is determined by reference to the number of votes conferred on each contributory by the company's articles.

4.63(2) **[Resolution for appointment of liquidator]** In the case of a resolution for the appointment of a liquidator–

(a) subject to paragraph (2A), if on any vote there are two nominees for appointment, the person who obtains the most support is appointed;

(b) if there are three or more nominees, and one of them has a clear majority over both or all the others together, that one is appointed; and

(c) in any other case, the chairman of the meeting shall continue to take votes (disregarding at each vote any nominee who has withdrawn and, if no nominee has withdrawn, the nominee who obtained the least support last time), until a clear majority is obtained for any one nominee.

4.63(2A) **[Majority in value]** In a winding up by the court the support referred to in paragraph (2)(a) must represent a majority in value of all those present (in person or by proxy) at the meeting and entitled to vote. (NO CVL APPLICATION).

4.63(3) **[Resolution for joint appointment]** The chairman may at any time put to the meeting a resolution for the joint appointment of any two or more nominees.

4.63(4) **[Resolution affecting liquidator etc.]** Where a resolution is proposed which affects a person in respect of his remuneration or conduct as liquidator, or as proposed or former liquidator, the vote of that person, and of any partner or employee of his, shall not be reckoned in the majority required for passing the resolution.

This paragraph applies with respect to a vote given by a person (whether personally or on his behalf by a proxy-holder) either as creditor or contributory or as proxy-holder for a creditor or a contributory (but subject to Rule 8.6 in Part 8 of the Rules).

(See General Note after r. 4.71.)

4.64 Chairman of meeting as proxy-holder

4.64 Where the chairman at a meeting of creditors or contributories holds a proxy which requires him to vote for a particular resolution, and no other person proposes that resolution–

(a) he shall himself propose it, unless he considers that there is good reason for not doing so, and

(b) if he does not propose it, he shall forthwith after the meeting notify his principal of the reason why not.

(See General Note after r. 4.71.)

4.65 Suspension and adjournment

4.65(1) **[Application of Rule]** This Rule applies to meetings of creditors and to meetings of contributories.

4.65(2) **[Suspension at chairman's discretion]** Once only in the course of any meeting, the chairman may, in his discretion and without an adjournment, declare the meeting suspended for any period up to one hour.

4.65(3) **[Adjournment]** The chairman at any meeting may in his discretion, and shall if the meeting so resolves, adjourn it to such time and place as seems to him to be appropriate in the circumstances.

This is subject to Rule 4.113(3) or, as the case may be, 4.114–CVL(3), in a case where the liquidator or his nominee is chairman, and a resolution has been proposed for the liquidator's removal.

4.65(4) **[Adjourned if inquorate]** If within a period of 30 minutes from the time appointed for the commencement of a meeting a quorum is not present, then the chairman may, at his discretion, adjourn the meeting to such time and place as he may appoint.

4.65(5) **[Period of adjournment]** An adjournment under this Rule shall not be for a period of more than 21 days; and Rule 4.60(1) and (2) applies.

4.65(6) **[If no chairman]** If there is no person present to act as chairman, some other person present (being entitled to vote) may make the appointment under paragraph (4), with the agreement of others present (being persons so entitled).

Failing agreement, the adjournment shall be to the same time and place in the next following week or, if that is not a business day, to the business day immediately following.

4.65(7) **[Use of proofs and proxies at adjourned meeting]** Where a meeting is adjourned under this Rule, proofs and proxies may be used if lodged at any time up to midday on the business day immediately before the adjourned meeting.

(See General Note after r. 4.71.)

4.66 Quorum

4.66 (Omitted by the Insolvency (Amendment) Rules 1987 (SI 1987/1919), r. 3(1), Sch., Pt. 1, para. 56 as from 11 January 1988).

4.67 Entitlement to vote (creditors)

4.67(1) **[Conditions for voting]** Subject as follows in this Rule and the next, at a meeting of creditors a person is entitled to vote as a creditor only if–

(a) there has been duly lodged (in a winding up by the court by the time and date stated in the notice of the meeting) a proof of the debt

  (i) claimed to be due to him from the company, or
  (ii) in relation to a member State liquidator, is claimed to be due to creditors in proceedings in relation to which he holds office,

and the claim has been admitted under Rule 4.70 for the purpose of entitlement to vote, and

(b) there has been lodged, by the time and date stated in the notice of the meeting, any proxy requisite for that entitlement.

4.67(2) **[Powers of court]** The court may, in exceptional circumstances, by order declare the creditors, or any class of them, entitled to vote at creditors' meetings, without being required to prove their debts.

Where a creditor is so entitled, the court may, on the application of the liquidator, make such consequential orders as it thinks fit (as for example an order treating a creditor as having proved his debt for the purpose of permitting payment of dividend).

4.67(3) **[Limitation on voting]** A creditor shall not vote in respect of a debt for an unliquidated amount, or any debt whose value is not ascertained, except where the chairman agrees to put upon the debt an estimated minimum value for the purpose of entitlement to vote and admits his proof for that purpose.

4.67(4) **[Secured creditor]** A secured creditor is entitled to vote only in respect of the balance (if any) of his debt after deducting the value of his security as estimated by him.

4.67(5) **[Further limitation on voting]** A creditor shall not vote in respect of a debt on, or secured by, a current bill of exchange or promissory note, unless he is willing–

(a) to treat the liability to him on the bill or note of every person who is liable on it antecedently to the company, and against whom a bankruptcy order has not been made (or, in the case of a company, which has not gone into liquidation), as a security in his hands, and

(b) to estimate the value of the security and (for the purpose of entitlement to vote, but not for dividend) to deduct it from his proof.

4.67(6) [**Still further limitation on voting**] No vote shall be cast by virtue of a debt more than once on any resolution put to the meeting.

4.67(7) [**Creditor's vote**] Where–

(a) a creditor is entitled to vote under this Rule and Rule 4.70 (admission of proof),

(b) has lodged his claim in one or more sets of other proceedings, and

(c) votes (either in person or by proxy) on a resolution put to the meeting,

only the creditor's vote shall be counted.

4.67(8) [**Member State liquidator**] Where–

(a) a creditor has lodged his claim in more than one set of other proceedings, and

(b) more than one member State liquidator seeks to vote by virtue of that claim,

the entitlement to vote by virtue of that claim is exercisable by the member State liquidator in main proceedings, whether or not the creditor has lodged his claim in the main proceedings.

4.67(9) [**"Other proceedings"**] For the purposes of paragraphs (7) and (8), "other proceedings" means main proceedings, secondary proceedings or territorial proceedings in another member State.

(See General Note after r. 4.71.)

4.68-CVL Chairman's discretion to allow vote

4.68-CVL At a creditors' meeting, the chairman may allow a creditor to vote, notwithstanding that he has failed to comply with Rule 4.67(1)(a), if satisfied that the failure was due to circumstances beyond the creditor's control.

(See General Note after r. 4.71.)

4.69 Entitlement to vote (contributories)

4.69 At a meeting of contributories, voting rights are as at a general meeting of the company, subject to any provision in the articles affecting entitlement to vote, either generally or at a time when the company is in liquidation.

(See General Note after r. 4.71.)

4.70 Admission and rejection of proof (creditors' meeting)

4.70(1) [**Power of chairman**] At any creditors' meeting the chairman has power to admit or reject a creditor's proof for the purpose of his entitlement to vote; and the power is exercisable with respect to the whole or any part of the proof.

4.70(2) [**Appeal from chairman's decision**] The chairman's decision under this Rule, or in respect of any matter arising under Rule 4.67, is subject to appeal to the court by any creditor or contributory.

4.70(3) [**Voting subject to objection**] If the chairman is in doubt whether a proof should be admitted or rejected, he shall mark it as objected to and allow the creditor to vote, subject to his vote being subsequently declared invalid if the objection to the proof is sustained.

4.70(4) [**If chairman's decision reversed etc.**] If on an appeal the chairman's decision is reversed or varied, or a creditor's vote is declared invalid, the court may order that another meeting be summoned, or make such other order as it thinks just.

4.70(5) [**Costs re application**] Neither the official receiver, nor any person nominated by him to be chairman, is personally liable for costs incurred by any person in respect of an application under this Rule;

and the chairman (if other than the official receiver or a person so nominated) is not so liable unless the court makes an order to that effect.

(NO CVL APPLICATION)

4.70(6) **[Costs re application]** The liquidator or his nominee as chairman is not personally liable for costs incurred by any person in respect of an application under this Rule, unless the court makes an order to that effect.

(See General Note after r. 4.71.)

4.71 Record of proceedings

4.71(1) **[Minutes of proceedings]** At any meeting, the chairman shall cause minutes of the proceedings to be kept. The minutes shall be signed by him, and retained as part of the records of the liquidation.

4.71(2) **[List of creditors or contributories attending]** The chairman shall also cause to be made up and kept a list of all the creditors or, as the case may be, contributories who attended the meeting.

4.71(3) **[Record of resolutions]** The minutes of the meeting shall include a record of every resolution passed.

4.71(4) **[Chairman's duty to deliver particulars]** It is the chairman's duty to see to it that particulars of all such resolutions, certified by him, are filed in court not more than 21 days after the date of the meeting.

(NO CVL APPLICATION)

GENERAL NOTE TO RR. 4.50–4.71

Rules 4.50(8) and 4.51(3) were substituted by the Financial Services and Markets Act 2000 (Consequential Amendments and Repeals) Order 2001 (SI 2001/3649) as from December 1, 2001.

Sub-paragraph (ii) was inserted into r. 4.67(1)(a) and paras (6)–(9) added by the Insolvency (Amendment) Rules 2002 (SI 2002/1307, effective May 31, 2002). A "liquidator" in insolvency proceedings which have been opened in any Member State is empowered by the EC Regulation, Art. 32(2), (3) to prove in proceedings in another Member State in respect of claims which have been lodged with him, and to attend meetings, etc. as a creditor. This rule, as amended, confirms his right to vote but includes provisions to ensure that a vote in respect of any particular debt is cast only once.

The official receiver has a discretion under IA 1986 whether to summon first meetings. If he decides to do so, the procedure to be followed in a winding up by the court is set out in rr. 4.50 and 4.52; rr. 4.51-CVL and 4.53-CVL deal with the first meeting of creditors in a creditors' voluntary winding up.

The remaining rules in this chapter provide for the summoning of other meetings and the conduct of creditors' and contributories' meetings generally. Voting at creditors' meetings is by a majority in *value* only, instead of the majority in *number* and *value* required under r. 134 of the former winding-up rules.

Note in regard to r. 4.57(1), (2) that the statutory power of the creditors and contributories to requisition meetings is contained in IA 1986, s. 168(2), which requires the support of at least one-tenth in value of the creditors or contributories, as the case may be.

Before a creditor may vote, a proof of his debt must have been lodged and admitted under r. 4.70 (subject to the court's powers under r. 4.67(1)); and, if he wishes to vote by proxy, his proxy must also have been duly lodged. The deadline for lodging a proof is fixed, in the case of a winding up by the court, by the notice convening the meeting (r. 4.67(1)), but there is no corresponding provision for the case of a creditors' voluntary winding up. It would appear that this may be done at any time up to the taking of the vote, or even (if the chairman exercises his discretion under r. 4.68) without lodging a proof at all. The chairman has no similar discretion in a compulsory winding up; but the court has power to grant a dispensation in either kind of winding up under r. 4.67(2). Rules 4.50(4), 4.51(2) and 4.54(4) specify varying times by which proxies must be lodged by creditors (and, where appropriate, contributories) for the different meetings.

Rule 4.53A-CVL brings back into operation a provision equivalent to the repealed CA 1985, s. 588(4), and allows the creditors to pass a resolution in anticipation of and conditionally upon the passing in due course of a resolution for winding up at an adjourned shareholders' meeting.

Rule 4.53B-CVL reflects a change in the form relating to the statement of affairs (Form 4.19). Previously, this had to be made up to the date of the creditors' meeting – a requirement which could not be met in practice. The date may now be anything up to 14 days before the meeting; and r. 4.53B-CVL imposes an obligation to make a report (which may be oral) to the meeting, bringing the statement up to date.

Rule 4.63(2A) prevents the election of a liquidator on a minority vote in the case where there are several nominees. The exclusion of its application to a creditors' voluntary winding up ensures that a liquidator who has the greatest support among the creditors (even if only a minority of them overall) is preferred to the company's nominee.

The repealed r. 4.66 has been replaced by the new r. 12.4A.

The language of r. 4.67(3) is similar to that formerly used in other rules, *e.g.* r. 1.17(3) and r. 5.17(3), and accordingly decisions on those provisions (such as *Re a Debtor (No. 222 of 1990) Ex p. Bank of Ireland* [1992] B.C.L.C. 137) are relevant to its interpretation. In *Re Bank of Credit & Commerce International SA (No. 5), Sheik Khalid v Bank of Credit & Commerce International SA* [1994] 1 B.C.L.C. 429 the court considered an application by a person claiming to be a creditor before any ruling had been given by the chairman (who had not yet been appointed).

A decision to accept a creditor's proof for voting purposes is not binding or conclusive for other purposes: *Re Assico Engineering Ltd* [2002] B.C.C. 481.

In considering an appeal from the decision of the chairman to allow or reject a creditor's proof for voting purposes, the evidence which the court may consider is not confined to that which was available to the chairman at the meeting: *Re a Company No. 004539 of 1993* [1995] B.C.C. 116. A similar approach was adopted by the court in reviewing the validity of proxies in *Re Philip Alexander Securities & Futures Ltd* [1998] B.C.C. 819.

Section B: winding up of recognised banks, etc.

4.72 Additional provisions as regards certain meetings

4.72(1) [Application of Rule] This Rule applies where a company goes, or proposes to go, into liquidation and it is an authorised deposit-taker or former authorised deposit-taker.

4.72(2) [Notice re proposed winding up] Notice of any meeting of the company at which it is intended to propose a resolution for its winding up shall be given by the directors to the Financial Services Authority and to the scheme manager established under section 212(1) of the Financial Services and Markets Act 2000.

4.72(3) [Form of notice] Notice to the Authority and the scheme manager shall be the same as given to members of the company.

4.72(4) [Where creditors' meeting summoned under s. 95 or 98] Where a creditors' meeting is summoned by the liquidator under section 95 or, in a creditors' voluntary winding up, is summoned under section 98, the same notice of the meeting must be given to the Authority and the scheme manager as is given to creditors under Rule 4.51–CVL.

4.72(5) [Where company being wound up by court] Where the company is being wound up by the court, notice of the first meetings of creditors and contributories shall be given to the Authority and the scheme manager by the official receiver.

4.72(6) [Where meeting to receive liquidator's resignation etc.] Where in the winding up (whether voluntary or by the court) a meeting of creditors or contributories or of the company is summoned for the purpose of–

(a) receiving the liquidator's resignation, or

(b) removing the liquidator, or

(c) appointing a new liquidator,

the person summoning the meeting and giving notice of it shall also give notice to the Authority and the scheme manager.

4.72(7) [Representation of Deposit Protection Board] The Board is entitled to be represented at any meeting of which it is required by this Rule to be given notice; and Schedule 1 to the Rules has effect with respect to the voting rights of the Board at such a meeting.

GENERAL NOTE

Rules 4.72(1)–(7) were substituted by the Financial Services and Markets Act 2000 (Consequential Amendments and Repeals) Order 2001 (SI 2001/3649) as from December 1, 2001. This rule ensures that the Financial Services Authority and the Deposit Protection Board are notified of meetings summoned in connection with the winding-up of an authorised deposit-taker under the Banking Act 1987.

CHAPTER 9

PROOF OF DEBTS IN A LIQUIDATION

Section A: procedure for proving

4.73 Meaning of "prove"

4.73(1) [Winding up by court] Where a company is being wound up by the court, a person claiming to be a creditor of the company and wishing to recover his debt in whole or in part must (subject to any order of the court under Rule 4.67(2)) submit his claim in writing to the liquidator.

(NO CVL APPLICATION)

4.73(2) [Voluntary winding up] In a voluntary winding up (whether members' or creditors') the liquidator may require a person claiming to be a creditor of the company and wishing to recover his debt in whole or in part, to submit the claim in writing to him.

4.73(3) ["Proving" and "proof"] A creditor who claims (whether or not in writing) is referred to as "proving" for his debt; and a document by which he seeks to establish his claim is his "proof".

4.73(4) ["Proof of debt"] Subject to the next paragraph, a proof must be in the form known as "proof of debt" (whether the form prescribed by the Rules, or a substantially similar form), which shall be made out by or under the directions of the creditor, and signed by him or a person authorised in that behalf.

(NO CVL APPLICATION)

[FORM 4.25]

4.73(5) [Debt due to Crown etc.] Where a debt is due to a Minister of the Crown or a Government Department, the proof need not be in that form, provided that there are shown all such particulars of the debt as are required in the form used by other creditors, and as are relevant in the circumstances.

(NO CVL APPLICATION)

4.73(6) [Creditor's proof] The creditor's proof may be in any form.

4.73(7) [Proof in form of affidavit] In certain circumstances, specified below in this Chapter, the proof must be in the form of an affidavit.

4.73(8) [Deemed proof in winding up] Where a winding up is immediately preceded by an administration, a creditor proving in the administration shall be deemed to have proved in the winding up.

(See General Note after r. 4.85.)

4.74 Supply of forms

(NO CVL APPLICATION)

4.74 A form of proof shall be sent to any creditor of the company by the liquidator where the creditor so requests.

(See General Note after r. 4.85.)

4.75 Contents of proof

(NO CVL APPLICATION)

4.75(1) **[Matters to be stated in creditor's proof]** Subject to Rule 4.73(5), the following matters shall be stated in a creditor's proof of debt –

(a) the creditor's name and address, and, if a company, its company registration number;

(b) the total amount of his claim (including any Value Added Tax) as at the date on which the company went into liquidation;

(c) whether or not that amount includes outstanding uncapitalised interest;

(d) particulars of how and when the debt was incurred by the company;

(e) particulars of any security held, the date when it was given and the value which the creditor puts upon it;

(f) details of any reservation of title in respect of goods to which the debt refers; and

(g) the name, and address and authority of the person signing the proof (if other than the creditor himself).

4.75(2) **[Specified documents]** There shall be specified in the proof any documents by reference to which the debts can be substantiated; but (subject as follows) it is not essential that such documents be attached to the proof or submitted with it.

4.75(3) **[Production of documents etc.]** The liquidator, or the chairman or convener of any meeting, may call for any document or other evidence to be produced to him, where he thinks it necessary for the purpose of substantiating the whole or any part of the claim made in the proof.

(See General Note after r. 4.85.)

4.76-CVL Particulars of creditor's claim

4.76-CVL The liquidator, or the convenor or chairman of any meeting, may, if he thinks it necessary for the purpose of clarifying or substantiating the whole or any part of a creditor's claim made in his proof, call for details of any matter specified in paragraphs (a) to (h) of Rule 4.75(1), or for the production to him of such documentary or other evidence as he may require.

(See General Note after r. 4.85.)

4.77 Claim established by affidavit

4.77(1) [Liquidator may require "affidavit of debt"] The liquidator may, if he thinks it necessary, require a claim of debt to be verified by means of an affidavit, for which purpose there shall be used the form known as "affidavit of debt", or a substantially similar form.

[FORM 4.26]

4.77(2) [In addition to proof] An affidavit may be required notwithstanding that a proof of debt has already been lodged.

4.77(3) [Swearing of affidavit] The affidavit may be sworn before an official receiver or deputy official receiver, or before an officer of the Department or of the court duly authorised in that behalf. (NO CVL APPLICATION)

(See General Note after r. 4.85.)

4.78 Cost of proving

4.78(1) [Creditor bears cost of proving own debt] Subject as follows, every creditor bears the cost of proving his own debt, including such as may be incurred in providing documents or evidence under Rule 4.75(3) or 4.76–CVL.

4.78(2) [Liquidator's costs] Costs incurred by the liquidator in estimating the quantum of a debt under Rule 4.86 (debts not bearing a certain value) are payable out of the assets, as an expense of the liquidation.

4.78(3) [Application of r. 4.78(1), (2)] Paragraphs (1) and (2) apply unless the court otherwise orders.

(See General Note after r. 4.85.)

4.79 Liquidator to allow inspection of proofs

4.79 The liquidator shall, so long as proofs lodged with him are in his hands, allow them to be inspected, at all reasonable times on any business day, by any of the following persons–

(a) any creditor who has submitted his proof of debt (unless his proof has been wholly rejected for purposes of dividend or otherwise);

(b) any contributory of the company;

(c) any person acting on behalf of either of the above.

(See General Note after r. 4.85.)

4.80 Transmission of proofs to liquidator

(NO CVL APPLICATION)

4.80(1) [On liquidator's appointment] Where a liquidator is appointed, the official receiver shall forthwith transmit to him all the proofs which he has so far received, together with an itemised list of them.

4.80(2) [Receipt for proofs] The liquidator shall sign the list by way of receipt for the proofs, and return it to the official receiver.

4.80(3) [All later proofs to liquidator] From then on, all proofs of debt shall be sent to the liquidator, and retained by him.

(See General Note after r. 4.85.)

4.81 New liquidator appointed

4.81(1) **[On appointment]** If a new liquidator is appointed in place of another, the former liquidator shall transmit to him all proofs which he has received, together with an itemised list of them.

4.81(2) **[Receipt for proofs]** The new liquidator shall sign the list by way of receipt for the proofs, and return it to his predecessor.

(See General Note after r. 4.85.)

4.82 Admission and rejection of proofs for dividend

4.82(1) **[Admission]** A proof may be admitted for dividend either for the whole amount claimed by the creditor, or for part of that amount.

4.82(2) **[Rejection]** If the liquidator rejects a proof in whole or in part, he shall prepare a written statement of his reasons for doing so, and send it forthwith to the creditor.

(See General Note after r. 4.85.)

4.83 Appeal against decision on proof

4.83(1) **[Application by creditor]** If a creditor is dissatisfied with the liquidator's decision with respect to his proof (including any decision on the question of preference), he may apply to the court for the decision to be reversed or varied.

The application must be made within 21 days of his receiving the statement sent under Rule 4.82(2).

4.83(2) **[Application by contributory etc.]** A contributory or any other creditor may, if dissatisfied with the liquidator's decision admitting or rejecting the whole or any part of a proof, make such an application within 21 days of becoming aware of the liquidator's decision.

4.83(3) **[Venue and notice]** Where application is made to the court under this Rule, the court shall fix a venue for the application to be heard, notice of which shall be sent by the applicant to the creditor who lodged the proof in question (if it is not himself) and to the liquidator.

4.83(4) **[Relevant proof etc. to be filed in court]** The liquidator shall, on receipt of the notice, file in court the relevant proof, together (if appropriate) with a copy of the statement sent under Rule 4.82(2).

4.83(5) **[Return of proof]** After the application has been heard and determined, the proof shall, unless it has been wholly disallowed, be returned by the court to the liquidator.

4.83(6) **[Costs re application]** The official receiver is not personally liable for costs incurred by any person in respect of an application under this Rule; and the liquidator (if other than the official receiver) is not so liable unless the court makes an order to that effect.

(See General Note after r. 4.85.)

4.84 Withdrawal or variation of proof

4.84 A creditor's proof may at any time, by agreement between himself and the liquidator, be withdrawn or varied as to the amount claimed.

(See General Note after r. 4.85.)

4.85 Expunging of proof by the court

4.85(1) **[Expunging or reduction of amount]** The court may expunge a proof or reduce the amount claimed–

(a) on the liquidator's application, where he thinks that the proof has been improperly admitted, or ought to be reduced; or

(b) on the application of a creditor, if the liquidator declines to interfere in the matter.

4.85(2) [Venue and notice] Where application is made to the court under this Rule, the court shall fix a venue for the application to be heard, notice of which shall be sent by the applicant–

(a) in the case of an application by the liquidator, to the creditor who made the proof, and

(b) in the case of an application by a creditor, to the liquidator and to the creditor who made the proof (if not himself).

GENERAL NOTE TO RR. 4.73–4.85

Here are set out the rules governing the proof of debts, the rights of inspection of proofs, appeals against a liquidator's decision with respect to a proof, etc. See generally the comment preceding s. 175.

Paragraph (ga) was inserted into r. 4.75(1) by the Insolvency (Amendment) Rules 2002 (SI 2002/1307, effective May 31, 2002). Paragraph (8) was inserted into r.4.73 by the Insolvency (Amendment) Rules 2003 (SI 2003/1730, effective September 15, 2003), Sch. 1, para. 18. Rules 4.74 and 4.75(1) were substituted by the Insolvency (Amendment) Rules 2004 (SI 2004/584), effective April 1, 2004. The liquidator is no longer obliged to send a form of proof to every creditor, but only to do so if a particular creditor requests. The details to be stated in a creditor's proof of debt have been revised.

The "rule against double proof" forbids more than one proof to be admitted in respect of the same debt (*e.g.* by a guarantor as well as a principal creditor). See *Re Oriental Commercial Bank* (1871) 7 Ch. App. 99, and the discussion in *Re Polly Peck International plc* [1996] B.C.C. 486, and contrast *Re Parkfield Group plc* [1997] B.C.C. 778.

In a proper case, a liquidator or the court may disallow a proof notwithstanding the fact that a judgment has been obtained in respect of the debt in question; but the court will do so only if it appears that there was some fraud, collusion or miscarriage of justice: *Re Menastar Finance Ltd* [2002] EWHC (Ch) 2610; [2003] B.C.C. 404.

The words "improperly admitted" in r. 4.85(1)(a) carry no connotation of impropriety. It is sufficient that the proof was admitted in error, and the burden of proof in establishing this is the balance of probabilities: see *Re Globe Legal Services Ltd* [2002] B.C.C. 858; *Re Allard Holdings Ltd* [2001] 1 B.C.L.C. 404 (in which the relevance of delay is also discussed).

The proper law of a debt is determined by its *lex situs*, and is not affected by the fact that the debtor is subsequently wound up in another jurisdiction: *Wight v Eckhardt Marine GmbH* [2003] UKPC 37, [2003] 3 W.L.R. 414, [2003] B.C.C. 702.

On the meaning of "went into liquidation", in r. 4.75, see IA 1986, s. 247.

Section B: quantification of claim

4.86 Estimate of quantum

4.86(1) [Estimating value of debts etc.] The liquidator shall estimate the value of any debt which, by reason of its being subject to any contingency or for any other reason, does not bear a certain value; and he may revise any estimate previously made, if he thinks fit by reference to any change of circumstances or to information becoming available to him.

He shall inform the creditor as to his estimate and any revision of it.

4.86(2) [Amount provable in winding up] Where the value of a debt is estimated under this Rule, or by the court under section 168(3) or (5), the amount provable in the winding up in the case of that debt is that of the estimate for the time being.

(See General Note after r. 4.89.)

4.87 Negotiable instruments, etc.

4.87 Unless the liquidator allows, a proof in respect of money owed on a bill of exchange, promissory note, cheque or other negotiable instrument or security cannot be admitted unless there is produced the instrument or security itself or a copy of it, certified by the creditor or his authorised representative to be a true copy.

(See General Note after r. 4.89.)

4.88 Secured creditors

4.88(1) **[Proving for balance of debt]** If a secured creditor realises his security, he may prove for the balance of his debt, after deducting the amount realised.

4.88(2) **[Proving for whole debt]** If a secured creditor voluntarily surrenders his security for the general benefit of creditors, he may prove for his whole debt, as if it were unsecured.

(See General Note after r. 4.89.)

4.89 Discounts

4.89 There shall in every case be deducted from the claim all trade and other discounts which would have been available to the company but for its liquidation, except any discount for immediate, early or cash settlement.

GENERAL NOTE TO RR. 4.86–4.89

These are the rules for assessing a debt for the purposes of proof in the special cases of contingent and secured debts, etc.

R. 4.88
A secured creditor who has been paid part of his debt as a result of realising his security may prove for the balance without bringing what he has received into hotchpot: *Cleaver v Delta American Reinsurance Co.* [2001] UKPC 6; [2001] 1 B.C.L.C. 482.

4.90 Mutual credit and set-off

4.90(1) **[Application of Rule]** This Rule applies where, before the company goes into liquidation there have been mutual credits, mutual debts or other mutual dealings between the company and any creditor of the company proving or claiming to prove for a debt in the liquidation.

4.90(2) **[Account of mutual dealings and set-off]** An account shall be taken of what is due from each party to the other in respect of the mutual dealings, and the sums due from one party shall be set off against the sums due from the other.

4.90(3) **[Sums not to be included in account]** Sums due from the company to another party shall not be taken into account under paragraph (2) if–

(a) that other party had notice at the time they became due that a meeting of creditors had been summoned under section 98 or (as the case may be) a petition for the winding up of the company was pending;

(b) the liquidation was immediately preceded by an administration and the sums became due during the administration; or

(c) the liquidation was immediately preceded by an administration and the other party had notice at the time that the sums became due that –

　　(i) an application for an administration order was pending; or
　　(ii) any person had given notice of intention to appoint an administrator.

4.90(4) **[Only balance (if any) provable etc.]** Only the balance (if any) of the account is provable in the liquidation. Alternatively (as the case may be) the amount shall be paid to the liquidator as part of the assets.

GENERAL NOTE

There is no provision in the Insolvency Act itself for the case of mutual credit and set-off in company insolvency corresponding to IA 1986, s. 323, which deals with individual bankruptcy. The present rule makes good this shortcoming. See the general comment on Pt IV, Ch. VIII preceding IA 1986, s. 175.

The present law removes some uncertainties that were not fully resolved previously. First, it is now clear that the rules as to mutual credit and set-off apply to all liquidations, irrespective of the solvency or otherwise of the company and whether the liquidation is voluntary or compulsory. Secondly, it is also clear that the relevant date (or time: see the note to s. 86) for all purposes of proof and set-off is that when the company goes into liquidation. (For the meaning of this expression, see s. 247(2).) On the other hand, some difficult questions remain to be resolved, *e.g.* the rules give inadequate guidance as to the set-off of contingent liabilities, and in particular how such liabilities of the company should be quantified. (On this point see Wood (1987) 8 Co Law 262; R M Goode, *Principles of Corporate Insolvency Law* (2nd edn, Ch. 8); *M S Fashions Ltd v Bank of Credit & Commerce International SA (No. 2)* [1993] Ch. 425 at p. 435; [1993] B.C.C. 70 at p. 75 and, especially, *Stein v Blake* [1996] A.C. 243 at p. 251ff., *per* Lord Hoffmann. The position is now reasonably clear: a contingent debt owed *by* the company is provable at its valuation pursuant to r. 4.86 (1) and may be set off accordingly. However a contingent debt owed *to* the company cannot be valued in a similar way, and so for as long as it remains contingent it is not available for set-off. There is no legal mechanism for accelerating the payment of such a debt. The court may, however, take into account events which have occurred since the date of the winding up and thus, with the benefit of hindsight, it may allow set-off where a debt ceases to be contingent after the date of the liquidation: the full amount is then deemed to have become due at that date. If the contingency occurs only after the company has been wound up and dissolved, it is possible for the company to be restored to the register for the purposes of bringing an action, and in that case the creditor could still claim a set-off (*M S Fashions* at p. 437; 75). A creditor whose proof has been rejected cannot reassert the debt by claiming to rely on it as a set-off: *Bank of Credit & Commerce International (Overseas) Ltd v Habib Bank Ltd* [1998] 2 B.C.L.C. 459. On similar reasoning, a claim that would be open to objection on the grounds of double proof cannot be set off: *Re Glen Express Ltd* [2000] B.P.I.R. 456. In the *Habib Bank* case it was also held that under r. 4.90 the court had to take account of the fact that debts owed to the creditor at the date of the liquidation had subsequently been paid by third parties. (Note that *Stein v Blake* was distinguished in *Re West End Networks Ltd* [2003] B.P.I.R. 496.)

The rules as to set-off in insolvency are different from those which apply between solvent parties: see the subject discussed by Lord Hoffmann in *Stein v Blake* (above). The object of the latter is to avoid cross-actions, and their scope is restricted. The former, in contrast, are intended to do substantial justice between the parties, and their application is not limited to particular categories of claim, but apply to all cross-claims provided that they are mutual and measurable in money terms (*Stein v Blake* [1993] B.C.C. 587 at p. 590, *per* Balcombe L.J.). Claims are only "mutual" if they are due between the same parties and in the same right – *e.g.* a debt owed by A to B as trustee for C and a debt owed to A by B personally cannot be set off: *Re ILG Travel Ltd* [1996] B.C.C. 21; *Re Griffin Trading Co.* [1999] B.P.I.R. 256. In the converse case, where B alleges that a debt owed by A to C is in fact held by C as trustee for B, the court will allow set-off only where it is satisfied that the debt is clear and ascertained and that B is the sole beneficiary and entitled without further inquiry to demand that the debt be transferred to him: *Ex parte Morier* (1879) 12 Ch.D. 491; *Bank of Credit and Commercial International SA (in liq.) v Prince Fahd Bin Salman Abdul Aziz Al-Saud* [1997] B.C.C. 63. The fact that one debt is secured and the other unsecured is not inconsistent with mutuality: *Re ILG Travel Ltd* (above). But there must have been "dealing" between the parties; and so (for instance) a debt cannot be set off against the creditor's liability to the company in damages for conversion: *Re Cosslett (Contractors) Ltd (No. 2), Smith v Bridgend County Borough Council* [2001] UKHL58; [2002] 1 A.C. 336; [2001] B.C.C. 740. The rules as to set-off are mandatory and cannot be excluded by agreement between the parties (*National Westminster Bank Ltd v Halesowen Presswork & Assemblies Ltd* [1972] A.C. 785); nor can they be disapplied by the court in the exercise of its discretion: *Re Bank of Credit & Commerce International SA (No. 10)* [1997] Ch. 213; [1996] B.C.C. 980. In the *M S Fashions* case (above, affirmed [1993] Ch. 425 at p. 439; sub nom. *High Street Services Ltd v Bank of Credit & Commerce International SA* [1993] B.C.C. 360), it was held that where several persons were each liable to the company as principal debtors in respect of the same debt, a set-off available against one of them operated automatically to reduce the debt for the benefit of them all. It was not open to a liquidator to seek to avoid this consequence by electing to claim the full amount in the first instance from the other debtors. (For earlier proceedings in the same case, see *M S Fashions Ltd v Bank of Credit & Commerce International SA* [1992] B.C.C. 571.) In contrast, in *Re Bank of Credit & Commerce International SA (No. 8), Morris v Rayners Enterprises Inc* [1988] A.C. 214; [1997] B.C.C. 965, the House of Lords held that the bank's liquidators could proceed first against the principal debtors concerned, without bringing into account the amounts of certain deposits made with the bank by other persons and allegedly charged to secure the debts. In this case the depositors had no personal liability for the principal debts, and accordingly there was no sum "due" from them on which a set-off could operate. It was observed that to permit the set-off of claims by third parties, even with their consent, would be to allow the parties by agreement to subvert the fundamental principle of pari passu distribution of assets in an insolvency.

A contributory's liability for calls cannot be set off in a liquidation against any liability of the company to him: *Re Overend Gurney, Grissell's case* (1864) 1 Ch. App. 528; *Re Pinecord Ltd* [1995] B.C.C. 483.

The holder of a secured debt is not required by r. 4.90 to set off money owed by the company to him against that debt, unless he elects to give up his security and prove his debt in the liquidation: *Re Norman Holding Co. Ltd (in liquidation)* [1991] 1 W.L.R. 10; [1991] B.C.C. 11.

For the exclusion of set-off in respect of post-insolvency VAT credits, see Value Added Tax Act 1994, s. 81(4)–(5).

In *Myles J. Callaghan Ltd (in receivership) v City of Glasgow District Council* (1987) 3 B.C.C. 337 it was held competent in Scots law for a creditor in a liquidation to set off a claim for damages for breach of a building contract against a claim by the company for the return of its plant and equipment or payment of its value, and to do so notwithstanding the appointment of a receiver.

On the application of r. 4.90 in the context of payment and securities settlement systems, see the Finality Regulations, reg. 15.

Under the original administration regime, there is no provision corresponding to r. 4.90, and the principle of insolvency set-off is not applicable: *Isovel Contracts Ltd v ABB Building Technologies Ltd* [2002] 1 B.C.L.C. 390. But under the new administration regime r. 2.85 provides for mutual credit and set-off in terms similar to r. 4.90. In keeping with this reform, paras (3)(a) and (3)(b) were inserted into r. 4.90 by the Insolvency (Amendment) Rules 2003 (SI 2003/1730, effective September 15, 2003), Sch. 1, para. 19.

4.91 Debt in foreign currency

4.91(1) **[Conversion into sterling]** For the purpose of proving a debt incurred or payable in a currency other than sterling, the amount of the debt shall be converted into sterling at the official exchange rate prevailing on the date when the company went into liquidation.

4.91(2) **["The official exchange rate"]** "The official exchange rate" is the middle exchange rate on the London Foreign Exchange Market at the close of business, as published for the date in question. In the absence of any such published rate, it is such rate as the court determines.

GENERAL NOTE

This confirms the ruling in *Re Lines Bros Ltd* [1983] Ch. 1 in which comments made (obiter) in the earlier decision of the House of Lords in *Miliangos v George Frank (Textiles) Ltd* [1976] A.C. 443 were not followed. For the meaning of "went into liquidation", see s. 247(2). Note that the rule refers to the *date*, rather than the *time*. (On this point, see the note to s. 86.)

4.92 Payments of a periodical nature

4.92(1) **[Rent etc.]** In the case of rent and other payments of a periodical nature, the creditor may prove for any amounts due and unpaid up to the date when the company went into liquidation.

4.92(2) **[If accruing from day to day]** Where at that date any payment was accruing due, the creditor may prove for so much as would have fallen due at that date, if accruing from day to day.

4.93 Interest

4.93(1) **[Where debt bears interest]** Where a debt proved in the liquidation bears interest, that interest is provable as part of the debt except in so far as it is payable in respect of any period after the company went into liquidation.

4.93(2) **[Where claim may include interest]** In the following circumstances the creditor's claim may include interest on the debt for periods before the company went into liquidation, although not previously reserved or agreed.

4.93(3) **[Debt due by written instrument]** If the debt is due by virtue of a written instrument, and payable at a certain time, interest may be claimed for the period from that time to the date when the company went into liquidation.

4.93(4) **[Debt due otherwise]** If the debt is due otherwise, interest may only be claimed if, before that date, a demand for payment of the debt was made in writing by or on behalf of the creditor, and notice given that interest would be payable from the date of the demand to the date of payment.

4.93(5) **[Claiming r. 4.93(4) interest]** Interest under paragraph (4) may only be claimed for the period from the date of the demand to that of the company's going into liquidation and for all the purposes of the Act and the Rules shall be chargeable at a rate not exceeding that mentioned in paragraph (6).

4.93(6) **[Rate of interest under r. 4.93(3) and (4)]** The rate of interest to be claimed under paragraphs (3) and (4) is the rate specified in section 17 of the Judgments Act 1838 on the date when the company went into liquidation.

GENERAL NOTE

See the notes to IA 1986, s. 189.

4.94 Debt payable at future time

4.94 A creditor may prove for a debt of which payment was not yet due on the date when the company went into liquidation, but subject to Rule 11.13 in Part 11 of the Rules (adjustment of dividend where payment made before time).

CHAPTER 10

SECURED CREDITORS

4.95 Value of security

4.95(1) **[Altering value]** A secured creditor may, with the agreement of the liquidator or the leave of the court, at any time alter the value which he has, in his proof of debt, put upon his security.

4.95(2) **[Limitation on re-valuation]** However, if a secured creditor–

(a) being the petitioner, has in the petition put a value on his security, or

(b) has voted in respect of the unsecured balance of his debt,

he may re-value his security only with leave of the court. (NO CVL APPLICATION)

(See General Note after r. 4.99.)

4.96 Surrender for non-disclosure

4.96(1) **[Omission to disclose security]** If a secured creditor omits to disclose his security in his proof of debt, he shall surrender his security for the general benefit of creditors, unless the court, on application by him, relieves him for the effect of this Rule on the ground that the omission was inadvertent or the result of honest mistake.

4.96(2) **[Relief from effect of r. 4.96(1)]** If the court grants that relief, it may require or allow the creditor's proof of debt to be amended, on such terms as may be just.

4.96(3) **[Rights protected under Art. 5]** Nothing in this Rule or the following two Rules may affect the rights in rem of creditors or third parties protected under Article 5 of the EC Regulation (third parties' rights in rem).

(See General Note after r. 4.99.)

4.97 Redemption by liquidator

4.97(1) [**Notice of proposed redemption**] The liquidator may at any time give notice to a creditor whose debt is secured that he proposes, at the expiration of 28 days from the date of the notice, to redeem the security at the value put upon it in the creditor's proof.

4.97(2) [**Time for revaluation etc.**] The creditor then has 21 days (or such longer period as the liquidator may allow) in which, if he so wishes, to exercise his right to re-value his security (with the leave of the court, where Rule 4.95(2) applies).

If the creditor re-values his security, the liquidator may only redeem at the new value.

4.97(3) [**If liquidator redeems**] If the liquidator redeems the security, the cost of transferring it is payable out of the assets.

4.97(4) [**Notice to liquidator to elect etc.**] A secured creditor may at any time, by a notice in writing, call on the liquidator to elect whether he will or will not exercise his power to redeem the security at the value then placed on it; and the liquidator then has 6 months in which to exercise the power or determine not to exercise it.

(See General Note after r. 4.99.)

4.98 Test of security's value

4.98(1) [**Offer for sale**] Subject as follows, the liquidator, if he is dissatisfied with the value which a secured creditor puts on his security (whether in his proof or by way of re-valuation under Rule 4.97), may require any property comprised in the security to be offered for sale.

4.98(2) [**Terms of sale**] The terms of sale shall be such as may be agreed, or as the court may direct; and if the sale is by auction, the liquidator on behalf of the company, and the creditor on his own behalf, may appear and bid.

(See General Note after r. 4.99.)

4.99 Realisation of security by creditor

4.99 If a creditor who has valued his security subsequently realises it (whether or not at the instance of the liquidator)–

(a) the net amount realised shall be substituted for the value previously put by the creditor on the security, and

(b) that amount shall be treated in all respects as an amended valuation made by him.

GENERAL NOTE TO RR. 4.95–4.99.

These rules deal with the valuation of his security by a secured creditor, the liquidator's right to redeem the security, the consequences of the realisation of a security, and various related matters.

Rule 4.96(3) was added by the Insolvency (Amendment) Rules 2002 (SI 2002/1307, effective May 31, 2002). The rights *in rem* referred to are those in respect of assets belonging to the debtor company which are situated within the territory of another Member State at the time of the opening of proceedings. See further the note to the European Regulation, Art. 5.

CHAPTER 11

The Liquidator

Section A: Appointment and associated formalities

4.100 Appointment by creditors or contributories
(NO CVL APPLICATION)

4.100(1) [Application of Rule] This Rule applies where a person is appointed as liquidator either by a meeting of creditors or by a meeting of contributories.

4.100(2) [Certification of appointment] The chairman of the meeting shall certify the appointment, but not unless and until the person appointed has provided him with a written statement to the effect that he is an insolvency practitioner, duly qualified under the Act to be the liquidator, and that he consents so to act.

[FORM 4.27]
[FORM 4.28]

4.100(3) [Date when appointment effective] The liquidator's appointment is effective from the date on which the appointment is certified, that date to be endorsed on the certificate.

4.100(4) [Certificate to official receiver] The chairman of the meeting (if not himself the official receiver) shall send the certificate to the official receiver.

4.100(5) [Certificate to liquidator, copyfiled] The official receiver shall in any case send the certificate to the liquidator and file a copy of it in court.

(See General Note after r. 4.106.)

4.101-CVL Appointment by creditors or by the company

4.101-CVL(1) [Application of Rule] This Rule applies where a person is appointed as liquidator either by a meeting of creditors or by a meeting of the company.

4.101-CVL(2) [Certification and effective date of appointment] Subject as follows, the chairman of the meeting shall certify the appointment, but not unless and until the person appointed has provided him with a written statement to the effect that he is an insolvency practitioner, duly qualified under the Act to be the liquidator, and that he consents so to act; the liquidator's appointment takes effect upon the passing of the resolution for that appointment.

[FORM 4.27]
[FORM 4.28]

4.101-CVL(3) [Certificate to liquidator] The chairman shall send the certificate forthwith to the liquidator, who shall keep it as part of the records of the liquidation.

4.101-CVL(4) [Where no need to comply with r. 4.101(2), (3)] Paragraphs (2) and (3) need not be complied with in case of a liquidator appointed by a company meeting and replaced by another liquidator appointed on the same day by a creditors' meeting.

(See General Note after r. 4.106.)

4.101A-CVL Power to fill vacancy in office of liquidator

4.101A-CVL Where a vacancy in the office of liquidator occurs in the manner mentioned in section 104 a meeting of creditors to fill the vacancy may be convened by any creditor or, if there were more liquidators than one, by the continuing liquidators.

(See General Note after r. 4.106.)

4.102 Appointment by the court

(NO CVL APPLICATION)

4.102(1) [**Application of Rule**] This Rule applies where the liquidator is appointed by the court under section 139(4) (different persons nominated by creditors and contributories) or section 140 (liquidation following administration or voluntary arrangement).

[FORM 4.29]
[FORM 4.30]

4.102(2) [**Issue of court order**] The court's order shall not issue unless and until the person appointed has filed in court a statement to the effect that he is an insolvency practitioner, duly qualified under the Act to be the liquidator, and that he consents so to act.

4.102(3) [**Copy of orders to official receiver etc.**] Thereafter, the court shall send 2 copies of the order to the official receiver. One of the copies shall be sealed, and this shall be sent to the person appointed as liquidator.

4.102(4) [**Commencement of appointment**] The liquidator's appointment takes effect from the date of the order.

4.102(5) [**Notice of appointment etc.**] The liquidator shall, within 28 days of his appointment, give notice of it to all creditors and contributories of the company of whom he is aware in that period. Alternatively, if the court allows, he may advertise his appointment in accordance with the court's directions.

4.102(6) [**Contents of notice etc.**] In his notice or advertisement under this Rule the liquidator shall–

(a) state whether he proposes to summon meetings of creditors and contributories for the purpose of establishing a liquidation committee, or proposes to summon only a meeting of creditors for that purpose, and

(b) if he does not propose to summon any such meeting, set out the powers of the creditors under the Act to require him to summon one.

4.103-CVL Appointment by the court

4.103-CVL(1) [**Application of Rule**] This Rule applies where the liquidator is appointed by the court under section 100(3) or 108.

[FORM 4.29]
[FORM 4.30]

4.103-CVL(2) [**Issue of court order**] The court's order shall not issue unless and until the person appointed has filed in court a statement to the effect that he is an insolvency practitioner, duly qualified under the Act to be the liquidator, and that he consents so to act.

4.103-CVL(3) [**Sealed copy to liquidator**] Thereafter, the court shall send a sealed copy of the order to the liquidator, whose appointment takes effect from the date of the order.

4.103-CVL(4) [**Notice etc. of appointment**] Not later than 28 days from his appointment, the liquidator shall give notice of it to all creditors of the company of whom he is aware in that period. Alternatively, if the court allows, he may advertise his appointment in accordance with the court's directions.

4.104 Appointment by Secretary of State

(NO CVL APPLICATION)

4.104(1) [**Application of Rule**] This Rule applies where the official receiver applies to the Secretary of

State to appoint a liquidator in place of himself, or refers to the Secretary of State the need for an appointment.

4.104(2) **[Copy of certificates to official receiver etc.]** If the Secretary of State makes an appointment, he shall send two copies of the certificate of appointment to the official receiver, who shall transmit one such copy to the person appointed, and file the other in court.

4.104(3) **[Content of certificate]** The certificate shall specify the date from which the liquidator's appointment is to be effective.

(See General Note after r. 4.106.)

4.105 Authentication of liquidator's appointment

4.105 A copy of the certificate of the liquidator's appointment or (as the case may be) a sealed copy of the court's order or a copy of the notice registered in accordance with paragraph 83(3) of Schedule B1 to the Act, may in any proceedings be adduced as proof that the person appointed is duly authorised to exercise the powers and perform the duties of liquidator in the company's winding up.

(See General Note after r. 4.106.)

4.106 Appointment to be advertised and registered

4.106(1) **[Where liquidator appointed by meeting]** Subject as follows, where the liquidator is appointed by a creditors' or contributories' meeting, or by a meeting of the company, he shall, on receiving his certificate of appointment, give notice of his appointment in such newspaper as he thinks most appropriate for ensuring that it comes to the notice of the company's creditors and contributories.

4.106(2) **[Where no need to comply with r. 4.106(1)]** Paragraph (1) need not be complied with in the case of a liquidator appointed by a company meeting and replaced by another liquidator appointed on the same day by a creditors' meeting.

4.106(3) **[Expense of giving notice]** The expense of giving notice under this Rule shall be borne in the first instance by the liquidator; but he is entitled to be reimbursed out of the assets, as an expense of the liquidation.

The same applies also in the case of the notice or advertisement required where the appointment is made by the court or the Secretary of State.

4.106(4) **[Notice to registrar]** In the case of a winding up by the court, the liquidator shall also forthwith notify his appointment to the registrar of companies.

This applies however the liquidator is appointed.

[FORM 4.31]

(NO CVL APPLICATION)

GENERAL NOTE TO RR. 4.100–4.106

These rules are concerned with the formalities relating to the appointment of a liquidator by the creditors or contributories (rr. 4.100, 4.101-CVL), by the court (rr. 4.102, 4.103-CVL), and by the Secretary of State (r. 4.104), and the certification, registration and notification of the appointment.

The liquidator's obligation to advertise his appointment under r. 4.106(1) is additional to the gazetting required by s. 109. Although the *Gazette* is arguably a "newspaper" for some purposes (*e.g.* postage), it would probably not be so treated in regard to this rule, and inconceivable that it would be "most appropriate" in the circumstances.

Rule 4.105 was amended by the insertion of the reference to the para. 83(3) notice by the Insolvency (Amendment) Rules 2003 (SI 2003/1730, effective September 15, 2003), Sch. 1, para. 20.

4.107 Hand-over of assets to liquidator

(NO CVL APPLICATION)

4.107(1) **[Application of Rule]** This Rule applies only where the liquidator is appointed in succession to the official receiver acting as liquidator.

4.107(2) **[On liquidator's appointment]** When the liquidator's appointment takes effect, the official receiver shall forthwith do all that is required for putting him into possession of the assets.

4.107(3) **[Discharge of balance due to official receiver]** On taking possession of the assets, the liquidator shall discharge any balance due to the official receiver on account of–

(a) expenses properly incurred by him and payable under the Act or the Rules, and

(b) any advances made by him in respect of the assets, together with interest on such advances at the rate specified in section 17 of the Judgments Act 1838 at the date of the winding-up order.

4.107(4) **[Undertaking to discharge]** Alternatively, the liquidator may (before taking office) give to the official receiver a written undertaking to discharge any such balance out of the first realisation of assets.

4.107(5) **[Official receiver's charge]** The official receiver has a charge on the assets in respect of any sums due to him under paragraph (3). But, where the liquidator has realised assets with a view to making those payments, the official receiver's charge does not extend in respect of sums deductible by the liquidator from the proceeds of realisation, as being expenses properly incurred therein.

4.107(6) **[Discharge of guarantees etc.]** The liquidator shall from time to time out of the realisation of assets discharge all guarantees properly given by the official receiver for the benefit of the estate, and shall pay all the official receiver's expenses.

4.107(7) **[Official receiver to give liquidator information]** The official receiver shall give to the liquidator all such information relating to the affairs of the company and the course of the winding up as he (the official receiver) considers to be reasonably required for the effective discharge by the liquidator of his duties as such.

4.107(8) **[Copy of Ch. 7 report]** The liquidator shall also be furnished with a copy of any report made by the official receiver under Chapter 7 of this Part of the Rules.

GENERAL NOTE

This rule applies following the appointment of a private liquidator under IA 1986, ss. 136 and 139, or s. 137.

Section B: Resignation and removal; vacation of office

4.108 Creditors' meeting to receive liquidator's resignation

4.108(1) **[Liquidator must call meeting etc.]** Before resigning his office, the liquidator must call a meeting of creditors for the purpose of receiving his resignation. The notice summoning the meeting shall indicate that this is the purpose, or one of the purposes, of it, and shall draw the attention of creditors to Rule 4.121 or, as the case may be, Rule 4.122–CVL with respect to the liquidator's release.

[FORM 4.22]

4.108(2) **[Copy of notice to official receiver]** A copy of the notice shall at the same time also be sent to the official receiver. (NO CVL APPLICATION)

4.108(3) **[Account of liquidator's administration]** The notice to creditors under paragraph (1) must be accompanied by an account of the liquidator's administration of the winding up, including–

(a) a summary of his receipts and payments, and

(b) a statement by him that he has reconciled his account with that which is held by the Secretary of State in respect of the winding up.

4.108(4) **[Grounds for proceeding under Rule]** Subject as follows, the liquidator may only proceed under this Rule on grounds of ill health or because–

(a) he intends ceasing to be in practice as an insolvency practitioner, or

(b) there is some conflict of interest or change of personal circumstances which precludes or makes impracticable the further discharge by him of the duties of liquidator.

4.108(5) **[Where joint liquidators]** Where two or more persons are acting as liquidator jointly, any one of them may proceed under this Rule (without prejudice to the continuation in office of the other or others) on the ground that, in his opinion and that of the other or others, it is no longer expedient that there should continue to be the present number of joint liquidators.

4.108(6) **[If no quorum]** If there is no quorum present at the meeting summoned to receive the liquidator's resignation, the meeting is deemed to have been held, a resolution is deemed to have been passed that the liquidator's resignation be accepted and the creditors are deemed not to have resolved against the liquidator having his release.

4.108(7) **[Application of r. 4.108(6)]** Where paragraph (6) applies any reference in the Rules to a resolution that the liquidator's resignation be accepted is replaced by a reference to the making of a written statement, signed by the person who, had there been a quorum present, would have been chairman of the meeting, that no quorum was present and that the liquidator may resign.

(See General Note after r. 4.112.)

4.109 Action following acceptance of resignation

(NO CVL APPLICATION)

4.109(1) **[Application of Rule]** This Rule applies where a meeting is summoned to receive the liquidator's resignation.

4.109(2) **[Copy of resolutions to official receiver etc.]** If the chairman of the meeting is other than the official receiver, and there is passed at the meeting any of the following resolutions–

(a) that the liquidator's resignation be accepted,

(b) that a new liquidator be appointed,

(c) that the resigning liquidator be not given his release,

the chairman shall, within 3 days, send to the official receiver a copy of the resolution.

If it has been resolved to accept the liquidator's resignation, the chairman shall send to the official receiver a certificate to that effect.

4.109(3) **[If creditors resolve to appoint new liquidator]** If the creditors have resolved to appoint a new liquidator, the certificate of his appointment shall also be sent to the official receiver within that time; and Rule 4.100 shall be complied with in respect of it.

4.109(4) **[If liquidator's resignation accepted]** If the liquidator's resignation is accepted, the notice of it required by section 172(6) shall be given by him forthwith after the meeting; and he shall send a copy of the notice to the official receiver.

The notice shall be accompanied by a copy of the account sent to creditors under Rule 4.108(3).

The Insolvency Rules 1986   Rule 4.112

[FORM 4.32]

4.109(5) **[Copy notice]** The official receiver shall file a copy of the notice in court.

4.109(6) **[Effective date of resignation]** The liquidator's resignation is effective as from the date on which the official receiver files the copy notice in court, that date to be endorsed on the copy notice.

(See General Note after r. 4.112.)

4.110-CVL Action following acceptance of resignation

4.110-CVL(1) **[Application of Rule]** This Rule applies where a meeting is summoned to receive the liquidator's resignation.

4.110-CVL(2) **[S. 171(5) notice]** If his resignation is accepted, the notice of it required by section 171(5) shall be given by him forthwith after the meeting.

[FORM 4.33]

4.110-CVL(3) **[Certificate of new liquidator's appointment]** Where a new liquidator is appointed in place of the one who has resigned, the certificate of his appointment shall be delivered forthwith by the chairman of the meeting to the new liquidator.

(See General Note after r. 4.112.)

4.111 Leave to resign granted by the court

4.111(1) **[If liquidator's resignation not accepted]** If at a creditors' meeting summoned to accept the liquidator's resignation it is resolved that it be not accepted, the court may, on the liquidator's application, make an order giving him leave to resign.

[FORM 4.34]

4.111(2) **[Extent of order under r. 4.111(1)]** The court's order may include such provision as it thinks fit with respect to matters arising in connection with the resignation, and shall determine the date from which the liquidator's release is effective.

4.111(3) **[Sealed copies of order]** The court shall send two sealed copies of the order to the liquidator, who shall send one of the copies forthwith to the official receiver. (NO CVL APPLICATION)

4.111(4) **[Sealed copies]** The court shall send two sealed copies of the order to the liquidator, who shall forthwith send one of them to the registrar of companies.

[FORM 4.35]

4.111(5) **[Copy notice to court and official receiver]** On sending notice of his resignation to the court, the liquidator shall send a copy of it to the official receiver.

(NO CVL APPLICATION)

[FORM 4.36]

4.112 Advertisement of resignation

4.112 Where a new liquidator is appointed in place of one who has resigned, the former shall, in giving notice of his appointment, state that his predecessor has resigned and (if it be the case) that he has been given his release.

GENERAL NOTE TO RR. 4.108–4.112

The circumstances in which a liquidator may resign are set out in r. 108(4), (5). These rules detail the procedure to be followed, and the date when the resignation takes effect. However, where an insolvency practitioner holds multiple offices and application is made to the court to remove him from all the offices and appoint a suitable replacement, the court has jurisdiction to by-pass the procedures laid down in these rules (and the corresponding rules for the removal of other office-holders) where it is satisfied that no useful purpose will be served by holding the meetings: see *Re Alt Landscapes Ltd* [1999] B.P.I.R. 459; *Re Equity Nominees Ltd* [2000] B.C.C. 84, and the note to s. 172(2). See the discussion at IR 6.126, and, on procedure, Appendix IV to this Guide, para. 1.1(6).

The question of the release of the liquidator is covered by rr. 4.121, 4.122-CVL.

4.113 Meeting of creditors to remove liquidator

(NO CVL APPLICATION)

4.113(1) **[Notice]** Where a meeting of creditors is summoned for the purpose of removing the liquidator, the notice summoning it shall indicate that this is the purpose, or one of the purposes, of the meeting; and the notice shall draw the attention of creditors to section 174(4) with respect to the liquidator's release.

[FORM 4.22]

4.113(2) **[Copy notice to official receiver]** A copy of the notice shall at the same time also be sent to the official receiver.

4.113(3) **[Chairman; if liquidator chairman etc.]** At the meeting, a person other than the liquidator or his nominee may be elected to act as chairman; but if the liquidator or his nominee is chairman and a resolution has been proposed for the liquidator's removal, the chairman shall not adjourn the meeting without the consent of at least one-half (in value) of the creditors present (in person or by proxy) and entitled to vote.

4.113(4) **[Copy resolutions to official receiver]** Where the chairman of the meeting is other than the official receiver, and there is passed at the meeting any of the following resolutions–

(a) that the liquidator be removed,

(b) that a new liquidator be appointed,

(c) that the removed liquidator be not given his release,

the chairman shall, within 3 days, send to the official receiver a copy of the resolution.

If it has been resolved to remove the liquidator, the chairman shall send to the official receiver a certificate to that effect.

[FORM 4.37]

4.113(5) **[If creditors resolve to appoint new liquidator]** If the creditors have resolved to appoint a new liquidator, the certificate of his appointment shall also be sent to the official receiver within that time; and Rule 4.100 above shall be complied with in respect of it.

(See General Note after r. 4.120-CVL.)

4.114-CVL Meeting of creditors to remove liquidator

4.114-CVL(1) **[S. 171(2)(b) meeting requested]** A meeting held under section 171(2)(b) for the removal of the liquidator shall be summoned by him if requested by 25 per cent in value of the company's creditors, excluding those who are connected with it.

4.114-CVL(2) **[Notice]** The notice summoning the meeting shall indicate that the removal of the liquidator is the purpose, or one of the purposes, of the meeting; and the notice shall draw the attention of creditors to section 173(2) with respect to the liquidator's release.

[FORM 4.22]

4.114-CVL(3) **[Chairman; if liquidator chairman etc.]** At the meeting, a person other than the liquidator or his nominee may be elected to act as chairman, but if the liquidator or his nominee is chairman and a resolution has been proposed for the liquidator's removal, the chairman shall not adjourn the meeting without the consent of at least one-half (in value) of the creditors present (in person or by proxy) and entitled to vote.

(See General Note after r. 4.120-CVL.)

4.115 Court's power to regulate meetings under Rules 4.113, 4.114–CVL

4.115 Where a meeting under Rule 4.113 or 4.114–CVL is to be held, or is proposed to be summoned, the court may, on the application of any creditor, give directions as to the mode of summoning it, the sending out and return of forms of proxy, the conduct of the meeting, and any other matter which appears to the court to require regulation or control under this Rule.

(See General Note after r. 4.120-CVL.)

4.116 Procedure on removal

(NO CVL APPLICATION)

4.116(1) **[Certificate of removal to be filed]** Where the creditors have resolved that the liquidator be removed, the official receiver shall file in court the certificate of removal.

4.116(2) **[Effective date of removal resolution]** The resolution is effective as from the date on which the official receiver files the certificate of removal in court, and that date shall be endorsed on the certificate.

4.116(3) **[Copy of certificate]** A copy of the certificate, so endorsed, shall be sent by the official receiver to the liquidator who has been removed and, if a new liquidator has been appointed, to him.

4.116(4) **[Reconciliation of accounts]** The official receiver shall not file the certificate in court unless and until the Secretary of State has certified to him that the removed liquidator has reconciled his account with that held by the Secretary of State in respect of the winding up.

(See General Note after r. 4.120-CVL.)

4.117-CVL Procedure on removal

4.117-CVL Where the creditors have resolved that the liquidator be removed, the chairman of the creditors' meeting shall forthwith–

(a) if at the meeting another liquidator was not appointed, send the certificate of the liquidator's removal to the registrar of companies, and

(b) otherwise, deliver the certificate to the new liquidator, who shall send it to the registrar.

[FORM 4.38]

(See General Note after r. 4.120-CVL.)

4.118 Advertisement of removal

4.118 Where a new liquidator is appointed in place of one removed, the former shall, in giving notice of his appointment, state that his predecessor has been removed and (if it be the case) that he has been given his release.

(See General Note after r. 4.120-CVL.)

4.119 Removal of liquidator by the court

(NO CVL APPLICATION)

4.119(1) **[Application of Rule]** This Rule applies where application is made to the court for the removal of the liquidator, or for an order directing the liquidator to summon a meeting of creditors for the purpose of removing him.

[FORM 4.39]

4.119(2) **[Court may dismiss application etc.]** The court may, if it thinks that no sufficient cause is shown for the application, dismiss it; but it shall not do so unless the applicant has had an opportunity to attend the court for an *ex parte* hearing, of which he has been given at least 7 days' notice.

If the application is not dismissed under this paragraph, the court shall fix a venue for it to be heard.

4.119(3) **[Deposit or security for costs]** The court may require the applicant to make a deposit or give security for the costs to be incurred by the liquidator on the application.

4.119(4) **[Notice etc.]** The applicant shall, at least 14 days before the hearing, send to the liquidator and the official receiver a notice stating the venue and accompanied by a copy of the application, and of any evidence which he intends to adduce in support of it.

4.119(5) **[Costs]** Subject to any contrary order of the court, the costs of the application are not payable out of the assets.

4.119(6) **[Where court removes liquidator]** Where the court removes the liquidator–

(a) it shall send copies of the order of removal to him and to the official receiver;

(b) the order may include such provision as the court thinks fit with respect to matters arising in connection with the removal; and

(c) if the court appoints a new liquidator, Rule 4.102 applies.

(See General Note after r. 4.120-CVL.)

4.120-CVL Removal of liquidator by the court

4.120-CVL(1) **[Application of Rule]** This Rule applies where application is made to the court for the removal of the liquidator, or for an order directing the liquidator to summon a creditors' meeting for the purpose of removing him.

[FORM 4.39]

4.120-CVL(2) **[Court may dismiss application etc.]** The court may, if it thinks that no sufficient cause is shown for the application, dismiss it; but it shall not do so unless the applicant has had an opportunity to attend the court for an *ex parte* hearing, of which he has been given at least 7 days' notice.

If the application is not dismissed under this paragraph, the court shall fix a venue for it to be heard.

4.120-CVL(3) **[Deposit or security for costs]** The court may require the applicant to make a deposit or give security for the costs to be incurred by the liquidator on the application.

4.120-CVL(4) **[Notice etc.]** The applicant shall, at least 14 days before the hearing, send to the liquidator a notice stating the venue and accompanied by a copy of the application, and of any evidence which he intends to adduce in support of it.

4.120-CVL(5) **[Costs]** Subject to any contrary order of the court, the costs of the application are not payable out of the assets.

4.120-CVL(6) **[Where court removes liquidator]** Where the court removes the liquidator–

(a) it shall send 2 copies of the order of removal to him, one to be sent by him forthwith to the registrar of companies, with notice of his ceasing to act;

(b) the order may include such provision as the court thinks fit with respect to matters arising in connection with the removal; and

(c) if the court appoints a new liquidator, Rule 4.103–CVL applies.

[FORM 4.40]

GENERAL NOTE TO RR. 4.113–4.120-CVL

The removal of a liquidator is dealt with in IA 1986, ss. 171, 172, which these rules supplement. On the liquidator's release, see rr. 4.121, 4.122-CVL. Costs on an indemnity basis may be awarded against a liquidator who unreasonably resists an application for his removal: *Shepheard v Lamey* [2001] B.P.I.R. 939.

See also the note to r. 4.112.

4.121 Release of resigning or removed liquidator

(NO CVL APPLICATION)

4.121(1) [Where liquidator's resignation accepted] Where the liquidator's resignation is accepted by a meeting of creditors which has not resolved against his release, he has his release from when his resignation is effective under Rule 4.109.

4.121(2) [Where liquidator removed by meeting] Where the liquidator is removed by a meeting of creditors which has not resolved against his release, the fact of his release shall be stated in the certificate of removal.

4.121(3) [Application to Secretary of State] Where–

(a) the liquidator resigns, and the creditors' meeting called to receive his resignation has resolved against his release, or

(b) he is removed by a creditors' meeting which has so resolved, or is removed by the court,

he must apply to the Secretary of State for his release.

[FORM 4.41]

4.121(4) [Certificate of release] When the Secretary of State gives the release, he shall certify it accordingly, and send the certificate to the official receiver, to be filed in court.

4.121(5) [Copy of certificate] A copy of the certificate shall be sent by the Secretary of State to the former liquidator, whose release is effective from the date of the certificate.

(See General Note after r. 4.122-CVL.)

4.122-CVL Release of resigning or removed liquidator

4.122-CVL(1) [Where liquidator's resignation accepted] Where the liquidator's resignation is accepted by a meeting of creditors which has not resolved against his release, he has his release from when he gives notice of his resignation to the registrar of companies.

[FORM 4.40]

4.122-CVL(2) [Where liquidator removed by meeting] Where the liquidator is removed by a creditors' meeting which has not resolved against his release, the fact of his release shall be stated in the certificate of removal.

4.122-CVL(3) [Application to Secretary of State] Where–

(a) the liquidator resigns, and the creditors' meeting called to receive his resignation has resolved against his release, or

(b) he is removed by a creditors' meeting which has so resolved, or is removed by the court,

he must apply to the Secretary of State for his release.

[FORM 4.41]

4.122-CVL(4) [Certificate of release] When the Secretary of State gives the release, he shall certify it accordingly, and send the certificate to the registrar of companies.

4.122-CVL(5) **[Copy of certificate]** A copy of the certificate shall be sent by the Secretary of State to the former liquidator, whose release is effective from the date of the certificate.

General Note to rr. 4.121, 4.122-CVL

These rules deal with the liquidator's release following his resignation or removal. On the question of release following completion of the administration of the winding up, see rr. 4.124ff.

4.123 Removal of liquidator by Secretary of State

(NO CVL APPLICATION)

4.123(1) **[Notice to liquidator etc.]** If the Secretary of State decides to remove the liquidator, he shall before doing so notify the liquidator and the official receiver of his decision and the grounds of it, and specify a period within which the liquidator may make representations against implementation of the decision.

4.123(2) **[On removal]** If the Secretary of State directs the removal of the liquidator, he shall forthwith—

(a) file notice of his decision in court, and

(b) send notice to the liquidator and the official receiver.

4.123(3) **[If liquidator removed]** If the liquidator is removed by direction of the Secretary of State—

(a) Rule 4.121 applies as regards the liquidator obtaining his release, as if he had been removed by the court, and

(b) the court may make any such order in his case as it would have power to make if he had been so removed.

General Note

The removal of a liquidator by the Secretary of State is provided for by IA 1986, s. 172(4).

Section C: Release on completion of administration

4.124 Release of official receiver

(NO CVL APPLICATION)

4.124(1) **[Notice of intention]** The official receiver shall, before giving notice to the Secretary of State under section 174(3) (that the winding up is for practical purposes complete), send out notice of his intention to do so to all creditors of which he is aware.

4.124(2) **[Accompanying summary of receipts and payments]** The notice shall in each case be accompanied by a summary of the official receiver's receipts and payments as liquidator.

4.124(2A) **[Summary to include amount paid under prescribed part]** The summary of receipts and payments referred to in paragraph (2) shall also include a statement as to the amount paid to unsecured creditors by virtue of the application of section 176A (prescribed part).

4.124(3) **[Notice to court of date of release]** The Secretary of State, when he has determined the date from which the official receiver is to have his release, shall give notice to the court that he has done so. The notice shall be accompanied by the summary referred to in paragraph (2).

(See General Note after r. 4.126-CVL.)

4.125 Final meeting

(NO CVL APPLICATION)

4.125(1) **[Notice to creditors etc.]** Where the liquidator is other than the official receiver, he shall give at least 28 days' notice of the final meeting of creditors to be held under section 146. The notice shall be sent to all creditors of which he is aware; and the liquidator shall cause it to be gazetted at least one month before the meeting is to be held.

[FORM 4.22]

4.125(2) **[Liquidator's report]** The liquidator's report laid before the meeting under that section shall contain an account of the liquidator's administration of the winding up, including–

(a) a summary of his receipts and payments, and

(b) a statement by him that he has reconciled his account with that which is held by the Secretary of State in respect of the winding up.

4.125(2A) **[Report to contain amount paid under prescribed part]** The liquidator's report shall also contain a statement as to the amount paid to unsecured creditors by virtue of the application of section 176A (prescribed part).

4.125(3) **[Questioning of liquidator]** At the final meeting, the creditors may question the liquidator with respect to any matter contained in his report, and may resolve against him having his release.

4.125(4) **[Notice to court]** The liquidator shall give notice to the court that the final meeting has been held; and the notice shall state whether or not he has been given his release, and be accompanied by a copy of the report laid before the final meeting. A copy of the notice shall be sent by the liquidator to the official receiver.

[FORM 4.42]

4.125(5) **[No quorum at final meeting]** If there is no quorum present at the final meeting, the liquidator shall report to the court that a final meeting was summoned in accordance with the Rules, but there was no quorum present; and the final meeting is then deemed to have been held, and the creditors not to have resolved against the liquidator having his release.

4.125(6) **[Release of liquidator]** If the creditors at the final meeting have not so resolved, the liquidator is released when the notice under paragraph (4) is filed in court. If they have so resolved, the liquidator must obtain his release from the Secretary of State and Rule 4.121 applies accordingly.

(See General Note after r. 4.126-CVL.)

4.125A Rule as to reporting

4.125A(1) **[Power of court]** The court may, on the liquidator or official receiver's application, relieve him of any duty imposed on him by Rule 4.124 or 4.125, or authorise him to carry out the duty in a way other than there required.

4.125A(2) **[Consideration in exercising power]** In considering whether to act under this Rule, the court shall have regard to the cost of carrying out the duty, to the amount of the assets available, and to the extent of the interest of creditors or contributories, or any particular class of them.

(See General Note after r. 4.126-CVL.)

4.126-CVL Final meeting

4.126-CVL(1) **[Notice to creditors]** The liquidator shall give at least 28 days' notice of the final meeting of creditors to be held under section 106. The notice shall be sent to all creditors who have proved their debts.

[FORM 4.22]

4.126-CVL(2) **[Questioning of liquidator]** At the final meeting, the creditors may question the liquidator with respect to any matter contained in the account required under the section or paragraph (4) of this Rule, and may resolve against the liquidator having his release.

4.126-CVL(3) **[Release of liquidator]** Where the creditors have so resolved, he must obtain his release from the Secretary of State; and Rule 4.122–CVL applies accordingly.

4.126-CVL(4) **[Account to include amount paid under prescribed part]** The account of the winding up required under section 106 shall also include a statement as to the amount paid to unsecured creditors by virtue of the application of section 176A (prescribed part).

GENERAL NOTE TO RR. 4.124–4.126-CVL

These rules deal with the liquidator's release following the completion of his administration of the estate. On the question of his release upon his resignation or removal, see rr. 4.121, 4.122-CVL.

New paragraphs (2A) were inserted into rr. 4.124 and 4.125, and para. 4.126(4) added, by the Insolvency (Amendment) Rules 2003 (SI 2003/1730, effective September 15, 2003), Sch. 1, paras 21-23. Rule 4.125A was inserted by the Insolvency (Amendment) Rules 2004 (SI 2004/584) effective April 1, 2004.

Section D: Remuneration

4.127 Fixing of remuneration

4.127(1) [Entitlement to remuneration] The liquidator is entitled to receive remuneration for his services as such.

4.127(2) [How fixed] The remuneration shall be fixed either–

(a) as a percentage of the value of the assets which are realised or distributed, or of the one value and the other in combination, or

(b) by reference to the time properly given by the insolvency practitioner (as liquidator) and his staff in attending to matters arising in the winding up.

4.127(3) [Determination under r. 4.127(2)] Where the liquidator is other than the official receiver, it is for the liquidation committee (if there is one) to determine whether the remuneration is to be fixed under paragraph (2)(a) or (b) and, if under paragraph (2)(a), to determine any percentage to be applied as there mentioned.

4.127(4) [Matters relevant r. 4.127(3) determination] In arriving at that determination, the committee shall have regard to the following matters–

(a) the complexity (or otherwise) of the case,

(b) any respects in which, in connection with the winding up, there falls on the insolvency practitioner (as liquidator) any responsibility of an exceptional kind or degree,

(c) the effectiveness with which the insolvency practitioner appears to be carrying out, or to have carried out, his duties as liquidator, and

(d) the value and nature of the assets with which the liquidator has to deal.

4.127(5) [If no committee or no determination] If there is no liquidation committee, or the committee does not make the requisite determination, the liquidator's remuneration may be fixed (in accordance with paragraph (2)) by a resolution of a meeting of creditors; and paragraph (4) applies to them as it does to the liquidation committee.

4.127(6) [Remuneration not otherwise fixed] Where the liquidator is not the official receiver and his remuneration is not fixed as above, the liquidator shall be entitled to remuneration fixed in accordance with the provisions of Rule 4.127A.

(See General Note after r. 4.131.)

4.127A Liquidator's entitlement to remuneration where it is not fixed under Rule 4.127

4.127A(1) [Application of r. 4.127A] This Rule applies where the liquidator is not the official receiver and his remuneration is not fixed in accordance with Rule 4.127

4.127A(2) [Realisation scale in Sch. 6] The liquidator shall be entitled by way of remuneration for his services as such, to such sum as is arrived at by –

(a) first applying the realisation scale set out in Schedule 6 to the monies received by him from the realisation of the assets of the company (including any Value Added Tax thereon but after deducting any sums paid to secured creditors in respect of their securities and any sums spent out of money received in carrying on the business of the company); and

(b) then by adding to the sum arrived at under sub-paragraph (a) such sum as is arrived at by applying the distribution scale set out in Schedule 6 to the value of assets distributed to creditors of the company (including payments made in respect of preferential debts) and to contributories.

(See General Note after r. 4.131.)

4.127B Liquidator's remuneration where he realises assets on behalf of chargeholder

4.127B(1) [**Application of r. 4.127B**] This Rule applies where the liquidator is not the official receiver and realises assets on behalf of a secured creditor.

4.127B(2) [**Mortgage or fixed charge**] Where the assets realised for a secured creditor are subject to a charge which when created was a mortgage or a fixed charge, the liquidator shall be entitled to such sum by way of remuneration as is arrived at by applying the realisation scale set out in Schedule 6 to the monies received by him in respect of the assets realised (including any sums received in respect of Value Added Tax thereon but after deducting any sums spent out of money received in carrying on the business of the company).

4.127B(3) [**Floating charge**] Where the assets realised for a secured creditor are subject to a charge which when created was a floating charge, the liquidator shall be entitled to such sum by way of remuneration as is arrived at by –

(a) first applying the realisation scale set out in Schedule 6 to monies received by him from the realisation of those assets (including any Value Added Tax thereon but ignoring any sums received which are spent in carrying on the business of the company); and

(b) then by adding to the sum arrived at under sub-paragraph (a) such sum as is arrived at by applying the distribution scale set out in Schedule 6 to the value of the assets distributed to the holder of the charge.

(See General Note after r. 4.131.)

4.128 Other matters affecting remuneration

4.128(1) [**Omitted.**]

4.128(2) [**Where joint liquidators**] Where there are joint liquidators, it is for them to agree between themselves as to how the remuneration payable should be apportioned. Any dispute arising between them may be referred–

(a) to the court, for settlement by order, or

(b) to the liquidation committee or a meeting of creditors, for settlement by resolution.

4.128(3) [**If liquidator is a solicitor**] If the liquidator is a solicitor and employs his own firm, or any partner in it, to act on behalf of the company, profit costs shall not be paid unless this is authorised by the liquidation committee, the creditors or the court.

(See General Note after r. 4.131.)

4.129 Recourse of liquidator to meeting of creditors

4.129 If the liquidator's remuneration has been fixed by the liquidation committee, and he considers the rate or amount to be insufficient, he may request that it be increased by resolution of the creditors.

(See General Note after r. 4.131.)

4.130 Recourse to the court

4.130(1) [**Liquidator may apply to court**] If the liquidator considers that the remuneration fixed for him by the liquidation committee, or by resolution of the creditors, or as under Rule 4.127(6), is insufficient, he may apply to the court for an order increasing its amount or rate.

4.130(2) [**Notice to committee etc.**] The liquidator shall give at least 14 days' notice of his application to the members of the liquidation committee; and the committee may nominate one or more members to appear or be represented, and to be heard, on the application.

4.130(3) [**Where no committee**] If there is no liquidation committee, the liquidator's notice of his application shall be sent to such one or more of the company's creditors as the court may direct, which creditors may nominate one or more of their number to appear or be represented.

4.130(4) [**Costs of application**] The court may, if it appears to be a proper case, order the costs of the liquidator's application, including the costs of any member of the liquidation committee appearing or being represented on it, or any creditor so appearing or being represented, to be paid out of the assets.

(See General Note after r. 4.131.)

4.131 Creditors' claim that remuneration is excessive

4.131(1) [**Creditor may apply to court**] Any creditor of the company may, with the concurrence of at least 25 per cent. in value of the creditors (including himself), apply to the court for an order that the liquidator's remuneration be reduced, on the grounds that it is, in all the circumstances, excessive.

4.131(2) [**Power of court to dismiss etc.**] The court may, if it thinks that no sufficient cause is shown for a reduction, dismiss the application; but it shall not do so unless the applicant has had an opportunity to attend the court for an *ex parte* hearing, of which he has been given at least 7 days' notice.

If the application is not dismissed under this paragraph, the court shall fix a venue for it to be heard, and give notice to the applicant accordingly.

4.131(3) [**Notice to liquidator**] The applicant shall, at least 14 days before the hearing, send to the liquidator a notice stating the venue and accompanied by a copy of the application, and of any evidence which the applicant intends to adduce in support of it.

4.131(4) [**Court order**] If the court considers the application to be well-founded, it shall make an order fixing the remuneration at a reduced amount or rate.

4.131(5) [**Costs of application**] Unless the court orders otherwise, the costs of the application shall be paid by the applicant, and are not payable out of the assets.

GENERAL NOTE TO RR. 4.127–4.131

Here are set out the provisions relating to fixing the liquidator's remuneration and the various ways in which a decision on this question may be reviewed or challenged. Rule 4.127(6) was amended, new rr. 4.127A, 4.127B inserted, and r. 4.128 omitted by the Insolvency (Amendment) Rules 2004 (SI 2004/584), effective April 1, 2004. The latter rules repeat in substance the provisions formerly set out in relation to the remuneration of official receivers by the Insolvency Regulations 1994 (SI 1994/2507), which have been repealed. Transitional provisions in reg. 3 of SI 2004/584 ensure that the former provisions continue to apply to cases which were already on foot on April 1, 2004.

A liquidator may not fix his own remuneration, and has no right to retain remuneration out of the assets if they are insufficient to pay other expenses of the liquidation ranking no lower than the remuneration in question: *Re Salters Hall School Ltd (in liq.)* [1998] B.C.C. 503. For an example of the exercise by the court of its jurisdiction under r. 4.130, see *Re Tony Rowse NMC Ltd* [1996] B.C.C. 196. On the remuneration of a liquidator in a members' voluntary winding up, see r. 4.148A and, where a compulsory winding up follows a voluntary winding up, r. 4.219.

A liquidator may, in an appropriate case, also be paid remuneration and allowed expenses for work done in relation to property which does not form part of the assets in the liquidation, for instance property held by the company on trust, or property subject to a fixed or floating charge where the chargee has not appointed a receiver (see *Re Leyland Daf Ltd, Buchler v Talbot* [2004] UKHL 9 at [63]). In *Re Berkeley Applegate (Investment Consultants) Ltd (No. 2)* (1988) 4 B.C.C. 279 the liquidator in a creditors' voluntary winding up discovered, after extensive investigations, that certain assets standing in the name of the company were held by it on trust for people who had paid money to the company for investment. Although there was no statutory authority for payment, the court held that fair compensation could be awarded to the liquidator on general equitable principles. In later proceedings (*Re Berkeley Applegate (Investment Consultants) Ltd (No. 3)* (1989) 5 B.C.C. 803), it was held that this remuneration could not properly be charged on the company's assets in the liquidation but only on the trust funds themselves. See also *Rye v Ashfield Nominees Ltd* (August 2, 2001, *British Company Law and Practice New Developments*, ¶96-471).

Section E: Supplementary provisions

4.132 Liquidator deceased
(NO CVL APPLICATION)

4.132(1) [**Notice to official receiver**] Subject as follows, where the liquidator (other than the official receiver) has died, it is the duty of his personal representatives to give notice of the fact to the official receiver, specifying the date of the death.

This does not apply if notice has been given under any of the following paragraphs of this Rule.

4.132(2) [**Notice by partner etc.**] If the deceased liquidator was a partner in a firm, notice may be given to the official receiver by a partner in the firm who is qualified to act as an insolvency practitioner, or is a member of any body recognised by the Secretary of State for the authorisation of insolvency practitioners.

4.132(3) [**Notice by others**] Notice of the death may be given by any person producing to the official receiver the relevant death certificate or a copy of it.

4.132(4) **[Notice by official receiver]** The official receiver shall give notice to the court, for the purpose of fixing the date of the deceased liquidator's release.

(See General Note after r. 4.138.)

4.133-CVL Liquidator deceased

4.133-CVL(1) **[Notice to registrar and committee]** Subject as follows, where the liquidator has died, it is the duty of his personal representatives to give notice of the fact, and of the date of death, to the registrar of companies and to the liquidation committee (if any) or a member of that committee.

[FORM 4.44]

4.133-CVL(2) **[Notice by others]** In the alternative, notice of the death may be given–

(a) if the deceased liquidator was a partner in a firm, by a partner qualified to act as an insolvency practitioner or who is a member of any body approved by the Secretary of State for the authorisation of insolvency practitioners, or

(b) by any person, if he delivers with the notice a copy of the relevant death certificate.

(See General Note after r. 4.138.)

4.134 Loss of qualification as insolvency practitioner
(NO CVL APPLICATION)

4.134(1) **[Application of Rule]** This Rule applies where the liquidator vacates office on ceasing to be qualified to act as an insolvency practitioner in relation to the company.

4.134(2) **[Notice to official receiver etc.]** He shall forthwith give notice of his doing so to the official receiver, who shall give notice to the Secretary of State.

The official receiver shall file in court a copy of his notice under this paragraph.

[FORM 4.45]

4.134(3) **[Application of r. 4.121]** Rule 4.121 applies as regards the liquidator obtaining his release, as if he had been removed by the court.

(See General Note after r. 4.138.)

4.135-CVL Loss of qualification as insolvency practitioner

4.135-CVL(1) **[Application of Rule]** This Rule applies where the liquidator vacates office on ceasing to be qualified to act as an insolvency practitioner in relation to the company.

4.135-CVL(2) **[Notice]** He shall forthwith give notice of his doing so to the registrar of companies and the Secretary of State.

[FORM 4.46]
[FORM 4.45]

4.135-CVL(3) **[Application of r. 4.122–CVL]** Rule 4.122–CVL applies as regards the liquidator obtaining his release, as if he had been removed by the court.

(See General Note after r. 4.138.)

4.136-CVL Vacation of office on making of winding-up order

4.136-CVL Where the liquidator vacates office in consequence of the court making a winding-up order against the company, Rule 4.122–CVL applies as regards his obtaining his release, as if he had been removed by the court.

(See General Note after r. 4.138.)

4.137 Notice to official receiver of intention to vacate office
(NO CVL APPLICATION)

4.137(1) **[Notice to official receiver]** Where the liquidator intends to vacate office, whether by resignation or otherwise, he shall give notice of his intention to the official receiver together with notice of any creditors' meeting to be held in respect of his vacation of office, including any meeting to receive his resignation.

4.137(2) **[Time limit for notice]** The notice to the official receiver must be given at least 21 days before any such creditors' meeting.

4.137(3) **[Details of property]** Where there remains any property of the company which has not been realised, applied, distributed or otherwise fully dealt with in the winding up, the liquidator shall include in his notice to the official receiver details of the nature of that property, its value (or the fact that it has no value), its location, any action taken by the liquidator to deal with that property or any reason for his not dealing with it, and the current position in relation to it.

(See General Note after r. 4.138.)

4.138 Liquidator's duties on vacating office

4.138(1) **[Obligation to deliver up assets etc.]** Where the liquidator ceases to be in office as such, in consequence of removal, resignation or cesser of qualification as an insolvency practitioner, he is under obligation forthwith to deliver up to the person succeeding him as liquidator the assets (after deduction of any expenses properly incurred, and distributions made, by him) and further to deliver up to that person–

(a) the records of the liquidation, including correspondence, proofs and other related papers appertaining to the administration while it was within his responsibility, and

(b) the company's books, papers and other records.

4.138(2) **[Omitted.]**

4.138(3) **[Vacation following creditors' final meeting]** Where the liquidator vacates office under section 172(8) (final meeting of creditors), he shall deliver up to the official receiver the company's books, papers and other records which have not already been disposed of in accordance with general regulations in the course of the liquidation. (NO CVL APPLICATION).

GENERAL NOTE TO RR. 4.132–4.138

Apart from resignation and removal, which are dealt with in rr. 4.108ff., the office of liquidator may be vacated by death or disqualification or in consequence of a court order. The present rules are concerned with these situations and with various other matters incidental to vacating office.

Rule 4.138(2) was omitted by the Insolvency (Amendment) Rules 2004 (SI 2004/584), effective April 1, 2004.

Section F: The liquidator in a members' voluntary winding up

4.139 Appointment by the company

4.139(1) **[Application of Rule]** This Rule applies where the liquidator is appointed by a meeting of the company.

4.139(2) **[Certifying appointment etc.]** Subject as follows, the chairman of the meeting shall certify the appointment, but not unless and until the person appointed has provided him with a written statement to the effect that he is an insolvency practitioner, duly qualified under the Act to be the liquidator, and that he consents so to act.

[FORM 4.27]
[FORM 4.28]

4.139(3) **[Certificate to liquidator]** The chairman shall send the certificate forthwith to the liquidator, who shall keep it as part of the records of the liquidation.

4.139(4) **[Notice to creditors]** Not later than 28 days from his appointment, the liquidator shall give notice of it to all creditors of the company of whom he is aware in that period.

(See General Note after r. 4.148B.)

4.140 Appointment by the court

4.140(1) **[Application of Rule]** This Rule applies where the liquidator is appointed by the court under section 108.

4.140(2) **[Issue of court order]** The court's order shall not issue unless and until the person appointed has filed in court a statement to the effect that he is an insolvency practitioner, duly qualified under the Act to be the liquidator, and that he consents so to act.

[FORM 4.29]
[FORM 4.30]

4.140(3) **[Copy of order to liquidator]** Thereafter, the court shall send a sealed copy of the order to the liquidator, whose appointment takes effect from the date of the order.

4.140(4) **[Notice to creditors]** Not later than 28 days from his appointment, the liquidator shall give notice of it all creditors of the company of whom he is aware in that period.

(See General Note after r. 4.148B.)

4.141 Authentication of liquidator's appointment

4.141 A copy of the certificate of the liquidator's appointment or (as the case may be) a sealed copy of the court's order appointing him may in any proceedings be adduced as proof that the person appointed is duly authorised to exercise the powers and perform the duties of liquidator in the company's winding up.

(See General Note after r. 4.148B.)

4.142 Company meeting to receive liquidator's resignation

4.142(1) **[Liquidator must call meeting etc.]** Before resigning his office, the liquidator must call a meeting of the company for the purpose of receiving his resignation. The notice summoning the meeting shall indicate that this is the purpose, or one of the purposes, of it.

4.142(2) **[Account of liquidator's administration]** The notice under paragraph (1) must be accompanied by an account of the liquidator's administration of the winding up, including–

(a) a summary of his receipts and payments, and

(b) a statement by him that he has reconciled his account with that which is held by the Secretary of State in respect of the winding up.

4.142(3) **[Grounds for proceeding under Rule]** Subject as follows, the liquidator may only proceed under this Rule on grounds of ill health or because–

(a) he intends ceasing to be in practice as an insolvency practitioner, or

(b) there is some conflict of interest or change of personal circumstances which precludes or makes impracticable the further discharge by him of the duties of liquidator.

4.142(4) **[Where joint liquidators]** Where two or more persons are acting as liquidator jointly, any one of them may proceed under this Rule (without prejudice to the continuation in office of the other or others) on the ground that, in his opinion or that of the other or others, it is no longer expedient that there should continue to be the present number of joint liquidators.

4.142(4A) **[If no quorum]** If there is no quorum present at the meeting summoned to receive the liquidator's resignation, the meeting is deemed to have been held.

4.142(5) **[S. 171(5) notice]** The notice of the liquidator's resignation required by section 171(5) shall be given by him forthwith after the meeting.

[FORM 4.33]

4.142(6) **[Where new liquidator appointed]** Where a new liquidator is appointed in place of one who has resigned, the former shall, in giving notice of his appointment, state that his predecessor has resigned.

(See General Note after r. 4.148B.)

4.143 Removal of liquidator by the court

4.143(1) [**Application of Rule**] This Rule applies where application is made to the court for the removal of the liquidator, or for an order directing the liquidator to summon a company meeting for the purpose of removing him.

4.143(2) [**Court may dismiss application etc.**] The court may, if it thinks that no sufficient cause is shown for the application, dismiss it; but it shall not do so unless the applicant has had an opportunity to attend the court for an *ex parte* hearing, of which he has been given at least 7 days' notice.

If the application is not dismissed under this paragraph, the court shall fix a venue for it to be heard.

4.143(3) [**Deposit or security for costs**] The court may require the applicant to make a deposit or give security for the costs to be incurred by the liquidator on the application.

4.143(4) [**Notice etc.**] The applicant shall, at least 14 days before the hearing, send to the liquidator a notice stating the venue and accompanied by a copy of the application, and of any evidence which he intends to adduce in support of it.

Subject to any contrary order of the court, the costs of the application are not payable out of the assets.

4.143(5) [**Where court removes liquidator**] Where the court removes the liquidator–

(a) it shall send 2 copies of the order of removal to him, one to be sent by him forthwith to the registrar of companies, with notice of his ceasing to act;

(b) the order may include such provision as the court thinks fit with respect to matters arising in connection with the removal; and

(c) if the court appoints a new liquidator, Rule 4.140 applies.

[FORM 4.39]
[FORM 4.40]

(See General Note after r. 4.148B.)

4.144 Release of resigning or removed liquidator

4.144(1) [**Where liquidator resigns**] Where the liquidator resigns, he has his release from the date on which he gives notice of his resignation to the registrar of companies.

[FORM 4.40]

4.144(2) [**Where removed by meeting**] Where the liquidator is removed by a meeting of the company, he shall forthwith give notice to the registrar of companies of his ceasing to act.

[FORM 4.40]

4.144(3) [**Where removed by court**] Where the liquidator is removed by the court, he must apply to the Secretary of State for his release.

[FORM 4.41]

4.144(4) [**Certifying release etc.**] When the Secretary of State gives the release, he shall certify it accordingly, and send the certificate to the registrar of companies.

4.144(5) [**Copy of certificate**] A copy of the certificate shall be sent by the Secretary of State to the former liquidator, whose release is effective from the date of the certificate.

(See General Note after r. 4.148B.)

4.145 Liquidator deceased

4.145(1) [**Duty to give notice**] Subject as follows, where the liquidator has died, it is the duty of his personal representatives to give notice of the fact, and of the date of death, to the company's directors, or any one of them, and to the registrar of companies.

[FORM 4.44]

4.145(2) **[Notice by partner or others]** In the alternative, notice of the death may be given–

(a) if the deceased liquidator was a partner in a firm, by a partner qualified to act as an insolvency practitioner or who is a member of any body approved by the Secretary of State for the authorisation of insolvency practitioners, or

(b) by any person, if he delivers with the notice a copy of the relevant death certificate.

(See General Note after r. 4.148B.)

4.146 Loss of qualification as insolvency practitioner

4.146(1) **[Application of Rule]** This Rule applies where the liquidator vacates office on ceasing to be qualified to act as an insolvency practitioner in relation to the company.

4.146(2) **[Notice]** He shall forthwith give notice of his doing so to the registrar of companies and the Secretary of State.

[FORM 4.45]
[FORM 4.46]

4.146(3) **[Application of r. 4.144]** Rule 4.144 applies as regards the liquidator obtaining his release, as if he had been removed by the court.

(See General Note after r. 4.148B.)

4.147 Vacation of office on making of winding-up order

4.147 Where the liquidator vacates office in consequence of the court making a winding-up order against the company. Rule 4.144 applies as regards his obtaining his release, as if he had been removed by the court.

(See General Note after r. 4.148B.)

4.148 Liquidator's duties on vacating office

4.148 Where the liquidator ceases to be in office as such, in consequence of removal, resignation or cesser of qualification as an insolvency practitioner, he is under obligation forthwith to deliver up to the person succeeding him as liquidator the assets (after deduction of any expenses properly incurred, and distributions made, by him) and further to deliver up to that person–

(a) the records of the liquidation, including correspondence, proofs and other related papers appertaining to the administration while it was within his responsibility, and

(b) the company's books, papers and other records.

(See General Note after r. 4.148B.)

4.148A Remuneration of liquidator in members' voluntary winding up

4.148A(1) **[Entitlement]** The liquidator is entitled to receive remuneration for his services as such.

4.148A(2) **[How fixed]** The remuneration shall be fixed either –

(a) as a percentage of the value of the assets which are realised or distributed, or of the one value and the other in combination, or

(b) by reference to the time properly given by the insolvency practitioner (as liquidator) and his staff in attending to matters arising in the winding up;

and the company in general meeting shall determine whether the remuneration is to be fixed under subparagraph (a) or (b) and, if under subparagraph (a), the percentage to be applied as there mentioned.

4.148A(3) **[Matters in determination]** In arriving at that determination the company in general meeting shall have regard to the matters set out in paragraph (4) of Rule 4.127.

4.148A(4) **[Otherwise fixed]** Where the liquidator's remuneration is not fixed as above, the liquidator shall be entitled to remuneration calculated in accordance with the provisions of Rule 4.148B.

4.148A(5) **[Application of r. 4.128]** Rule 4.128 shall apply in relation to the remuneration of the liquidator in respect of the matters there mentioned and for this purpose references in that Rule to "the liquidation committee" and "a meeting of creditors" shall be read as references to the company in general meeting.

4.148A(6) **[Liquidator may apply to court]** If the liquidator considers that the remuneration fixed for him by the company in general meeting, or as under paragraph (4), is insufficient, he may apply to the court for an order increasing its amount or rate.

4.148A(7) **[Notice to contributories]** The liquidator shall give at least 14 days' notice of an application under paragraph (6) to the company's contributories, or such one or more of them as the court may direct, and the contributories may nominate any one or more of their number to appear or be represented.

4.148A(8) **[Costs of application]** The court may, if it appears to be a proper case, order the costs of the liquidator's application, including the costs of any contributory appearing or being represented on it, to be paid out of the assets.

4.148B Liquidator's remuneration in members' voluntary liquidation where it is not fixed under Rule 4.148A

4.148B(1) **[Application of r. 4.148A]** This Rule applies where the liquidator's remuneration is not fixed in accordance with Rule 4.148A.

4.148B(2) **[Realisation scale in Sch.6]** The liquidator shall be entitled by way of remuneration for his services as such, to such sum as is arrived at by –

(a) first applying the realisation scale set out in Schedule 6 to the monies received by him from the realisation of the assets of the company (including any Value Added Tax thereon but after deducting any sums paid to secured creditors in respect of their securities and any sums spent out of money received in carrying on the business of the company); and

(b) then by adding to the sum arrived at under sub-paragraph (a) such sum as is arrived at by applying the distribution scale set out in Schedule 6 to the value of assets distributed to creditors of the company (including payments made in respect of preferential debts) and to contributories.

GENERAL NOTE TO RR. 4.139–4.148B

This is the only part of the rules which deals exclusively with a members' voluntary winding up. The rules set out here relate to the questions of the appointment of the liquidator and the vacation of his office, corresponding to earlier sections of this chapter which govern compulsory and insolvent liquidations. Rule 4.148A(4) was amended, and new r. 4.148B inserted, by the Insolvency (Amendment) Rules 2004 (SI 2004/584), effective April 1, 2004. This follows amendments made to the Insolvency Regulations 1994 (SI 1994/2507): see the note rr. 4.127–4.131.

In *Re AMF International Ltd* [1995] B.C.C. 439 a members' voluntary winding up was commenced but proved to be insolvent. A creditor applied to have the liquidator removed by the court, but before the application was heard he was replaced by a meeting of the creditors summoned under s. 95 of the Act. The court took the view that the liquidator had acted improperly in paying a contributory before all the creditors' claims had been satisfied and, acting under r. 4.143 (4), ordered him to bear the costs of all parties personally.

Section G: Rules applying in every winding up, whether voluntary or by the court

4.149 Power of court to set aside certain transactions

4.149(1) **[Liquidator's transaction with associate]** If in the administration of the estate the liquidator enters into any transaction with a person who is an associate of his, the court may, on the application of any person interested, set the transaction aside and order the liquidator to compensate the company for any loss suffered in consequence of it.

4.149(2) **[Where r. 4.149(1) does not apply]** This does not apply if either–

(a) the transaction was entered into with the prior consent of the court, or

(b) it is shown to the court's satisfaction that the transaction was for value, and that it was entered into by the liquidator without knowing, or having any reason to suppose, that the person concerned was an associate.

4.149(3) **[Effect of Rule]** Nothing in this Rule is to be taken as prejudicing the operation of any rule of law or equity with respect to a liquidator's dealings with trust property, or the fiduciary obligations of any person.

GENERAL NOTE

This rule imposes statutory duties of a quasi-fiduciary character on a liquidator, supplementing the rules of equity and the common law. For the meaning of "associate", see IA 1986, s. 435.

4.150 Rule against solicitation

4.150(1) **[Power of court]** Where the court is satisfied that any improper solicitation has been used by or on behalf of the liquidator in obtaining proxies or procuring his appointment, it may order that no remuneration out of the assets be allowed to any person by whom, or on whose behalf, the solicitation was exercised.

4.150(2) **[Effect of court order]** An order of the court under this Rule overrides any resolution of the liquidation committee or the creditors, or any other provision of the Rules relating to the liquidator's remuneration.

GENERAL NOTE

This rule similarly supplements principles of equity and the common law; and see also IA 1986, s. 164 (corrupt inducement affecting liquidator's appointment).

CHAPTER 12

THE LIQUIDATION COMMITTEE

4.151 Preliminary

(NO CVL APPLICATION)

For the purposes of this Chapter–

(a) an "insolvent winding up" is where the company is being wound up on grounds which include inability to pay its debts, and

(b) a "solvent winding up" is where the company is being wound up on grounds which do not include that one.

GENERAL NOTE

Note that this is a special use of the word "solvent": a company which is ordered to be wound up on grounds other than inability to pay debts may well be "insolvent" in any of the normal senses of that word, but the liquidation will be "solvent" within this definition, and conversely. See the general comment to IA 1986, Pt VI, preceding s. 230, and the note to IA 1986, s. 247.

For the meaning of "inability to pay its debts", see IA 1986, see s. 123.
For the rules which apply where a winding up follows immediately upon an administration, see rr. 4.173ff.

4.152 Membership of committee

4.152(1) **[Numbers to be elected]** Subject to Rule 4.154 below, the liquidation committee shall consist as follows–

(a) in any case of at least 3, and not more than 5, creditors of the company, elected by the meeting of creditors held under section 141 of the Act, and

(b) also, in the case of a solvent winding up, where the contributories' meeting held under that section so decides, of up to 3 contributories, elected by that meeting.

(NO CVL APPLICATION)

4.152(2) **[At least three members]** The committee must have at least 3 members before it can be established.

4.152(3) **[Eligibility]** Any creditor of the company (other than one whose debt is fully secured) is eligible to be a member of the committee, so long as–

(a) he has lodged a proof of his debt, and

(b) his proof has neither been wholly disallowed for voting purposes, nor wholly rejected for purposes of distribution or dividend.

4.152(4) **[No dual membership]** No person can be a member as both a creditor and a contributory.

4.152(5) **[Representation of body corporate]** A body corporate may be a member of the committee, but it cannot act as such otherwise than by a representative appointed under Rule 4.159.

4.152(6) **["Creditor members", "contributory members"]** Members of the committee elected or appointed to represent the creditors are called "creditor members"; and those elected or appointed to represent the contributories are called "contributory members".

4.152(7) **[Additional credit members]** The following categories of person are to be regarded as additional creditor members–

(a) a representative of the Financial Services Authority who exercises the right under section 371(4)(b) of the Financial Services and Markets Act 2000 to be a member of the committee;

(b) a representative of the scheme manager who exercises the right under section 215(4) of that Act to be a member of the committee.

(See General Note after r. 4.155.)

4.153 Formalities of establishment

4.153(1) **[Liquidator's certificate]** The liquidation committee does not come into being, and accordingly cannot act, until the liquidator has issued a certificate of its due constitution.

[FORM 4.47]

4.153(2) **[If chairman of meeting not liquidator]** If the chairman of the meeting which resolves to establish the committee is not the liquidator, he shall forthwith give notice of the resolution to the liquidator (or, as the case may be, the person appointed as liquidator by that same meeting), and inform him of the names and addresses of the persons elected to be members of the committee.

4.153(3) **[Agreement to act]** No person may act as a member of the committee unless and until he has agreed to do so and, unless the relevant proxy or authorisation contains a statement to the contrary, such agreement may be given by his proxy-holder or representative under section 375 of the Companies Act present at the meeting establishing the committee.

4.153(3A) **[No certificate without agreement]** The liquidator's certificate of the committee's due constitution shall not issue before the minimum number of persons (in accordance with Rule 4.152) who are to be members of the committee have agreed to act.

4.153(4) **[Amended certificate]** As and when the others (if any) agree to act, the liquidator shall issue an amended certificate.

4.153(5) **[Certificate to be filed in court]** The certificate, and any amended certificate, shall be filed in court by the liquidator.
(NO CVL APPLICATION)

4.153(6) **[Certificate to registrar]** The certificate, and any amended certificate, shall be sent by the liquidator to the registrar of companies.

[FORM 4.47]
[FORM 4.48]

4.153(7) **[Change in membership]** It after the first establishment of the committee there is any change in its membership, the liquidator shall report the change to the court.
(NO CVL APPLICATION)

[FORM 4.49]

4.153(8) **[Change in membership]** If after the first establishment of the committee there is any change in its membership, the liquidator shall report the change to the registrar of companies.

[FORM 4.49]
[FORM 4.48]

(See General Note after r. 4.155.)

4.154 Committee established by contributories

(NO CVL APPLICATION)

4.154(1) **[Application of Rule]** The following applies where the creditors' meeting under section 141 does not decide that a liquidation committee should be established, or decides that a committee should not be established.

4.154(2) **[Further creditors' meeting]** The meeting of contributories under that section may appoint one of their number to make application to the court for an order to the liquidator that a further creditors' meeting be summoned for the purpose of establishing a liquidation committee; and–

(a) the court may, if it thinks that there are special circumstances to justify it, make that order, and

(b) the creditors' meeting summoned by the liquidator in compliance with the order is deemed to have been summoned under section 141.

4.154(3) **[Meeting of contributories]** If the creditors' meeting so summoned does not establish a liquidation committee, a meeting of contributories may do so.

4.154(4) **[Constitution of committee]** The committee shall then consist of at least 3, and not more than 5, contributories elected by that meeting; and Rule 4.153 applies, substituting for the reference in paragraph (3A) of that Rule to Rule 4.152 a reference to this paragraph.

(See General Note after r. 4.155.)

4.155 Obligations of liquidator to committee

4.155(1) **[Liquidator's duty to report]** Subject as follows, it is the duty of the liquidator to report to the members of the liquidation committee all such matters as appear to him to be, or as they have indicated to him as being, of concern to them with respect to the winding up.

4.155(2) **[Non-compliance with request for information]** In the case of matters so indicated to him by the committee, the liquidator need not comply with any request for information where it appears to him that–

(a) the request is frivolous or unreasonable, or

(b) the cost of complying would be excessive, having regard to the relative importance of the information, or

(c) there are not sufficient assets to enable him to comply.

4.155(3) **[Report in summary form]** Where the committee has come into being more than 28 days after the appointment of the liquidator, he shall report to them, in summary form, what actions he has taken since his appointment, and shall answer all such questions as they may put to him regarding his conduct of the winding up hitherto.

4.155(4) **[Summary report for subsequent member]** A person who becomes a member of the committee at any time after its first establishment is not entitled to require a report to him by the liquidator, otherwise than in summary form, of any matters previously arising.

4.155(5) **[Access to liquidator's records]** Nothing in this Rule disentitles the committee, or any member of it from having access to the liquidator's records of the liquidation, or from seeking an explanation of any matter within the committee's responsibility.

GENERAL NOTE TO RR. 4.152–4.155

These rules deal with the membership of the liquidation committee in different circumstances (rr. 4.152, 4.154), and with the liquidator's reporting obligations (r. 4.155). Note that the contributories may be represented on the committee only in the case of a "solvent" winding up (as that term is defined by r. 4.151(b)). On the termination of membership, see rr. 4.160–4.164 and 4.171; and for further reporting obligations, see r. 4.168.

The amendment to r. 153(3) is intended to enable a meeting of the liquidation committee to be held immediately after the meeting at which the liquidator is appointed.

Rule 4.152(7) was substituted by the Financial Services and Markets Act 2000 (Consequential Provisions and Repeals) Order 2001 (SI 2001/3649) as from December 1, 2001.

Documents passing between the liquidator and the Department of Trade and Industry concerning possible disqualification of directors are not documents which are within any of the statutory rights of the liquidation committee to inspect, or in respect of which the committee can properly put questions to the liquidator and ask him to report to them: *Re W & A Glaser Ltd* [1994] B.C.C. 199.

4.156 Meetings of the committee

4.156(1) **[Holding of meetings]** Subject as follows, meetings of the liquidation committee shall be held when and where determined by the liquidator.

4.156(2) **[First and subsequent meetings]** The liquidator shall call a first meeting of the committee to take place within 3 months of his appointment or of the committee's establishment (whichever is the later); and thereafter he shall call a meeting–

(a) if so requested by a creditor member of the committee or his representative (the meeting then to be held within 21 days of the request being received by the liquidator), and

(b) for a specified date, if the committee has previously resolved that a meeting be held on that date.

4.156(3) **[Notice of venue]** The liquidator shall give 7 days' written notice of the venue of a meeting to every member of the committee (or his representative, if designated for that purpose), unless in any case the requirement of the notice has been waived by or on behalf of any member.

Waiver may be signified either at or before the meeting.

(See General Note after r. 4.159.)

4.157 The chairman at meetings

4.157(1) **[Liquidator or his nominee]** The chairman at any meeting of the liquidation committee shall be the liquidator, or a person nominated by him to act.

4.157(2) **[Nominated chairman]** A person so nominated must be either–

(a) one who is qualified to act as an insolvency practitioner in relation to the company, or

(b) an employee of the liquidator or his firm who is experienced in insolvency matters.

(See General Note after r. 4.159.)

4.158 Quorum

4.158(1) **[Two creditor members]** A meeting of the committee is duly constituted if due notice of it has been given to all the members, and at least 2 creditor members are present or represented.
(NO CVL APPLICATION)

4.158(2) **[Two members]** A meeting of the committee is duly constituted if due notice of it has been given to all the members, and at least 2 members are present or represented.

(See General Note after r. 4.159.)

4.159 Committee-members' representatives

4.159(1) **[Representation]** A member of the liquidation committee may, in relation to the business of the committee, be represented by another person duly authorised by him for that purpose.

4.159(2) **[Letter of authority]** A person acting as a committee-member's representative must hold a letter of authority entitling him so to act (either generally or specially) and signed by or on behalf of the committee-member, and for this purpose any proxy or any authorisation under section 375 of the Companies Act in relation to any meeting of creditors (or, as the case may be, members or contributories) of the company shall, unless it contains a statement to the contrary, be treated as such a letter of authority to act generally signed by or on behalf of the committee-member.

4.159(3) **[Production of letter of authority]** The chairman at any meeting of the committee may call on a person claiming to act as a committee-member's representative to produce his letter of authority, and may exclude him if it appears that his authority is deficient.

4.159(4) **[Who may not be a representative]** No member may be represented by a body corporate, or by a person who is an undischarged bankrupt or a disqualified director or is subject to a bankruptcy restrictions order, bankruptcy restrictions undertaking or an interim bankruptcy restrictions order.

4.159(5) **[No dual representation]** No person shall–

(a) on the same committee, act at one and the same time as representative of more than one committee-member, or

(b) act both as a member of the committee and as representative of another member.

4.159(6) **[Signing as representative]** Where a member's representative signs any document on the member's behalf, the fact that he so signs must be stated below his signature.

GENERAL NOTE TO RR. 4.156–4.159

Some of the rules regarding the holding and conduct of meetings of the liquidation committee are set out here. The remainder are at rr. 4.165–4.168. On the members' expenses, see r. 4.169, and on the role of representatives, see *Re W & A Glaser Ltd* [1994] B.C.C. 199 at p. 208. Rule 4.159(4) was amended by the Insolvency (Amendment) Rules 2004 (SI 2004/584), effective April 1, 2004, by the insertion of the reference to "a disqualified director", and also to take account of the changes made by the new bankruptcy regime.

4.160 Resignation

4.160 A member of the liquidation committee may resign by notice in writing delivered to the liquidator.

(See General Note after r. 4.164.)

4.161 Termination of membership

4.161(1) [Automatic termination] A person's membership of the liquidation committee is automatically terminated if—

(a) he becomes bankrupt, or

(b) at 3 consecutive meetings of the committee he is neither present nor represented (unless at the third of those meetings it is resolved that this Rule is not to apply in his case).

4.161(2) [Termination on bankruptcy] However, if the cause of termination is the member's bankruptcy, his trustee in bankruptcy replaces him as a member of the committee.

4.161(3) [Not a creditor] The membership of a creditor member is also automatically terminated if he ceases to be, or is found never to have been, a creditor.

(See General Note after r. 4.164.)

4.162 Removal

4.162(1) [Removal by resolution] A creditor member of the committee may be removed by resolution at a meeting of creditors; and a contributory member may be removed by a resolution of a meeting of contributories.

4.162(2) [Notice of intention] In either case, 14 days' notice must be given of the intention to move the resolution.

(See General Note after r. 4.164.)

4.163 Vacancy (creditor members)

4.163(1) [Application of Rule] The following applies if there is a vacancy among the creditor members of the committee.

4.163(2) [Agreement not to fill vacancy] The vacancy need not be filled if the liquidator and a majority of the remaining creditor members so agree, provided that the total number of members does not fall below the minimum required by Rule 4.152.

4.163(3) [Appointment by liquidator] The liquidator may appoint any creditor (being qualified under the Rules to be a member of the committee) to fill the vacancy, if a majority of the other creditor members agree to the appointment, and the creditor concerned consents to act.

4.163(4) [Appointment by resolution] Alternatively, a meeting of creditors may resolve that a creditor be appointed (with his consent) to fill the vacancy. In this case, at least 14 days' notice must have been given of the resolution to make such an appointment (whether or not of a person named in the notice).

4.163(5) [Report to liquidator] Where the vacancy is filled by an appointment made by a creditors' meeting at which the liquidator is not present, the chairman of the meeting shall report to the liquidator the appointment which has been made.

(See General Note after r. 4.164.)

4.164 Vacancy (contributory members)

4.164(1) [Application of Rule] The following applies if there is a vacancy among the contributory members of the committee.

4.164(2) **[Agreement not to fill vacancy]** The vacancy need not be filled if the liquidator and a majority of the remaining contributory members so agree, provided that, in the case of a committee of contributory members only, the total number of members does not fall below the minimum required by r. 4.154(4) or, as the case may be, 4.171(5).

4.164(3) **[Appointment by liquidator]** The liquidator may appoint any contributory member (being qualified under the Rules to be a member of the committee) to fill the vacancy, if a majority of the other contributory members agree to the appointment, and the contributory concerned consents to act.

4.164(4) **[Appointment by resolution]** Alternatively, a meeting of contributories may resolve that a contributory be appointed (with his consent) to fill the vacancy. In this case, at least 14 days' notice must have been given of the resolution to make such an appointment (whether or not of a person named in the notice).

4.164(5) **[Where contributories make r. 4.164(4) appointment]** Where the contributories make an appointment under paragraph (4), the creditor members of the committee may, if they think fit, resolve that the person appointed ought not to be a member of the committee; and–

(a) that person is not then, unless the court otherwise directs, qualified to act as a member of the committee, and

(b) on any application to the court for a direction under this paragraph the court may, if it thinks fit, appoint another person (being a contributory) to fill the vacancy on the committee.

4.164(6) **[Report to liquidator]** Where the vacancy is filled by an appointment made by a contributories' meeting at which the liquidator is not present, the chairman of the meeting shall report to the liquidator the appointment which has been made.

GENERAL NOTE TO RR. 4.160–4.164

Note also that the membership of the creditor members of the committee automatically ceases when it is certified that the creditors have been paid in full (r. 4.171).

4.165 Voting rights and resolutions

(NO CVL APPLICATION)

4.165(1) **[Creditor members' votes]** At any meeting of the committee, each member of it (whether present himself, or by his representative) has one vote; and a resolution is passed when a majority of the creditor members present or represented have voted in favour of it.

4.165(2) **[Contributory members' votes]** Subject to the next paragraph, the votes of contributory members do not count towards the number required for passing a resolution, but the way in which they vote on any resolution shall be recorded.

4.165(3) **[Only contributory members]** Paragraph (2) does not apply where, by virtue of Rule 4.154 or 4.171, the only members of the committee are contributories. In that case the committee is to be treated for voting purposes as if all its members were creditors.

4.165(4) **[Record of resolutions]** Every resolution passed shall be recorded in writing, either separately or as part of the minutes of the meeting. The record shall be signed by the chairman and kept with the records of the liquidation.

(See General Note after r. 4.169.)

4.166-CVL Voting rights and resolutions

4.166-CVL(1) **[Votes etc.]** At any meeting of the committee, each member of it (whether present himself, or by his representative) has one vote; and a resolution is passed when a majority of the members present or represented have voted in favour of it.

4.166-CVL(2) **[Record of resolutions]** Every resolution passed shall be recorded in writing, either separately or as part of the minutes of the meeting. The record shall be signed by the chairman and kept with the records of the liquidation.

(See General Note after r. 4.169.)

4.167 Resolutions by post

4.167(1) **[Sending proposed resolution]** In accordance with this Rule, the liquidator may seek to obtain the agreement of members of the liquidation committee to a resolution by sending to every member (or his representative designated for the purpose) a copy of the proposed resolution.

4.167(2) **[Copy of proposed resolution]** Where the liquidator makes use of the procedure allowed by this Rule, he shall send out to members of the committee or their representatives (as the case may be) a copy of any proposed resolution on which a decision is sought, which shall be set out in such a way that agreement with or dissent from each separate resolution may be indicated by the recipient on the copy so sent.

4.167(3) **[Creditor requiring meeting]** Any creditor member of the committee may, within 7 business days from the date of the liquidator sending out a resolution, require him to summon a meeting of the committee to consider the matters raised by the resolution. (NO CVL APPLICATION)

4.167(4) **[Member requiring meeting]** Any member of the committee may, within 7 business days from the date of the liquidator sending out a resolution, require him to summon a meeting of the committee to consider the matters raised by the resolution.

4.167(5) **[Deemed passing of resolution]** In the absence of such a request, the resolution is deemed to have been passed by the committee if and when the liquidator is notified in writing by a majority of the creditor members that they concur with it. (NO CVL APPLICATION)

4.167(6) **[Deemed passing of resolution where no request]** In the absence of such a request, the resolution is deemed to have been passed by the committee if and when the liquidator is notified in writing by a majority of the members that they concur with it.

4.167(7) **[Copy of resolutions]** A copy of every resolution passed under this Rule, and a note that the committee's concurrence was obtained, shall be kept with the records of the liquidation.

(See General Note after r. 4.169.)

4.168 Liquidator's reports

4.168(1) **[Liquidator directed to report]** The liquidator shall, as and when directed by the liquidation committee (but not more often than once in any period of 2 months), send a written report to every member of the committee setting out the position generally as regards the progress of the winding up and matters arising in connection with it, to which he (the liquidator) considers the committee's attention should be drawn.

4.168(2) **[If no directions to report]** In the absence of such directions by the committee, the liquidator shall send such a report not less often than once in every period of 6 months.

4.168(3) **[Effect of Rule]** The obligations of the liquidator under this Rule are without prejudice to those imposed by Rule 4.155.

4.169 Expenses of members, etc.

4.169 The liquidator shall defray out of the assets, in the prescribed order of priority, any reasonable travelling expenses directly incurred by members of the liquidation committee or their representatives in respect of their attendance at the committee's meetings, or otherwise on the committee's business.

General Note to rr. 4.165–4.167, 4.169

See also rr. 4.155–4.159 and, on the question of priority, r. 4.218(1)(m).

Rule 4.167(2), as now worded, removes the former requirement that each resolution be set out on a separate piece of paper.

4.170 Dealings by committee-members and others

4.170(1) [**Application of Rule**] This Rule applies to–

(a) any member of the liquidation committee,

(b) any committee-member's representative,

(c) any person who is an associate of a member of the committee or a committee-member's representative, and

(d) any person who has been a member of the committee at any time in the last 12 months.

4.170(2) [**Prohibited transactions**] Subject as follows, a person to whom this Rule applies shall not enter into any transaction whereby he–

(a) receives out of the company's assets any payment for services given or goods supplied in connection with the administration, or

(b) obtains any profit from the administration, or

(c) acquires any asset forming part of the estate.

4.170(3) [**Leave or sanction for r. 4.170(2) transaction**] Such a transaction may be entered into by a person to whom this Rule applies–

(a) with the prior leave of the court, or

(b) if he does so as a matter of urgency, or by way of performance of a contract in force before the date on which the company went into liquidation, and obtains the court's leave for the transaction, having applied for it without undue delay, or

(c) with the prior sanction of the liquidation committee, where it it satisfied (after full disclosure of the circumstances) that the person will be giving full value in the transaction.

4.170(4) [**Resolution to sanction transaction**] Where in the committee a resolution is proposed that sanction be accorded for a transaction to be entered into which, without that sanction or the leave of the court, would be in contravention of this Rule, no member of the committee, and no representative of a member, shall vote if he is to participate directly or indirectly in the transaction.

4.170(5) [**Powers of court**] The court may, on the application of any person interested–

(a) set aside a transaction on the ground that it has been entered into in contravention of this Rule, and

(b) make with respect to it such other order as it thinks fit, including (subject to the following paragraph) an order requiring a person to whom this Rule applies to account for any profit obtained from the transaction and compensate the estate for any resultant loss.

4.170(6) [**Member's or representative's associate**] In the case of a person to whom this Rule applies as an associate of a member of the committee or of a committee-member's representative, the court shall not make any order under paragraph (5), if satisfied that he entered into the relevant transaction without having any reason to suppose that in doing so he would contravene this Rule.

4.170(7) [**Costs of application**] The costs of an application to the court for leave under this Rule are not payable out of the assets, unless the court so orders.

General Note

This rule makes provision to guard against the risks of conflicts of interest on the part of committee members and their associates. (For the meaning of "associate", see IA 1986, s. 435.)

4.171 Composition of committee when creditors paid in full

4.171(1) **[Application of Rule]** This Rule applies if the liquidator issues a certificate that the creditors have been paid in full, with interest in accordance with section 189.

4.171(2) **[Liquidator to file certificate in court]** The liquidator shall forthwith file the certificate in court.
(NO CVL APPLICATION)

[FORM 4.50]

4.171(3) **[Copy of certificate to registrar]** The liquidator shall forthwith send a copy of the certificate to the registrar of companies.

[FORM 4.51]
[FORM 4.50]

4.171(4) **[Creditor members]** The creditor members of the liquidation committee cease to be members of the committee.

4.171(5) **[Contributory members]** The committee continues in being unless and until abolished by decision of a meeting of contributories, and (subject to the next paragraph) so long as it consists of at least 3 contributory members.

4.171(6) **[Cessation or suspension]** The committee does not cease to exist on account of the number of contributory members falling below 3, unless and until 28 days have elapsed since the issue of the liquidator's certificate under paragraph (1).

But at any time when the committee consists of less than 3 contributory members, it is suspended and cannot act.

4.171(7) **[Co-opting etc. of contributories]** Contributories may be co-opted by the liquidator, or appointed by a contributories' meeting, to be members of the committee; but the maximum number of members is 5.

4.171(8) **[Application of Rules]** The foregoing Rules in this Chapter continue to apply to the liquidation committee (with any necessary modifications) as if all the members of the committee were creditor members.

GENERAL NOTE

The liquidation committee continues in being without creditor members after the creditors have been paid in full, subject to r. 4.171(5), (6).

4.172 Committee's functions vested in Secretary of State

(NO CVL APPLICATION)

4.172(1) **[Liquidator's notices and reports]** At any time when the functions of the liquidation committee are vested in the Secretary of State under section 141(4) or (5), requirements of the Act or the Rules about notices to be given, or reports to be made, to the committee by the liquidator do not apply, otherwise than as enabling the committee to require a report as to any matter.

4.172(2) **[Exercise by official receiver]** Where the committee's functions are so vested under section 141(5), they may be exercised by the official receiver.

GENERAL NOTE

IA 1986, s. 141(4) applies when the official receiver is liquidator, and s. 141(5) where there is for the time being no liquidation committee.

4.172A Formal defects

4.172A The acts of the liquidation committee established for any winding up are valid notwithstanding any defect in the appointment, election or qualifications of any member of the committee or any committee-member's representative or in the formalities of its establishment.

GENERAL NOTE

This is a standard-form provision designed to prevent technical objections to the constitution of the committee. (See, however, *Re W & A Glaser Ltd* [1994] B.C.C. 199, which makes it clear that the court itself is free to go into this question.)

CHAPTER 13

THE LIQUIDATION COMMITTEE WHERE WINDING UP FOLLOWS IMMEDIATELY ON ADMINISTRATION
(NO CVL APPLICATION)

4.173 Preliminary

4.173(1) **[Application of Rules]** The Rules in this Chapter apply where–

(a) the winding-up order has been made by the court upon an application under paragraph 79 of Schedule B1 to the Act, and

(b) the court makes an order under section 140(1) of the Act appointing as liquidator the person who was previously the administrator.

4.173(2) **[Definitions]** In this Chapter, **"insolvent winding up"**, **"solvent winding up"**, **"creditor member"** and **"contributory member"** mean the same as in Chapter 12.

(See General Note after r. 4.178.)

4.174 Continuation of creditors' committee

4.174(1) **[Creditors' committee as liquidation committee]** If under paragraph 57 of Schedule B1 to the Act a creditors' committee has been established for the purposes of the administration, then (subject as follows in this Chapter) that committee continues in being as the liquidation committee for the purposes of the winding up, and–

(a) it is deemed to be a committee established as such under section 141, and

(b) no action shall be taken under subsections (1) to (3) of that section to establish any other.

4.174(2) **[Non-application of Rule]** This Rule does not apply if, at the time when the court's order under section 140(1) is made, the committee under paragraph 57 of Schedule B1 to the Act consists of less than 3 members; and a creditor who was, immediately before that date, a member of it, ceases to be a member on the making of the order if his debt is fully secured.

(See General Note after r. 4.178.)

4.175 Membership of committee

4.175(1) **[Three–five creditors]** Subject as follows, the liquidation committee shall consist of at least 3, and not more than 5, creditors of the company, elected by the creditors' meeting held under paragraph 57 of Schedule B1 to the Act or (in order to make up numbers or fill vacancies) by a creditors' meeting summoned by the liquidator after the company goes into liquidation.

4.175(2) **[In a solvent winding up]** In the case of a solvent winding up, the liquidator shall, on not less than 21 days' notice, summon a meeting of contributories, in order to elect (if it so wishes) contributory members of the liquidation committee, up to 3 in number.

(See General Note after r. 4.178.)

4.176 Liquidator's certificate

4.176(1) **[Certificate of continuance]** The liquidator shall issue a certificate of the liquidation committee's continuance, specifying the persons who are, or are to be, members of it.

[FORM 4.52]

4.176(2) **[Contents of certificate]** It shall be stated in the certificate whether or not the liquidator has summoned a meeting of contributories under Rule 4.175(2), and whether (if so) the meeting has elected contributories to be members of the committee.

4.176(3) **[Effect of certificate]** Pending the issue of the liquidator's certificate, the committee is suspended and cannot act.

4.176(4) **[Agreement to act]** No person may act, or continue to act, as a member of the committee unless and until he has agreed to do so; and the liquidator's certificate shall not issue until at least the minimum number of persons required under Rule 4.175 to form a committee have signified their agreement.

4.176(5) **[Amended certificate]** As and when the others signify their agreement, the liquidator shall issue an amended certificate.

[FORM 4.52]

4.176(6) **[Certificate to be filed in court]** The liquidator's certificate (or, as the case may be, the amended certificate) shall be filed by him in court.

4.176(7) **[Change in membership]** If subsequently there is any change in the committee's membership, the liquidator shall report the change to the court.

[FORM 4.49]

(See General Note after r. 4.178.)

4.177 Obligations of liquidator to committee

4.177(1) **[Liquidator's report]** As soon as may be after the issue of the liquidator's certificate under Rule 4.176, the liquidator shall report to the liquidation committee what actions he has taken since the date on which the company went into liquidation.

4.177(2) **[Summary report]** A person who becomes a member of the committee after that date is not entitled to require a report to him by the liquidator, otherwise than in a summary form, of any matters previously arising.

4.177(3) **[Access to records etc.]** Nothing in this Rule disentitles the committee, or any member of it, from having access to the records of the liquidation (whether relating to the period when he was administrator, or to any subsequent period), or from seeking an explanation of any matter within the committee's responsibility.

(See General Note after r. 4.178.)

4.178 Application of Chapter 12

4.178 Except as provided above in this Chapter, Rules 4.155 to 4.172A in Chapter 12 apply to the liquidation committee following the issue of the liquidator's certificate under Rule 4.176, as if it had been established under section 141.

General Note to rr. 4.173–4.178

These rules adapt those generally applicable to the liquidation committee (rr. 4.151–4.172A) for the special case where a winding up follows immediately on an administration. The creditors' committee appointed for the purpose of the administration continues in being as the liquidation committee, subject to the right of the contributories (where it is a "solvent" liquidation – see r. 4.151) to appoint their own members.

In rr. 4.173(1)(a), 4.174(1), (2) and 4.175(1) references to the original Pt II have been replaced by references to Sch. B1, which will of course apply only in the new administration regime: see the Insolvency (Amendment) Rules 2003 (SI 2003/1730, effective September 15, 2003), Sch. 1, paras 24–26.

Chapter 14

Collection and Distribution of Company's Assets by Liquidator

4.179 General duties of liquidator

(NO CVL APPLICATION)

4.179(1) [Officer of the court] The duties imposed on the court by the Act with regard to the collection of the company's assets and their application in discharge of its liabilities are discharged by the liquidator as an officer of the court subject to its control.

4.179(2) [Same powers as a receiver] In the discharge of his duties the liquidator, for the purposes of acquiring and retaining possession of the company's property, has the same powers as a receiver appointed by the High Court, and the court may on his application enforce such acquisition or retention accordingly.

General Note

For the statutory source of this rule, see IA 1986, ss. 148(1), 160(1)(b).

4.180 Manner of distributing assets

4.180(1) [Dividends] Whenever the liquidator has sufficient funds in hand for the purpose he shall, subject to the retention of such sums as may be necessary for the expenses of the winding up, declare and distribute dividends among the creditors in respect of the debts which they have respectively proved.

4.180(2) [Notice of intention] The liquidator shall give notice of his intention to declare and distribute a dividend.

4.180(3) [Notice of dividend] Where the liquidator has declared a dividend, he shall give notice of it to the creditors, stating how the dividend is proposed to be distributed. The notice shall contain such particulars with respect to the company, and to its assets and affairs, as will enable the creditors to comprehend the calculation of the amount of the dividend and the manner of its distribution.

(See General Note after r. 4.183.)

4.181 Debts of insolvent company to rank equally

(NO CVL APPLICATION)

4.181(1) [Ranking and priority] Debts other than preferential debts rank equally between themselves in the winding up and, after the preferential debts, shall be paid in full unless the assets are insufficient for meeting them, in which case they abate in equal proportions between themselves.

4.181(2) [Application of r. 4.181(1)] Paragraph (1) applies whether or not the company is unable to pay its debts.

(See General Note after r. 4.183.)

4.182 Supplementary provisions as to dividend

4.182(1) **[Calculation and distribution]** In the calculation and distribution of a dividend the liquidator shall make provision–

(a) for any debts which appear to him to be due to persons who, by reason of the distance of their place of residence, may not have had sufficient time to tender and establish their proofs,

(b) for any debts which are the subject of claims which have not yet been determined, and

(c) for disputed proofs and claims.

4.182(2) **[Proof after dividend declared]** A creditor who has not proved his debt before the declaration of any dividend is not entitled to disturb, by reason that he has not participated in it, the distribution of that dividend or any other dividend declared before his debt was proved, but–

(a) when he has proved that debt he is entitled to be paid, out of any money for the time being available for the payment of any further dividend, any dividend or dividends which he has failed to receive, and

(b) any dividend or dividends payable under sub-paragraph (a) shall be paid before that money is applied to the payment of any such further dividend.

4.182(3) **[Order for payment etc.]** No action lies against the liquidator for a dividend; but if he refuses to pay a dividend the court may, if it thinks fit, order him to pay it and also to pay, out of his own money–

(a) interest on the dividend, at the rate for the time being specified in section 17 of the Judgments Act 1838, from the time when it was withheld, and

(b) the costs of the proceedings in which the order to pay is made.

(See General Note after r. 4.183.)

4.182A Distribution in members' voluntary winding up

(NO CVL APPLICATION)

4.182A(1) **[Notice of intention]** In a members' voluntary winding up the liquidator may give notice in such newspaper as he considers most appropriate for the purpose of drawing the matter to the attention of the company's creditors that he intends to make a distribution to creditors.

4.182A(2) **["The last date for proving"]** The notice shall specify a date ("the last date for proving") up to which proofs may be lodged. The date shall be the same for all creditors and not less than 21 days from that of the notice.

4.182A(3) **[Proofs lodged out of time]** The liquidator is not obliged to deal with proofs lodged after the last date for proving; but he may do so, if he thinks fit.

4.182A(4) **[Distribution not to be disturbed]** A creditor who has not proved his debt before the last date for proving or after that date increases the claim in his proof is not entitled to disturb, by reason that he has not participated in it, either at all or, as the case may be, to the extent that his increased claim would allow, that distribution or any other distribution made before his debt was proved or his claim increased; but when he has proved his debt or, as the case may be, increased his claim, he is entitled to be paid, out of any money for the time being available for the payment of any further distribution, any distribution or distributions which he has failed to receive.

4.182A(5) **[Only or final distribution]** Where the distribution proposed to be made is to be the only or the final distribution in that winding up, the liquidator may, subject to paragraph (6), make that distribution without regard to the claim of any person in respect of a debt not already proved.

4.182A(6) **[Notice in r. 4.182A(5)]** Where the distribution proposed to be made is one specified in paragraph (5), the notice given under paragraph (1) shall state the effect of paragraph (5).

(See General Note after r. 4.183.)

4.183 Division of unsold assets

4.183 Without prejudice to provisions of the Act about disclaimer, the liquidator may, with the permission of the liquidation committee, divide in its existing form amongst the company's creditors, according to its estimated value, any property which from its peculiar nature or other special circumstances cannot be readily or advantageously sold.

GENERAL NOTE TO RR. 4.180–4.183

These rules deal with the distribution of dividends and the ranking of debts *inter se*. For further provisions regarding dividends, see rr. 4.186 and 11.1ff.; and on preferential debts see IA 1986, s. 386 and Sch. 6.

If the liquidator proposes to pay an interim dividend at a time when an application to the court to challenge the admission or rejection of a proof is outstanding, the leave of the court is required under IR 1986, r. 11.5(2).

Rule 4.181 was amended by the addition of para. (2) in 1987, but this amendment seems to have added more confusion that it has dispelled. If the new para. (2) was necessary at all, it ought to have been accompanied by the removal of the reference to insolvency in the heading to the rule. It appears that para. (2) was introduced to refer to the words "shall be paid in full" in para. (1); but there can hardly be any question of the "ranking" of debts that are all to be paid in full.

Note that a sum due to a member *qua* member is not deemed to be a debt, and ranks after the claims of the company's creditors: s. 74(2)(f).

Provision equivalent to r. 4.181 is made for a voluntary winding up by s. 107.

4.184 General powers of liquidator

4.184(1) **[Particular permission]** Any permission given by the liquidation committee or the court under section 167(1)(a), or under the Rules, shall not be a general permission but shall relate to a particular proposed exercise of the liquidator's power in question; and a person dealing with the liquidator in good faith and for value is not concerned to enquire whether any such permission has been given.

4.184(2) **[Ratification]** Where the liquidator has done anything without that permission, the court or the liquidation committee may, for the purpose of enabling him to meet his expenses out of the assets, ratify what he has done; but neither shall do so unless it is satisfied that the liquidator has acted in a case of urgency and has sought ratification without undue delay.

GENERAL NOTE

The powers referred to in IA 1986, s. 167(1)(a) are the payment of debts, the compromise of claims, the institution and defence of proceedings, and the carrying on of the business of the company.

4.185 Enforced delivery up of company's property

(NO CVL APPLICATION)

4.185(1) **[Powers under s. 234]** The powers conferred on the court by section 234 (enforced delivery of company property) are exercisable by the liquidator or, where a provisional liquidator has been appointed, by him.

4.185(2) **[Duty to comply]** Any person on whom a requirement under section 234(2) is imposed by the liquidator or provisional liquidator shall, without avoidable delay, comply with it.

GENERAL NOTE

For the statutory source of this rule, see IA 1986, ss. 160(1)(c), 234.

4.186 Final distribution

4.186(1) [Notice under Pt. 11] When the liquidator has realised all the company's assets or so much of them as can, in his opinion, be realised without needlessly protracting the liquidation, he shall give notice, under Part 11 of the Rules, either–

(a) of his intention to declare a final dividend, or

(b) that no dividend, or further dividend, will be declared.

4.186(2) [Contents of notice] The notice shall contain all such particulars as are required by Part 11 of the Rules and shall require claims against the assets to be established by a date specified in the notice.

4.186(3) [Final dividend] After that date, the liquidator shall–

(a) defray any outstanding expenses of the winding up out of the assets, and

(b) if he intends to declare a final dividend, declare and distribute that dividend without regard to the claim of any person in respect of a debt not already proved.

4.186(4) [Postponement] The court may, on the application of any person, postpone the date specified in the notice.

GENERAL NOTE

On dividends generally, see rr. 4.180–4.183 and 11.1ff.

CHAPTER 15

DISCLAIMER

4.187 Liquidator's notice of disclaimer

4.187(1) [Contents of notice] Where the liquidator disclaims property under section 178, the notice of disclaimer shall contain such particulars of the property disclaimed as enable it to be easily identified.

[FORM 4.53]

4.187(2) [Notice to be signed etc.] The notice shall be signed by the liquidator and filed in court, with a copy. The court shall secure that both the notice and the copy are sealed and endorsed with the date of filing.

4.187(3) [Copy of notice returned to liquidator] The copy notice, so sealed and endorsed, shall be returned by the court to the liquidator as follows–

(a) if the notice has been delivered at the offices of the court by the liquidator in person, it shall be handed to him,

(b) if it has been delivered by some person acting on the liquidator's behalf, it shall be handed to that person, for immediate transmission to the liquidator, and

(c) otherwise, it shall be sent to the liquidator by first class post.

The court shall cause to be endorsed on the original notice, or otherwise recorded on the file, the manner in which the copy notice was returned to the liquidator.

4.187(4) **[Date of notice]** For the purposes of section 178, the date of the prescribed notice is that which is endorsed on it, and on the copy, in accordance with this Rule.

(See General Note after r. 4.194.)

4.188 Communication of disclaimer to persons interested

4.188(1) **[Copy of notices]** Within 7 days after the day on which the copy of the notice of disclaimer is returned to him under Rule 4.187, the liquidator shall send or give copies of the notice (showing the date endorsed as required by that Rule) to the persons mentioned in paragraphs (2) to (4) below.

[FORM 4.53]

4.188(2) **[Leasehold property]** Where the property disclaimed is of a leasehold nature, he shall send or give a copy to every person who (to his knowledge) claims under the company as underlessee or mortgagee.

4.188(3) **[Giving notice]** He shall in any case send or give a copy of the notice to every person who (to his knowledge)–

(a) claims an interest in respect of the property, or

(b) is under any liability in respect of the property, not being a liability discharged by the disclaimer.

4.188(4) **[Unprofitable contract]** If the disclaimer is of an unprofitable contract, he shall send or give copies of the notice to all such persons as, to his knowledge, are parties to the contract or have interests under it.

4.188(5) **[Late communication]** If subsequently it comes to the liquidator's knowledge, in the case of any person, that he has such an interest in the disclaimed property as would have entitled him to receive a copy of the notice of disclaimer in pursuance of paragraphs (2) to (4), the liquidator shall then forthwith send or give to that person a copy of the notice.

But compliance with this paragraph is not required if–

(a) the liquidator is satisfied that the person has already been made aware of the disclaimer and its date, or

(b) the court, on the liquidator's application, orders that compliance is not required in that particular case.

(See General Note after r. 4.194.)

4.189 Additional notices

4.189 The liquidator disclaiming property may, without prejudice to his obligations under sections 178 to 180 and Rules 4.187 and 4.188, at any time give notice of the disclaimer to any persons who in his opinion ought, in the public interest or otherwise, to be informed of it.

[FORM 4.53]

(See General Note after r. 4.194.)

4.190 Duty to keep court informed

4.190 The liquidator shall notify the court from time to time as to the persons to whom he has sent or given copies of the notice of disclaimer under the two preceding Rules, giving their names and addresses, and the nature of their respective interests.

(See General Note after r. 4.194.)

4.191 Application by interested party under s. 178(5)

4.191 Where, in the case of any property, application is made to the liquidator by an interested party under section 178(5) (request for decision whether the property is to be disclaimed or not), the application–

(a) shall be delivered to the liquidator personally or by registered post, and

(b) shall be made in the form known as "notice to elect", or a substantially similar form.

[FORM 4.54]

4.192 Interest in property to be declared on request

4.192(1) [**Notice to declare interest**] If, in the case of property which the liquidator has the right to disclaim, it appears to him that there is some person who claims, or may claim, to have an interest in the property, he may give notice to that person calling on him to declare within 14 days whether he claims any such interest and, if so, the nature and extent of it.

[FORM 4.55]

4.192(2) [**Failing compliance with notice**] Failing compliance with the notice, the liquidator is entitled to assume that the person concerned has no such interest in the property as will prevent or impede its disclaimer.

(See General Note after r. 4.194.)

4.193 Disclaimer presumed valid and effective

4.193 Any disclaimer of property by the liquidator is presumed valid and effective, unless it is proved that he has been in breach of his duty with respect to the giving of notice of disclaimer, or otherwise under sections 178 to 180, or under this Chapter of the Rules.

(See General Note after r. 4.194.)

4.194 Application for exercise of court's powers under s. 181

4.194(1) [**Application of Rule**] This Rule applies with respect to an application by any person under section 181 for an order of the court to vest or deliver disclaimed property.

4.194(2) [**Time for application**] The application must be made within 3 months of the applicant becoming aware of the disclaimer, or of his receiving a copy of the liquidator's notice of disclaimer sent under Rule 4.188, whichever is the earlier.

4.194(3) [**Contents of affidavit**] The applicant shall with his application file in court an affidavit–

(a) stating whether he applies under paragraph (a) of section 181(2) (claim of interest in the property) or under paragraph (b) (liability not discharged);

(b) specifying the date on which he received a copy of the liquidator's notice of disclaimer, or otherwise became aware of the disclaimer; and

(c) specifying the grounds of his application and the order which he desires the court to make under section 181.

4.194(4) [**Venue for hearing**] The court shall fix a venue for the hearing of the application; and the applicant shall, not later than 7 days before the date fixed, give to the liquidator notice of the venue, accompanied by copies of the application and the affidavit under paragraph (3).

4.194(5) [**Directions for notice etc.**] On the hearing of the application, the court may give directions as to other persons (if any) who should be sent or given notice of the application and the grounds on which it is made.

4.194(6) [**Sealed copies of order**] Sealed copies of any order made on the application shall be sent by the court to the applicant and the liquidator.

4.194(7) [**Leasehold property**] In a case where the property disclaimed is of a leasehold nature, and section 179 applies to suspend the effect of the disclaimer, there shall be included in the court's order a direction giving effect to the disclaimer.

This paragraph does not apply if, at the time when the order is issued, other applications under section 181 are pending in respect of the same property.

GENERAL NOTE TO RR. 4.187–4.194

The statutory powers of disclaimer are contained in IA 1986, ss. 178–182. These rules supplement those provisions. On property "of a leasehold nature", see IA 1986, ss. 179, 182.

The period of three months specified in r. 4.194(2) may be extended at the discretion of the court: *W H Smith Ltd v Wyndham Investments Ltd* [1994] B.C.C. 699. In the same case it was held that, although a lease becomes ownerless following a disclaimer, it does not disappear, but ceases to exist only on the occurrence of one of the normal means of termination – effluxion of time, surrender or retaking of possession by the landlord.

CHAPTER 16

SETTLEMENT OF LIST OF CONTRIBUTORIES
(NO CVL APPLICATION)

4.195 Preliminary

4.195 The duties of the court with regard to the settling of the list of contributories are, by virtue of the Rules, delegated to the liquidator.

(See General Note after r. 4.196.)

4.196 Duty of liquidator to settle list

4.196(1) [**Settling list of contributories**] Subject as follows, the liquidator shall, as soon as may be after his appointment, exercise the court's power to settle a list of the company's contributories for the purposes of section 148 and, with the court's approval, rectify the register of members.

4.196(2) [**Officer of the court**] The liquidator's duties under this Rule are performed by him as an officer of the court subject to the court's control.

GENERAL NOTE TO RR. 4.195–4.196

For the statutory source of these rules, see IA 1986, ss. 148, 160(1)(b).

4.197 Form of list

4.197(1) [**Contents of list**] The list shall identify–

(a) the several classes of the company's shares (if more than one), and

(b) the several classes of contributories, distinguishing between those who are contributories in their own right and those who are so as representatives of, or liable for the debts of, others.

4.197(2) [**Further contents**] In the case of each contributory there shall in the list be stated–

(a) his address,

(b) the number and class of shares, or the extent of any other interest to be attributed to him, and

(c) if the shares are not fully paid up, the amounts which have been called up and paid in respect of them (and the equivalent, if any, where his interest is other than shares).

(See General Note after r. 4.201.)

4.198 Procedure for settling list

4.198(1) [**Notice**] Having settled the list, the liquidator shall forthwith give notice, to every person included in the list, that he has done so.

4.198(2) **[Contents of notice]** The notice given to each person shall state–

(a) in what character, and for what number of shares or what interest, he is included in the list,

(b) what amounts have been called up and paid up in respect of the shares or interest, and

(c) that in relation to any shares or interest not fully paid up, his inclusion in the list may result in the unpaid capital being called.

4.198(3) **[Objection to list]** The notice shall inform any person to whom it is given that, if he objects to any entry in, or omission from, the list, he should so inform the liquidator in writing within 21 days from the date of the notice.

4.198(4) **[Amendment of list]** On receipt of any such objection, the liquidator shall within 14 days give notice to the objector either–

(a) that he has amended the list (specifying the amendment), or

(b) that he considers the objection to be not well-founded and declines to amend the list.

The notice shall in either case inform the objector of the effect of Rule 4.199.

(See General Note after r. 4.201.)

4.199 Application to court for variation of the list

4.199(1) **[Application to court]** If a person objects to any entry in, or exclusion from, the list of contributories as settled by the liquidator and, notwithstanding notice by the liquidator declining to amend the list, maintains his objection, he may apply to the court for an order removing the entry to which he objects or (as the case may be) otherwise amending the list.

4.199(2) **[Time for application]** The application must be made within 21 days of the service on the applicant of the liquidator's notice under Rule 4.198(4).

(See General Note after r. 4.201.)

4.200 Variation of, or addition to, the list

4.200 The liquidator may from time to time vary or add to the list of contributories as previously settled by him, but subject in all respects to the preceding Rules in this Chapter.

(See General Note after r. 4.201.)

4.201 Costs not to fall on official receiver

4.201 The official receiver is not personally liable for any costs incurred by a person in respect of an application to set aside or vary his act or decision in settling the list of contributories, or varying or adding to the list; and the liquidator (if other than the official receiver) is not so liable unless the court makes an order to that effect.

GENERAL NOTE TO RR. 4.197–4.201

Here are set out the rules prescribing the form of the list of contributories and the procedure for settling it. Note that the power to rectify the register of members may be exercised only with the special leave of the court: IA 1986, s. 160(2), r. 4.196(1).

CHAPTER 17

CALLS (NO CVL APPLICATION)

4.202 Calls by liquidator

4.202 Subject as follows, the powers conferred by the Act with respect to the making of calls on contributories are exercisable by the liquidator as an officer of the court subject to the court's control.

(See General Note after r. 4.205.)

4.203 Control by liquidation committee

4.203(1) [**Meeting to sanction call**] Where the liquidator proposes to make a call, and there is a liquidation committee, he may summon a meeting of the committee for the purpose of obtaining its sanction.

4.203(2) [**Notice**] At least 7 days' notice of the meeting shall be given by the liquidator to each member of the committee.

4.203(3) [**Contents of notice**] The notice shall contain a statement of the proposed amount of the call, and the purpose for which it is intended to be made.

(See General Note after r. 4.205.)

4.204 Application to court for leave to make a call

4.204(1) [**Form of application**] For the purpose of obtaining the leave of the court for the making of a call on any contributories of the company, the liquidator shall apply *ex parte*, supporting his application by affidavit.

[FORM 4.56]

4.204(2) [**Contents of application**] There shall in the application be stated the amount of the proposed call, and the contributories on whom it is to be made.

4.204(3) [**Powers of court**] The court may direct that notice of the order be given to the contributories concerned, or to other contributories, or may direct that the notice be publicly advertised.

[FORM 4.57]

(See General Note after r. 4.205.)

4.205 Making and enforcement of the call

4.205(1) [**Notice of call**] Notice of the call shall be given to each of the contributories concerned, and shall specify–

(a) the amount or balance due from him in respect of it, and

(b) whether the call is made with the sanction of the court or the liquidation committee.

[FORM 4.58]

4.205(2) **[Enforcement by order]** Payment of the amount due from any contributory may be enforced by order of the court.

[FORM 4.59]

GENERAL NOTE TO RR. 4.202–4.205

For the statutory source of these rules, see IA 1986, ss. 150, 160(1)(d). The exercise of the power of the liquidator to make a call requires the special leave of the court or the sanction of the liquidation committee (s. 160(2), rr. 4.203, 4.204).

CHAPTER 18

SPECIAL MANAGER

4.206 Appointment and remuneration

4.206(1) **[Liquidator's report]** An application made by the liquidator under section 177 for the appointment of a person to be special manager shall be supported by a report setting out the reasons for the application.

The report shall include the applicant's estimate of the value of the assets in respect of which the special manager is to be appointed.

4.206(2) **[Application of Chapter]** This Chapter applies also with respect to an application by the provisional liquidator, where one has been appointed, and references to the liquidator are to be read accordingly as including the provisional liquidator. (NO CVL APPLICATION).

4.206(3) **[Duration of appointment]** The court's order appointing the special manager shall specify the duration of his appointment, which may be for a period of time, or until the occurrence of a specified event. Alternatively, the order may specify that the duration of the appointment is to be subject to a further order of the court.

[FORM 4.60]

4.206(4) **[Renewal]** The appointment of a special manager may be renewed by order of the court.

4.206(5) **[Remuneration]** The special manager's remuneration shall be fixed from time to time by the court.

4.206(6) **[Validation of acts]** The acts of the special manager are valid notwithstanding any defect in his appointment or qualifications.

(See General Note after r. 4.210.)

4.207 Security

4.207(1) **[Effect of giving security]** The appointment of the special manager does not take effect until the person appointed has given (or being allowed by the court to do so, undertaken to give) security to the person who applies for him to be appointed.

4.207(2) **[Special or general security]** It is not necessary that security shall be given for each separate company liquidation; but it may be given specially for a particular liquidation, or generally for any liquidation in relation to which the special manager may be employed as such.

4.207(3) **[Amount of security]** The amount of the security shall not be less than the value of the assets in respect of which he is appointed, as estimated by the applicant in his report under Rule 4.206.

4.207(4) **[Certificate of adequacy]** When the special manager has given security to the person applying for his appointment, that person shall file in court a certificate as to the adequacy of the security.

4.207(5) **[Cost of security]** The cost of providing the security shall be paid in the first instance by the special manager; but–

(a) where a winding-up order is not made, he is entitled to be reimbursed out of the property of the company, and the court may make an order on the company accordingly, and

(b) where a winding-up order is made, he is entitled to be reimbursed out of the assets in the prescribed order of priority.

(NO CVL APPLICATION)

4.207(6) **[Cost of providing security]** The cost of providing the security shall be paid in the first instance by the special manager; but he is entitled to be reimbursed out of the assets, in the prescribed order of priority.

(See General Note after r. 4.210.)

4.208 Failure to give or keep up security

4.208(1) **[Failure to give security]** If the special manager fails to give the required security within the time stated for that purpose by the order appointing him, or any extension of that time that may be allowed, the liquidator shall report the failure to the court, which may thereupon discharge the order appointing the special manager.

4.208(2) **[Failure to keep up security]** If the special manager fails to keep up his security, the liquidator shall report his failure to the court, which may thereupon remove the special manager, and make such order as it thinks fit as to costs.

4.208(3) **[Directions on removal]** If an order is made under this Rule removing the special manager, or discharging the order appointing him, the court shall give directions as to whether any, and if so what, steps should be taken for the appointment of another special manager in his place.

(See General Note after r. 4.210.)

4.209 Accounting

4.209(1) **[Contents of accounts]** The special manager shall produce accounts, containing details of his receipts and payments, for the approval of the liquidator.

4.209(2) **[Period of accounts]** The accounts shall be in respect of 3-month periods for the duration of the special manager's appointment (or for a lesser period, if his appointment terminates less than 3 months from its date, or from the date to which the last accounts were made up).

4.209(3) **[When accounts approved]** When the accounts have been approved, the special manager's receipts and payments shall be added to those of the liquidator.

(See General Note after r. 4.210.)

4.210 Termination of appointment

4.210(1) **[Automatic termination]** The special manager's appointment terminates if the winding-up petition is dismissed or if, a provisional liquidator having been appointed, the latter is discharged without a winding-up order having been made. (NO CVL APPLICATION).

4.210(2) **[Application to court]** If the liquidator is of opinion that the employment of the special manager is no longer necessary or profitable for the company, he shall apply to the court for directions, and the court may order the special manager's appointment to be terminated.

4.210(3) **[Resolution of creditors]** The liquidator shall make the same application if a resolution of the creditors is passed, requesting that the appointment be terminated.

GENERAL NOTE TO RR. 4.206–4.210

On the appointment of a special manager, see IA 1986, s. 177 and the notes thereto. A special manager need not be qualified to act as an insolvency practitioner. These rules deal with his appointment and remuneration, the furnishing of security, his obligation to keep accounts and the termination of his appointment.

CHAPTER 19

PUBLIC EXAMINATION OF COMPANY OFFICERS AND OTHERS

4.211 Order for public examination

4.211(1) **[Service of copy order]** If the official receiver applies to the court under section 133 for the public examination of any person, a copy of the court's order shall, forthwith after its making, be served on that person.

[FORM 4.61]

4.211(2) **[Official receiver's report]** Where the application relates to a person falling within section 133(1)(c) (promoters, past managers, etc.), it shall be accompanied by a report by the official receiver indicating–

(a) the grounds on which the person is supposed to fall within that paragraph, and

(b) whether, in the official receiver's opinion, it is likely that service of the order on the person can be effected by post at a known address.

4.211(3) **[Means of service]** If in his report the official receiver gives it as his opinion that, in a case to which paragraph (2) applies, there is no reasonable certainty that service by post will be effective, the court may direct that the order be served by some means other than, or in addition to, post.

4.211(4) **[Rescission of order]** In a case to which paragraphs (2) and (3) apply, the court shall rescind the order if satisfied by the person to whom it is directed that he does not fall within section 133(1)(c).

(See General Note after r. 4.217.)

4.212 Notice of hearing

4.212(1) **[Venue and direction to attend]** The court's order shall appoint a venue for the examination of the person to whom it is directed ("the examinee"), and direct his attendance thereat.

4.212(2) **[Notice of hearing]** The official receiver shall give at least 14 days' notice of the hearing–

(a) if a liquidator has been nominated or appointed, to him;

(b) if a special manager has been appointed, to him; and

(c) subject to any contrary direction of the court, to every creditor and contributory of the company who is known to the official receiver or is identified in the company's statement of affairs.

4.212(3) **[Advertisement]** The official receiver may, if he thinks fit, cause notice of the order to be given, by advertisement in one or more newspapers, at least 14 days before the date fixed for the hearing; but, unless the court otherwise directs, there shall be no such advertisement before at least 7 days have elapsed since the examinee was served with the order.

(See General Note after r. 4.217.)

4.213 Order on request by creditors or contributories

4.213(1) [**Form of request etc.**] A request to the official receiver by creditors or contributories under section 133(2) shall be made in writing and be accompanied by—

(a) a list of the creditors concurring with the request and the amounts of their respective claims in the liquidation or (as the case may be) of the contributories so concurring, with their respective values, and

(b) from each creditor or contributory concurring, written confirmation of his concurrence.

This paragraph does not apply if the requisitioning creditor's debt or, as the case may be, requisitioning contributory's shareholding is alone sufficient, without the concurrence of others.

[FORM 4.62]
[FORM 4.63]

4.213(2) [**Further contents**] The request must specify the name of the proposed examinee, the relationship which he has, or has had, to the company and the reasons why his examination is requested.

4.213(3) [**Security for expenses of hearing**] Before an application to the court is made on the request, the requisitionists shall deposit with the official receiver such sum as the latter may determine to be appropriate by way of security for the expenses of the hearing of a public examination, if ordered.

4.213(4) [**Time for application**] Subject as follows, the official receiver shall, within 28 days of receiving the request, make the application to the court required by section 133(2).

4.213(5) [**Relief from unreasonable request**] If the official receiver is of opinion that the request is an unreasonable one in the circumstances, he may apply to the court for an order relieving him from the obligation to make the application otherwise required by that subsection.

4.213(6) [**Notice of relief order etc.**] If the court so orders, and the application for the order was made *ex parte*, notice of the order shall be given forthwith by the official receiver to the requisitionists. If the application for an order is dismissed, the official receiver's application under section 133(2) shall be made forthwith on conclusion of the hearing of the application first mentioned.

(See General Note after r. 4.217.)

4.214 Witness unfit for examination

4.214(1) [**Application for stay etc.**] Where the examinee is suffering from any mental disorder or physical affliction or disability rendering him unfit to undergo or attend for public examination, the court may, on application in that behalf, either stay the order for his public examination or direct that it shall be conducted in such manner and at such place as it thinks fit.

[FORM 4.64]

4.214(2) [**Who may apply**] Application under this Rule shall be made—

(a) by a person who has been appointed by a court in the United Kingdom or elsewhere to manage the affairs of, or to represent, the examinee, or

(b) by a relative or friend of the examinee whom the court considers to be a proper person to make the application, or

(c) by the official receiver.

4.214(3) **[Application not by official receiver]** Where the application is made by a person other than the official receiver, then–

- (a) it shall, unless the examinee is a patient within the meaning of the Mental Health Act 1983, be supported by the affidavit of a registered medical practitioner as to the examinee's mental and physical condition;
- (b) at least 7 days' notice of the application shall be given to the official receiver and the liquidator (if other than the official receiver); and
- (c) before any order is made on the application, the applicant shall deposit with the official receiver such sum as the latter certifies to be necessary for the additional expenses of any examination that may be ordered on the application.

An order made on the application may provide that the expenses of the examination are to be payable, as to a specified proportion, out of the deposit under sub-paragraph (c), instead of out of the assets.

4.214(4) **[Application by official receiver]** Where the application is made by the official receiver it may be made *ex parte*, and may be supported by evidence in the form of a report by the official receiver to the court.

(See General Note after r. 4.217.)

4.215 Procedure at hearing

4.215(1) **[Examination on oath]** The examinee shall at the hearing be examined on oath; and he shall answer all such questions as the court may put, or allow to be put, to him.

4.215(2) **[Appearances etc.]** Any of the persons allowed by section 133(4) to question the examinee may, with the approval of the court (made known either at the hearing or in advance of it), appear by solicitor or counsel; or he may in writing authorise another person to question the examinee on his behalf.

4.215(3) **[Representation of examinee]** The examinee may at his own expense employ a solicitor with or without counsel, who may put to him such questions as the court may allow for the purpose of enabling him to explain or qualify any answers given by him, and may make representations on his behalf.

4.215(4) **[Record of examination]** There shall be made in writing such record of the examination as the court thinks proper. The record shall be read over either to or by the examinee, signed by him, and verified by affidavit at a venue fixed by the court.

[FORM 4.65]

4.215(5) **[Record as evidence]** The written record may, in any proceedings (whether under the Act or otherwise) be used as evidence against the examinee of any statement made by him in the course of his public examination.

4.215(6) **[Criminal proceedings etc.]** If criminal proceedings have been instituted against the examinee, and the court is of opinion that the continuance of the hearing would be calculated to prejudice a fair trial of those proceedings, the hearing may be adjourned.

(See General Note after r. 4.217.)

4.216 Adjournment

4.216(1) **[Adjourned by court]** The public examination may be adjourned by the court from time to time, either to a fixed date or generally.

[FORM 4.66]

The Insolvency Rules 1986 Rule 4.218

4.216(2) **[Resumption]** Where the examination has been adjourned generally, the court may at any time on the application of the official receiver or of the examinee–

(a) fix a venue for the resumption of the examination, and

(b) give directions as to the manner in which, and the time within which, notice of the resumed public examination is to be given to persons entitled to take part in it.

[FORM 4.67]

4.216(3) **[Deposit for expenses re application]** Where application under paragraph (2) is made by the examinee, the court may grant it on terms that the expenses of giving the notices required by that paragraph shall be paid by him and that, before a venue for the resumed public examination is fixed, he shall deposit with the official receiver such sum as the latter considers necessary to cover those expenses.

(See General Note after r. 4.217.)

4.217 Expenses of examination

4.217(1) **[Expenses paid out of r. 4.213 deposit]** Where a public examination of the examinee has been ordered by the court on a creditors' or contributories' requisition under Rule 4.213, the court may order that the expenses of the examination are to be paid, as to a specified proportion, out of the deposit under Rule 4.213(3), instead of out of the assets.

4.217(2) **[Official receiver not liable for costs]** In no case do the costs and expenses of a public examination fall on the official receiver personally.

GENERAL NOTE TO RR. 4.211–4.217

The power conferred on the official receiver to have company officers and others attend for public examination is conferred by the 1986 Act in more broadly drawn terms than under the former law: see the note to IA 1986, s. 133. The court has power under r. 4.215 to control the form of the examination and to give directions, or at least guidance, as to the hearing, but will not pre-empt questions which are a matter for the judge presiding at the hearing, *e.g.* as to the admissibility of questions and whether a particular question would be oppressive: *Re Richbell Strategic Holdings Ltd* [2001] B.C.C. 409.

On the *private* examination of persons connected with an insolvent company, see IA 1986, s. 236, and rr. 9.1ff., and the notes thereto.

Subject to r. 4.211(2)(a) and (4), the official receiver is entitled to an order *ipso facto*, *i.e.* he need not make out any case to the court.

In r. 4.211(1) the word "forthwith" means "as soon as is reasonably practicable": *Re Seagull Manufacturing Co. Ltd (in liquidation)* [1993] Ch. 345 at p. 359; [1993] B.C.C. 241 at p. 248.

CHAPTER 20

ORDER OF PAYMENT OF COSTS, ETC., OUT OF ASSETS

4.218 General rule as to priority

4.218(1) **[Priority of expenses]** The expenses of the liquidation are payable out of the assets in the following order of priority–

(a) expenses or costs which–

(i) are properly chargeable or incurred by the official receiver or the liquidator in preserving, realising or getting in any of the assets of the company or otherwise relating to the

conduct of any legal proceedings which he has power to bring or defend whether in his own name or the name of the company;
- (ii) relate to the employment of a shorthand writer, if appointed by an order of the court made at the instance of the official receiver in connection with an examination; or
- (iii) are incurred in holding an examination under Rule 4.214 (examinee unfit) where the application for it was made by the official receiver:

(b) any other expenses incurred or disbursements made by the official receiver or under his authority, including those incurred or made in carrying on the business of the company;

(c) the fees payable under any order made under section 414 or section 415A, including those payable to the official receiver (other than the fee referred to in sub-paragraph (d)(i) below), and any remuneration payable to him under general regulations;

(d) (i) the fee payable under any order made under section 414 for the performance by the official receiver of his general duties as official receiver;
(ii) any repayable deposit lodged under any such order as security for the fee mentioned in sub-paragraph (i);

(e) the cost of any security provided by a provisional liquidator, liquidator or special manager in accordance with the Act or the Rules;

(f) the remuneration of the provisional liquidator (if any);

(g) any deposit lodged on an application for the appointment of a provisional liquidator;

(h) the costs of the petitioner, and of any person appearing on the petition whose costs are allowed by the court;

(j) the remuneration of the special manager (if any);

(k) any amount payable to a person employed or authorised, under Chapter 6 of this Part of the Rules, to assist in the preparation of a statement of affairs or of accounts;

(l) any allowance made, by order of the court, towards costs on an application for release from the obligation to submit a statement of affairs, or for an extension of time for submitting such a statement;

(la) the costs of employing a shorthand writer in any case other than one appointed by an order of the court at the instance of the official receiver in connection with an examination;

(m) any necessary disbursements by the liquidator in the course of his administration (including any expenses incurred by members of the liquidation committee or their representatives and allowed by the liquidator under Rule 4.169, but not including any payment of corporation tax in circumstances referred to in sub-paragraph (p) below);

(n) the remuneration or emoluments of any person who has been employed by the liquidator to perform any services for the company, as required or authorised by or under the Act or the Rules;

(o) the remuneration of the liquidator, up to any amount not exceeding that which is payable to the official receiver under general regulations;

(p) the amount of any corporation tax on chargeable gains accruing on the realisation of any asset of the company (without regard to whether the realisation is effected by the liquidator, a secured creditor, or a receiver or manager appointed to deal with a security);

(q) the balance, after payment of any sums due under sub-paragraph (o) above, of any remuneration due to the liquidator;

(r) any other expenses properly chargeable by the liquidator in carrying out his functions in the liquidation.

4.218(2) [Omitted]

4.218(3) [Omitted]

(See General Note after r. 4.220.)

4.219 Winding up commencing as voluntary

4.219 In a winding up by the court which follows immediately on a voluntary winding up (whether members' voluntary or creditors' voluntary), such remuneration of the voluntary liquidator and costs and expenses of the voluntary liquidation as the court may allow are to rank in priority with the expenses specified in Rule 4.218(1)(a).

(See General Note after r. 4.220.)

4.220 Saving for powers of the court

4.220(1) [Powers of court under s. 156] In a winding up by the court, the priorities laid down by Rules 4.218 and 4.219 are subject to the power of the court to make orders under section 156, where the assets are insufficient to satisfy the liabilities.

4.220(2) [Powers of court re costs etc.] Nothing in those Rules applies to or affects the power of any court, in proceedings by or against the company, to order costs to be paid by the company, or the liquidator; nor do they affect the rights of any person to whom such costs are ordered to be paid.

GENERAL NOTE TO RR. 4.218–4.220

The present list giving the order of priority for payment of the expenses of the liquidation is longer and more detailed than under the old winding-up rules. The text as shown incorporates the change which was made, reversing the priority between subpara. (c) and (d) by SI 1995/586, as from April 1, 1995.

Paragraph (1)(a) was amended, paras (1)(l) and (1)(r) inserted, and the former paras (2) and (3) omitted, by the Insolvency (Amendment) (No. 2) Rules 2002 (SI 2002/2712, effective January 1, 2003), rr. 1, 4(1) and Sch. Pt 2, para. 23(a)–(c). These changes have had the effect of overruling the line of cases, from *Re MC Bacon Ltd (No. 2)* [1991] Ch. 127, [1990] B.C.C. 430 to *Re Floor Fourteen Ltd, Lewis v IRC* [2001] 3 All E.R. 499; [2002] B.C.C. 198, which had held that the expenses incurred by a liquidator in pursuing claims for wrongful trading and to recover preferences, etc. were not "expenses of the liquidation". The fact that such legal proceedings are now included in para. (1)(a)(i) puts beyond doubt any question that such costs are "expenses of the liquidation". (See also the notes to ss. 115 and 175(2)(a).)

Rule 4.218 applies to a creditors' voluntary winding up (including one that was originally a members' winding up): see r. 4.1(2).

The ruling in *Re Barleycorn Enterprises Ltd* [1970] Ch. 465 (which was followed in a number of cases including *Re Portbase Clothing Ltd, Mond v Taylor* [1993] Ch. 388, [1993] B.C.C. 96), that for the purposes of r. 4.218(1) the company's "assets" include assets covered by a floating charge, has been overruled by the House of Lords in *Re Leyland Daf Ltd, Buchler v Talbot* [2004] UKHL 9: see the note to s. 107. It follows that the liquidator's claims for expenses do not rank ahead of those of the holder of a floating charge.

In *Kahn v Commissioners of Inland Revenue, Re Toshoku Finance (UK) plc* [2002] UKHL 6; [2002] 1 W.L.R. 671; [2002] B.C.C. 110 the House of Lords held that corporation tax was payable out of the assets in priority to other claims as an expense of the liquidation even though the "income" in respect of which the tax was assessed had not been (and never would be) received by the company, and the tax debt had not arisen as a result of something done for the purposes of or with a view to obtaining a benefit for the estate.

In *Re W F Fearman Ltd (No. 2)* (1988) 4 B.C.C. 141 it was held that the costs of an administration petition (although bona fide presented and proving in the event to have been in the interests of the creditors) could not be allowed as a liquidation expense when the administration proceedings were terminated and a winding-up order was made. However, in the later case of *Re Gosscott (Groundworks) Ltd* (1988) 4 B.C.C. 372, an order was made in such circumstances.

In *Re Movitex Ltd* [1990] B.C.C. 491 the liquidators had continued an action, which had been commenced by the company before the winding up, to have certain property transactions set aside on the ground that they had been entered into without authority or in breach of directors' duty. Judgment had been given for the defendants with costs against the company, but the company's assets were insufficient to pay the costs order. It was held that the litigation costs were payable in full to the extent of the company's assets, but only after allowing the liquidators a deduction in respect of their costs in realising those assets.

Where rent is paid by a liquidator who has retained a lease in the hope of realising the company's assets to better advantage (as distinct from preserving the lease as an asset of the company) the rent does not rank as an expense of the liquidation under para. (a) of r. 4.218(1) but as a necessary disbursement under para. (m): *Re Linda Marie Ltd (in liq.)* (1988) 4 B.C.C. 463. In the same case, the court declined to exercise its discretion to confer priority on the liquidator's remuneration over the landlord's claim for rent.

A liquidator may seek guidance from the court in anticipation of making any particular expenditure in order to determine whether it will be treated as an expense of the liquidation: (*Re Demaglass Ltd* (above).

The court has power under r. 4.219 to allow, review or disallow in whole or in part the liquidator's remuneration, costs and expenses. However, if the liquidator seeks an increase of remuneration it is more appropriate to proceed under r. 4.130 than r. 4.219: *Re Tony Rowse NMC Ltd* [1996] B.C.C. 196.

CHAPTER 21

MISCELLANEOUS RULES

Section A: Return of capital
(NO CVL APPLICATION)

4.221 Application to court for order authorising return

4.221(1) **[Application of Rule]** This Rule applies where the liquidator intends to apply to the court for an order authorising a return of capital.

4.221(2) **[Accompanying list]** The application shall be accompanied by a list of the persons to whom the return is to be made.

4.221(3) **[Contents of list]** The list shall include the same details of those persons as appears in the settled list of contributories, with any necessary alterations to take account of matters after settlement of the list, and the amount to be paid to each person.

4.221(4) **[Copy order]** Where the court makes an order authorising the return, it shall send a sealed copy of the order to the liquidator.

(See General Note after r. 4.22.)

4.222 Procedure for return

4.222(1) **[Rate of return etc.]** The liquidator shall inform each person to whom a return is made of the rate of return per share, and whether it is expected that any further return will be made.

4.222(2) **[Method of payment]** Any payments made by the liquidator by way of the return may be sent by post, unless for any reason another method of making the payment has been agreed with the payee.

GENERAL NOTE TO RR. 4.221–4.222

In a winding up by the court, the court must "adjust the rights of the contributories among themselves and distribute any surplus among the persons entitled to it" (IA 1986, s. 154). Although it might have been thought from the language of IA 1986, ss. 143(1) and 160(1)(b), (2) that capital could be returned to contributories on the liquidator's own authority, these rules confirm that he must have the sanction of the court.

Section B: Conclusion of winding up

4.223-CVL Statements to registrar of companies under s. 192

4.223-CVL(1) **[Time limit for s. 192 statement]** Subject to paragraphs (3) and (3A), the statement which section 192 requires the liquidator to send to the registrar of companies, if the winding up is not concluded within one year from its commencement, shall be sent not more than 30 days after the expiration of that year, and thereafter 6-monthly until the winding up is concluded.

4.223-CVL(2) **[Conclusion of winding up etc.]** For this purpose the winding up is concluded at the date of the dissolution of the company, except that if at that date any assets or funds of the company remain unclaimed or undistributed in the hands or under the control of the liquidator, or any former liquidator, the winding up is not concluded until those assets or funds have either been distributed or paid into the Insolvency Services Account.

4.223-CVL(3) **[Final statement]** Subject as above, the liquidator's final statement shall be sent forthwith after the conclusion of the winding up.

4.223-CVL(3A) **[No statement required]** No statement shall be required to be delivered under this Rule where the return of the final meeting in respect of the company under sections 94 or 106 is delivered before the date at which the statement is to be delivered and that return shows that no assets or funds of the company remain unclaimed or undistributed in the hands or under the control of the liquidator or any former liquidator; but where this paragraph applies, the liquidator shall deliver a copy of that return to the Secretary of State.

4.223-CVL(4) **[Duplicate statements]** Every statement sent to the registrar of companies under section 192 shall be in duplicate.

GENERAL NOTE

The detailed reporting requirements imposed on the liquidator by IA 1986, s. 192 are spelt out in this rule, and in particular the statutory "intervals" are prescribed at six months. (Rule 4.223-CVL(1) was amended in 1987 in order to make it clear that shorter periods may not be substituted.) This rule applies to both a creditors' and a members' voluntary winding up; see r. 4.1(1)(g).

Rule 4.223-CVL(3A) avoids a duplication of returns where no assets remain at the end of the administration.

Section C: Dissolution after winding up

4.224 Secretary of State's directions under s. 203, 205

4.224(1) **[Copy of directions]** Where the Secretary of State gives a direction under–

(a) section 203 (where official receiver applies to registrar of companies for a company's early dissolution), or

(b) section 205 (application by interested person for postponement of dissolution),

he shall send two copies of the direction to the applicant for it.

4.224(2) **[Copy to registrar]** Of those copies one shall be sent by the applicant to the registrar of companies, to comply with section 203(5) or, as the case may be, 205(6).

(See General Note after r. 4.225.)

4.225 Procedure following appeal under s. 203(4) or 205(4)

4.225 Following an appeal under section 203(4) or 205(4) (against a decision of the Secretary of State under the applicable section) the court shall send two sealed copies of its order to the person in whose favour the appeal was determined; and that party shall send one of the copies to the registrar of companies to comply with section 203(5) or, as the case may be, 205(6).

[FORM 4.69]

GENERAL NOTE TO RR. 4.224–4.225

These rules provide machinery for the exercise of the official receiver's power under IA 1986, ss. 202ff., to apply to the registrar of companies for the early dissolution of the company where the assets are not worth the expense of administration.

CHAPTER 22

LEAVE TO ACT AS DIRECTOR, ETC., OF COMPANY WITH PROHIBITED NAME
(SECTION 216 OF THE ACT)

4.226 Preliminary

4.226 The Rules in this Chapter–

(a) relate to the leave required under section 216 (restriction on re-use of name of company in insolvent liquidation) for a person to act as mentioned in section 216(3) in relation to a company with a prohibited name,

(b) prescribe the cases excepted from that provision, that is to say, those in which a person to whom the section applies may so act without that leave, and

(c) apply to all windings up to which section 216 applies, whether or not the winding up commenced before the coming into force of the Rules.

(See General Note after r. 4.227.)

4.227 Application for leave under s. 216(3)

4.227 When considering an application for leave under section 216, the court may call on the liquidator, or any former liquidator, of the liquidating company for a report of the circumstances in which that company became insolvent, and the extent (if any) of the applicant's apparent responsibility for its doing so.

GENERAL NOTE TO RR. 4.226, 4.227

A former director or shadow director may not reuse a prohibited company name "except with the leave of the court or in such circumstances as may be prescribed" (IA 1986, s. 216(3)). Rule 4.227 deals with an application for such leave, while rr. 4.228–4.230 specify three sets of circumstances which are to be treated as excepted cases. Rule 4.226(c) makes this chapter coextensive with s. 216, so that the rules apply (for example) to a winding up where the petition was presented before December 29, 1986 (the commencement date for IR 1986) but the winding-up order was not made until after that date.

4.228 First excepted case

4.228(1) [Notice to creditors] Where a company ("the successor company") acquires the whole, or substantially the whole, of the business of an insolvent company, under arrangements made by an insolvency practitioner acting as its liquidator, administrator or administrative receiver, or as supervisor of a voluntary arrangement under Part I of the Act, the successor company may for the purposes of section 216 give notice under this Rule to the insolvent company's creditors.

4.228(2) [Time for notice and contents] To be effective, the notice must be given within 28 days from the completion of the arrangements, to all creditors of the insolvent company of whose addresses the successor company is aware in that period; and it must specify–

(a) the name and registered number of the insolvent company and the circumstances in which its business has been acquired by the successor company,

(b) the name which the successor company has assumed, or proposes to assume for the purpose of carrying on the business, if that name is or will be a prohibited name under section 216, and

(c) any change of name which it has made, or proposes to make, for that purpose under section 28 of the Companies Act.

4.228(3) [Notice may name director etc.] The notice may name a person to whom section 216 may apply as having been a director or shadow director of the insolvent company, and give particulars as to the nature and duration of that directorship, with a view to his being a director of the successor company or being otherwise associated with its management.

4.228(4) [Effect of notice] If the successor company has effectively given notice under this Rule to the insolvent company's creditors, a person who is so named in the notice may act in relation to the successor company in any of the ways mentioned in section 216(3), notwithstanding that he has not the leave of the court under that section.

GENERAL NOTE

The essential elements of this exception are:

- there must have been a transfer of the defunct company's business by its liquidator, etc., to a successor company;

- notice must be given to all known creditors of the insolvent company within 28 days of the completion of the arrangements, specifying the names used and proposed to be used by the two companies;

- the former director or shadow director must be named and the details in r. 4.228(3) also given.

4.229 Second excepted case

4.229(1) [Where director applies for leave] Where a person to whom section 216 applies as having been a director or shadow director of the liquidating company applies for leave of the court under that section not later than 7 days from the date on which the company went into liquidation, he may, during the period specified in paragraph (2) below, act in any of the ways mentioned in section 216(3), notwithstanding that he has not the leave of the court under that section.

4.229(2) [Period in r. 4.229(1)] The period referred to in paragraph (1) begins with the day on which the company goes into liquidation and ends either on the day falling six weeks after that date or on the day on which the court disposes of the application for leave under section 216, whichever of those days occurs first.

GENERAL NOTE

This exception enables a person who is seeking the leave of the court to act as a director, etc. of a company with a prohibited name for a brief period while his application is awaiting a hearing. Note the strict time limits. The six-week

4.230 Third excepted case

4.230 The court's leave under section 216(3) is not required where the company there referred to, though known by a prohibited name within the meaning of the section–

(a) has been known by that name for the whole of the period of 12 months ending with the day before the liquidating company went into liquidation, and

(b) has not at any time in those 12 months been dormant within the meaning of section 252(5) of the Companies Act.

GENERAL NOTE

This exception allows a former director to continue to act in the affairs of an established company even though it is known by a prohibited name, provided that it has been using that name for at least a year before his other company went into liquidation.

CHAPTER 23

EC REGULATION – MEMBER STATE LIQUIDATOR

4.231 Interpretation of creditor and notice to member State liquidator

4.231(1) [Application] This Rule applies where a member State liquidator has been appointed in relation to the company.

4.231(2) [Interpretation] For the purposes of the Rules referred to in paragraph (3) the member State liquidator is deemed to be a creditor.

4.231(3) [Rules referred to in r. 4.231(2)] The Rules referred to in paragraph (2) are Rules 4.43(1) (official receiver's report), 4.45(1) (report on statement of affairs), 4.46(2) (report where no statement of affairs), 4.47(2) (general rule on reporting), 4.48(2) (winding up stayed), 4.49 (information to creditors), 4.50(2) (notice of meetings), 4.51(2) (notice of creditors' meeting – CVL), 4.54 (power to call meetings), 4.57(1) (requisitioned meetings), 4.57(3), 4.67 (entitlement to vote (creditors)), 4.68 (chairman's discretion to allow vote – CVL), 4.70 (admission and rejection of proof (creditors' meeting)), 4.73 (meaning of "prove"), 4.74 (supply of forms), 4.75 (contents of proof), 4.76 (particulars of creditor's claim), 4.77 (claim established by affidavit), 4.78 (cost of proving), 4.79 (inspection of proofs), 4.82 (admission and rejection of proofs for dividend), 4.83(1) (appeal against decision in relation to proof), 4.83(2), 4.84 (withdrawal or variation of proof), 4.85(1) (expunging of proof), 4.86 (estimate of quantum), 4.87 (negotiable instruments, etc.), 4.88 (secured creditors), 4.89 (discounts), 4.90 (mutual credit and set-off), 4.91 (debt in foreign currency), 4.92 (payment of a periodical nature), 4.93 (interest), 4.94 (debt payable at future time), 4.101A (power to fill vacancy in office of liquidator), 4.102(5) (appointment by court), 4.103(4) (appointment by court), 4.113(1) (meeting of creditors to remove liquidator), 4.114(1) (meeting of creditors to remove liquidator), 4.115 (regulation of meetings), 4.124(1) (release of official receiver), 4.125(1) (final meeting), 4.125A(2) (rule on reporting), 4.126(1) (final meeting), 4.131(1) (challenge to liquidator's remuneration), 4.152(1) (liquidation committee), 4.152(3) (eligibility for liquidation committee), 4.163(3) (vacancy on liquidation committee), 4.175(1) (liquidation committee), 4.180 (notice of dividend) and 4.212(2) (notice of public examination hearing).

4.231(4) [Exercise of creditor's rights] Paragraphs (2) and (3) are without prejudice to the generality of the right to participate referred to in paragraph 3 of Article 32 of the EC Regulation (exercise of creditor's rights).

4.231(5) **[Notice, copies]** Where the liquidator is obliged to give notice to, or provide a copy of a document (including an order of court) to, the court, the registrar of companies or the official receiver, the liquidator shall give notice or provide copies, as the case may be, to the member State liquidator.

4.231(6) **[Duty to cooperate and communicate information]** Paragraph (5) is without prejudice to the generality of the obligations imposed by Article 31 of the EC Regulation (duty to cooperate and communicate information).

GENERAL NOTE

The new Chapter 23 was added by the Insolvency (Amendment) Rules 2002 (SI 2002/1307, effective May 31, 2002). It corresponds in a liquidation to Chapter 8, which makes similar provision for the rights of a Member State "liquidator" in an administration. See the note to r. *2.62*.

PART 5

INDIVIDUAL VOLUNTARY ARRANGEMENTS

CHAPTER 1

PRELIMINARY

GENERAL NOTE

A replacement Pt 5 was inserted by the Insolvency (Amendment) (No. 2) Rules 2002 (SI 2002/2712) with effect from January 1, 2003 to cater for the significant changes in the IVA regime brought about by IA 2000.

This new Part 5 only applies to IVAs agreed after January 1, 2003 – for existing IVAs the old Part 5 which is covered by the 6th edition of this work applies.

Further major changes/additions to Pt 5 were effected by the Insolvency (Amendment) Rules 2003 (SI 2003/1730) in response to the new requirements of EA 2002.

5.1 Introductory

5.1(1) **[Application of Pt. 5 Rules]** The Rules in this Part apply in relation to a voluntary arrangement under Part VIII of the Act, except in relation to voluntary arrangements under section 263A, in relation to which only Chapters 7, 10, 11 and 12 of this Part shall apply.

5.1(2) **[Application re voluntary arrangements other than under IA 1986, s. 263A]** In this Part, in respect of voluntary arrangements other than voluntary arrangements under section 263A–

    (a)   Chapter 2 applies in all cases;

    (b)   Chapter 3 applies in cases where an application for an interim order is made;

    (c)   Chapter 4 applies in cases where no application for an interim order is or is to be made;

    (d)   except where otherwise stated, Chapters 5 and 6 apply in all cases;

    (e)   Chapter 8 applies where a bankrupt makes an application under section 261(2)(a); and

    (f)   Chapter 9 applies where the official receiver makes an application under section 261(2)(b).

5.1(3) [Application re voluntary arrangements under IA 1986, s. 263A] In this Part, in respect of voluntary arrangements under section 263A–

(a) Chapter 7 applies in all cases; and

(b) Chapter 10 applies where the official receiver makes an application under section 263D(3).

5.1(4) [Application in all cases] In this Part, Chapters 11 and 12 apply in all cases.

R. 5.1
See general note to Pt 5. Rule 5.1 explains the structure of Pt 5 and reflects the growing complexity of IVA law.

This was further amended by Insolvency (Amendment) Rules 2003 (SI 2003/1730) in order to cater for the additional complications attendant upon reforms to IVA law made by EA 2002.

CHAPTER 2

PREPARATION OF THE DEBTOR'S PROPOSAL

5.2 Preparation of proposal

5.2 The debtor shall prepare for the intended nominee a proposal on which (with or without amendments to be made under Rule 5.3(3) below) to make his report to the court under section 256 or section 256A.

R. 5.2
See general note on Pt 5. This rule explains the debtor's responsibilities with regard to the preparation of the IVA proposal.

5.3 Contents of proposal

5.3(1) [Explanation why voluntary arrangement desirable] The debtor's proposal shall provide a short explanation why, in his opinion, a voluntary arrangement under Part VIII is desirable, and give reasons why his creditors may be expected to concur with such an arrangement.

5.3(2) [Other matters] The following matters shall be stated, or otherwise dealt with, in the proposal–

(a) the following matters, so far as within the debtor's immediate knowledge–

   (i) his assets, with an estimate of their respective values,
   (ii) the extent (if any) to which the assets are charged in favour of creditors,
   (iii) the extent (if any) to which particular assets are to be excluded from the voluntary arrangement;

(b) particulars of any property, other than assets of the debtor himself, which is proposed to be included in the arrangement, the source of such property and the terms on which it is to be made available for inclusion;

(c) the nature and amount of the debtor's liabilities (so far as within his immediate knowledge), the manner in which they are proposed to be met, modified, postponed or otherwise dealt with by means of the arrangement and (in particular)–

   (i) how it is proposed to deal with preferential creditors (defined in section 258(7)) and creditors who are, or claim to be, secured,
   (ii) how associates of the debtor (being creditors of his) are proposed to be treated under the arrangement, and
   (iii) in any case where the debtor is an undischarged bankrupt, whether, to the debtor's knowledge, claims have been made under section 339 (transactions at an undervalue),

section 340 (preferences) or section 343 (extortionate credit transactions), or where the debtor is not an undischarged bankrupt, whether there are circumstances which would give rise to the possibility of such claims in the event that he should be adjudged bankrupt,

and, where any such circumstances are present, whether, and if so how, it is proposed under the voluntary arrangement to make provision for wholly or partly indemnifying the insolvent estate in respect of such claims;

- (d) whether any, and if so what, guarantees have been given of the debtor's debts by other persons, specifying which (if any) of the guarantors are associates of his;
- (e) the proposed duration of the voluntary arrangement;
- (f) the proposed dates of distributions to creditors, with estimates of their amounts;
- (g) how it is proposed to deal with the claims of any person who is bound by the arrangement by virtue of section 260(2)(b)(ii);
- (h) the amount proposed to be paid to the nominee (as such) by way of remuneration and expenses;
- (j) the manner in which it is proposed that the supervisor of the arrangement should be remunerated, and his expenses defrayed;
- (k) whether, for the purposes of the arrangement, any guarantees are to be offered by any persons other than the debtor, and whether (if so) any security is to be given or sought;
- (l) the manner in which funds held for the purposes of the arrangement are to be banked, invested or otherwise dealt with pending distribution to creditors;
- (m) the manner in which funds held for the purpose of payment to creditors, and not so paid on the termination of the arrangement, are to be dealt with;
- (n) if the debtor has any business, the manner in which it is proposed to be conducted during the course of the arrangement;
- (o) details of any further credit facilities which it is intended to arrange for the debtor, and how the debts so arising are to be paid;
- (p) the functions which are to be undertaken by the supervisor of the arrangement;
- (q) the name, address and qualification of the person proposed as supervisor of the voluntary arrangement, and confirmation that he is, so far as the debtor is aware, qualified to act as an insolvency practitioner in relation to him or is an authorised person in relation to him; and
- (r) whether the EC Regulation will apply and, if so, whether the proceedings will be main proceedings or territorial proceedings.

5.3(3) **[Amendment of proposal]** With the agreement in writing of the nominee, the debtor's proposal may be amended at any time up to the delivery of the former's report to the court under section 256 or section 256A.

R. 5.3
See general note to Pt 5. Rule 5.3 details the required contents of the proposal – *e.g.* information on assets, liabilities, duration of IVA, proposed dividends, supervisor's remuneration, etc.

5.4 Notice to the intended nominee

5.4(1) **[Written notice]** The debtor shall give to the intended nominee written notice of his proposal.

5.4(2) **[Delivery of notice]** The notice, accompanied by a copy of the proposal, shall be delivered either to the nominee himself, or to a person authorised to take delivery of documents on his behalf.

5.4(3) [**Endorsement of receipt**] If the intended nominee agrees to act, he shall cause a copy of the notice to be endorsed to the effect that it has been received by him on a specified date.

5.4(4) [**Return of endorsed notice**] The copy of the notice so endorsed shall be returned by the nominee forthwith to the debtor at an address specified by him in the notice for that purpose.

5.4(5) [**Where debtor undischarged bankrupt**] Where the debtor is an undischarged bankrupt and he gives notice of his proposal to the official receiver and (if any) the trustee, the notice must contain the name and address of the insolvency practitioner or (as the case may be) authorised person who has agreed to act as nominee.

R. 5.4
See general note to Pt 5. This deals with the formal communication of the proposal by the debtor to his nominee.

5.5 Statement of Affairs

5.5(1) [**Delivery of statement**] Subject to paragraph (2), the debtor shall, within 7 days after his proposal is delivered to the nominee, or such longer time as the latter may allow, deliver to the nominee a statement of his (the debtor's) affairs.

5.5(2) [**Non-application of r. 5.5(1)**] Paragraph (1) shall not apply where the debtor is an undischarged bankrupt and he has already delivered a statement of affairs under section 272 (debtor's petition) or 288 (creditor's petition) but the nominee may require the debtor to submit a further statement supplementing or amplifying the statement of affairs already submitted.

5.5(3) [**Particulars in statement**] The statement of affairs shall comprise the following particulars (supplementing or amplifying, so far as is necessary for clarifying the state of the debtor's affairs, those already given in his proposal)–

(a) a list of his assets, divided into such categories as are appropriate for easy identification, with estimated values assigned to each category;

(b) in the case of any property on which a claim against the debtor is wholly or partly secured, particulars of the claim and its amount, and of how and when the security was created;

(c) the names and addresses of the debtor's preferential creditors (defined in section 258(7)), with the amounts of their respective claims;

(d) the names and addresses of the debtor's unsecured creditors, with the amounts of their respective claims;

(e) particulars of any debts owed by or to the debtor to or by persons who are associates of his;

(f) such other particulars (if any) as the nominee may in writing require to be furnished for the purposes of making his report to the court on the debtor's proposal.

5.5(4) [**Relevant date**] The statement of affairs shall be made up to a date not earlier than 2 weeks before the date of the notice to the nominee under Rule 5.4.

However, the nominee may allow an extension of that period to the nearest practicable date (not earlier than 2 months before the date of the notice under Rule 5.4); and if he does so, he shall give his reasons in his report to the court on the debtor's proposal.

5.5(5) [**Certification of statement**] The statement shall be certified by the debtor as correct, to the best of his knowledge and belief.

R. 5.5
See general note to Pt 5. After the proposal has been communicated the debtor has seven days to furnish the nominee with a formal statement of affairs. Rule 5.5 details the contents of this statement.

5.6 Additional disclosure for assistance of nominee

5.6(1) [**Nominee may request further information**] If it appears to the nominee that he cannot properly prepare his report on the basis of information in the debtor's proposal and statement of affairs, he may call on the debtor to provide him with–

(a) further and better particulars as to the circumstances in which, and the reasons why, he is insolvent or (as the case may be) threatened with insolvency;

(b) particulars of any previous proposals which have been made by him under Part VIII of the Act;

(c) any further information with respect to his affairs which the nominee thinks necessary for the purposes of his report.

5.6(2) [**Whether debtor concerned with insolvent company, bankrupt etc.**] The nominee may call on the debtor to inform him whether and in what circumstances he has at any time–

(a) been concerned in the affairs of any company (whether or not incorporated in England and Wales) which has become insolvent, or

(b) been adjudged bankrupt, or entered into an arrangement with his creditors.

5.6(3) [**Access to accounts and records**] For the purpose of enabling the nominee to consider the debtor's proposal and prepare his report on it, the latter must give him access to his accounts and records.

R. 5.6
See general note to Pt 5. This allows the nominee to call for further information from the debtor.

CHAPTER 3

CASES IN WHICH AN APPLICATION FOR AN INTERIM ORDER IS MADE

5.7 Application for interim order

5.7(1) [**Accompanying affidavit**] An application to the court for an interim order under Part VIII of the Act shall be accompanied by an affidavit of the following matters–

(a) the reasons for making the application;

(b) particulars of any execution or other legal process or levying of any distress which, to the debtor's knowledge, has been commenced against him;

(c) that he is an undischarged bankrupt or (as the case may be) that he is able to petition for his own bankruptcy;

(d) that no previous application for an interim order has been made by or in respect of the debtor in the period of 12 months ending with the date of the affidavit;

(e) that the nominee under the proposal (naming him) is willing to act in relation to the proposal and is a person who is either qualified to act as an insolvency practitioner in relation to the debtor or is authorised to act as nominee in relation to him; and

(f) that the debtor has not submitted to the official receiver either the document referred to at section 263B(1)(a) or the statement referred to at section 263B(1)(b).

5.7(2) [**Rule 5.4 notice to be exhibited**] A copy of the notice to the intended nominee under Rule 5.4, endorsed to the effect that he agrees so to act, and a copy of the debtor's proposal given to the nominee under that Rule, shall be exhibited to the affidavit.

5.7(3) [**Court to fix venue**] On receiving the application and affidavit, the court shall fix a venue for the hearing of the application.

5.7(4) [**Notice of hearing**] The applicant shall give at least 2 days' notice of the hearing–

(a) where the debtor is an undischarged bankrupt, to the bankrupt, the official receiver and the trustee (whichever of those three is not himself the applicant),

(b) where the debtor is not an undischarged bankrupt, to any creditor who (to the debtor's knowledge) has presented a bankruptcy petition against him, and

(c) in either case, to the nominee who has agreed to act in relation to the debtor's proposal.

R. 5.7
See general note to Pt 5. This explains the procedure to be followed on an application for an interim order.

This was then further amended in minor respects by Insolvency (Amendment) Rules 2003 (SI 2003/1730) to cater for modifications in the IVA regime made by EA 2002.

5.8 Court in which application to be made

5.8(1) [**Debtor not undischarged bankrupt**] Except in the case of an undischarged bankrupt, an application to the court under Part VIII of the Act shall be made to a court in which the debtor would be entitled to present his own petition in bankruptcy under Rule 6.40.

5.8(2) [**Information in application**] The application shall contain sufficient information to establish that it is brought in the appropriate court.

5.8(3) [**Debtor undischarged bankrupt**] In the case of an undischarged bankrupt, such an application shall be made to the court having the conduct of his bankruptcy and shall be filed with the bankruptcy proceedings.

R. 5.8
See the general note to Pt 5. This identifies the appropriate court where an application for an interim order is made.

5.9 Hearing of the application

5.9(1) [**Appearances etc.**] Any of the persons who have been given notice under Rule 5.7(4) may appear or be represented at the hearing of the application.

5.9(2) [**Representations re order**] The court, in deciding whether to make an interim order on the application, shall take into account any representations made by or on behalf of any of those persons (in particular, whether an order should be made containing such provision as is referred to in section 255(3) and (4)).

5.9(3) [**Consideration of nominee's report**] If the court makes an interim order, it shall fix a venue for consideration of the nominee's report. Subject to the following paragraph, the date for that consideration shall be not later than that on which the interim order ceases to have effect under section 255(6).

5.9(4) [**Extension of time under s. 256(4)**] If under section 256(4) an extension of time is granted for filing the nominee's report, the court shall, unless there appear to be good reasons against it, correspondingly extend the period for which the interim order has effect.

R. 5.9
See the general note to Pt 5. This explains the procedure to be followed on hearing an application for an interim order.

5.10 Action to follow making of order

5.10(1) [**Sealed copies**] Where an interim order is made, at least 2 sealed copies of the order shall be sent by the court to the person who applied for it; and that person shall serve one of the copies on the nominee under the debtor's proposal.

[FORM 5.2]

5.10(2) [**Notice of order**] The applicant shall also forthwith give notice of the making of the order to any person who was given notice of the hearing pursuant to Rule 5.7(4) and was not present or represented at it.

R. 5.10
See the general note to Pt 5. This rule deals with the dissemination of the fact that an interim order has been made.

5.11 Nominee's report on the proposal

5.11(1) [**Time for delivery**] Where the nominee makes his report to the court under section 256, he shall deliver 2 copies of it to the court not less than 2 days before the interim order ceases to have effect.

5.11(2) [**Accompanying documents**] With his report the nominee shall deliver–

(a) a copy of the debtor's proposal (with amendments, if any, authorised under Rule 5.3(3)); and

(b) a copy or summary of any statement of affairs provided by the debtor.

5.11(3) [**Nominee's opinion**] If the nominee makes known his opinion that the debtor's proposal has a reasonable prospect of being approved and implemented, and that a meeting of the debtor's creditors should be summoned under section 257, his report shall have annexed to it his comments on the debtor's proposal.
    If his opinion is otherwise, he shall give his reasons for that opinion.

5.11(4) [**Endorsement of date of filing**] The court shall upon receipt of the report cause one copy of the report to be endorsed with the date of its filing in court and returned to the nominee.

5.11(5) [**Inspection of file copy**] Any creditor of the debtor is entitled, at all reasonable times on any business day, to inspect the file.

5.11(6) [**Where debtor undischarged bankrupt**] Where the debtor is an undischarged bankrupt, the nominee shall send to the official receiver and (if any) the trustee–

(a) a copy of the debtor's proposal,

(b) a copy of his (the nominee's) report and his comments accompanying it (if any), and

(c) a copy or summary of the debtor's statement of affairs.

5.11(7) [**Where debtor not undischarged bankrupt**] Where the debtor is not an undischarged bankrupt, the nominee shall send a copy of each of the documents referred to in paragraph (6) to any person who has presented a bankruptcy petition against the debtor.

R. 5.11
See the general note to Pt 5. This regulates the nominee's report on the debtor's proposal and the communication of his views to the court. Note the right of creditors to inspect the court file.

5.12 Replacement of nominee

5.12(1) [**Notice of application**] Where the debtor intends to apply to the court under section 256(3) for the nominee to be replaced, he shall give to the nominee at least 7 days' notice of his application.

5.12(2) [**Replacement nominee to file statement of consent**] No appointment of a replacement nominee shall be made by the court unless there is filed in court a statement by the replacement nominee indicating his consent to act.

R. 5.12
See the general note to Pt 5. This provision supplements s. 265(3) on replacement of nominees.

5.13 Consideration of nominee's report

5.13(1) [**Appearances etc.**] At the hearing by the court to consider the nominee's report, any of the persons who have been given notice under Rule 5.7(4) may appear or be represented.

5.13(2) [**Application of r. 5.10**] Rule 5.10 applies to any order made by the court at the hearing.

R. 5.13
See the general note to Pt 5. This deals with procedural matters where the nominee's report is being considered.

CHAPTER 4

CASES WHERE NO INTERIM ORDER IS TO BE OBTAINED

5.14 Nominee's report to the court

5.14(1) [**Time for delivery**] The nominee shall deliver 2 copies of his report to the court (as defined in Rule 5.15) under section 256A within 14 days (or such longer period as the court may allow) after receiving from the debtor the document and statement mentioned in section 256A(2) but the court shall not consider the report unless an application is made under the Act or these Rules in relation to the debtor's proposal.

5.14(2) [**Accompanying documents**] With his report the nominee shall deliver–

(a) a copy of the debtor's proposal (with amendments, if any, authorised under Rule 5.3(3));

(b) a copy or summary of any statement of affairs provided by the debtor; and

(c) a copy of the notice referred to in Rule 5.4(3),

together with 2 copies of Form 5.5 listing the documents referred to in (a) to (c) above and containing a statement that no application for an interim order under section 252 is to be made.

5.14(3) [**Nominee's opinion**] If the nominee makes known his opinion that the debtor's proposal has a reasonable prospect of being approved and implemented, and that a meeting of the debtor's creditors should be summoned under section 257, his report shall have annexed to it his comments on the debtor's proposal.

If his opinion is otherwise, he shall give his reasons for that opinion.

5.14(4) [**Endorsement of date of filing**] The court shall upon receipt of the report and Form 5.5 cause one copy of the form to be endorsed with the date of its filing in court and returned to the nominee.

5.14(5) [**Inspection of file copy**] Any creditor of the debtor is entitled, at all reasonable times on any business day, to inspect the file.

5.14(6) [**Where debtor undischarged bankrupt**] Where the debtor is an undischarged bankrupt, the nominee shall send to the official receiver and (if any) the trustee–

(a) a copy of the debtor's proposal,

(b) a copy of his (the nominee's) report and his comments accompanying it (if any), and

(c) a copy or summary of the debtor's statement of affairs.

5.14(7) [**Where debtor not undischarged bankrupt**] Where the debtor is not an undischarged bankrupt, the nominee shall send a copy of each of the documents referred to in paragraph (6) to any person who has presented a bankruptcy petition against the debtor.

5.14(8) [**Filing to constitute insolvency proceeding**] The filing in court of the report under section 256A shall constitute an insolvency proceeding for the purpose of Rule 7.27 and Rule 7.30.

R. 5.14
See the general note to Pt 5. Chapter 4 deals with IVA procedure where no interim order is being sought. This provision explains the procedures operating where the nominee reports to the court on the proposal.

5.15 Filing of reports made under section 256A – appropriate court

5.15(1) **[Appropriate court]** Except where the debtor is an undischarged bankrupt, the court in which the nominee's report under section 256A is to be filed is the court in which the debtor would be entitled to present his own petition in bankruptcy under Rule 6.40.

5.15(2) **[Information in report]** The report shall contain sufficient information to establish that it is filed in the appropriate court.

5.15(3) **[Where debtor undischarged bankrupt]** Where the debtor is an undischarged bankrupt, such report shall be filed in the court having the conduct of his bankruptcy and shall be filed with the bankruptcy proceedings.

R. 5.15
See the general note to Pt 5. Rule 5.15 deals with procedures to be followed where reports are made under s. 256A and in particular it identifies the appropriate court.

5.16 Applications to the court

5.16(1) **[Application to court where nominee's report filed]** Any application to court in relation to any matter relating to a voluntary arrangement or a proposal for a voluntary arrangement shall be made in the court in which the nominee's report was filed.

5.16(2) **[Notice of debtor's application]** Where the debtor intends to apply to the court under section 256A(4)(a) or (b) for the nominee to be replaced, he shall give to the nominee at least 7 days' notice of the application.

5.16(3) **[Notice of nominee's application]** Where the nominee intends to apply to the court under section 256A(4)(b) for his replacement as nominee, he shall give to the debtor at least 7 days' notice of the application.

5.16(4) **[Replacement nominee to file statement of consent]** No appointment of a replacement nominee shall be made by the court unless there is filed in court a statement by the replacement nominee indicating his consent to act.

R. 5.16
See the general note to Pt 5. This deals with applications to court by identifying the appropriate court and defining notice periods.

CHAPTER 5

CREDITORS' MEETINGS

5.17 Summoning of creditors' meeting

5.17(1) **[Date of meeting]** If in his report the nominee states that in his opinion a meeting of creditors should be summoned to consider the debtor's proposal, the date on which the meeting is to be held shall be–

(a) in a case where an interim order has not been obtained, not less than 14 days and not more than 28 days from that on which the nominee's report is filed in court under Rule 5.14; and

(b) in a case where an interim order is in force, not less than 14 days from the date on which the nominee's report is filed in court nor more than 28 days from that on which the report is considered by the court.

5.17(2) **[Notice of meeting]** Notices calling the meeting shall be sent by the nominee, at least 14 days before the day fixed for it to be held, to all the creditors specified in the debtor's statement of affairs, and any other creditors of whom the nominee is otherwise aware.

5.17(3) **[Contents of notice and accompanying documents]** Each notice sent under this Rule shall specify the court to which the nominee's report on the debtor's proposal has been delivered and shall state the effect of Rule 5.23(1), (3) and (4) (requisite majorities); and with it there shall be sent–

(a) a copy of the proposal,

(b) a copy of the statement of affairs or, if the nominee thinks fit, a summary of it (the summary to include a list of the creditors and the amounts of their debts), and

(c) the nominee's comments on the proposal.

R. 5.17
See the general note to Pt 5. Chapter 5 is devoted to creditor meetings and r. 5.17 outlines procedures for summoning such meetings.

5.18 Creditors' meeting: supplementary

5.18(1) **[Convenience of venue]** Subject as follows, in fixing the venue for the creditors' meeting, the nominee shall have regard to the convenience of creditors.

5.18(2) **[Time of meeting]** The meeting shall be summoned for commencement between 10.00 and 16.00 hours on a business day.

5.18(3) **[Forms of proxy]** With every notice summoning the meeting there shall be sent out forms of proxy.

[FORM 8.1]

R. 5.18
See the general note to Pt 5. This rules deals with mundane matters such as venue.

5.19 The chairman at the meeting

5.19(1) **[Nominee to be chairman]** Subject as follows, the nominee shall be chairman of the creditors' meeting.

5.19(2) **[Other nominated chairman]** If for any reason the nominee is unable to attend, he may nominate another person to act as chairman in his place; but a person so nominated must be–

(a) a person qualified to act as an insolvency practitioner in relation to the debtor;

(b) an authorised person in relation to the debtor; or

(c) an employee of the nominee or his firm who is experienced in insolvency matters.

R. 5.19
See the general note to Pt 5. This particular rule regulates choice of chairman.

5.20 The chairman as proxy-holder

5.20 The chairman shall not by virtue of any proxy held by him vote to increase or reduce the amount of the remuneration or expenses of the nominee or the supervisor of the proposed arrangement, unless the proxy specifically directs him to vote in that way.

R. 5.20
See the general note to Pt 5. This is a sensible provision designed to curb any potential for abuse by a chair of a creditors' meeting.

5.21 Entitlement to vote

5.21(1) [**Entitlement**] Subject as follows, every creditor who has notice of the creditors' meeting is entitled to vote at the meeting or any adjournment of it.

5.21(2) [**Calculation of votes**] A creditor's entitlement to vote is calculated as follows–

(a) where the debtor is not an undischarged bankrupt and an interim order is in force, by reference to the amount of the debt owed to him as at the date of the interim order;

(b) where the debtor is not an undischarged bankrupt and an interim order is not in force, by reference to the amount of the debt owed to him at the date of the meeting; and

(c) where the debtor is an undischarged bankrupt, by reference to the amount of the debt owed to him as at the date of the bankruptcy order.

5.21(3) [**Limitation on voting**] A creditor may vote in respect of a debt for an unliquidated amount or any debt whose value is not ascertained, and for the purposes of voting (but not otherwise) his debt shall be valued at £1 unless the chairman agrees to put a higher value on it.

R. 5.21
See the general note to Pt 5. This important provision explains the calculation of voting entitlements. Note the nominal £1 valuation for unliquidated/unascertained debts.

5.22 Procedure for admission of creditors' claims for voting purposes

5.22(1) [**Procedure at creditor's meeting**] Subject as follows, at the creditors' meeting the chairman shall ascertain the entitlement of persons wishing to vote and shall admit or reject their claims accordingly.

5.22(2) [**Chairman's discretion**] The chairman may admit or reject a claim in whole or in part.

5.22(3) [**Appeal from chairman's decision**] The chairman's decision on any matter under this Rule or under paragraph (3) of Rule 5.21 is subject to appeal to the court by any creditor or by the debtor.

5.22(4) [**Voting subject to objection**] If the chairman is in doubt whether a claim should be admitted or rejected, he shall mark it as objected to and allow votes to be cast in respect of it, subject to such votes being subsequently declared invalid if the objection to the claim is sustained.

5.22(5) [**When chairman's decision reversed etc.**] If on an appeal the chairman's decision is reversed or varied, or votes are declared invalid, the court may order another meeting to be summoned, or make such order as it thinks just.

The court's power to make an order under this paragraph is exercisable only if it considers that the circumstances giving rise to the appeal are such as give rise to unfair prejudice or material irregularity.

5.22(6) [**Time for appeal**] An application to the court by way of appeal against the chairman's decision shall not be made after the end of the period of 28 days beginning with the first day on which the report required by section 259 is made to the court.

5.22(7) [**Costs of appeal**] The chairman is not personally liable for any costs incurred by any person in respect of an appeal under this Rule.

R. 5.22
See the general note to Pt 5. This deals with the sensitive matter of managing entitlement to vote. This has triggered much litigation in the past.

5.23 Requisite majorities

5.23(1) [**Three-quarters majority**] Subject as follows, at the creditors' meeting for any resolution to pass approving any proposal or modification there must be a majority in excess of three-quarters in value of the creditors present in person or by proxy and voting on the resolution.

5.23(2) [**One-half majority**] The same applies in respect of any other resolution proposed at the meeting, but substituting one-half for three-quarters.

5.23(3) [**Votes to be left out of account**] In the following cases there is to be left out of account a creditor's vote in respect of any claim or part of a claim–

(a) where written notice of the claim was not given, either at the meeting or before it, to the chairman or the nominee;

(b) where the claim or part is secured;

(c) where the claim is in respect of a debt wholly or partly on, or secured by, a current bill of exchange or promissory note, unless the creditor is willing–

   (i) to treat the liability to him on the bill or note of every person who is liable on it antecedently to the debtor, and against whom a bankruptcy order has not been made (or, in the case of a company, which has not gone into liquidation), as a security in his hands, and

   (ii) to estimate the value of the security and (for the purpose of entitlement to vote, but not of any distribution under the arrangement) to deduct it from his claim.

5.23(4) [**Votes rendering resolution invalid**] Any resolution is invalid if those voting against it include more than half in value of the creditors, counting in these latter only those–

(a) who have notice of the meeting;

(b) whose votes are not to be left out of account under paragraph (3); and

(c) who are not, to the best of the chairman's belief, associates of the debtor.

5.23(5) [**Chairman's powers**] It is for the chairman of the meeting to decide whether under this Rule–

(a) a vote is to be left out of account in accordance with the paragraph (3), or

(b) a person is an associate of the debtor for the purposes of paragraph (4)(c);

and in relation to the second of these cases the chairman is entitled to rely on the information provided by the debtor's statement of affairs or otherwise in accordance with this Part of the Rules.

5.23(6) [**Chairman's use of proxy**] If the chairman uses a proxy contrary to Rule 5.20, his vote with that proxy does not count towards any majority under this Rule.

5.23(7) [**Chairman's decision subject to appeal**] The chairman's decision on any matter under this Rule is subject to appeal to the court by any creditor or by the debtor and paragraphs (5) to (7) of Rule 5.22 apply as regards such an appeal.

R. 5.23
See the general note to Pt 5. The proposal must attract the support of the holders of 75 per cent of the debt and of more than 50 per cent of the independent debt. The voting position where debts are secured is also explained. Creditors who have not notified their claim before the meeting cannot vote.

5.24 Proceedings to obtain agreement on the proposal

5.24(1) [**Adjournments**] On the day on which the creditors' meeting is held, it may from time to time be adjourned.

5.24(2) **[Failure to obtain requisite majority]** If on that day the requisite majority for the approval of the voluntary arrangement (with or without modifications) has not been obtained, the chairman may, and shall if it is so resolved, adjourn the meeting for not more than 14 days.

5.24(3) **[Final adjournment]** If there are subsequently further adjournments, the final adjournment shall not be to a day later than 14 days after that on which the meeting was originally held.

5.24(4) **[Notice of adjournment]** If the meeting is adjourned under paragraph (2), notice of the fact shall be given by the chairman forthwith to the court.

5.24(5) **[Deemed rejection of proposal]** If following any final adjournment of the meeting the proposal (with or without modifications) is not agreed to, it is deemed rejected.

R. 5.24
See the general note to Pt 5. This deals with the possibility of adjournment, which is a common happening, in order to amend the proposal and win over doubters. Any adjournment(s) can only last for a maximum of 14 days after the initial meeting.

CHAPTER 6

IMPLEMENTATION OF THE ARRANGEMENT

5.25 Resolutions to follow approval

5.25(1) **[Resolution re supervisory acts]** If the voluntary arrangement is approved (with or without modifications), a resolution may be taken by the creditors, where two or more individuals are appointed to act as supervisor, on the question whether acts to be done in connection with the arrangement may be done by any one of them, or must be done by both or all.

5.25(2) **[Where supervisor to be other than nominee]** If at the creditors' meeting a resolution is moved for the appointment of some person other than the nominee to be supervisor of the arrangement, there must be produced to the chairman, at or before the meeting–

(a) that person's written consent to act (unless he is present and then and there signifies his consent), and

(b) his written confirmation that he is qualified to act as an insolvency practitioner in relation to the debtor or is an authorised person in relation to the debtor.

R. 5.25
See the general note to Pt 5. Chapter 6 deals with matters consequent upon approval of an IVA, including the powers of joint supervisors.

5.26 Hand-over of property, etc to supervisor

5.26(1) **[Putting supervisor into possession of assets]** Forthwith after the approval of the voluntary arrangement, the debtor or, where the debtor is an undischarged bankrupt, the official receiver or the debtor's trustee, shall do all that is required for putting the supervisor into possession of the assets included in the arrangement.

5.26(2) **[Discharge of official receiver's remuneration etc.]** On taking possession of the assets in any case where the debtor is an undischarged bankrupt, the supervisor shall discharge any balance due to the official receiver and (if other) the trustee by way of remuneration or on account of–

(a) fees, costs, charges and expenses properly incurred and payable under the Act or the Rules, and

(b) any advances made in respect of the insolvent estate, together with interest on such advances at the rate specified in section 17 of the Judgments Act 1838 at the date of the bankruptcy order.

5.26(3) **[Undertaking to discharge etc.]** Alternatively where the debtor is an undischarged bankrupt, the supervisor must, before taking possession, give the official receiver or the trustee a written undertaking to discharge any such balance out of the first realisation of assets.

5.26(4) **[Charge on assets]** Where the debtor is an undischarged bankrupt, the official receiver and (if other) the trustee has a charge on the assets included in the voluntary arrangement in respect of any sums due as above until they have been discharged, subject only to the deduction from realisations by the supervisor of the proper costs and expenses of realisation.

Any sums due to the official receiver take priority over those due to a trustee.

5.26(5) **[Discharge of guarantees etc.]** The supervisor shall from time to time out of the realisation of assets discharge all guarantees properly given by the official receiver or the trustee for the benefit of the estate, and shall pay all their expenses.

R. 5.26
See the general note to Pt 5. Chapter 6 deals with the implementation of the approved arrangement. Rule 5.26 addresses various matters consequential to approval, including the handing over of property to the supervisor. A properly drafted arrangement should carefully identify such property in order for it to become a trust asset protected from the claims of creditors outside the IVA.

5.27 Report of creditors' meeting

5.27(1) **[Chairman to prepare report]** A report of the creditors' meeting shall be prepared by the chairman of the meeting.

5.27(2) **[Contents of report]** The report shall–

(a) state whether the proposal for a voluntary arrangement was approved or rejected and, if approved, with what (if any) modifications;

(b) set out the resolutions which were taken at the meeting, and the decision on each one;

(c) list the creditors (with their respective values) who were present or represented at the meeting, and how they voted on each resolution;

(d) whether in the opinion of the supervisor,
  (i) the EC Regulation applies to the voluntary arrangement, and
  (ii) if so, whether the proceedings are main proceedings or territorial proceedings; and

(e) include such further information (if any) as the chairman thinks it appropriate to make known to the court.

5.27(3) **[Copy of report to be filed in court]** A copy of the chairman's report shall, within 4 days of the meeting being held, be filed in court; and the court shall cause that copy to be endorsed with the date of filing.

5.27(4) **[Notice of result]** The persons to whom notice of the result is to be given, under section 259(1), are all those who were sent notice of the meeting under this Part of the Rules and any other creditor of whom the chairman is aware, and where the debtor is an undischarged bankrupt, the official receiver and (if any) the trustee.

The notice shall be sent immediately after a copy of the chairman's report is filed in court under paragraph (3).

5.27(5) **[Where no interim order obtained]** In a case where no interim order has been obtained the court shall not consider the chairman's report unless an application is made to the court under the Act or the Rules in relation to it.

R. 5.27
See the general note to Pt 5. This rules explains the contents of the chairman's report on the creditor's meeting – this report, which has become more fulsome with successive reforms, must be filed in court within four days.

5.28 Register of voluntary arrangements

[Omitted]

R. 5.28
See the general note to Pt 5. A register of IVAs was to be maintained by the Secretary of State and be open for public inspection.

[This rule was then omitted by the Insolvency (Amendment) Rules 2003 (SI 2003/1730) – this register is now provided for by Pt 6A.]

5.29 Reports to Secretary of State

5.29(1) [Details of arrangement] Immediately after the chairman of the creditors' meeting has filed in court a report that the meeting has approved the voluntary arrangement, he shall report to the Secretary of State the following details of the arrangement–

(a) the name and address of the debtor;

(b) the date on which the arrangement was approved by the creditors;

(c) the name and address of the supervisor; and

(d) the court in which the chairman's report has been filed.

5.29(2) [Notice of appointment as supervisor etc.] A person who is appointed to act as supervisor of an individual voluntary arrangement (whether in the first instance or by way of replacement of another person previously appointed) shall forthwith give written notice to the Secretary of State of his appointment.

If he vacates office as supervisor, he shall forthwith give written notice of that fact also to the Secretary of State.

R. 5.29
See the general note to Pt 5. In addition to notifying the court the chairman of the creditors' meeting must notify approved voluntary arrangements to the Secretary of State. This is necessary to enable the latter to maintain the public register (see Pt 6A). The supervisor must also notify his appointment to the Secretary of State.

5.30 Revocation or suspension of the arrangement

5.30(1) [Application] This Rule applies where the court makes an order of revocation or suspension under section 262.

5.30(2) [Service of sealed copies] The person who applied for the order shall serve sealed copies of it–

(a) in a case where the debtor is an undischarged bankrupt, on the debtor, the official receiver and the trustee;

(b) in any other case, on the debtor; and

(c) in either case, on the supervisor of the voluntary arrangement.

5.30(3) [Notice re further creditors' meeting] If the order includes a direction by the court under section 262(4)(b) for any further creditors' meeting to be summoned, notice shall also be given (by the person who applied for the order) to whoever is, in accordance with the direction, required to summon the meeting.

5.30(4) [Notice of order and of intention re proposal] The debtor or (where the debtor is an undischarged bankrupt) the trustee or (if there is no trustee) the official receiver shall–

(a) forthwith after receiving a copy of the court's order, give notice of it to all persons who were sent notice of the creditors' meeting which approved the voluntary arrangement or who, not having been sent that notice, are affected by the order;

(b) within 7 days of their receiving a copy of the order (or within such longer period as the court may allow), give notice to the court whether it is intended to make a revised proposal to creditors, or to invite reconsideration of the original proposal.

5.30(5) **[Notice to Secretary of State]** The person on whose application the order of revocation or suspension was made shall, within 7 days after the making of the order, give written notice of it to the Secretary of State and shall, in the case of an order of suspension, within 7 days of the expiry of any suspension order, given written notice of such expiry to the Secretary of State.

R. 5.30
See the general note to Pt 5. This particular rule deals with revocation or suspension of the IVA under the terms of s. 262. Various consequential matters are addressed including the requirement imposed on the successful applicant to notify the Secretary of State within seven days.

5.31 Supervisor's accounts and reports

5.31(1) **[Obligation to keep accounts etc.]** Where the voluntary arrangement authorises or requires the supervisor–

(a) to carry on the debtor's business or to trade on his behalf or in his name, or

(b) to realise assets of the debtor or (in a case where the debtor is an undischarged bankrupt) belonging to the estate, or

(c) otherwise to administer or dispose of any funds of the debtor or the estate,

he shall keep accounts and records of his acts and dealings in and in connection with the arrangement, including in particular records of all receipts and payments of money.

5.31(2) **[Abstract of receipts and payments]** The supervisor shall, not less often than once in every 12 months beginning with the date of his appointment, prepare an abstract of such receipts and payments, and send copies of it, accompanied by his comments on the progress and efficacy of the arrangement, to–

(a) the court,

(b) the debtor, and

(c) all those of the debtor's creditors who are bound by the arrangement.

If in any period of 12 months he has made no payments and had no receipts, he shall at the end of that period send a statement to that effect to all who are specified in sub-paragraphs (a) to (c) above.

5.31(3) **[Abstract under r. 5.31(2)]** An abstract provided under paragraph (2) shall relate to a period beginning with the date of the supervisor's appointment or (as the case may be) the day following the end of the last period for which an abstract was prepared under this Rule; and copies of the abstract shall be sent out, as required by paragraph (2), within the 2 months following the end of the period to which the abstract relates.

5.31(4) **[If supervisor not authorised]** If the supervisor is not authorised as mentioned in paragraph (1), he shall, not less often than once in every 12 months beginning with the date of his appointment, send to all those specified in paragraph 2(a) to (c) a report on the progress and efficacy of the voluntary arrangement.

5.31(5) **[Powers of court]** The court may, on application by the supervisor, vary the dates on which the obligation to send abstracts or reports arises.

R. 5.31
See the general note to Pt 5. Rule 5.31 regulates the provision of accounts and reports from the supervisor.

5.32 Production of accounts and records to Secretary of State

5.32(1) **[Powers of Secretary of State]** The Secretary of State may at any time during the course of the voluntary arrangement or after its completion require the supervisor to produce for inspection–

(a) his records and accounts in respect of the arrangement, and

(b) copies of abstracts and reports prepared in compliance with Rule 5.31.

5.32(2) **[Production and duty to comply]** The Secretary of State may require production either at the premises of the supervisor or elsewhere; and it is the duty of the supervisor to comply with any requirement imposed on him under this Rule.

5.32(3) **[Audit of accounts and records]** The Secretary of State may cause any accounts and records produced to him under this Rule to be audited; and the supervisor shall give to the Secretary of State such further information and assistance as he needs for the purposes of his audit.

R. 5.32
See the general note to Pt 5. In addition to the general accounting requirements imposed by r. 5.31, the Secretary of State can at any time require further accounts and reports from the supervisor.

5.33 Fees, costs, charges and expenses

5.33 The fees, costs, charges and expenses that may be incurred for any purposes of the voluntary arrangement are–

(a) any disbursements made by the nominee prior to the approval of the arrangement, and any remuneration for his services as such agreed between himself and the debtor, the official receiver or the trustee;

(b) any fees, costs, charges or expenses which–

　　(i) are sanctioned by the terms of the arrangement, or
　　(ii) would be payable, or correspond to those which would be payable, in the debtor's bankruptcy.

R. 5.33
See the general note to Pt 5. This identifies the fees and expenses, etc., of an IVA.

5.34 Completion or termination of the arrangement

5.34(1) **[Supervisor to send notice]** Not more than 28 days after the final completion or termination of the voluntary arrangement, the supervisor shall send to all creditors of the debtor who are bound by the arrangement, and to the debtor, a notice that the arrangement has been fully implemented or (as the case may be) terminated.

5.34(2) **[Supervisor's report]** With the notice there shall be sent to each of those persons a copy of a report by the supervisor summarising all receipts and payments made by him in pursuance of the arrangement, and explaining any difference in the actual implementation of it as compared with the proposal as approved by the creditors' meeting or (in the case of termination of the arrangement) explaining the reasons why the arrangement has not been implemented in accordance with the proposal as approved by the creditors' meeting.

5.34(3) **[Copy of notice and report]** The supervisor shall, within the 28 days mentioned above, send to the Secretary of State and to the court a copy of the notice under paragraph (1), together with a copy of the report under paragraph (2), and he shall not vacate office until after such copies have been sent.

5.34(4) **[Extension of time]** The court may, on application by the supervisor, extend the period of 28 days under paragraphs (1) and (3).

R. 5.34
See the general note to Pt 5. The supervisor must notify all creditors of completion or termination and also must furnish them with a summary of receipts and payments. The Secretary of State must in addition be notified. The time limit for such notifications is fixed at 28 days.

CHAPTER 7

FAST-TRACK VOLUNTARY ARRANGEMENT

5.35 Application of Chapter

5.35 The Rules in this Chapter apply in relation to an individual debtor who intends to submit a proposal for a voluntary arrangement with his creditors to the official receiver in accordance with the provisions of section 263B.

GENERAL NOTE

This new Chapter 7 dealing with fast-track IVAs was inserted by the Insolvency (Amendment) Rules 2003 (SI 2003/1730) in the wake of the Enterprise Act 2002, which introduced this new IVA variant via s. 263B.

Under this model the official receiver is permitted to act as nominee/supervisor of an IVA proposed by an undischarged bankrupt. This is an exceptional scenario which has raised some concern in the minds of private practitioners but quite frankly its potential usage is likely to be limited particularly with discharge available after only one year.

The required contents of the undischarged bankrupt's proposal are mapped out by r. 5.37. The official receiver has 28 days to respond (r. 5.38). If his response is favourable he must as soon as practicable notify the creditors and the trustee in bankruptcy (r. 5.39). Voting is by post (r. 5.40) rather than through the medium of a meeting; this will save on costs. Rules on voting entitlements and majorities are detailed in rr. 5.41–5.43. There is an opportunity to challenge any approval given to such an IVA proposal (s. 263F and r. 5.46). Duties of the supervisor (who may be the official receiver) are explained in rr. 5.47–5.50. Paragraphs (3) and (4) of r. 5.43 were inserted by I(A)R 2004 (SI 2004/584) with effect from April 1, 2004 to clarify the position on calculating votes for the purposes of requisite majorities. Note the introduction of the standard IVA requirement that the support of the holders of 50 per cent of the independent debt must be obtained.

5.36 Interpretation

5.36 In this Chapter—

"voluntary arrangement" means an individual voluntary arrangement under section 263A;

"proposal" means the document setting out the terms of the voluntary arrangement which the debtor is proposing.

(See General Note after s. 5.35.)

5.37 Contents of proposal

5.37(1) **[Fees and contents]** The debtor's proposal submitted under section 263B(1) shall—

(a) be accompanied by any fee payable to the official receiver for acting as nominee; and

(b) contain—

    (i) a statement that the debtor is eligible to propose a voluntary arrangement;
    (ii) a short explanation why, in his opinion, a voluntary arrangement is desirable, and give reasons why his creditors may be expected to concur with such an arrangement; and
    (iii) a statement that the debtor is aware that he commits an offence under section 262A if, for the purpose of obtaining the approval of his creditors to his proposal, he makes any false representation, or fraudulently does, or omits to do, anything.

5.37(2) **[Matters to be stated]** The following matters shall be stated, or otherwise dealt with, in the proposal–

(a) the following matters, so far as within the debtor's immediate knowledge
 (i) his assets, with an estimate of their respective values;
 (ii) the extent (if any) to which the assets are charged in favour of creditors; and
 (iii) the extent (if any) to which particular assets are to be excluded from the voluntary arrangement;

(b) particulars of any property, other than assets of the debtor himself, which is proposed to be included in the voluntary arrangement, the source of such property and the terms on which it is to be made available for inclusion;

(c) the nature and amount of the debtor's liabilities (so far as within his immediate knowledge), the manner in which they are proposed to be met, modified, postponed or otherwise dealt with by means of the voluntary arrangement and (in particular)–
 (i) how it is proposed to deal with preferential creditors (defined in section 258(7)) and creditors who are, or claim to be, secured;
 (ii) how associates of the debtor (being creditors of his) are proposed to be treated under the voluntary arrangement; and
 (iii) whether, to the debtor's knowledge, claims have been made under section 339 (transactions at an undervalue), section 340 (preferences), section 343 (extortionate credit transactions), or whether there are circumstances giving rise to the possibility of such claims

and, where any such circumstances are present, whether, and if so how, it is proposed under the voluntary arrangement to make provision for wholly or partly indemnifying the insolvent estate in respect of such claims;

(d) whether any, and if so what, guarantees have been given of the debtor's debts by other persons, specifying which (if any) of the guarantors are associates of his;

(e) the proposed duration of the voluntary arrangement;

(f) the proposed dates of distributions to creditors, with estimates of their amounts;

(g) how it is proposed to deal with the claims of any person who is bound by the arrangement by virtue of section 263D(2)(c);

(h) an estimate of the fees and expenses that will be incurred in connection with the approval and implementation of the voluntary agreement;

(j) whether, for the purposes of the voluntary arrangement, any guarantees are to be offered by any persons other than the debtor and whether (if so) any security is to be given or sought;

(k) the manner in which funds held for the purpose of payment to creditors, and not so paid on the termination of the voluntary arrangement, are to be dealt with;

(l) the functions which are to be undertaken by the supervisor of the voluntary arrangement;

(m) an address of the official receiver to which correspondence with the official receiver is to be sent;

(n) the names and addresses of all the debtor's creditors so far as within his immediate knowledge; and

(o) whether the EC Regulation will apply and, if so, whether the proceedings will be main proceedings or territorial proceedings

and the proposal shall be signed and dated by the debtor.

5.37(3) **[Address of official receiver]** The official receiver shall on request supply to the debtor the address referred to in paragraph 2(m).

(See General Note after r. 5.35.)

Rule 5.38

5.38 Requirement for the official receiver's decision

5.38(1) [**Duty of official receiver to notify debtor**] Where the official receiver receives a proposal for a voluntary arrangement in accordance with Rule 5.37 he shall, within 28 days of its receipt, serve a notice on the debtor stating that–

(a) he agrees to act as nominee in relation to the proposal;

(b) he declines to act as nominee in relation to the proposal and specifying reasons for his decision; or

(c) on the basis of the information supplied to him he is unable to reach a decision as to whether to act and specifying what further information he requires.

5.38(2) [**Where a decision after further information**] Where the debtor, pursuant to a request under paragraph (1)(c), supplies the information requested, the official receiver shall, within 28 days of the receipt of the information, serve a notice on the debtor in accordance with paragraph (1).

(See General Note after r. 5.35.)

5.39 Arrangements for approval of fast-track voluntary arrangement

5.39(1) [**Duty of official receiver to creditors and trustee**] As soon as reasonably practicable after the official receiver agrees to act as nominee, he shall send to the creditors and any trustee who is not the official receiver–

(a) a copy of the proposal; and

(b) a notice inviting creditors to vote to approve or reject the debtor's proposal and stating that–

    (i) if a majority in excess of three-quarters in value of creditors who vote approve the proposal, the official receiver will, as soon as reasonably practicable, report to the court that the proposal has been approved;

    (ii) under section 263F–

        (aa) the debtor, a person who was entitled to participate in the arrangements made under section 263B(2), any trustee who is not the official receiver, or the official receiver, has 28 days from the date the official receiver reports to the court under section 263C that the proposal has been approved to apply to the court to have the proposal set aside on the grounds set out in section 263F(1);

        (bb) a creditor, who was not made aware of the arrangements under section 263B(2) at the time when they were made, has 28 days from the date on which he becomes aware of the voluntary arrangement, to apply to have the proposal set aside on the grounds set out in section 263F(1); and

    (iii) creditors cannot propose modifications to the debtor's proposal; and

(c) for the creditors, a copy of Form 5.6 for their use.

5.39(2) [**Final date for voting**] The notice shall include a date specified by the official receiver as the final date on which he will accept votes from creditors, being a date not less than 14 days and not more than 28 days from the date of the notice.

(See General Note after r. 5.35.)

5.40 Approval by creditors

5.40(1) [**Forms of notice re proposal**] All creditors who wish to vote shall give notice in Form 5.6 to the official receiver of their decision whether to accept or reject the debtor's proposal. Such notification shall be sent to the official receiver at the address specified in the notice.

[FORM 5.6]

5.40(2) [**Signature by representatives**] Votes may be signed by a representative of a creditor.

5.40(3) [**Written authority for representative**] Votes from a representative of a creditor shall be accompanied by written authority for that representation signed and dated by the creditor.

(See General Note after r. 5.35.)

5.41 Entitlement to vote

5.41(1) [**Entitlement to vote**] Subject as follows, any creditor who is sent a notice by the official receiver is entitled to vote for the approval or rejection of the proposal.

5.41(2) [**Calculation of voting entitlement**] A creditor's entitlement to vote is calculated by reference to the amount of the creditor's debt at the date of the bankruptcy order.

5.41(3) [**Valuation of unliquidated amounts**] A creditor may vote in respect of a debt for an unliquidated amount or any debt whose value is not ascertained, and for the purposes of voting (but not otherwise) his debt shall be valued at £1 unless the official receiver agrees to put a higher value on it.

(See General Note after r. 5.35.)

5.42 Procedure for admission of creditors' claims for voting purposes

5.42(1) [**Power of official receiver**] The official receiver has the power to admit or reject a creditor's claim for the purpose of his entitlement to vote, and the power is exercisable with respect to the whole or part of the claim.

5.42(2) [**Appeal**] The official receiver's decision on entitlement to vote is subject to appeal to the court by any creditor or the debtor.

5.42(3) [**Power of court**] If on appeal the official receiver's decision is reversed or varied, or votes are declared invalid, the court may order another vote to be held, or make such order as it thinks just.

The court's power to make an order under this paragraph is exercisable only if it considers that the circumstances giving rise to the appeal are such as give rise to unfair prejudice or material irregularity.

5.42(4) [**Time-limit for appeal**] An application to the court by way of appeal against the official receiver's decision shall not be made after the end of the period of 28 days beginning with the day on which the report required by section 263C is made to the court.

5.42(5) [**Liability for costs of appeal**] The official receiver is not personally liable for any costs incurred by any person in respect of an appeal under this Rule.

(See General Note after r. 5.35.)

5.43 Requisite majorities

5.43(1) [**Majority in excess of three-quarters in value**] A proposal is approved by the creditors if a majority in excess of three-quarters in value of the creditors who vote approve the proposal.

5.43(2) [**Votes to be left out of account**] In the following cases there is to be left out of account a creditor's vote in respect of any claim or part of a claim–

(a) where the claim or part is secured;

(b) where the claim is in respect of a debt wholly or partly on, or secured by, a current bill of exchange or promissory note, unless the creditor is willing–

    (i) to treat the liability to him on the bill or note of every person who is liable on it antecedently to the debtor, and against whom a bankruptcy order has not been made (or in the case of a company, which has not gone into liquidation), as a security in his hands and

    (ii) to estimate the value of the security and (for the purpose of entitlement to vote, but not of any distribution under the arrangement) to deduct it from his claim.

5.43(3) **[Proposal not approved]** A proposal is not approved if those voting against it include more than half in value of the creditors, counting in the latter only those –

(a) who gave notice to the official receiver in accordance with Rule 5.40;

(b) whose votes are not to be left out of account under paragraph (2); and

(c) who are not, to the best of the official receiver's belief, associates of the debtor.

5.43(4) **[Whether person associate of debtor]** It is for the official receiver to decide whether, under this Rule a person is an associate of the debtor for the purposes of paragraph (3)(c) and in relation to this he is entitled to rely on the information provided by the debtor's statement of affairs or otherwise in accordance with this Part of the Rules.

(See General Note after r. 5.35.)

5.44 Notification to the court

5.44 The official receiver shall, in his report to court for the purposes of section 263C, include a statement whether, in his opinion

(a) the EC Regulation applies to the voluntary arrangement; and

(b) if so, whether the proceedings are main proceedings or territorial proceedings.

5.45 Notice of appointment as supervisor etc

5.45(1) **[Duty of official receiver]** Where the official receiver is appointed to act as supervisor of a voluntary arrangement, he shall, as soon as reasonably practicable, give written notice of his appointment to the Secretary of State, and all creditors of whom he is aware, and the trustee (if any) who is not the official receiver.

5.45(2) **[Duty on vacation of office]** If the official receiver vacates office as supervisor he shall give written notice of that fact to the Secretary of State.

(See General Note after r. 5.35.)

5.46 Revocation of the fast-track voluntary arrangement

5.46(1) **[Application of r. 5.46]** This Rule applies where the court makes an order of revocation under section 263F.

5.46(2) **[Who to serve sealed copy of order]** Where the person who applied for the order is–

(a) the debtor, he shall serve a sealed copy of the order on the supervisor and any trustee of his estate who is not the official receiver;

(b) the supervisor, he shall serve a sealed copy of the order on the debtor, and any trustee who is not the official receiver;

(c) a trustee who is not the official receiver, he shall serve a sealed copy of the order on the debtor and the supervisor; and

(d) a creditor, he shall serve a sealed copy of the order on the debtor, the supervisor and any trustee who is not the official receiver.

5.46(3) **[Duty of supervisor to notify re order]** The supervisor shall, as soon as reasonably practicable after receiving a copy of the order, give notice of it, to all persons who were sent a copy of the debtor's proposal under Rule 5.39 and all other persons who are affected by the order.

5.46(4) **[Notice of order to Secretary of State]** The person on whose application the order was made shall, within 7 days after the making of the order, given written notice of it to the Secretary of State.

(See General Note after r. 5.35.)

5.47 Supervisor's accounts and reports

5.47(1) [**Duty to keep accounts and records**] The supervisor shall keep accounts and records of his acts and dealings in and in connection with the arrangement, including in particular records of all receipts and payments of money.

5.47(2) [**Duty to report progress**] The supervisor shall, not less than once in every 12 months beginning with the date of his appointment–

(a) prepare a report on the progress of the voluntary arrangement, including a summary of receipts and payments; and

(b) send copies of it to–

    (i) the debtor; and
    (ii) all of the debtor's creditors of whom he is aware

and if in any period of 12 months he has made no payments and had no receipts, he shall at the end of that period send a statement to that effect to those specified in sub-paragraphs (a) and (b) above.

5.47(3) [**Period for progress report**] A report provided under paragraph (2) shall relate to a period beginning with the date of the supervisor's appointment or (as the case may be) the day following the end of the last period for which a report was prepared under this Rule; and copies of the report shall be sent, as required by paragraph (2), within the 2 months following the end of the period to which the report relates.

(See General Note after r. 5.35.)

5.48 Fees, costs and expenses in respect of the performance of the functions of the official receiver

5.48 The fees, costs and expenses in respect of the performance by the official receiver of his functions in relation to the bankruptcy and those of the trustee who is not the official receiver (including those in connection with the employment of agents) shall be a first charge on any sums realised under the terms of the voluntary arrangement, and those of the official receiver in relation to the voluntary arrangement, shall be a second charge.

(See General Note after r. 5.35.)

5.49 Employment of agents by the supervisor

5.49 The supervisor may employ agents in connection with the realisation of any assets subject to the terms of the voluntary arrangement.

(See General Note after r. 5.35.)

5.50 Completion or termination of the fast-track voluntary arrangement

5.50(1) [**Duty of supervisor**] Not more than 28 days after the final completion or termination of the voluntary arrangement, the supervisor shall send to all creditors of the debtor who are bound by the arrangement, and to the debtor, a notice that the voluntary arrangement has been fully implemented, (or as the case may be) terminated.

5.50(2) [**Copy of supervisor's report**] With the notice there shall be sent to each of those persons a copy of a report by the supervisor summarising all receipts and payments made by him in pursuance of the voluntary arrangement, and explaining any difference in the actual implementation of it compared with the proposal as approved by the creditors.

5.50(3) [**Copies to Secretary of State**] The supervisor shall, within the 28 days mentioned above, send to the Secretary of State a copy of the notice under paragraph (1), together with a copy of the report under paragraph (2), and he shall not vacate office until after such copies have been sent.

5.50(4) **[Extension of time limits]** The court may, on application by the supervisor, extend the period of 28 days under paragraphs (1) and (3).

(See General Note after r. 5.35.)

CHAPTER 8

APPLICATION BY A BANKRUPT TO ANNUL A BANKRUPTCY ORDER UNDER SECTION 261(2)(A)

5.51 Application of this Chapter

5.51 The following Rules apply where a bankrupt applies for an annulment of a bankruptcy order under section 261(2)(a).

R. 5.51

This new Chapter 8 was inserted by the Insolvency (Amendment) Rules 2003 (SI 2003/1730). It deals with applications to annul a bankruptcy order pursuant to s. 261(2)(a) in order to allow an IVA to be promoted.

5.52 Application to court

5.52(1) **[Application to specify section made under]** An application to the court to annul a bankruptcy order under section 261(2)(a) shall specify the section under which it is made.

5.52(2) **[Affidavit in support]** The application shall be supported by an affidavit stating–

(a) that the voluntary arrangement has been approved at a meeting of creditors;

(b) the date of the approval by the creditors; and

(c) that the 28-day period in section 262(3)(a) for applications to be made under section 262(1) has expired and no applications or appeal remain to be disposed of.

5.52(3) **[Duty of court to fix venue]** The application and supporting affidavit shall be filed in court; and the court shall give to the bankrupt notice of the venue fixed for the hearing.

5.52(4) **[Duty of bankrupt to notify official receiver etc.]** The bankrupt shall give notice of the venue, accompanied by copies of the application and affidavit to the official receiver, any trustee who is not the official receiver, and the supervisor of the voluntary arrangement not less than 7 days before the date of the hearing.

5.52(5) **[Power of official receiver etc to attend hearing]** The official receiver, the supervisor of the voluntary arrangement and any trustee who is not the official receiver may attend the hearing or be represented and call to the attention of the court any matters which seem to him to be relevant.

5.52(6) **[Court to send copies of annulment order]** Where the court annuls a bankruptcy order, it shall send sealed copies of the order of annulment in Form 5.7 to the bankrupt, the official receiver, the supervisor of the voluntary arrangement and any trustee who is not the official receiver.

[FORM 5.7]

R. 5.52

This describes the manner of application and the procedure relating to the hearing of such application.

5.53 Notice to creditors

5.53(1) **[Duty of official receiver]** Where the official receiver has notified creditors of the debtor's bankruptcy, and the bankruptcy order is annulled, he shall, as soon as reasonably practicable, notify them of the annulment.

5.53(2) **[Notification expenses charge on former bankrupt's property]** Expenses incurred by the official receiver in giving notice under this Rule are a charge in his favour on the property of the former bankrupt, whether or not actually in his hands.

5.53(3) **[Where property not in former bankrupt's hands]** Where any property is in the hands of a trustee or any person other than the former bankrupt himself, the official receiver's charge is valid subject only to any costs that may be incurred by the trustee or that other person in effecting realisation of the property for the purpose of satisfying the charge.

R. 5.53
This deals with various consequential matters, including notification of the change of situation and expenses thereby incurred.

CHAPTER 9

APPLICATION BY OFFICIAL RECEIVER TO ANNUL A BANKRUPTCY ORDER UNDER SECTION 261(2)(B)

5.54 Application of this Chapter

5.54 The following Rules apply where the official receiver applies for an annulment of a bankruptcy order under section 261(2)(b).

R. 5.54
Chapter 9 was inserted by the Insolvency (Amendment) Rules 2003 (SI 2003/1730). It deals with applications to annul bankruptcy orders in cases covered by s. 261(2)(b).

5.55 Application to court

5.55(1) **[Application to specify section made under]** An application to the court to annul a bankruptcy order under section 261(2)(b) shall specify a section under which it is made.

5.55(2) **[Time limit]** An application under section 261(2)(b) shall not be made before the expiry of 14 days from the date that the time period in section 262(3)(a) for applications under section 262(1) has expired.

5.55(3) **[Affidavit in support]** The application shall be supported by a report stating the grounds on which it is made. It shall also state that–

(a) the time period for application in paragraph (2) above has expired; and

(b) the official receiver is not aware that any application or appeal remains to be disposed of.

5.55(4) **[Duty of court to fix venue]** The application and the report shall be filed in court and the court shall give to the official receiver notice of the venue fixed for the hearing.

5.55(5) **[Duty of official receiver to notify bankrupt]** The official receiver shall give notice of the venue, accompanied by copies of the application and the report to the bankrupt not less than 7 days before the date of the hearing.

5.55(6) **[Court to send copies of annulment order]** Where the court annuls a bankruptcy order, it shall send sealed copies of the order of annulment in Form 5.7 to the official receiver, any trustee who is not the official receiver, the supervisor of the voluntary arrangement and the bankrupt.

[FORM 5.7]

R. 5.55
This details the application procedure.

5.56 Notice to creditors

5.56(1) [**Duty of official receiver**] Where the bankruptcy order is annulled, the official receiver shall notify all creditors of whom he is aware of the annulment.

5.56(2) [**Notification expenses charge on former bankrupt's property**] Expenses incurred by the official receiver in giving notice under this Rule are a charge in his favour on the property of the former bankrupt, whether or not actually in his hands.

5.56(3) [**Where property not in former bankrupt's hands**] Where any property is in the hands of a trustee or any person other than the former bankrupt himself, the official receiver's charge is valid only to any costs that may be incurred by the trustee or that other person in effecting realisation of the property for the purpose of satisfying the charge.

R. 5.56
This rule explains the consequences of an annulment order made pursuant to the aforementioned procedure.

CHAPTER 10

APPLICATION BY OFFICIAL RECEIVER TO ANNUL A BANKRUPTCY ORDER UNDER SECTION 263D(3)

5.57 Application of this Chapter

5.57 The following Rules apply where the official receiver applies for an annulment of a bankruptcy order under section 263D(3).

R. 5.57
Chapter 10 was inserted by Insolvency (Amendment) Rules 2003 (SI 2003/1730). It deals with applications by the OR to annul bankruptcy orders under s. 263D(3) of the Act.

5.58 Application to court

5.58(1) [**Application to specify section made under**] An application to the court to annul a bankruptcy order under section 263D(3) shall specify the section under which it is made.

5.58(2) [**Time limit**] An application under section 263(d)(3) shall be made within 21 days of the expiry of the relevant period set out in section 263D(4).

5.58(3) [**Report in support**] The application shall be supported by a report stating the grounds on which it is made and a statement by the official receiver that he is not aware that any application or appeal under section 263F remains to be disposed of.

5.58(4) [**To accompany report**] The report shall be accompanied by a copy of the proposal for the voluntary arrangement and a copy of the report under section 263C.

5.58(5) [**Duty of court to fix venue**] The application, together with the report and the documents in support, shall be filed in court and the court shall give to the official receiver notice of the venue fixed for the hearing.

5.58(6) [**Duty of official receiver to notify bankrupt**] The official receiver shall give notice of the venue, accompanied by copies of the application and the report, to the bankrupt not less than 7 days before the date of the hearing.

5.58(7) [**Court to send copies of annulment order**] Where the court annuals a bankruptcy order, it shall send sealed copies of the order of annulment in Form 5.8 to the official receiver and the bankrupt.

[FORM 5.8]

R. 5.58
This details the application procedure. Note the 21-day deadline.

5.59 Notice to creditors

5.59(1) [**Duty of official receiver**] Where the official receiver has notified creditors of the debtor's bankruptcy, and the bankruptcy order is annulled, he shall, as soon as reasonably practicable, notify them of the annulment.

5.59(2) [**Notification expenses charge on former bankrupt's property**] Expenses incurred by the official receiver in giving notice under this Rule are a charge in his favour on the property of the former bankrupt, whether or not actually in his hands.

5.59(3) [**Where property not in former bankrupt's hands**] Where any property is in the hands of a trustee or any person other than the former bankrupt himself, the official receiver's charge is valid subject only to any costs that may be incurred by the trustee or that other person in effecting realisation of the property for the purpose of satisfying the charge.

R. 5.59
The consequences of a successful application are explained.

CHAPTER 11

OTHER MATTERS ARISING ON ANNULMENTS UNDER SECTIONS 261(2)(A), 261(2)(B) OR 263D(3)

5.60(1) [**Provision in order**] In an order under section 261(2)(a), 261(2)(b) or 263D(3) the court shall include provision permitting vacation of the registration of the bankruptcy petition as a pending action, and of the bankruptcy order, in the register of writs and orders affecting land.

5.60(2) [**Notice of order to Secretary of State**] The court shall as soon as reasonably practicable give notice of the making of the order to the Secretary of State.

5.60(3) [**Power of former bankrupt to require advertisement of order**] The former bankrupt may, in writing within 28 days of the date of the order, require the Secretary of State to give notice of the making of the order–

(a) in the Gazette;

(b) in any newspaper in which the bankruptcy order was advertised; or

(c) in both.

5.60(4) [**Omitted.**]

5.60(5) [**Former bankrupt deceased or unable to manage affairs**] Where the former bankrupt has died, or is a person incapable of managing his affairs (within the meaning of Chapter 7 in Part 7 of the Rules), the references to him in paragraphs (3) and (4) are to be read as referring to his personal representative or, as the case may be, a person appointed by the court to represent or act for him.

R. 5.60
This new Chapter 11 was inserted by the Insolvency (Amendment) Rules 2003 (SI 2003/1730). It deals with general matters relevant to applications made under Chapters 8–10. Rule 5.60 tidies up various loose ends attendant upon a successful application, including the clearing of registered entries and wide dissemination of the annulment. A 28-day time limit was inserted into para. (3) by I(A)R 2004 (SI 2004/584), which also deleted para. 4 on the cost of advertisement.

5.61 Trustee's final account

5.61(1) [**Trustee liable to account**] Where a bankruptcy order is annulled under section 261(2)(a), 261(2)(b) or 263D(3), this does not of itself release the trustee from any duty or obligation, imposed on him by or under the Act or the Rules, to account for all his transactions in connection with the former bankrupt's estate.

5.61(2) [**Duty of trustee to submit final account**] The trustee shall submit a copy of his final account to the Secretary of State as soon as reasonably practicable after the court's order annulling the bankruptcy order; and he shall file a copy of the final account in court.

5.61(3) [**Contents of final account**] The final account must include a summary of the trustee's receipts and payments in the administration, and contain a statement to the effect that he has reconciled his account with that held by the Secretary of State in respect of the bankruptcy.

5.61(4) [**Release of trustee**] The trustee is released from such time as the court may determine, having regard to whether paragraph (2) of this Rule has been complied with.

R. 5.61
The obligation of the trustee to produce a final account is not removed by the fact of annulment.

CHAPTER 12

EC REGULATION: CONVERSION OF VOLUNTARY ARRANGEMENT INTO BANKRUPTCY

5.62 Application for conversion of voluntary arrangement into bankruptcy

5.62(1) [**Application to be supported by affidavit**] Where a member State liquidator proposes to apply to the court for conversion under Article 37 of the EC Regulation (conversion of earlier proceedings) of a voluntary arrangement into a bankruptcy, an affidavit complying with Rule 5.63 must be prepared and sworn, and filed in court in support of the application.

5.62(2) [**Service**] The application and the affidavit required under this Rule shall be served upon—

(a) the debtor; and

(b) the supervisor.

R. 5.62
Chapter 12 was inserted by Insolvency (Amendment) Rules 2003 (SI 2003/1730). It deals with the impact of the EC Regulation on Insolvency Proceedings (1346/2000) and covers ground previously dealt with by IR 1986, rr. 5.35–5.38 in the former regime. Rule 5.62 deals with conversion of an IVA into a bankruptcy for the purposes of that Regulation.

5.63 Contents of affidavit

5.63(1) [**Contents**] The affidavit shall state—

(a) that the main proceedings have been opened in relation to the debtor in a member State other than the United Kingdom;

(b) the deponent's belief that the conversion of the voluntary arrangement into a bankruptcy would prove to be in the interests of the creditors in the main proceedings; and

(c) all other matters that, in the opinion of the member State liquidator, would assist the court—

   (i) in deciding whether to make an order under Rule 5.64; and
   (ii) if the court were to do so, in considering the need for any consequential provision that would be necessary or desirable.

5.63(2) [**Swearing of affidavit**] An affidavit under this Rule shall be sworn by, or on behalf of, the member State liquidator.

R. 5.63
This explains the contents of the affidavit which the member state liquidator must file.

5.64 Power of court

5.64(1) **[Order as thinks fit]** On hearing an application for conversion of a voluntary arrangement into a bankruptcy, the court may make such order as it thinks fit.

5.64(2) **[Consequential provisions]** If the court makes an order for conversion of a voluntary arrangement into a bankruptcy under paragraph (1), the order may contain all such consequential provisions as the court deems necessary or desirable.

5.64(3) **[Expenses incurred]** Where the court makes an order for conversion of a voluntary arrangement into a bankruptcy under paragraph (1), any expenses properly incurred as expenses of the administration of the voluntary arrangement in question shall be a first charge on the bankrupt's estate.

R. 5.64
The options open to the court are thus outlined.

5.65 Notices to be given to member State liquidator

5.65(1) **[Application of r. 5.65]** This Rule applies where a member State liquidator has been appointed in relation to the debtor.

5.65(2) **[Notice, copies]** Where the supervisor is obliged to give notice to, or provide a copy of a document (including an order of the court) to, the court or the official receiver, the supervisor shall give notice or provide copies, as appropriate, to the member State liquidator.

R. 5.65
This explains consequential matters resulting from a conversion.

PART 6

BANKRUPTCY

CHAPTER 1

THE STATUTORY DEMAND

6.1 Form and content of statutory demand

6.1(1) **[Must be dated and signed]** A statutory demand under section 268 must be dated, and be signed either by the creditor himself or by a person stating himself to be authorised to make the demand on the creditor's behalf.

[FORM 6.1]
or [FORM 6.2]
or [FORM 6.3]

6.1(2) [Whether s. 268(1) or (2)] The statutory demand must specify whether it is made under section 268(1) (debt payable immediately) or section 268(2) (debt not so payable).

6.1(3) [Further contents] The demand must state the amount of the debt, and the consideration for it (or, if there is no consideration, the way in which it arises) and–

(a) if made under section 268(1) and founded on a judgment or order of a court, it must give details of the judgment or order, and

(b) if made under section 268(2), it must state the grounds on which it is alleged that the debtor appears to have no reasonable prospect of paying the debt.

6.1(4) [Interest and accruing charges] If the amount claimed in the demand includes–

(a) any charge by way of interest not previously notified to the debtor as a liability of his, or

(b) any other charge accruing from time to time,

the amount or rate of the charge must be separately identified, and the grounds on which payment of it is claimed must be stated.

In either case the amount claimed must be limited to that which has accrued due at the date of the demand.

6.1(5) [If creditor holds security] If the creditor holds any security in respect of the debt, the full amount of the debt shall be specified, but–

(a) there shall in the demand be specified the nature of the security, and the value which the creditor puts upon it as at the date of the demand, and

(b) the amount of which payment is claimed by the demand shall be the full amount of the debt, less the amount specified as the value of the security.

GENERAL NOTE

See also *Practice Note (Bankruptcy: Prescribed Forms) (No. 2/88)* [1988] 1 W.L.R. 557. On who is an authorized signatory for the purposes of r. 6.1(1) see *Horne v Dacorum BC* [2000] B.P.I.R. 1047.

For judicial consideration of this provision see *Re a Debtor (No. 310 of 1988)* [1989] 1 W.L.R. 452. Here Knox J. held that the phrase "any security in respect of the debt" when used in r. 6.1(5) must have the same meaning as when used in IA 1986, ss. 383 and 385(1). Therefore the security that had to be referred to in the statutory demand was security over any property of the alleged debtor and not security provided by a third party. Failure to specify the security held as required under r. 6.1(5) may not always be fatal for the creditor, as the court now tends to consider whether the debtor has suffered any real injustice: see *Re a Debtor (No. 106 of 1992), The Independent* April 20, 1992 and the comments on s. 268. For the position where the incorrect form is used see *Cartwright v Staffordshire and Moorlands DC* [1998] B.P.I.R. 328.

(*See General Note after r. 6.2.*)

6.2 Information to be given in statutory demand

6.2(1) **[Explanation of demand generally]** The statutory demand must include an explanation to the debtor of the following matters–

(a) the purpose of the demand, and the fact that, if the debtor does not comply with the demand, bankruptcy proceedings may be commenced against him;

(b) the time within which the demand must be complied with, if that consequence is to be avoided;

(c) the methods of compliance which are open to the debtor; and

(d) his right to apply to the court for the statutory demand to be set aside.

6.2(2) **[Information re named individuals]** The demand must specify one or more named individuals with whom the debtor may, if he wishes, enter into communication with a view to securing or compounding for the debt to the satisfaction of the creditor or (as the case may be) establishing to the creditor's satisfaction that there is a reasonable prospect that the debt will be paid when it falls due.

In the case of any individual so named in the demand, his address and telephone number (if any) must be given.

GENERAL NOTE TO RR. 6.1, 6.2

These rules describe the statutory demand mentioned in IA 1986, s. 268(1)(a), (2)(a). The form and contents are detailed. Where the demand is made under s. 372(4)(a) of the FSMA 2000, r. 6.2 is disapplied (and substitute rules provided) by the Bankruptcy (Financial Services and Markets Act 2000) Rules 2001 (SI 2001/3634), rr. 1, 3 and 5 as from December 1, 2001.

6.3 Requirements as to service

6.3(1) **[Effect of r. 6.11]** Rule 6.11 in Chapter 2 below has effect as regards service of the statutory demand, and proof of that service by affidavit to be filed with a bankruptcy petition.

6.3(2) **[Creditor's obligation to effect personal service etc.]** The creditor is, by virtue of the Rules, under an obligation to do all that is reasonable for the purpose of bringing the statutory demand to the debtor's attention and, if practicable in the particular circumstances, to cause personal service of the demand to be effected.

6.3(3) **[Advertisement of demand for sum due under judgment etc.]** Where the statutory demand is for payment of a sum due under a judgment or order of any court and the creditor knows, or believes with reasonable cause–

(a) that the debtor has absconded or is keeping out of the way with a view to avoiding service, and

(b) there is no real prospect of the sum due being recovered by execution or other process,

the demand may be advertised in one or more newspapers; and the time limited for compliance with the demand runs from the date of the advertisement's appearance or (as the case may be) its first appearance.

GENERAL NOTE

The rules as to service of the statutory demand are hereby prescribed. Personal service is normally required, subject to r. 6.3(3). See also *Practice Note (Bankruptcy: Substituted Service)* [1987] 1 W.L.R. 82. For service out of the jurisdiction see *Practice Note (Bankruptcy: Service Abroad) (No. 1/88)* [1988] 1 W.L.R. 461.

In *Re a Debtor (No. 234 and 236 of 1991), The Independent* June 29, 1992 it was confirmed by Blackett-Ord Q.C. (sitting as a judge of the High Court) that in some cases it may be appropriate to serve the statutory demand upon the solicitors of the debtor. In *Regional Collection Services Ltd v Heald* [2000] B.P.I.R. 641 it was held that a creditor had failed to take all reasonable steps to bring the demand to the debtor's attention because it had failed to visit the debtor's business premises.

Rule 6.3 is modified so as to apply in relation to a demand made under s. 372(4)(a) FSMA 2000 as if (a) references to the debtors were references to an individual; (b) references (other than in rule 6.5(2) and (4)(c) to the creditor were references to the Authority; and (c) references to the creditor in rule 6.5(2) and (4)(c) were references to the person to whom the debt is owed by virtue of the Bankruptcy (Financial Services and Markets Act 2000) Rules 2001 (SI 2001/3634), rr. 1, 3 and 6(1) as from December 1, 2001.

6.4 Application to set aside statutory demand

6.4(1) [Time for application] The debtor may, within the period allowed by this Rule, apply to the appropriate court for an order setting the statutory demand aside.

[FORM 6.4]

That period is 18 days from the date of the service on him of the statutory demand or, where the demand is advertised in a newspaper pursuant to Rule 6.3, from the date of the advertisement's appearance or (as the case may be) its first appearance.

6.4(2) [Appropriate court where creditor is Minister etc.] Where the creditor issuing the statutory demand is a Minister of the Crown or a Government Department, and–

(a) the debt in respect of which the demand is made, or a part of it equal to or exceeding the bankruptcy level (within the meaning of section 267), is the subject of a judgment or order of any court, and

(b) the statutory demand specifies the date of the judgment or order and the court in which it was obtained, but indicates the creditor's intention to present a bankruptcy petition against the debtor in the High Court,

the appropriate court under this Rule is the High Court; and in any other case it is that to which the debtor would, in accordance with paragraphs (1) and (2) of Rule 6.40 in Chapter 3 below, present his own bankruptcy petition.

6.4(3) [Effect of filing application in court] As from (inclusive) the date on which the application is filed in court, the time limited for compliance with the statutory demand ceases to run, subject to any order of the court under Rule 6.5(6).

6.4(4) [Supporting affidavit] The debtor's application shall be supported by an affidavit–

(a) specifying the date on which the statutory demand came into his hands, and

(b) stating the grounds on which he claims that is should be set aside.

The affidavit shall have exhibited to it a copy of the statutory demand.

[FORM 6.5]

GENERAL NOTE

The debtor can, by using Forms 6.4 and 6.5, apply to the court to have the statutory demand set aside. He has 18 days after service to make such an application. If an application is made, the three weeks' deadline for compliance with the demand ceases to run.

See also *Practice Note (Bankruptcy: Statutory Demand: Setting Aside)* [1987] 1 W.L.R. 119 and *Morley IRC* [1996] B.P.I.R. 452. On the need for proper formal requirements to be satisfied see *Ariyo v Sovereign Leasing* [1998] B.P.I.R. 177.

Rule 6.4 is modified so as to apply in relation to a demand made under s. 372(4)(a) FSMA 2000 as if (a) references to the debtor were references to an individual; (b) the words in para. (2), "the creditor issuing the statutory demand is a Minister of the Crown or a Government Department, and" were omitted; and (c) the reference to the creditor in para. (2)(b) was a reference to the Authority, by virtue of the Bankruptcy (Financial Services and Markets Act 2000) Rules 2001 (SI 2001/3634), rr. 1, 3 and 7 as from December 1, 2001.

6.5 Hearing of application to set aside

6.5(1) [Court may dismiss application etc.] On receipt of an application under Rule 6.4, the court may, if satisfied that no sufficient cause is shown for it, dismiss it without giving notice to the creditor. As from (inclusive) the date on which the application is dismissed, the time limited for compliance with the statutory demand runs again.

6.5(2) **[Application not dismissed under r. 6.5(1)]** If the application is not dismissed under paragraph (1), the court shall fix a venue for it to be heard, and shall give at least 7 days' notice of it to–

(a) the debtor or, if the debtor's application was made by a solicitor acting for him, to the solicitor,

(b) the creditor, and

(c) whoever is named in the statutory demand as the person with whom the debtor may enter into communication with reference to the demand (or, if more than one person is so named, the first of them).

6.5(3) **[Summary determination or adjournment]** On the hearing of the application, the court shall consider the evidence then available to it, and may either summarily determine the application or adjourn it, giving such directions as it thinks appropriate.

6.5(4) **[Setting aside demand]** The court may grant the application if–

(a) the debtor appears to have a counterclaim, set-off or cross demand which equals or exceeds the amount of the debt or debts specified in the statutory demand; or

(b) the debt is disputed on grounds which appear to the court to be substantial; or

(c) it appears that the creditor holds some security in respect of the debt claimed by the demand, and either Rule 6.1(5) is not complied with in respect of it, or the court is satisfied that the value of the security equals or exceeds the full amount of the debt; or

(d) the court is satisfied, on other grounds, that the demand ought to be set aside.

[FORM 6.6]

6.5(5) **[Under-valued security]** Where the creditor holds some security in respect of his debt, and Rule 6.1(5) is complied with in respect of it but the court is satisfied that the security is under-valued in the statutory demand, the creditor may be required to amend the demand accordingly (but without prejudice to his right to present a bankruptcy petition by reference to the original demand).

6.5(6) **[On dismissal of application]** If the court dismisses the application, it shall make an order authorising the creditor to present a bankruptcy petition either forthwith, or on or after a date specified in the order.

A copy of the order shall be sent by the court forthwith to the creditor.

GENERAL NOTE

This rule outlines the hearing procedure for an application made under r. 6.4. If the application succeeds, the court's order should be in the style of Form 6.6. If the application fails the court can permit the immediate presentation of the bankruptcy petition. The leading case on r. 6.5(4) is *Re a Debtor (No. 1 of 1987)* [1989] 1 W.L.R. 271 where the Court of Appeal held that a document purporting to be a statutory demand was to be treated as such until set aside. In cases of setting aside under r. 6.5(4)(d) the debtor must not merely convince the court that the demand was perplexing but also prove what the true position was between himself and the creditor. See the general note after s. 268. For a useful comparison between the rules relating to set aside of statutory demands in corporate and personal insolvency law see *Re A Debtor (544/SD/98)* [2001] 1 B.C.L.C. 103 (also reported as *Garrow v The Society of Lloyds* [1999] B.P.I.R. 885).

A set-aside application is not a trial on the merits and fresh evidence can be adduced: *Royal Bank of Scotland v Binnell* [1996] B.P.I.R. 352; *Norman Laurier v United Overseas Bank* [1996] B.P.I.R. 635, *Salvidge v Hussein* [1999] B.P.I.R. 410. These cases confirm that the rule in *Ladd v Marshall* [1954] 1 W.L.R. 1489 does not apply. For further discussion in the context of appeals from decisions on set-aside applications see *AIB Finance Ltd v Alsop* [1998] B.C.C. 780. Such appeals are true appeals and subsequent events should not be taken into account – *Cozens v Customs and Excise* [2000] B.P.I.R. 252.

The jurisdiction to set aside statutory demands is permissive; the court is under no obligation to act, as was stressed in *Re a Debtor (No. 106 of 1992), The Independent* April 20, 1992. See also *Khan v Breezevale SARL* [1996] B.P.I.R. 190 (failure to refer to security).

The court cannot make a conditional order on a set-aside application. Either the demand must be set aside or the application rejected: *Re a Debtor (No. 90 of 1992)* [1993] T.L.R. 387 and *Re Debtor No. 32 of 1991 (No. 2)* [1994] B.C.C. 524. Equally the courts will not allow a petition to be presented and then adjourned simply in order to trigger time periods for transactional avoidance. Thus if the debtor has an arguable cross claim the proper course of action is to set aside the demand and not to allow this issue to be reserved for trial of the petition – *Garrow v The Society of Lloyds* [1999] B.P.I.R. 885. If a set-aside application fails the same issues cannot normally be relitigated on the hearing of the petition – *Turner v Royal Bank of Scotland* [2000] B.P.I.R. 683, *Atherton v Ogunlende* [2003] B.P.I.R. 21.

On r. 6.5(4)(a) see *Hofer v Strawson* [1999] B.P.I.R. 501 and *Re A Debtor (87 of 1999)* [2000] B.P.I.R. 589, which offer guidance on cross claims. Any counterclaim must be legally enforceable – *Re A Debtor (35 of 2000)* [2002] B.P.I.R. 75. Where there is a counterclaim within r. 6.5(4)(a) there appears to be a mutuality requirement – *Hurst v Bennett* [2001] EWCA Civ 182; [2001] B.P.I.R. 287, *Southward v Banham* [2002] B.P.I.R. 1253.

In *Re a Debtor (No. 960/SD/1992)* [1993] S.T.C. 218 Mummery J. refused to set aside a statutory demand under r. 6.5(4)(c) in a case where a tax assessment was being challenged by the taxpayer; the case did not appear to be covered by this provision.

A set-aside application also proved unsuccessful in *Re a Debtor (No. 415/SD/1993)* [1994] 1 W.L.R. 917. Here the debtor was seeking to set aside the demand by arguing that he had made a reasonable offer of security to the creditor. In discussing the meaning of "other grounds" in r. 6.5(4)(d) Jacob J. made it clear that set-aside applications were designed to deal with procedural flaws in the demand and were not meant to raise substantive issues of reasonableness – these issues could be considered when the petition was heard. Equally in *Platts v Western Trust and Savings Ltd* [1996] B.P.I.R. 339 the court indicated that it would not investigate such questions as whether the creditor was secured or not as these were issues best dealt with when the petition was heard. However see the comments of the Court of Appeal on r. 6.5(4)(d) in *Budge v Budge (Contractors) Ltd* [1997] B.P.I.R. 366. In *Re a Debtor (No. 90 of 1997), The Times* July 1, 1998, the High Court considered the position with regard to setting aside under r. 6.5(4)(d) when there were parallel bankruptcy and civil proceedings afoot. The importance of the general discretion vested in the court by r. 6.5(4)(d) was clearly illustrated in *City Electrical Factors v Hardingham* [1996] B.P.I.R. 541 where a statutory demand based upon a debt slightly in excess of £750 was set aside.

If the creditor bases his petition upon a judgment debt the court will not on a set-aside application look behind the earlier judgment: see Ferris J. in *Re a Debtor (657/SD/1991)* [1993] B.C.L.C. 1280 applying *Practice Direction* [1987] 1 W.L.R. 119. Note also *Neely v IRC* [1996] B.P.I.R. 473.

For the position where the debt is disputed within the context of r. 6.5(4)(b), see *Re a Debtor (No. 11 of 1987), The Independent* March 28, 1988; *Re a Debtor (No. 10 of 1988)* [1989] 1 W.L.R. 405 and *Cale v Assiudoman KPS (Harrow) Ltd* [1996] B.P.I.R. 245. On the standard of proof see *Kellar v BBR Graphic Engineers Ltd* [2002] B.P.I.R. 544. Another interesting case involving a disputed debt was *Re a Debtor (No. 49 and 50 of 1992)* [1995] Ch. 66. Here part of the debt upon which the statutory demand was based was disputed by the debtor. The undisputed element was for an amount less than the statutory minimum upon which a creditor could petition for bankruptcy. In those circumstances the Court of Appeal held that although the demand could not be set aside in its entirety under r. 6.5(4)(b) the court could set aside the whole demand using its residual discretion under r. 6.5(4)(d). For the dangers as to costs of a creditor using a statutory demand in cases where a trial of the action is pending see *Re a Debtor (No. 620 of 1997), The Times* June 18, 1998.

There is authority that the remedial r. 7.55 cannot apply in the context of defects in the statutory demand: *Re a Debtor (No. 190 of 1987), The Times* May 21, 1988.

Rule 6.5 is modified so as to apply in relation to a demand made under s. 372(4)(a) FSMA 2000 as if (a) references to the debtor were references to an individual; (b) references (other than in rule 6.5(2) and (4)(c)) to the creditor were references to the Authority; and (c) references to the creditor in rule 6.5(2) and (4)(c) were references to the person to whom the debt is owed by virtue of the Bankruptcy (Financial Services and Markets Act 2000) Rules 2001 (SI 2001/3634), rr. 1, 3 and 6(1) as from December 1, 2001.

CHAPTER 2

BANKRUPTCY PETITION (CREDITOR'S)

6.6 Preliminary

6.6 The Rules in this Chapter relate to a creditor's petition, and the making of a bankruptcy order thereon; and in those Rules **"the debt"** means, except where the context otherwise requires, the debt (or debts) in respect of which the petition is presented.

Those Rules also apply to a petition under section 264(1)(c) (supervisor of, or person bound by, voluntary arrangement), with any necessary modifications.

[FORM 6.7]
or [FORM 6.8]
or [FORM 6.9]
or [FORM 6.10]

GENERAL NOTE

See the guidance in *Practice Note (Bankruptcy: Petition)* [1987] 1 W.L.R. 81 and the *Practice Direction 3/86* noted in (1987) 3 *Insolvency Law & Practice* 101.

6.7 Identification of debtor

6.7(1) **[Contents of petition]** The petition shall state the following matters with respect to the debtor, so far as they are within the petitioner's knowledge–

(a) his name, place of residence and occupation (if any);

(b) the name or names in which he carries on business, if other than his true name, and whether, in the case of any business of a specified nature, he carries it on alone or with others;

(c) the nature of his business, and the address or addresses at which he carries it on;

(d) any name or names, other than his true name, in which he has carried on business at or after the time when the debt was incurred, and whether he has done so alone or with others;

(e) any address or addresses at which he has resided or carried on business at or after that time, and the nature of that business;

(f) whether the debtor has his centre of main interests or an establishment in another member State.

6.7(2) **[Title of proceedings]** The particulars of the debtor given under this Rule determine the full title of the proceedings.

6.7(3) **[Debtor's other names]** If to the petitioner's personal knowledge the debtor has used any name other than the one specified under paragraph (1)(a), that fact shall be stated in the petition.

(See General Note after r. 6.8.)

6.8 Identification of debt

6.8(1) [Contents of petition] There shall be stated in the petition, with reference to every debt in respect of which it is presented–

(a) the amount of the debt, the consideration for it (or, if there is no consideration, the way in which it arises) and the fact that it is owed to the petitioner;

(b) when the debt was incurred or became due;

(c) if the amount of the debt includes–

  (i) any charge by way of interest not previously notified to the debtor as a liability of his, or
  (ii) any other charge accruing from time to time,

  the amount or rate of the charge (separately identified) and the grounds on which it is claimed to form part of the debt, provided that such amount or rate must, in the case of a petition based on a statutory demand, be limited to that claimed in that demand;

(d) either–

  (i) that the debt is for a liquidated sum payable immediately, and the debtor appears to be unable to pay it, or
  (ii) that the debt is for a liquidated sum payable at some certain, future time (that time to be specified), and the debtor appears to have no reasonable prospect of being able to pay it,

and, in either case (subject to section 269) that the debt is unsecured.

6.8(2) [Where statutory demand served] Where the debt is one for which, under section 268, a statutory demand must have been served on the debtor–

(a) there shall be specified the date and manner of service of the statutory demand, and

(b) it shall be stated that, to the best of the creditor's knowledge and belief–

  (i) the demand has been neither complied with nor set aside in accordance with the Rules, and
  (ii) no application to set it aside is outstanding.

6.8(3) [If case within s. 268(1)(b)] If the case is within section 268(1)(b) (debt arising under judgment or order of court; execution returned unsatisfied), the court from which the execution or other process issued shall be specified, and particulars shall be given relating to the return.

GENERAL NOTE TO RR. 6.7, 6.8

These rules outline the contents of a creditor's petition. IR 6.7(1)(f) was inserted by the Insolvency (Amendment) Rules 2002 (SI 2002/1307) para. 8(1) with effect from May 31, 2002. This was required by the advent of EC Council Regulation (1346/2000) on Insolvency Proceedings.

See also *Practice Note (Bankruptcy) (No. 2/87)* dated September 30, 1987; [1987] 1 W.L.R. 1424 which amended the *Practice Note* in [1987] 1 W.L.R. 81. For the remedial effect of r. 7.55 in cases where the requirements of r. 6.8 have not been met see *Re a Debtor (No. 510 of 1997), The Times* June 18, 1998.

6.9 Court in which petition to be presented

6.9(1) [Presentation to High Court] In the following cases, the petition shall be presented to the High Court–

(a) if the petition is presented by a Minister of the Crown or a Government Department, and either in any statutory demand on which the petition is based the creditor has indicated the intention to present a bankruptcy petition to that Court, or the petition is presented under section 268(1)(b), or

(b) if the debtor has resided or carried on business within the London insolvency district for the greater part of the 6 months immediately preceding the presentation of the petition, or for a longer period in those 6 months than in any other insolvency district, or

(c) if the debtor is not resident in England and Wales, or

(d) if the petitioner is unable to ascertain the residence of the debtor, or his place of business.

6.9(2) [County court] In any other case the petition shall be presented to the county court for the insolvency district in which the debtor has resided or carried on business for the longest period during those 6 months.

6.9(3) [Insolvency districts] If the debtor has for the greater part of those 6 months carried on business in one insolvency district and resided in another, the petition shall be presented to the court for the insolvency district in which he has carried on business.

6.9(4) [Principal place of business] If the debtor has during those 6 months carried on business in more than one insolvency district, the petition shall be presented to the court for the insolvency district in which is, or has been for the longest period in those 6 months, his principal place of business.

6.9(4A) [Voluntary arrangement in force] Notwithstanding any other provision of this Rule, where there is in force for the debtor a voluntary arrangement under Part VIII of the Act, the petition shall be presented to the court to which the nominee's report under section 256 or section 256A or 263C was submitted.

6.9(5) [Establishing appropriate court] The petition shall contain sufficient information to establish that it is brought in the appropriate court.

GENERAL NOTE

The court to which the creditor's petition must be presented is hereby identified. Where the demand is made under s. 372(4)(a) FSMA 2000, r. 6.9 is disapplied and there is substituted the following "(a) if in any demand on which the petition is based the Authority has indicated the intention to present a bankruptcy petition to that Court", by virtue of the Bankruptcy (Financial Services and Markets Act 2000) Rules 2001 (SI 2001/3634), rr. 1, 3 and 8 as from December 1, 2001. Rule 6.9(4A) was amended by I(A)R 2003 (SI 2003/1730) with effect from April 1, 2004.

6.10 Procedure for presentation and filing

6.10(1) [Filing with verifying affidavit] The petition, verified by affidavit in accordance with Rule 6.12 (1) below, shall be filed in court.

6.10(2) [When petition not to be filed] No petition shall be filed unless there is produced on presentation of the petition a receipt for the deposit payable or paragraph (2A) applies.

6.10(2A) [Written notice of alternative arrangements] This paragraph applies in any case where the Secretary of State has given written notice to the court that the petitioner has made suitable alternative arrangements for the payment of the deposit to the official receiver and such notice has not been revoked in relation to the petitioner in accordance with paragraph (2B).

6.10(2B) [Revocation of r.6.10(2A) notice] A notice of the kind referred to in paragraph (2A) may be revoked in relation to the petitioner in whose favour it is given by a further notice in writing to the court stating that the earlier notice is revoked in relation to the petitioner.

6.10(3) **[Copies of petition]** The following copies of the petition shall also be delivered to the court with the petition–

(a) one for service on the debtor,

(b) one to be exhibited to the affidavit verifying that service, and

(c) if there is in force for the debtor a voluntary arrangement under Part VIII of the Act, and the petitioner is not the supervisor of the arrangement, one copy for him.

Each of these copies shall have applied to it the seal of the court, and shall be issued to the petitioner.

6.10(4) **[Endorsing of r. 6.10(3) copies]** The date and time of filing the petition shall be endorsed on the petition and on any copy issued under paragraph (3).

6.10(5) **[Venue for hearing]** The court shall fix a venue for hearing the petition, and this also shall be endorsed on the petition and on any copy so issued.

6.10(6) **[Former supervisor requested as trustee]** Where a petition contains a request for the appointment of a person as trustee in accordance with section 297(5) (appointment of former supervisor as trustee) the person whose appointment is sought shall, not less than 2 days before the day appointed for hearing the petition, file in court a report including particulars of–

(a) a date on which he gave written notification to creditors bound by the arrangement of the intention to seek his appointment as trustee, such date to be at least 10 days before the day on which the report under this paragraph is filed, and

(b) details of any response from creditors to that notice, including any objections to his appointment.

(See General Note after r. 6.12.)

6.11 Proof of service of statutory demand

6.11(1) **[Affidavit of service]** Where under section 268 the petition must have been preceded by a statutory demand, there must be filed in court, with the petition, an affidavit or affidavits proving service of the demand.

6.11(2) **[Copy of demand to be exhibited]** Every affidavit must have exhibited to it a copy of the demand as served.

6.11(3) **[Affidavit of personal service]** Subject to the next paragraph, if the demand has been served personally on the debtor, the affidavit must be made by the person who effected that service.

[FORM 6.11]

6.11(4) **[If service of demand acknowledged]** If service of the demand (however effected) has been acknowleged in writing either by the debtor himself, or by some person stating himself in the acknowledgement to be authorised to accept service on the debtor's behalf, the affidavit must be made either by the creditor or by a person acting on his behalf, and the acknowledgement of service must be exhibited to the affidavit.

6.11(5) **[If neither r. 6.11(3) or (4) applies]** If neither paragraph (3) nor paragraph (4) applies, the affidavit or affidavits must be made by a person or persons having direct personal knowledge of the means adopted for serving the statutory demand, and must–

(a) give particulars of the steps which have been taken with a view to serving the demand personally, and

(b) state the means whereby (those steps having been ineffective) it was sought to bring the demand to the debtor's attention, and

(c) specify a date by which, to the best of the knowledge, information and belief of the person making the affidavit, the demand will have come to the debtor's attention.

[FORM 6.12]

6.11(6) **[Sufficiency of r. 6.11(5)(a) particulars]** The steps of which particulars are given for the purposes of paragraph (5)(a) must be such as would have sufficed to justify an order for substituted service of a petition.

6.11(7) **[Deemed date of service]** If the affidavit specifies a date for the purposes of compliance with paragraph (5)(c), then unless the court otherwise orders, that date is deemed for the purposes of the Rules to have been the date on which the statutory demand was served on the debtor.

6.11(8) **[Newspaper advertisement]** Where the creditor has taken advantage of Rule 6.3(3) (newspaper advertisement), the affidavit must be made either by the creditor himself or by a person having direct personal knowledge of the circumstances; and there must be specified in the affidavit–

(a) the means of the creditor's knowledge or (as the case may be) belief required for the purposes of that Rule, and

(b) the date or dates on which, and the newspaper in which, the statutory demand was advertised under that Rule;

and there shall be exhibited to the affidavit a copy of any advertisement of the statutory demand.

6.11(9) **[Discharge of r. 6.3(2) obligation]** The court may decline to file the petition if not satisfied that the creditor has discharged the obligation imposed on him by Rule 6.3(2).

GENERAL NOTE

See *Practice Note (Bankruptcy: Statutory Demand)* [1987] 1 W.L.R. 85. See also general note after r. 6.12. Rule 6.11 is modified so as to apply in relation to a demand made under s. 372(4)(a) FSMA 2000 as if (a) references to the debtor were references to an individual; (b) references (other than in rule 6.5(2) and (4)(c)) to the creditor were references to the Authority; and (c) references to the creditor in rule 6.5(2) and (4)(c) were references to the person to whom the debt is owed by virtue of the Bankruptcy (Financial Services and Markets Act 2000) Rules 2001 (SI 2001/3634), rr. 1, 3 and 6(1) as from December 1, 2001.

6.12 Verification of petition

6.12(1) **[Verifying affidavit]** The petition shall be verified by an affidavit that the statements in the petition are true, or are true to the best of the deponent's knowledge, information and belief.

[FORM 6.13]

6.12(2) **[Debts due to different creditors]** If the petition is in respect of debts to different creditors, the debts to each creditor must be separately verified.

6.12(3) **[Petition to be exhibited]** The petition shall be exhibited to the affidavit verifying it.

6.12(4) **[Who shall make the affidavit]** The affidavit shall be made–

(a) by the petitioner (or if there are two or more petitioners, any one of them), or

(b) by some person such as a director, company secretary or similar company officer, or a solicitor, who has been concerned in the matters giving rise to the presentation of the petition, or

(c) by some responsible person who is duly authorised to make the affidavit and has the requisite knowledge of those matters.

6.12(5) **[Where deponent not petitioner]** Where the maker of the affidavit is not the petitioner himself, or one of the petitioners, he must in the affidavit identify himself and state–

(a) the capacity in which, and the authority by which, he makes it, and

(b) the means of his knowledge of the matters sworn to in the affidavit.

6.12(6) **[Affidavit as prima facie evidence]** The affidavit is prima facie evidence of the truth of the statements in the petition to which it relates.

Rule 6.13   *The Insolvency Rules 1986*

6.12(7) **[Delay between demand and petition]** If the petition is based upon a statutory demand, and more than 4 months have elapsed between the service of the demand and the presentation of the petition, the affidavit must also state the reasons for the delay.

GENERAL NOTE TO RR. 6.10–6.12

The procedure for filing a creditor's petition is described in these rules. The petition should be accompanied by proof of service of the statutory demand, and by an affidavit of verification. Paragraph (2) of r. 6.10 was substituted by paras (2)–(2B) by I(A)R 2004 (SI 2004/584) with effect from April 1, 2004. It introduces additional machinery for dealing with payment of the deposit.

6.13 Notice to Chief Land Registrar

6.13 When the petition is filed, the court shall forthwith send to the Chief Land Registrar notice of the petition together with a request that it may be registered in the register of pending actions.

[FORM 6.14]

GENERAL NOTE

Form 6.14 is now contained in modified form in I(A)R 1987 (SI 1987/1919), r. 3(1), Sch., Pt 5, s. 1.

6.14 Service of petition

6.14(1) **[Personal service]** Subject as follows, the petition shall be served personally on the debtor by an officer of the court, or by the petitioning creditor or his solicitor, or by a person instructed by the creditor or his solicitor for that purpose; and service shall be effected by delivering to him a sealed copy of the petition.

6.14(2) **[Substituted service]** If the court is satisfied by affidavit or other evidence on oath that prompt personal service cannot be effected because the debtor is keeping out of the way to avoid service of the petition or other legal process, or for any other cause, it may order substituted service to be effected in such manner as it thinks fit.

6.14(3) **[Deemed service]** Where an order for substituted service has been carried out, the petition is deemed duly served on the debtor.

[FORM 6.15]
[FORM 6.16]

6.14(4) **[If voluntary arrangement in force]** If to the petitioner's knowledge there is in force for the debtor a voluntary arrangement under Part VIII of the Act, and the petitioner is not himself the supervisor of the arrangement, a copy of the petition shall be sent by him to the supervisor.

6.14(5) **[Member State liquidator]** If, to the petitioner's knowledge, there is a member State liquidator appointed in main proceedings in relation to the bankrupt, a copy of the petition shall be sent by him to the member State liquidator.

GENERAL NOTE

Personal service of a creditor's petition is required unless it is a case where substituted service may be appropriate: see *Re a Debtor (No. 234 and 236 of 1991), The Independent* June 29, 1992 (Blackett-Ord Q.C. sitting as a judge of the High Court).

    See *Practice Note (Bankruptcy: Substituted Service)* [1987] 1 W.L.R. 82.
    For service outside the jurisdiction see r. 12.12(2).
    IR 6.14(5) was added by the Insolvency (Amendment) Rules 2002 (SI 2002/1307) para. 8(2) in consequence of the advent of EC Council Regulation on Insolvency Proceedings (1346/2000) on May 31, 2002.

6.15 Proof of service

6.15(1) **[Affidavit of service]** Service of the petition shall be proved by affidavit.

6.15(2) **[Exhibits]** The affidavit shall have exhibited to it–

    (a)   a sealed copy of the petition, and

(b) if substituted service has been ordered, a sealed copy of the order;

and it shall be filed in court immediately after service.

[FORM 6.17]
or [FORM 6.18]

General Note to rr. 6.14, 6.15

These map out the rules as to service of the creditor's petition. The courts will not waive proof of service – *Re Awan* [2000] B.P.I.R. 241. Note the use of substituted service (Forms 6.15, 6.16), and the requirement of proof of service by affidavit (Forms 6.17, 6.18).

6.16 Death of debtor before service

6.16 If the debtor dies before service of the petition, the court may order service to be effected on his personal representatives or on such other persons as it thinks fit.

6.17 Security for costs (s. 268(2) only)

6.17(1) [**Application of Rule**] This Rule applies where the debt in respect of which the petition is presented is for a liquidated sum payable at some future time, it being claimed in the petition that the debtor appears to have no reasonable prospect of being able to pay it.

6.17(2) [**Debtor's application for security**] The petitioning creditor may, on the debtor's application, be ordered to give security for the debtor's costs.

6.17(3) [**Court's discretion**] The nature and amount of the security to be ordered is in the court's discretion.

6.17(4) [**If order made**] If an order is made under this Rule, there shall be no hearing of the petition until the whole amount of the security has been given.

General Note

This imposes additional financial requirements for petitions based on IA 1986, s. 268(2).

6.18 Hearing of petition

6.18(1) [**Time for hearing**] Subject as follows, the petition shall not be heard until at least 14 days have elapsed since it was served on the debtor.

6.18(2) [**Expedited hearing**] The court may, on such terms as it thinks fit, hear the petition at an earlier date, if it appears that the debtor has absconded, or the court is satisfied that is is a proper case for an expedited hearing, or the debtor consents to a hearing within the 14 days.

6.18(3) [**Appearances**] Any of the following may appear and be heard, that is to say, the petitioning creditor, the debtor, the supervisor of any voluntary arrangement under Part VIII of the Act in force for the debtor and any creditor who has given notice under Rule 6.23 below.

General Note

Normally, 14 days must elapse between the petition being served and the hearing.

6.19 Petition against two or more debtors

6.19 (Omitted by the Insolvency (Amendment) Rules 1987 (SI 1987/1919), r. 3(1), Sch., Pt 1, para. 97 as from January 11, 1988).

General Note

This rule was omitted because it was felt that a joint petition against multiple debtors would create problems. The general rule of one petition for each debtor should prevail.

6.20 Petition by moneylender

6.20 A petition in respect of a moneylending transaction made before January 27, 1980 of a creditor who at the time of the transaction was a licensed moneylender shall at the hearing of the petition be supported by an affidavit incorporating a statement setting out in detail the particulars mentioned in section 9(2) of the Moneylenders Act 1927.

6.21 Petition opposed by debtor

6.21 Where the debtor intends to oppose the petition, he shall not later than 7 days before the day fixed for the hearing–

(a) file in court a notice specifying the grounds on which he will object to the making of a bankruptcy order, and

(b) send a copy of the notice to the petitioning creditor or his solicitor.

[FORM 6.19]

6.22 Amendment of petition

6.22 With the leave of the court (given on such terms, if any, as the court thinks fit to impose), the petition may be amended at any time after presentation by the omission of any creditor or any debt.

GENERAL NOTE

For the rationale see s. 271(5). This rule needs to be viewed in the light of the general rules on amendments to petitions laid down by RSC O. 20 r. 8: see *Aspinalls Club Ltd v Simone Halabi* [1998] B.P.I.R. 322.

6.23 Notice by persons intending to appear

6.23(1) [**Notice of intention**] Every creditor who intends to appear on the hearing of the petition shall give to the petitioning creditor notice of his intention in accordance with this Rule.

[FORM 6.20]

6.23(2) [**Contents of notice**] The notice shall specify–

(a) the name and address of the person giving it, and any telephone number and reference which may be required for communication with him or with any other person (to be also specified in the notice) authorised to speak or act on his behalf;

(b) whether his intention is to support or oppose the petition; and

(c) the amount and nature of his debt.

6.23(3) [**Time for sending notice**] The notice shall be sent so as to reach the addressee not later than 16.00 hours on the business day before that which is appointed for the hearing (or, where the hearing has been adjourned, for the adjourned hearing).

6.23(4) [**Effect of non-compliance**] A person failing to comply with this Rule may appear on the hearing of the petition only with the leave of the court.

(See General Note after r. 6.24.)

6.24 List of appearances

6.24(1) [**Petitioning creditor to prepare list**] The petitioning creditor shall prepare for the court a list of the creditors (if any) who have given notice under Rule 6.23, specifying their names and addresses and (if known to him) their respective solicitors.

[FORM 6.21]

6.24(2) [**Whether creditors support or oppose**] Against the name of each creditor in the list it shall be stated whether his intention is to support the petition, or to oppose it.

6.24(3) **[Copy list handed to court]** On the day appointed for the hearing of the petition, a copy of the list shall be handed to the court before the commencement of the hearing.

6.24(4) **[Leave under r. 6.23(4)]** If any leave is given under Rule 6.23(4), the petitioner shall add to the list the same particulars in respect of the person to whom leave has been given.

GENERAL NOTE TO RR. 6.23, 6.24

Creditors who wish to attend the hearing must notify the petitioning creditor, informing him of their attitude to the petition. The petitioning creditor must draw up a list of such persons (Form 6.21), and hand it to the court before the start of the hearing.

6.25 Decision on the hearing

6.25(1) **[Bankruptcy order]** On the hearing of the petition, the court may make a bankruptcy order if satisfied that the statements in the petition are true, and that the debt on which it is founded has not been paid, or secured or compounded for.

6.25(2) **[Stay or dismissal]** If the petition is brought in respect of a judgment debt, or a sum ordered by any court to be paid, the court may stay or dismiss the petition on the ground that an appeal is pending from the judgment or order, or that execution of the judgment has been stayed.

[FORM 6.22]

6.25(3) **[Debt over-stated in demand]** A petition preceded by a statutory demand shall not be dismissed on the ground only that the amount of the debt was over-stated in the demand, unless the debtor, within the time allowed for complying with the demand, gave notice to the creditor disputing the validity of the demand on that ground; but, in the absence of such notice, the debtor is deemed to have complied with the demand if he has, within the time allowed, paid the correct amount.

GENERAL NOTE

See *Practice Note (Bankruptcy: Certificate of Debt)* [1987] 1 W.L.R. 120 and *Eberhardt v Mair* [1995] B.C.C. 845. For a review of r. 6.25 see *Legal Services Commission v Leonard* [2002] EWCA Civ 744; [2002] B.P.I.R. 994. See also general note after r. 6.26. On the power of the court to go behind a judgment debt see *Dawodu v American Express Bank* [2001] B.P.I.R. 983.

Rule 6.25 is modified so as to apply in relation to a demand made under s. 372(4)(a) FSMA 2000 as if (a) references to the debtor were references to an individual; (b) references (other than in rule 6.5(2) and (4)(c)) to the creditor were references to the Authority; and (c) references to the creditor in rule 6.5(2) and (4)(c) were references to the person to whom the debt is owed by virtue of the Bankruptcy (Financial Services and Markets Act 2000) Rules 2001 (SI 2001/3634), rr. 1, 3 and 6(1) as from December 1, 2001.

6.26 Non-appearance of creditor

6.26 If the petitioning creditor fails to appear on the hearing of the petition, no subsequent petition against the same debtor, either alone or jointly with any other person, shall be presented by the same creditor in respect of the same debt, without the leave of the court to which the previous petition was presented.

GENERAL NOTE TO RR. 6.25, 6.26

These supplement IA 1986, s. 271. Note the sanction against non-appearance by a petitioning creditor. For guidance on the exercise of discretion under IR 6.26 see *Omgate Ltd v Gordon* [2001] B.P.I.R. 909.

6.27 Vacating registration on dismissal of petition

6.27 If the petition is dismissed or withdrawn by leave of the court, an order shall be made at the same time permitting vacation of the registration of the petition as a pending action; and the court shall send to the debtor two sealed copies of the order.

[FORM 6.22]

GENERAL NOTE

This should be viewed in the light of r. 6.13.

6.28 Extension of time for hearing

6.28(1) [If petition not served] The petitioning creditor may, if the petition has not been served, apply to the court to appoint another venue for the hearing.

6.28(2) [Why petition not served] The application shall state the reasons why the petition has not been served.

6.28(3) [Costs] No costs occasioned by the application shall be allowed in the proceedings except by order of the court.

6.28(4) [Notification of creditors] If the court appoints another day for the hearing, the petitioning creditor shall forthwith notify any creditor who has given notice under Rule 6.23.

GENERAL NOTE

"Venue" in r. 6.28(1) is defined in r. 13.6. See *Practice Direction (Bankruptcy 1/92)* [1992] 1 All E.R. 704.

6.29 Adjournment

6.29(1) [Application of Rule] If the court adjourns the hearing of the petition, the following applies.

[FORM 6.23]

6.29(2) [Notice of adjournment] Unless the court otherwise directs, the petitioning creditor shall forthwith send–

(a) to the debtor, and

(b) where any creditor has given notice under Rule 6.23 but was not present at the hearing, to him,

notice of the making of the order of adjournment. The notice shall state the venue for the adjourned hearing.

[FORM 6.24]

GENERAL NOTE

The order for adjournment is to take the style of Form 6.23, whereas Form 6.24 is to be used when giving notice of the adjournment to the debtor.

6.30 Substitution of petitioner

6.30(1) [Application of Rule] This Rule applies where a creditor petitions and is subsequently found not entitled to do so, or where the petitioner–

(a) consents to withdraw his petition or to allow it to be dismissed, or consents to an adjournment, or fails to appear in support of his petition when it is called on in court on the day originally fixed for the hearing, or on a day to which it is adjourned, or

(b) appears, but does not apply for an order in terms of the prayer of his petition.

6.30(2) [Substitution] The court may, on such terms as it thinks just, order that there be substituted as petitioner any creditor who–

(a) has under Rule 6.23 given notice of his intention to appear at the hearing,

(b) is desirous of prosecuting the petition, and

(c) was, at the date on which the petition was presented, in such a position in relation to the debtor as would have enabled him (the creditor) on that date to present a bankruptcy petition in respect of a debt or debts owed to him by the debtor (or in the case of the member State liquidator, owed to creditors in proceedings in relation to which he holds office), paragraphs (a) to (d) of section 267(2) being satisfied in respect of that debt or those debts.

[FORM 6.24A]

GENERAL NOTE

This allows the court to substitute petitioners in appropriate circumstances. The words in brackets in IR 6.30(2)(c) were added by Insolvency (Amendment) Rules 2002 (SI 2002/1307) para. 8(3) with effect from May 31, 2002 to cater for the advent of EC Council Regulation 1346/2000 on insolvency proceedings.

6.31 Change of carriage of petition

6.31(1) [**Application by creditor**] On the hearing of the petition, any person who claims to be a creditor of the debtor, and who has given notice under Rule 6.23 of his intention to appear at the hearing, may apply to the court for an order giving him carriage of the petition in place of the petitioning creditor, but without requiring any amendment of the petition.

6.31(2) [**Powers of court**] The court may, on such terms as it thinks just, make a change of carriage order if satisfied that–

(a) the applicant is an unpaid and unsecured creditor of the debtor, and

(b) the petitioning creditor either–

   (i) intends by any means to secure the postponement, adjournment or withdrawal of the petition, or
   (ii) does not intend to prosecute the petition, either diligently or at all.

[FORM 6.24B]

6.31(3) [**Where court not to make order**] The court shall not make the order if satisfied that the petitioning creditor's debt has been paid, secured or compounded for by means of–

(a) a disposition of property made by some person other than the debtor, or

(b) a disposition of the debtor's own property made with the approval of, or ratified by, the court.

6.31(4) [**Appearance by petitioning creditor**] A change of carriage order may be made whether or not the petitioning creditor appears at the hearing.

6.31(5) [**If order made**] If the order is made, the person given the carriage of the petition is entitled to rely on all evidence previously adduced in the proceedings (whether by affidavit or otherwise).

GENERAL NOTE

Other creditors can apply to the court for carriage of the petition. A formal amendment of the petition is not required. See *Re Purvis* [1998] B.P.I.R. 153.

6.32 Petitioner seeking dismissal or leave to withdraw

6.32(1) [**Affidavit specifying grounds of application etc.**] Where the petitioner applies to the court for the petition to be dismissed, or for leave to withdraw it, he must, unless the court otherwise orders, file in court an affidavit specifying the grounds of the application and the circumstances in which it is made.

Rule 6.33   *The Insolvency Rules 1986*

6.32(2) **[If payment made since petition filed]** If, since the petition was filed, any payment has been made to the petitioner by way of settlement (in whole or in part) of the debt or debts in respect of which the petition was brought, or any arrangement has been entered into for securing or compounding it or them, the affidavit must state–

(a) what dispositions of property have been made for the purposes of the settlement or arrangement, and

(b) whether, in the case of any disposition, it was property of the debtor himself, or of some other person, and

(c) whether, if it was property of the debtor, the disposition was made with the approval of, or has been ratified by, the court (if so, specifying the relevant court order).

6.32(3) **[No order before hearing]** No order giving leave to withdraw a petition shall be given before the petition is heard.

[FORM 6.22]

GENERAL NOTE

This restricts the right of a petitioner to change his mind, so to speak. Bankruptcy proceedings are essentially a class remedy for the benefit of all creditors.

6.33 Settlement and content of bankruptcy order

6.33(1) **[Order to be settled by court]** The bankruptcy order shall be settled by the court.

[FORM 6.25]

6.33(2) **[Contents of order]** The order shall–

(a) state the date of the presentation of the petition on which the order is made, and the date and time of the making of the order, and

(b) contain a notice requiring the bankrupt, forthwith after service of the order on him, to attend on the official receiver at the place stated in the order.

6.33(3) **[Order staying proceedings]** Subject to section 346 (effect of bankruptcy on enforcement procedures), the order may include provision staying any action or proceeding against the bankrupt.

6.33(4) **[Where petitioning creditor represented by solicitor]** Where the petitioning creditor is represented by a solicitor, the order shall be endorsed with the latter's name, address, telephone number and reference (if any).

GENERAL NOTE

This regulates the form of any bankruptcy order made under IA 1986, s. 271.

6.34 Action to follow making of order

6.34(1) **[Copies of order to official receiver etc.]** At least two sealed copies of the bankruptcy order shall be sent forthwith by the court to the official receiver, who shall forthwith send one of them to the bankrupt.

6.34(2) **[Official receiver to send notice etc.]** Subject to the next paragraph, the official receiver shall–

(a) send notice of the making of the order to the Chief Land Registrar, for registration in the register of writs and orders affecting land,

(b) cause the order to be advertised in such newspaper as the official receiver thinks fit, and

(c) cause the order to be gazetted.

[FORM 6.26]

6.34(3) **[Suspension of action under r. 6.34(2)]** The court may, on the application of the bankrupt or a creditor, order the official receiver to suspend action under paragraph (2) and Rule 6.223(B)(1), pending a further order of the court.

An application under this paragraph shall be supported by an affidavit stating the grounds on which it is made.

6.34(4) **[Where order made under r. 6.34(3)]** Where an order is made under paragraph (3), the applicant for the order shall forthwith deliver a copy of it to the official receiver.

GENERAL NOTE

This provides for the dissemination, advertisement and gazetting of the bankruptcy order.

Rule 6.34(2)
Formerly it was required that the notice be placed in a "local paper" but this restriction was removed by I(A)R 1991 (SI 1991/495). Any newspaper will now suffice. For the impact of bankruptcy upon registered land see Land Registration Rules 2003 (SI 2003/1417) rr. 165–170.

Rule 6.34(3)
Note the addition of the reference to Rule 6.223(B)(i) by the Insolvency (Amendment) Rules 1999 (SI 1999/359) with effect from March 22, 1999.

6.35 Amendment of title of proceedings

6.35(1) **[Application for amendment]** At any time after the making of a bankruptcy order, the official receiver or the trustee may apply to the court for an order amending the full title of the proceedings.

6.35(2) **[Where amendment order made]** Where such an order is made, the official receiver shall forthwith send notice of it to the Chief Land Registrar, for corresponding amendment of the register; and, if the court so directs he shall also cause notice of the order to be gazetted, and to be advertised in such newspaper as the official receiver thinks fit.

GENERAL NOTE

Rule 6.35(2)
The restriction that the newspaper had to be "local" was removed by I(A)R 1991 (SI 1991/495).

6.36 Old bankruptcy notices

6.36(1) **[Proceeding on old notice]** Subject as follows, a person who has before the appointed day for the purposes of the Act served a bankruptcy notice under the Bankruptcy Act 1914 may, on or after that day, proceed on the notice as if it were a statutory demand duly served under Chapter 1 of this Part of the Rules.

6.36(2) **[Conditions of application of Rule]** The conditions of the application of this Rule are that–

(a) the debt in respect of which the bankruptcy notice was served has not been paid, secured or compounded for in the terms of the notice and the Act of 1914;

(b) the date by which compliance with the notice was required was not more than 3 months before the date of presentation of the petition; and

(c) there has not, before the appointed day, been presented any bankruptcy petition with reference to an act of bankruptcy arising from non-compliance with the bankruptcy notice.

6.36(3) **[Application to set old notice aside]** If before, on or after the appointed day, application is made (under the Act of 1914) to set the bankruptcy notice aside, that application is to be treated, on and after that day, as an application duly made (on the date on which it was in fact made) to set aside a statutory demand duly served on the date on which the bankruptcy notice was in fact served.

GENERAL NOTE

This was a necessary transitional provision. See IA 1986, s. 443 for further guidance on "the appointed day". Note also r. 13.14(2).

CHAPTER 3

BANKRUPTCY PETITION (DEBTOR'S)

6.37 Preliminary

6.37 The Rules in this Chapter relate to a debtor's petition, and the making of a bankruptcy order thereon.

[FORM 6.27]

(See General Note after r. 6.39.)

6.38 Identification of debtor

6.38(1) [**Contents of petition**] The petition shall state the following matters with respect to the debtor–

(a) his name, place of residence and occupation (if any);

(b) the name or names in which he carries on business, if other than his true name, and whether, in the case of any business of a specified nature, he carries it on alone or with others;

(c) the nature of his business, and the address or addresses at which he carries it on;

(d) any name or names, other than his true name, in which he has carried on business in the period in which any of his bankruptcy debts were incurred and, in the case of any such business, whether he had carried it on alone or with others; and

(e) any address or addresses at which he has resided or carried on business during that period, and the nature of that business.

6.38(2) [**Title of proceedings**] The particulars of the debtor given under this Rule determine the full title of the proceedings.

6.38(3) [**Debtor's other names**] If the debtor has at any time used a name other than the one given under paragraph (1)(a), that fact shall be stated in the petition.

(See General Note after r. 6.39.)

6.39 Admission of insolvency

6.39(1) [**Contents of petition**] The petition shall contain the statement that the petitioner is unable to pay his debts, and a request that a bankruptcy order be made against him.

6.39(2) [**Particulars in preceding five-year period**] If within the period of 5 years ending with the date of the petition the petitioner has been adjudged bankrupt, or has made a composition with his creditors in satisfaction of his debts or a scheme of arrangement of his affairs, or he has entered into any voluntary arrangement or been subject to an administration order under Part VI of the County Courts Act 1984, particulars of these matters shall be given in the petition.

6.39(3) [**If voluntary arrangement in force**] If there is at the date of the petition in force for the debtor a voluntary arrangement under Part VIII of the Act, the particulars required by paragraph (2) above shall contain a statement to that effect and the name and address of the supervisor of the arrangement.

General Note to rr. 6.37–6.39

These rules map out the form and the contents of a debtor's petition (see IA 1986, s. 272). Form 6.27 should be employed for such a bankruptcy petition.

6.40 Court in which petition to be filed

6.40(1) [**Presentation to High Court**] In the following cases, the petition shall be presented to the High Court–

(a) if the debtor has resided or carried on business in the London insolvency district for the greater part of the 6 months immediately preceding the presentation of the petition, or for a longer period in those 6 months than in any other insolvency district, or

(b) if the debtor is not resident in England and Wales.

6.40(2) [**County court**] In any other case, the petition shall (subject to paragraph (3) below), be presented to the debtor's own county court, which is–

(a) the county court for the insolvency district in which he has resided or carried on business for the longest period in those 6 months, or

(b) if he has for the greater part of those 6 months carried on business in one insolvency district and resided in another, the county court for that in which he has carried on business, or

(c) if he has during those 6 months carried on business in more than one insolvency district, the county court for that in which is, or has been for the longest period in those 6 months, his principal place of business.

6.40(3) [**Case not falling within r. 6.40(1)**] If, in a case not falling within paragraph (1), it is more expedient for the debtor with a view to expediting his petition–

(a) it may in any case be presented to whichever court is specified by Schedule 2 to the Rules as being, in relation to the debtor's own court, the nearest full-time court, and

(b) it may alternatively, in a case falling within paragraph (2)(b), be presented to the court for the insolvency district in which he has resided for the greater part of the 6 months there referred to.

6.40(3A) [**Where voluntary arrangement in force**] Notwithstanding any other provision of this Rule, where there is in force for the debtor a voluntary arrangement under Part VIII of the Act the petition shall be presented to the court to which the nominee's report under section 256 or section 256A or 263C was submitted.

6.40(4) [**Establishing appropriateness of court**] The petition shall contain sufficient information to establish that it is brought in the appropriate court.

General Note

Compare r. 6.9.

Rule 6.40(3) was amended to facilitate the presentation of bankruptcy petitions by debtor traders. The possibility of using the court where one resides (as opposed to where one trades) is in addition to the alternatives in Sch. 2. Rule 6.40(3A) is equally sensible in its approach, in that it ensures that the court which dealt with the voluntary arrangement should be the one to hear the bankruptcy petition. Rule 6.40(3A) was amended by I(A)R 2003 (SI 2003/1730) with effect from April 1, 2004.

6.41 Statement of affairs

6.41(1) [**Accompanying statement etc.**] The petition shall be accompanied by a statement of the debtor's affairs, verified by affidavit.

[FORM 6.28]

Rule 6.42 *The Insolvency Rules 1986*

6.41(2) **[Application of Section B of Ch. 5]** Section B of Chapter 5 below applies with respect to the statement of affairs.

GENERAL NOTE

This supplements IA 1986, s. 272(2). Note also rr. 6.67, 6.68.

6.42 Procedure for presentation and filing

6.42(1) **[Filing in court]** The petition and the statement of affairs shall be filed in court, together with three copies of the petition, and two copies of the statement. No petition shall be filed unless there is produced with it the receipt for the deposit payable on presentation.

6.42(2) **[Powers of court]** Subject to paragraph (2A), the court may hear the petition forthwith. If it does not do so, it shall fix a venue for the hearing.

6.42(2A) **[If petition refers to voluntary arrangement]** If the petition contains particulars of a voluntary arrangement under Part VIII of the Act in force for the debtor, the court shall fix a venue for the hearing and give at least 14 days' notice of it to the supervisor of the arrangement; the supervisor may appear and be heard on the petition.

6.42(3) **[Copies of petition]** Of the three copies of the petition delivered–

(a) one shall be returned to the petitioner, endorsed with any venue fixed;

(b) another, so endorsed, shall be sent by the court to the official receiver; and

(c) the remaining copy shall be retained by the court, to be sent to an insolvency practitioner (if appointed under section 273(2)).

6.42(4) **[Copies of statement of affairs]** Of the two copies of the statement of affairs–

(a) one shall be sent by the court to the official receiver; and

(b) the other shall be retained by the court to be sent to the insolvency practitioner (if appointed).

6.42(5) **[Swearing verifying affidavit]** The affidavit verifying the debtor's statement of affairs may be sworn before an officer of the court duly authorised in that behalf.

6.42(6) **[Documents to official receiver]** Where the court hears a petition forthwith, or it will in the opinion of the court otherwise expedite the delivery of any document to the official receiver, the court may, instead of sending that document to the official receiver, direct the bankrupt forthwith to deliver it to him.

6.42(7) **[Former supervisor requested as trustee]** Where a petition contains a request for the appointment of a person as trustee in accordance with section 297(5) (appointment of former supervisor as trustee) the person whose appointment is sought shall, not less than 2 days before the day appointed for hearing the petition, file in court a report including particulars of–

(a) a date on which he gave written notification to creditors bound by the arrangement of the intention to seek his appointment as trustee, such date to be at least 10 days before the day on which the report under this paragraph is filed, and

(b) details of any response from creditors to that notice, including any objections to his appointment.

GENERAL NOTE

Rule 6.42 was substantially modified by I(A)R 1987. The change to r. 6.42(4) was to give the official receiver early access to the statement of affairs to facilitate his examination of the debtor. Note the addition of rr. 6.42(2A), 6.42(6) and 6.42(7).

6.43 Notice to Chief Land Registrar

6.43 When the petition is filed, the court shall forthwith send to the Chief Land Registrar notice of the petition, for registration in the register of pending actions.

[FORM 6.14]

6.44 Report of insolvency practitioner

6.44(1) **[If court appoints insolvency practitioner]** If the court under section 273(2) appoints an insolvency practitioner to act in the debtor's case, it shall forthwith–

(a) send to the person appointed–

(i) a sealed copy of the order of appointment, and
(ii) copies of the petition and statement of affairs,

(b) fix a venue for the insolvency practitioner's report to be considered, and

(c) send notice of the venue to the insolvency practitioner and the debtor.

[FORM 6.29]

6.44(2) **[Insolvency practitioner's report]** The insolvency practitioner shall file his report in court and send one copy of it to the debtor, so as to be in his hands not less than 3 days before the date fixed for consideration of the report, and a further copy to the official receiver.

6.44(3) **[Debtor's attendance etc.]** The debtor is entitled to attend when the report is considered, and shall attend if so directed by the court. If he attends, the court shall hear any representations which he makes with respect to any of the matters dealt with in the report.

6.44(4) (Omitted by the Insolvency (Amendment) Rules 1987 (SI 1987/1919), r. 3(1), Sch., Pt. 1, para. 101(2) as from January 11, 1988).

GENERAL NOTE

This adds to IA 1986, s. 273(2) (appointment of insolvency practitioner in small bankruptcies). It deals with the form of the court's order (see Form 6.29), and the production of the report under IA 1986, s. 274.

Rule 6.44(2) was amended to give the official receiver early access to the report.

6.45 Settlement and content of bankruptcy order

6.45(1) **[Order to be settled by court]** The bankruptcy order shall be settled by the court.

[FORM 6.30]

6.45(2) **[Contents of order]** The order shall–

(a) state the date of the presentation of the petition on which the order is made, and the date and time of the making of the order, and

(b) contain a notice requiring the bankrupt, forthwith after the service of the order on him, to attend on the official receiver at the place stated in the order.

6.45(3) **[Order staying proceedings]** Subject to section 346 (effect of bankruptcy on enforcement procedures), the order may include provision staying any action or proceeding against the bankrupt.

6.45(4) **[Where bankrupt represented by solicitor]** Where the bankrupt is represented by a solicitor, the order shall be endorsed with the latter's name, address, telephone number and reference.

6.46 Action to follow making of order

6.46(1) **[Copy orders to official receiver etc.]** At least two sealed copies of the bankruptcy order shall be sent forthwith by the court to the official receiver, who shall forthwith send one of them to the bankrupt.

6.46(2) **[Official receiver to send notice etc.]** Subject to the next paragraph, the official receiver shall–

(a) send notice of the making of the order to the Chief Land Registrar, for registration in the register of writs and orders affecting land,

(b) cause the order to be advertised in such newspaper as the official receiver thinks fit, and

(c) cause notice of the order to be gazetted.

[FORM 6.26]

6.46(3) **[Suspension of action under r. 6.46(2)]** The court may, on the application of the bankrupt or a creditor, order the official receiver to suspend action under paragraph (2) and Rule 6.223(B)(1), pending a further order of the court.

An application under this paragraph shall be supported by an affidavit stating the grounds on which it is made.

6.46(4) **[Where order made under r. 6.46(3)]** Where an order is made under paragraph (3), the applicant shall forthwith deliver a copy of it to the official receiver.

GENERAL NOTE

This regulates the dissemination, advertisement and gazetting of the order. Note the use of Form 6.26 and the connection with r. 6.43.

Formerly under r. 6.46(2)(b) the notice had to be placed in a "local paper" as such and not a national newspaper circulating in a local area: *Re a Bankrupt (No. 1273 of 1990), The Independent* February 26, 1990. This restriction was removed by I(A)R 1991 (SI 1991/495). For the impact of bankruptcy upon registered land see Land Registration Rules 2003 (SI 2003/1417) rr. 165–170.

The reference in 6.46(3) to r. 6.223(B)(1) was inserted by Insolvency (Amendment) Rules 1999 (SI 1999/359) as from March 22, 1999.

6.46A Expenses of voluntary arrangement

6.46A Where a bankruptcy order is made on a debtor's petition and there is at the time of the petition in force for the debtor a voluntary arrangement under Part VIII of the Act, any expenses properly incurred as expenses of the administration of the arrangement in question shall be a first charge on the bankrupt's estate.

6.47 Amendment of title of proceedings

6.47(1) **[Application for amendment]** At any time after the making of the bankruptcy order, the official receiver or the trustee may apply to the court for an order amending the full title of the proceedings.

6.47(2) **[Where amendment order made]** Where such an order is made, the official receiver shall forthwith send notice of it to the Chief Land Registrar, for corresponding amendment of the register; and, if the court so directs, he shall also–

(a) cause notice of the order to be gazetted, and

(b) cause notice of the order to be advertised in such newspaper as the official receiver thinks appropriate.

Rule 6.47(2)

The category of newspapers that can be used for placing notices has been extended by I(A)R 1991 (SI 1991/495). See the comment on r. 6.46(2)(b) above.

6.48 Certificate of summary administration [revoked]

6.48(1) **[S. 275 certificate]** If the court under section 275 issues a certificate for the summary administration of the bankrupt's estate, the certificate may be included in the bankruptcy order.

[FORM 6.30]

6.48(2) **[Copy of certificate]** If the certificate is not so included, the court shall forthwith send copies of it to the official receiver and the bankrupt.

(See General Note after r. 6.50.)

6.49 Duty of official receiver in summary administration [revoked]

6.49(1) **[Where trustee appointed]** Where a trustee has been appointed, the official receiver shall send a copy of the certificate of summary administration (whether or not included in the bankruptcy order) to him.

6.49(2) **[Notice to creditors]** Within 12 weeks after the issue of the certificate the official receiver shall (insofar as he has not already done so) give notice to creditors of the making of the bankruptcy order.

(See General Note after r. 6.50.)

6.50 Revocation of certificate of summary administration [revoked]

6.50(1) **[Powers of court]** The court may under section 275(3) revoke a certificate for summary administration, either of its own motion or on the application of the official receiver.

[FORM 6.31]

6.50(2) **[Notice to bankrupt]** If the official receiver applies for the certificate to be revoked, he shall give at least 14 days' notice of the application to the bankrupt.

6.50(3) **[Notice of revocation]** If the court revokes the certificate, it shall forthwith give notice to the official receiver and the bankrupt.

6.50(4) **[Copy of notice to trustee]** If at the time of revocation there is a trustee other than the official receiver, the official receiver shall send a copy of the court's notice to him.

GENERAL NOTE TO RR. 6.48–6.50

These rules provided guidance on the operation of summary administrations (see IA 1986, s. 275). Rule 6.50 was to be viewed in the light of s. 275(3). They were revoked by I(A)R 2003 (SI 2003/1730) with effect from April 1, 2004.

CHAPTER 4

THE INTERIM RECEIVER

6.51 Application for appointment of interim receiver

6.51(1) An application to the court for the appointment of an interim receiver under section 286 may be made by–

(a) a creditor;

(b) the debtor;

(c) an insolvency practitioner appointed under section 273(2);

(d) a temporary administrator, or

(e) a member State liquidator appointed in main proceedings.

6.51(2) [**Supporting affidavit**] The application must be supported by an affidavit stating–

(a) the grounds on which it is proposed that the interim receiver should be appointed,

(b) whether or not the official receiver has been informed of the application and, if so, has been furnished with a copy of it,

(c) whether to the applicant's knowledge there has been proposed or is in force a voluntary arrangement under Part VIII of the Act, and

(d) the applicant's estimate of the value of the property or business in respect of which the interim receiver is to be appointed.

6.51(3) [**If insolvency practitioner to be interim receiver**] If an insolvency practitioner has been appointed under section 273, and it is proposed that he (and not the official receiver) should be appointed interim receiver, and it is not the insolvency practitioner himself who is the applicant under this Rule, the affidavit under paragraph (2) must state that he has consented to act.

6.51(4) [**Copies of application and affidavit**] The applicant shall send copies of the application and the affidavit to the person proposed to be appointed interim receiver. If that person is the official receiver and an insolvency practitioner has been appointed under section 273 (and he is not himself the applicant), copies of the application and affidavit shall be sent by the applicant to the insolvency practitioner.

If, in any case where a copy of the application is to be sent to a person under this paragraph, it is for any reason not practicable to send a copy, that person must be informed of the application in sufficient time to enable him to be present at the hearing.

6.51(5) [**Appearances**] The official receiver and (if appointed) the insolvency practitioner may attend the hearing of the application and make representations.

6.51(6) [**Powers of court**] The court may on the application, if satisfied that sufficient grounds are shown for the appointment, make it on such terms as it thinks fit.

(See General Note after r. 6.57.) IR 6.51(1) was reconstituted by Insolvency (Amendment) Rules 2002 (SI 2002/1307) with effect from May 31, 2002 to cater for the advent of EC Council Regulation 1346/2000 on insolvency proceedings.

6.52 Order of appointment

6.52(1) [**Contents of order**] The order appointing the interim receiver shall state the nature and a short description of the property of which the person appointed is to take possession, and the duties to be performed by him in relation to the debtor's affairs.

[FORM 6.32]

6.52(2) [**Sealed copies**] The court shall, forthwith after the order is made, send 2 sealed copies of it to the person appointed interim receiver (one of which shall be sent by him forthwith to the debtor).

(See General Note after r. 6.57.)

6.53 Deposit

6.53(1) [**Security for official receiver's remuneration etc.**] Before an order appointing the official receiver as interim receiver is issued, the applicant for it shall deposit with him, or otherwise secure to his satisfaction, such sum as the court directs to cover his remuneration and expenses.

6.53(2) [**Sufficiency of deposit etc.**] If the sum deposited or secured subsequently proves to be insufficient, the court may, on application by the official receiver, order that an additional sum be deposited or secured. If the order is not complied with within 2 days after service on the person to whom the order is directed, the court may discharge the order appointing the interim receiver.

6.53(3) [**Repayment etc. of deposit**] If a bankruptcy order is made after an interim receiver has been appointed, any money deposited under this Rule shall (unless it is required by reason of insufficiency of assets for payment of remuneration and expenses of the interim receiver, or the deposit was made by the debtor out of his own property) be repaid to the person depositing it (or as that person may direct) out of the bankrupt's estate, in the prescribed order of priority.

(See General Note after r. 6.57.)

6.54 Security

6.54(1) [Application of Rule] The following applies where an insolvency practitioner is appointed to be interim receiver under section 286(2).

6.54(2) [Cost of providing security] The cost of providing the security required under the Act shall be paid in the first instance by the interim receiver; but–

(a) if a bankruptcy order is not made, the person so appointed is entitled to be reimbursed out of the property of the debtor, and the court may make an order on the debtor accordingly, and

(b) if a bankruptcy order is made, he is entitled to be reimbursed out of the estate in the prescribed order of priority.

(See General Note after r. 6.57.)

6.55 Failure to give or keep up security

6.55(1) [Powers of court] If the interim receiver fails to give or keep up his security, the court may remove him, and make such order as it thinks fit as to costs.

6.55(2) [Directions on removal etc.] If an order is made under this Rule removing the interim receiver, or discharging the order appointing him, the court shall give directions as to whether any, and if so what, steps should be taken for the appointment of another person in his place.

(See General Note after r. 6.57.)

6.56 Remuneration

6.56(1) [To be fixed by court] The remuneration of the interim receiver (other than the official receiver) shall be fixed by the court from time to time on his application.

6.56(2) [Matters to be taken into account] In fixing the interim receiver's remuneration, the court shall take into account–

(a) the time properly given by him (as interim receiver) and his staff in attending to the debtor's affairs,

(b) the complexity (or otherwise) of the case,

(c) any respects in which, in connection with the debtor's affairs, there falls on the interim receiver any responsibility of an exceptional kind or degree,

(d) the effectiveness with which the interim receiver appears to be carrying out, or to have carried out, his duties as such, and

(e) the value and nature of the property with which he has to deal.

Rule 6.57   *The Insolvency Rules 1986*

6.56(3) **[Source of payment of remuneration etc.]** Without prejudice to any order the court may make as to costs, the interim receiver's remuneration (whether the official receiver or another) shall be paid to him, and the amount of any expenses incurred by him (including the remuneration and expenses of any special manager appointed under section 370) reimbursed–

(a)   if a bankruptcy order is not made, out of the property of the debtor, and

(b)   if a bankruptcy order is made, out of the estate in the prescribed order of priority,

or, in either case (the relevant funds being insufficient), out of the deposit under Rule 6.53.

6.56(4) **[Power of retention]** Unless the court otherwise directs, in a case falling within paragraph (3)(a) above the interim receiver may retain out of the debtor's property such sums or property as are or may be required for meeting his remuneration and expenses.

(See General Note after r. 6.57.)

6.57 Termination of appointment

6.57(1) **[Termination by court]** The appointment of the interim receiver may be terminated by the court on his application, or on that of the official receiver, the debtor or any creditor.

6.57(2) **[Directions on termination]** If the interim receiver's appointment terminates, in consequence of the dismissal of the bankruptcy petition or otherwise, the court may give such directions as it thinks fit with respect to the accounts of his administration and any other matters which it thinks appropriate.

6.57(3) (Omitted by the Insolvency (Amendment) Rules 1987 (SI 1987/1919), r. 3(1), Sch., Pt 1, para. 104 as from January 11, 1988).

GENERAL NOTE TO RR 6.51–6.57

These rules all deal with the appointment of an interim receiver to protect the debtor's assets under IA 1986, s. 286. The application procedure is detailed. The order of appointment takes the style of Form 6.32. A deposit may be required from the applicant. The interim receiver may be required to give security; failure to do so could result in his removal by the court. The court is to determine the remuneration of an interim receiver. The question of the termination of his appointment is governed by r. 6.57, which should be cross-referenced to IA 1986, s. 286(7).

CHAPTER 5

DISCLOSURE BY BANKRUPT WITH RESPECT TO THE STATE OF HIS AFFAIRS

Section A: Creditor's petition

6.58 Preliminary

6.58 The Rules in this Section apply with respect to the statement of affairs required by section 288(1) to be submitted by the bankrupt, following a bankruptcy order made on a creditor's petition, and the further and other disclosure which is required of him in that case.

(See General Note after r. 6.59.)

6.59 The statement of affairs

6.59 The bankrupt's statement of affairs shall be in Form 6.33, and contain all the particulars required by that form.

[FORM 6.33]

General Note to rr. 6.58, 6.59

These rules expand upon the provisions of IA 1986, s. 288.

6.60 Verification and filing

6.60(1) [**Instructions for preparation of statement**] The bankrupt shall be furnished by the official receiver with instructions for the preparation of his statement of affairs, and the forms required for that purpose.

6.60(2) [**Verification and delivery**] The statement of affairs shall be verified by affidavit and delivered to the official receiver, together with one copy.

6.60(3) [**Filing in court**] The official receiver shall file the verified statement in court.

6.60(4) [**Swearing verifying affidavit**] The affidavit may be sworn before an official receiver or a deputy official receiver, or before an officer of the Department or the court duly authorised in that behalf.

6.61 Limited disclosure

6.61(1) [**Official receiver may apply to court**] Where the official receiver thinks that it would prejudice the conduct of the bankruptcy for the whole or part of the statement of affairs to be disclosed, he may apply to the court for an order of limited disclosure in respect of the statement, or any specified part of it.

6.61(2) [**Powers of court**] The court may on the application order that the statement or, as the case may be, the specified part of it be not filed in court, or that it is to be filed separately and not be open to inspection otherwise than with leave of the court.

General Note

This is the standard provision in the rules enabling the court to censor sensitive information.

6.62 Release from duty to submit statement of affairs; extension of time

6.62(1) [**Exercise of s. 288(3) power**] The power of the official receiver under section 288(3) to release the bankrupt from his duty to submit a statement of affairs, or to grant an extension of time, may be exercised at the official receiver's own discretion, or at the bankrupt's request.

6.62(2) [**Bankrupt may apply to court**] The bankrupt may, if he requests a release or extension of time and it is refused by the official receiver, apply to the court for it.

6.62(3) [**Court may dismiss application etc.**] The court may, if it thinks that no sufficient cause is shown for the application, dismiss it; but it shall not do so unless the bankrupt has had an opportunity to attend the court for an *ex parte* hearing, of which he has been given at least 7 days' notice.

If the application is not dismissed under this paragraph, the court shall fix a venue for it to be heard, and give notice to the bankrupt accordingly.

6.62(4) [**Bankrupt to send notice to official receiver**] The bankrupt shall, at least 14 days before the hearing, send to the official receiver a notice stating the venue and accompanied by a copy of the application, and of any evidence which he (the bankrupt) intends to adduce in support of it.

6.62(5) [**Appearance etc. by official receiver**] The official receiver may appear and be heard on the application; and, whether or not he appears, he may file a written report of any matters which he considers ought to be drawn to the court's attention.

If such a report is filed, a copy of it shall be sent by the official receiver to the bankrupt, not later than 5 days before the hearing.

6.62(6) **[Sealed copies of order]** Sealed copies of any order made on the application shall be sent by the court to the bankrupt and the official receiver.

6.62(7) **[Bankrupt's costs]** On any application under this Rule the bankrupt's costs shall be paid in any event by him and, unless the court otherwise orders, no allowance towards them shall be made out of the estate.

GENERAL NOTE

This builds upon IA 1986, s. 288(3).

6.63 Expenses of statement of affairs

6.63(1) **[Persons assisting in preparation of statement]** If the bankrupt cannot himself prepare a proper statement of affairs, the official receiver may, at the expense of the estate, employ some person or persons to assist in the preparation of the statement.

6.63(2) **[Allowance towards expenses]** At the request of the bankrupt, made on the grounds that he cannot himself prepare a proper statement, the official receiver may authorise an allowance payable out of the estate (in accordance with the prescribed order of priority) towards expenses to be incurred by the bankrupt in employing some person or persons to assist him in preparing it.

6.63(3) **[Estimate of expenses]** Any such request by the bankrupt shall be accompanied by an estimate of the expenses involved; and the official receiver shall only authorise the employment of a named person or a named firm, being in either case approved by him.

6.63(4) **[Authorisation subject to conditions]** An authorisation given by the official receiver under this Rule shall be subject to such conditions (if any) as he thinks fit to impose with respect to the manner in which any person may obtain access to relevant books and papers.

6.63(5) **[Effect of Rule]** Nothing in this Rule relieves the bankrupt from any obligation with respect to the preparation, verification and submission of his statement of affairs, or to the provision of information to the official receiver or the trustee.

GENERAL NOTE

This deals with the funding of the statement of affairs where the bankrupt is unable to prepare it himself.

6.64 Requirement to submit accounts

6.64(1) **[At request of official receiver]** The bankrupt shall, at the request of the official receiver, furnish him with accounts relating to his affairs of such nature, as at such date and for such period as he may specify.

6.64(2) **[Beginning of specified period]** The period specified may begin from a date up to 3 years preceding the date of the presentation of the bankruptcy petition.

6.64(3) **[Accounts for earlier period]** The court may, on the official receiver's application, require accounts in respect of any earlier period.

6.64(4) **[Application of r. 6.63]** Rule 6.63 applies (with the necessary modifications) in relation to accounts to be furnished under this Rule as it applies in relation to the statement of affairs.

(See General Note after r. 6.66.)

6.65 Submission and filing of accounts

6.65(1) **[Verification and delivery]** The accounts to be furnished under Rule 6.64 shall, if the official receiver so requires, be verified by affidavit, and (whether or not so verified) delivered to him within 21 days of the request under Rule 6.64(1), or such longer period as he may allow.

6.65(2) **[Copies of accounts etc. to official receiver]** Two copies of the accounts and (where required) the affidavit shall be delivered by the bankrupt to the official receiver, who shall file one copy in court (with the affidavit, if any).

(See General Note after r. 6.66.)

6.66 Further disclosure

6.66(1) **[Official receiver may require further information]** The official receiver may at any time require the bankrupt to submit (in writing) further information amplifying, modifying or explaining any matter contained in his statement of affairs, or in accounts submitted in pursuance of the Act or the Rules.

6.66(2) **[Verification and delivery]** The information shall, if the official receiver so directs, be verified by affidavit, and (whether or not so verified) delivered to him within 21 days of the requirement under this Rule, or such longer period as he may allow.

6.66(3) **[Copies to official receiver etc.]** Two copies of the documents containing the information and (where verification is directed) the affidavit shall be delivered by the bankrupt to the official receiver, who shall file one copy in court (with the affidavit, if any).

GENERAL NOTE TO RR. 6.64–6.66

These provisions clarify IA 1986, s. 288(2)(b). Note how far back the official receiver can request accounts for under r. 6.64(2).

Section B: Debtor's petition

6.67 Preliminary

6.67 The Rules in this Section apply with respect to the statement of affairs required in the case of a person petitioning for a bankruptcy order to be made against him, and the further disclosure which is required of him in that case.

GENERAL NOTE

This provision and r. 6.68 are to be linked with r. 6.41.

6.68 Contents of statement

6.68 The statement of affairs required by Rule 6.41 to accompany the debtor's petition shall be in Form 6.28, and contain all the particulars required by that form.

[FORM 6.28]

6.69 Requirement to submit accounts

6.69(1) **[At request of official receiver]** The bankrupt shall, at the request of the official receiver, furnish him with accounts relating to his affairs of such nature, as at such date and for such period as he may specify.

6.69(2) **[Beginning of specified period]** The period specified may begin from a date up to 3 years preceding the date of the presentation of the bankruptcy petition.

6.69(3) [**Accounts for earlier period**] The court may, on the official receiver's application, require accounts in respect of any earlier period.

(See General Note after r. 6.72.)

6.70 Submission and filing of accounts

6.70(1) [**Verification and delivery**] The accounts to be furnished under Rule 6.69 shall, if the official receiver so requires, be verified by affidavit, and (whether or not so verified) delivered to him within 21 days of the request under Rule 6.69, or such longer period as he may allow.

6.70(2) [**Copies of accounts etc. to official receiver**] Two copies of the accounts and (where required) the affidavit shall be delivered by the bankrupt to the official receiver, who shall file one copy in court (with the affidavit, if any).

(See General Note after r. 6.72.)

6.71 Expenses of preparing accounts

6.71(1) [**Persons assisting in preparation of accounts**] If the bankrupt cannot himself prepare proper accounts under Rule 6.69, the official receiver may, at the expense of the estate, employ some person or persons to assist in their preparation.

6.71(2) [**Allowance towards expenses**] At the request of the bankrupt, made on the grounds that he cannot himself prepare the accounts, the official receiver may authorise an allowance payable out of the estate (in accordance with the prescribed order of priority) towards expenses to be incurred by the bankrupt in employing some person or persons to assist him in their preparation.

6.71(3) [**Estimate of expenses**] Any such request by the bankrupt shall be accompanied by an estimate of the expenses involved; and the official receiver shall only authorise the employment of a named person or a named firm, being in either case approved by him.

6.71(4) [**Authorisation subject to conditions**] An authorisation given by the official receiver under this Rule shall be subject to such conditions (if any) as he thinks fit to impose with respect to the manner in which any person may obtain access to relevant books and papers.

6.71(5) [**Effect of Rule**] Nothing in this Rule relieves the bankrupt from any obligation with respect to the preparation and submission of accounts, or to the provision of information to the official receiver or the trustee.

(See General Note after r. 6.72.)

6.72 Further disclosure

6.72(1) [**Official receiver may require further information**] The official receiver may at any time require the bankrupt to submit (in writing) further information amplifying, modifying or explaining any matter contained in his statement of affairs, or in accounts submitted in pursuance of the Act or the Rules.

6.72(2) [**Verification and delivery**] The information shall, if the official receiver so directs, be verified by affidavit, and (whether or not so verified) delivered to him within 21 days from the date of the requirement under paragraph (1), or such longer period as he may allow.

6.72(3) [**Copies to official receiver etc.**] Two copies of the documents containing the information and (where verification is directed) the affidavit shall be delivered by the bankrupt to the official receiver, who shall file one copy in court, with the affidavit (if any).

GENERAL NOTE TO RR. 6.69–6.72

These provisions largely mirror rr. 6.63–6.66.

CHAPTER 6

INFORMATION TO CREDITORS

6.73 General duty of official receiver

6.73(1) [Report to creditors] In accordance with this Chapter, the official receiver shall, at least once after the making of the bankruptcy order, send a report to creditors with respect to the bankruptcy proceedings, and the state of the bankrupt's affairs.

6.73(2) [Copy of report] The official receiver shall file in court a copy of any report sent under this Chapter.

GENERAL NOTE

The rules in Ch. 6 impose additional duties upon the official receiver to keep creditors informed.

6.74 Those entitled to be informed

6.74 Any reference in this Chapter to creditors is to creditors of the bankrupt who are known to the official receiver or, where the bankrupt has submitted a statement of affairs, are identified in the statement.

GENERAL NOTE

This narrows the definition of "creditors".

6.75 Report where statement of affairs lodged

6.75(1) [Report to creditors] Where the bankrupt has submitted a statement of affairs, and it has been filed in court, the official receiver shall send out to creditors a report containing a summary of the statement (if he thinks fit, as amplified, modified or explained by virtue of Rule 6.66 or 6.72) and such observations (if any) as he thinks fit to make with respect to it or to the bankrupt's affairs generally.

6.75(2) [Where no need to comply with r. 6.75(1)] The official receiver need not comply with paragraph (1) if he has previously reported to creditors with respect to the bankrupt's affairs (so far as known to him) and he is of opinion that there are no additional matters which ought to be brought to their attention.

GENERAL NOTE

This develops IA 1986, s. 288 and relates to the dissemination of the statement of affairs.

6.76 Statement of affairs dispensed with

6.76(1) [Application of Rule] This Rule applies where the bankrupt has been released from the obligation to submit a statement of affairs.

6.76(2) [Report to creditors] As soon as may be after the release has been granted, the official receiver shall send to creditors a report containing a summary of the bankrupt's affairs (so far as within his knowledge), and his observations (if any) with respect to it or the bankrupt's affairs generally.

6.76(3) [Where no need to comply with r. 6.76(2)] The official receiver need not comply with paragraph (2) if he has previously reported to creditors with respect to the bankrupt's affairs (so far as known to him) and he is of opinion that there are no additional matters which ought to be brought to their attention.

GENERAL NOTE

If IA 1986, s. 288(3)(a) has been activated, the official receiver must supply a report to the creditors dealing with the financial position of the bankrupt.

6.77 General rule as to reporting

6.77(1) [Powers of court] The court may, on the official receiver's application, relieve him of any duty imposed on him by this Chapter of the Rules, or authorise him to carry out the duty in a way other than there required.

6.77(2) [Matters for court to consider] In considering whether to act as above, the court shall have regard to the cost of carrying out the duty, to the amount of the funds available in the estate, and to the extent of the interest of creditors or any particular class of them.

(See General Note after r. 6.78.)

6.78 Bankruptcy order annulled

6.78 If the bankruptcy order is annulled, the duty of the official receiver to send reports under the preceding Rules in this Chapter ceases.

GENERAL NOTE TO RR. 6.77, 6.78

These rules modify the above obligations which have been imposed on the official receiver. Note the court's power of waiver under r. 6.77.

CHAPTER 7

CREDITORS' MEETINGS

6.79 First meeting of creditors

6.79(1) [Venue for meeting etc.] If under section 293(1) the official receiver decides to summon a meeting of creditors, he shall fix a venue for the meeting, not more than 4 months from the date of the bankruptcy order.

6.79(2) [Notice of meeting] When a venue has been fixed, notice of the meeting shall be given–

(a) to the court, and

(b) to every creditor of the bankrupt who is known to the official receiver or is identified in the bankrupt's statement of affairs.

6.79(3) [Time for giving notice] Notice to the court shall be given forthwith; and the notice to creditors shall be given at least 21 days before the date fixed for the meeting.

6.79(4) **[Contents of notice]** The notice to creditors shall specify a time and date, not more than 4 days before the date fixed for the meeting, by which they must lodge proofs and (if applicable) proxies, in order to be entitled to vote at the meeting.

6.79(5) **[Public advertisement]** Notice of the meeting shall also be given by public advertisement.

6.79(6) **[Request by creditor under s. 294]** Where the official receiver receives a request by a creditor under section 294 for a meeting of creditors to be summoned, and it appears to him that the request is properly made in accordance with the Act, he shall–

(a) withdraw any notice already given by him under section 293(2) (that he has decided not to summon such a meeting), and

(b) fix the venue of the meeting for not more than 3 months from his receipt of the creditor's request, and

(c) act in accordance with paragraphs (2) to (5) above, as if he had decided under section 293(1) to summon the meeting.

[FORM 6.34]

6.79(7) **[Name of meeting]** A meeting summoned by the official receiver under section 293 or 294 is known as "the first meeting of creditors".

GENERAL NOTE

If the official receiver decides to call a first meeting of creditors under IA 1986, s. 293, it must take place within four months of the date of the bankruptcy order. The meeting must be properly notified to the court (immediately), and to creditors (who should have 21 days' notice). It should also be advertised. Creditors should be given an opportunity to lodge proofs. Rule 6.79(6) develops the provisions of IA 1986, s. 294. Note the use of Form 6.34 for the purposes of s. 294. For the meaning of "venue" see r. 13.6.

6.80 Business at first meeting

6.80(1) **[Limitation on resolutions]** At the first meeting of creditors, no resolutions shall be taken other than the following–

(a) a resolution to appoint a named insolvency practitioner to be trustee in bankruptcy or two or more named insolvency practitioners as joint trustees;

(b) a resolution to establish a creditors' committee;

(c) (unless it has been resolved to establish a creditors' committee) a resolution specifying the terms on which the trustee is to be remunerated, or to defer consideration of that matter;

(d) (if, and only if, two or more persons are appointd to act jointly as trustee) a resolution specifying whether acts are to be done by both or all of them, or by only one;

(e) (where the meeting has been requisitioned under section 294) a resolution authorising payment out of the estate, as an expense of the bankruptcy, of the cost of summoning and holding the meeting;

(f) a resolution to adjourn the meeting for not more than 3 weeks;

(g) any other resolution which the chairman thinks it right to allow for special reasons.

6.80(2) **[Further limitation]** No resolution shall be proposed which has for its object the appointment of the official receiver as trustee.

GENERAL NOTE

This restricts the agenda of the first meeting of creditors. Note the importance of securing the appointment of a trustee.

6.81 General power to call meetings

6.81(1) [General power, "the convener"] The official receiver or the trustee may at any time summon and conduct meetings of creditors for the purpose of ascertaining their wishes in all matters relating to the bankruptcy.

In relation to any meeting of creditors, the person summoning it is referred to as "the convener".

6.81(2) [Notice of meeting] When a venue for the meeting has been fixed, notice of the meeting shall be given by the convener to every creditor who is known to him or is identified in the bankrupt's statement of affairs.

The notice shall be given at least 21 days before the date fixed for the meeting.

[FORM 6.35]

6.81(3) [Contents of notice] The notice to creditors shall specify the purpose for which the meeting is summoned, and a time and date (not more than 4 days before the meeting) by which creditors must lodge proxies and those who have not already lodged proofs must do so, in order to be entitled to vote at the meeting.

6.81(4) [Public advertisement] Additional notice of the meeting may be given by public advertisement if the convener thinks fit, and shall be so given if the court so orders.

GENERAL NOTE

Subsequent meetings of creditors are held normally at the discretion of the official receiver, or trustee (subject to requisitions under r. 6.83).

6.82 The chairman at a meeting

6.82(1) [Where convener official receiver] Where the convener of a meeting is the official receiver, he, or a person nominated by him, shall be chairman.

A nomination under this paragraph shall be in writing, unless the nominee is another official receiver or a deputy official receiver.

6.82(2) [Where convener other than official receiver] Where the convener is other than the official receiver, the chairman shall be he, or a person nominated by him in writing to act.

A person nominated under this paragraph must be either–

(a) one who is qualified to act as an insolvency practitioner in relation to the bankrupt, or

(b) an employee of the trustee or his firm who is experienced in insolvency matters.

GENERAL NOTE

For the qualification of insolvency practitioners, see IA 1986, Pt XIII.

6.83 Requisitioned meetings

6.83(1) [Documents to accompany creditors' request] A request by creditors to the official receiver for a meeting of creditors to be summoned shall be accompanied by–

(a) a list of the creditors concurring with the request and the amount of their respective claims in the bankruptcy,

(b) from each creditor concurring, written confirmation of his concurrence, and

(c) a statement of the purpose of the proposed meeting.

Sub-paragraphs (a) and (b) do not apply if the requisitioning creditor's debt is alone sufficient, without the concurrence of other creditors.

[FORM 6.34]

6.83(2) **[Official receiver to fix venue etc.]** The official receiver, if he considers the request to be properly made in accordance with the Act, shall–

(a) fix a venue for the meeting, to take place not more than 35 days from the receipt of the request, and

(b) give 21 days' notice of the meeting, and of the venue for it, to creditors.

6.83(3) **[Application of Rule]** Where a request for a creditors' meeting is made to the trustee, this Rule applies to him as it does to the official receiver.

6.83(4) This Rule shall not apply to voluntary arrangements under section 263A.

GENERAL NOTE

This qualifies r. 6.81. No minimum level of support is specified here: but see IA 1986, s. 294. For the meaning of "venue" see r. 13.6.

A new para. (4) was introduced by the Insolvency (Amendment) Rules 2003 (SI 2003/1730) to exclude voluntary arrangements covered by s. 263A.

6.84 Attendance at meetings of bankrupt, etc.

6.84(1) **[Notice to bankrupt]** Whenever a meeting of creditors is summoned, the convener shall give at least 21 days' notice of the meeting to the bankrupt.

[FORM 6.36]

6.84(2) **[Notice of adjournment]** If the meeting is adjourned, the chairman of the meeting shall (unless for any reason it appears to him to be unnecessary or impracticable) give notice of the fact to the bankrupt, if the latter was not himself present at the meeting.

6.84(3) **[Notice that presence required]** The convener may, if he thinks fit, give notice to the bankrupt that he is required to be present, or in attendance.

6.84(4) **[Admission to meetings]** In the case of any meeting, the bankrupt or any other person may, if he has given reasonable notice of his wish to be present, be admitted; but this is at the discretion of the chairman.

The chairman's decision is final as to what (if any) intervention may be made by the bankrupt, or by any other person admitted to the meeting under this paragraph.

6.84(5) **[Adjournment for obtaining attendance]** If the bankrupt is not present, and it is desired to put questions to him, the chairman may adjourn the meeting with a view to obtaining his attendance.

6.84(6) **[Chairman's discretion re questions]** Where the bankrupt is present at a creditors' meeting, only such questions may be put to him as the chairman may in his discretion allow.

GENERAL NOTE

This is largely self-explanatory. Form 6.36 is used to notify the bankrupt. Bankrupts may be forced to attend. Note the wide powers of the chairman of the meeting.

6.85 Notice of meetings by advertisement only

6.85(1) **[Power of court]** In the case of any meeting to be held under the Act or the Rules, the court may order that notice of it be given by public advertisement, and not by individual notice to the persons concerned.

6.85(2) [**Matters for court to consider**] In considering whether to act under this Rule, the court shall have regard to the cost of public advertisement, to the amount of the funds available in the estate, and to the extent of the interest of creditors or any particular class of them.

GENERAL NOTE

This is an economy measure that the court may adopt in appropriate circumstances.

6.86 Venue of meetings

6.86(1) [**Convenience of venue**] In fixing the venue for a meeting of creditors, the person summoning the meeting shall have regard to the convenience of the creditors.

6.86(2) [**Time of meetings**] Meetings shall in all cases be summoned for commencement between the hours of 10.00 and 16.00 hours on a business day, unless the court otherwise directs.

6.86(3) [**Forms of proxy**] With every notice summoning a creditors' meeting there shall be sent out forms of proxy.

[FORM 8.5]

GENERAL NOTE

For the meaning of "venue" and "business day" see rr. 13.6 and 13.13(1).

6.87 Expenses of summoning meetings

6.87(1) [**Security for payment of expenses**] Subject to paragraph (3) below, the expenses of summoning and holding a meeting of creditors at the instance of any person other, than the official receiver or the trustee shall be paid by that person, who shall deposit security for their payment with the trustee or, if no trustee has been appointed, with the official receiver.

6.87(2) [**Appropriate security**] The sum to be deposited shall be such as the trustee or (as the case may be) the official receiver determines to be appropriate; and neither shall act without the deposit having been made.

6.87(3) [**Vote for expenses to be paid out of estate**] Where a meeting is so summoned, it may vote that the expenses of summoning and holding it shall be payable out of the estate, as an expense of the bankruptcy.

6.87(4) [**Repayment of deposit**] To the extent that any deposit made under this Rule is not required for the payment of expenses of summoning and holding the meeting, it shall be repaid to the person who made it.

GENERAL NOTE

This serves as a deterrent to persons wishing to requisition meetings under r. 6.83.

6.88 Resolutions

6.88(1) [**Resolution passed by majority in value**] Subject as follows, at a meeting of creditors, a resolution is passed when a majority (in value) of those present and voting, in person or by proxy, have voted in favour of the resolution.

6.88(2) **[Resolution for appointment of trustee]** In the case of a resolution for the appointment of a trustee–

(a) if on any vote there are two nominees for appointment, the person who obtains the most support is appointed, provided that such support represents a majority in value of all those present (in person or by proxy) at the meeting and entitled to vote;

(b) if there are three or more nominees, and one of them has a clear majority over both or all the others together, that one is appointed; and

(c) in any other case the chairman shall continue to take votes (disregarding at each vote any nominee who has withdrawn and, if no nominee has withdrawn, the nominee who obtained the least support last time), until a clear majority is obtained for any one nominee.

6.88(3) **[Resolution for joint appointment]** The chairman may at any time put to the meeting a resolution for the joint appointment of any two or more nominees.

6.88(4) **[Resolution affecting trustee etc.]** Where a resolution is proposed which affects a person in respect of his remuneration or conduct as trustee, or as proposed or former trustee, the vote of that person, and of any partner or employee of his, shall not be reckoned in the majority required for passing the resolution.

This paragraph applies with respect to a vote given by a person (whether personally or on his behalf by a proxy-holder) either as creditor or as proxy-holder for a creditor (but subject to Rule 8.6 in Part 8 of the Rules).

GENERAL NOTE

Simple majorities are required to pass resolutions.

6.89 Chairman of meeting as proxy-holder

6.89 Where the chairman at a meeting holds a proxy for a creditor, which requires him to vote for a particular resolution, and no other person proposes that resolution–

(a) he shall himself propose it, unless he considers that there is good reason for not doing so, and

(b) if he does not propose it, he shall forthwith after the meeting notify his principal of the reason why not.

6.90 Suspension of meeting

6.90 Once only in the course of any meeting, the chairman may, in his discretion and without an adjournment, declare the meeting suspended for any period up to one hour.

6.91 Adjournment

6.91(1) **[At chairman's discretion]** The chairman at any meeting may, in his discretion, and shall if the meeting so resolves, adjourn it to such time and place as seems to him to be appropriate in the circumstances.

This is subject to Rule 6.129(3) in a case where the trustee or his nominee is chairman and a resolution has been proposed for the trustee's removal.

6.91(2) **[Adjournment if inquorate]** If within a period of 30 minutes from the time appointed for the commencement of a meeting a quorum is not present, then the chairman may, at his discretion, adjourn the meeting to such time and place as he may appoint.

6.91(3) **[Period of adjournment]** An adjournment under this Rule shall not be for a period of more than 21 days; and Rule 6.86(1) and (2) applies with regard to the venue of the adjourned meeting.

6.91(4) [If no chairman] If there is no person present to act as chairman, some other person present (being entitled to vote) may make the appointment under paragraph (2), with the agreement of others present (being persons so entitled).

Failing agreement, the adjournment shall be to the same time and place in the next following week or, if that is not a business day, to the business day immediately following.

6.91(5) [Use of proof and proxies at adjourned meeting] Where a meeting is adjourned under this Rule, proofs and proxies may be used if lodged at any time up to midday on the business day immediately before the adjourned meeting.

GENERAL NOTE

For the meaning of "venue" and "business day" see rr. 13.6 and 13.13(1).
Rule 6.91(2) was amended to allow the chairman discretion to adjourn.

6.92 Quorum

6.92 (Omitted by the Insolvency (Amendment) Rules 1987 (SI 1987/1919), r. 3(1), Sch., Pt 1, para. 109 as from January 11, 1988).

GENERAL NOTE

See now r. 12.4A.

6.93 Entitlement to vote

6.93(1) [Conditions for voting] Subject as follows, at a meeting of creditors a person is entitled to vote as a creditor only if–

(a) there has been duly lodged, by the time and date stated in the notice of the meeting, a proof of the debt

  (i) claimed to be due to him from the bankrupt, or
  (ii) in relation to a member State liquidator, is claimed to be due to creditors in proceedings in relation to which he holds office, and

the claim has been admitted under Rule 6.94 for the purpose of entitlement to vote, and

(b) there has been lodged, by that time and date, any proxy requisite for that entitlement.

6.93(2) [Powers of court] The court may, in exceptional circumstances, by order declare the creditors, or any class of them, entitled to vote at creditors' meetings, without being required to prove their debts.

Where a creditor is so entitled, the court may, on the application of the trustee, make such consequential orders as it thinks fit (as for example an order treating a creditor as having proved his debt for the purpose of permitting payment of dividend).

6.93(3) [Limitation on voting] A creditor shall not vote in respect of a debt for an unliquidated amount, or any debt whose value is not ascertained, expect where the chairman agrees to put upon the debt an estimated minimum value for the purpose of entitlement to vote and admits his proof for that purpose.

6.93(4) [Secured creditor] A secured creditor is entitled to vote only in respect of the balance (if any) of his debt after deducting the value of his security as estimated by him.

6.93(5) [**Further limitation on voting**] A creditor shall not vote in respect of a debt on, or secured by, a current bill of exchange or promissory note, unless he is willing–

(a) to treat the liability to him on the bill or note of every person who is liable on it antecedently to the bankrupt, and against whom a bankruptcy order has not been made (or, in the case of a company, which has not gone into liquidation), as a security in his hands, and

(b) to estimate the value of the security and (for the purpose of entitlement to vote, but not for dividend) to deduct it from his proof.

6.93(6) [**Still further limitation on voting**] No vote shall be cast by virtue of a debt more than once on any resolution put to the meeting.

6.93(7) [**Creditor's vote**] Where–

(a) a creditor is entitled to vote under this Rule and Rule 6.94 (admission of proof),

(b) has lodged his claim in one or more sets of other proceedings, and

(c) votes (either in person or by proxy) on a resolution put to the meeting, only the creditor's vote shall be counted.

6.93(8) [**Member State liquidator**] Where–

(a) a creditor has lodged his claim in more than one set of other proceedings, and

(b) more than one member State liquidator seeks to vote by virtue of that claim,

the entitlement to vote by virtue of that claim is exercisable by the member State liquidator in main proceedings, whether or not the creditor has lodged his claim in the main proceedings.

6.93(9) [**"Other proceedings"**] For the purposes of paragraphs (7) and (8), "other proceedings" means main proceedings, secondary proceedings or territorial proceedings in another member State.

GENERAL NOTE

As a general rule, only creditors who have lodged proofs which have been admitted can vote. Note the special rules for persons claiming unliquidated amounts, etc. Note the amendment of r. 6.93(1)(a) and the insertion of r. 6.93(6)–(9) by the Insolvency (Amendment) Rules 2002 SI 2002/1307 with effect from May 31, 2002 to cater for the advent of EC Council Regulation 1346/2000 on insolvency proceedings.

6.94 Admission and rejection of proof

6.94(1) [**Power of chairman**] At any creditors' meeting the chairman has power to admit or reject a creditor's proof for the purpose of his entitlement to vote; and the power is exercisable with respect to the whole or any part of the proof.

6.94(2) [**Appeal from chairman's decision**] The chairman's decision under this Rule, or in respect of any matter arising under Rule 6.93, is subject to appeal to the court by any creditor, or by the bankrupt.

6.94(3) [**Voting subject to objection**] If the chairman is in doubt whether a proof should be admitted or rejected, he shall mark it as objected to and allow the creditor to vote, subject to his vote being subsequently declared invalid if the objection to the proof is sustained.

6.94(4) [**If chairman's decision reversed etc.**] If on an appeal the chairman's decision is reversed or varied, or a creditor's vote is declared invalid, the court may order that another meeting be summoned, or make such other order as it thinks just.

6.94(5) [**Costs re application**] Neither the official receiver nor any person nominated by him to be chairman is personally liable for costs incurred by any person in respect of an application to the court under this Rule; and the chairman (if other than the official receiver or a person so nominated) is not so liable unless the court makes an order to that effect.

GENERAL NOTE

Admission of proofs is a matter for the chairman (subject to an appeal to the court). On r. 6.94(2) see *Re Gunningham* [2002] B.P.I.R. 302.

6.95 Record of proceedings

6.95(1) [**Minutes of proceedings**] The chairman at any creditors' meeting shall cause minutes of the proceedings at the meeting, signed by him, to be retained by him as part of the records of the bankruptcy.

6.95(2) [**List of creditors attending**] He shall also cause to be made up and kept a list of all the creditors who attended the meeting.

6.95(3) [**Record of resolutions**] The minutes of the meeting shall include a record of every resolution passed; and it is the chairman's duty to see to it that particulars of all such resolutions, certified by him, are filed in court not more than 21 days after the date of the meeting.

CHAPTER 8

PROOF OF BANKRUPTCY DEBTS

Section A: Procedure for proving

6.96 Meaning of "prove"

6.96(1) [**Claim to be submitted in writing etc.**] A person claiming to be a creditor of the bankrupt and wishing to recover his debt in whole or in part must (subject to any order of the court under Rule 6.93(2)) submit his claim in writing to the official receiver, where acting as receiver and manager, or to the trustee.

6.96(2) [**"Proving" and "proof"**] The creditor is referred to as **"proving"** for his debt; and the document by which he seeks to establish his claim is his **"proof"**.

6.96(3) [**"Proof of debt"**] Subject to the next two paragraphs, the proof must be in the form known as **"proof of debt"** (whether the form prescribed by the Rules, or a substantially similar form), which shall be made out by or under the directions of the creditor, and signed by him or a person authorised in that behalf.

[FORM 6.37]

6.96(4) [**Debt due to Crown etc.**] Where a debt is due to a Minister of the Crown or a Government Department, the proof need not be in that form, provided that there are shown all such particulars of the debt as are required in the form used by other creditors, and as are relevant in the circumstances.

6.96(5) [**Proof under s. 335(5)**] Where an existing trustee proves in a later bankruptcy under section 335(5), the proof must be in Form 6.38.

[FORM 6.38]

6.96(6) [**Proof in form of affidavit**] In certain circumstances, specified below in this Chapter, the proof must be in the form of an affidavit.

[FORM 6.39]

GENERAL NOTE

This supplements IA 1986, s. 322.

6.97 Supply of forms

6.97 A form of proof shall be sent to any creditor of the bankrupt by the official receiver or trustee where the creditor so requests.

GENERAL NOTE

This rule, which deals with the supply of debt proof forms, was substituted by I(A)R 2004 (SI 2004/584) with effect from April 1, 2004 with a less complex version.

6.98 Contents of proof

6.98(1) [Matters to be stated] Subject to Rule 6.96(4), the following matters shall be stated in a creditor's proof of debt –

(a) the creditor's name and address, and, if a company, its company registration number;

(b) the total amount of his claim (including any Value Added Tax) as at the date of the bankruptcy order;

(c) whether or not that amount includes outstanding uncapitalised interest;

(d) particulars of how and when the debt was incurred by the debtor;

(e) particulars of any security held, the date when it was given and the value which the creditor puts upon it

(f) details of any reservation of title in respect of goods to which the debt refers; and

(g) the name, and address and authority of the person signing the proof (if other than the creditor himself).

6.98(2) [Specified documents] There shall be specified in the proof any documents by reference to which the debt can be substantiated; but (subject as follows) it is not essential that such documents be attached to the proof or submitted with it.

6.98(3) [Production of documents etc.] The trustee or the official receiver, acting as receiver and manager, or the convener or chairman of any meeting, may call for any document or other evidence to be produced to him, where he thinks it necessary for the purpose of substantiating the whole or any part of the claim made in the proof.

GENERAL NOTE

A new r. 6.98(1) was substituted by the Insolvency (Amendment No. 2) Rules 2004 (SI 2004/1070), r. 2 with effect from May 3, 2004 in substitution for r. 6.98(1) previously substituted by the Insolvency (Amendment) Rules 2004 (SI 2004/584), r. 28 as from 1 April 2004. The later substitution was to correct a drafting error which referred to companies rather than bankrupts.

6.99 Claim established by affidavit

6.99(1) [Trustee etc. may require "affidavit of debt"] The trustee or official receiver, acting as receiver and manager may, if he thinks it necessary, require a claim of debt to be verified by affidavit, for which purpose there shall be used the form known as **"affidavit of debt"**.

[FORM 6.39]

6.99(2) **[In addition to proof]** An affidavit may be required notwithstanding that a proof of debt has already been lodged.

6.99(3) **[Swearing of affidavit]** The affidavit may be sworn before an official receiver or a deputy official receiver, or before an officer of the Department or of the court duly authorised in that behalf.

GENERAL NOTE

Affidavits of debt (see Form 6.39) may be required to support proofs. "Department" is defined in r. 13.13(2). The reference to the official receiver, acting as receiver and manager was added by I(A)R 2004 (SI 2004/584) with effect from April 1, 2004.

6.100 Cost of proving

6.100(1) **[Creditor bears cost of proving own debt]** Subject as follows, every creditor bears the cost of proving his own debt, including such as may be incurred in providing documents or evidence under Rule 6.98.

6.100(2) **[Trustee's costs]** Costs incurred by the trustee in estimating the value of a bankruptcy debt under section 322(3) (debts not bearing a certain value) fall on the estate, as an expense of the bankruptcy.

6.100(3) **[Application of r. 6.100(1), (2)]** Paragraphs (1) and (2) apply unless the court otherwise orders.

6.101 Trustee to allow inspection of proofs

6.101 The trustee shall, so long as proofs lodged with him are in his hands, allow them to be inspected, at all reasonable times on any business day, by any of the following persons–

(a) any creditor who has submitted his proof of debt (unless his proof has been wholly rejected for purposes of dividend or otherwise),

(b) the bankrupt, and

(c) any person acting on behalf of either of the above.

GENERAL NOTE

Proofs are available for inspection by the creditors and the bankrupt and their representatives.

6.102 Proof of licensed moneylender

6.102 A proof of debt in respect of a moneylending transaction made before 27th January 1980, where the creditor was at the time of the transaction a licensed moneylender, shall have endorsed on or annexed to it a statement setting out in detail the particulars mentioned in section 9(2) of the Moneylenders Act 1927.

6.103 Transmissions of proofs to trustee

6.103(1) **[On trustee's appointment]** Where a trustee is appointed, the official receiver shall forthwith transmit to him all the proofs which he has so far received, together with an itemised list of them.

6.103(2) **[Receipt for proofs]** The trustee shall sign the list by way of receipt for the proofs, and return it to the official receiver.

6.103(3) **[All later proofs to trustee]** From then on, all proofs of debt shall be sent to the trustee and retained by him.

GENERAL NOTE

This deals with the transfer of responsibilities from the official receiver to the trustee.

6.104 Admission and rejection of proofs for dividend

6.104(1) **[Admission]** A proof may be admitted for dividend either for the whole amount claimed by the creditor, or for part of that amount.

6.104(2) **[Rejection]** If the trustee rejects a proof in whole or in part, he shall prepare a written statement of his reasons for doing so, and send it forthwith to the creditor.

GENERAL NOTE

For dividend distributions see IA 1986, s. 324. Note also Pt 11 of the rules.

6.105 Appeal against decision on proof

6.105(1) **[Application by creditor]** If a creditor is dissatisfied with the trustee's decision with respect to his proof (including any decision on the question of preference), he may apply to the court for the decision to be reversed or varied.

The application must be made within 21 days of his receiving the statement sent under Rule 6.104(2).

6.105(2) **[Application by bankrupt etc.]** The bankrupt or any other creditor may, if dissatisfied with the trustee's decision admitting or rejecting the whole or any part of a proof, make such an application within 21 days of becoming aware of the trustee's decision.

6.105(3) **[Venue and notice]** Where application is made to the court under this Rule, the court shall fix a venue for the application to be heard, notice of which shall be sent by the applicant to the creditor who lodged the proof in question (if it is not himself) and to the trustee.

6.105(4) **[Relevant proof etc. to be filed in court]** The trustee shall, on receipt of the notice, file in court the relevant proof, together (if appropriate) with a copy of the statement sent under Rule 6.104(2).

6.105(5) **[Return of proof]** After the application has been heard and determined, the proof shall, unless it has been wholly disallowed, be returned by the court to the trustee.

6.105(6) **[Costs re application]** The official receiver is not personally liable for costs incurred by any person in respect of an application under this Rule; and the trustee (if other than the official receiver) is not so liable unless the court makes an order to that effect.

GENERAL NOTE

Rejection of proof under r. 6.104 may be appealed against to the court. This is not a true appeal – *Cadwell v Jackson* [2001] B.P.I.R. 966. For the meaning of "venue" in r. 6.105(3) see r. 13.6. For the potential utility of r. 6.105 see *Barclays Bank v Henson* [2000] B.P.I.R. 941.

6.106 Withdrawal or variation of proof

6.106 A creditor's proof may at any time, by agreement between himself and the trustee, be withdrawn or varied as to the amount claimed.

6.107 Expunging of proof by the court

6.107(1) [**Expunging or reduction of amount**] The court may expunge a proof or reduce the amount claimed–

(a) on the trustee's application, where he thinks that the proof has been improperly admitted, or ought to be reduced; or

(b) on the application of a creditor, if the trustee declines to interfere in the matter.

6.107(2) [**Venue and notice**] Where application is made to the court under this Rule, the court shall fix a venue for the application to be heard, notice of which shall be sent by the applicant–

(a) in the case of an application by the trustee, to the creditor who made the proof, and

(b) in the case of an application by a creditor, to the trustee and to the creditor who made the proof (if not himself).

GENERAL NOTE

For the meaning of "venue" in r. 6.107(2) see r. 13.6

Section B: Quantification of claim

6.108 Negotiable instruments, etc.

6.108 Unless the trustee allows, a proof in respect of money owed on a bill of exchange, promissory note, cheque or other negotiable instrument or security cannot be admitted unless there is produced the instrument or security itself or a copy of it, certified by the creditor or his authorised representative to be a true copy.

6.109 Secured creditors

6.109(1) [**Proving for balance of debt**] If a secured creditor realises his security, he may prove for the balance of his debt, after deducting the amount realised.

6.109(2) [**Proving for whole debt**] If a secured creditor voluntarily surrenders his security for the general benefit of creditors, he may prove for his whole debt, as if it were unsecured.

GENERAL NOTE

This should be viewed in the light of IA 1986, ss. 269 and 383(2), and also rr. 6.15–6.19. For a useful discussion of the operation of this rule see Anderson (1989) 5 I.L. & P. 180.

6.110 Discounts

6.110 There shall in every case be deducted from the claim all trade and other discounts which would have been available to the bankrupt but for his bankruptcy, except any discount for immediate, early or cash settlement.

6.111 Debt in foreign currency

6.111(1) [**Conversion into sterling**] For the purpose of proving a debt incurred or payable in a currency other than sterling, the amount of the debt shall be converted into sterling at the official exchange rate prevailing on the date of the bankruptcy order.

6.111(2) [**"The official exchange rate"**] "The official exchange rate" is the middle exchange rate on the London Foreign Exchange Market at the close of business, as published for the date in question. In the absence of any such published rate, it is such rate as the court determines.

GENERAL NOTE

A similar rule applies in company law: *Re Dynamics Corporation of America (No. 2)* [1976] 1 W.L.R. 757. Note that conversion into sterling under r. 6.111(1) is not required at the stage when a statutory demand is presented: see the ruling of Morritt J. in *Re a Debtor (51/SD/1991)* [1992] 1 W.L.R. 1294. Rule 6.111(2) was modified by I(A)R 2003 (SI 2003/1730) with effect from April 1, 2004.

6.112 Payments of a periodical nature

6.112(1) [Rent etc.] In the case of rent and other payments of a periodical nature, the creditor may prove for any amounts due and unpaid up to the date of the bankruptcy order.

6.112(2) [If accruing from day to day] Where at that date any payment was accruing due, the creditor may prove for so much as would have fallen due at that date, if accruing from day to day.

6.113 Interest

6.113(1) [Where claim may include interest] In the following circumstances the creditor's claim may include interest on the debt for periods before the bankruptcy order, although not previously reserved or agreed.

6.113(2) [Debt due by written instrument] If the debt is due by virtue of a written instrument and payable at a certain time, interest may be claimed for the period from that time to the date of the bankruptcy order.

6.113(3) [Debt due otherwise] If the debt is due otherwise, interest may only be claimed if, before the presentation of the bankruptcy petition, a demand for payment was made in writing by or on behalf of the creditor, and notice given that interest would be payable from the date of the demand to the date of payment and for all the purposes of the Act and the Rules shall be chargeable at a rate not exceeding that mentioned in paragraph (5).

6.113(4) [Period of claim] Interest under paragraph (3) may only be claimed for the period from the date of the demand to that of the bankruptcy order.

6.113(5) [Rate of interest] The rate of interest to be claimed under paragraphs (2) and (3) is the rate specified in section 17 of the Judgments Act 1838 on the date of the bankruptcy order.

GENERAL NOTE

For further guidance on claims in respect of interest, see IA 1986, s. 328(4), (5).

Rule 6.113(4) and (5) substituted for the former second paragraph of r. 6.113(3) and the former r. 6.113(4) by the Insolvency (Amendment) Rules 1987 (SI 1987/1919), r. 3(1), Sch., Pt 1, para. 112(2) as from January 11, 1988. See also r. 4.93.

6.114 Debt payable at future time

6.114 A creditor may prove for a debt of which payment was not yet due at the date of the bankruptcy order, but subject to Rule 11.13 in Part 11 of the Rules (adjustment of dividend where payment made before time).

CHAPTER 9

SECURED CREDITORS

6.115 Value of security

6.115(1) [Altering value] A secured creditor may, with the agreement of the trustee or the leave of the court, at any time alter the value which he has, in his proof of debt, put upon his security.

6.115(2) **[Limitation on re-valuation]** However, if a secured creditor–

(a) being the petitioner, has in the petition put a value on his security, or

(b) has voted in respect of the unsecured balance of his debt,

he may re-value his security only with leave of the court.

(See General Note after r. 6.119.)

6.116 Surrender for non-disclosure

6.116(1) **[Omission to disclose security]** If a secured creditor omits to disclose his security in his proof of debt, he shall surrender his security for the general benefit of creditors, unless the court, on application by him, relieves him from the effect of this Rule on the ground that the omission was inadvertent or the result of honest mistake.

6.116(2) **[Relief from effect of r. 6.116(1)]** If the court grants that relief, it may require or allow the creditor's proof of debt to be amended, on such terms as may be just.

6.116(3) **[Third parties' rights *in rem*]** Nothing in this Rule or the following two Rules may affect the rights in rem of creditors or third parties protected under Article 5 of the EC Regulation (third parties' rights in rem).

(See General Note after r. 6.119.)

IR 6.116(3) was inserted by the Insolvency (Amendment) Rules 2002 (SI 2002/1307) with effect from May 31, 2002 to cater for the advent of the EC Regulation 1346/2000 on insolvency proceedings.

6.117 Redemption by trustee

6.117(1) **[Notice of proposed redemption]** The trustee may at any time give notice to a creditor whose debt is secured that he proposes, at the expiration of 28 days from the date of the notice, to redeem the security at the value put upon it in the creditor's proof.

6.117(2) **[Time for re-valuation]** The creditor then has 21 days (or such longer period as the trustee may allow) in which, if he so wishes, to exercise his right to re-value his security (with the leave of the court, where Rule 6.115(2) applies).

If the creditor re-values his security, the trustee may only redeem at the new value.

6.117(3) **[If trustee redeems]** If the trustee redeems the security, the cost of transferring it is borne by the estate.

6.117(4) **[Notice to trustee to elect etc.]** A secured creditor may at any time, by a notice in writing, call on the trustee to elect whether he will or will not exercise his power to redeem the security at the value then placed on it; and the trustee then has 6 months in which to exercise the power or determine not to exercise it.

(See General Note after r. 6.119.)

6.118 Test of security's value

6.118(1) **[Offer for sale]** Subject as follows, the trustee, if he is dissatisfied with the value which a secured creditor puts on his security (whether in his proof or by way of re-valuation under Rule 6.117), may require any property comprised in the security to be offered for sale.

6.118(2) **[Terms of sale]** The terms of sale shall be such as may be agreed, or as the court may direct; and if the sale is by auction, the trustee on behalf of the estate, and the creditor on his own behalf, may appear and bid.

6.118(3) **[Non-application of Rule]** This Rule does not apply if the security has been re-valued and the re-valuation has been approved by the court.

(See General Note after r. 6.119.)

6.119 Realisation of security by creditor

6.119 If a creditor who has valued his security subsequently realises it (whether or not at the instance of the trustee)–

(a) the net amount realised shall be substituted for the value previously put by the creditor on the security, and

(b) that amount shall be treated in all respects as an amended valuation made by him.

GENERAL NOTE TO RR. 6.115–6.119

These rules relate to secured creditors. Revaluation of security is permitted, subject to certain restrictions. Non-disclosure of security can lead to it being forfeited. Security may be redeemed by the trustee. If the secured creditor realises his security, the original valuation is replaced by the amount of the net proceeds of realisation.

CHAPTER 10

THE TRUSTEE IN BANKRUPTCY

Section A: Appointment and associated formalities

6.120 Appointment by creditors' meeting

6.120(1) [Application of Rule] This Rule applies where a person has been appointed trustee by resolution of a creditors' meeting.

6.120(2) [Certification of appointment] The chairman of the meeting shall certify the appointment, but not unless and until the person to be appointed has provided him with a written statement to the effect that he is an insolvency practitioner, duly qualified under the Act to act as trustee in relation to the bankrupt, and that he consents so to act.

[FORM 6.40]
or [FORM 6.41]

6.120(3) [Date when appointment effective] The trustee's appointment is effective from the date on which the appointment is certified, that date to be endorsed on the certificate.

6.120(4) [Certificate to official receiver] The chairman of the meeting (if not himself the official receiver) shall send the certificate to the official receiver.

6.120(5) [Certificate to trustee, copy to be filed] The official receiver shall in any case send the certificate to the trustee and file a copy of it in court.

GENERAL NOTE

This supplements IA 1986, s. 293.
Rules 6.120(3)–(5) were substituted to facilitate handovers to insolvency practitioners.

6.121 Appointment by the court

6.121(1) [Application of Rule] This Rule applies where the court under section 297 (4) or (5) appoints the trustee.

[FORM 6.42]
or [FORM 6.43]

6.121(2) **[Issue of court order]** The court's order shall not issue unless and until the person appointed has filed in court a statement to the effect that he is an insolvency practitioner, duly qualified under the Act to be the trustee, and that he consents so to act.

6.121(3) **[Copies of orders to official receiver etc.]** Thereafter, the court shall send 2 copies of the order to the official receiver. One of the copies shall be sealed, and this shall be sent by him to the person appointed as trustee.

6.121(4) **[Commencement of appointment]** The trustee's appointment takes effect from the date of the order.

GENERAL NOTE

This rule should be viewed in the light of IA 1986, s. 297(3), (4), (5). If the court appoints a trustee under these provisions, Forms 6.42 and 6.43 are to be adopted. Rule 6.121(1) was amended by I(A)R 2003 (SI 2003/1730) with effect from April 1, 2004.

6.122 Appointment by Secretary of State

6.122(1) **[Application of Rule]** This Rule applies where the official receiver–

(a) under section 295 or 300, refers to the Secretary of State the need for an appointment of a trustee, or

(b) under section 296, applies to the Secretary of State to make the appointment.

6.122(2) **[Copies of certificate to official receiver etc.]** If the Secretary of State makes an appointment he shall send two copies of the certificate of appointment to the official receiver, who shall transmit one such copy to the person appointed, and file the other copy in court.

The certificate shall specify the date which the trustee's appointment is to be effective.

GENERAL NOTE

This rule clarifies the provisions of IA 1986, ss. 295, 296 and 300.

6.123 Authentication of trustee's appointment

6.123 Where a trustee is appointed under any of the 3 preceding Rules, a sealed copy of the order of appointment or (as the case may be) a copy of the certificate of his appointment may in any proceedings be adduced as proof that he is duly authorised to exercise the powers and perform the duties of trustee of the bankrupt's estate.

GENERAL NOTE

This relates to rr. 6.120–6.122 by providing for the authentication of the trustee's appointment.

6.124 Advertisement of appointment

6.124(1) **[Where trustee appointed by meeting]** Where the trustee is appointed by a creditors' meeting, he shall, forthwith after receiving his certificate of appointment, give notice of his appointment in such newspaper as he thinks most appropriate for ensuring that it comes to the notice of the bankrupt's creditors.

6.124(2) **[Expense of giving notice]** The expense of giving the notice shall be borne in the first instance by the trustee; but he is entitled to be reimbursed by the estate, as an expense of the bankruptcy.

The same applies also in the case of the notice or advertisement under section 296(4) (appointment of trustee by Secretary of State), and of the notice or advertisement under section 297(7) (appointment by the court).

General Note

The onus is on the trustee to ensure that his appointment is advertised in the newspapers.

6.125 Hand-over of estate to trustee

6.125(1) [Application of Rule] This Rule applies only where–

(a) the bankrupt's estate vests in the trustee under Chapter IV of Part IX of the Act, following a period in which the official receiver is the receiver and manager of the estate according to section 287, or

(b) the trustee is appointed in succession to the official receiver acting as trustee.

6.125(2) [On trustee's appointment] When the trustee's appointment takes effect, the official receiver shall forthwith do all that is required for putting him into possession of the estate.

6.125(3) [Discharge of balance due to official receiver] On taking possession of the estate, the trustee shall discharge any balance due to the official receiver on account of–

(a) expenses properly incurred by him and payable under the Act or the Rules, and

(b) any advances made by him in respect of the estate, together with interest on such advances at the rate specified in section 17 of the Judgments Act 1838 on the date of the bankruptcy order.

6.125(4) [Undertaking to discharge] Alternatively, the trustee may (before taking office) give to the official receiver a written undertaking to discharge any such balance out of the first realisation of assets.

6.125(5) [Official receiver's charge] The official receiver has a charge on the estate in respect of any sums due to him under paragraph (3). But, where the trustee has realised assets with a view to making those payments, the official receiver's charge does not extend in respect of sums deductible by the trustee from the proceeds of realisation, as being expenses properly incurred therein.

6.125(6) [Discharge of guarantees etc.] The trustee shall from time to time out of the realisation of assets discharge all guarantees properly given by the official receiver for the benefit of the estate, and shall pay all the official receiver's expenses.

6.125(7) [Official receiver to give trustee information] The official receiver shall give to the trustee all such information, relating to the affairs of the bankrupt and the course of the bankruptcy, as he (the official receiver) considers to be reasonably required for the effective discharge by the trustee of his duties in relation to the estate.

6.125(8) [Ch. 6 report] The trustee shall also be furnished with any report of the official receiver under Chapter 6 of this Part of the Rules.

General Note

See IA 1986, ss. 287 and 306 for the relevant statutory provisions here.

Section B: Resignation and removal; vacation of office

6.126 Creditors' meeting to receive trustee's resignation

6.126(1) [Trustee must call meeting etc.] Before resigning his office, the trustee must call a meeting of creditors for the purpose of receiving his resignation. Notice of the meeting shall be sent to the official receiver at the same time as it is sent to creditors.

6.126(2) [Account of trustee's administration] The notice to creditors must be accompanied by an account of the trustee's administration of the bankrupt's estate, including–

(a) a summary of his receipts and payments and

(b) a statement by him that he has reconciled his accounts with that which is held by the Secretary of State in respect of the bankruptcy.

6.126(3) [Grounds for proceedings under Rule] Subject as follows, the trustee may only proceed under this Rule on grounds of ill health or because–

(a) he intends ceasing to be in practice as an insolvency practitioner, or

(b) there is some conflict of interest or change of personal circumstances which precludes or makes impracticable the further discharge by him of the duties of trustee.

6.126(4) [Where joint trustees] Where two or more persons are acting as trustee jointly, any one of them may proceed under this Rule (without prejudice to the continuation in office of the other or others) on the ground that, in his opinion and that of the other or others, it is no longer expedient that there should continue to be the present number of joint trustees.

6.126(5) [If no quorum] If there is no quorum present at the meeting summoned to receive the trustee's resignation, the meeting is deemed to have been held, a resolution is deemed to have been passed that the trustee's resignation be accepted and the creditors are deemed not to have resolved against the trustee having his release.

6.126(6) [Application of r. 6.126(5)] Where paragraph (5) applies any reference in the Rules to a resolution that the trustee's resignation be accepted is replaced by a reference to the making of a written statement, signed by the person who, had there been a quorum present, would have been chairman of the meeting, that no quorum was present and that the trustee may resign.

GENERAL NOTE

The relevant statutory provision here is IA 1986, s. 298(7). Note the restriction in r. 6.126(3) on the grounds for resignation. The concept of impracticability in r. 6.126(3) is to be construed narrowly – *Re Alt Landscapes Ltd* [1999] B.P.I.R. 459 where the court rejected *Re Sankey Furniture Ltd Ex parte Harding* [1995] 2 B.C.L.C. 594. For the facilitation of multiple resignations see *Re Equity Nominees Ltd* [2000] B.C.C. 84. Further explanation is provided by *HM Customs and Excise v Allen* [2003] B.P.I.R. 830. For procedure, see Appendix IV, para. 1.6.

6.127 Action following acceptance of resignation

6.127(1) [Notice of meeting to indicate purpose etc.] Where a meeting of creditors is summoned for the purpose of receiving the trustee's resignation, the notice summoning it shall indicate that this is the purpose, or one of the purposes, of the meeting; and the notice shall draw the attention of creditors to Rule 6.135 with respect to the trustee's release.

[FORM 6.35]

6.127(2) [Copy of notice to official receiver] A copy of the notice shall at the same time also be sent to the official receiver.

6.127(3) [Where chairman other than official receiver] Where the chairman of the meeting is other than the official receiver, and there is passed at the meeting any of the following resolutions–

(a) that the trustee's resignation be accepted,

(b) that a new trustee be appointed,

(c) that the resigning trustee be not given his release,

the chairman shall, within 3 days, send to the official receiver a copy of the resolution.

If it has been resolved to accept the trustee's resignation, the chairman shall send to the official receiver a certificate to that effect.

[FORM 6.44]

6.127(4) **[If creditors resolve to appoint new trustee]** If the creditors have resolved to appoint a new trustee, the certificate of his appointment shall also be sent to the official receiver within that time; and Rule 6.120 above shall be complied with in respect of it.

6.127(5) **[If trustee's resignation accepted]** If the trustee's resignation is accepted, the notice of it required by section 298(7) shall be given by him forthwith after the meeting; and he shall send a copy of the notice to the official receiver.

The notice shall be accompanied by a copy of the account sent to creditors under Rule 6.126(2).

6.127(6) **[Copy of notice]** The official receiver shall file a copy of the notice in court.

6.127(7) **[Effective date of resignation]** The trustee's resignation is effective as from the date on which the official receiver files the copy notice in court, that date to be endorsed on the copy notice.

GENERAL NOTE

Form 6.44 is to be used by the chairman of the creditors' committee to notify the official receiver of the resignation. The trustee must also notify the court.

6.128 Leave to resign granted by the court

6.128(1) **[If creditors resolve not to accept resignation]** If at a creditors' meeting summoned to accept the trustee's resignation it is resolved that it be not accepted, the court may, on the trustee's application, make an order giving him leave to resign.

[FORM 6.45]

6.128(2) **[Extent of order under r. 6.128(1)]** The court's order under this Rule may include such provision as it thinks fit with respect to matters arising in connection with the resignation, and shall determine the date from which the trustee's release is effective.

6.128(3) **[Sealed copies of order]** The court shall send two sealed copies of the order to the trustee, who shall send one of the copies forthwith to the official receiver.

6.128(4) **[Copy notice to court and official receiver]** On sending notice of his resignation to the court, as required by section 298(7), the trustee shall send a copy of it to the official receiver.

[FORM 6.46]

GENERAL NOTE

This allows the court to accept a trustee's resignation notwithstanding opposition from the creditors.

6.129 Meeting of creditors to remove trustee

6.129(1) **[Notice]** Where a meeting of creditors is summoned for the purpose of removing the trustee, the notice summoning it shall indicate that this is the purpose, or one of the purposes, of the meeting; and the notice shall draw the attention of creditors to section 299(3) with respect to the trustee's release.

[FORM 6.35]

6.129(2) **[Copy of notice to official receiver]** A copy of the notice shall at the same time also be sent to the official receiver.

6.129(3) **[Chairman, if trustee chairman etc.]** At the meeting, a person other than the trustee or his nominee may be elected to act as chairman; but if the trustee or his nominee is chairman and a resolution has been proposed for the trustee's removal, the chairman shall not adjourn the meeting without the consent of at least one-half (in value) of the creditors present (in person or by proxy) and entitled to vote.

6.129(4) **[Where chairman other than official receiver]** Where the chairman of the meeting is other than the official receiver, and there is passed at the meeting any of the following resolutions–

(a) that the trustee be removed,

(b) that a new trustee be appointed,

(c) that the removed trustee be not given his release,

the chairman shall, within 3 days, send to the official receiver a copy of the resolution.

If it has been resolved to remove the trustee, the chairman shall send to the official receiver a certificate to that effect.

[FORM 6.47]

6.129(5) **[If creditors resolve to appoint new trustee]** If the creditors have resolved to appoint a new trustee, the certificate of his appointment shall also be sent to the official receiver within that time; and Rule 6.120 shall be complied with in respect of it.

GENERAL NOTE

This develops IA 1986, s. 298(1).

6.130 Court's power to regulate meeting under Rule 6.129

6.130 Where a meeting under Rule 6.129 is to be held, or is proposed to be summoned, the court may on the application of any creditor give directions as to the mode of summoning it, the sending out and return of forms of proxy, the conduct of the meeting, and any other matter which appears to the court to require regulation or control.

6.131 Procedure on removal

6.131(1) **[Certificate of removal to be filed]** Where the creditors have resolved that the trustee be removed, the official receiver shall file the certificate of removal in court.

6.131(2) **[Effective date]** The resolution is effective as from the date on which the official receiver files the certificate of removal in court, and that date shall be endorsed on the certificate.

6.131(3) **[Copy of certificate]** A copy of the certificate, so endorsed, shall be sent by the official receiver to the trustee who has been removed and, if a new trustee has been appointed, to him.

6.131(4) **[Reconciliation of accounts]** The official receiver shall not file the certificate in court until the Secretary of State has certified to him that the removed trustee has reconciled his account with that held by the Secretary of State in respect of the bankruptcy.

GENERAL NOTE

The court enjoys power to remove trustees under IA 1986, s. 298(1). For the meaning of "venue" in r. 6.132(2) and (3), see r. 13.6

6.132 Removal of trustee by the court

6.132(1) **[Application of Rule]** This Rule applies where application is made to the court for the removal of the trustee, or for an order directing the trustee to summon a meeting of creditors for the purpose of removing him.

[FORM 6.48]

6.132(2) **[Court may dismiss application etc.]** The court may, if it thinks that no sufficient cause is shown for the application, dismiss it; but it shall not do so unless the applicant has had an opportunity to attend the court for an *ex parte* hearing, of which he has been given at least 7 days' notice.

If the application is not dismissed under this paragraph, the court shall fix a venue for it to be heard.

6.132(3) **[Notice etc.]** The applicant shall, at least 14 days before the hearing, send to the trustee and the official receiver notice stating the venue so fixed; and the notice shall be accompanied by a copy of the application, and of any evidence which the applicant intends to adduce in support of it.

6.132(4) **[Costs]** Subject to any contrary order of the court, the costs of the application do not fall on the estate.

6.132(5) **[Where court removes trustee]** Where the court removes the trustee–

(a) it shall send copies of the order of removal to him and to the official receiver;

(b) the order may include such provision as the court thinks fit with respect to matters arising in connection with the removal; and

(c) if the court appoints a new trustee, Rule 6.121 applies.

GENERAL NOTE

The court enjoys power to remove trustees under IA 1986, s. 298(1). For the meaning of "venue" in r. 6.132(2) and (3), see r. 13.6.

6.133 Removal of trustee by Secretary of State

6.133(1) **[Notice to trustee etc.]** If the Secretary of State decides to remove the trustee, he shall before doing so notify the trustee and the official receiver of his decision and the grounds of it, and specify a period within which the trustee may make representations against implementation of the decision.

6.133(2) **[On removal]** If the Secretary of State directs the removal of the trustee, he shall forthwith–

(a) file notice of his decision in court, and

(b) send notice to the trustee and the official receiver.

6.133(3) **[If trustee removed]** If the trustee is removed by direction of the Secretary of State, the court may make any such order in his case as it would have power to make if he had been removed by itself.

GENERAL NOTE

See IA 1986, s. 298(5).

6.134 Advertisement of resignation or removal

6.134 Where a new trustee is appointed in place of one who has resigned or been removed, the new trustee shall, in the advertisement of his appointment, state that his predecessor has resigned or, as the case may be, been removed and (if it be the case) that he has been given his release.

6.135 Release of resigning or removed trustee

6.135(1) **[Where trustee's resignation accepted]** Where the trustee's resignation is accepted by a meeting of creditors which has not resolved against his release, he has his release from when his resignation is effective under Rule 6.127.

6.135(2) **[Where trustee removed by meeting]** Where the trustee is removed by a meeting of creditors which has not resolved against his release, the fact of his release shall be stated in the certificate of removal.

6.135(3) **[Application to Secretary of State]** Where–

(a) the trustee resigns, and the creditor's meeting called to receive his resignation has resolved against his release, or

(b) he is removed by a creditors' meeting which has so resolved, or is removed by the court, he must apply to the Secretary of State for his release.

[FORM 6.49]

6.135(4) **[Certificate of release]** When the Secretary of State gives the release, he shall certify it accordingly, and send the certificate to the official receiver, to be filed in court.

6.135(5) **[Copy of certificate]** A copy of the certificate shall be sent by the Secretary of State to the former trustee, whose release is effective from the date of the certificate.

(See General Note after r. 6.136.)

Section C: Release on completion of administration

6.136 Release of official receiver

6.136(1) **[Notice of intention]** The official receiver shall, before giving notice to the Secretary of State under section 299(2) (that the administration of the estate is for practical purposes complete), send out notice of his intention to do so to all creditors of which he is aware, and to the bankrupt.

6.136(2) **[Accompanying summary]** The notice shall in each case be accompanied by a summary of the official receiver's receipts and payments as trustee.

6.136(3) **[Notice to court of date of release]** The Secretary of State, when he has under section 299(2) determined the date from which the official receiver is to have his release, shall give notice to the court that he has done so. The notice shall be accompanied by the summary referred to in paragraph (2).

GENERAL NOTE

These supplement IA 1986, s. 299 (release of trustees). The former reference to creditors proving for their debts has been dropped in favour of a modern terminology. See I(A)R 2004 (SI 2004/584) with effect from April 1, 2004.

6.137 Final meeting of creditors

6.137(1) **[Notice to creditors etc.]** Where the trustee is other than the official receiver, he shall give at least 28 days' notice of the final meeting of creditors to be held under section 331. The notice shall be sent to all creditors of which he is aware, and to the bankrupt.

[FORM 6.35]

6.137(2) **[Trustee's report]** The trustee's report laid before the meeting under that section shall include–

(a) a summary of his receipts and payments, and

(b) a statement by him that he has reconciled his account with that which is held by the Secretary of State in respect of the bankruptcy.

6.137(3) **[Questioning of trustee]** At the final meeting, the creditors may question the trustee with respect to any matter contained in his report, and may resolve against him having his release.

6.137(4) **[Notice to court]** The trustee shall give notice to the court that the final meeting has been held; and the notice shall state whether or not he has given his release, and be accompanied by a copy of the report laid before the final meeting. A copy of the notice shall be sent by the trustee to the official receiver.

[FORM 6.50]

6.137(5) **[No quorum at final meeting]** If there is no quorum present at the final meeting, the trustee shall report to the court that a final meeting was summoned in accordance with the Rules, but there was no quorum present; and the final meeting is then deemed to have been held, and the creditors not to have resolved against the trustee having his release.

6.137(6) **[Release of trustee]** If the creditors at the final meeting have not so resolved, the trustee is released when the notice under paragraph (4) is filed in court. If they have so resolved, the trustee must obtain his release from the Secretary of State, as provided by Rule 6.135.

GENERAL NOTE

See IA 1986, s. 331. 28 days' notice of the final meeting must be given. The change made by I(A)R 2004 (SI 2004/584) (effective from April 1, 2004) is along the same lines as that made for IR 6.136.

6.137A Rule as to reporting

6.137A(1) **[Power of court]** The court may, on the trustee or official receiver's application, relieve him of any duty imposed on him by Rules 6.136 or 6.137, or authorise him to carry out the duty in a way other than there required.

6.137A(2) **[Considerations in exercising power]** In considering whether to act as above, the court shall have regard to the cost of carrying out the duty, to the amount of the funds available in the estate, and to the extent of the interest of creditors or any particular class of them.

GENERAL NOTE

This new rule was added by I(A)R 2004 (SI 2004/584) with effect from April 1, 2004. It shows an awareness of the need for cost efficiencies by removing the automatic requirement to send out certain notices.

Section D: Remuneration

6.138 Fixing of remuneration

6.138(1) **[Entitlement to remuneration]** The trustee is entitled to receive remuneration for his services as such.

6.138(2) **[How fixed]** The remuneration shall be fixed either–

(a) as a percentage of the value of the assets in the bankrupt's estate which are realised or distributed, or of the one value and the other in combination, or

(b) by reference to the time properly given by the insolvency practitioner (as trustee) and his staff in attending to matters arising in the bankruptcy.

6.138(3) **[Determination under r. 6.138(2)]** Where the trustee is other than the official receiver, it is for the creditors' committee (if there is one) to determine whether his remuneration is to be fixed under paragraph (2)(a) or (b) and, if under paragraph (2)(a), to determine any percentage to be applied as there mentioned.

6.138(4) **[Matters relevant to r. 6.138(3) determination]** In arriving at that determination, the committee shall have regard to the following matters–

(a) the complexity (or otherwise) of the case,

(b) any respects in which, in connection with the administration of the estate, there falls on the insolvency practitioner (as trustee) any responsibility of an exceptional kind or degree,

(c) the effectiveness with which the insolvency practitioner appears to be carrying out, or to have carried out, his duties as trustee, and

(d) the value and nature of the assets in the estate with which the trustee has to deal.

6.138(5) **[If no committee or no determination]** If there is no creditors' committee, or the committee does not make the requisite determination, the trustee's remuneration may be fixed (in accordance with paragraph (2)) by a resolution of a meeting of creditors; and paragraph (4) applies to them as it does to the creditors' committee.

6.138(6) **[Otherwise fixed where not the official receiver]** Where the trustee is not the official receiver and his remuneration is not fixed as above, the trustee shall be entitled to remuneration calculated in accordance with Rule 6.138A.

GENERAL NOTE

The IA 1986 is silent on the question of the trustee's remuneration. This provision lays down the general rules for determining the rate of remuneration by the creditors' committee. For the meaning of "general regulations" in r. 6.138 (6), see r. 13.13(5). In a case decided under the 1914 Act the court decided that the use of the official receiver's scale was not suitable to be applied to value the work of a private practitioner – *Upton v Taylor and Colley* [1999] B.P.I.R. 168. For comment on assessment of a trustee's remuneration see *Mirror Group Newspapers v Maxwell* [1998] B.C.C. 324 at p. 336 *per* Ferris J. On taxation the claim for fees and disbursements was largely upheld – see the note in [1999] B.C.C. 684 (a rare instance of a determination on a matter of taxation of costs being reported). Matters in this area were reviewed by the Ferris Working Party in 1998 and a revised SIP 9 was published in December 2002. Paragraph (6) was remodelled by I(A)R 2004 (SI 2004/584) with effect from April 1, 2004. It anticipates the introduction of IR 6.138A.

6.138A Trustee's remuneration where it is not fixed in accordance with Rule 6.138

6.138A(1) **[Application of rule]** This Rule applies where the trustee is not the official receiver and his remuneration is not fixed in accordance with Rule 6.

6.138A(2) **[How fixed]** Subject to paragraph (3), the trustee shall be entitled by way of remuneration for his services as such, to such sum as is arrived at by –

(a) first applying the realisation scale set out in Schedule 6 to the monies received by him from the realisation of the assets of the bankrupt (including any Value Added Tax thereon but after deducting any sums paid to secured creditors in respect of their securities and any sums spent out of money received in carrying on the business of the bankrupt); and

(b) then by adding to the sum arrived at under sub-paragraph (a) such sum as is arrived at by applying the distribution scale set out in Schedule 6 to the value of assets distributed to creditors of the bankrupt (including sums paid in respect of preferential debts).

6.138A(3) **[Not to exceed bankruptcy debts and expenses]** That part of the trustee's remuneration calculated by reference to the realisation scale shall not exceed such sum as is arrived at by applying the realisation scale to such part of the bankrupt's assets as are required to pay the items referred to in paragraph (4).

6.138A(4) **[Bankruptcy debts and expenses]** The items referred to in paragraph (3) are –

(a) the bankruptcy debts (including any interest payable by virtue of section 328(4)) to the extent required to be paid by these Rules (ignoring those debts paid otherwise than out of the proceeds of the realisation of the bankrupt's assets or which have been secured to the satisfaction of the court);

(b) the expenses of the bankruptcy other than–

  (i) fees or the remuneration of the official receiver; and

  (ii) any sums spent out of money received in carrying on the business of the bankrupt;

(c) fees payable by virtue of any order made under section 415; and

(d) the remuneration of the official receiver.

GENERAL NOTE

This new rule was added by I(A)R 2004 (SI 2004/584) with effect from April 1, 2004. It deals with the fixing of remuneration in circumstances not covered by IR 6.138. Note the use of the realisation scale mapped out in the new Schedule 6.

6.139 Other matters affecting remuneration

6.139(1) [**Where trustee sells for secured creditor**] Where the trustee (not being the official receiver) realises assets on behalf of a secured creditor, the trustee is entitled to such sum by way of remuneration as is arrived at by applying the realisation scale set out in Schedule 6 to the monies received by him in respect of the assets realised (including any Value Added Tax thereon).

6.139(2) [**Where joint trustees**] Where there are joint trustees, it is for them to agree between themselves as to how the remuneration payable should be apportioned. Any dispute arising between them may be referred–

(a) to the court, for settlement by order, or

(b) to the creditors' committee or a meeting of creditors, for settlement by resolution.

6.139(3) [**If trustee is a solicitor**] If the trustee is a solicitor and employs his own firm, or any partner in it, to act on behalf of the estate, profit costs shall not be paid unless this is authorised by the creditors' committee, the creditors or the court.

Rule 6.139(1)
This relates to remuneration where the trustee is really acting for the benefit of a secured creditor.

GENERAL NOTE

A new paragraph (1) was substituted by I(A)R 2004 (SI 2004/584) with effect from April 1, 2004. This extends the use of the new Schedule 6 realisation scale to circumstances where the realisation is carried out on behalf of a secured creditor.

6.140 Recourse of trustee to meeting of creditors

6.140 If the trustee's remuneration has been fixed by the creditors' committee, and he considers the rate or amount to be insufficient, he may request that it be increased by resolution of the creditors.

GENERAL NOTE

The creditors can override any decision of their committee on remuneration.

6.141 Recourse to the court

6.141(1) [**Trustee may apply to court**] If the trustee considers that the remuneration fixed for him by the creditors' committee, or by resolution of the creditors, or as under Rule 6.138(6), is insufficient, he may apply to the court for an order increasing its amount or rate.

6.141(2) [**Notice to committee etc.**] The trustee shall give at least 14 days' notice of his application to the members of the creditors' committee; and the committee may nominate one or more members to appear or be represented, and to be heard, on the application.

6.141(3) [**If no committee**] If there is no creditors' committee, the trustee's notice of his application shall be sent to such one or more of the bankrupt's creditors as the court may direct, which creditors may nominate one or more of their number to appear or be represented.

6.141(4) [**Costs of application**] The court may, if it appears to be a proper case, order the costs of the trustee's application, including the costs of any member of the creditors' committee appearing or being represented on it, or any creditor so appearing or being represented, to be paid out of the estate.

(See General Note after r. 6.142.)

6.142 Creditor's claim that remuneration is excessive

6.142(1) [**Creditor may apply to court**] Any creditor of the bankrupt may, with the concurrence of at least 25 per cent. in value of the creditors (including himself), apply to the court for an order that the trustee's remuneration be reduced, on the grounds that it is, in all the circumstances, excessive.

6.142(2) **[Court may dismiss application etc.]** The court may, if it thinks that no sufficient cause is shown for the application, dismiss it; but it shall not do so unless the applicant has had an opportunity to attend the court for an *ex parte* hearing, of which he has been given at least 7 days' notice.

If the application is not dismissed under this paragraph, the court shall fix a venue for it to be heard.

6.142(3) **[Notice to trustee]** The applicant shall, at least 14 days before the hearing, send to the trustee a notice stating the venue so fixed; and the notice shall be accompanied by a copy of the application, and of any evidence which the applicant intends to adduce in support of it.

6.142(4) **[Court order]** If the court considers the application to be well-founded, it shall make an order fixing the remuneration at a reduced amount or rate.

6.142(5) **[Costs of application]** Unless the court orders otherwise, the costs of the application shall be paid by the applicant, and do not fall on the estate.

GENERAL NOTE TO RR. 6.141, 6.142

The court will always have the final say on issues of remuneration. If a creditor wishes to challenge the trustee's remuneration he must have the support of 25 per cent in value of the creditors.

Section E: Supplementary provisions

6.143 Trustee deceased

6.143(1) **[Notice to official receiver]** Subject as follows, where the trustee (other than the official receiver) has died, it is the duty of his personal representatives to give notice of the fact to the official receiver, specifying the date of the death.

This does not apply if notice has been given under any of the following paragraphs of this Rule.

6.143(2) **[Notice by partner etc.]** If the deceased trustee was a partner in a firm, which may be given to the official receiver by a partner in the firm who is qualified to act as an insolvency practitioner, or is a member of any body recognised by the Secretary of State for the authorisation of insolvency practitioners.

6.143(3) **[Notice by others]** Notice of the death may be giver by any person producing to the official receiver the relevant death certificate or a copy of it.

6.143(4) **[Notice to court by official receiver]** The official receiver shall give notice to the court, for the purpose of fixing the date of the deceased trustee's release in accordance with section 299(3)(a).

6.144 Loss of qualification as insolvency practitioner

6.144(1) **[Application of Rule]** This Rule applies where the trustee vacates office, under section 298(6), on his ceasing to be qualified to act as an insolvency practitioner in relation to the bankrupt.

6.144(2) **[Notice to official receiver etc.]** The trustee vacating office shall forthwith give notice of his doing so to the official receiver, who shall give notice to the Secretary of State.

The official receiver shall file in court a copy of his notice under this paragraph.

[FORM 6.51]

6.144(3) **[Application of r. 6.135]** Rule 6.135 applies as regards the trustee obtaining his release, as if he had been removed by the court.

GENERAL NOTE

This expands IA 1986, s. 298(6). On qualification, see IA 1986, Pt XIII.

6.145 Notice to official receiver of intention to vacate office

6.145(1) [**Notice of official receiver**] Where the trustee intends to vacate office, whether by resignation or otherwise, he shall give notice of his intention to the official receiver together with notice of any creditors' meeting to be held in respect of his vacation of office, including any meeting to receive his resignation.

6.145(2) [**Time limit for notice**] The notice to the official receiver must be given at least 21 days before any such creditors' meeting.

6.145(3) [**Details of property**] Where there remains in the bankrupt's estate any property which has not been realised, applied, distributed or otherwise fully dealt with in the bankruptcy, the trustee shall include in his notice to the official receiver details of the nature of that property, its value (or the fact that it has no value), its location, any action taken by the trustee to deal with that property or any reason for his not dealing with it, and the current position in relation to it.

GENERAL NOTE

Rule 6.145(3) makes it clear that valueless property must now be detailed in the report to the official receiver. The word "assets" used in the previous version of r. 6.145 has now been dropped to clarify matters.

6.146 Trustee's duties on vacating office

6.146(1) [**Obligation to deliver any assets etc.**] Where the trustee ceases to be in office as such, in consequence of removal, resignation or cesser of qualification as an insolvency practitioner, he is under obligation forthwith to deliver up to the person succeeding him as trustee the assets of the estate (after deduction of any expenses properly incurred, and distributions made, by him) and further to deliver up to that person–

(a) the records of the bankruptcy, including correspondence, proofs and other related papers appertaining to the bankruptcy while it was within his responsibility, and

(b) the bankrupt's books, papers and other records.

6.146(2) [**Omitted.**]

GENERAL NOTE

This ties up matters left unresolved by IA 1986, s. 298. Paragraph (2) was omitted by I(A)R 2004 (SI 2004/584) with effect from April 1, 2004. Again this appears to be a new cost cutting device.

6.147 Power of court to set aside certain transactions

6.147(1) [**Trustee's transaction with associate**] If in the administration of the estate the trustee enters into any transaction with a person who is an associate of his, the court may, on the application of any person interested, set the transaction aside and order the trustee to compensate the estate for any loss suffered in consequence of it.

6.147(2) [**Where r. 6.147(1) does not apply**] This does not apply if either–

(a) the transaction was entered into with the prior consent of the court, or

(b) it is shown to the court's satisfaction that the transaction was for value, and that it was entered into by the trustee without knowing, or having any reason to suppose, that the person concerned was an associate.

6.147(3) [**Effect of Rule**] Nothing in this Rule is to be taken as prejudicing the operation of any rule of law or equity with respect to a trustee's dealings with trust property, or the fiduciary obligations of any person.

GENERAL NOTE

This power is sufficiently important to have been located within the text of IA 1986. For "associate" see IA 1986, s. 435.

6.148 Rule against solicitation

6.148(1) [**Power of court**] Where the court is satisfied that any improper solicitation has been used by or on behalf of the trustee in obtaining proxies or procuring his appointment, it may order that no remuneration out of the estate be allowed to any person by whom, or on whose behalf, the solicitation was exercised.

6.148(2) [**Effect of court order**] An order of the court under this Rule overrides any resolution of the creditors' committee or the creditors, or any other provision of the Rules relating to the trustee's remuneration.

6.149 Enforcement of trustee's obligations to official receiver

6.149(1) [**Powers of court**] The court may, on the application of the official receiver, make such orders as it thinks necessary for enforcement of the duties of the trustee under section 305(3) (information and assistance to be given; production and inspection of books and records relating to the bankruptcy).

6.149(2) [**Extent of order**] An order of the court under this Rule may provide that all costs of and incidental to the official receiver's application shall be borne by the trustee.

GENERAL NOTE

See IA 1986, s. 305(3).

CHAPTER 11

THE CREDITORS' COMMITTEE

6.150 Membership of creditors' committee

6.150(1) [**Three-five members**] The creditors' committee shall consist of at least 3, and not more than 5, members.

6.150(2) [**Eligibility**] All the members of the committee must be creditors of the bankrupt; and any creditor (other than one who is fully secured) may be a member, so long as–

(a) he has lodged a proof of his debt, and

(b) his proof has neither been wholly disallowed for voting purposes, nor wholly rejected for the purposes of distribution or dividend.

6.150(3) [**Representation of body corporate**] A body corporate may be a member of the committee, but it cannot act as such otherwise than by a representative appointed under Rule 6.156.

GENERAL NOTE

This develops IA 1986, s. 301.

6.151 Formalities of establishment

6.151(1) [**Trustee's certificate of due constitution**] The creditors' committee does not come into being, and accordingly cannot act, until the trustee has issued a certificate of its due constitution.

[FORM 6.52]

6.151(2) [**If chairman of meeting not trustee**] If the chairman of the creditors' meeting which resolves to establish the committee is not the trustee, he shall forthwith give notice of the resolution to the trustee (or, as the case may be, the person appointed as trustee by that same meeting), and inform him of the names and addresses of the persons elected to be members of the committee.

6.151(3) [**Agreement to act**] No person may act as a member of the committee unless and until he has agreed to do so and, unless the relevant proxy contains a statement to the contrary, such agreement may be given by his proxy-holder present at the meeting establishing the committee.

6.151(3A) **[No certificate without agreement]** The trustee's certificate of the committee's due constitution shall not issue before at least 3 persons elected to be members of the committee have agreed to act.

6.151(4) **[Amended certificate]** As and when the others (if any) agree to act, the trustee shall issue an amended certificate.

[FORM 6.52]

6.151(5) **[Certificate to be filed]** The certificate, and any amended certificate, shall be filed in court by the trustee.

6.151(6) **[Change in membership]** If after the first establishment of the committee there is any change in its membership, the trustee shall report the change to the court.

[FORM 6.53]

GENERAL NOTE

This rule was amended to facilitate immediate committee meetings after the creditors' meeting. The original r. 6.151(3) has been broken down into (3) and (3A).

6.152 Obligations of trustee to committee

6.152(1) **[Trustee's duty to report]** Subject as follows, it is the duty of the trustee to report to the members of the creditors' committee all such matters as appear to him to be, or as they have indicated to him as being, of concern to them with respect to the bankruptcy.

6.152(2) **[Non-compliance with request for information]** In the case of matters so indicated to him by the committee, the trustee need not comply with any request for information where it appears to him that–

(a) the request is frivolous or unreasonable, or

(b) the cost of complying would be excessive, having regard to the relative importance of the information, or

(c) the estate is without funds sufficient for enabling him to comply.

6.152(3) **[Report in summary form]** Where the committee has come into being more than 28 days after the appointment of the trustee, the latter shall report to them, in summary form, what actions he has taken since his appointment, and shall answer such questions as they may put to him regarding his conduct of the bankruptcy hitherto.

6.152(4) **[Summary report for subsequent member]** A person who becomes a member of the committee at any time after its first establishment is not entitled to require a report to him by the trustee, otherwise than in summary form, of any matters previously arising.

6.152(5) **[Access to trustee's records]** Nothing in this Rule disentitles the committee, or any member of it, from having access to the trustee's records of the bankruptcy, or from seeking an explanation of any matter within the committee's responsibility.

GENERAL NOTE

This imposes a duty on the trustee to keep the committee informed (subject to r. 6.152(2)). Note also r. 6.163.

6.153 Meetings of the committee

6.153(1) **[Holding of meetings]** Subject as follows, meetings of the creditors' committee shall be held when and where determined by the trustee.

6.153(2) **[First and subsequent meetings]** The trustee shall call a first meeting of the committee to take place within 3 months of his appointment or of the committee's establishment (whichever is the later); and thereafter he shall call a meeting–

(a) if so requested by a member of the committee or his representative (the meeting then to be held within 21 days of the request being received by the trustee), and

(b) for a specified date, if the committee has previously resolved that a meeting be held on that date.

6.153(3) **[Notice of venue]** The trustee shall give 7 days' notice in writing of the venue of any meeting to every member of the committee (or his representative, if designated for that purpose), unless in any case the requirement of the notice has been waived by or on behalf of any member.

Waiver may be signified either at or before the meeting.

(See General Note after r. 6.156.)

6.154 The chairman at meetings

6.154(1) **[Trustee or his nominee]** The chairman at any meeting of the creditors committee shall be the trustee, or a person appointed by him in writing to act.

6.154(2) **[Nominated chairman]** A person so nominated must be either–

(a) one who is qualified to act as an insolvency practitioner in relation to the bankrupt, or

(b) an employee of the trustee or his firm who is experienced in insolvency matters.

(See General Note after r. 6.156.)

6.155 Quorum

6.155 A meeting of the committee is duly constituted if due notice of it has been given to all the members and at least 2 of the members are present or represented.

(See General Note after r. 6.156.)

6.156 Committee-members' representatives

6.156(1) **[Representation]** A member of the creditors' committee may, in relation to the business of the committee, be represented by another person duly authorised by him for that purpose.

6.156(2) **[Letter of authority]** A person acting as a committee-member's representative must hold a letter of authority entitling him so to act (either generally or specially) and signed by or on behalf of the committee-member, and for this purpose any proxy in relation to any meeting of creditors of the bankrupt shall, unless it contains a statement to the contrary, be treated as such a letter of authority to act generally signed by or on behalf of the committee-member.

6.156(3) **[Production of letter of authority]** The chairman at any meeting of the committee may call on a person claiming to act as a committee-member's representative to produce his letter of authority, and may exclude him if it appears that his authority is deficient.

6.156(4) **[Who may not be a representative]** No member may be represented by a body corporate, or by a person who is an undischarged bankrupt or a disqualified director or is subject to a bankruptcy restrictions order, bankruptcy restrictions undertaking or an interim bankruptcy restrictions order.

6.156(5) **[No dual representation]** No person shall–

(a) on the same committee, act at one and the same time as representative of more than one committee-member, or

(b) act both as a member of the committee and as representative of another member.

6.156(6) **[Signing as representative]** Where the representative of a committee-member signs any document on the latter's behalf, the fact that he so signs must be stated below his signature.

6.156(7) **[Validity of acts]** The acts of the committee are valid notwithstanding any defect in the appointment or qualifications of any committee-member's representative.

GENERAL NOTE TO RR. 6.153–6.156

These rules regulate meetings of the committee. Note that the quorum is fixed at two members. Committee members may appoint representatives to act on their behalf. The wording of paragraph (4) was modified by I(A)R 2004 (SI 2004/584) with effect from April 1, 2004 to include reference to disqualified directors and those subject to BROs, etc. The former reference to the exclusion of persons who had entered compositions with creditors was removed.

6.157 Resignation

6.157 A member of the creditors' committee may resign by notice in writing delivered to the trustee.

6.158 Termination of membership

6.158(1) **[Automatic termination]** A person's membership of the creditors committee is automatically terminated if–

(a) he becomes bankrupt, or

(b) at 3 consecutive meetings of the committee he is neither present nor represented (unless at the third of those meetings it is resolved that this Rule is not to apply in his case), or

(c) he ceases to be, or is found never to have been, a creditor.

6.158(2) **[Termination on bankruptcy]** However, if the cause of termination is the member's bankruptcy, his trustee in bankruptcy replaces him as a member of the committee.

GENERAL NOTE

Note the sanction against absenteeism. The former reference in paragraph (1)(a) to compositions or arrangements with creditors was removed by I(A)R 2004 (SI 2004/584) with effect from April 1, 2004.

6.159 Removal

6.159 A member of the creditors' committee may be removed by resolution at a meeting of creditors, at least 14 days' notice having been given of the intention to move that resolution.

6.160 Vacancies

6.160(1) **[Application of Rule]** The following applies if there is a vacancy in the membership of the creditors' committee.

6.160(2) **[Agreement not to fill vacancy]** The vacancy need not be filled if the trustee and a majority of the remaining committee-members so agree, provided that the number of members does not fall below the minimum required by Rule 6.150(1).

6.160(3) **[Appointment by trustee]** The trustee may appoint any creditor (being qualified under the Rules to be a member of the committee) to fill the vacancy, if a majority of the other members of the committee agree to the appointment and the creditor concerned consents to act.

6.160(4) **[Appointment by resolution]** Alternatively, a meeting of creditors may resolve that a creditor be appointed (with his consent) to fill the vacancy. In this case at least 14 days' notice must have been given of a resolution to make such an appointment (whether or not of a person named in the notice).

6.160(5) **[Report to trustee]** Where the vacancy is filled by an appointment made by a creditors' meeting at which the trustee is not present, the chairman of the meeting shall report to the trustee the appointment which has been made.

6.161 Voting rights and resolutions

6.161(1) **[Votes etc.]** At any meeting of the committee, each member (whether present himself, or by his representative) has one vote; and a resolution is passed when a majority of the members present or represented have voted in favour of it.

6.161(2) **[Record of resolutions]** Every resolution passed shall be recorded in writing, either separately or as part of the minutes of the meeting. The record shall be signed by the chairman and kept with the records of the bankruptcy.

GENERAL NOTE

Committee resolutions are to be passed by simple majority and there is to be no weighting of votes.

6.162 Resolutions by post

6.162(1) [**Sending proposed resolution**] In accordance with this Rule, the trustee may seek to obtain the agreement of members of the creditors' committee to a resolution by sending to every member (or his representative designated for the purpose) a copy of the proposed resolution.

6.162(2) [**Copy of proposed resolution**] Where the trustee makes use of the procedure allowed by this Rule, he shall send out to members of the committee or their representatives (as the case may be) a copy of any proposed resolution on which a decision is sought, which shall be set out in such a way that agreement with or dissent from each separate resolution may be indicated by the recipient on the copy so sent.

6.162(3) [**Member requiring meeting**] Any member of the committee may, within 7 business days from the date of the trustee sending out a resolution, require the trustee to summon a meeting of the committee to consider the matters raised by the resolution.

6.162(4) [**Deemed passing of resolution**] In the absence of such a request, the resolution is deemed to have been carried in the committee if and when the trustee is notified in writing by a majority of the members that they concur with it.

6.162(5) [**Copy resolutions**] A copy of every resolution passed under this Rule, and a note that the concurrence of the committee was obtained, shall be kept with the records of the bankruptcy.

GENERAL NOTE

This is to make life easy for committee members (and for the trustee).
The change to r. 6.162(2) is intended to prevent proliferation of documents. Rule 6.162(3) now refers to "business days" (for definition, see r. 13.13(1)).

6.163 Trustee's reports

6.163(1) [**Trustee directed to report**] The trustee shall, as and when directed by the creditors' committee (but not more often than once in any period of 2 months), send a written report to every member of the committee setting out the position generally as regards the progress of the bankruptcy and matters arising in connection with it, to which he (the trustee) considers the committee's attention should be drawn.

6.163(2) [**If no directions to report**] In the absence of any such directions by the committee, the trustee shall send such a report not less often than once in every period of 6 months.

6.163(3) [**Effect of Rule**] The obligations of the trustee under this Rule are without prejudice to those imposed by Rule 6.152.

GENERAL NOTE

The trustee can be required to submit two-monthly reports to the committee.

6.164 Expenses of members, etc.

6.164 The trustee shall defray out of the estate, in the prescribed order of priority, any reasonable travelling expenses directly incurred by members of the creditors' committee or their representatives in respect of their attendance at the committee's meetings, or otherwise on the committee's business.

6.165 Dealings by committee-members and others

6.165(1) [**Application of Rule**] This Rule applies to–

(a) any member of the creditors' committee,

(b) any committee-member's representative,

(c) any person who is an associate of a member of the committee or a committee-member's representative, and

(d) any person who has been a member of the committee at any time in the last 12 months.

6.165(2) **[Prohibited transactions]** Subject as follows, a person to whom this Rule applies shall not enter into any transaction whereby he–

(a) receives out of the estate any payment for services given or goods supplied in connection with the estate's administration, or

(b) obtains any profit from the administration, or

(c) acquires any asset forming part of the estate.

6.165(3) **[Leave or sanction for r. 6.165(2) transaction]** Such a transaction may be entered into by a person to whom this Rule applies–

(a) with the prior leave of the court, or

(b) if he does so as a matter of urgency, or by way of performance of a contract in force before the commencement of the bankruptcy, and obtains the court's leave for the transaction, having applied for it without undue delay, or

(c) with the prior sanction of the creditors' committee, where it is satisfied (after full disclosure of the circumstances) that the person will be giving full value in the transaction.

6.165(4) **[Resolution to sanction transaction]** Where in the committee a resolution is proposed that sanction be accorded for a transaction to be entered into which, without the sanction or the leave of the court, would be in contravention of this Rule, no member of the committee, and no representative of a member, shall vote if he is to participate directly or indirectly in the transaction.

6.165(5) **[Powers of court]** The court may, on application of any person interested–

(a) set aside a transaction on the ground that it has been entered into in contravention of this Rule, and

(b) make with respect to it such other order as it thinks fit, including (subject to the following paragraph) an order requiring a person to whom this Rule applies to account for any profit obtained from the transaction and compensate the estate for any resultant loss.

6.165(6) **[Member's or representative's associate]** In the case of a person to whom this Rule applies as an associate of a member of the committee or of a committee-member's representative the court shall not make any order under paragraph (5), if satisfied that he entered into the relevant transaction without having any reason to suppose that in doing so he would contravene this Rule.

6.165(7) **[Costs of application]** The costs of an application to the court for leave under this Rule do not fall on the estate, unless the court so orders.

GENERAL NOTE

This imposes strict controls on dealings between committee members, et al. and the estate. Full disclosure is required and the permission of the court or of the creditors must first be obtained. The court can set aside transactions contravening these rules. Once again, an important substantive provision like this would have been more appropriately placed in IA 1986 itself. See also *Re Gallard* [1896] 1 Q.B. 68 and *Re Bulmer Ex p. Greaves* [1937] Ch. 499.

6.166 Committee's functions vested in Secretary of State

6.166(1) **[Trustee's notices and reports]** At any time when the functions of the creditors' committee are bested in the Secretary of State under section 302(1) or (2), requirements of the Act or the Rules about notices to be given, or reports to be made, to the committee by the trustee do not apply, otherwise than as enabling the committee to require a report as to any matter.

6.166(2) **[Exercise by official receiver]** Where the committee's functions are so vested under section 302(2), they may be exercised by the official receiver.

GENERAL NOTE

See IA 1986, s. 302.

CHAPTER 12

SPECIAL MANAGER

6.167 Appointment and remuneration

6.167(1) **[Application under s. 370 to be supported by report]** An application made by the official receiver or trustee under section 370 for the appointment of a person to be special manager shall be supported by a report setting out the reasons for the application.

The report shall include the applicant's estimate of the value of the estate, property or business in respect of which the special manager is to be appointed.

6.167(2) **[Duration of appointment]** The court's order appointing the special manager shall specify the duration of his appointment, which may be for a period of time, or until the occurrence of a specified event. Alternatively, the order may specify that the duration of the appointment is to be subject to a further order of the court.

[FORM 6.54]

6.167(3) **[Renewal]** The appointment of a special manager may be renewed by order of the court.

6.167(4) **[Remuneration]** The special manager's remuneration shall be fixed from time to time by the court.

(See General Note after r. 6.171.)

6.168 Security

6.168(1) **[Effect of giving security]** The appointment of the special manager does not take effect until the person appointed has given (or, being allowed by the court to do so, undertaken to give) security to the person who applies for him to be appointed.

6.168(2) **[Special or general security]** It is not necessary that security shall be given for each separate bankruptcy; but it may be given either specially for a particular bankruptcy, or generally for any bankruptcy in relation to which the special manager may be employed as such.

6.168(3) **[Amount of security]** The amount of the security shall be not less than the value of the estate, property or business in respect of which he is appointed, as estimated by the applicant in his report under Rule 6.167(1).

6.168(4) **[Certificate of adequacy]** When the special manager has given security to the person applying for his appointment, that person's certificate as to the adequacy of the security shall be filed in court.

6.168(5) **[Cost of providing security]** The cost of providing the security shall be paid in the first instance by the special manager; but–

(a) where a bankruptcy order is not made, he is entitled to be reimbursed out of the property of the debtor, and the court may make an order on the debtor accordingly, and

(b) where a bankruptcy order is made, he is entitled to be reimbursed out of the estate in the prescribed order of priority.

(See General Note after r. 6.171.)

6.169 Failure to give or keep up security

6.169(1) **[Failure to give security]** If the special manager fails to give the required security within the time stated for that purpose by the order appointing him, or any extension of that time may be allowed, the official receiver or trustee (as the case may be) shall report the failure to the court, which may thereupon discharge the order appointing the special manager.

6.169(2) **[Failure to keep up security]** If the special manager fails to keep up his security, the official receiver or trustee shall report his failure to the court, which may thereupon remove the special manager, and make such order as it thinks fit as to costs.

6.169(3) **[Directions on removal]** If an order is made under this Rule removing the special manager, or discharging the order appointing him, the court shall give directions as to whether any, and if so what, steps should be taken for the appointment of another special manager in his place.

(See General Note after r. 6.171.)

6.170 Accounting

6.170(1) **[Contents of accounts]** The special manager shall produce accounts, containing details of his receipts and payments, for the approval of the trustee.

6.170(2) **[Period of accounts]** The accounts shall be in respect of 3-month periods for the duration of the special manager's appointment (or for a lesser period, if his appointment terminates less than 3 months from its date, or from the date to which the last accounts were made up).

6.170(3) **[When accounts approved]** When the accounts have been approved, the special manager's receipts and payments shall be added to those of the trustee.

(See General Note after r. 6.171.)

6.171 Termination of appointment

6.171(1) **[Automatic termination]** The special manager's appointment terminates if the bankruptcy petition is dismissed or if, an interim receiver having been appointed, the latter is discharged without a bankruptcy order having been made.

6.171(2) **[Application to court]** If the official receiver or the trustee is of opinion that the employment of the special manager is no longer necessary or profitable for the estate, he shall apply to the court for directions, and the court may order the special manager's appointment to be terminated.

6.171(3) **[Resolution of creditors]** The official receiver or the trustee shall make the same application if a resolution of the creditors is passed, requesting that the appointment be terminated.

GENERAL NOTE TO RR. 6.167–6.171

These rules develop the provisions of IA 1986, s. 370. If the court appoints a special manager, Form 6.54 is to be used. The court fixes his remuneration. Security is required. The special manager must provide three-monthly accounts for the trustee. The circumstances leading to the termination of the appointment of the special manager are mapped out.

CHAPTER 13

PUBLIC EXAMINATION OF BANKRUPT

6.172 Order for public examination

6.172(1) **[Copy of order to bankrupt]** If the official receiver applies to the court, under section 290, for the public examination of the bankrupt, a copy of the court's order shall, forthwith after its making, be sent by the official receiver to the bankrupt.

[FORM 6.55]

6.172(2) **[Venue and bankrupt's attendance]** The order shall appoint a venue for the hearing, and direct the bankrupt's attendance thereat.

6.172(3) **[Notice of hearing]** The official receiver shall give at least 14 days' notice of the hearing–

(a) if a trustee has been nominated or appointed, to him;

(b) if a special manager has been appointed, to him; and

(c) subject to any contrary direction of the court, to every creditor of the bankrupt who is known to the official receiver or is identified in the bankrupt's statement of affairs.

6.172(4) [Advertisement] The official receiver may, if he thinks fit, cause notice of the order to be given, by public advertisement in one or more newspapers, at least 14 days before the day fixed for the hearing.

(See General Note after r. 6.177.)

6.173 Order on request by creditors

6.173(1) [Form of request etc.] A request by a creditor to the official receiver, under section 290(2), for the bankrupt to be publicly examined shall be made in writing and be accompanied by–

(a) a list of the creditors concurring with the request and the amount of their respective claims in the bankruptcy,

(b) from each creditor concurring, written confirmation of his concurrence, and

(c) a statement of the reasons why the examination is requested.

Sub-paragraphs (a) and (b) do not apply if the requisitioning creditor's debt is alone sufficient, without the concurrence of others.

[FORM 6.56]

6.173(2) [Security for expenses of hearing] Before an application to the court is made on the request, the requisitionist shall deposit with the official receiver such sum as the latter may determine to be appropriate by way of security for the expenses of the hearing of a public examination, if ordered.

6.173(3) [Time for application] Subject as follows, the official receiver shall, within 28 days of receiving the request, make the application to the court required by section 290(2).

6.173(4) [Relief from unreasonable request] If the official receiver is of opinion that the request is an unreasonable one in the circumstances, he may apply to the court for an order relieving him from the obligation to make the application otherwise required by that subsection.

6.173(5) [Notice of relief order etc.] If the court so orders, and the application for the order was made *ex parte*, notice of the order shall be given forthwith by the official receiver to the requisitionist. If the application for an order is dismissed, the official receiver's application under section 290(2) shall be made forthwith on conclusion of the hearing of the application first mentioned.

(See General Note after r. 6.177.)

6.174 Bankrupt unfit for examination

6.174(1) [Application for stay etc.] Where the bankrupt is suffering from any mental disorder or physical affliction or disability rendering him unfit to undergo or attend for public examination, the court may, on application in that behalf, either stay the order for his public examination or direct that it shall be conducted in such manner and at such place as it thinks fit.

[FORM 6.57]

6.174(2) [Who may apply] Application under this Rule shall be made–

(a) by a person who has been appointed by a court in the United Kingdom or elsewhere to manage the affairs of, or to represent, the bankrupt, or

(b) by a relative or friend of the bankrupt whom the court considers to be a proper person to make the application, or

(c) by the official receiver.

6.174(3) **[Application not by official receiver]** Where the application is made by a person other than the official receiver, then–

(a) it shall, unless the bankrupt is a patient within the meaning of the Mental Health Act 1983, be supported by the affidavit of a registered medical practitioner as to the bankrupt's mental and physical condition;

(b) at least 7 days' notice of the application shall be given to the official receiver and the trustee (if any); and

(c) before any order is made on the application, the applicant shall deposit with the official receiver such sum as the latter certifies to be necessary for the additional expenses of any examination that may be ordered on the application.

An order made on the application may provide that the expenses of the examination are to be payable, as to a specified proportion, out of the deposit under sub-paragraph (c), instead of out of the estate.

6.174(4) **[Application by official receiver]** Where the application is made by the official receiver, it may be made *ex parte*, and may be supported by evidence in the form of a report by the official receiver to the court.

(See General Note after r. 6.177.)

6.175 Procedure at hearing

6.175(1) **[Examination on oath]** The bankrupt shall at the hearing be examined on oath; and he shall answer all such questions as the court may put, or allow to be put, to him.

6.175(2) **[Appearances etc.]** Any of the persons allowed by section 290(4) to question the bankrupt may, with the approval of the court (made known either at the hearing or in advance of it), appear by solicitor or counsel; or he may in writing authorise another person to question the bankrupt on his behalf.

6.175(3) **[Representation of bankrupt]** The bankrupt may at his own expense employ a solicitor with or without counsel, who may put to him such questions as the court may allow for the purpose of enabling him to explain or qualify any answers given by him, and may make representations on his behalf.

6.175(4) **[Record of examination]** There shall be made in writing such record of the examination as the court thinks proper. The record shall be read over either to or by the bankrupt, signed by him, and verified by affidavit at a venue fixed by the court.

[FORM 6.58]

6.175(5) **[Record as evidence]** The written record may, in any proceedings (whether under the Act or otherwise) be used as evidence against the bankrupt of any statement made by him in the course of his public examination.

6.175(6) **[Criminal proceedings etc.]** If criminal proceedings have been instituted against the bankrupt, and the court is of opinion that the continuance of the hearing would be calculated to prejudice a fair trial of those proceedings, the hearing may be adjourned.

(See General Note after r. 6.177.)

6.176 Adjournment

6.176(1) **[Adjourned by court]** The public examination may be adjourned by the court from time to time, either to a fixed date or generally.

[FORM 6.59]

6.176(2) **[Resumption]** Where the examination has been adjourned generally, the court may at any time on the application of the official receiver or of the bankrupt–

(a) fix a venue for the resumption of the examination, and

(b) give directions as to the manner in which, and the time within which, notice of the resumed public examination is to be given to persons entitled to take part in it.

[FORM 6.60]

6.176(3) **[Deposit for expenses re application]** Where application under paragraph (2) is made by the bankrupt, the court may grant it on terms that the expenses of giving the notices required by that paragraph shall be paid by him and that, before a venue for the resumed public examination is fixed, he shall deposit with the official receiver such sum as the latter considers necessary to cover those expenses.

6.176(4) **[Official receiver's application under s. 279(3)]** Where the examination is adjourned generally, the official receiver may, there and then, make application under section 279(3) (suspension of automatic discharge).

6.176(5) **[Copies of order to be sent by court]** If, on the hearing of an application pursuant to paragraph (4), the court makes an order suspending the bankrupt's discharge, copies of such order shall be sent by the court to the official receiver, the trustee and the bankrupt.

(See General Note after r. 6.177.)

6.177 Expenses of examination

6.177(1) **[Expenses paid out of r. 6.173(2) deposit]** Where a public examination of the bankrupt has been ordered by the court on a creditors' requisition under Rule 6.173, the court may order that the expenses of the examination are to be paid, as to a specified proportion, out of the deposit under Rule 6.173(2), instead of out of the estate.

6.177(2) **[Official receiver not liable for costs]** In no case do the costs and expenses of a public examination fall on the official receiver personally.

GENERAL NOTE TO RR. 6.172–6.177

These rules provide detailed guidance on the conduct of a public examination of a bankrupt under IA 1986, s. 290. If the official receiver applies to the court, Form 6.55 is to be used, whereas if a creditor applies to the official receiver for a public examination, Form 6.56 is the appropriate document. A creditor seeking a public examination must provide security. If the bankrupt is not fit to be publicly examined, the court can excuse him. Note the use of Form 6.57 in this context. The hearing procedure is mapped out by rr. 6.175 and 6.176. The public examination is normally to be funded out of the estate, unless the deposit furnished by a requisitioning creditor is made use of. The fee on public examination was abolished in 1995.

CHAPTER 14

DISCLAIMER

6.178 Trustee's notice of disclaimer

6.178(1) **[Contents of notice]** Where the trustee disclaims property under section 315, the notice of disclaimer shall contain such particulars of the property disclaimed as enable it to be easily identified.

[FORM 6.61]

6.178(2) **[Notice to be signed etc.]** The notice shall be signed by the trustee and filed in court, with a copy. The court shall secure that both the notice and the copy are sealed and endorsed with the date of filing.

6.178(3) **[Copy notice returned to trustee]** The copy notice, so sealed and endorsed, shall be returned by the court to the trustee as follows–

(a) if the notice has been delivered at the offices of the court by the trustee in person, it shall be handed to him,

(b) if it has been delivered by some person acting on the trustee's behalf, it shall be handed to that person, for immediate transmission to the trustee, and

(c) otherwise, it shall be sent to the trustee by first class post.

The court shall cause to be endorsed on the original notice, or otherwise recorded on the file, the manner in which the copy notice was returned to the trustee.

6.178(4) [**Date of notice**] For the purposes of section 315 the date of the prescribed notice is that which is endorsed on it, and on the copy, in accordance with this Rule.

(See General Note after r. 6.186.)

6.179 Communication of disclaimer to persons interested

6.179(1) [**Copy notices**] Within 7 days after the day on which a copy of the notice of disclaimer is returned to him, the trustee shall send or give copies of the notice (showing the date endorsed as required by Rule 6.178) to the persons mentioned in paragraphs (2) to (5) below.

6.179(2) [**Leasehold property**] Where the property disclaimed is of a leasehold nature, he shall send or give a copy to every person who (to his knowledge) claims under the bankrupt as underlessee or mortgagee.

6.179(3) [**Property in a dwelling-house**] Where the disclaimer is of property in a dwelling-house, he shall send or give a copy to every person who (to his knowledge) is in occupation of, or claims a right to occupy, the house.

6.179(4) [**Giving notice**] He shall in any case send or give a copy of the notice to every person who (to his knowledge)–

(a) claims an interest in the disclaimed property, or

(b) is under any liability in respect of the property, not being a liability discharged by the disclaimer.

6.179(5) [**Unprofitable contract**] If the disclaimer is of an unprofitable contract, he shall send or give copies of the notice to all such persons as, to his knowledge, are parties to the contract or have interests under it.

6.179(6) [**Late communication**] If subsequently it comes to the trustee's knowledge, in the case of any person, that he has such an interest in the disclaimed property as would have entitled him to receive a copy of the notice of disclaimer in pursuance of paragraphs (2) to (5), the trustee shall then forthwith send or give to that person a copy of the notice.

But compliance with this paragraph is not required if–

(a) the trustee is satisfied that the person has already been made aware of the disclaimer and its date, or

(b) the court, on the trustee's application, orders that compliance is not required in that particular case.

6.179(7) [**Notice to minor re dwelling-house**] A notice or copy notice to be served on any person under the age of 18 in relation to the disclaimer of property in a dwelling-house is sufficiently served if sent or given to the parent or guardian of that person.

GENERAL NOTE

Note the use of Pt 3 of Form 6.61 here.

(See also General Note after r. 6.186.)

6.180 Additional notices

6.180 The trustee disclaiming property may, without prejudice to his obligations under sections 315 to 319 and Rules 6.178 and 6.179, at any time give notice of the disclaimer to any persons who in his opinion ought, in the public interest or otherwise, to be informed of it.

GENERAL NOTE

Note the use of Pt 3 of Form 6.61 here.

(See also General Note after r. 6.186.)

6.181 Duty to keep court informed

6.181 The trustee shall notify the court from time to time as to the persons to whom he has sent or given copies of the notice of disclaimer under the two preceding Rules, giving their names and addresses, and the nature of their respective interests.

(See General Note after r. 6.186.)

6.182 Application for leave to disclaim

6.182(1) [**Applying ex parte**] Where under section 315(4) the trustee requires the leave of the court to disclaim property claimed for the bankrupt's estate under section 307 or 308, he may apply for that leave *ex parte*.

6.182(2) [**Accompanying report**] The application must be accompanied by a report–

(a) giving such particulars of the property proposed to be disclaimed as enable it to be easily identified,

(b) setting out the reasons why, the property having been claimed for the estate, the court's leave to disclaim is now applied for, and

(c) specifying the persons (if any) who have been informed of the trustee's intention to make the application.

6.182(3) [**Copy of consent to disclaimer**] If it is stated in the report that any person's consent to the disclaimer has been signified, a copy of that consent must be annexed to the report.

6.182(4) [**Court may grant leave etc.**] The court may, on consideration of the application, grant the leave applied for; and it may, before granting leave–

(a) order that notice of the application be given to all such persons who, if the property is disclaimed, will be entitled to apply for a vesting or other order under section 320, and

(b) fix a venue for the hearing of the application under section 315(4).

(See General Note after r. 6.186.)

6.183 Application by interested party under s. 316

6.183(1) [**Application of Rule**] The following applies where, in the case of any property, application is made to the trustee by an interested party under section 316 (request for decision whether the property is to be disclaimed or not).

6.183(2) [**Delivery and form of application**] The application–

(a) shall be delivered to the trustee personally or by registered post, and

(b) shall be made in the form known as "notice to elect", or a substantially similar form.

[FORM 6.62]

6.183(3) [**Where property cannot be disclaimed without leave of court**] This paragraph applies in a case where the property concerned cannot be disclaimed by the trustee without the leave of the court.

If within the period of 28 days mentioned in section 316(1) the trustee applies to the court for leave to disclaim, the court shall extend the time allowed by that section for giving notice of disclaimer to a date not earlier than the date fixed for the hearing of the application.

(See General Note after r. 6.186.)

6.184 Interest in property to be declared on request

6.184(1) [**Notice to declare interest**] If, in the case of property which the trustee has the right to disclaim, it appears to him that there is some person who claims, or may claim, to have an interest in the property, he may give notice to that person calling on him to declare within 14 days whether he claims any such interest and, if so, the nature and extent of it.

[FORM 6.63]

6.184(2) **[Failing compliance with notice]** Failing compliance with the notice, the trustee is entitled to assume that the person concerned has no such interest in the property as will prevent or impede its disclaimer.

(See General Note after r. 6.186.)

6.185 Disclaimer presumed valid and effective

6.185 Any disclaimer of property by the trustee is presumed valid and effective, unless it is proved that he has been in breach of his duty with respect to the giving of notice of disclaimer, or otherwise under sections 315 to 319, or under this Chapter of the Rules.

(See General Note after r. 6.186.)

6.186 Application for exercise of court's powers under s. 320

6.186(1) **[Application of Rule]** This Rule applies with respect to an application by any person under section 320 for an order of the court to vest or deliver disclaimed property.

6.186(2) **[Time for application]** The application must be made within 3 months of the applicant becoming aware of the disclaimer, or of his receiving a copy of the trustee's notice of disclaimer sent under Rule 6.179, whichever is the earlier.

6.186(3) **[Contents of affidavit]** The applicant shall with his application file an affidavit–

(a) stating whether he applies under paragraph (a) of section 320(2) (claim of interest in the property), under paragraph (b) (liability not discharged) or under paragraph (c) (occupation of dwelling-house);

(b) specifying the date on which he received a copy of the trustee's notice of disclaimer, or otherwise became aware of the disclaimer; and

(c) specifying the grounds of his application and the order which he desires the court to make under section 320.

6.186(4) **[Venue for hearing]** The court shall fix a venue for the hearing of the application; and the applicant shall, not later than 7 days before the date fixed, give to the trustee notice of the venue, accompanied by copies of the application and the affidavit under paragraph (3).

6.186(5) **[Directions for notice etc.]** On the hearing of the application, the court may give directions as to other persons (if any) who should be sent or given notice of the application and the grounds on which it is made.

6.186(6) **[Sealed copies of order]** Sealed copies of any order made on the application shall be sent by the court to the applicant and the trustee.

6.186(7) **[Leasehold property or property in a dwelling-house]** In a case where the property disclaimed is of a leasehold nature, or is property in a dwelling-house, and section 317 or (as the case may be) section 318 applies to suspend the effect of the disclaimer, there shall be included in the court's order a direction giving effect to the disclaimer.

This paragraph does not apply if, at the time when the order is issued, other applications under section 320 are pending in respect of the same property.

GENERAL NOTE TO RR. 6.178–6.186

These rules complement IA 1986, s. 315–321 (disclaimer of property, etc. by the trustee). This disclaimer is to take the style of Form 6.61 and must be filed with the court. Rules 6.179 and 6.180 relate to the dissemination of the notice of disclaimer. The court must always be kept informed of the dissemination process. Rule 6.182 develops IA 1986, s. 315 (4) (leave of court for certain notices of disclaimer). Section 316 must be read in the light of r. 6.183 and Form 6.62. The trustee can, under r. 6.184 and by using Form 6.63, compel persons to declare their interest in any property which he is considering disclaiming. The onus of proving that a disclaimer has been exercised improperly is naturally cast upon the person challenging it (r. 6.185). Section 320 is to be viewed in the light of r. 6.186. Note especially the time limitation upon applications under s. 320.

CHAPTER 15

REPLACEMENT OF EXEMPT PROPERTY

6.187 Purchase of replacement property

6.187(1) **[Time for purchase]** A purchase of replacement property under section 308(3) may be made either before or after the realisation by the trustee of the value of the property vesting in him under the section.

6.187(2) **[Sufficiency of funds in estate]** The trustee is under no obligation, by virtue of the section, to apply funds to the purchase of a replacement for property vested in him, unless and until he has sufficient funds in the estate for that purpose.

(See General Note after rr. 6.188.)

6.188 Money provided in lieu of sale

6.188(1) **[Application of Rule]** The following applies where a third party proposes to the trustee that he (the former) should provide the estate with a sum of money enabling the bankrupt to be left in possession of property which would otherwise be made to vest in the trustee under section 308.

6.188(2) **[Reasonableness of proposal]** The trustee may accept that proposal, if satisfied that it is a reasonable one, and that the estate will benefit to the extent of the value of the property in question less the cost of a reasonable replacement.

GENERAL NOTE TO RR. 6.187, 6.188

These rules provide further guidance on the operation of IA 1986, s. 308, which is a novel provision in the Act. A third party can provide funds for the estate to prevent a sale and replacement of assets.

CHAPTER 16

INCOME PAYMENTS ORDERS

6.189 Application for order

6.189(1) **[Court to fix venue]** Where the trustee applies for an income payments order under section 310, the court shall fix a venue for the hearing of the application.

6.189(2) **[Notice etc. to bankrupt]** Notice of the application, and of the venue, shall be sent by the trustee to the bankrupt at least 28 days before the day fixed for the hearing, together with a copy of the trustee's application and a short statement of the grounds on which it is made.

[FORM 6.64]

6.189(3) **[Contents of notice]** The notice shall inform the bankrupt that–

(a) unless at least 7 days before the date fixed for the hearing he sends to the court and to the trustee written consent to an order being made in the terms of the application, he is required to attend the hearing, and

(b) if he attends, he will be given an opportunity to show cause why the order should not be made, or an order should be made otherwise than as applied for by the trustee.

GENERAL NOTE

For the meaning of "venue" see r. 13.6.

(See General Note after r. 6.193.)

6.190 Action to follow making of order

6.190(1) **[Copy of order to bankrupt]** Where the court makes an income payments order, a sealed copy of the order shall, forthwith after it is made, be sent by the trustee to the bankrupt.

[FORM 6.65]
or [FORM 6.66]

6.190(2) **[Copy of order under s. 310(3)(b)]** If the order is made under section 310(3)(b), a sealed copy of the order shall also be sent by the trustee to the person to whom the order is directed.

(See General Note after r. 6.193.)

6.191 Variation of order

6.191(1) **[Non-compliance with s. 310(3)(a) order]** If an income payments order is made under section 310(3)(a), and the bankrupt does not comply with it, the trustee may apply to the court for the order to be varied, so as to take effect under section 310(3)(b) as an order to the payor of the relevant income.

[FORM 6.67]

6.191(2) **[*Ex parte* application]** The trustee's application under this Rule may be made *ex parte*.

6.191(3) **[Copy order to trustee and bankrupt]** Sealed copies of any order made on the application shall, forthwith after it is made, be sent by the court to the trustee and the bankrupt.

6.191(4) **[Variation, etc. of s. 310(3)(b) order]** In the case of an order varying or discharging an income payments order made under section 310(3)(b), an additional sealed copy shall be sent to the trustee, for transmission forthwith to the payor of the relevant income.

(See General Note after r. 6.193.)

6.192 Order to payor of income: administration

6.192(1) **[Compliance by payer]** Where a person receives notice of an income payments order under section 310(3)(b), with reference to income otherwise payable by him to the bankrupt, he shall make the arrangements requisite for immediate compliance with the order.

6.192(2) **[Costs of compliance]** When making any payment to the trustee, he may deduct the appropriate fee towards the clerical and administrative costs of compliance with the income payments order.

He shall give to the bankrupt a written statement of any amount deducted by him under this paragraph.

6.192(3) **[Where payer no longer liable etc.]** Where a person receives notice of an income payments order imposing on him a requirement under section 310(3)(b), and either–

(a) he is then no longer liable to make to the bankrupt any payment of income, or

(b) having made payments in compliance with the order, he ceases to be so liable,

he shall forthwith give notice of that fact to the trustee.

(See General Note after r. 6.193.)

6.193 Review of order

6.193(1) **[Application to court]** Where an income payments order is in force, either the trustee or the bankrupt may apply to the court for the order to be varied or discharged.

6.193(2) **[Application by trustee]** If the application is made by the trustee, Rule 6.189 applies (with any necessary modification) as in the case of an application for an income payments order.

6.193(3) **[Application by bankrupt]** If the application is made by the bankrupt, it shall be accompanied by a short statement of the grounds on which it is made.

6.193(4) **[Court may dismiss application etc.]** The court may, if it thinks that no sufficient cause is shown for the application, dismiss it; but it shall not do so unless the applicant has had an opportunity to attend the court for an *ex parte* hearing, of which he has been given at least 7 days' notice.

If the application is not dismissed under this paragraph, the court shall fix a venue for it to be heard.

6.193(5) **[Notice of venue etc.]** At least 28 days before the date fixed for the hearing, the applicant shall send to the trustee or the bankrupt (whichever of them is not himself the applicant) notice of the venue, accompanied by a copy of the application.

Where the applicant is the bankrupt, the notice shall be accompanied by a copy of the statement of grounds under paragraph (3).

6.193(6) **[Appearance etc. by trustee]** The trustee may, if he thinks fit, appear and be heard on the application; and, whether or not he intends to appear, he may, not less than 7 days before the date fixed for the hearing, file a written report of any matters which he considers ought to be drawn to the court's attention.

If such a report is filed, a copy of it shall be sent by the trustee to the bankrupt.

6.193(7) **[Sealed copies of order]** Sealed copies of any order made on the application shall, forthwith after the order is made, be sent by the court to the trustee, the bankrupt and the payor (if other than the bankrupt).

[FORM 6.66]

GENERAL NOTE TO RR. 6.189–6.193

Once again these rules develop an innovation introduced by IA 1986, s. 310, the income payments order. The trustee's application should adopt Form 6.64, whereas the court order should follow Forms 6.65 and 6.66. Variation of orders is provided for (see Form 6.67). Provision is made for third parties whose payments to the bankrupt may be diverted under IA 1986, s. 310(3)(b). Note the special fee, which is 50p, under r. 6.192(2): see r. 13.11(a).

CHAPTER 16A

INCOME PAYMENTS AGREEMENTS

6.193A Approval of income payments agreements

6.193A(1) **[Prior to discharge]** An income payments agreement can only be entered into prior to the discharge of the bankrupt.

6.193A(2) **[Where under IA 1986, s. 310A(1)]** Where an income payments agreement is to be entered into between the official receiver or trustee and the bankrupt under section 310A(1), the official receiver or trustee shall provide an income payments agreements to the bankrupt for his approval.

6.193A(3) **[Duty of bankrupt]** Within 14 days or such longer period as may be specified by the official receiver or trustee (whichever is appropriate) from the date on which the income payments agreement was sent, the bankrupt shall–

(a) if he decides to approve the draft income payments agreement, sign the agreement and return it to the official receiver or trustee (whichever is appropriate); or

(b) if he decides not to approve the agreement, notify the official receiver or trustee (whichever is appropriate) in writing of his decision.

6.193B Acceptance of income payments agreements

6.193B(1) **[Official receiver to sign and date]** On receipt by the official receiver or trustee of the signed income payments agreement, the official receiver or trustee shall sign and date it.

6.193B(2) **[Entry into force, copy to bankrupt]** When the official receiver or the trustee signs and dates the income payments agreement, it shall come into force. A copy shall be sent to the bankrupt.

6.193B(3) **[Notice of agreement where third party payments]** Where the agreement provides for payments by a third person to the official receiver or trustee who is not the official receiver in accordance with section 310A(1)(b), a notice of the agreement shall be sent by the official receiver or trustee to that person.

6.193B(4) **[Contents of notice]** The notice shall contain–

(a) the full name and address of the bankrupt;

(b) a statement that an income payments agreement has been made, the date of it, and that it provides for the payment by the third person of sums owed to the bankrupt (or a part thereof) to be paid to the official receiver or trustee;

(c) the full name and address of the third person;

(d) a statement of the amount of money to be paid to the official receiver or trustee from the bankrupt's income, the period over which the payments are to be made, and the intervals at which the sums are to be paid; and

(e) the full name and address of the official receiver or trustee and the address or details of where the sums are to be paid.

6.193B(5) **[Deduction of fee for clerical and administrative costs]** When making any payment to the trustee a person who has received notice of an income payments agreement with reference to income otherwise payable by him to the bankrupt may deduct the appropriate fee towards the clerical and administrative costs of compliance with the income payments agreement. He shall give to the bankrupt a written statement of any amount deducted by him under this paragraph.

6.193C Variation of income payments agreements

6.193C(1) **[Application accompanied by copy of agreement]** Where an application is made to court for variation of an income payments agreement, the application shall be accompanied by a copy of the agreement.

6.193C(2) **[Notice where application by bankrupt]** Where the bankrupt applies to the court for variation of an income payments agreement under section 310A(6)(b), he shall send a copy of the application and notice of the venue to the official receiver or trustee (whichever is appropriate) at least 28 days before the date fixed for the hearing.

6.193C(3) **[Notice where application by official receiver or trustee]** When the official receiver or trustee applies to the court for variation of an income payments agreement under section 310A(6)(b), he shall send a copy of the application and notice of the venue to the bankrupt at least 28 days before the date fixed for the hearing.

6.193C(4) **[Form of order]** The court may order in Form 6.81 the variation of an income payments agreement under section 310A.

[FORM 6.81]

6.193C(5) **[Notice where third party to make payments]** Where the court orders an income payments agreement under section 310A(1)(a) to be varied, so as to take the form of an agreement under section 310A(1)(b) as an agreement providing that a third person is to make payments to the trustee or the official receiver, the official receiver or trustee shall send a notice in accordance with Rule 6.193B(3).

6.193C(6) **[Deduction of fee for clerical and administrative costs]** When making any payment to the trustee a person who has received notice of an income payments agreement with reference to income otherwise payable by him to the bankrupt may deduct the appropriate fee towards the clerical and administrative costs of compliance with the income payments agreement. He shall give to the bankrupt a written statement of any amount deducted by him under this paragraph.

GENERAL NOTE

This new chapter was introduced by the Insolvency (Amendment) Rules 2003 (SI 2003/1730) to provide further regulations for the income payments agreements regime, which was introduced by EA 2002. See the note to s. 310A above.

CHAPTER 17

ACTION BY COURT UNDER SECTION 369
ORDER TO INLAND REVENUE OFFICIAL

6.194 Application for order

6.194(1) **[Application to specify documents etc.]** An application by the official receiver or the trustee for an order under section 369 (order to inland revenue official to produce documents) shall specify (with such particularity as will enable the order, if made, to be most easily complied with) the documents whose production to the court is desired, naming the official to whom the order is to be addressed.

6.194(2) **[Court to fix venue]** The court shall fix a venue for the hearing of the application.

6.194(3) **[Notice of venue etc. to Commissioners]** Notice of the venue, accompanied by a copy of the application, shall be sent by the applicant to the Commissioners of Inland Revenue ("the Commissioners") at least 28 days before the hearing.

6.194(4) **[Whether Commissioners consent or object]** The notice shall require the Commissioners, not later than 7 days before the date fixed for the hearing of the application, to inform the court whether they consent or object to the making of an order under the section.

6.194(5) **[If Commissioners consent]** If the Commissioners consent to the making of an order, they shall inform the court of the name of the official to whom it should be addressed, if other than the one named in the application.

6.194(6) **[If Commissioners object]** If the Commissioners object to the making of an order, they shall secure that an officer of theirs attends the hearing of the application and, not less than 7 days before it, deliver to the court a statement in writing of their grounds of objection.

A copy of the statement shall be sent forthwith to the applicant.

GENERAL NOTE

For the meaning of "venue" see r. 13.6

(See also General Note after r. 6.196.)

6.195 Making and service of the order

6.195(1) [Powers of court] If on the hearing of the application it appears to the court to be a proper case, the court may make the order applied for, with such modifications (if any) as appear appropriate having regard to any representations made on behalf of the Commissioners.

[FORM 6.69]

6.195(2) [Form and contents of order] The order–

(a) may be addressed to an inland revenue official other than the one named in the application,

(b) shall specify a time, not less than 28 days after service on the official to whom the order is addressed, within which compliance is required, and

(c) may include requirements as to the manner in which documents to which the order relates are to be produced.

6.195(3) [Service of copy of order] A sealed copy of the order shall be served by the applicant on the official to whom it is addressed.

6.195(4) [If official unable to comply] If the official is unable to comply with the order because he has not the relevant documents in his possession, and has been unable to obtain possession of them, he shall deliver to the court a statement in writing as to the reasons for his non-compliance.

A copy of the statement shall be sent forthwith by the official to the applicant.

(See General Note after r. 6.196.)

6.196 Custody of documents

6.196 Where in compliance with an order under section 369 original documents are produced, and not copies, any person who, by order of the court under section 369(2) (authorised disclosure to persons with right of inspection), has them in his possession or custody is responsible to the court for their safe keeping and return as and when directed.

GENERAL NOTE TO RR. 6.194–6.196

These rules provide further details on orders made under IA 1986, s. 369. Form 6.69 is to be used for orders against the Inland Revenue under s. 369. A maximum of 28 days after service is fixed for compliance with a s. 369 order.

CHAPTER 18

MORTGAGED PROPERTY

6.197 Claim by mortgagee of land

6.197(1) [Application for order for sale, "land"] Any person claiming to be the legal or equitable mortgagee of land belonging to the bankrupt may apply to the court for an order directing that the land be sold.

"Land" includes any interest in, or right over, land.

6.197(2) **[Court may direct accounts to be taken etc.]** The court, if satisfied as to the applicant's title, may direct accounts to be taken and enquiries made to ascertain–

(a) the principal, interest and costs due under the mortgage, and

(b) where the mortgagee has been in possession of the land or any part of it, the rents and profits, dividends, interest, or other proceeds received by him or on his behalf.

Directions may be given by the court under this paragraph with respect to any mortgage (whether prior or subsequent) on the same property, other than that of the applicant.

6.197(3) **[Powers of court]** For the purpose of those accounts and enquiries, and of making title to the purchaser, any of the parties may be examined by the court, and shall produce on oath before the court all such documents in their custody or under their control relating to the estate of the bankrupt as the court may direct.

The court may under this paragraph order any of the parties to clarify any matter which is in dispute in the proceedings or give additional information in relation to any such matter and CPR Part 18 (further information) shall apply to any such order.

6.197(4) **[In like manner as in High Court]** In any proceedings between a mortgagor and mortgagee, or the trustee of either of them, the court may order accounts to be taken and enquiries made in like manner as in the Chancery Division of the High Court.

(See General Note after r. 6.199.) In r. 6.197 the words from "The court may" to the end substituted for the former words "The court may under this paragraph authorise the service of interrogatories on any party." by the *Insolvency (Amendment) (No. 2) Rules* 1999 (SI 1999/1022), r. 3, Sch., para. 2 as from April 26, 1999.

6.198 Power of court to order sale

6.198(1) **[Order for sale etc.]** The court may order that the land, or any specified part of it, be sold; and any party bound by the order and in possession of the land or part, or in receipt of the rents and profits from it, may be ordered to deliver up possession or receipt to the purchaser or to such other person as the court may direct.

6.198(2) **[Directions re sale]** The court may permit the person having the conduct of the sale to sell the land in such manner as he thinks fit. Alternatively, the court may direct that the land be sold as directed by the order.

6.198(3) **[Contents of order]** The court's order may contain directions–

(a) appointing the persons to have the conduct of the sale;

(b) fixing the manner of sale (whether by contract conditional on the court's approval, private treaty, public auction, or otherwise);

(c) settling the particulars and conditions of sale;

(d) obtaining evidence of the value of the property, and fixing a reserve or minimum price;

(e) requiring particular persons to join in the sale and conveyance;

(f) requiring the payment of the purchase money into court, or to trustees or others;

(g) if the sale is to be by public auction, fixing the security (if any) to be given by the auctioneer, and his remuneration.

6.198(4) **[Sale by auction]** The court may direct that, if the sale is to be by public auction, the mortgagee may appear and bid on his own behalf.

6.198(5) **[Rights *in rem*]** Nothing in this Rule or the following Rule may affect the rights in rem of creditors or third parties protected under Article 5 of the EC Regulation (third parties' rights in rem).

(See General Note after r. 6.199.) Rule 6.198(5) was inserted by the *Insolvency (Amendment) Rules* 2002 (SI 2002/1307) para. 8(8) with effect from May 31, 2002 to cater for the advent of EC Council Regulation 1346/2000 on insolvency proceedings.

6.199 Proceeds of sale

6.199(1) [Application of proceeds] The proceeds of sale shall be applied–

(a) first, in payment of the expenses of the trustee, of and occasioned by the application to the court, of the sale and attendance thereat, and of any costs arising from the taking of accounts, and making of enquiries, as directed by the court under Rule 6.197; and

(b) secondly, in payment of the amount found due to any mortgagee, for principal, interest and costs;

and the balance (if any) shall be retained by or paid to the trustee.

6.199(2) [Where proceeds insufficient] Where the proceeds of the sale are insufficient to pay in full the amount found due to any mortgagee, he is entitled to prove as a creditor for any deficiency, and to receive dividends rateably with other creditors, but not so as to disturb any dividend already declared.

GENERAL NOTE TO RR. 6.197–6.199

These provisions regulate the rights of mortgagees of the bankrupt's land. The court can order the sale of the mortgage property. Note the priority of claims against the proceeds of sale (r. 6.199).

CHAPTER 19

AFTER-ACQUIRED PROPERTY

6.200 Duties of bankrupt in respect of after-acquired property

6.200(1) [Time for bankrupt to give notice] The notice to be given by the bankrupt to the trustee, under section 333(2), of property acquired by, or devolving upon, him, or of any increase of his income, shall be given within 21 days of his becoming aware of the relevant facts.

6.200(2) [Not to dispose of property] Having served notice in respect of property acquired by or devolving upon him, the bankrupt shall not, without the trustee's consent in writing, dispose of it within the period of 42 days beginning with the date of the notice.

6.200(3) [To identify etc. disponee] If the bankrupt disposes of property before giving the notice required by this Rule or in contravention of paragraph (2), it is his duty forthwith to disclose to the trustee the name and address of the disponee, and to provide any other information which may be necessary to enable the trustee to trace the property and recover it for the estate.

6.200(4) [Property to which r. 6.200 (1)–(3) do not apply] Subject as follows, paragraphs (1) to (3) do not apply to property acquired by the bankrupt in the ordinary course of a business carried on by him.

6.200(5) [If bankrupt carries on business] If the bankrupt carries on a business, he shall, not less often than 6-monthly, furnish to the trustee information with respect to it, showing the total of goods bought and sold (or, as the case may be, services supplied) and the profit or loss arising from the business.

The trustee may require the bankrupt to furnish fuller details (including accounts) of the business carried on by him.

(See General Note after r. 6.202.)

6.201 Trustee's recourse to disponee of property

6.201(1) [**Trustee may serve notice on disponee**] Where property has been disposed of by the bankrupt before giving the notice required by Rule 6.200 or otherwise in contravention of that Rule, the trustee may serve notice on the disponee, claiming the property as part of the estate by virtue of section 307(3).

6.201(2) [**Time for serving notice**] The trustee's notice under this rule must be served within 28 days of his becoming aware of the disponee's identity and an address at which he can be served.

(See General Note after r. 6.202.)

6.202 Expenses of getting in property for the estate

6.202 Any expenses incurred by the trustee in acquiring title to after-acquired property shall be paid out of the estate, in the prescribed order of priority.

GENERAL NOTE TO RR. 6.200–6.202

The key provision on after-acquired property is IA 1986, s. 307, which represents a new departure in bankruptcy law. Section 333(2) is also relevant. The bankrupt has 21 days after becoming aware that after-acquired property has become vested in him to notify the trustee. The bankrupt must then wait 42 days before disposing of that property. If property is wrongfully disposed of, it may be traced by the trustee at the expense of the estate.

6.202A In this Chapter a reference to a bankrupt includes a reference to a person in respect of whom a bankruptcy restrictions order is in force.

GENERAL NOTE

This was inserted by Insolvency (Amendment) Rules 2003 (SI 2003/1730) to widen the definition of a bankrupt to include those against whom a BRO or BRU is in force. A person may thus be discharged from bankruptcy but still be regarded as a bankrupt for the purposes of Chapter 19 if a BRO or BRU remains in force.

CHAPTER 20

LEAVE TO ACT AS DIRECTOR, ETC.

6.203 Application for leave

6.203(1) [**Application supported by affidavit**] An application by the bankrupt for leave, under section 11 of the Company Directors Disqualification Act 1986, to act as director of, or to take part or be concerned in the promotion, formation or management of a company, shall be supported by an affidavit complying with this Rule.

6.203(2) **[Contents of affidavit]** The affidavit must identify the company and specify–

(a) the nature of its business or intended business, and the place or places where that business is, or is to be, carried on,

(b) whether it is, or is to be, a private or a public company,

(c) the persons who are, or are to be, principally responsible for the conduct of its affairs (whether as directors, shadow directors, managers or otherwise),

(d) the manner and capacity in which the applicant proposes to take part or be concerned in the promotion or formation of the company or, as the case may be, its management, and

(e) the emoluments and other benefits to be obtained from the directorship.

6.203(3) **[If company in existence]** If the company is already in existence, the affidavit must specify the date of its incorporation and the amount of its nominal and issued share capital; and if not, it must specify the amount, or approximate amount, of its proposed commencing share capital, and the sources from which that capital is to be obtained.

6.203(4) **[Taking part in promotion etc.]** Where the bankrupt intends to take part or be concerned in the promotion or formation of a company, the affidavit must contain an undertaking by him that he will, within not less than 7 days of the company being incorporated, file in court a copy of its memorandum of association and certificate of incorporation under section 13 of the Companies Act.

6.203(5) **[Venue and notice]** The court shall fix a venue for the hearing of the bankrupt's application, and give notice to him accordingly.

(See General Note after r. 6.205.)

6.204 Report of official receiver

6.204(1) **[Notice of venue etc.]** The bankrupt shall, not less than 28 days before the date fixed for the hearing, give to the official receiver and the trustee notice of the venue, accompanied by copies of the application and the affidavit under Rule 6.203.

6.204(2) **[Official receiver's report]** The official receiver may, not less than 14 days before the date fixed for the hearing, file in court a report of any matters which he considers ought to be drawn to the court's attention. A copy of the report shall be sent by him, forthwith after it is filed, to the bankrupt and to the trustee.

6.204(3) **[Where bankrupt disputes report]** The bankrupt may, not later than 7 days before the date of the hearing, file in court a notice specifying any statements in the official receiver's report which he intends to deny or dispute.

If he gives notice under this paragraph, he shall send copies of it, not less than 4 days before the date of the hearing, to the official receiver and the trustee.

6.204(4) **[Appearances]** The official receiver and the trustee may appear on the hearing of the application, and may make representations and put to the bankrupt such questions as the court may allow.

(See General Note after r. 6.205.)

6.205 Court's order on application

6.205(1) **[If court grants application]** If the court grants the bankrupt's application for leave under section 11 of the Company Directors Disqualification Act 1986, its order shall specify that which by virtue of the order the bankrupt has leave to do.

6.205(2) **[Powers of court]** The court may at the same time, having regard to any representations made by the trustee on the hearing of the application–

(a) include in the order provision varying an income payments order already in force in respect of the bankrupt, or

(b) if no income payments order or an income payments agreement is in force, make one.

6.205(3) **[Copies of order]** Whether or not the application is granted, copies of the order shall be sent by the court to the bankrupt, the trustee and the official receiver.

GENERAL NOTE TO RR. 6.203–6.205

The placement of these provisions within the Insolvency Rules is puzzling. These rules relate to applications by a bankrupt for leave to participate in company management under CDDA 1986, s. 11. The official receiver is to be notified to give him a chance to put his views to the court.

Rule 6.205(2)(b) was amended by IAR 2003 (SI 2003/1730) to cater for the advent of ipas after April 1, 2004.

CHAPTER 21

ANNULMENT OF BANKRUPTCY ORDER

6.206 Application for annulment

6.206(1) **[Form of application]** An application to the court under section 282(1) for the annulment of a bankruptcy order shall specify whether it is made–

(a) under subsection (1)(a) of the section (claim that the order ought not to have been made), or

(b) under subsection (1)(b) (debts and expenses of the bankruptcy all paid or secured).

6.206(2) **[Supporting affidavit]** The application shall, in either case, be supported by an affidavit stating the grounds on which it is made; and, where it is made under section 282(1)(b), there shall be set out in the affidavit all the facts by reference to which the court is, under the Act and the Rules, required to be satisfied before annulling the bankruptcy order.

6.206(3) **[Copy of application etc.]** A copy of the application and supporting affidavit shall be filed in court; and the court shall give to the applicant notice of the venue fixed for the hearing.

6.206(4) **[Notice of venue]** The applicant shall give to the official receiver and (if other) the trustee notice of the venue, accompanied by copies of the application and the affidavit under paragraph (2)–

(a) where the application is made under section 282(1)(a), in sufficient time to enable them to be present at the hearing, and

(b) where the application is made under section 282(1)(b), not less than 28 days before the hearing.

6.206(5) **[Where application under s. 282(1)(a)]** Where the application is made under section 282(1)(a), paragraph (4) shall additionally be complied with in relation to the person on whose petition the bankruptcy order was made.

6.206(6) **[Where applicant not bankrupt]** In this Chapter, where the applicant is not the bankrupt all notices, documents and affidavits required to be given, sent or delivered to another party by the applicant shall also be given, sent or delivered to the bankrupt.

GENERAL NOTE

The general 28-day limit originally fixed by r. 6.206(4) was modified to deal with applications under s. 282(1)(a).
Sub-paragraph (6) was added by the Insolvency (Amendment) Rules 2003 (SI 2003/1730).

(See also General Note after r. 6.215.)

6.207 Report by trustee

6.207(1) [**Application of Rule**] The following applies where the application is made under section 282(1)(b) (debts and expenses of the bankruptcy all paid or secured).

6.207(2) [**Contents of report**] Not less than 21 days before the date fixed for the hearing, the trustee or, if no trustee has been appointed, the official receiver shall file in court a report with respect to the following matters–

(a) the circumstances leading to the bankruptcy;

(b) (in summarised form) the extent of the bankrupt's assets and liabilities at the date of the bankruptcy order and at the date of the present application;

(c) details of creditors (if any) who are known to him to have claims, but have not proved; and

(d) such other matters as the person making the report considers to be, in the circumstances, necessary for the information of the court.

6.207(3) [**Particulars of debts etc.**] The report shall include particulars of the extent (if any) to which, and the manner in which, the debts and expenses of the bankruptcy have been paid or secured.

In so far as debts and expenses are unpaid but secured, the person making the report shall state in it whether and to what extent he considers the security to be satisfactory.

6.207(4) [**Copy of report to applicant**] A copy of the report shall be sent to the applicant at least 14 days before the date fixed for the hearing; and he may, if he wishes, file further affidavits in answer to statements made in the report.

Copies of any such affidavits shall be sent by the applicant to the official receiver and (if other) the trustee.

6.207(5) [**If trustee not official receiver**] If the trustee is other than the official receiver, a copy of his report shall be sent to the official receiver at least 21 days before the hearing. The official receiver may then file an additional report, a copy of which shall be sent to the applicant at least 7 days before the hearing.

(See also General Note after r. 6.215.)

6.208 Power of court to stay proceedings

6.208(1) [**Interim order**] The court may, in advance of the hearing, make an interim order staying any proceedings which it thinks ought, in the circumstances of the application, to be stayed.

6.208(2) [*Ex parte* **application**] Except in relation to an application for an order staying all or any part of the proceedings in the bankruptcy, application for an order under this Rule may be made *ex parte*.

6.208(3) [**Copies of application**] Where application is made under this Rule for an order staying all or any part of the proceedings in the bankruptcy, the applicant shall send copies of the application to the official receiver and (if other) the trustee in sufficient time to enable them to be present at the hearing and (if they wish to do so) make representations.

6.208(4) [**Effect of staying order on annulment**] Where the court makes an order under this Rule staying all or any part of the proceedings in the bankruptcy, the rules in this Chapter nevertheless continue to apply to any application for, or other matters in connection with, the annulment of the bankruptcy order.

6.208(5) [**Copies of staying order**] If the court makes an order under this Rule, it shall send copies of the order to the applicant, the official receiver and (if other) the trustee.

GENERAL NOTE

Rule 6.208 was substantially expanded in 1988 to enable the official receiver to have an early warning of an application to stay. There is also provision for annulment proceedings.

(See also General Note after r. 6.215.)

Rule 6.209

6.209 Notice to creditors who have not proved

6.209 Where the application for annulment is made under section 282(1)(b) and it has been reported to the court Rule 6.207 that there are known creditors of the bankrupt who have not proved, the court may—

(a) direct the trustee or, if no trustee has been appointed, the official receiver to send notice of the application to such of those creditors as the court thinks ought to be informed of it, with a view to their proving their debts (if they so wish) within 21 days, and

(b) direct the trustee or, if no trustee has been appointed, the official receiver to advertise the fact that the application has been made, so that creditors who have not proved may do so within a specified time, and

(c) adjourn the application meanwhile, for any period not less than 35 days.

GENERAL NOTE

For the significance of r. 6.209 see the comments of Warner J. in *Re Robertson (a Bankrupt)* [1989] 1 W.L.R. 1139.

(See General Note after r. 6.215.)

6.210 The hearing

6.210(1) [Trustee to attend] The trustee shall attend the hearing of the application.

6.210(2) [Attendance of official receiver] The official receiver, if he is not the trustee, may attend, but is not required to do so unless he has filed a report under Rule 6.207.

6.210(3) [Copies of order] If the court makes an order on the application, it shall send copies of the order to the applicant, the official receiver and (if other) the trustee.

[FORM 6.71]

(See General Note after r. 6.215.)

6.211 Matters to be proved under s. 282(1)(b)

6.211(1) [Application of Rule] This rule applies with regard to the matters which must, in an application under section 282(1)(b), be proved to the satisfaction of the court.

6.211(2) [Debts paid in full] Subject to the following paragraph, all bankruptcy debts which have been proved must have been paid in full.

6.211(3) [If debt disputed etc.] If a debt is disputed, or a creditor who has proved can no longer be traced, the bankrupt must have given such security (in the form of money paid into court, or a bond entered into with approved sureties) as the court considers adequate to satisfy any sum that may subsequently be proved to be due to the creditor concerned and (if the court thinks fit) costs.

6.211(4) [Advertisement in case of untraced creditor] Where under paragraph (3) security has been given in the case of an untraced creditor, the court may direct that particulars of the alleged debt, and the security, be advertised in such manner as it thinks fit.

If advertisement is ordered under this paragraph, and no claim on the security is made within 12 months from the date of the advertisement (or the first advertisement, if more than one), the court shall, on application in that behalf, order the security to be released.

GENERAL NOTE

For the significance of r. 6.211 see *Re Robertson (a Bankrupt)* [1989] 1 W.L.R. 1139.

(See General Note after r. 6.215.)

6.212 Notice to creditors

6.212(1) [**Notice of annulment**] Where the official receiver has notified creditors of the debtor's bankruptcy, and the bankruptcy order is annulled, he shall forthwith notify them of the annulment.

6.212(2) [**Expenses of giving notice**] Expenses incurred by the official receiver in giving notice under this Rule are a charge in his favour on the property of the former bankrupt, whether or not actually in his hands.

6.212(3) [**Property in hands of trustee etc.**] Where any property is in the hands of a trustee or any person other than the former bankrupt himself, the official receiver's charge is valid subject only to any costs that may be incurred by the trustee or that other person in effecting realisation of the property for the purpose of satisfying the charge.

(See General Note after r. 6.215.)

6.212A Annulment under s. 261 [revoked]

6.212A Rules 6.206 to 6.212 apply to an application for annulment under section 261 as they apply to such an application under section 282(1)(a).

GENERAL NOTE

Rule 6.212A (which was added in 1988) was intended to fill a lacuna in the case of annulments following acceptance of a proposal for an individual voluntary arrangement. It was revoked by I(A)R 2003 (SI 2003/1730) with effect from April 1, 2004.

6.213 Other matters arising on annulment

6.213(1) [**Contents of s. 261 or 282 order**] In an order under section 282 the court shall include provision permitting vacation of the registration of the bankruptcy petition as a pending action, and of the bankruptcy order, in the register of writs and orders affecting land.

6.213(2) [**Notice of order**] The court shall forthwith give notice of the making of the order to the Secretary of State.

6.213(3) [**Requiring advertisement of order**] The former bankrupt may require within 28 days of the order the Secretary of State to give notice of the making of the order–

(a) in the Gazette, or

(b) in any newspaper in which the bankruptcy order was advertised, or

(c) in both.

6.213(4) [**Requirement under r. 6.213(3)**] Any requirement by the former bankrupt under paragraph (3) shall be addressed to the Secretary of State in writing.

6.213(5) [**Former bankrupt deceased etc.**] Where the former bankrupt has died, or is a person incapable of managing his affairs (within the meaning of Chapter 7 in Part 7 of the Rules), the references to him in paragraphs (3) and (4) are to be read as referring to his personal representative or, as the case may be, a person appointed by the court to represent or act for him.

GENERAL NOTE

A 28-day limit was inserted into paragraph (3) by I(A)R 2004 (SI 2004/584). The wording in paragraph (4) was truncated by I(A)R 2004 (SI 2004/584) with effect from April 1, 2004 by the removal of the second sentence dealing with notification by the Secretary of State to the bankrupt of the cost of advertisement.

6.214 Trustee's final account

6.214(1) [**Duty to account for all transactions**] Where a bankruptcy order is annulled under section 282, this does not of itself release the trustee from any duty or obligation, imposed on him by or under the Act or the Rules, to account for all his transactions in connection with the former bankrupt's estate.

6.214(2) **[Final account to Secretary of State etc.]** The trustee shall submit a copy of his final account to the Secretary of State, as soon as practicable after the court's order annulling the bankruptcy order; and he shall file a copy of the final account in court.

6.214(3) **[Contents of final account]** The final account must include a summary of the trustee's receipts and payments in the administration, and contain a statement to the effect that he has reconciled his account with that which is held by the Secretary of State in respect of the bankruptcy.

6.214(4) **[Release of trustee]** The trustee is released from such time as the court may determine, having regard to whether–

(a)   paragraph (2) of this Rule has been complied with, and

(b)   any security given under Rule 6.211(3) has been, or will be, released.

GENERAL NOTE TO RR. 6.206–6.214

The key provisions on annulment of bankruptcy orders, IA 1986, ss. 261 and 282, leave many questions unanswered. These rules provide the necessary answers. The form of the application to the court is prescribed and if the application is under s. 282(1)(b), a full report from the trustee is required. Proceedings can be stayed where an annulment application is pending. Notice of the application may have to be sent to known creditors who have not proved. Public advertisements may also be required. The court order for the annulment should be in the style of Form 6.71, which has been amended by I(A)R 1991 (SI 1991/495) to remove the word "local" before "newspaper". Rule 6.211 explains further s. 282(1)(b). Creditors must be notified of the annulment, entries in the Land Register, etc. will have to be vacated, the Secretary of State must be told and the former bankrupt can demand that the annulment be publicly advertised. Rule 6.214 is a necessary saving provision relating to the trustee's accounts. Note the amendments of rr. 6.213 and 6.214 to include annulments under s. 261.

Rule 6.212A and r. 6.214A were respectively deleted and inserted by SI 2003/1730. Rules 6.213 and 6.214 were also modified by that same SI with effect from April 1, 2004.

CHAPTER 21A

NOTICE UNDER SECTION 279(2)

6.214A   Notice under section 279(2) that an investigation of the conduct and affairs of a bankrupt is unnecessary or concluded

6.214A(1) **[Duty of official receiver to give notice]** Where the official receiver intends to file a notice that an investigation of the conduct and affairs of a bankrupt is unnecessary or concluded under section 279(2), he shall give notice in writing to all creditors of which he is aware and any trustee of his intention to file such a notice.

6.214A(2) **[Objections]** Where a creditor or a trustee receives written notice of the official receiver's intention to file a notice under section 279(2) and he has any objection to the official receiver filing such a notice, he may, within 28 days of the date of such written notice, inform the official receiver in writing of his objection and give reasons for that objection.

6.214A(3) **[Period for objections]** The official receiver shall not file a notice under section 279(2) until the period allowed for creditors or a trustee to object under paragraph (2) has expired.

6.214A(4) **[Form of notice where no objections]** Where the official receiver receives no objection from either a creditor or a trustee he may file a notice under section 279(2) by sending to the court two copies of Form 6.82. The court shall endorse each copy with the date of filing and shall return one copy to the official receiver. The official receiver shall send a copy of the endorsed form to the bankrupt.

[FORM 6.82]

6.214A(5) **[Rejection of objection]** Where the official receiver receives an objection under this Rule and he rejects that objection, he shall not file the notice under section 279(2) until he has–

(a) given notice of the rejection (and his reasons) to the complainant; and

(b) the period of time for an appeal by the complainant under Rule 7.50(2) has expired,

or an appeal under that Rule has been determined by the court.

GENERAL NOTE

Rule 6.214A was inserted by Insolvency (Amendment) Rules 2003 (SI 2003/1730) to cater for the liberal approach towards bankrupts favoured by EA 2002. It provides further details on how the new relaxed approach towards investigating the conduct of bankrupts will operate. The notification obligations of the OR under s. 279(2) are explained and rights of objection outlined. A new paragraph (4) rule was substituted by I(A)R 2004 (SI 2004/584) with effect from April 1, 2004. This expands on the bureaucratic role of the court.

CHAPTER 22

DISCHARGE

6.215 Application for suspension of discharge

6.215(1) **[Application of r. 6.215]** The following applies where the official receiver or any trustee who is not the official receiver applies to the court for an order under section 279(3) (suspension of automatic discharge), but not where the official receiver makes that application, pursuant to Rule 6.176(4), on the adjournment of the bankrupt's public examination.

6.215(2) **[Evidence in support]** The official receiver or any trustee who is not the official receiver shall, with his application, file evidence in support setting out the reasons why it appears to him that such an order should be made.

6.215(3) **[Court to fix venue]** The court shall fix a venue for the hearing of the application, and give notice of it to the official receiver, the trustee who is not the official receiver, and the bankrupt.

6.215(4) **[Copies of official receiver's report]** Copies of the official receiver's report under this Rule shall be sent by him to the bankrupt and any trustee who is not the official receiver, so as to reach them at least 21 days before the date fixed for the hearing.

6.215(5) **[Copies of the trustee's evidence in support]** Copies of the trustee's evidence in support under this Rule shall be sent by him to the official receiver and the bankrupt, so as to reach them at least 21 days before the date fixed for the hearing.

6.215(6) **[Where bankrupt intends to deny or dispute evidence]** The bankrupt may, not later than 7 days before the date of the hearing, file in court a notice specifying any statements in the official receiver's or trustee's evidence in support which he intends to deny or dispute.

6.215(7) **[Copies of notice]** If the bankrupt files a notice under paragraph (6), he shall send copies of it, not less than 4 days before the date of the hearing, to the official receiver and any trustee who is not the official receiver.

6.215(8) **[Copies of order]** If the court makes an order suspending the bankrupt's discharge, copies of the order shall be sent by the court to the official receiver, any trustee who is not the official receiver and the bankrupt.

[FORM 6.72]

6.216 Lifting of suspension of discharge

6.216(1) [**Bankrupt may apply to court**] Where the court has made an order under section 279(3) that the period specified in section 279(1) shall cease to run, the bankrupt may apply to it for the order to be discharged.

6.216(2) [**Venue and notice**] The court shall fix a venue for the hearing of the application; and the bankrupt shall, not less than 28 days before the date fixed for the hearing, give notice of the venue to the official receiver and any trustee who is not the official receiver, accompanied in each case by a copy of the application.

6.216(3) [**Appearances etc.**] The official receiver and the trustee may appear and be heard on the bankrupt's application; and, whether or not they appear, the official receiver and trustee may file in court evidence in support of any matters which either of them considers ought to be drawn to the court's attention.

6.216(4) [**Report on conditions in order**] If the court made an order under section 279(3)(b), the court may request a report from the official receiver or the trustee as to whether the conditions specified in the order have or have not been fulfilled.

6.216(5) [**Copies of report**] If a report if filed under paragraph (3) or (4), copies of it shall be sent by the official receiver or trustee to the bankrupt and to either the official receiver or trustee (depending on which has filed the report), not later than 14 days before the hearing.

6.216(6) [**Where bankrupt intends to deny or dispute report**] The bankrupt may, not later than 7 days before the date of the hearing, file in court a notice specifying any statements in the official receiver's or trustee's report which he intends to deny or dispute.

If he files a notice under this paragraph, he shall send copies of it, not less than 4 days before the date of the hearing, to the official receiver and the trustee.

6.216(7) [**If court discharges order**] If on the bankrupt's application the court discharges the order under section 279(3) (being satisfied that the period specified in section 279(1) should begin to run again), it shall issue to the bankrupt a certificate that it has done so, with effect from a specified date and shall send copies of the certificate to the official receiver and the trustee.

[FORM 6.73]
[FORM 6.74]

GENERAL NOTE TO RR. 6.215, 6.216

R. 6.215 was substituted by I(A)R 2003 (SI 2003/1730) with effect from April 1, 2004. The reference to "report" in r. 6.215(4) is unclear.

R. 6.216 was substituted by Insolvency (Amendment) Rules 2003 (SI 2003/1730). It deals with the scenario where discharge has been suspended and the bankrupt seeks to have that suspension lifted.

For the meaning of "venue" in r. 6.216(2) see r. 13.6. On alternative avenues open to the bankrupt see *Holmes v Official Receiver (Re a Debtor No. 26 of 1991)* [1996] B.C.C. 246. In r. 6.216(7) the words from "and shall send copies" to the end added by the Insolvency (Amendment) Rules 1999 (SI 1999/359), r. 1, Sch., para. 7 as from March 22, 1999.

(See also General Note after r. 6.233.)

6.217 Application by bankrupt for discharge

6.217(1) [**If bankrupt makes s. 280 application**] If the bankrupt applies under section 280 for an order discharging him from bankruptcy, he shall give to the official receiver notice of the application, and deposit with him such sum as the latter may require to cover his costs of the application.

6.217(2) [**Venue and notice**] The court, if satisfied that paragraph (1) has been complied with, shall fix a venue for the hearing of the application, and give at least 42 days' notice of it to the official receiver and the bankrupt.

6.217(3) **[Notice by official receiver]** The official receiver shall give notice accordingly–

(a) to the trustee, and

(b) to every creditor who, to the official receiver's knowledge, has a claim outstanding against the estate which has not been satisfied.

6.217(4) **[Time for r. 6.217(3) notice]** Notices under paragraph (3) shall be given not later than 14 days before the date fixed for the hearing of the bankrupt's application.

(See also General Note after r. 6.223.)

6.218 Report of official receiver

6.218(1) **[Contents etc. of report]** Where the bankrupt makes an application under section 280, the official receiver shall, at least 21 days before the date fixed for the hearing of the application, file in court a report containing the following information with respect to the bankrupt–

(a) any failure by him to comply with his obligations under Parts VIII to XI of the Act;

(b) the circumstances surrounding the present bankruptcy, and those surrounding any previous bankruptcy of his;

(c) the extent to which, in the present and in any previous bankruptcy, his liabilities have exceeded his assets; and

(d) particulars of any distribution which has been, or is expected to be, made to creditors in the present bankruptcy or, if such is the case, that there has been and is to be no distribution;

and the official receiver shall include in his report any other matters which in his opinion ought to be brought to the court's attention.

6.218(2) **[Copies of reports]** The official receiver shall send a copy of the report to the bankrupt and the trustee, so as to reach them at least 14 days before the date of the hearing of the application under section 280.

6.218(3) **[Where bankrupt disputes report]** The bankrupt may, not later than 7 days before the date of the hearing, file in court a notice specifying any statements in the official receiver's report which he intends to deny or dispute.

If he gives notice under this paragraph, he shall send copies of it, not less than 4 days before the date of the hearing, to the official receiver and the trustee.

[FORM 6.75]

6.218(4) **[Appearances]** The official receiver, the trustee and any creditor may appear on the hearing of the bankrupt's application, and may make representations and put to the bankrupt such questions as the court may allow.

(See General Note after r. 6.223.)

6.219 Order of discharge on application

6.219(1) **[Order to take effect when drawn up by court]** An order of the court under section 280(2)(b) (discharge absolutely) or (c) (discharge subject to conditions with respect to income or property) shall bear the date on which it is made, but does not take effect until such time as it is drawn up by the court.

[FORM 6.76]

6.219(2) **[Retrospective effect]** The order then has effect retrospectively to the date on which it was made.

6.219(3) **[Copies of order]** Copies of any order made by the court on an application by the bankrupt for discharge under section 280 shall be sent by the court to the bankrupt, the trustee and the official receiver.

(See General Note after r. 6.223.)

6.220 Certificate of discharge

6.220(1) [**Where bankrupt is discharged**] Where it appears to the court that a bankrupt is discharged, whether by expiration of time or otherwise, the court shall, on his application, issue to him a certificate of his discharge, and the date from which it is effective.

[FORM 6.77]

6.220(2) [**Requiring advertisement of discharge**] The discharged bankrupt may require the Secretary of State to give notice of the discharge–

(a) in the Gazette, or

(b) in any newspaper in which the bankruptcy was advertised, or

(c) in both.

6.220(3) [**Requirement in r. 6.220(2), cost of advertisement**] Any requirement by the former bankrupt under paragraph (2) shall be addressed to the Secretary of State in writing. The Secretary of State shall notify him forthwith as to the cost of the advertisement, and is under no obligation to advertise until that sum has been paid.

6.220(4) [**Former bankrupt deceased etc.**] Where the former bankrupt has died, or is a person incapable of managing his affairs (within the meaning of Chapter 7 in Part 7 of the Rules), the references to him in paragraphs (2) and (3) are to be read as referring to his personal representative or, as the case may be, a person appointed by the court to represent or act for him.

(See General Note after r. 6.223.)

6.221 Deferment of issue of order pending appeal

6.221 An order made by the court on an application by the bankrupt for discharge under section 280 shall not be issued or gazetted until the time allowed for appealing has expired or, if an appeal is entered, until the appeal has been determined.

(See General Note after r. 6.223.)

6.222 Costs under this Chapter

6.222 In no case do any costs or expenses arising under this Chapter fall on the official receiver personally.

(See General Note after r. 6.223.)

6.223 Bankrupt's debts surviving discharge

6.223 Discharge does not release the bankrupt from any obligation arising under a confiscation order made under section 1 of the Drug Trafficking Offences Act 1986 or section 1 of the Criminal Justice (Scotland) Act 1987 or section 71 of the Criminal Justice Act 1988 or under Parts 2, 3 or 4 of the Proceeds of Crime Act 2002.

GENERAL NOTE TO RR. 6.216–6.223

These rules provide additional information on the effect of IA 1986, ss. 279–281. Applications for suspension of automatic discharge under s. 279(3) are explained. If the court orders suspension, Form 6.72 is to be used. Suspension orders can be varied by the court. Note the use of Forms 6.73 and 6.74 here. Rules 6.217 and 6.218 are specially referable to applications by the bankrupt to the court for discharge under IA 1986, s. 280. The official receiver must be notified and he must file a report on the bankrupt's conduct. Form 6.76 is to be used for any court order under s. 280. Certificates of discharge must normally adopt the style of Form 6.77. Rule 6.223 is a specialised provision dealing with the enforcement of sanctions against drug dealers etc.: compare s. 281(4).

Rule 6.223 was modified by I(A)R 2003 (SI 2003/1730) with effect from April 1, 2004.

CHAPTER 22A **[revoked]**

REGISTER OF BANKRUPTCY ORDERS

Introduction
Chapter 22A was inserted by the Insolvency (Amendment) Rules 1999 (SI 1999/359) with effect from March 22, 1999. Chapter 22A established a public register of bankruptcy orders and therefore alleviated the difficulties involving bulk searches of court records as illustrated by cases such as *Re Austintel Ltd* [1997] 1 W.L.R. 616. This Chapter was revoked by I(A)R 2003 (SI 2003/1730). These matters are now dealt with by Part 6A.

6.223(A)   Register of bankruptcy orders *[revoked]*

6.223(A)(1) *[Secretary of State to maintain register] The Secretary of State shall maintain a register of bankruptcy orders ("the register") which shall contain the specified bankruptcy information entered in it by the official receiver in pursuance of Rule 6.223(B), any information entered in it by the official receiver in pursuance of Rule 6.223(C) and the information set out in paragraphs (2) and (3).*

6.223(A)(2) *[Notice of annulment order] The Secretary of State shall cause to be entered in the register notice of the making of an annulment order under section 261(1)(a) or 282(1)(b) given to him in pursuance of Rule 6.213(2).*

6.223(A)(3) *[Information to be entered in the register, etc.] The Secretary of State shall cause to be entered in the register such of the specified bankruptcy information and notice of the making of any annulment order under section 261(1)(a) or 282(1)(b) relating to any bankruptcy order where such bankruptcy order was made in the period of five years prior to March 22, 1999 as is in the possession of the Secretary of State on that date but excluding information relating to–*

(a)   *any bankruptcy order which has been annulled under section 282(1)(a) or which has been rescinded under section 375,*

(b)   *any bankruptcy order which has been annulled under section 261(1)(a) or 282(1)(b) more than two years prior to 22 March 1999, and*

(c)   *any bankruptcy order in respect of which an order made under Rule 6.34(3) or 6.46(3) is in force on that date and a copy of which has been delivered to the official receiver under Rule 6.34(4) or 6.46(4), provided that where after that date the order under Rule 6.34(3) or 6.46(3) expires, the Secretary of State shall enter in the register such of the specified bankruptcy information relating to the bankruptcy order previously the subject of the order under Rule 6.34(3) or 6.46(3) as is in his possession as at the date of expiry of such order, except where the official receiver receives a copy of any further order of the court under Rule 6.34(3) or 6.46(3) in respect of such bankruptcy order, in which event the Secretary of State shall not enter such specified bankruptcy information in the register until the expiry of such further order.*

6.223(A)(4) *[Deletion of bankruptcy information from register] Where a bankrupt in respect of whom specified bankruptcy information has been entered in the register is discharged from the bankruptcy or obtains an annulment order under section 261(1)(a) or 282(1)(b) in respect of the bankruptcy order, the Secretary of State shall, on the expiry of two years after the date of such discharge or annulment order (or where a certificate for the summary administration of the bankrupt's estate has been issued under section 275(1), on the expiry of three years after the date on which the bankrupt is discharged from the bankruptcy) delete from the register the specified bankruptcy information and any other information entered in the register in respect of such bankruptcy order.*

6.223(A)(5) **[Deletion from register upon annulment]** *If a bankruptcy order in respect of which specified bankruptcy information has been entered in the register is annulled by the court under section 282(1)(a), the Secretary of State shall delete from the register the specified bankruptcy information and any other information entered in the register in respect of such bankruptcy order upon receiving notice of such annulment under Rule 6.213(2).*

6.223(A)(6) **[Deletion from register upon rescission]** *If a bankruptcy order in respect of which specified bankruptcy information has been entered in the register is rescinded by the court under section 375 the Secretary of State shall delete from the register the specified bankruptcy information and any other information entered in the register in respect of such bankruptcy order upon receiving a copy of the order of the court rescinding the bankruptcy order.*

6.223(A)(7) **[Public inspection]** *The register shall be open to public inspection.*

GENERAL NOTE

Paragraphs (1), (2) and (7) provided that the Secretary of State was obliged to set up a public register of bankruptcy orders and annulment orders. Paragraph (3) indicated that the register was to include information already in the possession of the Secretary of State relating to existing bankruptcies occurring in the five years prior to March 22, 1999. Paragraphs (4) and (5) explained that on discharge or annulment a bankrupt could have his entry cleared after two years had elapsed or immediately if the annulment was granted under s. 282(1)(a) or a rescission was granted under s. 375.

6.223(B) **Specified bankruptcy information [revoked]**

6.223(B)(1) **[Entry in register by official receiver]** *Following the receipt by the official receiver pursuant to Rule 6.34 or 6.46 of a copy of the bankruptcy order from the court, the official receiver shall cause to be entered in the register the information listed in paragraph (5)(a) and shall cause to be entered in the register the information listed in paragraph 5(b) upon receipt by him of such information.*

6.223(B)(2) **[Entry of r. 6.223(B)(5)(c) information in register]** *Following the receipt by the official receiver–*

(a) *pursuant to Rule 6.50(3), of notice of the revocation of a certificate for summary administration,*

(b) *pursuant to Rule 6.176(5), of a copy of an order suspending the bankrupt's discharge,*

(c) *pursuant to Rule 6.215(6), of a copy of an order suspending the bankrupt's discharge,*

(d) *pursuant to Rule 6.216(7), of a copy of a certificate certifying the discharge of an order under section 279(3), or*

(e) *pursuant to Rule 6.219(3), of a copy of an order discharging the bankrupt absolutely or subject to conditions,*

the official receiver shall cause the information listed in paragraph (5)(c) to be entered in the register.

6.223(B)(3) **[Amendments to register on rescission of s. 279(3) order]** *Where an order referred to in paragraph 2(d) is subsequently rescinded by the court the official receiver shall cause the specified bankruptcy information relating to such bankruptcy to be amended to record the fact that the bankrupt is not discharged and, where the information in respect of such bankruptcy has been deleted from the register pursuant to paragraph (4) of Rule 6.223(A), shall cause such information to be restored to the register.*

6.223(B)(4) **[Discharge from bankruptcy noted in register]** *Where a bankrupt is discharged from bankruptcy under section 279(1)(b) the official receiver shall cause the fact and date of such discharge to be entered in the register.*

6.223(B)(5) *["Specified bankruptcy information"]* In this Chapter **"specified bankruptcy information"** means the following information–

(a)   (i) the matters listed in Rules 6.7 and 6.38 with respect to the debtor as stated in the bankruptcy petition;
             (ii) the bankruptcy order date, the court and court reference number;

(b)   (i) the name, gender, occupation (if any) and date of birth of the bankrupt;
             (ii) the bankrupt's last known address;
             (iii) where the bankrupt has been an undischarged bankrupt at any time in the period of 15 years ending with the date of the bankruptcy order in question, the date of the most recent of any previous bankruptcy orders (but excluding an order annulled under section 282(1)(a) or rescinded under section 375);
             (iv) any name by which the bankrupt is known other than his true name;
             (v) the name or names in which he carries on business if other than his true name and any address at which he carries on business;
             (vi) the contact address of the official receiver's office;
             (vii) the name and address of the insolvency practitioner (where appointed);
             (viii) the automatic discharge date under section 279(1)(b) or, where section 279(1)(a) applies, a statement that there is no automatic discharge date;
             (ix) where a certificate for summary administration has been issued, a statement to that effect; and

(c)   (i) the revised automatic discharge date where– (aa) the court has revoked a certificate for the summary administration of a bankrupt's estate under section 275(3), (bb) the court has made an order under section 279(3) that the relevant period under that section shall cease to run for the period specified in the order, or (cc) the court has discharged an order under section 279(3) being satisfied that the relevant period should begin to run again;
             (ii) a statement that discharge has been suspended where the court has made an order under section 279(3) that the relevant period under that section shall cease to run until the fulfilment of such conditions as may be specified in the order;
             (iii) the fact that and date on which the bankrupt is discharged.

GENERAL NOTE

This identified the circumstances under which the official receiver must register details on the register and specified what that information should be.

6.223(C) *Notification of changes [revoked]*

6.223(C)(1) *[Rectification of incorrect information on register]* If the official receiver becomes aware that the information which has been entered in the register is inaccurate he shall rectify the information entered in the register.

6.223(C)(2) *[Death of bankrupt to be entered in the register]* If the official receiver receives notice of the date of death of a bankrupt in respect of whom specified bankruptcy information has been entered in the register he shall cause such date to be entered in the register.

GENERAL NOTE

This dealt with procedures for changing inaccurate entries on the register.

CHAPTER 23

ORDER OF PAYMENT OF COSTS, ETC., OUT OF ESTATE

6.224 General rule as to priority

6.224(1) **[Priority of expenses]** The expenses of the bankruptcy are payable out of the estate in the following order of priority–

(a) expenses or costs which–

(i) are properly chargeable or incurred by the official receiver or the trustee in preserving, realising or getting in any of the assets of the bankrupt or otherwise relating to the conduct of any legal proceedings which he has power to bring (whether the claim on which the proceedings are based forms part of the estate or otherwise) or defend;

(ii) relate to the employment of a shorthand writer, if appointed by an order of the court made at the instance of the official receiver in connection with an examination; or

(iii) are incurred in holding an examination under Rule 6.174 (examinee unfit) where the application was made by the official receiver;

(b) any other expenses incurred or disbursements made by the official receiver or under his authority, including those incurred or made in carrying on the business of a debtor or bankrupt;

(c) the fees payable under any order made under section 415 or 415A, including those payable to the official receiver (other than the fee referred to in sub-paragraph (d)(i) below), and any remuneration payable to him under general regulations;

(d) (i) the fee payable under any order made under section 415 for the performance by the official receiver of his general duties as official receiver;

(ii) any repayable deposit lodged under any such order as security for the fee mentioned in sub-paragraph (i) (except where the deposit is applied to the payment of the remuneration of an insolvency practitioner appointed under section 273 (debtor's petition));

(e) the cost of any security provided by an interim receiver, trustee or special manager in accordance with the Act or the Rules;

(f) the remuneration of the interim receiver (if any);

(g) any deposit lodged on an application for the appointment of an interim receiver;

(h) the costs of the petitioner, and of any person appearing on the petition whose costs are allowed by the court;

(j) the remuneration of the special manager (if any);

(k) any amount payable to a person employed or authorised, under Chapter 5 of this Part of the Rules, to assist in the preparation of a statement of affairs or of accounts;

(l) any allowance made, by order of the court, towards costs on an application for release from the obligation to submit a statement of affairs, or for an extension of time for submitting such a statement;

(la) the costs of employing a shorthand writer in any case other than one appointed by an order of the court at the instance of the official receiver in connection with an examination;

(m) any necessary disbursements by the trustee in the course of his administration (including any expenses incurred by members of the creditors' committee or their representatives and allowed by the trustee under Rule 6.164, but not including any payment of capital gains tax in circumstances referred to in sub-paragraph (p) below);

(n) the remuneration or emoluments of any person (including the bankrupt) who has been employed by the trustee to perform any services for the estate, as required or authorised by or under the Act or the Rules;

(o) the remuneration of the trustee, up to any amount not exceeding that which is payable to the official receiver under general regulations;

(p) the amount of any capital gains tax on chargeable gains accruing on the realisation of any asset of the bankrupt (without regard to whether the realisation is effected by the trustee, a secured creditor, or a receiver or manager appointed to deal with a security);

(q) the balance, after payment of any sums due under sub-paragraph (o) above, of any remuneration due to the trustee.

(r) any other expenses properly chargeable by the trustee in carrying out his functions in the bankruptcy.

GENERAL NOTE

This is the normal priority regime though it is described in great detail here. Link this list with IA 1986, s. 328. For "general regulations" see r. 13.13(5).

The reform to sub-para. (1)(a) effected by the Insolvency (Amendment) (No. 2) Rules 2002 (SI 2002/2712) mirrors that made to r. 4.218 and allows recovery proceedings costs to be treated as bankruptcy costs. This amendment to r. 6.224 needs to be viewed in the light of the enhanced control of recovery proceedings imposed by EA 2002, s. 262, which introduces a new para. 2A into Sch. 5. Note also the insertion of sub-paras (la) and (r).

The priority as between sub-paras (c) and (d) was in the reverse order prior to April 1, 1995: see SI 1995/586.

The reference to s. 415A in paragraph (1)(c) was added by I(A)R 2004 (SI 2004/584) with effect from April 1, 2004. Fees orders are now being made under s. 415A.

CHAPTER 24

SECOND BANKRUPTCY

6.225 Scope of this Chapter

6.225(1) **[Application of Ch. 24 Rules]** The Rules in this Chapter relate to the manner in which, in the case of a second bankruptcy, the trustee in the earlier bankruptcy is to deal with property and money to which section 334(3) applies, until there is a trustee of the estate in the later bankruptcy.

6.225(2) **[Definitions]** "The earlier bankruptcy", "the later bankruptcy" and "the existing trustee" have the meanings given by section 334(1).

(See General Note after r. 6.228.)

6.226 General duty of existing trustee

6.226(1) **[Duty to get in property etc.]** Subject as follows, the existing trustee shall take into his custody or under his control all such property and money, in so far as he has not already done so as part of his duties as trustee in the earlier bankruptcy.

6.226(2) **[Power to sell perishable goods etc.]** Where any of that property consists of perishable goods, or goods the value of which is likely to diminish if they are not disposed of, the existing trustee has power to sell or otherwise dispose of those goods.

6.226(3) **[Proceeds of sale]** The proceeds of any such sale or disposal shall be held, under the existing trustee's control, with the other property and money comprised in the bankrupt's estate.

(See General Note after r. 6.228.)

6.227 Delivery up to later trustee

6.227 The existing trustee shall, as and when requested by the trustee for the purposes of the later bankruptcy, deliver up to the latter all such property and money as is in his custody or under his control in pursuance of Rule 6.226.

(See General Note after r. 6.228.)

6.228 Existing trustee's expenses

6.228 Any expenses incurred by the existing trustee in compliance with section 335(1) and this Chapter of the Rules shall be defrayed out of, and are a charge on, all such property and money as is referred to in section 334(3), whether in the hands of the existing trustee or of the trustee for the purposes of the later bankruptcy.

GENERAL NOTE TO RR. 6.225–6.228

These rules supplement IA 1986, s. 334 and deal with the complex relationship between the two successive bankruptcy regimes.

CHAPTER 25

CRIMINAL BANKRUPTCY

6.229 Presentation of petition

6.229(1) **[Presentation to High Court]** In criminal bankruptcy, the petition under section 264(1)(d) shall be presented to the High Court, and accordingly Rule 6.9 in Chapter 2 (court in which other petitions to be presented) does not apply.

[FORM 6.79]

6.229(2) **[Effect of Rule]** This does not affect the High Court's power to order that the proceedings be transferred.

(See General Note after r. 6.234.)

6.230 Status and functions of Official Petitioner

6.230(1) **[Official Petitioner as a creditor]** Subject as follows, the Official Petitioner is to be regarded for all purposes of the Act and the Rules as a creditor of the bankrupt.

6.230(2) **[Attendance, representation etc.]** He may attend or be represented at any meeting of creditors, and is to be given any notice under the Act or the Rules which is required or authorised to be given to creditors; and the requirements of the Rules as to the lodging or use of proxies do not apply.

(See General Note after r. 6.234.)

6.231 Interim receivership

6.231 Chapter 4 of this Part of the Rules applies in criminal bankruptcy only in so far as it provides for the appointment of the official receiver as interim receiver.

(See General Note after r. 6.234.)

6.232 Proof of bankruptcy debts and notice of order

6.232(1) [**Effect of order**] The making of a bankruptcy order on a criminal bankruptcy petition does not affect the right of creditors to prove for their debts arising otherwise than in consequence of the criminal proceedings.

6.232(2) [**Person suffering loss etc.**] A person specified in a criminal bankruptcy order as having suffered loss or damage shall be treated as a creditor of the bankrupt; and a copy of the order is sufficient evidence of his claim, subject to its being shown by any party to the bankruptcy proceedings that the loss or damage actually suffered was more or (as the case may be) less than the amount specified in the order.

6.232(3) [**Non-application of Rules**] The requirements of the Rules with respect to the proof of debts do not apply to the Official Petitioner.

6.232(4) [**Forms of proof**] In criminal bankruptcy, forms of proof shall be sent out by the official receiver within 12 weeks from the making of the bankruptcy order, to every creditor who is known to him, or is identified in the bankrupt's statements of affairs.

6.232(5) [**Notice to creditors**] The official receiver shall, within those 12 weeks, send to every such creditor notice of the making of the bankruptcy order.

GENERAL NOTE

The new r. 6.232(4) makes it clear that forms of proof do not have to be in a prescribed format. The deadline has been changed to within 12 weeks, which was what was originally intended but not conveyed by the language of the previous provision.

(See also General Note after r. 6.234.)

6.233 Meetings under the Rules

6.233(1) [**Non-application of Ch. 6 Rules**] The following Rules in Chapter 6 of this Part do not apply in criminal bankruptcy–

Rules 6.79 and 6.80 (first meeting of creditors, and business threat);

Rule 6.82(2) (the chairman, if other than the official receiver);

Rule 6.88(2) and (3) (resolution for appointment of trustee).

6.233(2) [**Non-application of r. 6.97**] Rule 6.97 (supply of forms for proof of debts) does not apply.

(See General Note after r. 6.234.)

6.234 Trustee in bankruptcy; creditors' committee; annulment of bankruptcy order

6.234(1) [**Non-application of Ch. 10 Rules**] Chapter 10 of this Part of the Rules does not apply in criminal bankruptcy, except Rules 6.136 (release of official receiver) and 6.147 (power of court to set aside transactions).

6.234(2) [**Non-application of Ch. 11 Rules**] Chapter 11 (creditors' committee) does not apply.

6.234(3) [**Application of Ch. 21 Rules**] Chapter 21 (annulment of bankruptcy order) applies to an application to the court under section 282(2) as it applies to an application under section 282(1), with any necessary modifications.

GENERAL NOTE TO RR. 6.229–6.234

The criminal bankruptcy regime (see IA 1986, s. 277) sits uneasily alongside the other facets of bankruptcy law. Further details of its operation are hereby provided. The form of the petition (Form 6.79) and the role of the official petitioner (see IA 1986, s. 402) are described. Proof of debts, meetings or creditors, etc., are also regulated by these rules.

The amendment to r. 6.232(4) by I(A)R 1987 is discussed above. Typographical errors in r. 6.234 have also been amended.

The criminal bankruptcy regime is to be abolished by CJA 1988: see the note to IA 1986, s. 277.

CHAPTER 26

MISCELLANEOUS RULES IN BANKRUPTCY

6.235 Bankruptcy of solicitors

6.235 Where a bankruptcy order is made against a solicitor, or such an order made against a solicitor is rescinded or annulled, the court shall forthwith give notice to the Secretary of the Law Society of the order that it has made.

6.236 Consolidation of petitions

6.236 Where two or more bankruptcy petitions are presented against the same debtor, the court may order the consolidation of the proceedings, on such terms as it thinks fit.

GENERAL NOTE

This provision would have been better located perhaps towards the beginning of this Part of the rules.

6.237 Bankrupt's dwelling-house and home [to be repealed]

6.237(1) *[Application of Rule]* This Rule applies where the trustee applies to the court under section 313 for an order imposing a charge on property consisting of an interest in a dwelling-house.

[FORM 6.79A]

6.237(2) *[Respondents to application]* The bankrupt's spouse or former spouse shall be made respondent to the application; and the court may, if it thinks fit, direct other persons to be made respondents also, in respect of any interest which they may have in the property.

6.237(3) *[Contents of trustee's report]* The trustee shall make a report to the court, containing the following particulars–

(a) the extent of the bankrupt's interest in the property which is the subject of the application; and

(b) the amount which, at the date of the application, remains owing to unsecured creditors of the bankrupt.

6.237(4) *[Terms of charge]* The terms of the charge to be imposed shall be agreed between the trustee and the bankrupt or, failing agreement, shall be settled by the court.

6.237(5) *[Rate of interest]* The rate of interest applicable under section 313(2) is the rate specified in section 17 of the Judgments Act 1838 on the day on which the charge is imposed, and the rate so applicable shall be stated in the court's order imposing the charge.

6.237(6) *[Contents of order] The court's order shall also–*

(a) *describe the property to be charged;*

(b) *state whether the title to the property is registered and, if it is, specify the title number;*

(c) *set out the extent of the bankrupt's interest in the property which has vested in the trustee;*

(d) *indicate, by reference to any, or the total, amount which is payable otherwise than to the bankrupt out of the estate and of interest on that amount, how the amount of the charge to be imposed is to be ascertained;*

(e) *set out the conditions (if any) imposed by the court under section 3(1) of the Charging Orders Act 1979;*

(f) *identify when any property charged under section 313 shall cease to be comprised in the bankrupt's estate and, subject to the charge (and any prior charge), to vest in the bankrupt.*

6.237(7) *[Date under r. 6.237(6)(f)] Unless the court is of the opinion that a different date is appropriate, the date under paragraph (6)(f) shall be that of the registration of the charge in accordance with section 3(2) of the Charging Orders Act 1979.*

6.237(8) *[Notice to Chief Land Registrar] The trustee shall, forthwith after the making of the court's order, send notice of it and its effect to the Chief Land Registrar.*

GENERAL NOTE

This is substituted by a new r. 6.237 (see below) from April 1, 2004.

6.237 Bankrupt's Home – Notification of property falling within section 283A

6.237(1) **[Form of notice]** Where it appears to a trustee that section 283A(1) applies, the trustee shall give notice in Form 6.83 as soon as reasonably practicable to–

(a) the bankrupt;

(b) the bankrupt's spouse (in a case falling within section 283A(1)(b)); and

[FORM 6.83]

(c) a former spouse of the bankrupt (in a case falling within section 283A(1)(c)).

6.237(2) **[Contents of notice]** A notice under paragraph (1) shall contain–

(a) the name of the bankrupt;

(b) the address of the dwelling-house; and

(c) if the dwelling-house is registered land, the title number.

6.237(3) **[Time limit for notice]** A trustee shall not give notice under paragraph (1) any later than 14 days before the expiry of the three year period under section 283A(2) or 283A(5).

6.237A Application in respect of the vesting of an interest in a dwelling-house (registered land)

6.237A(1) **[Application of r. 6.237A(2)]** Paragraph (2) applies where–

(a) property comprised in the bankrupt's estate consists of an interest in a dwelling-house which at the date of bankruptcy was the sole or principal residence of–
   (i) the bankrupt;
   (ii) the bankrupt's spouse; or
   (iii) a former spouse of the bankrupt; and

(b) the dwelling-house is registered land; and

(c) an entry has been made, or entries have been made, in the individual register or registers of the dwelling-house relating to the bankrupt's bankruptcy or the individual register or registers has or have been altered to reflect the vesting of the bankrupt's interest in a trustee in bankruptcy.

6.237A(2) **[Trustee to apply to register interest in bankrupt]** Where an interest of a kind mentioned in paragraph (1) ceases to be comprised in the bankrupt's estate and vests in the bankrupt under either section 283A(2) or 283A(4) of the Act, or under section 261(8) of the Enterprise Act 2002, the trustee shall, within 7 days of the vesting, make such application or applications to the Chief Land Registrar as shall be necessary to show in the individual register or registers of the dwelling house that the interest has vested in the bankrupt.

6.237A(3) **[Form of application]** An application under paragraph (2) shall be made in accordance with the Land Registration Act 2002 and shall be accompanied by–

(a) evidence of the trustee's appointment (where not previously provided to the Chief Land Registrar); and

(b) a certificate from the trustee stating that the interest has vested in the bankrupt under section 283A(2) or 283A(4) of the Act or section 261(8) of the Enterprise Act 2002 (whichever is appropriate).

6.237A(4) **[Notification of application]** As soon as reasonably practicable after making an application under paragraph (2), the trustee shall notify the bankrupt and if the dwelling-house was the sole or principal residence of his spouse or former spouse, such person, that the application has been made.

6.237A(5) **[Further notification of application]** The trustee shall notify every person who (to his knowledge) either claims an interest in the dwelling-house, or is under any liability in respect of the dwelling-house that an application has been made.

R. 6.237A
This deals with applications in respect of the vesting of an interest in a dwelling-house where the land is registered.

6.237B Vesting of bankrupt's interest (unregistered land)

6.237B(1) **[Certificate as to vesting]** Where an interest in a dwelling-house which at the date of the bankruptcy was the sole or principal residence of–

(a) the bankrupt;

(b) the bankrupt's spouse; or

(c) a former spouse of the bankrupt

ceases to be comprised in the bankrupt's estate and vests in the bankrupt under either section 283A(2) or 283A(4) of the Act or section 261(8) of the Enterprise Act 2002 and the dwelling-house is unregistered land, the trustee shall issue the bankrupt with a certificate as to the vesting in Form 6.84 as soon as reasonably practicable.

[FORM 6.84]

6.237B(2) **[Certificate conclusive proof of interest]** A certificate issued under paragraph (1) shall be conclusive proof that the interest mentioned in paragraph (1) has vested in the bankrupt.

6.237B(3) **[Notification of application]** As soon as reasonably practicable after issuing the certificate under paragraph (1) the trustee shall, if the dwelling-house was the sole or principal residence of the bankrupt's spouse or former spouse, notify such person, that the application has been made.

6.237B(4) **[Further notification of application]** The trustee shall notify every person who (to his knowledge) either claims an interest in the dwelling-house, or is under any liability in respect of the dwelling-house that an application has been made.

R. 6.237B
This covers the same matters as r. 6.237A but the land here is unregistered.

6.237C The court may substitute for the period of three years mentioned section 283A(2) such longer period as the court thinks just and reasonable in all the circumstances of the case.

R. 6.237C

The three-year time-limit may be extended at the discretion of the court.

6.237CA Vesting of bankrupt's estate – substituted period

6.237CA For the purposes of section 283A(2) for the period of three years set out therein there shall be substituted, where the trustee in bankruptcy has sent notice to the bankrupt that he considers–

(a) the continued vesting of the property in the bankrupt's estate to be of no benefit to creditors; or

(b) the re-vesting to the bankrupt will facilitate a more efficient administration of the bankrupt's estate,

the period of one month from the date of that notice.

GENERAL NOTE

This new rule was inserted by I(A)R 2004 (SI 2004/584) with effect from April 1, 2004. It provides further fine tuning for this new regime in dealing with the family home.

6.237D Charging Order

6.237D(1) [Application of r. 6.237D] This Rule applies where the trustee applies to the court under section 313 for an order imposing a charge on property consisting of an interest in a dwelling-house.

6.237D(2) [Respondents] The respondents to the application shall be–

(a) any spouse or former spouse of the bankrupt having or claiming to have an interest in the property;

[FORM 6.79A]

(b) any other person appearing to have an interest in the property; and

(c) such other persons as the court may direct.

6.237D(3) [Trustee's report to court] The trustee shall make a report to the court, containing the following particulars–

(a) the extent of the bankrupt's interest in the property which is the subject of the application;

(b) the amount which, at the date of the application, remains owing to unsecured creditors of the bankrupt; and

(c) an estimate of the cost of realising the interest.

6.237D(4) [Terms of change] The terms of the charge to be imposed shall be agreed between the trustee and the bankrupt or, failing agreement, shall be settled by the court.

6.237D(5) [Rate of interest] The rate of interest applicable under section 313(2) is the rate specified in section 17 of the Judgments Act 1838 on the day on which the charge is imposed, and the rate so applicable shall be stated in the court's order imposing the charge.

6.237D(6) [Court order] The court's order shall also–

(a) describe the property to be charged;

(b) state whether the title to the property is registered and, if it is, specify the title number;

(c) set out the extent of the bankrupt's interest in the property which has vested in the trustee;

(d) indicate, by reference to any, or the total, amount which is payable otherwise than to the bankrupt out of the estate and of interest on that amount, how the amount of the charge to be imposed is to be ascertained;

(e) set out the conditions (if any) imposed by the court under section 3(1) of the Charging Orders Act 1979; and

(f) identify the date any property charged under section 313 shall cease to be comprised in the bankrupt's estate and shall, subject to the charge (and any prior charge), vest in the bankrupt.

6.237D(7) **[Date in r. 6.237D(6)(f)]** Unless the court is of the opinion that a different date is appropriate, the date referred to in paragraph (6)(f) shall be that of the registration of the charge in accordance with section 3(2) of the Charging Orders Act 1979.

6.237D(8) **[Application for registration]** Where the court order is capable of giving rise to an application or applications under the Land Charges Act 1972 or the Land Registration Act 2002, the trustee shall, as soon as reasonably practicable after the making of the court order or at the appropriate time, make the appropriate application or applications to the Chief Land Registrar.

6.237D(9) **["Appropriate application"]** In paragraph (8) an "appropriate application" is—

(a) an application under section 6(1)(a) of the Land Charges Act 1972 (application for registration in the register of writs and orders affecting land); or

(b) an application under the Land Registration Act 2002 for an entry in the register in respect of the charge imposed by the order; and such application under that Act as shall be necessary to show in the individual register or registers of the dwelling-house that the interest has vested in the bankrupt.

6.237D(10) **[Determining the value of interest in property for r.6.237D(6)(c)]** In determining the value of the bankrupt's interest for the purposes of paragraph (6)(c), the court shall disregard that part of the value of the property in which the bankrupt's interest subsists which is equal to the value of –

(a) any loans secured by mortgage or other charge against the property;

(b) any other third party interest; and

(c) the reasonable costs of sale.

R. 6.237D
This deals with applications for charging orders pursuant to s. 313.

GENERAL NOTE

Paragraph (10) was added by I(A)R 2004 (SI 2004/584) with effect from April 1, 2004. Again this looks like a case of belated fleshing out of details.

6.237E Interpretation

6.237E(1) **["Registered land"]** In Rules 6.237 and 6.237A, "registered land" has the same meaning as in section 132(1) of the Land Registration Act 2002.

6.237E(2) **["Individual register"]** In Rules 6.237A and 6.237D, "individual register" has the same meaning as in the Land Registration Rules 2003.

R. 6.237E
This provides interpretation guidance.

GENERAL NOTE TO RR 6.237–6.237E

Rule 6.237 was substituted by Insolvency (Amendment) Rules 2003 (SI 2003/1730) to deal with the new law on the bankrupt's home. New rr. 6.237A–E were also inserted.

Rule 6.237 places the onus of notification on the trustee. Notification must be given before 14 days prior to the elapse of the three-year period.

CHAPTER 27

EC REGULATION – MEMBER STATE LIQUIDATOR

6.238 Interpretation of creditor and notice to member State liquidator

6.238(1) **[Application]** This Rule applies where a member State liquidator has been appointed in relation to the bankrupt.

6.238(2) **[Interpretation]** For the purposes of the Rules referred to in paragraph (3) a member State liquidator is deemed to be a creditor.

6.238(3) **[Rules referred to in r. 6.238(2)]** The Rules referred to in paragraph (2) are Rules 6.73(1) (duty of official receiver), 6.75(1) (report of official receiver), 6.76(2) (report of official receiver), 6.79(2) (creditors' meeting), 6.81 (power to call creditors' meeting), 6.83 (requisitioned meetings), 6.93 (entitlement to vote), 6.94 (admission and rejection of proof), 6.96 (meaning of "prove"), 6.97 (supply of forms), 6.98 (contents of proof), 6.99 (claim established by affidavit), 6.100 (cost of proving), 6.101 (inspection of proofs), 6.104 (admission and rejection of proofs for dividend), 6.105(1) (appeal against decision on proof), 6.105(2), 6.106 (withdrawal or variation of proofs), 6.107(1) (expunging of proof), 6.108 (negotiable instruments, etc.), 6.109 (secured creditors), 6.110 (discounts), 6.111 (debts in foreign currency), 6.112 (payments of a periodical nature), 6.113 (interest), 6.114 (debt payable at future time), 6.126(1) (resignation of trustee), 6.136(1) (release of official receiver), 6.137(1) (final meeting), 6.142(1) (challenge to remuneration), 6.150(2) (creditors' committee), 6.160(3) (vacancy on creditors' committee), 6.172(3) (request for public examination), 6.212(1) (notice of annulment) and 6.217(3) (application by bankrupt for discharge).

6.238(4) **[Exercise of creditor's rights]** Paragraphs (2) and (3) are without prejudice to the generality of the right to participate referred to in paragraph 3 of Article 32 of the EC Regulation (exercise of creditor's rights).

6.238(5) **[Notice, copies]** Where the trustee is obliged to give notice to, or provide a copy of a document (including an order of court) to, the court or the official receiver, the trustee shall give notice or provide copies, as the case may be, to the member State liquidator.

6.238(6) **[Duty to co-operate and communicate information]** Paragraph (5) is without prejudice to the generality of the obligations imposed by Article 31 of the EC Regulation (duty to cooperate and communicate information).

GENERAL NOTE

See note after r. 6.239.

6.239 Interpretation of creditor and notice to member State liquidator appointed in main proceedings

6.239(1) **[Application]** This Rule applies, in addition to Rule 6.238, where a member State liquidator has been appointed in main proceedings in relation to the bankrupt.

6.239(2) **[Interpretation]** For the purposes of the Rules referred to in paragraph (3) the member State liquidator is deemed to be a creditor.

6.239(3) **[Rules referred to in r. 6.239(2)]** The Rules referred to in paragraph (2) are Rules 6.18(3) (hearing of petition), 6.23(1) (notice of intention to appear), 6.28(4) (extension of time), 6.30(2) (substitution of petitioner), 6.31(1) (change of carriage of petition) and 6.218(4) (report of official receiver).

6.239(4) **[Exercise of creditor's rights]** Paragraphs (2) and (3) are without prejudice to the generality of the right to participate referred to in paragraph 3 of Article 32 of the EC Regulation (exercise of creditor's rights).

GENERAL NOTE

Chapter 27 (rr. 6.238 and 6.239) was introduced by Insolvency (Amendment) Rules 2002 (SI 2002/1307) para. 8(9) with effect from May 31, 2002 to cater for the introduction of EC Council Regulation on Insolvency Proceedings (1346/2000).

CHAPTER 28

BANKRUPTCY RESTRICTIONS ORDER

6.240 In this and the following two Chapters, "Secretary of State" includes the official receiver acting in accordance with paragraph 1(2)(b) of Schedule 4A to the Act.

R. 6.240
This Chapter 28 was inserted by Insolvency (Amendment) Rules 2003 (SI 2003/1730) to support the legislation on bankruptcy restriction orders, which were an innovation in EA 2002. Rule 6.240 is a curiously located interpretation provision.

6.241 Application for bankruptcy restrictions order

6.241(1) **[Report by Secretary of State]** Where the Secretary of State applies to the court for a bankruptcy restrictions order under paragraph 1 of Schedule 4A to the Act, the application shall be supported by a report by the Secretary of State.

6.241(2) **[Contents of report]** The report shall include–

(a) a statement of the conduct by reference to which it is alleged that it is appropriate for a bankruptcy restrictions order to be made; and

(b) the evidence on which the Secretary of State relies in support of the application.

6.241(3) **[Affidavit in support by other persons]** Any evidence in support of an application for a bankruptcy restrictions order provided by persons other than the Secretary of State shall be by way of affidavit.

6.241(4) **[Venue and date of hearing]** The date for the hearing shall be no earlier than 8 weeks from the date when the court fixes the venue for the hearing.

6.241(5) **[Application heard in public]** For the purposes of hearing an application under this Rule by a registrar, Rule 7.6(1) shall not apply and the application shall be heard in public.

R. 6.241
This outlines the procedure where an application is made for a BRO.

6.242 Service on the defendant

6.242(1) **[Time limit]** The Secretary of State shall serve notice of the application and the venue fixed by the court on the bankrupt not more than 14 days after the application is made at court.

6.242(2) **[Documents to accompany service]** Service shall be accompanied by a copy of the application, together with copies of the report by the Secretary of State, any other evidence filed with the court in support of the application, and an acknowledgement of service.

6.242(3) **[Acknowledgement of service]** The defendant shall file in court an acknowledgement of service of the application indicating whether or not he contests the application not more than 14 days after service on him of the application.

6.242(4) **[Failure to file acknowledgement of service]** Where the defendant has failed to file an acknowledgement of service and the time period for doing so has expired, the defendant may attend the hearing of the application but may not take part in the hearing unless the court gives permission.

R. 6.242
Notice of the application must be served on the bankrupt within 14 days of the application being lodged.

6.243 The bankrupt's evidence

6.243(1) **[Time limits etc.]** If the bankrupt wishes to oppose the application, he shall within 28 days of the service of the application and evidence of the Secretary of State, file in court any evidence which he wishes the court to take into consideration, and shall serve a copy of such evidence upon the Secretary of State within 3 days of filing it at court.

6.243(2) **[Time limit for Secretary of State's further evidence etc.]** The Secretary of State shall, within 14 days from receiving the copy of the bankrupt's evidence, file in court any further evidence in reply he wishes the court to take into consideration and shall as soon as reasonably practicable serve a copy of that evidence upon the bankrupt.

R. 6.243
This outlines the responsibilities of the bankrupt if he wishes to oppose the application for a BRO.

6.244 Making a bankruptcy restrictions order

6.244(1) **[Power of court]** The court may make a bankruptcy restrictions order against the bankrupt, whether or not the latter appears, and whether or not he has filed evidence in accordance with Rule 6.243.

6.244(2) **[Copies of order to Secretary of State]** Where the court makes a bankruptcy restrictions order, it shall send two sealed copies to the Secretary of State.

6.244(3) **[Copy of order to bankrupt]** As soon as reasonably practicable after receipt of the sealed copy of the order, the Secretary of State shall send a sealed copy of the order to the bankrupt.

R. 6.244
This deals with the making of the BRO and dissemination of the fact that it has been made.

CHAPTER 29

INTERIM BANKRUPTCY RESTRICTIONS ORDER

6.245 Application for interim bankruptcy restrictions order

6.245(1) **[Court to fix venue]** Where the Secretary of State applies for an interim bankruptcy restrictions order under paragraph 5 of Schedule 4A to the Act, the court shall fix a venue for the hearing.

6.245(2) **[Time limit for notice to bankrupt]** Notice of an application for an interim bankruptcy restrictions order shall be given to the bankrupt at least 2 business days before the date set for the hearing unless the court directs otherwise.

6.245(3) **[Application heard in public]** For the purposes of hearing an application under this Rule by a registrar, Rule 7.6(1) shall not apply and the application shall be heard in public.

R. 6.245
This Chapter 29 was inserted by Insolvency (Amendment) Rules 2003 (SI 2003/1730) to regulate interim BROs granted in cases of urgency before a full BRO hearing can be held. Rule 6.245 explains the mode of application.

6.246 The case against the defendant

6.246(1) **[Report by Secretary of State]** The Secretary of State shall file a report in court as evidence in support of any application for an interim bankruptcy restrictions order.

6.246(2) **[Contents of report]** The report shall include evidence of the bankrupt's conduct which is alleged to constitute the grounds for the making of an interim bankruptcy restrictions order and evidence of matters which relate to the public interest in making the order.

6.246(3) **[Affidavit in support by other persons]** Any evidence by persons other than the Secretary of State in support of an application for an interim bankruptcy restrictions order shall be by way of affidavit.

R. 6.246
This is how the case for an interim BRO is to be constructed.

6.247 Making an interim bankruptcy restrictions order

6.247(1) **[Power bankrupt to file evidence and appear]** The bankrupt may file in court any evidence which he wishes the court to take into consideration and may appear at the hearing for an interim bankruptcy restrictions order.

6.247(2) **[Power of court to make order]** The court may make an interim bankruptcy restrictions order against the bankrupt, whether or not the latter appears, and whether or not he has filed evidence.

6.247(3) **[Copies of order to Secretary of State]** Where the court makes an interim bankruptcy restrictions order, two sealed copies of the order shall be sent, as soon as reasonably practicable, to the Secretary of State.

6.247(4) **[Copy of order to bankrupt]** As soon as reasonably practicable after receipt of the sealed copies of the order, the Secretary of State shall send a copy of the order to the bankrupt.

R. 6.247

This explains the approach of the court to an application made under r. 6.245 and the consequences of any order being made.

6.248 Application to set aside an interim bankruptcy restrictions order

6.248(1) **[Power of bankrupt to apply]** A bankrupt may apply to the court to set aside an interim bankruptcy restrictions order.

6.248(2) **[Affidavit in support]** An application by the bankrupt to set aside an interim bankruptcy restrictions order shall be supported by an affidavit stating the grounds on which the application is made.

6.248(3) **[Documents to Secretary of State]** Where a bankrupt applies to set aside an interim bankruptcy restrictions order under paragraph (1), he shall send to the Secretary of State, not less than 7 days before the hearing–

(a) notice of his application;

(b) notice of the venue;

(c) a copy of his application; and

(d) a copy of the supporting affidavit.

6.248(4) **[Power of Secretary of State to attend hearing etc.]** The Secretary of State may attend the hearing and call the attention of the court to any matters which seem to him to be relevant, and may himself give evidence or call witnesses.

6.248(5) **[Copies of order to Secretary of State]** Where the court sets aside an interim bankruptcy restrictions order two sealed copies of the order shall be sent, as soon as reasonably practicable, to the Secretary of State.

6.248(6) **[Copy of order to bankrupt]** As soon as reasonably practicable after receipt of the sealed copies of the order, the Secretary of State shall send a sealed copy of the order to the bankrupt.

R. 6.248

A bankrupt wishing to have the interim BRO set aside must follow this procedure.

CHAPTER 30

BANKRUPTCY RESTRICTIONS UNDERTAKING

6.249 Acceptance of the bankruptcy restrictions undertaking

6.249 A bankruptcy restrictions undertaking signed by the bankrupt shall be deemed to have been accepted by the Secretary of State for the purposes of paragraph 9 of Schedule 4A of the Act when the undertaking is signed by the Secretary of State.

R. 6.249

This Chapter 30 was inserted by Insolvency (Amendment) Rules 2003 (SI 2003/1730) to permit bankruptcy restrictions to be established consensually by an undertakings procedure. This procedure bears many of the features of the director disqualification undertakings regime, which was introduced by IA 2000. Rule 6.249 explains when a BRU is deemed to have been agreed.

6.250 Notification to the court

6.250 As soon as reasonably practicable after a bankruptcy restrictions undertaking has been accepted by the Secretary of State, a copy shall be sent to the bankrupt and filed in court and sent to the official receiver if he is not the applicant.

R. 6.250
The court and the OR must be told of any BRU.

6.251 Application under paragraph 9(3) of Schedule 4A to the Act to annul a bankruptcy restrictions undertaking

6.251(1) [**Affidavit in support**] An application under paragraphs 9(3)(a) or (b) of Schedule 4A to the Act shall be supported by an affidavit stating the grounds on which it is made.

6.251(2) [**Time limit for notice of application to Secretary of State etc.**] The bankrupt shall give notice of the application and the venue, together with a copy of the affidavit supporting his application to the Secretary of State at least 28 days before the date fixed for the hearing.

6.251(3) [**Power of Secretary of State to attend hearing etc.**] The Secretary of State may attend the hearing and call the attention of the court to any matters which seem to him to be relevant, and may himself give evidence or call witnesses.

6.251(4) [**Copies of order to Secretary of State and bankrupt**] The court shall send a sealed copy of any order annulling or varying the bankruptcy restrictions undertaking to the Secretary of State and the bankrupt.

R. 6.251
This explains how and when a BRU may be annulled.

PART 6A

CHAPTER 1

GENERAL

GENERAL NOTE

This major insertion of Part 6A into the Insolvency Rules came about through the Insolvency (Amendment) Rules 2003 (SI 2003/1730). It seeks to bring together the scattered provisions in previous formulations of the rules and to enhance these in the light of the new information that now needs to be lodged on public registers.

6A.1 The individual insolvency register

6A.1(1) [**Duty of Secretary of State**] The Secretary of State shall create and maintain a register of matters relating to bankruptcies and individual voluntary arrangements in accordance with the provisions of this Part (referred to in this Part as "the individual insolvency register").

6A.1(2) [**Maintenance of bankruptcy restrictions register**] The register referred to in paragraph 12 of Schedule 4A to the Act (referred to in this Part as "the bankruptcy restrictions register") shall be maintained in accordance with the provisions of this Part.

6A.1(3) [**"Registers"**] In this Part the "registers" means the registers referred to in paragraphs (1) and (2).

6A.1(4) **[Register open to public inspection]** The registers shall be open to public inspection on any business day between the hours of 9.00 am and 5.00 pm.

6A.1(5) **[Amendment of register]** Where an obligation to enter information onto, or delete information from, the registers arises under this Part, that obligation shall be performed as soon as is reasonably practicable after it arises.

R. 6A.1
This explains the obligations of the Secretary of State with regard to the register of individual insolvencies.

CHAPTER 2

INDIVIDUAL INSOLVENCY REGISTER

6A.2 Entry of information onto the individual insolvency register – individual voluntary arrangements

6A.2(1) **[Duty of Secretary of State]** The Secretary of State shall enter onto the individual insolvency register–

(a) as regards any voluntary arrangement other than a voluntary arrangement under section 263A any information–

 (i) that was required to be held on the register of individual voluntary arrangements maintained by the Secretary of State immediately prior to the coming into force of this Rule and which relates to a voluntary arrangement which has not been completed or has not terminated on or before the date on which this Rule comes into force; or

 (ii) that is sent to him in pursuance of Rule 5.29 or Rule 5.34; and

(b) as regards any voluntary arrangement under section 263A of which notice is given to him pursuant to Rule 5.45–

 (i) the name and address of the debtor;
 (ii) the date on which the arrangement was approved by the creditors; and
 (iii) the court in which the official receiver's report has been filed.

6A.2(2) **[R. 6A.2 subject to r. 6A.3]** This Rule is subject to Rule 6A.3.

R. 6A.2
The rules governing the entry of information with regard to IVAs are outlined.

6A.3 Deletion of information from the individual insolvency register – individual voluntary arrangements

6A.3 The Secretary of State shall delete from the individual insolvency register all information concerning an individual voluntary arrangement where–

(a) he receives notice under Rule 5.30(5) or Rule 5.46(4) of the making of a revocation order in respect of the arrangement; or

(b) he receives notice under Rule 5.34(3) or Rule 5.50(3) of the full implementation or termination of the arrangement.

R. 6A.3
This covers deletion of entries with regard to IVAs.

6A.4 Entry of information onto the individual insolvency register – bankruptcy orders

6A.4(1) [**Duty of Secretary of State**] The Secretary of State shall enter onto the individual insolvency register any information that was required to be held on the register of bankruptcy orders maintained by the Secretary of State immediately prior to the coming into force of this Rule and which relates to a bankrupt who–

(a) has not received his discharge on or before the date that this Rule comes into force; or

(b) was discharged in the period of 3 months immediately preceding the coming into force of this Rule.

6A.4(2) [**Duty of official receiver**] Where the official receiver receives pursuant to Rule 6.34 or Rule 6.46 a copy of a bankruptcy order from the court, he shall cause to be entered onto the individual insolvency register–

(a) the matters listed in Rules 6.7 and 6.38 with respect to the debtor as they are stated in the bankruptcy petition;

(b) the date of the making of the bankruptcy order;

(c) the name of the court that made the order; and

(d) the court reference number as stated on the order.

6A.4(3) [**Further duty of official receiver**] The official receiver shall cause to be entered onto the individual insolvency register as soon as reasonably practicable after receipt by him, the following information–

(a) the name, gender, occupation (if any) and date of birth of the bankrupt;

(b) the bankrupt's last known address;

(c) the date of any bankruptcy order (or if more than one the latest of them) made in period of 6 years immediately prior to the date of the latest bankruptcy order made against the bankrupt (excluding for these purposes any order that was annulled);

(d) any name by which the bankrupt was known, not being the name in which he was adjudged bankrupt;

(e) the address of any business carried on by the bankrupt and the name in which that business was carried on if carried on in a name other than the name in which the bankrupt was adjudged bankrupt;

(f) the name and address of any insolvency practitioner appointed to act as trustee in bankruptcy;

(g) the address at which the official receiver may be contacted; and

(h) the automatic discharge date under section 279.

6A.4(4) [**Duty of official receiver when discharge of bankrupt suspended**] Where pursuant to Rule 6.176(5) or Rule 6.215(8) the official receiver receives a copy of an order suspending the bankrupt's discharge he shall cause to be entered onto the individual insolvency register–

(a) the fact that such an order has been made; and

(b) the period for which the discharge has been suspended or that the relevant period has ceased to run until the fulfilment of conditions specified in the order.

Rule 6A.5

6A.4(5) [Duty to re certificate of discharge of suspension of bankruptcy] Where pursuant to Rule 6.216(7) a copy of a certificate certifying the discharge of an order under section 279(3) is received by the official receiver, he shall cause to be entered onto the individual insolvency register–

(a) that the court has discharged the order made under section 279(3); and

(b) the new date of discharge of the bankrupt,

but where the order discharging the order under section 279(3) is subsequently rescinded by the court, the official receiver shall cause the register to be amended accordingly.

6A.4(6) [Duty re discharge from bankruptcy] Where a bankrupt is discharged from bankruptcy under section 279(1) or section 279(2), the official receiver shall cause the fact and date of such discharge to be entered in the individual insolvency register.

6A4.(7) [R. 6A.4 subject to r. 6A.5] This Rule is subject to Rule 6A.5.

R. 6A.4
Registration of bankruptcy details is described.

6A.5 Deletion of information from the individual insolvency register – bankruptcy orders

6A.5 The Secretary of State shall delete from the individual insolvency register all information concerning a bankruptcy where–

(a) the bankruptcy order has been annulled pursuant to section 261(2)(a), 261(2)(b), 263D (3) or section 282(1)(b);

(b) the bankrupt has been discharged from the bankruptcy and a period of 3 months has elapsed from the date of discharge;

(c) the bankruptcy order is annulled pursuant to section 282(1)(a) and he has received notice of the annulment under Rule 6.213(2); or

(d) the bankruptcy order is rescinded by the court under section 375 and the Secretary of State has received a copy of the order made by the court.

R. 6A.5
Deletion of information on bankruptcies is dealt with here.

GENERAL NOTE

The words "Subject to paragraph (2)," formerly appearing at the beginning were deleted by I(A)R 2004 (SI 2004/584) with effect from April 1, 2004. This is a sensible amendment in view of the fact that there is no paragraph (2)!

CHAPTER 3

BANKRUPTCY RESTRICTIONS REGISTER

6A.6 Bankruptcy restrictions orders and undertakings – entry of information onto the bankruptcy restrictions register

6A.6(1) [Duty of Secretary of State re order] Where an interim bankruptcy restrictions order or a bankruptcy restrictions order is made against a bankrupt, the Secretary of State shall enter onto the bankruptcy restrictions register

(a) the name, gender, occupation (if any) and date of birth of the bankrupt;

(aa) the bankrupt's last known address;

(b) a statement that an interim bankruptcy restrictions order or, as the case may be a bankruptcy restrictions order has been made against him;

(c) the date of the making of the order, the court and the court reference number; and

(d) the duration of the order.

6A.6(2) **[Duty of Secretary of State re undertaking]** Where a bankruptcy restrictions undertaking is given by a bankrupt the Secretary of State shall enter onto the bankruptcy restrictions register–

(a) the name, gender, occupation (if any) and date of birth of the bankrupt;

(aa) the bankrupt's last known address;

(b) a statement that a bankruptcy restrictions undertaking has been given;

(c) the date of the acceptance of the bankruptcy restrictions undertaking by the Secretary of State; and

(d) the duration of the bankruptcy restrictions undertaking.

6A.6(3) **[R. 6A.6 subject to r. 6A.7]** This Rule is subject to Rule 6A.7.

R. 6A.6
Entry of details of BROs and BRUs is outlined.

GENERAL NOTE

Amendments to paras (1) and (2) were made by I(A)R 2004 (SI 2004/584) with effect from April 1, 2004. The purpose of the change is to provide more information on the public register of the background of the bankrupt made subject to a BRO or BRU.

6A.7 Deletion of information from the bankruptcy restrictions register – bankruptcy restrictions orders and undertakings

6A.7 In any case where an interim bankruptcy restrictions order or a bankruptcy restrictions order is made or a bankruptcy restrictions undertaking has been accepted, the Secretary of State shall remove from the bankruptcy restrictions register all information regarding that order or, as the case may be undertaking after–

(a) receipt of notification that the order or, as the case may be the undertaking has ceased to have effect; or

(b) the expiry of the order or, as the case may be, undertaking.

R. 6A.7
Deletion of information about BROs and BRUs is regulated by this rule.

CHAPTER 4

RECTIFICATION OF REGISTERS

6A.8 Rectification of the registers

6A.8(1) **[Duty of Secretary of State re inaccurate information]** Where the Secretary of State becomes aware that there is any inaccuracy in any information maintained on the registers he shall rectify the inaccuracy as soon as reasonably practicable.

6A.8(2) **[Duty of Secretary of State on death of bankrupt]** Where the Secretary of State receives notice of the date of the death of a bankrupt in respect of whom information is held on the register, he shall cause the fact and date of the bankrupt's death to be entered onto the individual insolvency register and bankruptcy restrictions register.

R. 6A.8
This explains rectification procedures where there are errors on the register.

PART 7

COURT PROCEDURE AND PRACTICE

GENERAL COMMENT ON PT 7

Part 7 deals with the practice and procedure on all applications to the court, whether in corporate insolvency or individual bankruptcy, except for the three categories of petition listed in r. 7.1. Several of the rules in this Part were amended or replaced by the Insolvency Amendment (No. 2) Rules 1999 (SI 1999/1022) with effect from April 26, 1999 in order to bring insolvency proceedings into line with the CPR: see the note preceding r. 0.1.

CHAPTER 1

APPLICATIONS

7.1 Preliminary

7.1 This Chapter applies to any application made to the court under the Act or Rules except–

(a) an application for an administration order under Part II,

(b) a petition for a winding-up order under Part IV, or

(c) a petition for a bankruptcy order under Part IX

of the Act.

(See General Note after r. 7.18.)

7.2 Interpretation

7.2(1) [Definitions] In this Chapter, except in so far as the context otherwise requires–

"**originating application**" means an application to the court which is not an application in pending proceedings before the court; and

[FORM 7.1]

"**ordinary application**" means any other application to the court.

[FORM 7.2]

7.2(2) **[Form of application]** Every application shall be in the form appropriate to the application concerned.

(See General Note after r. 7.18.)

7.3 Form and contents of application

7.3(1) **[Contents etc. of application]** Each application shall be in writing and shall state–

(a) the names of the parties;

(b) the nature of the relief or order applied for or the directions sought from the court;

(c) the names and addresses of the persons (if any) on whom it is intended to serve the application or that no person is intended to be served;

(d) where the Act or Rules require that notice of the application is to be given to specified persons, the names and addresses of all those persons (so far as known to the applicant); and

(e) the applicant's address for service.

7.3(2) **[Grounds for application]** An originating application shall set out the grounds on which the applicant claims to be entitled to the relief or order sought.

7.3(3) **[Application must be signed etc.]** The application must be signed by the applicant if he is acting in person or, when he is not so acting, by or on behalf of his solicitor.

(See General Note after r. 7.18.)

7.3A Application under section 176A(5) to disapply section 176A

7.3A(1) **[Application accompanied by affidavit]** An application under section 176A(5) shall be accompanied by an affidavit prepared and sworn by the liquidator, administrator or receiver.

7.3A(2) **[Contents of affidavit]** The affidavit shall state–

(a) the type of insolvency proceedings in which the application arises;

(b) a summary of the financial position of the company;

(c) the information substantiating the applicant's view that the cost of making a distribution to unsecured creditors would be disproportionate to the benefits; and

(d) whether any other insolvency practitioner is acting in relation to the company and if so his address.

R. 7.3A
This was inserted by Insolvency (Amendment) Rules 2003 (SI 2003/1730) and deals with the obligations of the insolvency practitioner when seeking an order to disapply the special reserve fund for unsecured creditors – see the comment on s. 176A.

7.4 Filing and service of application

7.4(1) **[Filing etc.]** The application shall be filed in court, accompanied by one copy and a number of additional copies equal to the number of persons who are to be served with the application.

7.4(2) **[Venue]** Subject as follows in this Rule and the next, or unless the Rule under which the application is brought provides otherwise, or the court otherwise orders, upon the presentation of the documents mentioned in paragraph (1) above, the court shall fix a venue for the application to be heard.

7.4(3) **[Service]** Unless the court otherwise directs, the applicant shall serve a sealed copy of the application, endorsed with the venue for the hearing, on the respondent named in the application (or on each respondent if more than one).

7.4(4) [Directions] The court may give any of the following directions–

(a) that the application be served upon persons other than those specified by the relevant provision of the Act or Rules;

(b) that the giving of notice to any person may be dispensed with;

(c) that notice be given in some way other than that specified in paragraph (3).

7.4(5) [Time for service] Unless the provision of the Act or Rules under which the application is made provides otherwise, and subject to the next paragraph, the application must be served at least 14 days before the date fixed for the hearing.

7.4(6) [In case of urgency] Where the case is one of urgency, the court may (without prejudice to its general power to extend or abridge time limits)–

(a) hear the application immediately, either with or without notice to, or the attendance of, other parties, or

(b) authorise a shorter period of service than that provided for by paragraph (5);

and any such application may be heard on terms providing for the filing or service of documents, or the carrying out of other formalities, as the court thinks fit.

(See General Note after r. 7.18.)

On r. 7.4(6) see *Bagnall v Official Receiver* [2003] E.W.H.C. 1398 (Ch).

7.4A Notice of application under section 176A(5)

7.4A An application under section 176A(5) may be made without the application being served upon or notice being given to any other party, save that notice of the application shall be given to any other insolvency practitioner who acts as such in relation to the company including any member State liquidator.

R. 7.4A
This was inserted by Insolvency (Amendment) Rules 2003 (SI 2003/1730). This covers notice requirements where an application is made pursuant to s. 176A to disapply the reserve fund for unsecured creditors.

7.5 Other hearings *ex parte*

7.5(1) [Ex parte applications] Where the relevant provisions of the Act or Rules do not require service of the application on, or notice of it to be given to, any person, the court may hear the application *ex parte*.

7.5(2) [Power of court] Where the application is properly made *ex parte*, the court may hear it forthwith, without fixing a venue as required by Rule 7.4(2).

7.5(3) [Alternative power] Alternatively, the court may fix a venue for the application to be heard, in which case Rule 7.4 applies (so far as relevant).

(See General Note after r. 7.18.)

7.6 Hearing of application

7.6(1) [Hearing in chambers] Unless allowed or authorised to be made otherwise, every application before the registrar shall, and every application before the judge may, be heard in chambers.

7.6(2) [Registrar's jurisdiction] Unless either–

(a) the judge has given a general or special direction to the contrary, or

(b) it is not within the registrar's power to make the order required,

the jurisdiction of the court to hear and determine the application may be exercised by the registrar, and the application shall be made to the registrar in the first instance.

7.6(3) [Reference to judge] Where the application is made to the registrar he may refer to the judge any matter which he thinks should properly be decided by the judge, and the judge may either dispose of the matter or refer it back to the registrar with such directions as he thinks fit.

7.6(4) [Effect of Rule] Nothing in this Rule precludes an application being made directly to the judge in a proper case.

(See General Note after r. 7.18.)

7.7 Use of affidavit evidence

7.7(1) [Affidavit evidence, attendance for cross-examination] In any proceedings evidence may be given by affidavit unless by any provision of the Rules it is otherwise provided or the court otherwise directs; but the court may, on the application of any party, order the attendance for cross-examination of the person making the affidavit.

7.7(2) [Where attendance for cross-examination ordered] Where, after such an order has been made, the person in question does not attend, his affidavit shall not be used in evidence without the leave of the court.

(See General Note after r. 7.18.)

7.8 Filing and service of affidavits

7.8(1) [Filing in court etc.] Unless the provision of the Act or Rules under which the application is made provides otherwise, or the court otherwise allows–

(a) if the applicant intends to rely at the first hearing on affidavit evidence, he shall file the affidavit or affidavits (if more than one) in court and serve a copy or copies on the respondent, not less than 14 days before the date fixed for the hearing, and

(b) where a respondent to an application intends to oppose it and to rely for that purpose on affidavit evidence, he shall file the affidavit or affidavits (if more than one) in court and serve a copy or copies on the applicant, not less than 7 days before the date fixed for the hearing.

7.8(2) [Swearing of affidavits] Any affidavit may be sworn by the applicant or by the respondent or by some other person possessing direct knowledge of the subject matter of the application.

(See General Note after r. 7.18.)

7.9 Use of reports

7.9(1) [Filing report instead of affidavit] A report may be filed in court instead of an affidavit–

(a) in any case, by the official receiver (whether or not he is acting in any capacity mentioned in sub-paragraph (b)), or a deputy official receiver, or

(b) unless the application involves other parties or the court otherwise orders, by–

    (i) an administrator, a liquidator or a trustee in bankruptcy,
    (ii) a provisional liquidator or an interim receiver,
    (iii) a special manager, or
    (iv) an insolvency practitioner appointed under section 273(2).

7.9(2) [Report to be treated as affidavit] In any case where a report is filed instead of an affidavit, the report shall be treated for the purposes of Rule 7.8(1) and any hearing before the court as if it were an affidavit.

7.9(3) [Official receiver's report as prima facie evidence] Any report filed by the official receiver in accordance with the Act or the Rules is prima facie evidence of any matter contained in it.

(See General Note after r. 7.18.)

7.10 Adjournment of hearing; directions

7.10(1) [Powers of court] The court may adjourn the hearing of an application on such terms (if any) as it thinks fit.

7.10(2) [Directions] The court may at any time give such directions as it thinks fit as to–

(a) service or notice of the application on or to any person, whether in connection with the venue of a resumed hearing or for any other purpose;

(b) whether particulars of claim and defence are to be delivered and generally as to the procedure on the applications;

(c) the manner in which any evidence is to be adduced at a resumed hearing and in particular (but without prejudice to the generality of this sub-paragraph) as to–

    (i) the taking of evidence wholly or in part by affidavit or orally;

    (ii) the cross-examination either before the judge or registrar on the hearing in court or in chambers, of any deponents to affidavits;

    (iii) any report to be given by the official receiver or any person mentioned in Rule 7.9(1)(b);

(d) the matters to be dealt with in evidence.

(See General Note after r. 7.18.) On r. 7.10(2) see *Re Gunningham* [2002] B.P.I.R. 302.

CHAPTER 2

TRANSFER OF PROCEEDINGS BETWEEN COURTS

7.11 General power of transfer

7.11(1) [Transfer to county court] Where winding-up or bankruptcy proceedings are pending in the High Court, the court may order them to be transferred to a specified county court.

7.11(2) [Transfer to High Court etc.] Where winding-up or bankruptcy proceedings are pending in a county court, the court may order them to be transferred either to the High Court or to another county court.

7.11(3) [Transfer to county court with jurisdiction] In any case where proceedings are transferred to a county court, the transfer must be to a court which has jurisdiction to wind up companies or, as the case may be, jurisdiction in bankruptcy.

7.11(4) [Power of High Court judge] Where winding-up or bankruptcy proceedings are pending in a county court, a judge of the High Court may order them to be transferred to that Court.

7.11(5) [Order for transfer] A transfer of proceedings under this Rule may be ordered–

(a) by the court of its own motion, or

(b) on the application of the official receiver, or

(c) on the application of a person appearing to the court to have an interest in the proceedings.

7.11(6) [Proceedings commenced before coming into force of Rules] A transfer of proceedings under this Rule may be ordered notwithstanding that the proceedings commenced before the coming into force of the Rules.

GENERAL NOTE

See the *Practice Direction: Insolvency Proceedings* [2000] B.C.C. 927 (reproduced in Appendix IV to this *Guide*). See also general note after r. 7.18.

7.12 Proceedings commenced in wrong court

7.12 Where winding-up or bankruptcy proceedings are commenced in a court which is, in relation to those proceedings, the wrong court, that court may–

(a) order the transfer of the proceedings to the court in which they ought to have been commenced;

(b) order that the proceedings be continued in the court in which they have been commenced; or

(c) order the proceedings to be struck out.

(See General Note after r. 7.18.)

7.13 Applications for transfer

7.13(1) [**Official receiver's report**] An application by the official receiver for proceedings to be transferred shall be made with a report by him–

(a) setting out the reasons for the transfer, and

(b) including a statement either that the petitioner consents to the transfer, or that he has been given at least 14 days' notice of the official receiver's application.

7.13(2) [**More convenient conduct of proceedings**] If the court is satisfied from the official receiver's report that the proceedings can be conducted more conveniently in another court, the proceedings shall be transferred to that court.

7.13(3) [**Application not made by official receiver**] Where an application for the transfer of proceedings is made otherwise than by the official receiver, at least 14 days' notice of the application shall be given by the applicant–

(a) to the official receiver attached to the court in which the proceedings are pending, and

(b) to the official receiver attached to the court to which it is proposed that they should be transferred.

(See General Note after r. 7.18.)

7.14 Procedure following order for transfer

7.14(1) [**Copy of order etc. to transferee court**] Subject as follows, the court making an order under Rule 7.11 shall forthwith send to the transferee court a sealed copy of the order, and the file of the proceedings.

7.14(2) [**On receipt**] On receipt of these, the transferee court shall forthwith send notice of the transfer to the official receivers attached to that court and the transferor court respectively.

7.14(3) [**Non-application of r. 7.14(1)**] Paragraph (1) does not apply where the order is made by the High Court under Rule 7.11(4). In that case–

(a) the High Court shall send sealed copies of the order to the county court from which the proceedings are to be transferred, and to the official receivers attached to that court and the High Court respectively, and

(b) that county court shall send the file of the proceedings to the High Court.

7.14(4) [**Following compliance with Rule**] Following compliance with this Rule, if the official receiver attached to the court to which the proceedings are ordered to be transferred is not already, by virtue of directions given by the Secretary of State under section 399(6)(a), the official receiver in relation to those proceedings, he becomes, in relation to those proceedings, the official receiver in place of the official receiver attached to the other court concerned.

(See General Note after r. 7.18.)

7.15 Consequential transfer of other proceedings

7.15(1) [Application of Rule] This Rule applies where–

(a) an order for the winding up of a company, or a bankruptcy order in the case of an individual, has been made by the High Court, or

(b) in either such case, a provisional liquidator or (as the case may be) an interim receiver has been appointed, or

(c) winding-up or bankruptcy proceedings have been transferred to that Court from a county court.

7.15(2) [Power of High Court judge] A judge of any Division of the High Court may, of his own motion, order the transfer to that Division of any such proceedings as are mentioned below and are pending against the company or individual concerned ("the insolvent") either in another Division of the High Court or in a court in England and Wales other than the High Court.

7.15(3) [Proceedings which may be transferred] Proceedings which may be so transferred are those brought by or against the insolvent for the purpose of enforcing a claim against the insolvent estate, or brought by a person other than the insolvent for the purpose of enforcing any such claim (including in either case proceedings of any description by a debenture-holder or mortgagee).

7.15(4) [Where proceedings are transferred] Where proceedings are transferred under this Rule, the registrar may (subject to general or special directions of the judge) dispose of any matter arising in the proceedings which would, but for the transfer, have been disposed of in chambers or, in the case of proceedings transferred from a county court, by the registrar of that court.

(See General Note after r. 7.18.)

CHAPTER 3

SHORTHAND WRITERS

7.16 Nomination and appointment of shorthand writers

7.16(1) [Nomination] In the High Court the judge and, in a county court, the registrar may in writing nominate one or more persons to be official shorthand writers to the court.

[FORM 7.3]

7.16(2) [Appointment] The court may, at any time in the course of insolvency proceedings, appoint a shorthand writer to take down the evidence of a person examined under section 133, 236, 290 or 366.

[FORM 7.4]

7.16(3) [Application by official receiver etc.] Where the official receiver applies to the court for an order appointing a shorthand writer, he shall name the person he proposes for appointment; and that appointment shall be made, unless the court otherwise orders.

(See General Note after r. 7.18.)

7.17 Remuneration

7.17(1) [Payment] The remuneration of a shorthand writer appointed in insolvency proceedings shall be paid by the party at whose instance the appointment was made, or out of the insolvent estate, or otherwise, as the court may direct.

7.17(2) [Court's discretion] Any question arising as to the rates of remuneration payable under this Rule shall be determined by the court in its discretion.

(See General Note after r. 7.18.)

7.18 Cost of shorthand note

7.18 Where in insolvency proceedings the court appoints a shorthand writer on the application of the official receiver, in order that a written record may be taken of the evidence of a person to be examined, the cost of the written record is deemed an expense of the official receiver in the proceedings.

GENERAL NOTE TO RR. 7.1–7.18

There are only two forms of application: originating and ordinary. The distinction is relevant primarily in relation to the forms to be used (r. 7.2). In the case of an originating application, r. 7.3(2) also applies.

The procedure here laid down is largely similar to that prescribed by the CPR. The following provisions perhaps call for special note:

 r. 7.4(6) – hearings in case of urgency;

 r. 7.5 – other hearings without notice;

 r. 7.9 – use of reports of the official receiver or of an insolvency practitioner instead of affidavits;

 r. 7.15 – transfer to the insolvency court of other proceedings pending against the insolvent.

The meaning and nature of an "ordinary application" under r. 7.2 was discussed by Harman J. in *Port v Auger* [1994] 1 W.L.R. 862. He held that an ordinary application as defined in r. 7.2(1) could not be struck out under RSC O. 18, r. 19, since it was not within the definition of "pleadings" under the latter rule; but that the court might strike out such an application under its inherent jurisdiction to stay proceedings which are frivolous, vexatious or an abuse of its process (above). Similar reasoning would no doubt apply to an application to strike out an ordinary application under the CPR, which uses the term "statement of case" instead of "pleadings": see the CPR, r. 3.4 and, for the definition of "statement of case", r. 2.3(1).

Cross-examination was ordered under r. 7.7 and 7.10, and also discovery of documents, in *Re Bank of Credit and Commerce International SA (No. 6)* [1994] 1 B.C.L.C. 450.

In *Re Cover Europe Ltd* [2002] EWHC 799 (Ch); [2002] B.P.I.R. 931 it was held that the Companies Court could, under r. 7.10, deal with complicated issues of fact and give directions to the parties to serve details of statement of case and have witnesses cross-examined at trial; it was not necessary to remit the matter to the Queen's Bench Division.

R. 7.17
The rates of remuneration for shorthand writers were formerly fixed by Sch. 3. The court is now given a discretion to settle any disputed charge.

CHAPTER 4

ENFORCEMENT PROCEDURES

7.19 Enforcement of court orders

7.19(1) [Orders enforced as judgments] In any insolvency proceedings, orders of the court may be enforced in the same manner as a judgment to the same effect.

7.19(2) [**Enforcement etc. by any county court**] Where an order in insolvency proceedings is made, or any process is issued, by a county court ("the primary court"), the order or process may be enforced, executed and dealt with by any other county court ("the secondary court"), as if it had been made or issued for the enforcement of a judgment or order to the same effect made by the secondary court.

This applies whether or not the secondary court has jurisdiction to take insolvency proceedings.

(See General Note after r. 7.25.)

7.20 Orders enforcing compliance with the Rules

7.20(1) [**Application by competent person**] The court may, on application by the competent person, make such orders as it thinks necessary for the enforcement of obligations falling on any person in accordance with–

(a) paragraph 47 of Schedule B1 or section 47 or 131 (duty to submit statement of affairs in administration, administrative receivership or winding up),

(b) section 143(2) (liquidator to furnish information, books, papers, etc.), or

(c) section 235 (duty of various persons to co-operate with office-holder).

7.20(2) [**Who is competent person**] The competent person for this purpose is–

(a) under paragraph 47 of Schedule B1, the administrator,

(b) under section 47, the administrative receiver,

(c) under section 131 or 143(2), the official receiver, and

(d) under section 235, the official receiver, the administrator, the administrative receiver, the liquidator or the provisional liquidator, as the case may be.

7.20(3) [**Costs**] An order of the court under this Rule may provide that all costs of and incidental to the application for it shall be borne by the person against whom the order is made.

(See General Note after r. 7.25.)

7.21 Warrants (general provisions)

7.21(1) [**Address for warrant**] A warrant issued by the court under any provision of the Act shall be addressed to such officer of the High Court or of a county court (whether or not having jurisdiction in insolvency proceedings) as the warrant specifies, or to any constable.

7.21(2) [**Prescribed officer of the court**] The persons referred to in sections 134(2), 236(5), 364(1), 365(3) and 366(3) (court's powers of enforcement) as the prescribed officer of the court are–

(a) in the case of the High Court, the tipstaff and his assistants of the court, and

(b) in the case of a county court, the registrar and the bailiffs.

7.21(3) [**Definition**] In this Chapter references to property include books, papers and records.

(See General Note after r. 7.25.)

7.22 Warrants under s. 134, 364

7.22 When a person is arrested under a warrant issued by the court under section 134 (officer of company failing to attend for public examination), or section 364 (arrest of debtor or bankrupt)–

(a) the officer apprehending him shall give him into the custody of the governor of the prison named in the warrant, who shall keep him in custody until such time as the court otherwise orders and shall produce him before the court as it may from time to time direct; and

[FORM 7.9]

(b) any property in the arrested person's possession which may be seized shall be–
  (i) lodged with, or otherwise dealt with as instructed by, whoever is specified in the warrant as authorised to receive it, or
  (ii) kept by the officer seizing it pending the receipt of written orders from the court as to its disposal,

as may be directed by the court in the warrant.

[FORM 7.6]
[FORM 7.7]

(See General Note after r. 7.25.)

7.23 Warrants under s. 236, 366

7.23(1) [When person arrrested] When a person is arrested under a warrant issued under section 236 (inquiry into insolvent company's dealings) or 366 (the equivalent in bankruptcy), the officer arresting him shall forthwith bring him before the court issuing the warrant in order that he may be examined.

[FORM 7.8]

7.23(2) [If not brought before court immediately] If he cannot immediately be brought up for examination, the officer shall deliver him into the custody of the governor of the prison named in the warrant, who shall keep him in custody and produce him before the court as it may from time to time direct.

[FORM 7.9]

7.23(3) [Report of arrest etc.] After arresting the person named in the warrant, the officer shall forthwith report to the court the arrest or delivery into custody (as the case may be) and apply to the court to fix a venue for the person's examination.

7.23(4) [Time for examination etc.] The court shall appoint the earliest practicable time for the examination, and shall–

(a) direct the governor of the prison to produce the person for examination at the time and place appointed, and
(b) forthwith give notice of the venue to the person who applied for the warrant.

[FORM 7.9]

7.23(5) [Property in arrested person's possession] Any property in the arrested person's possession which may be seized shall be–

(a) lodged with, or otherwise dealt with as instructed by, whoever is specified in the warrant as authorised to receive it, or
(b) kept by the officer seizing it pending the receipt of written orders from the court as to its disposal,

as may be directed by the court.

(See General Note after r. 7.25.)

7.24 Execution of warrants outside court's district

7.24(1) [Application of Rule] This Rule applies where a warrant for a person's arrest has been issued in insolvency proceedings by a county court ("the primary court") and is addressed to another county court ("the secondary court") for execution in its district.

[FORM 7.10]

7.24(2) [Power of secondary court] The secondary court may send the warrant to the registrar of any other county court (whether or not having jurisdiction to take insolvency proceedings) in whose district the person to be arrested is or is believed to be, with a notice to the effect that the warrant is transmitted to that court under this Rule for execution in its district at the request of the primary court.

7.24(3) **[Court receiving warrant]** The court receiving a warrant transmitted by the secondary court under this Rule shall apply its seal to the warrant, and secure that all such steps are taken for its execution as would be appropriate in the case of a warrant issued by itself.

(See General Note after r. 7.25.)

7.25 Warrants under s. 365

7.25(1) **[Seizure]** A warrant issued under section 365(3) (search of premises not belonging to the bankrupt) shall authorise any person executing it to seize any property of the bankrupt found as a result of the execution of the warrant.

7.25(2) **[Seized property]** Any property seized under a warrant issued under section 365(2) or (3) shall be–

(a) lodged with, or otherwise dealt with as instructed by, whoever is specified in the warrant as authorised to receive it, or

(b) kept by the officer seizing it pending the receipt of written orders from the court as to its disposal,

as may be directed by the warrant.

[FORM 7.12]
[FORM 7.13]

GENERAL NOTE TO RR. 7.19–7.25

Chapter 4, as the title indicates, deals with the procedures for the enforcement of court orders, of statutory duties and of warrants issued under IA 1986. In particular, r. 7.20 sanctions with the backing of the court the general duty of corporate officers and others to co-operate with the official receiver and with insolvency practitioners holding office as liquidator, etc. Rule 7.20 was amended by I(A)R 2003 (SI 2003/1730) with effect from September 15, 2003 to cater for the new mode of administration.

CHAPTER 5

COURT RECORDS AND RETURNS

7.26 Title of proceedings

7.26(1) **[Proceedings under Pts I–VII]** Every proceeding under Parts I to VII of the Act shall, with any necessary additions, be intituled "IN THE MATTER OF ... (naming the company to which the proceedings relate) AND IN THE MATTER OF THE INSOLVENCY ACT 1986".

7.26(2) **[Proceedings under Pts IX–XI]** Every proceeding under Parts IX to XI of the Act shall be intituled "IN BANKRUPTCY".

(See General Note after r. 7.32.)

7.27 Court records

7.27 The court shall keep records of all insolvency proceedings, and shall cause to be entered in the records the taking of any step in the proceedings, and such decisions of the court in relation thereto, as the court thinks fit.

(See General Note after r. 7.32.)

7.28 Inspection of records

7.28(1) [**Open to inspection by any person**] Subject as follows, the court's records of insolvency proceedings shall be open to inspection by any person.

7.28(2) [**Application to inspect etc.**] If in the case of a person applying to inspect the records the registrar is not satisfied as to the propriety of the purpose for which inspection is required, he may refuse to allow it. The person may then apply forthwith and *ex parte* to the judge, who may refuse the inspection, or allow it on such terms as he thinks fit.

7.28(3) [**Judge's decision final**] The judge's decision under paragraph (2) is final.

(See General Note after r. 7.32.)

7.29 Returns to Secretary of State

7.29(1) [**Particulars of proceedings**] The court shall from time to time send to the Secretary of State the following particulars relating to winding-up and bankruptcy proceedings–

(a) the full title of the proceedings, including the number assigned to each case;

(b) where a winding-up or bankruptcy order has been made, the date of the order.

7.29(2) [**Request for particulars etc.**] The Secretary of State may, on the request of any person, furnish him with particulars sent by the court under this Rule.

(See General Note after r. 7.32.)

7.30 File of court proceedings

7.30(1) [**Court file**] In respect of all insolvency proceedings, the court shall open and maintain a file for each case; and (subject to directions of the registrar) all documents relating to such proceedings shall be placed on the relevant file.

7.30(2) [**No filing in Central Office**] No proceedings shall be filed in the Central Office of the High Court.

(See General Note after r. 7.32.)

7.31 Right to inspect the file

7.31(1) [**Who has right to inspect**] In the case of any insolvency proceedings, the following have the right, at all reasonable times, to inspect the court's file of the proceedings–

(a) the person who, in relation to those proceedings, is the responsible insolvency practitioner;

(b) any duly authorised officer of the Department; and

(c) any person stating himself in writing to be a creditor of the company to which, or the individual to whom, the proceedings relate.

7.31(2) [**Exercise of right**] The same right of inspection is exercisable–

(a) in proceedings under Parts I to VII of the Act, by every person who is, or at any time has been, a director or officer of the company to which the proceedings relate, or who is a member of the company or a contributory in its winding up;

(b) in proceedings with respect to a voluntary arrangement proposed by a debtor under Part VIII of the Act, by the debtor;

(c) in bankruptcy proceedings, by–

    (i) the bankrupt,
    (ii) any person against whom, or by whom, a bankruptcy petition has been presented, and
    (iii) any person who has been served, in accordance with Chapter 1 of Part 6 of the Rules, with a statutory demand.

7.31(3) [**Authority to inspect**] The right of inspection conferred as above on any person may be exercised on his behalf by a person properly authorised by him.

7.31(4) [**Leave to inspect**] Any person may, by special leave of the court, inspect the file.

7.31(5) [**When right not exercisable etc.**] The right of inspection conferred by this Rule is not exercisable in the case of documents, or parts of documents, as to which the court directs (either generally or specially) that they are not to be made open to inspection without the court's leave.

An application for a direction of the court under this paragraph may be made by the official receiver, by the person who in relation to any proceedings is the responsible insolvency practitioner, or by any party appearing to the court to have an interest.

7.31(6) [**If Secretary of State etc. requires to inspect**] If, for the purpose of powers conferred by the Act or the Rules, the Secretary of State, the Department or the official receiver requires to inspect the file of any insolvency proceedings, and requests the transmission of the file, the court shall comply with the request (unless the file is for the time being in use for the court's own purposes).

7.31(7) [**Application of r. 7.28**] Paragraphs (2) and (3) of Rule 7.28 apply in respect of the court's file of any proceedings as they apply in respect of court records.

(See General Note after r. 7.32.)

7.32 Filing of Gazette notices and advertisements

7.32(1) [**Filing by officer of the court**] In any court in which insolvency proceedings are pending, an officer of the court shall file a copy of every issue of the Gazette which contains an advertisement relating to those proceedings.

7.32(2) [**Filing by advertiser**] Where there appears in a newspaper an advertisement relating to insolvency proceedings pending in any court, the person inserting the advertisement shall file a copy of it in that court.

The copy of the advertisement shall be accompanied by, or have endorsed on it, such particulars as are necessary to identify the proceedings and the date of the advertisement's appearance.

7.32(3) [**Court officer's memorandum**] An officer of any court in which insolvency proceedings are pending shall from time to time file a memorandum giving the dates of, and other particulars relating to, any notice published in the Gazette, and any newspaper advertisements, which relate to proceedings so pending.

The officer's memorandum is prima facie evidence that any notice or advertisement mentioned in it was duly inserted in the issue of the newspaper or the Gazette which is specified in the memorandum.

GENERAL NOTE TO RR. 7.26–7.32

These rules give instructions about court records and files and the respective rights to inspect them; and also about the returns to be made by the court to the Secretary of State and the filing of Gazette notices. The *Practice Statement:*

Administration Orders – Reports [2002] B.C.C. 354 deals with the different forms of "restriction order" the court may make in exercise of the powers conferred by r. 7.31(5), and in particular the right to examine the r. 2.2 report.

For an analysis of the relationship between the various sub-rules in r. 7.31 see the judgment of Vinelott J. in *Astor Chemical Ltd v Synthetic Technology Ltd* [1990] B.C.C. 97.

An "insolvency consultant" who sought to search the records of insolvency proceedings for the names and addresses of potential customers for his services was not inspecting the records for a proper purpose, within r. 7.28(2), and was rightly refused inspection: *Re an Application pursuant to r. 7.28 of the Insolvency Rules 1986* [1994] B.C.C. 369. For a similar decision, see *Ex p. Creditnet Ltd* [1996] 1 W.L.R. 1291; [1996] B.C.C. 444. No appeal lies from the ruling of a judge under r. 7.28: see r. 7.28(3) and *Re Austintel Ltd* [1997] 1 W.L.R. 616; [1997] B.C.C. 362.

CHAPTER 6

COSTS AND DETAILED ASSESSMENT

INTRODUCTION

The whole of Chapter 6 (rr. 7.33–7.42) was replaced by the Insolvency Amendment (No. 2) Rules 1999 (SI 1999/1022) with effect from April 26, 1999 in order to bring these rules into line with the CPR.

7.33 Application of the CPR

7.33 Subject to provision to inconsistent effect made as follows in this Chapter, CPR Part 43 (scope of costs rules and definitions), Part 44 (general rules about costs), Part 45 (fixed costs), Part 47 (procedure for detailed assessment of costs and default provisions) and Part 48 (costs – special cases) shall apply to insolvency proceedings with any necessary modifications.

7.34 Requirement to assess costs by the detailed procedure

7.34(1) **[Costs, charges, expenses]** Subject as follows, where the costs, charges or expenses of any person are payable out of the insolvent estate, the amount of those costs, charges or expenses shall be decided by detailed assessment unless agreed between the responsible insolvency practitioner and the person entitled to payment, and in the absence of such agreement the responsible insolvency practitioner may serve notice in writing requiring that person to commence detailed assessment proceedings in accordance with CPR Part 47 (procedure for detailed assessment of costs and default provisions) in the court to which the insolvency proceedings are allocated or, where in relation to a company there is no such court, that in relation to any court having jurisdiction to wind up the company.

7.34(2) **[Assessment of costs, charges, expenses]** If a liquidation or creditors' committee established in insolvency proceedings (except administrative receivership) resolves that the amount of any such costs, charges or expenses should be decided by detailed assessment, the insolvency practitioner shall require detailed assessment in accordance with CPR Part 47.

7.34(3) **[Payments on account]** Where the amount of the costs, charges or expenses of any person employed by an insolvency practitioner in insolvency proceedings are required to be decided by detailed assessment or fixed by order of the court this does not preclude the insolvency practitioner from making payments on account to such person on the basis of an undertaking by that person to repay immediately any money which may, when detailed assessment is made, prove to have been overpaid, with interest at the rate specified in section 17 of the Judgments Act 1838 on the date payment was made and for the period from the date of payment to that of repayment.

7.34(4) **[Power of court re costs]** In any proceedings before the court, including proceedings on a petition, the court may order costs to be decided by detailed assessment.

7.34(5) **[Costs of trustee in bankruptcy, liquidator]** Unless otherwise directed or authorised, the costs of a trustee in bankruptcy or a liquidator are to be allowed on the standard basis for which provision is made in CPR rule 44.4 (basis of assessment) and rule 44.5 (factors to be taken into account in deciding the amount of costs).

7.34(6) **[Application of Rule]** This Rule applies additionally (with any necessary modifications) to winding-up and bankruptcy proceedings commenced before the coming into force of the Rules.

7.35 Procedure where detailed assessment required

7.35(1) **[Requirements of costs officer]** Before making a detailed assessment of the costs of any person employed in insolvency proceedings by a responsible insolvency practitioner, the costs officer shall require a certificate of employment, which shall be endorsed on the bill and signed by the insolvency practitioner.

7.35(2) **[Information on certificate]** The certificate shall include–

(a) the name and address of the person employed,

(b) details of the functions to be carried out under the employment, and

(c) a note of any special terms of remuneration which have been agreed.

7.35(3) **[Detailed assessment proceedings]** Every person whose costs in insolvency proceedings are required to be decided by detailed assessment shall, on being required in writing to do so by the insolvency practitioner, commence detailed assessment proceedings in accordance with CPR Part 47 (procedure for detailed assessment of costs and default provisions).

7.35(4) **[Commencement of detailed assessment proceedings within three months]** If that person does not commence detailed assessment proceedings within 3 months of the requirement under paragraph (3), or within such further time as the court, on application, may permit, the insolvency practitioner may deal with the insolvent estate without regard to any claim by that person, whose claim is forfeited by such failure to commence proceedings.

7.35(5) **[Failure to commence proceedings]** Where in any such case such a claim lies additionally against an insolvency practitioner in his personal capacity, that claim is also forfeited by such failure to commence proceedings.

7.35(6) **[Assessment of costs by High Court]** Where costs have been incurred in insolvency proceedings in the High Court and those proceedings are subsequently transferred to a county court, all costs of those proceedings directed by the court or otherwise required to be assessed may nevertheless, on the application of the person who incurred the costs, be ordered to be decided by detailed assessment in the High Court.

7.36 Costs of sheriff

7.36(1) **[Detailed assessment of sheriff's bill]** Where a sheriff–

(a) is required under section 184(2) or 346(2) to deliver up goods or money, or

(b) has under section 184(3) or 346(3) deducted costs from the proceeds of an execution or money paid to him,

the responsible insolvency practitioner may require in writing that the amount of the sheriff's bill of costs be decided by detailed assessment.

7.36(2) **[Application of r. 7.35(4)]** Where such a requirement is made, Rule 7.35(4) applies.

7.36(3) **[In case of r. 7.36(1)(b) deduction]** Where, in the case of a deduction under paragraph (1)(b), any amount deducted is disallowed at the conclusion of the detailed assessment proceedings, the sheriff shall forthwith pay a sum equal to that disallowed to the insolvency practitioner for the benefit of the insolvent estate.

7.37 Petitions presented by insolvents

7.37(1) **[Credit for security]** In any case where a petition is presented by a company or individual ("the insolvent") against himself, any solicitor acting for the insolvent shall in his bill of costs give credit for any sum or security received from the insolvent as a deposit on account of the costs and expenses to be incurred in respect of the filing and prosecution of the petition; and the deposit shall be noted by the costs officer on the final costs certificate.

7.37(2) [**Application of r. 7.37(3)**] Paragraph (3) applies where a petition is presented by a person other than the insolvent to whom the petition relates and before it is heard the insolvent presents a petition for the same order, and that order is made.

7.37(3) [**No costs allowed to insolvent, etc.**] Unless the court considers that the insolvent estate has benefited by the insolvent's conduct, or that there are otherwise special circumstances justifying the allowance of costs, no costs shall be allowed to the insolvent or his solicitor out of the insolvent estate.

7.38 Costs paid otherwise than out of the insolvent estate

7.38 Where the amount of costs is decided by detailed assessment under an order of the court directing that those costs are to be paid otherwise than out of the insolvent estate, the costs officer shall note on the final costs certificate by whom, or the manner in which, the costs are to be paid.

7.39 Award of costs against official receiver or responsible insolvency practitioner

7.39 Without prejudice to any provision of the Act or Rules by virtue of which the official receiver is not in any event to be liable for costs and expenses, where the official receiver or a responsible insolvency practitioner is made a party to any proceedings on the application of another party to the proceedings, he shall not be personally liable for costs unless the court otherwise directs.

7.40 Applications for costs

7.40(1) [**Application of Rule**] This Rule applies where a party to, or person affected by, any proceedings in an insolvency–

(a) applies to the court for an order allowing his costs, or part of them, incidental to the proceedings, and

(b) that application is not made at the time of the proceedings.

7.40(2) [**Copies of application**] The person concerned shall serve a sealed copy of his application on the responsible insolvency practitioner, and, in winding up by the court or bankruptcy, on the official receiver.

7.40(3) [**Appearances**] The insolvency practitioner and, where appropriate, the official receiver may appear on the application.

7.40(4) [**Costs**] No costs of or incidental to the application shall be allowed to the applicant unless the court is satisfied that the application could not have been made at the time of the proceedings.

7.41 Costs and expenses of witnesses

7.41(1) [**No allowance to bankrupt, etc.**] Except as directed by the court, no allowance as a witness in any examination or other proceedings before the court shall be made to the bankrupt or an officer of the insolvent company to which the proceedings relate.

7.41(2) [**Petitioner's expenses**] A person presenting any petition in insolvency proceedings shall not be regarded as a witness on the hearing of the petition, but the costs officer may allow his expenses of travelling and subsistence.

7.42 Final costs certificate

7.42(1) [**Certificate is final, etc.**] A final costs certificate of the costs officer is final and conclusive as to all matters which have not been objected to in the manner provided for under the rules of the court.

7.42(2) [**Duplicate certificate**] Where it is proved to the satisfaction of a costs officer that a final costs certificate has been lost or destroyed, he may issue a duplicate.

GENERAL NOTE TO RR. 7.33–7.42

Chapter 6 was rewritten by the Insolvency (Amendment) (No. 2) Rules 1999 (SI 1999/1022) r. 3 with effect from April 26, 1999 in order to cater for the new terminology used in the Civil Procedure Rules (which replace the Rules of the Supreme Court and County Court Rules). The changes appear to be more a question of semantics than substance.

CHAPTER 7

PERSONS INCAPABLE OF MANAGING THEIR AFFAIRS

7.43 Introductory

7.43(1) [**Application of Ch. 7 Rules**] The Rules in this Chapter apply where in insolvency proceedings it appears to the court that a person affected by the proceedings is one who is incapable of managing and administering his property and affairs either–

(a) by reason of mental disorder within the meaning of the Mental Health Act 1983, or

(b) due to physical affliction or disability.

7.43(2) [**"The incapacitated person"**] The person concerned is referred to as "the incapacitated person".

(See General Note after r. 7.46.)

7.44 Appointment of another person to act

7.44(1) [**Power of court**] The court may appoint such person as it thinks fit to appear for, represent or act for the incapacitated person.

[FORM 7.19]

7.44(2) [**General or particular appointment**] The appointment may be made either generally or for the purpose of any particular application or proceeding, or for the exercise of particular rights or powers which the incapacitated person might have exercised but for his incapacity.

7.44(3) [**Appointment by court or on application**] The court may make the appointment either of its own motion or on application by–

(a) a person who has been appointed by a court in the United Kingdom or elsewhere to manage the affairs of, or to represent, the incapacitated person, or

(b) any relative or friend of the incapacitated person who appears to the court to be a proper person to make the application, or

(c) the official receiver, or

(d) the person who, in relation to the proceedings, is the responsible insolvency practitioner.

7.44(4) [***Ex parte* application, powers of court**] Application under paragraph (3) may be made *ex parte*; but the court may require such notice of the application as it thinks necessary to be given to the person alleged to be incapacitated, or any other person, and may adjourn the hearing of the application to enable the notice to be given.

(See General Note after r. 7.46.)

7.45 Affidavit in support of application

7.45(1) [**Affidavit of registered medical practitioner**] Except where made by the official receiver, an application under Rule 7.44(3) shall be supported by an affidavit of a registered medical practitioner as to the mental or physical condition of the incapacitated person.

7.45(2) **[Official receiver's report]** In the excepted case, a report made by the official receiver is sufficient.

(See General Note after r. 7.46.)

7.46 Service of notices following appointment

7.46 Any notice served on, or sent to, a person appointed under Rule 7.44 has the same effect as if it had been served on, or given to, the incapacitated person.

GENERAL NOTE TO RR. 7.43–7.46

The court is empowered by these rules to make special provision for any person subject to a disability who is affected by insolvency proceedings.

CHAPTER 8

APPEALS IN INSOLVENCY PROCEEDINGS

7.47 Appeals and reviews of court orders (winding up)

7.47(1) **[Powers of courts]** Every court having jurisdiction under the Act to wind up companies may review, rescind or vary any order made by it in the exercise of that jurisdiction.

7.47(2) **[Appeal to High Court etc.]** An appeal from a decision made in the exercise of that jurisdiction by a county court or by a registrar of the High Court lies to a single judge of the High Court; and an appeal from a decision of that judge on such an appeal lies, with the leave of that judge or the Court of Appeal, to the Court of Appeal.

7.47(3) **[County court not to be restrained etc.]** A county court is not, in the exercise of its jurisdiction to wind up companies, subject to be restrained by the order of any other court, and no appeal lies from its decision in the exercise of that jurisdiction except as provided by this Rule.

7.47(4) **[Application for rescission of winding-up order]** Any application for the rescission of a winding-up order shall be made within 7 days after the date on which the order was made.

GENERAL NOTE

Appeals from a registrar's winding-up order go to the High Court, not the Court of Appeal: *Re Calahurst Ltd* (1989) 5 B.C.C. 318. This point was confirmed by the Court of Appeal in *Re Tasbian Ltd (No. 2)* [1990] B.C.C. 322. This is also true in relation to an order made by a district judge in the county court: *Re Langley Marketing Services Ltd* [1992] B.C.C. 585; and the rule applies to an order made under CDDA 1986. It applies also to administration orders: *Cornhill Insurance plc v Cornhill Financial Services Ltd* [1992] B.C.C. 818. The appeal may take the form either of an appeal against the original decision of the registrar, or of an appeal from the registrar's refusal to review his original decision (*Re S N Group plc* [1993] B.C.C. 808). The jurisdiction under r. 7.47 is very wide, and extends even to the review, rescission or variation by a High Court judge of a decision of any judge of that court: *Re W & A Glaser Ltd* [1994] B.C.C. 199 at p. 208, *per* Harman J. A judge can review his or her own decisions under r. 7.47(1) – *Re Thirty Eight Building Ltd (No. 2)* [2000] B.P.I.R. 158. Leave is not required for an appeal to the High Court (*Re Busytoday Ltd* [1992] B.C.C. 480), but is necessary for a further appeal to the Court of Appeal (*Midrome Ltd v Shaw* [1993] B.C.C. 659).

In spite of the wording of r. 7.47(2) (and also r. 7.48(2)) second appeals to the Court of Appeal require the leave of the Court of Appeal – Access to Justice Act 1999 s. 55.

Appeals under r. 7.47(2) are true appeals and do not require a hearing *de novo*. Thus a decision of the registrar will only be overturned if it was based on an error of law or wrongful exercise of discretion: *Re Probe Data Systems Ltd (No. 3)* [1991] B.C.C. 428 and *Re Tasbian Ltd (No. 3)* [1991] B.C.C. 435. See also *Re Industrial & Commercial*

Securities plc (1989) 5 B.C.C. 320. The court will review an exercise of discretion only if it is satisfied that no judge, properly instructed as to the law with regard to the relevant facts, could have reached the conclusion that was reached in the court below: *Re MTI Trading Systems Ltd* [1998] B.C.C. 400. However, the court may rescind a winding-up order made by the registrar notwithstanding the fact that there is no ground to allow an appeal from his decision: *Re Dollar Land (Feltham) Ltd* [1995] B.C.C. 740. In the latest of cases the High Court can hear both an appeal from and a request to review a registrar's order – *Re Piccadilly Property Management Ltd* [1998] B.P.I.R. 260.

The jurisdiction of the court under r. 7.47 is not inconsistent with CPR r. 40.12 (the "slip rule"); and an error in an order may be corrected under either provision, or under the court's inherent jurisdiction: *Re Brian Sheridan Cars Ltd* [1995] B.C.C. 1,035.

See further the General Note to IA 1986, s. 375.

(See also General Note after r. 7.50.)

7.48 Appeals in bankruptcy

7.48(1) **[Appeal at instance of Secretary of State]** In bankruptcy proceedings, an appeal lies at the instance of the Secretary of State from any order of the court made on an application for the rescission or annulment of a bankruptcy order, or for a bankrupt's discharge.

7.48(2) **[Appeal to High Court etc.]** In the case of an order made by a county court or by a registrar of the High Court, the appeal lies to a single judge of the High Court; and an appeal from a decision of that judge on such an appeal lies, with the leave of that judge or the Court of Appeal, to the Court of Appeal.

GENERAL NOTE

An appeal under r. 7.48(2) from either a county court judge or a registrar of the High Court to a single judge of the High Court is a true appeal and not a rehearing *de novo*: *Re Gilmartin (a Bankrupt)* [1989] 1 W.L.R. 513.

(See also General Notes to r. 7.47 and r. 7.50.)

7.49 Procedure on appeal

7.49(1) **[Application of Supreme Court procedure, etc.]** Subject as follows, the procedure and practice of the Supreme Court relating to appeals to the Court of Appeal apply to appeals in insolvency proceedings.

7.49(2) **[Re appeal to single judge]** In relation to any appeal to a single judge of the High Court under section 375(2) (individual insolvency) or Rule 7.47(2) above (company insolvency), any reference in the CPR to the Court of Appeal is replaced by a reference to that judge and any reference to the registrar of civil appeals is replaced by a reference to the registrar of the High Court who deals with insolvency proceedings of the kind involved.

7.49(3) **[Appeal by ordinary application]** In insolvency proceedings, the procedure under RSC Order 59 (appeals to the Court of Appeal) is by ordinary application and not by application notice.

GENERAL NOTE

The text of r. 7.49 was substituted by Insolvency (Amendment) (No. 2) Rules 1999 (SI 1999/1022) with effect from April 26, 1999. This change was to cater for the new Civil Procedure Rules terminology.

An appeal under r. 7.49 is a true appeal: see *Re Hitco 2000 Ltd* [1995] B.C.C. 161 and the note to r. 7.47.

(See also General Note after r. 7.50.)

7.50 Appeal against decision of Secretary of State or official receiver

7.50(1) An appeal under the Act or the Rules against a decision of the Secretary of State or the official receiver shall be brought within 28 days of the notification of the decision.

7.50(2) In respect of a decision under Rule 6.214A(5)(b), an appeal shall be brought within 14 days of the notification of the decision.

GENERAL NOTE TO RR. 7.47–7.50

The various procedures and time limits listed here govern reviews and appeals from decisions of the courts, the Secretary of State and the official receiver. For further details, see the General Note after r. 7.47. Note also the Practice Direction in Appendix IV.

R. 7.50
A new sub-para. (2) was inserted by Insolvency (Amendment) Rules 2003 (SI 2003/1730) to fix a 14-day time limit for appeals against decisions made under r. 6.214A(5)(b).

CHAPTER 9

GENERAL

7.51 Principal court rules and practice to apply

7.51(1) [**Application of CPR etc**] The CPR, the practice and procedure of the High Court and of the county court (including any practice direction) apply to insolvency proceedings in the High Court and county court as the case may be, in either case with any necessary modifications, except so far as inconsistent with the Rules.

7.51(2) [**Allocations to CPR multi-track etc**] All insolvency proceedings shall be allocated to the multi-track for which CPR Part 29 (the multi-track) makes provision, accordingly those provisions of the CPR which provide for allocation questionnaires and track allocation will not apply.

GENERAL NOTE

This amended rule provides for the application generally of the Civil Procedure Rules in insolvency proceedings. In regard to costs, see rr. 7.33–7.42. Rule 7.51 was replaced by a new version by the Insolvency (Amendment) (No. 2) Rules 1999 (SI 1999/1022) with effect from April 26, 1999. For discussion see *Jay Benning Peltz v Deutsch* [2001] B.P.I.R. 510, *Highberry Ltd v Colt Telecom Group plc* [2002] EWHC 2503 (Ch), [2003] B.P.I.R. 311 and Davis [2000] *Insolvency Lawyer* 33.

7.52 Right of audience

7.52(1) [**Official receivers and their deputies**] Official receivers and deputy official receivers have right of audience in insolvency proceedings, whether in the High Court or a county court.

7.52(2) [**Rights as obtained before Rules**] Subject as above, rights of audience in insolvency proceedings are the same as obtained before the coming into force of the Rules.

GENERAL NOTE

There appears to have been no express provision governing rights of audience in the former rules: the matter was presumably left to be settled by the ordinary rules of court and the common law.

7.53 Right of attendance (company insolvency)

7.53(1) [**Creditor or member or contributory**] Subject as follows, in company insolvency proceedings any person stating himself in writing, in records kept by the court for that purpose, to be a creditor or member of the company or, where the company is being wound up, a contributory, is entitled, at his own cost, to attend in court or in chambers at any stage of the proceedings.

7.53(2) **[Attendance in person etc.]** Attendance may be by the person himself, or his solicitor.

7.53(3) **[Notice of proceedings]** A person so entitled may request the court in writing to give him notice of any step in the proceedings; and, subject to his paying the costs involved and keeping the court informed as to his address, the court shall comply with the request.

7.53(4) **[Costs]** If the court is satisfied that the exercise by a person of his rights under this Rule has given rise to costs for the insolvent estate which would not otherwise have been incurred and ought not, in the circumstances, to fall on that estate, it may direct that the costs be paid by the person concerned, to an amount specified.

The person's rights under this Rule are in abeyance so long as those costs are not paid.

7.53(5) **[Power of court to appoint representatives etc.]** The court may appoint one or more persons to represent the creditors, the members or the contributories of an insolvent company, or any class of them, to have the rights conferred by this Rule, instead of the rights being exercisable by any or all of them individually.

If two or more persons are appointed under this paragraph to represent the same interest, they must (if at all) instruct the same solicitor.

GENERAL NOTE

The right of individual creditors, members and contributories to participate in company insolvency proceedings is here confirmed, subject to the power of the court to direct that such persons should be represented as a class under r. 7.53(5).

7.54 Insolvency practitioner's solicitor

7.54 Where in any proceedings the attendance of the responsible insolvency practitioner's solicitor is required, whether in court or in chambers, the insolvency practitioner himself need not attend, unless directed by the court.

7.55 Formal defects

7.55 No insolvency proceedings shall be invalidated by any formal defect or by any irregularity, unless the court before which objection is made considers that substantial injustice has been caused by the defect or irregularity, and that the injustice cannot be remedied by any order of the court.

GENERAL NOTE

This rule appears to have been based on BA 1914, s. 147(1), but is made to apply to all forms of insolvency proceedings. For its relevance in the context of setting aside a statutory demand, see *Re a Debtor (No. 1 of 1987)* [1988] 1 W.L.R. 419. In the later case of *Re a Debtor (No. 190 of 1987)*, *The Times* May 21, 1988, Vinelott J. held that r. 7.55 did not apply to cure defects in the statutory demand. He thereby followed *Re Cartwright* [1975] 1 W.L.R. 573, which was decided under the old law. In *Re Awan* [2000] B.P.I.R. 241 Judge Boggis refused to allow r. 7.55 to be invoked to justify failure to provide proof of service as this was regarded as such a fundamental flaw.

In *Re a Debtor (No. 340 of 1992)* [1996] 2 All E.R. 211 it was held that r. 7.55 did not validate an improperly executed writ of fieri facias as in the circumstances of the case the irregularity was so serious as to mean that the writ could not be said to have been served at all. Here apart from knocking on a debtor's door the bailiff had left the premises without any serious attempt to gain access.

Rule 7.55 did, however, come into play in *Re a Debtor (No. 22 of 1993)* [1994] 1 W.L.R. 46 (sometimes cited as *Focus Insurance v A Debtor*) where an omission by a creditor to state in his petition that there was an extant set-aside application by the debtor was waved through by Mummery J. See also *Re Continental Assurance Co. of London plc (in liq.) (No. 2)* [1998] 1 B.C.L.C. 583, where an application had been made in the wrong form but no prejudice had occurred. See also *Oben v Blackman* [2000] B.P.I.R. 302.

7.56 Restriction on concurrent proceedings and remedies

7.56 Where, in insolvency proceedings the court makes an order staying any action, execution or other legal process against the property of a company, or against the property or person of an individual debtor or bankrupt, service of the order may be effected by sending a sealed copy of the order to whatever is the address for service of the plaintiff or other party having the carriage of the proceedings to be stayed.

7.57 Affidavits

7.57(1) [**Application of High Court practice and procedure**] Subject to the following paragraphs of this Rule the practice and procedure of the High Court with regard to affidavits, their form and contents and the procedure governing their use are to apply to all insolvency proceedings.

7.57(2) [**Affidavit by official receiver or responsible insolvency practitioner**] Where, in insolvency proceedings, an affidavit is made by the official receiver or the responsible insolvency practitioner, the deponent shall state the capacity in which he makes it, the position which he holds, and the address at which he works.

7.57(3) [**Swearing creditor's affidavit of debt**] A creditor's affidavit of debt may be sworn before his own solicitor.

7.57(4) [**Power of official receiver, etc.**] The official receiver, any deputy official receiver, or any officer of the court duly authorised in that behalf, may take affidavits and declarations.

7.57(5) [**Witness statement, etc.**] Subject to paragraph (6), where the Rules provide for the use of an affidavit, a witness statement verified by a statement of truth may be used as an alternative.

7.57(6) [**Non application of r. 7.57(5)**] Paragraph (5) does not apply to Rules 3.4., 4.33., 6.60. (statement of affairs), 4.42., 6.66., 6.72. (further disclosure), 4.39., 4.40., 6.65; 6.70. (accounts), 4.73., 4.77., 6.96; 6.99. (claims) and 9.3., 9.4. (examinations).

7.57(7) [**Application of r. 7.57(5)**] Where paragraph (5) applies any form prescribed by Rule 12.7 of these Rules shall be modified as necessary.

GENERAL NOTE

Rule 7.57(6) was amended by I(A)R 2003 (SI 2003/1730) with effect from April 1, 2004.

7.58 Security in court

7.58(1) [**Form of security**] Where security has to be given to the court (otherwise than in relation to costs), it may be given by guarantee, bond or the payment of money into court.

7.58(2) [**Notice re bond**] A person proposing to give a bond as security shall give notice to the party in whose favour the security is required, and to the court, naming those who are to be sureties to the bond.

7.58(3) [**Court to give notice**] The court shall forthwith give notice to both the parties concerned of a venue for the execution of the bond and the making of any objection to the sureties.

7.58(4) [**Sureties' affidavits etc.**] The sureties shall make an affidavit of their sufficiency (unless dispensed with by the party in whose favour the security is required) and shall, if required by the court, attend the court to be cross-examined.

7.59 Payment into court

7.59 The CPR relating to payment into and out of court of money lodged in court as security for costs apply to money lodged in court under the Rules.

GENERAL NOTE

Rule 7.59 substituted by the Insolvency (Amendment) (No. 2) Rules 1999 (SI 1999/1022), r. 3, Sch., para. 7 as from April 26, 1999.

7.60 Further information and disclosure

7.60(1) **[Clarification, additional information, etc.]** Any party to insolvency proceedings may apply to the court for an order–

(a) that any other party

  (i) clarify any matter which is in dispute in the proceedings, or
  (ii) give additional information in relation to any such matter;

  in accordance with CPR Part 18 (further information); or

(b) to obtain disclosure from any other party in accordance with CPR Part 31 (disclosure and inspection of documents).

7.60(2) **[Application under Rule]** An application under this Rule may be made without notice being served on any other party.

GENERAL NOTE

Rule 7.60 substituted by the Insolvency (Amendment) (No. 2) Rules 1999 (SI 1999/1022), r. 3, Sch., para. 8 as from April 26, 1999. See *Highberry Ltd v Colt Telecom Group plc* [2002] EWHC 2503 (Ch), [2003] B.P.I.R. 311.

The operation of the predecessor of this rule was considered in detail by Harman J. in *Re Primlaks (UK) Ltd (No. 2)* [1990] B.C.L.C. 234. Here it was held that in an unfair prejudice application under s. 6 of the Act arising out of a corporate voluntary arrangement, discovery should be ordered if it was in the interests of justice to do so; and clearly if a particular creditor was making an application under s. 6 it was necessary for him to know the full facts of the transactions which he alleged were unfair.

7.61 Office copies of documents

7.61(1) **[Right to require office copy]** Any person who has under the Rules the right to inspect the court file of insolvency proceedings may require the court to provide him with an office copy of any document from the file.

7.61(2) **[Exercise of right]** A person's rights under this Rule may be exercised on his behalf by his solicitor.

7.61(3) **[Form of copy]** An office copy provided by the court under this Rule shall be in such form as the registrar thinks appropriate, and shall bear the court's seal.

CHAPTER 10

EC REGULATION – CREDITORS' VOLUNTARY WINDING UP – CONFIRMATION BY THE COURT

7.62 Application for confirmation

7.62(1) **[Application]** Where a company has passed a resolution for voluntary winding up, and no declaration under section 89 has been made, the liquidator may apply to court for an order confirming the creditors' voluntary winding up for the purposes of the EC Regulation.

7.62(2) [Requirements] The application shall be in writing and verified by affidavit by the liquidator (using [FORM 7.20] the same form) and shall state–

- (a) the name of the applicant,
- (b) the name of the company and its registered number
- (c) the date on which the resolution for voluntary winding up was passed,
- (d) that the application is accompanied by all of the documents required under paragraph (3) which are true copies of the documents required, and
- (e) that the EC Regulation will apply to the company and whether the proceedings will be main proceedings, territorial proceedings or secondary proceedings.

7.62(3) [Filing] The liquidator shall file in court two copies of the application, together with one copy of the following–

- (a) a copy of the resolution for voluntary winding up referred to by section 84(3),
- (b) evidence of his appointment as liquidator of the company, and
- (c) a copy of the statement of affairs required under section 99.

7.62(4) [Service not required] It shall not be necessary to serve the application on, or give notice of it to, any person.

7.62(5) [Confirmation] On an application under this Rule the court may confirm the creditors' voluntary winding up.

7.62(6) [Features of confirmation] If the court confirms the creditor's voluntary winding up–

- (a) it may do so without a hearing,
- (b) it shall affix its seal to the application.

7.62(7) [Authority] A member of the court staff may deal with an application under this Rule.

7.62(8) [Application of r. 7.62] This Rule shall also apply where a company has moved to a voluntary liquidation in accordance with paragraph 83 of Schedule B1.

GENERAL NOTE

Paragraph (8) was inserted by Insolvency (Amendment) Rules 2003 (SI 2003/1730). This extends the ambit of r. 7.62 to cover cases where a company moves from new-style administration to voluntary liquidation. This mode of exit is likely to be widely used.

7.63 Notice to member State liquidator and creditors in member States

7.63 Where the court has confirmed the creditors' voluntary winding up, the liquidator shall forthwith give notice–

- (a) if there is a member State liquidator in relation to the company, to the member State liquidator;
- (b) in accordance with Article 40 of the EC Regulation (duty to inform creditors).

GENERAL NOTE

Chapter 10 (IR 7.62 and 7.63) was introduced by Insolvency (Amendment) Rules 2002 (SI 2002/1307) para. 9(1) with effect from May 31, 2002 to cater for the introduction of EC Council Regulation 1346/2000 on Insolvency Proceedings. On the EC Regulation see p. 602 above.

CHAPTER 11

EC REGULATION – MEMBER STATE LIQUIDATOR

7.64 Interpretation of creditor

7.64(1) **[Application]** This Rule applies where a member State liquidator has been appointed in relation to a person subject to insolvency proceedings.

7.64(2) **[Interpretation]** For the purposes of the Rules referred to in paragraph (3) a member State liquidator appointed in main proceedings is deemed to be a creditor.

7.64(3) **[Rules referred to in r. 7.64(2)]** The Rules referred to in paragraph (2) are Rules 7.31(1) (right to inspect court file) and 7.53(1) (right of attendance).

7.64(4) **[Exercise of creditors' rights]** Paragraphs (2) and (3) are without prejudice to the generality of the right to participate referred to in paragraph 3 of Article 32 of the EC Regulation (exercise of creditor's rights).

GENERAL NOTE

Chapter 11 (IR 7.64) was introduced via the same mechanism as Chapter 10 above and for a similar reason.

PART 8

PROXIES AND COMPANY REPRESENTATION

8.1 Definition of "proxy"

8.1(1) **[Definition]** For the purposes of the Rules, a proxy is an authority given by a person (**"the principal"**) to another person (**"the proxy-holder"**) to attend a meeting and speak and vote as his representative.

[FORMS 8.1 to 8.5]

8.1(2) **[Use of proxies]** Proxies are for use at creditors', company or contributories' meetings summoned or called under the Act or the Rules.

8.1(3) **[Giving proxies]** Only one proxy may be given by a person for any one meeting at which he desires to be represented; and it may only be given to one person, being an individual aged 18 or over. But the principal may specify one or more other such individuals to be proxy-holder in the alternative, in the order in which they are named in the proxy.

8.1(4) **[Chairman etc. as proxy-holder]** Without prejudice to the generality of paragraph (3), a proxy for a particular meeting may be given to whoever is to be the chairman of the meeting; and for a meeting held as part of the proceedings in a winding up by the court, or in a bankruptcy, it may be given to the official receiver.

8.1(5) **[Chairman etc. cannot decline]** A person given a proxy under paragraph (4) cannot decline to be the proxy-holder in relation to that proxy.

8.1(6) **[Conduct of proxy-holder]** A proxy requires the holder to give the principal's vote on matters arising for determination at the meeting, or to abstain, or to propose, in the principal's name, a resolution to be voted on by the meeting, either as directed or in accordance with the holder's own discretion.

(See General Note after r. 8.6.)

8.2 Issue and use of forms

8.2(1) [**When forms are sent with notice**] When notice is given of a meeting to be held in insolvency proceedings, and forms of proxy are sent out with the notice, no form so sent out shall have inserted in it the name or description of any person.

8.2(2) [**Forms of proxy**] No form of proxy shall be used at any meeting except that which is sent out with the notice summoning the meeting, or a substantially similar form.

8.2(3) [**Proxy to be signed etc.**] A form of proxy shall be signed by the principal, or by some person authorised by him (either generally or with reference to a particular meeting). If the form is signed by a person other than the principal, the nature of the person's authority shall be stated.

(See General Note after r. 8.6.)

8.3 Use of proxies at meetings

8.3(1) [**Use at adjournment**] A proxy given for a particular meeting may be used at any adjournment of that meeting.

8.3(2) [**Official receiver etc. as proxy-holder**] Where the official receiver holds proxies for use at any meeting, his deputy, or any other official receiver, may act as proxy-holder in his place.

Alternatively, the official receiver may in writing authorise another officer of the Department to act for him at the meeting and use the proxies as if that other officer were himself proxy-holder.

8.3(3) [**Chairman etc. as proxy-holder**] Where the responsible insolvency practitioner holds proxies to be used by him as chairman of a meeting, and some other person acts as chairman, the other person may use the insolvency practitioner's proxies as if he were himself proxy-holder.

8.3(4) [**Appointment of responsible insolvency practitioner**] Where a proxy directs a proxy-holder to vote for or against a resolution for the nomination or appointment of a person as the responsible insolvency practitioner, the proxy-holder may, unless the proxy states otherwise, vote for or against (as he thinks fit) any resolution for the nomination or appointment of that person jointly with another or others.

8.3(5) [**Proposal by proxy-holder**] A proxy-holder may propose any resolution which, if proposed by another, would be a resolution in favour of which by virtue of the proxy he would be entitled to vote.

8.3(6) [**Specific directions to proxy-holder**] Where a proxy gives specific directions as to voting, this does not, unless the proxy states otherwise, preclude the proxy-holder from voting at his discretion on resolutions put to the meeting which are not dealt with in the proxy.

GENERAL NOTE

Rules 8.3(4), (5) and (6) were inserted to improve the effectiveness of the proxy system allowing a proxy more discretion (if his principal desires).
(See General Note after r. 8.6.)

8.4 Retention of proxies

8.4(1) [**Chairman to retain proxies**] Subject as follows, proxies used for voting at any meeting shall be retained by the chairman of the meeting.

8.4(2) [Delivery] The chairman shall deliver the proxies, forthwith after the meeting, to the responsible insolvency practitioner (where that is someone other than himself).

(See General Note after r. 8.6.)

8.5 Right of inspection

8.5(1) [Who may inspect] The responsible insolvency practitioner shall, so long as proxies lodged with him are in his hands, allow them to be inspected, at all reasonable times on any business day, by–

(a) the creditors, in the case of proxies used at a meeting of creditors, and

(b) a company's members or contributories, in the case of proxies used at a meeting of the company or of its contributories.

8.5(2) [Who are r. 8.5(1) creditors] The reference in paragraph (1) to creditors is–

(a) in the case of a company in liquidation or of an individual's bankruptcy, those creditors who have proved their debts, and

(b) in any other case, persons who have submitted in writing a claim to be creditors of the company or individual concerned;

but in neither case does it include a person whose proof or claim has been wholly rejected for purposes of voting, dividend or otherwise.

8.5(3) [Who may also inspect] The right of inspection given by this Rule is also exercisable–

(a) in the case of an insolvent company, by its directors, and

(b) in the case of an insolvent individual, by him.

8.5(4) [Person attending meeting] Any person attending a meeting in insolvency proceedings is entitled, immediately before or in the course of the meeting, to inspect proxies and associated documents (including proofs) sent or given, in accordance with directions contained in any notice convening the meeting, to the chairman of that meeting or to any other person by a creditor, member or contributory for the purpose of that meeting.

(See General Note after r. 8.6.)

8.6 Proxy-holder with financial interest

8.6(1) [Limitation on voting by proxy-holder] A proxy-holder shall not vote in favour of any resolution which would directly or indirectly place him, or any associate of his, in a position to receive any remuneration out of the insolvent estate, unless the proxy specifically directs him to vote in that way.

8.6(1A) [Written authorisation] Where a proxy-holder has signed the proxy as being authorised to do so by his principal and the proxy specifically directs him to vote in the way mentioned in paragraph (1), he shall nevertheless not vote in that way unless he produces to the chairman of the meeting written authorisation from his principal sufficient to show that the proxy-holder was entitled so to sign the proxy.

8.6(2) [Application of Rule] This Rule applies also to any person acting as chairman of a meeting and using proxies in that capacity under Rule 8.3; and in its application to him, the proxy-holder is deemed an associate of his.

GENERAL NOTE TO RR. 8.1–8.6

The use of proxies in insolvency proceedings is fairly strictly controlled by these rules.
　For the meaning of "associate" in r. 8.6, see IA 1986, s. 435.
　Rule 8.6(1A) was added to r. 8.6 to restrict the possibility of a proxy profiting from his position unless expressly authorised to do so by his principal.
　A faxed form of proxy may be accepted for the purposes of these rules: *IR Commrs v Conbeer* [1996] B.C.C. 189.

In accordance with general principles, a proxy may be varied or revoked by the party who has given it at any time prior to the relevant meeting or decision: *Re Cardona, IR Commrs v Cardona* [1997] B.C.C. 697.

8.7 Company representation

8.7(1) [**Production of copy of resolution**] Where a person is authorised under section 375 of the Companies Act to represent a corporation at a meeting of creditors or of the company or its contributories, he shall produce to the chairman of the meeting a copy of the resolution from which he derives his authority.

8.7(2) [**Copy of resolution to be sealed or certified**] The copy resolution must be under the seal of the corporation, or certified by the secretary or a director of the corporation to be a true copy.

8.7(3) [**Authority to sign proxy**] Nothing in this Rule requires the authority of a person to sign a proxy on behalf of a principal which is a corporation to be in the form of a resolution of that corporation.

GENERAL NOTE

Rule 8.7(3) was added to r. 8.7 to remove any doubt regarding the formality for a corporate proxy.

8.8 Interpretation of creditor

8.8(1) [**Application**] This Rule applies where a member State liquidator has been appointed in relation to a person subject to insolvency proceedings.

8.8(2) [**Interpretation**] For the purposes of rule 8.5(1) (right of inspection of proxies) a member State liquidator appointed in main proceedings is deemed to be a creditor.

8.8(3) [**Exercise of creditors' rights**] Paragraph (2) is without prejudice to the generality of the right to participate referred to in paragraph 3 of Article 32 of the EC Regulation (exercise of creditor's rights).

GENERAL NOTE

IR 8.8 was introduced by Insolvency (Amendment) Rules 2002 (SI 2002/1307) para. 9(2) with effect from May 31, 2002 to cater for the advent of the EC Council Regulation 1346/2000 on Insolvency Proceedings. On the EC Regulation see p. 602 above.

PART 9

EXAMINATION OF PERSONS CONCERNED IN COMPANY AND INDIVIDUAL INSOLVENCY

9.1 Preliminary

9.1(1) [**Application of Pt 9 Rules**] The Rules in this Part relate to applications to the court for an order under–

(a) section 236 (inquiry into company's dealings when it is, or is alleged to be, insolvent), or

[FORM 9.1]

(b) section 366 (inquiry in bankruptcy, with respect to the bankrupt's dealings).

[FORM 9.1]

9.1(2) [**Definitions**] The following definitions apply–

(a) the person in respect of whom an order is applied for is "the respondent";

(b) "the applicable section" is section 236 or section 366, according to whether the affairs of a company or those of a bankrupt or (where the application under section 366 is made by virtue of section 368) a debtor are in question;

(c) the company or, as the case may be, the bankrupt or debtor concerned is "the insolvent".

(See General Note after r. 9.6.)

9.2 Form and contents of application

9.2(1) [**In writing, statement of grounds**] The application shall be in writing, and be accompanied by a brief statement of the grounds on which it is made.

9.2(2) [**Respondent sufficiently identified**] The respondent must be sufficiently identified in the application.

9.2(3) [**Purpose to be stated**] It shall be stated whether the application is for the respondent–

  (a) to be ordered to appear before the court, or

  (b) to be ordered to clarify any matter which is in dispute in the proceedings or to give additional information in relation to any such matter and if so CPR Part 18 (further information) shall apply to any such order, or

  (c) to submit affidavits (if so, particulars to be given of the matters to which he is required to swear), or

  (d) to produce books, papers or other records (if so, the items in question to be specified),

or for any two or more of those purposes.

9.2(4) [*Ex parte* **application**] The application may be made *ex parte*.

(See General Note after r. 9.6.) Rule 9.2(3)(b) substituted by the Insolvency (Amendment) (No. 2) Rules 1999 (SI 1999/1022), r. 3, Sch., para. 9 as from April 26, 1999.

9.3 Order for examination, etc.

9.3(1) [**Powers of court**] The court may, whatever the purpose of the application, make any order which it has power to make under the applicable section.

9.3(2) [**Venue**] The court, if it orders the respondent to appear before it, shall specify a venue for his appearance, which shall be not less than 14 days from the date of the order.

9.3(3) [**Order to submit affidavits**] If he is ordered to submit affidavits, the order shall specify–

  (a) the matters which are to be dealt with in his affidavits, and

  (b) the time within which they are to be submitted to the court.

9.3(4) [**Order to produce books etc.**] If the order is to produce books, papers or other records, the time and manner of compliance shall be specified.

9.3(5) [**Service**] The order must be served forthwith on the respondent; and it must be served personally, unless the court otherwise orders.

GENERAL NOTE

For the meaning of "venue" see r. 13.6.
  (See General Note after r. 9.6.)

9.4 Procedure for examination

9.4(1) [**Applicant may attend etc.**] At any examination of the respondent, the applicant may attend in person, or be represented by a solicitor with or without counsel, and may put such questions to the respondent as the court may allow.

9.4(2) [**Other attendances etc.**] Any other person who could have applied for an order under the applicable section in respect of the insolvent's affairs may, with the leave of the court and if the applicant does not object, attend the examination and put questions to the respondent (but only through the applicant).

9.4(3) **[Clarification, additional information]** If the respondent is ordered to clarify any matter or to give additional information, the court shall direct him as to the questions which he is required to answer, and as to whether his answers (if any) are to be made on affidavit.

9.4(4) **[Attendance etc. of creditor]** Where application has been made under the applicable section on information provided by a creditor of the insolvent, that creditor may, with the leave of the court and if the applicant does not object, attend the examination and put questions to the respondent (but only through the applicant).

9.4(5) **[Representation of respondent]** The respondent may at his own expense employ a solicitor with or without counsel, who may put to him such questions as the court may allow for the purpose of enabling him to explain or qualify any answers given by him, and may make representations on his behalf.

9.4(6) **[Record of examination]** There shall be made in writing such record of the examination as the court thinks proper. The record shall be read over either to or by the respondent and signed by him at a venue fixed by the court.

9.4(7) **[Record as evidence]** The written record may, in any proceedings (whether under the Act or otherwise) be used as evidence against the respondent of any statement made by him in the course of his examination.

(See General Note after r. 9.6.) IR 9.4(3) was replaced by Insolvency (Amendment) (No. 2) Rules 1999 (SI 1999/1022) with effect from April 26, 1999.

9.5 Record of examination

9.5(1) **[Record etc. not to be filed]** Unless the court otherwise directs, the written record of the respondent's examination, and any answer given by him to interrogatories, and any affidavits submitted by him in compliance with an order of the court under the applicable section, shall not be filed in court.

9.5(2) **[Inspection]** The written record, answers and affidavits shall not be open to inspection, without an order of the court, by any person other than–

(a)   the applicant for an order under the applicable section, or

(b)   any person who could have applied for such an order in respect of the affairs of the same insolvent.

9.5(3) **[Application of r. 9.5(2)]** Paragraph (2) applies also to so much of the court file as shows the grounds of the application for an order under the applicable section and to any copy of proposed interrogatories.

9.5(4) **[Powers of court]** The court may from time to time give directions as to the custody and inspection of any documents to which this Rule applies, and as to the furnishing of copies of, or extracts from, such documents.

(See General Note after r. 9.6.)

9.6 Costs of proceedings under s. 236, 366

9.6(1) **[Power of court]** Where the court has ordered an examination of any person under the applicable section, and it appears to it that the examination was made necessary because information had been unjustifiably refused by the respondent, it may order that the costs of the examination be paid by him.

9.6(2) **[Further power]** Where the court makes an order against a person under–

(a)   section 237(1) or 367(1) (to deliver up property in his possession which belongs to the insolvent), or

(b)   section 237(2) or 367(2) (to pay any amount in discharge of a debt due to the insolvent),

the costs of the application for the order may be ordered by the court to be paid by the respondent.

9.6(3) [Applicant's costs] Subject to paragraphs (1) and (2) above, the applicant's costs shall, unless the court otherwise orders, be paid out of the insolvent estate.

9.6(4) [Travelling expenses etc.] A person summoned to attend for examination under this Chapter shall be tendered a reasonable sum in respect of travelling expenses incurred in connection with his attendance. Other costs falling on him are at the court's discretion.

9.6(5) [No order against official receiver] Where the examination is on the application of the official receiver otherwise than in the capacity of liquidator or trustee, no order shall be made for the payment of costs by him.

GENERAL NOTE TO RR. 9.1–9.6

Rules 9.2(3)(b) and 9.4(3) were substituted by the Insolvency (Amendment) (No. 2) Rules 1999 (SI 1999/1022) as from April 26, 1999, to coincide with the introduction of the CPR.

The examinations authorised by IA 1986, ss. 236, 366, to which this Part refers, are private examinations, in contrast to the public examinations which may be ordered under IA 1986, ss. 133, 134 and 290. For further discussion, see notes to those sections, and for the rules applicable in the latter case, see rr. 4.211ff. In addition, ss. 237 and 367, referred to in r. 9.6, empower the court to order a person to deliver up property to the liquidator or other office holder, or to pay money in discharge of a debt.

The explanatory words "when it is, or is alleged to be, insolvent" in r. 9.1(1)(a) are misleading. For the circumstances in which ss. 236 applies, reference should be made to ss. 236(1) and 234(1).

Under the former winding-up rules, it was the practice for an applicant seeking an order to support his application by a memorandum which was required to be verified by affidavit in every case except where the applicant, as a liquidator, was an officer of the court. Rule 9.2(1) has abolished this distinction, so that an unsworn statement is now sufficient in all cases. The statement is confidential: *Re Aveling Barford Ltd* [1989] 1 W.L.R. 360; (1988) 4 B.C.C. 548; but (in a departure from the previous practice) the court may order that it be disclosed in whole or in part to the person against whom the order is sought in a proper case: see the note to s. 236.

An order requiring a person to give "an account of full particulars of all dealings" by him with the company may be open to objection on the grounds that it lacks the particularity called for by rr. 9.2(3)(c) and 9.3(3)(a): *Re Aveling Barford Ltd* (above). It was held in the same case that the phrase "a person summoned to attend for examination under this Chapter" in r. 9.6(4) includes a person required to give information by the alternative methods permitted under s. 236. On the question of the examinee's costs, Hoffmann J. declined to make an order in advance or to say that there should be a presumption in favour of allowing costs, over and above the travelling expenses mentioned in r. 9.6(4).

For comments on the exercise of the discretion conferred on the court by r. 9.5(4), see *Hamilton v Naviede, Re Arrows Ltd (No. 4)* [1995] 2 A.C. 75; [1994] B.C.C. 641.

PART 10

OFFICIAL RECEIVERS

General comment on Pt 10
The rules in this Part supplement IA 1986, ss. 399–401.

10.1 Appointment of official receivers

10.1 Judicial notice shall be taken of the appointment under sections 399 to 401 of official receivers and deputy official receivers.

10.2 Persons entitled to act on official receiver's behalf

10.2(1) **[In absence of official receiver]** In the absence of the official receiver authorised to act in a particular case, an officer authorised in writing for the purpose by the Secretary of State, or by the official receiver himself, may, with the leave of the court, act on the official receiver's behalf and in his place–

(a) in any examination under section 133, 236, 290 or 366, and

(b) in respect of any application to the court.

10.2(2) **[In case of emergency]** In case of emergency, where there is no official receiver capable of acting, anything to be done by, to or before the official receiver may be done by, to or before the registrar of the court.

GENERAL NOTE

The possibility of a person acting on behalf of the official receiver would appear to be in addition to the appointment of a deputy under IA 1986, s. 401.

10.3 Application for directions

10.3 The official receiver may apply to the court for directions in relation to any matter arising in insolvency proceedings.

GENERAL NOTE

This is a standard facility for all insolvency practitioners.

10.4 Official receiver's expenses

10.4(1) **["Expenses"]** Any expenses incurred by the official receiver (in whatever capacity he may be acting) in connection with proceedings taken against him in insolvency proceedings are to be treated as expenses of the insolvency proceedings.

"Expenses" includes damages.

10.4(2) **[Official receiver's charge]** In respect of any sums due to him under paragraph (1), the official receiver has a charge on the insolvent estate.

GENERAL NOTE

Note the wide definition of "expenses".

PART 11

DECLARATION AND PAYMENT OF DIVIDEND (WINDING UP AND BANKRUPTCY)

General comment on Pt 11
The rules in this Part are to be viewed in light of the provisions of IA 1986 – *e.g.* see s. 324 and 330.

11.1 Preliminary

11.1(1) **[Application of Pt 11 Rules]** The Rules in this Part relate to the declaration and payment of dividends in companies winding up and in bankruptcy.

11.1(2) **[Definitions]** The following definitions apply–

(a) **"the insolvent"** means the company in liquidation or, as the case may be, the bankrupt; and

(b) **"creditors"** means those creditors of the insolvent of whom the responsible practitioner is aware, or who are identified in the insolvent's statement of affairs.

11.1(3) [**Interpretation**] For the purposes of this Part, a member State liquidator appointed in relation to an insolvent is deemed to be a creditor.

GENERAL NOTE

IR 11.1(3) was inserted by Insolvency (Amendment) Rules 2002 (SI 2002/1307) para. 10(1) with effect from May 31, 2002 to cater for the advent of EC Council Regulation 1346/2000 on insolvency proceedings. On the EC Regulation see p. 602 above.

11.2 Notice of intended dividend

11.2(1) [**Before declaring dividend**] Before declaring a dividend, the responsible insolvency practitioner shall give notice of his intention to do so

(a) to all creditors whose addresses are known to him and who have not proved their debts, and

(b) where a member State liquidator has been appointed in relation to the insolvent, to that person.

11.2(1A) [**Public advertisement**] Before declaring a first dividend, the responsible insolvency practitioner shall, unless he has previously by public advertisement invited creditors to prove their debts, give notice of the intended dividend by public advertisement.

11.2(2) [**"The last date for proving"**] Any notice under paragraph (1) and any notice of a first dividend under paragraph (1A) shall specify a date ("the last date for proving") up to which proofs may be lodged. The date shall be the same for all creditors, and not less than 21 days from that of the notice.

11.2(3) [**Contents of notice**] The insolvency practitioner shall in the notice state his intention to declare a dividend (specified as interim or final, as the case may be) within the period of 4 months from the last date for proving.

GENERAL NOTE

This is to give tardy creditors a last chance to lodge their proofs.

Notice need only be given under r. 11.2(1) to known creditors or member state liquidator – this latter requirement was introduced by Insolvency (Amendment) Rules 2002 (SI 2002/1307) para. 10(2) with effect from May 31, 2002 to cater for the advent of EC Council Regulation 1346/2000 on insolvency proceedings. Rule 11.2(1A) confers a discretion on the trustee to advertise for claims, in the case of a first dividend, where he has not previously advertised inviting creditors to prove.

11.3 Final admission/rejection of proofs

11.3(1) [**Dealing with every proof**] The responsible insolvency practitioner shall, within 7 days from the last date for proving, deal with every creditor's proof (in so far as not already dealt with) by admitting or rejecting it in whole or in part, or by making such provision as he thinks fit in respect of it.

11.3(2) [**Proofs lodged out of time**] The insolvency practitioner is not obliged to deal with proofs lodged after the date for proving; but he may do so, if he thinks fit.

11.3(3) [**Declaration of dividend**] In the declaration of a dividend no payment shall be made more than once by virtue of the same debt.

11.3(4) [**Payment**] Subject to Rule 11.11, where–

(a) a creditor has proved, and

(b) a member State liquidator has proved in relation to the same debt,

payment shall only be made to the creditor.

GENERAL NOTE

Late proofs may be accepted at the discretion of the insolvency practitioner. Rules 11.3(3) and (4) were inserted by the Insolvency (Amendment) Rules 2002 (SI 2002/1307) para. 10(3) with effect from May 31, 2002 to cater for the advent of EC Council Regulation 1346/2000 on insolvency proceedings.

The Insolvency Rules 1986   *Rule 11.6*

11.4 Postponement or cancellation of dividend

11.4 If in the period of 4 months referred to in Rule 11.2(3)–

(a) the responsible insolvency practitioner has rejected a proof in whole or in part and application is made to the court for his decision to be reversed or varied, or

(b) application is made to the court for the insolvency practitioner's decision on a proof to be reversed or varied, or for a proof to be expunged, or for a reduction of the amount claimed,

the insolvency practitioner may postpone or cancel the dividend.

GENERAL NOTE

An application to the court to have the decision of the insolvency practitioner on the admission or rejection of proofs varied is made, in the case of a winding up, under r. 4.83(1) or (2) and in a bankruptcy, under r. 6.105(1) or (2). There is a time-limit of 21 days in each case. If such an application has been made, the insolvency practitioner may postpone or cancel the dividend under this rule; but, if he proposes to pay a dividend, r. 11.5(2) applies.

11.5 Decision to declare dividend

11.5(1) [Proceeding to declare dividend] If the responsible insolvency practitioner has not, in the 4-month period referred to in Rule 11.2(3), had cause to postpone or cancel the dividend, he shall within that period proceed to declare the dividend of which he gave notice under that Rule.

11.5(2) [Pending application re proof etc.] Except with the leave of the court, the insolvency practitioner shall not declare the dividend so long as there is pending any application to the court to reverse or vary a decision of his on a proof, or to expunge a proof or to reduce the amount claimed.

If the court gives leave under this paragraph, the insolvency practitioner shall make such provision in respect of the proof in question as the court directs.

GENERAL NOTE

If no application has been made to the court to challenge a decision on the admission or rejection of a proof, the dividend must be declared within the four-month period. If the insolvency practitioner wishes to declare an interim dividend pending the outcome of such an application, the leave of the court is required under r. 11.5(2). Where this rule applies, the normal rules as to the payment of interim dividends (IA 1986, s. 324, IR 1986, rr. 4.180, 4.182) are displaced.

11.6 Notice of declaration

11.6(1) [Notice to all creditors who have proved] The responsible insolvency practitioner shall give notice of the dividend to

(a) all creditors who have proved their debts, and

(b) where a member State liquidator has been appointed in relation to the insolvent, to that person.

11.6(2) [Particulars in notice] The notice shall include the following particulars relating to the insolvency and the administration of the insolvent estate–

(a) amounts realised from the sale of assets, indicating (so far as practicable) amounts raised by the sale of particular assets;

(b) payments made by the insolvency practitioner in the administration of the insolvent estate;

(c) provision (if any) made for unsettled claims, and funds (if any) retained for particular purposes;

(d) the total amount to be distributed, and the rate of dividend;

(e) whether, and if so when, any further dividend is expected to be declared.

11.6(3) [Simultaneous distribution] The dividend may be distributed simultaneously with the notice declaring it.

11.6(4) [**Method of payment**] Payment of dividend may be made by post, or arrangements may be made with any creditor for it to be paid to him in another way, or held for his collection.

11.6(5) [**Endorsement in negotiable instrument**] Where a dividend is paid on a bill of exchange or other negotiable instrument, the amount of the dividend shall be endorsed on the instrument, or on a certified copy of it, if required to be produced by the holder for that purpose.

GENERAL NOTE

Creditors are to receive full information relating to the payment of dividends, etc. IR 11.6(1) was expanded by Insolvency (Amendment) Rules 2002 (SI 2002/1307) para. 10(4) with effect from May 31, 2002 to cater for the advent of EC Council Regulation 1346/2000 on insolvency proceedings.

11.7 Notice of no, or no further, dividend

11.7 If the responsible insolvency practitioner gives notice to creditors that he is unable to declare any dividend or (as the case may be) any further dividend, the notice shall contain a statement to the effect either–

(a) that no funds have been realised, or

(b) that the funds realised have already been distributed or used or allocated for defraying the expenses of administration.

11.8 Proof altered after payment of dividend

11.8(1) [**If amount claimed in proof increased**] If after payment of dividend the amount claimed by a creditor in his proof is increased, the creditor is not entitled to disturb the distribution of the dividend; but he is entitled to be paid, out of any money for the time being available for the payment of any further dividend, any dividend or dividends which he has failed to receive.

11.8(2) [**Payments under r. 11.8(1)**] Any dividend or dividends payable under paragraph (1) shall be paid before the money there referred to is applied to the payment of any such further dividend.

11.8(3) [**Proof withdrawn etc.**] If, after a creditor's proof has been admitted, the proof is withdrawn or expunged, or the amount of it is reduced, the creditor is liable to repay to the responsible insolvency practitioner, for the credit of the insolvent estate, any amount overpaid by way of dividend.

GENERAL NOTE

Here we have a "heads I win, tails you lose" situation.

11.9 Secured creditors

11.9(1) [**Application of Rule**] The following applies where a creditor re-values his security at a time when a dividend has been declared.

11.9(2) [**Reduction of unsecured claim**] If the revaluation results in a reduction of his unsecured claim ranking for dividend, the creditor shall forthwith repay to the responsible insolvency practitioner, for the credit of the insolvent estate, any amount received by him as dividend in excess of that to which he would be entitled having regard to the revaluation of the security.

11.9(3) [**Increase of unsecured claim**] If the revaluation results in an increase of his unsecured claim, the creditor is entitled to receive from the insolvency practitioner, out of any money for the time being available for the payment of a further dividend, before any such further dividend is paid, any dividend or dividends which he has failed to receive, having regard to the revaluation of the security.

However, the creditor is not entitled to disturb any dividend declared (whether or not distributed) before the date of the revaluation.

GENERAL NOTE

This again shows that the law will not disturb dividends that have already been declared.

11.10 Disqualification from dividend

11.10 If a creditor contravenes any provision of the Act or the Rules relating to the valuation of securities, the court may, on the application of the responsible insolvency practitioner, order that the creditor be wholly or partly disqualified from participation in any dividend.

GENERAL NOTE

This is a useful sanction.

11.11 Assignment of right to dividend

11.11(1) [Notice of assignment etc.] If a person entitled to a dividend gives notice to the responsible insolvency practitioner that he wishes the dividend to be paid to another person, or that he has assigned his entitlement to another person, the insolvency practitioner shall pay the dividend to that other accordingly.

11.11(2) [Contents of notice] A notice given under this Rule must specify the name and address of the person to whom payment is to be made.

GENERAL NOTE

The right to receive a dividend can be assigned.

11.12 Preferential creditors

11.12(1) [Application of Pt 11 Rules] Subject as follows, the Rules in this Part apply with respect to any distribution made in the insolvency to preferential creditors, with such adaptions as are appropriate considering that such creditors are of a limited class.

11.12(2) [Rule 11.2 notice] The notice by the responsible insolvency practitioner under Rule 11.2, where a dividend is to be declared for preferential creditors, need only be given to those creditors in whose case he has reason to believe that their debts are preferential and public advertisement of the intended dividend need only be given if the insolvency practitioner thinks fit.

GENERAL NOTE

This makes necessary modifications to the above rules where the declaration is for the benefit of preferential creditors – see IA 1986, Pt XII.

11.13 Debt payable at future time

11.13(1) [Entitlement to dividend] Where a creditor has proved for a debt of which payment is not due at the date of the declaration of dividend, he is entitled to dividend equally with other creditors, but subject as follows.

11.13(2) [Calculation of amount of reduction] For the purpose of dividend (and for no other purpose), the amount of the creditor's admitted proof (or, if a distribution has previously been made to him, the amount remaining outstanding in respect of his admitted proof) shall be reduced by a percentage calculated as follows–

$$\frac{I \times M}{12}$$

where I is 5 per cent. and M is the number of months (expressed, if need be, as, or as including, fractions of months) between the declaration of dividend and the date when payment of the creditor's debt would otherwise be due.

11.13(3) **[Other creditors' entitlement to interest]** Other creditors are not entitled to interest out of surplus funds under section 189(2) or (as the case may be) 328(4) until any creditor to whom paragraphs (1) and (2) apply has been paid the full amount of his debt.

GENERAL NOTE

This deals with interest payable on future debts. In *Re Park Air Services plc* [1996] 1 W.L.R. 649; [1996] B.C.C. 556 Ferris J. at first instance held that a landlord's claim for future loss under IA 1986, s. 178(6) following disclaimer of the lease carried interest at the rate fixed by this rule and not at that specified in the lease. This idea was rejected on appeal by the House of Lords [2000] 2 A.C. 172 which criticised the wording of r. 11.13.

PART 12

MISCELLANEOUS AND GENERAL

12.1 Power of Secretary of State to regulate certain matters

12.1(1) **[Power to make regulations]** Pursuant to paragraph 27 of Schedule 8 to the Act, and paragraph 30 of Schedule 9 to the Act, the Secretary of State may, subject to the Act and the Rules, make regulations with respect to any matter provided for in the Rules as relates to the carrying out of the functions of a liquidator, provisional liquidator, administrator or administrative receiver of a company, an interim receiver appointed under section 286, of the official receiver while acting as receiver or manager under section 287 or of a trustee of a bankrupt's estate, including, without prejudice to the generality of the foregoing, provision with respect to the following matters arising in companies winding up and individual bankruptcy–

(a) the preparation and keeping by liquidators, trustees, provisional liquidators, interim receivers and the official receiver, of books, accounts and other records, and their production to such persons as may be authorised or required to inspect them.

(b) the auditing of liquidators' and trustees' accounts;

(c) the manner in which liquidators and trustees are to act in relation to the insolvent company's or bankrupt's books, papers and other records, and the manner of their disposal by the responsible insolvency practitioner or others;

(d) the supply–

(i) in company insolvency, by the liquidator to creditors and members of the company, contributories in its winding up and the liquidation committee, and

(ii) in individual insolvency, by the trustee to creditors and the creditors' committee,

of copies of documents relating to the insolvency and the affairs of the insolvent company or individual (on payment, in such cases as may be specified by the regulations, of the specified fee);

(e) the manner in which insolvent estates are to be distributed by liquidators and trustees, including provision with respect to unclaimed funds and dividends;

(f) the manner in which moneys coming into the hands of a liquidator or trustee in the course of his administration are to be handled and invested, and the payment of interest on sums which, in pursuance of regulations made by virtue of this sub-paragraph, have been paid into the Insolvency Services Account;

(g) the amount (or the manner of determining the amount) to be paid to the official receiver by way of remuneration when acting as provisional liquidator, liquidator, interim receiver or trustee.

12.1(2) **[Reference to trustee in r. 12.1(1)]** Any reference in paragraph (1) to a trustee includes a reference to the official receiver when acting as receiver and manager under section 287.

12.1(3) **[Contents of regulations]** Regulations made pursuant to paragraph (1) may–

(a) confer a discretion on the court;

(b) make non-compliance with any of the regulations a criminal offence;

(c) make different provision for different cases, including different provision for different areas; and

(d) contain such incidental, supplemental and transitional provisions as may appear to the Secretary of State necessary or expedient.

GENERAL NOTE

This clarifies the power of the Secretary of State to make regulations to supplement the existing framework. Rule 12(1)(f) was amended by the *Insolvency (Amendment) Rules* 2001 (SI 2001/763) as from 2 April 2001 to cater for changes made by the *Insolvency Act* 2000.

12.2 Costs, expenses, etc.

12.2(1) **[Incidence of costs etc.]** All fees, costs, charges and other expenses incurred in the course of winding up, administration or bankruptcy proceedings are to be regarded as expenses of the winding up or the administration or, as the case may be, of the bankruptcy.

12.2(2) **[Prescribed part costs]** The costs associated with the prescribed part shall be paid out of the prescribed part.

GENERAL NOTE

Instalments of rates on non-domestic property which fell due for payment after the liquidation date were held to be liquidation expenses in *Re Nolton Business Centres Ltd* [1996] B.C.C. 500, even though the local authority had fixed the rates prior to that date. Contrast *Re Kentish Homes Ltd* [1993] B.C.C. 212, where post-liquidation community charges (and, by implication, council tax) were not so treated.

Amendments were made by Insolvency (Amendment) Rules 2003 (SI 2003/1730) to reflect the more expanded role of administration as a distributional regime and the coming into operation of the reserved fund for unsecured creditors (see IA 1986, s. 176A). Costs incurred with regard to the latter come exclusively out of that fund.

12.3 Provable debts

12.3(1) **[What is provable]** Subject as follows, in administration, winding up and bankruptcy, all claims by creditors are provable as debts against the company or, as the case may be, the bankrupt, whether they are present or future, certain or contingent, ascertained or sounding only in damages.

12.3(2) **[What is not provable]** The following are not provable–

(a) in bankruptcy, any fine imposed for an offence, and any obligation arising under an order made in family proceedings or under a maintenance assessment made under the Child Support Act 1991;

(b) in administration, winding up or bankruptcy, any obligation arising under a confiscation order made under section 1 of the Drug Trafficking Offences Act 1986 or section 1 of the Criminal Justice (Scotland) Act 1987 or section 71 of the Criminal Justice Act 1988 or under Parts 2, 3 or 4 of the Proceeds of Crime Act 2002.

"**Fine**" and "**family proceedings**" have the meanings given by section 281(8) of the Act (which applies the Magistrates' Courts Act 1980 and the Matrimonial and Family Proceedings Act 1984).

12.3(2A) **[Postponed debts]** The following are not provable except at a time when all other claims of creditors in the insolvency proceedings (other than any of a kind mentioned in this paragraph) have been paid in full with interest under section 189(2), Rule 2.88 or, as the case may be, section 328(4)–

(a) in an administration, winding up or a bankruptcy, any claim arising by virtue of section 382(1)(a) of the Financial Services and Markets Act 2000, not being a claim also arising by virtue of section 382(1)(b) of that Act;

(c) in an administration or winding up, any claim which by virtue of the Act or any other enactment is a claim the payment of which in a bankruptcy, an administration or a winding up is to be postponed.

12.3(3) **[Effect of Rule]** Nothing in this Rule prejudices any enactment or rule of law under which a particular kind of debt is not provable, whether on grounds of public policy or otherwise.

GENERAL NOTE

This provision complements IA 1986, ss. 322 and 382. It must be read in the light of r. 13.12. This was modified by Insolvency (Amendment) Rules 2003 (SI 2003/1730) to reflect the wider role of administration where issues of proof of debt will now become relevant. Note also the changes necessitated by POCA 2002. Not all debts are provable debts: see the discussion in *Woodley v Woodley (No. 2)* [1994] 1 W.L.R. 1167 at p. 1175. Note that fines are now regarded as not provable in a bankruptcy (reversing the former position as declared in *Re Pascoe* [1944] Ch. 310). The Cork Committee (Cmnd 8558, para. 1330) recommended that the law should be changed for all insolvency proceedings, but the legislators have done so only for bankruptcies.

Rule 12.3(2A) further restricts the categories of provable debt. Subparagraph (a) was replaced and (b) deleted by the Financial Services and Markets Act 2000 (Consequential Amendments and Repeals) Order 2001 (SI 2001/3649) reg. 380 with effect from December 1, 2001.

The legal status of r. 12.3 came under consideration in the Court of Appeal in *Woodley v Woodley (No. 2)* [1994] 1 W.L.R. 1167. Here the suggestion that r. 12.3 might be ultra vires the 1986 Act was considered and then dismissed. Authority for it was based upon para. 17 of Sch. 9 to IA 1986 and ultimately upon s. 412(2)(a). In spite of this reassuring finding the Court of Appeal suggested that the Insolvency Rules Committee should look at the question of whether lump-sum orders made in family proceedings should be restored as provable debts, which was the position before the 1986 rules came into effect. Costs orders in matrimonial proceedings fall within r. 12.3(2)(a) – *Levy v Legal Services Commission* [2000] B.P.I.R. 1065. Note also *Wehmeyer v Wehmeyer* [2001] B.P.I.R. 548. Compare *Cadwell v Jackson* [2001] B.P.I.R. 966. On r. 12.3 and foreign family proceedings see *Cartwright v Cartwright* [2002] EWCA Civ 931; [2002] B.P.I.R. 895.

Foreign tax debts provide an example of a debt which is regarded as non-provable on policy grounds: see *Government of India, Ministry of Finance (Revenue Division) v Taylor* [1955] A.C. 491 which is discussed by Miller in [1991] J.B.L. 144. See also *QRS 1 Aps v Frandsen* [1999] 1 W.L.R. 2169. This rule cannot be maintained where the EC Regulation on Insolvency Proceedings (1346/2000) applies.

12.4 Notices

12.4(1) **[Notices in writing etc.]** All notices required or authorised by or under the Act or the Rules to be given must be in writing, unless it is otherwise provided, or the court allows the notice to be given in some other way.

12.4(2) **[Proof of posting]** Where in any proceedings a notice is required to be sent or given by the official receiver or by the responsible insolvency practitioner, the sending or giving of it may be proved by means of a certificate–

(a) in the case of the official receiver, by him or a member of his staff, and

(b) in the case of the insolvency practitioner, by him, or his solicitor, or a partner or an employee of either of them,

that the notice was duly posted.

12.4(3) [**Certificates of posting**] In the case of a notice to be sent or given by a person other than the official receiver or insolvency practitioner, the sending or giving of it may be proved by means of a certificate by that person that he posted the notice, or instructed another person (naming him) to do so.

12.4(4) [**Certificate endorsed on copy of notice**] A certificate under this Rule may be endorsed on a copy or specimen of the notice to which it relates.

12.4A Quorum at meeting of creditors or contributories

12.4A(1) [**Meeting competent**] Any meeting of creditors or contributories in insolvency proceedings is competent to act if a quorum is present.

12.4A(2) [**Quorum**] Subject to the next paragraph, a quorum is–

- (a) in the case of a creditors' meeting, at least one creditor entitled to vote;
- (b) in the case of a meeting of contributories, at least 2 contributories so entitled, or all the contributories, if their number does not exceed 2.

12.4A(3) [**Persons present or represented**] For the purposes of this Rule, the reference to the creditor or contributories necessary to constitute a quorum is to those persons present or represented by proxy by any person (including the chairman) and in the case of any proceedings under Parts I–VII of the Act includes persons duly represented under section 375 of the Companies Act.

12.4A(4) [**Meeting to be delayed**] Where at any meeting of creditors or contributories–

- (a) the provisions of this Rule as to a quorum being present are satisfied by the attendance of–
    - (i) the chairman alone, or
    - (ii) one other person in addition to the chairman, and
- (b) the chairman is aware, by virtue of proofs and proxies received or otherwise, that one or more additional persons would, if attending, be entitled to vote,

the meeting shall not commence until at least the expiry of 15 minutes after the time appointed for its commencement.

GENERAL NOTE

In part r. 12.4A fills the void created by the deletion of rr. 3.13, 4.66 and 6.92. The quorum for creditors' meetings has been reduced from three creditors to one.

12.5 Evidence of proceedings at meetings

12.5(1) [**Minute of proceedings admissible**] A minute of proceedings at a meeting (held under the Act or the Rules) of a person's creditors, or of the members of a company, or of the contributories in a company's liquidation, signed by a person describing himself as, or appearing to be, the chairman of that meeting is admissible in insolvency proceedings without further proof.

12.5(2) [**Minute as prima facie evidence**] The minute is prima facie evidence that–

- (a) the meeting was duly convened and held,
- (b) all resolutions passed at the meeting were duly passed, and
- (c) all proceedings at the meeting duly took place.

12.6 Documents issuing from Secretary of State

12.6(1) [**Presumption re documents**] Any document purporting to be, or to contain, any order, directions or certificate issued by the Secretary of State shall be received in evidence and deemed to be or (as the case may be) contain that order or certificate, or those directions, without further proof, unless the contrary is shown.

12.6(2) [**Application of r. 12.6(1)**] Paragraph (1) applies whether the document is signed by the Secretary of State himself or an officer on his behalf.

12.6(3) [**Certificate as conclusive evidence**] Without prejudice to the foregoing, a certificate signed by the Secretary of State or an officer on his behalf and confirming–

(a) the making of any order,

(b) the issuing of any document, or

(c) the exercise of any discretion, power or obligation arising or imposed under the Act or the Rules,

is conclusive evidence of the matters dealt with in the certificate.

12.7 Forms for use in insolvency proceedings

12.7(1) [**Sch. 4 forms**] The forms contained in Schedule 4 to the Rules shall be used in and in connection with, insolvency proceedings, whether in the High Court or a county court.

12.7(2) [**Variations**] The forms shall be used with such variations, if any, as the circumstances may require.

12.7(3) [**Use of old forms**] Where any form contained in Schedule 4 is substantially the same as one used for a corresponding purpose under either–

(a) the law and practice obtaining before the coming into force of the Rules; or

(b) if the form was first required to be used after the coming into force of the Rules, the law and practice obtaining before the making of the requirement,

whichever shall be appropriate in any case, the latter may continue to be used (with the necessary modifications) until 1 March 1988.

GENERAL NOTE

The appropriate insolvency forms are in Sch. 4 but are not reproduced in this *Guide*, although a full list of the relevant names and numbers is included below at pp. 1103ff.

12.8 Insolvency practitioner's security

12.8(1) [**Duty re appointee's security**] Wherever under the Rules any person has to appoint, or certify the appointment of, an insolvency practitioner to any office, he is under a duty to satisfy himself that the person appointed or to be appointed has security for the proper performance of his functions.

12.8(2) [**Duty to review adequacy of security**] It is the duty–

(a) of the creditors' committee in companies administration, administrative receivership and bankruptcy,

(b) of the liquidation committee in companies winding up, and

(c) of any committee of creditors established for the purposes of a voluntary arrangement under Part I or VIII of the Act,

to review from time to time the adequacy of the responsible insolvency practitioner's security.

12.8(3) [**Cost of security**] In any insolvency proceedings the cost of the responsible insolvency practitioner's security shall be defrayed as an expense of the proceedings.

GENERAL NOTE

For the requirement of security, see IA 1986, s. 390(3). The provision of security is not a once and for all requirement, as r. 12.8(2) makes clear.

12.9 Time-limits

12.9(1) **[Application of CPR r. 2.8]** The provisions of CPR rule 2.8 (time) apply, as regards computation of time, to anything required or authorised to be done by the Rules.

12.9(2) **[Application of CPR r. 3.1(2)(a)]** The provisions of CPR rule 3.1(2)(a) (the court's general powers of management) apply so as to enable the court to extend or shorten the time for compliance with anything required or authorised to be done by the Rules.

GENERAL NOTE

Rule 12.9 substituted by the Insolvency (Amendment) (No. 2) Rules 1999 (SI 1999/1022), r. 3, Sch., para. 11 as from April 26, 1999. Under this rule, the court has power to abridge the period of five days' notice of a petition for an administration order that is normally required to be given to a floating chargeholder by r. 2.7(1): *Re a Company No. 00175 of 1987* (1987) 3 B.C.C. 124.

12.10 Service by post

12.10(1) **[Proper service by post]** For a document to be properly served by post, it must be contained in an envelope addressed to the person on whom service is to be effected, and pre-paid for either first or second class post.

12.10(1A) **[Where to be served]** A document to be served by post may be sent to the last known address of the person to be served.

12.10(2) **[First class post]** Where first class post is used, the document is treated as served on the second business day after the date of posting, unless the contrary is shown.

12.10(3) **[Second class post]** Where second class post is used, the document is treated as served on the fourth business day after the date of posting, unless the contrary is shown.

12.10(4) **[Presumed date of posting]** The date of posting is presumed, unless the contrary is shown, to be the date shown in the post-mark on the envelope in which the document is contained.

GENERAL NOTE

The requirements of r. 12.10 were not satisfied in *Skarzynski v Chalford Property Co. Ltd* [2001] B.P.I.R. 673.

12.11 General provisions as to service

12.11 Subject to Rule 12.10, CPR Part 6 (service of documents) applies as regards any matter relating to the service of documents and the giving of notice in insolvency proceedings.

GENERAL NOTE

Rule 12.11 substituted by the Insolvency (Amendment) (No. 2) Rules 1999 (SI 1999/1022), r. 3, Sch., para. 12 as from April 26, 1999.

12.12 Service outside the jurisdiction

12.12(1) **[Non-application of RSC, O.11 etc.]** RSC Order 11 (service of process, etc., out of the jurisdiction) does not apply in insolvency proceedings.

12.12(2) **[Service of bankruptcy petition outside England and Wales]** A bankruptcy petition may, with the leave of the court, be served outside England and Wales in such manner as the court may direct.

12.12(3) **[Service on a person not in England and Wales]** Where for the purposes of insolvency proceedings any process or order of the court, or other document, is required to be served on a person who is not in England and Wales, the court may order service to be effected within such time, on such person, at such place and in such manner as it thinks fit, and may also require such proof of service as it thinks fit.

12.12(4) [**Supporting affidavit**] An application under this Rule shall be supported by an affidavit stating–

(a) the grounds on which the application is made, and

(b) in what place or country the person to be served is, or probably may be found.

12.12(5) [**Leave of court not required**] Leave of the court is not required to serve anything referred to in this Rule on a member State liquidator.

GENERAL NOTE

The position under the old law (BR 1952, r. 86) was considered in *Re Jogia (a Bankrupt)* [1988] 1 W.L.R. 484; *Re Tucker (a Bankrupt)* [1988] 1 W.L.R. 497 and *Re Tucker (a Bankrupt) Ex p. Tucker* [1990] Ch. 148 at p. 162. For a case where a winding-up petition was served outside the jurisdiction, see *Re Baby Moon (UK) Ltd* (1985) 1 B.C.C. 99,298. Rule 12.12 is of growing importance as the UK courts strive to give extraterritorial effect to more and more provisions of IA 1986 and CDDA 1986. Recently the following judicial decisions have leaned in favour of extraterritoriality: *Re Paramount Airways Ltd (in Administration)* [1993] Ch. 223 (reported as *Re Paramount Airways Ltd (No. 2)* [1992] B.C.C. 416) (use of s. 238 of IA 1986); *Re Seagull Manufacturing Co. Ltd* [1993] Ch. 345; [1993] B.C.C. 241 (examinations of officers conducted under s. 133 of IA 1986); *Re Seagull Manufacturing Co. Ltd (No. 2)* [1994] Ch. 91; [1993] B.C.C. 833 (disqualification proceedings under CDDA 1986); and *McIsaac, Petitioners* [1994] B.C.C. 410 (orders under ss. 236, 237 and 426 of IA 1986). This drive towards extending the territorial scope of UK insolvency law is in response to the increasingly transnational nature of commercial activity and in particular the fact that with modern technology UK companies can be effectively managed from abroad.

Rule 12.12(5) was introduced by Insolvency (Amendment) Rules 2002 (SI 2002/1307) para. 10(5) with effect from May 31, 2002 to cater for the EC Council Regulation on Insolvency Proceedings 1346/2000.

12.13 Confidentiality of documents

12.13(1) [**Power of responsible insolvency practitioner**] Where in insolvency proceedings the responsible insolvency practitioner considers, in the case of a document forming part of the records of the insolvency, that–

(a) it should be treated as confidential, or

(b) it is of such a nature that its disclosure would be calculated to be injurious to the interests of the insolvent's creditors or, in the case of a company's insolvency, its members or the contributories in its winding up,

he may decline to allow it to be inspected by a person who would otherwise be entitled to inspect it.

12.13(2) [**Who may be refused inspection**] The persons to whom the insolvency practitioner may under this Rule refuse inspection include the members of a liquidation committee or a creditors' committee.

12.13(3) [**Application to court etc.**] Where under this Rule the insolvency practitioner determines to refuse inspection of a document, the person wishing to inspect it may apply to the court for that determination to be overruled; and the court may either overrule it altogether, or sustain it subject to such conditions (if any) as it thinks fit to impose.

12.13(4) [**Inspection of proof or proxy**] Nothing in this Rule entitles the insolvency practitioner to decline to allow the inspection of any proof or proxy.

GENERAL NOTE

This reinforces a theme reflected in several IA 1986 provisions (*e.g.* s. 48(6)), and also in many of the rules themselves (*e.g.* rr. 3.5 and 6.61).

Rule 12.13(4) was inserted in 1987 to curb refusal of inspection of proofs or proxy on grounds of confidentiality.

12.14 Notices sent simultaneously to the same person

12.14 Where under the Act or the Rules a document of any description is to be sent to a person (whether or not as a member of a class of persons to whom that same document is to be sent), it may be sent as an accompaniment to any other document or information which the person is to receive, with or without modification or adaption of the form applicable to that document.

12.15 Right to copy documents

12.15 Where the Act or the Rules confer a right for any person to inspect documents, the right includes that of taking copies of those documents, on payment–

(a) in the case of documents on the court's file of proceedings, of the fee chargeable under any order made under section 130 of the Supreme Court Act 1981 or under section 128 of the County Courts Act 1984, and

(b) otherwise, of the appropriate fee.

GENERAL NOTE

This is a standard provision where inspection is permitted. See also r. 12.17. For the meaning of "appropriate fee", see r. 13.11.

12.15A Charge for copy documents

12.15A Where the responsible insolvency practitioner or the official receiver is requested by a creditor, member, contributory or member of a liquidation or creditors' committee to supply copies of any documents he is entitled to require the payment of the appropriate fee in respect of the supply of the documents.

GENERAL NOTE

For details of "the appropriate fee", see r. 13.11. Apparently insolvency practitioners called for the insertion of r. 12.15A to enable them to charge for copies in cases where there is no right to inspect and so the case is not covered by r. 12.15.

12.16 Non-receipt of notice of meeting

12.16 Where in accordance with the Act or the Rules a meeting of creditors or other persons is summoned by notice, the meeting is presumed to have been duly summoned and held, notwithstanding that not all those to whom the notice is to be given have received it.

GENERAL NOTE

This is somewhat similar to art. 39 in Table A of the Companies (Tables A to F) Regulations 1985 (SI 1985/805). Compare BR 1952, r. 242. See *Re a Debtor No. 64 of 1992* [1994] 1 W.L.R. 264; [1994] B.C.C. 55 for a limitation on the utility of r. 12.16 – although in that case the creditor in question was held to have had constructive notice of the meeting, and that this was sufficient.

12.17 Right to have list of creditors

12.17(1) [Application of Rule] This Rule applies in any of the following proceedings–

(a) proceedings under Part II of the Act (company administration),

(b) a creditors' voluntary winding up, or a winding up by the court, and

(c) proceedings in bankruptcy.

12.17(2) [Creditor's right to list etc.] In any such proceedings a creditor who under the Rules has the right to inspect documents on the court file also has the right to require the responsible insolvency practitioner to furnish him with a list of the insolvent's creditors and the amounts of their respective debts.

This does not apply if a statement of the insolvent's affairs has been filed in court or, in the case of a creditors' voluntary winding up, been delivered to the registrar of companies.

12.17(2A) **[Member State liquidator]** For the purpose of this Rule a member State liquidator appointed in main proceedings in relation to a person is deemed to be a creditor.

12.17(3) **[Fee for sending list]** The insolvency practitioner, on being required by any person to furnish the list, shall send it to him, but is entitled to charge the appropriate fee for doing so.

GENERAL NOTE

This complements r. 12.15. Rule 12.17(2A) was inserted by Insolvency (Amendment) Rules 2002 (SI 2002/1307) para. 10(6) with effect from May 31, 2002 to cater for the EC Council Regulation or Insolvency Proceedings (1346/2000).
  For the meaning of "appropriate fee" in r. 12.17(3), see r. 13.11.

12.18 False claim of status as creditor, etc.

12.18(1) **[Offence]** Where the Rules provide for creditors, members of a company or contributories in a company's winding up a right to inspect any documents, whether on the court's file or in the hands of a responsible insolvency practitioner or other person, it is an offence for a person, with the intention of obtaining a sight of documents which he has not under the Rules any right to inspect, falsely to claim a status which would entitle him to inspect them.

12.18(2) **[Penalties]** A person guilty of an offence under this Rule is liable to imprisonment or a fine, or both.

GENERAL NOTE

This is a useful deterrent to restrict bogus claims to inspect. For the appropriate penalty, see r. 12.21 and Sch. 5.

12.19 Execution overtaken by judgment debtor's insolvency

12.19(1) **[Application of Rule]** This Rule applies where execution has been taken out against property of a judgment debtor, and notice is given to the sheriff or other officer charged with the execution–

(a) under section 184(1) (that a winding-up order has been made against the debtor, or that a provisional liquidator has been appointed, or that a resolution for voluntary winding up has been passed); or

(b) under section 184(4) (that a winding-up petition has been presented or a winding-up order made, or that a meeting has been called at which there is to be proposed a resolution for voluntary winding up, or that such a resolution has been passed); or

(c) under section 346(2) (that the judgment debtor has been adjudged bankrupt); or

(d) under section 346(3)(b) (that a bankruptcy petition has been presented in respect of him).

12.19(2) **[Notice]** Subject as follows, the notice shall be in writing and be delivered by hand at, or sent by recorded delivery to, the office of the under-sheriff or (as the case may be) of the officer charged with the execution.

12.19(3) **[Execution in county court etc.]** Where the execution is in a county court, and the officer in charge of it is the registrar of that court, then if–

(a) there is filed in that court in respect of the judgment debtor a winding-up or bankruptcy petition, or

(b) there is made by that court in respect of him a winding-up order or an order appointing a provisional liquidator, or a bankruptcy order or an order appointing an interim receiver,

section 184 or (as the case may be) 346 is deemed satisfied as regards the requirement of a notice to be served on, or given to, the officer in charge of the execution.

GENERAL NOTE

This provision supplements IA 1986, ss. 184 and 346 on procedural matters.

12.20 The Gazette

12.20(1) [**Gazetted notice as evidence**] A copy of the Gazette containing any notice required by the Act or the Rules to be gazetted is evidence of any facts stated in the notice.

12.20(2) [**Gazetted notice of court order as conclusive evidence**] In the case of an order of the court notice of which is required by the Act or the Rules to be gazetted, a copy of the Gazette containing the notice may in any proceedings be produced as conclusive evidence that the order was made on the date specified in the notice.

12.20(3) [**Where gazetted order varied etc.**] Where an order of the court which is gazetted has been varied, and where any matter has been erroneously or inaccurately gazetted, the person whose responsibility it was to procure the requisite entry in the Gazette shall forthwith cause the variation of the order to be gazetted or, as the case may be, a further entry to be made in the Gazette for the purpose of correcting the error or inaccuracy.

12.21 Punishment of offences

12.21(1) [**Effect of Sch. 5**] Schedule 5 to the Rules has effect with respect to the way in which contraventions of the Rules are punishable on conviction.

12.21(2) [**First, second and third columns of Schedule**] In relation to an offence under a provision of the Rules specified in the first column of the Schedule (the general nature of the offence being described in the second column), the third column shows whether the offence is punishable on conviction on indictment, or on summary conviction, or either in the one way or the other.

12.21(3) [**Fourth column**] The fourth column shows, in relation to an offence, the maximum punishment by way of fine or imprisonment which may be imposed on a person convicted of the offence in the way specified in relation to it in the third column (that is to say, on indictment or summarily), a reference to a period of years or months being to a term of imprisonment of that duration.

12.21(4) [**Fifth column**] The fifth column shows (in relation to an offence for which there is an entry in that column) that a person convicted of the offence after continued contravention is liable to a daily default fine; that is to say, he is liable on a second or subsequent conviction of the offence to the fine specified in that column for each day on which the contravention is continued (instead of the penalty specified for the offence in the fourth column of the Schedule).

12.21(5) [**Application of s. 431**] Section 431 (summary proceedings), as it applies to England and Wales, has effect in relation to offences under the Rules as to offences under the Act.

GENERAL NOTE

This explains the mechanics of Sch. 5. Note the connection with IA 1986, s. 431 for summary proceedings.

12.22 Notice of order under section 176A(5)

12.22(1) [**Court to send sealed copies**] Where the court makes an order under section 176A(5), it shall as soon as reasonably practicable send two sealed copies of the order to the applicant and a sealed copy to any other insolvency practitioner who holds office in relation to the company.

12.22(2) [**Liquidator, administrator or receiver to send copy to company**] Where the court has made an order under section 176A(5), the liquidator, administrator or receiver, as the case may be, shall, as soon as reasonably practicable, send a sealed copy of the order to the company.

12.22(3) [**Liquidator, administrator or receiver to send notice to creditors**] Where the court has made an order under section 176A(5), the liquidator, administrator or receiver, as the case may be, shall as soon as reasonably practicable, give notice to each creditor of whose claim and address he is aware.

12.22(4) [**Non-application of r. 12.22(3)**] Paragraph (3) shall not apply where the court directs otherwise.

12.22(5) **[R. 12.22(3) notice in newspaper]** The court may direct that the requirement in paragraph (3) is complied with by the liquidator, administrator or receiver, as the case may be, publishing a notice in such newspaper as he thinks most appropriate for ensuring that it comes to the notice of the company's unsecured creditors stating that the court has made an order disapplying the requirement to set aside the prescribed part.

12.22(6) **[Liquidator, administrator or receiver to send copy to registrar of companies]** The liquidator, administrator or receiver shall send a copy of the order to the registrar of companies as soon as reasonably practicable after the making of the order.

[FORM 12.1]

GENERAL NOTE

This new rule was added by Insolvency (Amendment) Rules 2003 (SI 2003/1730). It deals with the reserved fund for unsecured creditors (IA 1986, s. 176A). Orders made under s. 176A(5) cover cases where the reserve fund will not come into play because the costs of administering it would be disproportionate.

PART 13

INTERPRETATION AND APPLICATION

General comment on Pt 13
This interpretation Part should be viewed in the light of IA 1986 interpretation provisions, especially ss. 247–251, 380–385, and 435–436.

13.1 Introductory

13.1 This Part of the Rules has effect for their interpretation and application; and any definition given in this Part applies except, and in so far as, the context otherwise requires.

13.2 "The court"; "the registrar"

13.2(1) **["The court"]** Anything to be done under or by virtue of the Act or the Rules by, to or before the court may be done by, to or before a judge or the registrar.

13.2(2) **["The registrar"]** The registrar may authorise any act of a formal or administrative character which is not by statute his responsibility to be carried out by the chief clerk or any other officer of the court acting on his behalf, in accordance with directions given by the Lord Chancellor.

13.2(3) **["The registrar" in individual insolvency proceedings]** In individual insolvency proceedings, **"the registrar"** means a Registrar in Bankruptcy of the High Court, or the registrar or deputy registrar of a county court.

13.2(4) **[In company insolvency proceedings in High Court]** In company insolvency proceedings in the High Court, **"the registrar"** means–

(a) subject to the following paragraph, a Registrar in Bankruptcy of the High Court;

(b) where the proceedings are in the District Registry of Birmingham, Bristol, Cardiff, Leeds, Liverpool, Manchester, Newcastle-upon-Tyne or Preston, the District Registrar.

13.2(5) **[In a county court]** In company insolvency proceedings in a county court, **"the registrar"** means the officer of the court whose duty it is to exercise the functions which in the High Court are exercised by a registrar.

GENERAL NOTE

The registrar handles much of the day-to-day business of insolvency work.

Rule 13.2(2)
See *Practice Direction: Insolvency Proceedings* [2000] B.C.C. 927 (reproduced in Appendix IV to this *Guide*).

Rule 13.2(3)
See *Practice Direction: Insolvency Proceedings* [2000] B.C.C. 927.

13.3 "Give notice", etc.

13.3(1) **[Sending by post]** A reference in the Rules to giving notice, or to delivering, sending or serving any document, means that the notice or document may be sent by post, unless under a particular Rule personal service is expressly required.

13.3(2) **[Form of post]** Any form of post may be used, unless under a particular Rule a specified form is expressly required.

13.3(3) **[Personal service]** Personal service of a document is permissible in all cases.

13.3(4) **[Notice of venue]** Notice of the venue fixed for an application may be given by service of the sealed copy of the application under Rule 7.4(3).

13.4 Notice, etc. to solicitors

13.4 Where under the Act or the Rules a notice or other document is required or authorised to be given to a person, it may, if he has indicated that his solicitor is authorised to accept service on his behalf, be given instead to the solicitor.

GENERAL NOTE

Solicitors have no implied authority to receive notices: *Re Munro* [1981] 1 W.L.R. 1358.

13.5 Notice to joint liquidators, joint trustees, etc.

13.5 Where two or more persons are acting jointly as the responsible insolvency practitioner in any proceedings, delivery of a document to one of them is to be treated as delivery to them all.

13.6 "Venue"

13.6 References to the **"venue"** for any proceeding or attendance before the court, or for a meeting, are to the time, date and place for the proceeding, attendance or meeting.

13.7 "Insolvency proceedings"

13.7 **"Insolvency proceedings"** means any proceedings under the Act or the Rules.

GENERAL NOTE

See *Jyske Bank (Gibraltar) Ltd v Spjeldnaes*, [2000] B.C.C. 16 – s. 423 proceedings not insolvency proceedings.

13.8 "Insolvent estate"

13.8 References to **"the insolvent estate"** are–

(a) in relation to a company insolvency, the company's assets, and

(b) in relation to an individual insolvency, the bankrupt's estate or (as the case may be) the debtor's property.

13.9 "Responsible insolvency practitioner", etc.

13.9(1) [Definition] In relation to any insolvency proceedings, **"the responsible insolvency practitioner"** means–

(a) the person acting in a company insolvency, as supervisor of a voluntary arrangement under Part I of the Act, or as administrator, administrative receiver, liquidator or provisional liquidator;

(b) the person acting in an individual insolvency, as the supervisor of a voluntary arrangement under Part VIII of the Act, or as trustee or interim receiver;

(c) the official receiver acting as receiver and manager of a bankrupt's estate.

13.9(2) [Official receiver acting in relevant capacity] Any reference to the liquidator, provisional liquidator, trustee or interim receiver includes the official receiver when acting in the relevant capacity.

13.9(3) ["Authorised person"] A reference to an "authorised person" is a reference to a person who is authorised pursuant to section 389A of the Act to act as nominee or supervisor of a voluntary arrangement proposed or approved under Part I or Part VIII of the Act.

GENERAL NOTE

See IA 1986, Pt XIII.

13.10 "Petitioner"

13.10 In winding up and bankruptcy, references to **"the petitioner"** or **"the petitioning creditor"** include any person who has been substituted as such, or been given carriage of the petition.

GENERAL NOTE

See rr. 4.19, 6.30 and 6.31.

13.11 "The appropriate fee"

13.11 "The appropriate fee" means–

(a) in Rule 6.192(2) (payor under income payments order entitled to clerical etc. costs), or Rule 6.193C(4) (payor under income payments agreement entitled to clerical etc costs) 50 pence; and

(b) in other cases, 15 pence per A4 or A5 page, and 30 pence per A3 page.

GENERAL NOTE

Note the special higher fee for cases under r. 6.192(2). This definition provision was modified by Insolvency (Amendment) Rules 2003 (SI 2003/1730) to deal with the new income payments agreements regime in bankruptcy which was introduced by EA 2002 (see s. 310A of IA 1986).

13.12 "Debt", "liability" (winding up)

13.12(1) [Definition] "Debt", in relation to the winding up of a company, means (subject to the next paragraph) any of the following–

(a) any debt or liability to which the company is subject at the date on which it goes into liquidation;

(b) any debt or liability to which the company may become subject after that date by reason of any obligation incurred before that date; and

(c) any interest provable as mentioned in Rule 4.93(1).

The Insolvency Rules 1986 *Rule 13.12A*

13.12(2) [**Liability in tort**] In determining for the purposes of any provision of the Act or the Rules about winding up, whether any liability in tort is a debt provable in the winding up, the company is deemed to become subject to that liability by reason of an obligation incurred at the time when the cause of action accrued.

13.12(3) [**Debt or liability**] For the purposes of references in any provision of the Act or the Rules about winding up to a debt or liability, it is immaterial whether the debt or liability is present or future, whether it is certain or contingent, or whether its amount is fixed or liquidated, or is capable of being ascertained by fixed rules or as a matter of opinion; and references in any such provision to owing a debt are to be read accordingly.

13.12(4) [**"Liability"**] In any provision of the Act or the Rules about winding up, except in so far as the context otherwise requires, **"liability"** means (subject to paragraph (3) above) a liability to pay money or money's worth, including any liability under an enactment, any liability for breach of trust, any liability in contract, tort or bailment, and any liability arising out of an obligation to make restitution.

13.12(5) [**Application of r. 13.12**] This Rule shall apply where a company is in administration and shall be read as if references to winding-up were a reference to administration.

GENERAL NOTE

This important provision would have been better located in the Act itself. Compare IA 1986, s. 382 ("debt" in bankruptcy cases), and see also r. 12.3 (provable debts); and note that there are no corresponding definitions for other corporate insolvency proceedings, such as voluntary arrangements and administrations – a somewhat surprising omission in view of the references to "contingent and prospective creditors" in s. 9(1) and to "debts for an unliquidated amount ... or whose value is not ascertained" in rr. 1.17(3) and *2.22(5)*. These omissions have had to be made good by the case law. For references to the relevant cases and a general discussion of the terms "debt" and "creditor", see the note to s. 1(1), and also the notes to Sch. 8, paras 12 and 14. This definition provision was amended by the insertion of r. 13.12(5) to cater for the fact that these debt interpretation issues are now relevant in the context of administration because of the added distributional dimension of the new administration regime in the wake of the reforms introduced by EA 2002.

In *Re Kentish Homes Ltd* [1993] B.C.C. 212 a rare example of non-provable debt arose. In this case a Law of Property Act receiver had incurred community charges in respect of premises which had been constructed by the receiver in order to fulfil contractual obligations of the insolvent company, but which had remained unoccupied until they were sold. This property development company had gone into liquidation after the commencement of a Law of Property Act receivership but the liquidator had not been allowed into possession. On the subsequent liquidation of the company it was held by Nicholls V.-C. that the conditions laid down in r. 13.12(1) had not been satisfied in respect of this sum and the local authority could not prove in respect of it. The liability to pay the community charge did not exist at the date of entry into liquidation nor did it arise in respect of a pre-liquidation obligation. The receiver was empowered to settle this debt but he had no legal obligation under s. 109(8)(i) of LPA 1925 to do so nor would the court require him to do so. His Lordship made the point that the position would be the same in respect of the new council tax. These comments should be viewed with caution in view of *Re Toshoku Finance (UK) plc* [2002] UKHL 6, [2002] 1 W.L.R. 671.

By way of contrast it was held in *Tottenham Hotspur plc v Edennote plc* [1994] B.C.C. 681 that an order for costs was a debt for the purposes of r. 13.12(1)(b) and (3) and so could form the basis of a winding-up petition.

Rule 13.12(2)
This rule would appear to settle the inconsistency between *Re Berkeley Securities (Property) Ltd* [1980] 1 W.L.R. 1589 and *Re Islington Metal and Plating Works Ltd* [1984] 1 W.L.R. 14; (1983) 1 B.C.C. 98,933. The Cork Committee (*Report*, para. 1310) favoured the former decision. This new rule is not *ultra vires* but is authorised by IA 1986, Sch. 8, para. 12.

13.12A "Authorised deposit-taker" and "former authorised deposit-taker"

13.12A(1) [**"Authorised deposit-taker"**] **"Authorised deposit-taker"** means a person with permission under Part 4 of the Financial Services and Markets Act 2000 to accept deposits.

13.12A(2) **["Former authorised deposit-taker"]** "**Former authorised deposit-taker**" means a person who–

(a) is not an authorised deposit-taker,

(b) was formerly an authorised institution under the Banking Act 1987, or a recognised bank or a licensed institution under the Banking Act 1979, and

(c) continues to have liability in respect of any deposit for which it had a liability at a time when it was an authorised institution, recognised bank or licensed institution.

13.12A(3) **[Provisions r. 13.12A(1), (2) to be read with]** Paragraphs (1) and (2) must be read with–

(a) section 22 of the Financial Services and Markets Act 2000;

(b) any relevant order under that section; and

(c) Schedule 2 to that Act.

GENERAL NOTE

Rule 13.12A
This rule was inserted by the Financial Services and Markets Act 2000 (Consequential Amendments and Repeals) Order 2001 (SI 2001/3649) r. 381 with effect from December 1, 2001.

13.13 Expressions used generally

13.13(1) **["Business day"]** "**Business day**" means any day other than a Saturday, a Sunday, Christmas Day, Good Friday or a day which is a bank holiday in any part of Great Britain under or by virtue of the Banking and Financial Dealings Act 1971 except in Rules 1.7., 4.10., 4.11., 4.16., 4.20., 5.10. and 6.23. where "**business day**" shall include any day which is a bank holiday in Scotland but not in England and Wales.

13.13(2) **["The Department"]** "**The Department**" means the Department of Trade and Industry.

13.13(3) **["File in court"]** "**File in court**" and file with the court means deliver to the court for filing.

13.13(4) **["The *Gazette*"]** "**The Gazette**" means the London Gazette.

13.13(5) **["General regulations"]** "**General regulations**" means regulations made by the Secretary of State under Rule 12.1.

13.13(6) **["Practice direction"]** "**Practice direction**" means a direction as to the practice and procedure of any court within the scope of the CPR.

13.13(7) **["Prescribed order of priority"]** "**Prescribed order of priority**" means the order of priority of payments laid down by Chapter 20 of Part 4 of the Rules, or Chapter 23 of Part 6.

13.13(8) **["Centre of main interests"]** "**Centre of main interests**" has the same meaning as in the EC Regulation.

13.13(9) **["Establishment"]** "**Establishment**" has the meaning given by Article 2(h) of the EC Regulation.

13.13(10) **["Main proceedings"]** "**Main proceedings**" means proceedings opened in accordance with Article 3(1) of the EC Regulation and falling within the definition of insolvency proceedings in Article 2(a) of the EC Regulation and

in relation to England and Wales and Scotland set out in Annex A to the EC Regulation under the heading "United Kingdom", and

in relation to another member State, set out in Annex A to the EC Regulation under the heading relating to that member State;

13.13(11) ["Member State liquidator"] "Member State liquidator" means a person falling within the definition of liquidator in Article 2(b) of the EC Regulation appointed in proceedings to which it applies in a member State other than the United Kingdom.

13.13(12) ["Secondary proceedings"] "Secondary proceedings" means proceedings opened in accordance with Articles 3(2) and 3(3) of the EC Regulation and falling within the definition of winding-up proceedings in Article 2(c) of the EC Regulation, and

(a) in relation to England and Wales and Scotland, set out in Annex B to the EC Regulation under the heading "United Kingdom", and

(b) in relation to another member State, set out in Annex B to the EC Regulation under the heading relating to that member State.

13.13(13) ["Temporary administrator"] "Temporary administrator" means a temporary administrator referred to by Article 38 of the EC Regulation.

13.13(14) ["Territorial proceedings"] "Territorial proceedings" means proceedings opened in accordance with Articles 3(2) and 3(4) of the EC Regulation and falling within the definition of insolvency proceedings in Article 2(a) of the EC Regulation, and

(a) in relation to England and Wales and Scotland, set out in Annex A to the EC Regulation under the heading "United Kingdom", and

(b) in relation to another member State, set out in Annex A to the EC Regulation under the heading relating to that member State.

13.13(15) ["Prescribed part"] "Prescribed part" has the same meaning as it does in section 176A(2)(a).

GENERAL NOTE

Rules 13.13(1), (6) and (7) were substituted by the Insolvency (Amendment) (No. 2) Rules 1999 (SI 1999/1022) with effect from 26 April 1999. Rules 13.13(8)–(14) were introduced by Insolvency (Amendment) Rules 2002 (SI 2002/1307) para. 10(7) with effect from 31 May 2002 to cater for the advent of EC Council Regulation 1346/2000 on insolvency proceedings. Rule 13.13(3) was amended and r. 13.13(15) inserted by I(A)R 2003 (SI 2003/1730) with effect from September 15, 2003.

13.14 Application

13.14(1) [Application of Rules] Subject to paragraph (2) of this Rule, and save where otherwise expressly provided, the Rules apply–

(a) to receivers appointed on or after the day on which the Rules come into force,

(b) to bankruptcy proceedings where the bankruptcy petition is presented on or after the day on which the Rules come into force, and

(c) to all other insolvency proceedings commenced on or after that day.

13.14(2) [Further application] The Rules also apply to winding-up and bankruptcy proceedings commenced before that day to which provisions of the Act are applied by Schedule 11 to the Act, to the extent necessary to give effect to those provisions.

SCHEDULES

SCHEDULE 1

SCHEME MANAGER'S VOTING RIGHTS

Rule 4.72(7)

1   This Schedule applies as does Rule 4.72.

Schedule 2   *The Insolvency Rules 1986*

2   In relation to any meeting at which the scheme manager is under Rule 4.72 entitled to be represented, the Board may submit in the liquidation, instead of a proof, a written statement of voting rights ("the statement").

3   The statement shall contain details of–

    (a)   the names of creditors of the company in respect of whom an obligation of the scheme manager has arisen or may reasonably be expected to arise as a result of the liquidation or proposed liquidation;

    (b)   the amount of the obligation so arising; and

    (c)   the total amount of all such obligations specified in the statement.

4   The scheme manager's statement shall, for the purpose of voting at a meeting (but for no other purpose), be treated in all respects as if it were a proof.

5   Any voting rights which a creditor might otherwise exercise at a meeting in respect of a claim against the company are reduced by a sum equal to the amount of that claim in relation to which the scheme manager, by virtue of its having submitted a statement, is entitled to exercise voting rights at that meeting.

6   The scheme manager may from time to time submit a further statement, and, if it does so, that statement supersedes any statement previously submitted.

Schedule 2

Alternative Courts for Debtors' Petitions in Bankruptcy

Rule 6.40(3)

Debtor's own county court	*Nearest full-time court*
ABERDARE	CARDIFF
ABERYSTWYTH	CARDIFF
AYLESBURY	LUTON
BANBURY	LUTON or GLOUCESTER or READING
BANGOR	BIRKENHEAD or CHESTER
BARNSLEY	SHEFFIELD
BARNSTAPLE	EXETER
BARROW IN FURNESS	BLACKPOOL or PRESTON
BATH	BRISTOL
BEDFORD	LUTON
BLACKBURN	PRESTON
BLACKWOOD	CARDIFF
BOSTON	NOTTINGHAM
BRIDGEND	CARDIFF
BRIDGWATER	BRISTOL
BURNLEY	BOLTON or PRESTON
BURTON ON TRENT	LEICESTER or DERBY or NOTTINGHAM
BURY ST. EDMUNDS	CAMBRIDGE
CANTERBURY	CROYDON or THE HIGH COURT (LONDON)
CARLISLE	PRESTON or BLACKPOOL
CARMARTHEN	CARDIFF

Debtor's own county court	Nearest full-time court
CHELMSFORD	SOUTHEND or THE HIGH COURT (LONDON)
CHELTENHAM	GLOUCESTER
CHESTERFIELD	SHEFFIELD
COLCHESTER	SOUTHEND or THE HIGH COURT (LONDON)
COVENTRY	BIRMINGHAM
CREWE	STOKE or CHESTER
DARLINGTON	MIDDLESBROUGH
DEWSBURY	LEEDS
DONCASTER	SHEFFIELD
DUDLEY	BIRMINGHAM
DURHAM	NEWCASTLE
EASTBOURNE	BRIGHTON
GREAT GRIMSBY	HULL
GREAT YARMOUTH	NORWICH
GUILDFORD	CROYDON
HALIFAX	LEEDS
HARROGATE	LEEDS
HASTINGS	BRIGHTON
HAVERFORDWEST	CARDIFF
HEREFORD	GLOUCESTER
HERTFORD	LUTON
HUDDERSFIELD	LEEDS
IPSWICH	NORWICH or SOUTHEND
KENDAL	BLACKPOOL or PRESTON
KIDDERMINSTER	BIRMINGHAM
KING'S LYNN	NORWICH or CAMBRIDGE
LANCASTER	BLACKPOOL or PRESTON
LINCOLN	NOTTINGHAM
MACCLESFIELD	STOKE or MANCHESTER
MAIDSTONE	CROYDON or THE HIGH COURT (LONDON)
MEDWAY	CROYDON or THE HIGH COURT (LONDON)
MERTHYR TYDFIL	CARDIFF
MILTON KEYNES	LUTON
NEATH	CARDIFF
NEWBURY	READING
NEWPORT (GWENT)	CARDIFF
NEWPORT (I.O.W.)	SOUTHAMPTON or PORTSMOUTH
NORTHAMPTON	LUTON
OXFORD	READING
PETERBOROUGH	CAMBRIDGE
PONTYPRIDD	CARDIFF
PORTMADOC	BIRKENHEAD or STOKE or CHESTER
RHYL	BIRKENHEAD or CHESTER
ROCHDALE	OLDHAM or MANCHESTER
SALISBURY	BOURNEMOUTH or SOUTHAMPTON
SCARBOROUGH	YORK or HULL or MIDDLESBROUGH
SCUNTHORPE	HULL or SHEFFIELD

Schedule 3 *The Insolvency Rules 1986*

Debtor's own county court	*Nearest full-time court*
SHREWSBURY	STOKE
ST. ALBANS	LUTON
STAFFORD	STOKE
STOCKTON ON TEES	MIDDLESBROUGH
STOCKPORT	MANCHESTER
STOURBRIDGE	BIRMINGHAM
SUNDERLAND	NEWCASTLE
SWANSEA	CARDIFF
SWINDON	GLOUCESTER or READING
TAMESIDE	MANCHESTER
TAUNTON	EXETER or BRISTOL
TORQUAY	EXETER
TRURO	PLYMOUTH
TUNBRIDGE WELLS	CROYDON
WAKEFIELD	LEEDS
WARRINGTON	CHESTER or LIVERPOOL or MANCHESTER
WARWICK	BIRMINGHAM
WELSHPOOL	STOKE or CHESTER
WEST BROMWICH	BIRMINGHAM
WEYMOUTH	BOURNEMOUTH
WIGAN	BOLTON or MANCHESTER or PRESTON
WINCHESTER	SOUTHAMPTON
WORCESTER	GLOUCESTER
WORKINGTON	PRESTON or BLACKPOOL
WREXHAM	BIRKENHEAD or STOKE or CHESTER
YEOVIL	EXETER or BRISTOL

SCHEDULE 3

SHORTHAND WRITERS' REMUNERATION

Rule 7.17

(Deleted by the Insolvency (Amendment) Rules 1993 (SI 1993/602), r. 3, Sch., para. 4 as from April 5, 1993.)

GENERAL NOTE

Shorthand writers' remuneration is now a matter to be determined by the court in its discretion: see r. 7.17(2).

The Insolvency Rules 1986   *Schedule 4*

SCHEDULE 4

FORMS

Rule 12.7

Index

PART 1: COMPANY VOLUNTARY ARRANGEMENTS

FORM NO.	TITLE
1.1	Notice to registrar of companies of voluntary arrangement taking effect
1.2	Notice to registrar of companies of order of revocation or suspension of voluntary arrangement
1.3	Notice to registrar of companies of supervisor's abstract of receipts and payments
1.4	Notice to registrar of companies of completion or termination of voluntary arrangement
1.5	Nominee's statement of opinion
1.6	Statement of affairs
1.7	Statement of eligibility for a moratorium
1.8	Statement of consent to act by nominee
1.9	Documents to be submitted to court to obtain moratorium
1.10	Advertisement of coming into force or ending of moratorium
1.11	Notice to registrar of companies of commencement of moratorium
1.12	Notice to registrar of companies of extension or further extension or renewal or continuation of moratorium
1.13	Notice to court of extension or further extension of moratorium
1.14	Notice to the registrar of companies of ending of moratorium
1.15	Nominee's notice to court of end of moratorium
1.16	Notice to the registrar of companies of the withdrawal of nominee's consent to act
1.17	Notice to court by nominee of withdrawal of consent to act
1.18	Notice to the registrar of companies of the appointment of a replacement nominee
1.19	Notice to court of appointment of replacement nominee

FORMER PART 2: ADMINISTRATION PROCEDURE

2.1	*Petition for administration order*
2.2	*Consent of administrator(s) to act*
2.3	*Affidavit of service of petition for administration order*
2.4	*Administration order*
2.4A	*Notice to administrator of administration order*
2.5	*Notice of administration order (for newspaper or London Gazette)*
2.6	*Notice of administration order*
2.7	*Copy of administration order to registrar of companies*
2.8	*Notice requiring preparation and submission of administration statement of affairs*
2.9	*Statement of affairs*
2.10	*Notice to directors and others to attend meeting of creditors*
2.11	*Notice of creditors' meeting in administration proceedings*
2.12	*Report of meeting of creditors*
2.13	*Certificate of constitution [amended certificate] of creditors' committee*
2.14	*Notice by administrator of a change in committee membership*
2.15	*Administrator's abstract of receipts and payments*
2.16	*Notice to court of resignation by administrator under Rule 2.53(1) of the Insolvency Rules 1986*
2.17	*Notice to court of resignation by administrator under Rule 2.53(2) of the Insolvency Rules 1986*

Schedule 4 *The Insolvency Rules 1986*
FORM NO.   *TITLE*

2.18	*Notice of order to deal with charged property*
2.19	*Notice of discharge of administration order*
2.20	*Notice of variation of administration order*
2.21	*Statement of administrator's proposals*
2.22	*Statement of revised proposals and notice of meeting to consider them*
2.23	*Notice of result of meeting of creditors*

PART 2: ADMINISTRATION PROCEDURE

2.1B	Administration application
2.2B	Statement of proposed administrator
2.3B	Affidavit of service of administration application
2.4B	Administration order
2.5B	Notice of intention to appoint an administrator by holder of qualifying floating charge
2.6B	Notice of appointment of an administrator by holder of qualifying floating charge
2.7B	Notice of appointment of an administrator by holder of qualifying floating charge (For use in pursuance of Rule 2.19 of the Insolvency Rules 1986)
2.8B	Notice of intention to appoint an administrator by company or director(s)
2.9B	Notice of appointment of an administrator by company or director(s) (where a notice of intention to appoint has been issued)
2.10B	Notice of appointment of an administrator by company or director(s) (where a notice of intention to appoint has not been issued)
2.11B	Notification of appointment of administrator (for newspaper and London Gazette)
2.12B	Notice of administrator's appointment
2.13B	Notice requiring submission of a statement of affairs
2.14B	Statement of affairs
2.15B	Statement of concurrence
2.16B	Notice of statement of affairs
2.17B	Statement of administrator's proposals
2.18B	Notice of extension of time period
2.19B	Notice to attend meeting of creditors
2.20B	Notice of a meeting of creditors
2.21B	Creditor's request for a meeting
2.22B	Statement of administrator's revised proposals
2.23B	Notice of result of meeting of creditors
2.24B	Administrator's progress report
2.25B	Notice of conduct of business by correspondence
2.26B	[Amended] Certificate of constitution of creditors' committee
2.27B	Notice by administrator of a change in committee membership
2.28B	Notice of order to deal with charged property
2.29B	Affidavit of debt
2.30B	Notice of automatic end of administration
2.31B	Notice of extension of period of administration
2.32B	Notice of end of administration
2.33B	Notice of court order ending administration
2.34B	Notice of move from administration to creditors' voluntary liquidation
2.35B	Notice of move from administration to dissolution
2.36B	Notice to registrar of companies in respect of date of dissolution
2.37B	Notice of intention to resign as administrator
2.38B	Notice of resignation by administrator
2.39B	Notice of vacation of office by administrator
2.40B	Notice of appointment of replacement/additional administrator

The Insolvency Rules 1986   Schedule 4

FORM NO.	TITLE

PART 3: ADMINISTRATIVE RECEIVERSHIP

3.1	Written acceptance of appointment by receiver
3.1A	Notice of appointment of administrative receiver (for newspaper or London Gazette)
3.1B	Notice requiring preparation and submission of administrative receivership statement of affairs
3.2	Statement of affairs
3.3	Statement of affairs in administrative receivership following report to creditors
3.4	Certificate of constitution [amended certificate] of creditors' committee
3.5	Administrative receiver's report as to change in membership of creditors' committee
3.6	Receiver or manager or administrative receiver's abstract of receipts and payments
3.7	Notice of administrative receiver's death
3.8	Notice of order to dispose of charged property
3.9	Notice of resignation of administrative receiver pursuant to section 45(1) of Insolvency Act 1986
3.10	Administrative receiver's report

PART 4: COMPANIES WINDING UP

4.1	Statutory demand under section 123(1)(a) or 222(1)(a) of the Insolvency Act 1986
4.2	Winding-up petition
4.3	Affidavit verifying winding-up petition
4.4	Affidavit of service of winding-up petition at registered office
4.5	Affidavit of service of winding-up petition other than at registered office or on an oversea company
4.6	Advertisement of winding-up petition
4.7	Certificate that relevant provision of Rules have been complied with
4.8	Order for leave to withdraw winding-up petition
4.9	Notice of intention to appear on petition
4.10	List of persons intending to appear on the hearing of the petition
4.11	Order for winding up by the court
4.12	Order for winding up by the court following upon the cessation of the appointment of an administrator
4.13	Notice to official receiver of winding-up order
4.14	Petition by contributory
4.14A	Notice to official receiver of appointment of provisional liquidator
4.15	Order of appointment of provisional liquidator
4.16	Notice requiring preparation and submission of statement of company's affairs
4.17	Statement of affairs [s. 131 IA86–winding up by court]
4.18	Statement of affairs [s. 95 IA86–voluntary liquidator]
4.19	Statement of affairs [s. 99 IA86–creditors' voluntary winding up]
4.20	Statement of affairs under s. 95/s. 99 to registrar of companies
4.21	Request by creditors for a meeting of the company's creditors [and contributories]
4.22	Notice to creditors of meeting of creditors
4.23	Notice to contributories of meeting of contributories
4.24	Request by contributory/contributories for a meeting of the company's contributories
4.25	Proof of debt–general form
4.26	Affidavit of debt
4.27	Certificate of appointment of liquidator by meeting
4.28	Certificate of appointment of two or more liquidators by meeting
4.29	Order of court appointing liquidator
4.30	Order of court appointing two or more liquidators

Schedule 4 *The Insolvency Rules 1986*

FORM NO.	TITLE
4.31	Notice of appointment of liquidator in winding up by the court (for registrar of companies)
4.32	Notice to court of resignation of liquidator following meeting of creditors
4.33	Notice of resignation as voluntary liquidator under s. 171(5) of the Insolvency Act 1986
4.34	Order of court giving liquidator leave to resign
4.35	Order of court granting voluntary liquidator leave to resign
4.36	Notice to court of resignation of liquidator following leave of the court
4.37	Certificate of removal of liquidator
4.38	Certificate of removal of voluntary liquidator
4.39	Order of court removing liquidator or directing liquidator to summon a meeting of creditors for purpose of his removal
4.40	Notice of ceasing to act as voluntary liquidator
4.41	Liquidator's application to the Secretary of State for his release
4.42	Notice to court of final meeting of creditors
4.43	Notice to registrar of companies of final meeting of creditors
4.44	Notice of death of liquidator
4.45	Notice to official receiver or Secretary of State by liquidator on loss of qualification as insolvency practitioner
4.46	Notice of vacation of office by voluntary liquidator
4.47	Certificate of constitution [amended certificate] of liquidation committee
4.48	Notice of constitution of liquidation committee
4.49	Report by liquidator of any change in membership of liquidation committee
4.50	Liquidator's certificate that creditors paid in full
4.51	Certificate that creditors have been paid in full
4.52	Liquidator's certificate of continuance of liquidation committee
4.53	Notice of disclaimer under section 178 of the Insolvency Act 1986
4.54	Notice to elect
4.55	Notice of intended disclaimer to interested party
4.56	Affidavit of liquidator in support of application for call
4.57	Order giving leave to make a call
4.58	Notice of call sanctioned by the court or the liquidation committee to be sent to contributory
4.59	Order for payment of call due from contributory
4.60	Order of appointment of special manager
4.61	Order of public examination
4.62	Notice to official receiver by creditor requesting him to make application for the holding of a public examination
4.63	Notice to official receiver by contributory requesting him to make application for the holding of a public examination
4.64	Order as to examination of person who is suffering from mental disorder or physical affliction or disability
4.65	Affidavit of verification of record of the public examination
4.66	Order of adjournment of public examination
4.67	Order appointing time for proceeding with public examination adjourned generally
4.68	Liquidator's statement of receipts and payments
4.69	Order of court on appeal against Secretary of State's decision under section 203(4) or 205(4) of the Insolvency Act 1986
4.70	Members' voluntary winding up declaration of solvency embodying a statement of assets and liabilities
4.71	Return of final meeting in a members' voluntary winding up

FORM NO.	TITLE
4.72	Return of final meeting in a creditors' voluntary winding up

PART 5: INDIVIDUAL VOLUNTARY ARRANGEMENTS

5.1	Order for stay pending hearing of application for interim order
5.2	Interim order of court under section 252 of the Insolvency Act 1986
5.3	Order extending effect of interim order
5.4	Alternative orders to be made at hearing to consider chairman's report
5.5	Documents to be submitted to court under Rule 5.14
5.6	Voting form in relation to a proposal for a voluntary arrangement under section 263A of the Insolvency Act 1986
5.7	Order of annulment under section 261 of the Insolvency Act 1986
5.8	Order of annulment under section 263D of the Insolvency Act 1986

PART 6: BANKRUPTCY

6.1	Statutory demand under section 268(1)(a) of the Insolvency Act 1986–debt for liquidated sum payable immediately
6.2	Statutory demand under section 268(1)(a) of the Insolvency Act 1986–debt for liquidated sum payable immediately following a judgment or order of the court
6.3	Statutory demand under section 268(2) of the Insolvency Act 1986–debt payable at future date
6.4	Application to set aside statutory demand
6.5	Affidavit in support of application to set aside statutory demand
6.6	Order setting aside statutory demand
6.7	Creditor's bankruptcy petition on failure to comply with a statutory demand for a liquidated sum payable immediately
6.8	Creditor's bankruptcy petition on failure to comply with a statutory demand for a liquidated sum payable at a future date.
6.9	Creditor's bankruptcy petition where execution or other process on a judgment has been returned unsatisfied in whole or part
6.10	Bankruptcy petition for default in connection with voluntary arrangement
6.11	Affidavit of personal service of statutory demand
6.12	Affidavit of substituted service of statutory demand
6.13	Affidavit of truth of statements in bankruptcy petition
6.14	Application for registration of a petition in bankruptcy against an individual under Land Charges Act 1972
6.15	Order for substituted service of a bankruptcy petition
6.16	Substituted service of bankruptcy petition–notice in Gazette
6.17	Affidavit of personal service of bankruptcy petition
6.18	Affidavit of substituted service of bankruptcy petition
6.19	Notice by debtor of intention to oppose bankruptcy petition
6.20	Notice of intention to appear on bankruptcy petition
6.21	List of creditors intending to appear on hearing of the bankruptcy petition
6.22	Dismissal or withdrawal of bankruptcy petition
6.23	Order of adjournment of bankruptcy petition
6.24	Notice to debtor and creditors of order of adjournment of bankruptcy petition
6.24A	Order for substitution of petitioner on creditor's petition
6.24B	Change of carriage order
6.25	Bankruptcy order on creditor's petition
6.26	Application for registration of a bankruptcy order against an individual under the Land Charges Act 1972
6.27	Debtor's bankruptcy petition

Schedule 4   The Insolvency Rules 1986
FORM NO.   TITLE

6.28	Statement of affairs (debtor's petition)
6.29	Order of appointment of insolvency practitioner to prepare a report under section 274(1) of the Insolvency Act 1986
6.30	Bankruptcy order on debtor's petition
6.31	Revocation of certificate of summary administration
6.32	Order of appointment of interim receiver
6.33	Bankrupt's statement of affairs
6.34	Request by creditor(s) for a meeting of the bankrupt's creditors
6.35	Notice to creditors of meeting of creditors
6.36	Notice to bankrupt of meeting of creditors
6.37	Proof of debt
6.38	Proof by an existing trustee as a claim in later bankruptcy
6.39	Affidavit of debt
6.40	Certificate of appointment of trustee by creditors' meeting
6.41	Certificate of appointment of two or more trustees by creditors' meeting
6.42	Order of court appointing trustee
6.43	Order of court appointing two or more trustees
6.44	Notice to court of resignation of trustee following meeting of creditors
6.45	Order of court giving trustee leave to resign
6.46	Notice to court of resignation of trustee following leave of the court
6.47	Certificate of removal of trustee
6.48	Order of court removing trustee or directing trustee to summon a meeting of creditors for the purpose of his removal
6.49	Trustee's application to the Secretary of State for his release
6.50	Notice to court of final meeting of creditors
6.51	Notice to official receiver by trustee on loss of qualification as insolvency practitioner
6.52	Certificate of constitution [amended certificate] of creditors' committee
6.53	Report by trustee of any change in membership of creditors' committee
6.54	Order of appointment of special manager
6.55	Order for public examination of bankrupt
6.56	Request by creditor(s) for the holding of a public examination of the bankrupt
6.57	Order as to examination of bankrupt who is suffering from mental disorder or physical afflication or disability
6.58	Affidavit of verification of record of the public examination of the bankrupt
6.59	Order of adjournment of public examination of bankrupt
6.60	Order appointing time for proceeding with public examination of bankrupt adjourned generally
6.61	Notice of disclaimer under section 315 of the Insolvency Act 1986
6.62	Notice to elect
6.63	Notice of intended disclaimer to interested party
6.64	Notice to bankrupt of an application under section 310 of the Insolvency Act 1986 for an income payments order
6.65	Order for income claimed under section 310(3)(a) of the Insolvency Act 1986
6.66	Order for income claimed under section 310(3)(b) of the Insolvency Act1986
6.67	Order converting income payments order made under section 310(1)(a) to an order under section 310(3)(b) of the Insolvency Act 1986
6.68	Discharge or variation of order for income claimed under section 310 of the Insolvency Act 1986.
6.69	Order under section 369(1) of the Insolvency Act 1986
6.70	Order under section 369(2) of the Insolvency Act 1986
6.71	Order of annulment under section 282 of the Insolvency Act 1986

The Insolvency Rules 1986   *Schedule 4*

FORM NO.	TITLE
6.72	Order of suspension of discharge under section 279(3) of the Insolvency Act 1986
6.73	Order of court lifting suspension of discharge
6.74	Certificate that order suspending discharge has been lifted
6.75	Notice to court by bankrupt that he intends to dispute statements made by official receiver in his report under section 289(2) of the Insolvency Act 1986
6.76	Order granting absolute/suspended discharge under section 280(2)(b) or (c) of the Insolvency Act 1986
6.77	Certificate of discharge
6.78	Notice to existing trustee of the presentation of a petition for a later bankruptcy
6.79	Criminal bankruptcy petition
6.79A	Charging order under section 313 of the Insolvency Act 1986
6.80	Order to Post Office under section 371 of the Insolvency Act 1986
6.81	Variation of income payments agreement under section 310A of the Insolvency Act 1986
6.82	Notice under section 279(2) of the Insolvency Act 1986
6.83	Notice to interested parties of a dwelling-house falling within section 283A of the Insolvency Act 1986
6.84	Certificate issued pursuant to Rule 6.237B(1) of the Insolvency Rules 1986

PART 7: COURT PROCEDURE AND PRACTICE

7.1	Originating application
7.2	Ordinary application
7.3	Declaration by official shorthand writer
7.4	Appointment of shorthand writer to take examination under the Insolvency Act 1986
7.5	Declaration by shorthand writer
7.6	Warrant for failure to attend examination under section 133 of the Insolvency Act 1986
7.7	Warrant of arrest etc under section 364 of the Insolvency Act 1986
7.8	Warrant of arrest etc under section 236 or 366 of the Insolvency Act 1986
7.9	Order for production of person arrested under warrant issued under section 134, 236, 364 or 366 of the Insolvency Act 1986
7.10	Warrant to registrar of court in whose district a person against whom a warrant of arrest has been issued is believed to be
7.11	Endorsement of warrant of arrest issued by a court to which the same has been sent for execution by the court which originally issued it
7.12	Warrant of seizure of property under section 365 of the Insolvency Act 1986
7.13	Search warrant under section 365 of the Insolvency Act 1986
7.14	Order of discharge from custody under the Insolvency Act 1986 [General]
7.15	Affidavit in support of application for committal for contempt of court
7.17	Warrant of committal for contempt
7.18	Order of discharge from custody on contempt
7.19	Order appointing person to act for incapacitated person
7.20	Application, affidavit and order confirming creditors' voluntary winding up

PART 8: PROXIES AND COMPANY REPRESENTATION

8.1	Proxy–company or individual voluntary arrangements
8.2	Proxy–administration
8.3	Proxy–administrative receivership
8.4	Proxy–winding up by the court or bankruptcy
8.5	Proxy–members' or creditors' voluntary winding up

Schedule 4 *The Insolvency Rules 1986*
FORM NO. *TITLE*

PART 9: EXAMINATION OF PERSONS CONCERNED IN COMPANY AND INDIVIDUAL INSOLVENCY

9.1 Order under section 236 or 366 of the Insolvency Act 1986

PART 12: MISCELLANEOUS AND GENERAL

12.1 Notice to the Registrar of Companies in respect of order under section 176A.

GENERAL NOTE

This Schedule sets out the prescribed forms referred to in the above list. The use of the new prescribed forms of statutory demand and creditor's petition was made mandatory after March 31, 1988: see *Practice Note (Bankruptcy: Prescribed Forms)* [1988] 1 W.L.R. 557. The forms are not reproduced here. Form 7.20 was added by Insolvency (Amendment) Rules 2002 (SI 2002/1307) para. 11 with effect from May 31, 2002 to cater for the advent of EC Council Regulation 1346/2000 on insolvency proceedings. The 2002 Rules (*ibid*, para. 13) also substituted several amended forms to address the implications of the EC Regulation. Forms 1.1–1.19 were substituted and new Form 5.5 inserted by the Insolvency (Amendment) (No. 2) Rules 2002 (SI 2002/2712) as from January 1, 2003, and new Forms 2.1B–2.40B and 12.1 were added and Forms 3.2, 4.12, 4.17, 4.18, 4.19, 4.52, 5.2, 6.1, 6.2, 6.3 and 6.25 substituted by the Insolvency (Amendment) Rules 2003 (SI 2003/1730), r.14(1)(a), with effect from September 2003. The latter 2003 Rules, para. 14(1) also insert new Forms 5.6–5.8 and new Forms 6.81–6.84 as from April 1, 2004.

A number of the more important company insolvency forms are available on the Insolvency Service's website at *www.insolvency.gov.uk/information/forms*.

SCHEDULE 5

PUNISHMENT OF OFFENCES UNDER THE RULES

Rule 12.21

Rules creating offence	General nature of offence	Mode of prosecution	Punishment	Daily default fine (where applicable)
In Part 2, Rule 2.47(6).	Administrator failing to send notification as to progress of administration.	Summary.	One-fifth of the statutory maximum.	One-fiftieth of the statutory maximum.
Rule 2.111(3).	Administrator failing to file a notice of automatic end of administration.	Summary.	One-fifth of the statutory maximum.	One-fiftieth of the statutory maximum.
Rule 2.129(2).	Administrator's duties on vacating office.	Summary.	One-fifth of the statutory maximum.	One-fiftieth of the statutory maximum.
In Part 3, Rule 3.32(5).	Administrative receiver failing to send notification as to progress of receivership.	Summary.	One-fifth of the statutory maximum.	One-fiftieth of the statutory maximum.
In Part 12, Rule 12.18.	False representation of status for purpose of inspecting documents.	1. On indictment. 2. Summary.	2 years, or a fine, or both. 6 months or the statutory maximum, or both.	

GENERAL NOTE

This Schedule prescribes punishment for certain offences in various provisions of the Rules. It has been amended by IA 2000 and EA 2002. The "statutory maximum" means the prescribed sum under s. 32 of the Magistrates Courts Act 1980 – see the note to Sch. 10 to IA 1986 at p. 591.

Schedule 6   *The Insolvency Rules 1986*

SCHEDULE 6

DETERMINATION OF INSOLVENCY OFFICE HOLDER'S REMUNERATION

As regards the determination of the remuneration of trustees and liquidators the realisation and distribution scales are as set out in the table below –

The realisation scale

(i)	on the first £5000 or fraction thereof	20%
(ii)	on the next £5000 or fraction thereof	15%
(iii)	on the next £90000 or fraction thereof	10%
(iv)	on all further sums realised	5%

The distribution scale

(i)	on the first £5000 or fraction thereof	10%
(ii)	on the next £5000 or fraction thereof	7.5%
(iii)	on the next £90000 or fraction thereof	5%
(iv)	on all further sums distributed	2.5%.

Appendix I

Index to Statutory Definitions

The words and phrases listed below are given special meanings for the purpose of all or part of the insolvency legislation of 1986 which is the subject of this *Guide*. The numbers shown refer to the section of IA 1986 (or where indicated, the EC Regulation or EA 2002) in which the statutory definition appears and, in most cases, is discussed in the note adjoining that section. References to the original Pt II of IA 1986 are given in italics.

An asterisk (*) means that the term has a special meaning for only a limited part of the Act, as will be indicated in the section referred to. Some words or phrases have been used by the draftsman with more than one meaning and where this is the case, each reference has been separately asterisked or listed.

Where a definition applies to all the *bankruptcy* Parts of the Act, this is shown by *[b]; if it applies to all the *company* insolvency Parts, by *[c].

(An index to definitions in the Insolvency Rules 1986 is given in Appendix II.)

Statutory definition	*Provision*
acquired property	Sch. B1, para. 70(3)*
acquiring or receiving property	s. 359(5)*
acts as an insolvency practitioner	s. 388
administration application	Sch. B1, para. 12(1)*
administration order	s. 8(2)
administrative receiver	ss. 29(2),* 72A(3),* 251,*[c] 338(4),* Sch. B1, para. 111(1),* Sch. 11, para. 1(2)*
administrator	*s. 8*, Sch. B1, paras 1(1),* 75(5),* 111(1)*
affairs	s. 385(2)*[b]
agent	ss. 7A(8),* 19(3)*
agreement	Sch. A1, para. 4D(3),* Sch. 2A, para. 4*
appeal against a conviction is pending	s. 277(3)*
appears to be unable to pay a debt	s. 268(1)*
appears to have no reasonable prospect of being able to pay a debt	s. 268(2)*
appointed day	s. 436
appointment of a receiver or manager under powers contained in an instrument	s. 29(1)(b)*
appropriate amount	s. 342D(9)*
appropriate authority	s. 7A(2)*
approved pension arrangement	s. 342A(8)*
assignee	s. 215(3)*
assignment	s. 344(3)*
associate	ss. 249,* 435, 436
assurance	s. 190(1)*
attachment completed	s. 346(5)
authorised deposit taker	*s. 8(1B)*, Sch. B1, para. 9(4)*

Appendix I

Statutory definition	Provision
Authority (the)	Sch. A1, para. 44(18)*
bankrupt	s. 381(1),*b EA, s. 268(9)*
bankruptcy debt	s. 382*b
bankruptcy level	s. 667(4)*
bankruptcy restrictions regime	EA, s. 268(10)*
bankruptcy order	s. 381(2)*
bankruptcy petition	s. 381(3)*b
bankrupt obtaining credit	s. 360(2)*
bankrupt's estate	ss. 283,*b 385(1)*b
before petition	s. 351,* Sch. 4A, para. 2(4)*
beginning of the moratorium	Sch. A1, paras. 1,* 8(1)*
body	EA, s. 268(11)*
bond	Sch. A1, para. 4F(3),* Sch. 2A, para. 3(2)*
building	s. 72DA(3)*
building operations	s. 72DA(3)*
business	s. 436
business day	s. 251*c
business document	Sch. B1, para. 45(3)*
capital market arrangement	s. 72B(2),* Sch. 2A, para. 1(1)*
capital market investment	s. 72B(2),* Sch. 2A, paras. 2(1), 3(1)*
carrying on business	s. 265(2)*
centre of main interests	EC Reg., Preamble, para. 13
cessation	Sch. B1, para. 99(1)*
charged value	s. 313(2A)*
charitable purpose	s. 242(5)*
chattel leasing agreement	s. 251*c
collateral security	Sch. A1, para. 23(6)*
collateral security charge	Sch. A1, para. 23(6)*
commencement	EA, Sch. 19, para. 2*
commencement of winding up	ss. 86, 129, 185(3)*
commercial paper	Sch. A1, para. 4F(3),* Sch. B1, para. 3(2)*
Communication services	ss. 233(5)(d),* 372(5)(c)*
Companies Act	s. 436
company	ss. 70(1),* 111(4)(a),* 216(8),* 217(6),* 388(4),* 435(11),* Sch. B1, para. 111(1)*
company arrangement or administration provision	EA, s. 255(2)*
competent authority	s. 392(2)*
condition	s. 279(5)*
conditional sale agreement	s. 436
conduct and affairs of a bankrupt	s. 289(4)*
connected with a company	s. 249*c

1114

Appendix I

Statutory definition	*Provision*
consent	Sch. B1, paras. 78(1),* 78(2),* 108(2),* 108(3)*
contributory	ss. 79, 83(2), 226(1),* 251*c
control of a company	s. 435(10)*
conveyance	s. 190(3)*
correspondence	Sch. B1, para. 111(1)*
court	ss. 216(5),* 385(1),*b 423(4);* EC Reg., Art. 2(d)* (and see note below)
create a preference ... to the prejudice of the general body of creditors	s. 243(1)*
creditor	ss. 263B(3),* 383(1),*b Sch. B1, para. 12(4)*
creditors' committee	*ss. 26,* 49(1),* 68(1),* 301(1)*
creditors' meeting	Sch. B1, paras. 50(1),* 111(1)*
creditor's petition	ss. 264(1)(a),*b 385(1)*b
creditors' voluntary winding up	s. 90
criminal bankruptcy order	ss. 385(1),*b 402(5)*
daily default fine	s. 430(4)
date of filing	Sch. A1, para. 1*
day on which preference created	s. 243(3)*
debt	s. 385(1)*b
debt for a liquidated sum	s. 267(3)*
debtor	ss. 385(1),*b 386(2),* 423(5)*
debt or liability	s. 382(3), (4)*b
debtor's petition	ss. 264(1)(b),*b 385(1)*b
debtor's property	s. 286(8)*
deductions of income tax	Sch. 6, para. 1
default fine	s. 430(4)
designated disadvantaged area	s. 72DA(3)*
develop	s. 72DA(2)*
director	ss. 214(7),* 251*c
director or other officer employed by company	s. 435(9)*
discharged	s. 279ff.
disposing of property	s. 359(5)*
disqualification provision	EA, s. 268(2)*
dwelling house	s. 385(1)*b
earlier bankruptcy	s. 334(1),* Sch. 11, para. 16(1)*
EC Regulation	s. 436*c
effective date	ss. 233(4),* 235(4)*
employment	*ss. 22(2),* 47(3),* 66(3),* 131(6)*
enactment	s. 426C(2)*
engineering operations	s. 72DA(3)*
enters administration	Sch. B1, paras. 1(2)(b),* 111(1)*
enters into a transaction at an undervalue	ss. 238(4),* 339(3),* 423*
establishment	EC Reg., Art. 2(h)*
estate	ss. 283,*b 385(1)*b

1115

Appendix I

Statutory definition	Provision
excepted petition	Sch. A1, para. 12(5)*
excessive pension contribution	Sch. 4A, para. 2(4)*
execution commenced/continued	s. 10(5)*
execution completed	s. 346(5)
existing trustee	s. 334(1)*
extortionate	ss. 244(3),*c 343(3)*b
facts which a director ought to know or ascertain	s. 214(4)*
family	s. 385(1)*b
family proceedings	s. 281(8)*
final date	s. 330(2)*
financed	s. 72E(2)(a)*
fine	s. 281(8)*
fixed security	s. 70(1)*
floating charge	ss. 70(3),* 176A(9),* 251,*c Sch. B1, para. 111(1)*
foreign market	Sch. A1, para. 4E(3),* Sch. 2A, para. 2(3)*
foreign proceedings	IA 2000, s. 14(4)*
former administrator	Sch. B1, para. 99(2)*
former enactments	Sch. 11, para. 22*
former law	Sch. 11, para. 2(2),* 3(2),* 4(2)*
functions carried out in relation to a company by a director	s. 214(5)*
general assignment	s. 344(3)*
general prohibition	Sch. B1, para. 9(4)*
give a preference	ss. 239(4),* 340(3)*
go into insolvent liquidation	ss. 214(6),* 216(7)*
go into liquidation	s. 247(2)*c
goods	ss. 183(4),* 184(6)*
group	Sch. A1, para. 3(5)*
guaranteed minimum pension	s. 310(9)*
have no reasonable prospect of being able to pay a debt	s. 268(2)*
hire-purchase agreement	s. 10,* 15(9),* 436, Sch. A1, para. 1,* Sch. B1, para. 111(1)*
holder of a floating charge	s. 70(2)*
holder of a qualifying floating charge	Sch. B1, para. 111(1)*
holder of a qualifying floating charge in respect of a company's property	s. 72A(3)*
in administration	Sch. B1, paras. 1(2)(a),* 111(1)*
inability to pay: see "unable to pay"	
income of the bankrupt	s. 310(7)*

1116

Appendix I

Statutory definition	Provision
income payments agreement	s. 310A(1)*
income payments order	s. 310(1)*
individual	s. 388(3)*
individual carrying on business	s. 265(2)*
initial creditors' meeting	Sch. B1, para. 51(1)*
initial period	s. 351*
Inland Revenue Official	s. 369(6)*
insolvency	s. 247(1)*c
Insolvency Act	Sch. 13, Pt. II*
insolvency administration order	s. 421A(9)*
insolvency law	ss. 426(10),* IA 2000, s. 14(4)*
insolvency practitioner	s. 388(1)
insolvency proceedings	EC Reg., Art. 1(1), 2(a)*
insolvency services	s. 428(3)*
insolvent: see also "insolvency"	s. 341(3)*
insolvent estate of a deceased person	s. 421(4)*
instrument by which a floating charge was created	s. 70(4)*
instrument creating a charge	s. 70(3)*
instrument of appointment	ss. 53(1),* 70(1)*
insurance company	*s. 8(4)(a)*
interim liquidator	s. 138(2)*
interim order	s. 252*
interim trustee	s. 388(4)*
Investment Account	s. 403(2)*
involved in the management of a company	s. 217(4)*
judgment	EC Reg., Art. 2(e)*
landlord	Sch. B1, para. 43(8)*
later bankruptcy	s. 334(1)*
liability	s. 382(4),* Sch. A1, para. 4C(3)*
liquidating company	s. 216(1)*
liquidation committee	ss. 101(1),* 141(1),* 142(1)*
liquidator	s. 411(3);* EC Reg., Art. 2(b)*
listed	Sch. A1, para. 4E(2),* Sch. 2A, para. 2(2)*
local delivery services	ss. 233(5)(d),* 372(5)(c)*
making a charge on property	s. 357(2)*
making a transfer of property	s. 357(2)*
management power	Sch. B1, para. 64(2)(a)*
market charge	Sch. A1, para. 1*
market contract	Sch. A1, para. 1*
market value	Sch. B1, para. 111(1)*
member	s. 250*c
member[ship] of a recognised professional body	s. 391(3)*
Member State in which assets are situated	EC Reg., Art. 2(g)*

1117

Appendix I

Statutory definition	Provision
members' voluntary winding up	s. 90
minimum amount	s. 273(1)*
misfeasance or breach of fiduciary or any other duty	s. 212(2)*
model law on cross-border insolvency	IA 2000, s. 14(4)*
modifications	s. 436
moratorium	Sch. A1, para. 1*
name by which a company is known	s. 216(6)*
new law	Sch. 11, paras. 2(2),* 2(3),* 4(2)*
nominee	ss. 1(2),*c 253(2),*b Sch. A1, para. 1*
no reasonable prospect of being able to pay a debt	s. 268(2)*
notice of relevant proceedings	ss. 241(3A),* (3B),* (3C)*
not kept proper accounting records	s. 361(3)*
number of months or years before petition	s. 351*
obtaining credit	Sch. A1, para. 17(2)*
occupational pension scheme	s. 342C(5)*
office copy	s. 251*c (Scotland)
office holder	ss. 233(1),* 234(1),* 238(1),* 246(1),* 372(1)*
officer	ss. 6A(3),* 206(3),* 208(3),* 210(3),* 211(2),* Sch. A1, paras. 41(5),* 42(3)*
officer who is in default	s. 430(5)*
official name of trustee	s. 305(4)
official petitioner	s. 402
official rate	ss. 189(4), 251*c
official receiver	ss. 399, 401*
onerous property	ss. 178(3),* 315(2)*
onset of insolvency	ss. 240(3),* 245(5)*
opening of proceedings	EC Reg., Art. 2(f)*
order under s. 310	Sch. 11, para. 16*
party	Sch. A1, para. 4D(3)*
party to an arrangement	Sch. 2A, para. 1(3)*
pension-sharing transaction	s. 342D(9)*
permanent trustee	s. 388(4)*
person	Sch. A1, para. 4K*
personal injuries	s. 281(8)*
personally responsible for relevant debts of a company	s. 217(1)*
person connected with a company	s. 249*c
person liable to contribute to the assets	s. 79(2)*
person obtaining credit	s. 429(4)*
person's affairs	s. 385(2)*b
petitioning creditor	Sch. A1, para. 10(2)*

1118

Appendix I

Statutory definition	Provision
postal packet	s. 371(1)*
pre-commencement bankrupt	s. 313A(7),* EA, Sch. 19, para. 2*
preference	ss. 239(4),* 243,* 340(3),* Sch.4A, para. 2(4)*
preferential creditor(s)	ss. 4(7),* 258(7),* 386(1), Sch. A1, para. 31(8)*
preferential debt(s)	ss. 4(7),* 59(2),* 258(7),* 386(1), Sch. A1, para. 31(8),* Sch. 6
prescribed	ss. 38(4),* 70(1),* 176A(9),* 251,*c 342C(7),* 342F(9),* 384,*b 419*
prescribed amount	s. 418(1)*b
prohibited name	s. 216(2)*
project company	ss. 72C(3)*, 72D(2)(d),* 72DA(3),* 72E(2)(b),* Sch. A1, para. 4H(1), (2),* Sch. 2A, para. 7(1), (2)*
proper accounting records	s. 361(3)*
property	ss. 283(4),*b 307(5),* 351,* 436, 436A*
property comprised in the bankrupt's estate	s. 351*
property of the company	s. 42(2)(b),* Sch. 1*
property or goods of the bankrupt	s. 285(6)*
property possession of which is required to be delivered up	s. 351*
property vested in the existing trustee	s. 307(3),* Sch. 11, para. 16
proposal	ss. 1(2),* 253*
proprietor	ss. 180(1),* 319(1)*
prosecuting authority	s. 7A(8)*
protected rights	s. 310(9)*
provision	EA, s. 268(11)*
public body	Sch. A1, Para. 4I(3),* Sch. 2A, para. 9(1)*
public-private partnership project	s. 72C(2),* Sch. A1, para. 4I(1)*
public telecommunications operator	ss. 233(5),* 372(5)*
purpose of administration	Sch. B1, para. 111(1)*
qualified to act as an insolvency practitioner	s. 390
qualifying floating charge	Sch. B1, para. 14(2)*
qualifying liability	*ss. 19(7),* 44(2A)*
rash and hazardous speculations	s. 362(2)*
rated	Sch. A1, para. 4E(2),* Sch. 2A, para. 2(2)*
reasonable prospect that debtor will be able to pay a debt	s. 271(4)*b
reasonable replacement	s. 308(4)*

Appendix I

Statutory definition	Provision
receiver	ss. 51(6),* 70(1),* 72(2),* 251,*c Sch. A1, para. 43(2)*
receiver or manager of the property of a company	s. 29(1)(a)
recognised investment exchange	Sch. A1, para. 4E(3),* Sch. 2A, para. 2(3)*
recognised professional body	s. 391*
records	s. 436
recovery provisions	s. 342C(7)*
registered office	ss. 117(6),* 126(4)*
register of charges	s. 70(1)*
regulated business	s. 72D(2)(b),* Sch. 2A, para. 10(1)*
regulated company	Sch. A1, para. 44(18)*
regulations	ss. 342C(7),* 342F(9)*
relative	s. 435(8)*
relevant contributions	s. 342A(5)*
relevant country or territory	s. 426(11)*
relevant date	ss. 131(6),* 387*
relevant day	ss. 166(6),* 242(3),* 372(1)*
relevant debts	s. 217(3)*
relevant deposit	*s. 8(1B)*
relevant information about status	s. 360(4)*
relevant payment	s. 76(1)*
relevant period	ss. 95(7),* 98(5),* 279(2)
relevant person	Sch. B1, para. 47(3)*
relevant property	s. 43(7)*
relevant surrounding circumstances	ss. 241(3),* 342(4),* 425(3)*
relevant time	ss. 240,* 245(3), (4),* 341*
remuneration	Sch. B1, para. 41(4)*
resolution for voluntary winding up	s. 84(2)
resources	Sch. A1, para. 4I(2),* Sch. 2A, para. 8*
restoration amount	s. 342B(5)*
retention of title agreement	s. 251*c
rules	ss. 251,*c 384*b
secured [and related expressions]	ss. 383,*b 385(1)*b
secured creditor	ss. 67(9),* 248(a)*c
secured debenture	s. 70(1), (3)*
security	ss. 248(b),*c 425(4)*
series of secured debentures	ss. 70(1),* 70(3)*
setting aside a preference	Sch. 11, paras. 17(2),* 20(2)*
settlement finality regulations	Sch. A1, para. 1*
shadow director	s. 251*c
shared arrangement	s. 342D(9)*
sheriff	ss. 183(4),* 184(6)*
six-month period	Sch. 6, paras. 3,* 3A,* 3B*
small bankruptcies level	s. 273(1)
special Act	s. 111(4)*

Appendix I

Statutory definition	Provision
specified	s. 197(1)*
statutory demand	s. 268*
statutory maximum	Sch. 10, Note
step-in rights	ss. 72C(3),* 72D(2)(c),* 72DA(3),* 72E(2)(c),* Sch. A1, para. 4J(1),* Sch. 2A, para. 6(1)*
subordinate legislation	s. 436
substance	s. 72DA(3)*
sum payable by debtor by way of remuneration	Sch. 6, paras. 13(1)*
supervisor	ss. 7(2),* 263(2)*
system-charge	Sch. A1, para. 1*
time of the opening of proceedings	EC Reg., Art. 2(f)*
traded	Sch. A1, para. 4E(2),* Sch. 2A, para. 2(2)*
trading record	s. 355(5)*
transaction	s. 436
transaction at an undervalue	ss. 238(4),* 339(3),* 423*
transfer order	Sch. A1, para. 23(6)*
transferee	s. 342D(9)*
transferee company	s. 110(1)*
transferor	s. 342D(9)*
transferor company	s. 110(2)*
transitional period	s. 313A(7)*
Tribunal	s. 396, Sch. 7
trustee, trustee in bankruptcy, trustee of the estate of a bankrupt	s. 385(1)*[b]
trustees or managers	s. 342C(5)*
unable to pay a debt [individual]	s. 268(1)*
unable to pay its debts [company]	*ss.* 8,* 123, 222,* 223,* 224,* Sch. B1, para. 111(1)*
unapproved pension arrangement	s. 342A(8)*
undervalue	Sch. 4A, para. 2(4)*
unregistered company	s. 220(1)*
unsecured: see "secured"	
unsecured creditor	ss. 67(9),* 248(a)*[c]
utility project	s. 72D(2)(a)*
vacancy	s. 300(8)*
value lost to the estate	s. 421A(9)*
value of goods or services as consideration for floating charge	s. 245(6)*
victim of the transaction	s. 423(5)*
voluntary arrangement [company]	s. 1(1)
voluntary arrangement [individual]	s. 253(1)
wages or salary	Sch. B1, para. 99(6)*

Appendix I

Statutory definition	Provision
wages or salary payable in respect of a period of holiday/absence from work through sickness or other good cause	ss. 19(9),* 44(2C)
waste	s. 72DA(3)*
water authority	s. 233(5)*
willing to act on instructions	s. 217(5)*
winding-up proceedings	EC Reg., art. 2(c)

[Note that for the purposes of Pts I–VII of IA 1986, "the court" means, in relation to a company, the court having jurisdiction to wind up the company: CA 1985, s. 744, as incorporated by IA 1986, s. 251.]

Appendix II

Index to Definitions in the Rules

The words and phrases listed below have special definitions for all or part of the Insolvency Rules 1986. The numbers shown refer to the rule in which the definition appears. References to the original Pt 2 of the Rules are given in italics. An asterisk (*) means that the term has a special meaning for only a limited part of the Rules, as will be indicated in the rule referred to.

Definition in the Rules	*Rule*
Act, the	0.2
affidavit of debt	4.77(1),* 6.99(1)*
applicable section	9.1(2)*
appropriate application	6.237D(9)*
appropriate fee	13.11
authorised deposit taker	13.12A(1)
bankruptcy restrictions register	6A.1(2)*
business day	13.13(1)
Case 1	5.1(2)*
Case 2	5.1(2)*
centre of main interests	13.13(8)
Companies Act, the	0.2
company's personnel	4.58(2)
competent person	7.20(2)
Commissioners	6.194(3)
contributory members	4.152(6),* 4.173(2)*
convener	1.13(1),* 4.54(1),* 6.81(1)*
court	13.2
creditor members	4.152(6),* 4.173(2)*
creditors	4.44,* 11.1(2)*
CPR	0.2(1)
CVL	4.1(5)*
debt	6.6,* 13.12
Department, the	13.13(2)
deponents	*2.11(2),* 3.3(2),* 4.32(3)*
earlier bankruptcy	6.225(2)*
eligible company	1.1(4)*
establishment	13.13(9)
examinee	4.212(1)
existing trustee	6.225(2)*
expenses	10.4(1)
family proceedings	12.3(2)
file in court	13.13(3)
fine	12.3(2)
first meeting of contributories	4.50(7)*
first meeting of creditors	4.50(7),* 6.79(7)*
first meetings in the liquidation	4.50(7)*

Appendix II

Definition in the Rules	*Rule*
former authorised deposit taker	13.12A(2)
Gazette, the	13.13(4)
general regulations	13.13(5)
give notice	13.3
incapacitated person	7.43(2)*
individual insolvency register	6A.1(1)*
individual register	6.237E(2)*
insolvency proceedings	13.7
insolvent, the	7.15(2),* 7.37(1),* 9.1(2),* 11.1(2)*
insolvent estate	13.8
insolvent winding up	4.151(a),* 4.173(2)*
invalid resolution	*2.28(1A)*
land	6.197(1)
last date for proving	4.182A(2), 11.2(2)
later bankruptcy	6.225(2)*
liability	13.12
liquidation committee	4.148A(5)*
main proceedings	13.13(10)
meeting of creditors	4.148A(5)*
Member State liquidator	13.13(11)
mutual dealings	2.85(2)*
NO CVL APPLICATION	4.1(4)*
notice to elect	4.191(b),* 6.183(2)*
officer	1.30(2)*
official exchange rate	2.86(2),* 4.91(2),* 6.111(2)*
ordinary application	7.2(1)*
originating application	7.2(1)*
other proceedings	2.38(1)*
petitioner	13.10
petitioning creditor	13.10
prescribed officer of the court	7.21(2)*
prescribed order of priority	13.13(6)
prescribed part	13.13(15)*
primary court	7.19(2),* 7.24(1)*
principal	8.1(1)
proof, proof of debt	2.72(2),* 4.73,* 6.96*
proper address	*2.7(4),* *2.7(4A)*
proposal	5.36*
provable debts	12.3
property	7.21(3)*
prove, proving	2.72(2),* 4.73,* 6.96*
proxy	8.1(1)
proxy-holder	8.1(1)
registered land	6.237E(1)*
registers	6A.1(3)*
registrar	13.2
relevant person	2.28(1)*
respondent	9.1(2)*

1124

Appendix II

Definition in the Rules	*Rule*
responsible insolvency practitioner	1.1(3),* 1.23(6),* 13.9
return day	4.22(2)
RSC	0.2(1)
Rules, the	0.2
secondary court	7.19(2),* 7.24(1)*
secondary proceedings	13.13(12)
Secretary of State	6.240*
solvent winding up	4.151(b),* 4.173(2)*
statement	Sch. 1, para. 2*
statutory demand	4.4(1)
successor company	4.228(1)
temporary administrator	13.13(13)
territorial proceedings	13.13(14)
venue	13.6
voluntary arrangement	5.36*

Appendix III

Insolvency Service Information

The Insolvency Service (an Executive Agency within the Department of Trade and Industry) is responsible for much of the administration of insolvency law and (through its Disqualification Unit) the law relating to director disqualification. The address of the Service's London headquarters is:

The Insolvency Service
P.O. Box 203
21 Bloomsbury Street
London WC1B 3QW

Tel. 020 7291 6895

The Disqualification Unit's address is the same; tel. 020 7291 6807.

The Central Accounting Unit and Insolvency Practitioners Unit (IPU) is based in Birmingham. Its address is:

The Insolvency Service
Ladywood House
45/6 Stephenson Street
Birmingham B2 4DS

Tel. 0121 698 4103

The Service's website address is *www.insolvency.gov.uk*.

The Central Fax number for filing a notice of appointment of an administrator under IR 1986, r. 2.19 (which may only be used when the court office is closed for business) is 020 7947 6607. In Scotland, the form should be faxed directly to the relevant court. The numbers can be found on the Scottish Courts website, *www.scotcourts.gov.uk*.

Appendix IV

Practice Direction: Insolvency Proceedings [2000] B.C.C. 92

Set out below is the text of the Practice Direction ("PD") referred to above.

It should be noted that the statement in para. 1.2 that this PD "shall replace all previous Practice Notes and Practice Directions relating to insolvency proceedings" is probably misleading. For example, there is no overlap between the present PD and the Practice Note reported in [1994] 1 W.L.R. 160; [1994] B.C.C. 35 discussed above in the note to the original r. *2.2*; but it would be surprising if there had been any intention to repeal that Note and leave a void.

Attention should be drawn also to the Practice Direction: Applications under the Companies Act 1985 and the Insurance Companies Act 1982, reported at [1999] B.C.C. 741, dealing with petitions in which relief is sought under both CA 1985, s. 459 and IA 1986, s. 122(1)(g), which is discussed in the note to IA 1986, s. 127 and reproduced as Appendix V in this *Guide*.

Part One

1. *General*

    1.1 In this Practice Direction:

    (1) "The Act" means the Insolvency Act 1986 and includes the Act as applied to limited liability partnerships by the Limited Liability Partnerships Regulations 2001;

    (2) "The Insolvency Rules" means the rules for the time being in force and made under s. 411 and s. 412 of the Act in relation to insolvency proceedings;

    (3) "CPR" means the Civil Procedure Rules and "CPR" followed by a Part or rule by number means the Part or rule with that number in those Rules;

    (4) "RSC" followed by an Order by number means the Order with that number set out in Sch. 1 to the CPR;

    (5) "Insolvency proceedings" means any proceedings under the Act, the Insolvency Rules, the Administration of Insolvent Estates of Deceased Persons Order 1986 (SI 1986/1999), the Insolvent Partnerships Order 1986 (SI 1986/2124), the Insolvent Partnerships Order 1994 (SI 1994/2421) or the Limited Liability Partnerships Regulations 2001;

    (6) References to a "company" shall include a limited liability partnership and references to a "contributory" shall include a member of a limited liability partnership.

    1.2 This Practice Direction shall come into effect on April 26, 1999 and shall replace all previous Practice Notes and Practice Directions relating to insolvency proceedings.

    1.3 Except where the Insolvency Rules otherwise provide, service of documents in insolvency proceedings in the High Court will be the responsibility of the parties and will not be undertaken by the court.

    1.4 Where CPR Pt 2.4 provides for the court to perform any act, that act may be performed by a registrar in bankruptcy for the purpose of insolvency proceedings in the High Court.

    1.5 A writ of execution to enforce any order made in insolvency proceedings in the High Court may be issued on the authority of a registrar.

    1.6(1) This paragraph applies where an insolvency practitioner ("the outgoing office holder") holds office as a liquidator, administrator, trustee or supervisor in more than one case and dies, retires from practice as an insolvency practitioner or is otherwise unable or unwilling to continue in office.

    (2) A single application may be made to a judge of the Chancery Division of the High Court by way of ordinary application in Form 7.2 for the appointment of a substitute office holder or office holders in all

Part 2   Appendix IV

cases in which the outgoing office holder holds office, and for the transfer of each such case to the High Court for the purpose only of making such an order.

(3) The application may be made by any of the following:
    (i) the outgoing office holder (if he is able and willing to do so);
    (ii) any person who holds office jointly with the outgoing office holder;
    (iii) any person who is proposed to be appointed as a substitute for the outgoing office holder; or
    (iv) any creditor in the cases where the substitution is proposed to be made.

(4) The outgoing office holder (if he is not the applicant) and every person who holds office jointly with the office holder must be made a respondent to the application, but it is not necessary to join any other person as a respondent or to serve the application upon any other person unless the judge or registrar in the High Court so directs.

(5) The application should contain schedules setting out the nature of the office held, the identity of the court currently having jurisdiction over each case and its name and number.

(6) The application must be supported by evidence setting out the circumstances which have given rise to the need to make a substitution and exhibiting the written consent to act of each person who is proposed to be appointed in place of the outgoing office holder.

(7) The judge will in the first instance consider the application on paper and make such order as he thinks fit. In particular he may do any of the following:
    (i) make an order directing the transfer to the High Court of those cases not already within its jurisdiction for the purpose only of the substantive application;
    (ii) if he considers that the papers are in order and that the matter is straightforward, make an order on the substantive application;
    (iii) give any directions which he considers to be necessary including (if appropriate) directions for the joinder of any additional respondents or requiring the service of the application on any person or requiring additional evidence to be provided;
    (iv) if he does not himself make an order on the substantive application when the matter is first before him, give directions for the further consideration of the substantive application by himself or another judge of the Chancery Division or adjourn the substantive application to the registrar for him to make such order upon it as is appropriate.

(8) An order of the kind referred to in sub-paragraph (7)(i) shall follow the draft order in Form PDIP 3 set out in the Schedule hereto and an order granting the substantive application shall follow the draft order in Form PDIP 4 set out in the schedule hereto (subject in each case to such modifications as may be necessary or appropriate).

(9) It is the duty of the applicant to ensure that a sealed copy of every order transferring any case to the High Court and of every order which is made on a substantive application is lodged with the court having jurisdiction over each case affected by such order for filing on the court file relating to that case.

(10) It will not be necessary for the file relating to any case which is transferred to the High Court in accordance with this paragraph to be sent to the High Court unless a judge or registrar so directs.

Part Two – Companies

2. *Advertisement of winding-up petition*

2.1 Insolvency Rule 4.11(2)(b) is mandatory, and designed to ensure that the class remedy of winding up by the court is made available to all creditors, and is not used as a means of putting pressure on the company to pay the petitioner's debt. Failure to comply with the rule, without good reason accepted by the court, may lead to the summary dismissal of the petition on the return date (Insolvency Rule 4.11(5)). If the court, in its discretion, grants an adjournment, this will be on condition that the petition is advertised in due time for the adjourned hearing. No further adjournment for the purpose of advertisement will normally be granted.

2.2 Copies of every advertisement published in connection with a winding-up petition must be lodged with the court as soon as possible after publication and in any event not later than the day specified in Insolvency Rule 4.14 of the Insolvency Rules 1986. This direction applies even if the advertisement is defective in any way (*e.g.* is published at a date not in accordance with the Insolvency Rules, or omits or misprints some important words) or if the petitioner decides not to pursue the petition (*e.g.* on receiving payment).

3. *Certificate of compliance – time for filing*

3.1 In the High Court in order to assist practitioners and the court the time laid down by Insolvency Rule 4.14 of the Insolvency Rules 1986, for filing a certificate of compliance and a copy of the advertisement, is hereby extended to not later than 4.30 p.m. on the Friday preceding the day on which the petition is to be heard. Applications to file the certificate and the copy advertisement after 4.30 p.m. on the Friday will only be allowed if some good reason is shown for the delay.

4. *Errors in petitions*

4.1 Applications for leave to amend errors in petitions which are discovered subsequent to a winding-up order being made should be made to the court manager in the High Court and to the district judge in the county court.

4.2 Where the error is an error in the name of the company, the court manager in the High Court and the district judge in the county court may make any necessary amendments to ensure that the winding-up order is drawn with the correct name of the company inserted. If there is any doubt, *e.g.* where there might be another company in existence which could be confused with the company to be wound up, the court manager will refer the application to the registrar and the district judge may refer it to the judge.

4.3 Where an error is an error in the registered office of the company and any director or member of the company claims that the company was unaware of the petition by reason of it having been served at the wrong registered office, it will be open to them to apply to rescind the winding-up order in the usual way.

4.4 Where it is discovered that the company had been struck off the register of companies prior to the winding-up order being made, the matter must be restored to the list before the order is entered to enable an order for the restoration of the name to be made as well as the order to wind up.

5. *Distribution of business*

5.1 The following applications shall be made direct to the judge and, unless otherwise ordered, shall be heard in public:

(1) Applications to commit any person to prison for contempt;

(2) Applications for urgent interim relief (*e.g.* applications pursuant to s. 127 of the Act prior to any winding-up order being made);

(3) Applications to restrain the presentation or advertisement of a petition to wind up; or

(4) Applications for the appointment of a provisional liquidator;

(5) Petitions for administration orders or an interim order upon such a petition;

(6) Applications after an administration order has been made pursuant to s. 14(3) of the Act (for directions) or s. 18(3) of the Act (to vary or discharge the order);

(7) Petitions to discharge administration orders and to wind up;

(8) Applications pursuant to s. 5(3) of the Act (to stay a winding up or discharge an administration order or for directions) where a voluntary arrangement has been approved;

(9) Appeals from a decision made by a county court or by a registrar of the High Court.

5.2 Subject to para. 5.4 below all other applications shall be made to the registrar or the district judge in the first instance who may give any necessary directions and may, in the exercise of his discretion, either hear and determine it himself or refer it to the judge.

5.3 The following matters will also be heard in public:

(1) Petitions to wind up;

(2) Public examinations;

(3) All matters and applications heard by the judge, except those referred by the registrar or the district judge to be heard in private or so directed by the judge to be heard.

5.4 In accordance with directions given by the Lord Chancellor the registrar has authorised certain applications in the High Court to be dealt with by the court manager of the Companies Court, pursuant to Insolvency Rule 13.2(2). The applications are:

(1) To extend or abridge time prescribed by the Insolvency Rules in connection with winding up (Insolvency Rules 4.3 and 12.9);

(2) For substituted service of winding-up petitions (Insolvency Rule 4.8(6));

(3) To withdraw petitions (Insolvency Rule 4.15);

(4) For the substitution of a petitioner (Insolvency Rule 4.19);

(5) By the official receiver for limited disclosure of a statement of affairs (Insolvency Rule 4.35);

(6) By the official receiver for relief from duties imposed upon him by the rules (Insolvency Rule 4.47);

(7) By the official receiver for permission to give notice of a meeting by advertisement only (Insolvency Rule 4.59);

(8) To transfer proceedings from the High Court to a county court (Insolvency Rule 7.11);

(9) For permission to amend any originating application.

[N.B. In district registries all such applications must be made to the district judge.]

6. *Drawing up of orders*

6.1 The court will draw up all orders except orders on the application of the official receiver or for which the Treasury Solicitor is responsible under the existing practice.

7. *Rescission of a winding-up order*

7.1 Any application for the rescission of a winding-up order shall be made within seven days after the date on which the order was made (Insolvency Rule 7.47(4)). Notice of any such application must be given to the official receiver.

7.2 Applications will only be entertained if made (a) by a creditor, or (b) by a contributory, or (c) by the company jointly with a creditor or with a contributory. The application must be supported by written evidence of assets and liabilities.

7.3 In the case of an unsuccessful application the costs of the petitioning creditor, the supporting creditors and of the official receiver will normally be ordered to be paid by the creditor of the contributory making or joining in the application. The reason for this is that if the costs of an unsuccessful application are made payable by the company, they fall unfairly on the general body of creditors.

7.4 Cases in which the making of the winding-up order has not been opposed may, if the application is made promptly, be dealt with on a statement by the applicant's legal representative of the circumstances; but apart from such cases, the court will normally require any application to be supported by written evidence.

7.5 There is no need to issue a form of application (Form 7.2) as the petition is restored before the court.

8. *Restraint of presentation of a winding-up petition*

8.1 An application to restrain presentation of a winding-up petition must be made to the judge by the issue of an originating application (Form 7.1).

Part Three – Personal insolvency – Bankruptcy

9. *Distribution of business*

9.1 The following applications shall be made direct to the judge and unless otherwise ordered shall be heard in public:

(1) Applications for the committal of any person to prison for contempt;

(2) Application for injunctions or for the modification or discharge of injunctions;

(3) Applications for interlocutory relief or directions after the matter has been referred to the judge.

9.2 All other applications shall be made to the registrar or the district judge in the first instance. He shall give any necessary directions and may, if the application is within his jurisdiction to determine, in his discretion either hear and determine it himself or refer it to the judge.

9.3 The following matters shall be heard in public:

(1) The public examination of debtors;

(2) Opposed applications for discharge or for the suspension or lifting of the suspension of discharge;

(3) Opposed applications for permission to be a director;

(4) In any case where the petition was presented or the receiving order or order for adjudication was made before the appointed day, those matters and applications specified in r. 8 of the *Bankruptcy Rules* 1952;

(5) All matters and applications heard by the judge, except matters and applications referred by the registrar or the district judge to be heard by the judge in private or directed by the judge to be so heard.

9.4 All petitions presented will be listed under the name of the debtor.

9.5 In accordance with directions given by the Lord Chancellor the registrar has authorised certain applications in the High Court to be dealt with by the court manager of the Bankruptcy Court pursuant to Insolvency Rule 13.2(2). The applications are:

(1) by petitioning creditors: to extend time for hearing petitions (s. 376 of the Act).

(2) by the official receiver:

(a) To transfer proceedings from the High Court to a county court (Insolvency Rule 7.13);
(b) to amend the full title of the proceedings (Insolvency Rules 6.35 and 6.47).

[N.B. In district registries all such applications must be made to the district judge.]

10. *Service abroad of statutory demand*

10.1 A statutory demand is not a document issued by the court. Leave to serve out of the jurisdiction is not, therefore, required.

10.2 Insolvency Rule 6.3(2) ("Requirements as to service") applies to service of the statutory demand whether outside or within the jurisdiction.

10.3 A creditor wishing to serve a statutory demand outside the jurisdiction in a foreign country with which a civil procedure convention has been made (including the Hague Convention) may and, if the

Part Three *Appendix IV*

assistance of a British consul is desired, must adopt the procedure prescribed by CPR Pt. 6.25. In the case of any doubt whether the country is a "convention country", enquiries should be made of the Queen's Bench Masters' Secretary Department, Room E216, Royal Courts of Justice.

10.4 In all other cases, service of the demand must be effected by private arrangement in accordance with Insolvency Rule 6.3(2) and local foreign law.

10.5 When a statutory demand is to be served out of the jurisdiction, the time limits of 21 days and 18 days respectively referred to in the demand must be amended. For this purpose reference should be made to the table set out in the practice direction supplementing Section III of CPR Pt. 6.

10.6 A creditor should amend the statutory demand as follows:

(1) For any reference to 18 days there must be substituted the appropriate number of days set out in the table plus four days, and

(2) for any reference to 21 days there must be substituted the appropriate number of days in the table plus seven days.

Attention is drawn to the fact that in all forms of the statutory demand the figure 18 and the figure 21 occur in more than one place.

11. *Substituted service*

Statutory demands

11.1 The creditor is under an obligation to do all that is reasonable to bring the statutory demand to the debtor's attention and, if practicable, to cause personal service to be effected. Where it is not possible to effect prompt personal service, service may be effected by other means such as first class post or by insertion through a letter box.

11.2 Advertisement can only be used as a means of substituted service where:

(1) The demand is based on a judgment or order of any court;

(2) The debtor has absconded or is keeping out of the way with a view to avoiding service and,

(3) There is no real prospect of the sum due being recovered by execution or other process.

As there is no statutory form of advertisement, the court will accept an advertisement in the following form:

STATUTORY DEMAND

(Debt for liquidated sum payable immediately following a judgment or order of the court)

To (Block letters)

of

TAKE NOTICE that a statutory demand has been issued by:
Name of Creditor:

Address:

The creditor demands payment of £   the amount now due on a judgment or order of the (High Court of Justice   Division) (County Court) dated the   day of   199 .

The statutory demand is an important document and it is deemed to have been served on you on the date of the first appearance of this advertisement. You must deal with this demand within 21 days of the service upon you or you could be made bankrupt and your property and goods taken away from you. If you are in any doubt as to your position, you should seek advice immediately from a solicitor or your nearest Citizens' Advice Bureau. The statutory demand can be obtained or is available for inspection and collection from:

Appendix IV   *Part Three*

Name:

Address:

(Solicitor for) the Creditor

Tel. No.   Reference:

<u>You have only 21 days from the date of the first appearance of this advertisement before the creditor may present a bankruptcy petition. You have only 18 days from that date within which to apply to the court to set aside the demand.</u>

11.3 In all cases where substituted service is effected, the creditor must have taken all those steps which would justify the court making an order for substituted service of a petition. The steps to be taken to obtain an order for substituted service of a petition are set out below. Failure to comply with these requirements may result in the court declining to file the petition: Insolvency Rule 6.11(9).

Petitions

11.4 In most cases, evidence of the following steps will suffice to justify an order for substituted service:

(1) One personal call at the residence and place of business of the debtor where both are known or at either of such places as is known. Where it is known that the debtor has more than one residential or business address, personal calls should be made at all the addresses.

(2) Should the creditor fail to effect service, a first class prepaid letter should be written to the debtor referring to the call(s), the purpose of the same and the failure to meet with the debtor, adding that a further call will be made for the same purpose on the   day of   19   at   hours at   (place). At least two business days notice should be given of the appointment and copies of the letter sent to all known addresses of the debtor. The appointment letter should also state that

    (a) in the event of the time and place not being convenient, the debtor is to name some other time and place reasonably convenient for the purpose;
    (b) (statutory demands) if the debtor fails to keep the appointment the creditor proposes to serve the debtor by [advertisement] [post] [insertion through a letter box] or as the case may be, and that, in the event of a bankruptcy petition being presented, the court will be asked to treat such service as service of the demand on the debtor;
    (c) (petitions) if the debtor fails to keep the appointment, application will be made to the court for an order for substituted service either by advertisement, or in such other manner as the court may think fit.

(3) In attending any appointment made by letter, inquiry should be made as to whether the debtor has received all letters left for him. If the debtor is away, inquiry should also be made as to whether or not letters are being forwarded to an address within the jurisdiction (England and Wales) or elsewhere.

(4) If the debtor is represented by a solicitor, an attempt should be made to arrange an appointment for personal service through such solicitor. The Insolvency Rules enable a solicitor to accept service of a statutory demand on behalf of his client but there is no similar provision in respect of service of a bankruptcy petition.

(5) The written evidence filed pursuant to Insolvency Rule 6.11 should deal with all the above matters including all relevant facts as to the debtor's whereabouts and whether the appointment letter(s) have been returned.

11.5 Where the court makes an order for service by first class ordinary post, the order will normally provide that service be deemed to be effected on the seventh day after posting. The same method of calculating service may be applied to calculating the date of service of a statutory demand.

Part Three *Appendix IV*

12. *Setting aside a statutory demand*

12.1 The application (Form 6.4) and written evidence in support (Form 6.5) exhibiting a copy of the statutory demand must be filed in court within 18 days of service of the statutory demand on the debtor. Where service is effected by advertisement in a newspaper the period of 18 days is calculated from the date of the first appearance of the advertisement. Three copies of each document must be lodged with the application to enable the court to serve notice of the hearing date on the applicant, the creditor and the person named in Part B of the statutory demand.

12.2 Where, to avoid expense, copies of the documents are not lodged with the application in the High Court, any order of the registrar fixing a venue is conditional upon copies of the documents being lodged on the next business day after the registrar's order otherwise the application will be deemed to have been dismissed.

12.3 Where the statutory demand is based on a judgment or order, the court will not at this stage go behind the judgment or order and inquire into the validity of the debt nor, as a general rule, will it adjourn the application to await the result of an application to set aside the judgment or order.

12.4 Where the debtor (a) claims to have a counterclaim, set off or cross demand (whether or not he could have raised it in the action in which the judgment or order was obtained) which equals or exceeds the amount of the debt or debts specified in the statutory demand or (b) disputes the debt (not being a debt subject to a judgment or order) the court will normally set aside the statutory demand if, in its opinion, on the evidence there is a genuine triable issue.

12.5 A debtor who wishes to apply to set aside a statutory demand after the expiration of 18 days from the date of service of the statutory demand must apply for an extension of time within which to apply. If the applicant wishes to apply for an injunction to restrain presentation of a petition the application must be made to the judge. Paragraphs 1 and 2 of Form 6.5 (affidavit in support of application to set aside statutory demand) should be used in support of the application for an extension of time with the following additional paragraphs:

"3.   That to the best of my knowledge and belief the creditor(s) named in the demand has/have not presented a petition against me.
4.   That the reasons for my failure to apply to set aside the demand within 18 days after service are as follows:. . ."

If application is made to restrain presentation of a bankruptcy petition the following additional paragraph should be added.

"5.   Unless restrained by injunction the creditor(s) may present a bankruptcy petition against me."

13. *Proof of service of a statutory demand*

13.1 Insolvency Rule 6.11(3) provides that, if the statutory demand has been served personally, the written evidence must be provided by the person who effected that service. Insolvency Rule 6.11(4) provides that, if service of the demand (however effected) has been acknowledged in writing, the evidence of service must be provided by the creditor or by a person acting on his behalf. Insolvency Rule 6.11(5) provides that, if neither para. (3) or (4) apply, the written evidence must be provided by a person having direct knowledge of the means adopted for serving the demand.

13.2 Form 6.11 (evidence of personal service of the statutory demand): this form should only be used where the demand has been served personally and acknowledged in writing (see Insolvency Rule 6.11(4)). If the demand has not been acknowledged in writing, the written evidence should be provided by the process server and para. 2 and 3 (part of Form 6.11) should be omitted (see Insolvency Rule 6.11(3)).

13.3 Form 6.12 (evidence of substituted service of the statutory demand): this form can be used whether or not service of the demand has been acknowledged in writing. Paragraphs 4 and 5 (part) provide for the alternatives. Practitioners are reminded, however, that the appropriate person to provide the written evidence may not be the same in both cases. If the demand has been acknowledged in writing, the appropriate person is the creditor or a person acting on his behalf. If the demand has not been acknowledged, that person must be someone having direct knowledge of the means adopted for serving the demand.

Practitioners may find it more convenient to allow process servers to carry out the necessary investigation whilst reserving to themselves the service of the demand. In these circumstances para. 1 should be deleted and the following paragraph substituted:

"1. Attempts have been made to serve the demand, full details of which are set out in the accompanying affidavit of..."

13.4 "Written evidence" means an affidavit or a witness statement.

14. *Extension of hearing date of petition*

14.1 Late applications for extension of hearing dates under Insolvency Rule 6.28, and failure to attend on the listed hearing of a petition, will be dealt with as follows:

(1) If an application is submitted less than two clear working days before the hearing date (for example, later than Monday for Thursday, or Wednesday for Monday) the costs of the application will not be allowed under Insolvency Rule 6.28(3).

(2) If the petition has not been served and no extension has been granted by the time fixed for the hearing of the petition, and if no one attends for the hearing, the petition will be re-listed for hearing about 21 days later. The court will notify the petitioning creditor's solicitors (or the petitioning creditor in person), and any known supporting or opposing creditors or their solicitors, of the new date and times. Written evidence should then be filed on behalf of the petitioning creditor explaining fully the reasons for the failure to apply for an extension or to appear at the hearing, and (if appropriate) giving reasons why the petition should not be dismissed.

(3) On the re-listed hearing the court may dismiss the petition if not satisfied it should be adjourned or a further extension granted.

14.2 All applications for extension should include a statement of the date fixed for the hearing of the petition.

14.3 The petitioning creditor should attend (by solicitors or in person) on or before the hearing date to ascertain whether the application has reached the file and been dealt with. It should not be assumed that an extension will be granted.

15. *Bankruptcy petition*

To help in the completion of the form of a creditor's bankruptcy petition, attention is drawn to the following points:

15.1 The petition does not require dating, signing or witnessing.

15.2 In the title it is only necessary to recite the debtor's name, *e.g.* Re John William Smith or Re J. W Smith (Male). Any alias or trading name will appear in the body of the petition. This also applies to all other statutory forms other than those which require the "full title".

15.3 Where the petition is based on a statutory demand, only the debt claimed in the demand may be included in the petition.

15.4 In completing para. 2 of the petition, attention is drawn to Insolvency Rule 6.8(1)(a) to (c), particularly where the "aggregate sum" is made up of a number of debts.

Part Three Appendix IV

15.5 Date of service of the statutory demand (para. 4 of the petition):

(1) In the case of personal service, the date of service as set out in the affidavit of service should be recited and whether service is effected *before/after* 1700 hours on Monday to Friday or at any time on a Saturday or a Sunday: see CPR Pt. 6.7(2) and (3).

(2) In the case of substituted service (otherwise than by advertisement), the date alleged in the affidavit of service should be recited: see "11. Substituted service" above.

(3) In the strictly limited case of service by advertisement under Insolvency Rule 6.3, the date to be alleged is the date of the advertisement's appearance or, as the case may be, its first appearance: see Insolvency Rules 6.3(3) and 6.11(8).

15.6 There is no need to include in the petition details of the person authorised to present it.

15.7 Certificates at the end of the petition:

(1) The period of search for prior petitions has been reduced to eighteen months.

(2) Where a statutory demand is based wholly or in part on a county court judgment, the following certificate is to be added:

"I/We certify that on the   day of   19   I/We attended on the county court and was/were informed by an officer of the court that no money had been paid into court in the action or matter   v   Claim No   pursuant to the statutory demand."

This certificate will not be required when the demand also requires payment of a separate debt, not based on a county court judgment, the amount of which exceeds the bankruptcy level (at present £750).

15.8 Deposit on petition: the deposit will be taken by the court and forwarded to the official receiver. In the High Court, the petition fee and deposit should be handed to the Supreme Court Accounts Office, Fee Stamping Room, who will record the receipt and will impress two entries on the original petition, one in respect of the court fee and the other in respect of the deposit. In the county court, the petition fee and deposit should be handed to the duly authorised officer of the court's staff who will record its receipt.

In all cases cheque(s) for the whole amount should be made payable to "HM Paymaster General".

15.9 On the hearing of a petition for a bankruptcy order, in order to satisfy the court that the debt on which the petition is founded has not been paid or secured or compounded the court will normally accept as sufficient a certificate signed by the person representing the petitioning creditor in the following form:

"I certify that I have/my firm has made enquiries of the petitioning creditor(s) within the last business day prior to the hearing/adjourned hearing and to the best of my knowledge and belief the debt on which the petition is founded is still due and owing and has not been paid or secured or compounded save as to ....

Signed .... Dated ...."

For convenience in the High Court this certificate will be incorporated in the attendance slip, which will be filed after the hearing. A fresh certificate will be required on each adjourned hearing.

15.10 On the occasion of the adjourned hearing of a petition for a bankruptcy order, in order to satisfy the court that the petitioner has complied with Insolvency Rule 6.29, the petitioner will be required to file written evidence of the manner in which notice of the making of the order of adjournment and of the venue for the adjourned hearing has been sent to:

(i) the debtor, and

(ii) any creditor who has given notice under Insolvency Rule 6.23 but was not present at the hearing when the order for adjournment was made.

16. Orders without attendance

16.1 In suitable cases the court will normally be prepared to make orders under Pt. VIII of the Act (individual voluntary arrangements), without the attendance of either party, provided there is no bankruptcy order in existence and (so far as is known) no pending petition. The orders are:

(1) A 14-day interim order with the application adjourned 14 days for consideration of the nominee's report, where the papers are in order, and the nominee's signed consent to act includes a waiver of notice of the application or a consent by the nominee to the making of an interim order without attendance.

(2) A standard order on consideration of the nominee's report, extending the interim order to a date seven weeks after the date of the proposed meeting, directing the meeting to be summoned and adjourning to a date about three weeks after the meeting. Such an order may be made without attendance if the nominee's report has been delivered to the court and complies with s. 256(1) of the Act and Insolvency Rule 5.10(2) and (3) and proposes a date for the meeting not less than 14 days from that on which the nominee's report is filed in court under Insolvency Rule 5.10 nor more than 28 days from that on which that report is considered by the court under Insolvency Rule 5.12.

(3) A "concertina" order, combining orders as under (1) and (2) above. Such an order may be made without attendance if the initial application for an interim order is accompanied by a report of the nominee and the conditions set out in (1) and (2) above are satisfied.

(4) A final order on consideration of the chairman's report. Such an order may be made without attendance if the chairman's report has been filed and complies with Insolvency Rule 5.22(1). The order will record the effect of the chairman's report and may discharge the interim order.

16.2 Provided that the conditions as under 16.1(2) and (4) above are satisfied and that the appropriate report has been lodged with the court in due time the parties need not attend or be represented on the adjourned hearing for consideration of the nominee's report or of the chairman's report (as the case may be) unless they are notified by the court that attendance is required. Sealed copies of the order made (in all four cases as above) will be posted by the court to the applicant or his solicitor and to the nominee.

16.3 In suitable cases the court may also make consent orders without attendance by the parties. The written consent of the parties will be required. Examples of such orders are as follows:

(1) *On applications to set aside a statutory demand*, orders:

    (a) dismissing the application, with or without an order for costs as may be agreed (permission will be given to present a petition on or after the seventh day after the date of the order, unless a different date is agreed);

    (b) setting aside the demand, with or without an order for costs as may be agreed; or

    (c) giving permission to withdraw the application with or without an order for costs as may be agreed.

(2) *On petitions*: where there is a list of supporting or opposing creditors in Form 6.21, or a statement signed by or on behalf of the petitioning creditor that no notices have been received from supporting or opposing creditors, orders:

    (a) dismissing the petition, with or without an order for costs as may be agreed, or

    (b) if the petition has not been served, giving permission to withdraw the petition (with no order for costs).

(3) *On other applications*, orders:

    (a) for sale of property, possession of property, disposal of proceeds of sale

    (b) giving interim directions

    (c) dismissing the application, with or without an order for costs as may be agreed

    (d) giving permission to withdraw the application, with or without an order for costs as may be agreed.

Part Four *Appendix IV*

If, (as may often be the case with orders under sub-para. (3)(a) or (b) above) an adjournment is required, whether generally with liberty to restore or to a fixed date, the order by consent may include an order for the adjournment. If adjournment to a date is requested, a time estimate should be given and the court will fix the first available date and time on or after the date requested.

16.4 The above lists should not be regarded as exhaustive, nor should it be assumed that an order will be made without attendance as requested.

16.5 The procedure outlined above is designed to save time and costs but is not intended to discourage attendance.

16.6 Applications for consent orders without attendance should be lodged at least two clear working days (and preferably longer) before any fixed hearing date.

16.7 Whenever a document is lodged or a letter sent, the correct case number, code (if any) and year (for example 123/SD/99 or 234/99) should be quoted. A note should also be given of the date and time of the next hearing (if any).

16.8 Attention is drawn to para. 4.4(4) of the Practice Direction relating to CPR Pt. 44.

Part Four – Appeals

17. *Appeals in insolvency proceedings*

17.1 This Part shall come into effect on 2 May 2000 and shall replace and revoke para. 17 of, and be read in conjunction with the Practice Direction – Insolvency Proceedings [see [1999] B.C.C. 727] which came into effect on 26 April 1999 as amended.

17.2(1) An appeal from a decision of a county court (whether made by a district judge or a circuit judge) or of a registrar of the High Court in insolvency proceedings ("a first appeal") lies to a judge of the High Court pursuant to s. 375(2) of the Act and Insolvency Rules 7.47(2) and 7.48(2) (as amended by s. 55 of the Access to Justice Act 1999).

(2) The procedure and practice for a first appeal are governed by Insolvency Rule 7.49 which imports the procedure and practice of the Court of Appeal. The procedure and practice of the Court of Appeal is governed by CPR Pt. 52 and its Practice Direction, which are subject to the provisions of the Act, the Insolvency Rules and this Practice Direction: see CPR Pt. 52, r. 1(4).

(3) A first appeal (as defined above) does not include an appeal from a decision of a judge of the High Court.

17.3(1) Section 55 of the Access to Justice Act 1999 has amended s. 375(2) of the Act and Insolvency Rules 7.47(2) and 7.48(2) so that an appeal from a decision of a judge of the High Court made on a first appeal lies, with the permission of the Court of Appeal, to the Court of Appeal.

(2) An appeal from a judge of the High Court in insolvency proceedings which is not a decision on a first appeal lies, with the permission of the judge or of the Court of Appeal, to the Court of Appeal (see CPR Pt. 52, r. 3).

(3) The procedure and practice for appeals from a decision of a judge of the High Court in insolvency proceedings (whether made on a first appeal or not) are also governed by Insolvency Rule 7.49 which imports the procedure and practice of the Court of Appeal as stated at para. 17.2(2) above.

17.4 CPR Part 52 and its Practice Direction and Forms apply to appeals from a decision of a judge of the High Court in insolvency proceedings.

17.5 An appeal from a decision of a judge of the High Court in insolvency proceedings requires permission as set out in para. 17.3(1) and (2) above.

17.6 A first appeal does not require the permission of any court.

17.7 Except as provided in this Part, CPR Pt. 52 and its Practice Direction and Forms do not apply to first appeals, but para. 17.8 to 17.23 inclusive of this Part apply only to first appeals.

17.8 Interpretation:

(a) the expressions "appeal court", "lower court", "appellant", "respondent" and "appeal notice" have the meanings given in CPR Pt. 52.1(3);

(b) "registrar of appeals" means in relation to an appeal filed at the Royal Courts of Justice in London a bankruptcy registrar, and in relation to an appeal filed in a district registry in accordance with para. 17.10(2)and (3) below a district judge of the relevant district registry;

(c) "appeal date" means the date fixed by the appeal court for the hearing of the appeal or the date fixed by the appeal court upon which the period within which the appeal will be heard commences.

17.9 An appellant's notice and a respondent's notice shall be in Form PDIP 1 and PDIP 2 set out in the Schedule hereto.

17.10(1) An appeal from a decision of a registrar in bankruptcy shall, or from any decision made in any county court may, be filed at the Royal Courts of Justice in London.

(2) An appeal from a decision made in the county court exercising jurisdiction over an area within the Birmingham, Bristol, Cardiff, Leeds, Liverpool, Manchester, Newcastle upon Tyne or Preston Chancery District Registries may be filed in the Chancery District Registry of the High Court appropriate to the area in which the decision was made.

17.11(1) Where a party seeks an extension of time in which to file an appeal notice it must be requested in the appeal notice and the appeal notice should state the reason for the delay and the steps taken prior to the application being made; the court will fix a date for the hearing of the application and notify the parties of the date and place of hearing.

(2) The appellant must file the appellant's notice at the appeal court within–

(a) such period as may be directed by the lower court; or

(b) where the court makes no such direction, 14 days after the date of the decision of the lower court which the appellant wishes to appeal.

(3) Unless the appeal court orders otherwise, an appeal notice must be served by the appellant on each respondent–

(a) as soon as practicable; and

(b) in any event not later than seven days, after it is filed.

17.12(1) A respondent may file and serve a respondent's notice.

(2) A respondent who wishes to ask the appeal court to uphold the order of the lower court for reasons different from or additional to those given by the lower court must file a respondent's notice.

(3) A respondent's notice must be filed within–

(a) such period as may be directed by the lower court; or

(b) where the court makes no such direction, 14 days after the date on which the respondent is served with the appellant's notice.

(4) Unless the appeal court orders otherwise a respondent's notice must be served by the respondent on the appellant and any other respondent–

(a) a soon as practicable; and

(b) in any event not later than seven days, after it is filed.

17.13(1) An application to vary the time limit for filing an appeal notice must be made to the appeal court.

(2) The parties may not agree to extend any date or time limit set by–

(a) this Practice Direction; or

(b) an order of the appeal court or the lower court.

17.14 Unless the appeal court or the lower court orders otherwise an appeal shall not operate as a stay of any order or decision of the lower court.

17.15 An appeal notice may not be amended without the permission of the appeal court.

17.16 A judge of the appeal court may strike out the whole or part of an appeal notice where there is compelling reason for doing so.

17.17(1) In relation to an appeal the appeal court has all the powers of the lower court.

(2) The appeal court has power to–

(a) affirm, set aside or vary any order or judgment made or given by the lower court;

(b) refer any claim or issue for determination by the lower court;

(c) order a new trial or hearing;

(d) make a costs order.

(3) The appeal court may exercise its powers in relation to the whole or part of an order of the lower court.

17.18(1) Every appeal shall be limited to a review of the decision of the lower court.

(2) Unless it orders otherwise, the appeal court will not receive–

(a) oral evidence; or

(b) evidence which was not before the lower court.

(3) The appeal court will allow an appeal where the decision of the lower court was–

(a) wrong; or

(b) unjust because of a serious procedural or other irregularity in the proceedings in the lower court.

(4) The appeal court may draw any inference of fact which it considers justified on the evidence.

(5) At the hearing of the appeal a party may not rely on a matter not contained in his appeal notice unless the appeal court gives permission.

17.19 The following applications shall be made to a judge of the appeal court:

(1) for injunctions pending a substantive hearing of the appeal;

(2) for expedition or vacation of the hearing date of an appeal;

(3) for an order striking out the whole or part of an appeal notice pursuant to para. 17.16 above;

(4) for a final order on paper pursuant to para. 17.22(8) below.

17.20(1) All other interim applications shall be made to the registrar of appeals in the first instance who may in his discretion either hear and determine it himself or refer it to the judge.

(2) An appeal from a decision of a registrar of appeals lies to a judge of the appeal court and does not require the permission of either the registrar of appeals or the judge.

17.21 The procedure for interim applications is by way of ordinary application (see Insolvency Rule 12.7 and Sch 4, Form 7.2).

17.22 The following practice applies to all first appeals to a judge of the High Court whether filed at the Royal Courts of Justice in London, or filed at one of the other venues referred to in para. 17.10 above:

(1) On filing an appellant's notice in accordance with para. 17.11(2) above, the appellant must file:

> (a) two copies of the appeal notice for the use of the court, one of which must be stamped with the appropriate fee, and a number of additional copies equal to the number of persons who are to be served with it pursuant to para. 17.22(4) below;
> (b) a copy of the order under appeal; and
> (c) an estimate of time for the hearing;

Appendix IV *Part Four*

(2) The above documents may be lodged personally or by post and shall be lodged at the address of the appropriate venue listed below:

- (a) if the appeal is to be heard at the Royal Courts of Justice in London the documents must be lodged at Room 110, Thomas More Building, The Royal Courts of Justice, Strand, London WC2A 2LL;
- (b) if the appeal is to be heard in Birmingham, the documents must be lodged at the District Registry of the Chancery Division of the High Court, 33 Bull Street, Birmingham B4 6DS;
- (c) if the appeal is to be heard in Bristol the documents must be lodged at the District Registry of the Chancery Division of the High Court, Third Floor, Greyfriars, Lewins Mead, Bristol, BS1 2NR;
- (d) if the appeal is to be heard in Cardiff the documents must be lodged at the District Registry in the Chancery Division of the High Court, First Floor, 2 Park Street, Cardiff, CF10 1ET;
- (e) if the appeal is to be heard in Leeds the documents must be lodged at the District Registry of the Chancery Division of the High Court, The Court House, 1 Oxford Row, Leeds LS1 3BG;
- (f) if the appeal is to be heard in Liverpool the documents must be lodged at the District Registry of the Chancery Division of the High Court, Liverpool Combined Court Centre, Derby Square, Liverpool L2 1XA;
- (g) if the appeal is to be heard in Manchester the documents must be lodged at the District Registry of the Chancery Division of the High Court, Courts of Justice, Crown Square, Manchester, M60 9DJ;
- (h) if the appeal is to be heard at Newcastle upon Tyne the documents must be lodged at the District Registry of the Chancery Division of the High Court, The Law Courts, Quayside, Newcastle upon Tyne NE1 3LA;
- (i) if the appeal is to be heard in Preston the documents must be lodged at the District Registry of the Chancery Division of the High Court, The Combined Court Centre, Ringway, Preston PR1 2LL.

(3) If the documents are correct and in order the court at which the documents are filed will fix the appeal date and will also fix the place of hearing. That court will send letters to all the parties to the appeal informing them of the appeal date and of the place of hearing and indicating the time estimate given by the appellant. The parties will be invited to notify the court of any alternative or revised time estimates. In the absence of any such notification the estimate of the appellant will be taken as agreed. The court will also send to the appellant a document setting out the court's requirement concerning the form and content of the bundle of documents for the use of the judge. Not later than seven days before the appeal date the bundle of documents must be filed by the appellant at the address of the relevant venue as set out in sub-para. 17.22(2) above and a copy of it must be served by the appellant on each respondent. The bundle should include an approved transcript of the judgment of the lower court or, where there is no officially recorded judgment, the document(s) referred to in para. 5.12 of the Practice Direction to CPR Pt 52.

(4) The appeal notice must be served on all parties to the proceedings in the lower court who are directly affected by the appeal. This may include the official receiver, liquidator or trustee in bankruptcy.

(5) The appeal notice must be served by the appellant or by the legal representative of the appellant and may be effected by:

- (a) any of the methods referred to in CPR Pt 6, r. 2; or
- (b) with permission of the court, an alternative method pursuant to CPR Pt 6, r. 8.

Part Four *Appendix IV*

(6) Service of an appeal notice shall be proved by a Certificate of Service in accordance with CPR Pt 6, r. 10 (CPR Form N215) which must be filed at the relevant venue referred to at para. 17.22(2) above immediately after service.

(7) Skeleton arguments, accompanied by a written chronology of events relevant to the appeal, should be filed at the address of the appropriate venue as set out in sub-para. 17.22(2) above, at least two clear days before the date fixed for the hearing. Failure to lodge may result in an adverse costs order being made by the judge on the hearing of the appeal.

(8) Where an appeal has been settled or where an appellant does not wish to continue with the appeal, the appeal may be disposed of on paper without a hearing. It may be dismissed by consent but the appeal court will not make an order allowing an appeal unless it is satisfied that the decision of the lower court was wrong. Any consent order signed by each party or letters of consent from each party must be lodged not later than 24 hours before the date fixed for the hearing of the appeal at the address of the appropriate venue as set out in sub-para. 17.22(2) above and will be dealt with by the judge of the appeal court. Attention is drawn to para. 4.4(4) of the Practice Direction to CPR Pt 44 regarding costs where an order is made by consent without attendance.

17.23 Only the following paragraphs of the Practice Direction to CPR Pt 52, with any necessary modifications, shall apply to first appeals: 5.12 and 5.14 to 5.20 inclusive.

17.24(1) Where, under the procedure relating to appeals in insolvency proceedings prior to the coming into effect of this Part of this Practice Direction, an appeal has been set down in the High Court or permission to appeal to the Court of Appeal has been granted before 2 May 2000, the procedure and practice set out in this Part of this Practice Direction shall apply to such an appeal after that date.

(2) Where, under the procedure relating to appeals in insolvency proceedings prior to the coming into effect of this Part of this Practice Direction, any person has failed before 2 May 2000 either:

(a) in the case of a first appeal, to set down in the High Court an appeal which relates to an order made (county court) or sealed (High Court) after 27 March 2000 and before 2 May 2000, or

(b) in the case of an appeal from a decision of a judge of the High Court, to obtain any requisite permission to appeal to the Court of Appeal which relates to an order sealed in the same period,

the time for filing an appeal notice is extended to 16 May 2000 and application for any such permission should be made in the appeal notice.

17.25 This paragraph applies where a judge of the High Court has made a bankruptcy order or a winding-up order or dismissed an appeal against such an order and an application is made for a stay of proceedings pending appeal.

(1) The judge will not normally grant a stay of all proceedings but will confine himself to a stay of advertisement of the proceedings.

(2) Where the judge has granted permission to appeal any stay of advertisement will normally be until the hearing of the appeal but on terms that the stay will determine without further order if an appellant's notice is not filed within the period prescribed by the rules.

(3) Where the judge has refused permission to appeal any stay of advertisement will normally be for a period not exceeding 28 days.

Application for any further stay of advertisement should be made to the Court of Appeal.

Schedule

Forms—Insolvency Proceedings

PDIP 1 Appellant's Notice—Insolvency Proceedings

PDIP 2 Respondent's Notice—Insolvency Proceedings

PDIP 3 Draft Order—Multiple Transfer of Proceedings

PDIP 4 Draft Order—Multiple Appointments of Office Holder

Appendix V

Practice Direction: Applications under the Companies Act 1985 and the Insurance Companies Act 1982, [1999] B.C.C. 741, para. 9

9(1) Attention is drawn to the undesirability of asking as a matter of course for a winding up order as an alternative to an order under s. 459 of the Companies Act 1985. The petition should not ask for a winding up order unless that is the relief which the petitioner prefers or it is thought that it may be the only relief to which the petitioner is entitled.

(2) Whenever a winding up order is asked for in a contributory's petition, the petition must state whether the petitioner consents or objects to an order under s. 127 of the Act in the standard form. If he objects, the written evidence in support must contain a short statement of his reasons.

(3) If the petitioner objects to a s. 127 order in the standard form but consents to such an order in a modified form, the petition must set out the form of order to which he consents, and the written evidence in support must contain a short statement of his reasons for seeking the modification.

(4) If the petition contains a statement that the petitioner consents to a s. 127 order, whether in the standard or a modified form, but the petitioner changes his mind before the first hearing of the petition, he must notify the respondents and may apply on notice to a Judge for an order directing that no s. 127 order or a modified order only (as the case may be) shall be made by the registrar, but validating dispositions made without notice of the order made by the judge.

(5) If the petition contains a statement that the petitioner consents to a s. 127 order, whether in the standard or a modified form, the registrar shall without further enquiry make an order in such form at the first hearing unless an order to the contrary has been made by the judge in the meantime.

(6) If the petition contains a statement that the petitioner objects to a s. 127 order in the standard form, the company may apply (in the case of urgency, without notice) to the judge for an order.

(7) Section 127 order – standard form:

(Title etc.)

ORDER that notwithstanding the presentation of the said petition

(1) payments made into or out of the bank accounts of the company in the ordinary course of the business of the company and

(2) dispositions of the property of the company made in the ordinary course of its business for proper value

between the date of presentation of the petition and the date of judgment on the petition or further order in the meantime shall not be void by virtue of the provisions of s. 127 of the Insolvency Act 1986 in the event of an order for the winding up of the company being made on the said petition

Provided that (the relevant bank) shall be under no obligation to verify for itself whether any transaction through the company's bank accounts is in the ordinary course of business, or that it represents full market value for the relevant transaction.

This form of order may be departed from where the circumstances of the case require.

GENERAL NOTE

This Practice Direction, para. 9 replaces Practice Direction No. 1 of 1990 [1990] 1 W.L.R. 490, [1990] B.C.C. 292, and includes a standard form of order. See the note to IA 1986, s. 127.

Index

Abbreviations in the provision column are to the *Insolvency Act* 1986 (IA), the *Insolvency Act* 2000 (IA 2000), the *Enterprise Act* 2002 (EA), the *Insolvency Rules* 1986 (IR) and the *EC Regulation on Insolvency Proceedings* 2000 (ER). Where the provision is shown in italics, this denotes the system prior to the introduction of the Enterprise Act 2002.

                    Provision

A

Absconding
. bankruptcy offences, and, ...IA 358
. contributories, ...IA 158

Abstract of receipts and payments
. administrative receiver, and, ...IR 3.32
. administrator, by, ...*IR 2.52*

Accounts
. administrative receiver, and, ...IR 3.32
. administrator, by, ...*IR 2.52*
. company voluntary arrangements, and
. . access for nominee, ...IR 1.6(3)
. . audits, ...IR 1.27(3)
. . production to Secretary of
     State, ...IR 1.27
. creditor's petition for bankruptcy, and
. . requirement to submit, ...IR 6.64
. . submission and filing of, ...IR 6.65
. debtors' petition for bankruptcy, and
. . requirement to submit, ...IR 6.69
. . submission and filing of, ...IR 6.70
. individual voluntary arrangements, and
. . production to Secretary of
     State, ...IR 5.32
. . supervisor, of, ...IA 5.31
. public administration, ...IA 409
. receivers (England and Wales),
  and, ... IA 38
. special manager
. . bankruptcy, and, ...IR 6.170

                    Provision

. . winding up, and, ...IR 4.209
. trustees in bankruptcy
. . annulment of bankruptcy
     orders, and, ...IR 5.61
. winding up, and
. . creditors' voluntary
     liquidation, and, ... IR 4.40, IR 4.41
. . further disclosure, ...IR 4.42
. . requests for, ... IR 4.39

Adjournment
. applications for insolvency
  proceedings, and, ...IR 7.10
. creditors' meetings
. . bankruptcy, and, ...IR 6.91
. . receivership, and, ... IR 3.14
. . winding up, and, ...IR 4.65
. creditors' petition
. . bankruptcy, and, ...IR 6.29
. public examination
. . of bankrupt, ...IR 6.176
. . of company officers, ... IR 4.216

Adjustment of prior transactions
. bankruptcy, and
. . apprenticeships, and, ... IA 348
. . contracts to which bankrupt is
     party, ...IA 345
. . distress, and, ...IA 347
. . enforcement procedures, ...IA 346
. . excessive pension
     contributions, ... IA 342A—IA 342C
. . extortionate credit
     transactions, ... IA 343
. . general assignment of book
     debts, avoidance of, ... IA 344

Index

Adjustment of prior transactions—continued **Provision**
.. liens on books, unenforceability of, ... IA 349
.. pension-sharing, ... IA 342D—IA 342F
.. preferences, ... IA 340—IA 342
.. transactions at undervalue, ... IA 339, IA 341, IA 342
. company insolvency, and
.. extortionate credit transactions, ... IA 244
.. floating charges, avoidance of, ... IA 245
.. gratuitous alienations (Scotland), ... IA 242
.. liens on books, unenforceability of, ... IA 246
.. preferences (England and Wales), ... IA 239— IA 241
.. transactions at undervalue (England and Wales), IA 238, IA 240, IA 241
.. unfair preferences (Scotland), ... IA 243

Administration
. administration orders
.. advertisement of, ... *IR 2.10*
.. application, effect of, ... *IA 10*
.. application, procedure for, ... *IA 9*
.. content of, ... IR 2.13
.. effect of, ... *IA 11*
.. notification of, ... *IA 12, IR 2.10,* IR 2.14
.. power of court to make, ... *IA 8*
. administrator
.. advertisement of appointment, . IA Sch.B1, para.46, IR 2.27
.. appointment by company or directors, ... IA Sch.B1, paras 22—34, IR 2.20—IR 2.26
.. appointment by court, ... IA Sch.B1, paras 10—13, IR 2.2—IR 2.14
.. appointment by holder of floating charge, ... IA Sch.B1, paras 14—21, IR 2.10, IR 2.15—IR 2.19
.. appointment of, ... *IA 13*
.. charged property, disposal of, ..*IR 2.51,* IR 2.66
.. charged property, power to deal with, ... *IA 15*
.. company's affairs, investigation of, ... *IA 21—IA 22*
.. death of, ... *IR 2.54,* IR 2.124

Provision
.. debt or liabilities incurred by, ... *IA 19(5)—IA 19(6)*
.. discharge or variation of administration order, ... *IA 18*
.. duties of, ... *IA 17*
.. general powers of, ... *IA 14*
.. joint administrator, appointment of, ... IR 2.127
.. notification of appointment, ... IR 2.28
.. receipts and payments, abstract of, ... *IR 2.52*
.. release of, ... *IA 20*
.. remuneration of, ... *IA 19(4)*
.. remuneration, fixing of, . *IR 2.47—IR 2.50,* IR 2.106—IR 2.109
.. replacement of, ... IR 2.119—IR 2.126
.. resignation of, ... *IR 2.53*
.. role in Scotland, ... *IA 16*
.. role of, ... IA Sch.B1, paras 4—8
.. statement of administrator's proposals, ... IR 2.33
.. vacancy, court order filling, ... IR 2.55
.. vacation of office, ... *IA 19,* IR 2.129
. administrator's proposals
.. approval of substantial revisions, ... *IA 25*
.. creditors' meeting, consideration by, ... *IA 24*
.. failure to obtain approval of, ... IA Sch.B1, para.55
.. statement of, ...*IA 23,* IA Sch.B1, para.49
. company meetings, ...*IR 2.31,* IR 2.49
. company's affairs, investigation of
.. information supplied by administrator, ...*IA 21*
.. statement of affairs, ...*IA 22*
. creditors, distributions to
.. division of unsold assets, ... IR 2.71
.. notice of intention to declare and distribute dividend, ... IR 2.68
.. ranking of debts, ... IR 2.69
.. supplementary provisions, ... IR 2.70
. creditors' committee
.. administrator, summoning of, ... *IA 26*
.. appointment of, ...IA Sch.B1, para.57
.. chairman of, ...*IR 2.35,* IR 2.53
.. committee-members' representatives, ... *IR 2.37,* IR 2.55
.. constitution of, ... *IR 2.32,* IR 2.50

1146

Index

Provision

- . creditors' meeting,
  - establishment by, ... *IA 26*
- . . formal defects, ... *IR 2.46A*, IR 2.65
- . . formalities of establishment
  - of, ... *IR 2.33*, IR 2.51
- . . functions and meetings of, ... *IR 2.34*, IR 2.52
- . . information from
  - administrator, ... *IR 2.44*, IR 2.62
- . . members' dealings with
  - company, ... *IR 2.46*, IR 2.64
- . . members' expenses, ... *IR 2.45*, IR 2.63
- . . procedure at, ... *IR 2.42*, IR 2.60
- . . quorum of, ... *IR 2.36*, IR 2.54
- . . removal from, ... *IR 2.40*, IR 2.58
- . . resignation, ... *IR 2.38*, IR 2.56
- . . resolutions by post, ... *IR 2.43*, IR 2.61
- . . termination of membership, ... *IR 2.39*, IR 2.57
- . . vacancies on, ... *IR 2.41*, IR 2.59
- . creditors' interests, protection
  - of, ... *IA 27*
- . creditors' meetings
- . . administrator's proposals,
  - consideration of, ... IR 2.34
- . . administrator's proposals,
  - revision of, ... IA Sch.B1, para.54, IR 2.45
- . . admission of claims, ... *IR 2.23*, IR 2.39
- . . chairman at, ... *IR 2.20*, IR 2.36
- . . chattel leasing agreements
  - and, ... *IR 2.27*, IR 2.42
- . . conditional sale agreements,
  - and, ... *IR 2.27*, IR 2.42
- . . correspondence instead of, ... IA Sch.B1, para.58, IR 2.48
- . . generally, ... *IR 2.19*, IR 2.35
- . . hire-purchase agreements,
  - and, ... *IR 2.27*, IR 2.42
- . . initial meeting, requirement
  - for, ... IA Sch.B1, paras 51—53
- . . minutes of, ... *IR 2.28*, IR 2.44
- . . negotiable instrument holders, . *IR 2.25*, IR 2.41
- . . notices to creditors, ... *IR 2.30*, IR 2.46
- . . progress report to creditors, ... IR 2.47
- . . rejection of claims, ... *IR 2.23*, IR 2.39
- . . remuneration of administrator,
  - and, ... *IR 2.48*, IR 2.107
- . . reports and notices resulting
  - from, ... IR 2.29

Provision

- . . requisition of by creditors, ... *IR 2.21*, IR 2.37
- . . resolutions of, ... *IR 2.28*, IR 2.43
- . . retention of title creditors, ... *IR 2.26*
- . . secured creditors, ... *IR 2.24*, IR 2.40
- . . summoning, procedure for, ... *IR 2.18*
- . . voting rights, ... *IR 2.22*, IR 2.38
- . creditors' petition
- . . affidavit in support of, *IR 2.1(3)*, IR 2.2(3)
- . . form of, ... *IR 2.4*, IR 2.3
- . . service of, ... *IR 2.6(3)*
- . debts, proof of
- . . admission and rejection of
  - proofs for dividend, ... *IR 2.77*
- . . affidavit, establishment by, ... IR 2.73
- . . appeal against decision on, ... IR 2.78
- . . costs of, ... IR 2.74
- . . expunging of by court, ... *IR 2.80*
- . . inspection of proofs, ... *IR 2.75*
- . . making of proofs, ... *IR 2.72*
- . . new administrator,
  - appointment of, ... *IR 2.76*
- . . withdrawal or variation of, ... *IR 2.79*
- . director's petition
- . . affidavit in support of, *IR 2.1(2)*, IR 2.2(2)
- . . form of, ... *IR 2.4*, IR 2.3(1)
- . dividends, and
- . . alteration of proof after
  - payment of, ... IR 2.101
- . . assignment of right to, ... IR 2.104
- . . debts payable at future time, ... IR 2.89
- . . declaration of, ... IR 2.97
- . . disqualification from, ... IR 2.103
- . . notice of declaration of, ... IR 2.98
- . . notice of further, ... IR 2.100
- . . notice of no payment, ... IR 2.100
- . . payment of, ... IR 2.99
- . expenses of, ... IR 2.67
- . forms for, ... IR Sch.4
- . member State liquidator, notice
  - to, ... *IR 2.62*, IR 2.133
- . nature of, ... IA Sch.B1, paras 1—3
- . petition for
- . . affidavit, content of, ... *IR 2.3*, IR 2.4
- . . affidavit to support, ... *IR 2.1*, IR 2.2
- . . company in liquidation, and, ... IR 2.11
- . . content of, ... IR 2.4
- . . effect of, ... *IA 10*
- . . filing of, ... *IR 2.5*, IR 2.5
- . . form of, ... *IR 2.4*, IR 2.3
- . . hearing on, ... *IR 2.9*, IR 2.12
- . . manner of service, ... *IR 2.7*, IR 2.8

Index

Administration—continued   **Provision**
- . . notice to sheriff, ...*IR 2.6A*, IR 2.7
- . . procedure for, ... *IA 9*
- . . proof of service, ...*IR 2.8*, IR 2.9
- . . report on company's affairs, ... *IR 2.2*
- . . service of, ...*IR 2.6*, IR 2.6
- . proposals to creditors
- . . annexation of statement of affairs, ... *IR 2.16*
- . . notice to members of, ... *IR 2.17*
- . quantification of claims
- . . admission or rejection of proofs, ... IR 2.96
- . . debts payable at future time, ... IR 2.89
- . . discounts, ...IR 2.84
- . . estimate of, ... IR 2.81
- . . foreign currency debts, ... IR 2.86
- . . interest, ...IR 2.88
- . . mutual credit and set-off, ... IR 2.85
- . . negotiable instruments, and, ...IR 2.82
- . . non-disclosure, surrender for, ...IR 2.91
- . . notice of proposed distribution, ... IR 2.95
- . . periodical payments, ...IR 2.87
- . . redemption by administrator, ... IR 2.92
- . . revaluation of security, ... IR 2.102
- . . secured creditors, and, ... IR 2.83
- . . security, realisation by creditor, ...IR 2.94
- . . security, test of value, ...IR 2.93
- . . security, value of, ...IR 2.90
- . sisting for company voluntary arrangement, ... *IA 5(3)*
- . special administration regimes, ...EA 249
- . statement of affairs
- . . annexation to proposals, ... *IR 2.16*
- . . expenses of, ... *IR 2.15*, IR 2.32
- . . extension of time for submission, ...*IR 2.14*, IR 2.31
- . . limited disclosure, ... *IR 2.13*, IR 2.30
- . . notice requiring, ... *IR 2.11*
- . . release from duty to submit, ... *IR 2.14*, IR 2.31
- . . requirement for, . IA Sch.B1, paras 47—48
- . . verification and filing of, ..*IR 2.12*, IR 2.29
- . supervisor's petition
- . . affidavit in support of, ...*IR 2.1(4)*
- . termination of
- . . application by administrator, ... IA Sch.B1, para.79, IR 2.114
- . . application by creditor, ... IA Sch.B1, para.81, IR 2.115

    Provision
- . . application for extension, ...IR 2.112
- . . automatic termination, ...IA Sch.B1, paras 76—78
- . . Companies Registrar, notice to, ... IA Sch.B1, para.86
- . . discharge of administration order, ... IA Sch.B1, para.85
- . . final progress reports, ... IR 2.110
- . . move to creditors' voluntary liquidation, ... IA Sch.B1, para.83, IR 2.117
- . . move to dissolution, ...IA Sch.B1, para.84, IR 2.118
- . . notice of, ...IR 2.113
- . . notice where end automatic, ...IR 2.111
- . . notification of court order, ... IR 2.116
- . . public interest, and, ...IA Sch.B1, para.82
- . . where objective achieved, ... IA Sch.B1, para.80
- . VAT bad debt relief
- . . issue of certificate of insolvency, ...*IR 2.56*
- . . notice to creditors, ...*IR 2.57*
- . . preservation of certificate in company records, ... *IR 2.58*
- . winding up, conversion to
- . . affidavit, content of, ...*IR 2.60*, IR 2.131
- . . application for, ... *IR 2.59*, IR 2.130
- . . court powers, and, ... *IR 2.61*, IR 2.132
- . . liquidation committee, and, . IR 4.173—IR 4.178

Administration of bankrupt's estate by trustee
- . administration order, property under, ... IA 306C
- . after acquired property, and, ... IA 307, IA 309
- . charge on bankrupt's home, ...IA 313
- . income payment agreements, ... IA 310A
- . income payment orders, ... IA 310
- . items of excess value, ... IA 308, IA 309
- . low value home, ...IA 313A
- . property subject to restraint order, ... IA 306A
- . receivership, property under, ... IA 306B
- . vesting of bankrupt's estate in, ... IA 306

Administration orders
- . advertisement of, ...*IR 2.10*
- . application
- . . administrative receivership, and, ...IA Sch.B1, para.39
- . . by floating charge holder, ... IA Sch.B1, paras 35—36

1148

Index

Provision

. . company in liquidation, and, ... IA Sch.B1, paras 37—38
. . effect of, ... *IA 10*
. . procedure for, ... *IA 9*
. discharge or variation by administrator, .*IA 18*, IA Sch.B1, para.85
. effect of, ... *IA 11*, IA Sch.B1, paras 40—45
. notification of, ...*IA 12*, *IR 2.10*, IR 2.14
. power of court to make, ... *IA 8*
. property under
. . administration by trustee in bankruptcy, ... IA 306C
. revocation, disabilities on, ... IA 429

Administrative receiver
. and see **Receivers**
. abstract of receipts and payments, ... IR 3.32
. agency, and, ... IA 44
. appointment
. . acceptance of, ... IR 3.1
. . advertisement of, ...IR 3.2
. . confirmation of, ... IR 3.1
. . notice of, ... IR 3.2
. . prohibition on, ...IA 72A—IA 72H, IA Sch.2A
. application of IA 1986 s.176A, ... IR 3.39
. contracts, liability for, ... IA 44
. creditors' committee, and, ... IA 49
. death of, ... IR 3.34
. disposal of charged property, ... IA 43, IR 3.31
. general powers of, ... IA 42
. information to be given by, ... IA 46
. meaning, ...IA 29(2), IA 251
. powers of, ...IA Sch.1
. report of, ... IA 48, IR 3.8
. resignation of, ... IR 3.33
. statement of affairs
. . expenses of, ... IR 3.7
. . extension of time to submit, ...IR 3.6
. . limited disclosure in, ... IR 3.5
. . notice requiring, ... IR 3.3
. . release from duty to submit, ... IR 3.6
. . submission of, ... IA 47
. . verification and filing, ... IR 3.4
. vacation of office, . *IA 11(2)*, IA 45, IR 3.35
. VAT bad debt relief, and, IR 3.36—IR 3.38

Administrative receivership *see* **Receivership**

Administrator
. advertisement of appointment, ... IR 2.27
. agency, and, ... IA Sch.B1, para.69

Provision

. appointment by company or directors
. . notice of, ...IR 2.23—IR 2.26
. . notice of intention to appoint, IR 2.20—IR 2.22
. appointment by court, ...IR 2.2—IR 2.14
. appointment by holder of floating charge
. . application for, ... IR 2.10
. . court business hours, out of, ... IR 2.19
. . notice of, ...IR 2.16—IR 2.18
. . notice of intention to appoint, ... IR 2.15
. appointment of, ...*IA 13*
. challenges to conduct of company of, ... IA Sch.B1, para.74
. charged property
. . disposal of, ...IA Sch.B1, paras 70—71, *IR 2.51*, IR 2.66
. . power to deal with, ...*IA 15*
. company voluntary arrangements, and
. . proposals for, ... IA 1(3), IR 1.10—IR 1.12
. . summoning of meetings, ...IA 3(2)
. company's affairs, investigation of, ... IA 21—IA 22
. creditors' committee
. . information to, ... *IR 2.44*, IR 2.62
. . summoning by, ... IA 26
. death of, ...*IR 2.54*, IR 2.124
. debts or liabilities incurred by, IA 19(5)—IA 19(6)
. discharge or variation of administration order, ...*IA 18*
. distribution by, ... IA Sch.B1, paras 65—66
. duties of, ... *IA 17*, IA Sch.B1, paras 67—68
. general powers of, . *IA 14*, IA Sch.B1, paras 59—64
. hire purchase property, and, ... IA Sch.B1, para.72
. joint administrator, appointment of, IA Sch.B1, paras 100—103, IR 2.127
. misfeasance, and, ...IA Sch.B1, para.75
. notification of appointment, ... IR 2.28
. penalties, and, ... IA Sch.B1, para.106
. powers of, ...IA Sch.1
. qualification, loss of, ...IA Sch.B1, para.89
. quantification of claims, and, ... IR 2.92
. receipts and payments, abstract of, ... IR 2.52
. release of, ...*IA 20*
. removal of, ...IA Sch.B1, para.88
. remuneration of, ... IA 19(4)

1149

Index

Administrator—continued   **Provision**
. remuneration, fixing of, ... *IR 2.47—IR 2.50*, IR 2.106—IR 2.109
. resignation of, ..IA Sch.B1, para.87, *IR 2.53*
. role in Scotland, ...*IA 16*
. statement of administrator's proposals, ...IR 2.33
. substitution of, ...IA Sch.B1, paras 96—97
. termination of administration, ...IA Sch.B1, para.79, IR 2.114
. vacancy, court order filling, ... *IR 2.55*
. vacation of office, ..*IA 19*, IA Sch.B1, paras 90—95, , IA Sch.B1, paras 98—99, IR 2.129
. validity of acts of, ... IA Sch.B1, para.104

Administrator's proposal
. administration orders, and
.. annexation of statement of affairs, ... *IR 2.16*
.. approval of substantial revisions, ...*IA 25*
.. creditors' meeting, consideration by, ...*IA 24*, IR 2.34
.. creditors' meeting, revision by, ...IR 2.45
.. preferential creditors, and, ... IA Sch.B1, para.73
.. secured creditors, and, ...IA Sch.B1, para.73
.. statement of, ...*IA 23*
. company voluntary arrangement, for
.. notice to nominee, ...IR 1.12
.. preparation of, ...IR 1.10
.. summoning of meetings, ...IR 1.11

Admission or rejection of proofs
. creditors' meeting
.. bankruptcy, and, ...IR 6.94
.. winding up, and, ...IR 4.70
. proof of debts
.. administration, and, ... IR 2.77
.. bankruptcy, and, ...IR 6.104
.. winding up, and, ...IR 4.82

Advertisements
. appointment
.. of administrator, ...IR 2.27
.. of receiver, ... IR 3.2
. moratoriums, and, ... IR 1.40(2)
. petition for winding up, ... IR 4.11
. termination of administration, ...IR 2.113(6)

    Provision
Affairs, statement of
. administration orders, and
.. annexation to proposals, ... *IR 2.16*
.. expenses of, ... *IR 2.15*, IR 2.32
.. extension of time for submission, ...*IR 2.14*, IR 2.31
.. investigation of company affairs, ...*IA 22*
.. limited disclosure, ... *IR 2.13*, IR 2.30
.. notice requiring, ... *IR 2.11*
.. release from duty to submit, ... *IR 2.14*, IR 2.31
.. verification and filing of, ..*IR 2.12*, IR 2.29
. administrative receiver, and
.. expenses of, ... IR 3.7
.. extension of time to submit, ...IR 3.6
.. limited disclosure in, ... IR 3.5
.. notice requiring, ...IR 3.3
.. release from duty to submit, ... IR 3.6
.. submission of, ... IA 47
.. verification and filing, ... IR 3.4
. admissibility in evidence of, ... IA 433
. bankruptcy, and, ... IA 288
. company voluntary arrangements, and
.. directors' proposals, ... IR 1.5
.. moratoriums, proposals for, ... IR 1.37
. creditor's petition for bankruptcy, and
.. accounts, requirement to submit, ... IR 6.64
.. accounts, submission and filing of, ... IR 6.65
.. expenses of, ... IR 6.63
.. form of, ... IR 6.59
.. further disclosure, ...IR 6.66
.. limited disclosure, ... IR 6.62
.. verification and filing of, ... IR 6.60
. creditors' voluntary winding up, and, ... IA 99, IR 4.34, IR 4.34A, IR 4.38
. creditors, information to
.. bankruptcy, and, ...IR 6.75—IR 6.76
. debtors' petition for bankruptcy, and
.. accounts, requirement to submit, ... IR 6.69
.. accounts, submission and filing of, ... IR 6.70
.. content of, ...IR 6.68
.. expenses of, ... IR 6.71
.. limited disclosure, ... IR 6.72
. individual voluntary arrangement, and, ... IR 5.5

Index

Provision

. omissions from
.. malpractice during winding up, and, ...IA 210
. receivers (Scotland), and, ... IA 66
. winding up, and
.. creditors' voluntary liquidation, and, ... IR 4.34, IR 4.34A, IR 4.38
.. expenses of, ... IR 4.36
.. extension of time, ...IR 4.36
.. further disclosure, ...IR 4.42
.. limited disclosure, ...IR 4.35
.. notice requiring, ...IR 4.32
.. release for duty to submit, ... IR 4.36
.. verification and filing, ...IR 4.33
. winding up by court, and, ...IA 131

Affidavits
. administration
.. conversion to winding up, ... *IR 2.60*, IR 2.131
.. petition for, .. *IR 2.1*, *IR 2.3*, IR 2.2, IR 2.4
. company voluntary arrangements, and
.. conversion into winding up, ...IR 1.32
. court procedure, ...IR 7.57
. petition for winding up, opposition to, ...IR 4.18
. proof of debts
.. administration, and, ...IR 2.73
.. bankruptcy, and, ...IR 6.99
.. winding up, and, ...IR 4.77
. winding up (registered companies), ...IA 200

After-acquired property
. bankruptcy, and
.. administration by trustee in bankruptcy, ... IA 307, IA 309
.. bankrupt's duties in respect of, ... IR 6.200
.. expenses of ingathering, ... IR 6.202
.. trustee's recourse to disponees of, ... IR 6.201

Agency
. administrative receiver, and, ...IA 44
. administrator, and, ... *IA 14(5)*
. receivers (Scotland), and, ... IA 57

Agents
. fast track individual voluntary arrangement, and, ... IR 5.49

Provision

Annual report
. bankruptcy, and, ... IA 379

Appeals
. administration
.. admission and rejection of creditors' claims, ... IR 2.39(5)
.. expenses of statement of affairs, ...*IR 2.15(2)*
. bankruptcy, and, ...IR 7.48
. company voluntary arrangements, and
.. admission of creditors' claims, and, ... IR 1.17A, IR 1.50
.. decisions of creditors' meetings, ...IR 1.19(7)
. dissolution following, ... IR 4.225
. official receiver, decisions, of, ... IR 7.50
. procedure on, ... IR 7.49
. proof of debts in winding up, and, ...IR 4.83
. receivership, and
.. admission and rejection of claims, ... IR 3.12(2)
.. decisions of creditors' meetings, ...IR 3.12(2)
. Secretary of State, decisions of, ... IR 7.50
. winding up, and, ... IR 7.47
. winding up by court (Scotland), ... IA 162

Application for administration
see **Petition for administration**

Apprenticeships
. adjustment of prior transactions in bankruptcy, ... IA 348

Arrest, power of
. bankruptcy, and, ... IA 364

Assets
. administration, division to creditors on, ... IR 2.71
. collection and distribution by liquidator, ... IR 4.179—IR 4.186
. hand-over to liquidator, ... IR 4.107
. payment of costs of winding up out of, ...IR 4.218—IR 4.220
. power to make over to employees, ... IA 187

Associate
. meaning of, ... IA 435

Attachment
. avoidance of, ... IA 128

1151

Index

Attachment—continued   *Provision*
. effect of execution of
.. winding up, and, ... IA 183

Attendance, right of
. insolvency proceedings, ... IR 7.53

Audience, rights of
. insolvency proceedings, ... IR 7.52

Authorised deposit taker
. meaning, ... *IA 8(1B)*
. service of application for
    administration, ... IR 2.8(5)

B

Bad debt relief, VAT
. administration orders, and
.. issue of certificate of
    insolvency, ... *IR 2.56*
.. notice to creditors, ... *IR 2.57*
.. preservation of certificate in
    company records, ... *IR 2.58*
. administrative receiver, and, ... IR 3.36—IR 3.38

Bankrupt
. after-acquired property, and, ... IR 6.200
. annulment of bankruptcy orders,
    and, ... IR 5.51—IR 5.53
. debts surviving discharge, ... IR 6.223
. discharge of bankruptcy, and, ... IR 6.217
. disqualification from office
.. generally, ... EA 268
.. justice of the peace, ... EA 265
.. local government, ... EA 267
.. parliament, ... IA 426A, IA 427, EA 266
. evidence of for bankruptcy
    restriction order, ... IR 6.243
. official receiver, duties in
    relation to, ... IA 291
. public examination of
.. adjournment of, ... IR 6.176
.. bankrupt unfit for, ... IR 6.174
.. creditors' request for, ... IR 6.173
.. expenses of, ... IR 6.177
.. order for, ... IR 6.172
.. procedure at hearing, ... IR 6.175
. receivers (England and Wales),
    and, ... IA 31
. redirection of mail, ... IA 371
. undischarged bankrupts
.. receiver, power to appoint, ... IA 51(5)

Bankrupt's estate   *Provision*
. bankrupt's duties in relation to
    official receiver, ... IA 291
. bankrupt's home, ... IA 283A, IA 313, IR 6.237—IR 6.237E
. dispositions of property,
    restrictions of, ... IA 284
. interim receiver, appointment
    of, ... IA 286
. investigation by official
    receiver, ... IA 289
. meaning of, ... IA 283
. proceedings and remedies,
    restriction on, ... IA 285
. public examination of bankrupt, ... IA 290
. receivership pending
    appointment of trustee, ... IA 287
. seizure of, ... IA 365
. statement of affairs, ... IA 288
. vesting of property in trustee in
    bankruptcy, ... IA 306

Bankruptcy
. administration by trustee
.. administration order, property
    under, ... IA 306C
.. after acquired property, and, ... IA 307, IA 309
.. charge on bankrupt's home, ... IA 313
.. income payment agreements, ... IA 310A
.. income payment orders, ... IA 310
.. items of excess value, ... IA 308, IA 309
.. low value home, ... IA 313A
.. property subject to restraint
    order, ... IA 306A
.. receivership, property under, ... IA 306B
.. vesting of bankrupt's estate in, ... IA 306
. after-acquired property
.. bankrupt's duties in respect
    of, ... IR 6.200
.. expenses of ingathering, ... IR 6.202
.. trustee's recourse to disponees
    of, ... IR 6.201
. annual report, ... IA 379
. annulment of bankruptcy order, ... IA 282
. appeals from courts exercising
    insolvency jurisdiction, ... IA 375
. bankrupt's estate
.. bankrupt's duties in relation to
    official receiver, ... IA 291
.. bankrupt's home, . IA 283A, IR 6.237—IR 6.237E, EA 261
.. dispositions of property,
    restrictions of, ... IA 284
.. interim receiver, appointment
    of, ... IA 286

1152

Index

	Provision
. . investigation by official receiver,	IA 289
. . meaning of,	IA 283
. . proceedings and remedies, restriction on,	IA 285
. . public examination of bankrupt,	IA 290
. . receivership pending appointment of trustee,	IA 287
. . statement of affairs,	IA 288
. bankruptcy orders	
. . annulment of,	IR 6.206—IR 6.210
. . individual insolvency register, and,	IR 6A.4—IR 6A.5
. . register of,	IR 6.223A—IR 6.223C
. bankruptcy restriction order	
. . application for,	IR 6.241
. . bankrupt's evidence,	IR 6.243
. . interim orders,	IR 6.245—IR 6.248
. . making of,	IR 6.244
. . service on defendant,	IR 6.242
. bankruptcy restrictions register	
. . deletions from,	IR 6A.7
. . entries to,	IR 6A.6
. . rectification of,	IR 6A.8
. bankruptcy restrictions undertaking,	IR 6.249—IR 6.251
. commencement of,	IA 278
. contributories, of	
. . effect on winding up,	IA 82
. costs, payment out of estate of,	IR 6.224
. court powers in	
. . arrest, power of,	IA 364
. . general powers of,	IA 363
. . inquiry into bankrupt's dealings,	IA 366—IA 368
. . production of documents by inland revenue,	IA 369
. . redirection of bankrupt's letters,	IA 371
. . seizure of bankrupt's property,	IA 365
. . special manager, appointment of,	IA 370
. creditors, information to	
. . annulment of bankruptcy order, and,	IR 6.78
. . entitlement to be informed,	IR 6.74
. . generally,	IR 6.77
. . official receivers general duty,	IR 6.73
. . statement of affairs dispensed with,	IR 6.76
. . statement of affairs lodged,	IR 6.75

	Provision
. creditors' committee	
. . chairman at meetings of,	IR 6.154
. . committee-members representatives,	IR 6.156
. . dealings by members,	IR 6.165
. . expenses of members,	IR 6.164
. . formalities of establishment,	IR 6.151
. . functions vested in Secretary of State,	IR 6.166
. . meetings of,	IR 6.153
. . membership of,	*IR 2.39(2)*, IR 3.23(2), IR 6.150
. . obligations of trustee to,	IR 6.152
. . postal resolutions,	IR 6.162
. . quorum,	IR 6.155
. . removal from,	IR 6.159
. . resignation from,	IR 6.157
. . termination of membership,	IR 6.158
. . trustee's reports to,	IR 6.163
. . vacancies of,	IR 6.160
. . voting rights,	IR 6.161
. creditors' meetings, and	
. . adjournment of,	IR 6.91
. . admission and rejection of proofs,	IR 6.94
. . attendance of bankrupt,	IR 6.84
. . chairman as proxy holder,	IR 6.89
. . chairman at,	IR 6.82
. . expenses of summoning,	IR 6.87
. . first meeting of,	IR 6.79
. . first meeting, business of,	IR 6.80
. . notice by advertisement,	IR 6.85
. . power to call,	IR 6.81
. . quorum,	IR 6.92
. . record of proceedings,	IR 6.95
. . requisitioned meetings,	IR 6.83
. . resolutions,	IR 6.88
. . suspension of,	IR 6.90
. . venue of,	IR 6.86
. . voting rights,	IR 6.93
. creditors' petition	
. . action to follow making of order,	IR 6.34
. . adjournment of hearing on,	IR 6.29
. . amendment of title of proceedings,	IR 6.35
. . amendment of,	IR 6.22
. . change of carriage of,	IR 6.31
. . Chief Land Registrar, notice to,	IR 6.13
. . creditor with security,	IA 269
. . death of debtor,	IR 6.16

1153

Bankruptcy—continued   **Provision**
- . . decision on hearing, ... IR 6.25
- . . dismissal sought by petitioner, ... IR 6.32
- . . expedited petition, ...IA 270
- . . extension of time for hearing, ... IR 6.28
- . . grounds for, ... IA 267
- . . hearing of, ... IR 6.18
- . . identification of debt, ... IR 6.8
- . . identification of debtor, ... IR 6.7
- . . jurisdiction, ...IR 6.9
- . . list of appearances, ...IR 6.24
- . . moneylenders, and, ...IR 6.20
- . . multiple debtors, ... IR 6.19
- . . non-appearance of creditor, ...IR 6.26
- . . notice by persons intending to appear, ...IR 6.23
- . . old bankruptcy notices, ...IR 6.36
- . . opposition by debtor, ... IR 6.21
- . . procedure for presentation and filing, ...IR 6.10
- . . proceedings on, ...IA 271
- . . proof of service, ... IR 6.15
- . . security for costs, ... IR 6.17
- . . service of, ... IR 6.14
- . . settlement and content of bankruptcy order, ... IR 6.33
- . . statement of affairs, ... IR 6.58—IR 6.66
- . . statutory demand, ...IA 268
- . . substitution of petitioner, ... IR 6.30
- . . vacating registration on dismissal of, ...IR 6.27
- . . verification, ...IR 6.11
- . . withdrawal sought by petitioner, ... IR 6.32
- . criminal bankruptcy
- . . application of rules, ... IR 6.233—IR 6.234
- . . interim receivership, ... IR 6.231
- . . notice of bankruptcy order, ... IR 6.232
- . . Official Petitioner, status and functions of, ...IR 6.230
- . . pre-commencement bankruptcy, ...EA Sch.19, para.6
- . . presentation of petition, ... IR 6.229
- . . proof of debts, ...IR 6.232
- . debtor's petition
- . . action on report of insolvency practitioner, ... IA 274
- . . action to follow order, ... IR 6.46
- . . admission of insolvency, ... IR 6.39
- . . amendment of title of proceedings, ...IR 6.49
- . . appointment of insolvency practitioner, ...IA 273

    Provision
- . . certificate of summary administration, ...IR 6.48, IR 6.50
- . . Chief Land Registrar, notice to, ...IR 6.43
- . . expenses of voluntary arrangement, and, ... IR 6.46A
- . . grounds of, ... IA 272
- . . identification of debtor, ...IR 6.38
- . . insolvency practitioner, report of, ... IR 6.44
- . . jurisdiction, ...IR 6.40
- . . official receiver's duty in summary administration, ... IR 6.49
- . . presentation and filing of, ... IR 6.42
- . . settlement and content of bankruptcy order, ... IR 6.45
- . . statement of affairs, . IR 6.41, IR 6.68—IR 6.72
- . . summary administration, ... IA 275
- . default in connection with voluntary arrangement, ... IA 276
- . director, leave to act as
- . . application for, ... IR 6.203
- . . court's order on application, ... IR 6.205
- . . official receiver, report of, ... IR 6.204
- . discharge
- . . application by bankrupt, ... IR 6.217
- . . bankrupt's debts surviving, ... IR 6.223
- . . by order of court, ... IA 280
- . . certificate of, ... IR 6.220
- . . costs, ... IR 6.222
- . . deferment of issue pending appeal, ...IR 6.221
- . . effect of, ...IA 281
- . . lifting of suspension, ... IR 6.216
- . . official receiver, report of, ... IR 6.218
- . . order of, ... IR 6.219
- . . post-discharge restrictions, ...IA 281A
- . . suspension of, ... IR 6.215
- . disclaimers, and
- . . additional notices of, ... IR 6.180
- . . application for leave to disclaim, ... IR 6.182
- . . declaration of interest in property, ...IR 6.184
- . . duty to keep court informed, ... IR 6.181
- . . interested persons, application by, ...IR 6.183
- . . interested persons, communication to, ...IR 6.179
- . . trustee's notice of, ... IR 6.178
- . . validity, presumption of, ... IR 6.185

Index

Provision

. . vesting of disclaimed
property, ... IR 6.186
. duration of, ... IA 279, EA 256, EA Sch.19
. exempt property, replacement of
. . money in lieu of sale, ... IR 6.188
. . replacement property, purchase
of, ... IR 6.187
. formal defects, ... IA 377
. forms for, ... IR Sch.4
. income payment agreements
. . acceptance of, ... IR 6.193B
. . approval of, ... IR 6.193A
. . variation of, ... IR 6.194
. income payment orders
. . action to follow making of, ... IR 6.190
. . administration of, ... IR 6.192
. . application for, ... IR 6.189
. . pre-commencement
bankruptcy, ... EA Sch.19, para.7
. . review of order, ... IR 6.193
. . variation of, ... IR 6.191
. individual voluntary
arrangement, conversion of, IR 5.62—IR 5.64
. inland revenue official, order to
. . application for, ... IR 6.194
. . custody of documents, ... IR 6.196
. . making and service of, ... IR 6.195
. insolvency districts, ... IA 374
. interim receiver
. . application for appointment
of, ... IR 6.51
. . appointment, order of, ... IR 6.52
. . deposit, requirement for, ... IR 6.53
. . remuneration, ... IR 6.56
. . security, and, ... IR 6.54, IR 6.55
. . termination of appointment, ... IR 6.57
. interpretation, and, ... IA 380—IA 385
. jurisdiction, ... IA 373
. justice of the peace
. . disqualification from acting
as, ... EA 265
. Member State liquidator, notice
to, ... IR 6.238—IR 6.239
. mortgaged property
. . claim by mortgagee of land, ... IR 6.197
. . court power to order sale, ... IR 6.198
. . proceeds of sale, ... IR 6.199
. notice of conclusion of
investigations, ... IR 6.214A
. offences
. . absconding, ... IA 358
. . concealment of property, ... IA 354

Provision

. . false statements, ... IA 356
. . falsification of books, ... IA 355
. . fraudulent dealing with
property obtained on
credit, ... IA 359
. . fraudulent disposal of
property, ... IA 357
. . innocent intention, defence of, ... IA 352
. . non disclosure, ... IA 353
. . obtaining credit, ... IA 360
. official receiver
. . enforcement of trustee's
obligations to, ... IR 6.149
. . release of, ... IR 6.136, IR 6.137A
. petitions for
. . conditions to be satisfied, IA 265—IA 266
. . consolidation of, ... IR 6.236
. . criminal bankruptcy orders,
and, ... IA 277
. . persons entitled to present, ... IA 264
. pre-commencement bankruptcy,
discharge from, ... EA Sch.19, para.4
. prior transactions, adjustment of
. . apprenticeships, and, ... IA 348
. . contracts to which bankrupt is
party, ... IA 345
. . distress, and, ... IA 347
. . enforcement procedures, ... IA 346
. . excessive pension
contributions, ... IA 342A—IA 342C
. . extortionate credit
transactions, ... IA 343
. . general assignment of book
debts, avoidance of, ... IA 344
. . liens on books,
unenforceability of, ... IA 349
. . pension-sharing, ... IA 342D—IA 342F
. . preferences, ... IA 340—IA 342
. . transactions at undervalue, ...IA 339, IA 341, IA 342
. post-discharge restrictions, ... EA 257
. proof of debts
. . admission and rejection for
dividend, ... IR 6.104
. . appeal against decision, ... IR 6.105
. . claims established by
affidavit, ... IR 6.99
. . contents of, ... IR 6.98
. . costs of, ... IR 6.100
. . expunging of by court, ... IR 6.107
. . inspection of proof, ... IR 6.101
. . licensed moneylender, proof
of, ... IR 6.102

1155

Index

Bankruptcy—continued   **Provision**
- . . prove, meaning of, ... IR 6.96
- . . supply of forms, ... IR 6.97
- . . transmission of to trustee, ... IR 6.103
- . . variation of, ... IR 6.106
- . . withdrawal of, ... IR 6.106
- . protection of bankrupt's estate, IA 283—IA 291
- . public examination of bankrupt
- . . adjournment of, ... IR 6.176
- . . bankrupt unfit for, ... IR 6.174
- . . creditors' request for, ... IR 6.173
- . . expenses of, ... IR 6.177
- . . order for, ... IR 6.172
- . . procedure at hearing, ... IR 6.175
- . quantification of claims
- . . debts payable at future time, ... IR 6.114
- . . discounts, ... IR 6.110
- . . foreign currency debts, ... IR 6.111
- . . interest, ... IR 6.113
- . . negotiable instruments, ... IR 6.108
- . . periodical payments, ... IR 6.112
- . . secured creditors, ... IR 6.109
- . rights of occupation, and
- . . bankrupts, ... IA 337
- . . bankrupt's spouse, ... IA 336
- . . premises occupied by bankrupt, ... IA 338
- . rights under trusts of land, and, ... IA 335A
- . second bankruptcy
- . . delivery up to later trustee, ... IR 6.227
- . . duty of existing trustee, ... IR 6.226
- . . existing trustee's expenses, ... IR 6.228
- . . pre-commencement bankruptcy, ... EA Sch.19, para.5
- . secured creditors
- . . realisation of security by debtor, ... IR 6.119
- . . redemption by trustee, ... IR 6.117
- . . surrender for non-disclosure, ... IR 6.116
- . . test of security's value, ... IR 6.118
- . . value of security, ... IR 6.115
- . solicitors, and, ... IR 6.235
- . special manager
- . . accounting by, ... IR 6.170
- . . appointment of, ... IR 6.167
- . . remuneration of, ... IR 6.167
- . . security, and, ... IR 6.168, IR 6.169
- . . termination of appointment, ... IR 6.171
- . stamp duty, exemption from, ... IA 378
- . statement of affairs
- . . creditor's petition, and, .. IR 6.58—IR 6.66
- . . debtor's petition, ... IR 6.68—IR 6.72

        Provision
- . statutory demand
- . . application to set aside, ... IR 6.4
- . . form and content of, ... IR 6.1
- . . hearing of application to set aside, ... IR 6.5
- . . information to be given in, ... IR 6.2
- . . proof of service, ... IR 6.11
- . . service requirements, ... IR 6.3
- . time limits, ... IA 376
- . trustees in bankruptcy
- . . acquisition by trustee of control, ... IA 311
- . . adjustment between earlier and later bankruptcy estates, ... IA 335
- . . administration by, ... IA 306—IA 313A
- . . appointment, . IA 296, IR 6.120—IR 6.124
- . . bankrupt's estate, distribution of, ... IA 322—IA 322
- . . control of, ... IA 301—IA 304
- . . court power to set aside transactions of, ... IR 6.147
- . . creditors' power to requisition meetings, ... IA 294
- . . death of, ... IR 6.143
- . . duties of bankrupt in relation to, ... IA 333
- . . failure of meeting to appoint, ... IA 295
- . . general functions of, ... IA 305
- . . hand-over of property to, ... IR 6.125
- . . obligation to surrender control to, ... IA 312
- . . official receiver, enforcement of obligations to, ... IR 6.149
- . . onerous property, disclaimer of, ... IA 315—IA 321
- . . powers of, ... IA 314
- . . qualification, loss of, ... IR 6.144
- . . release of, . IA 299, IR 6.135, IR 6.137, IR 6.137A
- . . removal of, ... IA 298, IR 6.129—IR 6.134
- . . remuneration, ... IR 6.138—IR 6.142
- . . resignation of, ... IR 6.126—IR 6.128, IR 6.134
- . . second bankruptcy, stay of distribution in case of, ... IA 334
- . . solicitation, rule against, ... IR 6.148
- . . special cases, ... IA 297
- . . summoning of meeting to appoint, ... IA 293
- . . vacancy in office of, ... IA 300
- . . vacation of office, ... IA 298, IR 6.145, IR 6.146
- . utilities supplies, ... IA 372

1156

	Provision
Bankruptcy offences	
. absconding,	IA 358
. concealment of property,	IA 354
. false statements,	IA 356
. falsification of books,	IA 355
. fraudulent dealing with property obtained on credit,	IA 359
. fraudulent disposal of property,	IA 357
. innocent intention, defence of,	IA 352
. non disclosure,	IA 353
. obtaining credit,	IA 360
Bankruptcy orders	
. annulment of	
. . application for,	IR 6.206
. . by bankrupt,	IR 5.51—IR 5.53
. . by official receiver under s.261(2)(b),	IR 5.54—IR 5.56
. . by official receiver under s.263D(3),	IR 5.57—IR 5.59
. . court power to stay proceedings,	IR 6.208
. . court's power,	IA 282
. . creditors, information to,	IR 6.78
. . creditors, notice to,	IR 6.212
. . hearing on,	IR 6.210
. . notice to unproved creditors,	IR 6.209
. . registration, and,	IR 5.60
. . trustee's final account,	IR 5.6, IR 6.214
. . trustee's report,	IR 6.207
. creditor's petition for bankruptcy, and,	IR 6.33
. criminal bankruptcy, and,	IR 6.232
. debtor's petition for bankruptcy, and,	IR 6.45
. individual insolvency register	
. . deletion from,	IR 6A.5
. . entry to,	IR 6A.4
. register of,	IR 6.223A—IR 6.223C
Bankruptcy restriction order	
. application for,	IR 6.241
. bankrupt's evidence,	IR 6.243
. devolution, and,	IA 426B
. duration of,	IA Sch.4A, para.4
. grounds for making,	IA Sch.4A, para.2
. interim orders,	IA Sch.4A, paras 5—6, IR 6.245—IR 6.248
. making of,	IR 6.244
. pre-commencement bankruptcy,	EA Sch.19, para.8
. service on defendant,	IR 6.242
. timing of application for,	IA Sch.4A, para.3

	Provision
Bankruptcy restrictions register	
. deletions from,	IR 6A.7
. entries to,	IR 6A.6
. rectification of,	IR 6A.8
Bankruptcy restrictions undertaking	
. acceptance of,	IR 6.249
. annulment, effect of,	IA Sch.4A, paras 10—11
. application for annulment of,	IR 6.251
. devolution, and,	IA 426B
. notification to court,	IR 6.250
. offer of,	IA Sch.4A, paras 7—9
. pre-commencement bankruptcy,	EA Sch.19, para.8
. registration of,	IA Sch.4A, para.12
Banks	
. rule-making powers relating to,	IA 422
. winding up of,	IR 4.72
Bodies corporate	
. offences by,	IA 432
. receivers (England and Wales), and,	IA 30
Book debts, avoidance of	
. adjustment of prior transactions in bankruptcy,	IA 344
Books of company	
. use in evidence in winding up proceedings,	IA 191
Business day	
. meaning,	IA 251

C

	Provision
Calls on contributories	
. winding up, and	
. . by court,	IR 4.204
. . by liquidation committee,	IR 4.203
. . by liquidator,	IR 4.202
. . enforcement of,	IR 4.205
. . making of,	IR 4.205
Capital, return of	
. winding up, and,	IR 4.221—IR 4.222
Capital markets	
. prohibition on appointment of administrative receiver, and,	IA 72B
Certificate of compliance	
. petition for winding up,	IR 4.14

Index

Chairman   *Provision*
. company meetings
.. administration, and, ... *IR 2.31(2)*, 2.49(2)
.. winding up, and, ... IR 4.55, IR 4.64
. creditors' committee
.. administration, and, ... *IR 2.35*, IR 2.53
.. bankruptcy, and, ... IR 6.154
.. receivership, and, ... IR 3.19
. creditors' meetings
.. administration, and, ... *IR 2.20*, IR 2.36
.. bankruptcy, and, ... IR 6.82
.. company voluntary
    arrangements, and, ... IR 1.14, IR 1.15,
                                            IR 1.19(5)
.. individual voluntary
    arrangement, and, ... IR 5.19
.. receivership, and, ... IR 3.10
.. winding up, and, ... IR 4.55
. liquidation committee, ... IR 4.157

Charge, attachment of
. receiver
.. cessation of appointment of, ... IA 62(6)
.. mode of appointment of, ... IA 53(7)

Charged property
. administrative receiver, and
.. disposal by, ... IA 43, IR 3.31
. administration, and
.. disposal of, ... *IR 2.51*, IR 2.66
.. power to deal with, ... *IA 15*
. disposal during moratorium, ... IR 1.43
. receivers (England and Wales),
    and, ... IA 40

Chattel leasing agreements
. administration order, and
.. creditors' meetings, and, .. *IR 2.27*, IR 2.42
.. disposal of goods in Scotland, ... IA 16(2)
.. effect of application, ... *IA 10(4)*
. meaning, ... IA 251

Chief Land Registrar
. notice to
.. creditor's petition for
    bankruptcy, ... IR 6.13
.. debtor's petition for
    bankruptcy, and, ... IR 6.43

Claims
. admission or rejection of by
    creditors' meeting
.. administration, and, ... *IR 2.23*, IR 2.39
.. fast track individual voluntary
    arrangement, and, ... IR 5.42

                                                Provision
.. individual voluntary
    arrangement, and, ... IR 5.22
.. receivership, and, ... IR 3.12
. quantification of *See*
    Quantification of claims

Committee members'
    representatives
. creditors' committee
.. administration, and, ... *IR 2.37*, IR 2.55
.. bankruptcy, and, ... IR 6.156
.. receivership, and, ... IR 3.21
. liquidation committee, ... IR 4.159

Community patents
. EC Regulation on Insolvency
    Proceedings, and, ... ER 12

Companies Registrar
. termination of administration,
    and, ... IA Sch.B1, para.86

Company affairs
. investigation of in
    administration
.. information supplied by
    administrator, ... *IA 21*
.. statement of affairs, ... *IA 22*
. investigation of in winding up
.. official receiver, investigation
    by, ... IA 132
.. public examination of officers, ... IA
                                            133—IA
                                                134
.. statement of affairs, and, ... IA 131
. report on, ... *IR 2.2*
. statement of affairs *see*
    Statement of affairs

Company books
. falsification of
.. malpractice during winding up,
    and, ... IA 209
. inspection of, ... IA 155
. use as evidence in winding up
    proceedings, ... IA 191

Company in liquidation
. administration orders, and, ... *IA 8(4)*

Company insolvency
. *and see under individual*
    headings
. administration orders
.. administrator's proposals, ... IA 23—IA 25
.. administrators, ... IA 13—IA 20

1158

Index

	Provision
. . company's affairs, investigation of,	IA 21—IA 22
. . creditors' committee,	IA 26
. . creditors' interests, protection of,	IA 27
. . making of,	IA 8—IA 12
. company voluntary arrangements	
. . consideration and implementation of proposal,	IA 4—IA 7B
. . proposals for,	IA 1—IA 3
. management of insolvent companies,	IA 233—IA 237
. office holders,	IA 230—IA 232
. preferential debts,	IA 386—IA 387
. prior transactions, adjustment of,	IA 238—IA 246
. provisions capable of inclusion in rules,	IA Sch.8
. receivership	
. . administrative receivers, prohibition on appointment of,	IA 72A—IA 72H
. . receivers (Scotland),	IA 50—IA 71
. . receivers and managers (England and Wales),	IA 28—IA 49
. . receivers' powers,	IA 72
. rule-making powers, and,	IA 411
. winding up (registered companies)	
. . affidavits, and,	IA 200
. . application for leave to proceed, costs of,	IA 199
. . assets, power to make over to employees,	IA 187
. . attachment, effect of,	IA 183
. . commission for receiving evidence,	IA 197
. . company books, use in evidence,	IA 191
. . contributories,	IA 74—IA 83
. . contributories' meetings, and,	IA 195
. . court, by,	IA 117—IA 162
. . creditors' meetings, and,	IA 195
. . creditors' voluntary winding up,	IA 97—IA 106
. . diligence, effect of,	IA 185
. . disclaimers,	IA 178—IA 182
. . dissolution following,	IA 201—IA 205
. . examination of persons, court orders for,	IA 198

	Provision
. . execution, effect of,	IA 183
. . interest on debts,	IA 189
. . judicial notice of court documents,	IA 196
. . liquidators,	IA 163—IA 174
. . malpractice during,	IA 206—IA 219
. . members' voluntary winding up,	IA 91—IA 96
. . modes of,	IA 73
. . notification of,	IA 188
. . pending liquidations, information on,	IA 192
. . preferential debts,	IA 175—IA 176
. . rescission of contracts,	IA 186
. . resolutions passed at adjourned meetings,	IA 194
. . sheriff, duties of,	IA 184
. . special managers,	IA 177
. . stamp duty, exemption from,	IA 190
. . unclaimed dividends,	IA 193
. . voluntary winding up,	IA 84—IA 90, IA 107—IA 116
. winding up (unregistered companies),	IA 220—IA 229

Company meetings
. administration order, and,	IR 2.31, IR 2.49
. company voluntary arrangements, and	
. . attendance by company officers,	IR 1.16
. . chairman at,	IR 1.14
. . proxy holder as chairman,	IR 1.15
. . requisite majorities,	IR 1.20
. . summoning of,	IA 3, IR 1.13
. . voting rights,	IR 1.18
. evidence of proceedings,	IR 12.5
. winding up, and	
. . adjournment of,	IR 4.65
. . attendance of company personnel,	IR 4.58
. . chairman as proxy holder,	IR 4.64
. . chairman at,	IR 4.55
. . court power to call,	IA 195
. . expenses of summoning,	IR 4.61
. . first meeting,	IR 4.50, IR 4.52
. . notice by advertisement,	IR 4.59
. . power to call,	IR 4.54
. . quorum at,	IR 4.66
. . record of proceedings,	IR 4.71
. . requisitioned meetings,	IR 4.57
. . resolutions of,	IR 4.63
. . suspension of,	IR 4.65

Index

Company meetings—continued   **Provision**
  . venue, ...IR 4.60
  . voting rights, ...IR 4.69
. winding up by court, and, ...IA 157

Company name
. malpractice during winding up,
    and, . IA 216, IA 217, IR 4.22—IR 4.230

Company officers
. attendance at creditors' or
    members' meetings, ...IR 1.16, IR 4.58
. misconduct by
  . malpractice during winding up,
    and, ...IA 208
. prosecution of delinquent
  . company voluntary
    arrangements, and, ...IA 7A
  . malpractice during winding up,
    and, ... IA 218, IA 219

Company property
. *see also* **Assets**
. control of by administrator, ...*IA 17(1)*
. distribution of in voluntary
    winding up, ...IA 107
. management of insolvent
    companies, and, ...IA 234

Company voluntary
    arrangements
. administrator's proposal
  . notice to nominee, ...IR 1.12
  . preparation of, ...IR 1.10
  . summoning of meetings, ...IR 1.11
. approval of
  . by members meetings, IA Sch.A1, para.31
  . decisions, requirements for, ...IA 4A
  . effect of, ...IA 5, IA Sch.A1, para.37
  . revocation or suspension of, ...IA 6(5)
. challenge of decisions
    concerning, ... IA Sch.A1, para.38
. challenges to director's
    decisions, ...IA Sch.A1, para.40
. completion of, ...IR 1.29
. conversion into winding up
  . affidavits, ...IR 1.32
  . application for, ...IR 1.31
  . court powers, and, ...IR 1.33
. creditors' meetings
  . attendance by company
    officers, ... IR 1.16
  . chairman at, ...IR 1.14
  . proxy holder as chairman, ...IR 1.15
  . requisite majorities, ...IR 1.29

                       Provision
  . summoning of, ...IR 1.13
  . voting rights, ...IR 1.17
. directors' proposals
  . contents of, ... IR 1.3
  . disclosure for assistance of
    nominee, ... IR 1.6
  . nominee's report on, ... IR 1.7
  . notice to intended nominee, ... IR 1.4
  . preparation of, ...IR 1.2
  . replacement of, ... IR 1.8
  . statement of affairs, ...IR 1.5
  . summoning of meetings, ...IR 1.9
. effectiveness of decisions
    concerning, ... IA Sch.A1, para.36
. extension of, ...IA Sch.A1, paras 32—34
. forms for, ...IR Sch.4
. implementation of
  . accounts and records,
    production of to Secretary
    of State, ...IR 1.27
  . completion of arrangement, ... IR 1.29
  . costs, ...IR 1.28
  . expenses, ...IR 1.28
  . fees, ...IR 1.28
  . reports of meetings, ...IR 1.24
  . resolutions to follow proposal, ... IR 1.22
  . supervisor, and, ... IA Sch.A1, para.39
  . supervisor, hand-over of
    property to, ...IR 1.23
  . supervisor's accounts and
    reports, ... IR 1.26
. liquidator's proposals
  . notice to nominee, ...IR 1.12
  . preparation of, ...IR 1.10
  . summoning of meetings, ...IR 1.11
. Member State liquidator, notice
    to, ... IR 1.34
. members' meetings
  . attendance by company
    officers, ... IR 1.16
  . chairman at, ...IR 1.14
  . conduct of, ... IA Sch.A1, para.30
  . proxy holder as chairman, ...IR 1.15
  . requisite majorities, ... IR 1.20
  . summoning of, ...IA Sch.A1, para.29, IR 1.13
  . voting rights, ...IR 1.18
. moratorium committee, . IA Sch.A1, para.35
. moratoriums
  . consideration of proposals,
    and, ... IR 1.48—IR 1.54
  . directors' proposals, and, ... IA 2000 1

Provision	Provision
.. eligible companies, ... IA 1A	**Concealment of property**
.. Financial Services Authority,	. bankruptcy offences, and, ... IA 354
and, ... IA Sch.A1, para.44	**Concurrent insolvency**
.. floating charge documents,	**proceedings**
void provisions in, IA Sch.A1, para.43	. restrictions on, ... IR 7.56
.. nominees, and, ... IR 1.44—IR 1.47	**Conditional sale agreements**
.. obtaining of, ... IR 1.35—IR 1.42	. administration order, and
.. proceedings during, ... IR 1.43	.. creditors' meetings, and, ..IR 2.27, IR 2.42
. nominees	.. disposal of goods in Scotland, ... IA 16(2)
.. disclosure by directors for	.. effect of application, ... IA 10(4)
assistance of, ... IR 1.6	**Confidentiality**
.. meaning of, ... IA 1(2)	. documents, of, ...IR 12.13
.. notice of administrator's	**Consolidated Fund**
proposals, ... IR 1.12	. public administration, and, ... IA 408
.. notice of directors' proposals, ... IR 1.4	**Contracts**
.. notice of liquidator's proposals	. liability for
.. procedure where not	.. administrative receiver, ... IA 44
administrator or	.. receivers (England and Wales),
liquidator, ... IA 2	and, ...IA 37
.. report on directors' proposals, ... IR 1.7	.. receivers (Scotland), and, ... IA 57
.. summoning of meetings by, ... IA 3	. rescission of
. offences, ... IA Sch.A1, paras 41—42	.. winding up, and, ... IA 186
. proposals for	**Contributories**
.. administrator or liquidator, by, ... IR 1.10—IR 1.12	. arrest of absconding, ... IA 158
.. approval, effect of, ...IA 5	. bankruptcy of, ... IA 82
.. approval, revocation or	. call on
suspension of, ... IA 6(5)	.. by court, ... IR 4.204
.. challenging decisions, ... IA 6	.. by liquidation committee, ... IR 4.203
.. decisions of meetings, ... IA 4	.. by liquidator, ...IR 4.202
.. directors, by, ... IR 1.2—IR 1.9	.. enforcement of, ... IR 4.205
.. false representations, ... IA 6A, IR 1.30	.. making of, ...IR 4.205
.. implementation of, ...IA 7	.. winding up by court, ... IA 161
.. nominee procedure where not	. liquidation committee,
administrator or	establishment of, ...IR 4.154
liquidator, ... IA 2	. liquidator, appointment of, ... IA 139
.. persons entitled to propose, ... IA 1	. meaning, ...IA 251
.. premature end to arrangement, ...IA 7B	. prosecution of
.. proceedings to obtain	.. malpractice during winding up,
agreement on, ... IR 1.21	and, ... IA 218, IA 219
.. prosecution of delinquent	. winding up, and
officers, ... IA 7A	.. bankruptcy, effect of, ... IA 82
.. summoning of meetings, ... IA 3	.. calls on, ...IR 4.202—IR 4.205
. revocation or suspension of, ... IR 1.25	.. companies registered under
. supervisor	Companies Act s.680, ... IA 83
.. implementation of proposal	.. death of member, and, ...IA 81
by, ...IA 7	.. directors, liability of past, ...IA 76
. termination of, ... IR 1.29	.. directors with unlimited
Compliance, certificate of	liability, ...IA 75
. petition for winding up, ... IR 4.14	.. information to, ...IR 4.43—IR 4.49A
	.. liability, nature of, ... IA 80

Contributories—continued

.. limited company formerly unlimited, ...IA 77
.. list, settlement of, ... IR 4.195—IR 4.201
.. meaning, ... IA 79
.. members, liability of past and present, ... IA 74
.. petition for, ... IR 4.22—IR 4.24
.. shareholders, liability of past, ... IA 76
.. substitution for petitioner, ... IR 4.19
.. unlimited company formerly limited, ... IA 78
.. unregistered companies, ... IA 226
. winding up by court
.. adjustment of rights of, ... IA 154
.. debts due from, ... IA 149
.. list, settlement of, ...IA 148
.. orders on, ... IA 152

Contributories' meetings *See* **Company meetings**

Costs

. administration, and, ... IR 12.2
. application of CPR, ... IR 7.33
. applications for, ... IR 7.40
. assessment by detailed procedure, ... IR 7.34
. award against official receiver, ...IR 7.39
. bankruptcy, and, ... IR 6.224
. company voluntary arrangements, and, ... IR 1.28
. creditor's petition for bankruptcy, and, ... IR 6.17
. discharge of bankruptcy, ...IR 6.222
. EC Regulation on Insolvency Proceedings, and, ... ER 23
. fast track individual voluntary arrangement, and, ... IR 5.48
. final costs certificate, ... IR 7.42
. individual voluntary arrangements, and, ... IR 5.33
. insolvent estate, costs paid otherwise than, ... IR 7.38
. petitions presented by insolvents, ... IR 7.37
. procedure where detailed assessment required, ... IR 7.35
. proof of debts, ...IR 6.100
. sheriff, of, ... IR 7.36
. winding up, and, ... IR 12.2
. witnesses, and, ... IR 7.41

Court

. administration orders, and
.. appointment of administrator, ..IR 2.2—IR 2.14
.. duty where company in receivership, ...*IA 9(3)*
.. remuneration of administrator, and, ... IR 2.49, IR 2.108
. company voluntary arrangements, and
.. replacement of nominee, ... IA 2(4)
.. report by nominee, ... IA 2(2)
.. report of decisions of meetings, ... IA 4(6)
. cooperation between different courts, ...IA 426
. directions, application for
.. receivers (England and Wales), and, ...IA 35
. procedures *See* **Court procedure**
. proof of debts, expunging of
.. administration, and, ... IR 2.80
.. bankruptcy, and, ... IR 6.107
.. winding up, and, ... IR 4.85
. receivers
.. appointment in Scotland, ... IA 54
.. appointment in England and Wales, ... IA 32
.. power to appoint, ... IA 51(2)
.. remuneration, fixing of, ... IA 36
. trustees in bankruptcy, appointment of, ...IR 6.121
. winding up *See* **Winding up by court**

Court powers

. administration orders, and
.. appointment of administrator, ...*IA 13(2)*
.. conversion to winding up, ... *IR 2.61*, IR 2.132
.. expunging of proof of debts, ...IR 2.80(2)
.. petitions for, ... *IA 9(4)*
.. statement of affairs, ...IR 2.30(2)
. bankruptcy, and
.. arrest, power of, ...IA 364
.. general powers of, ...IA 363
.. inquiry into bankrupt's dealings, ...IA 366—IA 368
.. production of documents by inland revenue, ... IA 369
.. redirection of bankrupt's letters, ... IA 371
.. seizure of bankrupt's property, ... IA 365

1162

	Provision		Provision
. . special manager, appointment of,	IA 370	. confirmation of creditors' voluntary winding up,	IR 7.62
. company voluntary arrangements, and		. costs	
. . appointment of supervisor,	IA 7(5)	. . application of CPR,	IR 7.33
. . challenging decisions of meetings,	IA 6(4)	. . applications for,	IR 7.40
		. . assessment by detailed procedure,	IR 7.34
. . conversion into winding up,	IR 1.33	. . award against official receiver,	IR 7.39
. . revocation or suspension of approval,	IA 6(5)	. . final costs certificate,	IR 7.42
		. . insolvent estate, costs paid otherwise than,	IR 7.38
. . sisting of winding up or administration proceedings,	IA 5(3)	. . petitions presented by insolvents,	IR 7.37
. . supervisor's accounts and records,	IR 1.26(5)	. . procedure where detailed assessment required,	IR 7.35
. receivers (Scotland), and,	IA 63	. . sheriff, of,	IR 7.36
. receivership, and		. . witnesses, and,	IR 7.41
. . disclosure in statement of affairs,	IR 3.5(2)	. disclosure,	IR 7.60
		. enforcement procedures	
. voluntary winding up,	IA 113	. . compliance with rules,	IR 7.20
. winding up		. . court orders, and,	IR 7.19
. . *see also* **Winding up by court**		. . warrants,	IR 7.21—IR 7.25
. . disclaimers, and,	IA 181—IA 182, IR 4.194	. formal defects,	IR 7.55
		. forms for,	IR Sch.4
. . power to call company or creditors' meetings,	IA 195	. incapax	
		. . appointment of other persons to act for,	IR 7.44—IR 7.46
. winding up of unregistered companies,	IA 227	. insolvency practitioner's solicitor,	IR 7.54
Court procedure		. Member State liquidator, notice to,	IR 7.63
. affidavits,	IR 7.57	. office copies,	IR 7.61
. appeals in insolvency proceedings		. payment into court,	IR 7.59
. . bankruptcy, and,	IR 7.48	. records and returns	
. . official receiver, decisions, of,	IR 7.50	. . court records,	IR 7.27
. . procedure on,	IR 7.49	. . file of court proceedings,	IR 7.30
. . Secretary of State, decisions of,	IR 7.50	. . gazette notices and advertisements, filing of,	IR 7.32
. . winding up, and,	IR 7.47	. . inspection of records,	IR 7.28
. applications		. . returns by Secretary of State,	IR 7.29
. . adjournment of hearings,	IR 7.10	. . right to inspect the file,	IR 7.31
. . affidavit evidence, use of,	IR 7.7	. . title of proceedings,	IR 7.26
. . directions relating to,	IR 7.10	. right of attendance,	IR 7.53
. . disapplication of s.176A,	IR 7.3A	. rights of audience,	IR 7.52
. . ex parte hearings,	IR 7.5	. security in court,	IR 7.58
. . filing and service of affidavits,	IR 7.8	. shorthand writers	
. . filing and service of,	IR 7.4	. . cost of shorthand note,	IR 7.18
. . form and content of,	IR 7.3	. . nomination and appointment of,	IR 7.16
. . hearing of,	IR 7.6		
. . use of reports,	IR 7.9	. . remuneration,	IR 7.17, IR Sch.3
. concurrent proceedings, restrictions on,	IR 7.56	. transfer of proceedings between	
		. . applications for transfer,	IR 7.13

Court procedure—continued	**Provision**
. . consequential transfer of other proceedings,	IR 7.15
. . general powers of transfer,	IR 7.11
. . procedures following order for,	IR 7.14
. . proceedings commenced in wrong court,	IR 7.12

Creditors
- admission of claims, ... IR 1.50
- approval of
  - . . fast track individual voluntary arrangement, and, ... IR 5.40
- distributions to
  - . . division of unsold assets, ... IR 2.71
  - . . notice of intention to declare and distribute dividend, ... IR 2.68
  - . . ranking of debts, ... IR 2.69
  - . . supplementary provisions, ... IR 2.70
- EC Regulation on Insolvency Proceedings, and
  - . . content of lodgement of claim, ... ER 41
  - . . duty to inform, ... ER 40
  - . . language of information to, ... ER 42
  - . . right to lodge claims, ... ER 39
- exclusion where not proved on time, ... IA 153
- false claim to status of, ... IR 12.18
- false representations to
  - . . malpractice during winding up, and, ... IA 211
- information on bankruptcy, and
  - . . annulment of bankruptcy order, and, ... IR 6.78
  - . . entitlement to be informed, ... IR 6.74
  - . . generally, ... IR 6.77
  - . . official receiver's general duty, ... IR 6.73
  - . . statement of affairs dispensed with, ... IR 6.76
  - . . statement of affairs lodged, ... IR 6.75
- information on winding up, and, ... IR 4.43—IR 4.49A
- list of, right to have, ... IR 12.17
- notice to, ... *IR 2.30*, IR 2.46
- progress reports to, ... IR 2.47
- proposals to
  - . . annexation of statement of affairs, ... *IR 2.16*
  - . . notice to members of, ... *IR 2.17*
- protection of interests of, ... *IA 27*
- remuneration of administrator, and, ... *IR 2.50*, IR 2.109
- requisition of creditors' meeting by, ... *IR 2.21*, IR 2.37
- substitution for petitioner in winding up, ... IR 4.19
- termination of administration, ... IA Sch.B1, para.81, IR 2.115
- transactions in fraud of, ... IA 207, IA 423—IA 425
- voluntary winding up by, ... IA 97—IA 106

Creditors' committee
- administration, and
  - . . administrator, summoning of, ... *IA 26*
  - . . chairman of, ... *IR 2.35*, IR 2.53
  - . . committee-members' representatives, ... IR 2.37, IR 2.55
  - . . constitution of, ... *IR 2.32*, IR 2.50
  - . . creditors' meeting, establishment by, ... *IA 26*
  - . . formal defects, ... *IR 2.46A*, IR 2.65
  - . . formalities of establishment of, ... *IR 2.33*, IR 2.51
  - . . functions and meetings of, ... *IR 2.34*, IR 2.52
  - . . information from administrator, ... *IR 2.44*, IR 2.62
  - . . members' dealings with company, ... *IR 2.46*, IR 2.64
  - . . members' expenses, ... *IR 2.45*, IR 2.63
  - . . procedure at, ... *IR 2.42*, IR 2.60
  - . . quorum of, ... *IR 2.36*, IR 2.54
  - . . removal from, ... *IR 2.40*, IR 2.58
  - . . resignation, ... *IR 2.38*, IR 2.56
  - . . resolutions by post, ... *IR 2.43*, IR 2.61
  - . . termination of membership, ... *IR 2.39*, IR 2.57
  - . . vacancies on, ... *IR 2.41*, IR 2.59
- administrative receiver, and, ... IA 49
- bankruptcy, and
  - . . chairman at meetings of, ... IR 6.154
  - . . committee-members' representatives, ... IR 6.156
  - . . control of trustee, ... IA 301
  - . . dealings by members, ... IR 6.165
  - . . expenses of members, ... IR 6.164
  - . . formalities of establishment, ... IR 6.151
  - . . functions vested in Secretary of State, ... IR 6.166
  - . . meetings of, ... IR 6.153
  - . . membership of, ... *IR 2.39(2)*, IR 3.23(2), IR 6.150
  - . . obligations of trustee to, ... IR 6.152

	Provision		Provision
. . postal resolutions,	IR 6.162	. . remuneration of administrator, and,	*IR 2.48*, IR 2.107
. . quorum,	IR 6.155	. . reports and notices resulting from,	*IR 2.29*
. . removal from,	IR 6.159	. . requisition of by creditors,	*IR 2.21*, IR 2.37
. . resignation from,	IR 6.157	. . resolutions of,	*IR 2.28*, IR 2.43
. . termination of membership,	IR 6.158	. . retention of title creditors,	*IR 2.26*
. . trustee's reports to,	IR 6.163	. . secured creditors,	*IR 2.24*, IR 2.40
. . vacancies of,	IR 6.160	. . summoning, procedure for,	*IR 2.18*
. . voting rights,	IR 6.161	. . voting rights,	*IR 2.22*, IR 2.38
. receivers (Scotland), and,	IA 68	. administrators, summoning by,	*IA 17(3)*
. receivership, and		. bankruptcy, and	
. . chairman at,	IR 3.19	. . adjournment of,	IR 6.91
. . committee-members' representatives,	IR 3.21	. . admission and rejection of proofs,	IR 6.94
. . constitution of,	IR 3.16	. . attendance of bankrupt,	IR 6.84
. . formal defects, and,	IR 3.30A	. . chairman as proxy holder,	IR 6.89
. . formalities of establishment,	IR 3.17	. . chairman at,	IR 6.82
. . functions and meetings of,	IR 3.18	. . expenses of summoning,	IR 6.87
. . information from receiver,	IR 3.28	. . first meeting of,	IR 6.79
. . members' dealings with company,	IR 3.30	. . first meeting, business of,	IR 6.80
. . members' expenses,	IR 3.29	. . notice by advertisement,	IR 6.85
. . postal resolutions,	IR 3.27	. . power to call,	IR 6.81
. . procedure at meetings of,	IR 3.26	. . quorum,	IR 6.92
. . quorum,	IR 3.20	. . record of proceedings,	IR 6.95
. . removal from,	IR 3.24	. . removal of trustee,	IR 6.129, IR 6.130
. . resignation from,	IR 3.22	. . remuneration of trustee,	IR 6.140
. . termination of membership,	IR 3.23	. . requisitioned meetings,	IR 6.83
. . vacancies on,	IR 3.25	. . resignation of trustee,	IR 6.126

Creditors' meetings

. administration, and		. . resolutions,	IR 6.88
. . administrator's proposals, consideration of,	*IA 24*, IR 2.34	. . suspension of,	IR 6.90
. . administrator's proposals, revision of,	IR 2.45	. . venue of,	IR 6.86
. . admission of claims,	*IR 2.23*, IR 2.39	. . voting rights,	IR 6.93
. . chairman at,	*IR 2.20*, IR 2.36	. company voluntary arrangements, and	
. . chattel leasing agreements and,	*IR 2.27*, IR 2.42	. . attendance by company officers,	IR 1.16
. . conditional sale agreements, and,	*IR 2.27*, IR 2.42	. . chairman at,	IR 1.14
. . correspondence instead of,	IR 2.48	. . procedure at during moratorium,	IR 1.48
. . creditors' committee, establishment of,	*IA 26*	. . proxy holder as chairman,	IR 1.15
. . generally,	*IR 2.19*, IR 2.35	. . requisite majorities,	IR 1.29
. . hire-purchase agreements, and,	*IR 2.27*, IR 2.42	. . summoning of,	IA 3, IR 1.13
. . minutes of,	*IR 2.28*, IR 2.44	. . voting rights,	IR 1.17, IR 1.49
. . negotiable instrument holders,	*IR 2.25*, IR 2.41	. evidence of proceedings,	IR 12.5
. . notices to creditors,	*IR 2.30*, IR 2.46	. individual voluntary arrangements, and	
. . progress report to creditors,	IR 2.47	. . admission of claims,	IR 5.22
. . rejection of claims,	*IR 2.23*, IR 2.39	. . chairman as proxy holder,	IR 5.20
		. . chairman at,	IR 5.19
		. . challenges to decisions of,	IA 262

Index

Creditors' meetings—continued   **Provision**
.. decisions at, ... IA 258
.. majorities, ... IR 5.23
.. proceedings to obtain
     agreement on proposal, ... IR 5.24
.. reports to, ... IR 5.27
.. summoning of, ..IA 257, IR 5.17—IR 5.18
.. voting rights, ...IR 5.21
. individual voluntary
     arrangement, and
.. moratorium for insolvent
     debtors, and, ... IA 257
. liquidator, appointment of, ... IA 139
. receivership, and
.. adjournment, ... IR 3.14
.. admission and rejection of
     claim, ... IR 3.12
.. chairman at, ... IR 3.10
.. minutes, ... IR 3.15
.. quorum, ... IR 3.13
.. resolutions, ... IR 3.15
.. summoning, procedure for, ...IR 3.9
.. voting rights, ...IR 3.11
. trustees in bankruptcy,
     appointment of, ...IR 6.120
. winding up, and
.. adjournment of, ... IR 4.65
.. admission and rejection of
     proof, ... IR 4.70
.. attendance of company
     personnel, ... IR 4.58
.. chairman as proxy holder, ...IR 4.64
.. chairman at, ... IR 4.55
.. court power to call, ... IA 195
.. creditors' voluntary winding
     up, and, .. IA 98, IR 4.51, IR 4.53—IR
         4.53B, IR 4.56, IR 4.62, IR
         4.68
.. expenses of summoning, ...IR 4.61
.. first meeting, ...IR 4.50, IR 4.52
.. notice by advertisement, ... IR 4.59
.. power to call, ... IR 4.54
.. quorum at, ... IR 4.66
.. record of proceedings, ... IR 4.71
.. requisitioned meetings, ... IR 4.57
.. resolutions of, ... IR 4.63
.. suspension of, ... IR 4.65
.. venue, ...IR 4.60
.. voting rights, ...IR 4.67

**Creditor's petition for
     administration**
. affidavit in support of, .. *IR 2.1(3)*, IR 2.2(3)
. form of, ...*IR 2.4*, IR 2.3
. service of, ...*IR 2.6(3)*

                             Provision
**Creditor's petition for
     bankruptcy**
. action to follow making of
     order, ... IR 6.34
. adjournment of hearing on, ...IR 6.29
. amendment of title of
     proceedings, ... IR 6.35
. amendment of, ... IR 6.22
. change of carriage of, ... IR 6.31
. Chief Land Registrar, notice to, ... IR 6.13
. creditor with security, ... IA 269
. death of debtor, ... IR 6.16
. decision on hearing, ... IR 6.25
. dismissal sought by petitioner, ... IR 6.32
. expedited petition, ...IA 270
. extension of time for hearing, ... IR 6.28
. grounds for, ... IA 267
. hearing of, ... IR 6.18
. identification of debt, ... IR 6.8
. identification of debtor, ... IR 6.7
. jurisdiction, ...IR 6.9
. list of appearances, ...IR 6.24
. moneylenders, and, ...IR 6.20
. multiple debtors, ... IR 6.19
. non-appearance of creditor, ... IR 6.26
. notice by persons intending to
     appear, ... IR 6.23
. old bankruptcy notices, ...IR 6.36
. opposition by debtor, ...IR 6.21
. procedure for presentation and
     filing, ... IR 6.10
. proceedings on, ...IA 271
. proof of service, ... IR 6.15
. security for costs, ... IR 6.17
. service of, ... IR 6.14
. settlement and content of
     bankruptcy order, ...IR 6.33
. statement of affairs
.. accounts, requirement to
     submit, ... IR 6.64
.. accounts, submission and filing
     of, ... IR 6.65
.. expenses of, ... IR 6.63
.. form of, ... IR 6.59
.. further disclosure, ...IR 6.66
.. limited disclosure, ... IR 6.62
.. verification and filing of, ... IR 6.60
. statutory demand, ...IA 268
. substitution of petitioner, ... IR 6.30
. vacating registration on
     dismissal of, ... IR 6.27

1166

	Provision
. verification,	IR 6.11
. withdrawal sought by petitioner,	IR 6.32

Creditors' voluntary winding up
. accounts, submission of, ... IR 4.40, IR 4.41
. conclusion of, ...IR 4.223
. confirmation of, ...IR 7.62
. creditors' meetings, and, IA 98, IR 4.51, IR 4.53—IR 4.53B, IR 4.56, IR 4.62, IR 4.68
. directors' powers, cessation of, ...IA 103
. end of year meetings, ...IA 105
. final meeting, ...IA 106
. liquidation committee, appointment of, ...IA 101
. liquidator
.. appointment of, ...IA 100
.. powers of, ...IA 166
.. vacancy in office of, ...IA 104
. members' voluntary winding up
.. conversion from, ...IA 102
.. distinction from, ...IA 90
. proof of debts, and, ...IR 4.76
. statement of affairs, ...IA 99, IR 4.34, IR 4.34A, IR 4.38
. termination of administration, and, ... IA Sch.B1, para.83, IR 2.117

Criminal bankruptcy
. application of rules, ... IR 6.233—IR 6.234
. distribution of bankrupt's estate, ... IA 327
. interim receivership, ...IR 6.231
. notice of bankruptcy order, ...IR 6.232
. Official Petitioner, status and functions of, ... IR 6.230
. pre-commencement bankruptcy, ... EA Sch.19, para.6
. presentation of petition, ...IR 6.229
. proof of debts, ...IR 6.232

Cross-border insolvency
. model law on, ... IA 2000 14

Crown
. application of IA 1986 to, ... IA 434

D

Death
. administrative receiver, of, ... IR 3.34
. administrator, of, ... *IR 2.54*, IR 2.124

	Provision

Debenture, secured
. meaning, ... IA 70(1)

Debt
. avoidance of
.. transactions defrauding creditors, ... IA 423—IA 425
. identification of
.. creditor's petition for bankruptcy, and, ... IR 6.8
. priority of
.. receivers (Scotland), and, ...IA 59
. proof of *See* **Proof of debt**
. provable debt, ... IR 12.3
. quantification of claims *See* **Quantification of claims**

Debtor
. death of
.. creditor's petition for bankruptcy, and, ... IR 6.16
. honouring of obligations to, ...ER 24
. identification of
.. creditor's petition for bankruptcy, and, ... IR 6.7
.. debtor's petition for bankruptcy, and, ... IR 6.38
. prosecution of
.. individual voluntary arrangement, and, ... IA 262B

Debtor's petition for bankruptcy
. action on report of insolvency practitioner, ...IA 274
. action to follow order, ... IR 6.46
. admission of insolvency, ... IR 6.39
. alternative courts for, ...IR Sch.2
. amendment of title of proceedings, ... IR 6.49
. appointment of insolvency practitioner, ...IA 273
. certificate of summary administration, ...IR 6.48, IR 6.50
. Chief Land Registrar, notice to, ... IR 6.43
. expenses of voluntary arrangement, and, ...IR 6.46A
. grounds of, ... IA 272
. identification of debtor, ... IR 6.38
. insolvency practitioner, report of, ... IR 6.44
. jurisdiction, ...IR 6.40
. official receiver's duty in summary administration, ...IR 6.49
. presentation and filing of, ... IR 6.42

Debtor's petition for bankruptcy—continued   **Provision**
. settlement and content of bankruptcy order, ...IR 6.45
. statement of affairs
.. accounts, requirement to submit, ... IR 6.69
.. accounts, submission and filing of, ... IR 6.70
.. content of, ...IR 6.68
.. expenses of, ... IR 6.71
.. limited disclosure, ... IR 6.72
. summary administration, ... IA 275

Debtor's proposal
. consideration of
.. challenges to decisions at creditors' meetings, ... IA 262
.. decisions at creditors' meetings, ...IA 258
.. effect of approval, ... IA 260
.. false representations, and, ... IA 262A
.. premature end to arrangement, ... IA 262C
.. prosecution of delinquent debtors, ...IA 262B
.. report of decisions to court, ... IA 259
.. undischarged bankrupt, effect on, ... IA 261
. contents of, ... IR 5.3
. moratorium for insolvent debtors, and, ... IA 256A
. preparation of, ... IR 5.2

Deceased persons, insolvent estates of
. rule making powers, and, ... IA 421

Devolution
. bankruptcy restrictions orders, and, ... IA 426B

Diligence (Scotland)
. winding up, and, ... IA 185

Directors
. administration, and
.. admission or rejection of creditors' claims, ... *IR 2.23(2)*
.. appointment of administrator, ...IR 2.20—IR 2.26
.. notice of creditors' meetings, ...*IR 2.18(3)*
. bankrupt's leave to act as
.. application for, ... IR 6.203
.. court's order on application, ... IR 6.205
.. official receiver, report of, ... IR 6.204
. company voluntary arrangements, and

    Provision
.. exclusion of from creditors' or members' meetings, ... IR 1.16(2)
. meaning, ...IA 251
. unlimited liability
.. winding up, and, ... IA 75
. voluntary winding up, and, ... IA 114

Directors' petition
. affidavit in support of, .. *IR 2.1(2)*, IR 2.2(2)
. form of, ...*IR 2.4*, IR 2.3(1)

Directors' proposals
. company voluntary arrangements, and
.. contents of, ... IR 1.3
.. disclosure for assistance of nominee, ... IR 1.6
.. moratoriums, and, ... IA 2000 1
.. nominee's report on, ... IR 1.7
.. notice to intended nominee, ... IR 1.4
.. preparation of, ...IR 1.2
.. replacement of, ... IR 1.8
.. statement of affairs, ...IR 1.5
.. summoning of meetings, ...IR 1.9
. moratoriums, and, ... IR 1.35

Discharge of bankruptcy
. application by bankrupt, ... IR 6.217
. bankrupt's debts surviving, ... IR 6.223
. by order of court, ... IA 280
. certificate of, ... IR 6.220
. costs, ... IR 6.222
. deferment of issue pending appeal, ...IR 6.221
. effect of, ...IA 281
. lifting of suspension, ... IR 6.216
. official receiver, report of, ... IR 6.218
. order of, ...IR 6.219
. post-discharge restrictions, ...IA 281A
. suspension of, ... IR 6.215

Disclaimers (England and Wales)
. bankruptcy, and
.. additional notices of, ... IR 6.180
.. application for leave to disclaim, ... IR 6.182
.. declaration of interest in property, ... IR 6.184
.. duty to keep court informed, ... IR 6.181
.. interested persons, application by, ... IR 6.183
.. interested persons, communication to, ...IR 6.179

1168

Index

	Provision
. . trustee's notice of,	IR 6.178
. . validity, presumption of,	IR 6.185
. . vesting of disclaimed property,	IR 6.186
. winding up, and	
. . additional notices,	IR 4.189
. . applications by interested parties,	IR 4.191
. . communication of,	IR 4.188
. . court powers,	IA 181—IA 182, IR 4.194
. . declaration of interest in property,	IR 4.192
. . duty to keep court informed,	IR 4.190
. . leaseholds,	IA 179
. . liquidator's notice of,	IR 4.187
. . onerous property,	IA 178
. . rentcharges, land subject to,	IA 180
. . validity, presumption of,	IR 4.193

Disclosure
. court procedure, and,	IR 7.60
. statement of affairs, and	
. . administration, and,	*IR 2.13*, IR 2.30
. . administrative receiver, and,	IR 3.5
. . winding up, and,	IR 4.32, IR 4.35

Discounts
. creditor's petition for bankruptcy, and,	IR 6.62, IR 6.66
. debtor's petition for bankruptcy, and,	IR 6.72
. quantification of claims	
. . administration, and,	IR 2.84
. . bankruptcy, and,	IR 6.110
. . winding up, and,	IR 4.89

Dissolution
. termination of administration, and,	IA Sch.B1, para.84, IR 2.118
. winding up, following	
. . completion of winding up, and,	IA 205
. . early dissolution (England and Wales),	IA 202—IA 203
. . early dissolution (Scotland),	IA 204
. . procedures following appeals,	IR 4.225
. . Secretary of State's directions,	IR 4.224
. . voluntary winding up, and,	IA 201

Distress
. adjustment of prior transactions in bankruptcy,	IA 347

Dividends
. alteration of proof after payment of,	IR 2.101, IR 11.8

	Provision
. assignment of right to,	IR 2.104, IR 11.11
. cancellation of,	IR 11.4
. debts payable at future time,	IR 2.89, IR 11.13
. decision to declare,	IR 11.5
. declaration of,	IR 2.97
. disqualification from,	IR 2.103, IR 11.10
. distribution of bankrupt's estate,	IA 324
. final admission and rejection of proofs,	IR 11.3
. notice	
. . of declaration of,	IR 2.98, IR 11.6
. . of further,	IR 2.100
. . of intended,	IR 11.2
. . of intention to declare,	IR 2.68
. . of no dividend,	IR 2.100, IR 11.7
. payment of,	IR 2.99
. postponement of,	IR 11.4
. preferential creditors,	IR 11.12
. secured creditors,	IR 11.9
. unclaimed	
. . public administration, and,	IA 407

Documents
. charge for copies,	IR 12.15A
. confidentiality,	IR 12.13
. right to copy,	IR 12.15

Dwelling houses
. disclaimer of onerous property, and,	IA 318

E

EC Regulation on Insolvency Proceedings 2000
. applicable law,	ER 4
. application for administration orders, and,	IR 2.4(4)
. commencement,	ER 47
. community patents, and,	ER 12
. costs,	ER 23
. creditors	
. . content of lodgement of claim,	ER 41
. . duty to inform,	ER 40
. . language of information to,	ER 42
. . right to lodge claims,	ER 39
. debtor, honouring of obligations to,	ER 24
. detrimental acts,	ER 13
. employment contracts,	ER 10
. enforcement of judgments,	ER 25
. immoveable property, contracts relating to,	ER 8

EC Regulation on Insolvency Proceedings 2000—continued **Provision**
. international jurisdiction, ... ER 3
. interpretation, ... ER 2
. language of information to creditors, ... ER 42
. liquidator's appointment, proof of, ... ER 19
. liquidator's appointment, publication of, ... ER 21
. liquidator's powers, ... ER 18
. payments systems and financial markets, ... ER 9
. pending law suits, effect of insolvency proceedings on, ... ER 15
. principle, establishment of, ... ER 16
. public policy, ... ER 26
. recognition of judgments, ... ER 25
. recognition, effect of, ... ER 17
. registration of insolvency proceedings, ... ER 22
. relationship to conventions, ... ER 44
. reservation of title, ... ER 7
. return of assets, ... ER 20
. rights subject to registration, and, ... ER 11
. scope of, ... ER 1
. secondary insolvency proceedings
.. advanced payment of costs and expenses, ... ER 30
.. applicable law, ... ER 28
.. assets remaining in, ... ER 35
.. communication of information, ... ER 31
.. conversion of earlier proceedings, ... ER 37
.. cooperation, duty of, ... ER 31
.. creditors' rights, exercise of, ... ER 32
.. liquidation, stay of, ... ER 33
.. measures ending, ...ER 34
.. opening of proceedings, ... ER 27
.. preservation measures, ... ER 38
.. right to request opening of proceedings, ... ER 29
.. subsequent opening of main proceedings, ... ER 36
. set off, ... ER 6
. third parties' rights in rem, ... ER 5
. third party purchasers, protection of, ... ER 14
. trade marks, and, ... ER 12

Employment contracts
. insolvency proceedings, and, ... ER 10

Enforcement procedures **Provision**
. compliance with rules, ... IR 7.20
. court orders, and, ... IR 7.19
. warrants, ... IR 7.21—IR 7.25

Enterprise Act 2002
. amendments under, ... EA Sch.17

Ex parte hearings
. meaning, ... IR 0.2(2)

Examination of company officers
. court orders for, ... IA 198

Exchange rate
. foreign currency debts, ... IR 2.86(2)

Exempt property
. bankruptcy, and
.. money in lieu of sale, ... IR 6.188
.. replacement property, purchase of, ... IR 6.187

Expenses
. administration, of, ... IR 2.67
. company voluntary arrangements, and, ... IR 1.28, IR 1.33(4)
. creditors' committee
.. administration, and, ... *IR 2.45*, IR 2.63
.. bankruptcy, and, ... IR 6.164
.. receivership, and, ... IR 3.29
. statement of affairs
.. administration, and, ... *IR 2.15*, IR 2.32
.. administrative receiver, and, ... IR 3.7
.. creditor's petition for bankruptcy, and, ... IR 6.63
.. debtor's petition for bankruptcy, and, ... IR 6.71

Extortionate credit agreements
. adjustment of prior transactions, and, ... IA 244, IA 343

F

False representations
. bankruptcy offences, and, ... IA 356
. company voluntary arrangements, proposals for, ... IA 6A, IR 1.30
. individual voluntary arrangement, and, ... IA 262A
. malpractice during winding up, and, ... IA 211

	Provision
Falsification of books	
. bankruptcy offences, and,	IA 355
. malpractice during winding up, and,	IA 209
Fast track individual voluntary arrangement	
. agents, employment of,	IR 5.49
. approval by creditors,	IR 5.40
. approval of,	IA 263D, IR 5.39
. availability of,	IA 263A
. completion of,	IR 5.50
. costs and expenses of,	IR 5.48
. creditor's claims, admission of,	IR 5.42
. implementation of,	IA 263E
. majorities required,	IR 5.43
. notification to court,	IA 263C, IR 5.44
. offences,	IA 263G
. official receiver's decision, requirement for,	IR 5.38
. proposal for,	IA 263B, IR 5.37
. revocation of,	IA 263F, IR 5.46
. supervisor, notification of appointment of,	IR 5.45
. supervisor's accounts and reports,	IR 5.47
. termination of,	IR 5.50
. voting rights,	IR 5.41
Fees	
. company voluntary arrangements, and,	IR 1.28
Fees orders	
. company insolvency proceedings,	IA 414
. generally,	IA 415A
. individual insolvency proceedings,	IA 415
Financial markets	
. insolvency proceedings, and,	ER 9
. prohibition on appointment of administrative receiver, and,	IA 72F
Financial Services Authority	
. administration order, petition for,	IA 8(1A)
Fixed security	
. meaning,	IA 70(1)
Floating charge	
. adjustment of prior transactions, and,	IA 245
. company property,	IA 107
. meaning,	IA 251

	Provision
Floating charge holder	
. application for administration, and,	IR 2.4(3), IR 2.11(2)
. appointment of administrator	
. . application for,	IR 2.10
. . court business hours, out of,	IR 2.19
. . notice of,	IR 2.16—IR 2.18
. . notice of intention to appoint,	IR 2.15
. notice of application for administration, and,	IR 2.18
. receivers	
. . appointment in Scotland,	IA 53
. . mode of appointment,	IA 53(4)
. . power to appoint,	IA 51(1)
Foreign companies	
. winding up, and,	IA 225
Foreign currency debts	
. quantification of claims	
. . administration, and,	IR 2.86
. . bankruptcy, and,	IR 6.111
. . winding up, and,	IR 4.91
Fraudulent dealing	
. bankruptcy offences, and,	IA 359
Fraudulent disposal of property	
. bankruptcy offences, and,	IA 357
Fraudulent trading	
. malpractice during winding up, and,	IA 213, IA 215
Friendly societies	
. administration, and,	EA 255

G

	Provision
Gazette	
. advertisement in,	IR 12.20
Gratuitous alienations (Scotland)	
. adjustment of prior transactions, and,	IA 242
Guarantees	
. discharge by supervisor,	IR 1.23(5)

H

	Provision
Hire-purchase agreements	
. administration order, and	
. . creditors' meetings, and,	*IR 2.27*, IR 2.42
. . disposal of charged property,	IR 2.66(3)
. . disposal of goods in Scotland,	*IA 16(2)*
. . effect of application,	*IA 10(4)*

Index

Provision

Hire purchase property
. administration, and, ... IA Sch.B1, para.72

I

Immoveable property
. insolvency proceedings, and, ... ER 8

Incapax
. appointment of other persons to
    act for, ...IR 7.44—IR 7.46

Income payment agreements
. acceptance of, ... IR 6.193B
. administration by trustee in
    bankruptcy, ... IA 310A
. approval of, ... IR 6.193A
. variation of, ... IR 6.194

Income payment orders
. action to follow making of, ... IR 6.190
. administration by trustee in
    bankruptcy, ... IA 310
. administration of, ... IR 6.192
. application for, ... IR 6.189
. pre-commencement
    bankruptcy, ... EA Sch.19, para.7
. review of order, ... IR 6.193
. variation of, ... IR 6.191

Individual insolvency
. annual report, ...IA 379
. appeals, and, ...IA 375
. bankruptcy
. . administration by trustee, IA 305—IA 335
. . bankruptcy orders, ... IA 276—IA 282
. . court powers in, ... IA 363—IA 371
. . offences, ... IA 350—IA 362
. . petitions for, ... IA 264—IA 275
. . prior transactions, adjustment
    of, ... IA 339—IA 349
. . protection of bankrupt's
    estate, ...IA 283—IA 291
. . rights of occupation, and, IA 336—IA 338
. . rights under trusts of land,
    and, ... IA 335A
. . trustees in bankruptcy,
    appointment and role of, ..IA 292—IA 304
. formal defects, ... IA 377
. individual voluntary
    arrangements
. . debtor's proposal,
    consideration and
    implementation of, ...IA 258—IA 263

Provision

. . fast track voluntary
    arrangement, ... IA 263A—IA 263G
. . moratoriums for insolvent
    debtors, ... IA 252—IA 257
. insolvency districts, ...IA 374
. jurisdiction, and, ... IA 373
. preferential debts, ... IA 386—IA 387
. provisions capable of inclusion
    in rules, ...IA Sch.9
. rule-making powers, and, ... IA 412
. stamp duty, exemption from, ... IA 378
. time limits, ... IA 376
. utility supplies, ... IA 372

Individual insolvency register
. bankruptcy orders, and
. . deletion of, ...IR 6A.5
. . entry of, ... IR 6A.4
. creation of, ...IR 6A.1
. individual voluntary
    arrangements, and
. . deletion of, ...IR 6A.3
. . entry of, ... IR 6A.2
. rectification of, ... IR 6A.8

**Individual voluntary
arrangements**
. accounts
. . production to Secretary of
    State, ... IR 5.32
. . supervisor, of, ... IA 5.31
. approval, procedure for, ...IA 2000 3
. completion of, ...IR 5.34
. consideration of debtor's
    proposal
. . challenges to decisions at
    creditors' meetings, ... IA 262
. . decisions at creditors'
    meetings, ...IA 258
. . effect of approval, ...IA 260
. . false representations, and, ... IA 262A
. . premature end to arrangement, ... IA 262C
. . prosecution of delinquent
    debtors, ...IA 262B
. . report of decisions to court, ... IA 259
. . undischarged bankrupt, effect
    on, ... IA 261
. conversion into bankruptcy
. . affidavit, contents of, ... IR 5.63
. . application for, ...IR 5.62
. . court powers, and, ... IR 5.64
. costs and expenses of, ... IR 5.33
. creditors' meetings
. . admission of claims, ... IR 5.22
. . chairman as proxy holder, ...IR 5.20

1172

Index

	Provision
. . chairman at,	IR 5.19
. . majorities,	IR 5.23
. . proceedings to obtain agreement on proposal,	IR 5.24
. . summoning of,	IA 257, IR 5.17—IR 5.18
. . voting rights,	IR 5.21
. debtor's proposal	
. . contents of,	IR 5.3
. . preparation of,	IR 5.2
. expenses of	
. . debtor's petition for bankruptcy, and,	IR 6.46A
. fast track voluntary arrangement	
. . agents, employment of,	IR 5.49
. . approval by creditors,	IR 5.40
. . approval of,	IA 263D, IR 5.39
. . availability of,	IA 263A
. . completion of,	IR 5.50
. . costs and expenses of,	IR 5.48
. . creditors' claims, admission of,	IR 5.42
. . implementation of,	IA 263E
. . majorities required,	IR 5.43
. . notification to court,	IA 263C, IR 5.44
. . offences,	IA 263G
. . official receiver's decision, requirement for,	IR 5.38
. . proposal for,	IA 263B, IR 5.37
. . revocation of,	IA 263F, IR 5.46
. . Secretary of State's power to extend scheme for,	EA 264
. . supervisor, notification of appointment of,	IR 5.45
. . supervisor's accounts and reports,	IR 5.47
. . termination of,	IR 5.50
. . voting rights,	IR 5.41
. forms for,	IR Sch.4
. implementation of	
. . generally,	IA 263
. . hand-over of property to supervisor,	IR 5.26
. . report of creditors' meeting,	IR 5.27
. . reports to Secretary of State,	IR 5.29
. . resolutions to follow approval,	IR 5.25
. individual insolvency register, and	
. . deletion from,	IR 6A.3
. . entries to,	IR 6A.2
. interim orders	
. . action following making of,	IR 5.10
. . application for,	IR 5.7—IR 5.9

	Provision
. . consideration of nominee's report,	IR 5.13
. . nominee's report on,	IR 5.11
. . replacement of nominee, and,	IR 5.12
. Member State liquidator, notice to	IR 5.65
. moratoriums for insolvent debtors	
. . debtor's proposal,	IA 256A
. . interim orders for,	IA 252—IA 256
. . nominee's report,	IA 256A
. . summoning of creditors' meeting,	IA 257
. nominee	
. . disclosure for assistance of,	IR 5.6
. . interim orders, and,	IR 5.12—IR 5.13
. . notice of debtor's proposal,	IR 5.4
. . report for moratorium,	IA 256A
. . where no interim order made,	IR 5.14—IR 5.15
. revocation of,	IR 5.30
. statement of affairs, and,	IR 5.5
. supervision of,	IA 263
. supervisor's accounts and reports,	IR 5.31
. suspension of,	IR 5.30
. termination of,	IR 5.34
. where no interim order made	
. . applications to court,	IR 5.16
. . nominee's report to court,	IR 5.14—IR 5.15

Inland Revenue
. orders in bankruptcy to	
. . application for,	IR 6.194
. . custody of documents,	IR 6.196
. . making and service of,	IR 6.195
. production of documents in bankruptcy, and,	IA 369

Industrial and provident societies
. administration, and,	EA 255

Innocent intention, defence of
. bankruptcy offences, and,	IA 352

Insolvency
. meaning,	IA 247

Insolvency Act 1986
. amendment of enactments,	IA 439
. citation,	IA 444
. commencement,	IA 443
. extent (Northern Ireland),	IA 441

Index

Insolvency Act 1986—continued   **Provision**
. extent (other territories), ...IA 442
. extent (Scotland, ...IA 440
. foreign companies, and, ...EA 254
. repeals, ...IA 438
. subordinate legislation
.. deceased persons, and, ...IA 421
.. fees orders, ...IA 414—IA 415A
.. general insolvency rules, .IA 411—IA 413
.. insolvency practice
     regulations, ...IA 419
.. insolvent partnerships, ...IA 420
.. joint tenancies, and, ...IA 421A
.. monetary limits, ...IA 416—IA 418
.. recognised banks, ...IA 422
. transitional provisions and
     savings, ...IA 437

Insolvency Act 2000
. commencement, ...IA 2000 16
. extent, ...IA 2000 17
. short title, ...IA 2000 18

Insolvency districts
. individual insolvency, and, ...IA 374

Insolvency practitioners
. acting as, meaning of, ...IA 388
. acting without qualification, ...IA 389
. authorisation, grant, refusal and
     withdrawal of, ...IA 393
. charge over assets, ...IR 1.23(4)
. competent authority,
     authorisation by, ...IA 392
. debtor's petition for bankruptcy,
     and, ...IA 273, IA 274, IR 6.44
. discharge of remuneration, ... IR 1.23(2)
. loss of qualification as
.. administrator, ... IA Sch.B1, para.89
.. liquidator IR 4.134—IR 4.135
. nominees
.. authorisation of, ...IA 389A
.. official receiver as, ...IA 389B
. notices, and, ...IA 394
. office holders, and, ...IA 230
. qualifications required, ...IA 390
. recognised professional bodies, ...IA 391
. representations, right to make, ...IA 395
. responsible insolvency
     practitioner, meaning, ...IR 1.1(3)
. security, and, ...IR 12.8
. solicitor for, ...IR 7.54
. supervisor
.. authorisation of, ...IA 389A
.. official receiver as, ...IA 389B

Provision
. Tribunal, reference to, ...IA 396—IA 398
. trustee in bankruptcy
     qualification as, ...IR 6.144
. unqualified persons, restrictions
     on, ...IA 388—IA 389B

Insolvency Practitioners Tribunal
. panel of members, ...IA Sch.7, para.1
. procedure of, ...IA Sch.7, para.4
. reference to, ... IA 396—IA 398
. remuneration of members, .IA Sch.7, para.2
. sittings of, ...IA Sch.7, para.3

Insolvency proceedings
. forms for use in, ...IR 12.7
. registration of, ... ER 22
. secondary insolvency
     proceedings
.. advanced payment of costs and
     expenses, ...ER 30
.. applicable law, ...ER 28
.. assets remaining in, ...ER 35
.. communication of
     information, ...ER 31
.. conversion of earlier
     proceedings, ...ER 37
.. conversion to winding up, ...ER 37
.. cooperation, duty of, ...ER 31
.. creditors' rights, exercise of, ...ER 32
.. definition, ...ER 3(3)
.. liquidation, stay of, ...ER 33
.. measures ending, ...ER 34
.. opening of proceedings, ... ER 27
.. preservation measures, ...ER 38
.. right to request opening of
     proceedings, ... ER 29
.. subsequent opening of main
     proceedings, ...ER 36
.. territorial proceedings, ...ER 3(2)

Insolvency Rules 1986
. citation and commencement, ... IR 0.1
. construction and interpretation, ...IR 0.2
. extent, ... IR 0.3
. interpretation, ...IR 13.1—IR 13.14

Insolvency Rules Committee
. role and membership of, ...IA 413

Insolvency Services Account
. public administration, and, ... IA 403

Insolvent partnerships
. rule-making powers relating to, ... IA 420

	Provision
Instrument of appointment	
. receivers, and,	IA 53(1)
Interest	
. debts, on,	IA 189
. public administration, and,	IA 406
. quantification of claims	
.. administration, and,	IR 2.88
.. bankruptcy, and,	IR 6.113
.. winding up, and,	IR 4.93
Interest in property	
. declaration of	
.. bankruptcy, and,	IR 6.184
.. winding up, and,	IR 4.192
. disposal of	
.. receivers (Scotland), and,	IA 61
Interim moratorium	
. administration application, on making of,	IA Sch. B1, para. 44(1)
. appointment of administrator by floating charge holder,	IR 2.15(2)
. notice of intention to appoint administrator, on filing of,	IA Sch. B1, para. 44(2)
Interim receiver	
. appointment of,	IA 286, IR 6.51
. appointment, order of,	IR 6.52
. criminal bankruptcy, and,	IR 6.231
. deposit, requirement for,	IR 6.53
. remuneration,	IR 6.56
. security, and,	IR 6.54, IR 6.55
. termination of appointment,	IR 6.57
Investment Account	
. public administration, and,	IA 404
Invoices	
. notification of administration orders, and,	*IA 12(1)*
. notification of appointment of receiver,	IA 64(1)

J

Joint administrators	
. appointment of,	IA Sch.B1, paras 100—103, IR 2.127
. remuneration of,	*IR 2.47(7)*
Joint receivers	
. appointment of,	IA 33(2)
Joint tenancies, insolvent	
. rule-making powers relating to,	IA 421A

	Provision
Judicial notice of court documents	
. winding up, and,	IA 196
Jurisdiction	
. bankruptcy, and,	IA 373
. creditor's petition for bankruptcy, and,	IR 6.9
. cooperation between different courts,	IA 426
. debtor's petition for bankruptcy, and,	IR 6.40
. international,	ER 3
. service outside,	IR 12.12
. winding up by court,	IA 117—IA 121
Justice of the peace	
. disqualification of bankrupt from acting as,	EA 265

L

Leaseholds	
. disclaimer in bankruptcy, and,	IA 317
. disclaimers in winding up proceedings,	IA 179
Liens on books	
. adjustment of prior transactions, and,	IA 246, IA 349
Liquidation	
. meaning,	IA 247
. petition for administration,	IR 2.11
. stay of,	ER 33
Liquidation committee	
. calls on contributories,	IR 4.203
. chairman at meetings of,	IR 4.157
. committee-members' representatives,	IR 4.159
. composition when creditors paid in full,	IR 4.171
. dealings by members,	IR 4.170
. establishment by contributories,	IR 4.154
. expenses of members,	IR 4.169
. formal defects of,	IR 4.172A
. formalities of establishment,	IR 4.153
. functions vested in Secretary of State,	IR 4.172
. generally,	IR 4.151
. liquidator's reports, and,	IR 4.168
. meetings of,	IR 4.156
. membership of,	IR 4.152
. obligation of liquidator to,	IR 4.155
. quorum,	IR 4.158

Liquidation committee—continued   **Provision**
. removal from, ... IR 4.162
. resignation from, ... IR 4.160
. resolutions of, ...IR 4.165—IR 4.167
. termination of membership, ... IR 4.161
. vacancies, ...IR 4.163—IR 4.164
. voting rights, ... IR 4.165—IR 4.166
. winding up by court, and, ..IA 141—IA 142
. winding up following
    administration, and, .IR 4.173—IR 4.178

Liquidators
. appointment of, ... IA 135—IA 140, IR
    4.100—IR 4.106
. appointment, proof of, ...ER 19
. appointment, publication of, ... ER 21
. calls on contributories, ...IR 4.202
. collection and distribution of
    company assets by, ..IR 4.179—IR 4.186
. contributories, settlement of list
    of, ... IR 4.195—IR 4.210
. corrupt inducement affecting
    appointment of, ... IA 164
. creditors' voluntary winding up,
    powers on, ... IA 166
. death of, ...IR 4.132—IR 4.133
. delegation of court powers to, ...IA 160
. designation of, ... IA 163
. disclaimers, and, ... IR 4.187—IR 4.194
. duty to make returns,
    enforcement of, ... IA 170
. EC Regulation, special
    meaning, ... ER 2(b)
. final meeting, and, ... IR 4.125—IR 4.126
. functions of, ... IA 143—IA 146
. hand-over of assets to, ... IR 4.107
. liquidation committee
. . obligations to, ... IR 4.155
. . reports to, ...IR 4.168
. loss of qualification as
    insolvency practitioner, ... IR 4.134—IR
    4.135
. members' voluntary winding up,
    and
. . appointment by company, ... IR 4.139
. . appointment by court, ... IR 4.140
. . appointment of, ...IA 91
. . authentication of appointment, ... IR 4.141
. . death of , ...IR 4.145
. . loss of qualification as
    insolvency practitioner, ... IR 4.146
. . release of, ... IR 4.144
. . removal of, ...IR 4.143

    Provision
. . remuneration of, ... IR 4.148A—IR 4.148B
. . resignation of, ... IR 4.142
. . vacation of office, ... IR 4.147—IR 4.148
. power to set aside transactions, ... IR 4.149
. powers of, ... IA Sch.4, ER 18
. proof of debts, and
. . change of liquidator, ...IR 4.81
. . inspection of, ... IR 4.79
. . transmission of, ...IR 4.80
. release of, .. IA 173—IA 174, IR 4.121—IR
    4.122, IR 4.124, IR 4.125A
. removal from office, ...IA 171—IA 172, IR
    4.113—IR 4.120, IR
    4.123
. remuneration of, ... IR 4.127—IR 4.131
. resignation of, ... IR 4.108—IR 4.112
. solicitation, rule against, ... IR 4.150
. supplementary powers (England
    and Wales), ... IA 168
. supplementary powers
    (Scotland), ... IA 169
. vacation of office by, ... IR 4.136—IR 4.138
. voluntary winding up, and
. . appointment by court of, ... IA 108
. . notice of appointment of, ...IA 108
. . powers of, ...IA 165
. . removal by court of, ... IA 107
. winding up by court, and
. . by court, ... IA 140
. . by Secretary of State, ... IA 137
. . contributories, nomination by, ... IA 139
. . creditors' meetings,
    nomination by, ...IA 139
. . functions of official receiver,
    and, ...IA 136
. . in Scotland, ...IA 138
. . powers of, ...IA 167
. . provisional liquidator,
    appointment of, ... IA 135

Liquidator's proposals
. company voluntary
    arrangements, and
. . notice to nominee, ...IR 1.12
. . preparation of, ...IR 1.10
. . summoning of meetings, ..IA 3(2), IR 1.11

List of contributories
. settlement of, ...IR 4.195—IR 4.201

Local government
. disqualification of bankrupt
    from, ...EA 267

M

Malpractice during winding up
. company names, re-use of, . IA 216, IA 217, IR 4.22—IR 4.230
. false representations to creditors, ...IA 211
. falsification of company books, ... IA 209
. fraud in anticipation of winding up, ...IA 206
. fraudulent trading, ... IA 213, IA 215
. misconduct by officers, ... IA 208
. omissions from statement of affairs, ... IA 210
. prosecution of delinquent officers and members, ... IA 218, IA 219
. summary remedies, ... IA 212
. transactions in fraud of creditors, ...IA 207
. wrongful trading, ...IA 214, IA 215

Management of companies
. administrators, and, ...*IA 17(2)*
. company insolvency, and
.. company property, gathering in of, ...IA 234
.. co-operation with office holders, ... IA 235
.. inquiry into company dealings, ...IA 236—IA 237
.. utilities supplies, ... IA 233

Meetings *See* **Company meetings; Creditors' meetings**

Member of company
. meaning, ...IA 250

Member State liquidator
. notices to
.. court procedure, and, ... IR 7.63
.. of administration order, . IR *2.62*, IR 2.133
.. of bankruptcy, ... IR 6.238—IR 6.239
.. of company voluntary arrangement, ... IR 1.34
.. of individual voluntary arrangement, ...IR 5.65
.. of winding up, ...IR 4.231
. priority of creditors' vote, ... IR 2.38(7)

Members' meetings *See* **Company meetings**

Members' voluntary winding up
. creditors' voluntary winding up, conversion to, ...IA 96
. creditors' voluntary winding up, distinction from, ...IA 90
. effect of insolvency, ...IA 95
. end of year meeting, ... IA 93
. final meeting, ...IA 94
. liquidator
.. appointment by company, ... IR 4.139
.. appointment by court, ... IR 4.140
.. appointment of, ...IA 91
.. authentication of appointment, ... IR 4.141
.. death of , ...IR 4.145
.. loss of qualification as insolvency practitioner, ... IR 4.146
.. release of, ... IR 4.144
.. removal of, ...IR 4.143
.. remuneration of, ... IR 4.148A—IR 4.148B
.. resignation of, ... IR 4.142
.. vacation of office, ... IR 4.147—IR 4.148
. liquidator, power to fill vacancy in office of, ... IA 92

Minutes
. company meetings, ... IR 2.49(7)
. creditors' meetings, and
.. administration, and, ... *IR 2.28*, IR 2.44
.. receivership, and, ... IR 3.15

Misfeasance
. administrators, and, ...IA Sch.B1, para.75

Monetary limits
. bankruptcy, ...IA 418
. companies winding up, and, ... IA 416
. company moratoriums, ... IA 417
. winding up of unregistered companies, ... IA 417A

Moneylenders
. creditor's petition for bankruptcy, and, ... IR 6.19
. proof of debts, and, ... IR 6.102

Moratoriums
. company voluntary arrangements, and
.. admission of creditors' claims, ...IR 1.50
.. advertisement of, ... IR 1.40(2)
.. commencement of, ...IR 1.40(3)
.. company, effect on, ... IA Sch.A1, para.15
.. contracts, and, ... IA Sch.A1, para.23
.. creditors, effect on, ... IA Sch.A1, paras 12—14
.. creditors' voting rights, ... IR 1.49
.. delivery of documents to nominee, ...IR 1.36

Moratoriums—continued   **Provision**
.. disposal of charged property during, .. IA Sch.A1, paras 18—22, IR 1.43
.. documents to be submitted to court, ...IA Sch.A1, para.7, IR 1.39
.. duration of, ... IA Sch.A1, para.8
.. eligible companies, ...IA 1A, IA Sch.A1, paras 2—5, IR 1.1(4)
.. end of, notice of, ... IR 1.42
.. extension of, ... IR 1.41
.. Financial Services Authority, and, ... IA Sch.A1, para.44
.. floating charge documents, void provisions in, IA Sch.A1, para.43
.. implementation of arrangement during, ...IR 1.54
.. members' voting rights, ...IR 1.51
.. nominees, and, ...IA Sch.A1, paras 24—28
.. nominee's statement, ... IA Sch.A1, para.6
.. notice, service of, ...IR 1.40(1)
.. notification of end of, ..IA Sch.A1, para.11
.. notification of start of, ...IA Sch.A1, paras 9—10
.. obtaining credit during, ...IA Sch.A1, para.17
.. payments during, ... IA Sch.A1, para.19
.. procedure at creditors' or members' meetings, ... IR 1.48
.. proceedings during, ... IR 1.43
.. proceedings to obtain agreement on proposal for, ... IR 1.53
.. proposal for, ... IA 7A, IR 1.35
.. replacement nominee, notification of appointment of, ... IR 1.46
.. replacement of nominee by court, ...IR 1.45
.. requisite majorities, ... IR 1.52, IR 1.53
.. statement of affairs, delivery of, ... IR 1.37
.. statement on, ...IR 1.38
.. stationery of company, and, ... IA Sch.A1, para.16
.. withdrawal of consent to act, ... IR 1.44
. individual voluntary arrangements, and
.. debtor's proposal, ...IA 256A
.. interim orders for, ... IA 252—IA 256
.. nominee's report, ... IA 256A
.. summoning of creditors' meeting, ... IA 257

Mortgaged property   **Provision**
. bankruptcy, and
.. claim by mortgagee of land, ...IR 6.197
.. court power to order sale, ... IR 6.198
.. proceeds of sale, ...IR 6.199

Mutual credit
. distribution of bankrupt's estate, ... IA 323
. quantification of claims, and
.. administration, and, ... IR 2.85
.. winding up, and, ...IR 4.90

N

Negotiable instruments
. creditors' meetings, and, ...*IR 2.25*, IR 2.41
. endorsement of by administrator, ... IR 2.99(3)
. quantification of claims, and
.. administration, and, ... IR 2.82
.. bankruptcy, and, ... IR 6.108
.. winding up, and, ...IR 4.87

Nominees
. company voluntary arrangements, and
.. disclosure by directors for assistance of, ... IR 1.6
.. meaning of, ...IA 1(2)
.. notice of administrator's proposals, ... IR 1.12
.. notice of directors' proposals, ...IR 1.4
.. notice of liquidator's proposals, ... IR 1.12
.. procedure where not administrator or liquidator, ... IA 2
.. report on directors' proposals, ... IR 1.7
.. summoning of meetings by, ... IA 3
. individual voluntary arrangements, and
.. disclosure for assistance of, ... IR 5.6
.. interim orders, and, ... IR 5.12—IR 5.13
.. notice of debtor's proposal, ... IR 5.4
.. report for moratorium, ...IA 256A
.. where no interim order made, ...IR 5.14—IR 5.15
. insolvency practitioners, and
.. authorisation of, ... IA 389A
.. official receiver as, ... IA 389B
. moratoriums, and
.. advertisement of, ... IR 1.40(2)
.. challenge to nominee's actions, ... IA Sch.A1, paras 26—27

Index

	Provision
. . commencement of,	IR 1.40(3)
. . delivery of documents to nominee,	IR 1.36
. . documents to be submitted to court,	IR 1.39
. . end of, notice of,	IR 1.42
. . extension of,	IR 1.41
. . monitoring company activities,	IA Sch.A1, para.24
. . notice, service of,	IR 1.40(1)
. . procedure at creditors' or members' meetings,	IR 1.48
. . replacement nominee, notification of appointment of,	IR 1.46
. . replacement of nominee by court,	IA Sch.A1, para.28, IR 1.45
. . statement of affairs, delivery of,	IR 1.37
. . statement on,	IR 1.38
. . withdrawal of consent to act,	IA Sch.A1, para.25, IR 1.44

Non-disclosure
. bankruptcy offences, and,	IA 353
. quantification of claims, and,	IR 2.91

Northern Ireland
. application of Act,	IA 441
. co-operation of courts,	IA 426(12)

Notices
. requirements for,	IR 12.4
. simultaneous notices to same person,	IR 12.14
. non-receipt of,	IR 12.16

O

Occupation, rights of
. bankrupt, and,	IA 337
. bankrupt's spouse,	IA 336
. premises occupies by bankrupt,	IA 338

Offences
. bankruptcy, and	
. . absconding,	IA 358
. . concealment of property,	IA 354
. . false statements,	IA 356
. . falsification of books,	IA 355
. . fraudulent dealing with property obtained on credit,	IA 359
. . fraudulent disposal of property,	IA 357

	Provision
. . innocent intention, defence of,	IA 352
. . non disclosure,	IA 353
. . obtaining credit,	IA 360
. punishment of,	IA Sch.10, IR 12.21

Office copy
. meaning (Scotland),	IA 251

Office holders
. company insolvency, and	
. . appointment of two or more persons,	IA 231
. . insolvency practitioners, qualification as,	IA 230
. . validity of acts by,	IA 232
. management of insolvent companies, and,	IA 235

Official Petitioner
. criminal bankruptcy, and,	IR 6.230

Official Receiver
. administrator's proposal for company voluntary arrangement	
. . copy proposal to,	IR 1.12(6)
. . notice to,	IR 1.10(2)
. annulment of bankruptcy orders, and,	IR 5.54—IR 5.59
. appointment of,	IR 10.1
. bankruptcy, and	
. . bankrupt's duties in relation to,	IA 291
. . discharge of,	IR 6.218
. . enforcement of trustee's obligations to,	IR 6.149
. . information to creditors,	IR 6.73
. . investigation by,	IA 289
. . leave for bankrupt to act as director,	IR 6.204
. . release of,	IR 6.136, IR 6.137A
. directions, application for,	IR 10.3
. expenses of,	IR 10.4
. fast track individual voluntary arrangement, and,	IR 5.38
. insolvency practitioners, as,	IA 389B
. liquidator, functions in relation to,	IA 136
. persons entitled to act on behalf of,	IR 10.2
. summary administration, and,	IR 6.49
. winding up by court, and	
. . investigation of company affairs,	IA 132

Provision

Onerous property
. disclaimer in bankruptcy
.. court order vesting disclaimed
property, ...IA 320
.. dwelling houses, ...IA 318
.. general power, ...IA 315
.. leaseholds, ...IA 317
.. notice requiring trustees
decision, ...IA 316
.. rentcharges, ...IA 319, IA 321
. disclaimers in winding up
proceedings, ...IA 178

Orders pronounced in vacation
. winding up (Scotland), and, ...IA Sch.3

P

Parliament
. disqualification of bankrupt
from, ...IA 426A, IA 427, EA 266

Partnerships, insolvent
. rule-making powers relating to, ...IA 420

Payment systems
. insolvency proceedings, and, ...ER 9

Penalties
. administrators, and, ...IA Sch.B1, para.106
. provision for, ...IA 430

Pending liquidations
. information on, ...IA 192

Pension contributions
. adjustment of prior transactions
in bankruptcy, ...IA 342A—IA 342C

Pension sharing
. adjustment of prior transactions
in bankruptcy, ... IA 342D—IA 342F

Periodical payments
. quantification of claims, and
.. administration, and, ...IR 2.87
.. bankruptcy, and, ...IR 6.112
.. winding up, and, ...IR 4.92

**Petition (application) for
administration** *see*
**Application for
administration**
. affidavit
.. content of, ... *IR 2.3*, IR 2.4
.. in support of, ... *IR 2.1*, IR 2.2
. company in liquidation, and, ...IR 2.11

Provision

. content of, ... IR 2.4
. effect of, ... *IA 10*
. filing of, ... *IR 2.5*, IR 2.5
. form of, ... *IR 2.4*, IR 2.3
. hearing on, ... *IR 2.9*, IR 2.12
. manner of service, ...*IR 2.7*, IR 2.8
. notice to sheriff, ... *IR 2.6A*, IR 2.7
. procedure for, ... *IA 9*
. proof of service, ...*IR 2.8*, IR 2.9
. report on company's affairs, ... *IR 2.2*
. service of, ... *IR 2.6*, IR 2.6

Petition for bankruptcy
. conditions to be satisfied, .. IA 265—IA 266
. consolidation of, ...IR 6.236
. criminal bankruptcy orders,
and, ... IA 277
. persons entitled to present, ... IA 264

Petition for winding up
. advertisement of, ...IR 4.11
. affidavit in opposition, ...IR 4.18
. affidavit supporting petition for
administration, and, ... *IR 2.3(3)*
. by contributories, ... IR 4.22—IR 4.24
. certificate of compliance, ...IR 4.14
. leave for withdrawal, ...IR 4.15
. list of appearances, ...IR 4.17
. notice of appearance, ...IR 4.16
. persons to receive copies of, ... IR 4.10, IR
4.13
. presentation and filing of, ... IR 4.7
. proof of service, ...IR 4.9
. service of, ...IR 4.8
. substitution of creditor or
contributory for petitioner, ... IR 4.19
. termination of administration,
and, ...IR 2.114(4)
. verification of, ...IR 4.12

Precedence
. receivers (Scotland), and, ... IA 56

**Preferences (England and
Wales)**
. adjustment of prior transactions,
and, ...IA 239—IA 241, IA 340—IA 342

Preferences, undue (Scotland)
. adjustment of prior transactions,
and, ... IA 243

Preferential debts
. categories of, ... IA 386, IA Sch.6
. company insolvency, and, . IA 386—IA 387

1180

	Provision
. receivership, and	
. . payment out of charged assets,	IA 40(2)
. . priority of debts,	IA 59(2)
. relevant date for,	IA 387
. winding up, and,	IA 175—IA 176

Prescribed forms
. receivers (Scotland), and, ... IA 71

Prescribed part .... IA 176A

Prior transactions, adjustment of
. bankruptcy, and
. . apprenticeships, and, ... IA 348
. . contracts to which bankrupt is party, ... IA 345
. . distress, and, ... IA 347
. . enforcement procedures, ... IA 346
. . excessive pension contributions, ... IA 342A—IA 342C
. . extortionate credit transactions, ... IA 343
. . general assignment of book debts, avoidance of, ... IA 344
. . liens on books, unenforceability of, ...IA 349
. . pension-sharing, ... IA 342D—IA 342F
. . preferences, ... IA 340—IA 342
. . transactions at undervalue, ... IA 339, IA 341, IA 342
. company insolvency, and
. . extortionate credit transactions, ... IA 244
. . floating charges, avoidance of, ... IA 245
. . gratuitous alienations (Scotland), ...IA 242
. . liens on books, unenforceability of, ... IA 246
. . preferences (England and Wales), ... IA 239— IA 241
. . transactions at undervalue (England and Wales), IA 238, IA 240, IA 241
. . unfair preferences (Scotland), ... IA 243

Priority of debts
. receivers (Scotland), and, ... IA 59

Privilege
. irrelevance of, ... IA 426C

Progress report
. administrator's report to creditors, ... IR 2.47

	Provision
. termination of administration, and,	IR 2.110

Project finance
. prohibition on appointment of administrative receiver, and, ... IA 72E

Proof of debts
. administration, and
. . admission and rejection of proofs for dividend, ...IR 2.77
. . affidavit, establishment by, ... IR 2.73
. . alteration after payment of dividend, ...IR 2.101
. . appeal against decision on, ... IR 2.78
. . costs of, ... IR 2.74
. . expunging of by court, ...IR 2.80
. . inspection of proofs, ... IR 2.75
. . making of proofs, ... IR 2.72
. . new administrator, appointment of, ...IR 2.76
. . withdrawal or variation of, ...IR 2.79
. bankruptcy, and
. . admission and rejection for dividend, ...IR 6.104
. . appeal against decision, ... IR 6.105
. . claims established by affidavit, ... IR 6.99
. . contents of, ... IR 6.98
. . costs of, ... IR 6.100
. . expunging of by court, ...IR 6.107
. . inspection of proof, ... IR 6.101
. . licensed moneylender, proof of, ... IR 6.102
. . prove, meaning of, ... IR 6.96
. . supply of forms, ... IR 6.97
. . transmission of to trustee, ... IR 6.103
. . variation of, ...IR 6.106
. . withdrawal of, ... IR 6.106
. criminal bankruptcy, and, ... IR 6.232
. winding up, and
. . admission and rejection of for dividend, ... IR 4.82
. . appeal against decision on, ... IR 4.83
. . appointment of new liquidator, ... IR 4.81
. . claims established by affidavit, ... IR 4.77
. . contents of proof, ... IR 4.75
. . costs, ... IR 4.78
. . creditors' voluntary liquidation, and, ... IR 4.76
. . expunging of by court, ...IR 4.85
. . inspection allowed by liquidator, ... IR 4.79
. . meaning, ... IR 4.73

Proof of debts—continued   **Provision**
.. supply of forms, ...IR 4.74
.. transmission to liquidator, ...IR 4.80
.. withdrawal or variation of, ...IR 4.84

Proofs, admission or rejection of
. creditors' meeting
.. bankruptcy, and, ...IR 6.94
.. winding up, and, ...IR 4.70
. proof of debts
.. administration, and, ...IR 2.77
.. bankruptcy, and, ...IR 6.104
.. winding up, and, ...IR 4.82

Property in specie
. distribution of bankrupt's
    estate, ... IA 326

Proposals See **Company voluntary arrangements**

Provable debts
. nature of, ... IR 12.3

Provisional liquidator
. appointment of, ...IA 135, IR 4.25
. deposit, ...IR 4.27
. notice of appointment, ... IR 4.25A
. order of appointment, ... IR 4.26
. remuneration, ...IR 4.30
. security, ...IR 4.28, IR 4.29
. termination of appointment, ...IR 4.31

Proxies
. company representation, ...IR 8.7
. financial interests, and, ...IR 8.6
. forms for, ...IR Sch.4
. forms of, ...IR 8.2
. retention of, ...IR 8.4
. right of inspection, ...IR 8.5
. use of at meetings, ... IR 8.3

Proxy holder
. chairman of creditors' or members' meeting, as
.. administration, and, ...IR 1.15
.. bankruptcy, and, ...IR 6.89
.. individual voluntary arrangement, and, ...IR 5.20
.. winding up, and, ...IR 4.64

Public administration
. Insolvency Service finance
.. adjustment of balances, ... IA 408
.. annual financial statement and audit, ...IA 409
.. application of income from, ...IA 405

     Provision
.. Consolidated Fund, recourse to, ... IA 408
.. Insolvency Services Account, ... IA 403
.. interest on money invested, and, ...IA 406
.. Investment Account, ... IA 404
.. unclaimed dividends and undistributed balances, ...IA 407
. Official Petitioner, ...IA 402
. official receivers
.. appointment of, ...IA 399
.. deputy official receivers and staff, ...IA 401
.. functions and status of, ...IA 400

Public examination
. bankrupt
.. adjournment of, ...IR 6.176
.. bankrupt unfit for, ... IR 6.174
.. creditors' request for, ... IR 6.173
.. expenses of, ... IR 6.177
.. investigation of bankrupt's estate, ...IA 290
.. order for, ...IR 6.172
.. procedure at hearing, ... IR 6.175
. company officers
.. adjournment, ...IR 4.216
.. expenses of, ... IR 4.217
.. notice of hearing, ...IR 4.212
.. order for, ...IR 4.211
.. order on request of creditors or contributories, ...IR 4.213
.. procedure at hearings, ...IR 4.215
. winding up by court, and, IA 133—IA 134
.. witness unfit for examination, ... IR 4.214
. persons concerned
.. application, form and content of, ... IR 9.2
.. costs of, ... IR 9.6
.. forms for, ...IR Sch.4
.. order for, ... IR 9.3
.. procedure for, ... IR 9.4
.. record of, ... IR 9.5

Public interest
. termination of administration, and, ... IA Sch.B1, para.82

Public policy
. insolvency proceedings, ... ER 26

Public private partnership
. prohibition on appointment of administrative receiver, and, ...IA 72C

Q

Quantification of claims
. administration orders
.. admission or rejection of
  proofs, ... IR 2.96
.. debts payable at future time, ... IR 2.89
.. discounts, ...IR 2.84
.. estimate of, ... IR 2.81
.. foreign currency debts, ... IR 2.86
.. interest, ...IR 2.88
.. mutual credit and set off, ... IR 2.85
.. negotiable instruments, and, ...IR 2.82
.. non-disclosure, surrender for, ...IR 2.91
.. notice of proposed
  distribution, ... IR 2.95
.. periodical payments, ...IR 2.87
.. redemption by administrator, ... IR 2.92
.. revaluation of security, ... IR 2.102
.. secured creditors, and, ... IR 2.83
.. security, realisation by
  creditor, ...IR 2.94
.. security, test of value, ...IR 2.93
.. security, value of, ...IR 2.90
. bankruptcy, and
.. debts payable at future time, ... IR 6.114
.. discounts, ...IR 6.110
.. foreign currency debts, ... IR 6.111
.. interest, ...IR 6.113
.. negotiable instruments, ... IR 6.108
.. periodical payments, ...IR 6.112
.. secured creditors, ...IR 6.109
. winding up, and
.. debts payable at future time, ... IR 4.94
.. discounts, ...IR 4.89
.. estimate of quantum, ... IR 4.86
.. foreign currency debts, ... IR 4.91
.. interest, ...IR 4.93
.. mutual credit, ...IR 4.90
.. negotiable instruments, ...IR 4.87
.. periodical payments, ...IR 4.92
.. secured creditors, ...IR 4.88
.. set off, ...IR 4.90

Quorums
. company meetings
.. generally, ... IR 12.4A
.. winding up, and, ...IR 4.66
. creditors' committee
.. administration, and, ... *IR 2.36*, IR 2.54
.. bankruptcy, and, ...IR 6.155
.. receivership, and, ... IR 3.20
. creditors' meetings
.. bankruptcy, and, ...IR 6.92
.. generally, ... IR 12.4A

.. receivership, and, ... IR 3.13
.. winding up, and, ...IR 4.66
. liquidation committee, ... IR 4.158

R

Ranking
. administration, and, ... IR 2.69
. receivership, and
.. floating charges, and, ... IA 56(2)
.. ranking in winding up, and, ...IA 61(9)

Receipts and payments, abstract of
. administrative receiver, and, ... IR 3.32
. administrator, by, ... *IR 2.52*

Receivers (Scotland)
. agency, and, ... IA 57
. appointment
.. cessation of, ...IA 62
.. charge holder, by, ... IA 53
.. circumstances justifying, ... IA 52
.. court, by, ...IA 54
.. notification of, ... IA 64
.. power of, ...IA 51
. company's statement of affairs,
  and, ... IA 66
. contracts, liability for, ... IA 57
. court powers, ... IA 63
. creditors' committee, ... IA 68
. disposal of interest in property, ...IA 61
. distribution of money, ... IA 60
. duty to make returns,
  enforcement of, ... IA 69
. information to be given by, ... IA 65
. powers of, ... IA 55, IA Sch.2
. precedence amongst, ... IA 56
. prescribed forms, ... IA 71
. priority of debts, ... IA 59
. remuneration of, ... IA 58
. report by, ...IA 67

Receivers and managers (England and Wales)
. *and see* **Administrative receiver**
. accounts, delivery to registrar, ... IA 38
. appointment
.. court power of, ... IA 32
.. effective date of, ... IA 33
.. invalid, liability for, ... IA 34
.. notification of, ... IA 39
. bankrupts, disqualification of, ...IA 31
. bodies corporate,
  disqualification of, ... IA 30

1183

Index

Receivers and managers (England and Wales)—continued **Provision**
. contracts, liability for, ... IA 37
. directions, application to court for, ... IA 35
. duty to make returns, enforcement of, ... IA 41
. meaning, ...IA 251
. payment of debts from charged property, ... IA 40
. remuneration, court power to fix, ...IA 36
. undischarged bankrupt, disqualification of, ...IA 31
. vacation of office, ...IA 37(4)

Receivership
. administrative receiver
.. abstract of receipts and payments, ... IR 3.32
.. acceptance of appointment, ...IR 3.1
.. advertisement of appointment, ... IR 3.2
.. agency, and, ... IA 44
.. application of IA 1986 s.176A, ...IR 3.39
.. confirmation of appointment, ... IR 3.1
.. contracts, liability for, ... IA 44
.. creditors' committee, and, ... IA 49
.. death of, ...IR 3.34
.. disposal of charged property, ... IA 43, IR 3.31
.. general powers of, ...IA 42
.. information to be given by, ... IA 46
.. meaning, ... IA 29(2)
.. notice of appointment, ... IR 3.2
.. prohibition on appointment of, ... IA 72A—IA 72H
.. report of, ... IA 48, IR 3.8
.. resignation of, ... IR 3.33
.. statement of affairs, and, ... IR 3.3—IR 3.7
.. statement of affairs to be submitted by, ...IA 47
.. vacation of office, ... IA 45, IR 3.35
.. VAT bad debt relief, and, ...IR 3.36—IR 3.38
. creditors' committee, and
.. chairman at, ... IR 3.19
.. committee-members' representatives, ... IR 3.21
.. constitution of, ... IR 3.16
.. formal defects, and, ... IR 3.30A
.. formalities of establishment, ... IR 3.17
.. functions and meetings of, ... IR 3.18
.. information from receiver, ... IR 3.28

Provision
.. members' dealings with company, ...IR 3.30
.. members' expenses, ... IR 3.29
.. postal resolutions, ...IR 3.27
.. procedure at meetings of, ... IR 3.26
.. quorum, ... IR 3.20
.. removal from, ... IR 3.24
.. resignation from, ... IR 3.22
.. termination of membership, ... IR 3.23
.. vacancies on, ...IR 3.25
. creditors' meetings, and
.. adjournment, ... IR 3.14
.. admission and rejection of claim, ... IR 3.12
.. chairman at, ... IR 3.10
.. minutes, ... IR 3.15
.. quorum, ... IR 3.13
.. resolutions, ... IR 3.15
.. summoning, procedure for, ... IR 3.9
.. voting rights, ...IR 3.11
. cross border operation of provisions, ... IA 72
. forms for, ...IR Sch.4
. joint receivers, appointment of, ... IA 33(2)
. pending appointment of trustee in bankruptcy, ... IA 287
. receivers (Scotland)
.. agency, and, ... IA 57
.. cessation of appointment, ... IA 62
.. charge holder, appointment by, ... IA 53
.. circumstances justifying appointment, ... IA 52
.. company's statement of affairs, and, ... IA 66
.. contracts, liability for, ... IA 57
.. court powers, ...IA 63
.. court, appointment by, ... IA 54
.. creditors' committee, ... IA 68
.. disposal of interest in property, ... IA 61
.. distribution of money, ...IA 60
.. duty to make returns, enforcement of, ... IA 69
.. information to be given by, ... IA 65
.. notification of appointment, ...IA 64
.. power to appoint, ...IA 51
.. powers of, ... IA 55
.. precedence amongst, ... IA 56
.. prescribed forms, ... IA 71
.. priority of debts, ... IA 59
.. remuneration of, ... IA 58

Index

	Provision
. . report by,	IA 67

. property under
. . bankruptcy, and, ... IA 306B
. receivers and managers
    (England and Wales)
. . accounts, delivery to registrar, ... IA 38
. . bankrupts, disqualification of, ... IA 31
. . bodies corporate,
    disqualification of, ... IA 30
. . contracts, liability for, ... IA 37
. . court power to appoint, ... IA 32
. . directions, application to court
    for, ... IA 35
. . duty to make returns,
    enforcement of, ... IA 41
. . effective date of appointment, ... IA 33
. . invalid appointment, liability
    for, ... IA 34
. . notification of appointment, ... IA 39
. . payment of debts from charged
    property, ... IA 40
. . remuneration, court power to
    fix, ... IA 36
. . undischarged bankrupt,
    disqualification of, ... IA 31
. . vacation of office, ... IA 37(4)
. receivers' powers, ... IA 72

Registrar of Companies
. administration order
. . copy of, ... *IA 21(2)*
. . death of administrator, ... IR 2.124(4)
. . discharge of, ... *IA 27(6)*
. . disposal of charged property, ... IR 2.66(5)
. . removal of administrator, ... IR 2.122(5)
. . replacement administrator,
    appointment of, ... IR 2.128
. . revisions of administrator's
    proposals, ... *IA 25(6)*
. . statement of affairs, ... IR 2.30(3)
. . termination of, ... IR 2.111(2), IR 2.113(2)
. company voluntary
    arrangement, and
. . completion of, ... IR 1.29(3)
. . notice of end of moratorium, ... IR 1.42(2)
. . report of approval to, ... IR 1.24(5)
. . revocation or suspension, ... IR 1.25(5)
. receivership, and
. . disposal of charged assets, ... IA 43(5)
. . establishment of creditors'
    committee, ... IR 3.17(4)
. . vacation of office by receiver, ... IA 45(4)

	Provision

**Rejection of proofs, admission
or
. creditors' meeting**
. . bankruptcy, and, ... IR 6.94
. . winding up, and, ... IR 4.70
. proof of debts
. . administration, and, ... IR 2.77
. . bankruptcy, and, ... IR 6.104
. . winding up, and, ... IR 4.82

Relevant deposit
. meaning, ... *IA 8(1B)*

Rentcharges
. disclaimer in bankruptcy, and, ... IA 319, IA 321
. disclaimers in winding up
    proceedings, ... IA 180

Reservation of title
. insolvency proceedings, and, ... ER 7

**Reserve fund for unsecured
creditors,** .... IA 176A

Resignation
. creditors' committee, ... *IR 2.38*, IR 2.56

Resolutions
. adjourned meetings
. . winding up, and, ... IA 194
. company meetings
. . winding up, and, ... IR 4.63
. company voluntary
    arrangements, following
    proposals for, ... IR 1.22
. creditors' committee
. . administration, and, ... *IR 2.43*, IR 2.60(1), IR 2.61
. . bankruptcy, and, ... IR 6.162
. . receivership, and, ... IR 3.27
. creditors' meetings
. . administration, and, ... *IR 2.28*, IR 2.43
. . bankruptcy, and, ... IR 6.88
. . receivership, and, ... IR 3.15
. . winding up, and, ... IR 4.63
. individual voluntary
    arrangement, and, ... IR 5.25
. liquidation committee, . IR 4.165—IR 4.167

**Responsible insolvency
practitioner**
. meaning, ... IR 1.1(3)

Restraint order
. property under
. . bankruptcy, and, ... IA 306A

1185

Index

	Provision
Restrictive Trade Practices Act	
. exemptions from,	IA 428

Retention of title agreements
. administration order, and
. . creditors' meetings, and, ... *IR 2.26*
. . disposal of goods in Scotland, ... *IA 16(2)*
. . effect of application, ... *IA 10(4)*
. meaning, ...IA 251

Returns, duty to make
. liquidators, and, ... IA 170

Revocation
. company voluntary
   arrangement, and
. . of approval, ...IA 6(5)
. . of arrangement, ... IR 1.25

Right of attendance
. insolvency proceedings, ...IR 7.53

Rights of audience
. insolvency proceedings, ...IR 7.52

Rights of occupation
. bankrupt, and, ...IA 337
. bankrupt's spouse, ... IA 336
. premises occupies by bankrupt, ... IA 338

Rights under trusts of land
. bankruptcy, and, ...IA 335A

S

Scheme manager
. voting rights, ...IR Sch.1

Scotland
. role of administrator in, ... *IA 16*

Second bankruptcy
. delivery up to later trustee, ... IR 6.227
. duty of existing trustee, ... IR 6.226
. existing trustee's expenses, ... IR 6.228
. pre-commencement
   bankruptcy, ... EA Sch.19, para.5
. stay of distribution in case of, ...IA 344

Secretary of State
. bankruptcy, and
. . functions of creditors'
   committee, and, ...IR 6.166
. company voluntary
   arrangements, and
. . production of accounts and
   records to, ...IR 1.27

	Provision
. . supervisor's accounts and records,	IR 1.26(5)
. documents issuing from,	IR 12.6

. individual voluntary
   arrangements, and
. . production of accounts, ...IR 5.32
. dissolution, and, ... IR 4.224
. individual voluntary
   arrangement, and, ... IR 5.29
. liquidation committee, functions
   of, ... IR 4.153
. liquidator, appointment of, ... IA 137
. power to regulate certain
   matters, ... IR 12.1
. trustees in bankruptcy
. . appointment of, ...IA 296, IR 6.122
. . exercise of functions by, ...IA 302
. . removal of, ...IR 6.133

Secured creditors
. administration, and
. . creditors' meetings, and, ..*IR 2.24*, IR 2.40
. . meaning, ...IA 248
. . quantification of claims, and, ... IR 2.83
. bankruptcy, and
. . quantification of claims, ...IR 6.109
. . realisation of security by
   debtor, ... IR 6.119
. . redemption by trustee, ... IR 6.117
. . surrender for non-disclosure, ...IR 6.116
. . test of security's value, ... IR 6.118
. . value of security, ...IR 6.115
. dividends, and, ...IR 11.9
. winding up, and
. . quantification of claims, ... IR 4.88
. . realisation of security by
   creditor, ...IR 4.99
. . redemption by liquidator, ...IR 4.97
. . surrender for non-disclosure, ...IR 4.96
. . test of security's value, ...IR 4.98
. . value of security, ...IR 4.95

Secured debenture
. meaning, ... IA 70(1)

Security
. quantification of claims, and
. . realisation by creditor, ...IR 2.94
. . test of value, ... IR 2.93
. . value of, ...IR 2.90

Service
. by post, ...IR 12.10
. generally, ...IR 12.11
. outside jurisdiction, ... IR 12.12

Set off
. distribution of bankrupt's
  estate, ... IA 323
. insolvency proceedings, ... ER 6
. quantification of claims, and
.. administration, and, ... IR 2.85
.. winding up, and, ... IR 4.90

Shadow director
. meaning, ... IA 251

Shareholders
. liability on winding up, ... IA 76

Shares
. voluntary winding up, and
.. acceptance in consideration of
  sale, ... IA 110—IA 111
.. transfers of, ... IA 88

Sheriff
. duties in winding up, ... IA 184

Shorthand writers
. cost of shorthand note, ... IR 7.18
. nomination and appointment of, ... IR 7.16
. remuneration, ... IR 7.17, IR Sch.3

Social landlords
. prohibition on appointment of
  administrative receiver, and, ... IA 72G

Solicitation
. liquidators, and, ... IR 4.150
. trustee in bankruptcy, and, ... IR 6.148

Solicitors
. bankruptcy of, ... IR 6.235

Solvency, statutory declaration of
. voluntary winding up, and, ... IA 89

Special managers
. bankruptcy, and
.. accounting by, ... IR 6.170
.. appointment of, ... IA 370, IR 6.167
.. remuneration of, ... IR 6.167
.. security, and, ... IR 6.168, IR 6.169
.. termination of appointment, ... IR 6.171
. winding up, and
.. accounting, ... IR 4.209
.. appointment of, ... IR 4.206
.. power to appoint, ... IA 177
.. remuneration of, ... IR 4.206
.. security, and, ... IR 4.207—IR 4.208

.. termination of appointment, ... IR 4.210

Spouse, debts to
. distribution of bankrupt's
  estate, ... IA 329

Stamp duty
. bankruptcy, and, ... IA 378
. winding up, and, ... IA 190

Statement of affairs
. administration orders, and
.. annexation to proposals, ... IR 2.16
.. expenses of, ... IR 2.15, IR 2.32
.. extension of time for
  submission, ... IR 2.14, IR 2.31
.. investigation of company
  affairs, ... IA 22
.. limited disclosure, ... IR 2.13, IR 2.30
.. notice requiring, ... IR 2.11
.. release from duty to submit, ... IR 2.14, IR 2.31
.. verification and filing of, ..IR 2.12, IR 2.29
. administrative receiver, and
.. expenses of, ... IR 3.7
.. extension of time to submit, ...IR 3.6
.. limited disclosure in, ... IR 3.5
.. notice requiring, ... IR 3.3
.. release from duty to submit, ... IR 3.6
.. submission of, ... IA 47
.. verification and filing, ... IR 3.4
. admissibility in evidence of, ... IA 433
. bankruptcy, and, ... IA 288
. company voluntary
  arrangements, and
.. directors' proposals, ... IR 1.5
.. moratoriums, proposals for, ... IR 1.37
. creditor's petition for
  bankruptcy, and
.. accounts, requirement to
  submit, ... IR 6.64
.. accounts, submission and filing
  of, ... IR 6.65
.. expenses of, ... IR 6.63
.. form of, ... IR 6.59
.. further disclosure, ...IR 6.66
.. limited disclosure, ... IR 6.62
.. verification and filing of, ... IR 6.60
. creditors' voluntary winding up,
  and, ... IA 99, IR 4.34, IR 4.34A, IR 4.38
. creditors, information to
.. bankruptcy, and, ...IR 6.75—IR 6.76
. debtors' petition for bankruptcy,
  and

Statement of affairs—continued   Provision
  . . accounts, requirement to submit, ... IR 6.69
  . . accounts, submission and filing of, ... IR 6.70
  . . content of, ... IR 6.68
  . . expenses of, ... IR 6.71
  . . limited disclosure, ... IR 6.72
  . individual voluntary arrangement, and, ... IR 5.5
  . omissions from
  . . malpractice during winding up, and, ... IA 210
  . receivers (Scotland), and, ... IA 66
  . winding up, and
  . . creditors' voluntary liquidation, and, IR 4.34, IR 4.34A, IR 4.38
  . . expenses of, ... IR 4.36
  . . extension of time, ... IR 4.36
  . . further disclosure, ... IR 4.42
  . . limited disclosure, ... IR 4.35
  . . notice requiring, ... IR 4.32
  . . release for duty to submit, ... IR 4.36
  . . verification and filing, ... IR 4.33
  . winding up by court, and, ... IA 131

Statutory declaration of solvency
  . voluntary winding up, and, ... IA 89

Statutory demands
  . bankruptcy, and
  . . application to set aside, ... IR 6.4
  . . form and content of, ... IR 6.1
  . . hearing of application to set aside, ... IR 6.5
  . . information to be given in, ... IR 6.2
  . . proof of service, ... IR 6.11
  . . service requirements, ... IR 6.3
  . creditor's petition for bankruptcy, and, ... IA 268
  . winding up, and
  . . form and content of, ... IR 4.5
  . . generally, ... IR 4.4
  . . information to be given in, ... IR 4.6

Summary administration
  . debtor's petition for bankruptcy, and, ... IA 275, IR 6.48, IR 6.50
  . official receiver's duty in, ... IR 6.49

Summary proceedings
  . regulation of, ... IA 431

                               Provision
Summary remedies
  . malpractice during winding up, and, ... IA 212

Summoning of meetings
  . administrators, by, ... *IA 17(3)*
  . company meetings, ... IR 2.49(7)
  . company voluntary arrangements, and
  . . administrator's proposals, and, ... IR 1.11
  . . directors' proposals, and, ... IR 1.9
  . . liquidator's proposals, and, ... IA 3(2), IR 1.11
  . . members' meetings, ... IR 1.13
  . . proposals for, ... IA 3
  . creditors' meetings, and
  . . administration, and, ... *IR 2.18*
  . . bankruptcy, and, ... IR 6.87
  . . individual voluntary arrangement, and, ... IA 257, IR 5.17—IR 5.18
  . . receivership, and, ... IR 3.9
  . winding up, and
  . . expenses of, ... IR 4.61

Supervisors
  . administration, petition for
  . . affidavit in support of, ... *IR 2.1(4)*
  . company voluntary arrangements, and
  . . accounts and reports of, ... IR 1.26
  . . completion or termination of, ... IR 1.29
  . . hand-over of property to, ... IR 1.23
  . . role of, ... IA 7
  . fast track individual voluntary arrangement, and
  . . accounts and reports of, ... IR 5.47
  . . notification of appointment, ... IR 5.45
  . individual voluntary arrangements, and
  . . accounts and reports, and, ... IA 5.31
  . . hand-over of property to, ... IR 5.26
  . insolvency practitioners, and
  . . authorisation of, ... IA 389A
  . . official receiver as, ... IA 389B

Suspension
  . company voluntary arrangement, and
  . . of approval, ... IA 6(5)
  . . of arrangement, ... IR 1.25
  . individual voluntary arrangement, and, ... IR 5.30

	Provision

T

Tenancies, insolvent joint
. rule-making powers relating to, ...IA 421A

Termination of administration
. application by administrator, ...IR 2.114
. application by creditor, ...IR 2.115
. application for extension, ...IR 2.112
. final progress reports, ...IR 2.110
. move to creditors' voluntary
    liquidation, ...IR 2.117
. move to dissolution, ...IR 2.118
. notice of, ...IR 2.113
. notice where end automatic, ...IR 2.111
. notification of court order, ...IR 2.116

Territorial proceedings ....ER 3(2)

Third parties
. administrators, and, ...*IA 14(6)*
. protection of purchasers, ... ER 14
. rights in rem, ... ER 5

Time limits
. bankruptcy, and, ... IA 376
. winding up, ...IR 4.3

Title of proceedings
. amendment of
. . creditors' petition for
    bankruptcy, ...IR 6.35
. . debtor's petition for
    bankruptcy, and, ... IR 6.49

Trade marks
. insolvency proceedings, and, ... ER 12

Transactions at undervalue
. adjustment of prior transactions,
    and, IA 238, IA 240, IA 241, IA 339, IA
    341, IA 342

Trustee in bankruptcy
. accounts of
. . annulment of bankruptcy
    orders, and, ...IR 5.61
. acquisition by trustee of
    control, ... IA 311
. adjustment between earlier and
    later bankruptcy estates, ...IA 335
. administration by
. . administration order, property
    under, ... IA 306C
. . after acquired property, and, ... IA 307, IA 309
. . charge on bankrupt's home, ...IA 313
. . income payment agreements, ... IA 310A
. . income payment orders, ... IA 310

	Provision

. . items of excess value, ... IA 308, IA 309
. . low value home, ...IA 313A
. . property subject to restraint
    order, ...IA 306A
. . receivership, property under, ... IA 306B
. . vesting of bankrupt's estate in, ... IA 306
. after-acquired property, and, ... IR 6.201
. appointment
. . advertisement of, ...IR 6.124
. . authentication of, ...IR 6.123
. . by court, ... IR 6.121
. . by creditors' meeting, ...IR 6.120
. . by Secretary of State, ... IA 296, IR 6.122
. . power to make, ... IA 292
. bankrupt's estate, distribution of
. . bankrupt's home, saving for, ... IA 332
. . criminal bankruptcy, and, ... IA 327
. . debts to spouse, ...IA 329
. . dividend, by means of, ... IA 324
. . final distribution, ...IA 330
. . final meeting, ...IA 331
. . mutual credit, ...IA 323
. . priority of debts, ... IA 328
. . proof of debts, ...IA 322
. . property in specie, ...IA 326
. . set off, ...IA 323
. . unsatisfied creditors, claims
    by, ... IA 325
. control of
. . by court, ... IA 303
. . creditors' committee, and, ... IA 301
. . exercise of functions by
    Secretary of State, ...IA 302
. . liability of, ... IA 304
. court power to set aside
    transactions of, ... IR 6.147
. creditors' committee, and, ... IR 2.57(2), IR
    6.152, IR 6.153
. creditors' power to requisition
    meetings, ... IA 294
. death of, ...IR 6.143
. disclaimers, and, ...IR 6.178
. duties of bankrupt in relation
    to, ... IA 333
. failure of meeting to appoint, ...IA 295
. general functions of, ... IA 305
. hand-over of property to, ... IR 6.125
. obligation to surrender control
    to, ... IA 312
. official receiver, enforcement of
    obligations to, ... IR 6.149
. onerous property, disclaimer of

Index

Trustee in bankruptcy—continued   **Provision**
. . court order vesting disclaimed property, ...IA 320
. . dwelling houses, ... IA 318
. . general power, ... IA 315
. . leaseholds, ... IA 317
. . notice requiring trustee's decision, ...IA 316
. . rentcharges, ... IA 319, IA 321
. powers of, ... IA 314, IA Sch.5
. qualification, loss of, ... IR 6.144
. release of, ... IA 299, IR 6.135, IR 6.137, IR 6.137A
. removal of
. . advertisement of, ...IR 6.134
. . by court, ... IR 6.132
. . by creditors' meeting, ..IR 6.129, IR 6.130
. . by Secretary of State, ...IR 6.133
. . procedure on, ... IR 6.131
. remuneration
. . court, recourse to, ...IR 6.141
. . creditors' meetings, recourse to, ...IR 6.140
. . excessive remuneration, ...IR 6.142
. . fixing of, ...IR 6.138—IR 6.138A
. . matters affecting, ...IR 6.139
. resignation of
. . action following acceptance of, ... IR 6.127
. . advertisement of, ... IR 6.134
. . creditors' meeting to receive, ... IR 6.126
. . leave granted by court, ...IR 6.128
. second bankruptcy, stay of distribution in case of, ... IA 334
. solicitation, rule against, ... IR 6.148
. special cases, ... IA 297
. summoning of meeting to appoint, ...IA 293
. vacancy in office of, ...IA 300
. vacation of office, ...IA 298, IR 6.145, IR 6.146

Trusts of land, rights under
. bankruptcy, and, ...IA 335A

U

Unclaimed dividends
. winding up, and, ... IA 193

Undischarged bankrupts
. individual voluntary arrangement, and, ... IA 261
. receiver, power to appoint, ...IA 51(5)
. receivers (England and Wales), and, ... IA 31

Undue preferences (Scotland)   **Provision**
. adjustment of prior transactions, and, ... IA 243

Unqualified debts
. creditors' voting rights, ... IR 2.38(5)

Unsold assets, division of
. administration, division to creditors on, ... IR 2.71

Utilities
. bankruptcy, and, ... IA 372
. management of insolvent companies, and, ...IA 233
. prohibition on appointment of administrative receiver, and, ...IA 72D

V

Vacancies
. creditors' committee
. . administration, and, ... IR 2.41, IR 2.59
. . receivership, and, ... IR 3.25

Vacation of office
. administrator, by, ... IA 19, IR 2.129
. administrative receiver, by, IA 11(2), IA 45, IR 3.35
. receivers (England and Wales), and, ... IA 37(4)

VAT bad debt relief
. administration orders, and
. . issue of certificate of insolvency, ...IR 2.56
. . notice to creditors, ...IR 2.57
. . preservation of certificate in company records, ... IR 2.58
. administrative receiver, and, ...IR 3.36—IR 3.38

Voluntary arrangement
. expenses of, ... IR 4.21A

Voluntary winding up
. application of rules, ...IR 4.1
. circumstances enabling, ... IA 84
. commencement of, ...IA 86
. court powers (Scotland), ...IA 113
. creditors, by, ... IA 97—IA 106
. directors' powers where liquidator not appointed, ... IA 114
. dissolution, and, ...IA 201
. distribution of company property, ... IA 107
. effect of, ...IA 87

1190

Index

	Provision
. expenses of,	IA 115

. liquidator
.. appointment by court of, ... IA 108
.. notice of appointment of, ...IA 108
.. powers of, ...IA 165
.. removal by court of, ...IA 107
. members, by, ...IA 91—IA 96
. notice of resolution for, ...IA 85
. references to court, ...IA 112
. share transfers, and, ...IA 88
. shares, acceptance in
    consideration of sale, ...IA 110—IA 111
. statutory declaration of
    solvency, and, ...IA 89
. winding up by court,
    applications for, ...IA 116

Voting rights
. company meetings
.. company voluntary
    arrangements, and, ...IR 1.18, IR 1.51
.. winding up, and, ...IR 4.69
. creditors' committee
.. administration, and, ...IR 2.60(1)
.. bankruptcy, and, ...IR 6.161
. creditors' meetings
.. administration, and, ... *IR 2.22*, IR 2.38
.. bankruptcy, and, ...IR 6.93
.. company voluntary
    arrangements, and, ...IR 1.17, IR 1.49
.. individual voluntary
    arrangements, and, ... IR 5.21
.. receivership, and, ... IR 3.11
.. winding up, and, ...IR 4.67
. fast track individual voluntary
    arrangement, and, ... IR 5.41
. liquidation committee, . IR 4.165—IR 4.166
. scheme manager, ...IR Sch.1

W

Winding up (registered companies)
. accounts, submission of
.. creditors' voluntary
    liquidation, and, ...IR 4.40, IR 4.41
.. further disclosure, ...IR 4.42
.. requests for, ... IR 4.39
. administration, following
.. liquidation committee, and, . IR 4.173—IR 4.178
. affidavits, and, ... IA 200
. application for leave to proceed,
    costs of, ... IA 199

	Provision

. assets
.. collection and distribution by
    liquidator, ... IR 4.179—IR 4.186
.. payment of costs out of, ... IR 4.218—IR 4.220
.. power to make over to
    employees, ... IA 187
. attachment, effect of execution
    of, ...IA 183
. banks, winding up of, ...IR 4.72
. calls on contributories
.. by court, ... IR 4.204
.. by liquidation committee, ... IR 4.203
.. by liquidator, ...IR 4.202
.. enforcement of, ... IR 4.205
.. making of, ...IR 4.205
. capital, return of, ... IR 4.221—IR 4.222
. claims, quantification of
.. debts payable at future time, ... IR 4.94
.. discounts, ...IR 4.89
.. estimate of quantum, ... IR 4.86
.. foreign currency debts, ... IR 4.91
.. interest, ...IR 4.93
.. mutual credit, ... IR 4.90
.. negotiable instruments, ... IR 4.87
.. periodical payments, ...IR 4.92
.. secured creditors, ... IR 4.88
.. set off, ... IR 4.90
. commission for receiving
    evidence, ...IA 197
. company books, use in
    evidence, ...IA 191
. contracts, rescission of, ... IA 186
. contributories
.. bankruptcy, effect of, ... IA 82
.. calls on, ...IR 4.202—IR 4.205
.. companies registered under
    Companies Act s.680, ... IA 83
.. death of member, and, ...IA 81
.. directors, liability of past, ... IA 76
.. directors with unlimited
    liability, ... IA 75
.. information to, ...IR 4.43—IR 4.49A
.. liability, nature of, ... IA 80
.. limited company formerly
    unlimited, ...IA 77
.. list, settlement of, ... IR 4.195—IR 4.201
.. meaning, ... IA 79
.. members, liability of past and
    present, ... IA 74
.. shareholders, liability of past, ...IA 76
.. unlimited company formerly
    limited, ... IA 78

1191

Winding up (registered companies)—continued   **Provision**
. contributories' meetings, and
. . adjournment of, ...IR 4.65
. . attendance of company personnel, ...IR 4.58
. . chairman as proxy holder, ...IR 4.64
. . chairman at, ...IR 4.55
. . court power to call, ... IA 195
. . expenses of summoning, ...IR 4.61
. . first meeting, ...IR 4.50, IR 4.52
. . notice by advertisement, ...IR 4.59
. . power to call, ... IR 4.54
. . quorum at, ... IR 4.66
. . record of proceedings, ... IR 4.71
. . requisitioned meetings, ... IR 4.57
. . resolutions of, ... IR 4.63
. . suspension of, ... IR 4.65
. . venue, ...IR 4.60
. . voting rights, ...IR 4.69
. conversion of administration into
. . affidavit, content of, ...*IR 2.60*, IR 2.131
. . application for, ...*IR 2.59*, IR 2.130
. . court powers, and, ... *IR 2.61*, IR 2.132
. conversion of company voluntary arrangement into
. . affidavits, ...IR 1.32
. . application for, ...IR 1.31
. . court powers, and, ...IR 1.33
. costs, payment out of assets of, . IR 4.218—IR 4.220
. court, by
. . appeals from orders (Scotland), ...IA 162
. . application for, ...IA 124
. . application of rules, ...IR 4.1
. . attachments, avoidance of, ...IA 128
. . circumstances enabling, ...IA 122
. . commencement of, ...IA 129
. . company affairs, investigation of, ...IA 131—IA 134
. . consequences of, ...IA 130
. . contributories, orders for calls on (Scotland), ...IA 161
. . court powers, ... IA 125, IA 147—IA 160
. . inability to pay debts, meaning of, ...IA 123
. . jurisdiction (England and Wales), ... IA 117—IA 119
. . jurisdiction (Scotland), ...IA 120—IA 121
. . liquidation committees, ... IA 141—IA 142
. . liquidator, appointment of, ...IA 135—IA 140

   Provision
. . liquidator, functions of, ... IA 143—IA 146
. . petition, forms of, ...IR 4.2
. . proceedings against company, power to stay or restrain, ...IA 126
. . property dispositions, avoidance of, ...IA 127
. . public interest, petition on grounds of, ...IA 124A
. creditors, information to, ...IR 4.43—IR 4.49A
. creditors' meetings, and
. . adjournment of, ...IR 4.65
. . admission and rejection of proof, ... IR 4.70
. . attendance of company personnel, ... IR 4.58
. . chairman as proxy holder, ...IR 4.64
. . chairman at, ... IR 4.55
. . court power to call, ... IA 195
. . creditors' voluntary winding up, and, .. IA 98, IR 4.51, IR 4.53—IR 4.53B, IR 4.56, IR 4.62, IR 4.68
. . expenses of summoning, ...IR 4.61
. . first meeting, ...IR 4.50, IR 4.52
. . notice by advertisement, ... IR 4.59
. . power to call, ... IR 4.54
. . quorum at, ... IR 4.66
. . record of proceedings, ... IR 4.71
. . requisitioned meetings, ...IR 4.57
. . resolutions of, ... IR 4.63
. . suspension of, ... IR 4.65
. . venue, ...IR 4.60
. . voting rights, ...IR 4.67
. creditors' voluntary winding up
. . accounts, submission of, ..IR 4.40, IR 4.41
. . conclusion of, ...IR 4.223
. . creditors' meetings, and, ... IA 98, IR 4.51, IR 4.53—IR 4.53B,IR 4.56, IR 4.62, IR 4.68
. . directors' powers, cessation of, ... IA 103
. . end of year meetings, ... IA 105
. . final meeting, ...IA 106
. . liquidation committee, appointment of, ... IA 101
. . liquidator, appointment of, ... IA 100
. . liquidator, vacancy in office of, ... IA 104
. . members' voluntary winding up, conversion from, ... IA 102

1192

Provision

- . members' voluntary winding up, distinction from, ... IA 90
- . statement of affairs, ... IA 99, IR 4.34, IR 4.34A, IR 4.38
- debts, proof of
- . . admission and rejection of for dividend, ... IR 4.82
- . . appeal against decision on, ... IR 4.83
- . . appointment of new liquidator, ... IR 4.81
- . . claims established by affidavit, ... IR 4.77
- . . contents of proof, ... IR 4.75
- . . costs, ... IR 4.78
- . . creditors' voluntary liquidation, and, ... IR 4.76
- . . expunging of by court, ... IR 4.85
- . . inspection allowed by liquidator, ... IR 4.79
- . . meaning, ... IR 4.73
- . . supply of forms, ... IR 4.74
- . . transmission to liquidator, ... IR 4.80
- . . withdrawal or variation of, ... IR 4.84
- . diligence, effect of (Scotland), ... IA 185
- . disclaimers (England and Wales)
- . . additional notices, ... IR 4.189
- . . applications by interested parties, ... IR 4.191
- . . communication of, ... IR 4.188
- . . court powers, ... IA 181—IA 182, IR 4.194
- . . declaration of interest in property, ... IR 4.192
- . . duty to keep court informed, ... IR 4.190
- . . leaseholds, ... IA 179
- . . liquidator's notice of, ... IR 4.187
- . . onerous property, ... IA 178
- . . rentcharges, land subject to, ... IA 180
- . . validity, presumption of, ... IR 4.193
- . dissolution following
- . . completion of winding up, and, ... IA 205
- . . early dissolution (England and Wales), ... IA 202—IA 203
- . . early dissolution (Scotland), ... IA 204
- . . procedures following appeals, ... IR 4.225
- . . Secretary of State's directions, ... IR 4.224
- . . voluntary winding up, and, ... IA 201
- . examination of persons, court orders for, ... IA 198
- . execution, effect of, ... IA 183
- . forms for, ... IR Sch.4
- . information to creditors and contributories

Provision

- . . creditors' voluntary liquidation, and, ... IR 4.49
- . . liquidation following administration, and, ... IR 4.49A
- . . reports by Official Receiver, .. IR 4.43—IR 4.48
- . interest on debts, ... IA 189
- . judicial notice of court documents, ... IA 196
- . liquidation committee
- . . calls on contributories, ... IR 4.203
- . . chairman at meetings of, ... IR 4.157
- . . committee-members' representatives, ... IR 4.159
- . . composition when creditors paid in full, ... IR 4.171
- . . dealings by members, ... IR 4.170
- . . establishment by contributories, ... IR 4.154
- . . expenses of members, ... IR 4.169
- . . formal defects of, ... IR 4.172A
- . . formalities of establishment, ... IR 4.153
- . . functions vested in Secretary of State, ... IR 4.172
- . . generally, ... IR 4.151
- . . liquidator's reports, and, ... IR 4.168
- . . meetings of, ... IR 4.156
- . . membership of, ... IR 4.152
- . . obligation of liquidator to, ... IR 4.155
- . . quorum, ... IR 4.158
- . . removal from, ... IR 4.162
- . . resignation from, ... IR 4.160
- . . resolutions of, ... IR 4.165—IR 4.167
- . . termination of membership, ... IR 4.161
- . . vacancies, ... IR 4.163—IR 4.164
- . . voting rights, ... IR 4.165—IR 4.166
- . . winding up following administration, and, ... IR 4.173—IR 4.178
- . liquidators
- . . appointment of, ... IR 4.100—IR 4.106
- . . calls on contributories, ... IR 4.202
- . . collection and distribution of company assets by, ... IR 4.179—IR 4.186
- . . contributories, settlement of list of, ... IR 4.195—IR 4.210
- . . corrupt inducement affecting appointment of, ... IA 164
- . . creditors' voluntary winding up, powers on, ... IA 166
- . . death of, ... IR 4.132—IR 4.133

Index

Winding up (registered companies)—continued   *Provision*
- . . designation of, ... IA 163
- . . disclaimers, and, ... IR 4.187—IR 4.194
- . . duty to make returns, enforcement of, ... IA 170
- . . final meeting, and, ... IR 4.125—IR 4.126
- . . hand-over of assets to, ... IR 4.107
- . . loss of qualification as insolvency practitioner, . IR 4.134—IR 4.135
- . . members' voluntary winding up, and, ... IR 4.139—4.148B
- . . power to set aside transactions, ... IR 4.149
- . . release of, IA 173—IA 174, IR 4.121—IR 4.122, IR 4.124, IR 4.125A
- . . removal from office, .. IA 171—IA 172, IR 4.113—IR 4.120, IR 4.123
- . . remuneration of, ... IR 4.127—IR 4.131
- . . resignation of, ... IR 4.108—IR 4.112
- . . solicitation, rule against, ... IR 4.150
- . . supplementary powers (England and Wales), ... IA 168
- . . supplementary powers (Scotland), ... IA 169
- . . vacation of office by, . IR 4.136—IR 4.138
- . . voluntary winding up, powers on, ... IA 165
- . . winding up by court, powers on, ... IA 167
- . malpractice during
- . . company names, re-use of, ... IA 216, IA 217, IR 4.22—IR 4.230
- . . false representations to creditors, ... IA 211
- . . falsification of company books, ... IA 209
- . . fraud in anticipation of winding up, ... IA 206
- . . fraudulent trading, ... IA 213, IA 215
- . . misconduct by officers, ... IA 208
- . . omissions from statement of affairs, ... IA 210
- . . prosecution of delinquent officers and members, . IA 218, IA 219
- . . summary remedies, ... IA 212
- . . transactions in fraud of creditors, ... IA 207
- . . wrongful trading, ... IA 214, IA 215
- . Member State liquidator, and, ... IR 4.231
- . members' voluntary winding up

    Provision
- . . creditors' voluntary winding up, conversion to, ... IA 96
- . . creditors' voluntary winding up, distinction from, ... IA 90
- . . effect of insolvency, ... IA 95
- . . end of year meeting, ... IA 93
- . . final meeting, ... IA 94
- . . liquidator, appointment of, ... IA 91
- . . liquidator, power to fill vacancy in office of, ... IA 92
- . modes of, ... IA 73
- . notification of, ... IA 188
- . orders pronounced in vacation (Scotland), ... IA Sch.3
- . pending liquidations, information on, ... IA 192
- . petition for
- . . advertisement of, ... IR 4.11
- . . affidavit in opposition, ... IR 4.18
- . . affidavit supporting petition for administration, and, ... *IR 2.3(3)*
- . . by contributories, ... IR 4.22—IR 4.24
- . . certificate of compliance, ... IR 4.14
- . . leave for withdrawal, ... IR 4.15
- . . list of appearances, ... IR 4.17
- . . notice of appearance, ... IR 4.16
- . . persons to receive copies of, ... IR 4.10, IR 4.13
- . . presentation and filing of, ... IR 4.7
- . . proof of service, ... IR 4.9
- . . service of, ... IR 4.8
- . . substitution of creditor or contributory for petitioner, ... IR 4.19
- . . termination of administration, and, ... IR 2.114(4)
- . . verification of, ... IR 4.12
- . preferential debts, ... IA 175—IA 176
- . provisional liquidator
- . . appointment of, ... IR 4.25
- . . deposit, ... IR 4.27
- . . notice of appointment, ... IR 4.25A
- . . order of appointment, ... IR 4.26
- . . remuneration, ... IR 4.30
- . . security, ... IR 4.28, IR 4.29
- . . termination of appointment, ... IR 4.31
- . public examination of company officers
- . . adjournment, ... IR 4.216
- . . expenses of, ... IR 4.217
- . . notice of hearing, ...IR 4.212
- . . order for, ...IR 4.211
- . . order on request of creditors or contributories, ... IR 4.213

Provision

.. procedure at hearings, ... IR 4.215
.. witness unfit for examination, ... IR 4.214
. rescission of contracts, ... IA 186
. resolutions passed at adjourned
    meetings, ... IA 194
. secured creditors
.. realisation of security by
    creditor, ... IR 4.99
.. redemption by liquidator, ... IR 4.97
.. surrender for non-disclosure, ... IR 4.96
.. test of security's value, ... IR 4.98
.. value of security, ... IR 4.95
. sheriff, duties of (England and
    Wales), ... IA 184
. sisting for company voluntary
    arrangement, ... IA 5(3)
. special managers
.. accounting, ... IR 4.209
.. appointment of, ... IR 4.206
.. power to appoint, ... IA 177
.. remuneration of, ... IR 4.206
.. security, and, ... IR 4.207—IR 4.208
.. termination of appointment, ... IR 4.210
. stamp duty, exemption from, ... IA 190
. statement of affairs
.. creditors' voluntary
    liquidation, and, IR 4.34, IR 4.34A, IR
    4.38
.. expenses of, ... IR 4.36
.. extension of time, ... IR 4.36
.. further disclosure, ... IR 4.42
.. limited disclosure, ... IR 4.35
.. notice requiring, ... IR 4.32
.. release for duty to submit, ... IR 4.36
.. verification and filing, ... IR 4.33
. statutory demands
.. form and content of, ... IR 4.5
.. generally, ... IR 4.4
.. information to be given in, ... IR 4.6
. time limits, and, ... IR 4.3
. unclaimed dividends, ... IA 193
. voluntary arrangement,
    expenses of, ... IR 4.21A
. voluntary winding up
.. application of rules, ... IR 4.1
.. circumstances enabling, ... IA 84
.. commencement of, ... IA 86
.. court powers (Scotland), ... IA 113
.. creditors, by, ... IA 97—IA 106
.. directors' powers where
    liquidator not appointed, ... IA 114
.. distribution of company
    property, ... IA 107

Provision

.. effect of, ... IA 87
.. expenses of, ... IA 115
.. liquidator, appointment by
    court of, ... IA 108
.. liquidator, notice of
    appointment of, ... IA 108
.. liquidator, removal by court
    of, ... IA 107
.. members, by, ... IA 91—IA 96
.. notice of resolution for, ... IA 85
.. references to court, ... IA 112
.. share transfers, and, ... IA 88
.. shares, acceptance in
    consideration of sale, IA 110—IA 111
.. statutory declaration of
    solvency, and, ... IA 89
.. winding up by court,
    applications for, ... IA 116
. winding up order
.. notice and settling of, ... IR 4.20
.. transmission and advertisement
    of, ... IR 4.21

Winding up (unregistered companies)
. actions stayed on, ... IA 228
. application for, ... IA 221
. contributories, and, ... IA 226
. court power to stay, sist or
    restrain proceedings, ... IA 227
. cumulative effect of provisions, ... IA 229
. inability to pay debts, ... IA 222—IA 223
. overseas company, ... IA 225
. unregistered company, meaning
    of, ... IA 220

Winding up by court
. appeals from orders (Scotland), ... IA 162
. application for, ... IA 124
. application of rules, ... IR 4.1
. attachments, avoidance of, ... IA 128
. circumstances enabling, ... IA 122
. commencement of, ... IA 129
. company affairs, investigation
    of
.. official receiver, investigation
    by, ... IA 132
.. public examination of officers, ... IA 133—IA 134
.. statement of affairs, and, ... IA 131
. consequences of, ... IA 130
. contributories, orders for calls
    on (Scotland), ... IA 161

1195

Winding up by court—continued **Provision**
. court powers
. . arrest of absconding
    contributories, ... IA 158
. . attendance at company
    meetings (Scotland), ... IA 157
. . calls to satisfy debts, ... IA 150
. . contributories list, settlement
    of, ... IA 148
. . contributories, adjustment of
    rights of, ... IA 154
. . contributories, debts due from, ... IA 149
. . contributories, orders on, ... IA 152
. . cumulative nature of, ... IA 159
. . delegation of powers to
    liquidator, ... IA 160
. . exclusion of creditors not
    proving on time, ... IA 153
. . expenses, payment of, ... IA 156
. . inspection of books, ... IA 155
. . on hearing petition, ... IA 125
. . payment into bank of money
    due to company, ... IA 151
. . stay or sist winding up, ... IA 147
. inability to pay debts, meaning
    of, ... IA 123
. jurisdiction (England and
    Wales), ... IA 117—IA 119
. jurisdiction (Scotland), ... IA 120—IA 121
. liquidation committees, ... IA 141—IA 142
. liquidator, appointment of

Provision
. . by court, ... IA 140
. . by Secretary of State, ... IA 137
. . contributories, nomination by, ... IA 139
. . creditors' meetings,
    nomination by, ... IA 139
. . functions of official receiver,
    and, ... IA 136
. . in Scotland, ... IA 138
. . provisional liquidator,
    appointment of, ... IA 135
. liquidator, functions of
. . custody of company property, ... IA 144
. . final meeting, summoning of, ... IA 146
. . general functions, ... IA 143
. . vesting of company property
    in, ... IA 145
. proceedings against company,
    power to stay or restrain, ... IA 126
. property dispositions, avoidance
    of, ... IA 127
. public interest, petition on
    grounds of, ... IA 124A

Winding up orders
. notice and settling of, ... IR 4.20
. transmission and advertisement
    of, ... IR 4.21

Wrongful trading
. malpractice during winding up,
    and, ... IA 214, IA 215